Larry,

I pray that t[illegible]
will bless you in your
service to Him.

Your friend and Brother in Christ

Bob Harvey

Vine's Amplified Expository Dictionary of New Testament Words

REFERENCE EDITION

WORLD
Bible Publishers, Inc.

ISBN 0-529-06947-4

Manufactured in the U.S.A.

Vine's Amplified Expository Dictionary of New Testament Words
(REFERENCE EDITION)

(With a Comprehensive Key to Major Old & New Testament Reference Works)

INTRODUCTION

1. Nature and Purpose of the Key

For many years now, countless numbers of Bible students, pastors and lay workers from all sections of the Christian community the world over have greatly benefited from the labours of W.E. Vine in his *Expository Dictionary of New Testament Words*. This very useful reference work is now firmly established as a classic in its field, providing serious students of the Bible with valuable insights into the background, meaning and usage of every Greek term in the New Testament. In recent years there have been a number of new editions of this work which have extended the field of inquiry beyond the terms themselves. Primarily this has involved the keying of each Greek term to the corresponding reference number for that word in the index of *Strong's Concordance*. At least one other edition has also added to the Strong's listing, a reference to Colin Brown's *Dictionary of New Testament Theology*. To be sure, these additional references have considerably enhanced the usefulness of the work enabling students to further investigate the frequency of any given term throughout the New Testament, and to consider its theological significance in particular biblical contexts with much greater ease.

Realizing the valuable potential of such an approach, the editors of this latest edition have developed the idea of providing a Comprehensive Key to the Vine's Dictionary which will open up a great deal more reference material in an unparalleled way. The result of this venture means that the reader is now able to consult and cross-reference each Greek term listed in Vine's with up to 10 additional biblical reference works of major importance.

Over and above the expanded number of reference works in the New Testament component of the key, a unique element has been added in the references to Old Testament terms in Hebrew and Aramaic. Underlying this feature is the theological premise that the Bible is *one* book, and not two. The division of the Canon into Old and New Testaments has led in some ways to a false perception that the Bible is not a unified, integral work but one composed of two dissimilar, unrelated segments. It is the fervent prayerful hope of the editors that the discerning reader will come to understand and appreciate this underlying unity of scripture as he begins to use the key.

Before embarking on a specific explanation of the use of this latest reference tool (see below under 3.) it will be helpful to consider the rationale behind the Old Testament component of the key: Starting from the premise as stated above, it follows that for each Greek word in the New Testament there is likely to be a corresponding Hebrew (and/or Aramaic) word in the Old Testament. This is particularly the case where significant theological terms in the New Testament, such as redemption, justice, salvation, faith, atonement, judgment etc. will indeed have corresponding Hebrew terms in the Old. The reason for this is that themes like the ones sampled above are wholly biblical concepts and are not limited or restricted to the New Testament. Once this is realised and appreciated, then the careful student will be able to discover significant insights into important biblical themes from the perspective of *both* the Old and New Testaments and thus gain a richer understanding of Scriptural truth from a comprehensive perspective. One of the valuable fruits of such an exercise will be an enhanced appreciation of the unity of the Bible.

At this stage it is necessary to recognise a number of important factors emerging from this rationale. Careful reflection on, and attention to the following observations will guard against a possible misunderstanding and misuse of the key:

1.1 Not every Greek term in the New Testament does in fact have a corresponding Old Testament term in Hebrew (or Aramaic).

1.2 Where Old Testament Hebrew terms are listed as equivalents they are *not* to be perceived as precisely exact translations of the Greek word in every instance. In some cases there may in fact be a close one-to-one correspondence, but this is relatively rare. In most cases there will be multiple Hebrew terms approximating New Testament Greek words. Up to *three* of these "dynamic Hebrew equivalents" will be listed for each Greek entry, wherever they occur. Careful attention has been given in the key to assure that the equivalent Hebrew/Aramaic terms listed match as far as possible the meaning of the corresponding Greek term. Where more than three such correlations do exist, only the most significant of these are selected for the key.

1.3 Not every Greek word and its "dynamic Hebrew equivalent" will be theologically significant. At this point it needs to be noted that the key does not represent any theological function or intent, apart from the underlying premise mentioned above. Such an adjudication is left for the reader to determine in his study of each entry.

1.4 Before coming to any conclusions about the meaning, significance and interrelationship of Greek and Hebrew terminology from the key, it is of the utmost importance to thoroughly examine the scriptural context, both general and immediate, of every verse located in which the relevant word or words occur. Otherwise faulty conclusions are prone to emerge and the value of the whole exercise may be lost.

1.5 The General Reference section of the key will occasionally require a careful, judicious handling. In some cases, entries cited will often include discussion of Greek and Hebrew terms that may not occur in the key. When and where this occurs, the reader will need to be wisely selective in the way he harvests material from these sources.

2. Explanation of the Key: Listing of Works cited

NT (New Testament)

S. : *The New Strong's Exhaustive Concordance of the Bible* (Thomas Nelson Inc., Nashville, 1984). (N.B.: Other editions of *Strong's Concordance* will also match the key)

B. : *A Greek-English Lexicon of the New Testament*, W. F. Arndt and F. W. Gingrich — 2nd edition. [A translation and adaptation of W. Bauer's German work.] (University of Chicago Press, Chicago, 1979)

CB. : *The New International Dictionary of New Testament Theology* (3 vols.) Colin Brown — General Editor (Zondervan Pub. House, Grand Rapids, 1978)

K. : *Theological Dictionary of the New Testament* G. Kittel. Abridged in one volume by G. W. Bromiley (Eerdmans Pub. Co., Grand Rapids, 1985)

OT (Old Testament)

S. : *The New Strong's Exhaustive Concordance of the Bible* (Thomas Nelson Inc., Nashville, 1984). (N.B.: Other editions of *Strong's Concordance* will also match the key)

HR.: *A Concordance to the Septuagint* (3 vols.) E. Hatch & A. A. Redpath (Baker Book House, Grand Rapids, 1983)

H. : *Theological Wordbook of the Old Testament* (2 vols.) R. Laird Harris, G. J. Archer, B.K. Waltke (Moody Press, Chicago, 1980)

BD. : *A Hebrew & English Lexicon of the Old Testament* F. Brown, S. R. Driver, C. A. Briggs (Oxford University Press, Oxford, 1978)

GEN. REF. (General Reference)

IS. : *The International Standard Bible Encyclopedia* (4 vols.) G. W. Bromiley — General Editor (Eerdmans Pub. Co., Grand Rapids, 1988)

NB. : *The New Bible Dictionary* J. D. Douglas — Editor (Inter Varsity Press, London, 1972)

Z. : *The Zondervan Pictorial Encyclopedia of the Bible* (5 vols.) M. Tenney — Editor (Zondervan Pub. House, Grand Rapids, 1975, 1976)

3. Use of the Key

3.1. New Testament

3.1.1 Strong's (S)

The Strong's reference number for New Testament entries is regarded in the key as a basic starting point, and therefore this listing is placed next to the main entry in the body of the Vine's text. Simply check this number in the major New Testament Greek word index at the back of the concordance, and then turn to the main body of the work to locate the occurrences of the term throughout the New Testament.

Example: Vine's English entry: captain
Vine's Greek entry: *archēgos*
Strong's reference number: 747

When turning to entry under "captain" in the body of the *Strong's Concordance*, look for the number 747 to locate the frequency and occurrences of the term "archēgos" in the New Testament. Exactly the same procedure will be followed when locating the Old Testament Strong's reference number with respect to the Hebrew term. In this particular example the "dynamic

Hebrew equivalent" for "archēgos" is "rô'sh", whose corresponding reference number in *Strong's* is 7218 in the Old Testament Hebrew word index.

3.1.2 **Bauer (B)**

The reference here is to a page number in the Greek Lexicon (Arndt & Gingrich) followed by a letter: a, b, c or d. Each page in the lexicon is divided into two columns. The letter refers to a particular quadrant on the page, commencing at the top left-hand corner with the letter "a". Diagrammatically, the letter key operates as follows:

a	c
b	d

This has been done so that any reader unfamiliar with the Greek language may easily find the relevant term in the lexicon and examine the various shades of meanings along with their locations in the New Testament for himself.

Example: Vine's English entry: cage
Vine's Greek entry: *phulākē*
Bauer Lexicon reference number: 867c.

This tells the reader that the word "phulākē" will be found on p. 867 in the lexicon in the top right-hand quadrant of the second column.

3.1.3 **Colin Brown (CB)**

The reference number here is again a combined numeral/letter. The number refers to the page in the index of Greek words located at the back of Vol. 3. This index is divided into three columns on each page, and the letter a, b or c refers to the 1st, 2nd or 3rd column respectively, commencing on the left-hand side of each page. For easy access, the index in Colin Brown consists of each Greek word in transliterated form. The main body of this reference work also provides transliteration along with the Greek script.

Example: Vine's English entry: camel
Vine's Greek entry: *kamēlos*
Colin Brown reference number: 1253b.

This indicates that the term *kamēlos* may be found in the middle column on p. 1253 of the index to Greek words in Vol. 3. When this word is located in the index, the main reference listing will be given alongside it and the reader is then able to easily look up the term elsewhere in the dictionary.

3.1.4 **Kittel (K)**

In this case the reference is simply a straightforward page number where information on the particular term may be immediately located.

3.2. Old Testament

3.2.1 **Strongs (S)**

See above under 3.1.1.

3.2.2 **Hatch & Redpath (HR)**

This reference number in the key is crucial for the Old Testament listing since it is the prime source for discovering the "dynamic Hebrew equivalents" for each Greek term used in translating the Old Testament into Greek. The reference number is composed of *three* elements: The first of these is the page number in the concordance. The second is a letter — a, b or c, designating one of three columns into which each page of the concordance is divided. As with the Colin Brown reference, the letter "a" indicates the left-hand column, "b" the centre, "c" the right-hand one on each page. The third element is another number which may or may not be followed by a letter. In this case the number represents the designated Hebrew equivalent which is listed alongside the Greek entry. Frequently this Hebrew term may have more than one form, in which case the numeral will be followed by a, b, c . . . etc., depending on how many related forms there are to the root Hebrew word indicated by the number.

Example: Vine's English entry: captive, captivity: A. Nouns
Vine's Greek entry: 2. *aichmalōsia*
O.T. listing in key: gôlāh
H&R reference number: 38b.1a

This H&R reference indicates that the word *aichmalōsia* may be found on p. 38 of the Concordance in the second (i.e. middle) column. For those not familiar with Greek script, simply match the Vine's Greek script entry — always found in brackets alongside the transliterated form — with the Concordance listing. Then the reference "1a" informs the reader that the Hebrew equivalent term gôlāh is to be found adjacent to the Greek term *aichmalōsia* (*αιχμαλωσια*) as entry 1(a). In this case there happens to be two other variants of gôlāh viz. gālāh (1b) and gālût (1c). To discover the occurrences and frequency of the term gôlāh in the Old Testament, all one has to do is to look down the column for all the "1a" listings under the entry: *aichmalōsia*.

In addition to the instructions above there are two other important features of the Hatch & Redpath Concordance that require some explanation if confusion in the process of seeking the appropriate word entries is to be avoided.

First, in Vine's Dictionary all Greek verbs are listed in their 1st person singular present tense forms — a standard convention with New Testament Greek grammar. However, in Hatch and Redpath those same verbs are listed according to their corresponding present infinitive forms. These differences which occur at the end of each verb (i.e. as suffixes) are set out below in tabular form.

N.B.: This applies *only* to *verb forms*.

Verbal Suffixes

Vine's		**Hatch & Redpath**	
-*ω*	(-ō)	-*ειν*	(-ein)
-*εω*	(-eō)	-*εῖν*	(-ein)
-*αω*	(-aō)	-*ᾶν*	(-ān)
-*οω*	(-oō)	-*οῦν*	(-oun)
-*ομαι*	(-omai)	-*εσθαι*	(-esthai)
-*μι*	(-mi)	-*ναι*	(-nai)

Second, there are some differences in the ordering and naming of Old Testament books in the Septuagint as distinct from the English canonical listing. The result is that certain adjustments will need to be made when cross-referencing entries from the H&R Septuagint (LXX) Concordance to the English Bible. The following table lists the major variations.

LXX (H&R)	**English Bible**
1 Kings	1 Samuel
2 Kings	2 Samuel
3 Kings	1 Kings
4 Kings	2 Kings
2 Esdras (2 Es.)	Ezra

In connection with the above, whenever chapter numbers and verses in the H&R Concordance appear *in brackets* alongside other chapter/verse references this means that the LXX chapter and/or verse divisions are different from those in the English Bible. For English Bible references, the chapter/verse numbers in brackets are the correct ones to follow up. This will occur primarily in the Psalms and the Book of Jeremiah.

3.2.3 **Harris' Archer & Waltke (H)**

The reference number for the *Theological Wordbook of the Old Testament* refers not to a page number but to the corresponding *section or paragraph number* which contains a discussion or listing of the particular Hebrew term in question. The whole reference work is divided up along this organizing principle so there is little trouble in locating the word.

3.2.4 **Brown, Driver & Briggs (BD)**

In this Hebrew-English lexicon of the Old Testament the organizing principle is precisely the same as the Bauer lexicon of the Greek New Testament with the reference number plus letter a, b, c or d referring to the page number and quadrant respectively. The instructions given under 3.1.2 may be followed for this reference work in like manner.

3.3. General Reference

3.3.1 **The International Standard Bible Encyclopedia**

The reference number here is composed of *two* parts: The first refers to the particular volume of the Encyclopedia: 1, 2, 3 or 4; and the second is a page number for that particular volume.

3.3.2 **The New Bible Dictionary**

The reference here is a straightforward page reference.

3.3.3 **The Zondervan Pictorial Bible Encyclopedia**

As for 3.3.1 except that this work has *five* volumes, not four.

3.4. A Modified Hebrew Transliteration

In keeping with the format of the Greek word entries in *Vine's Dictionary*, every Hebrew word listed in the key has been transliterated into English script in order to greatly facilitate its use by those unfamiliar with the Hebrew language. The use of technical phonetic signs has been kept to a bare minimum here in order to avoid unnecessary difficulties in identifying the pronunciation and reading of the terms.

		Hebrew Letter	Transliteration	
Consonants:	א	āleph	’	
	ב	bēt	b	
	בּ		b or bb	
	ג	gîmel	g	
	גּ		g or gg	
	ד	dālet	d	
	דּ		d or dd	
	ה	hē	h	
	ו	wāw	w (pronounced ‘v’)	
	ז	zayin	z	
	ח	ḥēt	ḥ	
	ט	ṭēt	ṭ	
	י	yōd	y	
	כ	kaph	k	
	כּ		k or kk	
	ל	lāmed	l	
	מ	mēm	m	
	נ	nûn	n	
	ס	sāmek	(*)s	
	ע	ayin	c	
	פ	pēh	ph	
	פּ		p or pp	
	צ	ṣādēh	ṣ	
	ק	qōph	q	
	ר	rēsh	r	
	שׂ	sîn	(*)s	
	שׁ	shîn	(*)sh	
	ת	tāw	t	
	תּ		t or tt	
Vowels:	◌ָ		ā (long)	[e.g. father]
	◌ָ		o (short)	[e.g. top]
	◌ַ		a (short)	[e.g. hat]
	◌ֶ		e (short)	[e.g. gem]
	◌ֵ		ē (long)	[e.g. fete]
	◌ִ		i (short)	[e.g. bit]
	◌ֹ		ō (long)	[e.g. bone]
	◌ֻ		u (short)	[e.g. put]
	◌ָה		â (pure long)	
	◌ֵי ◌ֶי		ê (pure long)	
	◌ִי		î (pure long)	
	וֹ		ô (pure long)	
	וּ		û (pure long)	

N.B.: The “pure long” vowels are pronounced like the long form of English vowels.

(*) It needs to be noted that the "s" value for sāmek and sîn are not distinguished in the key. Technically the consonant is rendered "ś" in transliteration, but for the sake of simplicity this formal distinction has been discarded. Similarly the "sh" value for shîn is rendered "š" in a strict sense, but for easier recognition the form "sh" is included in preference to the technical phonetic transliteration.

S. D. Renn
N. J. Sandon
Editors

A

Notes: In the following pages † indicates that the word referred to (preposition, conjunction, or particle) is not dealt with in this volume.

¶ indicates that all the N.T. occurrences of the Greek word under consideration are mentioned under the heading or sub-heading.

ABASE

tapeinoō [ταπεινόω, 5013] signifies to make low, bring low, (*a*) of bringing to the ground, making level, reducing to a plain, as in Luke 3:5; (*b*) metaphorically in the Active Voice, to bring to a humble condition, to abase, 2 Cor. 11:7, and in the Passive, to be abased, Phil. 4:12; in Matt. 23:12; Luke 14:11; 18:14, the A.V. has "shall be abased," the R.V. "shall be humbled." It is translated "humble yourselves" in the Middle Voice sense in Jas. 4:10; 1 Pet. 5:6; "humble," in Matt. 18:4; 2 Cor. 12:21 and Phil. 2:8. See HUMBLE, LOW. ¶ Cp., *tapeinos*, lowly, *tapeinōsis*, humiliation, and *tapeinophrosunē*, humility.

NT: B.804c; CB.1271; K.1152-56.
OT: kāna': S.3665; HR.1334c.10; H.1001; BD.488b.
'ānāh: S.6031; HR.1334c.14; H.1651,1652; BD.776a.
shāphēl: S.8213; HR.1335a.20; H.2445; BD.1050a.
GEN. REF.: IS.1:3; NB.–; Z.–.

ABBA

abba [ἀββᾶ, 5] is an Aramaic word, found in Mark 14:36; Rom. 8:15 and Gal. 4:6. In the Gemara (a Rabbinical commentary on the Mishna, the traditional teaching of the Jews) it is stated that slaves were forbidden to address the head of the family by this title. It approximates to a personal name, in contrast to "Father," with which it is always joined in the N.T. This is probably due to the fact that, "Abba" having practically become a proper name, Greek-speaking Jews added the Greek word *patēr*, father, from the language they used. "Abba" is the word framed by the lips of infants, and betokens unreasoning trust; "father" expresses an intelligent apprehension of the relationship. The two together express the love and intelligent confidence of the child.

NT: B.1B; CB.1233; K.1-2.
OT: –.
GEN. REF.: IS.1:3; NB.2; Z.–.

ABHOR

1. *apostuegō* [ἀποστυγέω, 655] denotes to shudder (*apo*, from, here used intensively, *stugeō*, to hate); hence, to abhor, Rom. 12:9. ¶

NT: B.100c; CB.–; K.–.
OT: –.
GEN. REF.: IS.1:5; NB.–; Z.–.

2. *bdelussō* (βδελύσσω, 948), to render foul (from *bdeō*, to stink), to cause to be abhorred (in the Sept. in Ex. 5:21; Lev. 11:43; 20:25 etc.), is used in the Middle Voice, signifying to turn oneself away from (as if from a stench); hence to detest, Rom. 2:22. In Rev. 21:8 it denotes "to be abominable." See ABOMINABLE. ¶

NT: B.138A; CB.–; K.–.
OT: tā'ab: S.8581; HR.216a.8; H.2530; BD.1073a.
shiqqēṣ: S.8262; HR.216a.6; H.2459; BD.1055a.
GEN. REF.: IS.1:5; NB.–; Z.–.

ABIDE, ABODE

A. Verbs.

1. *menō* [μένω, 3306], used (*a*) of place, e.g. Matt. 10:11, metaphorically 1 John 2:19, is said of God, 1 John 4:15; Christ, John 6:56; 15:4, etc.; the Holy Spirit, John 1:32, 33; 14:17; believers, John 6:56; 15:4; 1 John 4:15, etc.; the Word of God, 1 John 2:14; the truth, 2 John 2, etc.; (*b*) of time; it is said of believers, John 21:22, 23; Phil. 1:25; 1 John 2:17; Christ, John 12:34; Heb. 7:24; the Word of God, 1 Pet. 1:23; sin, John 9:41; cities, Matt. 11:23; Heb. 13:14; bonds and afflictions, Acts 20:23; (*c*) of qualities; faith, hope, love, 1 Cor. 13:13; Christ's love, John 15:10; afflictions, Acts 20:23; brotherly love, Heb. 13:1; the love of God, 1 John 3:17; the truth, 2 John 2.

The R.V. usually translates it by "abide," but "continue" in 1 Tim. 2:15; in the following, the R.V. substitutes to abide for the K.J.V. to continue, John 2:12; 8:31; 15:9; 2 Tim, 3:14; Heb. 7:24; 13:14; 1 John 2:24. Cp. the noun *monē*, below. See CONTINUE, DWELL, ENDURE, REMAIN, STAND, TARRY.

NT: B.503c; CB.1258; K.581.
OT: 'āmad: S.5975; HR.910a.12; H.1637; BD.763c.
kûm: S.6965; HR.910a.15; H.1999; BD.877c.
yāshab: S.3427; HR.910a.7; H.922; BD.442a.
GEN. REF.: IS.1:7; NB.–; Z.–.

2. *epimenō* [ἐπιμένω, 1961], to abide in, continue in, tarry, is a strengthened form of

menō (*epi,* intensive), sometimes indicating perseverance in continuing, whether in evil, Rom. 6:1; 11:23; or good, Rom. 11:22; 1 Tim. 4:16. See CONTINUE, TARRY.
NT: B.296b; CB.1246; K.—.
OT: māhah: S.4102; HR.525c.1; H.1150; BD.554c.
GEN. REF.: IS.1:7; NB.—; Z.—.

3. *katamenō* [καταμένω, 2650], *kata*, down (intensive), and No. 1, is used in Acts 1:13. The word may signify constant residence, but more probably indicates frequent resort. In 1 Cor. 16:6, it denotes to wait. ¶
NT: B.414d; CB.—; K.—.
OT: yāshab: S.3427; HR.739a.3; H.922; BD.442a.
dûn: S.1777; HR.739a.1; H.426; BD.192b,c.
yā'al: S.2974; HR.739a.2; H.831; BD.383d.
GEN. REF.: IS.1:7; NB.—; Z.—.

4. *paramenō* [παραμένω, 3887], to remain beside (*para*, beside), to continue near, came to signify simply to continue, e.g., negatively, of the Levitical priests, Heb. 7:23. In Phil. 1:25, the Apostle uses both the simple verb *menō* and the compound *paramenō* (some mss. have *sumparamenō*), to express his confidence that he will "abide," and "continue to abide," with the saints. In 1 Cor. 16:6 some mss. have this word. In Jas. 1:25, of stedfast continuance in the law of liberty. See CONTINUE. ¶
NT: B.620c; CB.1262; K.581.
OT: yāshab: S.3427; HR.1062a.1; H.922; BD.442a.
'āmad: S.5975; HR.1062a.2; H.1637; BD.763c.
GEN. REF.: IS.1:7; NB.—; Z.—.

5. *hupomenō* [ὑπομένω, 5278), lit., to abide under (*hupo*, under), signifies to remain in a place instead of leaving it, to stay behind, e.g., Luke 2:43; Acts 17:14; or to persevere, Matt. 10:22; 24:13; Mark 13:13; in each of which latter it is used with the phrase "unto the end;" or to endure bravely and trustfully, e.g. Heb. 12: 2, 3, 7, suggesting endurance under what would be burdensome. See also Jas. 1:12; 5:11; 1 Pet. 2:20. Cp., *makrothumeō*, to be long-suffering. See ENDURE, SUFFER, TAKE, *Notes* (12), TARRY.
NT: B.845d; CB.1252; K.582-84.
OT: qāwāh: S.6960; HR.1415c.8; H.1994,1995; BD.875c.
yāḥal: S.3176; HR.1415c.4; H.859; BD.403d.
GEN. REF.: IS.1:7; NB.—; Z.—.

6. *prosmenō* [προσμένω, 4357], to abide still longer, continue with (*pros*, with) is used (*a*) of place, Matt. 15: 32; Mark 8:2; Acts 18:18; 1 Tim. 1:3; (*b*) metaphorically, of cleaving unto a person, Acts 11:23, indicating persistent loyalty; of continuing in a thing, Acts 13:43; 1 Tim. 5:5. See CLEAVE, CONTINUE, TARRY. ¶ In the Sept., Judg. 3:25. ¶
NT: B.717c; CB.1267; K.581-82.
OT: —.
GEN. REF.: IS.1:7; NB.—; Z.—.

7. *diatribō* [διατρίβω, 1304], lit., to wear through by rubbing, to wear away (*dia*, through, *tribō*, to rub), when used of time, to spend or pass time, to stay, is found twice in John's Gospel, 3:22 and 11:54, R.V., "tarried," instead of "continued;" elsewhere only in the Acts, eight times, 12:19; 14:3; 15:35; 16:12; 20:6; 25:6; 14. See CONTINUE, TARRY. ¶
NT: B.190a; CB.—; K.—.
OT: —.
GEN. REF.: IS.1:7; NB.—; Z.—.

8. *anastrephō* [ἀναστρέθω, 390], used once in the sense of abiding, Matt. 17:22, frequently denotes to behave oneself, to live a certain manner of life; here the most reliable mss. have *sustrephomai*, to travel about. See BEHAVE, CONVERSATION, LIVE, OVERTHROW, PASS, RETURN.
NT: B.618; CB.1235b; K.1094.
OT: shūb: S.7725; HR.82b.8; H.2340; BD.996d.
GEN. REF.: IS.1:7; NB.—; Z.—.

9. *aulizomai* [αὐλίζομαι, 835], to lodge, originally to lodge in the *aulē*, or courtyard, is said of shepherds and flocks; hence, to pass the night in the open air, as did the Lord, Luke 21:37; to lodge in a house, as of His visit to Bethany, Matt. 21:17. ¶
NT: B.121; CB.—; K.—.
OT: lûn, lîn: S.3885; HR.178b.3; H.1096; BD.533c.
GEN. REF.: IS.1:7; NB.—; Z.—.

10. *agrauleō* [ἀγραυλέω, 63], to lodge in a fold in a field (*agros*, a field, *aulē*, a fold), is used in Luke 2:8. ¶ See LODGE.
NT: B.121; CB.—; K.—.
OT: —.
GEN. REF.: IS.1:7; NB.—; Z.—.

11. *histēmi* [ἵστημι, 2476], to stand, to make to stand, is rendered "abode" in John 8:44, A.V.: "continue," in Acts 26:22. In these places the R.V. corrects to "stood" and "stand." This word is suggestive of fidelity and stability. It is rendered "lay . . . to the charge" in Acts 7:60. See APPOINT, CHARGE, ESTABLISH, HOLDEN, PRESENT, SET, STANCH, STAZ.
NT: B.381; CB.1250c; K.1082-84.
OT: 'āmad: S.5975; HR.689a.26; H.1637; BD.763c.
qûm: S.6965; HR.689a.28; H.1999; BD.877c.
nāṣab: S.5324; HR.689a.20; H.1398; BD.662a.
GEN. REF.: IS.1:7; NB.—; Z.—.

12. *poieō* [ποιέω, 4160], to do, make, is used of spending a time or tarrying, in a place, Acts 15:33; 20:3; in 2 Cor. 11:25 it is rendered "I have been (a night and a day);" a preferable translation is 'I have spent,' as in Jas. 4:13, "spend a year" (R.V.). So in Matt. 20:12. Cp., the English idiom "did one hour;" in Rev. 13:5 "continue" is perhaps the best rendering. See DO.
NT: B.680; CB.1265c; K.895-901.
OT: 'āsāh: S.6213; HR.1154a.33; H.1708,1709; BD.793c.
GEN. REF.: IS.1:7; NB.—; Z.—.

B. Noun.

monē [μονή, 3438], an abode (akin to No. 1)

is found in John 14:2, "mansions" (R.V. marg., "abiding places"), and 14:23, "abode." ¶

NT: B.527; CB.1259b; K.582.
OT: —.
GEN. REF.: IS.1:7; NB.—; Z.—.

ABILITY, ABLE

A. Nouns

1. *dunamis* [δύναμις, 1411] is (*a*) power, ability, physical or moral, as residing in a person or thing; (*b*) power in action, as, e.g., when put forth in performing miracles. It occurs 118 times in the N.T. It is sometimes used of the miracle or sign itself, the effect being put for the cause, e.g., Mark 6:5, frequently in the Gospels and Acts. In 1 Cor. 14:11 it is rendered "meaning"; "force" would be more accurate. Cp., the corresponding verbs, B. 1, 2, 3 and the adjective C. 1, below. See ABUNDANCE, DEED, MIGHT, POWER, STRENGTH, VIOLENCE, VIRTUE, WORK.

NT: B.207b; CB.1242b; K.186.
OT: ḥayil: S.2428; HR.350a.11; H.624a; BD. 298c.
ṣābā': S.6635; HR.350a.25; H.1865a,b; BD.838d.
GEN. REF.: IS.1:9; NB.—; Z.—.

2. *ischus* [ισχύς, 2479], connected with *ischō* and *echō*, to have, to hold (from the root *ech*—, signifying holding), denotes ability, force, strength; "ability" in 1 Pet. 4:11, A.V. (R.V., "strength"). In Eph. 1:19 and 6:10, it is said of the strength of God bestowed upon believers, the phrase "the power of His might" indicating strength afforded by power. In 2 Thess. 1:9, "the glory of His might" signifies the visible expression of the inherent Personal power of the Lord Jesus. It is said of angels in 2 Pet. 2:11 (cp., Rev. 18:2, A.V., "mightily"). It is ascribed to God in Rev. 5:12 and 7:12. In Mark 12:30, 33, and Luke 10:27 it describes the full extent of the power wherewith we are to love God. See MIGHT, POWER, STRENGTH. ¶

NT: B.383c; CB.1253a; K.378.
OT: kō'ah: S.3581; HR.694b.16; H.971.1; BD.470c.
'ōz: S.5794; HR.694b.21; H.1596a; BD.738d.
GEN. REF.: IS.1:9; NB.—; Z.—.

B. Verbs

1. *dunamai* [δύναμαι, 1410], to be able, to have power, whether by virtue of one's own ability and resources, e.g., Rom. 15:14; or through a state of mind, or through favourable circumstances, e.g., 1 Thess, 2:6; or by permission of law or custom, e.g., Acts 24:8, 11; or simply to be able, powerful, Matt. 3:9; 2 Tim. 3:15, etc. See CAN, MAY, POSSIBLE, POWER.

NT: B.207a; CB.1242b; K.186.
OT: yākōl: S.3201; HR.353a.4; H.866; BD.407b.
GEN. REF.: IS.1:9; NB.—; Z.—.

2. *dunamoō*, [δυναμόω, 1412], to make strong, confirm, occurs in Col. 1:11 (some authorities have the 1st aorist or momentary tense, in Heb. 11:34 also). Cp. *endunamoō*, to enable, strengthen. ¶

NT: B.208c; CB.1242b; K.186.
OT: 'āzaz: S.5810; HR.353a.2; H.1596; BD.738b.
gābar: S.1396; HR.353a.1; H.310; BD.149c.
GEN. REF.: IS.1:9; NB.—; Z.—.

3. *dunateō* [δυνατέω, 1414] signifies to be mighty, to show oneself powerful, Rom. 4:14; 2 Cor. 9:8; 13:3. See A, No. 1. ¶

NT: B.208c; CB.1242b; K.—.
OT: —.
GEN. REF.: IS.1:9; NB.—; Z.—.

4. *ischuō* [ἰσχύω, 2480], akin to A, No. 2, to be strong, to prevail, indicates a more forceful strength or ability than *dunamai*, e.g., Jas. 5:16, where it is rendered "availeth much" (i.e., "prevails greatly"). See AVAIL, CAN, DO, MAY, PREVAIL, STRENGTH, WORK.

NT: B.383d; CB.1253a; K.378.
OT: ḥāzaq: S.2388; HR.692c.6; H.636; BD.304a.
gābar: S.1396; HR.692c.5; H.310; BD.149c.
GEN. REF.: IS.1:9; NB.—; Z.—.

Note: Still stronger forms are *exischuō*, to be thoroughly strong, Eph. 3:18, "may be strong" (not simply "may be able," A.V.). ¶ ; *katischuō*, Matt. 16:18, and Luke 23:23, in the former, of the powerlessness of the gates of Hades to prevail against the Church; in the latter, of the power of a fierce mob to prevail over a weak ruler (see Notes on Galatians, by Hogg and Vine, p. 251); also Luke 21:36. The prefixed prepositions are intensive in each case. ¶

5. *echō* [ἔχω, 2192], to have, is translated "your ability" in 2 Cor. 8:11, and "ye may be able" in 2 Pet. 1:15, and is equivalent to the phrase 'to have the means of.' See CAN, HAVE.

NT: B.331d; CB.1242c; K.240.
OT: —.
GEN. REF.: IS.1:9; NB.—; Z.—.

6. *euporeō* [εὐπορέω, 2141], lit., to journey well (*eu*, well, *poreō*, to journey), hence, to prosper, is translated "according to (his) ability," in Acts 11:29. ¶

NT: B.324b; CB.—; K.—.
OT: māṣā': S.4672; HR.576a.1; H.2033; BD.592c.
GEN. REF.: IS.1:9; NB.—; Z.—.

Note: Hikanoō, corresponding to the adjective *hikanos* (see below) signifies to make competent, qualify, make sufficient; in 2 Cor. 3:6, A.V., "hath made (us) able;" R.V., "hath made us sufficient;" in Col. 1:12, "hath made (us) meet." See ENOUGH, SUFFICIENT. ¶

C. Adjectives

1. *dunatos* [δυνατός, 1415] corresponding to A, No. 1, signifies powerful. See, e.g. Rom. 4:21; 9:22; 11:23; 12:18; 15:1; 1 Cor. 1:26; 2 Cor. 9:8. See MIGHTY, POSSIBLE, POWER, STRONG.

NT: B.208c; CB.1242b; K.186.
OT: gibbōr: S.1368; HR.355c.6c; H.310b; BD.150a.
ḥayil: S.2428; HR.355c.9; H.624a; BD.298c.
GEN. REF.: IS.1:9; NB.—; Z.—.

2. *hikanos* [ἱκανός, 2426], translated "able,"

is to be distinguished from *dunatos*. While *dunatos* men as possessing power, *hikanos*, primarily, reaching to, has accordingly the meaning "sufficient." When said of things it signifies enough, e.g., Luke 22:38; when said of persons, it means "competent," "worthy," e.g., 2 Cor. 2:6, 16; 3:5; 2 Tim. 2:2. See CONTENT, ENOUGH, GOOD, GREAT, LARGE, LONG, MANY, MEET, MUCH, SECURITY, SUFFICIENT, WORTHY.

NT: B.374b; CB.1250c; K.361.
OT: day: S.1767; HR.683c.2; H.425; BD.191b.
shadday: S.7706; HR.683c.9; H.2333; BD.994d.
GEN. REF.: IS.1:9; NB.–; Z.–.

Note: Ischuros denotes strong, mighty; in an Active sense, mighty, in having inherent and moral power, e.g. Matt. 12:29; 1 Cor. 4:10; Heb. 6:18.

ABOARD

epibainō [ἐπιβαινω, 1910], to go upon (*epi*, upon, *bainō*, to go), is once translated "we went aboard," Acts 21:2, the single verb being short for going aboard ship. In ver. 6 it is rendered "we went on board;" in 27:2 "embarking;" in Matt. 21:5, "riding upon." See COME, No. 16.

NT: B.289d; CB.–; K.–.
OT: dārak: S.1869; HR.515c.1; H.453; BD.201d.
rākab: S.7392; HR.515c.10; H.2163; BD.938c.
GEN. REF.: –.

ABOLISH

katargeō [καταργέω, 2673], lit., to reduce to inactivity (*kata*, down, *argos*, inactive), is translated "abolish" in Eph. 2:15 and 2 Tim. 1:10, in the R.V. only in 1 Cor. 15:24, 26. It is rendered "is abolished" in the A.V. of 2 Cor. 3:13; the R.V. corrects to "was passing away" (marg., "was being done away"). In this and similar words no loss of being is implied, but loss of well being.

The barren tree was cumbering the ground, making it useless for the purpose of its existence, Luke 13:7; the unbelief of the Jews could not "make of none effect" the faithfulness of God, Rom. 3:3; the preaching of the Gospel could not make of none effect the moral enactments of the Law, 3:31; the Law could not make the promise of none effect, 4:14; Gal. 3:17; the effect of the identification of the believer with Christ in His death is to render inactive his body in regard to sin, Rom. 6:6; the death of a woman's first husband discharges her from the law of the husband, that is, it makes void her status as his wife in the eyes of the law, 7:2; in that sense the believer has been discharged from the Law, 7:6; God has chosen things that are not "to bring to nought things that are," i.e., to render them useless for practical purposes, 1 Cor. 1:28; the princes of this world are brought to nought, i.e., their wisdom becomes ineffective, 2:6; the use for which the human stomach exists ceases with man's death, 6:13; knowledge, prophesyings, and that which was in part were to be "done away," 1 Cor. 13:8, 10, i.e., they were to be rendered of no effect after their temporary use was fulfilled; when the Apostle became a man he did away with the ways of a child, verse 11; God is going to abolish all rule and authority and power, i.e., He is going to render them inactive, 1 Cor. 15:24; the last enemy that shall be abolished, or reduced to inactivity, is death, ver. 26; the glory shining in the face of Moses, "was passing away," 2 Cor. 3:7, the transitoriness of its character being of a special significance; so in verses 11, 13; the veil upon the heart of Israel is "done away" in Christ, ver. 14; those who seek justification by the Law are "severed" from Christ, they are rendered inactive in relation to Him, Gal. 5; 4; the essential effect of the preaching of the Cross would become inoperative by the preaching of circumcision, 5:11; by the death of Christ the barrier between Jew and Gentile is rendered inoperative as such, Eph. 2:15; the Man of Sin is to be reduced to inactivity by the manifestation of the Lord's Parousia with His people, 2 Thess. 2:8; Christ has rendered death inactive for the believer, 2 Tim. 1:10, death becoming the means of a more glorious life, with Christ; the Devil is to be reduced to inactivity through the death of Christ, Heb. 2:14. See CEASE, CUMBER, DESTROY, DO, *Note* (7), OF, NONE EFFECT, NOUGHT, PUT, No. 19, VOID. ¶

NT: B.417b; CB.1254b; K.76.
OT: –.
GEN. REF.: IS.1:13; NB.–; Z.–.

ABOMINABLE, ABOMINATION

A. Adjectives

1. *athemitos* [ἀθέμιτος, 111] occurs in Acts 10:28, "unlawful," and 1 Pet. 4:3, "abominable" (*a*, negative, *themitos*, an adjective from *themis*, "law"), hence, unlawful. See UNLAWFUL. ¶

NT: B.20d; CB.–; K.25.
OT: –.
GEN. REF.: IS.1:13; NB.5; Z.–.

2. *bdeluktos* [βδελυκτός, 947], Tit. 1:16, is said of deceivers who profess to know God, but deny Him by their works. ¶

NT: B.138a; CB.–; K.103.
OT: tō'ēbāh: S.8441; HR.215b.7; H.2530a; BD.1072d.
GEN. REF.: IS.1:13; NB.5; Z.1:19,20.

B. Verb.

bdelussō [βδελύσσω]: SEE ABHOR, No. 2.

C. Noun.

bdelugma [βδέλυγμα, 946], akin to A, No. 2 and B, denotes an object of disgust, an abomination. This is said of the image to be set up by Antichrist, Matt. 24:15; Mark 13:14; of that which is highly esteemed amongst men, in contrast to its real character in the sight of God, Luke 16:15. The constant association with idolatry suggests that what is highly esteemed among men constitutes an idol in the human heart. In Rev. 21:27, entrance is forbidden into the Holy City on the part of the unclean, or one who "maketh an abomination and a lie." It is also used of the contents of the golden cup in the hand of the evil woman described in Rev. 17:4, and of the name ascribed to her in the following verse. ¶

NT: B.137d; CB.1239a; K.103.
OT: tō'ēbāh: S.8441; HR.215b.7; H.2530a; BD.1072d.
shiqquṣ: S.8251; HR.215b.6; H.2459b; BD.1055a.
sheqeṣ: S.8263; HR.215b.6; H.2459a,b; BD.1054d.
GEN. REF.: IS.1:13; NB.5; Z.—.

For ABOUND see ABUNDANCE

ABOUT

A. Adverbs, etc.

Besides prepositions, the following signify "about":—

1. *kuklothen* [κυκλόθεν, 2943], round about, or all round (from *kuklos*, a circle; Eng., cycle), is found in the Apocalypse only, 4:3, 4, 8. ¶

NT: B.456d; CB.—; K.—.
OT: sābbîb: S.5439; HR.796b.2a; H.1456b; BD.686d.
GEN. REF.: —.

2. *kuklō* [κύκλῳ, 2944], the dative case of *kuklos* (see above), means round about, lit., in a circle. It is used in the same way as No. 1, Mark 3:34; 6:6, 36; Luke 9:12; Rom. 15:19; Rev. 4:6; 5:11; 7:11. ¶

NT: B.456d; CB.1256b; K.—.
OT: sābbîb: S.5439; HR: 796b.2a; H.1456b; BD.686d.
GEN. REF.: —.

3. *pou* [που, 4225], an indefinite particle, signifying "somewhere," somewhere about, nearly, has a limiting force, with numerals, e.g., Rom. 4:19. In referring to a passage in the O.T., it is translated "somewhere," in the R.V. of Heb. 2:6 and 4:4 (A.V., "in a certain place"); by not mentioning the actual passage referred to, the writer acknowledged the familiar acquaintance of his readers with the O.T. See PLACE.

NT: B.696b; CB.1266b; K.—.
OT: —.
GEN. REF.: —.

4. *hōs* [ὡσ, 5613], usually means "as." Used with numerals it signifies "about," e.g. Mark 5:13, 8:9; John 1:40; 6:19; 11:18; Acts 1:15; Rev. 8:1.

NT: B.897a; CB.1251b; K.—.
OT: —.
GEN. REF.: —.

5. *hōsei* [ὡσεί, 5616], "as if," before numerals, denotes about, nearly, something like, with perhaps an indication of greater indefiniteness than No. 4; e.g., Matt. 14:21; Luke 3:23; 9:14, 28; Acts 2:41; with a measure of space, Luke 22:41, "about a stone's cast." See LIKE.

NT: B.899b; CB.—; K.—.
OT: —.
GEN. REF.: —.

B. Verb.

mellō [μέλλω, 3195], signifies (*a*) of intention, to be about to do something, e.g., Acts 3:3; 18:14; 20:3; Heb. 8:5; (*b*) of certainty, compulsion or necessity, to be certain to act, e.g., John 6:71. See ALMOST, BEGIN, COME, INTEND, MEAN, MIND, POINT OF (at), READY, SHALL, SHOULD, TARRY.

NT: B.500d; CB.1258a; K.—.
OT: —.
GEN. REF.: —.

Note: Zēteō, to seek, is translated "were about" in the A.V. of Acts 27:30; R.V., correctly, "were seeking to."

ABOVE

The following adverbs have this meaning (prepositions are omitted here):—

1. *anō* [ἄνω, 507], denotes above, in a higher place, Acts 2:19 (the opposite to *katō*, below). With the article it means that which is above, Gal. 4:26; Phil. 3:14, "the high calling" (R.V. marg., "upward"); with the plural article, the things above, John 8: 23, lit., 'from the things above;' Col. 3:1, 2. With *heōs*, as far as, it is translated "up to the brim," in John 2:7. It has the meaning "upwards" in John 11:41 and Heb. 12:15. See BRIM, HIGH, UP. ¶

NT: B.76d; CB.—; K.63.
OT: —.
GEN. REF.: —.

2. *anōteron* [ἀνώτερον, 511], the comparative degree of No. 1, is the neuter of the adjective *anōteros*. It is used (*a*) of motion to a higher place, "higher," Luke 14:10; (*b*) of location in a higher place, i.e., in the preceding part of a passage, "above." Heb. 10:8. See HIGHER. ¶

NT: B.77c; CB.—; K.63.
OT: —.
GEN. REF.: —.

3. *epanō* [ἐπάνω, 1883], *epi*, over, *anō*, above, is used frequently as a preposition with a noun; adverbially, of number, e.g., Mark 14:5, R.V.; 1 Cor. 15:6.

NT: B.283b; CB.—; K.—.
OT: —.
GEN. REF.: —.

Note: In Acts 4:22, A.V., the adjective *pleion*, more, is translated "above," the R.V. corrects to "more than (forty years)."

4. *anōthen* [ἄνωθεν, 509], from above, is used of place, (*a*) with the meaning "from the top," Matt. 27:51; Mark 15:38, of the temple veil; in John 19:23, of the garment of Christ, lit., 'from the upper parts' (plural); (*b*) of things which come from heaven, or from God in Heaven, John 3:31; 19:11; Jas. 1:17; 3:15, 17. It is also used in the sense of "again." See AGAIN.

NT: B.77a; CB.1236a; K.63.
OT: –.
GEN. REF.: –.

For **ABROAD**, see the verbs with which it is used, **DISPERSE, NOISE, SCATTER, SHED, SPREAD**

ABSENCE, ABSENT

A. Noun.

apousia [ἀπουσία, 666], lit., a being away from, is used in Phil. 2:12, of the Apostle's absence from Philippi, in contrast to his *parousia*, his presence with the saints there (*parousia* does not signify merely a coming, it includes or suggests the presence which follows the arrival). ¶

NT: B.101d; CB.–; K.–.
OT: –.
GEN. REF.: –.

B. Verbs.

1. *apeimi* [ἄπειμι, 548], to be absent (*apo*, from, *eimi*, to be), is found in 1 Cor. 5:3; 2 Cor. 10:1, 11; 13:2, 10; Phil. 1:27; Col. 2:5. See GO. ¶

NT: B.83a; CB.–; K.–.
OT: –.
GEN. REF.: –.

2. *ekdēmeō* [ἐκδημέω, 1553], lit., to be away from people (*ek*, from, or out of, *dēmos*, people), hence came to mean either (*a*) to go abroad, depart; the Apostle Paul uses it to speak of departing from the body as the earthly abode of the spirit, 2 Cor. 5:8; or (*b*) to be away; in the same passage, of being here in the body and absent from the Lord (ver. 6), or being absent from the body and present with the Lord (ver. 8). Its other occurrence is in ver. 9. ¶

NT: B.238b; CB.1243c; K.149.
OT: –.
GEN. REF.: –.

C. Preposition.

ater [ἄτερ, 817], means without, Luke 22: 35, "without purse;" in ver. 6, "in the absence (of the multitude)," marg., "without tumult." See WITHOUT. ¶

NT: B.120a; CB.–; K.–.
OT: –.
GEN. REF.: –.

ABSTAIN, ABSTINENCE

apechō [ἀπέχω, 568], to hold oneself from (*apo*, from, *echomai*, the Middle Voice of *echō*, to have, i.e., to keep oneself from), in the N.T., invariably refers to evil practices, moral and ceremonial, Acts 15:20, 29; 1 Thess. 4:3; 5:22; 1 Tim. 4:3; 1 Pet. 2:11; so in the Sept. in Job 1:1; 2:3. See ENOUGH, RECEIVE. ¶

NT: B.84d; CB.1236b; K.286.
OT: sûr: S.5493; HR.122a.7; H.1480; BD.693b.
rāḥaq: S.7368; HR.122a.10; H.2151; BD.934d.
GEN. REF.: IS.1:19; NB.–; Z.–.

Note: The noun "abstinence" in Acts 27:21, A.V., translates *asitia*, "without food," R.V. (*a*, negative, *sitos*, food). Cp. *asitos*, fasting, ver. 33. ¶

ABUNDANCE, ABUNDANT, ABUNDANTLY, ABOUND

A. Nouns.

1. *hadrotēs* [ἁδρότης, 100], which, in 2 Cor. 8:20, in reference to the gifts from the church at Corinth for poor saints in Judaea, the R.V. renders "bounty" (A.V., abundance"), is derived from *hadros*, thick, fat, full-grown, rich (in the Sept. it is used chiefly of rich and great men, e.g., Jer. 5:5). In regard, therefore, to the offering in 2 Cor. 8:20 the thought is that of bountiful giving, a fat offering, not mere abundance. ¶

NT: B.18d; CB.–; K.–.
OT: –.
GEN. REF.: IS.1:15; NB.–; Z.–.

2. *perisseia* [περισσεία, 4050], an exceeding measure, something above the ordinary, is used four times; Rom. 5:17, of abundance of grace; 2 Cor. 8:2, of abundance of joy; 2 Cor. 10:15, of the extension of the Apostle's sphere of service through the practical fellowship of the saints at Corinth; in Jas. 1:21 it is rendered, metaphorically, "overflowing," A.V. "superfluity," with reference to wickedness. Some would render it "residuum," or what remains. See No. 3. ¶

3. *perisseuma* [περίσσευμα, 4051], denotes abundance in a slightly more concrete form, 2 Cor. 8:13, 14, where it stands for the gifts in kind supplied by the saints. In Matt. 12: 34 and Luke 6:45 it is used of the abundance of the heart; in Mark 8:8, of the broken pieces left after feeding the multitude "that remained over" (A.V. "that was left"). See REMAIN. ¶ In the Sept., Eccl. 2:15. ¶

4. *huperbolē* [ὑπερβολή, 5236], lit., a throwing beyond (*huper*, over, *ballō*, to throw), denotes excellence, exceeding greatness, of the power of God in His servants, 2 Cor. 4:7; of the

revelations given to Paul, 12:7 with the preposition *kata*, the phrase signifies "exceeding," Rom. 7:13; "still more excellent," 1 Cor. 12:31; "exceedingly," 2 Cor. 1:8; "beyond measure," Gal. 1:13; and, in a more extended phrase, "more and more exceedingly," 2 Cor. 4:17. See EXCELLENCY, EXCELLENT, MEASURE. ¶

NT: B.840b; CB.–; K.1230.
OT: –.
GEN. REF.: IS.1:15; NB.–; Z.–.

B. Verbs.

1. *perisseuō* [περισσεύω, 4052], akin to A, Nos. 2 and 3, is used intransitively (*a*) of exceeding a certain number, or measure, to be over, to remain, of the fragments after feeding the multitude (cp. *perisseuma*), Luke 9:17; John 6:12, 13; to exist in abundance; as of wealth, Luke 12:15; 21:4; of food, 15:17. In this sense it is used also of consolation, 2 Cor. 1:5; of the effect of a gift sent to meet the need of saints, 2 Cor. 9:12; of rejoicing, Phil. 1:26; of what comes or falls to the lot of a person in large measure, as of the grace of God and the gift by the grace of Christ, Rom. 5:15; of the sufferings of Christ, 2 Cor. 1:5. In Mark 12:14 and Luke 21:4, the R.V. has "superfluity."

(*b*) to redound to, or to turn out abundantly for something, as of the liberal effects of poverty, 2 Cor. 8:2; in Rom. 3:7, argumentatively, of the effects of the truth of God, as to whether God's truthfulness becomes more conspicuous and His glory is increased through man's untruthfulness; of numerical increase, Acts 16:5.

(*c*) to be abundantly furnished, to abound in a thing, as of material benefits, Luke 12:15; Phil. 4:18 of spiritual gifts, 1 Cor. 14:12, or to be pre-eminent, to excel, to be morally better off, as regards partaking of certain meats, 1 Cor. 8:8, "are we the better"; to abound in hope, Rom. 15:13; the work of the Lord, 1 Cor. 15:58; faith and grace, 2 Cor. 8:7; thanksgiving, Col. 2:7; walking so as to please God, Phil. 1:9; 1 Thess. 4:1, 10; of righteousness, Matt. 5:20; of the Gospel, as the ministration of righteousness, 2 Cor. 3:9, "exceed."

It is used transitively, in the sense of to make to abound, e.g., to provide a person richly so that he has abundance, as of spiritual truth, Matt. 13:12; the right use of what God has entrusted to us, 25:29; the power of God in conferring grace, 2 Cor. 9:8; Eph. 1:8; to make abundant or to cause to excel, as of the effect of grace in regard to thanksgiving, 2 Cor. 4:15; His power to make us to abound in love, 1 Thess. 3:12. See BETTER, ENOUGH, EXCEED, EXCEL, INCREASE,, REDOUND, REMAIN. ¶

NT: B.650c; CB.1263c; K.828.
OT: yātar: S.3498; HR.1126b.1; H.836; BD.451b.
GEN. REF.: IS.1:15; NB.–; Z.–.

2. *huperperisseuō* [ὑπερπερισσεύω, 5248], a strengthened form of No. 1, signifies to abound exceedingly, Rom. 5:20, of the operation of grace; 2 Cor. 7:4, in the Middle Voice, of the Apostle's joy in the saints. See JOYFUL. ¶

NT: B.841d; CB.1252a; K.828.
OT: –.
GEN. REF.: IS.1:15; NB.–; Z.–.

3. *pleonazō* [πλεονάζω, 4121], from *pleion*, or *pleon*, "more" (greater in quantity), akin to *pleō*, to fill, signifies, (*a*) intransitively, to superabound, of a trespass or sin, Rom. 5:20; of grace, Rom. 6:1; 2 Cor. 4:15; of spiritual fruit, Phil. 4:17; of love, 2 Thess. 1:3; of various fruits, 2 Pet. 1:8; of the gathering of the manna, 2 Cor. 8:15, "had . . . over"; (*b*) transitively, to make to increase, 1 Thess. 3:12. See INCREASE, OVER. ¶

NT: B.667; CB.1265b; K.864.
OT: ʿādaph: S.5736; HR.1141c.3; H.1568; BD.727a.
rābāh: S.7235; HR.1141c.4; H.2103, 2104; BD.915a.
GEN. REF.: IS.1:15; NB.–; Z.–.

4. *huperpleonazō* [ὑπερπλεονάζω, 5250], a strengthened form of No. 3, signifying to abound exceedingly, is used in 1 Tim. 1:14, of the grace of God. ¶

NT: B.842a; CB.1252a; K.864.
OT: –
GEN. REF.: IS.1:15; NB.–; Z.–.

5. *plēthunō* [πληθύνω, 4129], a lengthened form of *plēthō*, to fill, akin to No. 3, and to *plēthos*, a multitude, signifies to increase, to multiply, and, in the Passive Voice, to be multiplied, e.g., of iniquity, Matt. 24:12, R.V. See MULTIPLY.

NT: B.669a; CB.1265b; K.866.
OT: rābāh: S.7235; HR.1141c.4; H.2103, 2104; BD.915a.
GEN. REF.: IS.1:15; NB.–; Z.–.

Note: Huperballō, akin to A, No. 4, to excel, is translated "passeth" in Eph. 3:19. See also 2 Cor. 3:10 (R.V., "surpasseth;" A.V., "excelleth"); 9:14, "exceeding;" Eph. 1:19; 2:7. See EXCEED, EXCEL. ¶

C. Adjectives.

1. *perissos* [περισσός, 4053], akin to B, No. 1, "abundant," is translated "advantage" in Rom. 3:1, "superfluous" in 2 Cor. 9:1. See ADVANTAGE, MORE, B, No. 2, SUPERFLUOUS.

NT: B.651b; CB.1263c; K.828.
OT: yeter: S.3499; HR.1126c.1a; H.936a; BD.451d.
yātar: S.3498; HR.1126b.1; H.836; BD.451b.
GEN. REF.: IS.1:15; NB.–; Z.–.

2. *perissoteros* [περισσότερος, 4504], the comparative degree of No. 1, is translated as follows: in Matt. 11:9, and Luke 7:26, R.V., "much more" (A.V., "more"); in Mark 12:40,

"greater;" in Luke 12:4, 48, "more;" in 1 Cor. 12:23, 24, "more abundant;" in 2 Cor. 2:7, "overmuch;" in Cor. 10:8, R.V., "abundantly," A.V., "more." See GREATER, MORE, OVERMUCH.

NT: B.651c; CB.1263c; K.828.
OT: —.
GEN. REF.: IS.1:15; NB.—; Z.—.

D. Adverbs.

1. *perissōs* [περισσως, 4057], corresponding to Adjective No. 1 above, is found in Matt. 27:23, R.V., "exceedingly," A.V., "the more;" Mark 10:26, R.V., "exceedingly," A.V., "out of measure;" 15:14; Acts. 26:11, "exceedingly." See EXCEEDINGLY, B, No. 4, MEASURE, B, No. 2, MORE. ¶

NT: B.651d; CB.1263c; K.828.
OT: —.
GEN. REF.: IS.1:15; NB.—; Z.—.

2. *perissoteros* [περισσοτέρος, 4056], the adverbial form of No. 2, above, means 'more abundantly;' in Heb. 2:1, lit., 'we ought to give heed more abundantly.' It is most frequent in 2 Cor. In 11:23, see the R.V. See EARNEST, EXCEEDINGLY, RATHER.

NT: B.651d; CB.1263c; K.828.
OT: —.
GEN. REF.: IS.1:15; NB.—; Z.—.

3. *huperperissōs* [ὑπερπερισσως, 5249], a strengthened form of No. 1, signifies "exceeding abundantly," Mark 7:37. ¶

NT: B.842a; CB.1252a; K.828.
OT: —.
GEN. REF.: IS.1:15; NB.—; Z.—.

4. *huperekperissou* [ὑπερεκπερισσου, 5240], a still further strengthened form, is translated "exceeding abundantly" in Eph. 3:20; "exceedingly" in 1 Thess. 3:10; 5:13. See EXCEEDINGLY. ¶

NT: B.840c; CB.1252a; K.828.
OT: —.
GEN. REF.: IS.1:15; NB.—; Z.—.

Note: Huperballontōs, akin to A, No. 4, denotes "above measure," 2 Cor. 11:23. ¶

5. *plousiōs* [πλουσίως, 4146], connected with *ploutos*, riches, is rendered "abundantly," Tit. 3:6 and 2 Pet. 1:11; "richly," Col. 3:16 and 1 Tim. 6:17. It is used of (*a*) the gift of the Holy Spirit; (*b*) entrance into the coming Kingdom; (*c*) the indwelling of the Word of Christ; (*d*) material benefits. See RICHLY. ¶

NT: B.673d; CB.1265b; K.873.
OT: 'āshîr: S.6223; HR.1150b.3; H.1714b; BD.799b.
GEN. REF.: IS.1:15; NB.—; Z.—.

Notes: (1) *Dunamis*, power, is translated "abundance" in the A.V. of Rev. 18:3 (R.V. and A.V. marg., "power").

(2) *Polus*, much, many, is rendered "abundant" in 1 Pet. 1:3, A.V. (marg., "much"), R.V., "great."

(3) For the verbs *plouteō* and *ploutizō*, see RICH and ENRICH.

(4) For *ploutos*, wealth, riches, and *plousios*, rich, see RICH.

ABUSE, ABUSERS

A. Verb.

katachraomai [καταχράομαι, 2710], lit., to use overmuch (*kata*, down, intensive, *chraomai*, to use), is found in 1 Cor. 7:31, with reference to the believer's use of the world (marg., "use to the full"), and 1 Cor. 9:18, A.V., "abuse," R.V., "use to the full." See USE. ¶

B. Nown.

For the noun *arsenokoitēs*, see 1 Cor. 6:9, and 1 Tim. 1:10. ¶

For ABYSS see BOTTOM.

ACCEPT, ACCEPTED, ACCEPTABLE

A. Verbs.

1. *dechomai* [δέχομαι, 1209] signifies to accept, by a deliberate and ready reception of what is offered (cp. No. 4), e.g., 1 Thess. 2:13, R.V., "accepted;" 2 Cor. 8:17; 11:4. See RECEIVE, TAKE.

NT: B.177b; CB.1240b; K.146.
OT: lāqaḥ: S.3947; HR.294c.4; H.1124; BD.542c.
GEN. REF.: IS.1:22; NB.—; Z.—.

2. *apodechomai* [ἀποδέχομαι, 588], consisting of apo, from, intensive, and No. 1, expresses *dechomai* more strongly, signifying to receive heartily, to welcome, Luke 8:40 (R.V., "welcomed" A.V., "gladly received"); Acts 2:41; 18:27; 24:3; 28:30. See RECEIVE WELCOME.

NT: B.177b; CB.1240b; K.146.
OT: —.
GEN. REF.: IS.1:22; NB.8; Z.—.

3. *prosdechomai* [προσδέχομαι, 4327], *pros*, to, and No. 1, to accept favourably, or receive to oneself, is used of things future, in the sense of expecting; with the meaning of accepting, it is used negatively in Heb. 11:35, "not accepting their deliverance;" of receiving, e.g., Luke 15:2; Rom. 16:2; Phil. 2:29. See ALLOW, LOOK (for), RECEIVE, TAKE, WAIT.

NT: B.712b; CB.1267a; K.146.
OT: rāṣāh: S.7521; HR.1212c.7; H.2207; BD.953a.
GEN. REF. IS.1:22; NB.8; Z.—.

4. *lambanō* [λαμβάνω, 2983], almost synonymous with *dechomai*, is distinct from it, in that it sometimes means to receive as merely a self-prompted action, without necessarily signifying a favourable reception, Gal. 2:6. See ATTAIN, CALL, CATCH, HAVE, HOLD, OBTAIN, RECEIVE, TAKE.

NT: B.464a; CB.1256c; K.495.
OT: lāqaḥ: S.3947; HR.847c.11; H.1124; BD.542c.
nāśā': S.5375; HR.847a.17; H1421; BD.669d.
GEN. REF.: IS.1:22; NB.8; Z.—.

Note: The verb *charitoō*, to make acceptable, is translated "made accepted," in Eph. 1:6, A.V.; R.V., "freely bestowed."

B. Adjectives.

The following adjectives are translated "acceptable," or in some cases "accepted." The R.V. more frequently adopts the former rendering.

1. *dektos [δεκτός*, 1184], akin to No. 1, denotes a person or thing who has been regarded favourably, Luke 4:19, 24; Acts 10:35; 2 Cor. 6:2 (in this verse No. 3 is used in the second place); Phil. 4:18. ¶

NT: B.174b; CB.1240c; K.146.
OT: rāṣōn: S.5722; HR. 289c.2c; H.2207a; BD.953c.
GEN. REF.: IS.1:22; NB.8; Z.—.

2. *apodektos* [*ἀποδεκτός*, 587], a strengthened form of No. 1 (*apo*, from, used intensively), signifies acceptable, in the sense of what is pleasing and welcome, 1 Tim. 2:3; 5:4. ¶

NT: B.90a; CB.1236a; K.146.
OT: —.
GEN. REF.: IS.1.22; NB.8; Z.—.

3. *euprosdektos* [*εὐπρόσδεκτος*, 2144], a still stronger form of No. 1, signifies a very favourable acceptance (*eu*, well, *pros*, towards, No. 1), Rom. 15:16, 31; 2 Cor. 6:2; 8:12; 1 Pet. 2:5. ¶

NT: B.324c; CB.1247b; K.146.
OT: —.
GEN. REF.: IS.1:22; NB.8; Z.—.

4. *euarestos* [*εὐάρεστος*, 2101], *eu*, well, *arestos*, pleasing, is rendered "acceptable," in the A.V. of Rom. 12:1, 2; 14:18; in 2 Cor. 5:9, "accepted"; Eph. 5:10. The R.V. usually has "well-pleasing"; so A.V. and R.V. in Phil. 4:18; Col. 3:20; in Tit. 2:9, "please well," A.V.; Heb. 13:21. See PLEASING. ¶

NT: B.318d; CB.1247a; K.77.
OT: —.
GEN. REF.: IS.1:22; NB.8; Z.—.

C. Adverb.

euarestōs [*εὐαρέστως*, 2101], corresponding to B, No. 4, is used in Heb. 12:28, "so as to please." See PLEASE ¶

NT: B.318d; CB.—; K.77.
OT: —.
GEN. REF.: IS.1:22; NB.8; Z.—.

D. Nouns.

1. *apodochē* [*ἀποδοχή*, 594], akin to B, No. 2, signifies worthy to be received with approbation, acceptation, 1 Tim. 1:15; 4:9. The phrase in 1:15 is found in a writing in the 1st century expressing appreciation of a gift from a princess. ¶

NT: B.91a; CB.1236c; K.146.
OT: —.
GEN. REF.: IS.1:22; NB.8; Z.—.

2. *charis* [*χάρις*, 5485], grace, indicating favour on the part of the giver, thanks on the part of the receiver, is rendered "acceptable" in 1 Pet. 2:19, 20. See margin. See BENEFIT, FAVOUR, GRACE, LIBERALITY, PLEASURE, THANK.

NT: B.877b; CB.1239c; K.1298.
OT: ḥhēn: S.2580; HR.1455a.2; H.694a; BD.336b.
GEN. REF.: IS.2:547; NB.491; Z.—.

ACCESS

prosagōgē [*προσαγωγή*, 4318], lit., a leading or bringing into the presence of (*pros*, to, *ago*, to lead), denotes access, with which is associated the thought of freedom to enter through the assistance or favour of another. It is used three times, (*a*) Rom. 5:2, of the access which we have by faith, through our Lord Jesus Christ, into grace; (*b*) Eph. 2:18, of our access in one Spirit through Christ, unto the Father; (*c*) Eph. 3:12, of the same access, there said to be "in Christ," and which we have "in confidence through our faith in Him." This access involves the acceptance which we have in Christ with God, and the privilege of His favour towards us. Some advocate the meaning "introduction." ¶

NT: B.711c; CB.1267a; K.20.
OT: nāgash: S.5066; HR.1211a.6; H.1297; BD.620c.
qārab: S.7126; HR.1211b.111 H.2065; BD.897b.
GEN. REF.: IS.1:20; NB.9; Z.—.

ACCOMPANY

A. Verbs.

1. *sunepomai* [*συνέπομαι*, 4902], lit., to follow with (*sun*, with, *hepomai*, to follow), hence came to mean simply to accompany, Acts 20:4. ¶

NT: B.787c; CB.—; K.—.
OT: —.
GEN. REF.: —.

2. *sunerchomai* [*συνέρχομαι*, 4905], chiefly used of assembling together, signifies to accompany, in Luke 23:55; John 11:33; Acts 9:39; 10:45; 11:12; 15:38; 21:16. In Acts 1:21 it is said of men who had "companied with" the Apostles all the time the Lord Jesus was with them. See ASSEMBLE, COME, COMPANY, GO, RESORT.

NT: B.788a; CB.1270c; K.257.
OT: hālak: S.2505; HR.1314a.3; H.669; BD.229d.
'āsaph: S.622; HR. 1314a.1; H.140; BD.62a.
GEN. REF.: —.

3. *echō* [*ἔχω*, 2192], to have, is rendered "accompany," in Heb. 6:9, "things that accompany salvation." The margin gives perhaps the better sense, "things that are near to salvation."

NT: B.331d; CB.1242d; K.286.
OT: —.
GEN. REF.: —.

4. *propempō* [*προπέμπω*, 4311], translated "accompanied," in Acts 20:38, A.V., lit. means "to send forward"; hence, of assisting a person

on a journey either (*a*) in the sense of fitting him out with the requisites for it, or (*b*) actually accompanying him for part of the way. The former seems to be indicated in Rom. 15:24 and 1 Cor. 16:6, and ver. 11, where the R.V. has "set him forward." So in 2 Cor. 1:16 and Tit. 3:13, and of John' exhortation to Gaius concerning travelling evangelists, "whom thou wilt do well to set forward on their journey worthily of God," 3 John 6, R.V. While personal accompaniment is not excluded, practical assistance seems to be generally in view, as indicated by Paul's word to Titus to set forward Zenas and Apollos on their journey and to see "that nothing be wanting unto them." In regard tgo the parting of Paul from the elders of Ephesus at Miletus, personal accompaniment is especially in view, perhaps not without the suggestion of assistance, Acts 20:38, R.V., "brought him on his way; "accompaniment" is also indicated in 21:5; "they all with wives and children brought us on our way, till we were out of the city." In Acts 15:3, both ideas perhaps are suggested. See BRING, CONDUCT ¶

NT: B.709b; CB.–; K.–.
OT: –.
GEN. REF.: –.

ACCOMPLISH, ACCOMPLISHMENT

A. Verbs.

1. *exartizō* [ἐξαρτίζω, 1822], to fit out, (from *ek*, out, and a verb derived from *artos* a joint), hence means to furnish completely, 2 Tim. 3:17, or to accomplish, Acts 21:5, there said of a number of days, as if to render the days complete by what was appointed for them. See FURNISH ¶ In the Sept., Ex. 28:7. ¶

NT: B.273c; CB.1247c; K.80.
OT: ḥābar: S.2266; HR.490a.1; H.598; BD.287d.
GEN. REF.: IS.1:28; NB.–; Z.–.

2. *plēroō* [πληρόω, 4137], to fulfil, to complete, carry out to the full (as well as to fill), is translated "perfect" in Rev. 3:2, A.V.; R.V., "I have found no works of thine fulfilled before My God"; "accomplish" in Luke 9:31. See COMPLETE, END, EXPIRE, FILL, FULFIL, FULL, PREACH.

NT: B.670c; CB.1265b; K.867.
OT: mālē': S.4390; HR.1147c.2; H.1195; BD.569d.
GEN. REF.: IS.1:28; NB.–; Z.–.

Note: Its strengthened form, *ekplēroō*, to fulfil, lit., fill out, is used in Acts 13:33, of the fulfilment of a Divine promise of the resurrection of Christ.

3. *teleō* [τελέω, 5055], to finish, to bring an end (*telos*, an end), frequently signifies, not merely to terminate a thing, but to carry out a thing to the full. It is used especially in the Apocalypse, where it occurs eight times, and is rendered "finish" in 10:7; 11:7, and in the R.V. of 15:1, which rightly translates it "(in them) is finished (the wrath of God)." So in ver. 8; in 17:17, R.V., "accomplish," and "finish" in 20:3, 5, 7; in Luk3 2:39, R.V., "accomplish," for A.V., "performed." See END, EXPIRE, FILL, FINISH, FULFIL, GO, No. 5, PAY, PERFORM.

NT: B.810d; CB.1271b; K.1161.
OT: kālāh: S.3615; HR.1342c.3; H.982-984; BD.477b.
ṣamad: S.6775; HR.1342c.6; H.1927; BD.855a.
GEN. REF.: IS.1:28; NB.–; Z.–.

4. *epiteleō* [ἐπιτελέω, 2005], *epi*, up, intensive, and No. 3, is a strengthened form of that verb, in the sense of "accomplishing." The fuller meaning is to accomplish perfectly; in Rom. 15:28, R.V., "accomplish"; "perfecting" in 2 Cor. 7:1; "complete" in 8:6 and 11;"completion" in the latter part of this 11th verse, which is better than "performance"; "perfected" in Gal. 3:3; "perfect" in Phil. 1:6. In Heb. 8:5 the margin rightly has "complete" instead of "make," with regard to the Tabernacle. In Heb. 9:6 it is translated "accomplish" and in 1 Pet. 5:9. See COMPLETE, DO, FINISH, MAKE, PERFECT, PERFORM. ¶

NT: B.302b; CB.1246a; K.1161.
OT: 'āsāh: S.6213; HR.535a.5; H.1708,1709; BD.793c.
pā'al: S.6466; HR.535a.6; H.1792; BD.821b.
GEN. REF.: IS.1:28; NB.–; Z.–.

5. *teleioō* [τελειόω, 5048], through distinct grammatically from *teleō*, has much the same meaning. The main distinction is that *teleō* more frequently signifies to fulfil, *teleioō*, more frequently, to make perfect, one of the chief features of the Epistle to the Hebrews, where it occurs nine times. It is rendered "accomplish" in the R.V. of John 4:34; 5:36; 17:4, and Acts 20:24. See CONSECRATE, FINISH, FULFIL, PERFECT.

NT: B.809d; CB.1271b; K.1161.
OT: mālē': S.4390; HR.1343a.3; H.1195; BD.569d.
tāmam: S.8552; HR.1343a.7; H.2522; BD.1070b.
GEN. REF.: IS.1:28; NB.–; Z.–.

6. *plīyhō* [πλήθω, 4130], to fulfil, is translated "accomplished" in the A.V. of Luke 1:23; 2:6, 21, 22 (R.V., "fulfilled"). See FILL, No. 5, FURNISH, *Note*.

NT: B.658a; CB.1265a; K.–.
OT: mālē': S.4390; HR.1133b.1; H.1195; BD.569d.
sāba: S.7646; HR.1133b.3; H.2231; BD.956b.
GEN. REF.: –.

B. Noun.

ekplērōsis [ἐκπλήρωσις, 1604], see A, No.2, Note, means an entire fulfilment (*ek*, out, *plērosis*, Acts 21:26, of the fulfilment of days of purification. ¶

NT: B.244b; CB.–; K.867.
OT: –.
GEN. REF.: IS.1:28; NB.–; Z.–.

ACCORD

A. Adverb.

homothumadon [ὁμοθυμαδόν, 3661], of one accord (from *homos*, same, *thumos*, mind), occurs eleven times, ten in the Acts, 1:14; 2:46; 4:24; 5:12; 7:57; 8:6; 12:20; 15:25; 18:12; 19:29, and the other in Rom. 15:6, where, for A.V., "with one mind," the R.V. has "with one accord," as throughout the Acts. See MIND. ¶

NT: B.566c; CB.1251a; K.684.
OT: yaḥad: S.3162; HR.992b.1a; H.858b; BD.403a.
GEN. REF.: IS.1:28; NB.–; Z.–.

Note: In Acts 2:1, the adverb *homou*, "together," is so rendered in the R.V., for A.V., "of one accord."

B. Adjectives.

"Of one's own accord."

1. *authairetos* [αὐθάιρετος, 830], from *autos*, self, and *haireomai*, to choose, self-chosen, voluntary, of one's own accorfd, occurs in 2 Cor. 8:3, and 17, of the churches of Macedonia as to their gifts for the poor saints in Judaea, and of Titus in his willingness to go and exhort the church in Corinth concerning the matter. In 8:3 the R.V. translates it "(gave) of their own accord," consistently with the rendering in ver. 17. See WILLING. ¶

NT: B.121a; CB.–; K.–.
OT: –.
GEN. REF.: IS.1:28; NB.–; Z.–.

2. *automatos* [αὐτομάτος, 844], from *autos*, self, and a root *ma*—, signifying desire, denotes of oneself, moved by one's own impulse. It occurs in Mark 4:28, of the power of the earth to produce plants and fruits of itself; Acts 12:10, of the door which opened of its own accord. See SELF. ¶ In the Sept., Lev. 25:5, "spontaneous produce"; Ver. 11, "produce that comes of itself"; Josh. 6:5; 2 Kings 19:29, "(that which groweth) of itself"; Job 24:24, of an ear of corn "(falling off) of itself (from the stalk)." ¶

NT: B.122c; CB.1238b; K.–.
OT: sāphiyaḥ: S.5599; HR.179c.1; H.1533b; BD.705b.
GEN. REF.: IS.1:22; NB.–; Z.–.

3. *sumpsuchos* [σύμψυχος, 4861], lit., fellow-souled or minded (*sun*, with, *psuchē*, the soul), occurs in Phil. 2:2, "of one accord." ¶

NT: B.781b; CB.1270b; K.–.
OT: –.
GEN. REF.: –.

ACCORDING AS

1. *kathoti* [καθότι, 2530], from *kata*, according to, and *hoti*, that, lit., because that, Luke 1:7; 19:9; Acts 2:24, is translated "according as" in Acts 2:45, R.V. (A.V., "as") and in 4:35; "inasmuch as." 17:31. ¶

NT: B.391b; CB.–; K.–.
OT: –.
GEN. REF.: –.

2. *kathōs* [καθώς, 2531], from *kata*, according to, and *hōs*, as, signifies "according as" or "even as," e.g., 1 Cor. 1:31; 2 Cor. 9:7.

NT: B.391b; CB.1254c; K.–.
OT: –.
GEN. REF.: –.

3. *hōs* [ὡς, 5613], is sometimes rendered "according as," e.g., Rev. 22:12; in 2 Pet. 1:3, the R.V. has "seeing that," for the A.V. "according as."

NT: B.897a; CB.1251b; K.–.
OT: –.
GEN. REF.: –.

4. *katho* [καθό]: see INASMUCH AS.

ACCORDING TO: See Note † p. 9.

ACCOUNT (-ED) (Verbs and Noun)

A. Verbs.

1. *dokeō* [δοκέω, 1380], primarily, to be of opinion,, think, suppose, also signifies to seem, be accounted, reputed, translated "accounted" in Mark 10:42; Luke 22:24. It is not used ironically here, nor in Gal. 2:2, 6, 9, "those who were of repute." See REPUTE, SEEM, SUPPOSE, THINK.

NT: B.201d; CB.1242a; K.178.
OT: tôb: S.2896; HR.339b.4; H.793a; BD.373b.
nādab: S.5068; HR.339b.6; H.1299; BD.621c.
GEN. REF.: –.

2. *ellogeō (or-aō)* [ἐλλογέω, 1677], to put to a person's account, Philm. 18, is used of sin in Rom. 5:13, "reckon" (A.V., "impute"). See IMPUTE, No. 2. ¶

NT: B.252b; CB.1244b; K.229.
OT: –.
GEN. REF.: –.

3. *hēgeomai* [ἡγέομαι, 2233], primarily signifies to lead; then, to consider; it is translated "accounting" in Heb. 11:26, R.V. (A.V., "esteeming"); 2 Pet. 3:15, "account." See CHIEF, COUNT, ESTEEM, GOVERNOR, JUDGE, RULE, SUPPOSE, THINK.

NT: B.343c; CB.1249c; K.303.
OT: māshal: S.4910; HR.602c.20; H.1258,1259; BD.605c.
nāgîd: S.5051; HR.602c.21; H.1289b; BD.617d.
rō'sh: S.7218; HR.602c.31; H.2097; BD.910c.
GEN. REF.: –.

4. *logizomai* [λογίζομαι, 3049], primarily signifies to reckon, whether by calculation or imputation, e.g., Gal. 3:6 (R.V., "reckoned"); then, to deliberate, and so to suppose, account, Rom. 8:36; 14:14 (A.V., "esteemeth"); 1 Cor. 4:1; Heb. 11:19; John 11:50 (A.V., "consider"); Acts 19:27 ("made of no account"; A.V., "despised"); 1 Pet. 5:12 (A.V., "suppose"). It is used of love in 1 Cor. 13:5, as not taking account of evil, R.V. (A.V., "thinketh"). In 2 Cor. 3:5 the Apostle uses it in repudiation of the idea that he and fellow-servants of God are so self-sufficient as to "account anything" (R.V.)

as from themselves (A.V., "think"), i.e., as to attribute anything to themselves. Cp. 12:6. In 2 Tim. 4:16 it is used of laying to a person's "account" (R.V.) as a change against him (A.V., "charge").

NT: B.475d; CB.1257a; K.536.
OT: ḥashab: S.2803; HR.880a.2; H.767; BD.362d.
GEN. REF.: –.

Note: In Phil. 4:8 it signifies to think upon a matter by way of taking account of its character (R.V. margin). See CONCLUDE, COUNT, CHARGE, ESTEEM, IMPUTE, NUMBER, REASON, RECKON, THINK, SUPPOSE.

5. *kataxioō* [καταζιόω, 2661], denotes to account worthy (*kata*, intensive, *axios*, worthy), to judge worthy, Luke 20:35; some mss. have it in 21:36 (so the A.V.); the most authentic mss. have the verb *katischuō*, to prevail; Acts 5:41, "were counted worthy"; so 2 Thess. 1:5. ¶

NT: B.425c; CB.1254c; K.63.
OT: –.
GEN. REF.: –.

6. *exoutheneō* [ἐζουθενέω, 1418], to make of no account, frequently signifies to despise. In 1 Cor. 6:4, it is used, not in a contemptuous sense, but of Gentile judges, before whom the saints are not to go to law with one another, such magistrates having no place, and therefore being "of no account" (R.V.), in the church. The Apostle is not speaking of any believers as "least esteemed" (A.V.). In 2 Cor. 10:10, for A.V., "contemptible," the R.V. suitably has "of no account." See DESPISE.

NT: B.277c; CB.1247c; K.–.
OT: bûz: S.936; HR.500b.1; H.213; BD.100b.
bāzāh: S.959; HR.500b.3; H.224; BD.102b.
mā'as: S.3988; HR.500b.5; H.1139,1140; BD.549b.
GEN. REF.: –.

B. Noun.

logos [λόγος, 3056], a word or saying, also means an account which one gives by word of mouth (cp. No. 4), Matt. 12:36; Matt. 18:23, R.V., "reckoning"; 16:2; Acts 19:40; 20:24 (A.V., "count"); Rom. 14:12; Phil. 4:17; Heb. 13:17; 1 Pet. 4:5. See CAUSE, COMMUNICATION, DO, DOCTRINE, FAME, INTENT, MATTER, MOUTH, PREACHING, QUESTION, REASON, RECKONING, RUMOUR, SAYING, SHEW, SPEECH, TALK, THING, TIDINGS, TREATISE, UTTERANCE, WORD, WORK.

NT: B.477a; CB.1257a; K.505.
OT: dābār: S.1697; HR.881c.2; H.399a; BD.180b.
GEN. REF.: –.

ACCURATELY

akribōs [ἀκριβῶς, 199], is correctly translated in the R.V. of Luke 1:3, "having traced the course of all things accurately" (A.V., "having had perfect understanding"). It is used in Matt. 2:8, of Herod's command to the wise men as to searching for the young Child (R.V., "carefully," A.V., "diligently"); in Acts 18:25, of Apollos' teaching of "the things concerning Jesus" (R.V., "carefully," A.V., "diligently"); in Eph. 5:15, of the way in which believers are to walk (R.V., "carefully"; A.V., "circumspectly"); in 1 Thess. 5:2, of the knowledge gained by the saints through the Apostle's teaching concerning the Day of the Lord (R.V. and A.V., "perfectly). The word expresses that accuracy which is the outcome of carefulness. It is connected with *akros*, pointed.

This word and its other grammatical forms, *akribeia*, *akibēs*, *akribesteron* and *akriboō*, are used especially by Luke, who employs them eight times out of the thirteen in the N.T.; Matthew uses them three times, Paul twice. See CAREFUL, DILIGENT, EXACTLY, PERFECT. ¶

NT: B.33b; CB.–; K.–.
OT: yāṭab: S.3190; HR.50c.1; H.863; BD.405c.
GEN. REF.: –.

For **ACCURSED** see **CURSE,** A, No. 3

ACCUSATION, ACCUSE

A. Nouns.

1. *aitia* [αἰτία, 156], probably has the primary meaning of a cause, especially an occasion of something evil, hence a charge, an accusation. It is used in a forensic sense, of (*a*) an accusation, Acts 25:18 (R.V., "charge"), 27; (*b*) a crime, Matt. 27:37; March 15:26; John 18:38; 19:4, 6; Acts 13:28; 23:28; 28:18. See CASE, CAUSE, CHARGE, CRIME, FAULT.

NT: B.26b; CB.1234a; K.–.
OT: 'āwōn: S.5771; HR.38a.1; H.1577a; BD.730d.
'āshaq: S.6231; HR.38a.2; H.1713; BD.798d.
GEN. REF.: –.

2. *aitiōma* [αἰτιώμα, 157], an accusation, expressing No. 1 more concretely, is found in Acts 25:7, R.V., "charges," for A.V., "complaints." SEE COMPLAINT. ¶

NT: B.26d; CB.1234a; K.–.
OT: –.
GEN. REF.: –.

3. *enklēma* [ἔγκλημα, 1462], is an accusation made in public, but not necessarily before a tribunal. That is the case in Acts 23:39, "laid to his charge." In 25:16 it signifies a matter of complaint; hence the R.V. has "the matter laid against him" (A.V., "crime"). See CHARGE, CRIME. ¶

NT: B.216b; CB.1245a; K.394.
OT: –.
GEN. REF.: –.

4. *katēgoria* [κατηγορία, 2724], an accusation, is found in John 18:29; 1 Tim. 5:19

and Tit. 1:6, lit., 'not under accusation.' This and the verb *katēgoreō*, to accuse, and the noun *katēgoros*, an accuser (see below), all have chiefly to do with judicial procedure, as distinct from *diaballō*, to slander. it is derived from *agora*, a place of public speaking, prefixed by *kata*, against; hence it signifies a speaking against a person before a public tribunal. It is the opposite to *apologia*, a defence. ¶

NT: B.423c; CB.1254b; K.422.
OT: –
GEN. REF.: –.

Note: Krisis, which has been translated "accusation," in the A.V. of 2 Pet. 2:11 and Jude 9 (R.V., "judgement"), does not come under this category. It signifies a judgement, a decision given concerning anything.

B. Verbs.

1. *diaballō* [διαβάλλω, 1225], used in Luke 16:1, in the Passive Voice, lit. signifies to hurl across (*dia*, through, *ballō*, to throw), and hence suggests a verbal assault. It stresses the act rather than the author, as in the case of *aitia* and *kategoria*. *Diabolos* is connected. ¶

NT: B.181d; CB.1241a; K.150.
OT: sātān: S.7853; HR.298c.2; H.2252; BD.966c.
GEN. REF.: –.

2. *enkaleō* [ἐνκαλέω, 1458], — see A, No. 3, to bring a charge against, or to come forward as an accuser against, lit. denotes to call in (*en*, in, *kaleō*, to call), i.e., to call (something) in or against (someone); hence, to call to account, to accuse, Acts 19:38, R.V. (A.V., "implead"; in ver. 40, "accused" (A.V., "call in question"). It is used in four other places in the Acts, 23:28, 29; 26:2, 7, and elsewhere in Rom. 8:33, "shall lay to the charge." See CALL, IMPLEAD. ¶

NT: B.215c; CB.1245a; K.394.
OT: 'āmar: S.559; HR.365a.1; H.118; BD.55c.
pûaḥ: S.6315; HR.365a.2; H.1741; BD.806b.
GEN. REF.: –.

3. *epēreazō* [ἐπηρεάζω, 1908], besides its more ordinary meaning, to insult, treat abusively, despitefully, Luke 6:28, has the forensic significance to accuse falsely, and is used with this meaning in 1 Pet. 3:16, R.V., "revile." See DESPITEFULLY, REVILE. ¶

NT: B.285d; CB.–; K.–.
OT: –.
GEN. REF.: –.

4. *katēgoreō* [κατηγορέω, 2723], to speak against, accuse (cp. A, No. 4), is used (*a*) in a general way, to accuse, e.g., Luke 6:7, R.V., "how to accuse"; Rom. 2:15; Rev. 12:1; (*b*) before a judge, e.g. Matt. 12:10; Mark 15:4 (R.V., "witness against"); Acts 22:30; 25:16. In Acts 24:19, R.V. renders it "make accusation," for the A.V., "object." See OBJECT, WITNESS.

NT: B.423a; CB.1254b; K.422.
OT: –.
GEN. REF.: –.

5. *sukophanteō* [συκοφαντέω, 4811], Eng., sycophant, means (*a*) to accuse wrongfully, Luke 3:14 (A.V. and R.V. margin); R.V., "exact wrongfully"; (*b*) to exact money wrongfully, to take anything by false accusation, Luke 19:8, and the R.V. text of 3:14. It is more frequently found in the Sept.; see Gen. 43:18, to inform against; Lev. 19:11, "neither shall each falsely accuse his neighbour"; Job. 35:9, "they that are oppressed by false accusation"; Psalm 119:122, "let not the proud accuse me falsely"; Prov. 14:31 and 22:16, "he that oppresses the needy by false accusation."

The word is derived from *sukon*, a fig, and *phainō*, to show. At Athens a man whose business it was to give information against anyone who might be detected exporting figs out of the province, is said to have been called a *sukophantēs* (see Note (2) below). Probably, however, the word was used to denote one who brings figs to light by shaking the tree, and then in a metaphorical sense one who makes rich men yield up their fruit by false accusation. Hence in general parlance it was used to designate a malignant informer, one who accused from love of gain. See EXACT. ¶

NT: B.776c; CB.–; K.1100.
OT: gālal: S.1556; HR.1301c.1; H.353; BD.164b.
'āshaq: S.6231; HR.1301c.2; H.1713; BD.798d.
shāqar: S.8266; HR.1301c.3; H.2461; BD.1055d.
GEN. REF.: –.

Note: Proaitiaomai denotes to bring a previous charge against, Rom. 3:9, R.V. See CHARGE. ¶

ACCUSER

1. *diabolos* [διάβολος, 1228], an accuser (cp. Accuse, B, No. 1), is used 34 times as a title of Satan, "the Devil" (the English word is derived from the Greek); once of Judas, John 6:70, who, in his opposition to God, acted the part of the Devil. Apart from John 6:70, men are never spoken of as devils. it is always to be distinguished from *daimōn*, a demon. It is found three times, 1 Tim. 3:11; 2 Tim. 3:3; Tit. 2:3, of false accusers, slanderers.

NT: B.182a; CB.1241a; K.150.
OT: sātān: S.7853; HR.299b.2; H.2252; BD.966c.
GEN. REF.: IS.1:29; NB.–; Z.–.

2. *katēgoros* [κατηγόρος, 2725], an accuser (see p. 26), is used in John 8:10; Acts 23:30, 35; 24:8; 25:16, 18. In Rev. 12:10, it is used of Satan. ¶ In the Sept., Prov. 18:17. ¶

NT: B.423c; CB.1254b; K.422.
OT: rîb: S.7379; HR.751a.1; H.2159a; BD.936d.
GEN. REF.: IS.1:29; NB.–; Z.–.

Notes: (1) *Sukophantia*, a false accusation or oppression, is used in Eccl. 5:7; 7:8; Psa.

119:134 and Amos 2:8 (not in the N.T.). See No. 5, above.

(2) *Sukophantēs*, a false accuser, or oppressor, occurs in Psa. 72:4; Prov. 28:16 (not in the N.T.).

ACKNOWLEDGE (-MENT)

A. Verb.

epiginōskō [ἐπιγιν)ω, 1921], signifies (*a*) to know thoroughly (*epi*, intensive, *ginōskō*, to know); (*b*) to recognize a thing to be what it really is, to acknowledge, 1 Cor. 14:37 (R.V., "take knowledge of"); 16:18; 2 Cor. 1:13, 14. See KNOW, KNOWLEDGE, PERCEIVE.

NT: B.291a; CB.1245c; K.119.
OT: yāda': S.3045; HR.517c.2; H.848; BD.393b.
nākar: S.5234; HR.517c.3; H.1368; BD.647d.
GEN. REF.: –.

Note: In 1 John 2:23, "acknowledgeth" translates the verb *homologeō*, to confess, R.V., "confesseth."

B. Noun.

Epignōsis [ἐπίγνωσις, 1922], akin to A, full, or thorough knowledge, discernment, recognition, is translated "acknowledging" in the A.V. of 2 Tim. 2:25; Tit. 1:1 and Philm. 6 (in all three, R.V., "knowledge," properly, "thorough knowledge"). In Col. 2:2, A.V., "acknowledgement," R.V., "that they may know" (i.e., ':unto the full knowledge'). See KNOWLEDGE.

NT: B.291b; CB.1245c; K.119.
OT: da'at: S.1847; HR.518c.1; H.848c; BD.395c.
GEN. REF.: –.

ACQUAINTANCE

1. *gnōstos* [γνωστός, 1110], from *ginōskō*, to know, signifies known, or knowable; hence, one's acquaintance; it is used in this sense, in the plural, in Luke 2:44 and 23:49. See KNOWN, NOTABLE.

NT: B.164b; CB.1248b; K.119.
OT: yāda': S.3045; HR.274a.1; H.848; BD.393b.
GEN. REF.: –.

2. *idios* [ἴδιος, 2398], one's own, is translated "acquaintance" in the A.V. of Acts 24:23, "friends" (R.V.). See COMPANY.

NT: B.369c; CB.1252c; K.–.
OT: –.
GEN. REF.: –.

For **ACROSS** (Acts 27:5, R.V.), see Note 1 p. 1.

ACT

1. *epautophōrō* [ἐπαυτοφώρω, 1888], primarily signifies caught in the act of theft (*epi*, upon, intensive, *autos*, self, *phōr*, a thief); then, caught in the act of any other crime, John 8:4. In some texts the preposition *epi* is detached from the remainder of the adjective, and appears as *ep' autophōrō*. ¶

NT: B.125a; CB.–; K.–.
OT: –.
GEN. REF.: –.

2. *dikaiōma* [δικαίωμα, 1345], signifies an act of righteousness, a concrete expression of righteousness, as in the R.V. of Rom. 5:18, in reference to the Death of Christ; the A.V. wrongly renders it "the righteousness of One." The contrast is between the one trespass by Adam and the one act of Christ in His atoning Death. In Rev. 15:4 and 19:8, the word is used in the plural to signify, as in the R.V., "righteous acts," respectively, of God, and of the saints. See JUDGMENT, JUSTIFICATION, ORDINANCE, RIGHTEOUSNESS.

NT: B.198a; CB.1241c; K.168.
OT: ḥōq: S.2706; HR.334b.2a; H.728a; BD.349b.
mishpāṭ: S.4941; HR.334b.4; H.2443c; BD.1048b.
GEN. REF.: –.

3. *prassō* [πράσσω, 4238], to do, to practise, is translated "act" in the R.V. of Acts 17:7 (A.V., "do"). See COMMIT, DO, EXACT, KEEP, REQUIRE, USE.

NT: B.698b; CB.1266b; K.927.
OT: 'āsāh: S.6213; HR.1201a.3; H.1708,1709; BD.793c.
pā'al: S.6466; HR.1201a.4; H.1792; BD.821b.
GEN. REF.: –.

ACTIVE

energēs [ἐνεργ)ης, 1756], lit., 'in work' (cp. Eng., energetic), is used (*a*) of the Word of God, Heb. 4:12 (R.V., "active," A.V., "powerful"); (*b*) of a door for the Gospel, 1 Cor. 16:9, "effectual"; (*c*) of faith, Philm. 6, "effectual." See EFFECTUAL, POWERFUL. Cp. the synonymous words *dunatos* and *ischuros* (see ABLE. ¶

NT: B.265d; CB.1245a; K.251.
OT: –.
GEN. REF.: –.

ACTUALLY

holōs [ὅλως, 3654], from *holos*, all, whole, is translated "actually" in 1 Cor. 5:1, R.V. ("it is actually reported"); the A.V. "commonly" does not convey the meaning. In 6:7 it is translated "altogether" (A.V. "utterly"); in 15:29, "at all," as in Matt. 5:34. See ALL, ALTOGETHER. ¶

NT: B.565b; CB.1251a; K.682.
OT: –.
GEN. REF.: –.

ADD

1. *epitithēmi* [ἐπιτιθημι, 2007], lit., to put upon (*epi*, upon, *tithēmi*, to put), has a secondary and somewhat infrequent meaning,

to add to and is found in this sense in Mark 3:16, 17, lit., 'He added the name Peter to Simon,' 'He added to them the name Boanerges,' and Rev. 22:18, where the word is set in contrast to "take away from" (ver. 19). See LADE, LAY, PUT, SET.

NT: B.302d; CB.1246b; K.1176.
OT: sûm: S.7760; HR.535c.29; H.2243; BD.962c.
nātan: S.5414; HR.535c.14; H.1443; BD.678a.
GEN. REF.: –.

2. *prostithēmi* [προστίθημι, 4369], to put to (*pros*, to, *tithēmi*, to put), to add, or to place beside (the primary meaning), in Luke 17:15 is translated "increase," in the request "increase our faith"; in Luke 20:11, 12, "he sent yet" (A.V. "again he sent"), lit., 'he added and sent,' as in 19:11, "He added and spake." In Acts 12:3, R.V., "proceeded," A.V., "proceeded further" (of repeating or continuing the action mentioned by the following verb); in Acts 13:36, "was laid unto"; in Heb. 12:19, "more . . . be spoken," (lit., 'that no word should be added'). In Gal. 3:19, "What then is the law? It was added because of transgressions," there is no contradiction of what is said in verse 15, where the word is *epidiatassō* (see No. 4), for there the latter word conveys the idea of supplementing an agreement already made; here in ver. 19 the meaning is not that something had been added to the promise with a view to complete it, which the Apostle denies, but that something had been given in addition to the promise, as in Rom. 5:20, "The law came in beside." See GIVE, INCREASE, LAY, PROCEED, SPEAK.

NT: B.718d; CB.1267b.; K.1176.
OT: yāsaph: S.3254; HR.1221a.4; H.876; BD.414d.
GEN. REF.: –.

3. *prosanatithēmi* [προσανατίθημι, 4323], lit., to lay upon in addition, came to be used in the sense of putting oneself before another, for the purpose of consulting him; hence simply to take one into counsel, to confer. With this meaning it is used only in Gal. 1:16. In Gal. 2:2, a shorter form, *anatithēmi*, is used, which means to lay before (A.V., "communicated unto"). This less intensive word may have been purposely used there by the Apostle to suggest that he described to his fellow-apostles the character of his teaching, not to obtain their approval or their advice concerning it, but simply that they might have the facts of the case before them on which they were shortly to adjudicate.

It was also used to signify to communicate, to impart. With this meaning it is used only in Gal. 2:6, in the Middle Voice, the suggestion being to add from one's store of things. In regard to his visit to Jerusalem the Apostle says "those who were of repute imparted nothing to me" (A.V. "in conference added"), that is to say, they neither modified his teaching nor added to his authority. See CONFER. ¶

NT: B.711d; CB.–; K.57.
OT: –.
GEN. REF.: –.

4. *epidiatassō* [ἐπιδιατάσσω, 1928], lit., to arrange in addition (*epi*, upon, *dia*, through, *tassō*, to arrange), is used in Gal. 3:15 ("addeth," or rather, 'ordains something in addition'). If no one does such a thing in the matter of a human covenant, how much more is a covenant made by God inviolable! The Judaizers by their addition violated this principle, and, by proclaiming the Divine authority for what they did, they virtually charged God with a breach of promise. He gave the Law, indeed, but neither in place of the promise nor to supplement it. ¶

NT: B.292b; CB.–; K.–.
OT: –.
GEN. REF.: –.

5. *pareispherō* [παρεισφέρω, 3923], to bring in besides (*para*, besides, *eis*, in, *pherō*, to bring), means "to add," 2 Pet. 1:5, "adding on your part" (R.V.); the words "on your part" represent the intensive force of the verb; the A.V., "giving" does not provide an adequate meaning. ¶

NT: B.625a; CB.–; K.–.
OT: –.
GEN. REF.: –.

6. *epichorēgeō* [ἐπιχορηγέω, 2023], is translated "add" in the A.V. of 2 Pet. 1:5. Its meaning is to supply, to minister (*epi*, to, *chorēgeō*, to minister); R.V., "supply." See MINISTER.

NT: B.305a; CB.–; K.–.
OT: –.
GEN. REF.: –.

7. *didōmi* [δίδωμι, 1325], to give, is translated "add," in Rev. 8:3, R.V., for A.V., "offer" (marg., "add"). See GIVE.

NT: B.192c; CB.1241c; K.166.
OT: yāsaph: S.3254; HR.317b.11; H.876; BD.414d.
nātan: S.5414; HR.317b.26; H.1443; BD.678a.
GEN. REF.: –.

Note: In Phil. 1:17, R.V., *egeirō*, to raise, is translated "add" in the A.V. (R.V., "raise up"). See BRING, A, No. 6.

For **ADDICTED** (A.V. of 1 Cor. 16:15) see **SET**, No. 10.

ADJURE

1. *horkizō* [ὁρκίζω, 3726], to cause to swear, to lay under the obligation of an oath (*horkos*, Mark 5:7; Acts 19:13), is connected with the

Heb. word for a thigh, cp. Gen. 24:2, 9; 47:29. Some mss. have this word in 1 Thess. 5:27. The most authentic have No. 3 (below). See CHARGE. ¶

NT: B.581b; CB.1251b; K.729.
OT: shāba‘: S.7650; HR.1013b.1; H.2318; BD.989a.
GEN. REF.: –.

2. *exorkizō* [ἐξορκίζω, 1844], an intensive form of No. 1, signifies to appeal by an oath, to adjure, Matt. 26:63. ¶ In the Sept., Gen. 24:3; Judg. 17:2; 1 Kings 22:16. ¶

NT: B.277b; CB.1247c; K.729.
OT: shābā: S.7650; HR. 500a.2; H.2318; BD.989a.
'ālāh: S.422; HR.500a.1; H.94; BD.46d.
GEN. REF.: –.

3. *enorkizō* [ἐνορκίζω, —], to put under (or bind by) an oath, is translated "adjure" in the R.V. of 1 Thess. 5:27 (A.V., "charge"). ¶ In the Sept., Neh. 13:25. ¶

NT: B.267c; CB.–; K.729.
OT: shāba‘: S.7650; HR.476b.1; H.2318; BD.989a.
GEN. REF.: –.

Note: The synonymous verb *omnumi* signifies to make an oath, to declare or promise with an oath. See, e.g., Mark 6:23, in contrast to 5:7 (*horkizō*). See OATH and SWEAR.

For the A.V. **ADMINISTER** and **ADMINISTRATION** see **MINISTER** and **MINISTRATION, SERVE** and **SERVICE**

For the A.V. **ADMIRATION** and **ADMIRE** see **WONDER** and **MARVEL**

ADMONITION, ADMONISH

A. Noun.

nouthesia [νουθεσία, 3559], lit., a putting in mind (*nous*, mind, *tithēmi*, to put), is used in 1 Cor. 10:11, of the purpose of the Scriptures; in Eph. 6:4, of that which is ministered by the Lord: and in Tit. 3:10, of that which is to be administered for the correction of one who creates trouble in the church. *Nouthesia* is "the training by word," whether of encouragement, or, if necessary, by reproof or remonstrance. In contrast to this, the synonymous word *paideia* stresses training by act, though both words are used in each respect. ¶

NT: B.544a; CB.1260a; K.636.
OT: –.
GEN. REF.: IS.1:52; NB.–; Z.–.

B. Verbs

1. *noutheteō* [νουθετέω, 3560], cp. the noun above, means to put in mind, admonish, Acts 20:31 (A.V., "warn"); Rom. 15:14; 1 Cor. 4:14 (A.V., "warn"); Col. 1:28 (A.V., "warning"); Col. 3:16; 1 Thess. 5:12, 14 (A.V., "warn"); 2 Thess. 3:15.

It is used, (*a*) of instruction, (*b*) of warning. It is thus distinguished from *paideuō*, to correct by discipline, to train by act, Heb. 12:6; cp. Eph. 6:4.

"The difference between 'admonish' and 'teach' seems to be that, whereas the former has mainly in view the things that are wrong and call for warning, the latter has to do chiefly with the impartation of positive truth, cp. Col. 3:16; they were to let the word of Christ dwell richly in them, so that they might be able (1) to teach and admonish one another, and (2) to abound in the praises of God.

"Admonition differs from remonstrance, in that the former is warning based on instruction; the latter may be little more than expostulation. For example, though Eli remonstrated with his sons, 1 Sam. 2:24, he failed to admonish them, 3:13, LXX. Pastors and teachers in the churches are thus themselves admonished, i.e., instructed and warned, by the Scriptures, 1 Cor. 10:11, so to minister the Word of God to the saints, that, naming the Name of the Lord, they shall depart from unrighteousness, 2 Tim. 2:19".* See WARN. ¶

NT: B.544b; CB.1260a; K.636.
OT: bîn: S.995; HR.950b.1; H.239; BD.106c.
yāsar: S.3256; HR.950b.2; H.877; BD.415d.
kāhāh: S.3543; HR.950b.3; H.957; BD.462d.
GEN. REF.: IS.1:52; NB.–; Z.–.

2. *paraineō* [παραινέω, 3867], to admonish by way of exhorting or advising, is found in Acts 27:9 ("Paul admonished them") and ver. 22 ("and now I exhort you"). See EXHORT. ¶

NT: B.616b; CB.1262a; K.–.
OT: –.
GEN. REF.: IS.1:52; NB.–; Z.–.

3. *chrēmatizō* [χρηματίζω, 5537], primarily, to transact business, then, to give advice to enquirers (especially of official pronouncements of magistrates), or a response to those consulting an oracle, came to signify the giving of a Divine admonition or instruction or warning, in a general way; "admonished" in Heb. 8:5, A.V. (R.V. "warned"). Elsewhere it is translated by the verb to warn.

The word is derived from *chrēma*, an affair, business. Names were given to men from the nature of their business (see the same word in Acts 11:26; Rom. 7:3); hence the idea of dealing with a person and receiving instruction. In the case of oracular responses, the word is derived from *chrēsmos*, an oracle. See CALL, REVEAL, SPEAK, WARN.

NT: B.885; CB.1240a; K.1319.
OT: dābar: S.1697; HR.1474c.1; H.399a; BD.180b.
shā'ag: S.7580; HR.1474c.2; H.2300; BD.980c.
GEN. REF.: IS.1:52; NB.–; Z.–.

* From Notes on Thessalonians by Hogg and Vine, pp. 179, 180.

ADO

thorubeō [θορυβέω, 2350], to make an uproar, to throw into confusion, or to wail tumultuously, is rendered "make . . . ado," in Mark 5:39; elsewhere in Matt. 9:23; Acts 17:5; 20:10. See NOISE, TROUBLE, UPROAR. ¶

NT: B.362d; CB.1272d; K.–.
OT: rā'al: S.7477; HR.654a.3; H.2188; BD.947a.
GEN. REF.: IS.1:52; NB.–; Z.–.

Note: For the corresponding noun, *thorubos*, see TUMULT, UPROAR.

ADOPTION

huiothesia [υἱοθεσία, 5206], from *huios*, a son, and *thesis*, a placing, akin to *tithēmi*, to place, signifies the place and condition of a son given to one to whom it does not naturally belong. The word is used by the Apostle Paul only.

In Rom. 8:15, believers are said to have received "the Spirit of adoption," that is, the Holy Spirit who, given as the Firstfruits of all that is to be theirs, produces in them the realisation of sonship and the attitude belonging to sons. In Gal. 4:5 they are said to receive "the adoption of sons," i.e., sonship bestowed in distinction from a relationship consequent merely upon birth; here two contrasts are presented, (1) between the sonship of the believer and the unoriginated Sonship of Christ, (2) between the freedom enjoyed by the believer and bondage, whether of Gentile natural condition, or of Israel under the Law. In Eph. 1:5 they are said to have been foreordained unto "adoption as sons" through Jesus Christ, R.V.: the A.V., "adoption of children" is a mistranslation and misleading. God does not adopt believers as children; they are begotten as such by His Holy Spirit through faith. Adoption is a term involving the dignity of the relationship of believers as sons; it is not a putting into the family by spiritual birth, but a putting into the position of sons. In Rom. 8:23 the adoption of the believer is set forth as still future, as it there includes the redemption of the body, when the living will be changed and those who have fallen asleep will be raised. In Rom. 9:4 adoption is spoken of as belonging to Israel, in accordance with the statement in Ex. 4:12, "Israel is My Son." Cp. Hos. 11:1. Israel was brought into a special relation with God, a collective relationship, not enjoyed by other nations, Deut. 14:1; Jer. 31:9, etc. ¶

NT: B.833b; CB.1251c; K.1206.
OT: –.
GEN. REF.: IS.1:53; NB.15; Z.–.

ADORN, ADORNING

A. Verb.

kosmeō [κοσμέω, 2885], primarily to arrange, to put in order (Eng., cosmetic), is used of furnishing a room, Matt. 12:44; Luke 11:25, and of trimming lamps, Matt. 25:7. Hence, to adorn, to ornament, as of garnishing tombs, Matt. 23:29; buildings, Luke 21:5; Rev. 21:19; one's person; 1 Tim. 2:9; 1 Pet. 3:5; Rev. 21:2; metaphorically, of adorning a doctrine, Tit. 2:10. See GARNISH, TRIM. ¶

NT: B.445a; CB.1255c; K.459.
OT: 'adāh: S.5710; HR.780b.3; H.1565; BD.723c.
ṣāphāh: S.6823; HR.780b.5; H.1951; BD.860a.
tāqan: S.8626; HR.780b.6; H.2540; BD.1075b.
GEN. REF.: IS.1:57; NB.–; Z.–.

B. Noun.

kosmos [κόσμος, 2889], a harmonious arrangement or order, then, adornment, decoration, hence came to denote the world, or the universe, as that which is Divinely arranged. The meaning "adorning" is found in 1 Pet. 3:3. Elsewhere it signifies the world. Cp. *kosmios*, decent, modcst, 1 Tim. 2:9; 3:2. See WORLD.

NT: B.445d; CB.1255c; K.459.
OT: ṣābā': S.6635; HR.780c.6; H.1865a,b; BD.838d.
'adī: S.5716; HR.780c.4; H.1566a; BD.725d.
GEN. REF.: IS.1:57; NB.–; Z.–.

ADULTERER (-ESS), ADULTEROUS, ADULTERY

A. Nouns

1. *moichos* [μοιχός, 3432] denotes one who has unlawful intercourse with the spouse of another, Luke 18:11; 1 Cor. 6:9; Heb. 13:4. As to Jas. 4:4, see below. ¶

NT: B.526c; CB.1259a; K.605.
OT: nā'aph: S.5003; HR.932b.1; H.1273; BD.610c.
GEN. REF.: IS.1:58; NB.16; Z.–.

2. *moichalis* [μοιχαλίς, 3428], an adulteress, is used (*a*) in the natural sense, 2 Pet. 2:14; Rom. 7:3; (*b*) in the spiritual sense. Jas. 4:4; here the R.V. rightly omits the word "adulterers." It was added by a copyist. As in Israel the breach of their relationship with God through their idolatry, was described as adultery or harlotry (e.g., Ezek. 16:15, etc.; 23:43), so believers who cultivate friendship with the world, thus breaking their spiritual union with Christ, are spiritual adulteresses, having been spiritually united to Him as wife to husband, Rom. 7:4. It is used adjectivally to describe the Jewish people in transferring their affections from God, Matt. 12:39; 16:4; Mark 8:38. In 2 Pet. 2:14, the lit. translation is "full of an adulteress" (R.V. marg.). ¶

NT: B.526a; CB.1259a; K.605.
OT: nā'aph: S.5003; HR.932b.1; H.1273; BD.610c.
GEN. REF.: IS.1:58; NB.16; Z.–.

3. *moicheia* [μοιχεία, 3430], adultery, is found in Matt. 15:19; Mark 7:21; John 8:3 (A.V. only). ¶

NT: B.526b; CB.1259a; K.605.
OT: nā'āph: S.5003; HR.932b.1b,c; H.1273; BD.610c.
GEN. REF.: IS.1:58; NB.16; Z.–.

B. Verbs

1. *moichaō* [μοιχάω, 3429], used in the Middle Voice in the N.T., is said of men in Matt. 5:32; 19:9; Mark 10:11; of women in Mark 10:12. ¶

NT: B.526a; CB.1259a; K.605.
OT: nā'āph: S.5003; HR.932b.1; H.1273; BD.610c.
GEN. REF.: IS.1:58; NB.16; Z.–.

2. *moicheuō* [μοιχεύω, 3431] is used in Matt. 5:27, 28, 32 (in ver. 32 some texts have No. 1); 19:18; Mark 10:19; Luke 16:18; 18:20; John 8:4; Rom. 2:22; 13:9; Jas. 2:11; in Rev. 2:22, metaphorically, of those who are by a Jezebel's solicitations drawn away to idolatry. ¶

NT: B.526b; CB.1259b; K.605.
OT: nā'aph: S.5003; HR.932b.1; H.1273; BD.610c.
GEN. REF.: IS.1:58; NB.16; Z.–.

ADVANCE

prokoptō [προκόπτω, 4298], lit., to strike forward, cut forward a way, i.e., to make progress, is translated "advanced" in Luke 2:52, R.V., of the Lord Jesus (A.V., "increased"); in Gal. 1:14 "advanced," of Paul's former progress in the Jews' religion (A.V., "profited"); in Rom. 13:12, "is far spent," of the advanced state of the "night" of the world's spiritual darkness; in 2 Tim. 2:16, "will proceed further," of profane babblings; in 3:9 "shall proceed no further," of the limit Divinely to be put to the doings of evil men; in ver. 13, of the progress of evil men and impostors, "shall wax," lit., 'shall advance to the worse.' See INCREASE, PROCEED, PROFIT, SPENT, WAX. ¶

NT: B.707d; CB.1266c; K.939.
OT: –.
GEN. REF.: –.

Note: The corresponding noun *prokopē* is found in Phil. 1:12 and 25, "progress" (A.V., "furtherance"); 1 Tim. 4:15, "progress" (A.V., "profiting," an inadequate meaning). ¶

ADVANTAGE

A. Nouns

1. *perissos* [περισσός, 4053], primarily what is above and over, super-added, hence came to denote what is superior and advantageous, Rom. 3:1, in a comparison between Jew and Gentile; only here with this meaning. See ABUNDANT, C, No. 1.

NT: B.651b; CB.1263c; K.828.
OT: yeter: S.3499; HR.1126c.1; H.936a; BD.451d.
GEN. REF.: –.

2. *ophelos* [ὄφελος, 3786], akin to *ophellō*, to increase, comes from a root signifying to increase; hence, advantage, profit; it is rendered as a verb in its three occurrences, 1 Cor. 15:32 (A.V., "advantageth"; R.V., "doth it profit"); Jas. 2:14, 16, lit., 'What (is) the profit?' See PROFIT. ¶ In the Sept., Job 15:3. ¶

NT: B.599b; CB.–; K.–.
OT: yā'al: S.3276; HR.1039b.1; H.882; BD.418c.
GEN. REF.: –.

3. *ōpheleia* [ὠφέλεια, 5622], an alternative form to No. 2, akin to C, No. 1, is found in Rom. 3:1, "profit," and Jude 16, "advantage." (i.e., they shew respect of persons for the sake of what they may gain from them). See PROFIT. ¶

NT: B.900b; CB.1261a; K.–.
OT: beṣá: S.1215; HR.1497a.1; H.267a; BD.130c.
yā'al: S.3276; HR.1497a.2; H.882; BD.418c.
GEN. REF.: –.

Note: Ophelimos, profitable, is used only in the Pastoral Epistles, 1 Tim. 4:8; 2 Tim. 3:16; Tit. 3:8. See PROFIT. ¶

B. Verbs.

1. *ōpheleō* [ὠφελέω, 5623], signifies to be useful, do good, profit, Rom. 2:25; with a negative, to be of no use, to effect nothing, Matt. 27:24; John 6:63, "profiteth"; 12:19, "prevail"; in Luke 9:25, A.V., "(what is a man) advantaged?" R.V., "profited." See BETTERED (to be), PREVAIL, PROFIT.

NT: B.900c; CB.1261a; K.–.
OT: yā'āl: S.3276; HR.1497b.1; H.882; BD.418c.
nāshāh: S.5383; HR.1497b.2; H.1427; BD.674b.
'āzar: S.5826; HR.1497b.3; H.1598; BD.740a.
GEN. REF.: –.

2. *pleonekteō* [πλεονεκτέω, 4122], lit., to seek to get more (*pleon,* more, *echō,* to have); hence to get an advantage of, to take advantage of. In 2 Cor. 7:2 the A.V. has "defrauded," the R.V., "took advantage of"; in 1 Thess. 4:6, A.V., "defraud," R.V., "wrong." In the other three places the R.V. consistently translates it by the verb to take advantage of, 2 Cor. 2:11, of Satan's effort to gain an advantage over the church, through their neglect to restore the backslider; in 2 Cor. 12:17, 18, A.V., "make a gain of." See DEFRAUD, GAIN, WRONG. ¶

NT: B.667c; CB.1265b; K.864.
OT: bāṣá: S.1241; HR.1142a.1; H.267; BD.130b.
GEN. REF.: –.

Note: Cp. *pleonektēs*, a covetous person, *pleonexia*, covetousness.

ADVENTURE

didōmi [δίδωμι, 1325], to give, is once used of giving oneself to go into a place, to adventure into, Acts 19:31, of Paul's thought of going into the midst of the mob in the theatre at Ephesus. See BESTOW, COMMIT, DELIVER, GIVE.

NT: B.192c; CB.1241c; K.166.
OT: nātan: S.5414; HR.317b.26; H.1443; BD.678a.
GEN. REF.: IS.1:59; NB.–; Z.–.

ADVERSARY

A. Noun.

antidikos [ἀντίδικος, 476], firstly, an opponent in a lawsuit, Matt. 5:25 (twice); Luke 12:58; 18:3, is also used to denote an adversary or an enemy, without reference to legal affairs, and this is perhaps its meaning in 1 Pet. 5:8, where it is used of the Devil. Some would regard the word as there used in a legal sense, since the Devil accuses men before God. ¶

NT: B.74a; CB.1236a; K.62.
OT: rîb: S.7379; HR.110b.1; H.2159a; BD.936d.
GEN. REF.: IS.1:59; NB.–; Z.–.

B. Verb.

antikeimai [ἀντικεῖμαι, 480] is, lit., to lie opposite to, to be set over against. In addition to its legal sense it signifies to withstand; the present participle of the verb with the article, which is equivalent to a noun, signifies an adversary, e.g., Luke 13:17; 21:15; 1 Cor. 16:9; Phil. 1:28; 1 Tim. 5:14. This construction is used of the Man of Sin, in 2 Thess. 2:4, and is translated "He that opposeth," where, adopting the noun form, we might render by 'the opponent and self-exalter against . . .' In Gal. 5:17 it is used of the antagonism between the Holy Spirit and the flesh in the believer; in 1 Tim. 1:10, of anything, in addition to persons, that is opposed to the doctrine of Christ. In these two places the word is rendered "contrary to." ¶ In the Sept. it is used of Satan, Zech. 3:1, and of men, Job 13:24; Isa. 66:6. See CONTRARY, OPPOSE. ¶

NT: B.74b; CB.–; K.425.
OT: 'āyab: S.340; HR.110c.1; H.78; BD.33b.
qārāʿ: S.7121; HR.110c.6; H.2063; BD.894d.
sātan: S.7853; HR.110c.8; H.2252; BD.966c.
GEN. REF.: IS.1:59; NB.–; Z.–.

C. Adjective.

hupenantios [ὑπεναντίος, 5227], contrary, opposed, is a strengthened form of *enantios* (*en*, in, and *antios*, set against). The intensive force is due to the preposition *hupo*. It is translated "contrary to," in Col. 2:14, of ordinances; in Heb. 10:27, "adversaries." In each place a more violent form of opposition is suggested than in the case of *enantios*. See CONTRARY. ¶

NT: B.838b; CB.1252a; K.–.
OT: 'āyab: S.340; HR.1407b.1; H.78; BD.33b.
ṣar: S.6862; HR.1407b.2; H.1973-75; BD.865a.
sānē': S.8130; HR.1407b.4; H.2272; BD.971b.
GEN. REF.: IS.1:59; NB.–; Z.–.

For **ADVERSITY**, in Heb. 13:3, where the verb *kakoucheomai* is translated in the A.V., "suffer adversity," see **SUFFER**, (*b*), No. 6.

ADVICE, ADVISE

1. *gnōmē* [γνώμη, 1106], connected with *ginōskō*, to know, perceive, firstly means the faculty of knowledge, reason; then, that which is thought or known, one's mind. Under this heading there are various meanings: (1) a view, judgment, opinion, 1 Cor. 1:10; Philm. 14; Rev. 17:13, 17; (2) an opinion as to what ought to be done, either (*a*) by oneself, and so a resolve, or purpose, Acts 20:3; or (*b*) by others, and so, judgment, advice, 1 Cor. 7:25, 40; 2 Cor. 8:10. See AGREE, JUDGMENT, MIND, PURPOSE, WILL. ¶

NT: B.163a; CB.1248b; K.119.
OT: t^{e}ʿēm: S.2942; HR.273a.2b; H.2757a; BD.380d.
GEN. REF.: IS.1:60; NB.–; Z.–.

2. *boulē* [βουλή, 1012], from a root meaning a will, hence a counsel, a piece of advice, is to be distinguished from *gnōmē*; *boulē* is the result of determination, *gnōmē* is the result of knowledge. *Boulē* is everywhere rendered by "counsel" in the R.V. except in Acts 27:12, "advised," lit., 'gave counsel.' In Acts 13:36 the A.V. wrongly has "by the will of God fell on sleep;" the R.V., "after he had served the counsel of God, fell on sleep." The word is used of the counsel of God, in Luke 7:30; Acts 2:23; 4:28; 13:36; 20:27; Eph. 1:11; Heb. 6:17; in other passages, of the counsel of men, Luke 23:51; Acts 27:12, 42; 1 Cor. 4:5. See COUNSEL, WILL. ¶

NT: B.145d; CB.1239b; K.108.
OT: ʿēṣāh: S.6098; HR.227c.2e; H.887a; BD.420a.
GEN. REF.: IS.1:60; NB.–; Z.–.

For **ADVOCATE** see **COMFORTER**

AFAR

1. *makran* [μακράν, 3112], from *makros*, far, Matt. 8:30 (A.V., "a good way"; R.V., "afar"), a long way off, is used with *eis*, unto, in Acts 2:39, "afar off." With the article, in Eph. 2:13, 17, it signifies "the (ones) far off." See FAR and WAY.

NT: B.487c; CB.1257c; K.549.
OT: rāḥaq: S.7368; HR.892c.3; H.2151; BD.934d.
GEN. REF.: Z.–.

2. *makrothen* [μακρόθεν, 3113], also from *makros*, signifies afar off, from far, Matt. 26:58; 27:55, etc. It is used with *apo*, from, in Mark 5:6; 14:54; 15:40, etc.; outside the Synoptists, three times, Rev. 18:10, 15, 17.

NT: B.487; CB.1257c; K.549.
OT: rāḥaq: S.7368; HR.893b.1; H.2151; BD.934d.
GEN. REF.: –.

3. *porrōthen* [πόῤῥωθεν, 4207], afar off, from *porrō*, at a distance, a great way off, is found in Luke 17:12 and Heb. 11:13. ¶

NT: B.693d; CB.—; K.—.
OT: rāḥôq: S.7350; HR.1195b.1; H.2151b; BD.935b.
GEN. REF.: —.

Note: In 2 Pet. 1:9, *muōpazō*, to be shortsighted, is translated "cannot see afar off" (A.V.); R.V., "seeing only what is near."

AFFAIR (-S)

pragmatia, or *pragmateia* [πραγματία, 4230], from *pragma*, a deed, denotes a business, occupation, the prosecution of any affair; in the plural, purists, affairs (of life), 2 Tim. 2:4. ¶

NT: B.697b; CB.1266b; K.927.
OT: ḥēsheq: S.2837; HR.1200b.2; H.773a; BD.366a.
mᵉlā'kāh: S.4399; HR.1200b.3; H.1068b; BD.521d.
GEN. REF.: —.

Notes: (1) *Ta kata*, lit., the (things), with, or respecting a (person), is translated "affairs" in Eph. 6:21 and Col. 4:7, R.V.

(2) *Ta peri*, lit., the (things) concerning (a person), is translated "affairs" in the A.V. of Eph. 6:22 and Phil. 1:27 (R.V., "state," in each place).

AFFECT

kakoō [κακόω, 2559], from *kakos*, evil, to treat badly, to hurt, also means to make evil affected, to embitter, Acts 14:2. See EVIL, HARM, HURT.

NT: B.398b; CB.1253b; K.391.
OT: ʿānāh: S.6031; HR.711b.5; H.1651,1652; BD.776a.
rāʿā: S.7489; HR.711b.7; H.2191, 2192; BD.949b.
GEN. REF.: IS.1:60; NB.—; Z.—.

Note: Zēloō, akin to *zeō*, to boil (Eng., zeal), means (*a*) to be jealous, Acts 7:9; 17:5; to envy, 1 Cor. 13:4; to covet, Jas. 4:2; in a good sense ("jealous over"), in 2 Cor. 11:2; (*b*) to desire earnestly, 1 Cor. 12:31; 14:1, 39; to take a warm interest in, to seek zealously, Gal. 4:17, 18, A.V., "zealously affect," "to be zealously affected." The R.V. corrects this to "zealously seek," etc. See COVET, DESIRE, ENVY, JEALOUS, ZEALOUS. ¶

AFFECTION (-S), AFFECTED

1. *pathos* [πάφος, 3806], from *paschō*, to suffer, primarily denotes whatever one suffers or experiences in any way; hence, an affection of the mind, a passionate desire. Used by the Greeks of either good or bad desires, it is always used in the N.T. of the latter, Rom. 1:26 (A.V., "affections," R.V., "passions"); Col. 3:5 (A.V., "inordinate affection," R.V., "passion"); 1 Thess. 4:5 (A.V., "lust," R.V., "passion"). See LUST. ¶

NT: B.602d; CB.1262c; K.798.
OT: 'ēbel: S.60; HR.1045b.1; H.6a; BD.5c.
GEN. REF.: IS.1:60; NB.—; Z.—.

2. *splanchna* [σπλάγχνα, 4698], lit., the bowels, which were regarded by the Greeks as the seat of the more violent passions, by the Hebrews as the seat of the tender affections; hence the word denotes "tender mercies" and is rendered "affections" in 2 Cor. 6:12 (A.V., "bowels"); "inward affection," 2 Cor. 7:15. See BOWELS, COMPASSION, HEART, MERCY. Cp. *epithumia*, desire.

NT: B.763a; CB.1269c; K.1067.
OT: beṭen: S.990; HR.1284c.1; H.236a; BD.105d.
raḥam: S.7356; HR.1284c.2; H.2146a; BD.933a.
GEN. REF.: IS.1:60; NB.—; Z.—.

3. *pathēma* [πάθημα, 3804], akin to No. 1, translated "affections" in Gal. 5:24, A.V., is corrected to "passions" in the R.V. See AFFLICTION, B. No. 3.

NT: B.602b; CB.1262c; K.798.
OT: —.
GEN. REF.: IS.1:60; NB.—; Z.—.

B. Adjectives.

1. *astorgos* [ἄστοργος, 794], signifies without natural affection (*a*, negative, and *storgē*, love of kindred, especially of parents for children and children for parents; a fanciful etymology associates with this the "stork"), Rom. 1:31; 2 Tim. 3:3. ¶

NT: B.118a; CB.1238a; K.—.
OT: —.
GEN. REF.: IS.1:60; NB.—; Z.—.

2. *philostorgos* [φιλόστοργος, 5387], tenderly loving (from *philos*, friendly, *storgē*, see No. 1), is used in Rom. 12:10, R.V., "tenderly affectioned" (A.V., "kindly affectioned"). ¶

NT: B.861c; CB.1264b; K.—.
OT: —.
GEN. REF.: IS.1:60; NB.—; Z.—.

Notes: (1) *Phroneō*, to think, to set the mind on, implying moral interest and reflexion, is translated "set your affection on" in Col. 3:2, A.V. (R.V., "set your mind on"). See CAREFUL, MIND, REGARD, SAVOUR, THINK, UNDERSTAND.

(2) For *homeiromai* (or *himeiromai*), to be affectionately desirous of, 1 Thess. 2:8, see DESIRE. ¶

AFFIRM

1. *diabebaioomai* [διαβεβαιόομαι, 1226], *dia*, intensive, and *bebaioō*, to confirm, make sure, denotes to assert strongly, "affirm confidently," 1 Tim. 1:7; Tit. 3:8 (A.V., "affirm constantly"). ¶

NT: B.181d; CB.—; K.—.
OT: —.
GEN. REF.: —.

2. *diischurizomai* [διισχυρίζομαι, 1340], as in No. 1, and *ischurizomai*, to corroborate (*ischuros* "strong"; see ABILITY, A, No. 2 and C, No. 2, Note), primarily signifies to lean

upon, then, to affirm stoutly, assert vehemently, Luke 22:59; Acts 12:15. ¶

NT: B.195b; CB.–; K.–.
OT: –.
GEN. REF.: –.

3. *phaskō* [φάσκω, 5335], a frequentative form of the verb *phēmi* (No. 4), denotes to allege, to affirm by way of alleging or professing, Acts 24:9 (R.V., "affirming," A.V., "saying"); 25:19; Rom. 1:22, "professing." Some mss. have it in Rev. 2:2, instead of the verb *legō*, to say. See PROFESS, SAY. ¶

NT: B.854b; CB.–; K.–.
OT: 'āmar: S.559; HR.1425b.1; H.118; BD55c.
GEN. REF.: –.

4. *phēmi* [φημί, 5346], to say (primarily by way of enlightening, explaining), is rendered "affirm" in Rom. 3:8. See SAY.

NT: B.856b; CB.1264a; K.–.
OT: –.
GEN. REF.: –.

AFFLICT (-ED), AFFLICTION

1. *kakoō* [κακόω, 2559], is translated "afflict," in Acts 12:1, R.V. (A.V., "vex"). See AFFECT.

NT: B.398b; CB.1253b; K.391.
OT: 'ānāh: S.6031; HR.711b.5; H.1651,1652; BD.776a.
rā'a': S.7489; HR.711b.7; H.2191,2192; BD.949b.
GEN. REF.: IS.1:61; NB.–; Z.–.

2. *kakoucheō* [κακουχέω, 2558], from *kakos*, evil, and *echō*, to have, signifies, in the Passive Voice, to suffer ill, to be maltreated, tormented, Heb. 11:37 (A.V., "tormented," R.V., "afflicted"); 13:3, A.V., "suffer adversity," R.V., "evil entreated." See ENTREAT, TORMENT. ¶ In the Sept., I Kings, 2:26; 11:39. ¶

NT: B.398b; CB.–; K.–.
OT: 'ānāh: S.6031; HR.711c.1; H.1651,1652; BD.776a.
GEN. REF.: IS.1:61; NB.–; Z.–.

Note: Sunkakoucheō (*sun*, with, and No. 1), to be evil entreated with, is used in Heb. 11:25. ¶

3. *kakopatheō* [κακοπαθέω, 2553], from *kakos*, evil, *pathos*, suffering, signifies to suffer hardship. So the R.V. in 2 Tim. 2:9; and 4:5; in Jas. 5:13, "suffer" (A.V., "afflicted"). See ENDURE, SUFFER. ¶

NT: B.397c; CB.1253b; K.798.
OT: 'āmal: S.5998; HR.709a.1; H.1639; BD.765c.
GEN. REF.: IS.1:61; NB.–; Z.–.

Note: For *sunkakopatheō*, 2 Tim. 1:8, see HARDSHIP.

4. *thlibō* [θλίβω, 2346], to suffer affliction, to be troubled, has reference to sufferings due to the pressure of circumstances, or the antagonism of persons, 1 Thess. 3:4; 2 Thess. 1:6, 7; "straitened," in Matt. 7:14 (R.V.); "throng," Mark 3:9; "afflicted," 2 Cor. 1:6; 7:5 (R.V.); 1 Tim. 5:10; Heb. 11:37; "pressed," 2 Cor. 4:8. Both the verb and the noun (see B, No. 4), when used of the present experience of believers, refer almost invariably to that which comes upon them from without. See NARROW, PRESS, STRAITENED, THRONG, TRIBULATION, TROUBLE. ¶

NT: B.362a; CB.1272b; K.334.
OT: ṣārar: S.6887; HR.652b.10; H.1973,1974; BD.864c.
lāḥaṣ: S.3905; HR.652b.4; H.1106; BD.537d.
GEN. REF.: IS.1:61; NB.–; Z.–.

5. *talaipōreō* [ταλαιπωρέω, 5003], to be afflicted, is used in Jas. 4:9, in the Middle Voice ('afflict yourselves'). It is derived from *tlaō*, to bear, undergo, and *pōros*, a hard substance, a callus, which metaphorically came to signify that which is miserable. ¶

NT: B.803a; CB.1271a; K.–.
OT: shādad: S.7703; HR.1333a.2; H.2331; BD.994a.
GEN. REF.: IS.1:61; NB.–; Z.–.

Note: Talaipōria (akin to No. 5) denotes misery, hardship, Rom. 3:16; Jas. 5:1. ¶ The corresponding adjective is *talaipōros*, "wretched," Rom. 7:24; Rev. 3:17. ¶

B. Nouns.

1. *kakopatheia* [κακοπάθεια, 2552], from *kakos*, evil, and *pascho*, to suffer, is rendered "suffering" in Jas. 5:10, R.V. (A.V., "suffering affliction"). ¶ In Sept., Mal. 1:13. ¶

NT: B.397b; CB.1253b; K.798.
OT: tlā'āh: S.8513; HR.709a.1; H.1066a; BD.521b.
GEN. REF.: IS.1:61; NB.–; Z.–.

2. *kakōsis* [κάκωσις, 2561], affliction, ill treatment, is used in Acts 7:34. ¶

NT: B.398c; CB.1253b; K.391.
OT: –.
GEN. REF.: IS.1:61; NB.–; Z.–.

3. *pathēma* [πάθημα, 3804], from *pathos*, suffering, signifies affliction. The word is frequent in Paul's Epistles and is found three times in Hebrews, four in 1 Peter; it is used (*a*) of afflictions, Rom. 8:18 etc.; of Christ's sufferings, 1 Pet. 1:11; 5:1; Heb. 2:9; of those as shared by believers, 2 Cor. 1:5; Phil. 3:10; Pet. 4:13; 5:1; (*b*) of an evil emotion, passion, Rom. 7:5; Gal. 5:24. The connection between the two meanings is that the emotions, whether good or evil, were regarded as consequent upon external influences exerted on the mind (cp. the two meanings of the English "passion"). It is more concrete than No. 1, and expresses in sense (*b*) the uncontrolled nature of evil desires, in contrast to *epithumia*, the general and comprehensive term, lit., what you set your heart upon (Trench, Syn. § lxxxvii). Its concrete character is seen in Heb. 2:9. See AFFECTION, MOTION, PASSION, SUFFERING.

NT: B.602b; CB.1262c; K.798.
OT: –.
GEN. REF.: IS.1:61; NB.–; Z.–.

Note: The corresponding verbal form *pathētos*, used in Acts 26:23 of the sufferings of Christ, signifies destined to suffer. ¶

4. *thlipsis* [θλίψις, 2347], primarily means a

pressing, pressure (see A, No. 4), anything which burdens the spirit. In two passages in Paul's Epistles it is used of future retribution, in the way of affliction, Rom. 2:9; 2 Thess. 1:6. In Matt. 24:9, the A.V. renders it as a verb, "to be afflicted," (R.V., "unto tribulation'). It is coupled with *stenochōria*, anguish, in Rom. 2:9; 8:35; with *anankē*, distress, 1 Thess. 3:7; with *diōgmos*, persecution, Matt. 13:21; Mark 4:17; 2 Thess. 1:4. It is used of the calamities of war, Matt. 24:21, 29; Mark 13:19, 24; of want, 2 Cor. 8:13, lit., 'distress for you'; Phil. 4:14 (cp 1:16); Jas. 1:27; of the distress of woman in child-birth, John 16:21; of persecution, Acts 11:19; 14:22; 20:23; 1 Thess. 3:3, 7; Heb. 10:33; Rev. 2:10; 7:14; of the afflictions of Christ, from which (His vicarious sufferings apart) his followers must not shrink, whether sufferings of body or mind, Col. 1:24; of sufferings in general, 1 Cor. 7:28; 1 Thess. 1:6 etc. See ANGUISH, BURDENED, DISTRESS, PERSECUTION, TRIBULATION, TROUBLE.

NT: B.362b; CB.1272b; K.334.
OT: ṣārāh: S.6869; HR.652c.11; H.1973c,1974b; BD.865b.
GEN. REF.: IS.1:61; NB.–; Z.–.

AFFRIGHTED

A. Adjective.

emphobos [ἔμφοβος, 1719], lit., in fear (*en*, in, *phobos*, fear), means "affrighted," Luke 24:5, R.V. (A.V., "afraid"); 24:37; Acts 10:4, R.V. (A.V., "afraid"); Rev. 11:13. The R.V. omits it in Acts 22:9. See TREMBLE.

NT: B.257b; CB.–; K.–.
OT: –.
GEN. REF.: –.

B. Verbs.

1. *pturō* [πτύρω, 4426], to frighten, scare, is used in the Passive Voice in Phil 1:28, "be affrighted," R.V., "be terrified," A.V. See TERRIFY. ¶

NT: B.727d; CB.–; K.–.
OT: –.
GEN. REF.: –.

2. *ekthambeō* [ἐκθαμβέω, 1568], to throw into terror, is used in the Passive sense, to be amazed, "affrighted," Mark 16:5, 6, A.V. (R.V., "amazed"); Mark 9:15, "were greatly amazed"; 14:33, "to be greatly amazed" (R.V.), "to be sore amazed" (A.V.). See AMAZE, B, No. 4. ¶

NT: B.240b; CB.1244a; K.312.
OT: –.
GEN. REF.: –.

For **AFOOT** see **FOOT**, B, No. 2

AFORE, AFOREHAND

The Greek words with these meanings consist of prefixes to verbs, signifying to come, prepare, promise, write afore, etc. See under these words.

AFOREPROMISED

proepangellomai [προεπαγγέλλομαι, 4279], to promise before (*pro*, before, *epangellomai*, to promise), is translated by the one word "aforepromised," in the R.V. of 2 Cor. 9:5; in Rom. 1:2, "promised afore." ¶

NT: B.705b; CB.1266c; K.240.
OT: –.
GEN. REF.: –.

AFORETIME

1. *pote* [ποτέ, 4218], signifies once, at some time, John 9:13 (cp. *proteron*, in ver. 8); Eph. 2:2, 11; Col. 3:7; Tit. 3:3; Philm. 11; 1 Pet. 3:5, 20. In all these the R.V. translates it "aforetime." The A.V. varies it with "in time past," "some time," "sometimes," "in the old time."

NT: B.695a; CB.1266b; K.–.
OT: –.
GEN. REF.: –.

2. *proteron* [πρότερον, 4386], the comparative of *pro*, before, aforetime, as being definitely antecedent to something else, is more emphatic than *pote* in this respect. See, e.g., John 6:62; 7:50; 9:8; 2 Cor. 1:15; Gal. 4:13; 1 Tim. 1:13; Heb. 4:6; 7:27; 10:32; 1 Pet. 1:14. See BEFORE, FIRST, FORMER. ¶

NT: B.721d; CB.1267b; K.–.
OT: –.
GEN. REF.: –.

For **AFRAID** see **AFFRIGHTED**, A, **FEAR**, A, No. 2, B, No. 3, D, **SORE**

For **AFRESH** see under **CROSS, CRUCIFY**, B

AFTER, AFTERWARD (-S)

The following are adverbs only. For prepositions and conjunctions see Note †. p. 9.

1. *ekeithen* [ἐκειθεν, 1564], thence, is once used to signify "afterwards," in the sense of "then," from that time, Acts 13:21. See THENCE.

NT: B.239b; CB.–; K.–.
OT: –.
GEN. REF.: –.

2. *hexēs* [ἑξῆς, 1836] denotes "after" with the significance of a succession of events, an event

following next in order after another, Luke 7:11; 9:37; Acts 21:1; 25:17; 27:18. ¶
NT: B.276a; CB.–; K.–.
OT: –.
GEN. REF.: –.

3. *kathexēs* [καθεξῆς, 2517], a strengthened form of No. 2, denotes "afterward," or "in order" (*kata*, according to, and No. 2), Luke 1:3; 8:1; Acts 3:24; 11:4; 18:23. ¶
NT: B.388d; CB.–; K.–.
OT: –.
GEN. REF.: –.

4. *metepeita* [μετέπειτα, 3347], afterwards, without necessarily indicating an order of events, as in Nos. 1 and 2, is found in Heb. 12:17. ¶
NT: B.514a; CB.–; K.–.
OT: –.
GEN. REF.: –.

5. *husteron* [ὕστερον, 5305], afterwards, with the suggestion of at length, is found in Matt 4:2; 21:29; 32, 37 (A.V., "last of all"); 22:27; 25:11; 26:60 (A.V., "at the last"); Mark 16:14; Luke 4:2; 20:32 (A.V., "last"); John 13:36; Heb. 12:11. See LAST. ¶
NT: B.849c; CB.1252b; K.1240.
OT: –.
GEN. REF.: –.

Note: Eita and *epeita*, then, afterwards, or thereupon, are translated "afterward" or "afterwards" in the A.V. of Mark 4:17 (*eita*) and Gal. 1:21; 1 Cor. 15:23, 46 (*epeita*); always "then" in the R.V. See THEN.

AGAIN

1. *dis* [δίς, 1364], the ordinary numeral adverb signifying twice, is rendered "again" in Phil. 4:16, "ye sent once and again unto my need," and in 1 Thess. 2:18, where Paul states that he would have come to the Thessalonians "once and again," that is, twice at least he had attempted to do so. See TWICE.
NT: B.199d; CB.–; K.–.
OT: –.
GEN. REF.: –.

2. *palin* [πάλιν, 3825], the regular word for "again," is used chiefly in two senses, (*a*) with reference to repeated action; (*b*) rhetorically, in the sense of "moreover" or "further," indicating a statement to be added in the course of an argument, e.g., Matt. 5:33; or with the meaning 'on the other hand,' 'in turn,' Luke 6:43; 1 Cor. 12:21; 2 Cor. 10:7; 1 John 2:8. In the first chapter of Hebrews, ver. 5, *palin* simply introduces an additional quotation; in ver. 6 this is not so. There the R.V. rightly puts the word "again" in connection with "He bringeth in the firstborn into the world," "When He again bringeth etc." That is to say, *palin* is here set in contrast to the time when God *first* brought His Son into the world. This statement, then, refers to the future Second Advent of Christ. The word is used far more frequently in the Gospel of John than in any other book in the New Testament.
NT: B.606c; CB.1261c; K.–.
OT: –.
GEN. REF.: –.

Note: Other words are rendered "again" in the A.V., which the R.V. corrects, namely, *deuteros* and *anōthen. Deuteros* signifies "a second time," John 9:24; Acts 11:9. *Anōthen* signifies from above, or anew. See the R.V. of John 3:3, 7, and the A.V. and R.V. of ver. 31. Nicodemus was not puzzled about birth from Heaven; what perplexed him was that a person must be born a second time. This the context makes clear. This is really the meaning in Gal. 4:9, where it is associated with *palin*, "over again." The idea is "anew," for, though the bondage would be the same in essence and effect, it would be new in not being in bondage to idols but to the Law. See also Matt. 27:51; Mark 15:38; John 19:23, "from the top." *Anōthen* may mean "from the first," in Luke 1:3 and Acts 26:5. For the meaning "from above," see Jas. 1:17; 3:15, 17. ¶

AGAINST: see Note, † p. 1.

AGE

A. Nouns.

1. *aiōn* [αἰών, 165], an age, era (to be connected with *aei*, ever, rather than with *aō*, to breathe), signifies a period of indefinite duration, or time viewed in relation to what takes place in the period.

The force attaching to the word is not so much that of the actual length of a period, but that of a period marked by spiritual or moral characteristics. This is illustrated in the use of the adjective [see Note (1) below] in the phrase "life eternal," in John 17:3, in respect of the increasing knowledge of God.

The phrases containing this word should not be rendered literally, but consistently with its sense of indefinite duration. Thus *eis ton aiōna* does not mean "unto the age" but "for ever" (see, e.g., Heb. 5:6). The Greeks contrasted that which came to an end with that which was expressed by this phrase, which shows that they conceived of it as expressing interminable duration.

The word occurs most frequently in the Gospel of John, the Hebrews and Revelation. It is sometimes wrongly rendered "world."

See COURSE, ETERNAL, WORLD. It is a characteristic word of John's Gospel.

NT: B.27b; CB.1234a; K.31.
OT: ʿôlām: S.5769; HR.39b.5; H.1631a; BD.761d.
GEN. REF.: IS.1:67; NB.18; Z.—.

Notes: (1) *Aiōnios*, the adjective corresponding, denoting eternal, is set in contrast with *proskairos*, lit., 'for a season,' 2 Cor. 4:18. It is used of that which in nature is endless, as, e.g., of God, Rom. 16:26, His power, 1 Tim. 6:16, His glory, 1 Pet. 5:10, the Holy Spirit, Heb. 9:14, redemption, Heb. 9:12, salvation, 5:9, life in Christ, John 3:16, the resurrection body, 2 Cor. 5:1, the future rule of Christ, 2 Pet. 1:11, which is declared to be without end, Luke 1:33, of sin that never has forgiveness, Mark 3:29, the judgment of God, Heb. 6:2, and of fire, one of its instruments, Matt. 18:8; 25:41; Jude 7. See ETERNAL, EVERLASTING.

(2) In Rev. 15:3, the R.V. has "King of the ages," according to the texts which have *aiōnōn*; the A.V. has "of saints" (*hagiōn*, in inferior mss.). There is good ms. evidence for *ethnōn*, "nations," (A.V. marg.), probably a quotation from Jer. 10:7.

2. *genea* [γενεά, 1074], connected with *ginomai*, to become, primarily signifies a begetting, or birth; then that which has been begotten, a family; or successive members of a genealogy, Matt. 1:17, or of a race of people, possessed of similar characteristics, pursuits, etc., (of a bad character) Matt. 17:17; Mark 9:19; Luke 9:41; 16:8; Acts 2:40; or of the whole multitude of men living at the same time, Matt. 24:34; Mark 13:30; Luke 1:48; 21:32; Phil. 2:15, and especially of those of the Jewish race living at the same period, Matt. 11:16, etc. Transferred from people to the time in which they lived, the word came to mean an age, i.e., a period ordinarily occupied by each successive generation, say, of thirty or forty years, Acts 14:16; 15:21; Eph. 3:5; Col. 1:26; see also, e.g., Gen. 15:16. In Eph. 3:21 *genea* is combined with *aiōn* in a remarkable phrase in a doxology: "Unto Him be the glory in the church and in Christ Jesus, unto all generations for ever and ever (wrongly in A.V. 'all ages, world without end')." The word *genea* is to be distinguished from *aiōn*, as not denoting a period of unlimited duration. See GENERATION, NATION, TIME.

NT: B.153d; CB.1248a; K.114.
OT: dôr: S.1755; HR.236a.2; H.418b; BD.189c.
GEN. REF.: IS.1:67; NB.18; Z.—.

3. *hēlikia* [ἡλικία, 2244], primarily an age, as a certain length of life, came to mean (*a*) a particular time of life, as when a person is said to be "of age," John 9:21, 23, or beyond a certain stage of life, Heb. 11:11; (*b*) elsewhere only of stature, e.g., Matt. 6:27; Luke 2:52; 12:25; 19:3; Eph. 4:13. Some regard Matt. 6:27 and Luke 12:25 as coming under (*a*). It is to be distinguished from *aiōn* and *genea*, since it has to do simply with matters relating to an individual, either his time of life or his height. See STATURE. ¶

NT: B.345a; CB.1249c; K.—.
OT: qômāh: S.6967; HR.606b.2; H.1999a; BD.879b.
GEN. REF.: IS.1:67; NB.18; Z.—.

4. *hēmera* [ἡμέρα, 2250], a day, is rendered "age" in Luke 2:36, "of a great age" (lit., 'advanced in many days'). In Luke 3:23 there is no word in the original corresponding to age. The phrase is simply "about thirty years." See DAY, JUDGMENT, TIME, YEAR.

NT: B.345d; CB.1249c; K.309.
OT: yôm: S.3117; HR.607b.9; H.852; BD.398a.
GEN. REF.: IS.1:67; NB.18; Z.—.

B. Adjectives.

1. *huperakmos* [ὑπέρακμος, 5230] in 1 Cor. 7:36 is rendered "past the flower of her age"; more lit., 'beyond the bloom or flower (*acme*) of life.' ¶

NT: B.839d; CB.1252a; K.—.
OT: —.
GEN. REF.: IS.1:67; NB.18; Z.—.

2. *teleios* [τέλειος, 5046], complete, perfect, from *telos*, an end, is translated "of full age" in Heb. 5:14, A.V. (R.V., "fullgrown man").

NT: B.809a; CB.1271b; K.1161.
OT: shālēm: S.8003; HR.1342c.1b; H.2401; BD.1023d.
tāmîm: S.8549; HR.1342c.3a; H.2522d; BD.1071a.
GEN. REF.: IS.1:67; NB.18; Z.—.

Note: In Mark 5:42, R.V., "old," A.V., "of the age of," is, lit., 'of twelve years.' For "of great age," Luke 2:36, see STRICKEN. For "of mine own age," Gal. 1:14, R.V., see EQUAL, B, No. 2.

AGED

A. Nouns.

1. *presbutēs* [πρεσβύτης, 4246], an elderly man, is a longer form of *presbus*, the comparative degree of which is *presbuteros*, a senior, elder, both of which, as also the verb *presbeuō*, to be elder, to be an ambassador, are derived from *proeisbainō*, to be far advanced. The noun is found in Luke 1:18, "an old man"; Tit. 2:2, "aged men," and Philm. 9, where the R.V. marg., "Paul an ambassador," is to be accepted, the original almost certainly being *presbeutēs* (not *presbutēs*), an ambassador. So he describes himself in Eph. 6:20. As Lightfoot points out, he is hardly likely to have made his age a ground of appeal to Philemon, who, if he was the father of Archippus, cannot have been

much younger than Paul himself. See OLD.
NT: B.700d; CB.1266d; K.931.
OT: zāqēn: S.2205; HR.1202c.1; H.574b; BD.278c.
GEN. REF.: IS.1:67; NB.18; Z.–.

2. *presbutis* [πρεσβυτις, 4247], the feminine of No. 1, an aged woman, is found in Tit. 2:3. ¶
NT: B.700d; CB.1266b; K.931.
OT: –.
GEN. REF.: IS.1:67; NB.18; Z.–.

B. Verb.

gēraskō [γηράσκω, 1095], from *gēras*, old age, signifies to grow old, John 21:18 ("when thou shalt be old") and Heb. 8:13 (R.V., "that which . . . waxeth aged," A.V., "old"). See OLD. ¶
NT: B.158a; CB.1248b; K.–.
OT: zāqēn: S.2204; HR.256a.2; H.574; BD.278b.
GEN. REF.: IS.1:67; NB.18; Z.–.

For **AGO** see **LONG,** A, No. 5, and in combination with other words.

AGONY

agōnia [ἀγωνία, 74], Eng., agony, was used among the Greeks as an alternative to *agōn*, a place of assembly; then for the contests or games which took place there, and then to denote intense emotion. It was more frequently used eventually in this last respect, to denote severe emotional strain and anguish. So in Luke 22:44, of the Lord's agony in Gethsemane. ¶
NT: B.15a; CB.1233c; K.20.
OT: –.
GEN. REF.: –.

AGREE, AGREEMENT

A. Verbs.

1. *sumphōneō* [συμφωνέω, 4856], lit., to sound together (*sun*, together, *phōnē*, a sound), i.e., to be in accord, primarily of musical instruments, is used in the N.T. of the agreement (*a*) of persons concerning a matter, Matt. 18:19; 20:2, 13; Acts 5:9; (*b*) of the writers of Scripture, Acts 15:15; (*c*) of things that are said to be congruous in their nature, Luke 5:36. ¶
NT: B.780d; CB.–; K.1287.
OT: 'ût: S.225; HR.1306c.1; H.53; BD.22d.
ḥābar: S.2266; HR.1306c.2; H.598; BD.287d.
nûaḥ: S.5117; HR.1306c.3; H.1323; BD.628a.
GEN. REF.: IS.1:72; NB.–; Z.–.

Note: Cp. *sumphōnēsis*, concord, 2 Cor. 6:15, ¶ , and *sumphōnia*, music, Luke 15:25. ¶

2. *suntithēmi* [συντίθημι, 4934], lit., to put together (*sun*, with, *tithēmi*, to put), in the Middle Voice, means to make an agreement, or to assent to; translated "covenanted" in Luke 22:5, "agreed" in John 9:22, and Acts 23:20; "assented" in Acts 24:9. ¶
NT: B.790c; CB.–; K.–.
OT: qāshar: S.7194; HR.1320c.2; H.2090; BD.905a.
shālēm: S.8003; HR.1320c.3; H.2401; BD.1022b.
GEN. REF.: IS.1:72; NB.–; Z.–.

Note: For the synonym *sunkatatithēmi*, a strengthened form of No. 2, see CONSENT, No. 4.

3. *eunoeō* [εὐνοέω, 2132], lit., to be well-minded, well-disposed (*eu*, well, *nous*, the mind), is found in Matt. 5:25, "agree with," ¶
NT: B.323; CB.–; K.636.
OT: –.
GEN. REF.: IS.1:72; NB.–; Z.–.

4. *peithō* [πείθω, 3982], to persuade, is rendered "agreed" in Acts 5:40, where the meaning is "they yielded to him." See ASSURE, BELIEVE, CONFIDENT, FRIEND, OBEY, PERSUADE, TRUST, YIELD.
NT: B.639a; CB.1263a; K.818.
OT: bāṭaḥ: S.982; HR.1114b.2; H.233; BD.105a.
GEN. REF.: IS.1:72; NB.–; Z.–.

B. Nouns.

1. *gnōmē* [γνώμη, 1106], mind, will, is used with *poieō*, to make, in the sense of to agree, Rev. 17:17 (twice), lit., 'to do His mind, and to make one mind'; R.V., "to come to one mind," A.V., "to agree." See ADVICE, JUDGMENT, MIND, PURPOSE, WILL.
NT: B.163a; CB.1248b; K.119.
OT: –.
GEN. REF.: IS.1:72; NB.–; Z.–.

2. *sunkatathesis* [συνκατάθεσις, 4783], akin to A, No. 3, occurs in 2 Cor. 6:16. ¶
NT: B.773c; CB.–; K.–.
OT: –.
GEN. REF.: IS.1:72; NB.–; Z.–.

C. Adjectives.

1. *asumphōnos* [ἀσύμφωνος, 800], inharmonious (*a*, negative, *sumphōnos*, harmonious), is used in Acts 28:25, "they agreed not." ¶
NT: B.118c; CB.–; K.–.
OT: –.
GEN. REF.: IS.1:72; NB.–; Z.–.

2. *isos* [ἴσος, 2470], equal, is used with the verb to be, signifying to agree, Mark 14:56, 59, lit., 'their thought was not equal one with the other.' See EQUAL, LIKE, MUCH.
NT: B.381a; CB.1253a; K.370.
OT: –.
GEN. REF.: IS.1:72; NB.–; Z.–.

Note: Sumphōnos, harmonious, agreeing, is used only with the preposition *ek* in the phrase *ek sumphōnou*, by consent, lit., out of agreement, 1 Cor. 7:5. In Mark 14:70 some texts have the verb *homoiazō*, "agreeth," A.V.

For **AGROUND** see **RUN,** No. 11

AH!

1. *oua* [οὐά, 3758], an interjection of derision and insult, is translated Ha! in Mark 15:29, R.V. ¶
NT: B.591a; CB.–; K.–.
OT: –.
GEN. REF.: –.

2. *ea* [ἔα, 1436], an interjection of surprise, fear and anger, was the ejaculation of the man with the spirit of an unclean demon, Luke 4:34, R.V., the A.V. renders it "Let us alone" (see R.V. marg.). ¶

NT: B.211a; CB.–; K.–.
OT: –.
GEN. REF.: –.

AIM

philotimeomai [φιλοτιμέομαι, 5389], lit., to be fond of honour (*phileō*, to love, *timē*, honour), and so, actuated by this motive, to strive to bring something to pass; hence, to be ambitious, to make it one's aim, Rom. 15:20, of Paul's aim in Gospel pioneering, R.V. (A.V., "strive"); 2 Cor. 5:9, of the aim of believers "to be well-pleasing" unto the Lord, R.V. (A.V., "labour"); in 1 Thess. 4:11, of the aim of believers to be quiet, do their own business and work with their own hands; both Versions translate it "study." Some would render it, 'strive restlessly'; perhaps 'strive earnestly' is nearer the mark, but 'make it one's aim' is a good translation in all three places. See LABOUR, STRIVE, STUDY. ¶

NT: B.861c; CB.1264b; K.–.
OT: –.
GEN. REF.: IS.1:84; NB.–; Z.–.

AIR

1. *aēr* [ἀήρ, 109], (Eng., air), signifies the atmosphere, certainly in five of the seven occurrences, Acts 22:23; 1 Cor. 9:26; 14:9; Rev. 9:2; 16:17, and almost certainly in the other two, Eph. 2:2 and 1 Thess. 4:17. ¶

NT: B.20b; CB.1233a; K.25.
OT: shāḥaq: S.7834; HR.29a.1; H.2367a; BD.1007a.
GEN. REF.: IS.1:85; NB.–; Z.–.

2. *ouranos* [οὐρανός, 3772] denotes the heaven. The R.V. always renders it "heaven." The A.V. translates it "air" in Matt. 8:20. In the phrase "the fowls (or birds) of the heaven" the A.V. always has "air"; "sky" in Matt. 16:2, 3; Luke 12:56; in all other instances "heaven." The word is probably derived from a root meaning to cover or encompass. See HEAVEN, SKY.

NT: B.593d; CB.1261b; K.736.
OT: shāmayim: S.8065; HR.1031b.4; H.3038; BD.1029c.
GEN. REF.: IS.1:85; NB.–; Z.–.

For **ALABASTER** see **CRUSE**

For **ALAS!** see **WOE**

ALBEIT

hina [ἵνα, 2443], a conjunction, meaning "that," and so rendered in Philm. 19, R.V., for A.V., "albeit."

NT: B.376d; CB.1250c; K.366.
OT: –.
GEN. REF.: –.

ALIEN

allotrios [ἀλλότριος, 245], primarily, belonging to another (the opposite to *idios*, one's own), hence came to mean foreign, strange, not of one's own family, alien, an enemy; "aliens" in Heb. 11:34, elsewhere "strange," etc. See MAN'S, *Note* (1), STRANGE, STRANGER.

NT: B.40c; CB.1234c; K.43.
OT: nēkar: S.5236; HR.57a.4a; H.1368b; BD.648c.
zûr: S.2114; HR.57a.2; H.541; BD.266b.
nokrî: S.5237; HR.57a.4c; H.1368c; BD.648d.
GEN. REF.: IS.1:94; NB.–; Z.–.

ALIENATE

apallotrioō [ἀπαλλοτριόω, 526], consists of *apo*, from, and the above; it signifies to be rendered an alien, to be alienated. In Eph. 2:12 the R.V. corrects to the verbal form "alienated," for the noun "aliens"; elsewhere in Eph. 4:18 and Col. 1:21; the condition of the unbeliever is presented in a threefold state of alienation, (*a*) from the commonwealth of Israel, (*b*) from the life of God, (*c*) from God Himself. ¶ The word is used of Israelites in the Sept. of Ezek. 14:5 ("estranged") and of the wicked in general, Psa. 58:3.

NT: B.80b; CB.1236b; K.43.
OT: zûr: S.2114; HR.116c.1; H.541; BD.266b.
GEN. REF.: IS.1:94; NB.–; Z.–.

ALIKE

Note: In Rom. 14:5, this word is in italics. This addition is not needed in the translation.

For **ALIVE** see **LIFE, C, LIVE,** No. 6

ALL

A. Adjectives.

1. *pas* [πᾶς, 3956], radically means "all." Used without the article it means "every," every kind of variety. So the R.V. marg. in Eph. 2:21, "every building," and the text in 3:15, "every family," and the R.V. marg. of Acts 2:36, "every house"; or it may signify the highest degree, the maximum of what is referred to, as, "with all boldness" Acts 4:29. Before proper names of countries, cities and nations, and before collective terms, like "Israel," it signifies either "all" or "the whole," e.g., Matt. 2:3; Acts 2:36. Used with the article, it means the whole of one object. In the plural it signifies the totality of

the persons or things referred to. Used without a noun it virtually becomes a pronoun, meaning "everyone" or "anyone." In the plural with a noun it means "all." The neuter singular denotes "everything" or "anything whatsoever." One form of the neuter plural (*panta*) signifies wholly, together, in all ways, in all things, Acts 20:35; 1 Cor. 9:25. The neuter plural without the article signifies all things severally, e.g., John 1:3; 1 Cor. 2:10; preceded by the article it denotes all things, as constituting a whole, e.g., Rom. 11:36; 1 Cor. 8:6; Eph. 3:9. See EVERY, *Note* (1), WHOLE.

NT: B.631a; CB.1262c; K.795.
OT: kōl: S.3606; HR.1073a.1; H.2789; BD.481a.
GEN. REF.: IS.1:94; NB.–; Z.–.

2. *hapas* [ἅπας, 537], a strengthened form of *pas*, signifies quite all, the whole, and, in the plural, all, all things. Preceded by an article and followed by a noun it means the whole of. In 1 Tim. 1:16 the significance is 'the whole of His longsuffering,' or 'the fulness of His longsuffering.' See EVERY, WHOLE.

NT: B.81d; CB.1249b; K.795.
OT: kōl: S.3606; HR.118c.1; H.2789; BD.481a.
GEN. REF.: IS.1:94; NB.–; Z.–.

3. *holos* [ὅλος, 3650], the whole, all, is most frequently used with the article followed by a noun, e.g., Matt. 4:23. It is used with the article alone, in John 7:23, "every whit"; Acts 11:26; 21:31; 28:30; Tit. 1:11; Luke 5:5, in the best texts. See ALTOGETHER.

NT: B.564d; CB.1251a; K.682.
OT: kōl: S.3606; HR.989b.1a; H.2789; BD.481a.
GEN. REF.: IS.1:94; NB.–; Z.–.

Note: The adjective *holoklēros*, lit., whole-lot, entire, stresses the separate parts which constitute the whole, no part being incomplete. See ENTIRE.

B. Adverbs.

1. *holōs* [ὅλως, 3654] signifies "at all," Matt. 5:34; 1 Cor. 15:29; "actually," 1 Cor. 5:1, R.V. (A.V., wrongly, "commonly"); "altogether," 1 Cor. 6:7 (A.V., "utterly"). ¶

NT: B.565b; CB.1251a; K.682.
OT: –.
GEN. REF.: IS.1:94; NB.–; Z.–.

Notes: (1) *Holotelēs*, from A, No. 3, and *telos*, complete, signifies wholly, through and through, 1 Thess. 5:23, lit., 'whole complete'; there, not an increasing degree of sanctification is intended, but the sanctification of the believer in every part of his being. ¶

(2) The synonym *katholou*, a strengthened form of *holou* signifies "at all," Acts 4:18. ¶

2. *pantōs* [πάντως, 3843], when used without a negative, signifies wholly, entirely, by all means, Acts 18:21 (A.V.); 1 Cor. 9:22; altogether, 1 Cor. 9:10; no doubt, doubtless, Luke 4:23, R.V. (A.V., "surely"); Acts 28:4. In 21:22 it is translated "certainly," R.V., for A.V., "needs" (lit., 'by all means'). With a negative it signifies in no wise, Rom. 3:9; 1 Cor. 5:10; 16:12 ("at all"). See ALTOGETHER, DOUBT (NO), MEANS, SURELY, WISE. ¶

NT: B.609b; CB.–; K.–.
OT: –.
GEN. REF.: IS.1:95; NB.–; Z.–.

C. Pronoun.

hosa [ὅσα, 3745], the neuter plural of *hosos*, as much as, chiefly used in the plural, is sometimes rendered "all that," e.g., Acts 4:23; 14:27. It really means "whatsoever things." See Luke 9:10, R.V., "what things."

NT: B.586b; CB.1251b; K.–.
OT: –.
GEN. REF.: IS.1:95; NB.–; Z.–.

ALLEGE

paratithēmi [παρατίθημι, 3908], to place beside or to set before (*para*, beside, *tithēmi*, to put), while often used in its literal sense of material things, as well as in its more common significance, to commit, entrust, twice means to set before one in teaching, as in putting forth a parable, Matt. 13:24, 31, R.V. Once it is used of setting subjects before one's hearers by way of argument and proof, of Paul, in "opening and alleging" facts concerning Christ, Acts 17:3. See COMMEND, COMMIT, PUT, SET.

NT: B.622d; CB.–; K.1176.
OT: sûm, sîm: S.7760; HR.1065a.7; H.2243; BD.962c.
GEN. REF.: IS.1:95; NB.–; Z.–.

Note: Legō is rendered "put forth" in the A.V. of Luke 14:7; but *legō* signifies to speak; hence the R.V., "spake." The A.V. seems to be an imitation of *paratithēmi* in Matt. 13:24, 31. See SAY.

ALLEGORY

allēgoreō [ἀλληγορέω, 238], translated in Gal. 4:24 "contain an allegory" (A.V., "are an allegory"), formed from *allos*, other, and *agoreuō*, to speak in a place of assembly (*agora*, the market-place), came to signify to speak, not according to the primary sense of the word, but so that the facts stated are applied to illustrate principles. The allegorical meaning does not do away with the literal meaning of the narrative. There may be more than one allegorical meaning though, of course, only one literal meaning. Scripture histories represent or embody spiritual principles, and these are ascertained, not by the play of the imagination, but by the rightful application of the doctrines of Scripture. ¶

NT: B.39b; CB.1234c; K.42.
OT: –.
GEN. REF.: IS.1:95; NB.–; Z.–.

For **ALLELUIA** (which has been robbed of its initial aspirate) see **HALLELUJAH**

For **ALLOTTED** see **CHARGE,** A (*b*), No. 4

ALLOW

1. *dokimazō* [δοκιμάζω, 1381], to prove with a view to approving, is twice translated by the verb to allow in the A.V.; the R.V. corrects to "approveth" in Rom. 14:22, and "have been approved," 1 Thess. 2:4, of being qualified to be entrusted with the Gospel; in Rom. 1:28, with the negative, the R.V. has "refused," for A.V., "did not like." See APPROVE.

NT: B.202c; CB.1242a; K.181.
OT: bāḥan: S.974; HR.339c.1; H.230; BD.103c.
GEN. REF.: IS.1:97; NB.–; Z.–.

2. *ginōskō* [γινώσκω, 1097], to know, is rendered "allow" in Rom. 7:15 (A.V.); the R.V. has "that which I do I know not"; i.e., 'I do not recognize, as a thing for which I am responsible.' See AWARE, CAN, FEEL, KNOW, PERCEIVE, RESOLVE, SPEAK, SURE, UNDERSTAND.

NT: B.160d; CB.1248b; K.119.
OT: yāda': S.3045; HR.267a.4; H.848; BD.393b.
GEN. REF.: IS.1:97; NB.–; Z.–.

3. *suneudokeō* [συνευδοκέω, 4909], to consent or fully approve (*sun*, with, *eu*, well, *dokeō*, to think), is translated "allow" in Luke 11:48; "was consenting" in Acts 8:1; 22:20. See CONSENT.

NT: B.788d; CB.–; K.–.
OT: –.
GEN. REF.: IS.1:97; NB.–; Z.–.

4. *prosdechomai* [προσδέχομαι, 4327], mistranslated "allow" in Acts 24:15, A.V., means to wait for, in contrast to rejection, there said of entertaining a hope; hence the R.V., "look for." See ACCEPT, A, No. 3.

NT: B.712b; CB.1267a; K.146.
OT: rāṣāh: S.7521; HR.1212c.8; H.2207; BD.953a.
qābal: S.6901; HR.1212c.6; H.1980; BD.867a.
GEN. REF.: IS.1:97; NB.–; Z.–.

For **ALLURE** see **BEGUILE,** No. 4, **ENTICE**

ALMIGHTY

pantokratōr [παντοκράτωρ, 3841], almighty, or ruler of all (*pas*, all, *krateō*, to hold, or to have strength), is used of God only, and is found, in the Epistles, only in 2 Cor. 6:18, where the title is suggestive in connection with the context; elsewhere only in the Apocalypse, nine times. In one place, 19:6, the A.V. has "omnipotent," R.V., "(the Lord our God,) the Almighty." ¶ The word is introduced in the Sept. as a translation of "Lord (or God) of hosts," e.g., Jer. 5:14 and Amos 4:13.

NT: B.608d; CB.1261c; K.466.
OT: s^{e}bā'ōt: S.6635; HR.1053c.3; H.1865a,b; BD.839b.
shadday: S.7704; HR.1053c.4; H.2234a,b; BD.994d.
GEN. REF.: IS.1:97; NB.25; Z.–.

ALMOST

A. Adverb.

schedon [σχεδόν, 4975], is used either (*a*) of locality, Acts 19:26, or (*b*) of degree, Acts 13:44; Heb. 9:22. ¶

NT: B.797a; CB.–; K.–.
OT: –.
GEN. REF.: IS.1:97; NB.–; Z.–.

B. Verb.

mellō [μελλω, 3195], to be about to do anything, or to delay, is used in connection with a following verb in the sense of "almost," in Acts 21:27, lit., 'And when the seven days were about to be completed.' In Acts 26:28 the A.V., "Almost thou persuadest me to be a Christian" obscures the sense; the R.V. rightly has "with but little persuasion"; lit., 'in a little.' See ABOUT, B.

NT: B.500d; CB.1258a; K.–.
OT: –.
GEN. REF.: IS.1:97; NB.–; Z.–.

ALMS, ALMSDEEDS

eleēmosunē [ἐλεημοσύνη, 1654], connected with *eleēmōn*, merciful, signifies (*a*) mercy, pity, particularly in giving alms, Matt. 6:1 (see below), 2, 3, 4; Acts 10:2; 24:17; (*b*) the benefaction itself, the alms (the effect for the cause), Luke 11:41; 12:33; Acts 3:2, 3, 10; 9:36, "alms-deeds"; 10:2, 4, 31. ¶

NT: B.249d; CB.1244a; K.222.
OT: ṣ^{e}dāqāh: S.6666; HR.450b.3b; H.1879b; BD.842a.
ḥesed: S.2618; HR.450b.2; H.686a,699a; BD.338c.
GEN. REF.: IS.1:98; NB.26; Z.–.

Note: In Matt. 6:1, the R.V., translating *dikaiosunē*, according to the most authentic texts, has "righteousness," for A.V., "alms."

ALOES

aloē [ἀλόη, 250], an aromatic tree, the soft, bitter wood of which was used by Orientals for the purposes of fumigation and embalming, John 19:39 (see also Num. 24:6; Psa. 45:8; Prov. 7:17). ¶ In the Sept., S. of Sol. 4:14. ¶

NT: B.41b; CB.–; K.–.
OT: '^{a}hālōt: S.174; HR.59b.1; H.34; BD.14c.
GEN. REF.: IS.1:99; NB.26; Z.–.

ALONE (LET ALONE)

A. Adjective.

monos [μόνος] denotes single, alone, solitary, Matt. 4:4 etc. See ONLY, SELF.

B. Adverbs.

1. *monon* [μόνον, 3440], the neuter of A., meaning only, exclusively, e.g., Rom. 4:23; Acts 19:26, is translated "alone" in the A.V. of John 17:20; R.V., "only." See ONLY.

NT: B.527c; CB.1259b; K.–.
OT: lᵉbad: S.905; HR.933a.2; H.201a; BD.94c.
'ak: S.389; HR.933a.1; H.84; BD.36c.
GEN. REF.: –.

2. *kata monas* [κατὰ μόνας, 2651], signifies apart, in private, alone, Mark 4:10; Luke 9:18. Some texts have the phrase as one word. ¶

NT: B.527c (monas 3); CB.1253c; K.–.
OT: lᵉbad: S.905; HR.933b.4; H.201a; BD.94c.
GEN. REF.: –.

C. Verb.

aphiēmi [ἀφίημι, 863, 1438, 2398], signifies to send away, set free; also to let alone, Matt. 15:14; Mark 14:6; Luke 13:8; John 11:48; 12:7 (R.V., "suffer her"); in Acts 5:38 some texts have *easate* from *eaō*, to permit. See CRY, FORGIVE, FORSAKE, LAY, *Note* (2), LEAVE, LET, OMIT, PUT, No. 16, *Note*, REMIT, SEND, SUFFER, YIELD.

NT: B.125c; CB.1236b; K.88.
OT: nûaḥ: S.5117; HR.183b.4; H.1323; BD.628a.
nāsā': S.5375; HR.183b.6; H.1421; BD.669d.
nātan: S.5414; HR.183b.7; H.1443; BD.678a.
GEN. REF.: –.

Notes: (1) The phrase *kath' heautēn* means "by (or in) itself," Jas. 2:17, R.V., for A.V., "being alone" (see A.V., margin).

NT: B.211d; CB.1249b; K.–.
OT: –.
GEN. REF.: –.

(2) The phrase *kat' idian*, Mark 4:34, signifies in private, "privately," R.V. (A.V., "when they were alone").

NT: B.369c; CB.1252c; K.–.
OT: –.
GEN. REF.: –.

(3) For "let us alone" see AH!

For **ALONG** see the R.V. of Acts 17:23 and 27:13

For **ALOUD** see **CRY,** B, No. 2

ALREADY

ēdē [ἤδη, 2235, 5348], is always used of time in the N.T. and means now, at (or by) this time, sometimes in the sense of "already," i.e. without mentioning or insisting upon anything further, e.g., 1 Tim. 5:15. In 1 Cor. 4:8 and 1 John 2:8, the R.V. corrects the A.V. "now," and, in 2 Tim. 4:6, the A.V. "now ready to be," by the rendering "already."

See also John 9:27 (A.V., "already," R.V., "even now") and 1 Cor. 6:7 (A.V., "now," R.V., "already").

NT: B.344a; CB.1242a; K.–.
OT: kᵉbār: S.3528; HR.604b.2; H.947c; BD.460c.
'attāh: S.6258; HR.604b.3; H.1650c; BD.773d.
GEN. REF.: –.

Notes: (1) *Phthanō*, to anticipate, be beforehand with, signifies to attain already, in Phil. 3:16. See ATTAIN, COME, PRECEDE.

NT: B.856d; CB.1264c; K.1258.
OT: –.
GEN. REF.: –.

(2) *Proamartanō*, to sin before, or heretofore, is translated "have sinned already" in 2 Cor. 12:21, A.V.; both Versions have "heretofore" in 13:2.

ALSO

1. *kai* [καί, 2532], has three chief meanings, "and," "also," "even." When *kai* means "also" it precedes the word which it stresses. In English the order should be reversed. In John 9:40, e.g., the R.V. rightly has "are we also blind?" instead of "are we blind also?" In Acts 2:26 the R.V. has "moreover My flesh also," instead of "moreover also . . ." See EVEN.

NT: B.391d; CB.1253a; K.–.
OT: –.
GEN. REF.: –.

2. *eti* [ἔτι, 2089, 5037], "yet" or "further," is used (*a*) of time, (*b*) of degree, and in this sense is once translated "also," Luke 14:26, "his own life also." Here the meaning probably is 'and, further, even his own life' (the force of the *kai* being "even"). No other particles mean "also." See EVEN, FURTHER, LONGER, MORE, MOREOVER, STILL, THENCEFORTH, YET.

NT: B.315c; CB.1247a; K.–.
OT: 'ôd: S.5750; HR.561a.11; H.1576a; BD.728c.
GEN. REF.: –.

Note: The particle *te* means "both" or "and."

NT: B.807b; CB.–; K.–.
OT: –.
GEN. REF.: –.

ALTAR

1. *thusiastērion* [θυσιαστήριον, 2379], probably the neuter of the adjective *thusiastērios*, is derived from *thusiazō*, to sacrifice. Accordingly it denotes an altar for the sacrifice of victims, though it was also used for the altar of incense, e.g., Luke 1:11. In the N.T. this word is reserved for the altar of the true God, Matt. 5:23, 24; 23:18-20, 35; Luke 11:51; 1 Cor. 9:13; 10:18, in contrast to *bōmos*, No. 2, below. In the Sept. *thusiastērion* is mostly, but not entirely, used for the Divinely appointed altar; it is used for idol altars, e.g., in Judg. 2:2; 6:25; 2 Kings 16:10.

NT: B.366d; CB.1272c; K.342.
OT: mizbēaḥ: S.4196; HR.666b.3; H.522b; BD.258a.
GEN. REF.: IS.1:100; NB.27; Z.–.

2. *bōmos* [βωμός, 1041], properly, an elevated place, always denotes either a pagan altar or an altar reared without Divine appointment. In the N.T. the only place where this is

found is Acts 17:23, as this is the only mention of such. Three times in the Sept., but only in the Apocrypha, *bōmos* is used for the Divine altar. In Josh. 22 the Sept. translators have carefully observed the distinction, using *bōmos* for the altar which the two and a half tribes erected, verses 10, 11, 16, 19, 23, 26, 34, no Divine injunction being given for this; in verses 19, 28, 29, where the altar ordained of God is mentioned, *thusiastērion* is used. ¶

NT: B.148d; CB.1239b; K.–.
OT: mizbēaḥ: S.4196; HR.232c.2; H.522b; BD.258a.
GEN. REF.: IS.1:100; NB.27; Z.–.

For **ALTERED** see **OTHER**, No. 2

ALTHOUGH: see Note †, p. 1

ALTOGETHER

A. Adjective.

holos [ὅλος, 3650], whole, is rendered "altogether" in John 9:34. It is sometimes subjoined to an adjective or a verb, as in this case, to show that the idea conveyed by the adjective or verb belongs to the whole person or thing referred to. So here, lit., 'thou wast altogether (i.e., completely) born in sins.' Cp. Matt. 13:33, R.V.; Luke 11:36; 13:21; John 13:10, R.V. (rendered "every whit"). See ALL, and EVERY WHIT.

NT: B.564d; CB.1251a; K.682.
OT: kōl: S.3606; HR.989b.1a; H.2789; BD.481a.
GEN. REF.: –.

B. Adverbs.

1. *pantōs* [πάντως, 3843], from *pas*, "all," is translated in various ways. The rendering "altogether" is found only in 1 Cor. 5:10 (where the R.V. margin gives the alternative meaning, "not at all meaning the fornicators of this world") and 9:10 (marg., "doubtless"). The other renderings are, in Luke 4:23, "doubtless" (A.V., "surely"); in Acts 18:21, "by all means," (A.V., only); so in 1 Cor. 9:22, both R.V. and A.V.; in Acts 21:22, "certainly" (A.V., "needs," which does not give an accurate meaning); in Acts 28:4, "no doubt"; in Rom. 3:9, "in no wise" (lit., 'not at all'), so in 1 Cor. 16:12. In Acts 26:29 the A.V. has given a misleading rendering in the phrase "both almost and altogether"; there is no Greek word here which means "altogether"; the R.V. corrects to "whether with little or with much." See ALL. ¶

NT: B.609b; CB.–; K.–.
OT: –.
GEN. REF.: –.

2. *holōs* [3654] denotes altogether or actually, or assuredly. See ACTUALLY, and ALL, B, No. 1.

NT: B.565b; CB.1251a; K.–.
OT: –.
GEN. REF.: –.

ALWAY, ALWAYS

1. *aei* [ἀεί, 104], has two meanings: (*a*) perpetually, incessantly, Acts 7:51; 2 Cor. 4:11; 6:10; Tit. 1:12; Heb. 3:10; (*b*) invariably, at any and every time, of successive occurrences, when something is to be repeated, according to the circumstances, 1 Pet. 3:15; 2 Pet. 1:12. See EVER. ¶

NT: B.19c; CB.1233a; K.–.
OT: tāmîd: S.8548; HR.28b.2; H.1157a; BD.556b.
GEN. REF.: IS.1:104; NB.–; Z.–.

2. *hekastote* [ἑκάστοτε, 1539], from *hekastos*, each, is used in 2 Pet. 1:15, R.V., "at every time" (A.V., "always"). See TIME. ¶

NT: B.236d; CB.–; K.–.
OT: –.
GEN. REF.: IS.1:104; NB.–; Z.–.

3. *diapantos* [διαπαντός, 1275] is, lit., 'through all,' i.e., 'through all time,' (*dia*, through, *pas*, all). In the best texts the words are separated. The phrase, which is used of the time throughout which a thing is done, is sometimes rendered "continually," sometimes "always"; "always" or "alway" in Mk. 5:5; Acts 10:2; 24:16; Rom. 11:10; "continually" in Luke 24:53; Heb. 9:6; 13:15, the idea being that of a continuous practice carried on without being abandoned. See CONTINUALLY. ¶

NT: B.179b (A.II.1a); CB.–; K.–.
OT: –.
GEN. REF.: IS.1:104; NB.–; Z.–.

4 and 5. *pantē* [πάντῃ, 3839] and *pantote* [πάντοτε, 3842] are derived from *pas*, all. The former is found in Acts 24:3. ¶ The latter is the usual word for "always." See EVER, EVERMORE.

NT: pantē: B.608d; CB.–; K.–.
OT: –.
GEN. REF.: IS.1:104; NB.–; Z.–.

NT: pantote: B.609b; CB.1261c; K.–.
OT: –.
GEN. REF.: IS.1:104; NB.–; Z.–.

Note: Two phrases, rendered "always" or "alway" in the A.V., are *en panti kairō* [2540] (lit., 'in every season'), Luke 21:36, R.V., "at every season," Eph. 6:18, R.V., "at all seasons," and *pasas tas hēmeras* [2250], (lit., 'all the days'), Matt. 28:20, A.V. and R.V., "alway."

NT: kairos: B.394d; CB.1253a; K.389.
OT: –.
GEN. REF.: IS.1:104; NB.–; Z.–.

NT: hēmera: B.345d; CB.1249c; K.309.
OT: –.
GEN. REF.: IS.1:104; NB.–; Z.–.

AMAZE, AMAZEMENT

A. Nouns.

1. *ekstasis* [ἔκστασις, 1611] is, lit., 'a standing out (*ek*, out of, *stasis*, a standing).' Eng. "ecstasy" is a transliteration. It is translated "amazement" in Acts 3:10. It was said of any displacement, and hence, especially, with reference to the mind, of that alteration of the normal condition by which the person is thrown into a state of surprise or fear, or both; or again, in which a person is so transported out of his natural state that he falls into a trance, Acts 10:10; 11:5; 22:17. As to the other meaning, the R.V. has "amazement" in Mark 5:42 and Luke 5:26, but "astonishment" in Mark 16:8. See TRANCE. ¶

NT: B.245a; CB.1244a; K.217.
OT: hᵃrādāh: S.2731; HR.441b.4; H.735b; BD.353d.
paḥad: S.6342; HR.441b.6; H.1756; BD.808b.
timmāhôn: S.8541; HR.441b.10; H.2518a; BD.1069b.
GEN. REF.: –.

2. *thambos* [θάμβος, 2285], amazement, wonder, is probably connected with a root signifying to render immovable; it is frequently associated with terror as well as astonishment, as with the verb (No. 3, below) in Acts 9:6. It occurs in Luke 4:36; 5:9; Acts 3:10. See WONDER. ¶

NT: B.350c; CB.1271c; K.312.
OT: 'āyōm: S.366; HR.623b.1; H.80a; BD.33d.
paḥad: S.6342; HR.623b.3; H.1756; BD.808b.
GEN. REF.: –.

Note: Ptoēsis signifies "terror," not "amazement," 1 Pet. 3:6, R.V. ¶

B. Verbs.

1. *existēmi* [ἐξίστημι, 1839], akin to A, No. 1, lit. means to stand out from. Like the noun, this is used with two distinct meanings: (*a*) in the sense of amazement, the word should be invariably rendered "amazed," as in the R.V., e.g., in the case of Simon Magus (for A.V., "bewitched"), Acts 8:9 and 11. It is used, in the Passive Voice, of Simon himself in th 13th ver., R.V., "he was amazed," for A.V., "wondered." "Amaze" is preferable to "astonish" throughout; (*b*) in Mark 3:21 and 2 Cor. 5:13 it is used with its other meaning of being beside oneself. See BESIDE ONESELF (to be), BEWITCH, WONDER.

NT: B.276b; CB.1247c (exhi—); K.217.
OT: hārēd: S.2730; HR.496c.5; H.735a; BD.353d.
shāmēm: S.8074; HR.496c.28; H.2409; BD.1030d.
tāmāh: S.8539; HR.496c.29; H.2218; BD.1069b.
GEN. REF.: –.

2. *ekplēssō* [ἐκπλήσσω, 1605], from *ek*, out of, *plēssō*, to strike, lit., to strike out, signifies to be exceedingly struck in mind, to be astonished (*ek*, intensive). The English "astonish" should be used for this verb, and "amaze" for *existēmi*, as in the R.V.; see Matt. 19:25; Luke 2:48; 9:43.

NT: B.244b; CB.1243c; K.–.
OT: shāmēm: S.8074; HR.439b.1; H.2409; BD.1030d.
GEN. REF.: –.

3. *thambeō* [θαμβέω, 2284], akin to A, No. 2, is used in Mark 1:27; 10:24, 32 (and Acts 9:6, A.V.). The R.V. has "amazed" in each place; A.V., "astonished," in Mark 10:24. ¶

NT: B.350c; CB.1271c; K.312.
OT: bā'at: S.1204; HR.623b.1: H.265; BD.129d.
rāgaz: S.7264; HR.623b.4; H.2112; BD.919a.
GEN. REF.: –.

4. *ekthambeō* [ἐκθαμβέω, 1568], an intensive form of No. 3, is found in Mark's Gospel only; in 9:15, "were greatly amazed"; in 14:33, A.V., "were sore amazed"; in 16:5, R.V., "were amazed," A.V., "were affrighted"; in ver. 6, R.V., "be not amazed," A.V., "be not affrighted." See AFFRIGHTED. ¶

NT: B.240b; CB.1244a; K.312.
OT: –.
GEN. REF.: –.

C. Adjective.

ekthambos [ἔκθαμβος, 1569], a strengthened form of A, No. 2, is found in Acts 3:11. The intensive force of the word is brought out by the tendering "greatly wondering." See WONDER. ¶

NT: B.240b; CB.1244a; K.312.
OT: –.
GEN. REF.: –.

AMBASSADOR, AMBASSAGE

A. Verb.

presbeuō [πρεσβεύω, 4243] denotes (*a*) to be elder or eldest, prior in birth or age; (*b*) to be an ambassador, 2 Cor. 5:20, and Eph. 6:20; for Philm. 9 see under AGED. There is a suggestion that to be an ambassador for Christ involves the experience suggested by the word "elder." Elder men were chosen as ambassadors.

NT: B.699c; CB.1266b; K.931.
OT: –.
GEN. REF.: IS.1:109; NB.29; Z.–.

B. Noun.

presbeia [πρεσβεία, 4242], primarily, age, eldership, rank, hence, an embassy or ambassage, is used in Luke 14:32; in 19:14, R.V., "ambassage," for A.V., "message." ¶

NT: B.699b; CB.1266b; K.931.
OT: –.
GEN. REF.: IS.1:109; NB.29; Z.–.

AMEN

amēn [ἀμήν, 281] is transliterated from Hebrew into both Greek and English. "Its meanings may be seen in such passages as Deut. 7:9, 'the faithful (the Amen) God,' Isa. 49:7,

'Jehovah that is faithful,' 65:16, 'the God of truth,' marg., 'the God of Amen.' And if God is faithful His testimonies and precepts are 'sure (*amen*),' Psa. 19:7; 111:7, as are also His warnings, Hos. 5:9, and promises, Isa. 33:16; 55:3. 'Amen' is used of men also, e.g., Prov. 25:13.

"There are cases where the people used it to express their assent to a law and their willingness to submit to the penalty attached to the breach of it, Deut. 27:15, cp. Neh. 5:13. It is also used to express acquiescence in another's prayer, 1 Kings 1:36, where it is defined as '(let) God say so too,' or in another's thanksgiving, 1 Chron. 16:36, whether by an individual, Jer. 11:5, or by the congregation, Psa. 106:48.

"Thus 'Amen' said by God = 'it is and shall be so,' and by men, 'so let it be.'

"Once in the N.T. 'Amen' is a title of Christ, Rev. 3:14, because through Him the purposes of God are established, 2 Cor. 1:20.

"The early Christian churches followed the example of Israel in associating themselves audibly with the prayers and thanksgivings offered on their behalf, 1 Cor. 14:16, where the article 'the' points to a common practice. Moreover this custom conforms to the pattern of things in the Heavens, see Rev. 5:14, etc.

"The individual also said 'Amen' to express his 'let it be so' in response to the Divine 'thus it shall be,' Rev. 22:20. Frequently the speaker adds 'Amen' to his own prayers and doxologies, as is the case at Eph. 3:21, e.g.

"The Lord Jesus often used 'Amen,' translated 'verily,' to introduce new revelations of the mind of God. In John's Gospel it is always repeated, 'Amen, Amen,' but not elsewhere. Luke does not use it at all, but where Matthew, 16:28, and Mark, 9:1, have 'Amen,' Luke has 'of a truth'; thus by varying the translation of what the Lord said, Luke throws light on His meaning."* See VERILY.

NT: B.45c; CB.1234c; K.53.
OT: 'āmēn: S.543; HR.65c.1; H.116b; BD.53b.
GEN. REF.: IS.1:110; NB.29; Z.—.

* From Notes on Galatians by Hogg and Vine, pp.26, 27.

AMEND

echō kompsoteron [2866], lit., to have more finely, i.e., to be better, is used in John 4:52, "to amend." The latter word in the phrase is the comparative of *kompsos*, elegant, nice, fine. Cp. Eng., "he's doing nicely." ¶

NT: B.443a; CB.—; K.—.
OT: —.
GEN. REF.: —.

AMETHYST

amethustos [ἀμέθυστος, 271], primarily meaning "not drunken" (*a*, negative, and *methu*, wine), became used as a noun, being regarded as possessing a remedial virtue against drunkenness. Pliny, however, says that the reason for its name lay in the fact that in colour it nearly approached that of wine, but did not actually do so, Rev. 21:20. ¶

NT: B.44c; CB.1234c; K.—.
OT: 'aḥlāmāh: S.306; HR.65b.1; H.67b; BD.29a.
GEN. REF.: IS.1:110; NB.30; Z.—.

For AMIDST see MIDST

AMISS

A. Adjective.

atopos [ἄτοπος, 824], lit., out of place (*a*, negative, *topos*, a place), hence denotes unbecoming, not befitting. It is used four times in the N.T., and is rendered "amiss" three times in the R.V.; in the malefactor's testimony of Christ, Luke 23:41; in Festus's words concerning Paul, Acts 25:5, "if there is anything amiss in the man" (A.V., "wickedness"); in Acts 28:6, of the expected effect of the viper's attack upon Paul (A.V., "harm"); in 2 Thess. 3:2, of men capable of outrageous conduct, "unreasonable." See HARM, UNREASONABLE.

NT: B.120c; CB.—; K.—.
OT: 'āwen: S.205; HR.176b.1; H.48a; BD.19d.
shaw': S.7723; HR.176b.4; H.2338a; BD.996a.
GEN. REF.: —.

B. Adverb.

kakōs [κακῶς, 2560], akin to *kakos*, evil, is translated "amiss" in Jas. 4:3; elsewhere in various ways. See EVIL, GRIEVOUS, MISERABLE, SORE.

NT: B.398c; CB.1253b; K.391.
OT: —.
GEN. REF.: —.

AMONG: See Note †, p. 1

For ANATHEMA see under CURSE

ANCHOR

ankura [ἄγκυρα, 45], Eng., anchor, was so called because of its curved form (*ankos*, a curve), Acts 27:29, 30, 40; Heb. 6:19. In Acts 27:13 the verb *airō*, to lift, signifies to lift anchor (the noun being understood), R.V., "they weighed anchor" (A.V., "loosing thence"). ¶

NT: B.10c; CB.—; K.—.
OT: —.
GEN. REF.: IS.1:122; NB.—; Z.—.

ANEW

anōthen [ἄνωθεν, 509], lit., 'from above,' in the phrase rendered "anew" in the R.V. (A.V., "again") of John 3:3, 7. See AGAIN.

NT: B.77a; CB.1236a; K.63.
OT: 'al: S.5920; HR.112c.1a; H.1624p; BD.752b.
ma'al: S.4605; HR.112c.1b; H.1624k; BD.751c.
GEN. REF.: IS.1:123; NB.–; Z.–.

Note: In Phil. 3:21 "fashion anew" translates the verb *metaschēmatizō*, which signifies to change the form of.

ANGEL

angelos [ἄγγελος, 32], a messenger (from *angellō*, to deliver a message), sent whether by God or by man or by Satan, "is also used of a guardian or representative in Rev. 1:20, cp. Matt. 18:10; Acts 12:15 (where it is better understood as = 'ghost'), but most frequently of an order of created beings, superior to man, Heb. 2:7; Psa. 8:5, belonging to Heaven, Matt. 24:36; Mark 12:25; and to God, Luke 12:8, and engaged in His service, Psa. 103:20. Angels are spirits, Heb. 1:14, i.e., they have not material bodies as men have; they are either human in form, or can assume the human form when necessary, cp. Luke 24:4, with ver. 23, Acts 10:3 with ver. 30.

"They are called 'holy' in Mark 8:38, and 'elect,' 1 Tim. 5:21, in contrast with some of their original number, Matt. 25:41, who 'sinned,' 2 Pet. 2:4, 'left their proper habitation,' Jude 6, *oikētērion*, a word which occurs again, in the N.T., only in 2 Cor. 5:2. Angels are always spoken of in the masculine gender, the feminine form of the word does not occur."*

NT: B.7a; CB.1235c; K.12.
OT: mal'ak: S.4397; HR.7b.7; H.1068a; BD.521c.
GEN. REF.: IS.1:124; NB.37; Z.–.

Note: Isangelos, "equal to the angels," occurs in Luke 20:36. ¶

* From Notes on Thessalonians by Hogg and Vine, p. 229.

ANGER, ANGRY (to be)

A. Noun.

orgē [ὀργή, 3709], originally any natural impulse, or desire, or disposition, came to signify anger, as the strongest of all passions. It is used of the wrath of man, Eph. 4:31; Col. 3:8; 1 Tim. 2:8; Jas. 1:19, 20; the displeasure of human governments, Rom. 13:4, 5; the sufferings of the Jews at the hands of the Gentiles, Luke 21:23; the terrors of the Law, Rom. 4:15; the anger of the Lord Jesus, Mark 3:5; God's anger with Israel in the wilderness, in a quotation from the O.T., Heb. 3:11; 4:3; God's present anger with the Jews nationally, Rom. 9:22; 1 Thess. 2:16; His present anger with those who disobey the Lord Jesus in His Gospel, John 3:36; God's purposes in judgment, Matt. 3:7; Luke 3:7; Rom. 1:18; 2:5, 8; 3:5; 5:9; 12:19; Eph. 2:3; 5:6; Col. 3:6; 1 Thess. 1:10; 5:9. See INDIGNATION, VENGEANCE, WRATH. ¶

NT: B.578d; CB.1261c; K.716.
OT: 'aph: S.639; HR.1008b.1; H.133a; BD.60a.
ḥēmāh: S.2534; HR.1008b.4a; H.860a; BD.404b.
qāṣaph: S.7107; HR.1008b.13a; H.2058; BD.893b.
GEN. REF.: IS.1:127; NB.39; Z.–.

Notes: (1) *Thumos*, wrath (not translated "anger"), is to be distinguished from *orgē*, in this respect, that *thumos* indicates a more agitated condition of the feelings, an outburst of wrath from inward indignation, while *orgē* suggests a more settled or abiding condition of mind, frequently with a view to taking revenge. *Orgē* is less sudden in its rise than *thumos*, but more lasting in its nature. *Thumos* expresses more the inward feeling, *orgē* the more active emotion. *Thumos* may issue in revenge, though it does not necessarily include it. It is characteristic that it quickly blazes up and quickly subsides, though that is not necessarily implied in each case.

(2) *Parorgismos*, a strengthened form of *orgē*, and used in Eph. 4:26, R.V. margin, "provocation," points especially to that which provokes the wrath, and suggests a less continued state than No. (1). "The first keenness of the sense of provocation must not be cherished, though righteous resentment may remain" (Westcott). The preceding verb, *orgizō*, in this verse implies a just occasion for the feeling. This is confirmed by the fact that it is a quotation from Psa. 4:4 (Sept.), where the Hebrew word signifies to quiver with strong emotion.

Thumos is found eighteen times in the N.T., ten of which are in the Apocalypse, in seven of which the reference is to the wrath of God; so in Rom. 2:8, R.V., "wrath (*thumos*) and indignation" (*orgē*); the order in the A.V. is inaccurate. Everywhere else the word *thumos* is used in a bad sense. In Gal. 5:20, it follows the word jealousies, which when smouldering in the heart break out in wrath. *Thumos* and *orgē* are coupled in two places in the Apocalypse, 16:19, "the fierceness (*thumos*) of His wrath" (*orgē*); and 19:15, "the fierceness of the wrath of Almighty God." See WROTH (be).

(3) *Aganaktēsis* originally signified physical pain or irritation (probably from *agan*, very much, and *achomai*, to grieve), hence, annoyance, vexation, and is used in 2 Cor. 7:11, "indignation." ¶

B. Verbs.

1. *orgizō* [ὀργίζω, 3710], to provoke, to arouse to anger, is used in the Middle Voice in the eight places where it is found, and signifies to be angry, wroth. It is said of individuals, in Matt. 5:22; 18:34; 22:7; Luke 14:21; 15:28, and Eph. 4:26 (where a possible meaning is "be ye angry with yourselves"); of nations, Rev. 11:18; of Satan as the Dragon, 12:17. See WRATH. ¶

NT: B.579c; CB.1261a; K.716.
OT: ḥārāh: S.2734; HR.1010a.5a; H.736; BD.354a.
qāṣaph: S.7107; HR.1010a.9; H.2058; BD.893b.
rāgaz: S.7264; HR.1010a.10; H.2112; BD.919a.
GEN. REF.: IS.1:127; NB.39; Z.–.

2. *parorgizō* [παροργίζω, 3949], is to arouse to wrath, provoke (*para*, used intensively, and No. 1); Rom. 10:19, "will I anger"; Eph. 6:4, "provoke to wrath." See PROVOKE. ¶

NT: B.629d; CB.1262c; K.716.
OT: kā'as: S.3707; HR.1072b.2; H.1016; BD.494d.
qāsaph: S.7107; HR.1072b.6; H.2058; BD.893b.
rāgaz: S.7264; HR.1072b.8; H.2112; BD.919a.
GEN. REF.: IS.1:127; NB.39; Z.–.

3. *cholaō* [χολάω, 5520], connected with *cholē*, gall, bile, which became used metaphorically to signify bitter anger, means to be enraged, John 7:23, "wroth," R.V., in the Lord's remonstrance with the Jews on account of their indignation at His having made a man whole on the Sabbath Day. ¶

NT: B.883b; CB.–; K.–.
OT: –.
GEN. REF.: IS.1:127; NB.39; Z.–.

Notes: (1) *Thumomacheō* (from *thumos*, wrath, *machomai*, to fight) originally denoted to fight with great animosity, and hence came to mean to be very angry, to be exasperated, Acts 12:20, of the anger of Herod, "was highly displeased." ¶

(2) *Thumoō*, the corresponding verb, signifies to provoke to anger, but in the Passive Voice to be wroth, as in Matt. 2:16, of the wrath of Herod, "was exceeding wroth." ¶

(3) *Aganakteō*, see A, Note (3), is rendered in various ways in the seven places where it is used; "moved with indignation," Matt. 20:24 and 21:15, R.V. (A.V. "sore displeased"); "had indignation," Matt. 26:8; Mark 14:4. In Mark 10:14 the R.V. has "was moved with indignation" (A.V., "was much displeased"), said of the Lord Jesus. The same renderings are given in ver. 41. In Luke 13:14 (A.V., "with indignation"), the R.V. rightly puts "being moved with indignation." These words more particularly point to the cause of the vexation. See DISPLEASE, INDIGNATION. ¶

(4) In Col. 3:21 *erethizō* signifies to provoke. The R.V. correctly omits "to anger."

C. Adjective.

orgilos [ὀργίλος, 3711], angry, prone to anger, irascible (see B, Nos. 1, 2), is rendered "soon angry" in Tit. 1:7. ¶

NT: B.579d; CB.1261a; K.716.
OT: 'aph: S.639; HR.1010b; H.133a; BD.60a.
ḥēmah: S.2534; HR.1010b.2; H.860a; BD.404b.
ka'as: S.3707; HR.1010b.3; H.1016; BD.494d.
GEN. REF.: IS.1:127; NB.39; Z.–.

ANGUISH

A. Nouns.

1. *thlipsis* [θλιψις, 2347]; see AFFLICTION (No. 4).

NT: B.362b; CB.1272b; K.334.
OT: ṣar: S.6862; HR.652c.11a; H.1973a,b.1974a.1975a; BD.865a.
ṣārāh: S.6869; HR.652c.11b; H.1973c.1974b; BD.856b.
GEN. REF.: IS.1:127; NB.–; Z.–.

2. *stenochōria* [στενοχωρία, 4730], lit., narrowness of place (*stenos*, narrow, *chōra*, a place), metaphorically came to mean the distress arising from that condition, anguish. It is used in the plural, of various forms of distress, 2 Cor. 6:4 and 12:10, and of anguish or distress in general, Rom. 2:9; 8:35, R.V., "anguish" for A.V., "distress." The opposite state, of being in a large place, and so metaphorically in a state of joy, is represented by the word *platusmos* in certain Psalms as, e.g., Psa. 118:5; see also 2 Sam. 22:20. See DISTRESS. ¶

NT: B.766c; CB.1270a; K.1077.
OT: māṣôr: S.4692; HR.1288c.1; H.1898a; BD.596a.
ṣûqāh: S.6695; HR.1288c.2; H.1895a; BD.848a.
GEN. REF.: IS.1:127; NB.–; Z.–.

3. *sunochē* [συνοχή, 4928], lit., a holding together, or compressing (*sun*, together, *echō*, to hold), was used of the narrowing of a way. It is found only in its metahporical sense, of straits, distress, anguish, Luke 21:25, "distress of nations," and 2 Cor. 2:4, "anguish of heart." See DISTRESS. ¶

NT: B.791d; CB.–; K.1117.
OT: māṣôr: S.4692; HR.1318a.1; H.1898a; BD.596a.
shô'āh: S.7722; HR.1318a.2; H.2339,2339a; BD.996b.
GEN. REF.: IS.1:127; NB.–; Z.–.

Note: Anankē is associated with *thlipsis*, and signifies a condition of necessity arising from some form of compulsion. It is therefore used not only of necessity but of distress, Luke 21:23; 1 Thess. 3:7, and in the plural in 2 Cor. 6:4; 12:10.

B. Verbs.

1. *stenochōreō* [στενοχωρέω, 4729], akin to A, No. 2, lit., to crowd into a narrow space, or, in the Passive Voice to be pressed for room, hence, metaphorically, to be straitened, 2 Cor. 4:8 and 6:12 (twice), is found in its literal sense in two places in the Sept., in Josh. 17:15 and Isa. 49:19, and in two places in its metaphorical sense, in Judg. 16:16, where Delilah is said

to have pressed Samson sore with her words continually, and to have "straitened him," and in Isa. 28:20. See DISTRESS, STRAITENED. ¶

NT: B.766c; CB.1270a; K.1077.
OT: 'ûṣ: S.213; HR.1288c.1; H.51; BD.21a.
'ālaṣ: S.509; HR.1288c.2; H.110; BD.49b.
qāṣar: S.7114; HR.1288c.4; H.2061,2062; BD.894a.
GEN. REF.: IS.1:127; NB.–; Z.–.

2. *sunechō* [συνέχω, 4912], akin to A, No. 3, lit., to hold together, is used physically of being held, or thronged, Luke 8:45; 19:43; 22:63; of being taken with a malady, Matt. 4:24; Luke 4:38; Acts 28:8; with fear, Luke 8:37; of being straitened or pressed in spirit, with desire, Luke 12:50; Acts 18:5; Phil. 1:23; with the love of Christ, 2 Cor. 5:14. In one place it is used of the stopping of their ears by those who killed Stephen. See CONSTRAIN, HOLD, KEEP, PRESS, SICK (lie), STOP, STRAIT (be in a), STRAITENED, TAKE, THRONG.

NT: B.789a; CB.1270c; K.1117.
OT: ḥābar: S.2266; HR.1315b.6; H.598; BD.287d.
'āṣar: S.6113; HR.1315b.12; H.1675; BD.783c.
GEN. REF.: IS.1:127; NB.–; Z.–.

3. *odunaō* [ὀδυνάω, 3600], in the Middle and Passive Voices, signifies to suffer pain, be in anguish, be greatly distressed (akin to *odunē*, pain, distress); it is rendered "sorrowing" in Luke 2:48; in 16:24, 25, R.V., "in anguish," for A.V., "tormented"; in Acts 20:38, "sorrowing." See SORROW, TORMENT. ¶

NT: B.555a; CB.–; K.673.
OT: dāweh: S.1739; HR.967a.1; H.4116; BD.188c.
ḥîl: S.2342; HR.967a.2; H.623; BD.298c.
mārar: S.4843; HR.967a.3; H.2215h; BD.600a.
GEN. REF.: IS.1:127; NB.–; Z.–.

For **ANIMALS** (2 Pet. 2:12, R.V.), see **NATURAL**

ANISE

anēthon [ἄνηθον, 432], dill, anise, was used for food and for pickling, Matt. 23:23. ¶

NT: B.66a; CB.1235c; K.–.
OT: –.
GEN. REF.: IS.1:127; NB.39; Z.–.

ANKLE-BONES

sphuron [σφυρόν] or *sphudron* [σφυδρόν, 4974] denotes the ankle, or ankle-bone (from *sphura*, a hammer, owing to a resemblance in the shape), Acts 3:7. ¶

NT: B.797a; CB.–; K.–.
OT: tôtāḥ: S.8455; HR.1327c.1; H.933a; BD.450c.
GEN. REF.: –.

ANNOUNCE

anangellō [ἀναγγέλλω, 312], to declare, announce (*ana*, up *angellō*, to report), is used especially of heavenly messages, and is translated "announced" in the R.V. of 1 Pet. 1:12, for A.V., "reported," and in 1 John 1:5, R.V., "announce," for A.V., "declare." See DECLARE, REHEARSE, REPORT, SHOW, SPEAK, TELL.

NT: B.51b; CB.1235b; K.10.
OT: nāgad: S.5046; HR.74a.10; H.1289; BD.616c.
GEN. REF.: –.

ANOINT, ANOINTING

A. Verbs.

1. *aleiphō* [ἀλείφω, 218] is a general term used for an anointing of any kind, whether of physical refreshment after washing, e.g. in the Sept. of Ruth 3:3; 2 Sam. 12:20; Dan. 10:3; Micah 6:15; in the N.T., Matt. 6:17; Luke 7:38, 46; John 11:2; 12:3; or of the sick, Mark 6:13; Jas. 5:14; or a dead body, Mark 16:1. The material used was either oil, or ointment, as in Luke 7:38, 46. ¶ In the Sept. it is also used of anointing a pillar, Gen. 31:13, or captives, 2 Chron. 28:15, or of daubing a wall with mortar, Ezek. 13:10, 11, 12, 14, 15; and, in the sacred sense, of anointing priests, in Ex. 40:15 (twice), and Numb. 3:3.

NT: B.35b; CB.1234b; K.37.
OT: sûk: S.5480; HR.52c.3; H.1474; BD.691d.
tûaḥ: S.2902; HR.52c.1; H.795; BD.376b.
māshaḥ: S.4886; HR.52c.2; H.1255; BD.602d.
GEN. REF.: IS.1:129; NB.39; Z.–.

2. *chriō* [χρίω, 5548] is more limited in its use than No. 1; it is confined to sacred and symbolical anointings; of Christ as the Anointed of God, Luke 4:18; Acts 4:27; 10:38, and Heb. 1:9, where it is used metaphorically in connection with "the oil of gladness." The title Christ signifies "The Anointed One." The word (*Christos*) is rendered "(His) Anointed" in Acts 4:26, R.V. Once it is said of believers, 2 Cor. 1:21. *Chriō* is very frequent in the Sept., and is used of kings, 1 Sam. 10:1, and priests, Ex. 28:41, and prophets, 1 Kings 19:16. Among the Greeks it was used in other senses than the ceremonial, but in the Scriptures it is not found in connection with secular matters. ¶

NT: B.887c; CB.1240a; K.1322.
OT: māshaḥ: S.4886; HR.1475b.2; H.1255; BD.602d.
GEN. REF.: IS.1:129; NB.39; Z.–.

Note: The distinction referred to by Trench (Syn. § xxxviii), that *aleiphō* is the mundane and profane, *chriō*, the sacred and religious word, is not borne out by evidence. In a papyrus document *chrisis* is used of "a lotion for a sick horse" (Moulton and Milligan, Vocab. of Greek Test).

3. *enchriō* [ἐγχρίω, 1472], primarily, to rub in, hence, to besmear, to anoint, is used metaphorically in the command to the church in Laodicea to anoint their eyes with eyesalve, Rev. 3:18. ¶ In the Sept., Jer. 4:30, it is used of the

anointing of the eyes with a view to beautifying them.

NT: B.217a; CB.–; K.–.
OT: –.
GEN. REF.: IS.1:129; NB.39; Z.–.

4. *epichriō* [ἐπιχρίω, 2025], primarily, to rub on (*epi*, upon), is used of the blind man whose eyes Christ anointed, and indicates the manner in which the anointing was done, John 9:6, 11. ¶

NT: B.305b; CB.–; K.–.
OT: –.
GEN. REF.: IS.1:129; NB.39; Z.–.

5. *murizō* [μυρίζω, 3462] is used of anointing the body for burial, in Mark 14:8. ¶

NT: B.529d; CB.–; K.615.
OT: –.
GEN. REF.: IS.1:129; NB.39; Z.–.

B. Noun.

chrisma [χρίσμα, 5545], the corresponding noun to No. 2, above, signifies an unguent, or an anointing. It was prepared from oil and aromatic herbs. It is used only metaphorically in the N.T.; by metonymy, of the Holy Spirit, 1 John 2:20, 27, twice. The R.V. translates it "anointing" in all three places, instead of the A.V. "unction" and "anointing."

That believers have "an anointing from the Holy One" indicates that this anointing renders them holy, separating them to God. The passage teaches that the gift of the Holy Spirit is the all-efficient means of enabling believers to possess a knowledge of the truth. In the Sept., it is used of the oil for anointing the high priest, e.g., Ex. 29:7, lit., 'Thou shalt take of the oil of the anointing.' In Ex. 30:25, etc., it is spoken of as "a holy anointing oil." In Dan. 9:26 *chrisma* stands for the anointed one, "Christ," the noun standing by metonymy for the Person Himself, as for the Holy Spirit in 1 John 2. See UNCTION. ¶

NT: B.886c; CB.1240a; K.1322.
OT: mishḥāh: S.4888; HR.1475c.1a; H.1255a,b; BD.603b.
māshîaḥ: S.4899; HR.1475c.1c; H.1255c; BD.603c.
GEN. REF.: IS.1:129; NB.39; Z.–.

Notes: (1) *Aleimma*, akin to A, No. 1 (not in the N.T.), occurs three times in the Sept., Ex. 30:31, of the anointing of the priests; Isa. 61:3, metaphorically, of the oil of joy; Dan. 10:3, of physical refreshment.

(2) *Muron*, a word akin to A, No. 5, denotes ointment. The distinction between this and *elaion*, oil, is observable in Christ's reproof of the Pharisee who, while desiring Him to eat with him, failed in the ordinary marks of courtesy; "My head with oil (*elaion*) thou didst not anoint, but she hath anointed My feet with ointment" (*muron*), Luke 7:46.

ANON

Note: This is the A.V. rendering of *euthus*, in Matt. 13:20 and Mark 1:30, R.V., "straightway."

ANOTHER

allos [ἄλλος, 243] and *heteros* [ἕτερος, 2087] have a difference in meaning, which despite a tendency to be lost, is to be observed in numerous passages. *Allos* expresses a numerical difference and denotes another of the same sort; *heteros* expresses a qualitative difference and denotes another of a different sort. Christ promised to send "another Comforter" (*allos*, another like Himself, not *heteros*), John 14:16. Paul says "I see a different (A.V., 'another') law," *heteros*, a law different from that of the spirit of life (not *allos*, a law of the same sort), Rom. 7:23. After Joseph's death "another king arose," *heteros*, one of quite a different character, Acts 7:18. Paul speaks of "a different gospel (*heteros*), which is not another" (*allos*, another like the one he preached), Gal. 1:6, 7. See *heteros* (not *allos*) in Matt. 11:3, and Acts 27:1; in Luke 23:32 *heteroi* is used of the two malefactors crucified with Christ. The two words are only apparently interchanged in 1 Cor. 1:16 and 6:1; 12:8-10; 14:17 and 19, e.g., the difference being present, though not so readily discernible.

They are not interchangeable in 1 Cor. 15:39-41; here *heteros* is used to distinguish the heavenly glory from the earthly, for these differ in genus, and *allos* to distinguish the flesh of men, birds, and fishes, which in each case is flesh differing not in genus but in species. *Allos* is used again to distinguish between the glories of the heavenly bodies, for these also differ not in kind but in degree only. For *allos*, see MORE, OTHER, etc. For *heteros*, see OTHER, STRANGE.

NT: allos: B.39d; CB.2087; K.43.
OT: 'aḥēr: S.312; HR.56b.2; H.68a; BD.29c.
'eḥād: S.259; HR.56b.1; H.61; BD.25c.
'oḥorî: S.317; HR.56b.3a; H.2568a; BD.–.
GEN. REF.: –.

NT: heteros: B.315a; CB.1250a; K.265.
OT: 'aḥēr: S.312; HR.560a.4; H.68a; BD.29c.
'eḥād: S.259; HR.560a.2; H.61; BD.25c.
GEN. REF.: –.

Note: The distinction comes out in the compounds of *heteros*, viz., *heteroglōssos*, "strange tongues," 1 Cor. 14:21; ¶; *heterodidaskaleō*, "to teach a different doctrine," 1 Tim. 1:3; 6:3; ¶; *heterozugō*, "to be unequally yoked" (i.e., with those of a different character), 2 Cor. 6:14. ¶

ANSWER

A. Nouns.

1. *apokrisis* [ἀπόκρισις, 612], lit., a separation or distinction, is the regular word for "answer," Luke 2:47; 20:26; John 1:22 and 19:9. ¶

NT: B.93d; CB.–; K.469.
OT: 'ānāh: S.6030; HR.134b.3; H.1650,1653; BD.772c.
shûb: S.7725; HR.134b.4; H.2340; BD.996d.
GEN. REF.: –.

2. *apokrima* [ἀπόκριμα, 610], akin to No. 1, denotes a judicial "sentence," 2 Cor. 1:9, A.V., and R.V., margin, or an "answer" (R.V., text), an answer of God to the Apostle's appeal, giving him strong confidence. In an ancient inscription it is used of an official decision. In a papyrus document it is used of a reply to a deputation. See SENTENCE. ¶

NT: B.93b; CB.–; K.469.
OT: –.
GEN. REF.: IS.–; NB.–; Z.–.

3. *chrēmatismos* [χρηματισμός, 5538], a Divine response, an oracle, is used in Rom. 11:4, of the answer given by God to Elijah's complaint against Israel. ¶ See the verb under CALL.

NT: B.885d; CB.1240a; K.1319.
OT: massā': S.4853; HR.1474c.1; H.1421c; BD.672d.
GEN. REF.: –.

4. *apologia* [ἀπολογία, 627], a verbal defence, a speech in defence, is sometimes translated "answer," in the A.V., Acts 25:16; 1 Cor. 9:3; 2 Tim. 4:16, all which the R.V. corrects to "defence." See Acts 22:1; Phil. 1:7, 16; 2 Cor. 7:11, "clearing." Once it signifies an "answer," 1 Pet. 3:15. Cp. B, No. 4. See CLEARING, DEFENCE. ¶

NT: B.96a; CB.1237a; K.–.
OT: –.
GEN. REF.: –.

Note: Eperōtēma, 1 Pet. 3:21, is not, as in the A.V., an "answer." It was used by the Greeks in a legal sense, as a demand or appeal. Baptism is therefore the ground of an appeal by a good conscience against wrong doing.

B. Verbs.

1. *apokrinomai* [ἀποκρίνομαι, 611], akin to A, No. 1, above, signifies either to give an answer to a question (its more frequent use) or to begin to speak, but always where something has preceded, either statement or act to which the remarks refer, e.g., Matt. 11:25; Luke 14:3; John 2:18. The R.V. translates by "answered," e.g., Matt. 28:5; Mark 12:35; Luke 3:16, where some have suggested 'began to say' or 'uttered solemnly,' whereas the speaker is replying to the unuttered thought or feeling of those addressed by him.

NT: B.93b; CB.–; K.469.
OT: 'ānāh: S.6030; HR.133a.7; H.1650,1653; BD.772c.
shûb: S.7725; HR.133a.9; H.2340; BD.996d.
GEN. REF.: –.

2. *antapokrinomai* [ἀνταποκρίνομαι, 470], *anti*, against, and No. 1, a strengthened form, to answer by contradiction, to reply against, is found in Luke 14:6 and Rom. 9:20. ¶

NT: B.73b; CB.–; K.469.
OT: 'ānāh: S.6030; HR.109b.1; H.1650;1653; BD.772c.
GEN. REF.: –.

3. *hupolambanō* [ὑπολαμβάνω, 5274] signifies (*a*) to take or bear up from beneath, Acts 1:9; (*b*) to receive, 3 John 8; (*c*) to suppose, Luke 7:43; Acts 2:15; (*d*) to catch up (in speech), to answer, Luke 10:30; in sense (*d*) it indicates that a person follows what another has said either by controverting or supplementing it. See RECEIVE, SUPPOSE. ¶

NT: B.845b; CB.1252b; K.495.
OT: 'ānāh: S.6030; HR.1414c.7; H.1650,1653; BD.772c.
dāmāh: S.1819; HR.1414c.4; H.437; BD.197d.
GEN. REF.: –.

4. *apologeomai* [ἀπολογέομαι, 626], cp. A, No. 4, lit., to talk oneself off from (*apo*, from, *legō*, to speak), to answer by way of making a defence for oneself (besides its meaning to excuse, Rom. 2:15; 2 Cor. 12:19), is translated "answer" in Luke 12:11; 21:14; in Acts 19:33, A.V. and R.V. both have "made defence"; in Acts 24:10; 25:8; 26:1, 2, the R.V. has the verb to make a defence, for the A.V., to answer, and in 26:24 for the A.V., "spake for himself." See DEFENCE, EXCUSE, SPEAK. ¶

NT: B.95d; CB.1237a; K.–.
OT: rîb: S.7378; HR.138c.1; H.2159; BD.936d.
GEN. REF.: –.

5. *antilegō* [ἀντιλέγω, 483], to speak against, is rendered "answering again" in the A.V. of Tit. 2:9 (R.V., "gainsaying"). See CONTRADICT, DENY, GAINSAY, SPEAK.

NT: B.74d; CB.–; K.–.
OT: sûg: S.5472; HR.111a.1; H.1469; BD.690d.
rîb: S.7378; HR.111a.2; H.2159; BD.936d.
GEN. REF.: –.

6. *sustoicheo* [συστοιχέω, 4960], lit., to be in the same line or row with (*sun*, with, *stoichos*, a row), is translated "answereth to" in Gal. 4:25. ¶

NT: B.795b; CB.1271a; K.1087.
OT: –.
GEN. REF.: –.

Note: Cp. *stoicheō*, to walk (in line), 5:25; 6:16. For *hupakouō*, rendered to answer in Acts 12:13, R.V., see HEARKEN, No. 1, *Note*.

ANTICHRIST

antichristos [ἀντίχριστος, 500] can mean either against Christ or instead of Christ, or perhaps, combining the two, "one who, assuming the guise of Christ, opposes Christ"

(Westcott). The word is found only in John's Epistles, (*a*) of the many antichrists who are forerunners of the Antichrist himself, 1 John 2:18, 22; 2 John 7; (*b*) of the evil power which already operates anticipatively of the Antichrist, 1 John 4:3. ¶

What the Apostle says of him so closely resembles what he says of the first beast in Rev. 13, and what the Apostle Paul says of the Man of Sin in 2 Thess. 2, that the same person seems to be in view in all these passages, rather than the second beast in Rev. 13, the false prophet; for the latter supports the former in all his Antichristian assumptions.

NT: B.76b; CB.1236a; K.1322.
OT: —.
GEN. REF.: IS.1:139; NB.39; Z.—.

Note: The term *pseudochristos*, a false Christ, is to be distinguished from the above; it is found in Matt. 24:24 and Mark 13:22. The false Christ does not deny the existence of Christ, he trades upon the expectation of His appearance, affirming that he is the Christ. The Antichrist denies the existence of the true God (Trench, Syn. §, xxx). ¶

For **ANXIETY** and **ANXIOUS** see **CARE,** A, No. 1, B, No. 1

ANY: see Note †, p. 1

ANYTHING

Note: See the R.V. of Mark 15:5; John 16:23; 1 Tim. 6:7; in Luke 24:41, the R.V. suitably has "anything to eat," for, A.V., "any meat."

APART

1. *chōris* [χωρίς, 5565] is used both as an adverb and as a preposition. As an adverb it signifies separately, by itself, John 20:7, of the napkin which had been around the Lord's head in the tomb; as a preposition (its more frequent use), apart from, without, separate from. It is rendered "apart from" in the R.V. of John 15:5; Rom. 3:21, 28; 4:6; 2 Cor. 12:3; Heb. 9:22, 28; 11:40; Jas. 2:18, 20, 26. See BESIDE, WITHOUT.

NT: B.890c; CB.1240a; K.—.
OT: —.
GEN. REF.: IS.1:149; NB.—; Z.—.

Note: The opposite of *chōris* is *sun*, with. A synonymous preposition, *aneu*, denotes without, Matt. 10:29; 1 Pet. 3:1 and 4:9. ¶

2. *kat' idian* [κατ' ἰδίαν], lit., according to one's own, i.e., privately, alone, is translated "apart" in Matt. 14:13, 23; 17:1; 19; 20:17; Mark 6:31, 32 (A.V., "privately"); 9:2.

3. *kata monas* [κατὰ μόνας]: see ALONE.

APIECE

ana [ἀνά, 303], used with numerals or measures of quantity with a distributive force, is translated "apiece" in Luke 9:3, "two coats apiece," A.V.; in John 2:6, "two or three firkins apiece." In Matt. 20:9, 10, "every man a penny," is a free rendering for "a penny apiece"; in Luke 9:14, the R.V. adds "each" to translate the *ana*; in 10:1, *and duo* is "two by two." See Rev. 4:8, "each." See EACH, EVERY.

NT: B.49d; CB.1235a; K.—.
OT: —.
GEN. REF.: —.

APOSTLE, APOSTLESHIP

1. *apostolos* [ἀπόστολος, 652] is, lit., one sent forth (*apo*, from, *stellō*, to send). "The word is used of the Lord Jesus to describe His relation to God, Heb. 3:1; see John 17:3. The twelve disciples chosen by the Lord for special training were so called, Luke 6:13; 9:10. Paul, though he had seen the Lord Jesus, 1 Cor. 9:1; 15:8, had not 'companied with' the Twelve 'all the time' of His earthly ministry, and hence was not eligible for a place among them, according to Peter's description of the necessary qualifications, Acts 1:22. Paul was commissioned directly, by the Lord Himself, after His Ascension, to carry the Gospel to the Gentiles.

"The word has also a wider reference. In Acts 14:4, 14, it is used of Barnabas as well as of Paul; in Rom. 16:7 of Andronicus and Junias. In 2 Cor. 8:23 (R.V., margin) two unnamed brethren are called 'apostles of the churches'; in Phil. 2:25 (R.V., margin) Epaphroditus is referred to as 'your apostle.' It is used in 1 Thess. 2:6 of Paul, Silas and Timothy, to define their relation to Christ."*

NT: B.99c; CB.1237a; K.67.
OT: shālaḥ: S.7971; HR.145b.1; H.2394; BD.1018a.
GEN. REF.: IS.1:192; NB.48; Z.—.

2. *apostolē* [ἀποστολή], a sending, a mission, signifies an apostleship, Acts 1:25; Rom. 1:5; 1 Cor. 9:2; Gal. 2:8. ¶

NT: —.
OT: mishlaḥat: S.4917; HR.145a.1a; H.2394f; BD.1020a.
GEN. REF.: IS.1:192; NB.48; Z.—.

Note: Pseudapostoloi, "false apostles," occurs in 2 Cor. 11:13. ¶

* From Notes on Thessalonians by Hogg and Vine, pp. 59, 60.

APPAREL, APPARELLED

1. *esthēs* [ἐσθής, 2066(2067)] and *esthēsis* [ἔσθησις], connected with *hennumi*, to clothe, mean clothing, raiment, usually suggesting the ornate, the goodly. The former is found in Luke 23:11, R.V., "apparel" (A.V., "robe"); 24:4 (A.V., "garments"); Acts 10:30 (A.V., "clothing"); 12:21; Jas. 2:2 (R.V., "clothing," twice; A.V., "apparel" and "raiment"); 2:3 ("clothing"). *Esthēsis* is used in Acts 1:10, "apparel." See CLOTHING. ¶

NT: B.312b; CB.1246c; K.–.
OT: –.
GEN. REF.: IS.1:213; NB.–; Z.–.

2. *himation* [ἱμάτιον, 2440], a diminutive of *heima*, a robe, was used especially of an outer cloak or mantle, and in general of raiment, "apparel" in 1 Pet. 3:3. The word is not in the original in the next verse, but is supplied in English to complete the sentence. See CLOTHING, No. 2, GARMENT, RAIMENT, ROBE.

NT: B.376b; CB.1250c; K.–.
OT: beged: S.899; HR.685a.1; H.198a; BD.93d-94a.
simlāh: S.8071; HR.685a.11; H.2270a; BD.971a.
salmāh: S.8008; HR.685a.10; H.2270b; BD.971a.
GEN. REF.: IS.1:213; NB.–; Z.–.

3. *himatismos* [ἱματισμός, 2441], a collective word, i^r translated "apparelled" in Luke 7:25, and preceded by *en*, "in," lit., 'in apparel.' See CLOTHING, No. 4, RAIMENT, VESTURE.

NT: B.376d; CB.–; K.–.
OT: beged: S.899; HR.686a.1; H.198a; BD.93d-94a.
l^ebûsh: S.3831; HR.686a.4a; H.2810a; BD.528c.
salmāh: S.8008; HR.686a.6; H.2270b; BD.971a.
GEN. REF.: IS.1:213; NB.–; Z.–.

4. *katastolē* [καταστολή, 2689], connected with *katastellō*, to send or let down, to lower (*kata*, down, *stellō*, to send), was primarily a garment let down; hence, dress, attire, in general (cp. *stolē*, a loose outer garment worn by kings and persons of rank,—Eng., stole); 1 Tim. 2:9, "apparel." See CLOTHING. ¶

NT: B.419a; CB.–; K.1074.
OT: ma'ateh: S.4594; HR.745c.1; H.–; BD.742a.
GEN. REF.: IS.1:213; NB.–; Z.–.

APPARITION

phantasma [φάντασμα, 5326], a phantasm or phantom (from *phainō*, to appear), is translated "apparition" in the R.V. of Matt. 14:26 and Mark 6:49 (A.V., "spirit"). ¶ In the Sept., Job 20:8; Is. 28:7. ¶

NT: B.853c; CB.1263c; K.1244.
OT: ḥizāyôn: S.2384; HR.1424b.1; H.633e; BD.303b.
GEN. REF.: IS.1:213; NB.–; Z.–.

APPEAL

epikaleō [ἐπικαλέω, 1941(-OMAI)], to call upon, has the meaning appeal in the Middle Voice, which carries with it the suggestion of a special interest on the part of the doer of an action in that in which he is engaged. Stephen died "calling upon the Lord," Acts 7:59. In the more strictly legal sense the word is used only of Paul's appeal to Caesar, Acts 25:11, 12, 21, 25; 26:32; 28:19. See CALL (upon), SURNAME. See also *eperotēma*, under ANSWER.

NT: B.294a; CB.1245c(-OMAI); K.394.
OT: qārā': S.7121; HR.521b.5; H.2063; BD.894d.
shākan: S.7931; HR.521b.5; H.2387; BD.1014d.
GEN. REF.: IS.1:213; NB.–; Z.–.

APPEAR, APPEARING

1. *phainō* [φαίνω, 5316], signifies, in the Active Voice, to shine; in the Passive, to be brought forth into light, to become evident, to appear. In Rom. 7:13, concerning sin, the R.V. has "might be shewn to be," for A.V., "appear."

It is used of the appearance of Christ to the disciples, Mark 16:9; of His future appearing in glory as the Son of Man, spoken of as a sign to the world, Matt. 24:30; there the genitive is subjective, the sign being the appearing of Christ Himself; of Christ as the light, John 1:5; of John the Baptist, 5:35; of the appearing of an angel of the Lord, either visibly, Matt. 1:20, or in a dream, 2:13; of a star, 2:7; of men who make an outward show, Matt. 6:5; 6:18 (see the R.V.); 23:27, 28; 2 Cor. 13:7; of tares, Matt. 13:26; of a vapour, Jas. 4:14; of things physical in general, Heb. 11:3; used impersonally in Matt. 9:33, "it was never so seen"; also of what appears to the mind, and so in the sense of to think, Mark 14:64, or to seem, Luke 24:11 (R.V., "appeared"). See SEE, SEEM, SHINE, THINK.

NT: B.851b; CB.1263c; K.1244.
OT: ra'a': S.7490; HR.1423a.11b; H.3000; BD.949b.
'ôr: S.216; HR.1423a.1a; H.52a; BD.21a.
rā'āh: S.7200; HR.1423a.10; H.2095; BD.906b.
GEN. REF.: IS.1:214; NB.–; Z.–.

2. *epiphainō* [ἐπιφαίνω, 2014], a strengthened form of No. 1 but differing in meaning, *epi* signifying upon, is used in the Active Voice with the meaning to give light, Luke 1:79; in the Passive Voice, to appear, become visible. It is said of heavenly bodies, e.g., the stars, Acts 27:20 (R.V., "shone"); metaphorically, of things spiritual, the grace of God, Tit. 2:11; the kindness and the love of God, 3:4. See LIGHT. ¶ Cp. *epiphaneia*, B, No. 2.

NT: B.304a; CB.1246a; K.1244.
OT: 'ôr: S.215; HR.537c.1; H.52; BD.21a.
gālāh: S.1540; HR.537c.2; H.350; BD.162d.
GEN. REF.: IS.1:214; NB.–; Z.–.

3. *anaphainō* [ἀναφαίνω, 398], *ana*, forth, or up, perhaps originally a nautical term, to come up into view, hence, in general, to appear

suddenly, is used in the Passive Voice, in Luke 19:11, of the Kingdom of God; Active Voice, in Acts 21:3, to come in sight of, R.V.; "having sighted" would be a suitable rendering (A.V., "having discovered"). ¶
NT: B.63a; CB.–; K.–.
OT: ṣādaq: S.6663; HR.84c.2; H.1879; BD.841b.
GEN. REF.: IS.1:214; NB.–; Z.–.

4. *phaneroō* [φανερόω, 5319], akin to No. 1, signifies, in the Active Voice, to manifest; in the Passive Voice, to be manifested; so, regularly, in the R.V., instead of to appear. See 2 Cor. 7:12; Col. 3:4; Heb. 9:26; 1 Pet. 5:4; 1 John 2:28; 3:2; Rev. 3:18. To be manifested, in the Scriptural sense of the word, is more than to appear. A person may appear in a false guise or without a disclosure of what he truly is; to be manifested is to be revealed in one's true character; this is especially the meaning of *phaneroō*, see, e.g., John 3:21; 1 Cor. 4:5; 2 Cor. 5:10, 11; Eph. 5:13.
NT: B.852d; CB.1263; K.1244.
OT: gālāh: S.1540; HR.1424b.1; H.350; BD.162d.
GEN. REF.: IS.1:214; NB.–; Z.–.

5. *emphanizō* [ἐμφανίζω, 1718], from *en*, in, intensive, and *phainō*, to shine, is used, either of physical manifestation, Matt. 27:53; Heb. 9:24; cp. John 14:22, or, metaphorically, of the manifestation of Christ by the Holy Spirit in the spiritual experience of believers who abide in His love, John 14:21. It has another, secondary meaning, to make known, signify, inform. This is confined to the Acts, where it is used five times, 23:15, 22; 24:1; 25:2, 15. There is perhaps a combination of the two meanings in Heb. 11:14, i.e., to declare by oral testimony and to manifest by the witness of the life. See INFORM, MANIFEST, SHEW, SIGNIFY. ¶
NT: B.257d; CB.1244b; K.1244.
OT: yāda': S.3045; HR.460c.2; H.848; BD.393b.
rā'āh: S.7200; HR.460c.4; H.2095; BD.906b.
GEN. REF.: IS.1:214; NB.–; Z.–.

6. *optomai* [ὄπτομαι, 3708], to see (from *ōps*, the eye; cp. Eng. optical, etc.), in the Passive sense, to be seen, to appear, is used (*a*) objectively, with reference to the person or thing seen, e.g., 1 Cor. 15:5, 6, 7, 8, R.V. "appeared," for A.V., "was seen"; (*b*) subjectively, with reference to an inward impression or a spiritual experience, John 3:36, or a mental occupation, Acts 18:15, "look to it"; cp. Matt. 27:4, 24, "see (thou) to it," "see (ye) to it," throwing responsibility on others. *Optomai* is to be found in dictionaries under the word *horaō*, to see; it supplies some forms that are lacking in that verb.

These last three words, *emphanizō*, *phaneroō* and *optomai* are used with reference to the appearances of Christ in the closing verses of Heb. 9; *emphanizō* in ver. 24, of His presence before the face of God for us; *phaneroō* in ver. 26, of His past manifestation for "the sacrifice of Himself"; *optomai* in ver. 28, of His future appearance for His saints.
NT: B.577d; CB.1251a; K.–.
OT: –.
GEN. REF.: IS.1:214; NB.–; Z.–.

7. *optanō* [ὀπτάνω, 3700(-OMAI)], in the Middle Voice signifies to allow oneself to be seen. It is rendered "appearing" in Acts 1:3, R.V., for A.V., "being seen," of the Lord's appearances after His resurrection; the Middle Voice expresses the Personal interest the Lord took in this. ¶
NT: B.576c; CB.1261a; K.–.
OT: rā'āh: S.7200; HR.1004a.1; H.2095; BD.906b.
GEN. REF.: IS.1:214; NB.–; Z.–.

Note: In Acts 22:30 *sunerchomai* (in its aorist form), to come together, is translated "appear," A.V.; R.V., "come together."

B. Nouns.

1. *apokalupsis* [ἀποκάλυψις, 602], lit., an uncovering, unveiling (*apō*, from, *kaluptō*, to hide, cover), denotes a revelation, or appearing (Eng., apocalypse). It is translated "the appearing" in 1 Pet. 1:7, A.V. (R.V. "revelation"). See COMING, MANIFESTATION, REVELATION.
NT: B.92b; CB.1236c; K.405.
OT: 'erwāh: S.6172; HR.132b.1; H.1692b; BD.788d.
GEN. REF.: IS.1:214; NB.–; Z.–.

2. *epiphaneia* [ἐπιφάνεια, 2015], Eng., epiphany, lit., 'a shining forth,' was used of the appearance of a god to men, and of an enemy to an army in the field, etc. In the N.T. it occurs of (*a*) the advent of the Saviour when the Word became flesh, 2 Tim. 1:10; (*b*) the coming of the Lord Jesus into the air to the meeting with His saints, 1 Tim. 6:14; 2 Tim. 4:1, 8; (*c*) the shining forth of the glory of the Lord Jesus "as the lightning cometh forth from the east, and is seen even unto the west," Matt. 24:27, immediately consequent on the unveiling, *apokalupsis*, of His *Parousia* in the air with His saints, 2 Thess. 2:8; Tit. 2:13. ¶*
NT: B.304a; CB.1246a; K.1244.
OT: yāre': S.3372; HR.537c.1; H.907,908; BD.431a.
GEN. REF.: IS.1:214; NB.–; Z.–.

Notes: (1) *Phanerōsis*, akin to A, No. 4, a manifestation, is used in 1 Cor. 12:7 and 2 Cor. 4:2. ¶

(2) For *phaneros*, wrongly translated "may appear," in 1 Tim. 4:15, A.V. (R.V., "may be manifest," not mere appearance), see MANIFEST.

(3) *Emphanēs*, akin to A, No. 5, manifest, is used in Acts 10:40 and Rom. 10:20. See MANIFEST, OPENLY. ¶

(4) For *adēlos*, "which appear not," Luke 11:44, see UNCERTAIN.

APPEARANCE

A. Nouns.

1. *eidos* [εἶδος, 1491], properly that which strikes the eye, that which is exposed to view, signifies the external appearance, form, or shape, and in this sense is used of the Holy Spirit in taking bodily form, as a dove, Luke 3:22; of Christ, 9:29, "the fashion of His countenance." Christ used it, negatively, of God the Father, when He said "Ye have neither heard His voice at any time, nor seen His form," John 5:37. Thus it is used with reference to each Person of the Trinity. Probably the same meaning attaches to the word in the Apostle's statement, "We walk by faith, not by sight (*eidos*)," 2 Cor. 5:7, where eidos can scarcely mean the act of beholding, but the visible appearance of things which are set in contrast to that which directs faith. The believer is guided, then, not only by what he beholds but by what he knows to be true though it is invisible.

It has a somewhat different significance in 1 Thess. 5:22, in the exhortation "Abstain from every form of evil," i.e., every sort or kind of evil (not "appearance," A.V.). This meaning was common in the papyri, the Greek writings of the closing centuries, B.C., and the New Testament era. See FASHION, SHAPE, SIGHT. ¶ Cp. No. 4.

NT: B.221b; CB.1243a; K.202.
OT: mar'eh: S.4758; HR.375c.1; H.2095i; BD.909c.
tō'ar: S.8389; HR.375c.8; H.2491a; BD.1061b.
GEN. REF.: IS.1:214; NB.–; Z.–.

* From Notes on Thessalonians by Hogg and Vine, p. 263.

2. *prosōpon* [πρόσωπον, 4383], *pros*, towards, ōps, an eye, lit. the part round the eye, the face, in a secondary sense the look, the countenance, as being the index of the inward thoughts and feelings (cp. 1 Pet. 3:12, there used of the face of the Lord), came to signify the presentation of the whole person (translated "person," e.g., in Matt. 22:16). Cp. the expression in O.T. passages, as Gen. 19:21 (A.V. marg., "thy face"), where it is said by God of Lot, and 33:10, where it said by Jacob of Esau; see also Deut. 10:17 ("persons"), Lev. 19:15 ("person"). It also signifies the presence of a person, Acts 3:13; 1 Thess. 2:17; or the presence of a company, Acts 5:41. In this sense it is sometimes rendered "appearance," 2 Cor. 5:12. In 2 Cor. 10:7, A.V., "appearance," the R.V. corrects to "face." See COUNTENANCE, FACE, FASHION, PERSON, PRESENCE.

NT: B.720d; CB.1267b; K.950.
OT: panîm: S.6440; HR.1223c.6; H.1782a; BD.815d.
GEN. REF.: IS.1:214; NB.–; Z.–.

2. *opsis* [ὄψις, 3799], from ōps, the eye, connected with *horaō*, to see (cp. No. 2), primarily denotes seeing, sight; hence, the face, the countenance, John 11:44 ("face"); Rev. 1:16 ("countenance"); the outward "appearance," the look, John 7:24, only here, of the outward aspect of a person. See COUNTENANCE, FACE.

NT: B.601d; CB.1261a; K.–.
OT: mar'eh: S.4758; HR.1044b.3; H.2095i; BD.909c.
'ayin: S.5869; HR.1044b.4; H.1612a,1613; BD.744a.
GEN. REF.: IS.1:214; NB.–; Z.–.

4. *eidea* [εἰδέα, 2397], an aspect, appearance, is used in Matt. 28:3, R.V., "appearance"; A.V., "countenance." ¶

NT: B.369c; CB.–; K.202.
OT: d^emût: S.1823; HR.374b.1; H.437a; BD.198b.
GEN. REF.: IS.1:214; NB.–; Z.–.

B. Verb.

phantazō [φαντάζω, 5324], to make visible, is used in its participial form (Middle Voice), with the neuter article, as equivalent to a noun, and is translated "appearance," R.V., for A.V., "sight," Heb. 12:21. ¶

NT: B.853b; CB.1263c; K.1244.
OT: –.
GEN. REF.: IS.1:214; NB.–; Z.–.

APPEASE

katastellō [καταστέλλω, 2687], to quiet (lit., to send down, *kata*, down, *stellō*, to send), in the Passive Voice, to be quiet, or to be quieted, is used in Acts 19:35 and 36, in the former verse in the Active Voice, A.V., "appeased"; R.V., "quieted"; in the latter, the Passive, "to be quiet" (lit. 'to be quieted'). See QUIET. ¶

NT: B.419a; CB.–; K.1074.
OT: –.
GEN. REF.: –.

APPOINT, APPOINTED

1. *histēmi* [ἵστημι, 2476], to make to stand, means to appoint, in Acts 17:31, of the day in which God will judge the world by Christ. In Acts 1:23, with reference to Joseph and Barnabas, the R.V. has "put forward"; for these were not both appointed in the accepted sense of the term, but simply singled out, in order that it might be made known which of them the Lord had chosen. See ABIDE, No. 10.

NT: B.381d; CB.1250c; K.1082.
OT: 'āmad: S.5975; HR.689a.26; H.1637; BD.763c.
qûm: S.6965; HR.689a.28; H.1999; BD.877c.
nāṣab: S.5324; HR.689a.20; H.1398; BD.662a.
GEN. REF.: IS.1:215; NB.–; Z.–.

2. *kathistēmi* [*καθίστημι*, 2525], a strengthened form of No. 1, usually signifies to appoint a person to a position. In this sense the verb is often translated to make or to set, in appointing a person to a place of authority, e.g., a servant over a household, Matt. 24:45, 47; 25:21, 23; Luke 12:42, 44; a judge, Luke 12:14; Acts 7:27, 35; a governor, Acts 7:10; man by God over the work of His hands, Heb. 2:7. It is rendered "appoint," with reference to the so-called seven deacons in Acts 6:3. The R.V. translates it by "appoint" in Tit. 1:5, instead of "ordain," of the elders whom Titus was to appoint in every city in Crete. Not a formal ecclesiastical ordination is in view, but the appointment, for the recognition of the churches, of those who had already been raised up and qualified by the Holy Spirit, and had given evidence of this in their life and service (see No. 11). It is used of the priests of old, Heb. 5:1; 7:28; 8:3 (R.V., "appointed"). See CONDUCT, MAKE, ORDAIN, SET.

NT: B.390b; CB.1254c; K.387.
OT: nāṣab: S.5324; HR.702c.12; H.1398; BD.622a.
pāqad: S.6485; HR.702c.15; H.1802; BD.823a.
sûm, sîm: S.7760; HR.703c.19; H.2243; BD.962c.
GEN. REF.: IS.1:215; NB.—; Z.—.

3. *tithēmi* [*τίθημι*, 5087], to put, is used of appointment to any form of service. Christ used it of His followers, John 15:16 (R.V., "appointed" for A.V., "ordained"). "I set you" would be more in keeping with the metaphor of grafting. The verb is used by Paul of his service in the ministry of the Gospel, 1 Tim. 1:12 (R.V., "appointing" for "putting"); 2:7 (R.V., "appointed" for "ordained"); and 2 Tim. 1:11 (R.V., "appointing" for "putting"); of the overseers, or bishops, in the local church at Ephesus, as those appointed by the Holy Ghost, to tend the church of God, Acts 20:28 ("hath made"); of the Son of God, as appointed Heir of all things, Heb. 1:2. It is also used of appointment to punishment, as of the unfaithful servant, Matt. 24:51; Luke 12:46; of unbelieving Israel, 1 Pet. 2:8. Cp. 2 Pet. 2:6. See BOW, COMMIT, CONCEIVE, LAY, MAKE, ORDAIN, PURPOSE, PUT, SET, SINK.

NT: B.815d; CB.1272c; K.1176.
OT: nātan: S.5414; HR.1348c.16; H.1443; BD.678a.
sûm, sîm: S.7760; HR.1348c.25; H.2243; BD.962c.
GEN. REF.: IS.1:215; NB.—; Z.—.

Note: Akin to *tithēmi* is the latter part of the noun *prothesmia*, Gal. 4:2, of a term of period appointed. ¶

4. *diatithēmi* [*διατίθημι*, 1303(-EMAI)], a strengthened form of No. 3 (*dia*, through, intensive), is used in the Middle Voice only. The Lord used it of His disciples with reference to the Kingdom which is to be theirs hereafter, and of Himself in the same respect, as that which has been appointed for Him by His Father, Luke 22:29. For its use in connection with a covenant, see MAKE, and TESTATOR.

NT: B.189d; CB.1241b; K.157.
OT: kārat: S.3772; HR.313b.1; H.1048; BD.503c.
GEN. REF.: IS.1:215; NB.—; Z.—.

5. *tassō* [*τάσσω*, 5021], to place in order, arrange, signifies to appoint, e.g., of the place where Christ had appointed a meeting with His disciples after His resurrection, Matt. 28:16; of positions of military and civil authority over others, whether appointed by men, Luke 7:8, or by God, Rom. 13:1, "ordained." It is said of those who, having believed the Gospel, "were ordained to eternal life," Acts 13:48. The house of Stephanas at Corinth had "set themselves" to the ministry of the saints (A.V., "addicted"), 1 Cor. 16:15. Other instances of the arranging of special details occur in Acts 15:2; 22:10; 28:23. See DETERMINE, ORDAIN, SET ¶

NT: B.805d; CB.1271a; K.1156.
OT: sûm, sîm: S.7760; HR.1337a.11; H.2243; BD.962c.
nātan: S.5414; HR.1337a.6; H.1443; BD.678a.
GEN. REF.: IS.1:215; NB.—; Z.—.

6. *diatassō* [*διατάσσω*, 1299], a strengthened form of No. 5 (*dia*, through, intensive), frequently denotes to arrange, appoint, prescribe, e.g., of what was appointed for tax collectors to collect, Luke 3:13; of the tabernacle, as appointed by God for Moses to make, Acts 7:44; of the arrangements appointed by Paul with regard to himself and his travelling companions, Acts 20:13; of what the Apostle "ordained" in all the churches in regard to marital conditions, 1 Cor. 7:17; of what the Lord "ordained" in regard to the support of those who proclaimed the Gospel, 1 Cor. 9:14; of the Law as Divinely "ordained," or administered, through angels, by Moses, Gal. 3:19.

In Tit. 1:5, A.V., "had appointed thee," the sense is rather that of commanding, R.V., "gave thee charge." See COMMAND, No. 1, ORDAIN, ORDER.

NT: B.189c; CB.1241b; K.1156.
OT: sûm, sîm: S.7760; HR.313a.7; H.2243; BD.962c.
shāmar: S.8104; HR.313a.8; H.2414; BD.1036b.
GEN. REF.: IS.1:215; NB.—; Z.—.

7. *suntassō* [*συντάσσω*, 4929], *sun*, with, and No. 5, lit., arrange together with, hence to appoint, prescribe, is used twice, in Matt. 26:19 of what the Lord appointed for His disciples, and in 27:10, in a quotation concerning the price of the potter's field. ¶

NT: B.791d; CB.—; K.—.
OT: ṣāwāh: S.6680; HR.1318b.8; H.1887; BD.845b.
dābar: S.1697; HR.1318b.2; H.399a; BD.180b.
GEN. REF.: IS.1:215; NB.—; Z.—.

8. *protassō* [*προτάσσω*, 4384], *pro*, before, and No. 5, to appoint before, is used in Acts

17:26 (R.V., "appointed"), of the seasons arranged by God for nations, and the bounds of their habitation. ¶

NT: B.721d; CB.1267b; K.1156.
OT: —.
GEN. REF.: IS.1:215; NB.—; Z.—.

9. *keîmai* [κειμαι, 2749], to lie, is used in 1 Thess. 3:3 of the appointment of affliction for faithful believers. It is rendered "set" in Luke 2:34 and Phil. 1:16, R.V., where the sense is the same. The verb is a perfect tense, used for the perfect Passive of *tithēmi*, to place, 'I have been placed,' i.e., 'I lie.' See LAY, LIE, MADE (be), SET.

NT: B.426c; CB.1254c; K.425.
OT: yā'ad: S.3259; HR.758b.3; H.878; BD.416d.
sûm, sîm: S.7760; HR.758b.7; H.2243; BD.962c.
GEN. REF.: IS.1:215; NB.—; Z.—.

10. *apokeimai* [ἀποκεῖμαι, 606], *apo*, from, and No. 9, signifies to be laid, reserved, Luke 19:20; Col. 1:5; 2 Tim. 4:8; "appointed," in Heb. 9:27, where it is said of death and the judgment following (R.V., marg., "laid up"). See LAY. ¶

NT: B.92d; CB.—; K.425.
OT: ḥāsak: S.2820; HR.132b.1; H.765; BD.362b.
GEN. REF.: IS.1:215; NB.—; Z.—.

11. *cheirotoneō* [χειροτονέω, 5500], primarily used of voting in the Athenian legislative assembly and meaning to stretch forth the hands (*cheir*, the hand, *teinō*, to stretch), is not to be taken in its literal sense; it could not be so taken in its compound *procheirotoneō*, to choose before, since it is said of God, Acts 10:41. *Cheirotoneō* is said of the appointment of elders by apostolic missionaries in the various churches which they revisited, Acts 14:23, R.V., "had appointed," i.e., by the recognition of those who had been manifesting themselves as gifted of God to discharge the functions of elders (see No. 2). It is also said of those who were appointed (not by voting, but with general approbation) by the churches in Greece to accompany the Apostle in conveying their gifts to the poor saints in Judaea, 2 Cor. 8:19. See CHOOSE, ORDAIN. ¶

NT: B.881a; CB.1239a; K.1309.
OT: —.
GEN. REF.: IS.1:215; NB.—; Z.—.

12. *procheirizō* [προχειρίζω, 4400(-OMAI)], from *procheiros*, at hand, signifies (*a*) to deliver up, appoint, Acts 3:20 (R.V., "appointed"); (*b*) in the Middle Voice, to take into one's hand, to determine, appoint beforehand, translated "appointed" in Acts 22:14, R.V. (for A.V., "hath chosen"), and "to appoint" in 26:16 (for A.V., "to make"). ¶

NT: B.724c; CB.1266c; K.965.
OT: lāqaḥ: S.3947; HR.1234a.1; H.1124; BD.542c.
shālaḥ: S.7971; HR.1234a.2; H.2394; BD.1018a.
GEN. REF.: IS.1:215; NB.—; Z.—.

13. *horizō* [ὁρίζω, 3724], (Eng., horizon), lit., to mark by a limit, hence, to determine, ordain, is used of Christ as ordained of God to be a Judge of the living and the dead, Acts 17:31; of His being 'marked out' as the Son of God, Rom. 1:4; of Divinely appointed seasons, Acts 17:26, "having determined." See DEFINE.

NT: B.580d; CB.1251b; K.728.
OT: 'āsar: S.631; HR.1011c.1; H.141; BD.63c.
g^ebûl: S.1366; HR.1011c.2a; H.307a; BD.147d.
GEN. REF.: IS.1:215; NB.—; Z.—.

14. *anadeiknumi* [ἀναδείκνυμι, 322], lit., to show up, to show clearly, also signifies to appoint to a position or a service; it is used in this sense of the 70 disciples, Luke 10:1; for the meaning "show," see Acts 1:24. ¶

NT: B.53b; CB.1235a; K.141.
OT: —.
GEN. REF.: IS.1:215; NB.—; Z.—.

15. *poieō* [ποιέω, 4160], to do, to make, is rendered "appointed" in Heb. 3:2, of Christ. For Mark 3:14, R.V., see ORDAIN, *Note* (2).

NT: B.680d; CB.1265c; K.895.
OT: 'āsāh: S.6213; HR.1154a.33; H.1708,1709; BD.793c.
GEN. REF.: IS.1:215; NB.—; Z.—.

Note: Epithanatios, "appointed to death," doomed to it by condemnation, 1 Cor. 4:9, A.V., is corrected to "doomed to death" in the R.V. (*epi*, for, *thanatos*, death).

For **APPORTIONED** (R.V. in 2 Cor. 10:13) see **DISTRIBUTE**

APPREHEND

1. *katalambanō* [καταλαμβάνω, 2638], properly signifies to lay hold of; then, to lay hold of so as to possess as one's own, to appropriate. Hence it has the same twofold meaning as the Eng. "apprehend"; (*a*), to seize upon, take possession of, (1) with a beneficial effect, as of laying hold of the righteousness which is of faith, Rom. 9:30 (not there a matter of attainment, as in the Eng. Versions, but of appropriation); of the obtaining of a prize, 1 Cor. 9:24 (R.V., "attain"); of the Apostle's desire to apprehend, or lay hold of, that for which he was apprehended by Christ, Phil. 3:12, 13; (2) with a detrimental effect, e.g., of demon power, Mark 9:18; of human action in seizing upon a person, John 8:3, 4; metaphorically, with the added idea of overtaking, of spiritual darkness in coming upon people, John 12:35; of the day of the Lord, in suddenly coming upon unbelievers as a thief, 1 Thess. 5:4; (*b*), to lay hold of with the mind, to understand, perceive, e.g., metaphorically, of darkness with regard to light, John 1:5, though possibly here the sense is that of (*a*) as in 12:35; of mental perception,

Acts 4:13; 10:34; 25:25; Eph. 3:18. See ATTAIN No. 2, COME, *Note* (8), FIND, OBTAIN, OVERTAKE, PERCEIVE, TAKE. ¶

NT: B.412b; CB.1254a (-OMAI); K.495.
OT: lākad: S.3920; HR.735a.6; H.1115; BD.539d.
nāsag: S.5381; HR.735a.11; H.1422; BD.673b.
GEN. REF.: IS.1:216; NB.—; Z.—.

Note: Cp. *epilambanō*, to take hold of, always in the Middle Voice in the N.T. See HOLD.

2. *piazō* [πιάζω, 4084], to lay hold of, with the suggestion of firm pressure or force, is used in the Gospels only in John, six times of efforts to seize Christ, and is always rendered "take" in the R.V., 7:30, 32, 44; 8:20; 10:39; 11:57. The A.V. has "laid hands on" in 8:20. In Acts 12:4 and 2 Cor. 11:32 (A.V.), it is translated respectively "apprehended" and "apprehend" (R.V., "had taken," and "take"). In Rev. 19:20 it is used of the seizure of the Beast and the False Prophet. In John 21:3, 10 it is used of catching fish. Elsewhere in Acts 3:7. See CATCH, LAY HANDS ON, TAKE. ¶ In the Sept., S. of Sol. 2:15. ¶

NT: B.657a; CB.—; K.—.
OT: ʾāḥaz: S.270; HR.1132c.1; H.64; BD.28a
GEN. REF.: IS.1:216; NB.—; Z.—.

APPROACH

A. Verb.

engizō [ἐγγίζω, 1448], to draw near, to approach, from *engus*, near, is used (*a*) of place and position, literally and physically, Matt. 21:1; Mark 11:1; Luke 12:33; 15:25; figuratively, of drawing near to God, Matt. 15:8; Heb. 7:19; Jas. 4:8; (*b*) of time, with reference to things that are imminent, as the Kingdom of Heaven, Matt. 3:2; 4:17; 10:7; the Kingdom of God, Mark 1:15; Luke 10:9, 11; the time of fruit, Matt. 21:34; the desolation of Jerusalem, Luke 21:8; redemption, 21:28; the fulfilment of a promise, Acts 7:17; the Day of Christ in contrast to the present night of the world's spiritual darkness, Rom. 13:12; Heb. 10:25; the coming of the Lord, Jas. 5:8; the end of all things, 1 Pet. 4:7. It is also said of one who was drawing near to death, Phil. 2:30. See COME, *Note* (16), DRAW, *B*, No. 1, HAND (at), NIGH.

NT: B.213c; CB.1245a; K.194.
OT: nāgash: S.5066; HR.362b.11; H.1297; BD.620c.
qārab: S.7126; HR.362b.13; H.2065; BD.897b.
GEN. REF.: IS.1:216; NB.—; Z.—.

B. Adjective.

aprositos [ἀπρόσιτος, 676], unapproachable, inaccessible (*a*, negative, and an adjective formed from *proseimi*, to go to), is used, in 1 Tim. 6:16, of the light in which God dwells (A.V., "which no man can approach unto"; R.V., "unapproachable"). ¶

NT: B.102c; CB.—; K.—.
OT: —.
GEN. REF.: IS.1:216; NB.—; Z.—.

APPROVE, APPROVED

A. Verbs.

1. *dokimazō* [δοκιμάζω, 1381], primarily, of metals (e.g., the Sept. of Prov. 8:10; 17:3), signifies to prove, e.g., 1 John 4:1, more frequently to prove with a view to approval, e.g., Rom. 1:28, A.V., "they did not like to retain God in their knowledge"; R.V., "they refused"; marg., "did not approve," the true meaning. Their refusal was not the outcome of ignorance; they had the power to make a deliberate choice; they wilfully disapproved of having God in their knowledge.

In the next chapter, the Apostle speaks of the Jew as "approving things that are excellent," 2:18. The Jew knew God's will, and mentally approved of the things in which God had instructed him out of the Law.

In Rom. 14:22, he is said to be happy who "judgeth not himself in that which he approveth"; that is to say, in that which he approves of after having put the matter to the test. The A.V. "alloweth" has not now this meaning.

As to the gifts from the church at Corinth for poor saints in Judaea, those who were "approved" by the church to travel with the offering would be men whose trustworthiness and stability had been proved, 1 Cor. 16:3 (the R.V. margin seems right, "whomsoever ye shall approve, them will I send with letters"); cp. 2 Cor. 8:22.

In Phil. 1:10 the Apostle prays that the saints may "approve the things that are excellent" or 'things that differ,' i.e., approve after distinguishing and discerning.

In 1 Thess. 2:4, the Apostle and his fellow-missionaries were "approved of God to be entrusted with the Gospel" (not "allowed," A.V.). Not permission to preach, but Divine approval after Divine testing is intended. See ALLOW, DISCERN, EXAMINE, LIKE, PROVE, REFUSE, TRY.

NT: B.202c; CB.1242a; K.181.
OT: bāḥan: S.974; HR.339c.1; H.230; BD.103c.
GEN. REF.: IS.1:217; NB.—; Z.—.

Note: Cp. *dokimē*, proof, experience; see also B.

2. *sunistēmi* [συνίστημι, 4921], lit., to set together (*sun*, with, *histēmi*, to stand), hence signifies to set one person or thing with another by way of presenting and commending. This meaning is confined to Romans and 2 Corinthians. The saints at Corinth had 'approved themselves in everything to be pure,' in the matter referred to, 2 Cor. 7:11. The word

often denotes to commend, so as to meet with approval, Rom. 3:5; 5:8; 16:1; 2 Cor. 4:2; 6:4 (R.V.); 10:18; 12:11, etc. See COMMEND, COMPACTED, CONSIST (No. 2), STAND.

NT: B.709c; CB.1270c; K.1120.
OT: qāhal: S.6950; HR.1317a.10; H.1991; BD.874d.
ṣāwāh: S.6680; HR.1317a.9; H.1887; BD.845b.
pāqad: S.6485; HR.1317a.8; H.1802; BD.823a.
GEN. REF.: IS.1:217; NB.—; Z.—.

3. *apodeiknumi* [ἀποδείκνυμι, 584], lit., to point out, to exhibit (*apo*, forth, *deiknumi*, to show), is used once in the sense of proving by demonstration, and so bringing about an approval. The Lord Jesus was "a Man approved of God by mighty works and wonders and signs," Acts 2:22. See PROVE, SET, No. 17, SHEW.

NT: B.89c; CB.1236c; K.—.
OT: —.
GEN. REF.: IS.1:217; NB.—; Z.—.

B. Adjective.

dokimos [δόκιμος, 1384], akin to *dechomai*, to receive, always signifies "approved"; so the R.V. everywhere, e.g., in Jas. 1:12 for A.V., "when he is tried." The word is used of coins and metals in the Sept.; in Gen. 23:16, "four hundred didrachms of silver approved with merchants"; in Zech. 11:13, in regard to the 30 pieces of silver, "Cast them into a furnace and I will see if it is good (approved) metal."

NT: B.203a; CB.1242a; K.181.
OT: zāqaq: S.2212; HR.340a.1; H.576; BD.279b.
ṭāhor: S.2889; HR.340a.2; H.792d; BD.373a.
yᵉqar: S.3366; HR.340a.3; H.905b; BD.430b.
GEN. REF.: IS.1:217; NB.—; Z.—.

APRON

simikinthion [σιμικίνθιον, 4612], a thing girded round half the body (Latin, *semicinctium*), was a narrow apron, or linen covering, worn by workmen and servants, Acts 19:12. ¶

NT: B.751a; CB.—; K.—.
OT: —.
GEN. REF.: IS.1:217; NB.—; Z.—.

For **APT** see **TEACH,** B

ARCHANGEL

archangelos [ἀρχάγγελος, 743] "is not found in the O.T., and in the N.T. only in 1 Thess. 4:16 and Jude 9, where it is used of Michael, who in Daniel is called 'one of the chief princes,' and 'the great prince' (Sept., 'the great angel'), 10:13, 21; 12:1. Cp. also Rev. 12:7. . . . Whether there are other beings of this exalted rank in the heavenly hosts, Scripture does not say, though the description 'one of the chief princes' suggests that this may be the case; cp. also Rom. 8:38; Eph. 1:21; Col. 1:16, where the word translated 'principalities' is *archē*, the prefix in archangel."* In 1 Thess. 4:16 the meaning seems to be that the voice of the Lord Jesus will be of the character of an archangelic shout. ¶

NT: B.111a; CB.1237a; K.12.
OT: —.
GEN. REF.: IS.1:235; NB.37; Z.—.

For **ARIGHT** (R.V. of 2 Tim. 2:15) see **HANDLE,** No. 5

* From Notes on Thessalonians by Hogg and Vine, p. 142.

ARISE, AROSE, AROUSE, RAISE, RISE, ROUSE

1. *anistēmi* [ἀνίστημι, 450], to stand up or to make to stand up, according as its use is intransitive or transitive (*ana*, up, *histēmi*, to stand), is used (*a*) of a physical change of position, e.g., of rising from sleep, Mark 1:35; from a meeting in a synagogue, Luke 4:29; of the illegal rising of the high priest in the tribunal in Matt. 26:62; of an invalid rising from his couch, Luke 5:25; the rising up of a disciple from his vocation to follow Christ, Luke 5:28; cp. John 11:31; rising up from prayer, Luke 22:45; of a whole company, Acts 26:30; 1 Cor. 10:7; (*b*) metaphorically, of rising up antagonistically against persons, e.g., of officials against people, Acts 5:17; of a seditious leader, 5:36; of the rising up of Satan, Mark 3:26; of false teachers, Acts 20:30; (*c*) of rising to a position of pre-eminence or power; e.g., of Christ as a Prophet, Acts 3:22; 7:37; as God's servant in the midst of the nation of Israel, Acts 3:26; as the Son of God in the midst of the nation, 13:33 (not here of Resurrection, but with reference to the Incarnation: the A.V. "again" has nothing corresponding to it in the original, it was added as a misinterpretation: the mention of His Resurrection is in the next verse, in which it is stressed by way of contrast and by the addition, "from the dead"); as a Priest, Heb. 7:11, 15; as King over the nations, Rom. 15:12; (*d*) of a spiritual awakening from lethargy, Eph. 5:14; (*e*) of resurrection from the dead: (1) of the Resurrection of Christ, Matt. 17:9; 20:19; Mark 8:31; 9:9, 10, 31; 10:34; Luke 18:33; 24:7, 46; John 20:9; Acts 2:24, 32; 10:41; 13:34; 17:3, 31; 1 Thess. 4:14; (2) of believers, John 6:39, 40, 44, 54; 11:24; 1 Thess. 4:16; of unbelievers, Matt. 12:41. See LIFT, RAISE (up), STAND.

NT: B.70a; CB.1235c; K.60.
OT: qûm: S.6965; HR.102c.8; H.1999; BD.877c.
GEN. REF.: IS.1:298,4:36,37; NB.—; Z.—.

2. *exanistēmi* [ἐξανίστημι, 1817], a strengthened form of No. 1 (*ex*, i.e., *ek*, intensive), signifies to raise up, Mark 12:19; Luke 20:28; intransitively, to rise up, Acts 15:5. ¶

NT: B.272d; CB.1247c; K.60.
OT: qûm: S.6965; HR.487c.6; H.1999; BD.877c.
GEN. REF.: IS.1:298,4:36,37; NB.–; Z.–.

3. *egeirō* [ἐγείρω, 1453], is frequently used in the N.T. in the sense of raising (Active Voice), or rising (Middle and Passive Voices): (*a*) from sitting, lying, sickness, e.g., Matt. 2:14; 9:5, 7, 19; Jas. 5:15; Rev. 11:1; (*b*) of causing to appear, or, in the Passive, appearing, or raising up so as to occupy a place in the midst of people, Matt. 3:9; 11:11; Mark 13:22; Acts 13:22. It is thus said of Christ in Acts 13:23; cp. No. 1, (*c*); (*c*) of rousing, stirring up, or rising against, Matt. 24:7; Mark 13:8; (*d*) of raising buildings, John 2:19, 20; (*e*) of raising or rising from the dead; (1) of Christ, Matt. 16:21; and frequently elsewhere (but not in Phil., 2 Thess., 1 Tim., Tit., Jas., 2 Pet., Epp. of John and Jude); (2) of Christ's raising the dead, Matt. 11:5; Mark 5:41; Luke 7:14; John 12:1, 9, 17; (3) of the act of the disciples, Matt. 10:8; (4) of the resurrection of believers, Matt. 27:52; John 5:21; 1 Cor. 15:15, 16, 29, 32, 35, 42, 43, 44, 52; 2 Cor. 1:9; 4:14; of unbelievers, Matt. 12:42 (cp. ver. 41, No. 1).

Egeirō stands in contrast to *anistēmi* (when used with reference to resurrection) in this respect, that *egeirō* is frequently used both in the transitive sense of raising up and the intransitive of rising, whereas *anistēmi* is comparatively infrequent in the transitive use. See AWAKE.

NT: B.214c; CB.1242c; K.195.
OT: qûm: S.6965; HR.364a.12; H.1999; BD.877c.
'ûr: S.5782; HR.364a.8; H.1587; BD.734d.
GEN. REF.: IS.1:298,4:36,37; NB.–; Z.–.

4. *diegeirō* [διεγείρω, 1326], a strengthened form of No. 3 (*dia*, through, intensive), signifies to rouse, to awaken from sleep. The Active Voice is not used intransitively. In Matt. 1:24, R.V., "Joseph arose from his sleep," the Passive Participle is, lit., 'being aroused.' In Mark 4:39 (A.V., "he arose," R.V., "he awoke"), the lit. rendering is 'he being awakened.' In John 6:18 the imperfect tense of the Passive Voice is used, and the rendering should be, 'the sea was being aroused.' See AWAKE, No. 2.

NT: B.193d; CB.–; K.–.
OT: –.
GEN. REF.: IS.1:298,4:36,37; NB.–; Z.–.

5. *ginomai* [γίνομαι, 1096], to become, to take place, is sometimes suitably translated "arise"; e.g., Matt. 8:24; Mark 4:37, "there arose a great tempest." So of the arising of persecution, Matt. 13:21; Mark 4:17; this might be translated 'taketh place'; of a tumult, Matt. 27:24, R.V., "arising," for A.V., "made"; of a flood, Luke 6:48; a famine, 15:14; a questioning, John 3:25; a murmuring, Acts 6:1; a tribulation, 11:19 (R.V.); a stir in the city, 19:23; a dissension, 23:7; a great clamour, ver. 9. See BECOME.

NT: B.158a; CB.1248b; K.117.
OT: ḥāyāh: S.2421; HR.256b.6d; H.644; BD.310d.
GEN. REF.: IS.1:298; NB.–; Z.–.

6. *anabainō* [ἀναβαίνω, 305], to go up, to ascend, is once rendered "arise" in the R.V., Luke 24:38, of reasonings in the heart; in Rev. 13:1, R.V., "coming up," for A.V., "rise up," with reference to the beast; in 17:8, A.V., "ascend," for R.V., "to come up"; in 19:3, R.V., "goeth up," for A.V., "rose up." See CLIMB UP, COME, ENTER, GO, GROW, RISE, SPRING.

NT: B.50a; CB.1235a; K.90.
OT: 'ālāh: S.5927; HR.70a.11; H.1624; BD.748a.
GEN. REF.: IS.1:298; NB.–; Z.–.

7. *sunephistēmi* [συνεφίστημι, 4911], to rise up together (*sun*, together, *epi*, up, *histēmi*, to stand), is used in Acts 16:22, of the rising up of a multitude against Paul and Silas. ¶

NT: B.789b; CB.–; K.–.
OT: –.
GEN. REF.: IS.1:298; NB.–; Z.–.

8. *eiserchomai* [εἰσέρχομαι, 1525], lit., to go in (*eis*, in, *erchomai*, to go), to enter, is once rendered "arose," metaphorically, with reference to a reasoning among the disciples which of them should be the greatest, Luke 9:46. See COME, ENTER, GO.

NT: B.232c; CB.1243b; K.257.
OT: bō': S.935; HR.410b.4a; H.212; BD.97c.
GEN. REF.: IS.1:298; NB.–; Z.–.

9. *anatellō* [ἀνατέλλω, 393], to arise, is used especially of things in the natural creation, e.g., the rising of the sun, moon and stars; metaphorically, of light, in Matt. 4:16, "did spring up"; of the sun, Matt. 5:45; 13:6 (R.V.); Mark 4:6; James 1:11; in Mark 16:2 the R.V. has "when the sun was risen," keeping to the verb form, for the A.V., "at the rising of"; of a cloud, Luke 12:54; of the day-star, 2 Pet. 1:19; in Heb. 7:14 metaphorically, of the Incarnation of Christ: "Our Lord hath sprung out of Judah," more lit., 'Our Lord hath arisen out of Judah,' as of the rising of the light of the sun. See RISE, SPRING UP. ¶

NT: B.62a; CB.1235b; K.57.
OT: ṣāmaḥ: S.6779; HR.83a.10; H.1928; BD.855b.
zāraḥ: S.2224; HR.83a.2; H.580; BD.280b.
pāraḥ: S.6524; HR.83a.8; H.1813,1814,1815; BD.827a.
GEN. REF.: IS.1:298; NB.–; Z.–.

Notes: (1) A corresponding noun, *anatolē*, signifies the east, i.e., the place of the sunrising.

(2) In Acts 27:14, the verb *ballō*, to beat (intransitive), is translated "arose" in the A.V.; R.V., "beat."

ARK

kibōtos [κιβωτός, 2787], a wooden box, a chest, is used of (*a*) Noah's vessel, Matt. 24:38; Luke 17:27; Heb. 11:7; 1 Pet. 3:20; (*b*) the ark of the Covenant in the Tabernacle, Heb. 9:4; (*c*) the ark seen in vision in the Heavenly Temple, Rev. 11:19. ¶

NT: B.431d; CB.1255a; K.—.
OT: 'arôn: S.727; HR.763c.1; H.166a; BD.75b.
tēbāh: S.8392; HR.763c.3; H.2492; BD.1061c.
GEN. REF.: IS.1:291; NB.81; Z.—.

ARM (physical)

1. *ankalē* [ἀγκάλη, 43], used in the plural, in Luke 2:28, originally denoted the curve, or the inner angle, of the arm. The word is derived from a term signifying to bend, to curve; the Eng. "angle" is connected. ¶

NT: B.10c; CB.1235c; K.—.
OT: —.
GEN. REF.: IS.1:294; NB.82; Z.—.

Note: Enankalizomai (*en*, in, and a verb akin to No. 1), to take into the arms, to embrace, is used in Mark 9:36 and 10:16, of the tenderness of Christ towards little children. ¶

2. *brachiōn* [βραχίων, 1023], the shorter part of the arm, from the shoulder to the elbow, is used metaphorically to denote strength, power, and always in the N.T. of the power of God, Luke 1:51; John 12:38; Acts 13:17; frequently so in the O.T., especially in Deuteronomy, the Psalms and Isaiah; see, e.g., Deut. 4:34; 5:15; Psa. 44:3; 71:18, where "strength" is, lit., 'arm'; 77:15; Isa. 26:11, where "hand" is, lit., 'arm'; 30:30; 40:10, 11, etc. ¶

NT: B.147b; CB.—; K.110.
OT: z^{e}rôah: S.2220; HR.230a.1c; H.583a; BD.283d.
yad: S.3027; HR.230a.2; H.844; BD.388d.
shôq: S.7785; HR.230a.3; H.2350a; BD.1003b.
GEN. REF.: IS.1:294; NB.82; Z.—.

ARMS (weapons), ARMOUR, TO ARM

A. Nouns.

1. *hoplon* [ὅπλον, 3696], originally any tool or implement for preparing a thing, became used in the plural for weapons of warfare. Once in the N.T. it is used of actual weapons, John 18:3; elsewhere, metephorically, of (*a*) the members of the body as instruments of unrighteousness and as instruments of righteousness, Rom. 6:13; (*b*) the armour of light, Rom. 13:12; the armour of righteousness, 2 Cor. 6:7; the weapons of the Christian's warfare, 2 Cor. 10:4. ¶

NT: B.575c; CB.1251a; K.702.
OT: māgēn: S.4043; HR.1003c.3; H.367c; BD.171b.
nesheq: S.5402; HR.1003c.4; H.1436a; BD.676d.
GEN. REF.: IS.1:295; NB.82; Z.—.

2. *panoplia* [πανοπλία, 3833], Eng., panoply, lit., all armour, full armour, (*pas*, all, *hoplon*, a weapon), is used (*a*) of literal armour, Luke 11:22; (*b*) of the spiritual helps supplied by God for overcoming the temptations of the Devil, Eph. 6:11, 13. Among the Greeks the *panoplia* was the complete equipment used by heavily armed infantry. ¶

NT: B.607d; CB.1261c; K.702.
OT: halîṣāh: S.2488; HR.1053a.1; H.667a,668a; BD.322d.
GEN. REF.: IS.1:295; NB.82; Z.—.

B. Verbs.

1. *hoplizō* [ὁπλίζω, 3695], to arm oneself, is used in 1 Pet. 4:1, in an exhortation to arm ourselves with the same mind as that of Christ in regard to His sufferings. ¶

NT: B.575c; CB.1251a; K.702.
OT: —.
GEN. REF.: IS.1:295; NB.82; Z.—.

2. *kathoplizō* [καθοπλίζω, 2528] is an intensive form, to furnish fully with arms, *kata*, down, intensive, *hoplon*, a weapon, Luke 11:21, lit., 'a strong man fully armed.' ¶ In the Sept., Jer. 46:9. ¶

NT: B.391a; CB.—; K.—.
OT: tāphas: S.8610; HR.704b.1; H.2538; BD.1074c.
GEN. REF.: IS.1:295; NB.82; Z.—.

ARMY

1. *strateuma* [στράτευμα, 4753] denotes (*a*) an army of any size, large or small, Matt. 22:7; Rev. 9:16; 19:14, 19 (twice); (*b*) a company of soldiers, such as Herod's bodyguard, Luke 23:11 (R.V., "soldiers"), or the soldiers of a garrison, Acts 23:10, 27 (R.V., "the soldiers," for A.V., "an army"). See SOLDIER, WAR. ¶

NT: B.770b; CB.1270a; K.1091.
OT: —.
GEN. REF.: IS.1:295; NB.84; Z.—.

2. *stratopedon* [στρατόπεδον, 4760], from *stratos*, a military host, *pedon*, a plain, strictly denotes an army encamped, a camp; in Luke 21:20, of the soldiers which were to be encamped about Jerusalem in fulfilment of the Lord's prophecy concerning the destruction of the city; the phrase might be translated 'by camps' (or encampments). ¶

NT: B.771a; CB.1270b; K.1091.
OT: ḥayil: S.2428; HR.1296a.1; H.624a; BD.298c.
GEN. REF.: IS.1:295; NB.84; Z.—.

3. *parembolē* [παρεμβολή, 3925], lit., a casting in among, an insertion (*para*, among, *ballō*, to throw), in the Macedonian dialect, was a military term. In the N.T. it denotes the distribution of troops in army formation, "armies," Heb. 11:34; a camp, as of the Israelites, Ex. 19:17; 29:14; 32:17; hence, in Heb. 13:11, 13, of Jerusalem, since the city was to the Jews what the camp in the wilderness had been to the Israelites; in Rev. 20:9, the armies

or camp of the saints, at the close of the Millennium.

It is also denoted a castle or barracks, Acts 21:34, 37; 22:24; 23:10, 16, 32. ¶

NT: B.625b; CB.1262b; K.–.
OT: maḥaneh: S.4264; HR.1067b.2a; H.690e; BD.334a.
GEN. REF.: IS.1:295; NB.84; Z.–.

AROUND: see Note †, p. 1.

For ARRAY, see CLOTHE, No. 6, PUT

ARRIVE

1. *katantaō* [καταντάω, 2658], to come to, arrive at, is used (*a*) literally, of locality, Acts 16:1, "came to"; so 18:19, 24; 20:15 ("came"); 21:7; 25:13; 27:12 (A.V., "attain to," R.V., "reach"); 28:13; (*b*) metaphorically, of attainment, Acts 26:7, "attain"; so Eph. 4:13; Phil. 3:11. In 1 Cor. 10:11 ("upon whom the ends of the ages are come," R.V.), the metaphor is apparently that of an inheritance as coming down or descending to an heir, the "ends" (*telē*) being the spiritual revenues derived from taxes, and Rom. 13:7, where the singular, *telos*, "custom," is used); the inheritance metaphor is again seen in 1 Cor. 14:36, of the coming (or descending) of the word of God to the Corinthians. See ATTAIN.

NT: B.415b; CB.1254a; K.419.
OT: –.
GEN. REF.: IS.–; NB.–; Z.–.

2. *katapleō* [καταπλέω, 2668], denotes to sail down (*kata*, down, *pleō*, to sail), i.e., from the high sea to the shore, Luke 8:26. ¶

NT: B.416d; CB.; K..
OT: –.
GEN. REF.: –.

3. *paraginomai* [παραγίνομαι, 3854], lit., to become near, hence, to come on the scene, Matt. 3:1, of John the Baptist, is translated, "arrive" in the R.V. of 1 Cor. 16:3, for A.V., "come." See COME, GO, PRESENT.

NT: B.613c; CB.–; K.–.
OT: bô': S.935; HR.1056c.1a; H.212; BD.97c.
GEN. REF.: IS.–; NB.–; Z.–.

4. *paraballō* [παραβάλλω, 3846], *para*, alongside, *ballō*, to throw, signifies, nautically, "touched at"; so the R.V. of Acts 20:15 (A.V., "arrived"); or, perhaps, to strike across, from one place to another. In Mark 4:30, some mss. have this verb (A.V., "compare"); the most authentic have *tithēmi*, to set forth (with the word "parable"). See COMPARE.

NT: B.611d; CB.1262a; K.–.
OT: nāṭāh: S.5186; HR.1055c.1; H.1352; BD.640c.
GEN. REF.: –.

5. *phthanō* [φθάνω, 5348], to anticipate, reach to, is translated "did arrive at," Rom. 9:31, R.V., of Israel's failure to attain to the Law (A.V., "hath attained to"). See ATTAIN, COME, PRECEDE.

NT: B.856d; CB.1264c; K.1258.
OT: nāga': S.5060; HR.1429b.5; H.1293; BD.619a.
GEN. REF.: –.

ART, ARTS

1. *technē* [τέχνη, 5078], an art, handicraft, trade, is used in Acts 17:29, of the plastic art; in Acts 18:3, of a trade or craft (A.V., "occupation," R.V., "trade"); in Rev. 18:22, "craft" (cp. *technitēs*, a craftsman, Eng., technical). See CRAFT, OCCUPATION, TRADE. ¶

NT: B.814b; CB.1271a; K.–.
OT: ḥokmāh: S.2451; HR.1347c.1; H.647a; BD.315b.
ma'aseh: S.4639; HR.1347c.2; H.1708a; BD.795c.
'abôdāh: S.5656; HR.1347c.3; H.1553c; BD.715a.
GEN. REF.: IS.1:299; NB.86; Z.–.

2. *periergos* [περίεργος, 4021], lit., a work about (*peri*, about, *ergon*, a work), hence, 'busy about trifles.' is used, in the plural, of two things superfluous, "curious (or magical) arts," Acts 19:19; in 1 Tim. 5:13, "busybodies." See BUSYBODY. ¶

NT: B.646d; CB.–; K.–.
OT: –.
GEN. REF.: IS.1:299; NB.86; Z.–.

AS (and connected phrases): see Note †, p. 1.

For ASCEND see ARISE No. 6.

ASHAMED (to be), SHAME

A. Verbs.

1. *aischunō* [αἰσχύνω, 153(-OMAI)], from *aischos*, shame, always used in the Passive Voice, signifies (*a*) to have a feeling of fear or shame which prevents a person from doing a thing, e.g., Luke 16:3; (*b*) the feeling of shame arising from something that has been done, e.g., 2 Cor. 10:8; Phil. 1:20; 1 John 2:28, of the possibility of being ashamed before the Lord Jesus at His Judgment Seat in His Parousia with His saints; in 1 Pet. 4:16, of being ashamed of suffering as a Christian. ¶

NT: B.25c; CB.1234a(-OMAI); K.29.
OT: bôsh: S.954; HR.36c.2a; H.222; BD.101d.
GEN. REF.: IS.1:314; NB.1169; Z.–.

2. *epaischunomai* [ἐπαισχύνομαι, 1870], a strengthened form of No. 1 (*epi*, upon, intensive), is used only in the sense (*b*) in the preceding paragraph. It is said of being ashamed of persons, Mark 8:38; Luke 9:26; the Gospel, Rom. 1:16; former evil doing, Rom. 6:21; "the testimony of our Lord," 2 Tim. 1:8; suffering for the Gospel, ver. 12; rendering

assistance and comfort to one who is suffering for the Gospel's sake, ver. 16. It is used in Heb., of Christ in calling those who are sanctified His brethren, 2:11, and of God in His not being ashamed to be called the God of believers, 11:16. ¶ In the Sept., in Job 34:19; Ps.119:6; Is. 1:29. ¶

NT: B.282a; CB.1245b; K.29.
OT: bôsh: S.954; HR.505b.1; H.222; BD.101d.
ḥaphēr: S.2659; HR.505b.2; H.715; BD.344a.
GEN. REF.: IS.1:314; NB.1169; Z.–.

3. *kataischunō* [καταισχύνω, 2617], another strengthened form (*kata*, down, intensive), is used (*a*) in the Active Voice, to put to shame, e.g., Rom. 5:5; 1 Cor. 1:27 (A.V., "confound"); 11:4, 5 ("dishonoureth"), and ver. 22; (*b*) in the Passive Voice, Rom. 9:33; 10:11; 2 Cor. 7:14; 1 Pet. 2:6; 3:16. See CONFOUND, DISHONOUR, SHAME.

NT: B.410d; CB.1254a; K.29.
OT: bôsh: S.954; HR.731c.1; H.222; BD.101d.
kālam: S.3637; HR.731c.4; H.987; BD.483c.
GEN. REF.: IS.1:314; NB.1169; Z.–.

4. *entrepō* [ἐντρέπω, 1788], to put to shame, in the Passive Voice, to be ashamed, lit. means to turn in (*en*, in, *trepō*, to turn), that is, to turn one upon himself and so produce a feeling of shame, a wholesome shame which involves a change of conduct, 1 Cor. 4:14; 2 Thess. 3:14; Titus 2:8, the only places where it has this meaning. See also REGARD, REVERENCE.

NT: B.269d; CB.–; K.–.
OT: ḥaphēr: S.2659; HR.480c.1; H.715; BD.344a.
kālam: S.3637; HR.480c.2; H.987; BD.483c.
kāna': S.3665; HR.480c.4; H.1001; BD.488b.
GEN. REF.: IS.1:314; NB.1169; Z.–.

B. Nouns.

1. *aischunē* [αἰσχύνη, 152], shame, akin to A, No. 1, signifies (*a*) subjectively, the confusion of one who is ashamed of anything, a sense of shame, Luke 14:9; those things which shame conceals, 2 Cor. 4:2; (*b*) objectively, ignominy, that which is visited on a person by the wicked, Heb. 12:2; that which should arise from guilt, Phil. 3:19; (*c*) concretely, a thing to be ashamed of, Rev. 3:18; Jude 13, where the word is in the plural, lit., 'basenesses,' 'disgraces.' See DISHONESTY. ¶

NT: B.25b; CB.1234a; K.29.
OT: bōshet: S.1322; HR.37a.1c; H.222b; BD.102a.
'erᵉwāh: S.6172; HR.37b.7; H.1692b; BD.788d.
GEN. REF.: IS.1:314; NB.1169; Z.–.

2. *entropē* [ἐντροπή, 1791], akin to A, No. 4, lit., a turning in upon oneself, producing a recoil from what is unseemly or vile, is used in 1 Cor. 6:5; 15:34. It is associated with *aischunē* in the Psalms, in the Sept., e.g., 35:26, where it follows *aischunē*, "let them be clothed with shame (*aischunē*) and confusion (*entropē*)"; 44:15, "all the day my shame is before me and the confusion of my face has covered me"; 69:19, "Thou knowest my reproach and my shame and my confusion"; so in 71:13. In 109:29 the words are in the opposite order. ¶

NT: B.269d; CB.–; K.–.
OT: kᵉlimmāh: S.3639; HR.481a.1; H.987a; BD.484a.
GEN. REF.: IS.1:314; NB.1169; Z.–.

Note: Aidōs, used in 1 Tim. 2:9, denotes modesty, shamefastness (the right spelling for the A.V., "shamefacedness"). In comparison with *aischunē*, *aidōs* is "the nobler word, and implies the nobler motive: in it is involved an innate moral repugnance to the doing of the dishonourable act, which moral repugnance scarcely or not at all exists in *aischunē*" (Trench, Syn. § xix). See SHAMEFASTNESS. ¶

C. Adjectives.

1. *aischros* [αἰσχρός, 150], base (akin to No. 1), is used in 1 Cor. 11:6; 14:35; Eph. 5:12. See FILTHY, B, No. 1. ¶ Cp. *aischrotēs*, filthiness, Eph. 5:4. ¶

NT: B.25b; CB.1234a; K.29.
OT: ra': S.7451; HR.36c.1; H.2191; BD.948a.
GEN. REF.: IS.1:314; NB.1169; Z.–.

2. *anepaischuntos* [ἀνεπαίσχυντος, 422], an intensive adjective (*a*, negative, *n* euphonic, *epi*, upon, intensive, *aischunē*, shame), not ashamed, having no cause for shame, is used in 2 Tim. 2:15. ¶

NT: B.65a; CB.–; K.–.
OT: –.
GEN. REF.: IS.1:314; NB.1169; Z.–.

ASHES

A. Noun.

spodos [σποδός, 4700], ashes, is found three times, twice in association with sackcloth, Matt. 11:21 and Luke 10:13, as tokens of grief (cp. Esth. 4:1, 3; Isa. 58:5; 61:3; Jer. 6:26; Jonah 3:6); of the ashes resulting from animal sacrifices, Heb. 9:13; in the O.T., metaphorically, of one who describes himself as dust and ashes, Gen. 18:27, etc. ¶

NT: B.763b; CB.–; K.–.
OT: 'ēpher: S.665; HR.1285a.1; H.150a; BD.68a.
GEN. REF.: IS.1:318; NB.–; Z.–.

B. Verb.

tephroō [τεφρόω, 5077], to turn to ashes, is found in 2 Pet. 2:6, with reference to the destruction of Sodom and Gomorrah. ¶

NT: B.814b; CB.–; K.–.
OT: –.
GEN. REF.: IS.1:318; NB.–; Z.–.

Notes: (1) *Tephra*, frequently used of the ashes of a funeral pile, is not found in the N.T.

(2) The Hebrew verb, rendered "accept" in Psa. 20:3, "accept thy burnt sacrifice," signifies to turn to ashes (i.e., by sending fire from heaven). See also Ex. 27:3, and Num. 4:13, "shall take away the ashes."

For **ASHORE** (Acts 27:29), see **CAST,** A, No. 3

For **ASIDE** see **LAY,** No. 8. **TAKE,** No. 3, **TURN,** Nos. 3, 17, *Note* (1)

ASK

A. Verbs.

1. *aiteō* [αἰτέω, 154], to ask, is to be distinguished from No. 2. *Aiteō* more frequently suggests the attitude of a suppliant, the petition of one who is lesser in position than he to whom the petition is made; e.g., in the case of men in asking something from God, Matt. 7:7; a child from a parent, Matt. 7:9, 10; a subject from a king, Acts 12:20; priests and people from Pilate, Luke 23:23 (R.V., "asking" for A.V., "requiring"); a beggar from a passer by, Acts 3:2. With reference to petitioning God, this verb is found in Paul's Epistles in Eph. 3:20 and Col. 1:9; in James four times, 1:5, 6; 4:2, 3; in 1 John, five times, 3:22; 5:14, 15 (twice), 16. See BEG, CALL FOR, CRAVE, DESIRE, REQUIRE.

NT: B.25d; CB.1234a; K.30.
OT: shā'al: S.7592; HR.37c.3; H.2303; BD.981b.
GEN. REF.: IS.1:329; NB.–; Z.–.

2. *erōtaō* [ἐρωτάω, 2065], more frequently suggests that the petitioner is on a footing of equality or familiarity with the person whom he requests. It is used of a king in making request from another king, Luke 14:32; of the Pharisee who "desired" Christ that He would eat with him, an indication of the inferior conception he had of Christ, Luke 7:36; cp. 11:37; John 9:15; 18:19.

In this respect it is significant that the Lord Jesus never used *aiteō* in the matter of making request to the Father. "The consciousness of His equal dignity, of His potent and prevailing intercession, speaks out in this, that as often as He asks, or declares that He will ask anything of the Father, it is always *erōtaō*, an asking, that is, upon equal terms, John 14:16; 16:26; 17:9, 15, 20, never *aiteō*, that He uses. Martha, on the contrary, plainly reveals her poor unworthy conception of His person, that . . . she ascribes that *aiteō* to Him which He never ascribes to Himself, John 11:22" (Trench, Syn. § xl).

In passages where both words are used, the distinction should be noticed, even if it cannot be adequately represented in English. In John 16:23, "in that day ye shall ask Me nothing," the verb is *erōtaō*, whereas in the latter part of the verse, in the sentence, "If ye shall ask anything of the Father," the verb is *aiteō*. The distinction is brought out in the R.V. margin, which renders the former clause "Ye shall ask Me no question," and this meaning is confirmed by the fact that the disciples had been desirous of asking Him a question (*erōtaō*, ver. 19). If the Holy Spirit had been given, the time for asking questions from the Lord would have ceased. In John 14:14, where, not a question, but a request is made by the disciples, *aiteō* is used.

Both verbs are found in 1 John 5:16: in the sentence "he shall ask, and God will give him life for them that sin not unto death," the verb is *aiteō*, but with regard to the sin unto death, in the sentence "not concerning this do I say that he shall make request," the verb is *erōtaō*.

Later, the tendency was for *erōtaō* to approximate to *aiteō*. See BESEECH, DESIRE, INTREAT, PRAY, REQUEST.

NT: B.311d; CB.1246c; K.262.
OT: shā'al: S.7592; HR.553b.3; H.2303; BD.981b.
GEN. REF.: IS.1:329; NB.–; Z.–.

Note: In Matt. 19:17, the R.V., following the most authentic mss., has "Why askest (*erotaō*) thou Me concerning that which is good?"

3. *eperōtaō* [ἐπερωτάω, 1905], a strengthened form of No. 2 (*epi*, in addition), is frequently used in the Synoptic Gospels, but only twice in the Gospel of John, 18:7, 21. In Rom. 10:20 it is rendered "asked of" (A.V., "asked after"). The more intensive character of the asking may be observed in Luke 2:46; 3:14; 6:9; 17:20; 20:21, 27, 40; 22:64; 23:3, 6, 9. In Matt. 16:1, it virtually signifies to demand (its meaning in later Greek). See DEMAND, DESIRE, QUESTION.

NT: B.285b; CB.1245c; K.262.
OT: shā'al: S.7592; HR.510b.4; H.2303; BD.981b.
GEN. REF.: IS.1:329; NB.–; Z.–.

Note: For the corresponding noun *eperōtēma*, see ANSWER.

4. *punthanomai* [πυνθάνομαι, 4441], to ask by way of enquiry, not by way of making a request for something, is found in the Gospels and the Acts, five times in the former, seven in the latter; in Matt. 2:4, A.V., "demanded," R.V., "enquired," so Acts 21:33. See DEMAND, INQUIRE, UNDERSTAND.

NT: B.729c; CB.–; K.–.
OT: dārash: S.1875; HR.1242b.1; H.455; BD.205a.
GEN. REF.: IS.1:329; NB.–; Z.–.

5. *exetazō* [ἐξετάζω, 1833], to search out (*ek*, out, intensive, *etazō*, to examine), is translated "ask," in John 21:12, A.V. (R.V., "inquire"); in Matt. 2:8, A.V., "search"; R.V., "search out," expressing the intensive force of the verb, so Matt. 10:11 (A.V., "inquire"). See INQUIRE, SEARCH. ¶

NT: B.275c; CB.–; K.–.
OT: bāḥan: S.975; HR.495a.1; H.230b; BD.103c.
dārash: S.1875; HR.495a.2; H.455; BD.205a.
GEN. REF.: IS.1:329; NB.–; Z.–.

6. *legō* [λέγω, 3004], to say, occasionally signifies to ask, as of an enquiry, the reason being that *legō* is used for every variety of speaking, e.g., Acts 25:20, "I asked whether he would come to Jerusalem." See BID, BOAST, CALL, DESCRIBE, GIVE, NAME, PUT, *Note* (2), SAY, SPEAK, TELL, UTTER.

NT: B.468a; CB.1256c; K.505.
OT: 'āmar: S.559; HR.863c.1; H.118; BD.55c.
GEN. REF.: IS.1:329; NB.–; Z.–.

7. *anakrinō* [ἀνακρίνω, 350], to judge, sometimes has the meaning to ask a question; e.g., 1 Cor. 10:25, 27. See DISCERN, EXAMINE, JUDGE, SEARCH.

NT: B.56b; CB.1235a; K.469.
OT: ḥāqar: S.2713; HR.78c.1; H.729; BD.350c.
GEN. REF.: IS.1:329; NB.–; Z.–.

Notes: (1) For *apaiteō*, Luke 6:30, see REQUIRE, No. 3. (2) In Luke 22:31, R.V., *exaiteomai* is rendered "hath asked to have." ¶

B. Noun.

aitēma [αἴτημα, 155], akin to No. 1, lit., that which has been asked for, is used in Luke 23:24, R.V., "what they asked for" (A.V., "required"); Phil. 4:6, "requests"; 1 John 5:15, "petitions." See PETITION, REQUEST, REQUIRE. ¶

NT: B.26b; CB.1234a; K.30.
OT: she'ēlāh: S.7595; HR.38a.2a; H.3012a; BD.982c.
GEN. REF.: IS.1:329; NB.–; Z.–.

ASLEEP, SLEEP

1. *katheudō* [καθεύδω, 2518], to go to sleep, is chiefly used of natural sleep, and is found most frequently in the Gospels, especially Matthew and Luke. With reference to death it is found in the Lord's remark concerning Jairus' daughter, Matt. 9:24; Mark 5:39; Luke 8:52. In the Epistles of Paul it is used as follows: (*a*) of natural sleep, e.g., 1 Thess. 5:7; (*b*) of carnal indifference to spiritual things on the part of believers, Eph. 5:14; 1 Thess. 5:6, 10 (as in Mark 13:36), a condition of insensibility to Divine things involving conformity to the world (cp. *hupnos* below).

NT: B.388d; CB.1254c; K.384.
OT: shākab: S.7901; HR.700a.3; H.2381; BD.1011d.
GEN. REF.: IS.1:329; NB.–; Z.–.

2. *koimaomai* [κοιμάομαι, 2837], is used of natural sleep, Matt. 28:13; Luke 22:45; John 11:12; Acts 12:6; of the death of the body, but only of such as are Christ's; yet never of Christ Himself, though He is "the firstfruits of them that have fallen asleep." 1 Cor. 15:20; of saints who departed before Christ came, Matt. 27:52; Acts 13:36; of Lazarus, while Christ was yet upon the earth, John 11:11; of believers since the Ascension, 1 Thess. 4:13, 14, 15, and Acts 7:60; 1 Cor. 7:39; 11:30; 15:6, 18, 51; 2 Pet. 3:4. ¶

NT: B.437c; CB.1255b; K.–.
OT: shākab: S.7901; HR.773c.12; H.2381; BD.1011d.
GEN. REF.: IS.1:329; NB.–; Z.–.

Note: "This metaphorical use of the word sleep is appropriate, because of the similarity in appearance between a sleeping body and a dead body; restfulness and peace normally characterise both. The object of the metaphor is to suggest that, as the sleeper does not cease to exist while his body sleeps, so the dead person continues to exist despite his absence from the region in which those who remain can communicate with him, and that, as sleep is known to be temporary, so the death of the body will be found to be. . . .

"That the body alone is in view in this metaphor is evident, (*a*) from the derivation of the word *koimaomai*, from *keimai*, to lie down (cp. *enastasis*, resurrection, from *ana*, 'up,' and *histēmi*, to cause to stand); cp. Is. 14:8, where for 'laid down,' the Sept. has 'fallen asleep'; (*b*) from the fact that in the N.T. the word resurrection is used of the body alone; (*c*) from Dan. 12:2, where the physically dead are described as 'them that sleep (Sept. *katheudō*, as at 1 Thess. 5:6) in the dust of the earth,' language inapplicable to the spiritual part of man; moreover, when the body returns whence it came, Gen. 3:19, the spirit returns to God who gave it, Eccles. 12:7.

"When the physical frame of the Christian (the earthly house of our tabernacle, 2 Cor. 5:1) is dissolved and returns to the dust, the spiritual part of his highly complex being, the seat of personality, departs to be with Christ, Phil. 1:23. And since that state in which the believer, absent from the body, is at home with the Lord, 2 Cor. 5:6-9, is described as 'very far better' than the present state of joy in communion with God and of happy activity in His service, everywhere reflected in Paul's writings, it is evident the word 'sleep,' where applied to the departed Christians, is not intended to convey the idea that the spirit is unconscious. . . .

"The early Christians adopted the word *koimētērion* (which was used by the Greeks of a rest-house for strangers) for the place of interment of the bodies of their departed; thence the English word 'cemetery,' 'the sleeping place,' is derived."*

* From Notes on Thessalonians by Hogg and Vine, p. 172.

3. *exupnizō* [ἐξυπνίζω, 1852], to awake (*ek*, out, *hupnos*, sleep), to awake out of sleep, is used in John 11:11. ¶ In the Sept., Judg. 16:14, 20; 1 Kings 3:15; Job. 14:12. ¶

NT: B.279b; CB.–; K.1233.
OT: yāqaṣ: S.3364; HR.501b.1; H.904; BD.429c.
GEN. REF.: IS.1:329; NB.–; Z.–.

4. *aphupnoō* [ἀφυπνόω, 879], to fall asleep (*apo*, away), is used of natural sleep, Luke 8:23, of the Lord's falling asleep in the boat on the lake of Galilee. ¶

NT: B.127d; CB.–; K.1233.
OT: –.
GEN. REF.: IS.1:329; NB.–; Z.–.

B. Adjective.

exupnos [ἔξυπνος, 1853], Acts 16:27, signifies "out of sleep." ¶

NT: B.279b; CB.–; K.1233.
OT: –.
GEN. REF.: IS.1:329; NB.–; Z.–.

C. Noun.

hupnos [ὕπνος, 5258] is never used of death. In five places in the N.T. it is used of physical sleep; in Rom. 13:11, metaphorically, of a slumbering state of soul, i.e., of spiritual conformity to the world, out of which believers are warned to awake.

NT: B.843a; CB.1252a; K.1233.
OT: ḥ^{a}lōm: S.2472; HR.1411c.2a; H.663a; BD.321c.
shēnāh: S.8142; HR.1411c.4b; H.928c; BD446a.
GEN. REF.: IS.1:329; NB.–; Z.–.

ASP

aspis [ἀσπίς, 785], a small and very venomous serpent, the bite of which is fatal, unless the part affected is at once cut away, in Rom. 3:13 is said, metaphorically, of the conversation of the ungodly. ¶

NT: B.117b; CB.1238a; K.–.
OT: –.
GEN. REF.: IS.1:330; NB.99; Z.–.

ASS

1. *onos* [ὄνος, 3688], is the usual word. *Onarion*, the diminutive of *onos*, a young ass, or ass's colt, is used in John 12:14, together with *onos*. ¶

NT: B.574a; CB.1261a; K.700.
OT: 'ātôn: S.860; HR.1000a.1; H.190a; BD.87c.
ḥ^{a}mōr: S.2543; HR.1000a.2; H.685a; BD.331b.
GEN. REF.: IS.1:330; NB.99; Z.–.

2. *hupozugion* [ὑποζύγιον, 5268], lit., under a yoke (*hupo*, under, *zugos*, a yoke), is used as an alternative description of the same animal, in Matt. 21:5, where both words are found together, "Behold, thy king cometh unto thee, meek and riding upon an ass (*onos*), and upon a colt the foal of an ass (*hupozugion*)." It was upon the colt that the Lord sat, John 12:14. In 2 Pet. 2:16, it is used of Balaam's ass. ¶

NT: B.844c; CB.–; K.–.
OT: 'ātôn: S.860; HR.1413b.1; H.190a; BD.87c.
ḥ^{a}mōr: S.2543; HR.1413b.2; H.685a; BD.331b.
GEN. REF.: IS.1:330; NB.99; Z.–.

ASSASSIN

sikarios [σικάριος, 4607] is a Latin word (*sicarius*, from *sica*, a dagger? denoting one who carries a dagger or short sword under his clothing, an assassin, Acts 21:38, R.V. Here it is used as a proper name (see the R.V.) of the Sicarii, Assassins, the fanatical Jewish faction which arose in Judea after Felix had rid the country of the robbers referred to by Josephus (Ant., XX). They mingled with the crowds at Festivals and stabbed their political opponents unobserved (A.V., "murderers"). ¶

NT: B.750b; CB.–; K.1026.
OT: –.
GEN. REF.: IS.1:330; NB.99; Z.–.

ASSAULT

A. Verbs.

ephistēmi [ἐφίστημι, 2186], lit., to stand over (*epi*, over, *histēmi*, to stand), signifies to assault; and in Acts 17:5, of those who attacked the house of Jason. For its usual meanings see COME (in, to, upon), HAND (at), INSTANT, PRESENT, STAND.

NT: B.330d; CB.–; K.–.
OT: ḥāzaq: S.2388; HR.585c.1; H.636; BD.304a.
pāqad: S.6485; HR.585c.12; H.1802; BD.823a.
GEN. REF.: IS.–; NB.–; Z.–.

B. Noun.

hormē [ὁρμή, 3730], rendered "assault" in Acts 14:5, A.V.; R.V., "onset" corresponds to *hormaō*, to rush. See IMPULSE, ONSET. ¶

NT: B.581d; CB.1251b; K.730.
OT: ḥēmāh: S.2534; HR.1014a.1; H.860a; BD.404b.
massā: S.4853; HR.1014a.2; H.1421e; BD.672c.
qeṣeph: S.7110; HR.1014a.4; H.2058a; BD.893c.
GEN. REF.: IS.–; NB.–; Z.–.

For **ASSAY** see **TRY,** No. 2.

ASSEMBLE

1. *sunagō* [συνάγω, 4863], to assemble (*sun*, together, *agō*, to bring), is used of the gathering together of people or things; in Luke 12:17, 18, "bestow," with reference to the act of gathering one's goods; so in Luke 15:13, suggesting that the Prodigal, having gathered all his goods together, sold them off; in John 6:12, of gathering up fragments; in John 18:2, "resorted," with reference to the assembling of Christ with His disciples in the garden of Gethsemane, there in the Passive Voice (unsuitable, however, in an English translation). In Acts 11:26, the R.V. has "were gathered together (with the church)," for A.V., "assembled themselves" (possibly 'they were hospitably entertained by'). The verb is not found in the most authentic mss. in Rev. 13:10. See BESTOW, GATHER, LEAD, TAKE, No. 29.

NT: B.782a; CB.1270b; K.–.
OT: 'āsaph: S.622; HR.1307b.1; H.140; BD.62a.
qābaṣ: S.6908; HR.1307b.34; H.1983; BD.867b.
GEN. REF.: IS.1:331; NB.100; Z.–.

Note: Episunagō, to gather together, is found only in the Synoptic Gospels; twice of the gathering together of people, Mark 1:33; Luke 12:1; twice of the desire of the Lord to gather together the inhabitants of Jerusalem, Matt. 23:37; Luke 13:34; twice of His future act in gathering together His elect through the instrumentality of the angels, Matt. 24:31; Mark 13:27. See GATHER. ¶

2. *sunalizō* [συναλίζω, 1996B], to gather together, to assemble, with the suggestion of a crowded meeting (*sun*, with, *halizō*, to crowd, or mass: the corresponding adjective is *halēs*, thronged), is used in Acts 1:4. The meaning to eat with, suggested by some, as if the word were derived from *hais*, "salt," is not to be accepted. ¶

NT: B.301d; CB.1246a; K.—.
OT: —.
GEN. REF.: IS.1:331; NB.100; Z.—.

3. *sunerchomai* [συνέρχομαι, 4871], to come together (*sun*, together, *erchomai*, to come), is once rendered "assemble," Mark 14:53, A.V. It is frequently used of "coming together," especially of the gathering of a local church, 1 Cor. 11:17, 18, 20, 33, 34; 14:23, 26; it is rendered "resorted" in Acts 16:13, A.V., where the R.V. adheres to the lit. rendering, "came together." See ACCOMPANY.

NT: B.783d; CB.1270b; K.257.
OT: 'āsaph: S.622; HR.1314a.1; H.140; BD62a.
qābaṣ: S.6908; HR.1314a.7; H.1983; BD.867b.
GEN. REF.: IS.1:331; NB.100; Z.—.

Notes: (1) In Acts 15:25, *ginomai*, to become, is translated "having come to (one accord)," correcting the A.V., "being assembled with (one accord)."

(2) *Sunagōgē*, akin to A, No. 1, is, lit., a place where people assemble. In Acts 13:43 the R.V. suitably has "synagogue," for the A.V. "congregation," the building standing by metonymy for the people therein (cp. Matt. 10:17, etc.). In Jas. 2:2 (A.V., "assembly") the word is "synagogue" (R.V.). See SYNAGOGUE.

(3) *Episunagōgē*, akin to No. 1, *Note*, an assembling together, is used in 2 Thess. 2:1, of the Rapture of the saints into the air to meet the Lord, "our gathering together"; in Heb. 10:25; of the gatherings of believers on earth during the present period. See GATHERING.

ASSEMBLY

1. *ekklēsia* [ἐκκλησία, 4905], from *ek*, out of, and *klēsis*, a calling (*kaleō*, to call), was used among the Greeks of a body of citizens gathered to discuss the affairs of State, Acts 19:39. In the Sept. it is used to designate the gathering of Israel, summoned for any definite purpose, or a gathering regarded as representative of the whole nation. In Acts 7:38 it is used of Israel; in 19:32, 41, of a riotous mob. It has two applications to companies of Christians, (*a*) to the whole company of the redeemed throughout the present era, the company of which Christ said, "I will build My Church," Matt. 16:18, and which is further described as "the Church which is His Body," Eph. 1:22; 5:23, (*b*) in the singular number (e.g., Matt. 18:17, R.V. marg., "congregation"), to a company consisting of professed believers, e.g. Acts 20:28; 1 Cor. 1:2; Gal. 1:13; 1 Thess. 1:1; 2 Thess. 1:1; 1 Tim. 3:5, and in the plural, with reference to churches in a district.

There is an apparent exception in the R.V. of Acts 9:31, where, while the A.V. has "churches," the singular seems to point to a district; but the reference is clearly to the church as it was in Jerusalem, from which it had just been scattered, 8:1. Again, in Rom. 16:23, that Gaius was the host of "the whole church," simply suggests that the assembly in Corinth had been accustomed to meet in his house, where also Paul was entertained. See CHURCH.

NT: B.788a; CB.1270c; K.394.
OT: qāhāl: S.6951; HR.433a.1d; H.1991a; BD.874c.
GEN. REF.: IS.1:331; NB.100; Z.—.

2. *panēguris* [πανήγυρις, 3831], from *pan*, all, and *agora*, any kind of assembly, denoted, among the Greeks, an assembly of the people in contrast to the Council of National Leaders, or a gathering of the people in honour of a god, or for some public festival, such as the Olympic games. The word is used in Heb. 12:23, coupled with the word Church, as applied to all believers who form the Body of Christ. ¶

NT: B.607d; CB.1261c; K.770.
OT: mō'ēd: S.4150; HR.1052c.1; H.878b; BD.417b.
'ᵃṣārāh: S.6116; HR.1052c.2; H.1675c; BD.783d.
GEN. REF.: IS.1:331; NB.100; Z.—.

3. *plēthos* [πλῆθος, 4128], a multitude, the whole number, is translated "assembly" in Acts 23:7, R.V. See BUNDLE, COMPANY, MULTITUDE.

NT: B.668b; CB.1265b; K.866.
OT: hāmôn: S.1995; HR.1142c.3; H.505a; BD.242b.
rōb: S.7230; HR.1142c.11a; H.2099c; BD.913d.
GEN. REF.: IS.1:331; NB.100; Z.—.

Note: For *sunagōgē*, see ASSEMBLE, Note (2).

For **ASSENT** see **AGREE,** No. 2

For **ASSIST** see **HELP,** B, *Note*

ASSURANCE, ASSURE, ASSUREDLY

A. Nouns.

1. *pistis* [πίστις, 4102], faith, has the secondary meaning of an assurance or guarantee, e.g., Acts 17:31; by raising Christ from the dead, God has given "assurance" that the world will be judged by Him (the A.V. margin, "offered faith" does not express the meaning). Cp. 1 Tim. 5:12, where "faith" means "pledge." See BELIEF, FAITH, FIDELITY.

NT: B.662b; CB.1265a; K.849.
OT: ’^{e}mûnāh: S.530; HR.1138b.1b; H.116e; BD53c.
GEN. REF.: IS.1:332; NB.100; Z.—.

2. *plērophoria* [πληροφορία, 4136], a fulness, abundance, also means full assurance, entire confidence; lit., a 'full-carrying' (*plēros*, full, *pherō*, to carry). Some explain it as full fruitfulness (cp. R.V., "fulness" in Heb. 6:11). In 1 Thess. 1:5 it describes the willingness and freedom of spirit enjoyed by those who brought the Gospel to Thessalonica; in Col. 2:2, the freedom of mind and confidence resulting from an understanding in Christ; in Heb. 6:11 (A.V., "full assurance," R.V., "fulness"), the engrossing effect of the expectation of the fulfilment of God's promises; in Heb. 10:22, the character of the faith by which we are to draw near to God. See FULNESS. ¶

NT: B.670c; CB.1265b; K.867.
OT: —.
GEN. REF.: IS.1:332; NB.100; Z.—.

3. *hupostasis* [ὑπόστασις, 5287], lit., a standing under, support (*hupo*, under, *histēmi*, to stand), hence, an "assurance," is so rendered in Heb. 11:1, R.V., for A.V., "substance." It here may signify a title-deed, as giving a guarantee, or reality. See CONFIDENCE, PERSON, SUBSTANCE.

NT: B.847a; CB.1252b; K.—.
OT: maṣṣāb: S.4673; HR.1417a.6c; H.1398c; BD.662d.
t^{e}kûnāh: S.8498; HR.1417a.10; H.964e; BD.467d.
GEN. REF.: IS.1:332; NB.100; Z.—.

Note: In Acts 16:10, for the A.V. (of *sumbibazomai*), "assuredly gathering," see CONCLUDE.

B. Verbs.

1. *pistoō* [πιστόω, 4104], to trust or give assurance to (cp. A, No. 1), has a secondary meaning, in the Passive Voice, to be assured of, 2 Tim. 3:14. ¶

NT: B.665b; CB.1265a; K.849.
OT: ’āman: S.539; HR.1139a.1; H.116; BD.52d.
GEN. REF.: IS.1:332; NB.100; Z.—.

2. *plērophoreō* [πληροφορέω, 4135], akin to A, No. 2, to bring in full measure, to fulfil, also signifies to be fully assured, Rom. 4:21, R.V., of Abraham's faith. In 14:5 it is said of the apprehension of the will of God. So in Col. 4:12 in the best mss. In these three places it is used subjectively, with reference to an effect upon the mind. For its other and objective use, referring to things external, see FULFIL; see also BELIEVE, KNOW, PERSUADE, PROOF. ¶ In the Sept., Eccl. 8:11. ¶

NT: B.670b; CB.1265b; K.867.
OT: —.
GEN. REF.: IS.1:332; NB.100; Z.—.

3. *peithō* [πείθω, 3982], to persuade, is rendered "assure" in 1 John 3:19 (marg., "persuade"), where the meaning is that of confidence toward God consequent upon loving in deed and in truth. See BELIEVE, CONFIDENCE, FRIEND, OBEY, PERSUADE, TRUST, YIELD.

NT: B.639a; CB.1263a; K.818.
OT: bāṭah: S.982; HR.1114b.2a; H.233; BD.105a.
GEN. REF.: IS.1:332; NB.100; Z.—.

C. Adverb.

asphalōs [ἀσφαλῶς, 806] means (*a*) safely, Mark 14:44; Acts 16:23; (*b*) assuredly, Acts 2:36; the knowledge there enjoined involves freedom from fear of contradiction, with an intimation of the impossibility of escape from the effects. See SAFELY.

NT: B.119a; CB.1238a; K.87.
OT: beṭaḥ: S.983; HR.174c1; H.233a; BD.105b.
GEN. REF.: IS.1:332; NB.100; Z.—.

For **ASTONISH** and **ASTONISHMENT** see **AMAZE** and **AMAZEMENT**

For **ASTRAY** see **ERR**

For **ASUNDER** see **BREAK, BURST, CUT, PART, PUT, REND** and **SAW**

AT: see Note †, p. 1

For **ATHIRST** see **THIRST**

ATONEMENT

katallagē [καταλλαγή, 2643], translated "atonement" in the A.V. of Rom. 5:11, signifies, not "atonement," but "reconciliation," as in the R.V. See also Rom. 11:15; 2 Cor. 5:18, 19. ¶ So with the corresponding verb *katallassō*, see under RECONCILE. "Atonement" (the explanation of this English word as being at-one-ment is entirely fanciful) is frequently found in the O.T. See, for instance, Leviticus, chapters 16 and 17. The corresponding N.T. words are *hilasmos*, propitiation, 1 Jno. 2:2; 4:10, and *hilastērion*, Rom. 3:25; Heb. 9:5, "mercy-seat," the covering of the ark of the Covenant. These describe the means (in and through the Person and work of the Lord Jesus Christ, in His death on the Cross by the shedding of His blood in His vicarious sacrifice for sin) by which God shows mercy to sinners. See PROPITIATION.

NT: B.414a; CB.1254a; K.40.
OT: –.
GEN. REF.: IS.1:352; NB.107; Z.–.

ATTAIN

1. *katantaō* [καταντάω, 2658], a strengthened form of *antaō*, to come opposite to, signifies to reach, to arrive at. It is used in its local significance several times in the Acts, e.g., 27:12, R.V., "could reach."

In its metaphorical sense of attaining to something it is used in three places: Acts 26:7, of the fulfilment of the promise of God made to the ancestors of Israel, to which promise the twelve tribes "hope to attain" (R.V.); in Eph. 4:13, of attaining to the unity of the faith and of the knowledge of the Son of God; in Phil. 3:11, of the paramount aims of the Apostle's life, "if by any means," he says, "I might attain unto the resurrection from the dead," not the physical resurrection, which is assured to all believers hereafter, but to the present life of identification with Christ in His Resurrection. For the metaphorical sense in I Cor. 10:11 and 14:36, see ARRIVE, A, No. 1. See also COME, No. 28.

NT: B.415b; CB.1254a; K.419.
OT: –.
GEN. REF.: –.

2. *katalambanō* [καταλαμβάνω, 2638], to seize, to apprehend, whether physically or mentally, is rendered "attain" in the sense of making something one's own, appropriating a thing, Rom. 9:30, said of the Gentiles, who through the Gospel have attained to, or laid hold of, the righteousness which is of faith, in contrast to the present condition of Israel; in 1 Cor. 9:24, of securing a prize, R.V., "attain" for A.V., "obtain." See APPREHEND.

NT: B.412d; CB.1254a; K.495.
OT: lākad: S.3920; HR.735a.6; H.1115; BD.539d.
nāsag: S.5381; HR.735a.11; H.1422; BD.673b.
GEN. REF.: –.

3. *phthanō* [φθάνω, 5348], to anticipate, also means to reach, attain to a thing; negatively of Israel (see ARRIVE, No. 5). The only other passage where it has this significance is Phil. 3:16, "we have attained." See COME, PREVENT.

NT: B.856d; CB.1264c; K.1258.
OT: mᵉṭā', mᵉṭāh: S.4291; HR.1429b.4; H.2825; BD.592c.
nāga': S.5060; HR.1429b.5; H.1293; BD.619a.
GEN. REF.: –.

4. *tunchanō* [τυγχάνω, 5177], to reach, meet with, signifies to attain to, in Luke 20:35, R.V. (for A.V., "obtain"). See CHANCE, ENJOY, OBTAIN.

NT: B.829b; CB.–; K.1191.
OT: māṣā: S.4672; HR.1378a.1; H.2033; BD.592c.
GEN. REF.: –.

Notes: (1) *Parakoloutheō*, rendered "attained" in 1 Tim. 4:6, A.V. (R.V., "hast followed"), does not signify attainment, but following fully. It is an intensive form of *akoloutheō*, to follow. So in 2 Tim. 3:10, R.V., "didst follow" (A.V., "fully known"); 'follow fully' would be suitable. In Mark 16:17 it is translated "follow"; in Luke 1:3, "having traced" (R.V.). See FOLLOW, KNOW, *Notes* (1), UNDERSTAND. ¶

(2) *Lambanō*, incorrectly translated "attained" in the A.V. of Phil. 3:12, means "obtained" (R.V.).

ATTEND, ATTENDANCE, ATTENDANT

A. Verbs.

1. *prosechō* [προσέχω, 4337], to take heed, give heed, is said of the priests who "gave attendance at the altar," Heb. 7:13. It suggests devotion of thought and effort to a thing. In 1 Tim. 4:13 (in the exhortation regarding the public reading of the Scriptures), the R.V. translates it "give heed," for the A.V., "give attendance." In Acts 16:14, "to give heed," (for A.V., "attended"). See BEWARE, GIVE, No. 17, REGARD.

NT: B.714b; CB.–; K.–.
OT: qāshab: S.7181; HR.1215b.16; H.2084; BD.904a.
shāmar: S.8104; HR.1215b.19; H.2414; BD.1036b.
GEN. REF.: IS.1:363; NB.–; Z.–.

2. *proskartereō* [προσκαρτερέω, 4342], to be stedfast, a strengthened form of *kartereō* (*pros*, towards, intensive, *karteros*, strong), denotes to continue stedfastly in a thing and give unremitting care to it, e.g., Rom. 13:6, of rulers in the discharge of their functions. See CONTINUE, WAIT. In the Sept., Numb. 13:21. ¶

NT: B.715c; CB.1267a; K.417.
OT: –.
GEN. REF.: IS.1:363; NB.–; Z.–.

B. Adjective.

euparedros [εὐπάρεδρος], lit., sitting well beside (*eu*, well, *para*, beside, *hedra*, a seat), i.e., sitting constantly by, and so applying oneself diligently to, anything, is used in 1 Cor. 7:35, with *pros*, upon, "that ye may attend upon." Some mss. have *euprosedron*. ¶

NT: B.324a; CB.–; K.–.
OT: –.
GEN. REF.: IS.1:363; NB.–; Z.–.

C. Noun.

hupēretēs [ὑπηρέτης, 5257], lit., an under-rower; hence, a servant, is rendered "attendant" in Luke 4:20 and Acts 13:5, R.V. See MINISTER, OFFICER, SERVANT.

NT: B.842c; CB.1252c; K.1231.
OT: –.
GEN. REF.: IS.1:363; NB.–; Z.–.

For **ATTENTIVE,** in the A.V. of Luke 19:48, see **HANG,** No. 2

For **AUDIENCE** see **HEARING,** A, No. 1, B, No. 1

AUGHT

aught: See † page 1. It is wrongly spelt "ought" in the A.V. in some places, e.g., in John 4:33, "ought to eat" (there is no word in the original there for "aught").

AUSTERE

austēros [αὐστηρός, 840], akin to *auō,* to dry up (eng., austere), primarily denotes stringent to the taste, like new wine not matured by age, unripe fruit, etc.; hence, harsh, severe, Luke 19:21, 22. ¶

NT: B.122b; CB.–; K.–.
OT: –.
GEN. REF.: –.

Note: Synonymous with *austēros,* but to be distinguished from it, is *sklēros* (from *skellō,* to be dry). It was applied to that which lacks moisture, and so is rough and disagreeable to the touch, and hence came to denote harsh, stern, hard. It is used by Matthew to describe the unprofitable servant's remark concerning his master, in the parable corresponding to that in Luke 19 (see *austēros,* above). *Austēros* is derived from a word having to do with the taste, *sklēros,* with the touch. *Austēros* is not necessarily a term of reproach, whereas *sklēros* is always so, and indicates a harsh, even inhuman, character. *Austēros* is "rather the exaggeration of a virtue pushed too far, than an absolute vice" (Trench, Syn. § xiv). *Sklēros* is used of the character of a man, Matt. 25:24; of a saying, John 6:60; of the difficulty and pain of kicking against the ox-goads, Acts 9:5; 26:14; of rough winds, Jas. 3:4 and of harsh speeches, Jude 15. See FIERCE, HARD. ¶ Cp. *sklērotēs,* hardness, *sklērunō,* to harden, *sklērokardia,* hardness of heart, and *sklērotrachēlos,* stiff-necked.

AUTHOR

1. *aitios* [αἴτιος, 159], an adjective (cp. *aitia,* a cause), denotes that which causes something. This and No. 2 are both translated "author" in Hebrews. *Aitios,* in Heb. 5:9, describes Christ as the "Author of eternal salvation unto all them that obey Him," signifying that Christ, exalted and glorified as our High Priest, on the ground of His finished work on earth, has become the Personal mediating cause (R.V., margin) of eternal salvation. It is difficult to find an adequate English equivalent to express the meaning here. Christ is not the merely formal cause of our salvation. He is the concrete and active cause of it. He has not merely caused or effected it, He is, as His Name, "Jesus," implies, our salvation itself, Luke 2:30; 3:6.

NT: B.26d; CB.1234a; K.–.
OT: –.
GEN. REF.: IS.1:364; NB.–; Z.–.

2. *archēgos* [ἀρχηγός, 747], translated "Prince" in Acts 3:15 (marg., "Author") and 5:31, but "Author" in Heb. 2:10, R.V., "Captain," R.V. marg., and A.V., and "Author" in 12:2, primarily signifies one who takes a lead in, or provides the first occasion of, anything. In the Sept. it is used of the chief of a tribe or family, Num. 13:2 (R.V. prince); of the "heads" of the children of Israel, ver. 3; a captain of the whole people, 14:4; in Micah 1:13, of Lachish as the leader of the sin of the daughter of Sion: there, as in Heb. 2:10, the word suggests a combination of the meaning of leader with that of the source from whence a thing proceeds. That Christ is the Prince of life signifies, as Chrysostom says, that "the life He had was not from another; the Prince or Author of life must be He who has life from Himself." But the word does not necessarily combine the idea of the source or originating cause with that of leader. In Heb. 12:2 where Christ is called the "Author and Perfecter of faith," He is represented as the One who takes precedence in faith and is thus the perfect Exemplar of it. The pronoun "our" does not correspond to anything in the original, and may well be omitted. Christ in the days of His flesh trod undeviatingly the path of faith, and as the Perfecter has brought it to a perfect end in His own Person. Thus He is the leader of all others who tread that path. See PRINCE. ¶

NT: B.112c; CB.1237b; K.81.
OT: rō'sh: S.7218; HR.165a.8; H.2097; BD.910c.
GEN. REF.: IS.1:364; NB.–; Z.–.

Note: In 1 Cor. 14:33, the A.V., "the author," represents no word in the original; R.V. "a God of."

AUTHORITY

A. Nouns.

1. *exousia* [ἐξουσία, 1849], denotes authority (from the impersonal verb *exesti*, "it is lawful"). From the meaning of leave or permission, or liberty of doing as one pleases, it passed to that of the ability or strength with which one is endued, then to that of the power of authority, the right to exercise power, e.g., Matt. 9:6; 21:23; 2 Cor. 10:8; or the power of rule of government, the power of one whose will and commands must be obeyed by others, e.g., Matt. 28:18; John 17:2; Jude 25; Rev. 12:10; 17:13; more specifically of apostolic authority, 2 Cor. 10:8; 13:10; the power of judicial decision, John 19:10; of managing domestic affairs, Mark 13:34. By metonymy, or name-change (the substitution of a suggestive word for the name of the thing meant), it stands for that which is subject to authority or rule, Luke 4:6 (R.V. "authority," for the A.V. "power"); or, as with the English "authority," one who possesses authority, a ruler, magistrate, Rom. 13:1-3; Luke 12:11; Tit. 3:1; or a spiritual potentate, e.g. Eph. 3:10; 6:12; Col. 1:16; 2:10, 15; 1 Pet. 3:22. The R.V. usually translates it "authority."

In 1 Cor. 11:10 it is used of the veil with which a woman is required to cover herself in an assembly or church, as a sign of the Lord's authority over the Church. See JURISDICTION, LIBERTY, POWER, RIGHT, STRENGTH.

NT: B.277d; CB.1247c; K.238.
OT: shāllîṭ: S.7989; HR.500c.3; H.2396a; BD.1020c.
memshālāh: S.4475; HR.500c.2; H.1259c; BD.606a.
GEN. REF.: IS.1:364; NB.111; Z.–.

2. *epitagē* [ἐπιταγή, 2003], an injunction (from *epi*, upon, *tassō*, to order), is once rendered "authority," Tit. 2:15 (R.V., marg., "commandment"). See COMMANDMENT.
Note: The corresponding verb is *epitassō*, to command. See COMMAND.

NT: B.302a; CB.–; K.1156.
OT: –.
GEN. REF.: IS.1:364; NB.111; Z.–.

3. *huperochē* [ὑπεροχή, 5247], primarily, a projection, eminence, as a mountain peak, hence, metaphorically, pre-eminence, superiority, excellency, is once rendered "authority," 1 Tim. 2:2, A.V. (marg., "eminent place"), R.V., "high place," of the position of magistrates; in 1 Cor. 2:1, "excellency" (of speech). Cp. *huperechō*, to surpass. See EXCELLENCY. ¶

NT: B.841d; CB.–; K.1230.
OT: –.
GEN. REF.: IS.1:364; NB.111; Z.–.

4. *dunastēs* [δυνάστης, 1413], akin to *dunamis*, power, Eng., dynasty, signifies a potentate, a high officer; in Acts 8:27, of a high officer, it is rendered "of great authority"; in Luke 1:52, R.V., "princes," (A.V., "the mighty"); in 1 Tim. 6: 15 it is said of God ("Potentate"). See MIGHTY, POTENTATE. ¶

NT: B.208c; CB.1242b; K.186.
OT: –.
GEN. REF.: IS.1:364; NB.111; Z.–.

B. Verbs.

1. *exousiazō* [ἐξουσιάζω, 1850], akin to A, No. 1, signifies to exercise power, Luke 22:25; 1 Cor. 6:12; 7:4 (twice). See POWER. ¶

NT: B.279a; CB.1247c; K.238.
OT: shālaṭ: S.7980; HR.501b.2; H.2396; BD.1020c.
shāllîṭ: S.7989; HR.501b.2c; H.2396a; BD.1020c.
GEN. REF.: IS.1:364; NB.111; Z.–.

2. *katexousiazō* [κατεξουσιάζω, 2715], *kata*, down, intensive, and No. 1, to exercise authority upon, is used in Matt. 20:25, and Mark 10:42. ¶

NT: B.421c; CB.1254b; K.238.
OT: –.
GEN. REF.: IS.1:364; NB.111; Z.–.

3. *authenteō* [αὐθεντέω, 831], from *autos*, self, and a lost noun *hentēs*, probably signifying working (Eng., authentic), to exercise authority on one's own account, to domineer over, is used in 1 Tim. 2:12, A.V., "to usurp authority." R.V., "to have dominion." In the earlier usage of the word it signified one who with his own hand killed either others or himself. Later it came to denote one who acts on his own authority; hence, to exercise authority, dominion. See DOMINION, *Note*. ¶

NT: B.121a; CB.1238a; K.–.
OT: –.
GEN. REF.: IS.1:364; NB.111; Z.–.

AUTUMN

phthinopōrinos [φθινοπωρινός, 5352], an adjective signifying autumnal (from *phthinopōron*, late autumn, from *phthinō*, to waste away, or wane, and *opōra*, autumn), is used in Jude 12, where unfruitful and worthless men are figuratively described as trees such as they are at the close of autumn, fruitless and leafless (A.V., "trees whose fruit withereth"). ¶

NT: B.857c; CB.–; K.–.
OT: –.
GEN. REF.: IS.1:371; NB.–; Z.–.

AVAIL

ischuō [ἰσχύω, 2480], signifies (*a*) to be strong in body, to be robust, in sound health, Matt. 9:12; Mark 2:17; (*b*) to have power, as of the Gospel, Acts 19:20; to prevail against, said of spiritual enemies, Rev. 12:8; of an evil spirit against exorcists, Acts 19:16; (*c*) to be of force, to be effective, capable of producing results, Matt. 5:13 ("it is good for nothing;" lit., 'it availeth nothing'); Gal. 5:6; in Heb. 9:17 it apparently has the meaning to be valid (R.V., "for doth it ever avail . . .?"; for A.V., "it is of no strength"). It is translated "avail" with reference to prayer, in Jas. 5:16; cp. the strengthened form *exischuō* in Eph. 3:18. See ABLE, CAN, GOOD, MAY, PREVAIL, STRENGTH, WHOLE, WORK.

NT: B.383d; CB.1253a; K.378.
OT: gābar: S.1396; HR.692c.5; H.310; BD.149c.
ḥāzaq: S.2388; HR.692c.6; H.636; BD.304a.
GEN. REF.: —.

AVENGE, AVENGER

A. Verb.

ekdikeō [ἐκδικέω, 1556], *ek*, from, *dikē*, justice, i.e., that which proceeds from justice, means (*a*) to vindicate a person's right, (*b*) to avenge a thing. With the meaning (*a*), it is used in the parable of the unjust judge, Luke 18:3, 5, of the vindication of the rights of the widow; with the meaning (*b*) it is used in Rev. 6:10 and 19:2, of the act of God in avenging the blood of the saints; in 2 Cor. 10:6, of the Apostle's readiness to use his apostolic authority in punishing disobedience on the part of his readers; here the R.V. substitutes "avenge" for the A.V., "revenge;" in Rom 12:19 of avenging oneself, against which the believer is warned. ¶

Note: In Rev. 18:20, the A.V. mistranslates *krinō* and *krima* "hath avenged you"; R.V., "hath judged your judgement".

NT: B.238c; CB.1243c; K.215.
OT: nāqam: S.5358; HR.422b.3; H.1413; BD.667d.
pāqad: S.6485; HR.422b.4; H.1802; BD.823b.
GEN. REF.: IS.1:371; NB.—; Z.—.

B. Nouns.

1. *ekdikos* [ἔκδικος, 1558], primarily, without law, then, one who exacts a penalty from a person, an avenger, a punisher, is used in Rom. 13:4 of a civil authority in the discharge of his function of executing wrath on the evildoer (A.V., wrongly, "revenger"); in 1 Thess. 4:6, of God as the Avenger of the one who wrongs his brother, here particularly in the matter of adultery. ¶

NT: B.238d; CB.1243c; K.215.
OT: —.
GEN. REF.: IS.1:371; NB.—; Z.—.

2. *ekdikēsis* [ἐκδίκησις, 1557], vengeance, is used with the verb *poieō*, to make, i.e., to avenge, in Luke 18:7, 8; Acts 7:24; twice it is used in statements that "vengeance" belongs to God, Rom. 12:19; Heb. 10:30. In 2 Thess. 1:8 it is said of the act of Divine justice which will be meted out to those who know not God and obey not the Gospel, when the Lord comes in flaming fire at His Second Advent. In the Divine exercise of judgment there is no element of vindictiveness, nothing by way of taking revenge. In Luke 21:22, it is used of the days of vengeance upon the Jewish people; in 1 Pet. 2:14, of civil governors as those who are sent of God "for vengeance on evildoers" (A.V. "punishment"); in 2 Cor. 7:11, of the self-avenging of believers, in their godly sorrow for wrong doing, R.V., "avenging;" for A.V., "revenge." See PUNISHMENT, VENGEANCE. ¶

NT: B.238d; CB.1243c; K.215.
OT: n^{e}qāmāh: S. 5360, HR.423a.2c; H.1413b; BD.668c.
p^{e}quddah: S.6486; HR.423a.3b; H.1802a; BD.824b.
shephet: S.8201; HR.423a.4b; H.2443a; BD.1048a
GEN. REF.: IS.1:371; NB.—; Z.—.

AVOID

1. *ekklinō* [ἐκκλίνω, 1578], to turn away from, to turn aside, lit., to bend out of (*ek*, out, *klinō*, to bend), is used in Rom. 3:12, of the sinful condition of mankind, A.V., "gone out of the way;" R.V., "turned aside"; in Rom. 16:17, of turning away from those who cause offences and occasions of stumbling (A.V., "avoid"); in 1 Pet. 3:11 of turning away from evil (A.V., "eschew"). See ESCHEW, WAY. ¶

NT: B.241c; CB.—; K.—.
OT: nāṭāh: S.5186; HR.433c.11; H.1352; BD.639d.
sûr: S.5493; HR.433c.15; H.1480; BD.693b.
GEN. REF.: IS.1:372; NB.—; Z.—.

2. *ektrepō* [ἐκτρέπω, 1624], lit., to turn or twist out, is used in the Passive Voice in Heb. 12:13, "that which is lame be not turned out of the way" (or rather, 'put out of joint'); in the sense of the Middle Voice (though Passive in form) of turning aside, or turning away from, 2 Tim. 4:4 (A.V., "shall be turned unto fables;" R.V., "shall turn aside"); in 1 Tim. 1:6, of those who, having swerved from the faith, have turned aside unto vain talking; in 5:15, of those who have turned aside after Satan; in 6:20, R.V., of "turning away from (A.V., "avoiding") profane babblings and oppositions of the knowledge which is falsely so called." See TURN. In the Sept., Amos 5:8. ¶

NT: B.246b; CB.1244a; K.—.
OT: hāphak: S.2015; HR.443c.1; H.512; BD.245b.
GEN. REF.: IS.1:372; NB.—; Z.—.

3. *paraiteomai* [παραιτέομαι, 3868], lit., to ask aside (*para*, aside, *aiteō*, to ask), signifies (*a*) to beg of (or from) another, Mark 15:6, in the most authentic mss.; (*b*) to deprecate, (1) to entreat (that) not, Heb. 12:19; (2) to refuse, decline, avoid, 1 Tim. 4:7; 5:11; 2 Tim. 2:23; Tit. 3:10 (see No. 4 for ver. 9); Heb. 12:25; (*c*) to beg off, ask to be excused, Luke 14:18, 19 (some would put Heb. 12:25 here). See EXCUSE, INTREAT, REFUSE, REJECT. ¶

NT: B.616c; CB.1262a; K.30.
OT: shā'al: S.7592; HR.1060a3; H.2303; BD.981b.
GEN. REF.: IS.1:372; NB.—; Z.—.

4. *periistēmi* [περιίστημι, 4026], in the Active Voice, means to stand around (*peri*, around, *histēmi*, to stand), John 11:42; Acts 25:7; in the Middle Voice, to turn oneself about; for the purpose of avoiding something, to avoid, shun, said of profane babblings, 2 Tim. 2:16; of foolish questions, genealogies, strife, etc., Tit. 3:9 (A.V., "avoid"). See SHUN, STAND. ¶

NT: B.647c; CB.–; K.–.
OT: sābab: S.5437; HR.1123c.2; H.1456; BD.685b.
GEN. REF.: IS.1:372; NB.–; Z.–.

5. *stellō* [στέλλω, 4724], to place, sometimes signifies, in the Middle Voice, to take care against a thing, to avoid, 2 Cor. 8:20; in 2 Thess. 3:6, of withdrawing from a person. See WITHDRAW. ¶

NT: B.766a; CB.1270a; K.1074.
OT: –.
GEN. REF.: IS.1:372; NB.–; Z.–.

For **AWAIT** (A.V. of Acts 9:24; 20:3, 19; 23:30) see **PLOT**

AWAKE

1. *egeirō* [ἐγείρω, 1453], is used, (*a*) in the Active Voice, of arousing a person from sleep; in Matt. 8:25 of the act of the disciples in awaking the Lord; in Acts 12:7, of the awaking of Peter R.V., "awake him"; (*b*) in the Passive Voice, with a Middle significance, of the virgins, in arousing themselves from their slumber, Matt. 25:7; in Rom. 13:11, and Eph. 5:14, metaphorically, of awaking from a state of moral sloth. See ARISE, LIFT, RAISE, REAR, RISE, STAND, TAKE.

NT: B.214c; CB.1242c; K.195.
OT: 'ûr: S.5782; HR.364a.8; H.1587; BD.734d.
qûm: S.6965; HR. 364a.12; H.1999; BD.877c.
GEN. REF.: IS.1:373; NB.–; Z.–.

2. *diegeirō* [διεγείρω, 1326], is used of awaking from natural sleep, Matt. 1:24; Mark 4:38; of the act of the disciples in awaking the Lord, Luke 8:24 (cp. *egeirō*, in Matt. 8:25); metaphorically, of arousing the mind, 2 Pet. 1:13; 3:1. See ARISE, RAISE, STIR UP.

NT: B.193d; CB.–; K.–.
OT: –.
GEN. REF.: IS.1:373; NB.–; Z.–.

3. *eknēphō* [ἐκνήφω, 1594], primarily, to return to one's sense from drunkenness, to become sober, is so used in the Sept., e.g., Gen. 9:24; metaphorically, in Joel 1:5; Hab. 2:7; lit., in 2:19, of the words of an idolater to an image; in the N.T. in 1 Cor. 15:34, "Awake up righteously and sin not" (R.V.), suggesting a return to soberness of mind from the stupor consequent upon the influence of evil doctrine. ¶

NT: B.243b; CB.1243c; K.633.
OT: yāqaṣ: S.3364; HR.438b.2; H.904; BD.429c.
qîṣ, qûṣ: S.6974, HR.438b.3; H.904a, 2019; BD.884c.
GEN. REF.: IS.1:373; NB.–; Z.3:689, 708.

4. *exupnizō* [ἐξυπνίζω, 1852], from *ek*, out of, and *hupnos*, sleep, to rouse a person out of sleep, is used metaphorically, in John 11:11. ¶

NT: B.279b; CB.–; K.1233.
OT: yāqaṣ: S.3364; HR.501b.1; H.904; BD.429c
'ûr: S.5782; HR.501b.2; H.1587; BD.734d.
GEN. REF.: IS.1:373; NB.–; Z.–.

5. *diagrēgoreō* [διαγρηγορέω, 1235], *dia*, intensive, *grēgoreō*, to watch, is used in Luke 9:32, R.V., "were fully awake." A.V. "were awake." ¶

NT: B.182c; CB.–; K.–.
OT: –.
GEN. REF.: IS.1:373; NB.–; Z.–.

For **AWARE** see **KNOW,** A, No. 1, end of 1st par.

AWAY

Note: This word is to be taken in connection with various verbs. The verb *airō*, to seize, to lift up, take away, is translated "away with," in Luke 23:18; John 19:15; Acts 21:36; 22:22, implying a forcible removal for the purpose of putting to death. See BEAR, No. 9.

AWE

deos [δέος, 127], awe, is so rendered in Heb. 12:28, R.V.: the previous word "reverence" represents the inferior reading *aidōs* (see SHAMEFASTNESS).

NT: B.175b; CB.–; K.1272.
OT: –.
GEN. REF.: IS.1:373; NB.–; Z.–.

AXE

axinē [ἀξίνη, 513], an axe, akin to *agnumi*, to break, is found in Matt. 3:10, and Luke 3:9. ¶

NT: B.77d; CB.–; K.–.
OT: garzen: S.1631; HR.113a.1; H.379a; BD.173d.
qardōm: S.7134; HR.113a.2; H.2067; BD.899c.
GEN. REF.: IS.1:378; NB.–; Z.–.

B

BABBLER, BABBLINGS

1. *spermologos* [σπερμολόγος, 4691], a babbler, is used in Acts 17:18. Primarily an adjective, it came to be used as a noun signifying a crow, or some other bird, picking up seeds (*sperma*, a seed, *legō*, to collect). Then it seems to have been used of a man accustomed to hang about the streets and markets, picking up scraps which fall from loads; hence a parasite, who lives at the expense of others, a hanger on.

Metaphorically it became used of a man who picks up scraps of information and retails them secondhand, a plagiarist, or of those who make a show, in unscientific style of knowledge obtained from misunderstanding lectures. Prof. Ramsay points out that there does not seem to be any instance of the classical use of the word as a babbler or a mere talker. He finds in the word a piece of Athenian slang, applied to one who was outside any literary circle, an ignorant plagiarist. Other suggestions have been made, but without satisfactory evidence. ¶

NT: B.762b; CB.1269c; K.—.
OT: —.
GEN. REF.: IS.1:381; NB.—; Z.3:525.

2. *kenophōnia* [κενοφωνία, 2757], babbling (from *kenos*, empty, and *phonē*, a sound), signifies empty discussion, discussion on useless subjects, 1 Tim. 6:20 and 2 Tim. 2:16. ¶

NT: B.428a; CB.—; K.—.
OT: —.
GEN. REF.: IS.1:381; NB.—; Z.—.

BABE

1. *brephos* [βρεφος, 1025] denotes (*a*) an unborn child, as in Luke 1:41, 44; (*b*) a newborn child, or an infant still older, Luke 2:12, 16; 18:15; Acts 7:10; 2 Tim. 3:15; 1 Pet. 2:2. See CHILD, INFANT. ¶

NT: B.147b; CB.1239b; K.759.
OT: —.
GEN. REF.: IS.1:382; NB.—; Z.1:160, 280.

2. *nēpios* [νήπιος, 3516], lit., 'without the power of speech,' denotes a little child, the literal meaning having been lost in the general use of the word. It is used (*a*) of infants, Matt. 21:16; (*b*) metaphorically, of the unsophisticated in mind and trustful in disposition, Matt. 11:25 and Luke 10:21, where it stands in contrast to the wise; of those who are possessed merely of natural knowledge, Rom. 2:20; of those who are carnal, and have not grown, as they should have done, in spiritual understanding and power, the spiritually immature, 1 Cor. 3:1, those who are so to speak partakers of milk, and "without experience of the word of righteousness," Heb. 5:13; of the Jews who while the Law was in force, were in a state corresponding to that of childhood, or minority; just as the word "infant" is used of a minor, in English law, Gal. 4:3, "children"; of believers in an immature condition, impressionable and liable to be imposed upon instead of being in a state of spiritual maturity, Eph. 4:14, "children." Immaturity is always associated with this word. See CHILD, No. 7 ¶

NT: B.357c; CB.1259c; K.631.
OT: ṭaph: S.2945; HR.944b.1; H.—; BD.381d.
'ôlēl: S.5768; HR.944b.4; H.1579c; BD.760c.
GEN. REF.: IS.1:382; NB.—; Z.—.

BACK (Noun)

nōtos [νῶτος, 3577], the back, is derived from a root *nō—*, signifying to bend, curve. It is used in Rom. 11:10. ¶

NT: B.547c; CB.—; K.—.
OT: katēph: S.3802; HR.956b.3; H.1059; BD.509b.
'ōreph: S.6203; HR.956b.6; H.1700a; BD791b.
GEN. REF.: IS.—; NB.—; Z.3:1000, 1003.

BACK (Adverb), BACKSIDE, BACKWARD

1. *opisō* [ὀπίσω, 3694], connected with *hepomai*, to follow, is used adverbially, of place, with the meaning "back," "backward," in the phrase *eis ta opisō*, lit., unto the things behind, in Mark 13:16; Luke 9:62; 17:31; John 6:66; 18:6; 20:14. Cp. Phil. 3:13, "the things which are behind." See BEHIND.

NT: B.575a; CB.1261a; K.702.
OT: 'aḥar: S.310; HR.1001c.1a; H.68b; BD.29d.
GEN. REF.: —.

2. *opisthen* [ὄπισθεν, 3693], of place, behind, after, is rendered "backside" in Rev. 5:1, A.V. (R.V., "back"). See BEHIND.

NT: B.574d; CB.1261a K.702.
OT: 'aḥar: S.310; HR.1001b.1a; H.68b; BD.29d.
GEN. REF.: IS.—; NB.—; Z.1:492.

BACKBITER, BACKBITING

katalalos [κατάλαλος, 2637], a backbiter, and *katalalia* [καταλαλία], backbiting, are formed from *kata*, against, and *laleō*, to speak. *Katalalos* is used in Rom. 1:30. ¶ *Katalalia* is translated "evil speaking" in 1 Pet. 2:1, "backbiting" in 2 Cor. 12:20. ¶

NT: B.412d; CB.1254a; K.495.
OT: —.
GEN. REF.: —.

Note: The corresponding verb *katalaleō* the R.V. translates "speak against," in its five occurrences, Jas. 4:11 (three times); 1 Pet. 2:12, and 3:16; A.V. "speak evil," in all the passages except 1 Pet. 2:12. ¶

For **BADE** see **BID**

BAD

1. *kakos* [*κακός*, 2556], indicates the lack in a person or thing of those qualities which should be possessed; it means bad in character (*a*) morally, by way of thinking, feeling or acting, e.g., Mark 7:21, "thoughts"; 1 Cor. 15:33, "company"; Col. 3:5, "desire"; 1 Tim. 6:10, "all kinds of evil"; 1 Pet. 3:9, "evil for evil"; (*b*) in the sense of what is injurious or baneful, e.g., the tongue as "a restless evil," Jas. 3:8; "evil beasts," Tit. 1:12; "harm," Acts 16:28; once it is translated "bad," 2 Cor. 5:10. It is the opposite of *agathos*, good. See EVIL, HARM, ILL, NOISOME, WICKED.

NT: B.397d; CB.1253b; K.391.
OT: rā'a': S.7489; HR.709b.13; H.2191, 2192; BD.947d.
GEN. REF.: IS.—; NB.—; Z.1:561-65.

2. *ponēros* [*πονηρός*, 4190], connected with *ponos*, labour, expresses especially the active form of evil, and is practically the same in meaning as (*b*), under No. 1. It is used, e.g., of thoughts, Matt. 15:19 (cp. *kakos*, in Mark 7:21); of speech, Matt. 5:11 (cp. *kakos*, in 1 Pet. 3:10); of acts, 2 Tim. 4:18. Where *kakos* and *ponēros* are put together, *kakos* is always put first and signifies bad in character, base, *ponēros*, bad in effect, malignant: see 1 Cor. 5:8, and Rev. 16:2. *Kakos* has a wider meaning, *ponēros* a stronger meaning. *Ponēros* alone is used of Satan and might well be translated 'the malignant one,' e.g., Matt. 5:37 and five times in 1 John (2:13, 14; 3:12; 5:18, 19. R.V.); of demons, e.g., Luke 7:21. Once it is translated "bad," Matt. 22:10. See EVIL, GRIEVOUS, HARM, LEWD, MALICIOUS, WICKED.

NT: B.690d; CB.1266a; K.912.
OT: ra': S.7451; HR.1186c.4; H.2191; BD.947d.
GEN. REF.: IS.—; NB.—; Z.1:564-67.

3. *sapros* [*σαπρός*, 4550], corrupt, rotten (akin to *sēpō*, to rot), primarily, of vegetable and animal substances, expresses what is of poor quality, unfit for use, putrid. It is said of a tree and its fruit, Matt. 7:17, 18; 12:33; Luke 6:43; of certain fish, Matt. 13:48 (here translated "bad"); of defiling speech, Eph. 4:29. See CORRUPT. ¶

NT: B.742b; CB.1268b; K.1000.
OT: —.
GEN. REF.: IS.—; NB.—; Z.1:565, 722.

BAG

1. *glōssokomon* [*γλωσσόκομον*, 1101], from *glōssa*, a tongue, and *komeō*, to tend, was, firstly, a case in which to keep the mouthpiece of wind instruments; secondly, a small box for any purpose, but especially a casket or purse, to keep money in. It is used of the bag which Judas carried, John 12:6; 13:29; in the Sept. of 2 Chron. 24:8, 10, used of the box appointed by King Joash for offerings for the repair of the Temple. ¶

NT: B.162d; CB.1428b; K.—.
OT: 'ārôn: S.727; HR.272b.1; H.166a; BD.75b.
GEN. REF.: IS.1:403; NB.128; Z.1:142.

2. *ballantion* [*βαλλάντιον*, 905], from *ballō*, to cast, a money-box or purse, is found in Luke's Gospel, four times, 10:4; 12:33 (A.V., "bag"); 22:35, 36. See PURSE ¶

NT: B.1300; CB.1238d; K.—.
OT: kîm: S.3599; HR.189c.1; H.979; BD.476a.
GEN. REF.: IS.1:403; NB.128; Z.1:142.

Note: Zōnē, a girdle or belt, also served as a purse for money, Matt. 10:9, Mark 6:8. See GIRDLE.

BAGGAGE

episkeuazō [*ἐπισκευάζω*], to furnish with things necessary; in the Middle Voice, to furnish for oneself; it was used of equipping baggage animals for a journey; in Acts 21:15, R.V., it is translated "we took up our baggage" (A.V., "we took up our carriages"). The form is the 1st aorist participle, and lit. means 'having made ready (the things that were necessary for the journey).' ¶

NT: B.298c; CB.—; K.—.
OT: ḥādash: S.2318; HR.528b.2; H.613; BD.293d.
ḥāzaq: S.2388; HR.528b.3; H.636; BD.304c.
GEN. REF.: IS.1:403; NB.—; Z.—.

Note: Some mss. have the verb *aposkeuazō*, which has the same meaning.

BALANCE

zugos [*ζυγος*, 2218], a yoke, also has the meaning of a pair of scales, Rev. 6:5. So the Sept. of Lev. 19:36; Isa. 40:12. See YOKE. ¶

NT: B.339d; CB.1273c; K.301.
OT: 'ōl: S.5923; HR.599a.7; H.1628a; BD.760a.
mō'z^{e}nayim: S.3977; HR.599a.1; H.2819; BD.24d.
GEN. REF.: IS.1:405; NB.129; Z.3:1160-1162.

BAND

1. *speira* [*σπεῖρα*, 4686], primarily anything round, and so whatever might be wrapped round a thing, a twisted rope, came to mean a body of men at arms, and was the equivalent of the Roman *manipulus*. It was also used for a larger body of men, a cohort, about 600

infantry, commanded by a tribune. It is confined to its military sense. See, e.g., Matt. 27:27, and corresponding passages.

NT: B.761a; CB.–; K.–.
OT: –.
GEN. REF.: IS.1:407; NB.130; Z.–.

2. *desmos* [δεσμός, 1199], a band, fetter, anything for tying (from *deō*, to bind, fasten with chains etc.), is sometimes translated "band," sometimes "bond"; "bands," in Luke 8:29; Acts 16:26; 22:30, A.V. only. In the case of the deaf man who had an impediment in his speech, whom the Lord took aside, Mark 7:35, the A.V. says "the string of his tongue was loosed"; the R.V., more literally, "the bond of his tongue." See BOND, CHAIN, STRING.

NT: B.176a; CB.1240c; K.145.
OT: môsēr: S.4147; HR.292a.1e; H.141f; BD.64c.
ʿᵉbōt: S.5688; HR.292a.6; H.1558b; BD.721c.
GEN. REF.: IS.1:407; NB.130; Z.3:591.

3. *sundesmos* [σύνδεσμος, 4886], an intensive form of No. 2, denoting that which binds firmly together, is used metaphorically of the joints and bands of the mystic Body of Christ, Col. 2:19; otherwise in the following phrases, "the bond of iniquity," Acts 8:23; "the bond of peace," Eph. 4:3; "the bond of perfectness," Col. 3:14. See BOND ¶

NT: B.785b; CB.1270c; K.1114.
OT: ḥarṣubbôt: S.2784; HR.1312c.2; H.754a; BD.359b.
qesher: S.7195; HR.1312c.6; H.2090a; BD.905c.
GEN. REF.: IS.1:407; NB.130; Z.3:591.

4. *zeuktēria* [ζευκτηρία, 2202], a bond (connected with *zugos*, a yoke), is found once, of the rudder band of a ship, Acts 27:40. ¶

NT: B.337b; CB.–; K.–.
OT: –.
GEN. REF.: IS.1:407; NB.130; Z.–.

BANDED

poieō sustrophēn [ποιέω συστροφήν, 4963], Acts 23:12, of the Jews who "banded together" with the intention of killing Paul, consists of the verb *poieō*, to make, and the noun *sustrophē*, primarily a twisting up together, a binding together; then, a secret combination, a conspiracy. Accordingly it might be translated 'made a conspiracy.' The noun is used elsewhere in 19:40. See CONCOURSE. ¶

NT: B.795c; CB.–; K.895.
OT: qāshar: S.7194; HR.1324a.5; H.2090; BD.905a.
GEN. REF.: IS.–; NB.–; Z.3:1152-58.

BANK, BANKERS

1. *trapeza* [τράπεζα, 5132], primarily a table, denotes (*a*) an eating-table, e.g., Matt. 15:27; (*b*) food etc. placed on a table, Acts 6:2, 16:34; (*c*) a feast, a banquet, 1 Cor. 10:21; (*d*) the table or stand of a money changer, where he exchanged money for a fee, or dealt with loans and deposits, Matt. 21:12; Mark 11:15; Luke 19:23; John 2:15. See MEAT, TABLE.

NT: B.824b; CB.1273a; K.1148.
OT: shulᵉḥān: S.7979; HR.1369b.4; H.2395a; BD.1020b.
GEN. REF.: IS.1:408; NB.130; Z.2:520, 522.

2. *trapezitēs* [τραπεζίτης, 5133], a money-changer, broker, banker; translated "bankers" in Matt. 25:27, R.V. (A.V., "exchangers"). ¶

NT: B.824d; CB.–; K.–.
OT: –.
GEN. REF.: IS.1:408; NB.130; Z.–.

Note: for *charax*, Luke 19:43; see TRENCH.

For BANQUETING see CAROUSINGS

BAPTISM, BAPTIST, BAPTIZE

A. Nouns.

1. *baptisma* [βάπτισμα, 908], baptism, consisting of the processes of immersion, submersion and emergence (from *baptō*, to dip), is used (*a*) of John's baptism, (*b*) of Christian baptism, see B. below; (*c*) of the overwhelming afflictions and judgments to which the Lord voluntarily submitted on the Cross, e.g., Luke 12:50; (*d*) of the sufferings His followers would experience, not of a vicarious character, but in fellowship with the sufferings of their Master. Some mss. have the word in Matt. 20:22, 23; it is used in Mark 10:38, 39, with this meaning.

NT: B.132c; CB.1238b; K.92.
OT: –.
GEN. REF.: IS.1:410; NB.131; Z.1:144f.

2. *baptismos* [βαπτισμός, 909], as distinct from *baptisma* (the ordinance), is used of the ceremonial washing of articles, Mark 7:4, 8, in some texts; Heb. 9:10; once in a general sense, Heb. 6:2. ¶ See WASHING.

NT: B.132d; CB.1238c; K.92.
OT: –.
GEN. REF.: IS.1:410; NB.130; Z.1:144f.

3. *baptistēs* [βαπτιστής, 910], a baptist, is used only of John the Baptist, and only in the Synoptists, 14 times.

NT: B.132d; CB.1238c; K.92.
OT: –.
GEN. REF.: IS.1:410; NB.130; Z.1:144; 3:1208.

B. Verb.

baptizō [βαπτίζω, 907], to baptize, primarily a frequentative form of *baptō*, to dip, was used among the Greeks to signify the dyeing of a garment or the drawing of water by dipping a vessel into another, etc. Plutarchus uses it of the drawing of wine by dipping the cup into the bowl (*Alexis*, 67) and Plato, metaphorically, of being overwhelmed with questions (*Euthydemus*, 277 D).

It is used in the N.T. in Luke 11:38 of washing oneself (as in 2 Kings 5:14, "dipped himself," (Sept.); see also Isa. 21:4, lit., 'lawlessness overwhelms me.' In the early chapters of the four Gospels and in Acts 1:5; 11:16; 19:4, it is used of the rite performed by John the Baptist who called upon the people to repent that they might receive remission of sins. Those who obeyed came "confessing their sins," thus acknowledging their unfitness to be in the Messiah's coming Kingdom. Distinct from this is the baptism enjoined by Christ, Matt. 28:19, a baptism to be undergone by believers, thus witnessing to their identification with Him in death, burial and resurrection, e.g., Acts 19:5; Rom. 6:3, 4; 1 Cor. 1:13-17; 12:13; Gal. 3:27; Col. 2:12. The phrase in Matt. 28:19, "baptizing them into the Name" (R.V.; cp. Acts 8:16, R.V.), would indicate that the baptized person was closely bound to, or became the property of, the one into whose Name he was baptized.

In Acts 22:16 it is used in the Middle Voice, in the command given to Saul of Tarsus, "arise and be baptized," the significance of the Middle Voice form being 'get thyself baptized.' The experience of those who were in the ark at the time of the Flood was a figure or type of the facts of spiritual death, burial and resurrection, Christian baptism being an *antitupon*, "a corresponding type," a "like figure," 1 Pet. 3:21. Likewise the nation of Israel was figuratively baptized when made to pass through the Red Sea under the cloud, 1 Cor. 10:2. The verb is used metaphorically also in two distinct senses: firstly, of baptism by the Holy Spirit, which took place on the day of Pentecost; secondly, of the calamity which would come upon the nation of the Jews, a baptism of the fire of Divine judgment for rejection of the will and word of God, Matt. 3:11; Luke 3:16.

NT: B.131d; CB.1238c; K.92.
OT: ṭābal: S.2881; HR.190b.1; H.787, 788; BD.371b.
GEN. REF.: IS.1:410; NB.130; Z.1:143-146.

BARBARIAN, BARBAROUS

barbaros [*βάρβαρος*, 915], properly meant one whose speech is rude, or harsh; the word is onomatopoeic, indicating in the sound the uncouth character represented by the repeated syllable "bar-bar." Hence it signified one who speaks a strange or foreign language. See 1 Cor. 14:11. It then came to denote any foreigner ignorant of the Greek language and culture. After the Persian war it acquired the sense of rudeness and brutality. In Acts 28:2, 4, it is used unreproachfully of the inhabitants of Malta, who were of Phoenician origin. So in Rom. 1:14, where it stands in distinction from Greeks, and in implied contrast to both Greeks and Jews. Cp. the contrasts in Col. 3:11, where all such distinctions are shown to be null and void in Christ. "Berber" stood similarly in the language of the Egyptians for all non-Egyptian peoples. ¶

NT: B.133b; CB.1238c; K.94.
OT: bā'ar: S.1197; HR.190c.1; H.263; BD.129c.
GEN. REF.: IS.–; NB.–; Z.2:790.

BARE (Adjective)

gumnos [*γυμνός*, 1131], naked, is once translated "bare," 1 Cor. 15:37, where, used of grain, the meaning is made clearer by translating the phrase by "a bare grain," R.V. See NAKED.

NT: B.167d; CB.1248c; K.133.
OT: 'ērôm, 'ārôm: S.6174; HR.278a.4b,c; H.1698; BD.735d.
GEN. REF.: IS.–; NB.–; Z.1:312-314.

For **BARE** (Verb) see **BEAR**

BARLEY

A. Noun.

krithē [*κριθή*, 2915], barley, is used in the plural in Rev. 6:6. ¶

NT: B.450c; CB.–; K.–.
OT: s^{e}'ōrāh: S.8184; HR.786a.1; H.2274f.; BD.972d.
GEN. REF.: IS.1:431; NB.133; Z.–.

B. Adjective.

krithinos [*κρίθινος*, 2916], signifies made of barley, John 6:9, 13. ¶

NT: B.450c; CB.–; K.–.
OT: s^{e}'ōrāh: S.8184; HR.786a.1; H.2274f; BD.972d.
GEN. REF.: IS.1:431; NB.–; Z.–.

BARN

apothēkē [*ἀποθήκη*, 596], lit., a place where anything is stored (Eng., apothecary), hence denoted a garner, granary, barn, Matt. 3:12; 6:26; 13:30; Luke 3:17; 12:18, 24. See also under GARNER. ¶

NT: B.91a; CB.–; K.–.
OT: mishmeret: S.4931; HR.128a.6; H.2414g; BD.1038b.
'ôṣār: S.214; HR.128a.2; H.154a; BD.69d.
ḥeder: S.2315; HR.128a.4; H.612a; BD.293c.
GEN. REF.: IS.1:432; NB.–; Z.–.

Note: For *tameion*, a storehouse, store-chamber, more especially an inner chamber or secret room, Matt. 6:6; 24:26; Luke 12:3, 24, see CHAMBER ¶

BARREN

1. *steiros* [*στεῖρος*, 4723], from a root *ster*— meaning hard, firm (hence Eng., sterile), signifies barren, not bearing children, and is used with the natural significance three times in the Gospel of Luke, 1:7, 36; 23:29; and with a spiritual significance in Gal. 4:27, in a quota-

tion from Is. 54:1. The circumstances of Sarah and Hagar, which Isaiah no doubt had in mind, are applied by the Apostle to the contrast between the works of the Law and the promise by grace. ¶

NT: B.766a; CB.—; K.—.
OT: ʿᵃqeret: S.6135; HR.1288a.1; H.1682a; BD.785d.
(ʿāqār)
GEN. REF.: IS.1:432; NB.134; Z.—.

2. *argos* [ἀργός, 692], denoting idle, barren, yielding no return, because of inactivity, is found in the best mss. in Jas. 2:20 (R.V., "barren"); it is rendered "barren" in 2 Pet. 1:8, A.V., (R.V., "idle"). In Matt. 12:36, the "idle word" means the word that is thoughtless or profitless. See IDLE, SLOW; cp. *katargeō*, under ABOLISH.

NT: B.104c; CB.1237c; K.76.
OT: —.
GEN. REF.: IS.1:432; NB.134; Z.1:73, 2:96.

BASE, BASER

1. *agnēs* [ἀγενής, 36], of low birth (*a*, negative, *genos*, family, race), hence denoted that which is of no reputation, of no account, 1 Cor. 1:28, "the base things of the world," i.e., those which are of no account or fame in the world's esteem. That neuter plural of the adjective bears reference to persons is clear from verse 26. ¶

NT: B.8c; CB.—; K.—.
OT: —.
GEN. REF.: IS.1:436; NB.—; Z.—.

2. *tapeinos* [ταπεινός, 5011], primarily that which is low, and does not rise far from the ground, as in the Sept. of Ezek. 17:24, hence, metaphorically, signifies lowly, of no degree. So the R.V. in 2 Cor. 10:1. Cp. Luke 1:52 and Jas. 1:9, "of low degree." Cp. *tapeinophrosunē*, lowliness of mind, and *tapeinoō*, to humble. See CAST, *Note* (7), HUMBLE, LOW, LOWLY

NT: B.804a; CB.1271a; K.1152.
OT: ʿānî: S.6041; HR. 1334b.7a; H.1652d; BD.776d.
shāphāl: S.8217; HR.1334b.11a; H.2445c; BD.1050c.
GEN. REF.: IS.1:436; NB.—; Z.2:259-64.

3. *agoraios* [ἀγοραῖος, 60], translated in the A.V. of Acts 17:5 "of the baser sort," R.V., "of the rabble," signifies, lit., relating to the market place; hence, frequenting markets, and so sauntering about idly. It is also used of affairs usually transacted in the market-place, and hence of judicial assemblies, Acts 19:38, R.V., "courts" (A.V., "law"); the margin in both R.V. and A.V. has "court days are kept." See COURT. ¶

NT: B.13a; CB.1233c; K.—.
OT: —.
GEN. REF.: IS.—; NB.—; Z.1:267.

BASKET, BASKETFUL

1. *kophinos* [κόφινος, 2894], was a wicker basket, originally containing a certain measure of capacity, Matt. 14:20; 16:9; Mark 6:43 (R.V., "basketfuls"); 8:19; Luke 9:17; 13:8 in some mss.; John 6:13. ¶

NT: B.447c; CB.—; K.—.
OT: dûd: S.1731; HR.781b.1; H.410e; BD.188b.
sal: S.5536; HR.781b.2; H.1507a; BD.700d.
GEN. REF.: IS.1:437; NB.135; Z.—.

2. *spuris* [σπυρίς, 4711], or *sphuris*, signifies something round, twisted or folded together (connected with *speira*, anything rolled into a circle; Eng., sphere); hence a reed basket, plaited, a capacious kind of hamper, sometimes large enough to hold a man, Matt. 15:37; 16:10; Mark 8:8, 20 (R.V., "basketfuls"); Acts 9:25. ¶

NT: B.764a; CB.—; K.—.
OT: —.
GEN. REF.: IS.1:437; NB.135; Z.—.

3. *sarganē* [σαργάνη, 4553], denotes (*a*) a braided rope or band, (*b*) a large basket made of ropes, or a wicker basket made of entwined twigs, 2 Cor. 11:33. That the basket in which Paul was let down from a window in Damascus is spoken of by Luke as a *spuris*, and by Paul himself as a *sarganē*, is quite consistent, the two terms being used for the same article. ¶

NT: B.742c; CB.—; K.—.
OT: —.
GEN. REF.: IS.1:437; NB.135; Z.—.

BASON

niptēr [νιπτήρ, 3537], the vessel into which the Lord poured water to wash the disciples' feet, was a large ewer, John 13:5. The word is connected with the verb *niptō*, to wash. ¶

NT: B.540a; CB.—; K.—.
OT: —.
GEN. REF.: IS.1:437; NB.135; Z.—.

BASTARD

nothos [νόθος, 3541], denotes an illegitimate child, one born out of lawful wedlock, Heb. 12:8. ¶

NT: B.540d; CB.1260a; K.—.
OT: —.
GEN. REF.: IS.1:438; NB.—; Z.—.

BATHED

louō [λούω, 3068], signifies to bathe or to wash. In John 13:10 the R.V. "bathed" is necessary to distinguish the act from the washing of feet. See WASH.

NT: B.480d; CB.1257b; K.538.
OT: rāḥaṣ: S.7364; HR.888b.1; H.2150; BD.934b.
GEN. REF.: IS.1:439; NB.136; Z.1:150-154.

BATTLE

polemos [πόλεμος, 4171], a war, is incorrectly rendered "battle" in the A.V. of 1 Cor. 14:8; Rev. 9:7, 9; 16:14; 20:8; R.V., invariably, "war."

NT: B.685a; CB.1265c; K.904.
OT: milḥāmāh: S.4421; HR.1172a.4; H.1104c; BD.536A.
GEN. REF.: IS.1:440; NB.—; Z.3:958, 961-963.

BAY

kolpos [κόλπος, 2859], translated "bay" in the R.V. of Acts 27:39, is wider than a "creek" (A.V.). Eng., gulf, is connected. See BOSOM.

NT: B.442b; CB.1255c; K.452.
OT: ḥêq: S.2436; HR.777a.1; H.629a; BD.300b.
GEN. REF.: IS.1:441; NB.–; Z.1:240.

For BE see BEING

BEACH

aigialos [αἰγιαλός, 123], translated "shore" in the A.V. in each place where it is used, Matt. 13:2, 48; John 21:4; Acts 21:5; 27:39, 40, is always in the R.V. translated "beach." It is derived from a root signifying to press, drive; *aigis* denotes a wind-storm. ¶

NT: B.21d; CB.–; K.–.
OT: –.
GEN. REF.: IS.1:441; NB.–; Z.–.

BEAM

dokos [δοκός, 1385], a beam, is perhaps etymologically connected with the root *dek*–, seen in the word *dechomai*, to receive, beams being received at their ends into walls or pieces of timber. The Lord used it metaphorically, in contrast to a mote, of a great fault, or vice, Matt. 7:3, 4, 5; Luke 6:41, 42. ¶

NT: B.203a; CB.–; K.–.
OT: qōrāh: S.6982; HR.340a.4; H.2068d; BD.900a.
qîr: S.7023; HR.340a.3; H.2022; BD.885a.
GEN. REF.: IS.1:441; NB.–; Z.–.

BEAR

(*in the sense of carrying, supporting*)

For the verb to bear in the sense of begetting, see BEGET.

1. *bastazō* [βαστάζω, 941], signifies to support as a burden. It is used with the meaning (*a*) to take up, as in picking up anything, stones, John 10:31; (*b*) to carry something, Matt. 3:11; Mark 14:13; Luke 7:14; 22:10; Acts 3:2; 21:35; Rev. 17:7; to carry on one's person, Luke 10:4; Gal. 6:17; in one's body, Luke 11:27; to bear a name in testimony, Acts 9:15; metaphorically, of a root bearing branches, Rom. 11:18; (*c*) to bear a burden, whether physically, as of the Cross, John 19:17, or metaphoprically in respect of sufferings endured in the cause of Christ, Luke 14:27; Rev. 2:3; it is said of physical endurance, Matt. 20:12; of sufferings borne on behalf of others, Matt. 8:17; Rom. 15:1; Gal. 6:2; of spiritual truths not able to be borne. John 16:12; of the refusal to endure evil men, Rev. 2:2; of religious regulations imposed on others, Acts 15:10; of the burden of the sentence of God to be executed in due time, Gal. 5:10; of the effect at the Judgment Seat of Christ, to be borne by the believer for failure in the matter of discharging the obligations of discipleship, Gal. 6:5; (*d*) to bear by way of carrying off, John 12:6; 20:15. See CARRY, TAKE. ¶

NT: B.137b; CB.1238c; K.102.
OT: nāsā': S.5375; HR.215a.2; H.1421; BD.669d.
GEN. REF.: IS.1:442; NB.–; Z.1:403.

2. *pherō* [φέρω, 5342], to bring or bear, is translated in the R.V. by the latter verb in Luke 23:26; John 2:8 (twice); 12:24; 15:2 (twice); Heb. 13:13. See BRING, No. 1 and words there.

NT: B.854d; CB.1264a; K.1252.
OT: bô': S.935; HR.1426c.3b; H.212; BD.99a.
nāsā': S.5375; HR.1426c.17; H.1421; BD.671a.
GEN. REF.: IS.1:442; NB.–; Z.1:722; 3:1195.

3. *anapherō* [ἀναφέρω, 399], No. 2, with *ana*, up, is used of leading persons up to a higher place, and, in this respect, of the Lord's Ascension, Luke 24:51. It is used twice of the Lord's propitiatory sacrifice, in His bearing sins on the Cross, Heb. 9:28 and 1 Pet. 2:24; the A.V. margin, "to the tree," is to be rejected. The A.V. text, "on," and the R.V. "upon" express the phrase rightly. See BRING, CARRY, LEAD, OFFER.

NT: B.63a; CB.1235b; K.1252.
OT: 'ālāh: S.5927; HR.84c.10b; H.1624; BD.749b
qāṭar: S.6999; HR.84c.12; H.2011; BD.882d.
GEN. REF.: IS.1:442; NB.–; Z.3:435, 1195f.

4. *ekpherō* [ἐκφέρω, 1627], No. 2, with *ek*, out, is used, literally, of carrying something forth, or out, e.g., a garment, Luke 15:22; sick folk, Acts 5:15; a corpse, Acts 5:6, 9, 10; of the impossibility of carrying anything out from this world at death, 1 Tim. 6:7. The most authentic mss. have this word in Mark 8:23, of the blind man, whom the Lord brought out of the village (R.V.). It is also used of the earth, in bringing forth produce, Heb. 6:8. See BRING, CARRY. ¶

NT: B.246d; CB.–; K.–.
OT: yāṣā': S.3318; HR.444c.2b; H.893; BD.424b.
GEN. REF.: IS.1:442; NB.–; Z.–.

5. *peripherō* [περιφέρω, 4064], No. 2, with *peri*, about, signifies to carry about, or bear about, and is used literally, of carrying the sick, Mark 6:55, or of physical sufferings endured in fellowship with Christ, 2 Cor. 4:10; metaphorically, of being carried about by different evil doctrines, Eph. 4:14; Heb. 13:9; Jude 12. See CARRY.

NT: B.653b; CB.1263b; K.–.
OT: –.
GEN. REF.: IS.1:442; NB.–; Z.3:770.

6. *hupopherō* [ὑποφέρω, 5297], lit., to bear up under, is best rendered by "endure," as 1 Cor. 10:13, R.V., of enduring temptations; of

enduring persecutions, 2 Tim. 3:11; grief, 1 Pet. 2:19. See ENDURE. ¶

NT: B.848c; CB.–; K.–.
OT: yākōl: S.3201; HR.1418a.1; H.866; BD.407b.
nāsā': S.5375; HR.1418a.5; H.1421; BD.669d.
GEN. REF.: IS.1:442; NB.–; Z.–.

7. *phoreō* [φορέω, 5409], a frequentative form of *pherō*, is to be distinguished from it as denoting, not a simple act of bearing, but a continuous or habitual condition, e.g., of the civil authority in bearing the sword as symbolic of execution, Rom. 13:4; of a natural state of bodily existence in this life, spoken of as "the image of the earthy," and the spiritual body of the believer hereafter, "the image of the heavenly," 1 Cor. 15:49, the word "image" denoting the actual form and not a mere similitude. See WEAR.

NT: B.864d; CB.–; K.1252.
OT: –.
GEN. REF.: IS.1:442; NB.–; Z.–.

8. *tropophoreō* [τροποφορέω, 5159], from *tropos*, a manner, and *phoreō*, to endure, is found in Acts 13:18, where some ancient authorities have the verb *trophophoreō*, "He bare them as a nursing father," (from *trophos*, a feeder, a nurse, and *phoreō* to carry). ¶

NT: B.827c; CB.–; K.–.
OT: nāsā': S.5375; HR.1376b.1; H.1421; BD.669d.
GEN. REF.: IS.1:442; NB.–; Z.–.

9. *airō* [αἴρω, 142], signifies (*a*) to raise up, to lift, to take upon oneself and carry what has been raised, physically (its most frequent use), or as applied to the mind, to suspend, to keep in suspense, as in John 10:24, lit., 'How long doth thou suspend our souls?'; (*b*) to take away what is attached to anything, to remove, as of Christ, in taking (or bearing, marg.) away the sin of the world, John 1:29; Christ "was manifested to take away sins," 1 John 3:5, where, not the nature of the Atonement is in view, but its effect in the believer's life. See CARRY, DOUBT, No. 6, LIFT, LOOSE, PUT, No. 17, REMOVE, SUSPENSE, TAKE.

NT: B.24b; CB.1234a; K.28.
OT: nāsā': S.5375; HR.34c.14a; H.1421; BD.669d.
GEN. REF.: IS.1:442; NB.–; Z.1:701, 2:411.

10. *poieō* [ποιέω, 4160], to do, sometimes means to produce, bear, Luke 8:8; 13:9; Jas. 3:12 (A.V., "bear," R.V., "yield"); Rev. 22:2. See COMMIT, DO.

NT: B.680d; CB.1265c; K.895.
OT: 'āsāh: S.6213; HR.1154a.33; H.1708, 1709; BD.793c.
GEN. REF.: IS.1:442; NB.–; Z.3:1152-58.

11. *stegō* [στέγω, 4722], primarily to protect, or preserve by covering, hence means to keep off something which threatens, to bear up against, to hold out against, and so to endure, bear, forbear, 1 Cor. 9:12. The idea of supporting what is placed upon a thing is prominent in 1 Thess. 3:1, 5 ("forbear"), and 1 Cor. 13:7. See FORBEAR and SUFFER. ¶

NT: B.765d; CB.1270a; K.1073.
OT: –.
GEN. REF.: IS.1:442; NB.–; Z.3:887.

12. *anechomai* [ἀνέχομαι, 430], signifies to hold up against a thing and so to bear with (*ana*, up, and *echomai*, the Middle Voice of *echō*, to have, to hold), e.g., Matt. 17:7; 1 Cor. 4:12; 2 Cor. 11:1, 4, 19, 20; Heb. 13:22, etc. See ENDURE, FORBEAR, SUFFER.

NT: B.65d; CB.–; K.–.
OT: –.
GEN. REF.: IS.1:442; NB.–; Z.2:764-66.

13. *metriopatheō* [μετριοπαθέω, 3356], to treat with mildness, or moderation, to bear gently with (*metrios*, moderate, and *paschō*, to suffer), is used in Heb. 5:2 (R.V. and A.V. marg.). The idea is that of not being unduly disturbed by the faults and ignorance of others; or rather perhaps of feeling in some measure, in contrast to the full feeling with expressed in the verb *sumpatheō* in 4:15, with reference to Christ as the High Priest. See COMPASSION, No. 5. ¶

NT: B.514d; CB.–; K.798.
OT: –.
GEN. REF.: IS.1:442; NB.–; Z.–.

14. *makrothumeō* [μακροθυμέω, 3114], to be long-tempered (*makros*, long, *thumos*, temper), is translated "is longsuffering over" in Luke 18:7, R.V. (A.V., "bear long with"). See — PATIENT, SUFFER.

NT: B.488a; CB.1257a; K.550.
OT: –.
GEN. REF.: IS.1:442; NB.–; Z.2:768-772.

Notes: (1) For "bear (or give) witness," see WITNESS.

(2) For "bear up into," in Acts 27:15, see FACE.

(3) In 1 Cor. 10:13 the adjective *anthrōpinos*, human (from *anthrōpos*, man) is translated "is common to man," A.V. (R.V., "man can bear").

(4) For *karpophoreō*, to bear fruit, e.g., Mark 4:20 (*karpos*, fruit, and No. 7), A.V., "bring forth," see FRUIT.

(5) In Acts 20:9, R.V., *katapherō* is rendered "borne down." See GIVE. No. 12.

BEAR (animal)

ark(t)os [ἄρκος, 715], a bear, occurs in Rev. 13:2. ¶

NT: B.107b; CB.–; K.–.
OT: dōb: S.1678; HR.158a.1; H.2664., BD.179a.
GEN. REF.: IS.1:441; NB.136; Z.–.

BEAST

1. *zōon* [ζῷον, 2226], primarily denotes a living being (*zōē*, life). The Eng., "animal," is the equivalent, stressing the fact of life as the

characteristic feature. In Heb. 13:11 the A.V. and the R.V. translate it "beasts" ("animals" would be quite suitable). In 2 Pet. 2:12 and Jude 10, the A.V. has "beasts," the R.V. "creatures." In the Apocalypse, where the word is found some 20 times, and always of those beings which stand before the Throne of God, who give glory and honour and thanks to Him, 4:6, and act in perfect harmony with His counsels, 5:14; 6:1-7, e.g., the word "beasts" is most unsuitable; the R.V., "living creatures," should always be used; it gives to *zōon* its appropriate significance. See CREATURE.

NT: B.341c; CB.1273c; K.290.
OT: ḥayyāh: S.2416; HR.601b.1a; H.644a; BD.312c.
GEN. REF.: IS.1:442; NB.137; Z.2:476.

2. *thērion* [θηρίον, 2342], to be distinguished from *zōon*, almost invariably denotes a wild beast. In Acts 28:4, "a venomous beast" is used of the viper which fastened on Paul's hand. *Zōon* stresses the vital element, *thērion* the bestial. The idea of a beast of prey is not always present. Once, in Heb. 12:20, it is used of the animals in the camp of Israel, such, e.g., as were appointed for sacrifice. But in the Sept. *thērion* is never used of sacrificial animals; the word *ktēnos* (see below) is reserved for these.

Thērion, in the sense of wild beast, is used in the Apocalypse for the two Antichristian potentates who are destined to control the affairs of the nations with Satanic power in the closing period of the present era, 11:7; 13:1-18, 14:9, 11; 15:2; 16:2, 10, 13; 17:3-17; 19:19, 20; 20:4, 10.

NT: B.361a; CB.1272b; K.333.
OT: ḥay: S.2416; HR.650c.2a; H.644a; BD.311d.
ḥayyāh: S.2416; HR.650c.2b; H.644a; BD.312c.
GEN. REF.: IS.1:442; NB.137; Z.1:113-119.

3. *ktēnos* [κτῆνος, 2934], primarily denotes property (the connected verb *ktaomai* means to possess); then, property in flocks and herds. In Scripture it signifies, (*a*) a beast of burden, Luke 10:34; Acts 23:24, (*b*) beasts of any sort, apart from those signified by *thērion* (see above) 1 Cor. 15:39; Rev. 18:13, (*c*) animals for slaughter; this meaning is not found in the N.T., but is very frequent in the Sept. ¶

NT: B.455b; CB.1256a; K.—.
OT: bᵉhēmāh: S.929; HR.794a.1; H.208a; BD.96d.
miqneh: S.4735; HR.794a.6b; H.2039b; BD.889b.
GEN. REF.: IS.1:442; NB.136; Z.1:496.

4. *tetrapous* [τετράπους, 5074], a four-footed beast (*tetra*, four, and *pous*, a foot) is found in Acts 10:12; 11:6; Rom. 1:23. ¶

NT: B.814a; CB.—; K.—.
OT: bᵉhēmāh: S.929; HR.1347b.1; H.208a; BD.96d.
ḥayyāh: S.2416; HR.1347b.2; H.644a; BD.312c.
GEN. REF.: IS.1:442; NB.136; Z.1:496.

5. *sphagion* [σφάγιον, 4968], from *sphazō*, to slay, denotes a victim, slaughtered for sacrifice, a slain beast, Acts 7:42, in a quotation from Amos 5:25. ¶

NT: B.796a; CB.—; K.—.
OT: zebaḥ: S.2077; HR.1324b.1; H.525a; BD.257b.
ṭebaḥ: S.2874; HR.1324b.2; H.786a; BD.370d.
nᵉ'dābāh: S.5071; HR.1324b.3; H.1299a; BD.621d.
GEN. REF.: IS.1:442; NB.1:136; Z.1:496.

BEAT

1. *derō* [δέρω, 1194], from a root *der—*, skin (*derma*, a skin, cp. Eng., dermatology), primarily to flay, then to beat, thrash or smite, is used of the treatment of the servants of the owner of the vineyard by the husbandmen, in the parable in Matt. 21:35; Mark 12:3, 5; Luke 20:10, 11; of the treatment of Christ, Luke 22:63, R.V., "beat," for A.V., "smote"; John 18:23; of the followers of Christ, in the synagogues, Mark 13:9; Acts 22:19; of the punishment of unfaithful servants, Luke 12:47, 48; of the beating of apostles by the High Priest and the Council of the Sanhedrin, Acts 5:40; by magistrates, 16:37. The significance of flogging does not always attach to the word; it is used of the infliction of a single blow, John 18:23; 2 Cor. 11:20, and of beating the air, 1 Cor. 9:26. The usual meaning is that of thrashing or cudgelling, and when used of a blow it indicates one of great violence. See SMITE. ¶

NT: B.175d; CB.1240c; K.—.
OT: pāshaṭ: S.6584; HR.291b.1; H.1845; BD.832d.
GEN. REF.: —.

2. *tuptō* [τύπτω, 5180], from a root *tup—*, meaning a blow, (*tupos*, a figure or print: Eng., type) denotes to smite, strike, or beat, usually not with the idea of giving a thrashing as with *derō*. It frequently signifies a blow of violence and, when used in a continuous tense, indicates a series of blows. In Matt. 27:30 the imperfect tense signifies that the soldiers kept on striking Christ on the head. So Mark 15:19. The most authentic mss. omit it in Luke 22:64. In that verse the word *paiō*, to smite, is used of the treatment given to Christ (*derō* in the preceding verse). The imperfect tense of the verb is again used in Acts 18:17, of the beating given to Sosthenes. Cp. Acts 21:32, which has the present participle. It is used in the metaphorical sense of wounding, in 1 Cor. 8:12. See SMITE, STRIKE, WOUND.

NT: B.830b; CB.1273b; K.1195.
OT: nākāh: S.5221; HR.1378b.4; H.1364; BD.645a.
GEN. REF.: —.

3. *rhabdizō* [ῥαβδίζω, 4463], to beat with a rod, or stick, to cudgel, is the verbal form of *rhabdos*, a rod, or staff, Acts 16:22; 2 Cor. 11:25. ¶

NT: B.733b; CB.1268a; K.982.
OT: ḥābaṭ: S.2251; HR.1247a.1; H.591; BD.286a.
GEN. REF.: —.

4. *ballō* [βάλλω, 906], to throw or cast, is once rendered "beat," Acts 27:14 R.V., of the tempestuous wind that beat down upon the ship. So the A.V. margin. See CAST.

NT: B.130d; CB.1238b; K.91.
OT: nāphal: S.5307; HR.189c.6; H.1392; BD.656c.
GEN. REF.: –.

5. *epiballō* [ἐπιβάλλω, 1911], No. 4, with *epi*, upon, to cast upon, or lay hands upon, signifies to beat into, in Mark 4:37, of the action of the waves. See CAST, No. 7, FALL, No. 11, LAY, PUT, No. 8, STRETCH, THINK, No. 15.

NT: B.289d; CB.–; K.–.
OT: sîm, sûm: S.7760; HR.516a.15; H.2243; BD.962c.
shît: S.7896; HR.516a.17; H.2380; BD.1011a
shālaḥ: S.7971; HR.516a.18; H.2394; BD.1018a.
GEN. REF.: –.

6. *proskoptō* [προσκόπτω, 4350], to stumble, to strike against (*pros*, to or against, *koptō*, to strike), is once used of a storm beating upon a house, Matt. 7:27. See DASH, STUMBLE, and cp. *proskomma* and *proskopē*, a stumbling-block, offence.

NT: B.716b; CB.1267b; K.946.
OT: kāshal: S.3782; HR.1217b.1; H.1050; BD.505b.
nāgaph: S.5062; HR.1217b.2; H.1294; BD.619d.
GEN. REF.: –.

7. *prospiptō* [προσπίπτω, 4363], to fall upon (*pros*, to, *piptō*, to fall), is translated "beat" in Matt. 7:25; elsewhere, to fall down at or before. See FALL.

NT: B.718a; CB.–; K.–.
OT: nāphal: S.5307; HR.1219a.4; H.1392; BD.656c.
GEN. REF.: –.

8. *prosrēgnumi* [προσρήγνυμι, 4366], to break upon, is translated "beat vehemently upon," or against (*pros*, upon, *rhēgnumi*, to break), in Luke 6:48, 49, of the violent action of a flood (R.V., "brake"). ¶

NT: B.718b; CB.–; K.–.
OT: –.
GEN. REF.: –.

Note: In Luke 10:30, the phrase lit. rendered 'inflicting blows,' is translated "wounded" (A.V.), R.V., correctly, "beat."

BEAUTIFUL

1. *hōraios* [ὡραῖος, 5611], describes that which is seasonable, produced at the right time, as of the prime of life, or the time when anything is at its loveliest and best (from *kōra*, a season, a period fixed by natural laws and revolutions, and so the best season of the year). It is used of the outward appearance of whited sepulchres in contrast to the corruption within, Matt. 23:27; of the Jerusalem gate called "Beautiful," Acts 3:2, 10; of the feet of those that bring glad tidings, Rom. 10:15. ¶

In the Sept. it is very frequent, and especially in Genesis and the Song of Solomon. In Genesis it is said of all the trees in the garden of Eden, 2:9, especially of the tree of the knowledge of good and evil, 3:6; of the countenances of Rebekah, 26:7, Rachel, 29:17 and Joseph, 39:6. It is used five times in the Song of Solomon, 1:16; 2:14; 4:3 and 6:3, 5.

NT: B.896d; CB.1251a; K.–.
OT: nā'āh: S.4998; HR.1493c.5; H.1271; BD.610a.
ḥāmad: S.2530; HR.1493c.2a; H.673; BD.326b.
yāpheh: S.3303; HR.1493c.4; H.890a; BD.421c.
GEN. REF.: IS.1:444; NB.–; Z.1:503.

2. *asteios* [ἀστεῖος, 791], connected with *astu*, a city, was used primarily of that which befitted the town, town-bred (corresponding Eng. words are "polite," "polished," connected with *polis*, a town; cp. "urbane," from Lat., *urbs*, a city). Among Greek writers it is set in contrast to *agroikos*, rustic, and *aischros*, base, and was used, e.g., of clothing. It is found in the N.T. only of Moses, Acts 7:20, "(exceeding) fair," lit., 'fair (to God,' and Heb. 11:23, "goodly" (A.V., "proper"). See FAIR, GOODLY, *Note*, PROPER. ¶

NT: B.117c; CB.–; K.–.
OT: tôb: S.2895; HR.173b.2; H.793; BD.373b.
GEN. REF.: IS.1:444; NB.–; Z.1:503.

Notes: (1) In the Sept. it is far less frequent than *hōraios*. It is said of Moses in Ex. 2:2; negatively, of Balaam's procedure in the sight of God, Num. 22:32; of Eglon in Judg. 3:17.

(2) *Asteios* belongs to the realm of art, *hōraios*, to that of nature. *Asteios* is used of that which is beautiful because it is elegant; *hōraios* describes that which is beautiful because it is, in its season, of natural excellence.

(3) *Kalos*, good, describes that which is beautiful as being well proportioned in all its parts, or intrinsically excellent. See BETTER, FAIR, GOOD, etc.

For **BECAME** see **BECOME**

For **BECAUSE** see Note † p. 1

BECKON

1. *neuō* [νεύω, 3506], lit., to give a nod, to signify by a nod, is used in John 13:24, of Peter's beckoning to John to ask the Lord of whom He had been speaking; in Acts 24:10, of the intimation given by Felix to Paul to speak. ¶

NT: B.536d; CB.–; K.–.
OT: –.
GEN. REF.: IS.1:445; NB.–; Z.–.

2. *dianeuō* [διανεύω, 1269], to express one's meaning by a sign (No. 1, with *dia*, through, used intensively), is said of the act of Zacharias, Luke 1:22 (R.V., "continued making signs," for A.V., "beckoned"). In Sept., Psa. 35:19, "wink." ¶

NT: B.187a; CB.–; K.–.
OT: qāraṣ: S.7169; HR.306b.1; H.2075; BD.902d.
GEN. REF.: IS.1:445; NB.–; Z.–.

3. *kataneuō* [κατανεύω, 2656], No. 1, with *kata*, down, intensive, is used of the fishermen-partners in Luke 5:7, "beckoned." ¶
NT: B.415a; CB.–; K.–.
OT: –.
GEN. REF.: IS.1:445; NB.–; Z.–.

4. *kataseiō* [κατασείω, 2678], lit., to shake down (*kata*, down, *seiō*, to shake), of shaking the hand, or waving, expresses a little more vigorously the act of beckoning, Acts 12:17; 13:16; 19:33; 21:40. *Neuō* and its compounds have primary reference to a movement of the head; *kataseiō*, to that of the hand. ¶
NT: B.418a; CB.1254B; K.–.
OT: –.
GEN. REF.: IS.1:445; NB.–; Z.–.

BECOME (to be fitting)

A. Verb.

prepō [πρέπω, 4241], means to be conspicuous among a number, to be eminent, distinguished by a thing, hence, to be becoming, seemly, fit. The adornment of good works "becometh women professing godliness," 1 Tim. 2:10. Those who minister the truth are to speak "the things which befit the sound doctrine," Tit. 2:1. Christ, as a High Priest "became us," Heb. 7:26. In the impersonal sense, it signifies it is fitting, it becometh, Matt. 3:15; 1 Cor. 11:13; Eph. 5:3; Heb. 2:10. See Befit, Comely. ¶
NT: B.699b; CB.1266b; K.–.
OT: nā'āh: S.4998; HR.1201b.2a; H.1271; BD.610a.
nā'weh: S.5000; HR.1201b.2b; H.1271a; BD.610a.
GEN. REF.: IS.1:445; NB.–; Z.–.

B. Adjective.

hieroprepēs [ἱεροπρεπής, 2412], from *hieros*, sacred, with the adjectival form of *prepō*, denotes suited to a sacred character, that which is befitting in persons, actions or things consecrated to God, Tit. 2:3, R.V., "reverent," A.V., "as becometh holiness," (marg., "holy women"). Trench (Syn. §xcii) distinguishes this word from *kosmios*, modest, and *semnos*, grave, honourable. ¶
NT: B.372d; CB.1250b; K.34q.
OT: –.
GEN. REF.: IS.1:445; NB.–; Z.–.

Notes: (1) The A.V. translates the adverb *axiōs*, as "becometh," in Rom. 16:2; Phil. 1:27 (R.V. corrects to "worthily" and "worthy").

(2) *Ginomai*, to become, is mentioned under various other headings.

(3) For "become of no effect," Gal. 5:4, A.V., R.V., "severed from," see Abolish.

BED

1. *klinē* [κλίνη, 2825], akin to *klinō*, to lean (Eng., recline, incline etc.), a bed, e.g., Mark 7:30, also denotes a couch for reclining at meals, Mark 4:21, or a couch for carrying the sick, Matt. 9:2, 6. The metaphorical phrase 'to cast into a bed,' Rev. 2:22, signifies to afflict with disease (or possibly, to lay on a bier). In Mark 7:4 the A.V. curiously translates the word "tables" (Marg., "beds"), R.V., marg. only, "couches." See Couch.
NT: B.436b; CB.–; K.–.
OT: –.
GEN. REF.: IS.1:445; NB.137; Z.1:504.

2. *klinarion* [κλινάριον], a diminutive of No. 1, a small bed, is used in Acts 5:15. Some mss. have *klinōn*. See also No. 4. See Couch. ¶
NT: B.436b; CB.–; K.–.
OT: –.
GEN. REF.: IS.1:445; NB.137; Z.1:504.

3. *koitē* [κοίτη, 2845], primarily a place for lying down (connected with *keimai*, to lie), denotes a bed, Luke 11:7; the marriage bed, Heb. 13:4; in Rom. 13:13, it is used of sexual intercourse. By metonymy, the cause standing for the effect, it denotes conception, Rom. 9:10. ¶
NT: B.440a; CB.1255b; K.–.
OT: mishkāb: S.4904; HR.775b.6d; H.2381c; BD.1012d.
GEN. REF.: IS.1:445; NB.137; Z.1:504.

4. *krabbatos* [κράββατος, 2895], a Macedonian word (Lat. *grabatus*), is a somewhat mean bed, pallet, or mattress for the poor, Mark 2:4, 9, 11, 12; 6:55; John 5:8-11; Acts 5:15; 9:33. See also No. 2. See Couch. ¶
NT: B.447c; CB.–; K.–.
OT: –.
GEN. REF.: IS.1:445; NB.137; Z.1:504.

Note: The verb *strōnnuō* or *strōnnumi*, to spread, signifies, in Acts 9:34, to make a bed; elsewhere it has its usual meaning. See Furnish, Spread.

BEFALL

1. *ginomai* [γίνομαι, 1096], to become, is rendered "befell" in Mark 5:16; "hath befallen" in Rom. 11:25, R.V., for A.V., "is happened to;" so the R.V. in 2 Cor. 1:8; 2 Tim. 3:11.
NT: B.158a; CB.1248b; K.117.
OT: hāyāh: S.1961; HR.256b.6d; H.491; BD224a.
GEN. REF.: –.

2. *sumbainō* [συμβαίνω, 4819], lit., to walk, or go together (*sun*, with, *bainō*, to go), is used of things which happen at the same time; hence, to come to pass, "befall," Acts 20:19. In 21:35, it is translated "so it was." See Happen.
NT: B.77b; CB.–; K.–.
OT: qārā': S.7122; HR.1302c.5; H.2064; BD.894d.
GEN. REF.: –.

3. *sunantaō* [συναντάω, 4876], to meet with (*sun*, with, *antaō*, to meet), is used much in the

same way as *sumbainō*, of events which come to pass; "befall," Acts 20:22. See MEET.

NT: B.784c; CB.1270c; K.–.
OT: pāga': S.6293; HR.1311a.6; H.1731; BD.803b.
qārā': S.7122; HR.1311a.10; H.2064. BD.894d.
qārāh: S.7136; HR.1311a.11; H.2068,2068e; BD.899c.
GEN. REF.: –.

Note: The phrase in Matt. 8:33, "what was befallen to them that were possessed with demons," is, lit., 'the things of the demonized.'

BEFIT, BEFITTING

1. *prepō* [πρέπω, 4241], is translated "befit" in Tit. 2:1, R.V. (A.V., "become"). See BECOME.

NT: B.669b; CB.1266b; K.–.
OT: nā'āh: S.4998; HR.1201b.2a; H.1271; BD.610a.
nā'weh: S.5000; HR.1201b.2b; H.1271a; BD.610a.
GEN. REF.: –.

2. *anēkō* [ἀνήκω, 433], primarily, to have arrived at, reached to, pertained to, came to denote what is due to a person, one's duty, what is befitting. It is used ethically in the N.T.; Eph. 5:4, R.V., "are (not) befitting," for A.V., "are (not) convenient"; Col. 3:18, concerning the duty of wives towards husbands, R.V., "as is fitting," for A.V., "as it is fit." In Philm. 8, the participle is used with the article, signifying "that which is befitting," R.V. (A.V., "that which is convenient"). See CONVENIENT.

NT: B.66b; CB.1235c; K.–.
OT: –.
GEN. REF.: –.

For synonymous words see BECOME

BEFORE, BEFORETIME

A. Adverbs.

1. *prōton* [πρῶτον, 4412], the neuter of the adjective *prōtos* (the superlative degree of *pro*, before), signifies first, or at the first, (*a*) in order of time, e.g., Luke 10:5; John 18:13; 1 Cor. 15:46; 1 Thess. 4:16; 1 Tim. 3:10; (*b*) in enumerating various particulars, e.g., Rom. 3:2; 1 Cor. 11:18; 12:28; Heb. 7:2; Jas. 3:17. It is translated "before" in John 15:18. See CHIEFLY, FIRST.

NT: B.725b; CB.1267b; K.965.
OT: –.
GEN. REF.: –.

2. *proteron* [πρότερον, 4386], the neuter of *proteros*, the comparative degree of *pro*, is always used of time, and signifies aforetime, "before," e.g., John 6:62; 9:8; 2 Cor. 1:15; Heb. 7:27; in Gal. 4:13, "the first time" (R.V.)., 'the former time,' i.e., the former of two previous visits; in Heb. 10:32 it is placed between the article and the noun, "the former days;" so in 1 Pet. 1:14, "the former lusts," i.e., the lusts formerly indulged. See FIRST, FORMER.

NT: B.721; CB.1267b; K.–.
OT: lᵉpānîm: S. 6440; HR.1230b.1; H.1782a; BD.816b.
ri'shôn: S.7223; HR.1230b.2a; H.2097c; BD.911c.
GEN. REF.: –.

3. *prin* [πρίν, 4250], before, formerly (etymologically akin to *pro*, before), has the force of a conjunction, e.g., Matt. 1:18; 26:34, 75; John 14:29; Acts 7:2.

NT: B.701a; CB.–; K.–.
OT: –.
GEN. REF.: –.

4. *emprosthen* [ἔμπροσθεν, 1715], is used of place or position only; adverbally, signifying in front, Luke 19:28; Phil. 3:13; Rev. 4:6; as a preposition, e.g., Matt. 5:24; John 10:4; with the meaning 'in the sight of a person,' e.g., Matt. 5:16; 6:1; 17:2; Luke 19:27; John 12:37; 1 Thess. 2:19, R.V., "before;" A.V., "in the presence of;" Rev. 19:10, R.V., "before," especially in phrases signifying in the sight of God, as God wills, Matt. 11:26; 18:14 (lit., 'a thing willed before your Father,' R.V., marg.); Luke 10:21; in the sense of priority of rank or position or dignity, John 1:15, 30 (in some texts, ver. 27); in an antagonistic sense, "against," Matt. 23:13 (R.V., marg., "before").

NT: B.257a; CB.1244b; K.–.
OT: liphnē: S.3942; HR.459b.3c; H.1782b; BD.816d
GEN. REF.: –.

5. *enantion* [ἐναντίον, 1726], from *en*, in, and *anti*, over against, the neuter of the adjective *enantios*, and virtually an adverb, is also used as a preposition signifying in the presence of, in the sight of, Luke 20:26; Acts 7:10; 8:32; in the judgment of, Luke 24:19. ¶

NT: B.261d; CB.1244c; K.–.
OT: –.
GEN. REF.: –.

6. *enanti* [ἔναντι, 1725], an adverb, used as a preposition, has meanings like those of No. 5, "before," Luke 1:8; in the judgment of, Acts 8:21. Some texts have the word in Acts 7:10. ¶

NT: B.261d; CB.1244c; K.–.
OT: –.
GEN. REF.: –.

7. *apenanti* [ἀπέναντι, 561], *apo*, from, with No. 6, denotes (*a*) opposite, Matt. 27:61; (*b*) in the sight of, before, Matt. 27:24; Acts 3:16; Rom. 3:18; (*c*) against, Acts 17:7. See CONTRARY, PRESENCE. ¶

NT: B.84a; CB.–; K.–.
OT: –.
GEN. REF.: –.

8. *katenanti* [κατέναντι, 2713], *kata*, down, with No. 6, lit., down over against, is used (*a*) of locality, e.g., Mark 11:2; 13:3; Luke 19:30; (*b*) as 'in the sight of,' Rom. 4:17; in most mss. in 2 Cor. 2:17; 12:19.

NT: B.241b; CB.–; K.–.
OT: –.
GEN. REF.: –.

9. *enōpion* [ἐνώπιον, 1799], from *en*, in, and *ōps*, the eye, is the neuter of the adjective *enōpios*, and is used prepositionally, (*a*) of place, that which is before or opposite a person, towards which he turns his eyes, e.g. Luke

1:19; Acts 4:10; 6:6; Rev. 1:4; 4:10; 7:15; (*b*) in metaphorical phrases after verbs of motion, Luke 1:17; 12:9; Acts 9:15, etc.; signifying in the mind or soul of persons, Luke 12:6; Acts 10:31; Rev. 16:19; (*c*) in one's sight or hearing, Luke 24:43; John 20:30; 1 Tim. 6:12; metaphorically, Rom. 14:22; especially in Gal. 1:20; 1 Tim. 5:21; 6:13; 2 Tim. 2:14; 4:1; before, as having a person present to the mind, Acts 2:25; Jas. 4:10; in the judgment of a person, Luke 16:15; 24:11, R.V., "in their sight," for A.V., "to;" Acts 4:19; Rom. 3:20; 12:17; 2 Cor. 8:21; 1 Tim. 2:3; in the approving sight of God, Luke 1:75; Acts 7:46; 10:33; 2 Cor. 4:2; 7:12. See PRESENCE, SIGHT OF (in the).

NT: B.270c; CB.1245b; K.–.
OT: –.
GEN. REF.: –.

10. *katenōpion* [κατενώπιον, 2714], *kata*, against, with No. 9, signifies right over against, opposite; (*a*) of place, Jude 24; (*b*) before God as Judge, Eph. 1:4; Col. 1:22. See No. 8 (b). ¶

NT: B.241b; CB.1254b; K.–.
OT: –.
GEN. REF.: –.

B. Verb

prouparchō [προυπάρχω, 4391], to exist before, or be beforehand, is found in Luke 23:12, and Acts 8:9, "beforetime." ¶ In the Sept., Job 42:18. ¶

NT: B.722c; CB.–; K.–.
OT: –.
GEN. REF.: –.

BEG, BEGGAR, BEGGARLY

A. Verbs.

1. *epaiteō* [ἐπαιτέω, 1871], a strengthened form of *aiteō*, is used in Luke 16:3. ¶

NT: B.282b; CB.–; K.–.
OT: shā'al: S.7592; HR.505b.1; H.2303; BD.981b.
GEN. REF.: IS.1:451; NB.–; Z.1:509.

2. *prosaiteō* [προσαιτέω, 4319], lit., to ask besides (*pros*, towards, used intensively, and *aiteō*), to ask earnestly, to importune, continue asking, is said of the blind beggar in John 9:8. In Mark 10:46 and Luke 18:35 certain mss. have this verb; the most authentic have *prosaitēs*, a beggar, a word used in John 9:8, as well as the verb (see the R.V.). ¶

NT: B.711c; CB.–; K.–.
OT: –.
GEN. REF.: IS.1:451; NB.26; Z.1:509.

Note: "Begged" in Matt. 27:58 and Luke 23:52, R.V., "asked for," translates the verb *aiteō*; see ASK.

B. Adjective.

ptōchos [πτωχός, 4434], an adjective describing one who crouches and cowers, is used as a noun, a beggar (from *ptōssō*, to cower down or hide oneself for fear), Luke 14:13, 21 ("poor"); 16:20, 22; as an adjective, "beggarly" in Gal. 4:9, i.e., poverty-stricken, powerless to enrich, metaphorically descriptive of the religion of the Jews.

While *prosaitēs* is descriptive of a beggar, and stresses his begging, *ptōchos* stresses his poverty-stricken condition. See POOR.

NT: B.728b; CB.1268a; K.969.
OT: dal: S.1800; HR.1239b.2a; H.433a; BD.195d.
'ānī: S.6041; HR.1239b.4a; H.1652d; BD.776d.
GEN. REF.: IS.1:451; NB.26; Z.1:509.

For BEGAN see BEGIN

BEGET, BEAR (of begetting), BORN

A. Verbs.

1. *gennaō* [γεννάω, 1080], to beget, in the Passive Voice, to be born, is chiefly used of men begetting children, Matt. 1:2-16; more rarely of women begetting children, Luke 1:13, 57, "brought forth" (for "delivered," in this ver., see No. 4); 23:29; John 16:21, "is delivered of," and of the child, "is born" (for "is in travail" see No. 4). In Gal. 4:24, it is used allegorically, to contrast Jews under bondage to the Law, and spiritual Israel, A.V., "gendereth," R.V., "bearing children," to contrast the natural birth of Ishmael and the supernatural birth of Isaac. In Matt. 1:20 it is used of conception, "that which is conceived in her." It is used of the act of God in the Birth of Christ, Acts 13:33; Heb. 1:5; 5:5, quoted from Psalm 2:7, none of which indicates that Christ became the Son of God at His Birth.

It is used metaphorically (*a*) in the writings of the Apostle John, of the gracious act of God in conferring upon those who believe the nature and disposition of "children," imparting to them spiritual life, John 3:3, 5, 7; 1 John 2:29; 3:9; 4:7; 5:1, 4, 18; (*b*) of one who by means of preaching the Gospel becomes the human instrument in the impartation of spiritual life, 1 Cor. 4:15; Philm. 10; (*c*) in 2 Pet. 2:12, with reference to the evil men whom the Apostle is describing, the R.V. rightly has "born mere animals" (A.V., "natural brute beasts"); (*d*) in the sense of gendering strife, 2 Tim. 2:23. See A, No. 3, BRING, CONCEIVE, DELIVER, GENDER, SPRING.

NT: B.155b; CB.1248a; K.114.
OT: yālad: S.3205; HR.237b.6c; H.867; BD.408a.
GEN. REF.: IS.1:451; NB.–; Z.1:510.

2. *anagennaō* [ἀναγεννάω, 313], *ana*, again, or from above, with No. 1, is found in 1 Pet. 1:3, 23. ¶
NT: B.51c; CB.1235a; K.—.
OT: —.
GEN. REF.: IS.1:451; NB.—; Z.1:510.

Note: In John 3:3, 5, 7, the adverb *anōthen*, anew, or from above, accompanies the simple verb *gennaō*. See ABOVE.

3. *apokueō* [ἀποκυέω, 616], to give birth to, to bring forth (from *kueō*, to be pregnant), is used metaphorically of spiritual birth by means of the Word of God, Jas. 1:18, and of death as the offspring of sin (ver. 15; so in the best texts). See BRING, A, No. 30. ¶
NT: B.94a; CB.1237a; K.—.
OT: —.
GEN. REF.: IS.1:451; NB.—; Z.1:510.

4. *tiktō* [τίκτω, 5088], to bring forth, Luke 1:57; John 16:21; Heb. 11:11; Rev. 12:2, 4, or, to be born, said of the Child, Matt. 2:2; Luke 2:11, is used metaphorically in Jas. 1:15, of lust as bringing forth sin. See *apokueō* above, used in the same verse. See BRING, DELIVER, TRAVAIL (be in).
NT: B.816d; CB.1272c; K.—.
OT: yālad: S.3205; HR.1351c.2a; H.867; BD.408a.
GEN. REF.: IS.1:451; NB.—; Z.1:510.

B. Nouns.

1. *genos* [γένος, 1085], a generation, kind, stock, is used in the dative case, with the article, to signify "by race," in Acts 18:2 and 24, R.V., for the A.V., "born." See COUNTRYMEN, DIVERSITY, GENERATION, KIND, KINDRED, NATION, OFFSPRING, STOCK.
NT: B.156a; CB.1248b; K.117.
OT: mîn: S.4327; HR.239b.4; H.1191a; BD.568b.
'am: S.5972; HR.239b.6; H.2914; BD.766b.
GEN. REF.: IS.1:451; NB.—; Z.1:510.

2. *ektrōma* [ἔκτρωμα, 1626], denotes an abortion, an untimely birth; from *ektitrōskō*, to miscarry. In 1 Cor. 15:8 the Apostle likens himself to "one born out of due time;" i.e., in point of time, inferior to the rest of the Apostles, as an immature birth comes short of a mature one. ¶
NT: B.246c; CB.1244a; K.220.
OT: mût: S.4191; HR.444b.1; H.1169; BD.559b.
nēphel: S.5309; HR.444b.2; H.1392a; BD.658b.
GEN. REF.: IS.1:451; NB.—; Z.1:510.

C. Adjectives.

1. *gennētos* [γεννητός, 1084], born (related to *gennaō*, verb No. 1), is used in Matt. 11:11 and Luke 7:28 in the phrase "born of women," a periphrasis for "men," and suggestive of frailty. ¶
NT: B.156a; CB.—; K.114.
OT: yālad: S.3205; HR.239b.1; H.867; BD.408a.
GEN. REF.: IS.1:451; NB.—; Z.1:510.

2. *artigennētos* [ἀρτιγέννητος, 738], newborn (*arti*, newly, recently, and No. 1), is used in 1 Pet. 2:2. ¶
NT: B.110c; CB.—; K.114.
OT: —.
GEN. REF.: IS.1:451; NB.—; Z.1:510.

Notes: (1) For *prōtotokos* see FIRSTBORN. (2) For *monogenēs*, see ONLY BEGOTTEN.

For **BEGGAR** see **BEG**

BEGIN, BEGINNING, BEGINNER

A. Verbs.

1. *archomai* [ἄρχομαι, 756], denotes to begin. In Luke 3:23 the present participle is used in a condensed expression, lit., 'And Jesus Himself was beginning about thirty years.' Some verb is to be supplied in English. The R.V. has "when He began to teach, was about thirty years of age." The meaning seems to be that He was about thirty years when He began His public career (cp. Acts 1:1). The A.V. has "began to be about thirty years of age." In Acts 11:4 the R.V. suitably has "began, and expounded," instead of "from the beginning." See B, No. 1, below, and REIGN, RULE.
NT: B.113c; CB.—; K.114.
OT: ḥālal: S.2490; HR.163a.3; H.660, 661; BD.320a
GEN. REF.: IS.1:451; NB.—; Z.1:510.

2. *enarchomai* [ἐνάρχομαι, 1728], lit., to begin in (*en*, in, with No. 1), is used in Gal. 3:3 ("having begun in the Spirit"), to refer to the time of conversion; similarly in Phil. 1:6, "He which began a good work in you." The *en* may be taken in its literal sense in these places. ¶
NT: B.262b; CB.—; K.—.
OT: ḥālal: S.2490; HR.469a.1; H.660, 661; BD.320a.
bāri'shôn: S.7223; HR.469a.3; H.2097c; BD.911c.
GEN. REF.: IS.1:451; NB.—; Z.1:510.

3. *proenarchomai* [προενάρχομαι, 4278], lit., to begin in before (*pro*, with No. 2), is used in 2 Cor. 8:6, "he had made a beginning before;" and in ver. 10, "were the first to make a beginning" (R.V.). ¶
NT: B.705a; CB.—; K.—.
OT: —.
GEN. REF.: IS.1:451; NB.—; Z.1:510.

4. *mellō* [μέλλω, 3195], to be about to, is rendered "begin" in the A.V. of Rev. 10:7; R.V. suitably, "when he is about to sound." See COME, INTEND, MEAN, MIND, READY, SHALL, SHOULD, TARRY, WILL, WOULD.
NT: B.500d; CB.1258a; K.—.
OT: —.
GEN. REF.: IS.1:451; NB.—; Z.1:510.

Note: For "began to wax" in 1 Tim. 5:11, see WANTON, B, No. 2.

B. Noun.

archē [ἀρχή, 746], means a beginning. The root *arch* — primarily indicated what was of worth. hence the verb *archō* meant 'to be first,' and *archōn* denoted a ruler. So also arose the idea of a beginning, the origin, the active cause, whether a person or thing, e.g., Col. 1:18.

In Heb. 2:3 the phrase "having at the first been spoken" is, lit., 'having received a beginning to be spoken.' In 2 Thess. 2:13 ("God chose you from the beginning"), there is a well supported alternative reading, "chose you as first-fruits" (i.e., *aparchēn*, instead of *ap' archēs*). In Heb. 6:1, where the word is rendered "first principles," the original has 'let us leave the word of the beginning of Christ,' i.e., the doctrine of the elementary principles relating to Christ.

In John 8:25, Christ's reply to the question "Who art Thou?," "Even that which I have spoken unto you from the beginning," does not mean that He had told them before; He declares that He is consistently the unchanging expression of His own teaching and testimony from the first, the immutable embodiment of His doctrine. See CORNER, FIRST, MAGISTRATE, POWER, PRINCIPALITY, RULE.

NT: B.111d; CB.1237b; K.81.
OT: rō'sh: S.7218; HR.164a.20a; H.2097; BD.910c.
rēshît: S.7225; HR.164a.20c; H.2097e; BD.912a.
tᵉhillāh: S.8462; HR.164a.23; H.661d; BD.321a.
GEN. REF.: IS.1:451; NB.—; Z.1:510.

Note: In the following passages the A.V. faulty translations, "since the world began" etc. are rightly rendered in the R.V. by "before times eternal" and similar phrases, Rom. 16:25; Eph. 3:9; 2 Tim. 1:9; Tit. 1:2. The alteration has not been made, however, in Luke 1:70; John 9:32: Acts 3:21; 15:18.

C. Adverb.

prōton [πρῶτον, 4412], the neuter of *prōtos* (the superlative degree of *proteros*), first, at the first, is rendered "at the beginning" in John 2:10, A.V., R.V., "setteth on first." See BEFORE.

NT: B.725b; CB.1267b; K.965.
OT: —.
GEN. REF.: IS.1:451; NB.—; Z.1:510.

For **BEGOTTEN** see **BEGET**

BEGUILE

1. *apataō* [ἀπατάω, 538], to deceive, is rendered "beguiled" in the R.V. of 1 Tim. 2:14. See No. 2.

NT: B.81d; CB.1236b; K.805.
OT: pātāh: S.6601; HR.119b.3c; H.1853; BD.834c.
sût: S.5496; HR.119b.2; H.1481; BD.694d.
GEN. REF.: IS.1:451; NB.—; Z.1:510.

2. *exapataō* [ἐξαπατάω, 1818], a strengthened form of No. 1, is rendered "beguile," 2 Cor. 11:3; the more adequate rendering would be 'as the serpent thoroughly beguiled Eve.' So in 1 Tim. 2:14, in the best mss., this stronger form is used of Satan's deception of Eve, lit., 'thoroughly beguiled;' the simpler verb, No. 1, is used of Adam. In each of these passages the strengthened form is used. So of the influence of sin, Rom. 7:11 (R.V., "beguile"); of self-deception, 1 Cor. 3:18 (R.V., "deceive"); of evil men, who cause divisions, Rom. 16:18 (R.V., "beguile"); of deceitful teachers, 2 Thess. 2:3 (R.V., "beguile"). See DECEIVE ¶ In the Sept., Ex. 8:29. ¶

NT: B.273a; CB.1247c; K.65.
OT: tālal: S.—; HR.488a.1; H.—; BD.1068c.
GEN. REF.: IS.1:451; NB.—; Z.1:510.

3. *paralogizomai* [παραλογίζομαι, 3884], lit. and primarily, to reckon wrong, hence means to reason falsely (*para*, from, amiss, *logizomai*, to reason) or to deceive by false reasoning; translated "delude" in Col. 2:4, R.V. (A.V., "beguile") and Jas. 1:22 (A.V., "deceive"). See DECEIVE, DELUDE ¶

NT: B.620a; CB.1262a; K.—.
OT: rāmāh: S.7411; HR.1062a.2; H.2168, 2169; BD.941a.
tālal: S.—; HR.1062a.3; H.—; BD.1068c.
GEN. REF.: 1:451; NB.—; Z.1:510.

4. *deleazō* [δελεάζω, 1185], originally meant to catch by a bait (from *delear*, a bait);. hence to beguile, entice by blandishments: in Jas. 1:14, "entice;" in 2 Pet. 2:14, A.V., "beguile;" in ver. 18, A.V., "allure;" R.V., "entice" in both. See ENTICE. ¶

NT: B.174b; CB.—; K.—.
OT: —.
GEN. REF.: IS.1:451; NB.—; Z.1:510.

Note: In Col. 2:18, the verb *katabrabeuō*, to give judgment against, condemn, is translated "beguile . . . of your reward," A.V.; R.V., "rob . . . of your prize." The verb was used of an umpire's decision against a racer; hence the translations (or paraphrases) in the Eng. Versions. See ROB.

BEHALF

1. *meros* [μέρος, 3313], a part, is translated "behalf" in the A.V. of 2 Cor. 9:3 (R.V., "respect") and 1 Pet. 4:16; here the most authentic texts have *onoma*, a name; hence R.V., "in this name." See COAST, CRAFT, PART, PIECE, PORTION, RESPECT, SORT.

NT: B.505d; CB.1258b; K.585.
OT: qāṣeh: S.7097; HR.911c.16a; H.2053a, c; BD.892a.
GEN. REF.: —.

2. *huper* [ὑπέρ, 5228], on behalf of, is to be distinguished from *anti*, instead of. See Note †, p. 1.

NT: B.838b; CB.1252a; K.1228.
GEN. REF.: —.

BEHAVE, BEHAVIOUR

A. Verbs

1. *anastrephō* [ἀναστρέφω, 390], to turn back, return (*ana*, back, *strephō*, to turn), hence, to move about in a place, to sojourn, and, in the Middle and Passive Voices, to conduct oneself, indicating one's manner of life and character, is accordingly rendered "behave" in 1 Tim. 3:15, lit., 'how it is necessary to behave,' not referring merely to Timothy himself, but to all the members of the local church (see the whole Epistle); in Eph. 2:3, A.V., "we had our conversation," R.V., "we lived;" in 2 Cor. 1:12 "behaved ourselves," for A.V. "have had our conversation." See ABIDE, etc.

NT: B.61b; CB.1235b; K.1093.
OT: shûb: S. 7725; HR.82b.8a; H.2340; BD.996d.
GEN. REF.: IS.1:452; NB.–; Z.–.

2. *ginomai* [γίνομαι, 1096], to become, is rendered "behave" in 1 Thess. 2:10; lit., 'we became among you' (cp. 1:5).

NT: B.158a; CB.1248b; K.117.
OT: –.
GEN. REF.: IS.1:452; NB.–; Z.–.

3. *atakteō* [ἀτακτέω, 812], lit., to be disorderly (*a*, negative, and *taxis*, order), to lead a disorderly life, is rendered "behave disorderly" in 2 Thess. 3:7. ¶ Cp. *ataktos*, disorderly, unruly, and *ataktōs*, disorderly.

NT: B.–; CB.–; K.1156.
OT: –.
GEN. REF.: IS.1:452; NB.–; Z.–.

4. *aschemoneō* [ἀσχημονέω, 807], to be unseemly (*a*, negative, and *schēma*, a form), is used in 1 Cor. 7:36, "behave (himself) unseemly," i.e., so as to run the risk of bringing the virgin daughter into danger or disgrace, and in 13:5, "doth (not) behave itself unseemly." ¶

NT: B.119b; CB.–; K.–.
OT: qālāh: S.7034; HR.174c.2; H.2024; BD.885d.
GEN. REF.: IS.1:452; NB.–; Z.–.

B. Nouns.

1. *anastrophē* [ἀναστροφή, 390], lit., a turning back (cp. No. 1, above), is translated "manner of life," "living," etc. in the R.V., for A.V., "conversation," Gal. 1:13; Eph. 4:22; 1 Tim. 4:12; Heb. 13:7; Jas. 3:13; 1 Pet. 1:15, 18; 2:12 ("behaviour"); 3:1, 2, 16 (ditto); 2 Pet. 2:7; 3:11. See CONVERSATION, LIFE. ¶

NT: B.61c; CB.1235b; K.1093.
OT: –.
GEN. REF.: IS.1:452; NB.–; Z.–.

2. *katastēma* [κατάστημα, 2688], akin to *kathistēmi* (see APPOINT, No. 2), denotes a condition, or constitution of anything, or deportment, Tit. 2:3, "demeanour," R.V., for A.V., "behaviour." See DEMEANOUR. ¶

NT: B.419a; CB.–; K.–.
OT: –.
GEN. REF.: IS.1:452; NB.–; Z.–.

C. Adjective.

kosmios [κόσμιος, 2887], orderly, modest, is translated "orderly" in 1 Tim. 3:2, R.V., for A.V., "of good behaviour." Both have "modest" in 1 Tim. 2:9. Cp. *kosmeō*, to adorn, *kosmos*, adornment. ¶

NT: B.445c; CB.1255c; K.459.
OT: –.
GEN. REF.: IS.1:452; NB.–; Z.–.

BEHEAD

1. *apokephalizō* [ἀποκεφαλιζω, 607], *apo*, from, off, *kephalē*, a head, is found in Matt. 14:10; Mark 6:16, 27; Luke 9:9. ¶

NT: B.93a; CB.–; K.–.
OT: –.
GEN. REF.: IS.3:1051;; NB.–; Z.1:1030.

2. *pelekizō* [πελεκίζω, 3990], denotes, to cut with an axe (from *pelekus*, an axe), Rev. 20:4. ¶

NT: B.641c; CB.–; K.–.
OT: –.
GEN. REF.: IS.3:1051; NB.–; Z.1:1030.

BEHIND, COME BEHIND

A. Adverbs.

1. *opisthen* [ὄπισθεν, 3693], behind, is used only of place, e.g., Matt. 9:20; Mark 5:27; Luke 8:44; Rev. 4:6; as a preposition, Matt. 15:23 ("after"), and Luke 23:26; in Rev. 5:1, R.V., "on the back"; A.V., "backside." See BACK. ¶

NT: B.574d; CB.1261a; K.702.
OT: 'aḥar: S.310; HR.1001b.1a; H.68b; BD.29d.
GEN. REF.: –.

2. *opisō* [ὀπίσω, 3694], after (see BACK, adverb).

NT: B.575a; CB.1261a; K.702.
OT: 'aḥar: S.310; HR.1001c.1a; H.68b; BD.29d.
GEN. REF.: –.

B. Verbs.

1. *hustereō* [ὑστερέω, 5302], to come late, be behind, is translated "come behind," in 1 Cor. 1:7; "to be behind," 2 Cor. 11:5 and 12:11. See COME, No. 39, DESTITUTE, FAIL, LACK, NEED, B, *Note*, WANT, WORSE.

NT: B.849a; CB.1252b; K.1240.
OT: ḥāsēr: S.2637; HR.1418b.1; H.705a; BD.341a.
gāra': S.1639; HR.1418b.3; H.384; BD.175c.
GEN. REF.: –.

2. *hupomenō* [ὑπομένω, 5278], to abide, endure, is once rendered "tarry behind," Luke 2:43. See ABIDE.

NT: B.845d; CB.1252b; K.581.
OT: yāḥal: S.3176; HR.1415c.4; H.859; BD.403d.
kāwāh: S.6960; HR.1415c.8; H.1994, 1995; BD.875c.
GEN. REF.: –.

Note: In 1 Thess. 3:1, the R.V. "left behind" adequately expresses the verb *kataleipō*.

C. Noun.

husterēma [ὑστέρημα, 5303], akin to B.1, denotes that which is lacking, 1 Cor. 16:17; Phil. 2:30; Col. 1:24 (A.V., "that which is behind of the afflictions of Christ"), R.V., "that which is lacking"; 1 Thess. 3:10. For the other meaning, "want", see LACK, PENURY, WANT.

NT: B.849d; CB.1252b; K.1240.
OT: maḥsôr: S.4270, HR.1418c.1b; H.705e; BD.341d.
hesrôn: S.2642; HR.1418c.1a; H.705d; BD.341c.
GEN. REF.: –.

BEHOLD, BEHELD

1. *horaō* [ὁράω, 3708], with its aorist form *eidon*, to see (in a few places the A.V. uses the verb to behold), is said (*a*) of bodily vision, e.g., Mark 6:38; John 1:18, 46; (*b*) of mental perception, e.g., Rom. 15:21; Col. 2:18; (*c*) of taking heed, e.g., Matt. 8:4; 1 Thess. 5:15; (*d*) of experience, as of death, Luke 2:26; Heb. 11:5; life, John 3:36; corruption, Acts 2:27; (*e*) of caring for, Matt. 27:4; Acts 18:15 (here the form *opsomai* is used). See APPEAR, HEED, LOOK, PERCEIVE, SEE, SHEW.

NT: B.–; CB.1251a; K.706.
OT: rā'āh: S.7200; HR.1005a.8ab; H.2095; BD.906b.
GEN. REF.: IS.1:452; NB.–; Z.–.

2. *blepō* [βλέπω, 991], is also used of (*a*) bodily and (*b*) mental vision, (*a*) to perceive, e.g., Matt. 13:13; (*b*) to take heed, e.g., Mark 13:23, 33; it indicates greater vividness than *horaō*, expressing a more intent, earnest contemplation; in Luke 6:41, of beholding the mote in a brother's eye; Luke 24:12, of beholding the linen clothes in the empty tomb; Acts 1:9, of the gaze of the disciples when the Lord ascended. The greater earnestness is sometimes brought out by the rendering "regardest", Matt. 22:16. See BEWARE, HEED, LIE, LOOK, PERCEIVE, REGARD, SEE, SIGHT.

NT: B.143b; CB.1239a; K.706.
OT: rā'āh: S.7200; HR.221a.10a; H.2095; BD.906b.
pānāh: S.6437; HR.221a.7; H.1782; BD.815a.
pāneh: S.6440; HR.221a.8; H.1782a; BD.815d.
GEN. REF.: IS.1:452; NB.–; Z.–.

3. *emblepō* [ἐμβλέπω, 1689], from *en*, in (intensive), and No. 2, (not to be rendered literally), expresses earnest looking, e.g., in the Lord's command to behold the birds of the heaven, with the object of learning lessons of faith from them, Matt. 6:26. See also 19:26; Mark 8:25; 10:21, 27; 14:67; Luke 20:17; 22:61; John 1:36; of the Lord's looking upon Peter, John 1:42; Acts 1:11; 22:11. See GAZE, LOOK, SEE. ¶

NT: B.254c; CB.1244b; K.–.
OT: nābat: S.5027; HR.455c.1b; H.1282; BD.613c.
pānāh: S.6437; HR.455c.2; H.1782; BD.815a.
rā'āh: S.7200; HR.455c.3a,b; H.2095; BD.906b.
GEN. REF.: IS.1:452; NB.–; Z.–.

4. *ide* and *idou* [ἴδε and ἰδού, 2396, 2400], are Imperative Moods, Active and Middle Voices, respectively, of *eidon*, to see, calling attention to what may be seen or heard or mentally apprehended in any way. These are regularly rendered "behold". See especially the Gospels, Acts and the Apocalypse. See LO, SEE.

NT: B.370d; CB.1252c; K.–.
OT: hinnēh: S.2009, HR.673c.7b; H.510a; BD.243d.
GEN. REF.: –.

5. *epide* [ἔπιδε, 1896], a strengthened form of No. 4 (with *epi*, upon, prefixed), is used in Acts 4:29 of the entreaty made to the Lord to behold the threatenings of persecutors. ¶

NT: B.284b; CB.–; K.–.
OT: –.
GEN. REF.: –.

6. *theōreō* [θεωρέω, 2334], from *theōros*, a spectator, is used of one who looks at a thing with interest and for a purpose, usually indicating the careful observation of details; this marks the distinction from No. 2; see, e.g., Mark 15:47; Luke 10:18; 23:35; John 20:6 (R.V., "beholdeth", for A.V., "seeth"; so in verses 12 and 14; "consider", in Heb. 7:4. It is used of experience, in the sense of partaking of, in John 8:51; 17:24. See CONSIDER, LOOK, PERCEIVE, SEE. CP. *theōria*, sight, Luke 23:48, only.

NT: B.360a; CB.1272a; K.706.
OT: ḥāzāh: S.2372; HR.649b.2; H.633; BD.302b.
rā'āh: S.7200; HR.649b.4; H.2095; BD.906b.
GEN. REF.: –.

7. *anatheōreō* [ἀναθεωρέω, 333], *ana*, up (intensive), and No. 6, to view with interest, consider contemplatively, is translated "beheld", in Acts 17:23, R.V., "observed"; "Considering" in Heb. 13:7. See CONSIDER. ¶

NT: B.54c; CB.–; K.–.
OT: –.
GEN. REF.: –.

8. *theaomai* [θεάομαι, 2300], to behold, view attentively, contemplate, had, in earlier Greek usage, the sense of a wondering regard. This idea was gradually lost. It signifies a more earnest contemplation than the ordinary verbs for to see, "a careful and deliberate vision which interprets . . . its object," and is more frequently rendered "behold" in the R.V. than the A.V. Both translate it by "behold" in Luke 23:55 (of the sepulchre); "we beheld", in John 1:14, of the glory of the Son of God; "Beheld," R.V., in John 1:32; Acts 1:11; 1 John 1:1 (more than merely seeing); 4:12, 14. See LOOK, SEE.

NT: B.353a; CB.1271c; K.706.
OT: rā'āh: S.7200; HR.627c.1; H.2095; BD.906b.
GEN. REF.: –.

9. *epopteuō* [ἐποπτεύω, 2029], from *epi*, upon, and a form of *horaō*, to see, is used of witnessing as a spectator, or overseer, 1 Pet. 2:12; 3:2. ¶

NT: B.305c; CB.1246b; K.706.
OT: —.
GEN. REF.: —.

Note: The corresponding noun *epoptēs*, an eye-witness, found in 2 Pet. 1:16, was used by the Greeks of those who had attained to the highest grade of certain mysteries, and the word is perhaps purposely used here of those who were at the transfiguration of Christ. See EYE-WITNESS. ¶

10. *atenizō* [ἀτενίζω, 816], from *atenēs*, strained, intent, denotes to gaze upon, "beholding earnestly", or "steadfastly" in Acts 14:9; 23:1. See FASTEN, LOOK, SET, B, *Note* (5).

NT: B.119d; CB.1238a; K.—.
OT: —.
GEN. REF.: —.

11. *katanoeō* [κατανοέω, 2657], a strengthened form of *noeō*, to perceive, (*kata*, intensive), denotes the action of the mind in apprehending certain facts about a thing; hence, to consider; "behold", Acts 7:31, 32; Jas. 1:23, 24. See CONSIDER, DISCOVER, PERCEIVE.

NT: B.415a; CB.1254a; K.636.
OT: nābat: S.5027; HR.739c.3; H.1282; BD.613c.
rā'āh: S.7200; HR.739c.5; H.2095; BD.906b.
GEN. REF.: —.

12. *katoptrizō* [κατοπτρίζω, 2734], from *katoptron*, a mirror (*kata*, down, ōps, an eye or sight), in the Active Voice, signifies to make to reflect, to mirror; in the Middle Voice, to reflect as a mirror; so the R.V. in 2 Cor. 3:18, for A.V., "beholding as in a glass". The whole context in the 3rd chapter and the first part of the 4th bears out the R.V. ¶

NT: B.424d; CB.1254c; K.264.
OT: —.
GEN. REF.: IS.1:452; NB.—; Z.—.

Note: For *epeidon* (from *ephoraō*), Acts 4:29, see LOOK, No. 9. For *prooraō*, Acts 2:25, R.V., "behold", see FORESEE.

BEHOVE

1. *opheilō* [ὀφείλω, 3784], to owe, is once rendered "behove", Heb. 2:17; it indicates a necessity, owing to the nature of the matter under consideration; in this instance, the fulfilment of the justice and love of God, voluntarily exhibited in what Christ accomplished, that He might be a merciful and faithful High Priest. See BOUND, DEBT, DUE, DUTY, GUILTY, INDEBTED, MUST, NEED, OUGHT, OWE.

NT: B.598d; CB.1261a; K.746.
OT: ḥôb: S.2326; HR.1039a.2; H.614a; BD.295a.
GEN. REF.: —.

2. *dei* [δεῖ, 1163], "it is necessary", is rendered "behoved", in Luke 24:46; R.V., (that the Christ) "should" (suffer). *Dei* expresses a logical necessity, *opheilō*, a moral obligation; cp. *chrē*, Jas. 3:10, "ought", which expresses a need resulting from the fitness of things (Trench, § cvii). See MEET, MUST, NEED, OUGHT.

NT: B.172a; CB.1240b; K.140.
OT: —.
GEN. REF.: —.

BEING

When not part of another verb (usually the participle), or part of a phrase, this word translates one of the following:—

(*a*) the present participle of *eimi*, to be, the verb of ordinary existence;

(*b*) the participle of *ginomai*, to become, signifying origin or result;

(*c*) the present participle of *huparchō*, to exist, which always involves a pre-existent state, prior to the fact referred to, and a continuance of the state after the fact. Thus in Phil. 2:6, the phrase "who being (*huparchōn*) in the form of God", implies His pre-existent Deity, previous to His Birth, and His continued Deity afterwards.

In Acts 17:28 the phrase "we have our being" represents the present tense of the verb to be, "we are".

BELIAL

belial [βελίαλ, or βελίαρ, 955], is a word frequently used in the Old Testament, with various meanings, especially in the books of Samuel, where it is found nine times. See also Deut. 13:13; Judg. 19:22; 20:13; 1 Kings 21:10, 13; 2 Chron. 13:7. Its original meaning was either worthlessness or hopeless ruin (see the R.V., margin). It also had the meanings of extreme wickedness and destruction, the latter indicating the destiny of the former. In the period between the O.T. and the N.T. it came to be a proper name for Satan. There may be an indication of this in Nahum 1:15, where the word translated "the wicked one" is Belial.

The oldest form of the word is Beliar, possibly from a phrase signifying "Lord of the forest", or perhaps simply a corruption of the form Belial, due to harsh Syriac pronunciation. In the N.T., in 2 Cor. 6:15, it is set in contrast to Christ, and represents a personification of the system of impure worship connected especially with the cult of Aphrodite. ¶

NT: B.139a; CB.1239a; K.104.
OT: —.
GEN. REF.: IS.1:454; NB.138; Z.1:512.

BELIEF, BELIEVE, BELIEVERS

A. Verbs.

1. *pisteuō* [πιστεύω, 4100], to believe, also to be persuaded of, and hence, to place confidence in, to trust, signifies, in this sense of the word, reliance upon, not mere credence. It is most frequent in the writings of the Apostle John, especially the Gospel. He does not use the noun (see below). For the Lord's first use of the verb, see 1:50. Of the writers of the Gospels, Matthew uses the verb ten times, Mark ten, Luke nine, John ninety-nine. In Acts 5:14 the present participle of the verb is translated "believers". See COMMIT, INTRUST, TRUST.

NT: B.660b; CB.1265a; K.849.
OT: 'āman: S.539; HR.1137c.1b; H.116; BD.52d.
GEN. REF.: IS.2:270; NB.410ff; Z.2:479.

2. *peithō* [πείθω, 3982], to persuade, in the Middle and Passive voices signifies to suffer oneself to be persuaded, e.g., Luke 16:31; Heb. 13:18; it is sometimes translated "believe" in the R.V., but not in Acts 17:4, R.V., "were persuaded"; and 27:11, "gave (more) heed"; in Acts 28:24, "believed". See AGREE, ASSURE, OBEY, PERSUADE, TRUST, YIELD.

NT: B.639a; CB.1263a; K.818.
OT: bāṭaḥ: S.982; HR.1114b.2a; H.233; BD.105a.
GEN. REF.: IS.2:270; NB.410ff; Z.2:479.

Note: For *apisteō*, the negative of No. 1, and *apeitheō*, the negative of No. 2, see DISBELIEVE, DISOBEDIENT.

B. Noun.

pistis [πίστις, 4102], faith, is translated "belief" in Rom. 10:17; 2 Thess. 2:13. Its chief significance is a conviction respecting God and His Word and the believer's relationship to Him. See ASSURANCE, FAITH, FIDELITY.

NT: B.662b; CB.1265a; K.849.
OT: 'ēmûn: S.529; HR.1138b.1a; H.116d; BD.53c.
'ĕmûnāh: S.530; HR.1138b.1b; H.116e; BD.53c.
GEN. REF.: IS.2:270; NB.410ff; Z.2:479.

Note: In 1 Cor. 9:5 the word translated "believer" (R.V.), is *adelphē*, a sister, so 7:15; Rom. 16:1; Jas. 2:15, used, in the spiritual sense, of one connected by the tie of the Christian faith.

C. Adjective.

pistos [πιστός, 4103], (*a*) in the Active sense means believing, trusting; (*b*) in the Passive sense, trusty, faithful, trustworthy. It is translated "believer" in 2 Cor. 6:15; "them that believe" in 1 Tim. 4:12, R.V. (A.V., "believers"); in 1 Tim. 5:16, "if any woman that believeth", lit., 'if any believing woman'. So in 6:2, "believing masters". In 1 Pet. 1:21 the R.V., following the most authentic mss., gives the noun form, "are believers in God" (A.V., "do believe in God"). In John 20:27 it is translated "believing". It is best understood with significance (*a*), above, e.g., in Gal. 3:9; Acts 16:1; 2 Cor. 6:15; Tit. 1:6; it has significance (*b*), e.g., in 1 Thess. 5:24; 2 Thess. 3:3 (see Notes on Thess. p. 211, and Gal. p. 126, by Hogg and Vine). See FAITHFUL, SURE.

NT: B.664c; CB.1265a; K.849.
OT: 'āman: S.539; HR.1138c.1a; H.116; BD.52d.
GEN. REF.: IS.2:270; NB.410ff; Z.2:479.

Notes: (1) The corresponding negative verb is *apisteō*, 2 Tim. 2:13, A.V., "believe not" R.V., "are faithless", in contrast to the statement "He abideth faithful".

(2) The negative noun *apistia*, "unbelief", is used twice in Matthew (13:58; 17:20), three times in Mark (6:6; 9:24; 16:14), four times in Romans (3:3; 4:20; 11:20, 23); elsewhere in 1 Tim. 1:13 and Heb. 3:12, 19. ¶

(3) The adjective *apistos* is translated "unbelievers" in 1 Cor. 6:6, and 2 Cor. 6:14; in ver. 15, R.V., "unbeliever" (A.V., "infidel"); so in 1 Tim. 5:8; "unbelieving" in 1 Cor. 7:12, 13, 14, 15; 14:22, 23, 24; 2 Cor. 4:4; Tit. 1:15; Rev. 21:8; "that believe not" in 1 Cor. 10:27. In the Gospels it is translated "faithless" in Matt. 17:17; Mark 9:19; Luke 9:41; John 20:27, but in Luke 12:46, R.V., "unfaithful", A.V., "unbelievers". Once it is translated "incredible", Acts 26:8. See FAITHLESS, INCREDIBLE, UNBELIEVER. ¶

(4) *Plērophoreō*, in Luke 1:1 (A.V., "are most surely believed", lit., have had full course), the R.V. renders "have been fulfilled". See FULFIL, KNOW, PERSUADE, PROOF.

BELLY

1. *koilia* [κοιλία, 2836], from *koilos*, hollow (Lat., *coelum*, heaven, is connected), denotes the entire physical cavity, but most frequently was used to denote the womb. In John 7:38 it stands metaphorically for the innermost part of man, the soul, the heart. See WOMB.

NT: B.437b; CB.1255b; K.446.
OT: —.
GEN. REF.: IS.1:455; NB.—; Z.1:514.

2. *gastēr* [γαστήρ, 1064], (cp. Eng., gastritis), is used much as No. 1, but in Tit. 1:12, by synecdoche (a figure of speech in which the part is put for the whole, or vice versa), it is used to denote "gluttons", R.V., for A.V., "bellies". See GLUTTON, WOMB.

NT: B.152c; CB.—; K.—.
OT: beten: S.990; HR.234b.1; H.236a; BD.105d.
hārāh: S.2029; HR.234b.2; H.515; BD.247c.
GEN. REF.: IS.1:455; NB.—; Z.1:514.

BELONG

Note: This word represents (*a*) a phrase consisting of *eimi*, to be, with or without a preposition and a noun, and usually best rendered, as in the R.V., by the verb to be, Mark 9:41, lit., 'ye are of Christ'; Luke 23:7 and Heb. 5:14; cp. Rom. 12:19, "belongeth unto Me", R.V.; (*b*) a phrase consisting of the neuter plural of the definite article, either with the preposition *pros*, unto, as in Luke 19:42, where the phrase "the things which belong unto peace" (R.V.) is, lit., 'the (things) unto peace', or with the genitive case of the noun, as in 1 Cor. 7:32, A.V., "the things that belong to the Lord"; R.V., suitably, "the things of the Lord"; (*c*) a distinct verb, e.g., *metechō*, to partake of, share in, Heb. 7:13 R.V., "belongeth to (another tribe)", A.V., "pertaineth to".

BELOVED

A. Adjective.

agapētos [ἀγαπητός, 27], from *agapaō*, to love, is used of Christ as loved by God, e.g., Matt. 3:17; of believers (ditto), e.g., Rom. 1:7; of believers, one of another, 1 Cor. 4:14; often, as a form of address, e.g., 1 Cor. 10:14. Wherever the A.V. has "dearly beloved", the R.V. has "beloved"; so, "well beloved" in 3 John 1; in 1 John 2:7, A.V., "brethren" (*adelphos*), the R.V. has "beloved", according to the mss. which have *agapētos*. See DEAR.

NT: B.6b; CB.1233b; K.5.
OT: yādîd: S.3039; HR.7a.2; H.846a; BD.391d.
yaḥîd: S.3173; HR.7a.3; H.858a; BD.402d.
GEN. REF.: IS.1:455; NB.752; Z.1:514.

B. Verb.

agapaō [ἀγαπάω, 25], in its perfect participle Passive form, is translated "beloved" in Rom. 9:25; Eph. 1:6; Col. 3:12; 1 Thess. 1:4; 2 Thess. 2:13. In Jude 1 the best texts have this verb (R.V.); the A.V., "sanctified" follows those which have *hagiazō*. See LOVE.

NT: B.4b; CB.1233b; K.5.
OT: 'āhēb: S.157; HR.5b.1a; H.29; BD.12c.
GEN. REF.: IS.1:455; NB.752; Z.1:514.

Note: In Luke 9:35, the R.V., translating from the most authentic mss., has "My chosen" (*eklegō*), for A.V., "beloved" (*agapētos*); so in Philm. 2, "sister" (*adelphē*).

BENEATH

katō [κάτω, 2736], signifies (*a*) down, downwards, Matt. 4:6; Luke 4:9; John 8:6, 8; Acts 20:9; (*b*) below, beneath, of place, Mark 14:66; the realms that lie below in contrast to heaven, John 8:23; the earth, as contrasted with the heavens, Acts 2:19; with *heōs*, unto, Matt. 27:51; Mark 15:38. The comparative degree, *katōterō*, under, is used in Matt. 2:16. See BOTTOM, UNDER. ¶

NT: B.425a; CB.1254c; K.422.
OT: mittaḥat: S.8478; HR.756c.2a; H.2504; BD.1065b.
maṭṭāh: S.4294; HR.756c.1a; H.1352b; BD.641b.
lᵉmaṭṭāh: S.4294; HR.756c.1b; H.1352b; BD.641b.
GEN. REF.: –.

BENEFIT, BENEFACTOR

1. *euergesia* [εὐεργεσία, 2108], lit., 'good work (*eu*, well, *ergon*, work)', is found in Acts 4:9, "good deed", and 1 Tim. 6:2, "benefit". ¶

NT: B.319d; CB.1247a; K.251.
OT: 'ălîlāh: S.5949; HR.569c.1; H.1627c; BD.760a.
GEN. REF.: IS.1:457; NB.140; Z.1:518.

2. *euergetēs* [εὐεργέτης, 2110], a benefactor, expresses the agent, Luke 22:25. ¶

NT: B.320a; CB.1247a; K.251.
OT: –.
GEN. REF.: IS.1:457; NB.140; Z.1:518.

Note: Cp. *euergeteō*, to do good.

3. *charis* [χάρις, 5485], grace, is once rendered "benefit", 2 Cor. 1:15; it stresses the character of the benefit, as the effect of the gracious disposition of the benefactor. See ACCEPTABLE, FAVOUR, GRACE, LIBERALITY, PLEASURE, THANK.

NT: B.877b; CB.1239c; K.1298.
OT: ḥēn: S.2580; HR.1455a.2; H.694a; BD.336b.
GEN. REF.: IS.1:457; NB.491ff; Z.1:518.

4. *agathon* [ἀγαθόν, 18], the neuter of *agathos*, used as a noun in Philm. 14, is translated "benefit," A.V.; R.V., "goodness". See GOOD.

NT: B.2d; CB.1233b; K.3.
OT: ṭôb: S.2896; HR.2a.4b.; H793a; BD.373b.
GEN. REF.: IS.1:457; NB.481; Z.1:518.

BENEVOLENCE

eunoia [εὔνοια, 2133], good will (*eu*, well, *nous*, the mind), is rendered "benevolence" in 1 Cor. 7:3, A.V. The R.V., following the texts which have *opheilēn* ("due"), has "her due", a more comprehensive expression; in Eph. 6:7, "good will". ¶

NT: B.323b; CB.–; K.636.
OT: –.
GEN. REF.: IS.1:457; NB.–; Z.1:518.

BEREAVED, BEREFT

1. *aporphanizomai* [ἀπορφανίζομαι, 642], lit., to be rendered an orphan (*apo*, from, with the thought of separation, and *orphanos*, an orphan), is used metaphorically in 1 Thess. 2:17 (A.V., "taken from"; R.V., "bereaved"), in the sense of being bereft of the company of the saints through being compelled to leave them

(cp. the similes in 7 and 11). The word has a wider meaning than that of being an orphan. ¶
NT: B.98a; CB.–; K.–.
OT: –.
GEN. REF.: IS.1:461; NB.–; Z.–.

Note: The corresponding adjective, *orphanos*, is translated "desolate" in John 14:18 (A.V., "comfortless"); "fatherless" in Jas. 1:27; see DESOLATE, FATHERLESS. ¶

2. *apostereō* [ἀποστερέω, 650], to rob, defraud, deprive, is used in 1 Tim. 6:5, in the Passive Voice, of being deprived or "bereft" (of the truth), with reference to false teachers (A.V., "destitute"). See DEFRAUD, DESTITUTE, FRAUD.
NT: B.99a; CB.1237a; K.–.
OT: gāra': S.1639; HR.145a.1; H.384; BD.175c.
'āshaq: S.6231; HR.145a.2; H.1713; BD.798d.
GEN. REF.: IS.1:461; NB.–; Z.–.

BERYL

bērullos [βήρυλλος, 969], beryl, is a precious stone of a sea-green colour, Rev. 21:20 (cp. Ex. 28:20). ¶ See STONES (PRECIOUS).
NT: B.140b; CB.1239a; K.–.
OT: –.
GEN. REF.: IS.–; NB.631ff; Z.1:525.

BESEECH

1. *parakaleō* [παρακαλέω, 3870], the most frequent word with this meaning, lit. denotes to call to one's side, hence, to call to one's aid. It is used for every kind of calling to a person which is meant to produce a particular effect, hence, with various meanings, such as comfort, exhort, desire, call for, in addition to its significance to beseech, which has a stronger force than *aiteō* (see ASK). See, e.g., the R.V. "besought" in Mark 5:18; Acts 8:31; 19:31; 1 Cor. 16:12. See CALL, No. 6, Note (2), COMFORT, DESIRE, EXHORT, INTREAT, PRAY.
NT: B.617a; CB.1262a; K.778.
OT: nāḥam: S.5162; HR.1060a.10; H.1344; BD636d.
GEN. REF.: –.

2. *erōtaō* [ἐρωτάω, 2065], often translated by the verb to beseech, in the Gospels, is elsewhere rendered "beseech" in 1 Thess. 4:1; 5:12; 2 Thess. 2:1; 2 John 5. See under ASK, No. 2.
NT: B.311d; CB.1246c; K.262.
OT: shā'āl: S.7592; HR.553b,.3a; H.2303; BD.981b.
GEN. REF.: –.

3. *deomai* [δέομαι, 1189], to desire, to long for, usually representing the word "need"; is sometimes translated "beseech"; e.g., Luke 5:12; Acts 21:39; 2 Cor. 10:2; Gal. 4:12. It is used of prayer to God, in Matt. 9:38; Luke 10:2; 21:36; 22:32; Acts 4:31; 8:22, 24; 10:2; Rom. 1:10; 1 Thess. 3:10. See PRAY, REQUEST.
NT: B.175a; CB.1240c; K.144.
OT: –.
GEN. REF.: –.

Note: Proskuneō is wrongly rendered "besought" in the A.V. marg. of Matt. 18:26. The word signifies "to worship".

BESET

euperistatos [εὐπερίστατος, 2139], used in Heb. 12:1, and translated "which doth so easily beset"; lit. signifies 'standing well (i.e., easily) around' (*eu*, well, *peri*, around, *statos*, standing, i.e., easily encompassing). It describes sin as having advantage in favour of its prevailing. ¶
NT: B.324a; CB.–; K.–.
OT: –.
GEN. REF.: –.

BESIDE, BESIDES

1. *chōris* [χωρίς, 5565], separately, apart from, besides, is translated "beside" in Matt. 14:21; 15:38; 2 Cor. 11:28. See APART, SEPARATE, WITHOUT.
NT: B.890c; CB.1240a; K.–.
OT: –.
GEN. REF.: IS.1:462; NB.–; Z.–.

2. *loipon* [λοιπόν, 3063], is rendered "besides" in 1 Cor. 1:16. See FINALLY.
NT: B.479d; CB.1257b; K.–.
OT: –.
GEN. REF.: IS.1:462; NB.–; Z.–.

Notes: (1) *Pareiserchomai*, in Rom. 5:20 signifies to come in beside, i.e., of the Law, as coming in addition to sin committed previously apart from law, the prefix *par—* (i.e., *para*) denoting "beside" (the A.V., "entered" is inadequate); in Gal. 2:4 ("came in privily"). See COME. ¶

(2) In Philm. 19, *prosopheilō* signifies to owe in addition (*pros*, besides, amd *opheilō*, to owe); "thou owest (to me even thine own self) besides". ¶

(3) In 2 Pet. 1:5, the phrase, wrongly translated in the A.V., "beside this", means "for this very cause" (R.V.).

BESIDE ONESELF (to be)

1. *existēmi* [ἐξίστημι, 1839], primarily and lit. means to put out of position, displace; hence, (*a*) to amaze, Luke 24:22 (for A.V., "make . . . astonished"); Acts 8:9, 11 (A.V., "bewitched"); or to be amazed, astounded, Matt. 12:23; Mark 6:51; (*b*) to be out of one's mind, to be beside oneself, Mark 3:21; 2 Cor. 5:13, in the latter of which it is contrasted with *sōphroneō*, to be of a sound mind, sober. See AMAZE.
NT: B.276b; CB.1247c; K.217.
OT: ḥārēd: S.2730; HR.496c.5; H.735a; BD.353b.
shāmēm: S.8074; HR.496c.28; H.2409; BD.1030d.
tāmāh: S.8539; HR.496c.29; H.2218; BD.1069b.
GEN. REF.: –.

2. *mainomai* [μαίνομαι, 3105], to be mad, to rave, is said of one who so speaks that he appears to be out of his mind, Acts 26:24, translated "thou art beside thyself", A.V.; R.V., "thou art mad". In ver. 25; John 10:20; Acts 12:15; 1 Cor. 14:23, both Versions use the verb to be mad. See MAD. ¶

NT: B.486b; CB.1257b; K.548.
OT: hālal: S.1984; HR.892a.1; H.499, 500; BD.237c, 239d.
shāga': S.7696; HR.892a.2; H.2328; BD.993c.
GEN. REF.: –.

Note: For *paraphroneō*, 2 Cor. 11:23, R.V., see FOOL, B, No. 2.

BEST

1. *prōtos* [πρῶτος, 4413], is one of two words translated "best" in the A.V., but the only one so rendered in the R.V. In Luke 15:22 "the best (robe)" is, lit., 'the first (robe)', i.e., chief, principal, first in rank or quality. See BEFORE, BEGINNING, CHIEF, FIRST, FORMER.

NT: B.725b; CB.1267b; K.965.
OT: ri'shôn: S.7223; HR.1235c.3a; H.2097c; BD.911c.
GEN. REF.: –.

2. *meizōn* [μείζων, 3187], greater, is translated "best" in 1 Cor. 12:31, "the best gifts", greater, not in quality, but in importance and value. It is the comparative degree of *megas*, great; the superlative, *megistos*, is used only in 2 Pet. 1:4. See ELDER, GREATER and MORE.

NT: B.497c; CB.1258a; K.583.
OT: gādōl: S.1419; HR.902c.21b; H.315d; BD.152d.
GEN. REF.: –.

BESTOW

1. *didōmi* [δίδωμι, 1325], to give, is rendered "bestow" in 1 John 3:1, the implied idea being that of giving freely. The A.V. has it in 2 Cor. 8:1; the R.V. adheres to the lit. rendering, "the grace of God which hath been given in the churches of Macedonia". See ADVENTURE and especially GIVE.

NT: B.192c; CB.1241c; K.166.
OT: yāsaph: S.3254; HR.317b.11; H.876; BD.414d.
nātan: S.5414; HR.317b.26; H.1443; BD.678a.
GEN. REF.: IS.1:463; NB.–; Z.–.

2. *sunagō* [συνάγω, 4863], to bring together (*sun*, together, *agō*, to bring), is used in the sense of bestowing, or stowing, by the rich man who laid up his goods for himself, Luke 12:17, 18. See ASSEMBLE, COME, GATHER, LEAD, RESORT, TAKE.

NT: B.782a; CB.1270b; K.–.
OT: 'āsaph: S.622; HR.1307b.1; H.140; BD.62a.
qābaṣ: S.6908; HR.1307b.34; H.1983; BD.867c.
GEN. REF.: IS.1:463; NB.–; Z.–.

3. *kopiaō* [κοπιάω, 2872], (*a*) to grow tired with toil, Matt. 11:28; John 4:6; Rev. 2:3, also means (*b*) to bestow labour, work with toil, Rom. 16:6; Gal. 4:11; in John 4:38, A.V., "bestowed (no) labour", R.V., "have (not) laboured", and, in the same verse, A.V. and R.V., "laboured". See LABOUR, TOIL, WEARY.

NT: B.443c; CB.1255c; K.453.
OT: yāga': S.3021; HR.778b.6a; H.842; BD.388a.
GEN. REF.: IS.1:463; NB.–; Z.–.

4. *psōmizō* [ψωμίζω, 5595], primarily to feed by putting little bits into the mouths of infants or animals, came to denote simply to give out food, to feed, and is rendered by the phrase "bestow . . . to feed" in 1 Cor. 13:3; "feed", Rom. 12:20; there the person to be fed is mentioned; in 1 Cor. 13:3 the material to be given is specified, and the rendering "bestow . . . to feed" is necessary. See FEED. ¶

NT: B.894d; CB.–; K.–.
OT: 'ākal: S.398; HR.1490c.1b; H.85; BD.37a.
GEN. REF.: IS.1:463; NB.–; Z.–.

5. *peritithēmi* [περιτίθημι, 4060], to put around or on (*peri*, around, *tithēmi*, to put), is translated in 1 Cor. 12:23 (metaphorically) "bestow" (marg., "put on"). See PUT, SET, No. 5.

NT: B.652c; CB.–; K.–.
OT: sûm, sîm: S7760; HR.1127c.14; H.2243; BD.962c.
nātan: S.5414; HR.1127c.9; H.1443; BD.678a.
GEN. REF.: IS.1:463; NB.–; Z.–.

6. *charizomai* [χαρίζομαι, 5483], to show favour, grant, bestow, is rendered "bestowed" in Luke 7:21, R.V., for A.V., "gave". Here and in Gal. 3:18, the verb might be translated "graciously conferred". See DELIVER, FORGIVE, GIVE, GRANT.

NT: B.876c; CB.1239c; K.1298.
OT: nātan: S.5414; HR.1454c.1; H.1443; BD.678a.
GEN. REF.: IS.1:463; NB.–; Z.–.

Note: For "freely bestowed" see ACCEPT, A, *Note*.

BETRAY, BETRAYER

A. Verb.

paradidōmi [παραδίδωμι, 3860], to betray (*para*, up, *didōmi*, to give), lit., to give over, is used either (*a*) in the sense of delivering a person or thing to be kept by another, to commend, e.g., Acts 28:16; (*b*) to deliver to prison or judgment, e.g., Matt. 4:12; 1 Tim. 1:20; (*c*) to deliver over treacherously by way of betrayal, Matt. 17:22 (R.V., "delivered"); 26:16; John 6:64 etc.; (*d*) to hand on, deliver, e.g., 1 Cor. 11:23; (*e*) to allow of something being done, said of the ripening of fruit, Mark 4:29, R.V., "is ripe" (marg., "alloweth"). See BRING, p. 153, *Note* (4), CAST, COMMIT, DELIVER, GIVE, HAZARD, PUT (in prison), RECOMMEND.

NT: B.614b; CB.1262a; K.166.
OT: nātan: S:5414; HR.1058a.16; H.1443; BD.678a.
sāgar: S.5462; HR.1058a.17; H.1462; BD688d, 689a.
GEN. REF.: IS.1:480; NB.–; Z.–.

B. Noun.

prodotēs [προδότης, 4273], a betrayer (akin to A), is translated "betrayers" in Acts 7:52;

"traitor", "traitors", in Luke 6:16 and 2 Tim. 3:4. See TRAITOR. ¶
NT: B.704c; CB.1266c; K.–.
OT: –.
GEN. REF.: IS.1:480; NB.–; Z.–.

BETROTH

mnēsteuō [μνηστεύω, 3423], in the Active Voice, signifies to woo a woman and ask for her in marriage; in the N.T., only in the Passive Voice, to be promised in marriage, to be betrothed, Matt. 1:18; Luke 1:27; 2:5, R.V., "betrothed", (A.V., "espoused"). See ESPOUSED. ¶
NT: B.525c; CB.–; K.–.
OT: 'āras: S781; HR:932a.1; H.170; BD.76d.
GEN. REF.: IS.1:481; NB.–; Z.4:92.

BETTER

1. *kreissōn* [κρείσσων, 2909], from *kratos*, strong (which denotes power in activity and effect), serves as the comparative degree of *agathos*, good (good or fair, intrinsically). *Kreissōn* is especially characteristic of the Epistle to the Hebrews, where it is used 12 times; it indicates what is (*a*) advantageous or useful, 1 Cor. 7:9, 38; 11:17; Heb. 11:40; 12:24; 2 Pet. 2:21; Phil. 1:23, where it is coupled with *mallon*, more, and *pollō*, much, by far, "very far better" (R.V.); (*b*) excellent, Heb. 1:4; 6:9; 7:7, 19, 22; 8:6; 9:23; 10:34; 11:16, 35. ¶
NT: B.449d; CB.1256a; K.–.
OT: ṭôb: S.2896; HR.785a.2a; H:793a; BD.373b.
GEN. REF.: IS.2:525; NB.481; Z.–.

2. *kalon . . . mallon* [καλὸν . . . μᾶλλον], the neuter of *kalos*, with *mallon*, more, is used in Mark 9:42, "it were better (lit., much better) for him if a great millstone were hanged about his neck". In verses 43, 45, 47, *kalos* is used alone (R.V., "good", for A.V., "better"). See GOOD, 2. *kalos*.

Note: In Luke 5:39 the most authentic texts have *chrēstos*, good, instead of the comparative, *chrēstoteros*, better.

BETTER (be)

1. *diapherō* [διαφέρω, 1308], used (*a*) transitively, means to carry through or about (*dia*, through, *pherō*, to carry), Mark 11:16 ("carry . . . through"); Acts 13:49; 27:27 ("driven to and fro"); (*b*) intransitively, (1) to differ, Rom. 2:18; Gal. 2:6; Phil. 1:10; (2) to excel, be better, e.g., Matt. 6:26; 10:31 ("of more value"); 12:12; Luke 12:7, 24; 1 Cor. 15:41; Gal. 4:1; some would put Rom. 2:18 and Phil. 1:10 here (see marg.). See CARRY, DIFFER, DRIVE, EXCELLENT, MATTER (make), PUBLISH. ¶
NT: B.190b; CB.–; K.1252.
OT: –.
GEN. REF.: –.

2. *perisseuō* [περισσεύω, 4052], to be over or above (a number), to be more than enough, to be pre-eminent, superior, Matt. 5:20, is translated "are we the better", in 1 Cor. 8:8 (cp. 15:58; Rom. 15:13; 2 Cor. 3:9; 8:7; Phil. 1:9; Col. 2:7; 1 Thess. 4:1, 10). See ABOUND.
NT: B.650c; CB.1263c; K.828.
OT: yātar: S.3498; HR.1126b.1; H.836; BD.451b.
marbît: S.4768; HR.1126b.2; H.2103d; BD.916b.
GEN. REF.: –.

3. *lusiteleō* [λυσιτελέω, 3081], signifies to indemnify, pay expenses, pay taxes (from *luō*, to loose, *telos*, toll, custom); hence, to be useful, advantageous, to be better, Luke 17:2. ¶
NT: B.482b; CB.–; K.–.
OT: –.
GEN. REF.: –.

4. *huperechō* [ὑπερέχω, 5242], lit. means to hold or have above (*huper*, above, *echō*, to hold); hence, metaphorically, to be superior to, to be better than, Phil. 2:3; 1 Pet. 2:13, "supreme", in reference to kings; in Rom. 13:1, "higher"; Phil. 3:8, "excellency", more strictly 'the surpassing thing, (namely, the knowledge of Christ)'; in 4:7 "passeth". See EXCELLENCY, HIGHER, PASS, SUPREME. ¶
NT: B.840d; CB.1252a; K.1230.
OT: 'ādaph: S.5736; HR.1409b.5; H.1568; BD.727a.
'ārak: S.748; HR.1409b.3; H.162; BD.73c.
'āmēṣ: S.553; HR.1409b.2; H.117; BD.54d.
GEN. REF.: –.

Notes: (1) In Rom. 3:9 the R.V. rightly translates *proechō* (which there is used in the Passive Voice, not the Middle) "are we in worse case than . . .?," i.e., 'are we surpassed?' 'are we at a disadvantage?' The question is, are the Jews, so far from being better off than the Gentiles, in such a position that their very privileges bring them into a greater disadvantage or condemnation than the Gentiles? The A.V. "are we better" does not convey the meaning.

(2) *Sumpherō*, in Matt. 18:6, A.V., is translated "it were better for him", R.V., "profitable". See Matt. 5:29, 30 etc. See BRING, EXPEDIENT, GOOD, D. *Note* (2), PROFITABLE.

BETTERED (to be)

ōpheleō [ὠφελέω, 5623], in the Active Voice signifies to help, to succour, to be of service; in the Passive to receive help, to derive profit or advantage; in Mark 5:26, "was (nothing) bettered", of the woman who had an issue of blood. See under ADVANTAGE, C, No. 1, and cp. A, Nos. 2, 3 and B.
NT: B.900c; CB.1261a; K.–.
OT: yā'al: S.3276; HR.1497b.1; H.882; BD.418c.
GEN. REF.: –.

BETWEEN

In addition to the prepositions *en* and *pros* (see Note † p. 1), the following have this meaning:

1. *ana meson* [ἀνὰ μέσον], lit., up to the middle of, i.e., among, or in the midst of, hence, between, is used in 1 Cor. 6:5, of those in the church able to decide between brother and brother, instead of their going to law with one another in the world's courts.

NT: B.49c; CB.1235a; K.—.
OT: —.
GEN. REF.: —.

2. *metaxu* [μεταξύ, 3342], in the midst, or between (from *meta*, and *xun* i.e., *sun*, with), is used as a preposition, (*a*) of mutual relation, Matt. 18:15; Acts 15:9; Rom. 2:15, R.V., "one with another", lit., 'between one another', for A.V., "the meanwhile"; (*b*) of place, Matt. 23:35; Luke 11:51; 16:26; Acts 12:6; (*c*) of time, "meanwhile", John 4:31. In Acts 13:42, the A.V. marg. has "in the week between", the literal rendering. See WHILE. ¶

NT: B.512d; CB.—; K.—.
OT: —.
GEN. REF.: —.

Note: The phrase *ek meta* (*ek*, out of, *meta*, with) is translated "between . . . and" in the A.V. of John 3:25 (R.V., "on the part of . . . with").

BEWAIL

1. *klaiō* [κλαίω, 2799], to wail, whether with tears or any external expression of grief, is regularly translated "weep" in the R.V.; once in the A.V. it is rendered "bewail", Rev. 18:9. See WEEP.

NT: B.433a; CB.1255a; K.436.
OT: bākāh: S.1058; HR.766a.1a; H.243; BD.113b.
GEN. REF.: IS.1:481; NB.—; Z.—.

Note: The associated noun is *klauthmos*, weeping. Cp. *dakruō*, to weep, John 11:35. ¶

2. *koptō* [κόπτω, 2875], primarily, to beat, smite; then, to cut off, Matt. 21:8; Mark 11:8, is used in the Middle Voice, of beating oneself, beating the breast, as a token of grief; hence, to bewail, Matt. 11:17 (R.V., "mourn", for A.V., "lament"; 24:30, "mourn"; Rev. 1:7 (R.V., "mourn"; A.V., "wail"); in Luke 8:52; 23:27, "bewail"; in Rev. 18:9, "wail" (for A.V., "lament"). See CUT, MOURN. ¶ Cp. *kopetos*, lamentation, Acts 8:2. ¶

NT: B.444a; CB.1255c; K.453.
OT: sāphad: S.5594; HR.779a.10; H.1530; BD.704c.
nākāh: S.5221; HR.779a.9; H.1364; BD.645a.
kārat: S.3772; HR.779a.6; H.1048; BD.503c.
GEN. REF.: —.

3. *pentheō* [πενθέω, 3996], denotes to lament, mourn, especially for the dead; in 2 Cor. 12:21, R.V., "mourn" (A.V., "bewail"). See also Rev. 18:11, 15, 19. Cp. *penthos*, mourning. See MOURN.

NT: B.642c; CB.1263a; K.825.
OT: 'ābal: S.56; HR.1117b.1; H.6; BD.5b.
GEN. REF.: —.

Notes: (1) *Thrēneō*, to sing a dirge, to lament, is rendered "wail" in Matt. 11:17, R.V.; "mourned" in Luke 7:32; to lament in Luke 23:27 and John 16:20. ¶ *Thrēnos*, lamentation, occurs in Matt. 2:18. ¶

(2) *Odurmos* from *oduromai*, to wail (a verb not found in the N.T.), denotes "mourning", Matt. 2:18 and 2 Cor. 7:7. ¶

(3) Cp. *lupeomai*, to grieve, and see Trench, Syn. § lxv.

BEWARE

1. *blepō* [βλέπω, 991], to see, is applied to mental vision, and is sometimes used by way of warning to take heed against an object, Mark 8:15; 12:38; Acts 13:40; Phil. 3:2 (three times); in Col. 2:8, R.V., "take heed", marg., "see whether". See BEHOLD.

NT: B.143b; CB.1239a; K.706.
OT: pānāh: S.6437; HR.221a.7; H.1782; BD.815a.
rā'āh:S.7200; HR.221a.10; H.2095; BD.906b.
GEN. REF.: —.

2. *prosechō* [προσέχω, 4337], lit., to hold to (*pros*, to, *echō*, to have, to hold) hence, to turn one's mind or attention to a thing by being on one's guard against it, is translated "beware" in Matt. 7:15; 10:17; 16:6, 11, 12; Luke 12:1; 20:46. See ATTEND, HEED, REGARD.

NT: B.714b; CB.1267a; K.—.
OT: qāshab: S.7181; HR.1215b.16; H.2084; BD.904a.
shāmar: S.8104; HR.1215b.19; H.2414; BD.1036b.
GEN. REF.: —.

3. *phulassō* [φυλάσσω, 5442], to guard, watch, keep, is used, in the Middle Voice, of being on one's guard against (the Middle V. stressing personal interest in the action), Luke 12:15, "beware of", R.V., "keep yourselves from", as in Acts 21:25; in 2 Tim. 4:15, "be thou ware"; in 2 Pet. 3:17, "beware". See GUARD, KEEP, OBSERVE, SAVE.

NT: B.868b; CB.1264c; K.1280.
OT: shāmar: S.8104; HR.1441c.11; H.2414; BD.1036b.
GEN. REF.: —.

BEWITCH

1. *baskainō* [βασκαίνω, 940], primarily, to slander, to prate about anyone; then to bring evil on a person by feigned praise, or mislead by an evil eye, and so to charm, bewitch (Eng., fascinate is connected), is used figuratively in Gal. 3:1, of leading into evil doctrine. ¶

NT: B.137a; CB.1238c; K.102.
OT: rā'a': S.7489; HR.214c.1; H.2191,2192; BD.949b.
GEN. REF.: IS.1:481; NB.—; Z.1:553.

2. *existēmi* [ἐξίστημι, 1839], is rendered "bewitch" in Acts 8:9, 11, A.V., concerning Simon the sorcerer; it does not mean to bewitch, as in the case of the preceding verb, but to confuse, amaze (R.V.). See AMAZE, B. No. 1.

NT: –.
OT: shāmēm: S.8074; HR.496c.28; H.2409; BD.1030c.
tāmah:: S.8539; HR.496c.29; H.2218; BD.1069b
GEN REF.: IS.1:481; NB.–; Z.1:553.

BEWRAY

Note: The word "bewrayeth", Matt. 26:73, is a translation of *poieō*, to make, with *dēlos*, manifest, evident; lit., 'maketh thee manifest.'

BEYOND

In addition to the preposition *huper*, over, rendered "beyond" in 2 Cor. 8:3, the following adverbs have this meaning:

1. *epekeina* [ἐπέκεινα, 1900], *epi*, upon, and *ekeina*, those, the word "parts" being understood, is used in Acts 7:43. ¶

NT: B.284d; CB.–; K.–.
OT: hālᵉʼāh: S.1973; HR.509b.1a; H.496a; BD.229b.
GEN. REF.: –.

2. *peran* [πέραν, 4008], on the other side, across, is used with the definite article, signifying the regions beyond, the opposite shore, Matt. 8:18 etc. With verbs of going it denotes direction towards and beyond a place e.g., John 10:40. It frequently indicates "beyond", of locality, without a verb of direction, Matt. 16:5; Mark 10:1, R.V.; John 1:28; 3:26. See FARTHER, SIDE.

NT: B.643d; CB.–; K.–.
OT: ʻēber: S.5676; HR.1119b.2a; H.1556a; BD.719b.
GEN. REF.: IS.1:481; NB.–; Z.1:553.

Note: In 2 Cor. 10:14, the verb *huperekteinō*, to stretch overmuch, is so rendered in the R.V., for A.V., ". . . beyond our measure". ¶ In 2 Cor. 10:16 the adverb *huperekeina*, beyond, is used as a preposition.

BID, BIDDEN, BADE, BID AGAIN

1. *kaleō* [καλέω, 2564], to call, often means to bid, in the sense of invite, e.g., Matt. 22:3, 4, 8, 9; Luke 14:7, 8, 9, 10, 13, R.V.; Rev. 19:9, R.V. See CALL, NAME, SURNAME.

NT: B.398d; CB.1253b; K.394.
OT: qārāʼ: S.7121; HR.712c.9a; H.2063; BD.894d.
GEN. REF.: –.

2. *keleuō* [κελεύω, 2753], to command, is translated "bid" in Matt. 14:28, only. See COMMAND, No. 5. Compare the synonym *entellō*, to command.

NT: B.427b; CB.1254c; K.–.
OT: –.
GEN. REF.: –.

3. *eipon* [εἶπον], used as the aorist tense of *legō*, to speak, to say, sometimes has the meaning of commanding, or bidding, and is translated "bid", or "bade", e.g., in Matt. 16:12;23:3; Luke 10:40; 9:54, A.V., "command", R.V., "bid"; Acts 11:12; "bidding", Acts 22:24, R.V. See SAY, SPEAK.

NT: B.226a; CB.1243a; K.–.
OT: ʼāmar: S.559; HR.384a.1a; H.118; BD.55c.
GEN. REF.: –.

4. *antikaleō* [ἀντικαλέω, 479], to bid again, invite in turn, is found in Luke 14:12. ¶

NT: B.74b; CB.–; K.394.
OT: –.
GEN. REF.: –.

Notes: (1) *Legō*, to say, is translated "bid" and "biddeth" in the A.V. of 2 John 10, 11; R.V., "give (him no greeting)," "giveth (him greeting)." See GREETING.

(2). In Matt. 1:24, *prostassō*, to command, is translated "had bidden", A.V.; R.V., "commanded". See COMMAND.

BID FAREWELL

1. *apotassō* [ἀποτάσσω, 657], is used in the Middle Voice to signify to bid adieu to a person. It primarily means to set apart, separate (*apo*, from, *tassō*, to set, arrange); then, to take leave of, to bid farewell to, Mark 6:46 (R.V.); Luke 9:61; to give parting instructions to, Acts 18:18, 21; 2 Cor. 2:13; to forsake, renounce, Luke 14:33. See FORSAKE, RENOUNCE, SEND, *Note* (2) at end. ¶

NT: B.100d; CB.–; K.1156.
OT: –.
GEN. REF.: IS.2:283; NB.–; Z.–.

2. *apaspazomai* [ἀπασπάζομαι], to bid farewell (*apo*, from, *aspazomai*, to greet), is used in Acts 21:6, A.V., "had taken our leave of"; R.V., "bade . . . farewell". ¶

NT: B.81d; CB.–; K.84.
OT: –.
GEN. REF.: IS.2:283; NB.–; Z.–.

BIER

soros [σορός, 4673], originally denoted a receptacle for containing the bones of the dead, a cinerary urn; then a coffin, Gen. 50:26; Job 21:32; then, the funeral couch or bier on which the Jews bore their dead to burial, Luke 7:14. ¶

NT: B.759b; CB.–; K.–.
OT: ʼārôn: S.727; HR.1278c.1; H.166a; BD.75b.
GEN. REF.: IS.1:509; NB.–; Z.1:610.

BILL

1. *biblion* [βιβλίον, 975], primarily a small book, a scroll, or any sheet on which something has been written; hence, in connection with *apostasion*, divorce, signifies a bill of divorcement, Matt. 19:7 (A.V., "writing"); Mark 10:4. See BOOK, SCROLL, WRITING.

NT: B.141b; CB.1239a; K.106.
OT: sēpher: S.5612; HR.218b.4c; H.1540a; BD.706d.
GEN. REF.: IS.1:510; NB.–; Z.1:611.

2. *gramma* [γράμμα, 1121], from *graphō*, to write (Eng., graph, graphic etc.), in Luke 16:6, A.V., is translated "bill". It lit. signifies that which is drawn, a picture; hence, a written document; hence, a bill, or bond, or note of hand, showing the amount of indebtedness. In the passage referred to the word is in the plural, indicating perhaps, but not necessarily, various bills. The bonds mentioned in Rabbinical writings, were formal, signed by witnesses and the Sanhedrin of three, or informal, when only the debtor signed. The latter were usually written on wax, and easily altered. See LEARNING, LETTER, SCRIPTURE, WRITING.

NT: B.165b; CB.1248c; K.128.
OT: sēpher: S.5612; HR.275a.3; H.1540a; BD.706d.
GEN. REF.: IS.1:510; NB.–; Z.1:611.

For **BILLOWS,** Luke 21:25, R.V., see **WAVE**

BIND, BINDING (see also **BOUND**)

1. *deō* [δέω, 1210], to bind, is used (*a*) literally, of any sort of binding, e.g., Acts 22:5; 24:27, (*b*) figuratively, of the Word of God, as not being bound, 2 Tim. 2:9, i.e., its ministry, course and efficacy were not hindered by the bonds and imprisonment suffered by the Apostle. A woman who was bent together, had been "bound" by Satan through the work of a demon, Luke 13:16. Paul speaks of himself, in Acts 20:22, as being "bound in the spirit", i.e. compelled by his convictions, under the constraining power of the Spirit of God, to go to Jerusalem. A wife is said to be "bound" to her husband, Rom. 7:2; 1 Cor. 7:39; and the husband to the wife, 1 Cor. 7:27. The Lord's words to the Apostle Peter in Matt. 16:19, as to binding, and to all the disciples in 18:18, signify, in the former case, that the Apostle, by his ministry of the Word of Life, would keep unbelievers outside the kingdom of God, and admit those who believed. So with regard to 18:18, including the exercise of disciplinary measures in the sphere of the local church; the application of the Rabbinical sense of forbidding is questionable. See BOND, KNIT, *Note*, TIE.

NT: B.177c; CB.1240c; K.148.
OT: 'āsar: S.631; HR.287b.1a; H.141; BD.63c.
GEN. REF.: IS.1:511; NB.153; Z.1:611.

2. *perideō* [περιδέω, 4019], *peri*, around, with No. 1, to bind around, is used in John 11:44 of the napkin around the face of Lazarus. ¶ Cp. Job 12:18, Sept.

NT: B.646c; CB.–; K.–.
OT: 'āsar: S.631; HR.1122c.1; H.141; BD.63c.
GEN. REF.: IS.1:511; NB.153; Z.1:611.

3. *hupodeō* [ὑποδέω, 5265], *hupō*, under, with No. 1, to bind underneath, is used of binding of sandals, Acts 12:8; rendered "shod" in Mark 6:9 and Eph. 6:15. See SHOD. ¶

NT: B.844b; CB.–; K.702.
OT: na'al: S.5274; HR.1413b.1; H.1383; BD.653b.
GEN. REF.: IS.1:511; NB.153; Z.1:611.

4. *katadeō* [καταδέω, 2611], *kata*, down, with No. 1, to bind or tie down, or bind up, is used in Luke 10:34 of the act of the good Samaritan. ¶

NT: B.410b; CB.–; K.–.
OT: ḥābash: S.2280; HR.730b.1; H.599; BD.289c.
ḥāphas: S.2664; HR.730b.2; H.716; BD.344b.
GEN. REF.: IS.1:511; NB.153; Z.1:611.

5. *sundeō* [συνδέω, 4887], *sun*, together, and No. 1, to bind together, implying association, is used in Heb. 13:3 of those bound together in confinement. ¶

NT: B.785c; CB.–; K.–.
OT: dābaq: S.1692; HR.1312c.1; H.398; BD.179c.
qāshar: S.7194; HR.1312c.3; H.2090; BD.905a.
GEN. REF.: IS.1:511; NB.153; Z.1:611.

6. *desmeuō* or *desmeō* [δεσμεύω, 1195], signifies to put in fetters or any kind of bond, Luke 8:29; Acts 22:4, or to bind a burden upon a person, Matt. 23:4. The verb is connected with No. 1. ¶

NT: B.175d; CB.1240c; K.–.
OT: 'āsar: S.631; HR.292a.2; H.141; BD.63c.
ḥābash: S.2280; HR.292a.4; H.599; BD.289c.
ṣārar: S.6887; HR.292a.6; H.1973,1974; BD.864c.
GEN. REF.: IS.1:511; NB.153; Z.1:611.

Notes: (1) Cp. *desmos*, a band, bond, fetter, e.g., Luke 13:16, and *desmios*, "bound", Acts 25:14, A.V. (R.V., "a prisoner"); in Heb. 13:3, "them that are in bonds". See BOND, CHAIN, PRISONER, STRING.

(2) *Sundesmos* (see No. 5, above), that which binds together, is translated "bands", in Col. 2:19. See BONDS.

7. *proteinō* [προτείνω, 4385], lit., to stretch forth (*pro*, forth, *teinō*, to stretch), is used in Acts 22:25, A.V., "they bound"; R.V., "they had tied (him) up", in reference to the preparations made for scourging, probably, to stretch the body forward, to make it tense for severer punishment. See TIE. ¶

NT: B.721d; CB.–; K.–.
OT: –.
GEN. REF.: IS.1:511; NB.153; Z.1:611.

BIRD (Fowl)

1. *orneon* [ὄρνεον, 3732], is probably connected with a word signifying to perceive, to hear; Rev. 18:2; 19:17, 21. See FOWL. Cp. *ornis*, a hen. ¶

NT: B.581d; CB.–; K.–.
OT: 'ôph: S.5775; HR.1014a.1; H.1582a; BD.733d.
ṣippôr: S.6833; HR.1014a.3a; H.1959a; BD.861d.
GEN. REF.: IS.1:511; NB.154; Z.1:613;2:604.

2. *peteinon* [πετεινόν, 4071], signifies that which is able to fly, winged. It is connected

with *ptenon* signifying "feathered, winged", which is used in 1 Cor. 15:39. Cp. *petomai* and *petaomai*, to fly. In the Gospels the R.V. always translates it "birds", e.g., Matt. 6:26; but "fowls" in Acts 10:12; 11:6. The A.V. unsuitably has "fowls", in the Gospels, except Matt. 8:20; 13:32; Luke 9:58.

NT: B.654a; CB.1263c; K.–.
OT: 'ôph: S.5775; HR.1129a.2; H.1582a; BD.733d.
GEN. REF.: IS.1:511; NB.154; Z.1:613;2:604.

BIRTH

1. *gennēsis* [γέννησισ, 1083], a birth, begetting, producing (related to *gennaō*, beget), is used in Matt. 1:18 and Luke 1:14. Some mss. have *genesis*, lineage, birth (from *ginomai*, to become). ¶

NT: B.156a; CB.–; K.–.
OT: yālad: S.3205; HR.239b.1; H.867; BD.408a.
mishpāḥāh: S.4940; HR.239b.2; H.2442b; BD.1046d.
GEN. REF.: IS.1:514; NB.156; Z.1:616.

2. *genetē* [γενετή, 1084], a being born, or the hour of birth (related to *genea*, race, generation), is connected with *ginomai*, to become, to be born, and is used in John 9:1. ¶

NT: B.156a; CB.–; K.–.
OT: –.
GEN. REF.: IS.1:514; NB.156; Z.1:616.

Notes: (1) For *genesis* and *gennēma* see FRUIT, GENERATION, NATURE.

(2) In Gal. 4:19, ōdinō, to have birth pangs, is rendered "travail in birth", A.V.; R.V., "am in travail". See Rev. 12:2.

BIRTHDAY

genesia [γενέσια, 1077], a neuter plural (akin to *genesis*, lineage, from *ginomai*), primarily denoted the festivities of a birthday, a birthday feast, though among the Greeks it was also used of a festival in commemoration of a deceased friend. It is found in Matt. 14:6 and Mark 6:21. Some have regarded it as the day of the king's accession, but this meaning is not confirmed in Greek writings. ¶

NT: B.154c; CB.–; K.–.
OT: tôlēdôt: S.8435; HR.237a.3d; H.867g; BD.410a.
GEN. REF.: –.

BIRTHRIGHT

prōtotokia [πρωτοτόκια, 4415], a birthright (from *prōtos*, first, *tiktō*, to beget), is found in Heb. 12:16, with reference to Esau (cp. *prōtotokos*, firstborn). The birthright involved pre-eminence and authority, Gen. 27:29; 49:3. Another right was that of the double portion, Deut. 21:17; 1 Chron. 5:1, 2. Connected with the birthright was the progenitorship of the Messiah. Esau transferred his birthright to Jacob for a paltry mess of pottage, profanely despising this last spiritual privilege, Gen. 25 and 27. In the history of the nation God occasionally set aside the birthright, to show that the objects of His choice depended not on the will of the flesh, but on His own authority. Thus Isaac was preferred to Ishmael, Jacob to Esau, Joseph to Reuben, David to his elder brethren, Solomon to Adonijah. See FIRSTBORN. ¶

NT: B.726c; CB.–; K.965.
OT: –.
GEN. REF.: IS.1:515; NB.423; Z.1:617.

BISHOP (Overseer)

1. *episkopos* [ἐπίσκοπος, 1985], lit., an overseer (*epi*, over, *skopeō*, to look or watch), whence Eng. "bishop", which has precisely the same meaning, is found in Acts 20:28; Phil. 1:1; 1 Tim. 3:2; Tit. 1:7; 1 Pet. 2:25. See OVERSEER. ¶

NT: B.299; CB.1246a; K.244.
OT: pāqad: S.6485; HR.529a.3a; H.1802; BD.823b.
pᵉquddāh: S.6486; HR.529a.3d; H.1802a; BD.824a.
pāqîd: S.6496; HR.529a.3c; H.1802c; BD.824b.
GEN. REF.: IS.1:516; NB.158; Z.1:617.

Note: Presbuteros, an elder, is another term for the same person as bishop or overseer. See Acts 20:17 with verse 28. The term "elder" indicates the mature spiritual experience and understanding of those so described; the term "bishop", or "overseer", indicates the character of the work undertaken. According to the Divine will and appointment, as in the N.T., there were to be bishops in every local church, Acts 14:23; 20:17; Phil. 1:1; Tit. 1:5; Jas. 5:14. Where the singular is used, the passage is describing what a bishop should be, 1 Tim. 3:2; Tit. 1:7. Christ Himself is spoken of as "the . . . Bishop of our souls", 1 Pet. 2:25. See ELDER.

2. *episkopē* [ἐπισκοπή, 1984], besides its meaning, visitation, e.g., 1 Pet. 2:12 (cp. the Sept. of Ex. 3:16; Is. 10:3; Jer. 10:15), is rendered "office", in Acts 1:20, R.V. (A.V., "bishoprick"); in 1 Tim. 3:1, "the office of a bishop", lit., '(if any one seeketh) overseership', there is no word representing office.

NT: B.299c; CB.1246a; K.244.
OT: pāqad: S.6485; HR.528c.5a; H.1802; BD.823b.
pᵉquddāh: S.6486; HR.528c.5d; H.1802a; BD.824a.
GEN. REF.: IS.1:516; NB.158; Z.1:617.

Note: The corresponding verb is *episkopeō*, which, in reference to the work of an overseer, is found in 1 Pet. 5:2, R.V., "exercising the oversight", for A.V. "taking the oversight". See OVERSIGHT.

For **BIT** see **BRIDLE**

BITE

daknō [δάκνω, 1143], to bite, in Gal. 5:15, "if ye bite and devour one another"; is used metaphorically of wounding the soul, or rending with reproaches. ¶

NT: B.169d; CB.–; K.–.
OT: nāshak: S.–; HR.284a.1; H.–; BD.675a.
GEN. REF.: –.

BITTER, BITTERLY, BITTERNESS

A. Adjective.

pikros [πικρός, 4089], from a root *pik–*, meaning to cut, to prick, hence, lit., pointed, sharp, keen, pungent to the sense of taste, smell, etc., is found in Jas. 3:11, 14. In ver. 11 it has its natural sense, with reference to water; in ver. 14 it is used metaphorically of jealousy, R.V. ¶

NT: B.657c; CB.1265a; K.839.
OT: mar: S.4751; HR.1133a.1a; H.1248a,c; BD.600c.
GEN. REF.: IS.1:521; NB.158; Z.1:622.

B. Verb.

pikrainō [πικραίνω, 4087], related to A, signifies, in the Active Voice, to be bitter, Col. 3:19, or to embitter, irritate, or to make bitter, Rev. 10:9; the Passive Voice, to be made bitter, is used in Rev. 8:11; 10:10. ¶

NT: B.657b; CB.1265c; K.839.
OT: mārar: S.4843; HR.1132c.2; H.1248; BD.600a.
qāṣaph: S.7107; HR.1132c.3; H.2058; BD.893b.
rāgaz: S.7264; HR.1132c.4; H.2112; BD.919a.
GEN. REF.: IS.1:521; NB.158; Z.1:622.

C. Noun.

pikria [πικρία, 4088], denotes bitterness. It is used in Acts 8:23, metaphorically, of a condition of extreme wickedness, "gall of bitterness" or "bitter gall"; in Rom. 3:14, of evil speaking; in Eph. 4:31, of bitter hatred; in Heb. 12:15, in the same sense, metaphorically, of a root of bitterness, producing bitter fruit. ¶

NT: B.657c; CB.1265a; K.839.
OT: mārāh: S.4784; HR.1132c.4b; H.1242; BD.598a.
mar: S.4751; HR.1132c.4c; H.1248a,c; BD.600c.
GEN. REF.: IS.1:521; NB.158; Z.1:622.

D. Adverb.

pikrōs [πικρῶς, 4090], bitterly, is used of the poignant grief of Peter's weeping for his denial of Christ, Matt. 26:75; Luke 22:62. ¶

NT: B.657b; CB.1265a; K.839.
OT: mar: S.4751; HR.1133b.1a; H.1248a,c; BD.600c.
mārar: S.4843; HR.1133b.1b; H.1248; BD.600a.
GEN. REF.: IS.1:521; NB.158; Z.1:622.

Note: In the Sept., *pikris* (not in the N.T.), a bitter herb, is used in Ex. 12:8; Num. 9:11. ¶

BLACK, BLACKNESS

A. Adjective.

melas [μέλας, 3189], black, Matt. 5:36; Rev. 6:5, 12, is derived from a root *mal–*, meaning to be dirty; hence Latin, *malus*, bad. See INK.

NT: B.499d; CB.1258a; K.577.
OT: shāḥōr: S.7838; HR.908b.2; H.2368a,b; BD.1007b.
GEN. REF.: IS.1:729,731; NB.–; Z.1:624.

B. Nouns.

1. *gnophos* [γνόφος, 1105], Heb. 12:18, blackness, gloom, seems to have been associated with the idea of a tempest. It is related to *skotos*, darkness, in that passage, and in the Sept. of Ex. 10:22; Deut. 4:11; Zeph. 1:15. ¶

NT: B.163a; CB.–; K.–.
OT: 'ăphēlāh: S.–; HR.272c.1c; H.–; BD.66c.
'ărāphel: S.–; HR.272c.5; H.–; BD.791d.
GEN. REF.: IS.1:729,731; NB.–; Z.1:624.

2. *zophos* [ζόφος, 2217], akin to No. 1, especially the gloom of the regions of the lost, is used four times; 2 Pet. 2:4, "darkness" (R.V.); 2:17, R.V., "blackness," for A.V., "mist"; Jude 6, "darkness"; ver. 13, "blackness," suggesting a kind of emanation. See DARKNESS, MIST. ¶

NT: B.339d; CB.–; K.–.
OT: –.
GEN. REF.: IS.1:729,731; NB.–; Z.1:624.

For BLADE see GRASS

BLAME, BLAMELESS

A. Verb.

mōmaomai [μωμάομαι, 3469], to find fault with, to blame, or calumniate, is used in 2 Cor. 6:3, of the ministry of the Gospel; in 8:20, of the ministration of financial help. ¶

NT: B.531a; CB.–; K.–.
OT: mûm: S.3971; HR.938b.1; H.1137a; BD.548c.
GEN. REF.: –.

Notes: (1) Cp. the synonymous verb, *memphomai*, to find fault, Mark 7:2; Rom. 9:19; Heb. 8:8. See FAULT. ¶

(2) In Gal. 2:11, *kataginōskō* is rightly rendered "stood condemned," R.V., for A.V., "was to be blamed." See CONDEMN.

B. Adjectives.

1. *amōmos* [ἄμωμος, 299]: See BLEMISH, B.

NT: B.47d; CB.1234c; K.619.
OT: tāmîm: S.8549; HR.68b.2c; H.2522d; BD.1071a.
GEN. REF.: –.

2. *amōmētos* [ἀμώμητος, 298], translated in Phil. 2:15 "without blemish" (A.V., "without rebuke"), is rendered "blameless" in 2 Pet. 3:14 (A.V. and R.V.). ¶

NT: B.47d; CB.1234c; K.619.
OT: –.
GEN. REF.: –.

3. *amemptos* [ἄμεμπτος, 273], related to *memphomai* (A., Note), is translated "unblameable" in 1 Thess. 3:13; "blameless," in Luke 1:6; Phil. 2:15; 3:6; "faultless" in Heb. 8:7. See FAULTLESS, UNBLAMEABLE. ¶

NT: B.45a; CB.1234c; K.580.
OT: tām: S.8535; HR.65b.6; H.2522c; BD.1070d.
tāmîm: S.8549; HR.65b.7; H.2522d; BD.1071a.
GEN. REF.: –.

"If *amōmos* is the 'unblemished,' *amemptos* is the 'unblamed.' . . . Christ was *amōmos* in that there was in Him no spot or blemish, and He could say, 'Which of you convinceth (convicteth) Me of sin?' but in strictness of speech He was not *amemptos* (unblamed), nor is this epithet ever given to Him in the N.T., seeing that He endured the contradiction of sinners against Himself, who slandered His footsteps and laid to His charge 'things that He knew not' (i.e., of which He was guiltless)." Trench, Syn. § 103.

4. *anaitios* [ἀναίτιος, 338], guiltless (*a*, negative, *n*, euphonic, and *aitia*, a charge), is translated, "blameless" in the A.V. of Matt. 12:5, "guiltless" in 12:7. The R.V. has "guiltless" in both places. ¶ In the Sept., in Deut. 19:10, 13, and 21:8, 9. ¶ See GUILTLESS.

NT: B.55b; CB.1235a; K.–.
OT: nāqî: S.5355; HR.78a.1; H.1412b; BD.667d.
GEN. REF.: –.

5. *anepilēmptos* [ἀνεπίληπτος, 423], lit., that cannot be laid hold of, hence, not open to censure, irreproachable (from *a*, negative, *n*, euphonic, and *epilambanō*, to lay hold of), is used in 1 Tim. 3:2; 5:7; 6:14 (in all three places the R.V. has "without reproach"; in the first two, A.V., "blameless," in the last, "unrebukeable"; an alternative rendering would be 'irreprehensible'). See REPROACH, UNREBUKEABLE. ¶

NT: B.65b; CB.1235c; K.495.
OT: –.
GEN. REF.: –.

6. *anenklētos* [ἀνέγκλητος, 410], signifies that which cannot be called to account (from *a*, negative, *n*, euphonic, and *enkaleō*, to call in), i.e., with nothing laid to one's charge (as the result of public investigation); in 1 Cor. 1:8, R.V., "unreproveable," A.V., "blameless"; in Col. 1:22, A.V. and R.V., "unreproveable"; in 1 Tim. 3:10 and Tit. 1:6, 7, A.V. and R.V., "blameless." It implies not merely acquittal, but the absence of even a charge or accusation against a person. This is to be the case with elders. ¶

NT: B.64b; CB.1235c; K.58.
OT: –.
GEN. REF.: –.

C. Adverb.

amemptōs [ἀμέμπτως, 274], in 1 Thess. 2:10, "unblameably"; in 5:23, "without blame," A.V., "blameless," is said of believers at the Judgment-Seat of Christ in His Parousia (His presence after His coming), as the outcome of present witness and steadfastness. See B, No. 3, above. ¶

NT: B.45b; CB.1234c; K.58.
OT: –.
GEN. REF.: –.

BLASPHEME, BLASPHEMY, BLASPHEMER, BLASPHEMOUS

A. Noun.

blasphēmia [βλασφημία, 988], either from *blax*, sluggish, stupid, or, probably, from *blaptō*, to injure, and *phēmē*, speech, Eng. "blasphemy," is so translated thirteen times in the R.V., but "railing" in Matt. 15:19; Mark 7:22; Eph. 4:31; Col. 3:8; 1 Tim. 6:4; Jude 9. The word "blasphemy" is practically confined to speech defamatory of the Divine Majesty. See Note, below. See EVIL SPEAKING, RAILING.

NT: B.143a; CB.1239a; K.107.
OT: ne'āṣāh: S.5007; HR.221a.1; H.1274a,b; BD.611a.
GEN. REF.: IS.1:521; NB.159; Z.1:624.

B. Verb.

blasphēmeō [βλασφημέω, 987], to blaspheme, rail at or revile, is used (*a*) in a general way, of any contumelious speech, reviling, calumniating, railing at etc., as of those who railed at Christ, e.g., Matt. 27:39; Mark 15:29; Luke 22:65 (R.V., reviling); 23:39; (*b*) of those who speak contemptuously of God or of sacred things, e.g., Matt. 9:3; Mark 3:28; Rom. 2:24; 1 Tim. 1:20; 6:1; Rev. 13:6; 16:9, 11, 21; "hath spoken blasphemy," Matt. 26:65; "rail at," 2 Pet. 2:10; Jude 8, 10; "railing," 2 Pet. 2:12; "slanderously reported," Rom. 3:8; "be evil spoken of," Rom. 14:16; 1 Cor. 10:30; 2 Pet. 2:2; "speak evil of," Tit. 3:2; 1 Pet. 4:4; "being defamed," 1 Cor. 4:13. The verb (in the present participial form) is translated "blasphemers" in Acts 19:37; in Mark 2:7, "blasphemeth," R.V., for A.V., "speaketh blasphemies."

There is no noun in the original representing the English "blasphemer." This is expressed either by the verb, or by the adjective *blasphēmos*. See DEFAME, RAIL, REPORT, REVILE.

NT: B.142c; CB.1239a; K.107.
OT: nā'aṣ: S.5006; HR.221a.3; H.1274; BD.610d.
gādaph: S.1442; HR.221a.1; H.317; BD.154c.
GEN. REF.: IS.1:521; NB.159; Z.1:624.

C. Adjective.

blasphēmos [βλάσφημος, 989], abusive, speaking evil, is translated "blasphemous," in Acts 6:11, 13; "a blasphemer," 1 Tim. 1:13; "railers," 2 Tim. 3:2, R.V.; "railing," 2 Pet. 2:11. See RAIL. ¶

NT: B.143a; CB.1239a; K.107.
OT: –.
GEN. REF.: IS.1:521; NB.159; Z.1:624.

Note: As to Christ's teaching concerning blasphemy against the Holy Spirit, e.g., Matt. 12:32, that anyone, with the evidence of the Lord's power before His eyes, should declare it to be Satanic, exhibited a condition of heart beyond Divine illumination and therefore hopeless. Divine forgiveness would be inconsistent with the moral nature of God. As to the Son of Man, in his state of humiliation, there might be misunderstanding, but not so with the Holy Spirit's power demonstrated.

BLAZE ABROAD

diaphēmizō [διαφημίζω, 1310], to spread abroad (*dia*, throughout, *phēmizō*, to speak), is so translated in the R.V. in Matt. 9:31; 28:15 (A.V., "commonly reported"); Mark 1:45 (A.V., "blaze abroad"). ¶

NT: B.190c; CB.–; K.–.
OT: –.
GEN. REF.: IS.1:522; NB.–; Z.–.

BLEMISH

A. Noun.

mōmos [μῶμος, 3470], akin to *mōmaomai* (See BLAME, A), signifies (*a*) a blemish (Sept. only); (*b*) a shame, a moral disgrace, metaphorical of the licentious, 2 Pet. 2:13. ¶

NT: B.531a; CB.–; K.619.
OT: mûm: S.3971; HR.938b.1; H.1137a; BD.548c.
GEN. REF.: IS.1:522; NB.–; Z.1:625.

B. Adjective.

amōmos [ἄμωμος, 299], without blemish; is always so rendered in the R.V., Eph. 1:4; 5:27; Phil. 2:15; Col. 1:22; Heb. 9:14; 1 Pet. 1:19; Jude 24; Rev. 14:5. This meaning is to be preferred to the various A.V. renderings, "without blame", Eph. 1:4, "unblameable", Col. 1:22, "faultless", Jude 24, "without fault", Rev. 14:5. The most authentic mss. have *amōmōs*, "without blemish", in Phil. 2:15, for *amōmētos*, "without rebuke". ¶ In the Sept., in reference to sacrifices, especially in Lev. and Num., the Psalms and Ezek., of blamelessness in character and conduct. See BLAME, FAULT.

NT: B.47d; CB.1234c; K.619.
OT: tamîm: S.8549; HR.68b.2c; H.2522d; BD.1071a.
GEN. REF.: IS.1:522; NB.–; Z.1:625.

BLESS, BLESSED, BLESSEDNESS, BLESSING

A. Verbs.

1. *eulogeō* [εὐλογέω, 2127], lit., to speak well of (*eu*, well, *logos*, a word), signifies, (*a*) to praise, to celebrate with praises, of that which is addressed to God, acknowledging His goodness, with desire for His glory, Luke 1:64; 2:28; 24:51, 53; Jas. 3:9; (*b*) to invoke blessings upon a person, e.g., Luke 6:28; Rom. 12:14. The present participle Passive, blessed, praised, is especially used of Christ in Matt. 21:9; 23:39, and the parallel passages; also in John 12:13; (*c*) to consecrate a thing with solemn prayers, to ask God's blessing on a thing, e.g., Luke 9:16; 1 Cor. 10:16; (*d*) to cause to prosper, to make happy, to bestow blessings on, said of God, e.g., in Acts 3:26; Gal. 3:9; Eph. 1:3. Cp. the synonym *aineō*, to praise. See PRAISE.

NT: B.322b; CB.1247b; K.275.
OT: bārak: S.1288; HR.572a.1c; H.285; BD.138c.
GEN. REF.: IS.1:523; NB.160; Z.1:625.

2. *eneulogeomai* [ἐνευλογέομαι, 1757], to bless, is used in the Passive Voice, Acts 3:25, and Gal. 3:8. The prefix *en* apparently indicates the person on whom the blessing is conferred. ¶

NT: B.265d; CB.1245a; K.–.
OT: bārak: S.1288; HR.473a.2a,c; H.285; BD.138c.
GEN. REF.: IS.1:523; NB.160; Z.1:625.

3. *makarizō* [μακαρίζω, 3106], from a root *mak*–, meaning large, lengthy, found also in *makros*, long, *mēkos*, length, hence denotes to pronounce happy, blessed, Luke 1:48 and Jas. 5:11. See HAPPY. ¶

NT: B.486c; CB.1257c; K.548.
OT: 'āshar: S.833; HR.892a.1a; H.183; BD.80d.
GEN. REF.: IS.1:523; NB.160; Z.1:625.

B. Adjectives.

1. *eulogētos* [εὐλογητός, 2128], akin to A, 1, means blessed, praised; it is applied only to God, Mark 14:61; Luke 1:68; Rom. 1:25; 9:5; 2 Cor. 1:3; 11:31; Eph. 1:3; 1 Pet. 1:3. ¶ In the Sept. it is also applied to man, e.g., in Gen. 24:31; 26:29; Deut. 7:14; Judg. 17:2; Ruth 2:20; 1 Sam. 15:13.

NT: B.322d; CB.1247b; K.275.
OT: bārak: S.1288; HR.574a.1a; H.285; BD.138c.
GEN. REF.: IS.1:523; NB.160; Z.1:625.

2. *makarios* [μακάριος, 3107], akin to A, No. 3, is used in the beatitudes in Matt. 5 and Luke 6, is especially frequent in the Gospel of Luke, and is found seven times in Revelation, 1:3; 14:13; 16:15; 19:9; 20:6; 22:7, 14. It is said of God twice, 1 Tim. 1:11; 6:15. In the beatitudes the Lord indicates not only the characters that are blessed, but the nature of that which is the highest good.

NT: B.486c; CB.1257c; K.548.
OT: 'esher: S.835; HR.892b.1b; H.183a; BD.80d.
GEN. REF.: IS.1:523; NB.160; Z.1:625.

C. Nouns.

1. *eulogia* [εὐλογία, 2129], akin to A, 1, lit., good speaking, praise, is used of (*a*) God and Christ, Rev. 5:12, 13; 7:12; (*b*) the invocation of blessings, benediction, Heb. 12:17; Jas. 3:10; (*c*) the giving of thanks, 1 Cor. 10:16; (*d*) a blessing, a benefit bestowed, Rom. 15:29; Gal. 3:14; Eph. 1:3; Heb. 6:7; of a monetary gift sent to needy believers, 2 Cor. 9:5, 6; (*e*) in a bad sense, of fair speech, Rom. 16:18, R.V., where it is joined with *chrēstologia*, smooth speech, the latter relating to the substance, *eulogia* to the expression. See BOUNTY. ¶

NT: B.322d; CB.1247b; K.275.
OT: bᵉrākāh: S.1293; HR.574b.2d; H.285b; BD.139c.
GEN. REF.: IS.1:523; NB.160; Z.1:625.

2. *makarismos* [μακαρισμός, 3108], akin to A, 3, blessedness, indicates an ascription of blessing rather than a state; hence in Rom. 4:6, where the A.V. renders it as a noun, "(describeth) the blessedness"; the R.V. rightly puts "(pronounceth) blessing". So ver. 9. In Gal. 4:15 the A.V. has "blessedness", R.V., "gratulation". The Galatian believers had counted themselves happy when they heard and received the Gospel. Had they lost that opinion? See GRATULATION. ¶

NT: B.487a; CB.1257c; K.548.
OT: –.
GEN. REF.: IS.1:523; NB.160; Z.1:625.

Note: In Acts 13:34, *hosia*, lit., 'holy things', is translated "mercies" (A.V.), "blessings" (R.V.).

For **BLEW** see **BLOW**

BLIND, BLINDNESS

A. Verbs.

1. *tuphloō* [τυφλόω, 5186], to blind (from a root *tuph*—, to burn, smoke; cp. *tuphos*, smoke), is used metaphorically, of the dulling of the intellect, John 12:40; 2 Cor. 4:4; 1 John 2:11. ¶

NT: B.831a; CB.–; K.1196.
OT: 'iwwēr: S.5787; HR.1379c.1; H.1586a; BD.734c.
GEN. REF.: IS.1:523; NB.313; Z.2:132.

2. *pōroō* [πωρόω, 4456], signifies to harden (from *pōros*, a thick skin, a hardening); rendered "blinded", A.V., in Rom. 11:7 and 2 Cor. 3:14 (R.V., "hardened"); cp. 4:4. See HARDEN.

NT: B.732a; CB.1266a; K.816.
OT: kāhāh: S.3543; HR.1246c.1; H.957; BD.462c.
GEN. REF.: IS.1:525; NB.313; Z.2:132,133.

B. Adjective.

tuphlos [τυφλός, 5185], blind, is used both physically and metaphorically, chiefly in the Gospels; elsewhere four times; physically, Acts 13:11; metaphorically, Rom. 2:19; 2 Pet. 1:9; Rev. 3:17. The word is frequently used as a noun, signifying a blind man.

NT: B.830d; CB.1273a; K.1196.
OT: 'iwwēr: S.5787; HR.1379b.1a; H.1586a; BD.734c.
GEN. REF.: IS.1:525; NB.313; Z.2:132,133.

C. Noun.

pōrōsis [πώρωσις, 4457], akin to A. No. 2, primarily means a covering with a callus, a "hardening", Rom. 11:25 and Eph. 4:18, R.V., for A.V., "blindness", Mark 3:5, R.V., for A.V., "hardness". It is metaphorical of a dulled spiritual perception. See HARDNESS. ¶

NT: B.732a; CB.1266a; K.816.
OT: –.
GEN. REF.: IS.1:525; NB.313; Z.2:132,133.

Note: In John 9:8, the most authentic mss. have *prosaitēs*, a beggar, R.V., instead of *tuphlos*, blind.

BLINDFOLD

perikaluptō [περικαλύπτω, 4028], signifies to blindfold (*peri*, around, *kaluptō*, to hide), Luke 22:64. See COVER, OVERLAY.

NT: B.647d; CB.–; K.–.
OT: ḥaphas: S.2664; HR.1124a.1; H.716; BD.344b.
kāsāh: S.3680; HR.1124a.2; H.1008; BD.491b.
sākak: S.5526; HR.1124a.3; H.1492; BD.696d.
GEN. REF.: –.

BLOOD

A. Nouns.

1. *haima* [αἷμα, 129], (hence Eng., prefix *haem*—), besides its natural meaning, stands, (*a*) in conjunction with *sarx*, flesh, "flesh and blood", Matt. 16:17; 1 Cor. 15:50; Gal. 1:16; the original has the opposite order, blood and flesh, in Eph. 6:12 and Heb. 2:14; this phrase signifies, by *synecdoche*, man, human beings. It stresses the limitations of humanity; the two are essential elements in man's physical being; "the life of the flesh is in the blood", Lev. 17:11; (*b*) for human generation, John 1:13; (*c*) for blood shed by violence, e.g., Matt. 23:35; Rev. 17:6; (*d*) for the blood of sacrificial victims, e.g., Heb. 9:7; of the blood of Christ, which betokens His death by the shedding of His blood in expiatory sacrifice; to drink His blood is to appropriate the saving effects of His expiatory death, John 6:53. As "the life of the flesh is in the blood", Lev. 17:11 and was forfeited by sin, life eternal can be imparted only by the expiation made, in the giving up of the life by the sinless Saviour.

NT: B.22c; CB.1249a; K.26.
OT: dâm: S.1818; HR.31b.1; H.436; BD.196b.
GEN. REF.: IS.1:526; NB.160; Z.1:626.

2. *haimatekchusia* [αἱματεκχυσία, 130], denotes shedding of blood, Heb. 9:22 (*haima*, blood, *ekchunō*, to pour out, shed). ¶

NT: B.23b; CB.1249a; K.26.
OT: –.
GEN. REF.: IS.1:526; NB.160; Z.1:626.

B. Verb.

haimorrhoeō [αἱμορροέω, 131], from *haima*, blood, *rheō*, to flow (Eng., haemorrhage), signifies to suffer from a flow of blood, Matt. 9:20. ¶

NT: B.23c; CB.–; K.–.
OT: dâweh: S.1739; HR.33a.1; H.411b; BD.188c.
GEN. REF.: IS.1:526; NB.160; Z.1:626.

Notes: (1) In Mark 5:25 and Luke 8:43, different constructions are used, the translations respectively being "having a flowing of blood" and "being in (i.e., with) a flowing of blood".

(2) In Acts 17:26 (R.V., "of one"; A.V. "of one blood"), the most authentic mss. do not contain the noun *haima*, blood. So with the phrase "through His blood", in Col. 1:14.

(3) For "bloody flux" in Acts 28:8, A.V., see DYSENTERY (R.V.)

BLOT OUT

exaleiphō [ἐξαλείφω, 1813], from *ek*, out, used intensively, and *aleiphō*, to wipe, signifies to wash, or to smear completely. Hence, metaphorically, in the sense of removal, to wipe away, wipe off, obliterate; Acts 3:19, of sins; Col. 2:14, of writing; Rev. 3:5, of a name in a book; Rev. 7:17; 21:4, of tears. ¶

NT: B.272c; CB.1247b; K.—.
OT: māḥāh: S.4229; HR.486c.4a,b; H.1178, 1179; BD.562a.
shaḥat: S.7843; HR.486c.5a,b; H.2370; BD.1007d.
GEN. REF.: IS.—; NB.—; Z.1:629.

BLOW (Noun)

rhapisma [ῥάπισμα, 4475], (*a*) a blow with a rod or staff, (*b*) a blow with the hand, a slap or cuff, is found in three places, of the maltreatment of Christ by the officials or attendants of the high priest, Mark 14:65, R.V., "received (according to the most authentic mss.) Him with blows of their hands"; (A.V., "did strike Him with the palms of their hands"); that they received, or took, Him would indicate their rough handling of Him; John 18:22 and 19:3; in all three places the R.V. marg. gives the meaning (*a*), as to the use of a rod. ¶

So with the corresponding verb *rhapizō*, in Matt. 26:27. The soldiers subsequently beat him with a reed, 27:30, where *tuptō*, to beat, is used; *rhapizō* occurs elsewhere in Matt. 5:39. See SMITE. ¶

NT: B.734c; CB.1268a; K.—.
OT: māraṭ: S.4803; HR.1248a.1; H.1244; BD.598d.
GEN. REF.: —.

BLOW (Verb)

1. *pneō* [πνέω, 4154], signifies (*a*) to blow, e.g., Matt. 7:25; John 3:8; in Acts 27:40 the present participle is used as a noun, lit., 'to the blowing' (i.e., to the wind); (*b*) to breathe. See BREATHE.

NT: B.679c; CB.1265b; K.876.
OT: nāshab: S.5380; HR.1151c.1; H.1426; BD.674b.
nāshaph: S.5398; HR.1151c.2; H.1434; BD.676a.
GEN. REF.: IS.1:527; NB.—; Z.—.

2. *hupopneō* [ὑποπνέω, 5285], *hupo*, under (indicating repression), and No. 1, denotes to blow softly, Acts 27:13.

NT: B.846d; CB.—; K.—.
OT: —.
GEN. REF.: IS.1:527; NB.—; Z.—.

Note: In Acts 28:13, *epiginomai*, to come on, is used of the springing up of a wind, A.V., "blew"; R.V., "sprang up".

BOARD

sanis [σανίς, 4548], denotes a plank, or board, Acts 27:44. ¶

NT: B.742a; CB.—; K.—.
OT: delet: S.1817; HR.1259a.1; H.431a,e; BD.195a.
lûaḥ: S.3871; HR.1259a.2; H.1091a; BD.531d.
GEN. REF.: IS.3:882; NB.—; Z.1:630.

BOAST, BOASTER, BOASTFUL

A. Verbs.

1. *kauchaomai* [καυχάομαι, 2744], and its related words *katakauchaomai*, to glory or boast and the nouns *kauchēsis* and *kauchēma*, translated "boast", and "boasting", in the A.V., are always translated "glory", and "glorying" in the R.V., e.g., 2 Cor. 10:15; 11:10, 17; Eph. 2:9. See GLORY.

NT: B.425c; CB.1254c; K.423.
OT: hālal: S.1984; HR.757b.2; H.499,500; BD.239a.
GEN. REF.: IS.1:528; NB.—; Z.1:631.

2. *megalaucheō* [μεγαλαυχέω, 3166], from *megala*, great things, and *aucheō*, to lift up the neck, hence, to boast, is found in some texts of Jas. 3:5. The most authentic mss. have the two words separated. It indicates any kind of haughty speech which stirs up strife or provokes others. ¶

NT: B.496d; CB.—; K.—.
OT: gābah: S.1361; HR.901b.1; H.305; BD.146d.
'āraṣ: S.6206; HR.901b.2; H.1702; BD.791d.
GEN. REF.: IS.1:528; NB.—; Z.1:631.

Note: In Acts 5:36, the verb *legō*, to say, is rendered "boasting" in the A.V.; "giving out" (R.V.).

B. Nouns.

1. *alazōn* [ἀλαζών, 213], a boaster, Rom. 1:30 and 2 Tim. 3:2, A.V., "boasters", R.V., "boastful", primarily signifies a wanderer about the country (from *alē*, wandering), a vagabond; hence, an impostor. ¶

NT: B.34d; CB.1234b; K.36.
OT: yāhîr: S.3093; HR.52a.1; H.851a; BD.397d.
shaḥaṣ: S.7830; HR.52a.2; H.2366a; BD.1006d.
GEN. REF.: IS.1:528; NB.—; Z.1:631.

2. *alazoneia* [ἀλαζονεία, 212], the practice of an *alazōn*, denotes quackery; hence, arrogant display, or boastings, Jas. 4:16, R.V., "vauntings"; in 1 John 2:16, R.V., "vainglory"; A.V., "pride". See PRIDE,, VAUNT. ¶

NT: B.34c; CB.1234b; K.36.
OT: —.
GEN. REF.: IS.1:528; NB.—; Z.1:631.

Note: In 2 Cor. 9:4, *hupostasis*, a support, substance, means "confidence" (R.V.); A.V., "confident boasting".

BOAT

1. *ploiarion* [πλοιάριον, 4142], a skiff or small boat, is a diminutive of *ploion* (No. 2), Mark 3:9; 4:36; John 6:22 (but No. 2 in the 2nd part of the verse), 23 (here some texts have No. 2), 24; 21:8. ¶

NT: B.673b; CB.—; K.—.
OT: —.
GEN. REF.: IS.4:482; NB.1178; Z.1:631.

2. *ploion* [πλοῖον, 4143], A.V., "ship", is preferably translated "boat" (R.V.) in the Gospels, where it is of frequent use; it is found

18 times in Acts, where, as in Jas. 3:4; Rev. 8:9; 18:19, it signifies a ship. See SHIP.
NT: B.673b; CB.–; K.–.
OT: 'oniyyāh: S.591; HR.1150a.1b; H.125b; BD.58b.
GEN. REF.: IS.4:482; NB.1178; Z.1:631.

3. *skaphē* [σκάφη, 4627], is, lit., anything dug or scooped out (from *skaptō*, to dig), as a trough, a tub, and hence a light boat, or skiff, a boat belonging to a larger vessel, Acts 27:16, 30, 32. ¶
NT: B.753c; CB.–; K.–.
OT: –.
GEN. REF.: IS.4:482; NB.1178; Z.1:631.

BODY, BODILY

A. Nouns.

1. *sōma* [σῶμα, 4983], is the body as a whole, the instrument of life, whether of man living, e.g., Matt. 6:22, or dead, Matt. 27:52; or in resurrection, 1 Cor. 15:44; or of beasts, Heb. 13:11; of grain, 1 Cor. 15:37, 38; of the heavenly hosts, 1 Cor. 15:40. In Rev. 18:13 it is translated "slaves". In its figurative uses the essential idea is preserved.

Sometimes the word stands, by *synecdoche*, for the complete man, Matt. 5:29; 6:22; Rom. 12:1; Jas. 3:6; Rev. 18:13. Sometimes the person is identified with his or her body, Acts 9:37; 13:36, and this is so even of the Lord Jesus, John 19:40 with 42. The body is not the man, for he himself can exist apart from his body, 2 Cor. 12:2, 3. The body is an essential part of the man and therefore the redeemed are not perfected till the resurrection, Heb. 11:40; no man in his final state will be without his body, John 5:28, 29; Rev. 20:13.

The word is also used for physical nature, as distinct from *pneuma*, the spiritual nature, e.g., 1 Cor. 5:3, and from *psuchē*, the soul, e.g., 1 Thess. 5:23. "*Sōma*, body, and *pneuma*, spirit, may be separated; *pneuma* and *psuchē*, soul, can only be distinguished" (Cremer).

It is also used metaphorically of the mystic Body of Christ, with reference to the whole Church, e.g., Eph. 1:23; Col. 1:18, 22, 24; also of a local church, 1 Cor. 12:27.
NT: B.799a; CB.1269b; K.1140.
OT: bāsār: S.1320; HR.1330a.1; H.291a; BD.142b.
nᵉbēlāh: S.5038; HR.1330a.7; H.1286a; BD.615c.
GEN. REF.: IS.1:528; NB.162; Z.1:634.

2. *chrōs* [χρώς, 5559], signifies the surface of a body, especially of the human body, Acts 19:12, with reference to the handkerchiefs carried from Paul's body to the sick. ¶
NT: B.889a; CB.–; K.–.
OT: bāsār: S.1320; HR.1480a.1; H.291a; BD.142b.
GEN. REF.: IS.1:528; NB.162; Z.1:634.

3. *ptōma* [πτῶμα, 4430], denotes, lit., a fall (akin to *piptō*, to fall); hence, that which is fallen, a corpse, Matt. 14:12; 24:28, "carcase"; Mark 6:29; 15:45, "corpse"; Rev. 11:8, 9, "dead bodies" (Gk., "carcase", but plural in the 2nd part of ver. 9). See CARCASE, CORPSE ¶
NT: B.727d; CB.1268a; K.846.
OT: gᵉwîyyāh: S.1472; HR.1239a.2; H.326d; BD.156b.
mappelet: S.4658; HR.1239a.4; H.1392e; BD.658c.
peger: S.6297; HR.1239a.5; H.1732a; BD.803d.
GEN. REF.: IS.1:528; NB.162; Z.1:634.

B. Adjectives.

1. *sussōmos* [σύσσωμος, 4954], *sun*, with, and A, No. 1., means united in the same body, Eph. 3:6, of the Church. ¶
NT: B.794d; CB.–; K.1140.
OT: –.
GEN. REF.: IS.1:528; NB.162; Z.1:634.

2. *sōmatikos* [σωματικός, 4984], bodily, is used in Luke 3:22, of the Holy Spirit in taking a bodily shape; in 1 Tim. 4:8 of bodily exercise. ¶
NT: B.800b; CB.1269b; K.1140.
OT: –.
GEN. REF.: IS.1:528; NB.162; Z.1:634.

C. Adverb.

sōmatikōs [σωματικῶς], bodily, corporeally, is used in Col. 2:9. ¶
GEN. REF.: –.

BOISTEROUS

Note: The A.V. "boisterous" in Matt. 14:30 is a rendering of the word *ischuros*, "strong" (see margin); it is not in the most authentic mss.

BOLD, BOLDNESS, BOLDLY

A. Verbs.

1. *tharreō* [θαῤῥέω, 2292], a later form of *tharseō* (see CHEER, COMFORT), is connected with *therō*, to be warm (warmth of temperament being associated with confidence); hence, to be confident, bold, courageous; R.V., invariably, to be of good courage; 2 Cor. 5:6, 8 (A.V., to be confident); 7:16 (A.V., to have confidence); 10:1, 2 (A.V., to be bold); Heb. 13:6, A.V., "boldly"; R.V., "with good courage" (lit., 'being courageous'). See COURAGE.
NT: B.352a; CB.1271c; K.315.
OT: –.
GEN. REF.: IS.1:352; NB.–; Z.–.

2. *parrhēsiazomai* [παῤῥησιάζομαι, 3955], to speak boldly, or freely, primarily had reference to speech (see B, below), but acquired the meaning of being bold, or waxing bold, 1 Thess. 2:2; in Acts 13:46, R.V., "spake out boldly" (the aorist participle here signifies 'waxing bold'); Acts 9:27, 29, "preached boldly" (see also 18:26; 19:8) in 26:26, "speak freely". See FREELY.
NT: B.631a; CB.1262c; K.794.
OT: –.
GEN. REF.: IS.1:532; NB.–; Z.–.

3. *tolmaō* [τολμάω, 5111], signifies to dare to do, or to bear, something terrible or difficult; hence, to be bold, to bear oneself boldly, deal boldly; it is translated "be bold" in 2 Cor. 10:2, as contrasted with *tharreō* in verse 1, and the first line of verse 2, "shew courage" (see No. 1, above); in 10:12, R.V., "are not bold to", for A.V., "dare not make ourselves of". *Tharreō* denotes confidence in one's own powers, and has reference to character; *tolmaō* denotes boldness in undertaking and has reference to manifestation (Thayer). See COURAGE, DARE.

NT: B.821d; CB.1272c; K.1183.
OT: —.
GEN. REF.: IS.1:532; NB.—; Z.—.

4. *apotolmaō* [ἀποτολμάω, 662], *apo* (intensive), with No. 3, means to be very bold, to speak out boldly, and is used in Rom. 10:20. ¶

NT: B.101d; CB.—; K.1183.
OT: —.
GEN. REF.: IS.1:532; NB.—; Z.—.

B. Noun.

parrhēsia [παῤῥησία, 3954], from *pas*, all, *rhēsis*, speech (see A, No. 2), denotes (*a*), primarily, freedom of speech, unreservedness of utterance, Acts 4:29, 31; 2 Cor. 3:12; 7:4; Philm. 8; or to speak without ambiguity, plainly, John 10:24; or without figures of speech, John 16:25; (*b*) the absence of fear in speaking boldly; hence, confidence, cheerful courage, boldness, without any connection necessarily with speech; the R.V., has "boldness" in the following; Acts 4:13; Eph. 3:12; 1 Tim. 3:13; Heb. 3:6; 4:16; 10:19, 35; 1 John 2:28; 3:21; 4:17; 5:14; (*c*) the deportment by which one becomes conspicuous, John 7:4; 11:54, acts openly, or secures publicity, Col. 2:15. See CONFIDENCE, OPENLY, PLAINNESS.

NT: B.630c; CB.1262c; K.794.
OT: —.
GEN. REF.: IS.1:532; NB.—; Z.—.

C. Adverb.

tolmēroterōs [τολμηροτέρως, 5112], the comparative degree of *tolmērōs*, means the more boldly, Rom. 15:15; in some texts, *tolmēroteron*. Cp. A, No. 3. ¶ Cp. *tolmētēs*, presumptuous; R.V., "daring", 2 Pet. 2:10. ¶

NT: B.822a; CB.1272c; K.—.
OT: —.
GEN. REF.: IS.1:532; NB.—; Z.—.

BOND

1. *desmos* [δεσμός, 1199], from *deō*, to bind (see BAND), is usually found in the plural, either masculine or neuter; (*a*) it stands thus for the actual bonds which bind a prisoner, as in Luke 8:29; Acts 16:26; 20:23 (the only three places where the neuter plural is used); 22:30; (*b*) the masculine plural stands frequently in a figurative sense for a condition of imprisonment, Phil. 1:7, 13, i.e., 'so that my captivity became manifest as appointed for the cause of Christ'; verses 14, 16; Col. 4:18; 2 Tim. 2:9; Philm. 10, 13; Heb. 10:34.

In Mark 7:35 "the bond" (A.V., string) stands metaphorically the infirmity which caused an impediment in his speech. So in Luke 13:16, of the infirmity of the woman who was bowed together. See BAND, CHAIN, STRING.

NT: B.176a; CB.1240c; K.145.
OT: môsēr: S.4147; HR.292a.1e; H.141f; BD.64c.
'ăbôt: S.5688; HR.292a.6; H.1558b; BD.721c.
GEN. REF.: IS.1:533; NB.—; Z.1:636.

2. *desmios* [δέσμιος, 1198], a binding, denotes "a prisoner", e.g., Acts 25:14, R.V., for the A.V., "in bonds"; Heb. 13:3, "them that are in bonds". Paul speaks of himself as a prisoner of Christ, Eph. 3:1; 2 Tim. 1:8; Philm. 1, 9; "in the Lord", Eph. 4:1. See PRISONER.

NT: B.176b; CB.1240c; K.145.
OT: 'assîr: S.616; HR.292a.1b; H.141c; BD.64a.
GEN. REF.: IS.1:533; NB.—; Z.1:636.

3. *sundesmos* [σύνδεσμος, 4886], that which binds together (*sun*, with, and No. 1), is said of "the bond of iniquity", Acts 8:23; "the bond of peace", Eph. 4:3; "the bond of perfectness", Col. 3:14 (figurative of the ligaments of the body); elsewhere, Col. 2:19, "bands", figuratively of the bands which unite the Church, the Body of Christ. See BAND. ¶

NT: B.785b; CB.1270c—; K.1114.
OT: harṣubbôt: S.2784; HR.1312c.2; H.754a; BD.359b.
qesher: S.7195; HR.1312c.6; H.2090a; BD.905c.
GEN. REF.: IS.1:533; NB.—; Z.1:636.

4. *halusis* [ἅλυσις, 254], denotes a chain; so the R.V. in Eph. 6:20, for A.V., "bonds". See CHAIN.

NT: B.41c; CB.—; K.—.
OT: —.
GEN. REF.: IS.1:533; NB.—; Z.1:636.

5. *gramma* [γράμμα, 1121], in Luke 16:6, R.V., means a bill or note of hand. See BILL, No. 2.

NT: B.165b; CB.1248c; K.128.
OT: sēpher: S.5612; HR.275a.3; H.1540a; BD.706d.
GEN. REF.: IS.1:510; NB.—; Z.1:636.

6. *cheirographos* [χειρόγραφος, 5498], a handwriting, is rendered "bond" in Col. 2:14, R.V.

NT: B.880d; CB.1239c; K.1309.
OT: —.
GEN. REF.: IS.1:533; NB.—; Z.1:636.

BONDAGE

A. Noun.

douleia [δουλεία, 1397], akin to *deō*, to bind, primarily the condition of being a slave, came to denote any kind of bondage, as, e.g., of the condition of creation, Rom. 8:21; of that fallen condition of man himself which makes him dread God, ver. 15, and fear death, Heb. 2:15; of the condition imposed by the Mosaic Law, Gal. 4:24. See SERVE.

NT: B.205a; CB.1242b; K.182.
OT: 'ebed: S.5650; HR.345a.1a; H.1553a; BD.713d.
'ăbôdāh: S.5656; HR.345a.1b; H.1553c; BD.715a.
GEN. REF.: IS.1:533; NB.–; Z.1:636.

B. Verbs.

1. *douleuō* [δουλεύω, 1398], to serve as a slave, to be a slave, to be in bondage, is frequently used without any association of slavery, e.g., Acts 20:19; Rom. 6:6; 7:6; 12:11; Gal. 5:13. See SERVE.

NT: B.205a; CB.1242b; K.182.
OT: 'ābad: S.5647; HR.345a.1a; H.1553; BD.712b.
GEN. REF.: IS.1:533; NB.–; Z.1:636.

2. *douloō* [δουλόω, 1402], different from No. 1, in being transitive instead of intransitive, signifies to make a slave of, to bring into bondage, Acts 7:6; 1 Cor. 9:19, R.V.; in the Passive Voice, to be brought under bondage, 2 Pet. 2:19; to be held in bondage, Gal. 4:3 (lit., 'were reduced to bondage'); Tit. 2:3, of being enslaved to wine; Rom. 6:18, of service to righteousness (lit., 'were made bondservants'). As with the purchased slave there were no limitations either in the kind or the time of service, so the life of the believer is to be lived in continuous obedience to God. See ENSLAVED, GIVE, SERVANT.

NT: B.206a; CB.–; K.182.
OT: 'ābad: S.5647; HR.348b.1; H.1553; BD.712b.
GEN. REF.: IS.1:533; NB.–; Z.1:636.

3. *doulagōgeō* [δουλαγωγέω, 1396], to bring into bondage (from A, above, and *agō*, to bring), is used in 1 Cor. 9:27, concerning the body, R.V., "bondage", for A.V., "subjection". ¶

NT: B.205a; CB.1242a; K.182.
OT: –.
GEN. REF.: IS.1:533; NB.–; Z.1:636.

4. *katadouloō* [καταδουλόω, 2615], to bring into bondage, occurs in 2 Cor. 11:20; Gal. 2:4. ¶

NT: B.410c; CB.–; K.182.
OT: 'ābad: S.5647; HR.731a.1; H.1553; BD.712b.
GEN. REF.: IS.1:533; NB.–; Z.1:636.

BONDMAN, BONDMAID

1. *doulos* [δοῦλος, 1401], from *deō*, to bind, a slave, originally the lowest term in the scale of servitude, came also to mean one who gives himself up to the will of another, e.g., 1 Cor. 7:23; Rom. 6:17, 20, and became the most common and general word for "servant", as in Matt. 8:9, without any idea of bondage. In calling himself, however, a 'bondslave of Jesus Christ', e.g., Rom. 1:1, the Apostle Paul intimates (1) that he had been formerly a bondslave of Satan, and (2) that, having been bought by Christ, he was now a willing slave, bound to his new Master. See SERVANT.

The feminine, *doulē*, signifies a handmaid, Luke 1:38, 48; Acts 2:18. ¶

NT: B.205c; CB.1242b; K.182.
OT: 'ebed: S.5650; HR.346b.2b; H.1553a; BD.713d.
GEN. REF.: IS.1:534; NB.–; Z.–.

2. *paidiskē* [παιδίσκη, 3814], a young girl, maiden, also denoted a young female slave, bondwoman, or handmaid. For the A.V., "bondmaid" or "bondwoman", in Gal. 4:22, 23, 30, 31, the R.V. has "handmaid". See DAMSEL, HANDMAID, MAID.

NT: B.604b; CB.1261c; K.–.
OT: 'āmāh: S.519; HR.1048b.1; H.112; BD.51a.
shiphḥāh: S.8198; HR.1048b.4; H.2442a; BD.1046c.
GEN. REF.: IS.1:534; NB.–; Z.–.

For **BONDSERVANT** see **SERVANT**

BONE

osteon [ὀστέον,3747], probably from a word signifying strength, or firmness, sometimes denotes hard substances other than bones, e.g., the stone or kernel of fruit. In the N.T. it always denotes bones, Matt. 23:27; Luke 24:39; John 19:36; Heb. 11:22. ¶

NT: B.586c; CB.1261b; K.–.
OT: 'eṣem: S.6106; HR.1021c.2a; H.1673c; BD.782c.
GEN. REF.: IS.1:534; NB.–; Z.–.

Note: As to Eph. 5:30, R.V., "We are members of His body" (in contrast to the A.V.), "the words that follow in the common text are an unintelligent gloss, in which unsuccessful endeavour is made to give greater distinctness to the Apostle's statement" (Westcott).

BOOK

1. *biblos* [βίβλος, 976], Eng. "Bible," was the inner part, or rather the cellular substance, of the stem of the papyrus (Eng. "paper"). It came to denote the paper made from this bark in Egypt, and then a written book, roll, or volume. It is used in referring to books of Scripture, the book, or scroll, of Matthew's Gospel, Matt. 1:1; the Pentateuch, as the book of Moses, Mark 12:26; Isaiah, as "the book of the words of Isaiah," Luke 3:4; the Psalms, Luke 20:42 and Acts 1:20; "the prophets," Acts 7:42; to "the Book of Life," Phil. 4:3; Rev. 3:5; 20:15. Once only it is used of secular writings, Acts 19:19. ¶

NT: B.141c; CB.1239a; K.106.
OT: sēpher: S.5612; HR.219b.1a; H.1540a; BD.706d.
GEN. REF.: IS.4:1136; NB.1341; Z.1:637.

2. *biblion* [βιβλίον, 975], a diminutive of No. 1, had in Hellenistic Greek almost lost its diminutive force and was ousting *biblos* in ordinary use; it denotes a scroll or a small book. It is used in Luke 4:17, 20, of the book of Isaiah;

in John 20:30, of the Gospel of John; in Gal. 3:10 and Heb. 10:7, of the whole of the O.T.; in Heb. 9:19, of the book of Exodus; in Rev. 1:11; 22:7, 9, 10, 18 (twice), 19, of the Apocalypse; in John 21:25 and 2 Tim. 4:13, of books in general; in Rev. 13:8; 17:8; 20:12; 21:27, of the Book of Life (see Note, below); in Rev. 20:12, of other books to be opened in the Day of Judgment, containing, it would seem, the record of human deeds. In Rev. 5:1-9 the Book represents the revelation of God's purposes and counsels concerning the world. So with the "little book" in Rev. 10:8. In 6:14 it is used of a scroll, the rolling up of which illustrates the removal of the heaven.

In Matt. 19:7 and Mark 10:4 the word is used of a bill of divorcement. See BILL. ¶

NT: B.141b; CB.1239a; K.106.
OT: sēpher: S.5612; HR.218b.4c; H.1540a; BD.706d.
GEN. REF.: IS.4:1136; NB.1341; Z.1:637.

Note: In Rev. 22:19, the most authentic mss. have *xulon*, tree (of life), instead of "*biblion*".

3. *biblaridion* [βιβλαρίδιον, 974], another diminutive of No. 1, is always rendered "little book," in Rev. 10:2, 9, 10. Some texts have it also in verse 8, instead of *biblion* (but see beginning of No. 2). ¶

NT: B.141a; CB.—; K.—.
OT: —.
GEN. REF.: IS.4:1136; NB.1341; Z.1:637.

BOON

dōrēma [δώρημα, 1434], translated "boon" in Jas. 1:17, R.V., is thus distinguished, as the thing given, from the preceding word in the verse, *dosis*, the act of giving (A.V., "gift" in each case); elsewhere in Rom. 5:16. It is to be distinguished also from *dōron*, the usual word for a gift. See GIFT. ¶

NT: B.210d; CB.1242a; K.166.
OT: —.
GEN. REF.: —.

BORDER

1. *kraspedon* [κράσπεδον, 2899], was primarily the extremity or prominent part of a thing, an edge; hence the fringe of a garment, or a little fringe, hanging down from the edge of the mantle or cloak. The Jews had these attached to their mantles to remind them of the Law, according to Num. 15:38, 39; Deut. 22:12; Zech. 8:23. ¶ This is the meaning in Matt. 23:5. In Matt. 9:20; 14:36; Mark 6:56; Luke 8:44, it is used of the border of Christ's garment (A.V. "hem," in the first two places). See HEM. ¶

NT: B.448b; CB.—; K.466.
OT: kānāph: S.3671; HR.782a.1; H.1003a; BD.489b.
ṣîṣit: S.6734; HR.782a.2; H.1912; BD.851d.
GEN. REF.: IS.—; NB.—; Z.1:641.

2. *horion* [ὅριον, 3725], the border of a country or district (cp. Eng., horizon), is always used in the plural. The A.V. has "coasts," but "borders" in Matt. 4:13; the R.V. always "borders," Matt. 2:16; 4:13; 8:34; 15:22, 39; 19:1; Mark 5:17; 7:31 (twice); 10:1; Acts 13:50. In some of these it signifies territory. See COAST. ¶

NT: B.581b; CB.1251b; K.—.
OT: gᵉbûl: S.1366; HR.1012a; H.307a; BD.147d.
GEN. REF.: IS.1:535; NB.—; Z.1:641.

3. *methorion* [μεθόριον, 3181], *meta*, with, and No. 2, similar in meaning, is found, in some mss., in Mark 7:24. ¶ Cp. *horothesia*, under BOUND.

NT: B.499b; CB.—; K.—.
OT: —.
GEN. REF.: IS.—; NB.—; Z.1:641.

For BORN see BEGET

For BORNE see BEAR

BORROW

daneizō [δανείζω, 1155], in the Active Voice, signifies to lend money, as in Luke 6:34, 35; in the Middle Voice, to have money lent to oneself, to borrow, Matt. 5:42. ¶ Cp. *dan(e)ion*, a debt, Matt. 18:27, ¶ and *dan(e)istēs*, a creditor, Luke 7:41. ¶ See LEND.

NT: B.170d; CB.—; K.—.
OT: lāwāh: S.3867; HR.285a.1; H.1087,1088; BD.531a.
GEN. REF.: IS.3:102; NB.—; Z.1:641.

BOSOM

kolpos [κόλπος, 2859], signifies (*a*) the front of the body between the arms; hence, to recline in the bosom was said of one who so reclined at table that his head covered, as it were, the bosom of the one next to him, John 13:23. Hence, figuratively, it is used of a place of blessedness with another, as with Abraham in Paradise, Luke 16:22, 23 (plural in ver. 23), from the custom of reclining at table in the bosom, a place of honour; of the Lord's eternal and essential relation with the Father, in all its blessedness and affection as intimated in the phrase, "The Only-begotten Son, which is in the bosom of the Father" (John 1:18); (*b*) of the bosom of a garment, the hollow formed by the upper forepart of a loose garment, bound by a girdle and used for carrying or keeping things; thus figuratively of repaying one liberally, Luke 6:38; cp. Isa. 65:6; Jer. 39:18; (*c*) of an inlet of the sea, because of its shape, like a bosom, Acts 27:39. See BAY, CREEK. ¶

NT: B.442b; CB.1255c; K.452.
OT: ḥêq: S.2436; HR.777a.1; H.629a; BD.300c.
GEN. REF.: IS.1:18; NB.—; Z.1:642.

For **BOTH** see *Note* †, p. 1

For **BOTTLE** see **SKIN**

BOTTOM, BOTTOMLESS

A. Adverb.

katō [κάτω], for this see BENEATH.

NT: –.
OT: –.
GEN. REF.: –.

B. Adjective.

abussos [ἄβυσσος, 12], bottomless (from *a*, intensive, and *bussos*, a depth; akin to *bathus*, deep; Eng., (bath), is used as a noun denoting the abyss (A.V., "bottomless pit"). It describes an immeasurable depth, the underworld, the lower regions, the abyss of Sheol. In Rom. 10:7, quoted from Deut. 30:13, the abyss (the abode of the lost dead) is substituted for the sea (the change in the quotation is due to the facts of the Death and Resurrection of Christ); the A.V. has "deep" here and in Luke 8:31; the reference is to the lower regions as the abode of demons, out of which they can be let loose, Rev. 11:7; 17:8; it is found seven times in the Apocalypse, 9:1, 2, 11; 11:7; 17:8; 20:1, 3; in 9:1, 2 the R.V. has "the pit of the abyss." See DEEP. ¶

NT: B.2b; CB.1233a; K.2.
OT: t^ehôm: S.8415; HR.1b.1; H.2495a; BD.1062d.
GEN. REF.: –.

For **BOUGHT** see **BUY**

BOUND (Noun)

horothesia [ὁροθεσία, 3734], the fixing of a boundary, rather than the boundary itself (from *horos*, a boundary, and *tithēmi*, to place) is used in Acts 17:26, "bounds." ¶

NT: B.582a; CB.–; K.–.
OT: –.
GEN. REF.: –.

BOUND (to be)

(*a*) *of obligation:*

opheilō [ὀφείλω, 3784], to owe, whether of a debt or any obligation, is translated "we are bound," in 2 Thess. 1:3 and 2:13 (the Apostle expressing his obligation to give thanks for his readers). See BEHOVE.

NT: B.598d; CB.1261a; K.746.
OT: ḥôb: S.2326; HR.1039a.2; H.614a; BD.295a.
GEN. REF.: –.

Note: Dei, it is necessary (for which see MUST), expresses, not the obligation (as does *opheilō*) but the certainty or inevitableness of what is bound to happen, e.g., John 3:15, "must be lifted up" (i.e., inevitably), and Acts 4:12, "wherein we must be saved" (i.e., there is a certainty of salvation).

(*b*) *of binding:*

perikeimai [περίκειμαι, 4029], lit., to lie around (*peri*, around, *keimai*, to lie), to be compassed, is used of binding fetters around a person, Acts 28:20; in Mark 9:42, and Luke 17:2, to hang about a person's neck; in Heb. 5:2, to compass about, metaphorically of infirmities; in 12:1, of those who have witness borne to their faith. See COMPASS, HANG. ¶

NT: B.647d; CB.–; K.425.
OT: –.
GEN. REF.: –.

Note: For "bound" in Acts 22:5; 24:27, see BIND, No. 1; for Acts 22:25, A.V., see BIND, No. 7; for Luke 8:29, see BIND, No. 6.

BOUNTY, BOUNTIFULLY

1. *eulogia* [εὐλογία, 2129], a blessing, has the meaning of bounty in 2 Cor. 9:5, of the offering sent by the church at Corinth to their needy brethren in Judaea.

NT: B.322d; CB.1247b; K.275.
OT: b^erākāh: S.1293; HR.574b.2d; H.285b; BD.139c.
GEN. REF.: IS.–; NB.–; Z.1:642.

Note: In the next verse the adverb "bountifully" is a translation of the phrase *ep' eulogiais*, lit., 'with blessings' (R.V. marg.), that is, that blessings may accrue. See BLESSING.

2. *haplotēs* [ἁπλότης, 572], from *haplous*, simple, single, is translated "bountifulness" in 2 Cor. 9:11, A.V.; R.V., "liberality" (marg., "singleness"); cp. 8:2; 9:13; from sincerity of mind springs "liberality." The thought of sincerity is present in Rom. 12:8; 2 Cor. 11:3; Eph. 6:5; Col. 3:22. See LIBERAL, SIMPLICITY, SINGLENESS. ¶

NT: B.85d; CB.1249b; K.65.
OT: tôm: S.8537; HR.122c.2; H.2522a; BD.1070d.
GEN. REF.: IS.–; NB.–; Z.1:642.

3. *charis* [χάρις, 5485], grace, is rendered, "bounty" in 1 Cor. 16:3, R.V., (A.V., "liberality"), by metonymy for a material gift. See BENEFIT, No. 3.

NT: B.877b; CB.1239c; K.1298.
OT: ḥesed: S.2618; HR.1455a.3; H.686a,699a; BD.338c.
GEN. REF.: IS.–; NB.–; Z.1:643.

4. *hadrotēs* [ἁδρότης, 100], lit., fatness (from *hadros*, thick, well-grown), is used of a monetary gift, in 2 Cor. 8:20, A.V., "abundance;" R.V., "bounty." ¶

NT: B.18d; CB.–; K.–.
OT: –.
GEN. REF.: IS.–; NB.–; Z.1:643.

BOW, BOWED (Verb)

1. *kamptō* [κάμπτω, 2578], to bend, is used especially of bending the knees in religious

veneration, Rom. 11:4; 14:11; Eph. 3:14; Phil. 2:10. ¶

NT: B.402b; CB.1253b; K.413.
OT: kāra': S.3766; HR.718b.3a; H.1044; BD.502c.
GEN. REF.: –.

2. *sunkamptō* [συνκάμπτω, 4781] signifies to bend completely together, to bend down by compulsory force, Rom. 11:10. ¶

NT: B.773b; CB.–; K.–.
OT: gāhar: S.1457; HR.1299b.1; H.322; BD.155c.
kāra': S.3766; HR.718b.3a; H.1044; BD.502c.
GEN. REF.: –.

3. *sunkuptō* [συγκύπτω, 4794], to bow together (*sun*, together with, *kuptō*, to bow), is said, in Luke 13:11, of the woman crippled with a physical infirmity. ¶

NT: B.775a; CB.–; K.–.
OT: –.
GEN. REF.: –.

4. *klinō* [κλίνω, 2827], to incline, to bow down, is used of the women who in their fright bowed their faces to the earth at the Lord's empty tomb, Luke 24:5; of the act of the Lord on the Cross immediately before giving up His Spirit. What is indicated in the statement "He bowed His head," is not the helpless dropping of the head after death, but the deliberate putting of His head into a position of rest, John 19:30. The verb is deeply significant here. The Lord reversed the natural order. The same verb is used in His statement in Matt. 8:20 and Luke 9:58, "the Son of Man hath not where to lay His head." It is used, too, of the decline of day, Luke 9:12; 24:29; of turning enemies to flight, Heb. 11:34. See LAY, SPENT, No. 7, TURN, WEAR. ¶

NT: B.436c; CB.–; K.–.
OT: nāṭāh: S.5186; HR.771a.7; H.1352; BD.639d.
GEN. REF.: –.

5. *tithēmi* [τίθημι, 5087], to put, or place, is said of the soldiers who mockingly bowed their knees to Christ, Mark 15:19. See APPOINT.

NT: B.815d; CB.1272c; K.1176.
OT: sîm, sûm: S.7760; HR.1348c.25a; H.2243; BD.962c.
GEN. REF.: –.

Note: for *gonupeteō*, to bow the knee, Matt. 27:29, see KNEEL.

BOW (Noun)

toxon [τόχον, 5115], a bow, is used in Rev. 6:2. Cp. Hab. 3:8, 9. The instrument is frequently mentioned in the Sept., especially in the Psalms. ¶

NT: B.822b; CB.1273a; K.–.
OT: qeshet: S.7198; HR.1363c.3; H.2093; BD.905d.
GEN. REF.: IS.1:283; NB.82; Z.1:312, 318.

BOWELS

splanchnon [σπλάνχνον, 4698], always in the plural, properly denotes the physical organs of the intestines, and is once used in this respect, Acts 1:18 (for the use by Greeks and Hebrews, see AFFECTION, No. 2). The R.V. substitutes the following for the word "bowels": "affections," 2 Cor. 6:12; "affection," 2 Cor. 7:15; "tender mercies," Phil. 1:8; 2:1; "a heart (of compassion)," Col. 3:12; "heart," Philm. 12, 20; "hearts," Philm. 7; "compassion," 1 John 3:17. The word is rendered "tender" in the A.V. and R.V. of Luke 1:78, in connection with the word "mercy." See AFFECTION, No. 2, COMPASSION, A. No. 2 and B. No. 2. ¶

NT: B.763a; CB.1269c; K.1067.
OT: –.
GEN. REF.: IS.1:537; NB.164; Z.1:643.

BOWL

phialē [φιάλη, 5357], Eng., phial, denotes a bowl; so the R.V., for A.V., "vial," in Rev. 5:8; 15:7; 16:1, 2, 3, 4, 8, 10, 12, 17; 17:1; 21:9; the word is suggestive of rapidity in the emptying of the contents. While the seals (ch. 6) give a general view of the events of the last "week" or "hebdomad," in the vision given to Daniel, Dan. 9:23-27, the "trumpets" refer to the judgments which, in a more or less extended period, are destined to fall especially, though not only, upon apostate Christendom and apostate Jews. The emptying of the bowls betokens the final series of judgments in which this exercise of the wrath of God is "finished" (Rev. 15:1, R.V.). These are introduced by the 7th trumpet. See Rev. 11:15 and the successive order in ver. 18, "the nations were wroth, and Thy wrath came . . .;" see also 6:17; 14:19, 20; 19:11-21. ¶

NT: B.858b; CB.–; K.–.
OT: mizrāq: S.4219; HR.1430a.2; H.585f; BD.284d.
GEN. REF.: IS.1:537; NB.1309; Z.1:644.

BOX

alabastron [ἀλάβαστρον, 211], an alabaster vessel, is translated, in the A.V. of Matt. 26:7; Mark 14:3; Luke 7:37, "box," R.V., "cruse." The breaking refers to the seal, not to the box or cruse. See CRUSE. ¶

NT: B.34c; CB.–; K.–.
OT: ṣallaḥat: S.6747; HR.52a.1; H.1918b; BD.852c.
GEN. REF.: IS.1:85; NB.164; Z.–.

BOY

pais [παῖς, 3816], denotes a boy (in contrast to *paidion*, a diminutive of *pais*, and to *teknon*, a child). With reference to Christ, instead of the A.V. "child," the R.V. suitably translates otherwise as follows: Luke 2:43, "the boy Jesus"; Acts 4:27, 30, "Thy Holy Servant, Jesus." So in the case of others, Matt. 17:18

and Luke 9:42 ("boy"). See CHILD, MAID, MANSERVANT, SERVANT, SON, YOUNG MAN.
NT: B.604c; CB.1261c; K.759.
OT: na'ar: S.5288; HR.1049a.8a; H.—; BD.654d.
GEN. REF.: IS.1:538; NB.—; Z.1:645.

BRAIDED (A.V., BROIDED)

plegma [πλέγμα, 4117], signifies what is woven (from *plekō*, to weave, plait), whether a net or basket (Josephus uses it of the ark of bulrushes in which the infant Moses was laid), or of a web, plait, braid. It is used in 1 Tim. 2:9, of "braided hair," which the Vulgate signifies as ringlets, curls. ¶
NT: B.667a; CB.—; K.—.
OT: —.
GEN. REF.: IS.1:539; NB.—; Z.1:646.

Notes: (1) Cp. *emplokē*, 1 Pet. 3:3, "plaiting," i.e., intertwining the hair in ornament. ¶
(2) "Broided is to be distinguished from "broidered," which means to adorn with needlework (not to plait).

For BRAMBLE BUSH see BUSH

For BRAKE see BREAK

BRANCH

1. *klados* [κλάδος, 2798], from *klaō*, to break (cp. *klasma*, a broken piece), properly a young tender shoot, broken off for grafting, is used for any kind of branch, Matt. 13:32; 21:8; 24:32; Mark 4:32; 13:28; Luke 13:19; the descendants of Israel, Rom. 11:16-19, 21. ¶
NT: B.433a; CB.1255a; K.—.
OT: dālît: S.1808; HR.766a.1; H.431d; BD.194d.
pō'rāh: S.6288; HR.766a.7; H.1727a; BD.802d.
GEN. REF.: IS.1:539; NB.165; Z.1:646.

2. *klēma* [κλῆμα, 2814], akin to *klaō*, to break, denotes a tender, flexible branch, especially the shoot of a vine, a vine sprout, John 15:2, 4, 5, 6. ¶
NT: B.434c; CB.1255b; K.441.
OT: dālît: S.1808; HR.767c.1; H.431d; BD.194d.
z^e^môrāh: S.2156; HR.767c.2; H.559b; BD.274d.
GEN. REF.: IS.1:539; NB.165; Z.1:646.

3. *stoibas* or *stibas* [στοιβάς, 4746], from *steibō*, to tread on, primarily denoted a layer of leaves, reeds, twigs or straw, serving for a bed; then a branch full of leaves, soft foliage, which might be used in making a bed, or for treading upon, Mark 11:8. ¶
NT: B.768b; CB.—; K.—.
OT: —.
GEN. REF.: IS.1:539; NB.165; Z.1:646.

4. *baion* [βαΐον, 902], of Egyptian origin, frequent in the papyri writings, denotes a branch of the palm tree, John 12:13. ¶
NT: B.130c; CB.—; K.—.
OT: —.
GEN. REF.: IS.1:539; NB.165; Z.1:646.

Note: Matthew, Mark and John each use a different word for 'branch' in narrating Christ's entry into Jerusalem.

BRANDED

kaustēriazō [καυστηριάζω, 2743], to burn in with a branding iron (cp. Eng., caustic), is found, in the best mss., in 1 Tim. 4:2, R.V. "branded." Others have *kautēriazō* (from *kautērion*, a branding-iron, Eng., cauterize), to mark by branding, an act not quite so severe as that indicated by the former. The reference is to apostates whose consciences are branded with the effects of their sin. See SEARED. ¶
NT: B.425c; CB.1254c; K.423.
OT: —.
GEN. REF.: IS.—; NB.—; Z.1:647.

Note: in the R.V. of Gal. 6:17, "branded" does not represent a word in the original; it serves to bring out the force of the Apostle's metaphor of bearing in his body the *stigmata*, the marks, of the Lord Jesus. The reference is not to the branding of slaves, soldiers and criminals, but rather to the religious devotee, who branded himself with the mark of the god whom he specially worshipped. So Paul describes the physical marks due to the lictor's rods at Philippi and to the stones at Lystra, marks which, while not self-inflicted, betokened his devotion to Christ and his rejoicing therein.

BRASS, BRAZEN

1. *chalkos* [χαλκός, 5475], primarily, copper, became used for metals in general, later was applied to bronze, a mixture of copper and tin, then, by metonymy, to any article made of these metals, e.g., money, Matt. 10:9, Mark 6:8; 12:41, or a sounding instrument, 1 Cor. 13:1, figurative of a person destitute of love. See Rev. 18:12. See MONEY. ¶
NT: B.875a; CB.1239b; K.—.
OT: n^e^ḥōshet: S.5178; HR.1453b.1b; H.1349a, 1350a; BD.638d.
GEN. REF.: IS.1:539; NB.823, 825; Z.1:647.

2. *chalkeos* [χάλκεος, 5470], made of brass or bronze, is used of idols, Rev. 9:20. ¶
NT: B.875a; CB.—; K.—.
OT: n^e^ḥōshet: S.5178; HR.1453c.1c; H.1349a, 1350a; BD.638d.
GEN. REF.: IS.1:539; NB.823, 825; Z.1:647.

3. *chalkion* [χαλκίον, 5473], is used in Mark 7:4 of brazen vessels. ¶
NT: B.874d; CB.1239b; K.—.
OT: n^e^ḥûshah: S.5154; HR.1453a.1b; H.1349c; BD.639a.
n^e^ḥōshet: S.5178; HR.1453a.2; H.1349a, 1350a; BD.638d.
GEN. REF.: IS.1:539; NB.823; Z.1:647.

4. *chalkolibanon* [χαλκολίβανον, 5474], is used of white or shining copper or bronze, and describes the feet of the Lord, in Rev. 1:15 and 2:18. ¶
NT: B.875a; CB.1239b; K.—.
OT: —.
GEN. REF.: IS.1:539; NB.823; Z.1:647.

5. *chalkeus* [χαλκεύς, 5471], denotes a coppersmith, 2 Tim. 4:14. ¶

NT: B.874d; CB.1239b; K.—.
OT: ḥārāsh: S.2796; HR.1453a.1a; H.760a; BD.360d.
GEN. REF.: IS.1:539; NB.823; Z.1:647.

BRAWLER

1. *paroinos* [πάροινος, 3943], an adjective, lit., tarrying at wine (*para*, at, *oinos*, wine), "given to wine," 1 Tim. 3:3 and Tit. 1:7, A.V., probably has the secondary sense, of the effects of wine-bibbing, viz., abusive brawling. Hence R.V., "brawler". See WINE. ¶

NT: B.629b; CB.1262c; K.—.
OT: —.
GEN. REF.: —.

2. *amachos* [ἄμαχος, 269], an adjective, lit., not fighting (*a*, negative, *machē*, a fight), came to denote, metaphorically, not contentious, 1 Tim. 3:3, and Tit. 3:2, R.V., for A.V., "not a brawler," "not brawlers." See CONTENTIOUS. ¶

NT: B.44c; CB.1234c; K.573.
OT: —.
GEN. REF.: —.

BREAD (Loaf)

1. *artos* [ἄρτος, 740], bread (perhaps derived from *arō*, to fit together, or from a root *ar*—, the earth), signifies (*a*) a small loaf or cake, composed of flour and water, and baked, in shape either oblong or round, and about as thick as the thumb; these were not cut, but broken and were consecrated to the Lord every Sabbath and called the shewbread (loaves of presentation), Matt. 12:4; when the shewbread was reinstituted by Nehemiah (Neh. 10:32) a poll-tax of ⅓ shekel was laid on the Jews, Matt. 17:24; (*b*) the loaf at the Lord's Supper, e.g., Matt. 26:26 ("Jesus took a loaf," R.V., marg.); the breaking of bread became the name for this institution, Acts 2:42; 20:7; 1 Cor. 10:16; 11:23; (*c*) bread of any kind, Matt. 16:11; (*d*) metaphorically, of Christ as the Bread of God, and of Life, John 6:33, 35; (*e*) food in general, the necessities for the sustenance of life, Matt. 6:11; 2 Cor. 9:10, etc.

NT: B.110c; CB.1237c; K.80.
OT: leḥem: S.3899; HR.161b.3a; H.1105a; BD.536d.
GEN. REF.: IS.1:540; NB.165; Z.1:648.

2. *azumos* [ἄζυμος, 106], denotes unleavened bread, i.e., without any process of fermentation; hence, metaphorically, of a holy, spiritual condition, 1 Cor. 5:7, and of sincerity and truth (ver. 8). With the article it signifies the feast of unleavened bread, Matt. 26:17; Mark 14:1, 12; Luke 22:1, 7; Acts 12:3; 20:6. ¶

NT: B.19d; CB.1238b; K.302.
OT: maṣṣāh: S.4682; HR.28c.1; H.1234a; BD.595a.
GEN. REF.: IS.1:540; NB.165; Z.1:648.

For **BREADTH** see **BROAD**

BREAK, BREAKER, BREAKING, BRAKE

A. Verbs.

1. *klaō* or *klazō* [κλάω, κλαζω, 2806], to break, to break off pieces, is used of breaking bread, (*a*) of the Lord's act in providing for people, Matt. 14:19; 15:36; Mark 8:6, 19; (*b*) of the breaking of bread in the Lord's Supper, Matt. 26:26; Mark 14:22; Luke 22:19; Acts 20:7; 1 Cor. 10:16; 11:24; (*c*) of an ordinary meal, Acts 2:46; 20:11; 27:35; (*d*) of the Lord's act in giving evidence of His resurrection, Luke 24:30. ¶

NT: B.433d; CB.1255a; K.437.
OT: gāda': S.1438; HR.766c.1; H.316; BD.154b.
pāras: S.6536; HR.766c.2; H.1821; BD.828a.
raṣaṣ: S.7533; HR.766c.4; H.2212; BD.954c.
GEN. REF.: IS.1:544; NB.—; Z.—.

2. *ekklaō* [ἐκκλάω, 1575], *ek*, off, and No. 1, to break off, is used metaphorically of branches, Rom. 11:17, 19, 20. ¶

NT: B.240c; CB.1243c; K.—.
OT: shāsa': S.8156; HR.433a.1; H.2427; BD.1042d.
GEN. REF.: IS.1.544; NB.—; Z.—.

3. *kataklaō* [κατακλάω, 2622], *kata*, down, and No. 1, is used in Mark 6:41 and Luke 9:16, of Christ's breaking loaves for the multitudes. ¶

NT: B.411c; CB.—; K.—.
OT: nātash: S.5428; HR.733b.1; H.1451; BD.684c.
GEN. REF.: IS.1:544; NB.—; Z.—.

4. *luō* [λύω, 3089], to loosen, especially by way of deliverance, sometimes has the meaning of breaking, destructively, e.g., of breaking commandments, not only infringing them, but loosing the force of them, rendering them not binding, Matt. 5:19; John 5:18; of breaking the Law of Moses, John 7:23; Scripture, John 10:35; of the breaking up of a ship, Acts 27:41; of the breaking down of the middle wall of partition, Eph. 2:14; of the marriage tie, 1 Cor. 7:27. See DESTROY, DISSOLVE, LOOSE, MELT, PUT, *Note* (5), UNLOOSE.

NT: B.483c; CB.1257b; K.543.
OT: pātaḥ: S.6605; HR.889a.5; H.1854,1855; BD.834d.
nātar: S.5425; HR.889a.3; H.1448; BD.684a.
GEN. REF.: IS.1:544; NB.—; Z.—.

5. *suntribō* [συντρίβω, 4937], lit., to rub together, and so to shatter, shiver, break in pieces by crushing, is said of the bruising of a reed, Matt. 12:20 (No. 9 is used in the next clause); the breaking of fetters in pieces, Mark 5:4; the breaking of an alabaster cruse, Mark 14:3; an earthenware vessel, Rev. 2:27; of the physical bruising of a person possessed by a demon, Luke 9:39; concerning Christ, "a bone of Him shall not be broken," John 19:36; metaphorically of the crushed condition of a "broken-hearted" person, Luke 4:18 (A.V. only);

of the eventual crushing of Satan, Rom. 16:20. See BRUISE. ¶ This verb is frequent in the Sept. in the Passive Voice, e.g., Ps. 51:17; Is. 57:15, of a contrite heart, perhaps a figure of stones made smooth by being rubbed together in streams. Cp. *suntrimma*, destruction.

NT: B.793b; CB.—; K.1124.
OT: shābar: S.7665; HR.1321a.19; H.2321; BD.990c.
GEN. REF.: IS.1:544; NB.—; Z.—.

6. *rhēgnumi* [ῥήγνυμι, 4486], to tear, rend, as of garments etc., is translated "break" in the A.V. of Matt. 9:17, of wine-skins (R.V., "burst"); as in Mark 2:22 and Luke 5:37; "break forth" in Gal. 4:27. See BURST, REND, TEAR.

NT: B.735a; CB.—; K.—.
OT: bāqa': S.1234; HR.1248c.1; H.271; BD.131c.
qāra': S.7167; HR.1248c.5; H.2074; BD.902b.
GEN. REF.: IS.1:540; NB.—; Z.—.

7. *diarrhēgnumi* [διαῤῥήγνυμι, 1284], *dia*, through (intensive), and No. 6, to burst asunder, to rend, cleave, is said of the rending of garments, Matt. 26:65; Mark 14:63; Acts 14:14; of the breaking of a net, Luke 5:6; of fetters, 8:29. See REND. ¶

NT: B.188a; CB.1241b; K.—.
OT: qāra': S.7167; HR.309a.7a; H.2074; BD.902b.
bāqa': S.1234; HR.309a.2; H.271; BD.131c.
GEN. REF.: IS.1:540; NB.—; Z.—.

8. *prosrhēgnumi* [προσρήγνυμι, προσρησσω, 4366]: see BEAT, No. 8.

NT: B.718b; CB.—; K.—.
OT: —.
GEN. REF.: —.

9. *katagnumi* [κατάγνυμι, 2608], *kata*, down (intensive), and No. 6, is used of the breaking of a bruised reed, Matt. 12:20, and of the breaking of the legs of those who were crucified, John 19:31, 32, 33, ¶

NT: B.409d; CB.—; K.—.
OT: nākāh: S.5221; HR.730a.5; H.1364; BD.645a.
gāda': S.1438; HR.730a.1; H.316; BD.154b.
dûsh: S.1758; HR.730a.2; H.419; BD.190b.
GEN. REF.: IS.1:544; NB.—; Z.—.

10. *sunthlaō* [συνθλάω, 4917], *sun*, together (intensive), and *thlaō*, to break or crush, to break in pieces, to shatter, is used in Matt. 21:44 and Luke 20:18 of the physical effect of falling on a stone. ¶

NT: B.790a; CB.—; K.—.
OT: gāda': S.1438; HR.1316a.1; H.316; BD.154b.
māḥaṣ: S.4272; HR.1316a.2; H.1183; BD.563c.
rāṣaṣ: S.7533; HR.1316a.6; H.2212; BD.954c.
GEN. REF.: —.

11. *sunthruptō* [συνθρύπτω, 4919], *sun*, and *thruptō*, to crush, to break small, weaken, is used metaphorically of breaking one's heart, Acts 21:13. ¶

NT: B.790a; CB.—; K.—.
OT: —.
GEN. REF.: —.

12. *schizō* [σχίζω, 4977], to split, to rend open, is said of the veil of the temple, Matt. 27:51; the rending of rocks, Matt. 27:51; the rending of the heavens, Mark 1:10; a garment, Luke 5:36; John 19:24; a net, John 21:11; in the Passive Voice, metaphorically, of being divided into factions, Acts 14:4; 23:7. See DIVIDE, *Note*, OPEN, REND, RENT

NT: B.797b; CB.1268c; K.1130.
OT: bāqa': S.1234; HR.1327c.1; H.271; BD.131c.
qāra': S.7167; HR.1327c.2; H.2074; BD.902b.
GEN. REF.: —.

Note: Cp. *schisma* (Eng., schism), said of the rent in a garment, Matt. 9:16. See DIVISION, RENT, SCHISM.

13. *diorussō* [διορύσσω, 1358], lit., to dig through (*dia*, through, *orussō*, to dig), is used of the act of thieves in breaking into a house, Matt. 6:19, 20; 24:43; Luke 12:39. ¶

NT: B.199b; CB.1242a; K.—.
OT: ḥātar: S.2864; HR.336c.1; H.783; BD.369a.
GEN. REF.: —.

14. *exorussō* [ἐχορύσσω, 1846], lit., to dig out (cp. No. 13), is used of the breaking up of part of a roof, Mark 2:4, and, in a vivid expression, of plucking out the eyes, Gal. 4:15. See PLUCK. ¶

NT: B.277c; CB.—; K.—.
OT: nāqar: S.5365; HR.500a.1; H.1418; BD.669b.
GEN. REF.: —.

Note: For *aristaō*, to break one's fast, see DINE.

B. Nouns.

1. *klasis* [κλάσις, 2800], a breaking (akin to A, No. 1), is used in Luke 24:35 and Acts 2:42, of the breaking of bread. ¶

NT: B.433b; CB.1255a; K.437.
OT: —.
GEN. REF.: —.

2. *klasma* [κλάσμα, 2801], a broken piece, fragment, is always used of remnants of food, Matt. 14:20; 15:37 and corresponding passages. See PIECE.

NT: B.433b; CB.1255b; K.437.
OT: pelaḥ: S.6400; HR.766c.1; H.1773a; BD.812a.
pat: S.6595; HR.766c.2a; H.1862a; BD.837d.
GEN. REF.: —.

3. *parabasis* [παράβασις, 3847], a transgression (*para*, across, *bainō*, to go), is translated "breaking" in Rom. 2:23, A.V.; R.V., "transgression"; A.V. and R.V. ditto in 4:15; 5:14; Gal. 3:19; 1 Tim. 2:14; Heb. 2:2; 9:15. See TRANSGRESSION

NT: B.611d; CB.1262a; K.772.
OT: sēṭîm: S.7846; HR.1056a.1; H.2240a; BD.962b.
GEN. REF.: —.

4. *parabatēs* [παραβάτης, 3848], a transgressor (cp. No. 3), is translated "breaker," Rom. 2:25, A.V.; R.V. "transgressor." In ver. 27 the A.V. turns it into a verb, "dost transgress." See Gal. 2:18; Jas. 2:9, 11. ¶

NT: B.612a; CB.1262a; K.772.
OT: —.
GEN. REF.: —.

BREAST

1. *stēthos* [στῆθος, 4738], connected with *histēmi*, to stand, i.e., that which stands out, is used of mourners in smiting the breast, Luke 18:13; 23:48; of John in reclining on the breast of Christ, John 13:25; 21:20; of the breasts of the angels in Rev. 15:6. ¶

NT: B.767d; CB.—; K.—.
OT: gaḥôn: S.1512; HR.1290a.1; H.342a; BD.161a.
lēb: S.3820; HR.1290a.2; H.1071a; BD.524b.
GEN. REF.: IS.1:544; NB.166; Z.1:651.

2. *mastos* [μαστός, 3149], is used in the plural, "paps," Luke 11:27; 23:29; Rev. 1:13, A.V., is preferably rendered "breasts," in the R.V. ¶

NT: B.495b; CB.1258a; K.—.
OT: shad: S.7699; HR.898b.2a; H.2332a; BD.994c.
GEN. REF.: IS.1:544; NB.166; Z.1:651.

BREASTPLATE

thōrax [θώραχ, 2382], primarily, the breast, denotes a breastplate or corselet, consisting of two parts and protecting the body on both sides, from the neck to the middle. It is used metaphorically of righteousness, Eph. 6:14; of faith and love, 1 Thess. 5:8, with perhaps a suggestion of the two parts, front and back, which formed the coat of mail (an alternative term for the word in the N.T. sense); elsewhere in Rev. 9:9, 17. ¶

NT: B.367c; CB.1272b; K.702.
OT: shiryôn: S.8302; HR.668c.4b; H.2466a; BD.1056b.
GEN. REF.: IS.4:1041; NB.82; Z.1:320.

BREATH, BREATHE

A. Nouns.

1. *pnoē* [πνοή, 4157], akin to *pneō*, to blow, lit., a blowing, signifies (*a*) breath, the breath of life, Acts 17:25; (*b*) wind, Acts 2:2. See WIND. ¶

NT: B.680b; CB.1265c; K.876.
OT: nᵉshāmāh: S.5397; HR.1153b.2a; H.1433a; BD.675c.
GEN. REF.: IS.1:544; NB.—; Z.1:652.

2. *pneuma* [πνεῦμα, 4151], spirit, also denotes breath, Rev. 11:11 and 13:15, R.V. In 2 Thess. 2:8, the A.V. has "spirit" for R.V., "breath." See GHOST, LIFE, SPIRIT, WIND.

NT: B.674c; CB.1265b; K.876.
OT: rûaḥ: S.7307; HR.1151c.3; H.2131a; BD.924c.
GEN. REF.: IS.1:544; NB.—; Z.1:652.

B. Verbs.

1. *empneō* [ἐμπνέω, 1709], lit., to breathe in, or on, is used in Acts 9:1, indicating that threatening and slaughter were, so to speak, the elements from which Saul drew and expelled his breath. ¶

NT: B.256c; CB.1244b; K.876.
OT: nephesh: S.5315; HR.458c.1; H.1395a; BD.659b.
nᵉshāmāh: S.5397; HR.458c.2; H.1433a; BD.675c.
GEN. REF.: IS.1:545; NB.—; Z.1:652.

2. *emphusaō* [ἐμφυσάω, 1720], to breathe upon, is used of the symbolic act of the Lord Jesus in breathing upon His Apostles the communication of the Holy Spirit, John 20:22. ¶

NT: B.258a; CB.1244b; K.232.
OT: nāphaḥ: S.5301; HR.461a.2; H.1390; BD.655d.
pûaḥ: S.6315; HR.461a.3; H.1741; BD.806a.
GEN. REF.: IS.1:545; NB.—; Z.1:652.

BRIDE, BRIDECHAMBER, BRIDEGROOM

numphē [νύμφη, 3565], Eng. nymph, a bride, or young wife, John 3:29; Rev. 18:23; 21:2, 9; 22:17, is probably connected with the Latin *nubō*, to veil; the bride was often adorned with embroidery and jewels (see Rev. 21:2), and was led veiled from her home to the bridegroom. Hence the secondary meaning of daughter-in-law, Matt. 10:35; Luke 12:53. See DAUGHTER-IN-LAW. ¶ For the relationship between Christ and a local church, under this figure, see 2 Cor. 11:2; regarding the whole Church, Eph. 5:23-32; Rev. 22:17.

NT: B.545a; CB.1260a; K.657.
OT: kallāh: S.3618; HR.951a.2; H.986a; BD.483c.
GEN. REF.: IS.3:261; NB.168; Z.4:92.

numphios [νυμφίος, 3566], a bridegroom, occurs fourteen times in the Gospels, and in Rev. 18:23. "The friend of the bridegroom," John 3:29, is distinct from "the sons of the bride-chamber" who were numerous. When John the Baptist speaks of "the friend of the Bridegroom," he uses language according to the customs of the Jews.

NT: B.545b; CB.1260a; K.657.
OT: ḥātān: S.2860; HR.951b.1; H.781c; BD.368c.
GEN. REF.: IS.3:261; NB.168; Z.4:92.

numphōn [νυμφών, 3567], signifies (*a*) the room or dining hall in which the marriage ceremonies were held, Matt. 22:10; some mss. have *gamos*, a wedding, here; (*b*) the chamber containing the bridal bed, "the sons of the bride-chamber" being the friends of the bridegroom, who had the charge of providing what was necessary for the nuptials, Matt. 9:15; Mark 2:19; Luke 5:34. ¶

NT: B.545b; CB.1260a; K.—.
OT: —.
GEN. REF.: IS.3:261; NB.168; Z.4:92.

BRIDLE

A. Noun.

chalinos [χαλινός, 5469], a bridle, is used in Jas. 3:3 (A.V., "bits"), and Rev. 14:20. "The primitive bridle was simply a loop on the halter-cord passed round the lower jaw of the horse.

Hence in Ps. 32:9 the meaning is bridle and halter" (Hastings, Bib. Dic.). ¶
NT: B.874c; CB.–; K.–.
OT: meteg: S.4964; HR.1453a.1; H.1264a; BD.607c.
resen: S.7448; HR.1453a.2; H.2180a; BD.943d.
GEN. REF.: IS.1:519; NB.–; Z.1:655.

B. Verb.

chalinagōgeō [χαλιναγωγέω, 5468], from *chalinos* and *agō*, to lead, signifies to lead by a bridle, to bridle, to hold in check, restrain; it is used metaphorically of the tongue and of the body in Jas. 1:26 and 3:2. ¶
NT: B.874c; CB.–; K.–.
OT: –.
GEN. REF.: IS.1:519; NB.–; Z.1:655.

BRIEFLY

di' oligōn [δι' ὀλίγων, 3641], lit. means 'by few.' In 1 Pet. 5:12 it signifies by means of few words, "briefly." The R.V. of Rom. 13:9 omits "briefly," the meaning being "it is summed up." ¶
NT: B.563c; CB.1260c; K.682.
OT: –.
GEN. REF.: –.

For BRIER see THISTLE

BRIGHT, BRIGHTNESS

A. Adjectives.

1. *phōteinos* [φωτεινός, 5460], bright (from *phōs*, light), is said of a cloud, Matt. 17:5; metaphorically of the body, Matt. 6:22, "full of light"; Luke 11:34, 36. See LIGHT. ¶
NT: B.872d; CB.1264b; K.1293.
OT: –.
GEN. REF.: –.

2. *lampros* [λαμπρός, 2986], shining, brilliant, bright, is used of the clothing of an angel, Acts 10:30 and Rev. 15:6; symbolically, of the clothing of the saints in glory, Rev. 19:8, R.V., in the best texts (A.V., "white"); of Christ as the Morning Star, 22:16; of the water of life, 22:1, A.V., "clear." See CLEAR, GAY, GOODLY, GORGEOUS, WHITE.
NT: B.465d; CB.1256c; K.497.
OT: –.
GEN. REF.: –.

Note: Cp. *lamprōs*, sumptuously, Luke 16:19. ¶

B. Nouns.

1. *lamprotēs* [λαμπρότης, 2987], brightness, akin to A, No. 2, above, is found in Acts 26:13. ¶
NT: B.466a; CB.1256c; K.–.
OT: hādār: S.1926; HR.853a.1; H.477b; BD.214a.
zōhar: S.2096; HR.853a.2; H.531a; BD.264a.
GEN. REF.: –.

2. *apaugasma* [ἀπαύγασμα, 541], a shining forth (*apo*, from, *augē*, brightness, of a light coming from a luminous body, is said of Christ in Heb. 1:3, A.V., "brightness," R.V., "effulgence," i.e., shining forth (a more probable meaning than reflected brightness). ¶
NT: B.82b; CB.1236b; K.87.
OT: .
GEN. REF.: IS.1:547; NB.–; Z.–.

Note: Epiphaneia [ἐπιφάνεια], lit., shining forth or upon, is rendered "brightness" in the A.V. of 2 Thess. 2:8; R.V., "manifestation." See APPEARING.

BRIM

anō [ἄνω, 507], above, on high, in a higher place, in John 2:7 is used to denote the brim of a waterpot, lit., up to above, i.e., up to the higher parts, i.e., the brim. See ABOVE, HIGH, UP.
NT: B.76d; CB.1235c; K.63.
OT: –.
GEN. REF.: –.

BRIMSTONE

1. *theion* [φεῖον, 2303], originally denoted fire from heaven. It is connected with sulphur. Places touched by lightning were called *theia*, and, as lightning leaves a sulphurous smell, and sulphur was used in pagan purifications, it received the name of *theion*, Luke 17:29; Rev. 9:17, 18; 14:10; 19:20; 20:10; 21:8. ¶
NT: B.353d; CB.1271c; K.–.
OT: gophrît: S.1614; HR.628a.1; H.375; BD.172d.
GEN. REF.: IS.1:547; NB.169; Z.1:655.

2. *theiōdēs* [θειώδης, 2306], akin to No. 1, signifies brimstone-like, or consisting of brimstone, Rev. 9:17. ¶
NT: B.354a; CB.–; K.–.
OT: –.
GEN. REF.: IS.1:547; NB.169; Z.1:655.

BRING, BRINGING, BROUGHT

A. Verbs.

1. *pherō* [φέρω, 5342], to bear, or carry, is used also of bearing or bringing forth fruit, Mark 4:8; John 15:5, etc. To bring is the most frequent meaning. See BEAR, CARRY, DRIVE, ENDURE, GO, LEAD, MOVE, REACH, RUSHING, UPHOLD.
NT: B.854d; CB.1264a; K.1252.
OT: bô': S.935; HR.1426c.3b; H.212; BD.97c.
nāśā': S.5375; HR.1426c.17; H.1421; BD.669d.
GEN. REF.: –.

Compounds of No. 1, translated by the verb to bring, are as follows:

2. *anapherō* [ἀναφέρω, 399], denotes to bring up, Matt. 17:1. See BEAR, No. 3.
NT: B.63a; CB.1235b; K.1252.
OT: 'ālāh: S.5927; HR.84c.10b; H.1624; BD.748a.
qāṭar: S.6999; HR.84c.12; H.2011; BD.882d.
GEN. REF.: –.

3. *apopherō* [ἀποφέρω, 667], to carry forth, is rendered "bring;" in the A.V. of 1 Cor. 16:3; Acts 19:12 (R.V., "carried away"); some mss. have *epipherō* here. See CARRY.
NT: B.101d; CB.–; K.–.
OT: hālak: S.1980; HR.149c.2; H.498; BD.229d.
yābal: S.2986; HR.149c.3; H.835; BD.384d.
nāsā': S.5375; HR.149c.5; H.1421; BD.669d.
GEN. REF.: –.

4. *eispherō* [εἰσφέρω, 1533], denotes to bring to, Acts 17:20; to bring into, Luke 5:18, 19; 1 Tim. 6:7; Heb. 13:11. See LEAD, No. 11.
NT: B.233d; CB.1243b; K.1252.
OT: bô': S.935; HR.415a.2; H.212; BD.97c.
GEN. REF.: –.

5. *ekpherō* [ἐκφέρω, 1627], to bring forth. See BEAR, No. 4.
NT: B.246d; CB.–; K.–.
OT: yāṣā': S.3318; HR.444c.2b; H.893; BD.422b.
GEN. REF.: –.

6. *epipherō* [ἐπιφέρω, 2018], signifies (*a*) to bring upon, or to bring against, Jude 9; (*b*) to impose, inflict, visit upon, Rom. 3:5. Some mss. have it in Acts 25:18 (for No. 1); some in Phil. 1:16 (R.V., ver. 17, "raise up;" translating *egeirō*). ¶
NT: B.304c; CB.1246a; K.–.
OT: shālaḥ: S.7971; HR.538a.6; H.2394; BD.1018a.
GEN. REF.: –.

7. *propherō* [προφέρω, 4393], denotes to bring forth, Luke 6:45, twice. ¶
NT: B.722d; CB.–; K.–.
OT: –.
GEN. REF.: –.

8. *prospherō* [προσφέρω, 4374], means (*a*) to bring (in addition), Matt. 25:20; to bring unto, Matt. 5:23 (R.V., "art offering"); Mark 10:13; (*b*) to offer, Matt. 5:24. See DEAL WITH, DO, OFFER, PRESENT, PUT.
NT: B.719c; CB.1267b; K.1252.
OT: bô': S.935; HR.122c.1; H.212; BD.97c.
qārab: S.7126; HR.1222c.8a; H.2065; BD.897b.
GEN. REF.: –.

9. *sumpherō* [συμφέρω, 4851], to bring together, has this meaning in Acts 19:19. See BETTER (be), EXPEDIENT, GOOD, PROFIT.
NT: B.780b; CB.–; K.1252.
OT: –.
GEN. REF.: –.

10. *agō* [ἄγω, 71], to lead, to lead along, to bring, has the meaning to bring (besides its occurrences in the Gospels and Acts) in 1 Thess. 4:14, 2 Tim. 4:11, and Heb. 2:10. See CARRY, GO, KEEP, LEAD.
NT: B.14b; CB.1233c; K.–.
OT: bô': S.935; HR.9a.1b; H.212; BD.97c.
hālak: S.1980; HR.9a.3b; H.498; BD.229d.
nāhag: S.5090; HR.9a.14; H.1309,1310; BD.624a.
GEN. REF.: –.

Compounds of this verb are:

11. *anagō* [ἀνάγω, 321], to lead or bring up to, Luke 2:22; Acts 9:39 etc.; to bring forth, Acts 12:4; to bring again, Heb. 13:20; to bring up again, Rom. 10:7. See DEPART, LAUNCH, LEAD, LOOSE, OFFER, TAKE UP, SAIL.
NT: B.53a; CB.–; K.–.
OT: 'ālāh: S.5927; HR.75b.6b; H.1624; BD.748a.
GEN. REF.: –.

12. *apagō* [ἀπάγω, 520], to lead away, bring forth, bring unto, Acts 23:17. See CARRY, DEATH, LEAD, TAKE.
NT: B.79c; CB.–; K.–.
OT: hālak: S.1980; HR.115b.5; H.498; BD.229d.
nāhag: S.5090; HR.115b.8; H.1309,1310; BD.624a.
GEN. REF.: –.

13. *eisagō* [εἰσάγω, 1521], to bring in, into, Luke 2:27 etc. See LEAD.
NT: B.232b; CB.–; K.–.
OT: bô': S.935; HR.407c.2b; H.212; BD.97c.
GEN. REF.: –.

14. *exagō* [ἐχάγω, 1806], to lead out, bring forth, Acts 5:19; 7:36, 40 etc. See FETCH, LEAD.
NT: B.271c; CB.–; K.–.
OT: yāṣā': S.3318; HR.483a.4b; H.893; BD.422b.
GEN. REF.: –.

15. *epagō* [ἐπάγω, 1863], to bring upon, Acts 5:28; 2 Pet. 2:1, 5. ¶
NT: B.281b; CB.–; K.–.
OT: bô': S.935; HR.503b.2; H.212; BD.97c.
'ālāh: S. 5927; HR.503b.14; H.1624; BD.748a.
pāqad: S.6485; HR.503b.18a; H.1802; BD.823a.
GEN. REF.: –.

16. *katagō* [κατάγω, 2609], to bring down, Acts 9:30; 22:30; 23:15, 20; Rom. 10:6; to bring forth, Acts 23:28; of boats, to bring to land, Luke 5:11. See LAND, TOUCH.
NT: B.410a; CB.–; K.–.
OT: yārad: S.3381; HR.729b.3b; H.909; BD.432c.
GEN. REF.: –.

17. *pareisagō* [παρεισάγω, 3919], to bring in privily (lit., to bring in beside), to introduce secretly, 2 Pet. 2:1. ¶
NT: B.624c; CB.–; K.786.
OT: –.
GEN. REF.: –.

18. *proagō* [προάγω, 4254], to bring or lead forth, e.g., Acts 12:6; 16:30; 25:26. See GO, No. 10.
NT: B.702a; CB.–; K.20.
OT: nāgash: S.5066; HR.1203b.1; H.1297; BD.620c.
GEN. REF.: –.

19. *prosagō* [προσάγω, 4317], to bring to, or unto, Acts 16:20; 1 Pet. 3:18. For Acts 27:27 see DRAW (*B*) , No. 3. ¶
NT: B.711b; CB.–; K.20.
OT: nāgash: S.5066; HR.1211a.6; H.1297; BD.620c.
qārab: S.7126; HR.1211b.11; H.2065; BD.897b.
GEN. REF.: –.

Other verbs are:

20. *komizō* [κομίζω, 2865], usually, to receive, to bring in, Luke 7:37. See RECEIVE.
NT: B.442d; CB.1255c; K.–.
OT: lāqaḥ: S.3947; HR.777b.2; H.1124; BD.542c.
nāsā': S.5375; HR.777b.3; H.1421; BD.669d.
GEN. REF.: –.

21. *parechō* [παρέχω, 3930], usually, to offer, furnish, supply (lit., to have near), to bring, in the sense of supplying, Acts 16:16; 19:24. See DO, GIVE, KEEP, MINISTER, OFFER, SHEW, TROUBLE.
NT: B.626b; CB.—; K.—.
OT: —.
GEN. REF.: —.

22. *apostrephō* [ἀποστρέφω, 654], to turn, or put, back, is translated "brought back" in Matt. 27:3. See PERVERT, PUT, TURN.
NT: B.100b; CB.1237a; K.1093.
OT: shûb: S.7725; HR.145b.24a,d; H.2340; BD.996d.
sātar: S.5641; HR.145b.16b; H.1551; BD.711b.
GEN. REF.: —.

23. *katabibazō* [καταβιβάζω, 2601], in the Active Voice, to cause to go down, is used in the Passive in the sense of being brought down, Luke 10:15 (A.V., "thrust down"); "go down" in Matt. 11:23 (marg., "be brought down"). ¶
NT: B.409a; CB.—; K.—.
OT: yārad: S.3381; HR.729a.1b; H.909; BD.432c.
GEN. REF.: —.

24. *sumbibazō* [συμβιβάζω, 4822], rendered "brought" in Acts 19:33.
NT: B.777c; CB.—; K.1101.
OT: —.
GEN. REF.: —.

25. *propempō* [προπέμπω, 4311], to send forth, to bring on one's way, Acts 15:3; 20:38, R.V.; 21:5; Rom. 15:24; 1 Cor. 16:6, 11; 2 Cor. 1:16; Tit. 3:13; 3 John 6. See ACCOMPANY, CONDUCT. ¶
NT: B.709b; CB.—; K.—.
OT: —.
GEN. REF.: —.

26. *blastanō* [βλαστάνω, 985], to bud, spring up, translated "brought forth" (i.e., caused to produce), in Jas. 5:18. See BUD, SPRING.
NT: B.142b; CB.1239a; K.—.
OT: ṣāmaḥ: S.6779; HR.220c.6; H.1928; BD.855b.
dāshā': S.1876; HR.220c.2; H.456; BD.205d.
GEN. REF.: —.

27. *poieō* [ποιέω, 4160], to make, to do, used of the bringing forth of fruit, Matt. 3:8, 10; 7:17, 18. See DO.
NT: B.680d; CB.1265c; K.895.
OT: 'āsāh: S.6213; HR.1154a.33a; H.1708,1709; BD.793c.
GEN. REF.: —.

28. *ekballō* [ἐκβάλλω, 1544], to cast out, used of bringing forth good and evil things from the heart, Matt. 12:35. See CAST, No. 5.
NT: B.237b; CB.1243b; K.91.
OT: gārash: S.1644; HR.420c.3; H.388; BD.176c.
yāṣā': S.3318; HR.420c.8; H.893; BD.422b.
GEN. REF.: —.

29. *tiktō* [τίκτω, 5088], to beget, "bring forth," Matt. 1:21, 23, 25; Jas. 1:15 (first part of verse, according to the best mss.); Rev. 12:5 (R.V., "was delivered of"). See BEGET, BORN, DELIVER.
NT: B.816d; CB.1272c; K.—.
OT: yālad: S.3205; HR.1351c.2a; H.867; BD.408a.
GEN. REF.: —.

30. *apokueō* [ἀποκυέω, 616], to bear young, "bringeth forth" in Jas. 1:15 (end of verse) and "brought forth," ver. 18 (A.V., "begat"). See BEGET. ¶
NT: B.94a; CB.1237a; K.—.
OT: —.
GEN. REF.: —.

31. *gennaō* [γεννάω, 1080], to beget, translated "brought forth" in Luke 1:57. See BEGET, A, No. 1.
NT: B.155b; CB.1248a; K.114.
OT: yālad: S.3205; HR.237b.6c; H.867; BD.408a.
GEN. REF.: —.

32. *euphoreō* [εὐφορέω, 2164], to bear well, be productive, "brought forth plentifully," Luke 12:16. ¶ Cp. *karpophoreō*, Mark 4:20, R.V. "bear"; so, Col. 1:6.
NT: B.327c; CB.—; K.—.
OT: —.
GEN. REF.: —.

33. *trephō* [τρέφω, 5142], to rear, bring up, Luke 4:16. See FEED, NOURISH.
NT: B.825c; CB.—; K.—.
OT: ḥāyāh: S.2421; HR.1371b.5b; H.644; BD.310d.
kûl: S.3557; HR.1371b.6; H.962; BD.465a.
GEN. REF.: —.

34. *anatrephō* [ἀνατρέφω, 397], to nourish, Acts 7:20, 21; "brought up," Acts 22:3. ¶
NT: B.62d; CB.—; K.—.
OT: —.
GEN. REF.: —.

35. *ektrephō* [ἐκτρέφω, 1625], to nourish, Eph. 5:29; "bring up," 6:4, A.V.; R.V., "nurture." See NURTURE. ¶
NT: B.246c; CB.1244a; K.—.
OT: gādal: S.1431; HR.443c.1b; H.315; BD.152a.
ḥāyāh: S.242; HR.443c.3b; H.644; BD.310d.
kûl: S.3557; HR.443c.4; H.962; BD.465a.
GEN. REF.: —.

36. *apangellō* [ἀπαγγέλλω, 518], to announce, is translated "bring word" in Matt. 2:8, R.V. (the A.V. unnecessarily adds "again"); 28:8. See DECLARE, REPORT, SHEW, TELL.
NT: B.79b; CB.1236b; K.10.
OT: nāgad: S.5046; HR.113c.2a; H.1289; BD.616c.
GEN. REF.: —.

B. Noun.

epeisagōgē [ἐπεισαγωγή, 1898], lit., 'a bringing in besides,' is translated "a bringing in thereupon" in Heb. 7:19. ¶
NT: B.284c; CB.—; K.—.
OT: —.
GEN. REF.: —.

Notes: (1) In Mark 4:21, *erchomai*, to come, is translated "is brought," lit., '(does a lamp) come.'

(2) In Mark 13:9, the verb translated "be brought," A.V., is *histēmi*, to stand (R.V.); in Acts 27:24, *paristēmi*, to stand before (A.V., "be brought before").

(3) In Acts 5:36, *ginomai*, to become, is rendered "came (to nought)," R.V., for A.V., "were brought." So in 1 Cor. 15:54, "come to pass," for "shall be brought to pass."

(4) In Mark 4:29, *paradidōmi* is rendered "is ripe," R.V. and A.V. marg., for A.V., "brought forth".

(5) In Matt. 1:11, 12, 17, *metoikesia* signifies a removal, or carrying away (not "they were brought," ver. 12, A.V.).

(6) In Acts 13:1, *suntrophos* denotes a foster-brother, R.V. (A.V., marg.). ¶

(7) In 1 Cor. 4:17, for "bring you into remembrance" (R.V., "put . . ."), see REMEMBRANCE

(8) In Luke 1:19, for R.V., "bring you good tidings," and Acts 13:32, and Rom. 10:15 (end), see PREACH.

(9) In 1 Cor. 1:19, *atheteō*, to reject (R.V.), is rendered "bring to nothing" (A.V.). See DESPISE, Note (1).

(10) For *katargeō*, "bring to nought," R.V., "destroy," 1 Cor. 6:13 etc., See ABOLISH, DESTROY.

(11) For *eipon* in Matt. 2:13, A.V., "bring . . . word," see TELL.

(12) See also DESOLATION, No. 1, PERFECTION, B.

(13) For "bring into bondage" see BONDAGE, B.

(14) In Matt. 16:8 some mss. have *lambanō* (A.V., "ye have brought").

BROAD, BREADTH

A. Adjective.

euruchōros [εὐρύχωρος, 2149], from *eurus*, broad, and *chōra*, a place, signifies, lit., (with) a broad place, i.e., broad, spacious, Matt. 7:13. ¶

NT: B.326a; CB.–; K.–.
OT: rāḥab: S.7337; HR.580a.2; H.2143; BD.931b.
GEN. REF.: IS.1:547; NB.–; Z.–.

B.Verb.

platunō [πλατύνω, 4115], connected with *plak*, a flat, broad surface, signifies to make broad; said of phylacteries, Matt. 23:5; used figuratively in 2 Cor. 6:11, 13, "to be enlarged," in the ethical sense, of the heart. ¶

NT: B.667a; CB.1265a; K.–.
OT: rāḥab: S.7337; HR.1141b.5; H.2143; BD.931b.
GEN. REF.: IS.1:547; NB.–; Z.–.

C. Noun.

platos [πλάτος, 4114], denotes breadth, Eph. 3:18; Rev. 20:9; 21:16 (twice). ¶

NT: B.666d; CB.1265a; K.–.
OT: rōḥab: S.7341; HR.1141a.5a; H.2143b; BD.931d.
GEN. REF.: –.

For **BROIDED** see **BRAIDED**

For **BROKENHEARTED**, see **BREAK, A, No. 5.**

BROILED

optos [ὀπτός, 3702], broiled (from *optaō*, to cook, roast), is said of food prepared by fire, Luke 24:42. ¶

NT: B.576c; CB.–; K.–.
OT: sālî: S.6748; HR.1004b.1; H.1915a; BD.852a.
GEN. REF.: IS.1:548; NB.–; Z.–.

For **BROKEN** see **BREAK**

BROOD

nossia [νοσσιά, 3555], primarily, a nest, denotes a brood, Luke 13:34. Some texts have *nossion* in the plural, as Matt. 23:37, "chicken." ¶

NT: B.543d; CB.1260a; K.–.
OT: qēn: S.7064; HR.949b.2; H.2042a; BD.890a.
GEN. REF.: –.

BROOK

cheimarrhos [χείμαῤῥος, 5493], lit., winter-flowing (from *cheima*, winter, and *rheō*, to flow), a stream which runs only in winter or when swollen with rains, a brook, John 18:1. ¶

NT: B.879c; CB.–; K.–.
OT: naḥal: S.5158; HR.1457a.3; H.1343a,b; BD.636a.
GEN. REF.: IS.1:549; 4:197; NB.169; Z.1:656.

BROTHER, BRETHREN, BROTHERHOOD, BROTHERLY

adelphos [ἀδελφός, 80], denotes a brother, or near kinsman; in the plural, a community based on identity of origin or life. it is used of:—

(1) male children of the same parents, Matt. 1:2; 14:3; (2) male descendants of the same parents, Acts 7:23, 26; Heb. 7:5; (3) male children of the same mother, Matt. 13:55; 1 Cor. 9:5; Gal. 1:19; (4) people of the same nationality, Acts 3:17, 22; Rom. 9:3. With "men" (*anēr*, prefixed, it is used in addresses only, Acts 2:29, 37, etc.; (5) any man, a neighbour, Luke 10:29; Matt. 5:22; 7:3; (6) persons united by a common interest, Matt. 5:47; (7) persons united by a common calling, Rev. 22:9; (8) mankind, Matt. 25:40; Heb. 2:17; (9) the disciples, and so, by implication, all believers, Matt. 28:10; John 20:17; (10) believers, apart from sex, Matt. 23:8; Acts 1:15; Rom. 1:13; 1 Thess. 1:4; Rev. 19:10 (the word "sisters" is used of believers, only in 1 Tim. 5:2); (11) believers, with *anēr*, male, prefixed, and with "or sister" added, 1 Cor. 7:14 (R.V.),

15; Jas. 2:15, male as distinct from female, Acts 1:16; 15:7, 13, but not 6:3.*
NT: B.15d; CB.1233a; K.22.
OT: 'āḥ: S.251; HR.20a.1; H.62a; BD.26a.
GEN. REF.: IS.1:550; NB.–; Z.1:658.

Notes: (1) Associated words are *adelphotēs*, primarily, a brotherly relation, and so, the community possessed of this relation, a brotherhood, 1 Pet. 2:17 (see 5:9, marg.) ¶ ; *philadelphos*, (*phileō*, to love, and *adelphos*), fond of one's brethren, 1 Pet. 3:8; "loving as brethren," R.V. ¶ ; *philadelphia*, "brotherly love," Rom. 12:10; 1 Thess. 4:9; Heb. 13:1; "love of the brethren," 1 Pet. 1:22 and 2 Pet. 1:7, R.V., ¶ ; *pseudadelphos*, "false brethren," 2 Cor. 11:26; Gal. 2:4. ¶

(2) In Luke 6:16 and Acts 1:13, the R.V. has "son," for A.V., "brother."

(3) In Acts 13:1, for *suntrophos*, see BRING, B, Note (6).

For BROUGHT see BRING

BROW

ophrus [ὀφρύς, 3790], an eyebrow, stands for the brow of a hill, Luke 4:29, from the resemblance to an eyebrow, i.e., a ridge with an overhanging bank. ¶
NT: B.600b; CB.–; K.–.
OT: gab ('ayin): S.1354; HR.1042c.1; H.303a; BD.146b.
GEN. REF.: IS.1:552; NB.–; Z.–.

BRUISE

1. *suntribō* [συντρίβω], see BREAK, A, No. 5.

2. *thrauō* [θραύω, 2352], to smite through, shatter, is used in Luke 4:18, "them that are bruised," i.e., broken by calamity. ¶
NT: B.363b; CB.–; K.–.
OT: nāgaph: S.5062; HR.654b.5; H.1294; BD.619d.
rāṣas: S.7533; HR.654b.11; H.2212; BD.954c.
GEN. REF.: IS.1:553; NB.–; Z.1:666.

BRUTE

alogos [ἄλογος, 249], translated "brute" in the A.V. of 2 Pet. 2:12 and Jude 10, signifies "without reason," R.V., though, as J. Hastings points out, "brute beasts" is not at all unsuitable, as "brute" is from Latin *brutus*, which means dull, irrational; in Acts 25:27 it is rendered "unreasonable." ¶
NT: B.41a; CB.1234c; K.505.
OT: –.
GEN. REF.: –.

BUD

blastanō [βλαστάνω, 985], to bud, is said of Aaron's rod, Heb. 9:14; "spring up," Matt. 13:26, and Mark 4:27; elsewhere, in Jas. 5:18. See BRING, No. 26, SPRING, No. 6. ¶
NT: B.142b; CB.1239a; K.–.
OT: ṣāmah: S.6779; HR.220c.6; H.1928; BD.855b.
dāshā': S.187b; HR.220c.2; H.456; BD.205d.
GEN. REF.: –.

* From Notes on Thessalonians by Hogg and Vine, p. 32.

BUFFET

1. *kolaphizō* [κολαφίζω, 2852], signifies to strike with clenched hands, to buffet with the fist (*kolaphos*, a fist), Matt. 26:67; Mark 14:65; 1 Cor. 4:11; 2 Cor. 12:7; 1 Pet. 2:20. ¶
NT: B.441a; CB.1255b; K.451.
OT: –.
GEN. REF.: IS.1:553; NB.–; Z.1:667.

2. *hupōpiazō* [ὑπωπιάζω, 5299], lit., to strike under the eye (from *hupōpion*, the part of the face below the eye; *hupo*, under, *ōps*, an eye), hence, to beat the face black and blue (to give a black eye), is used metaphorically, and translated "buffet" in 1 Cor. 9:27 (A.V., "keep under"), of Paul's suppressive treatment of his body, in order to keep himself spiritually fit (R.V. marg., "bruise"); so R.V. marg. in Luke 18:5, of the persistent widow, text, "wear out" (A.V., "weary"). See KEEP, WEAR, WEARY. ¶
NT: B.848d; CB.1252b; K.1239.
OT: –.
GEN. REF.: IS.1:553; NB.–; Z.1:667.

BUILD, BUILDER, BUILDING

A. Verbs.

1. *oikodomeō* [οἰκοδομέω, 3618], lit., to build a house (*oikos*, a house, *domeō*, to build), hence, to build anything, e.g., Matt. 7:24; Luke 4:29; 6:48, R.V., "well builded" (last clause of verse); John 2:20; is frequently used figuratively, e.g., Acts 20:32 (some mss. have No. 3 here); Gal. 2:18; especially of edifying, Acts 9:31; Rom. 15:20; 1 Cor. 10:23; 14:4; 1 Thess. 5:11 (R.V.). In 1 Cor. 8:10 it is translated "emboldened" (marg., "builded up"). The participle with the article (equivalent to a noun) is rendered "builder," Matt. 21:42; Acts 4:11; 1 Pet. 2:7. See EDIFY, EMBOLDEN.
NT: B.558a; CB.1260b; K.674.
OT: bānāh: S.1129; HR.970c.1a; H.255; BD.124a.
GEN. REF.: IS.1:553; NB.89; Z.1:667.

2. *anoikodomeō* [ἀνοικοδομέω, 456], signifies to build again (*ana*, again), Acts 15:16. ¶
NT: B.71c; CB.–; K.–.
OT: bānāh: S.1129; HR.106a.1a; H.255; BD.124a.
GEN. REF.: IS.1:553; NB.89; Z.1:667.

3. *epoikodomeō* [ἐποικοδομέω, 2026], signifies to build upon (*epi*, upon), 1 Cor. 3:10, 12, 14; Eph. 2:20; Jude 20; or up, Acts 20:32; Col. 2:7. ¶
NT: B.305b; CB.1246b; K.674.
OT: –.
GEN. REF.: IS.1:553; NB.89; Z.1:667.

4. *sunoikodomeō* [συνοικοδομέω, 4925], to build together (*sun*, with), is used in Eph. 2:22, metaphorically, of the Church, as a spiritual dwelling-place for God. ¶
NT: B.791c; CB.1270c; K.674.
OT: –.
GEN. REF.: IS.1:553; NB.89; Z.1:667.

5. *kataskeuazō* [κατασκευάζω, 2680], to prepare, establish, furnish, is rendered "builded" and "built" in Heb. 3:3, 4. See MAKE, ORDAIN, PREPARE.
NT: B.418b; CB.1254b; K.–.
OT: bārā': S.1254; HR.744a.1; H.278; BD.135b.
'āsāh: S.6213; HR.744a.5; H.1708,1709; BD.793c.
yāṣar: S.3335; HR.744a.3; H.898; BD.427c.
GEN. REF.: IS.1:553; NB.89; Z.1:667.

B. Nouns.

1. *oikodomē* [οἰκοδομή, 3619], a building, or edification (see A, No. 1), is used (*a*) literally, e.g., Matt. 24:1; Mark 13:1, 2; (*b*) figuratively, e.g., Rom. 14:19 (lit., 'the things of building up'); 15:2; of a local church as a spiritual building, 1 Cor. 3:9, or the whole Church, the Body of Christ, Eph. 2:21. It expresses the strengthening effect of teaching, 1 Cor. 14:3, 5, 12, 26; 2 Cor. 10:8; 12:19; 13:10, or other ministry, Eph. 4:12, 16, 29 (the idea conveyed is progress resulting from patient effort). It is also used of the believer's resurrection body, 2 Cor. 5:1. See EDIFICATION, EDIFY. ¶
NT: B.558d; CB.1260b; K.674.
OT: bānāh: S.1129; HR.972c.2a; H.255; BD.124a.
GEN. REF.: IS.1:553; NB.89; Z.1:667.

2. *endōmēsis* [ἐνδώμησις, 1739], a thing built, structure (*en*, in, *dōmaō*, to build), is used of the wall of the heavenly city, Rev. 21:18 (some suggest that the word means a fabric; others, a roofing or coping; these interpretations are questionable; the probable significance is a building). ¶
NT: B.264b; CB.–; K.–.
OT: –.
GEN. REF.: IS.1:553; NB.89; Z.1:667.

3. *ktisis* [κτίσις, 2937], a creation, is so translated in the R.V. of Heb. 9:11 (A.V. "building,") See CREATION, B, No. 1, CREATURE, ORDINANCE.
NT: B.455d; CB.1256a; K.481.
OT: –.
GEN. REF.: IS.1:553; NB.89; Z.1:667.

4. *technitēs* [τεχνίτης, 5079], an artificer, one who does a thing by rules of art, is rendered "builder" in Heb. 11:10, marg., "architect," which gives the necessary contrast between this and the next noun in the verse. See CRAFTSMAN, No. 2.
NT: B.814b; CB.1271b; K.–.
OT: ḥārāsh: S.2796; HR.1347c.3; H.760a; BD.360d.
GEN. REF.: IS.1:553; NB.89; Z.1:667.

For **BULL** see **OX**

BUNDLE

1. *desmē* [δέσμη, 1197], from *deō*, to bind (similarly, Eng. "bundle" is akin to "bind"), is used in Matt. 13:30. ¶
NT: B.176a; CB.1240c; K.–.
OT: 'ᵃguddāh: S.92; HR.292a.1; H.15a; BD.8a.
GEN. REF.: IS.1:556; NB.–; Z.1:671.

2. *plēthos* [πλῆθος, 4128], a great number (akin to *pleō*, to fill), is the word for the bundle of sticks which Paul put on the fire, Acts 28:3. See COMPANY, MULTITUDE.
NT: B.668b; CB.1265b; K.866.
OT: hāmôn: S.1995; HR.1142c.3; H.505a; BD.242b.
rôb: S.7230; HR.1142c.11a; H.2099c; BD.913d.
GEN. REF.: IS.1:556; NB.–; Z.1:671.

BURDEN, BURDENED, BURDENSOME

A. Nouns.

1. *baros* [βάρος, 922], denotes a weight, anything pressing on one physically, Matt. 20:12, or that makes a demand on one's resources whether material, 1 Thess. 2:6 (to be burdensome), or spiritual, Gal. 6:2; Rev. 2:24, or religious, Acts 15:28. In one place it metaphorically describes the future state of believers as "an eternal weight of glory," 2 Cor. 4:17. See WEIGHT. ¶
NT: B.133b; CB.1238c; K.95.
OT: kābōd: S.3519; HR.190c.1; H.943d,e; BD.458c.
GEN. REF.: IS.1:556; NB.170; Z.1:671.

2. *phortion* [φορτίον, 5413], lit., something carried (from *pherō*, to bear), is always used metaphorically (except in Acts 27:10, of the lading of a ship); of that which, though "light," is involved in discipleship of Christ, Matt. 11:30; of tasks imposed by the Scribes, Pharisees and lawyers, Matt. 23:4; Luke 11:46; of that which will be the result, at the Judgment-Seat of Christ, of each believer's work, Gal. 6:5. ¶
NT: B.865a; CB.1264b; K.1252.
OT: massā': S.4853; HR.1438b.1; H.1421e; BD.672c.
GEN. REF.: IS.1:556; NB.170; Z.1:671.

Note: The difference between *phortion* and *baros* is, that *phortion* is simply something to be borne, without reference to its weight, but *baros* always suggests what is heavy or burdensome. Thus Christ speaks of His burden (*phortion*) as "light"; here *baros* would be inappropriate; but the burden of a transgressor is *baros*, "heavy". Contrast *baros* in Gal. 6:2, with *phortion* in ver. 5.

3. *gomos* [γόμος, 1117], from a root *gem*-, signifying full, or heavy, seen in *gemō*, to be full, *gemizō*, to fill, Lat. *gemo*, to groan, denotes the lading of freight of a ship, Acts 21:3, or

merchandise conveyed in a ship, and so merchandise in general, Rev. 18:11, 12. See MERCHANDISE. ¶
NT: B.164d; CB.–; K.–.
OT: massā': S.4853; HR.274b.1; H.1421e; BD.672c.
GEN. REF.: IS.1:556; NB.170; Z.1:671.

B. Verbs.

1. *bareō* [βαρέω, 916], akin to A, No. 1, is used of the effect of drowsiness, "were heavy," Matt. 26:43; Mark 14:40; Luke 9:32; of the effects of gluttony, Luke 21:34 ("overcharged"); of the believer's present physical state in the body, 2 Cor. 5:4; of persecution, 2 Cor. 1:8; of a charge upon material resources, 1 Tim. 5:16 (R.V.). See CHARGE, HEAVY, PRESS. ¶
NT: B.133c; CB.1238c; K.95.
OT: kābēd: S.3515; HR.190c.1; H.943a; BD.458a.
GEN. REF.: IS.1:556; NB.170; Z.1:671.

2. *epibareō* [ἐπιβαρέω, 1912], *epi*, upon (intensive), to burden heavily, is said of material resources, 1 Thess. 2:9 (R.V.); 2 Thess. 3:8, R.V., "burden," A.V., "be chargeable to"; of the effect of spiritual admonition and discipline, 2 Cor. 2:5, R.V., "press heavily," A.V., "overcharge". See CHARGEABLE, PRESS. ¶
NT: B.290b; CB.1245c; K.–.
OT: –.
GEN. REF.: IS.1:556; NB.170; Z.1:671.

3. *katabareō* [καταβαρέω, 2599], to weigh down (*kata*, down), overload, is used of material charges, in 2 Cor. 12:16. ¶
NT: B.408d; CB.1254a; K.–.
OT: –.
GEN. REF.: IS.1:556; NB.170; Z.1:671.

4. *katanarkaō* [καταναρκάω, 2655], to be a burden, to be burdensome, primarily signifies to be numbed or torpid, to grow stiff (*narkē* is the torpedo or cramp fish, which benumbs anyone who touches it); hence to be idle to the detriment of another person (like a useless limb), 2 Cor. 11:9; 12:13, 14. See CHARGEABLE. ¶
NT: B.414d; CB.–; K.–.
OT: –.
GEN. REF.: IS.1:556; NB.170; Z.1:671.

Note: For *thlipsis*, distress, affliction, "burdened" (A.V. of 2 Cor. 8:13), see AFFLICTION, B. No. 4.

C. Adjective.

abarēs [ἀβαρής, 4], without weight (*a*, negative, and *baros*, see A, No. 1), is used in 2 Cor. 11:9, lit. 'I kept myself burdensomeless.' ¶
NT: B.1b; CB.–; K.–.
OT: –.
GEN. REF.: IS.1:556 NB.170; Z.1:671.

BURIAL, BURY, BURYING

A. Nouns.

1. *entaphiasmos* [ἐνταφιασμός, 1780], lit., an entombing (from *en*, in, *taphos*, a tomb), "burying," occurs in Mark 14:8; John 12:7. Cp. B.1. ¶
NT: B.268b; CB.1245b; K.–.
OT: –: S.–; HR.–; H.–; BD.–.
GEN. REF.: IS.1:556 NB.170; Z.1:672.

2. *taphē* [ταφή, 5027], a burial (cp. No. 1, and Eng., epitaph), is found in Matt. 27:7, with *eis*, unto, lit. 'with a view to a burial (place) for strangers.' ¶
NT: B.806b; CB.1271a; K.–.
OT: qeber: S.6913; HR.1338a.2c; H.1984a; BD.868d.
qᵉbûrāh: S.6900; HR.1338a.2b; H.1984b; BD.869a.
GEN. REF.: IS.1:556; NB.170; Z.1:672.

B. Verbs.

1. *entaphiazō* [ἐνταφιάζω, 1779], see A, No. 1, to prepare a body for burial, is used of any provision for this purpose, Matt. 26:12; John 19:40. ¶
NT: B.268b; CB.1245b; K.–.
OT: hānaṭ: S.2590; HR.477a.1; H.691; BD.334c.
GEN. REF.: IS.1:556; NB.170; Z.1:672.

2. *thaptō* [θάπτω, 2290], occurs in Matt. 8:21, 22, and parallels in Luke; Matt. 14:12; Luke 16:22; Acts 2:29; 5:6, 9, 10; of Christ's burial, 1 Cor. 15:4. ¶
NT: B.351d; CB.1271c; K.–.
OT: qābar: S.6912; HR.625c.2a,b; H.1984; BD.868b.
GEN. REF.: IS.1:556; NB.170; Z.1:672.

3. *sunthaptō* [συνθάπτω, 4916], akin to A. 2, to bury with, or together (*sun*), is used in the metaphorical sense only, of the believer's identification with Christ in His burial, as set forth in baptism, Rom. 6:4; Col. 2:12. ¶
NT: B.789d; CB.1271a; K.1102.
OT: –.
GEN. REF.: IS.1:556; NB.170; Z.1:672.

BURN, BURNING

A. Verbs.

1. *kaiō* [καίω, 2545], to set fire to, to light; in the Passive Voice, to be lighted, to burn, Matt. 5:15; John 15:6; Heb. 12:18; Rev. 4:5; 8:8, 10; 19:20; 21:8; 1 Cor. 13:3, is used metaphorically of the heart, Luke 24:32; of spiritual light, Luke 12:35; John 5:35. See LIGHT. ¶
NT: B.396b; CB.1253a; K.390.
OT: bā'ar: S.1197; HR.705a.2; H.263; BD.128d.
yāqad: S.3344; HR.705a.5; H.901; BD.428d.
ṣāraph: S.8313; HR.705a.12; H.2292; BD.976d.
GEN. REF.: IS.1:561; NB.–; Z.1:674.

2. *katakaiō* [κατακαίω, 2618], from *kata*, down (intensive), and No. 1, signifies to burn up, burn utterly, as of chaff, Matt. 3:12; Luke 3:17; tares, Matt. 13:30, 40; the earth and its works, 2 Pet. 3:10; trees and grass, Rev. 8:7. This form should be noted in Acts 19:19; 1 Cor. 3:15; Heb. 13:11; Rev. 17:16. In each place the full rendering 'burn utterly' might be used, as in Rev. 18:8. ¶
NT: B.411a; CB.–; K.–.
OT: ṣāraph: S.8313; HR.732b.9; H.2292; BD.976d.
GEN. REF.: IS.1:561; NB.–; Z.1:674.

3. *ekkaiō* [ἐκκαίω, 1572], from *ek*, out (intensive), and No. 1, lit., to burn out, in the Passive Voice, to be kindled, burn up, is used of the lustful passions of men, Rom. 1:27. ¶
NT: B.240c; CB.–; K.–.
OT: bāʿar: S.1197; HR.432b.2; H.263; BD.128d.
GEN. REF.: IS.1:561; NB.–; Z.1:674.

4. *puroomai* [πυρόομαι, 4448], from *pur*, fire, to glow with heat, is said of the feet of the Lord, in the vision in Rev. 1:15; it is translated "fiery" in Eph. 6:16 (of the darts of the evil one); used metaphorically of the emotions, in 1 Cor. 7:9; 2 Cor. 11:29; elsewhere literally, of the heavens, 2 Pet. 3:12; of gold, Rev. 3:18 (R.V., "refined"). See FIERY, FIRE, TRY. ¶
NT: B.731a; CB.1268a; K.975.
OT: ṣāraph: S.6884; HR.1245c.3a; H.1972; BD.864a.
GEN. REF.: IS.1:561; NB.–; Z.1:674.

5. *empiprēmi* [ἐμπίπρημι, 1714], or *emprēthō*, to burn up, occurs in Matt. 2:7. ¶
NT: B.256b; CB.–; K.–.
OT: ṣāraph: S.8313; HR.457c.3a; H.2292; BD.976d.
GEN. REF.: IS.1:561; NB.–; Z.1:674.

B. Nouns.

1. *kausis* [καῦσις, 2740], akin to A, No. 1 (Eng., caustic), is found in Heb. 6:8, lit., 'whose end is unto burning.' ¶ Cp. BRANDED.
NT: B.425b; CB.–; K.423.
OT: bāʿar: S.1197; HR.757a.1; H.263; BD.128d.
GEN. REF.: IS.1:561; NB.–; Z.1:674.

2. *kausōn* [καύσων, 2742], is rendered "burning heat" in Jas. 1:11, A.V. (R.V., "scorching"). See HEAT.
NT: B.425c; CB.–; K.423.
OT: qādîm: S.6921; HR.757b.2; H.1988d; BD.870b.
GEN. REF.: IS.1:561; NB.–; Z.1:674.

3. *purōsis* [πύρωσις, 4451], akin to A. No. 4, is used literally in Rev. 18:9, 18; metaphorically in 1 Pet. 4:12, "fiery trial." See TRIAL. ¶
NT: B.731c; CB.1268a; K.975.
OT: kûr: S.3564; HR.1246a.1; H.967b; BD.468b.
GEN. REF.: IS.1:561; NB.–; Z.1:674.

BURNISHED

chalkolibanon [χαλκολίβανον]: see BRASS.

BURNT (offering)

holokautōma [ὁλοκαύτωμα, 3646], denotes a whole burnt offering (*holos*, whole, *kautos*, for *kaustos*, a verbal adjective from *kaiō*, to burn), i.e., a victim, the whole of which is burned, as in Ex. 30:20; Lev. 5:12; 23:8, 25, 27. It is used in Mark 12:33, by the scribe who questioned the Lord as to the first commandment of the Law, and in Heb. 10:6, 8, R.V., "whole burnt offerings." See OFFERING. ¶
NT: B.564b; CB.1251a; K.–.
OT: ʿōlāh: S.5930; HR.987c.5; H.1624c,d; BD.750b.
GEN. REF.: IS.4:260; NB.1113; Z.5:194.

BURST (asunder)

1. *rhēgnumi* [ῥήγνυμι]: see BREAK, A. No. 6.

2. *laschō* or *laskō* [λάσχω or λάσκω, 2997], primarily, to crack, or crash, denotes to burst asunder with a crack, crack open (always of making a noise), is used in Acts 1:18. ¶
NT: B.467b; CB.1256c; K.–.
OT: –.
GEN. REF.: –.

For BURY see BURIAL

BUSH

batos [βάτος, 942], denotes a bramble bush, as in Luke 6:44. In Mark 12:26 and Luke 20:37 the phrase "in the place concerning the Bush" signifies in that part of the book of Exodus concerning it. See also Acts 7:30, 35. ¶
NT: B.137c; CB.–; K.–.
OT: sᵉneh: S.5572; HR.215a.2; H.1520; BD.702d.
GEN. REF.: IS.1:561; NB.–; Z.–.

BUSHEL

modios [μόδιος, 3426], was a dry measure containing about a peck, Matt. 5:15; Mark 4:21; Luke 11:33. ¶
NT: B.525d; CB.–; K.–.
OT: –.
GEN. REF.: IS.1:562; NB.1325; Z.5:913.

BUSINESS

A. Nouns.

1. *chreia* [χρεία, 5532], translated "business' in Acts 6:3, of the distribution of funds, signifies a necessity, a need, and is used in this place concerning duty or business. See LACK, NECESSITY, NEED, USE, WANT.
NT: B.884d; CB.1240a; K.–.
OT: –.
GEN. REF.: IS.1:562; NB.–; Z.5:784.

2. *ergasia* [ἐργασία, 2039], denotes a business, Acts 19:24, 25, R.V., A.V., "gain" and "craft" (from *ergon*, work). See DILIGENCE
NT: B.307c; CB.1246b; K.251.
OT: mᵉlā'kāh: S.4399; HR.541b.1; H.1068b; BD.521d.
ʿᵃbôdāh: S.5656; HR.541b.3b; H.1553c; BD.715a.
GEN. REF.: IS.1:562; NB.–; Z.5:784.

B. Adjective.

idios [ἴδιος, 2398], expresses what is one's own (hence, Eng. "idiot," in a changed sense, lit., a person with his own opinions); the neuter plural with the article (*ta idia*) signifies one's own things. In 1 Thess. 4:11, the noun is not expressed in the original but is supplied in the English Versions by "business," "your own business". For the same phrase, otherwise expressed, see John 1:11, "His own (things)"; 16:32 and 19:27, "his own (home)"; Acts 21:6, "home". In Luke 2:49, the phrase "in My

Father's house" (R.V.), "about My Father's business" (A.V.), is, lit., 'in the (things, the neuter plural of the article) of my Father.' See ACQUAINTANCE, COMPANY No. 8, DUE, HOME, OWN, PRIVATE, PROPER, SEVERAL.

NT: B.369c; CB.1252c; K.—.
OT: —.
GEN. REF.: IS.1:562; NB.—; Z.5:784.

Notes: (1) In the A.V. of Rom. 16:2 *pragma* is translated "business," R.V., "matter." See MATTER, THING, WORK.

(2) In Rom. 12:11 *spoudē*, translated "business" (A.V.), signifies "diligence" (R.V.). See DILIGENCE.

BUSYBODY

A. Verb.

periergazomai [περιεργάζομαι, 4020], lit., to be working round about, instead of at one's own business (*peri*, around, *ergon*, work), signifies to take more pains than enough about a thing, to waste one's labour, to be meddling with, or bustling about, other people's matters. This is found in 2 Thess. 3:11, where, following the verb *ergazomai*, to work, it forms a paronomasia. This may be produced in a free rendering: 'some who are not busied in their own business, but are overbusied in that of others.' ¶

NT: B.646c; CB.1263b; K.—.
OT: —.
GEN. REF.: IS.1:562; NB.—; Z.—.

B. Adjective.

periergos [περίεργος, 4021], akin to A, denoting taken up with trifles, is used of magic arts in Acts 19:19; "busybodies" in 1 Tim. 5:13, i.e., meddling in other persons' affairs. See CURIOUS. ¶

NT: B.646d; CB.1263b; K.—.
OT: —.
GEN. REF.: IS.1:562; NB.—; Z.—.

C. Noun.

allotrioepiskopos [ἀλλοτριοεπίσκοπος, 244], from *allotrios*, belonging to another person, and *episkopos*, an overseer, translated "busybody" in the A.V. of 1 Pet. 4:15, "meddler," R.V., was a legal term for a charge brought against Christians as being hostile to civilized society, their purpose being to make Gentiles conform to Christian standards. Some explain it as a pryer into others' affairs. See MEDDLER. ¶

NT: B.40c; CB.1234c; K.244.
OT: —.
GEN. REF.: IS.1:562; NB.—; Z.—.

BUY, BOUGHT

1. *agorazō* [ἀγοράζω, 59], primarily, to frequent the market-place, the *agora*, hence to do business there, to buy or sell, is used lit., e.g., in Matt. 14:15. Figuratively Christ is spoken of as having bought His redeemed, making them His property at the price of His blood (i.e., His death through the shedding of His blood in expiation for their sins), 1 Cor. 6:20; 7:23; 2 Pet. 2:1; see also Rev. 5:9; 14:3, 4 (not as A.V., "redeemed"). *Agorazō* does not mean to redeem. See REDEEM.

NT: B.12d; CB.1233c; K.19.
OT: shābar: S.7666; HR.16b.5; H.2322; BD.991d.
qānāh: S.7069; HR.16b.4; H.2039; BD.888d.
GEN. REF.: IS.1:562; NB.—; Z.5:784.

2. *ōneomai* [ὠνέομαι, 5608], to buy, in contradistinction to selling, is used in Acts 7:16, of the purchase by Abraham of a burying place. ¶

NT: B.895d; CB.1260c; K.—.
OT: —.
GEN. REF.: IS.1:562; NB.—; Z.5:784.

Note: In Jas. 4:13 (A.V.) the verb *emporeuomai* (Eng., emporium) is rendered "buy and sell." Its meaning is to trade, traffic, R.V. It primarily denotes to travel, to go on a journey, then, to do so for traffic purposes; hence to trade; in 2 Pet. 2:3, "make merchandise of." See MERCHANDISE. ¶

BY See Note †, p. 1.

Note: The phrase "by and by" in the A.V. is in several places misleading. The three words *exautēs*, Mark 6:25, *euthus*, Matt. 13:21, and *eutheōs*, Luke 17:7; 21:9, mean "straightway," "immediately." See under these words.

C

CAGE

phulakē [φυλακή, 5438], from *phulassō*, to guard, denotes (*a*) a watching, keeping watch, Luke 2:8; (*b*) persons keeping watch, a guard, Acts 12:10; (*c*) a period during which watch is kept, e.g., Matt. 24:43; (*d*) a prison, a hold. In Rev. 18:2, A.V., Babylon is described figuratively, first as a "hold" and then as a "cage" of every unclean and hateful bird (R.V., "hold" in both clauses; marg., "prison"). The word is almost invariably translated "prison". See HOLD, IMPRISONMENT, PRISON, WARD, WATCH.

NT: B.867c; CB.1264c; K.1280.
OT: mishmār: S.4929; HR.1440c.2b; H.2414f; BD.1038b.
mishmeret: S.4931; HR.1440c.2c; H.2414g; BD.1038b.
maṭṭārāh: S.4307; HR.1440c.5; H.1356a; BD.643c.
GEN. REF.: IS.1:570; NB.—; Z.1:683.

CALF

moschos [μόσχος, 3448], primarily denotes anything young, whether plants or the offspring of men or animals, the idea being that which is tender and delicate; hence a calf, young bull, heifer, Luke 15:23, 27, 30; Heb. 9:12, 19; Rev. 4:7. ¶

NT: B.528c; CB.1259b; K.610.
OT: bāqār: S.1241; HR.934c.1a; H.274a; BD.133a.
par: S.6499; HR.934c.3; H.1831a; BD.830d.
shôr: S.7794; HR.934c.4; H.2355a; BD.1004a.
GEN. REF.: IS.1:578; NB.202; Z.1:764.

moschopoieō [μοσχοποιέω, 3447], signifies to make a calf (*moschos*, and *poieō*, to make), Acts 7:41. ¶

NT: B.528c; CB.—; K.—.
OT: —.
GEN. REF.: IS.1:578; NB.202; Z.1:764.

CALL, CALLED, CALLING

A. Verbs.

1. *kaleō* [καλέω, 2564], derived from the root *kal*—, whence Eng. "call" and "clamour" (see B. and C., below), is used (*a*) with a personal object, to call anyone, invite, summon, e.g., Matt. 20:8; 25:14; it is used particularly of the Divine call to partake of the blessings of redemption, e.g. Rom. 8:30; 1 Cor. 1:9; 1 Thess. 2:12; Heb. 9:15; cp. B. and C., below; (*b*) of nomenclature or vocation, to call by a name, to name; in the Passive Voice, to be called by a name, to bear a name. Thus it suggests either vocation or destination; the context determines which, e.g., Rom. 9:25, 26; "surname", in Acts 15:37, A.V., is incorrect (R.V., "was called"). See BID, NAME.

NT: B.398d; CB.1253b; K.394.
OT: qārā': S.7121; HR.712c.9; H.2063; BD.894d.
GEN. REF.: IS.1:580; NB.180; Z.1:694.

2. *eiskaleō* [εἰσκαλέω, 1528], lit., to call in, hence, to invite (*eis*, in, and No. 1), is found in Acts 10:23. ¶

NT: B.233b; CB.1243b; K.394.
OT: —.
GEN. REF.: IS.1:580; NB.180; Z.1:694.

3. *epikaleō* [ἐπικαλέω, 1941], *epi*, upon, and No. 1., denotes (*a*) to surname; (*b*) to be called by a person's name; hence it is used of being declared to be dedicated to a person, as to the Lord, Acts 15:17 (from Amos 9:12); Jas 2:7; (*c*) to call a person by a name by charging him with an offence, as the Pharisees charged Christ with doing His works by the help of Beelzebub, Matt. 10:25 (the most authentic reading has *epikaleō*, for *kaleō*); (*d*) to call upon, invoke; in the Middle Voice, to call upon for oneself (i.e., on one's behalf), Acts 7:59, or to call upon a person as a witness, 2 Cor. 1:23, or to appeal to an authority, Acts 25:11, etc.; (*e*) to call upon by way of adoration, making use of the Name of the Lord, Acts 2:21; Rom. 10:12, 13, 14; 2 Tim. 2:22. See APPEAL, SURNAME.

NT: B.294a; CB.1245c; K.394.
OT: qārā': S.7121; HR.521b.5a; H.2063; BD.894d.
GEN. REF.: IS.1:580; NB.180; Z.1:694.

4. *metakaleō* [μετακαλέω, 3333], *meta*, implying change, and No. 1, to call from one place to another, to summon (cp. the Sept. of Hos. 11:1), is used in the Middle Voice only, to call for oneself, to send for, call hither, Acts 7:14; 10:32; 20:17; 24:25. ¶

NT: B.511a; CB.—; K.394.
OT: qārā': S.7121; HR.916a.1; H.2063; BD.894d.
GEN. REF.: IS.1:580; NB.180; Z.1:694.

5. *proskaleō* [προσκαλέω, 4341], *pros*, to, and No. 1, signifies (*a*) to call to oneself, to bid to come; it is used only in the Middle Voice, e.g., Matt. 10:1; Acts 5:40; Jas. 5:14; (*b*) God's call to Gentiles through the Gospel, Acts 2:39; (*c*) the Divine call in entrusting men with the preaching of the Gospel, Acts 13:2; 16:10. ¶

NT: B.715c; CB.1267a; K.394.
OT: qārā': S.7121; HR.1216c.2a; H.2063; BD.894d.
GEN. REF.: IS.1:580; NB.180; Z.1:694.

6. *sunkaleō* [συνκαλέω, 4779], signifies to call together, Mark 15:16; Luke 9:1; 15:6, 9; 23:13; Acts 5:21; 10:24; 28:17. ¶

NT: B.773b; CB.—; K.394.
OT: qārā': S.7121; HR.1299a.1; H.2063; BD.894d.
GEN. REF.: IS.1:580; NB.180; Z.1:694.

Notes: (1) *Enkaleō*, Acts 19:40, A.V., "called in question", signifies to accuse, as always in the R.V., See ACCUSE, IMPLEAD.

(2) *Parakaleō*, to beseech, intreat, is rendered "have called for" in Acts 28:20, A.V.; R.V., "did intreat" (marg., "call for"). It is used only here with this meaning. See BESEECH.

7. *aiteō* [αἰτέω, 154], to ask, is translated "called for" in Acts 16:29 ("he called for lights"). See ASK, A. No. 1.
NT: B.25d; CB.1234a; K.30.
OT: —.
GEN. REF.: IS.1:580; NB.180; Z.1:694.

Note: For the R.V. of Matt. 19:17 (A.V., "callest"); see ASK (A, No. 2, *Note*).

8. *phōneō* [φωνέω, 5455], to sound (Eng., 'phone), is used of the crowing of a cock, e.g., Matt. 26:34; John 13:38; of calling out with a clear or loud voice, to cry out, e.g., Mark 1:26 (some mss. have *krazō* here); Acts 16:28; of calling to come to oneself, e.g., Matt. 20:32; Luke 19:15; of calling forth, as of Christ's call to Lazarus to come forth from the tomb, John 12:17; of inviting, e.g., Luke 14:12; of calling by name, with the implication of the pleasure taken in the possession of those called, e.g., John 10:3; 13:13. See CROW, CRY.
NT: B.870b; CB.1264b; K.1287.
OT: qārā': S.7121; HR.1447; H.2063; BD.894d.
GEN. REF.: IS.1:580; NB.180; Z.1:694.

9. *legō* [λέγω, 3004], to speak, is used of all kinds of oral communication, e.g., to call, to call by name, to surname, Matt. 1:16; 26:36; John 4:5; 11:54; 15:15; Rev. 2:2, R.V., "call themselves," etc. See ASK.
NT: B.468a; CB.1256c; K.505.
OT: 'āmar: S.559; HR.863c.1a; H.118; BD.55c.
GEN. REF.: IS.1:580; NB.180; Z.1:694.

10. *epilegō* [ἐπιλέγω, 1951], *epi*, upon, and No. 9, signifies to call in addition, i.e., by another name besides that already intimated, John 5:2; for its other meaning in Acts 15:40, see CHOOSE. ¶
NT: B.295c; CB.1246a; K.—.
OT: bāḥar: S.977; HR.524c.1; H.231; BD.103d.
GEN. REF.: IS.1:580; NB.180; Z.1:694.

11. *chrēmatizō* [χρηματίζω, 5537], occasionally means to be called or named, Acts 11:26 (of the name "Christians") and Rom. 7:3, the only places where it has this meaning. Its primary significance, to have business dealings with, led to this. They "were (publicly) called" Christians, because this was their chief business. See ADMONISH, REVEAL, SPEAK, WARN.
NT: B.885c; CB.1240a; K.1319.
OT: dābar: S.1696; HR.1474c.1; H.399; BD.180b.
GEN. REF.: IS.1:580; NB.180; Z.1:694.

12. *eipon* [εἶπον, 3004], to say, speak, means to call by a certain appellation, John 10:35. See BID, No. 3.
NT: B.226a; CB.1243a; K.—.
OT: —.
GEN. REF.: IS.1:580; NB.180; Z.1:694.

13. *krinō* [κρίνω, 2919], to judge, is translated to call in question, in Acts 23:6; 24:21.
NT: B.451b; CB.1256a; K.469.
OT: bāḥaz: S.974; HR.787b.2; H.230; BD.103c.
rîb: S.7378; HR.787b.8; H.2159; BD.936b.
GEN. REF.: IS.1:580; NB.180; Z.1:694.

Notes: (1) For *onoma*, a name, translated "called," A.V., in Luke 24:13, Acts 10:1, *onomazō*, to name, translated "called," A.V., 1 Cor. 5:11, and *eponomazō*, to surname, translated "art called," Rom. 2:17, see NAME and SURNAME.

(2) *Legō*, to say, is rendered "calleth" in 1 Cor. 12:3, A.V., which the R.V. corrects to "saith"; what is meant is not calling Christ "Anathema," but making use of the phrase "Anathema Jesus," i.e. 'Jesus is accursed.'

(3) *Prosagoreuō*, Heb. 5:10, means "to be named." See NAME. ¶

(4) *Metapempō*, rendered "call for," in Acts 10:5, A.V., and 11:13, signifies to fetch, R.V. See FETCH, SEND, No. 9.

(5) *Sunathroizō*, to assemble, is translated "he called together," in the A.V., of Acts 19:25; R.V., "he gathered together."

(6) *Lambanō*, to take or receive, is found with the noun *hupomnēsis*, remembrance, in 2 Tim. 1:5; R.V., "having been reminded" (lit., 'having received remembrance'), for A.V., "when I call to remembrance."

(7) In Acts 10:15 and 11:9, *koinoō*, to make common (R.V.) is translated "call common" in the A.V.

(8) For *prosphōneō*, to call unto, see SPEAK, No. 12.

B. Noun.

klēsis [κλῆσις, 2821], a calling (akin to A, No. 1), is always used in the N.T. of that calling the origin, nature and destiny of which are heavenly (the idea of invitation being implied); it is used especially of God's invitation to man to accept the benefits of salvation, Rom. 11:29; 1 Cor. 1:26; 7:20 (said there of the condition in which the calling finds one); Eph. 1:18, "His calling"; Phil. 3:14, the "high calling"; 2 Thess. 1:11 and 2 Pet. 1:10, "your calling"; 2 Tim. 1:9, a "holy calling"; Heb. 3:1, a "heavenly calling"; Eph. 4:1, "the calling wherewith ye were called"; 4:4, "in one hope of your calling." See VOCATION. ¶
NT: B.435d; CB.1255b; K.394.
OT: qārā': S.7121; HR.770c.1; H.2063; BD.894d.
GEN. REF.: IS.1:580; NB.180; Z.1:694.

C. Adjective.

klētos [κλητός, 2822], called, invited, is used, (*a*) of the call of the Gospel, Matt. 20:16; 22:14, not there an effectual call, as in the Epistles, Rom. 1:1, 6, 7; 8:28; 1 Cor. 1:2, 24; Jude 1; Rev. 17:14; in Rom. 1:7 and 1 Cor. 1:2 the meaning is 'saints by calling'; (*b*) of an appointment to apostleship, Rom. 1:1; 1 Cor. 1:1. ¶
NT: B.436a; CB.1255b; K.394.
OT: miqrā': S.4744; HR.771a.1b; H.2063d; BD.896d.
qārā': S.7121; HR.771a.1a; H.2063; BD.894d.
GEN. REF.: IS.1:580; NB.180; Z.1:694.

CALM

galēnē [γαλήνη, 1055], primarily signifies calmness, cheerfulness (from a root *gal*—, from which *gelaō*, to smile, is also derived; hence the calm of the sea, the smiling ocean being a favourite metaphor of the poets), Matt. 8:26; Mark 4:39; Luke 8:24. ¶

NT: B.150b; CB.1248a; K.—.
OT: —.
GEN. REF.: —.

CALVARY

kranion [κρανίον, 2898], *kara*, a head (Eng., cranium), a diminutive of *kranon*, denotes a skull (Latin *calvaria*, Matt. 27:33; Mark 15:22; Luke 23:33; John 19:17. The corresponding Aramaic word is Golgotha (Heb. *gulgōleth*; see Judg. 9:53; 2 Kings 9:35). ¶

NT: B.448a; CB.—; K.—.
OT: gulggōlet: S.1538; HR.782a.1; H.3531; BD.166b.
GEN. REF.: IS.2:523; NB.181; Z.2:772.

For CAME see COME

CAMEL

kamēlos [κάμηλος, 2574], from a Hebrew word signifying a bearer, carrier, is used in proverbs to indicate (*a*) something almost or altogether impossible, Matt. 19:24, and parallel passages, (*b*) the acts of a person who is careful not to sin in trivial details, but pays no heed to more important matters, Matt. 23:24.

NT: B.401c; CB.1253b; K.413.
OT: gāmāl: S.1581; HR.717c.2; H.360d; BD.168c.
GEN. REF.: IS.1:583; NB.181; Z.1:695.

For CAMP see ARMY

CAN (CANST, COULD, CANNOT)

1. *dunamai* [δύναμαι]; see ABILITY, B, No. 1.

2. *ischuō* [ἰσχύω, 2480], is translated "I can do" in Phil. 4:13; see ABLE, B, No. 4.

NT: B.383d; CB.1253a; K.378.
OT: yākōl: S.3201; HR.692c.8a; H.866; BD.407b.
GEN. REF.: —.

3. *echō* [ἔχω, 2192], to have, is translated "could" in Mark 14:8, lit., 'she hath done what she had'; in Luke 14:14, for the A.V., "cannot," the R.V. has "they have not wherewith"; in Acts 4:14, "could say nothing against" is, lit., 'had nothing to say against'; in Heb. 6:13, "he could swear" is, lit., 'He had (by none greater) to swear.' See ABLE, HAVE.

NT: B.331d; CB.1242c; K.286.
OT: —.
GEN. REF.: —.

4. *ginōskō* [γινώσκω, 1097], to know, is so rendered in the R.V. of Matt. 16:3, "ye know how to," for A.V., "ye can" (*dunamai* is used in the next sentence). This verb represents knowledge as the effect of experience. In Acts 21:37, for "canst thou speak Greek?" the R.V. has "dost . . ." See ALLOW, KNOW.

NT: B.160d; CB.1248b; K.119.
OT: yāda': S.3045; HR.267a.4a; H.848; BD.393b.
GEN. REF.: —.

5. *oida* [οἶδα, 1492], to know by perception, is the word in Pilate's remark "make it as sure as ye can" (marg. "sure, as ye know"), Matt. 27:65. The phrases "cannot tell," "canst not tell," etc., are in the R.V. rendered "know not" etc., Matt. 21:27; Mark 11:33; Luke 20:7; John 3:8; 8:14; 16:18; 2 Cor. 12:2, 3. See KNOW.

NT: B.555d; CB.1260b; K.673.
OT: —
GEN. REF.: —.

6. *esti* [ἐστί, 2076], meaning "it is," is translated "we cannot," in Heb. 9:5, lit., 'it is not possible (now to speak)'; so in 1 Cor. 11:20; see margin.

NT: B.222d; CB.1243a; K.206.
OT: —.
GEN. REF.: —.

7. *endechomai* [ἐνδέχομαι, 1735], to accept, admit, allow of, is used impersonally in Luke 13:33, "it can (not) be," i.e., it is not admissible. ¶

NT: B.262d; CB.—; K.—.
OT: —.
GEN. REF.: —.

For CANDLE and CANDLESTICK see LAMP and LAMPSTAND

For CANKER see GANGRENE and RUST

CAPTAIN

1. *chiliarchos* [χιλίαρχος, 5506], denoting a commander of 1000 soldiers (from *chilios*, a thousand, and *archō*, to rule), was the Greek word for the Persian vizier, and for the Roman military tribune, the commander of a Roman cohort, e.g., John 18:12; Acts 21:31-33, 37. One such commander was constantly in charge of the Roman garrison in Jerusalem. The word became used also for any military commander, e.g., a captain or chief captain, Mark 6:21; Rev. 6:15; 19:18.

NT: B.881d; CB.1239c; K.—.
OT: sar: S.8269; HR.1469a.1c; H.2295a; BD.978a.
GEN. REF.: IS.1:612; NB.200; Z.1:750.

2. *stratēgos* [στρατηγός, 4755], originally the commander of an army (from *stratos*, an army, and *agō*, to lead), came to denote a civil commander, a governor (Latin, *duumvir*), the highest magistrate, or any civil officer in chief command, Acts 16:20, 22, 35, 36, 38; also the chief captain of the Temple, himself a Levite, having command of the Levites who kept guard in and around the Temple, Luke 22:4, 52; Acts 4:1; 5:24, 26. Cp. Jer. 20:1. ¶

NT: B.770c; CB.1270a; K.1091.
OT: sāgān: S.5461; HR.1295b.3a; H.1461; BD.688c.
sar: S.8269; HR.1295b.5; H.2295a; BD.978a.
GEN. REF.: IS.1:612; NB.200; Z.1:750.

3. *archēgos* [ἀρχηγός, 747]: see AUTHOR (No. 2).
NT: B.112c; CB.1237b; K.81.
OT: rō'sh: S.7218; HR.165a.8a; H.2097; BD.910c.
GEN. REF.: IS.1:612; NB.200; Z.1:750.

Note: In Acts 28:16 some mss. have the word *stratopedarchēs* (lit., camp-commander), which some take to denote a praetorian prefect, or commander of the praetorian cohorts, the Emperor's bodyguard, "the captain of the praetorian guard." There were two praetorian prefects, to whose custody prisoners sent bound to the Emperor were consigned. But the word probably means the commander of a detached corps connected with the commissariat and the general custody of prisoners.

CAPTIVE, CAPTIVITY

A. Nouns.

1. *aichmalōtos* [αἰχμάλωτος, 164], lit., one taken by the spear (from *aichmē*, a spear, and *halōtos*, a verbal adjective, from *halōnai*, to be captured), hence denotes a captive, Luke 4:18. ¶
NT: B.27a; CB.1233c; K.31.
OT: gôlāh: S.1473; HR.39b.1a; H.350a; BD.163c.
shābāh: S.7617; HR.39b.2; H.2311; BD.985c.
GEN. REF.: IS.1:612; NB.582; Z.2:423.

2. *aichmalōsia* [αἰχμαλωσία, 161], captivity, the abstract noun in contrast to No. 1, the concrete, is found in Rev. 13:10 and Eph. 4:8, where "He led captivity captive" (marg., "a multitude of captives") seems to be an allusion to the triumphal procession by which a victory was celebrated, the captives taken forming part of the procession. See Judg. 5:12. The quotation is from Psa. 68:18, and probably is a forceful expression for Christ's victory, through His Death, over the hostile powers of darkness. An alternative suggestion is that at His Ascension Christ transferred the redeemed Old Testament saints from Sheol to His own presence in glory. ¶
NT: B.26d; CB.1233c; K.31.
OT: gôlāh: S.1473; HR.38b.1a; H.350a; BD.163c.
shᵉbî: S.7628; HR.38b.2c; H.2311a; BD.985d.
shibyāh: S.7633; HR.38b.2d; H.2311c; BD.986a.
GEN. REF.: IS.1:612; NB.582; Z.2:423.

B. Verbs.

1. *aichmalōteuō* [αἰχμαλωτεύω, 162], signifies (*a*) to be a prisoner of war, (*b*) to make a prisoner of war. The latter meaning is the only one used in the N.T., Eph. 4:8. ¶
NT: B.26d; CB.1233c; K.31.
OT: gālāh: S.1540; HR.39a.1a; H.350; BD.162d.
shābāh: S.7617; HR.39a.4a; H.2311; BD.985c.
GEN. REF.: IS.1:612; NB.582; Z.2:423.

2. *aichmalōtizō* [αἰχμαλωτίζω, 163], practically synonymous with No. 1, denotes either to lead away captive, Luke 21:24, or to subjugate, to bring under control, said of the effect of the Law in one's members in bringing the person into captivity under the law of sin, Rom. 7:23; or of subjugating the thoughts to the obedience of Christ, 2 Cor. 10:5; or of those who took captive "silly women laden with sins," 2 Tim. 3:6. ¶
NT: B.27a; CB.1233c; K.31.
OT: gālāh: S.1540; HR.39b.1; H.350; BD.162d.
shābāh: S.7617; HR.39b.2; H.2311; BD.985c.
GEN. REF.: IS.1:612; NB.582; Z.2:423.

3. *zōgreō* [ζωγρέω, 2221], lit. signifies to take men alive (from *zōos*, alive, and *agreuō*, to hunt or catch), Luke 5:10 (marg. "take alive"), there of the effects of the work of the Gospel; in 2 Tim. 2:26 it is said of the power of Satan to lead men astray. The verse should read 'and that they may recover themselves out of the snare of the Devil (having been taken captive by him), unto the will of God.' This is the probable meaning rather than to take alive or for life. See CATCH. ¶
NT: B.340b, CB.—, K.—.
OT: ḥāyāh: S.2421; HR.599b.1b; H.644; BD.310d.
GEN. REF.: IS.1:612; NB.582; Z.2:423.

CARCASE

1. *kōlon* [κῶλον, 2966], primarily denotes a member of a body, especially the external and prominent members, particularly the feet, and so, a dead body (see, e.g., the Sept., in Lev. 26:30; Num. 14:29, 32; Is. 66:24, etc.). The word is used in Heb. 3:17, from Num. 14:29, 32. ¶
NT: B.461b; CB.—; K.—.
OT: peger: S.6297; HR.839b.1; H.1732a; BD.803d.
GEN. REF.: IS.1:615; NB.—; Z.1:752.

2. *ptōma* [πτῶμα]: see BODY, No. 3.

CARE (noun and verb), CAREFUL, CAREFULLY, CAREFULNESS

A. Nouns.

1. *merimna* [μέριμνα, 3308], probably connected with *merizō*, to draw in different directions, distract, hence signifies that which causes this, a care, especially an anxious care, Matt. 13:22; Mark 4:19; Luke 8:14; 21:34; 2 Cor. 11:28 (R.V., "anxiety for"); 1 Pet. 5:7 (R.V., "anxiety"). See ANXIETY. ¶
NT: B.504d; CB.1258b; K.584.
OT: yᵉhāb: S.3053; HR.911a.1; H.849a; BD.396d.
GEN. REF.: IS.1:617; NB.—; Z.1:754.

Note: The negative adjective *amerimnos* (*a*, negative) signifies free from care, Matt. 28:14, R.V., "we will . . . rid you of care," A.V., "we will . . . secure you" ("secure" lit. means 'free from care'); 1 Cor. 7:32, A.V., "without carefulness." ¶

2. *spoudē* [σπουδή, 4710], primarily haste, zeal, diligence, hence means earnest care, carefulness, 2 Cor. 7:11, 12; 8:16 (R.V., "earnest care," in each place). *Merimna* conveys the thought of anxiety, *spoudē*, of watchful interest and earnestness. See BUSINESS, DILIGENCE (A, No. 2), EARNESTNESS, FORWARDNESS, HASTE.

NT: B.763d; CB.1269c; K.1069.
OT: bāhal: S.926; HR.1285c.1c; H.207; BD.96b.
ḥippāzôn: S.2649; HR.1285c.3; H.708a; BD.342a.
māhar: S.4116; HR.1285c.4; H.1152; BD.554d.
GEN. REF.: IS.1:617; NB.–; Z.1:754.

B. Verbs.

1. *merimnaō* [μεριμνάω, 3309], akin to A, No. 1, signifies to be anxious about, to have a distracting care, e.g., Matt. 6:25, 28, R.V., "be anxious," for A.V., "take thought"; 10:19; Luke 10:41 (R.V., "anxious," for A.V., "careful"); 12:11 (R.V., "anxious"); to be careful for, 1 Cor. 7:32, 33, 34; to have a care for, 1 Cor. 12:25; to care for, Phil. 2:20; "be anxious," Phil. 4:6, R.V. See THOUGHT (to take).

NT: B.505a; CB.1258b; K.584.
OT: rāgaz: S.7264; HR.911a.5; H.2112; BD.919a.
dā'ag: S.1672; HR.911a.1; H.393; BD.178b.
GEN. REF.: IS.1:617; NB.–; Z.1:754.

2. *melei* [μέλει, 3199], the third person sing. of *melō*, used impersonally, signifies that something is an object of care, especially the care of forethought and interest, rather than anxiety, Matt. 22:16; Mark 4:38; 12:14; Luke 10:40; John 10:13; 12:6; Acts 18:17; 1 Cor. 9:9 (R.V., "Is it for the oxen that God careth?" The A.V. seriously misses the point. God does care for oxen, but there was a Divinely designed significance in the O.T. passage, relating to the service of preachers of the Gospel); 7:21; 1 Pet. 5:7. ¶

NT: B.500a; CB.–; K.–.
OT: –.
GEN. REF.: IS.1:617; NB.–; Z.1:754.

3. *epimeleomai* [ἐπιμελέομαι, 1959], signifies to take care of, involving forethought and provision (*epi* indicating the direction of the mind toward the object cared for), Luke 10:34, 35, of the Good Samaritan's care for the wounded man, and in 1 Tim. 3:5, of a bishop's (or overseer's) care of a church — a significant association of ideas. ¶

NT: B.296a; CB.1246a; K.–.
OT: sîm ('ênayim): S.7760; HR.525b.1; H.2243; BD.963d.
GEN. REF.: IS.1:617; NB.–; Z.1:754.

4. *phrontizō* [φροντίζω, 5431], to think, consider, be thoughtful (from *phrēn*, the mind), is translated "be careful" in Tit. 3:8. ¶

NT: B.866d; CB.1264c; K.–.
OT: dā'ag: S.1672; HR.1439c.1; H.393; BD.178b.
GEN. REF.: IS.1:617; NB.–; Z.1:754.

5. *phroneō* [φρονέω, 5426], translated "be careful," in Phil. 4:10, A.V. [R.V., "(ye did) take thought"], has a much wider range of meaning than No. 5, and denotes to be minded, in whatever way. See AFFECTION, B, *Note* (1), MIND, REGARD, SAVOUR, THINK, UNDERSTAND.

NT: B.866a; CB.1264c; K.1277.
OT: ḥākam: S.2449; HR.1439a.2; H.647; BD.314b.
GEN. REF.: IS.1:617; NB.–; Z.1:754.

Note: Episkopeō, to oversee, is rendered "looking carefully," in Heb. 12:15, R.V. See OVERSIGHT. ¶

C. Adverbs.

1. *akribōs* [ἀκριβῶς, 199], carefully; see ACCURATELY.

NT: B.33b; CB.–; K.–.
OT: yāṭab: S.3190; HR.50c.1; H.863; BD.405c.
GEN. REF.: IS.1:617; NB.–; Z.1:754.

Note: For *akribesteron*, more carefully, see EXACTLY.

2. *spoudaioterōs* [σπουδαιοτερως, 4708], the comparative adverb corresponding to A, No. 2, signifies "the more diligently," Phil. 2:28, R.V. (A.V., "carefully"). ¶ The adverb *spoudaiōs* denotes "diligently," 2 Tim. 1:17 (some mss. have the comparative here); Tit. 3:13; or "earnestly," Luke 7:4 (A.V., "instantly"). See also *spoudaios* and its comparative, in 2 Cor. 8:17, 22, R.V., "earnest," "more earnest." ¶

NT: B.763c; CB.–; K.–.
OT: –.
GEN. REF.: IS.1:617; NB.–; Z.1:754.

CARNAL, CARNALLY

1. *sarkikos* [σαρκικός, 4559], from *sarx*, flesh, signifies (*a*) having the nature of flesh, i.e., sensual, controlled by animal appetites, governed by human nature, instead of by the Spirit of God, 1 Cor. 3:3 (for ver. 1, see below; some mss. have it in ver. 4); having its seat in the animal nature, or excited by it, 1 Pet. 2:11, "fleshly"; or as the equivalent of "human," with the added idea of weakness, figuratively of the weapons of spiritual warfare, "of the flesh" (A.V., "carnal"), 2 Cor. 10:4; or with the idea of unspirituality, of human wisdom, "fleshly," 2 Cor. 1:12; (*b*) pertaining to the flesh (i.e., the body), Rom. 15:27; 1 Cor. 9:11. ¶

NT: B.742d; CB.1268b; K.1000.
OT: –.
GEN. REF.: IS.1:619; NB.–; Z.1:756.

2. *sarkinos* [σάρκινος, 4560], (*a*) consisting of flesh, 2 Cor. 3:3, "tables that are hearts of flesh" (A.V., "fleshy tables of the heart"); (*b*) pertaining to the natural, transient life of the body, Heb. 7:16, "a carnal commandment"; (*c*) given up to the flesh, i.e., with almost the same significance as *sarkikos*, above, Rom. 7:14, "I am carnal, sold under sin"; 1 Cor. 3:1 (some texts have *sarkikos*, in both these places, and in those in (*a*) and (*b*) , but textual evidence is

against it). It is difficult to discriminate between *sarkikos* and *sarkinos* in some passages. In regard to 1 Pet. 2:11, Trench (Syn §§ lxxi, lxxii) says that *sarkikos* describes the lusts which have their source in man's corrupt and fallen nature, and the man is *sarkikos* who allows to the flesh a place which does not belong to it of right; in 1 Cor. 3:1 *sarkinos* is an accusation far less grave than *sarkikos* would have been. The Corinthian saints were making no progress, but they were not anti-spiritual in respect of the particular point with which the Apostle was there dealing. In vv. 3, 4, they are charged with being *sarkikos*. See FLESHLY, FLESHY. ¶

NT: B.743a; CB.1268c; K.1000.
OT: bāsār: S.1320; HR.1259b.1; H.291a; BD.142b.
GEN. REF.: IS.1:619; NB.–; Z.1:756.

CAROUSINGS

potos [πότος, 4224], lit., a drinking, signifies not simply a banquet but a drinking bout, a carousal, 1 Pet. 4:3 (R.V., "carousings," A.V., "banquetings"). ¶ Synonymous is *kraipalē*, "surfeiting," Luke 21:34. ¶

NT: B.696a; CB.1266b; K.841.
OT: mishteh: S.4960; HR.1198a.3a; H.2477c; BD.1059c.
GEN. REF.: IS.1:619; NB.–; Z.–.

CARPENTER

tektōn [τέκτων, 5045], denotes any craftsman, but especially a worker in wood, a carpenter, Matt. 13:55; Mark 6:3. ¶

NT: B.809a; CB.1271b; K.–.
OT: ḥārāsh: S.2790; HR.1342b.1a; H.760; BD.360b.
GEN. REF.: IS.1:619; NB.91; Z.1:757.

For CARRIAGE see BAGGAGE

CARRY

1. *sunkomizō* [συνκομίζω, 4792], to carry together, to help in carrying (*sun*, with, *komizō*, to carry), is used in Acts 8:2, R.V., "buried," for A.V., "carried to his burial." The verb has also the meaning of recovering or getting back a body. ¶

NT: B.774c; CB.–; K.–.
OT: –.
GEN. REF.: –.

2. *ekkomizō* [ἐκκομίζω, 1580], to carry out, is found in Luke 7:12. ¶

NT: B.241d; CB.–; K.–.
OT: –.
GEN. REF.: –.

3. *pherō* [φέρω, 5342], to bear, to bring, is translated "carry" only in John 21:18. See Note below.

NT: B.854d; CB.1264a; K.1252.
OT: bô': S.935; HR.1426c.3b; H.212; BD.97c.
nāsā': S.5375; HR.1426c.17; H.1421; BD.669d.
GEN. REF.: –.

4. *diapherō* [διαφέρω, 1308], has the meaning "to carry through" in Mark 11:16. See BETTER, DIFFER, DRIVE, EXCELLENT, MATTER, PUBLISH, VALUE.

NT: B.190b; CB.–; K.1252.
OT: –.
GEN. REF.: –.

5. *metatithēmi* [μετατίθημι, 3346], to place among, put in another place (*meta*, implying change, and *tithēmi*, to put), has this latter meaning in Acts 7:16, "carried over." See CHANGE, REMOVE, TRANSLATE, TURN.

NT: B.513c; CB.1258c; K.1176.
OT: sûg: S.5472; HR.917a.3; H.1469; BD.690d.
lāqaḥ: S.3947; HR.917c.1; H.1075; BD.542c.
GEN. REF.: –.

6. *apagō* [ἀπάγω, 520], to lead away (*apo*, from, *agō*, to lead) is rendered "carried" in 1 Cor. 12:2, A.V. (R.V., "were led"). See BRING.

NT: B.79c; CB.–; K.–.
OT: nāhag: S.5090; HR.115b.8; H.1309, 1310; BD.624a.
hālak: S.1980; HR.115b.5; H.498; BD.229d.
GEN. REF.: –.

7. *sunapagō* [συναπάγω, 4879], to carry away with (*sun*, with, and No. 6), is used in a bad sense, in Gal. 2:13 and 2 Pet. 3:17, "being carried away with" (R.V.); in a good sense in Rom. 12:16; the R.V. marg. "be carried away with" is preferable to the text "condescend" (R.V., and A.V.), and to the A.V. marg., "be contented (with mean things)." A suitable rendering would be 'be led along with.' ¶

NT: B.784d; CB.–; K.–.
OT: lāqaḥ: S.3947; HR.1312a.1; H.1075; BD.542c.
GEN. REF.: –.

Notes: (1) For *pherō*, to carry, or bring, *apopherō*, to carry away, *peripherō*, to carry about, *ekpherō*, to carry forth, *anapherō*, to carry up, *airō*, to lift and carry away, to take away, *bastazō*, to support, carry about, *agō*, to lead or carry, *apagō*, to carry away, see BEAR and BRING.

(2) For *elaunō*, rendered "carry" in 2 Pet. 2:17, see DRIVE.

CARRYING AWAY

A. Noun.

metoikesia [μετοικεσία, 3350], a change of abode, or a carrying away by force (*meta*, implying change, *oikia*, a dwelling), is used only of the carrying away to Babylon, Matt. 1:11, 12, 17. ¶

NT: B.514b; CB.1258c; K.–.
OT: gôlāh: S.1473; HR.917c.1b; H.350a; BD.163c.
gālāh: S.1540; HR.917c.1b; H.350; BD.162d.
GEN. REF.: IS.1:612; NB.582; Z.2:423.

B. Verb.

metoikizō [μετοικίζω, 3351], akin to A, is used of the removal of Abraham into Canaan, Acts 7:4, and of the carrying into Babylon, 7:43. ¶

NT: B.514b; CB.—; K.—.
OT: gālāh: S.1540; HR.918a.1b; H.350; BD.162d.
GEN. REF.: IS.1:612; NB.582; Z.2:423.

CASE

1. *aitia* [αἰτία]: see under ACCUSATION, A, No. 1.

2. *echō* [ἔχω, 2192], to have, is idiomatically used in the sense of being in a case or condition, as with the infirm man at the pool of Bethesda, John 5:6, lit., 'that he had already much time (in that case).'

NT: B.331d; CB.1242c; K.286.
OT: —.
GEN. REF.: —.

Note: In Acts 25:14 the phrase in the original is 'the things concerning Paul,' A.V., "cause" (as if translating *aitia*); R.V., "Festus laid Paul's case before the king."

3. *proechō* [προέχω, 4284], lit., to have before, in the Middle Voice, Rom. 3:9, is rightly translated "are we in worse case?" (R.V.), as is borne out by the context. See BETTER (be), Note (1). ¶

NT: B.705d; CB.—; K.—.
OT: —.
GEN. REF.: —.

4. The preposition *en*, followed by the dative of the pronoun, lit., 'in me,' is translated in the R.V., "in my case," in 1 Cor. 9:15; "unto me," in 1 Cor. 14:11 (marg. "in my case"). Similarly, in the plural, in 1 John 4:16, R.V. "in us" (marg., "in our case"); A.V., incorrectly, "to us."

Note: In Matt. 5:20 the strong double negative *ou mē* is translated "in no case" (A.V.): R.V., "in no wise."

CAST

A. Verbs.

1. *ballō* [βάλλω, 906], to throw, hurl, in contrast to striking, is frequent in the four Gospels and Revelation; elsewhere it is used only in Acts. In Matt. 5:30 some mss. have this verb (A.V., "should be cast"); the most authentic have *aperchomai*, to go away, R.V., "go." See ARISE, BEAT, DUNG, LAY, POUR, PUT, SEND, STRIKE, THROW, THRUST.

NT: B.130d; CB.1238b; K.91.
OT: nāphal: S.6307; HR.189c.6b; H.1735; BD.656d.
shālak: S.7993; HR.189c.1b; H.2398; BD.1020d.
GEN. REF.: IS.1:621; NB.—; Z.—.

2. *rhiptō* [ῥίπτω, 4496], denotes to throw with a sudden motion, to jerk, cast forth; "cast down," Matt. 15:30 and 27:5; "thrown down," Luke 4:35; "thrown," 17:2 (A.V., "cast"); [*rhipteō* in Acts 22:23 (A.V., "cast off"), of the casting off of clothes (in the next sentence *ballō*, No. 1, is used of casting dust into the air)]; in 27:19 "cast out," of the tackling of a ship; in ver. 29 "let go" (A.V., "cast"), of anchors; in Matt. 9:36, "scattered," said of sheep. See THROW, SCATTER. ¶

NT: B.736c; CB.—; K.987.
OT: shālak: S.7993; HR.1252b.10; H.2398; BD.1020d.
GEN. REF.: IS.1:621; NB.—; Z.—.

3. *ekpiptō* [ἐκπίπτω, 1601], lit., to fall out, is translated "be cast ashore," in Acts 27:29, R.V., A.V., "have fallen upon." See EFFECT, FAIL, FALL, NOUGHT.

NT: B.243d; CB.1243c; K.846.
OT: nābēl: S.5034; HR.439b.2; H.1286; BD.615b.
nāphal: S.6307; HR.439b.3a; H.1735; BD.656d.
shālak: S.7993; HR.439b.8a; H.2398; BD.1020d.
GEN. REF.: IS.1:621; NB.—; Z.—.

A number of compound verbs consisting of *ballō* or *rhiptō*, with prepositions prefixed, denote to cast, with a corresponding English preposition. Compounds of *ballō* are:

4. *apoballō* [ἀποβάλλω, 577], to throw off from, to lay aside, to cast away, Mark 10:50; Heb. 10:35. ¶

NT: B.88d; CB.—; K.—.
OT: nābēl: S.5034; HR.125c.1; H.1286; BD.615b.
GEN. REF.: IS.1:621; NB.—; Z.—.

Note: Apobolē, "casting away" (akin to No. 4), is used of Israel in Rom. 11:15; elsewhere, Acts 27:22, "loss" (of life). ¶

5. *ekballō* [ἐκβάλλω, 1544], to cast out of, from, forth, is very frequent in the Gospels and Acts; elsewhere, in Gal. 4:30; 3 John 10; in Jas. 2:25, "sent out"; in Rev. 11:2, "leave out" (marg., "cast without"). See BRING, No. 28, DRIVE, EXPEL, LEAVE, PLUCK, PULL, PUT, SEND, TAKE, THRUST.

NT: B.237b; CB.1243b; K.91.
OT: gārash: S.1644; HR.421c.3b; H.388; BD.176c.
yāṣā': S.3318; HR.421c.8; H.893; BD.422b.
shālak: S.7993; HR.421c.21a; H.2398; BD.1020d.
GEN. REF.: IS.1:621; NB.—; Z.—.

6. *emballō* [ἐμβάλλω, 1685], to cast into, is used in Luke 12:5. ¶

NT: B.254a; CB.1244b; K.—.
OT: sîm, sûm: S.7760; HR.455a.9; H.2243; BD.963d.
nātan: S.5414; HR.455a.5; H.1443; BD.678a.
GEN. REF.: IS.1:621; NB.—; Z.—.

7. *epiballō* [ἐπιβάλλω, 1911], to cast on, or upon, is used in this sense in Mark 11:7 and 1 Cor. 7:35. See BEAT (No. 5), FALL, No. 11, LAY, PUT, No. 8, STRETCH.

NT: B.289d; CB.—; K.91.
OT: sîm, sûm: S.7760; HR.516a.15; H.2243; BD.963d.
shît: S.7896; HR.516a.17; H.2380; BD.1011a.
shālaḥ: S.7971; HR.516a.18; H.2394; BD.1018a.
GEN. REF.: IS.1:621; NB.—; Z.—.

8. *kataballō* [καταβάλλω, 2598], signifies to cast down, 2 Cor. 4:9, A.V., "cast down," R.V.,

"smitten down"; Heb. 6:1, "laying." See LAY. ¶ Some mss. have this verb in Rev. 12:10 (for *ballō*).

NT: B.408d; CB.1253c; K.–.
OT: nāphal: S.6307; HR.728c.4b; H.1735; BD.656d.
GEN. REF.: IS.1:621; NB.–; Z.–.

9. *amphiballō* [ἀμφιβάλλω, 297, 906], to cast around, occurs Mark 1:16. ¶

NT: B.47b; CB.1234c; K.–.
OT: –.
GEN. REF.: IS.1:621; NB.–; Z.–.

10. *periballō* [περιβάλλω, 4016], to cast about, or around, is used in 23 of its 24 occurrences, of putting on garments, clothing, etc.; it is translated "cast about" in Mark 14:51; Acts 12:8; in Luke 19:43, used of casting up a bank or palisade against a city (see R.V. and marg.), A.V., "shall cast a trench about thee." See CLOTHE, No. 6, PUT.

NT: B.646a; CB.–; K.–.
OT: kāsāh: S.3680; HR.1121c.2a; H.1008; BD.491b.
lābash: S.3847; HR.1121c.3a; H.1075; BD.527d.
GEN. REF.: IS.1:621; NB.–; Z.–.

Compounds of *rhiptō* are:

11. *aporiptō* [ἀπορίπτω, 641], to cast off, Acts 27:43, of shipwrecked people in throwing themselves into the water. ¶

NT: B.97d; CB.–; K.987.
OT: shālak: S.7993; HR.140b.12a; H.2398; BD.1020d.
GEN. REF.: –.

12. *epiriptō* [ἐπιρίπτω, 1977], to cast upon, (*a*) lit., of casting garments on a colt, Luke 19:35; (*b*) figuratively, of casting care upon God, 1 Pet. 5:7. ¶

NT: B.298a; CB.–; K.987.
OT: shālak: S.7993; HR.527a.2a; H.2398; BD.1020d.
GEN. REF.: –.

Other verbs are:

13. *apōtheō* [ἀπωθέω, 683], to thrust away (*apo*, away, *ōtheō*, to thrust), in the N.T. used in the Middle Voice, signifying to thrust from oneself, to cast off, by way of rejection, Acts 7:27, 39; 13:46; Rom. 11:1, 2; 1 Tim. 1:19. See PUT and THRUST. ¶

NT: B.103b; CB.–; K.75.
OT: zānaḥ: S.2186; HR.151a.10; H.564; BD.276b.
mā'as: S.3988; HR.151a.11; H.1139, 1140; BD.549b.
nāṭash: S.5203; HR.151a.14; H.1357; BD.643c.
GEN. REF.: –.

14. *kathaireō* [καθαιρέω, 2507], *kata*, down, *haireō*, to take, to cast down, demolish, in 2 Cor. 10:5, of strongholds and imaginations. See DESTROY, PULL, PUT, TAKE.

NT: B.386c; CB.–; K.380.
OT: dûsh: S.1758; HR.697c.1; H.419; BD.190b.
GEN. REF.: –.

Note: The corresponding noun *kathairesis*, a casting down, is so rendered in 2 Cor. 10:4 (A.V., "pulling down") and 13:10 (A.V., "destruction").

15. *dialogizomai* [διαλογίζομαι, 1260], to reason (*dia*, through, *logizomai*, to reason), is translated "cast in (her) mind," Luke 1:29. See DISPUTE, MUSING, REASON, THINK.

NT: B.186a; CB.1241b; K.155.
OT: –.
GEN. REF.: IS.1:621; NB.–; Z.–.

16. *apotithēmi* [ἀποτίθημι, 659], to put off, lay aside, denotes in the Middle Voice, to put off from oneself, cast off, used figuratively of works of darkness, Rom. 13:12, "let us cast off," (aorist tense, denoting a definite act). See LAY, No. 8, PUT, No. 5.

NT: B.101a; CB.1237b; K.–.
OT: nûaḥ: S.5117; HR.148c.1; H.1323; BD.628a.
GEN. REF.: –.

17. *ektithēmi* [ἐκτίθημι, 1620], to expose, cast out (*ek*, out, *tithēmi*, to put), is said of a newborn child in Acts 7:21. In ver. 19 "cast out" translates the phrase *poieō*, to make, with *ekthetos*, exposed, a verbal form of *ektithēmi*, See EXPOUND.

NT: B.245d; CB.–; K.–.
OT: nātan: S.5414; HR.443a.4; H.–; BD.678a, 681b.
GEN. REF.: –.

18. *periaireō* [περιαιρέω, 4014], to take away, is used in Acts 27:40, as a nautical term, R.V., "casting off," A.V., "taken up." See TAKE.

NT: B.645d; CB.–; K.–.
OT: sûr: S.5493; HR.1121b.4b; H.1480; BD.693b.
GEN. REF.: –.

Notes: (1) For *zēmioō*, "cast away," Luke 9:25, see FORFEIT.

(2) For *katakrēmnizō*, Luke 4:29 (A.V., "cast down headlong"), see THROW. ¶

(3) For *oneidizō*, Matt. 27:44 (A.V., "cast in one's teeth"), see REPROACH.

(4) For *paradidōmi*, Matt. 4:12 (A.V., "cast into prison"), see DELIVER.

(5) For *atheteō*, 1 Tim. 5:12 (A.V., "cast off"), see REJECT.

(6) For *ekteinō*, Acts 27:30 (A.V., "cast out"), see LAY No. 13.

(7) For *tapeinos*, 2 Cor. 7:6 (A.V., "cast down"), see LOWLY.

B. Noun.

bole [βολή, 1000], denotes a throw (akin to *ballō*, to throw), and is used in Luke 22:21 in the phrase "a stone's cast," of the distance from which the Lord was parted from the disciples in the garden of Gethsemane. ¶

NT: B.144d; CB.–; K.–.
OT: ṭāḥāh: S.2909; HR.224b.1; H.800; BD.377b.
GEN. REF.: –.

Note: In Jas. 1:17, *aposkiasma* (from *aposkiazō*, to cast a shadow), is rendered "shadow that is cast," R.V. ¶

C. Adjective.

adokimos [ἀδόκιμος, 96], signifies not standing the test, rejected, (*a*, negative, and *dokimos*, tested, approved); it is said of things, e.g., the land, Heb. 6:8, "rejected," and of persons, Rom. 1:28, "reprobate"; 1 Cor. 9:27,

A.V., "castaway;" R.V. "rejected" (i.e., disapproved, and so rejected from present testimony, with loss of future reward); 2 Cor. 13:5, 6, 7, "reprobate" (sing. in R.V. in each verse), i.e., that will not stand the test; 2 Tim. 3:8, "reprobate (concerning the faith)," Tit. 1:16, "reprobate." See REJECT, REPROBATE. ¶

NT: B.18c; CB.1233a; K.181.
OT: sîg: S.5509; HR.27b.1; H.1469a; BD.691b.
GEN. REF.: –.

For CASTLE see ARMY (No. 3)

CATCH

1. *harpazō* [ἁρπάζω, 726], to snatch or catch away, is said of the act of the Spirit of the Lord in regard to Philip in Acts 8:39; of Paul in being caught up to Paradise, 2 Cor. 12:2, 4; of the Rapture of the saints at the return of the Lord, 1 Thess. 4:17; of the rapture of the man child in the vision of Rev. 12:5. This verb conveys the idea of force suddenly exercised, as in Matt. 11:12, "take (it) by force"; 12:29, "spoil" (some mss. have *diarpazō* here); in 13:19, R.V., "snatcheth"; for forceful seizure, see also John 6:15; 10:12, 28, 29; Acts 23:10; in Jude 23, R.V., "snatching." See PLUCK, PULL, SNATCH, TAKE (by force). ¶

NT: B.109a; CB.1249b; K.80.
OT: gāzal: S.1497; HR.160a.1; H.337; BD.159d.
ṭāraph: S.2963; HR.160a.3a; H.827; BD.382d.
GEN. REF.: –.

2. *lambanō* [λαμβάνω, 2983], to receive, is once used of catching by fraud, circumventing, 2 Cor. 12:16. In Matt. 21:39 and Mark 12:3, R.V. "took," for A.V. "caught." See ACCEPT, No. 4.

NT: B.464a; CB.1256c; K.495.
OT: lāqaḥ: S.3947; HR.847a.11a; H.1124; BD.542c.
nāśā': S.5375; HR.847a.17a; H.1421; BD.669d.
GEN. REF.: –.

3. *agreuō* [ἀγρεύω, 64], to take by hunting (from *agra*, a hunt, a catch), is used metaphorically, of the Pharisees and Herodians in seeking to catch Christ in His talk, Mark 12:13. ¶

NT: B.13b; CB.–; K.–.
OT: ṣûd: S.6679; HR.16c.4; H.1885; BD.844c.
lākad: S.3920; HR.16c.2; H.1115; BD.539d.
GEN. REF.: –.

4. *thēreuō* [θηρεύω, 2340], to hunt or catch wild beasts (*thērion*, a wild beast), is used by Luke of the same event as in No. 3, Luke 11:54. ¶

NT: B.360c; CB.–; K.–.
OT: ṣûd: S.6679; HR.650b.6; H.1885; BD.844c.
GEN. REF.: –.

5. *zōgreō* [ζωγρέω], to take alive: see CAPTIVE, B, No. 3.

6. *piazō* [πιάζω], to capture: see APPREHEND, No. 2.

7. *sunarpazō* [συναρπάζω, 4884], *sun*, used intensively, and No. 1, to snatch, to seize, to keep a firm grip of, is used only by Luke, and translated "caught" in the A.V. of Luke 8:29, of demon-possession; in Acts 6:12, of the act of the elders and scribes in seizing Stephen, R.V., more suitably, "seized." So in Acts 19:29. In 27:15, it is used of the effects of wind upon a ship. See SEIZE. ¶

NT: B.785b; CB.–; K.–.
OT: lāqaḥ: S.3947; HR.1312c.1; H.1124; BD.542c.
GEN. REF.: –.

8. *sullambanō* [συλλαμβάνω, 4815], *sun*, and No. 2, to seize, is used, similarly to No. 7, in Acts 26:21, of the act of the Jews in seizing Paul in the temple. See CONCEIVE, HELP, SEIZE, TAKE.

NT: B.776d; CB.1270b; K.1101.
OT: lākad: S.3920; HR.1301c.3; H.1115; BD.539d.
tāphas: S.8610; HR.1301c.7a; H.2538; BD.1074c.
GEN. REF.: –.

9. *epilambanō* [ἐπιλαμβάνω, 1949], to lay hold (*epi*, intensive, and No. 2), is translated "caught" in Acts 16:19, A.V.; R.V., "laid hold." See HOLD, TAKE.

NT: B.295a; CB.1246a; K.495.
OT: 'āḥaz: S.270; HR.523c.1; H.64; BD.28a.
ḥāzaq: S.2388; HR.523c.2; H.636; BD.304a.
GEN. REF.: –.

CATTLE

1. *thremma* [θρέμμα, 2353], whatever is fed or nourished (from *trephō*, to nourish, nurture, feed), is found in John 4:12. ¶

NT: B.363b; CB.1272b; K.–.
OT: –.
GEN. REF.: IS.1:623; NB.202; Z.1:764.

2. *ktēnos* [κτῆνος], cattle as property: see BEAST, No. 3.

Note: The verb *poimainō*, to act as a shepherd (*poimēn*), to keep sheep, is translated "keeping sheep" in Luke 17:7, R.V., for A.V., "feeding cattle."

CAUSE (Noun and Verb)

A. Nouns.

1. *aitia* [αἰτία], a cause: see ACCUSATION, A, No. 1.

2. *aition* [αἴτιον, 158], a fault (synonymous with No. 1, but more limited in scope), is translated "cause (of death)" in Luke 23:22; "cause" in Acts 19:40 (of a riot); "fault" in Luke 23:4, 14. See FAULT. ¶

NT: B.26c; CB.1234a; K.–.
OT: –.
GEN. REF.: –.

3. *logos* [λόγος, 3056], a word spoken for any purpose, denotes, in one place, a cause or reason assigned, Matt. 5:32.

NT: B.477a; CB.1257a; K.505.
OT: –.
GEN. REF.: –.

The following phrases are rendered by an English phrase containing the word "cause" (see WHEREFORE):

"For this cause"

1. *anti toutou* [ἀντὶ τούτου, 473], lit., instead of this, i.e., for this cause, signifying the principle or motive, Eph. 5:31.
NT: B.73c; CB.1236a; K.61.
OT: –.
GEN. REF.: –.

2. *dia touto* [διὰ τοῦτο, 1223], lit., on account of this, for this cause, signifying the ground or reason, e.g., R.V. in Mark 12:24; John 1:31; 5:16, 18; 6:65; 7:22; 8:47; 12:18, 27, 39; Rom. 1:26; 4:16; 13:6; 1 Cor. 4:17; 11:10, 30; Eph. 1:15; Col. 1:9; 1 Thess. 2:13; 3:5, 7; 2 Thess. 2:11; 1 Tim. 1:16; Heb. 9:15; 1 John 3:1.
NT: B.179b; CB.1241a; K.–.
OT: –.
GEN. REF.: –.

3. *heneken toutou* [ἕνεκεν τούτου, 1752], lit., for the sake of this, therefore, as a reason for, Matt. 19:5; Mark 10:7; *heneka toutōn*, 'for the sake of these things,' Acts 26:21; and *heneken tou*, for the cause of the (one) etc., 2 Cor. 7:12 (twice).
NT: B.264c; CB.1250a; K.–.
OT: –.
GEN. REF.: –.

4. *charin toutou*, or *toutou charin* [τούτου χάριν, 5484], for this cause, not simply as a reason, as in the preceding phrase, but in favour of, Eph. 3:1, 14; Tit. 1:5.
NT: B.877a; CB.–; K.–.
OT: –.
GEN. REF.: –.

"For this very cause"

auto touto [αὐτὸ τοῦτο, 846], lit., (as to) this very thing, 2 Pet. 1:5.
NT: B.122c; CB.1238b; K.–.
OT: –.
GEN. REF.: –.

Notes: (1) This phrase often represents one containing *aitia* (see above).

(2) In John 18:37, *eis touto*, unto this, denotes "unto this end," R.V. (A.V., "for this cause").

(3) For the phrase "for which cause" (*dio*), Rom. 15:22; 2 Cor. 4:16, see WHEREFORE, *Note* (2) (R.V.).

(4) In Phil. 2:18, *to auto*, is rendered "for the same cause," A.V.; R.V., "in the same manner."

"without a cause"

dōrean [δωρεάν, 1432], lit., as a gift, gratis, (connected with *dōron*, a gift), is rendered "without a cause," John 15:25; "for nought," 2 Cor. 11:7; Gal. 2:21; 2 Thess. 3:8; "freely," Matt. 10:8; Rom. 3:24; Rev. 21:6; 22:17. ¶
NT: B.210c; CB.1242a; K.166.
OT: ḥinām: S.2600; HR.358c.1; H.694b; BD.336c.
GEN. REF.: –.

Notes: (1) *Eikē*, "in vain," "without a cause," Matt. 5:22 (A.V.), is absent from the most authentic mss.

(2) For "cause," in Acts 25:14, A.V., see CASE.

(3) In 2 Cor. 5:13 (R.V., "unto you"), the A.V. has "for your cause."

B. Verbs.

1. *poieō* [ποιέω, 4160], to do, is translated by the verb to cause in John 11:37; Acts 15:3; Rom. 16:17; Col. 4:16; Rev. 13:15, 16. See DO.
NT: B.680d; CB.1265c; K.895.
OT: –.
GEN. REF.: –.

2. *didōmi* [δίδωμι, 1325], to give, is translated "cause" in 1 Cor. 9:12, R.V., for A.V., "(lest we) should."
NT: B.192c; CB.1241c; K.166.
OT: –.
GEN. REF.: –.

Notes: (1) In Matt. 5:32 the R.V. translates *poieō* "maketh (her an adulteress)"; in Rev. 13:12, R.V., "maketh," for A.V., "causeth."

(2) In 2 Cor. 9:11, *katergazomai*, to work, is translated "causeth" in the A.V.; R.V., "worketh."

(3) In 2 Cor. 2:14, *thriambeuō* is rendered "causeth us to triumph," A.V.; R.V., "leadeth us in triumph," the metaphor being taken from the circumstances of the procession of a Roman "triumph."

CAVE

1. *opē* [ὀπή, 3692], perhaps from *ōps*, sight, denotes a hole, an opening, such as a fissure in a rock, Heb. 11:38. In Jas. 3:11, the R.V. has "opening," of the orifice of a fountain (A.V., "place"). See PLACE. ¶
NT: B.574d; CB.–; K.–.
OT: ḥōr: S.2356; HR.1001b.3; H.758a; BD.359d.
sā'îph: S.5585; HR.1001b.5; H.1527a; BD.703d.
GEN. REF.: IS.1:625; NB.202; Z.1:767.

2. *spēlaion* [σπήλαιον, 4693], a grotto, cavern, den (Lat., *spelunca*), "cave," John 11:38, is said of the grave of Lazarus; in the R.V. in Heb. 11:38 and Rev. 6:15 (A.V., "dens"); in the Lord's rebuke concerning the defilement of the Temple, Matt. 21:13; Mark 11:17; Luke 19:46, "den" is used. ¶
NT: B.762c; CB.1269c; K.–.
OT: meʿārāh: S.4631; HR.1284b.1a; H.1704a; BD.792c.
GEN. REF.: IS.1:625; NB.202; Z.1:767.

CEASE

A. Verbs.

1. *pauō* [παύω, 3973], to stop, to make an end, is used chiefly in the Middle Voice in the N.T., signifying to come to an end, to take one's rest, a willing cessation (in contrast to the

Passive Voice which denotes a forced cessation), Luke 5:4, of a discourse; 8:24, of a storm; 11:1, of Christ's prayer; Acts 5:42, of teaching and preaching; 6:13, of speaking against; 13:10, of evil doing; 20:1, of an uproar; 20:31, of admonition; 21:32, of a scourging; 1 Cor. 13:8, of tongues; Eph. 1:16, of giving thanks; Col. 1:9, of prayer; Heb. 10:2, of sacrifices; 1 Pet. 4:1, of ceasing from sin. It is used in the Active Voice in 1 Pet. 3:10, 'let him cause his tongue to cease from evil.' See LEAVE, REFRAIN. ¶

NT: B.638a; CB.–; K.–.
OT: kālāh: S.3615; HR.1112b.3; H.982-4; BD.477b.
shābat: S.7673; HR.1112b.13; H.2323; BD.991d.
GEN. REF.: –.

2. *dialeipō* [διαλείπω, 1257], lit., to leave between, i.e., to leave an interval, whether of space or time (*dia*, between, *leipō*, to leave); hence, to intermit, desist, cease, in Luke 7:45 is used of the kissing of the Lord's feet. ¶

NT: B.185d; CB.1241a; K.–.
OT: ḥādal: S.2308; HR.304b.2; H.609; BD.292d.
mîsh: S.4185; HR.304b.4; H.1167; BD.559a.
māna‘: S.4513; HR.304b.5; H.1216; BD.586a.
GEN. REF.: –.

3. *hēsuchazō* [ἡσυχάζω, 2270], to be quiet, still, at rest, is said of Paul's friends in Caesarea, in ceasing to persuade him not to go to Jerusalem, Acts 21:14; it is used of silence (save in Luke 23:56 and 1 Thess. 4:11) in Luke 14:4 and Acts 11:18. See PEACE (hold one's), QUIET, REST. ¶

NT: B.349a; CB.1250a; K.–.
OT: shāqaṭ: S.8252; HR.620a.11a; H.2453; BD.1052d.
GEN. REF.: –.

4. *kopazō* [κοπάζω, 2869], to cease through being spent with toil, to cease raging (from *kopos*, labour, toil, *kopiaō*, to labour), is said of the wind only, Matt. 14:32; Mark 4:39; 6:51. ¶

NT: B.443b; CB.–; K.–.
OT: ḥādal: S.2308; HR.778a.1; H.609; BD.292d.
shādak: S.7918; HR.778a.6; H.2384; BD.1013c.
GEN. REF.: –.

5. *aphiēmi* [ἀφίημι, 863], to let go, is translated "let us cease to" in Heb. 6:1, R.V. (marg., "leave") for A.V., "leaving." See FORGIVE, LEAVE.

NT: B.125c; CB.1236b; K.88.
OT: nûaḥ: S.5117; HR.183b.4b; H.1323; BD.628a.
GEN. REF.: –.

6. *katapauō* [καταπαύω, 2664], to rest (*kata*, down, intensive, and No. 1), is so translated in Heb. 4:10, for the A.V. "hath ceased." See REST, RESTRAIN.

NT: B.416a; CB.1254a; K.419.
OT: nûaḥ: S.5117; HR.740c.7; H.1323; BD.628a.
shābat: S.7673; HR.740c.11; H.2323; BD.991d.
GEN. REF.: –.

Notes: (1) *Katargeō*, to render inactive, to bring to naught, to do away, is so rendered in Gal. 5:11, R.V., for the A.V. "ceased." See ABOLISH.

(2) *Akatapaustos*, incessant, not to be set at rest (from *a*, negative, *kata*, down, *pauō*, to cease), is used in 2 Pet. 2:14, of those who "cannot cease" from sin, i.e., who cannot be restrained from sinning. ¶

B. Adjective.

adialeiptos [ἀδιάλειπτος, 88], unceasing (from *a*, negative, *dia*, through, *leipō*, to leave), is used of incessant heart pain, Rom. 9:2, A.V., "continual," R.V., "unceasing," and in 2 Tim. 1:3, of remembrance in prayer; the meaning in each place is not that of unbroken continuity, but without the omission of any occasion. Cp. A, No. 2. See CONTINUAL. ¶

NT: B.17b; CB.1233a; K.–.
OT: –.
GEN. REF.: –.

C. Adverb.

adialeiptōs [ἀδιαλείπτως, 89], unceasingly, without ceasing, is used with the same significance as the adjective, not of what is not interrupted, but of that which is constantly recurring; in Rom. 1:9 and 1 Thess. 5:17, of prayer; in 1 Thess. 1:3, of the remembrance of the work, labour and patience of saints; in 1 Thess. 2:13, of thanksgiving. ¶

NT: B.17b; CB.1233a; K.–.
OT: –.
GEN. REF.: –.

Note: Ektenēs, lit., stretched out, signifies earnest, fervent; Acts 12:5, R.V., for A.V., "without ceasing." See 1 Pet. 4:8, "fervent." ¶

For **CELESTIAL** see **HEAVEN, HEAVENLY, B, No. 2**

CELL

oikēma [οἴκημα, 3612], lit., a habitation (akin to *oikeō*, to dwell), is euphemistically put for a prison, in Acts 12:7, R.V., "cell." See PRISON. ¶

NT: B.557a; CB.–; K.–.
OT: –.
GEN. REF.: IS.1:628; NB.–; Z.–.

CELLAR

kruptē [κρυπτή, 2926], — Eng., crypt — a covered way or vault (akin to *kruptos*, hidden, secret), is used in Luke 11:33, of lighting a lamp and putting it "in a cellar," R.V. See PLACE, *Note* (8). ¶

NT: B.454a; CB.–; K.476.
OT: –.
GEN. REF.: IS.1:628; NB.–; Z.1:770.

CENSER

1. *thumiatērion* [θυμιατήριον, 2369], a vessel for burning incense (2 Chron. 26:19; Ezek. 8:11), is found in Heb. 9:4. ¶

NT: B.365b; CB.1272c; K.–.
OT: miqṭeret: S.4730; HR.660c.1; H.2011f; BD.883b.
GEN. REF.: IS.1:628; NB.203; Z.1:711.

2. *libanōtos* [λιβανωτός, 3031], denotes frankincense, the gum of the *libanos*, the frankincense tree; in a secondary sense, a vessel in which to burn incense, Rev. 8:3, 5. ¶

NT: B.473c; CB.1257a; K.533.
OT: leḇônāh: S.3828; HR.876b.1; H.1074d; BD.526c.
GEN. REF.: IS.1:628; NB.203; Z.1:771.

Note: No. 1 derives its significance from the act of burning (*thumiaō*); No. 2 from that which was burned in the vessel.

CENTURION

1. *hekatontarchos* [ἑκατόνταρχος, 1543], a centurion, denotes a military officer commanding from 50 to 100 men, according to the size of the legion of which it was a part (*hekaton*, a hundred, *archō*, to rule), e.g., Matt. 8:5, 8.

NT: B.237a; CB.1249c; K.—.
OT: sar (hammē'ôt): S.8269; HR.420b.1a; H.2295a; BD.977d, 978c.
GEN. REF.: IS.1:629; NB.85; Z.1:772.

2. *hekatontarchēs* [ἑκατοντάρχης, 1543], has the same meaning as No. 1, e.g., Acts 10:1, 22. The Sept. has this word frequently, to denote captains of hundreds.

NT: B.237a; CB.—; K.—.
OT: sar (hammē'ô: S.8269; HR.420b.1a; H.2295a; BD.977d, 978c.
GEN. REF.: IS.1:629; NB.85; Z.1:772.

3. *kenturiōn* [κεντυρίων, 2760], is a Greek transliteration of the Latin *centurio*, signifying practically the same as No. 1, Mark 15:39, 44, 45. There were ten centurions to a cohort when the numbers were complete. There were several at Jerusalem under the chief captain mentioned in Acts 21:31. ¶

NT: B.428c; CB.1255a; K.—.
OT: —.
GEN. REF.: IS.1:629; NB.85; Z.1:772.

CERTAIN, CERTAINTY, CERTAINLY, CERTIFY

A. Noun.

asphaleia [ἀσφάλεια, 803], primarily, not liable to fall, stedfast, firm, hence denoting safety, Acts 5:23, and 1 Thess. 5:3, has the further meaning, "certainty," Luke 1:4. See SAFETY. ¶

NT: B.118d; CB.1238a; K.87.
OT: bāṭaḥ: S.982; HR.174b.1a; H.233; BD.105a.
beṭaḥ: S.983; HR.174b.1b; H.233a; BD.105b.
GEN. REF.: —.

B. Adjective.

asphalēs [ἀσφαλής, 804], safe, is translated "certainty," Acts 21:34; 22:30; "certain," Acts 25:26; "safe," Phil. 3:1; "sure," Heb. 6:19. See SAFE, SURE. ¶

NT: B.119a; CB.1238a; K.87.
OT: —.
GEN. REF.: —.

Notes: (1) *Dēlos*, evident, visible, is translated "certain" in 1 Tim. 6:7, A.V. The most authentic mss. omit it.

(2) The rendering "certain," is frequently changed in the R.V., or omitted, e.g., Luke 5:12; 8:22; Acts 23:17; Heb. 2:6; 4:4.

(3) The indefinite pronoun *tis* signifies anyone, some one, a certain one; the neuter, *ti*, a certain thing, e.g., Matt. 20:20; Mark 14:51.

(4) In the A.V. of Gal. 1:11, *gnōrizō* is rendered "certify," R.V., "to make known."

(5) For "a certain island," Acts 27:16, see the R.V., "small island."

(6) In 1 Cor. 4:11, the verb *astateō*, to be unsettled, to lead a homeless life, is rendered "we . . . have no certain dwelling place." The unsettlement conveyed by the word has suggested the meaning "we are vagabonds" or "we lead a vagabond life," a probable significance. ¶

C. Adverbs.

1. *ontōs* [ὄντως, 3689], really, actually, verily (from *eimi*, to be), is translated "certainly" in Luke 23:47. See CLEAN, INDEED, TRUTH, VERILY.

NT: B.574a; CB.—; K.—.
OT: 'ak: S.389; HR.1000c.1; H.84; BD.36c.
'ākēn: S.403; HR.1000c.2; H.86; BD.38c.
'umᵉnāh: S.552; HR.1000c.3; H.116i; BD.53d.
GEN. REF.: IS.1:629; NB.—; Z.—.

2. *pantōs* [πάντως]: see ALTOGETHER, B.

CHAFF

achuron [ἄχυρον, 892], chaff, the stalk of the grain from which the kernels have been beaten out, or the straw broken up by a threshing machine, is found in Matt. 3:12 and Luke 3:17. ¶

NT: B.129b; CB.—; K.—.
OT: teben: S.8401; HR.188a.5; H.2493; BD.1061d.
môṣ: S.4671; HR.188a.3; H.1162a; BD.558b.
GEN. REF.: IS.1:629; NB.203; Z.1:774.

CHAIN

halusis [ἅλυσις, 254], denotes a chain or bond for binding the body, or any part of it (the hands or feet). Some derive the word from *a*, negative, and *luō*, to loose, i.e., not to be loosed; others from a root connected with a word signifying to restrain. It is used in Mark 5:3, 4; Luke 8:29; Acts 12:6, 7; 21:33; 28:20; Eph. 6:20; 2 Tim. 1:16; Rev. 20:1. See BOND. ¶

NT: B.41c; CB.—; K.—.
OT: —.
GEN. REF.: IS.1:629; NB.—; Z.1:774.

Notes: (1) Some ancient authorities have *seira*, a cord, rope, band, chain, in 2 Pet. 2:4, instead of *seiros*, a cavern, R.V., "pits."

(2) In Jude 6 the R.V. renders *desmos* by "bonds" (for the A.V. "chains"). See BOND. ¶

CHALCEDONY

chalkēdōn [χαλκηδών, 5472], the name of a gem, including several varieties, one of which resembles a cornelian, is "supposed to denote a green silicate of copper found in the mines near Chalcedon" (*Swete, on the Apocalypse*), Rev. 21:19. ¶

NT: B.874d; CB.1239b; K.–.
OT: –.
GEN. REF.: IS.4:626; NB.632; Z.1:774.

CHAMBER (Store-chamber)

1. *tameion* [ταμεῖον, 5009], denotes, firstly, a store-chamber, then, any private room, secret chamber, Matt. 6:6; R.V., "inner chamber" (A.V., "closet"); 24:26, "inner (A.V., secret) chambers"; Luke 12:3, R.V., ditto, for A.V., "closets"; it is used in Luke 12:24 ("store-chamber") of birds. ¶

NT: B.803c; CB.–; K.–.
OT: ḥeder: S.2315; HR.1334a.2; H.6129; BD.293c.
GEN. REF.: IS.1:632; NB.–; Z.1:776.

2. *huperǭon* [ὑπερῷον, 5253], the neuter of *huperōos*, "above," denotes an upper room, upper chamber (*huper*, above), Acts 1:13; 9:37, 39; 20:8. See ROOM. ¶

NT: B.842b; CB.–; K.–.
OT: ʿalîyāh: S.5944; HR.1411b.1a; H.1624f; BD.751a.
GEN. REF.: IS.1:632; NB.–; Z.1:774.

CHAMBERING

koitē [κοίτη, 2845], primarily a place in which to lie down, hence, a bed, especially the marriage bed, denotes, in Rom. 13:13, illicit intercourse. See BED, CONCEIVE.

NT: B.440a; CB.1255b; K.–.
OT: mishkāb: S.4904; HR.775b.6d; H.2381c; BD.1012d.
GEN. REF.: IS.1:901; NB.–; Z.–.

CHAMBERLAIN

ho epi tou koitōnos [2846, *koitōn*], lit., the (one) over the bedchamber (*epi*, over, *koitōn*, a bedchamber), denotes a chamberlain, an officer who had various duties in the houses of kings and nobles. The importance of the position is indicated by the fact that the people of Tyre and Sidon sought the favour of Herod Agrippa through the mediation of Blastus, Acts 12:20.

NT: B.440b; CB.–; K.–.
OT: –.
GEN. REF.: IS.1:632; NB.204; Z.–.

Note: In Rom. 16:23, *oikonomos*, a person who manages the domestic affairs of a family, in general, a manager, a steward, is translated "chamberlain" in the A.V., which the R.V. corrects to "treasurer."

CHANCE

1. *sunkuria* [συνκυρία, 4795], lit., a meeting together with, a coincidence of circumstances, a happening, is translated "chance" in Luke 10:31. But concurrence of events is what the word signifies, rather than chance. ¶

NT: B.775a; CB.–; K.–.
OT: –.
GEN. REF.: IS.1:632; NB.–; Z.–.

Note: Some texts have *tucha* here (from *tunchanō*, to happen).

2. *ei tuchoi* [εἰ τύχοι, 5177], lit., 'if it may happen' (*ei*, if, *tunchanō*, to happen), signifies "it may chance," 1 Cor. 15:37. ¶

NT: B.829c; CB.–; K.–.
OT: –.
GEN. REF.: –.

CHANGE (Noun and Verb)

A. Noun.

metathesis [μετάθεσις, 3331], a transposition, or a transference from one place to another (from *meta*, implying change, and *tithēmi*, to put), has the meaning of change in Heb. 7:12, in connection with the necessity of a change of the Law (or, as margin, law), if the priesthood is changed (see B, No. 3). It is rendered "translation" in 11:5, "removing" in 12:27. See REMOVING, TRANSLATION. ¶

NT: B.511a; CB.1258c; K.1176.
OT: –.
GEN. REF.: –.

B. Verbs.

1. *allassō* [ἀλλάσσω, 236], to make other than it is (from *allos*, another), to transform, change, is used (*a*) of the effect of the Gospel upon the precepts of the Law, Acts 6:14; (*b*) of the effect, on the body of a believer, of Christ's Return, 1 Cor. 15:51, 52; (*c*) of the final renewal of the material creation, Heb. 1:12; (*d*) of a change in the Apostle's mode of speaking (or dealing), Gal. 4:20. In Rom. 1:23 it has its other meaning, to exchange. ¶

NT: B.39a; CB.1234c; K.40.
OT: ḥālaph: S.2498; HR.55b.2c; H.666; BD.322a.
ḥalîphāh: S.2487; HR.55b.2d; H.666c; BD.322b.
mûr: S.4171; HR.55b.3; H.1164; BD.558c.
GEN. REF.: IS.1:633; NB.–; Z.–.

2. *metallassō* [μεταλλάσσω, 3337], from *meta*, implying change, and No. 1, to change one thing for another, or into another, Rom. 1:25, 26, is translated "exchange" in ver. 25. See EXCHANGE. ¶

NT: B.511c; CB.1258c; K.40.
OT: –.
GEN. REF.: –.

3. *metatithēmi* [μετατίθημι, 3346], to place differently, to change, (akin to A, above), is said of priesthood, Heb. 7:12. See CARRY, No. 5.

NT: B.513c; CB.1258c; K.1176.
OT: –
GEN. REF.: –.

4. *metaballō* [μεταβάλλω, 3328], *meta*, as in No. 2, and *ballō*, to throw, signifies to turn quickly, or, in the Middle Voice, to change one's mind, and is found in Acts 28:6. ¶

NT: B.510d; CB.—; K.—.
OT: hāphak: S.2015; HR.915b.1; H.512; BD.245b.
GEN. REF.: —.

Notes: (1) In Phil. 3:21, for the A.V. rendering of *metaschēmatizō*, "change," the R.V. has "fashion anew"; in 2 Cor. 3:18 *metamorphoō* is rendered "change," in the A.V. (R.V., "transform").

(2) For *metanoia*, a change of mind, see REPENTANCE.

CHANGER (Money-changer)

1. *kollubistēs* [κολλυβιστής, 2855], from *kollubos* lit., clipped), a small coin or rate of change (*koloboō* signifies to cut off, to clip, shorten, Matt. 24:22), denotes a money-changer, lit., money-clipper, Matt. 21:12; Mark 11:15; John 2:15. ¶

NT: B.442a; CB.—; K.—.
OT: —.
GEN. REF.: IS.1:408; NB. —; Z. 1:778.

2. *kermatistēs* [κερματιστής, 2773], from *kermatizō* (not found in the N.T.), to cut into small pieces, to make small change (*kerma* signifies a small coin, John 2:15; akin to *keirō*, to cut short). In the court of the Gentiles, in the Temple precincts, were the seats of those who sold selected and approved animals for sacrifice, and other things. The magnitude of this traffic had introduced the bankers' or brokers' business, John 2:14. ¶

NT: B.429d; CB.—; K.—.
OT: —.
GEN. REF.: IS:—; NB.—; Z.1:778.

CHARGE (Nouns, Adjective and Verbs), CHARGEABLE

A. Nouns

(a) With the meaning of an accusation.

1. *aitia* [αἰτία, 156], a cause, accusation, is rendered "charges" in Acts 25:27 (A.V., "crimes"); cp. ver. 18. SEE ACCUSATION, CAUSE.

NT: B.26b; CB.1234a; K.—.
OT: 'āwôn: S.5771; HR.38a.1; H.1577a; BD.730d,731b
GEN. REF.: IS.1:634; NB.—; Z.—.

2. *aitiōma* [αἰτίωμα, 157], in some texts *aitiama*, denotes a charge, Acts 25:7. See ACCUSATION, A, No. 2.

NT: B.26d; CB.1234a; K.—.
OT: —.
GEN. REF.: IS.1:634; NB.—; Z.—.

3. *enklēma* [ἔνκλημα, 1462]: see ACCUSATION. A, No. 3.

NT: B.216b; CB.1245a; K.394.
OT: —.
GEN. REF.: IS.1:634; NB.—; Z.—.

(b) With the meaning of something committed or bestowed.

4. *klēros* [κλῆρως, 2819], a lot, allotment, heritage (whence Eng. "clergy"), is translated in 1 Pet. 5:3, R.V., "the charge allotted to you"; here the word is in the plural, lit., 'charges.' See INHERITANCE, LOT, PART.

NT: B.435b; CB.1255b; K.442.
OT: gôrāl: S.1486; HR.770a.1; H.—; BD.174a.
naḥ^{a}lāh: S.5159; HR.770a.6; H.—; BD.635a.
GEN. REF.: IS.1:634; NB.—; Z.—.

5. *opsōnion* [ὀψώνιον, 3800], from *opson*, meat, and *ōneomai*, to buy, primarily signified whatever is brought to be eaten with bread, provisions, supplies for an army, soldier's pay, "charges," 1 Cor. 9:7, of the service of a soldier. It is rendered "wages" in Luke 3:14; Rom. 6:23; 2 Cor. 11:8. See WAGES. ¶

NT: B.602a; CB.1261a; K.752.
OT: —.
GEN. REF.: IS.—; NB.—; Z.5:893.

6. *parangelia* [παραγγελία, 3852], a proclamation, a command or commandment, is strictly used of commands received from a superior and transmitted to others. It is rendered "charge" in Acts 16:24; 1 Thess. 4:2, R.V. (where the word is in the plural); 1 Tim. 1:5 (R.V.) and ver. 18. In Acts 5:28 the lit. meaning is 'Did we not charge you with a charge?' See also COMMANDMENT, STRAITLY. Cp. C, No. 8, below. ¶

NT: B.613b; CB.1262b; K.776.
OT: —.
GEN. REF.: —.

B. Adjective.

adapanos [ἀδάπανος, 77], lit., 'without expense' (*a*, negative, and *dapanē*, expense, cost), is used in 1 Cor. 9:18, "without charge" (of service in the Gospel). ¶

NT: B.15d; CB.—; K.—.
OT: —.
GEN. REF.: IS.1:634; NB.—; Z.—.

C. Verbs.

1. *diamarturomai* [διαμαρτύρομαι, 1263], a strengthened form of *marturomai* (*dia*, through, intensive), is used in the Middle Voice; primarily it signifies to testify through and through, bear a solemn witness; hence, to charge earnestly, 1 Tim. 5:21; 2 Tim. 2:14; 4:1. See TESTIFY, WITNESS.

NT: B.186c; CB.1241b; K.564.
OT: 'ûd: S.5749; HR.305b.3; H.1576; BD.729d.
GEN. REF.: IS.1:634; NB.—; Z.—.

2. *diastellomai* [διαστέλλομαι, 1291], lit., to draw asunder (*dia*, asunder, *stellō*, to draw), signifies to admonish, order, charge, Matt. 16:20; Mark 5:43; 7:36 (twice); 8:15; 9:9.

In Acts 15:24 it is translated "gave commandment"; in Heb. 12:20, A.V., "commanded," R.V., "enjoined." See COMMAND, *Note* (2). ¶
NT: B.188d; CB.1241b; K.1074.
OT: —.
GEN. REF.: IS.1:634; NB.—; Z.—.

3. *diatassō* [διατάσσω]: see APPOINT, No. 6.

4. *embrimaomai* [ἐμβριμάομαι, 1690], from *en*, in, intensive, and *brimē*, strength, primarily signifies to snort with anger, as of horses. Used of men it signifies to fret, to be painfully moved; then, to express indignation against; hence, to rebuke sternly, to charge strictly, Matt. 9:30; Mark 1:43; it is rendered "murmured against" in Mark 14:5; "groaned" in John 11:33; "groaning" in ver. 38. See GROAN, MURMUR. ¶
NT: B.254d; CB.1244b; K.—.
OT: —.
GEN. REF.: IS.1:634; NB.—; Z.—.

5. *enkaleō* [ἐνκαλέω]: see ACCUSE, B, No. 2.

6. *entellomai* [ἐντέλλομαι, 1781], to order, command, enjoin (from *en*, in, used intensively, and *teleō*, to fulfil), is translated by the verb to give charge, Matt. 4:6; 17:9 (A.V.); Luke 4:10. See COMMAND, ENJOIN.
NT: B.268b; CB.1245b; K.234.
OT: ṣāwāh: S.6680; HR.477a.7a; H.1887; BD.845b.
GEN. REF.: IS.1:634; NB.—; Z.—.

7. *epitimaō* [ἐπιτιμάω, 2008], signifies (*a*) to put honour upon (*epi*, upon, *timē*, honour); (*b*) to adjudge, to find fault with, rebuke; hence to charge, or rather, to charge strictly (*epi*, intensive), e.g., Matt. 12:16; Mark 3:12, "charged much"; Mark 8:30; in 10:48, R.V., "rebuked". See REBUKE.
NT: B.303b; CB.1246b; K.249.
OT: gā'ar: S.1605; HR.537a.1; H.370; BD.172a.
GEN. REF.: IS.1:634; NB.—; Z.—.

8. *parangellō* [παραγγέλλω, 3853], lit., to announce beside (*para*, beside, *angellō*, to announce), to hand on an announcement from one to another, usually denotes to command, to charge, Luke 5:14; 8:56; 1 Cor. 7:10 (A.V., "command"), "give charge," R.V.; 11:17, "in giving you this charge," R.V.; 1 Tim. 1:3; 6:13, R.V., and 6:17. It is rendered by the verb to charge in the R.V. of Acts 1:4; 4:18; 5:28; 15:5; 1 Thess. 4:11. See Acts 5:28 under A, No. 6. See COMMAND, DECLARE.
NT: B.613b; CB.1262b; K.776.
OT: shāma': S.8085; HR.1056b.6; H.2412; BD.1033b.
GEN. REF.: IS.1:634; NB.—; Z.—.

9. *proaitiaomai* [προαιτιάομαι, 4256], to accuse beforehand, to have already brought a charge (*pro*, before, *aitia*, an accusation), is used in Rom. 3:9, "we before laid to the charge." ¶
NT: B.702c; CB.—; K.—.
OT: —.
GEN. REF.: IS.1:634; NB.—; Z.—.

10. *tereō* [τηρέω, 5083], to keep, to guard, is translated "to be kept in charge," in Acts 24:23; 25:4, R.V. (A.V., "kept"). See HOLD, KEEP, OBSERVE, PRESERVE, WATCH.
NT: B.814d; CB.1271b; K.1174.
OT: shāmar: S.8104; HR.1348b.7; H.2414; BD.1036b.
nāṣar: S.5341; HR.1348b.2; H.1407; BD.665c.
GEN. REF.: IS.1:634; NB.—; Z.—.

Notes: (1) *Martureō*, to testify, translated "charged" in 1 Thess. 2:11, A.V., is found there in the most authentic mss. and translated "testifying" in the R.V.

(2) *Enorkizō*, to adjure (*en*, in, used intensively, *horkos*, an oath), is translated "I adjure," in 1 Thess. 5:27, R.V., for A.V., "I charge." Some mss. have *horkizō* here.

(3) The following are translated by the verb to charge or to be chargeable in the A.V., but differently in the R.V., and will be found under the word BURDEN: *bareō*, B, No. 1; *epibareō*, B, No. 2; *katanarkaō*, B, No. 5.

(4) *Epitassō*, to command, is so translated in Mark 9:25, R.V., for the A.V., "charge."

(5) *Dapanaō*, to be at the expense of anything (cp. B, above), is translated "be at charges," in Acts 21:24. See CONSUME, SPEND.

(6) In 2 Tim. 4:16, *logizomai* is rendered "laid to (their) charge," A.V.; R.V., ". . . account."

(7) In Acts 8:27, the R.V. translates the verb *eimi*, to be, with *epi*, over, "was over," A.V., "had the charge of."

(8) In Acts 7:60 *histēmi*, to cause to stand, is rendered "lay . . . to the charge."

CHARGER

pinax [πίναξ, 4094], primarily a board or plank, came to denote various articles of wood; hence, a wooden trencher, charger, Matt. 14:8, 11; Mark 6:25, 28; Luke 11:39. See PLATTER. ¶
NT: B.658c; CB.—; K.—.
OT: —.
GEN. REF.: —.

CHARIOT

1. *harma* [ἅρμα, 716], akin to *ararishō*, to join, denotes a war chariot with two wheels, Acts 8:28, 29, 38; Rev. 9:9. ¶
NT: B.107b; CB.1249b; K.—.
OT: rekeb: S.7393; HR.158b.1b; H.2163a; BD.939a.
merkābāh: S.4818; HR.158b.1e; H.2163f; BD.939d.
GEN. REF.: IS.1:635; NB.204; Z.1:780.

2. *rhedē* [ῥέδη, 4480], a wagon with four wheels, was chiefly used for travelling purposes, Rev. 18:13. ¶
NT: B.734d; CB.—; K.—.
OT: —.
GEN. REF.: IS.1:635; NB.204; Z.1:780.

For CHARITY see LOVE

CHASTE

hagnos [ἁγνός, 53], signifies (*a*) pure from every fault, immaculate, 2 Cor. 7:11 (A.V., "clear"); Phil. 4:8; 1 Tim. 5:22; Jas. 3:17; 1 John 3:3 (in all which the R.V. rendering is "pure"), and 1 Pet. 3:2, "chaste"; (*b*) pure from carnality, modest, 2 Cor. 11:2, R.V., "pure"; Tit. 2:5, "chaste." See CLEAR, HOLY, PURE. ¶

NT: B.11d; CB.1249a; K.19.
OT: ṭāhôr: S.2889; HR.16b.3; H.792d; BD.373a.
GEN. REF.: IS.–; NB.–; Z.1:784.

Note: Cp. *hagios*, holy, as being free from admixture of evil; *hosios*, holy, as being free from defilement; *eilikrinēs*, pure, as being tested, lit., judged by the sunlight; *katharos*, pure, as being cleansed.

CHASTEN, CHASTENING, CHASTISE, CHASTISEMENT

A. Verb.

paideuō [παιδεύω, 3811], primarily denotes to train children, suggesting the broad idea of education (*pais*, a child), Acts 7:22; 22:3; see also Tit. 2:12, "instructing" (R.V.), here of a training gracious and firm; grace, which brings salvation, employs means to give us full possession of it; hence, to chastise, this being part of the training, whether (*a*) by correcting with words, reproving, and admonishing, 1 Tim. 1:20 (R.V., "be taught"); 2 Tim. 2:25, or (*b*) by chastening by the infliction of evils and calamities, 1 Cor. 11:32; 2 Cor. 6:9; Heb. 12:6, 7, 10; Rev. 3:19. The verb also has the meaning to chastise with blows, to scourge, said of the command of a judge, Luke 23:16, 22. See CORRECTION, B, INSTRUCT, LEARN, TEACH, and cp. CHILD (Nos. 4 to 6). ¶

NT: B.603d; CB.1261c; K.753.
OT: yāsar: S.3256; HR.1047a.4b,c; H.877; BD.415d.
GEN. REF.: IS.1:635; NB.–; Z.1:783.

B. Noun.

paideia [παιδεία, 3809], denotes the training of a child, including instruction; hence, discipline, correction, "chastening," Eph. 6:4, R.V. (A.V., "nurture"), suggesting the Christian discipline that regulates character; so in Heb. 12:5, 7, 8 (in ver. 8 A.V., "chastisement," the R.V. corrects to "chastening"); in 2 Tim. 3:16, "instruction." See INSTRUCTION, NURTURE. ¶

NT: B.603b; CB.1261b; K.753.
OT: mûsār: S.4148; HR.1046c.5; H.877b; BD.416b.
GEN. REF.: IS.1:635; NB.–; Z.1:783.

CHEEK

siagōn (σιαγών, 4600], primarily denotes the jaw, the jaw-bone; hence "cheek," Matt. 5:39; Luke 6:29. ¶

NT: B.749c; CB.–; K.–.
OT: lᵉḥî: S.3895; HR.1265c.1; H.1101a; BD.534c.
GEN. REF.: IS.1:639; NB.207; Z.1:785.

CHEER, CHEERFUL, CHEERFULLY, CHEERFULNESS

A. Verbs.

1. *euthumeō* [εὐθυμέω, 2114], signifies, in the Active Voice, to put in good spirits, to make cheerful (*eu*, well, *thumos*, mind or passion); or, intransitively, to be cheerful, Acts 27:22, 25; Jas. 5:13 (R.V., "cheerful," for A.V., "merry"). See MERRY. ¶

NT: B.320d; CB.–; K.–.
OT: –.
GEN. REF.: –.

2. *tharseō* [θαρσέω, 2293], to be of good courage, of good cheer (*tharsos*, courage, confidence), is used only in the Imperative Mood, in the N.T.; "be of good cheer," Matt. 9:2, 22; 14:27; Mark 6:50; 10:49; Luke 8:48; John 16:33; Acts 23:11. See BOLD, A, No. 1, COMFORT, COURAGE. ¶

NT: B.352a; CB.1271c; K.315.
OT: –.
GEN. REF.: IS.1:788; NB.–; Z.–.

B. Adjectives.

1. *euthumos* [εὔθυμος, 2115], means of good cheer (see A, No. 1), Acts 27:36. ¶

NT: B.320d; CB.–; K.–.
OT: –.
GEN. REF.: –.

2. *hilaros* [ἱλαρός, 2431], from *hileōs*, propitious, signifies that readiness of mind, that joyousness, which is prompt to do anything; hence, cheerful (Eng., hilarious), 2 Cor. 9:7, "God loveth a cheerful (hilarious) giver." ¶

NT: B.375b; CB.1250c; K.362.
OT: –
GEN. REF.: –.

Note: In the Sept. the verb *hilarunō* translates a Hebrew word meaning "to cause to shine," in Ps. 104:15. ¶

C. Adverb.

euthumōs [εὐθύμως, 2115], cheerfully (see A, No. 1), is found in the most authentic mss., in Acts 24:10, instead of the comparative degree, *euthumoteron*. ¶

NT: B.320d; CB.–; K.–.
OT: –.
GEN. REF.: –.

D. Noun.

hilarotēs [ἱλαρότης, 2432], cheerfulness (akin to B, No. 2), is used in Rom. 12:8, in connection with shewing mercy. ¶

NT: B.375d; CB.–; K.362.
OT: rāṣôn: S.7522; HR.684b.1; H.2207a; BD.953c.
GEN. REF.: –.

CHERISH

thalpō [θάλπω, 2282], primarily means to heat, to soften by heat; then, to keep warm, as of birds covering their young with their feathers, Deut. 22:6, Sept.; metaphorically, to cherish with tender love, to foster with tender care, in Eph. 5:29 of Christ and the Church; 1 Thess. 2:7 of the care of the saints at Thessalonica by the Apostle and his associates, as of a nurse for her children. ¶

NT: B.350b; CB.—; K.—.
OT: rābaṣ: S.7250; HR.623b.3; H.2108; BD.918a.
GEN. REF.: IS.1:641; NB.—; Z.—.

CHERUBIM

cheroubim [χερουβίμ, 5502], are regarded by some as the ideal representatives of redeemed animate creation. In the Tabernacle and Temple they were represented by the two golden figures of two-winged living-creatures. They were all of one piece with the golden lid of the Ark of the Covenant in the Holy of Holies, signifying that the prospect of redeemed and glorified creatures as bound up with the sacrifice of Christ.

This in itself would indicate that they represent redeemed human beings in union with Christ, a union seen, figuratively, proceeding out of the Mercy Seat. Their faces were towards this Mercy Seat, suggesting a consciousness of the means whereby union with Christ has been produced.

The first reference to the cherubim is in Gen. 3:24, which should read ' . . . at the East of the Garden of Eden He caused to dwell in a tabernacle the cherubim, and the flaming sword which turned itself to keep the way of the Tree of Life.' This was not simply to keep fallen human beings out; the presence of the cherubim suggests that redeemed men, restored to God on God's conditions, would have access to the Tree of Life. (See Rev. 22:14).

Certain other references in the O.T. give clear indication that angelic beings are upon occasion in view, e.g., Psalm 18:10; Ezek. 28:4. So with the Vision of the Cherubim in Ezek. 10:1-20; 11:22. In the N.T. the word is found in Heb. 9:5, where the reference is to the Ark in the Tabernacle, and the thought is suggested of those who minister to the manifestation of the glory of God.

We may perhaps conclude, therefore, that, inasmuch as in the past and in the present angelic beings have have functioned and do function administratively in the service of God, and that redeemed man in the future is to act administratively in fellowship with Him, the Cherubim in Scripture represent one or other of these two groups of created beings according to what is set forth in the various passages relating to them. ¶

NT: B.881b; CB.1239c; K.1312.
OT: kᵉrûbîm: S.3742; HR.1467c.1; H.1033a; BD.500c.
GEN. REF.: IS.1:641; NB.208; Z.1:788.

For **CHICKEN** see **BROOD**

CHIEF, CHIEFEST, CHIEFLY

A. Adjective.

prōtos [πρῶτος, 4413], denotes the first, whether in time or place. It is translated "chief" in Mark 6:21, R.V., of men of Galilee; in Acts 13:50, of men in a city; in 28:7, of the chief man in the island of Melita; in 17:4, of chief women in a city; in 28:17, of Jews; in 1 Tim. 1:15, 16, of a sinner. In the following, where the A.V. has "chief," or "chiefest," the R.V. renderings are different: Matt. 20:27 and Mark 10:44, "first"; Luke 19:47 and Acts 25:2, "principal men"; Acts 16:12, said of Philippi, "the first (city) of the district," R.V., for incorrect A.V., "the chief city of that part of Macedonia." Amphipolis was the chief city of that part. *Prōtos* here must mean the first in the direction in which the Apostle came. See BEGINNING, BEFORE, BEST, FIRST, FORMER.

NT: B.725b; CB.1267b; K.965.
OT: ri'shôn: S.7223; HR.1235c.3a; H.2097c; BD.911c.
GEN. REF.: IS.1:644; NB.—; Z.1:793.

B. Nouns.

1. *kephalaion* [κεφάλαιον, 2774], akin to the adjective *kephalaios*, belonging to the head, and *kephalē*, the head, denotes the chief point or principal thing in a subject, Heb. 8:1, "the chief point is this" (A.V., "the sum"); elsewhere in Acts 22:28 (of principal, as to money), "(a great) sum." See SUM. ¶

NT: B.429d; CB.1255a; K.—.
OT: rō'sh: S.7218; HR.760c.1a; H.2097; BD.910c.
GEN. REF.: IS.1:644; NB.—; Z.1:793.

Certain compound nouns involving the significance of chief, are as follows:

2. *archiereus* [ἀρχιερεύς, 749], a chief priest, high priest (*archē*, first, *hiereus*, a priest), is frequent in the Gospels, Acts and Hebrews, but there only in the N.T. It is used of Christ, e.g., in Heb. 2:17; 3:1; of chief priests, including ex-high-priests and members of their families, e.g., Matt. 2:4; Mark 8:31.

NT: B.112d; CB.1237b; K.349.
OT: kāhan: S.3547; HR.165b.1; H.959; BD.464c.
GEN. REF.: IS.3:960; NB.—; Z.4:852.

3. *archipoimēn* [ἀρχιποίμην, 750], a chief shepherd (*archē*, chief, *poimēn*, a shepherd), is said of Christ only, 1 Pet. 5:4. Modern Greeks use it of tribal chiefs. ¶

NT: B.113a; CB.1237b; K.901.
OT: –.
GEN. REF.: –.

4. *architelōnēs* [ἀρχιτελώνης, 754], denotes a chief tax-collector, or publican, Luke 19:2. ¶

NT: B.113b; CB.1237b; K.–.
OT: –.
GEN. REF.: –.

5. *akrogōniaios* [ἀκρογωνιαῖος, 204], denotes a chief corner-stone (from *akros*, highest, extreme, *gōnia*, a corner, angle), Eph. 2:20 and 1 Pet. 2:6. ¶ In the Sept., Is. 28:16. ¶

NT: B.33d; CB.1234b; K.137.
OT: pinnāh: S.6438; HR.51a.1; H.1783a; BD.819c.
GEN. REF.: IS.1:644; NB.–; Z.–.

6. *prōtokathedria* [πρωτοκαθεδρία, 4410], a sitting in the first or chief seat (*prōtos*, first, *kathedra*, a seat), is found in Matt. 23:6; Mark 12:39; Luke 11:43; 20:46. ¶

NT: B.725b; CB.1267b; K.965.
OT: : –.
GEN. REF.: –.

7. *prōtoklisia* [πρωτοκλισία, 4411], the first reclining place, the chief place at table (from *prōtos*, and *klisia*, a company reclining at a meal; cp. *klinō*, to incline), is found in Matt. 23:6; Mark 12:39 (as with No. 6); Luke 14:7, 8; 20:46. ¶

NT: B.725b; CB.1267b; K.965.
OT: –.
GEN. REF.: –.

8. *chiliarchos* [χιλίαρχος], denotes a chief captain: see CAPTAIN, No. 1.

9. *asiarchēs* [Ἀσιαρχής, 775], an Asiarch, was one of certain officers elected by various cities in the province of Asia, whose function consisted in celebrating, partly at their own expense, the public games and festivals; in Acts 19:31, R.V., the word is translated "chief officers of Asia" (A.V., "chief of Asia").

It seems probable, according to Prof. Ramsay, that they were "the high priests of the temples of the Imperial worship in various cities of Asia"; further, that "the Council of the Asiarchs sat at stated periods in the great cities alternately . . . and were probably assembled at Ephesus for such a purpose when they sent advice to St. Paul to consult his safety." A festival would have brought great crowds to the city. ¶

NT: B.116a; CB.–; K.–.
OT: –.
GEN. REF.: IS.1:329; NB.–; Z.1:365.

10. *archōn* [ἄρχων, 758], a ruler, is rendered "chief" in the A.V. of Luke 14:1 (R.V., "ruler"); "chief rulers," in John 12:42, R.V., "rulers (of the people)," i.e., of members of the Sanhedrin; "chief," in Luke 11:15 (R.V., "prince"), in reference to Beelzebub, the prince of demons. See MAGISTRATE, PRINCE, RULER.

NT: B.113d; CB.1237b; K.81.
OT: nāsî': S.5387; HR.166b.17; H.1421b,c; BD.672b.
rō'sh: S.7218; HR.166b.26; H.2097; BD.910c.
sar: S.8269; HR.166b.30a; H.2295a; BD.978a.
GEN. REF.: IS.1:644; NB.–; Z.1:793.

11. *archisunagōgos* [ἀρχισυνάγωγος, 752], a ruler of a synagogue, translated "chief ruler of the synagogue," in Acts 18:8, 17, A.V., was the administrative officer supervising the worship.

NT: B.113b; CB.–; K.1108.
OT: –.
GEN. REF.: IS.4:681; NB.–; Z.5:554,566.

C. Verb.

hēgeomai [ἡγέομαι, 2233], to lead the way, to preside, rule, be the chief, is used of the ambition to be chief among the disciples of Christ, Luke 22:26; of Paul as the chief speaker in Gospel testimony at Lystra, Acts 14:12; of Judas and Silas, as chief (or rather, 'leading') men among the brethren at Jerusalem, Acts 15:22. See ACCOUNT, COUNT, ESTEEM, GOVERNOR, JUDGE, SUPPOSE, THINK.

NT: B.343c; CB.1249c; K.303.
OT: māshal: S.4910; HR.602c.20; H.1258,1259; BD.605c.
nāgîd: S.5057; HR.602c.21; H.1289b; BD.617d.
rō'sh: S.7218; HR.602c.31; H.2097; BD.910c.
GEN. REF.: –.

D. Adverbs.

1. *huperlian* [ὑπερλίαν, 5228, 3029], chiefest (*huper*, over, *lian*, exceedingly, pre-eminently, very much), is used in 2 Cor. 11:5; 12:11, of Paul's place among the Apostles. ¶

NT: B.841b; CB.–; K.–.
OT: –.
GEN. REF.: –.

2. *malista* [μάλιστα, 3122], the superlative of *mala*, very, very much, is rendered "chiefly" in 2 Pet. 2:10 and in the A.V. of Phil. 4:22 (R.V., "especially"). See ESPECIALLY, MOST.

NT: B.488d; CB.–; K.–.
OT: –.
GEN. REF.: –.

Note: In Rom. 3:2, R.V., the adverb *prōton* is translated "first of all" (A.V., "chiefly").

CHILD, CHILDREN, CHILD-BEARING, CHILDISH, CHILDLESS

1. *teknon* [τέκνον, 5043], a child (akin to *tiktō*, to beget, bear), is used in both the natural and the figurative senses. In contrast to *huios*, son (see below), it gives prominence to the fact of birth, whereas *huios* stresses the dignity and character of the relationship. Figuratively, *teknon* is used of children of (*a*) God, John 1:12; (*b*) light, Eph. 5:8; (*c*) obedience, 1 Pet. 1:14; (*d*) a promise, Rom. 9:8; Gal. 4:28; (*e*) the Devil,

1 John 3:10; (*f*) wrath, Eph. 2:3; (*g*) cursing, 2 Pet. 2:14; (*h*) spiritual relationship, 2 Tim. 2:1; Philm. 10. See DAUGHTER, SON, SEED.

NT: B.808b; CB.1271b; K.759.
OT: bēn: S.1121; HR.1340c.3; H.254; BD.119d.
GEN. REF.: IS.–; NB.416,1206; Z.1:793.

2. *teknion* [τεκνίον, 5040], a little child, a diminutive of No. 1, is used only figuratively in the N.T., and always in the plural. It is found frequently in 1 John, see 2:1, 12, 28; 3:7, 18; 4:4; 5:21; elsewhere, once in John's Gospel, 13:33, once in Paul's Epistles, Gal. 4:19. It is a term of affection by a teacher to his disciples under circumstances requiring a tender appeal, e.g., of Christ to the Twelve just before His death; the Apostle John used it in warning believers against spiritual dangers; Paul, because of the deadly errors of Judaism assailing the Galatian churches. Cp. his use of *teknon* in Gal. 4:28. ¶

NT: B.808a; CB.1271b; K.759.
OT: –.
GEN. REF.: IS.1:644; NB.–; Z.1:793.

3. *huios* [υἱός, 5207], a son, is always so translated in the R.V., except in the phrase "children of Israel," e.g., Matt. 27:9; and with reference to a foal, Matt. 21:5. The A.V. does not discriminate between *teknon* and *huios*. In the 1st Ep. of John, the Apostle reserves the word for the Son of God. See *teknia*, "little children" (above), and *tekna*, "children," in John 1:12; 11:52. See *paidion* (below). For the other use of *huios*, indicating the quality of that with which it is connected, see SON.

NT: B.833c; CB.1251c; K.1206.
OT: bēn: S.1121; HR.1384c.3; H.254; BD.119d.
GEN. REF.: IS.1:644; NB.1206; Z.–.

4. *pais* [παῖς, 3816], signifies (*a*) a child in relation to descent, (*b*) a boy or girl in relation to age, (*c*) a servant, attendant, maid, in relation to condition. As an instance of (*a*) see Matt. 21:15, "children," and Acts 20:12 (R.V., "lad"). In regard to (*b*) the R.V. has "boy" in Matt. 17:18 and Luke 9:42. In Luke 2:43 it is used of the Lord Jesus. In regard to (*c*) , see Matt. 8:6, 8, 13, etc. As to (*a*) note Matt. 2:16, R.V., "male children." See MAID, MANSERVANT, SERVANT, SON, YOUNG MAN.

NT: B.604c; CB.1261c; K.759.
OT: 'ebed: S.5650; HR.1049a.9a; H.1553a; BD.713d.
na'ar: S.5288; HR.1049a.8a; H.1389a; BD.654d.
GEN. REF.: IS.1:644; NB.–; Z.–.

5. *paidion* [παιδίον, 3813], a diminutive of *pais*, signifies a little or young child; it is used of an infant just born, John 16:21; of a male child recently born, e.g., Matt. 2:8; Heb. 11:23; of a more advanced child, Mark 9:24; of a son, John 4:49; of a girl, Mark 5:39, 40, 41; in the plural, of children, e.g., Matt. 14:21. It is used metaphorically of believers who are deficient in spiritual understanding, 1 Cor. 14:20, and in affectionate and familiar address by the Lord to His disciples, almost like the Eng., "lads," John 21:5; by the Apostle John to the youngest believers in the family of God, 1 John 2:13, 18; there it is to be distinguished from *teknia*, which term he uses in addressing all his readers (vv. 1, 12, 28: see *teknia*, above). See DAMSEL.

NT: B.604a; CB.1261c; K.759.
OT: bēn: S.1121; HR.1047c.2; H.254; BD.119d.
yeled: S.3206; HR.1047c.5a; H.867b; BD.409b.
na'ar: S.5288; HR.1047c.6a; H.1389a; BD.654d.
GEN. REF.: IS.1:644; NB.416; Z.1:793.

Note: The adverb *paidiothen*, "from (or of) a child," is found in Mark 9:21. ¶

6. *paidarion* [παιδάριον, 3808], another diminutive of *pais*, is used of boys and girls, in Matt. 11:16 (the best texts have *paidiois* here), and a lad, John 6:9; the tendency in colloquial Greek was to lose the diminutive character of the word. ¶

NT: B.603b; CB.1261b; K.759.
OT: yeled: S.3206; HR.1045c.1; H.867b; BD.409b.
na'ar: S.5288; HR.1045c.2a; H.1389a; BD.654d.
GEN. REF.: IS.1:644; NB.–; Z.1:793.

7. *nēpios* [νήπιος, 3516], lit., not-speaking (from *nē*, a negative, and *epos*, a word is rendered "childish" in 1 Cor. 13:11: see BABE.

NT: B.537c; CB.1259c; K.631.
OT: ṭaph: S.2945; HR.944b.1; H.–; BD.381d.
'ôlēl: S.5768; HR.944b.4; H.1579c; BD.760c.
GEN. REF.: IS.1:644; NB.–; Z.–.

8. *monogenēs* [μονογενής, 3439], lit., only-begotten, is translated "only child" in Luke 9:38. See ONLY, ONLY-BEGOTTEN.

NT: B.527b; CB.1259b; K.606.
OT: yaḥîd: S.3173; HR.933a.1a; H.858a; BD.402d.
GEN. REF.: IS.1:644; NB.–; Z.–.

9. *teknogonia* [τεκνογονία, 5042], *teknon* and a root *gen*—, whence *gennaō*, to beget, denotes bearing children, implying the duties of motherhood, 1 Tim. 2:15. ¶

NT: B.808b; CB.1271b; K.–.
OT: –.
GEN. REF.: –.

B. Verbs.

1. *nēpiazō* [νηπιάζω, 3515], to be a babe, is used in 1 Cor. 14:20, "(in malice) be ye babes" (akin to No. 7, above). ¶

NT: B.537c; CB.–; K.631.
OT: –.
GEN. REF.: IS.1:645. NB.–: Z.–.

2. *teknotropheō* [τεκνοτροφέω, 5044], to rear young, *teknon*, and *trephō*, to rear, signifies to bring up children, 1 Tim. 5:10. ¶

NT: B.808d; CB.1271b; K.–.
OT: –.
GEN. REF.: –.

3. *teknogoneō* [τεκνογονέω, 5041], to bear children (*teknon*, and *gennaō*, to beget), see No. 9 above, is found in 1 Tim. 5:14. ¶
NT: B.808a; CB.1271b; K.–.
OT: –.
GEN. REF.: –.

C. Adjectives.

1. *enkuos* [ἔγκυος, 1471], denotes "great with child" (*en*, in, and *kuō*, to conceive), Luke 2:5. ¶
NT: B.216d; CB.–; K.–.
OT: –.
GEN. REF.: –.

2. *philoteknos* [φιλότεκνος, 5388], from *phileō*, to love, and *teknon*, signifies loving one's children, Tit. 2:4. ¶
NT: B.861c; CB.1264b; K.–.
OT: –.
GEN. REF.: –.

3. *ateknos* [ἄτεκνος, 815], from *a*, negative, and *teknon*, signifies "childless," Luke 20:28, 29, 30. ¶
NT: B.119d; CB.–; K.–.
OT: ʿărîrî: S.6185; HR.175b.1; H.1705a; BD.792d.
shakkûl: S.7909; HR.175b.2b; H.2385b,c; BD.1014a.
GEN. REF.: –.

Notes: (1) For *brephos*, a new born babe, always rendered "babe" or "babes" in the R.V. (A.V., "young children", Acts 7:19; "child," 2 Tim. 3:15), see under BABE.

(2) *Huiothesia*, "adoption of children," in the A.V. of Eph. 1:5, is corrected to "adoption as sons" in the R.V. See on ADOPTION.

CHOKE

1. *pnigō* [πνίγω, 4155], is used, in the Passive Voice, of perishing by drowning, Mark 5:13; in the Active, to seize a person's throat, to throttle, Matt. 18:28. See THROAT. ¶
NT: B.679d; CB.1265c; K.895.
OT: –.
GEN. REF.: IS.1:650; NB.–; Z.–.

2. *apopnigō* [ἀποπνίγω, 638], a strengthened form of No. 1 (*apo*, from, intensive; cp. Eng., to choke off), is used metaphorically, of thorns crowding out seed sown and preventing its growth, Matt. 13:7; Luke 8:7. It is Luke's word for suffocation by drowning, Luke 8:33 (cp. Mark 5:13, above). ¶
NT: B.97c; CB.1237a; K.895.
OT: ḥānaq: S.2614; HR.139c.1; H.697; BD.338b.
GEN. REF.: IS.1:650; NB.–; Z.–.

3. *sumpnigō* [συμπνίγνω, 4846], gives the suggestion of choking together (*sun*, with), i.e., by crowding, Matt. 13:22; Mark 4:7, 19; Luke 8:14. It is used in Luke 8:42, of the crowd that thronged the Lord, almost, so to speak, to suffocation. ¶
NT: B.779d; CB.1270b; K.895.
OT: –.
GEN. REF.: IS.1:650; NB.–; Z.–.

CHOICE, CHOOSE, CHOSEN

A. Verbs.

1. *eklegō* [ἐκλέγω, 1586], to pick out, select, means, in the Middle Voice, to choose for oneself, not necessarily implying the rejection of what is not chosen, but choosing with the subsidiary ideas of kindness or favour or love, Mark 13:20; Luke 6:13; 9:35 (R.V.); 10:42; 14:7; John 6:70; 13:18; 15:16, 19; Acts 1:2, 24; 6:5; 13:17; 15:22, 25; in 15:7 it is rendered "made choice"; 1 Cor. 1:27, 28; Eph. 1:4; Jas. 2:5. ¶
NT: B.242b; CB.1243c; K.505.
OT: bāḥar: S.977; HR.435a.1; H.231; BD.103d.
GEN. REF.: IS.1:650; NB.–; Z.–.

2. *epilegō* [ἐπιλέγω, 1951], in the Middle Voice, signifies to choose, either in addition or in succession to another. It has this meaning in Acts 15:40, of Paul's choice of Silas. For its other meaning, to call or name, John 5:2, see CALL. ¶
NT: B.295c; CB.1246a; K.–.
OT: bāḥar: S.977; HR.524c.1; H.231; BD.103d.
GEN. REF.: IS.1:650, NB.–, Z.–.

3. *haireō* [αἱρέω, 138], to take, is used in the Middle Voice only, in the sense of taking for oneself, choosing, 2 Thess. 2:13, of a choice made by God (as in Deut. 7:6, 7; 26:18, Sept.); in Phil. 1:22 and Heb. 11:25, of human choice. Its special significance is to select rather by the act of taking, than by shewing preference or favour. ¶
NT: B.24a; CB.1249a; K.–.
OT: ʾāmar: S.559; HR.36a.1; H.118; BD.55c,56d.
bāḥar: S.977; HR.36a.2; H.231; BD.103d.
GEN. REF.: IS.1:650; NB.–; Z.–.

4. *hairetizō* [αἱρετίζω, 140], akin to the verbal adjective *hairetos*, that which may be taken (see No. 3), signifies to take, with the implication that what is taken is eligible or suitable; hence, to choose, by reason of this suitability, Matt. 12:18, of God's delight in Christ as His "chosen." ¶ It is frequent in the Sept., e.g., Gen. 30:20; Num. 14:8; Psa. 25:12; 119:30, 173; 132:13, 14; Hos. 4:18; Hag. 2:23 ("he hath chosen the Canaanites"); Zech. 1:17; 2:12; Mal. 3:17.
NT: B.24a; CB.1249a; K.–.
OT: bāḥar: S.977; HR.36a.2; H.231; BD.103d.
ʾāwāh: S.184; HR.36a.1; H.41; BD.16c.
GEN. REF.: IS.1:650; NB.–; Z.–.

5. *cheirotoneō* [χειροτονέω], see APPOINT, No. 11.

6. *procheirotoneō* [προχειροτονέω, 4401], signifies to choose before, Acts 10:41, where it is used of a choice made before by God. ¶
NT: B.724c; CB.1266c; K.–.
OT: –.
GEN. REF.: IS.1:651; NB.–; Z.–..

Notes: (1) For *procheirizō* see APPOINT, No. 12.

(2) *Stratologeō*, in 2 Tim. 2:4 (A.V., "chosen to be a soldier"), signifies to enrol as a soldier (R.V.). See SOLDIER.

B. Adjective.

eklektos [ἐκλεκτός, 1588], akin to A, No. 1, signifies chosen out, select, e.g., Matt. 22:14; Luke 23:35; Rom. 16:13 (perhaps in the sense of eminent); Rev. 17:14. In 1 Pet. 2:4, 9, the R.V. translates it "elect". See ELECT.

NT: B.242d; CB.1243; K.505.
OT: bāḥar: S.977; HR.437a.2a; H.231; BD.103d.
bāḥîr: S.972; HR.437a.2c; H.231c; BD.104c.
GEN. REF.: IS.1:650; NB.–; Z.–.

C. Noun.

eklogē [ἐκλογή, 1589], akin to A, No. 1 and B, a picking out, choosing (Eng., eclogue), is translated "chosen" in Acts 9:15, lit., 'he is a vessel of choice unto Me'. In the six other places where this word is found it is translated "election." See ELECTION.

NT: B.243a; CB.1243c; K.505.
OT: –.
GEN. REF.: IS.1:651; NB.–; Z.–.

CHRIST

christos [χριστός, 5547], anointed, translates, in the Sept., the word Messiah, a term applied to the priests who were anointed with the holy oil, particularly the High Priest, e.g., Lev. 4:3, 5, 16. The prophets are called *hoi christoi Theou*, "the anointed of God," Psa. 105:15. A king of Israel was described upon occasion as *christos tou Kuriou*, "the anointed of the Lord," 1 Sam. 2:10, 35; 2 Sam. 1:14; Ps. 2:2; 18:50; Hab. 3:13; the term is used even of Cyrus, Is. 45:1.

The title *ho Christos*, "the Christ," is not used of Christ in the Sept. Version of the Inspired Books of the O.T. In the N.T. the word is frequently used with the article, of the Lord Jesus, as an appellative rather than a title, e.g., Matt. 2:4; Acts 2:31; without the article, Luke 2:11; 23:2; John 1:41. Three times the title was expressly accepted by the Lord Himself, Matt. 16:17; Mark 14:61, 62; John 4:26.

It is added as an appellative to the proper name "Jesus," e.g., John 17:3, the only time when the Lord so spoke of Himself; Acts 9:34; 1 Cor. 3:11; 1 John 5:6. It is distinctly a proper name in many passages, whether with the article, e.g., Matt. 1:17; 11:2; Rom. 7:4; 9:5; 15:19; 1 Cor. 1:6, or without the article, Mark 9:41; Rom. 6:4; 8:9, 17; 1 Cor. 1:12; Gal. 2:16. The single title *Christos* is sometimes used without the article to signify the One who by His Holy Spirit and power indwells believers and moulds their character in conformity to His likeness, Rom. 8:10; Gal. 2:20; 4:19; Eph. 3:17. As to the use or absence of the article, the title with the article specifies the Lord Jesus as "the Christ"; the title without the article stresses His character and His relationship with believers. Again, speaking generally, when the title is the subject of a sentence it has the article; when it forms part of the predicate the article is absent. See also JESUS.

NT: B.886d; CB.1240a; K.1322.
OT: māshîaḥ: S.4899; HR.1475c.1a; H.1255c; BD.603c.
GEN. REF.: IS.1:652; NB.620,811; Z.3:497.

FALSE CHRISTS

pseudochristos [ψευδόχριστος, 5580], denotes one who falsely lays claim to the Name and office of the Messiah, Matt. 24:24; Mark 13:22. ¶ See Note under ANTICHRIST.

NT: B.892b; CB.1267c; K.–.
OT: –.
GEN. REF.: –.

CHRISTIAN

christianos [χριστιανός, 5546], Christian, a word formed after the Roman style, signifying an adherent of Jesus, was first applied to such by the Gentiles and is found in Acts 11:26; 26:28; 1 Pet. 4:16.

Though the word rendered "were called" in Acts 11:26 (see under CALL) might be used of a name adopted by oneself or given by others, the Christians do not seem to have adopted it for themselves in the times of the Apostles. In 1 Pet. 4:16, the Apostle is speaking from the point of view of the persecutor; cp. "as a thief," "as a murderer." Nor is it likely that the appellation was given by Jews. As applied by Gentiles there was no doubt an implication of scorn, as in Agrippa's statement in Acts 26:28. Tacitus, writing near the end of the first century, says, "The vulgar call them Christians. The author or origin of this denomination, Christus, had, in the reign of Tiberius, been executed by the Procurator, Pontius Pilate" (Annals xv. 44). From the second century onward the term was accepted by believers as a title of honour. ¶

NT: B.886c; CB.1240a; K.1322.
OT: –.
GEN. REF.: IS.1:657; NB.209; Z.1:802.

CHRYSOLITE

chrusolithos [χρυσόλιθος, 5555], lit., a gold stone (*chrusos*, gold, *lithos*, a stone), is the name of a precious stone of a gold colour, now called a topaz, Rev. 21:20 (see also Ex. 28:20 and Ezek. 28:13). ¶

NT: B.888c; CB.1240b; K.–.
OT: tarshîsh: S.8658; HR.1478b.1; H.2546; BD.1076d.
GEN. REF.: IS.4:626; NB.632; Z.1:845.

CHRYSOPRASUS

chrusoprasos [χρυσόπρασος, 5556], from *Chrusos*, gold, and *prasos*, a leek), is a precious stone like a leek in colour, a translucent, golden green. Pliny reckons it among the beryls. The word occurs in Rev. 21:20. ¶

NT: B.888d; CB.1240b; K.—.
OT: —.
GEN. REF.: IS.4:626; NB.632; Z.1:845.

For **CHURCH** see **ASSEMBLY** and **CONGREGATION**

CINNAMON

kinnamōn [κιννάμωμον, 2792], is derived from an Arabic word signifying to emit a smell; the substance was an ingredient in the holy oil for anointing, Ex. 30:23. See also Prov. 7:17 and S. of S. 4:14. In the N.T. it is found in Rev. 18:13. The cinnamon of the present day is the inner bark of an aromatic tree called *canella zeylanica*. ¶

NT: B.432; CB.—; K.—.
OT: qinnāmôn: S.7076; HR.765c.2; H.2041; BD.890a.
GEN. REF.: IS.1:699; NB.233; Z.1:866.

CIRCUIT

perierchomai [περιέρχομαι, 4022], to go about (*peri*, about, *erchomai*, to go), is said of navigating a ship under difficulty owing to contrary winds, Acts 28:13, R.V., "we made a circuit," for A.V., "we fetched a compass." See Compass, Strolling, Wander.

NT: B.646d; CB.1263b; K.257.
OT: sābab: S.5437; HR.1123a.1; H.1456; BD.685b.
GEN. REF.: IS.1:700; NB.—; Z.—.

CIRCUMCISION, UNCIRCUMCISION, CIRCUMCISE

A. Nouns.

1. *peritomē* [περιτομή, 4061], lit., a cutting round, circumcision (the verb is *peritemnō*), was a rite enjoined by God upon Abraham and his male descendants and dependents, as a sign of the covenant made with him, Gen. 17; Acts 7:8; Rom. 4:11. Hence Israelites termed Gentiles "the uncircumcised," Judg. 15:18; 2 Sam. 1:20. So in the N.T., but without the suggestion of contempt, e.g., Rom. 2:26; Eph. 2:11.

The rite had a moral significance, Ex. 6:12, 30, where it is metaphorically applied to the lips; so to the ear, Jer. 6:10, and the heart, Deut. 30:6; Jer. 4:4. Cp. Jer. 9:25, 26. It refers to the state of circumcision, in Rom. 2:25-28; 3:1; 4:10; 1 Cor. 7:19; Gal. 5:6; 6:15; Col. 3:11.

"In the economy of grace no account is taken of any ordinance performed on the flesh; the old racial distinction is ignored in the preaching of the Gospel, and faith is the sole condition upon which the favour of God in salvation is to be obtained, Rom. 10:11-13; 1 Cor. 7:19. See also Rom. 4:9-12."*

Upon the preaching of the Gospel to, and the conversion of, Gentiles, a sect of Jewish believers arose who argued that the Gospel, without the fulfilment of circumcision, would make void the Law and make salvation impossible, Acts 15:1. Hence this party was known as "the circumcision," Acts 10:45; 11:2; Gal. 2:12; Col. 4:11; Tit. 1:10 (the term being used by metonymy, the abstract being put for the concrete, as with the application of the word to Jews generally, Rom. 3:30; 4:9, 12; 15:8; Gal. 2:7-9; Eph. 2:11). It is used metaphorically and spiritually of believers with reference to the act, Col. 2:11 and Rom. 2:29; to the condition, Phil. 3:3.

The Apostle Paul's defence of the truth, and his contention against this propaganda, form the main subject of the Galatian Epistle. Cp. *katatomē*, "concision," Phil. 3:2. See Concision.

NT: B.652d; CB.1263c; K.831.
OT: mûl: S.4135; HR.1128a.1a; H.1161; BD.557d.
mûlāh: S.4139; HR.1128a.1b; H.1161a; BD.558a.
GEN. REF.: IS.1:700; NB.233; Z.1:866.

2. *akrobustia* [ἀκροβυστια, 203], uncircumcision, is used (*a*) of the physical state, in contrast to the act of circumcision, Acts 11:3 (lit., 'having uncircumcision'); Rom. 2:25, 26; 4:10, 11 ("though they be in uncircumcision," R.V.), 12; 1 Cor. 7:18, 19; Gal. 5:6; 6:15; Col. 3:11; (*b*) by metonymy, for Gentiles, e.g., Rom. 2:26, 27; 3:30; 4:9; Gal. 2:7; Eph. 2:11; (*d*) in a metaphorical or transferred sense, of the moral condition in which the corrupt desires of the flesh still operate, Col. 2:13. ¶

NT: B.33c; CB.1234b; K.36.
OT: ʻorlāh: S.6190; HR.51a.1; H.1695a; BD.790b.
GEN. REF.: IS.1:700,2:338; NB.—; Z.2:594.

Note: in Rom. 4:11, the phrase "though they be in uncircumcision" translates the Greek phrase *di' akrobustias*, lit., 'through uncircumcision'; here *dia* has the local sense of proceeding from and passing out.

* From Notes on Galatians by Hogg and Vine, p. 69.

B. Adjective.

aperitmētos [ἀπερίτμητος, 564], uncircumcised (*a*, negative, *peri*, around, *temnō*, to cut), is used in Acts 7:51, metaphorically, of "heart and ears." ¶

NT: B.84b; CB.1236b; K.831.
OT: ʿārēl: S.6189; HR.120c.2; H.1695b; BD.790c.
GEN. REF.: IS.1:700; NB.–; Z.–.

C. Verbs.

1. *peritemnō* [περιτέμνω, 4059], to circumcise, is used (*a*) lit., e.g., Luke 1:59; 2:21; of receiving circumcision, Gal. 5:2, 3; 6:13, R.V.; (*b*) metaphorically, of spiritual circumcision, Col. 2:11.

NT: B.652a; CB.1263c; K.831.
OT: mûl: S.4135; HR.1127b.3a,b; H.1161; BD.557d.
GEN. REF.: IS.1:700; NB.233; Z.1:866.

2. *epispaomai* [ἐπισπάομαι, 1986], lit., to draw over, to become uncircumcised, as if to efface Judaism, appears in 1 Cor. 7:18. ¶

NT: B.299d; CB.–; K.–.
OT: –.
GEN. REF.: –.

For **CIRCUMSPECTLY** see **ACCURATELY**

CITIZEN, CITIZENSHIP

1. *politēs* [πολίτης, 4177], a member of a city or state, or the inhabitant of a country or district, Luke 15:15, is used elsewhere in Luke 19:14; Acts 21:39, and, in the most authentic mss., in Heb. 8:11 (where some texts have *plēsion*, a neighbour). Apart from Heb. 8:11, the word occurs only in the writings of Luke (himself a Greek). ¶

NT: B.686d; CB.1265c; K.906.
OT: –.
GEN. REF.: IS.1:704; NB.–; Z.–.

2. *sumpolitēs* [συμπολίτης, 4847], *sun*, with, and No. 1, denotes a fellow-citizen, i.e., possessing the same citizenship, Eph. 2:19, used metaphorically in a spiritual sense. ¶

NT: B.780a; CB.1270b; K.–.
OT: –.
GEN. REF.: IS.1:704; NB.–; Z.–.

3. *politeia* [πολιτεία, 4174], signifies (*a*) the relation in which a citizen stands to the state, the condition of a citizen, citizenship, Acts 22:28, "with a great sum obtained I this citizenship" (A.V., "freedom"). While Paul's citizenship of Tarsus was not of advantage outside that city, yet his Roman citizenship availed throughout the Roman Empire and, besides private rights, included (1) exemption from all degrading punishments; (2) a right of appeal to the Emperor after a sentence; (3) a right to be sent to Rome for trial before the Emperor if charged with a capital offence. Paul's father might have obtained citizenship (1) by manumission; (2) as a reward of merit; (3) by purchase; the contrast implied in Acts 22:28 is perhaps against the last mentioned; (*b*) a civil polity, the condition of a state, a commonwealth, said of Israel, Eph. 2:12. See COMMONWEALTH. ¶

NT: B.686a; CB.1265c; K.906.
OT: –.
GEN. REF.: IS.1:704; NB.237; Z.1:873.

4. *politeuma* [πολίτευμα, 4175], signifies the condition, or life, of a citizen, citizenship; it is said of the heavenly status of believers, Phil. 3:20, "our citizenship (A.V., "conversation") is in Heaven." The R.V. marg. gives the alternative meaning, "commonwealth," i.e., community. See COMMONWEALTH, FREEDOM. ¶

NT: B.686b; CB.1265c; K.906.
OT: –.
GEN. REF.: IS.1:704; NB.237; Z.1:873.

Note: Politeuō, Phil. 1:27, signifies to be a *politēs* (see No. 1), and is used in the Middle Voice, signifying, metaphorically, conduct characteristic of heavenly citizenship, R.V., "let your manner of life (A.V., "conversation") be worthy (marg., 'behave as citizens worthily') of the Gospel of Christ." In Acts 23:1 it is translated "I have lived." See CONVERSATION, LIVE. ¶

CITY

polis [πόλις, 4172], primarily a town enclosed with a wall (perhaps from a root *plē*–, signifying fullness, whence also the Latin *plēo*, to fill, Eng., polite, polish, politic etc.), is used also of the heavenly Jerusalem, the abode and community of the redeemed, Heb. 11:10, 16; 12:22; 13:14. In the Apocalypse it signifies the visible capital of the Heavenly Kingdom, as destined to descend to earth in a coming age, e.g., Rev. 3:12; 21:2, 14, 19. By metonymy the word stands for the inhabitants, as in the English use, e.g., Matt. 8:34; 12:25; 21:10; Mark 1:33; Acts 13:44.

NT: B.685b; CB.1265c; K.906.
OT: ʿîr: S.5892; HR.1174a.4; H.1615; BD.746b.
GEN. REF.: IS.1:704; NB.237; Z.1:873.

Note: In Acts 16:13, the most authentic mss. have *pulē*, gate, R.V., "without the gate."

CLAMOUR

kraugē [κραυγή, 2906], an onomatopoeic word, imitating the raven's cry, akin to *krazō* and *kraugazō*, to cry, denotes an outcry, "clamour," Acts 23:9, R.V.; Eph. 4:31, where it signifies the tumult of controversy. See CRY.

NT: B.449c; CB.–; K.465.
OT: ṣᵉʿāqāh: S.6818; HR.784b.3b,6; H.1947a; BD.858c.
GEN. REF.: –.

CLANGING

alalazō [ἀλαλάζω, 214], an onomatopoeic word, from the battle-cry, *alala*, is used of raising the shout of battle, Josh. 6:20; hence, to make a loud cry or shout, e.g., Psa. 47:1; to wail, Jer. 29:2; in the N.T., in Mark 5:38, of wailing mourners; in 1 Cor. 13:1, of the "clanging" of cymbals (A.V., "tinkling"). ¶

NT: B.34d; CB.–; K.36.
OT: rûaʻ: S.7321; HR.52a.2; H.2135; BD.929c.
GEN. REF.: –.

CLAY

pēlos [πηλός, 4081], clay, especially such as was used by a mason or potter, is used of moist clay, in John 9:6, 11, 14, 15, in connection with Christ's healing the blind man; in Rom. 9:21, of potter's clay, as to the potter's right over it as an illustration of the prerogatives of God in His dealings with men. ¶

NT: B.656b; CB.–; K.838.
OT: ḥomer: S.2563; HR.1131a.1; H.683c; BD.330c.
ṭîm: S.2916; HR.1131a.2; H.796a; BD.376c.
GEN. REF.: IS.1:717; NB.–; Z.1:882.

CLEAN, CLEANNESS, CLEANSE, CLEANSING

A. Adjective.

katharos [καθαρός, 2513], free from impure admixture, without blemish, spotless, is used (*a*) physically, e.g., Matt. 23:26; 27:59; John 13:10 (where the Lord, speaking figuratively, teaches that one who has been entirely cleansed, needs not radical renewal, but only to be cleansed from every sin into which he may fall); 15:3; Heb. 10:22; Rev. 15:6; 19:8, 14; 21:18, 21; (*b*) in a Levitical sense, Rom. 14:20; Tit. 1:15, "pure"; (*c*) ethically, with the significance free from corrupt desire, from guilt, Matt. 5:8; John 13:10, 11; Acts 20:26; 1 Tim. 1:5; 3:9; 2 Tim 1:3; 2:22; Tit. 1:15; Jas. 1:27; blameless, innocent (a rare meaning for this word), Acts 18:6; (*d*) in a combined Levitical and ethical sense ceremonially, Luke 11:41, "all things are clean unto you." See CLEAR, C, Note (2), PURE. ¶

NT: B.388a; CB.1254b; K.381.
OT: ṭahôr: S.2889; HR.698c.5; H.792d; BD.373a.
ṭahēr: S.2891; HR.698c.15; H.792; BD.372a.
GEN. REF.: IS.1:718; NB.238; Z.1:886.

B. Verbs.

1. *katharizō* [καθαρίζω, 2511], akin to A, signifies (1) to make clean, to cleanse (*a*) from physical stains and dirt, as in the case of utensils, Matt. 23:25 (figuratively in verse 26); from disease, as of leprosy, Matt. 8:2; (*b*) in a moral sense, from the defilement of sin, Acts 15:9; 2 Cor. 7:1; Heb. 9:14; Jas. 4:8, "cleanse" from the guilt of sin, Eph. 5:26; 1 John 1:7; (2) to pronounce clean in a Levitical sense, Mark 7:19, R.V.; Acts 10:15; 11:9; to consecrate by cleansings, Heb. 9:22, 23; 10:2. See PURGE, PURIFY.

NT: B.387b; CB.1254b; K.381.
OT: ṭahēr: S.2891; HR.698a.5; H.792; BD.372a.
GEN. REF.: IS.1:718; NB.238; Z.1:886.

2. *diakatharizō* [διακαθαρίζω, 1245], to cleanse thoroughly, is used in Matt. 3:12, R.V. ¶

NT: B.183d; CB.–; K.–.
OT: –.
GEN. REF.: IS.1:718; NB.238; Z.1:886.

Note: For *kathairō*, John 15:2, R.V., see PURGE, No. 1. For *diakathairō*, Luke 3:17, R.V., see PURGE, No. 3.

C. Nouns.

1. *katharismos* [καθαρισμός, 2512], akin to A, denotes cleansing, (*a*) both the action and its results, in the Levitical sense, Mark 1:44; Luke 2:22, "purification"; 5:14, "cleansing"; John 2:6; 3:25, "purifying"; (*b*) in the moral sense, from sins, Heb. 1:3; 2 Pet. 1:9, R.V., "cleansing." See PURGE, PURIFICATION, PURIFYING. ¶

NT: B.387d; CB.1254b; K.381.
OT: ṭᵉhār: S.2892; HR.698c.2a; H.792a; BD.372d.
ṭāhᵃrāh: S.2893; HR.698c.2b; H.792c; BD.372d.
GEN. REF.: IS.1:718; NB.238; Z.1:886.

2. *katharotēs* [καθαρότης, 2514], akin to B, cleanness, purity, is used in the Levitical sense in Heb. 9:13, R.V., "cleanness." See PURIFY. ¶

NT: B.388b; CB.1254b; K.381.
OT: ṭōhar: S.2892; HR.699c.1; H.792a; BD.372d.
GEN. REF.: IS.1:718; NB.238; Z.1:886.

Note: In 2 Pet. 2:18, some inferior mss. have *ontōs*, "certainly" (A.V., "clean"), for *oligōs*, "scarcely" (R.V., "just").

CLEAR, CLEARING, CLEARLY

A. Verb.

krustallizō [κρυσταλλίζω, 2929], to shine like crystal, to be of crystalline brightness, or transparency, is found in Rev. 21:11, "clear as crystal." The verb may, however, have a transitive force, signifying to crystallize or cause to become like crystal. In that case it would speak of Christ (since He is the "Lightgiver," see the preceding part of the verse), as the One who causes the saints to shine in His own likeness. ¶

NT: B.454d; CB.1256a; K.–.
OT: –.
GEN. REF.: –.

B. Adjective.

lampros [λαμπρός, 2986], is said of crystal, Rev. 22:1, A.V., "clear," R.V., "bright." See BRIGHT, GAY, GOODLY, GORGEOUS, WHITE.

NT: B.465d; CB.1256c; K.497.
OT: –.
GEN. REF.: IS.–; NB.–; Z.1:887.

Note: The corresponding adverb *lamprōs* signifies "sumptuously."

C. Adverb.

tēlaugōs [τηλαυγῶς, 5081], from *tēle*, afar, and *augē*, radiance, signifies conspicuously, or clearly, Mark 8:25, of the sight imparted by Christ to one who had been blind. ¶ Some mss. have *dēlaugōs*, clearly (*dēlos*, clear).

NT: B.814c; CB.—; K.—.
OT: baheret: S.934; HR.1348b.1b; H.211a; BD.97b.
GEN. REF.: —.

Notes: (1) In 2 Cor. 7:11, A.V., *hagnos* is rendered "clear." See PURE.

(2) In Rev. 21:18, *katharos*, ("pure," R.V.) is rendered "clear," in the A.V., See CLEAN.

(3) *Apologia* (Eng., apology), a defence against an accusation, signifies, in 2 Cor. 7:11, a clearing of oneself.

(4) For *diablepō* to see clearly, Matt. 7:5; Luke 6:42, and *kathoraō*, ditto, Rom. 1:20, see SEE.

CLEAVE, CLAVE

1. *kollaō* [κολλάω, 2853], to join fast together, to glue, cement, is primarily said of metals and other materials (from *kolla*, glue). In the N.T. it is used only in the Passive Voice, with reflexive force, in the sense of cleaving unto, as of cleaving to one's wife, Matt. 19:5; some mss. have the intensive Verb No. 2, here; 1 Cor. 6:16, 17, "joined." In the corresponding passage in Mark 10:7, the most authentic mss. omit the sentence. In Luke 10:11 it is used of the cleaving of dust to the feet; in Acts 5:13; 8:29; 9:26; 10:28; 17:34, in the sense of becoming associated with a person so as to company with him, or be on his side, said, in the last passage, of those in Athens who believed: in Rom. 12:9, ethically, of cleaving to that which is good. For its use in Rev. 18:5 see REACH (R.V., marg. "clave together"). See COMPANY, JOIN. ¶

NT: B.441c; CB.1255c; K.452.
OT: dābaq: S.1692; HR.776b.1a; H.398; BD.179c.
GEN. REF.: IS.1:723; NB.—; Z.1:887.

2. *proskollaō* [προσκολλάω, 4347], in the Passive Voice, used reflexively, to cleave unto, is found in Eph. 5:31 (A.V. "joined to").

NT: B.716a; CB.1267a; K.452.
OT: dābaq: S.1692; HR.1217a.2; H.398; BD.179c.
GEN. REF.: IS.1:723; NB.—; Z.1:887.

3. *prosmenō* [προσμένω, 4357], lit., to abide with (*pros*, toward or with, and *menō*, to abide), is used of cleaving unto the Lord, Acts 11:23. See ABIDE.

NT: B.717c; CB.1267b; K.581.
OT: —.
GEN. REF.: —.

CLEMENCY

epieikeia [ἐπιείκεια, 1932], mildness, gentleness, kindness (what Matthew Arnold has called "sweet reasonableness"), is translated "clemency" in Acts 24:4; elsewhere, in 2 Cor. 10:1, of the gentleness of Christ. See GENTLENESS. ¶ Cp. *epieikēs* (see FORBEARANCE).

NT: B.292c; CB.1245c; K.243.
OT: —.
GEN. REF.: IS.1:723; NB.—; Z.—.

For **CLERK,** see under **TOWNCLERK**

CLIMB UP

anabainō [ἀναβαίνω, 305], to ascend, is used of climbing up, in Luke 19:4 and John 10:1. See ARISE.

NT: B.50a; CB.1235a; K.90.
OT: 'ālāh: S.5927; HR.70a.11a; H.1624; BD.748a.
GEN. REF.: —.

CLOKE (Pretence)

1. *epikalumma* [ἐπικάλυμμα, 1942], is a covering, a means of hiding (*epi*, upon, *kaluptō*, to cover); hence, a pretext, a cloke, for wickedness, 1 Pet. 2:16. ¶ In the Sept. it is used in Ex. 26:14; 39:21, "coverings"; 2 Sam. 17:19; Job 19:29, "deceit." ¶

NT: B.294b; CB.—; K.—.
OT: mikseh: S.4372; HR.522b.1; H.1008c; BD.492c.
māsāk: S.4539; HR.522b.2; H.1482a; BD.697a.
GEN. REF.: —.

2. *prophasis* [πρόφασις, 4392], either from *pro*, before, and *phainō*, to cause to appear, shine, or, more probably, from *pro*, and *phēmi*, to say, is rendered "cloke" (of covetousness) in 1 Thess. 2:5; "excuse" in John 15:22 (A.V. "cloke"); "pretence" in Matt. 23:14; Mark 12:40; Luke 20:47 (A.V. "shew"); Phil. 1:18; "colour" in Acts 27:30. It signifies the assuming of something so as to disguise one's real motives. See PRETENCE, SHEW. ¶

NT: B.722c; CB.—; K.—.
OT: —.
GEN. REF.: IS.1:724; NB.—; Z.—.

CLOKE (Garment)

For the various words for garments, see CLOTHING.

CLOSE (Verb)

1. *kammuō* [καμμύω, 2576], derived by syncope (i.e., shortening and assimilation of *t* to *m*) from *katamuō*, i.e., *kata*, down, and *muō*, from a root *mu*—, pronounced by closing the lips, denotes to close down; hence, to shut the eyes, Matt. 13:15 and Acts 28:27, in each place of the obstinacy of Jews in their opposition to the Gospel. ¶

NT: B.402a; CB.—; K.—.
OT: 'āṣam: S.6105; HR.718b.1; H.1674; BD.783b.
sha'a': S.8173; HR.718b.2; H.2435,2436; BD.1044a.
GEN. REF.: IS.1:724; NB.—; Z.—.

2. *ptussō* [πτύσσω, 4428], to fold, double up, is used of a scroll of parchment, Luke 4:20. ¶ Cp. *anaptussō*, to open up, ver. 17. ¶

NT: B.727d; CB.–; K.–.
OT: –.
GEN. REF.: IS.1:724; NB.–; Z.–.

Notes: (1) For "close-sealed," Rev. 5:1, see SEAL.

(2) In Luke 9:36, *sigaō*, to be silent, is translated "they kept it close," A.V., (R.V., "they held their peace").

CLOSE (Adverb)

asson [ἆσσον, 788], the comparative degree of *anchi*, near, is found in Acts 27:13, of sailing close by a place. ¶

NT: B.117b; CB.–; K.–.
OT: –.
GEN. REF.: –.

For the word CLOSET see CHAMBER

CLOTH

rhakos [ῥάκος, 4470], denotes a ragged garment, or a piece of cloth torn off, a rag; hence, a piece of undressed cloth, Matt. 9:16; Mark 2:21.

NT: B.734a; CB.–; K.–.
OT: beged: S.899; HR.1247c.1; H.198a; BD.93d.
GEN. REF.: IS.2:402; NB.–; Z.1:891.

Note: For other words, *othonion*, *sindon*, see LINEN, Nos. 1 and 3. ¶

CLOTHE

1. *amphiennumi* [ἀμφιέννυμι, 294], to put clothes round (*amphi*, around, *hennumi*, to clothe), to invest, signifies, in the Middle Voice, to put clothing on oneself, e.g., Matt. 6:30; 11:8; Luke 7:25; 12:28. ¶

NT: B.47c; CB.–; K.–.
OT: lābash: S.3847; HR.67c.3; H.1075; BD.527d.
GEN. REF.: –.

2. *enduō* [ἐνδύω, 1746], (Eng., "endue"), signifies to enter into, get into, as into clothes, to put on, e.g., Mark 1:6; Luke 8:27 (in the best mss.); 24:49 (A.V., "endued"); 2 Cor. 5:3; Rev. 1:13; 19:14. See ARRAY, ENDUE, PUT ON.

NT: B.264a; CB.1245a; K.192.
OT: lābash: S.3847; HR.471a.2a,b; H.1075; BD.527d.
GEN. REF.: –.

3. *endiduskō* [ἐνδιδύσκω, 1737], has the same meaning as No. 2; the termination, *—skō* suggests the beginning or progress of the action. The verb is used in the Middle Voice in Luke 16:19 (of a rich man). Some mss. have it in 8:27, for No. 2 (of a demoniac). In Mark 15:17 the best texts have this verb (some have No. 2). See WEAR. ¶

NT: B.263a; CB.–; K.–.
OT: lābash: S.3847; HR.470b.1; H.1075; BD.527d.
GEN. REF.: –.

4. *ependuō* [ἐπενδύω, 1902], a strengthened form of No. 2, used in the Middle Voice, to cause to be put on over, to be clothed upon, is found in 2 Cor. 5:2, 4, of the future spiritual body of the redeemed. ¶

NT: B.284d; CB.1245c; K.192.
OT: –
GEN. REF.: –.

5. *himatizō* [ἱματίζω, 2439], means to put on raiment (see *himation*, below), Mark 5:15; Luke 8:35. ¶

NT: B.376b; CB.–; K.–.
OT: –
GEN. REF.: –.

6. *periballō* [περιβάλλω, 4016], to cast around or about, to put on, array, or, in the Middle and Passive Voices, to clothe oneself, e.g., Matt. 25:36, 38, 43, is most frequent in the Apocalypse, where it is found some 12 times (see *peribolaion*, below). See CAST, No. 10. PUT, No. 9).

NT: B.646a; CB.–; K.–.
OT: kāsāh: S.3680; HR.1121c.2a; H.1008; BD.491b.
lābash: S.3847; HR.1121c.3a; H.1075; BD.527d.
GEN. REF.: –.

Note: The verb *enkomboomai*, to gird oneself with a thing, in 1 Pet. 5:5, is rendered in the A.V., "be clothed with."

CLOTHING, CLOTHS, CLOTHES, CLOKE, COAT

1. *phelonēs*, or *phailonēs* [φαιλόνης, 5341], probably by metathesis from *phainolēs* (Latin *paenula*), a mantle, denotes a travelling cloak for protection against stormy weather, 2 Tim. 4:13. Some, however, regard it as a Cretan word for *chitōn*, a tunic. It certainly was not an ecclesiastical vestment. The Syriac renders it a case for writings (some regard it as a book-cover), an explanation noted by Chrysostom, but improbable. It may have been "a light mantle like a cashmere dust-cloak, in which the books and parchments were wrapped" (Mackie in Hastings' Dic. of the Bible). ¶

NT: B.851a; CB.–; K.–.
OT: –.
GEN. REF.: IS.1:723; NB.–; Z.–.

2. *himation* [ἱμάτιον, 2440], an outer garment, a mantle, thrown over the *chitōn*. In the plural, clothes (the cloak and the tunic), e.g., Matt. 17:2; 26:65; 27:31, 35. See APPAREL, No. 2.

NT: B.376b; CB.1250c; K.–.
OT: beged: S.899; HR.685a.1; H.198a; BD.93d.
salmāh: S.8008; HR.685a.10; H.2270b; BD.971a.
simlāh: S.8071; HR.685a.11; H.2270a; BD.971a.
GEN. REF.: IS.2:402; NB.–; Z.1:890.

3. *chitōn* [χιτών, 5509], denotes the inner vest or under garment, and is to be distinguished, as such, from the *himation*. The distinction is made, for instance, in the Lord's

command in Matt. 5:40: "If any man would go to law with thee, and take away thy coat (*chitōn*), let him have thy cloke (*himation*) also." The order is reversed in Luke 6:29, and the difference lies in this, that in Matt. 5:40 the Lord is referring to a legal process, so the claimant is supposed to claim the inner garment, the less costly. The defendant is to be willing to let him have the more valuable one too. In the passage in Luke an act of violence is in view, and there is no mention of going to law. So the outer garment is the first one which would be seized.

When the soldiers had crucified Jesus they took His garments (*himation*, in the plural), His outer garments, and the coat, the *chitōn*, the inner garment, which was without seam, woven from the top throughout, John 19:23. The outer garments were easily divisible among the four soldiers, but they could not divide the *chitōn* without splitting it, so they cast lots for it.

Dorcas was accustomed to make coats (*chitōn*) and garments (*himation*), Acts 9:39, that is, the close fitting under garments and the long, flowing outer robes.

A person was said to be "naked" (*gumnos*), whether he was without clothing, or had thrown off his outer garment, e.g., his *epundutēs*, (No. 6, below), and was clad in a light undergarment, as was the case with Peter, in John 21:7. The High Priest, in rending his clothes after the reply the Lord gave him in answer to his challenge, rent his under garments (*chitōn*), the more forcibly to express his assumed horror and indignation, Mark 14:63. In Jude 23, "the garment spotted by the flesh" is the *chitōn*, the metaphor of the under garment being appropriate; for it would be that which was brought into touch with the pollution of the flesh.

NT: B.882b; CB.—; K.—.
OT: kuttōneh, k^e^tōneh: S.3801; HR.1471a.2; H.1058a; BD.509a.
GEN. REF.: IS.2:402; 1:724; NB.—; Z.1:894,896.

4. *himatismos* [ἱματισμός, 2441], in form a collective word, denoting vesture, garments, is used generally of costly or stately raiment, the apparel of kings, of officials, etc. See Luke 7:25, where "gorgeously apparelled" is, lit., 'in gorgeous vesture.' See also Acts 20:33 and 1 Tim. 2:9, "costly raiment." This is the word used of the Lord's white and dazzling raiment on the Mount of Transfiguration, Luke 9:29. It is also used of His *chitōn*, His under-garment (see note above), for which the soldiers cast lots, John 19:23, 24, "vesture"; in Matt. 27:35 it is also translated "vesture." See APPAREL, RAIMENT, VESTURE. ¶

NT: B.376d; CB.—; K.—.
OT: beged: S.899; HR.686a.1; H.198a; BD.93d.
salmāh: S.8008; HR.686a.6; H.2270b; BD.971a.
l^e^bûsh: S.3830; HR.686a.4; H.1075a; BD.528c.
GEN. REF.: IS.2:402; NB.—; Z.1:890.

5. *enduma* [ἔνδυμα, 1742], akin to *enduō* (see CLOTHE, No. 2), denotes anything put on, a garment of any kind. It was used of the clothing of ancient prophets, in token of their contempt of earthly splendour, 1 Kings 19:13; 2 Kings 1:8, R.V.; Zech. 13:4. In the N.T. it is similarly used of John the Baptist's raiment, Matt. 3:4; of raiment in general, Matt. 6:25, 28; Luke 12:23; metaphorically, of sheep's clothing, Matt. 7:15; of a wedding garment, 22:11, 12; of the raiment of the angel at the tomb of the Lord after His resurrection, 28:3. See GARMENT, RAIMENT.) ¶

NT: B.263c; CB.1245a; K.—.
OT: l^e^bûsh: S.3830; HR.471c.2a; H.1075a; BD.528c.
GEN. REF.: IS.2:402; NB.—; Z.—.

6. *ependutēs* [ἐπενδύτης, 1903], denotes an upper garment (*epi*, upon, *enduō*, to clothe). The word is found in John 21:7, where it apparently denotes a kind of linen frock, which fishermen wore when at their work. See No. 3. ¶

NT: B.285a; CB.—; K.—.
OT: m^e^'īl: S.4598; HR.509c.1; H.1230b; BD.591c.
GEN. REF.: IS.2:403; NB.—; Z.—.

7. *esthēs* [ἐσθής, 2066], "clothing," Acts 10:30; see APPAREL, No. 1.

NT: B.312b; CB.1246c; K.—.
OT: —.
GEN. REF.: IS.2:403; NB.—; Z.—.

8. *stolē [στολή,* 4749], (Eng., stole), denotes any stately robe, a long garment reaching to the feet or with a train behind. It is used of the long clothing in which the scribes walked, making themselves conspicuous in the eyes of men, Mark 12:38; Luke 20:46; of the robe worn by the young man in the Lord's tomb, Mark 16:5; of the best or, rather, the chief robe, which was brought out for the returned prodigal, Luke 15:22; five times in the Apocalypse, as to glorified saints, 6:11; 7:9, 13, 14; 22:14. ¶ In the Sept. it is used of the holy garments of the priests, e.g., Ex. 28:2; 29:21; 31:10.

NT: B.769c; CB.1270a; K.1088.
OT: beged: S.899; HR.1291c.3; H.198a; BD.93d.
simlāh: S.8071; HR.1291c.11; H.2270a; BD.971a.
l^e^bûsh: S.3830; HR.1291c.7; H.1075a; BD.528c.
GEN. REF.: IS.2:402; NB.—; Z.—.

Notes: (1) *Peribolaion*, from *periballō*, to throw around, lit., that which is thrown around, was a wrap or mantle. It is used in 1 Cor. 11:15, of the hair of a woman which is given to her as a veil; in Heb. 1:12, of the earth and the heavens, which the Lord will roll up "as a mantle," R.V., for A.V., "vesture." The other word in that verse rendered "garment," R.V., is *himation*. ¶

(2) *Endusis*, is "a putting on (of apparel)," 1 Pet. 3:3. Cp. No. 5. ¶

(3) *Esthēsis*. See APPAREL, No. 1.

(4) The *chlamus* was a short cloak or robe, worn over the *chitōn* (No. 3), by emperors, kings, magistrates, military officers, etc. It is used of the scarlet robe with which Christ was arrayed in mockery by the soldiers in Pilate's Judgment Hall, Matt. 27:28, 31.

What was known as purple was a somewhat indefinite colour. There is nothing contradictory about its being described by Mark and John as "purple," though Matthew speaks of it as "scarlet." The soldiers put it on the Lord in mockery of His Kingship. ¶

(5) The *podērēs* was another sort of outer garment, reaching to the feet (from *pous*, the foot, and *arō*, to fasten). It was one of the garments of the high priests, a robe (Hebrew, *chetoneth*), mentioned after the ephod in Ex. 28:4, etc. It is used in Ezek. 9:2, where instead of "linen" the Sept. reads "a long robe"; and in Zech. 3:4, "clothe ye him with a long robe"; in the N.T. in Rev. 1:13, of the long garment in which the Lord is seen in vision amongst the seven golden lampstands. There, *podērēs* is described as "a garment down to the feet," indicative of His High Priestly character and acts. ¶

(6) For *katastolē*, see APPAREL, No. 4.

CLOUD

1. *nephos* [νέφος, 3509], denotes a cloudy, shapeless mass covering the heavens. Hence, metaphorically, of a dense multitude, a throng, Heb. 12:1. ¶

NT: B.537a; CB.1259c; K.628.
OT: ʿāb: S.5645; HR.944a.2; H.1574a; BD.728a.
ʿānān: S.6051; HR.944a.3; H.1655a; BD.777d.
shaḥaq: S.7834; HR.944a.4; H.2367a; BD.1007a.
GEN. REF.: IS.1:725; NB.241; Z.1:894.

2. *nephelē* [νεφέλη, 3507], a definitely shaped cloud, or masses of clouds possessing definite form, is used, besides the physical element, (*a*) of the cloud on the mount of transfiguration, Matt. 17:5; (*b*) of the cloud which covered Israel in the Red Sea, 1 Cor. 10:1, 2; (*c*), of clouds seen in the Apocalyptic visions, Rev. 1:7; 10:1; 11:12; 14:14, 15, 16; (*d*) metaphorically in 2 Pet. 2:17, of the evil workers there mentioned; but R.V., "and mists" (*homichlē*), according to the most authentic mss.

In 1 Thess. 4:17, the clouds referred to in connection with the Rapture of the saints are probably the natural ones, as also in the case of those in connection with Christ's Second Advent to the earth. See Matt. 24:30; 26:64, and parallel passages. So at the Ascension, Acts 1:9.

NT: B.536d; CB.1259c; K.628.
OT: ʿāb: S.5645; HR.943b.4; H.1574a; BD.728a.
ʿānān: S.6051; HR.943b.6a; H.1655a; BD.777d.
shahaq: S.7834; HR.943b.7; H.2367a; BD.1007a.
GEN. REF.: IS.1:725; NB.–; Z.1:894.

CLOVEN

diamerizō [διαμερίζω, 1266], to part asunder (*dia*, asunder, *meros*, a part), is translated "cloven" in the A.V. of Acts 2:3, R.V., "parting asunder." See DIVIDE, PART.

NT: B.186d; CB.–; K.–.
OT: ḥālaq: S.2505; HR.305c.1; H.669; BD.323c.
GEN. REF.: IS.–; NB.241; Z.–.

CLUSTER

botrus [βότρυς, 1009], a cluster, or bunch, bunch of grapes, is found in Rev. 14:18. ¶

NT: B.145c; CB.–; K.–.
OT: ʾeshkōl: S.811; HR.226a.1; H.178; BD.79a.
GEN. REF.: IS.1:726; NB.–; Z.–.

Note: Cp. *staphulē*, a bunch of grapes, the ripe cluster, stressing the grapes themselves, Matt. 7:16; Luke 6:44; Rev. 14:18. ¶

COALS

1. *anthrax* [ἄνθραξ, 440], a burning coal (cp. Eng., *anthracite*), is used in the plural in Rom. 12:20, metaphorically in a proverbial expression, "thou shalt heap coals of fire on his head" (from Prov. 25:22), signifying retribution by kindness, i.e., that, by conferring a favour on your enemy, you recall the wrong he has done to you, so that he repents, with pain of heart. ¶

NT: B.67c; CB.1236a; K.–.
OT: gahelet: S.1513; HR.96a.3; H.341a; BD.160d.
GEN. REF.: IS.1:726; NB.242; Z.1:896.

2. *anthrakia* [ἀνθρακία, 439], akin to No. 1, is a heap of burning coals, or a charcoal fire, John 18:18; 21:9. ¶

NT: B.67c; CB.–; K.–.
OT: –.
GEN. REF.: IS.1:726; NB.241; Z.1:896.

COAST, COASTING

A. Noun.

horion [ὅριον, 3725], a bound, boundary, limit, frontier (akin to *horizō*, to bound, limit), is rendered "coasts" ten times in the A.V., but "borders" in Matt. 4:13, and is always translated "borders" in the R.V. See BORDER.

NT: B.581a; CB.1251b; K.–.
OT: gᵉbûl: S.1366; HR.1012a.3a; H.307a; BD.147d.
GEN. REF.: IS.1:727; NB.–; Z.1:896.

B. Adjective.

paralios [παράλιος, 3882], by the sea (*para*, by, *hals*, salt), hence denotes a sea coast, Luke 6:17. ¶ In the Sept., Gen. 49:13; Deut. 1:7; 33:19; Josh. 9:1; 11:3 (twice); Job 6:3; Is. 9:1.

NT: B.620a; CB.–; K.–.
OT: ḥôph: S.2348; HR.1061c.2a,3; H.710a; BD.342b.
yām: S.3220; HR.1061c.4; H.871a; BD.410d.
GEN. REF.: IS.1:727; NB.–; Z.–.

C. Verb.

paralegō [παραλέγω, 3881], is used, in the Middle Voice, as a nautical term, to sail past, Acts 27:8, "coasting along"; ver. 13, "sailed by." ¶

NT: B.619d; CB.–; K.–.
OT: –.
GEN. REF.: –.

Notes: (1) *Methorion* (*meta*, with, and A), in Mark 7:24, is translated "borders."

(2) The phrase "upon the sea coast," Matt. 4:13, A.V., translates *parathalassios* (*para*, by, *thalassa*, the sea), R.V. "by the sea." ¶

(3) *Meros*, a part, is translated "coasts" in Matt. 15:21; 16:13, A.V. (R.V., "parts,"); "country," R.V. in Acts 19:1, A.V. "coasts"; this refers to the high land in the interior of Asia Minor. See BEHALF, CRAFT, PART, PARTICULAR, PIECE, PORTION, RESPECT, SOMEWHAT, SORT.

(4) *Chōra*, a country, rendered "coasts" in Acts 26:20, A.V., is corrected in the R.V. to "country." See COUNTRY, FIELD, GROUND, LAND, REGION.

(5) In Acts 27:2 the phrase in the R.V., "on the coast of, "translates the preposition *kata*, along, and the complete clause, "unto the places on the coast of Asia," R.V., is curiously condensed in the A.V. to "by the coasts of Asia."

For **COAT** (*ependeutēs*) see **CLOKE, CLOTHING**

COCK, COCK-CROWING

1. *alektōr* [ἀλέκτωρ, 220], a cock, perhaps connected with a Hebrew phrase for the oncoming of the light, is found in the passages concerning Peter's denial of the Lord, Matt. 26:34, 74, 75; Mark 14:30, 68, 72; Luke 22:34, 60, 61; John 13:38; 18:27. ¶

NT: B.35c; CB.–; K.–.
OT: –.
GEN. REF.: IS.1:728; NB.156; Z.1:897.

2. *alektorophōnia* [ἀλεκτοροφωνία, 219], denotes cock-crowing (*alektōr*, and *phōnē*, a sound), Mark 13:35. There were two cock-crowings, one after midnight, the other before dawn. In these watches the Jews followed the Roman method of dividing the night. The first cock-crowing was at the third watch of the night. That is the one mentioned in Mark 13:35. Mark mentions both; see 14:30. The latter, the second, is that referred to in the other Gospels and is mentioned especially as "the cock-crowing." ¶

NT: B.35b; CB.1234b; K.–.
OT: –.
GEN. REF.: IS.1:728; NB.156; Z.1:897.

COLD

A. Noun.

psuchos [ψῦχος, 5592], coldness, cold, appears in John 18:18; Acts 28:2; 2 Cor. 11:27. ¶

NT: B.894c; CB.1267c; K.–.
OT: qôr: S.7120; HR.1490c.1a; H.2077b; BD.903b.
qārāh: S.7135; HR.1490c.1b; H.2077c; BD.903b.
GEN. REF.: IS.1:729; NB.–; Z.–.

B. Adjective.

psuchros [ψυχρός, 5593], cool, fresh, cold, chilly (fuller in expression than *psuchos*), is used in the natural sense in Matt. 10:42, "cold water"; metaphorically in Rev. 3:15, 16. ¶

NT: B.894c; CB.1267c; K.296.
OT: qar: S.7119; HR.1490c.1; H.2077a; BD.903b.
GEN. REF.: IS.1:729; NB.–; Z.–.

C. Verb.

psuchō [ψύχω, 5594], to breathe, blow, cool by blowing, Passive Voice, grow cool, is used metaphorically in Matt. 24:12, in the sense of waning zeal or love. ¶

NT: B.894d; CB.1267c; K.–.
OT: –.
GEN. REF.: IS.1:729; NB.–; Z.–.

COLLECTION

logia [λογία, 3048], akin to *legō*, to collect, is used in 1 Cor. 16:1, 2; in the latter verse, A.V. "gatherings," R.V., "collections," as in ver. 1. See GATHERING. ¶

NT: B.475d; CB.1257a; K.–.
OT: –.
GEN. REF.: –.

COLONY

kolōnia [κολωνία, 2862], transliterates the Latin *colonia*. Roman colonies belonged to three periods and classes, (*a*) those of the earlier republic before 100 B.C., which were simply centres of Roman influence in conquered territory; (*b*) agrarian colonies, planted as places for the overflowing population of Rome; (*c*) military colonies during the time of the Civil wars and the Empire, for the settlement of disbanded soldiers. This third class was established by the *imperator*, who appointed a legate to exercise his authority. To this class Philippi belonged as mentioned in Acts 16:12, R.V., "a Roman colony". They were watch-towers of the Roman State and formed on the model of Rome itself. The full organization of Philippi as such was the work of Augustus, who, after the battle of Actium, 31 B.C., gave his soldiers lands in Italy and transferred most of the inhabitants there to other quarters including Philippi. These communities possessed the right of Roman freedom, and of holding the soil under Roman law, as well as exemption from poll-tax and tribute. Most Roman colonies were established on the coast. ¶

NT: B.442c; CB.–; K.–.
OT: –.
GEN. REF.: IS.1:729; NB.242; Z.1:911.

For the word **COLOUR** (Acts 27:30) see **CLOKE**

COLT

pōlos [πῶλος, 4454], a foal, whether colt or filly, had the general significance of a young creature; in Matt. 21:2, and parallel passages, an ass's colt.

NT: B.731d; CB.1266a; K.981.
OT: 'ayir: S.5895; HR.1246b.3; H.1616a; BD.747a.
GEN. REF.: IS.1:735; NB.244; Z.1:918.

COME, CAME (see also COMING)

1. *erchomai* [ἔρχομαι, 2064], the most frequent verb, denoting either to come, or to go, signifies the act, in contrast with *hēkō* (see No. 22, below), which stresses the arrival, as, e.g., 'I am come and am here,' John 8:42 and Heb. 10:9. See BRING, B. *Note* (1) FALL, GO, GROW, LIGHT, PASS, RESORT.

NT: B.310b; CB.1246b; K.257.
OT: bô': S.935; HR.548b.5a; H.212; BD.97c.
GEN. REF.: –.

Compounds of this with prepositions are as follows (2 to 11):

2. *eiserchomai* [εἰσέρχομαι, 1525], to come into, or to go into (*eis*, into), e.g., Luke 17:7. See ENTER.

NT: B.232c; CB.1243b; K.257.
OT: bô': S.935; HR.410b.4a; H.212; BD.97c.
GEN. REF.: –.

3. *exerchomai* [ἐξέρχομαι, 1831], to come out, or go out or forth (*ek*, out), e.g., Matt. 2:6. See DEPART, ESCAPE, GET, (*b*), No. 3, GO, Note (1), PROCEED, SPREAD.

NT: B.274b; CB.1247c; K.247.
OT: yāṣā': S.3318; HR.491c.5a; H.893; BD.422b.
GEN. REF.: –.

4. *epanerchomai* [ἐπανέρχομαι, 1880], to come back again, return (*epi*, on, *ana*, again), Luke 10:35; 19:15. ¶

NT: B.283a; CB.–; K.–.
OT: shûb: S.7725; HR.506c.3; H.2340; BD.996d.
GEN. REF.: –.

5. *dierchomai* [διέρχομαι, 1330], to come or go through (*dia*, through), e.g., Acts 9:38. See DEPART, GO, PASS, PIERCE, TRAVEL, WALK.

NT: B.194c; CB.1241c; K.257.
OT: 'ābar: S.5674; HR.328c.10; H.1556; BD.716d.
hālak: S.1980; HR.328c.4a,c; H.498; BD.229d.
yāṣā': S.3318; HR.328c.6; H.893; BD.422b
GEN. REF.: –.

6. *eperchomai* [ἐπέρχομαι, 1904], to come or go upon (*epi*, upon), e.g., Luke 1:35; in Luke 21:26, used of coming events, suggesting their certainty; in Eph. 2:7, said of the on-coming of the ages; in Acts 14:19, of Jews coming to (lit., upon) a place.

NT: B.285a; CB.1245c; K.257.
OT: bô': S.935; HR.509c.3a; H.212; BD.97c.
'ābar: S.5674; HR.509c.14a; H.1556; BD.716d.
GEN. REF.: –.

7. *katerchomai* [κατέρχομαι, 2718], to come down (*kata*, down), e.g., Luke 9:37. See DEPART, DESCEND, GO, *Note* (1), LAND.

NT: B.422a; CB.–; K.–.
OT: –.
GEN. REF.: –.

8. *pareiserchomai* [παρεισέρχομαι, 3922], lit., to come in (*eis*) beside or from the side (*para*) so as to be present with, is used (*a*) in the literal sense, of the coming in of the Law in addition to sin, Rom. 5:20; (*b*) in Gal. 2:4, of false brethren, suggesting their coming in by stealth. See ENTER. ¶

NT: B.624d; CB.–; K.257.
OT: –.
GEN. REF.: –.

9. *parerchomai* [παρέρχομαι, 3928], (*para*, by or away), signifies (*a*) to come or go forth, or arrive, e.g., Luke 12:37; 17:7 (last part); Acts 24:7; (*b*) to pass by, e.g., Luke 18:37; (*c*) to neglect, e.g., Luke 11:42. See GO, PASS, TRANSGRESS.

NT: B.625d; CB.1262b; K.257.
OT: 'ābar: S.5674; HR.1068c.11a; H.1556; BD.716d.
GEN. REF.: –.

10. *proserchomai* [προσέρχομαι, 4334], denotes to come or go near to (*pros*, near to), e.g., Matt. 4:3; Heb. 10:1, A.V., "comers," R.V., "them that draw nigh." See CONSENT, DRAW, GO, *Note* (1).

NT: B.713a; CB.1267a; K.257.
OT: nāgash: S.5066; HR.1213c.7a; H.1297; BD.620c.
qārab: S.7126; HR.1213c.10a; H.2065; BD.897b.
GEN. REF.: –.

11. *sunerchomai* [συνέρχομαι, 4905], to come together (*sun*, with), e.g., John 18:20, is often translated by the verb to assemble; see the R.V. of 1 Cor. 11:20; 14:23. See ACCOMPANY, ASSEMBLE, COMPANY, GO WITH, RESORT.

NT: B.788a; CB.1270c; K.257.
OT: hālak: S.1980; HR.1314a.3; H.498; BD.229d.
qābaṣ: S.6908; HR.1314a.7; H.1983; BD.867c.
GEN. REF.: –.

Note: Aperchomai, to come away or from, is differently translated in the R.V.; see, e.g., Mark 3:13 where it signifies that they went from the company or place where they were to Him; it usually denotes to go away.

12. *ginomai* [γίνομαι, 1096], to become, signifies a change of condition, state or place, e.g., Mark 4:35. In Acts 27:33, the verb is used with *mellō*, to be about to, to signify the coming on of day.
NT: B.158a; CB.1248b; K.117.
OT: –.
GEN. REF.: –.

13. *paraginomai* [παραγίνομαι, 3854], near or by, denotes to arrive, to be present, e.g., Matt. 2:1. See GO, PRESENT.
NT: B.613c; CB.–; K.–.
OT: bô': S.935; HR.1056c.1a; H.212; BD.97c.
GEN. REF.: –.

14. *sumparaginomai* [συμπαραγίνομαι, 4836], (*sun*, with, *para*, near), to come together, is used in Luke 23:48; 2 Tim. 4:16, lit., 'stood at my side with me.' See STAND. ¶
NT: B.779a; CB.–; K.–.
OT: lāwāh: S.3867; HR.1304c.1; H.1087,1088; BD.530d.
GEN. REF.: –.

Note: For "come by" in Acts 27:16, A.V., the R.V. suitably has "secure."

Compounds of the verb bainō, to go, are as follows (15 to 21):

15. *anabainō* [ἀναβαίνω, 305], to come upon, to arrive in a place (*ana*, up or upon), is translated "come into" in Acts 25:1. See ARISE, ASCEND, ENTER, GO, CLIMB, GROW, RISE, SPRING.
NT: B.50a; CB.1235a; K.90.
OT: 'ālāh: S.5927; HR.70a.11a; H.1624; BD.748a.
GEN. REF.: –.

16. *epibainō* [ἐπιβαίνω, 1910], to come to or into, or go upon, is rendered, in Acts 20:18, R.V., "set foot in." See ENTER, GO, TAKE, *Note* (16).
NT: B.289b; CB.–; K.–.
OT: dārak: S.1869; HR.515c.1; H.453; BD.201d.
rākab: S.7392; HR.515c.10; H.2163; BD.938c.
GEN. REF.: –.

17. *ekbainō* [ἐκβαίνω, —], to come or go out, appears in the best mss. in Heb. 11:15; A.V., "came out," R.V., "went out." ¶
NT: B.237b; CB.–; K.–.
OT: 'ālāh: S.5927; HR.420c.1; H.1624; BD.748a.
GEN. REF.: –.

18. *diabainō* [διαβαινω, 1224], to pass through, is translated "come over" in Acts 16:9; "pass" in Luke 16:26; "pass through" in Heb. 11:29. See PASS. ¶
NT: B.185c; CB.–; K.–.
OT: 'ābar: S.5674; HR.298a.5a; H.1556; BD.716d.
GEN. REF.: –.

19. *katabainō* [καταβαίνω, 2597], signifies to come down, e.g., Matt. 8:1. See DESCEND, FALL, GET, GO, STEP (down).
NT: B.408b; CB.1253c; K.90.
OT: yārad: S.3381; HR.727a.8a; H.909; BD.432c.
GEN. REF.: –.

20. *sunanabainō* [συναναβαίνω, 4872], to come up with (*sun*, with, *ana*, up), is used in Mark 15:41; Acts 13:31. ¶
NT: B.784b; CB.–; K.–.
OT: 'ālāh: S.5927; HR.1311a.1; H.1624; BD.748a.
GEN. REF.: –.

21. *embainō* [ἐμβαίνω, 1684], to go into, is rendered, in Mark 5:18, A.V., "was come into," R.V., "was entering." See ENTER, GET, GO, STEP.
NT: B.254a; CB.–; K.–.
OT: bô: S.935; HR.455a.1; H.212; BD.97c.
GEN. REF.: –.

Note: Apobainō, to go away, is rendered, in the A.V. of John 21:9, "were come to"; R.V., "got out upon."

22. *hēkō* [ἥκω, 2240], means (*a*) to come, to be present (see above, on No. 1); (*b*) to come upon, of time and events, Matt. 24:14; John 2:4; 2 Pet. 3:10; Rev. 18:8; (*c*) metaphorically, to come upon one, of calamitous times, and evils, Matt. 23:36; Luke 19:43.
NT: B.344c; CB.1249c; K.306.
OT: bô': S.935; HR.605a.2a; H.212; BD.97c.
GEN. REF.: –.

23. *aphikneomai* [ἀφικνέομαι, 864], to arrive at a place, is used in Rom. 16:19, "come abroad" (of the obedience of the saints). ¶
NT: B.126c; CB.–; K.–.
OT: –.
GEN. REF.: –.

24. *chōreō* [χωρέω, 5562], lit., to make room (*chōra*, a place) for another, and so to have place, receive, is rendered "come" (followed by "to repentance") in 2 Pet. 3:9; the meaning strictly is 'have room (i.e., space of time) for repentance.' See CONTAIN, GO, PLACE, ROOM, RECEIVE.
NT: B.889c; CB.1240a; K.–.
OT: –.
GEN. REF.: –.

25. *eimi* [εἰμί, 1510], to be, is, in the Infinitive Mood, rendered "come," in John 1:46 and in the future Indicative "will come," in 2 Tim. 4:3.
NT: B.222d; CB.1243a; K.206.
OT: –.
GEN. REF.: –.

26. *enistēmi* [ἐνίστημι, 1764], lit., to stand in, or set in (*en*, in. *histēmi*, to stand), hence to be present or to be imminent, is rendered "shall come" in 2 Tim. 3:1; it here expresses permanence, 'shall settle in (upon you).' See AT HAND, PRESENT
NT: B.226d; CB.–; K.234.
OT: –.
GEN. REF.: –.

27. *ephistēmi* [ἐφίστημι, 2186], signifies to stand by or over (*epi*, upon), Luke 2:9, R.V.; Acts 12:7; "before," Acts 11:11; to come upon, Luke 20:1 (here with the idea of suddenness): Acts 4:1; 6:12; 23:27; 1 Thess. 5:3; "coming up," of the arrival of Anna at the Temple, Luke 2:38; "came up to (Him)," of Martha. Luke 10:40; "is come," 2 Tim. 4:6 (probably with the same idea as in Luke 20:1). The R.V. is significant

in all these places. See ASSAULT, AT HAND, PRESENT, STAND.

NT: B.330d; CB.–; K.–.
OT: nāṣab: S.5324; HR.585c.6; H.1398; BD.662a.
'āmad: S.5975; HR.585c.11; H.1637; BD.763c.
GEN. REF.: –.

28. *katantaō* [καταντάω, 2658], denotes (*a*) to come to, or over against, a place, arrive, Acts 16:1; 18:19, 24; 20:15 (in 21:7 and 25:13, R.V., "arrived"; in 27:12, "reach," for A.V., "attain to); 28:13; (*b*) of things or events, to arrive at a certain time, or come upon certain persons in the period of their lifetime, 1 Cor. 10:11; or to come to persons so that they partake of, as of the Gospel, 1 Cor. 14:36. For the remaining instances, Acts 26:7; Eph. 4:13; Phil. 3:11, see ATTAIN. ¶

NT: B.415b; CB.1254a; K.419.
OT: ḥûl: S.2342; HR.739c.1; H.623; BD.296d.
GEN. REF.: –.

29. *mellō* [μέλλω, 3195], to be about (to do something), often implying the necessity and therefore the certainty of what is to take place, is frequently rendered "to come," e.g., Matt. 3:7; 11:14; Eph. 1:21; 1 Tim. 4:8; 6:19; Heb. 2:5. See ALMOST, BEGIN, MEAN, MIND, SHALL, TARRY, WILL.

NT: B.500d; CB.1258a; K.–.
OT: –.
GEN. REF.: –.

30. *paristēmi* [παρίστημι, 3936], to stand by or near, to be at hand (*para*, near), is translated "is come," of the arrival of harvest, Mark 4:29. See BRING, COMMEND, GIVE, PRESENT, PROVE, PROVIDE, SHEW, STAND, YIELD.

NT: B.627c; CB.1262b; K.788.
OT: nāṣab: S.5324; HR.1070c.5a; H.1398; BD.662a.
'āmad: S.5975; HR.1070c.6a; H.1637; BD.763c.
GEN. REF.: –.

31. *pherō* [φέρω, 5342], to bear, carry, is rendered "came," in the sense of being borne from a place in 2 Pet 1:17, 18, 21. See BEAR, CARRY.

NT: B.854a; CB.1264a; K.1252.
OT: nāsā': S.5375; HR.1426c.17; H.1421; BD.669d.
GEN. REF.: –.

32. *phthanō* [φθάνω, 5348], denotes to anticipate, to come sooner than expected, 1 Thess. 2:16, "is come upon," of Divine wrath; cp. Rom. 9:31, "did not arrive at"; or to come in a different manner from what was expected, Matt. 12:28, "come upon"; Luke 11:20, of the Kingdom of God; so of coming to a place, 2 Cor. 10:14. See ATTAIN, PRECEDE, PREVENT. ¶

NT: B.856b; CB.1264c; K.1258.
OT: nāga': S.5060; HR.1429b.5; H.1293; BD.619a.
GEN. REF.: –.

Two of the compounds of the verb poreuomai, to go, proceed, are translated "come," with a preposition or adverb:

33. *ekporeuō* [ἐκπορεύω, 1607], in the Middle Voice, to come forth (*ek*, out of), Mark 7:15, 20; John 5:29. See DEPART, GO, ISSUE, PROCEED.

NT: B.244b; CB.1244a; K.915.
OT: yāṣā': S.3318; HR.439c.5a; H.893; BD.422b.
GEN. REF.: –.

34. *prosporeuomai* [προσπορεύομαι, 4365], in Mark 10:35, is translated "come near unto." ¶

NT: B.718b; CB.–; K.–.
OT: nāgash: S.5066; HR.1219b.4; H.1297; BD.620c.
qārab: S.7126; HR.1219b.5; H.2065; BD.897b.
GEN. REF.: –.

Notes: (1) No. 33 is rendered "proceed" in the R.V. of Mark 7:15, 20, 23 (A.V., "come").

(2) For *epiporeuomai*, in Luke 8:4, see RESORT. ¶

35. *prosengizō* [προσεγγίζω, 4331], denotes to come near (*pros*, to, *engizō*, to be near, to approach), Mark 2:4, used of those who tried to bring a palsied man to Christ. ¶

NT: B.712d; CB.–; K.194.
OT: nāgash: S.5066; HR.1213b.2; H.1297; BD.620c.
GEN. REF.: –.

36. *sumplēroō* [συμπληρόω, 4845], to fill completely (*sun*, with, intensive), is used, in the Passive Voice, of time to be fulfilled or completed, Luke 9:51, "the days were well-nigh come"; Acts 2:1, "the day . . . was now come" (A.V. "was fully come"). In Luke 8:23, it is used in the Active Voice, of the filling of a boat in a storm. See FILL. ¶

NT: B.779c; CB.1270b; K.867.
OT: malē': S.4390; HR.1305c.1; H.1195; BD.569d.
GEN. REF.: –.

37. *suntunchanō* [συντυγχάνω, 4940], to meet with (*sun*, with, and *tunchanō*, to reach), is rendered "to come at" in Luke 8:19, (of the efforts of Christ's mother and brethren to get at Him through a crowd). ¶

NT: B.793c; CB.–; K.–.
OT: –.
GEN. REF.: –.

38. *kukloō* [κυκλόω, 2944], to compass (Eng., cycle), is translated "came round about," in John 10:24. See COMPASS, ROUND, STAND

NT: B.456d; CB.–; K.–.
OT: sābab: S.5437; HR.798b.3; H.1456; BD.685b.
GEN. REF.: –.

39. *hustereō* [ὑστερέω, 5302], to be behind, is translated "to have come short," in Heb. 4:1. See BEHIND, B. No. 1.

NT: B.849a; CB.1252b; K.1240.
OT: ḥāsēr: S.2637; HR.1418b.3; H.705; BD.341a.
GEN. REF.: –.

Notes: (1) *Deuro*, hither, here, is used (sometimes with verbs of motion) in the singular number, in calling a person to come, Matt. 19:21; Mark 10:21; Luke 18:22; John 11:43; Acts 7:3, 34; Rev. 17:1; 21:9. For its other meaning, "hitherto," Rom. 1:13, see HITHERTO. ¶ It has a plural, *deute*, frequent in the Gospels; elsewhere in Rev. 19:17. *In the following the R.V. has a different rendering:—*

(2) In Mark 14:8, *prolambanō*, to anticipate, to be beforehand, A.V., "hath come aforehand to anoint My body," R.V., "hath anointed My body aforehand."

(3) In Acts 7:45, *diadechomai*, to succeed one, to take the place of, A.V., "who came after," R.V., "in their turn." ¶

(4) In Luke 8:55, *epistrephō*, to return to, A.V., "came again," R.V., "returned."

(5) In Acts 24:27, *lambanō*, with *diadochos*, a successor, A.V., "came into the room of," R.V., "was succeeded by."

(6) In Mark 9:23, for *episuntrechō*, to come running together, see under RUN. ¶

(7) In Acts 5:38, *kataluō*, to destroy, A.V., "will come to nought." R.V., "will be overthrown."

(8) In John 12:35, *katalambanō*, to seize, A.V., "come upon," R.V., "overtake."

(9) In 2 Corr. 11:28, *epistasis* (in some mss. *episustasis*), lit., a standing together upon, hence, a pressing upon, as of cares, A.V., "cometh upon," R.V., "presseth upon."

(10) In Acts 19:27, *erchomai*, with *eis apelegmon*, R.V., "come into disrepute," A.V., "be set at nought."

(11) For *pareimi*, John 7:6, see PRESENT, No. 1.

(12) *Sunagō*, to gather together, is always so rendered in R.V., e.g., Matt. 27:62; Mark 7:1; Luke 22:66; Acts 13:44; 15:6, 20:7. See GATHER, No. 1.

(13) For come to nought see NOUGHT.

(14) For *eisporeuomai* see ENTER, No. 4.

(15) For "was come again," Acts 22:17, A.V., see RETURN, No. 4.

(16) For *engizō*, to come near, see APPROACH, NIGH.

For **COME BEHIND,** see **BEHIND**

COMELINESS, COMELY

A. Noun.

euschēmosunē [εὐσχημοσύνη, 2157], elegance of figure, gracefulness, comeliness (*eu*, well, *schēma*, a form), is found in this sense in 1 Cor. 12:23.

NT: B.327a; CB.1247b; K.—.
OT: —.
GEN. REF.: —.

B. Adjective.

euschēmōn [εὐσχήμων, 2158], akin to A, elegant in figure, well formed, graceful, is used in 1 Cor. 12:24, of parts of the body (see above); in 1 Cor. 7:35, R.V., "(that which is) seemly," A.V., "comely"; "honourable," Mark 15:43; Acts 13:50; 17:12. See HONOURABLE. ¶

NT: B.327a; CB.—; K.278.
OT: —.
GEN. REF.: —.

Note: In 1 Cor. 11:13, *prepō*, to be becoming, is rendered in the A.V., "is it comely?" R.V., "is it seemly?" See BECOME, SEEMLY.

COMFORT, COMFORTER, COMFORTLESS

A. Nouns.

1. *paraklēsis* [παράκλησις, 3874], means a calling to one's side (*para*, beside, *kaleō*, to call); hence, either an exhortation, or consolation, comfort, e.g., Luke 2:25 (here "looking for the consolation of Israel" is equivalent to waiting for the coming of the Messiah); 6:24; Acts 9:31; Rom. 15:4, 5; 1 Cor. 14:3, "exhortation"; 2 Cor. 1:3, 4, 5, 6, 7; 7:4, 7, 13; 2 Thess. 2:16; Philm. 7. In 2 Thess. 2:16 it combines encouragement with alleviation of grief. The R.V. changes "consolation" into "comfort," except in Luke 2:25; 6:24; Acts 15:31; in Heb. 6:18, "encouragement"; in Acts 4:36, "exhortation." R.V. (A.V., "consolation"). See CONSOLATION, ENCOURAGEMENT, EXHORTATION, INTREATY.

NT: B.618a; CB.1262a; K.778.
OT: niḥûm: S.5150; HR.1061a.1a; H.1344b; BD.637b.
tanᵉḥûm: S.8575; HR.1061a.1c,d; H.1144d; BD.637c.
GEN. REF.: IS.1:735; NB.16; Z.1:918,952.

2. *paramuthia* [παραμυθία, 3889], primarily a speaking closely to anyone (*para*, near *muthos*, speech), hence denotes consolation, comfort, with a greater degree of tenderness than No. 1, 1 Cor. 14:3. ¶

NT: B.620d; CB.1262b; K.784.
OT: —.
GEN. REF.: IS.1:735; NB.—; Z.1:918.

3. *paramuthion* [παραμύθιον, 3890], has the same meaning as No. 2, the difference being that *paramuthia* stresses the process or progress of the act, *paramuthion* the instrument as used by the agent, Phil. 2:1. ¶

NT: B.620d; CB.1262b; K.784.
OT: —.
GEN. REF.: IS.1:735; NB.—; Z.1:918.

4. *parēgoria* [παρηγορία, 3931], primarily an addressing, address, hence denotes a soothing, solace, Col. 4:11. ¶ A verbal form of the word signifies medicines which allay irritation (Eng., paregoric).

NT: B.626d; CB.—; K.—.
OT: —.
GEN. REF.: IS.1:735; NB.—; Z.—.

5. *paraklētos* [παράκλητος, 3875], lit., called to one's side, i.e., to one's aid, is primarily a verbal adjective, and suggests the capability or adaptability for giving aid. It was used in a court of justice to denote a legal assistant, counsel for the defence, an advocate; then, generally, one

who pleads another's cause, an intercessor, advocate, as in 1 John 2:1, of the Lord Jesus. In the widest sense, it signifies a succourer, comforter. Christ was this to His disciples, by the implication of His word "another (*allos*, another of the same sort, not *heteros*, different) Comforter," when speaking of the Holy Spirit, John 14:16. In 14:26; 15:26; 16:7 He calls Him "the Comforter. ¶" "Comforter" or "Consoler" corresponds to the name "*Menaheri*," given by the Hebrews to the Messiah.

NT: B.618b; CB.1262a; K.782.
OT: —.
GEN. REF.: IS.1:735; NB.16; Z.1:918.

B. Verbs.

1. *parakaleō* [παρακαλέω, 3870], has the same variety of meanings as Noun, No. 1, above, e.g., Matt. 2:18; 1 Thess. 3:2, 7; 4:18. In 2 Cor. 13:11, it signifies to be comforted (so the R.V.). See BESEECH.

NT: B.617a; CB.1262a; K.778.
OT: nāḥam: S.5162; HR.1060a.10; H.1344; BD.636d.
GEN. REF.: IS.1:735; NB.16; Z.1:918.

2. *sumparakaleō* [συμπαρακαλέω, 4837], *sun*, with, and No. 1, signifies to comfort together, Rom. 1:12. ¶

NT: B.779a; CB.—; K.—.
OT: —.
GEN. REF.: IS.1:735; NB.16; Z.1:918.

3. *paramutheomai* [παραμυθέομαι, 3888], akin to Noun No. 2, to soothe, console, encourage, is translated, in John 11:31, "comforted"; in ver. 19, R.V. "console." In 1 Thess. 2:11 and 5:14, R.V., "encourage," as the sense there is that of stimulating to the earnest discharge of duties. See CONSOLE, ENCOURAGE ¶

NT: B.620d; CB.1262b; K.784.
OT: —.
GEN. REF.: IS.1:735; NB.—; Z.1:918.

4. *eupsucheō* [εὐψυχέω, 2174], signifies to be of good comfort (*eu*, well, *psuchē*, the soul), Phil. 2:19. ¶

NT: B.329b; CB.1247b; K.—.
OT: —.
GEN. REF.: IS.1:735; NB.—; Z.—.

Notes: (1) For the verb *tharseō*, "be of good comfort," see CHEER, No. 2.

(2) *Orphanos* is rendered "comfortless" in John 14:18, A.V.; R.V., "desolate," see DESOLATE, FATHERLESS.

COMING (Noun)

1. *eisodos* [εἴσοδος, 1529], an entrance (*eis*, in, *hodos*, a way), an entering in, is once translated "coming," Acts 13:24, of the coming of Christ into the nation of Israel. For its meaning "entrance" see 1 Thess. 1:9; 2:1; Heb. 10:19; 2 Pet. 1:11. See ENTER, ENTRANCE. ¶

NT: B.233b; CB.1243b; K.666.
OT: bô': S.935; HR.413c.1a; H.212; BD.97c.
mābô': S.872; HR.413c.1c; H.212a; BD.89d.
GEN. REF.: —.

2. *eleusis* [ἔλευσις, 1660], a coming (from *erchomai*, to come), is found in Acts 7:52. ¶

NT: B.251a; CB.1244b; K.257.
OT: —.
GEN. REF.: —.

3. *parousia* [παρουσία, 3952], lit., a presence, *para*, with, and *ousia*, being (from *eimi*, to be), denotes both an arrival and a consequent presence with. For instance, in a papyrus letter a lady speaks of the necessity of her *parousia* in a place in order to attend to matters relating to her property there. Paul speaks of his *parousia* in Philippi, Phil. 2:12 (in contrast to his *apousia*, his absence; see ABSENCE). Other words denote the arrival (see *eisodos* and *eleusis*, above). *Parousia* is used to describe the presence of Christ with His disciples on the Mount of Transfiguration, 2 Pet. 1:16. When used of the return of Christ, at the Rapture of the Church, it signifies, not merely His momentary coming for His saints, but His presence with them from that moment until His revelation and manifestation to the world. In some passages the word gives prominence to the beginning of that period, the course of the period being implied, 1 Cor. 15:23; 1 Thess. 4:15; 5:23; 2 Thess. 2:1; Jas. 5:7, 8; 2 Pet. 3:4. In some, the course is prominent, Matt. 24:3, 37; 1 Thess. 3:13; 1 John 2:28; in others the conclusion of the period, Matt. 24:27; 2 Thess. 2:8.

The word is also used of the Lawless One, the Man of Sin, his access to power and his doings in the world during his *parousia*, 2 Thess. 2:9. In addition to Phil. 2:12 (above), it is used in the same way of the Apostle, or his companions, in 1 Cor. 16:17; 2 Cor. 7:6, 7; 10:10; Phil. 1:26; of the Day of God, 2 Pet. 3:12. See PRESENCE.

NT: B.629d; CB.1262c; K.791.
OT: —.
GEN. REF.: IS.4:664; NB.386; Z.4:600.

Note: The word *apokalupsis*, rendered "coming" in 1 Cor. 1:7, A.V., denotes a "revelation" (R.V.). For a fuller treatment of *Parousia*, see *Notes on Thessalonians*, by Hogg and Vine, pp. 87, 88.

COMMAND (Verbs)

1. *diatassō* [διατάσσω, 1299], signifies to set in order, appoint, command, Matt. 11:1; Luke 8:55; 17:9, 10; Acts 18:2; 23:31; "gave order," 1 Cor. 16:1, R.V., So in Acts 24:23, where it is in the Middle Voice. See APPOINT, No. 6.

NT: B.189c; CB.1241b; K.1156.
OT: sîm, sûm: S.7760; HR.313a.7; H.2243; BD.962c.
shāmar: S.8104; HR.313a.8; H.2414; BD.1036b.
GEN. REF.: IS.1:215,736; NB.—; Z.—.

2. *epō* [ἔπω, 2036], denotes to speak (connected with *eipon*, to say); hence, among various renderings, to bid, command, Matt. 4:3; Mark 5:43; 8:7; Luke 4:3; 19:15. See BID.
NT: –.
OT: –.
GEN. REF.: –.

Note: In 2 Cor. 4:6, the R.V. rightly has "said," followed by the quotation "Light shall shine out of darkness."

3. *entellō* [ἐντέλλω, 1781], signifies to enjoin upon, to charge with; it is used in the Middle Voice in the sense of commanding, Matt. 19:7; 28:20; Mark 10:3; 13:34; John 8:5; 15:14, 17; Acts 13:47; Heb. 9:20; 11:22, "gave commandment." See CHARGE, ENJOIN.
NT: B.268b; CB.1245b; K.234.
OT: ṣāwāh: S.6680; HR.477a.7a; H.1887; BD.845b.
GEN. REF.: IS.1:736; NB.–; Z.–.

4. *epitassō* [ἐπιτάσσω, 2004], signifies to appoint over, put in charge (*epi*, over, *tassō*, to appoint); then, to put upon one as a duty, to enjoin, Mark 1:27; 6:27, 39; 9:25; Luke 4:36; 8:25, 31; 14:22; Acts 23:2; Philm. 8. See CHARGE, ENJOIN. ¶
NT: B.302b; CB.1246a; K.–.
OT: ṣāwāh: S.6680; HR.534c.4; H.1887; BD.845b.
GEN. REF.: IS.1:215; NB.–; Z.–.

5. *keleuō* [κελεύω, 2753], to urge, incite, order, suggests a stronger injunction than No. 6, Matt. 14:9, 19; 15:35; 18:25; 27:58, 64; Luke 18:40; Acts 4:15 (frequently in Acts, not subsequently in the N.T.). See BID.
NT: B.427b; CB.1254c; K.–.
OT: –.
GEN. REF.: –.

6. *parangellō* [παραγγέλλω, 3853], to announce beside (*para*, beside, *angellō*, to announce), to pass on an announcement, hence denotes to give the word, order, give a charge, command, e.g., Mark 6:8; Luke 8:29; 9:21; Acts 5:28; 2 Thess. 3:4, 6, 10, 12. See CHARGE, B, No. 8.
NT: B.613b; CB.1262b; K.776.
OT: shāma': S.8085; HR.1056b.6; H.2412; BD.1033b.
GEN. REF.: –.

7. *prostassō* [προστάσσω, 4367], denotes to arrange or set in order towards (*pros*, towards, *tassō*, to arrange); hence to prescribe, give command, Matt. 1:24; 8:4; Mark 1:44; Luke 5:14; Acts 10:33, 48. For Matt. 21:6 see Note (3) below. See BID. ¶
NT: B.718c; CB.1267b; K.1156.
OT: ṣāwāh: S.6680; HR.1220c.5a; H.1887; BD.845b.
GEN. REF.: IS.1:215; NB.–; Z.–.

Notes: (1) In Rev. 9:4, *rheō*, to speak, is translated "said" in the R.V. (A.V., "commanded").

(2) In Heb. 12:20 *diastellomai*, to charge, enjoin (so in the R.V.), is rendered "commanded" in the A.V.

(3) In Matt. 21:6, the R.V., translating *suntassō*, as in the best mss., has "appointed," A.V., "commanded."

COMMANDMENT

1. *diatagma* [διάταγμα, 1297], signifies that which is imposed by decree or law, Heb. 11:23. It stresses the concrete character of the commandment more than *epitagē* (No. 4). Cp. COMMAND, No. 1. For the verb in ver. 22 see No. 3 under COMMAND. ¶
NT: B.189b; CB.1241b; K.–.
OT: nishtᵉwān: S.5406; HR.312c.1; H.1439; BD.677a.
GEN. REF.: IS.–; NB.–; Z.1:919.

2. *entolē* [ἐντολή, 1785], akin to No. 3, above, denotes, in general, an injunction, charge, precept, commandment. It is the most frequent term, and is used of moral and religious precepts, e.g., Matt. 5:19; it is frequent in the Gospels, especially that of John, and in his Epistles. See also, e.g., Acts 17:15; Rom. 7:8-13; 13:9; 1 Cor. 7:19; Eph. 2:15; Col. 4:10. See PRECEPT.
NT: B.269a; CB.1245b; K.234.
OT: miṣwāh: S.4687; HR.479b.4; H.1887b; BD.846b.
GEN. REF.: IS.1:736; NB.–; Z.1:919.

3. *entalma* [ἔνταλμα, 1778], akin to No. 2, marks more especially the thing commanded, a commission; in Matt. 15:9; Mark 7:7; Col. 2:22, R.V. "precepts," A.V., "commandments." See PRECEPT. ¶
NT: B.268b; CB.–; K.–.
OT: miṣwāh: S.4687; HR.476c.2; H.1887b; BD.846b.
GEN. REF.: IS.1:736; NB.–; Z.1:919.

4. *epitagē* [ἐπιταγή, 2003], akin to No. 4, above, stresses the authoritativeness of the command; it is used in Rom. 16:26; 1 Cor. 7:6, 25; 2 Cor. 8:8; 1 Tim. 1:1; Tit. 1:3; 2:15. See AUTHORITY. ¶
NT: B.302a; CB.–; K.1156.
OT: –.
GEN. REF.: IS.1:736; NB.–; Z.1:919.

Notes: (1) For *parangelia* (cp. *parangellō*, above), a proclamation, see CHARGE.

(2) In Rev. 22:14 the R.V., "wash their robes" (for A.V., "do His commandments") follows the most authentic mss.

COMMEND, COMMENDATION

A. Verbs.

1. *epaineō* [ἐπαινέω, 1867], to praise, is an intensive form of *aineō*, Luke 16:8. It is elsewhere translated by the verb to praise, in the R.V., Rom. 15:11; 1 Cor. 11:2, 17, 22. See LAUD, PRAISE. ¶
NT: B.281c; CB.1245b; K.–.
OT: hālal: S.1984; HR.504c.1; H.499,500; BD.237d.
shābaḥ: S.7623; HR.504c.2; H.2312,2313; BD.986c.
GEN. REF.: IS.1:737; NB.–; Z.–.

2. *paradidōmi* [παραδίδωμι, 3860], lit., to give or deliver over (*para*, over, *didōmi*, to give),

is said of commending, or committing, servants of God to Him (A.V., "recommend"), Acts 14:26; 15:40. See BETRAY, BRING, B, *Note* (4), CAST, COMMIT, DELIVER, GIVE, HAZARD, PUT (in prison), RECOMMEND.

NT: B.614b; CB.1262a; K.166.
OT: nātan: S.5414; HR.1058a.16a; H.1443; BD.678a.
GEN. REF.: IS.1:737; NB.–; Z.–.

3. *paratithēmi* [παρατίθημι, 3908], lit., to put near (*para*, near), in the Middle Voice, denotes to place with someone, entrust, commit. In the sense of commending, it is said (*a*) of the Lord Jesus in commending His spirit into the Father's hands, Luke 23:46; (*b*) of commending disciples to God, Acts 14:23; (*c*) of commending elders to God, Acts 20:32. See ALLEGE, COMMIT, PUT, No. 3, Set, No. 4. Cp. No. 2.

NT: B.622d; CB.–; K.1176.
OT: sûm, sîm: S.7760; HR.1065a.7; H.2243; BD.962c.
GEN. REF.: IS.1:737; NB.–; Z.–.

4. *paristēmi* [παρίστημι, 3936], lit., to place near, set before, (*para*, near, *histēmi*, to set), is used of self-commendation, 1 Cor. 8:8. See ASSIST, BRING, COME, GIVE, PRESENT, PROVE, PROVIDE, SHEW, STAND, YIELD.

NT: B.627c; CB.1262b; K.788.
OT: nāṣab: S.5324; HR.1070c.5a; H.1398; BD.662a.
'āmad: S.5975; HR.1070c.6a; H.1637; BD.763c.
GEN. REF.: IS.1:737; NB.–; Z.–.

5. *sunistēmi* [συνίστημι, 4921], or *sunistanō* [συνιστάνω], lit., to place together, denotes to introduce one person to another, represent as worthy, e.g., Rom. 3:5; 5:8; 16:1; 2 Cor. 4:2; 6:4; 10:18; 12:11. In 2 Cor. 3:1; 5:12 and 10:12, the verb *sunistanō* is used. See APPROVE, CONSIST, MAKE, STAND.

NT: B.790c; CB.1270c; K.1120.
OT: –.
GEN. REF.: IS.1:737; NB.–; Z.–.

B. Adjective.

sustatikos [συστατικός, 4956], akin to A, No. 5, lit., placing together, hence, commendatory, is used of letters of commendation, 2 Cor. 3:1, lit., 'commendatory letters.' ¶

NT: B.795a; CB.–; K.–.
OT: –.
GEN. REF.: –.

COMMIT, COMMISSION

A. Verbs.

(I) *In the sense of doing or practising.*

1. *ergazomai* [ἐργαζομαι, 2038], to work, is translated by the verb to commit (of committing sin), in Jas. 2:9. This is a stronger expression than *poieō*, to do, or *prassō*, to practise (Nos. 2 and 3). See DO, LABOUR, MINISTER, TRADE, WORK.

NT: B.306d; CB.1246c; K.251.
OT: 'ābad: S.5647; HR.540c.8a; H.1553; BD.712b.
pā'al: S.6466; HR.540c.11a; H.1792; BD.821b.
GEN. REF.: IS.1:751; NB.–; Z.–.

2. *poieō* [ποιέω, 4160], to do, cause etc., sometimes signifies to commit, of any act, as of murder, Mark 15:7; sin, John 8:34; 2 Cor. 11:7; Jas. 5:15. See DO.

NT: B.680d; CB.1265c; K.895.
OT: 'āsāh: S.6213; HR.1154a.33; H.1708,1709; BD.793c.
GEN. REF.: –.

Note: In 1 John 3:4, 8, 9, the A.V. wrongly has "commit" (an impossible meaning in ver. 8); the R.V. rightly has "doeth," i.e., of a continuous habit, equivalent to *prassō*, to practise. The committal of an act is not in view in that passage.

3. *prassō* [πράσσω, 4238], to do, work, practise, is said of continuous action, or action not yet completed, Acts 25:11, 25; it is rendered "practise" in the R.V., for the incorrect A.V. "commit," in Rom. 1:32; 2:2. See DO, EXACT, KEEP, REQUIRE, USE.

NT: B.698b; CB.1266b; K.927.
OT: 'āsāh: S.6213; HR.1201a.3; H.1708,1709; BD.793c.
pā'al: S.6466; HR.1201a.4; H.1792; BD.821b.
GEN. REF.: –.

(II) *In the sense of delivering or entrusting something to a person.*

1. *paradidōmi* [παραδιδωμι, 3860], to give over, is often rendered by the verb to commit, e.g., to prison, Acts 8:3; to the grace of God, Acts 14:26; to God, 1 Pet. 2:23; by God to pits of darkness, 2 Pet. 2:4. See COMMEND, No. 2.

NT: B.614b; CB.1262a; K.166.
OT: nātan: S.5414; HR.1058a.16; H.1443; BD.678a.
GEN. REF.: IS.1:751; NB.–; Z.–.

2. *pisteuō* [πιστεύω, 4100], signifies to entrust, commit to, Luke 16:11; 1 Tim. 1:11, "committed to (my) trust." See BELIEVE.

NT: B.660b; CB.1265a; K.849.
OT: 'āman: S.539; HR.1137c.1b; H.116; BD.52d.
GEN. REF.: –.

3. *tithēmi* [τίθημι, 5087], to put, place, signifies, in the Middle Voice, to put for oneself, assign, place in, 2 Cor. 5:19, "having committed (unto us)."

NT: B.815d; CB.1272c; K.1176
OT: nātan: S.5414; HR.1348c.16; H.1443; BD.678a.
sûm, sîm: S.7760; HR.1348c.25; H.2243; BD.962c.
GEN. REF.: IS.1:751; NB.–; Z.–.

4. *paratithēmi* [παρατίθημι, 3908], see COMMEND, No. 3, signifies to entrust, commit to one's charge, e.g., in Luke 12:48; 1 Tim. 1:18; 2 Tim. 2:2; 1 Pet. 4:19 (A.V., "commit the keeping").

NT: B.622d; CB.–; K.1176.
OT: sûm, sîm: S.7760; HR.1065a.7; H.2243; BD.962c.
GEN. REF.: IS.1:751; NB.–; Z.–.

Notes: (1) *Didōmi*, to give, is rendered "committed" in the A.V. of John 5:22 (R.V., "given").

(2) For *porneuō* (to commit fornication) see FORNICATION.

(3) In Rom. 2:22, *hierosuleō*, to rob temples, is so rendered in the R.V., for A.V., "commit sacrilege."

(4) In Acts 27:40, *eaō*, to let, leave, is rendered in the R.V., "left the anchors) in"; for A.V., "committed themselves to."

B. Nouns.

1. *parathēkē* [παραθήκη, 3866], a putting with, a deposit (*para*, with, *tithēmi*, to put), and its longer form, *parakatathēkē*, are found, the former in 2 Tim. 1:12, "that which He hath committed unto me," R.V., marg., lit., 'my deposit' (perhaps, 'my deposit with Him'), the latter in 1 Tim. 6:20, where "guard that which is committed unto thee" is, lit., 'guard the deposit,' and 2 Tim. 1:14, "that good thing which was committed unto thee," i.e., the good deposit; R.V., marg., "the good deposit."
NT: B.616b; CB.1262b; K.1176.
OT: piqqādôr: S.6487; HR.1059c.1; H.1802f; BD.824c.
GEN. REF.: IS.1:751; NB.–; Z.–.

2. *epitropē* [ἐπιτροπή, 2011], denotes a turning over (to another), a referring of a thing to another (*epi*, over, *trepō*, to turn), and so a committal of full powers, a commission, Acts 26:12. ¶
NT: B.303d; CB.1246b; K.–.
OT: –.
GEN. REF.: –.

COMMODIOUS (not)

aneuthetos [ἀνεύθετος, 428], not commodious, lit., 'not-well-placed' (from *a*, not, *n*, euphonic, *eu*, well, *thetos*, from *tithēmi*, to put, place), is found in Acts 27:12, where it is said of the haven at the place called Fair Havens. ¶
NT: B.65c; CB.–; K.–.
OT: –.
GEN. REF.: –.

COMMON, COMMONLY

A. Adjective.

koinos [κοινός, 2839], denotes (*a*) common, belonging to several (Lat., *communis*), said of things had in common, Acts 2:44; 4:32; of faith, Tit. 1:4; of salvation, Jude 3; it stands in contrast to *idios*, one's own; (*b*) ordinary, belonging to the generality, as distinct from what is peculiar to the few; hence the application to religious practices of Gentiles in contrast with those of Jews; or of the ordinary people in contrast with those of the Pharisees; hence the meaning unhallowed, profane, Levitically unclean (Lat., *profanus*), said of hands, Mark 7:2 (A.V., "defiled,") R.V. marg., "common"; of animals, ceremonially unclean, Acts 10:14; 11:8; of a man, 10:28; of meats, Rom. 14:14, "unclean"; of the blood of the covenant, as viewed by an apostate, Heb. 10:29, "unholy" (R.V., marg., "common"); of everything unfit for the holy city, Rev. 21:27, R.V., "unclean" (marg., "common"). Some mss. have the verb here. See DEFILED, UNCLEAN, UNHOLY. ¶
NT: B.438a; CB.1255b; K.447.
OT: –.
GEN. REF.: IS.1:751; NB.–; Z.1:928.

B. Verb.

koinoō [κοινόω, 2840], to make, or count, common, has this meaning in Acts 10:15; 11:9. See DEFILE, POLLUTE, UNCLEAN.
NT: B.438b; CB.1255b; K.447.
OT: –.
GEN. REF.: IS.1:751; NB.–; Z.1:928.

Notes: (1) *Polus*, used of number, signifies many, numerous; used of space, it signifies wide, far reaching; hence, with the article it is said of a multitude as being numerous; it is translated "common" (people) in Mark 12:37 (see the R.V., marg.). It does not, however, mean the ordinary folk, but the many folk. See ABUNDANT, GREAT, LONG, MANY, MUCH, PLENTY.

(2) *Ochlos* denotes a crowd, a great multitude; with the article it is translated "the common people," in John 12:9, 12 (R.V., marg.). See COMPANY, CROWD, MULTITUDE, NUMBER, PEOPLE, PRESS.

(3) *Tunchanō*, to happen, is used as an adjective in Acts 28:2, of the kindness shown by the people of Melita to the shipwrecked company; A.V., "(no) little"; R.V., "(no) common"; the idea suggested by the verb is that which might happen anywhere or at all times; hence, little, ordinary, or casual. See CHANCE, ENJOY, OBTAIN.

(4) In Matt. 27:27, what the A.V. describes asd "the common hall," is the praetorium, R.V., "palace," the official residence of the Governor of a Province (marg., "praetorium").

(5) In Acts 5:18, *dēmosios* (A.V., "common," with reference to the prison) signifies "public," belonging to the people, *dēmos*, (R.V., "public").

(6) In 1 Cor. 5:1, *holōs*, altogether (A.V., "commonly") means "actually" (R.V.).

(7) In Matt. 28:15, *diaphēmizō*, to spread abroad (as in the R.V.), is rendered in the A.V., "is commonly reported." See SPREAD, *Note* (5).

COMMONWEALTH

1. *politeia* [πολιτεία]: see CITIZENSHIP, No. 3.

2. *politeuma* [πολίτευμα]: see CITIZENSHIP, No. 4.

For **COMMOTION** see **CONFUSION, TUMULT**

COMMUNE

1. *dialaleō* [διαλαλέω, 1255], signifies to speak with anyone (*dia*, by turns, *laleō*, to speak), Luke 6:11; in 1:65, to talk over, to noise abroad. The idea that *laleō* and its compounds bear no reference to the word spoken or the sentiment, is unfounded. See NOISE. ¶

NT: B.185c; CB.–; K.–.
OT: –.
GEN. REF.: IS.1:752; NB.–; Z.–.

2. *homileō* [ὁμιλέω, 3656], from *homos*, together, signifies to be in company, to associate with any one; hence, to have intercourse with, Luke 24:14 (R.V., "communed"; A.V., "talked"), 15; Acts 24:26; in 20:11, "talked with." See TALK. ¶

NT: B.565c; CB.–; K.–.
OT: –.
GEN. REF.: IS.1:752; NB.–; Z.–.

3. *sullaleō* [συλλαλέω, 4814], to talk together, is translated "communed" in Luke 22:4, of the conspiracy of Judas with the chief priests. See CONFER, SPEAK, TALK.

NT: B.776d; CB.–; K.–.
OT: dābar: S.1696; HR.1301c.1; H.399; BD.180b.
GEN. REF.: IS.1:752; NB.–; Z.–.

Note: Laleō and its compounds, and the noun *lalia*, speech, have a more dignified meaning in the Hellenistic Greek than to chatter, its frequent meaning in earlier times.

COMMUNICATE, COMMUNICATION

A. Verbs.

1. *koinōneō* [κοινωνέω, 2841], is used in two senses, (*a*) to have a share in, Rom. 15:27; 1 Tim. 5:22; Heb. 2:14; 1 Pet. 4:13; 2 John 11; (*b*) to give a share to, go shares with, Rom. 12:13, R.V., "communicating," for A.V., "distributing"; Gal. 6:6, "communicate"; Phil. 4:15. A.V., "did communicate," R.V., "had fellowship with." See DISTRIBUTE, FELLOWSHIP, PARTAKE. ¶

NT: B.438c; CB.1255b; K.447.
OT: ḥābar: S.2266; HR.775a.3; H.598; BD.287d.
GEN. REF.: IS.1:752; NB.245; Z.1:928.

2. *sunkoinōneō* [συγκοινωνέω, 4790], to share together with (*sun*, and No. 1), is translated "communicated with" in Phil. 4:14; "have fellowship with," Eph. 5:11; "be . . . partakers of," Rev. 18:4 (R.V., "have fellowship"). The thought is that of sharing with others what one has, in order to meet their needs. See FELLOWSHIP, B, No. 2, PARTAKE, B, No. 2. ¶

NT: B.774b; CB.1270c; K.447.
OT: –.
GEN. REF.: IS.1:752; NB.245; Z.1:928.

Note: Anatithēmi, to set forth, is rendered "laid before" in Gal. 2:2, R.V., for A.V., "communicated unto"; in Acts 25:14, R.V., "laid before," for A.V., "declared." ¶

B. Nouns.

1. *koinōnia* [κοινωνία, 2842], akin to A (which see), is translated in Heb. 13:16 "to communicate," lit., 'be not forgetful of good deed and of fellowship'; "fellowship" (A.V., "communication") in Philm. 6, R.V. See COMMUNION.

NT: B.438d; CB.1255b; K.447.
OT: –.
GEN. REF.: IS.1:752; NB.245; Z.1:928.

2. *logos* [λόγος, 3056], a word, that which is spoken (*legō*, to speak), is used in the plural with reference to a conversation; "communication," Luke 24:17. Elsewhere with this significance the R.V. renders it "speech," Matt. 5:37; Eph. 4:29. See ACCOUNT.

NT: B.477a; CB.1257a; K.505.
OT: dābār: S.1697; HR.881c.2a; H.399a; BD.182a.
GEN. REF.: –.

Note: In Col. 3:8, where the A.V. translates *aischrologia* by "filthy communication," the R.V. renders it "shameful speaking" (*aischros*, base, *legō*, to speak).

C. Adjective.

koinōnikos [κοινωνικός, 2843], akin to A, No. 1 and B, No. 1, means apt, or ready, to communicate, 1 Tim. 6:18. ¶

NT: B.439c; CB.1255b; K.447.
OT: –.
GEN. REF.: IS.1:752; NB.245; Z.1:928.

Note: Homilia, a company, association, or intercourse with (see COMMUNE, No. 2), is translated "company" in 1 Cor. 15:33, R.V. (A.V., "communications"); the word is in the plural, "evil companies," i.e., associations. See COMPANY, No. 6. ¶

COMMUNION

A. Noun.

koinōnia [κοινωνία, 2842], a having in common (*koinos*), partnership, fellowship (see COMMUNICATE), denotes (*a*) the share which one has in anything, a participation, fellowship recognized and enjoyed; thus it is used of the common experiences and interests of Christian men, Acts 2:42; Gal. 2:9; of participation in the knowledge of the Son of God, 1 Cor. 1:9; of sharing in the realization of the effects of the Blood (i.e., the Death) of Christ and the Body of Christ, as set forth by the emblems in the Lord's Supper, 1 Cor. 10:16; of participation in what is derived from the Holy Spirit, 2 Cor. 13:14 (R.V., "communion"); Phil. 2:1; of participation in the sufferings of Christ, Phil. 3:10; of sharing in the resurrection life possessed in Christ, and so of fellowship with the Father and the Son, 1 John 1:3, 6, 7; negatively, of the impossibility of communion between light and darkness, 2 Cor. 6:14; (*b*) fellowship manifested in acts, the practical effects of fellowship with God, wrought by the Holy Spirit in the lives of believers as the outcome of faith, Philm. 6, and finding expression in joint ministration to the needy, Rom. 15:26; 2 Cor. 8:4; 9:13; Heb. 13:16, and in the furtherance of the Gospel by gifts, Phil. 1:5. See COMMUNICATION, CONTRIBUTION, DISTRIBUTION, FELLOWSHIP. ¶

NT: B.438d; CB.1255b; K.447.
OT: –.
GEN. REF.: IS.1:752; NB.245; Z.1:928.

B. Adjective.

koinōnos [κοινωνός, 2844], having in common, is rendered "have communion with (the altar)," — the altar standing by metonymy for that which is associated with it — in 1 Cor. 10:18, R.V. (for A.V., "are partakers of"), and in ver. 20, for A.V., "have fellowship with (demons)." See COMPANION.

NT: B.439d; CB.1255b; K.447.
OT: ḥābēr: S.2270; HR.775a.1a; H.598c; BD.288d.
ḥᵃberet: S.2278; HR.775a.1b; H.598d; BD.289a.
GEN. REF.: IS.1:752; NB.245; Z.1:928.

COMPACTED

1. *sunistēmi* [συνίστημι, 4921], and transitively *sunistaō*, to stand together (*sun*, with, *histēmi*, to stand), is rendered "compacted," in 2 Pet. 3:5, of the earth as formerly arranged by God in relation to the waters. See APPROVE, COMMEND, CONSIST, MAKE, STAND.

NT: B.790c; CB.1270c; K.1120.
OT: 'āmad: S.5975; HR.1317a.7; H.1637; BD.763c.
qāhal: S.6950; HR.1317a.10; H.1991; BD.874d.
GEN. REF.: –.

2. *sumbibazō* [συμβιβάζω, 4822], to unite, to knit, is translated "compacted" in the A.V. of Eph. 4:16 (R.V., "knit together"), concerning the Church as the Body of Christ. See CONCLUDE, GATHER, INSTRUCT, KNIT, PROVE.

NT: B.777d; CB.–; K.1101.
OT: –.
GEN. REF.: IS.1:754; NB.–; Z.–.

COMPANION

1. *sunekdēmos* [συνέκδημος, 4898], a fellow-traveller (*sun*, with, *ek*, from *dēmos*, people; i.e. away from one's people), is used in Acts 19:29, of Paul's companions in travel; in 2 Cor. 8:19, "travel with"; a closer rendering would be '(as) our fellow-traveller.' See TRAVEL. ¶

NT: B.787a; CB.–; K.–.
OT: –.
GEN. REF.: IS.1:754; NB.–; Z.–.

2. *koinōnos* [κοινωνός, 2844], is rendered "companions" in the A.V. of Heb. 10:33 (R.V. "partakers"). So *sunkoinōnos* in Rev. 1:9, A.V., "companion"; R.V., "partaker with you." See B. above. PARTAKER, PARTNER. Cp. COMMUNICATE.

NT: B.439d; CB.1255b; K.447.
OT: ḥābēr: S.2270; HR.775a.1a; H.598c; BD.288d.
ḥᵃberet: S.2278; HR.775a.1b; H.598d; BD.289a.
GEN. REF.: IS.1:754; NB.245; Z.1:928.

3. *sunergos* [συνεργός, 4904], a fellow-worker (*sun*, with, *ergon*, work), is translated in Phil. 2:25 "companion in labour," A.V. (R.V., "fellow-worker"). See HELPER, LABOURER, WORKER.

NT: B.787d; CB.1270c; K.1116.
OT: –.
GEN. REF.: –.

COMPANY (Noun and Verb)

A. Nouns and Phrases.

1. *ochlos* [ὄχλος, 3793], a throng of people, an irregular crowd, most usually a disorganised throng; in Acts 6:7, however, it is said of a company of the priests who believed; the word here indicates that they had not combined to bring this about. The R.V. usually translates this word "company" or "multitude." Cp. B, *Note* 3. See COMMON, CROWD, MULTITUDE, and Trench, Syn. §xcviii.

NT: B.600c; CB.1260b; K.750.
OT: 'am: S.5971; HR.1043a.4; H.1640a,e; BD.766b.
qāhāl: S.6951; HR.1043a.5; H.1991a; BD.874c.
GEN. REF.: IS.1:754; NB.–; Z.1:931.

2. *sunodia* [συνοδία, 4923], lit., a way or journey together (*sun*, with, *hodos*, a way), denotes, by metonymy, a company of travellers; in Luke 2:44, of the company from which Christ was missed by Joseph and Mary. (Eng., synod). ¶

NT: B.791a; CB.–; K.–.
OT: yāḥas: S.3187; HR.1317b.1; H.862; BD.405b.
GEN. REF.: IS.1:754; NB.–; Z.1:931.

3. *sumposion* [συμποσίον, 4849], lit. denotes a drinking together (*sun*, with, *pinō*, to drink), a drinking-party; hence, by metonymy, any table party or any company arranged as a party. In Mark 6:39 the noun is repeated, in the plural, by way of an adverbial and distributive phrase, *sumposia sumposia*, lit., 'companies-companies' (i.e., by companies). ¶

NT: B.780a; CB.–; K.–.
OT: mishteh: S.4960; HR.1306a.1; H.2477c; BD.1059c.
GEN. REF.: IS.1:754; NB.–; Z.–.

4. *klisia* [κλισία, 2828], akin to *klinō*, to recline, primarily means a place for lying down in, and hence a reclining company, for the same purpose as No. 3. It is found in the plural in Luke 9:14, corresponding to Mark's word *sumposia* (No. 3, above), signifying companies reclining at a meal. ¶

NT: B.436d; CB.–; K.–.
OT: –.
GEN. REF.: IS.1:754; NB.–; Z.–.

5. *plēthos* [πλῆθος, 4128], lit., a fulness, hence denotes a multitude, a large or full company, Luke 23:1; "a multitude," ver. 27 (A.V., "a great company"). See BUNDLE, MULTITUDE.
NT: B.668b; CB.1265b; K.866.
OT: hāmôn: S.1995; HR.1142c.3; H.505a; BD.242b.
rōb: S.7230; HR.1142c.11; H.2099c; BD.913d.
GEN. REF.: IS.1:754; NB.–; Z.1:931.

6. *homilia* [ὁμιλία, 3657], an association of people, those who are of the same company (*homos*, same), is used in 1 Cor. 15:33, A.V., "(evil) communications"; R.V., "(evil) company." ¶
NT: B.565c; CB.–; K.–.
OT: –.
GEN. REF.: IS.1:754; NB.–; Z.–.

7. *homilos* [ὅμιλος, 3658], akin to No. 6, a throng or crowd, is found, in some mss., in Rev. 18:17, "all the company in ships," A.V. *Homilos* denotes the concrete; *homilia* is chiefly an abstract noun. ¶
NT: B.565b; CB.–; K.–.
OT: –.
GEN. REF.: IS.1:754; NB.–; Z.–.

8. *idios* [ἴδιος, 2398], one's own, is used in the plural with the article in Acts 4:23, to signify "their own (company)." See BUSINESS, B.
NT: B.369c; CB.1252c; K.–.
OT: –.
GEN. REF.: –.

Notes: (1) The preposition *ex* (i.e., *ek*), of, with the first personal pronoun in the genitive plural (*hēmōn*, us), signifies "of our company," lit., 'of us,' in Luke 24:22; so *ex autōn*, in Acts 15:22, "men out of their company," lit., 'men out of them.'

(2) The phrase in Acts 13:13, *hoi peri Paulon*, lit., 'the (ones) about Paul,' signifies "Paul and his company."

(3) *Murias*, a noun connected with the adjective *murios* (numberless, infinite), signifies a myriad (whence the English word), and is used hyperbolically, of vast numbers, e.g., Heb. 12:22, A.V., an innumerable company; R.V., "innumerable hosts." (Contrast *murioi*, 10,000, Matt. 18:24).

(4) In Acts 21:8, the phrase translated "that were of Paul's company" is absent from the best texts.

B. Verbs.

1. *sunanamignumi* [συναναμίγνυμι, 4874], lit., to mix up with (*sun*, with, *ana*, up, *mignumi*, to mix, mingle), signifies to have, or keep, company with, 1 Cor. 5:9, 11; 2 Thess. 3:14. ¶
NT: B.784b; CB.–; K.1113.
OT: bālal: S.1101; HR.1311a.1; H.248; BD.117b.
GEN. REF.: –.

2. *sunerchomai* [συνέρχομαι, 4905], to come, or go, with, is rendered "have companied" in Acts 1:21. See COME, No. 11.
NT: B.788a; CB.1270c; K.257.
OT: qābaṣ: S.6908; HR.1314a.7; H.1983; BD.867c.
hālak: S.1980; HR.1314a.3; H.498; BD.229d.
GEN. REF.: –.

Notes: (1) *Aphorizō*, to separate, is translated "separate (you) from (their) company," in Luke 6:22, the latter part being added in italics to supply the meaning of excommunication. See DIVIDE.

(2) *Kollaō*, to join, is rendered "keep company," in Acts 10:28, A.V.; R.V., "join himself." See CLEAVE, JOIN.

(3) *Ochlopoieō*, lit., to make a crowd (*ochlos*, a crowd, *poieō*, to make), is translated "gathered a company," in Acts 17:5, A.V.; the R.V. corrects this to "gathering a crowd." See CROWD. ¶

COMPARE, COMPARISON

1. *sunkrinō* [συνκρινω, 4793], denotes (*a*) to join fitly, to combine, 1 Cor. 2:13, either in the sense of combining spiritual things with spiritual, adapting the discourse to the subject, under the guidance of the Holy Spirit, or communicating spiritual things by spiritual things or words, or in the sense of interpreting spiritual things to spiritual men, R.V. and A.V., "comparing" (cp. the Sept. use, of interpreting dreams, etc. Gen. 40:8, 16, 22; 41:12, 15; Dan. 5:12); (*b*) to place together; hence, judge or discriminate by comparison, compare, with or among, 2 Cor. 10:12 (thrice). ¶
NT: B.774d; CB.1270c; K.469.
OT: pātar: S.6622; HR.1300b.2a; H.1860; BD.837c.
GEN. REF.: –.

2. *paraballō* [παραβάλλω, 3846], to place side by side, to set forth, and the noun *parabolē* (Eng., parable), occur in Mark 4:30, R.V., "In what parable shall we set it forth?", A.V., "with what comparison shall we compare it?" See ARRIVE.
NT: B.611d; CB.1262a; K.–.
OT: nāṭāh: S.5186; HR.1055c.1; H.1352; BD.639d.
GEN. REF.: –.

Note: The preposition *pros*, towards, is sometimes used of mental direction, in the way of estimation, or comparison, as in the phrase "(worthy) to be compared," or '(worthy) in comparison with,' Rom. 8:18.

COMPASS

1. *kukleuō* [κυκλεύω, 2944], denotes to encircle, surround, and is found in the best texts in John 10:24, "came round about," and Rev. 20:9, of a camp surrounded by foes; some mss. have No. 2 in each place. ¶
NT: B.456d; CB.–; K.–.
OT: sābab: S.5437; HR.796b.1; H.1456; BD.685b.
GEN. REF.: IS.1:755; NB.–; Z.–.

2. *kukloō* [κυκλόω, 2944], (cp. Eng., cycle), signifies to move in a circle, to compass about, as of a city encompassed by armies, Luke 21:20; Heb. 11:30; in Acts 14:20, "stood round about." See COME, No. 38, STAND. ¶
NT: B.456; CB.–; K.–.
OT: sābab: S.5437; HR.798b.3; H.1456; BD.685b.
GEN. REF.: IS.1:755; NB.–; Z.–.

3. *perikukloō* [περικυκλόω, 4033], *peri*, about, with No. 2, is used in Luke 19:43, "shall compass . . . round." ¶
NT: B.648b; CB.–; K.–.
OT: sābab: S.5437; HR.1124a.2; H.1456; BD.685b.
GEN. REF.: IS.1:755; NB.–; Z.–.

4. *periagō* [περιάγω, 4013], to lead about, 1 Cor. 9:5, or, intransitively, to go about, to go up and down, is so used in Matt. 4:23; 9:35; Mark 6:6; Acts 13:11; to compass regions, Matt. 23:15. See GO, LEAD. ¶
NT: B.645c; CB.–; K.–.
OT: sābab: S.5437; HR.1121b.2; H.1456; BD.685b.
'ābar: S.5674; HR.1121b.3; H.1556; BD.716d.
GEN. REF.: IS.1:755; NB.–; Z.–.

5. *perikeimai* [περίκειμαι, 4029], to be encompassed: see BOUND (*b*), HANG.
NT: B.647d; CB.–; K.425.
OT: –.
GEN. REF.: –.

6. *perierchomai* [περιέρχομαι, 4022], lit., to go, or come, about (*peri*, about, *erchomai*, to come), is translated in Acts 28:13, A.V., "fetched a compass." See CIRCUIT.
NT: B.646d; CB.1263b; K.257.
OT: –.
GEN. REF.: –.

COMPASSION, COMPASSIONATE

A. Verbs.

1. *oikteirō* [οἰκτείρω, 3627], to have pity, a feeling of distress through the ills of others, is used of God's compassion, Rom. 9:15. ¶
NT: B.561d; CB.1260c; K.680.
OT: ḥānan: S.2603; HR.982c.1; H.694,695; BD.335d.
rāḥam: S.7355; HR.982c.4; H.214b; BD.933c.
GEN. REF.: IS.1:755; NB.246; Z.1:932.

2. *splanchnizomai* [σπλαγχνίζομαι, 4697], to be moved as to one's inwards (*splanchna*), to be moved with compassion, to yearn with compassion, is frequently recorded of Christ towards the multitude and towards individual sufferers, Matt. 9:36; 14:14; 15:32; 18:27; 20:34; Mark 1:41; 6:34; 8:2; 9:22 (of the appeal of a father for a demon-possessed son); Luke 7:13; 10:33; of the father in the parable of the prodigal son, 15:20. (Moulton and Milligan consider the verb to have been coined in the Jewish Dispersion). ¶
NT: B.762d; CB.1269c; K.1067.
OT: –.
GEN. REF.: IS.1:755; NB.–; Z.1:932.

3. *sumpatheō* [συμπαθέω, 4834], to suffer with another (*sun*, with, *paschō*, to suffer), to be affected similarly (Eng., sympathy), to have compassion upon, Heb. 10:34, of compassionating those in prison, is translated "be touched with" in Heb. 4:15, of Christ as the High Priest. See TOUCH. ¶
NT: B.778d; CB.1270b; K.798.
OT: –.
GEN. REF.: IS.1:755; NB.–; Z.–.

4. *eleeō* [ἐλεέω, 1653], to have mercy (*eleos*, mercy), to show kindness, by beneficence, or assistance, is translated "have compassion" in Matt. 18:33 (A.V.); Mark 5:19 and Jude 22. See MERCY.
NT: B.249c; CB.1244a; K.222.
OT: ḥānan: S.2603; HR.449c.6a; H.694,695; BD.335d.
rāḥam: S.7355; HR.449c.14; H.2146; BD.933c.
GEN. REF.: IS.1:755; NB.246; Z.1:932.

5. *metriopatheō* [μετριοπαθέω, 3356], is rendered "have compassion," in Heb. 5:2, A.V. See BEAR, No. 13. ¶
NT: B.514d; CB.–; K.798.
OT: –.
GEN. REF.: –.

B. Nouns.

1. *oiktirmos* [οἰκτιρμός, 3628], akin to A, No. 1, is used with *splanchna* (see below), the viscera, the inward parts, as the seat of emotion, the "heart," Phil. 2:1; Col. 3:12, "a heart of compassion" (A.V., "bowels of mercies"). In Heb. 10:28 it is used with *chōris*, "without," (lit., 'without compassions'). It is translated "mercies" in Rom. 12:1 and 2 Cor. 1:3. See MERCY. ¶
NT: B.561d; CB.1260c; K.680.
OT: raḥam: S.7356; HR.983a.2a; H.2146a; BD.933b.
GEN. REF.: IS.1:755; NB.246; Z.1:932.

2. *splanchnon* [σπλάγχνον, 4698], always used in the plural, is suitably rendered "compassion," in the R.V. of Col. 3:12 and 1 John 3:17; "compassions" in Phil. 2:1. Cp. A, No. 2. See BOWELS.
NT: B.763a; CB.1269c; K.1067.
OT: –.
GEN. REF.: IS.1:755; NB.–; Z.–.

C. Adjective.

sumpathēs [συμπαθής, 4835], denotes suffering with, "compassionate," 1 Pet. 3:8, R.V. (A.V., "having compassion"). See A, No. 3. ¶
NT: B.779a; CB.–; K.798.
OT: 'ābēl: S.57; HR.1304c.1; H.6b; BD.5d.
GEN. REF.: IS.1:755; NB.–; Z.–.

COMPEL

1. *anankazō* [ἀναγκάζω, 315], denotes to put constraint upon (from *anankē*, necessity), to constrain, whether by threat, entreaty, force or persuasion; Christ "constrained" the disciples to get into a boat, Matt. 14:22; Mark 6:45; the servants of the man who made a great supper were to constrain people to come in, Luke 14:23 (R.V., "constrain"); Saul of Tarsus "strove"

to make saints blaspheme, Acts 26:11, R.V., (A.V., "compelled"); Titus, though a Greek, was not "compelled" to be circumcised, Gal. 2:3, as Galatian converts were, 6:12, R.V.; Peter was "compelling" Gentiles to live as Jews, Gal. 2:14; Paul was "constrained" to appeal to Caesar, Acts 28:19, and was "compelled" by the church at Corinth to become foolish in speaking of himself, 2 Cor. 12:11. See CONSTRAIN. ¶
NT: B.52a; CB.1235b; K.55.
OT: —.
GEN. REF.: IS.1:755; NB.—; Z.—.

2. *angareuō* [ἀγγαρεύω, 29], to despatch as an *angaros* (a Persian courier kept at regular stages with power of impressing men into service), and hence, in general, to impress into service, is used of compelling a person to go a mile, Matt. 5:41; of the impressing of Simon to bear Christ's Cross, Matt. 27:32; Mark 15:21. ¶
NT: B.6d; CB.—; K.—.
OT: —.
GEN. REF.: —.

COMPLAINER, COMPLAINT

1. *mempsimoiros* [μεμψίμοιρος, 3202], denotes one who complains, lit., complaining of one's lot (*memphomai*, to blame, *moira*, a fate, lot); hence, discontented, querulous, repining; it is rendered "complainers" in Jude 16. ¶
NT: B.502c; CB.1258b; K.580.
OT: —.
GEN. REF.: —.

2. *momphē* [μομφή, 3437], denotes blame (akin to *memphomai*, see No. 1), an occasion of complaint, Col. 3:13 (A.V., "quarrel"). See QUARREL. ¶
NT: B.527a; CB.—; K.580.
OT: —.
GEN. REF.: IS.1:755; NB.—; Z.—.

3. *aitiōma* [αἰτίωμα, 157], a charge, is translated "complaints" in Acts 25:7, A.V. See CHARGE. ¶
NT: B.26d; CB.1234a; K.—.
OT: —.
GEN. REF.: —.

COMPLETE, COMPLETION, COMPLETELY

A. Verbs.

1. *epiteleō* [ἐπιτελέω], to complete: see ACCOMPLISH, No. 4.

2. *exartizō* [ἐξαρτίζω, 1822], to fit out (*ek*, out, intensive, *artos*, a joint; or from *artios*, perfect, lit., exactly right), is said of the equipment of the man of God, 2 Tim. 3:17, "furnished completely" (A.V., "thoroughly furnished"); elsewhere in Acts 21:5, "accomplished." Cp. B. See FURNISH. ¶
NT: B.273c; CB.1247c; K.80.
OT: ḥābar: S.2266; HR.490a.1; H.598; BD.287d.
GEN. REF.: —.

3. *sunteleō* [συντελέω, 4931], to end together, bring quite to an end (*sun*, together, intensive, *telos*, an end), is said (*a*) of the completion of a period of days, Luke 4:2; Acts 21:27; (*b*) of completing something; some mss. have it in Matt. 7:28, of the Lord, in ending His discourse (the best mss. have *teleō* to finish); of God, in finishing a work, Rom. 9:28, in making a new covenant, Heb. 8:8, marg., "accomplish"; of the fulfilment of things foretold, Mark 13:4; of the Devil's temptation of the Lord, Luke 4:13. See END, FINISH, FULFIL, MAKE. ¶
NT: B.792a; CB.1271a; K.1161.
OT: kālāh: S.3615; HR.1319b.7; H.982-984; BD.477b.
tāmam: S.8552; HR.1319b.16a; H.2522; BD.1070b.
GEN. REF.: IS.2:366; NB.—; Z.—.

4. *plēroō* [πληρόω, 4137], to fill (in the Passive Voice, to be made full), is translated "complete" in the A.V. of Col. 2:10 (R.V., "made full"; cp. v. 9). See ACCOMPLISH.
NT: B.670c; CB.1265b; K.867.
OT: mālē': S.4390; HR.1147c.2a.b.c; H.1195; BD.569d.
GEN. REF.: IS.2:366; NB.—; Z.—.

5. *plerophoreō* [πληροφορέω, 4135], to be fully assured, is translated "complete" in Col. 4:12. See ASSURED, B, No. 2.
NT: B.670b; CB.1265b; K.867.
OT: mālē': S.4390; HR.1148b.1; H.1195; BD.569d.
GEN. REF.: IS.2:366; NB.—; Z.—.

B. Adjective.

artios [ἄρτιος, 739], fitted, complete (from *artos*, a limb, joint), is used in 2 Tim. 3:17, R.V., "complete;" A.V., "perfect." See PERFECT. ¶
NT: B.110c; CB.1237c; K.80.
OT: —.
GEN. REF.: —.

C. Noun.

apartismos [ἀπαρτισμός, 535], is rendered "complete" in Luke 14:28, R.V. ¶
NT: B.81b; CB.—; K.—.
OT: —.
GEN. REF.: —.

For **COMPREHEND** see **APPREHEND**, John 1:5, A.V., and **SUM UP**

CONCEAL

parakaluptō [παρακαλύπτω, 3871], to conceal thoroughly (*para*, beside, intensive, *kaluptō*, to hide), is found in Luke 9:45, of concealing from the disciples the fact of the delivering up of Christ.
NT: B.617d; CB.—; K.—.
OT: 'ālam: S.5956; HR.1060c.1; H.1629; BD.761a.
GEN. REF.: IS.1:756; NB.—; Z.—.

CONCEITS

1. *en heautois* [ἐν ἑαυτοῖς, 1438], lit., 'in yourselves,' is used with *phronimos*, "wise," in Rom. 11:25, "(wise) in your own conceits (i.e., opinions)."
NT: B.211d; CB.1249b; K.–.
OT: –.
GEN. REF.: –.

2. *par' heautois* [παρ' ἑαυτοῖς, 1438], (*para*, with, in the estimation of), in Rom. 12:16 has the same rendering as No. 1.
NT: B.211d; CB.1249b; K.–.
OT: –.
GEN. REF.: –.

CONCEIVE

1. *gennaō* [γεννάω], to conceive, beget: see BEGET, A, No. 1.

2. *sullambanō* [συλλαμβάνω, 4815], lit., to take together (*sun*, with, *lambanō*, to take or receive), is used (*a*) of a woman, to conceive, Luke 1:24, 31, 36; in the Passive Voice. Luke 2:21; (*b*) metaphorically, of the impulse of lust in the human heart, enticing to sin, Jas. 1:15. For its other meanings see CATCH, No. 8.
NT: B.776d; CB.1270b; K.1101.
OT: hārāh: S.2029; HR.1301c.1a; H.515; BD.247c.
GEN. REF.: IS.1:756; NB.–; Z.–.

3. *tithēmi* [τίθημι, 5087], to put, set, is used in Acts 5:4, of the sin of Ananias, in conceiving a lie in his heart.
NT: B.815d; CB.1272c; K.1176.
OT: sûm, sîm: S.7760; HR.1348c.25; H.2243; BD.962c.
GEN. REF.: –.

Notes: (1) The phrase *echō*, to have, with *koitē*, a lying down, a bed, especially the marriage bed, denotes to conceive, Rom. 9:10. ¶

(2) The phrase *eis katabolēn*, lit., for a casting down, or in, is used of conception in Heb. 11:11. ¶

CONCERN (-ETH)

1. The neuter plural of the article ('the things'), with the genitive case of a noun, is used in 2 Cor. 11:30 of Paul's infirmity, "the things that concern my infirmity," lit., 'the (things) of my infirmity.'

2. The neuter singular of the article, with the preposition *peri*, concerning, is used by the Lord in Luke 22:37, "that which concerneth," lit., 'the (thing) concerning (Me).' The same construction is found in Luke 24:27; Acts 19:8; 28:31.

CONCERNING: see Note †, p. 9.

CONCISION

katatomē [κατατομή, 2699], lit., a cutting off (*kata*, down, *temnō*, to cut), a mutilation, is a term found in Phil. 3:2, there used by the Apostle, by a paranomasia, contemptuously, for the Jewish circumcision with its Judaistic influence, in contrast to the true spiritual circumcision. ¶
NT: B.419d; CB.1254b; K.1169.
OT: –.
GEN. REF.: –.

CONCLUDE

sumbibazō [συμβιβάζω, 4822], lit., to make to come together, is translated "concluding" in Acts 16:10, R.V., for the A.V., "assuredly gathering." See COMPACTED, INSTRUCT, KNIT, PROVE.
NT: B.777d; CB.–; K.1101.
OT: –.
GEN. REF.: –.

Notes: (1) For *krinō*, to judge, give judgment, rendered "concluded" in the A.V. of Acts 21:25, R.V., "giving judgment," see JUDGMENT.

(2) For *logizomai*, to reckon, translated "conclude" in Rom. 3:28, A.V., R.V., "reckon," see RECKON.

(3) For *sunkleiō*, to shut up with, translated "concluded" in Rom. 11:32; Gal. 3:22, A.V., R.V., "shut up," see INCLOSE, SHUT

CONCORD

sumphōnēsis [συμφώνησις, 4857], lit., a sounding together (*sun*, with, *phōnē*, a sound; Eng., symphony), is found in 2 Cor. 6:15, in the rhetorical question "what concord hath Christ with Belial?" See AGREE, A, No. 1. ¶
NT: B.781a; CB.–; K.1287.
OT: –.
GEN. REF.: –.

CONCOURSE

suntrophē [συντροφή, 4963], a turning together (*sun*, with, *trepō*, to turn), signifies (*a*) that which is rolled together; hence (*b*) a dense mass of people, concourse, Acts 19:40. ¶ See BANDED.
NT: B.795c; CB.–; K.–.
OT: –.
GEN. REF.: IS.1:758; NB.–; Z.–.

For CONCUPISCENCE (A.V. of Rom. 7:8; Col. 3:5; 1 Thess. 4:5), see COVET, DESIRE, LUST

CONDEMN, CONDEMNATION

A. Verbs.

1. *kataginōskō* [καταγινώσκω, 2607], to know something against (*kata*, against, *ginōskō*,

to know by experience), hence, to think ill of, to condemn, is said, in Gal. 2:11, of Peter's conduct (R.V., "stood condemned"), he being self-condemned as the result of an exercised and enlightened conscience, and condemned in the sight of others; so of self-condemnation due to an exercise of heart, 1 John 3:20, 21. See BLAME. ¶

NT: B.409d; CB.1254a; K.—.
OT: ḥāqar: S.2713; HR.730a.1; H.729; BD.350c.
rāsha': S.7561; HR.730a.2; H.2222; BD.957d.
GEN. REF.: IS.1:759; NB.—; Z.1:935.

2. *katadikazō* [καταδικάζω, 2613], signifies to exercise right or law against anyone; hence, to pronounce judgment, to condemn (*kata*, down, or against, *dikē*, justice), Matt. 12:7, 37; Luke 6:37; Jas. 5:6. ¶

NT: B.410b; CB.1254a; K.418.
OT: ḥûb: S.2325; HR.730b.1; H.614; BD.295a.
rāsha': S.7561; HR.730b.3a; H.2222; BD.957d.
GEN. REF.: IS.1:759; NB.—; Z.1:935.

3. *krinō* [κρίνω, 2919], to distinguish, choose, give an opinion upon, judge, sometimes denotes to condemn, e.g., Acts 13:27; Rom. 2:27; Jas. 5:9 (in the best mss.). Cp. No. 1, below. See CALL (No. 13), CONCLUDE, DECREE, DETERMINE, ESTEEM, JUDGE, LAW (go to), ORDAIN, SUE, THINK.

NT: B.451b; CB.1256a; K.469.
OT: rîb: S.7378; HR.787b.8a; H.2159; BD.936b.
shāphaṭ: S.8199; HR.787b.10a; H.2443; BD.1047a.
GEN. REF.: IS.1:759; NB.—; Z.1:935.

4. *katakrinō* [κατακρίνω, 2632], a strengthened form of No. 3, signifies to give judgment against, pass sentence upon; hence to condemn, implying (*a*) the fact of a crime, e.g., Rom. 2:1; 14:23; 2 Pet. 2:6; some mss. have it in Jas. 5:9; (*b*) the imputation of a crime, as in the condemnation of Christ by the Jews, Matt. 20:18; Mark 14:64. It is used metaphorically of condemning by a good example, Matt. 12:41, 42; Luke 11:31, 32; Heb. 11:7.

In Rom. 8:3, God's condemnation of sin is set forth in that Christ, His own Son, sent by Him to partake of human nature (sin apart) and to become an offering for sin, died under the judgment due to our sin.

NT: B.412a; CB.1254a; K.469.
OT: gāzar: S.1504; HR.734c.1; H.340; BD.160b.
GEN. REF.: IS.1:759; NB.—; Z.1:935.

B. Nouns.

1. *krima* [κρίμα, 2917], denotes (*a*) the sentence pronounced, a verdict, a condemnation, the decision resulting from an investigation, e.g., Mark 12:40; Luke 23:40; 1 Tim. 3:6; Jude 4; (*b*) the process of judgment leading to a decision, 1 Pet. 4:17 ("judgment"), where *krisis* (see No. 3, below) might be expected. In Luke 24:20, "to be condemned" translates the phrase *eis krima*, "unto condemnation" (i.e., unto the pronouncement of the sentence of condemnation). For the rendering "judgment," see, e.g., Rom. 11:33; 1 Cor. 11:34; Gal. 5:10; Jas. 3:1. In these (*a*) the process leading to a decision and (*b*) the pronouncement of the decision, the verdict, are to be distinguished. In 1 Cor. 6:7 the word means a matter for judgment, a lawsuit. See JUDGMENT.

NT: B.450c; CB.1256a; K.469.
OT: mishpāṭ: S.4941; HR.786b.7b; H.2443c; BD.1048b.
GEN. REF.: IS.1:759; NB.—; Z.1:935.

2. *katakrima* [κατάκριμα, 2631], cp. No. 4, above, is the sentence pronounced, the condemnation with a suggestion of the punishment following; it is found in Rom. 5:16, 18; 8:1. ¶

NT: B.412a; CB.1254a; K.469.
OT: —.
GEN. REF.: IS.1:759; NB.—; Z.1:935.

3. *krisis* [κρίσις, 2920], (*a*) denotes the process of investigation, the act of distinguishing and separating (as distinct from *krima*, see No. 1 above); hence a judging, a passing of judgment upon a person or thing; it has a variety of meanings, such as judicial authority, John 5:22, 27; justice, Acts 8:33; Jas. 2:13; a tribunal, Matt. 5:21, 22; a trial, John 5:24; 2 Pet. 2:4; a judgment, 2 Pet. 2:11; Jude 9; by metonymy, the standard of judgment, just dealing, Matt. 12:18, 20; 23:23; Luke 11:42; Divine judgment executed, 2 Thess. 1:5; Rev. 16:7; (*b*) sometimes it has the meaning "condemnation," and is virtually equivalent to *krima* (*a*); see Matt. 23:33; John 3:19; Jas. 5:12, *hupo krisin*, "under judgment." See ACCUSATION, A (Note), DAMNATION, JUDGMENT.

NT: B.452c; CB.1256a; K.469.
OT: rîb: S.7379; HR.789c.7b; H.2159a; BD.936d.
mishpāṭ: S.4941; HR.789c.8d; H.2443c; BD.1048b.
GEN. REF.: IS.1:759; NB.—; Z.1:935.

Note: In John 9:39, "For Judgment (*krima*) came I into this world," the meaning would appear to be, 'for being judged' (as a touchstone for proving men's thoughts and characters), in contrast to 5:22, 'hath given all judging (*krisis*) to the Son'; in Luke 24:20, "delivered Him up to be condemned to death," the latter phrase is, lit., 'to a verdict (*krima*) of death' (which they themselves could not carry out); in Mark 12:40, "these shall receive greater condemnation" (*krima*), the phrase signifies a heavier verdict (against themselves).

4. *katakrisis* [κατάκρισις, 2633], a strengthened form of No. 3, denotes a judgment against, condemnation, with the suggestion of the process leading to it, as of "the ministration

of condemnation," 2 Cor. 3:9; in 7:3, "to condemn," more lit., 'with a view to condemnation.' ¶
NT: B.412b; CB.1254a; K.469.
OT: –.
GEN. REF.: IS.1:759; NB.–; Z.1:935.

C. Adjectives.

1. *autokatakritos* [αὐτοκατάκριτος, 843], self-condemned (*auto*, self, *katakrinō*, to condemn), i.e., on account of doing himself what he condemns in others, is used in Tit. 3:11. ¶
NT: B.122c; CB.1238b; K.469.
OT: –.
GEN. REF.: IS.1:759; NB.–; Z.–.

2. *akatagnōstos* [ἀκατάγνωστος, 176], akin to A, No. 1, with negative prefix, *a*, "not to be condemned," is said of sound speech, in Tit. 2:8. ¶
NT: B.29d; CB.–; K.119.
OT: –.
GEN. REF.: IS.–; NB.–; Z.1:935.

CONDESCEND

sunapagō [συναπάγω]: see **CARRY**, No. 7

CONDITIONS

Note: This translates the phrase *ta pros* in Luke 14:32, lit., 'the (things) towards,' i.e., the things relating to, or conditions of, (peace).

CONDUCT

A. Noun.

agōgē [ἀγωγή, 72], from *agō*, to lead, properly denotes a teaching; then, figuratively, a training, discipline, and so, the life led, a way or course of life, conduct, 2 Tim. 3:10, R.V., "conduct"; A.V., "manner of life." See LIFE. ¶
NT: B.14d; CB.1233c; K.–.
OT: –.
GEN. REF.: –.

B. Verbs.

1. *kathistēmi* [καθίστημι, 2525], lit., to stand down or set down (*kata*, down, *histēmi*, to stand), has, among its various meanings, the significance of bringing to a certain place, conducting, Acts 17:15 (so the Sept. in Josh. 6:23; 1 Sam. 5:3; 2 Chron. 28:15). See APPOINT.
NT: B.390b; CB.1254c; K.387.
OT: bô': S.935; HR.702c.2b; H.212; BD.97c.
nûaḥ: S.5117; HR.702c.10; H.1323; BD.628a.
shûb: S.7725; HR.703a.20b; H.2340; BD.996d.
GEN. REF.: –.

2. *propempō* [προπέμπω, 4311], signifies to set forward, conduct: see ACCOMPANY, No. 4.
NT: B.709b; CB.–; K.–.
OT: –.
GEN. REF.: –.

CONFER, CONFERENCE

1. *prosanatithēmi* [προσανατίθημι, 4323], lit., to put before (*pros*, towards, *ana*, up, and *tithēmi*, to put), i.e., to lay a matter before others so as to obtain counsel or instruction, is used of Paul's refraining from consulting human beings, Gal. 1:16 (translated "imparted" in 2:6; A.V., "added . . . in conference"). Cp. the shorter form *anatithēmi*, in 2:2, "laid before," the less intensive word being used there simply to signify the imparting of information, rather than conferring with others to seek advice. See ADD, IMPART. ¶
NT: B.711d; CB.–; K.57.
OT: –.
GEN. REF.:–.

2. *sullaleō* [συλλαλέω, 4814], to speak together with (*sun*, with, *laleō*, to speak), is translated "conferred" in Acts 25:12; elsewhere of talking with Matt. 17:3; Mark 9:4; Luke 4:36; 9:30; "communed" in Luke 22:4. See COMMUNE, SPEAK, TALK. ¶
NT: B.776d; CB.–; K.–.
OT: dābar: S.1696; HR.1301c.1; H.399; BD.180b.
sîaḥ: S.7878; HR.1301c.2; H.2255; BD.967a.
GEN. REF.: –.

3. *sumballō* [συμβάλλω, 4820], lit., to throw together (*sun*, with, *ballō*, to throw), is used of conversation, to discourse or consult together, confer, Acts 4:15. See ENCOUNTER, HELP, MEET WITH, PONDER.
NT: B.777b; CB.–; K.–.
OT: gārāh: S.1624; HR.1303a.1; H.378; BD.173b.
sûṭ: S.3249; HR.1303a.3; H.1480; BD.694c.
GEN. REF.: –.

Note: For the A.V., "conference" in Gal. 2:6, see No. 1, above.

CONFESS, CONFESSION

A. Verbs.

1. *homologeō* [ὁμολογέω, 3670], lit., to speak the same thing (*homos*, same, *legō*, to speak), to assent, accord, agree with, denotes, either (*a*) to confess, declare, admit, John 1:20; e.g., Acts 24:14; Heb. 11:13; (*b*) to confess by way of admitting oneself guilty of what one is accused of, the result of inward conviction, 1 John 1:9; (*c*) to declare openly by way of speaking out freely, such confession being the effect of deep conviction of facts, Matt. 7:23; 10:32 (twice) and Luke 12:8 (see next par.); John 9:22; 12:42; Acts 23:8; Rom. 10:9, 10 ("confession is made"); 1 Tim. 6:12 (R.V.); Tit. 1:16; 1 John 2:23; 4:2, 15; 2 John 7 (in John's Epp. it is the necessary antithesis to Gnostic doceticism); Rev. 3:5, in the best mss. (some have No. 2 here); (*d*) to confess by way of celebrating with

praise, Heb. 13:15; (*e*) to promise, Matt. 14:7.

In Matt. 10:32 and Luke 12:8 the construction of this verb with *en*, in, followed by the dative case of the personal pronoun, has a special significance, namely, to confess in a person's name, the nature of the confession being determined by the context, the suggestion being to make a public confession. Thus the statement, "every one . . . who shall confess Me (lit., in Me, i.e., in My case) before men, him (lit., in him, i.e., in his case) will I also confess before My Father . . .," conveys the thought of confessing allegiance to Christ as one's Master and Lord, and, on the other hand, of acknowledgment, on His part, of the faithful one as being His worshipper and servant, His loyal follower; this is appropriate to the original idea in *homologeō* of being identified in thought or language. See PROFESS, PROMISE, THANK. ¶

NT: B.568a; CB.–; K.–.
OT: yādāh: S.3034; HR.993c.1; H.847; BD.392b.
nādar: S.5087; HR.993c.2; H.1308; BD.623d.
shāba': S.7650; HR.993c.3; H.2318; BD.989a.
GEN. REF.: IS.1:759; NB.247; Z.–.

2. *exomologeō* [ἐξομολογέω, 1843], *ek*, out, intensive, and No. 1, and accordingly stronger than No. 1, to confess forth, i.e., freely, openly, is used (*a*) of a public acknowledgment or confession of sins, Matt. 3:6; Mark 1:5; Acts 19:18; jas. 5:16; (*b*) to profess or acknowledge openly, Matt. 11:25 (translated "thank," but indicating the fuller idea); Phil. 2:11 (some mss. have it in Rev. 3:5: see No. 1); (*c*) to confess by way of celebrating, giving praise, Rom. 14:11; 15:9. In Luke 10:21, it is translated "I thank," the true meaning being 'I gladly acknowledge.' In Luke 22:6 it signifies to consent (R.V.), for A.V., "promised." See CONSENT, PROMISE, THANK. ¶

NT: B.277a; CB.–; K.687.
OT: –.
GEN. REF.: IS.1:759; NB.247; Z.–.

B. Noun.

homologia [ὁμολογία, 3671], akin to A, No. 1, denotes confession, by acknowledgment of the truth, 2 Cor. 9:13; 1 Tim. 6:12, 13; Heb. 3:1; 4:14; 10:23 (A.V., incorrectly, "profession," except in 1 Tim. 6:13). ¶

NT: B.568d; CB.–; K.687.
OT: n^{e}dābāh: S.5071; HR.993c.1; H.1299a; BD.621d.
neder: S.5088; HR.993c.2; H.1308a; BD.623d.
GEN. REF.: IS.1:759; NB.247; Z.–.

Note: For the adverb *homologoumenōs*, confessedly, see CONTROVERSY.

CONFIDENCE (Noun, or Verb with "have"), CONFIDENT (-LY)

A. Nouns.

1. *pepoithēsis* [πεποίθησις, 4006], akin to *peithō*, B, No. 1 below, denotes persuasion, assurance, confidence, 2 Cor. 1:15; 3:4, A.V., "trust"; 8:22; 10:2; Eph. 3:12; Phil. 3:4. See TRUST. ¶

NT: B.643b; CB.1263b; K.818.
OT: biṭṭāḥôn: S.986; HR.1119b.1; H.233c; BD.105c.
GEN. REF.: IS.1:760; NB.–; Z.–.

2. *hupostasis* [ὑπόστασις, 5287], lit., a standing under (*hupo*, under, *stasis*, a standing), that which stands, or is set, under, a foundation, beginning; hence, the quality of confidence which leads one to stand under, endure, or undertake anything, 2 Cor. 9:4; 11:17; Heb. 3:14. Twice in Heb. it signifies substance, 1:3 (A.V., "Person") and 11:1. See SUBSTANCE. ¶

NT: B.847a; CB.1252b; K.1237.
OT: ma'amād: S.4613; HR.1417a.4; H.1637e; BD.765c.
nāṣab: S.5324; HR.1417a.6; H.1398; BD.662a.
tôtelet: S.8431; HR.1417a.9; H.859b; BD.404b.
GEN. REF.: IS.1:760; NB.–; Z.–.

3. *parrhēsia* [παῤῥησία, 3954], often rendered "confidence" in the A.V., is in all such instances rendered "boldness" in the R.V., Acts 28:31; Heb. 3:6; 1 John 2:28; 3:21; 5:14. See BOLDNESS, OPENLY, PLAINNESS.

NT: B.630c; CB.1262c; K.794.
OT: qom^{e}miyyût: S.6968; HR.1073a.1; H.1999e; BD.879c.
GEN. REF.: IS.1:760; NB.–; Z.–.

B. Verbs.

1. *peithō* [πείθω, 3982], to persuade, or, intransitively, to have confidence, to be confident (cp. A, No. 1), has this meaning in the following, Rom. 2:19; 2 Cor. 2:3; Gal. 5:10; Phil. 1:6, 14 (R.V., "being confident," for A.V., "waxing confident"), 25; 3:3, 4; 2 Thess. 3:4; Philm. 21. See AGREE, ASSURE, BELIEVE, OBEY, PERSUADE, TRUST, YIELD.

NT: B.639a; CB.1263a; K.818.
OT: bāṭaḥ: S.982; HR.1114b.2a; H.233; BD.105a.
beṭaḥ: S.983; HR.1114b.11a,b; H.233a; BD.105b.
GEN. REF.: IS.1:760; NB.–; Z.–.

2. *tharreō* [θαρρέω, 2292], to be of good courage, is so translated in the R.V. of 2 Cor. 5:6; 7:16 (A.V., to have confidence, or be confident). See COURAGE.

NT: B.352a; CB.1271c; K.315.
OT: yārē' (+ neg): S.3372; HR.626c.3; H.907,908; BD.431a.
GEN. REF.: IS.1:760; NB.–; Z.–.

Note: The adverb "confidently" is combined with the verb "affirm" to represent the verbs *diischurizomai*, Luke 22:59 and Acts 12:15, R.V. (A.V., "constantly affirmed"), ¶, and *diabebaioomai*, 1 Tim. 1:7, A.V., "affirm," and Tit. 3:8, A.V., "affirm constantly." See AFFIRM. ¶

CONFIRM, CONFIRMATION

A. Verbs.

1. *bebaioō* [βεβαιόω, 950], to make firm, establish, make secure (the connected adjective *bebaios* signifies stable, fast, firm), is used of

confirming a word, Mark 16:20; promises, Rom. 15:8; the testimony of Christ, 1 Cor. 1:6; the saints by the Lord Jesus Christ, 1 Cor. 1:8; the saints by God, 2 Cor. 1:21 ("stablisheth"); in faith, Col. 2:7; the salvation spoken through the Lord and confirmed by the Apostles, Heb. 2:3; the heart by grace, Heb. 13:9 ("stablished"). ¶

NT: B.138c; CB.1239a; K.103.
OT: nāṣab: S.5324; HR.216b.1; H.1398; BD.662a.
qûm: S.6965; HR.216b.2; H.1999; BD.877c,878c.
GEN. REF.: IS.1:760; NB.248; Z.1:939.

2. *epistērizō* [ἐπιστηρίζω, 1991], to make to lean upon, strengthen (*epi*, upon, *stērix*, a prop, support), is used of confirming souls, Acts 14:22; brethren, 15:32; churches, 15:41; disciples, 18:23, in some mss. ("stablishing," R.V., "strengthening," A.V.); the most authentic mss. have *stērizō* in 18:23. See STRENGTHEN. ¶

NT: B.300d; CB.1246a; K.1085.
OT: kûn: S.3559; HR.530b.2; H.964; BD.465c.
nāṣab: S.5324; HR.530b.4; H.1398; BD.877c,878c.
sāmak: S.5564; HR.530b.5; H.1514; BD.701d.
GEN. REF.: IS.2:155; NB.248; Z.1:939.

3. *kuroō* [κυρόω, 2964], to make valid, ratify, impart authority or influence (from *kuros*, might, *kurios*, mighty, a head, as supreme in authority), is used of spiritual love, 2 Cor. 2:8; a human covenant, Gal. 3:15. ¶ In the Sept., see Gen. 23:20, e.g.

NT: B.461a; CB.1256b; K.494.
OT: qûm: S.6965; HR.839a.1; H.1999; BD.877c.
GEN. REF.: IS.2:155; NB.248; Z.1:939.

4. *prokuroō* [προκυρόω, 4300], *pro*, before, and No. 3, to confirm or ratify before, is said of the Divine confirmation of a promise given originally to Abraham, Gen. 12, and confirmed by the vision of the furnace and torch, Gen. 15, by the birth of Isaac, Gen. 21, and by the oath of God, Gen. 22, all before the giving of the Law, Gal. 3:17. ¶

NT: B.708b; CB.1266c; K.494.
OT: –.
GEN. REF.: IS.–; NB.248; Z.1:939.

5. *mesiteuō* [μεσιτεύω, 3315], to act as a mediator, to interpose, is rendered "confirmed," in the A.V. of Heb. 6:17 (marg., and R.V., "interposed"). See INTERPOSED. ¶

NT: B.506d; CB.1258b; K.585.
OT: –.
GEN. REF.: IS.–; NB.248; Z.1:939.

B. Noun.

bebaiōsis [βεβαίωσις, 951], akin to A, No. 1, is used in two senses (*a*) of firmness, establishment, said of the confirmation of the Gospel, Phil. 1:7; (*b*) of authoritative validity imparted, said of the settlement of a dispute by an oath to produce confidence, Heb. 6:16. The word is found frequently in the Papyri of the settlement of a business transaction. ¶

NT: B.138d; CB.1239a; K.103.
OT: s^emîtut: S.6783; HR.2116b.1; H.1932a; BD.856c.
GEN. REF.: IS.1:760; NB.248; Z.1:939.

CONFLICT (Noun)

1. *agōn* [ἀγών, 73], from *agō*, to lead, signifies (*a*) a place of assembly, especially the place where the Greeks assembled for the Olympic and Pythian games; (*b*) a contest of athletes, metaphorically, 1 Tim. 6:12; 2 Tim. 4:7, "fight"; Heb. 12:1, "race"; hence, (*c*) the inward conflict of the soul; inward conflict is often the result, or the accompaniment, of outward conflict, Phil. 1:30; 1 Thess. 2:2, implying a contest against spiritual foes, as well as human adversaries; so Col. 2:1, "conflict," A.V.; R.V., "(how greatly) I strive," lit., 'how great a conflict I have.' See CONTENTION, FIGHT, RACE. ¶ Cp. *agōnizomai* (Eng., agonize), 1 Cor. 9:25 etc.

NT: B.15a; CB.1233c; K.20.
OT: –.
GEN. REF.: IS.1:760; NB.–; Z.–.

2. *athlēsis* [ἄθλησις, 119], denotes a combat, contest of athletes; hence, a struggle, fight, Heb. 10:32, with reference to affliction. See FIGHT. ¶ Cp. *athleō*, to strive, 2 Tim. 2:5 (twice). ¶

NT: B.21c; CB.1238a; K.25.
OT: –.
GEN. REF.: –.

CONFORMED, CONFORMABLE

A. Verb.

summorphizō [συμμορφιζω, 4833], to make of like form with another person or thing, to render like (*sun*, with, *morphē*, a form), is found in Phil. 3:10 (in the Passive Participle of the verb), "becoming conformed" (or 'growing into conformity') to the death of Christ, indicating the practical apprehension of the death of the carnal self, and fulfilling his share of the sufferings following upon the sufferings of Christ. Some texts have the alternative verb *summorphoō*, which has practically the same meaning.

NT: B.778d; CB.1270b; K.1102.
OT: –.
GEN. REF.: IS.1:760; NB.–; Z.–.

B. Adjectives.

1. *summorphos* [σύμμορφος, 4832], akin to A, signifies having the same form as another, conformed to; (*a*) of the conformity of children of God "to the image of His Son," Rom. 8:29; (*b*), of their future physical conformity to His body of glory, Phil. 3:21. See FASHION. ¶

NT: B.778d; CB.1270b; K.1102.
OT: –.
GEN. REF.: IS.1:760; NB.–; Z.–.

2. *suschēmatizō* [συσχηματίζω, 4964], to fashion or shape one thing like another, is translated "conformed" in Rom. 12:2, A.V.; R.V., "fashioned"; "fashioning" in 1 Pet. 1:14. This verb has more especial reference to that which is transitory, changeable, unstable; *summorphizō*, to that which is essential in character and thus complete or durable, not merely a form or outline. *Suschēmatizō* could not be used of inward transformation. See FASHION (*schēma*) and FORM (*morphē*). ¶

NT: B.795c; CB.1271a; K.–.
OT: –.
GEN. REF.: IS.1:760; NB.–; Z.–.

CONFOUND, CONFUSE, CONFUSION

A. Nouns.

1. *akatastasia* [ἀκαταστασία, 181], instability, (*a*, negative, *kata*, down, *stasis*, a standing), denotes a state of disorder, disturbance, confusion, tumult, 1 Cor. 14:33; Jas. 3:16, revolution or anarchy; translated "tumults" in Luke 21:9 (A.V., "commotions"); 2 Cor. 6:5; 12:20. See TUMULT. ¶

NT: B.30a; CB.1234b; K.387.
OT: midḥeh: S.4072; HR.44a.1; H.420b; BD.191a.
GEN. REF.: –.

2. *sunchusis* [σύγχυσις, 4799], a pouring or mixing together (*sun*, with, *cheō*, to pour); hence a disturbance, confusion, a tumultuous disorder, as of riotous persons, is found in Acts 19:29. ¶

NT: B.775c; CB.–; K.–.
OT: mᵉhûmāh: S.4103; HR.1301a.2; H.486a; BD.223b.
bābel: S.894; HR.1301a.1; H.197; BD.93c.
GEN. REF.: –.

B. Verbs.

1. *suncheō* [συγχέω, 4797], or *sunchunnō* or *sunchunō* (the verb form of A. 2), lit., to pour together, commingle, hence (said of persons), means to trouble or confuse, to stir up, Acts 19:32 (said of the mind); to be in confusion, 21:31, R.V. (A.V., "was in an uproar"); 21:27, "stirred up"; Acts 2:6; 9:22, "confounded." See STIR, UPROAR. ¶

NT: B.775a; CB.–; K.–.
OT: bālal: S.1101; HR.1301a.1; H.248; BD.117b.
rāgaz: S.7264; HR.1301a.9; H.2112; BD.919a.
GEN. REF.: –.

2. *kataischunō* [καταισχύνω, 2617], to put to shame, is translated "confound" in 1 Cor. 1:27, and 1 Pet. 2:6, A.V. (R.V., "put to shame"). See ASHAMED, DISHONOUR, SHAME.

NT: B.410d; CB.1254a; K.29.
OT: bôsh: S.954; HR.731c.1; H.222; BD.101c.
kālam: S.3637; HR.731c.4; H.987; BD.483d.
GEN. REF.: IS.4:447; NB.–; Z.–.

CONFUTE

diakatelenchomai [διακατελέγχομαι, 1246], to confute powerfully, is an intensive form of *elenchō*, to convict (*dia*, through, *kata*, down, both intensive), Acts 18:28, implying that he met the opposing arguments in turn (*dia*), and brought them down to the ground (*kata*). It carries also the thought that he brought home moral blame to them.

NT: B.184a; CB.–; K.–.
OT: –.
GEN. REF.: –.

CONGREGATION

1. *ekklēsia* [ἐκκλησία, 1577], is translated "congregation" in Heb. 2:12, R.V., instead of the usual rendering "church." See ASSEMBLY.

NT: B.240d; CB.1243c; K.394.
OT: qāhāl: S.6951; HR.433a.1d; H.1991a; BD.874c.
GEN. REF.: IS.1:760; NB.248; Z.1:939.

2. *sunagōgē* [συναγωγή, 4864], is translated "congregation" in Acts 13:43, A.V. (R.V., "synagogue"). See SYNAGOGUE.

NT: B.782d; CB.1270b; K.1108.
OT: ʿēdāh: S.5712; HR.1309b.13; H.878a; BD.417a.
qāhāl: S.6951; HR.1309b.17a; H.1991a; BD.874c.
GEN. REF.: IS.1:760; NB.248; Z.1:939.

CONQUER, CONQUEROR

1. *nikaō* [νικάω, 3528], to overcome (its usual meaning), is translated "conquering" and "to conquer" in Rev. 6:2. See OVERCOME, PREVAIL, VICTORY.

NT: B.539a; CB.1259c; K.634.
OT: nāṣaḥ: S.5329; HR.945b.3; H.1402; BD.663d.
GEN. REF.: IS.1:761; NB.–; Z.–.

2. *hupernikaō* [ὑπερνικάω, 5245], to be more than conqueror (*huper*, over, and No. 1), to gain a surpassing victory, is found in Rom. 8:37, lit., 'we are hyper-conquerors,' i.e., we are preeminently victorious. ¶

NT: B.841c; CB.1252a; K.634.
OT: –.
GEN. REF.: IS.1:761; NB.–; Z.–.

CONSCIENCE

suneidēsis [συνείδησις, 4893], lit., a knowing with (*sun*, with, *oida*, to know), i.e., a co-knowledge (with oneself), the witness borne to one's conduct by conscience, that faculty by which we apprehend the will of God, as that which is designed to govern our lives; hence (*a*) the sense of guiltiness before God; Heb. 10:2; (*b*) that process of thought which distinguishes what it considers morally good or bad, commending the good, condemning the bad, and so prompting to do the former, and avoid the latter; Rom. 2:15 (bearing witness with God's Law); 9:1; 2 Cor. 1:12; acting in a certain way because conscience requires it, Rom. 13:5; so as not to cause scruples of conscience in another, 1 Cor. 10:28, 29; not calling a thing in question unnecessarily, as if conscience demanded it, 1 Cor. 10:25, 27; 'commending oneself to every man's conscience,' 2 Cor. 4:2; cp. 5:11. There may be a conscience not strong enough to distinguish clearly between the lawful and the unlawful, 1 Cor. 8:7, 10, 12 (some regard consciousness as the meaning here). The phrase "conscience toward God," in 1 Pet. 2:19, signifies a conscience (or perhaps here, a consciousness) so controlled by the apprehension of God's presence, that the person realizes that griefs are to be borne in accordance with His will. Heb. 9:9 teaches that sacrifices under the Law could not so perfect a person that he could regard himself as free from guilt.

For various descriptions of conscience see Acts 23:1; 24:16; 1 Cor. 8:7; 1 Tim. 1:5, 19; 3:9; 4:2; 2 Tim. 1:3; Tit. 1:15; Heb. 9:14; 10:22; 13:18; 1 Pet. 3:16, 21. ¶

NT: B.786c; CB.1270c; K.1120.
maddā': S.4093; HR.1313b.1; H.848g; BD.396b.
GEN. REF.: IS.1:761; NB.248; Z.1:941.

CONSECRATE

Note: In Heb. 7:28 the verb *teleioō* is translated "perfected" in the R.V., for A.V., "consecrated"; so in 9:18 and 10:20, *enkainizō*, R.V., "dedicated." See DEDICATE, PERFECT.

CONSENT

A. Verbs.

1. *exmologeō* [ἐξομολογέω, 1843], to agree openly, to acknowledge outwardly, or fully (*ex*, for *ek*, out, intensive), is translated "consented" in the R.V. of Luke 22:6 (A.V., "promised"). See CONFESS, THANK.

NT: B.277a; CB.—; K.687.
OT: yādāh: S.3034; HR.499a.3b; H.847; BD.392a.
GEN. REF.: IS.1:759; NB.—; Z.—.

2. *epineuō* [ἐπινεύω, 1962], lit. signifies to nod to (*epi*, upon or to, *neuō*, to nod); hence, to nod assent, to express approval, consent, Acts 18:20.

NT: B.296c; CB.—; K.—.
OT: nākar: S.5234; HR.526a.1; H.1368; BD.647d.
GEN. REF.: —.

3. *proserchomai* [προσέρχομαι, 4334], to come to, signifies to consent, implying a coming to agreement with, in 1 Tim. 6:3. See COME, No. 10.

NT: B.713a; CB.1267a; K.257.
OT: nāgash: S.5066; HR.1213c.7a; H.1297; BD.620c.
qārab: S.7126; HR.1213c.10a; H.2065; BD.897a.
GEN. REF.: —.

4. *sunkatatithēmi* [συγκατατίθημι, 4784], lit., to put or lay down together with (*sun*, with, *kata*, down, *tithēmi*, to put), was used of depositing one's vote in an urn; hence, to vote for, agree with, consent to. It is said negatively of Joseph of Arimathaea, who had not "consented" to the counsel and deed of the Jews, Luke 23:51 (Middle Voice). ¶

NT: B.773c; CB.—; K.—.
OT: —.
GEN. REF.: —.

5. *sumphēmi* [συμφήμι, 4852], lit., to speak with (*sun*, with, *phēmi*, to speak), hence, to express agreement with, is used of consenting to the Law, agreeing that it is good, Rom. 7:16. ¶

NT: B.780c; CB.—; K.—.
OT: —.
GEN. REF.: —.

6. *suneudokeō* [συνευδοκέω, 4909], lit., to think well with (*sun*, with, *eu*, well, *dokeō*, to think), to take pleasure with others in anything, to approve of, to assent, is used in Luke 11:48, of consenting to the evil deeds of predecessors (A.V., "allow"); in Rom. 1:32, of consenting in doing evil; in Acts 8:1; 22:20, of consenting to the death of another. All these are cases of consenting to evil things. In 1 Cor. 7:.12, 13, it is used of an unbelieving wife's consent to dwell with her converted husband, and of an unbelieving husband's consent to dwell with a believing wife (A.V., "be pleased"; R.V., "be content"). See ALLOW, CONTENT, PLEASE. ¶

NT: B.788d; CB.—; K.—.
OT: —.
GEN. REF.: IS.1:765; NB.—; Z.—.

B. Phrases.

1. *apo mias* (575), lit., 'from one,' is found in Luke 14:18, some word like "consent" being implied; e.g., "with one consent." ¶

NT: B.232b,88c; CB.1236c; K.—.
OT: —.
GEN. REF.: —.

ek sumphōnou [ἐκ συγφωνου, 4859], lit., 'from (or by) agreement' (*sun*, with, *phōnē*, a sound), i.e., by consent, is found in 1 Cor. 7:5. Cp. AGREE. ¶

NT: B.781b; CB.1270b; K.1287.
OT: —.
GEN. REF.: IS.1:72; NB.—; Z.—.

CONSIDER

1. *eidon* [εἶδον, 3708], used as the aorist tense of *horaō*, to see, is translated "to consider" in Acts 15:6, of the gathering of the Apostles and elders regarding the question of circumcision in relation to the Gospel.

NT: B.220c; CB.1243a; K.706.
OT: yāda': S.3045; HR.374b.4a; H.848; BD.393b.
GEN. REF.: —.

2. *suneidon* [συνεῖδον, 4894], *sun*, with, and No. 1, used as the aorist tense of *sunoraō*, to see with one view, to be aware, conscious, as the result of mental perception, is translated "considered" in Acts 12:12, of Peter's consideration of the circumstances of his deliverance from. See KNOW, PRIVY.

NT: B.791c; CB.—; K.—.
OT: yāda': S.3045; HR.1313b.1; H.848; BD.393b.
GEN. REF.: —.

3. *katamanthanō* [καταμανθάνω, 2648], lit., to learn thoroughly (*kata*, down, intensive, *manthanō*, to learn), hence, to note accurately, consider well, is used in the Lord's exhortation to consider the lilies, Matt. 6:28. ¶

NT: B.414d; CB.—; K.552.
OT: shûr: S.7789; HR.739a.4; H.2354; BD.1003d.
rā'āh: S.7200; HR.739a.2; H.2095; BD.906b.
GEN. REF.: —.

4. *noeō* [νοέω, 3539], to perceive with the mind (*nous*), think about, ponder, is translated "consider," only in Paul's exhortation to Timothy in 2 Tim. 2:7. See PERCEIVE, THINK, UNDERSTAND.

NT: B.540b; CB.1259c; K.636.
OT: bîn: S.995; HR.946a.1; H.239; BD.106c.
sākal: S.7919; HR.946a.4; H.2263,2264; BD.968a.
GEN. REF.: IS.4:839; NB.—; Z.—.

5. *katanoeō* [κατανοέω, 2657], to perceive clearly (*kata*, intensive, and No. 4), to understand fully, consider closely, is used of not considering thoroughly the beam in one's own eye, Matt. 7:3 and Luke 6:41 (A.V., "perceivest"); of carefully considering the ravens, Luke 12:24; the lilies, ver. 27; of Peter's full consideration of his vision, Acts 11:6; of Abraham's careful consideration of his own body, and Sarah's womb, as dead, and yet accepting by faith God's promise, Rom. 4:19 (R.V.); of considering fully the Apostle and High Priest of our confession, Heb. 3:1; of thoughtfully considering one another to provoke unto love and good works, Heb. 10:24. It is translated by the verbs behold, Acts 7:31, 32; Jas. 1:23, 24; perceive, Luke 20:23; discover, Acts 27:39. See BEHOLD, DISCOVER, PERCEIVE. ¶

NT: B.415a; CB.1254a; K.636.
OT: bîn: S.995; HR.739c.1; H.239; BD.106c.
nābaṭ: S.5027; HR.739c.3; H.1282; BD.613c.
sākal: S.7919; HR.739c.7; H.2263,2264; BD.968a.
GEN. REF.: —.

6. *logizomai* [λογίζομαι, 3049], signifies to take account of, 2 Cor. 10:7 (R.V., "consider," A.V., "think"), the only place where the R.V. translates it "consider." See ACCOUNT.

NT: B.475d; CB.1257a; K.536.
OT: ḥāshab: S.2803; HR.880a.2a,b,c; H.767; BD.362d.
GEN. REF.: IS.4:839; NB.—; Z.—.

7. *theōreō* [θεωρέω]: see BEHOLD, No. 6.

8. *anatheōreō* [ἀναθεωρέω, 333], to consider carefully: see BEHOLD, No. 7.

NT: B.54c; CB.—; K.—.
OT: —.
GEN. REF.: —.

9. *analogizomai* [ἀναλογίζομαι, 357], to consider, occurs in Heb. 12:3. ¶

NT: B.57b; CB.—; K.—.
OT: —.
GEN. REF.: —.

Notes: (1) *Skopeō*, to look, is translated "looking to" in Gal. 6:1, R.V. (A.V., "considering"). See HEED, LOOK, MARK.

(2) *Suniēmi*, to understand, is translated "considered" in Mark 6:52 (A.V.), R.V., "understood."

(3) In John 11:50 (A.V., *dialogizomai*) the best texts have No. 6.

CONSIST

1. *eimi* [εἰμί, 1510], to be, is rendered "consist" (lit., 'is') in Luke 12:15.

NT: B.222d; CB.1243a; K.206.
OT: —.
GEN. REF.: —.

2. *sunistēmi* [συνίστημι, 4921], *sun*, with, *histēmi*, to stand, denotes, in its intransitive sense, to stand with or fall together, to be constituted, to be compact; it is said of the universe as upheld by the Lord, Col. 1:17, lit., 'by Him all things stand together,' i.e., "consist" (the Latin *consisto*, to stand together, is the exact equivalent of *sunistēmi*). See APPROVE, COMMEND, MAKE, STAND.

NT: B.790c; CB.1270c; K.1120.
OT: ḥātam: S.2856; HR.1317a.2; H.780; BD.367c.
kûn: S.3559; HR.1317a.4; H.964; BD.465c.
GEN. REF.: IS.1:765; NB.—; Z.—.

CONSOLATION, CONSOLE

A. Nouns.

1. *paraklēsis* [παράκλησις, 3874], is translated "consolation," in both A.V. and R.V., in Luke 2:25; 6:24; Acts 15:31; in 1 Cor. 14:3, A.V., "exhortation," R.V., "comfort"; in the following the A.V. has "consolation," the R.V., "comfort," Rom. 15:5; 2 Cor. 1:6, 7; 7:7; Phil. 2:1; 2 Thess. 2:16; Philm. 7; in Acts 4:36, R.V., "exhortation"; in Heb. 6:18, R.V., "encouragement." See COMFORT.

NT: B.618a; CB.1262a; K.778.
OT: nāḥam: S.5162; HR.1061a.1e; H.1344; BD.636d.
tanᵉḥûm: S.8575; HR.1061a.1a,c; H.1144d; BD.637c.
GEN. REF.: IS.1:735; NB.—; Z.1:952.

2. *paramuthia* [παραμυθία, 3889], a comfort, consolation: see COMFORT, A, No. 2.

NT: B.620d; CB.1262b; K.784.
OT: —.
GEN. REF.: IS.1:735; NB.—; Z.1:918.

3. *paramuthion* [παραμύθιον, 3890], an encouragement, "consolation," Phil. 2:1, R.V., in the phrase "consolation of love." See COMFORT, A, No. 3.
NT: B.620d; CB.1262b; K.784.
OT: –.
GEN. REF.: IS.1:735; NB.–; Z.1:918.

B. Verb.

paramutheomai [παραμυθέομαι, 3888], to speak soothingly to, is translated "console," John 11:19, R.V.; in ver. 31 "were comforting"; in 1 Thess. 2:11 and 5:14, A.V., "comforted" and "comfort," R.V., "encouraged" and "encourage."
NT: B.620d; CB.1262b; K.784.
OT: –.
GEN. REF.: IS.1:735; NB.–; Z.1:918.

CONSORT (with)

prosklēroō [προσκληρόω, 4345], lit., to assign by lot (*pros*, to, *klēros*, a lot), to allot, is found in Acts 17:4, "consorted with," imparting to the Passive Voice (the form of the verb there) a Middle Voice significance, i.e., 'they joined themselves to,' or 'threw in their lot with.' The Passive Voice significance can be retained by translating (in the stricter sense of the word), "they were allotted" (i.e., by God) to Paul and Silas, as followers or disciples. ¶
NT: B.716a; CB.1267a; K.442.
OT: –.
GEN. REF.: IS.1:766; NB.–; Z.–.

CONSPIRACY

sunōmosia [συνωμοσία, 4945], denotes, lit., a swearing together (*sun*, with, *omnumi*, to swear), a being leagued by oath, and so a conspiracy, Acts 23:13. ¶
NT: B.793d; CB.–; K.–.
OT: –.
GEN. REF.: IS.1:766; NB.–; Z.–.

For CONSTANTLY see AFFIRM

CONSTRAIN, CONSTRAINT

A. Verbs.

1. *anankazō* [ἀναγκάζω]: see COMPEL, No. 1.

2. *parabiazomai* [παραβιάζομαι, 3849], primarily denotes to employ force contrary to nature and right, to compel by using force (*para*, alongside, intensive, *biazō*, to force), and is used only of constraining by intreaty, as the two going to Emmaus did to Christ, Luke 24:29; as Lydia did to Paul and his companions, Acts 16:15. ¶
NT: B.612a; CB.–; K.–.
OT: pāṣar: S.6484; HR.1056a.3; H.1801; BD.823a.
GEN. REF.: –.

3. *sunechō* [συνέχω, 4912], to hold together, confine, secure, to hold fast (*echō*, to have or hold), to constrain, is said (*a*) of the effect of the word of the Lord upon Paul, Acts 18:5 (A.V., "was pressed in spirit," R.V., "was constrained by the word"); of the effect of the love of Christ, 2 Cor. 5:14; (*b*) of being taken with a disease, Matt. 4:24; Luke 4:38; Acts 28:8; with fear, Luke 8:37; (*c*) of thronging or holding in a person, Luke 8:45; being straitened, Luke 12:50; being in a strait betwixt two, Phil. 1:23; keeping a city in on every side, Luke 19:43; keeping a tight hold on a person, as the men who seized the Lord Jesus did, after bringing Him into the High Priest's house, Luke 22:63; (*d*) of stopping the ears in refusal to listen, Acts 7:57. Luke uses the word nine times out of its twelve occurrences in the N.T. See HOLD, KEEP, No. (1), PRESS, SICK (lie), STOP, STRAIT (be in a), TAKEN (be), THRONG. ¶
NT: B.789a; CB.1270c; K.1117.
OT: kālaʾ: S.3607; HR.1315b.8; H.980; BD.476b.
ʿāṣar: S.6113; HR.1315b.12; H.1675; BD.783c.
GEN. REF.: IS.1:766; NB.–; Z.–.

Note: The verb *echō*, to have, with *anankē*, a necessity, is translated "I was constrained," in Jude 3, R.V. (A.V., "it was needful").

B. Adverb.

anankastōs [ἀναγκαστῶς, 317], akin to A, No. 1, by force, unwillingly, by constraint, is used in 1 Pet. 5:2. ¶
NT: B.52b; CB.1235b; K.–.
OT: –.
GEN. REF.: IS.1:766; NB.–; Z.–.

CONSULT, CONSULTATION

A. Verbs.

1. *bouleuō* [βουλεύω, 1011], used in the Middle Voice, means (*a*) to consult, Luke 14:31; (*b*) to resolve, John 12:10, A.V., "consulted"; R.V., "took counsel." See COUNSEL.
NT: B.145c; CB.1239b; K.–.
OT: yāʿaṣ: S.3289; HR.227a.6; H.887; BD.419c.
ʿûṣ: S.5779; HR.227a.10a; H.1584; BD.734a.
ʿēṣāh: S.6098; HR.227a.10b; H.887a; BD.420a.
GEN. REF.: IS.1:766; NB.–; Z.1:953.

2. *sumbouleuō* [συμβουλεύω, 4823], to take counsel together, is translated "consulted together," in Matt. 26:4, A.V. (R.V., "took counsel.") See COUNSEL.
NT: B.777d; CB.1270b; K.–.
OT: yāʿaṣ: S.3289; HR.1303c.1; H.887; BD.419c.
GEN. REF.: IS.1:766; NB.–; Z.1:953.

B. Noun.

sumboulion [συμβούλιον, 4824], a word of the Graeco-Roman period (akin to A, No. 2), counsel, advice, is translated "consultation" in Mark 15:1 (with *poieō*, to make), to hold a consultation; elsewhere "counsel" in the R.V.,

except in Acts 25:12, where, by metonymy, it means a "council." See COUNCIL.
NT: B.778a; CB.1270b; K.–.
OT: –.
GEN. REF.: IS.–; NB.–; Z.1:953.

CONSUME

1. *analiskō* [ἀναλίσκω, 355], to use up, spend up, especially in a bad sense, to destroy, is said of the destruction of persons, (*a*) literally, Luke 9:54 and the R.V. marg. of 2 Thess. 2:8 (text, "shall slay"); (*b*) metaphorically, Gal. 5:15, "(that) ye be not consumed (one of another)." ¶
NT: B.57a; CB.–; K.–.
OT: 'ākal: S.398; HR.79b.1; H.85; BD.37a.
tāmam: S.8552; HR.79b.6; H.2522; BD.1070b.
kālāh: S.3615; HR.79b.3; H.982-984; BD.477b.
GEN. REF.: IS.1:766; NB.–; Z.–.

2. *katanaliskō* [καταναλίσκω, 2654], to consume utterly, wholly (*kata*, intensive), is said, in Heb. 12:29, of God as "a consuming fire." ¶
NT: B.414d; CB.–; K.–.
OT: 'ākal: S.398; HR.739b.1; H.85; BD.37a.
kāshal: S.3782; HR.739b.2; H.1050; BD.505b.
GEN. REF.: IS.1:766; NB.–; Z.–.

3. *aphanizō* [ἀφανίζω, 853], lit., to cause to disappear, put out of sight, came to mean to do away with (*a*, negative, *phainō*, to cause to appear), said of the destructive work of moth and rust, Matt. 6:19, 20 (R.V., "consume," A.V., "corrupt"). See CORRUPT, DISFIGURE, PERISH, VANISH.
NT: B.124c; CB.1236b; K.–.
OT: shāmad: S.8045; HR.181b.20; H.2406; BD.1029a.
shāmēm: S.8074; HR.181b.21; H.2409; BD.1030d.
ḥāram: S.2763; HR.181b.8; H.744; BD.355c.
GEN. REF.: IS.1:766; NB.–; Z.–.

Note: Dapanaō, to expend, be at an expense, is translated "consume" in the A.V. of James 4:3 (R.V., "spend"). See SPEND.

CONTAIN

1. *chōreō* [χωρέω, 5562], signifies (*a*) lit., to give space, make room (*chōra*, a place); hence, transitively, to have space or room for a thing, to contain, said of the waterpots as containing a certain quantity, John 2:6; of a space large enough to hold a number of people, Mark 2:2; of the world as not possible of containing certain books, John 21:25; (*b*) to go, Matt. 15:17; to have place, John 8:37; to come, 2 Pet. 3:9; (*c*) metaphorically, of receiving with the mind, Matt. 19:11, 12; or into the heart, 2 Cor. 7:2. See COME (No. 24), GO, PLACE, RECEIVE, ROOM. ¶
NT: B.889c; CB.1240a; K.–.
OT: nāsā': S.5375; HR.1482b.4; H.1421; BD.669d.
GEN. REF.: –.

2. *periechō* [περιέχω, 4023], lit., to have round (*peri*, around, *echō*, to have), means to encompass, enclose, contain, as a writing contains details, 1 Pet. 2:6. Some mss. have it in Acts 23:25, lit., 'having this form' (the most authentic have *echō*, to have). For the secondary meaning, amazed (A.V., "astonished"), Luke 5:9 (lit., amazement encompassed, i.e., seized, him). ¶
NT: B.647a; CB.1263b; K.–.
OT: nāqaph: S.5362; HR.1123a.6; H.1415,1416; BD.668c.
kātar: S.3803; HR.1123a.4; H.1060; BD.509c.
'āphaph: S.661; HR.1123a.2; H.148; BD.67d.
GEN. REF.: –.

Notes: (1) The verb *allēgoreō* in Gal. 4:24, R.V., is translated "contain an allegory" (A.V., "are an allegory"), i.e., they apply the facts of the narrative to illustrate principles.

(2) In Eph. 2:15 "the law of commandments contained in ordinances" is, lit., the law of commandments in ordinances.

(3) In Rom. 2:14, the R.V., translating literally, has "the things of the Law"; the A.V. inserts the words "contained in".

(4) In 1 Cor. 7:9, for the A.V., "if they cannot contain," see CONTINENCY.

For **CONTEMPTIBLE**, see **ACCOUNT** No. 6

CONTEND (-ING)

1. *athleō* [ἀθλέω, 118], to engage in a contest (cp. Eng., athlete), to contend in public games, is used in 2 Tim. 2:5, R.V., "contend in the games," for the A.V., "strive for the masteries." See STRIVE. ¶
NT: B.21b; CB.1238a; K.25.
OT: –.
GEN. REF.: IS.–; NB.–; Z.1:953.

Note: In 1 Cor. 9:25, the verb *agōnizomai*, to strive, is used in the same connection, R.V., "striveth in the games." Cp. No. 3.

2. *diakrinō* [διακρίνω, 1252], lit., to separate throughout or wholly (*dia*, asunder, *krinō*, to judge, from a root *kri*, meaning separation), then, to distinguish, decide, signifies, in the Middle Voice, to separate oneself from, or to contend with, as did the circumcisionists with Peter, Acts 11:2; as did Michael with Satan, Jude 9. See R.V. marg. of ver. 22, where the thought may be that of differing in opinion. See DIFFER, DISCERN, DOUBT, JUDGE, PARTIAL, STAGGER, WAVER.
NT: B.185a; CB.1241a; K.469.
OT: shāphat: S.8199; HR.304a.8; H.2443; BD.1047b.
rîb: S.7378; HR.304a.6; H.2159; BD.936b.
dîn: S.1777; HR.304a.4a; H.426; BD.192a.
GEN. REF.: IS.1:767; NB.–; Z.1:953.

3. *epagōnizomai* [ἐπαγωνίζομαι, 1864], signifies to contend about a thing, as a combatant (*epi*, upon or about, intensive, *agōn*, a contest), to contend earnestly, Jude 3. The word

"earnestly' is added to convey the intensive force of the preposition. ¶

NT: B.281b; CB.1245b; K.20.
OT: –.
GEN. REF.: IS.1:767; NB.–; Z.1:953.

CONTENT (to be), CONTENTMENT

A. Verb.

1. *arkeō* [ἀρκέω, 714], primarily signifies to be sufficient, to be possessed of sufficient strength, to be strong, to be enough for a thing; hence, to defend, ward off; in the Middle Voice, to be satisfied, contented with, Luke 3:14, with wages; 1 Tim. 6:8, with food and raiment; Heb. 13:5, with "such things as ye have"; negatively of Diotrephes, in 3 John 10, "not content therewith." See ENOUGH, SUFFICE, SUFFICIENT.

NT: B.107a; CB.1237c; K.78.
OT: hôn: S.1952; HR.158a.2; H.487a; BD.223c.
māṣā': S.4672; HR.158a.4; H.2033; BD.592c.
GEN. REF.: IS.1:767; NB.–; Z.–.

2. *suneudokeō* [συνευδοκέω, 4909], in 1 Cor. 7:12, 13, R.V., signifies to be content: see CONSENT, No. 6.

NT: B.788d; CB.–; K.–.
OT: –.
GEN. REF.: –.

B. Adjectives.

1. *autarkēs* [αὐτάρκης, 842], as found in the papyri writings, means sufficient in oneself (*autos*, self, *arkeō*, see A), self-sufficient, adequate, needing no assistance; hence, content, Phil. 4:11. ¶

NT: B.122b; CB.1238b; K.78.
OT: ḥōq: S.2706; HR.179b.1; H.728a; BD.349b.
GEN. REF.: IS.1:767; NB.250; Z.1:953.

2. *hikanos* [ἱκανός, 2425], sufficient, used with *poieō*, to do, in Mark 15:15, is translated "to content (the multitude)," i.e., to do sufficient to satisfy them. See ABLE.

NT: B.374b; CB.1250c; K.–.
OT: day: S.1767; HR.683c.2; H.425; BD.191b.
hôn: S.1952; HR.683c.3; H.487a; BD.223c.
GEN. REF.: –.

C. Noun.

autarkeia [αὐτάρκεια, 841], contentment, satisfaction with what one has, is found in 1 Tim. 6:6. For its other meaning "sufficiency," in 2 Cor. 9:8, see SUFFICIENCY. ¶

NT: B.122b; CB.1238b; K.78.
OT: –.
GEN. REF.: IS.1:767; NB.250; Z.1:953.

CONTENTION, CONTENTIOUS

A. Nouns.

1. *eris* [ἔρις, 2054], strife, quarrel, especially rivalry, contention, wrangling, as in the church in Corinth, 1 Cor. 1:11, is translated "contentions" in Tit. 3:9, A.V., See DEBATE, STRIFE, VARIANCE.

NT: B.309c; CB.1246c; K.–.
OT: –.
GEN. REF.: IS.4:637; NB.–; Z.1:953.

2. *paroxusmos* [παροξυσμός, 3948], Eng., paroxysm, lit., a sharpening, hence a sharpening of the feeling, or action (*para*, beside, intensive, *oxus*, sharp), denotes an incitement, a sharp contention, Acts 15:39, the effect of irritation; elsewhere in Heb. 10:24, "provoke," unto love. See PROVOKE. ¶

NT: B.629c; CB.1262c; K.791.
OT: qeṣeph: S.7110; HR.1072b.1; H.2058a; BD.893c.
GEN. REF.: IS.1:767; NB.–; Z.1:953.

3. *philoneikia* [φιλονεικία, 5379], lit., love of strife (*phileō*, to love, *neikos*, strife), signifies eagerness to contend; hence, a contention, said of the disciples, Luke 22:24. Cp. B, 2. ¶

NT: B.860d; CB.1264a; K.–.
OT: –.
GEN. REF.: –.

B. Adjectives.

1. *amachos* [ἄμαχος, 269], lit., not fighting (*a*, negative, *machē*, a fight, combat, quarrel), primarily signifying invincible, came to mean not contentious, 1 Tim. 3:3, R.V.; Tit. 3:2 (A.V., "not a brawler," "no brawlers"). ¶

NT: B.44c; CB.1234c; K.573.
OT: –.
GEN. REF.: –.

2. *philoneikos* [φιλόνεικος, 5380], akin to A, No. 3, is used in 1 Cor. 11:16. ¶ In the Sept., Ezek. 3:7, "stubborn." ¶

NT: B.860d; CB.1264a; K.–.
OT: mēṣaḥ: S.4696; HR.1431a.1; H.1233a; BD.594d.
GEN. REF.: IS.1:767; NB.–; Z.–.

Notes: (1) *Eritheia*, "contention," A.V., in Phil. 1:17, is translated "faction," in the R.V. The phrase *hoi ex eritheias*, Rom. 2:8, lit., 'those of strife,' is rendered "contentious," in the A.V.; R.V., "factious." See FACTIOUS, STRIFE.

(2) For *agōn*, a contest, "contention," 1 Thess. 2:2, A.V.; "conflict," R.V., see CONFLICT.

CONTINENCY

enkrateuomai [ἐγκρατεύομαι, 1467], *en*, in, *kratos*, power, strength, lit., to have power over oneself, is rendered "(if) they have (not) continency" (i.e., are lacking in self-control), in 1 Cor. 7:9, R.V.; A.V., "can (not) contain"; in 9:25, "is temperate." See TEMPERATE. ¶

NT: B.216c; CB.1245a; K.196.
OT: 'āphaq: S.662; HR.366c.1; H.149; BD.67c.
GEN. REF.: IS.–; NB.–; Z.1:953.

CONTINUAL, CONTINUALLY (see also CONTINUE)

A. Adverbial Phrases.

1. *eis telos* [εἰς τέλος, 5056], lit., 'unto (the) end,' signifies "continual," in Luke 18:5, of the importunate widow's applications to the unrighteous judge; see also Matt. 10:22; 24:13; Mark 13:13; John 13:1; 1 Thess. 2:16. Cp. *heōs telous*, lit., 'until the end,' 1 Cor. 1:8; 2 Cor. 1:13; ¶ *mechri telous*, ditto, Heb. 3:6, 14; ¶ *achri telous*, Heb. 6:11; Rev. 2:26. ¶

NT: B.811b; CB.1271b; K.1161.
OT: –.
GEN. REF.: –.

2. *dia pantos* [διὰ παντός, 1275], is used of a period throughout or during which anything is done; it is said of the disciples' continuance in the Temple after the Ascension of Christ, Luke 24:53; of the regular entrance of the priests into the first tabernacle, Heb. 9:6, R.V. (A.V. "always"); of the constant sacrifice of praise enjoined upon believers, Heb. 13:15. See also Matt. 18:10; Mark 5:5; Acts 10:2; 24:16; Rom. 11:10; 2 Thess. 3:16, "at all times." See ALWAYS, No. 3, and Note under No. 3 below). ¶

NT: B.179d; CB.–; K.–.
OT: –.
GEN. REF.: –.

3. *eis to diēnekes* [εἰς τὸ διηνεκές, 1336], lit., unto the carried-through (*dia*, through, *enenka*, to carry), i.e., unto (the) unbroken continuance, is used of the continuous Priesthood of Christ, Heb. 7:3, and of the continual offering of sacrifices under the Law, Heb. 10:1. It is translated "for ever," in Heb. 10:12, of the everlasting session of Christ at the right hand of God; and in 10:14, of the everlasting effects of His sacrifice upon "them that are sanctified." See EVER. ¶

NT: B.195a; CB.–; K.–.
OT: –.
GEN. REF.: –.

Note: No. 2 indicates that a certain thing is done frequently through-out a period; No. 3 stresses the unbroken continuity of what is mentioned.

B. Adjective.

adialeiptos [ἀδιάλειπτος, 88], continual, unceasing: see CEASE, B.

NT: B.17b; CB.1233a; K.–.
OT: –.
GEN. REF.: –.

CONTINUE, CONTINUANCE

1. *ginomai* [γίνομαι, 1096], signifies (*a*) to begin to be (suggesting origin); (*b*) to become (suggesting entrance on a new state); (*c*) to come to pass (suggesting effect); hence with the meaning (*c*) it is translated "continued" in Acts 19:10. See ARISE.

NT: B.158a; CB.1248b; K.117.
OT: –.
GEN. REF.: –.

2. *diateleō* [διατελέω, 1300], to bring through to an end (*dia*, through, *telos*, an end), to finish fully or, when used of time, continue right through, is said of continuing fasting up to the time mentioned, Acts 27:33. ¶

NT: B.189c; CB.–; K.–.
OT: hāyāh: S.1961; HR.313a.1; H.491; BD.224a.
kālāh: S.3615; HR.313a.2; H.982-984; BD.477b.
GEN. REF.: –.

3. *menō* [μένω]: see ABIDE.

Compounds of menō with this meaning, are as follows:

4. *diamenō* [διαμένω, 1265], to continue throughout, i.e., without interruption (No. 3 with *dia*, through), is said of the dumbness of Zacharias, Luke 1:22, A.V., "remained"; of the continuance of the disciples with Christ, Luke 22:28; of the permanency of the truth of the Gospel with churches, Gal. 2:5; of the unchanged course of things, 2 Pet. 3:4; of the eternal permanency of Christ, Heb. 1:11. See REMAIN. ¶

NT: B.186c; CB.–; K.–.
OT: 'āmad: S.5975; HR.305c.6; H.1637; BD.763c.
nāṣab: S.5324; HR.305c.5; H.1398; BD.662a.
GEN. REF.: –.

5. *emmenō* [ἐμμένω, 1696], to remain in (*en*, in), is used of abiding in a house, Acts 28:30 (in the best mss.); of continuing in the faith, Acts 14:22; in the Law, Gal. 3:10; in God's Covenant, Heb. 8:9. ¶

NT: B.255b; CB.1244b; K.581.
OT: qûm: S.6965; HR.456a.2; H.1999; BD.877c.
GEN. REF.: –.

6. *epimenō* [ἐπιμένω, 1961], lit., to remain on, i.e., in addition to (*epi*, upon and No. 3), to continue long, still to abide, is used of continuing to ask, John 8:7; to knock, Acts 12:16; in the grace of God, 13:43; in sin, Rom. 6:1; in God's goodness, 11:22; in unbelief, 11:23 (A.V., "abide"); in the flesh, Phil. 1:24; in the faith, Col. 1:23; in doctrine, 1 Tim. 4:16; elsewhere of abiding in a place. See ABIDE, TARRY.

NT: B.296b; CB.1246a; K.–.
OT: māhah: S.4102; HR.525c.1; H.1150; BD.554c.
GEN. REF.: –.

7. *paramenō* [παραμένω, 3887], to remain by or near (*para*, beside, and No. 3), hence, to continue or persevere in anything, is used of the inability of Levitical priests to continue, Heb. 7:23; of persevering in the law of liberty, Jas. 1:25; it is translated "abide" in Phil. 1:25 (2nd clause, in the best mss.), R.V. [see Note (1)], and in 1 Cor. 16:6. See ABIDE. ¶

NT: B.620c; CB.1262a; K.581.
OT: 'āmad: S.5975; HR.1062a.2; H.1637; BD.763c.
GEN. REF.: –.

8. *prosmenō* [προσμένω, 4357], to remain with (*pros*, with, and No. 3), to continue with a person, is said of the people with Christ, Matt. 15:32; Mark 8:2 (A.V., "been with"); of continuing in supplications and prayers, 1 Tim. 5:5. See ABIDE, CLEAVE (unto), TARRY.

NT: B.717c; CB.1267b; K.581.
OT: —.
GEN. REF.: —.

9. *proskartereō* [προσκαρτερέω, 4342], lit., to be strong towards (*pros*, towards, used intensively, and *kartereō*, to be strong), to endure in, or persevere in, to be continually stedfast with a person or thing, is used of continuing in prayer with others, Acts 1:14; Rom. 12:12; Col. 4:2; in the Apostles' teaching, Acts 2:42; in the Temple, 2:46 ("continuing stedfastly," R.V.), the adverb representing the intensive preposition; in prayer and the ministry, 6:4 (R.V., "will continue stedfastly"); of Simon Magus with Philip, 8:13. In Mark 3:9 and Acts 10:7, it signifies to wait on; in Rom. 13:6, to attend continually upon. See ATTEND, INSTANT, WAIT. ¶

NT: B.715c; CB.1267a; K.417.
OT: ḥāzaq: S.2388; HR.1216c.1; H.636; BD.304a.
GEN. REF.: —.

10. *dianuktereuō* [διανυκτερεύω, 1273], to pass the night through (*dia*, through, *nux*, a night), to continue all night, is found in Luke 6:12, of the Lord in spending all night in prayer. ¶

NT: B.187b; CB.1241b; K.—.
OT: —.
GEN. REF.: —.

Notes: (1) The following are translated by the verb to continue, in the A.V., in the places mentioned: *diatribō*, to tarry, (according to inferior mss.) John 11:54; Acts 15:35 (R.V., "tarried"); *histēmi*, to stand, Acts 26:22 (R.V., "stand"); *kathizō*, to sit down, Acts 18:11 (R.V., "dwelt"); *parateinō*, to extend, stretch, Acts 20:7 (R.V., "prolonged"); *paramenō*, to abide together with, Phil. 1:25, R.V., "abide with"; the A.V., "continue" translating *sumparamenō* (in some mss.), marks the difference from the preceding *menō*. See ABIDE, No. 4.

(2) In Rom. 2:7, for A.V., "patient continuance," the R.V. has "patience" (lit., 'according to patience').

(3) In Rev. 13:5 *poieō*, to do, is rendered "to continue."

CONTRADICT, CONTRADICTION

A. Verb.

antilegō [ἀντιλέγω, 483], lit., to speak against (*anti*, against, *legō*, to speak), is translated "contradict" in Acts 13:45. See ANSWER, GAINSAY, SPEAK (against).

NT: B.74d; CB.—; K.—.
OT: —.
GEN. REF.: IS.1:767.

B. Noun.

antilogia [ἀντιλογία, 485], akin to A, is translated "contradiction" in the A.V. of Heb. 7:7; 12:3, "dispute," and "gainsaying." See DISPUTE, GAINSAY, STRIFE.

NT: B.75a; CB.—; K.—.
OT: rîb: S.7379; HR.111b.4a; H.2159a; BD.936d.
m^{e}rîbāh: S.4808; HR.111b.4b; H.2159c; BD.937b.
GEN. REF.: IS.1:767; NB.—; Z.—.

CONTRARIWISE

t'ounantion [τοὐναντίον, 5121], for *to enantion*, the contrary, on the contrary or contrariwise, is used in 2 Cor. 2:7; Gal. 2:7; 1 Pet. 3:9. ¶

NT: B.262a; CB.—; K.—.
OT: —.
GEN. REF.: —.

CONTRARY

A. Verb.

antikeimai [ἀντίκειμαι, 480], to be contrary (*anti*, against, *keimai*, to lie), Gal. 5:17; 1 Tim. 1:10. See ADVERSARY.

NT: B.74b; CB.—; K.425.
OT: 'āyab: S.340; HR.110c.1; H.78; BD.33b.
sāṭan: S.7853; HR.110c.8a; H.2252; BD.966c.
sārar: S.6887; HR.110c.5; H.1973,1974; BD.865c.
GEN. REF.: —.

B. Prepositions.

1. *para* [παρά, 3844], beside, has the meaning "contrary to" in Acts 18:13; Rom. 11:24; 16:17; "other than" in Gal. 1:8.

NT: B.609c; CB.1261c; K.771.
OT: —.
GEN. REF.: —.

2. *apenanti* [ἀπέναντι, 561], lit., from over against, opposite to (*apo*, from, *enantios*, against), is translated "contrary to" in Acts 17:7; "before" in Matt. 27:24; Rom. 3:18; "over against," in Matt. 27:61; "in the presence of," in Acts 3:16. ¶

NT: B.84a; CB.—; K.—.
OT: —.
GEN. REF.: —.

Note: The most authentic mss. have *katenanti*, "over against," in Matt. 21:2.

C. Adjectives.

1. *enantios* [ἐναντίος, 1727], over against (*en*, in, *antios*, against), is used primarily of place, Mark 15:39; of an opposing wind, Matt. 14:24; Mark 6:48; Acts 27:4; metaphorically, opposed as an adversary, antagonistic, Acts 26:9; 1 Thess. 2:15; Tit. 2:8; Acts 28:17, "against." ¶

NT: B.262a; CB.1244c; K.—.
OT: liqra't: S.7125; HR.468b.9; H.2064; BD.896d.
GEN. REF.: —.

2. *hupenantios* [ὑπεναντίος, 5227], *hupo*, under, and No. 1, opposite to, is used of that which is contrary to persons, Col. 2:14, and as a noun, "adversaries," Heb. 10:27. See ADVERSARY. ¶

NT: B.838b; CB.1252a; K.—.
OT: 'āyab: S.340; HR.1407b.1; H.78; BD.33b.
ṣar: S.6862; HR.1407b.2; H.1973-1975; BD.865d.
sānē': S.8130; HR.1407b.4; H.2272; BD.971b.
GEN. REF.: —.

CONTRIBUTION

koinōnia [κοινωνία, 2842], is twice rendered "contribution," Rom. 15:26, and 2 Cor. 9:13, R.V., (A.V., "distribution"). See COMMUNION.

NT: B.438d; CB.1255b; K.447.
OT: tᵉsûmet: S.8667; HR.775a.1; H.2243a; BD.965a.
GEN. REF.: IS.1:767; NB.—; Z.1:954.

CONTROVERSY (without)

homologoumenōs [ὁμολογουμένως, 3672], confessedly, by common consent, akin to *homologeō*, to confess (*homos*, same, *legō*, to speak), is rendered in 1 Tim. 3:16 "without controversy"; some translate it "confessedly." See CONFESS, A, No. 1, and B. ¶

NT: B.569a; CB.—; K.687.
OT: —.
GEN. REF.: IS.1:768; NB.—; Z.—.

CONVENIENT, CONVENIENTLY

A. Adjective.

eukairos [εὔκαιρος, 2121], lit., well-timed (*eu*, well, *kairos*, a time, season), hence signifies timely, opportune, convenient; it is said of a certain day, Mark 6:21; elsewhere, Heb. 4:16, "in time of need." See NEED. ¶ Cp. *eukairia*, opportunity, Matt. 26:16; Luke 22:6; ¶ *eukaireō*, to have opportunity, Mark 6:31; Acts 17:21 ("they spent their time," marg. "had leisure for nothing else"); 1 Cor. 16:12. See OPPORTUNITY, NEED, C, *Note*. ¶

NT: B.321c; CB.1247b; K.389.
OT: 'ēt: S.6256; HR.571c.1; H.1650b; BD.773b.
GEN. REF.: IS.1:768; NB.—; Z.—.

B. Adverb.

eukairōs [εὐκαίρως, 2122], conveniently, Mark 14:11, is used elsewhere in 2 Tim. 4:2, "in season." ¶ See SEASON, C.

NT: B.321c; CB.147b; K.—.
OT: —.
GEN. REF.: IS.1:768; NB.—; Z.—.

C. Verbs.

1. *anēkō* [ἀνήκω, 433], is rendered "befitting" in Eph. 5:4, for A.V., "convenient"; so in Philm. 8. See BEFIT.

NT: B.66b; CB.1235c; K.—.
OT: —.
GEN. REF.: IS.1:768; NB.—; Z.—.

2. *kathēkō* [καθήκω, 2520], to be fitting, is so translated in Rom. 1:28, R.V.; A.V., "(not) convenient"; in Acts 22:22, "it is (not) fit." See FIT. ¶

NT: B.389a; CB.1254c; K.385.
OT: —.
GEN. REF.: IS.1:768; NB.—; Z.—.

CONVERSATION

This word is not used in the R.V., as it does not now express the meaning of the words so translated in the A.V. These are as follows:

A. Nouns.

1. *anastrophē* [ἀναστροφή]: see BEHAVIOUR, B. No. 1.

2. *tropos* [τρόπος, 5158], a turning, a manner, is translated simply "be ye," R.V. in Heb. 13:5, instead of "let your conversation be." See MANNER, MEANS, WAY.

NT: B.827b; CB.1273a; K.—.
OT: —.
GEN. REF.: IS.1:768; NB.250; Z.1:954.

3. *politeuma* [πολίτευμα]: see CITIZENSHIP, No. 4.

B. Verbs.

1. *anastrephō* [ἀναστρέφω]: see BEHAVE, A, No.1.

2. *politeuō* [πολιτεύω]: see CITIZENSHIP, No. 4, Note.

CONVERT, CONVERSION

A. Verbs.

1. *strephō* [στρέφω, 4762], to turn, is translated "be converted" in Matt. 18:3, A.V. See TURN.

NT: B.771a; CB.1270b; K.1093.
OT: hāphak: S.2015; HR.1296c.3; H.512; BD.245b.
sābab: S.5437; HR.1296c.4; H.1456; BD.685b.
shûb: S.7725; HR.1296c.7; H.2340; BD.996d.
GEN. REF.: IS.1:768; NB.250; Z.1:954.

2. *epistrephō* [ἐπιστρέφω, 1994], to turn about, turn towards (*epi*, towards and No. 1), is used transitively, and so rendered "convert" (of causing a person to turn) in Jas. 5:19, 20. Elsewhere, where the A.V. translates this verb, either in the Middle Voice and intransitive use, or the Passive, the R.V. adheres to the Middle Voice significance, and translates by "turn again," Matt. 13:15; Mark 4:12; Luke 22:32; Acts 3:19; 28:27. See COME (again), Note (4), GO (again), RETURN, TURN.

NT: B.301a; CB.1246a; K.1093.
OT: shûb: S.7725; HR.531a.18a; H.2340; BD.996d.
pānāh: S.6437; HR.531a.16a; H.1782; BD.815a.
sābab: S.5437; HR.531a.12; H.1456; BD.685b.
GEN. REF.: IS.1:768; NB.250; Z.1:954.

B. Noun.

epistrophē [ἐπιστροφή, 1995], akin to A, No. 2, a turning about, or round, conversion, is found in Acts 15:3. The word implies a turning from and a turning to; corresponding to these are repentance and faith; cp. "turned to God from idols" (1 Thess. 1:9). Divine grace is the efficient cause, human agency the responding effect. ¶

NT: B.301c; CB.1246a; K.1093.
OT: shûb: S.7725; HR.534a.2; H.2340; BD.996d.
GEN. REF.: IS.1:768; NB.250; Z.1:954.

CONVEY

ekneuō [ἐκνεύω, 1593], primarily, to bend to one side, to turn aside; then to take onself away, withdraw, is found in John 5:13, of Christ's conveying Himself away from one place to another. Some have regarded the verb as having the same meaning as *ekneō*, to escape, as from peril, slip away secretly; but the Lord did not leave the place where He had healed the paralytic in order to escape danger, but to avoid the applause of the throng. ¶

NT: B.243b; CB.—; K.—.
OT: sûr: S.5493; HR.438b.2; H.1480; BD.693b.
pānāh: S.6437; HR.438b.3; H.1782; BD.815a.
GEN. REF.: —.

CONVICT (*incl. the A.V., "convince"*)

1. *elenchō* [ἐλέγχω, 1651], signifies (*a*) to convict, confute, refute, usually with the suggestion of putting the convicted person to shame; see Matt. 18:15, where more than telling the offender his fault is in view; it is used of convicting of sin, John 8:46; 16:8; gainsayers in regard to the faith, Tit. 1:9; transgressors of the Law, Jas. 2:9; some texts have the verb in John 8:9; (*b*) to reprove, 1 Cor. 14:24, R.V. (for A.V., "convince"), for the unbeliever is there viewed as being reproved for, or convicted of, his sinful state; so in Luke 3:19; it is used of reproving works, John 3:20; Eph. 5:11, 13; 1 Tim. 5:20; 2 Tim. 4:2; Tit. 1:13; 2:15; all these speak of reproof by word of mouth. In Heb. 12:5 and Rev. 3:19, the word is used of reproving by action. See FAULT, REBUKE, REPROVE. ¶

NT: B.249b; CB.1244a; K.221.
OT: yākaḥ: S.3198; HR.449b.3a; H.865; BD.406d.
rāsha': S.7563; HR.449b.5; H.2222b; BD.957d.
GEN. REF.: IS.1:770; NB.—; Z.1:955.

2. *exelenchō* [ἐξελέγχω, 1827], an intensive form of No. 1, to convict thoroughly, is used of the Lord's future conviction of the ungodly, Jude 15. ¶

NT: B.274a; CB.—; K.—.
OT: yākaḥ: S.3198; HR.491a.1; H.865; BD.406d.
GEN. REF.: IS.1:770; NB.—; Z.—.

Note: For *diakatelenchō*, to confute powerfully in disputation, Acts 18:28 (A.V., "convinced"), see CONFUTE. ¶

COOL

katapsuchō [καταψύχω, 2711], Luke 16:24, denotes to cool off, make cool (*kata*, down, *psuchō*, to cool). ¶ In the Sept., Gen. 18:4. ¶

NT: B.421a; CB.—; K.—.
OT: —.
GEN. REF.: —.

For COPPERSMITH see under BRASS

COPY

hupodeigma [ὑπόδειγμα, 5262], from *hupō*, under, *deiknumi*, to show, properly denotes what is shown below or privately; it is translated "example," Heb. 8:5, A.V. (R.V., "copy"). It signifies (*a*) a sign suggestive of anything, the delineation or representation of a thing, and so, a figure, copy; in Heb. 9:23 the R.V. has "copies," for the A.V., "patterns"; (*b*) an example for imitation, John 13:15; Jas. 5:10; for warning, Heb. 4:11; 2 Pet. 2:6 (A.V. "ensample"). See EXAMPLE, PATTERN. ¶

NT: B.844a; CB.1252b; K.141.
OT: —.
GEN. REF.: IS.1:771; NB.—; Z.—.

Note: Cp. *hupogrammos* (*hupo*, under, *graphō*, to write), an underwriting, a writing copy, an example, is used in 1 Pet. 2:21.

CORBAN

korban [κορβᾶν, 2878], signifies (*a*) an offering, and was a Hebrew term for any sacrifice, whether by the shedding of blood or otherwise; (*b*) a gift offered to God, Mark 7:11. ¶ Jews were much addicted to rash vows; a saying of the Rabbis was, "It is hard for the parents, but the law is clear, vows must be kept." The Sept. translates the word by *dōron*, a gift. See *korbanas*, under TREASURY, Matt. 27:6. ¶

NT: B.444b; CB.1255c; K.459.
OT: qorbān: S.7133; HR.359a.13*; H.2065e; BD.898d.
GEN. REF.: IS.1:772; NB.1113; Z.1:959.
* cf. HR: Dōron

CORD

schoinion [σχοινίον, 4979], a cord or rope, a diminutive of *schoinos*, a rush, bulrush, meant a cord made of rushes; it denotes (*a*) a small cord, John 2:15 (plural), (*b*) a rope, Acts 27:32. See ROPE. ¶

NT: B.797d; CB.—; K.—.
OT: ḥebel: S.2256; HR.1328; H.592b; BD.286c.
GEN. REF.: IS.1:772; NB.252; Z.1:959.

CORN, CORNFIELD

1. *sitos* [σῖτος, 4621], wheat, corn; in the plural, grain, is translated "corn" in Mark 4:28; "wheat," Matt. 3:12; 13:25, 29, 30; Luke 3:17; 12:18 (some mss. have *genēmata*, "fruits," here); 16:7; 22:31; John 12:24; Acts 27:38; 1 Cor. 15:37; Rev. 6:6; 18:13. See WHEAT. ¶

NT: B.752b; CB.1269a; K.—.
OT: dāgān: S.1715; HR.1267b.3; H.403a; BD.186b.
ḥiṭṭāh: S.2406; HR.1267b.4; H.691b; BD.334d.
bar: S.1250; HR.1267b.2; H.288b; BD.141b.
GEN. REF.: IS.2:553; NB.258; Z.2:804.

2. *sition* [σίτιον, 4621], corn, grain, a diminutive of No. 1, is found in Acts 7:12. ¶

NT: B.752a; CB.—; K.—.
OT: leḥem: S.3899; HR.1267b.1; H.1105a; BD.536d.
GEN. REF.: —.

3. *sporimos* [σπόριμος, 4702], lit., sown, or fit for sowing (*speirō* to sow, scatter seed), denotes, in the plural, sown fields, fields of grain, cornfields, Matt. 12:1, R.V.; Mark 2:23; Luke 6:1 (cp. *spora*, 1 Pet. 1:23, ¶ and *sporos*, seed). ¶

NT: B.763b; CB.—; K.1065.
OT: zāra': S.2232; HR.1285b.1a; H.582; BD.281b.
zērûa': S.2221; HR.1285b.1b; H.582b; BD.283b.
GEN. REF.: IS.2:553; NB.—; Z.—.

4. *stachus* [στάχυς, 4719], means an ear of grain, Matt. 12:1; Mark 2:23; 4:28; Luke 6:1. Cp. the name *Stachys* in Rom. 16:9. ¶

NT: B.765d; CB.1269c; K.—.
OT: shibbōlet: S.7641; HR.1287b.3; H.2316b,c; BD.987c.
qāmāh: S.7054; HR.1287b.2; H.1999b; BD.879b.
GEN. REF.: IS.2:553; NB.—; Z.—.

Notes: (1) *Aloaō*, to thresh, from *alōn*, a threshing-floor, is translated "treadeth out (the) corn," in 1 Cor. 9:9, 10 and 1 Tim. 5:18. Cp. THRESH, TREAD. ¶

(2) *Kokkos*, a grain (its regular meaning), is translated "corn" in the A.V. of John 12:24 (R.V., "grain"). See GRAIN.

CORNER, CORNERSTONE

1. *gōnia* [γωνία, 1137], an angle (Eng., *coign*), signifies (*a*) an external angle, as of the corner of a street, Matt. 6:5; or of a building, 21:42; Mark 12:10; Luke 20:17; Acts 4:11; 1 Pet. 2:7, the corner stone or head-stone of the corner (see below); or the four extreme limits of the earth, Rev. 7:1; 20:8; (*b*) an internal corner, a secret place, Acts 26:26. See QUARTER. ¶

NT: B.168d; CB.1248c; K.137.
OT: pinnāh: S.6438; HR.283c.3a; H.1783a; BD.819c.
miqṣôa': S.4740; HR.283c.2a; H.2057a; BD.893a.
GEN. REF.: IS.1:783; NB.258; Z.1:979.

2. *archē* [ἀρχή, 746], a beginning (its usual meaning), first in time, order, or place, is used to denote the extremities or corners of a sheet, Acts 10:11; 11:5. See BEGINNING.

NT: B.111d; CB.1237b; K.81.
OT: pāneh: S.6440; HR.163c.16; H.1782a; BD.815d.
GEN. REF.: IS.1:783,784; NB.—; Z.1:979.

Note: For the adjective *akrogōniaios* (from *akros*, extreme, highest, and No. 1), a chief corner stone, see CHIEF. They were laid so as to give strength to the two walls with which they were connected. So Christ unites Jew and Gentile, Eph. 2:20; again, as one may carelessly stumble over the corner stone, when turning the corner, so Christ proved a stumbling stone to Jews, 1 Pet. 2:6.

CORPSE

ptōma [πτῶμα]: see BODY, No. 3.

CORRECT, CORRECTION, CORRECTOR, CORRECTING

A. Nouns.

1. *diorthōma* [διόρθωμα, —], signifies a reform, amendment, correction, lit., a making straight (*dia*, through, *orthoō*, to make straight). In Acts 24:2, lit., 'reformations come about (or take place, lit., 'become')', the R.V. has "evils are corrected," A.V., "worthy deeds are done"; there is no word for "worthy" or for "deeds" in the original. Some texts have *katorthōma*, which has the same meaning. ¶ See *diorthōsis*, "reformation," Heb. 9:10. ¶

NT: B.199a; CB.—; K.—.
OT: —.
GEN. REF.: —.

2. *epanorthōsis* [ἐπανόρθωσις, 1882], lit., a restoration to an upright or right state (*epi*, to, *ana*, up, or again, and *orthoō*, see No. 1), hence, "correction," is used of the Scripture in 2 Tim. 3:16, referring to improvement of life and character. ¶

NT: B.283a; CB.1245c; K.727.
OT: —.
GEN. REF.: IS.1:785; NB.—; Z.1:980.

3. *paideutēs* [παιδευτής, 3810], has two meanings, corresponding to the two meanings of the verb *paideuō* (see below) from which it is derived, (*a*) a teacher, preceptor, corrector, Rom. 2:20 (A.V., "instructor"), (*b*) a chastiser, Heb. 12:9, rendered "to chasten" (A.V., "which corrected"; lit., 'chastisers'). See INSTRUCTOR. ¶

NT: B.603d; CB.1261c; K.753.
OT: mûsār: S.4148; HR.1047c.1; H.877b; BD.416b.
GEN. REF.: IS.1:784; NB.—; Z.1:980.

B. Verb.

paideuō [παιδεύω, 3811], to train up a child (*pais*), is rendered "correcting" in 2 Tim. 2:25, R.V., A.V., "instructing." See CHASTEN.

NT: B.603d; CB.1261c; K.753.
OT: yāsar: S.3256; HR.1047a.4b,c,d; H.—; BD.415d.
GEN. REF.: IS.1:784; NB.—; Z.1:980.

CORRUPT, verb and adjective. CORRUPTION, CORRUPTIBLE, INCORRUPTION, INCORRUPTIBLE

A. Verbs.

1. *kapēleuō* [καπηλεύω, 2585], primarily signifies to be a retailer, to peddle, to hucksterize (from *kapēlos*, an inn-keeper, a petty retailer, especially of wine, a huckster, pedlar, in contrast to *emporos*, a merchant); hence, to get base gain by dealing in anything, and so, more generally, to do anything for sordid personal advantage. It is found in 2 Cor. 2:17, with reference to the ministry of the Gospel. The significance can be best ascertained by comparison and contrast with the verb *doloō* (δολόω) in 4:2 (likewise there only in the N.T.), to handle deceitfully. The meanings are not identical. While both involve the deceitful dealing of adulterating the word of truth, *kapēleuō* has the broader significance of doing so in order to make dishonest gain. Those to whom the Apostle refers in 2:17 are such as make merchandise of souls through covetousness (cp. Tit. 1:11; 2 Pet. 2:3, 14, 15; Jude 11, 16; Ezek. 13:19); accordingly "hucksterizing" would be the most appropriate rendering in this passage, while "handling deceitfully" is the right meaning in 4:2. See Trench, Syn. § lxii. ¶ In. Is. 1:22, the Sept. has "thy wine-merchants" (*kapēloi*, hucksterizers). ¶

NT: B.403a; CB.1253b; K.415.
OT: –.
GEN. REF.: –.

2. *phtheirō* [φθείρω, 5351], signifies to destroy by means of corrupting, and so bringing into a worse state; (*a*) with this significance it is used of the effect of evil company upon the manners of believers, and so of the effect of association with those who deny the truth and hold false doctrine, 1 Cor. 15:33 (this was a saying of the pagan poet Menander, which became a well known proverb); in 2 Cor. 7:2, of the effects of dishonourable dealing by bringing people to want (a charge made against the Apostle); in 11:3, of the effects upon the minds (or thoughts) of believers by corrupting them "from the simplicity and the purity that is toward Christ"; in Eph. 4:22, intransitively, of the old nature in waxing corrupt, "morally decaying, on the way to final ruin" (Moule), "after the lusts of deceit"; in Rev. 19:2, metaphorically, of the Babylonish harlot, in corrupting the inhabitants of the earth by her false religion.

(*b*) With the significance of destroying, it is used of marring a local church by leading it away from that condition of holiness of life and purity of doctrine in which it should abide, 1 Cor. 3:17 (A.V., "defile"), and of God's retributive destruction of the offender who is guilty of this sin (id.); of the effects of the work of false and abominable teachers upon themselves, 2 Pet. 2:12 (some texts have *kataphtheirō*; A.V., "shall utterly perish"), and Jude 10 (A.V., "corrupt themselves." R.V., marg., "are corrupted"). See DEFILE and DESTROY. ¶

NT: B.857b; CB.1264c; K.1259.
OT: shāḥat: S.7843; HR.1429c.5; H.2370; BD.1007d.
GEN. REF.: IS.1:785; NB.258; Z.1:980.

3. *diaphtheirō* [διαφθείρω, 1311], *dia*, through, intensive, and No. 2, to corrupt utterly, through and through, is said of men "corrupted in mind," whose wranglings result from the doctrines of false teachers, 1 Tim. 6:5 (the A.V. wrongly renders it as an adjective, "corrupt"). It is translated "destroyeth" instead of "corrupteth," in the R.V. of Luke 12:33, of the work of a moth; in Rev. 8:9, of the effect of Divine judgments hereafter upon navigation; in 11:18, of the Divine retribution of destruction upon those who have destroyed the earth; in 2 Cor. 4:16 it is translated "is decaying," said of the human body. See DESTROY, PERISH. ¶

NT: B.190c; CB.1241b; K.1259.
OT: shāḥat: S.7843; HR.314c.6; H.2370; BD.1007d.
GEN. REF.: IS.1:785; NB.258; Z.1:980.

4. *kataphtheirō* [καταφθείρω, 2704], *kata*, down, intensive, and No. 2, is said of men who are reprobate concerning the faith, "corrupted in mind" (A.V., "corrupt"). 2 Tim. 3:8. For 2 Pet. 2:12, R.V., "shall be destroyed," see No. 2. ¶

NT: B.420a; CB.–; K.1259.
OT: shāḥat: S.7843; HR.747c.5; H.2370; BD.1007d.
māqaq: S.4743; HR.747c.3; H.1237; BD.596d.
GEN. REF.: IS.1:785; NB.–; Z.1:980.

5. *sēpō* [σήπω, 4595], signifies to make corrupt, to destroy; in the Passive Voice with Middle sense, to become corrupt or rotten, to perish, said of riches, Jas. 5:2, of the gold and silver of the luxurious rich who have ground down their labourers. The verb is derived from a root signifying to rot off, drop to pieces. ¶

NT: B.749b; CB.–; K.1000.
OT: māqaq: S.4743; HR.1265b.2; H.1237; BD.596d.
GEN. REF.: –.

6. *aphanizō* [ἀφανίζω]: see CONSUME, No. 3.

B. Nouns.

1. *phthora* [φθορά, 5356], connected with *phtheirō*, No. 2, above, signifies a bringing or being brought into an inferior or worse condition, a destruction or corruption. It is used (*a*) physically, (1), of the condition of

creation, as under bondage, Rom. 8:21; (2) of the effect of the withdrawal of life, and so of the condition of the human body in burial, 1 Cor. 15:42; (3) by metonymy, of anything which is liable to corruption, 1 Cor. 15:50; (4) of the physical effects of merely gratifying the natural desires and ministering to one's own needs or lusts, Gal. 6:8, to the flesh in contrast to the Spirit, "corruption" being antithetic to "eternal life"; (5) of that which is naturally short-lived and transient, Col. 2:22, "perish"; (*b*) of the death and decay of beasts, 2 Pet. 2:12, R.V., "destroyed" (first part of verse; lit., 'unto . . . destruction'); (*c*) ethically, with a moral significance, (1) of the effect of lusts, 2 Pet. 1:4; (2) of the effect upon themselves of the work of false and immoral teachers, 2 Pet 2:12, R.V., "destroying"; A.V., "corruption," and verse 19. See DESTROY, PERISH. ¶

NT: B.858a; CB.1264c; K.1259.
OT: shāḥat: S.7843; HR.1430a.4; H.2370; BD.1007d.
GEN. REF.: IS.1:785; NB.258; Z.1:980.

Note: There is nothing in any of these words suggesting or involving annihilation.

2. *diaphthora* [διαφθορά, 1312], an intensified form of No. 1, utter or thorough corruption, referring in the N.T. to physical decomposition and decay, is used six times, five of which refer, negatively, to the body of God's "Holy One," after His death, which body, by reason of His absolute holiness, could not see corruption, Acts 2:27, 31; 13:34, 35, 37; once it is used of a human body, that of David, which, by contrast, saw corruption, Acts 13:36. ¶

NT: B.190d; CB.1241b; K.1259.
OT: shāḥat: S.7843; HR.315a.5; H.2370; BD.1007d.
GEN. REF.: IS.1:785; NB.258; Z.1:980.

3. *aphtharsia* [ἀφθαρσία, 861], incorruption, *a*, negative, with A, No. 2, is used (*a*) of the resurrection body, 1 Cor. 15:42, 50, 53, 54; (*b*) of a condition associated with glory and honour and life, including perhaps a moral significance, Rom. 2:7; 2 Tim. 1:10; this is wrongly translated "immortality" in the A.V.; (*c*) of love to Christ, that which is sincere and undiminishing, Eph. 6:24 (translated "uncorruptness"). See IMMORTALITY, SINCERITY. ¶

NT: B.125b; CB.1236c; K.1259.
OT: —.
GEN. REF.: IS.—; NB.258; Z.—.

Note: For Tit. 2:7 (where some texts have *aphtharsia*), see No. 4.

4. *aphthoria* [ἀφθορία, —], similar to No. 3, uncorruptness, free from (moral) taint, is said of doctrine, Tit. 2:7 (some texts have *adiaphthoria*, the negative form of No. 2, above). ¶

NT: B.125c; CB.—; K.1259.
OT: —.
GEN. REF.: —; NB.258; Z.—.

C. Adjectives.

1. *phthartos* [φθαρτός, 5349], corruptible, akin to A, No. 2, is used (*a*) of man as being mortal, liable to decay (in contrast to God), Rom. 1:23; (*b*) of man's body as death-doomed, 1 Cor. 15:53, 54; (*c*) of a crown of reward at the Greek games, 1 Cor. 9:25; (*d*) of silver and gold, as specimens of corruptible things, 1 Pet. 1:18; (*e*) of natural seed, 1 Pet. 1:23. ¶

NT: B.857a; CB.1264c; K.1259.
OT: māshḥāt: S.4893; HR.1429b.1; H.2370c; BD.1008c.
GEN. REF.: IS.—; NB.258; Z.—.

2. *aphthartos* [ἄφθατρος, 862], not liable to corruption or decay, incorruptible (*a*, negative, and A, No. 2) is used of (*a*) God, Rom. 1:23; 1 Tim 1:17 (A.V., "immortal"); (*b*) the raised dead, 1 Cor. 15:52; (*c*) rewards given to the saints hereafter, metaphorically described as a "crown," 1 Cor. 9:25; (*d*) the eternal inheritance of the saints, 1 Pet. 1:4; (*e*) the Word of God, as incorruptible seed, 1 Pet. 1:23; (*f*) a meek and quiet spirit, metaphorically spoken of as incorruptible apparel, 1 Pet. 3:4. See IMMORTAL. ¶

NT: B.125b; CB.1236c; K.1259.
OT: —.
GEN. REF.: IS.—; NB.258; Z.—.

3. *sapros* [σαπρ)ος, 4550], corrupt, akin to *sēpō*, A, No. 5; See BAD, No. 3.

NT: B.7426; CB.1268b; K.1000.
OT: —.
GEN. REF.: —.

Note: (1) Trench, Syn. § lxviii, contrasts this with *amarantos*, and *amarantinos*, unwithering, not fading away, 1 Pet. 1:4; 5:4. These are, however, distinct terms (see FADE) and are not strictly synonymous, though used in the same description of the heavenly inheritance.

COST, COSTLINESS, COSTLY

A. Nouns.

1. *dapanē* [δαπάνη, 1160], expense, cost (from *daptō*, to tear; from a root *dap* — meaning to divide), is found in Luke 14:28, in the Lord's illustration of counting the cost of becoming His disciple. Cp. *dapanaō*, to spend, and its compounds, under CHARGE, SPEND. ¶

NT: B.171a; CB.—; K.—.
OT: —.
GEN. REF.: —.

2. *timiotēs* [τιμιότης, 5094], costliness (from *timios*, valued at great price, precious; see

No. 3, below), is connected with *timē*, honour, price, and used in Rev. 18:19, in reference to Babylon. ¶

NT: B.818b; CB.–; K.–.
OT: –.
GEN. REF.: IS.1:786; NB.–; Z.–.

B. Adjectives.

1. *timios* [τίμιος, 5093], akin to A, No. 2, is translated "costly" in 1 Cor. 3:12, of costly stones, in a metaphorical sense (A.V., "precious"). Cp. Rev. 17:4; 18:12, 16; 21:19. See DEAR, HONOURABLE, PRECIOUS, REPUTATION.

NT: B.818a; CB.1272c; K.–.
OT: yāqār: S.3368; HR.1353c.2a; H.905a; BD.429d.
GEN. REF.: –.

2. *polutelēs* [πολυτελής, 4185], primarily, the very end or limit (from *polus*, much, *telos*, revenue), with reference to price, of highest cost, very expensive, is said of spikenard, Mark 14:3; raiment, 1 Tim. 2:9; metaphorically, of a meek and quiet spirit, 1 Pet. 3:4, "of great price"; cp. No. 1 and A, No. 2, above. See PRECIOUS, PRICE. ¶

NT: B.690a; CB.1266a; K.–.
OT: yāqār: S.3368; HR.1185c.1; H.905a; BD.429d.
GEN. REF.: –.

3. *polutimos* [πολύτιμος, 4186], lit., of great value (see A, No. 2 and B, No. 1), is used of a pearl, Matt. 13:46; of spikenard, John 12:3 (R.V., "very precious," A.V. "very costly"). See PRICE. ¶ The comparative *polutimo* (*v.l.iō*) *teros*, "much more precious," is used in 1 Pet. 1:7. ¶

NT: B.690a; CB.–; K.–.
OT: –.
GEN. REF.: –.

COUCH

1. *klinidion* [κλινίδιον, 2826], a small bed, a diminutive form of *klinē*, a bed (from *klinō*, to incline, recline), is used in Luke 5:19, 24 of the bed (*klinē*, in ver. 18) on which the palsied man was brought. See BED. ¶

NT: B.436c; CB.–; K.–.
OT: –.
GEN. REF.: IS.1:445; NB.–; Z.–.

2. *krabbatos* [κράββατος]: see BED, No. 4.

COULD

1. *echō* [ἔχω, 2192], to have, is rendered "could" in Mark 14:8, "she hath done what she could," lit., 'she hath done what she had.' See HAVE.

NT: B.331d; CB.1242c; K.286.
OT: –.
GEN. REF.: –.

2. *ischuō* [ἰσχύω, 2480], to have strength, is translated in Mark 14:37 "couldest thou not?" See ABLE.

NT: B.383d; CB.1253a; K.378.
OT: –.
GEN. REF.: IS.1:11; NB.–; Z.–.

Notes: (1) *Emblepō* in Acts 22:11, lit., 'I was not seeing,' is translated "I could not see." See BEHOLD.

(2) See CAN, when not used as part of another verb.

COUNCIL, COUNCILLOR

1. *sumboulion* [συμβούλιον, 4824], a uniting in counsel (*sun*, together, *boulē*, counsel, advice), denotes (*a*) counsel which is given, taken and acted upon, e.g., Matt. 12:14, R.V., "took counsel," for A.V., "held a council"; 22:15; hence (*b*) a council, an assembly of counsellors or persons in consultation, Acts 25:12, of the council with which Festus conferred concerning Paul. The governors and procurators of provinces had a board of advisers or assessors, with whom they took counsel, before pronouncing judgment. See CONSULTATION.

NT: B.778a; CB.1270b; K.–.
OT: –.
GEN. REF.: IS.1:787; NB.263; Z.1:990.

2. *sunedrion* [συνέδριον, 4892], properly, a settling together (*sun*, together, *hedra*, a seat), hence, (*a*) any assembly or session of persons deliberating or adjusting, as in the Sept. of Psa. 26:4 (lit., 'with a council of vanity'); Prov. 22:10; Jer. 15:17, etc.; in the N.T., e.g., Matt. 10:17; Mark 13:9; John 11:47, in particular, it denoted (*b*) the Sanhedrin, the Great Council at Jerusalem, consisting of 71 members, namely, prominent members of the families of the high priest, elders and scribes. The Jews trace the origin of this to Num. 11:16. The more important causes came up before this tribunal. The Roman rulers of Judaea permitted the Sanhedrin to try such cases, and even to pronounce sentence of death, with the condition that such a sentence should be valid only if confirmed by the Roman Procurator. In John 11:47, it is used of a meeting of the Sanhedrin; in Acts 4:15, of the place of meeting.

NT: B.786a; CB.1270c; K.1115.
OT: sôd: S.5475; HR.1313a.3; H.1147la; BD.691c.
qāhal: S.6950; HR.1313a.4; H.1991; BD.874d.
GEN. REF.: IS.1:787; NB.263; Z.1:991.

COUNSEL. For COUNSELLOR see above.

A. Nouns.

1. *boulē* [βουλή]: see under ADVICE.

2. *sumboulos* [σύμβουλος, 4825], a councillor with, occurs in Rom. 11:34. ¶

NT: B.778b; CB.1270b; K.–.
OT: yā'aṣ: S.3289; HR.1304a.1a; H.887; BD.419c.
'ēṣah: S.6098; HR.1304a.1b; H.887a; BD.420a.
GEN. REF.: IS.1:787; NB.–; Z.1:992.

B. Verbs.

1. *bouleuō* [βουλεύω, 1011], to take counsel, to resolve, is used in the Middle Voice in the N.T., "took counsel" in Acts 5:33, A.V. (R.V. translates *boulomai*); both in 27:39; in Luke 14:31, R.V. "take counsel" (A.V., "consulteth"); in John 11:53, A.V. and R.V. (so the best mss.); 12:10, R.V., "took counsel;" for A.V., "consulted"; in 2 Cor. 1:17 (twice), "purpose." See CONSULT, MINDED, PURPOSE. ¶

NT: B.145c; CB.–; K.–.
OT: yā'aṣ: S.3289; HR.227a.6; H.887; BD.419c.
zāmam: S.2161; HR.227a.3; H.556; BD.273a.
GEN. REF.: IS.1:787; NB.–; Z.–.

2. *sumbouleuō* [συμβουλεύω, 4823], in the Active Voice, to advise, to counsel, John 18:14, "gave counsel"; in Rev. 3:18, "I counsel"; in the Middle Voice, to take counsel, consult, Matt. 26:4, R.V., "took counsel together;" for A.V., "consulted"; Acts 9:23, "took counsel" (R.V. adds "together"); in some mss. John 11:53. See CONSULT. ¶

NT: B.777d; CB.1270b; K.–.
OT: yā'aṣ: S.3289; HR.1303c.1; H.887; BD.419c.
GEN. REF.: IS.1:787; NB.–; Z.–.

COUNT

1. *echō* [ἔχω, 2192], to have, to hold; then, to hold in the mind, to regard, to count, has this significance in Matt. 14:5, "they counted Him as a prophet"; Philm. 17, "If then thou countest me a partner"; Mark 11:32, A.V., (R.V., "hold"); Acts 20:24, A.V. See ABLE.

NT: B.331d; CB.1242c; K.286.
OT: –.
GEN. REF.: –.

2. *hēgeomai* [ἡγέομαι, 2233], primarily, to lead the way; hence, to lead before the mind, account, is found with this meaning in Phil. 2:3, R.V. (A.V., "esteem"); 2:6, R.V. (A.V., "thought"); 2:25 (A.V., "supposed"); Phil. 3:7, 8; 2 Thess. 3:15; 1 Tim. 1:12; 6:1; Heb. 10:29; Jas. 1:2; Heb. 11:11 (A.V., "judged"); 2 Pet. 2:13; 3:9. See ACCOUNT.

NT: B.343c; CB.1249c; K.303.
OT: –.
GEN. REF.: –.

3. *logizomai* [λογίζομαι, 3049], to reckon, is rendered "count" in 2 Cor. 10:2, R.V. (A.V., "think"); "counted" in the A.V. of Rom. 2:26; 4:3, 5; 9:8 (R.V., "reckoned").

NT: B.475d; CB.1257a; K.536.
OT: mānāh: S.4487; HR.880a.3; H.1213; BD.584a.1.
GEN. REF.: –.

4. *psēphizō* [ψηφίζω, 5585], akin to *psēphos*, a stone, used in voting, occurs in Luke 14:28; Rev. 13:18. ¶

NT: B.892d; CB.–; K.1341.
OT: sāphar: S.5608; HR.1485b.1; H.–; BD.707d.
GEN. REF.: –; NB.–; Z.–.

5. *sumpsēphizō* [συμψηφίζω, 4860], to count up, occurs in Acts 19:19. ¶

NT: B.781b; CB.–; K.1341.
OT: –.
GEN. REF.: –.

Note: In Jas. 5:11, *makarizō*, to pronounce blessed, is rendered "count . . . happy;" A.V. (R.V., "call . . ."). For *kataxioō* see ACCOUNT, No. 5. For "descent is counted" see GENEALOGY.

COUNTENANCE

1. *opsis* [ὄψις, 3799]: only Rev. 1:16 has "countenance." See APPEARANCE.

NT: B.601d; CB.1261a; K.–.
OT: 'ayin: S.5869; HR.1044b.4; H.1612a,1613; BD.744a.
GEN. REF.: –.

2. *prosōpon* [πρόσωπον, 4383], is translated "countenance" in Luke 9:29; Acts 2:28, and in the A.V. of 2 Cor. 3:7 (R.V., "face"). See APPEARANCE.

NT: B.720d; CB.1267b; K.950.
OT: pānîm: S.6440; HR.1223c.6; H.1782a; BD.815d.
GEN. REF.: IS.1:787; NB.–; Z.1:992.

3. *eidea* [εἰδέα, 2397], akin to *eidon*, to see: see APPEARANCE.

NT: B.220c; CB.–; K.202.
OT: dᵉmût: S.1823; HR.374b.1; H.437a; BD.198b.
GEN. REF.: –.

Notes: (1) In Acts 13:24 *prosōpon* is translated "before" (lit., 'before the presence of His coming').

(2) *Skuthrōpos*, "of a sad countenance" (*skuthros*, gloomy, sad, *ōps*, an eye), is used in Matt. 6:16 and Luke 24:17, "sad."

(3) *Stugnazō*, to be or become hateful, gloomy, in aspect, is translated "his countenance fell;" Mark 10:22, R.V. (A.V., "he was sad"). It is used of the heaven or sky in Matt. 16:3, "lowring." See LOWRING. ¶

COUNTRY

A. Nouns.

1. *agros* [ἀγρός, 68], denotes a field, especially a cultivated field; hence, the country in contrast to the town (Eng., agrarian, agriculture), e.g., Mark 5:14; 6:36; 15:21; 16:12; Luke 8:34; 9:12 (plural, lit., 'fields'); 23:26; a piece of ground, e.g., Mark 10:29; Acts 4:37. See FARM.

NT: B.13d; CB.1233c; K.–.
OT: sādeh: S.7704; HR.17a.7; H.2234a,b; BD.961b.
GEN. REF.: IS.1:787; NB.–; Z.1:992.

2. *patris* [πατρίς, 3968], primarily signifies one's fatherland, native country, of one's own town, Matt. 13:54, 57; Mark 6:1, 4; Luke 4:23, 24; John 4:44; Heb. 11:14. ¶

NT: B.636d; CB.1263a; K.–.
OT: ('ereṣ) môledet: S.4138; HR.1112a.1b; H.867f; BD.409d.
mishpāḥāh: S.4940; HR.1112a.2; H.2442b; BD.1046c.
GEN. REF.: IS.1:787; NB.–; Z.1:992.

3. *chōra* [χώρα, 5561], properly denotes the space lying between two limits or places; accordingly it has a variety of meanings: "country," Matt. 2:12; 8:28; Mark 1:5, R.V. (A.V., "land"); 5:1, 10; Luke 2:8; 8:26; 15:13, 14, R.V. (A.V., "land"), 15; 19:12; 21:21; Acts 10:39, R.V. (A.V., "land"); 12:20; 26:20, R.V. (A.V., "coasts"); 27:27; in Mark 6:55 (in the best mss.) and Acts 18:23, R.V., "region." See COAST, FIELD, GROUND, LAND, REGION.

NT: B.889b; CB.1240a; K.—.
OT: 'ereṣ: S.776; HR.1481a.4; H.167; BD.75d.
mᵉdînāh: S.4082; HR.1481a.5; H.426d; BD.193d.
GEN. REF.: IS.1:787; NB.—; Z.1:992.

4. *perichōros* [περίχωρος, 4066], *peri*, around, and No. 3, signifies "country round about," Luke 8:37; "country about," Luke 3:3, A.V. (R.V., "region round about"); in Matt. 14:35 and Luke 4:37, A.V., "country round about" (R.V., "region round about"); Matt. 3:5; Mark 1:28; Luke 4:14; 7:17; Acts 14:6. See REGION. ¶

NT: B.653c; CB.—; K.—.
OT: kikkār: S.3603; HR.1128b.2a; H.—; BD.503a.
migrāsh: S.4054; HR.1128b.3; H.388c; BD.177b.
GEN. REF.: IS.1:787; NB.—; Z.—.

5. *meros* [μέρος, 3313], a part, is rendered "country" in Acts 19:1, R.V.

NT: B.505d; CB.1258b; K.585.
OT: pelek: S.6418; HR.911c.12; H.1775a; BD.813a.
GEN. REF.: IS.1:787; NB.—; Z.—.

Note: Some inferior mss. have No. 4 in Mark 6:55, for No. 3.

B. Adjectives.

1. *anōterikos* [ἀνωτερικός, 510], upper, is used in the plural in Acts 19:1, to denote upper regions, with A.V., "coast," R.V., "country," i.e., the high central plateau, in contrast to the roundabout way by the river through the valley., See COAST. ¶

NT: B.77c; CB.—; K.—.
OT: —.
GEN. REF.: —.

2. *oreinos* [ὀρεινός, 3714], hilly (from *oros*, a hill, mountain), is translated "hill country" in Luke 1:39, 65. ¶

NT: B.580a; CB.1261a; K.—.
OT: har: S.2022; HR.1010c.1; H.517a; BD.249a.
GEN. REF.: —.

C. Verb.

apodēmeō [ἀποδημέω, 589], signifies to go or travel into a far country, lit., 'to be away from one's people' (*apo*, from, *dēmos*, a people), Matt. 21:33; 25:14; in ver. 15 the verb is translated in the R.V., "went on his journey" (A.V., "took his journey"); Mark 12:1; Luke 20:9, "went into another country," R.V. In Luke 15:13 both Versions translate by "took his journey" ("into a far country" being separately expressed); see JOURNEY. ¶

Cp. *apodēmos*, lit., away from one's own people, gone abroad, Mark 13:34. ¶

NT: B.90a; CB.1236c; K.—.
OT: —.
GEN. REF.: —.

Notes: (1) *Gē*, earth, land, is translated "country" in the A.V. of Matt. 9:31 and Acts 7:3; R.V., "land." See LAND.

(2) *Genos*, a race, is mistranslated "country" in the A.V. of Acts 4:36 (R.V., "by race"). See below.

COUNTRYMEN

1. *genos* [γένος, 1085], properly denotes an offspring; then, a family; then, a race, nation; otherwise, a kind or species; it is translated "countrymen," in 2 Cor. 11:26, in Paul's reference to his fellow-nationals; so in Gal. 1:14, R.V., for A.V., "nation." See BEGET.

NT: B.156a; CB.1248b; K.117.
OT: mîn: S.4327; HR.239b.4; H.1191a; BD.568b.
'am: S.5971; HR.239b.6; H.1640a,e; BD.766b.
GEN. REF.: —.

2. *sumphuletēs* [συμφυλέτης, 4853], lit., a fellow-tribesman (*sun*, with, *phulē*, a tribe, race, nation, people), hence, one who is of the same people, a fellow-countryman, is found in 1 Thess. 2:14. ¶

NT: B.780c; CB.—; K.—.
OT: —.
GEN. REF.: —.

COUPLED

Note: The word "coupled" is inserted in italics in 1 Pet. 3:2, the more adequately to express the original, which is, lit., 'your chaste behaviour in fear.'

COURAGE

A. Noun.

tharsos [θάρσος, 2294], akin to *tharseō*, to be of good cheer, is found in Acts 28:15. ¶

NT: B.352a; CB.—; K.—.
OT: 'ōmeṣ: S.555; HR.626c.1; H.117a; BD.55b.
'āmēṣ: S.553; HR.626c.3; H.117; BD.54d.
GEN. REF.: IS.1:788; NB.264; Z.—.

B. Verb.

tharreō [θαρρέω, 2292], is translated by some form of the verb to be of good courage, in the R.V. in five of the six places where it is used: 2 Cor. 5:6, "being of good courage" (A.V., "we are . . . confident"); 5:8, "we are of good courage" (A.V., "we are confident"); 7:16, "I am of good courage" (A.V., "I have confidence"); 10:1, "I am of good courage" (A.V., "I am bold"); 10:2, "show courage" (A.V., "be bold"); Heb. 13:6, "with good courage," lit., 'being of good courage' (A.V., "boldly"). See BOLD, CONFIDENCE. ¶

NT: B.352a; CB.1271c; K.315.
OT: bāṭaḥ: S.982; HR.626c.2; H.233; BD.105a.
yārē': S.3372; HR.626c.3; H.907,908; BD.431a.
(ω neg.)
GEN. REF.: IS.1:788; NB.–; Z.–.

Note: Tharreō is a later form of *tharseō*. Cp. *tolmaō*, to be bold.

COURSE

A. Nouns.

1. *aiōn* [αἰών, 165], an age (see AGE), is sometimes wrongly spoken of as a "dispensation," which does not mean a period of time, but a mode of dealing. It is translated "course" in Eph. 2:2, "the course of this world," i.e., the cycle or present round of things. See AGE, ETERNAL, EVER, WORLD.

NT: B.27a; CB.1234a; K.31.
OT: 'ôlām: S.5769; HR.39b.5; H.1631a; BD.761d.
GEN. REF.: –; NB.–; Z.1:993.

2. *dromos* [δρόμος, 1408], properly, a running, a race (from *edramon*, to run), hence, metaphorically, denotes a career, course of occupation, or of life, viewed in a special aspect, Acts 13:25; 20:24; 2 Tim. 4:7. ¶

NT: B.206d; CB.1242b; K.1189.
OT: m^e^rûṣāh: S.4794; HR.349a.1b; H.2137b; BD.930c.
GEN. REF.: IS.1:788; NB.–; Z.1:993.

3. *ephēmeria* [ἐφημερία, 2183], primarily, daily service, as, e.g., in the Sept. of 2 Chron. 13:11 (from *epi*, upon, or by, *hēmera*, a day, Eng., ephemeral), hence denoted a class, or course, into which the priests were divided for the daily service in the Temple, each class serving for seven days (see 1 Chron. 9:25). In the N.T. it is used in Luke 1:5, 8. ¶

NT: B.330c; CB.–; K.–.
OT: maḥ^a^lōqet: S.4256; HR.585b.1; H.669d; BD.324b.
mishmeret: S.4931; HR.585b.3b; H.2414g; BD.1038b.
GEN. REF.: IS.1:788; NB.–; Z.–.

Note: Cp. *ephēmeros*, "daily (food)," Jas. 2:15. ¶

4. *trochos* [τροχός, 5164], a wheel, is translated "wheel" in Jas. 3:6, R.V., with metaphorical reference to the round of human activity (A.V., "course"), as a glowing axle would set on fire the whole wooden wheel. ¶

NT: B.828a; CB.1273a; K.–.
OT: –.
GEN. REF.: IS.–; NB.–; Z.1:993.

B. Verb.

chōreō [χωρέω, 5562], to make room for, to go forward, is rendered "hath not free course," in John 8:37, R.V., (A.V., "hath no place"). See COME, No. 24.

NT: B.889c; CB.1240a; K.–.
OT: –.
GEN. REF.: –.

Notes: (1) Connected with *dromos*, A, No. 2, is *euthudromeō*, to make (or run) a straight course (*euthus*, straight), Acts 16:11 and 21:1. ¶

(2) In 2 Thess. 3:1, *trechō*, to run (R.V.), is translated "have free course" (A.V.) ¶

(3) In 1 Cor. 14:27, *ana meros*, "by turn," "in turn" (R.V.), is rendered "by course" (A.V.).

(4) For *ploos*, a sailing or voyage, "course," Acts 21:7, A.V. (R.V., "voyage"), see VOYAGE.

COURT

1. *agoraios* [ἀγοραῖος, 60], is an adjective, signifying pertaining to the *agora*, any place of public meeting, and especially where trials were held, Acts 19:38; the R.V. translates the sentence "the courts are open"; a more literal rendering is 'court days are kept.' In Acts 17:5 it is translated in the R.V., "rabble"; A.V., "baser sort," lit., frequenters of the markets. See BASER. ¶

NT: B.13a; CB.1233c; K.–.
OT: –.
GEN. REF.: –.

2. *aulē* [αὐλή, 833], primarily, an uncovered space around a house, enclosed by a wall, where the stables were, hence was used to describe (*a*) the courtyard of a house; in the O.T. it is used of the courts of the Tabernacle and Temple; in this sense it is found in the N.T. in Rev. 11:2; (*b*) the courts in the dwellings of well-to-do folk, which usually had two, one exterior, between the door and the street (called the *proaulion*, or porch, Mark 14:68. ¶), the other, interior, surrounded by the buildings of the dwellings, as in Matt. 26:69 (in contrast to the room where the judges were sitting); Mark 14:66; Luke 22:55; A.V., "hall"; R.V. "court" gives the proper significance, Matt. 26:3, 58; Mark 14:54; 15:16 (R.V., "praetorium"); Luke 11:21; John 18:15. It is here to be distinguished from the Praetorium, translated "palace." See HALL, PALACE. For the other meaning "sheepfold," John 10:1, 16, see FOLD. ¶

NT: B.121b; CB.1238b; K.–.
OT: ḥāṣēr: S.2691; HR.177b.2b; H.722a,723a; BD.346d.
'^a^zārāh: S.5835; HR.177b.5; H.1599a; BD.741c.
GEN. REF.: IS.1:789; NB.264; Z.1:994.

3. *basileion* [βασίλειον, 933], an adjective meaning "royal," signifies, in the neuter plural, a royal palace, translated "kings' courts" in Luke 7:25; in the singular, 1 Pet. 2:9, "royal." See ROYAL. ¶

NT: B.136a; CB.1238c; K.–.
OT: –.
GEN. REF.: –.

COURTEOUS, COURTEOUSLY

A. Adjective.

tapeinophrōn [ταπεινόφρων, —], lowly-minded, is used in 1 Pet. 3:8, "be courteous," A.V. (R.V., "humble-minded"). ¶

NT: B.804c; CB.1271a; K.1152.
OT: –.
GEN. REF.: –.

B. Adverbs.

1. *philophronōs* [φιλοφρόνως, 5390], lit., friendly, or, more fully, 'with friendly thoughtfulness' (*philos*, friend, *phrēn*, the mind), is found in Acts 28:7, of the hospitality showed by Publius to Paul and his fellow-shipwrecked travellers. ¶

NT: B.861d; CB.1264a; K.—.
OT: —.
GEN. REF.: —.

Note: Some mss. have the corresponding adjective *philophrōn*, "courteous," in 1 Pet. 3:8; the most authentic mss. have *tapeinophrōn*, "humble-minded."

2. *philanthrōpōs* [φιλανθρωπῶς, 5364], is translated "courteously" in Acts 27:3, A.V.; R.V., "kindly" (Eng., philanthropically). See KINDLY. ¶

NT: B.858d; CB.1264a; K.1261.
OT: —.
GEN. REF.: —.

COUSIN

1. *anepsios* [ἀνεψιός, 431], in Col. 4:10 denotes a cousin rather than a nephew (A.V., "sister's son"). "Cousin" is its meaning in various periods of Greek writers. ¶ In this sense it is used in the Sept., in Numb. 36:11. ¶ In later writings it denotes a nephew; hence the A.V. rendering. As Lightfoot says, there is no reason to suppose that the Apostle would have used it in any other than its proper sense. We are to understand, therefore, that Mark was the cousin of Barnabas. See SISTER.

NT: B.66a; CB.—; K.—.
OT: —.
GEN. REF.: IS.1:790; NB.264; Z.—.

2. *sungenis* [συγγενίς, —], in Luke 1:36 (so in the most authentic mss.) and *sungenēs* in ver. 58 (plural), A.V., "cousin" and "cousins," respectively signify "kinswoman" and "kinsfolk," (R.V.); so the R.V. and A.V. in 2:44 and 21:16. The word lit. signifies 'born with,' i.e., of the same stock, or descent; hence kinsman, kindred. See KIN, KINSFOLK, KINSWOMAN.

NT: B.772d; CB.—; K.—.
OT: —.
GEN. REF.: IS.1:790; NB.264; Z.1:995.

COVENANT (Noun and Verb)

diathēkē [διαθήκη, 1242], primarily signifies a disposition of property by will or otherwise. In its use in the Sept., it is the rendering of a Hebrew word meaning a covenant or agreement (from a verb signifying to cut or divide, in allusion to a sacrificial custom in connection with covenant-making, e.g., Gen. 15:10, "divided" Jer. 34:18, 19). In contradistinction to the English word "covenant" (lit., a coming together), which signifies a mutual undertaking between two parties or more, each binding himself to fulfil obligations, it does not in itself contain the idea of joint obligation, it mostly signifies an obligation undertaken by a single person. For instance, in Gal. 3:17 it is used as an alternative to a "promise" (vv. 16, 17, and 18). God enjoined upon Abraham the rite of circumcision, but His promise to Abraham, here called a covenant, was not conditional upon the observance of circumcision, though a penalty attached to its non-observance.

"The N.T. uses of the word may be analysed as follows: (*a*) a promise or undertaking, human or divine, Gal. 3:15; (*b*) a promise or undertaking on the part of God, Luke 1:72; Acts 3;25; Rom. 9:4; 11:27; Gal. 3:17; Eph. 2:12; Heb. 7:22; 8:6, 8, 10; 10:16; (*c*) an agreement, a mutual undertaking, between God and Israel, see Deut. 29 and 30 (described as a 'commandment,' Heb. 7:18, cp. ver. 22); Heb. 8:9; 9:20; (*d*) by metonymy, the token of the covenant, or promise, made to Abraham, Acts 7:8; (*e*) by metonymy, the record of the covenant, 2 Cor. 3:14; Heb. 9:4; cp. Rev. 11:19; (*f*) the basis, established by the death of Christ, on which the salvation of men is secured, Matt. 26:28; Mark 14:24; Luke 22:20; 1 Cor. 11:25; 2 Cor. 3:6; Heb. 10:29; 12:24; 13:20.

"This covenant is called the 'new,' Heb. 9:15, the 'second,' 8:7, the 'better,' 7:22. In Heb. 9:16, 17, the translation is much disputed. There does not seem to be any sufficient reason for departing in these verses from the word used everywhere else. The English word 'Testament' is taken from the titles prefixed to the Latin Versions."* ¶ See TESTAMENT.

NT: B.183a; CB.1241b; K.157.
OT: bᵉrîṯ: S.1285; HR.300c.2; H.282a; BD.136b.
GEN. REF.: IS.1:790; NB.264; Z.1:995.

B. Verb.

suntithēmi [συντίθημι, 4934], lit., to put together, is used only in the Middle Voice in the N.T., and, means to determine, agree, John 9:22 and Acts 23:20; to assent, Acts 24:9; to covenant, Luke 22:5. See AGREE, ASSENT. ¶

NT: B.792d; CB.—; K.—.
OT: qāshar: S.7194; HR.1320c.2; H.2090; BD.905a.
GEN. REF.: IS.1:790; NB.—; Z.1:995.

Note: In Matt. 26:15 the A.V. translates *histēmi*, to place (in the balances), i.e., to weigh, "they covenanted with;" R.V., "they weighed unto."

* From Notes on Galatians by Hogg and Vine, p. 144.

COVENANT-BREAKERS

asunthetos [ἀσύνθετος, 802], from *suntithēmi* (see above), with the negative prefix *a*, hence signifies "not covenant-keeping," i.e., refusing to abide by covenants made, covenant-breaking, faithless, Rom. 1:31. ¶ In the Sept. it is found in Jer. 3:8-11. ¶ Cp. the corresponding verb, *asuntithēmi*, in the Sept. of Ps. 73:15, to deal treacherously (R.V.), and the noun *asunthesia*, transgression, or covenant-breaking, e.g., Ezra 9:2, 4; 10:6.

NT: B.118d; CB.–; K.–.
OT: bāgad: S.898; HR.174b.1a; H.198; BD.93c.
GEN. REF.: –.

Note: Trench, Syn. § lii, notes the distinction between *asunthetos* and *aspondos*, "implacable," the latter, in 2 Tim. 3:3 only, being derived from *spondē*, a sacrificial libation, which accompanied treaty-making; hence, with the negative prefix *a*, "without a treaty or covenant," thus denoting a person who cannot be persuaded to enter into a covenant. He points out that *asunthetos* presumes a state of peace interrupted by the unrighteous, *aspondos* a state of war, which the implacable refuse to terminate equitably. The words are clearly not synonymous.

COVER, COVERING

A. Verbs.

1. *kaluptō* [καλύπτω, 2572], signifies to cover, Matt. 8:24; 10:26; Luke 8:16; 23:30; Jas. 5:20 (R.V.); 1 Pet. 4:8; to veil, in 2 Cor. 4:3 (R.V.; A.V., "hid"). See HIDE. ¶

NT: B.401a; CB.1253b; K.405.
OT: kāsāh: S.3680; HR.716c.1b; H.1008; BD.491b.
GEN. REF.: IS.1:797; NB.–; Z.–.

Note: Cp. the corresponding noun *kalumma*, a veil, 2 Cor. 3:13, 14, 15, 16. See VEIL. ¶

2. *epikaluptō* [ἐπικαλύπτω, 1943], to cover up or over (*epi*, over), is used in Rom. 4:7, lit., 'whose sins are covered over.' ¶ Cp. *epikalumma*, a cloke, 1 Pet. 2:16. ¶

NT: B.294c; CB.–; K.–.
OT: kāsāh: S.3680; HR.522b.2b; H.1008; BD.491b.
ḥāphāh: S.2645; HR.522b.1; H.707; BD.341d.
GEN. REF.: IS.1:797; NB.–; Z.–.

3. *perikaluptō* [περικαλύπτω, 4028], to cover around (*peri*, around), e.g., the face, and so, to blindfold, is translated "cover" in Mark 14:65, "blindfold" in Luke 22:64. In Heb. 9:4, it signifies to overlay. See BLINDFOLD, OVERLAY. ¶

NT: B.647d; CB.–; K.–.
OT: ḥāphas: S.2664; HR.1124a.1; H.716; BD.344b.
kāsāh: S.3680; HR.1124a.2; H.1008; BD.491b.
GEN. REF.: IS.1:797; NB.–; Z.–.

4. *sunkaluptō* [συγκαλύπτω, 4780], lit., to cover together; the *sun-*, however, is intensive, and the verb signifies to cover wholly, to cover up, Luke 12:2. ¶

NT: B.773b; CB.1270c; K.1098.
OT: kāsāh: S.3680; HR.1299a.3; H.1008; BD.491b.
ḥāphas: S.2664; HR.1299a.2; H.716; BD.344b.
GEN. REF.: IS.1:797; NB.–; Z.–.

5. *katakaluptō* [κατακαλύπτω, 2619], to cover up (*kata*, intensive), in the Middle Voice, to cover oneself, is used in 1 Cor. 11:6, 7 (R.V., "veiled"). ¶

NT: B.411a; CB.1254a; K.405.
OT: kāsāh: S.3680; HR.732c.3b; H.1008; BD.491b.
ḥāphas: S.2664; HR.732c.2; H.716; BD.344b.
GEN. REF.: IS.1:797; NB.–; Z.–.

Note: In 1 Cor. 11:4, "having his head covered" is, lit., 'having (something) down the head.'

B. Nouns.

1. *peribolaion* [περιβόλαιον, 4018], lit. denotes something thrown around (*peri*, around, *ballō*, to throw); hence, a veil, covering, 1 Cor. 11:15 (marg.), or a mantle around the body, a vesture, Heb. 1:12. See CLOTHING, Note (1), VESTURE. ¶

NT: B.646c; CB.1263b; K.–.
OT: kᵉsût: S.3682; HR.1122b.2a; H.1008b; BD.492b.
lᵉbûsh: S.3830; HR.1122b.3a; H.1075a; BD.528c.
GEN. REF.: IS.1:797; NB.–; Z.–.

2. *skepasma* [σκέπασμα, 4629], a covering (*skepazō*, to cover), strictly, a roofing, then, any kind of shelter or covering, is used in the plural in 1 Tim. 6:8 (A.V., "raiment"; R.V., "covering"). ¶

NT: B.753d; CB.–; K.–.
OT: –.
GEN. REF.: –.

COVET, COVETOUS, COVETOUSNESS

A. Verbs.

1. *epithumeō* [ἐπιθυμέω, 1937], to fix the desire upon (*epi*, upon, used intensively; *thumos*, passion), whether things good or bad; hence, to long for, lust after, covet, is used with the meaning to covet evilly in Acts 20:33, of coveting money and apparel; so in Rom. 7:7; 13:9. See DESIRE, FAIN, LUST.

NT: B.293a; CB.1246b; K.339.
OT: 'āwāh: S.183; HR.520b.1b; H.40; BD.16a.
hāphēṣ: S.2654; HR.520b.5; H.712; BD.342c.
ḥāmad: S.2530; HR.520b.4; H.673; BD.326a.
GEN. REF.: IS.1:797; NB.269; Z.1:1017.

2. *zēloō* [ζηλόω, 2206], is rendered "covet earnestly," in 1 Cor. 12:31, A.V.; R.V., "desire earnestly," as in 14:39 (A.V., "covet"). See AFFECT, DESIRE, ENVY, JEALOUS, ZEALOUS.

NT: B.338a; CB.1273b; K.297.
OT: qānā': S.7065; HR.594b.4a; H.2038; BD.888c.
GEN. REF.: IS.1:797; NB.–; Z.–.

3. *oregō* [ὀρέγω, 3713], to stretch after, is rendered "covet after" in 1 Tim. 6:10, A.V.; R.V., "reaching after." See DESIRE, REACH.

NT: B.579d; CB.1261a; K.–.
OT: –.
GEN. REF.: –.

B. Nouns.

1. *epithumētēs* [ἐπιθυμητής, 1938], a luster after (akin to A, No. 1), is translated in 1 Cor. 10:6, in verbal form, "should not lust after." See LUST ¶
NT: B.293b; CB.—; K.339.
OT: ʾāwāh: S.183; HR.520c.1; H.40; BD.16a.
ḥāmad: S.2530; HR.520c.2; H.673; BD.326a.
GEN. REF.: IS.1:797; NB.269; Z.1:1017.

2. *epithumia* [ἐπιθυμία, 1939], denotes "coveting," Rom. 7:7, 8, R.V.; A.V., "lust" and "concupiscence"; the commandment here referred to convicted him of sinfulness in his desires for unlawful objects besides that of gain. See DESIRE, LUST.
NT: B.293b; CB.1246b; K.339.
OT: taʾawāh: S.8378; HR.521a.1d; H.40d; BD.16b.
ḥāmad: S.2530; HR.521a.3a; H.673; BD.326a.
GEN. REF.: IS.1:797; NB.269; Z.1:1017.

3. *pleonexia* [πλεονεξία, 4124], covetousness, lit., a desire to have more (*pleon*, more, *echō*, to have), always in a bad sense, is used in a general way in Mark 7:22 (plural, lit., 'covetings,' i.e., various ways in which covetousness shows itself); Rom. 1:29; Eph. 5:3; 1 Thess. 2:5. Elsewhere it is used, (*a*) of material possessions, Luke 12:15; 2 Pet. 2:3; 2 Cor. 9:5 (R.V., "extortion"), lit., 'as (a matter of) extortion,' i.e., a gift which betrays the giver's unwillingness to bestow what is due; (*b*) of sensuality, Eph. 4:19, "greediness"; Col. 3:5 (where it is called idolatry); 2 Pet. 2:14 (A.V., "covetous practices"). See EXTORTION. ¶
NT: B.667d; CB.1265b; K.864.
OT: beṣaʿ: S.1215; HR.1142a.1; H.267a; BD.130c.
GEN. REF.: IS.1:797; NB.269; Z.1:1017.

Note: Cp. the corresponding verb *pleonekteō*, to gain, take advantage of, wrong. See ADVANTAGE, DEFRAUD, GAIN, B, *Note* (2), WRONG.

C. Adjectives.

1. *pleonektēs* [πλεονέκτης, 4123], lit., (eager) to have more (see B, No. 3), i.e., to have what belongs to others; hence, greedy of gain, covetous, 1 Cor. 5:10, 11; 6:10; Eph. 5:5 ("covetous man"). ¶
NT: B.667c; CB.1265b; K.864.
OT: —.
GEN. REF.: IS.1:797; NB.—; Z.1:1017.

2. *philarguros* [φιλάργυρος, 5366], lit., money-loving, is rendered "covetous" in the A.V. of Luke 16:14 and 2 Tim. 3:2; R.V., "lovers of money," the wider and due significance. ¶
NT: B.859b; CB.1264a; K.—.
OT: —.
GEN. REF.: IS.—; NB.—; Z.1:1017.

3. *aphilarguros* [ἀφιλάργυρος, 866], No. 2, with negative prefix, is translated "without covetousness" in Heb. 13:5, A.V.; R.V., "free from the love of money." In 1 Tim. 3:3, the A.V. has "not covetous," the R.V., "no lover of money."
NT: B.126c; CB.—; K.—.
OT: —.
GEN. REF.: —.

Note: Trench, Syn. § 24, points out the main distinction between *pleonexia* and *philarguria* as being that between covetousness and avarice, the former having a much wider and deeper sense, being "the genus of which *philarguria* is the species." The covetous man is often cruel as well as grasping, while the avaricious man is simply miserly and stinting.

CRAFT, CRAFTSMAN

1. *technē* [τέχνη], craft, Rev. 18:22: see ART.

2. *technitēs* [τεχνίτης, 5079], akin to No. 1, an artificer, artisan, craftsman, is translated "craftsman" in Acts 19:24, 38 and Rev. 18:22. It is found elsewhere in Heb. 11:10, "builder"; but this is practically the same as "maker" (*demiourgos*, the next noun in the verse; see No. 5, Note). Trench, Syn. § cv, suggests that *technitēs* brings out the artistic side of creation, viewing God as "moulding and fashioning . . . the materials which He called into existence." This agrees with the usage of the word in the Sept. See BUILDER. ¶
NT: B.814b; CB.1271b; K.—.
OT: ḥārāsh: S.2796; HR.1347c.3; H.—; BD.360d.
GEN. REF.: IS.—; NB.89; Z.1:1018.

3. *ergasia* [ἐργασία]: see DILIGENCE.

4. *homotechnos* [ὁμότεχνος, 3673], one of the same trade (from *homos*, same, and *technē*, see No. 1), is used in Acts 18:3 (R.V., "trade"). ¶ Cp. *architektōn*, "master-builder," 1 Cor. 3:10. ¶
NT: B.569b; CB.—; K.—.
OT: —.
GEN. REF.: —.

5. *meros* [μέρος, 3313], a part, portion, is translated "craft" in Acts 19:27, A.V.; "trade," R.V. (cp. *ergasia* in ver. 25). See BEHALF, COAST, PART, PIECE, PORTION, RESPECT, SORT.
NT: B.505d; CB.1258b; K.585.
OT: —.
GEN. REF.: —.

Note: Dēmiourgos, a maker, properly signifies one who works for the people, or whose work stands forth to the public gaze (*dēmos*, people, *ergon*, work), but this idea has been lost in the use of the word, which came to signify a maker, Heb. 11:10. This has reference to the structure, No. 2 to the design. Cp. *ktistēs*, a creator. ¶

CRAFTINESS, CRAFTY

A. Noun.

panourgia [πανουργία, 3834], lit., 'all-working,' i.e., doing everything (*pan*, all, *ergon*, work), hence, unscrupulous conduct, craftiness, is always used in a bad sense in the N.T., Luke 20:23; 1 Cor. 3:19; 2 Cor. 4:2; 11:3; Eph. 4:14, A.V., "cunning craftiness." See SUBTILTY. ¶ In the Sept. it is used in a good sense, Prov. 1:4; 8:5; indifferently in Numb. 24:22 and Josh. 9:4. ¶

NT: B.608a; CB.1261c; K.770.
OT: 'ārᵉmāh: S.6195; HR.1053a.1; H.1698b; BD.791a.
GEN. REF.: IS.1:800; NB.–; Z.–.

B. Adjective.

panourgos [πανοῦργος, 3835], cunning, crafty, is found in 2 Cor. 12:16, where the Apostle is really quoting an accusation made against him by his detractors. ¶ In the Sept. it is used in a good sense in Prov. 13:1; 28:2. ¶

NT: B.608a; CB.1261c; K.770.
OT: 'ārûm: S.6175; HR.1053a.2a; H.1698c; BD.791a.
'āram: S.6191; HR.1053a.2b; H.1698; BD.791a.
GEN. REF.: IS.1:800; NB.–; Z.–.

C. Noun.

dolos [δόλος, 1388], primarily, a bait, hence, fraud, guile, deceit, is rendered "craft" in the A.V. of Mark 14:1 (R.V. "subtilty"). See DECEIT, GUILE, SUBTILTY.

NT: B.203b; CB.–; K.–.
OT: mirmāh: S.4820; HR.340b.4a; H.2169b; BD.941b.
rᵉmiyyāh: S.7423; HR.340b.9; H.2169a; BD.941a.
GEN. REF.: –.

CRAVE

Note: The word "crave," found in the A.V. of Mark 15:43, translates the verb *aiteō*, to ask (R.V., "asked for"). See ASK.

CREATE, CREATION, CREATOR CREATURE

A. Verb.

ktizō [κτίζω, 2936], used among the Greeks to mean the founding of a place, a city or colony, signifies, in Scripture, to create, always of the act of God, whether (*a*) in the natural creation, Mark 13:19; Rom. 1:25 (where the title "The Creator" translates the article with the aorist participle of the verb); 1 Cor. 11:9; Eph. 3:9; Col. 1:16; 1 Tim. 4:3; Rev. 4:11; 10:6, or (*b*) in the spiritual creation, Eph. 2:10, 15; 4:24; Col. 3:10. See MAKE. ¶

NT: B.455c; CB.1256b; K.481.
OT: bārā': S.1254; HR.795b.1a; H.278; BD.135a.
yāṣar: S.3335; HR.795b.3; H.898; BD.427c.
GEN. REF.: IS.1:800; NB.269; Z.1:1020.

B. Nouns.

1. *ktisis* [κτίσις, 2937], primarily the act of creating, or the creative act in process, has this meaning in Rom. 1:20 and Gal. 6:15. Like the English word "creation," it also signifies the product of the creative act, the creature, as in Mark 16:15, R.V.; Rom. 1:25; 8:19; Col. 1:15 etc.; in Heb. 9:11, A.V., "building." In Mark 16:15 and Col. 1:23 its significance has special reference to mankind in general. As to its use in Gal. 6:15 and 2 Cor. 5:17, in the former, apparently, "the reference is to the creative act of God, whereby a man is introduced into the blessing of salvation, in contrast to circumcision done by human hands, which the Judaizers claimed was necessary to that end. In 2 Cor. 5:17 the reference is to what the believer is in Christ; in consequence of the creative act he has become a new creature."*

Ktisis is once used of human actions, 1 Pet. 2:13, "ordinance" (marg., "creation"). See BUILDING, ORDINANCE.

NT: B.455d; CB.1256a; K.481.
OT: qinyāw: S.7075; HR.795c.2; H.2039a; BD.889a.
GEN. REF.: IS.1:800; NB.269; Z.1:1020.

2. *ktisma* [κτίσμα, 2938], has the concrete sense, the created thing, the creature, the product of the creative act, 1 Tim. 4:4; Jas. 1:18; Rev. 5:13; 8:9. ¶

NT: B.456b; CB.1256a; K.481.
OT: –.
GEN. REF.: IS.1:800,804; NB.269; Z.1:1020.

3. *ktistēs* [κτίστης, 2939], among the Greeks, the founder of a city etc., denotes in Scripture the Creator, 1 Pet. 4:19 (cp. Rom. 1:20, under B, No. 1, above). ¶

NT: B.456b; CB.1256b; K.481.
OT: –.
GEN. REF.: IS.1:800; NB.269; Z.1:1020.

Note: It is a significant confirmation of Rom. 1:20, 21, that in all non-Christian Greek literature these words are never used by Greeks to convey the idea of a Creator or of a creative act by any of their gods. The words are confined by them to the acts of human beings.

4. *zōon* [ζῷον, 2226], a living creature: see BEAST.

NT: B.341c; CB.1273c; K.290.
OT: ḥayyāh: S.2416; HR.601b.1a; H.644a; BD.312c.
GEN. REF.: IS.1:804; NB.269; Z.1:1020.

For **CREDITOR** see **LEND, LENDER**

For **CREEK** see **BAY**

* From Notes on Galatians by Hogg and Vine, p. 339.

CREEP, CREEPING, CREPT

A. Verbs.

1. *endunō* [ἐνδύνω, 1744], properly, to envelop in (*en*, in, *dunō*, to enter), to put on, as of a garment, has the secondary and intransitive significance of creeping into, insinuating oneself into, and is found with this meaning in 2 Tim. 3:6. Cp. *enduō*, to clothe. ¶

NT: B.263d; CB.–; K.–.
OT: –.
GEN. REF.: –.

2. *pareisdunō* [παρεισδύνω, 3921], to enter in by the side (*para*, beside, *eis*, in), to insinuate onself into, by stealth, to creep in stealthily, is used in Jude 4.

NT: B.624d; CB.–; K.–.
OT: –.
GEN. REF.: –.

B. Noun.

herpeton [ἑρπετόν, 2062], signifies a creeping thing (*herpō*, to creep; Eng., "serpent" is from the same root), Jas. 3:7 (R.V., "creeping things," for A.V., "serpents," which form only one of this genus); it is set in contrast to quadrupeds and birds, Acts 10:12; 11:6; Rom. 1:23. See SERPENT. ¶

NT: B.310b; CB.–; K.–.
OT: –.
GEN. REF.: IS.–; NB.275; Z.1:1029.

For **CRIME** see **CHARGE**

For **CRIPPLE** see **HALT**

CROOKED

skolios [σκολιός, 4646], curved, crooked, was especially used (*a*) of a way, Luke 3:5, with spiritual import (see Prov. 28:18, Sept.); it is set in contrast to *orthos* and *euthus*, straight; (*b*) metaphorically, of what is morally crooked, perverse, froward, of people belonging to a particular generation, Acts 2:40 (A.V., "untoward"); Phil. 2:15; of tyrannical or unjust masters, 1 Pet. 2:18, "froward"; in this sense it is set in contrast to *agathos*, good. ¶

NT: B.756b; CB.–; K.1046.
OT: ʿiqqēsh: S.6141; HR.1275b.5a; H.1684a; BD.786a.
GEN. REF.: IS.1:825; NB.–; Z.–.

CROSS, CRUCIFY

A. Noun.

stauros [σταυρός, 4716], denotes, primarily, an upright pale or stake. On such malefactors were nailed for execution. Both the noun and the verb *stauroō*, to fasten to a stake or pale, are originally to be distinguished from the ecclesiastical form of a two beamed cross. The shape of the latter had its origin in ancient Chaldea, and was used as the symbol of the god Tammuz (being in the shape of the mystic Tau, the initial of his name) in that country and in adjacent lands, including Egypt. By the middle of the 3rd cent. A.D. the churches had either departed from, or had travestied, certain doctrines of the Christian faith. In order to increase the prestige of the apostate ecclesiastical system pagans were received into the churches apart from regeneration by faith, and were permitted largely to retain their pagan signs and symbols. Hence the Tau or T, in its most frequent form, with the cross-piece lowered, was adopted to stand for the cross of Christ.

As for the Chi, or X, which Constantine declared he had seen in a vision leading him to champion the Christian faith, that letter was the initial of the word "Christ" and had nothing to do with "the Cross" (for *xulon*, a timber beam, a tree, as used for the *stauros*, see under TREE).

The method of execution was borrowed by the Greeks and Romans from the Phoenicians. The *stauros* denotes (*a*) the cross, or stake itself, e.g., Matt. 27:32; (*b*) the crucifixion suffered, e.g., 1 Cor. 1:17, 18, where "the word of the cross," R.V., stands for the Gospel; Gal. 5:11, where crucifixion is metaphorically used of the renunciation of the world, that characterizes the true Christian life; 6:12, 14; Eph. 2:16; Phil. 3:18.

The judicial custom by which the condemned person carried his stake to the place of execution, was applied by the Lord to those sufferings by which His faithful followers were to express their fellowship with Him, e.g., Matt. 10:38.

NT: B.764d; CB.1270a; K.1071.
OT: –.
GEN. REF.: IS.1:825; NB.279; Z.1:1037.

B. Verbs

1. *stauroō* [σταυρόω, 4717], signifies (*a*) the act of crucifixion, e.g., Matt. 20:19; (*b*) metaphorically, the putting off of the flesh with its passions and lusts, a condition fulfilled in the case of those who are "of Christ Jesus," Gal. 5:24, R.V.; so the relationship between the believer and the world, 6:14.

NT: B.765b; CB.1270a; K.1071.
OT: tālāh: S.8518; HR.1287a.1; H.288d; BD.1067d.
GEN. REF.: IS.1:825; NB.279; Z.1:1037ff.

2. *sustauroō* [συσταυρόω, 4957], to crucify with (*su-*, for, *sun*, with), is used (*a*) of actual crucifixion in company with another, Matt.

27:44; Mark 15:32; John 19:32; (*b*) metaphorically, of spiritual identification with Christ in His death, Rom. 6:6, and Gal. 2:20. ¶

NT: B.765b; CB.1270a; K.1071.
OT: tālāh: S.8518; HR.1287a.1; H.288d; BD.1067d.
GEN. REF.: IS.1:825; NB.279; Z.1:1037ff.

3. *anastauroō* [ἀνασταυρόω, 388], (*ana*, again) is used in Heb. 6:6 of Hebrew apostates, who as merely nominal Christians, in turning back to Judaism, were thereby virtually guilty of crucifying Christ again. ¶

NT: B.61a; CB.1235b; K.1071.
OT: –.
GEN. REF.: IS.1:825; NB.279; Z.1:1037ff.

4. *prospēgnumi* [προσπήγνυμι, 4362], to fix or fasten to anything (*pros*, to, *pēgnumi*, to fix), is used of the crucifixion of Christ, Acts 2:23. ¶

NT: B.718a; CB.–; K.–.
OT: –.
GEN. REF.: –.

CROSS (Verb)

diaperaō [διαπεράω, 1276], to pass over, to cross over (*dia*, through, *peraō*, to pass: akin to this are *peran*, across, *peras*, a boundary, Latin, *porta*, a gate, Eng., portal, port, etc.), is translated by the verb to cross in the R.V., but differently in the A.V.; in Matt. 9:1; Mark 5:21; 6:53 (A.V., "passed"); Matt. 14:34 (A.V., "were gone"); Luke 16:26 (A.V., "neither can they pass"); Acts 21:2 (A.V., "sailing"). See GO, PASS, SAIL. ¶ In the Sept., Deut. 30:13; Is. 23:2. ¶

NT: B.187c; CB.–; K.–.
OT: ʿābar: S.5674; HR.307c.1; H.1556; BD.716d.
GEN. REF.: –.

For the verb **CROW (CREW)** see **CALL,** A, No. 8

CROWD

A. Noun.

ochlos [ὄχλος, 3793], a confused throng, is usually translated "multitude."

The R.V. translates it "crowd" (A.V., "press" in some) in Matt. 9:23, 25; Mark 2:4; 3:9; 5:27, 30; Luke 8:19; 19:3; Acts 21:34, 35; 24:12, 18; See COMPANY, MULTITUDE, NUMBER, PEOPLE.

NT: B.600c; CB.1260b; K.750.
OT: hāmôn: S.1995; HR.1043a.1; H.505a; BD.242b.
GEN. REF.: IS.1:830; NB.–; Z.–.

B. Verb.

ochlopoieō [ὀχλοποιέω, 3792], to make a crowd (A, with *poieō*, to make), is translated "gathered a crowd" in Acts 17:5, R.V. (A.V., "company").

NT: B.600c; CB.–; K.–.
OT: –.
GEN. REF.: –.

CROWN (Noun and Verb)

A. Nouns.

1. *stephanos* [στέφανος, 4735], primarily, that which surrounds, as a wall or crowd (from *stephō*, to encircle), denotes (*a*) the victor's crown, the symbol of triumph in the games or some such contest; hence, by metonymy, a reward or prize; (*b*) a token of public honour for distinguished service, military prowess etc., or of nuptial joy, or festal gladness, especially at the parousia of kings. It was woven as a garland of oak, ivy, parsley, myrtle or olive, or in imitation of these in gold. In some passages the reference to the games is clear, 1 Cor. 9:25; 2 Tim. 4:8 ("crown of righteousness"); it may be so in 1 Pet. 5:4, where the fadeless character of "the crown of glory" is set in contrast to the garlands of earth. In other passages it stands as an emblem of life, joy, reward and glory, Phil. 4:1; 1 Thess. 2:19; Jas. 1:12 ("crown of life"); Rev. 2:10 (ditto); 3:11; 4:4, 10; of triumph, 6:2; 9:7; 12:1; 14:14.

It is used of the crown of thorns which the soldiers plaited and put on Christ's head, Matt. 27:29; Mark 15:17; John 19:2, 5. At first sight this might be taken as an alternative for *diadēma*, a kingly crown (see below), but considering the blasphemous character of that masquerade, and the materials used, obviously *diadēma* would be quite unfitting and the only alternative was *stephanos* (see Trench § xxxii). ¶

NT: B.767a; CB.1270a; K.1078.
OT: ʿᵃṭārāh: S.5850; HR.1289c.4; H.1608a; BD.742d.
GEN. REF.: IS.1:831; NB.280; Z.1:1039.

2. *diadēma* [διάδημα, 1238], is never used as *stephanos* is; it is always the symbol of kingly or imperial dignity, and is translated "diadem" instead of "crown" in the R.V., of the claims of the Dragon, Rev. 12:3; 13:1; 19:12. See DIADEM. ¶

NT: B.182d; CB.1241a; K.–.
OT: keter: S.3804; HR.300a.1; H.1060a; BD.509d.
ṣāniph: S.6797; HR.300a.2b; H.1940a; BD.857b.
GEN. REF.: IS.1:831; NB.280; Z.1:1039.

B. Verb.

stephanoō [στεφανόω, 4737], to crown, conforms in meaning to *stephanos*; it is used of the reward of victory in the games, in 2 Tim. 2:5; of the glory and honour bestowed by God upon man in regard to his position in creation Heb. 2:7; of the glory and honour bestowed upon the Lord Jesus in His exaltation, ver. 9. ¶

NT: B.767c; CB.1270a; K.1078.
OT: ʿāṭar: S.5849; HR.1290a.1; H.1608,1608b; BD.742d.
GEN. REF.: IS.1:831; NB.280; Z.1:1039.

For **CRUCIFY** see **CROSS**

CRUMB

psichion [ψιχίον, 5589], a small morsel, a diminutive of *psix*, a bit, or crumb; of bread or meat, it is used in Matt. 15:27 and Mark 7:28; some mss. have it in Luke 16:21. ¶

NT: B.893a; CB.–; K.–.
OT: –.
GEN. REF.: –.

CRUSE

alabastron [ἀλάβαστρον, 211], was a vessel for holding ointment or perfume; it derived its name from the alabaster stone, of which it was usually made. "Cruse," R.V., is a more suitable rendering than "box"; Matt. 26:7; Mark 14:3; Luke 7:37. ¶

NT: B.34c; CB.–; K.–.
OT: ṣallaḥat: S.6747; HR.52a.1; H.1918b; BD.852c.
GEN. REF.: IS.1:832; NB.1309; Z.1:1042.

CRUSH

apothlibō [ἀποθλίβω, 598], a strengthened form of *thlibō*, to throng (*apo*, intensive), is used in Luke 8:45, R.V., "crush," for A.V., "press," of the multitude who were pressing around Christ (cp. the preceding word *sunechō*, to press). ¶ In the Sept., Numb. 22:25. ¶

NT: B.91b; CB.–; K.–.
OT: lāḥaṣ: S.3905; HR.128a.1; H.1106; BD.537d.
GEN. REF.: –.

CRY (Noun and Verb), CRYING

A. Nouns.

1. *kraugē* [κραυγή, 2906], an onomatopoeic word, is used in Matt. 25:6; Luke 1:42 (some mss. have *phōnē*); Acts 23:9, R.V., "clamour"; Eph. 4:31, "clamour"; Heb. 5:7; Rev. 21:4, "crying." Some mss. have it in Rev. 14:18 (the most authentic have *phōnē*). See CLAMOUR. ¶

NT: B.449c; CB.–; K.465.
OT: zā'aq: S.2199; HR.784b.3a; H.570; BD.277a.
ṣᵉ'āqāh: S.6818; HR.784b.6; H.1947a; BD.858c.
GEN. REF.: IS.1:832; NB.–; Z.1:1042.

2. *boē* [βοή, 995], especially a cry for help, an onomatopoeic word (cp. Eng., boo), connected with *boaō* (see B, No. 1), is found in Jas. 5:4. ¶

NT: B.144c; CB.1239b; K.–.
OT: ṣᵉ'āqāh: S.6818; HR.222c.3; H.1947a; BD.858c.
shaw'āh: S.7775; HR.222c.6; H.2348c; BD.1003a.
GEN. REF.: IS.1:832; NB.–; Z.1:1042.

B. Verbs.

1. *boaō* [βοάω, 994], akin to A, No. 2, signifies (*a*) to raise a cry, whether of joy, Gal. 4:27, or vexation, Acts 8:7; (*b*) to speak with a strong voice, Matt. 3:3; Mark 1:3; 15:34; Luke 3:4; 9:38 (some mss. have *anaboaō* here: see No. 2); John 1:23; Acts 17:6; 25:24 (some mss. have *epiboaō*, No. 3, here); (*c*) to cry out for help, Luke 18:7, 38. ¶ For Acts 21:34, see No. 8.

NT: B.144b; CB.1239a; K.108.
OT: ṣā'aq: S.6817; HR.222a.12a; H.1947; BD.858b.
qārā': S.7121; HR.222a.14a; H.2063; BD.894d.
shāwa': S.7768; HR.222a.18; H.2348; BD.1002d.
GEN. REF.: IS.1:832; NB.–; Z.1:1042.

2. *anaboaō* [ἀναβοάω, 310], *ana*, up, intensive, and No. 1, to lift up the voice, cry out, is said of Christ at the moment of His Death, a testmony to His supernatural power in giving up His life, Matt. 27:46; in some mss. in Mark 15:8, of the shouting of a multitude; in some mss. in Luke 9:38, of the crying out of a man in a company (see No. 1). ¶

NT: B.51a; CB.1235a; K.–.
OT: ṣā'aq: S.6817; HR.73c.3a; H.1947; BD.858b.
qārā: S.7121; HR.73c.4; H.2063; BD.894d.
GEN. REF.: IS.1:832; NB.–; Z.1:1042.

3. *epiboaō* [ἐπιβοάω, 1916], *epi*, upon, intensive, and No. 1, to cry out, exclaim vehemently, is used in some mss. in Acts 25;24 (see No. 1. ¶)

NT: B.290c; CB.–; K.–.
OT: –.
GEN. REF.: IS.–; NB.–; Z.1:1042.

4. *krazō* [κράζω, 2896], akin to A, No. 1, to cry out, an onomatopoeic word, used especially of the cry of the raven; then, of any inarticulate cries, from fear, pain etc.; of the cry of a Canaanitish woman, Matt. 15:22 (so the best mss., instead of *kraugazō*); of the shouts of the children in the Temple, Matt. 21:15; of the people who shouted for Christ to be crucified, 27:23; Mark 15:13, 14; of the cry of Christ on the Cross at the close of His sufferings, Matt. 27:50; Mark 15:39 (see No. 2, above).

In John's Gospel it is used three times, out of the six, of Christ's utterances, 7:28, 37; 12:44. In the Acts it is not used of cries of distress, but chiefly of the shouts of opponents; in the Apocalypse, chiefly of the utterances of heavenly beings concerning earthly matters; in Rom. 8:15 and Gal. 4:6, of the appeal of believers to God the Father; in Rom. 9:27, of a prophecy concerning Israel; in Jas. 5:4, metaphorically, of hire kept back by fraud.

NT: B.447c; CB.1256a; K.465.
OT: ṣā'aq: S.6817; HR.781b.3a; H.1947; BD.858b.
qārā: S.7121; HR.781b.4a; H.2063; BD.894d.
shāwa': S.7768; HR.781b.7; H.2348; BD.1002d.
GEN. REF.: IS.1:832; NB.–; Z.1:1042.

Note: A recent translator renders this verb in Matt. 27:50 "uttered a scream," an utterly deplorable mistranslation, and a misrepresentation of the nature of the Lord's cry.

5. *anakrazō* [ἀνακράζω, 349], *ana*, up, intensive, and No. 4, signifies to cry out loudly, Mark 1:23; 6:49; Luke 4:33; 8:28; 23:18. ¶

NT: B.56b; CB.–; K.465.
OT: rûa': S.7321; HR.78b.3; H.2135; BD.929c.
qārā: S.7121; HR.78b.2; H.2063; BD.894d.
zā'aq: S.2199; HR.78b.1; H.570; BD.277a.
GEN. REF.: IS.1:832; NB.–; Z.1:1042.

6. *kraugazō* [κραυγάζω, 2905], a stronger form of No. 4, to make a clamour or outcry (A, No. 1), is used in Matt. 12:19, in a prophecy from Isaiah of Christ; in Luke 4:41 (in the best mss., instead of *krazō*); John 11:43; 12:13 (in the best mss.); 18:40; 19:6, 12, 15; Acts 22:23. ¶

NT: B.449b; CB.1256a; K.465.
OT: rûa: S.7321; HR.784b.1; H.2135; BD.929c.
GEN. REF.: –; NB.–; Z.1:1042.

7. *phōneō* [φωνέω, 5455], to utter a loud sound or cry, whether of animals, e.g., Matt. 26:34; or persons, Luke 8:8; 16:24; this is the word which Luke uses to describe the cry of the Lord at the close of His sufferings on the Cross, Luke 23:46 (see under *anaboaō* and *krazō*, above); also, e.g., Acts 16:28; Rev. 14:18. See CALL, A, No. 8, CROW.

NT: B.870b; CB.1264b; K.1287.
OT: qārā: S.7121; HR.1447b.4; H.2063; BD.894d.
GEN. REF.: 1:832; NB.–; Z.1:1042.

8. *epiphōneō* [ἐπιφωνέω, 2019], No. 7, with *epi*, upon, or against, signifies to shout, either against, Luke 23:21; Acts 21:34 (in the best mss., No. 1); 22:24, or in acclamation, Acts 12:22. See SHOUT. ¶

NT: B.304d; CB.1246a; K.–.
OT: –.
GEN. REF.: IS.–; NB.–; Z.1:1042.

Note: For *aphiēmi*, Mark 15:37, see UTTER.

Comparing the various verbs, *kaleō*, denotes to call out for any purpose, *boaō*, to cry out as an expression of feeling, *krazō*, to cry out loudly. *Kaleō* suggests intelligence, *boaō*, sensibilities, *krazō*, instincts.

CRYSTAL

A. Noun.

krustallos [κρύσταλλος, 2930], from *kruos*, ice, and hence properly anything congealed and transparent, denotes crystal, a kind of precious stone, Rev. 4:6; 22:1. Rock-crystal is pure quartz; it crystallizes in hexagonal prisms, each with a pyramidical apex. ¶

NT: B.454d; CB.1256a; K.–.
OT: qeraḥ: S.7140; HR.792c.4; H.6070a; BD.901c.
'eqdāh: S.688; HR.792c.1; H.1987b; BD.869b.
GEN. REF.: IS.1:832; NB.632; Z.1:1042.

B. Verb.

krustallizō [κρυσταλλίζω, 2929], to be of crystalline brightness and transparency, to shine like crystal, is found in Rev. 21:11, where it is said of Christ as the "Light-giver" (*phōstēr*) of the Heavenly City (not *phōs*, light, R.V. and A.V.). Possibly there the verb has a transitive force, to transform into crystal splendour, as of the effect of Christ upon His saints. ¶

NT: B.454d; CB.1256a; K.–.
OT: –.
GEN. REF.: IS.1:832; NB.632; Z.1:1042.

CUBIT

pēchus [πῆχυς, 4083], denotes the fore-arm, i.e., the part between the hand and the elbow-joint; hence, a measure of length, not from the wrist to the elbow, but from the tip of the middle finger to the elbow joint, i.e., about a foot and a half, or a little less than two feet, Matt. 6:27; Luke 12:25; John 21:8; Rev. 21:17. ¶

NT: B.656d; CB.–; K.–.
OT: 'ammāh: S.520; HR.1131b.1; H.115c; BD.52a.
GEN. REF.: IS.1:832; NB.1321,1324; Z.5:914.

CUMBER

1. *katargeō* [καταργέω, 2673], lit., to reduce to idleness or inactivity (*kata*, down, and *argos*, idle), is once rendered "cumber," Luke 13:7. See ABOLISH. ¶

NT: B.417b; CB.1254b; K.76.
OT: –.
GEN. REF.: IS.1:833; NB.–; Z.–.

2. *perispaō* [περισπάω, 4049], lit., to draw around (*peri*), draw away, distract, is used in the Passive Voice in the sense of being over-occupied about a thing, to be cumbered, Luke 10:40. ¶

NT: B.650b; CB.–; K.–.
OT: –.
GEN. REF.: –.

CUMMIN

kuminon [κύμινον, 2951], is an umbelliferous plant with aromatic seeds, used as a condiment, Matt. 23:23.

NT: B.457c; CB.1256b; K.–.
OT: kammōn: S.3646; HR.799b.1; H.991,991b; BD.485a.
GEN. REF.: IS.1:833; NB.282; Z.1:1043.

For the A.V. **CUNNING** see **CRAFTINESS.** For **CUNNINGLY** see **DEVISED**

CUP

potērion [ποτήριον, 4221], a diminutive of *potēr*, denotes, primarily, a drinking vessel; hence, a cup (*a*) literal, as, e.g., in Matt. 10:42. The cup of blessing, 1 Cor. 10:16, is so named from the third (the fourth according to Edersheim) cup in the Jewish Passover Feast, over which thanks and praise were given to God. This connection is not to be rejected on the ground that the church at Corinth was unfamiliar with Jewish customs. That the contrary was the case, see 5:7; (*b*) figurative, of one's lot or experience, joyous or sorrowful (frequent in the Psalms; cp. Ps. 116:18, "cup of salvation"); in the N.T. it is used most frequently of the sufferings of Christ, Matt.

20:22, 23; 26:39; Mark 10:38, 39; 14:36; Luke 22:42; John 18:11; also of the evil deeds of Babylon, Rev. 17:4; 18:6; of Divine punishments to be inflicted, Rev. 14:10; 16:19. Cp. Ps. 11:6; 75:8; Is. 51:17; Jer. 25:15; Ezek. 23:32-34; Zech. 12:2.

NT: B.695b; CB.1266b; K.841.
OT: kôs: S.3563; HR.1197b.1a; H.965,966; BD.468a.
GEN. REF.: IS.1:836; NB.282; Z.1:1044.

CURE (Noun and Verb)

A. Noun.

iasis [ἴασις, 2392], a healing, a cure (akin to *iaomai*, to heal, and *iatros*, a physician), is used in the plural in Luke 13:32; in Acts 4:22, "healing"; in 4:30 with the preposition *eis*, unto, lit., 'unto healing,' translated "heal." See HEALING. ¶

NT: B.368c; CB.1252c; K.344.
OT: marpē': S.4832; HR.668c.4a; H.2196c; BD.951b.
'^{a}rûkāh: S.724; HR.668c.1; H.162d; BD.74a.
GEN. REF.: IS.2:640; NB.—; Z.—.

B. Verb.

therapeuō [θεραπεύω, 2323], Eng., therapeutics, etc., denotes (*a*) primarily, to serve (cp. *therapeia* and *therapōn*), Actgs 17:25 (A.V., "worshipped"); then, (*b*) to heal, restore to health, to cure; it is usually translated "to heal," but "cure" in Matt. 17:16, 18; Luke 7:21; 9:1; John 5:10, Acts 28:9, R.V. see HEAL, WORSHIP.

NT: B.359a; CB.1272b; K.331.
OT: —.
GEN. REF.: IS.2:640; NB.—; Z.—.

CURIOUS

Note: For the adjective *periergos*, busy about trifles, see BUSYBODY: it is used of magic arts in Acts 19:19 (lit, 'things that are around work,' and thus superfluous), i.e., the arts of those who pry into forbidden things, with the aid of evil spirits. See also 1 Tim. 5:13, where the meaning is "inquisitive," prying into other people's affairs.

CURSE, CURSING (Noun and Verb), CURSED, ACCURSED

A. Nouns.

1. *ara* [ἀρά, 685], in its most usual meaning, a malediction, cursing (its other meaning is "a prayer"), is used in Rom. 3:14 (often in the Sept.). ¶

NT: B.103d; CB.1237b; K.75.
OT: 'ālāh: S.423; HR.152b,2b; H.91a; BD.46d.
q^{e}lālāh: S.7045; HR.152b.3; H.2028d; BD.887a.
GEN. REF.: IS.1:837; NB.283; Z.1:1045.

2. *katara* [κατάρα, 2671], *kata*, down, intensive, and No. 1, denotes an execration, imprecation, curse, uttered out of malevolence, Jas. 3:10; 2 Pet. 2:14; or pronounced by God in His righteous judgment, as upon a land doomed to barrenness, Heb. 6:8; upon those who seek for justification by obedience, in part or completely, to the Law, Gal. 3:10, 13; in this 13th verse it is used concretely of Christ, as having "become a curse" for us, i.e., by voluntarily undergoing on the Cross the appointed penalty of the curse. He thus was identified, on our behalf, with the doom of sin. Here, not the verb in the Sept. of Deut. 21:23 is used (see B, No. 3), but the concrete noun. ¶

NT: B.417a; CB.1254b; K.75.
OT: q^{e}lālāh: S.7045; HR.742b.5; H.2028d; BD.887a.
m^{e}'ērāh: S.3994; HR.742b.3; H.168a; BD.76d.
GEN. REF.: IS.1:837; NB.283; Z.1:1045.

3. *anathema* [ἀνάθεμα, 331], transliterated from the Greek, is frequently used in the Sept., where it translates the Heb. *cherem*, a thing devoted to God, whether (*a*) for His service, as the sacrifices, Lev. 27:28 (cp. *anathēma*, a votive offering, gift), or (*b*) for its destruction, as an idol, Deut. 7:26, or a city, Josh. 6:17. Later it acquired the more general meaning of the disfavour of Jehovah, e.g., Zech. 14:11. This is the meaning in the N.T. It is used of (*a*) the sentence pronounced, Acts 23:14 (lit., 'cursed themselves with a curse'; see *anathematizō* below); (*b*) of the object on which the curse is laid, "accursed"; in the following, the R.V. keeps to the word "anathema," Rom. 9:3; 1 Cor. 12:3; 16:22; Gal. 1:8, 9, all of which the A.V. renders by "accursed" except 1 Cor. 16:22, where it has "Anathema." In Gal. 1:8, 9, the Apostle declares in the strongest manner that the Gospel he preached was the one and only way of salvation, and that to preach another was to nullify the Death of Christ. ¶

NT: B.54a; CB.1235b; K.57.
OT: ḥērem: S.2764; HR.77a.1a; H.744a; BD.356a.
GEN. REF.: IS.1:837; NB.283; Z.—.

4. *katahtema* [κατάθεμα, 2652], or, as in some mss., the longer form *katanathema*, is stronger than No. 3 (*kata*, intensive), and denotes, by metonymy, an accursed thing (the object cursed being put for the curse pronounced), Rev. 22:3. ¶

NT: B.410c; CB.1254b; K.57.
OT: —.
GEN. REF.: IS.—; NB.283; Z.—.

B. Verbs.

1. *anathematizō* [ἀναθεματίζω, 332], akin to No. 3, signifies to declare anathema, i.e., devoted to destruction, accursed, to curse, Mark 14:71, or to bind by a curse, Acts 23:12, 14, 21. ¶

NT: B.54c; CB.1235b; K.57.
OT: ḥāram: S.2763; HR.77a.1a; H.744; BD.355c.
GEN. REF.: IS.1:837; NB.283; Z.—.

2. *katanathematizō* [καταναθεματίζω, 2653], a strengthened form of No. 1, denotes to

utter curses against, Matt. 26:74; cp. Mark's word concerning the same occasion (No. 1). ¶

NT: B.414d; CB.1254b; K.57.
OT: —.
GEN. REF.: IS.1:837; NB.283; Z.—.

3. *kataraomai* [καταράομαι, 2672], akin to A, No. 2, primarily signifies to pray against, to wish evil against a person or thing; hence to curse, Matt. 25:41; Mark 11:21; Luke 6:28; Rom. 12:14; Jas. 3:9. Some mss. have it in Matt. 5:44. ¶

NT: B.417a; CB.1254b; K.75.
OT: 'ārar: S.779; HR.742c.1a; H.168; BD.76d.
qālal: S.7043; HR.742c.6a,b; H.2028; BD.886b.
GEN. REF.: IS.1:837; NB.283; Z.1:1045.

4. *kakologeō* [κακολογέω, 2551], to speak evil (*kakos*, evil, *legō*, to speak), is translated by the verb to curse in Matt. 15:4, and Mark 7:10, to speak evil of father and mother, not necessarily to curse, is what the Lord intended (R.V.). A.V. and R.V. have the verb to speak evil in Mark 9:39 and Acts 19:9. See EVIL.

NT: B.397b; CB.1253b; K.391.
OT: qālal: S.7043; HR.709a.1; H.2028; BD.886b.
GEN. REF.: IS.1:837; NB.283; Z.1:1045.

C. Adjectives.

1. *epikataratos* [ἐπικατάρατος, 1944], cursed, accursed (*epi*, upon, and A, No. 2), is used in Gal. 3:10, 13. ¶

NT: B.294c; CB.1245c; K.75.
OT: 'ārar: S.779; HR.522c.1; H.168; BD.76d.
GEN. REF.: IS.1:837; NB.283; Z.1:1045.

2. *eparatos* [ἐπάρατος, —], accursed, is found, in the best mss., in John 7:49, R.V., "accursed," instead of No. 1.

NT: B.283c; CB.1245c; K.75.
OT: —.
GEN. REF.: —.

For **CUSHION** see **PILLOW**

CUSTOM (Usage), ACCUSTOM (Verb)

A. Nouns.

1. *ethos* [ἔθος, 1485], denotes (*a*) a custom, usage, prescribed by law, Acts 6:14; 15:1; 25:16; a rite or ceremony Luke 2:42; (*b*) a custom, habit, manner, Luke 22:39; John 19:40; Heb. 10:25 (A.V., "manner"). See MANNER, WONT.

NT: B.218d; CB.1247a; K.202.
OT: —.
GEN. REF.: IS.1:840; NB.—; Z.1:1049.

2. *sunētheia* [συνήθεια, 4914], *sun*, with, *ethos* (see No. 1), denotes (*a*) an intercourse, intimacy, a meaning not found in the N.T. (*b*) a custom, customary usage, John 18:39; 1 Cor. 11:16; or force of habit, 1 Cor. 8:7, R.V., "being used to" (some mss. here have *suneidēsis*, conscience; whence A.V., "with conscience of"). ¶

NT: B.789c; CB.—; K.—.
OT: —.
GEN. REF.: IS.1:840; NB.—; Z.1:1049.

B. Verbs.

1. *ethizō* [ἐθίζω, 1480], akin to A, No. 1, signifies to accustom, or in the Passive Voice, to be accustomed. In the participial form it is equivalent to a noun, "custom," Luke 2:27. ¶

NT: B.218b; CB.—; K.—.
OT: —.
GEN. REF.: IS.1:840; NB.—; Z.1:1049.

2. *ethō* [ἔθω, 1486], to be accustomed, as in the case of No. 1, is used in the Passive participle as a noun, signifying a custom, Luke 4:16; Acts 17:2 (A.V., "manner"; R.V., "custom"); in Matt. 17:15 and Mark 10:1, "was wont." See MANNER, WONT. ¶

NT: B.234a; CB.—; K.—.
OT: —.
GEN. REF.: IS.1:840; NB.—; Z.1:1049.

CUSTOM (Toll)

1. *telos* [τέλος, 5056], an end, termination, whether of time or purpose, denotes, in its secondary significance, what is paid for public ends, a toll, tax, custom, Matt. 17:25 (R.V., "toll"); Rom. 13:7 (R.V. and A.V., "custom"). In Palestine the Herods of Galilee and Peraea received the custom; in Judaea it was paid to the Procurator for the Roman Government. See END, FINALLY, UTTERMOST

NT: B.811b; CB.1271b; K.1161.
OT: mekem: S.4371; HR.1344a.1a; H.1014a; BD.493d.
GEN. REF.: IS.4:739; NB.—; Z.1:1049.

2. *telōnion* [τελώνιον, 5058], denotes a custom-house, for the collection of the taxes, Matt., 9:9; Mark 2:14; Luke 5:27 (R.V., "place of toll").

NT: B.812c; CB.1271b; K.—.
OT: —.
GEN. REF.: IS.4:739; NB.—; Z.1:1049.

CUT

1. *koptō* [κόπτω, 2875], denotes to cut by a blow, e.g., branches, Matt. 21:8; Mark 11:8. See BEWAIL, LAMENT, MOURN, WAIL

NT: B.444a; CB.1255c; K.453.
OT: kārat: S.3772; HR.779a.6a; H.1048; BD.503c.
GEN. REF.: IS.1:840; NB.—; Z.1:1049.

2. *apokoptō* [ἀποκόπτω, 609], to cut off, or cut away (*apo* from, and No. 1), is used (*a*) literally, of members of the body, Mark 9:43, 45; John 18:10, 26; of ropes, Acts 27:32; (*b*) metaphorically, in the Middle Voice, of cutting off oneself, to excommunicate, Gal. 5:12, of the Judaizing teachers, with a reference, no doubt, to circumcision. ¶

NT: B.93a; CB.1237a; K.453.
OT: qāṣaṣ: S.7112; HR.133a.4; H.2060; BD.893c.
kārat: S.3772; HR.133a.3; H.1048; BD.503c.
GEN. REF.: IS.1:840; NB.—; Z.1:1049.

3. *ekkoptō* [ἐκκόπτω, 1581], lit., to cut or strike out (*ek*, out or off, and No. 1), to cut down, is used (*a*) literally, Matt. 5:30 (in 3:10

and 7:19) and Luke 3:9, "hewn down"); 18:8; Luke 13:7, 9; (*b*) metaphorically, of cutting off from spiritual blessing, Rom. 11:22, 24; of depriving persons of an occasion for something, 2 Cor. 11:12. See HEW. ¶

NT: B.241d; CB.1243c; K.453.
OT: kārat: S.3772; HR.434c.4; H.1048; BD.503c.
gāda': S.1438; HR.434c.2; H.316; BD.154b.
nākāh: S.5221; HR.434c.5; H.1364; BD.645a.
GEN. REF.: IS.1:840; NB.–; Z.1:1049.

Note: In 1 Pet. 3:7 the best mss. have *enkoptō*, to hinder; some have *ekkoptō*.

4. *katakoptō* [*κατακόπτω*, 2629], lit., to cut down, cut in pieces (*kata*, down, intensive), Mark 5:5, of the demoniac. ¶

NT: B.412a; CB.–; K.–.
OT: gāda': S.1438; HR.734b.1; H.316; BD.154b.
nākāh: S.5221; HR.734b.6; H.1364; BD.645a.
qāṣaṣ: S.7112; HR.734b.8; H.2060; BD.893c.
GEN. REF.: IS.1:840; NB.–; Z.1:1049.

5. *diapriō* [*διαπρίω*, 1282], signifies to saw asunder (*dia*, asunder, *priō*, to saw), to divide by a saw (as in 1 Chron. 20:3, Sept.), hence, metaphorically, to be sawn through mentally, to be rent with vexation, to be cut to the heart, is used in Acts 5:33; 7:54. ¶

NT: B.187d; CB.–; K.–.
OT: sûr: S.7787; HR.308c.1; H.2245; BD.965a.
GEN. REF.: –.

6. *dichotomeō* [*διχοτομέω*, 1371], lit., to cut into two parts (*dicha*, apart, *temnō*, to cut, *tomē*, a cutting), Matt. 24:51, to cut asunder, is used in Luke 12:46. Some take the reference to be to the mode of punishment by which criminals and captives were cut in two; others, on account of the fact that in these passages the delinquent is still surviving after the treatment, take the verb to denote to cut up by scourging to scourge severely, the word being used figuratively.

As to Matt. 24:51, it has been remarked that the cutting asunder was an appropriate punishment for one who had lived a double life. In both passages the latter part of the sentence applies to retribution beyond this life. ¶ In the Sept. the verb is used in Ex. 29:17 of the dividing of the ram as a whole burnt offering at the consecration of the priests. ¶ The corresponding noun is found in Gen. 15:11, 17; Ex. 29:17; Lev. 1:8; Ezek. 24:4. ¶

NT: B.200c; CB.–; K.177.
OT: nātaḥ: S.5408; HR.338a.1; H.1441; BD.677c.
GEN. REF.: –.

7. *suntemnō* [*συντέμνω*, 4932], lit., to cut together (*sun*, with, *temnō*, to cut; the simple verb *temnō* is not found in the N.T.), signifies to contract by cutting, to cut short; thus, to bring to an end or accomplish speedily; it is said of a prophecy or decree, Rom. 9:28 (twice), from the Sept. of Is. 10:23. See SHORT. ¶

NT: B.792b; CB.–; K.–.
OT: ḥāraṣ: S.2782; HR.1320b.1; H.752; BD.358c.
GEN. REF.: –.

8. *aphaireō* [*ἀφαιρέω*, 851], to take away, remove, is translated "cut off "in Mark 14:47, A.V., and Luke 22:50, and "smote off" in Matt. 26:51; R.V., "struck off" in each place. See SMITE, TAKE.

NT: B.124b; CB.1236b; K.–.
OT: rûm: S.7311; HR.180a.32; H.2133; BD.927b.
sûr: S.5493; HR.180a.23; H.1480; BD.693b.
GEN. REF.: –.

CYMBAL

kumbalon [*κύμβαλον*, 2950], a cymbal, was so called from its shape (akin to *kumbos*, a hollow basin, *kumbē*, a cup), and was made of bronze, two being struck together, 1 Cor. 13:1. ¶

NT: B.457c; CB.–; K.486.
OT: m^{e}ṣēlet: S.4700; HR.799b.2; H.1919f; BD.853a.
GEN. REF.: IS.1:842; NB.855; Z.4:319.

D

DAILY (Adjective)

1. *epiousios* [ἐπιούσιος, 1967], is found in Matt. 6:11 and Luke 11:3. Some would derive the word from *epi*, upon, and *eimi*, to be, as if to signify "(Bread) present," i.e., sufficient bread, but this formation is questionable. The same objection applies to the conjecture, that it is derived from *epi*, and *ousia*, and signifies "(bread) for sustenance." The more probable derivation is from *epi*, and *eimi*, to go, (bread) for going on, i.e., for the morrow and after, or (bread) coming (for us). See the R.V. marg. This suits the added *sēmeron*, "to-day," i.e., the prayer is to be for bread that suffices for this day and next, so that the mind may conform to Christ's warning against anxiety for the morrow. Confirmation of this derivation is also to be found in the word *epiousē*, in the phrase "the next day," Act 7:26; 16:11. ¶

NT: B.296d; CB.1246a; K.243.
OT: —.
GEN. REF.: IS.1:851; NB.—; Z.—.

2. *ephēmeros* [ἐφήμερος, 2184], signifies "for the day" (*epi*, upon, or for, *hēmera*, a day, Eng., ephermeral), Jas. 2:15. ¶

NT: B.330c; CB.—; K.—.
OT: —.
GEN. REF.: IS.—

3. *kathēmerinos* [καθημερινός, 2522], means, lit., according to (*kata*) the day (*hēmera*), day by day, daily, Acts 6:1. ¶

NT: B.389d.
OT: —.
GEN. REF.: IS.—.

Notes: The following phrases contain the word *hēmera*, day, and are translated "daily" or otherwise: (*a*) *kath' hēmeran*, lit., according to, or for, (the) day, or throughout the day, "day by day," e.g., Luke 11:3; Acts 3:2; 16:5; 1 Cor. 15:31; Heb. 7:27; (*b*) *hēmera kai hēmera*, lit., day and day, "day by day," 2 Cor. 4:16; (*c*) *hēmeran ex hēmeras*, lit., day from day, "from day to day," 2 Pet. 2:8; (*d*) *sēmeron*, "this day," or "to-day," used outside the Synoptists and the Acts, in 2 Cor. 3:14, 15, eight times in Hebrews, and in Jas. 4:13; (*e*) *tēs sēmeron hēmeras*, "(unto) this very day," Rom. 11:8 (R.V.); (*f*) *tas hēmeras*, Luke 21:37, R.V., "every day," for A.V., "in the daytime;" (*g*) *pasan hēmeran*, Acts 5:42, R.V., "every day;" preceded by *kata* in Acts 17:17, R.V., "every day"; (*h*) *kath' hekastēn hēmeran*, lit., 'according to each day,' Heb. 3:13, "day by day," R.V.

DAINTY

liparos [λιπαρός, 3045], properly signifies oily, or anointed with oil (from *lipos*, grease, connected with *aleiphō*, to anoint); it is said of things which pertain to delicate and sumptuous living; hence, "dainty," Rev. 18:14. ¶ In the Sept., Judg. 3:29; Neh. 9:35; Is. 30:23. ¶

NT: B.475c; CB.—; K.—.
OT: shāmēn: S.8082; HR.879b.1; H.2410a; BD.1032a.
GEN. REF.: IS.1:852; NB.—; Z.—.

For DAMAGE see LOSS

For DAMNABLE, DAMNATION and DAMNED, see CONDEMNATION, DESTRUCTION, JUDGE, JUDGMENT

DAMSEL

1. *korasion* [κοράσιον, 2877], a diminutive of *korē*, a girl, denotes a little girl (properly a colloquial word, often used disparagingly, but not so in later writers); in the N.T. it is used only in familiar conversation, Matt. 9:24, 25 (A.V., "maid"); 14:11; Mark 5:41, 42; 6:22, 28.

NT: B.444b; CB.1255c; K.—.
OT: naʿarāh: S.5291; HR.799c.2b; H.1389c; BD.655a.
GEN. REF.: IS.1:855; NB.—; Z.—.

2. *paidion* [παίδιον, 3813], a diminutive of *pais*, denotes a young child (male or female) in the A.V. of Mark 5:39, 40, 41 (1st line); the R.V. corrects "damsel" to "child," so as to distinguish between the narrative of facts, and the homely address to the little girl herself, in which, and in the following sentence, *korasion* is used. (See No. 1). See CHILD.

NT: B.604a; CB.1261c; K.759.
OT: —.
GEN. REF.: IS.1:855; NB.—; Z.—.

3. *paidiskē* [παιδίσκη, 3814], denotes a young girl, or a female slave; "damsel," A.V., in John 18:17; Acts 12:13; 16:16; R.V. "maid" in each case. See BONDMAID, BONDWOMAN, MAID, MAIDEN.

NT: B.604b; CB.1261c; K.—.
OT: 'āmāh: S.519; HR.1048b.1; H.112; BD.51a.
shiphhah: S.8198; HR.1048b.4; H.2442a; BD.1046c
GEN. REF.: IS.1:855; NB.—; Z.—.

DANCE

orcheō [ὀρχέω, 3738], cp. Eng. orchestra, probably originally signified to lift up, as of the feet; hence, to leap with regularity of motion. It is always used in the Middle Voice, Matt. 11:17; 14:6; Mark 6:22; Luke 7:32. The performance by the daughter of Herodias is the only clear instance of artistic dancing, a form introduced from Greek customs. ¶

NT: B.583b; CB.1261a; K.–.
OT: rāqad: S.7540; HR.1018a.3; H.2214; BD.955a.
GEN. REF.: IS.1:856; NB.–; Z.2:11.

DANCING

choros [χορός, 5525], Eng., chorus, primarily denoted an enclosure for dancing; hence, a company of dancers and singers. The supposition that the word is connected with *orcheō* by metathesis (i.e., change of place, of the letters *ch* and *o*) seems to be without foundation. The word is used in Luke 15:25. ¶

NT: B.883d; CB.–; K.–.
OT: māhôl: S.4234; HR.1472c.3a; H.623g; BD.298b.
mᵉḥôlāh: S.4246; HR.1472c.3b; H.623h; BD.298b.
GEN. REF.: IS.1:856; NB.–; Z.2:11.

DANGER, DANGEROUS

A. Verb.

kinduneuō [κινδυνεύω, 2793], properly signifies to run a risk, face danger, but is used in the N.T. in the sense of being in danger, jeopardy, Acts 19:27, 40. It is translated "were in jeopardy" in Luke 8:23, and "stand we in jeopardy," 1 Cor. 15:30. ¶

NT: B.432b; CB.1255a; K.–.
OT: yāqash: S.3369; HR.765a.3; H.906; BD.430b.
sākan: S.5533; HR. 765a.4; H.1495,1496; BD.698b.
GEN. REF.: IS.1:858; NB.–; Z.–.

Note: Kindunos, akin to A, peril, danger, is always rendered "peril," Rom. 8:35 and 2 Cor. 11:26 (eight times). ¶

B. Adjectives.

1. *enochos* [ἔνοχος, 1777], lit. held in, contained in (*en*, in, *echō*, to have, hold), hence, bound under obligation to, liable to, subject to, is used in the sense of being in danger of the penal effect of a misdeed, i.e., in a forensic sense, signifying the connection of a person with (*a*) his crime, "guilty of an eternal sin," Mark 3:29, R.V.; (*b*) the trial or tribunal, as a result of which sentence is passed, Matt. 5:21, 22, "the judgment," "the council;" *enochos* here has the obsolete sense of control (J. Hastings); (*c*) the penalty itself, 5:22, "the hell of fire," and, with the translation "worthy" (A.V., "guilty"), of the punishment determined to be inflicted on Christ, Matt. 26:66 and Mark 14:64, "death;" (*d*) the person or thing against whom or which the offence is committed, 1 Cor. 11:27, "guilty," the crime being against "the body and blood of the Lord;" Jas. 2:10, "guilty" of an offence against all the Law, because of a breach of one commandment.

Apart from the forensic sense, this adjective is used of the thing by which one is bound, "subject to" (bondage), in Heb. 2:15. See GUILTY, SUBJECT, WORTHY. ¶

NT: B.267d; CB.1245b; K.286.
OT: dām: S.1818; HR.476c.2; H.436; BD.196b.
GEN. REF.: IS.1:858; NB.–; Z.–.

2. *episphalēs* [ἐπισφαλής, 2000], lit., prone to fall (*epi*, upon, i.e., near upon, *sphallō*, to fall), hence, insecure, dangerous, is used in Acts 27:9. ¶

NT: B.302a; CB.–; K.–.
OT: –.
GEN. REF.:–.

DARE, DARING, DURST

A. Verb.

tolmaō [τολμάω, 5111], signifies to dare, (*a*) in the sense of not dreading or shunning through fear, Matt. 22:46; Mark 12:34; Mark 15:43, "boldly," lit., 'having dared, went in;' Luke 20:40; John 21:12; Acts 5:13; 7:32; Rom. 15:18; 2 Cor. 10:2, R.V., "shew courage," (A.V., "be bold"); 10:12, R.V., "are (not) bold;" 11:21; Phil. 1:14, "are bold;" Jude 9; (*b*) in the sense of bearing, enduring, bringing oneself to do a thing, Rom. 5:7; 1 Cor. 6:1. ¶ Cp. *apotolmaō*, to be very bold, Rom. 10:20. ¶ SEE BOLD.

NT: B.821d; CB.1272c; K.1183.
OT: –.
GEN. REF.:–.

B. Adjective.

tolmētēs [τολμητής, 5113], akin to A, daring, is used in 2 Pet. 2:10, R.V., "daring" (A.V., "presumptuous"), shameless and irreverent daring. ¶

NT: B.822a; CB.1272c; K.1183.
OT: –.
GEN. REF.: –.

DARK, DARKEN, DARKLY, DARKNESS

A. Adjectives.

1. *skoteinos* [σκοτειυος, 4652], full of darkness, or covered with darkness, is translated "dark" in Luke 11:36; "full of darkness," in Matt. 6:23 and Luke 11:34, where the physical condition is figurative of the moral. The group of *skot*-words is derived from a root *ska*—, meaning to cover. The same root is to be found in *skēnē*, a tent. ¶

NT: B.757b; CB.1269b; K.1049.
OT: ḥōshek: S.2822; HR.1276a.2; H.769a; BD.365a.
GEN. REF.: IS.1:868; NB.–; Z.2:29.

Note: Contrast *phōteinos*, full of light, e.g., Matt. 6:22.

2. *auchmēros* [αὐχμηρός, 850], from *auchmos*, drought produced by excessive heat, hence signifies dry, murky, dark, 2 Pet. 1:19 (R.V. marg., "squalid"). No. 1 signifies darkness produced by covering; No. 2, darkness produced by being squalid or murky. ¶

NT: B.124b; CB.–; K.–.
OT: –.
GEN. REF.: IS.1:868; NB.–; Z.–.

B. Nouns.

2. *skotia* [σκοτία, 4653], is used (*a*) of physical darkness, "dark," John 6:17, lit., 'darkness had come on,' and 20:1, lit., 'darkness still being;' (*b*) of secrecy, in general, whether what is done therein is good or evil, Matt. 10:27; Luke 12:3; (*c*) of spiritual or moral darkness, emblematic of sin, as a condition of moral or spiritual depravity, Matt. 4;16; John 1:5; 8:12; 12:35, 46; 1 John 1:5; 2:8, 9, 11. ¶

NT: B.757b; CB.1269b; K.1049.
OT: 'ōphel: S.652; HR.1276b.1; H.145a; BD.66c.
ḥāshak: S.2821; HR.1276b.2; H.769; BD.364d
GEN. REF.: IS.1:868; NB.–; Z.2:29.

2. *skotos* [σκότος, 4655], an older form than No. 1, grammatically masculine, is found in some mss. in Heb. 12:18. ¶ See *skotos* below.

3. *skotos* [σκότος, 4655], a neuter noun, frequent in the Sept., is used in the N.T. as the equivalent of No. 1; (*a*) of physical darkness, Matt. 27:45; 2 Cor. 4:6; (*b*) of intellectual darkness, Rom. 2:19 (cp. C. No. 1); (*c*) of blindness, Acts 13:11; (*d*) by metonymy, of the place of punishment, e.g., Matt. 8:12; 2 Pet. 2:17; Jude 13; (*e*) metaphorically, of moral and spiritual darkness, e.g., Matt. 6:23; Luke 1:79; 11:35; John 3:19; Acts 26:18; 2 Cor. 6:14; Eph. 6:12; Col. 1:13; 1 Thess. 5:4, 5; 1 Pet. 2:9; 1 John 1:6; (*f*) by metonymy, of those who are in moral or spiritual darkness, Eph. 5:8; (*g*) of evil works, Rom. 13;12; Eph. 5:11; (*h*) of the evil powers that dominate the world, Luke 22;53; (*i*) of secrecy [as in No. 1, (*b*)]. While *skotos* is used more than twice as many times as *skotia* in the N.T., the Apostle John uses *skotos* only once, 1 John 1:6, but *skotia* 15 times out of the 18.

"With the exception of the significance of secrecy [No. 1, (*b*) and No. 3 (*i*)], darkness is always used in a bad sense. Moreover the different forms of darkness are so closely allied, being either cause and effect, or else concurrent effects of the same cause, that they cannot always be distinguished; 1 John 1:5; 2:8, e.g., are passages in which both spiritual and moral darkness are intended."*

NT: B.757c; CB.1269b; K.1049.
OT: ḥōshek: S.2822; HR.1276b.2a; H.769a; BD.365a.
'ōphel: S.652; HR.1276b.1a; H.145a; BD.66c.
'ᵃphēlāh: S.653; HR.1276b.1b; H.145c; BD.66c.
GEN. REF.: IS.1:868; NB.–; Z.2:29.

4. *zophos* [ζόφος, 2217], denotes the gloom of the nether world; hence, thick darkness, darkness that may be felt; it is rendered "darkness in Heb. 12;18; 2 Pet. 2;4 and Jude 6; in 2 Pet. 2:17, R.V., "blackness," A.V., "mists;" in Jude 13, R.V. and A.V., "blackness." see BLACKNESS, B, NOS. 1 and 2, MIST. ¶

NT: B.339d; CB.–; K.–.
OT: –.
GEN. REF.: –.

C. Verbs.

1. *skotizō* [σκοτίζω, 4654], to deprive of light, to make dark, is used in the N.T. in the Passive Voice only, (*a*) of the heavenly bodies, Matt. 24:29; Mark 13:24; Rev. 8:12; (*b*) metaphorically, of the mind, Rom. 1:21; 11:10; (some mss. have it in Luke 23:45). ¶

NT: B.757c; CB.1269b; K.1049.
OT: ḥāshak: S.2821; HR.1276b.1a,b; H.769; BD.364d.
maḥshāk: S.4255; HR.1276b.1c; H.2732b; BD.365b
GEN. REF.: IS.1:868; NB.–; Z.2:29.

2. *skotoō* [σκοτόω, 4656], to darken, is used (*a*) of the heavenly bodies, Rev. 9:2; 16:10; (*b*) metaphorically, of the mind, Eph. 4:18. ¶

NT: B.758c; CB.1269b; K.1049.
OT: qādar: S.6937; HR.1277a.2; H.1989; BD.871a.
ḥāshak: S.2821; HR.1277a.1a; H.769; Bd.364d
maḥshāk: S.4255; HR.1277a.1b; H.2732b; BD.365b
GEN. REF.: IS.1:868; NB.–; Z.2:29.

Note: The phrase *en ainigmati*, lit., 'in an enigma,' is rendered "darkly" in 1 Cor. 13;12. *Ainigma* is akin to the verb *ainissomai*, to hint obscurely. The allusion is to Numb. 12:8 (Sept.), "not in (*dia*, by means of) dark speeches" (lit., enigmas); God's communications to Moses were not such as in the case of dreams, etc. After the same analogy, what we see and know now is seen "darkly" compared with the direct vision in the presence of God hereafter. The riddles of seeming obscurity in life will all be made clear.

DART

belos [βέλος, 956], akin to *ballō*, to throw, denotes a missile, an arrow, javelin, dart, etc., Eph. 6:16 (see FIERY). ¶ Cp. *bolē*, a stone's throw or cast, Luke 22:41, ¶; *bolizō*, to sound (to fathom the depth of water), Acts 27:28. ¶

NT: B.139b; CB.1239a; K.104.
OT: ḥēṣ: S.2671; HR.217a.1a; H.721b; BD.346b.
GEN. REF.: IS.1:869; NB.84; Z.2:30.

Note: The noun *bolis*, a dart, is found in some texts in Heb. 12:20 (see A.V.). ¶

* From Notes on Thessalonians, by Hogg and Vine, pp. 157-148.

DASH

1. *proskoptō* [προσκόπτω, 4350], denotes to beat upon or against, to strike against, dash against (*pros*, to or against, *koptō*, to strike, beat); hence, of the foot, to stumble, "dash" (A.V. and R.V.), Matt. 4:6; Luke 4:11. See BEAT, STUMBLE.

NT: B.716b; CB.1267b; K.946.
OT: kāshal: S.3782; HR.1217b.1; H.1050; BD.505b.
nāgaph: S5062; HR.1217b.2; H.1294; BD.619d
GEN. REF.: IS.1:869; NB.—; Z.—.

2. *rhēgnumi* [ῥήγνυμι, 4486], to tear, rend, break, is used of the action of a demon upon a human victim, Mark 9:18, "dasheth . . . down," R.V.; (A.V., marg.: A.V., text, "teareth"); Luke 9:42, R.V., "dashed . . . down" (A.V., "threw . . . down"). See BREAK, No. 6.

NT: B.735a; CB.—; K.—.
OT: bāgaʻ: S.1234; HR.1248c.1; H.271; BD.131d.
qāraʻ: S.7167; HR.1248c.5; H.2074; BD.902b
GEN. REF.: IS.1:869; NB.—; Z.—.

3. *edaphizō* [ἐδαφίζω, 1474], to beat level with the earth, e.g., as a threshing floor (cp. *edaphos*, the ground), Luke 19:44; R.V., "shall dash (thee) to the ground;" (A.V., "shall lay (thee) even with the ground"). See GROUND. ¶

NT: B.217c; CB.—; K.—.
OT: nāphaṣ: S.5310; HR.367c.3; H.1394; BD.658c.
rāṭash: S.7376; HR.367c.4; H.2158; BD936b
GEN. REF.: IS.1:869; NB.—; Z.—.

DAUGHTER, DAUGHTER-IN-LAW

1. *thugatēr* [θυγάτηρ, 2364], a daughter, (etymologically, Eng., daughter is connected), is used of (*a*) the natural relationship (frequent in the Gospels); (*b*) spiritual relationship to God, 2 Cor. 6:18, in the sense of the practical realization of acceptance with, and the approval of, God (cp. Isa. 43:6), the only place in the N.T. where it applies to spiritual relationship; (*c*) the inhabitants of a city or region, Matt. 21:5; John 12:15 ("of Zion"); cp. Is. 37:22; Zeph. 3:14 (Sept.); (*d*) the women who followed Christ to Calvary, Luke 23:28; (*e*) women of Aaron's posterity, Luke 1:5; (*f*) a female descendant of Abraham, Luke 13:16.

NT: B.364d; CB.1272c; K.—.
OT: bat: S.1323; HR.656b.2; H.254b; BD.123a.
GEN. REF.: IS.1:870; NB.416; Z.2:31.

2. *thugatrion* [θυγάτριον, 2365], a diminutive of No. 1, denotes a little daughter, Mark 5:23; 7:25. ¶

NT: B.365a; CB.—; K.—.
OT: —.
GEN. REF.: IS.1:870; NB.416; Z.2:31.

3. *parthenos* [παρθένος, 3933], a maiden, virgin, e.g., Matt. 1:23, signifies a virgin-daughter in 1 Cor. 7:36, 37,38 (R.V.); in Rev. 14:4, it is used of chaste persons. See VIRGIN

NT: B.627a; CB.1262c; K.786.
OT: bᵉtûlāh: S.1330; HR.1070a.la; H.295a; BD.143d.
ʿalmāh: S.5959; HR.1070a.3; H.1630b; BD.761c.
GEN. REF.: —.

4. *numphē* [νύμφη, 3565], Eng. nymph, denotes a bride, John 3:29; also a daughter-in-law, Matt. 10:35; Luke 12:53. See BRIDE.

NT: B.545b; CB.1260a; K.657.
OT: kallāh: S.3618; HR.95la.2; H.986a; BD.483c.
GEN. REF.: IS.—; NB.—; Z.2:31.

Note: In 1 Pet. 3:6, *teknon*, a child, is translated "daughters" (A.V.), "children" (R.V.).

DAWN

A. Verbs

1. *augazō* [αὐγάζω, 826], to shine, is used metaphorically of the light of dawn, in 2 Cor. 4:4 (some texts have *kataugazō*). Cp. *augē*, brightness or break of day, Acts 20:11. The word formerly meant to see clearly, and it is possible that this meaning was continued in general usage. ¶

NT: B.120c; CB.1238b; K.87.
OT: —.
GEN. REF.: —.

2. *diaugazō* [διαυγάζω, 1306], signifies to shine through (*dia*, through, *augē*, brightness); it describes the breaking of daylight upon the darkness of night, metaphorically in 2 Pet. 1:19, of the shining of spiritual light into the heart. A probable reference is to the Day to be ushered in at the Second Coming of Christ: 'until the Day gleam through the present darkness, and the Light-bringer dawn in your hearts.' ¶

NT: B.190a; CB.1241b; K.—.
OT: —.
GEN. REF.: IS.1:876; NB.—; Z.—.

Note: Cp. *diaugēs*, translucent, transparent, Rev. 21:21 (some texts have *diaphanēs*, "transparent"). ¶

3. *epiphōskō* [ἐπιφώσκω, 2020], to grow light (*epi*, upon, *phōs*, light), in the sense of shining upon, is used in Matt. 28:1; in Luke 23:54, "drew on" (of the Sabbath-day); R.V., marg., "began to dawn." See DRAW. ¶

NT: B.304d; CB.—; K.1293.
OT: hālal: S.1984; HR.538b.1; H.499,500; BD.237d.
GEN. REF.: IS.1:877; NB.—; Z.—.

B. Noun.

orthros [ὄρθρος, 3722], daybreak, denotes "at early dawn," Luke 24:1 (R.V.), "early in the morning" (A.V.), and John 8:2 (A.V. and R.V.); in Acts 5:21, R.V., "about daybreak," for A.V., "early in the morning." ¶

NT: B.580c; CB.—; K.—.
OT: shaḥar: S.7837; HR.1011b.3; H.2369a; BD.1007b.
GEN. REF.: IS.1:876; NB.—; Z.—.

Note: Cp. *orthrios*, "early," in some texts in Luke 24:22; ¶ *orthrinos*, a later form of *orthros*, in some mss. in Rev. 22:16; ¶ *orthrizō*, to do anything early in the morning, in Luke 21:38. ¶

DAY

A. Nouns.

1. *hēmera* [ἡμέρα, 2250], a day, is used of (*a*) the period of natural light, Gen. 1:5; Prov. 4:18; Mark 4:35; (*b*) the same, but figuratively, for a period of opportunity for service, John 9:4; Rom. 13:13; (*c*) one period of alternate light and darkness, Gen. 1:5; Mark 1:13; (*d*) a period of undefined length marked by certain characteristics, such as "the day of small things," Zech. 4:10; of perplexity and distress, Isa. 17:11; Obad. 12-14; of prosperity and of adversity, Ecc. 7:14; of trial or testing, Psa. 95:8; of salvation, Isa. 49:8; 2 Cor. 6:2; cp. Luke 19:42; of evil, Eph. 6:13; of wrath and revelation of the judgments of God, Rom. 2:5; (*e*) an appointed time, Ecc. 8:6; Eph. 4:30; (*f*) a notable defeat in battle, etc. Isa. 9:4; Psa. 137:7; Ezek. 30:9; Hos. 1:11; (*g*) by metonymy = 'when,' 'at the time when'; (1), of the past, Gen. 2:4; Numb. 3:13; Deut. 4:10, (2), of the future, Gen. 2:17; Ruth 4:5; Matt. 24:50; Luke 1:20; (*h*) a judgment or doom, Job 18:20.* (i) of a time of life, Luke 1:17, 18 ("years").

As the day throws light upon things that have been in darkness, the word is often associated with the passing of judgment upon circumstances. In 1 Cor. 4:3, "man's day," A.V., "man's judgment," R.V., denotes mere human judgment upon matters ("man's" translates the adjective *anthrōpinos*, human), a judgment exercised in the present period of human rebellion against "God"; probably therefore "the Lord's Day," Rev. 1:10, or 'the Day of the Lord' (where an adjective, *kuriakos*, is similarly used), is the Day of His manifested judgment on the world.

The phrases "the day of Christ," Phil. 1:10; 2:16; "the day of Jesus Christ," 1:6; "the day of the Lord Jesus," 1 Cor. 5:5; 2 Cor. 1:14; "the day of our Lord Jesus Christ," 1 Cor. 1:8, denote the time of the Parousia of Christ with His saints, subsequent to the Rapture, 1 Thess. 4:16, 17. In 2 Pet. 1:19 this is spoken of simply as "the day," (see DAY-STAR).

From these the phrase "the day of the Lord" is to be distinguished; in the O.T. it had reference to a time of the victorious interposition by God for the overthrow of the foes of Israel, e.g., Isa. 2:12; Amos 5:18; if Israel transgressed in the pride of their hearts, the Day of the Lord would be a time of darkness and judgment. For their foes, however, there would come 'a great and terrible day of the Lord,' Joel 2:31; Mal. 4:5. That period, still future, will see the complete overthrow of Gentile power and the establishment of Messiah's Kingdom, Isa. 13:9-11; 34:8; Dan. 2:34, 44; Obad. 15; cp. Isa. 61:2; John 8:56.

In the N.T. "the day of the Lord" is mentioned in 1 Thess. 5:2 and 2 Thess. 2:2, R.V., where the Apostle's warning is that the church at Thessalonica should not be deceived by thinking that "the Day of the Lord is now present." This period will not begin till the circumstances mentioned in verses 3 and 4 take place.

For the eventual development of the Divine purposes in relation to the human race see 2 Pet. 3:12, "the Day of God."

NT: B.345d; CB.1249c; K.309.
OT: yôm: S.3117; HR.607b.9; H.852; BD.398a.
GEN. REF.: IS.1:877; NB.179; Z.2:45.

2. *augē* [αὐγή, 827], brightness, bright, shining, as of the sun; hence, the beginning of daylight, is translated "break of day" in Acts 20:11. ¶

NT: B.120c; CB.1238b; K.—.
OT: nᵉgōhāh: S.5054; HR.176c.1; H.1290b; BD.618c.
GEN. REF.: —.

B. Adverb.

ennucha [ἔννυχα, 1773], the neuter plural of *ennuchos*, used adverbially, lit., in night (*en*, in, *nux*, night, with *lian*, "very"), signifies very early, yet in the night, "a great while before day," Mark 1:35. ¶

NT: B.267b; CB.—; K.—.
OT: —.
GEN. REF.: —.

Notes: (1) For phrases, see DAILY.

(2) In Mark 6:35, the clause "the day was far spent" is, lit., 'a much hour (i.e., a late hour) having become,' or, perhaps, 'many an hour having become,' i.e. many hours having passed. In the end of the ver., R.V., "day," for A.V., "time."

(3) In Mark 2:26, A.V., "in the days of," there is no word for "days" in the original; R.V. (from best mss.), "when"; in Acts 11:28, "in the days of".

(4) In John 21:4, the adjective *prōios*, at early morn, is translated "day" (R.V., for A.V., "the morning"); see Matt. 27:1. ¶

* From Notes on Thessalonians by Hogg and Vine, pp. 150-151.

(5) In 2 Thess. 2:3, "that day shall not come" (A.V.) translates nothing in the original; it is inserted to supply the sense (see the R.V.); cp. Luke 7:11 (R.V., "soon afterwards"); 1 Cor. 4:13 (R.V., "even until now").

(6) For "day following" see MORROW.

For **DAYBREAK** (R.V., in Acts 5:21), see **DAWN, B**

DAYSPRING

anatolē [ἀνατολή, 395], lit., a rising up (cp. *anatellō*, to cause to rise), is used of the rising of the sun and stars; it chiefly means the east, as in Matt. 2:1, etc.; rendered "dayspring" in Luke 1:78. Its other meaning, "a shoot," is found in the Sept. in Jer. 23:5; Zech. 6:12. See also the margin of Luke 1:78, "branch." See EAST.

NT: B.62b; CB.1235b; K.57.
OT: qedem: S.6924; HR.83c.5; H.1988a; BD.869c.
ṣemaḥ: S.6780; HR.83c.4; H.1928a; BD.855c.
mizrāḥ: S.4217; HR.83c.2; H.580c; BD.280d.
GEN. REF.: IS.1:880; NB.297; Z.2:45,47.

DAY-STAR

phōsphoros [φωσφόρος, 5459], Eng., phosphorus, lit., light-bearing (*phōs*, light, *phērō*, to bear), is used of the morning star, as the light-bringer, 2 Pet. 1:19, where it indicates the arising of the light of Christ as the Personal fulfilment, in the hearts of believers, of the prophetic Scriptures concerning His Coming to receive them to Himself. ¶

NT: B.872d; CB.1264b; K.1293.
OT: –.
GEN. REF.: IS.1:879; NB.–; Z.2:48.

DAZZLING

1. *astrapto* [ἀστράπτω, 797], to flash forth, lighten, is said of lightning, Luke 17:24, and of the apparel of the two men by the Lord's sepulchre, 24:4, A.V., "shining." See LIGHTEN, SHINE. ¶

NT: B.118b; CB.–; K.–.
OT: bāraq: S.1299; HR.173c.1; H.287; BD.140b.
GEN. REF.: –.

2. *exastraptō* [ἐξαστράπτω, 1823], a strengthened form of No. 1 (*ek*, out of), signifies to flash like lightning, gleam, be radiant, in Luke 9:29 of the Lord's raiment at His transfiguration, R.V., "dazzling"; A.V., "glistering." ¶ In the Sept., Ezek. 1:4, 7; Nahum 3:3. ¶

NT: B.273d; CB.–; K.–.
OT: bārāq: S.1300; HR.490a.1; H.287a; BD.140c.
lāqaḥ: S.3947; HR.490a.2; H.1124; BD.542c,544a.
GEN. REF.: –.

DEACON

diakonos [διάκονος, 1249], whence Eng. deacon, primarily denotes a servant, whether as doing servile work, or as an attendant rendering free service, without particular reference to its character. The word is probably connected with the verb *diōkō*, to hasten after, pursue (perhaps originally said of a runner). "It occurs in the N.T. of domestic servants, John 2:5, 9; the civil ruler, Rom. 13:4; Christ, Rom. 15:8; Gal. 2:17; the followers of Christ in relation to their Lord, John 12:26; Eph. 6:21; Col. 1:7; 4:7; the followers of Christ in relation to one another, Matt. 20:26; 23:11; Mark 9:35; 10:43; the servants of Christ in the work of preaching and teaching, 1 Cor. 3:5; 2 Cor. 3:6; 6:4; 11:23; Eph. 3:7; Col. 1:23, 25; 1 Thess. 3:2; 1 Tim. 4:6; those who serve in the churches, Rom. 16:1 (used of a woman here only in N.T.); Phil. 1:1; 1 Tim. 3:8, 12; false apostles, servants of Satan, 2 Cor. 11:15. Once *diakonos* is used where, apparently, angels are intended, Matt. 22:13; in ver. 3, where men are intended, *doulos* is used."*

Diakonos is, generally speaking, to be distinguished from *doulos*, a bondservant, slave; *diakonos* views a servant in relationship to his work; *doulos* views him in relationship to his master. See, e.g., Matt. 22:2-14; those who bring in the guests (vv. 3, 4, 6, 8, 10) are *douloi*; those who carry out the king's sentence (v. 13) are *diakonoi*. ¶

NT: B.1249; CB.1241a; K.152.
OT: shārat: S.8334; HR.302b.2; H.2472; BD.1058a.
GEN. REF.: IS.1:880; NB.297; Z.2:48.

Note: As to synonymous terms, *leitourgos* denotes one who performs public duties; *misthios* and *misthōtos*, a hired servant; *oiketēs*, a household servant; *hupēretēs*, a subordinate official waiting on his superior (originally an under-rower in a war-galley); *therapōn*, one whose service is that of freedom and dignity. See MINISTER, SERVANT.

The so-called Seven Deacons in Acts 6 are not there mentioned by that name, though the kind of service in which they were engaged was of the character of that committed to such.

DEAD

A. Noun and Adjective.

nekros [νεκρός, 3498], is used of (*a*) the death of the body, cp. Jas. 2:26, its most frequent sense; (*b*) the actual spiritual condition

* From Notes on Thessalonians by Hogg and Vine, p. 91.

of unsaved men, Matt. 8:22; John 5:25; Eph. 2:1, 5; 5:14; Phil. 3:11; Col. 2:13; cp. Luke 15:24; (*c*) the ideal spiritual condition of believers in regard to sin, Rom. 6:11; (*d*) a church in declension, inasmuch as in that state it is inactive and barren, Rev. 3:1; (*e*) sin, which apart from law cannot produce a sense of guilt, Rom. 7:8; (*f*) the body of the believer in contrast to his spirit, Rom. 8:10; (*g*) the works of the Law, inasmuch as, however good in themselves, Rom. 7:13, they cannot produce life, Heb. 6:1; 9:14; (*h*) the faith that does not produce works, Jas. 2:17, 26; cp. ver. 20.*

NT: B.534d; CB.1259c; K.627.
OT: mût: S.4191; HR.941b.3; H.1169; BD.559b.
nᵉbēlāh: S.5038; HR.941b.4; H.1286a; BD.615c.
GEN. REF.: IS.1:898; NB.301; Z.2:49.

B. Verbs.

1. *nekroō* [νεκρόω, 3499], to put to death, is used in the Active Voice in the sense of destroying the strength of, depriving of power, with reference to the evil desires which work in the body, Col. 3:5. In the Passive Voice it is used of Abraham's body as being "as good as dead," Rom. 4:19 with Heb. 11:12. ¶

NT: B.535c; CB.1259c; K.627.
OT: –.
GEN. REF.: IS.1:898; NB.301; Z.2:49.

2. *thanatoō* [θανατόω, 2289], to put to death: see DEATH, C. No. 1.

NT: B.351c; CB.1271c; K.312.
OT: mût: S.4191; HR.625a.4a,c,d; H.1169; BD.559b.
GEN. REF.: IS.1:898; NB.301; Z.–.

DEADLY

1. *thanatēphoros* [θανατηφόρος, 2287], lit., death-bearing, deadly (*thanatos*, death, *pherō*, to bear), is used in Jas. 3:8. ¶ In the Sept., Numb. 18:22; Job 33:23. ¶

NT: B.350d; CB.–; K.–.
OT: mût: S.4191; HR.623b.1; H.1169; BD.559b.
GEN. REF.: IS.1:898; NB.301; Z.–.

2. *thanasimos* [θανάσιμος, 2286], from *thanatos* (see No. 1), belonging to death, or partaking of the nature of death, is used in Mark 16:18. ¶

NT: B.350d; CB.–; K.–.
OT: –.
GEN. REF.: –.

HALF DEAD

hēmithanēs [ἡμιθανής], from *hēmi*, half, and *thnēskō*, to die, is used in Luke 10:30. ¶

DEADNESS

nekrōsis [νέκρωσις, 3500], a putting to death (cp. DEAD, A and B), is rendered "dying" in 2 Cor. 4:10; "deadness" in Rom. 4:19, i.e., the state of being virtually dead. ¶

NT: B.535c; CB.–; K.627.
OT: –.
GEN. REF.: –.

DEAF

kōphos [κωφός, 2974], akin to *koptō*, to beat, and *kopiaō*, to be tired (from a root *kop*—, to cut), signifies blunted, dull, as of a weapon; hence, blunted in tongue, dumb, Matt. 9:32 etc.; in hearing, deaf, Matt. 11:5; Mark 7:32, 37; 9:25; Luke 7:22. See DUMB.

NT: B.462a; CB.–; K.–.
OT: ḥērēsh: S.2795; HR.840c.2; H.761a; BD.361b.
GEN. REF.: IS.1:897; NB.316; Z.2:70.

For a GREAT DEAL see GREAT

DEAL

merizō [μερίζω, 3307], signifies to divide into parts (*meros*, a portion, part) hence, to distribute, divide out, deal out to, translated "hath dealt" in Rom. 12:3. See DIFFERENCE, DISTRIBUTE, DIVIDE.

NT: B.504c; CB.1258b; K.–.
OT: ḥālaq: S.2505; HR.910c.2; H.669; BD.323c.
nāḥal: S.5157; HR.910c.5; H.1342; BD.635c.
GEN. REF.: –.

DEAL WITH, HAVE DEALINGS WITH

1. *poieō* [ποιέω, 4160], to do, used to describe almost any act, whether complete or repeated, like the Eng. "do," is translated to deal with, in Luke 2:48. In Luke 1:25, A.V., 'hath dealt with (me),' the R.V., adhering to the ordinary meaning, translates by "hath done unto (me)."

NT: B.680d; CB.1265c; K.895.
OT: –.
GEN. REF.: –.

2. *prospherō* [προσφέρω, 4374], to bring or bear to (*pros*, to, *pherō*, to bear), signifies, in the Middle Voice, to bear oneself towards anyone, to deal with anyone in a certain manner, Heb. 12:7, "God dealeth with you." See BRING, OFFER, PRESENT.

NT: B.719c; CB.1267b; K.1252.
OT: –.
GEN. REF.: –.

3. *sunchraomai* [συγχράομαι, 4798], lit., to use with (*sun*, with, *chraomai*, to use), to have in joint use, and hence to have dealings with, is said, in John 4:9, of Jews and Samaritans. ¶

NT: B.775b; CB.–; K.–.
OT: –.
GEN. REF.: IS.1:897; NB.–; Z.–.

Notes: (1) In Acts 25:24, *entunchanō*, to fall in with, meet and talk with, and hence to make suit to a person by way of pleading with him, is translated "have dealt with" in the A.V.; correctly in the R.V., "have made suit to," of the Jews in appealing to Festus against Paul. See INTERCESSION.

* From Notes on Thessalonians by Hogg and Vine, p. 143.

(2) *Katasophizomai*, to circumvent by fraud, conquer by subtle devices (*kata*, down, intensive, and *sophizō*, to devise cleverly or cunningly; cp. Eng., sophist, sophistry), is translated "dealt subtilly," in Acts 7:19, of Pharaoh's dealings with the Israelites. ¶ This is the word in the Sept. of Ex. 1:10. See SUBTILLY. ¶

(3) In 1 Thess. 2:11 the italicised phrase "we dealt with" (R.V.), has no corresponding word in the original, but is inserted in order to bring out the participial forms of the verbs "exhorting," "encouraging," "testifying," as showing the constant practice of the apostles at Thessalonica. The incompleteness of the sentence in the original illustrates the informal homeliness of the Epistle.

(4) In 2 Cor. 13:10, the verb *chraomai*, to use, is rendered, in the R.V., "deal (sharply)," A.V., "use (sharpness)."

DEAR

1. *timios* [τίμιος, 5093], from *timē*, honour, price, signifies (*a*), primarily, accounted as of great price, precious, costly, 1 Cor. 3:12; Rev. 17:4; 18:12, 16; 21:19, and in the superlative degree, 18:12; 21:11; the comparative degree is found in 1 Pet. 1:7 (*polutimoteros*, in the most authentic mss., "much more precious"); (*b*) in the metaphorical sense, held in honour, esteemed, very dear, Acts 5:34, "had in honour," R.V. (A.V., "had in reputation"); so in Heb. 13:4, R.V., "let marriage be had in honour"; A.V., "is honourable"; Acts 20:24, "dear," negatively of Paul's estimate of his life; Jas. 5:7, "precious" (of fruit); 1 Pet. 1:19, "precious" (of the blood of Christ); 2 Pet. 1:4 (of God's promises). See COSTLY, HONOURABLE, REPUTATION, PRECIOUS. ¶ Cp. *timiōtes*, preciousness, Rev. 18:19. ¶

NT: B.818a; CB.1272c; K.—.
OT: yāqār: S.3368; HR.1353c.2a; H.905a; BD.429c.
GEN. REF.: —.

2. *entimos* [ἔντιμος, 1784], held in honour (*timē*, see above), precious, dear, is found in Luke 7:2, of the centurion's servant; 14:8, "more honourable"; Phil. 2:29, "honour" (A.V., "reputation"), of devoted servants of Christ; in 1 Pet. 2:4, 6, "precious," of stones, metaphorically. See HONOURABLE, REPUTATION, PRECIOUS. ¶

NT: B.268d; CB.1245b; K.—.
OT: yāqar: S.3365; HR.479a.3; H.—; BD.429c.
kābēd: S.3513; HR.479a.4; H.—; BD.457a,c.
GEN. REF.: —.

3. *agapētos* [ἀγαπητός, 27], from *agapē*, love, signifies beloved; it is rendered "very dear" in 1 Thess. 2:8 (A.V., "dear"), of the affection of Paul and his fellow-workers for the saints at Thessalonica; in Eph. 5:1 and Col. 1:7, A.V., "dear"; R.V., "beloved." See BELOVED.

NT: B.6b; CB.1233b; K.5.
OT: yādîd: S.3039; HR.7a.2; H.846a; BD.391d.
yaḥîd: S.3173; HR.7a.3; H.858a; BD.402d.
GEN. REF.: —.

Note: In Col. 1:13, *agapē* is translated "dear" in the A.V.; the R.V., adhering to the noun, has "the Son of His love."

For **DEARLY** see **BELOVED**

For **DEARTH** see **FAMINE**

DEATH, DEATH-STROKE (See also **DIE**)

A. Nouns.

1. *thanatos* [θάνατος, 2288], death, is used in Scripture of:

(*a*) the separation of the soul (the spiritual part of man) from the body (the material part), the latter ceasing to function and turning to dust, e.g., John 11:13; Heb. 2:15; 5:7; 7:23. In Heb. 9:15, the A.V., "by means of death" is inadequate; the R.V., "a death having taken place" is in keeping with the subject. In Rev. 13:3, 12, the R.V., "death-stroke" (A.V., "deadly wound") is, lit., the stroke of death:

(*b*) the separation of man from God; Adam died on the day he disobeyed God, Gen. 2:17, and hence all mankind are born in the same spiritual condition, Rom. 5:12, 14, 17, 21, from which, however, those who believe in Christ are delivered, John 5:24; 1 John 3:14. Death is the opposite of life; it never denotes non-existence. As spiritual life is "conscious existence in communion with God," so spiritual death is "conscious existence in separation from God."

"Death, in whichever of the abovementioned sense it is used, is always, in Scripture, viewed as the penal consequence of sin, and since sinners alone are subject to death, Rom. 5:12, it was as the Bearer of sin that the Lord Jesus submitted thereto on the Cross, 1 Pet. 2:24. And while the physical death of the Lord Jesus was of the essence of His sacrifice, it was not the whole. The darkness symbolised, and His cry expressed, the fact that He was left alone in the Universe, He was 'forsaken'; cp. Matt. 27:45, 46."*

NT: B.350b; CB.1271c; K.312.
OT: mût: S.4191; HR.623b.4a,d; H.1169; BD.559b.
ṣalmāwet: S.6757; HR.623b.10; H.1921b; BD.853c.
GEN. REF.: IS.1:898; NB.301; Z.2:70.

* From Notes on Thessalonians by Hogg and Vine, p. 134.

2. *anairesis* [ἀναίρεσις, 336], another word for death, lit. signifies a taking up or off (*ana*, up, *airō*, to take), as of the taking of a life, or putting to death; it is found in Acts 8:1, of the murder of Stephen. Some mss. have it in 22:20. See *anaireō*, under KILL. ¶ In the Sept., Numb. 11:15; Judg. 15:17, "the lifting of the jawbone." ¶

NT: B.54d; CB.–; K.–.
OT: hārag: S.2026; HR.77c.1; H.514; BD.246d.
GEN. REF.: IS.1:898; NB.301; Z.2:70.

3. *teleutē* [τελευτή, 5054], an end, limit (cp. *telos*, see END), hence, the end of life, death, is used of the death of Herod, Matt. 2:15. ¶

NT: B.810c; CB.1271b; K.–.
OT: māwet: S.4194; HR.1344a.2a; H.1169a; BD.560c.
mût: S.4191; HR.1344a.2b; H.1169; BD.559b.
GEN. REF.: IS.1:898; NB.301; Z.2:70.

B. Adjective.

epithanatios [ἐπιθανάτιος, 1935], doomed to death (*epi*, upon, *thanatos*, A, No. 1), is said of the apostles, in 1 Cor. 4:9. ¶

NT: B.292d; CB.–; K.–.
OT: –.
GEN. REF.: IS.1:898; NB.301; Z.–

C. Verbs.

1. *thanatoō* [θανατόω, 2289], to put to death (akin to A, No. 1), in Matt. 10:21; mark 13:12; Luke 21:16, is translated "shall . . . cause (them) to be put to death," lit., 'shall put (them) to death' (R.V. marg.). It is used of the Death of Christ in Matt. 26:59; 27:1; Mark 14:55 and 1 Pet. 3:18. In Rom. 7:4 (Passive Voice) it is translated "ye . . . were made dead," R.V. (for A.V., "are become"), with reference to the change from bondage to the Law to union with Christ; in 8:13, "mortify" (marg., "make to die"), of the act of the believer in regard to the deeds of the body; in 8:36, "are killed"; so in 2 Cor. 6:9. See KILL, MORTIFY. ¶

NT: B.351c; CB.1271c; K.312.
OT: mût: S.4191; HR.625a.4c,d; H.1169; BD.559b.
hārag: S.2026; HR.625a.2; H.514; BD.246d.
GEN. REF.: IS.1:898; NB.301; Z.2:70.

2. *anaireō* [ἀναιρέω, 337], lit., to take or lift up or away (see A, No. 2), hence, to put to death, is usually translated to kill or slay; in two places "put to death," Luke 23:32; Acts 26:10. it is used 17 times, with this meaning, in Acts. See KILL, SLAY, TAKE.

NT: B.54d; CB.–; K.–.
OT: hārag: S.2026; HR.77b.2a; H.514; BD.246d.
mût: S.4191; HR.77b.4; H.1169; BD.559b.
nākāh: S.5221; HR.77b.6; H.1364; BD.645a.
GEN. REF.: IS.1:898; NB.301; Z.2:70.

3. *apagō* [ἀπάγω, 520], lit., to lead away (*apo*, away, *agō*, to lead), is used especially in a judicial sense, to put to death, e.g., Acts 12:19. See BRING, CARRY, LEAD, TAKE.

NT: B.79c; CB.–; K.–.
OT: nāhag: S.5090; HR.115b.8; H.1309,1310; BD.624a,b.
hālak: S.1980; HR.115b.5; H.498; BD.229d,236c.
GEN. REF.: IS.–; NB.301; Z.–.

4. *apokteinō* [ἀποκτείνω, 615], to kill, is so translated in the R.V., for the A.V., "put to death," in Mark 14:1; Luke 18:33; in John 11:53; 12:10 and 18:31, R.V., "put to death." See KILL, SLAY.

NT: B.93d; CB.1237a; K.–.
OT: hārag: S.2026; HR.135a.2a; H.514; BD.246d.
mût: S.4191; HR.135a.4c; H.1169; BD.559b.
GEN. REF.: IS.1:898; NB.301; Z.2:70.

Note: The phrase *eschatōs echō*, lit., to have extremely, i.e., to be in extremity, *in extremis*, at the last (gasp), to be at the point of death, is used in Mark 5:23. ¶

For the A.V., **DEBATE** (Rom. 1:29 and 2 Cor. 12:20), see **STRIFE**

DEBT

1. *opheilē* [ὀφειλή, 3782], that which is owed (see Note, below), is translated "debt" in Matt. 18:32; in the plural, "dues," Rom. 13:7; "(her) due," 1 Cor. 7:3, of conjugal duty: some texts here have *opheilomenēn* (*eunoian*) "due (benevolence)," A.V.; the context confirms the R.V. See DUE. ¶

NT: B.598c; CB.1261a; K.746.
OT: –.
GEN. REF.: IS.1:905; NB.304; Z.2:79.

2. *opheilēma* [ὀφείλημα, 3783], a longer form of No. 1, expressing a debt more concretely, is used (*a*) literally, of that which is legally due, Rom. 4:4; (*b*) metaphorically, of sin as a debt, because it demands expiation, and thus payment by way of punishment, Matt. 6:12. ¶

NT: B.598c; CB.1261a; K.746.
OT: mashshā'āh: S.4859; HR.1039b.1; H.1421d; BD.673d.
GEN. REF.: IS.1:905; NB.304; Z.2:79.

3. *daneion* [δάνειον, 1156], a loan (akin to *danos*, a gift), is translated "debt" in Matt. 18:27 (R.V., marg., "loan"), of the ten thousand talents debtor. ¶ Cp. *daneizō*, to lend, and *daneistēs*, a money-lender, a creditor.

NT: B.170d; CB.–; K.–.
OT: nāshā': S.5378; HR.285a.1; H.1424; BD.673d.
GEN. REF.: IS.1:905; NB.304; Z.2:79.

Note: In Matt. 18:30, *opheilō*, to owe, is translated "debt" in the A.V. (R.V., "that which was due."). See DUE.

DEBTOR

1. *opheiletēs* [ὀφειλέτης, 3781], one who owes anything to another, primarily in regard to money; in Matt. 18:24, "who owed" (lit., 'one was brought, a debtor to him of ten thousand talents'). The slave could own property, and so become a debtor to his master, who might seize him for payment.

It is used metaphorically,

(*a*) of a person who is under an obligation, Rom. 1:14, of Paul, in the matter of preaching the Gospel; in Rom. 8:12, of believers, to mortify the deeds of the body; in Rom. 15:27, of Gentile believers, to assist afflicted Jewish believers; in Gal. 5:3, of those who would be justified by circumcision, to do the whole Law;

(*b*) of those who have not yet made amends to those whom they have injured, Matt. 6:12, "our debtors"; of some whose disaster was liable to be regarded as a due punishment, Luke 13:4 (R.V., "offenders"; A.V., "sinners"; marg., "debtors"). ¶

NT: B.598b; CB.1261a; K.746.
OT: —.
GEN. REF.: IS.1:905; NB.304; Z.2:79.

2. *chreōpheiletēs* [χρεωφειλέτης, 5533], lit., a debt-ower (*chreōs*, a loan, a debt, and No. 1), is found in Luke 7:41, of the two debtors mentioned in the Lord's parable addressed to Simon the Pharisee, and in 16:5, of the debtors in the parable of the unrighteous steward. This parable indicates a system of credit in the matter of agriculture. ¶ In the Sept., Job 31:37, "having taken nothing from the debtor"; Prov. 29:13, "when the creditor and the debtor meet together." ¶ The word is more expressive than No. 1.

NT: B.885b; CB.—; K.—.
OT: —.
GEN. REF.: IS.1:905; NB.304; Z.—.

Note: In Matt. 23:16 *opheilō*, to owe (see DEBT), is translated "he is a debtor." The R.V. marg., keeping the verbal form, has "bound by his oath" (A.V., marg., "bound"). In the 18th verse the A.V., "he is guilty," means that he is under obligation to make amends for his misdeeds.

DECAY

1. *palaioō* [παλαιόω, 3822], to make old (*palaios*), is translated in Heb. 8:13, firstly, "hath made . . . old," secondly (Passive Voice), R.V. "is becoming old" (A.V., "decayeth"); "wax old," Luke 12:33 and Heb. 1:11. See OLD. ¶

NT: B.606a; CB.1261c; K.769.
OT: bālāh: S.1086; HR.1051b.,1a,b; H.246; BD.115a.
GEN. REF.: —.

2. *diaphtheirō* [διαφθείρω, 1311], to destroy utterly, as used in 2 Cor. 4:16 (here in the Passive Voice, lit., 'is being destroyed'), is rendered "is decaying" (R.V., for A.V., "perish"). See CORRUPT, DESTROY.

NT: B.190c; CB.1241b; K.1259.
OT: shāḥat: S.7843; HR.314c.6; H.2370; BD.1007d.
GEN. REF.: —.

DECEASE

A. Noun.

exodos [ἔξοδος, 1841], Eng., exodus, lit. signifies a way out (*ex*, out, *hodos*, a way); hence, a departure, especially from life, a decease; in Luke 9:31, of the Lord's Death, "which He was about to accomplish"; in 2 Pet. 1:15, of Peter's death (marg., "departure" in each case); "departure" in Heb. 11:22, R.V., See DEPARTURE. ¶

NT: B.27c; CB.1247c; K.666.
OT: —.
GEN. REF.: —.

B. Verb.

teleutaō [τελευτάω, 5053], lit., to end, is used intransitively and translated "deceased" in Matt. 22:25. See DEATH, A, No. 3, DIE.

NT: B.810c; CB.1271b; K.—.
OT: mût: S.4191; HR.1343b.2a; H.1169; BD.559b.
gāwa': S.1478; HR.1343b.1; H.328; BD.157b.
GEN. REF.: IS.1:898; NB.301, Z.—.

DECEIT, DECEITFUL, DECEITFULLY, DECEITFULNESS, DECEIVE, DECEIVABLENESS

A. Nouns.

1. *apatē* [ἀπάτη, 539], deceit or deceitfulness (akin to *apataō*, to cheat, deceive, beguile), that which gives a false impression, whether by appearance, statement or influence, is said of riches, Matt. 13:22; Mark 4:19; of sin, Heb. 3:13. The phrase in Eph. 4:22, "deceitful lusts," A.V., "lusts of deceit," R.V. signifies lusts excited by deceit of which deceit is the source of strength, not lusts deceitful in themselves. In 2 Thess. 2:10, "all deceit of unrighteousness," R.V., signifies all manner of unscrupulous words and deeds designed to deceive (see Rev. 13: 13-15). In Col. 2:8, "vain deceit" suggests that deceit is void of anything profitable. ¶

NT: B.82a; CB.1236b; K.65.
OT: —.
GEN. REF.: IS.1:908; NB.305; Z.2:84.

Note: In 2 Pet. 2:13, the most authentic texts have "revelling in their love-feasts," R.V. (*agapais*), for A.V., "deceivings" (*apatais*).

2. *dolos* [δόλος, 1388], primarily a bait, snare; hence, craft, deceit, guile, is translated "deceit" in Mark 7:22; Rom. 1:29. See CRAFT, GUILE, SUBTILTY.

NT: B.203b; CB.—; K.—.
OT: mirmāh: S.4820; HR.340b.4a; H.2169b; BD.941b.
rᵉmiyyāh: S.7423; HR.340b.6; H.2169a; BD.941a.
GEN. REF.: IS.1:908; NB.305; Z.2:84.

Notes: (1) *Planē*, rendered "deceit" in 1 Thess. 2:3, A.V., signifies wandering (cp. Eng., "planet"), hence, "error" (R.V.), i.e., a wandering from the right path; in Eph. 4:14, "wiles of error," A.V., "to deceive," See DELUDE, ERROR.

(2) For *dolioō*, to use deceit, see C, No. 4.

B. Adjective.

dolios [δόλιος, 1386], deceitful, is used in 2 Cor. 11:13, of false apostles as "deceitful workers"; cp. A, No. 2 and Note (2). ¶

NT: B.203b; CB.—; K.—.
OT: mirmāh: S.4820; HR.340b.4; H.2169b; BD.941b.
rᵉmiyyāh: S.7423; HR.340b.6; H.2169a; BD.941a.
sheqer: S.8263; HR.340b.7; H.2459a,b; BD.1054d.
GEN. REF.: IS.1:908; NB.305; Z.2:84.

C. Verbs.

1. *apataō* [ἀπατάω, 538], to beguile, deceive (see A, No. 1), is used (*a*) of those who deceive "with empty words," belittling the true character of the sins mentioned, Eph. 5:6; (*b*) of the fact that Adam was "not beguiled," 1 Tim. 2:14, R.V. (cp. what is said of Eve; see No. 2 below); (*c*) of the self-deceit of him who thinks himself religious, but bridles not his tongue, Jas. 1:26. ¶

NT: B.81b; CB.1236b; K.65.
OT: pātāh: S.6601; HR.119b.3; H.1853; BD.834c.
sût: S.3249; HR.119b.2; H.1480; BD.694c.
GEN. REF.: IS.1:908; NB.305; Z.2:84.

2. *exapataō* [ἐξαπατάω, 1818], *ek* (*ex*), intensive, and No. 1, signifies to beguile thoroughly, to deceive wholly, 1 Tim. 2:14, R.V. See BEGUILE.

NT: B.273a; CB.1247c; K.65.
OT: tātal: S.2048; HR.488a.1; H.518; BD.1068c.
GEN. REF.: IS.1:908; NB.305; Z.2:84.

3. *phrenapataō* [φρεναπατάω, 5422], lit., to deceive in one's mind (*phrēn*, the mind, and No. 1), "to deceive by fancies" (Lightfoot), is used in Gal. 6:3, with reference to self-conceit, which is self-deceit, a sin against common sense. Cp. Jas. 1:26 (above). ¶

NT: B.865d; CB.—; K.—.
OT: —.
GEN. REF.: IS.1:908; NB.305; Z.—.

Note: Cp. *phrenapatēs*, No. 2, under DECEIVER.

4. *dolioō* [δολιόω, 1387], to lure, as by a bait (see A, No. 2), is translated "have used deceit" in Rom. 3:13. ¶

NT: B.203b; CB.—; K.—.
OT: nākal: S.5230; HR.340b.2; H.1366; BD.647d.
ḥālaq: S.2505; HR.340b.1; H.669; BD.325a.
GEN. REF.: IS.1:908; NB.305; Z.—.

5. *doloō* [δολόω, 1389], a short form of No. 4, primarily signifies to ensnare; hence, to corrupt, especially by mingling the truths of the Word of God with false doctrines or notions, and so handling it deceitfully, 2 Cor. 4:2. ¶ Cp. *kapēleuō*, to corrupt by way of huckstering, 2:17. ¶ For the difference between the words see CORRUPT, A, No. 1.

NT: B.203b; CB.1242a; K.—.
OT: hālaq: S.2505; HR.340c.1; H.669; BD.325a.
GEN. REF.: IS.—; NB.305; Z.2:84.

6. *planaō* [πλανάω, 4105], akin to *planē*, A, Note (1) (Eng., planet), in the Passive form sometimes means to go astray, wander, Matt. 18:12; 1 Pet. 2:25; Heb. 11:38; frequently Active, to deceive, by leading into error, to seduce, e.g., Matt. 24:4, 5, 11, 24; John 7:12, "leadeth astray," R.V. (cp. 1 John 3:7). In Rev. 12:9 the present participle is used with the definite article, as a title of the Devil, "the Deceiver," lit., 'the deceiving one.' Often it has the sense of deceiving oneself, e.g., 1 Cor. 6:9; 15:33; Gal. 6:7; Jas. 1:16, "be not deceived," R.V., "do not err," A.V. See ERR, LEAD (astray), SEDUCE, WANDER, WAY (be out of the).

NT: B.665b; CB.1265a; K.887.
OT: tāʿāh: S.8582; HR.1139b.16c; H.2531; BD.1073b.
pātāh: S.6601; HR.1139b.11; H.1853; BD.834c.
GEN. REF.: IS.1:908; NB.305; Z.2:84.

7. *paralogizomai* [παραλογίζομαι]; see BEGUILE, No. 3.

DECEIVER

1. *planos* [πλάνος, 4108], is, properly, an adjective, signifying wandering, or leading astray, seducing, 1 Tim. 4:1, "seducing (spirits)"; used as a noun, it denotes an impostor of the vagabond type, and so any kind of deceiver or corrupter, Matt. 27:63; 2 Cor. 6:8; 2 John 7 (twice), in the last of which the accompanying definite article necessitates the translation "the deceiver," R.V. See SEDUCE ¶

NT: B.666b; CB.1265a; K.857.
OT: —.
GEN. REF.: IS.1:908; NB.—; Z.2:84.

2. *phrenapatēs* [φρεναπάτης, 5423], akin to C, No. 3, under DECEIVE, lit., a mind-deceiver, is used in Tit. 1:10. ¶

NT: B.865d; CB.—; K.—.
OT: —.
GEN. REF.: IS.1:908; NB.—; Z.—.

Note: For "the deceiver," in Rev. 12:9, see DECEIVE, C. No. 6.

DECENTLY

euschēmonōs [εὐσχημόνως, 2156], denotes gracefully, becomingly, in a seemly manner (*eu*, well, *schēma*, a form, figure); "honestly," in Rom. 13:13 (marg., "decently"), in contrast to the shamefulness of Gentile social life; in 1 Thess. 4:12, the contrast is to idleness and its concomitant evils and the resulting bad testimony to unbelievers; in 1 Cor. 14:40, "decently," where the contrast is to disorder in oral testimony in the churches. See HONESTLY. ¶

NT: B.327a; CB.—; K.—.
OT: —.
GEN. REF.: IS.1:908; NB.—; Z.—.

Note: Cp. *euschēmosunē*, comeliness, 1 Cor. 12:23 ¶, and *euschēmōn*, comely, honourable. See COMELY.

DECIDE, DECISION

A. Verb.

diakrinō [διακρίνω, 1252], primarily signifies to make a distinction, hence, to decide, especially judicially, to decide a dispute, to give judgment, 1 Cor. 6:5, A.V., "judge"; R.V., "decide", where church members are warned against procuring decisions by litigation in the world's law courts. See CONTEND.

NT: B.185a; CB.1241a; K.469.
OT: dîn: S.1777; HR.304a.4; H.426; BD.192a.
rîb: S.7378; HR.304a.b; H.2159; BD.936b.
shāphaṭ: S.8199; HR.304a.8; H.2443; BD.1047a.
GEN. REF.: –.

B. Nouns.

1. *diagnōsis* [διάγνωσις, 1233], transliterated in English, primarily denotes a discrimination (*dia*, apart, *ginōskō*, to know), hence, a judicial decision, which is its meaning in Acts 25:21, R.V., "for the decision of the Emperor" (A.V., "hearing"). ¶

NT: B.182c; CB.–; K.–.
OT: –.
GEN. REF.: IS.1:908; NB.–; Z.–.

Note: Cp. *diaginōskō*, to distinguish, Acts 23:15, to judge (A.V., "enquire"), or "determine," 24:22, R.V. (A.V., "know the uttermost of"). ¶

2. *diakrisis* [διάκρισις, 1253], a distinguishing, and so a decision (see A), signifies "discerning" in 1 Cor. 12:10; Heb. 5:14, lit., 'unto a discerning of good and evil' (translated "to discern"); in Rom. 14:1, "not to (doubtful) disputations" is more literally rendered in the margin "not for decisions (of doubts)." See DISCERN. Cp. JUDGE. ¶ In the Sept., Job. 37:16. ¶

NT: B.185b; CB.1241a; K.469.
OT: –.
GEN. REF.: –.

DECK (Verb)

chrusoō [χρυσόω, 5558], lit., to gild with gold (*chrusos*, gold), is used in Rev. 17:4; 18:16. ¶

NT: B.889a; CB.1240b; K.–.
OT: ṣāphāh: S.6823; HR.1478c.2; H.1951; BD.860a.
GEN. REF.: IS.–; NB.–; Z.2:84.

DECLARE, DECLARATION

A. Verbs.

1. *anangellō* [ἀναγγέλλω, 312], signifies to announce, report, bring back tidings (*ana*, back, *angellō*, to announce). Possibly the *ana* carries the significance of upward, i.e., heavenly, as characteristic of the nature of the tidings. In the following, either the A.V., or the R.V. translates the word by the verb to declare; in John 4:25, R.V., "declare," A.V., "tell"; in 16:13, 14, 15, R.V., "declare," A.V., "shew"; in Acts 15:4, R.V., "rehearsed," A.V., "declared"; in 19:18, R.V., "declaring," A.V., "shewed" (a reference, perhaps, to the destruction of their idols, in consequence of their new faith); in 20:20, R.V., "declaring," A.V., "have shewed"; in 1 John 1:5, R.V., "announce," A.V., "declare." See REHEARSE, REPORT, SHEW, SPEAK, TELL.

NT: B.51b; CB.1235b; K.10.
OT: nāgad: S.5046; HR.74a.10a; H.1289; BD.616c.
GEN. REF.: IS.1:909; NB.–; Z.–.

2. *apangellō* [ἀπαγγέλλω, 518], signifies to announce or report from a person or place (*apo*, from); hence, to declare, publish; it is rendered "declare" in Luke 8:47; Heb. 2:12; 1 John 1:3. It is very frequent in the Gospels and Acts; elsewhere, other than the last two places mentioned, only in 1 Thess. 1:9 and 1 John 1:2. See BRING, A, No. 36.

NT: B.79b; CB.1236b; K.10.
OT: nāgad: S.5046; HR.113c.2a; H.1289; BD.616c.
GEN. REF.: IS.1:909; NB.–; Z.–.

3. *diangellō* [διαγγέλλω, 1229], lit., to announce through, hence, to declare fully, or far and wide (*dia*, through), is translated "declaring" in Acts 21:26, R.V. (A.V., "to signify"); in Luke 9:60, R.V., "publish abroad" (for A.V. "preach"), giving the verb its fuller significance; so in Rom. 9:17, for A.V., "declared." See PREACH, SIGNIFY. ¶

NT: B.182a; CB.1241b; K.10.
OT: sāphar: S.5608; HR.299b.2; H.1540; BD.707d,708a.
GEN. REF.: IS.1:909; NB.–; Z.–.

4. *katangellō* [καταγγέλλω, 2605], lit., to report down (*kata*, intensive), is ordinarily translated to preach; "declare" in Acts 17:23, A.V. (R.V., "set forth"); in 1 Cor. 2:1, R.V., "proclaiming," for A.V., "declaring." It is nowhere translated by "declare" in the R.V. See PREACH, SHEW, SPEAK, TEACH.

NT: B.409b; CB.1254a; K.10.
OT: –.
GEN. REF.: –.

5. *parangellō* [παραγγέλλω]: see CHARGE, B. No. 8.

6. *diēgeomai* [διηγέομαι, 1334], to conduct a narration through to the end (*dia*, through, intensive, *hegēomai*, to lead), hence denotes to recount, to relate in full, Mark 5:16; Luke 8:39; 9:10; Acts 8:33; 9:27; 12:17; in Mark 9:9 and Heb. 11:32, "tell." See SHEW, TELL. ¶

NT: B.195a; CB.1241c; K.–.
OT: sāphar: S.5608; HR.329c.5b; H.1540; BD.707d,708a.
GEN. REF.: IS.1:908; NB.–; Z.–.

7. *ekdiēgeomai* [ἐκδιηγέομαι, 1555], properly, to narrate in full, came to denote, to tell, declare; it is used in Acts 13:41; 15:3. ¶
NT: B.238c; CB.1243c; K.—.
OT: sāphar: S.5608; HR.422b.1a; H.1540; BD.707d,708a.
GEN. REF.: IS.1:908; NB.—; Z.—.

8. *exēgeomai* [ἐξηγέομαι, 1834], lit., to lead out, signifies to make known, rehearse, declare, Luke 24:35 (A.V., "told"; R.V., "rehearsed"); Acts 10:8; 15:12, 14; 21:19. In John 1:18, in the sentence "He hath declared Him," the other meaning of the verb is in view, to unfold in teaching, to declare by making known. See TELL. ¶
NT: B.275d; CB.1247c; K.303.
OT: sāphar: S.5608; HR.495b.3; H.1540; BD.707d,708a.
GEN. REF.: IS.1:908; NB.—; Z.—.

9. *horizō* [ὁρίζω, 3724], to mark off by boundaries, signifies to determine, usually of time; in Rom. 1:4, Christ is said to have been marked out as the Son of God, by the fact of His resurrection; "declared" (R.V., marg., "determined"). See DEFINE.
NT: B.580d; CB.1251b; K.728.
OT: 'āsar: S.631; HR.1011c.1; H.141; BD.63d.
gābal: S.1379; HR.1011c.2b; H.307; BD.148b.
gᵉbûl: S.1366; HR.1011c.2a; H.307a; BD.147d.
GEN. REF.: —.

10. *dēloō* [δηλόω, 1213], to make plain, is rendered to declare in 1 Cor. 1:11, A.V.; 3:13; Col. 1:8. See SIGNIFY.
NT: B.178c; CB.1240c; K.148.
OT: yāda': S.3045; HR.295c.3; H.848; BD.393b.
GEN. REF.: IS.1:909; NB.—; Z.—.

11. *phrazō* [φράζω, 5419], to declare, occurs in Matt. 15:15 and (in some texts) in 13:36 (as A.V.).
NT: B.865c; CB.—; K.—.
OT: —.
GEN. REF.: —.

Note: For *gnōrizō*, to make known, rendered to declare in John 17:26; 1 Cor. 15:1 and Col. 4:7, see KNOW, A, No. 8. For *emphanizō*, to declare plainly, Heb. 11:14, A.V., see MANIFEST, B, No. 2. For *phaneroō*, see MANIFEST, B, No. 1. For *anatithēmi*, Acts 25:14, A.V., see COMMUNICATE. For "declare glad tidings" see TIDINGS.

B. Noun.

endeixis [ἔνδειχις, 1732], a showing, pointing out (*en*, in, *deiknumi*, to show), is said of the showing forth of God's righteousness, in Rom. 3:25, 26, A.V., "to declare"; R.V., "to shew," and "(for) the shewing." In 2 Cor. 8:24, "proof"; Phil. 1:28, "an evident token." See SHEW, TOKEN. ¶
NT: B.262d; CB.1244c; K.—.
OT: —.
GEN. REF.: —.

Notes: (1) In Luke 1:1, *diēgēsis* is a "narrative" (R.V.), not a "declaration" (A.V.).

(2) In 2 Cor. 8:19, "declaration" does not represent any word in the original.

DECREASE (Verb)

elattoō [ἐλαττόω, 1642], signifies to make less or inferior, in quality, position or dignity; "madest . . . lower" and "hast made . . . lower," in Heb. 2:7, 9. In John 3:30, it is used in the Middle Voice, in John the Baptist's "I must decrease," indicating the special interest he had in his own decrease, i.e., in authority and popularity. See LOWER. ¶
NT: B.248b; CB.—; K.—.
OT: ḥasēr: S.2637; HR.448b.1a,b; H.705; BD.341a.
mā'aṭ: S.4591; HR.448b.2; H.1228; BD.589b.
GEN. REF.: —.

DECREE (Noun and Verb)

dogma [δόγμα, 1378], transliterated in English, primarily denoted an opinion or judgment (from *dokeō*, to be of opinion), hence, an opinion expressed with authority, a doctrine, ordinance, decree; "decree," Luke 2:1; Acts 16:4; 17:7; in the sense of ordinances, Eph. 2:15; Col. 2:14. See ORDINANCE. ¶
NT: B.201c; CB.1242a; K.178.
OT: dāt: S.1881; HR.339b.2; H.458; BD.206c.
GEN. REF.: IS.1:909; NB.—; Z.2:84.

Note: Krinō, to determine, is translated "hath decreed" in 1 Cor. 7:37, A.V.; R.V., "hath determined."

DEDICATE, DEDICATION

A. Verb.

enkainizō [ἐγκαινίζω, 1457], primarily means to make new, to renew (*en*, in, *kainos*, new) as in the Sept. of 2 Chron. 15:8; then, to initiate or dedicate, Heb. 9:18, with reference to the first Covenant, as not dedicated without blood; in 10:20, of Christ's dedication of the new and living way (A.V., "consecrated"; R.V., "dedicated"). See CONSECRATE. ¶ In the Sept. it has this meaning in Deut. 20:5; 2 Chron. 7:5; Isa. 16:11; 41:1; 45:16, "keep a feast (to Me)."
NT: B.215b; CB.1245a; K.388.
OT: ḥādash: S.2318; HR.364c.1; H.613; BD.293d.
ḥānak: S.2596; HR.364c.2; H.693; BD.335b.
GEN. REF.: IS.1:909; NB.305; Z.2:85.

B. Noun.

enkainia [ἐγκαίνια, 1456], akin to A, frequent in the Sept., in the sense of dedication, became used particularly for the annual eight days' feast beginning on the 25th of Chisleu (mid. of Dec.), instituted by Judas Maccabaeus, 164, B.C., to commemorate the cleansing of the

Temple from the pollutions of Antiochus Epiphanes; hence it was called the Feast of the Dedication, John 10:22. This Feast could be celebrated anywhere. The lighting of lamps was a prominent feature; hence the description "Feast of Lights." Westcott suggests that John 9:5 refers to this. ¶

NT: B.215b; CB.–; K.–.
OT: ḥ^{a}nukāh: S.2598; HR.364c.1; H.693b; BD.335c.
GEN. REF.: IS.1:910; NB.305; Z.2:85.

DEED, DEEDS

1. *ergon* [ἔργον, 2041], denotes a work (Eng., "work" is etymologically akin), deed, act. When used in the sense of a deed or act, the idea of working is stressed, e.g., Rom. 15:18; it frequently occurs in an ethical sense of human actions, good or bad, e.g., Matt. 23:3; 26:10; John 3:20, 21; Rom. 2:7, 15; 1 Thess. 1:3; 2 Thess. 1:11, etc.; sometimes in a less concrete sense, e.g., Tit. 1:16; Jas. 1:25 (R.V., "that worketh," lit., 'of work'). See LABOUR, WORK.

NT: B.307d; CB.1246c; K.251.
OT: m^{e}la'kāh: S.4399; HR.541c.10; H.1068b; BD.521d.
'^{a}bōdāh: S.5656; HR.541c.16b; H.1553c; BD.715a.
ma'^{a}seh: S.4639; HR.541c.19b; H.1708a; BD.795d.
GEN. REF.: –.

2. *praxis* [πρᾶξις, 4234], denotes a doing, transaction, a deed the action of which is looked upon as incomplete and in progress (cp. *prassō*, to practise); in Matt. 16:27, R.V., "deeds," for A.V., "works"; in Luke 23:51, "deed"; in ver. 41, the verb is used [see Note (2) below]; Acts 19:18; Rom. 8:13; Col. 3:9. In Rom. 12:4 it denotes an action, business, or function, translated "office." See OFFICE, WORK. ¶

NT: B.697d; CB.1266b; K.927.
OT: pō'al: S.6467; HR.1200c.2; H.–; BD.821c.
GEN. REF.: –.

Note: Contrast *pragma*, that which has been done, an accomplished act, e.g., Jas. 3:16, R.V., "deed," A.V., "work."

3. *poiēsis* [ποίησις, 4162], a doing (akin to *poieō*, to do), is translated "deed" in Jas. 1:25, A.V. (R.V., "doing"). ¶

NT: B.683b; CB.1265c; K.895.
OT: ma'^{a}seh: S.4639; HR.1168c.2a; H.1708a; BD.795d.
derek: S.1870; HR.1168c.1; H.453a; BD.202c,203c.
GEN. REF.: –.

Note: Cp, *poiēma*, a work done, Rom. 1:20; Eph. 2:10. ¶

4. *euergesia* [εὐεργεσία]: see BENEFIT, No. 1.

Notes: (1) *Katergazomai*, to work out, bring about something, to perpetrate a deed, is used with the neuter demonstrative pronoun *touto*, this, in 1 Cor. 5:3, "hath (so) done this deed," A.V.; R.V., "hath (so) wrought this thing."

(2) *Prassō* (see No. 2), is used in Luke 23:41, with the neuter plural of the relative pronoun, "of our deeds"; lit., '(the things) which we practised.'

(3) In 2 Cor. 12:12 the phrase "mighty deeds" (R.V., "mighty works") translates *dunameis*, "powers" (marg.). See WORK.

(4) In Acts 24:2, *diorthōma*, a straightening, with *ginomai*, to become, is translated in the A.V., "very worthy deeds are done," R.V., "evils are corrected"; more lit., 'reforms take place.' ¶ For the variant reading *katorthōma* see CORRECTION, No. 1.

DEEM

huponoeō [ὑπονοέω, 5282], to suppose, conjecture, surmise, is translated "deemed" in Acts 27:27, A.V. (R.V., "surmised"); in 13:25, "think ye" (A.V.); R.V., "suppose ye"; in 25:18, "supposed." See SUPPOSE, THINK. ¶

NT: B.846d; CB.–; K.636.
OT: –.
GEN. REF.: –.

DEEP (Noun and Adjective), DEEPNESS, DEEPLY, DEPTH

A. Nouns.

1. *bathos* [βάθος, 899], is used (*a*) naturally, in Matt. 13:5, "deepness"; Mark 4:5, A.V., "depth," R.V., "deepness"; Luke 5:4, of deep water; Rom. 8:39 (contrasted with *hupsōma*, height); (*b*) metaphorically, in Rom. 11:33, of God's wisdom and knowledge; in 1 Cor. 2:10, of God's counsels; in Eph. 3:18, of the dimensions of the sphere of the activities of God's counsels, and of the love of Christ which occupies that sphere; in 2 Cor. 8:2, of deep poverty; some mss. have it in Rev. 2:24. ¶

NT: B.130a; CB.1238; K.89.
OT: ma'^{a}maqîm: S.4615; HR.189a.3; H.1644e; BD.771b.
m^{e}ṣûlāh: S.4688; HR.189a.4; H.1889b; BD.846d.
taḥtî: S.8482; HR.189a.8; H.2504b; BD.1066b.
GEN. REF.: IS.1:910; NB.–; Z.2:86.

2. *buthos* [βυθός, 1037], a depth, is used in the N.T. only in the natural sense, of the sea, 2 Cor. 11:25. ¶

NT: B.148c; CB.–; K.–.
OT: m^{e}ṣûlāh: S.4688; HR.232b.1b; H.1889b; BD.846d.
GEN. REF.: IS.1:910; NB.–; Z.2:86.

Notes: (1) Cp. *buthizō*, to sink (intransitive), Middle Voice, Luke 5:7; (transitive) to drown, 1 Tim. 6:9. ¶

(2) *Abussos*, Eng., abyss, is translated "the deep" in Luke 8:31 and Rom. 10:7, A.V. See ABYSS, BOTTOM.

B. Adjective and Adverb.

bathus [βαθύς, 901], akin to A, No. 1, deep, is said in John 4:11, of a well; in Acts 20:9, of sleep; in Rev. 2:24 the plural is used, of the deep things, the evil designs and workings, of Satan.

NT: B.130b; CB.1238c; K.—.
OT: ʽāmōq: S.6009; HR.189b.1b; H.1644; BD.770d.
GEN. REF.: IS.1:910; NB.—; Z.—.

Notes: (1) In Luke 24:1, some mss. have *batheos*, the genitive case, with *orthros*, dawn; the most authentic mss. have *batheōs*, deeply, i.e., very early.

(2) In Mark 8:12, "He sighed deeply" represents *anastenazō*, to fetch a deep-drawn sigh (*ana*, up, *stenazō*, to sigh or groan). See SIGH. ¶

C. Verb.

bathunō [βαθύνω, 900], to deepen, make deep, is used in Luke 6:48 (A.V., "digged deep"). The original has two separate verbs, *skaptō*, to dig, and *bathunō*; the R.V. therefore has "digged and went deep." ¶

NT: B.130b; CB.—; K.—.
OT: ʽāmaq: S.6009; HR.189a.1; H.1644; BD.770d.
GEN. REF.: IS.1:910; NB.—; Z.—.

DEFAME

dusphēmeō [δυσφημέω, 1418, 5346], lit., to speak injuriously (from *dus—*, an inseparable prefix signifying opposition, injury etc., and *phēmi*, to speak), is translated "defamed," 1 Cor. 4:13. Some mss. have *blasphēmeō*. See BLASPHEME. ¶

NT: B.209d; CB.—; K.—.
OT: —.
GEN. REF.: —.

DEFECT

hēttēma [ἥττημα, 2275], primarily a lessening, a decrease, diminution, denotes a loss. It is used of the loss sustained by the Jewish nation in that they had rejected God's testimonies and His Son and the Gospel, Rom. 11:12, the reference being not only to national diminution but to spiritual loss; R.V., "loss," for A.V., "diminishing." Here the contrasting word is *plērōma*, fulness. In 1 Cor. 6:7 the reference is to the spiritual loss sustained by the church at Corinth because of their discord and their litigious ways in appealing to the world's judges. Here the R.V. has "defect" (marg. "loss"), for A.V., "fault." The preceding adverb "altogether" shows the comprehensiveness of the defect; the loss affected the whole church, and was "an utter detriment."

In the Sept. of Isa. 31:8 the word signifies the loss of a defeat, with reference to the overthrow of the Assyrians; lit. 'his young men shall be for loss' (i.e., "tributary"). See DIMINISHING, FAULT, LOSS. ¶

NT: B.349c; CB.1250b; K.—.
OT: mas: S.4522; HR.620c.1; H.1218; BD.586d.
GEN. REF.: —.

Note: Cp. *hēttaō*, to make inferior, used in the Passive Voice, to be overcome (of spiritual defeat, 2 Pet. 2:20), and the adjective *hēttōn* or *hēssōn*, less, worse.

DEFENCE

A. Noun.

apologia [ἀπολογία], a speech made in defence. See ANSWER.

B. Verb.

apologeomai [ἀπολογέομαι]: see ANSWER, B, No. 4.

DEFEND

amunō [ἀμύνω, 292], to ward off, is used in the Middle Voice in Acts 7:24, of the assistance given by Moses to his fellow-Israelite against an Egyptian (translated "defended"). The Middle Voice indicates the special personal interest Moses had in the act. ¶

NT: B.47a; CB.—; K.—.
OT: yāshaʽ: S.3467; HR.67c.1; H.929; BD.446b.
nāqam: S.5358; HR.67c.3; H.1413; BD.667d.
GEN. REF.: —.

DEFER

anaballō [ἀναβάλλω, 306], lit., to throw up (*ana*, up, *ballō*, to throw), hence to postpone, is used in the Middle Voice in Acts 24:22, in the forensic sense of deferring the hearing of a case. ¶

NT: B.50c; CB.—; K.—.
OT: —.
GEN. REF.: —.

Note: Cp. *anabolē*, a putting off, delay, Acts 25:17. ¶

DEFILE, DEFILEMENT

A. Verbs.

1. *koinoō* [κοινόω, 2840], denotes (*a*) to make common; hence, in a ceremonial sense, to render unholy, unclean, to defile, Matt. 15:11, 18, 20; Mark 7:15, 18, 20, 23; Acts 21:28 (R.V., "defiled"; A.V., "polluted"); Heb. 9:13 (R.V., "them that have been defiled," A.V., "the unclean"); (*b*) to count unclean, Acts 10:15; 11:9. In Rev. 21:27, some mss. have this verb, "defileth"; the most authentic have the adjective, *koinos*, "unclean." See CALL, COMMON. ¶

NT: B.438b; CB.1255b; K.447.
OT: —.
GEN. REF.: IS.1:912; NB.—; Z.2:87.

2. *miainō* [μιαίνω, 3392], primarily, to stain, to tinge or dye with another colour, as in the staining of a glass, hence, to pollute, contaminate, soil, defile, is used (*a*) of ceremonial defilement, John 18:28; so in the Sept., in Lev. 22:5, 8; Num. 19:13, 20 etc.; (*b*) of moral defilement, Tit. 1:15 (twice); Heb. 12:15; of moral and physical defilement, Jude 8. See B, Nos. 1 and 2. ¶

NT: B.520d; CB.1258c; K.593.
OT: ṭāmē': S.2930; HR.925c.5a-e; H.809; BD.379a.
GEN. REF.: IS.1:912; NB.238; Z.2:87.

3. *molunō* [μολύνω, 3435], properly denotes to besmear, as with mud or filth, to befoul. It is used in the figurative sense, of a conscience defiled by sin, 1 Cor. 8:7; of believers who have kept themselves (their "garments") from defilement, Rev. 3:4, and of those who have not soiled themselves by adultery or fornication, Rev. 14:4. ¶

NT: B.526d; CB.1259a; K.606.
OT: ḥānēph: S.2610; HR.932c.4; H.696; BD.337d.
piggûl: S.6292; HR.932c.7; H.1730a; BD.803b.
GEN. REF.: IS.1:912; NB.–; Z.2:87.

Note: The difference between *miainō* and *molunō* is that the latter is not used in a ritual or ceremonial sense, as *miainō* is (Trench, Syn. xxxi).

4. *spiloō* [σπιλόω, 4695], to make a stain or spot, and so to defile, is used in Jas. 3:6 of the defiling effects of an evil use of the tongue; in Jude 23, "spotted," with reference to moral defilement. See SPOT. ¶

NT: B.762d; CB.–; K.–.
OT: –.
GEN. REF.: –.

Note: (1) Cp. *spilos*, a spot, a moral blemish, Eph. 5:27; 2 Pet. 2:13; ¶ *aspilos*, without spot, spotless, 1 Tim. 6:14; Jas. 1:27; 1 Pet. 1:19; 2 Pet. 3:14; ¶ *spilas*, Jude 12, "hidden rocks," R.V. (A.V. "spots," a late meaning, equivalent to *spilos*). ¶

5. *phtheirō* [φθείω]: see CORRUPT, A, No. 2.

B. Nouns.

1. *miasma* [μίασμα, 3393], whence the Eng. word, denotes defilement (akin to A, No. 2), and is found in 2 Pet. 2:20, A.V., "pollutions," R.V., "defilements," the vices of the ungodly which contaminate a person in his intercourse with the world. ¶

NT: B.521a; CB.1258c; K.593.
OT: piggûl: S.6292; HR.926c.2; H.1730a; BD.803b.
shiqqûṣ: S.8351; HR.926c.3; H.2301d; BD.1055b.
GEN. REF.: IS.1:912; NB.–; Z.–.

2. *miasmos* [μιασμός, 3394], also akin to A, No. 2, primarily denotes the act of defiling, the process, in contrast to the defiling thing (No. 1). It is found in 2 Pet. 2:10 (A.V., "uncleanness," R.V., "defilement.") ¶

NT: B.521a; CB.1258c; K.593.
OT: –.
GEN. REF.: IS.1:912; NB.–; Z.–.

3. *molusmos* [μολυσμός, 3436], akin to A, No. 3, denotes defilement, in the sense of an action by which anything is defiled, 2 Cor. 7:1. ¶ Cp. the synonymous word *spilos*, A, No. 4, Note.

NT: B.527a; CB.1259a; K.606.
OT: ḥ^{a}nuppāh: S.2613; HR.932c.1; H.696c; BD.338b.
GEN. REF.: IS.1:912; NB.–; Z.–.

C. Adjective.

koinos [κοινός, 2839], akin to A, No. 1, common, and, from the idea of coming into contact with everything, "defiled," is used in the ceremonial sense in Mark 7:2; in ver. 5, R.V., "defiled," for A.V., "unwashen" (the verb is used in 7:15). See COMMON, UNCLEAN.

NT: B.438a; CB.1255b; K.447.
OT: –.
GEN. REF.: IS.1:912; NB.–; Z.2:87.

DEFINE

horizō [ὁρίζω, 3724], Eng., horizon, primarily means to mark out the boundaries of a place (as in the Sept. of Numb. 34:6; Josh. 13:27); hence to determine, appoint. In Heb. 4:7, where the reference is to the time of God's invitation to enter into His rest, in contrast to Israel's failure to do so, the word may mean either the appointing of the day (i.e., the period), or the defining of the day, i.e., marking its limits. So the R.V. (A.V., "limiteth"). See DECLARE, DETERMINE, LIMIT, ORDAIN.

NT: B.580d; CB.1251b; K.728.
OT: g^{e}bûl: S.1366; HR.1011c.2a; H.307a; BD.147d.
GEN. REF.: –.

DEFRAUD

1. *apostereō* [ἀποστερέω, 650], signifies to rob, despoil, defraud, Mark 10:19; 1 Cor. 6:8; 7:5 (of that which is due to the condition of natural relationship of husband and wife); in the Middle Voice, to allow one-self to be defrauded, 1 Cor. 6:7; in the Passive Voice, "bereft," 1 Tim. 6:5, R.V., with reference to the truth, with the suggestion of being retributively robbed of the truth, through the corrupt condition of the mind. Some mss. have this verb in Jas. 5:4 for *aphustereō*, to keep back by fraud. See BEREFT, DESTITUTE, FRAUD. ¶ In the Sept., Ex. 21:10; in some mss., Deut. 24:14. ¶

NT: B.99a; CB.1237a; K.–.
OT: 'āshaq: S.6231; HR.145a.2; H.1713; BD.798d.
GEN. REF.: –.

2. *pleonekteō* [πλεονεκτέω, 4122], translated "defraud" in 1 Thess. 4:6, A.V. (R.V. "wrong"),

the reference being to the latter part of the Tenth Commandment. See ADVANTAGE, C, No. 2.

NT: B.667c; CB.1265b; K.864.
OT: bāṣa': S.1214; HR.1142a.1; H.267; BD.130b.
GEN. REF.: –.

DEGREE

bathmos [βαθμός, 898], denotes a step, primarily of a threshold or stair, and is akin to *bainō*, to go; figuratively, a standing, a stage in a career, position, degree, 1 Tim. 3:13, of faithful deacons. ¶

NT: B.130a; CB.–; K.–.
OT: –.
GEN. REF.: IS.–; NB.305; Z.2:88.

Note: Tapeinos, low, humble, whether in condition or mind, is translated "of low degree" in Luke 1:52 and Jas. 1:9. ¶

DELAY

A. Verbs.

1. *okneō* [ὀκνέω, 3635], akin to *oknos*, a shrinking, to be loath or slow to do a thing, to hesitate, delay, is used in Acts 9:38. ¶ In the Sept. in Numb. 22:16, "do not delay"; Judg. 18:9. ¶

NT: B.563a; CB.–; K.–.
OT: māna': S.4513; HR.985b.1; H.1216; BD.586a.
'āṣal: S.6101; HR.985b.2; H.1672; BD.782b.
GEN. REF.: –.

2. *chronizō* [χρονίζω, 5549], from *chronos*, time, lit. means to while away time, i.e., by way of lingering, tarrying, delaying; "delayeth," Matt. 24:48; Luke 12:45; "tarried," Matt. 25:5; "tarried so long," Luke 1:21; "will (not) tarry," Heb. 10:37. See TARRY. ¶

NT: B.887d; CB.1240b; K.–.
OT: 'āḥar: S.309; HR.1476a.1b; H.68; BD.29b.
GEN. REF.: IS.1:914; NB.–; Z.–.

B. Noun.

anabolē [ἀναβολή, 311], lit. signifies that which is thrown up (*ana*, up, *ballō*, to throw); hence a delay, Acts 25:17. See DEFER. ¶

NT: B.51a; CB.–; K.–.
OT: –.
GEN. REF.: –.

Note: In Rev. 10:6, *chronos* is translated "delay" in R.V. marg., and is to be taken as the true meaning.

DELICACIES

Note: For *strēnos*, rendered "delicacies" in Rev. 18:3, A.V., denoting "wantonness" (R.V.), i.e., arrogant luxury, see WANTON. ¶ Cp. the verb *strēniaō*, below, under DELICATELY.

DELICATELY (live)

A. Verbs.

truphaō [τρυφάω, 5171], from *thruptō*, to enervate, signifies to lead a voluptuous life, to give oneself up to pleasure, Jas. 5:5, R.V., "ye have lived delicately"; A.V., "ye have lived in pleasure." ¶

NT: B.828c; CB.–; K.–.
OT: 'ādan: S.5727; HR.1377c.1; H.1568; BD.726c.
'ānag: S.6026; HR.1377c.2; H.1648; BD.772b.
GEN. REF.: –.

Notes: (1) Cp. *spatalaō*, from *spatalē*, wantonness, to live riotously, used with A in Jas. 5:5, "ye have lived in pleasure" (R.V., "have taken your . . ."); cp. 1 Tim. 5:6, of carnal women in the church, A.V., "liveth in pleasure," R.V., "giveth herself to pleasure." See PLEASURE. ¶

(2) Cp. also *strēniaō*, to run riot, translated "lived deliciously," in Rev. 18:7, 9, A.V. (R.V., "waxed wanton" and "lived wantonly"). Cp. DELICACIES (above). See WANTON. ¶ Cp. the intensive form *katastrēniaō*, to wax utterly wanton, 1 Tim. 5:11. ¶

(3) *Spatalaō* "might properly be laid to the charge of the prodigal, scattering his substance in riotous living, Luke 15:13; . . . *truphaō* to the charge of the rich man, faring sumptuously every day, Luke 16:19; *strēniaō* to Jeshurun, when, waxing fat, he kicked, Deut. 32:15" (Trench, Syn. § liv).

B. Noun.

truphē [τρυφή, 5172], akin to A, is used with *en*, in the phrase *en truphē*, luxuriously, "delicately," Luke 7:25, and denotes effiminacy, softness; "to revel" in 2 Pet. 2:13 (A.V., "riot"), lit., 'counting revelling in the day time a pleasure.' See REVEL, RIOT. ¶

NT: B.828d; CB.–; K.–.
OT: 'ēden: S.5730; HR.1377c.1a; H.1568a; BD.726c.
ta'ănûg: S.8588; HR.1377c.2; H.1648c; BD.772c.
GEN. REF.: –.

Note: Entruphaō, to revel luxuriously, is used in 2 Pet. 2:13, R.V., "revelling" (A.V., "sporting themselves"). ¶

For **DELICIOUSLY**, Rev. 18:7, 9, A.V., see Note (1) above.

DELIGHT IN

sunēdomai [συνήδομαι, 4913], lit., to rejoice with (anyone), to delight in (a thing) with (others), signifies to delight with oneself inwardly in a thing, in Rom. 7:22. ¶

NT: B.789c; CB.–; K.–.
OT: –.
GEN. REF.: IS.1:914; NB.–; Z.–.

Note: Cp. *hēdonē*, desire, pleasure.

DELIVER, DELIVERANCE, DELIVERER

A. Verbs.

1. *didōmi* [δίδωμι, 1325], to give, is translated "delivered" in Luke 7:15; R.V., "gave"; so 19:13. See GIVE.
NT: B.192c; CB.1241c; K.166.
OT: –.
GEN. REF.: IS.–; NB.–; Z.2:89.

2. *anadidōmi* [ἀναδίδωμι, 325], *ana*, up, and No. 1, to deliver over, give up, is used of delivering the letter mentioned in Acts 23:33. ¶
NT: B.53c; CB.–; K.–.
OT: –.
GEN. REF.: –.

Note: For the different verb in Acts 15:30, see No. 4.

3. *apodidōmi* [ἀποδίδωμι, 591], *apo*, from, and No. 1, lit., to give away, hence, to give back or up, is used in Pilate's command for the Lord's body to be given up, Matt. 27:58; in the sense of giving back, of the Lord's act in giving a healed boy back to his father, Luke 9:42. See GIVE, PAY, PAYMENT, PERFORM, RECOMPENSE, RENDER, REPAY, REQUITE, RESTORE, REWARD, SELL, YIELD.
NT: B.90b; CB.1236c; K.166.
OT: shûb: S.7725; HR.126b.8b; H.2340; BD.996d,998c.
mākar: S.4376; HR.126b.3a; H.1194; BD.569a.
GEN. REF.: IS.1:916; NB.–; Z.–.

4. *epididōmi* [ἐπιδίδωμι, 1929], lit., to give upon or in addition, as from oneself to another, hence, to deliver over, is used of the delivering of the roll of Isaiah to Christ in the synagogue, Luke 4:17; of the delivering of the epistle from the elders at Jerusalem to the church at Antioch, Acts 15:30. See DRIVE (let), GIVE, OFFER.
NT: B.292b; CB.–; K.–.
OT: bô': S.935; HR.519b.1; H.212; BD.97c,98d.
nātan: S.5414; HR.519b.3; H.1443; BD.678a.
GEN. REF.: IS.1:916; NB.–; Z.2:89.

5. *paradidōmi* [παραδίδωμι, 3860], to deliver over, in Rom. 6:17, R.V. "that form of teaching whereunto ye were delivered," the figure being that of a mould which gives its shape to what is cast in it (not as the A.V.). In Rom. 8:32 it is used of God in delivering His Son to expiatory Death; so 4:25; see Mark 9:31; of Christ in delivering Himself up, Gal. 2:20; Eph. 5:2, 25. See BETRAY, A. In Mark 1:14, R.V., it is used of delivering John the Baptist to prison. See PUT, No. 12.
NT: B.614b; CB.1262a; K.166.
OT: nātan: S.5414; HR.1058a.16; H.1443; BD.678a.
GEN. REF.: IS.1:916; NB.–; Z.2:89.

6. *apallassō* [ἀπαλλάσσω, 525], lit., to change from (*apo*, from, *allassō*, to change), to free from, release, is translated "might deliver" in Heb. 2:15; in Luke 12:58, it is used in a legal sense of being quit of a person, i.e., the opponent being appeased and withdrawing his suit. For its other meaning, to depart, in Acts 19:12, see DEPART. ¶
NT: B.80a; CB.1236b; K.40.
OT: –.
GEN. REF.: IS.1:915; NB.–; Z.–.

7. *eleutheroō* [ἐλευθερόω, 1659], to set free, is translated "deliver" in Rom. 8:21. In six other places it is translated "make free," John 8:32, 36; Rom. 6:18, 22; 8:2; Gal. 5:1, R.V., "set free." See FREE ¶
NT: B.250d; CB.1244b; K.224.
OT: –.
GEN. REF.: –.

8. *exaireō* [ἐξαιρέω, 1807], lit., to take out, denotes, in the Middle Voice, to take out for oneself, hence, to deliver, to rescue, the person who does so having a special interest in the result of his act. Thus it is used, in Gal. 1:4, of the act of God in delivering believers "out of this present evil world," the Middle Voice indicating His pleasure in the issue of their deliverance. It signifies to deliver by rescuing from danger, in Acts 12:11; 23:27; 26:17; from bondage, Acts 7:10, 34. For its other meaning, to pluck out of, Matt. 5:29; 18:9, see PLUCK. ¶
NT: B.271d; CB.–; K.–.
OT: nāṣal: S.5337; HR.484b.8a; H.1404; BD.664c.
ḥālaṣ: S.2502; HR.484b.3; H.667; BD.322c.
GEN. REF.: IS.1:915; NB.–; Z.–.

9. *katargeō* [καταργέω]: see ABOLISH.

10. *rhuomai* [ῥύομαι, 4506], to rescue from, to preserve from, and so, to deliver, the word by which it is regularly translated, is largely synonymous with *sōzō*, to save, though the idea of rescue from is predominant in *rhuomai* (see Matt. 27:43), that of preservation from, in *sōzō*. In Rom. 11:26 the present participle is used with the article, as a noun, "the Deliverer." This is the construction in 1 Thess. 1:10, where Christ is similarly spoken of. Here the A.V. wrongly has "which delivered" (the tense is not past); R.V., "which delivereth"; the translation might well be (as in Rom. 11:26), 'our Deliverer,' that is, from the retributive calamities with which God will visit men at the end of the present age. From that wrath believers are to be delivered. The verb is used with *apo*, away from, in Matt. 6:13; Luke 11:4 (in some mss.); so also in 11:4; Rom. 15:31; 2 Thess. 3:2; 2 Tim. 4:18; and with *ek*, from, out of, in Luke 1:74; Rom. 7:24; 2 Cor. 1:10; Col. 1:13, from bondage; in 2 Pet. 2:9, from temptation; in 2 Tim. 3:11, from persecution; but *ek* is used of ills impending, in 2 Cor. 1:10; in 2 Tim. 4:17, *ek* indicates that the danger was more imminent than in ver. 18, where *apo* is used. Accordingly

the meaning 'out of the midst of' cannot be pressed in 1 Thess. 1:10. ¶

NT: B.737c; CB.1268b; K.988.
OT: gā'al: S.1350; HR.1254b.1; H.300; BD.145b.
nāṣal: S.5337; HR.1254b.5b; H.1404; BD.664c.
mālaṭ: S.4422; HR.1254b.4b; H.1197b; BD.572b.
GEN. REF.: IS.1:915; NB.1078; Z.2:89.

11. *charizomai* [χαρίζομαι, 5483], to gratify, to do what is pleasing to anyone, is translated "deliver" in the A.V. of Acts 25:11, 16; R.V., "give up" (marg., "grant by favour," i.e., to give over to the Jews so as to gratify their wishes). See FORGIVE, GIVE, GRANT.

NT: B.876c; CB.1239c; K.1298.
OT: ḥātan: S.5414; HR.1454c.1; H.1443; BD.678a.
GEN. REF.: IS.1:916; NB.–; Z.2:89.

Note: For *gennaō* and *tiktō*, to bear, to be delivered (said of women at childbirth), see BEGET.

B. Nouns.

1. *apolutrōsis* [ἀπολύτρωσις, 629], denotes redemption (*apo*, from, *lutron*, a price of release). In Heb. 11:35 it is translated "deliverance"; usually the release is effected by the payment of a ransom, or the required price, the *lutron* (ransom). See REDEMPTION.

NT: B.96b; CB.1237a; K.543.
OT: –.
GEN. REF.: IS.1:915; NB.1078; Z.–.

2. *aphesis* [ἄφεσις, 859], denotes a release, from bondage, imprisonment etc. (the corresponding verb is *aphiēmi*, to send away, let go); in Luke 4:18 it is used of liberation from captivity (A.V., "deliverance," R.V., "release"). See FORGIVENESS, REMISSION.

NT: B.125a; CB.1236b; K.88.
OT: yôbēl: S.3104; HR.182b.6; H.835e; BD.385c.
d^{e}rôr: S.1865; HR.182b.3; H.454b; BD.204d.
shāmaṭ: S.8058; HR.182b.11; H.2408; BD.1030c.
GEN. REF.: –.

3. *lutrōtēs* [λυτρωτής, 3086], a redeemer, one who releases (see No. 1), is translated "deliverer" in Acts 7:35 (R.V. marg., "redeemer"). ¶

NT: B.483a; CB.1257b; K.543.
OT: gā'al: S.1350; HR.891a.1; H.300; BD.145b.
GEN. REF.: IS.1:915,4:61; NB.1078; Z.2:90.

Note: See also DELIVER, A, No. 10.

C. Verbal Adjective.

ekdotos [ἔκδοτος, 1560], lit., given up (*ek*, out of, *didōmi*, to give), delivered up (to enemies, or to the power or will of someone), is used of Christ in Acts 2:23. ¶

NT: B.239a; CB.1243c; K.–.
OT: –.
GEN. REF.: IS.1:915; NB.–; Z.–.

DELUDE, DELUSION

A. Verb.

paralogizomai [παραλογίζομαι]: see BEGUILE.

B. Noun.

planē [πλάνη, 4106], lit., a wandering, whereby those who are led astray roam hither and thither, is always used in the N.T., of mental straying, wrong opinion, error in morals or religion. In 2 Thess. 2:11, A.V., it is translated "delusion," R.V., "error." See DECEIT, ERROR.

NT: B.665d; CB.1265a; K.857.
OT: mirmāh: S.4820; HR.1140a.1; H.2169b; BD.941b.
GEN. REF.: IS.1:917; NB.–; Z.–.

DEMAND

Note: For **DEMAND** (Matt. 2:4 and Acts 21:33), see INQUIRE; for its use in Luke 3:14 and 17:20, see under ASK.

DEMEANOUR

katastēma [κατάστημα]: see BEHAVIOUR, B, No. 2.

DEMON, DEMONIAC

A. Nouns.

1. *daimōn* [δαίμων, 1142], a demon, signified, among pagan Greeks, an inferior deity, whether good or bad. In the N.T. it denotes an evil spirit. It is used in Matt. 8:31, mistranslated "devils."

Some would derive the word from a root *da*—, meaning to distribute. More probably it is from a similar root *da*—, meaning to know, and hence means a knowing one. ¶

NT: B.169d; CB.1240b; K.137.
OT: –.
GEN. REF.: IS.1:919; NB.310; Z.2:92.

2. *daimonion* [δαιμόνιον, 1140], not a diminutive of *daimōn*, No. 1, but the neuter of the adjective *daimonios*, pertaining to a demon, is also mistranslated "devil," "devils." In Acts 17:18, it denotes an inferior pagan deity. Demons are the spiritual agents acting in all idolatry. The idol itself is nothing, but every idol has a demon associated with it who induces idolatry, with its worship and sacrifices, 1 Cor. 10:20, 21; Rev. 9:20; cp. Deut. 32:17; Isa. 13:21; 34:14; 65:3, 11. They disseminate errors among men, and seek to seduce believers, 1 Tim. 4:1. As seducing spirits they deceive men into the supposition that through mediums (those who have "familiar spirits," Lev. 20:6, 27, e.g.) they can converse with deceased human beings. Hence the destructive deception of Spiritism, forbidden in Scripture, Lev. 19:31; Deut. 18:11; Isa. 8:19. Demons tremble before God, Jas. 2:19; they recognized Christ as Lord and as their future Judge, Matt. 8:29; Luke 4:41.

Christ cast them out of human beings by His own power. His disciples did so in His Name, and by exercising faith, e.g., Matt. 17:20.

Acting under Satan (cp. Rev. 16:13, 14), demons are permitted to afflict with bodily disease, Luke 13:16. Being unclean they tempt human beings with unclean thoughts, Matt. 10:1; Mark 5:2; 7:25; Luke 8:27-29; Rev. 16:13; 18:2, e.g. They differ in degrees of wickedness, Matt. 12:45. They will instigate the rulers of the nations at the end of this age to make war against God and His Christ, Rev. 16:14. See DEVIL.

NT: B.169a; CB.1240b; K.137.
OT: shēd: S.7700; HR.283b.5a; H.2330; BD.993d.
GEN. REF.: IS.1:919; NB.310; Z.2:92.

B. Verb.

daimonizomai [δαιμονίζομαι, 1139], signifies to be possessed of a demon, to act under the control of a demon. Those who were thus afflicted expressed the mind and consciousness of the demon or demons indwelling them, e.g., Luke 8:28. The verb is found chiefly in Matt. and Mark; Matt. 4:24; 8:16, 28, 33; 9:32; 12:22; 15:22; Mark 1:32; 5:15, 16, 18; elsewhere in Luke 8:36 and John 10:21, "him that hath a devil (demon)." ¶

NT: B.169a; CB.1240b; K.137.
OT: –.
GEN. REF.: IS.1:919; NB.310; Z.2:91.

C. Adjective.

diamoniōdēs [δαιμονιώδης, 1141], signifies proceeding from, or resembling, a demon, "demoniacal"; see marg. of Jas. 3:15, R.V. (text, "devilish"). ¶

NT: B.169c; CB.–; K.137.
OT: –.
GEN. REF.: IS.1:919; NB.310; Z.2:91.

DEMONSTRATION

apodeixis [ἀπόδειξις, 585], lit., a pointing out (*apo, forth, deiknumi*, to show), a showing or demonstrating by argument, is found in 1 Cor. 2:4, where the Apostle speaks of a proof, a showing forth or display, by the operation of the Spirit of God in him, as affecting the hearts and lives of his hearers, in contrast to the attempted methods of proof by rhetorical arts and philosophic arguments. ¶

NT: B.89d; CB.1236c; K.–.
OT: –.
GEN. REF.: –.

DEN

spēlaion [σπήλαιον]: See CAVE.

DENY

1. *arneomai* [ἀρνέομαι, 720], signifies (*a*) to say . . . not, to contradict, e.g., Mark 14:70; John 1:20; 18:25, 27; 1 John 2:22; (*b*) to deny by way of disowning a person, as, e.g., the Lord Jesus as Master, e.g., Matt. 10:33; Luke 12:9; John 13:38 (in the best mss.); 2 Tim. 2:12; or, on the other hand, of Christ Himself, denying that a person is His follower, Matt. 10:33; 2 Tim. 2:12; or to deny the Father and the Son, by apostatizing and by disseminating pernicious teachings, to deny Jesus Christ as Master and Lord by immorality under a cloak of religion, 2 Pet. 2:1; Jude 4; (*c*) to deny oneself, either in a good sense, by disregarding one's own interests, Luke 9:23, or in a bad sense, to prove false to oneself, to act quite unlike oneself, 2 Tim. 2:13; (*d*) to abrogate, forsake, or renounce a thing, whether evil, Tit. 2:12, or good, 1 Tim. 5:8; 2 Tim. 3:5; Rev. 2:13; 3:8; (*e*) not to accept, to reject something offered, Acts 3:14; 7:35, "refused"; Heb. 11:24, "refused." See REFUSE.

NT: B.107d; CB.1237c; K.79.
OT: kāḥash: S.3584; HR.159b.1; H.975; BD.471a.
GEN. REF.: IS.–; NB.–; Z.2:101.

2. *aparneomai* [ἀπαρνέομαι, 533], a strengthened form of No. 1, with *apo*, from, prefixed (Lat., *abnego*), means (*a*) to deny utterly, to abjure, to affirm that one has no connection with a person, as in Peter's denial of Christ, Matt. 26:34, 35, 75; Mark 14:30, 31, 72; Luke 22:34, 61 (some mss. have it in John 13:38). This stronger form is used in the Lord's statements foretelling Peter's denial, and in Peter's assurance of fidelity; the simple verb (No. 1) is used in all the records of his actual denial. The strengthened form is the verb used in the Lord's warning as to being "denied" in the presence of the angels, Luke 12:9; in the preceding clause, "he that denieth Me," the simple verb *arneomai* is used; the rendering therefore should be 'he that denieth Me in the presence of men, shall be utterly denied in the presence of the angels of God'; (*b*) to deny oneself as a follower of Christ, Matt. 16:24; Mark 8:34; Luke 9:23. ¶

NT: B.81a; CB.1236b; K.–.
OT: mā'as: S.3988; HR.118a.1; H.1139,1140; BD.548d.
GEN. REF.: IS.–; NB.–; Z.2:101.

3. *antilegō* [ἀντιλέγω, 483], means to speak against, contradict. In Luke 20:27, the R.V., "they which say that there is no resurrection," follows the texts which have the simple verb *legō*; for the A.V., which translates the verb *antilegō*, "which deny that there is any

resurrection." See ANSWER, CONTRADICT, GAINSAY, SPEAK, No. 6.

NT: B.74d; CB.–; K.–.
OT: rîb: S.7378; HR.111a.2; H.2159; BD.936b.
GEN. REF.: –.

DEPART

(*a*) *Compounds of agō.*

1. *anagō* [ἀνάγω, 321], lit., to lead up (*ana*, up, *agō*, to lead), is used, in the Middle Voice, as a nautical term, signifying to set sail, put to sea; "to depart," Acts 27:12, A.V. (R.V., "put to sea"); 28:10 (R.V., "sailed"); ver. 11 (R.V., "set sail"). Cp. *epanagō*, in Luke 5:3, to put out. See BRING, No. 11.

NT: B.53a; CB.–; K.–.
OT: 'ālāh: S.5927; HR.75b.6; H.1624; BD.748a.
GEN. REF.: –.

2. *paragō* [παράγω, 3855], used intransitively, means to pass by (*para*, by, beside), and is so translated everywhere in the Gospels, except in the A.V. of Matt. 9:27, "departed"; R.V., "passed by." Outside the Gospels it is used in its other meaning, to pass away, 1 Cor. 7:31; 1 John 2:8 (R.V.), 17. See PASS.

NT: B.613d; CB.–; K.20.
OT: 'ābar: S.5674; HR.1056b.2; H.1556; BD.716d.
GEN. REF.: –.

3. *hupagō* [ὑπάγω, 5217], to go, translated "depart" in Jas. 2:16, A.V., primarily and lit. meant to lead under (*hupo*, under); in its later use, it implied a going, without noise or notice, or by stealth. In this passage the idea is perhaps that of a polite dismissal, 'Go your ways.' See GET, GO.

NT: B.836c; CB.–; K.1227.
OT: hālak: S.1980; HR.1405c.1; H.498; BD.229d,236c.
GEN. REF.: IS.1:923; NB.–; Z.–.

(*b*) *Compounds of erchomai.*

4. *aperchomai* [ἀπέρχομαι, 565], lit., to come or go away (*apo*), hence, to set off, depart, e.g., Matt. 8:18, is frequent in the Gospels and Acts; Rev. 18:14, R.V., "are gone." See COME, No. 11 (Note), GO, PASS.

NT: B.84c; CB.1236b; K.257.
OT: hālak: S.1980; HR.121a.5a; H.498; BD.229d.
GEN. REF.: IS.1:923; NB.–; Z.–.

5. *dierchomai* [διέρχομαι, 1330], to come or go through, to pass through to a place, is translated "departed" in Acts 13:14, A.V.; R.V., "passing through"; elsewhere it is usually translated "pass through" or "go through." See COME, No. 5.

NT: B.194c; CB.1241c; K.257.
OT: hālak: S.1980; HR.328c.4a,c; H.498; BD.229d.
yāṣā': S.3318; HR.328c.6; H.893; BD.422b.
'ābar: S.5674; HR.328c.10a; H.1556; BD.716d.
GEN. REF.: IS.1:923; NB.–; Z.–.

6. *exerchomai* [ἐξέρχομαι, 1831], denotes to come out, or go out of, to go forth. It is frequently translated by the verb to depart, e.g., Matt. 9:31; in Luke 4:42, for the A.V., "He departed and went (No. 8)," the R.V. has "He came out and went"; in 9:6 the A.V. and R.V. agree. See COME, No. 3.

NT: B.274b; CB.1247c; K.257.
OT: yāṣā': S.3318; HR.491c.5a; H.893; BD.422b.
GEN. REF.: –.

7. *katerchomai* [κατέρχομαι, 2718], to come down (its usual meaning), is translated "departed" in Acts 13:4, A.V. (R.V., "went down"). See COME, No. 7.

NT: B.422a; CB.–; K.–.
OT: –.
GEN. REF.: –.

(*c*) *Poreuō and a compound.*

8. *poreuō* [πορεύω, 4198], akin to *poros*, a passage, in the Middle Voice signifies to go on one's way, to depart from one place to another. In some places, where the A.V. has the verb to depart, the R.V. translates by to go one's way, e.g., Matt. 2:9, "went their way"; 11:7; 24:1, "was going on His way." In the following the R.V. has the verb to go, for the A.V. depart, Luke 4:42 (latter part of verse); 13:31; John 16:7; 2 Tim. 4:10. In Luke 21:8, "go (after)," is said of disciples or partisans. In some places both A.V. and R.V. translate by the verb to depart, e.g., Matt. 19:15; 25:41; Acts 5:41; Acts 22:21. This verb is to be distinguished from others signifying to go. It is best rendered, as often as possible, to go on one's way. See GO, JOURNEY, WALK.

NT: B.692b; CB.1266a; K.–.
OT: hālak: S.1980; HR.1189a.3a; H.498; BD.229d.
GEN. REF.: IS.1:923; NB.–; Z.–.

9. *ekporeuō* [ἐκπορεύω, 1607], *ek*, from, in the Middle and Passive, to proceed from or forth, more expressive of a definite course than simply to go forth, is translated "go forth," in Mark 6:11; "went out" in Matt. 20:29, R.V., (A.V., "departed"); both have "depart" in Acts 25:4. It is frequently translated by the verb to proceed, and is often best so rendered, e.g., in Rev. 9:17, 18, R.V., for A.V., "issued." See COME, No. 33.

NT: B.244b; CB.1244a; K.–.
OT: yāṣā': S.3318; HR.439c.5a; H.893; BD.422b.
GEN. REF.: –.

(*d*) *Compounds of chōreō.*

10. *anachōreō* [ἀναχωρέω, 402], to go back, recede, retire (*ana*, back or up, *chōreō*, to make room for, betake oneself, *chōros*, a place), is translated "departed" in Matt. 2:12, 13, 14; 4:12 (R.V., "withdrew"); so in 14:13 and 15:21, but "departed" in 27:5; "withdrew" in John 6:15. In Matt. 2:22 the R.V. has "withdrew," which is preferable to the A.V., "turned aside." The most suitable translation wherever possible, is

by the verb to withdraw. See PLACE, B, No. 1, GO, No. 15, TURN, *Note* (1), WITHDRAW.

NT: B.63c; CB.1235a; K.–.
OT: bāraḥ: S.1272; HR.85c.1; H.284; BD.137d.
hûs: S.5127; HR.85c.3; H.1327; BD.630c.
GEN. REF.: –.

11. *apochōreō* [ἀποχωρέω, 672], to depart from (*apo*), is so translated in Matt. 7:23; Luke 9:39; Acts 13:13 (both A.V. and R.V.). Some mss. have it in Luke 20:20. ¶

NT: B.102a; CB.–; K.–.
OT: sûg: S.5472; HR.150a.1; H.1469; BD.690d.
GEN. REF.: –.

12. *ekchōreō* [ἐκχωρέω, 1633], signifies to depart out (*ek*), to leave a place, Luke 21:21. ¶

NT: B.247c; CB.–; K.–.
OT: bāraḥ: S.1272; HR.446c.1; H.284; BD.137d.
GEN. REF.: –.

(*e*) *Chōrizō and compounds.*

13. *chōrizō* [χωρίζω, 5563], to put apart, separate, means, in the Middle Voice, to separate oneself, to depart from, Acts 1:4; 18:1, 2; in marital affairs, 1 Cor. 7:10, 11, 15; "departed" (R.V. corrects to "was parted"), Phlm. 15. The verb is also used in Matt. 19:6; Mark 10:9; Rom. 8:35, 39; Heb. 7:26. See PUT, No. 14, SEPARATE. ¶

NT: B.890a; CB.1240a; K.–.
OT: bādal: S.914; HR.1482b.2; H.203; BD.95a.
pārad: S.6504; HR.1482b.4; H.1806; BD.825b.
GEN. REF.: –.

14. *apochōrizō* [ἀποχωρίζω, 673], signifies to separate off (*apo*); in the Middle Voice, to depart from, Acts 15:39, A.V., "departed asunder"; R.V., "parted asunder"; Rev. 6:14, R.V., "was removed." See PART, REMOVE, ¶

NT: B.102b; CB.–; K.–.
OT: miphqād: S.4662; HR.150a.1; H.1802g; BD.824c.
GEN. REF.: –.

15. *diachōrizō* [διαχωρίζω, 1316], lit., to separate throughout (*dia*), i.e., completely, in the Middle Voice, to separate oneself definitely from, is used in Luke 9:33, R.V., "were parting from." ¶

NT: B.191a; CB.1241a; K.–.
OT: pārad: S.6504; HR.316a.4a; H.1806; BD.825b.
bādal: S.914; HR.316a.1b; H.203; BD.95a.
GEN. REF.: –.

(*f*) *Various other verbs.*

16. *analuō* [ἀναλύω, 360], lit., to unloose, undo (*ana*, up, or again), signifies to depart, in the sense of departing from life, Phil. 1:23, a metaphor drawn from loosing moorings preparatory to setting sail, or, according to some, from breaking up an encampment, or from the unyoking of baggage animals. See DEPARTING, No. 1. In Luke 12:36, it has its other meaning, to return. See RETURN. ¶

NT: B.57a; CB.1235a; K.543.
OT: –.
GEN. REF.: –.

17. *apoluō* [ἀπολύω, 630], to loose from (*apo*), in the Middle Voice, signifies to depart, Luke 2:29; Acts 23:22, R.V., "let go"; 28:25. See DISMISS.

NT: B.96c; CB.1237a; K.–.
OT: –.
GEN. REF.: –.

18. *exeimi* [ἔξειμι, 1826], to go out (*ex*, out, *eimi*, to go) is rendered "went out" in Acts 13:42; in 27:43, "got," of mariners getting to shore; in 17:15, "departed"; in 20:7, "to depart." See GET, GO. ¶

NT: B.273d; CB.1247c; K.–.
OT: yāṣā': S.3318; HR.490c.2; H.893; BD.422b.
GEN. REF.: –.

19. *metairō* [μεταίρω, 3332], to make a distinction, to remove, to lift away (in its transitive sense), is used intransitively in the N.T., signifying to depart, and is said of Christ, in Matt. 13:53; 19:1. It could be well translated "removed." ¶

NT: B.511a; CB.–; K.–.
OT: sûr: S.5493; HR.916a.4; H.1480; BD.693b.
GEN. REF.: –.

20. *aphistēmi* [ἀφίστημι, 868], in the Active Voice, used transitively, signifies to cause to depart, to cause to revolt, Acts 5:37; used intransitively, to stand off, or aloof, or to depart from anyone, Luke 4:13; 13:27; Acts 5:38 ("refrain from"); 12:10; 15:38; 19:9; 22:29; 2 Cor. 12:8; metaphorically, to fall away, 2 Tim. 2:19; in the Middle Voice, to withdraw or absent oneself from, Luke 2:37; to apostatize, Luke 8:13; 1 Tim. 4:1; Heb. 3:12, R.V., "falling away." See DRAW (away), FALL, No. 14, REFRAIN, WITHDRAW. ¶

NT: B.126d; CB.1236b; K.88.
OT: sûr: S.5493; HR.184b.27; H.1480; BD.693b.
mārad: S.4775; HR.184b.17; H.1240; BD.597c.
GEN. REF.: –.

21. *apallassō* [ἀπαλλάσσω, 525], lit., to change from (*apo*, from, *allassō*, to change), is used once of departing, said of the removal of diseases, Acts 19:12. In Heb. 2:15 it signifies to deliver, release. In Luke 12:58, it is used in a legal sense, to be quit of. See DELIVER. ¶

NT: B.80a; CB.1236b; K.40.
OT: sûr: S.5493; HR.116c.3; H.1480; BD.693b.
GEN. REF.: –.

22. *metabainō* [μεταβαίνω, 3327], is rendered to depart in Matt. 8:34; 11:1; 12:9; 15:29; John 7:3; 13:1; Acts 18:7.

NT: B.510c; CB.1258b; K.90.
OT: –.
GEN. REF.: –.

DEPARTING, DEPARTURE

1. *analusis* [ἀνάλυσις, 359], an unloosing (as of things woven), a dissolving into separate parts (Eng., analysis), is once used of departure from life, 2 Tim. 4:6, where the metaphor is either nautical, from loosing from moorings

(thus used in Greek poetry), or military, from breaking up an encampment; cp. *kataluō* in 2 Cor. 5:1 (cp. DEPART, No. 16). ¶
NT: B.57b; CB.–; K.543.
OT: –.
GEN. REF.: –.

2. *aphixis* [ἄφιξις, 867], most frequently an arrival (akin to *aphikneomai*, see COME), also signifies a departure (*apo*, from, *hikneomai*, to come: etymologically, to come far enough, reach; cp. *hikanos*, sufficient), the departure being regarded in relation to the end in view. Thus Paul speaks of his "departing," Acts 20:29. ¶
NT: B.126d; CB.–; K.–.
OT: –.
GEN. REF.: IS.1:923; NB.–; Z.–.

3. *exodos* [ἔξοδος]: see DECEASE.

DEPOSE

kathaireō [καθαιρέω, 2507], lit., signifies to take down (*kata*, down, *haireō*, to take), the technical term for removing a body after crucifixion, e.g., Mark 15:36; hence, to pull down, demolish; in Acts 19:27, according to the most authentic mss., the translation is (as the R.V.) "that she (Diana) should even be deposed from her magnificence" (possibly, in the partitive sense of the genitive, 'destroyed from, or diminished in, somewhat of her magnificence'). See CAST, DESTROY, PULL, PUT, TAKE (down).
NT: B.386c; CB.–; K.380.
OT: –.
GEN. REF.: –.

For **DEPOSIT** see **COMMIT**, B, No. 1

DEPTH

1. *bathos* [βάθος]: see DEEP.

2. *pelagos* [πέλαγος, 3989], the sea, Acts 27:5, denotes also "the depth" (of the sea), Matt. 18:6. The word is most probably connected with a form of *plēssō*, to strike, and *plēgē*, a blow, suggestive of the tossing of the waves. Some would connect it with *plax*, a level board, but this is improbable, and less applicable to the general usage of the word, which commonly denotes the sea in its restless character. See SEA. ¶
NT: B.641b; CB.–; K.–.
OT: –.
GEN. REF.: –.

For **DEPUTY** see **PROCONSUL**

DERIDE

Note: For *ekmuktērizō*, lit., to turn up the nose at, to deride out and out, Luke 16:14; 23:35, see SCOFF. ¶

DESCEND

1. *katabainō* [καταβαίνω, 2597], to go down (*kata*, down, *bainō*, to go), used for various kinds of motion on the ground (e.g., going, walking, stepping), is usually translated to descend. The R.V. uses the verb to come down, for A.V., descend, in Mark 15:32; Acts 24:1; Rev. 21:10. See COME, No. 19.
NT: B.408b; CB.1253c; K.90.
OT: yārad: S.3381; HR.727a.8a; H.909; BD.432c.
GEN. REF.: IS.1:925; NB.–; Z.2:103.

2. *katerchomai* [κατέρχομαι, 2718], to come or go down, is translated "descendeth," in Jas. 3:15, A.V.; R.V., "cometh down." See COME, No. 7.
NT: B.422a; CB.–; K.–.
OT: –.
GEN. REF.: –.

DESCENT

katabasis [κατάβασις, 2600], denotes a going down, akin to No. 1 under DESCEND, a way down, Luke 19:37. ¶
NT: B.409a; CB.–; K.–.
OT: yārad: S.3381; HR.729a.2; H.909; BD.432c.
GEN. REF.: IS.1:926; NB.–; Z.2:103.

Note: For "descent" (A.V. in Heb. 7:3, 6), see GENEALOGY (the R.V. rendering).

DESCRIBE

1. *graphō* [γράφω, 1125], to write, is rendered "describeth" in Rom. 10:5, A.V., "For Moses describeth the righteousness which is of the Law . . ."; this the R.V. corrects to "For Moses writeth that the man that doeth the righteousness which is of the Law . . ." See WRITE.
NT: B.166c; CB.1248c; K.128.
OT: kātab: S.3789; HR.276a.3a,b; H.1053; BD.507a.
GEN. REF.: IS.1:927; NB.–; Z.–.

2. *legō* [λέγω, 3004], to say, is rendered "describeth" in Rom. 4:6, A.V., "David describeth the blessedness . . ."; this the R.V. corrects to, "David pronounceth blessing upon . . ." This might be regarded as the meaning, if David is considered as the human agent acting for God as the real pronouncer of blessing. Otherwise the verb *legō* is to be taken in its ordinary sense of telling or relating; especially as the blessedness (*makarismos*) is not an act, but a state of felicity resulting from God's act of justification.
NT: B.468a; CB.1256c; K.505.
OT: –.
GEN. REF.: –.

DESERT (Noun and Adjective)

A. Noun.

eremia [ἐρημία, 2047], primarily a solitude, an uninhabited place, in contrast to a town or village, is translated "deserts" in Heb. 11:38; "the wilderness" in Matt. 15:33, A.V., "a desert place," R.V.; so in Mark 8:4; "wilderness" in 2 Cor. 11:26. It does not always denote a barren region, void of vegetation; it is often used of a place uncultivated, but fit for pasturage. See WILDERNESS. ¶

NT: B.308d; CB.1246b; K.255.
OT: ḥārēb: S.2717; HR.545a.1a; H.731,732; BD.351c.
ḥārbāh: S.2723; HR.545a.1b; H.731d; BD.352a.
GEN. REF.: IS.1:927; NB.1327; Z.2:106.

B. Adjective.

erēmos [ἔρημος, 2048], used as a noun, has the same meaning as *erēmia*; in Luke 5:16 and 8:29, R.V., "deserts," for A.V., "wilderness"; in Matt. 24:26 and John 6:31, R.V., "wilderness," for A.V., "desert." As an adjective, it denotes (*a*), with reference to persons, "deserted," desolate, deprived of the friends and kindred, e.g., of a woman deserted by a husband, Gal. 4:27; (*b*) so of a city, as Jerusalem, Matt. 23:38; or uninhabited places, "desert," e.g., Matt. 14:13, 15; Acts 8:26; in Mark 1:35, R.V., "desert," for A.V., "solitary." See DESOLATE, WILDERNESS.

NT: B.309a; CB.1246b; K.255.
OT: midbār: S.4057; HR.545a.5; H.399k,l; BD.184d.
shᵉmāmāh: S.8077; HR.545a.11d; H.2409b,c; BD.1031b.
shāmēm: S.8074; HR.545a.11a,b; H.2409; BD.1030c.
GEN. REF.: IS.1:927; NB.1327; Z.2:106.

DESIRE (Noun and Verb), DESIROUS

A. Nouns.

1. *epithumia* [ἐπιθυμία, 1939], a desire, craving, longing, mostly of evil desires, frequently translated "lust," is used in the following, of good desires: of the Lord's wish concerning the last Passover, Luke 22:15; of Paul's desire to be with Christ, Phil. 1:23; of his desire to see the saints at Thessalonica again, 1 Thess. 2:17.

With regard to evil desires, in Col. 3:5 the R.V. has "desire," for the A.V., "concupiscence"; in 1 Thess. 4:5, R.V., "lust," for A.V., "concupiscence"; there the preceding word *pathos* is translated "passion," R.V., for A.V., "lust" (see AFFECTION); also in Col. 3:5 *pathos* and *epithumia* are associated, R.V., "passion," for A.V., "inordinate affection." *Epithumia* is combined with *pathēma*, in Gal. 5:24; for the A.V., "affections and lusts," the R.V. has "passions, and the lusts thereof." *Epithumia* is the more comprehensive term, including all manner of lusts and desires; *pathēma* denotes suffering; in the passage in Gal. (l.c.) the sufferings are those produced by yielding to the flesh; *pathos* points more to the evil state from which lusts spring. Cp. *orexis*, lust, Rom. 1:27. See CONCUPISCENCE, LUST, and Trench, Syn. lxxxvii.

NT: B.293b; CB.1246b; K.339.
OT: 'āwāh: S.183; HR.521a.1; H.40; BD.16a.
ḥāmad: S.2530; HR.521a.3a; H.673; BD.326b.
ḥᵃmudôt: S.2530; HR.521a.3c; H.673; BD.326d.
GEN. REF.: IS.1:929; NB.307; Z.2:107.

2. *eudokia* [εὐδοκία, 2107], lit., good pleasure (*eu*, well, *dokeō*, to seem), implies a gracious purpose, a good object being in view, with the idea of a resolve, shewing the willingness with which the resolve is made. It is often translated "good pleasure," e.g., Eph. 1:5, 9; Phil. 2:13; in Phil. 1:15, "good will"; in Rom. 10:1, "desire," (marg., "good pleasure"); in 2 Thess. 1:11, R.V., "desire," A.V. and R.V., marg., "good pleasure."

It is used of God in Matt. 11:26 ("well pleasing," R.V., for A.V., "seemed good"); Luke 2:14, R.V., "men in whom He is well pleased," lit., 'men of good pleasure' (the construction is objective); 10:21; Eph. 1:5, 9; Phil. 2:13. See PLEASURE, SEEM, WILL. ¶

NT: B.319c; CB.1247a; K.273.
OT: rāṣôn: S.7522; HR.569b.1a; H.2207a; BD.953c.
GEN. REF.: IS.1:929; NB.307; Z.2:107.

3. *epipothēsis* [ἐπιπόθησις, 1972], an earnest desire, a longing for (*epi*, upon, intensive, *potheō*, to desire), is found in 2 Cor. 7:7, 11, A.V., "earnest desire," and "vehement desire"; R.V., "longing" in both places. See LONGING. ¶

NT: B.298a; CB.1246a; K.—.
OT: —.
GEN. REF.: —.

4. *epipothia* [ἐπιποθία, 1974], with the same meaning as No. 3, is used in Rom. 15:23, R.V., "longing," A.V., "great desire." ¶ Cp. *epipothētos*, Phil. 4:1, "longed for" ¶, and *epipotheō*, to long for [see B, Note (4)]. See LONGING.

NT: B.298a; CB.1246a; K.—.
OT: —.
GEN. REF.: —.

5. *thelēma* [θέλημα, 2307], denotes a will, that which is willed (akin to B, No. 6). It is rendered "desires," in Eph. 2:3. See PLEASURE, WILL.

NT: B.354b; CB.1271c; K.318.
OT: ḥēpheṣ: S.2656; HR.629a.1c; H.712b; BD.343a.
rāṣôn: S.7522; HR.629a.4; H.2207a; BD.953c.
GEN. REF.: IS.1:929; NB.307; Z.2:107.

Note: In 1 Pet. 4:3, R.V., *boulēma* is rendered "desire." See WILL.

B. Verbs.

1. *axioō* [ἀξιόω, 515], to deem worthy, is translated "desire" in Acts 28:22, where a suitable rendering would be 'We think it meet (or good) to hear of thee'; so in 15:38. See THINK.

NT: B.78c; CB.1238b; K.63.
OT: –.
GEN. REF.: –.

2. *epithumeō* [ἐπιθυμέω, 1937], to desire earnestly (as with A, No. 1), stresses the inward impulse rather than the object desired. It is translated to desire in Luke 16:21; 17:22; 22:15; 1 Tim. 3:1; Heb. 6:11; 1 Pet. 1:12; Rev. 9:6. See COVET.

NT: B.293a; CB.1246b; K.339.
OT: 'āwāh: S.183; HR.520b.1a,b; H.40; BD.16a.
ḥāmad: S.2530; HR.520b.4; H.673; BD.326b.
ḥāphēṣ: S.2654; HR.520b.5; H.712; BD.342c.
GEN. REF.: IS.1:929; NB.–; Z.2:107.

3. *erōtaō* [ἐρωτάω, 2065], in Luke 7:36 is translated "desired"; in 14:32, R.V., "asketh," for A.V., "desireth"; so in John 12:21; Acts 16:39; 18:20; 23:20; in ver. 18 "asked," for A.V., "prayed." See ASK.

NT: B.311d; CB.1246c; K.262.
OT: shā'al: S.7592; HR.553b.3a; H.2303; BD.981b.
GEN. REF.: IS.1:929; NB.–; Z.2:107.

4. *homeiromai*, or *himeiromai* [ὁμείρομαι, 2442], to have a strong affection for, a yearning after, is found in 1 Thess. 2:8, "being affectionately desirous of you." It is probably derived from a root indicating remembrance.¶

NT: B.565b; CB.–; K.683.
OT: –.
GEN. REF.: IS.1:929; NB.–; Z.–.

5. *oregō* [ὀρέγω, 3713], to reach or stretch out, is used only in the Middle Voice, signifying the mental effort of stretching oneself out for a thing, of longing after it, with stress upon the object desired (cp. No. 2); it is translated "desire" in Heb. 11:16; in 1 Tim. 3:1, R.V., "seeketh," for A.V., "desireth"; in 1 Tim. 6:10, R.V., "reached after," for A.V., "coveted after." In Heb. 11:16, a suitable rendering would be 'reach after.' See COVET, SEEK. ¶ Cp. *orexis*, lust, Rom. 1:27. ¶

NT: B.579d; CB.1261a; K.–.
OT: –.
GEN. REF.: IS.1:929; NB.–; Z.–.

6. *thelō* [θέλω, 2309], to will, to wish, implying volition and purpose, frequently a determination, is most usually rendered to will. It is translated to desire in the R.V. of the following: Matt. 9:13; 12:7; Mark 6:19; Luke 10:29; 14:28; 23:20; Acts 24:27; 25:9; Gal. 4:17; 1 Tim. 5:11; Heb. 12:17; 13:18. See DISPOSED, FORWARD, INTEND, LIST, LOVE, MEAN, PLEASED, RATHER, VOLUNTARY, WILL.

NT: B.354d; CB.1271c; K.318.
OT: 'ābāh: S.14; HR.628b.1; H.3; BD.2c.
ḥāphēṣ: S.2654; HR.628b.8a; H.712; BD.342c.
GEN. REF.: IS.1:929; NB.–; Z.2:107.

7. *boulomai* [βούλομαι, 1014], to wish, to will deliberately, expresses more strongly than *thelō* (No. 6) the deliberate exercise of the will; it is translated to desire in the R.V. of the following: Acts 22:30; 23:38; 27:43; 28:18; 1 Tim. 2:8; 5:14; 6:9 and Jude 5. See DISPOSED, INTEND, LIST, MINDED, WILLING, WISH, WOULD.

NT: B.146a; CB.1239b; K.108.
OT: ḥāphēṣ: S.2654; HR.226b.5a,b; H.712; BD.342c.
'ābāh: S.14; HR.226b.1; H.3; BD.2c.
GEN. REF.: IS.1:929; NB.–; Z.2:107.

8. *zēloō* [ζηλόω, 2206], to have a zeal for, to be zealous towards, whether in a good or evil sense, the former in 1 Cor. 14:1, concerning spiritual gifts R.V., "desire earnestly," A.V., "desire"; in an evil sense, in Jas. 4:2, R.V., "covet," for A.V., "desire to have."

NT: B.338a; CB.1273b; K.297.
OT: qānā': S.7065; HR.594b.4a; H.2038; BD.888c.
GEN. REF.: IS.1:929; NB.–; Z.–.

9. *aiteō* [αἰτέω, 154], to ask, is rendered to desire in A.V., e.g., in Matt. 20:20; Luke 23:25 [R.V., always 'to ask (for)'].

NT: B.25d; CB.1234a; K.30.
OT: shā'al: S.7592; HR.37c.3; H.2303; BD.981b.
GEN. REF.: IS.1:929; NB.–; Z.2:107.

10. *speudō* [σπεύδω] is translated "earnestly desiring" in 2 Pet. 3:12, R.V. See HASTE.

Note: The following are translated by the verb to desire in the A.V.

(1) *Eperōtaō*, No. 3, with *epi*, intensive, to ask, interrogate, inquire of, consult, or to demand of a person; in Matt. 16:1, R.V., "asked." See ASK.

(2) *Zēteō*, to seek; in Matt. 12:46, 47, R.V., "seeking"; in Luke 9:9, R.V., "sought." See ENDEAVOUR, GO, *Note* (2), (*a*), INQUIRE, REQUIRE, SEEK.

(3) *Epizēteō*, to seek earnestly (No. 2, with *epi*, intensive), in Acts 13:7, R.V., "sought"; in Phil. 4:17, R.V., "seek for" (twice). See INQUIRE, SEEK.

(4) *Epipotheō*, to long after, to lust; in 2 Cor. 5:2, R.V., "longing"; in 1 Thess. 3:6 and 2 Tim. 1:4, R.V., "longing"; in 1 Pet. 2:2, R.V., "long for." See A, Nos. 3, 4. See LONG, LUST.

(5) *Exaiteomai*, intensive of No. 9, occurs in Luke 22:31. ¶

(6) For *parakaleō*, see BESEECH, EXHORT, INTREAT.

(7) For "desirous of vain glory," see VAINGLORY.

DESOLATE (Verb and Adjective), DESOLATION

A. Verbs.

1. *erēmoō* [ἐρημόω, 2049], signifies to make desolate, lay waste. From the primary sense of

making quiet comes that of making lonely. It is used only in the Passive Voice in the N.T.; in Rev. 17:16, "shall make desolate" is, lit., 'shall make her desolated'; in 18:17, 19, "is made desolate"; in Matt. 12:25 and Luke 11:17, "is brought to desolation." See NOUGHT (come to). ¶ Cp. DESERT.

NT: B.309b; CB.1246b; K.255.
OT: ḥārēb: S.2717; HR.546c.2a-e; H.731,732; BD.351c.
ḥārbāh: S.2723; HR.546c.2g; H.731d; BD.352a.
shāmēm: S.8074; HR.546c.10a-d; H.2409; BD.1030d.
GEN. REF.: IS.1:927; NB.1327; Z.2:106.

2. *monoō* [μονόω, 3443], to leave alone (akin to *monos*, alone), is used in 1 Tim. 5:5, in the Passive Voice, but translated "desolate," lit., 'was made desolate' or 'left desolate.' ¶

NT: B.528b; CB.—; K.—.
OT: —.
GEN. REF.: —.

B. Adjectives.

1. *erēmos* [ἔρημος, 2048], is translated "desolate" in the Lord's words against Jerusalem, Matt. 23:38; some mss. have it in Luke 13:35; in reference to the habitation of Judas, Acts 1:20, and to Sarah, from whom, being barren, her husband had turned, Gal. 4:27. See DESERT.

NT: B.309a; CB.1246b; K.255.
OT: midbār: S.4057; HR.545a.5; H.399k,l; BD.184c.
shᵉmāmāh: S.8077; HR.545a.11d; H.2409b,c; BD.1031b.
GEN. REF.: IS.1:927; NB.1327; Z.2:106.

2. *orphanos* [ὀρφανός, 3737], (Eng., orphan; Lat., *orbus*), signifies bereft of parents or of a father. In Jas. 1:27 it is translated "fatherless." It was also used in the general sense of being friendless or desolate. In John 14:18 the Lord uses it of the relationship between Himself and His disciples, He having been their Guide, Teacher and Protector; R.V., "desolate," A.V., "comfortless." Some mss. have the word in Mark 12:40. See FATHERLESS. ¶

NT: B.583a; CB.1261b; K.734.
OT: yātôm: S.3490; HR.1018a; H.934a; BD.450c.
GEN. REF.: —.

C. Noun.

erēmōsis [ἐρήμωσις, 2050], akin to A, No. 1, denotes desolation, (*a*) in the sense of making desolate, e.g., in the phrase "the abomination of desolation," Matt. 24:15; Mark 13:14; the genitive is objective, 'the abomination that makes desolate'; (*b*) with stress upon the effect of the process, Luke 21:20, with reference to the desolation of Jerusalem. ¶

NT: B.309b; CB.1246b; K.255.
OT: ḥārbāh: S.2723; HR.547a.1; H.731d; BD.352a.
shāmēm: S.8074; HR.547a.2a-c; H.2409; BD.1030d.
GEN. REF.: IS.1:927; NB.1327; Z.2:106.

DESPAIR

1. *exaporeō* [ἐξαπορέω, 1820], is used in the N.T. in the Passive Voice, with Middle sense, to be utterly without a way (*ek*, out of, intensive, *a*, negative, *poros*, a way through; cp. *poreuō*, to go through; Eng., 'ferry' is connected), to be quite at a loss, without resource, in despair. It is used in 2 Cor. 1:8, with reference to life; in 4:8, in the sentence "perplexed, yet not unto (A.V. 'in') despair," the word "perplexed" translates the verb *aporeō*, and the phrase "unto despair" translates the intensive form *exaporeō*, a play on the words. ¶ In the Sept., Ps. 88:15, where the translation is "having been lifted up, I was brought low and into despair." ¶

NT: B.273a; CB.—; K.—.
OT: —.
GEN. REF.: IS.1:932; NB.—; Z.—.

2. *apelpizō* [ἀπελπίζω, 560], lit., to hope away (*apo*, away from, *elpizō*, to hope), i.e., to give up in despair, to despair, is used in Luke 6:35, R.V., "nothing despairing," i.e., without anxiety as to the result, or not despairing of the recompense from God; this is probably the true meaning; A.V., "hoping for nothing again." The marg., "of no man," is to be rejected. ¶

NT: B.83a; CB.1236b; K.229.
OT: —.
GEN. REF.: —.

DESPISE, DESPISER

A. Verbs.

1. *exoutheneō* [ἐξουθενέω, 1848], to make of no account (*ex*, out, *oudeis*, nobody, alternatively written, *outheis*), to regard as nothing, to despise utterly, to treat with contempt. This is usually translated to set at nought, Luke 18:9, R.V., A.V., "despised." So in Rom. 14:3. Both have "set at nought" in Luke 23:11; Acts 4:11; Rom. 14:10. Both have "despise" in 1 Cor. 16:11; Gal. 4:14, and 1 Thess. 5:20; in 2 Cor. 10:10, R.V., "of no account," for A.V., "contemptible"; in 1 Cor. 1:28, A.V. and R.V., "despised." For the important rendering in 1 Cor. 6:4, R.V., see ACCOUNT. ¶

NT: B.277c; CB.1247c; K.—.
OT: bûz: S.936; HR.500b.1; H.213; BD.100b.
bāzāh: S.959; HR.500b.3; H.224; BD.102b.
mā'as: S.3988; HR.500b.5; H.1139,1140; BD.549b.
GEN. REF.: —.

Note: In Mark 9:12 some mss. have this verb; the most authentic have the alternative spelling *exoudeneō*, "set at nought."

2. *kataphroneō* [καταφρονέω, 2706], lit., to think down upon or against anyone (*kata*, down, *phrēn*, the mind), hence signifies to think slightly of, to despise, Matt. 6:24; 18:10; Luke 16:13; Rom. 2:4; 1 Cor. 11:22; 1 Tim. 4:12; 6:2; Heb. 12:2; 2 Pet. 2:10. ¶

NT: B.420b; CB.1254b; K.421.
OT: bûz: S.936; HR.748a.2; H.213; BD.100b.
GEN. REF.: —.

3. *periphroneō* [περιφρονέω, 4065], lit. denotes to think round a thing, to turn over in the mind; hence, to have thoughts beyond, to despise, Tit. 2:15. ¶
NT: B.653b; CB.1263b; K.421.
OT: –.
GEN. REF.: –.

Notes: The following verbs, translated to despise etc. in the A.V., are given suitable meanings in the R.V.:

(1) *Atheteō*, lit., to displace, to set aside, R.V., to reject, Luke 10:16; 1 Thess. 4:8; in 1 Tim. 5:12, "rejected," for A.V., "cast off"; in Heb. 10:28, "hath set at nought"; so Jude 8. See DISANNUL, REJECT, VOID, No. 2.

(2) *Atimazō*, to dishonour (*a*, negative, *timē*, honour); in Jas. 2:6, R.V., "have dishonoured." See DISHONOUR, ENTREAT, SHAME, C, No. 1, SHAMEFULLY.

(3) *Oligōreō*, to care little for, regard lightly (*oligos*, little); in Heb. 12:5, R.V., "regard lightly." See REGARD. ¶

(4) The phrase *logizomai eis ouden* signifies to reckon as nothing; in the Passive Voice, to be counted as nothing; in Acts 19:27, R.V., "be made of no account."

B. Adjective.

atimos [ἄτιμος, 820], without honour, see Note (2), above, is translated as a verb in 1 Cor. 4:10, A.V., "are despised"; R.V., "have dishonour," lit., '(we are) without honour'; "without honour" in Matt. 13:57; Mark 6:4. The comparative degree *atimoteros*, "less honourable," is used in 1 Cor. 12:23. ¶
NT: B.120b; CB.1238b; K.–.
OT: bāzāh: S.959; HR.176a.1; H.224; BD.102b.
GEN. REF.: –.

Note: Aphilagathos, not loving the good (*a*, negative, *phileō*, to love, *agathos*, good), is used in 2 Tim. 3:3, A.V., "despisers of those that are good," R.V., "no lovers of good." See LOVER. ¶

C. Noun.

kataphronētēs [καταφρονητής, 2707], lit., one who thinks down against, hence, a despiser (see A, No. 2), is found in Acts 13:41. ¶ In the Sept., Hab. 1:5; 2:5 and Zeph. 3:4. ¶
NT: B.420c; CB.1254b; K.421.
OT: –.
GEN. REF.: –.

DESPITE, DESPITEFUL, DESPITEFULLY (use)

1. *enubrizō* [ἐνυβρίζω, 1796], to treat insultingly, with contumely (*en*, intensive, *hubrizō*, to insult; some connect it with *huper*, above, over, Lat. *super*, which suggests the insulting disdain of one who considers himself superior), is translated "hath done despite" in Heb. 10:29. ¶
NT: B.270b; CB.–; K.1200.
OT: –.
GEN. REF.: IS.1:932; NB.–; Z.–.

Notes: (1) *Hubrizō*, to insult, act with insolence, is translated "to use despitefully" in Acts 14:5, A.V.; R.V., "to entreat . . . shamefully." See (ENTREAT) SHAMEFULLY, (ENTREAT) SPITEFULLY, REPROACH, B, No. 2.

(2) The noun *hubristēs*, a violent man, is translated "despiteful" in Rom. 1:30, A.V.; R.V., "insolent"; in 1 Tim. 1:13, "injurious." ¶

2. *epēreazō* [ἐπηρεάζω, 1908], for which see ACCUSE, B, No. 3, is found in some mss. in Matt. 5:44, and translated "despitefully use," A.V. (the R.V. follows the mss. which omit the sentence). In the corresponding passage in Luke 6:28, the A.V. and R.V. have "despitefully use"; in 1 Pet. 3:16, A.V., "falsely accuse," R.V., "revile." See ACCUSE, REVILE. ¶
NT: B.285d; CB.–; K.–.
OT: –.
GEN. REF.: IS.1:932; NB.–; Z.–.

DESTITUTE (be, etc.)

1. *apostereō* [ἀποστερέω]: see DEFRAUD.

2. *hustereō* [ὑστερέω, 5302], primarily, to be behind, to be last, hence, to lack, fail of, come short of, is translated "being destitute" in Heb. 11:37. See BEHIND, B, No. 1.
NT: B.849a; CB.1252b; K.1240.
OT: ḫāsēr: S.2638; HR.1418b.3a; H.705c; BD.341c.
GEN. REF.: –.

3. *leipō* [λείπω, 3007], signifies to leave, forsake; in the Passive Voice, to be left, forsaken, destitute; in Jas. 2:15, A.V., "destitute," R.V., "be in lack." See LACK, WANT.
NT: B.470b; CB.1256c; K.–.
OT: lûz: S.3868; HR.872c.1; H.1090; BD.531b.
GEN. REF.: –.

DESTROY, DESTROYER, DESTRUCTION, DESTRUCTIVE

A. Verbs.

1. *apollumi* [ἀπόλλυμι, 622], a strengthened form of *ollumi*, signifies to destroy utterly; in Middle Voice, to perish. The idea is not extinction but ruin, loss, not of being, but of well-being. This is clear from its use, as, e.g., of the marring of wine skins, Luke 5:37; of lost sheep, i.e., lost to the shepherd, metaphorical of spiritual destitution, Luke 15:4, 6, etc.; the lost son, 15:24; of the perishing of food, John 6:27; of gold, 1 Pet. 1:7. So of persons, Matt. 2:13, "destroy"; 8:25, "perish"; 22:7; 27:20; of the loss of well-being in the case of the unsaved hereafter, Matt. 10:28; Luke 13:3, 5;

John 3:16 (ver. 15 in some mss.); 10:28; 17:12; Rom. 2:12; 1 Cor. 15:18; 2 Cor. 2:15, "are perishing"; 4:3; 2 Thess. 2:10; Jas. 4:12; 2 Pet. 3:9. Cp. B, II, No. 1. See DIE, LOSE, MARRED, PERISH.

NT: B.95a; CB.1237a; K.67.
OT: 'ābad: S.6; HR.136c.1a-d; H.2; BD.1a.
kārat: S.3772; HR.136c.13; H.1048; BD.503c,504a.
shāḥat: S.7843; HR.136c.33a,b; H.2370; BD.1007d.
GEN. REF.: IS.1:932; NB.—; Z.—.

2. *katargeō* [καταργέω]: See ABOLISH.

3. *kathaireō* [καθαιρέω, 2507], to cast down, pull down by force, etc., is translated to destroy in Acts 13:19. In Acts 19:27, A.V., "should be destroyed," the R.V. suitably has "should be deposed." See CAST, No. 13, PULL, PUT, TAKE.

NT: B.386c; CB.—; K.380.
OT: —.
GEN. REF.: —.

4. *luō* [λύω, 3089], to loose, dissolve, sever, break, demolish, is translated "destroy," in 1 John 3:8, of the works of the Devil. See BREAK, A, No. 4.

NT: B.483c; CB.1257b; K.543.
OT: —.
GEN. REF.: —.

5. *kataluō* [καταλύω, 2647], *kata*, down, intensive, and No. 4, to destroy utterly, to overthrow completely, is rendered "destroy," in Matt. 5:17, twice, of the Law; Matt. 24:2; 26:61; 27:40; Mark 13:2; 14:58; 15:29; Luke 21:6, of the Temple; in Acts 6:14, of Jerusalem; in Gal. 2:18, of the Law as a means of justification; in Rom. 14:20 (A.V., "destroy," R.V., "overthrow"), of the marring of a person's spiritual well-being (in ver. 15 *apollumi*, No. 1, is used in the same sense); in Acts 5:38 and 39 (R.V., "overthrow") of the failure of purposes; in 2 Cor. 5:1, of the death of the body ("dissolved"). See DISSOLVE, NOUGHT (come to), OVERTHROW, THROW.

For its other meaning, to lodge, see Luke 9:12 and 19:7. See GUEST, LODGE. ¶

NT: B.414b; CB.1254a; K.543.
OT: —.
GEN. REF.: —.

6. *olothreuō* [ὀλοθρεύω, 3645], to destroy, especially in the sense of slaying, is found in Heb. 11:28, where the R.V. translates the present participle with the article by the noun "destroyer." ¶ See B, below. The verb occurs frequently in the Sept., e.g., Ex. 12:23; Josh. 3:10; 7:25; Jer. 2:30; 5:6; 22:7.

NT: B.564b; CB.1260c; K.—.
OT: kārat: S.3772; HR.986a.2; H.1048; BD.503c,504a.
shāḥat: S.7843; HR.986a.5; H.2370; BD.1007d.
GEN. REF.: IS.1:932; NB.—; Z.—.

7. *exolothreuō* [ἐξολοθρεύω, 1842], *ek*, out of (intensive), and No. 6, to destroy utterly, to slay wholly, is found in Acts 3:23, R.V., "utterly destroyed," referring to the destruction of one who would refuse to hearken to the voice of God through Christ. ¶ This verb is far more abundantly used in the Sept. than No. 6; it occurs 35 times in Deut.; 34 in Josh.; 68 in the Psalms.

NT: B.276d; CB.—; K.681.
OT: kārat: S.3772; HR.497c.10b,c; H.1048; BD.503c,504a.
ḥāram: S.2763; HR.497c.6; H.744; BD.355c.
shāmad: S.8045; HR.497c.19; H.2406; BD.1029a.
GEN. REF.: IS.1:932; NB.—; Z.—.

8. *phtheirō* [φθείρω]: see CORRUPT, A, No. 2.

9. *diaphtheirō* [διαφθείρω]: see CORRUPT, A, No. 3.

Note: Portheō, to ruin by laying waste, to make havock of, is translated "destroyed" in Acts 9:21, of the attacks upon the church in Jerusalem by Saul of Tarsus; "wasted," in Gal. 1:13, with reference to the same; "destroyed" in Gal. 1:23, where "the faith" is put by metonymy (one thing being put for another associated with it), for those who held the faith. In each of these places the R.V. consistently translates by "made havock of." See HAVOCK, WASTE.

B. Nouns.

(I) (*Personal: DESTROYER*)

olothreutēs [ὀλοθρευτής, 3644], akin to A, No. 6, a destroyer, is found in 1 Cor. 10:10. ¶

NT: B.564b; CB.1260c; K.681.
OT: —.
GEN. REF.: IS.1:932; NB.—; Z.2:108.

Note: For the construction in Heb. 11:28, "the destroyer," see A, No. 6. Cp. *apolluōn*, in Rev. 9:11, the present participle of *apollumi*, A, No. 1, used as a proper noun. ¶

(II) (*Abstract: DESTRUCTION*)

1. *apōleia* [ἀπώλεια, 684], akin to A, No. 1, and likewise indicating loss of well-being, not of being, is used (*a*) of things, signifying their waste, or ruin; of ointment, Matt. 26:8; Mark 14:4; of money, Acts 8:20 ("perish"); (*b*) of persons, signifying their spiritual and eternal perdition, Matt. 7:13; John 17:12; 2 Thess. 2:3, where "son of perdition" signifies the proper destiny of the person mentioned; metaphorically of men persistent in evil, Rom. 9:22, where "fitted" is in the Middle Voice, indicating that the vessels of wrath fitted themselves for destruction; of the adversaries of the Lord's people, Phil. 1:28 ("perdition"); of professing Christians, really enemies of the Cross of Christ, Phil. 3:19 (R.V., "perdition"); of those who are subjects of foolish and hurtful lusts, 1 Tim. 6:9 (for the preceding word "destruction" see No. 3, below); of professing Hebrew adherents who shrink back into unbelief, Heb. 10:39; of false teachers, 2 Pet. 2:1, 3; of ungodly men, 3:7; of those who wrest the Scriptures,

3:16; of the Beast, the final head of the revived Roman Empire, Rev. 17:8, 11; (*c*) of impersonal subjects, as heresies, 2 Pet. 2:1, where "destructive heresies" (R.V.; A.V., "damnable") is, lit., 'heresies of destruction' (marg., "sects of perdition"); in ver. 2 the most authentic mss. have *aselgeiais*, "lascivious," instead of *apōleiais*. See PERDITION, PERNICIOUS, WASTE. ¶

NT: B.103b; CB.1237a; K.67.
OT: 'ᵃbaddôn: S.11; HR.151c.1d; H.2d; BD.2b.
'ābad: S.6; HR.151c.1a,b; H.2; BD.1a.
'ēd: S.343; HR.151c.2; H.38c; BD.15c.
GEN. REF.: IS.1:932; NB.–; Z.–.

2. *kathairesis* [καθαίρεσις, 2506], akin to A, No. 3, a taking down, a pulling down, is used three times in 2 Cor., "casting down" in the R.V. in each place; in 10:4 (A.V., "pulling down"); in 10:8 and 13:10 (A.V., "destruction"). see PULL. ¶

NT: B.386b; CB.–; K.380.
OT: ḥāram: S.2040; HR.697c.1; H.516; BD.248c.
GEN. REF.: IS.1:932; NB.–; Z.–.

3. *olethros* [ὄλεθρος, 3639], ruin, destruction, akin to A, No. 6, always translated "destruction," is used in 1 Cor. 5:5, of the effect upon the physical condition of an erring believer for the purpose of his spiritual profit; in 1 Thess. 5:3 and 2 Thess. 1:9, of the effect of the Divine judgments upon men at the ushering in of the Day of the Lord and the revelation of the Lord Jesus; in 1 Tim. 6:9, of the consequences of the indulgence of the flesh, referring to physical ruin and possibly that of the whole being, the following word *apōleia* (see No. 1) stressing the final, eternal and irrevocable character of the ruin. ¶

NT: B.563b; CB.1260c; K.681.
OT: shôd: S.7701; HR.986a.6a; H.2331a; BD.994c.
shādad: S.7703; HR.986a.6b; H.2331; BD.994a.
shᵉmāmah: S.8077; HR.986a.3b; H.2409b,c; BD.1031b.
GEN. REF.: IS.1:932; NB.–; Z.–.

4. *phthora* [φθορά, 5356], akin to A, No. 8, denotes the destruction that comes with corruption. In 2 Pet. 2:12 it is used twice; for the A.V., "made to be taken and destroyed . . . shall utterly perish (*phtheirō*) in their own corruption," the R.V. has "to be taken and destroyed (lit., unto capture and destruction, *phthora*) . . . shall in their destroying (*phthora*) surely be destroyed," taking the noun in the last clause in the sense of their act of destroying others. See CORRUPT, CORRUPTION.

NT: B.858a; CB.1264c; K.1259.
OT: shāḥat: S.7843; HR.1430a.4a; H.2370; BD.1007d.
ḥebel: S.2256; HR.1430a.2a; H.592b; BD.287c.
GEN. REF.: IS.1:932; NB.–; Z.–.

5. *suntrimma* [σύντριμμα, 4938], a breaking in pieces, shattering (the corresponding verb is *suntribō*; see under BREAK, BRUISE), hence, ruin, destruction, is compounded of *sun*, together and *trimma*, a rubbing or wearing away. The latter, and *tribō*, to beat, are derived from a root, signifying to rub, wear away; hence Eng., tribulation and trouble. It is used, metaphorically, of destruction, in Rom. 3:16 (from Isa. 59:7), which, in a passage setting forth the sinful state of mankind in general, suggests the wearing process of the effects of cruelty. ¶ The word is frequent in the Sept., especially in Isaiah and Jeremiah.

NT: B.793c; CB.–; K.1124.
OT: sheber: S.7667; HR.1322b.3a; H.2321a; BD.991a.
GEN. REF.: –.

DETERMINE, DETERMINATE

1. *krinō* [κρίνω, 2919], primarily, to separate, hence, to be of opinion, approve, esteem, Rom. 14:5, also to determine, resolve, decree, is used in this sense in Acts 3:13; 20:16; 25:25; 27:1; 1 Cor. 2:2; 2 Cor. 2:1; Tit. 3:12. See CONDEMN, JUDGE, JUDGMENT, LAW, B, No. 2.

NT: B.451b; CB.1256a; K.469.
OT: rîb: S.7378; HR.787b.8a; H.2159; BD.936b.
shāphaṭ: S.8199; HR.787b.10a; H.2443; BD.1047a.
dîn: S.1777; HR.787b.3a; H.426; BD.192a.
GEN. REF.: IS.1:934; NB.–; Z.–.

2. *horizō* [ὁρίζω, 3724], denotes to bound, to set a boundary (Eng., horizon); hence, to mark out definitely, determine; it is translated to determine in Luke 22:22, of the fore-ordained pathway of Christ; Acts 11:29; of a determination to send relief; 17:26, where it is used of fixing the bounds of seasons. In Acts 2:23 the verb is translated "determinate," with reference to counsel. Here the verbal form might have been adhered to by the translation 'determined'; that is to say, in the sense of 'settled.'

In Rom. 1:4 it is translated "declared," where the meaning is that Christ was marked out as the Son of God by His Resurrection and that of others (see under DECLARE. In Acts 10:42 and 17:31 it has its other meaning of ordain, that is, to appoint by determined counsel. In Heb. 4:7, it is translated "limiteth," but preferably in the R.V., "defineth," with reference to a certain period; here again it approaches its primary meaning of marking out the bounds of. See DECLARE, No. 9, LIMIT, ORDAIN.

NT: B.580d; CB.1251b; K.728.
OT: gᵉbûl: S.1366; HR.1011c.2a; H.307a; BD.147d.
GEN. REF.: IS.1:934; NB.–; Z.–.

3. *proorizō* [προορίζω, 4309], *pro*, beforehand, and No. 2, denotes to mark out beforehand, to determine before, foreordain; in Acts 4:28, A.V., "determined before," R.V., "foreordained"; so the R.V. in 1 Cor. 2:7, A.V., "ordained"; in Rom. 8:29, 30 and Eph. 1:5, 11,

A.V., "predestinate;" R.V., "foreordain." See ORDAIN, *Note* (1), PREDESTINATE. ¶
NT: B.709b; CB.–; K.728.
OT: –.
GEN. REF.: –.

4. *epiluō* [ἐπιλύω, 1956], lit., to loosen upon, denotes to solve, expound, Mark 4:34; to settle, as of a controversy, Acts 19:39, A.V., "it shall be determined;" R.V., "it shall be settled." See EXPOUND, SETTLE. ¶
NT: B.295d; CB.1246a; K.543.
OT: –.
GEN. REF.: –.

5. *diaginōskō* [διαγινώσκω, 1231], besides its meaning to ascertain exactly, Acts 23:15, was an Athenian law term signifying to determine, so used in 24:22, R.V., "determine"; A.V., "know the uttermost of." ¶
NT: B.182b; CB.–; K.–.
OT: yāda': S.3045; HR.299c.2; H.848; BD.393b.
GEN. REF.: IS.1:934; NB.–; Z.–.

6. *tassō* [τάσσω]: see APPOINT, No. 5.

Note: Boulomai, to be minded, to purpose, is translated "determined" in Acts 15:37; R.V., "was minded." See MINDED, No. 2.

DEVICE

1. *enthumēsis* [ἐνθύμησις, 1761], a cogitation, an inward reasoning (generally, evil surmising or supposition), is formed from *en*, in, and *thumos*, strong feeling, passion (cp. *thumoō*, in the Middle Voice, to be wroth, furious); Eng., fume is akin; the root, *thu*, signifies to rush, rage. The word is translated "device" in Acts 17:29, of man's production of images; elsewhere, "thoughts," Matt. 9;4; 12:25; Heb. 4:12, where the accompanying word *ennoia* denotes inward intentions. See THOUGHT. ¶
NT: B.266b; CB.1245b; K.339.
OT: –.
GEN. REF.: –.

2. *noēma* [νόημα, 3540], denotes thought, that which is thought out (cp. *noeō*, to understand); hence, a purpose, device; translated "devices" in 2 Cor. 2:11; "minds" in 2 Cor. 3:14; 4:4; 11:3; in 2 Cor. 10:5, "thought"; in Phil. 4:7, A.V., "minds," R.V., "thoughts." See MIND, THOUGHT. ¶
NT: B.540d; CB.1259c; K.636.
OT: –.
GEN. REF.: –.

DEVIL, DEVILISH

diabolos [διάβολος, 1228], an accuser, a slanderer (from *diaballō*, to accuse, to malign), is one of the names of Satan. From it the English word "Devil" is derived, and should be applied only to Satan, as a proper name. *Daimōn*, a demon, is frequently, but wrongly, translated "devil"; it should always be translated "demon," as in the R.V. margin. There is one Devil, there are many demons. Being the malignant enemy of God and man, he accuses man to God, Job 1:6-11; 2:1-5; Rev. 12:9, 10, and God to man, Gen. 3. He afflicts men with physical sufferings, Acts 10:38. Being himself sinful, 1 John 3:8, he instigated man to sin, Gen. 3, and tempts man to do evil, Eph. 4:27; 6:11, encouraging him thereto by deception, Eph. 2:2. Death having been brought into the world by sin, the Devil had the power of death, but Christ through His own Death, has triumphed over him, and will bring him to nought, Heb. 2:14; his power over death is intimated in his struggle with Michael over the body of Moses, Jude 9. Judas, who gave himself over to the Devil, was so identified with him, that the Lord described him as such, John 6:70 (see 13:2). As the Devil raised himself in pride against God and fell under condemnation, so believers are warned against similar sin, 1 Tim. 3:6; for them he lays snares, ver. 7, seeking to devour them as a roaring lion, 1 Pet. 5:8; those who fall into his snare may be recovered therefrom unto the will of God, 2 Tim. 2:26, "having been taken captive by him (i.e., by the Devil);" "by the Lord's servant" is an alternative, which some regard as confirmed by the use of *zōgreō* (to catch alive) in Luke 5:10; but the general use is that of taking captive in the usual way. If believers resist he will flee from them, Jas. 4:7. His fury and malignity will be especially exercised at the end of the present age, Rev. 12:12. His doom is the lake of fire, Matt. 25:41; Rev. 20:10. The noun is applied to slanderers, false accusers, 1 Tim. 3:11; 2 Tim. 3:3; Tit. 2:3.
NT: B.182a; CB.1241a; K.150.
OT: sāṭān: S.7854; HR.299b.2; H.2252a; BD.966b.
GEN. REF.: IS.1:919; NB.310; Z.2:116.

Note: For "devilish," Jas. 3:17, see DEMON, C.

DEVISED (cunningly)

sophizō [σοφίζω, 4679], from *sophos*, wise (connected etymologically with *sophēs*, tasty), in the Active Voice signifies to make wise, 2 Tim. 3:15 (so in the Sept. of Ps. 19:7, e.g., "making babes wise"; in 119:98, "Thou hast made me wiser than mine enemies"). In the Middle Voice it means (*a*) to become wise; it is not used thus in the N.T., but is so found in the Sept., e.g. in Eccles. 2:15, 19; 7:17; (*b*) to play the sophist, to devise cleverly; it is used with this meaning in the Passive Voice in 2 Pet. 1:16, "cunningly devised fables." See WISE. ¶

NT: B.760b; CB.1269b; K.1056.
OT: ḥākam: S.2449; HR.1280a.2; H.647; BD.314b.
GEN. REF.: IS.1:940; NB.–; Z.–.

Note: Cp. *katasophizomai*, to deal subtilly. See DEAL WITH, *Note* (2).

DEVOTION

Note: For this word, in Acts 17:23, A.V., which translates *sebasma*, "devotions," marg., "gods that ye worship," R.V., "objects of your worship," in 2 Thess. 2:4, "that is worshipped," see WORSHIP. ¶ Cp. Acts 14:15, where, in translating *mataia*, the A.V. has "vanities," the abstract for the concrete (R.V., "vain things").

DEVOUR

1. *esthiō* [ἐσθίω, 2068], is a strengthened form of an old verb *edō*, from the root *ed*—, whence Lat., *edo*, Eng., eat. The form *ephagon*, used as the 2nd Aorist Tense of this verb, is from the root *phag*—, to eat up. It is translated "devour" in Heb. 10:27; elsewhere, by the verb to eat. See Eat.

NT: B.312b; CB.1246c; K.262.
OT: 'ākal: S.398; HR.554a.1a; H.85; BD.37a.
GEN. REF.: –.

2. *katesthiō* and *kataphagō* [κατεσθίω and καταφάγω, 2719], *kata*, down, intensive, and No. 1, signifies (*a*) to consume by eating, to devour, said of birds, Matt. 13:4; Mark 4:4; Luke 8:5; of the Dragon, Rev. 12:4; of a prophet, eating up a book, suggestive of spiritually eating and digesting its contents, Rev. 10:9 (cp. Ezek. 2:8; 3:1-3; Jer. 15:16); (*b*) metaphorically, to squander, to waste, Luke 15:30; to consume one's physical powers by emotion, John 2:17; to devour by forcible appropriation, as of widows' property, Matt. 23:14 (A.V. only); Mark 12:40; to demand maintenance, as false apostles did to the church at Corinth, 2 Cor. 11:20; to exploit or prey on one another, Gal. 5:15, where "bite . . . devour . . . consume" form a climax, the first two describing a process, the last the act of swallowing down; to destroy by fire, Rev. 11:5; 20:9. See EAT. ¶

NT: B.422a; CB.–; K.–.
OT: 'ākal: S.398; HR.749b.1a; H.85; BD.37a.
GEN. REF.: –.

3. *katapinō* [καταπίνω, 2666], from *kata*, down, intensive, *pinō*, to drink, in 1 Pet. 5:8 is translated "devour," of Satan's activities against believers. The meaning to swallow is found in Matt. 23:24; 1 Cor. 15:54; 2 Cor. 2:7; 5:4; Heb. 11:29, R.V. (for A.V., "drowned"); Rev. 12:16. See SWALLOW. ¶

NT: B.416b; CB.1254b; K.841.
OT: bāla': S.1104; HR.741c.1a-c; H.251; BD.118a.
GEN. REF.: –.

DEVOUT

1. *eulabēs* [εὐλαβής, 2126], lit., taking hold well (*eu*, well, *lambanō*, to take hold), primarily, cautious, signifies in the N.T., careful as to the realization of the presence and claims of God, reverencing God, pious, devout; in Luke 2:25 it is said of Simeon; in Acts 2:5, of certain Jews; in 8:2, of those who bore Stephen's body to burial; of Ananias, 22:12 (see No. 2), "In that mingled fear and love which, combined, constitute the piety of man toward God, the Old Testament placed its emphasis on the fear, the New places it on the love (though there was love in the fear of God's saints then, as there must be fear in their love now)," Trench, Syn., § xlviii. ¶

NT: B.322a; CB.1247b; K.275.
OT: ḥāsîd: S.2623; HR.572a.1; H.698b; BD.339c.
GEN. REF.: IS.1:941; NB.–; Z.2:118.

Note: Cp. the noun *eulabeia*, reverence, and the verb *eulabeomai*, to reverence.

2. *eusebēs* [εὐσεβής, 2152], from *eu*, well, *sebomai*, to reverence, the root *seb*— signifying sacred awe, describes reverence exhibited especially in actions, reverence or awe well directed. Among the Greeks it was used, e.g., of practical piety towards parents. In the N.T. it is used of a pious attitude towards God, Acts 10:2,7; (in some mss. in 22:12); "godly," in 2 Pet. 2:9. See GODLY. ¶ In the Sept., Prov. 12:12; Is. 24:16; 26:7; 32:8; Mic. 7:2. ¶

NT: B.326b; CB.1247b; K.1010.
OT: ṣāddîq: S.6662; HR.580b.3; H.1879c; BD.843a.
ḥāsîd: S.2623; HR.580b.1; H.698b; BD.339c.
GEN. REF.: IS.1:941; NB.–; Z.2:118.

Notes: (1) While *eulabēs* especially suggests the piety which characterizes the inner being, the soul, in its attitude towards God, *eusebēs* directs us rather to the energy which, directed by holy awe of God, finds expression in devoted activity. ¶

(2) Cp. *theosebeia*, and *theosebēs*, which, by their very formation (*theos*, God, and *sebomai*), express reverence towards God. See Trench (§ xlviii).

3. *sebomai* [σέβομαι, 4576], to feel awe, whether before God or man, to worship, is translated "devout," in Acts 13:43, R.V., (A.V., "religious"); 13:50; 17:4, 17. See WORSHIP.

NT: B.746a; CB.1268c; K.1010.
OT: –.
GEN. REF.: IS.1:941; NB.–; Z.2:118.

DIADEM

diadēma [διάδημα, 1238], is derived from *diadeō*, to bind round. It was the kingly ornament for the head, and especially the blue band marked with white, used to bind on the turban or tiara of Persian kings. It was adopted by Alexander the Great and his successors. Among the Greeks and Romans it was the distinctive badge of royalty. Diocletian was the first Roman Emperor to wear it constantly. The word is found in Rev. 12:3; 13:1; 19:12, in which passages it symbolises the rule respectively of the Dragon, the Beast, and Christ. ¶ In the Sept., Esth. 1:11; 2:17; in some mss. in 6:8 and 8:15; also in Is. 62:3. ¶ For the distinction between this and *stephanos*, see CROWN.

NT: B.182d; CB.1241a; K.—.
OT: keter: S.3804; HR.300a.1; H.1060a; BD.509d.
ṣānîph: S.6797; HR.300a.2b; H.1940a; BD.857b.
GEN. REF.: IS.1:941; NB.280; Z.2:119.

DIE, DEAD (to be, become), DYING

1. *thnēskō* [θνήσκω, 2348], to die (in the perf. tense, to be dead), in the N.T. is always used of physical death, except in 1 Tim. 5:6, where it is metaphorically used of the loss of spiritual life. The noun *thanatos*, and the verb *thanatoō* (below) are connected. The root of this group of words probably had the significance of the breathing out of the last breath. Cp. words under DEATH.

NT: B.362c; CB.1272b; K.312.
OT: mût: S.4191; HR.653c.3a; H.1169; BD.559b.
GEN. REF.: IS.1:898; NB.301; Z.2:70.

2. *apothnēskō* [ἀποθνήσκω, 599], lit., to die off or out, is used (*a*) of the separation of the soul from the body, i.e., the natural death of human beings, e.g., Matt. 9:24; Rom. 7:2; by reason of descent from Adam, 1 Cor. 15:22; or of violent death, whether of men or animals; with regard to the latter it is once translated "perished," Matt. 8:32; of vegetation, Jude 12; of seeds, John 12:24; 1 Cor. 15:36; it is used of death as a punishment in Israel under the Law, in Heb. 10:28; (*b*) of the separation of man from God; all who are descended from Adam not only die physically, owing to sin, see (*a*) but are naturally in the state of separation from God, 2 Cor. 5:14. From this believers are freed both now and eternally, John 6:50; 11:26, through the Death of Christ, Rom. 5:8, e.g.; unbelievers, who die physically as such, remain in eternal separation from God, John 8:24. Believers have spiritually died to the Law as a means of life, Gal. 2:19; Col. 2:20; to sin, Rom. 6:2, and in general to all spiritual association with the world and with that which pertained to their unregenerate state, Col. 3:3, because of their identification with the Death of Christ, Rom. 6:8 (see No. 3, below). As life never means mere existence, so death, the opposite of life, never means non-existence. See PERISH.

NT: B.91b; CB.1237b; K.312.
OT: mût: S.4191; HR.128a.4a; H.1169; BD.559b.
GEN. REF.: IS.1:898; NB.301; Z.2:70.

3. *sunapothnēskō* [συναποθνήσκω, 4880], to die with, to die together, is used of association in physical death, Mark 14:31; in 2 Cor. 7:3, the Apostle declares that his love to the saints makes separation impossible, whether in life or in death. It is used once of association spiritually with Christ in His death, 2 Tim. 2:11. See No. 2 (*b*). ¶

NT: B.784d; CB.1270c; K.312,1102.
OT: —.
GEN. REF.: IS.1:898; NB.—; Z.—.

4. *teleutaō* [τελευτάω, 5053], to end (from *telos*, an end), hence, to end one's life, is used (*a*) of the death of the body, Matt. 2:19; 9:18; 15:4, where "die the death" means "surely die," R.V., marg., lit., 'let him end by death'; Mark 7:10; Matt. 22:25, "deceased"; Luke 7:2; John 11:39, some mss. have verb No. 1 here; Acts 2:29; 7:15; Heb. 11:22 (R.V., "his end was nigh"); (*b*) of the gnawings of conscience in self reproach, under the symbol of a worm, Mark 9:48 (vv. 44 and 46, A.V.). See DECEASE. ¶

NT: B.810c; CB.1271b; K.—.
OT: mût: S.4191; HR.1343b.2a; H.1169; BD.559b.
gāwaʻ: S.1478; HR.1343b.1; H.328; BD.157b.
GEN. REF.: IS.1:898; NB.301; Z.2:70.

5. *koimaō* [κοιμάω, 2837], in the Middle and Passive Voices, its only use in the N.T., signifies to fall asleep. It is connected etymologically with *keimai*, to lie down, the root *ki*— signifying to lie. Hence it is used metaphorically of death, Matt. 27:52, etc. It is translated "be dead" in 1 Cor. 7:39. See ASLEEP.

NT: B.437c; CB.1255b; K.—.
OT: shākab: S.7901; HR.773b.12a; H.2381; BD.1011d.
GEN. REF.: IS.1:898; NB.—; Z.—.

6. *apoginomai* [ἀπογίνομαι, 581], lit., to be away from (*apo*, from, *ginomai*, to be, become; *apo* here signifies separation), is used in 1 Pet. 2:24 of the believer's attitude towards sin as the result of Christ's having borne our sins in His body on the Tree; R.V., "Having died unto sins," the aorist or momentary tense, expressing an event in the past. ¶

NT: B.89b; CB.1236c; K.117.
OT: —.
GEN. REF.: IS.1:898; NB.—; Z.—.

Note: Apollumi, to destroy, is found in the Middle Voice in some mss. in John 18:14, and translated "die." The most authentic mss. have *apothnēskō* (No. 2, above).

DIFFER, DIFFERING, DIFFERENT, DIFFERENCE

A. Verbs.

1. *diapherō* [διαφέρω, 1308], lit., to bear through, carry different ways, hence, to be different from, is said of the stars, 1 Cor. 15:41; of a child under age in comparison with a servant, Gal. 4:1; in Phil. 1:10, marg., "things that differ," for "things that are excellent." See BETTER (be).

NT: B.190b; CB.–; K.1252.
OT: shᵉnā' (Aramaic): S.8133; HR.314b.1; H.3043.1; BD.1116c.
GEN. REF.: –.

2. *merizō* [μερίζω, 3307], denotes to divide (from *meros*, a part: the root *mer*— indicates distribution, or measuring out, and is seen in *meris*, a district). In 1 Cor. 7:34 the perfect tense of the Passive Voice is translated "there is a difference." Some take the verb with what precedes, with reference to the married brother, and translate "he has been divided." See DEAL, DISTRIBUTE, DIVIDE, GIVE, PART.

NT: B.504c; CB.1258b; K.–.
OT: –.
GEN. REF.: –.

3. *diakrinō* [διακρίνω, 1252], lit., to separate throughout, to make a distinction, Acts 15:9, R.V., is translated to make to differ, in 1 Cor. 4:7. In Jude 22, where the Middle Voice is used, the A.V. has "making a difference"; the R.V., adopting the alternative reading, the accusative case, has "who are in doubt," a meaning found in Matt. 21:21; Mark 11:23; Acts 10:20; Rom. 14:23; Jas. 1:6; 2:4. See CONTEND.

NT: B.185a; CB.1241a; K.469.
OT: –.
GEN. REF.: –.

B. Nouns.

1. *diairesis* [διαίρεσις, 1243], lit. signifies to take asunder, from *dia*, apart, and *haireō*, to take (Eng., diaeresis, i.e., distinguishing two successive vowels as separate sounds); it is rendered in the A.V., "diversities" in 1 Cor. 12:4 and 6; "differences" in ver. 5; R.V., "diversities," in each place. ¶

NT: B.183c; CB.1241a; K.27.
OT: –.
GEN. REF.: –.

2. *diastolē* [διαστολή, 1293], signifies a setting asunder (*dia*, asunder, *stellō*, to set, place, arrange), hence, a distinction; in Rom. 3:22 and 10:12, A.V., "difference"; R.V., "distinction"; in 1 Cor. 14:7 it is used of the distinction in musical sounds. ¶

NT: B.188d; CB.–; K.1074.
OT: –.
GEN. REF.: –.

C. Adjectives.

1. *diaphoros* [διάφορος, 1313], akin to A, No. 1, signifies varying in kind, different, diverse. It is used of spiritual gifts, Rom. 12:6; of ceremonial washings, Heb. 9:10 ("divers"). See DIVERS, and for its other meaning, in Heb. 1:4; 8:6, see EXCELLENT. ¶

NT: B.190d; CB.–; K.1252.
OT: shᵉnā' (Aramaic): S.8133; HR.315b.2; H.3043.1; BD.1116c.
GEN. REF.: –.

2. *heteros* [ἕτερος, 2087], R.V., "different," for A.V., "another," in Rom. 7:23; 2 Cor. 11:4; Gal. 1:6; cp. 1 Tim. 1:3; 6:3. See ANOTHER.

NT: B.315a; CB.1250a; K.265.
OT: 'ahēr: S.312; HR.560a.4a; H.68a; BD.29c.
GEN. REF.: –.

DIFFICULTY

molis [μόλις, 3433], signifies with difficulty, hardly (from *molos*, toil). In Luke 9:39, it is rendered "hardly," of the difficulty in the departure of a demon. In Acts 27:7, 8, 16, where the A.V. has three different renderings, "scarce," "hardly," and "much work," respectively, the R.V. has "with difficulty" in each place. For its other meanings, scarce, scarcely, see Acts 14:18; Rom. 5:7; 1 Pet. 4:18. See HARDLY, No. 3. ¶

NT: B.526d; CB.–; K.606.
OT: –.
GEN. REF.: –.

DIG, DIG DOWN

1. *orussō* [ὀρύσσω, 3736], to dig, dig up soil, dig a pit, is said of a place for a winepress, Matt. 21:33; Mark 12:1; of digging a pit for hiding something, Matt. 25:18. ¶

NT: B.582d; CB.–; K.–.
OT: ḥāphar: S.2658; HR.1017c.2; H.714; BD.343c.
kārāh: S.3738; HR.1017c.5a; H.1035-1037; BD.500a.
ḥātar: S.2864; HR.1017c.4; H.783; BD.369a.
GEN. REF.: IS.1:943; NB.–; Z.–.

Notes: (1) *Diorussō*, lit., to dig through (*dia*, through), is translated to break through (or up) in Matt. 6:19, 20; 24:43; Luke 12:39. See BREAK. ¶

(2) *Exorussō*, lit., to dig out, is translated to break up in Mark 2:4; to pluck out (the eyes) in Gal. 4:15. See BREAK, PLUCK. ¶

2. *skaptō* [σκάπτω, 4626], primarily, to dig, by way of hollowing out, hence, denotes to dig. The root *skap* is seen in *skapanē*, a spade, *skapetos*, a ditch, *skaphē*, a boat, and in Eng., scoop, skiff, and ship (i.e. something hollowed out). The verb is found in Luke 6:48; 13:8; 16:3. ¶

NT: B.753b; CB.–; K.–.
OT: 'ādar: S.5737; HR.1268b.1; H.1570-1572; BD.727b.
GEN. REF.: IS.1:943; NB.–; Z.–.

3. *kataskaptō* [κατασκάπτω, 2679], to dig down (*kata*, down, and No. 2), is found in Rom. 11:3, of altars, and in some mss. in Acts 15:16, "ruins," lit., 'the things dug down.' Here the best texts have *katastrephō*, to overthrow, overturn. ¶

NT: B.418b; CB.—; K.—.
OT: hāṯaṣ: S.5422; HR.743c.5a-c; H.1446; BD.683a.
hāram: S.2040; HR.743c.3a,b; H.516; BD.248c.
GEN. REF.: —.

DIGNITY, DIGNITIES

doxa [δόξα, 1391], primarily denotes an opinion, estimation, repute; in the N.T., always good opinion, praise, honour, glory, an appearance commanding respect, magnificence, excellence, manifestation of glory; hence, of angelic powers, in respect of their state as commanding recognition, "dignities," 2 Pet. 2:10; Jude 8. See GLORY, HONOUR, PRAISE, WORSHIP.

NT: B.203c; CB.1242b; K.178.
OT: kābôd: S.3519; HR.341b,13b; H.943d,e; BD.458c,459a.
GEN. REF.: —.

DILIGENCE, DILIGENT, DILIGENTLY

A. Nouns.

1. *ergasia* [ἐργασία, 2039], (*a*) lit., a working (akin to *ergon*, work), is indicative of a process, in contrast to the concrete, *ergon*, e.g., Eph. 4:19, lit., 'unto a working' (R.V. marg., 'to make a trade of'); contrast *ergon* in ver. 12; (*b*) "business," Acts 19:25, R.V. (for A.V., "craft"); or gain got by work, Acts 16:16, 19; 19:24; (*c*) endeavour, pains, "diligence," Luke 12:58. See CRAFT, GAIN, WORK. ¶

NT: B.307c; CB.1246b; K.251.
OT: mᵉlā'kāh: S.4399; HR.541b.1; H.1068b; BD.521d.
ᵃbōdāh: S.5656; HR.541b.3b; H.1553c; BD.715a.
GEN. REF.: —.

2. *spoudē* [σπουδή, 4710], earnestness, zeal, or sometimes the haste accompanying this, Mark 6:25; Luke 1:39, is translated "diligence" in Rom. 12:8; in ver. 11, A.V., "business" (R.V., "diligence"); in 2 Cor. 8:7, A.V., "diligence," R.V., "earnestness"; both have "diligence" in Heb. 6:11; 2 Pet. 1:5; Jude 3; in 2 Cor. 7:11, 12, R.V., "earnest care," A.V., "carefulness," and "care." See CARE. ¶

NT: B.763d; CB.1269c; K.1069.
OT: —.
GEN. REF.: —.

B. Verbs.

1. *spoudazō* [σπουδάζω, 4704], has meanings corresponding to A, No. 2; it signifies to hasten to do a thing, to exert oneself, endeavour, give diligence; in Gal. 2:10, of remembering the poor, A.V., "was forward," R.V., "was zealous"; in Eph. 4:3, of keeping the unity of the Spirit, A.V. "endeavouring," R.V., "giving diligence"; in 1 Thess. 2:17, of going to see friends, "endeavoured"; in 2 Tim. 4:9; 4:21, "do thy diligence"; in the following the R.V. uses the verb to give diligence: 2 Tim. 2:15, A.V., "study"; Tit. 3:12, A.V., "be diligent"; Heb. 4:11, of keeping continuous Sabbath rest, A.V., "let us labour"; in 2 Pet. 1:10, of making our calling and election sure; in 2 Pet. 1:15, of enabling believers to call Scripture truth to remembrance, A.V., "endeavour"; in 2 Pet. 3:14, of being found in peace without fault and blameless, when the Lord comes, A.V., "be diligent." See ENDEAVOUR, FORWARD, LABOUR, STUDY, ZEALOUS. ¶

NT: B.763c; CB.1269c; K.1069.
OT: —.
GEN. REF.: —.

2. *meletaō* [μελετάω, 3191], signifies to care for, attend carefully (from *meletē*, care); in 1 Tim. 4:15, A.V., "meditate," R.V., "be diligent in"; in Acts 4:25, "imagine" (marg., "meditate"); in Mark 13:11, the most authentic mss. have *promerimnaō*. See IMAGINE, MEDITATE. ¶

NT: B.500b; CB.—; K.—.
OT: siaḥ: S.7878; HR.908b.4; H.2255; BD.967a.
GEN. REF.: —.

C. Adjectives.

1. *spoudaios* [σπουδαῖος, 4705], akin to A, No. 2 and B, No. 1, primarily signifies in haste; hence, diligent, earnest, zealous, 2 Cor. 8:22, A.V., "diligent," R.V., "earnest." See EARNEST, FORWARD. ¶ In the Sept., Ezek. 41:25, "stout (planks)." ¶

NT: B.763c; CB.1269c; K.1069.
OT: —.
GEN. REF.: —.

2. *spoudaioteros* [σπουδαιότερος, 4707], the comparative degree of No. 1, 2 Cor. 8:22, A.V., "more diligent," R.V., "more earnest"; in ver. 17, A.V., "more forward," R.V., "very earnest." See EARNEST; cp. FORWARD. ¶

NT: B.763c; CB.—; K.—.
OT: —.
GEN. REF.: —.

D. Adverbs.

1. *epimelōs* [ἐπιμελῶς, 1960], from *epi*, intensive, and an adverbial form of the impersonal verb *melei*, it is a care (cp. B, No. 2), signifies carefully, diligently, Luke 15:8. ¶

NT: B.296a; CB.—; K.—.
OT: —.
GEN. REF.: IS.1:943; NB.—; Z.—.

2. *pugmē* [πυγμῇ, 4435], the dative case of *pugmē*, a fist, lit. means 'with the fist' (one hand being rubbed with the clenched fist of the other), a metaphorical expression for thoroughly, in contrast to what is superficial; Mark 7:3, R.V. and A.V. marg., "diligently" (A.V.,

text, "oft"). It also signified boxing (not in the N.T.); cp. *puktēs* and *pugmachos*, a boxer (Lat., *pugnus* and *pugno*; Eng., pugilist). ¶ In the Sept., Ex. 21:18; Is. 58:4. ¶
NT: B.728c; CB.1268a; K.973.
OT: –.
GEN. REF.: –.

3. *spoudaiōs* [σπουδαίως, 4709], speedily, earnestly, diligently (cp. the corresponding noun, verb and adjective above), is translated "earnestly" in the R.V. of Luke 7:4 (A.V., "instantly"); "diligently" in Tit. 3:13. See INSTANTLY.
NT: B.763d; CB.–; K.–.
OT: –.
GEN. REF.: –.

4. *spoudaioterōs* [σπουδαιοτέρως, 4708], the comparative degree of No. 3, "more diligently," is used in Phil. 2:28, R.V., "the more diligently" (A.V., "the more carefully"). See CAREFULLY. ¶
NT: B.763d; CB.–; K.–.
OT: –.
GEN. REF.: –.

Notes: (1) Some mss. have the neuter of the comparative adjective *spoudaioteron* in 2 Tim. 1:17. The most authentic texts have the adverb, No. 4.

(2) *Akribōs* (ἀκριβῶς) means accurately, exactly. The A.V. translates it "diligently" in Matt. 2:8 and Acts 18:25; "perfectly" in 1 Thess. 5:2 (cp. Luke 1:3). See ACCURATELY, CAREFUL, CIRCUMSPECTLY, PERFECTLY.

DIMINISHING

hēttēma [ἥττημα]: see DEFECT.

DINE, DINNER

A. Verb.

aristaō [ἀριστάω, 709], primarily, to breakfast (see B), was later used also with the meaning to dine, e.g., Luke 11:37; in John 21:12, 15, R.V., "break your fast," and "had broken their fast," for A.V., "dine"; obviously there it was the first meal in the day. ¶ In the Sept., Gen. 43:25; 1 Sam. 14:24; 1 Chron. 13:7. ¶
NT: B.106c; CB.–; K.–.
OT: sā'ad: S.5584; HR.157b.2; H.1526; BD.703c.
GEN. REF.: IS.–; NB.–; Z.2:586.

B. Noun.

ariston [ἄριστον, 712], primarily, the first food, taken early in the morning before work; the meal in the Pharisee's house, in Luke 11:37, was a breakfast or early meal (see R.V., marg.); the dinner was called *deipnon*. Later the breakfast was called *akratisma* (not in N.T.), and dinner, *ariston*, as in Matt. 22:4; Luke 11:38; 14:12. ¶
NT: B.106d; CB.–; K.–.
OT: –.
GEN. REF.: IS.1:944; NB.–; Z.2:586.

DIP, DIPPED, DIPPETH

1. *baptō* [βάπτω, 911], to immerse, dip (derived from a root signifying deep), also signified to dye, which is suggested in Rev. 19:13, of the Lord's garment "dipped (i.e., dyed) in blood" (R.V., "sprinkled" translates the verb *rhantizō*: see SPRINKLED. It is elsewhere translated to dip, Luke 16:24; John 13:26. Cp. the longer form *baptizō* (primarily a frequentative form). See BAPTIZE ¶
NT: B.132d; CB.1238c; K.92.
OT: ṭābal: S.2881; HR.190b.2a; H.787,788; BD.371a.
GEN. REF.: IS.1:946; NB.–; Z.–.

2. *embaptō* [ἐμβάπτω, 1686], *en*, in, and No. 1, to dip into, is used of the act of Judas in dipping his hand with that of Christ in the dish, Matt. 26:23; Mark 14:20. ¶
NT: B.254b; CB.–; K.–.
OT: –.
GEN. REF.: IS.1:946; NB.–; Z.–.

DIRECT

kateuthunō [κατευθύνω, 2720], to make straight (*kata*, down, intensive, *euthus*, straight, *euthunō*, to straighten), is translated "guide" in Luke 1:79, of the Lord's guidance of the feet of His people; "direct," in 1 Thess. 3:11, of His directing the way of His servants; in 2 Thess. 3:5, of His directing the hearts of His saints into the love of God. See GUIDE. ¶
NT: B.422b; CB.–; K.–.
OT: kûn: S.3559; HR.750b.4; H.964; BD.465c.
GEN. REF.: IS.1:946; NB.–; Z.–.

DISALLOW

apodokimazō [ἀποδοκιμάζω, 593], to reject as the result of disapproval (*apo*, away from, *dokimazō*, to approve), is always translated to reject, except in the A.V. of 1 Pet. 2:4 and 7. See REJECT.
NT: B.90d; CB.1236c; K.181.
OT: mā'as: S.3988; HR.127c.1a; H.1139,1140; BD.549b.
GEN. REF.: IS.1:946; NB.–; Z.–.

DISANNUL, DISANNULLING

A. Verbs.

1. *atheteō* [ἀθετέω, 114], signifies to put as of no value (*a*, negative, *theton*, what is placed, from *tithēmi*, to put, place); hence, (*a*) to act towards anything as though it were annulled; e.g., to deprive a law of its force by opinions or acts contrary to it, Gal. 3:15, A.V., "disannulleth," R.V., "maketh void"; (*b*) to thwart the efficacy of anything, to nullify, to frustrate it, Luke 7:30, "rejected"; 1 Cor. 1:19, "will I reject"; to make void, Gal. 2:21; to set at nought, Jude 8, R.V. (A.V., "despised"); the parallel passage, in 2 Pet. 2:10, has *kataphroneō*.

In Mark 6:26, the thought is that of breaking faith with. See DESPISE, A, Note (1).

NT: B.21a; CB.1238a; K.1176.
OT: pāsha': S.6586; HR.29b.12; H.1846; BD.833b.
bāgad: S.898; HR.29b.1; H.198; BD.93c.
GEN. REF.: IS.1:128; NB.—; Z.—.

2. *akuroō* [ἀκυρόω, 208], to deprive of authority (*a*, negative, *kuros*, force, authority; cp. *kurios*, a lord, *kuroō*, to strengthen), hence, to make of none effect, Matt. 15:6; Mark 7:13, with reference to the commandment or word of God, R.V., to make void, is translated "disannul" in Gal. 3:17, of the inability of the Law to deprive of force God's covenant with Abraham. This verb stresses the effect of the act, while No. 1 stresses the attitude of the rejector. See VOID. ¶

NT: B.34b; CB.—; K.494.
OT: —.
GEN. REF.: IS.1:128; NB.—; Z.—.

B. Noun.

athetēsis [ἀθέτησις, 115], akin to A, No. 1, a setting aside, abolition, is translated "disannulling" in Heb. 7:18, with reference to a commandment; in 9:26 "to put away," with reference to sin, lit., 'for a putting away.' See PUTTING, *Note*. ¶

NT: B.21b; CB.1238a; K.1176.
OT: —.
GEN. REF.: —.

DISBELIEVE

apisteō [ἀπιστέω, 569], to be unbelieving (*a*, negative, *pistis*, faith; cp. *apistos*, unbelieving), is translated "believed not," etc. in the A.V. (except in 1 Pet. 2:7, "be disobedient"); "disbelieve" (or "disbelieved") in the R.V., in Mark 16:11, 16; Luke 24:11, 41; Acts 28:24; "disbelieve" is the best rendering, implying that the unbeliever has had a full opportunity of believing and has rejected it; some mss. have *apeitheō*, to be disobedient, in 1 Pet. 2:7; Rom. 3:3, R.V., "were without faith"; 2 Tim. 2:13, R.V., "are faithless." Cp. DISOBEDIENT, C. See BELIEVE. ¶

NT: B.85b; CB.1236c; K.849.
OT: —.
GEN. REF.: —.

DISCERN, DISCERNER, DISCERNMENT

A. Verbs.

1. *anakrinō* [ἀνακρίνω, 350], to distinguish, or separate out so as to investigate (*krinō*) by looking throughout (*ana*, intensive) objects or particulars, hence signifies to examine, scrutinize, question, to hold a preliminary judicial examination preceding the trial proper (this first examination, implying more to follow, is often present in the non-legal uses of the word), e.g., Luke 23:14; figuratively, in 1 Cor. 4:3; it is said of searching the Scriptures in Acts 17:11; of discerning or determining the excellence or defects of a person or thing, e.g., 1 Cor. 2:14, A.V., "discerned"; R.V., "judged"; in 1 Cor. 10:27, "asking (no) question" (i.e., not raising the question as to whether the meat is the residue from an idolatrous sacrifice). Except in Luke 23:14, this word is found only in Acts and 1 Cor. See EXAMINE, JUDGE.

NT: B.56b; CB.1235a; K.469.
OT: ḥāqar: S.2713; HR.78c.1; H.729; BD.350c.
GEN. REF.: IS.1:946; NB.—; Z.—.

2. *diakrinō* [διακρίνω, 1252], signifies to separate, discriminate; then, to learn by discriminating, to determine, decide. It is translated "discern" in Matt. 16:3, of discriminating between the varying conditions of the sky (see *dokimazō*, No. 3, below, in Luke 12:56), and in 1 Cor. 11:29, with reference to partaking of the bread and the cup of the Lord's Supper unworthily, by not discerning or discriminating what they represent; in ver. 31, the R.V. has "discerned," for the A.V., "would judge," of trying oneself, discerning one's condition, and so judging any evil before the Lord; in 14:29, regarding oral testimony in a gathering of believers, it is used of discerning what is of the Holy Spirit, R.V., "discern" (A.V., "judge"). See CONTEND, DECIDE, DIFFER, etc.

NT: B.185a; CB.1241a; K.469.
OT: dîn: S.1777; HR.304a.4a; H.426; BD.192a.
rîb: S.7378; HR.304a.6; H.2159; BD.936b.
shāphaṭ: S.8199; HR.304a.8a; H.2443; BD.1047a.
GEN. REF.: IS.1:946; NB.—; Z.—.

3. *dokimazō* [δοκιμάζω, 1381], signifies to test, prove, scrutinize, so as to decide. It is translated "discern" in the A.V. of Luke 12:56; R.V., "interpret" (marg., "prove"). See APPROVE.

NT: B.202c; CB.1242a; K.181.
OT: bāḥan: S.974; HR.339c.1; H.230; BD.103c.
GEN. REF.: —.

B. Noun.

diakrisis [διάκρισις, 1253], cp. A, No. 2, a distinguishing, a clear discrimination, discerning, judging, is translated "discernings" in 1 Cor. 12:10, of discerning spirits, judging by evidence whether they are evil or of God. In Heb. 5:14 the phrase consisting of *pros*, with this noun, lit., 'towards a discerning,' is translated "to discern," said of those who are capable of discriminating between good and evil. In Rom. 14:1 the word has its other sense of decision or judgment and the phrase "doubtful disputations" is, lit., 'judgments of reasonings' (marg., "not for decisions of doubts," i.e., not to act as a judge of the weak brother's scruples). See DECISION, B, No. 2. ¶

NT: B.185b; CB.1241a; K.469.
OT: –.
GEN. REF.: IS.1:946; NB.–; Z.–.

Note: For "discernment," Phil. 1:19, see JUDGMENT, *Note* (4).

C. Adjective.

kritikos [κριτικός, 2924], signifies that which relates to judging (*krinō,* to judge), fit for, or skilled in, judging (Eng., critical), found in Heb. 4:12, of the Word of God as "quick to discern the thoughts and intents of the heart," (lit., 'critical of etc.'), i.e., discriminating and passing judgment on the thoughts and feelings. ¶

NT: B.453d; CB.1256a; K.469.
OT: –.
GEN. REF.: IS.1:946; NB.–; Z.–.

DISCHARGED

katargeō [καταργέω, 2673], means to reduce to inactivity. "Discharged" is the R.V. translation of the word in Rom. 7:2 and 6 (A.V., "is loosed," and "are delivered"). In ver. 2 the meaning is that the death of a woman's first husband makes void her status as a wife in the eyes of the Law; she is therefore discharged from the prohibition against remarrying; the prohibition is rendered ineffective in her case. So in ver.6, with the believer in relation to the Law, he has been made dead to the Law as a means of justification and life. It is not the Law that has died (.A.V), but the believer (see the R.V.), who has been discharged, through being put to death, as to the old nature, in identification with the Death of Christ, that he might have life in Christ. See ABOLISH.

NT: B.417b; CB.1254b; K.76.
OT: bᵉṭēl (Aramaic): S.989; HR.743a.1; H.2625; BD.1084b.
GEN. REF.: –.

DISCIPLE

A. Nouns.

1. *mathētēs* [μαθητής, 3101], lit., a learner (from *manthanō,* to learn, from a root *math*—, indicating thought accompanied by endeavour), in contrast to *didaskalos*, a teacher; hence it denotes one who follows one's teaching, as the disciples of John, Matt. 9:14; of the Pharisees, Matt. 22:16; of Moses, John 9:28; it is used of the disciples of Jesus (*a*) in a wide sense, of Jews who became His adherents, John 6:66; Luke 6:17, some being secretly so, John 19:38; (*b*) especially of the twelve Apostles, Matt. 10:1; Luke 22:11, e.g.; (*c*) of all who manifest that they are His disciples by abiding in His Word, John 8:31; cp. 13:35; 15:8; (*d*) in the Acts, of those who believed upon Him and confessed Him, 6:1, 2, 7; 14:20, 22, 28; 15:10; 19:1 etc.

A disciple was not only a pupil, but an adherent; hence they are spoken of as imitators of their teacher; cp. John 8:31; 15:8.

NT: B.485c; CB.1258a; K.552.
OT: –.
GEN. REF.: IS.1:947; NB.312; Z.2:129.

2. *mathētria* [μαθήτρια, 3102], a female disciple, is said of Tabitha, Acts 9:36. ¶

NT: B.486a; CB.–; K.552.
OT: –
GEN. REF.: IS.–; NB.312; Z.2:129.

3. *summathētēs* [συμμαθητής, 4827], means a fellow-disciple (*sun*, with, and No. 1), John 11:16. ¶

NT: B.778b; CB.–; K.552.
OT: –
GEN. REF.: IS.–; NB.312; Z.2:129.

Note: In Acts 1:15, the R.V. translates the mss. which have *adelphōn*, "brethren"; in 20:7, R.V., "we," for A.V., "disciples."

B. Verb.

mathēteuō [μαθητεύω, 3100], is used in the Active Voice, intransitively, in some mss., in Matt. 27:57, in the sense of being the disciple of a person; here, however, the best mss. have the Passive Voice, lit., 'had been made a disciple,' as in Matt. 13:52, R.V., "who hath been made a disciple." It is used in this transitive sense in the Active Voice in 28:19 and Acts 14:21. ¶

NT: B.485c; CB.1258a; K.552.
OT: –
GEN. REF.: IS.1:947; NB.312; Z.2:129.

DISCIPLINE

sōphronismos [σωφρονισμός, 4995], from *sōphrōn*, lit., saving the mind, from *saos*, contracted to *sōs*, safe (cp. *sōzō*, to save), *phrēn*, the mind, primarily, an admonishing or calling to soundness of mind, or to self-control, is used in 2 Tim. 1:7, A.V., "a sound mind"; R.V., "discipline." Cp. *sōphroneō* (to be of sound mind), *sōphronizō* (to admonish), *sōphronōs* (soberly), and *sōphrōn*, of sound mind. See MIND. ¶ Cp. CHASTISEMENT.

NT: B.802b; CB.–; K.1150.
OT: –
GEN. REF.: –.

DISCOURAGE (-D)

athumeō [ἀθυμέω, 120], to be disheartened, dispirited, discouraged (*a*, negative, *thumos*, spirit, courage, from the root *thu*, found in *thuō*, to rush, denoting feeling, passion; hence Eng., fume), is found in Col. 3:21. ¶

NT: B.21c; CB.—; K.—.
OT: ’ebyôn: S.34; HR.30a.1; H.3a; BD.2d.
rāgaz: S.7264; HR.30a.5; H.2112; BD.919a.
GEN. REF.: —.

DISCOURSE

dialegomai [διαλέγομαι, 1256], primarily denotes to ponder, resolve in one's mind (*dia*, through, *legō*, to say); then, to converse, dispute, discuss, discourse with; most frequently, to reason or dispute with. In Heb. 12:5 the R.V., "reasoneth with" is to be preferred to the A.V., "speaketh unto." The A.V. translates it "preached," in Acts 20:7 and 9; this the R.V. corrects to "discoursed," lit., 'dialogued,' i.e., not by way of a sermon, but by a discourse of a more conversational character. See DISPUTE, PREACH, REASON, SPEAK. In the sept., Ex. 6:27; Judg. 8:1; Is. 63:1.

NT: B.185c; CB.1241a; K.155.
OT: dābar: S.1696; HR.304b.1; H.399; BD.180b,d.
rîb: S.7378; HR.304b.2; H.2159; BD.936b.
GEN. REF.: —.

DISCOVER

Two verbs are translated by the verb to discover, in the A.V. The R.V. translates differently in each case.

1. *anaphainō* [ἀναφαίνω]: see APPEAR, A, No. 3.

2. *katanoeō* [κατανοέω, 2657], to perceive distinctly, discern clearly, descry, is translated "discovered" in Acts 27:39, A.V., of finding a bay with a creek (R.V., "perceived"). See BEHOLD.

NT: B.415a; CB.1254a; K.636.
OT: —
GEN. REF.: —.

DISCREET, DISCREETLY

A. Adjective.

sōphrōn [σώφρων, 4998], of sound mind, self-controlled (for the derivation, see DISCIPLINE), is translated "sober-minded," in its four occurrences in the R.V., 1 Tim. 3:2 (A.V., "sober"); Tit. 1:8 (A.V., ditto); 2:2 (A.V., "temperate"); 2:5 (A.V., "discreet"). See SOBER, TEMPERATE. ¶

NT: B.802c; CB.1269b; K.—.
OT: —
GEN. REF.: —.

B. Adverb.

nounechōs [νουνεχῶς, 3562], lit., mind-possessing (*nous*, mind, understanding, *echō*, to have), hence denotes discreetly, sensibly, prudently. Mark 12:34. ¶

NT: B.544b; CB.—; K.286.
OT: —
GEN. REF.: —.

DISEASE, DISEASED (BE)

A. Nouns.

1. *astheneia* [ἀσθένεια, 769], lit., lacking strength (*a*, negative, *sthenos*, strength), weakness, infirmity, is translated "diseases" in Matt. 8:17, R.V., for A.V., "sicknesses," and in Acts 28:9. Its usual rendering is "infirmity" or "infirmities"; "sickness," in John 11:4. Cp. B, No. 1. See INFIRMITY, SICKNESS, WEAKNESS.

NT: B.115a; CB.1238a; K.83.
OT: ‘aṣṣebet: S.6094; HR.172a.2; H.1666d; BD.781a.
GEN. REF.: IS.1:953; NB.313; Z.—.

2. *malakia* [μαλακία, 3119], primarily denotes softness (cp. *malakos*, soft, Matt. 11:8 etc.); hence, debility, disease. It is found in Matthew only, 4:23; 9:35; 10:1. ¶ It is frequent in the Sept., e.g., Gen. 42:4; 44:29; Deut. 7:15; 28:61; Is. 38:9; 53:3.

NT: B.488c; CB.1257c; K.655.
OT: ḥ^{o}lî: S.2483; HR.894b.2a; H.655a; BD.318b.
GEN. REF.: IS.1:953; NB.313; Z.2:132.

3. *nosos* [νόσος, 3554], akin to Lat. *nocere*, to injure (Eng., nosology), is the regular word for disease, sickness, Matt. 4:23; 8:17; 9:35; 10:1, R.V., "disease," A.V., "sickness"; in Matt. 4:24; Mark 1:34; Luke 4:40; 6:17; 9:1; Acts 19:12, A.V. and R.V. render it "diseases." In Luke 7:21, A.V. has "infirmities." The most authentic mss. omit the word in Mark 3:15. See SICKNESS. ¶

NT: B.543c; CB.1260a; K.655.
OT: ḥ^{o}lî: S.2483; HR.949b.1a; H.655a; BD.318b.
maḥ^{a}leh: S.4245; HR.949b.1c; H.655b,c; BD.318b.
maḥ^{a}lāh: S.4246; HR.949b.1b; H.623h; BD.318b.
GEN. REF.: IS.1:953; NB.313; Z.2:132.

4. *nosēma* [νόσημα, 3553], an alternative form of No. 3, is found in some mss. in John 5:4. ¶ Cp. *noseō*, to dote about, have a diseased craving for, 1 Tim. 6:4. ¶

NT: B.543c; CB.1260a; K.655.
OT: —.
GEN. REF.: IS.—; NB.313; Z.2:132.

B. Verbs.

1. *astheneō* [ἀσθενέω, 770], akin to A, No. 1, to lack strength, to be weak, sick, is translated "were diseased" in John 6:2, A.V. (R.V., "were sick"). See IMPOTENT, SICK, WEAK.

NT: B.115b; CB.1238a; K.83.
OT: —
GEN. REF.: IS.1:953; NB.313; Z.—.

2. *echō kakōs* [ἔχω κακῶς, 2560 (*kakōs*)], lit., to have badly, i.e., to be ill or in an evil case, is used in Matt. 14:35 (A.V., "were diseased," R.V., "were sick"); so in Mark 1:32; Luke 7:2. See SICK. ¶

NT: B.398c; CB.1253b; K.391.
OT: —
GEN. REF.: IS.1:953; NB.313; Z.—.

DISFIGURE

aphanizō [ἀφανίζω, 853], primarily means to cause to disappear, hence (*a*) to make unsightly, to disfigure, as of the face, Matt. 6:16; (*b*) to cause to vanish away, consume, Matt. 6:19, 20; (*c*) in the Passive Voice, to perish, Acts 13:41, or to vanish away, Jas. 4:14. See CONSUME. ¶

NT: B.124c; CB.1236b; K.–.
OT: shāmēm: S.8074; HR.181b.21a-c; H.2409; BD.1030d.
GEN. REF.: –.

DISH

trublion [τρύβλιον, 5165], denotes a bowl, somewhat deep, Matt. 26:23; Mark 14:20; among the Greeks it was a measure in medical prescriptions. ¶

NT: B.828b; CB.–; K.–.
OT: qeʿārāh: S.7086; HR.1377a.2; H.2047a; BD.891a.
GEN. REF.: IS.1:960; NB.–; Z.2:142.

DISHONESTY

aischunē [αἰσχύνη, 152], shame, so the R.V. in 2 Cor. 4:2 (for A.V., "dishonesty"), is elsewhere rendered "shame," Luke 14:9; Phil. 3:19; Heb. 12:2; Jude 13; Rev. 3:18. See SHAME. ¶

NT: B.25b; CB.1234a; K.29.
OT: –
GEN. REF.: –.

DISHONOUR

A. Noun.

atimia [ἀτιμία, 819], from *a*, negative, *timē*, honour, denotes dishonour, ignominy, disgrace, in Rom. 1:26, "vile passions" (R.V.), lit., 'passions of dishonour'; in Rom. 9:21, "dishonour," of vessels designed for meaner household purposes (in contrast to *timē*, honour, as in 2 Tim. 2:20); in 1 Cor. 11:14, said of long hair, if worn by men, R.V., "dishonour," for A.V., "shame," in contrast to *doxa*, glory, ver. 15; so in 1 Cor. 15:43, of the "sowing" of the natural body, and in 2 Cor. 6:8, of the Apostle Paul's ministry. In 2 Cor. 11:21 he uses it in self-disparagement, A.V., "reproach," R.V., "disparagement." See DISPARAGEMENT, REPROACH, SHAME, VILE. ¶

NT: B.120a; CB.1238b; K.–.
OT: qālôn: S.7036; HR.175c.5c; H.2024a; BD.885d.
kelimmāh: S.3639; HR.175c.3b; H.987a; BD.484a.
GEN. REF.: –.

B. Adjective.

atimos [ἄτιμος], akin to A: See DESPISE, B.

C. Verbs.

1. *atimazō* [ἀτιμάζω, 818], akin to A, signifies to dishonour, treat shamefully, insult, whether in word, John 8:49, or deed, Mark 12:4; Luke 20:11, R.V., "handled (him) shamefully," (A.V. "entreated . . . shamefully"); Rom. 1:24; 2:23, "dishonourest"; Jas. 2:6, R.V., "ye have dishonoured (the poor)," (A.V. "despised"); in the Passive Voice, to suffer dishonour, Acts 5:41 (A.V., "suffer shame"). See DESPISE, A, Note (2). ¶

NT: B.120a; CB.1238b; K.–.
OT: qālāh: S.7034; HR.175c.6a,b; H.2024; BD.885c.
bāzāh: S.959; HR.175c.1b; H.224; BD.102b.
GEN. REF.: –.

Note: Atimaō is found in some mss. in Mark 12:4.

2. *kataischunō* [καταισχύνω]: see ASHAMED, No. 3.

DISMISS (-ED)

apoluō [ἀπολύω, 630], lit., to loose from (*apo*, from, *luō*, to loose), is translated "dismiss" in Acts 15:30, 33, R.V. (A.V., "let go") and 19:41. See DEPART, DIVORCE, FORGIVE, GO, LIBERTY, LOOSE, PUT, No. 16, RELEASE, SEND.

NT: B.96c; CB.1237a; K.–.
OT: –
GEN. REF.: –.

DISOBEDIENCE, DISOBEDIENT

A. Nouns.

1. *apeitheia* [ἀπείθεια, 543], lit., the condition of being unpersuadable (*a*, negative, *peithō*, to persuade), denotes obstinacy, obstinate rejection of the will of God; hence, "disobedience"; Eph. 2:2; 5:6; Col. 3:6, and in the R.V. of Rom. 11:30, 32 and Heb. 4:6, 11 (for A.V., "unbelief"), speaking of Israel, past and present. See UNBELIEF. ¶

NT: B.82c; CB.1236b; K.818.
OT: –
GEN. REF.: IS.1:961; NB.–; Z.–.

2. *parakoē* [παρακοή, 3876], primarily, hearing amiss (*para*, aside, *akouō*, to hear), hence signifies a refusal to hear; hence, an act of disobedience, Rom. 5:19; 2 Cor. 10:6; Heb. 2:2. It is broadly to be distinguished from No. 1, as an act from a condition, though *parakoē* itself is the effect, in transgression, of the condition of failing or refusing to hear. Carelessness in attitude is the precursor of actual disobedience. In the O.T. disobedience is frequently described as a refusing to hear, e.g., Jer. 11:10; 35:17; cp. Acts 7:57. See Trench, Syn. § lxvi. ¶

NT: B.618d; CB.1262a; K.34.
OT: –
GEN. REF.: IS.1:961; NB.–; Z.–.

B. Adjective.

apeithēs [ἀπειθής, 545], akin to A, No. 1, signifies unwilling to be persuaded, spurning belief, disobedient, Luke 1:17; Acts 26:19; Rom. 1:30; 2 Tim. 3:2; Tit. 1:16; 3:3. ¶

NT: B.82d; CB.1236b; K.818.
OT: m^erî: S.1805; HR.119c.2; H.431c; BD.598b.
mārāh: S.4784; HR.119c.1; H.1242; BD.598a.
GEN. REF.: IS.1:961; NB.–; Z.–.

Note: In 1 Tim. 1:9 *anupotaktos*, insubordinate, unsubjected (*a*, negative, *n*, euphonic, *hupo*, under, *tassō*, to order), is translated "disobedient" in the A.V.; the R.V. has "unruly," as in Tit. 1:6, 10; in Heb. 2:8, "not subject" (R.V.), "not put under" (A.V.). See PUT, UNRULY. ¶

C. Verb.

apeitheō [ἀπειθέω, 544], akin to A, No. 1, and B, to refuse to be persuaded, to refuse belief, to be disobedient, is translated "disobedient," or by the verb to be disobedient, in the R.V. of Acts 14:2 (A.V., "unbelieving"), and 19:9 (A.V., "believed not"); it is absent from the most authentic mss. in Acts 17:5; in John 3:36 "obeyeth not," R.V. (A.V., "believeth not"); in Rom. 2:8 "obey not"; in 10:21 "disobedient"; in 11:30, 31, "were disobedient" (A.V., "have not believed"); so in 15:31; Heb. 3:18; 11:31; in 1 Pet. 2:8, "disobedient"; so in 3:20; in 3:1 and 4:17, "obey not." In 2:7 the best mss. have *apisteō*, to disbelieve. See OBEY, B, No. 4, UNBELIEVING. ¶

NT: B.82c; CB.1236b; K.818.
OT: mārāh: S.4784; HR.119c.6; H.1242; BD.598a.
GEN. REF.: IS.1:961; NB.–; Z.–.

DISORDERLY

A. Adjective.

ataktos [ἄτακτος, 813], signifies not keeping order (*a*, negative, *tassō*, to put in order, arrange); it was especially a military term, denoting not keeping rank, insubordinate; it is used in 1 Thess. 5:14, describing certain church members who manifested an insubordinate spirit, whether by excitability or officiousness or idleness. See UNRULY. ¶

NT: B.119c; CB.–; K.1156.
OT: –.
GEN. REF.: –.

B. Adverb.

ataktōs [ἀτάκτως, 814], signifies disorderly, with slackness (like soldiers not keeping rank), 2 Thess. 3:6; in ver. 11 it is said of those in the church who refused to work, and became busybodies (cp. 1 Tim. 5:13). ¶

NT: B.119d; CB.–; K.1156.
OT: –
GEN. REF.: –.

C. Verb.

atakteō [ἀτακτέω, 812], signifies to be out of rank, out of one's place, undisciplined, to behave disorderly: in the military sense, to break rank; negatively in 2 Thess. 3:7, of the example set by the Apostle and his fellow-missionaries, in working for their bread while they were at Thessalonica so as not to burden the saints. See BEHAVE. ¶

NT: B.119c; CB.–; K.1156.
OT: –
GEN. REF.: –.

DISPARAGEMENT

For this R.V. translation of *atimia* in 2 Cor. 11:21, see DISHONOUR, A.

DISPENSATION

oikonomia [οἰκονομία, 3622], primarily signifies the management of a household or of household affairs (*oikos*, a house, *nomos*, a law); then the management or administration of the property of others, and so a stewardship, Luke 16:2, 3, 4; elsewhere only in the Epistles of Paul, who applies it (*a*) to the responsibility entrusted to him of preaching the Gospel, 1 Cor. 9:17 (R.V., "stewardship," A.V., "dispensation"); (*b*) to the stewardship committed to him "to fulfil the Word of God," the fulfilment being the unfolding of the completion of the Divinely arranged and imparted cycle of truths which are consummated in the truth relating to the Church as the Body of Christ, Col. 1:25 (R.V. and A.V., "dispensation"); so in Eph. 3:2, of the grace of God given him as a stewardship ("dispensation") in regard to the same "mystery"; (*c*) in Eph. 1:10 and 3:9, it is used of the arrangement or administration by God, by which in "the fulness of the times" (or seasons) God will sum up all things in the heavens and on earth in Christ. In Eph. 3:9 some mss. have *koinōnia*, "fellowship," for *oikonomia*, "dispensation." In 1 Tim. 1:4 *oikonomia* may mean either a stewardship in the sense of (*a*) above, or a dispensation in the sense of (*c*). The reading *oikodomia*, "edifying," in some mss., is not to be accepted. See STEWARDSHIP. ¶

NT: B.559c; CB.1260b; K.674.
OT: memshālāh: S.4475; HR.973a.1; H.1259c; BD.606a.
GEN. REF.: IS.1:962; NB.–; Z.2:142.

Note: A dispensation is not a period or epoch (a common, but erroneous, use of the word), but a mode of dealing, an arrangement or administration of affairs. Cp. *oikonomos*, a steward, and *oikonomeō*, to be a steward.

DISPERSE, DISPERSION

A. Verbs.

1. *dialuō* [διαλύω, 1262], to dissolve, is used in Acts 5:36 of the breaking up and dispersion

of a company of men, R.V., "dispersed," A.V., "scattered." See SCATTER. ¶
NT: B.186b; CB.1241b; K.—.
OT: —.
GEN. REF.: —.

2. *skorpizō* [σκορπίζω, 4650], to scatter (probably from a root, *skarp*—, signifying to cut asunder, akin to *skorpios*, a scorpion), is used in Matt. 12:30; Luke 11:23; John 10:12; 16:32; in the R.V. of 2 Cor. 9:9, "scattered abroad" (A.V., "he hath dispersed abroad"), of one who liberally dispenses benefits. See SCATTER. ¶
NT: B.757a; CB.1269b; K.1048.
OT: pûṣ: S.6327; HR.1275c.4; H.1745,1746,1800; BD.806d.
zārāh: S.2219; HR.1275c.2; H.579; BD.279d.
GEN. REF.: —.

3. *diaskorpizō* [διασκορπίζω, 1287], *dia*, through, and No. 2, signifies to scatter abroad, in Matt. 26:31; Mark 14:27, metaphorically of sheep; in Luke 1:51, of the proud; in John 11:52, of the scattering of the children of God; in Acts 5:37, of the followers of Judas of Galilee (A.V., "were dispersed"); cp. No. 1, re ver. 36; of scattering grain by winnowing, Matt. 25:24, 26; in Luke 15:13 and 16:1, it signifies to waste. See SCATTER, STRAWED, WASTE. ¶
NT: B.188b; CB.1241b; K.1048.
OT: pûṣ: S.6327; HR.310b.10; H.1745,1746,1800; BD.806d.
zārāh: S.2219; HR.310b.4; H.579; BD.279d.
nāphaṣ: S.5310; HR.310b.9a; H.1394; BD.659a.
GEN. REF.: —.

4. *diaspeirō* [διασπείρω, 1289], to scatter abroad (*dia*, through, *speirō*, to sow), is used in Acts 8:1, 4; 11:19. ¶
NT: B.188c; CB.1241b; K.—.
OT: pûṣ: S.6327; HR.310c.6; H.1745,1746,1800; BD.806d.
zārāh: S.2219; HR.310c.1; H.579; BD.279d.
nāphaṣ: S.5310; HR.310c.4; H.1394; BD.659a.
GEN. REF.: —.

B. Noun.

diaspora [διασπορά], akin to A, No. 4, a scattering, a dispersion, was used of the Jews who from time to time had been scattered among the Gentiles, John 7:35; later with reference to Jews, so scattered, who had professed, or actually embraced, the Christian faith, "the Dispersion," Jas. 1:1, R.V.; especially of believers who were converts from Judaism and scattered throughout certain districts, "sojourners of the Dispersion," 1 Pet. 1:1, R.V. ¶ In the Sept., of Israelites, scattered and exiled, e.g., Deut. 28:25; 30:4; Neh. 1:9.

DISPLEASED

1. *aganakteō* [ἀγανακτέω, 23], from *agan*, much, and *achomai*, to grieve, primarily meant to feel a violent irritation, physically; it was used, too, of the fermenting of wine; hence, metaphorically, to show signs of grief, to be displeased, to be grieved, vexed; it is translated "sore displeased" in Matt. 21:15, A.V.; "much displeased," in Mark 10:14, 41; the R.V. always renders it to be moved with, or to have, indignation, as the A.V. elsewhere, Matt. 20:24; 26:8; Mark 14:4; Luke 13:14. See INDIGNATION. ¶
NT: B.4b; CB.—; K.—.
OT: —.
GEN. REF.: —.

2. *prosochthizō* [προσοχθίζω, 4360], to be wroth or displeased with (*pros*, toward, or with, *ochtheō*, to be sorely vexed), is used in Heb. 3:10, 17 (A.V., "grieved"; R.V., "displeased"). "Grieved" does not adequately express the righteous anger of God intimated in the passage. See GRIEVE. ¶
NT: B.717d; CB.—; K.—.
OT: gāʻal: S.1602; HR.1218c.1a; H.369; BD.171d.
qûṣ: S.6973; HR.1218c.5; H.2002; BD.880d.
GEN. REF.: —.

3. *thumomacheō* [θυμομαχέω, 2371], lit., to fight with great animosity (*thumos*, passion, *machomai*, to fight), hence, to be very angry, to be highly displeased, is said of Herod's displeasure with the Tyrians and Sidonians, Acts 12:20. ¶
NT: B.365b; CB.—; K.—.
OT: —.
GEN. REF.: —.

DISPOSED (to be)

1. *boulomai* [βούλομαι, 1014], to wish, to purpose, to will deliberately, indicating a predisposition acting through the deliberate will, is translated "was disposed" in Acts 18:27, A.V. (R.V., "was minded"). It expresses more strongly than *thelō* (No. 2) the deliberate exercise of the will. See DESIRE, B, No. 7.
NT: B.146a; CB.1239b; K.108.
OT: ʼābāh: S.14; HR.226b.1; H.3; BD.2c.
ḥāphēṣ: S.2654; HR.226b.5; H.712; BD.342c.
GEN. REF.: —.

2. *thelō* [θέλω, 2309], means to will; it signifies more especially the natural impulse or volition, and indicates a less formal or deliberate purpose than No. 1. It is translated "are disposed" in 1 Cor. 10:27. See DESIRE, B, No. 6.
NT: B.354d; CB.1271c; K.318.
OT: ʼābāh: S.14; HR.628b.1; H.3; BD.2c.
ḥāphēṣ: S.2654; HR.628b.8; H.712; BD.342c.
GEN. REF.: —.

DISPOSITION

diatagē [διαταγή, 1296], an ordinance, e.g., Rom. 13:2 (cp. *diatassō* to appoint, ordain), is rendered "disposition" in Acts 7:53; R.V., "as it (the law) was ordained by angels" (marg., "as the ordinance of angels"; lit., 'unto ordinances of angels'). Angels are mentioned in connection with the giving of the Law of Moses in Deut. 33:2. In Gal. 3:19 and Heb. 2:2 the purpose of the reference to them is to show the superiority of the Gospel to the Law. In Acts 7:53 Stephen mentions the angels to stress the majesty of the Law. See ORDAIN, ORDINANCE. ¶

NT: B.189b; CB.–; K.1156.
OT: –.
GEN. REF.: –.

DISPUTATION

1. *zētēsis* [ζήτησις, 2214], denotes, firstly, a seeking (*zēteō*, to seek), then, a debate, dispute, questioning, Acts 15:2, 7 (some texts have *suzētēsis*, reasoning, in both verses), R.V., "questioning," for A.V., "disputation" and "disputing"; for John 3:25; Acts 25:20; 1 Tim. 1:4; 6:4; 2 Tim 2:23; Tit. 3:9, see QUESTION, QUESTIONING. ¶

NT: B.339b; CB.1273c; K.300.
OT: –.
GEN. REF.: IS.1:968; NB.–; Z.–.

2. *diaglogismos* [διαλογισμός] is translated "disputations" in Rom. 14:1. See below.

DISPUTE, DISPUTER, DISPUTING

A. Nouns.

1. *dialogismos* [διαλογισμός, 1261], denotes, primarily, an inward reasoning, an opinion (*dia*, through, suggesting separation, *logismos*, a reasoning), e.g., Luke 2:35; 5:22; 6:8; then, a deliberating, questioning, Luke 24:38; (more strongly) a disputing, Phil. 2:14; 1 Tim. 2:8 (A.V., "doubtings"); in Rom. 14:1, "disputations"; marg., "(not for decisions) of doubts" (lit., 'not unto discussions of doubts,' which is perhaps a suitable rendering). Cp. *dialogizomai*, to reason. See DOUBTING, IMAGINATION, REASONING, THOUGHT.

NT: B.186a; CB.1241b; K.155.
OT: –.
GEN. REF.: IS.1:968; NB.–; Z.–.

2. *logomachia* [λογομαχία, 3055], denotes a dispute about words (*logos*, a word, *machē*, a fight), or about trivial things, 1 Tim. 6:4, R.V., "disputes," A.V., "strifes." See STRIFE. ¶

NT: B.477a; CB.1257a; K.505.
OT: –.
GEN. REF.: IS.1:968; NB.–; Z.–.

3. *diaparatribē* [διαπαρατριβή, 3859], denotes a constant or incessant wrangling (*dia*, through, *para*, beside, *tribō*, to wear out, suggesting the attrition or wearing effect of contention), 1 Tim. 6:5, R.V., "wranglings," A.V., "perverse disputings." Some mss. have the word *paradiatribē*, in the opposite order of the prefixed prepositions. See WRANGLING. ¶

NT: B.187c; CB.–; K.–.
OT: –.
GEN. REF.: –.

4. *antilogia* [ἀντιλογία, 485], denotes a gainsaying, contradiction (*anti*, against, *legō*, to speak), Heb. 6:16 (A.V., "strife," R.V., "dispute,"); 7:7, a gainsaying (R.V., "dispute"; A.V., "contradiction"); 12:3 (R.V., "gainsaying"; A.V., "contradiction"); Jude 11 ("gainsaying"). See CONTRADICTION, B. ¶

NT: B.75a; CB.–; K.–.
OT: rîb: S.7378; HR.111b.4a; H.2159; BD.936b.
GEN. REF.: IS.1:968; NB.–; Z.–.

5. *suzētētēs* [συζητητής, 4804], from *sun*, with, *zēteō*, to seek, denotes a disputer, 1 Cor. 1:20, where the reference is especially to a learned disputant, a sophist. ¶

NT: B.775d; CB.–; K.1099.
OT: –.
GEN. REF.: IS.1:968; NB.–; Z.–.

B. Verbs.

1. *dialegomai* [διαλέγομαι, 1256], akin to A, No. 1, primarily signifies to think different things with oneself, to ponder; then, with other persons, to converse, argue, dispute; it is translated to dispute in Mark 9:34 (for ver. 33 see No. 2), the R.V. and A.V. "had disputed" is somewhat unsuitable here, for the delinquency was not that they had wrangled, but that they had reasoned upon the subject at all; in Acts 17:17, A.V. (R.V., "reasoned," as in the A.V. of 18:4, 19); in 19:8, 9 (R.V., "reasoning"); in 24:12, "disputing"; in Jude 9, "disputed." See DISCOURSE.

NT: B.185c; CB.1241a; K.155.
OT: dābar: S.1696; HR.304b.1; H.399; BD.180b,d.
rîb: S.7378; HR.304b.2; H.2159; BD.936b.
GEN. REF.: IS.1:968; NB.–; Z.–.

2. *dialogizomai* [διαλογίζομαι, 1260], akin to A, No. 1, to bring together different reasons, to reckon them up, to reason, discuss, in Mark 9:33 is translated "ye disputed among yourselves," A.V.; R.V., "were reasoning." See CAST, No. 15, REASON.

NT: B.186a; CB.1241b; K.155.
OT: ḥāshab: S.2803; HR.304c.2; H.767; BD.362d.
GEN. REF.: IS.1:968; NB.–; Z.–.

3. *suzēteō* [συζητέω, 4802], akin to A, No. 5, lit., to seek or examine together, signifies to discuss, but is translated to dispute in Acts 6:9, and 9:29; elsewhere only in Mark and Luke. See INQUIRE, QUESTION, REASON.

NT: B.775c; CB.–; K.1099.
OT: –.
GEN. REF.: IS.1:968; NB.–; Z.–.

DISREPUTE

apelegmos [ἀπελεγμός, 557], from *apo*, from, and *elenchō*, to refute, denotes censure, repudiation (of something shown to be worthless), hence, contempt, "disrepute," Acts 19:27, R.V., "(come into) disrepute," for A.V., "(to be) set at nought." It is akin to *apelenchō*, to convict, refute (not in the N.T.), *elenchō*, to convict, *elenxis*, rebuke, and *elegmos*, reproof. See NOUGHT. ¶

NT: B.83d; CB.–; K.–.
OT: –.
GEN. REF.: IS.1:969; NB.–; Z.–.

For DISSEMBLE see DISSIMULATION

DISSENSION

stasis [στάσις, 4714], akin to *histēmi*, to stand, denotes (*a*) a standing, stability, Heb. 9:8, "(while as the first tabernacle) is yet standing"; (*b*) an insurrection, uproar, Mark 15:7; Luke 23:19, 25; Acts 19:40; 24:5; (*c*) a dissension, Acts 15:2; 23:7, 10. See INSURRECTION, SEDITION, STANDING, UPROAR. ¶

NT: B.764c; CB.1270a; K.1070.
OT: –.
GEN. REF.: IS.1:969; NB.–; Z.–.

DISSIMULATION, DISSEMBLE

A. Noun.

hupokrisis [ὑπόκρισις, 5272], primarily, a reply, came to mean the acting of a stage-player, because such answered one another in dialogue; hence the meaning dissembling or pretence. It is translated "dissimulation" in Gal. 2:13 (see B). See HYPOCRISY.

NT: B.845a; CB.1252b; K.1235.
OT: –.
GEN. REF.: IS.2:790; NB.–; Z.–.

B. Verb.

sunupokrinomai [συνυποκρίνομαι, 4942], *sun*, with, *hupokrinomai*, akin to A, to join in acting the hypocrite, in pretending to act from one motive, whereas another motive really inspires the act. So in Gal. 2:13, Peter with other believing Jews, in separating from believing Gentiles at Antioch, pretended that the motive was loyalty to the Law of Moses, whereas really it was fear of the Judaizers. ¶

NT: B.793d; CB.1270c; K.1235.
OT: –.
GEN. REF.: –.

C. Adjective.

anupokritos [ἀνυπόκριτος, 505], from *a*, negative, *n*, euphonic, and an adjectival form corresponding to A, signifies unfeigned; it is said of love, 2 Cor. 6:6; 1 Pet. 1:22; Rom. 12:9, A.V., "without dissimulation," R.V., "without hypocrisy"; of faith, 1 Tim. 1:5; 2 Tim. 1:5, "unfeigned"; of the wisdom that is from above, Jas. 3:17, "without hypocrisy." See HYPOCRISY. ¶

NT: B.76d; CB.–; K.1235.
OT: –.
GEN. REF.: –.

DISSOLVE

1. *luō* [λύω, 3089], to loose, is used of the future demolition of the elements or heavenly bodies, 2 Pet. 3:10, 11, 12; in ver. 10, A.V., "shall melt;" R.V., "shall be dissolved"; in verses 11, 12, A.V. and R.V., "dissolved." See BREAK.

NT: B.483c; CB.1257b; K.543.
OT: –.
GEN. REF.: IS.1:969; NB.–; Z.–.

2. *kataluō* [καταλύω]: see DESTROY, A, No. 5.

For DISTINCTION (*diastolē*) see DIFFERENCE

DISTRACTION (without)

aperispastōs [ἀπερισπάστως, 563], from *a*, negative, *perispaō*, to draw around, draw away, distract (for which see CUMBER), is found in 1 Cor. 7:35. ¶

NT: B.84b; CB.–; K.–.
OT: –.
GEN. REF.: –.

DISTRESS, DISTRESSED

A. Nouns.

1. *ananke* [ἀνάγκη, 318], denotes (*a*) a necessity, imposed whether by external circumstances, e.g., Luke 23:17, or inward pressure, e.g., 1 Cor. 9:16; (*b*) straits, distress, Luke 21:23 (in ver. 25, "distress" translates No. 3); 1 Cor. 7:26; 1 Thess. 3:7; the last two refer to the lack of material things. See NECESSARY, NECESSITY, NEEDS.

NT: B.52b; CB.1235b; K.55.
OT: mᵉṣûqāh: S.4691; HR.76a.6b; H.1895e; BD.848a.
ṣar: S.6862; HR.76a.7a; H.1973-1975; BD.865a.
ṣārāh: S.6869; HR.76a.7b; H.1973c,1974b; BD.865b.
GEN. REF.: IS.1:970; NB.–; Z.–.

2. *stenochōria* [στενοχωρία]: see ANGUISH.

3. *sunochē* [συνοχή]: see ANGUISH.

4. *thlipsis* [θλίψις]: see AFFLICTION, B, No. 5.

B. Verbs.

1. *basanizō* [βασανίζω, 928], properly signifies to test by rubbing on the touchstone (*basanos*, a touchstone), then, to question by applying torture; hence to vex, torment; in the Passive Voice, to be harassed, distressed; it is said of men struggling in a boat against wind and waves, Matt. 14:24, R.V., "distressed" (A.V., "tossed"); Mark 6:48, R.V., "distressed" (A.V., "toiling"). See PAIN, TOIL, TORMENT, VEX.

NT: B.134c; CB.1238c; K.96.
OT: –.
GEN. REF.: IS.1:970; NB.–; Z.–.

2. *skullō* [σκύλλω, 4660], primarily signifies to skin, to flay; then to rend, mangle; hence, to vex, trouble, annoy; it is found in the most authentic mss. in Matt. 9:36, R.V., "distressed" (of the multitudes who applied to the Lord for healing); A.V., "fainted;" translating the alternative reading, *ekluō*, lit., to loosen out. It is also used in Mark 5:35; Luke 7:6; 8:49. See TROUBLE. ¶

NT: B.758b; CB.—; K.—.
OT: —.
GEN. REF.: —.

3. *stenochōreō* [στενοχωρέω]: see ANGUISH.

4. *kataponeō* [καταπονέω, 2669], primarily, to tire down with toil, exhaust with labour (*kata*, down, *ponos*, labour), hence signifies to afflict, oppress; in the Passive Voice, to be oppressed, much distressed; it is translated "oppressed" in Acts 7:24, and "sore distressed" in 2 Pet. 2:7, R.V., (A.V., "vexed"). See OPPRESS, VEX. ¶

NT: B.416d; CB.—; K.—.
OT: —.
GEN. REF.: IS.1:970; NB.—; Z.—.

DISTRIBUTE, DISTRIBUTION

A. Verbs.

1. *diadidōmi* [διαδίδωμι, 1239], lit., to give through, (*dia*, through, *didōmi*, to give), as from one to another, to deal out, is said of distributing to the poor, Luke 18:22; Acts 4:35, "distribution was made;" or to a company of people, John 6:11. It is translated "divideth" in Luke 11:22. In Rev. 17:13 the most authentic mss. have the verb *didōmi*, to give, instead of the longer form. ¶

NT: B.182d; CB.—; K.—.
OT: ḥālaq: S.2505; HR.300b.1; H.669; BD.323c.
nātan: S.5414; HR.300b.3; H.1443; BD.678a.
GEN. REF.: —.

2. *merizō* [μερίζω, 3307], is translated "hath distributed" in 1 Cor. 7:17, and in the A.V. of 2 Cor. 10:13, where, however, this rendering is unsuitable, as it is not a case of distributing among a number, but apportioning a measure to the Apostle and his co-workers; hence the R.V., "apportioned." See DIFFER, A, No. 2.

NT: B.504c; CB.1258b; K.—.
OT: ḥālaq: S.2505; HR.910c.2a-c; H.669; BD.323c.
nāḥal: S.5157; HR.910c.5a,b; H.1342; BD.635c.
GEN. REF.: —.

Note: Koinōneō, to share in common with, is translated "distributing" in Rom. 12:13, A.V. The verb does not mean to distribute; hence R.V., "communicating." Similarly *koinōnia*, fellowship, communion, is translated "distribution" in 2 Cor. 9:13, A.V.; R.V., "contribution."

B. Adjective.

eumetadotos [εὐμετάδοτος, 2130], ready to impart (*eu*, well, *meta*, with, *didōmi*, to give: see A, No. 1) is used in 1 Tim. 6:18, "ready to distribute." ¶

NT: B.323a; CB.—; K.—.
OT: —.
GEN. REF.: —.

DISTRICT

meris [μερίς, 3310], denotes a part (akin to *merizō*, DISTRIBUTE, A., No. 2), Luke 10:42; Acts 8:21; 2 Cor. 6:15; Col. 1:12 (lit., 'unto the part,' or share, of the inheritance). In Acts 16:12 the R.V. translates it "district," with reference to Macedonia. See PART. ¶

NT: B.505a; CB.1258b; K.—.
OT: ḥēleq: S.2506; HR.911a.1a; H.669a; BD.324a.
maḥᵃlōqet: S.4256; HR.911a.1d; H.669d; BD.324d.
GEN. REF.: IS.1:970; NB.—; Z.—.

DITCH

bothunos [βόθυνος, 999], any kind of deep hole or pit (probably connected with *bathos*, deep), is translated "ditch" in the A.V. of Matt. 15:14 and Luke 6:39, R.V., "pit" in each place, as in both Versions of Matt. 12:11. See PIT. ¶

NT: B.144d; CB.—; K.—.
OT: paḥat: S.6354; HR.224b.3; H.1761a; BD.809b.
GEN. REF.: —.

DIVERS

A. Adjectives.

1. *diaphoros* [διάφορος] is rendered "divers" in Heb. 9:10. See DIFFER, C.

2. *poikilos* [ποικίλος, 4164], denotes particoloured, variegated (*poikillō* means to make gay: the root of the first syllable is *pik*—, found in Eng., picture), hence "divers," Matt. 4:24; Mark 1:34; Luke 4:40; 2 Tim. 3:6; Tit. 3:3; Heb. 2:4 (R.V., "manifold"); 13:9; Jas. 1:2 (R.V., "manifold"); in 1 Pet. 1:6 and 4:10, "manifold," both A.V. and R.V. See MANIFOLD. ¶

NT: B.683c; CB.—; K.901.
OT: riqmāh: S.7553; HR.1168c.5; H.2216a; BD.955d.
GEN. REF.: IS.1:970; NB.—; Z.—.

Notes: (1) Cp. *polupoikilos*, Eph. 3:10, "manifold" (lit., 'much varied').

(2) The pronoun *tines*, "some" (the plural of *tis*, someone), is translated "divers" in the A.V. of Mark 8:3 and Acts 19:9; R.V., "some."

(3) In 1 Cor. 12:28, *genos*, in the plural, is rendered "divers kinds." See DIVERSITIES.

B. Adverb.

polutropōs [πολυτρόπως, 4187], means in many ways (*polus*, much, *tropos*, a manner, way; Eng., trope), "in divers manners," Heb. 1:1. ¶

NT: B.690a; CB.—; K.—.
OT: —.
GEN. REF.: —.

Note: The phrase *kata topous*, lit., throughout places (*kata*, down, or throughout, in a distributive sense, *topos*, a place), is translated "in divers places," in Matt. 24:7; Mark 13:8 and Luke 21:11.

DIVERSITY, DIVERSITIES

diairesis [διαίρεσις]: See DIFFER, B, No. 1.

Note; Genos, a kind, class, sort (Eng., genus), is translated "diversities" in the A.V. of 1 Cor. 12:28 (marg., "kinds"); R.V., "divers kinds."

DIVIDE, DIVIDER, DIVIDING

A. Verbs.

1. *aphorizō* [ἀφορίζω, 873], lit., to mark off by boundaries or limits (*apo*, from, *horizō*, to determine, mark out), denotes to separate; "divideth," Matt. 25:32, A.V.; R.V., "separateth," as in the preceding part of the verse. See SEPARATE, SEVER.

NT: B.127b; CB.1236c; K.728.
OT: bādal: S.914; HR.185c.1a; H.203; BD.95a.
gābal: S.1379; HR.185c.3; H.307; BD.148b.
GEN. REF.: IS.1:971; NB.—; Z.—.

2. *diaireō* [διαιρέω, 1244], lit., to take asunder (see DIFFER, B, No. 1), to divide into parts, to distribute, is found in Luke 15:12 and 1 Cor. 12:11. ¶

NT: B.183d; CB.—; K.27.
OT: —.
GEN. REF.: IS.1:971; NB.—; Z.—.

3. *diadidōmi* [διαδίδωμι]: see DISTRIBUTE, A, No. 1.

4. *diakrinō* [διακρίνω, 1252], to separate, discriminate, hence, to be at variance with oneself, to be divided in one's mind, is rendered "divided" in Jas. 2:4, R.V.; A.V., "partial." See DISCERN.

NT: B.185b; CB.1241a; K.469.
OT: dîn: S.1777; HR.304a.4a; H.426; BD.192a.
rîb: S.7378; HR.304a.6; H.2159; BD.936b.
shāphaṭ: S.8199; HR.304a.8a; H.2443; BD.1047a.
GEN. REF.: —.

5. *ginomai* [γίνομαι, 1096], to become, is translated "was divided" in Rev. 16:19 (of "the great city"), lit., 'became into three parts.'

NT: B.158a; CB.1248b; K.117.
OT: —.
GEN. REF.: —.

6. *merizō* [μερίζω, 3307], akin to *meros*, a part, to part, divide into, in the Middle Voice means to divide anything with another, to share with. The usual meaning is to divide, Matt. 12:25, 26; Mark 3:24, 25, 26; 6:41; Luke 12:13 (Middle Voice); Rom. 12:3, "hath dealt"; 1 Cor. 1:13; Heb. 7:2, R.V. (A.V., "gave a part"). Elsewhere with other meanings, 1 Cor. 7:17, 34; 2 Cor. 10:13. See DEAL, DIFFER, A, No. 2, DISTRIBUTE, A, No. 2, GIVE. ¶

NT: B.504c; CB.1258b; K.—.
OT: ḥālaq: S.2505; HR.910c.2a-c; H.669; BD.323c.
nāḥal: S.5157; HR.910c.5a,b; H.1342; BD.635c.
GEN. REF.: IS.1:971; NB.—; Z.—.

7. *diamerizō* [διαμερίζω, 1266], *dia*, through, and No. 6, to divide through, i.e., completely, to divide up, is translated to divide in Luke 11:17, 18; 12:52, 53; 22:17; "parted" in Matt. 27:35; Mark 15:24; Luke 23:34; John 19:24; Acts 2:45; in Acts 2:3, A.V., "cloven," R.V., "parting asunder." See CLOVEN. ¶

NT: B.186d; CB.—; K.—.
OT: ḥālaq: S.2505; HR.305c.1a-c; H.669; BD.323c.
GEN. REF.: IS.1:971; NB.—; Z.—.

8. *orthotomeō* [ὀρθοτομέω, 3718], lit., to cut straight (*orthos*, straight, *temnō*, to cut), is found in 2 Tim. 2:15, A.V., "rightly dividing," R.V., "handling aright" (the word of truth); the meaning passed from the idea of cutting or dividing, to the more general sense of rightly dealing with a thing. What is intended here is not dividing Scripture from Scripture, but teaching Scripture accurately. ¶ In the Sept., of directing one's paths, Prov. 3:6 and 11:5 ("righteousness traces out blameless paths"). ¶

NT: B.580b; CB.1261b; K.1169.
OT: yāshar: S.3474; HR.1011a.1; H.930; BD.448c.
GEN. REF.: —.

Note: In Acts 13:19, the A.V., "He divided their land . . . by lot," represents the verb *kataklērodoteō*, from *kata*, suggesting distribution, *klēros*, a lot, *didōmi*, to give. The most authentic mss. have *kataklēronomeō*, to distribute, as an inheritance, from *klēronomia*, an inheritance; hence R.V., "He gave them their land for an inheritance." ¶ For *Schizō*, Acts 14:4; 23:7, see BREAK, No. 12.

B. Nouns.

1. *meristēs* [μεριστής, 3312], a divider, is found in Luke 12:14. ¶

NT: B.505d; CB.—; K.—.
OT: —.
GEN. REF.: IS.1:971; NB.—; Z.—.

2. *merismos* [μερισμός, 3311], akin to No. 1, primarily denotes a division, partition (*meros*, a part); hence, (*a*) a distribution, Heb. 2:4, "gifts" (marg. of R.V., "distributions"); (*b*) a dividing or separation, Heb. 4:12, "dividing" (A.V., "dividing asunder"). Some take this in the Active sense, "as far as the cleaving asunder or separation of soul and spirit"; others in the Passive sense, "as far as the division (i.e., the dividing line) between soul and spirit," i.e., where one differs from the other. The former seems more in keeping with the meaning of the word. See GIFT. ¶

NT: B.505c; CB.—; K.—.
OT: maḥ^{a}lōqet: S.4256; HR.911c.1a; H.669d; BD.324d.
GEN. REF.: —.

DIVINATION

puthōn [πύθων, 4436], Eng., python, in Greek mythology was the name of the Pythian serpent or dragon, dwelling in Pytho, at the foot of Mount Parnassus, guarding the oracle of Delphi, and slain by Apollo. Thence the name was transferred to Apollo himself. Later the word was applied to diviners or soothsayers, regarded as inspired by Apollo. Since demons are the agents inspiring idolatry, 1 Cor. 10:20, the young woman in Acts 16:16 was possessed by a demon instigating the cult of Apollo, and thus had "a spirit of divination." ¶

NT: B.728d; CB.1268a; K.973.
OT: –.
GEN. REF.: IS.–; NB.320,321; Z.–.

DIVINE

A. Adjective.

theios [θεῖος, 2304], divine (from *theos*, God), is used of the power of God, 2 Pet. 1:3, and of His nature, ver. 4, in each place, as that which proceeds from Himself. In Acts 17:29 it is used as a noun with the definite article, to denote "the Godhead," the Deity (i.e., the one true God). This word, instead of *theos*, was purposely used by the Apostle in speaking to Greeks on Mars Hill, as in accordance with Greek usage. Cp. DIVINITY. ¶ In the Sept., Ex. 31:3; 35:31; Job 27:3; 33:4; Prov. 2:17. ¶

NT: B.353d; CB.1271c; K.322.
OT: ʼēl: S.410; HR.628a.1; H.93a; BD.42a.
ʼᵉlōah: S.433; HR.628a.2a; H.93b; BD.43a.
ʼᵉlōhîm: S.430; HR.628a.2b; H.93c; BD.43b.
GEN. REF.: IS.2:504; NB.474; Z.–.

B. Noun.

latreia [λατρεία, 2999], akin to *latreuō*, to serve, primarily, any service for hire, denotes in Scripture the service of God according to the requirements of the Levitical Law, Rom. 9:4; Heb. 9:1, 6, "Divine service." It is used in the more general sense of service to God, in John 16:2; Rom. 12:1. See SERVICE. ¶

NT: B.467b; CB.1256c; K.503.
OT: ʻᵃbodāh: S.5656; HR.863a.1; H.1553c; BD.715a.
GEN. REF.: IS.4:1117; NB.1340; Z.–.

DIVINITY

theiotēs [θειότης, 2305], divinity, the R.V. rendering in Rom. 1:20 (A.V., "Godhead"), is derived from *theios* (see DIVINE, A), and is to be distinguished from *theotēs*, in Col. 2:9, "Godhead." In Rom. 1:20 the Apostle "is declaring how much of God may be known from the revelation of Himself which He has made in nature, from those vestiges of Himself which men may everywhere trace in the world around them. Yet it is not the personal God whom any man may learn to know by these aids; He can be known only by the revelation of Himself in His Son; . . . But in the second passage (Col. 2:9), Paul is declaring that in the Son there dwells all the fulness of absolute Godhead; they were no mere rays of Divine glory which gilded Him, lighting up His Person for a season and with a splendour not His own; but He was, and is, absolute and perfect God; and the Apostle uses *theotēs* to express this essential and personal Godhead of the Son" (Trench, Syn. § ii). *Theotēs* indicates the Divine essence of Godhood, the Personality of God; *theiotēs*, the attributes of God, His Divine nature and properties. See GODHEAD. ¶

NT: B.354a; CB.1271c; K.322.
OT: –.
GEN. REF.: IS.1:493; NB.1340; Z.2:88.

DIVISION

1. *diamerismos* [διαμερισμός, 1267], primarily, a parting, distribution, denotes a discussion, dissension, division or discord, breaking up as of family ties (*dia*, asunder, *meros*, a part), it is found in Luke 12:51, where it is contrasted with *eirēnē*, peace. Cp. DIVIDE, A, No. 7.

NT: B.186d; CB.1241b; K.–.
OT: –.
GEN. REF.: IS.1:974; NB.–; Z.–.

2. *dichostasia* [διχοστασία, 1370], lit., a standing apart (*dichē*, asunder, apart, *stasis*, a standing; the root *di*— indicating division, is found in many words in various languages), is used in Rom. 16:17, where believers are enjoined to mark those who cause division and to turn away from them; and in Gal. 5:20, R.V. (A.V., "seditions"), where divisions are spoken of as "works of the flesh." Some mss. have this noun in 1 Cor. 3:3. ¶

NT: B.200b; CB.1241b; K.88.
OT: –.
GEN. REF.: –.

3. *schisma* [σχίσμα, 4978], Eng., schism, denotes a cleft, a rent, Matt. 9:16; Mark 2:21; then, metaphorically, a division, dissension, John 7:43; 9:16; 10:19; 1 Cor. 1:10; 11:18; in 1 Cor. 12:25 it is translated "schism" (marg., "division"). The root is *skid*—, seen in the corresponding verb *schizō*, to cleave (Lat. *scindo*). See SCHISM. Cp. *hairesis*, a sect. ¶

NT: B.797c; CB.1268c; K.1130.
OT: –.
GEN. REF.: IS.1:974; NB.–; Z.–.

DIVORCE, DIVORCEMENT

A. Verb.

apoluō [ἀπολύω, 630], to let loose from, let go free (*apo*, from, *luō*, to loose), is translated "is divorced" in the A.V. of Matt. 5:32 (R.V., "is put away"); it is further used of divorce in Matt. 1:19; 19:3, 7-9; Mark 10:2, 4, 11; Luke 16:18. The Lord also used it of the case of a wife putting away her husband, Mark 10:12, a usage among Greeks and Romans, not among Jews. See DISMISS.

NT: B.96c; CB.1237a; K.–.
OT: gārash: S.1644; HR.138c.2; H.388; BD.176c.
GEN. REF.: IS.1:975; NB.790; Z.–.

B. Noun.

apostasion [ἀποστάσιον, 647], primarily, a defection, lit., a standing off (*apo*, from, *stasis*, a standing; cp. *aphistēmi*, to cause to withdraw), denotes, in the N.T., a writing or bill of divorcement, Matt. 5:31; 19:7; Mark 10:4. ¶ In Sept., Deut. 24:3; Isa. 50:1; Jer. 3:8. ¶

NT: B.98b; CB.1237a; K.–.
OT: k^{e}rîtût: S.3748; HR.141b.1; H.1048a; BD.504d.
GEN. REF.: IS.1:975; NB.790; Z.2:149.

DO, DONE

In English the verb to do serves the purpose of a large number of verbs, and has a large variety of meanings. It therefore translates a considerable number of Greek verbs. These, with their specific meanings, are as follows:

1.*poieō* [ποιέω, 4160], signifies (*a*) to make, (*b*) to do, i.e., to adopt a way of expressing by act the thoughts and feelings. It stands for a number of such acts, chiefly to make, produce, create, cause, e.g., Matt. 17:4. See ABIDE, APPOINT, BEAR, BRING, CAUSE, COMMIT, CONTINUE, DEAL, EXECUTE, EXERCISE, FULFIL, GAIN, GIVE, HOLD, KEEP, MAKE, MEAN, OBSERVE, ORDAIN, PERFORM, PROVIDE, PURPOSE, PUT, SHEW, SHOOT FORTH, SPEND, TAKE, TARRY, WORK, YIELD.

NT: B.680d; CB.1265c; K.895.
OT: ‘āsāh: S.6213; HR.1154a.33a; H.1708,1709; BD.793c.
GEN. REF.: –.

2. *prassō* [πράσσω, 4238], signifies to practise, though this is not always to be pressed. The Apostle John, in his Epistles, uses the continuous tenses of *poieō*, to indicate a practice, the habit of doing something, e.g., 1 John 3:4 (the A.V., "committeth" and "commit" in 1 John 3:8 and 9, e.g., is wrong, "doeth," R.V., in the sense of practising, is the meaning). He uses *prassō* twice in the Gospel, 3:20 and 5:29. The Apostle Paul uses *prassō* in the sense of practising, and the R.V. so renders the word in Rom. 1:32; 2:2, instead of A.V., "commit," though, strangely enough, the R.V. translates it "committed," instead of "practised," in 2 Cor. 12:21.

Generally speaking, in Paul's Epistles *poieō* denotes an action complete in itself, while *prassō* denotes a habit. The difference is seen in Rom. 1:32, R.V. Again, *poieō* stresses the accomplishment, e.g., "perform," in Rom. 4:21; *prassō* stresses the process leading to the accomplishment, e.g., "doer," in 2:25. In Rom. 2:3 he who does, *poieō*, the things mentioned, is warned against judging those who practise them, *prassō*.

The distinction in John 3:20, 21 is noticeable: "Every one that doeth (*prassō*, practiseth) ill . . . he that doeth (*poieō*) the truth." While we cannot draw the regular distinction, that *prassō* speaks of doing evil things, and *poieō* of doing good things, yet very often "where the words assume an ethical tinge, there is a tendency to use the verbs with this distinction" (Trench, Syn., § xcvi). See COMMIT, EXACT, KEEP, REQUIRE, USE.

NT: B.698b; CB.1266b; K.927.
OT: ‘āsāh: S.6213; HR.1201a.3; H.1708,1709; BD.793c.
pā‘al: S.6466; HR.1201a.4; H.1792; BD.821b.
GEN. REF.: –.

3. *ginomai* [γίνομαι, 1096], to become, is sometimes translated "do" or "done," e.g., Luke 4:23, "done (at Capernaum)," followed by *poieō* in the next clause. In Matt. 21:42 and Mark 12:11, this verb is translated, in the A.V., "(the Lord's) doing"; R.V., "this was from the Lord." See BECOME.

NT: B.158a; CB.1248b; K.117.
OT: –.
GEN. REF.: –.

4. *ergazomai* [ἐργάζομαι, 2038], denotes to work (*ergon*, work). In Gal. 6:10 the R.V. renders it "let us work," for A.V., "let us do"; in 3 John 5, "thou doest." See COMMIT, LABOUR, MINISTER, TRADE, WORK.

NT: B.306d; CB.1246c; K.251.
OT: ‘ābad: S.5647; HR.540c.8a; H.1553; BD.712b.
pā‘al: S.6466; HR.540c.11a; H.1792; BD.821b.
GEN. REF.: –.

5. *katergazomai* [κατεργάζομαι, 2716], *kata* (intensive), is a more emphatic verb than No. 4. In Rom. 2:9 the R.V. has "worketh" for A.V., "doeth." In Rom. 7:15, 17, both translate it "I do" (R.V. marg., "work"); so in ver. 20, "I that do." In 1 Cor. 5:3 the R.V. has "wrought," for A.V., "done." In Eph. 6:13 both render it "having done (all)"; more suitably, 'having wrought (all)'; the A.V. marg. "having overcome" does not give the correct meaning.

See CAUSE, B, *Note* (2), PERFORM, WORK, WROUGHT.

NT: B.421c; CB.–; K.421.
OT: ʿābad: S.5647; HR.749b.4; H.1553; BD.712b.
ʿāsāh: S.6213; HR.749b.5; H.1708,1709; BD.793c.
pāʿal: S.6466; HR.749b.6; H.1792; BD.821b.
GEN. REF.: –.

6. *ischuō* [ἰσχύω, 2480], signifies to be strong, to prevail. It is translated "I can do," in Phil. 4:13. See ABLE, etc.

NT: B.383d; CB.1253a; K.378.
OT: gābar: S.1396; HR.692c.5a; H.310; BD.149c.
ḥāzaq: S.2388; HR.692c.6; H.636; BD.304a.
GEN. REF.: –.

7. *parechō* [παρέχω, 3930], lit. means to hold near (*para*, beside, and *echō*, to have), i.e., to present, offer, supply. It is translated "do for" in Luke 7:4. See BRING, No. 21.

NT: B.626b; CB.–; K.–.
OT: –.
GEN. REF.: –.

Notes: (1) In Phil. 2:13 *energeō*, to work, is translated "to do," A.V.; R.V., "to work."

(2) In Luke 13:32 *apoteleō*, to complete, perform, is translated "I . . . do," A.V.; R.V., "I perform" (some mss. have *epiteleō* here).

(3) In Acts 15:36, *echō*, to have, to hold, sometimes used to express the condition in which a person is, how he is faring, is translated "(how) they do," A.V.; R.V., "how they fare." It is often used of a physical condition, e.g., Matt. 4:24 (see SICK).

(4) In Acts 25:9 *katatithēmi*, to deposit, or lay up, for future use, to lay up favour for oneself with a person, is translated "to do (the Jews a pleasure)," A.V.; R.V., "to gain (favour with the Jews)."

(5) In John 16:2 *prospherō*, to bring near, offer, present, is translated "doeth (service)," A.V.; R.V., "offereth (service)."

(6) In Heb. 4:13 the phrase *hēmin ho logos*, rendered "(with whom) we have to do," is, lit., '(with whom is) the account to us.'

(7) In 1 Cor. 13:10, *katargeō*, to render inactive, abolish, so is translated "shall be done away"; 2 Cor. 3:7, A.V., "was to be done away," R.V., "was passing away"; ver. 11. See ABOLISH, DESTROY.

(8) For "done aforetime," Rom. 3:25, R.V., see PAST. For "did," 2 Tim. 4:14, A.V., see SHEW, no. 3. For "do good" see GOOD.

For **DOING** see **DEED,** No. 3, **DO,** No. 3

DOCTOR

1. *didaskalos* [διδάσκαλος, 1320], a teacher (from *didaskō*, to teach), cp. *didaskalia*, teaching, doctrine, instruction, is translated "doctors," with reference to the teachers of the Jewish religion, Luke 2:46. Cp. *paideutēs*, a teacher. See MASTER, TEACHER.

NT: B.191c; CB.1241b; K.161.
OT: –.
GEN. REF.: IS.1:980; NB.–; Z.2:151.

2. *nomodidaskalos* [νομοδιδάσκαλος, 3547], a teacher of the Law (*nomos*, a law, and No. 1), with reference to the teachers of the Mosaic Law, is used in the same sense as No. 1, Luke 5:17; Acts 5:34; also of those who went about among Christians, professing to be instructors of the Law, 1 Tim. 1:7. See TEACHER. ¶ See under LAW.

NT: B.541d; CB.1260a; K.161.
OT: –.
GEN. REF.: IS.1:980; NB.–; Z.2:151.

DOCTRINE

1. *didachē* [διδαχή, 1322], akin to No. 1, under DOCTOR, denotes teaching, either (*a*) that which is taught, e.g., Matt. 7:28, A.V., "doctrine," R.V., "teaching"; Tit. 1:9, R.V.; Rev. 2:14, 15, 24, or (*b*) the act of teaching, instruction, e.g., Mark 4:2, A.V., "doctrine," R.V., "teaching"; the R.V. has "the doctrine" in Rom. 16:17. See Note (1) below.

NT: B.192d; CB.1241b; K.161.
OT: lāmad: S.3925; HR.317b.1; H.1116; BD.540c.
GEN. REF.: IS.1:980; NB.321; Z.2:151.

2. *didaskalia* [διδασκαλία, 1319], denotes, as No. 1 (from which, however, it is to be distinguished), (*a*) that which is taught, doctrine, Matt. 15:9; Mark 7:7; Eph. 4:14; Col. 2:22; 1 Tim. 1:10; 4:1, 6; 6:1, 3; 2 Tim. 4:3; Tit. 1:9 ("doctrine," in last part of verse: see also No. 1); 2:1, 10; (*b*) teaching, instruction, Rom. 12:7, "teaching"; 15:4, "learning"; 1 Tim. 4:13, A.V., "doctrine," R.V., "teaching"; ver. 16, A.V., "the doctrine," R.V., (correctly) "thy teaching"; 5:17, A.V., "doctrine," R.V. "teaching"; 2 Tim. 3:10, 16 (ditto); Tit. 2:7, "thy doctrine." Cp. No. 1, under DOCTOR. See LEARNING. ¶

NT: B.191c; CB.1241b; K.161.
OT: lāmad: S.3925; HR.316c.2; H.1116; BD.540c.
GEN. REF.: IS.1:980; NB.321; Z.2:151.

Notes: (1) Whereas *didachē* is used only twice in the Pastoral Epistles, 2 Tim. 4:2, and Tit. 1:9, *didaskalia* occurs fifteen times. Both are used in the active and passive senses (i.e., the act of teaching and what is taught), the passive is predominant in *didachē*, the active in *didaskalia*; the former stresses the authority, the latter the act (Cremer). Apart from the Apostle Paul, other writers make use of *didachē* only, save in Matt. 15:9 and Mark 7:7 (*didaskalia*).

(2) In Heb. 6:1, *logos*, a word, is translated "doctrine," A.V.; the R.V. margin gives the lit. rendering, "the word (of the beginning of

Christ)," and, in the text, "the (first) principles (of Christ)."

DOER

poiētēs [ποιητής, 4163], akin to *poieō*, see Do, No. 1, signifies a doer, Rom. 2:13; Jas. 1:22, 23, 25; 4:11. Its meaning "poet" is found in Acts 17:28. ¶

NT: B.683b; CB.1265c; K.895.
OT: –.
GEN. REF.: –.

Notes: (1) For *prassō*, rendered "doer" in Rom. 2:25, see Do, No. 2.

(2) In 2 Tim. 2:9, *kakourgos* is rendered "evil doer" (R.V., "malefactor").

DOG

1. *kuōn* [κύων, 2965], is used in two senses, (*a*) natural, Matt. 7:6; Luke 16:21; 2 Pet. 2:22, (*b*) metaphorical, Phil. 3:2; Rev. 22:15, of those whose moral impurity will exclude them from the New Jerusalem. The Jews used the term of Gentiles, under the idea of ceremonial impurity. Among the Greeks it was an epithet of impudence. Lat., *canis*, and Eng., hound are etymologically akin to it. ¶

NT: B.461b; CB.1256b; K.494.
OT: keleb: S.3611; HR.839a.1; H.981a; BD.476d.
GEN. REF.: IS.1:980; NB.321; Z.2:153.

2. *kunarion* [κυνάριον, 2952], a diminutive of No. 1, a little dog, a puppy, is used in Matt. 15:26, 27; Mark 7:27, 28. ¶

NT: B.457c; CB.1256b; K.494.
OT: –.
GEN. REF.: IS.1:980; NB.321; Z.2:153.

DOMINION (have . . . over)

A. Nouns.

1. *kratos* [κράτος, 2904], force, strength, might, more especially manifested power, is derived from a root *kra—*, to perfect, to complete: "creator" is probably connected. It also signifies dominion, and is so rendered frequently in doxologies, 1 Pet. 4:11; 5:11; Jude 25; Rev. 1:6; 5:13 (R.V.); in 1 Tim. 6:16, and Heb. 2:14 it is translated "power." See Might, Power, Strength.

NT: B.449a; CB.1256a; K.466.
OT: 'ōz: S.5797; HR.784a.6; H.1596b; BD.738d.
ḥāzqāh: S.2394; HR.784a.2b; H.636d; BD.306a.
'ammîṣ: S.533; HR.784a.2; H.117d; BD.55c.
GEN. REF.: IS.1:983; NB.—; Z.2:154.

(*Note:* Synonymous words are *bia*, force, often oppressive, *dunamis*, power, especially inherent power; *energeia*, power especially in exercise, operative power; *exousia*, primarily liberty of action, then authority either delegated or arbitrary; *ischus*, strength, especially physical, power as an endowment.

2. *kuriotēs* [κυριότης, 2963], denotes lordship (*kurios*, a lord), power, dominion, whether angelic or human, Eph. 1:21; Col. 1:16; 2 Pet. 2:10 (R.V., for A.V., "government"); Jude 8. In Eph. and Col. it indicates a grade in the angelic orders, in which it stands second. ¶

NT: B.460d; CB.1256b; K.486.
OT: –.
GEN. REF.: IS.1:983; NB.—; Z.2:154.

B. Verbs.

1. *kurieuō* [κυριεύω, 2961], to be lord over, rule over, have dominion over (akin to A, No. 2), is used of (*a*) Divine authority over men, Rom. 14:9, "might be Lord"; (*b*) human authority over men, Luke 22:25, "lordship," 1 Tim. 6:15, "lords" (R.V., marg., "them that rule as lords"); (*c*) the permanent immunity of Christ from the dominion of death, Rom. 6:9; (*d*) the deliverance of the believer from the dominion of sin, Rom. 6:14; (*e*) the dominion of law over men, Rom. 7:1; (*f*) the dominion of a person over the faith of other believers, 2 Cor. 1:24 (R.V., "lordship"). See Lord. ¶

NT: B.458c; CB.1256b; K.486.
OT: māshal: S.4910; HR.800a.4; H.1258,1259; BD.605c.
sheleṭ (Aramaic): S.7981; HR.800a.9; H.3034; BD.1115c.
GEN. REF.: IS.1:983; NB.—; Z.2:154.

2. *katakurieuō* [κατακυριεύω, 2634], *kata*, down (intensive), and No. 1, to exercise, or gain, dominion over, to lord it over, is used of (*a*) the lordship of Gentile rulers, Matt. 20:25, A.V., "exercise dominion," R.V., "lord it"; Mark 10:42, A.V., "exercise lordship," R.V., "lord it"; (*b*) the power of demons over men, Acts 19:16, A.V., "overcame," R.V., "mastered"; (*c*) of the evil of elders in lording it over the saints under their spiritual care, 1 Pet. 5:3. See Lordship, Overcome.

NT: B.412c; CB.1254a; K.486.
OT: kābash: S.3533; HR.735a.3; H.951; BD.461b.
rādāh: S.7287; HR.735a.6; H.2121,2122; BD.921d.
māshal: S.4910; HR.735a.4; H.1258,1259; BD.605c.
GEN. REF.: IS.1:983; NB.—; Z.2:154.

Note: For *authenteō*, to have dominion, 1 Tim. 2:12, R.V., see Authority, No. 3.

DOOMED

For R.V. in 1 Cor. 4:9, see Appoint (Note at end), Death, B.

DOOR

thura [θύρα, 2374], a door, gate (Eng., door is connected), is used (*a*) literally, e.g., Matt. 6:6; 27:60; (*b*) metaphorically, of Christ, John 10:7, 9; of faith, by acceptance of the Gospel, Acts 14:27; of openings for preaching and teaching the Word of God, 1 Cor. 16:9; 2 Cor. 2:12; Col. 4:3; Rev. 3:8; of entrance into the

Kingdom of God, Matt. 25:10; Luke 13:24, 25; of Christ's entrance into a repentant believer's heart, Rev. 3:20; of the nearness of Christ's Second Advent, Matt. 24:33; Mark 13:29; cp. Jas. 5:9; of access to behold visions relative to the purposes of God, Rev. 4:1.

NT: B.365d; CB.1272c; K.340.
OT: delet: S.1817; HR.662c.1b; H.431a,e; BD.195a.
petaḥ: S.6607; HR.662c.4a; H.1854a; BD.835d.
GEN. REF.: IS.1:983; NB.544; Z.2:155.

Note: For the phrase "that kept the door," *thurōros*, John 18:16, 17 ("porter" in Mark 13:34; John 10:3), see PORTER. ¶

DOTE

noseō [νοσέω, 3552], signifies to be ill, to be ailing, whether in body or mind; hence, to be taken with such a morbid interest in a thing as is tantamount to a disease, to dote, 1 Tim. 6:4 (marg., "sick"). The primary meaning of dote is to be foolish (cp. Jer. 50:36), the evident meaning of *noseō*, in this respect, is to be unsound. ¶

NT: B.543c; CB.1260a; K.655.
OT: –.
GEN. REF.: –.

DOUBLE

A. Adjective.

diplous [διπλοῦς, 1362], denotes twofold, double, 1 Tim. 5:17; Rev. 18:6 (twice). ¶ The comparative degree *diploteron* (neuter) is used adverbially in Matt. 23:15, "twofold more." ¶

NT: B.199c; CB.1242a; K.–.
OT: kāphal: S.3717; HR.337a.1a; H.1019; BD.495c.
mishneh: S.4932; HR.337a.2a; H.2421c; BD.1041c.
shᵉnayim: S.8147; HR.337a.2b; H.2421a; BD.1040d.
GEN. REF.: IS.1:986; NB.–; Z.–.

B. Verb.

diploō [διπλόω, 1363], signifies to double, to repay or render twofold, Rev. 18:6. ¶

NT: B.199d; CB.–; K.–.
OT: –.
GEN. REF.: –.

DOUBLE-MINDED

dipsuchos [δίψυχος, 1374], lit. means two-souled (*dis*, twice, *psuchē*, a soul), hence, double-minded, Jas. 1:8; 4:8. ¶

NT: B.201a; CB.1242a; K.1342.
OT: –.
GEN. REF.: IS.1:986; NB.–; Z.2:160.

DOUBLE-TONGUED

dilogos [δίλογος, 1351], primarily means saying the same thing twice, or given to repetition (*dis*, twice, *logos*, a word, or speech); hence, saying a thing to one person and giving a different view of it to another, double-tongued, 1 Tim. 3:8. ¶

NT: B.198d; CB.–; K.–.
OT: –.
GEN. REF.: IS.1:986; NB.–; Z.2:160.

DOUBT (be in, make to), DOUBTFUL, DOUBTING

A. Verbs.

1. *aporeō* [ἀπορέω, 639], always used in the Middle Voice, lit. means to be without a way (*a*, negative, *poros*, a way, transit), to be without resources, embarrassed, in doubt, perplexity, at a loss, as was Herod regarding John the Baptist, Mark 6:20 (R.V., following the most authentic mss., "was much perplexed"); as the disciples were, regarding the Lord's betrayal, John 13:22, "doubting"; and regarding the absence of His body from the tomb, Luke 24:4, "were perplexed"; as was Festus, about the nature of the accusations brought against Paul, Acts 25:20, A.V. "doubted," R.V., "being perplexed"; as Paul was, in his experiences of trial, 2 Cor. 4:8, "perplexed," and, as to the attitude of the believers of the churches in Galatia towards Judaistic errors, Gal. 4:20, A.V., "I stand in doubt," R.V., "I am perplexed." Perplexity is the main idea. See PERPLEX. ¶ Cp. the noun *aporia*, "distress," Luke 21:25. ¶

NT: B.97c; CB.–; K.–.
OT: ṣārar: S.6887; HR.140a.6; H.1973,1974; BD.864d.
GEN. REF.: –.

2. *diaporeō* [διαπορέω, 1280], *dia*, asunder (intensive), and No. 1, signifies to be thoroughly perplexed, with a perplexity amounting to despair, Acts 2:12; 5:24 and 10:17, A.V., "were in doubt," "doubted," R.V., "were (was) perplexed." See also Luke 9:7 (some mss. have it in Luke 24:4, where the most authentic have No. 1). See PERPLEX. ¶

NT: B.187d; CB.–; K.–.
OT: –.
GEN. REF.: –.

3. *diakrinō* [διακρίνω, 1252]: see CONTEND and DIFFER, A, No. 2; in Acts 11:12, A.V., "nothing doubting," R.V., "making no distinction"; in Jude 22, R.V., "who are in doubt" (A.V., "making a difference," R.V., marg., "while they dispute"); in Jas. 1:6, A.V., "wavereth," R.V., "doubteth." This verb suggests, not so much weakness of faith, as lack of it, (contrast, Nos. 4 and 5).

NT: B.185a; CB.1241a; K.469.
OT: –.
GEN. REF.: IS.1:987; NB.–; Z.–.

4. *distazō* [διστάζω, 1365], to stand in two ways (*dis*, double, *stasis*, a standing), implying uncertainty which way to take, is used in Matt.

14:31 and 28:17; said of believers whose faith is small. Cp. No. 5. ¶

NT: B.200a; CB.1242a; K.–.
OT: –.
GEN. REF.: IS.1:987; NB.–; Z.–.

5. *meteōrizō* [μετεωρίζω, 3349], from *meteōros* (Eng., meteor), signifying in mid air, raised on high, was primarily used of putting a ship out to sea, or of raising fortifications, or of the rising of the wind. In the Sept., it is used, e.g., in Micah 4:1, of the exaltation of the Lord's house; in Ezek. 10:16, of the lifting up of the wings of the cherubim; in Obad. 4, of the mounting up of the eagle; in the N.T. metaphorically, of being anxious, through a distracted state of mind, of wavering between hope and fear, Luke 12:29, "neither be ye of doubtful mind" (A.V., marg., "live not in careful suspense"), addressed to those who have little faith. Cp. No. 4. The interpretation "do not exalt yourselves" is not in keeping with the context. ¶

NT: B.514a; CB.–; K.590.
OT: –.
GEN. REF.: –.

6. *psuchēn airō* [ψυχὴν αἴρω, 5590, 412], lit., to raise the breath, or to lift the soul, signifies to hold in suspense, R.V. of John 10:24 (A.V., "make us to doubt"), suggestive of "an objective suspense due to lack of light" (Warfield), through a failure of their expectations, rather than, subjectively, through unbelief. The meaning may thus be, 'How long dost Thou raise our expectations without satisfying them?'

NT: B.893b,24b; CB.1267c; K.1342.
OT: –.
GEN. REF.: –.

B. Noun.

dialogismos [διαλογισμός, 1261], expresses reasoning or questioning hesitation, 1 Tim. 2:8. See DISPUTE, A, No. 1.

NT: B.186a; CB.1241b; K.155.
OT: mahᵃshābāh: S.4284; HR.305a.2; H.767d; BD.364b.
GEN. REF.: –.

Note: For A.V., "doubtful" in Rom. 14:1 see DECISION, B, No. 2.

DOUBT (No), DOUBTLESS

pantōs [πάντως]: see ALTOGETHER, B.

Notes: (1) In 2 Cor. 12:1 the best texts have no word representing "doubtless."

(2) In Luke 11:20, the particle *ara*, A.V., "no doubt," means "then" (R.V.).

(3) In 1 Cor. 9:10 the conjunction *gar*, A.V., "no doubt," here means "assuredly," or "yea" (R.V.).

(4) In Phil. 3:8, the opening phrase means "yea, verily," as R.V.

(5) In 1 Cor. 9:2, the R.V., "at least," gives the right sense (not "doubtless," A.V.).

DOVE, TURTLE-DOVE

1. *peristera* [περιστερά, 4058], denotes a dove or pigeon, Matt. 3:16; 10:16 (indicating its proverbial harmlessness); 21:12; Mark 1:10; 11:15; Luke 2:24 ("pigeons"); 3:22; John 1:32; 2:14, 16. ¶

NT: B.651d; CB.1263c; K.830.
OT: yônāh: S.3123; HR.1126c.2a; H.854a; BD.401c.
GEN. REF.: IS.1:987; NB.156; Z.2:160.

2. *trugōn* [τρυγών, 5167], denotes a turtle-dove (from *truzō*, to murmur, to coo), Luke 2:24. ¶

NT: B.828b; CB.–; K.830.
OT: tôr: S.8449; HR.1377b.1; H.2500c; BD.1076a.
GEN. REF.: IS.1:987; NB.156; Z.–.

DOWN: see Note † p. 1

DRAG

1. *surō* [σύρω, 4951], to draw, drag, haul, is used of a net, John 21:8; of violently dragging person along, Acts 8:3, "haling"; 14:19, R.V., "dragged," A.V., "drew"; 17:6 (ditto); Rev. 12:4, A.V., "drew," R.V., "draweth." See DRAW, HALE. ¶

NT: B.794c; CB.–; K.–.
OT: –.
GEN. REF.: –.

Note: Cp. the strengthened form *katasurō*, to hale, used in Luke 12:58. ¶

2. *helkuō* (or *helkō*) [ἑλκύω or ἕλκώ, 1670], to draw, differs from *surō*, as drawing does from violent dragging. It is used of drawing a net, John 21:6, 11 (cp. No. 1, in ver. 8); Trench remarks, "At vv. 6 and 11 *helkō* (or *helkuō*) is used; for there a *drawing* of the net to a certain point is intended; by the disciples to themselves in the ship, by Peter to himself upon the shore. But at ver. 8 *helkō* gives place to *surō*: for nothing is there intended but the *dragging* of the net, which had been fastened to the ship, after it through the water" (Syn., § xxi).

This less violent significance, usually present in *helkō*, but always absent from *surō*, is seen in the metaphorical use of *helkō*, to signify drawing by inward power, by Divine impulse, John 6:44; 12:32. So in the Sept., e.g., S. of S., 1:4, and Jer. 31:3, "with lovingkindness have I drawn thee." It is used of a more vigorous action, in John 18:10, of drawing a sword; in Acts 16:19; 21:30, of forcibly drawing men to or from a place; so in Jas. 2:6, A.V., "draw," R.V., "drag." See DRAW. ¶

NT: B.251c; CB.–; K.227.
OT: shālaph: S.8025; HR.453a.9; H.2402; BD.1025b.
māshak: S.4900; HR.453a.4a; H.1257; BD.604a.
GEN. REF.: –.

DRAGON

drakōn [δράκων, 1404], denoted a mythical monster, a dragon; also a large serpent, so called because of its keen power of sight (from a root *derk—*, signifying to see). Twelve times in the Apocalypse it is used of the Devil, 12:3, 4, 7, 9, 13, 16, 17; 13:2, 4, 11; 16:13; 20:2. ¶

NT: B.206b; CB.1242b; K.186.
OT: tannîn: S.8577; HR.348b.6b; H.2528b; BD.1072c.
GEN. REF.: IS.1:990; NB.322; Z.2:162.

For **DRANK** see **DRINK**

DRAUGHT

1. *agra* [ἄγρα, 61], a hunting, catching (from *agō*, to lead), is used only in connection with fishing. In Luke 5:4 it signifies the act of catching fish; in ver. 9 it stands for the catch itself. ¶

NT: B.13a; CB.—; K.—.
OT: —.
GEN. REF.: —.

2. *aphedrōn* [ἀφεδρών, 856], a latrine, a sink, drain, is found in Matt. 15:17 and Mark 7:19. ¶

NT: B.124d; CB.—; K.—.
OT: —.
GEN. REF.: —.

For **DRAVE** and **DROVE** see **DRIVE**

DRAW (Away, Back, Nigh, On, Out, Up)

(*A*) *In the sense of dragging, pulling, or attracting:*

1. *anabibazō* [ἀναβιβάζω, 307], a causal form of *anabainō*, to go up, denotes, lit., to make go up, cause to ascend (*ana*, up, *bibazō*, to cause to mount), hence, to draw a boat up on land, Matt. 13:48. ¶

NT: B.50d; CB.—; K.—.
OT: ʿālāh: S.5927; HR.73a.3b; H.1624; BD.748a,749b.
GEN. REF.: —.

2. *helkō* [ἕλκω] is translated to draw in the A.V., of Acts 21:30 and Jas. 2:6; see DRAG, No. 2.

3. *surō* [σύρω]: see DRAG, No. 1.

4. *spaō* [σπάω, 4685], to draw or pull, is used, in the Middle Voice, of drawing a sword from its sheath, Mark 14:47; Acts 16:27. ¶

NT: B.761a; CB.—; K.—.
OT: shālaph: S.8025; HR.1281b.5; H.2402; BD.1025b.
GEN. REF.: —.

5. *anaspaō* [ἀνασπάω, 385], *ana*, up, and No. 4, to draw up, is used of drawing up an animal out of a pit, Luke 14:5 (R.V., "draw up"; A.V., "pull out"), and of the drawing up of the sheet into heaven, in the vision in Acts 11:10. ¶

NT: B.60b; CB.—; K.—.
OT: ʿālāh: S.5927; HR.82a.2; H.1624; BD.748a,749b.
GEN. REF.: —.

6. *apospaō* [ἀποσπάω, 645], *apo*, from, and No. 4, to draw away, lit., to wrench away from, is used of a sword, Matt. 26:51; of drawing away disciples into error, Acts 20:30; of Christ's withdrawal from the disciples, in Gethsemane, Luke 22:41, A.V., "was withdrawn," R.V., "was parted" (or 'was reft away from them'); of parting from a company, Acts 21:1 (A.V., "were gotten," R.V., "were parted"). See GET, PART. ¶

NT: B.98a; CB.—; K.—.
OT: nātaq: S.5423; HR.141a.2; H.1447; BD.683c.
nātash: S.5428; HR.141a.3; H.1451; BD.684c.
GEN. REF.: —.

7. *antleō* [ἀντλέω, 501], signified, primarily, to draw out a ship's bilge-water, to bale or pump out (from *antlos*, bilge-water), hence, to draw water in any way (*ana*, up, and a root, *tel—*, to lift, bear), John 2:8, 9; 4:7, 15. ¶

NT: B.76b; CB.—; K.—.
OT: shā'ab: S.7579; HR.112a.3; H.2299; BD.980b.
GEN. REF.: —.

Note: In John 4:11, "to draw with" translates the corresponding noun *antlēma*, a bucket for drawing water by a rope. ¶

8. *exelkō* [ἐξέλκω, 1828], *ek*, out of, and No. 2, to draw away, or lure forth, is used metaphorically in Jas. 1:14, of being drawn away by lust. As in hunting or fishing the game is lured from its haunt, so man's lust allures him from the safety of his self-restraint. ¶

NT: B.274a; CB.—; K.—.
OT: māshak: S.4900; HR.491a.3; H.1257; BD.604a.
nātaq: S.5423; HR.491a.4; H.1447; BD.683c.
GEN. REF.: —.

9. *anatassomai* [ἀνατάσσομαι, 392], to arrange in order, is used in Luke 1:1; R.V., "to draw up" (some interpret the word to mean to bring together from memory assisted by the Holy Spirit). ¶

NT: B.61d; CB.1235b; K.1156.
OT: —.
GEN. REF.: —.

(*B*) *In the sense of approaching or withdrawing:*

1. *engizō* [ἐγγίζω, 1448], to come near, draw night (akin to *engus*, near), is translated by the verb draw near or nigh, in the R.V., Luke 12:33, A.V., "approacheth"; Heb. 10:25, A.V., "approaching"; Luke 18:35; 19:29, 37; Acts 22:6, A.V., "was come nigh"; Luke 7:12, "came nigh"; Acts 9:3, "came near." See APPROACH.

NT: B.213c; CB.1245a; K.194.
OT: nāgash: S.5066; HR.362b.11; H.1297; BD.620c.
qārab: S.7126; HR.362b.13; H.2065; BD.897a.
GEN. REF.: —.

2. *proserchomai* [προσέρχομαι, 4334], is translated "draw near" in Heb. 4:16; 7:25, R.V., and 10:22, A.V. and R.V.; in Acts 7:31, "drew near." See COME, GO.

NT: B.713a; CB.1267a; K.257.
OT: nāgash: S.5066; HR.1213c.7; H.1297; BD.620c.
qārab: S.7126; HR.1213c.10a,b; H.2065; BD.897a.
GEN. REF.: —.

3. *prosagō* [προσάγω, 4317], used transitively, to bring to; intransitively, to draw near, is so rendered in Acts 27:27. See BRING.

NT: B.711b; CB.—; K.20.
OT: nāgash: S.5066; HR.1211a.6; H.1297; BD.620c.
qārab: S.7126; HR.1211b.11; H.2065; BD.897a.
GEN. REF.: —.

4. *hupostellō* [ὑποστέλλω, 5288], to draw back, withdraw, perhaps a metaphor from lowering a sail and so slackening the course, and hence of being remiss in holding the truth; in the Active Voice, rendered "drew back" in Gal. 2:12, R.V. (A.V., "withdrew"); in the Middle, in Heb. 10:38, "shrink back" R.V. (A.V., "draw back"); the prefix *hupo*, underneath, is here suggestive of stealth. In verse 39 the corresponding noun, *hupostolē*, is translated "of them that shrink back," R.V.; A.V., "draw back" (lit., 'of shrinking back'). In Acts 20:20, 27, "shrank," R.V. See KEEP, *Note* (6), SHRINK, SHUN, WITHDRAW. ¶

NT: B.847b; CB.—; K.1074.
OT: —.
GEN. REF.: —.

5. *aphistēmi* [ἀφίστημι]: see DEPART, A, No. 20.

6. *ginomai* [γίνομαι, 1096], to become, begin to be, is translated "drawing nigh," in John 6:19. See BECOME.

NT: B.158a; CB.1248b; K.117
OT: —.
GEN. REF.: —.

7. *epiphōskō* [ἐπιφώσκω, 2020], to dawn (lit., to make to shine upon), is said of the approach of the Sabbath, Luke 23:54 (marg., "began to dawn"); cp. Matt. 28:1. ¶ See DAWN, A, No. 3.

NT: B.304d; CB.—; K.1293.
OT: hālal: S.1984; HR.538b.1; H.499,500; BD.237c.
GEN. REF.: —.

Notes: (1) In Mark 6:53, *prosormizō*, to bring a ship (or boat), to anchor, cast anchor, land at a place (*pros*, to, *hormizō*, to moor, bring to anchorage), is translated "moored to the shore," in the R.V., for A.V., "drew." ¶

(2) In Acts 19:33, where the most authentic mss. have *sumbibazō*, the R.V. translates it "brought" (marg., "instructed"), A.V., "draw out." Some mss. have *probibazō*, to bring or drag forward. See BRING, No. 24.

DREAM (noun and verb), DREAMER

A. Nouns.

1. *onar* [ὄναρ, 3677], is a vision in sleep, in distinction from a waking vision, Matt. 1:20; 2:12, 13, 19, 22; 27:19. ¶

NT: B.569d; CB.1260c; K.690.
OT: —.
GEN. REF.: IS.1:991; NB.323; Z.2:162.

2. *enupnion* [ἐνύπνιον, 1798], is, lit., what appears in sleep (*en*, in, *hupnos*, sleep), an ordinary dream, Acts 2:17. For synonymous nouns see VISION. ¶

NT: B.270c; CB.1245b; K.1233.
OT: ḥªlôm: S.2472; HR.481b.1a; H.662; BD.321c.
ḥēlem (Aramaic): S.2493; HR.481b.1b; H.662; BD.1093a.
GEN. REF.: IS.1:991; NB.323; Z.2:162.

B. Verb.

enupniazō [ἐνυπνιάζω, 1797], akin to A, No. 2, is used in Acts 2:17, in the Passive Voice, in a phrase (according to the most authentic mss.) which means 'shall be given up to dream by dreams,' translated "shall dream dreams"; metaphorically in Jude 8, of being given over to sensuous "dreamings," R.V., A.V., "dreamers," and so defiling the flesh. ¶

NT: B.270b; CB.1245b; K.1233.
OT: ḥālam: S.2492; HR.481b.2a; H.662; BD.321b.
GEN. REF.: IS.1:991; NB.323; Z.2:162.

DRESSED

Note: This is the A.V. translation of the Passive of *geōrgeō*, Heb. 6:7, to till the ground, to practise as a farmer; R.V., "is tilled." See TILL. ¶

DRESSER

Note: For *ampelourgos*, "dresser," Luke 13:7, A.V. (R.V., "vinedresser"), see VINEDRESSER.

For DRIED see DRY, B

DRIFT

pararheō [παραρέω, 3901], lit., to flow past, glide by (*para*, by, *rheō*, to flow), is used in Heb. 2:1, where the significance is to find oneself flowing or passing by, without giving due heed to a thing, here "the things that were heard," or perhaps the salvation of which they spoke; hence the R.V., "lest haply we drift away from them," for A.V., "let them slip." The A.V. marg. "run out as leaking vessels," does not give the meaning. ¶ In the Sept., Prov. 3:21; Isa. 44:4. ¶

NT: B.621d; CB.1262b; K.—.
OT: —.
GEN. REF.: —.

DRINK (-ETH, -ER, -ING), DRANK

A. Nouns.

1. *poma* [πόμα, 4188], akin to B, No. 1, denotes the thing drunk (from a root *po*—, found in the Eng., potion; it is connected with the root *pi*—; see B, No. 3), 1 Cor. 10:4; Heb. 9:10. ¶

NT: B.690b; CB.1266a; K.840.
OT: mishteh: S.4960; HR.1186a.1; H.2477c; BD.1059c.
GEN. REF.: IS.1:992; NB.—; Z.2:170.

2. *posis* [πόσις, 4213], akin to B, No. 1, suggests the act of drinking, John 6:55 (where it is practically equivalent to No. 1); Rom. 14:17, "drinking," R.V.; Col. 2:16. ¶

NT: B.694b; CB.1266a; K.841.
OT: mishteh: S.4960; HR.1195c.1; H.2477c; BD.1059c.
GEN. REF.: IS.1:992; NB.–; Z.2:170.

3. *sikera* [σίκερα, 4608], is a strong, intoxicating drink, made from any sweet ingredients, whether grain, vegetables, or the juice of fruits, or a decoction of honey; "strong drink," Luke 1:15. ¶ In the Sept., Lev. 10:9; Num. 6:3; 28:7; Deut. 14:26; 29:6; Isa. 5:11, 22; 24:9; 28:7; 29:9.

NT: B.750b; CB.–; K.–.
OT: shēkār: S.7941; HR.1266c.1; H.2388a; BD.1016b.
GEN. REF.: IS.1:992; NB.1332; Z.2:170.

B. Verbs.

1. *pinō* [πίνω, 4095], to drink, is used chiefly in the Gospels and in 1 Cor., whether literally (most frequently), or figuratively, (*a*) of drinking of the Blood of Christ, in the sense of receiving eternal life, through His Death, John 6:53, 54, 56; (*b*) of receiving spiritually that which refreshes, strengthens and nourishes the soul, John 7:37; (*c*) of deriving spiritual life from Christ, John 4:14, as Israel did typically, 1 Cor. 10:4; (*d*) of sharing in the sufferings of Christ humanly inflicted, Matt. 20:22, 23; Mark 10:38, 39; (*e*) of participating in the abominations imparted by the corrupt religious and commercial systems emanating from Babylon, Rev. 18:3; (*f*) of receiving Divine judgment, through partaking unworthily of the Lord's Supper, 1 Cor. 11:29; (*g*) of experiencing the wrath of God, Rev. 14:10; 16:6; (*h*) of the earth's receiving the benefits of rain, Heb. 6:7.

NT: B.658c; CB.1265a; K.840.
OT: shātāh: S.8354; HR.1134a.3; H.2477; BD.1059a.
GEN. REF.: IS.1:992; NB.–; Z.2:170.

2. *methuō* [μεθύω, 3184], from *methu*, wine, to be drunk, is used in John 2:10 in the Passive Voice, and is translated in the R.V., "have drunk freely"; A.V., "have well drunk." See DRUNK.

NT: B.499c; CB.1258c; K.576.
OT: shākar: S.7937; HR.907c.4a-d; H.2388; BD.1016a.
GEN. REF.: IS.1:992; NB.1332; Z.2:170.

3. *potizō* [ποτίζω, 4222], to give to drink, to make to drink, is used (*a*) in the material sense, in Matt. 10:42; 25:35, 37, 42 (here of ministering to those who belong to Christ and thus doing so virtually to Him); 27:48; Mark 9:41; 15:36; Luke 13:15 ("to watering"); Rom. 12:20; 1 Cor. 3:7, 8; (*b*) figuratively, with reference to teaching of an elementary character, 1 Cor. 3:2, "I fed (you with milk)"; of spiritual watering by teaching the word of God, 3:6; of being provided and satisfied by the power and blessing of the Spirit of God, 1 Cor. 12:13; of the effect upon the nations of partaking of the abominable mixture, provided by Babylon, of paganism with details of the Christian faith, Rev. 14:8. See FEED, WATER. ¶

NT: B.695d; CB.1266b; K.841.
OT: shāqāh: S.8248; HR.1197c.3; H.2452; BD.1052b.
GEN. REF.: IS.1:992; NB.–; Z.2:170.

4. *sumpinō* [συμπίνω, 4844], to drink together (*sun*, with, and B, No. 1), is found in Acts 10:41. ¶

NT: B.779c; CB.–; K.–.
OT: shātāh: S.8354; HR.1305b.1; H.2477; BD.1059a.
GEN. REF.: IS.1:992; NB.–; Z.2:170.

5. *hudropoteō* [ὑδροποτέω, 5202], to drink water (*hudōr*, water, *poteō*, to drink), is found in 1 Tim. 5:23, R.V., "be (no longer) a drinker of water." ¶

NT: B.832d; CB.–; K.–.
OT: shātāḥ: S.8354; HR.1381a.1; H.2477; BD.1059a.
GEN. REF.: IS.1:992; NB.–; Z.2:170.

DRIVE, DRIVEN, DRAVE, DROVE

1. *ekballō* [ἐκβάλλω, 1544], denotes, lit., to cast forth, with the suggestion of force (*ek*, out, *ballō*, to cast); hence to drive out or forth. It is translated "driveth" in Mark 1:12, R.V., "driveth forth." In John 2:15 for the A.V., "drove," the R.V. has "cast," the more usual translation. See CAST, No. 5.

NT: B.237b; CB.1243b; K.91.
OT: gārash: S.1644; HR.420c.3a,b; H.388; BD.176c.
shālak: S.7993; HR.420c.21a; H.2398; BD.1020d.
GEN. REF.: –.

2. *ekdiōkō* [ἐκδιώκω, 1559], to chase away, drive out (*ek*, out, *diōkō*, to pursue), is used in 1 Thess. 2:15, R.V., "drave out," A.V., "have persecuted." Some mss. have this verb for *diōkō*, in Luke 11:49. ¶

NT: B.239a; CB.1243c; K.–.
OT: –.
GEN. REF.: –.

3. *elaunō* [ἐλαύνω, 1643], signifies to drive, impel, urge on. It is used of rowing, Mark 6:48 and John 6:19; of the act of a demon upon a man, Luke 8:29; of the power of winds upon ships, Jas. 3:4; and of storms upon mists, 2 Pet. 2:17, A.V., "carried," R.V., "driven." See also CARRY, Note (2), ROW.

NT: B.248c; CB.–; K.–.
OT: shayiṭ: S.7885; HR.448c.4; H.2344c; BD.1002b.
GEN. REF.: –.

4. *apelaunō* [ἀπελαύνω, 556], *apo*, from, and No. 3, to drive from, is used in Acts 18:16. ¶

NT: B.83c; CB.–; K.–.
OT: shālaḥ: S.7971; HR.120b.2; H.2394; BD.1018a.
GEN. REF.: –.

5. *exōtheō* [ἐξωθέω, 1856], to thrust out (*ek*, out, *ōtheō*, to push, thrust), is translated "thrust" in Acts 7:45, R.V. (A.V., "drave"); in 27:39, of driving a storm-tossed ship ashore (R.V., "drive," A.V., "thrust"). Cp. No. 6. See THRUST. ¶

NT: B.280a; CB.—; K.—.
OT: nādaḥ: S.5080; HR.502b.7b,c; H.1304; BD.623a.
GEN. REF.: —.

6. *pherō* [φέρω, 5342], to bear, is translated "driven" in Acts 27:15, 17, of being borne in a storm-tossed ship. See BEAR, etc.

NT: B.854d; CB.1264a; K.1252.
OT: —.
GEN. REF.: —.

7. *diapherō* [διαφέρω, 1308], lit., to bear through (*dia*, through, and No. 6), in Acts 27:27 signifies to be borne hither and thither (R.V., "were driven to and fro"; A.V., "up and down"). See BETTER (be), No. 1.

NT: B.190b; CB.—; K.1252.
OT: —.
GEN. REF.: —.

8. *anemizō* [ἀνεμίζω, 416], to drive by the wind (*anemos*, wind), is used in Jas. 1:6. ¶

NT: B.64c; CB.—; K.—.
OT: —.
GEN. REF.: —.

Note: For "let . . . drive," Acts 27:15, see GIVE, No. 3.

DROP (Noun)

thrombos [θρόμβος, 2361], a large, thick drop of clotted blood (etymologically akin to *trephō*, to curdle), is used in Luke 22:44, in the plural, in the narrative of the Lord's agony in Gethsemane. ¶

NT: B.364b; CB.—; K.—.
OT: —.
GEN. REF.: IS.1:993; NB.—; Z.—.

DROPSY

hudrōpikos [ὑδρωπικός, 5203], dropsical, suffering from dropsy (*hudrops*, dropsy), is found in Luke 14:2, the only instance recorded of the healing of this disease by the Lord. ¶

NT: B.832d; CB.—; K.—.
OT: —.
GEN. REF.: IS.1:994; NB.—; Z.2:134.

DROWN

1. *buthizō* [βυθίζω, 1036], to plunge into the deep, to sink (*buthos*, bottom, the deep, the sea), akin to *bathos*, depth, and *abussos*, bottomless, and Eng., bath, is used in Luke 5:7 of the sinking of a boat; metaphorically in 1 Tim. 6:9, of the effect of foolish and hurtful lusts, which "drown men in destruction and perdition." See SINK ¶

NT: B.148c; CB.—; K.—.
OT: —.
GEN. REF.: —.

2. *katapinō* [καταπίνω, 2666], lit., to drink down (*pinō*, to drink, prefixed by *kata*, down), signifies to swallow up (R.V., in Heb. 11:29, for A.V., "were drowned"). It is elsewhere translated by the verb to swallow or swallow up, except in 1 Pet. 5:8, "devour." See DEVOUR, No. 3, SWALLOW.

NT: B.416b; CB.1254b; K.841.
OT: bāla': S.1104; HR.741c.1a-e; H.251; BD.118a.
GEN. REF.: —.

3. *katapontizō* [καταποντίζω, 2670], to throw into the sea (*kata*, down, *pontos*, the open sea), in the Passive Voice, to be sunk in, to be drowned, is translated "were drowned," in Matt. 18:6, A.V. (R.V., "should be sunk"); elsewhere in 14:30, "(beginning) to sink." See SINK. ¶

NT: B.417a; CB.—; K.—.
OT: bāla': S.1104; HR.742a.1; H.251; BD.118a.
ṭāba': S.2883; HR.742a.2; H.789; BD.371c.
shāṭaph: S.7857; HR.742a.3; H.2373; BD.1009a.
GEN. REF.: IS.1:994; NB.—; Z.—.

DRUNK (-EN, be), DRUNKARD, DRUNKENNESS

A. Verbs.

1. *methuō* [μεθύω, 3184], signifies to be drunk with wine (from *methu*, mulled wine; hence Eng., mead, honey-wine; originally it denoted simply a pleasant drink). For John 2:10 see under DRINK. The verb is used of being intoxicated in Matt. 24:49; Acts 2:15; 1 Cor. 11:21; 1 Thess. 5:7*b*; metaphorically, of the effect upon men of partaking of the abominations of the Babylonish system, Rev. 17:2; of being in a state of mental intoxication, through the shedding of men's blood profusely, ver. 6. ¶

NT: B.499c; CB.1258c; K.576.
OT: shākar: S.7937; HR.907c.4a-d; H.2388; BD.1016a.
GEN. REF.: IS.1:993,994; NB.1331; Z.2:170.

2. *methuskō* [μεθύσκω, 3182], signifies to make drunk, or to grow drunk (an inceptive verb, marking the process of the state expressed in No. 1), to become intoxicated, Luke 12:45; Eph. 5:18; 1 Thess. 5:7*a*. ¶

NT: B.499b; CB.1258c; K.576.
OT: shākar: S.7937; HR.907c.4a-d; H.2388; BD.1016a.
GEN. REF.: IS.1:993,994; NB.1331; Z.2:170.

B. Adjective.

methusos [μέθυσος, 3183], drunken (cp. No. 2), is used as noun, in the singular, in 1 Cor. 5:11, and in the plural, in 6:10, "drunkard," "drunkards." ¶

NT: B.499b; CB.1258c; K.576.
OT: sābā': S.5433; HR.908a.1; H.1455; BD.684d.
shikkôr: S.7910; HR.908a.2; H.2388b; BD.1016c.
GEN. REF.: IS.1:993,994; NB.1331; Z.2:170.

C. Noun.

methē [μέθη, 3178], strong drink (akin to *methu*, wine, see under A. 1, above), denotes drunkenness, habitual intoxication, Luke 21:34; Rom. 13:13; Gal. 5:21. ¶

NT: B.498d; CB.1258c; K.576.
OT: –.
GEN. REF.: IS.1:993,994; NB.1331; Z.2:170.

DRY

A. Adjectives.

1. *xēros* [ξηρός, 3584], is used (*a*) naturally, of dry land, Heb. 11:29; or of land in general, Matt. 23:15, "land"; or of physical infirmity, "withered," Matt. 12:10; Mark 3:3; Luke 6:6, 8; John 5:3; (*b*) figuratively, in Luke 23:31, with reference to the spiritual barrenness of the Jews, in contrast to the character of the Lord. Cp. Ps. 1:3; Isa. 56:3; Ezek. 17:24; 20:47. See LAND, WITHERED. ¶

NT: B.548c; CB.1273b; K.–.
OT: ḥārābāh: S.2724; HR.957b.1; H.731e; BD.351c.
yabbāshāh: S.3004; HR.957b.2a; H.837b; BD.387a.
GEN. REF.: –.

2. *anudros* [ἄνυδρος, 504], waterless (*a*, negative, *n*, euphonic, *hudōr*, water), is rendered "dry" in Matt. 12:43, A.V., and Luke 11:24 (R.V., "waterless"); "without water" in 2 Pet. 2:17 and Jude 12. See WATER. ¶

NT: B.76c; CB.–; K.–.
OT: ṣiyyāh: S.6723; HR.112a.6; H.1909a; BD.851a.
yᵉshîmôn: S.3452; HR.112a.3; H.927b; BD.445b.
yabbāshāh: S.3004; HR.112a.2; H.837b; BD.387a.
GEN. REF.: –.

B. Verb.

xērainō [ξηραίνω, 3583], akin to A. 1, to dry, dry up, make dry, wither, is translated "dried" (of physical infirmity), in Mark 5:29; of a tree, in the A.V. of Mark 11:20 (R.V., "withered away"); of water, in Rev. 16:12. It is translated "ripe" (R.V., "over-ripe") in Rev. 14:15, of a harvest (used figuratively of the gathered nations against Jerusalem at the end of this age); "pineth away," in Mark 9:18. See OVER-RIPE, PINE AWAY, RIPE, WITHER.

NT: B.548c; CB.1273b; K.–.
OT: yābēsh: S.3001; HR.957a.2; H.837; BD.386b.
ḥārēb: S.2717; HR.957a.1; H.731,732; BD.351a.
GEN. REF.: –.

DUE

A. Adjective.

idios [ἴδιος, 2398], one's own, is applied to *kairos*, a season, in Gal. 6:9, "in due season," i.e., in the season Divinely appointed for the reaping. So in 1 Tim. 2:6, "the testimony to be borne in its own (A.V., 'due') times (seasons)"; 6:15, "in its own (*idios*) times (seasons)"; similarly in Tit. 1:3. See BUSINESS, B.

NT: B.369c; CB.1252c; K.–.
OT: –.
GEN. REF.: –.

Note: For *axios*, "the due reward," see REWARD, *Note* (1).

B. Verbs.

1. *opheilō* [ὀφείλω, 3784], signifies to owe, to be indebted, especially financially, Matt. 18:30, R.V., "that which was due"; 18:34, "all that was due." See BEHOVE, BOUND (to be).

NT: B.598d; CB.1261a; K.746.
OT: ḥôb: S.2326; HR.1039a.2; H.614a; BD.295a.
GEN. REF.: –.

2. *dei* [δεῖ, 1163], an impersonal verb signifying "it is necessary," is translated "was due" in Rom. 1:27, R.V. (A.V., "was meet"). See BEHOVE.

NT: B.172a; CB.1240b; K.140.
OT: –.
GEN. REF.: –.

C. Noun.

opheilē [ὀφειλή, 3782], akin to B, No. 1, is rendered "dues" in Rom. 13:7. In 1 Cor. 7:3, R.V., it is translated "her due" (the A.V. "due benevolence" follows another reading).

NT: B.598c; CB.1261a; K.746.
OT: –.
GEN. REF.: –.

Notes: (1) In the phrases "in due season" in Matt. 24:45; Luke 12:42; Rom. 5:6 (lit., 'according to time'), and "in due time," 1 Pet. 5:6, there is no word representing "due" in the original, and the phrases are, lit., "in season," "in time."

(2) For the phrase "born out of due time," in 1 Cor. 15:8, see BEGET, B, No. 2.

DULL

A. Adjective.

nōthros [νωθρός, 3576], slow, sluggish, indolent, dull (the etymology is uncertain), is translated "dull" in Heb. 5:11 (in connection with *akoē*, hearing; lit., 'in hearings'); "sluggish," in 6:12. See SLOTHFUL, SLUGGISH. ¶ In the Sept., Prov. 22:29. ¶ Cp. *nōthrokardios*, "slow of heart" (*kardia*, the heart), Prov. 12:8. ¶

NT: B.547c; CB.–; K.661.
OT: ḥāshōk: S.2823; HR.956b.1; H.769b; BD.365b.
GEN. REF.: –.

Note: In Luke 24:25 "slow (of heart)" translates the synonymous word *bradus*. Of these Trench says (Syn. § civ), "*Bradus* differs from the words with which it is here brought into comparison, in that no moral fault or blame is necessarily involved in it; so far indeed is it from this, that of the three occasions on which it is used in the N.T. two are in honour; for to be 'slow' to evil things, to rash speaking, or to anger (Jas. 1:19, twice), is a grace, and not the contrary. . . . There is a deeper, more inborn sluggishness implied in *nōthros*, and this bound up as it were in the very life, more than in either of the other words of this group." Trench compares and contrasts *argos*, idle, but this word is not strictly synonymous with the other two. ¶

B. Adverb.

bareōs [βαρέως, 917], heavily, with difficulty (*barus*, heavy), is used with *akouō*, to hear, in Matt. 13:15, and Acts 28:27 (from Isa. 6:10), lit., to hear heavily, to be dull of hearing. ¶ In the Sept., Gen. 31:35 (lit., 'bear it not heavily'); Isa. 6:10. ¶

NT: B.133c; CB.1238c; K.—.
OT: kābēd: S.3513; HR.190c.2; H.943; BD.457a.
GEN. REF.: —.

DUMB

A. Adjectives.

1. *alalos* [ἄλαλος, 216], lit., speechless (*a*, negative, and *laleō*, to speak), is found in Mark 7:37; 9:17, 25. ¶ In the Sept., Ps. 38:13. ¶

NT: B.34d; CB.1234b; K.—.
OT: 'ālam: S.481; HR.52b.1a; H.102; BD.47d.
'illēm: S.483; HR.52b.1b; H.102c; BD.48a.
GEN. REF.: IS.1:995; NB.316; Z.2:134.

2. *aphōnos* [ἄφωνος, 880], lit., voiceless, or soundless (*a*, negative, and *phōnē*, a sound), has reference to voice, Acts 8:32; 1 Cor. 12:2; 2 Pet. 2:16, while *alalos* has reference to words. In 1 Cor. 14:10 it is used metaphorically of the significance of voices or sounds, "without signification." ¶ In the Sept. Isa. 53:7. ¶

NT: B.128a; CB.—; K.—.
OT: 'ālam: S.481; HR.187b.1; H.102; BD.47d.
GEN. REF.: IS.1:995; NB.316; Z.2:134.

3. *kophos* [κωφός], denotes blunted or dulled; see DEAF.

B. Verb.

siōpaō [σιωπάω, 4623], from *siōpē*, silence, to be silent, is used of Zacharias' dumbness, Luke 1:20. See PEACE (hold one's).

NT: B.752c; CB.—; K.—.
OT: ḥāshāh: S.2814; HR.1267c.7; H.768; BD.364c.
ḥārash: S.2790; HR.1267c.6; H.760; BD.361a.
dāmam: S.1826; HR.1267c.3; H.439; BD.198d.
GEN. REF.: IS.1:995; NB.316; Z.2:134.

DUNG

1. *skubalon* [σκύβαλον, 4657], denotes refuse, whether (*a*) excrement, that which is cast out from the body, or (*b*) the leavings of a feast, that which is thrown away from the table. Some have derived it from *kusibalon* (with *metathesis* of k and s), "thrown to dogs"; others connect it with a root meaning "shred." Judaizers counted Gentile Christians as dogs, while they themselves were seated at God's banquet. The Apostle, reversing the image, counts the Judaistic ordinances as refuse upon which their advocates feed, Phil. 3:8. ¶

NT: B.758a; CB.1269b; K.1052.
OT: —.
GEN. REF.: IS.—; NB.328; Z.2:171.

2. *koprion* [κόπριον, —], manure, Luke 13:8, used in the plural with *ballō*, to throw, is translated by the verb to dung. Some mss. have the accusative case of the noun *kopria*, a dunghill. See below. ¶

NT: B.443d; CB.1255c; K.—.
OT: dōmen: S.1828; HR.779a.1; H.441a; BD.199b.
GEN. REF.: IS.1:995; NB.328; Z.2:171.

DUNGHILL

kopria [κοπρία], a dunghill, is found in Luke 14:35. ¶

For **DURE** see under **WHILE,** *Note* (1)

DURING: see Note †, p. 1.

For **DURST** see **DARE**

DUST

A. Nouns.

1. *chous*, or *choos* [χοῦς or χόος, 5522], from *cheō*, to pour, primarily, earth dug out, an earth heap, then, loose earth or dust, is used in Mark 6:11 and Rev. 18:19. ¶

NT: B.884b; CB.1240a; K.—.
OT: 'āphār: S.6083; HR.1473b.3; H.1664a; BD.779c.
GEN. REF.: IS.1:998; NB.328; Z.2:172.

2. *koniortos* [κονιορτός, 2868], raised or flying dust (*konia*, dust, *ornumi*, to stir up), is found in Matt. 10:14; Luke 9:5; 10:11; Acts 13:51; 22:23. ¶

NT: B.443b; CB.—; K.—.
OT: 'ābāq: S.80; HR.777c.1a; H.11a; BD.7b.
'āphār: S.6083; HR.777c.6; H.1664a; BD.779c.
GEN. REF.: IS.1:998; NB.328; Z.2:172.

B. Verb.

likmaō [λικμάω, 3039], primarily, to winnow (from *likmos*, a winnowing-fan), hence, to scatter as chaff or dust, is used in Matt. 21:44 and Luke 20:18, R.V., "scatter as dust," A.V., "grind to powder." There are indications in the papyri writings that the word came to denote to ruin, to destroy. ¶

NT: B.474d; CB.—; K.535.
OT: zārāh: S.2219; HR.878b.1a-c; H.579; BD.279d.
GEN. REF.: —.

DUTY

opheilō [ὀφείλω, 3784], to owe, to be indebted, is translated "it was our duty," in Luke 17:10, lit., 'we owe (ought) to do'; so in Rom. 15:27, A.V., "their duty is"; R.V., "they owe it." See BEHOVE, BOUND.

NT: B.598d; CB.1261a; K.746.
OT: ḥôb: S.2326; HR.1039a.2; H.614a; BD.295a.
GEN. REF.: IS.1:998; NB.—; Z.—.

DWELL, DWELLERS, DWELLING (place)

A. Verbs.

1. *oikeō* [οἰκέω, 3611], to dwell (from *oikos*, a house), to inhabit as one's abode, is derived from the Sanskrit, *viç*, a dwelling place (the Eng. termination —wick is connected). It is used (*a*) of God as dwelling in light, 1 Tim. 6:16; (*b*) of the indwelling of the Spirit of God in the believer, Rom. 8:9, 11, or in a church, 1 Cor. 3:16; (*c*) of the indwelling of sin, Rom. 7:20; (*d*) of the absence of any good thing in the flesh of the believer, Rom. 7:18; (*e*) of the dwelling together of those who are married, 1 Cor. 7:12, 13. ¶

NT: B.557a; CB.1260b; K.674.
OT: yāshab: S.3427; HR.968a.4a; H.922; BD.442a.
tēbel: S.8398; HR.968a.7d; H.835h; BD.385c.
GEN. REF.: IS.1:999; NB.—; Z.2:172.

2. *katoikeō* [κατοικέω, 2730], *kata*, down, and No. 1, the most frequent verb with this meaning, properly signifies to settle down in a dwelling, to dwell fixedly in a place. Besides its literal sense, it is used of (*a*) the indwelling of the totality of the attributes and powers of the Godhead in Christ, Col. 1:19; 2:9; (*b*) the indwelling of Christ in the hearts of believers ('may make a home in your hearts'), Eph. 3:17; (*c*) the dwelling of Satan in a locality, Rev. 2:13; (*d*) the future indwelling of righteousness in the new heavens and earth, 2 Pet. 3:13. It is translated "dwellers" in Acts 1:19; 2:9; "inhabitants" in Rev. 17:2, A.V. (R.V.. "they that dwell"), "inhabiters" in Rev. 8:13 and 12:12, A.V. (R.V., "them that dwell").

Cp. the nouns *katoikēsis* (below), *katoikia*, habitation, Acts 17:26 ¶; *katoikētērion*, a habitation, Eph. 2:22; Rev. 18:2. ¶ Contrast *paroikeō*, to sojourn, the latter being temporary, the former permanent. See HABITATION, INHABITANT.

NT: B.424a; CB.1254c; K.674.
OT: yāshab: S.3427; HR.751c.11a; H.922; BD.442a.
GEN. REF.: IS.1:999; NB.—; Z.2:172.

3. *katoikizō* [κατοικίζω, —], to cause to dwell, is said of the act of God concerning the Holy Spirit in Jas. 4:5, R.V. (some mss. have No. 2). ¶

NT: B.424c; CB.1254c; K.674.
OT: yāshab: S.3427; HR.755c.2a-c; H.922; BD.442a.
shākan: S.7931; HR.755c.5; H.2387; BD.1014d.
GEN. REF.: IS.1:999; NB.—; Z.2:172.

4. *enoikeō* [ἐνοικέω, 1774], lit., to dwell in (*en*, in, and No. 1), is used, with a spiritual significance only, of (*a*) the indwelling of God in believers, 2 Cor. 6:16; (*b*) the indwelling of the Holy Spirit, Rom. 8:11; 2 Tim. 1:14; (*c*) the indwelling of the word of Christ, Col. 3:16; (*d*) the indwelling of faith, 2 Tim. 1:5; (*e*) the indwelling of sin in the believer, Rom. 7:17. ¶

NT: B.267b; CB.1245b; K.—.
OT: yāshab: S.3427; HR.476a.4; H.922; BD.442a.
mishkān: S.4908; HR.476a.6; H.2387c; BD.1015c.
gûr: S.1481; HR.476a.3; H.330,332; BD.157c.
GEN. REF.: IS.1:999; NB.—; Z.2:172.

5. *perioikeō* [περιοικέω, 4039], *peri*, around, and No. 1, to dwell around, be a neighbour, is used in Luke 1:65. ¶ Cp. *perioikos*, a neighbour, Luke 1:58. ¶

NT: B.648d; CB.—; K.—.
OT: —.
GEN. REF.: IS.1:999; NB.—; Z.—.

6. *sunoikeō* [συνοικέω, 4924], *sun*, with, and No. 1, to dwell with, is used in 1 Pet. 3:7. ¶

NT: B.791c; CB.—; K.—.
OT: yābam: S.2992; HR.1317c.4; H.836; BD.386a.
GEN. REF.: IS.1:999; NB.—; Z.—.

7. *enkatoikeō* [ἐγκατοικέω, 1460], *en*, in, and No. 2, to dwell among, is used in 2 Pet. 2:8. ¶

NT: B.216a; CB.—; K.—.
OT: —.
GEN. REF.: IS.1:999; NB.—; Z.—.

8. *menō* [μένω, 3306], to abide, remain, is translated to dwell, in the A.V. of John 1:38, 39; 6:56; 14:10, 17; Acts 28:16. The R.V. adheres throughout to the verb to abide. See ABIDE.

NT: B.503c; CB.1258b; K.581.
OT: yāshab: S.3427; HR.910a.7; H.922; BD.442a.
GEN. REF.: IS.1:999; NB.—; Z.2:172.

9. *skēnoō* [σκηνόω, 4637], to pitch a tent (*skēnē*), to tabernacle, is translated "dwelt," in John 1:14, A.V., R.V. marg., "tabernacled"; in Rev. 7:15, A.V., "shall dwell," R.V. "shall spread (His) tabernacle"; in Rev. 12:12; 13:6; 21:3, "dwell." See TABERNACLE.

NT: B.755c; CB.1269a; K.1040.
OT: shākēn: S.7931; HR.1273a.2; H.2387; BD.1014d.
GEN. REF.: IS.1:999; NB.—; Z.2:172.

10. *kataskēnoō* [κατασκηνόω, 2681], to pitch one's tent (*kata*, down, *skēnē*, a tent), is translated "lodge" in Matt. 13:32; Mark 4:32; Luke 13:19; in Acts 2:26, R.V., "dwell," A.V., "rest." ¶

NT: B.418c; CB.1254b; K.1040.
OT: shākēn, shākan: S.7931; HR.744b.5a,b; H.2387; BD.1014d.
GEN. REF.: IS.1:999; NB.—; Z.2:172.

11. *embateuō* [ἐμβατεύω, 1687], primarily, to step in, or on (from *embainō*, to enter), hence (*a*) to frequent, dwell in, is used metaphorically in Col. 2:18, R.V., "dwelling in" (marg., "taking

his stand upon"); (*b*) with reference to the same passage, alternatively, to invade, to enter on; perhaps used in this passage as a technical term of the mystery religions denoting the entrance of the initiated into the new life (A.V., "intruding into"). A suggested alternative reading involves the rendering "treading on air," i.e., indulging in vain speculations, but evidences in the papyri writings make the emendation unnecessary. ¶

NT: B.254b; CB.–; K.232.
OT: –.
GEN. REF.: –.

12. *kathēmai* [κάθημαι, 2521], to sit down, is translated "dwell," in Luke 21:35. See SET, SIT.

NT: B.389b; CB.1254c; K.386.
OT: yāshab: S.3427; HR.700b.3a; H.922; BD.442a.
GEN. REF.: IS.1:999; NB.–; Z.2:172.

13. *kathizō* [καθίζω, 2523], to sit down, denotes to dwell, in Acts 18:11 (R.V., "dwelt," for A.V., "continued").

NT: B.389d; CB.1254c; K.386.
OT: yāshab: S.3427; HR.701c.4a,b; H.922; BD.442a.
GEN. REF.: IS.1:999; NB.–; Z.2:172.

14. *astateō* [ἀστατέω, 790], to wander about (*a*, negative, *histēmi*, to stand), to have no fixed dwelling-place, is used in 1 Cor. 4:11. ¶ Cp. *akatastatos*, unstable, Jas. 1:8; 3:8. ¶ *akatastasia*, revolution, confusion, e.g., 1 Cor. 14:33.

NT: B.117b; CB.–; K.86.
OT: –.
GEN. REF.: –.

B. Nouns.

1. *paroikia* [παροικία, 3940], denotes a sojourning, Acts 13:17, lit., 'in the sojourning,' translated "when they sojourned," R.V. (A.V., "dwelt as strangers"); in 1 Pet. 1:17, "sojourning." ¶

NT: B.629a; CB.1262b; K.788.
OT: māgôr: S.4033; HR.1071c.2a; H.330c; BD.158c.
GEN. REF.: IS.1:999; NB.–; Z.–.

2. *katoikēsis* [κατοίκησις, 2731], akin to A, No. 2, a dwelling, a habitation, is used in Mark 5:3. ¶

NT: B.424c; CB.–; K.–.
OT: môshāb: S.4186; HR.755b.1a; H.922c; BD.444b.
yāshab: S.3427; HR.755b.1b; H.922; BD.442a.
GEN. REF.: IS.1:999; NB.–; Z.2:172.

Note: Cp. *oikia*, and *oikos*, a house, *oekēma*, a prison, *katoikia*, a habitation (see A, No. 2).

3. *misthōma* [μίσθωμα, 3410], primarily, a price, a hire (akin to *misthos*, wages, hire, and *misthoō*, to let out for hire), is used in Acts 28:30 to denote a hired dwelling. ¶

NT: B.523d; CB.1259a; K.–.
OT: –.
GEN. REF.: –.

For **DYING** see **DEADNESS**

DYSENTERY

dusenterion [δυσεντέριον, 1420], whence Eng., dysentery, is so translated in Acts 28:8, R.V., for A.V. "bloody flux" (*enteron* denotes an intestine), ¶

NT: B.209c; CB.–; K.–.
OT: –.
GEN. REF.: IS.1:1000; NB.328; Z.2:135.

E

EACH, EACH MAN, EACH ONE

1. *hekastos* [ἕκαστος, 1538], each or every, is used of any number separately, either (*a*) as an adjective qualifying a noun, e.g., Luke 6:44; John 19:23; Heb. 3:13, where "day by day," is, lit., 'according to each day;' or, more emphatically with *heis,* one, in Matt. 26:22; Luke 4:40; 16:5; Acts 2:3,6; 20:31; 1 Cor. 12:18; Eph. 4:7, 16, R.V., "each (several)," for A.V., "every"; Col. 4:6; 1 Thess. 2:11; 2 Thess. 1:3; (*b*) as a distributive pronoun, e.g., Acts 4:35; Rom. 2:6; Gal. 6:4; in Phil. 2:4, it is used in the plural; some mss. have it thus in Rev. 6:11. The repetition in Heb. 8:11 is noticeable, "every man" (i.e., everyone). Prefixed by the preposition *ana,* apiece (a colloquialism), it is used, with stress on the individuality, in Rev. 21:21, of the gates of the heavenly city, "each one of the several," R.V.; in Eph. 5:33, preceded by *kath' hena*, 'by one,' it signifies "each (one) his own."

NT: B.236C; CB.1249c; K.–.
OT: –
GEN. REF.: IS.–

2. The phrase *hen kath' hen,* lit., 'one by one,' is used in Rev. 4:8, "each one of them."

EACH OTHER

allēlōn [ἀλλήλων, 240], a reciprocal pronoun, preceded by the preposition *meta,* with, signifies "with each other," Luke 23:12, R.V., for A.V., "together." Similarly in 24:14 *pros allēlous*, where *pros* suggests greater intimacy. See One Another.

NT: B.39c; CB.1234c; K.–.
OT: –.
GEN. REF.: –.

EAGLE

aetos [ἀετός, 105], an eagle (also a vulture), is perhaps connected with *aēmi*, to blow, as of the wind, on account of its windlike flight. In Matt. 24:28 and Luke 17:37 the vultures are probably intended. The meaning seems to be that, as these birds of prey gather where the carcase is, so the judgments of God will descend upon the corrupt state of humanity. The figure of the eagle is used in Ezek. 17 to represent the great powers of Egypt and Babylon, as being employed to punish corrupt and faithless Israel. Cp. Job 39:30; Prov. 30:17. The eagle is mentioned elsewhere in the N.T. in Rev. 4:7; 8:13 (R.V.); 12:14. There are eight species in Palestine. ¶

NT: B.19d; CB.1233b; K.–.
OT: nesher: S.5404; HR.28c.1a; H.1437; BD.676d.
GEN. REF.: IS.2:1; NB.154; Z.2:175.

EAR (of the body)

1. *ous* [οὖς, 3775], Latin *auris,* is used (*a*) of the physical organ, e.g., Luke 4:21; Acts 7:57; in Acts II:22, in the plural with *akouō,* to hear, lit., 'was heard into the ears of someone,' i.e., came to the knowledge of; similarly, in the singular, Matt. 10:27, in familiar private conversation; in Jas. 5:4 the phrase is used with *eiserchomai,* to enter into; in Luke 1:44, with *ginomai,* to become, to come; in Luke 12:3, with *lalein,* to speak and *pros,* to; (*b*) metaphorically, of the faculty of perceiving with the mind, understanding and knowing, Matt. 13:16; frequently with *akouō,* to hear, e.g., Matt. 11:15; 13:9, 43; Rev. 2 and 3, at the close of each of the messages to the churches; in Matt. 13:15 and Acts 28:27, with *bareōs*, heavily, of being slow to understand and obey; with a negative in Mark 8:18; Rom. 11:8; in Luke 9:44 the lit. meaning is 'put those words into your ears,' i.e., take them into your mind and keep them there; in Acts 7:51 it is used with *aperitmētos,* uncircumcised. As seeing is metaphorically associated with conviction, so hearing is with obedience (*hupakoē,* lit., hearing under; the Eng., "obedience" is etymologically 'hearing over against,' i.e., with response in the hearer).

NT: B.595c; CB.1261b; K.744.
OT: ōzen: S.241; HR.1034c.1a; H.57a; BD.23d.
GEN. REF.: IS.2:2; NB.329; Z.2:176.

2. *ōtion* [ὠτίον, 5621], a diminutive of No. 1, but without the diminutive force, it being a common tendency in everyday speech to apply a diminutive form to most parts of the body, is used in Matt. 26:51; Mark 14;47 (in some mss.); Luke 22:51; John 18:10 (in some mss.) and ver. 26, all with reference to the ear of Malchus. ¶

NT: B.900b; CB.–; K.744.
OT: 'ōzen: S.241; HR.1496c.1; H.57a; BD.23d.
GEN. REF.: IS.2:2; NB.329; Z.2:176.

Note: The most authentic mss. have the authentic mss. have the alternative diminutive *ōtarion,* in Mark 14:47 and John 18:10. ¶

3. *akoē* [ἀκοη, 189], hearing, akin to *akouō,* denotes (*a*) the sense of hearing, e.g., 1 Cor. 12:17; 2 Pet. 2:8; (*b*) that which is heard, a report, e.g., Matt. 4:24; (*c*) the physical organ, Mark 7:35, standing for the sense of hearing;

so in Luke 7:1, R.V., for A.V., "audience"; Acts 17:20; 2 Tim. 4:3, 4 (in ver. 3, lit., 'being tickled as to the ears'); (*d*) a message or teaching, John 12:38; Rom. 10:16, 17; Gal. 3:2, 5; 1 Thess. 2:13; Heb. 4:2, R.V., "(the word) of hearing," for A.V., "(the word) preached." See FAME, HEARING, PREACH, REPORT, RUMOUR.

NT: B.30d; CB.1234b; K.34.
OT: shāma: S.8085; HR.44b.1a; H.2412; BD.1033b.
sh^{e}mûāh: S.8052; HR.44b.1a; H.2412d; BD.1035b.
shēma': S.8088; HR.44b.1f; H.2412b; BD.1034d.
GEN. REF.: IS.2.2; NB.329; Z.2:176.

Note: In Matt. 28:14, the verb *akouō* is used with the preposition *epi*, upon or before (or *hupo*, by, in some mss.), lit., 'if this comes to a hearing before the governor.'

EAR (of corn)

stachus [στάχυς, 4719], is found in Matt. 12:1; Mark 2:23; 4:28 ("ear," twice); Luke 6:1. The first part of the word is derived from the root *sta*— found in parts of the verb *histēmi*, to cause to stand. it is used as a proper name in Rom. 16:9. ¶

NT: B.765c; CB.1269c; K.—.
OT: shibbōlet: S.7641; HR.1287b.3; H.2316b,c; BD.987c.
qāmāh: S.7054; HR.1287b.2; H.1999b; BD.876b.
GEN. REF.: IS.—; NB.—; Z.2:177.

EARLY

A. Noun.

orthros [ὄρθρος, 3722], denotes daybreak, dawn (cp. Lat. *orior*, to rise). Used with the adverb *batheōs*, deeply, in Luke 24:1, it means "at early dawn" (R.V.). In John 8:2 it is used in the genitive case, *orthrou*, at dawn, i.e., "early in the morning." In Acts 5:21, it is used with the article and preceded by the preposition *hupo*, under, or about, lit., 'about the dawn,' "about daybreak," R.V. (for A.V., "early in the morning."). ¶

NT: B.580c; CB.—; K.—.
OT: shaḥar: S.7837; HR.1011b.3; H.2369a; BD.1007b.
shākam: S.7925; HR.1011b.5e; H.2386; BD.1014c.
GEN. REF.: IS.2:3; NB.—; Z.—.

B. Adjectives.

1. *orthrinos* [ὀρθρινός, 3720], early, akin to A., is a later form of *orthrios*. It is found, in the most authentic mss., in Luke 24:22, of the women at the sepulchre, lit., 'early ones' (some texts have the form *orthrios*, at daybreak). ¶

NT: B.580c; CB.—; K.—.
OT: shākam: S.7925; HR.1011b.1; H.2386; BD.1014c.
GEN. REF.: IS.2:3; NB.—; Z.—.

2. *prōimos* [πρώϊμος, 4406], or *proimos*, a longer and later form of *proios*, pertaining to the morning, is formed from *prō*, before (cp. *prōtos*, first), and used in Jas. 5:7, of the early rain. ¶

NT: B.706d; CB.1266c; K.—.
OT: yôreh: S.3138; HR.1235a.2b; H.910a; BD.435c.
GEN. REF.: IS.2:3; NB.—; Z.—.

C. Adverb.

prōi [πρωΐ, 4404], early in the day, at morn, is derived from *prō*, before (see B, No. 2, above). In Mark 16:2, A.V., it is translated "early in the morning"; in Mark 16:9 and John 18:28; 20:1, "early"; in Matt. 16:3; 20:1; 21:18; Mark 1:35; 11:20; 13:35; 15:1, "in the morning"; in Acts 28:23, "(from) morning." See MORNING. ¶

NT: B.724d; CB.1266c; K.—.
OT: bōqer: S.1242; HR.1234b.1; H.274c; BD.133c.
GEN. REF.: IS.2:3; NB.—; Z.—.

Note: In Matt. 20:1, hama, at once, is rendered "early."

EARNEST (Noun)

arrabōn [ἀρραβών, 728], originally, earnest-money deposited by the purchaser and forfeited if the purchase was not completed, was probably a Phœnician word, introduced into Greece. In general usage it came to denote a pledge or earnest of any sort; in the N.T. it is used only of that which is assured by God to believers; it is said of the Holy Spirit as the Divine pledge of all their future blessedness, 2 Cor. 1:22; 5:5; in Eph. 1:14, particularly of their eternal inheritance. ¶ In the Sept., Gen. 38:17, 18, 20. ¶ In modern Greek *arrabōna* is an engagement ring.

NT: B.109b; CB.1237c; K.80.
OT: 'ērābôn: S.6162; HR.160a.1; H.1686b; BD.786d.
GEN. REF.: IS.2:577; NB.329; Z.2:177.

EARNEST, EARNESTNESS, EARNESTLY

A. Noun.

spoudē [σπουδή, 4710], akin to *speudō*, denotes haste, Mark 6:25; Luke 1:39; hence, "earnestness," 2 Cor. 8:7, R.V., for A.V., "diligence," and ver. 8, for A.V., "forwardness"; in 7:12, "earnest care," for A.V., "care"; in 8:16, "earnest care." See BUSINESS, CARE, CAREFULNESS, DILIGENCE, FORWARDNESS, HASTE.

NT: B.763d; CB.1269c; K.1069.
OT: —.
GEN. REF.: —.

B. Adjective.

spoudaios [σπουδαῖος, 4705], akin to A, denotes active, diligent, earnest, 2 Cor. 8:22, R.V., "earnest," for A.V., "diligent"; in the latter part of the verse the comparative degree, *spoudaioteros*, is used, R.V., "more earnest," for A.V., "more diligent"; in ver. 17, R.V., in the superlative sense, "very earnest," for A.V., "more forward." See DILIGENT, FORWARD. ¶

NT: B.763c; CB.1269c; K.1069.
OT: —.
GEN. REF.: —.

C. Adverbs.

1. *ektenōs* [ἐκτενῶς, 1619], earnestly (*ek*, out, *teinō*, to stretch; Eng., tension, etc.), is used in Acts 12:5, "earnestly," R.V., for A.V., "without ceasing" (some mss. have the adjective *ektenēs*, earnest; in 1 Pet. 1:22, "fervently." The idea suggested is that of not relaxing in effort, or acting in a right spirit. See FERVENTLY. ¶

NT: B.245d; CB.1244a; K.—.
OT: ḥāzqāh: S.2394; HR.443a.1; H.636d; BD.306a.
GEN. REF.: —.

2. *ektenesteron* [ἐκτενέστερον, 1617], the comparative degree of No. 1, used as an adverb in this neuter form, denotes more earnestly, fervently, Luke 22:44. ¶

NT: B.245c; CB.—; K.219.
OT: —.
GEN. REF.: —.

3. *spoudaiōs* [σπουδαίως, 4709], akin to B, signifies with haste, or with zeal, earnestly, Luke 7:4, R.V., "earnestly," for A.V., "instantly"; in 2 Tim. 1:17, R.V., and Tit. 3:13, "diligently"; ¶ in Phil. 2:28, the comparative *spoudaioterōs*, R.V., "the more diligently," A.V., "the more carefully." See CAREFULLY, DILIGENTLY, INSTANTLY. ¶

NT: B.763d; CB.—; K.—.
OT: —
GEN. REF.: —.

D. Adverbial Phrase.

en ekteneia [ἐν ἐκτενείᾳ, 1616], lit., 'in earnestness,' cp. C, No. 1, is translated "earnestly" in Acts 26:7, R.V., for A.V., "instantly." See INSTANTLY. ¶

NT: B.245c; CB.—; K.219.
OT: —
GEN. REF.: —.

Notes: (1) For the phrase "earnest expectation," Rom. 8:19 and Phil. 1:20, see EXPECTATION.

(2) In 1 Cor. 12:31; 14:1, 39, *zēloō*, to be zealous about, is translated "desire earnestly." See DESIRE.

(3) In 2 Pet. 3:12, *speudō* is translated "earnestly desiring," for A.V., "hasting unto." See HASTEN.

(4) In Jude 3, *epagōnizō*, to contend earnestly, is so translated. ¶

(5) In Jas. 5:17 the dative case of the noun *proseuchē* is translated "earnestly" (A.V.), in connection with the corresponding verb, lit., 'he prayed with prayer' (R.V., "fervently"), implying persevering continuance in prayer with fervour. Cp., e.g., Ps. 40:1, lit., 'in waiting I waited.' See FERVENT.

(6) *Atenizō*, akin to C, No. 1, to fix the eyes upon, gaze upon, is translated "earnestly looked" in Luke 22:56, A.V. (R.V., "looking stedfastly"); in Acts 3:12, A.V., "look ye earnestly," R.V., "fasten ye your eyes on"; in Acts 23:1, A.V., "earnestly beholding," R.V., "looking stedfastly on."

(7) In Heb. 2:1, *prosechō*, to give heed, is used with the adverb *perissoterōs*, more abundantly, to signify "to give the more earnest heed"; lit., 'to give heed more exceedingly.' For the verb see ATTEND, GIVE, No. 16, HEED, REGARD.

EARTH

1. *gē* [γῆ, 1093], denotes (*a*) earth as arable land, e.g., Matt. 13:5, 8, 23; in 1 Cor. 15:47 it is said of the earthly material of which "the first man" was made, suggestive of frailty; (*b*) the earth as a whole, the world, in contrast, whether to the heavens, e.g., Matt. 5:18, 35, or to Heaven, the abode of God, e.g., Matt. 6:19, where the context suggests the earth as a place characterized by mutability and weakness; in Col. 3:2 the same contrast is presented by the word "above"; in John 3:31 (R.V., "of the earth," for A.V., "earthly") it describes one whose origin and nature are earthly and whose speech is characterized thereby, in contrast with Christ as the One from heaven; in Col. 3:5 the physical members are said to be "upon the earth," as a sphere where, as potential instruments of moral evils, they are, by metonymy, spoken of as the evils themselves; (*c*) the inhabited earth, e.g., Luke 21:35; Acts 1:8; 8:33; 10:12; 11:6; 17:26; 22:22; Heb. 11:13; Rev. 13:8. In the following the phrase "on the earth" signifies 'among men,' Luke 12:49; 18:8; John 17:4; (*d*) a country, territory, e.g., Luke 4:25; John 3:22; (*e*) the ground, e.g., Matt. 10:29; Mark 4:26, R.V., "(upon the) earth," for A.V., "(into the) ground"; (*f*) land, e.g., Mark 4:1; John 21:8, 9, 11. Cp. Eng. words beginning with *ge*—, e.g., geodetic, geodesy, geology, geometry, geography. See COUNTRY, GROUND, LAND, WORLD.

NT: B.157c; CB.1248a; K.116.
OT: ʼereṣ: S.776; HR.240c.2c; H.167; BD.75d.
GEN. REF.: IS.2:3; NB.329; Z.2:177.

2. *oikoumenē* [οἰκουμένη, 3625], the present participle, Passive Voice, of *oikeō*, to dwell, inhabit, denotes the inhabited earth. It is translated "world" in every place where it has this significance, save in Luke 21:26, A.V., where it is translated "earth." See WORLD.

NT: B.561b; CB.1260c; K.674.
OT: —.
GEN. REF.: IS.2:3; NB.—; Z.—.

Note: For *epigeios*, translated "on earth" in Phil. 2:10, *ostrakinos*, "of earth," 2 Tim. 2:20, and *katachthonios*, "under the earth," Phil. 2:10, ¶ see EARTHEN.

EARTHEN, EARTHLY, EARTHY

1. *ostrakinos* [ὀστράκινος, 3749], signifies made of earthenware or clay (from *ostrakon*, baked clay, potsherd, shell; akin to *osteon*, a bone), 2 Tim. 2:20, "of earth"; 2 Cor. 4:7, "earthen." ¶

NT: B.587c; CB.1261b; K.—.
OT: ḥeres: S.2789; HR.1023b.2; H.759a; BD.360a.
GEN. REF.: IS.2:4; NB.—; Z.—.

2. *epigeios* [ἐπίγειος, 1919], on earth (*epi*, on, *gē*, the earth), is rendered "earthly" in John 3:12; 2 Cor. 5:1; Phil. 3:19; Jas. 3:15; in Phil. 2:10, "on earth," R.V.; "terrestrial" in 1 Cor. 15:40 (twice). See TERRESTRIAL. ¶

NT: B.290c; CB.1245c; K.116.
OT: —.
GEN. REF.: IS.2:4; NB.—; Z.—.

3. *choïkos* [χοϊκός, 5517], denotes "earthy," made of earth, from *chous*, soil, earth thrown down or heaped up, 1 Cor. 15:47, 48, 49. ¶

NT: B.883a; CB.1240a; K.1318.
OT: —.
GEN. REF.: —.

4. *katachthonios* [καταχθόνιος, 2709], under the earth, subterranean (*kata*, down, *chthōn*, the ground, from a root signifying that which is deep), is used in Phil. 2:10. ¶

NT: B.420c; CB.1254a; K.421.
OT: —.
GEN. REF.: —.

EARTHQUAKE

seismos [σεισμός, 4578], a shaking, a shock, from *seiō*, to move to and fro, to shake, chiefly with the idea of concussion (Eng., seismic, seismology, seismometry), is used (*a*) of a tempest in the sea, Matt. 8:24; (*b*) of earthquakes, Matt. 24:7; 27:54; 28:2; Mark 13:8; Luke 21:11; Acts 16:26; Rev. 6:12; 8:5; 11:13 (twice), 19; 16:18 (twice). See TEMPEST. ¶

NT: B.746b; CB.1268c; K.1014.
OT: ra'ash: S.7494; HR.1262b.2; H.2195a; BD.950b.
GEN. REF.: IS.2:4; NB.330; Z.2:178.

EASE, EASED

A. Verb.

anapauō [ἀναπαύω, 373], signifies to cause or permit one to cease from any labour or movement so as to recover strength. It implies previous toil and care. Its chief significance is that of taking, or causing to take, rest; it is used in the Middle Voice in Luke 12:19, "take (thine) ease," indicative of unnecessary, self-indulgent relaxation. In the papyri it is used technically, as an agricultural term. Cp. *anapausis*, rest. See REFRESH, REST.

NT: B.58d; CB.1235b; K.56.
OT: nûaḥ: S.5117; HR.80b.3a-c; H.1323; BD.628a.
rābaṣ: S.7257; HR.80b.6; H.2109; BD.918b.
GEN. REF.: IS.2:5; NB.—; Z.—.

B. Noun.

anesis [ἄνεσις, 425], denotes a letting loose, relaxation, easing, it is connected with *aniēmi*, to loosen, relax (*ana*, back, and *hiēmi*, to send). It signifies rest, not from toil, but from endurance and suffering. Thus it is said (*a*) of a less vigorous condition in imprisonment, Acts 24:23, "indulgence," A.V., "liberty"; (*b*) relief from anxiety, 2 Cor. 2:13; 7:5, "relief" (A.V., "rest"); (*c*) relief from persecutions, 2 Thess. 1:7, "rest"; (*d*) of relief from the sufferings of poverty, 2 Cor. 8:13, "be eased," lit., '(that there should be) easing for others (trouble to you).' Cp. the synonymous word *anapausis*, cessation or rest (akin to A). See INDULGENCE, LIBERTY, RELIEF, REST. ¶ In the Sept., 2 Chron. 23:15. ¶

NT: B.65b; CB.—; K.60.
OT: —.
GEN. REF.: IS.2:5; NB.—; Z.—.

For **EASILY** see **EASY**

EAST

anatole [ἀνατολή, 395], primarily a rising, as of the sun and stars, corresponds to *anatellō*, to make to rise, or, intransitively, to arise, which is also used of the sunlight, as well as of other objects in nature. In Luke 1:78 it is used metaphorically of Christ as "the Dayspring," the One through Whom light came into the world, shining immediately into Israel, to dispel the darkness which was upon all nations. Cp. Mal. 4:2. Elsewhere it denotes the east, as the quarter of the sun's rising, Matt. 2:1, 2, 9; 8:11; 24:27; Luke 13:29; Rev. 7:2; 16:12; 21:13. The east in general stands for that side of things upon which the rising of the sun gives light. In the heavenly city itself, Rev. 21:13, the reference to the east gate points to the outgoing of the influence of the city eastward. See DAYSPRING. ¶

NT: B.62b; CB.1235b; K.57.
OT: mizrāḥ: S.4217; HR.83c.2; H.580c; BD.280d.
qādîm: S.6921; HR.83c.5a; H.1988d; BD.870b.
qedem: S.6924; HR.83c.5c; H.1988a; BD.868d.
GEN. REF.: IS.2:5; NB.330; Z.2:180.

EASTER

pascha [πάσχα, 3957], mistranslated "Easter" in Acts 12:4, A.V., denotes the Passover (R.V.). The phrase "after the Passover" signifies after the whole festival was at an end. The term Easter is not of Christian origin. It is another form of *Astarte*, one of the titles of the Chaldean goddess, the queen of heaven.

The festival of Pasch held by Christians in post-apostolic times was a continuation of the Jewish feast, but was not instituted by Christ, nor was it connected with Lent. From this Pasch the Pagan festival of Easter was quite distinct and was introduced into the apostate Western religion, as part of the attempt to adapt Pagan festivals to Christianity. See PASSOVER.

NT: B.633b; CB.1262c; K.797.
OT: pesaḥ: S.6453; HR.1103a.1; H.1786a; BD.820a.
GEN. REF.: IS.2:6; NB.330; Z.2:180.

EASY, EASIER, EASILY

1. *chrēstos* [χρηστός, 5543], primarily signifies fit for use, able to be used (akin to *chraomai*, to use), hence, good, virtuous, mild, pleasant (in contrast to what is hard, harsh, sharp, bitter). It is said (*a*) of the character of God as kind, gracious, Luke 6:35; 1 Pet. 2:3; good, Rom. 2:4, where the neuter of the adjective is used as a noun, "the goodness" (cp. the correspoonding noun *chrēstotēs*, "goodness," in the same verse); of the yoke of Christ, Matt. 11:30, "easy" (a suitable rendering would be 'kindly'); (*c*) of believers, Eph. 4:32; (*d*) of things, as wine, Luke 5:39, R.V., "good," for A.V., "better" (cp. Jer. 24:3, 5, of figs); (*e*) ethically, of manners, 1 Cor. 15:33. See GOOD, GRACIOUS, KIND. ¶

NT: B.886a; CB.1240a; K.1320.
OT: ṭôb: S.2896; HR.1475a.1a; H.793a; BD.373c.
GEN. REF.: –.

2. *eukopōteros* [εὐκοπώτερος, 2123], the comparative degree of *eukopos*, easy, with easy labour (*eu*, well, *kopos*, labour), hence, of that which is easier to do, is found in the Synoptists only, Matt. 9:5; 19:24; Mark 2:9; 10:25; Luke 5:23; 16:17; 18:25. ¶

NT: B.321d; CB.–; K.–.
OT: –.
GEN. REF.: –.

Notes: (1) The adverb "easily" is included in the translation of *euperistatos* in Heb. 12:1, "easily beset," lit., "the easily besetting sin," probably a figure from a garment, 'easily surrounding,' and therefore easily entangling. See BESET.

(2) In 1 Cor. 13:5, A.V., "is not easily provoked," there is no word in the original representing "easily"; R.V., "is not provoked."

(3) For "easy to be entreated" see INTREAT. For "easy to be understood" see UNDERSTAND.

EAT, EAT WITH, EATING

A. Verbs.

1. *esthiō* [ἐσθίω, 2068], signifies to eat (as distinct from *pinō*, to drink); it is a lengthened form from *edō* (Lat., *edō*; cp. Eng., edible); in Heb. 10:27, metaphorically, "devour"1 it is said of the ordinary use of food and drink, 1 Cor. 9:7; 11:22; of partaking of food at table, e.g., Mark 2:16; of revelling, Matt. 24:49; Luke 12:45. Cp. the strengthened form *katesthiō*, and the verb *sunesthiō*, below. See DEVOUR.

NT: B.312b; CB.1246c; K.262.
OT: 'ākal: S.398; HR.554a.1a; H.85; BD.37a.
GEN. REF.: IS.2:6; NB.–; Z.2:581.

2. *phagō* [φάγω, 5315], to eat, devour, consume, is obsolete in the present and other tenses, but supplies certain tenses which are wanting in No. 1, above. In Luke 8:55 the A.V. has "(to give her) meat," the R.V. "(that something be given her) to eat." The idea that this verb combines both eating and drinking, while No. 1 differentiates the one from the other, is not borne out in the N.T. The word is very frequent in the Gospels and is used eleven times in 1 Cor. See also No. 3. See MEAT.

NT: B.312b; CB.–; K.–.
OT: 'ākal: S.398; HR.554a.1a; H.85; BD.37a.
GEN. REF.: IS.2:6; NB.–; Z.2:581.

3. *trōgō* [τρώγω, 5176], primarily, to gnaw, to chew, stresses the slow process; it is used metaphorically of the habit of spiritually feeding upon Christ, John 6:54, 56, 57, 58 (the aorists here do not indicate a definite act, but view a series of acts seen in perspective); of the constant custom of eating in certain company, John 13:18; of a practice unduly engrossing the world, Matt. 24:38.

In John 6, the change in the Lord's use from the verb *esthiō* (*phagō*) to the stronger verb *trōgō*, is noticeable. The more persistent the unbelief of His hearers, the more difficult His language and statements became. In vv. 49 to 53 the verb *phagō* is used; in 54, 58, *trōgō* (in ver. 58 it is put into immediate contrast with *phagō*). The use of *trōgō* in Matt. 24:38 and John 13:18 is a witness against pressing into the meaning of the word the sense of munching or gnawing; it had largely lost this sense in its common usage. ¶

NT: B.829b; CB.1273a; K.1191.
OT: –.
GEN. REF.: IS.–; NB.–; Z.2:581.

4. *geuō* [γεύω, 1089], primarily, to cause to taste, to give one a taste of, is used in the Middle Voice and denotes (*a*) to taste, its usual meaning; (*b*) to take food, to eat, Acts 10:10; 20:11; 23:14; the meaning to taste must not be pressed in these passages, the verb having acquired the more general meaning. As to whether Acts 20:11 refers to the Lord's Supper or to an ordinary meal, the addition of the words "and eaten" is perhaps a sufficient indication that the latter is referred to here, whereas ver. 7, where the

single phrase "to break bread" is used, refers to the Lord's Supper. A parallel instance is found in Acts 2:43, 46. In the former verse the phrase "the breaking of bread," unaccompanied by any word about taking food, clearly stands for the Lord's Supper; whereas in ver. 46 the phrase "breaking bread at home" is immediately explained by "they did take their food," indicating their ordinary meals. See TASTE.

NT: B.153d; CB.—; K.—.
OT: ṭā'am: S.2938; HR.240a.2; H.815; BD.380d.
GEN. REF.: —.

5. *bibrōskō* [*βιβρώσκω*, 977], to eat, is derived from a root, *bor*—, to devour (likewise seen in the noun *brōma*, food, meat; cp. Eng., carnivorous, voracious, from Lat. *vorax*. This verb is found in John 6:13. The difference between this and *phagō*, No. 2, above, may be seen perhaps in the fact that whereas in the Lord's question to Philip in ver. 5, *phagō* intimates nothing about a full supply, the verb *bibrōskō*, in ver. 13, indicates that the people had been provided with a big meal, of which they had partaken eagerly. ¶

NT: B.141c; CB.—; K.—.
OT: 'ākal: S.398; HR.219c.1; H.85; BD.37a.
GEN. REF.: IS.2:6; NB.—; Z.2:581.

6. *kataphagō* [*καταφάγω*, 2719], signifies to eat up (*kata*, used intensively, and No. 2), John 2:17; Rev. 10:9, 10; elsewhere it is translated "devour," as also is *katesthiō* (see No. 1). See DEVOUR.

NT: B.422c; CB.—; K.—.
OT: 'ākal: S.398; HR.749b.1a; H.85; BD.37a.
GEN. REF.: IS.2:6; NB.—; Z.2:581.

7. *korennumi* [*κορέννυμι*, 2880], to satiate, to satisfy, as with food, is used in the Middle Voice in Acts 27:38, "had eaten enough"; in 1 Cor. 4:8, "ye are filled." See FILL. ¶

NT: B.444c; CB.—; K.—.
OT: —.
GEN. REF.: —.

8. *sunesthiō* [*συνεσθίω*, 4906], to eat with (*sun*, with, and No. 1), is found in Luke 15:2; Acts 10:41; 11:3; 1 Cor. 5:11; Gal. 2:12. ¶

NT: B.788b; CB.—; K.—.
OT: 'ākal: S.398; HR.1314a.1; H.85; BD.37a.
bārāh: S.1262; HR.1314a.2; H.281; BD.136a.
GEN. REF.: IS.2:6; NB.—; Z.2:581.

9. *nomēn echō* [*νομὴν ἔχω* (*nomē*), 3542], is a phrase consisting of the noun *nomē*, denoting (*a*) pasturage, (*b*) growth, increase, and *echō*, to have. In John 10:9 the phrase signifies to find pasture (*a*). In 2 Tim. 2:17, with the meaning (*b*), the phrase is, lit., 'will have growth,' translated "will eat," i.e., 'will spread like a gangrene.' It is used in Greek writings, other than the N.T., of the spread of a fire, and of ulcers. See PASTURE. ¶

NT: B.541a; CB.1260a; K.—.
OT: —.
GEN. REF.: —.

Note: The verb *metalambanō*, to take a part or share of anything with others, to partake of, share, is translated "did eat," in Acts 2:46, corrected in the R.V. to "did take"; a still more suitable rendering would be 'shared,' the sharing of food being suggested; cp. *metadidōmi*, to share, e.g., Luke 3:11.

B. Nouns.

1. *brōsis* [*βρῶσις*, 1035], akin to A, No. 5, denotes (*a*) the act of eating, e.g., Rom. 14:17; said of rust, Matt. 6:19, 20; or, more usually, (*b*) that which is eaten, food (like *brōma*, food), meat, John 4:32; 6:27, 55; Col. 2:16; Heb. 12:16 ("morsel of meat"); "food," 2 Cor. 9:10; "eating," 1 Cor. 8:4. See FOOD, MEAT, RUST. ¶

NT: B.148b; CB.1239b; K.111.
OT: 'ākal: S.398; HR.231c.1b; H.85; BD.37a.
ma'akāl: S.3978; HR.231c.1f; H.85d; BD.38b.
GEN. REF.: IS.2:6; NB.—; Z.2:581.

2. *prosphagion* [*προσφάγιον*, 4371], primarily a dainty or relish (especially cooked fish), to be eaten with bread (*pros*, to, and A, No. 2), then, fish in general, is used in John 21:5, "Have ye aught to eat?" (A.V., "have ye any meat)"). Moulton remarks that the evidences of the papyri are to the effect that *prosphagion*, "is not so broad a word as 'something to eat.' The apostles had left even loaves behind them once, Mark 8:14; they might well have left the 'relish' on this occasion. It would normally be fish; cp. Mark 6:38" (Gram. of N.T. Greek, Vol. 1, p. 170). ¶

NT: B.719c; CB.—; K.—.
OT: —.
GEN. REF.: IS.2:6; NB.—; Z.—.

C. Adjective.

brōsimos [*βρώσιμος*, 1034], akin to A, No. 5, and B., signifying eatable, is found in Luke 24:41, R.V., appropriately, "to eat," for the A.V., "meat." ¶ In the Sept., Lev. 19:23; Neh. 9:25; Ezek. 47:12. ¶

NT: B.148b; CB.1239b; K.—.
OT: ma'akāl: S.3978; HR.231c.1; H.85d; BD.38b.
GEN. REF.: IS.2:6; NB.—; Z.2:581.

EDGE, EDGED

A. Noun.

stoma [*στόμα*, 4750], the mouth (cp. Eng., stomach, from *stomachos*, 1 Tim. 5:23), has a secondary and figurative meaning in reference to the edge of a sharp instrument, as of a sword, Luke 21:24; Heb. 11:34 (cp. the Sept., e.g., Gen. 34:26; Jud. 18:27). See FACE, MOUTH.

NT: B.769d; CB.1270a; K.1089.
OT: peh: S.6310; HR.1292b.1; H.1738; BD.804d.
GEN. REF.: IS.2:18; NB.—; Z.—.

B. Adjective.

distomos [δίστομος, 1366], lit., double-mouthed (*dis*, twice, and A.), two-edged, is used of a sword with two edges, Heb. 4:12; Rev. 1:16; 2:12. ¶ In the Sept., Judg. 3:16; Psa. 149:6; Prov. 5:4. ¶

NT: B.200a; CB.1242a; K.—.
OT: piyyôt: S.6366; HR.337b.2a; H.1738; BD.805b.
GEN. REF.: —.

EDIFICATION, EDIFY, EDIFYING

A. Noun.

oikodomē [οἰκοδομή, 3619], denotes (*a*) the act of building (*oikos*, a home, and *demō*, to build); this is used only figuratively in the N.T., in the sense of edification, the promotion of spiritual growth (lit., the things of building up), Rom. 14:19; 15:2; 1 Cor. 14:3, 5, 12, 26, e.g.; (*b*) a building, edifice, whether material, Matt. 24:1, e.g., or figurative, of the future body of the believer, 2 Cor. 5:1, or of a local church, 1 Cor. 3:9, or the whole Church, "the body of Christ," Eph. 2:21. See BUILDING.

NT: B.558a; CB.1260b; K.674.
OT: bānāh: S.1129; HR.972c.2a; H.255; BD.124a.
mibneh: S.4011; HR.972c.2b; H.255c; BD.125d.
GEN. REF.: IS.2:18; NB.—; Z.2:201.

B. Verb.

oikodomeō [οἰκοδομέω, 3618], lit., to build a house (see above), (*a*) usually signifies to build, whether literally, or figuratively; the present participle, lit., 'the (ones) building,' is used as a noun, "the builders," in Matt. 21:42; Mark 12:10; Luke 20:17; Acts 4:11 (in some mss.; the most authentic have the noun *oikodomos*); 1 Pet. 2:7; (*b*) is used metaphorically, in the sense of edifying, promoting the spiritual growth and development of character of believers, by teaching or by example, suggesting such spiritual progress as the result of patient labour. It is said (1) of the effect of this upon local churches, Acts 9:31; 1 Cor. 14:4; (2) of the individual action of believers towards each other, 1 Cor. 8:1; 10:23; 14:17; 1 Thess. 5:11; (3) of an individual in regard to himself, 1 Cor. 14:4. In 1 Cor. 8:10, where it is translated "emboldened," the Apostle uses it with pathetic irony, of the action of a brother in "building up" his brother who had a weak conscience, causing him to compromise his scruples; 'strengthened,' or 'confirmed,' would be suitable renderings. See BUILD, EMBOLDEN.

NT: B.558a; CB.1260b; K.674.
OT: bānāh: S.1129; HR.970c.1a; H.255; BD.124a.
GEN. REF.: IS.2:18; NB.—; Z.2:201.

EFFECT (of none)

1. *akuroō* [ἀκυρόω, 208], signifies to render void, deprive of force and authority (from *a*, negative, and *kuros*, might, authority; *kurios*, a lord, is from the same root), the opposite to *kuroō*, to confirm (see CONFIRM). It is used of making void the Word of God, Matt. 15:6; Mark 7:13 (A.V., "making of none effect"), and of the promise of God to Abraham as not being deprived of authority by the Law 430 years after, Gal. 3:17, "disannul." *Kuroō* is used in verse 15. See DISANNUL, VOID. ¶

NT: B.34b; CB.—; K.494.
OT: —.
GEN. REF.: —.

2. *katargeō* [καταργέω, 2673], to reduce to inactivity, to render useless, is translated to make of none effect, in Rom. 3:3, 31; 4:14; Gal. 3:17 (cp. *akuroō*, No. 1, in the same verse), and in the A.V. of Gal. 5:4, R.V., "ye are severed" (from Christ). For the meaning and use of the word see ABOLISH and DESTROY.

NT: B.417b; CB.1254b; K.76.
OT: —.
GEN. REF.: —.

3. *kenoō* [κενόω, 2758], to make empty, to empty, is translated "should be made of none effect" in 1 Cor. 1:17, A.V. (R.V. "made void"); it is used (*a*) of the Cross of Christ, there; (*b*) of Christ, in emptying Himself, Phil. 2:7; (*c*) of faith, Rom. 4:14; (*d*) of the Apostle Paul's glorying in the Gospel ministry, 1 Cor. 9:15; (*e*) of his glorying on behalf of the church at Corinth, 2 Cor. 9:3. See EMPTY, VAIN, VOID. ¶

NT: B.428a; CB.1255a; K.426.
OT: 'āmal: S.535; HR.759b.1; H.114; BD.51b.
GEN. REF.: —.

Note: In Rom. 9:6 the verb *ekpiptō*, lit., to fall out of, as of a ship falling out of its course (cp. the same word in Acts 27:17, "were driven"), is translated "hath taken none effect," A.V. (R.V., "hath come to nought"). See NOUGHT.

EFFECTUAL

A. Adjective.

energēs [ἐνεργής, 1756), denotes active, powerful in action (*en*, in, *ergon*, work; Eng. "energy"; the word "work" is derived from the same root). It is translated "effectual" in 1 Cor. 16:9, of the door opened for the Gospel in Ephesus, and made effectual in the results of entering it; and in Philm. 6, of the fellowship of Philemon's faith "in the knowledge of every good thing" (R.V.). In Heb. 4:12 it describes the Word of God as "active," R.V. (A.V.,

"powerful"), i.e., full of power to achieve results. See ACTIVE, POWERFUL. ¶
NT: B.265d; CB.1245a; K.251.
OT: —.
GEN. REF.: —.

B. Verb.

energeō [ἐνεργέω, 1754], to put forth power, be operative, to work (its usual meaning), is rendered by the verb to work effectually, or to be effectual, in the A.V. of 2 Cor. 1:6; Gal. 2:8 and 1 Thess. 2:13; in each case the R.V. translates it by the simple verb to work (past tense, "wrought"). In Jas. 5:16 the R.V. omits the superfluous word "effectual," and translates the sentence "the supplication of a righteous man availeth much in its working," the verb being in the present participial form. Here the meaning may be 'in its inworking,' i.e., in the effect produced in the praying man, bringing him into line with the will of God, as in the case of Elijah. For a fuller treatment of the word see WORK. See also DO, MIGHTY, SHEW, *Note* (11).
NT: B.265b; CB.1245a; K.251.
OT: pā'al: S.6466; HR.473a.2a; H.1792; BD.821b.
pō'al: S.6467; HR.473a.2b; H.1792a; BD.821c.
GEN. REF.: —.

Note: The noun *energeia*, working, is translated "effectual working," in the A.V. of Eph. 3:7, and 4:16.

EFFEMINATE

malakos [μαλακός, 3120], soft, soft to the touch (Lat., *mollis*, Eng., mollify, emollient, etc., are from the same root), is used (*a*) of raiment, Matt. 11:8 (twice); Luke 7:25; (*b*) metaphorically, in a bad sense, 1 Cor. 6:9, "effeminate," not simply of a male who practises forms of lewdness, but persons in general, who are guilty of addiction to sins of the flesh, voluptuous. ¶
NT: B.488d; CB.—; K.—.
OT: —.
GEN. REF.: —.

EFFULGENCE

apaugasma [ἀπαύγασμα, 541], radiance, effulgence, is used of light shining from a luminous body (*apo*, from, and *augē*, brightness). The word is found in Heb. 1:3, where it is used of the Son of God as "being the effulgence of His glory." The word "effulgence" exactly corresponds (in its Latin form) to *apaugasma*. The glory of God expresses all that He is in His nature and His actings and their manifestation. The Son, being one with the Father in Godhood, is in Himself, and ever was, the shining forth of the glory, manifesting in Himself all that God is and does, all, for instance, that is involved in His being "the very image of His substance," and in His creative acts, His sustaining power, and in His making purification of sins, with all that pertains thereto and issues from it. ¶
NT: B.82b; CB.1236b; K.87.
OT: —.
GEN. REF.: —.

EGG

ōon [ᾠόν, 5609], denotes an egg (Lat., *ovum*), Luke 11:12. ¶
NT: B.896a; CB.—; K.—.
OT: bêṣāh: S.1000; HR.1493b.1; H.218a; BD.101b.
GEN. REF.: IS.2:27; NB.—; Z.2:223.

EIGHT, EIGHTEEN, EIGHTH

oktō [ὀκτώ, 3638], eight (Lat., *octo, octavus*; cp. Eng., octagon, octave, octavo, October, etc.), is used in Luke 2:21; 9:28; John 20:26; Acts 9:33; 25:6; 1 Pet. 3:20; in composition with other numerals, *oktō kai deka*, lit., eight and ten, eighteen, Luke 13:4, 11, 16; *triakonta kai oktō*, thirty and eight, John 5:5. ¶
NT: B.563a; CB.1260c; K.—.
OT: —.
GEN. REF.: —.

ogdoos [ὄγδοος, 3590], eighth (connected with the preceding), is used in Luke 1:59; Acts 7:8; 2 Pet. 2:5; Rev. 17:11; 21:20. ¶
NT: B.552d; CB.1260c; K.—.
OT: shᵉmînî: S.8066; HR.960a.1a; H.2411c; BD.1033b.
shᵉmōneh: S.8083; HR.960a.1c; H.2411a; BD.1032d.
GEN. REF.: —.

oktaēmeros [ὀκταήμερος, 3637], an adjective, signifying an eighth-day person or thing, eight days old (*oktō*, and *hēmera*, a day), is used in Phil. 3:5. This, and similar numerical adjectives not found in the N.T., indicate duration rather than intervals. The Apostle shows by his being an 'eighth-day' person as to circumcision, that his parents were neither Ishmaelites (circumcised in their thirteenth year) nor other Gentiles, converted to Judaism (circumcised on becoming Jews). ¶
NT: B.563a; CB.—; K.—.
OT: —.
GEN. REF.: —.

EITHER

ē [ἤ, 2228], is a disjunctive particle. One of its uses is to distinguish things which exclude each other, or one of which can take the place of another. It is translated "either" in Matt. 6:24; 12:33; Luke 16:13; Acts 17:21; 1 Cor. 14:6. The R.V. rightly omits it in Luke 6:42, and

translates it by "or" in Luke 15:8; Phil. 3:12 and Jas. 3:12.
NT: B.342a; CB.–; K.–.
OT: –.
GEN. REF.: –.

Note: The adverb *enteuthen*, denoting "hence," is repeated in the phrase rendered "on either side," (lit., 'hence and hence') in John 19:18. The R.V. of Rev. 22:2 translates it "on this side," distinguishing it from *ekeithen*, "on that side"; the A.V., following another reading for the latter adverb, has "on either side." See HENCE.

ELDER, ELDEST

A. Adjectives.

1. *presbuteros* [πρεσβύτερος, 4245], an adjective, the comparative degree of *presbus*, an old man, an elder, is used (*a*) of age, whether of the elder of two persons, Luke 15:25, or more, John 8:9, "the eldest"; or of a person advanced in life, a senior, Acts 2:17; in Heb. 11:2, the "elders" are the forefathers in Israel; so in Matt. 15:2; Mark 7:3, 5; the feminine of the adjective is used of elder women in the churches, 1 Tim. 5:2, not in respect of position but in seniority of age; (*b*) of rank or positions of responsibility, (1) among Gentiles, as in the Sept. of Gen. 50:7; Num. 22:7; (2) in the Jewish nation, firstly those who were the heads or leaders of the tribes and families, as of the seventy who assisted Moses, Num. 11:16; Deut. 27:1, and those assembled by Solomon; secondly, members of the Sanhedrin, consisting of the chief priests, elders and scribes, learned in Jewish Law, e.g., Matt. 16:21; 26:47; thirdly, those who managed public affairs in the various cities, Luke 7:3; (3) in the Christian churches, those who, being raised up and qualified by the work of the Holy Spirit, were appointed to have the spiritual care of, and to exercise oversight over, the churches. To these the term bishops, *episkopoi*, or overseers, is applied (see Acts 20, ver. 17 with ver. 28, and Tit. 1:5 and 7), the latter term indicating the nature of their work, *presbuteroi* their maturity of spiritual experience. The Divine arrangement seen throughout the N.T. was for a plurality of these to be appointed in each church, Acts 14:23; 20:17; Phil. 1:1; 1 Tim. 5:17; Tit. 1:5. The duty of elders is described by the verb *episkopeō*. They were appointed according as they had given evidence of fulfilling the Divine qualifications, Tit. 1:6 to 9; cp. 1 Tim. 3:1-7 and 1 Pet. 5:2; (4) the twenty-four elders enthroned in Heaven around the throne of God, Rev. 4:4, 10; 5:5-14; 7:11, 13; 11:16; 14:3; 19:4. The number twenty-four is representative of earthly conditions. The word "elder" is nowhere applied to angels. See OLD.
NT: B.699c; CB.1266b; K.931.
OT: zāqēn: S.2205; HR.1201c.3; H.574b; BD.278c.
GEN. REF.: IS.2:54; NB.356; Z.2:266.

2. *sumpresbuteros* [συμπρεσβύτερος, 4850], a fellow-elder (*sun*, with), is used in 1 Pet. 5:1. ¶
NT: B.780a; CB.–; K.931.
OT: –.
GEN. REF.: IS.2:54; NB.356; Z.2:266.

3. *meizōn* [μείζων, 3187], greater, the comparative degree of *megas*, great, is used of age, and translated "elder" in Rom. 9:12, with reference to Esau and Jacob. See GREATER, GREATEST, MORE.
NT: B.497c; CB.1258a; K.–.
OT: –.
GEN. REF.: –.

B. Noun.

presbuterion [πρεσβυτέριον, 4244], an assembly of aged men, denotes (*a*) the Council or Senate among the Jews, Luke 22:66; Acts 22:5; (*b*) the elders or bishops in a local church, 1 Tim. 4:14, "the presbytery." For their functions see A, No. 1, (3).
NT: B.699c; CB.1266b; K.931.
OT: –.
GEN. REF.: IS.2:54; NB.356; Z.2:266.

ELECT, ELECTED, ELECTION

A. Adjectives.

1. *eklektos* [ἐκλεκτός, 1588], lit. signifies picked out, chosen (*ek*, from, *legō*, to gather, pick out), and is used of (*a*) Christ, the chosen of God, as the Messiah, Luke 23:35 (for the verb in 9:35 see Note below), and metaphorically as a "living Stone," "a chief corner Stone," 1 Pet. 2:4, 6; some mss. have it in John 1:34, instead of *huios*, Son; (*b*) angels, 1 Tim. 5:21, as chosen to be of especially high rank in administrative association with God, or as His messengers to human beings, doubtless in contrast to fallen angels (see 2 Pet. 2:4 and Jude 6); (*c*) believers (Jews or Gentiles), Matt. 24:22, 24, 31; Mark 13:20, 22, 27; Luke 18:7; Rom. 8:33; Col. 3:12; 2 Tim. 2:10; Tit. 1:1; 1 Pet. 1:1; 2:9 (as a spiritual race); Matt. 20:16; 22:14 and Rev. 17:14, "chosen"; individual believers are so mentioned in Rom. 16:13; 2 John 1, 13. ¶

Believers were chosen "before the foundation of the world" (cp. "before times eternal," 2 Tim. 1:9), in Christ, Eph. 1:4, to adoption, Eph. 1:5; good works, 2:10; conformity to Christ, Rom. 8:29; salvation from the delusions of the Antichrist and the doom of the deluded, 2 Thess. 2:13; eternal glory, Rom. 9:23.

The source of their election is God's grace, not human will, Eph. 1:4, 5; Rom. 9:11; 11:5. They are given by God the Father to Christ as the fruit of His Death, all being foreknown and foreseen by God, John 17:6 and Rom. 8:29. While Christ's Death was sufficient for all men, and is effective in the case of the elect, yet men are treated as responsible, being capable of the will and power to choose. For the rendering 'being chosen as firstfruits,' an alternative reading in 2 Thess. 2:13, see FIRSTFRUITS. See CHOICE, B.

NT: B.242d; CB.1243c; K.505.
OT: bāḥar: S.977; HR.437a.2a; H.231; BD.103c.
baḥîr: S.972; HR.437a.2c; H.231c; BD.104c.
GEN. REF.: IS.2:54; NB.357; Z.2:270.

2. *sunekletos* [συνεκλεκτός, 4899], means "elect together with," 1 Pet. 5:13. ¶

NT: B.787b; CB.—; K.—.
OT: —.
GEN. REF.: IS.2:54; NB.357; Z.2:270.

B. Noun.

eklogē [ἐκλογή, 1589], denotes a picking out, selection (Eng., eclogue), then, that which is chosen; in Acts 9:15, said of the choice of God of Saul of Tarsus, the phrase is, lit., 'a vessel of choice.' It is used four times in Romans; in 9:11, of Esau and Jacob, where the phrase "the purpose . . . according to election" is virtually equivalent to 'the electing purpose'; in 11:5, the "remnant according to the election of grace" refers to believing Jews, saved from among the unbelieving nation; so in ver. 7; in ver. 28, "the election" may mean either the act of choosing or the chosen ones; the context, speaking of the fathers, points to the former, the choice of the nation according to the covenant of promise. In 1 Thess. 1:4, "your election" refers not to the church collectively, but to the individuals constituting it; the Apostle's assurance of their election gives the reason for his thanksgiving. Believers are to give 'the more diligence to make their calling and election sure,' by the exercise of the qualities and graces which make them fruitful in the knowledge of God, 2 Pet. 1:10. ¶ For the corresponding verb *eklegomai*, see CHOOSE.

NT: B.243a; CB.1243c; K.505.
OT: —.
GEN. REF.: IS.2:54; NB.357; Z.2:270.

ELEMENTS

stoicheion [στοιχεῖον, 4747], used in the plural, primarily signifies any first things from which others in a series, or a composite whole, take their rise; the word denotes an element, first principle (from *stoichos*, a row, rank, series; cp. the verb *stoicheō*, to walk or march in rank; see WALK); it was used of the letters of the alphabet, as elements of speech. In the N.T. it is used of (*a*) the substance of the material world, 2 Pet. 3:10, 12; (*b*) the delusive speculations of Gentile cults and of Jewish theories, treated as elementary principles, "the rudiments of the world," Col. 2:8, spoken of as "philosophy and vain deceit"; these were presented as superior to faith in Christ; at Colossae the worship of angels, mentioned in ver. 18, is explicable by the supposition, held by both Jews and Gentiles in that district, that the constellations were either themselves animated heavenly beings, or were governed by them; (*c*) the rudimentary principles of religion, Jewish or Gentile, also described as "the rudiments of the world," Col. 2:20, and as "weak and beggarly rudiments," Gal. 4:3, 9, R.V., constituting a yoke of bondage; (*d*) the elementary principles (the A.B.C.) of the O.T., as a revelation from God, Heb. 5:12, R.V., "rudiments," lit., 'the rudiments of the beginning of the oracles of God,' such as are taught to spiritual babes. See PRINCIPLES, RUDIMENTS. ¶

NT: B.768d; CB.1270a; K.1087.
OT: —.
GEN. REF.: IS.2:57; NB.361; Z.2:275.

ELEVEN, ELEVENTH

hendeka [ἕνδεκα, 1733], lit., one ten (Lat., *undecim*), is used only of the eleven Apostles remaining after the death of Judas Iscariot, Matt. 28:16; Mark 16:14; Luke 24:9, 33; Acts 1:26; 2:14. ¶

NT: B.262d; CB.—; K.—.
OT: —.
GEN. REF.: IS.2:61; NB.—; Z.—.

hendekatos [ἑνδέκατος, 1734], an adjective derived from the above, is found in Matt. 20:6, 9; Rev. 21:20. ¶

NT: B.262d; CB.—; K.—.
OT: 'ashtê: S.6249; HR.469c.2; H.1717c; BD.799d.
GEN. REF.: —.

ELOQUENT

logios [λόγιος, 3052], an adjective, from *logos*, a word, primarily meant learned, a man skilled in literature and the arts. In the A.V. of Acts 18:24, it is translated "eloquent," said of Apollos; the R.V. is almost certainly right in translating it "learned." It was much more frequently used among the Greeks of one who was erudite than of one who was skilled in words. He had stores of learning and could use it convincingly. ¶

NT: B.476d; CB.1257a; K.505.
OT: —.
GEN. REF.: IS.2:74; NB.—; Z.—.

ELSE

epei [ἐπεί, 1893], a conjunction, when used of cause, meaning "since," "otherwise," "for then," "because"; in an ellipsis, "else," as in 1 Cor. 7:14, where the ellipsis would be 'if the unbelieving husband were not sanctified in the wife, your children would be unclean'; cp. Rom. 11:6, 22; 1 Cor. 5:10; Heb. 9:26. Sometimes it introduces a question, as in Rom. 3:6; 1 Cor. 14:16; 15:29; Heb. 10:2. It is translated "else" in 1 Cor. 14:16 and in the R.V. in Heb. 9:26 and 10:2, for A.V., "for then."

NT: B.284a; CB.—; K.—.
OT: —.
GEN. REF.: —.

ELSEWHERE

allachou [ἀλλαχοῦ, —], connected with *allos*, another, is used in Mark 1:38 (R.V. only). ¶

NT: B.39b; CB.—; K.—.
OT: —.
GEN. REF.: —.

For **EMBARK** (R.V., in Acts 27:2) see **ABOARD**

EMBOLDEN

oikodomeō [οἰκοδομέω, 3618], is rendered "embolden" in 1 Cor. 8:10, in reference to blameworthy actions (see marg.), the delinquent being built up, so to speak, to do what is contrary to his conscience. See BUILD, EDIFICATION.

NT: B.558a; CB.1260b; K.674.
OT: bānāh: S.1129; HR.970c.1a; H.255; BD.124a.
GEN. REF.: —.

EMBRACE

1. *aspazomai* [ἀσπάζομαι, 782], lit. signifies to draw to oneself; hence, to greet, salute, welcome, the ordinary meaning, e.g., in Rom. 16, where it is used 21 times. It also signifies to bid farewell, e.g., Acts 20:1, R.V., "took leave of" (A.V., "embraced"). A salutation or farewell was generally made by embracing and kissing (see Luke 10:4, which indicates the possibility of delay on the journey by frequent salutation). In Heb. 11:13 it is said of those who greeted the promises from afar, R.V., "greeted," for A.V., "embraced." Cp. *aspasmos*, a salutation. See GREET, LEAVE (take), SALUTE.

NT: B.116c; CB.1238a; K.84.
OT: shā'al (+ lᵉshalôm): S.7592; HR.173a.1; H.2303; BD.981b,d.
GEN. REF.: —.

Note: In Acts 21:6 the most authentic texts have *apaspazomai* (*apo*, and No. 1), to bid farewell.

2. *sumperilambanō* [συμπεριλαμβάνω, 4843], lit., to take around with; (*sun*, with, *peri*, around, *lambanō*, to take), to embrace, is used in Acts 20:10, in connection with Paul's recovery of Eutychus. ¶ In the Sept., Ezra 5:3, "to enclose." ¶

NT: B.779c; CB.—; K.—.
OT: —.
GEN. REF.: IS.2:76; NB.—; Z.—.

EMPEROR

sebastos [σεβαστός, 4575], august, reverent, the masculine gender of an adjective (from *sebas*, reverential awe), became used as the title of the Roman Emperor, Acts 25:21, 25, R.V., for A.V., "Augustus"; then, taking its name from the Emperor, it became a title of honour applied to certain legions or cohorts or battalions, marked for their valour, Acts 27:1. ¶ Cp. *sebazomai*, to worship, Rom. 1:25; ¶ *sebasma*, an object of worship, Acts 17:23; 2 Thess. 2:4. ¶

NT: B.745d; CB.1268c; K.1010.
OT: —.
GEN. REF.: IS.2:74; NB.—; Z.—.

EMERALD

A. Noun.

smaragdos [σμάραγδος, 4665], is a transparent stone of a light green colour, occupying the first place in the second row on the high priest's breastplate, Ex. 28:18. Tyre imported it from Syria, Ezek. 27:16. It is one of the foundations of the Heavenly Jerusalem, Rev. 21:19. The name was applied to other stones of a similar character, such as the carbuncle. ¶

NT: B.758c; CB.1269b; K.—.
OT: shōham: S.7718; HR.1278b.4; H.2337; BD.995d.
bāreqet: S.1304; HR.1278b.2; H.287d; BD.140c.
yahᵃlōm: S.3095; HR.1278b.3; H.502b; BD.240d.
GEN. REF.: IS.4:627; NB.632; Z.2:299.

B. Adjective.

smaragdinos [σμαράγδινος, 4664], emerald in character, descriptive of the rainbow round about the Throne in Rev. 4:3, is used in the papyri to denote emerald green. ¶

NT: B.758c; CB.1269b; K.—.
OT: —.
GEN. REF.: IS.4:627; NB.632; Z.2:299.

EMPTY

A. Verbs.

1. *kenoō* [κενόω, 2758], to empty, is so translated in Phil. 2:7, R.V., for A.V., "made . . . of no reputation." The clauses which follow the verb are exegetical of its meaning, especially the phrases "the form of a servant," and "the likeness of men." Christ did not empty Himself

of Godhood. He did not cease to be what He essentially and eternally was. The A.V., while not an exact translation, goes far to express the act of the Lord (see GIFFORD on the Incarnation). For other occurrences of the word see Rom. 4:14; 1 Cor. 1:17; 9:15; 2 Cor. 9:3. ¶ In the Sept., Jer. 14:2; 15:9. ¶

NT: B.428a; CB.1255a; K.426.
OT: 'āmal: S.535; HR.759b.1; H.114; BD.51b.
GEN. REF.: IS.2:77; NB.–; Z.3:784.

2. *scholazō* [σχολάζω, 4980], from *scholē*, leisure, that for which leisure is employed, such as a lecture (hence, the place where lectures are given; Eng., school), is used of persons, to have time for anything and so to be occupied in, 1 Cor. 7:5; of things, to be unoccupied, empty, Matt. 12:44 (some mss. have it in Luke 11:25). See GIVE (oneself to). ¶

NT: B.797d; CB.–; K.–.
OT: rāphāh: S.7503; HR.1328b.1; H.2198; BD.951c.
GEN. REF.: IS.2:77; NB.–; Z.–.

B. Adjective.

kenos [κενός, 2756], expresses the hollowness of anything, the absence of that which otherwise might be possessed. It is used (*a*) literally, Mark 12:3; Luke 1:53; 20:10, 11; (*b*) metaphorically, of imaginations, Acts 4:25; of words which convey erroneous teachings, Eph. 5:6; of deceit, Col. 2:8; of a person whose professed faith is not accompanied by works, Jas. 2:20; negatively, concerning the grace of God, 1 Cor. 15:10; of refusal to receive it, 2 Cor. 6:1; of faith, 1 Cor. 15:14; of preaching (id.); and other forms of Christian activity and labor, 1 Cor. 15:58; Gal. 2:2; Phil. 2:16; 1 Thess. 2:1; 3:5. ¶ The synonymous word *mataios*, vain, signifies void of result, it marks the aimlessness of anything. The vain (*kenos*) man in Jas. 2:20 is one who is empty of Divinely imparted wisdom; in 1:26 the vain (*mataios*) religion is one that produces nothing profitable. *Kenos* stresses the absence of quality, *mataios*, the absence of useful aim or effect. Cp. the corresponding adverb *kenōs*, "in vain," in Jas. 4:5, ¶ the noun *kenodoxia*, vainglory, Phil. 2:3, ¶ the adjective *kenodoxos*, vainglorious, Gal. 5:26, ¶ and the noun *kenophōnia*, vain, or empty, babblings, 1 Tim. 6:20; 2 Tim. 2:16. ¶

NT: B.427d; CB.1255a; K.426.
OT: rîq: S.7324; HR.759a.9a; H.2161; BD.937d.
rêq: S.7386; HR.759a.9b; H.2161a; BD.938a.
rêqām: S.7387; HR.759a.9c; H.2161c; BD.938b.
GEN. REF.: IS.2:77; NB.–; Z.3:784.

For **EMULATION**, A.V. (Rom. 11:14; Gal. 5:20) see **JEALOUSY**

ENABLE

endunamoō [ἐνδυναμόω, 1743], to render strong (*en*, in, *dunamis*, power), is translated "enabled" in 1 Tim. 1:12, more lit., 'in-strengthened,' 'inwardly strengthened,' suggesting strength in soul and purpose (cp. Phil. 4:13). See STRENGTH, STRONG. (In the Sept., Judg. 6:34; 1 Chron. 12:18; Psa. 52:7. ¶)

NT: B.263d; CB.1245a; K.186.
OT: 'āzaz: S.5810; HR.472a.2; H.1596; BD.738b.
GEN. REF.: IS.2:78; NB.–; Z.–.

ENACT

nomotheteō [νομοθετέω, 3549], to ordain by law, to enact (*nomos*, a law, *tithēmi*, to put), is used in the Passive Voice, and rendered "enacted" in Heb. 8:6, R.V., for A.V., "established"; in 7:11, used intransitively, it is rendered "received the Law." See ESTABLISH, LAW. ¶

NT: B.541d; CB.1260a; K.646.
OT: yārāh: S.3384; HR.947a.1; H.910; BD.434d,435b.
GEN. REF.: –.

For **ENCLOSE** see **INCLOSE**

ENCOUNTER

sumballō [συμβάλλω, 4820], lit., to throw together (*sun*, with, *ballō*, to throw), is used of encountering in war, Luke 14:31, R.V., "to encounter . . . (in war)," for A.V., "to make war against"; of meeting in order to discuss, in Acts 17:18, "encountered," of the philosophers in Athens and the Apostle. See CONFER, HELP, MAKE, MEET, PONDER.

NT: B.777b; CB.–; K.–.
OT: gārāh: S.1624; HR.1303a.1; H.378; BD.173b.
sût: S.3249; HR.1303a.3; H.1480; BD.694c.
GEN. REF.: –.

ENCOURAGE, ENCOURAGEMENT

A. Verbs.

1. *protrepō* [προτρέπω, 4389], to urge forward, persuade, is used in Acts 18:27 in the Middle Voice, R.V., "encouraged," indicating their particular interest in giving Apollos the encouragement mentioned; the A.V., "exhorting," wrongly connects the verb. ¶

NT: B.722b; CB.–; K.–.
OT: –.
GEN. REF.: IS.2:78; NB.–; Z.–.

2. *paramutheomai* [παραμυθέομαι, 3888], from *para*, with, and *muthos*, counsel, advice, is translated "encouraging" in 1 Thess. 2:11, R.V., and "encourage" in 5:14, R.V., there signifying to stimulate to the discharge of the

ordinary duties of life. In John 11:19, 31, it means to comfort. See COMFORT. ¶

Cp. the nouns *paramuthia*, 1 Cor. 14:3, ¶ and *paramuthion*, Phil. 2:1, comfort. ¶

NT: B.620d; CB.1262b; K.784.
OT: —.
GEN. REF.: IS.2:78; NB.—; Z.—.

B. Noun.

paraklēsis [παράκλησις, 3874], a calling to one's aid (*para*, by the side, *kaleō*, to call), then, an exhortation, encouragement, is translated "encouragement" in Heb. 6:18, R.V., for A.V., "consolation"; it is akin to *parakaleō*, to beseech or exhort, encourage, comfort, and *paraklētos*, a paraclete or advocate. See COMFORT, CONSOLATION, EXHORTATION, INTREATY.

NT: B.618a; CB.1262a; K.778.
OT: niḥûmîm: S.5150; HR.1061a.1a; H.1344b; BD.637b.
tanᵉhûmîm: S.8575; HR.1061a.1d; H.1144d; BD.637c.
GEN. REF.: IS.2:78; NB.—; Z.—.

END, ENDING

A. Nouns.

1. *telos* [τέλος, 5056], signifies (*a*) the limit, either at which a person or thing ceases to be what he or it was up to that point, or at which previous activities were ceased, 2 Cor. 3:13; 1 Pet. 4:7; (*b*) the final issue or result of a state or process, e.g., Luke 1:33; in Rom. 10:4, Christ is described as "the end of the Law unto righteousness to everyone that believeth"; this is best explained by Gal. 3:23-26; cp. Jas. 5:11; the following more especially point to the issue or fate of a thing, Matt. 26:58; Rom. 6:21; 2 Cor. 11:15; Phil. 3:19; Heb. 6:8; 1 Pet. 1:9; (*c*) a fulfilment, Luke 22:37, A.V. "(have) an end"; (*d*) the utmost degree of an act, as of the love of Christ towards His disciples, John 13:1; (*e*) the aim or purpose of a thing, 1 Tim. 1:5; (*f*) the last in a succession or series Rev. 1:8 (A.V., only, "ending"); 21:6; 22:13. See CONTINUAL, CUSTOM (Toll), FINALLY, UTTERMOST.

NT: B.811d; CB.1271b; K.1161.
OT: lamᵉnaṣṣēaḥar: S.5329; HR.1344a.6e; H.1402; BD.663d.
lāneṣaḥ: S.5331; HR.1344a.6f; H.1402a; BD.664b.
qēṣ: S.7093; HR.1344a.4a; H.2060a; BD.893d.
GEN. REF.: IS.2:79; NB.—; Z.2:304.

Note: The following phrases contain *telos* (the word itself coming under one or other of the above): *eis telos*, unto the end," e.g., Matt. 10:22; 24:13; Luke 18:5, "continual"; John 13:1 (see above); 2 Cor. 3:13, "on the end" (R.V.); *heōs telous*, "unto the end," 1 Cor. 1:8; 2 Cor. 1:13; ¶ *achri telous*, "even to the end" (a stronger expression than the preceding), Heb. 6:11; Rev. 2:26 (where 'even' might well have been added); ¶ *mechri telous*, with much the same meaning as *achri telous*, Heb. 3:6, 14. ¶ See other expressions in the Notes after C.

2. *sunteleia* [συντέλεια, 4930], signifies a bringing to completion together (*sun*, with, *teleō*, to complete, akin to No. 1), marking the completion or consummation of the various parts of a scheme. In Matt. 13:39, 40, 49; 24:3; 28:20, the rendering "the end of the world" (A.V. and R.V., text) is misleading; the R.V. marg., "the consummation of the age," is correct. The word does not denote a termination, but the heading up of events to the appointed climax. *Aiōn* is not the world, but a period or epoch or era in which events take place. In Heb. 9:26, the word translated "world" (A.V.) is in the plural, and the phrase is 'the consummation of the ages.' It was at the heading up of all the various epochs appointed by Divine counsels that Christ was manifested (i.e., in His Incarnation) "to put away sin by the sacrifice of Himself." ¶

NT: B.792a; CB.1271a; K.1161.
OT: kālāh: S.3617; HR.1318c.5b; H.982a; BD.478d.
qēṣ: S.7093; HR.1318c.9; H.2060a; BD.893d.
GEN. REF.: IS.2:79; NB.—; Z.2:304.

3. *peras* [πέρας, 4009], a limit, boundary (from *pera*, beyond), is used (*a*) of space, chiefly in the plural, Matt. 12:42, R.V., "ends," for A.V., "uttermost parts"; so Luke 11:31 (A.V., "utmost"); Rom. 10:18 (A.V. and R.V., "ends"); (*b*) of the termination of something occurring in a period, Heb. 6:16, R.V., "final," for A.V., "an end," said of strife. See UTTERMOST. ¶

NT: B.644a; CB.1263b; K.—.
OT: qēṣ: S.7093; HR.1120a.6a; H.2060a; BD.893d.
'ephem: S.657; HR.1120a.1; H.147a; BD.67a.
GEN. REF.: IS.2:79; NB.—; Z.—.

4. *ekbasis* [ἔκβασις, 1545], denotes a way out (*ek*, out, *bainō*, to go), 1 Cor. 10:13, "way of escape"; or an issue, Heb. 13:7 (A.V., "end," R.V., "issue"). See ISSUE. ¶

NT: B.237d; CB.—; K.—.
OT: —.
GEN. REF.: —.

B. Verbs.

1. *teleō* [τελέω, 5055], to complete, finish, bring to an end, is translated "had made an end," in Matt. 11:1. See ACCOMPLISH.

NT: B.810d; CB.1271b; K.1161.
OT: kālāh: S.3615; HR.1342c.3; H.982-984; BD.477b.
GEN. REF.: IS.2:79; NB.—; Z.2:304.

2. *sunteleō* [συντελέω, 4931], cp. A, No. 2, signifies (*a*) to bring to an end, finish completely (*sun*, together, imparting a perfective significance to *teleō*), Matt. 7:28 (in some mss.); Luke 4:2, 13; Acts 21:27, R.V., "completed"; (*b*) to bring to fulfilment, Mark 13:4; Rom. 9:28; (*c*) to effect, make, Heb. 8:8. See FINISH, FULFIL, MAKE. ¶

NT: B.792a; CB.1271a; K.1161.
OT: kālāh: S.3615; HR.1319b.7a,b; H.982-984; BD.477b.
tāmam: S.8552; HR.1319b.16; H.2522; BD.1070b.
GEN. REF.: IS.2:79; NB.—; Z.2:304.

3. *plēroō* [πληρόω, 4137], (*a*) to fill, (*b*) to fulfil, complete, end, is translated "had ended" in Luke 7:1; "were ended" (Passive) in Acts 19:21. See ACCOMPLISH.
NT: B.670c; CB.1265b; K.867.
OT: mālē': S.4390; HR.1147c.2a-c; H.1195; BD.569d.
GEN. REF.: –.

Note: In John 13:2, the verb *ginomai*, there signifying to be in progress, and used in the present participle, is translated "during supper" (R.V.). A less authentic reading, is *genomenou*, "being ended" (A.V.).

C. Adjective.

eschatos [ἔσχατος, 2078], last, utmost, extreme, is used as a noun (*a*) of time, rendered "end" in Heb. 1:2, R.V., "at the end of these days," i.e., at the end of the period under the Law, for A.V., "in these last days"; so in 1 Pet. 1:20, "at the end of the times." In 2 Pet. 2:20, the plural, *ta eschata*, lit., 'the last things,' is rendered "the latter end," A.V., (R.V., "the last state"); the same phrase is used in Matt. 12:45; Luke 11:26; (*b*) of place, Acts 13:47, A.V., "ends (of the earth)," R.V., "uttermost part." See LAST, LOWEST, UTTERMOST.
NT: B.313d; CB.1246c; K.264.
OT: 'aḥarôn: S.314; HR.558a.1c; H.68e; BD.30d.
'aḥarît: S.319; HR.558a.1d; H.68f; BD.31a.
GEN. REF.: IS.2:130; NB.–; Z.2:342.

Notes: (1) In Matt. 28:1, *opse*, late (in the evening), is rendered "in the end (of)," A.V., R.V., "late (on)."

(2) In 1 Pet. 1:13, *teleiōs*, "perfectly," R.V. is rendered "to the end," in A.V.

(3) The phrase *eis touto*, lit., 'unto this,' signifies "to this end," John 18:37, R.V. (twice; A.V., "for this cause," in the second clause); so Mark 1:38; Acts 26:16; Rom. 14:9; 2 Cor. 2:9; 1 Tim. 4:10 (A.V., "therefore"); 1 Pet. 4:6; 1 John 3:8 (A.V., "for this purpose").

(4) *Eis*, unto, followed by the article and the infinitive mood of a verb, signifies "to the end that . . .," marking the aim of an action, Acts 7:19; Rom. 1:11; 4:16, 18; Eph. 1:12; 1 Thess. 3:13; 2 Thess. 1:5; 2:2, 6; 1 Pet. 3:7. In Luke 18:1, *pros*, to, has the same construction and meaning.

(5) The conjunction *hina*, in order that, is sometimes rendered "to the end that," Eph. 3:17; 2 Thess. 3:14; Tit. 3:8.

(6) In Matt. 24:31, the prepositions *apo*, from, and *heōs*, unto, are used with the plural of *akros*, highest, extreme, signifying "from one end . . . to the other," lit., 'from extremities . . . to extremities.'

ENDEAVOUR

1. *spoudazō* [σποθδάζω, 4704], to make haste, to be zealous, and hence, to be diligent, is rendered "endeavouring" in Eph. 4:3, A.V.; R.V., "giving diligence." In 2 Pet. 1:15, A.V., "endeavour," R.V., "give diligence." Both have "endeavoured" in 1 Thess. 2:17. See DILIGENCE.
NT: B.763c; CB.1269c; K.1069.
OT: –.
GEN. REF.: IS.2:80; NB.–; Z.–.

2. *zēteō* [ζητέω, 2212], to seek after, is translated "endeavour" in Acts 16:10, A.V., R.V., "sought." See ABOUT (to be), DESIRE, INQUIRE, SEEK.
NT: B.338d CB.1273c; K.300.
OT: bāqash: S.1245; HR.597a.6a; H.276; BD.134c.
dārash: S.1875; HR.597a.8a; H.455; BD.205c.
GEN. REF.: IS.2:80; NB.–; Z.–.

ENDLESS

1. *akatalutos* [ἀκατάλυτος, 179], denotes indissoluble (from *a*, negative, *kata*, down, *luō*, to loose), Heb. 7:16, "endless"; see the R.V., marg., i.e., a life which makes its Possessor the holder of His priestly office for evermore. ¶
NT: B.30a; CB.1234a; K.543.
OT: –.
GEN. REF.: –.

2. *aperantos* [ἀπέραντος, 562], from *a*, negative and *perainō*, to complete, finish, signifies interminable, endless; it is said of genealogies, 1 Tim. 1:4. ¶ In the Sept., Job 36:26. ¶
NT: B.84a; CB.–; K.–.
OT: –.
GEN. REF.: IS.2:80; NB.–; Z.–.

ENDUE

enduō [ἐνδύω, 1746], in the Middle Voice, to put on oneself, be clothed with, is used metaphorically of power, Luke 24:49, R.V., "clothed." See CLOTHE. ¶
NT: B.264a; CB.1245a; K.192.
OT: lābash: S.3847; HR.471a.2; H.1075; BD.527d.
GEN. REF.: –.

Note: In Jas. 3:13 the adjective *epistēmōn*, knowing, skilled, is translated "endued with knowledge," A.V., R.V., "understanding." ¶

ENDURE, ENDURING

A. Verbs.

1. *menō* [μένω, 3306], to abide, is rendered to endure in the A.V. of John 6:27 and 1 Pet. 1:25 (R.V., "abideth"); Heb. 10:34, A.V., "enduring (substance)," R.V., "abiding." See ABIDE.
NT: B.503c; CB.1258b; K.581.
OT: 'āmad: S.5975; HR.910a.12; H.1637; BD.763c.
qûm: S.6965; HR.910a.15; H.1999; BD.877c.
yāshab: S.3427; HR.910a.7; H.922; BD.442a.
GEN. REF.: IS.2:80; NB.–; Z.–.

2. *hupomenō* [ὑπομένω, 5278], a strengthened form of No. 1, denotes to abide under, to bear up courageously (under suffering), Matt. 10:22; 24:13; Mark 13:13; Rom. 12:12, translated "patient"; 1 Cor. 13:7; 2 Tim. 2:10, 12 (A.V., "suffer"); Heb. 10:32; 12:2, 3, 7; Jas. 1:12; 5:11; 1 Pet. 2:20, "ye shall take it patiently." It has its other significance, to tarry, wait for, await, in Luke 2:43; Acts 17:14 (in some mss., Rom. 8:24). ¶ Cp. B. See ABIDE, PATIENT, SUFFER, TARRY. Cp. *makrothumeō*, to be longsuffering (see No. 7).

NT: B.845d; CB.1252b; K.581.
OT: qûm: S.6965; HR.1415c.9; H.1999; BD.877c.
qāwāh: S.6960; HR.1415c.8; H.1994,1995; BD.875c.
GEN. REF.: IS.2:80; NB.–; Z.–.

3. *pherō* [φέρω, 5342], to bear, is translated "endured" in Rom. 9:22 and Heb. 12:20. See BEAR.

NT: B.854d; CB.1264a; K.1252.
OT: –.
GEN. REF.: IS.2:80; NB.–; Z.–.

4. *hupopherō* [ὑποφέρω, 5297], a strengthened form of No. 3, to bear or carry, by being under, is said metaphorically of enduring temptation, 1 Cor. 10:13, A.V., "bear"; persecutions, 2 Tim. 3:11; griefs, 1 Pet. 2:19. See BEAR. ¶

NT: B.848c; CB.–; K.–.
OT: yākōl: S.3201; HR.1418a.1; H.866; BD.407b.
kûn: S.3559; HR.1418a.3; H.964; BD.465c.
GEN. REF.: IS.2:80; NB.–; Z.–.

5. *anechō* [ἀνέχω, 430], to hold up (*ana*, up, *echō*, to hold or have), always in the Middle Voice in the N.T., is rendered "endure" in 2 Thess. 1:4, of persecutions and tribulations; in 2 Tim. 4:3, of sound doctrine. See BEAR.

NT: B.65d; CB.1235b; K.58.
OT: yākōl: S.3201; HR.87c.4; H.866; BD.407b.
'ārak: S.748; HR.87c.2; H.162; BD.73c.
GEN. REF.: IS.2:80; NB.–; Z.–.

6. *kartereō* [καρτερέω, 2594], to be stedfast, patient, is used in Heb. 11:27, "endured," of Moses in relation to Egypt. ¶ In the Sept., Job 2:9; Isa. 42:14. ¶

NT: B.405b; CB.1253c; K.417.
OT: ḥāzaq: S.2388; HR.725a.1; H.636; BD.304a.
GEN. REF.: IS.2:80; NB.–; Z.–.

7. *makrothumeō* [μακροθυμέω, 3114], to be long-tempered (*makros*, long, *thumos*, mind), is rendered "patiently endured" in Heb. 6:15, said of Abraham. See B. below. See BEAR, LONGSUFFERING, PATIENCE, SUFFER.

NT: B.488a; CB.1257c; K.550.
OT: 'ārak: S.748; HR.893b.1a; H.162; BD.73c.
GEN. REF.: IS.2:80; NB.–; Z.–.

Note: In 2 Tim. 2:9, *kakopatheō*, to suffer evil, (*kakos*, evil, *paschō*, to suffer), is translated "endure hardness," A.V.; R.V., "suffer hardship"; so in 4:5, A.V., "endure afflictions"; elsewhere in Jas. 5:13. ¶ In 2 Tim. 2:3 the most authentic mss. have *sunkakopatheō*, to suffer hardship with, as in 1:8. ¶ See HARDSHIP, SUFFER.

B. Noun.

hupomonē [ὑπομονή, 5281], patience, lit., a remaining under (akin to A, No. 2), is translated "patient enduring" in 2 Cor. 1:6, R.V., for A.V., "enduring." Cp. *makrothumia*, longsuffering (akin to A, No. 7). See PATIENCE.

NT: B.846b; CB.1252b; K.581.
OT: miqweh: S.4723; HR.1416b.1a; H.1994c; BD.876a.
tiqwāh: S.8615; HR.1416b.1b; H.1994d,e; BD.876b.
GEN. REF.: IS.2:80; NB.–; Z.–.

ENEMY

echthros [ἐχθρός, 2190], an adjective, primarily denoting hated or hateful (akin to *echtos*, hate; perhaps associated with *ektos*, outside), hence, in the Active sense, denotes hating, hostile; it is used as a noun signifying an enemy, adversary, and is said (*a*) of the Devil, Matt. 13:39; Luke 10:19; (*b*) of death, 1 Cor. 15:26; (*c*) of the professing believer who would be a friend of the world, thus making Himself an enemy of God, Jas. 4:4; (*d*) of men who are opposed to Christ, Matt. 13:25, 28; 22:44; Mark 12:36; Luke 19:27; 20:43; Acts 2:35; Rom. 11:28; Phil. 3:18; Heb. 1:13; 10:13; or to His servants, Rev. 11:5, 12; to the nation of Israel, Luke 1:71, 74; 19:43; (*e*) of one who is opposed to righteousness, Acts 13;10; (*f*) of Israel in its alienation from God, Rom. 11:28; (*g*) of the unregenerate in their attitude toward God, Rom. 5:10; Col. 1:21; (*h*) of believers in their former state, 2 Thess. 3:15; (*i*) of foes, Matt. 5:43, 44; 10:36; Luke 6:27, 35; Rom. 12:20; 1 Cor. 15:25; of the Apostle Paul because he told converts "the truth," Gal. 4:16. See FOE. Cp. *echthra*, enmity. ¶

NT: B.331b; CB.1242c; K.285.
OT: 'āyab: S.340; HR.589c.1; H.78; BD.33b.
ṣar: S.6862; HR.589c.10; H.1973-1975; BD.865d.
GEN. REF.: IS.2:81; NB.–; Z.2:305.

ENGRAFTED

Note: This is the A.V. rendering of *emphutos*, Jas. 1:21, an adjective derived from *emphuō*, to implant; the R.V. has "implanted." ¶ The metaphor is that of a seed rooting itself in the heart; cp. Matt. 13:21; 15:13; 1 Cor. 3:6, and the kindred word *sumphutos*, Rom. 6:5, "planted together" (*sun*, with). ¶ The A.V. "engrafted" would translate the word *emphuteuton* (from *emphuteuō*, to graft), which is not found in the N.T.; it uses *enkentrizō* in Rom. 11. Cp. *ekphuō*, to cause to grow out, put forth (leaves), Matt. 24:32; Mark 13:28.

ENGRAVE

entupoō [ἐντυπόω, 1795], to imprint, engrave (*en*, in, *tupos*, a mark, impression, form, type), is used of the engraving of the Law on the two stones, or tablets, 2 Cor. 3:7. ¶ In the Sept., Ex. 36:39 (some texts have *ektupoō*). ¶ See also GRAVEN.

NT: B.270b; CB.—; K.—.
OT: pittûaḥ: S.6603; HR.481b.1; H.1855a; BD.836c.
GEN. REF.: IS.1:620; NB.—; Z.—.

ENJOIN

1. *entellomai* [ἐντέλλομαι, 1781], is translated "hath enjoined" in the A.V. of Heb. 9:20. See COMMAND (R.V.).

NT: B.268b; CB.1245b; K.234.
OT: ṣāwāh: S.6680; HR.477a.7a; H.1887; BD.845b.
GEN. REF.: IS.2:102; NB.—; Z.—.

2. *epitassō* [ἐπιτάσσω, 2004], lit., to set or arrange over, to charge, command, is rendered "enjoin" in Philm. 8. See COMMAND. Cp. *keleuō*, to order.

NT: B.302b; CB.1246a; K.—.
OT: ṣāwāh: S.6680; HR.534c.4a,b; H.1887; BD.845b.
GEN. REF.: IS.2:102; NB.—; Z.—.

ENJOY

A. Verb.

tunchanō [τυγχάνω, 5177], used transitively, denotes to hit upon, meet with; then, to reach, get, obtain; it is translated "enjoy" (i.e., obtain to our satisfaction) in Acts 24:2. See CHANCE, COMMON, *Note* (3), OBTAIN.

NT: B.829b; CB.—; K.1191.
OT: —.
GEN. REF.: IS.2:102; NB.—; Z.—.

B. Noun.

apolausis [ἀπόλαυσις, 619], enjoyment (from *apolauō*, to take hold of, enjoy a thing), suggests the advantage or pleasure to be obtained from a thing (from a root, *lab—* seen in *lambanō*, to obtain); it is used with the preposition *eis*, in 1 Tim. 6:17, lit., 'unto enjoyment,' rendered "to enjoy"; with *echō*, to have, in Heb. 11:25, lit., 'to have pleasure (of sin),' translated "to enjoy the pleasures." ¶ See PLEASURE.

NT: B.94d; CB.—; K.—.
OT: —.
GEN. REF.: IS.2:102; NB.—; Z.—.

ENLARGE

1. *megalunō* [μεγαλύνω, 3170], denotes to make great (from *megas*, great), Matt. 23:5, "enlarge"; 2 Cor. 10:15, A.V., "enlarged," R.V., "magnified"; elsewhere in the A.V. it is rendered by the verb to magnify, except in Luke 1:58, A.V., "had shewed great (mercy)," R.V., "had magnified (His mercy); see Luke 1:46; Acts 5:13; 10:46; 19:17; Phil. 1:20. See MAGNIFY. ¶

NT: B.497; CB.1258a; K.573.
OT: gādal: S.1431; HR.902a.2a-d; H.315; BD.152a.
rābāh: S.7235; HR.902a.5a; H.2103,2104; BD.915a.
rᵉbāh (Aramaic): S.7236; HR.902a.5b,c; H.2985; BD.1112b.
GEN. REF.: IS.2:103; NB.—; Z.—.

2. *platunō* [πλατύνω, 4115], to make broad, from *platus*, broad, is translated "enlarged" in 2 Cor. 6:11, 13 (metaphorically), "make broad," Matt. 23:5 (literally). From the primary sense of freedom comes that of the joy that results from it. See BROAD. ¶ Cp. *platos*, breadth, and *plateia*, a street.

NT: B.667a; CB.1265a; K.—.
OT: rāḥab: S.7337; HR.1141b.5; H.2143; BD.931b.
GEN. REF.: IS.2:103; NB.—; Z.—.

ENLIGHTEN

phōtizō [φωτίζω, 5461], from *phōs*, light, (*a*) used intransitively, signifies to give light, shine, Rev. 22:5; (*b*), used transitively, to enlighten, illumine, is rendered "enlighten" in Eph. 1:18, metaphorically of spiritual enlightenment; so John 1:9, i.e., "lighting every man" by reason of His coming); Eph. 3:9, "to make (all men) see" (R.V. marg., "to bring to light"); Heb. 6:4, "were enlightened"; 10:32, R.V., "enlightened," A.V., "illuminated." See ILLUMINATED, LIGHT. Cp. *phōtismos*, light, and *phōteinos*, full of light.

NT: B.872d; CB.1264b; K.1293.
OT: 'ôr: S.215; HR.1451b.1a-c; H.52; BD.21a.
yārāh: S.3384; HR.1451b.2; H.910; BD.434d.
GEN. REF.: IS.2:103; NB.—; Z.2:308.

ENMITY

echthra [ἔχθρα, 2189], from the adjective *echthros* (see ENEMY) is rendered "enmity" in Luke 23:12; Rom. 8:7; Eph. 2:15, 16; Jas. 4:4; "enmities," Gal. 5:20, R.V., for A.V., "hatred." It is the opposite of *agapē*, love. ¶

NT: B.331b; CB.1242c; K.285.
OT: 'āyab: S.340; HR.589b.1a; H.78; BD.33b.
'ēbāh: S.342; HR.589b.1b; H.78a; BD.33c.
sin'āh: S.8135; HR.589b.4; H.2272b; BD.971d.
GEN. REF.: IS.2:103; NB.—; Z.—.

ENOUGH

A. Adjectives.

1. *arketos* [ἀρκετός, 713], sufficient, akin to *arkeō* (see B, No. 1), is rendered "enough" in Matt. 10:25; "sufficient" in Matt. 6:34; "suffice" in 1 Pet. 4:3, lit., "(is) sufficient." See SUFFICE, SUFFICIENT. ¶

NT: B.107a; CB.1237c; K.78.
OT: —.
GEN. REF.: —.

2. *hikanos* [ἱκανός, 2425], sufficient, competent, fit (akin to *hikanō* and *hikō*, to reach, to attain and *hikanoō*, to make sufficient), is

translated "enough" in Luke 22:38, of the Lord's reply to Peter concerning the swords. See ABLE.

NT: B.374b; CB.1250c; K.361.
OT: hôn: S.1951; HR.683c.3; H.487; BD.223b.
day: S.1767; HR.683c.2; H.425; BD.191b.
GEN. REF.: –.

Note: In Luke 15:17 the verb *perisseuō*, to have abundance, is translated "have enough and to spare." In Acts 27:38 the verb *korennumi*, to satisfy, is translated "had eaten enough."

B. Verbs.

1. *arkeō* [ἀρκέω, 714], to ward off; hence, to aid, assist; then, to be strong enough, i.e., to suffice, to be enough (cp. A, No. 1), is translated "be enough" in Matt. 25:9. See CONTENT.

NT: B.107a; CB.1237c; K.78.
OT: hôn: S.1951; HR.158a.2; H.487; BD.223b.
māṣā': S.4672; HR.158a.4; H.2033; BD.592c,594b.
GEN. REF.: –.

2. *apechō* [ἀπέχω, 568], lit., to hold off from, to have off or out (*apō*, from, *echō*, to have), i.e., to have in full, to have received, is used impersonally in Mark 14:41, it is enough," in the Lord's words to His slumbering disciples in Gethsemane. It is difficult, however, to find examples of this meaning in Greek usage of the word, and *apechō* may here refer, in its commercial significance, to Judas (who is mentioned immediately afterwards), with the meaning 'he hath received' (his payment); cp. the same use in Matt. 6:2, 5, 16 (see Deissmann, *Light from the Ancient East*, pp. 110 ff). See ABSTAIN, HAVE, RECEIVE.

NT: B.84d; CB.1236b; K.286.
OT: –.
GEN. REF.: –.

For ENQUIRE see INQUIRE

ENRICH

ploutizō [πλουτίζω, 4148], to make rich (from *ploutos*, wealth, riches), is used metaphorically, of spiritual riches, in 1 Cor. 1:5, "ye were enriched"; 2 Cor. 6:10, "making rich"; 2 Cor. 9:11, "being enriched." See RICH. ¶

NT: B.674a; CB.1265b; K.873.
OT: 'āshar: S.6238; HR.1150c.1; H.1714; BD.799b.
GEN. REF.: –.

ENROL, ENROLMENT

A. Verb.

apographō [ἀπογράφω, 583], primarily signifies to write out, to copy; then, to enrol, to inscribe, as in a register. It is used of a census, Luke 2:1, R.V., "be enrolled," for A.V., "be taxed"; in the Middle Voice, vv. 3, 5, to enrol oneself, A.V., "be taxed." Confirmation that this census (not taxation) was taken in the domin ions of the Roman Empire is given by the historians Tacitus and Suetonius. Augustus himself drew up a sort of Roman Doomsday Book, a Rationarium, afterwards epitomized into a Breviarium, to include the allied kingdoms, appointing twenty commissioners to draw up the lists. In Heb. 12:23 the members of the Church of the firstborn are said to be "enrolled," R.V. ¶

NT: B.89c; CB.1236c; K.–.
OT: kātab: S.3789; HR.126a.1; H.1053; BD.507a.
GEN. REF.: –.

Note: For R.V., 1 Tim. 5:9, *katalegō*, see TAKE, *Note* (18); for R.V., 2 Tim. 2:4, *stratologeō*, see SOLDIER, B, *Note* (2).

B. Noun.

apographē [ἀπογραφή, 582], primarily denotes a written copy, or, as a law term, a deposition; then, a register, census, enrolment, Luke 2:2; Acts 5:37, R.V., for A.V., "taxing." Luke's accuracy has been vindicated, as against the supposed inconsistency that as Quirinius was Governor of Syria in A.D. 6, ten years after the birth of Christ, the census, as "the first" (R.V.), could not have taken place. At the time mentioned by Luke, Cilicia, of which Quirinius was Governor, was separated from Cyprus and joined to Syria. His later direct governorship of Syria itself accounts for the specific inclusion of, and reference to, his earlier connection with that Province. Justin Martyr, a native of Palestine, writing in the Middle of the 2nd century, asserts thrice that Quirinius was present in Syria at the time mentioned by Luke (see Apol., 1:34, 46; Trypho 78). Noticeable, too, are the care and accuracy taken by Luke in his historical details, 1:3, R.V.

As to charges made against Luke's accuracy, Moulton and Milligan say as follows:— "The deduction so long made . . . about the census apparently survives the demonstration that the blunder lay only in our lack of information: the microbe is not yet completely expelled. Possibly the salutary process may be completed by our latest inscriptional evidence that Quirinius was a legate in Syria for census purposes in 8-6 B.C." ¶

NT: B.89b; CB.–; K.–.
OT: kᵉtāb (Aramaic): S.3792; HR.126a.1; H.2805a; BD.1098a.
GEN. REF.: –.

ENSAMPLE

1. *tupos* [τύπος, 5179], primarily denoted a blow (from a root *tup*—, seen also in *tuptō*, to strike), hence, (*a*) an impression, the mark of a blow, John 20:25; (*b*) the impress of a seal, the

stamp made by a die, a figure, image, Acts 7:43; (*c*) a form or mould, Rom. 6:17 (see R.V.); (*d*) the sense or substance of a letter, Acts 23:25; (*e*) an ensample, pattern, Acts 7:44; Heb. 8:5, "pattern"; in an ethical sense, 1 Cor. 10:6; Phil. 3:17; 1 Thess. 1:7; 2 Thess. 3:9; 1 Tim. 4:12, R.V., "ensample"; Tit. 2:7, R.V., "ensample," for A.V., "pattern"; 1 Pet. 5:3; in a doctrinal sense, a type, Rom. 5:14. See EXAMPLE, FASHION, FIGURE, FORM, MANNER, PATTERN, PRINT. ¶

NT: B.829d; CB.1273b; K.1193.
OT: ṣelem: S.6754; HR.1378b.1; H.1923a; BD.853d.
tabnîṯ: S.8403; HR.1378b.2; H.255d; BD.125d.
GEN. REF.: IS.2:217; NB.—; Z.—.

2. *hupotupōsis* [ὑποτύπωσις, 5296], an outline, sketch, akin to *hupotupoō*, to delineate, is used metaphorically to denote a pattern, an ensample, 1 Tim. 1:16, R.V., "ensample," for A.V., "pattern"; 2 Tim. 1:13, R.V., "pattern," for A.V., "form." See FORM, PATTERN. ¶

NT: B.848c; CB.1252b; K.1193.
OT: —.
GEN. REF.: IS.2:217; NB.—; Z.—.

3. *hupodeigma* [ὑπόδειγμα, 5262], lit., that which is shown (from *hupo*, under, and *deiknumi*, to show), hence, (*a*) a figure, copy, Heb. 8:5, R.V., "copy," for A.V., "example"; 9:23; (*b*) an example, whether for imitation, John 13:15; Jas. 5:10, or for warning, Heb. 4:11; 2 Pet. 2:6, R.V., "example." See EXAMPLE, PATTERN. ¶

NT: B.844a; CB.1252b; K.141.
OT: —.
GEN. REF.: IS.2:217; NB.—; Z.—.

ENSLAVED

douloō [δουλόω, 1402], to make a slave of, is rendered "enslaved" (to much wine) in Tit. 2:3, R.V., for A.V., "given to." See BONDAGE.

NT: B.206b; CB.—; K.182.
OT: ʿābad: S.5647; HR.348b.1; H.1553; BD.712b.
GEN. REF.: —.

ENSNARE

pagideuō [παγιδεύω, 3802], to entrap, lay snares for (from *pagis*, anything which fixes or grips, hence, a snare), is used in Matt. 22:15, of the efforts of the Pharisees to entrap the Lord in His speech, A.V., "entangle." See ENTANGLE. ¶

NT: B.602a; CB.—; K.752.
OT: yāqash: S.3369; HR.1044a.1; H.906; BD.430b.
GEN. REF.: —.

For ENSUE see PURSUE

ENTANGLE

1. *pagideuō: see* ENSNARE.

2. *emplekō* [ἐμπλέκω, 1707], to weave in (*en*, in, *plekō*, to weave), hence, metaphorically, to be involved, entangled in, is used in the Passive Voice in 2 Tim. 2:4, "entangleth himself"; 2 Pet. 2:20, "are entangled." ¶ In the Sept., Prov. 28:18. ¶

NT: B.256c; CB.—; K.—.
OT: nāphal: S.5307; HR.458b.1; H.1392; BD.656c.
GEN. REF.: IS.2:105; NB.—; Z.—.

3. *enechō* [ἐνέχω, 1758], to hold in, is said (*a*) of being entangled in a yoke of bondage, such as Judaism, Gal. 5:1. Some mss. have the word in 2 Thess. 1:4, the most authentic have *anechō*, to endure; (*b*) with the meaning to set oneself against, be urgent against, said of the plotting of Herodias against John the Baptist, Mark 6:19, R.V., "set herself against," A.V., "had a quarrel against"; of the effort of the Scribes and Pharisees to provoke the Lord to say something which would provide them with a ground of accusation against Him, Luke 11:53, R.V., "to press upon," marg., "to set themselves vehemently against," A.V., "to urge." ¶

NT: B.265d; CB.1245a; K.286.
OT: sāṭam: S.7852; HR.473a.1; H.2251; BD.966b.
GEN. REF.: IS.2:105; NB.—; Z.—.

ENTER, ENTERING, ENTRANCE

A. Verbs.

1. *eiserchomai* [εἰσέρχομαι, 1525], to come into (*eis*, in, *erchomai*, to come), is frequently rendered "entered" in the R.V. for A.V., "went into," e.g., Matt. 9:25; 21:12; or "go in," e.g., Matt. 7:13; Luke 8:51; "go," Luke 18:25; "was coming in," Acts 10:25. See COME, No. 2, GO (Notes).

NT: B.232c; CB.1243b; K.257.
OT: bôʾ: S.935; HR.410b.4a; H.212; BD.97c.
GEN. REF.: —.

2. *suneiserchomai* [συνεισέρχομαι, 4897], to enter together, is used in John 6:22 (in the best mss.; see No. 6) and 18:15. ¶

NT: B.787a; CB.1270c; K.—.
OT: bôʾ: S.935; HR.1313b.1; H.212; BD.97c.
GEN. REF.: —.

3. *pareiserchomai* [παρεισέρχομαι, 3922], (*a*) to come in beside (*para*, beside, and No. 1), is rendered "entered" in Rom. 5:20, A.V., for R.V., "came in beside," the meaning being that the Law entered in addition to sin; (*b*) to enter secretly, by stealth, Gal. 2:4, "came in privily," to accomplish the purposes of the circumcision party. See COME, No. 8. ¶ Cp. *pareisduō* (or *—dunō*), Jude 4, "crept in privily." ¶

NT: B.624d; CB.1262b; K.257.
OT: —.
GEN. REF.: —.

4. *eisporeuomai* [εἰσπορεύομαι, 1531], to go into, found only in the Synoptists and Acts, is translated to enter, in the R.V. of Mark 1:21; 6:56; 11:2; Luke 8:16; 11:33 (A.V., "come in"); 19:30 (A.V., "at your entering"); 22:10; in the following the R.V. has the verb to go, for the A.V., to enter, Matt. 15:17; Mark 5:40; 7:15, 18, 19; in Acts 28:30, "went," A.V., "came"; in 9:28, R.V., "going," A.V., "coming"; in the following both A.V. and R.V. have the verb to enter, Mark 4:19; Luke 18:24 (in the best mss.); Acts 3:2; 8:3. See GO, No. 5. ¶

NT: B.233c; CB.—; K.915.
OT: bô': S.935; HR.414a.1a; H.212; BD.97c.
GEN. REF.: —.

5. *anabainō* [ἀναβαίνω, 305], to go up (*ana*, up, *bainō*, to go), is translated "entered" in 1 Cor. 2:9, metaphorically, of coming into the mind. In John 21:3, the best mss. have No. 6. See ARISE, No. 6.

NT: B.50a; CB.1235a; K.90.
OT: 'ālāh: S.5927; HR.70a.11a; H.1624; BD.748a.
GEN. REF.: —.

6. *embainō* [ἐμβαίνω, 1684], to go in (*en*, in), is used only in the Gospels, of entering a boat, Matt. 8:23; 9:1; 13:2; 14:22, 32; 15:39; Mark 4:1; 5:18; 6:45; 8:10, 13; Luke 5:3; 8:22, 37; John 6:17, (in some mss., in ver. 22), 24, R.V., "got into the boats," for A.V., "took shipping"; 21:3 (some mss. have No. 5 here); Acts 21:6 (in the best mss.); of stepping into water, John 5:4 (R.V. omits the verb). See COME, No. 21, GET, No. 5, GO, *Note* (2), *m*, STEP, TAKE, *Note* (3). ¶

NT: B.254a; CB.—; K.—.
OT: 'ālāh: S.5927; HR.455a.3; H.1624; BD.748a.
bô': S.935; HR.455a.1; H.212; BD.97c.
GEN. REF.: —.

7. *epibainō* [ἐπιβαίνω, 1910], to go upon (*epi*, upon), is used of going on board ship, Acts 21:2; 27:2, A.V., "entering into," R.V., "embarking in." See ABOARD, COME, No. 16, SIT, *Note*.

NT: B.289d; CB.—; K.—.
OT: 'ālāh: S.5927; HR.515c.7; H.1624; BD.748a.
rākab: S.7392; HR.515c.10; H.2163; BD.938c.
GEN. REF.: —.

8. *eiseimi* [εἴσειμι, 1524], to go into (*eis*, into, *eimi*, to go), Acts 3:3; 21:18, 26, A.V., "entered"; Heb. 9:6, R.V., "go in," for A.V., "went into." See GO, No. 12. ¶

NT: B.232c; CB.—; K.—.
OT: —.
GEN. REF.: —.

Notes: (1) *Erchomai*, to come, is never translated to enter, in the R.V.; in the A.V., Mark 1:29; Acts 18:7.

(2) In 2 John 7, the most authentic mss. have the verb *exerchomai*, "gone forth," R.V., for A.V. (No. 1), "entered."

(3) In Luke 16:16, *biazō*, to force, to enter in violently, is so rendered in the R.V., for A.V., "presseth."

B. Noun.

eisodos [εἴσοδος, 1529], lit., a way in (*eis*, in, *hodos*,a way), an entrance, is used (*a*) of the coming of Christ into the midst of the Jewish nation, Acts 13:24, R.V., marg., "entering in"; (*b*) of entrance upon Gospel work in a locality, 1 Thess. 1:9; 2:1; (*c*) of the present access of believers into God's presence, Heb. 10:19, lit., 'for entrance into'; (*d*) of their entrance into Christ's eternal Kingdom, 2 Pet. 1:11. See COMING. ¶

NT: B.233b; CB.1243b; K.666.
OT: bô': S.935; HR.413c.1a,b; H.212; BD.97c.
mābô': S.872; HR.413c.1c; H.212a; BD.99d.
GEN. REF.: —.

ENTERTAIN

xenizō [ξενίζω, 3579], signifies (*a*) to receive as a guest (*xenos*, a guest), rendered "entertained" in Acts 28:7, R.V., for A.V., "lodged"; in Heb. 13:2, "have entertained"; (*b*) to be astonished by the strangeness of a thing, Acts 17:20; 1 Pet. 4:4, 12. See LODGE, STRANGE (think).

NT: B.547d; CB.1273b; K.661.
OT: —.
GEN. REF.: IS.2:105; NB.—; Z.—.

Note: In Heb. 13:2 (first part), *philoxenia*, lit., love of strangers (*phileō*, to love, and *xenos*, a stranger or guest), is translated to show love to, R.V., for A.V., "entertain." See HOSPITALITY.

ENTICE, ENTICING

A. Verb.

deleazō [δελεάζω, 1185], primarily, to lure by a bait (from *delear*, a bait), is used metaphorically in Jas. 1:14, of the enticement of lust; in 2 Pet. 2:14, of seducers, R.V., "enticing," for A.V., "beguiling"; in ver. 18, R.V., "entice (in)," for A.V., "allure (through)." ¶

NT: B.174b; CB.—; K.—.
OT: —.
GEN. REF.: —.

B. Adjective.

peithos [πειθός, 3981], apt to persuade (from *peithō*, to persuade), is used in 1 Cor. 2:4, A.V., "enticing," R.V., "persuasive." ¶

NT: B.639a; CB.1263a; K.818.
OT: —.
GEN. REF.: —.

Note: In Col. 2:4, *pithanologia*, persuasive speech (from *pithanos*, persuasive, plausible, akin to the above, and *logos*, speech), is rendered "enticing" in the A.V. (R.V., "persuasiveness of.") It signifies the employment of plausible arguments, in contrast to demonstration. ¶ Cp. *eulogia*, "fair speech," Rom. 16:18, i.e., 'nice style.' ¶

ENTIRE

holoklēros [ὁλόκληρος, 3648], complete, sound in every part (*holos*, whole, *klēros*, a lot, i.e., with all that has fallen by lot), is used ethically in 1 Thess. 5:23, indicating that every grace present in Christ should be manifested in the believer; so Jas. 1:4. ¶ In the Sept. the word is used, e.g., of a full week, Lev. 23:15; of altar stones unhewn, Deut. 27:6 and Josh. 8:31; of a full-grown vine tree, useless for work, Ezek. 15:5; of the sound condition of a sheep, Zech. 11:16.

The corresponding noun *holoklēria* is used in Acts 3:16, "perfect soundness." ¶ The synonymous word *teleios*, used also in Jas. 1:4, "perfect," indicates the development of every grace into maturity.

The Heb. *shalom*, peace, is derived from a root meaning "wholeness." See, e.g., Is. 42:19, marg., "made perfect," for text, "at peace"; cp. 26:3. Cp. also Col. 1:28 with 2 Pet. 3:14.

NT: B.564c; CB.—; K.442.
OT: shālēm: S.7999; HR.989a.2; H.2401c; BD.1022a.
tāmîm: S.8549; HR.989a.3; H.2522d; BD.1071a.
GEN. REF.: —.

For ENTREAT, to request, see INTREAT; for ENTREATY see INTREATY

ENTREAT (to deal with, to treat)

Note: The distinction between this and the preceding word is maintained in the R.V., which confines the initial "e" to the sense of dealing with, or uses the Verb to treat.

chraomai [χράομαι, 5531], denotes (*a*) to use (of things); (*b*) to use well or ill, to treat, deal with (of persons); "treated (kindly)," Acts 27:3, R.V., A.V., "(courteously) entreated." The remaining ten instances come under (*a*). See USE.

NT: B.884b; CB.1240a; K.—.
OT: ṣālēah: S.6743; HR.1473c.4; H.1916,1917; BD.852b.
ʿāsāh: S.6213; HR.1473c.3; H.1708,1709; BD.793c.
shāʾal: S.7592; HR.1473c.5; H.2303; BD.981b.
GEN. REF.: —.

Note: In Luke 20:11, *atimazō*, to dishonour (*a*, negative, *timē*, honour), is translated "entreated shamefully," A.V. (R.V., "handled shamefully"). For *kakoucheō*, Heb. 11:37, R.V., and *sunkakoucheomai*, Heb. 11:25, R.V., see SUFFER, Nos. 6 and 7.

ENVY, ENVYING

A. Noun.

phthonos [φθόνος, 5355], envy, is the feeling of displeasure produced by witnessing or hearing of the advantage or prosperity of others; this evil sense always attaches to this word, Matt. 27:18; Mark 15:10; Rom. 1:29; Gal. 5:21; Phil. 1:15; 1 Tim. 6:4; Tit. 3:3; 1 Pet. 2:1; so in Jas. 4:5, where the quesion is rhetorical and strongly remonstrative, signifying that the Spirit (or spirit) which God made to dwell in us was certainly not so bestowed that we should be guilty of envy. ¶

NT: B.857d; CB.1264c; K.—.
OT: —.
GEN. REF.: IS.2:108; NB.378; Z.2:314.

Note: Zēlos, zeal or jealousy, translated "envy" in the A.V., in Acts 13:45; Rom. 13:13; 1 Cor. 3:3; 2 Cor. 12:20; Jas. 3:14, 16, is to be distinguished from *phthonos*, and, apart from the meanings "zeal" and "indignation," is always translated "jealousy" in the R.V. The distinction lies in this, that envy desires to deprive another of what he has, jealousy desires to have the same or the same sort of thing for itself. See FERVENT, INDIGNATION, JEALOUSY, ZEAL.

B. Verbs.

1. *phthoneō* [φθονέω, 5354], to envy (akin to A.), is used in Gal. 5:26. ¶

NT: B.857c; CB.1264c; K.—.
OT: —.
GEN. REF.: IS.2:108; NB.378; Z.2:314.

2. *zēloō* [ζηλόω, 2206], denotes to be zealous, moved with jealousy, Acts 7:9 and 17:5, R.V., "moved with jealousy" (A.V., "moved with envy"); both have "envieth" in 1 Cor. 13:4. See the Note under A. See AFFECT, COVET, DESIRE, JEALOUS, ZEALOUS.

NT: B.338a; CB.1273b; K.297.
OT: qānāʾ: S.7065; HR.594; H.2038; BD.888c.
GEN. REF.: IS.2:108; NB.378; Z.2:314.

EPHPHATHA

Note: Ephphatha [2188] is an Aramaic word signifying to open, used in the Imperative Mood, "be opened," Mark 7:34; while the application in this case was to the ears, the tongue was remedially affected.

NT: B.331a; CB.1245c; K.—.
OT: pᵉtaḥ: S.6606; HR.—; H.2951; BD.1109b.
GEN. REF.: IS.2:118; NB.382; Z.2:333.

EPILEPTIC

selēniazō [σεληνιάζω, 4583], lit., to be moon struck (from *selēnē*, the moon), is used in the Passive Voice with Active significance, R.V., "epileptic," for A.V., "lunatick," Matt. 4:24;

17:15; the corresponding English word is lunatic. Epilepsy was supposed to be influenced by the moon. ¶

NT: B.746d; CB.1268c; K.—.
OT: —.
GEN. REF.: IS.2:122; NB.—; Z.2:135.

EPISTLE

epistolē [ἐπιστολή, 1992], primarily a message (from *epistellō*, to send to), hence, a letter, an epistle, is used in the singular, e.g., Acts 15:30; in the plural, e.g., Acts 9:2; 2 Cor. 10:10. "Epistle is a less common word for a letter. A letter affords a writer more freedom, both in subject and expression, than does a formal treatise. A letter is usually occasional, that is, it is written in consequence of some circumstance which requires to be dealt with promptly. The style of a letter depends largely on the occasion that calls it forth."* "A broad line is to be drawn between the letter and the epistle. The one is essentially a spontaneous product dominated throughout by the image of the reader, his sympathies and interests, instinct also with the writer's own soul: it is virtually one half of an imaginary dialogue, the suppressed responses of the other party shaping the course of what is actually written . . .; the other has a general aim, addressing all and sundry whom it may concern: it is like a public speech and looks towards publication" (J. V. Bartlet, in *Hastings' Bib. Dic.*).

In 2 Pet. 3:16 the Apostle includes the Epistles of Paul as part of the God-breathed Scriptures.

NT: B.300d; CB.1246a; K.1074.
OT: 'iggeret: S.107; HR.530c.1a; H.23b; BD.8d.
GEN. REF.: IS.2:122; NB.383; Z.2:137.

EQUAL, EQUALITY

A. Adjective.

isos [ἴσος, 2470], the same in size, number, quality, etc., is translated "equal" in John 5:18; Phil. 2:6; in the latter the word is in the neuter plural, lit., 'equalities'; "in the R.V. the words are translated 'on an equality with God,' instead of 'equal with God,' as in the A.V. The change is of great importance to the right interpretation of the whole passage. The rendering 'equal with God,' is evidently derived from the Latin Version . . . It was apparently due at first to the fact that the Latin language had no adequate mode of representing the exact form and meaning of the Greek. The neuter plural denotes the various modes or states in which it was possible for the nature of Deity to exist and manifest itself as Divine."†

NT: B.381a; CB.1253a; K.370.
OT: 'eḥād: S.259; HR.688c.1; H.61; BD.25c.
GEN. REF.: IS.2:125; NB.—; Z.—.

Note: Cp. *isotimos*, equally precious, 2 Pet. 1:1; ¶ *isopsuchos*, of equal soul, like-minded, Phil. 2:20; ¶ also Eng. words beginning with the prefix *iso—*.

B. Nouns.

1. *isotēs* [ἰσοτής, 2471], equality (akin to A.), is translated "equality" in 2 Cor. 8:14, twice; in Col. 4:1, with the article, "that which is . . . equal," (lit., 'the equality,' as marg.), i.e., equity, fairness, what is equitable. ¶ In the Sept., Job 36:29; Zech. 4:7. ¶

NT: B.381b; CB.1253a; K.370.
OT: —.
GEN. REF.: IS.2:125; NB.—; Z.—.

2. *sunēlikiōtēs* [συνηλικιώτης, 4915], denotes one of the same age, an equal in age (*sun*, with, *hēlikia*, age), a contemporary, Gal. 1:14, R.V., "of mine own age," for A.V. "mine equals," the reference being to the Apostle's good standing among his fellow-students in the Rabbinical Schools; cp. Acts 22:3. ¶

NT: B.789d; CB.—; K.—.
OT: —.
GEN. REF.: —.

ERE: See Note † p. 1.

ERR

1. *planaō* [πλανάω, 4105], in the Active Voice, signifies to cause to wander, lead astray, deceive (*planē*, a wandering; cp. Eng., planet); in the Passive Voice, to be led astray, to err. It is translated "err," Matt. 22:29; Mark 12:24, 27; Heb. 3:10; Jas. 1:16 (A.V., "do not err," R.V., "be not deceived"); 5:19. See DECEIVE, SEDUCE, WANDER, WAY, *Note* (5).

NT: B.665b; CB.1265a; K.857.
OT: tā'āh: S.8582; HR.1139b.16; H.2531; BD.1073b.
pātāh: S.6601; HR.1139b.11; H.1853; BD.834c.
GEN. REF.: IS.2:127; NB.—; Z.—.

2. *apoplanaō* [ἀποπλανάω, 635], to cause to wander away from, to lead astray from (*apō*, from, and No. 1), is used metaphorically of leading into error, Mark 13:22, A.V., "seduce," R.V., "lead astray"; 1 Tim. 6:10, in the Passive Voice, A.V., "have erred," R.V., "have been led astray." See SEDUCE. ¶

NT: B.97b; CB.1237a; K.857.
OT: nāṭāh: S.5186; HR.139c.2; H.1352; BD.639d,640c.
GEN. REF.: —.

* From Notes on Thessalonians by Hogg and Vine, p. 5.

† Gifford, The Incarnation, p. 20.

3. *astocheō* [ἀστοχέω, 795], to miss the mark, fail (*a*, negative, *stochos*, a mark), is used only in the Pastoral Epistles, 1 Tim. 1:6, "having swerved"; 6:21 and 2 Tim. 2:18, "have erred." See SWERVE. ¶
NT: B.118a; CB.1238a; K.—.
OT: —.
GEN. REF.: —.

ERROR

1. *planē* [πλάνη, 4106], akin to *planaō* (see ERR, No. 1), "a wandering, a forsaking of the right path, see Jas. 5:20, whether in doctrine, 2 Pet. 3:17; 1 John 4:6, or in morals, Rom. 1:27; 2 Pet. 2:18; Jude 11, though, in Scripture, doctrine and morals are never divided by any sharp line. See also Matt. 27:64, where it is equivalent to 'fraud'"*

Errors in doctrine are not infrequently the effect of relaxed morality, and vice versa.

In Eph. 4:14 the R.V. has "wiles of error," for A.V., "they lie in wait to deceive"; in 1 Thess. 2:3, R.V., "error," for A.V., "deceit"; in 2 Thess. 2:11, R.V., "a working of error," for A.V., "strong delusion." See DECEIT. ¶ Cp. *planētēs*, a wandering, Jude 13, ¶ and the adjective *planos*, leading astray, deceiving, a deceiver.
NT: B.665d; CB.1265a; K.857.
OT: mirmāh: S.4820; HR.1140a.1; H.2169b; BD.941b.
GEN. REF.: IS.2:127; NB.—; Z.—.

2. *agnoēma* [ἀγνόημα, 51], a sin of ignorance (cp. *agnoia*, ignorance, and *agnoeō*, to be ignorant), is used in the plural in Heb. 9:7. ¶
NT: B.11c; CB.1233b; K.18.
OT: mishgeh: S.4870; HR.16a.1; H.2325b; BD.993b.
GEN. REF.: IS.2:127; NB.—; Z.—.

ESCAPE

A. Verbs.

1. *pheugō* [φεύγω, 5343], to flee (Lat., *fuga*, flight, etc.; cp. Eng., fugitive, subterfuge), is rendered "escape" in Matt. 23:33; Heb. 11:34. See FLEE.
NT: B.855d; CB.1264a; K.—.
OT: bāraḥ: S.1272; HR.1428b.1a; H.284; BD.137d.
nûs: S.5127; HR.1428b.4a; H.1327; BD.630c.
GEN. REF.: IS.2:130; NB.—; Z.—.

2. *apopheugō* [ἀποφεύγω, 668], to flee away from (*apo*, from, and No. 1), is used in 2 Pet. 1:4; 2:18, 20. ¶
NT: B.101d; CB.1237a; K.—.
OT: —.
GEN. REF.: IS.2:130; NB.—; Z.—.

3. *diapheugō* [διαφεύγω, 1309], lit., to flee through, is used of the escaping of prisoners from a ship, Acts 27:42. For the word in verse 44 see No. 5. ¶
NT: B.190c; CB.—; K.—.
OT: sārîd: S.8300; HR.314b.7; H.2285a; BD.975a.
nûs: S.5127; HR.314b.3; H.1327; BD.630c.
pālîṭ: S.6412; HR.314b.5; H.1774b,c; BD.812c.
GEN. REF.: IS.2:130; NB.—; Z.—.

4. *ekpheugō* [ἐκφεύγω, 1628], to flee out of a place (*ek*, out of, and No. 1), is said of the escape of prisoners, Acts 16:27; of Sceva's sons, fleeing from the demoniac, 19:16; of Paul's escape from Damascus, 2 Cor. 11:33; elsewhere with reference to the judgments of God, Luke 21:36; Rom. 2:3; Heb. 2:3; 12:25; 1 Thess. 5:3. See FLEE. ¶
NT: B.246d; CB.1243c; K.—.
OT: nûs: S.5127; HR.445b.3; H.1327; BD.630c.
GEN. REF.: IS.2:130; NB.—; Z.—.

5. *diasōzō* [διασώζω, 1295], in the Active Voice, to bring safely through a danger (*dia*, through, intensive, *sōzō*, to save), to make completely whole, to heal, Luke 7:3; to bring safe, Acts 23:24; to save, 27:43; in the Passive Voice, Matt. 14:36, "were made whole"; 1 Pet. 3:20. It is also used in the Passive Voice, signifying to escape, said of shipwrecked mariners, Acts 27:44; 28:1, 4. See HEAL, SAFE, SAVE. ¶
NT: B.189a; CB.1241b; K.—.
OT: mālaṭ: S.4422; HR.312b.3; H.1198; BD.572b.
sārîd: S.8300; HR.312b.6b; H.2285a; BD.975a.
pālîṭ: S.6412; HR.312b.5d; H.1774b,c; BD.812c.
GEN. REF.: IS.2:130; NB.—; Z.—.

Note: Exerchomai, to come or go out of a place, is rendered "He escaped," in John 10:39, A.V., an unsuitable translation, both in meaning and in regard to the circumstances of the Lord's departure from His would-be captors. The R.V. "went forth" is both accurate and appropriate to the dignity of the Lord's actions.

B. Noun.

ekbasis [ἔκβασις, 1545], a way out (*ek*, out, *bainō*, to go), denotes (*a*) an escape, 1 Cor. 10:13, used with the definite article and translated "the way of escape," as afforded by God in case of temptation; (*b*) an issue or result, Heb. 13:7. See END, ISSUE. ¶ Cp. *ekbainō*, to go out, Heb. 11:15 (some mss. have *exerchomai*). ¶
NT: B.237d; CB.—; K.—.
OT: —.
GEN. REF.: IS.2:130; NB.—; Z.—.

ESCHEW

ekklinō [ἐκκλίνω, 1578], to turn aside (*ek*, from, *klinō*, to turn, bend), is used metaphorically (*a*) of leaving the right path, Rom. 3:12, R.V., "turned aside," for A.V., "gone out of the way"; (*b*) of turning away from division-makers, and errorists, 16:17, R.V., "turn away from"; (*c*) of turning away from evil, 1 Pet. 3:11, R.V., "turn away from," A.V., "eschew." See AVOID, TURN. ¶ In the Sept. the verb is frequently

* From Notes on Thessalonians by Hogg and Vine, p. 53.

used of declining or swerving from God's ways, e.g., Job 23:11; Psa. 44:18; 119:51, 157.

NT: B.241c; CB.—; K.—.
OT: nāṭāh: S.5186; HR.433c.11a,b; H.1352; BD.639d.
 sûr: S.5493; HR.433c.15; H.1480; BD.693b.
GEN. REF.: —.

ESPECIALLY

malista [μάλιστα, 3122], most, most of all, above all, is the superlative of *mala*, very much; translated "especially" in Acts 26:3; Gal. 6:10; 1 Tim. 5:17; 2 Tim. 4:13; Phil. 4:22, R.V. (for A.V., "chiefly"); "specially," Acts 25:26; 1 Tim. 4:10; 5:8; Tit. 1:10; Philm. 16; in Acts 20:38, "most of all." See CHIEFLY, MOST.

NT: B.488d; CB.—; K.—.
OT: —.
GEN. REF.: —.

ESPOUSED

1. *harmozō* [ἁρμόζω, 718], to join (from *harmos*, a joint, joining; the root *ar*—, signifying to fit, is in evidence in various languages; cp. *arthron*, a joint, *arithmos*, a number, etc.), is used in the Middle Voice, of marrying or giving in marriage; in 2 Cor. 11:2 it is rendered "espoused," metaphorically of the relationship established between Christ and the local church, through the Apostle's instrumentality. The thought may be that of fitting or joining to one Husband, the Middle Voice expressing the Apostle's interest or desire in doing so. ¶

NT: B.107c; CB.1249b; K.—.
OT: —.
GEN. REF.: —.

2. *mnēsteuō* [μνηστεύω, 3423], to woo and win, to espouse or promise in marriage, is used in the Passive Voice in Matt. 1:18; Luke 1:27; 2:5, all with reference to the Virgin Mary, R.V., "betrothed," for A.V., "espoused," in each case. See BETROTH. ¶

NT: B.525c; CB.—; K.—.
OT: 'āras: S.781; HR.932a.1; H.170; BD.76d.
GEN. REF.: —.

ESTABLISH

1. *stērizō* [στηρίζω, 4741], to fix, make fast, to set (from *stērix*, a prop), is used of establishing or stablishing (i.e., the confirmation) of persons; the Apostle Peter was called by the Lord to establish his brethren, Luke 22:32, translated "strengthen"; Paul desired to visit Rome that the saints might be "established," Rom. 1:11; cp. Acts 8:23; so with Timothy at Thessalonica, 1 Thess. 3:2; the confirmation of the saints is the work of God, Rom. 16:25, "to stablish (you)"; 1 Thess. 3:13, "stablish (your hearts)"; 2 Thess. 2:17, "stablish them (in every good work and word)"; 1 Pet. 5:10, "stablish"; the means used to effect the confirmation is the ministry of the Word of God, 2 Pet. 1:12, "are established (in the truth which is with you)"; James exhorts Christians to "stablish" their hearts, Jas. 5:8; cp. Rev. 3:2, R.V.

The character of this confirmation may be learned from its use in Luke 9:51, "stedfastly set"; 16:26, "fixed," and in the Sept. in Ex. 17:12, "stayed up" (also from its strengthened form *epistērizō*, to confirm, in Acts 14:22; 15:32, 41; in some mss. to strengthen, in 18:23; see CONFIRM ¶). Neither the laying on of hands nor the impartation of the Holy Spirit is mentioned in the N.T. in connection with either of these words, or with the synonymous verb *bebaioō* (see 1 Cor. 1:8; 2 Cor. 1:21, etc.). See FIX, SET, STRENGTHEN. ¶

NT: B.768a; CB.1270a; K.1085.
OT: sāmak: S.5564; HR.1290c.6a,b; H.1514; BD.701d.
 sûm, sîm: S.7760; HR.1290c.9; H.2243; BD.962c.
GEN. REF.: IS.2:155; NB.—; Z.—.

2. *stereoō* [στερεόω, 4732], to make firm, or solid (akin to *stereos*, hard, firm, solid; cp. Eng., stereotype), is used only in Acts, (*a*) physically, 3:7, "received strength"; 3:16, "hath made strong"; (*b*) metaphorically, of establishment in the faith, 16:5, R.V., "strengthened," for A.V., "established." ¶

NT: B.766d; CB.—; K.1077.
OT: ḥāzaq: S.2388; HR.1289a.2; H.636; BD.304a.
 kûn: S.3559; HR.1289a.4; H.964; BD.465c.
GEN. REF.: IS.2:155; NB.—; Z.—.

3. *histēmi* [ἵστημι, 2476], to cause to stand, is translated "establish" in Rom. 3:31; 10:3; Heb. 10:9. See ABIDE, APPOINT, STAND, etc.

NT: B.381d; CB.1250c; K.1082.
OT: 'āmad: S.5975; HR.689a.26a-c; H.1637; BD.763c.
 qûm: S.6965; HR.689a.28a-c; H.1999; BD.877c.
GEN. REF.: IS.2:155; NB.—; Z.—.

4. *bebaioō* [βεβαιόω, 950], to confirm, is rendered "stablish," 2 Cor. 1:21; "stablished," Col. 2:7; "be established," Heb. 13:9: see CONFIRM.

NT: B.138c; CB.1239a; K.103.
OT: nāṣab: S.5324; HR.216b.1; H.1398; BD.662a.
 qûm: S.6965; HR.216b.2; H.1999; BD.877c.
GEN. REF.: IS.2:155; NB.—; Z.—.

5. *nomotheteō* [νομοθετέω]: see ENACT.

ESTATE, STATE

1. *euschēmōn* [εὐσχήμων, 2158], signifying elegant, graceful, comely (*eu*, well, *schēma*, figure, fashion), is used (*a*) in a moral sense, seemly, becoming, 1 Cor. 7:35; (*b*) in a physical sense, comely, 1 Cor. 12:24; (*c*) with reference to social degree, influential, a meaning developed in later Greek, and rendered of "honourable estate" in the R.V. of Mark 15:43; Acts 13:50; 17:12 (for A.V., "honourable"). See COMELY, HONOURABLE. ¶

NT: B.327a; CB.—; K.—.
OT: —.
GEN. REF.: IS.2:156; NB.—; Z.—.

2. *tapeinōsis* [ταπείνωσις, 5014], denotes abasement, humiliation, low estate (from *tapeinos*, lowly), Luke 1:48, "low estate"; Acts 8:33, "humiliation"; Phil. 3:21, R.V., "of humiliation," for A.V., "vile; Jas. 1:10, "is made low," lit., 'in his low estate.' See HUMILIATION, LOW, VILE. ¶

NT: B.805a; CB.1271a; K.1152.
OT: ʿonî: S.6040; HR.1335c.2a; H.1652e; BD.777a.
GEN. REF.: –.

3. *hupsos* [ὕψος, 5311], signifying height, is rendered "(in his) high estate," Jas. 1:9, R.V., for A.V., "in that he is exalted"; "on high," Luke 1:78; 24:49; Eph. 4:8; "height," Eph. 3:18; Rev. 21:16. See EXALT, HEIGHT, HIGH. ¶

NT: B.850c; CB.1252b; K.1241.
OT: qômāh: S.6967; HR.1421b.7; H.1999a; BD.879b.
mārôm: S.4791; HR.1421b.6a; H.2133h; BD.928d.
rûm: S.7312; HR.1421b.6b; H.2133a; BD.927d.
GEN. REF.: –.

Notes: (1) In Acts 22:5, *presbuterion*, presbytery, a body of elders, is translated "estate of the elders," lit., 'the presbytery,' i.e., the Sanhedrin.

(2) In Col. 4:7 the plural of the definite article with the preposition *kata*, and the singular personal pronoun with *panta*, all, is rendered "all my state," A.V., R.V., "all my affairs"; in ver. 8 the preposition *peri*, with the personal pronoun, lit., 'the things concerning us,' is translated "our estate," i.e., 'how we fare'; so in Phil. 2:19, 20, "your state," i.e., 'your condition.'

(3) In Mark 6:21 *prōtos*, lit., first, is rendered "chief estates," A.V., R.V., "the chief men," i.e., the men to whom belongs the dignity.

(4) In Rom. 12:16 *tapeinos*, in the plural with the article, lit., the lowly, is translated "men of low estate," A.V., R.V., "things that are lowly."

(5) In Jude 6 *archē*, "principality," R.V., A.V. has "first estate."

(6) For "last state" see LAST, P. 311, ll. 4-6.

ESTEEM

1. *hēgeomai* [ἡγέομαι, 2233], signifies to lead; then, to lead before the mind, to suppose, consider, esteem; translated "esteem" in Phil. 2:3, A.V., R.V., "counting"; in 1 Thess. 5:13, "esteem"; in Heb. 11:26, A.V., "esteeming," R.V., "accounting."

NT: B.343c; CB.1249c; K.303.
OT: –.
GEN. REF.: –.

2. *krinō* [κρίνω, 2919], signifies to separate, choose; then, to approve, esteem; translated "esteemeth" in Rom. 14:5 (twice), said of days, here the word "alike" (A.V.) is rightly omitted in the R.V., the meaning being that every day is especially regarded as sacred. See DETERMINE.

NT: B.451b; CB.1256a; K.469.
OT: –.
GEN. REF.: IS.2:156; NB.–; Z.–.

3. *logizomai* [λογίζομαι, 3049], to reckon, is translated "esteemeth" in Rom. 14:14 (R.V., "accounteth"). See ACCOUNT.

NT: B.475d; CB.1257a; K.536.
OT: ḥāshab: S.2803; HR.880a.2a-c; H.767; BD.362d.
GEN. REF.: –.

Notes: (1) In 1 Cor. 6:4, A.V., *exoutheneō*, to set at nought, is rendered "are least esteemed"; the meaning is that judges in the world's tribunals have no place (are not of account) in the church. See ACCOUNT.

(2) In the A.V. marg. of 1 Pet. 2:17, *timaō*, to honour, is rendered "esteem."

(3) For "highly esteemed," Luke 16:15, A.V., see EXALT, B.

ETERNAL

1. *aion* [αἰών, 165], an age, is translated "eternal" in Eph. 3:11, lit., '(purpose) of the ages' (marg.), and 1 Tim. 1:17, lit. '(king) of the ages' (marg.). See AGE.

NT: B.27b; CB.1234a; K.31.
OT: ʿôlām: S.5769; HR.39b.5a; H.1631a; BD.761d.
GEN. REF.: IS.2:160; NB.–; Z.2:380.

2. *aiōnios* [αἰώνιος, 166], "describes duration, either undefined but not endless, as in Rom. 16:25; 2 Tim. 1:9; Tit. 1:2; or undefined because endless as in Rom. 16:26, and the other sixty-six places in the N.T.

"The predominant meaning of *aiōnios*, that in which it is used everywhere in the N.T., save the places noted above, may be seen in 2 Cor. 4:18, where it is set in contrast with *proskairos*, lit., 'for a season,' and in Philm. 15, where only in the N.T. it is used without a noun. Moreover it is used of persons and things which are in their nature endless, as, e.g., of God, Rom. 16:26; of His power, 1 Tim. 6:16, and of His glory, 1 Pet. 5:10; of the Holy Spirit, Heb. 9:14; of the redemption effected by Christ, Heb. 9:12, and of the consequent salvation of men, 5:9, as well as of His future rule, 2 Pet. 1:11, which is elsewhere declared to be without end, Luke 1:33; of the life received by those who believe in Christ, John 3:16, concerning whom He said, 'they shall never perish,' 10:28, and of the resurrection body, 2 Cor. 5:1, elsewhere said to be 'immortal,' 1 Cor. 15:53, in which that life will be finally realized, Matt. 25:46; Tit. 1:2.

"*Aiōnios* is also used of the sin that 'hath never forgiveness,' Mark 3:29, and of the judgment of God, from which there is no appeal, Heb. 6:2, and of the fire, which is one of its instruments, Matt. 18:8; 25:41; Jude 7, and which is elsewhere said to be 'unquenchable,' Mark 9:43.

"The use of *aiōnios* here shows that the punishment referred to in 2 Thess. 1:9, is not temporary, but final, and, accordingly, the phraseology shows that its purpose is not remedial but retributive."*

NT: B.28b; CB.1234a; K.31.
OT: 'ôlām: S.5769; HR.41c.1a; H.1631a; BD.761d.
GEN. REF.: IS.2:160; NB.—; Z.2:380.

3. *aidios* [ἀΐδιος]: see EVERLASTING.

EUNUCH

A. Noun.

eunouchos [εὐνοῦχος, 2135], denotes (*a*) an emasculated man, a eunuch, Matt. 19:12; (*b*) in the 3rd instance in that verse, one naturally incapacitated for, or voluntarily abstaining from, wedlock; (*c*) one such, in a position of high authority in a court, a chamberlain, Acts 8:27-39. ¶

NT: B.323c; CB.1247b; K.277.
OT: sārîs: S.5631; HR.575b.1; H.1545; BD.710b.
GEN. REF.: IS.2:200; NB.398; Z.2:415.

B. Verb.

eunouchizō [εὐνουχίζω, 2134], to make a eunuch (from A.), is used in Matt. 19:12, as under (*b*) in A.; and in the Passive Voice, "were made eunuchs," probably an allusion by the Lord to the fact that there were eunuchs in the courts of the Herods, as would be well known to His hearers. ¶

NT: B.323c; CB.1247b; K.277.
OT: —.
GEN. REF.: IS.2:200; NB.398; Z.2:415.

EVANGELIST

euangelistēs [εὐαγγελιστής, 2099], lit., a messenger of good (*eu*, well, *angelos*, a messenger), denotes a preacher of the Gospel, Acts 21:8; Eph. 4:11, which makes clear the distinctiveness of the function in the churches; 2 Tim. 4:5. ¶ Cp. *euangelizō*, to proclaim glad tidings, and *euangelion*, good news, gospel. Missionaries are evangelists, as being essentially preachers of the Gospel.

NT: B.318c; CB.1247a; K.267.
OT: —.
GEN. REF.: IS.2:204; NB.400; Z.2:418.

EVEN (Noun), EVENING, EVENTIDE

A. Nouns.

1. *hespera* [ἑσπέρα, 2073], properly, the feminine of the adjective *hesperos*, of, or at, evening, western (Lat., *vesper*, Eng., vespers), is used as a noun in Luke 24:29; Acts 4:3, "eventide"; 28:23. Some mss. have the word in 20:15, 'in the evening (we touched),' instead of *hetera*, "next (day)."

NT: B.313c; CB.—; K.—.
OT: 'ereb: S.6153; HR.557a.2b; H.1689a; BD.787d.
GEN. REF.: IS.2:205; NB.—; Z.—.

2. *opsia* [ὀψία, 3798], the feminine of the adjective *opsios*, late, used as a noun, denoting evening, with *hora*, understood (see No. 1), is found seven times in Matthew, five in Mark, two in John, and in these places only in the N.T. (some mss. have it in Mark 11:11, see B.). The word really signifies the late evening, the latter of the two evenings as reckoned by the Jews, the first from 3 p.m. to sunset, the latter after sunset; this is the usual meaning. It is used, however, of both, e.g., Mark 1:32 (cp. *opsimos*, latter, said of rain, Jas. 5:7).

NT: B.601c; CB.—; K.—.
OT: —.
GEN. REF.: IS.2:205; NB.—; Z.—.

B. Adverb.

opse [ὀψέ, 3796], long after, late, late in the day, at evening (in contrast to *prōi*, early, e.g., Matt. 20:1), is used practically as a noun in Mark 11:11, lit., 'the hour being at eventide'; 11:19; 13:35; in Matt. 28:1 it is rendered "late on," R.V., for A.V., "in the end of." Here, however, the meaning seems to be "after," a sense in which the word was used by late Greek writers. See LATE. ¶ In the Sept., Gen. 24:11; Ex. 30:8; Jer. 2:23; Isa. 5:11. ¶

NT: B.601b; CB.1261a; K.—.
OT: 'ereb: S.6153; HR.1044a.2a; H.1689a; BD.787d.
nesheph: S.5399; HR.1044a.1; H.1434a; BD.676a.
GEN. REF.: —.

Note: In Luke 12:38 some mss. have the adjective *hesperinos*, of the evening (see A, No. 1), lit., 'in the evening watch.'

EVEN (Adjective)

Notes: (1) In Luke 19:44 (A.V., "shall lay thee even with the ground"), there is no word representing "even"; the verb *edaphizō* signifies to beat level (like a threshing floor); hence, to dash to the ground. See DASH. ¶

(2) In Heb. 12:13 the adjective *orthos*, straight, is rendered "even" in the A.V., marg.

EVEN (Adverb, etc.), EVEN AS, EVEN SO

1. *kai* [καί, 2532], a conjunction, is usually a mere connective, meaning "and"; it

* From Notes on Thessalonians by Hogg and Vine, pp. 232, 233.

frequently, however, has an ascensive or climactic use, signifying "even," the thing that is added being out of the ordinary, and producing a climax. The determination of this meaning depends on the context. Examples are Matt. 5:46, 47; Mark 1:27; Luke 6:33 (R.V.); 10:17; John 12:42; Gal. 2:13, 17, where "also" should be "even"; Eph. 5:12. Examples where the R.V. corrects the A.V. "and" or "also," by substituting "even," are Luke 7:49; Acts 17:28; Heb. 11:11; in 1 John 4:3 the R.V. rightly omits "even."

When followed by "if" or "though," *kai* often signifies "even," e.g., Matt. 26:35; John 8:14. So sometimes when preceded by "if," e.g., 1 Cor. 7:11, where "but and if" should be "but even if."

The epexegetic or explanatory use of *kai* followed by a noun in apposition, and meaning "namely," or "even" is comparatively rare. Wincr's cautionary word needs heeding, that "this meaning has been introduced into too many passages" (Gram. of the N.T., p. 546.). Some think it has this sense in John 3:5, "water, even the Spirit," and Gal. 6:16, "even the Israel of God."

NT: B.391c; CB.1253a; K.–.
OT: –.
GEN. REF.: –.

2. *de* [δέ, 1161], usually signifying "but," is sometimes used for emphasis, signifying "even," e.g., Rom. 3:22; 9:30, "even the righteousness"; Phil. 2:8 (R.V., "yea"). This is to be distinguished from No. 1.

NT: B.171c; CB.–; K.–.
OT: –.
GEN. REF.: –.

3. *eti* [ἔτι, 2089], an adverb, as yet, still, is rendered "even" in Luke 1:15.

NT: B.315c; CB.1247a; K.–.
OT: –.
GEN. REF.: –.

4. *hōs* [ὡς, 5613], "as," in comparative sentences, is sometimes translated "even as," Matt. 15:28; Mark 4:36; Eph. 5:33; 1 Pet. 3:6 (A.V. only); Jude 7.

NT: B.897a; CB.1251b; K.–.
OT: –.
GEN. REF.: –.

5. *houtōs* [οὕτως, 3779], or *houtō*, so, thus, is frequently rendered "even so," e.g., Matt. 7:17; 12:45; 18:14; 23:28; "so" in 1 Cor. 11:12 and 1 Thess. 2:4, R.V.

NT: B.597c; CB.–; K.–.
OT: –.
GEN. REF.: –.

6. *kathōs* [καθώς, 2531], according as (*kāta*, according to, and No. 4), is frequently translated "even as," e.g., Mark 11:6; Luke 1:2; 1 Thess. 5:11.

NT: B.391b; CB.1254c; K.–.
OT: –.
GEN. REF.: –.

7. *hōsper* [ὥσπερ, 5618], No. 4, strengthened by *per*, is translated "even as" in Matt. 20:28.

NT: B.899c; CB.1251b; K.–.
OT: –.
GEN. REF.: –.

8. *kathaper* [καθάπερ, 2509], just as, even as, is rendered "even as" in Rom. 4:6; 9:13; 10:15; 12:4 (R.V.); 2 Cor. 3:18; 1 Thess. 3:6, 12; 4:5; Heb. 4:2; "according as," Rom. 11:8; elsewhere simply "as."

NT: B.387a; CB.–; K.–.
OT: –.
GEN. REF.: –.

9. *nai* [ναί, 3483], a particle of strong affirmation, yea, verily, even so, is rendered "even so" in the A.V., "yea" in the R.V., in Matt. 11:26; Luke 10:21; Rev. 16:7; both A.V. and R.V. have it in Rev. 1:7; the most authentic mss. omit it in 22:20. See SURELY, TRUTH, VERILY, YEA, YES.

NT: B.532d; CB.–; K.–.
OT: ʾabal: S.61; HR.939a.1; H.8; BD.6a.
GEN. REF.: –.

10. *homōs* [ὅμως, 3676], yet, nevertheless, is translated "even" in 1 Cor. 14:7 (A.V., "and even"); elsewhere John 12:42, "nevertheless"; Gal. 3:15, "yet" (i.e., 'nevertheless,' an example of hyperbaton, by which a word is placed out of its true position). ¶

NT: B.569c; CB.–; K.–.
OT: –.
GEN. REF.: –.

Notes: (1) In Rom. 1:26, there is no word representing "even" in the original. The A.V. seems to have put it for the particle *te*, which simply annexes the statement to the preceding and does not require translation.

(2) In 1 Thess. 2:18 the A.V. renders the particle *men* by "even"; if translated, it signifies "indeed."

(3) In 1 Cor. 12:2, *hōs* (see No. 4, above), followed by the particle *an*, means "howsoever" (R.V., for A.V., "even as").

(4) In Matt. 23:37, "even as" translates the phrase *hon tropon*, lit., '(in) what manner.'

(5) In 1 Tim. 3:11, *hōsautōs*, a strengthened form of No. 4, likewise, in like manner, is rendered "even so," A.V. (R.V., "in like manner").

(6) *Kàgō*, for *kai egō*, means either "even I" or "even so I" or "I also." In John 10:15, the R.V. has "and I" for the A.V., "even so . . . I"; in 17:18 and 20:21, A.V. and R.V., "even so I"; in the following, *kàgō* is preceded by *hōs*, or *kathōs*, "even as I," 1 Cor. 7:8; 10:33; "even as

I also," 11:1; "as I also," Rev. 2:27.

(7) In Luke 12:7 the R.V. renders *kai* by "very" (for A.V., "even the very").

(8) In John 6:57 *kàkeinos* (for *kai ekeinos*, "also he"), is translated "he also," R.V., for A.V., "even he."

(9) In Eph. 1:10 there is no word in the original for "even." The R.V. expresses the stress on the pronoun by "in Him, I say."

EVER, FOR EVER, EVERMORE

A. Adverbs.

1. *pantote* [πάντοτε, 3842], at all times, always (akin to *pas*, all), is translated "ever" in Luke 15:31; John 18:20; 1 Thess. 4:17; 5:15; 2 Tim. 3:7; Heb. 7:25; "evermore" in John 6:34; in 1 Thess. 5:16, R.V., "alway," for A.V., "evermore." It there means 'on all occasions,' as, e.g., in 1 Thess. 1:2; 3:6; 5:15; 2 Thess. 1:3, 11; 2:13. See ALWAYS.

NT: B.609a; CB.1261c; K.—.
OT: —.
GEN. REF.: —.

2. *aei* [ἀεί, 104], ever, is used (*a*) of continuous time, signifying unceasingly, perpetually, Acts 7:51; 2 Cor. 4:11; 6:10; Tit. 1:12; Heb. 3:10; (*b*) of successive occurrences, signifying 'on every occasion,' 1 Pet. 3:15; 2 Pet. 1:12. Some texts have the word in Mark 15:8. See ALWAYS. ¶

NT: B.19c; CB.1233a; K.—.
OT: tāmîd: S.8548; HR.28b.2; H.1157a; BD.556b.
mē'ôlām: S.5769; HR.28b.1; H.1631a; BD.761d,762a.
GEN. REF.: IS.2:162; NB.—; Z.—.

Note: The adjective *diēnekēs*, unbroken, continuous, is used in a phrase with *eis*, unto, and the article, signifying perpetually, for ever, Heb. 7:3; 10:1, 12, 14. ¶

B. Phrases.

The following phrases are formed in connection with *aiōn*, an age: they are idiomatic expressions betokening undefined periods and are not to be translated literally: (*a*) *eis aiōna*, lit., 'unto an age,' Jude 13, "for ever"; (*b*) *eis ton aiōna*, lit., 'unto the age,' "for ever" (or, with a negative, "never"), Matt. 21:19; Mark 3:29; 11:14; Luke 1:55; John 4:14; 6:51, 58; 8:35 (twice), 51; 52; 10:28; 11:26; 12:34; 13:8; 14:16; 1 Cor. 8:13; 2 Cor. 9:9; Heb. 5:6; 6:20; 7:17, 21, 24, 28; 1 Pet. 1:25; 1 John 2:17; 2 John 2; (*c*) *eis tous aiōnas*, lit., 'unto the ages,' "for ever," Matt. 6:13 (A.V. only); Luke 1:33; Rom. 1:25; 9:5; 11:36; 16:27 (some mss. have the next phrase here); 2 Cor. 11:31; Heb. 13:8; (*d*) *eis tous aiōnas tōn aiōnōn*, lit. 'unto the ages of the ages,' "for ever and ever," or "for evermore," Gal. 1:5; Phil. 4:20; 1 Tim. 1:17; 2 Tim. 4:18; Heb. 13:21; 1 Pet. 4:11; 5:11 [(*c*) in some mss.]; Rev. 1:6 [(*c*) in some mss.]; 1:18, "for evermore"; 4:9, 10; 5:13; 7:12; 10:6; 11:15; 15:7; 19:3; 20:10; 22:5; (*e*) *eis aiōnas aiōnōn*, lit., 'unto ages of ages,' "for ever and ever," Rev. 14:11; (*f*) *eis ton aiōna tou aiōnos*, lit., 'unto the age of the age,' "for ever and ever," Heb. 1:8; (*g*) *tou aiōnos tōn aiōnōn*, lit., 'of the age of the ages,' "for ever and ever," Eph. 3:21; (*h*) *eis pantas tous aiōnas*, lit., 'unto all the ages,' Jude 25 ("for evermore," R.V.; "ever," A.V.); (*i*) *eis hēmeran aiōnos*, lit., 'unto a day of an age,' "for ever," 2 Pet. 3:18.

EVERLASTING

1. *aiōnios* [αἰώνιος]: see ETERNAL.

2. *aidios* [ἀΐδιος, 126], denotes everlasting (from *aei*, ever), Rom. 1:20, R.V., "everlasting," for A.V., "eternal"; Jude 6, A.V. and R.V., "everlasting." *Aiōnios*, should always be translated "eternal" and *aidios*, "everlasting." "While *aiōnios* . . . negatives the end either of a space of time or of unmeasured time, and is used chiefly where something future is spoken of, *aidios* excludes interruption and lays stress upon permanence and unchangeableness" (Cremer). ¶

NT: B.22a; CB.1233c; K.25.
OT: —.
GEN. REF.: IS.2:162; NB.—; Z.2:381.

EVERY, EVERYONE (MAN), EVERYTHING

1. *pas* [πᾶς, 3956], signifies (1) with nouns without the article, (*a*) every one of the class denoted by the noun connected with *pas*, e.g., Matt. 3:10, "every tree"; Mark 9:49, "every sacrifice"; see also John 2:10; Acts 2:43; Rom. 2:9; Eph. 1:21; 3:15; 2 Thess. 2:4; 2 Tim. 3:16, R.V.; (*b*) any and every, of every kind, "all manner of," e.g., Matt. 4:23; "especially with nouns denoting virtues or vices, emotions, condition, indicating every mode in which a quality manifests itself; or any object to which the idea conveyed by the noun belongs" (Grimm-Thayer). This is often translated "all," e.g., Acts 27:20; Rom. 15:14; 2 Cor. 10:6; Eph. 4:19, 31; Col. 4:12, "all the will of God," i.e., everything God wills; (2) without a noun, every one, everything, every man (i.e., person), e.g., Luke 16:16; or with a negative, not everyone, e.g., Mark 9:49; with a participle and the article, equivalent to a relative clause, everyone who, e.g., 1 Cor. 9:25; Gal. 3:10, 13; 1 John 2:29; 3:3, 4, 6, 10, 15, rendered "whosoever." So in the neuter, 1 John 2:16; 5:4, often rendered "whatsoever"; governed by the preposition *en*, in, without a noun following,

it signifies in every matter, or condition, Phil. 4:6; 1 Thess. 5:18; in every way or particular, 2 Cor. 4:8, translated "on every side"; so 2 Cor. 7:5; "in everything," Eph. 5:24; Phil. 4:12, lit., 'in everything and (perhaps "even") in all things.' See THOROUGHLY, WHOLE.

NT: B.631a; CB.1262c; K.795.
OT: kōl: S.3605; HR.1073a.1; H.985a; BD.481a.
GEN. REF.: –.

2. *hapas* [ἅπας, 537], a strengthened form of No. 1, signifies all, the whole, altogether; it is translated "every one" in Acts 5:16, where it occurs in the plural. In Mark 8:25, the A.V., "every man" translates the text with the masculine plural; the best mss. have the neuter plural, R.V., "all things." See ALL, WHOLE.

NT: B.81d; CB.1249b; K.795.
OT: kōl: S.3605; HR.118c.1a; H.985a; BD.481a.
GEN. REF.: –.

3. *hekastos* [ἕκαστος, 1538]: see EACH, No. 1. It is used with *heis*, one, in Acts 2:6, "every man," and in Eph. 4:16, "each several (part)," for A.V., "every (part)." In Rev. 22:2 the most authentic mss. omit the numeral in the phrase "every month." It is preceded by *kath hena* (*kata*, according to, *hena*, one), a strengthened phrase, in Eph. 5:33, A.V., "everyone . . . in particular," R.V., "severally, each one." The same kind of phrase with *ana*, each, before the numeral, is used in Rev. 21:21, R.V., "each one of the several (gates)," for A.V., "every several (gate)." See EACH, PARTICULAR, SEVERAL.

NT: B.236c; CB.1249c; K.–.
OT: 'îsh: S.376; HR.418a.3a; H.83a; BD.35c.
GEN. REF.: –.

Notes: (1) The preposition *kata*, down, is sometimes found governing a noun, in the sense of "every," e.g., Luke 2:41, "every year"; 16:19, "every day"; Heb. 9:25, "every year" (R.V., "year by year"); so 10:3. This construction sometimes signifies "in every . . .," e.g., Acts 14:23, "in every church"; 15:21, "in every city"; so 20:23; Tit. 1:5; Acts 22:19, "in every synagogue" (plural); Acts 8:3 "(into) every house." In Luke 8:1 the phrase means "throughout every city," as in the A.V.; in ver. 4 "of every city," R.V. In Acts 5:42 the R.V. renders *kat' oikon* "at home," for A.V., "in every house"; in 2:46, for A.V., "from house to house" (marg., "at home"). In Acts 15:21 (last part) the adjective *pas* (all) is placed between the preposition and the noun for the sake of emphasis. In Acts 26:11, *kata*, followed by the plural of *pas* and the article before the noun, is rendered "in all the synagogues," R.V., for A.V., "in every synagogue." The presence of the article confirms the R.V. See SEVERALLY.

(2) In Matt. 20:9, 10, the preposition *ana*, upward (used distributively), governing the noun *dēnarion*, is translated "every man (a penny)." There is no word for "every man," and an appropriate rendering would be 'a penny apiece'; cp. Luke 9:14, "fifty each," R.V.; 10:1, "two and two"; John 2:6, "two or three . . . apiece"; Rev. 4:8, "each . . . six wings."

(3) The pronoun *tis*, anyone, is rendered "any" in Acts 2:45, R.V., for the incorrect A.V., "every." In Mark 15:24, the interrogative form is rendered "what each (should take)" (A.V., "every man"), lit., 'who (should take) what.'

EVERYWHERE, EVERY QUARTER, EVERY SIDE

1. *pantachē* [πανταχῇ], everywhere, is used in Acts 21:28. ¶

2. *pantachou* [πανταχοῦ, 3837], a variation of No. 1, is translated "everywhere" in Mark 1:28, R.V., of the report throughout Galilee concerning Christ; in Mark 16:20, of preaching; Luke 9:6, of healing; Acts 17:30, of a Divine command for repentance; 28:22, of disparagement of Christians; 1 Cor. 4:17, of apostolic teaching; in Acts 24:3, it is rendered "in all places." ¶ In the Sept., Isa. 42:22. ¶ See PLACE.

NT: B.608b; CB.–; K.–.
OT: –.
GEN. REF.: –.

3. *pantothen* [πάντοθεν, 3840], or *pantachothen*, from all sides, is translated "from every quarter," Mark 1:45; in Luke 19:43, "on every side"; in Heb. 9:4, "round about." ¶

NT: B.608d; CB.–; K.–.
OT: –.
GEN. REF.: –.

Notes: (1) In Phil. 4:12, the phrase *en panti*, A.V., "everywhere," is corrected to "in everything," in the R.V.; in 2 Cor. 4:8, "on every side."

(2) In 1 Tim. 2:8, *en panti topǭ*, "in every place," R.V., is translated "everywhere" in the A.V.

EVERY WHIT

holos [ὅλος, 3650], all, whole, complete, is rendered "every whit" in John 7:23; 13:10. See ALL.

NT: B.564d; CB.1251a; K.682.
OT: kōl: S.3605; HR.989b.1a; H.985a; BD.481a.
GEN. REF.: –.

For **EVIDENCE** (Heb. 11:1) see **REPROOF,** A

EVIDENT, EVIDENTLY

A. Adjectives.

1. *dēlos* [δῆλος, 1212], properly signifying visible, clear to the mind, evident, is translated "evident" in Gal. 3:11 and 1 Cor. 15:27, R.V. (A.V., "manifest"); "bewrayeth," Matt. 26:73; "certain," 1 Tim. 6:7, A.V. Cp. *dēloō*, to declare, signify. See BEWRAY, CERTAIN, MANIFEST. ¶

NT: B.178b; CB.1240c; K.–.
OT: –.
GEN. REF.: –.

2. *katadēlos* [κατάδηλος, 2612], a strengthened form of No. 1, quite manifest, evident, is used in Heb. 7:15 (A.V., "more evident"). ¶ For the preceding verse see No. 3.

NT: B.410b; CB.–; K.–.
OT: –.
GEN. REF.: –.

3. *prodēlos* [πρόδηλος, 4271], manifest beforehand (*pro*, before, and No. 1), is used in Heb. 7:14 in the sense of 'clearly evident.' So in 1 Tim. 5:24, 25, R.V., "evident," for A.V., "open beforehand," and "manifest beforehand." The *pro* is somewhat intensive. ¶

NT: B.704b; CB.–; K.–.
OT: –.
GEN. REF.: –.

Note: Phaneros, visible, manifest (akin to *phainomai*, to appear), is synonymous with the above, but is not translated "evident" in the N.T. For "evident token" see TOKEN.

B. Adverb.

phanerōs [φανερῶς, 5320], manifestly (see note above), is rendered "openly" in Mark 1:45; "publicly" in John 7:10, R.V. (opposite to "in secret"); in Acts 10:3, R.V., "openly," for A.V., "evidently." See OPENLY, PUBLICLY. ¶

NT: B.853a; CB.1263c; K.–.
OT: –.
GEN. REF.: IS.2:206; NB.–; Z.–.

Note: For the A.V. "evidently" in Gal. 3:1, see OPENLY.

EVIL, EVIL-DOER

A. Adjectives.

1. *kakos* [κακός, 2556], stands for whatever is evil in character, base, in distinction (wherever the distinction is observable) from *ponēros* (see No. 2), which indicates what is evil in influence and effect, malignant. *Kakos* is the wider term and often covers the meaning of *ponēros*. *Kakos* is antithetic to *kalos*, fair, advisable, good in character, and to *agathos*, beneficial, useful, good in act; hence it denotes what is useless, incapable, bad; *ponēros* is essentially antithetic to *chrēstos*, kind, gracious, serviceable; hence it denotes what is destructive, injurious, evil. As evidence that *ponēros* and *kakos* have much in common, though still not interchangeable, each is used of thoughts, cp. Matt. 15:19 with Mark 7:21; of speech, Matt. 5:11 with 1 Pet. 3:10; of actions, 2 Tim. 4:18 with 1 Thess. 5:15; of man, Matt. 18:32 with 24:48.

The use of *kakos* may be broadly divided as follows: (*a*) of what is morally or ethically evil, whether of persons, e.g., Matt. 21:41; 24:48; Phil. 3:2; Rev. 2:2, or qualities, emotions, passions, deeds, e.g., Mark 7:21; John 18:23, 30; Rom. 1:30; 3:8; 7:19, 21; 13:4; 14:20; 16:19; 1 Cor. 13:5; 2 Cor. 13:7; 1 Thess. 5:15; 1 Tim. 6:10; 2 Tim. 4:14; 1 Pet. 3:9, 12; (*b*) of what is injurious, destructive, baneful, pernicious, e.g., Luke 16:25; Acts 16:28; 28:5; Tit. 1:12; Jas. 3:8; Rev. 16:2, where *kakos* and *ponēros* come in that order, "noisome and grievous." See B, No. 3. For compounds of *kakos*, see below.

NT: B.397d; CB.1253b; K.391.
OT: ra': S.7451; HR.709b,13b; H.2191; BD.948c.
ra'āh: S.7451; HR.709b.13c; H.2191; BD.949a.
GEN. REF.: IS.2:206; NB.400; Z.2:420.

2. *ponēros* [πονηρός, 4190], akin to *ponos*, labour, toil, denotes evil that causes labour, pain, sorrow, malignant evil (see No. 1); it is used (*a*) with the meaning bad, worthless, in the physical sense, Matt. 7:17, 18; in the moral or ethical sense, evil, wicked; of persons, e.g., Matt. 7:11; Luke 6:45; Acts 17:5; 2 Thess. 3:2; 2 Tim. 3:13; of evil spirits, e.g., Matt. 12:45; Luke 7:21; Acts 19:12, 13, 15, 16; of a generation, Matt. 12:39, 45; 16:4; Luke 11:29; of things, e.g., Matt. 5:11; 6:23; 20:15; Mark 7:22; Luke 11:34; John 3:19; 7:7; Acts 18:14; Gal. 1:4; Col. 1:21; 1 Tim. 6:4; 2 Tim. 4:18; Heb. 3:12; 10:22; Jas. 2:4; 4:16; 1 John 3:12; 2 John 11; 3 John 10; (*b*) with the meaning toilsome, painful, Eph. 5:16; 6:13; Rev. 16:2. Cp. *ponēria*, iniquity, wickedness. For its use as a noun see B, No. 2.

NT: B.690d; CB.1266a; K.912.
OT: ra': S.7451; HR.1186c.4a; H.2191; BD.948c.
ra'āh: S.7451; HR.1186c.4c; H.2191; BD.949a.
GEN. REF.: IS.2:206; NB.400; Z.2:420.

3. *phaulos* [φαῦλος, 5337], primarily denotes slight, trivial, blown about by every wind; then, mean, common, bad, in the sense of being worthless, paltry or contemptible, belonging to a low order of things; in John 5:29, those who have practised evil things, R.V., "ill" (*phaula*), are set in contrast to those who have done good things (*agatha*); the same contrast is presented in Rom. 9:11 and 2 Cor. 5:10, in each of which the most authentic mss. have *phaulos* for *kakos*; he who practises evil things (R.V., "ill") hates the light, John 3:20; jealousy and strife are accompanied by "every vile deed," Jas. 3:16. It

is used as a noun in Tit. 2:8 (see B, No. 4). See BAD, ILL, VILE. ¶

NT: B.854c; CB.1264a; K.—.
OT: 'ᵉwîl: S.191; HR.1425c.1; H.44a; BD.17b.
GEN. REF.: IS.2:206; NB.400; Z.2:420.

B. Nouns.

1. *kakia* [κακία, 2549], primarily, badness in quality (akin to A, No. 1), denotes (*a*) wickedness, depravity, malignity, e.g., Acts 8:22, "wickedness"; Rom. 1:29, "maliciousness"; in Jas. 1:21, A.V., "naughtiness"; (*b*) the evil of trouble, affliction, Matt. 6;34, only, and here alone translated "evil." See MALICE, MALICIOUSNESS, NAUGHTINESS, WICKEDNESS.

NT: B.397a; CB.1253a; K.391.
OT: rā'āh: S.7451; HR.708a.11d; H.2191; BD.949a.
GEN. REF.: IS.2:206; NB.400; Z.2:420.

2. *ponēros* [πονηρός, 4190], the adjective (A, No. 2), is used as a noun, (*a*) of Satan as the evil one, Matt. 5:37; 6:13; 13:19, 38; Luke 11:4 (in some texts); John 17:15; Eph. 6:16; 2 Thess. 3:3; 1 John 2:13, 14; 3:12; 5:18, 19; (*b*) of human beings, Matt. 5:45; (probably ver. 39); 13:49; 22:10; Luke 6:35; 1 Cor. 5:13; (*c*) neuter, "evil (things)," Matt. 9:4; 12:35; Mark 7:23; Luke 3:19; "that which is evil," Luke 6:45; Rom. 12:9; Acts 28:21, "harm."

NT: B.690d; CB.1266a; K.912.
OT: ra': S.7451; HR.1186c.4a; H.2191; BD.948c.
rā'āh: S.7451; HR.1186c.4c; H.2191; BD.949a.
GEN. REF.: IS.2:206; NB.400; Z.2:420.

3. *kakon* [κακόν, 2556], the neuter of A, No. 1, is used with the article, as a noun, e.g., Acts 23:9; Rom. 7:21; Heb. 5:14; in the plural, "evil things," e.g., 1 Cor. 10:6; 1 Tim. 6:10, "all kinds of evil," R.V.

NT: B.397d; CB.1253b; K.391.
OT: —.
GEN. REF.: IS.2:206; NB.400; Z.2:420.

4. *phaulon* [φαῦλον, 5337], the neuter of A, No. 3, is used as a noun in Tit. 2:8.

NT: B.854c; CB.1264a; K.—.
OT: —.
GEN. REF.: IS.2:206; NB.400; Z.2:420.

5. *kakopoios* [κακοποιός, 2555], properly the masculine gender of the adjective, denotes an evil-doer (*kakon*, evil, *poieō*, to do), 1 Pet. 2:12, 14; 4:15; in some mss. in 3:16 and John 18:30 (so the A.V.). ¶ For a synonymous word see *Note* (1). Cp. the verb below. In the Sept., Prov. 12:4; 24:19. See MALEFACTOR. ¶

NT: B.397c; CB.1253b; K.391.
OT: rā'a': S.7489; HR.709b.2; H.2191,2192; BD.949b.
GEN. REF.: IS.2:206; NB.400; Z.2:420.

Notes: (1) Kakourgos, an evil-worker (*kakon*, evil, *ergon*, a work), is translated "evil-doer" in 2 Tim. 2:9, A.V. (R.V., "malefactor"). Cp. Luke 23:32, 33, 39. ¶

(2) *Adikēma*, an injustice (*a*, negative, *dikaios*, just), is translated "evil-doing," in Acts 24:20, A.V., R.V., "wrong-doing." See INIQUITY, WRONG.

C. Verbs.

1. *kakoō* [κακόω, 2559], to ill-treat (akin to A, No. 1), is rendered to entreat evil in Acts 7:6, 19; "made (them) evil affected," 14:2. See AFFECT, AFFLICT, HARM, HURT, VEX.

NT: B.398b; CB.1253b; K.391.
OT: 'ānāh: S.6031; HR.711b.5c; H.1651,1652; BD.776a.
ra'a': S.7489; HR.711b.7b; H.2191,2192; BD.949b.
GEN. REF.: IS.2:206; NB.400; Z.2:420.

2. *kakopoieō* [κακοποιέω, 2554], signifies to do evil (cp. B, No. 5), Mark 3:4 (R.V., "to do harm"); so, Luke 6:9; in 3 John 11, "doeth evil"; in 1 Pet. 3:17, "evil doing." See HARM. ¶

NT: B.397c; CB.1253b; K.391.
OT: ra'a': S.7489; HR.709a.3; H.2191,2192; BD.949b.
GEN. REF.: IS.2:206; NB.400; Z.2:420.

Note: Cp. *kakologeō*, to speak evil (see CURSE, SPEAK); *kakopatheō*, to endure evil (see ENDURE, SUFFER); *kakopatheia*, suffering affliction (see SUFFER); *kakoucheō*, to suffer adversity (see SUFFER).

D. Adverb.

kakōs [κακῶς, 2560], badly, evilly, akin to A, No. 1, is used in the physical sense, to be sick, e.g., Matt. 4:24; Mark 1:32, 34; Luke 5:31 (see DISEASE). In Matt. 21:41 this adverb is used with the adjective, "He will miserably destroy those miserable men," more lit., 'He will evilly destroy those men (evil as they are),' with stress on the adjective; (*b*) in the moral sense, to speak evilly, John 18:23; Acts 23:5; to ask evilly, Jas. 4:3. See AMISS, GRIEVOUSLY, SICK, SORE.

NT: B.398c; CB.1253b; K.—.
OT: 'ārar: S.779; HR.712a.2a; H.168; BD.76c.
qālal: S.7043; HR.712a.2b; H.2028; BD.886b.
GEN. REF.: IS.—; NB.400; Z.2:420.

EVIL SPEAKING

1. *blasphēmia* [βλασφημία, 988], is translated "evil speaking" in Eph. 4:31, A.V. (R.V., "railing"). See BLASPHEMY.

NT: B.142c; CB.1239a; K.107.
OT: ne'āṣāh: S.5007; HR.221a.1; H.1274a,b; BD.611a.
GEN. REF.: IS.1:521; NB.401; Z.1:624.

2. *katalalia* [καταλαλία], "evil speaking," 1 Pet. 2:1: see BACKBITING.

EXACT (Verb)

1. *prassō* [πράσσω, 4238], to do, to practise, also has the meaning of transacting, or managing in the matter of payment, to exact, to get money from a person, Luke 3:13 (R.V., "extort"). Cp. the English idiom "to do a person." This verb is rendered "required," in 19:23.

NT: B.698b; CB.1266b; K.927.
OT: nāgas: S.5065; HR.1201a.2; H.1296; BD.620b.
GEN. REF.: IS.2:215; NB.—; Z.—.

2. *sukophanteō* [συκοφαντέω, 4811], to accuse falsely, Luke 3:14, has its other meaning, to exact wrongfully, in 19:8. See ACCUSE. ¶

NT: B.776c; CB.—; K.1100.
OT: ʿāshaq: S.6231; HR.1301c.2a; H.1713; BD.798d.
ʿashûqîm: S.6217; HR.1301c.2b; H.1713d; BD.799a.
GEN. REF.: —.

EXACT, EXACTLY

akribesteron [ἀκριβέστερον, 197], the comparative degree of *akribōs*, accurately, carefully, is used in Acts 18:26, A.V., "more perfectly," R.V., "more carefully"; 23:15, A.V., "more perfectly," R.V., "more exactly"; so ver. 20; 24:22, A.V., "more perfect," R.V., "more exact" (lit., 'knowing more exactly'). See CAREFULLY, PERFECTLY. ¶

Cp. *akribeia*, precision, exactness, Acts 22:3, ¶ and *akriboō*, to learn carefully, to enquire with exactness, Matt. 2:7, 16. ¶

NT: B.33b; CB.—; K.—.
OT: —.
GEN. REF.: —.

EXALT, EXALTED

A. Verbs.

1. *hupsoō* [ὑψόω, 5312], to lift up (akin to *hupsos*, height), is used (*a*) literally of the lifting up of Christ in His crucifixion, John 3:14; 8:28; 12:32, 34; illustratively, of the serpent of brass, John 3:14; (*b*) figuratively, of spiritual privileges bestowed on a city, Matt. 11:23; Luke 10:15; of raising to dignity and happiness, Luke 1:52; Acts 13:17; of haughty self-exaltation, and, contrastingly, of being raised to honour, as a result of self-humbling, Matt. 23:12; Luke 14:11; 18:14; of spiritual uplifting and revival, Jas. 4:10; 1 Pet. 5:6; of bringing into the blessings of salvation through the Gospel, 2 Cor. 11:7; (*c*) with a combination of the literal and metaphorical, of the exaltation of Christ by God the Father, Acts 2:33; 5:31. See LIFT. ¶

NT: B.850d; CB.1252b; K.1241.
OT: rûm: S.7311; HR.1422a.13; H.2133; BD.926c.
gādal: S.1431; HR.1422a.5a-c; H.315; BD.152a.
gābah: S.1361; HR.1422a.3; H.305; BD.146d.
GEN. REF.: IS.2:215; NB.—; Z.—.

2. *huperupsoō* [ὑπερυψόω, 5251], to exalt highly (*huper*, over, and No. 1), is used of Christ, as in No. 1, (*c*), in Phil. 2:9. ¶

NT: B.842a; CB.1252a; K.1241.
OT: rûm: S.7311; HR.1411a.3; H.2133; BD.926c.
GEN. REF.: IS.2:215; NB.—; Z.—.

3. *epairō* [ἐπαίρω, 1869], to lift up (*epi*, up, *airō*, to raise), is said (*a*) literally, of a sail, Acts 27:40; hands, Luke 24:50; 1 Tim. 2:8; heads, Luke 21:28; eyes, Matt. 17:8, etc.; (*b*) metaphorically, of exalting oneself, being lifted up with pride, 2 Cor. 10:5; 11:20. See LIFT.

NT: B.281d; CB.—; K.28.
OT: nāsāʾ: S.5375; HR.505a.14; H.1421; BD.669d.
rûm: S.7311; HR.505a.20; H.2133; BD.926c.
GEN. REF.: IS.2:215; NB.—; Z.—.

4. *huperairō* [ὑπεραίρω, 5229], to raise over (*huper*, above, and *airō*, see No. 3), is used in the Middle Voice, of exalting oneself exceedingly, 2 Cor. 12:7; 2 Thess. 2:4. ¶

NT: B.839d; CB.—; K.—.
OT: nāsāʾ: S.5375; HR.1408b.1; H.1421; BD.669d,671c.
GEN. REF.: IS.2:215; NB.—; Z.—.

B. Adjective.

hupsēlos [ὑψηλός, 5308], high, lofty, is used metaphorically in Luke 16:15, as a noun with the article, R.V., "that which is exalted," A.V., "that which is highly esteemed." See ESTEEM, HIGH.

NT: B.849d; CB.1252b; K.—.
OT: bāmāh: S.1116; HR.1419b.1; H.253; BD.119a.
qābôah: S.1364; HR.1419b.3a; H.305a; BD.147a.
mārôm: S.4791; HR.1419b.12b; H.2133h; BD.928d.
GEN. REF.: IS.2:215; NB.—; Z.—.

Note: For Jas. 1:9, R.V., "in his high estate," see ESTATE, No. 3.

EXAMINATION, EXAMINE

A. Noun.

anakrisis [ἀνάκρισις, 351], from *ana*, up or through, and *krinō*, to distinguish, was a legal term among the Greeks, denoting the preliminary investigation for gathering evidence for the information of the judges, Acts 25:26. ¶

NT: B.56c; CB.—; K.469.
OT: —.
GEN. REF.: IS.2:217; NB.—; Z.—.

B. Verbs.

1. *anakrinō* [ἀνακρίνω, 350], to examine, investigate, is used (*a*) of searching or enquiry, Acts 17:11; 1 Cor. 9:3; 10:25, 27; (*b*) of reaching a result of the enquiry, judging, 1 Cor. 2:14, 15; 4:3, 4; 14:24; (*c*) forensically, of examining by torture, Luke 23:14; Acts 4:9; 12:19; 24:8; 28:18. See ASK, DISCERN, JUDGE, SEARCH. ¶

NT: B.56b; CB.1235a; K.469.
OT: ḥāqar: S.2713; HR.78c.1; H.729; BD.350c.
GEN. REF.: IS.2:217; NB.—; Z.—.

2. *anetazō* [ἀνετάζω, 426], to examine judicially (*ana*, up, *etazō*, to test), is used in Acts 22:24, 29. ¶ Cp. the synonymous verb *exetazō*, to search or enquire carefully, Matt. 2:8; 10:11; John 21:12. ¶

NT: B.65c; CB.—; K.—.
OT: dārash: S.1875; HR.87b.1; H.455; BD.205a.
bāqash: S.1245; HR.87b.2; H.276; BD.134c.
GEN. REF.: IS.2:217; NB.—; Z.—.

3. *dokimazō* [δοκιμάζω, 1381], to prove, test, approve, is rendered "examine" in 1 Cor. 11:28, A.V. (R.V., "prove"). See APPROVE.
NT: B.202c; CB.1242a; K.181.
OT: bāḥan: S.974; HR.339c.1; H.230; BD.103c.
GEN. REF.: IS.2:217; NB.–; Z.–.

4. *peirazō* [πειράζω, 3985], to tempt, try, is rendered "examine" in 2 Cor. 13:5, A.V. (R.V., "try"). See GO, PROVE, TEMPT, TRY.
NT: B.640b; CB.1263a; K.822.
OT: nāsāh: S.5254; HR.1115c.1; H.1373; BD.650a.
GEN. REF.: IS.2:217; NB.–; Z.–.

EXAMPLE

A. Nouns.

1. *deigma* [δεῖγμα, 1164], primarily a thing shown, a specimen (akin to *deiknumi*, to show), denotes an example given as a warning, Jude 7. ¶
NT: B.172c; CB.1240b; K.–.
OT: –.
GEN. REF.: IS.2:217; NB.–; Z.–.

Note: The corresponding word in 2 Pet. 2:6 is No. 2.

2. *hupodeigma* [ὑπόδειγμα]: see ENSAMPLE, No. 3.

3. *tupos* [τύπος]: See ENSAMPLE, No. 1.

4. *hupogrammos* [ὑπογραμμός, 5261], lit., an under-writing (from *hupographō*, to write under, to trace letters for copying by scholars); hence, a writing-copy, an example, 1 Pet. 2:21, said of what Christ left for believers, by His sufferings (not expiatory, but exemplary), that they might "follow His steps."
NT: B.843d; CB.1252b; K.128.
OT: –.
GEN. REF.: IS.2:218; NB.–; Z.–.

B. Verbs.

1. *deigmatizō* [δειγματίζω, 1165], to make a show of, to expose (akin to A, No. 1), is translated "to make a public example," in Matt. 1:19 (some mss. have the strengthened form *paradeigmatizō* here; "put . . . to an open shame," Heb. 6:6, ¶); in Col. 2:15, "made a show of." ¶
NT: B.172c; CB.1240c; K.141.
OT: –.
GEN. REF.: IS.2:218; NB.–; Z.–.

2. *hupodeiknumi* [ὑποδείκνυμι, 5263], primarily, to show secretly (*hupo*, under, *deiknumi*, to show), to show by tracing out (akin to A, No. 2); hence, to teach, to show by example, Acts 20:35, R.V., "I gave you an example," for A.V., "I shewed you." Elsewhere, to warn, Matt. 3:7; Luke 3:7; 12:5, R.V., for A.V. "forewarn"; to show, Luke 6:47; Acts 9:16. See FOREWARN, SHEW, WARN. ¶
NT: B.844b; CB.–; K.–.
OT: nāgad: S.5046; HR.1413a.5; H.1289; BD.616c.
GEN. REF.: IS.2:218; NB.–; Z.–.

EXCEED, EXCEEDING, EXCEEDINGLY

A. Verbs.

1. *huperballō* [ὑπερβάλλω, 5235], to throw over or beyond (*huper*, over, *ballō*, to throw), is translated "exceeding" in 2 Cor. 9:14; Eph. 1:19; 2:7; "excelleth" (R.V., "surpasseth") in 2 Cor. 3:10; "passeth" in Eph. 3:19 ("surpasseth" might be the meaning here). See EXCEL, SURPASS. ¶ Cp. *huperbolē*, under EXCEL, B, No. 1.
NT: B.840b; CB.–; K.1230.
OT: –.
GEN. REF.: –.

2. *perisseuō* [περισσεύω, 4052], to be over and above, over a certain number or measure, to abound, exceed, is translated "exceed" in Matt. 5:20; 2 Cor. 3:9. See ABUNDANCE, B, No. 1.
NT: B.650c; CB.1263c; K.828.
OT: –.
GEN. REF.: –.

B. Adverbs and Adverbial Phrases.

1. *lian* [λίαν, 3029], very, exceedingly, is translated "exceeding" in Matt. 2:16 (for ver. 10, see No. 2); 4:8; 8:28; Mark 9:3; Luke 23:8. See GREATLY (GREAT), SORE, VERY.
NT: B.473b; CB.1257a; K.–.
OT: me'ōd: S.3966; HR.876a.1; H.1134; BD.547a.
GEN. REF.: –.

2. *sphodra* [σφόδρα, 4970], properly the neuter plural of *sphodros*, excessive, violent (from a root indicating restlessness), signifies very, very much, exceedingly, Matt. 2:10; 17:6, "sore"; 17:23; 18:31, R.V., "exceeding," for A.V., "very"; 19:25; 26:22; 27:54, R.V., "exceedingly" for A.V., "greatly"; Mark 16:4, "very"; Luke 18:23 (ditto); Acts 6:7, R.V., "exceedingly," for A.V., "greatly"; Rev. 16:21. See GREATLY, SORE, VERY. ¶
NT: B.796a; CB.1269c; K.–.
OT: me'ōd: S.3966; HR.1325a.2a; H.1134; BD.547a.
GEN. REF.: –.

3. *sphodrōs* [σφοδρῶς], exceedingly (see No. 2), is used in Acts 27:18. ¶

4. *perissōs* [περισσῶς, 4057], is used in Matt. 27:23, R.V., "exceedingly," for A.V., "the more"; Mark 10:26, R.V., "exceedingly," for A.V., "out of measure"; in Acts 26:11, "exceedingly." In Mark 15:14, the most authentic mss. have this word (R.V., "exceedingly") for No. 5 (A.V., "the more exceedingly"). See MORE. ¶
NT: B.651b; CB.1263c; K.–.
OT: –.
GEN. REF.: –.

5. *perissoterōs* [περισσοτέρως, 4056], the comparative degree of No. 4, abundantly, exceedingly (akin to A, No. 2), Gal. 1:14, "more exceedingly"; 1 Thess. 2:17, R.V., "the more

exceedingly," for A.V., "the more abundantly"; see ABUNDANCE, D, No. 2.

NT: B.651c; CB.1263c; K.828.
OT: –.
GEN. REF.: –.

6. *huperekperissou* [ὑπερεκπερισσοῦ, 4053], denotes superabundantly (*huper*, over, *ek*, from, *perissos*, abundant); in 1 Thess. 3:10, "exceedingly"; Eph. 3:20, "exceeding abundantly." ¶ Another form, *huperekperissōs* (*huper*, and *ek* and No. 4), is used in 1 Thess. 5:13 (in the best mss.), "exceeding highly." ¶ Cp. the verb *huperperisseuō*, to abound more exceedingly, Rom. 5:21; in 2 Cor. 7:4, "I overflow (with joy)," R.V., for A.V., "I am exceeding (joyful). See ABUNDANT, D, No. 2.

NT: B.840c; CB.1252a; K.828.
OT: –.
GEN. REF.: –.

Notes: (1) In Acts 7:20, the phrase "exceeding fair" (*asteios*) is, lit., 'fair to God' (see marg.).

(2) In Matt. 26:7, *barutimos* (*barus*, weighty, *timē*, value), is rendered "exceeding precious," R.V., for A.V., "very precious."

(3) In Mark 4:41, "they feared exceedingly" is, lit., 'they feared a great fear.' See FEAR.

(4) For other combinations of the adverb, see GLAD, GREAT, JOYFUL, SORROWFUL, SORRY.

EXCEL, EXCELLENCY, EXCELLENT

A. Verbs.

1. *huperballō* [ὑπερβάλλω], lit., to throw over: see EXCEED, No. 1.

2. *perisseuō* [περισσεύω, 4052], to be over and above, is rendered "abound" in 1 Cor. 14:12, R.V., for A.V., "excel." See ABUNDANCE, B, No. 1, and EXCEED, A, No. 2.

NT: B.650c; CB.1263c; K.828.
OT: –.
GEN. REF.: –.

3. *huperechō* [ὑπερέχω, 5242], lit., to have over (*huper*, over, *echō*, to have), is translated "excellency" in Phil. 3:8, 'the surpassingness' (Moule); the phrase could be translated 'the surpassing thing, which consists in the knowledge of Christ Jesus,' and this is the probable meaning. This verb is used three times in Philippians, here and in 2:3; 4:7. See also Rom. 13:1; 1 Pet. 2:13. See BETTER, No. 4. ¶

NT: B.840d; CB.1252a; K.1230.
OT: gādal: S.1431; HR.1409b.4; H.1431; BD.152a.
GEN. REF.: –.

4. *diapherō* [διαφέρω, 1308], to differ, is used in the neuter plural of the present participle with the article, in Phil. 1:10, "the things that are excellent" (marg., "the things that differ"), lit., 'the excellent things.' See DIFFER.

NT: B.190b; CB.–; K.1252.
OT: –.
GEN. REF.: –.

B. Nouns.

1. *huperbolē* [ὑπερβολή, 5236], lit., a throwing beyond, hence, a surpassing, an excellence, is translated "excellency" in 2 Cor. 4:7, A.V.; R.V., "exceeding greatness." It always betokens pre-eminence. It is used with *kata*, according to, in the phrase *kath' huperbolēn*, signifying beyond measure, exceedingly, Rom. 7:13, "exceeding sinful"; in 2 Cor. 1:8, R.V., "exceedingly," for A.V., "out of measure"; in Gal. 1:13, "beyond measure"; in 1 Cor. 12:31, "more excellent." In 2 Cor. 4:17, there is an expanded phrase *kath' huperbolēn eis huperbolēn*, lit., 'according to a surpassing unto a surpassing,' R.V., "more and more exceedingly," which corrects the A.V., "a far more exceeding"; the phrase refers to "worketh," showing the surpassing degree of its operation, and not to the noun "weight" (nor does it qualify "eternal"). In 2 Cor. 12:7, the R.V. has "exceeding greatness," the A.V., "abundance." See ABUNDANCE. ¶

NT: B.840b; CB.–; K.1230.
OT: –.
GEN. REF.: IS.2:218; NB.–; Z.–.

2. *huperochē* [ὑπεροχή, 5247], akin to A, No. 3, strictly speaking, the act of overhanging (*huper*, and *echō*, to hold) or the thing which overhangs, hence, superiority, pre-eminence, is translated "excellency (of speech)" in 1 Cor. 2:1; elsewhere, in 1 Tim. 2:2, R.V., "high place," for A.V., "authority." See AUTHORITY, PLACE. ¶

NT: B.841d; CB.–; K.1230.
OT: –.
GEN. REF.: –.

Note: In 1 Pet. 2:9 R.V. renders *aretē* (virtue) "excellencies."

C. Adjectives.

1. *megaloprepēs* [μεγαλοπρεπής, 3169], signifies magnificent, majestic, that which is becoming to a great man (from *megas*, great, and *prepō*, to be fitting or becoming), in 2 Pet. 1:17, "excellent." ¶

NT: B.497a; CB.–; K.573.
OT: ga'awāh: S.1346; HR.901c.1; H.299d; BD.144d.
GEN. REF.: –.

2. *diaphorōteros* [διαφορώτερος, 1313], comparative degree of *diaphoros*, excellent, akin to A, No. 4, is used twice, in Heb. 1:4, "more excellent (name)," and 8:6, "more excellent (ministry)." ¶ For the positive degree see Rom. 12:6; Heb. 9:10. See under DIFFER. ¶

NT: B.190d; CB.–; K.–.
OT: –.
GEN. REF.: IS.2:218; NB.–; Z.–.

3. *pleiōn* [πλείων, 4119], more, greater, the comparative degree of *polus*, much, is translated "more excellent" in Heb. 11:4, of Abel's

sacrifice; *pleiōn* is used sometimes of that which is superior by reason of inward worth, cp. 3:3, "more (honour)"; in Matt. 6:25, of the life in comparison with meat.

NT: B.687a; CB.–; K.–.
OT: rab: S.7227; HR.1181b.9a; H.2099a,b; BD.912d.
rōb: S.7230; HR.1181b.9b; H.2099c; BD.913d.
rābab: S.7231; HR.1181b.9c; H.2099; BD.912c.
GEN. REF.: –.

4. *kratistos* [κράτιστος, 2903], mightiest, noblest, best, the superlative degree of *kratus*, strong (cp. *kratos*, strength), is used as a title of honour and respect, "most excellent," Luke 1:3 (Theophilus was quite possibly a man of high rank); Acts 23:26; 24:3 and 26:25, R.V., for A.V., "most noble." ¶

NT: B.449a; CB.1256a; K.–.
OT: ṭôb: S.2896; HR.785a.2a; H.793a; BD.375a.
GEN. REF.: IS.2:218; NB.–; Z.–.

Note: The phrase *kath' huperbolēn* (for which see B, No. 1) is translated "more excellent" in 1 Cor. 12:31.

EXCEPT, EXCEPTED

Note: For the negative conjunctions *ean mē* and *ei mē*, see † p. 1.

1. *ektos* [ἐκτός, 1622], an adverb, lit., outside, is used with *ei mē*, as an extended conjunction signifying "except"; so in 1 Cor. 14:5; in 15:2, R.V., for A.V., "unless"; in 1 Tim. 5:19, R.V., for A.V., "but." It has the force of a preposition in the sense of (*a*) outside of, in 1 Cor. 6:18, "without"; in 2 Cor. 12:2, "out of"; (*b*) besides, except, in Acts 26:22, R.V., "but," for A.V., "other than"; in 1 Cor. 15:27 "excepted." For its use as a noun see Matt. 23:26, "(the) outside." See OTHER, OUT OF, OUTSIDE, UNLESS, WITHOUT. ¶

NT: B.246a; CB.–; K.–.
OT: –.
GEN. REF.: –.

2. *parektos* [παρεκτός, 3924], a strengthened form of No. 1 (*para*, beside), is used (*a*) as an adverb, signifying "without," 2 Cor. 11:28; lit., 'the things without,' i.e., the things happening without; (*b*) as a preposition signifying "except"; in Matt. 5:32, "saving"; in Acts 26:29, "except." ¶

NT: B.625a; CB.1262b; K.–.
OT: –.
GEN. REF.: –.

Note: In Matt. 19:9, the A.V. and R.V., translating the mss. which have the negative *mē*, followed by *epi*, render it "except for." The authorities mentioned in the R.V. marg. have *parektos*, followed by *logou*, i.e., 'saving for the cause of.'

3. *plēn* [πλήν, 4133], an adverb, most frequently signifying yet, howbeit, or only, sometimes has the meaning "except (that)," "save (that)," Acts 20:23; Phil. 1:18, R.V., "only that," for A.V., "notwithstanding." It is also used as a preposition, signifying except, save, Mark 12:32, "but"; John 8:10, "but" (A.V. only); Acts 8:1, "except"; Acts 15:28, "than"; 27:22, "but (only)."

NT: B.669b; CB.1265b; K.–.
OT: –.
GEN. REF.: –.

EXCESS

1. *akrasia* [ἀκρασία, 192], lit. denotes want of strength (*a*, negative, *kratos*, strength), hence, want of self-control, incontinence, Matt. 23:25, "excess"; 1 Cor. 7:5, "incontinency." ¶ Cp. *akratēs*, powerless, incontinent, 2 Tim. 3:3, R.V., "without self-control." ¶

NT: B.33a; CB.1234b; K.196.
OT: –.
GEN. REF.: –.

2. *anachusis* [ἀνάχυσις, 401], lit., a pouring out, overflowing (akin to *anacheō*, to pour out), is used metaphorically in 1 Pet. 4:4, "excess," said of the riotous conduct described in ver. 3. ¶

NT: B.63c; CB.–; K.–.
OT: –.
GEN. REF.: –.

Notes: (1) *Asōtia* denotes prodigality, profligacy, riot (from *a*, negative, and *sōzō*, to save); it is translated "riot" in Eph. 5:18, R.V., for A.V., "excess"; in Tit. 1:6 and 1 Pet. 4:4, "riot" in A.V. and R.V. See RIOT. ¶ Cp. the adverb *asōtōs*, wastefully, "in riotous living," Luke 15:13. ¶ A synonymous noun is *aselgeia*, lasciviousness, outrageous conduct, wanton violence.

(2) In 1 Pet. 4:3, *oinophlugia*, drunkenness, debauchery (*oinos*, wine, *phluō*, to bubble up, overflow), is rendered "excess of wine," A.V. (R.V., "winebibbings"). ¶

EXCHANGE

A. Noun.

antallagma [ἀντάλλαγμα, 465], the price received as an equivalent of, or in exchange for, an article, an exchange (*anti*, instead of, *allassō*, to change, akin to *allos*, another), hence denotes the price at which the exchange is effected, Matt. 16:26; Mark 8:37. ¶ Connected with this is the conception of atonement, as in the word *lutron*, a ransom. Cp. *allagma* in the Sept., e.g., in Isa. 43:3.

NT: B.72d; CB.1236a; K.40.
OT: m^{e}ḥîr: S.4242; HR.108c.2; H.1185c; BD.564b.
kōpher: S.3724; HR.108c.4; H.1025b; BD.497a.
GEN. REF.: –.

B. Verb.

metallassō [μεταλλάσσω, 3337], denotes (*a*) to exchange, *meta*, with, implying change, and *allassō* (see A.), Rom. 1:25, of exchanging the truth for a lie, R.V., for A.V., "changed"; (*b*) to change, ver. 26, a different meaning from that in the preceding verse. See CHANGE. ¶ In the Sept., Esth. 2:7, 20. ¶

NT: B.511c; CB.1256c; K.40.
OT: –.
GEN. REF.: –.

Note: In Luke 24:17, "what communications are these that ye have one with another?" the verb *antiballō*, to throw in turn, to exchange, is used of conversation, lit., 'what words are these that ye exchange one with another?'

For **EXCHANGERS** see **BANKERS**

EXCLUDE

ekkleiō [ἐκκλείω, 1576], to shut out (*ek*, from, *kleiō*, to shut), is said of glorying in works as a means of justification, Rom. 3:27; of Gentiles, who by Judaism would be excluded from salvation and Christian fellowship, Gal. 4:17. ¶

NT: B.240c; CB.–; K.–.
OT: nāṭāh: S.5186; HR.433a.1; H.1352; BD.639d,640c.
GEN. REF.: –.

EXCUSE

prophasis [πρόφασις, 4392], a pretence, pretext (from *pro*, before, and *phēmi*, to say), is translated "excuse" in John 15:22, R.V., for A.V., "cloke"; "cloke" in 1 Thess. 2:5, A.V. and R.V. See CLOKE, PRETENCE, SHOW (Noun).

NT: B.722c; CB.–; K.–.
OT: –.
GEN. REF.: IS.2:220; NB.–; Z.–.

B. Adjective (*negative*).

anapologētos [ἀναπολόγητος, 379], without excuse, inexcusable (*a*, negative, *n*, euphonic, and *apologeomai*, see C, No. 1, below), is used, Rom. 1:20, "without excuse," of those who reject the revelation of God in creation; 2:1, R.V., for A.V., "inexcusable," of the Jew who judges the Gentile. ¶

NT: B.60a; CB.1235b; K.–.
OT: –.
GEN. REF.: IS.2:220; NB.–; Z.–.

C. Verbs.

1. *apologeomai* [ἀπολογέομαι, 626], lit., to speak oneself off, hence to plead for oneself, and so, in general, (*a*) to defend, as before a tribunal; in Rom. 2:15, R.V., "excusing them," means one excusing others (not themselves); the preceding phrase "one with another" signifies one person with another, not one thought with another; it may be paraphrased, 'their thoughts with one another, condemning or else excusing one another'; conscience provides a moral standard by which men judge one another; (*b*) to excuse oneself, 2 Cor. 12:19; cp. B. See ANSWER.

NT: B.95d; CB.1237a; K.–.
OT: rīb: S.7378; HR.138c.1; H.2159; BD.936b.
GEN. REF.: IS.2:220; NB.–; Z.–.

2. *paraiteomai* [παραιτέομαι, 3868], is used in the sense of begging off, asking to be excused or making an excuse, in Luke 14:18 (twice) and ver. 19. In the first part of ver. 18 the verb is used in the Middle Voice, "to make excuse" (acting in imagined self-interest); in the latter part and in ver. 19 it is in the Passive Voice, "have me excused."

NT: B.616c; CB.1262a; K.30.
OT: shā'al: S.7592; HR.1060a.3; H.2303; BD.981b.
ḥāuan: S.2603; HR.1060a.2; H.694,695; BD.335d,336b.
GEN. REF.: IS.2:220; NB.–; Z.–.

EXECUTE

1. *poieō* [ποιέω, 4160], to do, to make, is thrice rendered "execute," of the Lord's authority and acts in executing judgment, (*a*) of His authority as the One to whom judgment is committed, John 5:27; (*b*) of the judgment which He will mete out to all transgressors at His Second Advent, Jude 15; (*c*) of the carrying out of His word (not "work," as in the A.V.) in the earth, especially regarding the nation of Israel, the mass being rejected, the remnant saved, Rom. 9:28. That He will "execute His word finishing and cutting it short," is expressive of the summary and decisive character of His action. See DO.

NT: B.680d; CB.1265c; K.895.
OT: 'āsāh: S.6213; HR.1154a.33a; H.1708,1709; BD.793c.
shāphaṭ: S.8199; HR.1154a.45; H.2443; BD.1047a.
GEN. REF.: IS.2:221; NB.–; Z.2:423.

2. *hierateuō* [ἱερατεύω, 2407], to be a priest, to officiate as such, is translated "executed the priest's office," in Luke 1:8. ¶ It occurs frequently in the Sept., and in Inscriptions. Cp. *hierateuma*, priesthood, 1 Pet. 2:5, 9, ¶ *hierateia*, a priest's office, Luke 1:9; Heb. 7:5, ¶ *hiereus*, a priest, and *hieros*, sacred.

NT: B.371d; CB.1250b; K.349.
OT: kāhan: S.3547; HR.679a.1b; H.959; BD.464c.
GEN. REF.: –.

For **EXECUTIONER**, Mark 6:27, see **GUARD**, A, No. 2

EXERCISE

A. Verbs.

1. *gumnazō* [γυμνάζω, 1128], primarily signifies to exercise naked (from *gumnos*, naked); then, generally, to exercise, to train the body or

mind (Eng., gymnastic), 1 Tim. 4:7, with a view to godliness; Heb. 5:14, of the senses, so as to discern good and evil; 12:11, of the effect of chastening, the spiritual exercise producing the fruit of righteousness; 2 Pet. 2:14, of certain evil teachers with hearts "exercised in covetousness," R.V. ¶

NT: B.167c; CB.1248c; K.133.
OT: –.
GEN. REF.: IS.2:221; NB.–; Z.–.

2. *askeō* [ἀσκέω, 778], signifies to form by art, to adorn, to work up raw material with skill; hence, in general, to take pains, endeavour, exercise by training or discipline, with a view to a conscience void of offence, Acts 24:16. ¶

NT: B.116b; CB.1238a; K.84.
OT: –.
GEN. REF.: –.

3. *poieō* [ποιέω, 4160], to do, is translated "exerciseth" in Rev. 13:12, said of the authority of the second, "Beast." Cp. EXECUTE. See DO

NT: B.680d; CB.1265c; K.895.
OT: 'āsāh: S.6213; HR.1154a.33a; H.1708,1709; BD.793c.
GEN. REF.: –.

Notes: The following verbs contain in translation the word "exercise" but belong to other headings: *exousiazō*, to exercise authority over, Luke 22:25 (*exousia*, authority); in the first part of this verse, the verb *kurieuō*, to be lord, is translated "exercise lordship," A.V. (R.V., "have lordship"); *katexousiazō*, a strengthened form of the preceding (*kata*, down, intensive), Matt. 20:25; Mark 10:42, "exercise authority" (in the first part of these verses the synonymous verb *katakurieuō*, is rendered "lord it," R.V., for A.V., "exercise dominion," and "exercise lordship," respectively); *episkopeō*, to look over or upon (*epi*, over, *skopeō*, to look), to care for, 1 Pet. 5:2 (absent in some mss.), R.V., "exercising the oversight," for A.V. "taking etc."

B. Noun.

gumnasia [γυμνασία, 1129], primarily denotes gymnastic exercise (akin to A, No. 1), 1 Tim. 4:8, where the immediate reference is probably not to mere physical training for games but to discipline of the body such as that to which the Apostle refers in 1 Cor. 9:27, though there may be an allusion to the practices of asceticism.

NT: B.167d; CB.1248c; K.133.
OT: –.
GEN. REF.: IS.2:221; NB.–; Z.–.

EXHORT, EXHORTATION

A. Verbs.

1. *parakaleō* [παρακαλέω, 3870], primarily, to call to a person (*para*, to the side, *kaleō*, to call), denotes (*a*) to call on, entreat; see BESEECH; (*b*) to admonish, exhort, to urge one to pursue some course of conduct (always prospective, looking to the future, in contrast to the meaning to comfort, which is retrospective, having to do with trial experienced), translated "exhort" in the R.V. of Phil. 4:2; 1 Thess. 4:10; Heb. 13:19, 22, for A.V., "beseech"; in 1 Tim. 5:1, for A.V., "intreat"; in 1 Thess. 5:11, for A.V., "comfort"; "exhorted" in 2 Cor. 8:6 and 12:18, for A.V., "desired"; in 1 Tim. 1:3, for A.V., "besought." See BESEECH.

NT: B.617a; CB.1262a; K.778.
OT: 'āmēṣ: S.553; HR.1060a.1; H.117; BD.54d.
nāham: S.5162; HR.1060a.10a,b; H.1344; BD.636d.
GEN. REF.: IS.2:221; NB.–; Z.–.

2. *paraineō* [παραινέω, 3867], primarily, to speak of near (*para*, near, and *aineō*, to tell of speak of, then, to recommend), hence, to advise, exhort, warn, is used in Acts 27:9, "admonished," and ver. 22, "I exhort." See ADMONISH. ¶

NT: B.616b; CB.1262a; K.–.
OT: –.
GEN. REF.: –.

3. *protrepō* [προτρέπω, 4389], lit., to turn forward, propel (*pro*, before, *trepō*, to turn); hence, to impel morally, to urge forward, encourage, is used in Acts 18:27, R.V., "encouraged him" (Apollos), with reference to his going into Achaia; A.V., "exhorting the disciples"; while the encouragement was given to Apollos, a letter was written to the disciples in Achaia to receive him. ¶

NT: B.722b; CB.–; K.–.
OT: –.
GEN. REF.: –.

B. Noun.

paraklēsis [παράκλησις, 3874], akin to A, No. 1, primarily a calling to one's side, and so to one's aid, hence denotes (*a*) an appeal, "entreaty," 2 Cor. 8:4; (*b*) encouragement, exhortation, e.g., Rom. 12:8; in Acts 4:36, R.V., "exhortation," for A.V., "consolation"; (*c*) consolation and comfort, e.g., Rom. 15:4. See COMFORT. Cp. *paraklētos*, an advocate, comforter.

NT: B.618a; CB.1262a; K.778.
OT: niḥûm: S.5150; HR.1061a.1a; H.1344b; BD.637b.
tanᵉḥûm: S.8575; HR.1061a.1c,d; H.1144d; BD.637c.
GEN. REF.: IS.2:221; NB.–; Z.–.

EXIST

huparchō [ὑπάρχω, 5225], primarily, to make a beginning (*hupo*, under, *archē*, a beginning), denotes to be, to be in existence, involving an existence or condition both previous to the circumstances mentioned and continuing after it. This is important in Phil. 2:6; concerning the Deity of Christ. The phrase "being (existing) in the form (*morphē*, the essential and specific form and character) of God," carries with it the two facts of the antecedent Godhood of Christ, previous to His Incarnation, and the continuance of His Godhood at and after the event of His Birth (see Gifford, on the Incarnation, pp. 11, sqq.). It is translated "exist" in 1 Cor. 11:18, R.V., for A.V., "there be." Cp. Luke 16:14; 23:50; Acts 2:30; 3:2; 17:24; 22:3 etc. See BEING, GOODS, LIVE, POSSESS, SUBSTANCE.

NT: B.838a; CB.–; K.–.
OT: –.
GEN. REF.: –.

EXORCIST

exorkistēs [ἐξορκιστής, 1845], denotes (*a*) one who administers an oath; (*b*) an exorcist (akin to *exorkizō*, to adjure, from *orkos*, an oath), one who employs a formula of conjuration for the expulsion of demons, Acts 19:13. The practice of exorcism was carried on by strolling Jews, who used their power in the recitation of particular names. ¶

NT: B.277b; CB.–; K.729.
OT: –.
GEN. REF.: IS.2:242; NB.–; Z.2:450.

EXPECT, EXPECTATION

A. Verbs.

1. *ekdechomai* [ἐκδέχομαι, 1551], lit. and primarily, to take or receive from (*ek*, from, *dechomai*, to receive), hence denotes to await, expect, the only sense of the word in the N.T.; it suggests a reaching out in readiness to receive something; "expecting," Heb. 10:13; "expect," 1 Cor. 16:11, R.V. (A.V., "look for"); to wait for, John 5:3 (A.V. only); Acts 17:16; 1 Cor. 11:33, R.V. (A.V., "tarry for"); Jas. 5:7; to wait, 1 Pet. 3:20 in some mss.; "looked for," Heb. 11:10. Cp. B, No. 1. See LOOK, TARRY, WAIT. ¶

NT: B.238b; CB.1243c; K.146.
OT: –.
GEN. REF.: IS.2:245; NB.–; Z.–.

2. *prosdokaō* [προσδοκάω, 4328], to watch toward, to look for, expect (*pros*, toward, *dokeō*, to think: *dokaō* does not exist), is translated "expecting" in Matt. 24:50 and Luke 12:46, R.V. (A.V., "looketh for"); Luke 3:15, "were in expectation"; Acts 3:5, "expecting" (A.V. and R.V.); 28:6 (twice), "expected that," R.V. (A.V., "looked when") and "when they were long in expectation" (A.V., "after they had looked a great while"). See LOOK, TARRY, WAIT.

NT: B.712c; CB.1267a; K.943.
OT: sābar: S.7663; HR.1213a.2; H.2232; BD.960b.
qāwāh: S.6960; HR.1213a.1; H.1994,1995; BD.875c.
GEN. REF.: IS.2:245; NB.–; Z.–.

B. Nouns.

1. *apokaradokia* [ἀποκαραδοκία, 603], primarily a watching with outstretched head (*apo*, from, *kara*, the head, and *dokeō*, to look, to watch), signifies strained expectancy, eager longing, the stretching forth of the head indicating an expectation of something from a certain place, Rom. 8:19 and Phil. 1:20. The prefix *apo* suggests "abstraction and absorption" (Lightfoot), i.e., abstraction from anything else that might engage the attention, and absorption in the object expected "till the fulfilment is realized" (Alford). The intensive character of the noun, in comparison with No. 2 (below), is clear from the contexts; in Rom. 8:19 it is said figuratively of the creation as waiting for the revealing of the sons of God ("waiting" translates the verb *apekdechomai*, a strengthened form of A, No. 1; see WAIT FOR). In Phil. 1:20 the Apostle states it as his "earnest expectation" and hope, that, instead of being put to shame, Christ shall be magnified in his body, "whether by life, or by death," suggesting absorption in the Person of Christ, abstraction from aught that hinders. ¶

NT: B.92c; CB.1236c; K.66.
OT: –.
GEN. REF.: IS.2:245; NB.–; Z.–.

2. *prosdokia* [προσδοκία, 4329], a watching for, expectation (akin to A, No. 2, which see), is used in the N.T. only of the expectation of evil, Luke 21:26, R.V., "expectation," A.V., "looking for," regarding impending calamities; Acts 12:11, "the expectation," of the execution of Peter.¶

NT: B.712d; CB.–; K.943.
OT: sēber: S.7664; HR.1213a.2; H.2232a; BD.960c.
GEN. REF.: IS.2:245; NB.–; Z.–.

3. *ekdochē* [ἐκδοχή, 1561], primarily a receiving from, hence, expectation (akin to A, No. 1), is used in Heb. 10:27 (R.V., "expectation"; A.V., "looking for"), of judgment. ¶

NT: B.239a; CB.1243c; K.–.
OT: –.
GEN. REF.: IS.2:245; NB.–; Z.–.

EXPEDIENT

sumpherō [συμφέρω, 4851], signifies (*a*) transitively, lit., to bring together, (*sun*, with, *pherō*, to bring), Acts 19:19; (*b*) intransitively, to be an advantage, profitable, expedient (not merely 'convenient'); it is used mostly impersonally, "it is (it was) expedient"; so in Matt. 19:10, R.V. (negatively), A.V., "it is (not) good"; John 11:50; 16:7; 18:14; 1 Cor. 6:12; 10:23; 2 Cor. 8:10; 12:1; "it is profitable," Matt. 5:29, 30; 18:6, R.V.; "was profitable," Acts 20:20; "to profit withal," 1 Cor. 12:7; in Heb. 12:10, used in the neuter of the present participle with the article as a noun, "for (our) profit." See PROFIT. ¶ Cp. the adjective *sumphoros* (or *sumpheron*), profitable, used with the article as a noun, 1 Cor. 7:35; 10:33. ¶

NT: B.780b; CB.–; K.1252.
OT: nā'weh: S.5000; HR.1306b.2; H.1271a; BD.610a.
ṭôb: S.2896; HR.1306b.1a; H.793a; BD.373c.
ṭôbāh: S.2896; HR.1306b.1b; H.793a; BD.375c.
GEN. REF.: IS.2:246; NB.–; Z.–.

For **EXPELLED**, Acts 13:50, A.V., see **CAST**, No. 5

EXPERIENCE (without) EXPERIMENT

1. *apeiros* [ἄπειρος, 552], without experience (*a*, negative, *peira*, a trial, experiment), is used in Heb. 5:13, R.V., "without experience," A.V., "unskilful," with reference to "the word of righteousness." ¶ In the Sept., Numb. 14:23, of youths; Jer. 2:6, of a land, "untried"; Zech. 11:15, of a shepherd. ¶

NT: B.83b; CB.1236b; K.–.
OT: ʿarābāh: S.6160; HR.120b.2; H.1688d; BD.787b.
GEN. REF.: –.

2. *dokimē* [δοκιμή, 1382], means (*a*) the process of proving; it is rendered "experiment" in 2 Cor. 9:13, A.V., R.V., "the proving (of you)"; in 8:2, A.V., "trial," R.V., "proof"; (*b*) the effect of proving, approval, approvedness, R.V., "probation," Rom. 5:4 (twice), for A.V., "experience"; A.V. and R.V., "proof" in 2 Cor. 2:9; 13:3 and Phil. 2:22. See EXPERIENCE, PROOF. ¶ Cp. *dokimos*, approved, *dokimazō*, to prove, approve; see APPROVE.

NT: B.202d; CB.1242a; K.181.
OT: –.
GEN. REF.: –.

EXPERT

gnōstēs [γνώστης, 1109], one who knows (akin to *ginōskō*, to know), denotes an expert, a connoisseur, Acts 26:3. ¶ Cp. *gnōstos*, known.

NT: B.164a; CB.–; K.–.
OT: yāda': S.3045; HR.274a.1a; H.848; BD.393b.
yiddeʿōnî: S.3049; HR.274a.1b; H.848d; BD.396b.
GEN. REF.: –.

EXPIRE

Note: In Acts 7:30, the A.V. "were expired" translates the verb *plēroō*, to fulfil (R.V.). See FULFIL. In Rev. 20:7, the A.V. "are expired" translates the verb *teleō*, to finish (R.V.). See FINISH.

EXPLAIN

diasapheō [διασαφέω, 1285], to make clear, explain fully (*dia*, through, intensive, and *saphēs*, clear), is translated "explain" in Matt. 13:36 R.V. (A.V., "declare") translates *phrazō*; in 18:31, told," of the account of the unforgiving debtor's doings, given by his fellow-servants. The preferable rendering would be 'they made clear' or 'they explained,' suggesting a detailed explanation of the circumstances. ¶

NT: B.188a; CB.–; K.–.
OT: bā'ar: S.874; HR.309c; H.194; BD.91b.
GEN. REF.: IS.2:248; NB.–; Z.–.

EXPOUND

1. *ektithēmi* [ἐκτίθημι, 1620], to set out, expose (*ek*, out, *tithēmi*, to place) is used (*a*) literally, Acts 7:21, (*b*) metaphorically, in the Middle Voice, to set forth, expound, of circumstances, Acts 11:4; of the way of God, 18:26; of the Kingdom of God, 28:23. ¶

NT: B.245d; CB.–; K.–.
OT: nātan: S.5414; HR.443a.4; H.1443; BD.678a,681b.
GEN. REF.: IS.2:248; NB.–; Z.–.

2. *epiluō* [ἐπιλύω, 1956], primarily, to loose, release, a strengthened form of *luō*, to loose, signifies to solve, explain, expound, Mark 4:34, "expounded"; in Acts 19:39, of settling a controversy, R.V., "it shall be settled," for A.V., "it shall be determined." See DETERMINE. ¶ Cp. *epilusis*, an interpretation, 2 Pet. 1:20. ¶

NT: B.295d; CB.1246a; K.543.
OT: –.
GEN. REF.: –.

3. *diermēneuō* [διερμηνεύω, 1329], to interpret fully (*dia*, through, intensive, *hermēneuō*, to interpret; Eng., hermeneutics), is translated "He expounded" in Luke 24:27, A.V., R.V., "interpreted"; in Acts 9:36, "by interpretation," lit., 'being interpreted'; see also 1 Cor. 12:30; 14:5, 13, 27. See INTERPRET. ¶

NT: B.194b; CB.1241c; K.256.
OT: –.
GEN. REF.: –.

For **EXPRESS**, Heb. 1:3, A.V., see **IMAGE**, No. 2

EXPRESSLY

rhētōs [ῥητῶς, 4490], meaning 'in stated terms' (from *rhētos*, stated, specified; from *rheō*, or *erō*, to say; cp. *rhēma*, a word), is used in 1 Tim. 4:1, "expressly." ¶

NT: B.736a; CB.–; K.–.
OT: dābār: S.1697; HR.1251c.1; H.399a; BD.182a.
GEN. REF.: –.

EXTORT, EXTORTION, EXTORTIONER

A. Verb.

prassō [πράσσω, 4238], to practise, has the special meaning "extort" in Luke 3:13, R.V.

(A.V., "exact"). In Luke 19:23 it is translated "required"; it may be that the master, in addressing the slothful servant, uses the word 'extort' or 'exact' (as in 3:13), in accordance with the character attributed to him by the servant.

NT: B.698b; CB.1266b; K.927.
OT: —.
GEN. REF.: —.

B. Nouns.

1. *harpagē* [ἁρπαγή, 724], denoted pillage, plundering, robbery, extortion [akin to *harpazō*, to seize, carry off by force, and *harpagmos*, a thing seized, or the act of seizing; from the root *arp* (sic), seen in Eng., rapacious; an associated noun, with the same spelling, denoted a rake, or hook for drawing up a bucket]; it is translated "extortion" in Matt. 23:25; Luke 11:39, R.V., A.V., "ravening"; Heb. 10:34, "spoiling." See RAVENING, SPOILING. ¶ Cp. C. below.

NT: B.108b; CB.1249b; K.—.
OT: gāzēl: S.1498; HR.159c.1a; H.337a; BD.160a.
gᵉzēlāh: S.1500; HR.159c.1b; H.337b; BD.160a.
shālāl: S.7998; HR.159c.3; H.2400a; BD.1021d.
GEN. REF.: IS.2:248; NB.—; Z.2:452.

2. *pleonexia* [πλεονεξία, 4124], covetousness, desire for advantage, is rendered "extortion" in 2 Cor. 9:5, R.V. (A.V. and R.V. marg., "covetousness"). See COVET,

NT: B.667d; CB.1265b; K.864.
OT: beṣa': S.1215; HR.1142a.1; H.267a; BD.130c.
GEN. REF.: —.

C. Adjective.

harpax [ἅρπαξ, 727], rapacious (akin to No. 1), is translated as a noun, "extortioners," in Luke 18:11; 1 Cor. 5:10, 11; 6:10; in Matt. 7:15 "ravening" (of wolves). ¶ In the Sept., Gen. 49:27. ¶

NT: B.109b; CB.1249b; K.—.
OT: ṭāraph: S.2963; HR.160a.1; H.827; BD.382d.
GEN. REF.: IS.2:248; NB.—; Z.2:452.

EYE

1. *ophthalmos* [ὀφθαλμός, 3788], akin to *opsis*, sight, probably from a root signifying penetration, sharpness (Curtius, Gk. Etym.) (cp. Eng., ophthalmia, etc.), is used (*a*) of the physical organ, e.g., Matt. 5:38; of restoring sight, e.g., Matt. 20:33; of God's power of vision, Heb. 4:13; 1 Pet. 3:12; of Christ in vision, Rev. 1:14; 2:18; 19:12; of the Holy Spirit in the unity of the Godhood with Christ, Rev. 5:6; (*b*) metaphorically, of ethical qualities, evil, Matt. 6:23; Mark 7:22 (by metonymy, for envy); singleness of motive, Matt. 6:22; Luke 11:34; as the instrument of evil desire, "the principal avenue of temptation," 1 John 2:16; of adultery, 2 Pet. 2:14; (*c*) metaphorically, of mental vision, Matt. 13:15; John 12:40; Rom. 11:8; Gal. 3:1, where the metaphor of the "evil eye" is altered to a different sense from that of bewitching (the posting up or placarding of an eye was used as a charm, to prevent mischief); by Gospel-preaching Christ had been, so to speak, placarded before their eyes; the question may be paraphrased, 'What evil teachers have been malignly fascinating you?'; Eph. 1:18, of the "eyes of the heart," as a means of knowledge.

NT: B.599b; CB.1261a; K.706.
OT: 'ayin: S.5869; HR.1039b.2; H.1612a,1613; BD.744a.
GEN. REF.: IS.2:249; NB.406; Z.2:452.

2. *omma* [ὄμμα, 3659], sight, is used in the plural in Matt. 20:34 (No. 1 is used in ver. 33); Mark 8:23 (No. 1 is used in ver. 25). The word is more poetical in usage than No. 1, and the writers may have changed the word with a view to distinguishing the simple desire of the blind man from the tender act of the Lord Himself. ¶

NT: B.565d; CB.1260c; K.—.
OT: 'ayin: S.5869; HR.991b.1; H.1612a,1613; BD.744a.
GEN. REF.: IS.2:249; NB.406; Z.2:452.

3. *trumalia* [τρυμαλιά, 5168], is used of the eye of a needle, Mark 10:25 (from *trumē*, a hole, *truō*, to wear away). ¶ Cp. *trēma*, a hole, perforation, Matt. 19:24 (some texts have *trupēma*, a hole, from *trupaō*, to bore a hole) and Luke 18:25, as in the most authentic mss. (some texts have *trumalia* here). ¶

NT: B.828b; CB.—; K.—.
OT: —.
GEN. REF.: IS.2:249; NB.—; Z.—.

EYE (with one)

monophthalmos [μονόφθαλμος, 3442], one-eyed, deprived of one eye (*monos*, only, and No. 1, above), is used in the Lord's warning in Matt. 18:9; Mark 9:47. ¶

NT: B.528b; CB.—; K.—.
OT: —.
GEN. REF.: IS.2:249; NB.406; Z.—.

EYE-SALVE

kollourion [κολλούριον, 2854], primarily a diminutive of *kollura*, and denoting a coarse bread roll (as in the Sept. of 1 Kings 12: after ver. 24, lines 30, 32, 39; Eng. Version, 14:3 ¶), hence an eye-salve, shaped like a roll, Rev. 3:18, of the true knowledge of one's condition and of the claims of Christ. The word is doubtless an allusion to the Phrygian powder used by oculists in the famous medical school at Loadicea (Ramsay, *Cities and Bishoprics of Phrygia*, Vol. 1, p. 52).

NT: B.441d; CB.1255c; K.—.
OT: —.
GEN. REF.: IS.4:295; NB.—; Z.2:454.

EYE-SERVICE

ophthalmodoulia [ὀφθαλμοδουλία, 3787], denotes service performed only under the master's eye (*ophthalmos*, an eye, *doulos*, a slave), diligently performed when he is looking, but neglected in his absence, Eph. 6:6 and Col. 3:22. ¶

NT: B.599b; CB.–; K.182.
OT: –.
GEN. REF.: IS.2:250; NB.–; Z.2:454.

EYE-WITNESS

1. *autoptēs* [αὐτόπτης, 845], signifies seeing with one's own eyes (*autos*, self, and a form, *optanō*, to see), Luke 1:2. ¶

NT: B.122c; CB.–; K.706.
OT: –.
GEN. REF.: IS.2:250; NB.–; Z.2:454.

2. *epoptēs* [ἐπόπτης, 2030], primarily an overseer (*epi*, over), then, a spectator, an eye-witness of anything, is used in 2 Pet. 1:16 of those who were present at the Transfiguration of Christ. Among the Greeks the word was used of those who had attained to the third grade, the highest, of the Eleusinian mysteries, a religious cult at Eleusis, with its worship, rites, festival and pilgrimages; this brotherhood was open to all Greeks. ¶ In the Sept., Esth. 5:1, where it is used of God as the Overseer and Preserver of all things. ¶ Cp. *epopteuō*, to behold, 1 Pet. 2:12 and 3:2. ¶

NT: B.305d; CB.1246b; K.706.
OT: –.
GEN. REF.: IS.2:250; NB.–; Z.2:454.

F

FABLE

muthos [μῦθος, 3454], primarily signifies speech, conversation. The first syllable comes from a root *mu–*, signifying to close, keep secret, be dumb; whence, *muō*, to close (eyes, mouth) and *mustērion*, a secret, a mystery; hence, a story, narrative, fable, fiction (Eng., myth). The word is used of Gnostic errors and of Jewish and profane fables and genealogies, in 1 Tim. 1:4; 4:7; 2 Tim. 4:4; Tit. 1:14; of fiction, in 2 Pet. 1:16. ¶

Muthos is to be contrasted with *alētheia*, truth, and with *logos*, a story, a narrative purporting to set forth facts, e.g., Matt. 28:15, a "saying" (i.e., an account, story, in which actually there is a falsification of facts); Luke 5:15, R.V., "report."

NT: B.529a; CB.1259b; K.610.
OT: –.
GEN. REF.: IS.2:267; NB.410; Z.2:477.

FACE

1. *prosōpon* [πρόσωπον, 4383], denotes the countenance, lit., the part towards the eyes (from *pros*, towards, *ōps*, the eye), and is used (*a*) of the face, Matt. 6:16, 17; 2 Cor. 3:7, 2nd part (A.V., "countenance"); in 2 Cor. 10:7, in the R.V., "things that are before your face" (A.V., "outward appearance"), the phrase is figurative of superficial judgment; (*b*) of the look, i.e., the face, which by its various movements affords an index of inward thoughts and feelings, e.g., Luke 9:51, 53; 1 Pet. 3:12; (*c*) the presence of a person, the face being the noblest part, e.g., Acts 3:13, R.V., "before the face of," A.V., "in the presence of"; 5:41, "presence"; 2 Cor. 2:10, "person"; 1 Thess. 2:17 (first part), "presence"; 2 Thess. 1:9, R.V., "face," A.V., "presence"; Rev. 12:14, "face"; (*d*) the person himself, e.g., Gal. 1:22; 1 Thess. 2:17 (second part); (*e*) the appearance one presents by his wealth or poverty, his position or state, Matt. 22:16; Mark 12:14; Gal. 2:6; Jude 16; (*f*) the outward appearance of inanimate things, Matt. 16:3; Luke 12:56; 21:35; Acts 17:26.

To spit in a person's face was an expression of the utmost scorn and aversion, e.g., Matt. 26:67 (cp. 27:30; Mark 10:34; Luke 18:32). See APPEARANCE.

NT: B.720d; CB.1267b; K.950.
OT: pānîm: S.6440; HR.1223c.6; H.1782a; BD.815d.
GEN. REF.: IS.2:267; NB.410; Z.2:478.

2. *opsis* [ὄψις, 3799], is primarily the act of seeing; then, (*a*) the face; of the body of Lazarus, John 11:44; of the countenance of Christ in a vision, Rev. 1:16; (*b*) the outward appearance of a person or thing, John 7:24. See APPEARANCE. ¶

NT: B.601d; CB.1261a; K.–.
OT: mar'eh: S.4758; HR.1044b.3; H.2095i; BD.909c.
'ayin: S.5869; HR.1044b.4; H.1612a,1613; BD.744a.
GEN. REF.: IS.2:267; NB.–; Z.2:478.

Note: The phrase "face to face" translates two phrases in Greek:

(1) *kata prosōpon* (*kata*, over against, and No. 1), Acts 25:16;

(2) *stoma pros stoma*, lit., 'mouth to mouth' (*stoma*, a mouth), 2 John 12; 3 John 14. See MOUTH.

(3) For *antophthalmeō*, Acts 27:15, R.V. has 'to face.'

FACTION, FACTIOUS

erithia (or —*eia*) [ἐριθία, 2052], denotes ambition, self-seeking, rivalry, self-will being an underlying idea in the word; hence it denotes party-making. It is derived, not from *eris*, strife, but from *erithos*, a hireling; hence the meaning of seeking to win followers, "factions," so rendered in the R.V. of 2 Cor. 12:20, A.V., "strifes"; not improbably the meaning here is rivalries, or base ambitions (all the other words in the list express abstract ideas rather than factions); Gal. 5:20 (ditto); Phil. 1:17 (R.V.; A.V., ver. 16, "contention"); 2:3 (A.V., "strife"); Jas. 3:14, 16 (ditto); in Rom. 2:8 it is translated as an adjective, "factious" (A.V., "contentious"). The order strife, jealousy, wrath, faction, is the same in 2 Cor. 12:20 and Gal. 5:20. Faction is the fruit of jealousy. ¶ Cp. the synonymous adjective *hairetikos*, Tit. 3:10, causing division (marg., "factious"), not necessarily "heretical," in the sense of holding false doctrine. ¶

NT: B.309b; CB.1246c; K.256.
OT: —.
GEN. REF.: IS.2:268; NB.—; Z.—.

FADE (away)

A. Verb.

marainō [μαραίνω, 3133], was used (*a*) to signify to quench a fire, and in the Passive Voice, of the dying out of a fire; hence (*b*) in various relations, in the Active Voice, to quench, waste, wear out; in the Passive, to waste away, Jas. 1:11, of the fading away of a rich man, as illustrated by the flower of the field. ¶ In the Sept., Job 15:30; 24:24. ¶

NT: B.491b; CB.—; K.—.
OT: yabēsh: S.3001; HR.896a.1; H.837; BD.386b.
GEN. REF.: IS.2:268; NB.—; Z.—.

B. Adjectives (negative).

1. *amarantos* [ἀμάραντος, 263], unfading (*a*, negative, and A., above), whence the "amaranth," an unfading flower, a symbol of perpetuity (see *Paradise Lost*, iii. 353), is used in 1 Pet. 1:4 of the believer's inheritance, "that fadeth not away." It is found in various writings in the language of the *Koinē*, e.g., on a gladiator's tomb; and as a proper name (Moulton and Milligan, Vocab.). ¶

NT: B.42b; CB.—; K.—.
OT: —.
GEN. REF.: —.

2. *amarantinos* [ἀμαράντινος, 262], primarily signifies composed of amaranth (see No. 1); hence, unfading, 1 Pet. 5:4, of the crown of glory promised to faithful elders. ¶ Cp. *rhodinos*, made of roses (*rhodon*, a rose).

NT: B.42b; CB.—; K.—.
OT: —.
GEN. REF.: —.

FAIL

A. Verbs.

1. *ekleipō* [ἐκλείπω, 1587], to leave out (*ek*, out, *leipō*, to leave), used intransitively, means to leave off, cease, fail; it is said of the cessation of earthly life, Luke 16:9; of faith, 22:32; of the light of the sun, 23:45 (in the best mss.); of the years of Christ, Heb. 1:12. ¶

NT: B.242c; CB.1243c; K.—.
OT: kālāh: S.3615; HR.435c.24a,b; H.982-984; BD.477b.
tāmam: S.8552; HR.435c.47; H.2522; BD.1070b.
GEN. REF.: IS.2:268; NB.—; Z.—.

2. *epileipō* [ἐπιλείπω, 1952], not to suffice for a purpose (*epi*, over), is said of insufficient time, in Heb. 11:32. ¶

NT: B.295c; CB.—; K.—.
OT: shā'ar: S.7604; HR.525a.1; H.2307,2308; BD.983d.
GEN. REF.: IS.2:268; NB.—; Z.—.

3. *piptō* [πίπτω, 4098], to fall, is used of the Law of God in its smallest detail, in the sense of losing its authority or ceasing to have force, Luke 16:17. In 1 Cor. 13:8 it is used of love (some mss. have *ekpiptō*, to fall off). See FALL.

NT: B.659b; CB.1265a; K.846.
OT: nāphal: S.5307; HR.1135c.12a; H.1392; BD.656c.
GEN. REF.: IS.2:268; NB.—; Z.—.

Notes: (1) In 1 Cor. 13:8, *katargeō*, to reduce to inactivity (see ABOLISH), in the Passive Voice, to be reduced to this condition, to be done away, is translated "shall fail," A.V. This, however, misses the distinction between what has been previously said of love and what is here said of prophecies (see No. 3); the R.V. has "shall be done away"; so also as regards knowledge (same verse).

(2) In Heb. 12:15, *hustereō*, to come behind, fall short, miss, is rendered "fail" in the A.V., R.V., "falleth short."

(3) In Luke 21:26, *apopsuchō*, lit., to breathe out life, hence, to faint, is translated "hearts failing," in the A.V., R.V., "fainting." See FAINT. ¶

B. Adjective.

anekleiptos [ἀνέκλειπτος, 413], unfailing (*a*, negative, and A, No. 1), is rendered "that faileth not," in Luke 12:33. ¶ In a Greek document dated A.D. 42, some contractors undertake to provide unfailing heat for a bath during the current year (Moulton and Milligan, Vocab.).

NT: B.64b; CB.—; K.—.
OT: —.
GEN. REF.: IS.2:269; NB.—; Z.—.

FAIN

1. *boulomai* [βούλομαι, 1014], to will deliberately, wish, desire, be minded, implying the deliberate exercise of volition (contrast No. 3), is translated "would fain" in Philm. 13 (in the best mss.). See DISPOSED.

NT: B.146a; CB.1239b; K.108.
OT: 'ābāh: S.14; HR.226b.1; H.3; BD.2c.
ḥāphēṣ: S.2654; HR.226b.5; H.712; BD.342c.
GEN. REF.: –.

2. *epithumeō* [ἐπιθυμέω, 1937], to set one's heart upon, desire, is translated "would fain" in Luke 15:16, of the prodigal son. See DESIRE.

NT: B.293a; CB.1246b; K.339.
OT: 'āwāh: S.183; HR.520b.1; H.40; BD.16a.
ḥāmad: S.2530; HR.520b.4; H.673; BD.326a.
ḥāphēṣ: S.2654; HR.520b.5; H.712; BD.342c.
GEN. REF.: IS.2:269; NB.–; Z.–.

3. *thelō* [θέλω, 2309], to wish, to design to do anything, expresses the impulse of the will rather than the intention (see No. 1); the R.V. translates it "would fain" in Luke 13:31, of Herod's desire to kill Christ, A.V., "will (kill)"; in 1 Thess. 2:18, of the desire of the missionaries to return to the church in Thessalonica. See DISPOSED.

NT: B.354d; CB.1271c; K.318.
OT: 'ābāh: S.14; HR.628b.1; H.3; BD.2c.
ḥāphēṣ: S.2654; HR.628b.8; H.712; BD.342c.
GEN. REF.: –.

Note: In Acts 26:28, in Agrippa's statement to Paul, the R.V. rendering is "with but little persuasion thou wouldest fain make me a Christian." The lit. rendering is 'with (or in) little (labour or time) thou art persuading me so as to make (me) a Christian.' There is no verb for "wouldest" in the original, but it brings out the sense.

FAINT

1. *ekluō* [ἐκλύω, 1590], denotes (*a*) to loose, release (*ek*, out, *luō*, to loose); (*b*) to unloose, as a bow-string, to relax, and so, to enfeeble, and is used in the Passive Voice with the significance to be faint, grow weary, (1) of the body, Matt. 15:32; (some mss. have it in 9:36); Mark 8:3; (2) of the soul, Gal. 6:9 (last clause), in discharging responsibilities in obedience to the Lord; in Heb. 12:3, of becoming weary in the strife against sin; in ver. 5, under the chastening hand of God. ¶ It expresses the opposite of *anazōnnumi*, to gird up, 1 Pet. 1:13. ¶

NT: B.243a; CB.1243c; K.–.
OT: rāphāh: S.7495; HR.438a.17a-d; H.2196; BD.950c.
yā'ēph: S.3286; HR.438a.4; H.885; BD.419b.
'āṭaph: S.5848; HR.438a.8; H.1605-1607; BD.742c.
GEN. REF.: IS.2:269; NB.–; Z.–.

2. *enkakeō* or *ekkakeō* [ἐνκακέω, 1573], to lack courage, lose heart, be fainthearted (*en*, in, *kakos*, base), is said of prayer, Luke 18:1; of Gospel ministry, 2 Cor. 4:1, 16; of the effect of tribulation, Eph. 3:13; as to well doing, 2 Thess. 3:13, "be not weary" (A.V. marg., "faint not"). Some mss. have this word in Gal. 6:9 (No. 1). ¶

NT: B.215c; CB.1245a; K.391.
OT: –.
GEN. REF.: –.

3. *kamnō* [κάμνω, 2577], primarily signified to work; then, as the effect of continued labour, to be weary; it is used in Heb. 12:3, of becoming weary (see also No. 1), R.V., "wax not weary"; in Jas. 5:15, of sickness; some mss. have it in Rev. 2:3, A.V., "hast (not) fainted," R.V., "grown weary." See SICK, WEARY. ¶

NT: B.402a; CB.–; K.–.
OT: –.
GEN. REF.: –.

Note: For *apopsuchō*, Luke 21:26, R.V., see FAIL, *Note* (3). ¶

FAINTHEARTED

oligopsuchos [ὀλιγόψυχος, 3642], lit., small-souled (*oligos*, small, *psuchē*, the soul), denotes despondent; then, "fainthearted," 1 Thess. 5:14, R.V., for the incorrect A.V., "feeble-minded." ¶ In the Sept., similarly, in a good sense, Isa. 57:15, 'who giveth endurance to the fainthearted,' for R.V. "to revive the spirit of the humble"; in a bad sense, Prov. 18:14, 'who can endure a fainthearted man?'

NT: B.564a; CB.1260c; K.1342.
OT: –.
GEN. REF.: –.

FAIR

1. *asteios* [ἀστεῖος, 791], lit., of the city (from *astu*, a city; like Lat. *urbanus*, from *urbs*, a city; Eng., urbane; similarly, polite, from *polis*, a town), hence, fair, elegant (used in the papyri writings of clothing), is said of the external form of a child, Acts 7:20, of Moses "(exceeding) fair," lit., 'fair to God'; Heb. 11:23 (R.V., "goodly," A.V., "proper"). See BEAUTIFUL, GOODLY, *Note*. ¶

NT: B.117c; CB.–; K.–.
OT: ṭôb: S.2896; HR.173b.2; H.793a; BD.373c.
GEN. REF.: IS.2:269; NB.–; Z.2:478.

2. *eudia* [εὐδία, 2105], denotes fair weather, Matt. 16:2, from *eudios*, calm; from *eu*, good, and *dios*, divine, among the pagan Greeks, akin to the name for the god Zeus, or Jupiter. Some would derive *Dios* and the Latin *deus* (god) and *dies* (day) from a root meaning bright. Cp. the Latin *sub divo*, 'under a bright, open sky.' ¶

NT: B.319a; CB.1247a; K.–.
OT: –.
GEN. REF.: –.

3. *kalos* [καλός, 2570], beautiful, fair, in appearance, is used as part of the proper name, Fair Havens, Acts 27:8. See BETTER, GOOD.

NT: B.400b; CB.1253b; K.402.
OT: ṭôb: S.2896; HR.715b.2a; H.793a; BD.373c.
yāpheh: S.3303; HR.715b.3a; H.890a; BD.421c.
GEN. REF.: IS.2:269; NB.–; Z.2:478.

Notes: (1) In Rom. 16:18 *eulogia*, which generally signifies blessing, is used in its more literal sense, "fair speech," i.e., a fine style of utterance, giving the appearance of reasonableness.

(2) In Gal. 6:12 the verb *euprosōpeō*, to look well, lit., to be fair of face (*eu*, well, and *prosōpon*, a face), signifies to make a fair or plausible show, used there metaphorically of making a display of religious zeal. ¶

FAITH

pistis [πίστις, 4102], primarily, firm persuasion, a conviction based upon hearing (akin to *peithō*, to persuade), is used in the N.T. always of faith in God or Christ, or things spiritual.

The word is used of (*a*) trust, e.g., Rom. 3:25 [see Note (4) below]; 1 Cor. 2:5; 15:14, 17; 2 Cor. 1:24; Gal. 3:23 [see Note (5) below]; Phil. 1:25; 2:17; 1 Thess. 3:2; 2 Thess. 1:3; 3:2; (*b*) trustworthiness, e.g., Matt. 23:23; Rom. 3:3, R.V., "the faithfulness of God"; Gal. 5:22 (R.V., "faithfulness"); Tit. 2:10, "fidelity"; (*c*) by metonymy, what is believed, the contents of belief, the faith, Acts 6:7; 14:22; Gal. 1:23; 3:25 [contrast 3:23, under (*a*)]; 6:10; Phil. 1:27; 1 Thess. 3:10; Jude 3, 20 (and perhaps 2 Thess. 3:2); (*d*) a ground for faith, an assurance, Acts 17:31 (not as in A.V., marg., "offered faith"); (*e*) a pledge of fidelity, plighted faith, 1 Tim. 5:12.

The main elements in faith in its relation to the invisible God, as distinct from faith in man, are especially brought out in the use of this noun and the corresponding verb, *pisteuō*; they are (1) a firm conviction, producing a full acknowledgement of God's revelation or truth, e.g., 2 Thess. 2:11, 12; (2) a personal surrender to Him, John 1:12; (3) a conduct inspired by such surrender, 2 Cor. 5:7. Prominence is given to one or other of these elements according to the context. All this stands in contrast to belief in its purely natural exercise, which consists of an opinion held in good faith without necessary reference to its proof. The object of Abraham's faith was not God's promise (that was the occasion of its exercise); his faith rested on God Himself, Rom. 4:17, 20, 21. See ASSURANCE, BELIEF, FAITHFULNESS, FIDELITY.

NT: B.662b; CB.1265a; K.849.
OT: 'ēmûn: S.529; HR.1138b.1a; H.116d; BD.53c.
'ᵉmûnāh: S.530; HR.1138b.1b; H.116e; BD.53c.
'ᵉmet: S.571; HR.1138b.1d; H.116k; BD.54a.
GEN. REF.: IS.2:270; NB.410; Z.2:479.

Notes: (1) In Heb. 10:23, *elpis*, hope, is mistranslated "faith" in the A.V. (R.V., "hope").

(2) In Acts 6:8 the most authentic mss. have *charis*, grace, R.V., for *pistis*, faith.

(3) In Rom. 3:3, R.V., *apistia*, is rendered "want of faith," for A.V., "unbelief" (so translated elsewhere). See UNBELIEF. The verb *apisteō* in that verse is rendered "were without faith," R.V., for A.V., "did not believe."

(4) In Rom. 3:25, the A.V. wrongly links "faith" with "in His blood," as if faith is reposed in the blood (i.e., the Death) of Christ; the *en* is instrumental; faith rests in the living Person; hence the R.V. rightly puts a comma after "through faith," and renders the next phrase "by His blood," which is to be connected with "a propitiation." Christ became a propitiation through His blood (i.e., His death in expiatory sacrifice for sin).

(5) In Gal. 3:23, though the article stands before "faith" in the original, faith is here to be taken as under (*a*) above, and as in ver. 22, and not as under (*c*), the faith; the article is simply that of renewed mention.

(6) For the difference between the teaching of Paul and that of James, on faith and works, see Notes on Galations, by Hogg and Vine, pp. 117-119.

FAITH (of little)

oligopistos [ὀλιγόπιστος, 3640], lit., little of faith (*oligos*, little, *pistis*, faith), is used only by the Lord, and as a tender rebuke, for anxiety, Matt. 6:30 and Luke 12:28; for fear, Matt. 8:26; 14:31; 16:8. ¶

NT: B.563b; CB.–; K.849.
OT: –.
GEN. REF.: IS.–; NB.–; Z.2:483.

FAITHFUL, FAITHFULLY, FAITHLESS

1. *pistos* [πιστός, 4103], a verbal adjective, akin to *peithō* (see FAITH), is used in two senses, (*a*) Passive, faithful, to be trusted, reliable, said of God, e.g., 1 Cor. 1:9; 10:13; 2 Cor. 1:18 (A.V., "true"); 2 Tim. 2:13; Heb. 10:23; 11:11; 1 Pet. 4:19; 1 John 1:9; of Christ, e.g., 2 Thess. 3:3; Heb. 2:17; 3:2; Rev. 1:5; 3:14; 19:11; of the words of God, e.g. Acts 13:34, "sure"; 1 Tim. 1:15; 3:1 (A.V., "true"); 4:9;

2 Tim. 2:11; Tit. 1:9; 3:8; Rev. 21:5; 22:6; of servants of the Lord, Matt. 24:45; 25:21, 23; Acts 16:15; 1 Cor. 4:2, 17; 7:25; Eph. 6:21; Col. 1:7; 4:7, 9; 1 Tim. 1:12; 3:11; 2 Tim. 2:2; Heb. 3:5; 1 Pet. 5:12; 3 John 5; Rev. 2:13; 17:14; of believers, Eph. 1:1; Col. 1:2; (*b*) Active, signifying believing, trusting, relying, e.g., Acts 16:1 (feminine); 2 Cor. 6:15; Gal. 3:9 seems best taken in this respect, as the context lays stress upon Abraham's faith in God, rather than upon his faithfulness. In John 20:27 the context requires the Active sense, as the Lord is reproaching Thomas for his want of faith. See No. 2.

With regard to believers, they are spoken of sometimes in the Active sense, sometimes in the Passive, i.e., sometimes as believers, sometimes as faithful. See Lightfoot on Galations, p. 155.

NT: B.664c; CB.1265a; K.849.
OT: 'āman: S.539; HR.1138c.1a; H.116; BD.52d.
'ĕmûn: S.529; HR.1138c.1c; H.116d; BD.53c.
'ᵉmet: S.571; HR.1138c.1d; H.116k; BD.54a.
GEN. REF.: IS.2:273; NB.410; Z.2:483.

Note: In 3 John 5 the R.V. has "thou doest a faithful work," for A.V., "thou doest faithfully." The lit. rendering is 'thou doest (*poieō*) a faithful thing, whatsoever thou workest (*ergazō*).' That would not do as a translation. To do a faithful work is to do what is worthy of a faithful man. The A.V. gives a meaning but is not exact as a translation. Westcott suggests 'thou makest sure (*piston*) whatsoever thou workest' (i.e., it will not lose its reward). The change between *poieō*, to do, and *ergazō*, to work, must be maintained. Cp. Matt. 26:10 (*ergazō* and *ergon*).

2. *apistos* [ἄπιστος, 571], is used with meanings somewhat parallel to No. 1; (*a*) untrustworthy (*a*, negative, and No. 1), not worthy of confidence or belief, is said of things "incredible," Acts 26:8; (*b*) unbelieving, distrustful, used as a noun, "unbeliever," Luke 12:46; 1 Tim. 5:8 (R.V., for A.V., "infidel"); in Tit. 1:15 and Rev. 21:8, "unbelieving"; "faithless" in Matt. 17:17; Mark 9:19; Luke 9:41; John 20:27. The word is most frequent in 1 and 2 Corinthians. See BELIEVE, INCREDIBLE, INFIDEL, UNBELIEVER, UNFAITHFUL. (In the Sept., Prov. 17:6; 28:25; Is. 17:10. ¶).

NT: B.85d; CB.1236c; K.849.
OT: —.
GEN. REF.: IS.2:276; NB.—; Z.2:483.

FAITHFULNESS

Note: This is not found in the A.V. The R.V. corrects the A.V. "faith" to "faithfulness" in Rom. 3:3; Gal. 5:22. See FAITH.

FALL, FALLEN, FALLING, FELL

A. Nouns.

1. *ptōsis* [πτῶσις, 4431], a fall (akin to B, No. 1), is used (*a*) literally, of the overthrow of a building, Matt. 7:27; (*b*) metaphorically, Luke 2:34, of the spiritual fall of those in Israel who would reject Christ; the word "again" in the A.V. of the next clause is misleading; the "rising up" (R.V.) refers to those who would acknowledge and receive Him, a distinct class from those to whom the "fall" applies. The fall would be irretrievable, cp. (*a*) ; such a lapse as Peter's is not in view. ¶

NT: B.728a; CB.1268a; K.846.
OT: mappelet: S.4658; HR.1239b.2d; H.1392e; BD.658c.
mappālāh: S.4654; HR.1239b.2a; H.1392d; BD.658c.
nāphal: S.5307; HR.1239b.2b; H.1392; BD.656c.
GEN. REF.: —.

2. *paraptōma* [παράπτωμα, 3900], primarily a false step, a blunder (*para*, aside, *piptō*, to fall), then a lapse from uprightness, a sin, a moral trespass, misdeed, is translated "fall" in Rom. 11:11, 12, of the sin and downfall of Israel in their refusal to acknowledge God's claims and His Christ; by reason of this the offer of salvation was made to Gentiles; cp. *ptaiō*, to stumble, in ver. 11. See FAULT, OFFENCE, SIN, TRESPASS.

NT: B.621d; CB.1262b; K.846.
OT: pesha': S.6588; HR.1063c.4; H.1846a; BD.833b.
'āwel: S.5766; HR.1063c.3; H.1580a,b; BD.732b.
GEN. REF.: —.

3. *apostasia* [ἀποστασία, 646], a defection, revolt, apostasy, is used in the N.T. of religious apostasy; in Acts 21:21, it is translated "to forsake," lit., 'thou teachest apostasy from Moses.' In 2 Thess. 2:3 "the falling away" signifies apostasy from the faith. In papyri documents it is used politically of rebels. ¶.

NT: B.98b; CB.1237a; K.88.
OT: mered: S.4777; HR.141a.3; H.1240a; BD.597d.
mā'al: S.4603; HR.141a.2; H.1230; BD.591a.
GEN. REF.: —.

Note: For "mighty fall," Rev. 18:21, R.V., see VIOLENCE.

B. Verbs.

1. *piptō* [πίπτω, 4098], to fall, is used (*a*) of descent, to fall down from, e.g., Matt. 10:29; 13:4; (*b*) of a lot, Acts 1:26; (*c*) of falling under judgment, Jas. 5:12 (cp. Rev. 18:2, R.V.); (*d*) of persons in the act of prostration, to prostrate oneself, e.g., Matt. 17:6; John 18:6; Rev. 1:17; in homage and worship, e.g., Matt. 2:11; Mark 5:22; Rev. 5:14; 19:4; (*e*) of things, falling into ruin, or failing, e.g., Matt. 7:25; Luke 16:17, R.V., "fall," for A.V., "fail"; Heb. 11:30; (*f*) of falling in judgment upon persons, as of the sun's heat, Rev. 7:16, R.V., "strike," A.V., "light"; of a mist and darkness, Acts 13:11

(some mss. have *epipiptō*); (*g*) of persons, in falling morally or spiritually, Rom. 14:4; 1 Cor. 10:8, 12; Rev. 2:5 (some mss. have No. 3 here). See FAIL, LIGHT (upon), STRIKE.

NT: B.659b; CB.1265a; K.846.
OT: nāphal: S.5307; HR.1135c.12a; H.1392; BD.656c.
GEN. REF.: –.

2. *apopipto* [ἀποπίπτω, 634], to fall from (*apo*, from), is used in Acts 9:18, of the scales which fell from the eyes of Saul of Tarsus. ¶

NT: B.97b; CB.–; K.–.
OT: nāphal: S.5307; HR.139c.5; H.1392; BD.656c.
GEN. REF.: –.

3. *ekpiptō* [ἐκπίπτω, 1601], to fall out of (*ek*, out, and No. 1), "is used in the N.T., literally, of flowers that wither in the course of nature, Jas. 1:11; 1 Pet. 1:24; of a ship not under control, Acts 27:17, 26, 29, 32; of shackles loosed from a prisoner's wrist, 12:7; figuratively, of the Word of God (the expression of His purpose), which cannot fall away from the end to which it is set, Rom. 9:6; of the believer who is warned lest he fall away from the course in which he has been confirmed by the Word of God, 2 Pet. 3:17."* So of those who seek to be justified by law, Gal. 5:4, "ye are fallen away from grace." Some mss. have this verb in Mark 13:25, for No. 1; so in Rev. 2:5. See CAST, EFFECT. ¶

NT: B.243d; CB.1243c; K.846.
OT: nāphal: S.5307; HR.439b.3a; H.1392; BD.656c.
nābēl: S.5034; HR.439b.2; H.1286; BD.615b.
GEN. REF.: –.

4. *empiptō* [ἐμπίπτω, 1706], to fall into, or among (*en*, in, and No. 1), is used (*a*) literally, Matt. 12:11; Luke 6:39 (some mss. have No. 1 here); 10:36; some mss. have it in 14:5; (*b*) metaphorically, into condemnation, 1 Tim. 3:6; reproach, 3:7; temptation and snare, 6:9; the hands of God in judgment, Heb. 10:31. ¶

NT: B.256b; CB.–; K.–.
OT: nāphal: S.5307; HR.458a.3; H.1392; BD.656c.
GEN. REF.: –.

5. *epipiptō* [ἐπιπίπτω, 1968], to fall upon (*epi*, upon, and No. 1), is used (*a*) literally, Mark 3:10, "pressed upon"; Acts 20:10, 37; (*b*) metaphorically, of fear, Luke 1:12; Acts 19:17; Rev. 11:11 (No. 1, in some mss.); reproaches, Rom. 15:3; of the Holy Spirit, Acts 8:16; 10:44; 11:15.

NT: B.297c; CB.–; K.–.
OT: nāphal: S.5307; HR.526b.4a,b; H.1392; BD.656c.
GEN. REF.: –.

Note: Some mss. have this verb in John 13:25; Acts 10:10; 13:11. See PRESS. ¶

6. *katapiptō* [καταπίπτω, 2667], to fall down (*kata*, down, and No. 1), is used in Luke 8:6 (in the best mss.); Acts 26:14; 28:6. ¶

NT: B.416c; CB.1254b; K.846.
OT: nāphal: S.5307; HR.741c.1; H.1392; BD.656c.
GEN. REF.: –.

7. *parapiptō* [παραπίπτω, 3895], akin to A, No. 2, properly, to fall in one's way (*para*, by), signifies to fall away (from adherence to the realities and facts of the faith), Heb. 6:6. ¶

NT: B.621b; CB.1262b; K.846.
OT: 'āsham: S.816; HR.1063b.1; H.180; BD.79c.
mā'al: S.4603; HR.1063b.2; H.1230; BD.591a.
nāphal: S.5307; HR.1063b.3; H.1392; BD.656c.
GEN. REF.: –.

8. *peripiptō* [περιπίπτω, 4045], to fall around (*peri*, around), hence signifies to fall in with, or among, to light upon, come across, Luke 10:30, "among (robbers)"; Acts 27:41, A.V., "falling into," R.V., "lighting upon," a part of a shore; Jas. 1:2, into temptation (i.e., trials). See LIGHT (to l. upon). ¶ In the Sept., Ruth 2:3; 2 Sam. 1:6; Prov. 11:5. ¶

NT: B.649d; CB.1263b; K.846.
OT: qārāh: S.7136; HR.1125b.2; H.2068,2068e; BD.899c.
nāphal: S.5307; HR.1125b.1; H.1392; BD.656c.
GEN. REF.: –.

9. *prospiptō* [προσπίπτω, 4363], to fall towards anything (*pros*, towards), to strike against, is said of "wind," Matt. 7:25; it also signifies to fall down at one's feet, fall prostrate before, Mark 3:11; 5:33; 7:25; Luke 5:8; 8:28, 47; Acts 16:29. ¶

NT: B.718a; CB.–; K.–.
OT: nāphal: S.5307; HR.1219a.4; H.1392; BD.656c.
nāga': S.5060; HR.1219a.3; H.1293; BD.619a.
kāra': S.3766; HR.1219a.2; H.1044; BD.502c.
GEN. REF.: –.

10. *hustereō* [ὑστερέω, 5302], to come late, to be last, behind, inferior, is translated "falleth short" in Heb. 12:15, R.V., for A.V., "fail," and "fall short" in Rom. 3:23, for A.V., "come short," which, in view of the preceding "have," is ambiguous, and might be taken as a past tense. See BEHIND.

NT: B.849b; CB.1252b; K.1240.
OT: ḥāsēr: S.2637; HR.1418b.3a,b; H.705; BD.341a.
GEN. REF.: –.

11. *epiballō* [ἐπιβάλλω, 1911], to cast upon (*epi*, on, *ballō*, to throw), also signifies to fall to one's share, Luke 15:12, "that falleth." The phrase is frequently found in the papyri documents as a technical formula. See CAST, A, No. 7.

NT: B.289d; CB.–; K.91.
OT: –.
GEN. REF.: –.

12. *erchomai* [ἔρχομαι, 2064], to come, is translated "have fallen out," in Phil. 1:12, of the issue of circumstances. See COME.

NT: B.310b; CB.1246b; K.257.
OT: –.
GEN. REF.: –.

13. *ginomai* [γίνομαι, 1096], to become, is translated "falling" (headlong) in Acts 1:18. See Note (1) below. See BECOME.

NT: B.158a; CB.1248b; K.117.
OT: –.
GEN. REF.: –.

*From Notes on Galatians by Hogg and Vine, p. 242.

14. *aphistēmi* [ἀφίστημι, 868], when used intransitively, signifies to stand off (*apo*, from, *histēmi*, to stand), to withdraw from; hence, to fall away, to apostatize, 1 Tim. 4:1, R.V., "shall fall away," for A.V., "shall depart"; Heb. 3:12, R.V., "falling away." See DEPART, No. 20.

NT: B.126d; CB.1236b; K.88.
OT: mā'al: S.4603; HR.184b.16; H.1230; BD.591a.
sûr: S.5493; HR.184b.27a,b; H.1480; BD.693b.
mārad: S.4775; HR.184b.17; H.1240; BD.597c.
GEN. REF.: –.

15. *parabainō* [παραβαίνω, 3845], to transgress, fall (*para*, away, across, *bainō*, to go), is translated "fell away" in Acts 1:25, R.V., for A.V., "by transgression fell." See TRANSGRESS.

NT: B.611c; CB.1262a; K.772.
OT: sûr: S.5493; HR.1055b.3; H.1480; BD.693b.
'ābar: S.5674; HR.1055b.4; H.1556; BD.716d.
sāṭāh: S.7847; HR.1055b.7; H.2250; BD.966a.
GEN. REF.: –.

16. *katabainō* [καταβαίνω, 2597], denotes to come (or fall) down, Luke 22:44; in Rev. 16:21, "cometh down," R.V. See COME, DESCEND.

NT: B.408b; CB.1253c; K.90.
OT: yārad: S.3381; HR.727a.8a; H.909; BD.432c.
GEN. REF.: –.

Notes: (1) In Rev. 16:2, *ginomai*, to become, is translated "it became," R.V., for A.V., "there fell."

(2) In 2 Pet. 1:10, *ptaiō*, to stumble, is translated "stumble," R.V., for A.V., "fall."

(3) In Rom. 14:13, *skandalon*, a snare, a means of doing wrong, is rendered "an occasion of falling," R.V., for A.V. "an occasion to fall."

(4) *Koimaō*, in the Middle Voice, signifies to fall asleep, Matt. 27:52, R.V., "had fallen asleep," for A.V., "slept." See ASLEEP.

(5) In Acts 27:34, *apollumi*, to perish, is translated "shall . . . perish," R.V., for A.V., "shall . . . fall."

(6) In Jude 24 the adjective *aptaistos*, without stumbling, sure footed (*a*, negative, and *ptaiō*, to stumble), is translated "from stumbling," R.V., for A.V., "from falling."

(7) In Acts 1:18 the phrase *prēnēs*, headlong, with the aorist participle of *ginomai*, to become, "falling headlong," lit., 'having become headlong,' is used of the suicide of Judas Iscariot. Some would render the word (it is a medical term) "swollen," (as connected with a form of the verb *pimprēmi*, to burn), indicating the condition of the body of certain suicides.

(8) In Acts 20:9, A.V., *katapherō*, to bear down, is translated "being fallen into" (R.V., "borne down"), and then "he sunk down" (R.V., ditto), the first of gradual oppression, the second (the aorist tense) of momentary effect.

(9) In Acts 19:35 *diopetēs*, from *dios*, heaven, *piptō*, to fall, i.e., fallen from the sky, is rendered "image which fell down from Jupiter" (R.V. marg., "heaven").

FALSE, FALSEHOOD, FALSELY

A. Adjectives.

1. *pseudēs* [ψευδής, 5571], is used of false witnesses, Acts 6:13; false apostles, Rev. 2:2, R.V., "false," A.V., "liars"; Rev. 21:8, "liars." ¶

NT: B.891c; CB.1267c; K.1339.
OT: kāzab: S.3577; HR.1484b.1b; H.970a; BD.469c.
shāw': S.7723; HR.1484b.3; H.2338a; BD.996a.
sheqer: S.8267; HR.1484b.4; H.2461a; BD.1055b.
GEN. REF.: –.

Note: For compound words with this adjective, see APOSTLE, BRETHREN, CHRIST, PROPHET, WITNESS.

2. *pseudōnumos* [ψευδώνυμος, 5581], under a false name (No. 1, and *onoma*, a name; Eng., pseudonym), is said of the knowledge professed by the propagandists of various heretical cults, 1 Tim. 6:20. ¶

NT: B.892c; CB.1267c; K.694.
OT: –.
GEN. REF.: –.

B. Noun.

pseudos [ψεῦδος, 5579], a falsehood (akin to A, No. 1), is so translated in Eph. 4:25, R.V. (A.V., "lying"); in 2 Thess. 2:9, "lying wonders" is lit. 'wonders of falsehood,' i.e., wonders calculated to deceive; it is elsewhere rendered "lie," John 8:44; Rom. 1:25; 2 Thess. 2:11; 1 John 2:21, 27; Rev. 14:5, R.V.; 21:27; 22:15. See GUILE, LIE. ¶

NT: B.892b; CB.1267c; K.1339.
OT: kāzab: S.3577; HR.1485a.1b; H.970a; BD.469c.
kāḥash: S.3584; HR.1485a.2; H.975; BD.471a.
sheqer: S.8267; HR.1485a.4; H.2461a; BD.1055b.
GEN. REF.: –.

C. Verb.

pseudō [ψεύδω, -ουαι, 5574], to deceive by lies, is used in the Middle Voice, translated "to say . . . falsely," in Matt. 5:11; it is elsewhere rendered to lie, Acts 5:3, 4; Rom. 9:1; 2 Cor. 11:31; Gal. 1:20; Col. 3:9; 1 Tim. 2:7. See LIE.

NT: B.891d; CB.1267c; K.1339.
OT: kāzab: S.3577; HR.1484b.2; H.970a; BD.469c.
kāḥash: S.3584; HR.1484b.4; H.975; BD.471a.
GEN. REF.: –.

FAME

A. Noun.

phēmē [φήμη, 5345], originally denoted a Divine voice, an oracle; hence, a saying or report (akin to *phēmi*, to say, from a root meaning to shine, to be clear; hence, Lat., *fama*, Eng., fame), is rendered "fame" in Matt. 9:26 and Luke 4:14. ¶

NT: B.856b; CB.–; K.–.
OT: sh^{e}mû'āh: S.8052; HR.1429b.1; H.2412d; BD.1035b.
GEN. REF.: IS.2:279; NB.–; Z.–.

Notes: (1) In Luke 5:15, R.V., *logos*, a word, report, account, is translated "report," for A.V., "fame." See REPORT.

(2) *Akoē*, a hearing, is translated "report" in the R.V. of Matt. 4:24; 14:1; Mark 1:28, for A.V., "fame." See EAR, No. 3, HEARING.

(3) *Ēchos*, a noise, report, sound, is translated "rumour," in the R.V. of Luke 4:37, for A.V., "fame"; "sound" in Acts 2:2; Heb. 12:19. See RUMOUR, SOUND. ¶

B. Verb.

diaphēmizō [διαφημίζω, 1310], signifies to spread abroad a matter, Matt. 28:15, R.V.; Mark 1:45, R.V. (from *dia*, throughout, and *phēmi*, to say); hence, to spread abroad one's fame, Matt. 9:31. All the passages under this heading relate to the testimony concerning Christ in the days of His flesh. ¶

NT: B.190c; CB.–; K.–.
OT: –.
GEN. REF.: IS.2:279; NB.–; Z.–.

FAMILY

1. *oikos* [οἶκος, 3624], signifies (*a*) a dwelling, a house (akin to *oikeō*, to dwell); (*b*) a household, family, translated "family" in 1 Tim. 5:4, R.V., for A.V., "at home." See HOME, HOUSE, HOUSEHOLD, TEMPLE.

NT: B.560b; CB.1260b; K.674.
OT: bayit: S.1004; HR.973a.5; H.241; BD.108c.
GEN. REF.: IS.2:279; NB.415; Z.2:497.

2. *patria* [πατριά, 3965], primarily an ancestry, lineage, signifies in the N.T. a family or tribe (in the Sept. it is used of related people, in a sense wider than No. 1, but narrower than *phulē*, a tribe, e.g., Ex. 12:3; Numb. 32:28); it is used of the family of David, Luke 2:4, R.V., for A.V., "lineage"; in the wider sense of nationalities, races, Acts 3:25, R.V., "families," for A.V., "kindreds"; in Eph. 3:15, R.V., "every family," for A.V., "the whole family," the reference being to all those who are spiritually related to God the Father, He being the Author of their spiritual relationship to Him as His children, they being united to one another in family fellowship (*patria* is akin to *patēr*, a father); Luther's translation, "all who bear the name of children," is advocated by Cremer, p. 474. The phrase, however, is lit., 'every family.' ¶ See KINDRED. ¶

NT: B.636d; CB.1263a; K.805.
OT: 'āb: S.1; HR.1111a.1a; H.4a; BD.3a.
mishpāḥāh: S.4940; HR.1111a.2; H.2442b; BD.1046c.
GEN. REF.: IS.2:279; NB.415; Z.2:497.

FAMINE

limos [λιμός, 3042], is translated "hunger" in Luke 15:17; 2 Cor. 11:27; elsewhere it signifies a famine, and is so translated in each place in the R.V.; the A.V. has the word "dearth" in Acts 7:11 and 11:28, and "hunger" in Rev. 6:8; the R.V. "famine" is preferable there; see Matt. 24:7; Mark 13:8; Luke 4:25; 15:14; 21:11; Rom. 8:35; Rev. 18:8. See HUNGER. ¶

NT: B.475a; CB.1257a; K.820.
OT: rā'āb: S.7458; HR.878c.2a; H.2183a; BD.944b.
GEN. REF.: IS.2:281; NB.418; Z.2:501.

FAN

ptuon [πτύον, 4425], denotes a winnowing shovel or fan, with which grain is thrown up against the wind, in order to separate the chaff, Matt. 3:12; Luke 3:17. ¶

NT: B.727c; CB.1268a; K.–.
OT: –.
GEN. REF.: IS.2:344; NB.418; Z.2:501.

FAR

A. Adjective.

makros [μακρός, 3117], is used (*a*) of space and time, long, said of prayers (in some mss., Matt. 23:14), Mark 12:40; Luke 20:47; (*b*) of distance, far, far distant, Luke 15:13; 19:12. See LONG. ¶

NT: B.488c; CB.–; K.–.
OT: 'ōrek: S.753; HR.893c.1b; H.162a; BD.78d.
'ārēk: S.750; HR.893c.1d; H.162b; BD.74a.
'ārōk: S.752; HR.893c.1a; H.162c; BD.74a.
GEN. REF.: –.

B. Adverbs.

1. *makran* [μακράν, 3112], properly a feminine form of the adjective above, denotes a long way, far, (*a*) literally, Matt. 8:30, R.V., "afar off." Luke 7:6; 15:20, R.V., "afar off"; John 21:8; Acts 17:27; 22:21; (*b*) metaphorically, "far (from the kingdom of God)," Mark 12:34; in spiritual darkness, Acts 2:39; Eph. 2:13, 17. See AFAR. ¶

NT: B.487c; CB.1257c; K.549.
OT: rāḥaq: S.7368; HR.892c.3a,b; H.2151; BD.934d.
rāḥōq: S.7350; HR.892c.3c; H.2151b; BD.935b.
GEN. REF.: IS.2:283; NB.–; Z.–.

2. *makrothen* [μακρόθεν], from far (akin to No. 1), Mark 8:3; see AFAR.

3. *porrō* [πόρρω, 4206], is used (*a*) literally, Luke 14;32, "a great way off"; the comparative degree *porrōteron*, "further," is used in 24:28; (*b*) metaphorically, of the heart in separation from God, Matt. 15:8; Mark 7:6. See FURTHER, WAY. ¶ Cp. *porrōthen*, afar off; see AFAR.

NT: B.693d; CB.1266a; K.–.
OT: rāḥaq: S.7368; HR.1195b.1a; H.2151; BD.934d.
rāḥōq: S.7350; HR.1195b.1d; H.2151b; BD.935b.
GEN. REF.: IS.2:283; NB.–; Z.–.

Notes: (1) In Matt. 16:22, Peter's word to the Lord "be it far from Thee" translates the phrase *hileōs soi*, lit., '(God be) propitious to Thee,' R.V., marg., "God have mercy on Thee." Some would translate it "God avert this from Thee!"

Others render it "God forbid!" Luther's translation is 'spare Thyself.' Lightfoot suggests 'Nay, verily!' or 'Away with the thought!' It was the vehement and impulsive utterance of Peter's horrified state of mind. *Hileōs* signifies propitious, "merciful," Heb. 8:12. See MERCY, C. ¶

(2) In Luke 22:51, "thus far" translates the phrase *heōs toutou*, lit., 'unto this.'

(3) In Gal. 6:14 the R.V. "far be it" translates the phrase *mē genoito*, lit., 'let it not be,' elsewhere translated idiomatically "God forbid," e.g., Luke 20:16. See FORBID.

(4) In Heb. 7:15 the A.V. "far more" translates *perissoteron*, R.V., "more abundantly"; see ABUNDANT.

(5) In the following the verb *apodēmeō*, to go abroad, is rendered, in the A.V., to go into a far country, R.V., to go into another country, Matt. 21:33; 25:14; Mark 12:1; in Matt. 25:15, R.V., "he went on his journey" (A.V., "took etc."). In Luke 15:13 the A.V. and R.V. have "took (his) journey into a far country"; in Luke 20:9, R.V., "another country," for A.V., "a far country." ¶ The adjective *apodēmos* in Mark 13:34 is rendered in the A.V., "taking a far journey," R.V., "sojourning in another country." See JOURNEY. ¶

(6) In 2 Cor. 4:17 the phrase *kath' huperbolēn* is translated "more and more," R.V. for A.V., "a far more."

(7) In the following, *heōs*, used as a preposition, is translated "as far as" in the R.V., for different words in the A.V.; Acts 17:14, in the best mss., instead of *hōs*, which the A.V. renders "as it were"; 17:15, "unto"; 23:23, "to." Both Versions have "as far as" in 11:19, 22; in Luke 24:50, the R.V. has "until they were over against," for A.V., "as far as to."

(8) In Rev. 14:20, the preposition *apo*, from, is translated "as far as" in the R.V., for A.V., "by the space of."

FARE, FAREWELL

1. *euphrainō* [εὐφραίνω, 2165], in the Active Voice, signifies to cheer, gladden, 2 Cor. 2:2; in the Passive, to rejoice, make merry; translated "faring sumptuously" in Luke 16:19, especially of food (R.V., marg., "living in mirth and splendour"). See GLAD, MERRY, REJOICE.

NT: B.327d; CB.1247b; K.278.
OT: sāmaḥ: S.8055; HR.581b.19a; H.2268; BD.970a.
GEN. REF.: —.

2. *rhōnnumi* [ῥώννυμι, 4517], to strengthen, to be strong, is used in the Imperative Mood as a formula at the end of letters, signifying "Farewell," Acts 15:29; some mss. have it in 23:30 (the R.V. omits it, as do most Versions). ¶

NT: B.738d; CB.—; K.—.
OT: —.
GEN. REF.: IS.2:283; NB.—; Z.—.

3. *echō* [ἔχω, 2192], to have, is used idiomatically in Acts 15:36, R.V., "(how) they fare," A.V., "how they do."

NT: B.331d; CB.1242c; K.286.
OT: —.
GEN. REF.: —.

4. *chairō* [χαίρω, 5463], to joy, rejoice, be glad, is used in the Imperative Mood in salutations, (*a*) on meeting, "Hail," e.g., Matt. 26:49; or with *legō*, to say, to give a greeting, 2 John 11; in letters, "greeting," e.g., Acts 15:23; (*b*) at parting, the underlying thought being joy, 2 Cor. 13:11 (R.V., marg., "rejoice); (*c*) on other occasions, see the R.V. marg. in Phil. 3:1; 4:4. See GLAD, GREETING, No. 2, HAIL, JOY, JOYFULLY.

NT: B.873b; CB.1239b; K.1298.
OT: sāmaḥ: S.8055; HR.1452a.7a; H.2268; BD.970a.
gîl: S.1523; HR.1452a.2; H.346; BD.162a.
GEN. REF.: IS.2:283; NB.—; Z.—.

Note: As "farewell" is inadequate to express *chairō*, which always conveys the thought of joy or cheer, (*b*) properly comes under (*c*).

5. *apotassō* [ἀποτάσσω, 657], primarily denotes to set apart; then, in the Middle Voice, (*a*) to take leave of, bid farewell to, Mark 6:46, "had taken leave of"; cp. Acts 18:18, 21; 2 Cor. 2:13 (in these three verses, the verb may signify to give final instructions to); Luke 9:61, "to bid farewell"; (*b*) to forsake, Luke 14:33. In the papyri, besides saying goodbye, the stronger meaning is found of getting rid of a person (Moulton and Milligan). See FORSAKE, LEAVE (take), RENOUNCE, SEND (away). ¶

NT: B.100d; CB.—; K.—.
OT: —.
GEN. REF.: IS.2:283; NB.—; Z.—.

Note: For *aspazomai*, to bid farewell, see LEAVE (*c*), No. 2.

FARM

agros [ἀγρός, 68], denotes (*a*) a field (cp. Eng., agriculture), e.g., Matt. 6:28; (*b*) the country, e.g., Mark 15:21, or, in the plural, country places, farms, Mark 5:14; 6:36, 56; Luke 8:34; 9:12; (*c*) a piece of ground, e.g., Mark 10:29; Acts 4;37; a farm, Matt. 22:5. See COUNTRY, FIELD, GROUND, LAND

NT: B.13d; CB.1233c; K.—.
OT: sādeh: S.7740; HR.17a.7; H.2342a; BD.961b.
GEN. REF.: IS.2:283; NB.—; Z.—.

Note: For the synonymous word *chōra*, a country, land, see COUNTRY. Moulton and Milligan point out that *agros* is frequent in the Sept., and in the Synoptic Gospels, but that Luke uses *chōra* especially, and that possibly *agros* was a favourite word with translators from Hebrew and Aramaic.

For **FARTHER SIDE,** Mark 10:1, see **BEYOND,** No. 2

FARTHING

1. *assarion* [ἀσσάριον, 787], a diminutive of the Latin *as*, was one-tenth of a drachma, or one-sixteenth of a Roman *denarius*, i.e., about three farthings, Matt. 10:29; Luke 12:6. ¶
NT: B.117b; CB.—; K.—.
OT: —.
GEN. REF.: IS.3:409; NB.839; Z.—.

2. *kodrantēs* [κοδράντης, 2835], was the Latin *quadrans*, the fourth part of an *as* (see No. 1), about two thirds of a farthing, Matt. 5:26; Mark 12:42. ¶
NT: B.437a; CB.—; K.—.
OT: —.
GEN. REF.: IS.3:409; NB.840; Z.—.

FASHION

A. Nouns.

1. *eidos* [εἶδος, 1491], that which is seen, an appearance, is translated "fashion" in Luke 9:29, of the Lord's countenance at the Transfiguration. See APPEARANCE, and Note under IMAGE, No. 1.
NT: B.221b; CB.1243a; K.202.
OT: mar'eh: S.4758; HR.375c.1; H.2095i; BD.909c.
tō'ar: S.8389; HR.375c.8; H.2491a; BD.1061b.
GEN. REF.: —.

2. *prosōpon* [πρόσωπον, 4383], the face, countenance, is translated "fashion" in Jas. 1:11, of the flower of grass. See COUNTENANCE. Cp. ver. 24, "what manner of man," which translates *hopoios*, of what sort.
NT: B.720d; CB.1267b; K.950.
OT: —.
GEN. REF.: —.

3. *schēma* [σχῆμα, 4976], a figure, fashion (akin to *echō*, to have), is translated "fashion" in 1 Cor. 7:31, of the world, signifying that which comprises the manner of life, actions, etc. of humanity in general; in Phil. 2:8 it is used of the Lord in His being found "in fashion" as a man, and signifies what He was in the eyes of men, "the entire outwardly perceptible mode and shape of His existence, just as the preceding words *morphē*, form, and *homoiōma*, likeness, describe what he was in Himself as Man" (Gifford on the Incarnation, p. 44). "Men saw in Christ a human form, bearing, language, action, mode of life . . . in general the state and relations of a human being, so that in the entire mode of His appearance He made Himself known and was recognized as a man" (Meyer).
NT: B.797b; CB.1268c; K.1129.
OT: —.
GEN. REF.: —.

4. *tupos* [τύπος, 5179], a type, figure, example, is translated "fashion" in the A.V. of Acts 7:44, R.V., "figure," said of the Tabernacle. See ENSAMPLE.
NT: B.829d; CB.1273b; K.1193.
OT: tabnît: S.8403; HR.1378b.2; H.255d; BD.125d.
ṣelem: S.6754; HR.1378b.1; H.1923a; BD.853d.
GEN. REF.: —.

B. Adverb.

houtōs [οὕτως, 3779], thus, so, in this way, is rendered "on this fashion" in Mark 2:12. See EVEN, No. 5, LIKEWISE, MANNER, SO, THUS, WHAT.
NT: B.597c; CB.—; K.—.
OT: kōh: S.3541; HR.1035c.9a; H.955; BD.462a.
kēn: S.3651; HR.1035c.13a; H.964a,b; BD.485d.
GEN. REF.: —.

C. Verbs.

1. *metaschēmatizō* [μετασχηματίζω, 3345], to change in fashion or appearance (*meta*, after, here implying change, *schēma*, see A, No. 3), is rendered "shall fashion anew" in Phil. 3:21, R.V.; A.V., "shall change," of the bodies of believers as changed or raised at the Lord's Return; in 2 Cor. 11:13, 14, 15, the R.V. uses the verb to fashion oneself, for A.V., to transform, of Satan and his human ministers, false apostles; in 1 Cor. 4:6 it is used by way of a rhetorical device, with the significance of transferring by a figure. See CHANGE, TRANSFORM. ¶
NT: B.513b; CB.1258c; K.1129.
OT: —.
GEN. REF.: —.

2. *suschēmatizō* [συσχηματίζω, 4964], to give the same figure or appearance as, to conform to (*sun*, with, *schēma*, cp. No. 1), used in the Passive Voice, signifies to fashion oneself, to be fashioned, Rom. 12:2, R.V., "be not fashioned according to," for A.V., "be not conformed to"; 1 Pet. 1:14, "(not) fashioning yourselves." See CONFORMED. ¶
NT: B.795c; CB.1271a; K.—.
OT: —.
GEN. REF.: —.

Note: In Rom. 12:2 being outwardly conformed to the things of this age is contrasted with being transformed (or transfigured) inwardly by the renewal of the thoughts through the Holy Spirit's power. A similar distinction holds good in Phil. 3:21; the Lord will "fashion anew," or change outwardly, the body of our humiliation, and conform it in its nature (*summorphos*) to the body of His glory.

D. Adjective.

summorphos [σύμμορφος, 4832], having like form with (*sun*, with, *morphē*, form), is used in Rom. 8:29 and Phil. 3:21 (A.V., "fashioned;" R.V., "conformed"). See CONFORM. ¶

NT: B.778d; CB.1270b; K.1102.
OT: –.
GEN. REF.: –.

FAST, FASTING

A. Nouns.

1. *nēsteia* [νηστεία, 3521], a fasting, fast (from *nē*, a negative prefix, and *esthiō*, to eat), is used (*a*) of voluntary abstinence from food, Luke 2:37; Acts 14:23 (some mss. have it in Matt. 17:21 and Mark 9:29); fasting had become a common practice among Jews, and was continued among Christians; in Acts 27:9, "the Fast" refers to the Day of Atonement, Lev. 16:29; that time of the year would be one of dangerous sailing; (*b*) of involuntary abstinence (perhaps voluntary is included), consequent upon trying circumstances, 2 Cor. 6:5; 11:27. ¶

NT: B.538a; CB.1259c; K.632.
OT: ṣôm: S.6685; HR.945a.1; H.1890a; BD.847b.
GEN. REF.: IS.2:284; NB.418; Z.2:501.

2. *nēstis* [νῆστις, 3523], not eating (see No. 1), fasting, is used of lack of food, Matt. 15:32; Mark 8:3. ¶

NT: B.538d; CB.1259c; K.632.
OT: ṭᵉwāt (Aramaic): S.2908; HR.945b.1; H.2753; BD.1094a.
GEN. REF.: IS.2:284; NB.418; Z.2:501.

Note: Asitia, Acts 27:21, means "without food" (not through lack of supplies), i.e., abstinence from food. See ABSTINENCE, and cp. C, below.

B. Verb.

nēsteuō [νηστεύω, 3522], to fast, to abstain from eating (akin to A, Nos. 1 and 2), is used of voluntary fasting, Matt. 4:2; 6:16, 17, 18; 9:14, 15; Mark 2:18, 19, 20; Luke 5:33, 34, 35; 18:12; Acts 13:2, 3. Some of these passages show that teachers to whom scholars or disciples were attached, gave them special instructions as to fasting. Christ taught the need of purity and simplicity of motive.

The answers of Christ to the questions of the disciples of John and of the Pharisees reveal His whole purpose and method. No doubt He and His followers observed such a Fast as that on the Day of Atonement, but He imposed no frequent fasts in addition. What He taught was suitable to the change of character and purpose which He designed for His disciples. His claim to be the Bridegroom, Matt. 9:15, and the reference there to the absence of fasting, virtually involved a claim to be the Messiah (cp. Zech. 8:19). ¶ Some mss. have the verb in Acts 10:30.

NT: B.538b; CB.1259c; K.632.
OT: ṣûm: S.6684; HR.945b.1; H.1890; BD.847a.
GEN. REF.: IS.2:284; NB.418; Z.2:501.

C. Adjective.

asitos [ἄσιτος, 777], without food (*a*, negative, *sitos*, corn, food), is used in Acts 27:33, "fasting." Cp. *asitia*, Note under A, No. 2. ¶

NT: B.116b; CB.–; K.–.
OT: –.
GEN. REF.: IS.–; NB.419; Z.2:501.

FAST (to make)

asphalizō [ἀσφαλίζω, 805], to make secure, safe, firm (akin to *asphalēs*, safe), (*a*, negative, and *sphallō*, to trip up), is translated "make . . . fast," in Acts 16:24, of prisoners' feet in the stocks. In Matt. 27:64, 65, 66, it is rendered 'to make sure.' See SURE. ¶

NT: B.119a; CB.1238a; K.87.
OT: ḥāzaq: S.2388; HR.174b.1; H.636; BD.304a.
GEN. REF.: –.

Note: For HOLD (fast) and STAND (fast), see HOLD and STAND, No. 7.

FASTEN

1. *atenizō* [ἀτενίζω, 816], from *atenēs*, strained, intent, and *teinō*, to stretch, strain (from a root *ten*—, seen in Eng., tension, tense etc.), signifies to look fixedly, gaze, fasten one's eyes upon, and is found twelve times in the writings of Luke (ten in the Acts), out of its fourteen occurrences. It always has a strongly intensive meaning, and is translated to fasten the eyes upon in the A.V. and R.V. in Luke 4:20; Acts 3:4; 11:6; so in the R.V., where the A.V. has different renderings, in Acts 6:15 (for A.V., "looking steadfastly"); 10:4 ("looked"); 13:9 ("set his eyes"); 14:9 ("steadfastly beholding"). In Acts 7:55, both have "looked up steadfastly." In the following the R.V. also varies the translation, Luke 22:56; Acts 1:10; 3:12; 23:1; 2 Cor. 3:7, 13. See BEHOLD, LOOK. ¶

NT: B.119d; CB.1238a; K.–.
OT: –.
GEN. REF.: –.

2. *kathaptō* [καθάπτω, 2510], to fasten on, lay hold of, attack, is used of the serpent which fastened on Paul's hand, Acts 28:3. ¶

NT: B.387a; CB.–; K.–.
OT: –.
GEN. REF.: –.

FATHER

A. Noun.

patēr [πατήρ, 3962], from a root signifying a nourisher, protector, upholder (Lat., *pater*,

Eng., father, are akin), is used (*a*) of the nearest ancestor, e.g., Matt. 2:22; (*b*) of a more remote ancestor, the progenitor of the people, a forefather, e.g., Matt. 3:9; 23:30; 1 Cor. 10:1; the patriarchs, 2 Pet. 3:4; (*c*) one advanced in the knowledge of Christ, 1 John 2:13; (*d*) metaphorically, of the originator of a family or company of persons animated by the same spirit as himself, as of Abraham, Rom. 4:11, 12, 16, 17, 18, or of Satan, John 8:38, 41, 44; (*e*) of one who, as a preacher of the Gospel and a teacher, stands in a father's place, caring for his spiritual children, 1 Cor. 4:15 (not the same as a mere title of honour, which the Lord prohibited, Matt. 23:9); (*f*) of the members of the Sanhedrin, as of those who exercised religious authority over others, Acts 7:2; 22:1; (*g*) of God in relation to those who have been born anew (John 1:12, 13), and so are believers, Eph. 2:18; 4:6 (cp. 2 Cor. 6:18), and imitators of their Father, Matt. 5:45, 48; 6:1, 4, 6, 8, 9, etc. Christ never associated Himself with them by using the personal pronoun "our"; He always used the singular, "My Father," His relationship being unoriginated and essential, whereas theirs is by grace and regeneration, e.g., Matt. 11:27; 25:34; John 20:17; Rev. 2:27; 3:5, 21; so the Apostles spoke of God as the Father of the Lord Jesus Christ, e.g., Rom. 15:6; 2 Cor. 1:3; 11:31; Eph. 1:3; Heb. 1:5; 1 Pet. 1:3; Rev. 1:6; (*h*) of God, as the Father of lights, i.e., the Source or Giver of whatsoever provides illumination, physical and spiritual, Jas. 1:17; of mercies, 2 Cor. 1:3; of glory, Eph. 1:17; (*i*) of God, as Creator, Heb. 12:9 (cp. Zech. 12:1).

NT: B.635a; CB.1262c; K.805.
OT: 'āb: S.1; HR.1105a.1a; H.4a; BD.3a.
GEN. REF.: IS.2:284; NB.415; Z.2:497.

Note: Whereas the everlasting power and Divinity of God are manifest in creation, His Fatherhood in spiritual relationship through faith is the subject of N.T. revelation, and waited for the presence on earth of the Son, Matt. 11:27; John 17:25. The spiritual relationship is not universal, John 8:42, 44 (cp. John 1:12 and Gal. 3:26).

B. Adjectives.

1. *patrōos* [πατρῷος, 3971], signifies of one's fathers, or received from one's fathers (akin to A), Acts 22:3; 24:14; 28:17. ¶ In the Sept., Prov. 27:10. ¶

NT: B.637b; CB.–; K.805.
OT: 'āb: S.1; HR.1112; H.4a; BD.3a.
GEN. REF.: IS.2:284; NB.415; Z.2:504.

2. *patrikos* [πατρικός, 3967], from one's fathers, or ancestors, is said of that which is handed down from one's forefathers, Gal. 1:14. ¶

NT: B.636d; CB.1263a; K.805.
OT: 'āb: S.1; HR.1111c.1; H.4a; BD.3a.
GEN. REF.: IS.2:284; NB.415; Z.2:504.

3. *apatōr* [ἀπάτωρ, 540], without father (*a*, negative, and *patēr*), signifies, in Heb. 7:3, with no recorded genealogy. ¶

NT: B.82b; CB.1236b; K.805.
OT: –.
GEN. REF.: –.

4. *patroparadotos* [πατροπαράδοτος, 3970], handed down from one's fathers (*patēr*, and *paradidomi*, to hand down), is used in 1 Pet. 1:18. ¶

NT: B.637a; CB.–; K.–.
OT: –.
GEN. REF.: –.

FATHER-IN-LAW

pentheros [πενθερός, 3995], a wife's father (from a root signifying a bond, union), is found in John 18:13. ¶

NT: B.642c; CB.–; K.–.
OT: ḥām: S.2524; HR.1117c.1; H.674a; BD.327a.
ḥōtēn: S.2859; HR.1117c.2; H.781b; BD.368c.
GEN. REF.: IS.4:77; NB.–; Z.–.

FATHERLESS

orphanos [ὀρφανός, 3737], properly, an orphan, is rendered "fatherless" in Jas. 1:27; "desolate" in John 14:18, for A.V., "comfortless." See COMFORTLESS. ¶

NT: B.583a; CB.1261b; K.734.
OT: yātôm: S.3490; HR.1018a.1; H.934a; BD.450c.
GEN. REF.: IS.2:286; NB.–; Z.2:506.

FATHOM

orguia [ὀργυιά, 3712], akin to *oregō*, to stretch, is the length of the outstretched arms, about six feet, Acts 27:28 (twice). ¶

NT: B.579d; CB.–; K.–.
OT: –.
GEN. REF.: IS.2:287; NB.1324; Z.5:915.

FATLING, FATTED

1. *sitistos* [σιτιστός, 4619], fattened, lit., 'fed with grain' (from *siteuō*, to feed, to fatten), is used as a neuter plural noun, "fatlings," in Matt. 22:4. ¶ Cp. *asitos*, under FASTING.

NT: B.752a; CB.–; K.–.
OT: –.
GEN. REF.: IS.2:287; NB.–; Z.2:506.

2. *siteutos* [σιτευτός, 4618], fed (with grain), denotes "fatted," Luke 15:23, 27, 30. ¶

NT: B.752a; CB.1269a; K.–.
OT: 'ābas: S.75; HR.1267b.1; H.10; BD.7b.
marbēk: S.4770; HR.1267b.2; H.2110a; BD.918c.
GEN. REF.: IS.2:287; NB.–; Z.–.

FATNESS

piotēs [πιότης, 4096], from *piōn*, fat, from a root, *pi*–, signifying swelling, is used metaphorically in Rom. 11:17. The Gentile believer had become a sharer in the spiritual life and blessing bestowed by Divine covenant upon Abraham and his descendants as set forth under the figure of "the root of (not 'and') the fatness of the olive tree." ¶

NT: B.659a; CB.1265a; K.—.
OT: deshen: S.1880; HR.1135b.1; H.457a; BD.206b.
GEN. REF.: IS.2:289; NB.—; Z.—.

FAULT, FAULTLESS

A. Noun.

aition [αἴτιον, 158], properly the neuter of *aitios*, causative of, responsible for, is used as a noun, a crime, a legal ground for punishment, translated "fault" in Luke 23:4, 14; in ver. 22, "cause." See AUTHOR, CAUSE.

NT: B.26d; CB.1234a; K.—.
OT: —.
GEN. REF.: —.

Notes: (1) For *aitia*, rendered "fault" in John 18:38; 19:4, 6, A.V. (Like *aition*, denoting a ground for punishment), see ACCUSATION, CAUSE, CHARGE.

(2) For *hēttēma*, a loss, translated "fault" in 1 Cor. 6:7, A.V., see DEFECT (R.V.).

(3) For *paraptōma*, a false step, a trespass, translated "fault" in Gal. 6:1, A.V., and "faults" in Jas. 5:16, A.V., see SIN, A, No. 2, *Note* (1), TRESPASS.

B. Adjective.

amemptos [ἄμεμπτος, 273], without blame, is rendered "faultless," in Heb. 8:7. See BLAMELESS.

NT: B.45a; CB.1234c; K.580.
OT: zākāh: S.2135; HR.65b.2a; H.549; BD.269a.
zākak: S.2141; HR.65b.2b; H.550; BD.269a.
tām: S.8535; HR.65b.6; H.2522c; BD.1070d.
GEN. REF.: IS.2:288; NB.—; Z.—.

Note: for *amōmos*, without blemish, rendered "faultless," i.e., without any shortcoming, in Jude 24, and "without fault" in Rev. 14:5, A.V., see BLEMISH.

C. Verbs.

1. *memphomai* [μέμφομαι, 3201], to blame, is translated "to find fault" in Rom. 9:19 and Heb. 8:8. Some mss. have the verb in Mark 7:2. See BLAME.

NT: B.502b; CB.1258b; K.580.
OT: —.
GEN. REF.: IS.2:288; NB.—; Z.—.

2. *elenchō* [ἐλέγχω, 1651], to convict, reprove, rebuke, is translated "shew (him) his fault" in Matt. 18:15. See CONVICT.

NT: B.249b; CB.1244a; K.221.
OT: yākaḥ: S.3198; HR.449b.3a; H.865; BD.406d.
GEN. REF.: IS.2:288; NB.—; Z.—.

Note: In 1 Pet. 2:20, A.V., the verb *hamartanō*, to sin (strictly, to miss the mark) is rendered "for your faults." The R.V. corrects to "when ye sin (and are buffeted for it)."

FAVOUR, FAVOURED

A. Noun.

charis [χάρις, 5485], denotes (*a*) objectively, grace in a person, graciousness, (*b*) subjectively, (1) grace on the part of a giver, favour, kindness, (2) a sense of favour received, thanks. It is rendered "favour" in Luke 1:30; 2:52; Acts 2:47; 7:10, 46; 24:27 and 25:9, R.V. (for A.V., "pleasure"); 25:3; see more fully under GRACE.

NT: B.877b; CB.1239c; K.1298.
OT: ḥēn: S.2580; HR.1455a.2; H.694a; BD.336b.
GEN. REF.: IS.2:288; NB.491; Z.—.

B. Verb.

charitoō [χαριτόω, 5487], akin to A., to endow with *charis*, primarily signified to make graceful or gracious, and came to denote, in Hellenistic Greek, to cause to find favour, Luke 1:28, "highly favoured" (marg., "endued with grace"); in Eph. 1:6, it is translated "made . . . accepted," A.V., "freely bestowed," R.V. (lit., 'graced'); it does not here mean to endue with grace. Grace implies more than favour; grace is a free gift, favour may be deserved or gained. ¶

NT: B.879a; CB.1239c; K.1298.
OT: —.
GEN. REF.: IS.2:288; NB.491; Z.—.

FEAR, FEARFUL, FEARFULNESS

A. Nouns.

1. *phobos* [φόβος, 5401], first had the meaning of flight, that which is caused by being scared; then, that which may cause flight, (*a*) fear, dread, terror, always with this significance in the four Gospels; also e.g., in Acts 2:43; 19:17; 1 Cor. 2:3; 1 Tim. 5:20 (lit., 'may have fear'); Heb. 2:15; 1 John 4:18; Rev. 11:11; 18:10, 15; by metonymy, that which causes fear, Rom. 13:3; 1 Pet. 3:14, R.V., "(their) fear," A.V. "(their) terror," an adaptation of the Sept. of Isa. 8:12, "fear not their fear"; hence some take it to mean, as there, 'what they fear,' but in view of Matt. 10:28, e.g., it seems best to understand it as that which is caused by the intimidation of adversaries; (*b*) reverential fear, (1) of God, as a controlling motive of the life, in matters spiritual and moral, not a mere fear of His power and righteous retribution, but a wholesome dread of displeasing Him, a fear which banishes the terror that shrinks from His presence, Rom. 8:15, and which influences the disposition and attitude of one whose circumstances are guided by trust in God, through the indwelling Spirit of God, Acts 9:31; Rom. 3:18; 2 Cor. 7:1; Eph. 5:21 (R.V., "the fear of

Christ"); Phil. 2:12; 1 Pet. 1:17 (a comprehensive phrase: the reverential fear of God will inspire a constant carefulness in dealing with others in His fear); 3:2, 15; the association of "fear and trembling," as e.g., in Phil. 2:12, has in the Sept. a much sterner import, e.g., Gen. 9:2; Ex. 15:16; Deut. 2:25; 11:25; Ps. 55:5; Is. 19:16; (2) of superiors, e.g., Rom. 13:7; 1 Pet. 2:18. See TERROR.

NT: B.863c; CB.1264b; K.1272.
OT: 'êmāh: S.367; HR.1435c.1a; H.80b; BD.33d.
yir'āh: S.3374; HR.1435c.4a; H.907b; BD.432a.
paḥad: S.6343; HR.1435c.6; H.1756a; BD.808b.
GEN. REF.: IS.2:289; NB.419; Z.2:518.

2. *deilia* [δειλία, 1167], fearfulness (from *deos*, fright), is rightly rendered "fearfulness" in 2 Tim. 1:7, R.V. (for A.V., "fear"). That spirit is not given us of God. The word denotes cowardice and timidity and is never used in a good sense, as No. 1 is. ¶ Cp. *deilos*, B, No. 2, below, and *deiliaō*, to be fearful (A.V., "afraid"), John 14:27. ¶

NT: B.173a; CB.1240c; K.—.
OT: 'êmāh: S.367; HR.286c.1; H.80b; BD.33d.
mōrek: S.4816; HR.286c.3; H.2164c; BD.940b.
GEN. REF.: —.

3. *eulabeia* [εὐλάβεια, 2124], signifies, firstly, caution; then, reverence, godly fear, Heb. 5:7; 12:28, in best mss., "reverence"; in general, apprehension, but especially holy fear, "that mingled fear and love which, combined, constitute the piety of man toward God; the O.T. places its emphasis on the fear, the N.T. . . . on the love, though there was love in the fear of God's saints then, as there must be fear in their love now" (Trench, Syn. § xlviii). ¶ In the Sept., Josh. 22:24; Prov. 28:14. ¶

NT: B.321d; CB.1247b; K.275.
OT: deʾāgāh: S.1674; HR.572a.1; H.393a; BD.178c.
GEN. REF.: IS.2:292; NB.—; Z.—.

Note: In Luke 21:11, *phobētron* (akin to No. 1) denotes a terror, R.V., "terrors," for A.V., "fearful sights," i.e., 'objects or instruments of terror.' ¶

B. Adjectives.

1. *phoberos* [φοβερός, 5398], fearful (akin to A, No. 1), is used only in the Active sense in the N.T., i.e., causing fear, terrible, Heb. 10:27, 31; 12:21, R.V., "fearful," for A.V., "terrible." ¶

NT: B.862b; CB.1264b; K.—.
OT: yārēʾ: S.3372; HR.1435c.3a; H.907,908; BD.431a.
GEN. REF.: IS.2:289; NB.419; Z.2:518.

2. *deilos* [δειλός, 1169], cowardly (see A, No. 2), timid, is used in Matt. 8:26; Mark 4:40; Rev. 21:8 (here "the fearful" are first in the list of the transgressors). ¶

NT: B.173a; CB.—; K.—.
OT: rak: S.7390; HR.287a.3; H.2164a; BD.940a.
GEN. REF.: —.

3. *ekphobos* [ἔκφοβος, 1630], signifies frightened outright (*ek*, out, intensive, and A, No. 1), Heb. 12:21 (with *eimi*, I am), "I exceedingly fear" (see No. 4); Mark 9:6, "sore afraid." ¶

NT: B.247a; CB.—; K.—.
OT: yāgōr: S.3025; HR.445c.1; H.843; BD.388c.
GEN. REF.: IS.2:289,292; NB.—; Z.—.

4. *entromos* [ἔντρομος, 1790], trembling with fear (*en*, in, intensive, and *tremō*, to tremble, quake; Eng., tremor, etc.), is used with *ginomai*, to become, in Acts 7:32, "trembled"; 16:29, R.V., "trembling for fear"; with *eimi*, to be, in Heb. 12:21, "quake" (some mss. have *ektromos* here). See QUAKE, TREMBLE. ¶ The distinction between No. 3 and No. 4. as in Heb. 12:21, would seem to be that *ekphobos* stresses the intensity of the fear, *entromos* the inward effect, 'I inwardly tremble (or quake).'

NT: B.269d; CB.—; K.—.
OT: rāʿad: S.7460; HR.481a.1; H.2184; BD.914c.
GEN. REF.: —.

C. Adverb.

aphobōs [ἀφόβως, 870], denotes "without fear" (*a*, negative, and A, No. 1), and is said of serving the Lord, Luke 1:74; of being among the Lord's people as His servant, 1 Cor. 16:10; of ministering the Word of God, Phil. 1:14; of the evil of false spiritual shepherds, Jude 12. ¶ In the Sept., Prov. 1:33. ¶

NT: B.127a; CB.1236b; K.—.
OT: —.
GEN. REF.: IS.2:292; NB.—; Z.—.

D. Verbs.

1. *phobeō* [φοβέω, 5399], in earlier Greek, to put to flight (see A, No. 1), in the N.T. is always in the Passive Voice, with the meanings either (*a*) to fear, be afraid, its most frequent use, e.g., Acts 23:10, according to the best mss. (see No. 2); or (*b*) to show reverential fear [see A, No. 1, (*b*)], (1) of men, Mark 6:20; Eph. 5:33, R.V., "fear," for A.V., "reverence"; (2) of God, e.g., Acts 10:2, 22; 13:16, 26; Col. 3:22 (R.V., "the Lord"); 1 Pet. 2:17; Rev. 14:7; 15:4; 19:5; (*a*) and (*b*) are combined in Luke 12:4, 5, where Christ warns His followers not to be afraid of men, but to fear God. See MARVEL, B, No. 1, *Note*.

NT: B.862b; CB.1264b; K.1272.
OT: yārēʾ: S.3372; HR.1433b.9a,b; H.907,908; BD.431a.
GEN. REF.: IS.2:289; NB.419; Z.2:518.

2. *eulabeomai* [εὐλαβέομαι, 2125], to be cautious, to beware (see A, No. 3), signifies to act with the reverence produced by holy fear, Heb. 11:7, "moved with godly fear."

NT: B.321d; CB.1247b; K.275.
OT: yāgōr: S.3025; HR.572a.9; H.843; BD.388c.
yārēʾ: S.3372; HR.572a.10; H.907,908; BD.431a.
pāḥad: S.6342; HR.572a.14; H.1756; BD.808b.
GEN. REF.: IS.2:289; NB.419; Z.2:518.

Notes: (1) In Acts 23:10 some mss. have this verb with the meaning (*a*) under No. 1.

(2) In Luke 3:14, *diaseiō*, to shake violently, to intimidate, to extort by violence, blackmail, is rendered "put no man in fear" in A.V. marg. See VIOLENCE.

FEAST

A. Nouns.

1. *heortē* [ἑορτή, 1859], a feast or festival, is used (*a*) especially of those of the Jews, and particularly of the Passover; the word is found mostly in John's Gospel (seventeen times); apart from the Gospels it is used in this way only in Acts 18:21; (*b*) in a more general way, in Col. 2:16, A.V., "holy day," R.V., "a feast day."

NT: B.280b; CB.1250a; K.—.
OT: ḥag: S.2282; HR.503a.1; H.602a; BD.290d.
mô'ēd: S.4150; HR.503a.3a; H.878b; BD.417b.
GEN. REF.: IS.2:292; NB.420; Z.2:521.

2. *deipnon* [δεῖπνον, 1173], denotes (*a*) the chief meal of the day, dinner or supper, taken at or towards evening; in the plural "feasts," Matt. 23:6; Mark 6:21; 12:39; Luke 20:46; otherwise translated "supper," Luke 14:12, 16, 17, 24; John 12:2; 13:2, 4; 21:20; 1 Cor. 11:21 (of a social meal); (*b*) the Lord's Supper, 1 Cor. 11:20; (*c*) the supper or feast which will celebrate the marriage of Christ with His spiritual Bride, at the inauguration of His Kingdom, Rev. 19:9; (*d*) figuratively, of that to which the birds of prey will be summoned after the overthrow of the enemies of the Lord at the termination of the war of Armageddon, 19:17 (cp. Ezek. 39:4, 17-20). See SUPPER. ¶

NT: B.173b; CB.1240c; K.143.
OT: patbāg: S.6598; HR.288a.2; H.1851; BD.834a.
GEN. REF.: —.

3. *dochē* [δοχή, 1403], a reception feast, a banquet (from *dechomai*, to receive), Luke 5:29; 14:13 (not the same as No. 2; see ver. 12). ¶

NT: B.206b; CB.1242a; K.146.
OT: mishteh: S.4960; HR.348b.2; H.2477c; BD.1059c.
GEN. REF.: IS.—; NB.—; Z.2:521.

4. *gamos* [γάμος, 1062], a wedding, especially a wedding feast (akin to *gameō*, to marry); it is used in the plural in the following passages (the R.V. rightly has "marriage feast" for the A.V., "marriage," or "wedding"), Matt. 22:2, 3, 4, 9 (in verses 11, 12, it is used in the singular, in connection with the wedding garment); 25:10; Luke 12:36; 14:8; in the following it signifies a wedding itself, John 2:1, 2; Heb. 13:4; and figuratively in Rev. 19:7, of the marriage of the Lamb; in ver. 9 it is used in connection with the supper, the wedding supper (or what in English is termed breakfast), not the wedding itself, as in ver. 7.

NT: B.151b; CB.1248a; K.111.
OT: mishteh: S.4960; HR.234a.1; H.2477c; BD.1059c.
GEN. REF.: IS.—; NB.—; Z.2:521.

5. *agapē* [ἀγάπη, 26], love, is used in the plural in Jude 12, signifying "love feasts," R.V. (A.V., "feasts of charity"); in the corresponding passage, 2 Pet. 2:13, the most authentic mss. have the word *apatē*, in the plural, "deceivings."

NT: B.5b; CB.1233b; K.5.
OT: —.
GEN. REF.: IS.2:296; NB.—; Z.2:521.

Notes: (1) In 1 Cor. 10:27 the verb *kaleō*, to call, in the sense of inviting to one's house, is translated "biddeth you (to a feast)"; in the most authentic texts there is no separate phrase representing "to a feast," as in some mss., *eis deipnon* (No. 2).

(2) In Mark 14:2 and John 2:23 the A.V. translates *heortē* (see No. 1) by "feast day" (R.V., "feast").

(3) For the Feast of the Dedication, John 10:22, see DEDICATION.

B. Verbs.

1. *heortazō* [ἑορτάζω, 1858], to keep festival (akin to A, No. 1) is translated "let us keep the feast," in 1 Cor. 5:8. This is not the Lord's Supper, nor the Passover, but has reference to the continuous life of the believer as a festival or holy-day (see A.V., margin), in freedom from "the leaven of malice and wickedness, but with the unleavened bread of sincerity and truth." ¶

NT: B.280a; CB.1250a; K.—.
OT: ḥāgag: S.2287; HR.502c.1a; H.602,602b; BD.290c.
GEN. REF.: IS.2:292; NB.419; Z.2:521.

2. *suneuōcheō* [συνευωχέω, 4910], to entertain sumptuously with, is used in the Passive Voice, denoting to feast sumptuously with (*sun*, together, and *euōchia*, good cheer), to revel with, translated "feast with" in 2 Pet. 2:13 and Jude 12. ¶

NT: B.789a; CB.—; K.—.
OT: —.
GEN. REF.: —.

FEEBLE

asthenēs [ἀσθενής, 772], without strength (*a*, negative, and *sthenos*, strength), is translated feeble in 1 Cor. 12:22, of members of the body. See IMPOTENT, SICK, STRENGTH, B, *Note* (5), WEAK.

NT: B.115c; CB.1238a; K.83.
OT: dal: S.1800; HR.172b.3; H.433a; BD.195d.
'ānî: S.6041; HR.172b.7a; H.1652d; BD.776d.
rāpheh: S.7504; HR.172b.10; H.2198a; BD.952a.
GEN. REF.: —.

Notes: (1) In Heb. 12:12 *paraluō*, to weaken, enfeeble, in the Passive Voice, to be enfeebled, as by a paralytic stroke, is translated "feeble" in the A.V. (R.V., "palsied").

(2) For "feeble-minded" in 1 Thess. 5:14, A.V., see FAINTHEARTED.

FEED, FED

1. *boskō* [βόσκω, 1006], to feed, is primarily used of a herdsman (from *boō*, to nourish, the special function being to provide food; the root is *bo*, found in *botēr*, a herdsman or herd, and *botanē*, fodder, pasture); its uses are (*a*) literal, Matt. 8:30; in ver. 33, the R.V. corrects the A.V., "they that kept," to "they that fed," as in Mark 5:14 (A.V. and R.V.) and Luke 8:34; in Mark 5:11 and Luke 8:32, "feeding"; Luke 15:15; (*b*) metaphorical, of spiritual ministry, John 21:15, 17 (see note on No. 2). See KEEP. ¶

NT: B.145b; CB.1239b; K.—.
OT: —.
GEN. REF.: IS.2:297; NB.—; Z.—.

2. *poimainō* [ποιμαίνω, 4165], to act as a shepherd (from *poimēn*, a shepherd), is used (*a*) literally, Luke 17:7, R.V., "keeping sheep," for A.V., "feeding cattle"; 1 Cor. 9:7; (*b*) metaphorically, to tend, to shepherd; said of Christ, Matt. 2:6, R.V., "shall be Shepherd of" (for A.V., "shall rule"); of those who act as spiritual shepherds under Him, John 21:16, R.V., "tend" (for A.V. "feed"); so 1 Pet. 5:2; Acts 20:28, "to feed" ('to tend' would have been a consistent rendering; a shepherd does not only feed his flock); of base shepherds, Jude 12. See RULE.

NT: B.683d; CB.1265c; K.901.
OT: rā'āh: S.7462; HR.1169a.2; H.2185,2186; BD.944d.
GEN. REF.: IS.2:297; NB.—; Z.—.

Note: In John 21:15, 16, 17, the Lord, addressing Peter, first uses No. 1, *boskō* (ver. 15), then No. 2, *poimainō* (ver.16), and then returns to *boskō* (ver. 17). These are not simply interchangeable (nor are other variations in His remarks); a study of the above notes will show this. Nor, again, is there a progression of ideas. The lesson to be learnt, as Trench points out (Syn. § xxv), is that, in the spiritual care of God's children, the feeding of the flock from the Word of God is the constant and regular necessity; it is to have the foremost place. The tending (which includes this) consists of other acts, of discipline, authority, restoration, material assistance of individuals, but they are incidental in comparison with the feeding.

3. *trephō* [τρέφω, 5142], signifies (*a*) to make to grow, bring up, rear, Luke 4:16, "brought up"; (*b*) to nourish, feed, Matt. 6:26; 25:37; Luke 12:24; Acts 12:20; Rev. 12:6, 14; of a mother, to give suck, Luke 23:29 (some mss. here have *thēlazō*, to suckle); to fatten, as of fattening animals, Jas. 5:5, "ye have nourished (your hearts)." See BRING, A, No. 33. ¶

NT: B.825c; CB.—; K.—.
OT: ḥāyāh: S.2421; HR.1371b.5; H.644; BD.310d.
kûl: S.3557; HR.1371b.6; H.962; BD.465a.
GEN. REF.: IS.2:297; NB.—; Z.—.

4. *chortazō* [χορτάζω, 5526], to feed, to fatten, is used (*a*) primarily of animals, Rev. 19:21; (*b*) of persons, to fill or satisfy with food. It is usually translated by the verb "to fill," but is once rendered "to be fed," in Luke 16:21, of Lazarus, in his desire for the crumbs (he could be well supplied with them) that fell from the rich man's table, a fact which throws light upon the utter waste that went on at the table of the latter. The crumbs that fell would provide no small meal. See FILL, SATISFY.

NT: B.883d; CB.1240a; K.—.
OT: sāba': S.7646; HR.1472c.1; H.2231; BD.959b.
GEN. REF.: IS.2:297; NB.—; Z.—.

5. *psōmizō* [ψωμίζω, 5595], primarily denotes to feed with morsels, as nurses do children; then, to dole out or supply with food, Rom. 12:20; 1 Cor. 13:3. ¶ Cp. *psōmion*, a fragment, morsel, John 13:26, 27, 30 ("sop"). ¶

NT: B.894d; CB.—; K.—.
OT: 'ākal: S.398; HR.1490c.1b; H.85; BD.37a.
GEN. REF.: IS.2:297; NB.—; Z.—.

6. *potizō* [ποτίζω, 4222], to give to drink, is translated "I fed (you with milk)" in 1 Cor. 3:2. See DRINK, WATER.

NT: B.695c; CB.1266b; K.841.
OT: shāqāḥ: S.8248; HR.1197c.3; H.2452; BD.1052b.
GEN. REF.: IS.2:297; NB.—; Z.—.

FEEL, FEELING, FELT

1. *ginōskō* [γινώσκω, 1097], to know, perceive, is translated "she felt (in her body)," of the woman with the issue of blood, Mark 5:29, i.e., she became aware of the fact. See KNOW.

NT: B.160d; CB.1248b; K.119.
OT: yāda': S.3045; HR.267a.4a-e; H.848; BD.393b.
GEN. REF.: IS.2:297; NB.—; Z.—.

2. *phroneō* [φρονέω, 5426], to think, to be minded, is translated "I felt" in the R.V. of 1 Cor. 13:11 (for A.V., "I understood"). See CAREFUL.

NT: B.866a; CB.1264c; K.1277.
OT: ḥākam: S.2449; HR.1439a.2; H.647; BD.314b.
GEN. REF.: IS.2:297; NB.—; Z.—.

3. *psēlaphaō* [ψηλαφάω, 5584], to feel or grope about (from *psaō*, to touch), expressing the motion of the hands over a surface, so as to feel it, is used (*a*) metaphorically, of seeking after God, Acts 17:27; (*b*) literally, of physical handling or touching, Luke 24:39 with 1 John 1:1; Heb. 12:18. See HANDLE, TOUCH ¶

NT: B.892c; CB.—; K.—.
OT: mûsh: S.4184; HR.1485b.3a; H.1168; BD.559b.
māshash: S.4959; HR.1485b.4; H.1262; BD.606d.
GEN. REF.: IS.2:297; NB.—; Z.—.

4. *sumpatheō* [συμπαθέω, 4834], to have a fellow-feeling for or with, is rendered "touched with the feeling of" in Heb. 4:15; "have compassion" in 10:34. See COMPASSION. ¶

NT: B.778d; CB.1270b; K.798.
OT: —.
GEN. REF.: —.

5. *apalgeō* [ἀπαλγέω, 524], signifies to cease to feel pain for (*apo*, from, *algeō*, to feel pain; cp. Eng., neuralgia); hence, to be callous, "past feeling," insensible to honour and shame, Eph. 4:19. ¶

NT: B.80a; CB.—; K.—.
OT: —.
GEN. REF.: —.

Note: In Acts 28:5 *paschō*, to suffer, is rendered "felt (no harm)," R.V., "took," lit., 'suffered no ill (effect).'

For FEET see FOOT

FEIGN, FEIGNED

A. Verb.

hupokrinomai [ὑποκρίνομαι, 5271], primarily denotes to answer; then, to answer on the stage, play a part, and so, metaphorically, to feign, pretend, Luke 20:20. ¶ Cp. *hupokritēs*, a hypocrite, and *hupokrisis*, hypocrisy.

NT: B.845a; CB.1252b; K.1235.
OT: —.
GEN. REF.: —.

B. Adjective.

plastos [πλαστός, 4112], primarily denotes formed, moulded (from *plassō*, to mould; Eng., plastic); then, metaphorically, made up, fabricated, feigned, 2 Pet. 2:3. ¶ Cp. *plasma*, that which is moulded, Rom. 9:20 ¶

NT: B.666c; CB.—; K.862.
OT: —.
GEN. REF.: —.

For FELL see FALL

FELLOW

1. *anēr* [ἀνήρ, 435], denotes a man, in relation to his sex or age; in Acts 17:5 (plural) it is rendered "fellows," as more appropriate to the accompanying description of them. See HUSBAND, MAN, SIR.

NT: B.66c; CB.1235c; K.59.
OT: 'îsh: S.376; HR.88a.2; H.83a; BD.35d.
'ᵉnôsh: S.582; HR.88a.3a; H.136a; BD.60d.
GEN. REF.: IS.2:298; NB.—; Z.2:528.

2. *hetairos* [ἑταῖρος, 2083], a companion, comrade, is translated "fellows" in Matt. 11:16 [where, however, the most authentic mss. have *heterois*, "(the) others"]. The word is used only by Matthew and is translated "friend" in 20:13; 22:12; 26:50. See FRIEND. ¶

NT: B.314c; CB.—; K.265.
OT: rēa': S.7453; HR.559c.2a; H.2186a; BD.945d.
rē'eh: S.7463; HR.559c.2b; H.2186b; BD.946b.
rā'āh: S.7462; HR.559c.3; H.2185,2186; BD.946b.
GEN. REF.: IS.2:298; NB.—; Z.—.

3. *metochos* [μέτοχος, 3353], properly an adjective, signifying sharing in, partaking of, is translated "partners" in Luke 5:7; "partakers" in Heb. 3:1, 14; 6:4; 12:8; "fellows" in Heb. 1:9, of those who share in a heavenly calling, or have held, or will hold, a regal position in relation to the earthly, Messianic Kingdom. (Cp. *summetochos*, "fellow-partakers," in Eph. 3:6, R.V.). See PARTAKER, PARTNER.

NT: B.514c; CB.1258c; K.286.
OT: ḥābēr: S.2270; HR.918a.1a; H.598c; BD.288d.
ḥābar: S.2266; HR.918a.1b,c; H.598; BD.287d.
GEN. REF.: IS.—; NB.—; Z.2:528

Notes: (1) In Acts 24:5 *loimos*, a plague, a pest, is rendered "a pestilent fellow." This is a sample of the strongest use of the epithet "fellow."

(2) *Toioutos*, an adjective, "such a one," is often used as a noun, e.g., Acts 22:22, where it is translated "such a fellow."

(3) *Houtos*, this, is translated "this fellow" in the A.V. of Luke 23:2 (R.V., "this man"). So in John 9:29. Both Versions have "this man," e.g., in Mark 2:7; John 6:52, in the same contemptuous sense.

(4) For the word in combination with various nouns see CITIZEN, DISCIPLE, ELDER, HEIR, HELPER, LABOURER, MEMBER, PARTNER, PRISONER, SERVANT, SOLDIER, WORK, WORKER.

FELLOWSHIP

A. Nouns.

1. *koinōnia* [κοινωνία, 2842], (*a*) communion, fellowship, sharing in common (from *koinos*, common), is translated "communion" in 1 Cor. 10:16; Philm. 6, R.V., "fellowship," for A.V., "communication"; it is most frequently translated "fellowship"; (*b*) that which is the outcome of fellowship, a contribution, e.g., Rom. 15:26; 2 Cor. 8:4. See COMMUNION, CONTRIBUTION, etc.

NT: B.438d; CB.1255b; K.447.
OT: —.
GEN. REF.: IS.1:752; NB.245; Z.2:528.

Note: In Eph. 3:9, some mss. have *koinōnia*, instead of *oikonomia*, dispensation, R.V.

2. *metochē* [μετοχή, 3352], partnership (akin to No. 3, under FELLOW), is translated "fellowship" in 2 Cor. 6:14. ¶ In the Sept., Ps. 122:3, "Jerusalem is built as a city whose fellowship is complete." ¶ The word seems to have a more restricted sense than *koinōnia*. Cp. the verb form in Heb. 2:14.

NT: B.514c; CB.1258c; K.286.
OT: ḥābar: S.2266; HR.918a.1; H.598; BD.287d.
GEN. REF.: IS.1:752; NB.—; Z.2:528.

3. *koinōnos* [κοινωνός, 2844], denotes a partaker or partner (akin to No. 1); in 1 Cor.

10:20 it is used with *ginomai*, to become, "that ye should have communion with," R.V. (A.V., "fellowship with"). See COMPANION, PARTAKER, PARTNER.

NT: B.439c; CB.1255b; K.447.
OT: ḥābēr: S.2270; HR.775c.1a; H.598c; BD.288d.
GEN. REF.: IS.1:752; NB.245; Z.2:528.

B. Verbs.

1. *koinōneō* [κοινωνέω, 2841], to have fellowship, is so translated in Phil. 4:15, R.V., for A.V., "did communicate." See COMMUNICATE.

NT: B.438c; CB.1255b; K.447.
OT: ḥābar: S.2266; HR.775a.3a,b; H.598; BD.287d.
ḥebᵉrāh: S.2274; HR.775a.3c; H.598b; BD.288d.
GEN. REF.: IS.1:752; NB.245; Z.2:528.

2. *sunkoinōneō* [συγκοινωνέω, 4790], to have fellowship with or in (*sun*, with, and No. 1), is used in Eph. 5:11; Phil. 4:14, R.V., "ye had fellowship," for A.V., "ye did communicate"; Rev. 18:4, R.V., "have (no) fellowship with," for A.V., "be (not) partakers of." See COMMUNICATE, PARTAKER. ¶

NT: B.774b; CB.1270c; K.447.
OT: —.
GEN. REF.: IS.1:752; NB.245; Z.2:528.

For **FELT** see **FEEL**

FEMALE

thēlus [θῆλυς, 2338], an adjective (from *thēlē*, a breast), is used in the form *thēlu* (grammatically neuter) as a noun, "female," in Matt. 19:4; Mark 10:6; Gal. 3:28; in the feminine form *thēleia*, in Rom. 1:26, "women"; ver. 27 "woman." See WOMAN. ¶

NT: B.360c; CB.1271c; K.—.
OT: nᵉqēbāh: S.5347; HR.650a.4; H.1409b; BD.666c.
'ishshāh: S.802; HR.650a.2; H.137a; BD.61a.
GEN. REF.: IS.2:299; NB.—; Z.2:528.

FERVENT, FERVENTLY

A. Adjective.

ektenēs [ἐκτενής, 1618], denotes strained, stretched (*ek*, out, *teinō*, to stretch); hence, metaphorically, "fervent," 1 Pet. 4:8. Some mss. have it in Acts 12:5, for the adverb (see B). ¶ Cp. *ekteneia* (with *en*), intently, strenuously, in Acts 26:7, A.V., "instantly," R.V., "earnestly." Cp. EARNEST.

NT: B.245c; CB.—; K.219.
OT: —.
GEN. REF.: —.

B. Adverb.

ektenōs [ἐκτενῶς, 1619], fervently (akin to A.), is said of love, in 1 Pet. 1:22; of prayer, in some mss., Acts 12:5 (see under A.); for the comparative degree in Luke 22:44, see EARNESTLY. ¶

NT: B.245d; CB.1244a; K.—.
OT: bᵉḥāzqāh: S.2394; HR.443a.1; H.636d; BD.306a.
GEN. REF.: —.

C. Verb.

zeō [ζέω, 2204], to be hot, to boil (Eng., "zeal" is akin), is metaphorically used of fervency of spirit, Acts 18:25; Rom. 12:11. ¶

NT: B.337c; CB.1273c; K.296.
OT: rātaḥ: S.7570; HR.593a.2a; H.2225; BD.958b.
retaḥ: S.7571; HR.593a.2b; H.2225a; BD.958c.
GEN. REF.: —.

Notes: (1) In Col. 4:12, the verb *agōnizomai*, to strive, is translated "labouring fervently," A.V. (R.V., "striving").

(2) In 2 Cor. 7:7, the noun *zēlos*, zeal (akin to C.), is translated "fervent mind," A.V. (R.V., "zeal").

(3) In Jas. 5:17, "he prayed fervently" (A.V., "earnestly") translates the noun *proseuchē*, followed by the corresponding verb, lit., 'he prayed with prayer.' In ver. 16 *deēsis*, supplication, is so translated in the R.V., for the A.V., "effectual fervent prayer." There is nothing in the original corresponding to the word "effectual." The phrase, including the verb *energeomai*, to work in, is, lit., 'the inworking supplication,' suggesting a supplication consistent with inward conformity to the mind of God.

(4) For "fervent heat" see HEAT, B.

FETCH

metapempō [μεταπέμπω, 3343], to send after or for (*meta*, after, *pempō*, to send), in the Middle Voice, is translated "fetch" in the R.V. of Acts 10:5 and 11:13. See CALL.

NT: B.513b; CB.—; K.—.
OT: —.
GEN. REF.: —.

Notes: (1) In Acts 16:37, the R.V. gives to *exagō*, to bring out, the adequate meaning "let them . . . bring us out," for the A.V., "let them fetch us out." "Fetch" is not sufficiently dignified for the just demand made.

(2) For Acts 28:13, A.V., "fetched a compass," see CIRCUIT.

FETTER

pedē [πέδη, 3976], a fetter (akin to *peza*, the instep, and *pous*, a foot; cp. Eng. prefix *ped*—), occurs in Mark 5:4 and Luke 8:29. Cp. FOOT. ¶

NT: B.638c; CB.—; K.—.
OT: nᵉḥōshet: S.5178; HR.1113a.3,4; H.1349a,1350a; BD.638d.
GEN. REF.: IS.2:300; NB.—; Z.2:533.

FEVER (to be sick of)

A. Noun.

puretos [πυρετός, 4446], feverish heat (from *pur*, fire), hence, a fever, occurs in Matt. 8:15;

Mark 1:31; John 4:52; Acts 28:8; in Luke 4:38, with *megas*, great, a high fever; ver. 39. Luke, as a physician, uses the medical distinction by which the ancients classified fevers into great and little. ¶ In the Sept., Deut. 28:22. ¶

NT: B.730d; CB.1268a; K.981.
OT: qaddaḥat: S.6920; HR.1245b.1; H.1987a; BD.869b.
GEN. REF.: IS.2:300; NB.421; Z.–.

B. Verb.

puressō [πυρέσσω, 4445], signifies to be ill of a fever (akin to A.), Matt. 8:14; Mark 1:30. ¶

NT: B.730d; CB.1268a; K.981.
OT: –.
GEN. REF.: IS.2:300; NB.421; Z.–.

FEW

A. Adjectives.

1. *oligos* [ὀλίγος, 3641], used of number, quantity, and size, denotes few, little, small, slight, e.g., Matt. 7:14; 9:37; 15:34; 20.16; neuter plural, "a few things," Matt. 25:21, 23; Rev. 2:14 (20 in some mss.); in Eph. 3:3, the phrase *en oligō*, in brief, is translated " in a few words."

NT: B.563c; CB.1260c; K.682.
OT: mᵉʿaṭ: S.4592; HR.986b.4; H.1228a; BD.589d.
GEN. REF.: –.

2. *brachus* [βραχύς, 1024], denotes (*a*) short, in regard to time, e.g., Heb. 2:7; or distance, Acts 27:28; (*b*) few, in regard to quantity, Heb. 13:22, in the phrase *dia bracheōn*, lit., 'by means of few,' i.e., "in few words." See LITTLE.

NT: B.147b; CB.1239b; K.–.
OT: mᵉʿaṭ: S.4592; HR.230c.1; H.1228a; BD.589d.
GEN. REF.: –.

Note: In Luke 10:42, in the Lord's words to Martha, many ancient authorities provide the rendering, 'but there is need of few things (neuter plural) or one.'

B. Adverb.

suntomōs [συντόμως, 4935], concisely, briefly, cut short (from *suntemnō*, to cut in pieces, *sun*, used intensively, *temnō*, to cut), occurs in the speech of Tertullus, Acts 24:4. ¶

NT: B.793a; CB.–; K.–.
OT: –.
GEN. REF.: –.

FICKLENESS

elaphria [ἐλαφρία, 1644], denotes lightness, levity, "fickleness," 2 Cor. 1:17, R.V. (for A.V., "lightness"). ¶ The corresponding adjective is *elaphros*, light, Matt. 11:30; 2 Cor. 4:17. ¶

NT: B.248c; CB.–; K.–.
OT: –.
GEN. REF.: –.

FIDELITY

pistis [πίστις], faith, faithfulness, is translated "fidelity" in Tit. 2:10. See FAITH (*b*).

FIELD, CORNFIELD

1. *agros* [ἀγρός, 68], a cultivated field, or fields in the aggregate, e.g., Matt. 6:28; Mark 11:8 (some mss. here have *dendrōn*, trees); Luke 15:15. See FARM.

NT: B.13d; CB.1233c; K.–.
OT: śādeh: S.7704; HR.17a.7; H.2234a,b; BD.961b.
GEN. REF.: IS.2:300; NB.421; Z.2:533.

2. *chōra* [χώρα, 5561], (*a*) a space, place, then, (*b*) land, country, region, is translated "fields" in John 4:35; Jas. 5:4. See COUNTRY.

NT: B.889b; CB.1240a; K.–.
OT: 'ereṣ: S.776; HR.1481a.4; H.167; BD.75d.
mᵉdînāh: S.4082; HR.1481a.5; H.426d; BD.193d.
GEN. REF.: IS.2:300; NB.421; Z.2:533.

3. *chōrion* [χωρίον, 5564], a diminutive of No. 2, denotes (*a*) a place, region, (*b*) a piece of land, property, rendered "field" in Acts 1:18, 19. See LAND, PARCEL, PLACE, POSSESSION.

NT: B.890b; CB.1240a; K.–.
OT: kerem: S.3754; HR.1482c.1; H.1040a; BD.501c.
GEN. REF.: IS.2:300; NB.421; Z.2:533.

4. *sporimos* [σπόριμος, 4702], signifies fit for sowing (from *speirō*, to sow), and denotes a cornfield, Matt. 12:1; Mark 2:23; Luke 6:1. ¶ In the Sept., Gen. 1:29; Lev. 11:37. ¶

NT: B.763b; CB.–; K.1065.
OT: zāraʿ: S.2232; HR.1285b.1a; H.582; BD.281b.
zērûaʿ: S.2221; HR.1285b.1b; H.582b; BD.283b.
GEN. REF.: –.

FIERCE, FIERCENESS

A. Adjectives.

1. *anēmeros* [ἀνήμερος, 434], signifies 'not tame,' savage (from *a*, negative, and *hēmeros*, gentle), 2 Tim. 3:3. Epictetus describes those who forget God as their Creator, as resembling lions, 'wild, savage and fierce (*anēmeroi*)' (Moulton and Milligan, Greek Test. Vocab.). ¶

NT: B.66c; CB.–; K.–.
OT: –.
GEN. REF.: IS.2:301; NB.–; Z.–.

2. *chalepos* [χαλεπός, 5467], hard, (*a*) hard to do or deal with, difficult, fierce, is said of the Gadarene demoniacs, Matt. 8:28; (*b*) hard to bear, painful, grievous, said of the last times, 2 Tim. 3:1, R.V., "grievous," for A.V., "perilous." See GRIEVOUS. ¶

NT: B.874c; CB.1239b; K.–.
OT: yārēʾ: S.3372; HR.1453a.1; H.907,908; BD.431a.
GEN. REF.: IS.2:300; NB.–; Z.–.

Notes: (1) In Jas.3:4, *sklēros*, hard, rough, violent, is said of winds, R.V., "rough," for A.V., "fierce."

(2) In Luke 23:5, the verb *epischuō*, to make or grow stronger (from *epi*, over, intensive, and *ischus*, strength), is used metaphorically, "they were the more urgent," R.V., for A.V., "the more fierce." ¶

B. Nouns.

1. *thumos* [θυμός, 2372], hot anger, wrath, is rendered "fierceness" in Rev. 16:19; 19:15, of the wrath of God. See ANGER (A, Notes), INDIGNATION, WRATH.
NT: B.365b; CB.1272c; K.339.
OT: 'aph: S.639; HR.660c.1; H.133a; BD.60a.
ḥēmāh: S.2534; HR.660c.5a; H.860a; BD.404b.
GEN. REF.: IS.4:1134; NB.—; Z.5:990.

2. *zēlos* [ζῆλος, 2205], zeal, jealousy, is rendered "fierceness" in Heb. 10:27, R.V. (of fire).
NT: B.337d; CB.1273b; K.297.
OT: qin'āh: S.7068; HR.594a.1; H.2038a; BD.888b.
GEN. REF.: IS.4:1175; NB.—; Z.—.

FIERY

puroō [πυρόω, 4448], to set on fire, burn up (from *pur*, fire), always used in the Passive Voice in the N.T., is translated "fiery" in Eph. 6:16, metaphorically of the darts of the evil one; 'fire-tipped' would perhaps bring out the verbal force of the word. The most ancient mss. have the article repeated, lit., 'the darts of the evil one, the fiery (darts)', marking them as particularly destructive. Some mss. omit the repeated article. In ancient times, darts were often covered with burning material. See BURN, FIRE, TRY, *Note* (1).
NT: B.731a; CB.1268a; K.975.
OT: ṣāraph: S.6884; HR.1243c.3a; H.1972; BD.864a.
GEN. REF.: IS.2:305; NB.—; Z.—.

Notes: (1) For Heb. 10:27, R.V., see FIRE (cp. FIERCE, B, No. 2).

(2) For *purōsis*, a fiery trial, 1 Pet. 4:12, (lit., a burning, as in Rev. 18:9, 18) a refining, or trial by fire, see TRIAL.

FIFTEEN, FIFTEENTH

dekapente [δεκαπέντε, 1178], lit., ten-five, occurs in John 11:18; Acts 27:28; Gal. 1:18. ¶
NT: B.173d; CB.—; K.—.
OT: —.
GEN. REF.: —.

Notes: (1) In Acts 7:14, "threescore and fifteen" translates a different numeral, lit., 'seventy-five'. This refers to all Joseph's kindred whom he sent for. There is no discrepancy between this and Gen. 46:26. The Sept., translations give the number as 75 in Gen. 46:27 and in Ex. 1:5, and this Stephen follows, being a Grecian Jew.

(2) The corresponding ordinal numeral *pentekaidekatos*, fifteenth (lit., five and tenth) is found in Luke 3:1, where Luke dates the reign of Tiberias from the period of his joint rule with Augustus.

FIFTH

pemptos [πέμπτος, 3991], akin to *pente*, five, is found only in the Apocalypse, 6:9; 9:1; 16:10; 21:20. ¶
NT: B.641c; CB.—; K.—.
OT: ḥ^{a}mîshî: S.2549; HR.1116c.1a; H.686d; BD.332c.
ḥāmēsh: S.2568; HR.1116c.1b; H.686a; BD.331c.
GEN. REF.: —.

FIFTY

pentēkonta [πεντήκοντα, 4004], is found in Luke 7:41; 16:6; John 8:57; 21:11; Acts 13:20; in Mark 6:40 with *kata* (in the most authentic mss.), according to, "by fifties"; in Luke 9:14, with *ana*, up, used distributively, "fifty each," R.V. (Luke adds *hōsei*, "about"). ¶
NT: B.643a; CB.—; K.—.
OT: —.
GEN. REF.: —.

FIG

1. *sukon* [σῦκον, 4810], denotes the ripe fruit of a *sukē*, a fig-tree (see below; cp. No. 2), Matt. 7:16; Mark 11:13; Luke 6:44; Jas. 3:12. ¶
NT: B.776b; CB.—; K.1100.
OT: t^e'ēnāh: S.8384; HR.1301b.1; H.94b; BD.1061a.
GEN. REF.: IS.2:301; NB.422; Z.2:534.

2. *olunthos* [ὄλυνθος, 3653], denotes an unripe fig, which grows in winter and usually falls off in the Spring, Rev. 6:13. ¶ In the Sept., S. of Sol., 2:13. ¶
NT: B.565a; CB.—; K.1100.
OT: paggāh: S.6291; HR.990c.1; H.1729a; BD.803a.
GEN. REF.: IS.2:301; NB.422; Z.2:534.

FIG-TREE

sukē, or *sukea* [συκῆ, 4808], a fig tree, is found in Matt. 21:19, 20, 21; 24:32; Mark 11:13, 20, 21; 13:28; Luke 13:6, 7; 21:29; John 1:48, 50; Jas. 3:12; Rev. 6:13 (see *sukon*, above). ¶
NT: B.776b; CB.1270b; K.1100.
OT: t^e'ēnāh: S.8384; HR.1301b.1; H.94b; BD.1061a.
GEN. REF.: IS.2:301; NB.422; Z.2:534.

Note: A fig tree with leaves must have young fruits already, or it will be barren for the season. The first figs ripen in late May or early June. The tree in Mark 11:13 should have had fruit, unripe indeed, but existing. In some lands fig-trees bear the early fruit under the leaves and the later fruit above the leaves. In that case the leaves were a sign that there should have been fruit, unseen from a distance, underneath the leaves. The condemnation of this fig-tree lay in the absence of any sign of fruit.

FIGHT

A. Nouns.

1. *agōn* [ἀγών, 73], akin to *agō*, to lead, primarily a gathering, then, a place of assembly,

and hence, a contest, conflict, is translated "fight" in 1 Tim. 6:12; 2 Tim. 4:7. See CONFLICT.
NT: B.15a; CB.1233c; K.20.
OT: –.
GEN. REF.: IS.1:68; NB.–; Z.–.

2. *athlēsis* [ἄθλησις, 119], is translated "fight" in Heb. 10:32, A.V. See CONFLICT. ¶
NT: B.21c; CB.1238a; K.–.
OT: –.
GEN. REF.: –.

Note: In Heb. 11:34, *polemos*, war, is translated "fight," A.V. (R.V., "war"); it is misrendered "battle" in the A.V. of 1 Cor. 14:8; Rev. 9:7, 9; 16:14; 20:8.

B. Verbs.

1. *agōnizomai* [ἀγωνίζομαι, 75], from A, No. 1, denotes (*a*) to contend in the public games, 1 Cor. 9:25 ("striveth in the games," R.V.); (*b*) to fight, engage in conflict, John 18:36; (*c*) metaphorically, to contend perseveringly against opposition and temptation, 1 Tim. 6:12; 2 Tim. 4:7 (cp. A, No. 1; in regard to the meaning there, the evidence of *Koinē* inscriptions is against the idea of games-contests); to strive as in a contest for a prize, straining every nerve to attain to the object, Luke 13:24; to put forth every effort, involving toil, Col. 1:29; 1 Tim. 4:10 (some mss. have *oneidizomai* here, to suffer reproach); to wrestle earnestly in prayer, Col. 4:12 (cp. *sunagōnizomai*, Rom. 15:30). See LABOUR, STRIVE. ¶
NT: B.15b; CB.1233c; K.20.
OT: –.
GEN. REF.: IS.1:68; NB.–; Z.–.

2. *pukteuō* [πυκτεύω, 4438], to box (from *puktēs*, a pugilist), one of the events in the Olympic games, is translated "fight" in 1 Cor. 9:26. ¶
NT: B.729a; CB.–; K.973.
OT: –.
GEN. REF.: –.

3. *machomai* [μάχομαι, 3164], to fight, is so rendered in Jas. 4:2 (cp. "fightings," ver. 1, see below), and translated "strive" in 2 Tim. 2:24; "strove" in John 6:52; Acts 7:26. See STRIVE. ¶
NT: B.496c; CB.1257b; K.573.
OT: rîb: S.7378; HR.900c.6; H.2159; BD.936b.
lāḥam: S.3898; HR.900c.3; H.1104; BD.535b.
nāṣāh: S.5327; HR.900c.5; H.1399-1401; BD.663c.
GEN. REF.: IS.4:637; NB.–; Z.–.

4. *thēriomacheō* [θηριομαχέω, 2341], signifies to fight with wild beasts (*thērion*, a beast, and No. 3), 1 Cor. 15:32. Some think that the Apostle was condemned to fight with wild beasts; if so, he would scarcely have omitted it from 2 Cor. 11:23-end. Moreover, he would have lost his status as a Roman citizen. Probably he uses the word figuratively of contending with ferocious men. Ignatius so uses it in his Ep. to the Romans. ¶
NT: B.360d; CB.–; K.–.
OT: –.
GEN. REF.: –.

Notes: (1) In Rev. 2:16 and 12:7, A.V., *polemeō*, to war, is translated "to fight," R.V., "will make war," "*going forth* to war," and "warred."

(2) In Acts 23:9 some mss. have the verb *theomacheō*, to fight against God. Cp. the corresponding adjective, below, under FIGHTING.

FIGHTING

A. Noun.

machē [μάχη, 3163], a fight, strife (akin to B, No. 3, under FIGHT), is always used in the plural in the N.T., and translated "fightings" in 2 Cor. 7:5; Jas. 4:1; and Tit. 3:9, R.V. (for A.V., "strivings"); "strifes" in 2 Tim. 2:23. See STRIFE. ¶
NT: B.496c; CB.1257b; K.573.
OT: rîb: S.7379; HR.901a.5a; H.2159a; BD.936d.
mᵉrîbāh: S.4808; HR.901a.5b; H.2159c; BD.937b.
GEN. REF.: IS.4:637; NB.–; Z.–.

B. Adjective.

theomachos [θεομάχος, 2314], fighting against God (*theos*, God, and A, occurs in Acts 5:39 (A.V., "to fight"), lit., 'God-fighters.' ¶
NT: B.356c; CB.1272a; K.–.
OT: –.
GEN. REF.: –.

FIGURE

1. *tupos* [τύπος, 5179], a type, figure, pattern, is translated "figures" (i.e., representations of gods) in Acts 7:43; in the R.V. of ver. 44 (for A.V., "fashion") and in Rom. 5:14, of Adam as a "figure" of Christ. See ENSAMPLE.
NT: B.829d; CB.1273b; K.1193.
OT: tabᵉnît: S.8403; HR.1378b.2; H.255d; BD.125d.
ṣelem: S.6754; HR.1378b.1; H.1923a; BD.853d.
GEN. REF.: IS.2:302,4:930; NB.–; Z.2:535.

2. *antitupos* [ἀντίτυπος, 499], an adjective, used as a noun, denotes, lit., a striking back; metaphorically, resisting, adverse; then, in a Passive sense, struck back; in the N.T. metaphorically, 'corresponding to,' (*a*) a copy of an archetype (*anti*, corresponding to, and No. 1), i.e. the event or person or circumstance corresponding to the type, Heb. 9:24, R.V., "like in pattern" (A.V., "the figure of"), of the Tabernacle, which, with its structure and appurtenances, was a pattern of that "holy place," "Heaven itself," "the true," into which Christ entered, "to appear before the face of God for us." The earthly Tabernacle anticipatively represented what is now made good in Christ; it was a "figure" or "parable" (9:9), "for

the time now present," R.V., i.e., pointing to the present time, not "then present," A.V. (see below); (*b*) a corresponding type, 1 Pet. 3:21, said of baptism; the circumstances of the flood, the ark and its occupants, formed a type, and baptism forms 'a corresponding type' (not an antitype), each setting forth the spiritual realities of the death, burial, and resurrection of believers in their identification with Christ. It is not a case of type and antitype, but of two types, that in Genesis, the type, and baptism, the corresponding type. ¶

NT: B.76a; CB.1236a; K.1193.
OT: —.
GEN. REF.: IS.4:930; NB.—; Z.2:535.

3. *parabolē* [παραβολή, 3850], a casting or placing side by side (*para*, beside, *ballō*, to throw) with a view to comparison or resemblance, a parable, is translated "figure" in the A.V. of Heb. 9:9 (R.V., "a parable for the time now present") and 11:19, where the return of Isaac was (parabolically, in the lit. sense of the term) figurative of resurrection (R.V., "parable"). See No. 2 (*a*). See PARABLE.

NT: B.612b; CB.1262a; K.773.
OT: māshāl: S.4912; HR.1056a.1a; H.1258a; BD.605a.
GEN. REF.: IS.3:655; NB.932; Z.2:535.

Notes: (1) The synonymous noun *hupotupōsis*, an example, pattern, 1 Tim. 1:16; 2 Tim. 1:13, denotes simply a delineation or outline. ¶

(2) For *metaschēmatizō*, rendered "I have in a figure transferred" in 1 Cor. 4:6, where the fact stated is designed to change its application, i.e., from Paul and Apollos to circumstances in Corinth, see FASHION.

FILL, FILL UP

A. Verbs.

1. *plēroō* [πληρόω, 4137], denotes (1) to make full, to fill to the full; in the Passive Voice, to be filled, made full; it is used (1) of things: a net, Matt. 13:48; a building, John 12:3; Acts 2:2; a city, Acts 5:28; needs, Phil. 4:19, A.V., "supply," R.V., "fulfil"; metaphorically, of valleys, Luke 3:5; figuratively, of a measure of iniquity, Matt. 23:32; (2) of persons: (*a*) of the members of the Church, the Body of Christ, as filled by Him, Eph. 1:23 ('all things in all the members'); 4:10; in 3:19, of their being filled 'into' (*eis*), R.V., "unto," A.V., "with" (all the fulness of God); of their being "made full" in Him, Col. 2:10 (R.V., for A.V., "complete"); (*b*) of Christ Himself: with wisdom, in the days of His flesh, Luke 2:40; with joy, in His return to the Father, Acts 2:28; (*c*) of believers: with the Spirit, Eph. 5:18; with joy, Acts 13:52; 2 Tim. 1:4; with joy and peace, Rom. 15:13; [from these are to be distinguished those passages which speak of joy as being fulfilled or completed, which come under FULFIL, John 3:29; 15:11 (R.V.); 16:24 (R.V.); Phil. 2:2; 1 John 1:4 (R.V.); 2 John 12 (R.V.)]; with knowledge, Rom. 15:14; with comfort, 2 Cor. 7:4; with the fruits of righteousness, Phil. 1:11 (Gk. 'fruit'); with the knowledge of God's will, Col. 1:9; with abundance through material supplies by fellow-believers, Phil. 4:18; (*d*) of the hearts of believers as the seat of emotion and volition, John 16:6 (sorrow); Acts 5:3 (deceitfulness); (*e*) of the unregenerate who refuse recognition of God, Rom. 1:29; (11) to accomplish, complete, fulfil. See ACCOMPLISH, FULFIL.

NT: B.670c; CB.1265b; K.867.
OT: mālē': S.4390; HR.1147c.2a-c; H.1195; BD.569d.
GEN. REF.: IS.2:369; NB.—; Z.—.

2. *anaplēroō* [ἀναπληρόω, 378], to fill up adequately, completely (*ana*, up, and No. 1), is twice translated by the verbs to fill, to fill up, in 1 Cor. 14:16, R.V. (for A.V., "occupieth"), of a believer as a member of an assembly, who fills the position or condition (not one who fills it by assuming it) of being unable to understand the language of him who had the gift of tongues; in 1 Thess. 2:16, "to fill up their sins," of the Jews who persisted in their course of antagonism and unbelief. See FULFIL.

NT: B.59c; CB.1235b; K.867.
OT: mālē': S.4390; HR.81b.1; H.1195; BD.569d.
shālēm: S.7999; HR.81b.5b; H.2401c; BD.1022a.
GEN. REF.: IS.2:369; NB.—; Z.—.

3. *antanaplēroō* [ἀνταναπληρόω, 466], to fill up in turn (or on one's part; *anti*, corresponding to, and No. 2), is used in Col. 1:24, of the Apostle's responsive devotion to Christ in filling up, or undertaking on his part a full share of, the sufferings which follow after the sufferings of Christ, and are experienced by the members of His Body, the Church. "The point of the Apostle's boast is that Christ, the sinless Master, should have left something for Paul, the unworthy servant, to suffer" (Lightfoot, on Col. p. 165). ¶

NT: B.72d; CB.1236a; K.867.
OT: —.
GEN. REF.: IS.2:369; NB.—; Z.—.

4. *sumplēroō* [συμπληρόω, 4845], to fill completely (*sun*, with, and No. 1), is used in the Passive Voice (*a*) of a boat filling with water, and, by metonymy, of the occupants themselves, Luke 8:23 (R.V., "were filling"); (*b*) of fulfilling, with regard to time, "when the days were well-nigh come," R.V., for A.V., "when the time was come" (R.V., marg., "were being

fulfilled"), Luke 9:51; Acts 2:1, see R.V., marg. See COME. ¶ In the Sept. Jer. 25:12. ¶

NT: B.779c; CB.1270b; K.867.
OT: mālē': S.4390; HR.1305c.1; H.1195; BD.569d.
GEN. REF.: IS.2:369; NB.–; Z.–.

5. *pimplēmi* [πίμπλημι, 4130], and *plēthō* [πλήθω], lengthened forms of *pleō*, to fill (*plēthō* supplies certain tenses of *pimplēmi*), is used (1) of things; boats, with fish, Luke 5:7; a sponge, with vinegar, Matt. 27:48 (some mss. have this verb in John 19:29); a city, with confusion, Acts 19:29; a wedding, with guests, Matt. 22:10; (2) of persons (only in Luke's writings): (*a*) with the Holy Spirit, Luke 1:15, 41, 67; Acts 2:4; 4:8, 31; 9:17; 13:9; (*b*) with emotions: wrath, Luke 4:28; fear, 5:26; madness, 6:11; wonder, amazement, Acts 3:10; jealousy, 5:17, R.V., for A.V., "indignation," and 13:45 (A.V., "envy"). For its other significance, to complete, see ACCOMPLISH.

NT: B.658a; CB.1265a; K.840.
OT: mālē': S.4390; HR.1133b.1a-c; H.1195; BD.569d.
sāba': S.7646; HR.1133b.3; H.2231; BD.959c.
GEN. REF.: IS.2:369; NB.–; Z.–.

6. *empiplēmi* [ἐμπίπλημι, 1705], or *emplēthō* (as in No. 5), to fill full, to satisfy, is used (*a*) of filling the hungry, Luke 1:53; John 6:12; of the abundance of the rich, Luke 6:25; (*b*) metaphorically, of a company of friends, Rom. 15:24, R.V., "satisfied," for A.V., "filled." ¶

NT: B.256a; CB.1244b; K.840.
OT: mālē: S.4390; HR.457a.3a-c; H.1195; BD.569d.
sāba': S.7646; HR.457a.6a-c; H.2231; BD.959c.
GEN. REF.: IS.2:369; NB.–; Z.–.

7. *empiplaō* [ἐμπιπλάω], an alternative form of No. 6, is found in Acts 14:17, "filling (your hearts)," of God's provision for mankind. ¶

8. *chortazō* [χορτάζω, 5526], to fill or satisfy with food, e.g., Matt. 15:33; Phil. 4:12, is used metaphorically in Matt. 5:6; Luke 6:21. See FEED.

NT: B.883d; CB.1240a; K.–.
OT: sāba': S.7646; HR.1472c.1; H.2231; BD.959c.
GEN. REF.: IS.2:369; NB.–; Z.–.

9. *gemizō* [γεμίζω, 1072], to fill or load full, is used of a boat, Mark 4:37 (R.V., "was filling"); a sponge, Mark 15:36 (cp. No. 5, Matt. 27:48); a house, Luke 14:23; the belly, Luke 15:16; waterpots, John 2:7; baskets, 6:13; bowls, with fire, Rev. 8:5; the Temple, with smoke, 15:8. ¶ Cp. *gemō*, to be full. See FULL.

NT: B.153c; CB.1248a; K.–.
OT: tā'an: S.2943; HR.236a.1; H.816; BD.381b.
GEN. REF.: IS.2:369; NB.–; Z.–.

10. *korennumi* [κορέννυμι, 2880], to satisfy (akin to *koros*, a surfeit), is used metaphorically of spiritual things, in 1 Cor. 4:8, R.V., "ye are filled"; in Acts 27:38, "had eaten enough," lit., 'having being satisfied with food.' See EAT, ENOUGH.

NT: B.444c; CB.–; K.–.
OT: –.
GEN. REF.: –.

11. *mestoō* [μεστόω, 3325], to fill full, from *mestos*, full, is used of being filled with wine, Acts 2:13, R.V., "are filled with." ¶

NT: B.508c; CB.–; K.–.
OT: –.
GEN. REF.: –.

B. Noun.

plērōma [πλήρωμα, 4138], fulness, has two meanings, (*a*) in the active sense, that which fills up, a piece of undressed cloth on an old garment, Matt. 9:16; Mark 2:21, lit., 'the filling' (R.V., "that which should fill it up"), i.e., the patch, which is probably the significance; (*b*) that which has been completed, the fulness, e.g., Mark 8:20. See FULNESS.

NT: B.672a; CB.1265b; K.867.
OT: m^elō: S.4393; HR.1148b.2a; H.1195b; BD.571a.
GEN. REF.: IS.2:370; NB.442; Z.–.

Notes: (1) In Rev. 18:6, A.V., *kerannumi*, to mix, is incorrectly rendered to fill full (R.V., to mingle).

(2) In Rev. 15:1, A.V., *teleō*, to finish, complete, is incorrectly rendered "filled up" (R.V., "finished"); the contents of the seven bowls are not the sum total of the Divine judgments; they form the termination of them; there are many which precede (see previous chapters), which are likewise comprised under "the wrath of God," to be executed at the closing period of the present age, e.g., 6:17; 11:18; 14:10, 19.

FILTH

1. *perikatharma* [περικάθαρμα, 4027], denotes offscouring, refuse (lit., cleanings, i.e., that which is thrown away in cleansing; from *perikathairō*, to purify all around, i.e., completely, as in the Sept. of Deut. 18:10; Josh. 5:4. ¶) It is once used in the Sept. (Prov. 21:18) as the price of expiation; among the Greeks the term was applied to victims sacrified to make expiation; they also used it of criminals kept at the public expense, to be thrown into the sea, or otherwise killed, at the outbreak of a pestilence, etc. It is used in 1 Cor. 4:13 much in this sense (not of sacrificial victims), "the filth of the world," representing "the most abject and despicable men" (Grimm-Thayer), the scum or rubbish of humanity. ¶

NT: B.647d; CB.1263b; K.381.
OT: –.
GEN. REF.: –.

2. *rhupos* [ῥύπος], denotes dirt, filth, 1 Pet. 3:21. ¶ Cp. *rhuparia*, filthiness (see A, No. 2, below); *rhuparos*, vile, Jas. 2:2; Rev. 22:11, in the best mss. (see B, No. 3, below); ¶ *rhupoō*, to make filthy, Rev. 22:11; ¶ *rhupainō* (see D. below).

FILTHINESS, FILTHY (to make)

A. Nouns.

1. *aischrotēs* [αἰσχρότης, 151], baseness (from *aischos*, shame, disgrace), is used in Eph. 5:4, of obscenity, all that is contrary to purity. ¶
NT: B.25b; CB.1234a; K.29.
OT: –.
GEN. REF.: IS.2:303; NB.–; Z.2:536.

2. *rhuparia* [ῥυπαρία, 4507], denotes dirt, filth (cp, No. 2, under FILTH), and is used metaphorically of moral defilement in Jas. 1:21. ¶
NT: B.738a; CB.1268b; K.–.
OT: –.
GEN. REF.: IS.2:303; NB.–; Z.2:536.

3. *molusmos* [μολυσμός, 3436], a soiling, defilement, is used in 2 Cor. 7:1. See DEFILEMENT. ¶
NT: B.527a; CB.1259a; K.606.
OT: ḥᵃnuphāh: S.2613; HR.932c.1; H.696c; BD.338b.
GEN. REF.: IS.1:912; NB.–; Z.–.

4. *aselgeia* [ἀσέλγεια, 766], wantonness, licentiousness, lasciviousness, is translated "filthy (conversation)," in 2 Pet. 2:7, A.V.; R.V., "lascivious (life)." See LASCIVIOUSNESS, WANTONNESS.
NT: B.114d; CB.1238a; K.83.
OT: –.
GEN. REF.: IS.3:128; NB.–; Z.–.

Notes: (1) Broadly speaking, *aischrotēs* signifies whatever is disgraceful; *rhuparia*, that which is characterized by moral impurity; *molusmos*, that which is defiling by soiling the clean; *aselgeia*, that which is an insolent disregard of decency.

(2) In Col. 3:8 *aischrologia*, which denotes any kind of base utterance, the utterance of an uncontrolled tongue, is rendered "filthy communication" in the A.V.; but this is only part of what is included in the more comprehensive R.V. rendering, "shameful speaking." In the papyri writings the word is used of abuse. In general it seems to have been associated more frequently with foul or filthy, rather than abusive, speaking (Moulton and Milligan). ¶

B. Adjectives.

1. *aischros* [αἰσχρός, 150], base, shameful (akin to A, No. 1), is used of base gain, "filthy (lucre)," Tit. 1:11, and translated "shame" in 1 Cor. 11:6, with reference to a woman with shorn hair; in 14:35, of oral utterances of women in a church gathering (R.V., "shameful"); in Eph. 5:12, of mentioning the base and bestial practices of those who live lascivious lives. See SHAME. ¶
NT: B.25b; CB.1234a; K.29.
OT: raʿ: S.7451; HR.36c.1a; H.2191; BD.948a.
GEN. REF.: IS.2:303; NB.–; Z.2:536.

2. *aischrokerdēs* [αἰσχροκερδής, 146], greedy of base gain (No. 1, and *kerdos*, gain), is used in 1 Tim. 3:8 and Tit. 1:7, "greedy of filthy lucre"; some mss. have it also in 1 Tim. 3:3. ¶
NT: B.25a; CB.1234a; K.–.
OT: –.
GEN. REF.: IS.–; NB.–; Z.2:536.

3. *rhuparos* [ῥυπαρός, 4508], akin to A, No. 2 (see also FILTH, No. 2), dirty, is said of shabby clothing, Jas. 2:2; metaphorically, of moral defilement, Rev. 22:11 (in the best mss.). ¶
NT: B.738a; CB.1268b; K.–.
OT: sōʾ: S.6674; HR.1255b.1; H.1884; BD.844b.
GEN. REF.: IS.2:303; NB.–; Z.2:536.

Note: For *akathartos* see UNCLEAN, No. 1.

C. Adverb.

aischrokerdōs [αἰσχροκερδῶς, 147], eagerness for base gain (akin to B, No. 2), is used in 1 Pet. 5:2, "for filthy lucre." ¶
NT: B.25b; CB.–; K.–.
OT: –.
GEN. REF.: –.

D. Verb.

rhupainō [ῥυπαίνω, 4510], to make filthy, defile (from A, No. 2), is used in the Passive Voice, in an ethical sense, in Rev. 22:11 (cp. B, No. 3, in the same verse), "let him be made filthy," R.V. The tense (the aorist) marks the decisiveness of that which is decreed. Some texts have *rhupareuomai*, here, with the same meaning; some have *rhupoō*, in the Middle Voice, to make oneself filthy. ¶
NT: B.737d; CB.1268b; K.–.
OT: –.
GEN. REF.: IS.2:303; NB.–; Z.–.

FINAL, FINALLY

A. Nouns.

1. *peras* [πέρας, 4009], a limit, end, is translated "final" in Heb. 6:16, R.V., "an oath is final for confirmation" (the A.V. connects the clauses differently). See END.
NT: B.644a; CB.1263b; K.–.
OT: qēṣ: S.7093; HR.1120a.6a; H.2060a; BD.893d.
ʾephes: S.657; HR.1120a.1; H.147a; BD.67a.
GEN. REF.: IS.2:79; NB.–; Z.–.

2. *telos* [τέλος, 5056], an end, most frequently of the termination of something, is used with the article adverbially, meaning "finally" or 'as to the end,' i.e., as to the last detail, 1 Pet. 3:8. See END.
NT: B.811b; CB.1271b; K.1161.
OT: qēṣ: S.7093; HR.1344a.4a; H.2060a; BD.893d.
GEN. REF.: IS.2:79; NB.–; Z.–.

B. Adverb.

loipon [λοιπόν, 3063], is the neuter of the adjective *loipos*, remaining (which is used in its different genders as a noun, 'the rest'), and is used either with the article or without, to signify "finally," lit., 'for the rest.' The Apostle Paul uses it frequently in the concluding portion of his Epistles, introducing practical exhortations, not necessarily implying that the letter is drawing to a close, but marking a transition in the subject-matter, as in Phil. 3:1, where the actual conclusion is for the time postponed and the farewell injunctions are resumed in 4:8. See also 1 Thess. 4:1 (A.V., "furthermore"); 2 Thess. 3:1.

NT: B.479d; CB.1257a; K.—.
OT: —.
GEN. REF.: —.

FIND, FOUND

1. *heuriskō* [εὑρίσκω, 2147], denotes (*a*) to find, either with previous search, e.g., Matt. 7:7, 8, or without, e.g., Matt. 27:32; in the Passive Voice, of Enoch's disappearance, Heb. 11:5; of mountains, Rev. 16:20; of Babylon and its occupants, 18:21, 22; (*b*) metaphorically, to find out by enquiry, or to learn, discover, e.g., Luke 19:48; John 18:38; 19:4, 6; Acts 4:21; 13:28; Rom. 7:10; Gal. 2:17, which indicates "the surprise of the Jew;; who learned for the first time that before God he had no moral superiority over the Gentiles whom he superciliously dubbed "sinners," while he esteemed himself to be 'righteous'; 1 Pet. 1:7; Rev. 5:4; (*c*) in the Middle Voice, to find for oneself, gain, procure, obtain, e.g., Matt. 10:39; 11:29, "ye shall find (rest)"; Luke 1:30; Acts 7:46; 2 Tim. 1:18. See GET, OBTAIN.

NT: B.324d; CB.1250b; K.—.
OT: māṣā': S.4672; HR.576c.8a,b; H.2033; BD.592c.
GEN. REF.: IS.2:303; NB.—; Z.—.

2. *aneuriskō* [ἀνευρίσκω, 429], to find out (by search), discover (*ana*, up, and No. 1), implying diligent searching, is used in Luke 2:16, of the shepherds in searching for and finding Mary and Joseph and the Child; in Acts 21:4, of Paul and his companions, in searching for and finding "the disciples" at Tyre (in ver. 2, No. 1, is used). ¶

NT: B.65c; CB.—; K.—.
OT: —.
GEN. REF.: IS.2:303; NB.—; Z.—.

3. *lambanō* [λαμβάνω, 2983], to take, receive, is translated "finding (occasion)" in Rom. 7:11, R.V. (A.V., "taking"). See ACCEPT.

NT: B.464a; CB.1256c; K.495.
OT: —.
GEN. REF.: —.

4. *katalambanō* [καταλαμβάνω, 2638], to lay hold of, said of mental action, to comprehend by laying hold of or finding facts, is translated "I found," of Festus regarding charges made against Paul, Acts 25:25. See APPREHEND.

NT: B.412d; CB.1254a; K.495.
OT: —.
GEN. REF.: IS.1:216; NB.—; Z.—.

Notes: (1) For *sunanapauomai*, to be refreshed in spirit, in Rom. 15:32, R.V., "find rest with," see FIND, REFRESH.

(2) In Rom. 7:18, there is no word in the original for "find." Hence the R.V. has "is not."

(3) In Rom. 11:33, *anexichniastos*, untraceable, is rendered "past finding out," A.V., R.V., "past tracing out" (*ichniazō*, to track out); in Eph. 3:8, "unsearchable." See TRACE, UNSEARCHABLE ¶

For FINE see BRASS, No. 4, FLOUR, GOODLY, Note, LINEN

FINGER

daktulos [δάκτυλος, 1147], Matt. 23:4; Mark 7:33; Luke 11:46; 16:24; John 8:6; 20:25, 27, is used metaphorically in Luke 11:20, for the power of God, the effects of which are made visible to men (cp. Matt. 12:28, "by the Spirit of God"; cp. also Ex. 8:19). ¶

NT: B.170a; CB.1240b; K.140.
OT: 'eṣba': S.676; HR.284b.1; H.1873a; BD.840c.
GEN. REF.: IS.2:304; NB.—; Z.2:536.

FINISH

1. *teleō* [τελέω, 5055], to bring to an end (*telos*, an end), in the Passive Voice, to be finished, is translated by the verb to finish in Matt. 13:53; 19:1; 26:1; John 19:28, where the R.V. "are . . . finished" brings out the force of the perfect tense (the same word as in ver. 30, "It is finished"), which is missed in the A.V.; as Stier says, "the word was in His heart before He uttered it"; 2 Tim. 4:7; Rev. 10:7; 11:7; 20:3, R.V., "should be finished" (A.V., "fulfilled"), 5, 7, R.V., "finished" (A.V., "expired"). In Rev. 15:1 the verb is rightly translated "is finished," R.V., see FILL, Note (2). In 15:8 the R.V., "should be finished" corrects the A.V., "were fulfilled." See ACCOMPLISH.

NT: B.810d; CB.1271b; K.1161.
OT: kālāh: S.3615; HR.1342c.3; H.982-984; BD.477b.
GEN. REF.: IS.2:304; NB.—; Z.—.

2. *teleioō* [τελειόω, 5048], akin to the adjective *teleios*, complete, perfect, and to No. 1, denotes to bring to an end in the sense of

completing or perfecting, and is translated by the verb to finish in John 4:34; 5:36; 17:4; Acts 20:24. See CONSECRATE, FULFIL, PERFECT.
NT: B.809d; CB.1271b; K.1161.
OT: mālē': S.4390; HR.1343a.3; H.1195; BD.569d,570c.
tāmam: S.8552; HR.1343a.7; H.2522; BD.1070b.
GEN. REF.: IS.2:304; NB.–; Z.–.

3. *ekteleō* [ἐκτελέω, 1615], lit., to finish out, i.e., completely (*ek*, out, intensive, and No. 1), is used in Luke 14:29, 30. ¶
NT: B.245c; CB.–; K.–.
OT: kālāh: S.3615; HR.442c.1; H.982-984; BD.477b.
GEN. REF.: IS.2:304; NB.–; Z.–.

4. *epiteleō* [ἐπιτελέω, 2005], to bring through to an end, is rendered "finish" in 2 Cor. 8:6, A.V. (R.V., "complete"). See ACCOMPLISH.
NT: B.302b; CB.–; K.1161.
OT: kālāh: S.3615; HR.535a.4; H.982-984; BD.477b.
'āsāh: S.6213; HR.535a.5; H.1708,1709; BD.793c.
GEN. REF.: IS.2:304; NB.–; Z.–.

5. *sunteleō* [συντελέω, 4931], to bring to fulfilment, to effect, is translated "finishing" (A.V., "will finish") in Rom. 9:28. See COMPLETE.
NT: B.792a; CB.1271a; K.1161.
OT: kālāh: S.3615; HR.1319b.7a,b; H.982-984; BD.477b.
tāmam: S.8552; HR.1319b.16; H.2522; BD.1070b.
GEN. REF.: IS.2:304; NB.–; Z.–.

6. *dianuō* [διανύω, 1274], is translated "had finished," in Acts 21:7, of the voyage from Tyre to Ptolemais. As this is so short a journey, and this verb is intensive in meaning, some have suggested the rendering 'but we having (thereby) completed our voyage (i.e., from Macedonia, 20:6), came from Tyre to Ptolemais.' In late Greek writers, however, the verb is used with the meaning to continue, and this is the probable sense here. ¶
NT: B.187b; CB.–; K.–.
OT: –.
GEN. REF.: –.

7. *ginomai* [γίνομαι, 1096], to become, to come into existence, is translated "were finished" in Heb. 4:3, i.e., were brought to their predestined end.
NT: B.158a; CB.1248b; K.117.
OT: –.
GEN. REF.: –.

Notes: (1) In Luke 14:28, *apartismos* denotes a completion, and the phrase is, lit., 'unto a completion.' The A.V. has "to finish" (R.V., "to complete"). See COMPLETE. ¶

(2) In Jas. 1:15, *apoteleō*, to perfect, to bring to maturity, to become "fullgrown." R.V. (A.V., "is finished"), is said of the full development of sin.

(3) In Heb. 12:2, the R.V. suitably translates *teleiōtēs* "perfecter," for A.V., "finisher."

FIRE

A. Nouns.

1. *pur* [πῦρ, 4442], (akin to which are No. 2, *pura*, and *puretos*, a fever, Eng., fire, etc.) is used (besides its ordinary natural significance):

(*a*) of the holiness of God, which consumes all that is inconsistent therewith, Heb. 10:27; 12:29; cp. Rev. 1:14; 2:18; 10:1; 15:2; 19:12; similarly of the holy angels as His ministers, Heb. 1:7; in Rev. 3:18 it is symbolic of that which tries the faith of saints, producing what will glorify the Lord:

(*b*) of the Divine judgment, testing the deeds of believers, at the Judgment-Seat of Christ, 1 Cor. 3:13 and 15:

(*c*) of the fire of Divine judgment upon the rejectors of Christ, Matt. 3:11 (where a distinction is to be made between the baptism of the Holy Spirit at Pentecost and the fire of Divine retribution; Acts 2:3 could not refer to baptism); Luke 3:16:

(*d*) of the judgments of God at the close of the present age previous to the establishment of the Kingdom of Christ in the world, 2 Thess. 1:8; Rev. 18:8:

(*e*) of the fire of Hell, to be endured by the ungodly hereafter, Matt. 5:22; 13:42, 50; 18:8, 9; 25:41; Mark 9:43, 48; Luke 3:17:

(*f*) of human hostility both to the Jews and to Christ's followers, Luke 12:49:

(*g*) as illustrative judgment upon the luxurious and tyrannical rich, Jas. 5:3:

(*h*) of the future overthrow of the Babylonish religious system at the hands of the Beast and the nations under him, Rev. 17:16:

(*i*) of turning the heart of an enemy to repentance by repaying his unkindness by kindness, Rom. 12:20:

(*j*) of the tongue, as governed by a fiery disposition and as exercising a destructive influence over others, Jas. 3:6:

(*k*) as symbolic of the danger of destruction, Jude 23.
NT: B.729d; CB.1268a; K.975.
OT: 'ēsh: S.784; HR.1242b.2a; H.172; BD.77b.
GEN. REF.: IS.2:305; NB.422; Z.2:538.

Note: See also under FLAME.

2. *pura* [πυρά, 4443], from No. 1, denotes a heap of fuel collected to be set on fire (hence Eng., pyre), Acts 28:2, 3. ¶
NT: B.730c; CB.1268b; K.–.
OT: –.
GEN. REF.: IS.2:305; NB.422; Z.2:538.

Note: In Mark 14:54, the italicised phrase "of the fire" is added in the Eng. Versions to indicate the light as coming from the fire.

B. Adjective.

purinos [πύρινος, 4447], "fiery" (akin to A, No. 1), is translated "of fire" in Rev. 9:17. ¶ In the Sept., Ezek. 28:14, 16. ¶

NT: B.731a; CB.1268b; K.975.
OT: 'ēsh: S.784; HR.1245b.1; H.172; BD.77b.
GEN. REF.: IS.2:305; NB.422; Z.2:538.

C. Verbs.

1. *puroō* [πυρόω, 4448], is translated "being on fire" (Middle Voice) in 2 Pet. 3:12. See FIERY.

NT: B.731a; CB.1268a; K.975.
OT: ṣāraph: S.6884; HR.1245c.1; H.1972; BD.864a.
GEN. REF.: IS.2:305; NB.422; Z.2:538.

2. *phlogizō* [φλογίζω, 5394], to set on fire, burn up, is used figuratively, in both Active and Passive Voices, in Jas. 3:6, of the tongue, firstly, of its disastrous effects upon the whole round of the circumstances of life; secondly, of Satanic agency in using the tongue for this purpose. ¶

NT: B.862a; CB.—; K.—.
OT: lāhaṭ: S.3857; HR.1432c.2; H.1081; BD.529c.
lāqaḥ: S.3947; HR.1432c.3; H.1124; BD.542c,544a.
GEN. REF.: IS.2:305; NB.—; Z.—.

FIRKIN

metrētēs [μετρητής, 3355], is a liquid measure (akin to *metreō*, to measure), equivalent to one and a half Roman *amphorae*, or about nine gallons, John 2:6. ¶

NT: B.514d; CB.1258c; K.—.
OT: bat: S.1324; HR.918a.1; H.298a; BD.144c.
s^e'āh: S.5429; HR.918a.2; H.1452; BD.684b.
GEN. REF.: IS.2:306;4:1050; NB.1325; Z.5:918.

FIRM

1. *bebaios* [βέβαιος, 949], firm, steadfast, secure (from *bainō*, to go), is translated "firm" in Heb. 3:6, of the maintenance of the boldness of the believer's hope, and in 3:14, R.V., of "the beginning of our confidence" (A.V., "steadfast"). See STEADFAST, SURE.

NT: B.138b; CB.1239a; K.103.
OT: —.
GEN. REF.: IS.2:306; NB.—; Z.—.

2. *stereos* [στερεός, 4731], solid, hard, stiff, is translated "firm" in 2 Tim 2:19, R.V., "the firm (foundation of God)," A.V., "(standeth) sure"; *stereos* is not part of the predicate; "solid (food)" in Heb. 5:12, 14, R.V.; "steadfast" in 1 Pet. 5:9. See SOLID, STEADFAST, STRONG. ¶

NT: B.766c; CB.1270a; K.1077.
OT: ḥāzāq: S.2389; HR.1289a.4; H.636a; BD.305c.
GEN. REF.: IS.2:306; NB.—; Z.—.

Note: Cp. *stereoō*, to make strong, establish, Acts 3:7, 16; 16:5, and *stereōma*, steadfastness, Col. 2:5. ¶

FIRST

A. Adjective.

prōtos [πρῶτος, 4413], the superlative degree of *pro*, before, is used (I) of time or place, (*a*) as a noun, e.g., Luke 14:18; Rev. 1:17; opposite to 'the last,' in the neuter plural, Matt. 12:45; Luke 11:26; 2 Pet. 2:20; in the neuter singular, opposite to 'the second,' Heb. 10:9; in 1 Cor. 15:3, *en prōtois*, lit., 'in the first (things, or matters)' denotes "first of all"; (*b*) as an adjective, e.g., Mark 16:9, used with "day" understood, lit., 'the first (day) of (i.e., after) the Sabbath,' in which phrase the "of" is objective, not including the Sabbath, but following it (cp. B, No. 3); in John 20:4, 8; Rom. 10:19, e.g., equivalent to an English adverb; in John 1:15, lit., 'first of me,' i.e., "before me" (of superiority); (II) of rank or dignity, see CHIEF. Cp. B, Nos. 3 and 4.

NT: B.725b; CB.1267b; K.965.
OT: ri'shôn: S.7223; HR.1235c.3a; H.2097c; BD.911c.
GEN. REF.: IS.2:307; NB.—; Z.—.

B. Adverbs.

1. *proteron* [πρότερον, 4386], the comparative degree of *pro* (see No. 1), former, before, denotes "first" in Heb. 7:27; in 4:6, R.V., "before" (A.V., "first"), speaking of Israel as having heard God's good tidings previously to the ministry of the Gospel; in Gal. 4:13, "I preached . . . unto you the first time" means on the former of his two previous visits.

NT: B.721d; CB.1267b; K.—.
OT: ri'shôn: S.7223; HR.1230b.2a; H.2097c; BD.911c.
GEN. REF.: IS.2:307; NB.—; Z.—.

2. *anōthen* [ἄνωθεν, 509], from above, is rendered "from the first" in Luke 1:3, R.V.; it may mean 'from their beginning, or source.'

NT: B.77a; CB.1236a; K.63.
OT: —.
GEN. REF.: —.

3. *prōtōs* [πρώτως, 4413], firstly, is used in Acts 11:26, "first" (some mss. have No. 4 here). ¶

NT: B.727a; CB.—; K.—.
OT: —.
GEN. REF.: IS.2:307; NB.—; Z.—.

4. *prōton* [πρῶτον, 4412], the neuter of the adjective *prōtos*, is used as an adverb, signifying first, firstly, e.g., of time, Matt. 8:21; of order, Rom. 3:2 (A.V., "chiefly"); in John 7:51, R.V., "except it first hear from himself" (the A.V., "before it hear him," follows the mss. which have No. 1).

NT: B.725b; CB.1267b; K.965.
OT: —.
GEN. REF.: IS.2:307; NB.—; Z.—.

C. Numeral.

mia [μία, 3391], a grammatically feminine form of *heis*, one, is translated "first" in certain occurrences of the phrase "on the first day of the week," e.g., Luke 24:1; 1 Cor. 16:2; cp. A. and see DAY; also in Tit. 3:10, of a first admonition to a heretical man. See ONE.

NT: B.230d; CB.1249c; K.214.
OT: —.
GEN. REF.: IS.2:307; NB.—; Z.—.

D. Noun.

archē [ἀρχή, 746], a beginning, is translated "first" in Heb. 5:12, "of the first (principles of the oracles of God)," lit., '(the principles) of the beginning (of the oracles of God)'; in 6:1 "the first (principles) of Christ," lit., '(the account) of the beginning of Christ,' i.e., the elementary teaching concerning Christ. In Acts 26:4, where the word is preceded by *apo*, from, the A.V. has "at the first," the R.V., "from the beginning."

NT: B.111d; CB.1237b; K.81.
OT: rō'sh: S.7218; HR.164a.20a; H.2097; BD.910c.
rē'shît: S.7225; HR.164a20c; H.2097e; BD.912a.
GEN. REF.: IS.2:307; NB.—; Z.1:510.

Notes: (1) In Jude 6 *archē* has the meaning "principality," as in the R.V. and the A.V. margin.

(2) In 2 Cor. 8:12 *prokeimai*, to be present, lit., to lie beforehand (*pro*, before, *keimai*, to lie), R.V. renders "(if the readiness) is there," for A.V., "if there be first (a willing mind)." See SET, A, No. 23.

FIRST-BEGOTTEN, FIRSTBORN

prōtotokos [πρωτότοκος, 4416], firstborn (from *prōtos*, first, and *tiktō*, to beget), is used of Christ as born of the Virgin Mary, Luke 2:7; further, in His relationship to the Father, expressing His priority to, and pre-eminence over, creation, not in the sense of being the first to be born. It is used occasionally of superiority of position in the O.T.; see Ex. 4:22; Deut. 21:16, 17, the prohibition being against the evil of assigning the privileged position of the firstborn to one born subsequently to the first child.

The five passages in the N.T. relating to Christ may be set forth chronologically thus: (*a*) Col. 1:15, where His eternal relationship with the Father is in view, and the clause means both that He was the Firstborn before all creation and that He Himself produced creation (the genitive case being objective, as ver. 16 makes clear); (*b*) Col. 1:18 and Rev. 1:5, in reference to His resurrection; (*c*) Rom. 8:29, His position in relationship to the Church; (*d*) Heb. 1:6, R.V., His Second Advent (the R.V. "when He again bringeth in," puts "again" in the right place, the contrast to His First Advent, at His Birth, being implied); cp. Psa. 89:27. The word is used in the plural, in Heb. 11:28, of the firstborn sons in the families of the Egyptians, and in 12:23, of the members of the Church. ¶

NT: B.726c; CB.1267b; K.965.
OT: bᵉkōr: S.1060; HR.1237a.1a; H.244a; BD.114a.
GEN. REF.: IS.—; NB.—; Z.2:540.

Note: With (*a*) cp. John 1:30, "He was before me," lit., 'He was first (*prōtos*) of me,' i.e., 'in regard to me,' expressing all that is involved in His pre-existence and priority.

FIRSTFRUIT(S)

aparchē [ἀπαρχή, 536], denotes, primarily, an offering of firstfruits (akin to *aparchomai*, to make a beginning; in sacrifices, to offer firstfruits). "Though the English word is plural in each of its occurrences save Rom. 11:16, the Greek word is always singular. Two Hebrew words are thus translated, one meaning the chief or principal part, e.g., Num. 18:12; Prov. 3:9; the other, the earliest ripe of the crop or of the tree, e.g., Ex. 23:16; Neh. 10:35; they are found together, e.g., in Ex. 23:19, "the first of the firstfruits."

"The term is applied in things spiritual, (*a*) to the presence of the Holy Spirit with the believer as the firstfruits of the full harvest of the Cross, Rom. 8:23; (*b*) to Christ Himself in resurrection in relation to all believers who have fallen asleep, 1 Cor. 15:20, 23; (*c*) to the earliest believers in a country in relation to those of their countrymen subsequently converted, Rom. 16:5; 1 Cor. 16:15; (*d*) to the believers of this age in relation to the whole of the redeemed, 2 Thess. 2:13 (see Note below) and Jas. 1:18. Cp. Rev. 14:4." ¶ *

NT: B.81b; CB.1236b; K.81.
OT: rē'shît: S.7225; HR.118b.3; H.2097e; BD.912a.
tᵉrûmāh: S.8641; HR.118b.5; H.2133i; BD.929a.
GEN. REF.: IS.2:307; NB.1117; Z.2:541.

Notes: (1) In Jas. 1:15 the qualifying phrase, "a kind of," may suggest a certain falling short, on the part of those mentioned, of what they might be.

(2) In 2 Thess. 2:13, instead of *ap' archēs*, "from the beginning," there is an alternative reading, well supported, viz., *aparchēn*, '(God chose you) as firstfruits.'

FISH

1. *ichthus* [ἰχθύς, 2486], denotes a fish, Matt. 7:10; Mark 6:38, etc.; apart from the Gospels, only in 1 Cor. 15:39.

NT: B.384b; CB.1252c; K.—.
OT: dāg: S.1709; HR.696a.1a; H.401a; BD.185c.
dāgāh: S.1710; HR.696a.1b; H.401b; BD.185d.
GEN. REF.: IS.2:308; NB.424; Z.2:541.

2. *ichthudion* [ἰχθύδιον, 2485], is a diminutive of No. 1, a little fish, Matt. 15:34; Mark 8:7. ¶

NT: B.384b; CB.1252c; K.—.
OT: —.
GEN. REF.: IS.2:308; NB.424; Z.2:541.

* From Notes on Thessalonians by Hogg and Vines, p. 271.

3. *opsarion* [ὀψάριον, 3795], is a diminutive of *opson*, cooked meat, or a relish, a dainty dish, especially of fish; it denotes a little fish, John 6:9, 11; 21:9, 10, 13. ¶
NT: B.601b; CB.1261a; K.–.
OT: –.
GEN. REF.: IS.2:308; NB.424; Z.2:541.

FISH (Verb), FISHER, FISHERMAN

A. Noun.

halieus [ἁλιεύς, 231], a fisherman, fisher (from *hals*, the sea), occurs in Matt. 4:18, 19; Mark 1:16, 17; Luke 5:2. ¶
NT: B.37c; CB.–; K.–.
OT: dāg: S.1709; HR.54b.1a; H.401d; BD.185c.
dawwāg: S.1728; HR.54b.1b; H.401d; BD.186a.
GEN. REF.: IS.2:309; NB.424; Z.541,543.

B. Verb.

halieuō [ἁλιεύω, 232], to fish (akin to A.), occurs in John 21:3. ¶ In the Sept., Jer. 16:16. ¶
NT: B.37d; CB.–; K.–.
OT: dîg: S.1770; HR.54b.1; H.401c; BD.185d.
GEN. REF.: IS.2:309; NB.424; Z.2:541,543.

FIT (Adjective and Verb), FITLY, FITTING

A. Adjectives.

1. *euthetos* [εὔθετος, 2111], ready for use, fit, well adapted, lit., well placed (*eu*, well, *tithēmi*, to place), is used (*a*) of persons, Luke 9:62, negatively, of one who is not fit for the Kingdom of God; (*b*) of things, Luke 14:35, of salt that has lost is savour; rendered "meet" in Heb. 6:7, of herbs. See MEET. ¶
NT: B.320b; CB.–; K.–.
OT: māṣā': S.4672; HR.570b.1; H.2033; BD.592c.
GEN. REF.: IS.2:311; NB.–; Z.–.

2. *arestos* [ἀρεστός, 701], pleasing (akin to *areskō*, to please), is translated "(it is not) fit," R.V. (A.V., "reason"), in Acts 6:2. See PLEASE, REASON.
NT: B.105d; CB.1237c; K.77.
OT: yāshār: S.3477; HR.156a.3; H.930a; BD.449a.
GEN. REF.: IS.3:885; NB.–; Z.–.

B. Verbs.

1. *anēkō* [ἀνήκω, 433], properly, to have come up to (*ana*, up, and *hēkō*, to arrive), is translated "is fitting," in Col. 3:18, R.V. See BEFITTING.
NT: B.66b; CB.1235c; K.58.
OT: –.
GEN. REF.: IS.2:311; NB.–; Z.–.

2. *kathēkō* [καθήκω, 2520], to come or reach down to (*kata*, down), hence, to befit, be proper, is translated "is (not fit)," in Acts 22:22; in Rom. 1:28, R.V., "fitting" (A.V., "convenient"). See CONVENIENT. ¶
NT: B.389a; CB.1254c; K.385.
OT: –.
GEN. REF.: –.

3. *katartizō* [καταρτίζω, 2675], to make fit, to equip, prepare (*kata*, down, *artos*, a joint), is rendered "fitted" in Rom. 9:22, of vessels of wrath; here the Middle Voice signifies that those referred to fitted themselves for destruction (as illustrated in the case of Pharaoh, the self-hardening of whose heart is accurately presented in the R.V. in the first part of the series of incidents in the Exodus narrative, which records Pharaoh's doings; only after repeated and persistent obstinancy on his part is it recorded that God hardened his heart.) See FRAME, JOIN, PERFECT, PREPARE, RESTORE.
NT: B.417d; CB.1254b; K.80.
OT: kûn: S.3559; HR.743b,3a,c; H.964; BD.465c.
GEN. REF.: IS.2:311; NB.–; Z.–.

4. *sunarmologeō* [συναρμολογέω, 4883], to fit or frame together (*sun*, with, *harmos*, a joint, in building, and *legō*, to choose), is used metaphorically of the various parts of the Church as a building, Eph. 2:21, "fitly framed together"; also of the members of the Church as the Body of Christ, 4:16, R.V., "Fitly framed . . . together." ¶
NT: B.785b; CB.–; K.1114.
OT: –.
GEN. REF.: –.

FIVE, FIVE TIMES

pente [πέντε, 4002], is derived by some from words suggesting the fingers of a hand, or a fist. The word is frequent in the Gospels. *Pentakis*, five times, is found in 2 Cor. 11:24; ¶ *pentakosioi*, five hundred, in Luke 7:41; 1 Cor. 15:6; ¶ *pentakischilioi*, five thousand (*chilios*, a thousand), in Matt. 14:21; 16:9 and corresponding passages. See FIFTEENTH, FIFTH, FIFTY.
NT: B.643a; CB.1263a; K.–.
OT: ḥāmēsh: S.2568; HR.1118c; H.686a; BD.331c.
GEN. REF.: IS.3:559; NB.–; Z.–.

FIX

stērizō [στηρίζω, 4741], to set forth, make fast, fix, is translated "fixed" in Luke 16:26, of the great gulf separating Hades or Sheol from the region called "Abraham's bosom." See ESTABLISH.
NT: B.768a; CB.1270a; K.1085.
OT: sûm, sîm: S.7760; HR.1290c.9; H.2243; BD.962c.
GEN. REF.: –.

FLAME, FLAMING

phlox [φλόξ, 5395], akin to Lat. *fulgeō*, to shine, is used apart from *pur*, fire, in Luke 16:24; with *pur*, it signifies a fiery flame, lit., a flame of fire, Acts 7:30; 2 Thess. 1:8, where the fire is to be understood as the instrument of Divine judgment; Heb. 1:7, where the meaning probably is that God makes His angels as active and powerful as a flame of fire; in Rev. 1:14; 2:18; 19:12, of the eyes of the Lord Jesus as emblematic of penetrating judgment, searching out evil. ¶

NT: B.862a; CB.–; K.–.
OT: lahab: S.3851; HR.1433a.4a; H.1077,1077a; BD.529a.
lehābāh: S.3852; HR.1433a.4b; H.1077b; BD.529b.
GEN. REF.: IS.2:312; NB.–; Z.–.

FLATTERY (-ING)

kolakia (or *-eia*) [κολακία, 2850], akin to *kolakeuō*, to flatter, is used in 1 Thess. 2:5 of "words of flattery" (R.V.), adopted as "a cloke of covetousness," i.e., words which flattery uses, not simply as an effort to give pleasure, but with motives of self-interest. ¶

NT: B.440d; CB.–; K.451.
OT: –.
GEN. REF.: IS.2:312; NB.–; Z.–.

FLAX

linon [λίνον, 3043], primarily denotes flax (Eng., linen); then, that which is made of it, a wick of a lamp, Matt. 12:20; several ancient mss. have the word in Rev. 15:6 (A.V. only, "linen"). See LINEN. ¶

NT: B.475b; CB.–; K.–.
OT: pēshet: S.6593; HR.879b.2a; H.1849; BD.833d.
pishtāh: S.6594; HR.879b.2b; H.1849; BD.834a.
GEN. REF.: IS.2:313; NB.425; Z.2:545.

FLEE, FLED

1. *pheugō* [φεύγω, 5343], to flee from or away (Lat., *fugio*; Eng., fugitive, etc.), besides its literal significance, is used metaphorically, (*a*) transitively, of fleeing fornication, 1 Cor. 6:18; idolatry, 10:14; evil doctrine, questionings, disputes of words, envy, strife, railings, evil surmisings, wranglings, and the love of money, 1 Tim. 6:11; youthful lusts, 2 Tim. 2:22; (*b*) intransitively, of the flight of physical matter, Rev. 16:20; 20:11; of death, 9:6. See ESCAPE.

NT: B.855d; CB.1264a; K.–.
OT: bāraḥ: S.1272; HR.1428b.1a; H.284; BD.137d.
nûs: S.5127; HR.1428b.4a; H.1327; BD.630c.
GEN. REF.: IS.2:313; NB.–; Z.–.

2. *ekpheugō* [ἐκφεύγω, 1628], to flee away, escape (*ek*, from, and No. 1), is translated "fled" in Acts 16:27 (A.V. only); 19:16. In Heb. 12:25 the best mss. have this verb instead of No. 1. See ESCAPE.

NT: B.246d; CB.1243c; K.–.
OT: nûs: S.5127; HR.445b.3; H.1327; BD.630c.
GEN. REF.: IS.2:313; NB.–; Z.–.

3. *katapheugō* [καταφεύγω, 2703], to flee for refuge (*kata*, used intensively, and No. 1), is used (*a*) literally in Acts 14:6; (*b*) metaphorically in Heb. 6:18, of fleeing for refuge to lay hold upon hope. ¶

NT: B.420a; CB.1254b; K.–.
OT: nûs: S.5127; HR.747b.5; H.1327; BD.630c.
rûṣ: S.7323; HR.747b.7; H.2137; BD.930a.
GEN. REF.: IS.2:313; NB.–; Z.–.

Note: For *apopheugō* and *diapheugō*, See ESCAPE.

FLESH

1. *sarx* [σάρξ, 4561], has a wider range of meaning in the N.T. than in the O.T. Its uses in the N.T. may be analysed as follows:

"(*a*) the substance of the body, whether of beasts or of men, 1 Cor. 15:39; (*b*) the human body, 2 Cor. 10:3a; Gal. 2:20; Phil. 1:22; (*c*) by synecdoche, of mankind, in the totality of all that is essential to manhood, i.e., spirit, soul, and body, Matt. 24:22; John 1:13; Rom. 3:20; (*d*) by synecdoche, of the holy humanity of the Lord Jesus, in the totality of all that is essential to manhood, i.e., spirit, soul, and body, John 1:14; 1 Tim. 3:16; 1 John 4:2; 2 John 7; in Heb. 5:7, 'the days of His flesh,' i.e., His past life on earth in distinction from His present life in resurrection; (*e*) by synecdoche, for the complete person, John 6:51-57; 2 Cor. 7:5; Jas. 5:3; (*f*) the weaker element in human nature, Matt. 26:41; Rom. 6:19; 8:3a; (*g*) the unregenerate state of men, Rom. 7:5; 8:8, 9; (*h*) the seat of sin in man (but this is not the same thing as in the body), 2 Pet. 2:18; 1 John 2:16; (*i*) the lower and temporary element in the Christian, Gal. 3:3; 6:8, and in religious ordinances, Heb. 9:10; (*j*) the natural attainments of men, 1 Cor. 1:26; 2 Cor. 10:2, 3b; (*k*) circumstances, 1 Cor. 7:28; the externals of life, 2 Cor. 7:1; Eph. 6:5; Heb. 9:13; (*l*) by metonymy, the outward and seeming, as contrasted with the spirit, the inward and real, John 6:63; 2 Cor. 5:16; (*m*) natural relationship, consanguine, 1 Cor. 10:18; Gal. 4:23, or marital, Matt. 19:5."*

In Matt. 26:41; Rom. 8:4, 13; 1 Cor. 5:5; Gal. 6:8 (not the Holy Spirit, here), flesh is contrasted with spirit; in Rom. 2:28, 29, with heart and spirit; in Rom. 7:25, with the mind; cp. Col. 2:1, 5. It is coupled with the mind in Eph. 2:3, and with the spirit in 2 Cor. 7:1.

NT: B.743b; CB.1268c; K.1000.
OT: bāsār: S.1320; HR.1259b.1a; H.291a; BD.142b.
GEN. REF.: IS.2:313; NB.425; Z.2:546,548.

Note: In Col. 2:18 the noun *sarx* is used in the phrase "(by his) fleshly mind," lit., 'by the

* From Notes on Galatians by Hogg and Vine, pp. 111, 112.

mind of his flesh' [see (*h*) above], whereas the mind ought to be dominated by the Spirit.

2. *kreas* [κρέας, 2907], denotes flesh in the sense of meat. It is used in the plural in Rom. 14:21; 1 Cor. 8:13. ¶

NT: B.449c; CB.1256a; K.—.
OT: bāsār: S.1320; HR.784c.1; H.291a; BD.142b.
GEN. REF.: IS.2:313; NB.425; Z.2:546,548.

FLESHLY, FLESHY

1. *sarkikos* [σαρκικός, 4559], akin to No. 1, under FLESH, signifies (*a*) associated with or pertaining to, the flesh, carnal, Rom. 15:27; 1 Cor. 9:11; (*b*) of the nature of the flesh, sensual, translated "fleshly" in 2 Cor. 1:12, of wisdom; in 1 Pet. 2:11, of lusts; in 2 Cor. 10:4, negatively, of the weapons of the Christian's warfare, R.V., "of the flesh" (A.V., "carnal"). See CARNAL.

NT: B.742d; CB.1268b; K.1000.
OT: —.
GEN. REF.: IS.2:313; NB.425; Z.2:548.

2. *sarkinos* [σάρκινος, 4560], denotes 'of the flesh,' fleshly (the termination *—inos* signifying the substance or material of a thing); in 2 Cor. 3:3, R.V., "(tables that are hearts) of flesh," A.V., "Fleshy (tables)," etc. See CARNAL.

NT: B.743a; CB.1268c; K.1000.
OT: bāsār: S.1320; HR.784c.1; H.291a; BD.142b.
GEN. REF.: IS.2:313; NB.425; Z.2:546,548.

Note: The adjectives "fleshly," "carnal" are contrasted with spiritual qualities in Rom. 7:14; 1 Cor. 3:1, 3, 4; 2 Cor. 1:12; Col. 2:18 (lit., 'mind of flesh'). Speaking broadly, the carnal denotes the sinful element in man's nature, by reason of descent from Adam; the spiritual is that which comes by the regenerating operation of the Holy Spirit.

FLIGHT

A. Noun.

phugē [φυγή, 5437], akin to *pheugō* (see FLEE), is found in Matt. 24:20. Some inferior mss. have it in Mark 13:18. ¶

NT: B.867c; CB.1264c; K.—.
OT: nûs: S.5127; HR.1440b.2a; H.1327; BD.630c.
mānôs: S.4498; HR.1440b.2b; H.1327a; BD.631a.
m^enûsāh: S.4499; HR.1440b.2c; H.1327b; BD.631a.
GEN. REF.: IS.2:313; NB.—; Z.—.

B. Verb.

klinō [κλίνω, 2827], to make to bend, is translated "turned to flight" in Heb. 11:34. See BOW.

NT: B.436c; CB.—; K.—.
OT: —.
GEN. REF.: —.

FLOCK

1. *poimnē* [ποίμνη, 4167], akin to *poimēn*, a shepherd, denotes a flock (properly, of sheep), Matt. 26:31; Luke 2:8; 1 Cor. 9:7; metaphorically, of Christ's followers, John 10:16, R.V., for the erroneous A.V., "fold." What characterizes Christ's sheep is listening to His voice, and the flock must be one as He is one. ¶

NT: B.684c; CB.1265c; K.901.
OT: 'ēder: S.5739; HR.1169c.1; H.1572a; BD.727c.
GEN. REF.: IS.4:463; NB.—; Z.2:550.

2. *poimnion* [ποίμνιον, 4168], possibly a diminutive of No. 1, is used in the N.T. only metaphorically, of a group of Christ's disciples, Luke 12:32; of local churches cared for by elders, Acts 20:28, 29; 1 Pet. 5:2, 3. ¶

NT: B.684c; CB.1265c; K.901.
OT: 'ēder: S.5739; HR.1169c.1; H.1572a; BD.727c.
ṣō'n: S.6629; HR.1169c.6; H.1864a; BD.838a.
GEN. REF.: IS.4:463; NB.—; Z.2:550.

FLOOD

A. Nouns.

1. *kataklusmos* [κατακλυσμός, 2627], a deluge (Eng., cataclysm), akin to *katakluzō*, to inundate, 2 Pet. 3:6, is used of the flood in Noah's time, Matt. 24:38, 39; Luke 17:27; 2 Pet. 2:5. ¶

NT: B.411d; CB.1254a; K.—.
OT: mābbûl: S.3999; HR.734a.1; H.1142; BD.550a.
GEN. REF.: IS.2:315; NB.426; Z.—.

2. *plēmmura* [πλήμμυρα, 4132], akin to *plēthō* and *pimplēmi*, to fill, a flood of sea or river, the latter in Luke 6:48. ¶ In the Sept., Job 40:18 (ver. 23 in the E.V.). ¶

NT: B.669b; CB.—; K.—.
OT: —.
GEN. REF.: IS.2:315; NB.426; Z.—.

3. *potamos* [ποταμός, 4215], a river, stream, torrent, is translated "flood" in Matt. 7:25, 27; in Rev. 12:15, 16, A.V., "flood," R.V., "river." See RIVER, WATER.

NT: B.694c; CB.1266b; K.921.
OT: y^e'ōr: S.2975; HR.1196a.1; H.832; BD.384b.
nāhār: S.5104; HR.1196a.2a; H.1315a; BD.625c.
GEN. REF.: IS.2:315; NB.426; Z.—.

B. Adjective.

potamophorētos [ποταμοφόρητος, 4216], signifies carried away by a stream or river (A, No. 3, and *pherō*, to carry), Rev. 12:15, R.V., "carried away by the stream" (A.V., "of the flood"). ¶

NT: B.694d; CB.1266a; K.921.
OT: —.
GEN. REF.: IS.2:315; NB.426; Z.—.

For FLOOR see THRESHING-FLOOR

FLOUR

semidalis [σεμίδαλις, 4585], denotes the finest wheaten flour, Rev. 18:13. ¶

NT: B.746d; CB.—; K.—.
OT: sōlet: S.5560; HR.1262b.2; H.1512; BD.701c.
GEN. REF.: —.

For **FLOURISH** in Phil. 4:10, see **REVIVE**

FLOW

rheō [ῥέω, 4483], to flow, is used figuratively in John 7:38 of the Holy Spirit, acting in and through the believer. ¶

NT: B.735a; CB.1268a; K.–.
OT: zûb: S.2100; HR.1248b.2; H.534; BD.264c.
GEN. REF.: IS.2:325; NB.–; Z.–.

FLOWER

A. Noun.

anthos [ἄνθος, 438], a blossom, flower (used in certain names of flowers), occurs in Jas. 1:10, 11; 1 Pet. 1:24 (twice). ¶

NT: B.67c; CB.1236a; K.–.
OT: ṣîṣ: S.6731; HR.96a; H.1911; BD.847c.
GEN. REF.: IS.2:325; NB.–; Z.2:580.

B. Adjective.

huperakmos [ὑπέρακμος, 5230], past the bloom of youth (from *huper*, beyond, and *akmē*, the highest point of anything, the full bloom of a flower: Eng., acme), is used in 1 Cor. 7:36, "past the flower of her age"; Lightfoot prefers the rendering "of full age."

NT: B.839d; CB.1252a; K.–.
OT: –.
GEN. REF.: –.

For **FLUX** see **DYSENTERY**

FLUTE-PLAYERS

aulētēs [αὐλητής, 834], a flute-player (from *auleō*, to play the flute), occurs in Matt. 9:23 (A.V., "minstrel"), and Rev. 18:22 (A.V., "pipers"). In the papyri writings of the time the word is chiefly associated with religious matters (Moulton and Milligan, Vocab.). Cp. MINSTREL. ¶

NT: B.121b; CB.–; K.–.
OT: –.
GEN. REF.: –.

FLY

petomai [πέτομαι, 4072], to fly (the root of which is seen in *pteron* and *pterux*, a wing, *ptilon*, a feather, etc.), is confined to the Apocalypse, 4:7; 8:13; 12:14; 14:6; 19:17. Some mss. have the verb *petaomai*, a frequentative form. ¶

NT: B.654a; CB.1263c; K.–.
OT: 'ûph: S.5774; HR.1129b.2a,b; H.1582,1583; BD.733b.
GEN. REF.: IS.2:325; NB.–; Z.–.

FOAL

huios [υἱός, 5207], a son, primarily signifying the relation of offspring to parent, is used of the foal of an ass in Matt. 21:5. See SON.

NT: B.833c; CB.1251c; K.1206.
OT: –.
GEN. REF.: IS.1:735; NB.–; Z.–.

FOAM

A. Verbs.

1. *aphrizō* [ἀφρίζω, 875], denotes to foam at the mouth (akin to *aphros*, foam; see B.), Mark 9:18, 20. ¶

NT: B.127c; CB.–; K.–.
OT: –.
GEN. REF.: IS.2:326; NB.–; Z.–.

2. *epaphrizō* [ἐπαφρίζω, 1890], to foam out, or up (*epi*, up, and No. 1), is used metaphorically in Jude 13, of the impious libertines, who had crept in among the saints, and foamed out their own shame with swelling words. The metaphor is drawn from the refuse borne on the crest of waves and cast up on the beach. ¶

NT: B.283d; CB.–; K.–.
OT: –.
GEN. REF.: IS.2:326; NB.–; Z.–.

B. Noun.

aphros [ἀφρός, 876], foam, occurs in Luke 9:39, where it is used with the preposition *meta*, with, lit., '(teareth him) with (accompanied by) foam.' ¶

NT: B.127d; CB.–; K.–.
OT: –.
GEN. REF.: IS.2:326; NB.–; Z.–.

FOE

echthros [ἐχθρός, 2190], an adjective signifying hated, hateful, or hostile, is used also as a noun denoting an enemy, translated "foes" in Matt. 10:36 and the A.V. of Acts 2:35. See ENEMY.

NT: B.331b; CB.1242c; K.285.
OT: 'āyab: S.340; HR.589c.1; H.78; BD.33b.
GEN. REF.: IS.2:81; NB.–; Z.2:305.

FOLD

aulē [αὐλή, 833], first signifies an open courtyard before a house; then, an enclosure in the open, a sheepfold, John 10:1, 16. In the papyri "the word is extremely common, denoting the court attached to a house" (Moulton and Milligan, Vocab.). The sheepfold was usually surrounded by a stone wall, Numb. 32:16, preferably near a well, Ex. 2:16; Psa. 23:2, and often protected by a tower, 2 Chron. 26:10; Mic. 4:8. See COURT, HALL, PALACE.

NT: B.121b; CB.1238b; K.–.
OT: ḥāṣēr: S.2691; HR.177b.2b; H.722a,723a; BD.347b.
GEN. REF.: IS.2:326; NB.–; Z.2:581.

Note: For the erroneous A.V. rendering, "fold," of *poimnē*, a flock, in John 10:16, see FLOCK.

For **FOLD UP** see **ROLL,** A, No. 4

For **FOLK** see **IMPOTENT,** B, **SICK,** B, No. 2

FOLLOW, FOLLOW AFTER

1. *akoloutheō* [ἀκολουθέω, 190], to be an *akolouthos*, a follower, or companion (from the prefix *a*, here expressing union, likeness, and *keleuthos*, a way; hence, one going in the same way), is used (*a*) frequently in the literal sense, e.g., Matt. 4:25; (*b*) metaphorically, of discipleship, e.g., Mark 8:34; 9:38; 10:21. It is used 77 times in the Gospels, of following Christ, and only once otherwise, Mark 14:13.

NT: B.31a; CB.1234b; K.33.
OT: hālak: S.1980; HR.44c.3b; H.498; BD.229d.
GEN. REF.: IS.2:326; NB.–; Z.–.

2. *exakoloutheō* [ἐξακολουθέω, 1811], to follow up, or out to the end (*ek*, out, used intensively, and No. 1), is used metaphorically, and only by the Apostle Peter in his Second Epistle: in 1:16, of cunningly devised fables; 2:2, of lascivious doings; 2:15, of the way of Balaam. ¶ In the Sept., Job 31:9; Is. 56:11; Jer. 2:2; Amos 2:4. ¶

NT: B.272b; CB.1247b; K.33.
OT: hālak: S.1980; HR.486c.1; H.498; BD.229d,231c.
GEN. REF.: IS.2:326; NB.–; Z.–.

3. *epakoloutheō* [ἐπακολουθέω, 1872], to follow after, close upon (*epi*, upon, and No. 1), is used of signs following the preaching of the Gospel, Mark 16:20; of following good works, 1 Tim. 5:10; of sins following after those who are guilty of them, 5:24; of following the steps of Christ, 1 Pet. 2:21. ¶

NT: B.282b; CB.1245b; K.33.
OT: pānāh: S.6437; HR.505b.3; H.1782; BD.815a.
hālak: S.1980; HR.505b.2; H.498; BD.229d.
GEN. REF.: IS.2:326; NB.–; Z.–.

4. *katakoloutheō* [κατακολουθέω, 2628], to follow behind or intently after (*kata*, after, used intensively, and No. 1), is used of the women on their way to Christ's tomb, Luke 23:55; of the demon-possessed maid in Philippi in following the missionaries, Acts 16:17. ¶

NT: B.412a; CB.–; K.–.
OT: hālak: S.1980; HR.734a.1; H.498; BD.229d.
GEN. REF.: IS.2:326; NB.–; Z.–.

5. *parakoloutheō* [παρακολουθέω, 3877], lit. signifying to follow close up, or side by side, hence, to accompany, to conform to (*para*, beside, and No. 1), is used of signs accompanying "them that believe," Mark 16:17; of tracing the course of facts, Luke 1:3, R.V.; of following the good doctrine, 1 Tim. 4:6, R.V. (A.V., "attained"); similarly of following teaching so as to practise it, 2 Tim. 3:10, R.V., "didst follow" (A.V., "hast fully known"). See ATTAIN, KNOW, TRACE, UNDERSTAND. ¶

NT: B.618d; CB.1262a; K.33.
OT: –.
GEN. REF.: IS.2:326; NB.–; Z.–.

6. *sunakoloutheō* [συνακολουθέω, 4870], to follow along with, to accompany a leader (*sun*, with, and No. 1), is given its true rendering in the R.V. of Mark 5:37, "He suffered no man to follow with Him"; in 14:51, of the young man who "followed with" Christ (inferior mss. have No. 1 here); Luke 23:49, of the women who "followed with" Christ from Galilee. ¶

NT: B.783d; CB.1270b; K.33.
OT: –.
GEN. REF.: IS.2:326; NB.–; Z.–.

7. *diōkō* [διώκω, 1377], denotes (*a*) to drive away, Matt. 23:34; (*b*) to pursue without hostility, to follow, follow after, said of righteousness, Rom. 9:30; the Law, 9:31; 12:13, hospitality ("given to") lit., 'pursuing' (as one would a calling); the things which make for peace, 14:19; love, 1 Cor. 14:1; that which is good, 1 Thess. 5:15; righteousness, godliness, faith, love, patience, meekness, 1 Tim. 6:11; righteousness, faith, love, peace, 2 Tim. 2:22; peace and sanctification, Heb. 12:14; peace, 1 Pet. 3:11; (*c*) to follow on (used intransitively), Phil. 3:12, 14, R.V., "I press on"; 'follow after,' is an inadequate meaning. See GIVE, PERSECUTE, PRESS, PURSUE.

NT: B.201b; CB.1242a; K.177.
OT: rādaph: S.7291; HR.338b.10a-c; H.2124; BD.922c.
GEN. REF.: IS.2:326; NB.–; Z.–.

8. *katadiōkō* [καταδιώκω, 2614], to follow up or closely, with the determination to find (*kata*, down, intensive, giving the idea of a hard, persistent search, and No. 7), Mark 1:36, "followed after (Him)," is said of the disciples in going to find the Lord who had gone into a desert place to pray. ¶ The verb is found, e.g., in 1 Sam. 30:22; Psa. 23:6, and with hostile intent in Gen. 31:36.

NT: B.410c; CB.1254a; K.–.
OT: rādaph: S.7291; HR.730b.6a; H.2124; BD.922c.
GEN. REF.: IS.2:326; NB.–; Z.–.

9. *ginomai* [γίνομαι, 1096], to become, to come into existence, is used in Rev. 8:17; 11:15, 19, in the sense of taking place after, translated "there followed." See BECOME.

NT: B.158a; CB.1248b; K.117.
OT: –.
GEN. REF.: IS.2:326; NB.–; Z.–.

10. *epeimi* [ἔπειμι, 1966 (*epiousa*)], to come upon, or, of time, to come on or after (*epi*, upon, and *eimi*, to go), is used in the present participle as an adjective, in reference to a day, in Acts 7:26; 16:11; 20:15; 21:18; a night, 23:11, R.V., "following," in each place (A.V., "next"). ¶

NT: B.284c; CB.1245c; K.–.
OT: –.
GEN. REF.: –.

Notes: (1) In Luke 13:33, the present participle, Middle Voice, of the verb *echō*, to have, to be next, is used with the article, the word *hēmera*, a day, being understood, signifying "the day following."

(2) In John 1:43 and 6:22 the adverb *epaurion* with the article, "on the morrow," is translated "the day following" in the A.V. See MORROW.

(3) In Acts 21:1 the adverb *hexēs*, in order, next, is translated "the day following" (A.V.).

(4) *Mimeomai*, to imitate, be an imitator, is so translated always in the R.V., where the A.V. uses the verb to follow; it is always used in a good sense, 2 Thess. 3:7, 9; Heb. 13:7; 3 John 11. So with the nouns *mimētēs*, an imitator, and *summimētēs*, an imitator together. See IMITATE, IMITATOR.

(5) In Matt. 4:19, *deute*, come hither, with *opisō*, after, is translated "come ye after," R.V. (A.V., "follow").

(6) In Matt. 27:62, R.V., the phrase *eimi meta*, to be after, is translated "(which) is (the day) after" (A.V., "that followed").

(7) In 1 Pet. 1:11, the phrase *meta tauta*, lit., 'after these things,' is translated "that should follow," said of glories after the sufferings of Christ.

(8) In Luke 22:49, the phrase *to esomenon*, lit., 'the (thing) about to be' (from *eimi*, to be), is translated "what would follow."

(9) In Acts 3:24, the adverb *kathexēs*, successively, in order, is translated "(them) that followed after," i.e., those who succeeded (him), lit., 'the (ones) successively (to him).' Cp. Note (3) above. See AFTERWARD.

FOLLY

anoia [ἄνοια, 454), lit. signifies 'without understanding' (*a*, negative, *nous*, mind); hence, folly, or, rather, senselessness, 2 Tim. 3:9; in Luke 6:11 it denotes violent or mad rage, "madness." See MADNESS. ¶ Cp. *anoētos*, foolish.

NT: B.70d; CB.1235c; K.636.
OT: 'iwwelet: S.200; HR.105a.1; H.44c; BD.17c.
GEN. REF.: IS.2:331; NB.—; Z.2:581.

Note: For *aphrosunē*, rendered "folly" in 2 Cor. 11:1, A.V., see FOOLISHNESS (R.V.).

FOOD

1. *trophē* [τροφή, 5160], denotes nourishment, food (akin to *trephō*, to rear, nourish, feed); it is used literally, in the Gospels, Acts and Jas. 2:15; metaphorically, in Heb. 5:12, 14, R.V., "(solid) food," A.V., "(strong) meat," i.e., deeper subjects of the faith than that of elementary instruction. The word is always rendered "food" in the R.V., where the A.V. has "meat"; e.g., Matt. 3:4; 6:25; 10:10; 24:45; Luke 12:23; John 4:8; Acts 2:46, "did take their food," R.V. (A.V., "did eat their meat"); 9:19, "took food"; 27:33, 34, 36. The A.V. also has "food" in Acts 14:17 and Jas. 2:15. ¶

NT: B.827d; CB.—; K.—.
OT: 'ōkel: S.400; HR.1376b.1; H.85a; BD.38a.
leḥem: S.3899; HR.1376b.4; H.1105a; BD.536d.
GEN. REF.: IS.2:327; NB.429; Z.2:581.

2. *diatrophē* [διατροφή, 1305], sustenance, food, a strengthened form of No. 1 (*dia*, through, suggesting a sufficient supply), is used in 1 Tim. 6:8. ¶

NT: B.190a; CB.—; K.—.
OT: —.
GEN. REF.: IS.2:327; NB.429; Z.2:581.

3. *brōsis* [βρῶσις, 1035], eating, the act of eating (akin to *bibrōskō*, to eat) is translated "food" in 2 Cor. 9:10. See EATING, MEAT, RUST.

NT: B.148b; CB.1239b; K.111.
OT: 'ākal: S.398; HR.231c.1b; H.85; BD.37a.
ma'ᵃkāl: S.3978; HR.231c.1f; H.85d; BD.38b.
GEN. REF.: IS.2:327; NB.429; Z.2:581.

4. *sitometrion* [σιτομέτριον, 4620], a measured "portion of food" (*sitos*, corn, *metreō*, to measure), is used in Luke 12:42, R.V. ¶

NT: B.752a; CB.—; K.—.
OT: —.
GEN. REF.: —.

5. *brōma* [βρῶμα, 1033], akin to No. 3, frequently translated "meat," and always so in the A.V. except in Matt. 14:15, "victuals," is rendered "food" in the R.V. in Matt. 14:15; Luke 3:11; 9:13.

NT: B.148a; CB.1239b; K.111.
OT: 'ōkel: S.400; HR.231c.1b; H.85a; BD.38a.
ma'ᵃkāl: S.3978; HR.231c.1f; H.85d; BD.38b.
GEN. REF.: IS.2:327; NB.429; Z.2:581.

Note: For *asitia*, without food, see ABSTINENCE.

FOOL, FOOLISH, FOOLISHLY, FOOLISHNESS

A. Adjectives.

1. *aphrōn* [ἄφρων, 878], signifies 'without reason' (*a*, negative, *phrēn*, the mind), "want of mental sanity and sobriety, a reckless and inconsiderate habit of mind" (Hort), or "the lack of commonsense perception of the reality of things natural and spiritual . . . or the imprudent ordering of one's life in regard to salvation" (G. Vos, in Hastings' Bible Dic.); it is mostly translated "foolish" or "foolish ones" in the R.V.; Luke 11:40; 12:20; Rom. 2:20; 1 Cor. 15:36; 2 Cor. 11:16 (twice), 19 (contrasted with *phronimos*, prudent); 12:6, 11; Eph. 5:17; 1 Pet. 2:15. ¶

NT: B.127d; CB.1236c; K.1277.
OT: 'ᵉwîl: S.191; HR.186c.1a; H.44a; BD.17b.
kᵉsîl: S.3685; HR.186c.8a; H.—; BD.493a.
nābāl: S.5036; HR.186c.10; H.1285a; BD.614d.
GEN. REF.: IS.2:331; NB.433; Z.2:581.

2. *anoētos* [ἀνόητος, 453], signifies not understanding (*a*, negative, *noeō*, to perceive, understand), not applying *nous*, the mind, Luke 24:25; in Rom. 1:14 and Gal. 3:1, 3 it signifies senseless, an unworthy lack of understanding; sometimes it carries a moral reproach (in contrast with *sōphrōn*, sober-minded, self-controlled) and describes one who does not govern his lusts, Tit. 3:3; in 1 Tim. 6:9 it is associated with evil desires, lusts. See UNWISE. ¶

NT: B.70c; CB.1235c; K.636.
OT: 'ewîl: S.191; HR.105a.1a; H.44a; BD.17b.
'iwwelet: S.200; HR.105a.1b; H.44c; BD.17c.
GEN. REF.: IS.2:331; NB.433; Z.2:581.

3. *mōros* [μωρός, 3474], primarily denotes dull, sluggish (from a root *muh*, to be silly); hence, stupid, foolish; it is used (*a*) of persons, Matt. 5:22, "Thou fool"; here the word means morally worthless, a scoundrel, a more serious reproach than "Raca"; the latter scorns a man's mind and calls him stupid; *mōros* scorns his heart and character; hence the Lord's more severe condemnation; in 7:26, "a foolish man"; 23:17, 19, "fools"; 25:2, 3, 8, "foolish"; in 1 Cor. 3:18, "a fool"; the Apostle Paul uses it of himself and his fellow-workers, in 4:10, "fools" (i.e., in the eyes of opponents); (*b*) of things, 2 Tim. 2:23, "foolish and ignorant questionings"; so Tit. 3:9; in 1 Cor. 1:25, "the foolishness of God," not *mōria*, foolishness as a personal quality (see C, No. 1), but adjectivally, that which is considered by the ignorant as a foolish policy or mode of dealing, lit., 'the foolish (thing)'; so in ver.27, "the foolish (things) of the world." ¶

NT: B.531c; CB.1259b; K.620.
OT: 'ewîl: S.191; HR.938c.1; H.44a; BD.17b.
nābāl: S.5036; HR.938c.2a; H.1285a; BD.614d.
GEN. REF.: IS.2:331; NB.433; Z.2:581.

4. *asunetos* [ἀσύνετος, 801], denotes without discernment, or understanding (*a*, negative, *suniēmi*, to understand); hence "senseless," as in the R.V. of Rom. 1:21 (A.V., "foolish"), of the heart; in 10:19, A.V., "foolish," R.V., "void of understanding." See UNDERSTANDING.

NT: B.118c; CB.1238a; K.1119.
OT: kesîl: S.3685; HR.174a.1; H.1011c; BD.493a.
nābāl: S.5036; HR.174a.2; H.1285a; BD.614d.
GEN. REF.: IS.2:331; NB.433; Z.2:581.

Note: For "fools," Eph. 5:15, see UNWISE, No. 3.

B. Verbs.

1. *mōrainō* [μωραίνω, 3471], is used (*a*) in the causal sense, to make foolish, 1 Cor. 1:20; (*b*) in the passive sense, to become foolish, Rom. 1:22; in Matt. 5:13 and Luke 14:34 it is said of salt that has lost its flavour, becoming tasteless. See SAVOUR. ¶

NT: B.531b; CB.1259b; K.620.
OT: bā'ar: S.1198; HR.938b.1; H.264; BD.129c.
sākal: S.5528; HR.938b.2; H.1493; BD.698a.
GEN. REF.: IS.2:331; NB.433; Z.2:581.

2. *paraphroneō* [παραφρονέω, 3912], to be beside oneself (from *para*, contrary to, and *phrēn*, the mind), to be deranged, 2 Cor. 11:23, R.V., "as one beside himself," for A.V., "as a fool." ¶

NT: B.623c; CB.—; K.—.
OT: sārar: S.5639; HR.1065b.1; H.1549; BD.710d.
GEN. REF.: —.

C. Nouns.

1. *mōria* [μωρία, 3472], denotes foolishness (akin to A, No. 3 and B, No. 1), and is used in 1 Cor. 1:18, 21, 23; 2:14; 3:19. ¶

NT: B.531b; CB.1259b; K.620.
OT: —.
GEN. REF.: IS.2:331; NB.433; Z.2:581.

2. *aphrosunē* [ἀφροσύνη, 877], senselessness, is translated "foolishness" in Mark 7:22; 2 Cor. 11:1, 17, 21, "foolishness," R.V. (A.V., "folly" and "foolishly"). See FOLLY. ¶

NT: B.127d; CB.1236c; K.1277.
OT: 'iwwelet: S.200; HR.186b.1; H.44c; BD.17c.
nebālāh: S.5039; HR.186b.3; H.1285b; BD.615a.
sikelût: S.5531; HR.186b.4b; H.1493c,d; BD.698b.
GEN. REF.: IS.2:331; NB.433; Z.2:581.

Note: Mōrologia denotes foolish talking, Eph. 5:4. See TALKING. ¶

FOOT, FEET

A. Nouns.

1. *pous* [πούς, 4228], besides its literal meaning, is used, by metonymy, of a person in motion, Luke 1:79; Acts 5:9; Rom. 3:15; 10:15; Heb. 12:13. It is used in phrases expressing subjection, 1 Cor. 15:27, R.V.; of the humility and receptivity of discipleship, Luke 10:39; Acts 22:3; of obeisance and worship, e.g., Matt. 28:9; of scornful rejection, Matt. 10:14; Acts 13:51. Washing the feet of another betokened the humility of the service and the comfort of the guest, and was a feature of hospitality, Luke 7:38; John 13:5; 1 Tim. 5:10 (here figuratively).

NT: B.696c; CB.1266b; K.925.
OT: regel: S.7272; HR.1198b.6a; H.2113a; BD.919c.
GEN. REF.: IS.2:332; NB.433; Z.2:587.

Note: In Acts 7:5 *bēma*, a step, is used with *podos*, the genitive case of *pous*, lit., 'the step of a foot,' i.e., a foot breadth, what the foot can stand on, "(not so much as) to set his foot on."

2. *basis* [βάσις, 939], lit., a step (akin to *bainō*, to go), hence denotes that with which one steps, a foot, and is used in the plural in Acts 3:7. ¶

NT: B.137a; CB.1238c; K.—.
OT: 'eden: S.134; HR.214b.1; H.27a; BD.10d.
yesôd: S.3247; HR.214b.5; H.875b; BD.414b.
GEN. REF.: IS.2:332; NB.—; Z.—.

B. Adjectives.

1. *podērēs* [ποδήρης, 4158], signifies reaching to the feet, from *pous*, and *arō*, to fit (akin to A, No. 1), and is said of a garment, Rev. 1:13. ¶ In the Sept. it is used of the high priest's garment, e.g., Ex. 28:4.

NT: B.680b; CB.—; K.—.
OT: meʿîl: S.4598; HR.1153c.5; H.1230b; BD.591c.
GEN. REF.: —.

2. *pezos* [πεζός, 3978], an adjective, "on foot," is used in one of its forms as an adverb in Matt. 14:13, and Mark 6:33, in each place signifying 'by land,' in contrast to 'by sea.' ¶

Cp. *pezeuō*, to go on foot, Acts 20:13, R.V., "to go by land" (marg., "on foot").

NT: B.638d; CB.—; K.—.
OT: raglî: S.7273; HR.1114b.1; H.2113b; BD.920b.
GEN. REF.: IS.2:332; NB.433; Z.2:587.

Notes: (1) In Acts 20:18, the R.V. "set foot in" expresses more literally the verb *epibainō* (lit., to go upon) than the A.V. "came into." So again in 21:4 (some mss. have *anabainō* here).

(2) In Luke 8:5, *katapateō*, to tread down (*kata*, down, *pateō*, to tread, trample), is translated "was trodden under foot," R.V. (A.V., "was trodden down").

FOOTSTOOL

hupopodion [ὑποπόδιον, 5286], from *hupo*, under, and *pous*, a foot, is used (*a*) literally in Jas. 2:3, (*b*) metaphorically, of the earth as God's footstool, Matt. 5:35; of the foes of the Lord, Matt. 22:44 (in some mss.); Mark 12:36, "underneath" (in some mss.); Luke 20:43; Acts 2:35; 7:49; Heb. 1:13; 10:13. The R.V., adhering to the literal rendering, translates the phrase "the footstool of My (Thy, His) feet," for the A.V., "My (etc.) footstool," but in Matt. 22:44, "(till I put Thine enemies) underneath thy feet." ¶

NT: B.846d; CB.—; K.—.
OT: hadôm: S.1916; HR.1416c.1; H.474; BD.213b.
GEN. REF.: IS.2:333; NB.434; Z.2:588.

FOR and FORASMUCH:
see Note †, p.1.

For FORBADE see FORBID

FORBEAR, FORBEARANCE

A. Verbs.

1. *anechō* [ἀνέχω, 430], to hold up (*ana*, up, *echō*, to have or hold), is used in the Middle Voice in the N.T., signifying to bear with, endure; it is rendered "forbearing (one another)" in Eph. 4:2 and Col. 3:13. See BEAR. Cp. B, No. 1, below.

NT: B.65d; CB.1235b; K.58.
OT: ʾāphaq: S.662; HR.87a.1; H.149; BD.67c.
GEN. REF.: IS.2:334; NB.—; Z.2:588.

2. *aniēmi* [ἀνίημι, 447], lit., to send up or back (*ana*, up, *hiēmi*, to send), hence, to relax, loosen, or, metaphorically, to desist from, is translated "forbearing" (threatening) in Eph. 6:9 ('giving up your threatening,' T. K. Abbott). See LEAVE, LOOSE.

NT: B.69d; CB.—; K.60.
OT: rāphāh: S.7503; HR.102b.11a,c; H.2198; BD.951d.
GEN. REF.: IS.2:334; NB.—; Z.2:588.

3. *pheidomai* [φείδομαι, 5339], to spare (its usual meaning), to refrain from doing something, is rendered "I forbear" in 2 Cor. 12:6. See SPARE.

NT: B.854d; CB.—; K.—.
OT: ḥûs: S.2347; HR.1426a.1a; H.626; BD.299b.
ḥāmal: S.2550; HR.1426a.2a; H.676; BD.328a.
GEN. REF.: IS.2:334; NB.—; Z.2:589.

4. *stegō* [στέγω, 4722], properly denotes to protect by covering; then to conceal; then, by covering, to bear up under; it is translated "forbear" in 1 Thess. 3:1, 5. See BEAR.

NT: B.765d; CB.1270a; K.1073.
OT: —.
GEN. REF.: IS.—; NB.—; Z.2:589.

Note: In 1 Cor. 9:6, the verb *ergazomai*, to work, is used in the present infinitive, with a negative, and translated "to forbear working" (lit., 'not working').

B. Noun.

anochē [ἀνοχή, 463], a holding back (akin to A, No. 1), denotes forbearance, a delay of punishment, Rom. 2:4; 3:25, in both places of God's forbearance with men; in the latter passage His forbearance is the ground, not of His forgiveness, but of His praetermission of sins, His withholding punishment. In 2:4 it represents a suspense of wrath which must eventually be exercised unless the sinner accepts God's conditions; in 3:25 it is connected with the passing over of sins in times past, previous to the atoning work of Christ. ¶

NT: B.72c; CB.1235c; K.58.
OT: —.
GEN. REF.: IS.2:334; NB.—; Z.2:588.

Note: Cp. the noun *epieikeia*, Acts 24:4, "clemency"; 2 Cor. 10:1, "gentleness." Synonymous with this are *makrothumia*, longsuffering, and *hupomonē*, patience (see Col. 1:11). *Anochē* and *makrothumia* are used together in Rom. 2:4. See also Eph. 4:2 (where A, No. 1, is used in this combination). Trench (Syn.) and Abbott-Smith (Lex.) state that *hupomonē* expresses patience with regard to adverse things, *makrothumia* patience with regard to antagonistic persons. It must be observed, however, that in Heb. 6:15 the verb *makrothumeō* is used of Abraham's patience under the pressure of trying circumstances (cp. also Jas. 5:7, 8). *Makrothumia* and *hupomonē* are often found together, e.g., 2 Cor. 6:4 and 6; 2 Tim. 3:10.

"Longsuffering is that quality of self-restraint in the face of provocation which does not hastily retaliate or promptly punish; it is the opposite of anger and is associated with mercy, and is used of God, Ex. 34:6, Sept.; Rom. 2:4; 1 Pet. 3:20. Patience is the quality that does not surrender to circumstances or succumb under trial; it is the opposite of despondency and is associated with hope, in 1 Thess. 1:3; it is not used of God."*

C. Adjectives.

1. *anexikakos* [ἀνεξίκακος, 420], denotes patiently forbearing evil, lit., 'patient of wrong,' (from *anechō*, A, No. 1 and *kakos*, evil), enduring; it is rendered "forbearing" in 2 Tim. 2:24. ¶

NT: B.65a; CB.—; K.391.
OT: —.
GEN. REF.: IS.2:334; NB.—; Z.—.

2. *epieikēs* [ἐπιεικής, 1933], an adjective (from *epi*, used intensively, and *eikos*, reasonable), is used as a noun with the article in Phil. 4:5, and translated "forbearance" in the R.V.; A.V., "moderation," R.V., marg., "gentleness," 'sweet reasonableness' (Matthew Arnold). See GENTLE.

NT: B.292c; CB.1245c; K.243.
OT: sallāḥ: S.5546; HR.519c.1; H.1505a; BD.699c.
GEN. REF.: —.

FORBID, FORBADE

A. Verb.

kōluō [κωλύω, 2967], to hinder, restrain, withhold, forbid (akin to *kolos*, docked, lopped, clipped), is most usually translated to forbid, often an inferior rendering to that of hindering or restraining, e.g., 1 Thess. 2:16; Luke 23:2; 2 Pet. 2:16, where the R.V. has "stayed"; in Acts 10:47 "forbid." In Luke 6:29, the R.V. has "withhold not (thy coat also)." See HINDER, KEEP, *Note* (7), STAY, SUFFER, A, *Note* (3), WITHHOLD, WITHSTAND, No. 1.

NT: B.461b; CB.1255c; K.—.
OT: kālā': S.3607; HR.839b.1; H.980; BD.476b.
māna': S.4513; HR.839b.3; H.1216; BD.586a.
GEN. REF.: IS.2:334; NB.—; Z.—.

Notes: (1) The strengthened form *diakōluō* (*dia*, through, used intensively) is used in Matt. 3:14, where, for the A.V., "forbad" the R.V. has "would have hindered him" ["forbad" is unsuitable with reference to the natural and persistent (*dia*) effort to prevent Christ from being baptized.] ¶

(2) The phrase *mē genoito*, lit., 'let it not be' (*mē*, negative, and *ginomai*, to become), is idiomatically translated "God forbid" in Luke 20:16; Rom. 3:4, 6, 31; 6:2, 15; 7:7, 13; 9:14; 11:1, 11; 1 Cor. 6:15; Gal. 2:17; 3:21, and in the A.V. of 6:14; here the R.V. has "far be it from me (to glory)," which the American R.V. uses in the O.T. In Paul's Epistles it is almost entirely used to express the Apostle's repudiation of an inference which he apprehends may be drawn from his argument.

B. Adverb.

akōlutōs [ἀκωλύτως, 209], without hindrance (*a*, negative, and A, No. 1), is translated "none forbidding him," in Acts 28:31. From the 2nd century A.D. onwards the word is found constantly in legal documents (Moulton and Milligan, Vocab., who draw attention to the triumphant note on which the word brings the Acts to a close). ¶

NT: B.34b; CB.—; K.—.
OT: —.
GEN. REF.: —.

FORCE

A. Adjective.

bebaios [βέβαιος, 949], firm, secure, is translated "of force" (present usage would translate it 'in force') in Heb. 9:17, of a testament, or covenant, in relation to a death. See FIRM.

NT: B.138c; CB.1239a; K.103.
OT: —.
GEN. REF.: —.

B. Verb.

1. *harpazō* [ἁρπάζω, 726], to snatch away, carry off by force, is used in the next sentence in Matt. 11:12, to that referred to under No. 1, "men of violence (A.V. 'the violent') take it by force," the meaning being, as determined by the preceding clause, that those who are possessed of eagerness and zeal, instead of yielding to the opposition of religious foes, such as the Scribes and Pharisees, press their way into the Kingdom, so as to possess themselves of it. It is elsewhere similarly rendered in John 6:15, of those who attempted to seize the Lord, and in Acts 23:10, of the chief captain's command to the soldiers to rescue Paul. See CATCH, PLUCK, PULL. Cp. *diarpazō*, to plunder, e.g., Matt. 12:29, and *sunarpazō*, to seize and carry away, e.g., Acts 6:12, and *harpax*, rapacious, ravening, e.g., Matt. 7:15.

NT: B.109a; CB.1249b; K.80.
OT: gāzal: S.1497; HR.160a.1; H.337; BD.159d.
ṭāraph: S.2963; HR.160a.3a; H.827; BD.382d.
GEN. REF.: IS.2:334; NB.—; Z.—.

Notes: (1) *Biazō*, to force (from *bia*, force), is used in the Passive Voice in Matt. 11:12, of the Kingdom of Heaven as 'suffering violence'; so in Luke 16:16, "entereth violently into it," here

* From Notes on Thessalonians by Hogg and Vine, pp. 183, 184.

in the Middle Voice, expressive of the special interest which the doer of the act has in what he is doing. This meaning is abundantly confirmed by the similar use in the papyri. Moulton and Milligan (Vocab.) remark that Luke's statement can be naturally rendered 'everyone is entering it violently.' See VIOLENCE.

(2) In Matt. 11:12, the corresponding noun, *biastēs*, violence, is rendered "men of violence," R.V. (see No. 2). See VIOLENCE.

FOREFATHER

1. *progonos* [πρόγονος, 4269], an adjective, primarily denoting born before (*pro*, before, and *ginomai*, to become), is used as a noun in the plural, 2 Tim. 1:3, "forefathers" (in 1 Tim. 5:4, "parents"). See PARENTS. ¶

NT: B.704a; CB.—; K.—.
OT: —.
GEN. REF.: —.

2. *propatōr* [προπάτωρ, 4253, 3962], a forefather (*pro*, before, *patēr*, a father), is used of Abraham in Rom. 4:1. ¶

NT: B.709b; CB.1266c; K.—.
OT: —.
GEN. REF.: IS.2:335; NB.—; Z.—.

FOREGOING

proagō [προάγω, 4254], when used intransitively, signifies either to lead the way, or to go before, precede; in Heb. 7:18, it is used of the commandment of the Law (ver. 16), as preceding the bringing in of "a better hope" (R.V., "foregoing"). See BRING, GO.

NT: B.702a; CB.—; K.20.
OT: nāgash: S.5066; HR.1203b.1; H.1297; BD.620c.
GEN. REF.: —.

FOREHEAD

metōpon [μέτωπον, 3359], from *meta*, with, and *ōps*, an eye, occurs only in the Apocalypse, 7:3; 9:4; 13:16; 14:1, 9; 17:5; 20:4; 22:4. ¶

NT: B.515b; CB.—; K.591.
OT: mēṣaḥ: S.4696; HR.918c.1; H.1233a; BD.594d.
GEN. REF.: IS.2:335; NB.434; Z.2:589.

FOREIGN, FOREIGNER

exō [ἔξω, 1854], an adverb, signifying outside, without, is used in Acts 26:11, R.V., "foreign," for A.V. "strange," of cities beyond the limits of Palestine, lit., 'unto (the) cities without,' including Damascus. See FORTH, OUTWARD, STRANGE, WITHOUT.

NT: B.279b; CB.—; K.240.
OT: ḥûṣ: S.2351; HR.501c.2; H.627a; BD.299c.
GEN. REF.: —.

Note: In Eph. 2:19, *paroikos*, lit., dwelling near (*para*, near, *oikos*, a dwelling), denotes an alien, a sojourner, in contrast to fellow-citizens, R.V., "sojourners" (A.V., "foreigners"); in 1 Pet. 2:11, A.V., "strangers"; see also Acts 7:6, 29. See SOJOURNER, STRANGER. Cp. *allotrios*, e.g., Acts 7:6; Heb. 11:9, 34; *allophulos*, Acts 10:28; ¶ *xenos*, Matt. 25:35, 38, 43; 27:7; Acts 17:21, etc.

FOREKNOW, FOREKNOWLEDGE

A. Verb.

proginōskō [προγινώσκω, 4267], to know before (*pro*, before, *ginoskō*, to know), is used (*a*) of Divine knowledge, concerning (1) Christ, 1 Pet. 1:20, R.V., "foreknown" (A.V., "foreordained"); (2) Israel as God's earthly people, Rom. 11:2; (3) believers, Rom. 8:29; the foreknowledge of God is the basis of His foreordaining counsels; (*b*) of human knowledge, (1) of persons, Acts 26:5; (2) of facts, 2 Pet. 3:17. ¶

NT: B.703d; CB.1266c; K.119.
OT: —.
GEN. REF.: IS.2:336; NB.1024; Z.2:590.

B. Noun.

prognōsis [πρόγνωσις, 4268], a foreknowledge (akin to A.), is used only of Divine foreknowledge, Acts 2:23; 1 Pet. 1:2. ¶ Foreknowledge is one aspect of omniscience; it is implied in God's warnings, promises and predictions. See Acts 15:18. God's foreknowledge involves His electing grace, but this does not preclude human will. He foreknows the exercise of faith which brings salvation. The Apostle Paul stresses especially the actual purposes of God rather than the ground of the purposes, see e.g., Gal. 1:16; Eph. 1:5, 11. The Divine counsels will ever be unthwartable. Cp. FORESHEW.

NT: B.703d; CB.1266c; K.119.
OT: —.
GEN. REF.: IS.2:336; NB.1024; Z.2:590.

For **FOREORDAIN** see **DETERMINE**, No. 3, **FOREKNOW**, A

For **FOREPART** see **FORESHIP**

FORERUNNER

prodromos [πρόδρομος, 4274], an adjective signifying running forward, going in advance, is used as a noun, of those who were sent before to take observations, acting as scouts, especially in military matters; or of one sent before a king to see that the way was prepared, Isa. 40:3; (cp.

Luke 9:52; and, of John the Baptist, Matt. 11:10, etc.). In the N.T. it is said of Christ in Heb. 6:20, as going in advance of His followers who are to be where He is, when he comes to receive them to Himself. ¶ In the Sept., Numb. 13:21, "forerunners (of the grape)"; Is. 28:4, "an early (fig)." ¶

NT: B.704c; CB.1266c; K.1189.
OT: bikkûrîm: S.1061; HR.1206a.1; H.244e; BD.114c.
bikkûrāh: S.1063; HR.1206a.2; H.244f; BD.114c.
GEN. REF.: IS.2:337; NB.434; Z.2:594.

FORESAIL

artemōn [ἀρτέμων, 736], from *artaō*, to fasten to, is rendered "mainsail" in Acts 27:40, A.V.; R.V., "foresail." As to the particular kind of sail there mentioned, Sir William Ramsay, quoting from Juvenal concerning the entrance of a disabled ship into harbour by means of a prow-sail, indicates that the *artemōn* would be a sail set on the bow. ¶

NT: B.110a; CB.—; K.—.
OT: —.
GEN. REF.: —.

FORESEE, FORESEEN

1. *prooraō* [προοράω, 4308], with the aorist form *proeidon* (used to supply tenses lacking in *prooraō*), to see before (*pro*, before, *horaō*, to see), is used with reference (*a*) to the past, of seeing a person before, Acts 21:29; (*b*) to the future, in the sense of foreseeing a person or thing, Acts 2:25, with reference to Christ and the Father, R.V., "beheld" (here the Middle Voice is used). ¶

NT: B.709a; CB.—; K.706.
OT: —.
GEN. REF.: IS.—; NB.1024; Z.—.

2. *proeidon* [προεῖδον, 4308], an aorist tense form without a present, to foresee, is used of David, as foreseeing Christ, in Acts 2:31, R.V., "foreseeing" (A.V., "seeing before"); in Gal. 3:8, it is said of the Scripture, personified, personal activity being attributed to it by reason of its Divine source (cp. ver. 22). "What saith the Scripture?" was a common formula among the Rabbis. ¶ In the Sept., Gen. 37:18; Ps. 16:8 (*prooraō*); 139:3. ¶

NT: B.709a; CB.—; K.706.
OT: —.
GEN. REF.: IS.—; NB.1024; Z.—.

3. *problepō* [προβλέπω, 4265], from *pro*, before, and *blepō*, to see, perceive, is translated "having provided" in Heb. 11:40 (Middle Voice), marg., "foreseen," which is the lit. meaning of the verb, as with Eng. 'provide.' ¶ In the Sept., Psa. 37:13. ¶

NT: B.703c; CB.—; K.—.
OT: rā'āh: S.7200; HR.1205c.1; H.2095; BD.906b.
GEN. REF.: —.

FORESHEW

prokatangellō [προκαταγγέλλω, 4293], to announce beforehand (*pro*, before, *katangellō*, to proclaim), is translated "foreshewed" in Acts 3:18, R.V. (A.V., "before had shewed"); in 7:52, A.V. and R.V., "shewed before." ¶

NT: B.707b; CB.1266c; K.10.
OT: —.
GEN. REF.: —.

FORESHIP

prōra [πρῶρα, 4408], denotes the forward part of a ship, the prow, Acts 27:30; in ver. 41 (A.V., "forepart") in contrast to *prumna*, the stern. ¶

NT: B.725a; CB.—; K.—.
OT: —.
GEN. REF.: —.

FORETELL

prolegō [προλέγω, 4302], with the aorist form *proeipon*, and a perfect form *proeirēka* (from *proereō*), signifies (1) to declare openly or plainly, or to say or tell beforehand (*pro*, before, *legō*, to say), translated in 2 Cor. 13:2 (in the first sentence), R.V., "I have said beforehand," A.V., "I told . . . before"; in the next sentence, A.V., "I foretell," R.V., "I do say beforehand" (marg., "plainly"); not prophecy is here in view, but a warning given before and repeated (see under FOREWARN); (2) to speak before, of prophecy, as foretelling the future, Mark 13:23, A.V., "have foretold," R.V., "have told . . . beforehand"; Acts 1:16 (of the prophecy concerning Judas); Rom. 9:29; 2 Pet. 3:2; Jude 17; some inferior mss. have it in Heb. 10:15. See FOREWARN, SPEAK, TELL.

NT: B.708b; CB.1266c; K.—.
OT: nāgad: S.5046; HR.1207c.1; H.1289; BD.616c.
GEN. REF.: IS.—; NB.—; Z.2:595.

Note: In Acts 3:24 some mss. have *prokatangellō* (see FORESHEW); the most authentic have *katangellō*, R.V., "told."

FOREWARN

prolegō [προλέγω, 4302], with verbal forms as mentioned above, is translated "I forewarn" and "I did forewarn," in the R.V. of Gal. 5:21, A.V., "I tell (you) before" and "I have told (you) in time past"; here, however, as in 2 Cor. 13:2 and 1 Thess. 3:4 (see below), the R.V. marg., "plainly" is to be preferred to "beforehand" or "before" (see under FORETELL); the meaning in Gal. 5:21 is not so much that Paul prophesied the result of the practice of the evils mentioned, but that he had told them before of the consequence and was now repeating his warning, as leaving no possible room for doubt or misunderstanding; in 1 Thess. 3:4, the subject told before was the affliction consequent upon the preaching of the Gospel; in 1 Thess. 4:6, "we forewarned," the warning was as to the consequences of whatsoever violates chastity.

NT: B.708b; CB.1266c; K.—.
OT: nāgad: S.5046; HR.1207c.1; H.1289; BD.616c.
GEN. REF.: IS.—; NB.—; Z.2:595.

Note: In Luke 12:5 the verb *hupodeiknumi*, to shew, teach, make known, is translated "will warn" in the R.V. (A.V., "forewarn"). See EXAMPLE (B, No. 2), SHEW, WARN.

FORFEIT

zēmioō [ζημιόω, 2210], in the Active Voice, signifies to damage; in the Passive, to suffer loss, forfeit, Matt. 16:26 and Mark 8:36, of the "life," R.V.; A.V., AND R.V. marg., "soul"; in each place the R.V. has "forfeit," for A.V., "lose"; Luke 9:25, "his own self" (R.V., "forfeit," A.V., "be cast away"; here the preceding word "lose" translates *apollumi*, to destroy). What is in view here is the act of forfeiting what is of the greatest value, not the casting away by Divine judgment, though that is involved, but losing or penalising one's own self, with spiritual and eternal loss. The word is also used in 1 Cor. 3:15; 2 Cor. 7:9; Phil. 3:8. See CAST, LOSE, LOSS (suffer). ¶

NT: B.338c; CB.1273c; K.299.
OT: 'ānash: S.6064; HR.594c.2; H.1659; BD.778d.
GEN. REF.: IS.2:339; NB.—; Z.2:595.

FORGET, FORGETFUL

A. Verbs.

1. *lanthanō* [λανθάνω, 2990], to escape notice, is translated "they (wilfully) forget" in 2 Pet. 3:5, R.V., lit., 'this escapes them (i.e., their notice, wilfully on their part),' A.V., "they willingly are ignorant of"; in ver. 8, R.V., "forget not," lit., 'let not this one thing escape you' (your notice), A.V., "be not ignorant of." See HIDE, IGNORANT, UNAWARES.

NT: B.466b; CB.1256c; K.—.
OT: 'ālam: S.5956; HR.853a.4; H.1629; BD.761a.
GEN. REF.: —.

2. *epilanthanomai* [ἐπιλανθάνομαι, 1950], to forget, or neglect (*epi*, upon, used intensively, and No. 1), is said (*a*) negatively of God, indicating His remembrance of sparrows, Luke 12:6, and of the work and labour of love of His saints, Heb. 6:10; (*b*) of the disciples regarding taking bread, Matt. 16:5; Mark 8:14; (*c*) of Paul regarding "the things which are behind," Phil. 3:13; (*d*) of believers, as to shewing love to strangers, Heb. 13:2, R.V., and as to doing good and communicating, ver. 16; (*d*) of a person who, after looking at himself in a mirror, forgets what kind of person he is, Jas. 1:24. ¶

NT: B.295b; CB.—; K.—.
OT: shākaḥ: S.7911; HR.524a.3a-c; H.2383; BD.1013a.
GEN. REF.: IS.2:339; NB.—; Z.—.

3. *eklanthanomai* [ἐκλανθάνομαι, 1585], to forget utterly (*ek*, out, intensive), is used in the Middle Voice in Heb. 12:5, of forgetting an exhortation. ¶

NT: B.242b; CB.—; K.—.
OT: —.
GEN. REF.: IS.2:339; NB.—; Z.—.

B. Nouns.

1. *lēthē* [λήθη, 3024], forgetfulness (from *lēthō*, to forget, an old form of *lanthanō*, see A, No. 1; cp. Eng. lethal, lethargy, and the mythical river Lethe, which was supposed to cause forgetfulness of the past to those who drank of it), is used with *lambanō*, to take, in 2 Pet. 1:9, "having forgotten," lit., 'having taken forgetfulness' (cp. 2 Tim. 1:5, lit., 'having taken reminder'), a periphrastic expression for a single verb. ¶

NT: B.472d; CB.1256c; K.—.
OT: shākaḥ: S.7911; HR.875c.2; H.2383; BD.1013a.
GEN. REF.: IS.2:339; NB.—; Z.—.

2. *epilēsmonē* [ἐπιλησμονή, 1953], forgetfulness (akin to A, No. 2), is used in Jas. 1:25, "a forgetful hearer," R.V., "a hearer that forgetteth," lit., 'a hearer of forgetfulness,' i.e., a hearer characterized by forgetfulness. ¶

NT: B.295d; CB.—; K.—.
OT: —.
GEN. REF.: IS.2:339; NB.—; Z.—.

FORGIVE, FORGAVE, FORGIVENESS

A. Verbs.

1. *aphiēmi* [ἀφίημι, 863], primarily, to send forth, send away (*apo*, from, *hiēmi*, to send), denotes, besides its other meanings, to remit or forgive (*a*) debts, Matt. 6:12; 18:27, 32, these being completely cancelled; (*b*) sins, e.g., Matt. 9:2, 5, 6; 12:31, 32; Acts 8:22 ("the thought of thine heart"); Rom. 4:7; Jas. 5:15; 1 John 1:9; 2:12. In this latter respect the verb, like its corresponding noun (below), firstly signifies the remission of the punishment due to sinful conduct, the deliverance of the sinner from the penalty Divinely, and therefore righteously, imposed; secondly, it involves the complete removal of the cause of offence; such remission is based upon the vicarious and propitiatory sacrifice of Christ. In the O.T. atoning sacrifice and forgiveness are often associated, e.g., Lev. 4:20, 26. The verb is used in the N.T. with reference to trespasses (*paraptōma*), e.g., Matt. 6:14, 15; sins (*hamartia*), e.g., Luke 5:20; debts

(see above) (*opheilēma*), Matt. 6:12; (*opheilē*, 18:32; (*daneion*), 18:27; the thought (*dianoia*) of the heart, Acts 8:22. Cp. *kaluptō*, to cover, 1 Pet. 4:8; Jas. 5:20; and *epikaluptō*, to cover over, Rom. 4:7, representing the Hebrew words for atonement.

Human forgiveness is to be strictly analogous to Divine forgiveness, e.g., Matt. 6:12. If certain conditions are fulfilled, there is no limitation to Christ's law of forgiveness, Matt. 18:21, 22. The conditions are repentance and confession, Matt. 18:15-17; Luke 17:3.

As to limits to the possibility of Divine forgiveness, see Matt. 12:32, 2nd part (see Blasphemy) and 1 John 5:16 (see Death). See Forsake, Lay, *Note* (2) at end, Leave, Let, Omit, Put, No. 16, *Note*, Remit, Send, *Note* (1), Suffer, Yield.

NT: B.125c; CB.1236b; K.88.
OT: sālaḥ: S.5545; HR.183b.8a,b; H.1505; BD.699b.
nāsā': S.5375; HR.183b.6; H.1421; BD.669d.
kāphar: S.3722; HR.183b.3; H.1023-1026; BD.497b.
GEN. REF.: IS.2:340; NB.435; Z.2:596.

2. *charizomai* [χαρίζομαι, 5483], to bestow a favour unconditionally, is used of the act of forgiveness, whether Divine, Eph. 4:32; Col. 2:13; 3:13; or human, Luke 7:42, 43 (debt); 2 Cor. 2:7, 10; 12:13; Eph. 4:32 (1st mention). Paul uses this word frequently, but No. 1 only, in Rom. 4:7, in this sense of the word. See Deliver.

NT: B.876c; CB.1239c; K.1298.
OT: nātan: S.5414; HR.1454c.1; H.1443; BD.678a.
GEN. REF.: IS.2:340; NB.435; Z.2:596.

Note: Apoluō, to let loose from (*apo*, from, *luō*, to loose), to release, is translated "forgive," "ye shall be forgiven," Luke 6:37, A.V. (R.V., "release," "ye shall be released"), the reference being to setting a person free as a quasi-judicial act. The verb does not mean to forgive. See Dismiss, Release.

B. Noun.

aphesis [ἄφεσις, 859], denotes a dismissal, release (akin to A, No. 1); it is used of the remission of sins, and translated "forgiveness' in Mark 3:29; Eph. 1:7; Col. 1:14, and in the A.V. of Acts 5:31; 13:38; 26:18, in each of which the R.V. has "remission." Eleven times it is followed by "of sins," and once by "of trespasses." It is never used of the remission of sins in the Sept., but is especially connected with the year of Jubilee (Lev. 25:10, etc.). Cp. the R.V. of Luke 4:18, "release" (A.V., "liberty"). For the significance in connection with remission of sins and the propitiatory sacrifice of Christ, see A, No. 1. See Deliverance, Liberty, Release, Remission. Cp. the different word *paresis*, a passing over, a remission, of sins committed under the old Covenant, Rom. 3:25. The R.V. should be used here. This passing over, or by, was neither forgetting nor forgiving; it was rather a suspension of the just penalty; cp. Acts 17:30, "the times of ignorance God overlooked," R.V.; see also, e.g., Ps. 78:38.

NT: B.125a; CB.1236b; K.88.
OT: yôbēl: S.3104; HR.182b.6; H.835e; BD.385c.
d^{e}rôd: S.1865; HR.182b.3; H.454b; BD.204d.
shāmaṭ: S.8058; HR.182b.11; H.2408; BD.1030c.
GEN. REF.: IS.2:340; NB.435; Z.2:596.

FORM (Noun)

morphē [μορφή, 3444], denotes the special or characteristic form or feature of a person or thing; it is used with particular significance in the N.T., only of Christ, in Phil. 2:6, 7, in the phrases "being in the form of God," and "taking the form of a servant." An excellent definition of the word is that of Gifford: "*morphē* is therefore properly the nature or essence, not in the abstract, but as actually subsisting in the individual, and retained as long as the individual itself exists. . . . Thus in the passage before us *morphē Theou* is the Divine nature actually and inseparably subsisting in the Person of Christ. . . . For the interpretation of 'the form of God' it is sufficient to say that (1) it includes the whole nature and essence of Deity, and is inseparable from them, since they could have no actual existence without it; and (2) that it does not include in itself anything 'accidental' or separable, such as particular modes of manifestation, or conditions of glory and majesty, which may at one time be attached to the 'form,' at another separated from it. . . .

The true meaning of *morphē* in the expression 'form of God' is confirmed by its recurrence in the corresponding phrase, 'form of a servant.' It is universally admitted that the two phrases are directly antithetical, and that 'form' must therefore have the same sense in both."*

The definition above mentioned applies to its use in Mark 16:12, as to the particular ways in which the Lord manifested Himself.

NT: B.528b; CB.1259b; K.607.
OT: zîw (Aramaic): S.2122; HR.934b.1; H.2707; BD.1091b.
tō'ar: S.8389; HR.934b.3; H.2491a; BD.1061b.
tabnît: S.8403; HR.934b.4; H.255d; BD.125d.
GEN. REF.: IS.2:344; NB.—; Z.—.

Note: For the synonymous word *schēma*, see Fashion. For the verb *morphoō*, see Formed, No. 1, below.

2. *morphōsis* [μόρφωσις, 3446], a form or outline, denotes, in the N.T., an image or

* From Gifford, "The Incarnation," pp. 16, 19, 39.

impress, an outward semblance, Rom. 2:20, of knowledge of the truth; 2 Tim. 3:5, of godliness. it is thus to be distinguished from *morphē* (No. 1); it is used in almost the same sense as *schēma*, fashion (which see), but is not so purely the outward form as *schēma* is. ¶

NT: B.528c; CB.1259b; K.607.
OT: –.
GEN. REF.: IS.2:344; NB.–; Z.–.

3. *tupos* [τύπος, 5179], the representation or pattern of anything (for which see ENSAMPLE, is rendered "form" in Rom. 6:17, "that form (or mould) of teaching whereunto ye were delivered," R.V. The metaphor is that of a cast or frame into which molten material is poured so as to take its shape. The Gospel is the mould; those who are obedient to its teachings become conformed to Christ, whom it presents. In Acts 23:25, it is used of a letter, R.V., "form" (A.V., "manner"), with reference to the nature of the contents.

NT: B.829d; CB.1273b; K.1193.
OT: ṣelem: S.6754; HR.1378b.1; H.1923a; BD.853d.
tabnît: S.8403; HR.1378b.2; H.255d; BD.125d.
GEN. REF.: –.

4. *eidos* [εἶδος, 1491], lit., that which is seen (*eidon*, to see), an appearance or external form, is rendered "form" in the R.V. of Luke 3:22, of the Holy Spirit's appearance at the baptism of Christ; in John 5:37, in the Lord's testimony concerning the Father; in Luke 9:29 it is said of Christ Himself; it is translated "sight" in 2 Cor. 5:7, the Christian being guided by what he knows to be true, though unseen; in 1 Thess. 5:22 Christians are exhorted to abstain from "every form of evil," R.V. (the A.V., "appearance" is inadequate), i.e., from every kind of evil. See FASHION, SHAPE, SIGHT. ¶

NT: B.221b; CB.1243a; K.202.
OT: mar'eh: S.4758; HR.375c.1; H.2095i; BD.909c.
tō'ar: S.8389; HR.375c.8; H.2491a; BD.1061b.
GEN. REF.: IS.2:344; NB.–; Z.–.

5. *hupotupōsis* [ὑποτύπωσις, 5296], an outline, sketch (akin to *hupotupoō*, to delineate, *delineate, hupo*, under, and No. 3), is used metaphorically to denote a pattern, example, "form," in 2 Tim. 1:13, "of sound words" (R.V., "pattern"); in 1 Tim. 1:16, "pattern" and "ensample." See ENSAMPLE. ¶

NT: B.848c; CB.1252b; K.1193.
OT: –.
GEN. REF.: –.

FORMED

A. Verbs.

1. *morphoō* [μορφόω, 3445], like the noun (A, No. 1), refers, not to the external and transient, but to the inward and real; it is used in Gal. 4:19, expressing the necessity of a change in character and conduct to correspond with inward spiritual condition, so that there may be moral conformity to Christ. ¶

Cp. *metamorphoō*, to transform, transfigure, *summorphizō* and *suschematizō*, to conform to.

NT: B.528c; CB.1259b; K.607.
OT: –.
GEN. REF.: IS.2:344; NB.–; Z.–.

2. *plassō* [πλάσσω, 4111], to mould, to shape, was used of the artist who wrought in clay or wax (Eng., plastic, plasticity), and occurs in Rom. 9:20; 1 Tim. 2:13. ¶

NT: B.666c; CB.1265a; K.862.
OT: yāsar: S.3335; HR.1140c.3; H.898; BD.427c.
GEN. REF.: IS.2:344; NB.–; Z.–.

B. Noun.

plasma [πλάσμα, 4110], denotes anything moulded or shaped into a form (akin to A, No. 2), Rom. 9:20, "the thing formed." ¶ Cp. the adjective *plastos*, made up, fabricated, feigned, 2 Pet. 2:3. ¶

NT: B.666b; CB.–; K.862.
OT: yēṣer: S.3336; HR.1140b.2; H.898a; BD.428a.
GEN. REF.: –.

FORMER

1. *prōtos* [πρῶτος, 4413], first, is translated "former" in Acts 1:1, of Luke's first treatise; in Rev. 21:4, R.V., "first" (A.V., "former."). See BEFORE, FIRST.

NT: B.725b; CB.1267b; K.965.
OT: ri'shôn: S.7223; HR.1235c.3a; H.2097c; BD.911c.
GEN. REF.: IS.2:345; NB.–; Z.–.

2. *proteros* [πρότερος, 4387], before, former, is translated "former" in Eph. 4:22; Heb. 10:32; 1 Pet. 1:14. See BEFORE.

NT: B.721d; CB.–; K.–.
OT: lᵉpānîm: S.6440; HR.1230c.1a; H.1782a; BD.815d, 816d.
GEN. REF.: IS.2:345; NB.–; Z.–.

FORNICATION, FORNICATOR

A. Nouns.

1. *porneia* [πορνεία, 4202], is used (*a*) of illicit sexual intercourse, in John 8:41; Acts 15;20, 29; 21:25; 1 Cor. 5:1; 6:13, 18; 2 Cor. 12:21; Gal. 5:19; Eph. 5:3; Col. 3:5; 1 Thess. 4;3; Rev. 2:21; 9:21; in the plural in 1 Cor. 7:2; in Matt. 5:32 and 19:9 it stands for, or includes, adultery; it is distinguished from it in 15:19 and Mark 7:21; (*b*) metaphorically, of the association of pagan idolatry with doctrines of, and professed adherence to, the Christian faith, Rev. 14:8; 17:2, 4; 18:3; 19:2; some suggest this as the sense in 2:21. ¶

NT: B.693a; CB.1266a; K.918.
OT: zᵉnûnîm: S.2183; HR.1194c.1a; H.563a; BD.276a.
zᵉnût: S.2184; HR.1194c.1b; H.563b; BD.276a.
taznût: S.8457; HR.1194c.1d; H.563c; BD.276b.
GEN. REF.: IS.2:345; NB.–; Z.2:601.

2. *pornos* [πόρνος, 4205], denotes a man who indulges in fornication, a fornicator, 1 Cor. 5:9,

10, 11; 6:9; Eph. 5:5, R.V.; 1 Tim. 1:10, R.V.; Heb. 12:16; 13:4, R.V.; Rev. 21:8 and 22:15, R.V. (A.V., "whoremonger"). ¶

NT: B.693d; CB.1266a; K.918.
OT: —.
GEN. REF.: IS.2:345; NB.—; Z.2:601.

B. Verbs.

1. *porneuō* [πορνεύω, 4203], to commit fornication, is used (*a*) literally, Mark 10:19; 1 Cor. 6:18; 10:8; Rev. 2:14, 20, see (*a*) and (*b*) above; (*b*) metaphorically, Rev. 17:2; 18:3, 9. ¶

NT: B.693c; CB.1266a; K.918.
OT: zānāh: S.2181; HR.1194c.1; H.563; BD.275c.
GEN. REF.: IS.2:345; NB.—; Z.2:601.

2. *ekporneuō* [ἐκπορνεύω, 1608], a strengthened form of No. 1, (*ek*, used intensively), to give oneself up to fornication, implying excessive indulgence, Jude 7. ¶

NT: B.244d; CB.—; K.918.
OT: zānāh: S.2181; HR.440c.1; H.563; BD.275c.
GEN. REF.: IS.2:345; NB.—; Z.2:601.

FORSAKE

A. Verbs.

1. *kataleipō* [καταλείπω, 2641], a strengthened form of *leipō*, to leave, signifies (*a*) to leave, to leave behind, e.g., Matt. 4:13; (*b*) to leave remaining, reserve, e.g., Luke 10:40; (*c*) to forsake, in the sense of abandoning, translated to forsake in the R.V. of Luke 5:28 and Acts 6:2; in Heb. 11:27 and 2 Pet. 2:15, A.V. and R.V. In this sense it is translated to leave, in Mark 10:7; 14:52; Luke 15:4; Eph. 5:31. See LEAVE, RESERVE.

NT: B.413c; CB.1254a; K.523.
OT: 'āzab: S.5800; HR.736a.11; H.1594,1595; BD.736d.
yātar: S.3498; HR.736a.5a,b; H.836; BD.451b.
GEN. REF.: IS.2:345; NB.—; Z.—.

2. *enkataleipō* [ἐγκαταλείπω, 1459], from *en*, in and No. 1, denotes (*a*) to leave behind, among, leave surviving, Rom. 9:29; (*b*) to forsake, abandon, leave in straits, or helpless, said by, or of, Christ, Matt. 27:46; Mark 15:34; Acts 2:27, 31 (No. 1 in some mss.); of men, 2 Cor. 4:9; 2 Tim. 4:10, 16; by God, Heb. 13:5; of things, by Christians (negatively), Heb. 10:25. See LEAVE. ¶

NT: B.215d; CB.—; K.—.
OT: 'āzab: S.5800; HR.365a.8a; H.1594,1595; BD.736d.
bāgad: S.898; HR.365a.1; H.198; BD.93c.
GEN. REF.: IS.2:345; NB.—; Z.—.

3. *aphiēmi* [ἀφίημι, 863], sometimes has the significance of forsaking, Mark 1:18; 14:50 (R.V., "left"); so Luke 5:11. See FORGIVE.

NT: B.125c; CB.1236b; K.88.
OT: 'āzab: S.5800; HR.183b.9a; H.1594,1595; BD.736d.
GEN. REF.: IS.2:345; NB.—; Z.—.

4. *apotassō* [ἀποτάσσω, 657], primarily, to set apart (*apo*, off, from, *tassō*, to arrange), is used in the Middle Voice, meaning (*a*) to take leave of, e.g., Mark 6:46, (*b*) to renounce, forsake, Luke 14:33, A.V., "forsaketh," R.V., "renounceth" ("all that he hath"). See BID FAREWELL, RENOUNCE, SEND, *Note* (2) at end, TAKE, *Note* (14).

NT: B.100d; CB.—; K.1156.
OT: —.
GEN. REF.: IS.2:345; NB.—; Z.—.

B. Noun.

apostasia [ἀποστασία, 646], an apostasy, defection, revolt, always in N.T. of religious defection, is translated "to forsake" in Acts 21:21, lit., '(thou teachest) apostasy (from Moses)'; in 2 Thess. 2:3, "falling away." See FALL. ¶

NT: B.98a; CB.1237a; K.88.
OT: ma'al: S.4603; HR.141a.2; H.1230; BD.591a.
mered: S.4777; HR.1141a.3; H.1240a; BD.597d.
GEN. REF.: IS.2:345; NB.—; Z.—.

FORSOMUCH: see † p.1

FORSWEAR

epiorkeō [ἐπιορκέω, 1964], signifies to swear falsely, to undo one's swearing, forswear oneself (*epi*, against, orkos, an oath), Matt. 5:33. ¶ Cp. *epiorkos*, a perjured person, a perjurer, 1 Tim. 1:10, "false swearers." ¶

NT: B.296d; CB.—; K.729.
OT: —.
GEN. REF.: —.

FORTH

exō [ἔξω, 1854], outside, without (from, *ek*, out of, from), frequently signifies "forth," especially after verbs of motion, e.g., John 11:43; 19:4, 13. See OUTWARD, STRANGE, WITHOUT.

NT: B.279b; CB.1247c; K.240.
OT: ḥûṣ: S.2351; HR.501c.2; H.627a; BD.299c.
GEN. REF.: IS.2:346; NB.—; Z.—.

Notes: (1) For the word "forth" in combination with various verbs, see, e.g., BREAK, BRING, COME, PUT.

(2) In Matt. 26:16, the R.V. omits "forth," as the phrase *apo tote*, 'from then,' simply means "from that time"; in the similar phrase "from that day forth," Matt. 22:46; John 11:53, there is no word in the original representing "forth."

(3) In John 2:11 the R.V. rightly omits "forth."

FORTHWITH

1. *exautēs* [ἐξαυτῆς, 1824], at once (from, *ek*, out of, and *autēs*, the genitive case of *autos*, self or very, agreeing with "hour" understood, i.e., 'from that very hour'), is translated "forthwith" in the R.V. in Mark 6:25 (A.V., "by and by"); Acts 10;33 (A.V., "immediately"); 11:11 (ditto); 21:32 (ditto); 23:30 (A.V., "straightway"); Phil.

2:23 (A.V., "presently"). The word is frequent in the period of the *koinē* Greek (see Preface). See IMMEDIATELY, PRESENTLY, STRAIGHTWAY. ¶

NT: B.273d; CB.—; K.—.
OT: —.
GEN. REF.: —.

2. *eutheōs* [εὐθέως, 2112], at once, straightway (from the adjective, *euthus*, straight), is translated "forthwith," in the A.V. of Matt. 13:5; 26:49; (it occurs in some mss. in Mark 5:13; the R.V. omits it); Acts 12:10; 21:30 (R.V., "straightway," in each place). See IMMEDIATELY, SHORTLY, STRAIGHTWAY.

NT: B.320b; CB.1247b; K.—.
OT: pit'ōm: S.6597; HR.570b.1; H.1859a; BD.837b.
GEN. REF.: —.

3. *euthus* [εὐθύς, 2117], an alternative adverb to No. 2, is translated "forthwith" in the A.V. of Mark 1:29; 1:43 (in the best mss.), and John 19:34 (R.V., "straightway"). See ANON, IMMEDIATELY, STRAIGHTWAY. ¶

NT: B.321a; CB.1247b; K.—.
OT: pit'ōm: S.6597; HR.571b.2; H.1859a; BD.837b.
GEN. REF.: —.

Note: Parachrēma, a synonymous word denoting instantly, on the spot, is not translated "forthwith" in A.V. or R.V. See IMMEDIATELY.

FORTY

tessarakonta [τεσσαράκοντα, 5062], is used in circumstances in Scripture which indicate the number as suggesting probation, separation or judgment, e.g., Matt. 4:2; Acts 1:3; Heb. 3:9, 17.

NT: B.813a; CB.1271b; K.1172.
OT: —.
GEN. REF.: IS.3:558; NB.—; Z.2:602.

Note: Tessarakontaetēs, forty years (*etos*, a year), is found in Acts 7:23; 13:18. ¶

FORWARD (be), FORWARDNESS

Notes: (1) The verb *thelō*, to will, wish, is translated "to be forward," in the A.V. of 2 Cor. 8:10, which the R.V. corrects to "to will."

(2) In Gal. 2:10, *spoudazō*, to be zealous, is so rendered in the R.V. (A.V., "I was forward").

(3) In 2 Cor. 8:17, the corresponding adjective *spoudaios*, earnest, is so rendered in the R.V. (A.V., "forward"). So in ver. 8, the noun *spoudē*, earnestness, is thus rendered in the R.V. (A.V., "forwardness").

(4) In 9:2, R.V., the noun *prothumia*, "readiness" (*pro*, before, *thumos*, impulse), is so rendered (A.V., "forwardness of mind").

(5) For the combination of this word with verbs see GO, PUT, SET, STRETCH.

FOSTER-BROTHER

suntrophos [σύντροφος, 4939], primarily denotes one nourished or brought up with another (*sun*, with, *trephō*, to rear); it is rendered "foster-brother" in Acts 13:1, R.V. It has, however, been found in Hellenistic usage as a court term, signifying an intimate friend of a king (Deissmann), and this would seem to be the meaning regarding Manaen and Herod the Tetrarch.

NT: B.793c; CB.—; K.—.
OT: —.
GEN. REF.: —.

FOUL

akathartos [ἀκάθαρτος, 169], denotes unclean, impure (*a*, negative, and *kathairō*, to purify), (*a*) ceremonially, e.g., Acts 10:14, 28; (*b*) morally, always in the Gospels, of unclean spirits; it is translated "foul" in the A.V. of Mark 9:25 and Rev. 18:2, but always "unclean" in the R.V. Since the word primarily had a ceremonial significance, the moral significance is less prominent as applied to a spirit, than when *ponēros*, wicked, is so applied. Cp. *akatharsia*, uncleanness. See UNCLEAN.

NT: B.29a; CB.1234b; K.381.
OT: ṭāmē': S.2930; HR.42c.3a-c; H.809; BD.379a.
GEN. REF.: IS.2:355; NB.—; Z.—.

Note: In Rev. 17:4 the best mss. have this word in the plural, R.V., "the unclean things" (*akathartēs*, filthiness, in some mss.).

FOUNDATION (to lay), FOUNDED

A. Nouns.

1. *themelios*, or *themelion* [θεμέλιος, 2310], is properly an adjective denoting belonging to a foundation (connected with *tithēmi*, to place). It is used (1) as a noun, with *lithos*, a stone, understood, in Luke 6:48, 49; 14:29; Heb. 11:10; Rev. 21:14, 19; (2) as a neuter noun in Acts 16:26, and metaphorically, (*a*) of the ministry of the gospel and the doctrines of the faith, Rom. 15:20; 1 Cor. 3:10, 11, 12; Eph. 2:20, where the "of" is not subjective (i.e., consisting of the apostles and prophets), but objective, (i.e., laid by the apostles, etc.); so in 2 Tim. 2:19, where "the foundation of God" is 'the foundation laid by God,' — not the Church (which is not a foundation), but Christ Himself, upon whom the saints are built; Heb. 6:1; (*b*) of good works, 1 Tim. 6:19. ¶

NT: B.355d; CB.1272a; K.322.
OT: yᵉsôd: S.3247; HR.629b.3d; H.875b; BD.414b.
môsād: S.4144; HR.629b.3f; H.875f; BD.414c.
GEN. REF.: IS.2:355; NB.439; Z.2:602.

2. *katabolē* [καταβολή, 2602], lit., a casting down, is used (*a*) of conceiving seed, Heb. 11:11;

(*b*) of a foundation, as that which is laid down, or in the sense of founding; metaphorically, of the foundation of the world; in this respect two phrases are used, (1) "from the foundation of the world," Matt. 25:34 (in the most authentic mss. in 13:35 there is no phrase representing "of the world"); Luke 11:50; Heb. 4:3; 9:26; Rev. 13:8; 17:8; (2) "before the foundation of the world," John 17:24; Eph. 1:4; 1 Pet. 1:20. The latter phrase looks back to the past eternity. ¶

NT: B.409a; CB.1254a; K.418.
OT: –.
GEN. REF.: IS.2:356; NB.439; Z.2:602.

B. Verb.

themelioō [θεμελιόω, 2311], to lay a foundation, to found (akin to A, No. 1), is used (*a*) literally, Matt. 7:25; Luke 6:48; Heb. 1:10; (*b*) metaphorically, Eph. 3:17, "grounded (in love)"; Col. 1:23 (ditto, "in the faith"); 1 Pet. 5:10, A.V., "settle." See GROUND, SETTLE. ¶

NT: B.356a; CB.1272a; K.322.
OT: yāsad: S.3245; HR.629c.3a-d; H.875; BD.413d.
GEN. REF.: IS.2:356; NB.439; Z.2:602.

FOUNTAIN

pēgē [πηγή, 4077], a spring or fountain, is used of (*a*) an artificial well, fed by a spring, John 4:6; (*b*) metaphorically (in contrast to such a well), the indwelling Spirit of God, 4:14; (*c*) springs, metaphorically in 2 Pet. 2:17, R.V., for A.V., "wells"; (*d*) natural fountains or springs, Jas. 3:11, 12; Rev. 8:10; 14:7; 16:4; (*e*) metaphorically, eternal life and the future blessings accruing from it, Rev. 7:17; 21:6; (*f*) a flow of blood, Mark 5:29. ¶

NT: B.655d; CB.1263a; K.837.
OT: 'ayin: S.5869; HR.1130b.5a; H.1612a,1613; BD.745a.
ma'yān: S.4599; HR.1130b.5b; H.1613a; BD.745d.
GEN. REF.: IS.2:356; NB.440; Z.2:604.

FOUR (-TH), FOURTEEN (-TH), FOUR HUNDRED

tessares [τέσσαρες, 5064], four, is not found in the N.T. outside the Gospels, the Acts and Apocalypse; in the last it is very frequent. *Tetartos*, fourth, is found in Matt. 14:25; Mark 6:48 and seven times in the Apocalypse; also in Acts 10:30, "four days ago," lit., 'from a fourth day.' *Dekatessares*, fourteen (lit., ten-four), is found in Matt. 1:17; 2 Cor. 12:2; Gal. 2:1; ¶ *tessareskaidekatos*, fourteenth (lit., four-and-tenth), Acts 27:27, 33; ¶ *tetrakosia*, four hundred, Acts 5:36; 7:6; 13:20; Gal. 3:17. ¶ In Acts 7:6 the 400 years refers to Abraham's descendants and to the sojourning and the bondage. This agrees with Gen. 15:13. In Ex. 12:40 the 430 years dates from the call of Abraham himself. Likewise the giving of the Law was 430 years from the promise in Gen. 12:3, which agrees with Gal. 3:17. In John 11:39 *tetartaios*, lit., 'a fourth day (one),' is rendered "four days."

NT: B.813b; CB.1271b; K.1172.
OT: –.
GEN. REF.: IS.3:558; NB.–; Z.–.

FOURFOLD

tetraploos [τετραπλόος, 5073], an adjective, is found in Luke 19:8. ¶

NT: B.813d; CB.–; K.–.
OT: –.
GEN. REF.: IS.2:357; NB.–; Z.–.

FOURFOOTED

tetrapous [τετράπους, 5074], from *tetra*, four (used in compound words), and *pous*, a foot, is used of beasts, Acts 10:12; 11:6; Rom. 1:23. ¶

NT: B.814a; CB.–; K.–.
OT: b^{e}hēmāh: S.929; HR.1347b.1; H.208a; BD.96d.
GEN. REF.: –.

FOURSCORE

ogdoēkonta [ὀγδοήκοντα, 3589], from *ogdoos*, eighth, is found in Luke 2:37; 16:7. ¶

NT: B.552d; CB.–; K.–.
OT: –.
GEN. REF.: IS.2:357; NB.–; Z.–.

FOURSQUARE

tetragōnos [τετράγωνος, 5068], four-cornered (from *tetra*, see above, and *gōnia*, a corner, or angle), is found in Rev. 21:16. ¶

NT: B.813c; CB.–; K.–.
OT: rāba': S.7251; HR.1347a.1a-b; H.2107; BD.917c.
GEN. REF.: IS.2:357; NB.–; Z.2:604.

For FOWL see BIRD

FOX

alōpēx [ἀλώπηξ, 258], is found in Matt. 8:20; Luke 9:58; metaphorically, of Herod, in Luke 13:32. ¶

NT: B.41d; CB.1234c; K.–.
OT: shû'āl: S.7776; HR.60b.1; H.2433a; BD.1043c.
GEN. REF.: IS.2:358; NB.440; Z.2:605.

For FRAGMENTS see PIECE, No. 4

FRAME (Verb)

1. *katartizō* [καταρτίζω, 2675], to fit, to render complete, is translated "have been framed" in Heb. 11:3, of the worlds or ages. See FIT.

NT: B.417d; CB.1254b; K.80.
OT: kûn: S.3559; HR.743b.3; H.964; BD.465b.
k^{e}lal (Aramaic): S.3635; HR.743b.4a; H.2788; BD.1097a.
GEN. REF.: IS.–; NB.–; Z.2:606.

2. *sunarmologeō* [συναρμολογέω, 4883], to fit or frame together (*sun*, with, *harmos*, a joint, *legō*, to choose), is used metaphorically of the Church as a spiritual temple, the parts being "fitly framed together," Eph. 2:21; as a body, 4:16, R.V., "fitly framed," (for A.V., "fitly joined"). ¶
NT: B.785b; CB.—; K.1114.
OT: —.
GEN. REF.: IS.—; NB.—; Z.2:606.

FRANKINCENSE

libanos [λίβανος, 3030], from a Semitic verb signifying to be white, is a vegetable resin, bitter and glittering, obtained by incisions in the bark of the *arbor thuris*, the incense tree, and especially imported through Arabia; it was used for fumigation at sacrifices, Ex. 30:7 etc., or for perfume, S. of Sol., 3:6. The Indian variety is called *looban*. It was among the offerings brought by the wise men, Matt. 2:11. In Rev. 18:13 it is listed among the commodities of Babylon. The "incense" of Rev. 8:3 should be "frankincense." Cp. INCENSE. ¶
NT: B.473c; CB.1257a; K.533.
OT: l^ebônāh: S.3828; HR.876b.1; H.1074d; BD.526c.
GEN. REF.: IS.2:360; NB.440; Z.2:606.

FRANKLY

Note: In Luke 7:42, the verb *charizomai*, to forgive (as a matter of grace), is rendered "frankly forgave," so as to bring out the force of the grace in the action. Older versions had "forgave," and to this the R.V. returns.

FRAUD

aphustereō [ἀφυστερέω, 575, 5302], to keep back, deprive (*apo*, from, *hustereō*, to be lacking), is used in Jas. 5:4, "is kept back by fraud" (some mss. have *apostereō*, to defraud). The word is found in a papyrus writing of A.D. 42, of a bath insufficiently warmed (Moulton and Milligan, Vocab.). The Law required the prompt payment of the labourer, Deut. 24:15. ¶
NT: B.128a; CB.—; K.1240.
OT: māna‘: S.4513; HR.187b.1; H.1216; BD.586a.
GEN. REF.: —.

FREE, FREEDOM, FREELY, FREEMAN, FREEDMAN, FREEWOMAN

A. Adjective.

eleutheros [ἐλεύθερος, 1658], primarily of freedom to go wherever one likes, is used (*a*) of freedom from restraint and obligation in general, Matt. 17:26; Rom. 7:3; 1 Cor. 7:39, R.V., "free," of the second marriage of a woman; 9:1, 19; 1 Pet. 2:16; from the Law, Gal. 4:26; from sin, John 8:36; with regard to righteousness, Rom. 6:20 (i.e., righteousness laid no sort of bond upon them, they had no relation to it); (*b*) in a civil sense, free from bondage or slavery, John 8:33; 1 Cor. 7:21, 22, 2nd part (for ver. 22, 1st part, see C. No. 2); 12:13; Gal. 3:28; Eph. 6:8; Rev. 13:16; 19:18; as a noun, "freeman," Col. 3:11, R.V.; Rev. 6:15; "freewoman," Gal. 4:22, 23, 30, and ver. 31. R.V. ¶
NT: B.250d; CB.1244b; K.224.
OT: ḥāphshî: S.2670; HR.452b.1; H.717c; BD.344d.
GEN. REF.: IS.3:119; NB.733; Z.3:920.

Notes: (1) In Matt. 15:6 and Mark 7:11, the words "he shall be free," A.V., have nothing to represent them in the Greek.

(2) In Heb. 13:5, R.V., "be ye free from the love of money," is an abbreviated rendering of the adjective *aphilarguros* (not loving money) with the noun *tropos*, turn (of mind); hence the marg., "let your turn of mind be free etc.," for A.V., "let your conversation be without covetousness."

B. Verb.

eleutheroō [ἐλευθερόω, 1659], to make free (akin to A.), is used of deliverance from (*a*) sin, John 8:32, 36; Rom. 6:18, 22; (*b*) the Law, Rom. 8:2; Gal. 5:1 (see, however, under C.); (*c*) the bondage of corruption, Rom. 8:21. See DELIVER. ¶
NT: B.250d; CB.1244a; K.224.
OT: —.
GEN. REF.: IS.3:119; NB.733; Z.3:920.

Note: In Rom. 6:7, the verb *dikaioō*, translated "is freed," signifies to justify, as in the R.V., "is justified," i.e., in the legal sense; death annuls all obligations. The death penalty which Christ endured holds good for the believer, through his identification with Christ in His death; having been crucified as to his unregenerate nature, and justified from sin, he walks in newness of life in Christ.

C. Nouns.

1. *eleutheria* [ἐλευθερία, 1657], liberty (akin to A. and B.), is rendered "freedom" in Gal. 5:1, "with freedom did Christ set us free." The combination of the noun with the verb stresses the completeness of the act, the aorist (or point) tense indicating both its momentary and comprehensive character; it was done once for all. The R.V. margin "for freedom" gives perhaps the preferable meaning, i.e., 'not to bring us into another form of bondage did Christ liberate us from that in which we were born, but in order to make us free from bondage.'

The word is twice rendered "freedom" in the R.V. of Gal. 5:13 (A.V., "liberty"). The phraseology is that of manumission from slavery, which among the Greeks was effected by a legal fiction, according to which the manumitted slave was purchased by a god; as the slave could not provide the money, the master paid it into the temple Treasury in the presence of the slave, a document being drawn up containing the words "for freedom." No one could enslave him again, as he was the property of the god. Hence the word *apeleutheros*, No. 2. The word is also translated "freedom" in 1 Pet. 2:16, R.V. In 2 Cor. 3:17 the word denotes freedom of access to the presence of God. See LIBERTY.

NT: B.250c; CB.1244b; K.224.
OT: huphshāh: S.2668; HR.452b.1; H.717b; BD.344d.
GEN. REF.: IS.3:119; NB.733; Z.3:920.

2. *apeleutheros* [ἀπελεύθερος, 558], a freed man (*apo*, from, and A.), is used in 1 Cor. 7:22, "the Lord's freedman." See the illustration above under No. 1. Here the fuller word brings out the spiritual emancipation in contrast to the natural freedman.

NT: B.83d; CB.1236b; K.224.
OT: –.
GEN. REF.: IS.3:119; NB.733; Z.3:920.

Note: In Acts 22:28, the word *politeia*, rendered "freedom" (A.V.), denotes citizenship, as in the R.V. (see CITIZENSHIP); in the next sentence the Greek is, lit., 'But I was even born'; the necessary word to be supplied is "Roman," from the previous verse; hence the R.V., "But I am a Roman born."

(2) For "free gift" (*charisma*), Rom. 5:15, 16; 6:23, see GIFT.

D. Adverb.

dōrean [δωρεάν, 1432], from *dōrea*, a gift, is used as an adverb in the sense "freely," in Matt. 10:8; Rom. 3:24; 2 Cor. 11:7 (R.V., "for nought"); Rev. 21:6; 22:17. Here the prominent thought is the grace of the Giver. See CAUSE.

NT: B.210c; CB.1242a; K.166.
OT: ḥinnām: S.2600; HR.358c.1; H.694b; BD.336c.
GEN. REF.: –.

Notes: (1) In Acts 26:26 *parrhēsiazomai*, to be bold in speech, is translated, to speak freely.

(2) In Acts 2:29 the noun *parrhēsia* with the preposition *meta*, with, is rendered "freely," lit., 'with free-spokenness.'

(3) For *charizomai*, to give freely, Rom. 8:32; 1 Cor. 2:12, see GIVE.

(4) In 2 Thess. 3:1, A.V., the verb *trechō*, to run, is rendered "may have free course"; this the R.V. corrects to "may run."

(5) For *charitoō*, to bestow freely, Eph. 1:6, see ACCEPT, *Note.*

(6) For "have drunk freely," John 2:10, R.V., see DRINK, B, No. 2.

FREIGHT

ekbolē [ἐκβολή, 1546], lit., a throwing out (from *ekballō*, to throw out), denotes a jettison, a throwing out of cargo, Acts 27:18, lit., 'they made a throwing out,' R.V., "they began to throw the freight overboard," A.V., "they lightened the ship." ¶ In the Sept., Ex. 11:1; Jonah 1:5. ¶

NT: B.238a; CB.–; K.–.
OT: gārash: S.1644; HR.421b.1; H.388; BD.176c.
tûl: S.2904; HR.421b.2; H.797; BD.376c.
GEN. REF.: –.

For FREQUENT, 2 Cor. 11:23, see ABUNDANT, D

FRESH

neos [νέος, 3501], new (in respect of time, as distinct from *kainos*, new, in respect of quality), is translated "fresh" in the R.V. of Matt. 9:17; Mark 2:22; Luke 5:38, with reference to wineskins. See NEW.

NT: B.535d; CB.1259c; K.628.
OT: 'ābîb: S.24; HR.942a.1; H.1b; BD.1.
ḥādāsh: S.2319; HR.942a.3; H.613a; BD.294a.
GEN. REF.: IS.2:361; NB.–; Z.–.

Note: Glukus, sweet, is used in Jas. 3:11, 12 (in this verse, A.V., "fresh," R.V., "sweet," as in both elsewhere); Rev. 10:9, 10. See SWEET. ¶

FRIEND (make one's)

A. Nouns.

1. *philos* [φίλος, 5384], primarily an adjective, denoting loved, dear, or friendly, became used as a noun, (*a*) masculine, Matt. 11:19; fourteen times in Luke (once feminine, 15:9); six in John; three in Acts; two in James, 2:23, "the friend of God"; 4:4, "a friend of the world"; 3 John 14 (twice); (*b*) feminine, Luke 15:9, "her friends."

NT: B.861a; CB.1264a; K.1262.
OT: 'āhēb: S.157; HR.1431b.1a; H.29; BD.12c.
rēa': S.7453; HR.1431b.5b; H.2186a; BD.945d.
GEN. REF.: IS.2:361; NB.441; Z.2:608.

2. *hetairos* [ἑταῖρος, 2083], a comrade, companion, partner, is used as a term of kindly address in Matt. 20:13; 22:12; 26:50. This, as expressing comradeship, is to be distinguished from No. 1, which is a term of endearment. Some mss. have the word in Matt. 11:16; the best have *heterois*, others, A.V. and R.V., "fellows." See FELLOW.

NT: B.314c; CB.–; K.265.
OT: rēa': S.7453; HR.559c.2a; H.2186a; BD.945d.
rē'eh: S.7463; HR.559c.2b; H.2186b; BD.946b.
GEN. REF.: IS.2:361; NB.441; Z.2:608.

Notes: (1) The phrase *hoi para autou*, in Mark 3:21, "his friends," lit. means 'the (ones) besdie Him,' i.e., those belonging to him.

(2) In Mark 5:19, "thy friends" represents the phrase *hoi soi*, lit., 'the (ones) to thee,' i.e., 'thine own.'

B. Verb.

peithō [πείθω, 3982], to persuade, influence, is rendered "having made . . . their friend" in Acts 12:20, of the folks of Tyre and Sidon in winning the good will of Blastus, Herod's chamberlain, possibly with bribes. See ASSURE, B, No. 3.

NT: B.639a; CB.1263a; K.818.
OT: bāṭāḥ: S.982; HR.1114b.2a; H.233; BD.105a.
GEN. REF.: —.

FRIENDSHIP

philia [φιλία, 5373], akin to *philos*, a friend (see above), is rendered in Jas. 4:4, "the friendship (of the world)." It involves "the idea of loving as well as being loved" (Mayor); cp. the verb in John 15:19. ¶

NT: B.859d; CB.1264a; K.1262.
OT: 'ahᵃbāh: S.160; HR.1430c.1a; H.29c; BD.13b.
GEN. REF.: IS.2:361; NB.—; Z.2:608.

FRO and FROM: see † p. 1.

FROG

batrachos [βάτραχος, 944], is mentioned in Rev. 16:13. Quacks were represented as frogs and were associated metaphorically with serpents. ¶

NT: B.137c; CB.—; K.—.
OT: ṣᵉphardēa': S.6854; HR.215a.1; H.1963; BD.862c.
GEN. REF.: IS.2:363; NB.441; Z.2:609.

For FROWARD see CROOKED

FRUIT (bear), FRUITFUL, UNFRUITFUL

A. Nouns.

1. *karpos* [καρπός, 2590], fruit, is used (I) of the fruit of trees, fields, the earth, that which is produced by the inherent energy of a living organism, e.g., Matt. 7:17; Jas. 5:7, 18; plural, e.g., in Luke 12:17 [for the next verse, see Note (1) below] and 2 Tim. 2:6; of the human body, Luke 1:42; Acts 2:30; (II) metaphorically, (*a*) of works or deeds, fruit being the visible expression of power working inwardly and invisibly, the character of the fruit being evidence of the character of the power producing it, Matt. 7:16. As the visible expressions of hidden lusts are the works of the flesh, so the invisible power of the Holy Spirit in those who are brought into living union with Christ (John 15:2-8, 16) produces "the fruit of the Spirit," Gal. 5:22, the singular form suggesting the unity of the character of the Lord as reproduced in them, namely, "love, joy, peace, longsuffering, kindness, goodness, faithfulness, meekness, temperance," all in contrast with the confused and often mutually antagonistic "works of the flesh." So in Phil. 1:11, marg., "fruit of righteousness." In Heb. 12:11, the fruit of righteousness is described as "peaceable fruit," the outward effect of Divine chastening; "the fruit of righteousness is sown in peace," Jas. 3:18, i.e., the seed contains the fruit; those who make peace, produce a harvest of righteousness; in Eph. 5:9, "the fruit of the light" (R.V., and see context) is seen in "goodness and righteousness and truth," as the expression of the union of the Christian with God (Father, Son and Holy Spirit); for God is good, Mark 10:18, the Son is "the righteous One," Acts 7:52, the Spirit is "the Spirit of truth," John 16:13; (*b*) of advantage, profit, consisting (1) of converts as the result of evangelistic ministry, John 4:36; Rom. 1:13; Phil. 1:22; (2) of sanctification, through deliverance from a life of sin and through service to God, Rom. 6:22, in contrast to (3) the absence of anything regarded as advantageous as the result of former sins, ver. 21; (4) of the reward for ministration to servants of God, Phil. 4:17; (5) of the effect of making confession to God's Name by the sacrifice of praise, Heb. 13:15.

NT: B.404c; CB.1253b; K.416.
OT: pᵉrî: S.6529; HR.723c.7a; H.1809a; BD.826b.
GEN. REF.: IS.2:364; NB.441; Z.2:609.

2. *genēma* [γένημα, 1096], from *ginomai*, to come into being, denotes fruit (*a*) as the produce of the earth, e.g., the vine; in the following the best mss. have this noun, Matt. 26:29; Mark 14:25; Luke 22:18; [12:18 in some mss.; see Note (1)]; (*b*) metaphorically, as "the fruits of . . . righteousness" (i.e., of material ministrations to the needy), 2 Cor. 9:10. ¶

NT: B.155a; CB.1248a; K.117.
OT: tᵉbû'āh: S.8398; HR.238c.9; H.835h; BD.100a.
pᵉrî: S.6529; HR.238c.8b; H.1809a; BD.826b.
GEN. REF.: IS.2:364; NB.441; Z.2:609.

Notes: (1) In Luke 12:18 some mss. have *gennēmata*, a mistake for *genēmata*; the best have *sitos*, corn.

(2) *Genēma* is to be distinguished from *gennēma*, offspring (from *gennaō*, to beget), Matt. 3:7; 12:34; 23:33; Luke 3:7. ¶

3. *opōra* [ὀπώρα, 3703], primarily denotes late summer or early autumn, i.e., late July, all August and early September. Since that is the

time of fruit-bearing, the word was used, by metonymy, for the fruits themselves, Rev. 18:14. ¶

NT: B.576d; CB.—; K.—.
OT: qayiṣ: S.7019; HR.1004b.1; H.2020a; BD.884c.
GEN. REF.: IS.2:364; NB.441; Z.2:609.

Note: Cp. *phthinopōrinos*, autumnal, in Jude 12, "autumn trees," bearing no fruit when fruit should be expected. ¶

B. Adjectives.

1. *karpophoros* [καρποφόρος, 2593], denotes fruitful (A, No. 1, and *pherō*, to bear), Acts 14:17. ¶ Cp. C. below.

NT: B.405b; CB.—; K.—.
OT: zeraʿ: S.2233; HR.724c.1; H.582a; BD.282a.
pᵉrî: S.6529; HR.724c.2; H.1809a; BD.826b.
GEN. REF.: IS.2:364; NB.441; Z.2:609.

2. *akarpos* [ἄκαρπος, 175], unfruitful (*a*, negative, and A, No. 1), is used figuratively (*a*) of "the word of the Kingdom," rendered unfruitful in the case of those influenced by the cares of the world and the deceitfulness of riches, Matt. 13:22; Mark 4:19; (*b*) of the understanding of one praying with a "tongue," which effected no profit to the church without an interpretation of it, 1 Cor. 14:14; (*c*) of the works of darkness, Eph. 5:11; (*d*) of believers who fail "to maintain good works," indicating the earning of one's living so as to do good works to others, Tit. 3:14; of the effects of failing to supply in one's faith the qualities of virtue, knowledge, temperance, patience, godliness, love of the brethren, and love, 2 Pet. 1:8. In Jude 12 it is rendered "without fruit," of ungodly men, who oppose the Gospel while pretending to uphold it, depicted as "autumn trees" (see Note under A, No. 3). ¶ In the Sept., Jer. 2:6. ¶

NT: B.29d; CB.1234a; K.416.
OT: ṣalmāwet: S.6757; HR.43c.1; H.1921b; BD.853c.
GEN. REF.: IS.2:364; NB.441; Z.2:609.

C. Verb.

karpophoreō [καρποφορέω, 2592], to bear or bring forth fruit (see B, No. 1), is used (*a*) in the natural sense, of the fruit of the earth, Mark 4:28; (*b*) metaphorically, of conduct, or that which takes effect in conduct, Matt. 13;23; Mark 4:20; Luke 8:15; Rom. 7:4, 5 (the latter, of evil fruit, borne "unto death," of activities resulting from a state of alienation from God); Col. 1:6, in the Middle Voice; Col. 1:10. ¶

NT: B.405a; CB.1253b; K.416.
OT: pāraḥ: S.6524; HR.724c.1; H.1813-1815; BD.827a.
GEN. REF.: IS.2:364; NB.441; Z.2:609.

Note: For "bring forth fruit to perfection," Luke 8:14, see PERFECTION, B.

For **FRUSTRATE**, Gal. 2:21, see **VOID**

FULFIL, FULFILLING, FULFILMENT

A. Verbs.

1. *plēroō* [πληρόω, 4137], signifies (1) to fill (see FILL); (2) to fulfil, complete, (*a*) of time, e.g., Mark 1:15; Luke 21:24; John 7:8 (A.V., "full come"); Acts 7:23, R.V., "he was well-nigh forty years old" (A.V., "was full" etc.), lit., 'the time of forty years was fulfilled to him'; ver. 30, A.V., "were expired"; 9:23; 24:27 (A.V., "after two years"; R.V., "when two years were fulfilled"); (*b*) of number, Rev. 6:11; (*c*) of good pleasure, 2 Thess. 1:11; (*d*) of joy, Phil. 2:2; in the Passive Voice, 'to be fulfilled,' John 3:29 and 17:13; in the following the verb is rendered "fulfilled" in the R.V., for the A.V., "full," John 15:11; 16:24; 1 John 1:4; 2 John 12; (*e*) of obedience, 2 Cor. 10:6; (*f*) of works, Rev. 3:2; (*g*) of the future Passover, Luke 22:16; (*h*) of sayings, prophecies, etc., e.g., Matt. 1:22 (twelve times in Matt., two in Mark, four in Luke, eight in John, two in Acts); Jas. 2:23; in Col. 1:25 the word signifies to preach fully, to complete the ministry of the Gospel appointed. See FILL.

NT: B.670c; CB.1265b; K.867.
OT: mālēʾ: S.4390; HR.1147c.2a-c; H.1195; BD.569d.
GEN. REF.: IS.2:366; NB.442; Z.2:611.

2. *anaplēroō* [ἀναπληρόω, 378], to fill up, fill completely (*ana*, up, up to, and No. 1), is used (*a*) of Isaiah's prophecy of Israel's rejection of God, fulfilled in the rejection of His Son, Matt. 13;14; (*b*) of the status of a person in a church, R.V., "filleth the place," for A.V., "occupieth the room," 1 Cor. 14:16; (*c*) of an adequate supply of service, 1 Cor. 16:17, "supplied"; Phil. 2:30, "to supply"; (*d*) of sins, 1 Thess. 2:16; (*e*) of the law of Christ, Gal. 6:2. See FILL, OCCUPY, SUPPLY. ¶

NT: B.59c; CB.1235b; K.867.
OT: mālēʾ: S.4390; HR.81b.1; H.1195; BD.569d.
GEN. REF.: IS.2:366; NB.442; Z.2:611.

3. *teleō* [τελέω, 5055], to end (akin to *telos*, an end), signifies, among its various meanings, to give effect to, and is translated "fulfil," of the Law, intentionally, Jas. 2:8, or unconsciously, Rom. 2:27; of the prophetic Scriptures concerning the Death of Christ, Acts 13:29; prohibitively, of the lust of the flesh, Gal. 5:16. See ACCOMPLISH, FINISH.

NT: B.810d; CB.1271b; K.1161.
OT: kālāh: S.3615; HR.1342c.3; H.982-984; BD.477b.
GEN. REF.: IS.2:364; NB.—; Z.2:611.

Notes: (1) In regard to this word in Rev. 15:1 and 8, the R.V., "finished," corrects the A.V., "filled up," and "fulfilled," as the judgments there indicated finish the whole series of those consisting of the wrath of God; so in 20:3, of the thousand years of the Millennium (cp. vv. 5, 7).

(2) In 17:17, the R.V. has "should be accomplished," for A.V., "shall be fulfilled."

(3) In Luke 22:37 the A.V. has "be accomplished" (R.V., "be fulfilled").

4. *sunteleō* [συντελέω, 4931], to complete, is translated "fulfilled" in the A.V. of Mark 13:4 (R.V., "accomplished"). See COMPLETE.

NT: B.792a; CB.1271a; K.1161.
OT: kālāh: S.3615; HR.1319b.7a,b; H.982-984; BD.477b.
tāmam: S.8552; HR.1319b.16; H.2522; BD.1070b.
GEN. REF.: IS.2:364; NB.—; Z.2:611.

5. *teleioō* [τελειόω, 5048], to bring to an end, fulfil, is rendered to fulfil, of days, Luke 2:43; of the Scripture, John 19:28. See FINISH.

NT: B.809d; CB.1271b; K.1161.
OT: mālē': S.4390; HR.1343a.3; H.1195; BD.569d.
tāmam: S.8552; HR.1343a.7; H.2522; BD.1070d.
GEN. REF.: IS.2:364; NB.—; Z.2:611.

6. *plērophoreō* [πληροφορέω, 4135], to bring in full measure, from *plēroō* (see No. 1), and *phoreō*, to bring; hence, to fulfil, of circumstances relating to Christ, Luke 1:1, R.V., "have been fulfilled" (A.V. "are most surely believed"); of evangelical ministry, 2 Tim. 4:5, "fulfil" (A.V., "make full proof"); so in ver. 17, R.V., "fully proclaimed" (A.V., "fully known"). See ASSURE, PERSUADE.

NT: B.670b; CB.1265b; K.867.
OT: mālē': S.4390; HR.1148b.1; H.1195; BD.569d.
GEN. REF.: IS.2:364; NB.—; Z.2:611.

7. *ekplēroō* [ἐκπληρόω, 1603], a strengthened form of No. 1, occurs in Acts 13:33. ¶

NT: B.244a; CB.1243c; K.867.
OT: —.
GEN. REF.: IS.2:364; NB.—; Z.2:611.

Notes: (1) *Poieō*, to do, is so rendered in the R.V., for A.V. "fulfil," in Acts 13;22; Eph. 2:3; Rev. 17:17 [for the end of this verse see *Note* (2) under *teleō*, above].

(2) *Ginomai*, to become, to take place, is rendered "fulfilled" in the A.V. of Matt. 5:18; 24:34; Luke 21:32, R.V., "accomplished," in each place.

B. Nouns.

1. *plērōma* [πλήρωμα, 4138], stands for the result of the action expressed in *pleroō*, to fill. It is used to signify (*a*) that which has been completed, the complement, fulness, e.g., John 1:16; Eph. 1:23; some suggest that the "fulness" here points to the Body as the filled receptacle of the power of Christ (words terminating in —*ma* are frequently concrete in character; cp. *dikaiōma* in Rom. 5:18, act of righteousness); in Mark 8:20 the rendering "basketfuls" (R.V.) represents the plural of this word, lit., 'the fulnesses of (how many baskets)'; (*b*) that which fills up, Matt. 9:16; Mark 2:21 (see FILL); (*c*) a filling up, fulfilment, Rom. 13:10, of the fulfilling of the Law. See FULNESS (below).

NT: B.672a; CB.1265b; K.867.
OT: m^e^lō: S.4393; HR.1148b.2a; H.1195b; BD.571a.
GEN. REF.: IS.2:364; NB.442; Z.2:611.

2. *teleiōsis* [τελείωσις, 5058], a fulfilment, is so rendered in Luke 1:45, R.V. (A.V., "performance"). See PERFECTION.

NT: B.810b; CB.1271b; K.1161.
OT: millu'îm: S.4394; HR.1343a.1; H.1195e; BD.571b.
GEN. REF.: IS.2:364; NB.—; Z.2:611.

FULL

A. Adjectives.

1. *plērēs* [πλήρης, 4134], denotes full, (*a*) in the sense of being filled, materially, Matt. 14:20; 15:37; Mark 8:19 (said of baskets full of bread crumbs); of leprosy, Luke 5:12; spiritually, of the Holy Spirit, Luke 4:1; Acts 6:3; 7:55; 11:24; grace and truth, John 1:14; faith, Acts 6:5; grace and power, 6:8; of the effects of spiritual life and qualities, seen in good works, Acts 9:36; in an evil sense, of guile and villany, Acts 13:10; wrath, 19:28; (*b*) in the sense of being complete, "full corn in the ear," Mark 4:28; of a reward, hereafter, 2 John 8. ¶

NT: B.669d; CB.1265b; K.867.
OT: mālē' (Adj): S.4392; HR.1147a.2a; H.1195a; BD.570d.
m^e^lō': S.4393; HR.1147a.2b; H.1195b; BD.571a.
mālē' (Vb): S.4390; HR.1147a.2c; H.1195; BD.569d.
GEN. REF.: IS.2:364; NB.442; Z.2:611.

2. *mestos* [μεστός, 3324], probably akin to a root signifying to measure, hence conveys the sense of having full measure, (*a*) of material things, a vessel, John 19:29; a net, 21:11; (*b*) metaphorically, of thoughts and feelings, exercised (1) in evil things, hypocrisy, Matt. 23:28; envy, murder, strife, deceit, malignity, Rom. 1:29; the utterances of the tongue, Jas. 3:8; adultery, 2 Pet. 2:14; (2) in virtues, goodness, Rom. 15:14; mercy, etc., Jas. 3:17. ¶

NT: B.508b; CB.1258b; K.—.
OT: mālē' (Adj): S.4392; HR.913c.1; H.1195a; BD.570d.
GEN. REF.: IS.2:364; NB.—; Z.2:611.

B. Verb.

gemō [γέμω, 1073], to be full, to be heavily laden with, was primarily used of a ship; it is chiefly used in the N.T. of evil contents, such as extortion and excess, Matt. 23:25; dead men's bones, ver. 27; extortion and wickedness, Luke 11:39; cursing, Rom. 3:14; blasphemy, Rev. 17:3; abominations, ver. 4; of Divine judgments, 15:17; 21:9; (R.V., "laden," A.V., "full"); of good things, 4:6, 8; 5:8. ¶

NT: B.153d; CB.1248a; K.—.
OT: mālē' (Vb): S.4390; HR.235c.1a; H.1195; BD.569d.
mālē' (Adj): S.4392; HR.235c.1b; H.1195a; BD.570d.
GEN. REF.: IS.2:364; NB.—; Z.2:611.

Notes: (1) *Gemizō* (see FILL, A, No. 9) is always rendered to fill in R.V.

(2) For Acts 2:13, A.V., see FILL, No. 11.

(3) For "fullgrown," Heb. 5:14, R.V. see Age, No. 2; for Jas. 1:15, R.V., see Finish, *Note* (2).

FULLER

gnapheus [γναφεύς, 1102], akin to *knaptō*, to card wool, denotes a cloth-carder, or dresser (*gnaphos*, the prickly teasel-cloth; hence, a carding comb); it is used of the raiment of the Lord in Mark 9:3. ¶

NT: B.162d; CB.–; K.–.
OT: kābas: S.3526; HR.272c.1; H.946; BD.460a.
GEN. REF.: IS.2:370; NB.93; Z.2:613.

FULLGROWN: see AGE, B, No. 2, FINISH, *Note* (2)

FULLY: see ASSURED, COME, KNOW, PERSUADE, PREACH, RIPE

FULNESS

plerōma [πλήρωμα, 4138], denotes fulness, that of which a thing is full; it is thus used of the grace and truth manifested in Christ, John 1:16; of all His virtues and excellencies, Eph. 4:13; "the blessing of Christ," Rom. 15:29, R.V. (not as A.V.); the conversion and restoration of Israel, Rom. 11:12; the completion of the number of Gentiles who receive blessing through the Gospel, ver. 25; the complete products of the earth, 1 Cor. 10:26; the end of an appointed period, Gal. 4:4; Eph. 1:10; God, in the completeness of His Being, Eph. 3:19; Col. 1:19; 2:9; the Church as the complement of Christ, Eph. 1:23. In Mark 6:43, "basketfuls," R.V., is, lit., 'fulnesses of baskets.' For Matt. 9:16; Mark 2:21 see Fill, (B); for 8:20 see Fulfil, B.

NT: B.672a; CB.1265b; K.867.
OT: m^{e}lō’: S.4393; HR.1148b.2; H.1195b; BD.571a.
GEN. REF.: IS.2:369; NB.442; Z.2:611.

Note: For *plērophoria*, "fulness," Heb. 6:11, R.V., see Assurance.

FURLONG

stadion [στάδιον, 4712], denotes (*a*) a stadium, i.e., a measure of length, 600 Greek feet, or one-eighth of a Roman mile, Matt. 14:24 (in the best mss.); Luke 24:13; John 6:19; 11:18; Rev. 14:20; 21:16; (*b*) a race course, the length of the Olympic course, 1 Cor. 9:24. ¶

NT: B.764a; CB.–; K.–.
OT: –.
GEN. REF.: IS.2:371; NB.1324; Z.5:915.

FURNACE

kaminos [κάμινος, 2575], an oven, furnace, kiln (whence Lat. *caminus*, Eng., chimney), used for smelting, or for burning earthenware, occurs in Matt. 13:42, 50; Rev. 1:15; 9:2. ¶

NT: B.401d; CB.–; K.–.
OT: ’attûn (Aramaic): S.861; HR.718a.1; H.2619; BD.1083c.
kûr: S.3564; HR.718a.4; H.967b; BD.468b.
GEN. REF.: IS.2:371; NB.443; Z.2:613.

FURNISH

1. *strōnnumi* [στρώννυμι, 4766], or *strōnnuō*, to spread, is used of furnishing a room, Mark 14:15; Luke 22:12; of making a bed, Acts 9:34; in Matt. 21:8; Mark 11:8, "spread" (A.V., "strawed," twice). See Spread. ¶

NT: B.771c; CB.–; K.–.
OT: –.
GEN. REF.: IS.2:371; NB.–; Z.–.

2. *exartizō* [ἐξαρτίζω, 1822], to fit out, to prepare perfectly, to complete for a special purpose (*ex*, out, used intensively, and *artios*, joined, *artos*, a joint), is used of accomplishing days, Acts 21:5, i.e., of terminating a space of time; of being "completely furnished," by means of the Scriptures, for spiritual service, 2 Tim. 3:17. See Accomplish.

NT: B.273c; CB.1247c; K.80.
OT: ḥābar: S.2266; HR.490a.1; H.598; BD.287d.
GEN. REF.: –.

3. *plēthō* [πλήθω, 4130 (see *pimplēmi*)], Matt. 21:10, "furnished" R.V., "filled." See Fill, No. 5.

NT: B.658a; CB.1265a; K.840.
OT: mālē’: S.4390; HR.1133b.1a-c; H.1195; BD.569d.
GEN. REF.: IS.2:364; NB.–; Z.–.

FURTHER

1. *eti* [ἔτι, 2089], yet, still, further, is used (*a*) of time, most usually translated "yet," e.g., Matt. 12:46; or negatively, "any more," "no more," e.g., Heb. 8:12; (*b*) of degree, translated "further," or "any further," Matt. 26:65; Mark 5:35; 14:63; Luke 22:71; Heb. 7:11; in Acts 21:28, R.V., "moreover" (A.V., "further"). See Longer, More, Moreover, Still, Thenceforth, Yet.

NT: B.315c; CB.1247a; K.–.
OT: ‘ôd: S.5750; HR.561a.11; H.1576a; BD.728c.
GEN. REF.: –.

2. *porrōteron* [πορρώτερον, 4208], the comparative degree of *porrō*, far off, signifies "further," Luke 24:28. See Far.

NT: B.693d; CB.–; K.–.
OT: –.
GEN. REF.: –.

Note: In Acts 27:28, *brachu*, a little, is rendered "a little further," A.V., (R.V., "after a little space").

FURTHERANCE

Notes: (1) In Phil. 1:12, 25, A.V., *prokopē*, a striking forward (*pro*, forward, *koptō*, to cut), is translated "furtherance"; "progress" in R.V., as in 1 Tim. 4:15. Originally the word was used of a pioneer cutting his way through brushwood. See PROGRESS. ¶

(2) In Phil. 1:5 the R.V. "(for your fellowship) in furtherance of the Gospel," and in 2:22, "in furtherance of the Gospel," are, lit., 'unto the Gospel.'

FURTHERMORE

eita [εἶτα, 1534], which is chiefly used of time or enumerations, signifying 'then' or 'next,' is once used in argument, signifying 'furthermore,' Heb. 12:9. See AFTERWARD, THEN.

NT: B.233d; CB.1243b; K.—.
OT: —.
GEN. REF.: —.

Note: In 1 Thess. 4:1 the A.V. "furthermore" translates the the phrase *to loipon*, lit., 'for the rest,' R.V., "finally." See FINALLY.

G

GAIN (Noun and verb)

A. Nouns.

1. *ergasia* [ἐργασία, 2039], signifies (*a*) work, working, performance (from *ergon*, work), Eph. 4:19; in Luke 12:58, "diligence"; (*b*) business or gain got by work, Acts 16:16, 19; in 19:24, 25, the R.V. adheres to the meaning "business" (A.V., "gain" and "craft"). See CRAFT, DILIGENCE. ¶

NT: B.307c; CB.1246b; K.251.
OT: m^e^lā'kāh: S.4399; HR.541b.1; H.1068b; BD.521d.
GEN. REF.: IS.2:377; NB.—; Z.2:624.

2. *porismos* [πορισμός, 4200], primarily denotes a providing (akin to *porizō*, to procure), then, a means of gain, 1 Tim. 6:5 (R.V., "a way of gain"); 6:6. ¶

NT: B.693a; CB.—; K.—.
OT: —.
GEN. REF.: IS.2:377; NB.—; Z.2:624.

3. *kerdos* [κέρδος, 2771], gain (akin to *kerdainō*, see below), occurs in Phil. 1:21; 3:7; Tit. 1:11. See LUCRE. ¶

NT: B.429c; CB.1255a; K.428.
OT: —.
GEN. REF.: IS.2:377; NB.—; Z.2:624.

B. Verbs.

1. *kerdainō* [κερδαίνω, 2770], akin to A, No. 3, signifies (I), literally, (*a*) to gain something, Matt. 16:26; 25:16 (in the best mss.), 17, 20, 2; Mark 8:36; Luke 9:25; (*b*) to get gain, make a profit, Jas. 4:13; (II), metaphorically, (*a*) to win persons, said (1) of gaining an offending brother who by being told privately of his offence, and by accepting the representations, is won from alienation and from the consequences of his fault, Matt. 18:15; (2) of winning souls into the Kingdom of God by the Gospel, 1 Cor. 9:19, 20 (twice), 21, 22, or by godly conduct, 1 Pet. 3:1 (R.V., "gained"); (3) of so practically appropriating Christ to oneself that He becomes the dominating power in and over one's whole being and circumstances, Phil. 3:8 (R.V., "gain"); (*b*) to gain things, said of getting injury and loss, Acts 27:21, R.V., "gotten." See GET. ¶

NT: B.429c; CB.1255a; K.428.
OT: —.
GEN. REF.: IS.2:377; NB.—; Z.2:624.

2. *diapragmateuomai* [διαπραγματεύομαι, 1281], signifies to gain by trading, Luke 19:15 (from *dia*, through, used intensively, and *pragmateuomai*, to busy oneself, to be engaged in business). ¶

NT: B.187d; CB.1241b; K.927.
OT: —.
GEN. REF.: —.

3. *peripoieō* [περιποιέω, 4046], to save for oneself, gain, is in the Middle Voice in the best mss. in Luke 17:33, R.V., "gain." See PURCHASE.

NT: B.650a; CB.1263b; K.—.
OT: yātar: S.3498; HR.1125c.4; H.836; BD.451a.
GEN. REF.: IS.2:377; NB.—; Z.—.

Notes: (1) In Luke 19:16, A.V., *prosergazomai*, to work out in addition, or to earn in addition, is translated "gained" (R.V., "made"); in ver. 18 the verb *poieō*, to make, is translated in the same way, the English verb "make" standing both for earning and for producing.

(2) In 2 Cor. 12:17, 18, *pleonekteō*, to claim unduly, to overreach, is translated "make a gain of," A.V. (R.V., "take advantage of").

(3) For *ergazomai*, Rev. 18:17, R.V., see TRADE.

(4) In Acts 25:9, R.V., *katatithēmi*, Middle Voice, to lay up for oneself, is rendered "to gain."

GAINSAY, GAINSAYER, GAINSAYING

A. Verbs.

1. *antilegō* [ἀντιλέγω, 483], to contradict, oppose, lit., say against, is translated "gainsaying" in Rom. 10:21 and Tit. 2:9, R.V. (A.V., "answering again"), of servants in regard to masters; in Tit. 1:9 "gainsayers." Moulton and Milligan (Vocab.) illustrate from the papyri "the strong sense of *antilegō* in Rom. 10:21, 'contradict,' 'oppose'." See ANSWER, CONTRADICT.

NT: B.74d; CB.—; K.—.
OT: rîb: S.7378; HR.111a.2; H.2159; BD.936b.
GEN. REF.: IS.2:377; NB.—; Z.—.

2. *anteipon* [ἀντεῖπον, as for *antilegō*], which serves as an aorist tense of No. 1, is rendered "gainsay" in Luke 21:15; "say against" in Acts 4:14. See SAY. ¶

NT: B.74d; CB.—; K.—.
OT: rîb: S.7378; HR.111a.2; H.2159; BD.936b.
GEN. REF.: IS.2:377; NB.—; Z.—.

B. Noun.

antilogia [ἀντιλογία, 485], akin to A, No. 1, is rendered "gainsaying," in Heb. 12:3, R.V., and Jude 11. Opposition in act seems to be implied in these two places; though this sense has been questioned by some, it is confirmed by instances from the papyri (Moulton and Milligan, Vocab.). See CONTRADICTION, DISPUTE, STRIFE.

NT: B.75a; CB.—; K.—.
OT: rîb: S.7378; HR.111b.4a; H.2159; BD.936b.
mᵉrîbāh: S.4808; HR.111b.4b; H.2159c; BD.937b.
GEN. REF.: IS.2:377; NB.—; Z.—.

C. Adjective.

anantirrhētos [ἀναντίρρητος, 368], lit., not to be spoken against (*a*, negative, *n*, euphonic, *anti*, against, *rhētos*, spoken), is rendered "cannot be gainsaid" in Acts 19:36, R.V. ¶

NT: B.58c; CB.—; K.—.
OT: —.
GEN. REF.: IS.2:377; NB.—; Z.—.

D. Adverb.

anantirrhētōs [ἀναντιρρήτως, 369], corresponding to C, is translated "without gainsaying" in Acts 10:29; it might be rendered 'unquestioningly.' ¶

NT: B.58c; CB.—; K.—.
OT: —.
GEN. REF.: IS.2:377; NB.—; Z.—.

GALL

cholē [χολή, 5521], a word probably connected with *chloē*, yellow, denotes gall, (*a*) literal, Matt. 27:34 (cp. Ps. 69:21); some regard the word here as referring to myrrh, on account of Mark 15:23; (*b*) metaphorical, Acts 8:23, where "gall of bitterness" stands for extreme wickedness, productive of evil fruit. ¶ In the O.T. it is used (*a*) of a plant characterized by bitterness (probably wormwood), Deut. 29:18; Hos. 10:4; Amos 6:12; (*b*) as the translation of the word *mererah*, bitterness, Job. 13:26, e.g.; (*c*) as the translation of *rôsh*, venom; in Deut. 32:32 "(grapes) of gall." In Job 20:25, the gall bladder is referred to (the receptacle of bile). The ancients supposed that the poison of serpents lay in the gall (see Job 20:14).

NT: B.883b; CB.1240a; K.—.
OT: rōsh: S.7219; HR.1472a.3; H.2098; BD.912c.
mᵉrōrāh: S.4846; HR.1472a.2b; H.1248f; BD.601a.
mᵉrērāh: S.4845; HR.1472a.2a; H.1248g; BD.601a.
GEN. REF.: IS.2:392; NB.450; Z.2:648.

GAMES, see CONTEND

GANGRENE

gangraina [γάγγραινα, 1044], an eating sore, spreading corruption and producing mortification, is used, in 2 Tim. 2:17, of errorists in the church, who, pretending to give true spiritual food, produce spiritual gangrene (A.V., "canker," R.V., "gangrene"). ¶

NT: B.149a; CB.—; K.—.
OT: —.
GEN. REF.: IS.2:399; NB.—; Z.—.

GARDEN

kēpos [κῆπος, 2779], a garden, occurs in Luke 13:19, in one of the Lord's parables; in John 18:1, 26, of the garden of Gethsemane; in 19:41, of the garden near the place of the Lord's crucifixion. ¶

NT: B.430d; CB.—; K.—.
OT: gan: S.1588; HR.763a.1a; H.367a; BD.171a.
gannāh: S.1593; HR.763a.1c; H.367b; BD.171b.
GEN. REF.: IS.2:399; NB.453; Z.2:652.

GARDENER

kēpouros [κηπουρός, 2780], lit., a garden-keeper (from *kēpos*, see above, and *ouros*, a watcher), occurs in John 20:15. ¶

NT: B.430d; CB.—; K.—.
OT: —.
GEN. REF.: IS.2:400; NB.—; Z.2:653.

GARLAND

stemma [στέμμα, 4725], denotes a wreath (from *stephō*, to put around, enwreath), as used in sacrifices, Acts 14:13. ¶

NT: B.766a; CB.1270a; K.—.
OT: —.
GEN. REF.: IS.2:401; NB.—; Z.2:654.

GARMENT

Note: For *himation*, the usual word for "garment," see CLOTHING, where see also *esthēsis* (translated "garments" in the A.V. of Luke 24:4, R.V., "apparel"), *enduma, chitōn*, and *stolē* (R.V., "robe" in Mark 16:5). The fact of the wedding garment, *enduma* in Matt. 22, vv. 11, 12, indicates that persons of high rank showed their magnificence by providing the guests with festal garments. See APPAREL.

GARNER

apothēkē [ἀποθήκη, 596], a storehouse, granary (from *apo*, away, and *tithēmi*, to put), is translated "garner" in Matt. 3:12 and Luke 3:17. See BARN.

NT: B.91a; CB.—; K.—.
OT: 'ôṣār: S.214; HR.128a.2; H.154a; BD.69d.
GEN. REF.: IS.—; NB.—; Z.2:654.

GARNISH

kosmeō [κοσμέω, 2885], is translated by the verb to garnish in Matt. 12:44; 23:29; Luke 11:25; and in the A.V. of Rev. 21:19. See ADORN.

NT: B.445a; CB.1255c; K.459.
OT: —.
GEN. REF.: IS.2:407; NB.—; Z.—.

For **GARRISON** see **GUARD**, B, No. 3

GATE

1. *pulē* [πύλη, 4439], is used (*a*) literally, for a larger sort of gate, in the wall either of a city or palace or temple, Luke 7:12, of Nain (burying places were outside the gates of cities); Acts 3:10; 9:24; 12:10; Heb. 13:12; (*b*) metaphorically, of the gates at the entrances of the ways leading to life and to destruction, Matt. 7:13, 14; some mss. have *pulē*, for *thura*, a door, in Luke 13:24 (see the R.V.); of the gates of Hades, Matt. 16:18, than which nothing was regarded as stronger. The importance and strength of gates made them viewed as synonymous with power. By metonymy, the gates stood for those who held government and administered justice there. ¶

NT: B.729b; CB.1268a; K.974.
OT: sha'ar: S.8179; HR.1240b.4; H.2437a; BD.1044c.
GEN. REF.: IS.2:408; NB.236; Z.2:655.

2. *pulōn* [πυλών, 4440], akin to No. 1, primarily signifies a porch or vestibule, e.g., Matt. 26:71; Luke 16:20; Acts 10:17; 12:13, 14; then, the gateway or gate tower of a walled town, Acts 14:13; Rev. 21:12, 13, 15, 21, 25; 22:14. ¶

NT: B.729c; CB.1268a; K.974.
OT: petah: S.6607; HR.1242a.2; H.1854a; BD.835d.
sha'ar: S.8179; HR.1242a.3; H.2437a; BD.1044c.
GEN. REF.: IS.2:408; NB.236; Z.2:655.

Notes: (1) In Acts 3:2 *thura* denotes, not a gate, but a door, R.V. See DOOR.

(2) *Probatikos*, signifying of, or belonging to, sheep, denotes a sheep gate in John 5:2, R.V., and A.V. marg.

(3) The conjectural emendation which suggests the idea of "floods" for "gates" in Matt. 16:18 is not sufficiently substantiated to be accepted.

GATHER, GATHERING

A. Verbs.

1. *sunagō* [συνάγω, 4863], to gather or bring together, is said of (*a*) persons, e.g., Matt. 2:4; (*b*) things, e.g., Matt. 13:30; in Luke 15:13 the idea is that of gathering his goods together for sale, i.e., 'having sold off all.' See ASSEMBLE, BESTOW, COME, RESORT.

NT: B.782a; CB.1270b; K.—.
OT: 'āsaph: S.622; HR.1307b.1; H.140; BD.62a.
qābaṣ: S.6908; HR.1307b.34; H.1983; BD.867c.
GEN. REF.: IS.2:414; NB.—; Z.—.

2. *episunagō* [ἐπισυνάγω, 1996], to gather together, suggesting stress upon the place at which the gathering is made (*epi*, to), is said of a hen and her chickens, Matt. 23:37; and so of the Lord's would-be protecting care of the people of Jerusalem, *id.*, and Luke 13:34; of the gathering together of the elect, Matt. 24:31; Mark 13:27; of the gathering together of a crowd, Mark 1:33; Luke 12:1. ¶

NT: B.301d; CB.1246a; K.—.
OT: 'āsaph: S.622; HR.534a.1; H.140; BD.62a.
qābaṣ: S.6908; HR.534a.10; H.1983; BD.867c.
GEN. REF.: IS.2:414; NB.—; Z.—.

3. *sullegō* [συλλέγω, 4816], to collect, gather up or out (*sun*, with, *legō*, to pick out), is said of gathering grapes and figs, Matt. 7:16; Luke 6:44 (cp. No. 5); tares, Matt. 13:28, 29, 30, 40; good fish, 13:48; "all things that cause stumbling, and them that do iniquity," 13:41. ¶

NT: B.777a; CB.1270b; K.—.
OT: lāqaṭ: S.3950; HR.1302b.3; H.1125; BD.544c.
GEN. REF.: IS.2:414; NB.—; Z.—.

4. *sustrephō* [συστρέφω, 4962], signifies (*a*) to twist together or roll into a mass (*sun*, together, *strephō*, to turn), said of the bundle of sticks gathered by Paul, Acts 28:3; (*b*) to assemble or gather together (possibly, to journey about together), of persons, Matt. 17:22 (in the best mss.), R.V., marg. ¶

NT: B.795c; CB.1271a; K.—.
OT: qāshar: S.7194; HR.1323c.7; H.2090; BD.905a.
lāqaṭ: S.3950; HR.1323c.4; H.1125; BD.544c.
qābaṣ: S.6908; HR.1323c.6; H.1983; BD.867c.
GEN. REF.: IS.2:414; NB.—; Z.—.

5. *trugaō* [τρυγάω, 5166], signifies to gather in, of harvest, vintage, ripe fruits (*trugē* denotes fruit, etc., gathered in autumn), Luke 6:44, of grapes (last part of ver.; for the previous clause, as to figs, see No. 3); metaphorically, of the clusters of "the vine of the earth," Rev. 14:18; of that from which they are gathered, ver. 19. ¶

NT: B.828b; CB.1273a; K.—.
OT: bāṣar: S.1219; HR.1377a.2; H.270; BD.130d.
qāṣar: S.7114; HR.1377a.6a; H.2061,2062; BD.894b.
qāṣîr: S.7105; HR.1377a.6b; H.2062a,b; BD.894c.
GEN. REF.: IS.2:414; NB.—; Z.—.

6. *athroizō* [ἀθροίζω, —], denotes to assemble, gather together, Luke 24:33 (according to the best mss.); the word is akin to *athroos*, assembled in crowds (not found in the N.T.). ¶
NT: B.21c; CB.1238b; K.–.
OT: qābaṣ: S.6908; HR.30a.2; H.1983; BD.867c.
GEN. REF.: IS.2:414; NB.–; Z.–.

7. *sunathroizō* [συναθροίζω, 4867], *sun*, together, and No. 6, signifies (*a*) to gather together, Acts 19:25, R.V. (A.V., "called together"); in the Passive Voice, 12:12. ¶
NT: B.783b; CB.1270c; K.–.
OT: qābaṣ: S.6908; HR.1310a.5; H.1983; BD.867c.
GEN. REF.: IS.2:414; NB.–; Z.–.

8. *epathroizō* [ἐπαθροίζω, 1865], to assemble besides (*epi*), said of multitudes, Luke 11:29, is rendered "were gathering together" (Middle Voice), R.V. (A.V., "were gathered thick together"). ¶
NT: B.281b; CB.–; K.–.
OT: –.
GEN. REF.: –.

Notes: (1) In Eph. 1:10, A.V., the verb *anakephalaioō*, to sum up, head up, is rendered "might gather together in one" (R.V., "sum up").

(2) In Luke 8:4, A.V. (*suneimi*, to come together) as "were gathered together" (see R.V.).

(3) For "assuredly gathering" see CONCLUDE.

B. Noun.

episunagōgē [ἐπισυναγωγή, 1997], a gathering together, is used in 2 Thess. 2:1, of the 'rapture' of the saints; for Heb. 10:25, see ASSMBLE.
NT: B.301d; CB.1246a; K.1108.
OT: –.
GEN. REF.: IS.2:414; NB.–; Z.–.

Note: For *Logia*, 1 Cor. 16:2, A.V., see COLLECTION.

For **GAY** SEE **GOODLY**, A, *Note*

For **GAZE** see **BEHOLD**, No. 3

GAZINGSTOCK

theatrizō [θεατρίζω, 2301], signifies to make a spectacle (from *theatron*, a theatre, spectacle, show); it is used in the Passive Voice in Heb. 10:33, "being made a gazingstock." ¶
NT: B.353c; CB.–; K.–.
OT: –.
GEN. REF.: IS.2:419; NB.–; Z.–.

GEAR

skeuos [σκεῦος, 4632], an implement, vessel, utensil, is used of the tackling or gear of a ship, Acts 27:17, R.V. (A.V., "sail").
NT: B.754a; CB.1269a; K.1038.
OT: kᵉlî: S.3627; HR.1269b.1; H.982g; BD.479b.
GEN. REF.: IS.2:420; NB.–; Z.2:666.

For **GENDER** see **BEGET**, No. 1

GENEALOGY

A. Noun.

genealogia [γενεαλογία, 1076], is used in 1 Tim. 1:4 and Tit. 3:9, with reference to such genealogies as are found in Philo, Josephus and the book of Jubilees, by which Jews traced their descent from the patriarchs and their families, and perhaps also to Gnostic genealogies and orders of aeons and spirits. Amongst the Greeks, as well as other nations, mythological stories gathered round the birth and genealogy of their heroes. Probably Jewish genealogical tales crept into Christian communities. Hence the warnings to Timothy and Titus. ¶
NT: B.154b; CB.1248a; K.114.
OT: –.
GEN. REF.: IS.2:424; NB.–; Z.2:673.

B. Verb.

genealogeō [γενεαλογέω, 1075], to reckon or trace a genealogy (from *genea*, a race, and *legō*, to choose, pick out), is used, in the Passive Voice, of Melchizedek in Heb. 7:6, R.V., "whose genealogy (A.V., 'descent') is not counted." ¶
NT: B.154b; CB.1248a; K.114.
OT: yāḥash: S.3187; HR.237a.1; H.862; BD.405b.
GEN. REF.: IS.2:424; NB.456; Z.2:673.

C. Adjective (*negative*).

agenealogētos [ἀγενεαλόγητος, 35], denoting without recorded pedigree (*a*, negative, and an adjectival form from B.), is rendered "without genealogy" in Heb. 7:3. The narrative in Gen. 14 is so framed in facts and omissions as to foreshadow the Person of Christ. ¶
NT: B.8c; CB.1233b; K.114.
OT: –.
GEN. REF.: IS.2:424; NB.456; Z.2:673.

For **GENERAL** (Assembly) see **ASSEMBLY**, No. 2

GENERATION

1. *genea* [γενεά]: see AGE, No. 2.

2. *genesis* [γένεσις, 1078], denotes an origin, a lineage, or birth, translated "generation" in Matt. 1:1. See NATURAL, NATURE.
NT: B.154c; CB.1248a; K.117.
OT: tôlēdôt: S.8435; HR.237a.3d; H.867g; BD.410a.
GEN. REF.: IS.2:431; NB.460; Z.2:678.

Notes: (1) For *gennēma*, translated "generation" in the A.V. of Matt. 3:7; 12:34; 23:33; Luke 3:7, see OFFSPRING. ¶

(2) For *genos*, translated "generation" in 1 Pet. 2:9, A.V., see KIND.

GENTILES

A. Nouns.

1. *ethnos* [ἔθνος, 1484], whence Eng., "heathen," denotes, firstly, a multitude or company; then, a multitude of people of the same nature or genus, a nation, people; it is used in the singular, of the Jews, e.g., Luke 7:5; 23:2; John 11:48, 50-52; in the plural, of nations (Heb., *goïim*) other than Israel, e.g., Matt. 4:15; Rom. 3:29; 11:11; 15:10; Gal. 2:8; occasionally it is used of Gentile converts in distinction from Jews, e.g., Rom. 11:13; 16:4; Gal. 2:12, 14; Eph. 3:1.

NT: B.218b; CB.1246c; K.201.
OT: gôy: S.1471; HR.368b.4; H.326e; BD.156c.
'am: S.5971; HR.368b.13; H.1640a,e; BD.766b.
GEN. REF.: IS.2:443; NB.462; Z.2:696.

2. *hellēn* [ἕλλην, 1672], originally denoted the early descendants of Thessalian Hellas; then, Greeks as opposed to barbarians, Rom. 1:14. It became applied to such Gentiles as spoke the Greek language, e.g., Gal. 2:3; 3:28. Since that was the common medium of intercourse in the Roman Empire, Greek and Gentile became more or less interchangeable terms. For this term the R.V. always adheres to the word "Greeks," e.g., John 7:35; Rom. 2:9, 10; 3:9; 1 Cor. 10:32, where the local church is distinguished from Jews and Gentiles; 12:13.

NT: B.251d; CB.1249c; K.227.
OT: —.
GEN. REF.: IS.2:443; NB.462; Z.—.

B. Adjective.

ethnikos [ἐθνικός, 1482], is used as noun, and translated "Gentiles" in the R.V. of Matt. 5:47; 6:7; "the Gentile" in 18:17 (A.V., "an heathen man"); "the Gentiles" in 3 John 7, A.V. and R.V. ¶

NT: B.218b; CB.1246c; K.201.
OT: —.
GEN. REF.: IS.2:443; NB.462; Z.—.

C. Adverb.

ethnikōs [ἐθνικῶς, 1483], in Gentile fashion, in the manner of Gentiles, is used in Gal. 2:14, "as do the Gentiles," R.V. ¶

NT: B.218b; CB.1246c; K.—.
OT: —.
GEN. REF.: —.

Notes: (1) For the synonymous word *laos*, a people, see PEOPLE.

(2) When, under the new order of things introduced by the Gospel the mystery of the Church was made known, the word *ethnos* was often used in contrast to the local church, 1 Cor. 5:1; 10:20; 12:2; 1 Thess. 4:5; 1 Pet. 2:12.

GENTLE, GENTLENESS, GENTLY

A. Adjectives.

1. *epieikēs* [ἐπιεικής, 1933], from *epi*, unto, and *eikos*, likely, denotes seemly, fitting; hence, equitable, fair, moderate, forbearing, not insisting on the letter of the law; it expresses that considerateness that looks "humanely and reasonably at the facts of a case"; it is rendered "gentle" in 1 Tim. 3:3, R.V. (A.V., "patient"), in contrast to contentiousness; in Tit. 3:2, "gentle," in association with meekness; in Jas. 3:17, as a quality of the wisdom from above; in 1 Pet. 2:18, in association with the good; for the R.V. rendering "forbearance" in Phil. 4:5, R.V., see FORBEARANCE. Cp. B. See PATIENT. ¶ In the Sept., Esth. 8:13; Ps. 86:5. ¶

NT: B.292c; CB.1245c; K.243.
OT: sallāḥ: S.5546; HR.519c; H.1505a; BD.699c.
GEN. REF.: IS.2:444; NB.462; Z.—.

2. *ēpios* [ἤπιος, 2261], mild, gentle, was frequently used by Greek writers as characterizing a nurse with trying children or a teacher with refractory scholars, or of parents toward their children. In 1 Thess. 2:7, the Apostle uses it of the conduct of himself and his fellow-missionaries towards the converts at Thessalonica (cp. 2 Cor. 11:13, 20); in 2 Tim. 2:24, of the conduct requisite for a servant of the Lord. ¶

NT: B.348b; CB.1246a; K.—.
OT: —.
GEN. REF.: IS.2:444; NB.—; Z.—.

B. Noun.

epieikeia [ἐπιείκεια, 1932], or *epieikia*, denotes fairness, moderation, gentleness, "sweet reasonableness" (Matthew Arnold); it is said of Christ, 2 Cor. 10:1, where it is coupled with *praütēs*, "meekness"; for its meaning in Acts 24:4, see CLEMENCY. ¶ Trench (Syn. § xlviii) considers that the ideas of equity and justice, which are essential to the meaning, do not adequately express it in English. In contrast with *praütēs* (meekness), which is more especially a temperament or habit of mind, *epieikeia* expresses an active dealing with others.

NT: B.292c; CB.1245c; K.243.
OT: —.
GEN. REF.: IS.2:444; NB.462; Z.—.

Notes: (1) For *chrēstotēs*, kindness, goodness of heart, rendered "gentleness" in Gal. 5:22, A.V., see KINDNESS. The corresponding adjective *chrēstos* is translated "good," "kind," "easy," "gracious."

(2) For *metriopatheō*, to bear gently with, Heb. 5:2, see BEAR, No. 13.

GET, GOT, GOTTEN

(*a*) *In the sense of acquiring:*

1. *heuriskō* [εὑρίσκω, 2147], to find, is translated "get" in Luke 9:12, of victuals. See FIND.
NT: B.324d; CB.1250b; K.—.
OT: māṣā': S.4672; HR.576c.8; H.2033; BD.592c.
GEN. REF.: IS.2:457; NB.—; Z.—.

2. *ktaomai* [κτάομαι, 2932], to acquire, procure for oneself, gain, is rendered "get" in the R.V. of Matt. 10:9 and A.V. marg. (A.V., text, "provide"); in Luke 18:12 (for A.V., "possess"). See OBTAIN, POSSESS, PROVIDE, PURCHASE
NT: B.455a; CB.1256a; K.—.
OT: qānāh: S.7069; HR.793b.9a-c; H.2039; BD.888d.
GEN. REF.: IS.2:457; NB.—; Z.—.

3. *kerdainō* [κερδαίνω, 2770], to gain, is rendered "have gotten" in Acts 27:21, R.V. (of injury and loss); the word is there used metaphorically, however, of avoiding, or saving oneself from. For the meaning, to get gain, Jas. 4:13, see GAIN.
NT: B.429c; CB.1255a; K.428.
OT: —.
GEN. REF.: —.

Notes: (1) For *pleonekteō*, to get an advantage of (A.V., in 2 Cor. 2:11; R.V., "an advantage may be gained over;"), see ADVANTAGE.

(2) In Rev. 15:2, A.V., *nikaō*, to conquer, prevail over, is translated "had gotten the victory" (R.V., "come victorious").

(3). In Rev. 3:17, R.V., *plouteō*, to become rich, is rendered "I have gotten riches."

(*b*) *In the sense of going:*

1. *exeimi* [ἔξειμι, 1826], to go or come out, is used in Acts 27:43 of getting to land. See DEPART, GO, No. 23.
NT: B.273d; CB.1247c; K.—.
OT: yāṣā': S.3318; HR.495c.1; H.893; BD.422b.
GEN. REF.: IS.2:457; NB.—; Z.—.

2. *hupagō* [ὑπάγω, 5217], to go away, withdraw, is rendered "get," "get . . . hence," in Matt. 4:10; 16:23; Mark 8:33; some mss. have it in Luke 4:8. See DEPART, GO, No. 8.
NT: B.836c; CB.—; K.1227.
OT: hālak: S.1980; HR.1405c.1; H.498; BD.229d.
GEN. REF.: IS.2:457; NB.—; Z.—.

3. *exerchomai* [ἐξέρχομαι, 1831], to come or go out, is translated "get . . . out" in Luke 13:31; Acts 7:3; 22:18. See COME, No. 3, GO (Notes).
NT: B.274b; CB.1247c; K.257.
OT: yāṣā': S.3318; HR.491c.5a; H.893; BD.422b.
GEN. REF.: IS.2:457; NB.—; Z.—.

4. *katabainō* [καταβαίνω, 2597], to descend, is translated "get . . . down," in Acts 10:20. See COME, No. 19.
NT: B.408b; CB.1253c; K.90.
OT: yārad: S.3381; HR.727a.8a; H.909; BD.432c.
GEN. REF.: —.

5. *embainō* [ἐμβαίνω, 1684], to enter, is translated "they got into" in John 6:24 (of boats), R.V. [A.V., "took (shipping)."]. See COME, No. 21.
NT: B.254a; CB.—; K.—.
OT: bô: S.935; HR.455a.1; H.212; BD.97c.
'ālāh: S.5927; HR.455a.3; H.1624; BD.748a.
GEN. REF.: —.

6. *apobainō* [ἀποβαίνω, 576], to go from, is translated "they got out" in John 21:9, R.V. (A.V., "were come to"). See COME, 21 (note).
NT: B.88c; CB.—; K.—.
OT: —.
GEN. REF.: —.

Note: In Acts 21:1, A.V., *apospaō*, to withdraw or part from, is rendered "we had gotten (from," R.V., "had parted (from)." After the scene described at the end of ch. 20, it may well have the force of being reft away (or tearing themselves away) from them. Cp. the same verb in Luke 22:41 ('He was reft away from them'). See DRAW, PART, WITHDRAW.

For GHOST see SPIRIT

GHOST (give up the)

1. *ekpneō* [ἐκπνέω, 1606], lit., to breathe out (*ek*, out, *pneō*, to breathe), to expire, is used in the N.T., without an object, "soul" or "life" being understood, Mark 15:37, 39, and Luke 23:46, of the Death of Christ. In Matt. 27:50 and John 19:30, where different verbs are used, the act is expressed in a way which stresses it as of His own volition: in the former, "Jesus . . . yielded up His spirit (*pneuma*); in the latter, "He gave up His spirit." ¶
NT: B.244b; CB.1243c; K.876.
OT: —.
GEN. REF.: —.

2. *ekpsuchō* [ἐκψύχω, 1634], to expire, lit., to breathe out the soul (or life), to give up the ghost (*ek*, out, *psuchē*, the soul), is used in Acts 5:5, 10; 12:23. ¶
NT: B.247c; CB.—; K.—.
OT: kāhāh: S.3543; HR.446c.1; H.957; BD.462c.
GEN. REF.: —.

GIFT, GIVING

1. *dōron* [δῶρον, 1435], akin to *didōmi*, to give, is used (*a*) of gifts presented as an expression of honour, Matt. 2:11; (*b*) of gifts for the support of the temple and the needs of the poor, Matt. 15:5; Mark 7:11; Luke 21:1, 4; (*c*) of gifts offered to God, Matt. 5:23, 24; 8:4; 23:18, 19; Heb. 5:1; 8:3, 4; 9:9; 11:4; (*d*) of salvation by grace as the gift of God, Eph. 2:8; (*e*) of presents for mutual celebration of an occasion, Rev. 11:10. See OFFERING. ¶
NT: B.210c; CB.1242a; K.166.
OT: qorbān: S.7133; HR.359a.13a; H.2065e; BD.898d.
minḥāh: S.4503; HR.359a.9; H.1214a; BD.585a.
GEN. REF.: IS.2:465; NB.468; Z.2:721.

2. *dōrea* [δωρεά, 1431], denotes a free gift, stressing its gratuitous character; it is always used in the N.T. of a spiritual or supernatural gift, John 4:10; Acts 8:20; 11:17; Rom. 5;15; 2 Cor. 9:15; Eph. 3:7; Heb. 6:4; in Eph. 4:7, "according to the measure of the gift of Christ," the gift is that given by Christ; in Acts 2:28, "the gift of the Holy Ghost," the clause is epexegetical, the gift being the Holy Ghost Himself; cp. 10:45; 11:17, and the phrase, "the gift of righteousness," Rom. 5:17. ¶

NT: B.210d; CB.1242a; K.166.
OT: ḥinnām: S.2600; HR.358c.1; H.694b; BD.336c.
GEN. REF.: IS.2:465; NB.468; Z.2:721.

Note: For *dōrean*, a form of this noun, used adverbially, see FREELY.

3. *dōrēma* [δώρημα]: see BOON.

4. *doma* [δόμα, 1390], lends greater stress to the concrete character of the gift, than to its beneficent nature, Matt. 7:11; Luke 11:13; Eph. 4:8; Phil. 4:17. ¶

NT: B.203c; CB.1242a; K.—.
OT: mattānāh: S.4979; HR.341a.6b; H.1443c; BD.682b.
nātan: S.5414; HR.341a.9; H.1443; BD.678a.
GEN. REF.: IS.2:465; NB.468; Z.2:721.

5. *dosis* [δόσις, 1394], denotes, properly, the act of giving, Phil. 4:15, euphemistically referring to gifts as a matter of debt and credit accounts; then, objectively, a gift, Jas. 1:17 (1st mention; see BOON). ¶

NT: B.204d; CB.1242a; K.—.
OT: mattān: S.4976; HR.344c.2a; H.1443b; BD.682b.
mattat: S.4991; HR.344c.2b; H.1443d; BD.682c.
GEN. REF.: IS.2:465; NB.468; Z.2:721.

6. *charisma* [χάρισμα, 5486], a gift of grace, a gift involving grace (*charis*) on the part of God as the Donor, is used (*a*) of His free bestowments upon sinners, Rom. 5;15, 16; 6:23; 11:29; (*b*) of His endowments upon believers by the operation of the Holy Spirit in the churches, Rom. 12:6; 1 Cor. 1:7; 12:4, 9, 28, 30, 31; 1 Tim. 4:14; 2 Tim. 1:6; 1 Pet. 4:10; (*c*) of that which is imparted through human instruction, Rom. 1:11; (*d*) of the natural gift of continence, consequent upon the grace of God as Creator, 1 Cor. 7:7; (*e*) of gracious deliverances granted in answer to the prayers of fellow-believers, 2 Cor. 1:11. ¶

NT: B.878d; CB.1239c; K.1298.
OT: —.
GEN. REF.: IS.2:465; NB.468; Z.2:721.

Note: In the A.V. of 2 Cor. 8:4 *charis*, grace, is translated "gift." The R.V., "in regard of this grace," adheres to the true meaning, as in ver. 6.

7. *merismos* [μερισμός, 3311], a dividing (from *meros*, a part), is translated "gifts" in Heb. 2:4, "gifts of the Holy Ghost" (marg., "distributions"); in 4:12, "dividing." See DIVIDING. ¶

NT: B.505c; CB.—; K.—.
OT: maḥ^{a}lōqet: S.4256; HR.911c.1a; H.669d; BD.324d.
GEN. REF.: IS.2:465; NB.—; Z.—.

Note: In the A.V. of Luke 21:5 *anathēma*, a votive offering, is translated "gifts" (R.V., "offerings"). ¶

GIRD, GIRDED, GIRT (about, up)

1. *zōnnumi* [ζώννυμι, 2224], or *zōnnuō*, to gird, in the Middle Voice, to gird oneself, is used of the long garments worn in the east, John 21:18;; Acts 12:8 (*perizōnnumi* in some mss.). ¶

NT: B.341c; CB.1273c; K.702.
OT: ḥāgar: S.2296; HR.601a.4a; H.604; BD.291c.
GEN. REF.: —.

2. *anazōnnumi* [ἀναζώννυμι, 328], to gird up (*ana*, up, and No. 1), is used metaphorically of the loins of the mind, 1 Pet. 1:13; cp. Luke 12:35 (see No. 4). The figure is taken from the circumstances of the Israelites as they ate the passover in readiness for their journey, Ex. 12:11; the Christian is to have his mental powers alert in expectation of Christ's Coming. The verb is in the Middle Voice, indicating the special interest the believer is to take in so doing. ¶

NT: B.53d; CB.—; K.—.
OT: ḥāgar: S.2296; HR.77a.1; H.604; BD.291c.
GEN. REF.: —.

3. *diazōnnumi* [διαζώννυμι, 1241], to gird round, i.e., firmly (*dia*, throughout, used intensively), is used of the Lord's act in girding Himself with a towel, John 13:4, 5, and of Peter's girding himself with his coat, 21:7. ¶

NT: B.182d; CB.1241b; K.702.
OT: ḥăgôr: S.2289; HR.300b.1; H.604b; BD.292a.
GEN. REF.: —.

4. *perizōnnumi* [περιζώννυμι, 4024], to gird around or about, is used (*a*) literally, of girding oneself for service, Luke 12:37; 17:8; for rapidity of movement, Acts 12:8; (*b*) figuratively, of the condition for service on the part of the followers of Christ, Luke 12;35; Eph. 6:14; (*c*) emblematically, of Christ's Priesthood, Rev. 1:13, indicative of majesty of attitude and action, the Middle Voice suggesting the particular interest taken by Christ in girding Himself thus; so of the action of the angels mentioned in 15:6. ¶

NT: B.647b; CB.1263c; K.702.
OT: ḥāgar: S.2289; HR.1123b.3a; H.604b; BD.292a.
'āzar: S.247; HR.1123b.1; H.59; BD.25a.
GEN. REF.: —.

GIRDLE

zōnē [ζώνη, 2223], Eng., zone, denotes a belt or girdle, Matt. 3:4; Mark 1:6; Acts 21:11; Rev.

1:13; 15:6; it was often hollow, and hence served as a purse, Matt. 10:9; Mark 6:8. ¶

NT: B.341b; CB.1273c; K.702.
OT: 'abnēṭ: S.73; HR.601a.1; H.256a; BD.126a.
ḥ^{a}gôrāh: S.2290; HR.601a.4b; H.604a,c; BD.292a.
GEN. REF.: IS.2:404; NB.470; Z.2:728.

GIVE

1. *didōmi* [*διδωμι*, 1325], to give, is used with various meanings according to the context; it is said, e.g., of seed yielding fruit, Mark 4:7, 8; of giving (i.e., exercising) diligence, Luke 12:58; of giving lots, Acts 1:26, R.V. (A.V., "gave forth"); of rendering vengeance, 2 Thess. 1:8; of striking or smiting Christ, John 18:22 (lit., 'gave a blow') and 19:3 (lit., 'they gave Him blows'); of putting a ring on the hand, Luke 15:22; of Paul's adventuring himself into a place, Acts 19:31. (In Rev. 17:13 some mss. have *diadidōmi*, to divide). See ADVENTURE, BESTOW, No. 1, COMMIT, *Note* (1), DELIVER, GRANT, MAKE, MINISTER, OFFER, PUT, SET, SHEW, SUFFER, TAKE, UTTER, YIELD.

NT: B.192c; CB.1241c; K.166.
OT: nātan: S.5414; HR.317b.26a; H.1443; BD.678a.
GEN. REF.: IS.2:473; NB.—; Z.—.

Note: In the following the R.V. gives the correct rendering: Acts 7:25, "was giving them deliverance" (A.V., "would deliver them"); Acts 10:40, "gave Him to be made manifest" (A.V., "shewed Him openly"); Rev. 13:14, 15, "it was given him" (A.V., "he had power").

2. *apodidōmi* [*ἀποδίδωμι*, 591], signifies to give up or back, to restore, return, render what is due, to pay, give an account (*apo*, back, and No. 1), e.g., of an account, Matt. 5:26; 12:36; Luke 16:2; Acts 19:40; Heb. 13:17; 1 Pet. 4:5; of wages, etc., Matt. 18:25-34; 20:8; of conjugal duty, 1 Cor. 7:3; of a witness, Acts 4:33; frequently of recompensing or rewarding, 1 Tim. 5:4; 2 Tim. 4:8, 14; 1 Pet. 3:9; Rev. 18:6; 22:12. In the Middle Voice it is used of giving up what is one's own; hence, to sell, Acts 5:8; 7:9; Heb. 12:16. See DELIVER

NT: B.90b; CB.1236c; K.166.
OT: shûb: S.7725; HR.126b.8b; H.2340; BD.996d,998c.
shālēm: S.7999; HR.126b.9; H.2401c; BD.1022b.
mākar: S.4376; HR.126b.3a; H.1194; BD.569a.
GEN. REF.: IS.2:473; NB.—; Z.—.

3. *epididōmi* [*ἐπιδίδωμι*, 1929], signifies (*a*) to give by handing, to hand (*epi*, over), e.g., Matt. 7:9, 10; Luke 4:17; 24:30, here of the Lord's act in handing the broken loaf to the two at Emmaus, an act which was the means of the revelation of Himself as the crucified and risen Lord; the simple verb, No. 1, is used of His handing the bread at the institution of the Lord's Supper, Matt. 26:26; Mark 14:22; Luke 22:19; this meaning of the verb *epididōmi* is found also in Acts 15;30, "they delivered"; (*b*) to give in, give way, Acts 27:15, R.V., "we gave way to it." See DELIVER.

NT: B.292b; CB.—; K.—.
OT: nātan: S.5414; HR.519b.3; H.1443; BD.678a.
GEN. REF.: IS.2:473; NB.—; Z.—.

4. *metadidōmi* [*μεταδίδωμι*, 3330], to give a share of, impart (*meta*, with), as distinct from giving. The Apostle Paul speaks of sharing some spiritual gift with Christians at Rome, Rom. 1:11, "that I may impart," and exhorts those who minister in things temporal, to do so as sharing, and that generously, 12:8, "he that giveth"; so in Eph. 4:28; Luke 3:11; in 1 Thess. 2:8 he speaks of himself and his fellow-missionaries as having been well pleased to impart to the converts both God's Gospel and their own souls (i.e., so sharing those with them as to spend themselves and spend out their lives for them). See IMPART. ¶

NT: B.510d; CB.1258b; K.—.
OT: —.
GEN. REF.: IS.2:473; NB.—; Z.—.

5. *paradidōmi* [*παραδίδωμι*, 3860], to give or hand over, is said of giving up the ghost, John 19:30; of giving persons up to evil, Acts 7:42; Rom. 1:24, 26; of giving one's body to be burned, 1 Cor. 13:3; of Christ's giving Himself up to death, Gal. 2:20; Eph. 5:2, 25. See BETRAY, COMMIT, DELIVER.

NT: B.614b; CB.1262a; K.166.
OT: nātan: S.5414; HR.1058a.16a; H.1443; BD.678a.
GEN. REF.: IS.2:473; NB.—; Z.—.

6. *prodidōmi* [*προδίδωμι*, 4272], to give before, or first (*pro*, before), is found in Rom. 11:35. ¶

NT: B.704c; CB.—; K.—.
OT: nātan: S.5414; HR.1206a.1; H.1443; BD.678a.
GEN. REF.: IS.2:473; NB.—; Z.—.

7. *charizomai* [*χαρίζομαι*, 5483], primarily denotes to show favour or kindness, as in Gal. 3:18, R.V., "hath granted"(A.V., "gave"); then, to give freely, bestow graciously; in this sense it is used almost entirely of that which is given by God, Acts 27:24, "God hath granted thee all them that sail with thee" (R.V.); in Rom. 8:32, "shall . . . freely give"; 1 Cor. 2:12, "are freely given"; Phil. 1:29, "it hath been granted" (said of believing on Christ and suffering for Him); 2:9, "hath given" (said of the Name of Jesus as given by God); Philm. 22, "I shall be granted unto you" (R.V.). In Luke 7:21, it is said in regard to the blind, upon whom Christ "bestowed" sight (R.V.). The only exceptions, in this sense of the word, as to Divinely imparted gifts, are Acts 3:14, of the granting of Barabbas by Pilate to the Jews, and Acts 25:11,

16, of the giving up of a prisoner to his accusers or to execution. See DELIVER, FORGIVE, GRANT.

NT: B.876c; CB.1239c; K.1298.
OT: nātan: S.5414; HR.1454c.1; H.1443; BD.678a.
GEN. REF.: IS.2:473; NB.–; Z.–.

8. *parechō* [παρέχω, 3930], in the Active Voice, signifies to afford, furnish, provide, supply (lit., to hold out or towards; *para*, near, *echō*, to hold); it is translated "hath given" in Acts 17:31; "giveth" in 1 Tim. 6:17 (in the sense of affording); in Col. 4:1, R.V., "render" (A.V., "give"). See BRING, DO, KEEP, MINISTER, OFFER, RENDER, SHEW, TROUBLE.

NT: B.626b; CB.–; K.–.
OT: –.
GEN. REF.: –.

9. *dōreō* [δωρέω, 1433], akin to No. 1, and used in the Middle Voice, to bestow, make a gift of, is translated in the R.V. by the verb to grant, instead of the A.V., to give, Mark 15:45; 2 Pet. 1:3, 4. See GRANT. ¶

NT: B.210c; CB.–; K.–.
OT: nātan: S.5414; HR.359a.2; H.1443; BD.678a.
qorbān: S.7133; HR.359a.3; H.2065e; BD.898d.
GEN. REF.: IS.2:473; NB.–; Z.–.

10. *aponemō* [ἀπονέμω, 632], to assign, apportion (*apo*, away, *nemō*, to distribute), is rendered "giving" in 1 Pet. 3:7, of giving honour to the wife. In the papyri writings it is said of a prefect who gives to all their dues. ¶ In the Sept., Deut. 4:19. ¶

NT: B.97a; CB.–; K.–.
OT: –.
GEN. REF.: –.

11. *poieō* [ποιέω, 4160], to do, is used in Jude 3 of giving diligence (the Middle Voice indicating Jude's especial interest in his task).

NT: B.680d; CB.1265c; K.895.
OT: –.
GEN. REF.: –.

12. *katapherō* [καταφέρω, 2702], to bring down or against (*kata*, down), said of an accusation in Acts 25:7 (in the best mss.), and of being "borne down" with sleep, 20:9, R.V., is used of casting a ballot of giving a vote in 26:10. See FALL, *Note* (8); SINK. ¶

NT: B.419d; CB.–; K.–.
OT: yārad: S.3381; HR.747b.3; H.909; BD.432c.
GEN. REF.: –.

13. *prostithēmi* [προστίθημι, 4369], lit., to put in addition (*pros*, to, *tithēmi*, to put), to give more, is translated "shall more be given," in Mark 4:24 (Passive Voice). See ADD.

NT: B.718d; CB.1267b; K.1176.
OT: yāsaph: S.3254; HR.1221a.4c; H.876; BD.414d.
GEN. REF.: –.

14. *scholazō* [σχολάζω, 4980], to be at leisure, hence, to have time or opportunity for, to be occupied in, is said of 'giving oneself' to prayer, 1 Cor. 7:5; of an "empty" house, 'lying vacant,' Matt. 12:44. ¶

NT: B.797d; CB.–; K.–.
OT: rāphāh: S.7503; HR.1328b.1; H.2198; BD.951c.
GEN. REF.: –.

15. *legō* [λέγω, 3004], to say, is rendered "giving out," of the self-advertisement of Simon Magus, Acts 8:9. See SAY.

NT: B.468a; CB.1256c; K.505.
OT: –.
GEN. REF.: –.

16. *prosechō* [προσέχω, 4337], to turn one's mind to, attend to, is used of giving oneself up to, 1 Tim. 3:8 (to wine); of giving heed to, Acts 8:6, 10, 11 (R.V.); 1 Tim. 1:4; 4:1, 13 (R.V.); Tit. 1:14; Heb. 2:1. See ATTEND.

NT: B.714b; CB.1267a; K.–.
OT: shāmar: S.8104; HR.1215b.19; H.2414; BD.1036b.
qāshab: S.7181; HR.1215b.16a; H.2084; BD.904a.
GEN. REF.: –.

17. *diōkō* [διώκω, 1377], to pursue, is translated "given to" in Rom. 12:13, lit., 'pursuing hospitality,' See FOLLOW.

NT: B.201b; CB.1242a; K.177.
OT: rādaph: S.7291; HR.338b.10a-c; H.2124; BD.922c.
GEN. REF.: –.

Notes: (1) In John 10:11, R.V., *tithēmi*, to put, lay down etc., is rendered "layeth down," for the A.V., "giveth."

(2) For *pareispherō*, to add, rendered "giving" in 2 Pet. 1:5, A.V., see ADD.

(3) For *martureō*, to bear witness, A.V., "gave (record)" in 1 John 5:10, R.V., "hath borne (witness)," see WITNESS.

(4) For *chorēgeō*, to supply, minister, rendered "giveth" (R.V., "supplieth") in 1 Pet. 4:11, see MINISTER.

(5) For *merizō*, to divide into parts, rendered "gave a part" (R.V., "divided") in Heb. 7:2, see DIVIDE.

(6) For *paristēmi*, to place by, rendered "give" in Matt. 26:53, A.V. (R.V., "send"), see SEND.

(7) For *douloō*, in the Passive Voice, to be enslaved, rendered "given to" in Tit. 2:3, A.V., see ENSLAVE.

(8) In 1 Tim. 4:15, the Imperative Mood of *eimi*, to be, with *en*, in, lit., 'be in,' is translated "give thyself wholly to."

(9) In Luke 10:7, the phrase, lit., 'the (things) by them,' is rendered "such things as they give."

(10) For *epikrinō*, see SENTENCE.

(11) For *proskartereō*, to give oneself continually, Acts 6:4; see CONTINUE.

(12) See CHARGE, COMMANDMENT, DRINK, HOSPITALITY, LAW, LIGHT, MARRIAGE, PLACE, PLEASURE, SUCK, THANKS.

GIVER

dotēs [δότης, 1395], akin to *didōmi*, to give, is used in 2 Cor. 9:7 of him who gives cheerfully (hilariously) and is thereby loved of God. ¶

NT: B.205a; CB.1242a; K.—.
OT: —.
GEN. REF.: —.

GLAD (be, make), GLADLY

A. Verbs.

1. *chairō* [χαίρω, 5463], is the usual word for rejoicing, being glad; it is rendered by the verb to be glad in Mark 14:11; Luke 15:32; 22:5; 23:8; John 8:56; 11:15; 20:20; Acts 11:23; 13:48; in the following the R.V. has 'to rejoice' for A.V., 'to be glad,' Rom. 16:19; 1 Cor. 16:17; 2 Cor. 13:9; 1 Pet. 4:13; Rev. 19:7. See FAREWELL, No. 4, GREETING, HAIL, JOY, REJOICE.

NT: B.873b; CB.1239b; K.1298.
OT: gîl: S.1523; HR.1452a.2; H.346; BD.162a.
sāmaḥ: S.8055; HR.1452a.7a; H.2268; BD.970a.
GEN. REF.: IS.2:474; NB.—; Z.—.

2. *agalliaō* [ἀγαλλιάω, 21], to exult, rejoice greatly, is chiefly used in the Middle Voice (Active in Luke 1:47; some mss. have the Passive in John 5:35, 'to be made glad'). In the O.T., it is found abundantly in the Psalms, from 2:11 onward to 149:2, 5 (Sept.). It conveys the idea of jubilant exultation, spiritual gladness, Matt. 5:12, "be exceeding glad," the Lord's command to His disciples; Luke 1:47, in Mary's song; 10:21, of Christ's exultation ("rejoiced"); cp. Acts 2:26, "(My tongue) was glad," A.V. (R.V., "rejoiced"); John 8:56, of Abraham; Acts 16:34, R.V., "rejoiced greatly" (of the Philippian jailor); 1 Pet. 1:6, 8; 4:13 ("with exceeding joy"), of believers in general; in Rev. 19:7, R.V., "be exceeding glad" (A.V., "rejoice"). See REJOICE. ¶

NT: B.3d; CB.1233b; K.—.
OT: gîl: S.1523; HR.4c.1; H.346; BD.162a.
rānan: S.7442; HR.4c.6b; H.2134,2179; BD.943b.
GEN. REF.: IS.2:474; NB.—; Z.—.

3. *euphrainō* [εὐφραίνω, 2165], to cheer, gladden, is rendered "maketh . . . glad" in 2 Cor. 2:2. See FARE, MERRY, REJOICE.

NT: B.327c; CB.1247b; K.278.
OT: sāmaḥ: S.8055; HR.581b.19a,b; H.2268; BD.970a.
GEN. REF.: IS.2:474; NB.—; Z.—.

B. Adverbs.

1. *hēdeōs* [ἡδέως, 2234], gladly (from *hēdus*, sweet), is used in Mark 6:20; 12:37; 2 Cor. 11:19. ¶

NT: B.343d; CB.1249c; K.—.
OT: —.
GEN. REF.: IS.2:474; NB.—; Z.—.

2. *hēdista* [ἥδιστα, 2236], the superlative degree of No. 1, most gladly, most delightedly, with great relish, is rendered "most gladly" in 2 Cor. 12:9, and in ver. 15 (R.V.; A.V., "very gladly"). ¶

NT: B.343d; CB.—; K.—.
OT: —.
GEN. REF.: —.

3. *asmenōs* [ἀσμένως, 780], with delight, delightedly, gladly, is found in Acts 21:17. It is absent from the best texts in 2:41 (see the R.V.). ¶

NT: B.116c; CB.—; K.—.
OT: —.
GEN. REF.: IS.2:474; NB.—; Z.—.

GLADNESS

1. *chara* [χαρά, 5479], joy, delight (akin to A, No. 1 above), is rendered "gladness" in the A.V. of Mark 4:16; Acts 12:14 and Phil. 2:29 (R.V. "joy," as elsewhere in both Versions). See JOY.

NT: B.875c; CB.1239b; K.1298.
OT: simḥāh: S.8057; HR.1454b.5; H.2268b; BD.970d.
sāśôn: S.8342; HR.1454b.6a; H.2246a; BD.965b.
GEN. REF.: IS.2:474; NB.—; Z.—.

2. *agalliasis* [ἀγαλλίασις, 20], exultation, exuberant joy (akin to A, No. 2), is translated "gladness" in Luke 1:14; Acts 2:6; Heb. 1:9; "joy" in Luke 1:44; "exceeding joy" in Jude 24. It indicates a more exultant joy than No. 1. In the Sept. this word is found chiefly in the Psalms, where it denotes joy in God's redemptive work, e.g., 30:5; 42:4; 45:7, 15. See JOY.

NT: B.3d; CB.1233b; K.4.
OT: rinnāh: S.7440; HR.5b.3a; H.2179c; BD.943c.
sāśôn: S.8342; HR.5b.4; H.2246a; BD.965b.
GEN. REF.: IS.2:474; NB.—; Z.—.

3. *euphrosunē* [εὐφροσύνη, 2167], good cheer, joy, mirth, gladness of heart (akin to A, No. 3), from *eu*, well, and *phrēn*, the mind, is rendered "gladness" in Acts 2:28, R.V. (A.V., "joy") and 14:17. See JOY. ¶

NT: B.328a; CB.1247b; K.278.
OT: simḥāh: S.8057; HR.582c.15d; H.2268b; BD.970d.
GEN. REF.: IS.2:474; NB.—; Z.—.

GLASS, GLASSY

A. Nouns.

1. *hualos* [ὕαλος, 5194], primarily denoted anything transparent, e.g., a transparent stone or gem, hence, a lens of crystal, a glass, Rev. 21:18, 21. ¶

NT: B.831d; CB.—; K.—.
OT: zᵉkûkît: S.2137; HR.1379c.1; H.550b; BD.269b.
GEN. REF.: IS.2:475; NB.471; Z.2:729.

2. *esoptron* [ἔσοπτρον, 2072], a mirror, is rendered "glass" in the A.V. of 1 Cor. 13:12 and Jas. 1:23. See MIRROR. ¶

NT: B.313b; CB.1246c; K.27,264.
OT: —.
GEN. REF.: —.

Note: For the corresponding verb *katoptrizō* in 2 Cor. 3:18 (Middle Voice), see BEHOLD, No. 12.

B. Adjective.

hualinos [ὑάλινος, 5193], signifies glassy, made of glass (akin to A, No. 1), Rev. 4:6; 15:2 (twice), R.V., "glassy." ¶

NT: B.831d; CB.1251b; K.—.
OT: —.
GEN. REF.: IS.2:475; NB.—; Z.2:729.

For GLISTERING see DAZZLING and SHINE, No. 4

GLORIFY

1. *doxazō* [δοξάζω, 1392], primarily denotes "to suppose" (from *doxa*, an opinion); in the N.T. (*a*) to magnify, extol, praise (see DOXA below), especially of glorifying God, i.e., ascribing honour to Him, acknowledging Him as to His being, attributes and acts, i.e., His glory (see GLORY), e.g., Matt. 5:16; 9:8; 15:31; Rom. 15:6, 9; Gal. 1:24; 1 Pet. 4:16; the word of the Lord, Acts 13:48; the Name of the Lord, Rev. 15:4; also of glorifying oneself, John 8:54; Rev. 18:7; (*b*) to do honour to, to make glorious, e.g., Rom. 8:30; 2 Cor. 3:10; 1 Pet. 1:8, "full of glory," Passive Voice (lit., 'glorified'); said of Christ, e.g., John 7:39; 8:54, R.V., "glorifieth," for A.V., "honour" and "honoureth" (which would translate *timaō*, to honour); of the Father, e.g., John 13:31, 32; 21:19; 1 Pet. 4:11; of glorifying one's ministry, Rom. 11:13, R.V., "glorify" (A.V., "magnify"); of a member of the body, 1 Cor. 12:26, "be honoured" (R.V. marg., "be glorified").

"As the glory of God is the revelation and manifestation of all that He has and is . . ., it is said of a Self-revelation in which God manifests all the goodness that is His, John 12:28. So far as it is Christ through whom this is made manifest, He is said to glorify the Father, John 17:1, 4; or the Father is glorified in Him, 13:31; 14:13; and Christ's meaning is analogous when He says to His disciples, 'Herein is My Father glorified, that ye bear much fruit; and so shall ye be My disciples,' John 15:8. When *doxazō* is predicated of Christ . . ., it means simply that His innate glory is brought to light, is made manifest; cp. 11:4. So 7:39; 12:16, 23; 13:31; 17:1, 5. It is an act of God the Father in Him. . . . As the revelation of the Holy Spirit is connected with the glorification of Christ, Christ says regarding Him, 'He shall glorify Me,' 16:14" (Cremer).

NT: B.204c; CB.1242b; K.178.
OT: kābēd: S.3513; HR.343b.7a-c; H.943; BD.457a.
pā'ar: S.6286; HR.343b.11a; H.1726,1727; BD.802b.
GEN. REF.: IS.2:478; NB.472; Z.2:730.

2. *endoxazō* [ἐνδοξάζω, 1740], No. 1 prefixed by *en*, "in," signifies, in the Passive Voice, to be glorified, i.e., to exhibit one's glory; it is said of God, regarding His saints in the future, 2 Thess. 1:10, and of the Name of the Lord Jesus as glorified in them in the present, ver. 12. ¶

NT: B.263b; CB.1245a; K.178.
OT: kābēd: S.3513; HR.470c.2; H.943; BD.457a.
pā'ar: S.6286; HR.470c.4; H.1726,1727; BD.802b.
hālal: S.1984; HR.470c.1; H.499,500; BD.237d,239a.
GEN. REF.: IS.2:478; NB.472; Z.2:730.

3. *sundoxazō* [συνδοξάζω, 4888], to glorify together (*sun*, with), is used in Rom. 8:17. ¶

NT: B.785d; CB.1270c; K.178,1102.
OT: —.
GEN. REF.: IS.2:478; NB.472; Z.—.

GLORY, GLORIOUS

A. Nouns.

1. *doxa* [δόξα, 1391], glory (from *dokeō*, to seem), primarily signifies an opinion, estimate, and hence, the honour resulting from a good opinion. It is used (I) (*a*) of the nature and acts of God in self-manifestation, i.e., what He essentially is and does, as exhibited in whatever way he reveals Himself in these respects and particularly in the Person of Christ, in whom essentially His glory has ever shone forth and ever will do, John 17:5, 24; Heb. 1:3; it was exhibited in the character and acts of Christ in the days of His flesh, John 1:14; John 2:11; at Cana both His grace and His power were manifested, and these constituted His glory; so also in the resurrection of Lazarus, 11:4, 40; the glory of God was exhibited in the resurrection of Christ, Rom. 6:4, and in His ascension and exaltation, 1 Pet. 1:21, likewise on the Mount of Transfiguration, 2 Pet. 1:17. In Rom. 1:23 His "everlasting power and Divinity" are spoken of as His glory, i.e., His attributes and power as revealed through creation; in Rom. 3:23 the word denotes the manifested perfection of His character, especially His righteousness, of which all men fall short; in Col. 1:11 "the might of His glory" signifies the might which is characteristic of His glory; in Eph. 1:6, 12, 14, "the praise of the glory of His grace" and "the praise of His glory" signify the due acknowledgement of the exhibition of His attributes and ways; in Eph. 1:17, "the Father of glory" describes Him as the source from whom all Divine splendour and perfection proceed in their manifestation, and to whom they belong; (*b*) of the character and ways of God as exhibited through Christ to and through believers, 2 Cor. 3:18 and 4:6; (*c*) of the state of blessedness into which believers are to enter

hereafter through being brought into the likeness of Christ, e.g., Rom. 8:18, 21; Phil. 3:21 (R.V., "the body of His glory"); 1 Pet. 5:1, 10; Rev. 21:11; (*d*) brightness or splendour, (1) supernatural, emanating from God (as in the Shekinah glory, in the pillar of cloud and in the Holy of Holies, e.g., Ex. 16:10; 25:22), Luke 2:9; Acts 22:11; Rom. 9:4; 2 Cor. 3:7; Jas. 2:1; in Tit. 2:13 it is used of Christ's return, "the appearing of the glory of our great God and Saviour Jesus Christ" (R.V.); cp. Phil. 3:21, above; (2) natural, as of the heavenly bodies, 1 Cor. 15:40, 41; (II) of good reputation, praise, honour, Luke 14:10 (R.V., "glory," for A.V., "worship"); John 5:41 (R.V., "glory," for A.V., "honour"); 7:18; 8:50; 12:43 (R.V., "glory," for A.V., "praise"); 2 Cor. 6:8 (R.V., "glory," for A.V. "honour"); Phil. 3:19; Heb. 3:3; in 1 Cor. 11:7, of man as representing the authority of God, and of woman as rendering conspicuous the authority of man; in 1 Thess. 2:6, "glory" probably stands, by metonymy, for material gifts, an honorarium, since in human estimation glory is usually expressed in things material.

The word is used in ascriptions of praise to God, e.g., Luke 17:18; John 9:24, R.V., "glory" (A.V., "praise"); Acts 12:23; as in doxologies (lit., glory-words), e.g., Luke 2:14; Rom. 11:36; 16:27; Gal. 1:5; Rev. 1:6. See DIGNITY, HONOUR, PRAISE, WORSHIP.

NT: B.203c; CB.1242b; K.178.
OT: kābōd: S.3519; HR.341b.13b; H.943d,e; BD.458c.
GEN. REF.: IS.2:478; NB.472; Z.2:730.

2. *kleos* [κλέος, 2811], good report, fame, renown, is used in 1 Pet. 2:20. ¶ The word is derived from a root signifying hearing; hence, the meaning 'reputation.'

NT: B.434b; CB.1255b; K.—.
OT: shēma‘: S.8088; HR.767b.1; H.2412b; BD.1034d.
GEN. REF.: IS.—; NB.—; Z.2:731.

Note: In 2 Cor. 3:11 the phrase *dia doxēs*, through (i.e., by means of) glory, is rendered "with glory" in the R.V. (A.V., "glorious"); in the same verse *en doxē*, "in glory" (R.V.), i.e., accompanied by glory, is rendered "glorious" in the A.V. The first is said of the ministration of the Law, the second of that of the Gospel.

B. Adjective.

endoxos [ἔνδοξος, 1741], signifies (*a*) held in honour (*en*, in, *doxa*, honour), of high repute, 1 Cor. 4:10, R.V., "have glory" (A.V., "are honourable"); (*b*) splendid, glorious, said of apparel, Luke 7:25, "gorgeously"; of the works of Christ, 13:17; of the Church, Eph. 5:27. See GORGEOUSLY, HONOURABLE. ¶

NT: B.263b; CB.1245a; K.178.
OT: kābēd: S.3513; HR.470c.3a; H.943; BD.457a.
GEN. REF.: IS.2:482; NB.472; Z.2:730.

GLORY (to boast), GLORYING

A. Verbs.

1. *kauchaomai* [καυχάομαι, 2744], to boast or glory, is always translated in the R.V. by the verb to glory, where the A.V. uses the verb to boast (see, e.g., Rom. 2:17, 23; 2 Cor. 7:14; 9:2; 10:8, 13, 15, 16); it is used (*a*) of vainglorying, e.g., 1 Cor. 1:29; 3:21; 4:7; 2 Cor. 5:12; 11:12, 18; Eph. 2:9; (*b*) of valid glorying, e.g., Rom. 5:2, "rejoice"; 5:3, 11 (R.V., "rejoice"); 1 Cor. 1:31; 2 Cor. 9:2; 10:8; 12:9; Gal. 6:14; Phil. 3:3 and Jas. 1:9, R.V., "glory" (A.V., "rejoice"). See BOAST, JOY, REJOICE.

NT: B.425c; CB.1254c; K.423.
OT: hālal: S.1984; HR.757b.2; H.499,500; BD.237d,239a.
‘ālaz: S.5937; HR.757b.3; H.1625; BD.759c.
GEN. REF.: —.

katakauchaomai [κατακαυχάομαι, 2620], a strengthened form of No. 1 (*kata*, intensive), signifies to boast against, exult over, Rom. 11:18, R.V., "glory" (A.V., "boast"); Jas. 2:13, R.V., "glorieth" (A.V., "rejoiceth"); 3:14, "glory (not)." See BOAST, REJOICE. ¶

NT: B.411b; CB.1254a; K.423.
OT: hālal: S.1984; HR.733a.2; H.499,500; BD.237d,239b.
‘ālaz: S.5937; HR.733a.3; H.1625; BD.759c.
GEN. REF.: —.

3. *enkauchaomai* [ἐνκαυχάομαι, —], *en*, in, and No. 1, to glory in, is found, in the most authentic mss., in 2 Thess. 1:4. ¶

NT: B.216a; CB.1245a; K.423.
OT: —.
GEN. REF.: —.

Note: Cp. *perpereuomai*, to vaunt oneself, to be *perperos*, vainglorious, 1 Cor. 13:4. ¶

B. Nouns.

1. *kauchēma* [καύχημα, 2745], akin to A, No. 1, denotes (*a*) that in which one glories, a matter or ground of glorying, Rom. 4:2 and Phil. 2:16, R.V., "whereof to glory" (for Rom. 3:27, see No. 2); in the following the meaning is likewise a ground of glorying: 1 Cor. 5:6; 9:15, "glorying," 16, "to glory of"; 2 Cor. 1:14, R.V.; 9:3, R.V.; Gal. 6:4, R.V. (A.V., "rejoicing"); Phil. 1:26 (ditto); Heb. 3:6 (ditto). In 2 Cor. 5:12 and 9:3 the word denotes the boast itself, yet as distinct from the act (see No. 2). ¶

NT: B.426a; CB.1254c; K.423.
OT: tᵉhillāh: S.8416; HR.757c.4; H.500c; BD.239d.
tiph'eret: S.8597; HR.757c.6; H.1726b; BD.802c.
GEN. REF.: —.

2. *kauchēsis* [καύχησις, 2746], denotes the act of boasting, Rom. 3:27; 15:17, R.V., "(my) glorying" (A.V., "whereof I may glory"); 1 Cor. 15:31, R.V., "glorying"; 2 Cor. 1:12 (ditto); 7:4,

14 (A.V., "boasting"); 8:24; 11:10, and 17 (ditto); 1 Thess. 2:19 (A.V., "rejoicing"); Jas. 4:16 (ditto). The distinction between this and No. 1 is to be observed in 2 Cor. 8:24, speaking of the Apostle's act of glorying in the liberality of the Corinthians, while in 9:3 he exhorts them not to rob him of the ground of his glorying (No. 1). Some take the word in 2 Cor. 1:12 (see above) as identical with No. 1, a boast, but there seems to be no reason for regarding it as different from its usual sense, No. 2. ¶

NT: B.426a; CB.1254c; K.423.
OT: tiph'eret: S.8597; HR.757c.1; H.1726b; BD.802c.
GEN. REF.: –.

Note: Cp. *alazoneia* (or *-ia*), vainglory, ostentatious (or arrogant) display, Jas. 4:16 and 1 John 2:16, ¶ and *alazōn*, a boaster, Rom. 1:30 and 2 Tim. 3:2. ¶

GLUTTON

gastēr [γαστήρ, 1064], denotes a belly; it is used in Tit. 1:12, with the adjective *argos*, idle, metaphorically, to signify a glutton, R.V., "(idle) gluttons" [A.V. "(slow) bellies"]; elsewhere, Luke 1:31. See WOMB. ¶

NT: B.152a; CB.–; K.–.
OT: beṭen: S.990; HR.234b.1; H.236a; BD.105d.
GEN. REF.: IS.2:483; NB.–; Z.–.

GLUTTONOUS

phagos [φάγος, 5314], akin to *phagō*, to eat, a form used for the aorist or past tense of *esthiō*, denotes a glutton, Matt. 11:19; Luke 7:34. ¶

NT: B.851a; CB.–; K.–.
OT: –.
GEN. REF.: IS.2:483; NB.–; Z.2:735.

GNASH, GNASHING

A. Verbs.

1. *bruchō* [βρύχω, 1031], primarily, to bite or eat greedily (akin to *brukō*, to chew), denotes to grind or gnash with the teeth, Acts 7:54. ¶

NT: B.148a; CB.1239b; K.110.
OT: ḥāraq: S.2786; HR.231b.1; H.755; BD.359b.
GEN. REF.: IS.2:483; NB.–; Z.2:735.

2. *trizō* [τρίζω, 5149], primarily used of the sounds of animals, to chirp, cry, squeak, came to signify to grind or gnash with the teeth, Mark 9:18. ¶

NT: B.826b; CB.–; K.–.
OT: –.
GEN. REF.: IS.2:483; NB.–; Z.2:735.

B. Noun.

brugmos [βρυγμός, 1030], akin to A, No. 1, denotes "gnashing" ("of teeth" being added), Matt. 8:12; 13:42, 50; 22:13; 24:51; 25:30; Luke 13:28. ¶

NT: B.147d; CB.1239b; K.110.
OT: naham: S.5099; HR.231b.1; H.1313a; BD.625b.
GEN. REF.: IS.2:483; NB.–; Z.2:735.

GNAT

kōnōps [κώνωψ, 2971], denotes the wine-gnat or midge, which breeds in fermenting or evaporating wine, Matt. 23:24, where the A.V., "strain at" is corrected to "strain out," in the R.V. ¶

NT: B.462a; CB.1255c; K.–.
OT: –.
GEN. REF.: IS.2:483; NB.473; Z.2:735.

GNAW

masaomai or *massaomai* [μασάομαι, 3145], denotes to bite or chew, Rev. 16:10. ¶ In the Sept., Job. 30:4. ¶

NT: B.495a; CB.–; K.570.
OT: –.
GEN. REF.: –.

GO (WENT), GO ONWARD, etc.

1. *poreuomai* [πορεύομαι, 4198], to go on one's way, to proceed from one place to another (from *poros*, a passage, a ford, Eng., pore), is always used in the Middle Voice in the N.T. and the Sept., and is the most frequent verb signifying to go; it is more distinctly used to indicate procedure or course than the verb *eimi*, to go (not found in the N.T.). It is often rendered "go thy (your) way," in Oriental usage the customary dismissal, marking the close of a case in court. Hence, in ordinary parlance, marking the end of a conversation, etc., e.g., Luke 7:22; 17:19; John 4:50; Acts 9:15; 24:25; cp. Dan. 12:9; in Rom. 15:24 (1st part), R.V., "go" (A.V., "take my journey"); in Acts 9:3 and 26:13, "journeyed" (A.V. and R.V.). See DEPART, JOURNEY, WALK.

NT: B.692b; CB.1266a; K.915.
OT: hālak: S.1980; HR.1189a.3a; H.498; BD.229d.
GEN. REF.: IS.2:490; NB.–; Z.–.

2. *paraporeuomai* [παραπορεύομαι, 3899], denotes to go past, to pass by (*para*, by, and No. 1), Mark 2:23, A.V., "went (through)," R.V., "was going (through)"; some mss. have No. 4 here. See PASS.

NT: B.621c; CB.–; K.–.
OT: 'ābar: S.5674; HR.1063b.2; H.1556; BD.716d.
GEN. REF.: IS.2:490; NB.–; Z.–.

3. *proporeuomai* [προπορεύομαι, 4313], to go before (*pro*, and No. 1), is used in Luke 1:76 and Acts 7:40. ¶

NT: B.709c; CB.–; K.–.
OT: hālak: S.1980; HR.1208c.2a-c; H.498; BD.229d.
'ābar: S.5674; HR.1208c.4; H.1556; BD.716d.
GEN. REF.: IS.2:490; NB.–; Z.–.

4. *diaporeuomai* [διαπορεύομαι, 1279], to go through (*dia*, through, and No. 1), to pass across, is translated to go through, in Luke 6:1; 13:22, "went on His way through," R.V.; Acts 16:4; "going by" in Luke 18:36, R.V. (A.V.,

"pass by"); "in my journey" in Rom. 15:24 (2nd part). For Mark 2:23 see No. 2. See JOURNEY.

NT: B.187d; CB.–; K.–.
OT: hālak: S.1980; HR.308b.4a-c; H.498; BD.229d.
'ābar: S.5674; HR.308b.6; H.1556; BD.716d.
GEN. REF.: IS.2:490; NB.–; Z.–.

5. *eisporeuomai* [εἰσπορεύομαι, 1531], to go in, enter, is never rendered by the verb to come in, in the R.V. See, e.g., Luke 11:33, "enter"; Acts 9:28, "going in"; 28:30, "went in." See ENTER.

NT: B.233c; CB.–; K.915.
OT: bô': S.935; HR.414a.1a; H.212; BD.97c.
GEN. REF.: IS.2:490; NB.–; Z.–.

6. *sumporeuomai* [συμπορεύομαι, 4848], to go together with (*sun*, with), is used in Mark 10:1, R.V., "come together" (A.V., "resort"); Luke 7:11; 14:25; 24:15. See RESORT. ¶

NT: B.780a; CB.–; K.–.
OT: hālak: S.1980; HR.1305c.2; H.498; BD.229d.
GEN. REF.: IS.2:490; NB.–; Z.–.

7. *agō* [ἄγω, 71], to bring, lead, is used intransitively, signifying "let us go" (as if to say, 'let us be leading on,' with the point of departure especially in view), Matt. 26:46; Mark 1:38; 14:42; John 11:7, 15, 16; 14:31. See BRING.

NT: B.14b; CB.–; K.–.
OT: bô': S.935; HR.9a.1b; H.212; BD.97c.
hālak: S.1980; HR.9a.3b; H.498; BD.229d.
GEN. REF.: IS.2:490; NB.–; Z.–.

8. *hupagō* [ὑπάγω, 5217], to go away or to go slowly away, to depart, withdraw oneself, often with the idea of going without noise or notice (*hupo*, under, and No. 7), is very frequent in the Gospels; elsewhere it is used in Jas. 2:16; 1 John 2:11; Rev. 10:8; 13:10; 14:4; 16:1; 17:8, 11. It is frequently rendered "go your (thy) way," See DEPART.

NT: B.836c; CB.–; K.1227.
OT: hālak: S.1980; HR.1405c.1; H.498; BD.229d.
GEN. REF.: IS.2:490; NB.–; Z.–.

9. *periagō* [περιάγω, 4013], to lead about (*peri*, about, and No. 7), as in 1 Cor. 9:5, is used intransitively with the meaning to go about; "went about," Matt. 4:23; 9:35; Mark 6:6; Acts 13:11; in Matt. 23:15, "ye compass." See COMPASS, LEAD. ¶

NT: B.645c; CB.–; K.–.
OT: sābab: S.5437; HR.1121b.2; H.1456; BD.685b.
'ābar: S.5674; HR.1121b.2; H.1556; BD.716d.
GEN. REF.: IS.2:490; NB.–; Z.–.

10. *proagō* [προάγω, 4254], to lead forth, used intransitively signifies to go before, usually of locality, e.g., Matt. 2:9; figuratively, in 1 Tim. 1:18, "went before" (R.V., marg., "led the way to"), of the exercise of the gifts of prophecy which pointed to Timothy as one chosen by God for the service to be committed to him; in 5:24, of sins "going before unto judgment." In 2 John 9, where the best mss. have this verb (instead of *parabainō*, to transgress, A.V.), the R.V. renders it "goeth onward" (marg., "taketh the lead"), of not abiding in the doctrine of Christ. Cp. Mal. 4:4. See BRING.

NT: B.702a; CB.–; K.20.
OT: nāgash: S.5065; HR.1203; H.1296; BD.620a.
GEN. REF.: IS.2:490; NB.–; Z.–.

11. *apeimi* [ἄπειμι, 549], to go away, is found in Acts 17:10. ¶

NT: B.83a; CB.–; K.–.
OT: –.
GEN. REF.: –.

12. *eiseimi* [εἴσειμι, 1524], to go into, enter, is used in Acts 3:3; 21:18, 26; Heb. 9:6, R.V., "go in" (A.V., "went . . . into"). See ENTER. ¶

NT: B.232c; CB.–; K.–.
OT: bô': S.935; HR.413c.1; H.212; BD.97c.
GEN. REF.: IS.2:490; NB.–; Z.–.

13. *metabainō* [μεταβαίνω, 3327], to go or pass over from one place to another, is translated "go" in Luke 10:7. See DEPART.

NT: B.510c; CB.1258b; K.90.
OT: –.
GEN. REF.: –.

14. *aperchomai* [ἀπέρχομαι, 565], to go away (*apo*, from), is chiefly used in the Gospels; it signifies to go aside in Acts 4:15. See DEPART.

NT: B.84c; CB.1236b; K.257.
OT: hālak: S.1980; HR.121a.5a; H.498; BD.229d.
GEN. REF.: IS.2:490; NB.–; Z.–.

15. *anachōreō* [ἀναχωρέω, 402], signifies to withdraw, often in the sense of avoiding danger, e.g., Acts 23:19, R.V., "going aside" (A.V., "went . . . aside"). See DEPART.

NT: B.63c; CB.1235a; K.–.
OT: nûs: S.5127; HR.85c.3; H.1327; BD.630c.
GEN. REF.: –.

16. *hupochōreō* [ὑποχωρέω, 5298], to go back, retire (*hupo*, under, suggesting privacy), Luke 5:16; 9:10, A.V., "went aside" (R.V., "withdrew apart"). See WITHDRAW. ¶

NT: B.848c; CB.–; K.–.
OT: –.
GEN. REF.: –.

17. *proerchomai* [προέρχομαι, 4281], to go before, precede, go forward or farther (*pro*, before), is used of (*a*) place, e.g., Matt. 26:39; Acts 12:10, "passed on through"; (*b*) time, Luke 1:17; Acts 20:5, 13; 2 Cor. 9:5. See OUTGO, PASS.

NT: B.705b; CB.1266c; K.–.
OT: 'ābar: S.5674; HR.1206a.1; H.1556; BD.716d.
GEN. REF.: IS.2:490; NB.–; Z.–.

18. *epiduo* [ἐπιδύω, 1931], signifies to go down, and is said of the sun in Eph. 4:26; i.e., put wrath away before sunset (see ANGER, A, *Note* (2). In the Sept., Deut. 24:15; Josh. 8:29; Jer. 15:9. ¶

NT: B.292c; CB.–; K.–.
OT: bô': S.935; HR.519c.1; H.212; BD.97c.
GEN. REF.: IS.2:490; NB.–; Z.–.

19. *sunkatabainō* [συνκαταβαίνω, 4782], to go down with, is used in Acts 25:5. ¶ In the Sept., Psa. 49:17. ¶

NT: B.773c; CB.–; K.–.
OT: yārad: S.3381; HR.1299b.1; H.909; BD.432c.
GEN. REF.: IS.2:490; NB.–; Z.–.

20. *probainō* [προβαίνω, 4260], to go on, forwards, advance, is used of locality, Matt. 4:21; Mark 1:19; for the metaphorical use with reference to age, Luke 1:7, 18; 2:36, see AGE, STRICKEN. ¶

NT: B.702d; CB.1266c; K.—.
OT: bô': S.935; HR.1204a.1; H.212; BD.97c.
hālak: S.1980; HR.1204a.2; H.498; BD.229d.
GEN. REF.: IS.2:490; NB.—; Z.—.

21. *apobainō* [ἀποβαίνω, 576], to go away or from, is translated "had gone out," in Luke 5:2, i.e., disembarked. See COME, 21, *Note*, TURN.

NT: B.88c; CB.—; K.—.
OT: —.
GEN. REF.: —.

22. *prosanabainō* [προσαναβαίνω, 4320], to go up higher (*pros*, towards), is used of moving to a couch of greater honour at a feast, Luke 14:10. ¶

NT: B.711c; CB.—; K.—.
OT: 'ālāh: S.5927; HR.1212a.1; H.1624; BD.748a.
GEN. REF.: IS.2:490; NB.—; Z.—.

23. *exeimi* [ἔξειμι, 1826], to go out, is so rendered in Acts 13:42. See DEPART, GET.

NT: B.275b; CB.1247c; K.—.
OT: yāṣā': S.3318; HR.495c.1; H.893; BD.422b.
GEN. REF.: IS.2:490; NB.—; Z.—.

24. *sbennumi* [σβέννυμι, 4570], to quench, is used in the Passive Voice, of the going out of the light of a torch or lamp, Matt. 25:8, "are going out" (R.V.). See QUENCH.

NT: B.745b; CB.1268c; K.1009.
OT: kābāh: S.3518; HR.1261a.2; H.944; BD.459c.
dā'ak: S.1846; HR.1261a.1; H.445; BD.200b.
GEN. REF.: —.

25. *teleō* [τελέω, 5055], to finish, is rendered to go through or over in Matt. 10:23, of going through the cities of Israel (A.V., marg., "end," or "finish"). See END, FINISH.

NT: B.810d; CB.1271b; K.1161.
OT: kālāh: S.3615; HR.1342c.3; H.982-984; BD.477b.
GEN. REF.: —.

26. *diodeuō* [διοδεύω, 1353], to travel throughout or along (*dia*, through, *hodos*, a way), is used in Luke 8:1, of going throughout (A.V.) or about through (R.V.) cities and villages; of passing through towns, Acts 17:1. See PASS.

NT: B.198d; CB.—; K.—.
OT: 'ābar: S.5674; HR.336a.3; H.1556; BD.716d.
GEN. REF.: IS.2:490; NB.—; Z.—.

27. *apodēmeō* [ἀποδημέω, 589], to be abroad, is translated "going into another country," in Matt. 25:14 (A.V., "travelling etc."). See JOURNEY.

NT: B.90a; CB.1236c; K.—.
OT: —.
GEN. REF.: —.

28. *anerchomai* [ἀνέρχομαι, 424], to go up (*ana*), occurs in John 6:3; Gal. 1:17, 18. ¶

NT: B.65b; CB.—; K.—.
OT: hālak: S.1980; HR.87b.1; H.498; BD.229d.
GEN. REF.: IS.2:490; NB.—; Z.—.

29. *perierchomai* [περιέρχομαι, 4022], to go around, or about, is translated "going about" in 1 Tim. 5:13, R.V. (A.V., "wandering about"); "went about" in Heb. 11:37, R.V. (A.V., "wandered about"). See CIRCUIT.

NT: B.646d; CB.1263b; K.257.
OT: sābab: S.5437; HR.1123a.1; H.1456; BD.685b.
GEN. REF.: —.

30. *epicheireō* [ἐπιχειρέω, 2021], lit., to put the hand to (*epi*, to, *cheir*, the hand), to take in hand, undertake, occurs in Luke 1:1, "have taken in hand"; in Acts 9:29, "they went about"; in 19:13, "took upon them." See TAKE. ¶

NT: B.304d; CB.—; K.—.
OT: —.
GEN. REF.: IS.2:490; NB.—; Z.—.

Notes: (1) The following verbs signify both to come and to go, with prefixed prepositions accordingly, and are mentioned under the word COME: *erchomai* (No. 1); *eiserchomai* (No. 2); *exerchomai* (No. 3); *dierchomai* (No. 5); *katerchomai* (No. 7); Luke 17:7, *parerchomai* (No. 9); *proserchomai*, "go near," Acts 8:29 (No. 10); *sunerchomai*, "went with," Acts 9:39; 15:38; 21:16 (No. 11); *anabainō*, (No. 15); *katabainō* (No. 19); *paraginomai*, Acts 23:16, A.V., "went," R.V. "entered" (No. 13); *ekporeuō* (No. 33); *chōreō*, Matt. 15:17, A.V., "goeth," R.V., "passeth" (No. 24); *anabainō*, Luke 19:28, R.V., "going up"; *ekbainō* (No. 17).

(2) In the following, the verbs mentioned, translated in the A.V. by some form of the verb to go, are rendered in the R.V. more precisely in accordance with their true meaning: (*a*) *zēteō*, to seek, so the R.V. in John 7:19, 20; Acts 21:31; Rom. 10:3 (A.V., to go about); (*b*) *peirazō*, to make an attempt, Acts 24:6, R.V., "assayed" (A.V., "have gone about"); (*c*) *peiraō*, to attempt, Acts 26:21, R.V., "assayed" A.V., "went about"); (*d*) *epistrephō*, to return, Acts 15:16, R.V., "let us return" (A.V., "let us go again"); (*e*) *huperbainō*, to overstep, 1 Thess. 4:6, R.V., "transgress" (A.V., "go beyond"); (*f*) *diistēmi*, to set apart, make an interval, Acts 27:28, R.V., "(after) a space" (A.V., "had gone further"); (*g*) *suneiserchomai*, to go in with, John 6:22 and 18:15, R.V., "entered (in) with" (A.V., "went . . . with"); (*h*) *pherō*, in the Middle Voice, lit., to bear oneself along, Heb. 6:1, R.V., "let us press on" (A.V., "let us go on"); (*i*) *ekklinō*, to bend or turn away, Rom. 3:12, R.V., "have turned aside" (A.V., "have gone out of the way"); (*j*) *diaperaō*, to pass through, or across, Matt. 14:34, R.V., "had crossed over" (A.V., "were gone over"); (*k*) *strateuomai*, to serve in war, 1 Cor. 9:7, R.V., "(what) soldier . . . serveth" (A.V., "goeth a warfare"); (*l*) *hodoiporeō*, to be on a journey, Acts 10:9, R.V., "as they were on their journey" (A.V., "as they went etc."); (*m*)

embainō, to enter, Matt. 13:2 and Luke 8:22, R.V., "entered" (A.V., "went into"); in ver. 37 (A.V., "went up into"); (*n*) *apoluō*, to set free, Luke 23:22 and John 19:12, R.V., "release" (A.V., "let . . . go"); Acts 15:33, R.V. "dismissed" (A.V., ditto); Acts 28:18, R.V., "set at liberty" (A.V., ditto); (*o*) *epibainō*, to go upon, Acts 21:4, R.V., "set foot" (A.V., "go"); some mss. have *anabainō*; (*p*) *apangellō*, to announce, Acts 12:17, R.V., "tell" (A.V., "go shew"); (*q*) *aperchomai*, to go away, Matt. 5:30, R.V., "go" (A.V., "be cast"); some mss. have *ballō*, to cast; (*r*) *peripateō*, to walk, Mark 12:38, R.V., "walk" (A.V. "go"); (*s*) *For* "gone by," Acts 14:16, R.V., see PASS, No. 17.

GOAD

kentron [κέντρον, 2759], from *kenteō*, to prick, denotes (*a*) a sting, Rev. 9:10; metaphorically, of sin as the sting of death, 1 Cor. 15:55, 56; (*b*) a goad, Acts 26:14, R.V., "goad" (marg., "goads"), for A.V., "pricks" (in some mss. also in 9:5), said of the promptings and misgivings which Saul of Tarsus had resisted before conversion. ¶

NT: B.428b; CB.1255a; K.427.
OT: meteg: S.4964; HR.759b.1; H.1264a; BD.607c.
qōṭeb: S.6987; HR.759b.2; H.2007a; BD.881c.
GEN. REF.: IS.2:491; NB.474; Z.2:739.

GOAL

skopos [σκοπός, 4649], primarily, a watcher (from *skopeō*, to look at; Eng., scope), denotes a mark on which to fix the eye, and is used metaphorically of an aim or object in Phil. 3:14, R.V., "goal" (A.V.,) "mark"), See MARK.

NT: B.756d; CB.1269b; K.1047.
OT: ṣāphāh: S.6822; HR.1275c.3; H.1950; BD.859b.
GEN. REF.: –.

GOAT

1. *eriphos* [ἔριφος, 2056], denotes a kid or goat, Matt. 25:32 (R.V., marg., "kids"); Luke 15:29, "a kid"; some mss. have No. 2 here, indicating a sneer on the part of the elder son, that his father had never given him even a tiny kid. ¶

NT: B.309d; CB.1246c; K.–.
OT: gᵉdî: S.1423; HR.547c.1; H.314b; BD.152a.
sā'îr: S.8163; HR.547c.5; H.2274c,e; BD.972d.
GEN. REF.: IS.2:491; NB.474; Z.2:739.

2. *eriphion* [ἐρίφιον, 2055], a diminutive of No. 1, is used in Matt. 25:33. In ver. 32 *eriphos* is purely figurative; in ver. 33, where the application is made, though metaphorically, the change to the diminutive is suggestive of the contempt which those so described bring upon themselves by their refusal to assist the needy. ¶

NT: B.309d; CB.1246c; K.–.
OT: –.
GEN. REF.: IS.2:491; NB.474; Z.2:739.

3. *tragos* [τράγος, 5131], denotes a he-goat, Heb. 9:12, 13, 19; 10:4, the male prefiguring the strength by which Christ laid down His own life in expiatory sacrifice.

NT: B.824a; CB.1273a; K.–.
OT: 'attûd: S.6260; HR.1369a.1; H.1719b; BD.800c.
ṣāphîr: S.6842; HR.1369a.2; H.1962a; BD.862b.
tayish: S.8495; HR.1369a.3; H.2506; BD.1066d.
GEN. REF.: IS.2:491; NB.474; Z.2:739.

GOATSKIN

Note: The adjective *aigeios* signifies belonging to a goat (from *aix*, a goat); it is used with *derma*, a skin, in Heb. 11:37.

GOD

theos [θεός, 2316], (A) in the polytheism of the Greeks, denoted a god or deity, e.g., Acts 14:11; 19:26; 28:6; 1 Cor. 8:5; Gal. 4:8.

(B) (*a*) Hence the word was appropriated by Jews and retained by Christians to denote the one true God. In the Sept. *theos* translates (with few exceptions) the Hebrew words Elohim and Jehovah, the former indicating His power and pre-eminence, the latter His unoriginated, immutable, eternal and self-sustained existence.

In the N.T., these and all the other Divine attributes are predicated of Him. To Him are ascribed, e.g., His unity, or monism, e.g., Mark 12:29; 1 Tim. 2:5; self-existence, John 5:26; immutability, Jas. 1:17; eternity, Rom. 1:20; universality, Matt. 10:29; Acts 17:26-28; almighty power, Matt. 19:26; infinite knowledge, Acts 2:23, 15:18; Rom. 11:33; creative power, Rom. 11:36; 1 Cor. 8:6; Eph. 3:9; Rev. 4:11; 10:6; absolute holiness, 1 Pet. 1:15; 1 John 1:5; righteousness, John 17:25; faithfulness, 1 Cor. 1:9; 10:13; 1 Thess. 5:24; 2 Thess. 3:3; 1 John 1:9; love, 1 John 4:8, 16; mercy, Rom. 9:15, 18; truthfulness, Tit. 1:2; Heb. 6:18. See GOOD, No. 1 (*b*).

(*b*) The Divine attributes are likewise indicated or definitely predicated of Christ, e.g., Matt. 20:18-19; John 1:1-3; 1:18, R.V., marg.; 5:22-29; 8:58; 14:6; 17:22-24; 20:28; Rom. 1:4; 9:5; Phil. 3:21; Col. 1:15; 2:3; Tit. 2:13, R.V.; Heb. 1:3; 13:8; 1 John 5:20; Rev. 22:12, 13.

(*c*) Also of the Holy Spirit, e.g., Matt. 28:19; Luke 1:35; John 14:16; 15:26; 16:7-14; Rom. 8:9, 26; 1 Cor. 12:11; 2 Cor. 13:14.

(*d*) *Theos* is used (1) with the definite article, (2) without (i.e., as an anarthrous noun). "The English may or may not have need of the article in translation. But that point cuts no figure in the Greek idiom. Thus in Acts 27:23 ('the God whose I am,' R.V.) the article points out the special God whose Paul is, and is to be preserved in English. In the very next verse (*ho theos*) we in English do not need the article" (A. T. Robertson, Gram. of Greek, N.T., p. 758).

As to this latter it is usual to employ the article with a proper name, when mentioned a second time. There are, of course, exceptions to this, as when the absence of the article serves to lay stress upon, or give precision to, the character or nature of what is expressed in the noun. A notable instance of this is in John 1:1, "and the Word was God"; here a double stress is on *theos*, by the absence of the article and by the emphatic position. To translate it literally, 'a god was the Word,' is entirely misleading. Moreover, that "the Word" is the subject of the sentence, exemplifies the rule that the subject is to be determined by its having the article when the predicate is anarthrous (without the article). In Rom. 7:22, in the phrase "the law of God," both nouns have the article; in ver. 25, neither has the article. This is in accordance with a general rule that if two nouns are united by the genitive case (the "of" case), either both have the article, or both are without. Here, in the first instance, both nouns, "God" and "the law" are definite, whereas in ver. 25 the word "God" is not simply titular, the absence of the article stresses His character as Lawgiver.

Where two or more epithets are applied to the same person or thing, one article usually serves for both (the exceptions being when a second article lays stress upon different aspects of the same person or subject, e.g., Rev. 1:17). In Tit. 2:13 the R.V. correctly has "our great God and Saviour Jesus Christ," Moulton (Prol., p. 84) shows, from papyri writings of the early Christian era, that among Greek-speaking Christians this was "a current formula" as applied to Christ. So in 2 Pet. 1:1 (cp. 1:11; 3:18).

In the following titles God is described by certain of His attributes; the God of glory, Acts 7:2; of peace, Rom. 15:33; 16:20; Phil. 4:9; 1 Thess. 5:23; Heb. 13:20; of love and peace, 2 Cor. 13:11; of patience and comfort, Rom. 15:5; of all comfort, 2 Cor. 1:3; of hope, Rom. 15:13; of all grace, 1 Pet. 5:10. These describe Him, not as in distinction from other persons, but as the Source of all these blessings; hence the employment of the definite article. In such phrases as 'the God of a person,' e.g., Matt. 22:32, the expression marks the relationship in which the person stands to God and God to him.

(*e*) In the following the nominative case is used for the vocative, and always with the article; Mark 15:34; Luke 18:11, 13; John 20:28; (Acts 4:24 in some mss.); Heb. 1:8; 10:7.

(*f*) The phrase "the things of God" (translated literally or otherwise) stands for (1) His interests, Matt. 16:23; Mark 8:33; (2) His counsels, 1 Cor. 2:11; (3) things which are due to Him, Matt. 22:21; Mark 12:17; Luke 20:25. The phrase "things pertaining to God," Rom. 15:17; Heb. 2:17; 5:1, describes, in the Heb. passages, the sacrificial service of the priest; in the Rom. passage the Gospel ministry as an offering to God.

(C) The word is used of Divinely appointed judges in Israel, as representing God in His authority, John 10:34, quoted from Psa. 82:6, which indicates that God Himself sits in judgment on those whom He has appointed. The application of the term to the Devil, 2 Cor. 4:4, and the belly, Phil. 3:19, virtually places these instances under (A).

NT: B.356d; CB.1272a; K.322.
OT: ʼelōhîm: S.430; HR.630a.4b; H.93c; BD.43b.
yehōwāh: S.3068; HR.630a.7a; H.484a; BD.217d.
GEN. REF.: IS.2:493; NB.474; Z.2:742.

For **GOD-SPEED** see **GREETING**

GOD (without)

atheos [ἄθεος, 112], cp. Eng., atheist, primarily signifies godless (*a*, negative), i.e., destitute of God; in Eph. 2:12 the phrase indicates, not only that the Gentiles were void of any true recognition of God, and hence became morally godless (Rom. 1:19-32), but that, being given up by God, they were excluded from communion with God and from the privileges granted to Israel (see the context and cp. Gal. 4:8). As to pagan ideas, the popular cry against the early Christians was "away with the atheists" (see the account of the martyrdom of Polycarp, in Eusebius, Eccles. Hist. iv. 15, 19). ¶

NT: B.20d; CB.1238a; K.322.
OT: —.
GEN. REF.: —.

GODDESS

thea [θεά] is found in Acts 19:27 (in some mss. in vv. 35, 37). ¶

For **GODHEAD** see **DIVINE, DIVINITY**

GODLINESS, GODLY

A. Nouns.

1. *eusebeia* [εὐσέβεια, 2150], from *eu*, well, and *sebomai*, to be devout, denotes that piety which, characterized by a Godward attitude, does that which is well-pleasing to Him. This and the corresponding verb and adverb (see below) are frequent in the Pastoral Epistles, but do not occur in previous Epistles of Paul. The Apostle Peter has the noun four times in his 2nd Epistle, 1:3, 6, 7; 3:11. Elsewhere it occurs in Acts 3:12; 1 Tim. 2:2; 3:16; 4:7, 8; 6:3, 5, 6, 11; 2 Tim. 3:5; Tit. 1:1. In 1 Tim. 6:3 "the doctrine which is according to godliness" signifies that which is consistent with godliness, in contrast to false teachings; in Tit. 1:1, "the truth which is according to godliness" is that which is productive of godliness; in 1 Tim. 3:16, "the mystery of godliness" is godliness as embodied in, and communicated through, the truths of the faith concerning Christ; in 2 Pet. 3:11, the word is in the plural, signifying acts of godliness. ¶

NT: B.326a; CB.1247b; K.1010.
OT: yir'āh: S.3374; HR.580a.1; H.907b; BD.432a.
GEN. REF.: IS.2:516; NB.—; Z.2:767.

2. *theosebeia* [θεοσέβεια, 2317], denotes the fear or reverence of God, from *theos*, god, and *sebomai* (see No. 1), 1 Tim. 2:10. ¶ Cp. the adjective *theosebēs*, God-fearing, John 9:31. ¶ In the Sept., Gen. 20:11 and Job 28:28. ¶

NT: B.358b; CB.1272a; K.331.
OT: yir'āh: S.3374; HR.648a.1,2; H.907b; BD.432a.
GEN. REF.: IS.—; NB.—; Z.2:767.

Note: For *eulabeia*, godly fear, Heb. 5:7; 12:28, see FEAR, A, No. 3; for *eulabeomai*, to reverence, Heb. 11:7 ("for His godly fear"), see FEAR, D, No. 2; for the verb *eusebeō*, to show piety, 1 Tim. 5:4; to worship, Acts 17:23, see PIETY and WORSHIP. ¶

B. Adjective.

eusebēs [εὐσεβής, 2152], akin to A, No. 1, denotes pious, devout, godly, indicating reverence manifested in actions; it is rendered "godly" in 2 Pet. 2:9. See DEVOUT.

NT: B.326b; CB.1247b; K.1010.
OT: ṣaddîq: S.6662; HR.580b.3; H.1879c; BD.843a.
GEN. REF.: IS.2:516; NB.—; Z.2:767.

C. Adverb.

eusebōs [εὐσεβῶς, 2153], denotes piously, godly; it is used with the verb to live (of manner of life) in 2 Tim. 3:12; Tit. 2:12. ¶

NT: B.326c; CB.1247b; K.—.
OT: —.
GEN. REF.: —.

Notes: (1) In the following the word "godly" translates the genitive case of the noun *theos*, lit., 'of God,' 2 Cor. 1:12, A.V., "godly (sincerity)," R.V., "(sincerity) of God"; 2 Cor. 11:2, "a godly jealousy," lit., 'a jealousy of God' (R.V., marg.); 1 Tim. 1:4, R.V., "a dispensation of God" (*oikonomia*, in the best mss.), A.V., "godly edifying" (*oikodomē*, lit., 'an edifying of, i.e., by, God').

(2) In 2 Cor. 7:10, "godly (sorrow)," and in vv. 9 and 11, "after a godly sort," are in all three places, lit., 'according to God.'

(3) In 3 John 6, where the A.V. translates the adverb *axiōs*, with the noun *theos*, "after a godly sort," the R.V. rightly substitutes "worthily of God."

GODWARD

Note: This translates the phrase *pros ton theon*, lit., 'toward God,' in 2 Cor. 3:4, and 1 Thess. 1:8.

GOLD, GOLDEN

A. Nouns.

1. *chrusos* [χρυσός, 5557], is used (*a*) of coin, Matt. 10:9; Jas. 5:3; (*b*) of ornaments, Matt. 23:16, 17; Jas. 5:3 (perhaps both coin and ornaments); Rev. 18:12; some mss. have it instead of No. 2 in 1 Cor. 3:12; (*c*) of images, Acts 17:29; (*d*) of the metal in general, Matt. 2:11; Rev. 9:7 (some mss. have it in Rev. 18:16). ¶

NT: B.888d; CB.1240b; K.—.
OT: zāhāb: S.2091; HR.1478c.1a; H.520a; BD.262c.
GEN. REF.: IS.2:520; NB.824; Z.2:771.

2. *chrusion* [χρυσίον, 5553], a diminutive of No. 1, is used (*a*) of coin, primarily smaller than those in No. 1 (*a*), Acts 3:6; 20:33; 1 Pet. 1:18; (*b*) of ornaments, 1 Pet. 3:3, and the following (in which some mss. have No. 1), 1 Tim. 2:9; Rev. 17:4; 18:16; (*c*) of the metal in general, Heb. 9:4; 1 Pet. 1:7; Rev. 21:18, 21; metaphorically, (*d*) of sound doctrine and its effects, 1 Cor. 3:12; (*e*) of righteousness of life and conduct, Rev. 3:18. ¶

NT: B.888c; CB.1240b; K.—.
OT: zāhāb: S.2091; HR.1477a.1a; H.520a; BD.262c.
GEN. REF.: IS.2:521; NB.824; Z.2:771.

B. Adjective.

chruseos [χρυσέος, 5552], denotes golden, i.e., made of, or overlaid with, gold, 2 Tim. 2:20; Heb. 9:4, and fifteen times in the Apocalypse.

NT: B.888d; CB.—; K.—.
OT: zāhāb: S.2091; HR.1478c.1a; H.520a; BD.262c.
GEN. REF.: IS.2:521; NB.824; Z.2:771.

GOLD RING

chrusodaktulios [χρυσοδακτύλιος, 5554], an adjective denoting 'with a gold ring' (*daktulos*, a finger), occurs in Jas. 2:2. ¶

NT: B.888c; CB.—; K.—.
OT: —.
GEN. REF.: IS.2:521; NB.—; Z.—.

GOOD, GOODLY, GOODNESS

A. Adjectives.

1. *agathos* [ἀγαθός, 18], describes that which, being good in its character or constitution, is beneficial in its effect; it is used (*a*) of things physical, e.g., a tree, Matt. 7:17; ground, Luke 8:8; (*b*) in a moral sense, frequently of persons and things. God is essentially, absolutely and consummately good, Matt. 19:17; Mark 10:18; Luke 18:19. To certain persons the word is applied in Matt. 20:15; 25:21, 23; Luke 19:17; 23:50; John 7:12; Acts 11:24; Tit. 2:5; in a general application, Matt. 5:45; 12:35; Luke 6:45; Rom. 5:7; 1 Pet. 2:18.

The neuter of the adjective with the definite article signifies that which is good, lit., 'the good,' as being morally honourable, pleasing to God, and therefore beneficial. Christians are to prove it, Rom. 12:2; to cleave to it, 12:9; to do it, 13:3; Gal. 6:10; 1 Pet. 3:11 (here, and here only, the article is absent); John 5:29 (here, the neuter plural is used, 'the good things); to work it, Rom. 2:10; Eph. 4:28; 6:8; to follow after it, 1 Thess. 5;15; to be zealous of it, 1 Pet. 3:13; to imitate it, 3 John 11; to overcome evil with it, Rom. 12:21. Governmental authorities are ministers of good, i.e., that which is salutary, suited to the course of human affairs, Rom. 13:4. In Philm. 14, "thy goodness," R.V. (lit., 'thy good'), means 'thy benefit.' As to Matt. 19:17, "why askest thou Me concerning that which is good?" the R.V. follows the most ancient mss.

The neuter plural is also used of material goods, riches, etc., Luke 1:53; 12:18, 19; 16:25; Gal. 6:6 (of temporal supplies); in Rom. 10:15; Heb. 9:11; 10:1, the good things are the benefits provided through the sacrifice of Christ, in regard both to those conferred through the Gospel and to those of the coming Messianic Kingdom. See further under No. 2. See BENEFIT, GOODS.

NT: B.2d; CB.1233b; K.3.
OT: ṭôb: S.2895; HR.2a.4b; H.793; BD.373b.
GEN. REF.: IS.2:525; NB.481; Z.2:775.

2. *kalos* [καλός, 2570], denotes that which is intrinsically good, and so, goodly, fair, beautiful, as (*a*) of that which is well adapted to its circumstances or ends, e.g., fruit, Matt. 3:10; a tree, 12:33; ground, 13:8, 23; fish, 13:48; the Law, Rom. 7:16; 1 Tim. 1:8; every creature of God, 1 Tim. 4:4; a faithful minister of Christ and the doctrine he teaches, 4:6; (*b*) of that which is ethically good, right, noble, honourable, e.g., Gal. 4:18; 1 Tim. 5:10, 25; 6:18; Tit. 2:7, 14; 3:8, 14. The word does not occur in the Apocalypse, nor indeed after 1 Peter.

Christians are to "take thought for things honourable" (*kalos*), 2 Cor. 8:21, R.V.; to do that which is honourable, 13:7; not to be weary in well doing, Gal. 6:9; to hold fast "that which is good," 1 Thess. 5:21; to be zealous of good works, Tit. 2:14; to maintain them, 3:8; to provoke to them, Heb. 10:24; to bear testimony by them, 1 Pet. 2:12.

Kalos and *agathos* occur together in Luke 8:15, an "honest" (*kalos*) heart, i.e., the attitude of which is right towards God; a "good" (*agathos*) heart, i.e., one that, instead of working ill to a neighbour, acts beneficially towards him. In Rom. 7:18, "in me . . . dwelleth no good thing" (*agathos*) signifies that in him is nothing capable of doing good, and hence he lacks the power "to do that which is good" (*kalos*). In 1 Thess. 5:15, "follow after that which is good" (*agathos*), the good is that which is beneficial; in ver. 21, "hold fast that which is good (*kalos*)," the good describes the intrinsic value of the teaching. See BETTER, FAIR, HONEST, MEET, WORTHY.

NT: B.400b; CB.1253b; K.402.
OT: ṭôb: S.2895; HR.715b.2a; H.793; BD.373b.
yāpheh: S.3303; HR.715b.3a; H.890a; BD.421c.
GEN. REF.: IS.2:525; NB.481; Z.2:775.

3. *chrēstos* [χρηστός, 5543], said of things, that which is pleasant, said of persons, kindly, gracious, is rendered "good" in 1 Cor. 15:33; "goodness" in Rom. 2:4. See EASY.

NT: B.886a; CB.1240a; K.1320.
OT: ṭôb: S.2895; HR.1475a.la; H.793; BD.373b.
GEN. REF.: IS.2:525; NB.481; Z.2:775.

Note: Lampros denotes gay, bright, "goodly" in Jas. 2:2, A.V., (R.V., "fine"); in 2:3, A.V., "gay"; in Rev. 18:14 (R.V., "sumptuous"). See GORGEOUS, SUMPTUOUS. For *asteios*, "goodly," Heb. 11:23, R.V., see BEAUTIFUL. For *hikanos*, Acts 18:18, A.V., "a good while" see WHILE. *Note* (16).

B. Nouns.

1. *chrēstotēs* [χρηστότης, 5544], akin to A, No. 3, denotes goodness (*a*) in the sense of what is upright, righteous, Rom. 3:12 (translated "good"); (*b*) in the sense of kindness of heart or act, said of God, Rom. 2:4; 11:22 (thrice); Eph. 2:7 ("kindness"); Tit. 3:4 ("kindness"); said of believers and rendered "kindness,"

2 Cor. 6:6; Col. 3:12; Gal. 5:22 (R.V.; A.V., "gentleness"). It signifies "not merely goodness as a quality, rather it is goodness in action, goodness expressing itself in deeds; yet not goodness expressing itself in indignation against sin, for it is contrasted with severity in Rom. 11:22, but in grace and tenderness and compassion."* See GENTLENESS, KINENESS. ¶

NT: B.886b; CB.1240a; K.1320.
OT: ṭôb: S.2895; HR.1475a.1b; H.793; BD.373b.
ṭôbāh: S.2896; HR.1475a.1c; H.793a; BD.375c.
GEN. REF.: IS.2:525; NB.481; Z.2:775.

2. *agathōsunē* [ἀγαθωσύνη, 19], goodness, signifies that moral quality which is described by the adjective *agathos* (see A, No. 1). It is used, in the N.T., of regenerate persons, Rom. 15:14; Gal. 5:22; Eph. 5:9; 2 Thess. 1:11; in the last, the phrase "every desire of goodness" (R.V.; the addition of "His" in the A.V. is an interpolation; there is no pronoun in the original) may be either subjective, i.e., desire characterised by goodness, good desire, or objective, i.e., desire after goodness, to be and do good. ¶

Trench, following Jerome, distinguishes between *chrēstotēs* and *agathōsunē* in that the former describes the kindlier aspects of goodness, the latter includes also the sterner qualities by which doing good to others is not necessarily by gentle means. He illustrates the latter by the act of Christ in cleansing the temple, Matt. 21:12, 13, and in denouncing the Scribes and Pharisees, 23:13-29; but *chrēstotēs* by His dealings with the penitent woman, Luke 7:37;50. Lightfoot regards *chrēstotēs* as a kindly disposition towards others; *agathōsunē* as a kindly activity on their behalf.

J. A. Robertson (on Eph. 5:9) remarks that *agathōsunē* is "the kindlier, as *dikaiosunē* (righteousness) the sterner element in the ideal character."

NT: B.3d; CB.1233b; K.3.
OT: ṭôb: S.2895; HR.4c.1b; H.793; BD.373b.
ṭôbāh: S.2896; HR.4c.1c; H.793a; BD.375c.
GEN. REF.: IS.2:525; NB.481; Z.2:775.

3. *eupoiia* [εὐποιΐα, 2140], beneficence, doing good (*eu*, well, *poieō*, to do), is translated as a verb in Heb. 13:16, "to do good." ¶

NT: B.324a; CB.–; K.–.
OT: –.
GEN. REF.: –.

C. Adverbs.

1. *kalōs* [καλῶς, 2573], well, finely, is used in some mss. in Matt. 5:44, with *poieō*, to do, and translated "do good." In Jas. 2:3 it is rendered "in a good place" (A.V. marg., "well" or "seemly"). See WELL

NT: B.401b; CB.1253b; K.–.
OT: yāṭab: S.3190; HR.717b.1a,2b; H.863; BD.405c.
ṭôb: S.2895; HR.717b.1b,2a,3b; H.793; BD.373b.
GEN. REF.: IS.2:525; NB.481; Z.2:775.

2. *eu* [εὖ, 2095], well, used with *poieō*, is translated "do . . . good" in Mark 14:7. See WELL.

NT: B.317b; CB.1247a; K.–.
OT: yāṭab: S.3190; HR.568a.1a,3a; H.863; BD.405c.
ṭôb: S.2895; HR.568a.2b; H.793; BD.373b.
GEN. REF.: IS.2:525; NB.481; Z.2:775.

D. Verbs (to do, or be, good).

1. *agathopoieō* [ἀγαθοποιέω, 15], from A, No. 1, and *poieō*, to do, is used (*a*) in a general way, to do well, 1 Pet. 2:15, 20; 3:6, 17; 3 John 11; (*b*) with pointed reference to the benefit of another, Luke 6:9, 33, 35; in Mark 3:4 the parts of the word are separated in some mss. Some mss. have it in Acts 14:17, for No. 2. ¶ Cp. the noun *agathopoiia*, well-doing, 1 Pet. 4:19, and the adjective *agathopoios*, doing well, 1 Pet. 2:14.

NT: B.2c; CB.1233b; K.3.
OT: yāṭab: S.3190; HR.1c.1; H.863; BD.405c.
GEN. REF.: IS.2:525; NB.481; Z.–.

2. *agathourgeō, agathoergeō* [ἀγαθουργέω, 14], for *agathoergeō*, to do good (from A, No. 1, and *ergon*, a work), is used in Acts 14:17 (in the best mss.; see No. 1), where it is said of God's beneficence towards man, and 1 Tim. 6:18, where it is enjoined upon the rich. ¶

NT: B.2b; CB.1233b; K.3.
OT: –.
GEN. REF.: –.

3. *euergeteō* [εὐεργετέω, 2109], to bestow a benefit, to do good (*eu*, well, and a verbal form akin to *ergon*), is used in Acts 10:38. ¶

NT: B.320a; CB.1247a; K.251.
OT: gāmal: S.1580; HR.569c.1; H.360; BD.168a.
GEN. REF.: –.

Notes: (1) The verb *ischuō*, to be strong (*ischus*, strength), to have efficacy, force or value, is said of salt in Matt. 5:13, negatively, "it is good for nothing."

(2) In Matt. 19:10, A.V., *sumpherō*, to be profitable, expedient (*sun*, together, *pherō*, to bring), is rendered with a negative "it is not good" (R.V., "it is not expedient").

(3) In Mark 14:7, the two words *eu*, well, and *poieō*, to do, are in some mss. treated as one verb *eupoieō*, to do good.

GOODMAN

oikodespotēs [οἰκοδεσπότης, 3617], denotes the master of a house (*oikos*, a house, *despotēs*, a master), a householder. It occurs only in the Synoptists, and there 12 times. It is rendered

* From Notes on Galatians, by Hogg and Vine, p. 252.

"goodman" in Luke 22:11, where "of the house" is put separately; in Matt. 20:11, where A.V. has "the goodman of the house" for the one word, the R.V. renders it by "householder," as in ver. 1; in 24:43, "master"; so in Luke 12:39; in Mark 14:14, both have "the goodman of the house." See HOUSEHOLDER, MASTER.

NT: B.558a; CB.1260b; K.145.
OT: —.
GEN. REF.: IS.2:527; NB.—; Z.2:776.

GOODS

1. For the neuter plural of *agathos*, used as a noun, "goods," see Luke 12:18, 19, where alone this word is so rendered.

2. *huparxis* [ὕπαρξις, 5223], primarily, subsistence, then, substance, property, goods (akin to *huparchō*, to exist, be, belong to), is translated "goods" in Acts 2:45; "possession," R.V. (A.V., "substance") in Heb. 10:34. ¶

NT: B.837d; CB.1252a; K.—.
OT: rᵉkûsh: S.7399; HR.1406b.4; H.2167b; BD.940d.
hôn: S.1952; HR.1406b.1; H.487a; BD.223c.
GEN. REF.: IS.2:528; NB.—; Z.2:776.

3. *bios* [βίος, 979], which denotes (*a*) life, lifetime, (*b*) livelihood, living, means of living, is translated "goods" in 1 John 3:17, R.V. (A.V., "good"). See LIFE, No. 2.

NT: B.141d; CB.1239a; K.290.
OT: yôm: S.3117; HR.220a.3a; H.852; BD.398a,399a.
GEN. REF.: IS.2:528; NB.—; Z.—.

4. *skeuos* [σκεῦος, 4632], a vessel, denotes "goods" in Matt. 12:29; Mark 3:27; Luke 17:31, R.V. (A.V., "stuff"). See VESSEL.

NT: B.754a; CB.1269a; K.1038.
OT: kᵉlî: S.3627; HR.1269b.1; H.982g; BD.479b.
GEN. REF.: IS.2:528; NB.—; Z.2:776.

Notes: (1) The neuter plural of the present participle of *huparchō*, is used as a noun denoting goods, in Matt. 24:47, A.V. "his goods," R.V. "that he hath"; "goods" in Matt. 25:14; Luke 11:21; 16:1; 19:8; 1 Cor. 13:3; in Heb. 10:34 (1st part).

(2) In Luke 6:30 "thy goods" translates the neuter plural of the possessive pronoun with the article, lit., 'thy things,' or possessions.

(3) In Rev. 3:17, the A.V. "I am . . . increased with goods" translates the perfect tense of the verb *plouteō*, to be rich; R.V., "I have gotten riches."

(4) See SUBSTANCE

GORGEOUS, GORGEOUSLY

lampros [λαμπρός, 2986], bright, splendid, is rendered "gorgeous" in Luke 23:11, of the apparel in which Herod and his soldiers arrayed Christ. See BRIGHT.

NT: B.465d; CB.1256c; K.497.
OT: —.
GEN. REF.: IS.2:528; NB.—; Z.—.

Note: For the A.V., "gorgeously apparelled" in Luke 7:25, see GLORIOUS, B.

GOSPEL
(Noun and Verb: to preach)

A. Noun.

euangelion [εὐαγγέλιον, 2098], originally denoted a reward for good tidings; later, the idea of reward dropped, and the word stood for the good news itself. The Eng. word gospel, i.e. good message, is the equivalent of *euangelion* (Eng. evangel). In the N.T. it denotes the good tidings of the Kingdom of God and of salvation through Christ, to be received by faith, on the basis of His expiatory death, His burial, resurrection, and ascension, e.g., Acts 15:7; 20:24; 1 Pet. 4:17. Apart from those references and those in the Gospels of Matthew and Mark, and Rev. 14:6, the noun is confined to Paul's Epistles. The Apostle uses it of two associated yet distinct things, (*a*) of the basic facts of the death, burial and resurrection of Christ, e.g., 1 Cor. 15:1-3; (*b*) of the interpretation of these facts, e.g., Rom. 2:16; Gal. 1:7, 11; 2:2; in (*a*) the Gospel is viewed historically, in (*b*) doctrinally, with reference to the interpretation of the facts, as is sometimes indicated by the context.

The following phrases describe the subjects or nature or purport of the message; it is the gospel of God, Mark 1:14; Rom. 1:1; 15:16; 2 Cor. 11:7; 1 Thess. 2:2, 9; 1 Pet. 4:17; God, concerning His Son, Rom. 1:1-3; His Son, Rom. 1:9; Jesus Christ, the Son of God, Mark 1:1; our Lord Jesus, 2 Thess. 1:8; Christ, Rom. 15:19, etc.; the glory of Christ, 2 Cor. 4:4; the grace of God, Acts 20:24; the glory of the blessed God, 1 Tim. 1:11; your salvation, Eph. 1:13; peace, Eph. 6:15. Cp. also "the gospel of the Kingdom," Matt. 4:23; 9:35; 24:14; "an eternal gospel," Rev. 14:6.

In Gal. 2:14, "the truth of the gospel" denotes, not the true gospel, but the true teaching of it, in contrast to perversions of it.

The following expressions are used in connection with the Gospel: (*a*) with regard to its testimony; (1) *kērussō*, to preach it as a herald, e.g., Matt. 4:23; Gal. 2:2 (see PREACH); (2) *laleō*, to speak, 1 Thess. 2:2; (3) *diamarturomai*, to testify (thoroughly), Acts 20:24; (4) *euangelizō*, to preach, e.g., 1 Cor. 15:1; 2 Cor. 11:7; Gal. 1:11 (see B, No. 1 below); (5) *katangellō*, to proclaim, 1 Cor. 9:14; (6) *douleuō eis*, to serve unto ("in furtherance of"), Phil. 2:22; (7) *sunathleō en*, to labour with in, Phil.

4:3; (8) *hierourgeō*, to minister, Rom. 15:16; (8) *plēroō*, to preach fully, Rom. 15:19; (10) *sunkakopatheō*, to suffer hardship with, 2 Tim. 1:8; (*b*) with regard to its reception or otherwise: (1) *dechomai*, to receive, 2 Cor. 11:4; *hupakouō*, to hearken to, or obey, Rom. 10:16; 2 Thess. 1:8; *pisteuō en*, to believe in, Mark 1:15; *metastrephō*, to pervert, Gal. 1:7.

NT: B.317d; CB.1247a; K.267.
OT: bᵉsôrāh: S.1309; HR.568c.1; H.291b; BD.142d.
GEN. REF.: IS.2:529; NB.484; Z.2:779.

Note: In connection with (*a*), the Apostle's statement in 1 Cor. 9:23 is noticeable, "I do all things for the Gospel's sake, that I may be a joint partaker thereof," R.V., for the incorrect A.V., "that I might be partaker thereof with you."

B. Verbs.

1. *euangelizō* [εὐαγγελίζω, 2097], to bring or announce glad tidings (Eng., evangelize), is used (*a*) in the Active Voice in Rev. 10:7 ("declared") and 14:6 ("to proclaim," R.V., A.V., "to preach"); (*b*) in the Passive Voice, of matters to be proclaimed as glad tidings, Luke 16:16; Gal. 1:11; 1 Pet. 1:25; of persons to whom the proclamation is made, Matt. 11:5; Luke 7:22; Heb. 4:2, 6; 1 Pet. 4:6; (*c*) in the Middle Voice, especially of the message of salvation, with a personal object, either of the Person preached, e.g., Acts 5:42; 11:20; Gal. 1:16, or, with a preposition, of the persons evangelized, e.g., Acts 13:32, "declare glad tidings"; Rom. 1:15; Gal. 1:8; with an impersonal object, e.g., "the word," Acts 8:4; "good tidings," 8:12; "the word of the Lord," 15:35; "the gospel," 1 Cor. 15:1; 2 Cor. 11:7; "the faith," Gal. 1:23; "peace," Eph. 2:17; "the unsearchable riches of Christ," 3:8. See PREACH, SHEW, TIDINGS.

NT: B.317b; CB.1247a; K.267.
OT: bāsar: S.1319; HR.586b.1; H.291; BD.142a.
GEN. REF.: IS.2:529; NB.–; Z.2:779.

2. *proeuangelizomai* [προευαγγελίζομαι, 4283], to announce glad tidings beforehand, is used in Gal. 3:8. ¶

NT: B.705d; CB.–; K.267.
OT: –.
GEN. REF.: IS.2:529; NB.–; Z.–.

Note: For other verbs see above.

For **GOT** and **GOTTEN** see **GET**

GOVERNMENT

kubernēsis [κυβέρνησις, 2941], from *kubernaō*, to guide (whence Eng., govern), denotes (*a*) steering, pilotage; (*b*) metaphorically, governments or governings, said of those who act as guides in a local church, 1 Cor. 12:28. ¶ Cp. *kubernētes*, a pilot, Acts 27:11; Rev. 18:17. ¶

NT: B.456c; CB.1256b; K.486.
OT: taḥbulôt: S.8458; HR.796a.1; H.596a; BD.287a.
GEN. REF.: –.

Note: For *kuriotēs*, lordship, dominion, rendered "government" in 2 Pet. 2:10, A.V., see DOMINION.

GOVERNOR

A. Nouns.

1. *hēgemōn* [ἡγεμών, 2232], is a term used (*a*) for rulers generally, Mark 13:9; 1 Pet. 2:14; translated "princes" (i.e., leaders) in Matt. 2:6; (*b*) for the Roman Procurators, referring, in the Gospels to Pontius Pilate, e.g., Matt. 27:2; Luke 20:20 (so designated by Tacitus, Annals, xv. 44); to Felix, Acts 23:26. Technically the Procurator was a financial official under a proconsul or propraetor, for collecting the Imperial revenues, but entrusted also with magistrial powers for decisions of questions relative to the revenues. In certain provinces, of which Judaea was one (the Procurator of which was dependent on the Legate of Syria), he was the general administrator and supreme judge, with sole power of life and death. Such a governor was a person of high social standing. Felix, however, was an ex-slave, a freedman, and his appointment to Judaea could not but be regarded by the Jews as an insult to the nation. The headquarters of the governor of Judaea was Caesarea, which was made a garrison town. See PRINCE, RULER. For *anthupatos*, a proconsul, see PROCONSUL.

NT: B.343b; CB.1249c; K.–.
OT: allûph: S.441; HR.603c.2; H.109b; BD.49b.
sar: S.8269; HR.603c.5; H.2295a; BD.978a.
GEN. REF.: IS.2:546; NB.491; Z.2:798.

2. *ethnarchēs* [ἐθνάρχης, 1481], an ethnarch, lit. a ruler of a nation (*ethnos*, a people, *archē*, rule), is translated "governor" in 2 Cor. 11:32; it describes normally the ruler of a nation possessed of separate laws and customs among those of a different race. Eventually it denoted a ruler of a Province, superior to a tetrarch, but inferior to a king (e.g., Aretas). ¶

NT: B.218b; CB.–; K.–.
OT: –.
GEN. REF.: IS.2:546; NB.491; Z.2:798.

3. *oikonomos* [οἰκονόμος, 3623], lit., one who rules a house (*oikos*, a house, *nomos*, a law), Gal. 4:2, denotes a superior servant responsible for the family housekeeping, the direction of other servants, and the care of the children under age. See CHAMBERLAIN, STEWARD.

NT: B.560a; CB.1260b; K.674.
OT: –.
GEN. REF.: IS.–; NB.491; Z.2:798.

4. *architriklinos* [ἀρχιτρίκλινος, 755], from *archē*, rule, and *triklinos*, a room with three couches, denotes the ruler of a feast, John 2:8, R.V. (A.V., "the governor of the feast"), a man appointed to see that the table and couches were duly placed and the courses arranged, and to taste the food and wine. ¶

NT: B.113b; CB.–; K.–.
OT: –.
GEN. REF.: IS.–; NB.491; Z.2:798.

B. Verbs.

1. *hēgeomai* [ἡγέομαι, 2233], akin to A, No. 1, is used in the present participle to denote a governor, lit., '(one) governing,' Matt. 2:6; Acts 7:10.

NT: B.343c; CB.1249c; K.303.
OT: nāgîd: S.5057; HR.602c.21; H.1289b; BD.617d.
rō'sh: S.7218; HR.602c.31; H.2097; BD.910c.
GEN. REF.: IS.2:546; NB.491; Z.2:798.

2. *hēgemoneuō* [ἡγεμονεύω, 2230], to be a *hēgemōn*, to lead the way, came to signify to be a governor of a Province; it is used of Quirinius, governor of Syria, Luke 2:2, R.V. (for the circumstances see under ENROLMENT); of Pontius Pilate, governor of Judaea, 3:1. ¶ In the first clause of this verse the noun *hēgemonia*, a rule or sovereignty, is translated "reign"; Eng., hegemony. ¶

NT: B.343a; CB.–; K.–.
OT: –.
GEN. REF.: IS.2:546; NB.491; Z.2:798.

Note: In Jas. 3:4, the verb *euthunō*, to make or guide straight, is used in the present participle, as a noun, denoting the "steersman" (R.V.) or pilot of a vessel, A.V., "governor."

GRACE

1. *charis* [χάρις, 5485], has various uses, (*a*) objective, that which bestows or occasions pleasure, delight, or causes favourable regard; it is applied, e.g., to beauty, or gracefulness of a person, Luke 2:40; act, 2 Cor. 8:6, or speech, Luke 4:22, R.V., "words of grace" (A.V., "gracious words"); Col. 4:6; (*b*) subjective, (1) on the part of the bestower, the friendly disposition from which the kindly act proceeds, graciousness, loving-kindness, goodwill generally, e.g., Acts 7:10; especially with reference to the Divine favour or grace, e.g., Acts 14:26; in this respect there is stress on its freeness and universality, its spontaneous character, as in the case of God's redemptive mercy, and the pleasure or joy He designs for the recipient; thus it is set in contrast with debt, Rom. 4:4, 16, with works, 11:6, and with law, John 1:17; see also, e.g., Rom 6:14, 15; Gal. 5:4; (2) on the part of the receiver, a sense of the favour bestowed, a feeling of gratitude, e.g., Rom. 6:17 ("thanks"); in this respect it sometimes signifies to be thankful, e.g., Luke 17:9 ("doth he thank the servant?" lit., 'hath he thanks to'); 1 Tim. 1:12; (*c*) in another objective sense, the effect of grace, the spiritual state of those who have experienced its exercise, whether (1) a state of grace, e.g., Rom. 5;2; 1 Pet. 5:12; 2 Pet. 3:18, or (2) a proof thereof in practical effects, deeds of grace, e.g., 1 Cor. 16:3, R.V., "bounty" (A.V., "liberality"); 2 Cor. 8:6, 19 (in 2 Cor. 9:8 it means the sum of earthly blessings); the power and equipment for ministry, e.g., Rom. 1:5; 12:6; 15:15; 1 Cor. 3:10; Gal. 2:9; Eph. 3:2, 7.

To be in favour with is to find grace with, e.g., Acts 2:47; hence it appears in this sense at the beginning and the end of several Epistles, where the writer desires grace from God for the readers, e.g., Rom. 1:7; 1 Cor. 1:3; in this respect it is connected with the imperative mood of the word *chairō*, to rejoice, a mode of greeting among Greeks, e.g., Acts 15:23; Jas. 1:1 (marg.); 2 John 10, 11, R.V., "greeting" (A.V., "God speed").

The fact that grace is received both from God the Father, 2 Cor. 1:12, and from Christ, Gal. 1:6; Rom. 5:15 (where both are mentioned), is a testimony to the Deity of Christ. See also 2 Thess. 1:12, where the phrase "according to the grace of our God and the Lord Jesus Christ" is to be taken with each of the preceding clauses, "in you," "and ye in Him."

In Jas. 4:6, "But He giveth more grace" (Greek, 'a greater grace,' R.V., marg.), the statement is to be taken in connection with the preceding verse, which contains two remonstrating, rhetorical questions, "Think ye that the Scripture speaketh in vain?" and "Doth the Spirit (the Holy Spirit) which He made to dwell in us long unto envying?" (see the R.V.). The implied answer to each is 'it cannot be so.' Accordingly, if those who are acting so flagrantly, as if it were so, will listen to the Scripture instead of letting it speak in vain, and will act so that the Holy Spirit may have His way within, God will give even 'a greater grace,' namely, all that follows from humbleness and from turning away from the world. See BENEFIT, BOUNTY, LIBERALITY, THANK.

NT: B.877b; CB.1239c; K.1298.
OT: ḥēn: S.2580; HR.1455a.2; H.694a; BD.336b.
ḥesed: S.2617; HR.1455a.3; H.686a,699a; BD.338c.
GEN. REF.: IS.2:547; NB.491; Z.2:799.

Note: The corresponding verb *charitoō*, to endue with Divine favour or grace, is used in Luke 1:28, "highly favoured" (marg., "endued with grace") and Eph. 1:6, A.V., "hath made . . . accepted"; R.V. "freely bestowed" (marg., "endued."). ¶

2. *euprepeia* [εὐπρέπεια, 2143], comeliness, goodly appearance, is said of the outward appearance of the flower of the grass, Jas. 1:11. ¶

NT: B.324b; CB.–; K.–.
OT: hādār: S.1926; HR.576b.2; H.477b; BD.214a.
GEN. REF.: –.

GRACIOUS

chrēstos [χρηστός, 5543], is rendered "gracious" in 1 Pet. 2:3, as an attribute of the Lord. See EASY, GOOD, KIND.

NT: B.886a; CB.1240; K.1320.
OT: ṭôb: S.2895; HR.1475a.1a; H.793; BD.373b.
yāqār: S.3368; HR.1475a.2; H.905a; BD.429d.
GEN. REF.: IS.2:552; NB.–; Z.–.

Note: Euphēmos, fair-sounding (*eu*, well, *phēmē*, a saying, or report), "of good report," Phil. 4:8, is rendered "gracious" in the R.V. marg.

GRAFF, GRAFT (R.V.)

enkentrizō [ἐνκεντρίζω, 1461], denotes to graft in (*en*, in, *kentrizō*, to graft), to insert a slip of a cultivated tree into a wild one. In Rom. 11:17, 19, 23, 24, however, the metaphor is used "contrary to nature" (ver. 24), of grafting a wild olive branch (the Gentile) into the good olive tree (the Jews); that unbelieving Jews (branches of the good tree) were broken off that Gentiles might be grafted in, afforded no occasion for glorying on the part of the latter. Jew and Gentile alike must enjoy the Divine blessings by faith alone. So Jews who abide not in unbelief shall, as "the natural branches, be grafted into their own olive tree." ¶

NT: B.216a; CB.1245a; K.–.
OT: –.
GEN. REF.: IS.2:553; NB.–; Z.2:804.

GRAIN

kokkos [κόκκος, 2848], denotes a grain, Matt. 13:31; 17:20; Mark 4:31; Luke 13:19; 17:6; John 12:24 (A.V., "corn"); 1 Cor. 15:37 (where the R.V. has "a . . . grain," to distinguish it from grain in general). See CORN. ¶

NT: B.440c; CB.–; K.450.
OT: –
GEN. REF.: IS.2:553; NB.493; Z.2:804.

GRANDCHILDREN

ekgonos [ἔκγονος, 1549], an adjective, denoting born of (*ek*, from, *ginomai*, to become or be born), was used as a noun, signifying a child; in the plural, descendants, "grandchildren," 1 Tim. 5:4, R.V. (A.V., "nephews"). ¶

NT: B.238a; CB.–; K.–.
OT: yālîd: S.3211; HR.867e; H.421c.5a; BD.409c.
môledet: S.4138; HR.867f; H.421c.5b; BD.409d.
ṣe'ᵉṣā'îm: S.6631; HR.893b; H.421c.7; BD.425c.
GEN. REF.: IS.2:554; NB.–; Z.–.

GRANDMOTHER

mammē [μάμμη, 3125], an onomatopoeic word, was primarily a child's name for its mother; later it denoted a grandmother, 2 Tim. 1:5. ¶

NT: B.490a; CB.–; K.–.
OT: –.
GEN. REF.: –.

GRANT

1. *didōmi* [δίδωμι, 1325], to give, is rendered "grant" in Mark 10:37; Luke 1:74; Acts 4:29; 11:18; 14:3. See GIVE.

NT: B.192c; CB.1241c; K.166.
OT: nātan: S.5414; HR.317b.26a; H.1443; BD.678a.
GEN. REF.: –.

2. *dōreō* [δωρέω, 1433], to present, bestow (akin to No. 1), is rendered "granted" in Mark 15:45, R.V., (A.V., "gave"); in 2 Pet. 1:3, 4, "hath granted," "He hath granted," R.V. (A.V., "hath given" and "are given"); in each place Middle Voice. See GIVE. ¶

NT: B.210d; CB.1242a; K.166.
OT: nātan: S.5414; HR.359a.2; H.1443; BD.678a.
qorbān: S.7133; HR.359a.3; H.2065e; BD.898d.
GEN. REF.: –.

3. *charizomai* [χαρίζομαι, 5483], primarily signifies to show favour or kindness (akin to *charis*, see GRACE), Gal. 3:18, R.V., "hath granted" (A.V., "gave"; it signifies more than to give); then, to give freely, bestow, rendered to grant in Acts 3:14; 27:24, R.V. (A.V., "given"); Phil. 1:29, R.V.; Philm. 22, R.V. See DELIVER.

NT: B.876c; CB.1239c; K.1298.
OT: nātan: S.5414; HR.1454c.1; H.1443; BD.678a.
GEN. REF.: –.

GRAPE

staphulē [σταφυλή, 4718], denotes a bunch of grapes, or a grape, Matt. 7:16; Luke 6:44; Rev. 14:18. It is to be distinguished from *omphax*, an unripe grape (not in N.T.), e.g., in the Sept. of Job 15:33, and from *botrus*, a cluster, used together with *staphulē* in Rev. 14:18. ¶

NT: B.765c; CB.–; K.–.
OT: 'ēnāb: S.6025; HR.1287a.1; H.1647a; BD.772a.
GEN. REF.: IS.2:554; NB.–; Z.–.

GRASS

chortos [χόρτος, 5528], primarily denoted a feeding enclosure (whence Latin *hortus*, a garden; Eng., yard, and garden); then, food, especially grass for feeding cattle; it is translated "grass" in Matt. 6:30; 14:19; Mark 6:39 (where "the green grass" is the first evidence of early spring); Luke 12:28; John 6:10; Jas. 1:10, 11; 1 Pet. 1:24; Rev. 8:7; 9:4; "blade" in Matt. 13:26; Mark 4:28; "hay" in 1 Cor. 3:12, used figuratively. In Palestine or Syria there are 90 genera and 243 species of grass. ¶

NT: B.884a; CB.1240a; K.—.
OT: ḥāṣîr: S.2682; HR.1473a.2; H.724a,725a; BD.348b.
ʿēsheb: S.6212; HR.1473a.3a; H.1707a; BD.793b.
GEN. REF.: IS.2:555; NB.—; Z.2:805.

GRATULATION

makarismos [μακαρισμός, 3108], denotes a declaration of blessedness, a felicitation; it is translated "gratulation" in Gal. 4:15, R.V. (A.V., "blessedness"); the Galatian converts had counted themselves happy when they heard and received the Gospel from Paul; he asks them rhetorically what had become of that spirit which had animated them; the word is rendered "blessing" in Rom. 4:6, 9. See BLESSING, C, No. 2. ¶

NT: B.487a; CB.1257c; K.548.
OT: —.
GEN. REF.: —.

GRAVE (Noun)

1. *mnēmeion* [μνημεῖον, 3419], primarily denotes a memorial (akin to *mnaomai*, to remember), then, a monument (the significance of the word rendered "tombs," A.V., "sepulchres," in Luke 11:47), anything done to preserve the memory of things and persons; it usually denotes a tomb, and is translated either "tomb" or "sepulchre" or "grave." Apart from the Gospels, it is found only in Acts 13:29. Among the Hebrews it was generally a cavern, closed by a door or stone, often decorated. Cp. Matt. 23:29. See TOMB.

NT: B.524c; CB.1259a; K.596.
OT: qeber: S.6913; HR.931b.1a; H.1984a; BD.868d.
GEN. REF.: IS.—; NB.170; Z.2:807.

2. *mnēma* [μνῆμα, 3418], akin to No. 1, like which it signified a memorial or record of a thing or a dead person, then a sepulchral monument, and hence a tomb; it is rendered "graves" in the A.V. of Rev. 11:9 (R.V., "a tomb"); "tomb" or "tombs," Mark 5:3, 5 (some mss. have No. 1, as in 15:46, A.V., "Sepulchre") and 16:2 (A.V., "sepulchre"); Luke 8:27; Acts 2:29 and 7:16 (A.V., "sepulchre"). See TOMB.

NT: B.524c; CB.1259a; K.596.
OT: qeber: S.6913; HR.931b.1a; H.1984a; BD.868d.
GEN. REF.: IS.1:556; NB.170; Z.2:807.

Note: In 1 Cor. 15:55, where some texts have "Hades," A.V., "grave," the most authentic have *thanatos*, death.

GRAVE (Adjective)

semnos [σεμνός, 4586], first denoted reverend, august, venerable (akin to *sebomai*, to reverence); then, serious, grave, whether of persons, 1 Tim. 3:8, 11 (deacons and their wives); Tit. 2:2 (aged men); or things, Phil. 4:8, R.V., "honourable" (marg., "reverend"), A.V., "honest." Trench (Syn. § xcii) points out that "grave" and "gravity" fail to cover the full meaning of their original; "the word we want is one in which the sense of gravity and dignity is combined." Cremer describes it as denoting what inspires reverence and awe, and says that *semnos* and *hosios*, holy, consecrated, are only secondary designations of the conception of holiness. "The word points to seriousness of purpose and to self-respect in conduct" (Moule). ¶ Cp. *semnotēs*, gravity (see below).

NT: B.746d; CB.1269a; K.1010.
OT: —.
GEN. REF.: —.

GRAVE-CLOTHES

keiria [κειρία, 2750], denotes, firstly, a band either for a bed girth, or bed sheets themselves (Sept. of Prov. 7:16. ¶); then, the swathings wrapped round a corpse; it is used in the plural in John 11:44. ¶

NT: B.427a; CB.—; K.—.
OT: marbaddîm: S.4765; HR.758b.1; H.2102a; BD.915a.
GEN. REF.: —.

GRAVEN

charagma [χάραγμα, 5480], from *charassō*, to engrave (akin to *charaktēr*, an impress, R.V., marg., of Heb. 1:3), denotes (*a*) a mark or stamp, e.g., Rev. 13:16, 17; 14:9, 11; 16:2; 19:20; 20:4; 15:2 in some mss.; (*b*) a thing graven, Acts 17:29. ¶

NT: B.876a; CB.1239b; K.1308.
OT: —.
GEN. REF.: —.

GRAVITY

semnotēs [σεμνότης, 4587], denotes venerableness, dignity; it is a necessary characteristic of the life and conduct of Christians, 1 Tim. 2:2, R.V., "gravity" (A.V., "honesty"), a qualification of a bishop or overseer in a church, in regard to his children, 1 Tim. 3:4; a necessary characteristic of the teaching imparted by a servant of God, Tit. 2:7. ¶ Cp. the adjective *semnos*, under GRAVE.

NT: B.747a; CB.1269a; K.1010.
OT: —.
GEN. REF.: —.

GREAT

1. *megas* [μέγας, 3173], is used (*a*) of external form, size, measure, e.g., of a stone, Matt. 27:60; fish, John 21:11; (*b*) of degree and intensity, e.g., of fear, Mark 4:41; wind, John 6:18; Rev. 6:13, R.V., "great" (A.V., "mighty"); of a circumstance, 1 Cor. 9:11; 2 Cor. 11:15; in Rev. 5:2, 12, the R.V. has "great" (A.V., "loud"), of a voice; (*c*) of rank, whether of persons, e.g., God, Tit. 2:13; Christ as a "great Priest," Heb. 10:21, R.V.; Diana, Acts 19:27; Simon Magus, Acts 8:9 "(some) great one"; in the plural, "great ones," Matt. 20:25; Mark 10:42, those who hold positions of authority in Gentile nations; or of things, e.g., a mystery, Eph. 5:32. Some mss. have it in Acts 8:8, of joy (see No. 2). See also *Note* (2) below. See GREATEST, HIGH, LOUD, MIGHTY, STRONG.

NT: B.497c; CB.1258a; K.573.
OT: gādôl: S.1419; HR.902c.2a; H.315d; BD.152d.
rab: S.7227; HR.902c.12a; H.2099a,b; BD.912d.
GEN. REF.: IS.2:556; NB.—; Z.2:810.

2. *polus* [πολύς, 4183], much, many, great, is used of number, e.g., Luke 5:6; Acts 11:21; degree, e.g., of harvest, Matt. 9:37 [See *Note* (8)]; mercy, 1 Pet. 1:3, R.V., "great" (A.V., "abundant"); glory, Matt. 24:30; joy, Philm. 7, R.V., "much" (A.V., "great"); peace, Acts 24:2. The best mss. have it in Acts 8:8 (R.V., "much"), of joy. See ABUNDANT, COMMON, *Note* (1), LONG, MANY, MUCH, OFT, SORE, STRAITLY.

NT: B.687c; CB.1266a; K.—.
OT: rab: S.7227; HR.1181b.9a; H.2099a,b; BD.912d.
rōb: S.7230; HR.1181b.9b; H.2099c; BD.913d.
rābab: S.7231; HR.1181b.9c; H.2099; BD.912c.
GEN. REF.: IS.2:556; NB.—; Z.2:810.

3. *hikanos* [ἱκανός, 2425], lit., reaching to (from *hikanō*, to reach), denotes sufficient, competent, fit, and is sometimes rendered "great," e.g., of number (of people), Mark 10:46; of degree (of light), Acts 22:6; See ABLE, ENOUGH, GOOD, LARGE, LONG, MANY, MEET, MUCH, SECURITY, SUFFICIENT, WORTHY.

NT: B.374b; CB.1250c; K.361.
OT: day: S.1767; HR.683c.2; H.425; BD.191b.
GEN. REF.: —.

4. *hēlikos* [ἡλίκος, 2245], primarily denotes as big as, as old as (akin to *hēlikia*, an age); then, as an indirect interrogation, what, what size, how great, how small (the context determines the meaning), said of a spiritual conflict, Col. 2:1, A.V., "what great (conflict) I have"; R.V., "how greatly (I strive)"; of much wood as kindled by a little fire, Jas. 3:5 (twice in the best mss.), "how much (wood is kindled by) how small (a fire)," R.V., said metaphorically of the use of the tongue. Some mss. have No. 4 in Gal. 6:11; the most authentic have No. 5. ¶

NT: B.345c; CB.—; K.—.
OT: —.
GEN. REF.: —.

5. *pēlikos* [πηλίκος, 4080], primarily a direct interrogative, how large? how great? is used in exclamations, indicating magnitude, like No. 4 (No. 6 indicates quantity), in Gal. 6:11, of letter characters (see No. 4, Note); in Heb. 7:4, metaphorically, of the distinguished character of Melchizedek. ¶

NT: B.656b; CB.—; K.—.
OT: kammāh: S.4100; HR.1131a.1; H.1149; BD.552b,553d.
GEN. REF.: —.

6. *posos* [πόσος, 4214], an adjective of number, magnitude, degree etc., is rendered "how great" in Matt. 6:23. See MANY, MUCH

NT: B.694b; CB.—; K.—.
OT: kammāh: S.4100; HR.1195c.1; H.1149; BD.552b,553d.
GEN. REF.: —.

7. *hosos* [ὅσος, 3745], how much, how many, is used in the neuter plural to signify how great things, Mark 5:19, 20; Luke 8:39 (twice); Acts 9:16, A.V. (R.V., "how many things"); in Rev. 21:16 (in the best mss.), "as great as," R.V. (A.V., "as large as," said of length). See ALL, MANY, No. 5, WHATSOEVER.

NT: B.586b; CB.1251b; K.—.
OT: —.
GEN. REF.: —.

8. *tosoutos* [τοσοῦτος, 5118], so great, so many, so much, of quantity, size, etc., is rendered "so great," in Matt. 8:10, and Luke 7:9, of faith; Matt. 15:33, of a multitude; Heb. 12:1, of a cloud of witnesses; Rev. 18:17, of riches. See LARGE, LONG, MANY, MUCH.

NT: B.823b; CB.—; K.—.
OT: —.
GEN. REF.: —.

9. *tēlikoutos* [τηλικοῦτος, 5082], so great, is used in the N.T. of things only, a death, 2 Cor. 1:10; salvation, Heb. 2:3; ships, Jas. 3:4; an earthquake, Rev. 16:18, A.V., "so mighty," corrected in the R.V. to "so great." See MIGHTY. ¶

NT: B.814c; CB.—; K.—.
OT: —.
GEN. REF.: —.

Notes: (1) In Mark 7:36, "so much the more a great deal" translates a phrase lit. signifying 'more abundantly'; in 10:48, "the more a great deal" translates a phrase lit. signifying 'more by much.'

(2) For the noun *megistan*, in the plural, rendered "Lords" in the A.V. of Mark 6:21, see LORD; in Rev. 6:15 and 18:23, see PRINCE.

(3) In Luke 1:58, the verb *megalunō*, to magnify, make great (akin to No. 1), is rendered "had magnified (His mercy)," R.V. [A.V., "had shewed great (mercy)"]

(4) In Luke 10:13, the adverb *palai*, of old, long ago, is so rendered in the R.V. (A.V., "a great while ago").

(5) In 2 Pet. 1:4, *megistos*, the superlative of *megas* (No. 1), said of the promises of God, is rendered "exceeding great." ¶

(6) In Matt. 21:8, *pleistos*, the superlative of *polus* (No. 2), said of a multitude, is rendered "very great" in the A.V. (R.V., "the most part").

(7) In Rev. 21:10, the most authentic mss. omit "that great" [R.V., "the holy (city)"].

(8) In Luke 10:2, the R.V. renders *polus* by "plenteous" (A.V., "great").

(9) In Mark 1:35, the adverb *lian*, exceedingly (see GREATLY), is rendered "a great while." See DAY, B.

(10) In Luke 1:49 some texts have *megaleia*, "great things"; the best have No. 1.

GREATER

1. *meizōn* [μείζων, 3187], is the comparative degree of *megas* (see GREAT, No. 1), e.g., Matt. 11:11; in Matt. 13:32, the R.V. rightly has "greater than" (A.V., "the greatest among"); 23:17; in Luke 22:26, R.V., "the greater (among you)" (A.V., "greatest"); in Jas. 3:1, R.V., "the heavier (marg., greater) judgment" (A.V., "the greater condemnation"); it is used in the neuter plural in John 1:50, "greater things"; in 14:12, "greater works" (lit., 'greater things'); in 1 Cor. 12:31, R.V., "the greater," A.V., "the best." See GREATEST, No. 2.

NT: B.497c; CB.1258a; K.—.
OT: gādôl: S.1419; HR.902c.21b; H.315d; BD.152d.
GEN. REF.: IS.2:556; NB.—; Z.2:810.

Note: In Matt. 20:31, the neuter of *meizōn*, used as an adverb, is translated "the more." See MORE.

2. *meizoteros* [μειζότερος, 3186], a double comparative of *megas* (cp. No. 1, above), is used in 3 John 4, of joy. ¶

NT: B.497c; CB.—; K.—.
OT: —.
GEN. REF.: —.

3. *pleiōn* [πλείων, 4119], the comparative of *polus* (see GREAT, No. 2), is used (*a*) as an adjective, greater, more, e.g., Acts 15:28; (*b*) as a noun, e.g., Matt. 12:41, "a greater (than Jonah)"; ver. 42, "a greater (than Solomon)"; in these instances the neuter *pleion*, 'something greater,' is "a fixed or stereotyped form" of the word; in 1 Cor. 15:6, "the greater part" (masculine plural); (*c*) as an adverb, e.g., Matt. 5:20, lit., '(except your righteousness abound) more greatly (than of scribes and Pharisees)'; so 26:53, "more"; Luke 9:13. See ABOVE, LONGER, MANY, MORE, MOST, YET.

NT: B.689a; CB.1265b; K.—.
OT: rab: S.7227; HR.1181b.9a; H.2099a,b; BD.912d.
rōb: S.7230; HR.1181b.9b; H.2099c; BD.913d.
rābab: S.7311; HR.1181b.9c; H.2099; BD.912c.
GEN. REF.: IS.2:556; NB.—; Z.2:810.

4. *perissoteros* [περισσότερος, 4055], the comparative of *perissos*, over and above, abundant, signifies more abundant, greater, e.g., of condemnation, Mark 12:40; Luke 20:47. See ABUNDANT, C, No. 2.

NT: B.651c; CB.1263c; K.—.
OT: —.
GEN. REF.: IS.2:556; NB.—; Z.—.

GREATEST

1. *megas* [μέγας, 3173], for which see GREAT, No. 1, is translated "the greatest," in Acts 8:10 and Heb. 8:11. The whole phrase, lit., 'from small to great,' is equivalent to the Eng. idiom "one and all." It is used in the Sept., e.g., in 1 Sam. 5:9 ('God smote the people of Gath from the least to the greatest,' "both small and great"). So 1 Sam. 30:19; 2 Chron. 34:30, etc. See GREAT.

NT: B.497c; CB.1258a; K.573.
OT: gādôl: S.1419; HR.902c.2a; H.315d; BD.152d.
rab: S.7227; HR.902c.12a; H.2099a,b; BD.912d.
GEN. REF.: IS.2:556; NB.—; Z.2:810.

2. *meizōn* [μείζων, 3187], the comparative of No. 1, is sometimes translated "greatest"; besides the two cases given under GREATER, No. 1, where the R.V. corrects the A.V., "greatest" to "greater" (Matt. 13:32 and Luke 22:26), the R.V. itself has "greatest" for this comparative in the following, and relegates "greater" to the margin, Matt. 18:1, 4; 23:11; Mark 9:34; Luke 9:46; 22:24. See GREATER, MORE.

NT: B.497c; CB.1258a; K.—.
OT: gādôl: S.1419; HR.902c.21b; H.315d; BD.152d.
GEN. REF.: IS.2:556; NB.—; Z.2:810.

GREATLY

1. *lian* [λίαν, 3029], very, exceedingly, is rendered "greatly" in Matt. 27:14, of wonder; 2 Tim. 4:15, of opposition; 2 John 4 and 3 John 3, of joy. See EXCEEDING, SORE, VERY.

NT: B.473b; CB.1257a; K.—.
OT: m^{e}ôd: S.3966; HR.876a.1; H.1134; BD.547a.
GEN. REF.: IS.2:556; NB.—; Z.—.

2. *polus* [πολύς, 4183], is used in the neuter singular (*polu*) or the plural (*polla*), as an adverb; in the sing., e.g., Mark 12:27; in the plur., e.g., Mark 1:45, "much"; 5:23, "greatly" (R.V.,

"much"); ver. 38, A.V. and R.V. "greatly"; 1 Cor. 16:12 (R.V., "much"). See LONG, MUCH.

NT: B.687c; CB.1266a; K.–.
OT: rab: S.7227; HR.1181b.9a; H.2099a,b; BD.912d.
rōb: S.7230; HR.1181b.9b; H.2099c; BD.913d.
rābab: S.7311; HR.1181b.9c; H.2099; BD.912c.
GEN. REF.: IS.2:556; NB.–; Z.2:810.

Note: In Acts 28:6, A.V., *polu* is rendered "a great while" (R.V., "long").

3. *megalōs* [μεγάλως, 3171], from *megas* (GREAT, No. 1), is used of rejoicing, Phil. 4:10. ¶

NT: B.497b; CB.–; K.–.
OT: gādôl: S.1419; HR.902b.1; H.315d; BD.152d.
rōb: S.7230; HR.902b.3; H.2099c; BD.913d.
GEN. REF.: IS.2:556; NB.–; Z.2:810.

4. *chara* [χαρά, 5479], joy, is used in the dative case adverbially with the verb *chairō*, to rejoice, in John 3:29, "rejoiceth greatly," lit., 'rejoiceth with joy.'

NT: B.875c; CB.1239b; K.1298.
OT: simḥāh: S.8057; HR.1454b.5; H.2268b; BD.970d.
sāsôn: S.8342; HR.1454b.6a; H.2246a; BD.965b.
GEN. REF.: –.

Notes: (1) For *sphodra*, R.V., "exceedingly," in Matt. 27:54 and Acts 6:7, see EXCEED, B, No. 2.

(2) In the following the R.V. omits "greatly," as the verbs are adequately translated without, Phil. 1:8; 1 Thess. 3:6; 2 Tim. 1:4. In the following the R.V. adds "greatly" to express the fuller force of the verb, Luke 1:29; Acts 16:34; 1 Pet. 1:8.

(3) In 1 Pet. 1:6, "ye greatly rejoice," the adverb is not separately expressed, but is incorporated in the rendering of the verb *agalliaō*, to rejoice much, to exult.

GREATNESS

1. *megethos* [μέγεθος, 3174], akin to *megas* (see GREAT, No. 1), is said of the power of God, in Eph. 1:19. ¶

NT: B.498c; CB.–; K.573.
OT: qômāh: S.6967; HR.907a.3; H.1999a; BD.879b.
GEN. REF.: IS.2:556; NB.–; Z.–.

2. *huperbolē* [ὑπερβολή, 5236], denotes "exceeding greatness," 2 Cor. 4:7; 12:7. See EXCEL, B, No. 1.

NT: B.840b; CB.–; K.1230.
OT: –.
GEN. REF.: –.

For **GREEDILY** see **RUN,** No. 9

For **GREEDINESS** see **COVETOUSNESS,** B, No. 3

For **GREEDY** see **LUCRE**

GREEN

1. *chlōros* [χλωρός, 5515], akin to *chloē*, tender foliage (cp. the name Chloe, 1 Cor. 1:11, and Eng., chlorine), denotes (*a*) pale green, the colour of young grass, Mark 6:39; Rev. 8:7; 9:4, "green thing"; hence, (*b*) pale, Rev. 6:8, the colour of the horse whose rider's name is Death. See PALE. ¶

NT: B.882d; CB.1240a; K.–.
OT: yereq: S.3418; HR.1471c.2a; H.918a; BD.438d.
yārāq: S.3419; HR.1471c.2b; H.918b; BD.438d.
GEN. REF.: IS.1:731; NB.–; Z.2:849.

2. *hugros* [ὑγρός, 5200], denotes wet, moist (the opposite of *xēros*, dry); said of wood, sappy, "green," Luke 23:31, i.e., if they thus by the fire of their wrath treated Christ, the guiltless, holy, the fruitful, what would be the fate of the perpetrators, who were like the dry wood, exposed to the fire of Divine wrath. ¶

NT: B.832c; CB.1251c; K.–.
OT: laḥ: S.3892; HR.1380c.1; H.1102a; BD.535a.
rāṭōb: S.7372; HR.1380c.2; H.2154; BD.936a.
GEN. REF.: IS.–; NB.–; Z.2:849.

GREET, GREETING

A. Verbs.

1. *aspazomai* [ἀσπάζομαι, 782], signifies to greet, welcome, or salute. In the A.V. it is chiefly rendered by either of the verbs to greet or to salute. "There is little doubt that the Revisers have done wisely in giving 'salute' . . . in the passages where A.V. has 'greet.' For the cursory reader is sure to imagine a difference of Greek and of meaning when he finds, e.g., in Phil. 4:21, 'Salute every saint in Christ Jesus. The brethren which are with me greet you,' or in 3 John 14, 'Our friends salute thee. Greet the friends by name' " (Hastings, Bible Dic.). In Acts 25:13 the meaning virtually is 'to pay his respects to.'

In two passages the renderings vary otherwise; in Acts 20:1, of bidding farewell, A.V., "embraced them," R.V., "took leave of them," or, as Ramsay translates it, 'bade them farewell'; in Heb. 11:13, of welcoming promises, A.V., "embraced," R.V., "greeted."

The verb is used as a technical term for conveying greetings at the close of a letter, often by an amanuensis, e.g., Rom. 16:22, the only instance of the use of the first person in this respect in the N.T.; see also 1 Cor. 16:19, 20; 2 Cor. 13:13; Phil. 4:22; Col. 4:10-15; 1 Thess. 5:26; 2 Tim. 4:21; Tit. 3:15; Philm. 23; Heb. 13:24; 1 Pet. 5:13, 14; 2 John 13. This special use is largely illustrated in the papyri, one example of this showing how keenly the absence of the greeting was felt. The papyri also illustrate the use of the addition "by name," when several persons are included in the greeting, as in 3 John 14 (Moulton and Milligan, Vocab). See EMBRACE, LEAVE, SALUTE.

NT: B.116c; CB.1238a; K.84.
OT: —.
GEN. REF.: IS.2:574; NB.1126; Z.—.

2. *chairō* [χαίρω, 5463], to rejoice, is thrice used as a formula of salutation in Acts 15:23, A.V., "send greeting," R.V., "greeting"; so 23:26; Jas. 1:1. In 2 John 10, 11, the R.V. substitutes the phrase (to give) greeting, for the A.V. (to bid) God speed. See FAREWELL, GLAD, HAIL, JOY, REJOICE.

NT: B.873b; CB.1239b; K.1298.
OT: —.
GEN. REF.: IS.2:574; NB.1126; Z.—.

B. Noun

aspasmos [ἀσπασμός, 783], a salutation, is always so rendered in the R.V.; A.V., "greetings" in Matt. 23:7; Luke 11:43; 20:46; it is used (*a*) orally in those instances and in Mark 12:38; Luke 1:29, 41, 44; (*b*) in written salutations, 1 Cor. 16:21 (cp. A, No. 1, in ver. 20); Col. 4:18; 2 Thess. 3:17. ¶

NT: B.117a; CB.1238a; K.84.
OT: —.
GEN. REF.: IS.2:574; NB.1126; Z.—.

GRIEF, GRIEVE

A. Noun.

lupē [λύπη, 3077], signifies pain, of body or mind; it is used in the plural in 1 Pet. 2:19 only, R.V., "griefs" (A.V., "grief"); here, however, it stands, by metonymy, for 'things that cause sorrow,' grievances; hence Tyndale's rendering, "grief," for Wycliffe's "sorews"; everywhere else it is rendered "sorrow," except in Heb. 12:11, where it is translated "grievous" (lit., 'of grief'). See HEAVINESS, SORROW.

NT: B.482a; CB.1257b; K.540.
OT: 'eṣeb: S.6089; HR.889c.3a; H.1666a,1667a; BD.780d.
'aṣṣebet: S.6094; HR.889c.3c; H.1666d; BD.781a.
'iṣṣābôn: S.6093; HR.889c.3b; H.1666e; BD.781a.
GEN. REF.: IS.2:574; NB.—; Z.2:849.

B. Verbs.

1. *lupeō* [λυπέω, 3076], akin to A, denotes (*a*), in the Active Voice, to cause pain, or grief, to distress, grieve, e.g., 2 Cor. 2:2 (twice, Active and Passive Voices); ver. 5 (twice), R.V., "hath caused sorrow" (A.V., "have caused grief," and "grieved"); 7:8, "made (you) sorry"; Eph. 4:30, of grieving the Holy Spirit of God (as indwelling the believer); (*b*) in the Passive Voice, to be grieved, to be made sorry, to be sorry, sorrowful, e.g., Matt. 14:9, R.V., "(the king) was grieved" (A.V., "was sorry"); Mark 10:22, R.V., "(went away) sorrowful" (A.V., "grieved"); John 21:17, "(Peter) was grieved"; Rom. 14:15, "(if . . . thy brother) is grieved"; 2 Cor. 2:4, "(not that) ye should be made sorry," R.V., A.V., "ye should be grieved." See HEAVINESS, SORROW, SORROWFUL, SORRY.

NT: B.481c; CB.1257b; K.540.
OT: qāṣaph: S.7107; HR.889b.9; H.2058; BD.893b.
'āṣab: S.6087; HR.889b.8; H.1666,1667; BD.780c.
GEN. REF.: IS.2:574; NB.—; Z.2:849.

2. *sunlupeō* [συνλυπέω, 4818], or *sullupeō*, is used in the Passive Voice in Mark 3:5, to be grieved or afflicted together with a person, said of Christ's grief at the hardness of heart of those who criticised His healing on the Sabbath Day; it here seems to suggest the sympathetic nature of His grief because of their self-injury. Some suggest that the *sun* indicates the mingling of grief with His anger. ¶

NT: B.777a; CB.—; K.—.
OT: —.
GEN. REF.: IS.2:574; NB.—; Z.—.

3. *stenazō* [στενάζω, 4727], to groan (of an inward, unexpressed feeling of sorrow), is translated "with grief" in Heb. 13:17 (marg. "groaning"). It is rendered "sighed" in Mark 7:34; "groan," in Rom. 8:23; 2 Cor. 5:2, 4; "murmur," in Jas. 5:9, R.V. (A.V., "grudge"). See GROAN, MURMUR, SIGH. ¶

NT: B.766b; CB.1270a; K.1076.
OT: 'ānaḥ: S.584; HR.1288b.3; H.127; BD.58c.
'ānaq: S.602; HR.1288b.4; H.134; BD.60b.
GEN. REF.: —.

Notes: (1) *Diaponeō*, to work out with labour, in the Passive Voice, to be sore troubled, is rendered "being grieved" in Acts 4:2 and 16:18, A.V. (R.V., "sore troubled"). See TROUBLE. ¶ In some mss., Mark 14:4.

(2) *Prosochthizō*, to be angry with, is rendered "was grieved" in Heb. 3:10, 17, A.V. (R.V., "was displeased"). See DISPLEASE. ¶

GRIEVOUS, GRIEVOUSLY

A. Adjectives.

1. *barus* [βαρύς, 926], denotes heavy, burdensome; it is always used metaphorically in the N.T., and is translated "heavy" in Matt. 23:4, of Pharisaical ordinances; in the comparative degree "weightier," 23:23, of details of the Law of God; "grievous," metaphorically of wolves, in Acts 20:29; of charges, 25:7; negatively of God's commandments, 1 John 5:3 (causing a burden on him who fulfils them); in 2 Cor. 10:10, "weighty," of Paul's letters. See HEAVY, WEIGHTY. ¶

NT: B.134b; CB.1238c; K.95.
OT: kābēd: S.3513; HR.191b.2a; H.943; BD.457a.
GEN. REF.: IS.2:575; NB.—; Z.—.

2. *ponēros* [πονηρός, 4190], painful, bad, is translated "grievous" in Rev. 16:2, of a sore inflicted retributively. See BAD.
NT: B.690d; CB.1266a; K.912.
OT: ra': S.7451; HR.1186c.4a; H.2191; BD.948a.
GEN. REF.: IS.2:575; NB.–; Z.–.

3. *dusbastaktos* [δυσβάστακτος, 1419], hard to be borne (from *dus*, an inseparable prefix, like Eng. mis-, and un-, indicating difficulty, injuriousness, opposition, etc., and *bastazō*, to bear), is used in Luke 11:46 and, in some mss., in Matt. 23:4, "grievous to be borne"; in the latter the R.V. marg. has "many ancient authorities omit." ¶
NT: B.209b; CB.–; K.–.
OT: nēṭel: S.5192; HR.357b.1; H.1353a; BD.642b.
GEN. REF.: –.

4. *chalepos* [χαλεπός, 5467], hard, signifies (*a*) hard to deal with, Matt. 8:28 (see FIERCE); (*b*) hard to bear, grievous, 2 Tim. 3:1, R.V., "grievous" (A.V., "perilous"), said of a characteristic of the last days of this age. See FIERCE ¶
NT: B.874c; CB.1239b; K.–.
OT: yārē': S.3372; HR.1453a.1; H.907,908; BD.431a.
GEN. REF.: –.

Notes: (1) For the noun *lupē*, "grievous," in Heb. 12:11, see GRIEF.

(2) In Phil. 3:1, the adjective *oknēros*, shrinking, or causing shrinking, hence, tedious (akin to *okneō*, to shrink), is rendered "irksome" in the R.V. (A.V., "grievous"); the Apostle intimates that, not finding his message tedious, he has no hesitation in giving it. In Matt. 25:26 and Rom. 12:11, "slothful." ¶

B. Adverbs.

1. *deinōs* [δεινῶς, 1171], akin to *deos*, fear, signifies (*a*) terribly, Matt. 8:6, "grievously (tormented)"; (*b*) vehemently, Luke 11:53. See VEHEMENTLY. ¶
NT: B.173b; CB.–; K.–.
OT: –.
GEN. REF.: –.

2. *kakōs* [κακῶς, 2560], badly, ill, is translated "grievously (vexed)," in Matt. 15:22. See AMISS, EVIL, MISERABLY, SORE.
NT: B.398c; CB.1253b; K.655.
OT: –.
GEN. REF.: –.

Notes: (1) In Mark 9:20 and Luke 9:42, the R.V. renders the verb *susparassō* tare (him) grievously," the adverb bringing out the intensive force of the prefix *su*– (i.e., *sun*); the meaning may be 'threw violently to the ground.'

(2) In Matt. 17:15, the idiomatic phrase, consisting of No. 2 (above) with *echō*, to have, (lit., 'hath badly'), is rendered "suffereth grievously," R.V. (A.V., "is . . . sore vexed").

GRIND

1. *alēthō* [ἀλήθω, 229], signifies to grind at the mill, Matt. 24:41; Luke 17:35. ¶ The Sept. has both the earlier form *aleō*, Is. 47:2, ¶, and the later one *alēthō*, used in the *Koinē* period, Numb. 11:8; Judg. 16:21; Eccles. 12:3, 4. ¶
NT: B.37b; CB.–; K.–.
OT: ṭāḥan: S.2912; HR.53c.1a; H.802; BD.377c.
GEN. REF.: IS.2:575; NB.494; Z.2:851.

2. *trizō* [τρίζω, 5149], primarily of animal sounds, to chirp, cry, etc., is used of grinding the teeth, Mark 9.18, R.V., "grindeth" (A.V., "gnasheth with"). See GNASH. ¶
NT: B.826b; CB.–; K.–.
OT: –.
GEN. REF.: IS.2:575; NB.–; Z.2:851.

Note: In Matt. 21:44 and Luke 20:18, *likmaō*, to winnow, as of grain, by throwing it up against the wind, to scatter the chaff and straw, hence has the meaning to scatter, as chaff or dust, and is translated "will scatter . . . as dust," R.V. (A.V., "will grind . . . to powder"). In the Sept. it is used of being scattered by the wind or of sifting (cp. Amos 9:9). The use of the verb in the papyri writings suggests the meaning, to ruin, destroy (Deissmann). ¶

GROAN, GROANING

A. Verbs.

1. *embrimaomai* [ἐμβριμάομαι, 1690], from *en*, in, and *brimē*, strength, is rendered "groaned" in John 11:33 (preferable to the R.V. marg., "He had indignation"); so in ver. 38. The Lord was deeply moved doubtless with the combination of circumstances, present and in the immediate future. Indignation does not here seem to express His feelings. See CHARGE.
NT: B.254d; CB.1244b; K.–.
OT: –.
GEN. REF.: IS.2:576; NB.–; Z.–.

2. *stenazō* [στενάζω]: see GRIEVE, B, No. 3.

3. *sustenazō* [συστενάζω, 4959], to groan together (*sun*, with, and No. 2), is used of the creation in Rom. 8:22. In ver. 23, No. 2 is used. ¶
NT: B.795b; CB.–; K.1076.
OT: –.
GEN. REF.: IS.2:575; NB.–; Z.–.

B. Noun.

stenagmos [στεναγμός, 4726], akin to A, No. 2, is used in Acts 7:34, in a quotation from Ex. 3:7, but not from the Sept., which there has *kraugē*, a cry; the word is used, however, in Ex. 2:24; in Rom. 8:26, in the plural, of the intercessory groanings of the Holy Spirit. ¶
NT: B.766b; CB.1270a; K.1076.
OT: 'anāḥāh: S.585; HR.1288a.1; H.127a; BD.58d.
n°'āqāh: S.5009; HR.1288a.4; H.1313a; BD.611a.
GEN. REF.: IS.2:575; NB.–; Z.–.

GROSS (to wax)

pachunō [παχύνω, 3975], from *pachus*, thick, signifies to thicken, fatten; in the Passive Voice, to grow fat; metaphorically said of the heart, to wax gross or dull, Matt. 13:15; Acts 28:27. ¶

NT: B.638b; CB.1261b; K.816.
OT: shāmēn: S.8080; HR.1112c.4; H.2410; BD.1031d.
dāshēn: S.1878; HR.1112c.1; H.457; BD.206a.
GEN. REF.: IS.2:576; NB.—; Z.—.

GROUND, GROUNDED

A. Nouns.

1. *gē* [γῆ, 1093], the earth, land, etc., often denotes the ground, e.g., Matt. 10:29; Mark 8:6. See EARTH.

NT: B.157c; CB.1248a; K.116.
OT: 'ereṣ: S.776; HR.240c.2c; H.167; BD.75d.
GEN. REF.: IS.2:576; NB.—; Z.—.

2. *edaphos* [ἔδαφος, 1475], a bottom, base, is used of the ground in Acts 22:7, suggestive of that which is level and hard. ¶ Cp. B, No. 1, below.

NT: B.217d; CB.—; K.—.
OT: qarqa': S.7172; HR.367c.5; H.2076; BD.903a.
'āphār: S.6083; HR.367c.4; H.1664a; BD.779c.
GEN. REF.: IS.2:576; NB.—; Z.—.

3. *chōra* [χώρα, 5561], land, country, is used of property, ground, in Luke 12:16, "the ground (of a certain rich man)." See COUNTRY.

NT: B.889b; CB.1240a; K.—.
OT: 'ereṣ: S.776; HR.1481a.4; H.167; BD.75d.
m^e^dînāh: S.4082; HR.1481a.5; H.426d; BD.193d.
GEN. REF.: IS.2:576; NB.—; Z.—.

4. *chōrion* [χωρίον, 5564], a diminutive of No. 3, a piece of land, a place, estate, is translated "parcel of ground" in John 4:5. See FIELD.

NT: B.890b; CB.1240a; K.—.
OT: —.
GEN. REF.: —.

5. *hedraiōma* [ἑδραίωμα, 1477], a support, bulwark, stay (from *hedraios*, stedfast, firm; from *hedra*, a seat), is translated "ground" in 1 Tim. 3:15 (said of a local church); the R.V. marg., "stay" is preferable.¶

NT: B.218a; CB.—; K.200.
OT: —.
GEN. REF.: —.

Notes: (1) In Mark 4:16 the R.V. rightly has "rocky places" (*petrōdēs*) for A.V., "stony ground."

(2) In Acts 27:29, for the A.V., "rocks" the R.V. has "rocky ground," lit., 'rough places,' i.e., a rocky shore.

(3) In Luke 14:18, *agros*, a field, is translated "a piece of ground," A.V., R.V., "a field." See FIELD.

B. Verbs.

1. *edaphizō* [ἐδαφίζω], akin to A, No. 2: see DASH.

2. *themelioō* [θεμελιόω, 2311], signifies to lay the foundation of, to found (akin to *themelios*, a foundation; from *tithēmi*, to put), and is rendered "grounded" in Eph. 3:17, said of the condition of believers with reference to the love of Christ; in Col. 1:23, of their continuance in the faith. See FOUND.

NT: B.356a; CB.1272a; K.322.
OT: y^e^sôd: S.3247; HR.629b.3d; H.875b; BD.414b.
môsād: S.4144; HR.629b.3f; H.875f; BD.414c.
'ar^e^môn: S.759; HR.629b.1; H.164a; BD.74d.
GEN. REF.: —.

C. Adverb.

chamai [χαμαί, 5476], akin to Lat., *humi*, on the ground, and *homo*, man), signifies "on the ground," John 9:6, of the act of Christ in spitting on the ground before anointing the eyes of a blind man; in 18:6, "to the ground," of the fall of the rabble that had come to seize Christ in Gethsemane. ¶

NT: B.875b; CB.—; K.—.
OT: —.
GEN. REF.: —.

GROW

1. *auxanō* [αὐξάνω, 837], to grow or increase, of the growth of that which lives, naturally or spiritually, is used (*a*) transitively, signifying to make to increase, said of giving the increase, 1 Cor. 3:6, 7; 2 Cor. 9:10, the effect of the work of God, according to the analogy of His operations in nature; to grow, become greater, e.g. of plants and fruit, Matt. 6:28; used in the Passive Voice in 13:32 and Mark 4:8, "increase"; in the Active in Luke 12:27; 13:19; of the body, Luke 1:80; 2:40; of Christ, John 3:30, "increase"; of the work of the Gospel of God, Acts 6:7, "increased"; 12:24; 19:20; of people, Acts 7:17; of faith, 2 Cor. 10:15 (Passive Voice), R.V., "groweth" (A.V., "is increased"); of believers individually, Eph. 4:15; Col. 1:6, R.V., 10 (Passive Voice), "increasing"; 1 Pet. 2:2; 2 Pet. 3:18; of the Church, Col. 2:19; of churches, Eph. 2:21. See INCREASE. ¶

NT: B.121c; CB.1238b; K.1229.
OT: gādal: S.1431; HR.178c.1; H.315; BD.152a.
pārāh: S.6509; HR.178c.4a,b; H.1809; BD.826a.
GEN. REF.: —.

Note: Cp. *auxēsis*, increase, Eph. 4:16; Col. 2:19. ¶

2. *ginomai* [γίνομαι, 1096], to become or come to be, is translated "grow" in Acts 5:24, of the development of apostolic work. See ARISE, No. 5.

NT: B.158a; CB.1248b; K.117.
OT: —.
GEN. REF.: —.

Notes: (1) In Matt. 21:19, for A.V., "let (no fruit) grow," the R.V., more strictly, has "let there be (no fruit)."

(2) In Heb. 11:24, *ginomai* is used with *megas*, great, of Moses, lit., 'had become great;' R.V., "had grown up" (A.V., "had come to years").

3. *erchomai* [ἔρχομαι, 2064], to come or go, is translated "grew (worse);" in Mark 5:26. See COME, No. 1.

NT: B.310b; CB.1246b; K.257.
OT: —.
GEN. REF.: —.

4. *anabainō* [ἀναβαίνω, 305], to ascend, when used of plants, signifies to grow up, Mark 4:7, 32; in 4:8, of seed, "growing up;" R.V., A.V., "that sprang up;" (for the next word, "increasing;" see No. 1). See ARISE, No. 6.

NT: B.50a; CB.1235a; K.90.
OT: pārāh: S.6509; HR.70a.13; H.1809; BD.826a.
GEN. REF.: —.

5. *mēkunomai* [μηκύνομαι, 3373], to grow long, lengthen, extend (from *mēkos*, length), is used of the growth of plants, in Mark 4:27. ¶

NT: B.518d; CB.—; K.—.
OT: gādal: S.1431; HR.921c.1; H.315; BD.152a.
māshak: S.4900; HR.921c.2; H.1257; BD.604a.
GEN. REF.: —.

Note: Three different words are used in Mark 4 of the growth of plants or seed, Nos. 1, 4, 5.

6. *huperauxanō* [ὑπεραυξάνω, 5232], to increase beyond measure (*huper*, over, and No. 1), is used of faith and love, in their living and practical effects, 2 Thess. 1:3. Lightfoot compares this verb and the next in the verse (*pleonazō*, to abound) in that the former implies "an internal, organic growth, as of a tree;" the latter "a diffusive or expansive character, as of a flood irrigating the land." ¶

NT: B.840a; CB.1252a; K.1229.
OT: —.
GEN. REF.: —.

7. *sunauxanō* [συναυξάνω, 4885], to grow together, is in Matt. 13:30. ¶

NT: B.785b; CB.—; K.—.
OT: —.
GEN. REF.: —.

8. *phuō* [φύω, 5453], to produce, is rendered "grew" (Passive V.) in Luke 8:6. See SPRING.

NT: B.870b; CB.1264c; K.—.
OT: nāta': S.5193; HR.1440c.1; H.1354; BD.642b.
pārāh: S.6509; HR.1440c.3; H.1809; BD.826a.
ṣāmaḥ: S.6779; HR.1440c.4; H.1928; BD.855b.
GEN. REF.: —.

9. *sumphuō* [συμφύω, 4855], is used in Luke 8:7, R.V., "grow with." ¶

NT: B.780d; CB.—; K.—.
OT: —.
GEN. REF.: —.

For GRUDGE (Jas. 5:9), GRIEVE, B, No. 3, GRUDGING (1 Pet. 4:9) see MURMUR

GRUDGINGLY

Note: In 2 Cor. 9:7, the phrase *ek lupēs*, lit., 'out of sorrow' (*ek*, out of, or from, *lupē*, sorrow, grief), is translated "grudgingly" (R.V. marg., "of sorrow"); the grudging regret is set in contrast to cheerfulness enjoined in giving, as is the reluctance expressed in "of necessity."

GUARD (Noun and Verb)

A. Nouns.

1. *koustōdia* [κουστωδία, 2892], a guard, (Latin, *custodia*; Eng., custodian), is used of the soldiers who guarded Christ's sepulchre, Matt. 27:65, 66 and 28:11, and is translated "(ye have) a guard;" "the guard (being with them);" and "(some of) the guard;" R.V., A.V., ". . . a watch;" "(setting a) watch;" and ". . . the watch." This was the Temple Guard, stationed under a Roman officer in the Tower of Antonia, and having charge of the high priestly vestments. Hence the significance of Pilate's words "Ye have a guard." See WATCH. ¶

NT: B.447b; CB.—; K.—.
OT: —.
GEN. REF.: IS.2:578; NB.—; Z.2:851.

2. *spekoulatōr* [σπεκουλάτωρ, 4688], Latin, *speculator*, primarily denotes a lookout officer, or scout, but, under the Emperors, a member of the bodyguard; these were employed as messengers, watchers and executioners; ten such officers were attached to each legion; such a guard was employed by Herod Antipas, Mark 6:27, R.V., "a soldier of his guard" (A.V., "executioner"). ¶

NT: B.761c; CB.—; K.—.
OT: —.
GEN. REF.: IS.2:578; NB.494; Z.2:851.

3. *phulax* [φύλαξ, 5441], a guard, keeper (akin to *phulassō*, to guard, keep), is translated "keepers" in Acts 5:23; in 12:6, 19, R.V., "guards" (A.V., "keepers"). See KEEPER. ¶

NT: B.868b; CB.1264c; K.—.
OT: sûr: S.6696; HR.1441b.1; H.1898-1900; BD.848d.
shāmar: S.8104; HR.1441b.2; H.2414; BD.1036b.
GEN. REF.: IS.2:578; NB.494; Z.2:851.

Notes: (1) In Acts 28:16, some mss. have the sentence containing the word *stratopedarchēs*, a captain of the guard. See CAPTAIN

(2) In Phil. 1:13, the noun *praitōrion*, the "Praetorian Guard;" is so rendered in the R.V. (A.V., "palace").

B. Verbs.

1. *phulassō* [φυλάσσω, 5442], to gaurd, watch, keep (akin to A, No. 3), is rendered by the verb to guard in the R.V. (A.V., to keep) of Luke 11:21; John 17:12; Acts 12:4; 28:16; 2 Thess. 3:3; 1 Tim. 6:20; 2 Tim. 1:12, 14; 1 John 5:21; Jude 24. In Luke 8:29, "was kept under

guard," R.V. (A.V., "kept"). See BEWARE, KEEP, OBSERVE, PRESERVE, SAVE, WARE OF, WATCH.

NT: B.868b; CB.1264c; K.1280.
OT: shāmar: S.8104; HR.1441c.11a; H.2414; BD.1036b.
GEN. REF.: IS.2:578; NB.494; Z.—.

2. *diaphulassō* [διαφυλάσσω, 1314], a strengthened form of No. 1 (*dia*, through, used intensively), to guard carefully, defend, is found in Luke 4:10 (from the Sept. of Psa. 91:11), R.V., "to guard" (A.V., "to keep"). ¶

NT: B.191a; CB.—; K.—.
OT: shāmar: S.8104; HR.315c.3; H.2414; BD.1036b.
GEN. REF.: IS.2:578; NB.494; Z.—.

3. *phroureō* [φρουρέω, 5432], a military term, to keep by guarding, to keep under guard, as with a garrison (*phrouros*, a guard, or garrison), is used, (*a*) of blocking up every way of escape, as in a siege; (*b*) of providing protection against the enemy, as a garrison does; see 2 Cor. 11:32, "guarded," A.V., "kept," i.e., kept the city, "with a garrison." It is used of the security of the Christian until the end, 1 Pet. 1:5, R.V., "are guarded," and of the sense of that security that is his when he puts all his matters into the hand of God, Phil. 4:7, R.V., "shall guard." In these passages the idea is not merely that of protection, but of inward garrisoning as by the Holy Spirit; in Gal. 3:23 ("were kept in ward"), it means rather a benevolent custody and watchful guardianship in view of world-wide idolatry (cp. Is. 5:2). See KEEP. ¶

NT: B.867b; CB.1264c; K.—.
OT: —.
GEN. REF.: IS.2:578; NB.—; Z.—.

GUARDIAN

epitropos [ἐπίτροπος, 2012], lit., one to whose care something is committed (*epi*, upon, *trepō*, to turn or direct), is rendered "guardians" in Gal. 4:2, R.V., A.V., "tutors" (in Matt. 20:8 and Luke 8:3, "steward"). ¶

"The corresponding verb, *epitrepō*, is translated 'permit,' 'give leave,' 'suffer'; see 1 Cor. 14:34; 16:7; 1 Tim. 2:12, e.g., . . . An allied noun, *epitropē*, is translated 'commission' in Acts 26:12 (¶) and refers to delegated authority over persons. This usage of cognate words suggests that the *epitropos* was a superior servant responsible for the persons composing the household, whether children or slaves."*

NT: B.303d; CB.1246b; K.—.
OT: —.
GEN. REF.: IS.2:578; NB.—; Z.2:851.

GUEST

anakeimai [ἀνάκειμαι, 345], to recline at table, frequently rendered to sit at meat, is used in its present participial form (lit., 'reclining ones as a noun denoting "guests," in Matt. 22:10, 11. See LEAN, LIE, SIT.

NT: B.55d; CB.1235a; K.425.
OT: —.
GEN. REF.: IS.2:579; NB.—; Z.2:852.

Note: For *kataluō*, to unloose, rendered to be a guest in Luke 19:7, A.V., (R.V., to lodge), see LODGE.

GUEST-CHAMBER

kataluma [κατάλυμα, 2646], akin to *kataluō* (see *Note* above), signifies (*a*) an inn, lodging-place, Luke 2:7; (*b*) a guest-room, Mark 14:14; Luke 22:11. The word lit. signifies a loosening down (*kata*, down, *luō*, to loose), used of the place where travellers and their beasts untied their packages, girdles and sandals. "In the East, no figure is more invested with chivalry than the guest. In his own right he cannot cross the threshold, but when once he is invited in, all do him honour and unite in rendering service; cp. Gen. 18:19; Judg. 19:9, 15." These two passages in the N.T. "concern a room in a private house, which the owner readily placed at the disposal of Jesus and His disciples for the celebration of the Passover . . . At the festivals of Passover, Pentecost and Tabernacles the people were commanded to repair to Jerusalem; and it was a boast of the Rabbis that, notwithstanding the enormous crowds, no man could truthfully say to his fellow, 'I have not found a fire where to roast my paschal lamb in Jerusalem,' or 'I have not found a bed in Jerusalem to lie in,' or 'My lodging is too strait in Jerusalem' " (Hastings, Bib. Dic., GUEST-CHAMBER and INN). See INN. ¶

NT: B.414b; CB.1254a; K.543.
OT: lûn: S.3885; HR.738a.2a; H.1096; BD.533c.
mālôn: S.4411; HR.738a.2b; H.1096a; BD.533d.
GEN. REF.: IS.2:579; NB.541; Z.2:852.

GUIDE (Noun and Verb)

A. Noun.

hodēgos [ὁδηγός, 3595], a leader on the way (*hodos*, a way, *hēgeomai*, to lead), a guide, is used (*a*) literally, in Acts 1:16; (*b*) figuratively, Matt. 15:14, R.V., "guides" (A.V., "leaders"); Matt. 23:16, 24, "guides"; Rom. 2:19, "a guide." Cp. B, No. 1. ¶

NT: B.553c; CB.1251a; K.666.
OT: —.
GEN. REF.: IS.2:579; NB.—; Z.—.

B. Verbs.

1. *hodēgeō* [ὁδηγέω, 3594], to lead the way (akin to A), is used (*a*) literally, R.V., "guide"

* From Notes on Galatians, by Hogg and Vine, p. 180.

(A.V., "lead"), of guiding the blind, in Matt. 15:14; Luke 6:39; of guiding unto fountains of waters of life, Rev. 7:17; (*b*) figuratively, in John 16:13, of guidance into the truth by the Holy Spirit; in Acts 8:31, of the interpretation of Scripture. See LEAD. ¶

NT: B.553b; CB.1251a; K.666.
OT: nāḥāh: S.5148; HR.962a.6; H.1341; BD.634d.
GEN. REF.: IS.2:579; NB.–; Z.–.

2. *kateuthunō* [κατευθύνω, 2720], to make straight, is said of guiding the feet into the way of peace, Luke 1:79. See DIRECT.

NT: B.422b; CB.–; K.–.
OT: kûn: S.3559; HR.750b.4a-d; H.964; BD.465c.
ṣālēaḥ: S.6743; HR.750b.7a,b; H.1916,1917; BD.852b.
GEN. REF.: IS.2:579; NB.–; Z.–.

Notes: (1) In 1 Tim. 5:14, the R.V. rightly translates the verb *oikodespoteō* by "rule the household" (A.V., "guide the house"), the meaning being that of the management and direction of household affairs. See RULE. ¶

(2) *Hēgeomai*, to lead, in Heb. 13:7, 24, is rendered "that had the rule over" and "that have etc.," more lit., 'them that were (are) your leaders,' or guides.

GUILE

dolos [δόλος, 1388], a bait, snare, deceit, is rendered "guile" in John 1:47, negatively of Nathanael; Acts 13:10, R.V., A.V., "subtlety" (of Bar-Jesus); 2 Cor. 12:16, in a charge made against Paul by his detractors, of catching the Corinthian converts by guile (the Apostle is apparently quoting the language of his critics); 1 Thess. 2:3, negatively, of the teaching of the Apostle and his fellow-missionaries; 1 Pet. 2:1, of that from which Christians are to be free; 2:22, of the guileless speech of Christ (cp. GUILELESS, No. 2); 3:10, of the necessity that the speech of Christians should be guileless. See also Matt. 26:4; Mark 7:22; 14:1. See CRAFT, DECEIT, SUBTILTY. ¶

NT: B.203b; CB.–; K.–.
OT: mirmāh: S.4820; HR.340b.4a; H.2169b; BD.941b.
rᵉmiyyāh: S.7423; HR.340b.9; H.2169a; BD.941a.
GEN. REF.: IS.2:580; NB.–; Z.2:852.

Note: In Rev. 14:15, some mss. have *dolos*; the most authentic have *pseudos*, a "lie."

GUILELESS (WITHOUT GUILE)

1. *adolos* [ἄδολος, 97], without guile (*a*, negative, and *dolos*, see GUILE), pure, unadulterated, is used metaphorically of the teaching of the Word of God, 1 Pet. 2:2, R.V. It is used in the papyri writings of seed, corn, wheat, oil, wine, etc. ¶

NT: B.18c; CB.1233a; K.–.
OT: –.
GEN. REF.: –.

2. *akakos* [ἄκακος, 172], lit., without evil (*a*, negative, *kakos*, evil), signifies simple, guileless, Rom. 16:18, "simple," of believers (perhaps = unsuspecting, or, rather, innocent, free from admixture of evil); in Heb. 7:26, R.V., "guileless" (A.V., "harmless"), the character of Christ (more lit., 'free from evil'). ¶ Cp. Sept., Job 2:3; 8:20; Prov. 1:4; 14:15. See HARMLESS.

NT: B.29b; CB.1234a; K.391.
OT: petî: S.6612; HR.43b.2; H.1853a; BD.834b.
tām: S.8535; HR.43b.3a; H.2522c; BD.1070d.
tōm: S.8537; HR.43b.3b; H.2522a; BD.1070d.
GEN. REF.: –.

GUILTLESS

anaitios [ἀναίτιος, 338], innocent, guiltless (*a*, negative, *n*, euphonic, *aitai*, a charge of crime), is translated "blameless" in Matt. 12:5, A.V., "guiltless" in ver. 7; R.V., "guiltless" in each place. See BLAMELESS. ¶

NT: B.55b; CB.1235a; K.–.
OT: nāqî: S.5355; HR.78a.1; H.1412b; BD.667c.
GEN. REF.: –.

GUILTY (Adjective)

enochos [ἔνοχος, 1777], lit., held in, bound by, liable to a charge or action at law: see DANGER.

NT: B.267d; CB.1245b; K.286.
OT: dām: S.1818; HR.476c.2a; H.436; BD.196b.
GEN. REF.: IS.2:580; NB.–; Z.2:852.

Notes: (1) In Rom. 3:19, A.V., *hupodikos*, brought to trial, lit., 'under judgment' (*hupo*, under, *dikē*, justice), is incorrectly rendered "guilty"; R.V., "under the judgement of." See JUDGMENT.

(2) In Matt. 23:18, *opheilō*, to owe, to be indebted, to fail in duty, be a delinquent, is misrendered "guilty" in the A.V.; R.V., "a debtor."

GULF

chasma [χάσμα, 5490], akin to *chaskō*, to yawn (Eng., chasm), is found in Luke 16:26. ¶ In the Sept., 2 Sam. 18:17, two words are used with reference to Absalom's body, *bothunos* which signifies a great pit, and *chasma*, a yawning abyss, or precipice, with a deep pit at the bottom, into which the body was cast. ¶

NT: B.879b; CB.–; K.–.
OT: paḥat: S.6354; HR.1456a.1; H.1761a; BD.809b.
GEN. REF.: IS.2:581; NB.495; Z.–.

GUSH OUT

ekchunō, or *ekchunnō* [ἐκχύνω, 1632], a Hellenistic form of *ekcheō* to pour forth, is translated "gushed out" in Acts 1:18, of the bowels of Judas Iscariot. See POUR, RUN, SHED, SPILL.

NT: B.247b; CB.1243b; K.220.
OT: –.
GEN. REF.: –.

H

For **HA** (Mark 15:29, R.V.) see **AH**

HABITATION

1. *oikētērion* [οἰκητήριον, 3613], a habitation (from *oikētēr*, an inhabitant, and *oikos*, a dwelling), is used in Jude 6, of the heavenly region appointed by God as the dwelling place of angels; in 2 Cor. 5:2, R.V., "habitation," A.V., "house," figuratively of the spiritual bodies of believers when raised or changed at the return of the Lord. See HOUSE. ¶

NT: B.557b; CB.1260b; K.674.
OT: –.
GEN. REF.: –.

2. *katoikētērion* [κατοικητήριον, 2732], (*kata*, down, used intensively, and No. 1), implying more permanency than No. 1, is used in Eph. 2:22 of the Church as the dwelling-place of the Holy Spirit; in Rev. 18:2 of Babylon, figuratively, as the dwelling-place of demons. ¶

NT: B.424c; CB.1254c; K.674.
OT: môshāb: S.4186; HR.755b.2b; H.922c; BD.444a.
mā'ôn: S.4583; HR.755b.4a; H.1581a; BD.732d.
m^{e}'ônāh: S.4585; HR.755b.4b; H.1581b; BD.733a.
GEN. REF.: IS.2:590; NB.–; Z.–.

3. *katoikia* [κατοικία, 2733], a settlement, colony, dwelling (*kata*, and *oikos*, see above), is used in Acts 17:26, of the localities Divinely appointed as the dwelling-places of the nations. ¶

NT: B.424c; CB.–; K.–.
OT: môshāb: S.4186; HR.755b.1b; H.922c; BD.444a.
GEN. REF.: IS.2:590; NB.–; Z.–.

4. *epaulis* [ἔπαυλις, 1886], a farm, a dwelling (*epi*, upon, *aulis*, a place in which to pass the night, a country-house, cottage or cabin, a fold), is used in Acts 1:20 of the habitation of Judas. ¶

NT: B.283d; CB.–; K.–.
OT: ḥāṣēr: S.2691; HR.508c.4; H.722a,723a; BD.347b.
GEN. REF.: IS.2:590; NB.–; Z.–.

5. *skēnē* [σκηνή, 4633], akin to *skēnoō*, to dwell in a tent or tabernacle, is rendered "habitations" in Luke 16:9, A.V. (R.V., "tabernacles"), of the eternal dwelling-places of the redeemed. See TABERNACLE.

NT: B.754c; CB.1269a; K.1040.
OT: 'ōhel: S.168; HR.1271a.1; H.32a; BD.13d.
mishkān: S.4908; HR.1271a.3; H.2387c; BD.1015c.
GEN. REF.: IS.2:590; NB.–; Z.–.

6. *skēnōma* [σκήνωμα, 4638], a booth, or tent pitched (akin to No. 5), is used of the Temple as God's dwelling, as that which David desired to build, Acts 7:46 (R.V., "habitation," A.V., "tabernacle"); metaphorically of the body as a temporary tabernacle, 2 Pet. 1:13, 14. ¶ See TABERNACLE.

NT: B.755c; CB.1269a; K.1040.
OT: 'ōhēl: S.168; HR.1273b.1; H.32a; BD.13d.
mishkān: S.4908; HR.1273b.3; H.2387c; BD.1015c.
GEN. REF.: IS.2:590; NB.–; Z.–.

HADES

hadēs [ᾅδης, 86], the region of departed spirits of the lost (but including the blessed dead in periods preceding the Ascension of Christ). It has been thought by some that the word etymologically meant the unseen (from *a*, negative, and *eidō*, to see), but this derivation is questionable; a more probable derivation is from *hadō*, signifying all-receiving. It corresponds to "Sheol" in the O.T. In the A.V. of the O.T. and N.T., it has been unhappily rendered "Hell," e.g., Psa. 16:10; or "the grave," e.g., Gen. 37:35; or "the pit," Num. 16:30, 33; in the N.T. the Revisers have always used the rendering "Hades"; in the O.T. they have not been uniform in the translation, e.g., in Isa. 14:15, "hell" (marg., "Sheol"); usually they have "Sheol" in the text and "the grave" in the margin. It never denotes the grave, nor is it the permanent region of the lost; in point of time it is, for such, intermediate between decease and the doom of Gehenna. For the condition, see Luke 16:23-31.

The word is used four times in the Gospels, and always by the Lord, Matt. 11:23; 16:18; Luke 10:15; 16:23; it is used with reference to the soul of Christ, Acts 2:27, 31; Christ declares that He has the keys of it, Rev. 1:18; in Rev. 6:8 it is personified, with the signification of the temporary destiny of the doomed; it is to give up those who are therein, 20:13, and is to be cast into the lake of fire, ver. 14. ¶

NT: B.16d; CB.1248c; K.22.
OT: sh^{e}'ôl: S.7585; HR.24a.6; H.2303c; BD.982d.
GEN. REF.: IS.2:591; NB.518; Z.3:7.

Note: In 1 Cor. 15:55 the most authentic mss. have *thanatos*, death, in the 2nd part of the verse, instead of *Hades*, which the A.V. wrongly renders "grave" ("hell," in the marg.).

HAIL (Noun)

chalaza [χάλαζα, 5464], akin to *chalaō*, to let loose, let fall, is always used as an instrument of Divine judgment, and is found in the N.T. in Rev. 8:7; 11:19; 16:21. ¶

NT: B.874b; CB.1239b; K.—.
OT: bārād: S.1259; HR.1452b.2a; H.280a; BD.135d.
GEN. REF.: IS.2:596; NB.—; Z.3:15.

HAIL (Verb)

chairō [χαίρω, 5463], to rejoice, is used in the imperative mood, (*a*) as a salutation, only in the Gospels; in this respect it is rendered simply "hail," in mockery of Christ, Matt. 26:49; 27:29; Mark 15:18; John 19:3; (*b*) as a greeting, by the angel Gabriel to Mary, Luke 1:28, and, in the plural, by the Lord to the disciples after His resurrection, Matt. 28:9.

NT: B.873b; CB.1239b; K.1298.
OT: gîl: S.1523; HR.1452a.2; H.346; BD.162a.
sāmaḥ: S.8055; HR.1452a.7a; H.2268; BD.970a.
GEN. REF.: IS.2:596; NB.—; Z.—.

HAIR

A. Nouns.

1. *thrix* [θρίξ, 2359], denotes the hair, whether of beast, as of the camel's hair which formed the raiment of John the Baptist, Matt. 3:4; Mark 1:6; or of man. Regarding the latter (*a*) it is used to signify the minutest detail, as that which illustrates the exceeding care and protection bestowed by God upon His children, Matt. 10:30; Luke 12:7; 21:18; Acts 27:34; (*b*) as the Jews swore by the hair, the Lord used the natural inability to make one hair white or black, as one of the reasons for abstinence from oaths, Matt. 5:36; (*c*) while long hair is a glory to a woman (see B), and to wear it loose or dishevelled is a dishonour, yet the woman who wiped Christ's feet with her hair (in place of the towel which Simon the Pharisee omitted to provide), despised the shame in her penitent devotion to the Lord (slaves were accustomed to wipe their masters' feet), Luke 7:38, 44 (R.V., "hair"); see also John 11:2; 12:3; (*d*) the dazzling whiteness of the head and hair of the Son of Man in the vision of Rev. 1 (ver. 14) is suggestive of the holiness and wisdom of "the Ancient of Days"; (*e*) the long hair of the spirit-beings described as locusts in Rev. 9:8 is perhaps indicative of their subjection to their Satanic master (cp. 1 Cor. 11:10, R.V.); (*f*) Christian women are exhorted to refrain from adorning their hair for outward show, 1 Pet. 3:3. ¶

NT: B.363d; CB.1272b; K.—.
OT: s^{e}ʿār: S.8181; HR.655b.2a; H.2274a; BD.972b.
GEN. REF.: IS.2:596; NB.499; Z.3:15.

Note: Goat's hair was used in tent-making, as, e.g., in the case of Paul's occupation, Acts 18:3; the haircloth of Cilicia, his native province was noted, being known in commerce as *cilicium*.

2. *komē* [κόμη, 2864], is used only of human hair, but not in the N.T. of the ornamental. The word is found in 1 Cor. 11:15, where the context shows that the "covering" provided in the long hair of the woman is as a veil, a sign of subjection to authority, as indicated in the headships spoken of in vers. 1-10. ¶

NT: B.442d; CB.—; K.—.
OT: peraʿ: S.6545; HR.777b.4; H.1823a; BD.828d.
p^{e}ʾēr: S.6287; HR.777b.3; H.1726a; BD.802c.
GEN. REF.: IS.2:596; NB.499; Z.—.

B. Verb.

komaō [κομάω, 2863], signifies to let the hair grow long, to wear long hair, a glory to a woman, a dishonour to a man (as taught by nature), 1 Cor. 11:14, 11:14, 15. ¶

NT: B.442d; CB.—; K.—.
OT: —.
GEN. REF.: IS.2:596; NB.499; Z.—.

C. Adjective.

trichinos [τρίχινος, 5155], akin to A, No. 1, signifies hairy, made of hair, Rev. 6:12, lit., 'hairy sackcloth.' Cp. SACKCLOTH. ¶

NT: B.827a; CB.—; K.—.
OT: s^{e}ʿār: S.8181; HR.1375c.1; H.2274a; BD.972b.
GEN. REF.: IS.2:596; NB.499; Z.3:15.

HALE (Verb)

1. *surō* [σύρω, 4951], to drag, haul, is rendered "haling" in Acts 8:3, of taking to trial or punishment. See DRAG.

NT: B.794c; CB.—; K.—.
OT: zāḥal: S.2119; HR.1322c.1; H.545; BD.267b.
sāḥab: S.5498; HR.1322c.2; H.1482; BD.694d.
GEN. REF.: IS.2:599; NB.—; Z.—.

2. *katasurō* [κατασύρω, 2694], an intensive form of No. 1, lit., to pull down (*kata*), hence, to drag away, is used in Luke 12:58, of haling a person before a judge. ¶

NT: B.419b; CB.—; K.—.
OT: —.
GEN. REF.: IS.2:599; NB.—; Z.—.

HALF

hēmisus [ἥμισυς, 2255], an adjective, is used (*a*) as such in the neuter plural, in Luke 19:8, lit., 'the halves (of my goods)'; (*b*) as a noun, in the neuter sing., "the half," Mark 6:23; "half (a time)," Rev. 12:14; "a half," 11:9, 11, R.V. ¶

NT: B.348a; CB.—; K.—.
OT: ḥ^{a}ṣî: S.2677; HR.618c.1a; H.719b; BD.345c.
GEN. REF.: IS.2:599; NB.—; Z.—.

For **HALF-SHEKEL** see **SHEKEL**

HALL

1. *aulē* [αὐλή, 833], a court, most frequently the place where a governor dispensed justice, is rendered "hall" in Mark 15:16 and Luke 22:55, A.V. (R.V., "court"). See COURT, FOLD, PALACE.

NT: B.121b; CB.1238b; K.—.
OT: hāsēr: S.2691; HR.177b.2b; H.722a,723a; BD.347b.
GEN. REF.: —.

2. *praitōrion* [πραιτώριον, 4232], is translated "common hall" in Matt. 27:27, A.V. (R.V., "palace"); "Praetorium" in Mark 15:16; "hall of judgment" or "judgment hall" in John 18:28, 33; 19:9; Acts 23:35 (R.V., "palace," in each place); "praetorian guard," Phil. 1:13 (A.V., "palace"). See PALACE. ¶

NT: B.697c; CB.—; K.—.
OT: —.
GEN. REF.: IS.—; NB.1018; Z.3:17.

HALLELUJAH

hallēlouia [Ἀλληλουιά, 239], signifies "Praise ye Jah." It occurs as a short doxology in the Psalms, usually at the beginning, e.g., 111, 112, or the end, e.g., 104, 105, or both, e.g., 106, 135 (where it is also used in ver. 3), 146-150. In the N.T. it is found in Rev. 19:1, 3, 4, 6, as the keynote in the song of the great multitude in Heaven. Alleluia, without the initial H, is a misspelling. ¶

NT: B.39c; CB.1249a; K.—.
OT: halᵉlû-yāh: S.1984; HR.55c.1; H.499,500; BD.237d,238b.
GEN. REF.: IS.2:600; NB.500; Z.3:19.

HALLOW

hagiazō [ἁγιάζω, 37], to make holy (from *hagios*, holy), signifies (*a*) to set apart for God, to sanctify, to make a person or thing the opposite of *koinos*, common; it is translated "Hallowed," with reference to the Name of God the Father in the Lord's Prayer, Matt. 6:9; Luke 11:2. See SANCTIFY.

NT: B.8c; CB.1249a; K.14.
OT: qādash: S.6942; HR.10c.7; H.1990; BD.872d.
GEN. REF.: IS.2:600; NB.—; Z.3:20.

HALT

chōlos [χωλός, 5560], lame, is translated "halt" in Matt. 18:8; Mark 9:45; John 5:3; in Acts 14:8, "cripple"; in Luke 14:21, A.V., "halt," R.V., "lame"; elsewhere, "lame," Matt. 11:5; 15:30, 31; 21:14; Luke 7:22; 14:13; Acts 3:2; 8:7; Heb. 12:13; some mss. have it in Acts 3:11 (A.V., "the lame man"), R.V., "he," translating *autou*, as in the best texts. ¶

NT: B.889a; CB.1240a; K.—.
OT: pissēaḥ: S.6455; HR.1480b.1; H.1787a; BD.820c.
GEN. REF.: IS.2:601; NB.—; Z.—.

Note: For *kullos*, Matt. 18:8, R.V., "halt," see MAIMED, No. 2.

HAND

cheir [χείρ, 5495], the hand (cp. Eng., chiropody), is used, besides its ordinary significance, (*a*) in the idiomatic phrases, by the hand of, at the hand of, etc., to signify by the agency of, Acts 5:12; 7:35; 17:25; 14:3; Gal. 3:19 (cp. Lev. 26:46); Rev. 19:2; (*b*) metaphorically, for the power of God, e.g., Luke 1:66; 23:46; John 10:28, 29; Acts 11:21; 13:11; Heb. 1:10; 2:7; 10:31; (*c*) by metonymy, for power, e.g., Matt. 17:22; Luke 24:7; John 10:39; Acts 12:11.

NT: B.879d; CB.1239c; K.1309.
OT: yād: S.3027; HR.1457c.2a; H.844; BD.388d.
GEN. REF.: IS.2:610; NB.503; Z.3:28.

AT HAND

A. Adverb.

engus [ἐγγύς, 1451], near, nigh, frequently rendered "at hand," is used (*a*) of place, e.g., of the Lord's sepulchre, John 19:42, "nigh at hand"; (*b*) of time, e.g., Matt. 26:18; Luke 21:30, 31, R.V., "nigh," A.V., "nigh at hand"; in Phil. 4:5, "the Lord is at hand," it is possible to regard the meaning as that either of (*a*) or (*b*); the following reasons may point to (*b*) : (1) the subject of the preceding context has been the return of Christ, 3:20, 21; (2) the phrase is a translation of the Aramaic Maranatha, 1 Cor. 16:22, a Christian watchword, and the use of the title "the Lord" is appropriate; (3) the similar use of the adverb in Rev. 1:3 and 22:10; (4) the similar use of the corresponding verb (see B) in Rom. 13:12; Heb. 10:25, "drawing nigh," R.V.; Jas. 5:8; cp. 1 Pet. 4:7. See NEAR, NIGH, READY.

NT: B.214a; CB.1245a; K.194.
OT: qārôb: S.7138; HR.363c.4; H.2065d; BD.898b.
GEN. REF.: —.

B. Verb.

engizō [ἐγγίζω]: See APPROACH, A.

Notes: (1) In 2 Thess. 2:2, A.V., the verb *enistēmi*, to be present (*en*, in, *histēmi*, to cause to stand), is wrongly translated "is at hand"; the R.V. correctly renders it, "is (now) present"; the Apostle is counteracting the error of the supposition that "the Day of the Lord" (R.V.), a period of Divine and retributive judgments upon the world, had already begun.

(2) In 2 Tim. 4:6, A.V., the verb *ephistēmi*, to stand by, to come to or upon (*epi*, upon, *histēmi*, to make to stand), is rendered "is at hand," of the Apostle's departure from this life; the R.V. "is come" represents the vivid force of the statement, expressing suddenness or imminence.

HAND (lead by the)

A. Adjective.

cheiragōgos [χειραγωγός, 5497], lit., a hand-leader (*cheir*, the hand, *agō*, to lead), is used as a noun (plural) in Acts 13:11, "some to lead him by the hand." ¶

NT: B.880d; CB.–; K.1309.
OT: –.
GEN. REF.: –.

B. Verb.

cheiragōgeō [χειραγωγέω, 5496], to lead by the hand, is used in Acts 9:8; 22:11. ¶

NT: B.880d; CB.–; K.1309.
OT: –.
GEN. REF.: –.

HANDED DOWN

patroparadotos [πατροπαράδοτος, 3970], an adjective, denoting handed down from one's fathers, is used in 1 Pet. 1:18, R.V., for A.V., "*received* by tradition from your fathers" (from *patēr*, a father, and *paradidōmi*, to hand down). ¶

NT: B.637a; CB.–; K.–.
OT: –.
GEN. REF.: –.

HAND (with one's own)

autocheir [αὐτόχειρ, 849], a noun (*autos*, self, *cheir*, the hand), is used in the plural in Acts 27:19, "with their own hands." ¶

NT: B.124a; CB.–; K.–.
OT: –.
GEN. REF.: –.

HAND (take in)

epicheireō [ἐπιχειρέω, 2021], to put the hand to (*epi*, to, *cheir*, the hand), is rendered "have taken in hand" in Luke 1:1. See TAKE.

NT: B.304d; CB.–; K.–.
OT: ḥāshab: S.2803; HR.538c.2; H.767; BD.362d.
GEN. REF.: –.

For **LAY HANDS ON** (*krateō* in Matt. 18:28; 21:46; *piazō* in John 8:20), see HOLD and APPREHEND.

HANDS (made by, not made with)

1. *cheiropoiētos* [χειροποίητος, 5499], made by hand, of human handiwork (*cheir*, and *poieō*, to make), is said of the temple in Jerusalem, Mark 14:58; temples in general, Acts 7:48 (R.V., "houses"); 17:24; negatively, of the heavenly and spiritual tabernacle, Heb. 9:11; of the holy place in the earthly tabernacle, ver. 24; of circumcision, Eph. 2:11. ¶ In the Sept., of idols, Lev. 26:1, 30; Isa. 2:18; 10:11; 16:12; 19:1; 21:9; 31:7; 46:6. ¶

NT: B.880d; CB.1239c; K.1309.
OT: ʾělîl: S.457; HR.1467a.1; H.99a; BD.47b.
GEN. REF.: IS.–; NB.503; Z.–.

2. *acheiropoiētos* [ἀχειροποίητος, 886], not made by hands (*a*, negative, and No. 1), is said of an earthly temple, Mark 14:58; of the resurrection body of believers, metaphorically as a house, 2 Cor. 5:1; metaphorically, of spiritual circumcision, Col. 2:11. ¶ This word is not found in the Sept.

NT: B.128b; CB.1233a; K.1309.
OT: –.
GEN. REF.: –.

HANDKERCHIEF

soudarion [σουδάριον, 4676], a Latin word, *sudarium* (from *sudor*, sweat), denotes (*a*) a cloth for wiping the face, etc., Luke 19:20; Acts 19:12; (*b*) a head-covering for the dead, John 11:44; 20:7. See NAPKIN. ¶

NT: B.759c; CB.–; K.–.
OT: –.
GEN. REF.: IS.2:610; NB.504; Z.3:28.

HANDLE

1. *psēlaphaō* [ψηλαφάω, 5584], to feel, touch, handle, is rendered by the latter verb in Luke 24:39, in the Lord's invitation to the disciples to accept the evidence of His resurrection in His being bodily in their midst; in 1 John 1:1, in the Apostle's testimony (against the Gnostic error that Christ had been merely a phantom) that he and his fellow-apostles had handled Him. See FEEL.

NT: B.892c; CB.–; K.–.
OT: mûsh: S.4184; HR.1485b.3; H.1168; BD.559b.
māshash: S.4959; HR.1485b.4; H.1262; BD.606d.
GEN. REF.: IS.2:611; NB.–; Z.3:29.

2. *thinganō* [θιγγάνω, 2345], signifies (*a*) to touch, to handle (though to handle is rather stronger than the actual significance compared with No. 1). In Col. 2:21 the R.V. renders it "touch," and the first verb (*haptō*, to lay hold of) "handle," i.e., 'handle not, nor taste, nor touch'; "touch" is the appropriate rendering; in Heb. 12:20 it is said of a beast's touching Mount Sinai; (*b*) to touch by way of injuring, Heb. 11:28. See TOUCH. ¶ In the Sept., Ex. 19:12. ¶

NT: B.361d; CB.–; K.–.
OT: nāgaʿ: S.5060; HR.652a.1; H.1293; BD.619a.
GEN. REF.: IS.–; NB.–; Z.3:29.

Note: The shortened form found in the passages mentioned is an aorist (or point) tense of the verb.

3. *doloō* [δολόω, 1389], to corrupt, is used in 2 Cor. 4:2, "handling (the Word of God) deceitfully," in the sense of using guile (*dolos*);

the meaning approximates to that of adulterating (cp. *kapēleuō*, in 2:17). ¶
NT: B.203b; CB.1242a; K.–.
OT: ḥālaq: S.2505; HR.340c.1; H.669; BD.325a.
GEN. REF.: –.

4. *atimazō* [ἀτιμάζω, 818], to dishonour, insult, is rendered "handled shamefully" in Mark 12:4. Some mss. have the alternative verb *atimaō*. See DESPISE, DISHONOUR.
NT: B.120a; CB.1238b; K.–.
OT: bāzāh: S.959; HR.175c.1b; H.224; BD.102b.
qālāh: S.7034; HR.175c.6a,b; H.2024; BD.885d.
GEN. REF.: –.

5. *orthotomeō* [ὀρθοτομέω, 3718], to cut straight, as in road-making (*orthos*, straight, *temnō*, to cut), is used metaphorically in 2 Tim. 2:15, of 'handling aright (the word of truth),' R.V. (A.V., "rightly dividing"). The stress is on *orthos*; the Word of God is to be handled strictly along the lines of its teaching. If the metaphor is taken from ploughing, cutting a straight furrow, the word would express a careful cultivation, the Word of God viewed as ground designed to give the best results from its ministry and in the life. See DIVIDE. ¶

In the Sept., in Prov. 3:6 and 11:5, the knowledge of God's wisdom and the just dealing of the upright are enjoined as producing a straight walk in the life. ¶
NT: B.580b; CB.1261b; K.1169.
OT: yāshar: S.3474; HR.1011a.1; H.930; BD.448c.
GEN. REF.: IS.2:611; NB.–; Z.–.

For **HANDMAID** and **HANDMAIDEN** see under **BONDMAN**

For **HANDWRITING** see **BOND**

HANG

1. *kremannumi* [κρεμάννυμι, 2910], is used (*a*) transitively in Acts 5:30; 10:39; in the Passive Voice, in Matt. 18:6, of a millstone about a neck, and in Luke 23:39, of the malefactors; (*b*) intransitively, in the Middle Voice, in Matt. 22:40, of the dependence of "the Law and the prophets" (i.e., that which they enjoin) upon the one great principle of love to God and one's neighbour (as a door hangs on a hinge, or as articles hang on a nail); in Acts 28:4, of the serpent hanging from Paul's hand; in Gal. 3:13 the word is used in a quotation from the Sept. of Deut. 21:23. ¶
NT: B.450a; CB.1256a; K.468.
OT: tālāh: S.8518; HR.785c.4; H.2512; BD.1067d.
GEN. REF.: IS.2:612; NB.–; Z.3:30.

2. *ekkremannumi* [ἐκκρεμάννυμι, 1582], to hang from, or upon (*ek*, and No. 1), is used in the Middle Voice (*ekkremamai*) metaphorically in Luke 19:48, R.V., "(the people all) hung upon (Him, listening)," A.V., "were very attentive." ¶ In the Sept., Gen. 44:30. ¶
NT: B.242a; CB.–; K.468.
OT: qāshar: S.7194; HR.435a.1; H.2090; BD.905a.
GEN. REF.: –.

3. *pariēmi* [παρίημι, 3935], signifies (*a*) to disregard, leave alone, leave undone, Luke 11:42 (some mss. have *aphiēmi*, here); (*b*) to relax, loosen, and, in the Passive Voice, to be relaxed, exhausted, said of hands that hang down in weakness, Heb. 12:12. ¶
NT: B.627c; CB.1262b; K.88.
OT: –.
GEN. REF.: –.

4. *perikeimai* [περίκειμαι, 4029], signifies to lie round (*peri*, around, *keimai*, to lie); then, to be hanged round, said of "a great millstone" (lit., 'a millstone turned by an ass'), Mark 9:42, R.V., and marg., to be hung round the neck of him who causes one of Christ's "little ones" to stumble; in Luke 17:2, "a millstone." See BOUND (to be).
NT: B.647d; CB.–; K.425.
OT: –.
GEN. REF.: –.

5. *apanchō* [ἀπάγχω, 519], signifies to strangle; in the Middle Voice, to hang oneself, Matt. 27:5. ¶ In the Sept. it is said of Ahithophel (2 Sam. 17:23). ¶
NT: B.79c; CB.–; K.–.
OT: ḥānaq: S.2614; HR.115c.1; H.697; BD.338b.
GEN. REF.: IS.2:612; NB.–; Z.–.

HAPLY (if, lest)

1. *ei ara* [εἰ ἄρα, 686], denotes if therefore, if accordingly (i.e., if in these circumstances), e.g., Mark 11:13, of Christ and the fig tree (not 'if perchance,' but marking a correspondence in point of fact).
NT: B.104a; CB.1237b; K.75.
OT: –.
GEN. REF.: IS.2:613; NB.–; Z.–.

2. *ei arage* [εἰ ἄραγε, —], denotes if in consequence, e.g., Acts 17:27, "if haply" they might feel after God, in consequence of seeking Him.
NT: B.104a; CB.–; K.–.
OT: –.
GEN. REF.: IS.2:613; NB.–; Z.–.

3. *mē pote* [μή ποτε, 3379], lit., lest ever, "lest haply," e.g., Luke 14:29, of laying a foundation, with the possibility of being unable to finish the building; Acts 5:39, of the possibility of being found fighting against God; Heb. 3:12, R.V., "lest haply," of the possibility of having an evil heart of unbelief. The R.V., usually has "lest haply" (A.V. "lest at any time"), e.g., Matt. 4:6; 5:25; 13:15; Mark 4:12; Luke 4:11; 21:34; Heb. 2:1; in Matt. 25:9, the R.V. has "peradventure"; in 2 Tim. 2:25, A.V. and R.V., have "if

peradventure"; in John 7:26 the R.V. has "Can it be that," for the word "Do" in the A.V.
NT: B.695a; CB.1266b; K.–.
OT: –.
GEN. REF.: IS.2:613; NB.–; Z.–.

4. *mē pōs* [μή πως, 3381], denotes lest in any way, by any means, e.g., 2 Cor. 9:4, A.V., "lest haply," R.V., "lest by any means."
NT: B.732a; CB.–; K.–.
OT: –.
GEN. REF.: –.

5. *mē pou* [μή που], denotes lest somehow; the R.V. has "lest haply" in Acts 27:29 (some mss. have No. 4, here).
NT: B.696b; CB.1266b; K.–.
OT: –.
GEN. REF.: –.

HAPPEN

1. *sumbainō* [συμβαίνω, 4819], lit., to go or come together (*sun*, with, *bainō*, to go), signifies to happen together, of things or events, Mark 10:32; Luke 24:14; Acts 3:10; 1 Cor. 10:11; 1 Pet. 4:12; 2 Pet. 2:22; "befell" in Acts 20:19; in Acts 21:35, "so it was." See BEFALL. ¶
NT: B.777b; CB.–; K.–.
OT: qārā': S.7121; HR.1302c.5; H.2063; BD.894d.
GEN. REF.: –.

Notes: (1) In Phil. 1:12, the phrase *ta kat'* (i.e., *kata*) *eme*, lit., 'the things relating to me,' is rendered "the things *which happened* unto me."

(2) In Luke 24:35, the phrase "the things *that happened* in the way," R.V. (A.V., "what things were done in the way"), is, lit., 'the things in the way.'

HAPPY, HAPPIER

A. Adjective.

makarios [μακάριοσ, 3107], blessed, happy, is rendered "happy" in the R.V., in two places only, as in the A.V., Acts 26:2 and Rom. 14:22 (where "blessed" would have done); also the comparative "happier" in 1 Cor. 7:40. Elsewhere the R.V. uses "blessed" for A.V. "happy," e.g., John 13:17; 1 Pet. 3:14; 4:14. See BLESSED.
NT: B.486c; CB.1257c; K.548.
OT: 'esher: S.835; HR.892b.1b; H.183a; BD.80d.
GEN. REF.: IS.–; NB.–; Z.3:31.

B. Verb.

makarizō [μακαρίζω, 3106], to call blessed, Luke 1:48, is rendered "we count . . . happy" in Jas. 5:11. See BLESSED. ¶
NT: B.486c; CB.1257c; K.548.
OT: 'āshar: S.833; HR.892a.1a,b; H.183; BD.80d.
GEN. REF.: IS.–; NB.–; Z.3:31.

HARD, HARDEN, HARDENING, HARDNESS

A. Adjectives.

1. *sklēros* [σκληρός, 4642], from *skellō*, to dry, signifies trying, exacting; see AUSTERE.
NT: B.756a; CB.1269a; K.816.
OT: qāsheh: S.7186; HR.1274b.4a; H.2085a; BD.904c.
GEN. REF.: IS.2:614; NB.–; Z.3:33.

2. *duskolos* [δύσκολος, 1422], primarily means hard to satisfy with food (*dus*, a prefix like Eng., *un*— or *mis*—, indicating difficulty, opposition, injuriousness, etc., the opposite of, *eu*, well, and *kolon*, food); hence, difficult, Mark 10:24, of the difficulty, for those who trust in riches, to enter into the Kingdom of God. ¶
NT: B.209c; CB.–; K.–.
OT: 'ēd: S.343; HR.357b.1; H.38c; BD.15c.
GEN. REF.: IS.2:614; NB.–; Z.–.

B. Nouns.

1. *sklērotēs* [σκληρότης, 4643], akin to A, No. 1, is rendered "hardness" in Rom. 2:5. ¶
NT: B.756b; CB.1269a; K.816.
OT: qᵉshî: S.7190; HR.1274c.3; H.2085b; BD.904d.
GEN. REF.: IS.2:614; NB.–; Z.3:33.

2. *pōrōsis* [πώρωσις, 4457], denotes a hardening, a covering with a *pōros*, a kind of stone, indicating a process (from *pōroō*, C, No. 1), and is used metaphorically of dulled spiritual perception, Mark 3:5, R.V., "at the hardening of their hearts"; Rom. 11:25, R.V., "a hardening" (A.V., "blindness"), said of the state of Israel; Eph. 4:18, R.V., "hardening," of the heart of Gentiles. See BLINDNESS. ¶
NT: B.732a; CB.1266a; K.816.
OT: –.
GEN. REF.: IS.2:614; NB.–; Z.3:33.

Note: See also under HARDSHIP and HEART (hardness of).

C. Verbs.

1. *pōroō* [πωρόω, 4456], to make hard, callous, to petrify (akin to B, No. 2), is used metaphorically, of the heart, Mark 6:52; 8:17; John 12:40; of the mind (or thoughts), 2 Cor. 3:14, of those in Israel who refused the revealed will and ways of God in the Gospel, as also in Rom. 11:7, R.V., "hardened" (A.V., "blinded"), in both places. See BLINDNESS. ¶
NT: B.732a; CB.1266a; K.816.
OT: kāhāh: S.3543; HR.1246c.1; H.957; BD.462c.
GEN. REF.: IS.2:614; NB.–; Z.3:33.

2. *sklērunō* [σκληρύνω, 4645], to make dry or hard (akin to A, No. 1 and B, No. 1), is used in Acts 19:9; in Rom. 9:18, illustrated by the case of Pharaoh, who first persistently hardened his heart (see the R.V. marg. of Ex. 7:13, 22; 8:19; text of ver. 32 and 9:7), all producing the retributive hardening by God, after His much long-suffering, 9:12, etc.; in Heb. 3:8, 13, 15;

4:7, warnings against the hardening of the heart. ¶

NT: B.756b; CB.1269a; K.816.
OT: qāshāh: S.7186; HR.1275a,3a,b; H.2085a; BD.904c.
ḥāzaq: S.2388; HR.1275a.1; H.636; BD.304a.
GEN. REF.: IS.2:614; NB.–; Z.3:33.

HARDLY

1. *duskolōs* [δυσκόλως, 1423], the adverbial form of HARD, A, No. 2, is used in Matt. 19:23; Mark 10:23; Luke 18:24 of the danger of riches. ¶

NT: B.209d; CB.–; K.–.
OT: –.
GEN. REF.: –.

2. *mogis* [μόγις, 3425], with labour, pain, trouble (akin to *mogos*, toil), is found in some mss. in Luke 9:39, instead of No. 3. ¶

NT: B.525d; CB.–; K.606.
OT: –.
GEN. REF.: –.

3. *molis* [μόλις, 3433], with difficulty, scarcely, hardly (akin to *molos*, toil), is used as an alternative for No. 2, and occurs in the most authentic mss. in Luke 9:39; it is rendered "hardly" in Acts 27:8, A.V. See DIFFICULTY.

NT: B.526d; CB.–; K.606.
OT: –.
GEN. REF.: –.

HARDSHIP (to suffer)

1. *kakopatheō* [κακοπαθέω, 2553], to suffer evil, is translated "suffer hardship" in three places in the R.V., 2 Tim. 2:3 (in some mss.; see No. 2), A.V., "endure hardness"; 2:9, A.V., "suffer trouble"; 4:5, A.V., "endure affliction"; in Jas. 5:13, R.V., "suffering" (A.V., "afflicted"). See AFFLICT, ENDURE, SUFFER. ¶ In the Sept., Jonah 4:10. ¶

NT: B.397c; CB.1253b; K.798.
OT: 'āmal: S.5998; HR.709a.1; H.1639; BD.765c.
GEN. REF.: –.

2. *sunkakopatheō* [συγκακοπαθέω, 4777], to suffer hardship with, is so rendered in 2 Tim. 1:8, R.V., A.V., "be thou partaker of the afflictions" (of the Gospel), and, in the best mss., in 2:3, "suffer hardship with me." See AFFLICTION, No. 3, *Note.* ¶

NT: B.773b; CB.1270c; K.798.
OT: –.
GEN. REF.: –.

HARLOT

pornē [πόρνη, 4204], a prostitute, harlot (from *pernēmi*, to sell), is used (*a*) literally, in Matt. 21:31, 32, of those who were the objects of the mercy shown by Christ; in Luke 15:30, of the life of the prodigal; in 1 Cor. 6:15, 16, in a warning to the Corinthian church against the prevailing licentiousness which had made Corinth a byword; in Heb. 11:31 and Jas. 2:25, of Rahab; (*b*) metaphorically, of mystic Babylon, Rev. 17:1, 5 (A.V., "harlots"), 15, 16; 19:2, R.V., for A.V., "whore." ¶

NT: B.693c; CB.1266a; K.918.
OT: zānāh: S.2181; HR.1195a.1; H.563; BD.275c.
GEN. REF.: IS.2:616; NB.1048; Z.3:34.

HARM

A. Nouns.

1. *kakos* [κακός, 2556], evil, is rendered "harm" in Acts 16:28; 28:5. See EVIL.

NT: B.397d; CB.1253b; K.391.
OT: ra': S.7451; HR.709b.13b; H.2191; BD.948c.
rā'āh: S.7451; HR.709b.13c; H.2191; BD.949a.
GEN. REF.: –.

2. *ponēros* [πονηρός, 4190], evil, generally of a more malignant sort than No. 1, is translated "harm" in Acts 28:21. See EVIL.

NT: B.690d; CB.1266a; K.912.
OT: ra': S.7451; HR.1186c.4a; H.2191; BD.948c.
GEN. REF.: –.

3. *atopos* [ἄτοπος]: see AMISS.

4. *hubris* [ὕβρις, 5196], primarily denotes wantonness, insolence; then, an act of wanton violence, an outrage, injury, 2 Cor. 12:10, R.V., "injuries," A.V., "reproaches" (more than reproach is conveyed by the term); metaphorically of a loss by sea, Acts 27:10, R.V., "injury," A.V., "hurt," and ver. 21, R.V., "injury," A.V., "harm." See HURT, INJURY, REPROACH. ¶

NT: B.832a; CB.1251b; K.1200.
OT: ga'ᵃwāh: S.1346; HR.1380a.1b; H.299d; BD.144d.
gā'wôn: S.1347; HR.1380a.1c; H.299e; BD.144d.
GEN. REF.: –.

B. Verb.

1. *kakoō* [κακόω, 2559], to do evil to a person (akin to A, No. 1), is rendered "harm" in 1 Pet. 3:13, and in the R.V. of Acts 18:10 (A.V., "hurt"). See AFFECT, EVIL.

NT: B.398b; CB.1253b; K.391.
OT: 'ānāh: S.6031; HR.711b.5c; H.1651,1652; BD.776a.
rā'a': S.7489; HR.711b.7a,b; H.2191,2192; BD.949b.
GEN. REF.: –.

2. *kakopoieō* [κακοποιέω, 2554], to do harm (A, No. 1, and *poieō*, to do), is so rendered in the R.V. of Mark 3:4 and Luke 6:9 (A.V., "to do evil"), with reference to the moral character of what is done; in 1 Pet. 3:17, "evil doing"; 3 John 11, "doeth evil." ¶

NT: B.397c; CB.1253b; K.798.
OT: rā'a': S.7489; HR.709a.3a; H.2191,2192; BD.949b.
GEN. REF.: –.

HARMLESS

1. *akeraios* [ἀκέραιος, 185], lit., unmixed, with absence of foreign mixture (from *a*, negative, and *kerannumi*, to mix), pure, is used metaphorically in the N.T. of what is guileless, sincere, Matt. 10:16, "harmless" (marg., "simple"), i.e., with the simplicity of a single eye, discerning what is evil, and choosing only what glorifies God; Rom. 16:19, "simple (unto

that which is evil);" A.V. marg., "harmless"; Phil. 2:15, "harmless;" A.V. marg., "sincere." The Greeks used it of wine unmixed with water, of unalloyed metal; in the papyri writings it is used of a loan the interest of which is guaranteed (Moulton and Milligan, Vocab.). Trench compares it and synonymous words as follows: "as the *akakos* (see No. 2, below) has no harmfulness in him, and the *adolos* no guile, so the *akeraios* no foreign mixture, and the *haplous* no folds" (Syn. § lvi). *Haplous* is said of the single eye, Matt. 6:22; Luke 11:34. ¶

NT: B.30b; CB.—; K.33.
OT: —.
GEN. REF.: —.

2. *akakos* [ἄκακος, 172], the negative of *kakos* (see Harm, A, No. 1), void of evil, is rendered "harmless" in Heb. 7:26 (R.V., "guileless"), of the character of Christ as a High Priest; in Rom. 16:18, R.V., "innocent;" A.V., "simple." ¶

NT: B.29b; CB.1234a; K.391.
OT: tām: S.8535; HR.43b.3a; H.2522c; BD.1070d.
tōm: S.8537; HR.43b.3b; H.2522a; BD.1070d.
GEN. REF.: —.

HARP

A. Noun.

kithara [κιθάρα, 2788], whence Eng., guitar, denotes a lyre or harp; it is described by Josephus as an instrument of ten strings, played by a plectrum (a smaller instrument was played by the hand); it is mentioned in 1 Cor. 14:7; Rev. 5:8; 14:2; 15:2. ¶

NT: B.432a; CB.—; K.—.
OT: kinnôr: S.3658; HR.765a.1; H.1004a; BD.490a.
GEN. REF.: IS.2:618; NB.852; Z.4:320.

B. Verb.

kitharizō [κιθαρίζω, 2789], signifies to play on the harp, 1 Cor. 14:7; Rev. 14:2. ¶ In the Sept., Isa. 23:16. ¶

NT: B.432a; CB.—; K.—.
OT: nāgan: S.5059; HR.765a.1; H.1291.1; BD.618d.
GEN. REF.: IS.2:618; NB.852; Z.4:320.

HARPER

kitharōdos [κιθαρωδός, 2790], denotes one who plays and sings to the lyre (from *kithara*, a lyre, and *aoidos*, a singer), Rev. 14:2; 18:22. ¶

NT: B.432a; CB.—; K.—.
OT: —.
GEN. REF.: —.

HARVEST

therismos [θερισμός, 2326], akin to *therizō*, to reap, is used (*a*) of the act of harvesting, John 4:35; (*b*) the time of harvest, figuratively, Matt. 13:30, 39; Mark 4:29; (*c*) the crop, figuratively, Matt. 9:37, 38; Luke 10:2; Rev. 14:15. The beginning of harvest varied according to natural conditions, but took place on the average about the middle of April in the eastern lowlands of Palestine, in the latter part of the month in the coast plains and a little later in high districts. Barley harvest usually came first and then wheat. Harvesting lasted about seven weeks, and was the occasion of festivities. ¶

NT: B.359c; CB.1272b; K.332.
OT: qāṣîr: S.7105; HR.649a.4; H.2062a,b; BD.894c.
GEN. REF.: IS.2:619; NB.—; Z.3:36.

HASTE, WITH HASTE, HASTILY

A. Noun.

spoudē [σπουδή, 4710], denotes (*a*) haste, speed, accompanied by "with;" Mark 6:25; Luke 1:39; (*b*) zeal, diligence, earnestness; see Business, Care, Carefulness, Diligence, Forwardness.

NT: B.763d; CB.1269c; K.1069.
OT: behālāh: S.928; HR.1285c.1b; H.207a; BD.96d.
bāhal: S.926; HR.1285c.1c; H.207; BD.96b.
ḥippāzôn: S.2649; HR.1285c.3; H.708a; BD.342a.
GEN. REF.: IS.2:628; NB.—; Z.—.

B. Verb.

speudō [σπεύδω, 4692], denotes (*a*) intransitively, to hasten, Luke 2:16, "with haste;" lit., '(they came) hastening'; Luke 19:5, 6; Acts 20:16; 22:18; (*b*) transitively, to desire earnestly, 2 Pet. 3:12, R.V., "earnestly desiring" (marg., "hastening"), A.V., "hasting" (the day of God), i.e., in our practical fellowship with God as those who are appointed by Him as instruments through prayer and service for the accomplishment of His purposes, purposes which will be unthwartably fulfilled both in time and manner of accomplishment. In this way the earnest desire will find its fulfilment. ¶

NT: B.762b; CB.1269c; K.—.
OT: māhar: S.4116; HR.1284a.6a; H.1152; BD.554d.
bāhal: S.926; HR.1284a.2a-c; H.207; BD.96b.
GEN. REF.: IS.2:628; NB.—; Z.—.

C. Adverb.

tacheōs [ταχέως, 5030], quickly, is used in a warning to lay hands "hastily" on no man (with a suggestion of rashness), 1 Tim. 5:22, R.V. (A.V., "suddenly"); in John 11:31, R.V., "(she rose up) quickly" (A.V., "hastily"). See Quickly, Shortly, Suddenly.

NT: B.806d; CB.—; K.—.
OT: māhar: S.4116; HR.1338b.1a; H.1152; BD.554d.
mᵉhērāh: S.4120; HR.1338b.1b; H.1152d; BD.555b.
GEN. REF.: IS.2:628; NB.—; Z.—.

HATE, HATEFUL, HATER, HATRED

A. Verb.

miseō [μισέω, 3404], to hate, is used especially (*a*) of malicious and unjustifiable feelings towards others, whether towards the innocent or by mutual animosity, e.g., Matt. 10:22;

24:10; Luke 6:22, 27; 19:14; John 3:20, of hating the light (metaphorically); 7:7; 15:18, 19, 23-25; Tit. 3:3; 1 John 2:9, 11; 3:13, 15; 4:20; Rev. 18:2, where "hateful" translates the perfect participle Passive Voice of the verb, lit., 'hated,' or 'having been hated'; (*b*) of a right feeling of aversion from what is evil; said of wrong doing, Rom. 7:15; iniquity, Heb. 1:9; "the garment (figurative) spotted by the flesh," Jude 23; "the works of the Nicolaitans," Rev. 2:6 (and ver. 15, in some mss.; see the A.V.); (*c*) of relative preference for one thing over another, by way of expressing either aversion from, or disregard for, the claims of one person or thing relatively to those of another, Matt. 6:24, and Luke 16:13, as to the impossibility of serving two "masters"; Luke 14:26, as to the claims of parents relatively to those of Christ; John 12:25, of disregard for one's life relatively to the claims of Christ; Eph. 5:29, negatively, of one's flesh, i.e., of one's own, and therefore a man's wife as one with him.

NT: B.522c; CB.1259a; K.597.
OT: sānē': S.8130; HR.929a.5a-c; H.2272; BD.971b.
GEN. REF.: IS.2:629; NB.506; Z.3:46.

Note: In 1 John 3:15, he who hates his brother is called a murderer; for the sin lies in the inward disposition, of which the act is only the outward expression.

B. Adjective.

stugētos [στυγητός, 4767], hateful (from *stugeō*, to hate, not found in the N.T.), is used in Tit. 3:3. ¶

NT: B.771d; CB.—; K.—.
OT: —.
GEN. REF.: IS.2:629; NB.506; Z.—.

C. Nouns.

1. *echthra* [ἔχθρα], hatred: see ENMITY.

2. *theostugēs* [θεοστυγής, 2319], from *theos*, God, and *stugeō* (see B), is used in Rom. 1:30, A.V., and R.V., marg., "haters of God," R.V., "hateful to God"; the former rendering is appropriate to what is expressed by the next words, "insolent," "haughty," but the R.V. text seems to give the true meaning. Lightfoot quotes from the Epistle of Clement of Rome, in confirmation of this, "those who practise these things are hateful to God." ¶

NT: B.358c; CB.1272b; K.—.
OT: —.
GEN. REF.: —.

HAUGHTY

huperēphanos [ὑπερήφανος, 5244], showing oneself above others (*huper*, over, *phainomai*, to appear), though often denoting pre-eminent, is always used in the N.T. in the evil sense of arrogant, disdainful, haughty; it is rendered "haughty" in Rom. 1:30 and 2 Tim. 3:2, R.V., A.V., "proud," but "proud" in both Versions in Luke 1:51; Jas. 4:6, and 1 Pet. 5:5; in the last two it is set in opposition to *tapeinos*, humble, lowly. Cp. the noun *huperēphania*, Mark 7:22, pride. ¶

NT: B.841b; CB.1252a; K.1231.
OT: zēd: S.2086; HR.1410a.3; H.547a; BD.267d.
gē'eh: S.1343; HR.1410a.1a; H.299b; BD.144b.
GEN. REF.: IS.2:633; NB.—; Z.—.

HAVE

(*Note:* The following are distinct from the word when it is auxiliary to the tenses of other verbs.)

1. *echō* [ἔχω, 2192], the usual verb for to have, is used with the following meanings: (*a*) to hold, in the hand, etc., e.g., Rev. 1:16; 5:8; (*b*) to hold fast, keep, Luke 19:20; metaphorically, of the mind and conduct, e.g., Mark 16:8; John 14:21; Rom. 1:28; 1 Tim. 3:9; 2 Tim. 1:13; (*c*) to hold on, cling to, be next to, e.g., of accompaniment, Heb. 6:9. "things that accompany (salvation)," lit., 'the things holding themselves of salvation' (R.V., marg., "are near to"); of place, Mark 1:38, "next (towns)," lit., 'towns holding nigh'; of time, e.g., Luke 13:33, "(the day) following," lit., 'the holding (day)'; Acts 13:44; 20:15; 21:26; (*d*) to hold, to count, consider, regard, e.g., Matt. 14:5; 21:46; Mark 11:32; Luke 14:18; Philm. 17; (*e*) to involve, Heb. 10:35; Jas. 1:4; 1 John 4:18; (*f*) to wear, of clothing, arms, etc., e.g., Matt. 3:4; 22:12; John 18:10; (*g*) to be (with child), of a woman, Mark 13:17; Rom. 9:10 (lit., 'having conception'); (*h*) to possess, the most frequent use, e.g., Matt. 8:20; 19:22; Acts 9:14; 1 Thess. 3:6; (*i*) of complaints, disputes, Matt. 5:23; Mark 11:25; Acts 24:19; Rev. 2:4, 20; (*j*) of ability, power, e.g., Luke 12:4; Acts 4:14 (lit., 'had nothing to say'); (*k*) of necessity, e.g., Luke 12:50; Acts 23:17-19; (*l*) to be in a certain condition, as, of readiness, Acts 21:13 (lit., 'I have readily'); of illness, Matt. 4:24, "all that were sick" (lit., 'that had themselves sickly'); Mark 5:23, "lieth (lit., 'hath herself') at the point of death"; Mark 16:18, "they shall recover" (lit., 'shall have themselves well'); John 4:52, "he began to amend" (lit., 'he had himself better'); of evil works, 1 Tim. 5:25, "they that are otherwise," (lit., 'the things having otherwise'); to be so, e.g., Acts 7:1, "are these things so?" (lit., 'have these things thus?'); of

time, Acts 24:25, "for this time" (lit., 'the thing having now').
NT: B.331d; CB.1242c; K.286.
OT: –.
GEN. REF.: IS.–.

2. *apechō* [ἀπέχω, 568], denotes to have in full, to have received (*apo*, from, and No. 1), Matt. 6:2, 5, 16, R.V., "have received," for A.V., "have"; Luke 6:24, A.V. and R.V., "have received," but Phil. 4:18, "I have"; Philm. 15, "(that) thou shouldest have (him)" (A.V., "receive"). Deissmann, in *Light from the Ancient East*, and Moulton and Milligan (Vocab. of Gk. Test.) show that the verb was constantly used "as a technical expression in drawing up a receipt. Consequently in the Sermon on the Mount we are led to understand 'they have received their reward' as 'they have signed the receipt of their reward: their right to receive their reward is realised, precisely as if they had already given a receipt for it.' "

Is there not a hint of this in Paul's word to Philemon concerning receiving Onesimus (ver. 17)? Philemon would give the Apostle a receipt for his payment in sending him. This is in keeping with the metaphorical terms of finance in vv. 18, 19. See ABSTAIN.
NT: B.84d; CB.1236b; K.286.
OT: –.
GEN. REF.: –.

3. *ginomai* [γίνομαι, 1096], to begin to be, come to pass, happen, is rendered "have" in Matt. 18:12; "had" in Acts 15:2; "shall have" in 1 Cor. 4:5, lit., 'praise shall be,' or come to pass. See BECOME.
NT: B.158a; CB.1248b; K.117.
OT: –.
GEN. REF.: –.

4. *metalambanō* [μεταλαμβάνω, 3335], to have, or get a share of, is rendered "I have (a convenient season)," in Acts 24:25. See EAT, PARTAKE, RECEIVE, TAKE.
NT: B.511b; CB.1258b; K.495.
OT: –.
GEN. REF.: –.

5. *huparchō* [ὑπάρχω, 5225], to be in existence, to be ready, at hand, is translated by the verb to have in Acts 3:6, lit., 'silver and gold is not to me' (in the next clause, "such as I have," *echō* is used); 4:37, "having (land)," lit., '(land) being (to him)'; Matt. 19:21, "that (thou) hast," lit., '(things that) are (thine),' i.e., 'thy belongings'; similarly Luke 12:33, 44; 14:33. See BEING.
NT: B.838a; CB.–; K.–.
OT: –.
GEN. REF.: –.

6. *antiballō* [ἀντιβάλλω, 474], lit., to throw in turn, exchange (*anti*, corresponding to, *ballō*, to throw), hence, metaphorically, to exchange thoughts, is used in Luke 24:27, "ye have," i.e., 'ye exchange.' ¶
NT: B.74a; CB.–; K.–.
OT: –.
GEN. REF.: –.

7. *eimi* [εἰμί, 1510], to be, is often used in its various forms with some case of the personal pronoun, to signify to be to, or of, a person, e.g., Matt. 19:27, "(what then) shall we have," lit., 'what then shall be to us?'; Acts 21:23, "we have four men," lit., 'there are to us, etc.'
NT: B.222d; CB.1243a; K.206.
OT: –.
GEN. REF.: –.

8. *enduō* [ἐνδύω, 1746], to put on, is rendered "having on" in Eph. 6:14. See CLOTHE.
NT: B.264a; CB.1245a; K.192.
OT: –.
GEN. REF.: –.

Notes: (1) In John 5:4 (in those mss. which contain the passage), *katechō*, to hold fast, is used in the Passive Voice, in the phrase "whatsoever disease he had," lit., '(by whatsoever disease) he was held.'

(2) In Mark 12:22, in some mss., *lambanō*, to take or receive, is translated "had," in the statement "the seven had her"; in Acts 25:16, R.V., "have had" (A.V., "have"); in Heb. 11:36, "had."

(3) In Matt. 27:19, "Have thou nothing to do with that righteous man" translates what is lit. 'nothing to thee and that righteous man,' the verb being omitted. Similarly with the phrase, "What have I to do with thee?" lit., 'what (is) to me and thee?' Mark 5:7; Luke 8:28; John 2:4, where Westcott translates it 'What is there to Me and to thee?'; Ellicott, 'What is that to Me and to thee,' i.e., 'What is My concern and thine in the matter?' There is certainly nothing disparaging in the question. On the contrary, it answers what must have been the thought in Mary's heart, and suggests that while there is no obligation either on Him or her, yet the need is a case for rendering help. For the construction with the plural pronoun see Matt. 8:29; Mark 1:24; Luke 4:34.

(4) In Heb. 4:13, "with whom we have to do" is, lit., 'with whom (is) the account (*logos*) to us.'

(5) In Heb. 13:5, "such things as ye have" is, lit., 'the (things) present.'

(6) In Mark 5:26, "all that she had" is, lit., 'all the (things) with her.'

(7) For Luke 15:31, A.V., "all that I have," lit., 'all my (things),' see R.V.

(8) For *eneimi*, Luke 11:41, "ye have," see WITHIN, *Note* (*h*).

HAVEN

limēn [λιμήν, 3040], is mentioned in Acts 27:8, "Fair Havens," and ver. 12; for the first of these see FAIR. The first mention in the Bible is in Gen. 49:13 (see R.V. marg.). ¶

NT: B.475a; CB.—; K.—.
OT: māḥôz: S.4231; HR.878c.1; H.1180; BD.562c.
GEN. REF.: IS.2:634; NB.—; Z.3:33.

HAVOCK

1. *portheō* [πορθέω, 4199], to destroy, ravage, lay waste, is used of the persecution inflicted by Saul of Tarsus on the church in Jerusalem, Acts 9:21, and Gal. 1:23, R.V., "made havock," for A.V., "destroyed"; Gal. 1:13, ditto, for A.V., "wasted." See DESTROY, *Note.* ¶

NT: B.693a; CB.—; K.—.
OT: —.
GEN. REF.: IS.2:634; NB.—; Z.—.

2. *lumainomai* [λυμαίνομαι, 3075], to maltreat, outrage (*lumē*, an outrage), is translated "made havock" in Acts 8:3, A.V. (R.V., "laid waste.") ¶

NT: B.481c; CB.—; K.540.
OT: shāḥat: S.7843; HR.889b.6; H.2370; BD.1007d.
GEN. REF.: —.

For **HAY** see **GRASS**

HAZARD

1. *paradidōmi* [παραδίδωμι, 3860], to give over, deliver, signifies to risk, to hazard, in Acts 15:26, of Barnabas and Paul, who hazarded their lives for the Name of the Lord Jesus. See BETRAY.

NT: B.614b; CB.1262a; K.166.
OT: —.
GEN. REF.: —.

2. *paraboleuomai* [παραβολεύομαι, 3851], lit., to throw aside (*para*, aside, *ballō*, to throw), hence, to expose oneself to danger, to hazard one's life, is said of Epaphroditus in Phil. 2:30, R.V., "hazarding." Some mss. have *parabouleuomai* here, to consult amiss, A.V., "not regarding." ¶

NT: B.612b; CB.—; K.—.
OT: —.
GEN. REF.: —.

HE

Note: This pronoun is generally part of the translation of a verb. Frequently it translates the article before nouns, adjectives, numerals, adverbs, prepositional phrases and the participial form of verbs. Apart from these it translates one of the following:

1. *autos* [αὐτός, 846], he himself and no other, emphatic, e.g., Matt. 1:21, where the R.V. brings out the emphasis by the rendering "it is He"; 3:11 (last clause), where the repeated "He" brings out the emphasis; in some cases it can be marked only by a circumlocution which would not constitute a translation, e.g., 8:24; this use is very frequent, especially in the Gospels, the Epistles of John and the Apocalypse; see also, e.g., Eph. 2:14; 4:11; 5:23, 27; See SAME, SELF, THIS, VERY.

NT: B.122c; CB.1238b; K.—.
OT: —.
GEN. REF.: —.

2. *houtos* [οὗτος, 3778], this, this person here, is always emphatic; it is used with this meaning, sometimes to refer to what precedes, e.g., Matt. 5:19, "he (shall be called great)"; John 6:46, "he (hath seen)"; often rendered "this," e.g., Rom. 9:9, or "this man," e.g., Matt. 27:58, R.V.; Jas. 1:25; "the same," e.g., Luke 9:48. See THAT, THIS, THESE.

NT: B.596b; CB.1251b; K.—.
OT: —.
GEN. REF.: —.

3. *ekeinos* [ἐκεῖνος, 1565], denotes that one, that person (in contrast to No. 2); its use marks special distinction, favourable or unfavourable; this form of emphasis should always be noted; e.g., John 2:21 "(But) He (spake)"; 5:19, "(what things soever) He (doeth)"; 7:11; 2 Cor. 10:18, lit., 'for not he that commendeth himself, he (*ekeinos*) is approved'; 2 Tim. 2:13. "He (in contrast to "we") abideth faithful"; 1 John 3:3, "(even as) He (is pure)"; ver. 5, "He (was manifested)"; ver. 7, "He (is righteous)"; ver. 16, "He laid down"; 4:17, "(as) He (is)." See OTHER, THAT, THIS.

NT: B.239b; CB.1243c; K.—.
OT: —.
GEN. REF.: —.

Note: The indefinite pronoun *tis*, anyone, any man, is rendered "he" in Acts 4:35, A.V. (R.V., rightly, "any one"); in Heb. 10:28, R.V. "a man."

HE HIMSELF

1. *autos* [αὐτός]: see No. 1, above.

2. *heauton* [ἑαυτόν, 1438], oneself, himself, a reflexive of No. 1, is rendered "he himself" in Luke 23:2 and Acts 25:4.

NT: B.211d; CB.1249b; K.—.
OT: —.
GEN. REF.: —.

HE THAT

1. *hos* [ὅς, 3739], the relative pronoun who, is sometimes rendered "he that," e.g., Matt. 10:38; with the particle *an*, expressing possibility, uncertainty or a condition, signifying whosoever, Mark 3:29, A.V. (R.V., "whoso-

ever"); 4:25 and 9:40 (with *an*, in the best mss.). See WHATSOEVER, WHICH, WHO, WHOSOEVER.
NT: B.583b; CB.1251b; K.—.
OT: —.
GEN. REF.: —.

2. *hosge* [ὅσγε, —], who even (No. 1, and the particle *ge*), indicates a greater in regard to a less, Rom. 8:32, "He that (spared not)."
NT: B.585a; CB.—; K.—.
OT: —.
GEN. REF.: —.

Notes: (1) In Rev. 13:10, *ei tis*, if anyone, is rendered "if any man" in the R.V., for A.V., "he that."

(2) In Matt. 23:12, *hostis*, No. 1, combined with the indefinite pronoun *tis* (see preceding note), is properly rendered "whosoever," R.V., for A.V., "he that."

HEAD

kephalē [κεφαλή, 2776], besides its natural significance, is used (*a*) figuratively in Rom. 12:20, of heaping coals of fire on a head (see COALS); in Acts 18:6, "Your blood be upon your own heads," i.e., 'your blood-guiltiness rest upon your own persons,' a mode of expression frequent in the O.T., and perhaps here directly connected with Ezek. 3:18, 20; 33:6, 8; see also Lev. 20:16; 2 Sam. 1:16; 1 Kings 2:37; (*b*) metaphorically, of the authority or direction of God in relation to Christ, of Christ in relation to believing men, of the husband in relation to the wife, 1 Cor. 11:3; of Christ in relation to the Church, Eph. 1:22; 4:15; 5:23; Col. 1:18; 2:19; of Christ in relation to principalities and powers, Col. 2:10. As to 1 Cor. 11:10, taken in connection with the context, the word "authority" probably stands, by metonymy, for a sign of authority (R.V.), the angels being witnesses of the pre-eminent relationship as established by God in the creation of man as just mentioned, with the spiritual significance regarding the position of Christ in relation to the Church; cp. Eph. 3:10; it is used of Christ as the foundation of the spiritual building set forth by the Temple, with its "corner stone," Matt. 21:42; symbolically also of the Imperial rulers of the Roman power, as seen in the Apocalyptic visions, Rev. 13:1, 3; 17:3, 7, 9.
NT: B.430a; CB.1255a; K.429.
OT: rō'sh: S.7218; HR.760c.5a; H.2097; BD.910c.
GEN. REF.: IS.2:639; NB.508; Z.3:52.

HEAD (to wound in the)

kephalioō or *kephalaioō* [κεφαλιόω, 2775], from *kephalion*, a diminutive of *kephalē*, usually meant to sum up, to bring under heads; in Mark 12:4 it is used for wounding on the head, the only place where it has this meaning. ¶
NT: B.430c; CB.—; K.—.
OT: —.
GEN. REF.: IS.2:639; NB.—; Z.—.

HEADLONG (to cast, to fall)

1. *katakrēmnizō* [κατακρημνίζω, 2630], signifies to throw over a precipice (*kata*, down, *krēmnos*, a steep bank, etc.), said of the purpose of the people of Nazareth to destroy Christ, Luke 4:29. ¶
NT: B.412a; CB.—; K.—.
OT: shālak: S.7993; HR.734c.1; H.2398; BD.1020d.
GEN. REF.: —.

2. *prēnēs* [πρηνής, 4248], an adjective denoting headlong, prone, is used with the verb *ginomai*, to become, in Acts 1:18, of the death of Judas, "falling headlong"; various suggestions have been made as to the actual details; some ascribe to the word the meaning "swelling up." ¶
NT: B.700d; CB.1266b; K.—.
OT: —.
GEN. REF.: —.

HEADSTRONG (R.V.), HEADY (A.V.)

propetēs [προπετής, 4312], lit. means falling forwards (from *pro*, forwards, and *piptō*, to fall); it is used metaphorically to signify precipitate, rash, reckless, and is said (*a*) of persons, 2 Tim. 3:4; "headstrong" is the appropriate rendering; (*b*) of things, Acts 19:36, R.V., "(nothing) rash" (A.V., "rashly"). ¶
NT: B.709c; CB.—; K.—.
OT: 'ewîl: S.191; HR.1208b.1; H.44a; BD.17b.
GEN. REF.: —.

HEAL, HEALING

A. Verbs.

1. *therapeuō* [θεραπεύω, 2323], primarily signifies to serve as a *therapōn*, an attendant; then, to care for the sick, to treat, cure, heal (Eng., therapeutics). It is chiefly used in Matthew and Luke, once in John (5:10), and, after the Acts, only Rev. 13:3 and 12. See CURE.
NT: B.359a; CB.1272b; K.331.
OT: —.
GEN. REF.: IS.2:640; NB.—; Z.3:54.

2. *iaomai* [ἰάομαι, 2390], to heal, is used (*a*) of physical treatment 22 times; in Matt. 15:28, A.V., "made whole," R.V., "healed"; so in Acts 9:34; (*b*) figuratively, of spiritual healing, Matt. 13:15; John 12:40; Acts 28:27; Heb. 12:13; 1 Pet. 2:24; possibly, Jas. 5:16 includes both (*a*) and (*b*); some mss. have the word, with sense

(*b*), in Luke 4:18. Apart from this last, Luke, the physician, uses the word fifteen times. See WHOLE.

NT: B.368b; CB.1252c; K.344.
OT: rāphā': S.7495; HR.668a.3a-c; H.2196; BD.950c.
GEN. REF.: IS.2:640; NB.509; Z.3:54.

3. *sōzō* [σώζω, 4982], to save, is translated by the verb to heal in the A.V. of Mark 5:23 and Luke 8:36 (R.V., to make whole; so A.V. frequently); the idea is that of saving from disease and its effects. See SAVE.

NT: B.798a; CB.1269c; K.1132.
OT: yāsha': S.3467; HR.1328b.5b; H.929; BD.446a.
mālaṭ: S.4422; HR.1328b.6b; H.1198; BD.572b.
nāṣal: S.5337; HR.1328b.7a; H.1404; BD.664c.
GEN. REF.: IS.2:640; NB.—; Z.—.

4. *diasōzō* [διασώζω, 1295], to save thoroughly (*dia*, through, and No. 3), is translated "heal" in Luke 7:3, A.V. (R.V., "save"). See ESCAPE.

NT: B.189a; CB.1241b; K.—.
OT: mālaṭ: S.4422; HR.312b.3a; H.1198; BD.572b.
GEN. REF.: IS.2:640; NB.—; Z.—.

B. Nouns.

1. *therapeia* [θεραπεία, 2322], akin to A, No. 1, primarily denotes care, attention, Luke 12:42 (see HOUSEHOLD); then, medical service, healing (Eng., therapy), Luke 9:11; Rev. 22:2, of the effects of the leaves of the tree of life, perhaps here with the meaning "health." ¶

NT: B.358d; CB.1272b; K.331.
OT: —.
GEN. REF.: IS.2:640; NB.—; Z.3:54.

2. *iama* [ἴαμα, 2386], akin to A, No. 2, formerly signified a means of healing; in the N.T., a healing (the result of the act), used in the plural, in 1 Cor. 12:9, 28, 30, R.V., "healings"; of Divinely imparted gifts in the churches in Apostolic times. ¶

NT: B.368a; CB.1252c; K.344.
OT: marpē': S.4832; HR.668a.3a; H.2196c; BD.951b.
GEN. REF.: IS.2:640; NB.—; Z.3:54.

3. *iasis* [ἴασις, 2392], akin to A, No. 2, stresses the process as reaching completion, Luke 13:32, "cures," of the acts of Christ in the days of His flesh; Acts 4:22, 30, "to heal," lit. 'unto healing.' ¶

NT: B.368c; CB.1252c; K.344.
OT: marpē': S.4832; HR.668c.4a; H.2196c; BD.951b.
GEN. REF.: IS.2:640; NB.—; Z.3:54.

HEALTH (to be in)

hugiainō [ὑγιαίνω, 5198], denotes to be healthy, sound, in good health (Eng., hygiene), rendered "mayest be in health," in 3 John 2; rendered "safe and sound" in Luke 15:27. See SAFE, D, No. 2, SOUND, WHOLE, B, No. 1.

NT: B.832b; CB.1251c; K.1202.
OT: shālôm: S.7965; HR.1380b.1b; H.2401a; BD.1022c.
GEN. REF.: IS.—; NB.509; Z.—.

Note: In Acts 27:34, *sōtēria*, salvation, safety, is translated "health" in the A.V.; the R.V., gives the right meaning, "safety."

HEAP (to)

1. *sōreuō* [σωρεύω, 4987], to heap one thing on another, is said of heaping coals of fire on the head, Rom. 12:20 (for the meaning see COALS); in 2 Tim. 3:6 it is used metaphorically of women "laden" (or overwhelmed) with sins. See LADEN. ¶ In the Sept., Prov. 25:22. ¶

NT: B.800c; CB.—; K.1150.
OT: ḥātāh: S.2846; HR.1331a.1; H.777; BD.367a.
GEN. REF.: IS.2:648; NB.—; Z.—.

2. *episōreuō* [ἐπισωρεύω, 2002], to heap upon or together (*epi*, upon, and No. 1), is used metaphorically in 2 Tim. 4:3 of appropriating a number of teachers to suit the liking of those who do so. The reference may be to those who, like the Athenians, run about to hear and follow those who proclaim new ideas of their own invention. ¶

NT: B.302a; CB.—; K.1150.
OT: —.
GEN. REF.: —.

HEAR, HEARING

A. Verbs.

1. *akouō* [ἀκούω, 191], the usual word denoting to hear, is used (*a*) intransitively, e.g., Matt. 11:15; Mark 4:23; (*b*) transitively when the object is expressed, sometimes in the accusative case, sometimes in the genitive. Thus in Acts 9:7, "hearing the voice," the noun "voice" is in the partitive genitive case [i.e., hearing (something) of], whereas in 22:9, "they heard not the voice," the construction is with the accusative. This removes the idea of any contradiction. The former indicates a hearing of the sound, the latter indicates the meaning or message of the voice (this they did not hear). "The former denotes the sensational perception, the latter (the accusative case) the thing perceived" (Cremer). In John 5:25, 28, the genitive case is used, indicating a "sensational perception" that the Lord's voice is sounding; in 3:8, of hearing the wind, the accusative is used, stressing "the thing perceived."

That God hears prayer signifies that He answers prayer, e.g., John 9:31; 1 John 5:14, 15. Sometimes the verb is used with *para* (from beside), e.g., John 1:40, "one of the two which heard John speak," lit., 'heard from beside John,' suggesting that he stood beside him; in John 8:26, 40, indicating the intimate fellowship of the Son with the Father; the same construction is used in Acts 10:22 and 2 Tim. 2:2, in the latter case, of the intimacy between Paul and Timothy. See HEARKEN.

NT: B.31d; CB.1234b; K.34.
OT: shāma': S.8085; HR.45a.8a; H.2412; BD.1033b.
GEN. REF.: IS.2:649; NB.—; Z.—.

2. *eisakouō* [εἰσακούω, 1522], to listen to (*eis*, to, and No. 1), has two meanings, (*a*) to hear and to obey, 1 Cor. 14:21, "they will not hear"; (*b*) to hear so as to answer, of God's answer to prayer, Matt. 6:7; Luke 1:13; Acts 10:31; Heb. 5:7. ¶
NT: B.232b; CB.1243b; K.34.
OT: shāma': S.8085; HR.408b.10a; H.2412; BD.1033b.
'ānāh: S.6030; HR.408b.6a; H.1650,1653; BD.772c.
GEN. REF.: IS.2:649; NB.–; Z.–.

3. *diakouō* [διακούω, 1251], to hear through, hear fully (*dia*, through, and No. 1), is used technically, of hearing judicially, in Acts 23:35, of Felix in regard to the charges against Paul. ¶ In the Sept., Deut. 1:16; Job 9:33. ¶
NT: B.185a; CB.–; K.–.
OT: shāma': S.8085; HR.304a.2; H.2412; BD.1033b.
GEN. REF.: IS.2:649; NB.–; Z.–.

4. *epakouō* [ἐπακούω, 1873], to listen to, hear with favour, at or upon an occasion (*epi*, upon, and No. 1), is used in 2 Cor. 6:2 (R.V., "hearken"). ¶
NT: B.282c; CB.1245b; K.34.
OT: shama': S.8085; HR.505c.9a; H.2412; BD.1033b.
'anah: S.6030; HR.505c.4a; H.1650,1653; BD.772c.
GEN. REF.: IS.2:649; NB.–; Z.–.

5. *epakroaomai* [ἐπακροάομαι, 1874], to listen attentively to (*epi*, used intensively, and a verb akin to No. 1), is used in Acts 16:25, "(the prisoners) were listening to (them)," R.V., expressive of rapt attention. ¶
NT: B.282c; CB.1245b; K.–.
OT: –.
GEN. REF.: –.

6. *proakouō* [προακούω, 4257], signifies to hear before (*pro*), Col. 1:5, where Lightfoot suggests that the preposition contrasts what they heard before, the true Gospel, with the false gospel of their recent teachers. ¶
NT: B.702c; CB.–; K.–.
OT: –.
GEN. REF.: –.

7. *parakouō* [παρακούω, 3878], primarily signifies to overhear, hear amiss or imperfectly (*para*, beside, amiss, and No. 1); then (in the N.T.) to hear without taking heed, to neglect to hear, Matt. 18:17 (twice); in Mark 5:36 the best mss. have this verb, which the R.V. renders "not heeding" (marg., "overhearing"); some mss. have No. 1, A.V., "hearing." It seems obvious that the Lord paid no attention to those from the ruler's house and their message that his daughter was dead. ¶ Cp. the noun *parakoē*, disobedience.
NT: B.619a; CB.1262a; K.34.
OT: ḥārash: S.2790; HR.1061b.1; H.760; BD.361a.
GEN. REF.: –.

B. Nouns.

1. *akoē* [ἀκοή, 189], akin to A, No. 1, denotes (*a*) the sense of hearing, 1 Cor. 12:17; 2 Pet. 2:8; a combination of verb and noun is used in phrases which have been termed Hebraic as they express somewhat literally an O.T. phraseology, e.g., "By hearing ye shall hear," Matt. 13:14; Acts 28:26, R.V., a mode of expression conveying emphasis; (*b*) the organ of hearing, Mark 7:35, "ears"; Luke 7:1, R.V., "ears," for A.V., "audience"; Acts 17:20; 2 Tim. 4:3, 4; Heb. 5:11, "dull of hearing," lit., 'dull as to ears'; (*c*) a thing heard, a message or teaching, John 12:38, "report"; Rom. 10:16; 1 Thess. 2:13, "the word of the message," lit., 'the word of hearing' (A.V., "which ye heard"); Heb. 4:2, "the word of hearing," R.V., for A.V., "the word preached"; in a somewhat similar sense, a rumour, report, Matt. 4:24; 14:1; Mark 1:28, A.V., "fame," R.V., "report"; Matt. 24:6; Mark 13:7, "rumours (of wars)"; (*d*) the receiving of a message, Rom. 10:17, something more than the mere sense of hearing [see (*a*)]; so with the phrase "the hearing of faith," Gal. 3:2, 5, which it seems better to understand so than under (*c*). See EAR, FAME, PREACH, REPORT, RUMOUR. ¶
NT: B.30d; CB.1234b; K.34.
OT: shāma': S.8085; HR.44b.1a; H.2412; BD.1033b.
sh'mû'āh: S.8052; HR.44b.1d; H.2412d; BD.1035b.
shēma': S.8088; HR.44b.1f; H.2412b; BD.1034d.
GEN. REF.: IS.2:649; NB.–; Z.–.

Notes: (1) For *diagnōsis* (investigation, followed by decision), rendered "hearing" in Acts 25:21, A.V., see DECISION.

(2) For the phrase to be dull of hearing, lit., 'to hear heavily,' Matt. 13:15; Acts 28:27, see DULL.

(3) For *akroatērion*, a place of hearing, Acts 25:23, see PLACE. ¶

HEARER

akroatēs [ἀκροατής, 202], from *akroaomai*, to listen, is used in Rom. 2:13, "of a law"; Jas. 1:22, 23, "of the word"; ver. 25, "a (forgetful) hearer." ¶
NT: B.33c; CB.1234b; K.–.
OT: –.
GEN. REF.: –.

Note: In Eph. 4:29 and 2 Tim. 2:14, the verb *akouō*, to hear, is rendered "hearers" in the A.V. (R.V., "them that hear").

HEARKEN

1. *akouō* [ἀκούω, 191], to hear, is rendered "hearken" in the A.V. and R.V., in Mark 4:3; Acts 4:19; 7:2; 15:13; Jas. 2:5; in the R.V. only, in Acts 3:22, 23; 13:16 (A.V., "give audience");

15:12, "hearkened" (A.V. "gave audience"). See HEAR, No. 1.

NT: B.31d; CB.1234b; K.34.
OT: shāma‘: S.8085; HR.45a.8a; H.2412; BD.1033b.
GEN. REF.: IS.2:649; NB.–; Z.–.

Note: In Acts 12:13, *hupakouō*, lit., to hearken, with the idea of stillness, or attention (*hupo*, under, *akouō*, to hear), signifies to answer a knock at a door, R.V., "to answer" (A.V., "to hearken"). See OBEY.

2. *epakouō* [ἐπακούω, 1873], denotes to hearken to, 2 Cor. 6:2, R.V. (see HEAR, A, No. 4). ¶

NT: B.282c; CB.1245b; K.34.
OT: shāma‘: S.8085; HR.505c.9a; H.2412; BD.1033b.
‘ānāh: S.6030; HR.505c.4a; H.1650,1653; BD.772c.
GEN. REF.: IS.2:649; NB.–; Z.–.

3. *enōtizomai* [ἐνωτίζομαι, 1801], to give ear to, to hearken (from *en*, in, and *ous*, an ear), is used in Acts 2:14, in Peter's address to the men of Israel. ¶

NT: B.271a; CB.1245b; K.744.
OT: 'āzan: S.238; HR.482b.1; H.57; BD.24b.
GEN. REF.: –.

4. *peitharcheō* [πειθαρχέω, 3980], to obey one in authority, be obedient (*peithomai*, to be persuaded, *archē*, rule), is translated to hearken unto in Acts 27:21, in Paul's reminder to the shipwrecked mariners that they should have given heed to his counsel. See OBEY.

NT: B.638d; CB.1263a; K.818.
OT: sh^{e}ma‘ (Aramaic): S.8086; HR.1114b.1; H.3040; BD.1116b.
GEN. REF.: –.

HEART, HEARTILY

kardia [καρδία, 2588], the heart (Eng., cardiac, etc.), the chief organ of physical life ("for the life of the flesh is in the blood," Lev. 17:11), occupies the most important place in the human system. By an easy transition the word came to stand for man's entire mental and moral activity, both the rational and the emotional elements. In other words, the heart is used figuratively for the hidden springs of the personal life. "The Bible describes human depravity as in the 'heart,' because sin is a principle which has its seat in the centre of man's inward life, and then 'defiles' the whole circuit of his action, Matt. 15:19, 20. On the other hand, Scripture regards the heart as the sphere of Divine influence, Rom. 2:15; Acts 15:9. . . . The heart, as lying deep within, contains 'the hidden man,' 1 Pet. 3:4, the real man. It represents the true character but conceals it" (J. Laidlaw, in Hastings; Bible Dic.).

As to its usage in the N.T. it denotes (*a*) the seat of physical life, Acts 14:17; Jas. 5:5; (*b*) the seat of moral nature and spiritual life, the seat of grief, John 14:1; Rom. 9:2; 2 Cor. 2:4; joy, John 16:22; Eph. 5:19; the desires, Matt. 5:28; 2 Pet. 2:14; the affections, Luke 24:32; Acts 21:13; the perceptions, John 12:40; Eph. 4:18; the thoughts, Matt. 9:4; Heb. 4:12; the understanding, Matt. 13:15; Rom. 1:21; the reasoning powers, Mark 2:6; Luke 24:38; the imagination, Luke 1:51; conscience, Acts 2:37; 1 John 3:20; the intentions, Heb. 4:12, cp. 1 Pet. 4:1; purpose, Acts 11:23; 2 Cor. 9:7; the will, Rom. 6:17; Col. 3:15; faith, Mark 11:23; Rom. 10:10; Heb. 3:12.

The heart, in its moral significance in the O.T., includes the emotions, the reason and the will.

NT: B.403b; CB.1253b; K.415.
OT: lēb: S.3820; HR.719a.4a; H.1071a; BD.524b.
lēbāb: S.3824; HR.719a.4b; H.1071a; BD.523a.
GEN. REF.: IS.2:650; NB.509; Z.3:58.

2. *psuchē* [ψυχή, 5590], the soul, or life, is rendered "heart" in Eph. 6:6 (marg., "soul"), "doing the will of God from the heart." In Col. 3:23, a form of the word *psuchē* preceded by *ek*, from, lit., 'from (the) soul,' is rendered "heartily."

NT: B.893b; CB.1267c; K.1342.
OT: nephesh: S.5315; HR.1486a.4; H.1395a; BD.659b.
GEN. REF.: IS.2:650; NB.509; Z.3:58.

Notes: (1) The R.V., "heart" is substituted for A.V., "bowels," in Col. 3:12; Philm. 7, 12, 20.

(2) In 2 Cor. 3:3, the R.V. has "tables that are hearts of flesh," for A.V., "fleshy tables of the heart."

(3) In Eph. 1:18, the best mss. have *kardia*, "(the eyes of your) heart"; some have *dianoia*, "understanding" (A.V.).

(4) In Heb. 8:10 and 10:16, the A.V. has "in their hearts" and "into their hearts"; R.V., "on their heart."

(5) In Luke 21:26, where there is no word for "hearts" in the original, the R.V. has "men fainting (for fear)."

(6) In 2 Cor. 7:2, the verb *chōreō*, to make room for, "receive" (A.V.), is translated, or rather, interpreted, "open your hearts," R.V., marg., "make room for (us)."

HEART (hardness of)

sklērokardia [σκληροκαρδία, 4641], hardness of heart (*sklēros*, hard, and *kardia*), is used in Matt. 19:8; Mark 10:5; 16:14. ¶ In the Sept., Deut. 10:16; Jer. 4:4. ¶

NT: B.756a; CB.1269a; K.415.
OT: ‘ar^{e}lāh: S.6190; HR.1274b.1; H.1695a; BD.790b.
GEN. REF.: –.

HEART (knowing the)

kardiognōstēs [καρδιογνώστης, 2589], a knower of hearts (*kardia* and *ginōskō*, to know), is used in Acts 1:24; 15:8. ¶
NT: B.404c; CB.1253b; K.415.
OT: –.
GEN. REF.: –.

HEAT

A. Nouns.

1. *kausōn* [καύσων, 2742], denotes a burning heat (from *kaiō*, to burn; cp. Eng., caustic, cauterize), Matt. 20:12; Luke 12:55 (A.V., "heat"), R.V., in each place, "scorching heat" (marg., "hot wind"); in Jas. 1:11, "a burning heat," A.V., R.V., "the scorching wind," like the Sirocco. Cp. Amos 4:9, where the Sept. has *purōsis*, burning (*pur*, fire). See BURNING.
NT: B.425c; CB.–; K.423.
OT: qādîm: S.6921; HR.757b.2; H.1988d; BD.870b.
ḥōreb: S.2721; HR.757b.1; H.731b; BD.351b.
GEN. REF.: IS.2:653; NB.–; Z.–.

2. *kauma* [καῦμα, 2738], heat (akin to No. 1), signifies the result of burning, or the heat produced, Rev. 7:16; 16:9; ¶ cp. *kaumatizō*, to scorch, *kausis*, burning, *kautēriazomai*, to brand, sear.
NT: B.425b; CB.1254c; K.423.
OT: ḥōm: S.2527; HR.757a.1; H.677a; BD.328d.
ḥōreb: S.2721; HR.757a.2; H.731b; BD.351b.
GEN. REF.: IS.2:653; NB.–; Z.–.

3. *thermē* [θέρμη, 2329], denotes warmth, heat, Acts 28:3 (Eng., thermal, etc.). ¶
NT: B.359c; CB.1272b; K.–.
OT: –.
GEN. REF.: IS.2:653; NB.–; Z.–.

B. Verb.

kausoō [καυσόω, 2741], was used as a medical term, of a fever; in the N.T., to burn with great heat (akin to A, No. 1), said of the future destruction of the natural elements, 2 Pet. 3:10, 12, "with fervent heat," Passive Voice, lit., 'being burned.' ¶
NT: B.425b; CB.–; K.423.
OT: –.
GEN. REF.: IS.2:653; NB.–; Z.–.

For **HEATHEN** see **GENTILES**

HEAVEN, HEAVENLY (-IES)

A. Nouns.

1. *ouranos* [οὐρανός, 3772], probably akin to *ornumi*, to lift, to heave, is used in the N.T. (*a*) of the aërial heavens, e.g., Matt. 6:26; 8:20; Acts 10:12; 11:6 (R.V., "heaven," in each place, A.V., "air"); Jas. 5:18; (*b*) the sidereal, e.g., Matt. 24:29, 35; Mark 13:25, 31; Heb. 11:12, R.V., "heaven," A.V., "sky"; Rev. 6:14; 20:11; they, (*a*) and (*b*), were created by the Son of God, Heb. 1:10, as also by God the Father, Rev. 10:6; (*c*) the eternal dwelling place of God, Matt. 5:16; 12:50; Rev. 3:12; 11:13; 16:11; 20:9. From thence the Son of God descended to become Incarnate, John 3:13, 31; 6:38, 42. In His ascension Christ "passed through the heavens," Heb. 4:14, R.V., He "ascended far above all the heavens," Eph. 4:10, and was "made higher than the heavens," Heb. 7:26; He "sat down on the right hand of the throne of the Majesty in the heavens," Heb. 8:1; He is "on the right hand of God," having gone into Heaven, 1 Pet. 3:22. Since His Ascension it is the scene of His present life and activity, e.g., Rom. 8:34; Heb. 9:24. From thence the Holy Spirit descended at Pentecost, 1 Pet. 1:12. It is the abode of the angels, e.g., Matt. 18:10; 22:30; cp. Rev. 3:5. Thither Paul was "caught up," whether in the body or out of the body, he knew not, 2 Cor. 12:2. It is to be the eternal dwelling place of the saints in resurrection glory, 2 Cor. 5:1. From thence Christ will descend to the air to receive His saints at the Rapture, 1 Thess. 4:16; Phil. 3:20, 21, and will subsequently come with His saints and with His holy angels at His Second Advent, Matt. 24:30; 2 Thess. 1:7. In the present life heaven is the region of the spiritual citizenship of believers, Phil. 3:20. The present heavens, with the earth, are to pass away, 2 Pet. 3:10, "being on fire," ver. 12 (see ver. 7); Rev. 20:11, and new heavens and earth are to be created, 2 Pet. 3:13; Rev. 21:1, with Is. 65:17, e.g.

In Luke 15:18, 21, heaven is used, by metonymy, for God. See AIR.
NT: B.593d; CB.1261b; K.736.
OT: shāmayim: S.8064; HR.1031b.4a; H.2407a; BD.1029c.
GEN. REF.: IS.2:654; NB.510; Z.3:60.

Notes: (1) For the phrase in Luke 11:13, see *Note* on B, No. 2.

(2) In Luke 11:2, the A.V., "as in heaven," translates a phrase found in some mss.

2. *mesouranēma* [μεσουράνημα, 3321], denotes mid-heaven, or the midst of the heavens (*mesos*, middle, and No. 1), Rev. 8:13; 14:6; 19:17. ¶
NT: B.508a; CB.–; K.–.
OT: –.
GEN. REF.: –.

B. Adjectives.

1. *ouranios* [οὐράνιος, 3770], signifying of heaven, heavenly, corresponding to A, No. 1, is used (*a*) as an appellation of God the Father, Matt. 6:14, 26, 32, "your heavenly Father"; 15:13, "My heavenly Father"; (*b*) as descriptive

of the holy angels, Luke 2:13; (*c*) of the vision seen by Paul, Acts 26:19. ¶
NT: B.593c; CB.1261b; K.736.
OT: shāmayim: S.8064; HR.1031b.1a; H.2407a; BD.1029c.
GEN. REF.: IS.2:655; NB.510; Z.3:60.

2. *epouranios* [ἐπουράνιος, 2032], heavenly, what pertains to, or is in, heaven (*epi*, in the sense of 'pertaining to,' not here, 'above'), has meanings corresponding to some of the meanings of *ouranos*, A, No. 1. It is used (*a*) of God the Father, Matt. 18:35; (*b*) of the place where Christ "sitteth at the right hand of God" (i.e., in a position of Divine authority), Eph. 1:20, and of the present position of believers in relationship to Christ, 2:6; where they possess 'every spiritual blessing,' 1:3; (*c*) of Christ as "the Second Man," and all those who are related to Him spiritually, 1 Cor. 15:48; (*d*) of those whose sphere of activity or existence is above, or in contrast to that of earth, of "principalities and powers," Eph. 3:10; of "spiritual hosts of wickedness," 6:12, R.V., "in heavenly places," for A.V., "in high places"; (*e*) of the Holy Spirit, Heb. 6:4; (*f*) of "heavenly things," as the subjects of the teaching of Christ, John 3:12, and as consisting of the spiritual and heavenly Sanctuary and "true tabernacle" and all that appertains thereto in relation to Christ and His sacrifice as antitypical of the earthly tabernacle and sacrifices under the Law, Heb. 8:5; 9:23; (*g*) of the "calling" of believers, Heb. 3:1; (*h*) of Heaven as the abode of the saints, "a better country" than that of earth, Heb. 11:16, and of the spiritual Jerusalem, 12:22; (*i*) of the Kingdom of Christ in its future manifestation, 2 Tim. 4:18; (*j*) of all beings and things, animate and inanimate, that are "above the earth," Phil. 2:10; (*k*) of the resurrection and glorified bodies of believers, 1 Cor. 15:49; (*l*) of the heavenly orbs, 1 Cor. 15:40 ("celestial," twice, and so rendered here only). ¶
NT: B.305d; CB.1246b; K.736.
OT: shadday: S.7706; HR.539b.1; H.2333; BD.994d.
shᵉmayim: S.8065; HR.539b.2; H.3038; BD.1116a.
GEN. REF.: IS.2:655; NB.510; Z.3:60.

Note: In connection with (*a*), the word "heavenly," used of God the Father in Luke 11:13, represents the phrase *ex ouranou*, 'from heaven.'

C. Adverb.

ouranothen [οὐρανόθεν, 3771], formed from A, No. 1, and denoting 'from heaven,' is used of (*a*) the aërial heaven, Acts 14:17; (*b*) heaven, as the uncreated sphere of God's abode, 26:13. ¶
NT: B.593d; CB.1261b; K.736.
OT: –.
GEN. REF.: –.

HEAVY, HEAVINESS

A. Nouns.

1. *lupē* [λύπη, 3077], grief, sorrow, is rendered "heaviness" in the A.V. of Rom. 9:2; 2 Cor. 2:1 (R.V., "sorrow," in both places). See GRIEF, SORROW.
NT: B.482a; CB.1257b; K.540.
OT: 'eṣeb: S.6089; HR.889c.3a; H.1666a,1667a; BD.780d.
'iṣṣabôn: S.6093; HR.889c.3b; H.1666e; BD.781a.
'aṣṣebet: S.6094; HR.889c.3c; H.1666d; BD.781a.
GEN. REF.: –.

2. *katēpheia* [κατήφεια, 2726], probably denotes a downcast look, expressive of sorrow; hence, dejection, heaviness; it is used in Jas. 4:9. ¶
NT: B.423c; CB.–; K.–.
OT: –.
GEN. REF.: –.

B. Verbs.

1. *adēmoneō* [ἀδημονέω, 85], to be troubled, much distressed, is used of the Lord's sorrow in Gethsemane, Matt. 26:37; Mark 14:33, A.V., "to be very heavy," R.V., "to be sore troubled"; of Epaphroditus, because the saints at Philippi had received news of his sickness, Phil. 2:26, A.V., "was full of heaviness," R.V., "was sore troubled." See TROUBLE, B, No. 12. ¶
NT: B.16d; CB.–; K.–.
OT: –.
GEN. REF.: –.

2. *lupeō* [λυπέω, 3076], to distress, grieve (akin to A, No. 1), is rendered "are in heaviness" in 1 Pet. 1:6, A.V. (R.V., "have been put to grief"); here, as frequently, it is in the Passive Voice. See GRIEF, SORROWFUL.
NT: B.481c; CB.1257b; K.540.
OT: rā'a: S.7489; HR.889b.12a; H.2191,2192; BD.949b.
ḥārāh: S.2734; HR.889b.5; H.736; BD.354a.
GEN. REF.: –.

3. *bareō* [βαρέω, 916], always in the Passive Voice in the N.T., is rendered "were heavy" in Matt. 26:43; Mark 14:40; Luke 9:32. See BURDEN.
NT: B.133c; CB.1238c; K.95.
OT: kābēd: S.3513; HR.190c.1; H.943; BD.457a.
GEN. REF.: –.

Note: For "heavy laden," Matt. 11:28, see LADE, No. 3.

C. Adjective.

barus [βαρύς, 926], heavy (akin to B, No. 3), is so rendered in Matt. 23:4. See GRIEVOUS.
NT: B.134b; CB.1238c; K.95.
OT: kābēd: S.3515; HR.191b.2a; H.943a; BD.458a.
GEN. REF.: –.

HEDGE

phragmos [φραγμός, 5418], denotes any sort of fence, hedge, palings or wall (akin to *phrassō*, to fence in, stop). It is used (*a*) in its literal sense, in Matt. 21:33, lit. '(he put) a hedge (around)'; Mark 12:1; Luke 14:23; (*b*) metaphorically, of the "partition" which separated Gentile from Jew, which was broken down by Christ through the efficacy of His expiatory sacrifice, Eph. 2:14. ¶

NT: B.865c; CB.1264b; K.—.
OT: gādēr: S.1447; HR.1438b.1a; H.318a; BD.154d.
pereṣ: S.6556; HR.1438b.4; H.1826a; BD.829c.
GEN. REF.: IS.2:671; NB.—; Z.3:110.

HEED (to give, to take)

1. *blepō* [βλέπω, 991], to look, see, usually implying more especially an intent, earnest contemplation, is rendered "take heed" in Matt. 24:4; Mark 4:24; 13:5, 9, 23, 33; Luke 8:18; 21:8; 1 Cor. 3:10; 8:9; 10:12; Gal. 5:15; Col. 2:8 (A.V., "beware"); 4:17; Heb. 3:12. See BEHOLD, BEWARE, LIE, LOOK, PERCEIVE, REGARD, SEE.

NT: B.143b; CB.1239a; K.706.
OT: rā'āh: S.7200; HR.221a.10a; H.2095; BD.906b.
pānāh: S.6437; HR.221a.7a; H.1782; BD.815a.
pāneh: S.6440; HR.221a.8; H.1782a; BD.815d.
GEN. REF.: IS.2:671; NB.—; Z.—.

2. *horaō* [ὁράω, 3708], to see, usually expressing the sense of vision, is rendered "take heed" in Matt. 16:6; 18:10, A.V. (R.V., "see"); Mark 8:15; Luke 12:15; Acts 22:26 (A.V. only). See BEHOLD, SEE.

NT: B.577c; CB.1251a; K.706.
OT: rā'āh: S.7200; HR.1005a.8a,b; H.2095; BD.906b.
GEN. REF.: IS.2:671; NB.—; Z.—.

3. *prosechō* [προσέχω, 4337], lit., to hold to, signifies to turn to, turn one's attention to; hence, to give heed; it is rendered "take heed" in Matt. 6:1; Luke 17:3; 21:34; Acts 5:35; 20:28; 2 Pet. 1:19; to give heed to, in Acts 8:6, 10; in ver. 11 (A.V., "had regard to"); 16:14 (A.V., "attended unto"); 1 Tim. 1:4; 4:1, 13 (A.V., "give attendance to"); Tit. 1:14; Heb. 2:1, lit., 'to give heed more earnestly.' See ATTEND, BEWARE, GIVE, REGARD.

NT: B.714b; CB.1267a; K.—.
OT: qāshab: S.7181; HR.1215b.16a; H.2084; BD.904a.
shāmar: S.8104; HR.1215b.19; H.2414; BD.1036b.
GEN. REF.: IS.2:671; NB.—; Z.—.

4. *epechō* [ἐπέχω, 1907], lit., to hold upon, then, to direct towards, to give attention to, is rendered "gave heed," in Acts 3:5; "take heed," in 1 Tim. 4:16. See HOLD (forth), MARK, STAY.

NT: B.285c; CB.—; K.—.
OT: —.
GEN. REF.: IS.2:671; NB.—; Z.—.

Notes: (1) In Luke 11:35, A.V., *skopeō*, to look, is translated "take heed (that)," R.V., "look (whether)."

(2) Nos. 2 and 3 are used together in Matt. 16:6; Nos. 2 and 1, in that order, in Mark 8:15; but in Luke 12:15 the R.V. rightly follows No. 2 by "keep yourselves from" (*phulassō*, to guard).

(3) For the R.V. of Mark 5:36, "not heeding," see under HEAR, No. 7.

(4) In Rom. 11:21 the A.V. adds "take heed," because of a variant reading which introduces the clause by a conjunctive phrase signifying "lest."

HEEL

pterna [πτέρνα, 4418], is found in John 13:18, where the Lord quotes from Ps. 41:9; the metaphor is that of tripping up an antagonist in wrestling. ¶ Cp. the verb in Gen. 27:36; Jer. 9:4; Hos. 12:3.

NT: B.727b; CB.1267c; K.—.
OT: 'āqēb: S.6119; HR.1237c.1a; H.1676a; BD.784b.
GEN. REF.: IS.2:671; NB.—; Z.3:110.

HEIFER

damalis [δάμαλις, 1151], etymologically one of fit age to be tamed to the yoke (*damaō*, to tame), occurs in Heb. 9:13, with reference to the "red heifer" of Numb. 19. ¶

NT: B.170b; CB.1240b; K.—.
OT: 'eglāh: S.5697; HR.284c.2b; H.1560b; BD.722b.
'ēgel: S.5695; HR.284c.2a; H.1560a; BD.722a.
pārāh: S.6509; HR.284c.3a; H.1809; BD.826a.
GEN. REF.: IS.2:672; NB.517; Z.1:764.

HEIGHT

1. *hupsos* [ὕψος, 5311], a summit, top, is translated "height" in Eph. 3:18, where it may refer either to "the love of Christ" or to "the fulness of God"; the two are really inseparable, for they who are filled into the fulness of God thereby enter appreciatively into the love of Christ, which 'surpasseth knowledge'; in Rev. 21:16, of the measurement of the Heavenly Jerusalem. See ESTATE, HIGH.

NT: B.850c; CB.1252b; K.1241.
OT: mārôm: S.4791; HR.1421b.6a; H.2133h; BD.928d.
rûm: S.7312; HR.1421b.6b; H.2133a; BD.927d.
qômāh: S.6967; HR.1421b.7; H.1999a; BD.879b.
GEN. REF.: IS.2:673; NB.—; Z.—.

2. *hupsōma* [ὕψωμα, 5313], more concrete than No. 1, is used (*a*) of a height, as a mountain or anything definitely termed a height, Rom. 8:39 (metaphorically); (*b*) of a high thing lifted up as a barrier or in antagonistic exaltation, 2 Cor. 10:5. See HIGH. ¶ Cp. *hupsoō*, to exalt.

NT: B.851c; CB.1252b; K.1241.
OT: —.
GEN. REF.: IS.2:673; NB.—; Z.—.

HEIR

A. Noun.

1. *klēronomos* [κληρονόμος, 2818], lit. denotes one who obtains a lot or portion (*klēros*, a lot, *nemomai*, to possess), especially of an inheritance. The N.T. usage may be analysed as under: "(*a*) the person to whom property is to pass on the death of the owner, Matt. 21:38; Mark 12:7; Luke 20:14; Gal. 4:1; (*b*) one to

whom something has been assigned by God, on possession of which, however, he has not yet entered, as Abraham, Rom. 4:13, 14; Heb. 6:17; Christ, Heb. 1:2; the poor saints, Jas. 2:5; (*c*) believers, inasmuch as they share in the new order of things to be ushered in at the return of Christ, Rom. 8:17; Gal. 3:29; 4:7; Tit. 3:7; (*d*) one who receives something other than by merit, as Noah, Heb. 11:7."* ¶

In the Sept., Judg. 18:7; 2 Sam. 14:7; Jer. 8:10; Mic. 1:15. ¶

NT: B.435b; CB.1255b; K.442.
OT: yārash: S.3423; HR.770a.1; H.920; BD.439a.
GEN. REF.: IS.2:673; NB.562; Z.3:111.

2. *sunklēronomos* [συγκληρονόμος, 4789], a joint-heir, co-inheritor (*sun*, with, and No. 1), "is used of Isaac and Jacob as participants with Abraham in the promises of God, Heb. 11:9; of husband and wife who are also united in Christ, 1 Pet. 3:7; of Gentiles who believe, as participants in the gospel with Jews who believe, Eph. 3:6; and of all believers as prospective participants with Christ in His glory, as recompense for their participation in His sufferings, Rom. 8:17."† ¶

NT: B.774a; CB.1270c; K.442,1102.
OT: –.
GEN. REF.: IS.2:673; NB.562; Z.3:111.

B. Verb.

klēronomeō [κληρονομέω, 2816], to be an heir to, to inherit (see A, No. 1), is rendered "shall (not) inherit with" in Gal. 4:30, R.V., A.V., "shall (not) be heir with"; in Heb. 1:14, R.V., "shall inherit," A.V., "shall be heirs of." See INHERIT. Cp. *klēroomai*, to be taken as an inheritance, *klēronomia*, an inheritance, *klēros*, a lot, an inheritance.

NT: B.434d; CB.1255b; K.442.
OT: yārash: S.3423; HR.768a.5a; H.920; BD.439a.
nāhal: S.5157; HR.768a.7a; H.1342; BD.635c.
GEN. REF.: IS.2:673; NB.562; Z.3:111.

HELL

1. *geenna* [γεέννα, 1067], represents the Hebrew Gê-Hinnom (the valley of Tophet) and a corresponding Aramaic word; it is found twelve times in the N.T., eleven of which are in the Synoptists, in every instance as uttered by the Lord Himself. He who says to his brother, Thou fool (see under FOOL), will be in danger of "the hell of fire," Matt. 5:22; it is better to pluck out (a metaphorical description of irrevocable law) an eye that causes its possessor to stumble, than that his "whole body be cast into hell," ver. 29; similarly with the hand, ver. 30; in Matt. 18:8, 9, the admonitions are repeated, with an additional mention of the foot; here, too, the warning concerns the person himself (for which obviously the "body" stands in chapt. 5); in ver. 8, "the eternal fire" is mentioned as the doom, the character of the region standing for the region itself, the two being combined in the phrase "the hell of fire," ver. 9. To the passage in Matt. 18, that in Mark 9:43-47, is parallel; here to the word "hell" are applied the extended descriptions "the unquenchable fire" and "where their worm dieth not and the fire is not quenched."

That God, "after He hath killed, hath power to cast into hell," is assigned as a reason why He should be feared with the fear that keeps from evil doing, Luke 12:5; the parallel passage to this in Matt. 10:28 declares, not the casting in, but the doom which follows, namely, the destruction (not the loss of being, but of well-being) of "both soul and body."

In Matt. 23 the Lord denounces the Scribes and Pharisees, who in proselytizing a person "make him two-fold more a son of hell" than themselves (ver. 15), the phrase here being expressive of moral characteristics, and declares the impossibility of their escaping "the judgment of hell," ver. 33. In Jas. 3:6 hell is described as the source of the evil done by misuse of the tongue; here the word stands for the powers of darkness, whose characteristics and destiny are those of hell. ¶

For terms descriptive of hell, see e.g., Matt. 13:42; 25:46; Phil. 3:19; 2 Thess. 1:9; Heb. 10:39; 2 Pet. 2:17; Jude 13; Rev. 2:11; 19:20; 20:6, 10, 14; 21:8.

NT: B.153b; CB.1248a; K.113.
OT: hinnōm: S.2011; HR.–; H.–; BD.244d.
GEN. REF.: IS.2:677; NB.518; Z.3:114.

Notes: (1) For the rendering "hell" as a translation of Hades, corresponding to Sheol, wrongly rendered "the grave" and "hell," see HADES.

(2) The verb *tartaroō*, translated "cast down to hell" in 2 Pet. 2:4, signifies to consign to Tartarus, which is neither Sheol nor Hades nor Hell, but the place where those angels whose special sin is referred to in that passage are confined "to be reserved unto judgment"; the region is described as "pits of darkness," R.V. ¶

For HELM (Jas. 3:4) see RUDDER

* From Notes on Galatians, by Hogg and Vine, pp. 177, 178.

† ditto, p. 178.

HELMET

perikephalaia [περικεφαλαία, 4030], from *peri*, around, and *kephalē*, a head, is used figuratively in Eph. 6:17, with reference to salvation, and 1 Thess. 5:8, where it is described as "the hope of salvation." The head is not to be regarded here as standing for the seat of the intellect; the word is not so used elsewhere in Scripture. In Eph. 6:17 salvation is a present experience of the Lord's deliverance of believers as those who are engaged in spiritual conflict; in 1 Thess. 5:8, the hope is that of the Lord's Return, which encourages the believer to resist the spirit of the age in which he lives. ¶

NT: B.648a; CB.1263b; K.702.
OT: kôba': S.3553; HR.1124a.1; H.960; BD.464d.
qôba': S.6959; HR.1124a.2; H.1993; BD.875c.
GEN. REF.: IS.4:1041; NB.83; Z.3:118.

HELP

A. Nouns.

1. *antilēpsis* or *antilēmpsis* [ἀντίληψις, 484], properly signifies a laying hold of, an exchange (*anti*, in exchange, or, in its local sense, in front, and *lambanō*, to take, lay hold of, so as to support); then, a help (akin to B, No. 1); it is mentioned in 1 Cor. 12:28, as one of the ministrations in the local church, by way of rendering assistance, perhaps especially of help ministered to the weak and needy. So Theophylact defines the injunction in 1 Thess. 5:14, "support the weak"; cp. Acts 20:35; not official functionaries are in view in the term "helps," but rather the functioning of those who, like the household of Stephanas, devote themselves to minister to the saints. Hort defines the ministration as "anything that would be done for poor or weak or outcast brethren." ¶

NT: B.75a; CB.—; K.62.
OT: —.
GEN. REF.: IS.2:682; NB.—; Z.3:119.

2. *boētheia* [βοήθεια, 996], from *boē*, a shout, and *theō*, to run, denotes help, succour, Heb. 4:16, lit., '(grace) unto (timely) help'; in Acts 27:17, where the plural is used, the term is nautical, 'frapping.' ¶

NT: B.144c; CB.—; K.108.
OT: 'ēzer: S.5828; HR.222c.6c; H.1598a; BD.740c.
'ezrāh: S.5833; HR.222c.6d; H.1598b; BD.740d.
GEN. REF.: IS.2:682; NB.—; Z.—.

3. *epikouria* [ἐπικουρία, 1947], strictly denotes such aid as is rendered by an *epikouros*, an ally, an auxiliary; Paul uses it in his testimony to Agrippa, "having therefore obtained the help that is from God," Acts 26:22, R.V. ¶

NT: B.294d; CB.—; K.—.
OT: —.
GEN. REF.: —.

B. Verbs.

1. *antilambanō* [ἀντιλαμβάνω, 482], lit., to take instead of, or in turn (akin to A, No. 1), is used in the Middle Voice, and rendered "He hath holpen" in Luke 1:54; "to help," R.V., "to support," A.V., in Acts 20:35; its other meaning, to partake of, is used of partaking of things, 1 Tim. 6:2, "that partake of," for A.V., "partakers of." See PARTAKE, SUPPORT. ¶

NT: B.74c; CB.—; K.62.
OT: ḥāzaq: S.2388; HR.110c.2b; H.636; BD.304a.
'āzar: S.5826; HR.110c.9; H.1598; BD.740b.
GEN. REF.: IS.2:682; NB.—; Z.3:119.

2. *sullambanō* [συλλαμβάνω, 4815], to assist, take part with (*sun*, with, and *lambanō*), is used, in the Middle Voice, of rendering help in what others are doing, Luke 5:7, of bringing in a catch of fish; in Phil. 4:3, in an appeal to Synzygus ("yokefellow") to help Euōdia and Syntychē (ver. 2). See CATCH, CONCEIVE.

NT: B.776d; CB.1270b; K.1101.
OT: —.
GEN. REF.: IS.2:682; NB.—; Z.—.

3. *sunantilambanō* [συναντιλαμβάνω, 4878], signifies to take hold with at the side for assistance (*sun*, with, and No. 1); hence, to take a share in, help in bearing, to help in general. It is used, in the Middle Voice, in Martha's request to the Lord to bid her sister help her, Luke 10:40; and of the ministry of the Holy Spirit in helping our infirmities, Rom. 8:26. ¶ In the Sept., Ex. 18:22; Num. 11:17; Ps. 89:21.

NT: B.784c; CB.—; K.62.
OT: nāsā': S.5375; HR.1312a.2; H.1421; BD.669d.
kûn: S.3559; HR.1312a.1; H.964; BD.465c.
GEN. REF.: IS.2:682; NB.—; Z.—.

4. *boētheō* [βοηθέω, 997], to come to the aid of anyone, to succour (akin to A, No. 2), is used in Matt. 15:25; Mark 9:22, 24; Acts 16:9; 21:28; 2 Cor. 6:2, "did I succour"; Heb. 2:18, "to succour"; Rev. 12:16. ¶

NT: B.144c; CB.—; K.108.
OT: 'āzar: S.5826; HR.223b.6; H.1598; BD.740b.
yāsha': S.3467; HR.223b.3; H.929; BD.446a.
GEN. REF.: IS.2:682; NB.—; Z.—.

5. *sumballō* [συμβάλλω, 4820], lit., to throw together (*sun*, with, *ballō*, to throw), is used in the Middle Voice in Acts 18:27, of helping or benefiting believers by discussion or ministry of the Word of God. See CONFER, ENCOUNTER, MAKE (war), MEET, PONDER.

NT: B.777b; CB.—; K.—.
OT: —.
GEN. REF.: IS.2:682; NB.—; Z.—.

6. *sunupourgeō* [συνυπουργέω, 4943], denotes to help together, join in helping, to serve with anyone as an underworker (*sun*, with, *hupourgeō*, to serve; *hupo*, under, *ergon*, work); it is used in 2 Cor. 1:11. ¶

NT: B.793d; CB.—; K.—.
OT: —.
GEN. REF.: IS.2:682; NB.—; Z.—.

7. *sunergeō* [συνεργέω, 4903], to help in work, to co-operate, be a co-worker, is rendered "that helpeth with" in 1 Cor. 16:16. See WORK.

NT: B.787c; CB.1270c; K.1116.
OT: –.
GEN. REF.: –.

Note: Paristēmi, to place beside (*para*, by, *histēmi*, to cause to stand), to stand by, be at hand, is used of standing up for help, in Rom. 16:2, "that ye assist," and 2 Tim. 4:17, "stood with." See BRING, COME, COMMEND, GIVE, PRESENT, PROVE, PROVIDE, SHEW, STAND, YIELD.

HELPER, FELLOW-HELPER

1. *boēthos* [βοηθός, 998], an adjective, akin to A, No. 2, and B, No. 4, under HELP, signifying helping, is used as a noun in Heb. 13:6, of God as the Helper of His saints. ¶

NT: B.144d; CB.1239b; K.108.
OT: ʿēzer: S.5828; HR.223c.6b; H.1598a; BD.740c.
ʿezrāh: S.5833; HR.223c.6c; H.1598b; BD.740d.
GEN. REF.: IS.2:682; NB.–; Z.–.

2. *sunergos* [συνεργός, 4904], an adjective, akin to B, No. 7, under HELP, a fellow-worker, is translated "helper" in the A.V. of Rom. 16:3, 9, R.V., "fellow-worker"; in 2 Cor. 1:24, A.V. and R.V., "helpers"; in 2 Cor. 8:23, A.V., "fellow-helper," R.V. "fellow-worker"; so the plural in 3 John 8: See COMPANION, LABOURER, etc.

NT: B.787d; CB.1270c; K.1116.
OT: –.
GEN. REF.: –.

For **HEM** see **BORDER**

HEN

ornis [ὄρνις, 3733], a bird, is used, in the N.T., only of a hen, Matt. 23:37; Luke 13:34. ¶

NT: B.582a; CB.1261b; K.–.
OT: barburîm: S.1257; HR.1014b.1; H.288g; BD.141b.
GEN. REF.: IS.1:643; NB.156; Z.3:120.

HENCE

1. *enthen* [ἔνθεν, —], is found in the best mss. in Matt. 17:20; Luke 16:26. ¶

NT: B.–; CB.266a; K.–.
OT: –: S.–.
GEN. REF.: –.

2. *enteuthen* [ἐντεῦθεν, 1782], akin to No. 1, is used (*a*) of place, "hence," or "from hence," Luke 4:9; 13:31; John 2:16; 7:3; 14:31; 18:36; in John 19:18, "on either side (one)," lit., 'hence and hence'; in Rev. 22:2, it is contrasted with *ekeithen* thence, R.V., "on this side . . . on that" (A.V., "on either side"), lit. 'hence . . . thence'; (*b*) causal, Jas. 4:1, "(come they not) hence," ie., 'owing to.' ¶

NT: B.268c; CB.–; K.–.
OT: –.
GEN. REF.: –.

Notes: (1) For *makran*, far hence," in Acts 22:21, see FAR.

(2) In Acts 1:5, the phrase "not many days hence" is, lit., 'not after (*meta*) many days.'

HENCEFORTH (from, and negatives), HENCEFORWARD

Notes: (1) Positively, "henceforth" stands for the following: (*a*) *ap; arti* (i.e., *apo arti*), lit., 'from now,' e.g., Matt. 26:64; Luke 22:69; John 13:19, R.V., and A.V. marg., "from henceforth"; Rev. 14:13 (where *aparti* is found as one word in the best mss.); (*b*) *to loipon*, lit., (for) the remaining (time), Heb. 10:13; *tou loipou*, Gal. 6:17; (*c*) *apo tou nun*, lit., 'from the now,' e.g., Luke 1:48; 5:10; 12:52; Acts 18:6; 2 Cor. 5:16 (1st part).

(2) negatively, "henceforth . . . not" (or "no more") translates one or other of the negative adverbs *ouketi* and *mēketi*, no longer, e.g., Acts 4:17, A.V., and R.V., "henceforth (to no man)"; in the following the R.V. has "no longer" for the A.V., "henceforth" (with a negative), John 15:15; Rom. 6:6; 2 Cor. 5:15; Eph. 4:17; in 2 Cor. 5:16 (last part), R.V., "no more"; in Matt. 21:19 and Mark 11:14, "no (fruit . . .) henceforward"; A.V. in the latter, "hereafter." See HEREAFTER.

For **HER** and **HERSELF** see the forms under **HE**

HERB

1. *lachanon* [λάχανον, 3001], denotes a garden herb, a vegetable (from *lachainō*, to dig), in contrast to wild plants, Matt. 13:32; Mark 4:32; Luke 11:42; Rom. 14:2. ¶

NT: B.467d; CB.1256b; K.504.
OT: yereq: S.3418; HR.863b.1a; H.918a; BD.438d.
yārāq: S.3419; HR.863b.1b; H.918b; BD.438d.
GEN. REF.: IS.2:684; NB.519; Z.3:121.

2. *botanē* [βοτάνη, 1008], denotes grass, fodder, herbs (from *boskō*, to feed; Eng., botany), Heb. 6:7. ¶

NT: B.145b; CB.1239b; K.–.
OT: ʿēseb: S.6212; HR.225c.3; H.1707a; BD.793b.
GEN. REF.: IS.2:684; NB.519; Z.3:121.

HERD

agelē [ἀγέλη, 34], from *agō*, to lead, is used, in the N.T., only of swine, Matt. 8:30, 31, 32; Mark 5:11, 13; Luke 8:32, 33. ¶

NT: B.8b; CB.–; K.–.
OT: ʿēder: S.5739; HR.10b.2; H.1572a; BD.727c.
GEN. REF.: –.

HERE

1. *hōde* [ὧδε, 5602], an adverb signifying (*a*) here (of place), e.g., Matt. 12:6; Mark 9:1; used with the neuter plural of the article, Col. 4:9, "(all) things (that are done) here" lit., '(all) the (things) here'; in Matt. 24:23, *hōde* is used in both parts, hence the R.V., "Lo, here (is the Christ, or) Here"; in Mark 13:21 *hōde* is followed by *ekei*, "there." The word is used metaphorically in the sense of in this circumstance, or connection, in 1 Cor. 4:2; Rev. 13:10, 18; 14:12; 17:9. See HITHER.

NT: B.895b; CB.—; K.—.
OT: pōh: S.6311; HR.1491b.5; H.1739; BD.805d.
hēnnāh: S.2008; HR.1491b.3; H.510b; BD.244c.
GEN. REF.: —.

2. *enthade* [ἐνθάδε, 1759], has the same meanings as No. 1; "here" in Luke 24:41; Acts 16:28; 25:24. See HITHER (John 4:15, 16; Acts 25:17). ¶

NT: B.266a; CB.—; K.—.
OT: —.
GEN. REF.: —.

3. *autou* [αὐτοῦ, 847], the genitive case of *autos*, self, signifies 'just here' in Matt. 26:36. See THERE, No. 5.

NT: B.124a; CB.—; K.—.
OT: —.
GEN. REF.: —.

HERE (to be, be present)

pareimi [πάρειμι, 3918], to be by or beside or here (*para*, by, and *eimi*, to be), is rendered "to have been here" in Acts 24:19. See COME, PRESENT.

NT: B.624a; CB.1262b; K.791.
OT: —.
GEN. REF.: —.

Note: For *sumpareimi*, to be here present, see PRESENT.

HEREAFTER

Notes: (1) This adverb translates the phrase *meta tauta*, lit., 'after these things,' John 13:7; Rev. 1:19, and frequently in the Apocalypse, see 4:1 (twice); 7:9; 9:12; 15:5; 18:1; 19:1; 20:3.

(2) For Matt. 26:64 and Luke 22:69 (A.V., "hereafter") see HENCEFORTH; for Mark 11:14 see HENCEFORWARD.

(3) In John 14:30, *ouk eti* is rendered "no more" in the R.V. (A.V., "Hereafter . . . not").

(4) In 1 Tim. 1:16, "hereafter" translates the verb *mellō*, to be about to.

HEREBY

Notes: (1) This translates the phrase *en toutō̧*, lit., 'in this,' 1 Cor. 4:4; 1 John 2:3, 5; 3:16, 19, 24; 4:2, 13; 5:2 (R.V., "hereby," A.V., "by this").

(2) In 1 John 4:6, A.V., *ek toutou*, lit., 'out of this,' i.e., in consequence of this, is rendered "hereby" (R.V., "by this"). ¶

HEREIN

Note: This translates the phrase *en toutō̧*, 'in this,' in John 4:37; 9:30; 15:8; Acts 24:16; 2 Cor. 8:10; 1 John 4:9 (A.V., "in this"), 10, 17. ¶

HEREOF

Notes: (1) This translates the word *hautē*, this, the feminine of *houtos*, this, in Matt. 9:26, lit., 'this (fame),' A.V., and R.V. marg.

(2) In Heb. 5:3, A.V., *dia tautēn*, lit., 'by reason of (*dia*) this' (i.e., this infirmity), is rendered "hereof"; the best texts have *autēn*, R.V., "thereof."

HERESY

hairesis [αἵρεσις, 139], denotes (*a*) a choosing, choice (from *haireomai*, to choose); then, that which is chosen, and hence, an opinion, especially a self-willed opinion, which is substituted for submission to the power of truth, and leads to division and the formation of sects, Gal. 5:20 (marg., "parties"); such erroneous opinions are frequently the outcome of personal preference or the prospect of advantage; see 2 Pet. 2:1, where "destructive" (R.V.) signifies leading to ruin; some assign even this to (*b*); in the papyri the prevalent meaning is "choice" (Moulton and Milligan, Vocab.); (*b*) a sect; this secondary meaning, resulting from (*a*), is the dominating significance in the N.T., Acts 5:17; 15:5; 24:5, 14; 26:5; 28:22; "heresies" in 1 Cor. 11:19 (see marg.). See SECT. ¶

NT: B.23d; CB.1249a; K.27.
OT: n[e]dābāh: S.5071; HR.36a.1; H.1299a; BD.621d.
GEN. REF.: IS.2:684; NB.519; Z.3:122.

HERETICAL

hairetikos [αἱρετικός, 141], akin to the above, primarily denotes capable of choosing (*haireomai*); hence, causing division by a party spirit, factious, Tit. 3:10, R.V., "heretical." ¶

NT: B.24a; CB.1249a; K.27.
OT: —.
GEN. REF.: IS.2:687; NB.—; Z.3:122.

For **HERETOFORE** see **SIN**, C, No. 2

HEREUNTO

Note: This translates the phrase *eis touto*, lit., 'unto this,' in 1 Pet. 2:21.

For **HEREWITH** see **TRADE**, A, No. 2

HERITAGE

klēroō [κληρόω, 2820], primarily, to cast lots or to choose by lot, then, to assign a portion, is used in the Passive Voice in Eph. 1:11, "we were made a heritage," R.V. (A.V., "we have obtained an inheritance"). The R.V. is in agreement with such O.T. passages as Deut. 4:20, "a people of inheritance"; 9:29; 32:9; Psa. 16:6. The meaning 'were chosen by lot,' as in the Vulgate, and in 1 Sam. 14:41, indicating the freedom of election without human will (so Chrysostom and Augustine), is not suited to this passage. ¶

NT: B.435d; CB.1255b; K.442.
OT: –.
GEN. REF.: IS.2:687; NB.562; Z.3:122.

HEW, HEW DOWN, HEWN

A. Verbs.

1. *ekkoptō* [ἐκκόπτω, 1581], to cut out or down (*ek*, out of, *koptō*, to cut), is rendered to hew down, of trees, Matt. 3:10; 7:19 (a similar testimony by John the Baptist and Christ); Luke 3:9. See CUT, HINDER.

NT: B.241d; CB.1243c; K.453.
OT: kārat: S.3772; HR.434c.4; H.1048; BD.503d.
GEN. REF.: IS.2:702; NB.–; Z.–.

2. *latomeō* [λατομέω, 2998], signifies to hew out stones (from *latomos*, a stone-cutter; *las*, a stone, *temnō*, to cut), and is used of the sepulchre which Joseph of Arimathaea had hewn out of a rock for himself, where the body of the Lord was buried, Matt. 27:60; Mark 15:46. ¶

NT: B.467b; CB.–; K.–.
OT: ḥāṣab: S.2672; HR.862c.1; H.718; BD.345a.
GEN. REF.: IS.2:702; NB.–; Z.–.

B. Adjective.

laxeutos [λαξευτός, 2991], denotes hewn in stone (*las*, a stone, *xeō*, to scrape; cp. A, No. 2), is used of Christ's tomb, in Luke 23:53. ¶

NT: B.466c; CB.–; K.–.
OT: –.
GEN. REF.: –.

HIDE, HID, HIDDEN

A. Verbs.

1. *kruptō* [κρύπτω, 2928], to cover, conceal, keep secret (Eng., crypt, cryptic, etc.), is used (*a*) in its physical significance, e.g., Matt. 5:14; 13:44; 25:18 (some mss. have No. 2); (*b*) metaphorically, e.g., Matt. 11:25 (some mss. have No. 2 here); 13:35, R.V., "(things) hidden"; A.V., "(things) which have been kept secret"; Luke 18:34; 19:42; John 19:38, "secretly." See SECRET.

NT: B.454b; CB.1256a; K.476.
OT: ḥābā': S.2244; HR.791c.1a-d; H.588a; BD.285a.
sātar: S.5641; HR.791c.9; H.1551; BD.711b.
GEN. REF.: IS.2:705; NB.–; Z.–.

2. *apokruptō* [ἀποκρύπτω, 613], to conceal from, to keep secret (*apo*, from, and No. 1), is used metaphorically, in Luke 10:21, of truths hidden from the wise and prudent and revealed to babes; 1 Cor. 2:7, of God's wisdom; Eph. 3:9, of the mystery of the unsearchable riches of Christ, revealed through the gospel; Col. 1:26, of the mystery associated with the preceding. ¶

NT: B.93d; CB.1237a; K.476.
OT: sātar: S.5641; HR.134b.3; H.1551; BD.711b.
GEN. REF.: IS.2:705; NB.–; Z.–.

3. *enkruptō* [ἐγκρύπτω, 1470], to hide in anything (*en*, in, and No. 1), is used in Matt. 13:33, of leaven hidden in meal. ¶

NT: B.216d; CB.1245b; K.–.
OT: ṭāman: S.2934; HR.367a.2; H.811; BD.380b.
ḥābā': S.2244; HR.367a.1; H.588a; BD.285a.
GEN. REF.: IS.2:705; NB.–; Z.–.

4. *perikruptō* [περικρύπτω, 4032], signifies to hide by placing something around, to conceal entirely, to keep hidden (*peri*, around, used intensively, and No. 1), Luke 1:24. ¶

NT: B.648b; CB.–; K.–.
OT: –.
GEN. REF.: IS.2:705; NB.–; Z.–.

5. *kaluptō* [καλύπτω, 2572], signifies to cover, conceal, so that no trace of it can be seen (hence somewhat distinct from No. 1); it is not translated to hide in the R.V.; in 2 Cor. 4:3 it is rendered "veiled," suitably continuing the subject of 3:13-18; in Jas. 5:20, "shall hide," A.V. (R.V., "shall cover"). See COVER.

NT: B.401a; CB.1253b; K.405.
OT: kāsāh: S.3680; HR.716c.1b; H.491b; BD.1008.
GEN. REF.: IS.2:705; NB.–; Z.–.

6. *parakaluptō* [παρακαλύπτω, 3871], lit., to cover with a veil, A.V., "hid," in Luke 9:45, 'it was veiled from them'; see CONCEAL. ¶

NT: B.617d; CB.–; K.–.
OT: 'ālam: S.5956; HR.1060c.1; H.1629; BD.761a.
GEN. REF.: IS.2:705; NB.–; Z.–.

7. *lanthanō* [λανθάνω, 2990], to escape notice, to be hidden from, is rendered "(could not) be hid" in Mark 7:24, of Christ; "was (not) hid," Luke 8:47, of the woman with the issue of blood; "is hidden," Acts 26:26, of the facts concerning Christ; the sentence might be rendered 'none of these things has escaped the king's notice.' See FORGET, UNAWARES.

NT: B.466b; CB.1256c; K.–.
OT: 'ālam: S.5956; HR.853a.4; H.1629; BD.761a.
GEN. REF.: IS.2:705; NB.–; Z.–.

B. Adjectives.

1. *kruptos* [κρυπτός, 2927], akin to A, No. 1, hidden, secret, is translated "hid" in Matt. 10:26; Mark 4:22; Luke 8:17, R.V., for A.V.,

"secret"; 12:2 (last part); in 1 Cor. 4:5, "hidden (things of darkness)"; 2 Cor. 4:2, "hidden (things of shame)"; 1 Pet. 3:4, "hidden (man of the heart)." See INWARDLY, SECRET.
NT: B.454a; CB.1256a; K.476.
OT: sātar: S.5641; HR.792c.5a; H.1551; BD.711b.
mistār: S.4565; HR.792c.5b; H.1551d; BD.712c.
GEN. REF.: IS.2:705; NB.–; Z.–.

2. *apokruphos* [ἀπόκρυφος, 614], hidden away from (corresponding to A, No. 2; cp. Eng., apocryphal), is translated, "made (A.V., kept) secret," in Mark 4:22; in Luke 8:17, R.V., "secret," for A.V., "hid"; in Col. 2:3, R.V., "hidden," A.V., "hid." See SECRET. ¶
NT: B.93d; CB.1237a; K.476.
OT: sēter: S.5643; HR.134c.3a; H.1551a; BD.712a.
mistār: S.4565; HR.134c.3c; H.1551d; BD.712c.
GEN. REF.: IS.2:705; NB.–; Z.–.

HIGH (from on, most), HIGHLY

A. Adjectives.

1. *hupsēlos* [ὑψηλός, 5308], high, lofty, is used (*a*) naturally, of mountains, Matt. 4:8; 17:1; Mark 9:2; Rev. 21:10; of a wall, Rev. 21:12; (*b*) figuratively, of the arm of God, Acts 13:17; of heaven, "on high," plural, lit., 'in high (places),' Heb. 1:3; (*c*) metaphorically, Luke 16:15, R.V., "exalted" (A.V., "highly esteemed"); Rom. 11:20, in the best texts, "high-minded" [lit., 'mind (not) high things']; 12:16. ¶
NT: B.849d; CB.1252b; K.–.
OT: bāmāh: S.1116; HR.1419b.1; H.253; BD.119a.
gābōah: S.1364; HR.1419b.3a; H.305a; BD.147a.
rûm: S.7311; HR.1419b.12a; H.2133; BD.926c.
GEN. REF.: IS.2:708; NB.525; Z.3:155.

2. *hupsistos* [ὕψιστος, 5310], most high, is a superlative degree, the positive not being in use; it is used of God in Luke 1:32, 35, 76; 6:35, in each of which the R.V. has "the most High," for A.V., "the highest"; A.V. and R.V. in Mark 5:7; Luke 8:28; Acts 7:48; 16:17; Heb. 7:1. See HIGHEST (below).
NT: B.850b; CB.1252b; K.1241.
OT: 'elᵉyôn: S.5945; HR.1420b.3a; H.1624g,h; BD.751b.
GEN. REF.: IS.2:506; NB.–; Z.–.

3. *megas* [μέγας, 3173], great, is translated "high" in John 19:31, of the Sabbath Day at the Passover season; here the meaning is virtually equivalent to 'holy.' See GREAT.
NT: B.497c; CB.1258a; K.573.
OT: gādôl: S.1419; HR.902c.2a; H.315d; BD.152d.
GEN. REF.: –.

Note: In Heb. 10:21, the R.V. rightly has "a great (priest)," A.V., "high." For "high places," Eph. 6:12, A.V., see HEAVENLY, B, No. 2.

B. Nouns.

1. *hupsos* [ὕψος, 5311], height, is used with *ex* (*ek*) from, in the phrase "on high," Luke 1:78; 24:49; with *eis*, in or into, Eph. 4:8. See ESTATE, HEIGHT, No. 1.
NT: B.850c; CB.1252b; K.1241.
OT: mārôm: S.4791; HR.1421b.6a; H.2133h; BD.928d.
qômāh: S.6967; HR.1421b.7; H.1999a; BD.879b.
GEN. REF.: –.

2. *hupsōma* [ὕψωμα, 5313], high thing, 2 Cor. 10:5; in Rom. 8:39, "height." See HEIGHT, No. 2. ¶
NT: B.851c; CB.1252b; K.1241.
OT: –.
GEN. REF.: –.

C. Adverb.

anō [ἄνω, 507], above, upward, is used in Phil. 3:14, of the "high calling of God in Christ Jesus," the prize of which is set before believers as their goal, lit., 'calling upward' (R.V., marg.), a preferable rendering to 'heavenly calling.' See ABOVE.
NT: B.69d; CB.1235c; K.63.
OT: –.
GEN. REF.: –.

HIGHER

A. Adverb.

1. *anōteron* [ἀνώτερον, 511], the neuter of *anōteros*, higher, the comparative of *anō* (see C, under HIGH), is used as an adverb of place in Luke 14:10; for the meaning "above," in Heb. 10:8, see ABOVE. ¶
NT: B.77c; CB.–; K.63.
OT: 'elᵉyôn: S.5945; HR.112c.2; H.1624g,h; BD.751b.
GEN. REF.: –.

B. Verb.

huperechō [ὑπερέχω, 5242], lit., to hold over anything, as being superior, is used metaphorically in Rom. 13:1, of rulers, as the "higher" powers; cp. 1 Pet. 2:13, "supreme." See BETTER, EXCELLENCY, PASS, SUPREME.
NT: B.840d; CB.1252a; K.1230.
OT: 'ādaph: S.5736; HR.1409b.5; H.1568; BD.727a.
GEN. REF.: –.

HIGHEST

hupsistos [ὕψιστος, 5310], is used in the plural in the phrase "in the highest," i.e., in the highest regions, the abode of God, Matt. 21:9; Mark 11:10; Luke omits the article, Luke 2:14; 19:38; for its use as a title of God, see HIGH, A, No. 2.
NT: B.850b; CB.1252b; K.1241.
OT: 'elᵉyôn: S.5945; HR.1420b.3a; H.1624g,h; BD.751b.
GEN. REF.: –.

For **HIGHLY** see **DISPLEASE, EXALT, EXCEEDING, FAVOUR, THINK**

HIGH-MINDED

1. *tuphoō* [τυφόω, 5187], properly means to wrap in smoke (from *tuphos*, smoke; metaphorically, for conceit); it is used in the Passive Voice, metaphorically in 1 Tim. 3:6, "puffed up," R.V. (A.V., "lifted up with pride"); so 6:4, A.V., "proud," and 2 Tim. 3:4, A.V., "high-minded." See PROUD, PUFF (up). ¶ Cp. *tuphomai*, to smoke, Matt. 12:20, ¶ and *tuphōnikos*, tempestuous (with *anemos*, wind, understood), Acts 27:14. ¶

NT: B.831a; CB.—; K.—.
OT: —.
GEN. REF.: IS.2:713; NB.—; Z.—.

2. *hupsēlophroneō* [ὑψηλοφρονέω, 5309], to be highminded, is used in 1 Tim. 6:17. ¶

NT: B.850a; CB.1252b; K.—.
OT: —.
GEN. REF.: IS.2:713; NB.—; Z.—.

HIGHWAY, HIGHWAYSIDE

hodos [ὁδός, 3598], a way, path, road, is rendered "highways" in Matt. 22:10; Luke 14:23; in Mark 10:46, R.V., "way side," A.V., "highway side"; in Matt. 22:9, the word is used with *diexodoi* (ways out through), and the phrase is rightly rendered in the R.V., "the partings of the highways" (i.e., the crossroads), A.V., "the highways." See WAY.

NT: B.553d; CB.1251a; K.666.
OT: derek: S.1870; HR.962b.3a; H.453a; BD.202c.
GEN. REF.: IS.4:199; NB.—; Z.—.

HILL

1. *oros* [ὄρος, 3735], a hill or mountain, is translated "hill" in Matt. 5:14; Luke 4:29; "mountain" in Luke 9:37, R.V., A.V., "hill" (of the mount of transfiguration) as in ver. 28. See MOUNTAIN.

NT: B.582b; CB.1261b; K.732.
OT: har: S.2022; HR.1014b.2b; H.517a; BD.249a.
GEN. REF.: IS.2:713; NB.527; Z.3:158.

2. *oreinos* [ὀρεινός, 3714], an adjective meaning mountainous, hilly, is used in the feminine, *orienē*, as a noun, and rendered "hill country" in Luke 1:39, 65. See COUNTRY. ¶

NT: B.580a; CB.1261a; K.—.
OT: har: S.2022; HR.1010c.1; H.517a; BD.249a.
GEN. REF.: IS.2:713; NB.527; Z.3:158.

3. *bounos* [βουνός, 1015], a mound, heap, height, is translated "hill" in Luke 3:5; "hills" in 23:30. ¶

NT: B.146c; CB.—; K.—.
OT: gib'āh: S.1389; HR.228b.2; H.309a; BD.148d.
GEN. REF.: IS.2:713; NB.527; Z.3:158.

Note: In Acts 17:22, A.V., *pagos* is translated "hill." "The Areopagus," R.V., stands for the Council (not hill) held near by.

For **HIM** and **HIMSELF** see **HE**

HINDER, HINDRANCE

A. Verbs.

1. *enkoptō* [ἐνκόπτω, 1465], lit., to cut into (*en*, in, *koptō*, to cut), was used of impeding persons by breaking up the road, or by placing an obstacle sharply in the path; hence, metaphorically, of detaining a person unnecessarily, Acts 24:4; of hindrances in the way of reaching others, Rom. 15:22; or returning to them, 1 Thess. 2:18; of hindering progress in the Christian life, Gal. 5:7 (*anakoptō* in some mss.), where the significance virtually is 'who broke up the road along which you were travelling so well?'; of hindrances to the prayers of husband and wife, through low standards of marital conduct, 1 Pet. 3:7 (*ekkoptō*, to cut out, repulse, in some mss.). ¶

NT: B.216c; CB.1245a; K.453.
OT: —.
GEN. REF.: —.

2. *kōluō* [κωλύω, 2967], to hinder, forbid, restrain, is translated to hinder in Luke 11:52; Acts 8:36; Rom. 1:13, R.V., (A.V., "was let"); Heb. 7:23, R.V. (A.V., "were not suffered"). See FORBID.

NT: B.461b; CB.1255c; K.—.
OT: kālā': S.3607; HR.839c.1; H.980; BD.476b.
GEN. REF.: —.

3. *diakōluō* [διακωλύω, 1254], a strengthened form of No. 2, to hinder thoroughly, is used in Matt. 3:14, of John the Baptist's endeavour to hinder Christ from being baptized, A.V., "forbad," R.V., "would have hindered," lit., 'was hindering.' ¶

NT: B.185c; CB.—; K.—.
OT: —.
GEN. REF.: —.

B. Noun.

enkopē [ἐγκοπή, 1464], a hindrance, lit., a cutting in, akin to A, No. 1, with corresponding significance, is used in 1 Cor. 9:12, with *didōmi*, to give, R.V., "(that) we may cause (no) hindrance," A.V., "(lest) we should hinder." ¶

NT: B.216b; CB.1245a; K.453.
OT: —.
GEN. REF.: —.

For **HINDER (part)** see **STERN**

HIRE, HIRED

A. Noun.

misthos [μισθός, 3408], denotes (*a*) wages, hire, Matt. 20:8; Luke 10:7; Jas. 5:4; in 1 Tim. 5:18; 2 Pet. 2:13; Jude 11, R.V., "hire" (A.V., "reward"); in 2 Pet. 2:15, R.V., "hire" (A.V., "wages"). See REWARD.

NT: B.523b; CB.1259a; K.599.
OT: sākār: S.7939; HR.930a.6a; H.2264.1b; BD.969a.
maskōret: S.7958; HR.930a.6b; H.2265; BD.969b.
GEN. REF.: IS.2:718; NB.528; Z.3:162.

B. Verb.

misthoō [μισθόω, 3409], to let out for hire, is used in the Middle Voice, signifying to hire, to engage the services of anyone by contract, Matt. 20:1, 7. ¶

NT: B.523d; CB.1259a; K.599.
OT: sākar: S.7939; HR.930b.3a; H.2264.1b; BD.969a.
GEN. REF.: IS.2:718; NB.528; Z.3:162.

Note: In ver. 9 there is no word for "hired" in the original.

HIRED HOUSE

misthōma [μίσθωμα, 3410], akin to A and B, above, primarily denotes a hire, as in the Sept. of Deut. 23:18; Prov. 19:13; Ezek. 16:31, 34, 41, etc.; in the N.T., it is used of a hired dwelling, Acts 28:30. ¶

NT: B.523d; CB.1259a; K.–.
OT: 'etnan: S.868; HR.930c.2; H.2529a; BD.1072c.
GEN. REF.: IS.2:718; NB.–; Z.–.

HIRED SERVANT, HIRELING

1. *misthōtos* [μισθωτός, 3411], an adjective denoting hired, is used as a noun, signifying one who is hired, "hired servants," Mark 1:20; "hireling," John 10:12, 13; here, it expresses, not only one who has no real interest in his duty (that may or may not be present in its use in Mark 1:20, and in *misthios*, No. 2), but one who is unfaithful in the discharge of it; that sense attaches always to the word rendered "hireling." ¶

NT: B.523d; CB.1259a; K.599.
OT: sākîr: S.7916; HR.930c.1; H.2264.1c; BD.969b.
GEN. REF.: IS.2:719; NB.528; Z.3:162.

2. *misthios* [μίσθιος, 3407], an adjective, akin to No. 1, and similarly signifying a hired servant, is used in Luke 15:17, 19 (in some texts, ver. 21). ¶

NT: B.523a; CB.1259a; K.599.
OT: sākîr: S.7916; HR.930a.1; H.2264.1c; BD.969b.
GEN. REF.: IS.2:719; NB.528; Z.3:162.

HIS, HIS OWN

Note: These translate (*a*) forms of pronouns under HE, No. 1 (a frequent use: in 1 Pet. 2:24, "His own self"); the form *autou*, "his," becomes emphatic when placed between the article and the noun, e.g., 1 Thess. 2:19; Tit. 3:5; Heb. 2:4; also under HE, No. 3 (in which "his" is emphasized), e.g., John 5:47; 9:28; 1 Cor. 10:28; 2 Cor. 8:9; 2 Tim. 2:26; Tit. 3:7; 2 Pet. 1:16; (*b*) *heautou*, of himself, his own; the R.V. rightly puts "his own," for the A.V., "his," in Luke 11:21; 14:26; Rom. 4:19; 5:8, "His own (love)"; 1 Cor. 7:37; Gal. 6:8; Eph. 5:28, 33; 1 Thess. 2:11, 12; 4:4; in Rev. 10:7 the change has not been made; it should read 'his own servants'; (*c*) *idios*, one's own, "his own," in the R.V., in Matt. 22:5; John 5:18; 2 Pet. 2:16; in Matt. 25:15, it is rendered "his several"; in John 19:27, "his own home," lit., 'his own things'; in 1 Tim. 6:15, R.V., "its own (times)," referring to the future appearing of Christ; in Heb. 4:10 (end of verse), both A.V. and R.V. have "his," where it should be 'his own'; so in Acts 24:23, for A.V. and R.V., "his"; in 1 Cor. 7:7, R.V., "his own," A.V., "his proper"; (*d*) in Acts 17:28, the genitive case of the definite article, "His (offspring)," lit., 'of the' (i.e., the one referred to, namely, God).

HITHER

1. *hōde* [ὧδε, 5602], primarily an adverb of manner, then, of place, (*a*) of motion or direction towards a place, e.g., Matt. 8:29; Mark 11:3; Luke 9:41; John 6:25; (*b*) of position; see HERE, PLACE.

NT: B.895b; CB.–; K.–.
OT: pōh: S.6311; HR.1491b.5; H.1739; BD.805d.
hēnnāh: S.2008; HR.1491b.3; H.510b; BD.244c.
GEN. REF.: –.

2. *enthade* [ἐνθάδε, 1759], has the same meaning as No. 1; "hither," John 4:15, 16; Acts 17:6; 25:17. See HERE.

NT: B.266a; CB.–; K.–.
OT: –.
GEN. REF.: –.

Note: For *deuro*, "come hither," see COME, and HITHERTO, *Note* (2).

HITHERTO

Notes: (1) The phrase *heōs arti*, until now, is rendered "hitherto" in John 16:24, A.V., and R.V.; in 5:17, R.V., "even until now," which more definitely expresses the meaning than the A.V., "hitherto"; the rest of the Father and the Son having been broken by man's sin, they were engaged in the accomplishment of their counsels of grace with a view to redemption.

(2) the phrase *achri tou deuro*, lit., 'until the hither,' or 'the present,' is used of time in Rom. 1:13, "hitherto."

(3) In 1 Cor. 3:2, A.V., *oupō*, not yet, is translated "hitherto . . . not," R.V., "not yet."

HOISE UP, HOIST UP

1. *airō* [αἴρω, 142], to raise, is used of hoisting up a skiff, or little boat, before undergirding the ship, Acts 27:17, R.V., "had hoisted up," for A.V., "had taken up." See AWAY, TAKE.

NT: B.24b; CB.1234a; K.20.
OT: nāsā': S.5375; HR.34c.14a; H.1421; BD.669d.
GEN. REF.: –.

2. *epairō* [ἐπαίρω, 1869], to raise up (*epi*, up, and No. 1), is used of hoisting up the foresail of a vessel, Acts 27:40, R.V., "hoisting up." See EXALT, LIFT.
NT: B.281d; CB.—; K.28.
OT: nāsā': S.5375; HR.505a.14a-c; H.1421; BD.669d.
GEN. REF.: IS.2:725; NB.—; Z.—.

HOLD (Noun)

1. *tērēsis* [τήρησις, 5084], translated "hold" in Acts 4:3, A.V., "prison" in 5:18 (R.V., "ward") signifies (*a*) a watching, guarding; hence, imprisonment, ward (from *tēreō*, to watch, keep); the R.V., has "ward" in both places; (*b*) a keeping, as of commandments, 1 Cor. 7:19. See KEEPING, WARD. ¶
NT: B.815c; CB.1271b; K.1174.
OT: —.
GEN. REF.: —.

2. *phulakē* [φυλακή, 5438], a guarding or guard (akin to *phulassō*, to guard or watch), also denotes a prison, a hold, Rev. 18:2 (twice), R.V., "hold" in both places, A.V., "cage," in the second (R.V., marg., "prison," in both). See CAGE, IMPRISONMENT, PRISON.
NT: B.867c; CB.1264c; K.1280.
OT: mishmār: S.4929; HR.1440c.2b; H.2414f; BD.1038a.
mishmeret: S.4931; HR.1440c.2c; H.2414g; BD.1038a.
GEN. REF.: —.

HOLD (down, fast, forth, on, to, up), HELD, (take) HOLD

1. *echō* [ἔχω, 2192], to have or hold, is used of mental conception, to consider, account, e.g., Matt. 21:26; of stedfast adherence to faith, or the faith, e.g., 1 Tim. 1:19; 3:9; 2 Tim. 1:13. See HAVE.
NT: B.331d; CB.1242a; K.286.
OT: —.
GEN. REF.: IS.2:725; NB.—; Z.—.

2. *katechō* [κατέχω, 2722], to hold firmly, hold fast (*kata*, down, and No. 1), is rendered "hold fast" in 1 Cor. 11:2, R.V. (A.V., "keep"); 1 Thess. 5:21; Heb. 3:6, 14 (R.V.); 10:23; "hold down," Rom. 1:18, R.V., of unrighteous men who restrain the spread of truth by their unrighteousness, or, as R.V. marg., "who hold the truth in (or with) unrighteousness," contradicting their profession by their conduct (cp. 2:15, R.V.); in Rom. 7:6, R.V., "holden," A.V., "held," of the Law as that which had held in bondage those who through faith in Christ were made dead to it as a means of life. See KEEP, MAKE (toward), POSSESS, RESTRAIN, RETAIN, SEIZE, STAY, TAKE.
NT: B.422c; CB.1254b; K.286.
OT: 'āḥaz: S.270; HR.750c.1; H.64; BD.28a.
ḥāzaq: S.2388; HR.750c.5; H.636; BD.304a.
GEN. REF.: IS.2:725; NB.—; Z.—.

3. *antechō* [ἀντέχω, 472], *anti*, against, or to, and No. 1, signifies in the Middle Voice, (*a*) to hold firmly to, cleave to, of holding or cleaving to a person, Matt. 6:24; Luke 16:13; of holding to the faithful word, Tit. 1:9, R.V., A.V., "holding fast"; (*b*) to support, 1 Thess. 5:14 (the weak). See SUPPORT. ¶
NT: B.73b; CB.—; K.—.
OT: 'āḥaz: S.270; HR.109c.1; H.64; BD.28a.
ḥāzaq: S.2388; HR.109c.4; H.636; BD.304a.
GEN. REF.: IS.2:725; NB.—; Z.—.

4. *sunechō* [συνέχω, 4912], *sun*, with, intensive, and No., 1, is used of holding a prisoner, in Luke 22:63. See CONSTRAIN, KEEP, PRESS, STOP, STRAIT, STRAITENED, TAKE.
NT: B.789a; CB.1270c; K.1117.
OT: 'āṣar: S.6113; HR.1315b.12a; H.1675; BD.783c.
GEN. REF.: —.

5. *epechō* [ἐπέχω, 1907], is used in Phil. 2:16, of holding forth the word of life (*epi*, forth, and No. 1). See (give) HEED, (take) HEED, MARK, STAY.
NT: B.285c; CB.—; K.—.
OT: —.
GEN. REF.: —.

6. *krateō* [κρατέω, 2902], to be strong, mighty, to prevail, (1) is most frequently rendered to lay or take hold on (*a*) literally, e.g., Matt. 12:11; 14:3; 18:28 and 21:46, R.V. (A.V., "laid hands on"); 22:6, R.V. (A.V., "took"); 26:55, A.V. (R.V., "took"); 28:9, R.V., "took hold of" (A.V., "held by"); Mark 3:21; 6:17; 12:12; 14:51; Acts 24:6, R.V. (A.V., "took"); Rev. 20:2; (*b*) metaphorically, of laying hold of the hope of the Lord's return, Heb. 6:18; (2) also signifies to hold or hold fast, i.e., firmly, (*a*) literally, Matt. 26:48, A.V. (R.V., "take"); Acts 3:11; Rev. 2:1; (*b*) metaphorically, of holding fast a tradition or teaching, in an evil sense, Mark 7:3, 4, 8; Rev. 2:14, 15; in a good sense, 2 Thess. 2:15; Rev. 2:25; 3:11; of holding Christ, i.e., practically apprehending Him, as the Head of His Church, Col. 2:19; a confession, Heb. 4:14; the Name of Christ, i.e., abiding by all that His Name implies, Rev. 2:13; of restraint, Luke 24:16, "(their eyes) were holden"; of the winds, Rev. 7:1; of the impossibility of Christ's being holden of death, Acts 2:24. See KEEP, RETAIN (of sins), TAKE.
NT: B.448c; CB.1256a; K.466.
OT: 'āḥaz: S.270; HR.783a.2; H.64; BD.28a.
ḥāzaq: S.2388; HR.783a.6a-c; H.636; BD.304a.
GEN. REF.: IS.2:725; NB.—; Z.—.

7. *epilambanō* [ἐπιλαμβάνω, 1949], to lay hold of (*epi*, upon, *lambanō*, to take), with a special purpose, always in the Middle Voice, is so translated in Luke 20:20, 26, of taking hold of Christ's words; in 23:26 and Acts 21:33, R.V., of laying hold of persons; in 1 Tim. 6:12, 19,

of laying hold on eternal life, i.e., practically appropriating all the benefits, privileges and responsibilities involved in the possession of it; in Heb. 2:16, R.V. "He taketh hold" (A.V., "took on"), perhaps to be viewed in connection with "deliver" (v. 15) and "succour" (v. 18). See APPREHEND, CATCH, TAKE.

NT: B.295a; CB.1246a; K.495.
OT: 'āḥaz: S.270; HR.523c.1; H.64; BD.28a.
ḥāzaq: S.2388; HR.523c.2; H.636; BD.304a.
GEN. REF.: IS.2:725; NB.—; Z.—.

8. *tēreō* [τηρέω, 5083], akin to A, No. 1, under HOLD (Noun), to watch over, keep, give heed to, observe, is rendered "hold fast" in Rev. 3:3, A.V. (R.V., "keep"). See KEEP, OBSERVE, RESERVE, WATCH.

NT: B.814d; CB.1271b; K.1174.
OT: nāṣar: S.5341; HR.1348b.2; H.1407; BD.665c.
shāmar: S.8104; HR.1348b.7; H.2414; BD.1036b.
GEN. REF.: —.

9. *eimi* [εἰμί, 1510], to be, is used in the imperfect tense, with the preposition, *sun*, with, in the idiomatic phrase "held with," in Acts 14:4, lit., 'were with.'

NT: B.222d; CB.1243a; K.206.
OT: —.
GEN. REF.: —.

Notes: (1) In Rom. 14:4, *histēmi*, to cause to stand, in the Passive Voice, to be made to stand, is used in both forms, the latter in the first part, R.V., "he shall be made to stand" (A.V., "he shall be holden up"), the Active Voice in the second part, A.V., and R.V., "to make stand."

(2) In Matt. 12:14, R.V., *lambanō*, to take, is translated "took (counsel)," A.V., "held (a council)."

(3) In Mark 15:1, some mss. have the verb *poieō*, to make, rendered "held (a consultation)"; the most authentic have *hetoimazō*, to prepare, also translated "held."

HOLE

1. *phōleos* [φωλεός, 5454], a lair, burrow, den or hole, is used of foxes in Matt. 8:20 and Luke 9:58. ¶

NT: B.870b; CB.—; K.—.
OT: —.
GEN. REF.: —.

2. *opē* [ὀπή, 3692], is translated "holes" in Heb. 11:38, R.V., A.V. "caves." See CAVE, OPENING.

NT: B.574d; CB.—; K.—.
OT: ḥōr: S.2356; HR.1001b.3; H.758a; BD.359d.
GEN. REF.: —.

HOLINESS, HOLY, HOLILY

A. Nouns.

1. *hagiasmos* [ἁγιασμός, 38], translated "holiness" in the A.V. of Rom. 6:19, 22; 1 Thess. 4:7; 1 Tim. 2:15; Heb. 12:14, is always rendered "sanctification" in the R.V. It signifies (*a*) separation to God, 1 Cor. 1:30; 2 Thess. 2:13; 1 Pet. 1:2; (*b*) the resultant state, the conduct befitting those so separated, 1 Thess. 4:3, 4, 7, and the four other places mentioned above. Sanctification is thus the state predetermined by God for believers, into which in grace He calls them, and in which they begin their Christian course and so pursue it. Hence they are called "saints" (*hagioi*). See SANCTIFICATION. ¶

NT: B.9a; CB.1249a; K.14.
OT: miqdāsh: S.4720; HR.11c.1; H.1990f; BD.874a.
qādash: S.6942; HR.11c.4; H.1990; BD.872d.
qōdesh: S.6944; HR.11c.5; H.1990a; BD.871c.
GEN. REF.: IS.2:725; NB.529; Z.3:173.

Note: The corresponding verb *hagiazō* denotes to set apart to God. See HALLOW, SANCTIFY.

2. *hagiōsunē* [ἁγιωσύνη, 42], denotes the manifestation of the quality of holiness in personal conduct; (*a*) it is used in Rom. 1:4, of the absolute holiness of Christ in the days of His flesh, which distinguished Him from all merely human beings; this (which is indicated in the phrase "the spirit of holiness") and (in vindication of it) His resurrection from the dead, marked Him out as (He was "declared to be") the Son of God; (*b*) believers are to be "perfecting holiness in the fear of God," 2 Cor. 7:1, i.e., bringing holiness to its predestined end, whereby (*c*) they may be found "unblameable in holiness" in the Parousia of Christ, 1 Thess. 3:13. ¶

"In eachplace character is in view, perfect in the case of the Lord Jesus, growing toward perfection in the case of the Christian. Here the exercise of love is declared to be the means God uses to develop likeness to Christ in His children. The sentence may be paraphrased thus:— 'The Lord enable you more and more to spend your lives in the interests of others, in order that He may so establish you in Christian character now, that you may be vindicated from every charge that might possibly be brought against you at the Judgment-seat of Christ'; cp. 1 John 4:16, 17."*

NT: B.10b; CB.1249a; K.14.
OT: qōdesh: S.6944; HR.15b.3; H.1990a; BD.871c.
GEN. REF.: IS.2:725; NB.529; Z.3:173.

3. *hagiotēs* [ἁγιότης, 41], sanctity, the abstract quality of holiness, is used (*a*) of God, Heb. 12:10; (*b*) of the manifestation of it in the conduct of the Apostle Paul and his fellow-

* From Notes on Thessalonians by Hogg and Vine, pp. 108, 115.

labourers, 2 Cor. 1:12 (in the best mss., for *haplotēs*). ¶

NT: B.10b; CB.1249a; K.14.
OT: —.
GEN. REF.: IS.2:725; NB.529; Z.3:173.

4. *hosiotēs* [ὁσιότης, 3742], is to be distinguished from No. 3, as denoting that quality of holiness which is manifested in those who have regard equally to grace and truth; it involves a right relation to God; it is used in Luke 1:75 and Eph. 4:24, and in each place is associated with righteousness. ¶

NT: B.585d; CB.1251b; K.734.
OT: —.
GEN. REF.: IS.—; NB.529; Z.3:177.

Notes: (1) In Acts 3:12, the A.V. translates *eusebeia*, by "holiness," R.V., "godliness," as everywhere, the true meaning of the word. See GODLINESS.

(2) In Tit. 2:3, A.V., *hieroprepēs*, which denotes suited to a sacred character, reverent, is rendered "as becometh holiness," R.V., "reverent." See REVERENT. ¶

B. Adjectives.

1. *hagios* [ἅγιος, 40], akin to A, Nos. 1 and 2, which are from the same root as *hagnos* (found in *hazō*, to venerate), fundamentally signifies separated (among the Greeks, dedicated to the gods), and hence, in Scripture in its moral and spiritual significance, separated from sin and therefore consecrated to God, sacred.

(*a*) It is predicated of God (as the absolutely Holy One, in His purity, majesty and glory); of the Father, e.g., Luke 1:49; John 17:11; 1 Pet. 1:15, 16; Rev. 4:8; 6:10; of the Son, e.g., Luke 1:35; Acts 3:14; 4:27, 30; 1 John 2:20; of the Spirit, e.g., Matt. 1:18 and frequently in all the Gospels, Acts, Romans, 1 and 2 Cor., Eph., 1 Thess.; also in 2 Tim. 1:14; Tit. 3:5; 1 Pet. 1:12; 2 Pet. 1:21; Jude 20.

(*b*) It is used of men and things (see below) in so far as they are devoted to God. Indeed the quality, as attributed to God, is often presented in a way which involves Divine demands upon the conduct of believers. These are called *hagioi*, saints, i.e., 'sanctified' or 'holy ones.'

This sainthood is not an attainment, it is a state into which God in grace calls men; yet believers are called to sanctify themselves (consistently with their calling, 2 Tim. 1:9), cleansing themselves from all defilement, forsaking sin, living a holy manner of life, 1 Pet. 1:15; 2 Pet. 3:11, and experiencing fellowship with God in His holiness. The saints are thus figuratively spoken of as "a holy temple," 1 Cor. 3:17 (a local church); Eph. 2:21 (the whole Church), cp. 5:27; "a holy priesthood," 1 Pet. 2:5; "a holy nation," 2:9.

"It is evident that *hagios* and its kindred words . . . express something more and higher than *hieros*, sacred, outwardly associated with God; . . . something more than *semnos*, worthy, honourable; something more than *hagnos*, pure, free from defilement. *Hagios* is . . . more comprehensive. . . . It is characteristically godlikeness" (G. B. Stevens, in Hastings' Bib. Dic.).

The adjective is also used of the outer part of the Tabernacle, Heb. 9:2 (R.V., "the Holy place"); of the inner sanctuary, 9:3, R.V., "the Holy of Holies"; 9:24, "a holy place," R.V.; ver. 25 (plural), of the Presence of God in Heaven, where there are not two compartments as in the Tabernacle, all being "the holy place"; 9:8, 12 (neuter plural); 10:19, "the holy place," R.V. (A.V., "the holiest," neut. plural), see SANCTUARY; of the city of Jerusalem, Rev. 11:2; its temple, Acts 6:13; of the faith, Jude 20; of the greetings of saints, 1 Cor. 16:20; of angels, e.g., Mark 8:38; of apostles and prophets, Eph. 3:5; of the future heavenly Jerusalem, Rev. 21:2, 10; 22:19.

NT: B.9b; CB.1249a; K.14.
OT: qōdesh: S.6944; HR.12a.15; H.1990a; BD.871c.
miqdāsh: S.4720; HR.12a.6; H.1990f; BD.874a.
GEN. REF.: IS.2:725; NB.529; Z.3:173.

2. *hosios* [ὅσιος, 3741], akin to A, No. 4, signifies religiously right, holy, as opposed to what is unrighteous or polluted. It is commonly associated with righteousness (see A, No. 4). It is used "of God, Rev. 15:4; 16:5; and of the body of the Lord Jesus, Acts 2:27; 13:35, citations from Ps. 16:10, Sept.; Heb. 7:26; and of certain promises made to David, which could be fulfilled only in the resurrection of the Lord Jesus, Acts 13:34. In 1 Tim. 2:8 and Tit. 1:8, it is used of the character of Christians. . . . In the Sept., *hosios* frequently represents the Hebrew word *chasid*, which varies in meaning between 'holy' and 'gracious,' or 'merciful'; cp. Ps. 16:10 with 145:17."*

NT: B.585c; CB.1251b; K.734.
OT: yōsher: S.3476; HR.1018c.1; H.930b; BD.449c.
tôm: S.8537; HR.1018c.2a; H.2522a; BD.1070d.
tāmîm: S.8549; HR.1018c.2b; H.2522d; BD.1071a.
GEN. REF.: IS.—; NB.529; Z.3:177.

Notes: (1) For Acts 13:34, see the R.V. and the A.V. marg.; the R.V. in Rev. 16:5, "Thou Holy One," translates the most authentic mss. (A.V., "and shalt be").

* From Notes on Thessalonians by Hogg and Vine, p. 64.

(2) For *hieros* (see No. 1), subserving a sacred purpose, translated "holy" in 2 Tim. 3:15, A.V. (of the Scriptures), see SACRED.

C. Adverb.

hosiōs [ὁσίως, 3743], akin to A, No. 4, and B No. 2, "holily," i.e., pure from evil conduct, and observant of God's will, is used in 1 Thess. 2:10, of the conduct of the Apostle and his fellow-missionaries. ¶

NT: B.585d; CB.–; K.734.
OT: –.
GEN. REF.: IS.–; NB.529; Z.3:177.

D. Verb.

hagiazō [ἁγιάζω, 37], to hallow, sanctify, in the Passive Voice, to be made holy, be sanctified, is translated "let him be made holy" in Rev. 22:11, the aorist or point tense expressing the definiteness and completeness of the Divine act; elsewhere it is rendered by the verb to sanctify. See HALLOW, SANCTIFY.

NT: B.8c; CB.1249a; K.14.
OT: qādash: S.6942; HR.10c.7; H.1990; BD.872d.
GEN. REF.: IS.2:725; NB.529; Z.3:173.

For **HOLY GHOST** see under **SPIRIT** and **HOLY**, B, No. 1 (a)

HOLYDAY

heortē [ἑορτή, 1859], denotes a feast, festival; it is translated "a holyday" in the A.V. of Col. 2:16; R.V., "a feast day." See FEAST.

NT: B.280b; CB.1250a; K.–.
OT: ḥāg: S.2282; HR.503a.1; H.602a; BD.290d.
mô'ēd: S.4150; HR.503a.3a; H.878b; BD.417b.
GEN. REF.: IS.2:729; NB.–; Z.3:196.

HOME, AT HOME (to be; workers)

A. Noun and Phrases.

1. *oikos* [οἶκος, 3624], a house, dwelling, is used (*a*) with the preposition *eis*, unto, with the meaning 'to home,' lit., to a house, in Mark 8:3, R.V., "to (their) home," A.V., "to (their own) houses"; so 8:26, "to (his) home"; Luke 15:6, "home," lit., 'into the house'; (*b*) with the preposition *en*, in, 1 Cor. 11:34, "(let him eat) at home"; 14:35, "(let them ask . . .) at home"; (*c*) with the preposition *kata*, down, Acts 2:46, "(breaking bread) at home," R.V. (A.V., "from house to house"); so in 5:42 (A.V., "in every house").

NT: B.560b; CB.1260b; K.674.
OT: bayit: S.1004; HR.973a.5; H.241; BD.108c.
GEN. REF.: IS.2:747; NB.–; Z.–.

Notes: (1) In Mark 3:19, the A.V. and R.V. marg., have "home," for the text "to a house"; the latter seems the more probable. See HOUSE.

(2) In 1 Tim. 5:4, the phrase *ton idion oikon*, is rendered "at home," of the necessity that children should show piety there; R.V., "towards their own family," the house being put by metonymy for the family.

2. The neuter plural of *idios*, one's own, with the article, preceded by *eis*, unto, lit., 'unto one's own (things),' is translated "home" in Acts 21:6; in John 19:27, "unto his own home" ("home" being italicised).

Note: In John 16:32, this phrase is rendered "to his own" (of the predicted scattering of the dsciples), A.V. marg., "his own home"; cp. John 1:11, "His own things," R.V., marg. (i.e. 'His possessions').

For *oikia* in Matt. 8:6, A.V., "at home," see HOUSE.

3. In Luke 24:12 the reflexive pronoun *hauton* (in some mss. *heauton*), preceded by *pros*, to, is rendered "to his home," R.V. (lit., 'to himself'), of the departure of Peter from the Lord's tomb; in John 20:10, the same construction is used, in the plural, of Peter and John on the same occasion, and rendered "unto their own home."

B. Adjective.

oikourgos [οἰκουργός, 3626], working at home (*oikos*, and a root of *ergon*, work), is used in Tit. 2:5, "workers at home," R.V. in the injunction given to elder women regarding the training of the young women. Some mss. have *oikouros*, watching or keeping the home (*oikos*, and *ouros* a keeper), A.V., "keepers at home." ¶

NT: B.561c; CB.–; K.–.
OT: –.
GEN. REF.: –.

C. Verb.

endēmeō [ἐνδημέω, 1736], lit., to be among one's people (*en*, in, *dēmos*, people; *endēmos*, one who is in his own place or land), is used metaphorically of the life on earth of believers, 2 Cor. 5:6, "at home (in the body)"; in ver. 8 of the life in Heaven of the spirits of believers, after their decease, "at home (with the Lord)," R.V. (A.V., "present"); in ver. 9, "at home" (A.V., "present") refers again to the life on earth. In each verse the verb is contrasted with *ekdēmeō*, to be away from home, to be absent; in ver. 6, "we are absent," i.e., away from home (from the Lord); in ver. 8, "to be absent" (i.e., away from the home of the body); so in ver. 9, "absent." The implication in being "at home with the Lord" after death is a testimony against the doctrine of the unconsciousness of the spirit, when freed from the natural body. ¶

NT: B.263a; CB.1244c; K.149.
OT: –.
GEN. REF.: IS.2:747; NB.–; Z.–.

HONEST, HONESTLY, HONESTY

A. Adjectives.

1. *kalos* [καλός, 2570], good, admirable, becoming, has also the ethical meaning of what is fair, right, honourable, of such conduct as deserves esteem; it is translated "honest" [cp. Latin *honestus* (from *honos*, honour)], which has the same double meaning as "honest" in the A.V., namely, regarded with honour, honourable, and bringing honour, becoming; in Luke 8:15 (A.V., and R.V.), "an honest and good (*agathos*) heart"; Rom. 12:17; 2 Cor. 8:21 and 13:7, R.V., "honourable" (A.V., "honest"), of things which are regarded with esteem; in 1 Pet. 2:12, of behaviour, R.V., "seemly," A.V., "honest" (i.e., becoming). See GOOD.

NT: B.400b; CB.1253b; K.402.
OT: ṭôb: S.2896; HR.715b.2a; H.793a; BD.373c.
yāpheh: S.3303; HR.715b.3a; H.890a; BD.421c.
GEN. REF.: IS.2:749; NB.–; Z.–.

Note: In Tit. 3:14, the R.V. and A.V. margins give what is probably the accurate meaning, "(to profess) honest occupations" (A.V., "trades"); in the texts "(to maintain) good works."

2. *semnos* [σεμνός, 4586], august, venerable, is rendered "honest" in Phil. 4:8, A.V. (marg., "venerable"), R.V., "honourable" (marg., "reverent"). Matthew Arnold suggests 'nobly serious.' See GRAVE.

NT: B.746b; CB.1269a; K.1010.
OT: –.
GEN. REF.: –.

Note: In Acts 6:3, "men of honest (R.V., good) report" translates the Passive Voice of *martureō*, lit., 'having had witness borne.'

B. Adverbs.

1. *kalōs* [καλῶς, 2573], corresponding to A, No. 1, is used in Heb. 13:18, "honestly," i.e., honourably. See PLACE, C, *Note* (4), WELL.

NT: B.401b; CB.1253b; K.–.
OT: yāṭab: S.3190; HR.717b.1a; H.863; BD.405c.
ṭôb: S.2896; HR.717b.1b; H.793a; BD.373c.
GEN. REF.: IS.2:749; NB.–; Z.–.

2. *euschēmonōs* [εὐσχημόνως, 2156], becomingly, decently, is rendered "honestly" in Rom. 13:13, where it is set in contrast with the confusion of Gentile social life, and in 1 Thess. 4:12, of the manner of life of believers as a witness to "them that are without"; in 1 Cor. 14:40, "decently," in contrast with confusion in the churches. See DECENTLY. ¶

NT: B.327a; CB.–; K.–.
OT: –.
GEN. REF.: –.

C. Noun.

semnotēs [σεμνότης, 4587], denotes gravity, dignified seriousness; it is rendered "honesty" in the A.V. of 1 Tim. 2:2, R.V., "gravity." See GRAVITY.

NT: B.747a; CB.1269a; K.1010.
OT: –.
GEN. REF.: –.

HONEY

meli [μέλι, 3192], occurs with the adjective *agrios*, wild, in Matt. 3:4; Mark 1:6; in Rev. 10:9, 10, as an example of sweetness. ¶ As honey is liable to ferment, it was precluded from offerings to God, Lev. 2:11. The liquid honey mentioned in Psa. 19:10 and Prov. 16:24 is regarded as the best; a cruse of it was part of the present brought to Ahijah by Jeroboam's wife, 1 Kings 14:3.

NT: B.500c; CB.–; K.577.
OT: d^ebash: S.1706; HR.908c.1; H.400a; BD.185a.
GEN. REF.: IS.2:749; NB.534; Z.3:196.

HONEY-COMB

melissios [μελίσσιος, 3193], signifying made by bees from *melissa*, a bee, is found, with *kerion*, a comb, in some mss. in Luke 24:42. ¶

NT: B.500c; CB.–; K.–.
OT: –.
GEN. REF.: IS.–; NB.534; Z.–.

HONOUR (Noun and Verb)

A. Nouns.

1. *timē* [τιμή, 5092], primarily a valuing, hence, objectively, (*a*) a price paid or received, e.g., Matt. 27:6, 9; Acts 4:34; 5:2, 3; 7:16, R.V., "price" (A.V., "sum"); 19:19; 1 Cor. 6:20; 7:23; (*b*) of the preciousness of Christ unto believers, 1 Pet. 2:7, R.V., i.e., the honour and inestimable value of Christ as appropriated by believers, who are joined, as living stones, to Him the Corner-Stone; (*c*) in the sense of value, of human ordinances, valueless against the indulgence of the flesh, or, perhaps of no value in attempts at asceticism, Col. 2:23 (see extended note under INDULGENCE, No. 2); (*d*) honour, esteem, (1) used in ascriptions of worship to God, 1 Tim. 1:17; 6:16; Rev. 4:9, 11; 5:13; 7:12; to Christ, 5:12, 13; (2) bestowed upon Christ by the Father, Heb. 2:9; 2 Pet. 1:17; (3) bestowed upon man, Heb. 2:7; (4) bestowed upon Aaronic priests, Heb. 5:4; (5) to be the reward hereafter of "the proof of faith" on the part of tried saints, 1 Pet. 1:7, R.V.; (6) used of the believer who as a vessel is "meet for the Master's use," 2 Tim. 2:21; (7) to be the reward of patience in well-doing, Rom. 2:7, and of working good (a perfect life to which man cannot attain, so as to be justified before God thereby), 2:10; (8) to be given to all to whom it is due, Rom. 13:7 (see 1 Pet. 2:17, under B,

No. 1); (9) as an advantage to be given by believers one to another instead of claiming it for self, Rom. 12:10; (10) to be given to elders that rule well ("double honour"), 1 Tim. 5:17 (here the meaning may be an honorarium); (11) to be given by servants to their master, 1 Tim. 6:1; (12) to be given to wives by husbands, 1 Pet. 3:7; (13) said of the husband's use of the wife, in contrast to the exercise of the passion of lust, 1 Thess. 4:4 (some regard the "vessel" here as the believer's body); (14) of that bestowed upon parts of the body, 1 Cor. 12:23, 24; (15) of that which belongs to the builder of a house in contrast to the house itself, Heb. 3:3; (16) of that which is not enjoyed by a prophet in his own country, John 4:44; (17) of that bestowed by the inhabitants of Melita upon Paul and his fellow-passengers, in gratitude for his benefits of healing, Acts 28:10; (18) of the festive honour to be possessed by nations, and brought into the Holy City, the Heavenly Jerusalem, Rev. 21:26 (in some mss., ver. 24); (19) of honour bestowed upon things inanimate, a potters' vessel, Rom. 9:21; 2 Tim. 2:20. See PRECIOUSNESS, PRICE, SUM, VALUE. ¶

NT: B.817b; CB.1272c; K.1181.
OT: yᵉqār: S.3366; HR.1353a.4a; H.905b; BD.430b.
ʿēreq: S.6187; HR.1353a.10; H.1694a; BD.789d.
GEN. REF.: IS.2:750; NB.–; Z.3:197.

Note: For *entimos*, 'in honour,' see HONOURABLE, No. 2.

2. *doxa* [δοξά], glory, is translated "honour" in the A.V. of John 5:41, 44 (twice); 8:54; 2 Cor. 6:8, and Rev. 19:7; the R.V. keeps to the word "glory," as the A.V. everywhere else. See GLORY.

B. Verbs.

1. *timaō* [τιμάω, 5091], to honour (akin to A, No. 1), is used of (*a*) valuing Christ at a price, Matt. 27:9, cp. A, No. 1, (*a*); (*b*) honouring a person: (1) the honour done by Christ to the Father, John 8:49; (2) honour bestowed by the Father upon him who serves Christ, John 12:26; (3) the duty of all to honour the Son equally with the Father, 5:23; (4) the duty of children to honour their parents, Matt. 15:4; 19:19; Mark 7:10; 10:19; Luke 18:20; Eph. 6:2; (5) the duty of Christians to honour the king, and all men, 1 Pet. 2:17; (6) the respect and material assistance to be given to widows "that are widows indeed," 1 Tim. 5:3; (7) the honour done to Paul and his companions by the inhabitants of Melita, Acts 28:10; (8) mere lip profession of honour to God, Matt. 15:8; Mark 7:6. ¶

NT: B.817b; CB.1272c; K.1181.
OT: kābēd: S.3513; HR.1353a.3a; H.943; BD.457a.
ʿārak: S.6186; HR.1353a.5a; H.1694; BD.789b.
GEN. REF.: IS.2:750; NB.–; Z.3:197.

2. *doxazō* [δοξάζω, 1392], to glorify (from *doxa*, A. No. 2), is rendered "honour" and "honoureth" in the A.V. of John 8:54; in 1 Cor. 12:26, however, in reference to the members of the body, both A.V. and R.V. have "honoured" (R.V. marg., "glorified"). Everywhere else it is translated by some form of the verb to glorify, have glory, or be made glorious, except in Rom. 11:13, "magnify," A.V. See GLORIFY.

NT: B.204c; CB.1242b; K.178.
OT: kābēd: S.3513; HR.343b.7b,c; H.943; BD.457a.
pā'ar: S.6286; HR.343b.11a-c; H.1726,1727; BD.802b.
GEN. REF.: IS.2:750; NB.–; Z.3:197.

HONOURABLE, WITHOUT HONOUR

1. *endoxos* [ἔνδοξος, 1741], denotes (*a*) held in honour (*en*, in, *doxa*, honour; cp. HONOUR, A, No. 2), of high repute, 1 Cor. 4:10, A.V. "(are) honourable," R.V., "(have) glory," in contrast to *atimos*, without honour (see No. 6 below). See GLORIOUS, GORGEOUSLY.

NT: B.263b; CB.1245a; K.178.
OT: kābēd: S.3513; HR.470c.3a; H.943; BD.457a.
GEN. REF.: IS.2:750; NB.–; Z.3:197.

2. *entimos* [ἔντιμος, 1784], lit., in honour (*en*, in, *timē*, honour: see HONOUR, A, No. 1), is used of the centurion's servant in Luke 7:2, "dear" (R.V. marg., "precious . . . or honourable"); of self-sacrificing servants of the Lord, said of Epaphroditus, Phil. 2:29, R.V. "(hold such) in honour" (A.V., "in reputation"; marg., "honour such"); of Christ, as a precious stone, 1 Pet. 2:4, 6 (R.V. marg., "honourable"). Cp. *timios* in 1:7, 19; see No. 4. ¶

The comparative degree, *entimoteros*, is used (in the best mss.) of degrees of honour attached to persons invited to a feast, a marriage feast, Luke 14:8, "a more honourable man." See PRECIOUS. ¶

NT: B.268d; CB.1245b; K.–.
OT: ḥōr: S.2715; HR.479a.2; H.757a; BD.359c.
yᵉqār: S.3366; HR.479a.3d; H.905b; BD.430b.
GEN. REF.: IS.2:750; NB.–; Z.–.

3. *euschēmōn* [εὐσχήμων, 2158], signifies elegant, comely, of honourable position, A.V., "honourable," R.V., "of honourable estate," Mark 15:43; Acts 13:50; 17:12; for other renderings in 1 Cor. 7:35 and 12:24 see COMELY, B.

NT: B.327a; CB.–; K.278.
OT: –.
GEN. REF.: –.

4. *timios* [τίμιος, 5093], precious, valuable, honourable (akin to *timē*, honour; see No. 2), is used of marriage in Heb. 13:4, A.V., as a statement, "(marriage) is honourable (in all)," R.V., as an exhortation, "let (marriage) be had

in honour (among all)." See DEAR, PRECIOUS, REPUTATION.

NT: B.818a; CB.1272c; K.—.
OT: yāqār: S.3368; HR.1353c.2a; H.905a; BD.429d.
GEN. REF.: IS.2:750; NB.—; Z.—.

5. *kalos* [καλός, 2570], good, fair, is translated "honourable" in Rom. 12:17; 2 Cor. 8:21; 13:7, R.V. (A.V., "Honest"). See GOOD, HONEST.

NT: B.400b; CB.1253b; K.402.
OT: ṭôb: S.2896; HR.715b.2a; H.793a; BD.373c.
GEN. REF.: IS.2:750; NB.—; Z.—.

6. *atimos* [ἄτιμος, 820], without honour (*a*, negative, or privative, *timē*, honour), despised, is translated "without honour" in Matt. 13:57; Mark 6:4; "dishonour" in 1 Cor. 4:10, R.V. (A.V., "despised"). See DESPISE. ¶

The comparative degree *atimoteros* is used in the best mss. in 1 Cor. 12:23, "less honourable." ¶

NT: B.120a; CB.1238b; K.—.
OT: bāzāh: S.959; HR.176a.1; H.224; BD.102b.
qālāh: S.7034; HR.176a.3; H.2024; BD.885d.
GEN. REF.: IS.2:750; NB.—; Z.—.

Note: For *semnos*, honourable, Phil. 4:8, R.V., see GRAVE.

HOOK

ankistron [ἄγκιστρον, 44], a fish-hook (from *ankos*, a bend; Lat. *angulus*; Eng., anchor and angle are akin), is used in Matt. 17:27. ¶ In the Sept., 2 Kings 19:28; Job 40:20; Is. 19:8; Ezek. 32:3; Hab. 1:15. ¶

NT: B.10c; CB.—; K.—.
OT: ḥakkāh: S.2443; HR.15b.2; H.693c; BD.335c.
ḥaḥ: S.2397; HR.15b.1; H.620b; BD.296b.
GEN. REF.: IS.2:751; NB.535; Z.3:197.

HOPE (Noun and Verb), HOPE (for)

A. Noun.

elpis [ἐλπίς, 1680], in the N.T., favourable and confident expectation (contrast the Sept. in Isa. 28:19, "an evil hope"). It has to do with the unseen and the future, Rom. 8:24, 25. Hope describes (*a*) the happy anticipation of good (the most frequent significance), e.g., Tit. 1:2; 1 Pet. 1:21; (*b*) the ground upon which hope is based, Acts 16:19; Col. 1:27, "Christ in you the hope of glory"; (*c*) the object upon which the hope is fixed, e.g., 1 Tim. 1:1.

Various phrases are used with the word hope, in Paul's Epistles and speeches: (1) Acts 23:6, "the hope and resurrection of the dead"; this has been regarded as a hendiadys (one by means of two), i.e., the hope of the resurrection; but the *kai*, "and," is epexegetic, defining the hope, namely, the resurrection; (2) Acts 26:6, 7, "the hope of the promise (i.e., the fulfilment of the promise) made unto the fathers"; (3) Gal. 5:5, "the hope of righteousness"; i.e., the believer's complete conformity to God's will, at the Coming of Christ; (4) Col. 1:23, "the hope of the Gospel," i.e., the hope of the fulfilment of all the promises presented in the Gospel; cp. 1:5; (5) Rom. 5:2, "(the) hope of the glory of God," i.e., as in Tit. 2:13, "the blessed hope and appearing of the glory of our great God and Saviour Jesus Christ"; cp. Col. 1:27; (6) 1 Thess. 5:8, "the hope of salvation," i.e., of the Rapture of believers, to take place at the opening of the Parousia of Christ; (7) Eph. 1:18, "the hope of His (God's) calling," i.e., the prospect before those who respond to His call in the Gospel; (8) Eph. 4:4, "the hope of your calling," the same as (7), but regarded from the point of view of the called; (9) Tit. 1:2, and 3:7, "the hope of eternal life," i.e., the full manifestation and realization of that life which is already the believer's possession; (10) Acts 28:20, "the hope of Israel," i.e., the expectation of the coming of the Messiah. See Notes on Galatians by Hogg and Vine, pp. 248, 249.

In Eph. 1:18; 2:12 and 4:4, the hope is objective. The objective and subjective use of the word need to be distinguished; in Rom. 15:4, e.g., the use is subjective.

In the N.T. three adjectives are descriptive of hope: "good," 2 Thess. 2:16; "blessed," Tit. 2:13; "living," 1 Pet. 1:3. To these may be added Heb. 7:19, "a better hope," i.e., additional to the commandment, which became disannulled (v. 18), a hope centred in a new Priesthood.

In Rom. 15:13 God is spoken of as "the God of hope," i.e., He is the Author, not the Subject, of it. Hope is a factor in salvation, Rom. 8:24; it finds its expression in endurance under trial, which is the effect of waiting for the Coming of Christ, 1 Thess. 1:3; it is "an anchor of the soul," staying it amidst the storms of this life, Heb. 6:18, 19; it is a purifying power, "every one that hath this hope set on Him (Christ) purifieth himself, even as He is pure," 1 John 3:3, R.V. (the Apostle John's one mention of hope).

The phrase "fulness of hope," Heb. 6:11, R.V., expresses the completeness of its activity in the soul; cp. "fulness of faith," 10:22, and "of understanding," Col. 2:2 (R.V., marg.).

NT: B.252d; CB.1244b; K.229.
OT: bāṭṭaḥ: S.982; HR.454a.1a; H.233; BD.105a.
beṭaḥ: S.983; HR.454a.1b; H.233a; BD.105b.
GEN. REF.: IS.2:751; NB.535; Z.3:198.

B. Verbs.

1. *elpizō* [ἐλπίζω, 1679], to hope, is not infrequently translated in the A.V., by the verb to trust; the R.V. adheres to some form of the

verb to hope, e.g., John 5:45, "Moses, on whom ye have set your hope"; 2 Cor. 1:10, "on whom we have set our hope"; so in 1 Tim. 4:10; 5:5; 6:17; see also, e.g., Matt. 12:21; Luke 24:21; Rom. 15:12, 24.

The verb is followed by three prepositions: (1) *eis*, rendered "on" in John 5:45 (as above); the meaning is really "in" as in 1 Pet. 3:5, "who hoped in God"; the hope is thus said to be directed to, and to centre in, a Person; (2) *epi*, "on" Rom. 15:12. "On Him shall the Gentiles hope," R.V.; so 1 Tim. 4:10; 5:5 (in the best mss.); 6:17, R.V.; this expresses the ground upon which hope rests; (3) *en*, "in," 1 Cor. 15:19, "we have hoped in Christ," R.V., more lit., 'we are (men) that have hoped in Christ,' the preposition expresses that Christ is not simply the ground upon whom, but the sphere and element in whom, the hope is placed. The form of the verb (the perfect participle with the verb to be, lit., 'are having hoped') stresses the character of those who hope, more than the action; hope characterizes them, showing what sort of persons they are. See TRUST.

NT: B.252c; CB.1244; K.229.
OT: bāṭaḥ: S.982; HR.453c.1a; H.233; BD.105a.
ḥāsāh: S.2620; HR.453c.5; H.700; BD.340a.
tiqwāh: S.8615; HR.453c.15; H.1994d,e; BD.876b.
GEN. REF.: IS.2:751; NB.535; Z.3:198.

2. *proelpizō* [προελπίζω, 4276], to hope before (*pro*, before, and No. 1), is found in Eph. 1:12. ¶

NT: B.705a; CB.1266c; K.229.
OT: –.
GEN. REF.: –.

3. *apelpizō* [ἀπελπίζω, 560], lit., to hope from (*apo*, and No. 1): see DESPAIR.

NT: B.83d; CB.1236b; K.229.
OT: –.
GEN. REF.: –.

HORN

keras [κέρας, 2768], a horn, is used in the plural, as the symbol of strength, (*a*) in the Apocalyptic visions; (1) on the head of the Lamb as symbolic of Christ, Rev. 5:6; (2) on the heads of beasts as symbolic of national potentates, Rev. 12:3; 13:1, 11; 17:3, 7, 12, 16 (cp. Dan. 7:8; 8:9; Zech. 1:18, etc.); (3) at the corners of the golden altar, Rev. 9:13 (cp. Ex. 30:2; the horns were of one piece with the altar, as in the case of the brazen altar, 27:2, and were emblematic of the efficacy of the ministry connected with it); (*b*) metaphorically, in the singular, "a horn of salvation," Luke 1:69 (a frequent metaphor in the O.T., e.g., Psa. 18:2; cp. 1 Sam. 2:10; Lam. 2:3). ¶

NT: B.429a; CB.1255a; K.428.
OT: qeren: S.7161; HR.759c.3; H.2072a; BD.901d.
GEN. REF.: IS.2:757; NB.537; Z.4:320.

HORSE

hippos [ἵππος, 2462], apart from the fifteen occurrences in the Apocalypse, occurs only in Jas. 3:3; in the Apocalypse horses are seen in visions in 6:2, 4, 5, 8; 9:7, 9, 17 (twice); 14:20; 19:11, 14, 19, 21; otherwise in 18:13; 19:18. ¶

NT: B.380c; CB.1250c; K.369.
OT: sûs: S.5483; HR.687b.1a; H.1476,1477; BD.692b.
GEN. REF.: IS.2:759; NB.538; Z.3:203.

HORSEMEN

1. *hippeus* [ἱππεύς, 2460], a horseman, is used in the plural in Acts 23:23, 32. ¶

NT: B.380c; CB.–; K.–.
OT: pārāsh: S.6571; HR.687a.2; H.1836a; BD.832a.
GEN. REF.: IS.2:759; NB.538; Z.3:203.

2. *hippikos* [ἱππικός, 2461], an adjective signifying 'of a horse' or 'of horsemen,' equestrian, is used as a noun denoting cavalry, in Rev. 9:16, "horsemen," numbering "twice ten thousand times ten thousand," R.V. ¶

NT: B.380c; CB.–; K.–.
OT: –.
GEN. REF.: –.

HOSANNA

hōsanna [ὡσαννά, 5614], in the Hebrew, means "save, we pray." The word seems to have become an utterance of praise rather than of prayer, though originally, probably, a cry for help. The people's cry at the Lord's triumphal entry into Jerusalem (Matt. 21:9, 15; Mark 11:9, 10; John 12:13) was taken from Psa. 118, which was recited at the Feast of Tabernacles (see FEAST) in the great Hallel (Psalms 113 to 118) in responses with the priest, accompanied by the waving of palm and willow branches. "The last day of the feast" was called "the great Hosanna"; the boughs also were called hosannas. ¶

NT: B.899a; CB.1251b; K.1356.
OT: yāsha': S.3467; HR.–; H.929; BD.446b.
GEN. REF.: IS.2:761; NB.539; Z.3:206.

HOSPITALITY

A. Noun.

philoxenia [φιλοξενία, 5381], love of strangers (*philos*, loving, *xenos*, a stranger), is used in Rom. 12:13; Heb. 13:2, lit. '(be not forgetful of) hospitality.' See ENTERTAIN, *Note*. ¶

NT: B.860d; CB.1264b; K.661.
OT: –.
GEN. REF.: IS.2:105; NB.–; Z.3:214.

B. Adjective.

philoxenos [φιλόξενος, 5382], hospitable, occurs in 1 Tim. 3:2; Tit. 1:8; 1 Pet. 4:9. ¶

NT: B.860d; CB.1264b; K.661.
OT: –.
GEN. REF.: IS.2:105; NB.–; Z.3:214.

Note: For *xenodocheō*, 1 Tim. 5:10, see STRANGER, B. ¶

HOST (of guests)

1. *xenos* [ξένος, 3581], in addition to the meaning stranger, mentioned above under A, denotes one or other of the parties bound by ties of hospitality, (*a*) the guest (not in the N.T.), (*b*) the host, Rom. 16:23. ¶

NT: B.548a; CB.1273b; K.661.
OT: –.
GEN. REF.: IS.2:105; NB.–; Z.3:214.

2. *pandocheus* [πανδοχεύς, 3830], lit., one who receives all (*pas*, all, *dechomai*, to receive), denotes an innkeeper, host, Luke 10:35. ¶

NT: B.607d; CB.–; K.–.
OT: –.
GEN. REF.: IS.–; NB.542; Z.3:214.

HOST (of angels, etc.)

stratia [στρατιά, 4756], an army, is used of angels, Luke 2:13; of stars, Acts 7:42; some mss. have it instead of *strateia*, in 2 Cor. 10:4 ("warfare"). ¶ Cp. *strateuma*, an army.

NT: B.770d; CB.1270a; K.1091.
OT: ṣābā': S.6635; HR.1295c.4; H.1865a,b; BD.838d.
ḥayil: S.2428; HR.1295c.1; H.624a; BD.298c.
GEN. REF.: IS.2:768; NB.543; Z.3:215.

HOT

zestos [ζεστός, 2200], boiling hot (from *zeō*, to boil, be hot, fervent; Eng., zest), is used, metaphorically, in Rev. 3:15, 16. ¶

NT: B.337b; CB.1273b; K.296.
OT: –.
GEN. REF.: –.

HOUR

hōra [ὥρα, 5610], whence Lat., *hora*, Eng., hour, primarily denoted any time or period, especially a season. In the N.T. it is used to denote (*a*) a part of the day, especially a twelfth part of day or night, an hour, e.g., Matt. 8:13; Acts 10:3, 9; 23:23; Rev. 9:15; in 1 Cor. 15:30, "every hour" stands for 'all the time'; in some passages it expresses duration, e.g., Matt. 20:12; 26:40; Luke 22:59; inexactly, in such phrases as "for a season," John 5:35; 2 Cor. 7:8; "for an hour," Gal. 2:5; "for a short season," 1 Thess. 2:17, R.V. (A.V., "for a short time," lit., 'for the time of an hour'); (*b*) a period more or less extended, e.g., 1 John 2:18, "it is the last hour," R.V.; (*c*) a definite point of time, e.g., Matt. 26:45, "the hour is at hand"; Luke 1:10; 10:21; 14:17, lit., 'at the hour of supper'; Acts 16:18; 22:13; Rev. 3:3; 11:13; 14:7; a point of time when an appointed action is to begin, Rev. 14:15; in Rom. 13:11, "it is high time," lit., 'it is already an hour,' indicating that a point of time has come later than would have been the case had responsibility been realised. In 1 Cor. 4:11, it indicates a point of time previous to which certain circumstances have existed.

NT: B.896a; CB.1251a; K.1355.
OT: 'ēt: S.6256; HR.1493b.5; H.1650b; BD.773b.
GEN. REF.: IS.2:769; NB.543; Z.3:217.

Notes: (1) In 1 Cor. 8:7, A.V., "unto this hour," the phrase in the original is simply, "until now," as R.V.

(2) In Rev. 8:1, *hēmiōron*, half an hour (*hēmi*, half, and *hōra*), is used with *hōs*, "about," of a period of silence in Heaven after the opening of the 7th seal, a period corresponding to the time customarily spent in silent worship in the Temple during the burning of incense. ¶

HOUSE

A. Nouns.

1. *oikos* [οἶκος, 3624], denotes (*a*) a house, a dwelling, e.g., Matt. 9:6, 7; 11:8; it is used of the Tabernacle, as the House of God, Matt. 12:4, and the Temple similarly, e.g., Matt. 21:13; Luke 11:51, A.V., "temple," R.V., "sanctuary"; John 2:16, 17; called by the Lord "your house" in Matt. 23:38 and Luke 13:35 (some take this as the city of Jerusalem); metaphorically of Israel as God's house, Heb. 3:2, 5, where "his house" is not Moses', but God's; of believers, similarly, ver. 6, where Christ is spoken of as "over God's House" (the word "own" is rightly omitted in the R.V.); Heb. 10:21; 1 Pet. 2:5; 4:17; of the body, Matt. 12:44; Luke 11:24; (*b*) by metonymy, of the members of a household or family, e.g., Luke 10:5; Acts 7:10; 11:14; 1 Tim. 3:4, 5, 12; 2 Tim. 1:16; 4:19, R.V. (A.V., "household"); Tit. 1:11 (plural); of a local church, 1 Tim. 3:15; of the descendants of Jacob (Israel) and David, e.g., Matt. 10:6; Luke 1:27, 33; Acts 2:36; 7:42. See HOME, A, No. 1, *Note* (1), HOUSEHOLD.

NT: B.560b; CB.1260b; K.674.
OT: bayit: S.1004; HR.973a.5; H.241; BD.108c.
GEN. REF.: IS.2:770; NB.544; Z.3:217.

2. *oikia* [οἰκία, 3614], is akin to No. 1, and used much in the same way; in Attic law *oikos* denoted the whole estate, *oikia* stood for the dwelling only; this distinction was largely lost in later Greek. In the N.T. it denotes (*a*) a house, a dwelling, e.g., Matt. 2:11; 5:15; 7:24-27; 2 Tim. 2:20; 2 John 10; it is not used of the Tabernacle or the Temple, as in the case of No. 1; (*b*) metaphorically, the heavenly abode, spoken of by the Lord as "My Father's house," John 14:2, the eternal dwelling place of believers; the body as the dwelling place of the soul, 2 Cor. 5:1; similarly the resurrection body of believers (*id*); property, e.g., Mark 12:40; by metonymy, the inhabitants of a house, a

household, e.g., Matt. 12:25; John 4:53; 1 Cor. 16:15. See HOUSEHOLD.

NT: B.557b; CB.1260b; K.674.
OT: bayit: S.1004; HR.969b.2; H.241; BD.108c.
GEN. REF.: IS.2:770; NB.544; Z.3:217.

B. Adverb.

panoikei [πανοικεί, 3832], denotes 'with all the house,' Acts 16:34, i.e., the household. ¶

NT: B.607d; CB.–; K.–.
OT: –.
GEN. REF.: –.

Notes: (1) In 2 Cor. 5:2, *oikētērion*, a habitation (see R.V.) is translated "house" in the A.V., of the resurrection body (cp. *oikia* in the preceding verse; see above).

(2) In 1 Tim. 5:13, "from house to house" is, lit., 'the houses.'

(3) For "in every house," Acts 5:42 (cp. 2:46), see HOME.

(4) For "them which are of the house," 1 Cor. 1:11, A.V., see HOUSEHOLD.

For GOODMAN of the HOUSE see HOUSEHOLDER

For MASTER of the HOUSE see HOUSEHOLDER

HOUSEHOLD

A. Nouns.

1. *oikos* [οἶκος, 3624], is translated "household" in Acts 16:15; 1 Cor. 1:16; in the A.V. of 2 Tim. 4:19 (R.V., "house"). See HOUSE, No. 1.

NT: B.560b; CB.1260b; K.674.
OT: bayit: S.1004; HR.973a.5; H.241; BD.108c.
GEN. REF.: IS.2:770; NB.544; Z.–.

2. *oikia* [οἰκία, 3614], is translated "household" in Phil. 4:22. See HOUSE, No. 2.

NT: B.557b; CB.1260b; K.674.
OT: bayit: S.1004; HR.969b.2; H.241; BD.108c.
GEN. REF.: IS.2:770; NB.544; Z.–.

3. *oiketeia* [οἰκετεία, —], denotes a household of servants, Matt. 24:45 (some mss. have No. 4 here). ¶

NT: B.556d; CB.–; K.–.
OT: –.
GEN. REF.: –.

4. *therapeia* [θεραπεία, 2322], service, care, attention, is also used in the collective sense of a household, in Luke 12:42 (see No. 3). See HEALING.

NT: B.358d; CB.1272b; K.331.
OT: –.
GEN. REF.: –.

Notes: (1) In Rom. 16:10, 11, the phrase "those of the household" translates a curtailed phrase in the original, lit., 'the (persons) of (*ek*, consisting of) the (members of the household of).'

(2) In 1 Cor. 1:11, "they which are of the household (A.V., house) of Chloe" is, lit., 'the . . . of Chloe,' the Eng. translation being necessary to express the idiom.

B. Adjectives.

1. *oikeios* [οἰκεῖος, 3609], akin to A, No. 1, primarily signifies of, or belonging to, a house, hence, of persons, one's household, or kindred, as in 1 Tim. 5:8, R.V., "household," A.V. "house," marg., "kindred"; in Eph. 2:19, "the household of God" denotes the company of the redeemed; in Gal. 6:10, it is called "the household of the faith," R.V. In these two cases *oikeios* is used in the same sense as those mentioned under *oikos* (A, No. 1). ¶

NT: B.556d; CB.1260b; K.674.
OT: sh^e'ār: S.7607; HR.968c.5a; H.2308a; BD.984d.
dôd: S.1730; HR.968c.4; H.410a; BD.187c.
GEN. REF.: –.

2. *oikiakos* [οἰκιακός, 3615], from A, No. 2, denotes belonging to one's household, one's own; it is used in Matt. 10:25, 36. ¶

NT: B.557d; CB.–; K.–.
OT: –.
GEN. REF.: –.

HOUSEHOLDER

A. Noun.

oikodespotēs [οἰκοδεσπότης, 3617], a master of a house (*oikos*, a house, *despotēs*, a master), is rendered "master of the house" in Matt. 10:25; Luke 13:25, and 14:21, where the context shows that the authority of the householder is stressed; in Matt. 24:43 and Luke 12:39, the R.V. "master of the house" (A.V., "goodman of the house," does not give the exact meaning); "householder" is the rendering in both Versions in Matt. 13:27, 52; 20:1; 21:33; so the R.V. in 20:11 (for A.V., "goodman of the house"); both have "goodman of the house" in Mark 14:14; in Luke 22:11, "goodman." See GOODMAN. ¶

NT: B.558a; CB.1260b; K.145.
OT: –.
GEN. REF.: IS.2:773; NB.–; Z.3:222.

B. Verb.

oikodespoteō [οἰκοδεσποτέω, 3616], corresponding to A, to rule a house, is used in 1 Tim. 5:14, R.V., "rule the household" (A.V., "guide the house"). ¶

NT: B.558a; CB.1260b; K.145.
OT: –.
GEN. REF.: IS.2:773; NB.–; Z.3:222.

HOUSEHOLD-SERVANT

oiketēs [οἰκέτης, 3610], a house-servant, is translated "household-servants" in Acts 10:7;

elsewhere, "servant" or "servants," Luke 16:13; Rom. 14:4; 1 Pet. 2:18. See SERVANT. ¶

NT: B.557a; CB.1260b; K.—.
OT: 'ebed: S.5650; HR.969a.1; H.1553a; BD.713d.
GEN. REF.: —.

HOUSETOP

dōma [δῶμα, 1430], akin to *demō*, to build, denotes a housetop. The housetop was flat, and guarded by a low parapet wall (see Deut. 22:8). It was much frequented and used for various purposes, e.g., for proclamations, Matt. 10:27; Luke 12:3; for prayer, Acts 10:9. The house was often built round a court, across the top of which cords were fixed from the parapet walls for supporting a covering from the heat. The housetop could be reached by stairs outside the building; the paralytic in Luke 5:19 could be let down into the court or area by rolling back the covering. External flight from the housetop in time of danger is enjoined in Matt. 24:17; Mark 13:15; Luke 17:31. ¶

NT: B.210b; CB.1242a; K.—.
OT: gāg: S.1406; HR.358b.1; H.312; BD.150d.
GEN. REF.: IS.2:771; NB.—; Z.—.

HOW and HOWBEIT, see † p. 1.

For HOW GREAT see GREAT, Nos. 4, 5, 6

HOWL

ololuzō [ὀλολύζω, 3649], an onomatopoeic verb (expressing its significance in its sound), to cry aloud (the Sept. uses it to translate the Heb. *yālal*, e.g., Is. 13:6; 15:3; Jer. 4:8; Ezek. 21:12; Lat., *ululare*, and Eng., howl are akin), was primarily used of crying aloud to the gods; it is found in Jas. 5:1 in an exhortation to the godless rich. ¶

NT: B.564c; CB.—; K.—.
OT: yālal: S.3213; HR.989b.1; H.868; BD.410a.
GEN. REF.: —.

HUMBLE (Adjective and Verb)

A. Adjectives.

1. *tapeinos* [ταπεινός, 5011], primarily signifies low-lying. It is used always in a good sense in the N.T., metaphorically, to denote (*a*) of low degree, brought low, Luke 1:52; Rom. 12:16, A.V., "(men) of low estate," R.V., "(things that are) lowly" (i.e., of low degree); 2 Cor. 7:6, A.V., "cast down," R.V., "lowly"; the preceding context shows that this occurrence belongs to (*a*) ; Jas. 1:9, "of low degree"; (*b*) humble in spirit, Matt. 11:29; 2 Cor. 10:1, R.V., "lowly," A.V. "base"; Jas. 4:6; 1 Pet. 5:5. See BASE, CAST, *Note* (7), DEGREE (Note), LOWLY. ¶

NT: B.804a; CB.1271a; K.1152.
OT: 'ānî: S.6041; HR.1334b.7a; H.1652d; BD.776d.
shāphāl: S.8217; HR.1334b.11a; H.2445c; BD.1050c.
GEN. REF.: IS.2:775; NB.547; Z.—.

2. *tapeinophrōn* [ταπεινόφρων, —], "humble-minded" (*phrēn*, the mind), 1 Pet. 3:8; see COURTEOUS. ¶

NT: B.804c; CB.1271a; K.1152.
OT: shāphāl rûaḥ: S.6041; HR.1335c.1; H.2445c; BD.1050c.
GEN. REF.: IS.2:775; NB.—; Z.—.

B. Verb.

tapeinoō [ταπεινόω, 5013], akin to A, signifies to make low, (*a*) literally, of mountains and hills, Luke 3:5 (Passive Voice); (*b*) metaphorically, in the Active Voice, Matt. 18:4; 23:12 (2nd part); Luke 14:11 (2nd part); 18:14 (2nd part); 2 Cor. 11:7 ("abasing"); 12:21; Phil. 2:8; in the Passive Voice, Matt. 23:12 (1st part), R.V., "shall be humbled," A.V., "shall be abased"; Luke 14:11 (ditto); 18:14 (ditto); Phil. 4:12, "to be abased"; in the Passive, with Middle Voice sense, Jas. 4:10, "humble yourselves"; 1 Pet. 5:6 (ditto). See ABASE, LOW (to bring). ¶

NT: B.804c; CB.1271a; K.1152.
OT: 'ānāh: S.6031; HR.1334c.14a-c; H.1651,1652; BD.776a.
shāphēl: S.8213; HR.1335a.20a,b; H.2445; BD.1050a.
GEN. REF.: IS.2:775; NB.547; Z.—.

HUMBLENESS OF MIND, HUMILITY

tapeinophrosunē [ταπεινοφροσύνη, 5012], lowliness of mind (*tapeinos*, see A, above, under HUMBLE, and *phrēn*, the mind), is rendered "humility of mind" in Acts 20:19, A.V. (R.V., "lowliness of mind"); in Eph. 4:2, "lowliness"; in Phil. 2:3, "lowliness of mind"; in Col. 2:18, 23, of a false humility; in Col. 3:12, A.V., "humbleness of mind," R.V., "humility"; 1 Pet. 5:5, "humility." See LOWLINESS. ¶

NT: B.804c; CB.1271a; K.1152.
OT: —.
GEN. REF.: IS.2:775; NB.—; Z.3:223.

HUMILIATION

tapeinōsis [ταπείνωσις, 5014], akin to *tapeinos* (see above), is rendered "low estate" in Luke 1:48; "humiliation," Acts 8:33; Phil. 3:21, R.V. "(the body of our) humiliation," A.V., "(our) vile (body)"; Jas. 1:10, where "in that he is made low," is, lit., 'in his humiliation.' See ESTATE, LOW. ¶

NT: B.805a; CB.1271a; K.1152.
OT: 'ᵃnî: S.6040; HR.1335c.2a; H.1652e; BD.777a.
GEN. REF.: IS.2:775; NB.547; Z.—.

HUNDRED, HUNDREDFOLD

1. *hekaton* [ἑκατόν, 1540], an indeclinable numeral, denotes a hundred, e.g., Matt. 18;12, 28; it also signifies a hundredfold, Matt. 13:8, 23, and the R.V. in the corresponding passage, Mark 4:8, 20 (for A.V., "hundred"), signifying the complete productiveness of sown seed. In the passage in Mark the phrase is, lit., 'in thirty and in sixty and in a hundred.' In Mark 6:40 it is used with the preposition *kata*, in the phrase "by hundreds." It is followed by other numerals in John 21:11; Acts 1:15; Rev. 7:4; 14:1, 3; 21:17.

NT: B.236c; CB.–; K.–.
OT: –.
GEN. REF.: –.

2. *hekatontaplasiōn* [ἑκατονταπλασίων, 1542], an adjective, denotes a hundredfold, Mark 10:30; Luke 8:8; the best mss. have it in Matt. 19:29 for *pollaplasiōn*, many times more. See the R.V. margin. ¶

NT: B.237a; CB.–; K.–.
OT: mēʾāh pᵉʿāmîm: S.3967; HR.420b.1; H.1135; BD.547c,548b.
GEN. REF.: –.

For multiples of a hundred, see under the numerals TWO, THREE, etc. For "a hundred years," see YEARS.

HUNGER (Noun and Verb), HUNGERED, HUNGRY

A. Noun.

limos [λιμός, 3042], has the meanings famine and hunger; hunger in Luke 15:17; 2 Cor. 11:27; in Rev. 6:8, R.V. "famine" (A.V., "hunger"). See FAMINE.

NT: B.475a; CB.1257a; K.820.
OT: rāʿāb: S.7458; HR.878c.2a; H.2183a; BD.944b.
GEN. REF.: IS.2:781; NB.–; Z.3:226.

B. Verb.

peinaō [πεινάω, 3983], to hunger, be hungry, hungered, is used (*a*) literally, e.g., Matt. 4:2; 12:1; 21:18; Rom. 12:20; 1 Cor. 11:21, 34; Phil. 4:12; Rev. 7:16; Christ identifies Himself with His saints in speaking of Himself as suffering in their sufferings in this and other respects, Matt. 25:35, 42; (*b*) metaphorically, Matt. 5:6; Luke 6:21, 25; John 6:35.

NT: B.640a; CB.1263a; K.820.
OT: rāʿēb: S.7456; HR.1115b.4; H.2183; BD.944b.
GEN. REF.: IS.2:781; NB.–; Z.3:226.

C. Adjective.

prospeinos [πρόσπεινος, 4361], signifies hungry (*pros*, intensive, *peina*, hunger), Acts 10:10, A.V., "very hungry," R.V., "hungry." ¶

NT: B.718a; CB.–; K.–.
OT: –.
GEN. REF.: IS.2:781; NB.–; Z.–.

HURT (Noun and Verb), HURTFUL

A. Noun.

hubris [ὕβρις, 5196], is rendered "hurt" in Acts 27:10, A.V. only. See HARM.

NT: B.832a; CB.1251b; K.–.
OT: –.
GEN. REF.: –.

B. Verbs.

1. *adikeō* [ἀδικέω, 91], signifies, intransitively, to do wrong, do hurt, act unjustly (*a*, negative, and *dikē*, justice), transitively, to wrong, hurt or injure a person. It is translated to hurt in the following: (*a*), intransitively, Rev. 9:19; (*b*) transitively, Luke 10:19; Rev. 2:11 (Passive); 6:6; 7:2, 3; 9:4, 10; 11:5. See INJURE, OFFENDER, UNJUST, UNRIGHTEOUSNESS, WRONG, WRONG-DOER.

NT: B.17c; CB.1233a; K.22.
OT: ʿāwāh: S.5753; HR.24c.11c; H.1577; BD.730c,731c.
āshaq: S.6231; HR.24c.15a; H.1713; BD.798d.
GEN. REF.: IS.2:786; NB.–; Z.–.

2. *blaptō* [βλάπτω, 984], signifies to injure, mar, do damage to, Mark 16:18, "shall (in no wise) hurt (them)"; Luke 4:35, "having done (him no) hurt," R.V. *Adikeō* stresses the unrighteousness of the act, *blaptō* stresses the injury done. ¶

NT: B.142b; CB.1239a; K.–.
OT: –.
GEN. REF.: –.

3. *kakoō* [κακόω, 2559], to do evil to anyone: see HARM.

NT: B.398b; CB.1253b; K.391.
OT: ʿānāh: S.6031; HR.711b.5c; H.1651,1652; BD.776a.
rāʿa: S.7489; HR.711b.7a,b; H.2191,2192; BD.949b.
GEN. REF.: IS.2:786; NB.–; Z.–.

C. Adjective.

blaberos [βλαβερός, 983], akin to B, No. 2, signifies hurtful, 1 Tim. 6:9, said of lusts. ¶ In the Sept., Prov. 10:26. ¶

NT: B.142b; CB.–; K.–.
OT: –.
GEN. REF.: –.

HUSBAND

A. Noun.

anēr [ἀνήρ, 435], denotes, in general, a man, an adult male (in contrast to *anthrōpos*, which generically denotes a human being, male or female); it is used of man in various relations, the context deciding the meaning; it signifies a husband, e.g., Matt. 1:16, 19; Mark 10:12; Luke 2:36; 16:18; John 4:16, 17, 18; Rom. 7:23. See MAN.

NT: B.66c; CB.1235c; K.59.
OT: ʾîsh: S.376; HR.88a.2; H.83a; BD.35d.
ʾᵉnôsh: S.582; HR.88a.3a; H.136a; BD.60d.
baʿal: S.1166; HR.88a.5a; H.262; BD.127b.
GEN. REF.: IS.4:76; NB.786; Z.3:229.

B. Adjectives.

1. *philandros* [φίλανδρος, 5362], primarily, loving man, signifies 'loving a husband,' Tit. 2:4, in instruction to young wives to love their husbands, lit., '(to be) lovers of their husbands.' ¶ The word occurs frequently in epitaphs.

NT: B.858c; CB.1264a; K.—.
OT: —.
GEN. REF.: —.

2. *hupandros* [ὕπανδρος, 5220], lit., 'under (i.e. subject to) a man,' married, and therefore, according to Roman law under the legal authority of the husband, occurs in Rom. 7:2, "that hath a husband." ¶

NT: B.837c; CB.—; K.—.
OT: taḥat 'îsh: S.376; HR.1406b.1; H.83a; BD.35d,1065c.
GEN. REF.: IS.4:76; NB.—; Z.—.

HUSBANDMAN

geōrgos [γεωργός, 1092], from *gē*, land, ground, and ergō (or *erdō*), to do (Eng., George), denotes (*a*) a husbandman, a tiller of the ground, 2 Tim. 2:6; Jas. 5:7; (*b*) a vinedresser, Matt. 21:33-35, 38, 40, 41; Mark 12:1, 2, 7, 9; Luke 20:9, 10, 14, 16; John 15:1, where Christ speaks of the Father as the Husbandman, Himself as the Vine, His disciples as the branches, the object being to bear much fruit, life in Christ producing the fruit of the Spirit, i.e., character and ways in conformity to Christ. ¶

NT: B.157b; CB.—; K.—.
OT: 'ikkār: S.406; HR.240b.3; H.88a; BD.38d.
GEN. REF.: IS.2:786; NB.548; Z.3:230.

HUSBANDRY

geōrgion [γεώργιον, 1091], akin to the above, denotes tillage, cultivation, husbandry, 1 Cor. 3:9, where the local church is described under this metaphor (A.V., marg., "tillage," R.V., marg., "tilled land"), suggestive of the diligent toil of the Apostle and his fellow-missionaries, both in the ministry of the gospel, and the care of the church at Corinth; suggestive, too, of the effects in spiritual fruitfulness. ¶ Cp. *geōrgeomai*, to till the ground, Heb. 6:7. ¶

NT: B.157b; CB.—; K.—.
OT: ʿᵃbuddāh: S.5657; HR.240b.1; H.1553d; BD.715c.
sādeh: S.7704; HR.240b.3; H.2234a,b; BD.961b.
GEN. REF.: IS.2:786; NB.—; Z.3:230.

HUSKS

keration [κεράτιον, 2769], a little horn (a diminutive of *keras*, a horn; see HORN), is used in the plural in Luke 15:16, of carob-pods, given to swine, and translated "husks."

NT: B.429b; CB.—; K.—.
OT: —.
GEN. REF.: IS.3:891; NB.548; Z.3:232.

HYMN (Noun and Verb)

A. Noun.

humnos [ὕμνος, 5215], denotes a song of praise addressed to God (Eng., hymn), Eph. 5:19; Col. 3:16, in each of which the punctuation should probably be changed; in the former "speaking to one another" goes with the end of ver. 18, and should be followed by a semi-colon; similarly in Col. 3:16, the first part of the verse should end with the words "admonishing one another," where a semi-colon should be placed. ¶

NT: B.836b; CB.1251c; K.1225.
OT: —.
GEN. REF.: IS.2:788; NB.549; Z.—.

Note: The *psalmos* denoted that which had a musical accompaniment; the *ōdē* (Eng., ode) was the generic term for a song; hence the accompanying adjective "spiritual."

B. Verb.

humneō [ὑμνέω, 5214], akin to A, is used (*a*) transitively, Matt. 26:30; Mark 14:26, where the hymn was that part of the Hallel consisting of Psalms 113-118; (*b*) intransitively, where the verb itself is rendered to sing praises or praise, Acts 16:25; Heb. 2:12. The Psalms are called in general, "hymns," by Philo; Josephus calls them "songs and hymns." ¶

NT: B.836b; CB.1251c; K.1225.
OT: hālal: S.1984; HR.1405a.1; H.499,500; BD.237d.
shîr: S.7891; HR.1405a.6; H.2378; BD.1010c.
GEN. REF.: IS.2:788; NB.549; Z.—.

HYPOCRISY

hupokrisis [ὑπόκρισις, 5272], primarily denotes a reply, an answer (akin to *hupokrinomai*, to answer); then, play-acting, as the actors spoke in dialogue; hence, pretence, hypocrisy; it is translated "hypocrisy" in Matt. 23:28; Mark 12:15; Luke 12:1; 1 Tim. 4:2; the plural in 1 Pet. 2:1. For Gal. 2:13 and *anupokritos*, "without hypocrisy," in Jas. 3:17, see DISSIMULATION. ¶

NT: B.845a; CB.1252b; K.1235.
OT: —.
GEN. REF.: IS.2:790; NB.549; Z.3:234.

HYPOCRITE

hupokritēs [ὑποκριτής, 5273], corresponding to the above, primarily denotes one who answers; then, a stage-actor; it was a custom for Greek and Roman actors to speak in large masks with mechanical devices for augmenting the force of the voice; hence the word became used metaphorically of a dissembler, a hypocrite. It is found only in the Synoptists, and always used

by the Lord, fifteen times in Matthew; elsewhere, Mark 7:6; Luke 6:42; 11:44 (in some mss.); 12:56; 13:15.
NT: B.845b; CB.1252b; K.1235.
OT: ḥānēph: S.2611; HR.1414c.1; H.696b; BD.338a.
GEN. REF.: IS.2:790; NB.549; Z.3:234.

HYSSOP

hussōpos [ὕσσωπος, 5301], a bunch of which was used in ritual sprinklings, is found in Heb. 9:19; in John 19:29 the reference is apparently to a branch or rod of hyssop, upon which a sponge was put and offered to the Lord on the Cross. The suggestion has been made that the word in the original may have been *hussos*, a javelin; there seems to be no valid reason for the supposition. ¶
NT: B.849a; CB.—; K.—.
OT: 'ēzôb: S.231; HR.1418b.1; H.55; BD.23c.
GEN. REF.: IS.2:790; NB.1004; Z.3:235.

I

I

egō [ἐγώ, 1473], is the nominative case of the first personal pronoun. The pronoun, "I," however, generally forms a part of the verb itself in Greek; thus *luō* itself means "I loose," the pronoun being incorporated in the verb form. Where the pronoun *egō* is added to the verb, it is almost invariably, if not entirely, emphatic. The emphasis may not be so apparent in some instances, as e.g., Matt. 10:16, but even here it may be taken that something more of stress is present than if the pronoun were omitted. By far the greater number of instances are found in the Gospel of John, and there in the utterances of the Lord concerning Himself, e.g., 4:14, 26, 32, 38; 5:34, 36, 43, 45; 6:35, 40, 41, 48, 51 (twice), 63, 70; instances in the Epistles are Rom. 7:9, 14, 17, 20 (twice), 24, 25; there are more in that chapter than in any other outside the Gospel of John.

In other cases of the pronoun than the nominative, the pronoun is usually more necessary to the meaning, apart from any stress.

For *k'agō* (i.e., *kai egō*), see EVEN, *Note* (6).
NT: B.217a; CB.1242c; K.196.
OT: 'ᵃnî: S.589; HR.367c.1a; H.129; BD.58d.
'ānôkî: S.595; HR.367c.1b; H.130; BD.59a.
GEN. REF.: —.

IDLE

argos [ἀργός, 692], denotes inactive, idle, unfruitful, barren (*a*, negative, and *ergon*, work; cp. the verb *katargeō*, to reduce to inactivity: see ABOLISH); it is used (*a*) literally, Matt. 20:3, 6; 1 Tim. 5:13 (twice); Tit. 1:12, R.V., "idle (gluttons)"; 2 Pet. 1:8, R.V., "idle," A.V., "barren"; (*b*) metaphorically in the sense of ineffective, worthless, as of a word, Matt. 12:36; of faith unaccompanied by works, Jas. 2:20 (some mss. have *nekra*, dead). ¶
NT: B.104c; CB.1237c; K.76.
OT: —.
GEN. REF.: IS.2:793; NB.—; Z.3:241.

For **IDLE TALES** (Luke 24:11, R.V., "idle talk") see **TALK**

IDOL

eidōlon [εἴδωλον, 1497], primarily a phantom or likeness (from *eidos*, an appearance, lit., that which is seen), or an idea, fancy, denotes in the N.T. (*a*) an idol, an image to represent a false god, Acts 7:41; 1 Cor. 12:2; Rev. 9:20; (*b*) the false god worshipped in an image, Acts 15:20; Rom. 2:22; 1 Cor. 8:4, 7; 10:19; 2 Cor. 6:16; 1 Thess. 1:9; 1 John 5:21. ¶
NT: B.221c; CB.1243a; K.202.
OT: 'ᵉlôah: S.433; HR.376a.2a; H.93b; BD.43a.
gillûlîm: S.1544; HR.376a.6; H.353h; BD.165c.
'āṣāb: S.6091; HR.376a.10b; H.1667c; BD.781b.
GEN. REF.: IS.2:794; NB.551; Z.3:242.

IDOLS (full of)

kateidōlos [κατείδωλος, 2712], an adjective denoting "full of idols" (*kata*, throughout, and *eidōlon*), is said of Athens in Acts 17:16, R.V., and A.V., marg. (A.V., "wholly given to idolatry"). ¶
NT: B.421a; CB.1254b; K.202.
OT: —.
GEN. REF.: IS.2:794; NB.—; Z.—.

IDOLS (offered to, sacrificed to)

1. *eidōlothutos* [εἰδωλόθυτος, 1494], is an adjective signifying sacrificed to idols (*eidōlon*, as above, and *thuō*, to sacrifice), Acts 15:29; 21:25; 1 Cor. 8:1, 4, 7, 10; 10:19 (in all these the R.V. substitutes "sacrificed" for the A.V.); Rev. 2:14, 20 (in these the R.V. and A.V. both

have "sacrificed"). Some inferior mss. have this adjective in 1 Cor. 10:28; see No. 2. The flesh of the victims, after sacrifice, was eaten or sold. ¶
NT: B.221b; CB.1243a; K.202.
OT: —.
GEN. REF.: IS.—; NB.554; Z.—.

2. *hierothutos* [ἱερόθυτος, —], "offered in sacrifice" (*hieros*, sacred, and *thuō*, to sacrifice), is found in the best mss. in 1 Cor. 10:28 (see No. 1). ¶
NT: B.372b; CB.1250c; K.349.
OT: —.
GEN. REF.: —.

IDOL'S TEMPLE

eidōlion (or *eidōleion*) [εἰδώλιον, 1493], an idol's temple, is mentioned in 1 Cor. 8:10; feasting in the temple usually followed the sacrifice. ¶
NT: B.221b; CB.1243a; K.202.
OT: —.
GEN. REF.: IS.2:794; NB.—; Z.—.

IDOLATER

eidōlolatrēs [εἰδωλολάτρης, 1496], an idolater (from *eidōlon*, and *latris*, a hireling), is found in 1 Cor. 5:10, 11; 6:9; 10:7; the warning is to believers against turning away from God to idolatry, whether "openly or secretly, consciously or unconsciously" (Cremer); Eph. 5:5; Rev. 21:8; 22:15. ¶
NT: B.221c; CB.1243a; K.202.
OT: —.
GEN. REF.: IS.2:794; NB.—; Z.—.

IDOLATRY

eidōlolatria (or *-eia*) [εἰδωλολατρία, 1495], whence Eng., idolatry, (from *eidōlon*, and *latreia*, service), is found in 1 Cor. 10:14; Gal. 5:20; Col. 3:5; and, in the plural, in 1 Pet. 4:3. ¶

Heathen sacrifices were sacrificed to demons, 1 Cor. 10:19; there was a dire reality in the cup and table of demons and in the involved communion with demons. In Rom. 1:22-25, idolatry, the sin of the mind against God (Eph. 2:3), and immorality, sins of the flesh, are associated, and are traced to lack of the acknowledgement of God and of gratitude to Him. An idolater is a slave to the depraved ideas his idols represent, Gal. 4:8, 9; and thereby, to divers lusts, Tit. 3:3 (see Notes on Thess. by Hogg and Vine, p. 44).
NT: B.221c; CB.1243a; K.202.
OT: —.
GEN. REF.: IS.2:794; NB.551; Z.3:245.

For **IDOLATRY (wholly given to)** see **IDOLS (full of)**

IF: See † p. 1.

IGNORANCE, IGNORANT, IGNORANTLY

A. Nouns.

1. *agnoia* [ἄγνοια, 52], lit., want of knowledge or perception (akin to *agnoeō*, to be ignorant), denotes ignorance on the part of the Jews regarding Christ, Acts 3:17; of Gentiles in regard to God, 17:30; Eph. 4:18 (here including the idea of wilful blindness: see Rom. 1:28, not the ignorance which mitigates guilt); 1 Pet. 1:14, of the former unregenerate condition of those who became believers (R.V., " in *the time of* your ignorance"). The semantic range of this term denotes a lack of knowledge morally based. ¶
NT: B.11c; CB.1233b; K.18.
OT: 'āshām: S.817; HR.16a.1; H.180b; BD.79d.
'ash^{e}māh: S.819; HR.16a.2; H.180c; BD.80a.
sh^{e}gāgāh: S.7684; HR.16a.5; H.2324a; BD.993a.
GEN. REF.: IS.2:801; NB.555; Z.3:251.

2. *agnōsia* [ἀγνωσία, 56], denotes ignorance as directly opposed to *gnōsis*, which signifies knowledge as a result of observation and experience (*a*, negative, *ginōskō*, to know; cp. Eng., agnostic); 1 Cor. 15:34 ("no knowledge"); 1 Pet. 2:15. In both these passages reprehensible ignorance is suggested. See KNOWLEDGE. ¶
NT: B.12d; CB.1233c; K.18.
OT: b^{e}lî (-da'at): S.1097; HR.16b.1; H.246e; BD.115c.
GEN. REF.: IS.2:801; NB.555; Z.3:251.

3. *agnoēma* [ἀγνόημα, 51], a sin of ignorance, occurs in Heb. 9:7, "errors" (R.V. marg., "ignorances"). ¶ For the corresponding verb in Heb. 5:2 see B, No. 1. What is especially in view in these passages is unwitting error. For Israel a sacrifice was appointed, greater in proportion to the culpability of the guilty, greater, for instance, for a priest or ruler than for a private person. Sins of ignorance, being sins, must be expiated. A believer guilty of a sin of ignorance needs the efficacy of the expiatory sacrifice of Christ, and finds "grace to help." Yet, as the conscience of the believer receives enlightenment, what formerly may have been done in ignorance becomes a sin against the light and demands a special confession, to receive forgiveness, 1 John 1:8, 9. ¶
NT: B.11c; CB.1233b; K.18.
OT: mishgeh: S.4870; HR.16a.1; H.2325b; BD.993b.
GEN. REF.: IS.—; NB.555; Z.3:251.

4. *idiōtēs* [ἰδιώτης, 2399], primarily a private person in contrast to a State official, hence, a person without professional knowledge, unskilled, uneducated, unlearned, is translated "unlearned" in 1 Cor. 14:16, 23, 24, of those who have no knowledge of the facts relating to the testimony borne in and by a local church;

"rude" in 2 Cor. 11:6, of the Apostle's mode of speech in the estimation of the Corinthians; "ignorant men," in Acts 4:13, of the speech of the Apostle Peter and John in the estimation of the rulers, elders and scribes in Jerusalem.

While *agrammatoi* ("unlearned") may refer to their being unacquainted with Rabbinical learning, *idiōtai* would signify 'laymen,' in contrast with the religious officials. See RUDE, UNLEARNED. ¶

NT: B.370c; CB.1252c; K.348.
OT: –.
GEN. REF.: –; NB.555; Z.–.

B. Verbs.

1. *agnoeō* [ἀγνοέω, 50], signifies (*a*) to be ignorant, not to know, either intransitively, 1 Cor. 14:38 (in the 2nd occurrence in this verse, the R.V. text translates the Active Voice, the margin the Passive); 1 Tim. 1:13, lit., 'being ignorant (I did it)'; Heb. 5:2, "ignorant"; or transitively, 2 Pet. 2:12, A.V., "understand not," R.V., "are ignorant (of)"; Acts 13:27, "knew (Him) not"; 17:23, R.V., "(what ye worship) in ignorance," for A.V., "(whom ye) ignorantly (worship)," lit., '(what) not knowing (ye worship)'; also rendered by the verb to be ignorant that, or to be ignorant of, Rom. 1:13; 10:3; 11:25; 1 Cor. 10:1; 12:1; 2 Cor. 1:8; 2:11; 1 Thess 4:13; to know not, Rom. 2:4; 6:3; 7:1; to be unknown (Passive Voice), 2 Cor. 6:9; Gal. 1:22; (*b*) not to understand, Mark 9:32; Luke 9:45. See KNOW, UNDERSTAND. ¶

NT: B.11b; CB.1233b; K.18.
OT: shāgāh: S.7686; HR.16a.6; H.2325; BD.993b.
shāgag: S.7683; HR.16a.5; H.2324; BD.992d.
'āsham: S.817; HR.16a.1; H.180b; BD.79d.
GEN. REF.: IS.2:801; NB.555; Z.3:251.

2. *lanthanō* [λανθάνω]; for 2 Pet. 3:5, 8, A.V., see FORGET.

Note: For adjectives see UNLEARNED.

ILL

kakos [κακός, 2556], bad, is used in the neuter as a noun in Rom. 13:10, and translated "ill." See BAD.

NT: B.397d; CB.1253b; K.391.
OT: ra': S.7451; HR.709b.13b; H.2191; BD.948a.
rā'āh: S.7451; HR.709b.13c; H.2191; BD.949a.
GEN. REF.: –.

Note: For *phaulos*, John 5:29, R.V., see EVIL, A, No. 3.

For **ILLUMINATED** (Heb. 10:32) see **ENLIGHTEN**

IMAGE

1. *eikōn* [εἰκών, 1504], denotes an image; the word involves the two ideas of representation and manifestation. "The idea of perfection does not lie in the word itself, but must be sought from the context" (Lightfoot); the following instances clearly show any distinction between the imperfect and the perfect likeness.

The word is used (1) of an image or a coin (not a mere likeness), Matt. 22:20; Mark 12:16; Luke 20:24; so of a statue or similar representation (more than a resemblance), Rom. 1:23; Rev. 13:14, 15 (thrice); 14:9, 11; 15:2; 16:2; 19:20; 20:4; of the descendants of Adam as bearing his image, 1 Cor. 15:49, each a representation derived from the prototype; (2) of subjects relative to things spiritual, Heb. 10:1, negatively of the Law as having "a shadow of the good things to come, not the very image of the things," i.e., not the essential and substantial form of them; the contrast has been likened to the difference between a statue and the shadow cast by it; (3) of the relations between God the Father, Christ, and man, (*a*) of man as he was created as being a visible representation of God, 1 Cor. 11:7, a being corresponding to the Original; the condition of man as a fallen creature has not entirely effaced the image; he is still suitable to bear responsibility, he still has Godlike qualities, such as love of goodness and beauty, none of which are found in a mere animal; in the Fall man ceased to be a perfect vehicle for the representation of God; God's grace in Christ will yet accomplish more than what Adam lost; (*b*) of regenerate persons, in being moral representations of what God is, Col. 3:10; cp. Eph. 4:24; (*c*) of believers, in their glorified state, not merely as resembling Christ but representing Him, Rom. 8:29; 1 Cor. 15:49; here the perfection is the work of Divine grace; believers are yet to represent, not something like Him, but what He is in Himself, both in His spiritual body and in His moral character; (*d*) of Christ in relation to God, 2 Cor. 4:4, "the image of God," i.e., essentially and absolutely the perfect expression and representation of the Archetype, God the Father; in Col. 1:15, "the image of the invisible God" gives the additional thought suggested by the word "invisible," that Christ is the visible representation and manifestation of God to created beings; the likeness expressed in this manifestation is involved in the essential relations in the Godhead, and is therefore unique and perfect; "he that hath seen Me hath seen the Father," John 14:9. "The epithet 'invisible' . . . must not be confined to the apprehension of the bodily senses, but will include the cognisance of the inward eye also" (Lightfoot). ¶

As to synonymous words, *homoiōma*, likeness, stresses the resemblance to an archetype, though the resemblance may not be derived, whereas *eikōn* is a derived likeness (see LIKENESS); *eidos*, a shape, form, is an appearance, "not necessarily based on reality" (see FORM); *skia*, is "a shadowed resemblance" (see SHADOW); *morphē* is "the form, as indicative of the inner being" (Abbott-Smith); See FORM. For *charaktēr*, see No. 2.

NT: B.222b; CB.1243a; K.203.
OT: ṣelem: S.6754; HR.377b.4a; H.1923a; BD.853d.
s^elēm (Aramaic): S.6755; HR.377b.4b; H.2961; BD.1109d.
GEN. REF.: IS.2:803; NB.556; Z.3:242.

2. *charaktēr* [χαρακτήρ, 5481], denotes, firstly, a tool for graving (from *charassō*, to cut into, to engross; cp. Eng., character, characteristic); then, a stamp or impress, as on a coin or a seal, in which case the seal or die which makes an impression bears the image produced by it, and, *vice versa*, all the features of the image correspond respectively with those of the instrument producing it. In the N.T. it is used metaphorically in Heb. 1:3, of the Son of God as "the very image (marg., 'the impress') of His substance," R.V. The phrase expresses the fact that the Son "is both personally distinct from, and yet literally equal to, Him of whose essence He is the adequate imprint" (Liddon). The Son of God is not merely his image (His *charaktēr*), He is the image or impress of His substance, or essence. It is the fact of complete similarity which this word stresses in comparison with those mentioned at the end of No. 1. ¶ In the Sept., Lev. 13:28, 'the mark (of the inflammation).' ¶

"In John 1:1-3, Col. 1:15-17, and Heb. 1:2, 3, the special function of creating and upholding the universe is ascribed to Christ under His titles of Word, Image, and Son, respectively. The kind of Creatorship so predicated of Him is not that of a mere instrument or artificer in the formation of the world, but that of One 'by whom, in whom, and for whom' all things are made, and through whom they subsist. This implies the assertion of His true and absolute Godhood" (Laidlaw, in Hastings' Bib. Dic.).

NT: B.876a; CB.1239c; K.1308.
OT: sārebet: S.6867; HR.1454c.1; H.1966b; BD.863a.
GEN. REF.: —.

Note: The similar word *charagma*, a mark (see GRAVEN and MARK), has the narrower meaning of the thing impressed, without denoting the special characteristic of that which produces it, e.g., Rev. 13:16, 17. In Acts 17:29 the meaning is not "graven (*charagma*) by art," but 'an engraved work of art.'

IMAGINATION

1. *logismos* [λογισμός, 3053], a reasoning, a thought (akin to *logizomai*, to count, reckon), is translated "thoughts" in Rom. 2:15, suggestive of evil intent, not of mere reasonings; "imaginations" in 2 Cor. 10:5 (R.V., marg., "reasonings," in each place). The word suggests the contemplation of actions as a result of the verdict of conscience. See THOUGHT. ¶

NT: B.476d; CB.1257a; K.536.
OT: maḥ^ashābāh: S.4284; HR.881a.1a; H.767d; BD.364b.
GEN. REF.: IS.—; NB.—; Z.3:256.

2. *dialogismos* [διαλογισμός, 1261], *dia*, and No. 1, is rendered "imaginations" in Rom. 1:21, carrying with it the idea of evil purposes, R.V., "reasonings"; it is most frequently translated "thoughts." See DISPUTE.

NT: B.186a; CB.1241b; K.155.
OT: maḥ^ashābāh: S.4284; HR.305a.2; H.767d; BD.364b.
rayōn (Aramaic): S.7476; HR.305a.4b; H.2998b; BD.1113b.
GEN. REF.: IS.—; NB.—; Z.3:256.

3. *dianoia* [διάνοια, 1271], strictly, a thinking over, denotes the faculty of thinking; then, of knowing; hence, the understanding, and in general, the mind, and so, the faculty of moral reflection; it is rendered "imagination" in Luke 1:51, "the imagination of their heart" signifying their thoughts and ideas. See MIND, UNDERSTANDING.

NT: B.187a; CB.1241a; K.636.
OT: lēb: S.3820; HR.306c.3a; H.1071a; BD.524b.
lēbāb: S.3824; HR.306c.3b; H.1071a; BD.523a.
GEN. REF.: —.

IMAGINE

meletaō [μελετάω, 3191], signifies to care for (*meletē*, care); then, to attend to, "be diligent in," 1 Tim. 4:15, R.V., i.e., to practise as the result of devising or planning; thirdly, to ponder, "imagine," Acts 4:25, R.V., marg., "meditate." Some inferior mss. have it in Mark 13:11. See DILIGENT, MEDITATE. ¶

NT: B.500b; CB.—; K.—.
OT: hāgāh: S.1897; HR.908b.3; H.467; BD.211c.
GEN. REF.: IS.2:806; NB.—; Z.3:256.

IMITATE, IMITATOR

A. Verb.

mimeomai [μιμέομαι, 3401], a mimic, an actor (Eng., mime, etc.), is always translated to imitate in the R.V., for A.V., to follow, (*a*) of imitating the conduct of missionaries, 2 Thess. 3:7, 9; the faith of spiritual guides, Heb. 13:7; (*b*) that which is good, 3 John 11. The verb is always used in exhortations, and always in the continuous tense, suggesting a constant habit or practice. See FOLLOW.

NT: B.521d; CB.1259a; K.594.
OT: —.
GEN. REF.: IS.2:806; NB.—; Z.—.

B. Nouns.

1. *mimētēs* [μιμητής, 3402], akin to A, an imitator, so the R.V. for A.V., "follower," is always used in a good sense in the N.T. In 1 Cor. 4:16; 11:1; Eph. 5:1; Heb. 6:12, it is used in exhortations, accompanied by the verb *ginomai*, to be, become, and in the continuous tense (see A) except in Heb. 6:12, where the aorist or momentary tense indicates a decisive act with permanent results; in 1 Thess. 1:6; 2:14, the accompanying verb is in the aorist tense, referring to the definite act of conversion in the past. These instances, coupled with the continuous tenses referred to, teach that what we became at conversion we must diligently continue to be thereafter. See FOLLOW, *Note* (4). ¶

NT: B.522a; CB.1259a; K.594.
OT: –.
GEN. REF.: –.

2. *summimētēs* [συμμιμητής, 4831], denotes a fellow-imitator (*sun*, with, and No. 1), Phil. 3:17, R.V., "imitators together" (A.V., "followers together"). See FOLLOW, *Note* (4). ¶

NT: B.778c; CB.1270b; K.594.
OT: –.
GEN. REF.: –.

IMMEDIATELY

1. *parachrēma* [παραχρῆμα, 3916], lit., with the matter (or business) itself (*para*, with *chrēma*, a business, or event), and so, immediately, Matt. 21:19 (A.V., "presently"), 20; Luke 1:64; 4:39; 5:25; 8:44, 47, 55; 13:13; 18:43; 19:11; 22:60; Acts 3:7; 5:10; 12:23; 13:11; 16:26, 33; it is thus used by Luke only, save for the two instances in Matthew. See FORTHWITH. It is also rendered "presently," "soon," "straightway." ¶

NT: B.623d; CB.–; K.–.
OT: pit'ōm: S.6597; HR.1065c.1; H.1859a; BD.837b.
GEN. REF.: –.

2. *euthus* [εὐθύς]: see FORTHWITH.

3. *eutheōs* [εὐθέως]: ditto.

4. *exautēs* [ἐξαυτῆς]: ditto.

IMMORTAL, IMMORTALITY

athanasia [ἀθανασία, 110], lit., deathlessness (*a*, negative, *thanatos*, death), is rendered "immortality" in 1 Cor. 15:53, 54, of the glorified body of the believer; 1 Tim. 6:16, of the nature of God. Moulton and Milligan (Vocab.) show that in early times the word had the wide connotation of freedom from death; they also quote Ramsey (*Luke the Physician*, p. 273), with reference to the use of the word in sepulchral epitaphs. In a papyrus writing of the sixth century, "a petitioner says that he will send up 'unceasing (*athanatous*)' hymns to the Lord Christ for the life of the man with whom he is pleading." In the N.T., however, *athanasia* expresses more than deathlessness, it suggests the quality of the life enjoyed, as is clear from 2 Cor. 5:4; for the believer what is mortal is to be "swallowed up of life." ¶

NT: B.20c; CB.1238a; K.312.
OT: –.
GEN. REF.: IS.2:809; NB.–; Z.3:262.

Note: The adjective *aphthartos*, translated "immortal" in 1 Tim. 1:17, A.V., does not bear that significance, it means 'incorruptible.' So with the noun *aphtharsia*, incorruption, translated "immortality," in the A.V. of Rom. 2:7 and 2 Tim. 1:10. See CORRUPT, B, No. 3, and C, No. 2.

IMMUTABLE, IMMUTABILITY

ametathetos [ἀμετάθετος, 276], an adjective signifying immutable (*a*, negative, *metatithēmi*, to change), Heb. 6:18, where the "two immutable things" are the promise and the oath. In ver. 17 the word is used in the neuter with the article, as a noun, denoting "the immutability," with reference to God's counsel. Examples from the papyri show that the word was used as a technical term in connection with wills, "The connotation adds considerably to the force of Heb. 6:17 (and foll.)" (Moulton and Milligan). ¶

NT: B.45b; CB.1234c; K.–.
OT: –.
GEN. REF.: IS.–; NB.–; Z.3:264.

IMPART

1. *prosanatithēmi* [προσανατίθημι, 4323], is used in the Middle Voice in the N.T., in Gal. 1:16, "conferred," or 'had recourse to,' and 2:6, R.V., "imparted." See CONFER. ¶

NT: B.711d; CB.–; K.57.
OT: –.
GEN. REF.: –.

2. *metadidōmi* [μεταδίδωμι]: see GIVE, No. 4.

IMPEDIMENT

mogilalos [μογιλάλος, 3424], denotes speaking with difficulty (*mogis*, hardly, *laleō*, to talk), stammering, Mark 7:32; some mss. have *moggilalos*, thick-voiced (from *moggos*, with a hoarse, hollow voice). ¶ In the Sept., Isa. 35:6 "(the tongue) of stammerers." ¶

NT: B.525d; CB.1259a; K.–.
OT: 'illēm: S.483; HR.932b.1; H.102c; BD.48a.
GEN. REF.: IS.2:811; NB.–; Z.–.

IMPENITENT

ametanoētos [ἀμετανόητος, 279], lit., without change of mind (*a*, negative, *metanoeō*, to change one's mind, *meta*, signifying change, *nous*, the mind), is used in Rom. 2:5, "impenitent" (or 'unrepentant'). ¶ Moulton and Milligan show from the papyri writings that the word is also used "in a passive sense, 'not affected by change of mind,' like *ametamelētos* in Rom. 11:29," "without repentance."

NT: B.45c; CB.1234c; K.636.
OT: –.
GEN. REF.: –.

IMPLACABLE

aspondos [ἄσπονδος, 786], lit. denotes without a libation (*a*, negative, *spondē*, a libation), i.e., without a truce, as a libation accompanied the making of treaties and compacts; then, one who cannot be persuaded to enter into a covenant, "implacable," 2 Tim. 3:3 (A.V., "truce-breakers"). Some mss. have this word in Rom. 1:31. ¶

NT: B.117b; CB.–; K.–.
OT: –.
GEN. REF.: –.

Note: Trench (Syn., § lii) contrasts *aspondos* with *asunthetos*; see Note under COVENANT-BREAKERS. *Aspondos* may signify untrue to one's promise, *asunthetos* not abiding by one's covenant, treacherous.

For IMPLEAD see ACCUSE, B, No. 2

IMPLANTED

emphutos [ἔμφυτος, 1721], implanted, or rooted (from *emphuō*, to implant), is used in Jas. 1:21, R.V., "implanted," for A.V., "engrafted," of the word of God, "as the 'rooted word,' i.e., a word whose property it is to root itself like a seed in the heart. "The A.V. seems to identify it with *emphuteuton*, which however would be out of place here, since the word is sown, not grafted, in the heart" (Mayor). ¶

NT: B.258a; CB.1244a; K.–.
OT: –.
GEN. REF.: IS.2:811; NB.–; Z.–.

IMPORTUNITY

anaidia (or *anaideia*) [ἀναιδία, 335], denotes shamelessness, importunity (*a*, negative, *n*, euphonic, and *aidōs*, shame, modesty), and is used in the Lord's illustration concerning the need of earnestness and perseverance in prayer, Luke 11:8. If shameless persistence can obtain a boon from a neighbour, then certainly earnest prayer will receive our Father's answer. ¶

NT: B.54c; CB.–; K.–.
OT: –.
GEN. REF.: IS.2:811; NB.–; Z.–.

IMPOSED

epikeimai [ἐπίκειμαι, 1945], denotes to be placed on, to lie on, (*a*) literally, as of the stone on the sepulchre of Lazarus, John 11:38; of the fish on the fire of coals, 21:9; (*b*) figuratively, of a tempest (to press upon), Acts 27:20; of a necessity laid upon the Apostle Paul, 1 Cor. 9:16; of the pressure of the multitude upon Christ to hear Him, Luke 5:1, "pressed upon"; of the insistence of the chief priests, rulers and people that Christ should be crucified, Luke 23:23, "were instant"; of carnal ordinances "imposed" under the Law until a time of reformation, brought in through the High-Priesthood of Christ, Heb. 9:10. See INSTANT, LIE, PRESS. ¶

NT: B.294c; CB.–; K.425.
OT: –.
GEN. REF.: –.

IMPOSSIBLE

A. Adjectives.

1. *adunatos* [ἀδύνατος, 102], from *a*, negative, and *dunatos*, able, strong, is used (*a*) of persons, Acts 14:8, "impotent"; figuratively, Rom. 15:1, "weak"; (*b*) of things, "impossible," Matt. 19:26; Mark 10:27; Luke 18:27; Heb. 6:4, 18; 10:4; 11:6; in Rom. 8:3, "for what the Law could not do," is, more lit., 'the inability of the law'; the meaning may be either 'the weakness of the Law,' or 'that which was impossible for the Law'; the latter is perhaps preferable; literalism is ruled out here, but the sense is that the Law could neither justify nor impart life. ¶

NT: B.19a; CB.1233a; K.186.
OT: 'ebyôn: S.34; HR.28a.1; H.3a; BD.2d.
dal: S.1800; HR.28a.3; H.433a; BD.195c.
pālā': S.6381; HR.28a.7; H.1768; BD.810c.
GEN. REF.: IS.2:812; NB.–; Z.–.

2. *anendektos* [ἀνένδεκτος, 418], signifies inadmissible (*a*, negative, *n*, euphonic, and *endechomai*, to admit, allow), Luke 17:1, of occasions of stumbling, where the meaning is 'it cannot be but that they will come.' ¶

NT: B.65a; CB.–; K.–.
OT: –.
GEN. REF.: –.

B. Verb.

adunateō [ἀδυνατέω, 101], signifies to be impossible (corresponding to A, No. 1), unable; in the N.T. it is used only of things, Matt. 17:20, "(nothing) shall be impossible (unto you)"; Luke 1:37, A.V. "(with God nothing) shall be impossible"; R.V., "(no word from God — a different construction in the best mss.) shall be void of power"; *rhēma* may mean either "word" or "thing" (i.e., fact). ¶ In the Sept.

the verb is always used of things and signifies either to be impossible or to be impotent, e.g., Gen. 18:14; Lev. 25:35, "he fail"; Deut. 17:8; Job 4:4, "feeble"; 42:2; Dan. 4:6; Zech. 8:6.

NT: B.19a; CB.–; K.186.
OT: pālā': S.6381; HR.27c.5; H.1768; BD.810c.
mûṭ: S.4131; HR.27c.4; H.1158; BD.556d.
GEN. REF.: IS.2:812; NB.–; Z.–.

IMPOSTORS

goēs [γόης, 1114], primarily denotes a wailer (*goaō*, to wail); hence, from the howl in which spells were chanted, a wizard, sorcerer, enchanter, and hence, a juggler, cheat, impostor, rendered "impostors" in 2 Tim. 3:13, R.V. (A.V., "seducers"); possibly the false teachers referred to practised magical arts; cp. ver. 8. ¶

NT: B.164d; CB.1248c; K.126.
OT: –.
GEN. REF.: IS.2:812; NB.–; Z.–.

IMPOTENT

A. Adjectives.

1. *adunatos* [ἀδύνατος]: see IMPOSSIBLE, A, No. 1.

2. *asthenēs* [ἀσθενής, 772], without strength (*a*, negative, *sthenos*, strength), is translated "impotent" in Acts 4:9. See FEEBLE, SICK, WEAK.

NT: B.115c; CB.1238a; K.83.
OT: dal: S.1800; HR.172b.3; H.433a; BD.195c.
'ānî: S.6041; HR.172b.7a; H.1652d; BD.776d.
rāpheh: S.7504; HR.172b.10; H.2198a; BD.952a.
GEN. REF.: IS.2:812; NB.–; Z.–.

B. Verb.

astheneō [ἀσθενέω], to be without strength (akin to A, No. 2), is translated "impotent folk" in John 5:3, A.V.; cp. ver. 7 (the present participle, lit., 'being impotent'). See DISEASED, SICK, WEAK.

IMPRISON, IMPRISONMENT

A. Verb.

phulakizō [φυλακίζω, 5439], to imprison, akin to *phulax*, a guard, a keeper, and *phulassō*, to guard, and B, below, is used in Acts 22:19. ¶

NT: B.868a; CB.1264c; K.–.
OT: –.
GEN. REF.: IS.3:973; NB.1035; Z.–.

B. Noun.

phulakē [φυλακή, 5438], besides its other meanings, denotes imprisonment, in 2 Cor. 6:5 (plural) and Heb. 11:36. See CAGE.

NT: B.867d; CB.1264c; K.1280.
OT: mishmār: S.4929; HR.1440c.2b; H.2414f; BD.1038b.
mishmeret: S.4931; HR.1440c.2c; H.2414g; BD.1038b.
maṭṭārāh: S.4307; HR.1440c.5; H.1356a; BD.643c.
GEN. REF.: IS.3:973; NB.1035; Z.–.

IMPULSE

hormē [ὁρμή, 3730], denotes (*a*) an impulse or violent motion, as of the steersman of a vessel, Jas. 3:4, R.V., "impulse" (A.V. omits); (*b*) an assault, onset, Acts 14:5. See ASSAULT ¶

NT: B.581d; CB.1251b; K.730.
OT: ḥēmāh: S.2534; HR.1014a.1; H.860a; BD.404b.
qeṣeph: S.7110; HR.1014a.4; H.2058a; BD.893c.
GEN. REF.: –.

IMPUTE

1. *logizomai* [λογίζομαι, 3049], to reckon, take into account, or, metaphorically, to put down to a person's account, is never rendered in the R.V. by the verb to impute. In the following, where the A.V. has that rendering, the R.V. uses the verb to reckon, which is far more suitable; Rom. 4:6, 8, 11, 22, 23, 24; 2 Cor 5:19; Jas. 2:23. See ACCOUNT, and especially, in the above respect, RECKON.

NT: B.475d; CB.1257a; K.536.
OT: ḥāshab: S.2803; HR.880a.2a-c; H.767; BD.362d.
GEN. REF.: IS.2:812; NB.–; Z.3:265.

2. *ellogaō*, or *-eō* [ἐλλογάω, 1677], (the *-ao* termination is the one found in the *Koinē*, the language covering the N.T. period), denotes to charge to one's account, to lay to one's charge, and is translated "imputed" in Rom. 5:13, of sin as not being "imputed when there is no law." This principle is there applied to the fact that between Adam's transgression and the giving of the Law at Sinai, sin, though it was in the world, did not partake of the character of transgression; for there was no law. The law of conscience existed, but that is not in view in the passage, which deals with the fact of external commandments given by God. In Philm. 18 the verb is rendered "put (that) to (mine) account." See ACCOUNT ¶

NT: B.252b; CB.1244b; K.229.
OT: –.
GEN. REF.: –.

IN: See † p. 1.

INASMUCH AS

1. *katho* [καθό, 2526], lit., according to what (*kata*, according to, and *ho*, the neuter of the relative pronoun), is translated "inasmuch as" in 1 Pet. 4:13, A.V. (R.V., "insomuch as"); in Rom. 8:26, "as (we ought)"; in 2 Cor. 8:12, R.V., "according as" (A.V., "according to that"). See INSOMUCH. ¶

NT: B.390d; CB.–; K.–.
OT: –.
GEN. REF.: –.

2. *eph'hoson* [ἐφ'ὅσον, —], lit., upon how much (*epi*, upon, *hosos*, how much), is translated "inasmuch as" in Matt. 25:40, 45; Rom. 11:13. ¶

NT: B.586b; CB.—; K.—.
OT: —.
GEN. REF.: —.

3. *kathoti* [καθότι]: see ACCORDING AS, No. 1.

4. *kath' hoson* [καθ' ὅσον, —], *kata*, according to, and *hosos*, how much, is translated "inasmuch as" in Heb. 3:3, A.V. (R.V., "by so much as"); 7:20; 9:27, R.V. (A.V., "as").

NT: B.586b; CB.—; K.—.
OT: —.
GEN. REF.: —.

Note: In Phil. 1:7, the phrase "inasmuch as" translates the present participle of the verb *eimi*, to be, lit., '(ye) being (all partakers)'.

INCENSE (burn)

A. Noun.

thumiama [θυμίαμα, 2368], denotes fragrant stuff for burning, incense (from *thuō*, to offer in sacrifice), Luke 1:10, 11; in the plural, Rev. 5:8 and 18:13, R.V. (A.V., "odours"); 8:3, 4, signifying frankincense here. In connection with the Tabernacle, the incense was to be prepared from stacte, onycha, and galbanum, with pure frankincense, an equal weight of each; imitation for private use was forbidden, Ex. 30:34-38. See ODOUR. ¶ Cp. *thumiatērion*, a censer, Heb. 9:4, and *libanos*, frankincense, Rev. 18:13; see FRANKINCENSE. ¶

NT: B.365a; CB.1272c; K.—.
OT: qᵉṭōret: S.7004; HR.660b.7d; H.2011c; BD.882c.
GEN. REF.: IS.2:816; NB.561; Z.3:274.

B. Verb.

thumiaō [θυμιάω, 2370], to burn incense (see A), is found in Luke 1:9. ¶

NT: B.365b; CB.1272c; K.—.
OT: qāṭar: S.6999; HR.660a.2a-c; H.2011; BD.882d.
GEN. REF.: IS.2:816; NB.561; Z.3:274.

INCLOSE

sunkleiō [συγκλείω, 4788], to shut together, shut in on all sides (*sun*, with, *kleiō*, to shut), is used of a catch of fish, Luke 5:6; metaphorically in Rom. 11:32, of God's dealings with Jew and Gentile, in that He has "shut up (A.V., concluded) all unto disobedience, that He might have mercy upon all." There is no intimation in this of universal salvation. The meaning, from the context, is that God has ordered that all should be convicted of disobedience without escape by human merit, that He might display His mercy, and has offered the Gospel without national distinction, and that when Israel is restored, He will, in the resulting Millennium, show His mercy to all nations. The word "all' with reference to Israel, is to be viewed in the light of ver. 26, and, in reference to the Gentiles, in the light of verses 12-25; in Gal. 3:22, 23 ("the Scripture hath shut up all things under sin"), the Apostle shows that, by the impossibility of being justified by keeping the Law, all Jew and Gentile, are under sin, so that righteousness might be reckoned to all who believe. See CONCLUDE, SHUT. ¶

NT: B.774a; CB.1270c; K.1098.
OT: sāgar: S.5462; HR.1299c.2a-d; H.1462; BD.688d.
GEN. REF.: —.

INCONTINENCY, INCONTINENT

A. Noun.

akrasia [ἀκρασία, 192], denotes want of power (*a*, negative, *kratos*, power); hence, want of self-control, incontinency, 1 Cor. 7:5; in Matt. 23;25, "excess." See EXCESS. ¶

NT: B.33a; CB.1234b; K.196.
OT: —.
GEN. REF.: IS.2:819; NB.—; Z.—.

B. Adjective.

akratēs [ἀκρατής, 193], denotes powerless, impotent; in a moral sense, unrestrained, "without self-control," 2 Tim. 3:3, R.V. (A.V., "incontinent"). See SELF-CONTROL. ¶

NT: B.33a; CB.1234b; K.196.
OT: —.
GEN. REF.: IS.2:819; NB.—; Z.—.

For **INCORRUPTIBLE** and **INCORRUPTION,** see under **CORRUPT**

For the noun **INCREASE,** see **GROW,** No. 1, Note

INCREASE (Verb)

1. *auxanō* [αὐξάνω]: see GROW, No. 1.

2. *perisseuō* [περισσεύω, 4052], to be over and above, to abound, is translated "increased" in Acts 16:5, of churches; "increase" in the A.V. of 1 Thess. 4:10 (R.V., "abound"). See ABOUND, under ABUNDANCE, B, No. 1.

NT: B.650c; CB.1263c; K.828.
OT: yātar: S.3498; HR.1126b.1a; H.836; BD.451a.
yôtēr: S.3148; HR.1126b.1b; H.936d; BD.452b.
marbît: S.4768; HR.1126b.2; H.2103d; BD.916b.
GEN. REF.: IS.2:819; NB.561; Z.—.

3. *pleonazō* [πλεονάζω, 4121], to make to abound, is translated "make (you) to increase" in 1 Thess. 3:12, with No. 2. See ABUNDANCE, B, No. 3.

NT: B.667b; CB.1265b; K.864.
OT: rābāh: S.7235; HR.1141c.4a,b; H.2103,2104; BD.915a.
'ādaph: S.5736; HR.1141c.3a; H.1568; BD.727b.
GEN. REF.: IS.2:819; NB.561; Z.—.

4. *prokoptō* [προκόπτω, 4298], is translated by the verb to increase in Luke 2:52 and in the A.V. of 2 Tim. 2:16 (R.V., "will proceed further"). See ADVANCE, PROCEED.
NT: B.707d; CB.1266c; K.939.
OT: –.
GEN. REF.: IS.2:819; NB.–; Z.–.

5. *prostithēmi* [προστίθημι, 4369], to put to, add to, is translated "increase" in Luke 17:5. See ADD, No. 2.
NT: B.718d; CB.1267b; K.1176.
OT: yāsaph: S.3254; HR.1221a,4a-c; H.876; BD.414d.
GEN. REF.: IS.2:819; NB.–; Z.–.

Note: For "increased in strength" see STRENGTH.

INCREDIBLE

apistos [ἄπιστος, 571], is once rendered "incredible," Acts 26:8, of the doctrine of resurrection; elsewhere it is used of persons, with the meaning unbelieving. See BELIEVE, C, *Note* (3).
NT: B.85d; CB.1236c; K.849.
OT: –.
GEN. REF.: –.

INDEBTED (to be)

opheilō [ὀφείλω, 3784], to owe, to be a debtor, is translated "is indebted" in Luke 11:4. Luke does not draw a parallel between our forgiving and God's; he speaks of God's forgiving sins, or our forgiving debts, moral debts, probably not excluding material debts. Matthew speaks of our sins as *opheilēmata*, debts, and uses parallel terms. Ellicott and others suggest that Luke used a term more adapted to the minds of Gentile readers. The inspired language provides us with both, as intended by the Lord.
NT: B.598d; CB.1261a; K.746.
OT: ḥôb: S.2326; HR.1039a.2; H.614a; BD.295a.
nāshā': S.5378; HR.1039a.4; H.1424; BD.673d.
GEN. REF.: –.

INDEED

1. *men* [μέν, 3303], a conjunctive particle (originally a form of *mēn*, verily, truly, found in Heb. 6:14. ¶), usually related to an adversative conjunction or particle, like *de*, in the following clause, which is placed in opposition to it. Frequently it is untranslateable; sometimes it is rendered "indeed," e.g., Matt. 3:11; 13:32; 17:11, R.V. (A.V., "truly"); 20:23; 26:41; (some mss. have it in Mark 1:8); Mark 9:12, R.V. (A.V., "verily").
NT: B.502c; CB.1258b; K.591.
OT: –.
GEN. REF.: –.

2. *alēthēs* [ἀληθής, 227], true, is rendered "indeed" in John 6:55 (twice), see R.V. marg.; some mss. have No. 3 here.
NT: B.36d; CB.1234b; K.37.
OT: 'emet: S.571; HR.53c.1; H.116k; BD.54a.
GEN. REF.: –.

3. *alēthōs* [ἀληθῶς, 230], truly (from No. 2), is translated "indeed" in John 1:47; 4:42; 8:31.
NT: B.37b; CB.1234b; K.–.
OT: 'umᶜnāh: S.552; HR.54b.1d; H.116i; BD.53d.
'emet: S.571; HR.54b.1e; H.116k; BD.54a.
GEN. REF.: –.

4. *ontōs* [ὄντως, 3689], an adverb from *ōn*, the present participle of *eimi*, to be, denotes really, actually; it is translated "indeed" in Mark 11:32 (R.V., "verily"); Luke 24:34; John 8:36; 1 Cor. 14:25, R.V. (A.V., "of a truth"); 1 Tim. 5:3, 5, 16, 6:19, R.V., where some mss. have *aiōnios*, "eternal" (A.V.); in Gal. 3:21, "verily."
NT: B.574a; CB.–; K.–.
OT: –.
GEN. REF.: –.

5. *kai gar* [καὶ γάρ, 1063 (gar)], signifies 'and in fact,' 'for also' (*kai*, and, or even, or also; *gar*, for; *gar*, always comes after the first word in the sentence); it is translated "For indeed" in the R.V. of Acts 19:40; 2 Cor. 5:4; 1 Thess. 4:10 (A.V., "And indeed"); A.V. and R.V. in Phil. 2:27. This phrase has a confirmatory sense, rather than a modifying effect, e.g., Matt. 15:27, R.V., "for even," instead of the A.V. "yet"; the woman confirms that her own position as a Gentile 'dog' brings privilege, 'for indeed the dogs, etc.'
NT: B.151c; CB.1248a; K.–.
OT: –.
GEN. REF.: –.

6. *oude gar* [οὐδὲ γάρ, 1063], for neither, is rendered "neither indeed" in Rom. 8:7.
NT: B.151c; CB.1248a; K.–.
OT: –.
GEN. REF.: –.

7. *alla kai* [ἀλλὰ καί, —], but even, or but also, is rendered "nay indeed" in 2 Cor. 11:1, R.V. (A.V., "and indeed"; R.V. marg., "but indeed").
NT: B.391c; CB.1253a; K.–.
OT: –.
GEN. REF.: –.

8. *kai* [καί, 2532], preceded by the particle *ge*, 'at least,' 'ever,' is rendered "indeed" in Gal. 3:4, R.V. (A.V., "yet"). *Kai* alone is rendered "indeed" in Phil. 4:10, R.V. (A.V., "also").
NT: B.391c; CB.1253a; K.–.
OT: –.
GEN. REF.: –.

9. *ei mēti* [εἰ μήτι, 3385 (mēti)], if not indeed, is rendered "unless indeed" in 2 Cor. 13:5, R.V. (A.V., "except").
NT: B.520b; CB.–; K.–.
OT: –.
GEN. REF.: –.

INDIGNATION

A. Noun.

aganaktēsis [ἀγανάκτησις, 24], is rendered "indignation" in 2 Cor. 7:11. See ANGER, A, *Note* (3). ¶

NT: B.4b; CB.—; K.—.
OT: —.
GEN. REF.: IS.2:820; NB.—; Z.—.

Notes: (1) *Orgē*, wrath, is translated "indignation" in Rev. 14:10, A.V.; R.V., "anger." See ANGER, A, No. 1.

(2) For *thumos*, see ANGER, A, *Notes* (1) and (2).

(3) In Acts 5:17, the A.V. translates *zēlos* by "indignation" (R.V. "jealousy"); in Heb. 10:27, A.V., "indignation" (R.V., "fierceness"; marg., "jealousy"). See JEALOUSY.

B. Verb.

aganakteō [ἀγανακτέω, 23], to be indignant, to be moved with indignation (from *agan*, much, *achomai*, to grieve), is translated "were moved with indignation" of the ten disciples against James and John, Matt. 20:24; in Mark 10:41, R.V. (A.V., "they began to be much displeased"); in Matt. 21:15, of the chief priests and scribes, against Christ and the children, R.V., "they were moved with indignation" (A.V., "they were sore displeased"); in 26:8, of the disciples against the woman who anointed Christ's feet, "they had indignation"; so Mark 14:4; in Mark 10:14, of Christ, against the disciples, for rebuking the children, "He was moved with indignation," R.V. (A.V., "he was much displeased"); in Luke 13:14, of the ruler of the synagogue against Christ for healing on the Sabbath, "being moved with indignation," R.V., A.V., "(answered) with indignation." See ANGER, B, Note (3). ¶

NT: B.4b; CB.—; K.—.
OT: —.
GEN. REF.: IS.2:820; NB.—; Z.—.

INDULGENCE

1. *anesis* [ἄνεσις, 425], a loosening, relaxation of strain (akin to *aniēmi*, to relax, loosen), is translated "indulgence" in Acts 24:23, R.V. (A.V., "liberty"), in the command of Felix to the centurion, to moderate restrictions upon Paul. The papyri and inscriptions illustrate the use of the word as denoting relief (Moulton and Milligan, Vocab.). In the N.T. it always carries the thought of relief from tribulation or persecution; so 2 Thess. 1:7, "rest"; in 2 Cor. 2:13 and 7:5 it is rendered "relief," R.V. (A.V., "rest"); in 8:13, "eased." Josephus speaks of the rest or relief (*anesis*) from ploughing and pillage, given to the land in the year of Jubilee. See EASE, LIBERTY, RELIEF, REST. ¶

NT: B.65b; CB.—; K.60.
OT: shālû (Aramaic): S.7960; HR.87b.1; H.3032c; BD.1115c.
GEN. REF.: —.

2. *plēsmonē* [πλησμονή, 4140], a filling up, satiety (akin to *pimplēmi*, to fill), is translated "indulgence (of the flesh)" in Col. 2:23, R.V. (A.V., "satisfying"). Lightfoot translates the passage "yet not really of any value to remedy indulgence of the flesh." A possible meaning is, 'of no value in attempts at asceticism.' Some regard it as indicating that the ascetic treatment of the body is not of any honour to the satisfaction of the flesh (the reasonable demands of the body); this interpretation is unlikely. The following paraphrase well presents the contrast between the asceticism which "practically treats the body as an enemy, and the Pauline view which treats it as a potential instrument of a righteous life"; ordinances, 'which in fact have a specious look of wisdom (where there is no true wisdom), by the employment of self-chosen acts of religion and humility (and) by treating the body with brutality instead of treating it with due respect, with a view to meeting and providing against over-indulgence of the flesh' (Parry, in the Camb. Greek Test.). ¶

NT: B.673a; CB.—; K.840.
OT: sōba‘: S.7648; HR.1149c.4b; H.2231a; BD.959d.
sāba‘: S.7646; HR.1149c.4c; H.2231; BD.959b.
sāb^{e}‘āh: S.7654; HR.1149c.4e; H.2231b; BD.960a.
GEN. REF.: —.

For **INEXCUSABLE** see **EXCUSE**

For **INFALLIBLE** see **PROOF**

For **INFANT** see **BABE**

INFERIOR

hēttaomai, or *hēssaomai* [ἡττάομαι, 2270], to be less or inferior, is used in the Passive Voice, and translated "ye were made inferior," in 2 Cor. 12:13, R.V., for A.V., "ye were inferior," i.e., were treated with less consideration than other churches, through his independence in not receiving gifts from them. In 2 Pet. 2:19, 20, it signifies to be overcome, in the sense of being subdued and enslaved. See OVERCOME. ¶ Cp. *hēssōn*, less, 2 Cor. 12:15; in 1 Cor. 11:17, "worse"; ¶ *hēttēma*, a loss, a spiritual defect, Rom. 11:12; 1 Cor. 6:7. ¶ Also *elattoō*, to decrease, make lower, John 3:30; Heb. 2:7, 9. ¶

NT: B.349c; CB.—; K.—.
OT: ḥātat: S.2865; HR.620b.3; H.784; BD.368d.
GEN. REF.: —.

For **INFIDEL** (R.V., **UNBELIEVER**), see **BELIEF**, C, *Note* (3)

INFIRMITY

1. *astheneia* [ἀσθένεια, 769], lit., want of strength (*a*, negative, *sthenos*, strength), weakness, indicating inability to produce results, is most frequently translated "infirmity," or "infirmities"; in Rom. 8:26, the R.V. has "infirmity" (A.V., "infirmities"); in 2 Cor. 12:5, 9, 10, "weaknesses" and in 11:30, "weakness" (A.V., "infirmities"); in Luke 13:11 the phrase "a spirit of infirmity" attributes her curvature directly to Satanic agency. The connected phraseology is indicative of trained medical knowledge on the part of the writer.

NT: B.115a; CB.1238a; K.83.
OT: 'aṣṣebet: S.6094; HR.172a.2; H.1666d; BD.781a.
GEN. REF.: IS.1:953; NB.–; Z.–.

2. *asthenēma* [ἀσθένημα, 771], akin to No. 1, is found in the plural in Rom. 15:1, "infirmities," i.e., those scruples which arise through weakness of faith. The strong must support the infirmities of the weak (*adunatos*) by submitting to self-restraint. ¶

NT: B.115c; CB.–; K.83.
OT: –.
GEN. REF.: IS.1:953; NB.–; Z.–.

Note: In Luke 7:21, A.V., *nosos*, a disease, is translated "infirmities" (R.V., "diseases").

INFLICTED

Note: This is inserted in 2 Cor. 2:6 to complete the sentence; there is no corresponding word in the original, which lit. reads 'this punishment, the (one) by the majority.'

INFORM

1. *emphanizō* [ἐμφανίζω, 1718], to manifest, exhibit, in the Middle and Passive Voices, to appear, also signifies to declare, make known, and is translated "informed" in Acts 24:1; 25:2, 15. For all the occurrences of the word see APPEAR, A, No. 5.

NT: B.257c; CB.1244b; K.1244.
OT: yāda': S.3045; HR.460c.2; H.848; BD.393b.
rā'āh: S.7200; HR.460c.4; H.2095; BD.906b,908d.
GEN. REF.: –.

2. *katēcheō* [κατηχέω, 2727], primarily denotes to resound (*kata*, down, *ēchos*, a sound); then, to sound down the ears, to teach by word of mouth, instruct, inform (Eng., catechize, catechumen); it is rendered, in the Passive Voice, by the verb to inform, in Acts 21:21, 24. Here it is used of the large numbers of Jewish believers at Jerusalem whose zeal for the Law had been stirred by information of accusations made against the Apostle Paul, as to certain anti-Mosaic teaching he was supposed to have given the Jews. See INSTRUCT, TEACH.

NT: B.423d; CB.1254b; K.422.
OT: –.
GEN. REF.: –.

For **INHABITANTS, INHABITERS**, see **DWELL**, A, No. 2

INHERIT, INHERITANCE

A. Verbs.

1. *klēronomeō* [κληρονομέω, 2816], strictly means to receive by lot (*klēros*, a lot, *nemomai*, to possess); then, in a more general sense, to possess oneself of, to receive as one's own, to obtain. The following list shows how in the N.T. the idea of inheriting broadens out to include all spiritual good provided through and in Christ, and particularly all that is contained in the hope grounded on the promises of God.

The verb is used of the following objects:

"(*a*) birthright, that into the possession of which one enters in virtue of sonship, not because of a price paid or of a task accomplished, Gal. 4:30; Heb. 1:4; 12:17;

(*b*) that which is received as a gift, in contrast with that which is received as the reward of law-keeping, Heb. 1:14; 6:12 ('through,' i.e., 'through experiences that called for the exercise of faith and patience,' but not 'on the ground of the exercise of faith and patience.');

(*c*) that which is received on condition of obedience to certain precepts, 1 Pet. 3:9, and of faithfulness to God amidst opposition, Rev. 21:7;

(*d*) the reward of that condition of soul which forbears retaliation and self-vindication, and expresses itself in gentleness of behaviour . . ., Matt. 5:5. The phrase "inherit the earth"; or "land," occurs several times in O.T. See especially Psa. 37:11, 22;

(*e*) the reward (in the coming age, Mark 10:30) of the acknowledgment of the paramountcy of the claims of Christ, Matt. 19:29. In the three accounts given of this incident, see Mark 10:17-31, Luke 18:18-30, the words of the question put to the Lord are, in Matthew, 'that I may have,' in Mark and Luke, 'that I may inherit.' In the report of the Lord's word to Peter in reply to his subsequent question, Matthew has 'inherit eternal life,' while Mark and Luke have 'receive eternal life.' It seems to follow that the meaning of the word 'inherit' is here ruled by the words 'receive' and 'have,' with which it is interchanged in each of the three Gospels, i.e., the less common word 'inherit' is to be regarded as equivalent to the more common words 'receive' and 'have.' Cp. Luke 10:25;

(*f*) the reward of those who have shown kindness to the 'brethren' of the Lord in their distress, Matt. 25:34;

(*g*) the Kingdom of God, which the morally corrupt cannot inherit, 1 Cor. 6:9, 10, the inheritance of which is likewise impossible to the present physical constitution of man, 1 Cor. 15:50;

(*h*) incorruption, impossible of inheritance by corruption, 1 Cor. 15:50."*

See HEIR. ¶

NT: B.434d; CB.1255b; K.442.
OT: yārash: S.3423; HR.768a.5a,b; H.920; BD.439a.
nāḥal: S.5157; HR.768a.7a-c; H.1342; BD.635b.
GEN. REF.: IS.2:823; NB.562; Z.3:277.

Note: In regard to (*e*), the word clearly signifies entrance into eternal life without any previous title; it will not bear the implication that a child of God may be divested of his inheritance by the loss of his right of succession.

2. *klēroō* [κληρόω, 2820], is used in the Passive Voice in Eph. 1:11, A.V., "we have obtained an inheritance"; R.V., "we were made a heritage." See HERITAGE. ¶

NT: B.435d; CB.1255b; K.442.
OT: lākad: S.3920; HR.770c.1; H.1115; BD.539d.
qārā': S.7121; HR.770c.3; H.2063; BD.894d.
GEN. REF.: IS.2:823; NB.562; Z.3:277.

B. Nouns.

1. *klēronomia* [κληρονομία, 2817], a lot (see A), properly an inherited property, an inheritance. "It is always rendered inheritance in N.T., but only in a few cases in the Gospels has it the meaning ordinarily attached to that word in English, i.e., that into possession of which the heir enters only on the death of an ancestor. The N.T. usage may be set out as follows: (*a*) that property in real estate which in ordinary course passes from father to son on the death of the former, Matt. 21:38; Mark 12:7; Luke 12:13; 20:14; (*b*) a portion of an estate made the substance of a gift, Acts 7:5; Gal. 3:18, which also is to be included under (*c*); (*c*) the prospective condition and possessions of the believer in the new order of things to be ushered in at the return of Christ, Acts 20:32; Eph. 1:14; 5:5; Col. 3:24; Heb. 9:15; 1 Pet. 1:4; (*d*) what the believer will be to God in that age, Eph. 1:18."†

NT: B.435a; CB.1255b; K.442.
OT: naḥ^{a}lāh: S.5159; HR.769a.6a; H.1342a; BD.635a.
GEN. REF.: IS.2:823; NB.562; Z.3:277.

Note: In Gal. 3:18, "if the inheritance is of the Law," the word "inheritance" stands for 'the title to the inheritance.'

2. *klēros* [κλῆρος, 2819], (whence Eng., clergy), denotes (*a*) a lot, given or cast (the latter as a means of obtaining Divine direction), Matt. 27:35; Mark 15:24; Luke 23:24; John 19:24; Acts 1:26; (*b*) a person's share in anything, Acts 1:17, R.V., "portion" (A.V., "part"); 8:21, "lot"; (*c*) a charge (lit., 'charges') "allotted," to elders, 1 Pet. 5:3, R.V. [A.V., "(God's) heritage"]; the figure is from portions of lands allotted to be cultivated; (*d*) an inheritance, as in No. 1 (*c*); Acts 26:18; Col. 1:12. See CHARGE, A, No. 4, LOT(S), PART, PORTION. ¶

NT: B.435b; CB.1255b; K.442.
OT: naḥ^{a}lāh: S.5159; HR.770a.6; H.1342a; BD.635a.
gôrāl: S.1486; HR.770a.1; H.381a; BD.174a.
GEN. REF.: IS.2:823; NB.562; Z.3:277.

INIQUITY

1. *anomia* [ἀνομία, 458], lit., lawlessness (*a* negative, *nomos*, law), is used in a way which indicates the meaning as being lawlessness or wickedness. Its usual rendering in the N.T. is "iniquity," which lit. means unrighteousness. It occurs very frequently in the Sept., especially in the Psalms, where it is found about 70 times. It is used (*a*) of iniquity in general, Matt. 7:23; 13:41; 23:28; 24:12; Rom. 6:19 (twice); 2 Cor. 6:14, R.V., "iniquity" (A.V., "unrighteousness"); 2 Thess. 2:3, in some mss.; the A.V. and R.V. follow those which have *hamartia*, "(man of) sin"; 2:7, R.V., "lawlessness" (A.V., "iniquity"); Tit. 2:14; Heb. 1:9; 1 John 3:4 (twice), R.V., "(doeth) . . . lawlessness" and "lawlessness" (A.V., "transgresseth the law" and "transgression of the law"); (*b*) in the plural, of acts or manifestations of lawlessness, Rom. 4:7; Heb. 10:17 (some inferior mss. have it in 8:12, for the word *hamartia*). See LAWLESSNESS, TRANSGRESSION, UNRIGHTEOUSNESS. ¶

NT: B.71d; CB.1235c; K.646.
OT: 'āwen: S.205; HR.106b.1; H.48a; BD.19d.
'āwōn: S.5771; HR.106b.15; H.1577a; BD.730d.
tô'ēbāh: S.8441; HR.106b.22; H.2530a; BD.1072d.
GEN. REF.: IS.2:825; NB.—; Z.5:444.

Note: In the phrase "man of sin," 2 Thess. 2:3, the word suggests the idea of contempt of Divine law, since the Antichrist will deny the existence of God.

2. *adikia* [ἀδικία, 93], denotes unrighteousness, lit., 'unrightness' (*a*, negative, *dikē*, right), a condition of not being right, whether with God, according to the standard of His holiness and righteousness, or with man, according to the standard of what man knows to be right by his conscience. In Luke 16:8 and 18:6, the phrases lit. are, 'the steward of unrighteousness'

* From Notes on Galatians, by Hogg and Vine, pp. 286-289.

† From Notes on Galatians, by Hogg and Vine, pp. 146, 147.

and 'the judge of injustice,' the subjective genitive describing their character; in 18:6 the meaning is 'injustice' and so perhaps in Rom. 9:14. The word is usually translated "unrighteousness," but is rendered "iniquity" in Luke 13:27; Acts 1:18; 8:23; 1 Cor. 13:6, A.V. (R.V., "unrighteousness"); so in 2 Tim. 2:19; Jas. 3:6.

NT: B.17d; CB.1233a; K.22.
OT: 'āwōn: S.5771; HR.25b.21; H.1577a; BD.730d.
sheqer: S.8267; HR.25b.34; H.2461a; BD.1055b.
GEN. REF.: IS.2:825; NB.—; Z.5:444.

3. *adikēma* [ἀδίκημα, 92], denotes a wrong, injury, misdeed (akin to No. 2; from *adikeō*, to do wrong), the concrete act, in contrast to the general meaning of No. 2, and translated "a matter of wrong," in Acts 18:14; "wrong-doing," 24:20 (A.V., "evil-doing"); "iniquities," Rev. 18:5. See EVIL, WRONG. ¶

NT: B.17d; CB.1233a; K.22.
OT: 'āwōn: S.5771; HR.25a.4; H.1577a; BD.730d.
pesha': S.6588; HR.25a.6; H.1846a; BD.833b.
GEN. REF.: IS.2:825; NB.—; Z.5:444.

4. *ponēria* [πονηρία, 4189], akin to *poneō*, to toil (cp. *ponēros*, bad, worthless; see BAD), denotes wickedness, and is so translated in Matt. 22:18; Mark 7:22 (plural); Luke 11:39; Rom. 1:29; 1 Cor. 5:8; Eph. 6:12; in Acts 3:26, "iniquities." See WICKEDNESS. ¶ Cp. *kakia*, evil.

NT: B.690c; CB.1266a; K.912.
OT: ra': S.7451; HR.1186b.4a; H.2191; BD.948d.
rōa': S.7455; HR.1186b.4b; H.2191b; BD.947d.
rā'āh: S.7451; HR.1186b.4c; H.2191; BD.949a.
GEN. REF.: —.

5. *paranomia* [παρανομία, 3892], law-breaking (*para*, against, *nomos*, law), denotes transgression, so rendered in 2 Pet. 2:16, for A.V., "iniquity." ¶

NT: B.621a; CB.—; K.646.
OT: 'āwōn: S.5771; HR.1062b.1; H.1577a; BD.730d.
m^{e}zimmāh: S.4209; HR.1062b.2; H.556c; BD.273c.
GEN. REF.: IS.2:825; NB.—; Z.5:444.

INJURE, INJURIOUS, INJURY

A. Verb.

adikeō [ἀδικέω, 91], akin to Nos. 2 and 3, under INIQUITY, is usually translated either to hurt, or by some form of the verb to do wrong. In the A.V. of Gal. 4:12, it is rendered "ye have (not) injured me," which the R.V. corrects, both in tense and meaning, to "ye did (me no) wrong." See HURT.

NT: B.17c; CB.1233a; K.22.
OT: 'āwāh: S.5753; HR.24c.11c; H.1577; BD.731c.
'āshaq: S.6231; HR.24c.15; H.1713; BD.798d.
GEN. REF.: IS.1:815; NB.—; Z.—.

B. Adjective.

hubristēs [ὑβριστής, 5197], a violent, insolent man (akin to C), is translated "insolent" in Rom. 1:30, R.V., for A.V., "despiteful"; in 1 Tim. 1:13, "injurious." See DESPITEFUL, INSOLENT. ¶

NT: B.832a; CB.1251c; K.1200.
OT: gē'eh: S.1343; HR.1380a.1b; H.299b; BD.144b.
GEN. REF.: IS.2:856; NB.—; Z.—.

C. Noun.

hubris [ὕβρις]: see HARM, A, No. 4.

INK

melan [μέλαν, 3188], the neuter of the adjective *melas*, black (see Matt. 5:36; Rev. 6:5, 12), denotes ink, 2 Cor. 3:3; 2 John 12; 3 John 13. ¶

NT: B.499d; CB.1258a; K.—.
OT: —.
GEN. REF.: IS.2:825; NB.1344; Z.3:279.

INN

1. *kataluma* [κατάλυμα]: see GUEST-CHAMBER.

2. *pandocheion* [πανδοχεῖον, 3829], lit., a place where all are received (*pas*, all, *dechomai*, to receive), denotes a house for the reception of strangers, a *caravanserai*, translated "inn," in Luke 10:34, in the parable of the Good Samaritan. Cattle and beasts of burden could be sheltered there, and this word must thereby be distinguished from No. 1. ¶ Cp. *pandocheus* in the next verse, "(the) host." ¶

NT: B.607c; CB.—; K.—.
OT: —.
GEN. REF.: IS.2:826; NB.543; Z.3:279.

INNER

1. *esō* [ἔσω, 2080], an adverb connected with *eis*, into, is translated "inner" in the A.V. of Eph. 3:16 (R.V., "inward"); after verbs of motion, it denotes 'into,' Mark 15:16; after verbs of rest, "within." See WITHIN.

NT: B.314b; CB.1246c; K.265.
OT: p^{e}nîmāh: S.6441; HR.558c.2b; H.1782c; BD.819b.
GEN. REF.: —.

2. *esōteros* [ἐσώτερος, 2082], the comparative degree of No. 1, denotes "inner," Acts 16:24 (of a prison); Heb. 6:19, with the article, and practically as a noun, "that which is within (the veil)," lit., 'the inner (of the veil).' ¶ Cp. Eng., esoteric.

NT: B.314c; CB.1246c; K.—.
OT: p^{e}nîmî: S.6442; HR.559a.3d; H.1782d; BD.819b.
GEN. REF.: —.

Note: For "inner chamber(s)" see CHAMBER, No. 1.

INNOCENT

1. *athōos* [ἀθῷος, 121], primarily denotes unpunished (*a*, negative, *thōē*, a penalty); then, innocent, Matt. 27:4, "innocent blood," i.e., the blood of an innocent person, the word "blood"

being used both by synecdoche (a part standing for the whole), and by metonymy (one thing standing for another), i.e., for death by execution (some mss. have *dikaion*, righteous); ver. 24, where Pilate speaks of himself as "innocent." ¶

NT: B.21d; CB.—; K.—.
OT: nāqāh: S.5352; HR.30a.2; H.1412; BD.667b.
nāqî: S.5355; HR.30a.3; H.1412b; BD.667c.
GEN. REF.: IS.2:827; NB.—; Z.3:281.

2. *akakos* [ἄκακος, 172], lit., not bad (*a*, negative, *kakos*, bad), denotes guileless, innocent, Rom. 16:18, R.V., "innocent" (A.V., "simple"); "harmless" in Heb. 7:26. See HARMLESS. ¶

NT: B.29b; CB.1234a; K.391.
OT: tām: S.8535; HR.43b.3a; H.2522c; BD.1070d.
tōm: S.8537; HR.43b.3b; H.2522a; BD.1070d.
GEN. REF.: IS.—; NB.—; Z.3:281.

INNUMERABLE

1. *anarithmētos* [ἀναρίθμητος, 382], *a*, negative, *n*, euphonic, *arithmeō*, to number, is used in Heb. 11:12. ¶

NT: B.60a; CB.—; K.—.
OT: 'ên mispār: S.4557; HR.81c.1a; H.1540e; BD.708d.
GEN. REF.: —.

2. *murias* [μυριάς, 3461], denotes either ten thousand, or, indefinitely, a myriad, a numberless host, in the plural, Acts 19:19; lit. 'five ten-thousands,' Rev. 5:11; 9:16; in the following, used of vast numbers, Luke 12:1, A.V., "an innumerable multitude," R.V., "the many thousands" (R.V. marg., "the myriads"); Acts 21:20, "thousands"; Heb. 12:22, "innumerable hosts"; Jude 14, "ten thousands" (R.V., marg., in each place, "myriads"). See COMPANY, THOUSANDS. ¶ Cp. the adjective *murios*, ten thousand, Matt. 18:24; 1 Cor. 4:15; 14:19. ¶

NT: B.529c; CB.—; K.—.
OT: r^{e}bābāh: S.7233; HR.937a.1a; H.2099d; BD.914b.
ribbô': S.7239; HR.937a.1b; H.2099e; BD.914b.
GEN. REF.: —.

For **INORDINATE** see **AFFECTION**, No. 1

INQUIRE, INQUIRY (make)

A. Verbs.

1. *punthanomai* [πυνθάνομαι, 4441], to inquire, is translated "inquired" in Matt. 2:4, and Acts 21:33, R.V. (A.V., "demanded"); in Luke 15:26; 18:36 and Acts 4:7 (A.V., "asked"); "inquired" (A.V., "enquired") in John 4:52; "inquire" (A.V., "enquire") in Acts 23:20; in Acts 23:34 it denotes to learn by enquiry, A.V., and R.V., "when (he) understood"; elsewhere it is rendered by the verb to ask, Acts 10:18, 29; 23:19. See ASK, UNDERSTAND. ¶

NT: B.729c; CB.—; K.—.
OT: dārash: S.1875; HR.1242b.1; H.455; BD.205a.
GEN. REF.: IS.2:830; NB.—; Z.3:282.

2. *zēteō* [ζητέω, 2212], to seek, is rendered "inquire" in John 16:19; "inquire . . . for" in Acts 9:11. See ABOUT, B, *Note*, DESIRE, ENDEAVOUR, GO, *Note* (2), *a*, REQUIRE, SEEK.

NT: B.338d; CB.1273a; K.300.
OT: bāqash: S.1245; HR.597a.6a; H.276; BD.134c.
dārash: S.1875; HR.597a.8; H.455; BD.205a.
GEN. REF.: IS.2:830; NB.—; Z.3:282.

3. *dierōtaō* [διερωτάω, 1331], to find by inquiry, to inquire through to the end (*dia*, intensive, *erōtaō*, to ask), is used in Acts 10:17. ¶

NT: B.194d; CB.—; K.—.
OT: —.
GEN. REF.: IS.2:830; NB.—; Z.—.

4. *exetazō* [ἐξετάζω, 1833], to examine, seek out, inquire thoroughly, is translated "enquire" in Matt. 10:11, A.V. (R.V., "search out"); in John 21:12, "(durst) inquire," R.V. [A.V., "(durst) ask"]; in Matt. 2:8, R.V., "search out" (A.V., "search"). See ASK, SEARCH. ¶

NT: B.275c; CB.—; K.—.
OT: dārash: S.1875; HR.495a.2; H.455; BD.205a.
bāḥan: S.974; HR.495a.1; H.230; BD.103c.
GEN. REF.: IS.2:830; NB.—; Z.3:282.

Notes: (1) *Epizēteō*, to seek after or for (*epi*, after, *zēteō*, to seek), is rendered "enquire" in Acts 19:39, A.V. (R.V., "seek").

(2) *Sunzēteō*, to search or examine together, is rendered "to enquire" in Luke 22:23. A.V. (R.V., "to question").

(3) *Ekzēteō*, to seek out, search after, is rendered "have inquired" in 1 Pet. 1:10, A.V. (R.V., "sought").

(4) *Diaginōskō*, to ascertain exactly, or to determine, is rendered "enquire" in Acts 23:15, A.V. (R.V., "judge").

(5) *Akriboō*, to learn by diligent or exact inquiry, is rendered "enquired diligently" and "had diligently enquired" respectively, in Matt. 2:7, 16, A.V. (R.V., "learned carefully," and "had carefully learned").

(6) In 2 Cor. 8:23, the words "any inquire" are inserted to complete the meaning, lit., 'whether about Titus.'

B. Noun.

zētēsis [ζήτησις, 2214], primarily denotes a search; then, an inquiry, a questioning, debate; it forms part of a phrase translated by the verb to inquire, in Acts 25:20, R.V., "how to inquire," lit. '(being perplexed as to) the inquiry.' See QUESTION.

NT: B.339b; CB.1273c; K.300.
OT: —.
GEN. REF.: IS.2:830; NB.—; Z.3:282.

INSCRIPTION

epigraphō [ἐπιγράφω, 1924], to write upon, inscribe (*epi*, upon, *graphō*, to write), is usually rendered by the verb to write upon, over, or in,

Mark 15:26; Heb. 8:10; 10:16; Rev. 21:12; it is translated by a noun phrase in Acts 17:23, "(with this) inscription," lit., '(on which) had been inscribed.' ¶ Cp. the noun *epigraphē*, a superscription.

NT: B.291c; CB.1245c; K.—.
OT: kātab: S.3789; HR.518c.1; H.1053; BD.507a.
GEN. REF.: IS.2:831; NB.—; Z.3:282.

INSIDE

1. *entos* [ἐντός, 1787], an adverb denoting within, or among, is once used with the article, as a noun, of "the inside (of the cup and of the platter)," Matt. 23:26, R.V. (A.V., "that which is within etc."); elsewhere, Luke 17:21. See WITHIN. ¶

NT: B.269b; CB.1245b; K.—.
OT: —.
GEN. REF.: —.

2. *esōthen* [ἔσωθεν, 2081], an adverb denoting from within, or within, is used with the article, as a noun, of the inner being, the secret intents of the heart, which, the Lord declared, God made, as well as the visible physical frame, Luke 11:40. In ver. 39, it is rendered "inward part." See INWARD, WITHIN.

NT: B.314b; CB.—; K.—.
OT: mibbayit: S.1004; HR.559a.1c; H.241; BD.108c,110a.
mippᵉnîmāh: S.6441; HR.559a.2d; H.1782c; BD.819b.
pᵉnîmî: S.6442; HR.559a.2e; H.1782d; BD.819b.
GEN. REF.: —.

INSOLENT

hubristēs [ὑβριστής, 5197], violent, injurious, insolent, is rendered "insolent" in Rom. 1:30, R.V. (A.V., "despiteful"). See DESPITEFUL, INJURIOUS.

NT: B.832a; CB.1251c; K.1200.
OT: gē'eh: S.1343; HR.1380a.1b; H.299b; BD.144b.
GEN. REF.: IS.2:839; NB.—; Z.—.

INSOMUCH THAT, or AS

1. *hōste* [ὥστε, 5620], a consecutive particle, is used with the meaning "insomuch that," or "so that," or "that," to express the effect or result of anything, e.g., Matt. 8:24; 13:54; 15:31; 27:14; Acts 1:19 (A.V., "insomuch as"); 5:15; 19:12 (A.V., "so that"); 2 Cor. 1:8; Gal. 2:13. See WHEREFORE.

NT: B.899d; CB.1251b; K.—.
OT: —.
GEN. REF.: —.

2. *eis to* [εἰς τό, 1519 (*eis*)], lit., unto the, followed by the infinitive mood, is sometimes used of result, and is rendered "insomuch that" in 2 Cor. 8:6.

NT: B.228a; CB.—; K.—.
OT: —.
GEN. REF.: —.

3. *katho* [καθό, 2526], is translated "insomuch as" in 1 Pet. 4:13, R.V. (A.V., "inasmuch as"). See INASMUCH.

NT: B.390d; CB.—; K.—.
OT: —.
GEN. REF.: —.

INSPIRATION OF GOD, INSPIRED OF GOD

theopneustos [θεόπνευστος, 2315], inspired by God (*Theos*, God, *pneō*, to breathe), is used in 2 Tim. 3:16, of the Scriptures as distinct from non-inspired writings. Wycliffe, Tyndale, Coverdale and the Great Bible have the rendering "inspired of God." ¶

NT: B.356c; CB.1272a; K.876.
OT: —.
GEN. REF.: IS.2:839; NB.564; Z.3:290.

INSTANT, BE INSTANT, INSTANTLY

A. Verbs.

1. *epikeimai* [ἐπίκειμαι, 1945], to lie or press upon, is rendered "they were instant" in Luke 23:23 (Amer. R.V., "they were urgent"). See IMPOSE.

NT: B.294c; CB.—; K.425.
OT: —.
GEN. REF.: —.

2. *ephistēmi* [ἐφίστημι, 2186], to set upon or by, is used in the N.T. intransitively, either in the Middle Voice, or in certain tenses of the Active, signifying to stand by , be present, be at hand, come on or upon, and is translated "be instant" in 2 Tim. 4:2. See ASSAULT, COME, etc.

NT: B.330c; CB.—; K.—.
OT: —.
GEN. REF.: —.

Note: For *proskartereō*, in Rom. 12:12, A.V., rendered "continuing instant," R.V., "stedfastly," see CONTINUE, No. 9.

B. Noun.

Note: The word *hōra*, an hour, is translated "instant" in Luke 2:38, A.V.; the R.V. renders it "hour." See HOUR.

C. Adverb.

spoudaiōs [σπουδαίως, 4709], earnestly, diligently, is rendered "instantly" in Luke 7:4, A.V. (R.V., "earnestly"). See EARNEST.

NT: B.763d; CB.—; K.—.
OT: —.
GEN. REF.: —.

Note: For the phrase *en ekteneia*, rendered "instantly" in Acts 26:7, A.V., see EARNEST, D.

INSTRUCT, INSTRUCTION INSTRUCTOR

A. Verbs.

1. *katēcheō* [κατηχέω, 2727], to teach orally, inform, instruct, is translated by the verb to instruct in Luke 1:4; Acts 18:25 (R.V. marg., "taught by word of mouth"); Rom. 2:18; 1 Cor. 14:19, R.V. (A.V., "teach"). See INFORM, TEACH.

NT: B.423d; CB.1254b; K.422.
OT: –.
GEN. REF.: IS.2:854; NB.–; Z.–.

2. *paideuō* [παιδεύω, 3811], to train children, teach, is rendered "was instructed," in Acts 7:22, R.V. (A.V., "learned"); "instructing" in 2 Tim. 2:25, A.V. (R.V., "correcting"); Tit. 2:12, R.V., "instructing" (A.V., "teaching"). The verb is used of the family discipline, as in Heb. 12:6, 7, 10; cp. 1 Cor. 11:32; 2 Cor. 6:9; Rev. 3:19. In 1 Tim. 1:20 (Passive Voice) it is translated "might be taught," R.V. (A.V., "may learn"), but, "however the passage is to be understood, it is clear that not the impartation of knowledge but severe discipline is intended. In Luke 23:16, 22, Pilate, since he had declared the Lord guiltless of the charge brought against Him, and hence could not punish Him, weakly offered, as a concession to the Jews, to 'chastise, *paideuō*, Him, and let Him go.' "*

This sense of *paideuō* is confirmed by Heb. 12:6, where it is joined (in a quotation from the Sept. of Prov. 3:12) with to lash or scourge. Cp. the scene in the *Pilgrim's Progress* where a shining one with a whip of small cords "chastised sore" the pilgrims foolishly caught in the net of the flatterer and said to them, "As many as I love I rebuke and chasten" (*paideuō*). See CORRECT, TEACH ¶

NT: B.603d; CB.1261c; K.753.
OT: yāsar: S.3256; HR.1047a.4a-d; H.877; BD.415d.
GEN. REF.: IS.2:854; NB.–; Z.–.

3. *mathēteuō* [μαθητεύω, 3100], used transitively, to make a disciple, is translated "which is instructed" in Matt. 13:52, A.V. (R.V., "who hath been made a disciple"). See DISCIPLE.

NT: B.485c; CB.1258a; K.552.
OT: –.
GEN. REF.: –.

4. *mueō* [μυέω, 3453], to initiate into the mysteries, is used in the Passive Voice, in Phil. 4:12, A.V., "I am instructed," R.V., "have I learned the secret." See LEARN. ¶

NT: B.529a; CB.1259b; K.615.
OT: –.
GEN. REF.: –.

5. *probibazō* [προβιβάζω, 4264], to lead forward, lead on (the causal of *probainō*, to go forward; *pro*, forward, *bibazō*, to lift up), is used in the Passive Voice in Matt. 14:8, and translated, A.V., "being before instructed," R.V., "being put forward." Some mss. have it in Acts 19:33, instead of No. 6. ¶

NT: B.703c; CB.–; K.–.
OT: yārāh: S.3384; HR.1205c.1; H.910; BD.434d.
GEN. REF.: IS.2:854; NB.–; Z.–.

6. *sumbibazō* [συμβιβάζω, 4822], to join, knit, unite (*sun*, with), then, to compare, and so, to prove, hence, to teach, instruct, is so rendered in 1 Cor. 2:16; it is found in the best mss. in Acts 19:33 (R.V. marg., "instructed"). See COMPACTED, CONCLUDE, KNIT TOGETHER, PROVE.

NT: B.777c; CB.–; K.1101.
OT: yāda': S.3045; HR.303b.2; H.848; BD.393b.
yārāh: S.3384; HR.130b.3; H.910; BD.434d.
GEN. REF.: IS.2:854; NB.–; Z.–.

B. Nouns.

(INSTRUCTION)

paideia [παιδεία, 3809], training, instruction, is translated "instruction" in 2 Tim. 3:16. See CHASTEN.

NT: B.603b; CB.1261b; K.753.
OT: mûsār: S.4148; HR.1046b.5; H.877b; BD.416b.
GEN. REF.: IS.2:854; NB.–; Z.–.

(INSTRUCTOR)

1. *paidagōgos* [παιδαγωγός, 3807], a guide, or guardian or trainer of boys, lit., a child-leader (*pais*, a boy, or child, *agō*, to lead), a tutor, is translated "instructors" in 1 Cor. 4:15, A.V. (R.V., "tutors"); here the thought is that of pastors rather than teachers; in Gal. 3:24, 25, A.V., "schoolmaster" (R.V., "tutor,"), but here the idea of instruction is absent. "In this and allied words the idea is that of training, discipline, not of impartation of knowledge. The *paidagōgos* was not the instructor of the child; he exercised a general supervision over him and was responsible for his moral and physical well-being. Thus understood, *paidagōgos* is appropriately used with 'kept in ward' and 'shut up,' whereas to understand it as equivalent to 'teacher' introduces an idea entirely foreign to the passage, and throws the Apostle's argument into confusion."* ¶ Cp. *epitropos*, a steward, guardian, tutor.

NT: B.603a; CB.1261b; K.753.
OT: –.
GEN. REF.: IS.2:854; NB.–; Z.–.

2. *paideutēs* [παιδευτής, 3810], akin to A, No. 2, denotes (*a*) an instructor, a teacher, Rom. 2:20, A.V., "an instructor" (R.V., "a corrector"); (*b*) one who disciplines, corrects, chastens, Heb. 12:9, R.V., "to chasten" [A.V., "which corrected" (lit., 'correctors')]. In (*a*) the discipline of the school is in view; in (*b*) that of the family.

* From Notes on Galatians, by Hogg and Vine, pp. 163, 164.

See CORRECTOR ¶. Cp. *epitropos*, a steward, guardian, tutor.
NT: B.603d; CB.1261c; K.753.
OT: mûsār: S.4148; HR.1047c.1; H.877b; BD.416b.
GEN. REF.: IS.2:854; NB.–; Z.–.

INSTRUMENTS

hoplon [ὅπλον, 3696], a tool, instrument, weapon, is used metaphorically in Rom. 6:13 of the members of the body as "instruments" (marg., "weapons"), negatively, of unrighteousness, positively, of righteousness. The metaphor is probably military (cp. ver. 23, "wages," i.e., soldiers' pay); Moule renders it 'implements'; 'weapons' seems to be the meaning. See ARMOUR, WEAPONS.
NT: B.575c; CB.1251a; K.702.
OT: māgēn: S.4043; HR.1003c.3; H.367c; BD.171b.
nesheq: S.5402; HR.1003c.4; H.2877; BD.676d.
GEN. REF.: IS.2:856; NB.–; Z.–.

INSURRECTION

A. Nouns.

1. *stasis* [στάσις, 4714], akin to *histēmi*, to make to stand, denotes (*a*) primarily, a standing or place, Heb. 9:8; (*b*) an insurrection, sedition, translated "insurrection" in Mark 15:7; "insurrections" in Acts 24:5, R.V. (A.V., "sedition"); in Luke 23:19, 25 (A.V. "sedition"); "riot," Acts 19:40, R.V. (A.V., "uproar"); (*c*) a dissension, Acts 15:2; in Acts 23:7, 10, "dissension." See DISSENSION. ¶
NT: B.764c; CB.1270a; K.1070.
OT: ʿāmod: S.5975; HR.1286c.6d; H.1637; BD.763c.
rîb: S.7379; HR.1286c.8; H.2159a; BD.936b.
GEN. REF.: IS.2:857; NB.–; Z.–.

2. *stasiastēs* [στασιαστής, 4955], denotes a rebel, revolutionist, one who stirs up sedition (from *stasiazō*, to stir up sedition), Mark 15:7, "had made insurrection." Some mss. have *sustasiastēs*, a fellow-rioter, a fellow-mover of sedition, A.V., "had made insurrection with (him)." ¶
NT: B.764b; CB.–; K.–.
OT: –.
GEN. REF.: –.

B. Verb.

katephistēmi [κατεφίστημι, 2721], signifies to rise up against (lit., to cause to stand forth against, *kata*, against, *epi*, forth, *histēmi*, to cause to stand), Acts 18:12, A.V., "made insurrection" (R.V., "rose up against)." ¶
NT: B.422c; CB.–; K.–.
OT: –.
GEN. REF.: –.

INTEND

1. *boulomai* [βούλομαι, 1014], to will, wish, desire, purpose (expressing a fixed resolve, the deliberate exercise of volition), is translated "intend" in Acts 5:28, and "intending" in 12:4. See DESIRE.
NT: B.146a; CB.1239b; K.108.
OT: ʾābāh: S.14; HR.226b.1; H.3; BD.2c.
ḥāpheṣ: S.2654; HR.226b.5; H.712; BD.343a.
GEN. REF.: IS.2:857; NB.–; Z.–.

2. *thelō* [φέλω, 2309], to will, be willing, desire, (less strong, and more frequent than No. 1), is translated "intending" in Luke 14:28, A.V. (R.V., "desiring"). See DESIRE.
NT: B.354d; CB.1271c; K.318.
OT: ʾābāh: S.14; HR.628b.1; H.3; BD.2c.
ḥāphēṣ: S.2654; HR.628b.8; H.712; BD.343a.
GEN. REF.: –.

3. *mellō* [μέλλω, 3195], to be about to do a thing, indicating simply the formation of a design, is translated "intend" in Acts 5:35, A.V. (R.V., "are about"); "intending," in Acts 20:7, R.V. (A.V., "ready"); 20:13 (1st part); in the 2nd part of the ver., R.V., "intending" (A.V., "minding").
NT: B.500d; CB.1258a; K.–.
OT: –.
GEN. REF.: –.

INTENT

1. *ennoia* [ἔννοια, 1771], primarily a thinking, idea, consideration, denotes purpose, intention, design (*en*, in, *nous*, mind); it is rendered "intents" in Heb. 4:12; "mind," in 1 Pet. 4:1 (R.V., marg., "thought"). See MIND. ¶ Cp. *Enthumēsis*, thought (see DEVICE).
NT: B.267a; CB.1245b; K.636.
OT: bînāh: S.998; HR.475c.1a; H.239b; BD.108a.
mᵉzimmāh: S.4209; HR.475c.4; H.556c; BD.273c.
GEN. REF.: IS.2:857; NB.–; Z.–.

2. *logos* [λόγος, 3056], a word, account, etc., sometimes denotes a reason, cause, intent, e.g., Matt. 5:32, "cause"; it is rendered "intent" in Acts 10:29. See CAUSE.
NT: B.477a; CB.1257a; K.505.
OT: dābār: S.1697; HR.881c.2a; H.399a; BD.182a.
GEN. REF.: –.

Notes: (1) The phrase *eis touto*, lit., 'unto this,' i.e., for this purpose, is rendered "for this (A.V., 'that') intent" in Acts 9:21, R.V.

(2) The phrase *eis to*, 'unto the,' followed by a verb in the infinitive mood, is translated "to the intent" in 1 Cor. 10:6.

(3) The phrase *pros ti*, lit., 'in reference to what,' is rendered "for what intent" in John 13:28.

(4) In John 11:15 the conjunction *hina*, to the end that, is translated "to the intent," and in Eph. 3:10, "to the intent that."

INTERCESSIONS

A. Noun.

enteuxis [ἔντευξις, 1783], primarily denotes a lighting upon, meeting with (akin to B); then, a conversation; hence, a petition, a meaning

frequent in the papyri; it is a technical term for approaching a king, and so for approaching God in intercession; it is rendered "prayer" in 1 Tim. 4:5; in the plural in 2:1 (i.e., seeking the presence and hearing of God on behalf of others). ¶ For the synonymous words, *proseuchē*, *deēsis*, see PRAYER.
NT: B.268d; CB.1245b; K.1191.
OT: —.
GEN. REF.: IS.2:858; NB.1021; Z.—.

B. Verbs.

1. *entunchanō* [ἐντυγχάνω, 1793], primarily to fall in with, meet with in order to converse; then, to make petition, especially to make intercession, plead with a person, either for or against others; (*a*) against, Acts 25:24, "made suit to (me)," R.V. [A.V., "have dealt with (me)"], i.e., against Paul; in Rom. 11:2, of Elijah in 'pleading' with God, R.V. (A.V., "maketh intercession to"), against Israel; (*b*) "for," in Rom. 8:27, of the intercessory work of the Holy Spirit for the saints; ver. 34, of the similar intercessory work of Christ; so Heb. 7:25. See DEAL WITH, PLEAD, SUIT. ¶
NT: B.270a; CB.1245b; K.1191.
OT: qᵉrēb (Aramaic): S.7127; HR.481b.1; H.2978; BD.1111c.
GEN. REF.: IS.2:858; NB.1021; Z.—.

2. *huperentunchanō* [ὑπερεντυγχάνω, 5241], to make a petition or intercede on behalf of another (*huper*, on behalf of, and No. 1), is used in Rom. 8:26 of the work of the Holy Spirit in making intercession (see No. 1, ver. 27). ¶
NT: B.840d; CB.1252a; K.1191.
OT: —.
GEN. REF.: IS.2:858; NB.1021; Z.—.

INTEREST

tokos [τόκος, 5110], primarily a bringing forth, birth (from *tiktō*, to beget), then, an offspring, is used metaphorically of the produce of money lent out, interest, usury, Matt. 25:27; Luke 19:23. See USURY ¶.
NT: B.821d; CB.1272c; K.—.
OT: nēshek: S.5392; HR.1363b.3; H.1430a; BD.675b.
GEN. REF.: IS.2:860; NB.304; Z.3:295.

INTERPOSED

mesiteuō [μεσιτεύω, 3315], to mediate, give surety (akin to *mesitēs*, a mediator), is translated "interposed" in Heb. 6:17, R.V. See CONFIRM, No. 5. ¶
NT: B.506d; CB.1258b; K.585.
OT: —.
GEN. REF.: —.

INTERPRET, INTERPRETATION, INTERPRETER

A. Verbs.

1. *hermēneuō* [ἑρμηνεύω, 2059], (cp. *Hermēs*, the Greek name of the pagan god Mercury, who was regarded as the messenger of the gods), denotes to explain, interpret (Eng., hermeneutics), and is used of explaining the meaning of words in a different language, John 1:38 (in some mss.), see No. 3; 9:7 ("Siloam," interpreted as "sent"); Heb. 7:2 (Melchizedec, "by interpretation," lit., 'being interpreted,' King of righteousness). ¶
NT: B.310a; CB.1250a; K.256.
OT: targēm: S.8638; HR.547c.1; H.2543; BD.1076a.
GEN. REF.: IS.2:861; NB.566; Z.3:297.

2. *diermēneuō* [διερμηνεύω, 1329], a strengthened form of No. 1 (*dia*, through, used intensively), signifies to interpret fully, to explain. In Luke 24:27, it is used of Christ in interpreting to the two on the way to Emmaus "in all the Scriptures the things concerning Himself," R.V., "interpreted" (A.V., "expounded"); in Acts 9:36, it is rendered "is by interpretation," lit., 'being interpreted' (of Tabitha, as meaning Dorcas); in 1 Cor. 12:30 and 14:5, 13, 27, it is used with reference to the temporary gift of tongues in the churches; this gift was inferior in character to that of prophesying, unless he who spoke in a "tongue" interpreted his words, 14:5; he was, indeed, to pray that he might interpret, ver. 13; only two, or at the most three, were to use the gift in a gathering, and that "in turn" (R.V.); one was to interpret; in the absence of an interpreter, the gift was not to be exercised, ver. 27. See EXPOUND. ¶
NT: B.194b; CB.1241c; K.256.
OT: —.
GEN. REF.: IS.2:861; NB.566; Z.3:297.

3. *methermēneuō* [μεθερμηνεύω, 3177], to change or translate from one language to another (*meta*, implying change, and No. 1), to interpret, is always used in the Passive Voice in the N.T., "being interpreted," of interpreting the names, Immanuel, Matt. 1:23; Golgotha, Mark 15:22; Barnabas, Acts 4:36; in Acts 13:8, of Elymas, the verb is rendered "is . . . by interpretation," lit., 'is interpreted'; it is used of interpreting or translating sentences in Mark 5:41; 15:34; in the best mss., John 1:38 (Rabbi, interpreted as "Master"); ver. 41 (Messiah, interpreted as "Christ"); see No. 1. ¶
NT: B.498d; CB.1258c; K.—.
OT: —.
GEN. REF.: —.

B. Nouns.
(INTERPRETATION)

1. *hermēneia* (or *-ia*) [ἑρμηνία, 2058], akin to A, No. 1, is used in 1 Cor. 12:10; 14:26 (see A, No. 2). ¶

NT: B.310a; CB.1250a; K.256.
OT: —.
GEN. REF.: IS.2:861; NB.566; Z.3:297.

2. *epilusis* [ἐπίλυσις, 1955], from *epiluō*, to loose, solve, explain, denotes a solution, explanation, lit., a release (*epi*, up, *luō*, to loose), 2 Pet. 1:20, "(of private) interpretation"; i.e., the writers of Scripture did not put their own construction upon the 'God-breathed' words they wrote. ¶

NT: B.295d; CB.1246a; K.543.
OT: —.
GEN. REF.: IS.2:861; NB.566; Z.3:297.

Note: For "hard of interpretation," Heb. 5:11, R.V., see UTTER, *Note* (1).

(INTERPRETER)

diermēneutēs [διερμηνευτής, 1328], lit., a thorough interpreter (cp. A. No. 2), is used in 1 Cor. 14:28 (some mss. have *hermēneutēs*). ¶

NT: B.194b; CB.1241c; K.256.
OT: —.
GEN. REF.: IS.2:861; NB.566; Z.3:297.

INTERROGATION

eperōtēma [ἐπερώτημα, 1906], primarily a question or enquiry, denotes a demand or appeal; it is found in 1 Pet. 3:21, R.V., "interrogation" (A.V., "answer"). See ANSWER, *Note*. Some take the word to indicate that baptism affords a good conscience, an appeal against the accuser. ¶

NT: B.285c; CB.1245c; K.262.
OT: sheʾēlā': S.7595,7596; HR.511a.1; H.3012a,2303a; BD.982c,1114a.
GEN. REF.: —.

INTO: see † p. 1.

INTREAT, INTREATY

A. Verbs.

1. *erōtaō* [ἐρωτάω, 2065], to ask, beseech, is rendered "intreat," e.g., in Phil. 4:3, A.V. (R.V., "beseech"). See ASK.

NT: B.311d; CB.1246c; K.262.
OT: shā'al: S.7592; HR.553b.3a; H.2303; BD.981b.
GEN. REF.: —.

2. *parakaleō* [παρακαλέω, 3870], to beseech, comfort, exhort, is rendered by the verb to intreat in Luke 8:31, R.V., "intreated" (A.V., "besought"); 15:28; Acts 9:38, R.V., "intreating" (A.V., "desiring"); 28:20, R.V. (A.V., "called for"); 1 Cor. 4:13; 2 Cor. 9:5, R.V. (A.V., "exhort"); 10:1, R.V. (A.V., "beseech"); 1 Tim. 5:1, A.V. (R.V., "exhort"). See BESEECH.

NT: B.617a; CB.1262a; K.778.
OT: nāḥam: S.5162; HR.1060a.10a-d; H.1344; BD.636d.
GEN. REF.: IS.2:107; NB.—; Z.—.

3. *paraiteomai* [παραιτέομαι, 3868], to ask to be excused, to beg, etc., is rendered "intreated" in Heb. 12:19. See AVOID.

NT: B.616c; CB.1262a; K.30.
OT: shā'al: S.7592; HR.1060a.3; H.2303; BD.981b.
ḥānan: S.2603; HR.1060a.2; H.694,695; BD.335d,336b.
GEN. REF.: IS.2:107; NB.—; Z.—.

B. Adjective.

eupeithēs [εὐπειθής, 2138], ready to obey (*eu*, well, *peithomai*, to obey, to be persuaded), compliant, is translated "easy to be intreated" in Jas. 3:17, said of the wisdom that is from above. ¶

NT: B.324a; CB.—; K.—.
OT: —.
GEN. REF.: IS.2:107; NB.—; Z.—.

C. Noun.

paraklēsis [παράκλησις, 3874], an appeal, a comfort, exhortation, etc., is translated "intreaty" in 2 Cor. 8:4.

NT: B.618a; CB.1262a; K.778.
OT: tanᵉḥûm: S.8575; HR.1061a.1d; H.1144d; BD.637c.
nāḥam: S.5162; HR.1061a.1e; H.1344; BD.636d.
GEN. REF.: IS.2:107; NB.—; Z.—.

For **INTRUDE** (Col. 2:18) see **DWELL**, A. No. 11

INTRUST

pisteuō [πιστεύω, 4100], to believe, also means to entrust, and in the Active Voice is translated to commit, in Luke 16:11; John 2:24; in the Passive Voice, to be intrusted with, Rom. 3:2, R.V., "they were intrusted with" (A.V., "unto them were committed"), of Israel and the oracles of God; 1 Cor. 9:17, R.V., "I have . . . intrusted to me" (A.V., "is committed unto me"), of Paul and the stewardship of the Gospel; so Gal. 2:7; Tit. 1:3; in 1 Thess. 2:4, where he associates with himself his fellow-missionaries, R.V., "to be intrusted with" (A.V., "to be put in trust with"). See BELIEVE, COMMIT.

NT: B.660b; CB.1265a; K.849.
OT: 'āman: S.539; HR.1137c.1b; H.116; BD.52d.
GEN. REF.: IS.2:107; NB.—; Z.—.

INVENTORS

epheuretēs [ἐφευρετής, 2182], an inventor, contriver (akin to *epheuriskō*, to find out; *epi*, on, used intensively, *heuriskō*, to find), occurs in the plural in Rom. 1:30. ¶

NT: B.330b; CB.—; K.—.
OT: —.
GEN. REF.: —.

INVISIBLE

aoratos [ἀόρατος, 517], lit., unseen (*a*, negative, *horaō*, to see), is translated "invisible" in Rom. 1:20, of the power and Divinity of

God; of God Himself, Col. 1:15; 1 Tim. 1:17; Heb. 11:27; of things unseen, Col. 1:16. ¶ In the Sept., Gen. 1:2; Is. 45:3, "unseen (treasures)." ¶

NT: B.79a; CB.1236a; K.706.
OT: mistār: S.4565; HR.113c.1; H.1551d; BD.712c.
tōhû: S.8414; HR.113c.2; H.2494a; BD.1062c.
GEN. REF.: IS.2:878; NB.—; Z.—.

INWARD (man, part), INWARDLY

1. *esō* [*ἔσω*, 2080], within, inward, is used adjectivally in Rom. 7:22, "(the) inward (man)"; 2 Cor. 4:16, with "man" expressed in the preceding clause, but not repeated in the original, "(our) inward (man)" (some mss. have *esōthen*, from within); Eph. 3:16, R.V., "(the) inward (man)" (A.V., "inner"). See INNER, WITHIN.

NT: B.314b; CB.1246c; K.265.
OT: pᵉnîmāh: S.6441; HR.558c.2b; H.1782c; BD.819b.
GEN. REF.: —.

2. *esōthen* [*ἔσωθεν*, 2081], is used in Luke 11:39, as a noun with the article, "part" being understood, "(your) inward part"; in Matt. 7:15 it has its normal use as an adverb, "inwardly." See WITHIN.

NT: B.314b; CB.—; K.—.
OT: mibbayit: S.1004; HR.559a.1c; H.241; BD.108c,110a.
mippᵉnîmāh: S.6441; HR.559a.2d; H.1782c; BD.819b.
pᵉnîmî: S.6442; HR.559a.2e; H.1782d; BD.819b.
GEN. REF.: —.

Note: In Rom. 2:29 the phrase *en tǭ kruptǭ*, lit., in (the) secret, or hidden ('part' being understood), is rendered "inwardly," said of a spiritual Jew, in contrast to the one who is merely naturally circumcised and so is one outwardly. See HIDE, SECRET.

IRKSOME

oknēros [*ὀκνηρός*, 3636], shrinking, timid (from *okneō*, to shrink, delay), is used negatively in Phil. 3:1, R.V., "irksome" (A.V., "grievous"), i.e., 'I do not hesitate'; in Matt. 25:26, and Rom. 12:11, "slothful." See GRIEVOUS, SLOTHFUL. ¶

NT: B.563a; CB.—; K.681.
OT: 'āṣēl: S.6102; HR.985b.1a; H.1672a; BD.782b.
GEN. REF.: —.

IRON

A. Noun.

sidēros [*σίδηρος*, 4604], iron, occurs in Rev. 18:12. ¶

NT: B.750a; CB.1269a; K.—.
OT: barzel: S.1270; HR.1266a.1; H.283a; BD.137b.
GEN. REF.: IS.2:880; NB.825; Z.3:307.

B. Adjective.

sidēreos [*σιδήρεος*, 4603], of iron, occurs in Acts 12:10, of an iron gate; "of iron," Rev. 2:27; 9:9; 12:5; 19:15. ¶

NT: B.750a; CB.1269a; K.—.
OT: barzel: S.1270; HR.1266b.1; H.283a; BD.137b.
GEN. REF.: IS.2:880; NB.825; Z.3:307.

ISLAND, ISLE

1. *nēsos* [*νῆσος*, 3520], an island, occurs in Acts 13:6; 27:26; 28:1, 7, 9, 11; Rev. 1:9; 6:14; 16:20. ¶

NT: B.538a; CB.—; K.—.
OT: 'î: S.339; HR.944c.1; H.39a; BD.15d.
GEN. REF.: IS.2:907; NB.578; Z.3:335.

2. *nēsion* [*νησίον*, 3519], a diminutive of No. 1, a small island, occurs in Acts 27:16, Cauda, R.V. ¶

NT: B.538a; CB.—; K.—.
OT: —.
GEN. REF.: IS.2:907; NB.578; Z.3:335.

ISSUE

A. Nouns.

1. *ekbasis* [*ἔκβασις*, 1545], a way out, "way of escape," 1 Cor. 10:13 (*ek*, out, *bainō*, to go), is rendered "issue" in Heb. 13:7, R.V., for A.V., "end," regarding the manner of life of deceased spiritual guides. See END. ¶

NT: B.237b; CB.—; K.—.
OT: —.
GEN. REF.: —.

2. *rhusis* [*ῥύσις*, 4511], a flowing (akin to *rheō*, to flow), an issue, is used in Mark 5:25; Luke 8:43, 44. ¶

NT: B.738b; CB.1268b; K.—.
OT: zôb: S.2101; HR.1255c.1b; H.534a; BD.264d.
GEN. REF.: IS.—; NB.589; Z.—.

Note: In Matt. 22:25, A.V., *sperma*, seed, is translated "issue" (RV., "seed").

B. Verb.

ekporeuō [*ἐκπορεύω*, 1607], to cause to go forth (*ek*, out, *poreuō*, to cause to go), is used in the Middle Voice in Rev. 9:17, 18, of the coming forth of fire, smoke and brimstone from the mouths of the symbolic horses in a vision, A.V., "issued" (the R.V. renders it by the verb to proceed). See COME, DEPART, GO, PROCEED

NT: B.244b; CB.1244a; K.915.
OT: yāṣā': S.3318; HR.439b.5a; H.893; BD.422b.
GEN. REF.: —.

IT

Note: The pronouns used are the same, in their neuter forms, as Nos. 1, 2, 3 under HE.

ITCHING

knēthō [*κνήθω*, 2833] to scratch, tickle, is used in the Passive Voice, metaphorically, of an eagerness to hear, in 2 Tim. 4:3, lit., 'itched (as to the hearing),' of those who, not enduring sound doctrine, heap to themselves teachers. ¶

NT: B.437a; CB.—; K.—.
OT: —.
GEN. REF.: —.

ITSELF

Note: The pronouns used are the same in their neuter forms, as those under HIMSELF.

IVORY

elephantinos [ἐλεφάντινος, 1661], an adjective from *elephas* (whence Eng., elephant), signifies 'of ivory,' Rev. 18:12. ¶

NT: B.251a; CB.—; K.—.
OT: shēn: S.8127; HR.452c.1; H.2422a; BD.1042a.
GEN. REF.: IS.2:940; NB.590; Z.3:376.

J

JACINTH

A. Noun.

huakinthos [ὑάκινθος, 5192], primarily denoted a hyacinth, probably the dark blue iris; then, a precious stone, most likely the sapphire, Rev. 21:20. ¶

NT: B.831b; CB.1251b; K.—.
OT: t[e]kēlet: S.8504; HR.1379b.2; H.2510; BD.1067a.
GEN. REF.: IS.4:627; NB.632; Z.3:383.

B. Adjective.

huakinthinos [ὑακίνθινος, 5191], signifies hyacinthine, perhaps primarily having the colour of the hyacinth. Some regard its colour as that of the martagon lily, a dusky red. According to Swete, the word in Rev. 9:17 is "doubtless meant to describe the blue smoke of a sulphurous flame." ¶

NT: B.831b; CB.—; K.—.
OT: t[e]kēlet: S.8504; HR.1379a.2; H.2510; BD.1067a.
taḥash: S.8476; HR.1379a.1; H.2503; BD.1065a.
GEN. REF.: IS.4:627; NB.632; Z.3:383.

JAILOR

desmophulax [δεσμοφύλαξ, 1200], a prison-keeper, gaoler (*desmos*, a band, *phulax*, a guard, keeper), occurs in Acts 16:23, 27, 36. ¶

NT: B.176b; CB.1240c; K.—.
OT: —.
GEN. REF.: IS.3:973; NB.—; Z.—.

For **JANGLING** (1 Tim. 1:6, A.V.) see **TALKING (vain)**

JASPER

iaspis [ἴασπις, 2393], a Phoenician word (cp. Heb. *yāsh'pheh*, e.g., Ex. 28:20; 39:16), seems to have denoted a translucent stone of various colours, especially that of fire, Rev. 4:3; 21:11, 18, 19. The sardius and the jasper, of similar colour, were the first and last stones on the breastplate of the High Priest, Ex. 28:17, 20. ¶

NT: B.368d; CB.1252c; K.—.
OT: yah[a]lōm: S.3095; HR.669a.1; H.502b; BD.240d.
yash[e]pheh: S.3471; HR.669a.2; H.929.1; BD.448c.
kadkōd: S.3539; HR.669a.3; H.953c; BD.461d.
GEN. REF.: IS.4:627; NB.632; Z.3:408.

JEALOUS, JEALOUSY

A. Noun.

zēlos [ζῆλος, 2205], zeal, jealousy, is rendered "jealousy" in the R.V. (A.V., "envying") in Rom. 13:13; 1 Cor. 3:3; Jas. 3:14, 16; in 2 Cor. 12:20 (A.V., "envyings"); in Gal. 5:20, R.V. "jealousies" (A.V., "emulations"); in Acts 5:17 (A.V., "indignation"); in 13:45 (A.V., "envy"); in 2 Cor. 11:2 it is used in the phrase "with a godly jealousy," lit., 'with a jealousy of God' (R.V., marg.). See ENVY.

NT: B.337c; CB.1273b; K.297.
OT: qin'āh: S.7068; HR.594a.1; H.2038a; BD.888b.
GEN. REF.: IS.2:971; NB.601; Z.3:410.

B. Verbs.

1. *zēloō* [ζηλόω, 2206], akin to A, to be jealous, to burn with jealousy (otherwise, to seek or desire eagerly), is rendered "moved with jealousy," in Acts 7:9 and 17:5, R.V. (A.V., "moved with envy"); in 1 Cor. 13:4, "envieth (not)," A.V. and R.V.; in Jas. 4:2, R.V. marg., "are jealous" (text "covet"; A.V., "desire to have"). See AFFECT, *Note*, DESIRE.

NT: B.338a; CB.1273b; K.297.
OT: qānā': S.7065; HR.594b.4a; H.2038; BD.888c.
GEN. REF.: IS.2:971; NB.601; Z.3:410.

2. *parazēloō* [παραζηλόω, 3863], to provoke to jealousy (*para*, beside, used intensively, and No. 1), is found in Rom. 10:19 and 11:11, of God's dealings with Israel through his merciful dealings with Gentiles; in 11:14, R.V., "I may provoke to jealousy" (A.V., ". . . emulation"), of the Apostle's evangelical ministry to Gentiles with a view to stirring his fellow-nationals to a sense of their need and responsibilities regarding the Gospel; in 1 Cor. 10:22, of the provocation of God on the part of believers who compromise their Divine relationship by partaking of the table of demons; in Gal. 5:20, of the works of the flesh. ¶

NT: B.616a; CB.—; K.297.
OT: qānā': S.7065; HR.1059c.2; H.2038; BD.888c.
GEN. REF.: IS.2:971; NB.601; Z.3:410.

For JEOPARDY see DANGER

JESTING

eutrapelia [εὐτραπελία, 2160], properly denotes wit, facetiousness, versatility (lit., easily turning, from *eu*, well, *trepō*, to turn). It was used in the literal sense to describe the quick movements of apes and persons. Pericles speaks of the Athenians of his day (430 B.C.) as distinguished by a happy and gracious 'flexibility.' In the next century Aristotle uses it of 'versatility' in the give and take of social intercourse, quick repartee. In the sixth century, B.C., the poet Pindar speaks of one Jason as never using a word of 'vain lightness,' a meaning approaching to its latest use. Its meaning certainly deteriorated, and it came to denote coarse jesting, ribaldry, as in Eph. 5:4, where it follows *mōrologia*, foolish talking. ¶

NT: B.327c; CB.–; K.–.
OT: –.
GEN. REF.: IS.2:1034; NB.–; Z.–.

JESUS

iēsous [Ἰησοῦς, 2424], is a transliteration of the Heb. "Joshua," meaning 'Jehovah is salvation,' i.e., 'is the Saviour,' "a common name among the Jews, e.g., Ex. 17:9; Luke 3:29 (R.V.); Col. 4:11. It was given to the Son of God in Incarnation as His personal name, in obedience to the command of an angel to Joseph, the husband of His Mother, Mary, shortly before He was born, Matt. 1:21. By it He is spoken of throughout the Gospel narratives generally, but not without exception, as in Mark 16:19, 20; Luke 7:13, and a dozen other places in that Gospel, and a few in John.

" 'Jesus Christ' occurs only in Matt. 1:1, 18; 16:21, marg.; Mark 1:1; John 1:17; 17:3. In Acts the name 'Jesus' is found frequently. 'Lord Jesus' is the normal usage, as in Acts 8:16; 19:5, 17; see also the reports of the words of Stephen, 7:59, of Ananias, 9:17, and of Paul, 16:31; though both Peter, 10:36, and Paul, 16:18, also used 'Jesus Christ.'

"In the Epp. of James, Peter, John and Jude, the personal name is not once found alone, but in Rev. eight times (R.V.), 1:9; 12:17; 14:12; 17:6; 19:10 (twice); 20:4; 22:16.

"In the Epp. of Paul 'Jesus' appears alone just thirteen times, and in the Hebrews eight times; in the latter the title 'Lord' is added once only, at 13:20. In the Epp. of James, Peter, John, and Jude, men who had companied with the Lord in the days of His flesh, 'Jesus Christ' is the invariable order (in the R.V.) of the Name and Title, for this was the order of their experience; as 'Jesus' they knew Him first, that He was Messiah they learnt finally in His resurrection. But Paul came to know Him first in the glory of heaven, Acts 9:1-6, and his experience being thus the reverse of theirs, the reverse order, 'Christ Jesus,' is of frequent occurrence in his letters, but, with the exception of Acts 24:24, does not occur elsewhere in the R.V.

"In Paul's letters the order is always in harmony with the context. Thus 'Christ Jesus' describes the Exalted One who emptied Himself, Phil. 2:5, and testifies to His preexistence; 'Jesus Christ' describes the despised and rejected One Who was afterwards glorified, Phil. 2:11, and testifies to His resurrection. 'Christ Jesus' suggests His grace, 'Jesus Christ' suggests His glory."*

NT: B.373d; CB.1252c; K.360.
OT: yᵉshû'āh: S.3444; HR.–; H.929b; BD.447b.
GEN. REF.: IS.2:1034; NB.620; Z.3:497.

JEW(-S) (live as do the), JEWESS, JEWISH, JEWRY, JEWS' RELIGION

A. Adjectives.

1. *ioudaios* [Ἰουδαῖος, 2453], is used (*a*) adjectivally, with the lit. meaning, 'Jewish,' sometimes with the addition of *anēr*, a man, Acts 10:28; 22:3; in 21:39 with *anthrōpos*, in some mss. (a man in the generic sense); the best mss. omit the phrase here; in 13:6, lit., 'a Jewish false-prophet'; in John 3:22, with the word *chōra*, land or country, signifying 'Judaean,' lit., 'Judaean country'; used by metonymy for the people of the country; (*b*) as a noun, a Jew, Jews, e.g., Matt. 2:2; Mark 7:3. The name 'Jew' is primarily "tribal" (from 'Judah'). It is first found in 2 Kings 16:6, as distinct from Israel, of the Northern Kingdom. After the Captivity it was chiefly used to distinguish the race from Gentiles, e.g., John 2:6; Acts 14:1; Gal. 2:15, where it denotes Christians of Jewish race; it distinguishes Jews from Samaritans, in John 4:9; from proselytes, in Acts 2:10. The word is most frequent in John's Gospel and the Acts; in the former "it especially denotes the typical representatives of Jewish thought contrasted with believers in Christ . . . or with other Jews of less pronounced opinions, e.g., John 3:25; 5:10; 7:13; 9:22" (Lukyn Williams, in Hastings' Bib. Dic.); such representatives were found,

* From Notes on Thessalonians, by Hogg and Vine, pp. 26, 29.

generally, in opposition to Christ; in the Acts they are chiefly those who opposed the apostles and the Gospel. In Rom. 2:28, 29 the word is used of ideal Jews, i.e., Jews in spiritual reality, believer, whether Jews or Gentiles by natural birth. The feminine, "Jewess," is found in Acts 16:1; 24:24.

It also denotes Judaea, e.g., Matt. 2:1; Luke 1:5; John 4:3, the word 'country' being understood [cp. (*a*) above]. In Luke 23:5 and John 7:1, where the A.V. has "Jewry," the R.V. translates it as usual "Judaea."

NT: B.379b; CB.1252c; K.372.
OT: yᵉhûdāh: S.3063; HR.–; H.850c; BD.397a.
GEN. REF.: IS.2:1056; NB.670; Z.3:585,727.

2. *ioudaikos* ['Ἰουδαϊκός, 2451], denotes "Jewish," Tit. 1:14. ¶

NT: B.379d; CB.1252c; K.372.
OT: –.
GEN. REF.: IS.2:1056; NB.670; Z.3:585,727.

B. Noun.

ioudaismos ['Ἰουδαϊσμός, 2454], Judaism, denotes "the Jews' religion," Gal. 1:13, 14, and stands, not for their religious beliefs, but for their religious practices, not as instituted by God, but as developed and extended from these by the traditions of the Pharisees and scribes. In the Apocrypha it denotes comprehensively "the Government, laws, institutions and religion of the Jews." ¶

NT: B.379d; CB.1252c; K.372.
OT: –.
GEN. REF.: IS.2:1056; NB.670; Z.3:727.

C. Verb.

ioudaizō ['Ἰουδαΐζω, 2450], lit. to Judaize, i.e., to conform to Jewish religious practices and manners, is translated "to live as do the Jews," in Gal. 2:14. ¶

NT: B.379b; CB.1252c; K.372.
OT: yāhad: S.3054; HR.687a.1; H.850; BD.397c.
GEN. REF.: IS.2:1056; NB.670; Z.3:727.

D. Adverb.

ioudaikōs ['Ἰουδαϊκῶς, 2452], in Jewish fashion, is translated "as do the Jews," in Gal. 2:14. ¶

NT: B.379b; CB.1252c; K.–.
OT: –.
GEN. REF.: IS.2:1056; NB.670; Z.3:727.

JEWELS

chrusion [χρυσίον, 5553], gold, is used of ornaments in 1 Pet. 3:3, R.V., "jewels." See GOLD, No. 2.

NT: B.888c; CB.1240b; K.–.
OT: zāhāb: S.2091; HR.1477a.1a; H.520a; BD.262c.
GEN. REF.: IS.2:520; NB.–; Z.–.

JOIN

1. *kollaō* [κολλάω, 2853], primarily, to glue or cement together, then, generally, to unite, to join firmly, is used in the Passive Voice signifying to join oneself to, to be joined to, Luke 15:15; Acts 5:13; 8:29; 9:26; 10:28, R.V. (A.V., "to keep company with"); 1 Cor. 6:16, 17; elsewhere, to cleave to, Luke 10:11; Acts 17:34; Rom. 12:9. See CLEAVE. ¶

NT: B.441c; CB.1255c; K.452.
OT: dābaq: S.1692; HR.776b.1a; H.398; BD.179c.
GEN. REF.: IS.2:1111; NB.–; Z.–.

2. *proskollaō* [προσκολλάω, 4347], to stick to, a strengthened form of No. 1, with *pros*, to, intensive, is used in the Passive Voice, reflexively in a metaphorical sense, with the meanings (*a*) to join oneself to, in Acts 5:36; (*b*) to cleave to, of the husband with regard to the wife, Matt. 19:5; Mark 10:7; in Eph. 5:31, R.V., "shall cleave to" (A.V., "shall be joined to"). See CLEAVE. ¶

NT: B.716a; CB.1267a; K.–.
OT: dābaq: S.1692; HR.1217a.2a-c; H.398; BD.179c.
GEN. REF.: IS.2:1111; NB.–; Z.–.

3. *su(n)zeugnumi* [συνζεύγνυμι, 4801], to yoke together (*sun*, with, *zugos*, a yoke), is used metaphorically of union-in wedlock, in Matt. 19:6; Mark 10:9. ¶

NT: B.775c; CB.1271a; K.–.
OT: ḥābar: S.2266; HR.1301a.1; H.598; BD.287d.
GEN. REF.: IS.2:1111; NB.–; Z.–.

4. *sunomoreō* [συνομορέω, 4927], to border on, is used of a house as being contiguous with a synagogue, in Acts 18:7, "joined hard to." ¶

NT: B.791c; CB.–; K.–.
OT: –.
GEN. REF.: –.

Notes: (1) In 1 Cor. 1:10, *katartizō*, to render complete, to perfect, (*kata*, down, intensive, and *artios*, complete, jointed), to restore, is translated "be perfectly joined together," A.V. (R.V., "be perfected together"); see FIT.

(2) In Eph. 4:16, *sunarmologeō*, to fit or frame together, is translated "fitly joined together," A.V. (R.V., fitly framed . . . together"); cp. 2:21. ¶

JOINT

1. *harmos* [ἁρμός, 719], a joining, joint (akin to *harmozō*, to fit, join), is found in Heb. 4:12, figuratively (with the word "marrow") of the inward moral and spiritual being of man, as just previously expressed literally in the phrase "soul and spirit." ¶

NT: B.107d; CB.1249b; K.–.
OT: –.
GEN. REF.: –.

2. *haphē* [ἁφή, 860], a ligature, joint (akin to *haptō*, to fit, to fasten), occurs in Eph. 4:16 and Col. 2:19. ¶

NT: B.125a; CB.1249b; K.–.
OT: negaʻ: S.5061; HR.182c.1; H.1293a; BD.619b.
GEN. REF.: –.

For JOINT-HEIR see HEIR

JOT

iōta [ἰῶτα, 2503], from the Heb. *yod*, the smallest Hebrew letter, is mentioned by the Lord in Matt. 5:18 (together with *keraia*, a little horn, a tittle, the point or extremity which distinguishes certain Hebrew letters from others), to express the fact that not a single item of the Law will pass away or remain unfulfilled. ¶

NT: B.386a; CB.1252c; K.–.
OT: –.
GEN. REF.: IS.2:879; NB.665; Z.3:713.

JOURNEY (Noun and Verb), JOURNEYINGS

A. Nouns.

1. *hodos* [ὁδός, 3598], a way, path, road, used of a traveller's way, a journey, is rendered "journey" in Matt. 10:13; Mark 6:8; Luke 2:44, "a day's journey" (probably to Beeroth, six miles north of Jerusalem); 9:3; 11:6; Acts 1:12, "a Sabbath day's journey," i.e., the journey which a Jew was allowed to take on the Sabbath, viz., about 2,000 yards or cubits (estimates vary). The regulation was not a Mosaic enactment, but a Rabbinical tradition, based upon an exposition of Ex. 16:29, and a comparison of the width of the suburb of a Levitical city as enjoined in Num. 35:4, 5, and the distance between the Ark and the people at the crossing of the Jordan, Josh. 3:4. In regard to Acts 1:12, there is no discrepancy between this and Luke 24:50, where the R.V. rightly translates by "over against Bethany," which does not fix the exact spot of the Ascension. See HIGHWAY, WAY.

NT: B.553d; CB.1251a; K.666.
OT: derek: S.1870; HR.962b.3a; H.453a; BD.202c.
GEN. REF.: IS.1:879; NB.–; Z.–.

2. *hodoiporia* [ὁδοιπορία, 3597], a wayfaring, journeying (No. 1, and *poros*, a way, a passage), is used of the Lord's journey to Samaria, John 4:6, and of Paul's "journeyings," 2 Cor. 11:26. Cp. B, No. 3.

NT: B.553d; CB.–; K.–.
OT: –.
GEN. REF.: –.

Note: In Luke 13:22 the noun *poreia*, a journey, a going (cp. *poros*, No. 2, above), is used with the verb *poieō*, to make, with the meaning 'to journey,' lit., 'making (for Himself, Middle Voice) a way,' "journeying." In Jas. 1:11, "ways." See WAY. ¶

B. Verbs.

1. *poreuomai* [πορεύομαι, 4198], is used in the Middle Voice in the N.T., signifying to go, proceed, go on one's way; it is translated by the verb to journey in Acts 9:3; 22:6, "as I made (my) journey"; 26:13; Rom. 15:24 (1st part), A.V., "I take my journey," R.V., "I go" (for the 2nd part, "in my journey," see No. 2). See GO, No. 1.

NT: B.692b; CB.1266a; K.915.
OT: hālak: S.1980; HR.1189a.3a; H.498; BD.229d.
GEN. REF.: –.

2. *diaporeuō* [διαπορεύω, 1279], to carry over, used in the Passive Voice with the meaning to pass by, to journey through, is translated "in my journey," in Rom. 15:24, lit., 'journeying through'; in Luke 18:36, R.V., "going by" (A.V. "pass by"). See GO, No. 4.

NT: B.187d; CB.–; K.–.
OT: hālak: S.1980; HR.308b.4a-c; H.498; BD.229d.
'abar: S.5674; HR.308b.6; H.1556; BD.716d.
GEN. REF.: –.

3. *hodoiporeō* [ὁδοιπορέω, 3596], to travel, journey (akin to A, No. 2), is found in Acts 10:9. ¶

NT: B.553c; CB.1251a; K.–.
OT: –.
GEN. REF.: –.

4. *hodeuō* [ὁδεύω, 3593], to be on the way, journey (from *hodos*, a way), the simplest form of the verbs denoting to journey, is used in the parable of the Good Samaritan, Luke 10:33. ¶

NT: B.553b; CB.–; K.–.
OT: hālak: S.1980; HR.961c.1; H.498; BD.229d.
GEN. REF.: –.

5. *sunodeuō* [συνοδεύω, 4922], *sun*, with, and No. 4, to journey with, occurs in Acts 9:7. ¶ In the Sept., Zech. 8:21. ¶

NT: B.791a; CB.–; K.–.
OT: hālak: S.1980; HR.1317b.1; H.498; BD.229d.
GEN. REF.: –.

6. *euodoō* [εὐοδόω, 2137], to help on one's way (*eu*, well, and *hodos*), is used in the Passive Voice with the meaning 'to have a prosperous journey'; so the A.V. of Rom. 1:10; the R.V., "I may be prospered" rightly expresses the metaphorical use which the verb acquired, without reference to a journey; see 1 Cor. 16:2; 3 John 2. ¶

NT: B.323d; CB.–; K.666.
OT: ṣālēaḥ: S.6743; HR.575c.3b; H.1916,1917; BD.852b.
GEN. REF.: –.

7. *propempō* [προπέμπω, 4311], to send before or forth (*pro*, before, *pempō*, to send), also means to set forward on a journey, to escort; in 1 Cor. 16:6, "may set (me) forward on my journey," R.V. [A.V., "may bring (me) etc."]; so Tit. 3:13, and 3 John 6. See ACCOMPANY, CONDUCT, WAY.

NT: B.709b; CB.–; K.–.
OT: –.
GEN. REF.: –.

8. *apodēmeō* [ἀποδημέω, 589], denotes to go on a journey to another country, go abroad, Matt. 21:33; 25:14, 15; Mark 12:1; Luke 15:13; 20:9. See COUNTRY. ¶

NT: B.90a; CB.1236c; K.—.
OT: —.
GEN. REF.: —.

Note: For the adjective *apodēmos*, Mark 13:34, A.V., "taking a far journey," R.V., "sojourning in another country," See COUNTRY.

JOY (Noun and Verb), JOYFULNESS, JOYFULLY, JOYOUS

A. Nouns.

1. *chara* [χαρά, 5479], joy, delight (akin to *chairō*, to rejoice), is found frequently in Matthew and Luke, and especially in John, once in Mark (4:16, R.V., "joy," A.V., "gladness"); it is absent from 1 Cor. (though the verb is used three times), but is frequent in 2 Cor., where the noun is used five times (for 7:4, R.V., see Note below), and the verb eight times, suggestive of the Apostle's relief in comparison with the circumstances of the 1st Epistle; in Col. 1:11, A.V., "joyfulness," R.V., "joy." The word is sometimes used, by metonymy, of the occasion or cause of joy, Luke 2:10 (lit., 'I announce to you a great joy'); in 2 Cor. 1:15, in some mss., for *charis*, "benefit"; Phil. 4:1, where the readers are called the Apostle's joy; so 1 Thess. 2:19, 20; Heb. 12:2, of the object of Christ's joy; Jas. 1:2, where it is connected with falling into trials; perhaps also in Matt. 25:21, 23, where some regard it as signifying, concretely, the circumstances attending co-operation in the authority of the Lord. See also the Note following No. 3.

NT: B.875c; CB.1239b; K.1298.
OT: simḥāh: S.8057; HR.1454b.5; H.2268b; BD.970d.
sāsôn: S.8342; HR.1454b.6a; H.2246a; BD.965b.
GEN. REF.: IS.2:1140; NB.665; Z.3:714.

Note: In Heb. 12:11, "joyous" represents the phrase *meta*, with, followed by *chara*, lit., 'with joy.' So in 10:34, "joyfully"; in 2 Cor.7:4 the noun is used with the Middle Voice of *huperperisseuō*, to abound more exceedingly, and translated "(I overflow) with joy," R.V. (A.V., "I am exceeding joyful").

2. *agalliasis* [ἀγαλλίασις, 20], exultation, exuberant joy. Cp. B, No. 3, below. See GLADNESS.

NT: B.3d; CB.1233b; K.4.
OT: rinnāh: S.7440; HR.5b.3a; H.2179c; BD.943c.
sāsôn: S.8342; HR.5b.4; H.2246a; BD.965b.
GEN. REF.: IS.2:1140; NB.665; Z.3:714.

3. *euphrosunē* [εὐφροσύνη, 2167], is rendered "joy" in the A.V. of Acts 2:28, R.V., "gladness," as in 14:17. See GLADNESS. ¶

NT: B.328a; CB.1247b; K.278.
OT: simḥāh: S.8057; HR.582c.15d; H.2268b; BD.970d.
GEN. REF.: IS.2:1140; NB.665; Z.3:714.

Note: Joy is associated with life, e.g., 1 Thess. 3:8, 9. Experiences of sorrow prepare for, and enlarge, the capacity for joy, e.g., John 16:20; Rom. 5:3, 4; 2 Cor. 7:4; 8:2; Heb. 10:34; Jas. 1:2. Persecution for Christ's sake enhances joy, e.g., Matt. 5:11, 12; Acts 5:41. Other sources of joy are faith, Rom. 15:13; Phil. 1:25; hope, Rom. 5:2 (*kauchaomai*, see B, No. 2); 12:12 (*chairō*, see B, No. 1); the joy of others, 12:15, which is distinctive of Christian sympathy. Cp. 1 Thess. 3:9. In the O.T. and the N.T. God Himself is the ground and object of the believer's joy, e.g., Ps. 35:9; 43:4; Is. 61:10; Luke 1:47; Rom. 5:11; Phil. 3:1; 4:4.

B. Verbs.

1. *chairō* [χαίρω, 5463], to rejoice, be glad, is translated "joyfully" in Luke 19:6, lit., 'rejoicing'; "we joyed," 2 Cor. 7:13; "I joy," Phil. 2:17; "do ye joy," 2:18; "joying," Col. 2:5; "we joy," 1 Thess. 3:9. It is contrasted with weeping and sorrow, e.g., in John 16:20, 22; Rom. 12:15; 1 Cor. 7:30 (cp. Ps. 30:5). See FAREWELL, GLAD, GREETING, HAIL, REJOICE.

NT: B.873c; CB.1239b; K.1298.
OT: sāmaḥ: S.8055; HR.1452a.7a; H.2268; BD.970a.
gîl: S.1524; HR.1452a.2; H.346a; BD.162b.
GEN. REF.: IS.2:1140; NB.665; Z.3:714.

2. *kauchaomai* [καυχάομαι, 2744], to boast, glory, exult, is rendered "we joy," in Rom. 5:11, A.V. (R.V., "we rejoice"). It would have been an advantage to translate this word distinctively by the verbs to glory or to exult.

NT: B.425c; CB.1254c; K.423.
OT: hālal: S.1984; HR.757b.2; H.499,500; BD.237d.
GEN. REF.: IS.2:1140; NB.665; Z.3:714.

3. *agalliaō* [ἀγαλλιάω, 21], to exult, rejoice greatly, is translated "with exceeding joy" in 1 Pet. 4:13 (Middle Voice), lit., '(ye rejoice, *chairō*) exulting.' Cp. A, No. 2. See GLAD, REJOICE.

NT: B.3d; CB.1233b; K.4.
OT: gîl: S.1524; HR.4c.1; H.346a; BD.162b.
rānan: S.7442; HR.4c.6a-c; H.2134,2179; BD.943a.
GEN. REF.: IS.2:1140; NB.665; Z.3:714.

4. *oninēmi* [ὀνίνημι, 3685], to benefit, profit, in the Middle Voice, to have profit, derive benefit, is translated "let me have joy" in Philm. 20 (R.V. marg., "help"); the Apostle is doubtless continuing his credit and debit metaphors and using the verb in the sense of 'profit.' ¶

NT: B.570d; CB.1260c; K.—.
OT: —.
GEN. REF.: —.

JUDGE (Noun and Verb)

A. Nouns.

1. *kritēs* [κριτής, 2923], a judge (from *krino*, see B, No. 1), is used (*a*) of God, Heb. 12:23, where the order in the original is 'to a Judge who is God of all'; this is really the significance; it suggests that He who is the Judge of His people is at the same time their God; that is the order in 10:30; the word is also used of God in Jas. 4:12, R.V.; (*b*) of Christ, Acts 10:42; 2 Tim. 4:8; Jas. 5:9; (*c*) of a ruler in Israel in the times of the Judges, Acts 13:20; (*d*) of a Roman procurator, Acts 24:10; (*e*) of those whose conduct provides a standard of judging, Matt. 12:27; Luke 11:19; (*f*) in the forensic sense, of one who tries and decides a case, Matt. 5:25 (twice); Luke 12:14 (some mss. have No. 2 here); 12:58 (twice); 18:2; 18:6 (lit., 'the judge of unrighteousness,' expressing subjectively his character); Acts 18:15; (*g*) of one who passes, or arrogates to himself, judgment on anything, Jas. 2:4 (see the R.V.); 4:11.

NT: B.453c; CB.1256a; K.469.
OT: shāphaṭ: S.8199; HR.791a.5a; H.2443; BD.1047a.
GEN. REF.: IS.2:1156; NB.676; Z.3:739.

2. *dikastēs* [δικαστής, 1348], denotes a judge (from *dikē*, right, a judicial hearing, justice; akin to *dikazō*, to judge), Acts 7:27, 35; some mss. have it in Luke 12:14 (see No. 1); while *dikastēs* is a forensic term, *kritēs* "gives prominence to the mental process" (Thayer). At Athens the *dikastēs* acted as a juryman, the *kritēs* being the presiding judge. ¶

NT: B.198b; CB.—; K.—.
OT: shāphaṭ: S.8199; HR.335b.1; H.2443; BD.1047a.
GEN. REF.: IS.2:1156; NB.676; Z.3:739.

B. Verbs.

1. *krinō* [κρίνω, 2919], primarily denotes to separate, select, choose; hence, to determine, and so to judge, pronounce judgment. "The uses of this verb in the N.T. may be analysed as follows: (*a*) to assume the office of a judge, Matt. 7:1; John 3:17; (*b*) to undergo process of trial, John 3:18; 16:11; 18:31; Jas. 2:12; (*c*) to give sentence, Acts 15:19; 16:4; 21:25; (*d*) to condemn, John 12:48; Acts 13:27; Rom. 2:27; (*e*) to execute judgment upon, 2 Thess. 2:12; Acts 7:7; (*f*) to be involved in a lawsuit, whether as plaintiff, Matt. 5:40; 1 Cor. 6:1; or as defendant, Acts 23:6; (*g*) to administer affairs, to govern, Matt. 19:28; cp. Judg. 3:10; (*h*) to form an opinion, Luke 7:43; John 7:24; Acts 4:19; Rom. 14:5; (*i*) to make a resolve, Acts 3:13; 20:16; 1 Cor. 2:2"*

See CALL, No. 13, CONCLUDE, CONDEMN, DECREE, DETERMINE, ESTEEM, LAW (go to), ORDAIN, SENTENCE, THINK.

NT: B.451b; CB.1256a; K.469.
OT: shāphaṭ: S.8199; HR.787b.10a; H.2443; BD.1047a.
rîb: S.7378; HR.787b.8a; H.2159; BD.936b.
GEN. REF.: IS.2:1156; NB.676; Z.3:758.

Note: In Acts 21:25, the R.V. has "giving judgement" (A.V., "concluded"); see JUDGMENT, *Note* (5).

2. *anakrinō* [ἀνακρίνω, 350], to examine, investigate, question (*ana*, up, and No. 1), is rendered "judged" in 1 Cor. 2:14, R.V. (A.V., "are . . . discerned"; R.V. marg., "examined"), said of the things of the Spirit of God; in ver. 15, "judgeth" (R.V. marg., "examineth"), said of the exercise of a discerning judgment of all things as to their true value, by one who is spiritual; in the same verse, "is judged (of no man)," R.V. marg., "examined," i.e., the merely natural mind cannot estimate the motives of the spiritual; in 4:3, "I should be judged," i.e., as to examining and passing sentence on the fulfilment or non-fulfilment of the Apostle's stewardship; so in the same verse, "I judge (not mine own self)," and in ver. 4 "(he that) judgeth (me is the Lord)"; in 14:24, "he is judged (of all)," i.e., the light of the heart-searching testimony of the assembly probes the conscience of the unregenerate, sifting him judicially, See ASK, No. 7, DISCERN, A, No. 1.

NT: B.56b; CB.1235a; K.469.
OT: ḥāqar: S.2713; HR.78c.1; H.729; BD.350c.
GEN. REF.: IS.2:1156; NB.676; Z.3:758.

3. *diakrinō* [διακρίνω, 1252], denotes to separate throughout (*dia*, and No. 1), discriminate, discern, and hence, to decide, to judge (also to contend, to hesitate, to doubt); it is rendered "to judge" in 1 Cor. 6:5, in the sense of arbitrating; in 11:31 (1st part), the R.V. has "(if we) discerned (ourselves)," A.V. "(if we would) judge" (*krinō*, No. 1, is used in the 2nd part); so in 14:29, R.V., "discern" (A.V., "judge"). See DECIDE, A, DISCERN, A. No. 2.

NT: B.185a; CB.1241a; K.469.
OT: shāphaṭ: S.8199; HR.304a.8a,b; H.2443; BD.1047a.
GEN. REF.: IS.2:1156; NB.676; Z.3:758.

Notes: (1) In 1 Cor. 6:2 (last clause) "to judge" represents the noun *kritērion*, which denotes a tribunal, a law court, and the meaning thus is 'are ye unworthy of sitting upon tribunals of least importance?' (see R.V. marg.), i.e., to judge matters of smallest importance. Some would render it 'cases,' but there is no clear instance elsewhere of this meaning. See JUDGMENT-SEAT.

* From Notes on Thessalonians by Hogg and Vine, p. 267.

(2) In Heb. 11:11, the verb *hēgeomai*, to consider, think, account, is rendered "she judged (Him faithful)," A.V. (R.V., "she counted"). See COUNT, No. 2.

JUDGMENT

1. *krisis* [κρίσις, 2920], primarily denotes a separating, then, a decision, judgment, most frequently in a forensic sense, and especially of Divine judgment. For the variety of its meanings, with references, see CONDEMNATION, B, No. 3.

NT: B.452c; CB.1256a; K.469.
OT: mishpāṭ: S.4941; HR.789c.8d; H.2443c; BD.1048b.
GEN. REF.: IS.2:1161; NB.–; Z.3:758.

Notes: (1) The Holy Spirit, the Lord said, would convict the world of (*peri*, in respect of), i.e., of the actuality of, God's judgment, John 16:8, 11. Cp. 2 Thess. 1:5.

(2) In Rom. 2:5 the word *dikaiokrisia*, "righteous judgment," combines the adjective *dikaios*, righteous, with *krisis*, the two words which are used separately in 2 Thess. 1:5. ¶

2. *krima* [κρίμα, 2917], denotes the result of the action signified by the verb *krinō*, to judge; for its general significance see CONDEMNATION, B, No. 1; it is used (*a*) of a decision passed on the faults of others, Matt. 7:2; (*b*) of judgment by man upon Christ, Luke 24:20; (*c*) of God's judgment upon men, e.g., Rom. 2:2, 3; 3:8; 5:16; 11:33; 13:2; 1 Cor. 11:29; Gal. 5:10; Heb. 6:2; Jas. 3:1; through Christ, e.g., John 9:39; (*d*) of the right of judgment, Rev. 20:4; (*e*) of a law-suit, 1 Cor. 6:7.

NT: B.450c; CB.1256a; K.469.
OT: mishpāṭ: S.4941; HR.786b.7b; H.2443c; BD.1048b.
GEN. REF.: IS.2:1161; NB.–; Z.3:758.

3. *hēmera* [ἡμέρα, 2250], a day, is translated "judgment" in 1 Cor. 4:3, where "man's judgment" (lit., 'man's day,' marg.) is used of the present period in which man's mere judgment is exercised, a period of human rebellion against God. The adjective *anthrōpinos*, human, belonging to man (*anthrōpos*),is doubtless set in contrast here to *kuriakos*, belonging to the Lord (*kurios*, a lord), which is used in the phrase "the Day of the Lord," in Rev. 1:10, "The Lord's Day," a period of Divine judgments. See DAY.

NT: B.345d; CB.1249c; K.309.
OT: yôm: S.3117; HR.607b.9; H.852; BD.398a.
GEN. REF.: –.

4. *gnōmē* [γνώμη, 1106], primarily a means of knowing (akin to *ginōskō*, to know), came to denote a mind, understanding; hence (*a*) a purpose, Acts 20:3, lit., '(it was his) purpose'; (*b*) a royal purpose, a decree, Rev. 17:17, R.V., "mind" (A.V., "will"); (*c*) judgment, opinion, 1 Cor. 1:10, "(in the same) judgment"; Rev. 17:13, "mind"; (*d*) counsel, advice, 1 Cor. 7:25, "(I give my) judgment"; 7:40, "(after my) judgment"; Philm. 14, "mind." See MIND, PURPOSE, WILL. ¶

NT: B.163a; CB.1248b; K.119.
OT: ṭᵉʿēm (Aramaic): S.2942; HR.273a.2a; H.2757a; BD.1094c.
GEN. REF.: –.

Notes: (1) In 1 Cor. 6:4, A.V., *kritērion*, a tribunal, is rendered "judgments" (R.V., "to judge," marg., "tribunals"). See JUDGE, B, No. 3, Note (1).

(2) In Rom. 1:32, A.V., *dikaiōma*, an ordinance, righteous act, is translated "judgment" (R.V. "ordinance"); in Rev. 15:4, "judgments" (R.V., "righteous acts").

(3) In Acts 25:15, A.V., *katadikē*, a sentence, condemnation, is translated "judgment" (R.V., "sentence"). Some mss. have *dikē*. See SENTENCE.

(4) In Phil. 1:9, A.V., *aisthēsis*, perception, discernment, is translated "judgment" (R.V., "discernment").

(5) In Acts 21:25, in the record of the decree from the Apostles and elders at Jerusalem to the churches of the Gentiles, the verb *krinō* (see JUDGE, B, No. 1), is translated "giving judgment," R.V. (A.V., "concluded").

B. Adjective.

hupodikos [ὑπόδικος, 5267], brought to trial, answerable to (*hupo*, under, *dikē*, justice), Rom. 3:19, is translated "under the judgment," R.V. (A.V., "guilty"). ¶

NT: B.844c; CB.–; K.1235.
OT: –.
GEN. REF.: –.

For HALL OF JUDGMENT, JUDGMENT HALL, see HALL

JUDGMENT-SEAT

1. *bēma* [βῆμα, 968], primarily, a step, a pace (akin to *bainō*, to go), as in Acts 7:5, translated "to set (his foot) on," lit., 'foot-room,' was used to denote a raised place or platform, reached by steps, originally that at Athens in the Pnyx Hill, where was the place of assembly; from the platform orations were made. The word became used for a tribune, two of which were provided in the law-courts of Greece, one for the accuser and one for the defendant; it was applied to the tribunal of a Roman magistrate or ruler, Matt. 27:19; John 19:13; Acts 12:21, translated "throne"; 18:12, 16, 17; 25:6, 10, 17.

In two passages the word is used of the Divine tribunal before which all believers are hereafter to stand. In Rom. 14:10 it is called "The judgment-seat of God," R.V. (A.V., "of Christ"), according to the most authentic mss. The same tribunal is called "the judgment-seat of Christ," 2 Cor. 5:10, to whom the Father has given all judgment, John 5:22, 27. At this *bēma* believers are to be made manifest, that each may 'receive the things done in (or through) the body,' according to what he has done, 'whether it be good or bad.' There they will receive rewards for their faithfulness to the Lord. For all that has been contrary in their lives to His will they will suffer loss, 1 Cor. 3:15. This judgment-seat is to be distinguished from the pre-millennial, earthly Throne of Christ, Matt. 25:31, and the post-millennial "Great White Throne," Rev. 20:11, at which only "the dead" will appear. The judgment-seat of Christ will be a tribunal held 'in His Parousia,' i.e., His presence with His saints after His return to receive them to Himself. ¶

NT: B.140b; CB.1239a; K.—.
OT: migdāl: S.4026; HR.217c.1; H.315f,g; BD.153d.
midrāk: S.4096; HR.217c.2; H.453b; BD.204a.
GEN. REF.: IS.2:1161; NB.—; Z.3:760.

2. *kritērion* [κριτήριον, 2922], primarily a means of judging (akin to *krinō*, to judge: Eng., criterion), then, a tribunal, law-court, or lawsuit, 1 Cor 6:2 (last clause), for which see JUDGE, B, No. 3, Note (1); 6:4, for which see JUDGMENT, *Note* (1) at end; Jas. 2:6, ¶

NT: B.453b; CB.—; K.469.
OT: dîn (Aramaic): S.1710; HR.791a.1; H.2674; BD.1088b.
mishpāṭ: S.4941; HR.791a.2; H.2443c; BD.1048b.
GEN. REF.: IS.2:1161,1163; NB.—; Z.—.

JURISDICTION

exousia [ἐξουσία, 1849], power, authority, is used, by metonymy, to denote jurisdiction, in Luke 23:7. For the different meanings of the word and other instances of its use by metonymy, see AUTHORITY, A, No. 1.

NT: B.277d; CB.1247c; K.238.
OT: memshālāh: S.4475; HR.500c.2; H.1259c; BD.606b.
shallîṭ: S.7990; HR.500c.3a; H.3034b; BD.1115d.
GEN. REF.: IS.2:1166; NB.—; Z.—.

JUST, JUSTLY

A. Adjectives.

1. *dikaios* [δίκαιος, 1342], was first used of persons observant of *dikē*, custom, rule, right, especially in the fulfilment of duties towards gods and men, and of things that were in accordance with right. The Eng. word "righteous" was formerly spelt 'rightwise,' i.e., (in a) straight way. In the N.T. it denotes righteous, a state of being right, or right conduct, judged whether by the Divine standard, or according to human standards, of what is right. Said of God, it designates the perfect agreement between His nature and His acts (in which He is the standard for all men). See RIGHTEOUSNESS. It is used (1) in the broad sense, of persons: (*a*) of God, e.g., John 17:25; Rom. 3:26; 1 John 1:9; 2:29; 3:7; (*b*) of Christ, e.g., Acts 3:14; 7:52; 22:14; 2 Tim. 4:8; 1 Pet. 3:18; 1 John 2:1; (*c*) of men, Matt. 1:19; Luke 1:6; Rom. 1:17; 2:13; 5:7. (2) of things; blood (metaphorical), Matt. 23:35; Christ's judgment, John 5:30; any circumstance, fact or deed, Matt. 20:4 (v. 7, in some mss.); Luke 12:57; Acts 4:19; Eph. 6:1; Phil. 1:7; 4:8; Col. 4:1; 2 Thess. 1:6; "the commandment" (the Law), Rom. 7:12; works, 1 John 3:12; the ways of God, Rev. 15:3. See RIGHTEOUS.

NT: B.195c; CB.1241c; K.168.
OT: ṣaddiq: S.6662; HR.330c.10b; H.1879c; BD.843a.
GEN. REF.: IS.2:1166; NB.680; Z.—.

2. *endikos* [ἔνδικος, 1738], just, righteous (*en*, in, *dikē*, right), is said of the condemnation of those who say "Let us do evil, that good may come," Rom. 3:8; of the recompense of reward of transgressions under the Law, Heb. 2:2. ¶

NT: B.263b; CB.—; K.—.
OT: —.
GEN. REF.: IS.2:1166; NB.680; Z.—.

Note: As to the distinction between No. 1 and No. 2, "*dikaios* characterizes the subject so far as he or it is (so to speak) one with *dikē*, right; *endikos*, so far as he occupies a due relation to *dikē*; . . . in Rom. 3:8 *endikos* presupposes that which has been decided righteously, which leads to the just sentence." (Cremer).

B. Adverb.

dikaiōs [δικαίως, 1346], justly, righteously, in accordance with what is right, is said (*a*) of God's judgment, 1 Pet. 2:23; (*b*) of men, Luke 23:41; "justly"; 1 Cor. 15:34, R.V., "righteously" (A.V., "to righteousness"); 1 Thess. 2:10, R.V., "righteously"; Tit. 2:12. ¶

NT: B.198b; CB.1241c; K.—.
OT: ṣedeq: S.6664; HR.335a.2; H.1879a; BD.841c.
GEN. REF.: IS.2:1166; NB.680; Z.—.

JUSTICE

dikē [δίκη, 1349], primarily custom, usage, came to denote what is right; then, a judicial hearing; hence, the execution of a sentence, "punishment," 2 Thess. 1:9, R.V.; Jude 7, "punishment," R.V. (A.V., "vengeance"). In Acts 28:4 (A.V., "vengeance") it is personified and denotes the goddess Justice or Nemesis (Lat., *Justitia*), who the Melita folk supposed was about to inflict the punishment of death upon Paul by means of the viper. See PUNISHMENT, VENGEANCE. ¶

NT: B.198c; CB.1242a; K.168.
OT: rîb: S.7379; HR.335b.6b; H.2159a; BD.936d.
nāqām: S.5359; HR.335b.5b; H.1413a; BD.668b.
GEN. REF.: IS.2:1166; NB.680; Z.—.

JUSTIFICATION, JUSTIFIER, JUSTIFY

A. Nouns.

1. *dikaiōsis* [δικαίωσις, 1347], denotes the act of pronouncing righteous, justification, acquittal; its precise meaning is determined by that of the verb *dikaioō*, to justify (see B); it is used twice in the Ep. to the Romans, and there alone in the N.T., signifying the establishment of a person as just by acquittal from guilt. In Rom. 4:25 the phrase "for our justification," is, lit., 'because of our justification' (parallel to the preceding clause "for our trespasses," i.e., because of trespasses committed), and means, not with a view to our justification, but because all that was necessary on God's part for our justification had been effected in the Death of Christ. On this account He was raised from the dead. The propitiation being perfect and complete, His resurrection was the confirmatory counterpart. In 5:18, "justification of life" means 'justification which results in life' (cp. ver. 21). That God justifies the believing sinner on the ground of Christ's Death, involves His free gift of life. On the distinction between *dikaiōsis* and *dikaiōma*, see below. ¶ In the Sept., Lev. 24:22. ¶

NT: B.198b; CB.1241c; K.168.
OT: mishpāṭ: S.4941; HR.335b.1; H.2443c; BD.1048b.
GEN. REF.: IS.2:1168; NB.683; Z.3:765.

2. *dikaiōma* [δικαίωμα, 1345], has three distinct meanings, and seems best described comprehensively as "a concrete expression of righteousness"; it is a declaration that a person or thing is righteous, and hence, broadly speaking, it represents the expression and effect of *dikaiōsis* (No. 1). It signifies (*a*) an ordinance, Luke 1:6; Rom. 1:32, R.V., "ordinance," i.e., what God has declared to be right, referring to His decree of retribution (A.V., "judgment"); Rom. 2:26, R.V., "ordinances of the Law" (i.e., righteous requirements enjoined by the Law); so 8:4, "ordinance of the Law," i.e., collectively, the precepts of the Law, all that it demands as right; in Heb. 9:1, 10, ordinances connected with the Tabernacle ritual; (*b*) a sentence of acquittal, by which God acquits men of their guilt, on the conditions (1) of His grace in Christ, through His expiatory sacrifice, (2) the acceptance of Christ by faith, Rom 5:16; (*c*) a righteous act, Rom. 5:18, "(through one) act of righteousness," R.V., not the act of justification, nor the righteous character of Christ (as suggested by the A.V.: *dikaiōma* does not signify character, as does *dikaiosunē*, righteousness), but the Death of Christ, as an act accomplished consistently with God's character and counsels; this is clear as being in antithesis to the "one trespass" in the preceding statement. Some take the word here as meaning a decree of righteousness, as in ver. 16; the Death of Christ could indeed be regarded as fulfilling such a decree, but as the Apostle's argument proceeds, the word, as is frequently the case, passes from one shade of meaning to another, and here stands not for a decree, but an act; so in Rev. 15:4, R.V., "righteous acts" (A.V., "judgments"), and 19:8, "righteous acts (of the saints)" (A.V., "righteousness"). ¶

NT: B.198a; CB.1241c; K.168.
OT: ḥōq: S.2706; HR.334b.2a; H.728a; BD.349b.
ḥuqqāh: S.2708; HR.334b.2b; H.728b; BD.349d.
mishpaṭ: S.4941; HR.334b.4; H.2443c; BD.1048b.
GEN. REF.: IS.2:1168; NB.683; Z.3:765.

Note: For *dikaiosunē*, always translated "righteousness," see RIGHTEOUSNESS.

B. Verb.

dikaioō [δικαιόω, 1344], primarily, to deem to be right, signifies, in the N.T., (*a*) to show to be right or righteous; in the Passive Voice, to be justified, Matt. 11:19; Luke 7:35; Rom. 3:4; 1 Tim. 3:16; (*b*) to declare to be righteous, to pronounce righteous, (1) by man, concerning God, Luke 7:29 (see Rom. 3:4, above); concerning himself, Luke 10:29; 16:15; (2) by God concerning men, who are declared to be righteous before Him on certain conditions laid down by Him.

Ideally the complete fulfilment of the Law of God would provide a basis of justification in His sight, Rom. 2:13. But no such case has occurred in mere human experience, and therefore no one can be justified on this ground, Rom. 3:9-20; Gal. 2:16; 3:10, 11; 5:4. From this negative presentation in Rom. 3, the Apostle proceeds to show that, consistently with God's own righteous character, and with a view to its manifestation, He is, through Christ, as "a propitiation . . . by (*en*, instrumental) His blood," 3:25, R.V., "the Justifier of him that hath faith in Jesus" (ver. 26), justification being the legal and formal acquittal from guilt by God as Judge, the pronouncement of the sinner as righteous, who believes on the Lord Jesus Christ. In ver. 24, "being justified" is in the present continuous tense, indicating the constant process of justification in the succession of those who believe and are justified. In 5:1, "being justified" is in the aorist, or point, tense, indicating the definite time at which each person, upon the exercise of faith, was justified. In 8:1, justification is presented as "no condemnation." That justification is in view here is confirmed by the preceding chapters and by verse 34. In 3:26, the word rendered "Justifier" is the present participle of the verb, lit., 'justifying'; similarly in 8:33 (where the article is used), "God that justifieth," is, more lit., 'God is the (One) justifying,' with stress upon the word "God."

Justification is primarily and gratuitously by faith, subsequently and evidentially by works. In regard to justification by works, the so-called contradiction between James and the Apostle Paul is only apparent. There is harmony in the different views of the subject. Paul has in mind Abraham's attitude toward God, his acceptance of God's word. This was a matter known only to God. The Romans Epistle is occupied with the effect of this Godward attitude, not upon Abraham's character or actions, but upon the contrast between faith and the lack of it, namely, unbelief, cp. Rom. 11:20. James (2:21-26) is occupied with the contrast between faith that is real and faith that is false, a faith barren and dead, which is not faith at all.

Again, the two writers have before them different epochs in Abraham's life — Paul, the event recorded in Gen. 15, James, that in Gen. 22. Contrast the words 'believed' in Gen. 15:6 and 'obeyed' in 22:18.

Further, the two writers use the words 'faith' and 'works' in somewhat different senses. With Paul, faith is acceptance of God's word; with James, it is acceptance of the truth of certain statements about God, (ver. 19), which may fail to affect one's conduct. Faith, as dealt with by Paul, results in acceptance with God., i.e., justification, and is bound to manifest itself. If not, as James says 'Can that faith save him?' (ver. 14). With Paul, works are dead works; with James they are life works. The works of which Paul speaks could be quite independent of faith: those referred to by James can be wrought only where faith is real, and they will attest its reality.

So with righteousness, or justification: Paul is occupied with a right relationship with God, James, with right conduct. Paul testifies that the ungodly can be justified by faith, James that only the right-doer is justified. See also under RIGHTEOUS, RIGHTEOUSNESS.

NT: B.197c; CB.1241c; K.168.
OT: ṣādēq: S.6663; HR.334b.3a-d; H.1879; BD.842c.
rîb: S.7379; HR.334b.4; H.2159a; BD.936d.
GEN. REF.: IS.2:1168; NB.683; Z.3:765.

K

KEEP, KEEPING (Noun)

A. Verbs.

1. *tēreō* [τηρέω, 5083], denotes (*a*) to watch over, preserve, keep, watch, e.g., Acts 12:5, 6; 16:23; in 25:21, R.V. (1st part), "kept" (A.V., "reserved"); the present participle is translated "keepers" in Matt. 28:4, lit. 'the keeping (ones)'; it is used of the keeping power of God the Father and Christ, exercised over His people, John 17:11, 12, 15; 1 Thess. 5:23, "preserved"; 1 John 5:18, where "He that was begotten of God," R.V., is said of Christ as the Keeper ("keepeth him," R.V., for A.V., "keepeth himself"); Jude 1, R.V., "kept for Jesus Christ" (A.V., "preserved in Jesus Christ"); Rev. 3:10; of their inheritance, 1 Pet. 1:4 ("reserved"); of judicial reservation by God in view of future doom, 2 Pet. 2:4, 9, 17; 3:7; Jude 6, 13; of keeping the faith, 2 Tim. 4:7; the unity of the Spirit, Eph. 4:3; oneself, 2 Cor. 11:9; 1 Tim. 5:22; Jas. 1:27; figuratively, one's garments, Rev. 16:15; (*b*) to observe, to give heed to, as of keeping commandments, etc., e.g., Matt. 19:17; John 14:15; 15:10; 17:6; Jas. 2:10; 1 John 2:3, 4, 5; 3:22, 24; 5:2 (in some mss.), 3; Rev. 1:3; 2:26; 3:8, 10; 12:17; 14:12; 22:7, 9. See RESERVE.

NT: B.814d; CB.1271b; K.1174.
OT: nāṣar: S.5341; HR.1348b.2; H.1407; BD.665c.
shāmar: S.8104; HR.1348b.7; H.2414; BD.1036b.
GEN. REF.: IS.2:578; NB.—; Z.3:781.

2. *diatēreō* [διατηρέω, 1301], to keep carefully (*dia*, intensive, and No. 1), is said of "the Mother of Jesus," in keeping His sayings in her

heart, Luke 2:51, and of the command of the Apostles and elders in Jerusalem to Gentile converts in the churches to keep themselves from the evils mentioned in Acts 15:29. ¶

NT: B.189d; CB.1241b; K.1174.
OT: shāmar: S.8104; HR.313a.5a; H.2414; BD.1036b.
GEN. REF.: IS.2:578; NB.—; Z.3:781.

3. *suntēreō* [συντηρέω, 4933], denotes to preserve, keep safe, keep close (*sun*, together with, used intensively, and No. 1), in Luke 2:19, as in ver. 51 (see No. 2, above), of the Mother of Jesus in regard to the words of the shepherds; in Mark 6:20 it is used of Herod's preservation of John the Baptist from Herodias, R.V., "kept (him) safe," A.V., "observed (him)" (marg., "kept"); in Matt. 9:17 (in some mss., Luke 5:38), of the preservation of wine-skins. See OBSERVE, PRESERVE. ¶

NT: B.792c; CB.—; K.1174.
OT: shāmar: S.8104; HR.1320c.3; H.2414; BD.1036b.
GEN. REF.: IS.2:578; NB.—; Z.3:781.

4. *phulassō* [φυλάσσω, 5442], denotes (*a*) to guard, watch, keep watch, e.g., Luke 2:8; in the Passive Voice, 8:29; (*b*) to keep by way of protection, e.g., Luke 11:21; John 12:25; 17:12 (2nd part; No. 1 in 1st part and in ver. 11); (*c*) metaphorically, to keep a law, precept, etc., e.g., Matt. 19:20 and Luke 18:21, "have observed"; Luke 11:28; John 12:47 (in the best mss.); Acts 7:53; 16:4; 21:24; Rom. 2:26; Gal. 6:13; 1 Tim. 5:21 ("observe"); in the Middle Voice, Mark 10:20 ("have observed"); (*d*) in the Middle Voice, to keep oneself from, Acts 21:25; elsewhere translated by the verb to beware. See BEWARE, No. 3, GUARD, B, No. 1.

NT: B.868b; CB.1264c; K.1280.
OT: shāmar: S.8104; HR.1441c.11a; H.2414; BD.1036b.
GEN. REF.: IS.2:578; NB.—; Z.3:781.

5. *diaphulassō* [διαφυλάσσω], an intensive form of No. 4, to guard thoroughly; see GUARD.

6. *phroureō* [φρουρέω, 5432], to keep with a military guard, e.g., Gal. 3:23, R.V., "kept in ward"; see GUARD, B, No. 3.

NT: B.867b; CB.1264c; K.—.
OT: —.
GEN. REF.: IS.2:578; NB.—; Z.3:781.

7. *poieō* [ποιέω, 4160], to do, make, signifies to keep, in Matt. 26:18, in the Lord's statement, "I will keep the passover"; so in Acts 18:21, in some mss.; in John 7:19, where the A.V. has "keepeth (the law)," the R.V. adheres to the usual meaning "doeth."

NT: B.680d; CB.1265c; K.895.
OT: —.
GEN. REF.: —.

8. *echō* [ἔχω, 2192], to have, to hold, is rendered "I kept" in Luke 19:20, R.V. (A.V., "I have kept"), of keeping a pound laid up in a napkin. See HAVE.

NT: B.331d; CB.1242c; K.286.
OT: —.
GEN. REF.: —.

9. *krateō* [κρατέω, 2902], to be strong, get possession of, hold fast, is used in mark 9:10, "(and) they kept (the saying)," i.e., they held fast to the Lord's command to refrain from telling what they had seen in the mount of Transfiguration. See HOLD.

NT: B.448c; CB.1256a; K.466.
OT: 'āḥaz: S.270; HR.783a.2a; H.64; BD.28a.
ḥāzaq: S.2388; HR.783a.6a-c; H.636; BD.304a.
GEN. REF.: —.

10. *nosphizō* [νοσφίζω, 3557], to set apart, remove, signifies, in the Middle Voice, to set apart for oneself, to purloin, and is rendered "purloining" in Tit. 2:10; "kept back" (and "keep") in Acts 5:2, 3, of the act of Ananias and his wife in retaining part of the price of the land. ¶

NT: B.543d; CB.—; K.—.
OT: —.
GEN. REF.: —.

11. *sunechō* [συνέχω, 4912], to hold together, is translated "shall . . . keep (thee) in," in Luke 19:43. See also *Note* (8) below. See CONSTRAIN.

NT: B.789a; CB.1270c; K.1117.
OT: ḥābar: S.2266; HR.1315b.6; H.598; BD.287d.
'āṣar: S.6113; HR.1315b.12; H.1675; BD.783c.
GEN. REF.: —.

Notes: (1) In Acts 22:2, A.V., *parechō*, to afford, give, cause, is rendered "kept (the more silence)," R.V., "were (the more quiet)."

(2) In Matt. 14:6 some mss. have the verb *agō*, to lead, hold (of a feast), of keeping Herod's birthday; the most authentic have *ginomai*, to become, take place; hence the R.V., "when Herod's birthday came." The verb *agō* is used in Acts 19:38 of keeping certain occasions, as of the holding of law courts, R.V. "(the courts) are open," A.V. marg., "court days are kept"; Moulton and Milligan illustrate from the papyri the use of the adjective *agoraios*, in the plural with *hēmerai*, days, understood, in regard to certain market days; certain court days are what are indicated here. The conjecture that the meaning is 'courts are now being held' (*sunodoi* being understood as meetings of the court instead of 'days') is scarcely so appropriate to the circumstances.

(3) In Matt. 8:33, *boskō*, to feed (swine etc.), is translated "(they that) fed," R.V. for A.V. "(they that) kept."

(4) In Acts 9:33, *katakeimai*, to lie down, is used with *epi*, upon, with the meaning to keep one's bed (see LIE, No. 2).

(5) In Rom. 2:25, *prassō*, to do (continuously), to practise, is rendered "be a doer of," R.V. (A.V., "keep").

(6) In Acts 20:20, *hupostellō*, to shrink, draw back from, is translated "I shrank (not)" (Middle Voice), R.V., A.V., "I kept back (nothing)."

(7) In Acts 27:43, *kōluō*, to hinder, is translated "stayed (them from)," R.V., A.V., "kept (them from)."

(8) In Luke 8:15 and 1 Cor. 11:2, *katechō*, to hold fast (a strengthened form of *echō*, No. 8), is translated "hold fast," R.V., A.V., "keep"; in 15:2, R.V., "hold fast," A.V., "keep in memory."

(9) For keep secret, see SECRET.

(10) For keep under, see BUFFET.

(11) *Paratithēmi* is rendered "commit the keeping" in 1 Pet. 4:19, A.V.

(12) For "keep the feast" see FEAST, B, No. 2.

B. Noun.

tērēsis [τήρησις, 5084], akin to A, No. 1, denotes (*a*) a watching, and hence, imprisonment, prison, Acts 4:3 and 5:18, "ward," R.V. (A.V., "hold" and "prison"); (*b*) "keeping," 1 Cor. 7:19. See HOLD, PRISON. ¶

NT: B.815c; CB.1271b; K.1174.
OT: —.
GEN. REF.: —.

KEEPER

phulax [φύλαξ, 5441], akin to A, No. 4, above, a guard: see GUARD.

NT: B.868b; CB.1264c; K.—.
OT: shāmar: S.8104; HR.1441b.2; H.2414; BD.1036b.
ṣûr: S.6697; HR.1441b.1; H.1901a; BD.849c.
GEN. REF.: IS.3:6; NB.—; Z.3:781.

Note: For *tēreō*, in Matt. 28:4, see A, No. 1, above.

KEY

kleis [κλείς, 2807], a key, is used metaphorically (*a*) of "the keys of the kingdom of heaven," which the Lord committed to Peter, Matt. 16:19, by which he would open the door of faith, as he did to Jews at Pentecost, and to Gentiles in the person of Cornelius, acting as one commissioned by Christ, through the power of the Holy Spirit; he had precedence over his fellow-disciples, not in authority, but in the matter of time, on the ground of his confession of Christ (ver. 16); equal authority was committed to them (18:18); (*b*) of "the key of knowledge," Luke 11:52, i.e., knowledge of the revealed will of God, by which men entered into the life that pleases God; this the religious leaders of the Jews had presumptuously 'taken away,' so that they neither entered in themselves, nor permitted their hearers to do so; (*c*) of "the keys of death and of Hades," Rev. 1:18, R.V. (see HADES), indicative of the authority of the Lord over the bodies and souls of men; (*d*) of "the key of David," Rev. 3:7, a reference to Is. 22:22, speaking of the deposition of Shebna and the investiture of Eliakim, in terms evidently Messianic, the metaphor being that of the right of entrance upon administrative authority; the mention of David is symbolic of complete sovereignty; (*e*) of "the key of the pit of the abyss," Rev. 9:1; here the symbolism is that of competent authority; the pit represents a shaft or deep entrance into the region (see ABYSS), from whence issued smoke, symbolic of blinding delusion; (*f*) of "the key of the abyss," Rev. 20:1; this is to be distinguished from (*e*): the symbolism is that of the complete supremacy of God over the region of the lost, in which, by angelic agency, Satan is destined to be confined for a thousand years. ¶

NT: B.433d; CB.1255b; K.439.
OT: maphtēaḥ: S.4668; HR.767b.1; H.1854f; BD.836b.
GEN. REF.: IS.3:10; NB.690; Z.3:785.

KICK

laktizō [λακτίζω, 2979], to kick (from *lax*, an adverb signifying 'with the foot'), is used in Acts 26:14 (some mss. have it in 9:5).

NT: B.463a; CB.—; K.495.
OT: —.
GEN. REF.: IS.3:13; NB.—; Z.—.

For **KID** see **GOAT**

KILL

1. *apokteinō* [ἀποκτείνω, 615], to kill, is used (*a*) physically, e.g., Matt. 10:28; 14:5, "put . . . to death," similarly rendered in John 18:31; often of Christ's Death; in Rev. 2:13, R.V., "was killed" (A.V., "was slain"); 9:15, R.V., "kill' (A.V., "slay"); 11:13, R.V., "were killed" (A.V., "were slain"); so in 19:21; (*b*) metaphorically, Rom. 7:11, of the power of sin, which is personified, as "finding occasion, through the commandment," and inflicting deception and spiritual death, i.e., separation from God, realized through the presentation of the commandment to conscience, breaking in upon the fancied state of freedom; the argument shows the power of the Law, not to deliver from sin, but to enhance its sinfulness; in 2 Cor. 3:6, "the letter killeth," signifies not the literal meaning of Scripture as contrasted with the spiritual, but the power of the Law to bring home the knowledge of guilt and its punishment; in Eph.

2:16 "having slain the enmity" describes the work of Christ through His death in annulling the enmity, "the Law" (ver. 15), between Jew and Gentile, reconciling regenerate Jew and Gentile to God in spiritual unity "in one body." See DEATH, C, No. 4, SLAY.

NT: B.93d; CB.1237a; K.–.
OT: hārag: S.2026; HR.135a.2a; H.514; BD.246d.
mût: S.4191; HR.135a.4c; H.1169; BD.559b,560b.
GEN. REF.: IS.3:15; NB.–; Z.–.

2. *anaireō* [ἀναιρέω, 337], denotes (*a*) to take up (*ana*, up, *haireō*, to take), said of Pharaoh's daughter, in taking up Moses, Acts 7:21; (*b*) to take away in the sense of removing, Heb. 10:9, of the legal appointment of sacrifices, to bring in the will of God in the sacrificial offering of the Death of Christ; (*c*) to kill, used physically only (not metaphorically as in No. 1), e.g., Luke 22:2; in 2 Thess. 2:8, instead of the future tense of this verb, some texts (followed by R.V. marg.) read the future of *analiskō*, to consume. See DEATH, C, No. 2, SLAY.

NT: B.54d; CB.–; K.–.
OT: hārag: S.2026; HR.77b.2a; H.514; BD.246d.
mût: S.4191; HR.77b.4; H.1169; BD.559b,560b.
GEN. REF.: IS.3:15; NB.–; Z.–.

3. *thuō* [θύω, 2380], primarily denotes to offer first fruits to a god; then (*a*) to sacrifice by slaying a victim, Acts 14:13, 18, to do sacrifice; 1 Cor. 10:20, to sacrifice; 1 Cor. 5:7, "hath been sacrificed," of the Death of Christ as our Passover; (*b*) to slay, kill, Matt. 22:4; Mark 14:12; Luke 15:23, 27, 30; 22:7; John 10:10; Acts 10:13; 11:7. ¶

NT: B.367a; CB.1272c; K.342.
OT: zābaḥ: S.2076; HR.659a.1; H.525; BD.256d.
shāḥaṭ: S.7819; HR.659a.4a; H.2362; BD.1006a.
GEN. REF.: IS.3:15; NB.–; Z.–.

4. *phoneuō* [φονεύω, 5407], to murder, akin to *phoneus*, a murderer, is always rendered by the verb to kill (except in Matt. 19:18, A.V., "do . . . murder," and in Matt. 23:35, A.V. and R.V., "ye slew"); Matt. 5:21 (twice); 23:31; Mark 10:19; Luke 18:20; Rom. 13:9; Jas. 2:11 (twice); 4:2; 5:6. ¶

NT: B.864c; CB.–; K.–.
OT: rāṣaḥ: S.7523; HR.1437a.4a; H.2208; BD.953d.
hārag: S.2026; HR.1437a.1a; H.514; BD.246d.
GEN. REF.: IS.3:15; NB.–; Z.–.

5. *thanatoō* [θανατόω, 2289], to put to death (from *thanatos*, death), is translated "are killed" in Rom. 8:36; "killed" in 2 Cor. 6:9. See DEATH, C, No. 1.

NT: B.351c; CB.1271c; K.312.
OT: hārag: S.2026; HR.625a.2; H.514; BD.246d.
mût: S.4191; HR.625a.4c,d; H.1169; BD.559b,560b.
GEN. REF.: IS.3:15; NB.–; Z.–.

6. *diacheirizō* [διαχειρίζω, 1315], primarily, to have in hand, manage (*cheir*, the hand), is used in the Middle Voice, in the sense of laying hands on with a view to kill, or of actually killing, Acts 5:30, "ye slew"; 26:21, "to kill." See SLAY.

NT: B.191a; CB.–; K.–.
OT: –.
GEN. REF.: IS.3:15; NB.–; Z.–.

7. *sphazō*, or *sphattō* [σφάζω, 4969], to slay, to slaughter, especially victims for sacrifice, is most frequently translated by the verb to slay; so the R.V. in Rev. 6:4 (A.V., "should kill"); in 13:3, R.V., "smitten unto death" (A.V., "wounded"). See SLAY, WOUND. Cp. *katasphazō*, to kill off, Luke 19:27; ¶ *sphagē*, slaughter, e.g., Acts 8:32, and *sphagion*, a victim for slaughter, Acts 7:42. ¶

NT: B.796a; CB.1269c; K.1125.
OT: shāḥaṭ: S.7819; HR.1324b.4a; H.2362; BD.1006a.
GEN. REF.: IS.3:15; NB.–; Z.–.

KIN, KINSFOLK, KINSMAN, KINSWOMAN

A. Adjective.

sungenēs [συγγενής, 4773], primarily denoting congenital, natural, innate (*sun*, with, *genos*, a family, race, offspring), then, 'akin to,' is used as a noun, denoting (*a*) of family relationship, kin, a kinsman, kinsfolk(s), Luke 1:58, R.V., "kinsfolk" (A.V., "cousins"); 14:12; 21:16; John 18:26; Acts 10:24; (*b*) of tribal or racial kinship, fellow-nationals, Rom. 9:3; 16:7, 11, 21. ¶

NT: B.772c; CB.1270c; K.1097.
OT: dôd: S.1732; HR.1298c.1a; H.410c; BD.187c.
dōdāh: S.1733; HR.1298c.1b; H.410b; BD.187c.
GEN. REF.: IS.3:17; NB.–; Z.–.

B. Nouns.

1. *sungenis* [συγγενίς, —], a late feminine form of A (some mss. have *sungenēs*), denotes a kinswoman, Luke 1:36, R.V., "kinswoman" (A.V., "cousin"). Cp. *sungeneia* (see KINDRED). ¶

NT: B.772d; CB.–; K.–.
OT: –.
GEN. REF.: IS.3:17; NB.–; Z.–.

2. *sungeneus* [συγγενεύς, 4773], an alternative form of A, is used in Mark 6:4, "kin," and Luke 2:44, "kinsfolk." ¶

NT: B.772c; CB.–; K.–.
OT: –.
GEN. REF.: IS.3:17; NB.–; Z.–.

KIND (Noun)

1. *genos* [γένος, 1085], akin to *ginomai*, to become, denotes (*a*) a family, Acts 4:6, "kindred"; 7:13, R.V., "race" (A.V., "kindred"); 13:26, "stock"; (*b*) an offspring, Acts 17:28; Rev. 22:16; (*c*) a nation, a race, Mark 7:26, R.V., "race" (A.V., "nation"); Acts 4:36, R.V. "(a man of Cyprus) by race," A.V., "of the country (of Cyprus)"; *genos* does not mean a country, the

word here signifies parentage (Jews had settled in Cyprus from, or even before, the reign of Alexander the Great); 7:19, R.V., "race" (A.V., "kindred"); 18:2, 24, R.V., "by race" (A.V., "born"); 2 Cor. 11:26, "countrymen"; Gal. 1:14, R.V., "countrymen" (A.V., "nation"); Phil. 3:5, "stock"; 1 Pet. 2:9, R.V., "race" (A.V., "generation"); (*d*) a kind, sort, class, Matt. 13:47, "kind"; in some mss. in 17:21, A.V., "kind"; Mark 9:29, "kind"; 1 Cor. 12:10, 28, "kinds" (A.V., "diversities"); 14:10 (ditto). ¶ See BEGET, B.

NT: B.156a; CB.1248b; K.117.
OT: mîn: S.4327; HR.239b.4; H.1191a; BD.568b.
ʿam: S.5971; HR.239b.6; H.1640a,e; BD.766b.
GEN. REF.: IS.3:19; NB.—; Z.—.

2. *phusis* [φύσις, 5449], among its various meanings denotes the nature, the natural constitution or power of a person or thing, and is translated "kind" in Jas. 3:7 (twice), "kind" (of beasts etc.), and "(man)kind," lit., 'human kind.' See NATURE, NATURAL.

NT: B.869b; CB.1264c; K.1280.
OT: —.
GEN. REF.: —.

Notes: (1) The indefinite pronoun *tis*, some, a certain, one, is used adjectively with the noun *aparchē*, firstfruits, in Jas. 1:18, "a kind of."

(2) In 1 Cor. 15:37, R.V., "some other kind" (A.V., "some other grain") translates a phrase which, lit., rendered, is 'some (one) of the rest (*loipos*).'

(3) In 2 Cor. 6:13, "(for a recompense) in like kind," R.V. (A.V., "in the same"), is, lit., '(as to) the same (recompense).'

KIND (Adjective), KIND (be), KINDLY, KINDNESS

A. Adjectives.

1. *chrēstos* [χρηστός, 5543], serviceable, good, pleasant (of things), good, gracious, kind (of persons), is translated "kind" in Luke 6:35, of God; in Eph. 4:32, enjoined upon believers. See BETTER, EASY, GOOD, GOODNESS, GRACIOUS.

NT: B.886a; CB.1240a; K.1320.
OT: ṭôb: S.2896; HR.1475a.1a; H.793a; BD.373c.
yāqār: S.3368; HR.1475a.2; H.905a; BD.429d.
GEN. REF.: IS.3:19; NB.—; Z.3:794.

2. *agathos* [ἀγαθός, 18], good, is translated "kind" in Tit. 2:5, R.V. See GOOD.

NT: B.2d; CB.1233b; K.3.
OT: ṭôb: S.2896; HR.2a.4b; H.793a; BD.373c.
GEN. REF.: IS.3:19; NB.—; Z.—.

B. Verb.

chrēsteuomai [χρηστεύομαι, 5541], akin to A, No. 1, to be kind, is said of love, 1 Cor. 13:4. ¶

NT: B.886a; CB.1240a; K.1320.
OT: —.
GEN. REF.: IS.3:19; NB.—; Z.—.

C. Nouns.

1. *chrēstotēs* [χρηστότης, 5544], akin to A, No. 1, and B, used of goodness of heart, kindness, is translated "kindness" in 2 Cor. 6:6; Gal. 5:22, R.V. (A.V., "gentleness"); Eph. 2:7; Col. 3:12; Tit. 3:4. See GOODNESS.

NT: B.886b; CB.1240a; K.1320.
OT: ṭôb: S.2896; HR.1475a.1b; H.793a; BD.373c.
ṭôbāh: S.2896; HR.1475a.1c; H.793a; BD.373c.
GEN. REF.: IS.3:19; NB.—; Z.3:794.

2. *philanthrōpia* [φιλανθρωπία, 5363], from *philos*, loving, *anthrōpos*, man (Eng., philanthropy), denotes kindness, and is so translated in Acts 28:2, of that which was shown by the inhabitants of Melita to the shipwrecked voyagers; in Tit. 3:4, of the kindness of God, translated "(His) love toward man." See LOVE. ¶

NT: B.858d; CB.1264a; K.1261.
OT: —.
GEN. REF.: IS.3:19; NB.—; Z.3:794.

D. Adverb.

philanthrōpōs [φιλανθρώπως, 5364], akin to C, No. 2, humanely, kindly, is translated "kindly" in Acts 27:3 (A.V., "courteously"). See COURTEOUSLY. ¶

NT: B.858d; CB.1264a; K.1261.
OT: —.
GEN. REF.: —.

KINDLE

1. *haptō* [ἅπτω, 681], properly, to fasten to, is used in Acts 28:2 (in the most authentic mss., some mss. have No. 3), of kindling a fire. See No. 2.

NT: B.102c; CB.1249b; K.—.
OT: ʿālāh: S.5927; HR.150b.1; H.1624; BD.748a,749c.
GEN. REF.: —.

Note: Haptō is used of lighting a lamp, in Luke 8:16, 11:33; 15:8. For the Middle Voice see TOUCH.

2. *periaptō* [περιάπτω, —], properly, to tie about, attach (*peri*, around, and No. 1), is used of lighting a fire in the midst of a court in Luke 22:55 (some mss. have No. 1). ¶

NT: B.645d; CB.—; K.—.
OT: —.
GEN. REF.: —.

3. *anaptō* [ἀνάπτω, 381], to light up (*ana*, up, and No. 1), is used (*a*) literally, in Jas. 3:5, "kindleth"; (*b*) metaphorically, in the Passive Voice, in Luke 12:49, of the kindling of the fire of hostility; see FIRE, A, (*f*). For Acts 28:2, see No. 1, above. ¶

NT: B.60a; CB.—; K.—.
OT: yāṣat: S.3341; HR.81c.4b; H.899; BD.428b.
bāʿar: S.1197; HR.81c.2; H.263; BD.128d.
GEN. REF.: —.

KINDRED

1. *sungeneia* [συγγένεια, 4772], primarily denotes kinship; then, kinsfolk, kindred (cp. *sungenēs*, a kinsman; see KIN), Luke 1:16; Acts 7:3, 14. ¶

NT: B.772c; CB.1270c; K.1097.
OT: mishpāḥah: S.4940; HR.1298b.4; H.2442b; BD.1046c.
tôlēdōt: S.8435; HR.1298b.6; H.867g; BD.410a.
GEN. REF.: –.

2. *genos* [γένος; see KIND (Noun), No. 1.

Notes: (1) *Phulē*, a tribe, rendered "kindreds" in the A.V. of Rev. 1:7; 7:9; 11:9; 13:7, "kindred' in 5:9; 14:6, and elsewhere, "tribe," "tribes," is always translated by the latter in the R.V. See TRIBE.

(2) For *patria*, rendered "kindreds" in Acts 3:25, A.V., see FAMILY.

KING

A. Noun.

basileus [βασιλεύς, 935], a king (cp. Eng., Basil), e.g., Matt. 1:6, is used of the Roman Emperor in 1 Pet. 2:13, 17 (a command of general application); this reference to the Emperor is illustrated frequently in the *koinē* (for which see Preface to Vol. 1); of Herod the Tetrach (used by courtesy), Matt. 14:9; of Christ, as the King of the Jews, e.g., Matt. 2:2; 27:11, 29, 37; as the King of Israel, Mark 15:32; John 1:49; 12:13; as King of kings, Rev. 17:14; 19:16; as "the King" in judging nations and men at the establishment of the Millennial Kingdom, Matt. 25:34, 40; of God, "the great King," Matt. 5:35; "the King eternal, incorruptible, invisible," 1 Tim. 1:17; "King of kings," 1 Tim. 6:15, see *Note* (2) below; "King of the ages," Rev. 15:3, R.V. (A.V., "saints"). Christ's Kingship was predicted in the O.T., e.g., Psa. 2:6, and in the N.T., e.g., Luke 1:32, 33; He came as such, e.g., Matt. 2:2; John 18:37; was rejected and died as such, Luke 19:14; Matt. 27:37; is now a King Priest, after the order of Melchizedek, Heb. 5:6; 7:1, 17; and will reign for ever and ever, Rev. 11:15.

NT: B.136a; CB.1238c; K.–.
OT: melek: S.4428; HR.197a.2d; H.1199a; BD.572d.
GEN. REF.: IS.3:20; NB.692; Z.3:795.

Notes: (1) In Rev. 1:6 and 5:10, the most authentic mss. have the word *basileia*, kingdom, instead of the plural of *basileus*, A.V., "kings"; R.V., "a kingdom (to be priests)," and "a kingdom (and priests)." The kingdom was conditionally offered by God to Israel, that they should be to Him "a kingdom of priests," Ex. 19:6, the entire nation fulfilling priestly worship and service. Their failure to fulfil His covenant resulted in the selection of the Aaronic priesthood. The bringing in of the new and better covenant of grace has constituted all believers a spiritual Kingdom, a holy and royal priesthood, 1 Pet. 2:5, 9.

(2) In 1 Tim. 6:15, the word "kings" translates the present participle of the verb *basileuō*, to be king, to have kingship, lit., 'of (those) who are kings.' See REIGN.

(3) Deissmann has shown that the title "king of kings" was "in very early eastern history a decoration of great monarchs and also a divine title." (*Light from the Ancient East*, pp. 367, f.). Moulton and Milligan illustrate the use of the title among the Persians, from documents discovered in Media.

B. Adjectives.

1. *basileios* [βασίλειος, 934], denoting royal, as in 1 Pet. 2:9, is used in the plural, of the courts or palaces of kings, Luke 7:25, "kings' courts"; a possible meaning is 'among royal courtiers or persons.' ¶

NT: B.136a; CB.1238c; K.97.
OT: mamlākāh: S.4467; HR.194c.1; H.1199f; BD.575a.
GEN. REF.: IS.3:20; NB.692; Z.3:795.

2. *basilikos* [βασιλικός, 937], royal, belonging to a king, is used in Acts 12:20 with 'country' understood, "their country was fed from the king's," lit., 'the royal (country).' See NOBLEMAN, ROYAL.

NT: B.136d; CB.1238c; K.97.
OT: melek: S.4428; HR.214a.1a; H.1199a; BD.572d.
GEN. REF.: IS.3:20; NB.692; Z.3:795.

KINGDOM

basileia [βασιλεία, 932], is primarily an abstract noun, denoting sovereignty, royal power, dominion, e.g., Rev. 17:18, translated" (which) reigneth," lit., 'hath a kingdom' (R.V. marg.); then, by metonymy, a concrete noun, denoting the territory or people over whom a king rules, e.g., Matt. 4:8; Mark 3:24. It is used especially of the Kingdom of God and of Christ.

"The Kingdom of God is (*a*) the sphere of God's rule, Ps. 22:28; 145:13; Dan. 4:25; Luke 1:52; Rom. 13:1, 2. Since, however, this earth is the scene of universal rebellion against God, e.g., Luke 4:5, 6; 1 John 5:19; Rev. 11:15-18, the Kingdom of God is (*b*) the sphere in which, at any given time, His rule is acknowledged. God has not relinquished His sovereignty in the face of rebellion, demoniac and human, but has declared His purpose to establish it, Dan. 2:44; 7:14; 1 Cor. 15:24, 25. Meantime, seeking willing obedience, He gave His law to a nation and appointed kings to administer His Kingdom over it, 1 Chron. 28:5. Israel, however, though declaring still a nominal allegiance shared in the common rebellion, Isa. 1:2-4, and, after they had rejected the Son of God, John 1:11 (cp. Matt. 21:33-43), were "cast away," Rom. 11:15, 20, 25. Henceforth God calls upon men everywhere, without distinction of race or nationality, to submit voluntarily to His rule. Thus the Kingdom is said to be 'in mystery' now, Mark 4:11, that is, it does not come within the range of the natural powers of observation, Luke 17:20, but is spiritually discerned, John 3:3 (cp. 1 Cor. 2:14). When, hereafter, God asserts His rule universally, then the Kingdom will be in glory, that is, it will be manifest to all; cp. Matt. 25:31-34; Phil. 2:9-11; 2 Tim. 4:1, 18.

"Thus, speaking generally, references to the Kingdom 'fall into two classes, the first, in which it is viewed as present and involving suffering for those who enter it, 2 Thess. 1:5; the second, in which it is viewed as future and is associated with reward, Matt. 25:34, and glory, 13:43. See also Acts 14:22.

"The fundamental principle of the Kingdom is declared in the words of the Lord spoken in the midst of a company of Pharisees, "the Kingdom of God is in the midst of you," Luke 17:21, marg., that is, where the King is, there is the Kingdom. Thus at the present time and so far as this earth is concerned, where the King is and where His rule is acknowledged, is, first, in the heart of the individual believer, Acts 4:19; Eph. 3:17; 1 Pet. 3:15; and then in the churches of God, 1 Cor., 12:3, 5, 11; 14:37; cp. Col. 1:27, where for "in" read 'among.'

"Now, the King and His rule being refused, those who enter the Kingdom of God are brought into conflict with all who disown its allegiance, as well as with the desire for ease, and the dislike of suffering and unpopularity, natural to all. On the other hand, subjects of the Kingdom are the objects of the care of God, Matt. 6:33, and of the rejected King, Heb. 13:5.

"Entrance into the Kingdom of God is by the new birth, Matt. 18:3; John 3:5, for nothing that a man may be by nature, or can attain to by any form of self-culture, avails in the spiritual realm. And as the new nature, received in the new birth, is made evident by obedience, it is further said that only such as do the will of God shall enter into His Kingdom, Matt. 7:21, where, however, the context shows that the reference is to the future, as in 2 Pet. 1:10, 11. Cp. also 1 Cor. 6:9, 10; Gal. 5:21; Eph. 5:5.

"The expression 'Kingdom of God' occurs four times in Matthew, 'Kingdom of the Heavens' usually taking its place. The latter (cp. Dan. 4:26) does not occur elsewhere in N.T., but see 2 Tim. 4:18, "His heavenly Kingdom." . . . This Kingdom is identical with the Kingdom of the Father (cp. Matt. 26:29, with Mark 14:25), and with the Kingdom of the Son (cp. Luke 22:30). Thus there is but one Kingdom, variously described: of the Son of Man, Matt. 13:41; of Jesus, Rev. 1:9; of Christ Jesus, 2 Tim. 4:1; "of Christ and God," Eph. 5:5; "of our Lord, and of His Christ," Rev. 11:15; "of our God, and the authority of His Christ," 12:10; "of the Son of His love," Col. 1:13.

"Concerning the future, the Lord taught His disciples to pray, "Thy Kingdom come," Matt. 6:10, where the verb is in the point tense, precluding the notion of gradual progress and development, and implying a sudden catastrophe as declared in 2 Thess. 2:8.

"Concerning the present, that a man is of the Kingdom of God is not shown in the punctilious observance of ordinances, which are external and material, but in the deeper matters of the heart, which are spiritual and essential, viz., 'righteousness, and peace, and joy in the Holy Spirit,' Rom. 14:17."*

"With regard to the expressions 'the Kingdom of God' and the 'Kingdom of the Heavens,' while they are often used interchangeably, it does not follow that in every case they mean exactly the same and are quite identical.

"The Apostle Paul often speaks of the Kingdom of God, not dispensationally but morally, e.g., in Rom. 14:17; 1 Cor. 4:20, but never so of the Kingdom of Heaven. 'God' is not the equivalent of 'the heavens.' He is everywhere and above all dispensations, whereas 'the heavens' are distinguished from the earth, until the Kingdom comes in judgment and power and glory (Rev. 11:15, R.V.) when rule in heaven and on earth will be one.

"While, then, the sphere of the Kingdom of God and the Kingdom of Heaven are at times identical, yet the one term cannot be used indiscriminately for the other. In the 'Kingdom of Heaven' (32 times in Matt.), heaven is in antithesis to earth, and the phrase is limited to the Kingdom in its earthly aspect for the time being, and is used only dispensationally and in connection with Israel. In the 'Kingdom of

* From Notes on Thessalonians by Hogg and Vine, pp. 68-70.

God," in its broader aspect, God is in antithesis to 'man' or 'the world," and the term signifies the entire sphere of God's rule and action in relation to the world. It has a moral and spiritual force and is a general term for the Kingdom at any time. The Kingdom of Heaven is always the Kingdom of God, but the Kingdom of God is not limited to the Kingdom of Heaven, until in their final form, they become identical; e.g., Rev. 11:15, R.V.; John 3:5; Rev. 12:10." (*An Extract*).

NT: B.134d; CB.1238c; K.97.
OT: mamlākāh: S.4467; HR.192a.4f; H.1199f; BD.575a.
malᵉkût: S.4438; HR.192a.4e; H.1199e; BD.574d.
malᵉkû (Aramaic): S.4437; HR.192a.4d; H.2829c; BD.1100b.
GEN. REF.: IS.3:20; NB.692,693; Z.3:795.

For **KINSFOLK** and **KINSMAN** see **KIN**

KISS (Noun and Verb)

A. Noun.

philēma [φίλημα, 5370], a kiss (akin to B), Luke 7:45; 22:48, was a token of Christian brotherhood, whether by way of welcome or farewell, "a holy kiss," Rom. 16:16; 1 Cor. 16:20; 2 Cor. 13:12; 1 Thess. 5:26, "holy" (*hagios*), as free from anything inconsistent with their calling as saints (*hagioi*); "a kiss of love," 1 Pet. 5:14. There was to be an absence of formality and hypocrisy, a freedom from prejudice arising from social distinctions, from discrimination against the poor, from partiality towards the well-to-do. In the churches masters and servants would thus salute one another without any attitude of condescension on the one part or disrespect on the other. The kiss took place thus between persons of the same sex. In the "Apostolic Constitutions," a writing compiled in the 4th century, A.D., there is a reference to the custom whereby men sat on one side of the room where a meeting was held, and women on the other side of the room (as is frequently the case still in parts of Europe and Asia), and the men are bidden to salute the men, and the women the women, with "the kiss of the Lord." ¶

NT: B.859c; CB.1264a; K.1262.
OT: nᵉshîqāh: S.5390; HR.1430c.1; H.1435a; BD.676c.
GEN. REF.: IS.3:43; NB.701; Z.3:831.

B. Verbs.

1. *phileō* [φιλέω, 5368], to love, signifies to kiss, in Matt. 26:48; Mark 14:44; Luke 22:47.

NT: B.859b; CB.1264a; K.1262.
OT: nāshaq: S.5401; HR.1430b.2a; H.1435,1436; BD.676b.
'āhēb: S.157; HR.1430b.1a; H.29; BD.12c.
GEN. REF.: IS.3:43; NB.701; Z.3:831.

2. *kataphileō* [καταφιλέω, 2705], denotes to kiss fervently (*kata*, intensive, and No. 1); the stronger force of this verb has been called in question, but the change from *phileō* to *kataphileō* in Matt. 26:49 and Mark 14:45 can scarcely be without significance, and the act of the traitor was almost certainly more demonstrative than the simple kiss of salutation. So with the kiss of genuine devotion, Luke 7:38, 45; 15:20; Acts 20:37, in each of which this verb is used. ¶

NT: B.420b; CB.1254b; K.1262.
OT: nāshaq: S.5401; HR.747c.1; H.1435,1436; BD.676b.
GEN. REF.: IS.3:43; NB.701; Z.3:831.

KNEE

gonu [γόνυ, 1119], a knee (Latin, *genu*) is used (*a*) metaphorically in Heb. 12:12, where the duty enjoined is that of "courageous self-recovery in God's strength"; (*b*) literally, of the attitude of a suppliant, Luke 5:8; Eph. 3:14; of veneration, Rom. 11:4; 14:11; Phil. 2:10; in mockery, Mark 15:19. See KNEEL.

NT: B.165a; CB.1248c; K.126.
OT: berek: S.1290; HR.274c.2; H.285a; BD.139c.
GEN. REF.: IS.3:46; NB.702; Z.3:835.

KNEEL

1. *gonupeteō* [γονυπετέω, 1120], denotes to bow the knees, kneel, from *gonu* (see above) and *piptō*, to fall prostrate, the act of one imploring aid, Matt. 17:14; Mark 1:40; of one expressing reverence and honour, Mark 10:17; in mockery, Matt. 27:29. ¶

NT: B.165b; CB.1248c; K.126.
OT: –.
GEN. REF.: IS.–; NB.702; Z.3:835.

2. A phrase consisting of *tithēmi*, to put, with *gonata*, the plural of *gonu*, the knee (see above), signifies to kneel, and is always used of an attitude of prayer; Luke 22:41 (lit., 'placing the knees'); Acts 7:60; 9:40; 20:36; 21:5. ¶

KNIT TOGETHER

sumbibazō [συμβιβάζω, 4822], signifies to cause to coalesce to join or knit tgether, Eph. 4:16, R.V., "knit together" (A.V., "compacted"); Col. 2:2, where some would assign the alternative meaning, to instruct as, e.g., in 1 Cor. 2:16; in Col. 2:19, "knit together," it is said of the Church, as the Body of which Christ is the head. See COMPACTED.

NT: B.777c; CB.–; K.1101.
OT: yārāh: S.3384; HR.1303b.3; H.910; BD.434b.
yāda': S.3045; HR.1303b.2; H.848; BD.393b.
GEN. REF.: IS.3:47; NB.–; Z.–.

Note: In Acts 10:11 some mss. have the verb *deō*, to bind, translated "knit," of the four corners of the sheet in Peter's vision. The R.V. "let down" translates the verb *kathiēmi*, found in the best texts.

KNOCK

krouō [κρούω, 2925], to strike, knock, is used in the N.T. of knocking at a door, (*a*) literally, Luke 12:36; Acts 12;13, 16; (*b*) figuratively, Matt. 7:7, 8; Luke 11:9, 10 (of importunity in dealing with God); 13:25; Rev. 3:20. ¶

NT: B.453d; CB.1256a; K.475.
OT: dāphaq: S.1849; HR.791c.1; H.447; BD.200c.
GEN. REF.: IS.3:47; NB.–; Z.–.

KNOW, KNOWN, KNOWLEDGE, UNKNOWN

A. Verbs.

1. *ginōskō* [γινώσκω, 1097], signifies to be taking in knowledge, to come to know, recognize, understand, or to understand completely, e.g., Mark 13:28, 29; John 13:12; 15:18; 21:17; 2 Cor. 8:9; Heb. 10:34; 1 John 2:5; 4:2, 6 (twice), 7, 13; 5:2, 20; in its past tenses it frequently means to know in the sense of realising, the aorist or point tense usually indicating definiteness, Matt. 13:11; Mark 7:24; John 7:26; in 10:38 "that ye may know (aorist tense) and understand, (present tense)"; 19:4; Acts 1:7; 17:19; Rom. 1:21; 1 Cor. 2:11 (2nd part) 14; 2 Cor. 2:4; Eph. 3:19; 6:22; Phil. 2:19; 3:10; 1 Thess. 3:5; 2 Tim. 2:19; Jas. 2:20; 1 John 2:13 (twice), 14; 3:6; 4:8; 2 John 1; Rev. 2:24; 3:3, 9. In the Passive Voice, it often signifies to become known, e.g., Matt. 10:26; Phil. 4:5. In the sense of complete and absolute understanding on God's part, it is used, e.g., in Luke 16:15; John 10:15 (of the Son as well as the Father); 1 Cor. 3:20. In Luke 12:46, A.V., it is rendered "he is . . . aware."

In the N.T. *ginōsko* frequently indicates a relation between the person knowing and the object known; in this respect, what is known is of value or importance to the one who knows, and hence the establishment, of the relationship, e.g., especially of God's knowledge, 1 Cor. 8:3, "if any man love God, the same is known of Him"; Gal. 4:9, "to be known of God"; here the knowing suggests approval and bears the meaning 'to be approved'; so in 2 Tim. 2:19; cp. John 10:14, 27; Gen. 18:19; Nahum 1:7; the relationship implied may involve remedial chastisement, Amos 3:2. The same idea of appreciation as well as knowledge underlies several statements concerning the knowledge of God and His truth on the part of believers, e.g., John 8:32; 14:20, 31; 17:3; Gal. 4:9 (1st part); 1 John 2:3, 13, 14; 4:6, 8, 16; 5:20; such knowledge is obtained, not by mere intellectual activity, but by operation of the Holy Spirit consequent upon acceptance of Christ. Nor is such knowledge marked by finality; see, e.g., 2 Pet. 3:18; Hos. 6:3, R.V.

The verb is also used to convey the thought of connection or union, as between man and woman, Matt. 1:25; Luke 1:34.

NT: B.160d; CB.1248b; K.119.
OT: yāda': S.3045; HR.267a.4a; H.848; BD.393b.
GEN. REF.: IS.3:48; NB.702; Z.3:836.

2. *oida* [οἶδα, —], from the same root as *eidon*, to see, is a perfect tense with a present meaning, signifying, primarily, to have seen or perceived; hance, to know, to have knowledge of, whether absolutely, as in Divine knowledge, e.g., Matt. 6:8, 32; John 6:6, 64; 8:14; 11:42; 13:11; 18:4; 2 Cor. 11:31; 2 Pet. 2:9; Rev. 2:2, 9, 13, 19; 3:1, 8, 15; or in the case of human knowledge, to know from observation, e.g., 1 Thess. 1:4, 5; 2:1; 2 Thess. 3:7.

The differences between *ginōskō* (No. 1) and *oida* demand consideration: (*a*) *ginōsko*, frequently suggests inception or progress in knowledge, while *oida* suggests fulness of knowledge, e.g., John 8:55, "ye have not known Him" (*ginōskō*), i.e., begun to know, "but I know Him" (*oida*), i.e., 'know Him perfectly'; 13:7, "What I do thou knowest not now," i.e. Peter did not yet perceive (*oida*) its significance. "but thou shalt understand," i.e., 'get to know (*ginōskō*), hereafter'; 14:7, "If ye had known Me" (*ginōskō*), i.e., 'had definitely come to know Me,' "ye would have known My Father also" (*oida*), i.e., 'would have had perception of': "from henceforth ye know Him" (*ginōskō*), i.e., having unconsciously been coming to the Father, as the One who was in Him, they would now consciously be in the constant and progressive experience of knowing Him; in Mark 4:13, "Know ye not (*oida*) this parable? and how shall ye know (*ginōskō*) all the parables?" (R.V.), i.e., 'Do ye not understand this parable? How shall ye come to perceive all . . .' the intimation being that the first parable is a leading and testing one; (*b*) while *ginōskō* frequently implies an active relation between the one who knows and the person or thing known (see No. 1, above), *oida* expresses the fact that the object has simply come within the scope of the knower's perception; thus in Matt. 7:23 "I never knew you" (*ginōskō*) suggests 'I have never been in approving connection with you,' whereas in 25:12, "I know you not" (*oida*) suggests 'you stand in no relation to Me.'

NT: B.555d; CB.1260b; K.673.
OT: –.
GEN. REF.: IS.3:48; NB.–; Z.3:836.

3. *epiginōskō* [ἐπιγινώσκω, 1921], denotes (*a*) to observe, fully perceive, notice attentively, discern, recognize (*epi*, upon, and No. 1); it suggests generally a directive, a more special, recognition of the object known than does No. 1; it also may suggest advanced knowledge or special appreciation; thus, in Rom. 1:32, "knowing the ordinance of God" (*epiginōskō*) means 'knowing full well,' whereas in verse 21 "knowing God" (*ginōskō*) simply suggests that they could not avoid the perception. Sometimes *epiginōskō* implies a special participation in the object known, and gives greater weight to what is stated; thus in John 8:32, "ye shall know the truth," *ginōskō* is used, whereas in 1 Tim. 4:3, "them that believe and know the truth," *epiginōskō* lays stress on participation in the truth. Cp. the stronger statement in Col. 1:6 (*epiginōskō*) with that in 2 Cor. 8:9 (*ginōskō*), and the two verbs in 1 Cor. 13:12, "now I know in part (*ginōskō*); but then shall I know (*piginōskō*) even as also I have been known (*epiginōskō*)," a knowledge "which perfectly unites the subject with the object"; (*b*) to discover, ascertain, determine, e.g., Luke 7:37; 23:7; Acts 9:30; 19:34; 22:29; 28:1; in 24:11 the best mss. have this verb instead of No. 1; hence the R.V., "take knowledge." J. Armitage Robinson (on Ephesians) points out that *epignōsis* is "knowledge directed towards a particular object, perceiving, discerning," whereas *gnōsis* is knowledge in the abstract. See ACKNOWLEDGE.

NT: B.291a; CB.1245c; K.—.
OT: yāda': S.3045; HR.517c.2a-c; H.848; BD.393b.
nākar: S.5234; HR.517c.3; H.1368; BD.647d.
GEN. REF.: IS.3:48; NB.702; Z.3:836.

4. *proginōskō* [προγινώσκω, 4267], to know beforehand, is used (*a*) of the Divine foreknowledge concerning believers, Rom. 8:29; Israel, 11:2; Christ as the Lamb of God, 1 Pet. 1:20, R.V., "foreknown" (A.V., "foreordained"); (*b*) of human previous knowledge, of a person, Acts 26:5, R.V., "having knowledge of" (A.V., "which knew"); of facts, 2 Pet. 3:17. See FOREKNOW. ¶

NT: B.703d; CB.1266c; K.119.
OT: —.
GEN. REF.: —.

5. *epistamai* [ἐπίσταμαι, 1987], to know, know of, understand (probably an old Middle Voice form of *ephistēmi*, to set over), is used in Mark 14:68, "understand," which follows *oida* "I (neither) know"; most frequently in the Acts, 10:28; 15:7; 18:25; 19:15, 25; 20:18; 22:19; 24:10; 26:26; elsewhere, 1 Tim. 6:4; Heb. 11:8; Jas. 4:14; Jude 10. See UNDERSTAND. ¶

NT: B.300a; CB.1246a; K.—.
OT: yāda': S.3045; HR.529b.2a; H.848; BD.393b.
GEN. REF.: IS.3:48; NB.702; Z.3:836.

6. *sunoida* [σύνοιδα, —], *sun*, with, and No. 2, a perfect tense with a present meaning, denotes (*a*) to share the knowledge of, be privy to, Acts 5:2; (*b*) to be conscious of, especially of guilty consciousness, 1 Cor. 4:4, "I know nothing against (A.V., by) myself." The verb is connected with *suneidon*, found in Acts 12:12; 14:6 (in the best texts). See CONSIDER, PRIVY, WARE. ¶

NT: B.791b; CB.1270c; K.1120.
OT: —.
GEN. REF.: —.

7. *agnoeō* [ἀγνοέω], not to know, to be ignorant: see IGNORANT.

8. *gnōrizō* [γνωρίζω, 1107], signifies (*a*) to come to know, discover, know, Phil. 1:22, "I wot (not)," i.e., 'I know not,' 'I have not come to know' (the R.V. marg. renders it, as under (*b*), "I do not make known"); (*b*) to make known, whether (I) communicating things before unknown, Luke 2:15, 17; in the latter some mss. have the verb *diagnōrizō* (hence the A.V., "made known abroad)"; John 15:15, "I have made known"; 17:26; Acts 2:28; 7:13 (1st part), see *Note* (3) below; Rom. 9:22, 23; 16:26 (Passive Voice); 2 Cor. 8:1, "we make known (to you)," R.V., A.V., "we do (you) to wit"; Eph. 1:9; 3:3, 5, 10 (all three in the Passive Voice); 6:19, 21; Col. 1:27; 4:7, 9, "shall make known" (A.V., "shall declare"); 2 Pet. 1:16; or (II) reasserting things already known, 1 Cor. 12:3, "I give (you) to understand" (the Apostle reaffirms what they knew); 15:1, of the Gospel; Gal. 1:11 (he reminds them of what they well knew, the ground of his claim to Apostleship); Phil. 4:6 (Passive Voice), of requests to God. See CERTIFY, DECLARE (*Note*), UNDERSTAND, WIT, WOT. ¶

NT: B.163b; CB.1248b; K.119.
OT: yāda': S.3045; HR.273a.2c; H.848; BD.393b.
GEN. REF.: IS.3:48; NB.702; Z.3:836.

Notes: (1) In 2 Tim. 3:10, A.V., *parakoloutheō*, to follow closely, follow as a standard of conduct, is translated "hast fully known" (R.V., "didst follow"). See FOLLOW.

(2) In 2 Tim. 4:17, A.V., *plērophoreō*, to fulfil, accomplish, is translated "might be fully known" (R.V., "might be fully proclaimed"). See FULFIL.

(3) In Acts 7:13, some mss. have the verb *anagnōrizō*, to make oneself known, "was made known," instead of No. 8 (which see). ¶

(4) In Acts 7:13 (2nd part) the A.V., "was made known" translates the phrase *phaneros ginomai*, to become manifest (R.V., "became manifest"). See MANIFEST.

(5) For *diagnōrizō*, to make known, in Luke 2:17, see No. 8.

(6) For *diaginōskō*, in Acts 24:22. "I will know the uttermost of," see DETERMINE, No. 5.

B. Adjectives.

1. *gnōstos* [γνωστός, 1110], a later form of *gnōtos* (from No. 1), most frequently denotes "known"; it is used ten times in the Acts, always with that meaning (save in 4:16, where it means "notable"); twice in the Gospel of John, 18:15, 16; in Luke 2:44 and 23:49 it denotes "acquaintance"; elsewhere only in Rom. 1:19, "(that which) may be known (of God)," lit., 'the knowable of God,' referring to the physical universe, in the creation of which God has made Himself knowable, that is, by the exercise of man's natural faculties, without such supernatural revelations as those given to Israel. See ACQUAINTANCE.

NT: B.164b; CB.1248b; K.119.
OT: yāda': S.3045; HR.274a.1a,b; H.848; BD.393b.
GEN. REF.: IS.3:48; NB.702; Z.3:836.

2. *phaneros* [φανερός, 5318], visible, manifest, is translated "known" in Matt. 12:16 and Mark 3:12. See APPEAR, MANIFEST, OPENLY, OUTWARDLY.

NT: B.852b; CB.1263c; K.1244.
OT: yāda': S.3045; HR.1424a.3a; H.848; BD.393b.
GEN. REF.: IS.3:48; NB.702; Z.3:836.

3. *epistēmōn* [ἐπιστήμων, 1990], akin to A, No. 5, knowing, skilled, is used in Jas. 3:13, A.V., "endued with knowledge" (R.V. "understanding"). ¶

NT: B.300c; CB.—; K.—.
OT: bîn: S.995; HR.530b.1; H.239; BD.106c.
yāda': S.3045; HR.530b.2; H.848; BD.393b.
GEN. REF.: IS.3:48; NB.702; Z.3:836.

4. *agnōstos* [ἄγνωστος, 57], the negative of No. 1, "unknown," is found in Acts 17:23. ¶

NT: B.12b; CB.1233c; K.18.
OT: —.
GEN. REF.: —.

C. Nouns.

1. *gnōsis* [γνῶσις, 1108], primarily a seeking to know, an enquiry, investigation (akin to A, No. 1), denotes, in the N.T., knowledge, especially of spiritual truth; it is used (*a*) absolutely, in Luke 11:52; Rom. 2:20; 15:14; 1 Cor. 1:5; 8:1 (twice), 7, 10, 11; 13:2, 8; 14:6; 2 Cor. 6:6; 8:7; 11:6; Eph. 3:19; Col. 2:3; 1 Pet. 3:7; 2 Pet. 1:5, 6; (*b*) with an object: in respect of (1) God, 2 Cor. 2:14; 10:5; (2) the glory of God, 2 Cor. 4:6; (3) Christ Jesus, Phil. 3:8; 2 Pet. 3:18; (4) salvation, Luke 1:77; (*c*) subjectively, of God's knowledge, Rom. 11:33; the word of knowledge, 1 Cor. 12:8; knowledge falsely so called, 1 Tim. 6:20. ¶

NT: B.163b; CB.1248b; K.119.
OT: da'at: S.1847; HR.273c.1b; H.848c; BD.395c.
GEN. REF.: IS.3:48; NB.702; Z.3:836.

2. *epignōsis* [ἐπίγνωσις, 1922], akin to A, No. 3, denotes exact or full knowledge, discernment, recognition, and is a strengthened form of No. 1, expressing a fuller or a full knowledge, a greater participation by the knower in the object known, thus more powerfully influencing him. It is not found in the Gospels and Acts. Paul uses it 15 times (16 if Heb. 10:26 is included) out of the 20 occurrences; Peter 4 times, all in his 2nd Epistle. Contrast Rom. 1:28 (*epignōsis*) with the simple verb in ver. 21. "In all the four Epistles of the first Roman captivity it is an element in the Apostle's opening prayer for his correspondents' well-being, Phil. 1:9; Eph. 1:17; Col. 1:9; Philm. 6" (Lightfoot).

It is used with reference to God in Rom. 1:28; 10:2; Eph. 1:17; Col. 1:10; 2 Pet. 1:3; God and Christ, 2 Pet. 1:2; Christ, Eph. 4:13; 2 Pet. 1:8; 2:20; the will of the Lord, Col. 1:9; every good thing, Philm. 6, R.V. (A.V., "acknowledging"); the truth, 1 Tim. 2:4; 2 Tim. 2:25, R.V.; 3:7; Tit. 1:1, R.V.; the mystery of God, Col. 2:2, R.V., "(that they) may know" (A.V., "to the acknowledgment of"), lit., 'into a full knowledge.' It is used without the mention of an object in Phil. 1:9; Col. 3:10, R.V., "(renewed) unto knowledge." See ACKNOWLEDGE. ¶

NT: B.291b; CB.1245c; K.119.
OT: da'at: S.1847; HR.518c.1; H.848c; BD.395c.
GEN. REF.: IS.3:48; NB.702; Z.3:836.

3. *agnōsia* [ἀγνωσία, 56], the negative of No. 1, ignorance, is rendered "no knowledge" in 1 Cor. 15:34, R.V. (A.V., "not the knowledge"); in 1 Pet. 2:15, "ignorance." See IGNORANCE. ¶

NT: B.12b; CB.1233c; K.18.
OT: —.
GEN. REF.: —.

Note: In Eph. 3:4, A.V., *sunesis*, understanding, is translated 'knowledge'; R.V., "understanding." For *kardiognōstēs* see p. 383.

L

LABOUR (Noun and Verb)

A. Nouns.

1. *kopos* [κόπος, 2873], primarily denotes a striking, beating (akin to *koptō*, to strike, cut); then, toil resulting in weariness, laborious toil, trouble, it is translated "labour" or "labours" in John 4:38; 1 Cor. 3:8; 15:58; 2 Cor. 6:5; 10:15; 11:23, 27, R.V., "labour" (A.V., "weariness"); 1 Thess. 1:3; 2:9; 3:5; 2 Thess. 3:8; (in some mss., Heb. 6:10); Rev. 2:2 (R.V. "toil"); 14:13. In the following the noun is used as the object of the verb *parechō*, to afford, give, cause, the phrase being rendered to trouble, lit., to cause toil or trouble, to embarrass a person by giving occasion for anxiety, as some disciples did to the woman with the ointment, perturbing her spirit by their criticisms, Matt. 26:10; Mark 14:6; or by distracting attention or disturbing a person's rest, as the importunate friend did, Luke 11:7; 18:5; in Gal. 6:17, "let no man trouble me," The Apostle refuses, in the form of a peremptory prohibition, to allow himself to be distracted further by the Judaizers, through their proclamation of a false gospel and by their malicious attacks upon himself. ¶

NT: B.443d; CB.1255c; K.453.
OT: ʿāmāl: S.5999; HR.778b.7; H.1639a; BD.765d.
GEN. REF.: IS.3:54; NB.—; Z.3:847.

2. *ponos* [πόνος, 4192], denotes (*a*) labours, toil, Col. 4:13, in the best mss. (some have *zēlos*, zeal, A.V.); (*b*) the consequence of toil, viz., distress, suffering, pain, Rev. 16:10, 11; 21:4. See PAIN. ¶

NT: B.691c; CB.1266a; K.—.
OT: ʿāmāl: S.5999; HR.1188b.9; H.1639a; BD.765d.
ʾāwen: S.205; HR.1188b.1; H.48a; BD.19d.
GEN. REF.: IS.3:54; NB.—; Z.3:847.

Notes: (1) In Phil. 1:22, A.V., *ergon*, work, is translated "labour" (R.V., "work"); work refers to what is done, and may be easy and pleasant; *kopos* suggests the doing, and the pains taken therein.

(2) A synonymous word is *mochthos*, toil, hardship, distress, 2 Cor. 11:27; 1 Thess. 2:9; 2 Thess. 3:8. ¶

B. Verbs.

1. *kopiaō* [κοπιάω, 2872], akin to A, No. 1, has the two different meanings (*a*) growing weary, (*b*) toiling; it is sometimes translated to bestow labour (see under BESTOW, No. 3). It is translated by the verb to labour in Matt. 11:28; John 4:38 (2nd part); Acts 20:35; Rom. 16:12 (twice); 1 Cor. 15:10; 16:16; Eph. 4:28; Phil. 2:16; Col. 1:29; 1 Thess. 5:12; 1 Tim. 4:10; 5:17; 2 Tim. 2:6; Rev. 2:3; 1 Cor. 4:12, R.V., "toil" (A.V., "labour"). See TOIL.

NT: B.443c; CB.1255c; K.453.
OT: yāgaʿ: S.3021; HR.778b.6a; H.842; BD.388a.
ʿāmāl: S.5999; HR.778b.11a; H.1639a; BD.765d.
GEN. REF.: IS.3:54; NB.—; Z.3:847.

2. *cheimazō* [χειμάζω, 5492], from *cheima*, winter-cold, primarily, to expose to winter cold, signifies to drive with a storm; in the Passive Voice, to be driven with storm, to be tempest-tossed, Acts 27:18, R.V., "as (we) laboured with th storm" (A.V., "being . . . tossed with a tempest"). ¶

NT: B.879c; CB.—; K.—.
OT: —.
GEN. REF.: —.

3. *sunathleō* [συναθλέω, 4866], to contend along with a person (*sun*, with, *athleō*, to contend), is said in Phil. 4:3 of two women who "laboured with" the Apostle in the Gospel; in 1:27, R.V., "striving (for)," marg., "with," A.V., "striving together (for)." See STRIVE. ¶

NT: B.783b; CB.1270c; K.25.
OT: —.
GEN. REF.: IS.3:54; NB.—; Z.—

Notes: (1) In John 6:27 and 1 Thess. 2:9, A.V., *ergazomai*, to work, is translated respectively "labour" and "labouring" (R.V., "working"). It is used of manual work here and in 4:11 and Eph. 4:28; of work for Christ in general, in 1 Cor. 16:10. See COMMIT.

(2) In Heb. 4:11, A.V., *spoudazō*, to be diligent, is translated "let us labour" (R.V., "let us give diligence").

(3) In Col. 4:12, A.V., *agōnizomai*, to strive, wrestle, is translated "labouring fervently" (R.V., and A.V., marg., "striving").

(4) In 2 Cor. 5:9, A.V., *philotimeomai*, to seek after honour, and hence, to be ambitious, is translated "we labour," marg., "endeavour" (R.V., "we make it our aim," marg., "are ambitious"); cp. Rom. 15:20; 1 Thess. 4:11, R.V., marg. ¶

LABOURER, FELLOW-LABOURER

ergatēs [ἐργάτης, 2040], akin to *ergazomai*, to work, and *ergon*, work, denotes (*a*) a field-labourer, a husbandman, Matt. 9:37, 38; 20:1, 2, 8; Luke 10:2 (twice); Jas. 5:4; (*b*) a workman, labourer, in a general sense, Matt. 10:10; Luke 10:7; Acts 19:25; 1 Tim. 5:18; it is used (*c*) of false apostles and evil teachers, 2 Cor. 11:13;

Phil. 3:2; (*d*) of a servant of Christ, 2 Tim. 2:15; (*e*) of evildoers, Luke 13:27. ¶

NT: B.307c; CB.1246c; K.251.
OT: –.
GEN. REF.: IS.3:54; NB.–; Z.–.

Note: In the A.V. of Philm. 1 and 24, *sunergos*, a fellow-worker, is translated "fellow-labourer," R.V., "fellow-worker"; in Phil. 4:3, the plural, R.V., "fellow-workers"; in Phil. 2:25, A.V., "companion in labour," R.V., "fellow-worker"; in 1 Cor. 3:9, A.V., "labourers together (with God)," R.V., "God's fellow-workers," i.e., fellow-workers belonging to and serving God; in 3 John 8, A.V., "fellow-helpers" (to the truth), R.V., "fellow-workers (with the truth)," i.e., acting together with the truth as an operating power; in 1 Thess. 3:2, some ancient authorities have the clause "fellow-worker (with God)," R.V., marg.; it is absent from the most authentic mss. See HELPER.

LACK, LACKING

A. Noun.

husterēma [ὑστέρημα, 5303], denotes (*a*) that which is lacking, deficiency, shortcoming (akin to *hustereō*, to be behind, in want), 1 Cor. 16:17; Phil. 2:30; Col. 1:24, R.V., "that which is lacking" [A.V., "that which is behind" (of the afflictions of Christ)], where the reference is not to the vicarious sufferings of Christ, but to those which He endured previously, and those which must be endured by His faithful servants; 1 Thess. 3:10, where "that which is lacking" means that which Paul had not been able to impart to them, owing to the interruption of his spiritual instruction among them; (*b*) need, want, poverty, Luke 21:4, R.V., "want" (A.V., "penury"); 2 Cor. 8:14 (twice), "want"; 9:12, "wants" (A.V., "want"); 11:9, R.V., "(the measure of my) want" [A.V., "that which was lacking (to me)"]. See BEHIND, PENURY, WANT. ¶

NT: B.849b; CB.1252b; K.1240.
OT: maḥsôr: S.4270; HR.1418c.1b; H.705e; BD.341d.
GEN. REF.: –.

Note: In 1 Thess. 4:12, A.V., *chreia*, need, is translated "lack" [R.V., "need"). See NEED.

B. Adjective.

endeēs [ἐνδεής, 1729], from *endeō*, to lack, signifies needy, in want, translated "that lacked" in Acts 4:34. ¶

NT: B.262c; CB.–; K.–.
OT: 'ebyôn: S.34; HR.469b.1; H.3a; BD.2d.
ḥāsēr: S.2637; HR.469b.3b; H.705; BD.341a.
GEN. REF.: –.

C. Verbs.

1. *hustereō* [ὑστερέω, 5302], akin to A, to come or be behind, is used in the sense of lacking certain things, Matt. 19:20; Mark 10:21 ("one thing"; cp. No. 3 in Luke 18:22); Luke 22:35; in the sense of being inferior, 1 Cor. 12:24 (Middle Voice). Elsewhere it is translated in various ways; see BEHIND, B, No. 1, COME, No. 39, DESTITUTE, FAIL, *Note* (2), NEED, WANT, WORSE.

NT: B.849a; CB.1252b; K.1240.
OT: ḥāsēr: S.2637; HR.1418b.3a; H.705; BD.341a.
GEN. REF.: –.

2. *elattoneō* [ἐλαττονέω, 1641], to be less (from *elattōn*, less), is translated "had no lack," 2 Cor. 8:15 (quoted from the Sept. of Ex. 16:18), the circumstance of the gathering of the manna being applied to the equalising nature of cause and effect in the matter of supplying the wants of the needy. ¶

NT: B.248b; CB.–; K.–.
OT: ḥāsēr: S.2637; HR.448a.1; H.705; BD.341a.
GEN. REF.: –.

3. *leipō* [λείπω, 3007], to leave, denotes (*a*) transitively, in the Passive Voice, to be left behind, to lack, Jas. 1:4, "ye may be lacking in (nothing)," R.V. (A.V., "wanting"); ver. 5, "lacketh" (A.V., "lack"); 2:15, R.V., "be . . . in lack" (A.V., "be . . . destitute"); (*b*) intransitively, Active Voice, Luke 18:22, "(one thing thou) lackest," is, lit., '(one thing) is lacking (to thee)'; Tit. 1:5, "(the things) that were wanting"; 3:13, "(that nothing) be wanting." See DESTITUTE, WANTING. ¶

NT: B.470b; CB.1256c; K.–.
OT: –.
GEN. REF.: –.

Note: In 2 Pet. 1:9, "he that lacketh" translates a phrase the lit. rendering of which is '(he to whom these things) are not present' (*pareimi*, to be present).

For **LAD**, in John 6:9, see **CHILD**, A, No. 6

LADE, LADEN

1. *sōreuō* [σωρεύω, 4987], signifies (*a*) to heap on (from *sōros*, a heap, not in the N.T.; in the Sept., e.g., Josh. 7:26; 8:29; 2 Sam. 18:17; 2 Chron. 31:6-9), Rom. 12:20, of coals of fire; 2 Tim. 3:6, said of silly women ('womanlings') laden with sins. See HEAP. ¶ In the Sept., Prov. 25:22. ¶

NT: B.800c; CB.–; K.1150.
OT: ḥātāh: S.2846; HR.1331a.1; H.777; BD.367a.
GEN. REF.: –.

2. *gemō* [γέμω, 1073], to be full, is translated "laden" in Rev. 21:9, R.V. See FULL.

NT: B.153d; CB.1248a; K.–.
OT: mālē': S.4390; HR.235c.1; H.1195; BD.569d.
GEN. REF.: –.

3. *phortizō* [φορτίζω, 5412], to load (akin to *pherō*, to bear), is used in the Active Voice in Luke 11:46, "ye lade"; in the Passive Voice, metaphorically, in Matt. 11:28, "heavy laden." See BURDEN. ¶ In the Sept., Ezek. 16:33. ¶

NT: B.865a; CB.1264b; K.1252.
OT: –.
GEN. REF.: IS.3:148; NB.–; Z.–.

Note: In Acts 28:10, A.V., *epitithēmi*, to put on (*epi*, on, *tithēmi*, to put), is translated "they laded (us) with," R.V., "they put on (board)."

LADING

phortion [φορτίον, 5413], a burden, load (a diminutive of *phortos*, a load, from *pherō*, to bear), is used of the cargo of a ship, Acts 27:10, "lading," (some mss. have *phortos*). See BURDEN, A, No. 2.

NT: B.865a; CB.1264b; K.1252.
OT: –.
GEN. REF.: IS.3:148; NB.–; Z.–.

LADY

kuria [κυρία, 2959], is the person addressed in 2 John 1 and 5. Not improbably it is a proper name (Eng., Cyria), in spite of the fact that the full form of address in ver. 1 is not quite in accord, in the original, with those in ver. 13 and in 3 John 1. The suggestion that the Church is addressed is most unlikely. Possibly the person is one who had a special relation with the local church. ¶

NT: B.458b; CB.1256b; K.486.
OT: g[e]beret: S.1404; HR.799c.2; H.310e; BD.150c.
GEN. REF.: IS.3:60; NB.–; Z.–.

For LAID see LAY

LAKE

limnē [λίμνη, 3041], a lake, is used (*a*) in the Gospels, only by Luke, of the Sea of Galilee, Luke 5:2; 8:22, 23, 33, called Gennesaret in 5:1 (Matthew and Mark use *thalassa*, a sea); (*b*) of the lake of fire, Rev. 19:20; 20:10, 14, 15; 21:8. ¶

NT: B.475a; CB.1257a; K.–.
OT: 'agam: S.98; HR.878c.1; H.18a; BD.8b.
GEN. REF.: IS.3:61; NB.–; Z.3:859.

LAMA

lama [λαμά, 2982], is the Hebrew word for "Why?" (the variant *lema* is the Aramaic form), Matt. 27:46; Mark 15:34. ¶

NT: B.464a; CB.–; K.–.
OT: –.
GEN. REF.: –.

LAMB

1. *arēn* [ἀρήν, 704], a noun the nominative case of which is found only in early times, occurs in Luke 10:3. In normal usage it was replaced by *arnion* (No. 2), of which it is the equivalent. ¶

NT: B.106a; CB.1237c; K.54.
OT: –.
GEN. REF.: IS.3:61; NB.–; Z.3:859.

2. *arnion* [ἀρνίον, 721], is a diminutive in form, but the diminutive force is not to be pressed (see Note under No. 3). The general tendency in the vernacular was to use nouns in *-ion* freely, apart from their diminutive significance. It is used only by the Apostle John, (*a*) in the plural, in the Lord's command to Peter, John 21:15, with symbolic reference to young converts; (*b*) elsewhere, in the singular, in the Apocalypse, some 28 times, of Christ as the Lamb of God, the symbolism having reference to His character and His vicarious Sacrifice, as the basis both of redemption and of Divine vengeance. He is seen in the position of sovereign glory and honour, e.g., 7:17, which He shares equally with the Father, 22:1, 3, the centre of angelic beings and of the redeemed and the object of their veneration, e.g. 5:6, 8, 12, 13; 15:3, the Leader and Shepherd of His saints, e.g., 7:17; 14:4, the head of His spiritual Bride, e.g., 21:9, the luminary of the heavenly and eternal city, 21:23, the One to whom all judgment is committed, e.g., 6:1, 16; 13:8, the Conqueror of the foes of God and His people, 17:14; the song that celebrates the triumph of those who 'gain the victory over the Beast,' is the song of Moses . . . and the song of the Lamb, 15:3. His sacrifice, the efficacy of which avails for those who accept the salvation thereby provided, forms the ground of the execution of Divine wrath for the rejector, and the defier of God, 14:10; (*c*) in the description of the second "Beast," Rev. 13:11, seen in the vision "like a lamb," suggestive of his acting in the capacity of a false Messiah, a travesty of the true. For the use in the Sept. see Note under No. 3.

NT: B.108b; CB.1237c; K.54.
OT: bēn: S.1121; HR.159b.1; H.254; BD.119d.
kebes: S.3532; HR.159b.2; H.949; BD.461a.
GEN. REF.: IS.3:61; NB.706; Z.3:859.

3. *amnos* [ἀμνός, 286], a lamb, is used figuratively of Christ, in John 1:29, 36 with the article, pointing Him out as the expected One, the One to be well known as the Personal fulfilment and embodiment of all that had been indicated in the O.T., the One by whose sacrifice deliverance from Divine judgment was to be obtained; in Acts 8:32 (from the Sept. of Is. 53:7) and 1 Pet. 1:19, the absence of the article stresses the nature and character of His sacrifice as set forth in the symbolism. The reference in each case is to the lamb of God's providing, Gen. 22:8, and the Paschal lamb of God's

appointment for sacrifice in Israel, e.g., Ex. 12:5, 14, 27 (cp. 1 Cor. 5:7. ¶
NT: B.46c; CB.1234c; K.54.
OT: kebes: S.3532; HR.66b.2a; H.949; BD.461a.
GEN. REF.: IS.3:61; NB.706; Z.3:859.

Note: The contrast between *arnion* and *amnos* does not lie in the diminutive character of the former as compared with the latter. As has been pointed out under No. 2, *arnion* lost its diminutive force. The contrast lies in the manner in which Christ is presented in the two respects. The use of *amnos* points directly to the fact, the nature and character of His sacrifice; *arnion* (only in the Apocalypse) presents Him, on the ground, indeed, of His Sacrifice, but in His acquired majesty, dignity, honour, authority and power.

In the Sept. *arnion* is used in Ps. 114:4, 6; in Jer. 11:19, with the adjective *akakos*, innocent; in Jer. 27:45, "lambs." There is nothing in these passages to suggest a contrast between a lamb in the general sense of the term and the diminutive; the contrast is between lambs and sheep. Elsewhere in the Sept. *amnos* is in general used some 100 times in connection with lambs for sacrifice.

For **LAME** see **HALT**

For **LAMENT** and **LAMENTATION** see **BEWAIL**

LAMP

1. *lampas* [λαμπάς, 2985], denotes a torch (akin to *lampō*, to shine), frequently fed, like a lamp, with oil from a little vessel used for the purpose (the *angeion* of Matt. 25:4); they held little oil and would frequently need replenishing. Rutherford (*The New Phrynichus*) points out that it became used as the equivalent of *luchnos* (No. 2), as in the parable of the Ten Virgins, Matt. 25:1, 3, 4, 7, 8; John 18:3, "torches"; Acts 20:8, "lights"; Rev. 4:5; 8:10 (R.V., "torch," A.V., "lamp"). See *Note* below. ¶ Cp. *phanos*, a torch, John 18:3 (translated "lanterns"). ¶
NT: B.465c; CB.1256c; K.497.
OT: lappîd: S.3940; HR.852c.1; H.1122a; BD.542a.
GEN. REF.: IS.3:68; NB.708; Z.3:865.

2. *luchnos* [λύχνος, 3088], frequently mistranslated "candle," is a portable lamp usually set on a stand (see LAMPSTAND); the word is used ((*a*) literally, Matt. 5:15; Mark 4:21; Luke 8:16; 11:33, 36; 15:8; Rev. 18:23; 22:5; (*b*) metaphorically, of Christ as the Lamb, Rev. 21:23, R.V., "lamp" (A.V., "light"); of John the Baptist, John 5:35, R.V., "the lamp" (A.V., "a . . . light"); of the eye, Matt. 6:22, and Luke 11:34, R.V., "lamp"; of spiritual readiness, Luke 12:35, R.V., "lamps"; of "the word of prophecy," 2 Pet. 1:19, R.V., "lamp." See LIGHT. ¶

"In rendering *luchnos* and *lampas* our Translators have scarcely made the most of the words at their command. Had they rendered *lampas* by 'torch' not once only (John 18:3), but always, this would have left 'lamp,' now wrongly appropriated by *lampas*, disengaged. Altogether dismissing 'candle,' they might then have rendered *luchnos* by 'lamp' wherever it occurs. At present there are so many occasions where 'candle' would manifestly be inappropriate, and where, therefore, they are obliged to fall back on 'light,' that the distinction between *phōs* and *luchnos* nearly, if not quite, disappears in our Version. The advantages of such a redistribution of the words would be many. In the first place, it would be more accurate. *Luchnos* is not a 'candle' (candela,' from 'candeo,' the white wax light, and then any kind of taper), but a handlamp, fed with oil. Neither is *lampas* a 'lamp,' but a 'torch' " (Trench Syn., § xlvi).
NT: B.483b; CB.1257b; K.542.
OT: nēr: S.5216; HR.891b.1b; H.1333b; BD.632d.
GEN. REF.: IS.3:68; NB.708; Z.3:865.

Note: There is no mention of a candle in the original either in the O.T. or in the N.T. The figure of that which feeds upon its own substance to provide its light would be utterly inappropriate. A lamp is supplied by oil, which in its symbolism is figurative of the Holy Spirit.

LAMPSTAND

luchnia [λυχνία, 3087], is mistranslated "candlestick" in every occurrence in the A.V. and in certain places in the R.V.; the R.V. has "stand" in Matt. 5:15; Mark 4:21; Luke 8:16; 11:33; "candlestick" in Heb. 9:2; Rev. 1:12, 13, 20 (twice); 2:1, 5; 11:4; the R.V. marg., gives "lampstands" in the passages in Rev., but not in Heb. 9:2. ¶
NT: B.483a; CB.1257b; K.542.
OT: mᵉnôrāh: S.4501; HR.891a.1; H.1333c; BD.633a.
GEN. REF.: IS.3:68; NB.708; Z.3:865.

LAND

A. Nouns.

1. *gē* [γῆ, 1093], in one of its usages, denotes (*a*) land as distinct from sea or other water, e.g., Mark 4:1; 6:47; Luke 5:3; John 6:21; (*b*) land as subject to cultivation, e.g., Luke 14:35 (see GROUND); (*c*) land as describing a country or region, e.g., Matt. 2:20, 21; 4:15; Luke 4:25; in 23:44, R.V., "(the whole) land," A.V., "(all

the) earth"; Acts 7:29; Heb. 11:9, R.V., "a land (not his own)," A.V. "a (strange) country"; Jude 5. In Acts 7:11 the A.V. follows a reading of the noun with the definite article which necessitates the insertion of "land." See EARTH.

NT: B.157c; CB.1248a; K.116.
OT: ’ereṣ: S.776; HR.240c.2a; H.167; BD.75d.
’^{a}dāmāh: S.127; HR.240c.1; H.25b; BD.9c.
GEN. REF.: IS.3:71; NB.—; Z.—.

2. *chōra* [χώρα, 5561], is used with the meaning land, (*a*) of a country, region, e.g., Mark 1:5; Luke 15:14; sometimes translated "region," e.g., Matt. 4:16; Luke 3:1; Acts 8:1; 13:49; 16:6; (*b*) of property, Luke 12:16, "ground." See COUNTRY, A, No. 3.

NT: B.889b; CB.1240a; K.—.
OT: ’ereṣ: S.776; HR.1481a.4; H.167; BD.75d.
m^{e}dînāh: S.4082; HR.1481a.5; H.426d; BD.193d.
GEN. REF.: IS.3:71; NB.—; Z.—.

3. *chōrion* [χωρίον, 5564], a diminutive of No. 2, in form, but not in meaning, is translated "land" in the sense of property, in Acts 4:34; 5:3, 8; 28:7, R.V., "lands" (A.V., "possessions"). See FIELD, GROUND, A, No. 4, PLACE, POSSESSION.

NT: B.890b; CB.1240a; K.—.
OT: kerem: S.3754; HR.1482c.1; H.1040a; BD.501c.
GEN. REF.: IS.3:71; NB.—; Z.—.

4. *agros* [ἀγρός, 68], a field, or piece of ground, or the country as distinct from the town, is translated "lands" in Matt. 19:29; Mark 10:29, 30; Acts 4:37 (cp. No. 3 in ver. 34). See COUNTRY, A, No. 1, FARM, FIELD, GROUND.

NT: B.13d; CB.1233c; K.—.
OT: sādeh: S.7704; HR.17a.7; H.2234a,b; BD.961b.
GEN. REF.: IS.3:71; NB.—; Z.—.

B. Adjective.

xēros [ξηρός, 3584], dry, "dry land," Matt. 23:15 (*gē*, land, being understood); Heb. 11:29: see DRY.

NT: B.548c; CB.1273b; K.—.
OT: yabbāshāh: S.3004; HR.957b.2a; H.837b; BD.387a.
yābēsh: S.3002; HR.957b.2c; H.837a; BD.386d.
ḥārābāh: S.2724; HR.957b.1; H.731e; BD.351c.
GEN. REF.: IS.3:71; NB.—; Z.—.

Note: In Luke 4:26, the R.V., "in the land (of)" and A.V., "a city (of)," represent no word in the original, but give the sense of the phrase.

C. Verb.

katerchomai [κατέρχομαι, 2718], to come down, or go down, descend, is used of coming to port by ship, in Acts 18:22, "landed"; 21:3 (ditto); 27:5, "came to." See COME, No. 7, GO, Note (1).

NT: B.422a; CB.—; K.—.
OT: —.
GEN. REF.: —.

Notes: (1) In Acts 28:12, R.V., *katagō*, to bring down, used as a nautical term in the Passive Voice, is translated "touching" (A.V., "landing").

(2) In Acts 21:3, some mss. have the verb *katagō*, with reference to Cyprus.

(3) In Acts 20:13, *pezeuō*, to travel by land or on foot (*pezos*, on foot; *pous*, a foot), is translated "to go by land," R.V., A.V., "to go afoot," and R.V. marg., "to go on foot." ¶

LANE

rhumē [ῥύμη, 4505], in earlier Greek meant the force or rush or swing of a moving body; in later times, a narrow road, lane or street; it is translated "lanes" in Luke 14:21; "streets" in Matt. 6:2; "street" in Acts 9:11; 12:10. See STREET. ¶ In the Sept., Is. 15:3. ¶

NT: B.737c; CB.—; K.—.
OT: r^{e}ḥôb: S.7339; HR.1255b.1; H.2143d; BD.932a.
GEN. REF.: —.

LANGUAGE

dialektos [διάλεκτος, 1258], primarily a conversation, discourse (akin to *dialegomai*, to discourse or discuss), came to denote the language or dialect of a country or district; in the A.V. and R.V. of Acts 2:6 it is translated "language"; in the following R.V. retains "language," for A.V., "tongue," Acts 1:19; 2:8; 21:40; 22:2; 26:14. See TONGUE. ¶ In the Sept., Esth. 9:26. ¶

NT: B.185d; CB.1241a; K.—.
OT: lāshôn: S.3956; HR.304c.1; H.1131a; BD.546a.
GEN. REF.: IS.3:72; NB.—; Z.—.

LANTERN

phanos [φανός, 5322], denotes either a torch or a lantern (from *phainō*, to cause to shine, to give light), John 18:3, where it is distinguished from *lampas* (see LAMP, No. 1); it was "a link or torch consisting of strips of resinous wood tied together" (Rutherford). "Torch" would seem to be the meaning. ¶

NT: B.853b; CB.—; K.—.
OT: —.
GEN. REF.: IS.3:72; NB.716; Z.3:877.

LARGE

1. *megas* [μέγας, 3173], great, large, of physical magnitude, is translated "large" in Mark 14:15 and Luke 22:12, of the upper room. See GREAT, No. 1.

NT: B.497c; CB.1258a; K.573.
OT: gādôl: S.1419; HR.902c.2a; H.315d; BD.152d.
rab: S.7227; HR.902c.12a; H.2099a,b; BD.912d.
GEN. REF.: —.

2. *hikanos* [ἱκανός, 2425], of persons, denotes sufficient, competent, fit; of things, sufficient, enough, much, many (so of time); it is translated "large" in Matt. 28:12, of money. See ABLE, C, No. 2.

NT: B.374d; CB.1250c; K.361.
OT: shadday: S.7706; HR.683c.9; H.2333; BD.994d.
day: S.1767; HR.683c.2; H.425; BD.191b.
GEN. REF.: —.

3. *pēlikos* [πηλίκος, 4080], how large, is used of letters of the alphabet, characters in writing, Gal. 6:11, "with how large (letters)"; it is said of personal greatness in Heb. 7:4. See GREAT, No. 5. ¶

NT: B.656d; CB.—; K.—.
OT: kammāh: S.4100; HR.1131a.1; H.1149; BD.552b,553d.
GEN. REF.: —.

LASCIVIOUS, LASCIVIOUSNESS

aselgeia [ἀσέλγεια, 766], denotes excess, licentiousness, absence of restraint, indecency, wantonness; "lasciviousness" in Mark 7:22, one of the evils that proceed from the heart; in 2 Cor. 12:21, one of the evils of which some in the church at Corinth had been guilty; in Gal. 5:19, classed among the works of the flesh; in Eph. 4:19, among the sins of the unregenerate who are "past feeling"; so in 1 Pet. 4:3; in Jude 4, of that into which the grace of God had been turned by ungodly men; it is translated "wantonness" in Rom. 13:13, one of the sins against which believers are warned; in 2 Pet. 2:2, according to the best mss., "lascivious (doings)," R.V. (the A.V. "pernicious ways" follows those texts which have *apōleiais*); in ver. 7, R.V., "lascivious (life)," A.V., "filthy (conversation)," of the people of Sodom and Gomorrah; in 2:18, R.V., "lasciviousness" (A.V., "wantonness"), practised by the same persons as mentioned in Jude. The prominent idea is shameless conduct. Some have derived the word from *a*, negative, and *selgē*, a city in Pisidia. Others, with similar improbability, trace it to *a*, negative, and *selgō*, or *thelgō*, to charm. See WANTONNESS. ¶

NT: B.114d; CB.1238a; K.—.
OT: —.
GEN. REF.: IS.3:128; NB.—; Z.3:880.

LAST

A. Adjective.

eschatos [ἔσχατος, 2078], last, utmost, extreme, is used (*a*) of place, e.g., Luke 14:9, 10, "lowest"; Acts 1:8 and 13:47, "uttermost part"; (*b*) of rank, e.g., Mark 9:35; (*c*) of time, relating either to persons or things, e.g., Matt. 5:26, "the last (farthing)," R.V. (A.V., "uttermost"); Matt. 20:8, 12, 14; Mark 12:6, 22; 1 Cor. 4:9, of apostles as last in the programme of a spectacular display; 1 Cor. 15:45, "the last Adam"; Rev. 2:19; of the last state of persons, Matt. 12:45, neuter plural, lit., 'the last (things)'; so Luke 11:26; 2 Pet. 2:20, R.V., "the last state" (A.V., "the latter end"); of Christ as the Eternal One, Rev. 1:17 (in some mss. ver. 11); 2:8; 22:13; in eschatological phrases as follows: (*a*) "the last day," a comprehensive term including both the time of the resurrection of the redeemed, John 6:39, 40, 44, 54 and 11:24, and the ulterior time of the judgment of the unregenerate, at the Great White Throne, John 12:48; (*b*) "the last days," Acts 2:17, a period relative to the supernatural manifestation of the Holy Spirit at Pentecost and the resumption of the Divine interpositions in the affairs of the world at the end of the present age, before "the great and notable Day of the Lord," which will usher in the Messianic Kingdom; (*c*) in 2 Tim. 3:1, "the last days" refers to the close of the present age of world conditions; (*d*) in Jas. 5:3, the phrase "in the last days" (R.V.) refers both to the period preceding the Roman overthrow of the city and the land in A.D. 70, and to the closing part of the age in consummating acts of Gentile persecution including "the time of Jacob's trouble" (cp. verses 7, 8); (*e*) in 1 Pet. 1:5, "the last time" refers to the time of the Lord's Second Advent; (*f*) in 1 John 2:18, "the last hour" (R.V.) and, in Jude 18, "the last time" signify the present age previous to the Second Advent.

NT: B.313d; CB.1246c; K.264.
OT: aḥarôn: S.314; HR.558a.1c; H.68e; BD.30d.
aḥarît: S.319; HR.558a.1d; H.68f; BD.31a.
GEN. REF.: IS.2:130; NB.—; Z.2:342.

Notes: (1) In Heb. 1:2, R.V., "at the end of these days" (A.V., "in these last days"), the reference is to the close of the period of the testimony of the prophets under the Law, terminating with the presence of Christ and His redemptive sacrifice and its effects, the perfect tense "hath spoken" indicating the continued effects of the message embodied in the risen Christ; so in 1 Pet. 1:20, R.V., "at the end of the times" (A.V., "in these last times").

B. Adverb.

husteron [ὕστερον, 5305], the neuter of the adjective *husteros*, is used as an adverb signifying 'afterwards,' 'later,' see AFTER, No. 5. Cp. the adjective, under LATER.

NT: B.849c; CB.1252b; K.1240.
OT: 'aḥarê: S.310; HR.1418c.1b; H.68b; BD.29d,30a.
hā'aḥarôn: S.314; HR.1418c.1c; H.68e; BD.30d.
GEN. REF.: IS.2:130; NB.—; Z.2:342.

Note: In Phil. 4:10 the particle *pote*, sometime, used after *ēdē*, now, already, to signify "now at length," is so rendered in the R.V., A.V., "(now) at the last."

LATCHET

himas [ἱμάς, 2438], denotes a thong, strap, whether for binding prisoners, Acts 22:25, "(the) thongs" (for scourging; see BIND, No. 7), or for fastening sandals, Mark 1:7; Luke 3:16; John 1:27. "Among the Orientals everything connected with the feet and shoes is defiled and debasing, and the stooping to unfasten the dusty latchet is the most insignificant in such service" (Mackie, in Hastings' Bib. Dic.). ¶

NT: B.376b; CB.–; K.–.
OT: S^e^rôk: S.8288; HR.685a.1; H.2290a; BD.976c.
 ^a^bōt: S.5688; HR.685a.2; H.1558b; BD.721c.
GEN. REF.: IS.4:842; NB.–; Z.3:881.

LATE

opse [ὀψέ, 3796], an adverb of time, besides its meaning at evening or at eventide, denotes late in, or on, Matt. 28:1, R.V., "late on (the Sabbath day)" (A.V., "in the end of"); it came also to denote 'late after,' which seems to be the meaning here. See EVENING.

NT: B.601b; CB.1261a; K.–.
OT: 'ereb: S.6153; HR.1044a.2a; H.1689a; BD.787d.
GEN. REF.: –.

Note: In John 11:8, A.V., *nun*, now, is translated "of late" (R.V., "but now").

LATELY

prosphatōs [προσφάτως, 4373], denotes recently, lately, from the adjective *prosphatos*, new, fresh, recent; primarily, newly slain, Heb. 10:20 (*phatos*, slain), is also found in Acts 18:2. ¶ In the Sept., Deut. 24:5; Ezek. 11:3. ¶

NT: B.719c; CB.–; K.950.
OT: ḥādāsh: S.2319; HR.1222c.1; H.613a; BD.294a.
GEN. REF.: –.

LATER

husteros [ὕστερος, 5306], denotes later or latter and is used in 1 Tim. 4:1, R.V., "in later (times)," A.V., "in (the) latter (times)." Several mss. have it in Matt. 21:31, 'the former,' for *prōtos*, "the first." ¶

NT: B.849c; CB.1252b; K.1240.
OT: 'aḥ^a^rôn: S.314; HR.1418c.1; H.68e; BD.30d.
GEN. REF.: IS.2:130; NB.–; Z.–.

LATIN

rhōmaisti [ῥωμαϊστί, 4515], an adverb, "in Latin," occurs in John 19:20, lit., 'in Roman.' ¶

NT: B.738c; CB.–; K.–.
OT: –.
GEN. REF.: IS.3:75; NB.717; Z.3:881.

Note: In Luke 23:38, some mss. have the adjective *Rhōmaikos*, 'of Latin,' agreeing with "letters."

LATTER

opsimos [ὄψιμος, 3797], akin to *opse* and *opsios* (see LATE), denotes late, or latter, and is used of "the latter rain" in Jas. 5:7 (the most authentic mss. omit *huetos*, rain; some have *karpos*, fruit); this rain falls in March and April, just before the harvest, in contrast to the early rain, in October. ¶ In the Sept., Deut. 11:14; Prov. 16:15; Jer. 5:24; Hos. 6:3; Joel 2:23; Zech. 10:1. ¶

NT: B.601c; CB.1261a; K.–.
OT: malqōsh: S.4456; HR.1044b.2; H.1127b; BD.545b.
GEN. REF.: –.

Note: For "latter" (*husteros*) in the A.V., of 1 Tim. 4:1 see LATER, and for 2 Pet. 2:20 see LAST.

For **LAUD** (Rom. 15:11, A.V.) see **PRAISE**, B, No. 1

LAUGH, LAUGH TO SCORN

1. *gelaō* [γελάω, 1070], to laugh, is found in Luke 6:21, 25. This signifies loud laughter in contrast to demonstrative weeping. ¶

NT: B.153c; CB.1248a; K.113.
OT: ṣāḥaq: S.6711; HR.235b.1; H.1905; BD.850b.
 sāḥaq: S.7832; HR.235b.2; H.1905c; BD.965d.
GEN. REF.: IS.3:75; NB.–; Z.3:881.

2. *katagelaō* [καταλεγάω, 2606], denotes to laugh scornfully at, more emphatic than No. 1 (*kata*, down, used intensively, and No. 1), and signifies derisive laughter, Matt. 9:24; Mark 5:40; Luke 8:53. ¶ Cp. *ekmuktērizō*, to deride.

NT: B.409c; CB.1254a; K.113.
OT: sāḥaq: S.7832; HR.729c.5a; H.1905c; BD.965d.
GEN. REF.: IS.3:75; NB.–; Z.3:881.

Note: The laughter of incredulity, as in Gen. 17:17 and 18:12, is not mentioned in the N.T.

LAUGHTER

gelōs [γέλως, 1071], denotes laughter, Jas. 4:9. ¶ This corresponds to the kind of laughter mentioned above (see LAUGH, No. 1).

NT: B.153c; CB.1248a; K.113.
OT: s^e^hôq: S.7814; HR.235c.2a; H.1905d; BD.966a.
GEN. REF.: IS.3:75; NB.–; Z.3:881.

LAUNCH

1. *anagō* [ἀνάγω, 321], to bring up (*ana*, up, *agō*, to lead), is used in the Middle Voice as a nautical term signifying to put to sea; it is translated "launch forth" in Luke 8:22; "set sail" in Acts 13:13, R.V. (A.V., "loosed"); similarly in 16:11; in 18:21, for A.V., "sailed"; similarly in 20:3, 13; in 21:1, R.V., "set sail," (A.V., "launched"), and in ver. 2, for A.V., "set forth"; in 27:2 and 4 the R.V. has the verb to put to sea, for A.V. to launch; in ver. 12 for A.V., "depart"; in ver. 21, R.V., "set sail" (A.V., "loosed"); in 28:10, 11, "sailed" and "set sail" (A.V., "departed"). See BRING, DEPART, LEAD, LOOSE, OFFER, PUT, SAIL, SET.

NT: B.53a; CB.–; K.–.
OT: 'ālāh: S.5927; HR.75b.6b; H.1624; BD.748a.
GEN. REF.: –.

2. *epanagō* [ἐπανάγω, 1877], to lead up upon (*epi*, upon, and No. 1), is used as a nautical term with *ploion*, a ship, understood, denoting to put

out to sea, translated in Luke 5:3, "put out," R.V. (A.V., "thrust out"); in ver. 4, for A.V., "launch." For the non-nautical significance to return, see Matt. 21:18. See PUT, RETURN, THRUST. ¶ In the Sept., Zech. 4:12, "that communicate with (the golden oil vessels)."

NT: B.282d; CB.–; K.–.
OT: –.
GEN. REF.: –.

LAW

A. Nouns.

1. *nomos* [νόμος, 3551], akin to *nemō*, to divide out, distribute, primarily meant that which is assigned; hence, usage, custom, and then, law, law as prescribed by custom, or by statute; the word *ēthos*, custom, was retained for unwritten law, while *nomos* became the established name for law as decreed by a state and set up as the standard for the administration of justice.

In the N.T. it is used (*a*) of law in general, e.g., Rom. 2:12, 13, "a law" (R.V.), expressing a general principle relating to law; ver. 14, last part; 3:27, "By what manner of law?" i.e., 'by what sort of principle (has the glorying been excluded)?'; 4:15 (last part); 5:13, referring to the period between Adam's trespass and the giving of the Law; 7:1 (1st part, R.V. marg., "law"); against those graces which constitute the fruit of the Spirit "there is no law," Gal. 5:23; "the ostensible aim of the law is to restrain the evil tendencies natural to man in his fallen estate; yet in experience law finds itself not merely ineffective, it actually provokes those tendencies to greater activity. The intention of the gift of the Spirit is to constrain the believer to a life in which the natural tendencies shall have no place, and to produce in him their direct contraries. Law, therefore, has nothing to say against the fruit of the Spirit; hence the believer is not only not under law, ver. 18, the law finds no scope in his life, inasmuch as, and in so far as, he is led by the Spirit";*

(*b*) of a force or influence impelling to action, Rom. 7:21, 23 (1st part), "a different law," R.V.;

(*c*) of the Mosaic Law, the Law of Sinai, (1) with the definite article, e.g., Matt. 5:18; John 1:17; Rom. 2:15, 18, 20, 26, 27; 3:19; 4:15; 7:4, 7, 14, 16, 22; 8:3, 4, 7; Gal. 3:10, 12, 19, 21, 24; 5:3; Eph. 2:15; Phil. 3:6; 1 Tim. 1:8; Heb. 7:19; Jas. 2:9; (2) without the article, thus stressing the Mosaic Law in its quality as law, e.g., Rom. 2:14 (1st part); 5:20; 7:9, where the stress on the quality lies in this, that "the commandment which was unto (i.e., which he thought would be a means of) life," he found to be "unto (i.e., to have the effect of revealing his actual state of) death"; 10:4; 1 Cor. 9:20; Gal. 2:16, 19, 21; 3:2, 5, 10 (1st part), 11, 18, 23; 4:4, 5, 21 (1st part); 5:4, 18; 6:13; Phil. 3:5, 9; Heb. 7:16; 9:19; Jas. 2:11; 4:11; (in regard to the statement in Gal. 2:16, that "a man is not justified by the works of the Law," the absence of the article before *nomos* indicates the assertion of a principle, 'by obedience to law,' but evidently the Mosaic law is in view. Here the Apostle is maintaining that submission to circumcision entails the obligation to do the whole Law. Circumcision belongs to the ceremonial part of the Law, but, while the Mosaic Law is actually divisible into the ceremonial and the moral, no such distinction is made or even assumed in Scripture. The statement maintains the freedom of the believer from the law of Moses in its totality as a means of justification);

(*d*) by metonymy, of the books which contain the law, (1) of the Pentateuch, e.g., Matt. 5:17; 12:5; Luke 16:16; 24:44; John 1:45; Rom. 3:21; Gal. 3:10; (2) of the Psalms, John 10:34; 15:25; of the Psalms, Isaiah, Ezekiel and Daniel, 12:34; the Psalms and Isaiah, Rom. 3:19 (with vv. 10-18); Isaiah, 1 Cor. 14:21; from all this it may be inferred that "the law" in the most comprehensive sense was an alternative title to "The Scriptures."

The following phrases specify laws of various kinds:

(*a*) "the law of Christ," Gal. 6:2, i.e., either given by Him (as in the Sermon on the Mount and in John 13:14, 15; 15:4), or the law or principle by which Christ Himself lived (Matt. 20:28; John 13:1); these are not actual alternatives, for the law imposed by Christ was always that by which He Himself lived in the "days of His flesh." He confirmed the Law as being of Divine authority (cp. Matt. 5:18); yet He presented a higher standard of life than perfunctory obedience to the current legal rendering of the Law, a standard which, without annulling the Law, He embodied in His own character and life (see, e.g., Matt. 5:21-48; this breach with legalism is especially seen in regard to the ritual or ceremonial part of the Law in its wide scope); He showed Himself superior to all human interpretations of it;

* From Notes on Galatians by Hogg and Vine, p. 298.

(*b*) "a law of faith," Rom. 3:27, i.e., a principle which demands only faith on man's part;

(*c*) "the law of my mind," Rom. 7:23, that principle which governs the new nature in virtue of the new birth;

(*d*) "the law of sin," Rom. 7:23, the principle by which sin exerts its influence and power despite the desire to do what is right; "of sin and death," 8:2, death being the effect;

(*e*) "the law of liberty," Jas. 1:25; 2:12, a term comprehensive of all the Scriptures, not a law of compulsion enforced from without, but meeting with ready obedience through the desire and delight of the renewed being who is subject to it; into it he looks, and in its teaching he delights; he is "under law (*ennomos*, 'in law,' implying union and subjection) to Christ," 1 Cor. 9:21; cp., e.g., Ps. 119:32, 45, 97; 2 Cor. 3:17;

(*f*) "the royal law," Jas. 2:8, i.e., the law of love, royal in the majesty of its power, the law upon which all others hang, Matt. 22:34-40; Rom. 13:8; Gal. 5:14;

(*g*) "the law of the Spirit of life," Rom. 8:2, i.e., the animating principle by which the Holy Spirit acts as the Imparter of life (cp. John 6:63);

(*h*) "a law of righteousness," Rom. 9:31, i.e., a general principle presenting righteousness as the object and outcome of keeping a law, particularly the Law of Moses (cp. Gal. 3:21);

(*i*) "the law of a carnal commandment," Heb. 7:16, i.e., the law respecting the Aaronic priesthood, which appointed men conditioned by the circumstances and limitations of the flesh. In the Epistle to the Hebrews the Law is treated of especially in regard to the contrast between the Priesthood of Christ and that established under the Law of Moses, and in regard to access to God and to worship. In these respects the Law "made nothing perfect," 7:19. There was "a disannulling of a foregoing commandment . . . and a bringing in of a better hope." This is established under the "new Covenant," a covenant instituted on the basis of "better promises," 8:6.

NT: B.542a; CB.1260a; K.646.
OT: tôrāh: S.8451; HR.947b.7; H.910d; BD.435d.
dāt: S.1881; HR.947b.2; H.458; BD.206c.
GEN. REF.: IS.3:76,85; NB.718; Z.3:883.

Notes: (1) In Gal. 5:3, the statement that to receive circumcision constitutes a man a debtor to do "the whole Law," views the Law as made up of separate commands, each essential to the whole, and predicates the unity of the Law; in ver. 14, the statement that "the whole law" is fulfilled in the one commandment concerning love, views the separate commandments as combined to make a complete law.

(2) In Rom. 8:3, "what the law could not do," is lit., 'the inability (*adunaton*, the neuter of the adjective *adunatos*, unable, used as a noun) of the Law'; this may mean either 'the weakness of the Law' or 'that which was impossible for the Law'; the latter is preferable; the significance is the same in effect; the Law could neither give freedom from condemnation nor impart life.

(3) For the difference between the teaching of Paul and that of James in regard to the Law, see under JUSTIFICATION.

(4) For Acts 19:38, A.V., "the law is open" (R.V., "courts" etc.) see COURT, No. 1.

(5) For *nomodidaskaloi*, "doctors of the law," Luke 5:17, singular in Acts 5:34, "teachers of the law," 1 Tim. 1:7, see DOCTOR.

2. *nomothesia* [νομοθεσία, 3548], denotes legislation, lawgiving (No. 1, and *tithēmi*, to place, to put), Rom. 9:4, "(the) giving of the law." Cp. B, No. 1. ¶

NT: B.541d; CB.1260a; K.646.
OT: —.
GEN. REF.: IS.—; NB.718; Z.—.

B. Verbs.

1. *nomotheteō* [νομοθετέω, 3549], (*a*) used intransitively, signifies to make laws (cp. A, No. 2, above); in the Passive Voice, to be furnished with laws, Heb. 7:11, "received the law," lit., 'was furnished with (the) law'; (*b*) used transitively, it signifies to ordain by law, to enact, in the Passive Voice, Heb. 8:6. See ENACT. ¶

NT: B.541d; CB.1260a; K.646.
OT: yārāh: S.3384; HR.947a.1; H.910; BD.434d.
GEN. REF.: IS.3:76; NB.718; Z.3:883.

2. *krinō* [κρίνω, 2919], to esteem, judge, etc., signifies to go to law, and is so used in the Middle Voice in Matt. 5:40, R.V., "go to law" (A.V., "sue . . . at the law"); 1 Cor. 6:1, 6. See ESTEEM.

NT: B.451a; CB.1256a; K.469.
OT: shāphaṭ: S.8199; HR.787b.10a; H.2443; BD.1047a.
rîb: S.7378; HR.787b.8a; H.2159; BD.936b.
GEN. REF.: IS.3:93; NB.—; Z.—.

Note: In 1 Cor. 6:7, the A.V., "go to law," is a rendering of the phrase *echō krimata*, to have lawsuits, as in the R.V.

3. *paranomeō* [παρανομέω, 3891], to transgress law (*para*, contrary to, and *nomos*), is used in the present participle in Acts 23:3, and translated "contrary to the law," lit., 'transgressing the law.' ¶

NT: B.621a; CB.1262b; K.646.
OT: 'āwal: S.5765; HR.1062b.3; H.1580; BD.732c.
GEN. REF.: —.

C. Adjectives.

1. *nomikos* [νομικός, 3544], denotes relating to law; in Tit. 3:9 it is translated "about the law," describing "fightings" (A.V., "strivings"); see LAWYER.

NT: B.541b; CB.1260a; K.646.
OT: —.
GEN. REF.: IS.3:76; NB.718; Z.—.

2. *ennomos* [ἔννομος, 1772], (*a*) lawful, legal, lit., in law (*en*, in, and *nomos*), or, strictly, what is within the range of law, is translated "lawful" in Acts 19:39, A.V. (R.V., "regular"), of the legal tribunals in Ephesus; (*b*) "under law" (R.V.), in relation to Christ, 1 Cor. 9:21, where it is contrasted with *anomos* (see No. 3 below); the word as used by the Apostle suggests not merely the condition of being under law, but the intimacy of a relation established in the loyalty of a will devoted to his Master. See LAWFUL.

NT: B.267a; CB.1245b; K.646.
OT: —.
GEN. REF.: IS.—; NB.718; Z.—.

3. *anomos* [ἄνομος, 459], signifies "without law" (*a*, negative) and has this meaning in 1 Cor. 9:21 (four times). See LAWLESS, TRANSGRESSOR, UNLAWFUL, WICKED.

NT: B.72a; CB.1235c; K.646.
OT: rāshā': S.7563; HR.107c.16a; H.2222b; BD.957b.
resha': S.7562; HR.107c.16b; H.2222a; BD.957c.
'āwen: S.205; HR.107c.1; H.48a; BD.19d.
GEN. REF.: IS.3:92; NB.—; Z.3:894.

D. Adverb.

anomōs [ἀνόμως, 460], without law (the adverbial form of C, No. 3), is used in Rom. 2:12 (twice), where "(have sinned) without law" means in the absence of some specifically revealed law, like the law of Sinai; "(shall perish) without law" predicates that the absence of such a law will not prevent their doom; the law of conscience is not in view here. The succeeding phrase "under law" is lit., 'in law,' not the same as the adjective *ennomos* (C, No. 2), but two distinct words. ¶

NT: B.72b; CB.1235c; K.—.
OT: —.
GEN. REF.: —.

LAWFUL, LAWFULLY

A. Verb.

exesti [ἔξεστι, 1832], an impersonal verb, signifying it is permitted, it is lawful (or interrogatively, is it lawful?), occurs most frequently in the Synoptic Gospels and the Acts; elsewhere in John 5:10; 18:31; 1 Cor. 6:12; 10:23; 2 Cor. 12:4; in Acts 2:29, it is rendered "let me (speak)," lit., 'it being permitted'; in the A.V. of 8:37, "thou mayest," lit., 'it is permitted'; 16:21; in 21:37, "may I?" lit., 'is it permitted?' See LET, MAY.

NT: B.275b; CB.1247c; K.—.
OT: —.
GEN. REF.: IS.3:92; NB.—; Z.—.

Note: For *ennomos*, see C, No. 2, (under LAW).

B. Adverb.

nomimōs [νομίμως, 3545], lawfully, is used in 1 Tim. 1:8, "the Law is good, if a man use it lawfully," i.e., agreeably to its design; the meaning here is that, while no one can be justified or obtain eternal life through its instrumentality, the believer is to have it in his heart and to fulfil its requirements; walking "not after the flesh but after the spirit," Rom. 8:4, he will "use it lawfully." In 2 Tim. 2:5 it is used of contending in the games and adhering to the rules. ¶

NT: B.541c; CB.1260a; K.—.
OT: —.
GEN. REF.: IS.3:92; NB.—; Z.—.

LAWGIVER

nomothetēs [νομοθέτης, 3550], a lawgiver (see LAW, A, No. 2, and B, No. 1), occurs in Jas. 4:12, of God, as the sole Lawgiver; therefore, to criticize the Law is to presume to take His place, with the presumption of enacting a better law. ¶

NT: B.542a; CB.1260a; K.646.
OT: —.
GEN. REF.: IS.3:92; NB.723; Z.3:896.

LAWLESS, LAWLESSNESS

A. Adjective.

anomos [ἄνομος, 459], without law, also denotes lawless, and is so rendered in the R.V. of Acts 2:23, "lawless (men)," marg., "(men) without the law," A.V., "wicked (hands)"; 2 Thess. 2:8, "the lawless one" (A.V., "that wicked"), of the man of sin (ver. 4); in 2 Pet. 2:8, of deeds (A.V., "unlawful"), where the thought is not simply that of doing what is unlawful, but of flagrant defiance of the known will of God. See LAW, C, No. 3.

NT: B.72a; CB.1235c; K.646.
OT: rāshā': S.7563; HR.107c.16a; H.2222b; BD.957b.
resha': S.7562; HR.107c.16b; H.2222a; BD.957c.
'āwen: S.205; HR.107c.1; H.48a; BD.19d.
GEN. REF.: IS.3:92; NB.—; Z.—.

B. Noun.

anomia [ἀνομία, 458], lawlessness, akin to A, is most frequently translated "iniquity"; in 2 Thess. 2:7, R.V., "lawlessness" (A.V., "iniquity"); "the mystery of lawlessness" is not recognized by the world, for it does not consist merely in confusion and disorder (see A); the display of lawlessness by the lawless one (ver. 8) will be the effect of the attempt by the powers of darkness to overthrow the Divine government. In 1 John 3:4, the R.V. adheres to the real meaning of the word, "every one that doeth sin (a practice, not the committal of an act) doeth also lawlessness: and sin is lawlessness." This definition of sin sets forth its essential character as the rejection of the law, or will, of God and the substitution of the will of self. See INIQUITY and synonymous words.

NT: B.71d; CB.1235c; K.646.
OT: 'āwôn: S.5771; HR.107c.15; H.1577a; BD.730d.
'āwen: S.205; HR.107c.1; H.48a; BD.19d.
tô'ēbāh: S.8441; HR.107c.22; H.2530a; BD.1072d.
GEN. REF.: IS.3:92; NB.—; Z.—.

LAWYER

nomikos [νομικός, 3544], an adjective, learned in the law (see Tit. 3:9, under LAW, C, No. 1), is used as a noun, a lawyer, Matt. 22:35; Luke 7:30; 10:25; 11:45, 46, 52 (ver. 53 in some mss.); 14:3; Tit. 3:13, where Zenas is so named. As there is no evidence that he was one skilled in Roman jurisprudence, the term may be regarded in the usual N.T. sense as applying to one skilled in the Mosaic Law. ¶

The usual name for a scribe is *grammateus*, a man of letters; for a doctor of the law, *nomodidaskalos* (see DOCTOR). "A comparison of Luke 5:17 with ver. 21 and Mark 2:6 and Matt. 9:3 shows that the three terms were used synonymously, and did not denote three distinct classes. The scribes were originally simply men of letters, students of Scripture, and the name first given to them contains in itself no reference to the law; in course of time, however, they devoted themselves mainly, though by no means exclusively, to the study of the law. They became jurists rather than theologians, and received names which of themselves called attention to that fact. Some would doubtless devote themselves more to one branch of activity than to another; but a 'lawyer' might also be a 'doctor,' and the case of Gamaliel shows that a 'doctor' might also be a member of the Sanhedrin, Acts 5:34" (Eaton, in Hastings' Bib. Dic.).

NT: B.541b; CB.1260a; K.646.
OT: —.
GEN. REF.: IS.3:93; NB.723; Z.3:896.

LAY

1. *tithēmi* [τίθημι, 5087], to put, place, set, frequently signifies to lay, and is used of (*a*) laying a corpse in a tomb, Matt. 27:60; Mark 6:29; 15:47; 16:6; Luke 23:53, 55; John 11:34; 19:41, 42; 20:2, 13, 15; Acts 7:16; 13:29; Rev. 11:9, R.V., "to be laid" (A.V., "to be put"); in an upper chamber, Acts 9:37; (*b*) laying the sick in a place, Mark 6:56; Luke 5:18; Acts 3:2; 5:15; (*c*) laying money at the Apostles' feet, Acts 4:35, 37; 5:2; (*d*) Christ's laying His hands upon children, Mark 10:16, R.V., "laying" (A.V., "put"); upon John, Rev. 1:17 (in the best mss.); (*e*) laying down one's life, (1) of Christ, John 10:11, R.V., "layeth down" (A.V., "giveth"); vers. 17, 18 (twice); 1 John 3:16; (2) of Peter for Christ's sake, John 13:37, 38; (3) of Christ's followers, on behalf of others, 1 John 3:16; (4) of anyone, for his friends, John 15:13; (*f*) laying up sayings in one's heart, Luke 1:66 (Middle Voice, in the sense of 'for themselves'); in 9:44, of letting Christ's words "sink" (Middle Voice, in the sense of 'for oneself'; A.V., "sink down") into the ears; (*g*) laying a foundation (1) literally, Luke 6:48; 14:29; (2) metaphorically, of Christ in relation to an assembly, 1 Cor. 3:10, 11; (*h*) God in laying Christ as a "stone of stumbling" for Israel, Rom. 9:33; (*i*) Christ's laying aside His garments, John 13:4; (*j*) Christians, in laying money in store for the help of the needy, 1 Cor. 16:2 (lit., 'let him put'); (*k*) depositing money, Luke 19:21, 22. See APPOINT.

NT: B.815d; CB.1272c; K.1176.
OT: nātan: S.5414; HR.1348c.16; H.1443; BD.678a.
sûm, sîm: S.7760; HR.1348c.25a; H.2243; BD.962c.
GEN. REF.: IS.3:94; NB.—; Z.—.

2. *katatithēmi* [κατατίθημι, 2698], to lay down (*kata*), is used in Mark 15:46 of the act of Joseph of Arimathaea in laying Christ's body in the tomb (some mss. have No. 1 here). See DO, Note (4), SHEW.

NT: B.419c; CB.—; K.—.
OT: shûb: S.7725; HR.746c.3; H.2340; BD.996d.
nātan: S.5414; HR.746c.2; H.1443; BD.678a.
GEN. REF.: IS.3:94; NB.—; Z.—.

3. *ballō* [βάλλω, 906], to cast, throw, place, put, is used in the Passive Voice signifying to be laid, e.g., Mark 7:30; Luke 16:20; for Matt. 8:14, R.V., "lying" (A.V., "laid") and 9:2, see LIE, No. (3). See CAST.

NT: B.130d; CB.1238b; K.91.
OT: sûm, sîm: S.7760; HR.189c.14; H.2243; BD.962c.
shālak: S.7993; HR.189c.16; H.2398; BD.1020d.
GEN. REF.: IS.3:94; NB.—; Z.—.

4. *epiballō* [ἐπιβάλλω, 1911], to lay upon, is used of seizing men, to imprison them, Acts 4:3. See CAST.

NT: B.289d; CB.—; K.91.
OT: sum, sûm: S.7760; HR.516a.15; H.2243; BD.962c.
shît: S.7896; HR.516a.17; H.2380; BD.1011a.
shālaḥ: S.7971; HR.516a.18a; H.2394; BD.1018a.
GEN. REF.: IS.3:94; NB.—; Z.—.

5. *kataballō* [καταβάλλω, 2598], to cast down (*kata*), is used metaphorically in Heb. 6:1, in the Middle Voice, negatively, of laying a foundation of certain doctrines. See CAST.

NT: B.408d; CB.1253c; K.—.
OT: nāphal: S.5307; HR.728c.4b; H.1392; BD.656c.
GEN. REF.: —.

6. *klino* [κλίνω, 2827], to make to bend, to bow, or to make to lean, to rest, is used in Matt. 8:20 and Luke 9:58, in the Lord's statement, "the Son of man hath not where to lay His head"; it is significant that this verb is used in

John 19:30 of the Lord's act at the moment of His Death in placing His head into a position of rest, not a helpless drooping of the head as in all other cases of crucifixion. He reversed the natural order, by first reclining His head (indicative of His submission to His Father's will), and then 'giving up His spirit.' The rest he found not on earth in contrast to His creatures the foxes and birds, He found in this consummating act on the Cross. See BOW.

NT: B.436c; CB.–; K.–.
OT: nāṭāh: S.5186; HR.771a.7a; H.1352; BD.639d.
GEN. REF.: –.

7. *anaklinō* [ἀνακλίνω, 347], to lay down, make to recline (in the Passive Voice, to lie back, recline), is used in Luke 2:7, of the act of the Virgin Mary in laying her Child in a manger. See SIT.

NT: B.56a; CB.–; K.–.
OT: –.
GEN. REF.: –.

8. *apotithēmi* [ἀποτίθημι, 659], to put off from oneself (*apo*, from, and No. 1), always in the Middle Voice in the N.T., is used metaphorically in Heb. 12:1, "laying aside (every weight)"; in Jas. 1:21, A.V., "lay apart," R.V., "putting away"; in Acts 7:58 of laying down garments, after taking them off, for the purpose of stoning Stephen. See CAST, PUT

NT: B.101a; CB.1237b; K.–.
OT: nûaḥ: S.5117; HR.148c.1; H.1323; BD.628a.
GEN. REF.: –.

9. *hupotithēmi* [ὑποτίθημι, 5294], to place under, lay down (*hupo*, under, and No. 1), is used metaphorically in Rom. 16:4, of risking one's life, "laid down" (their own necks). In the Middle Voice in 1 Tim. 4:6 it is used of putting persons in mind, R.V., (A.V., "in remembrance"). See REMEMBERANCE. ¶

NT: B.848b; CB.–; K.–.
OT: sûm, sîm: S.7760; HR.1417c.4; H.2243; BD.962c.
GEN. REF.: IS.3:94; NB.–; Z.–.

10. *epitithēmi* [ἐπιτίθημι, 2007], to add to, lay upon, etc., is used of laying hands on the sick, for healing, Matt. 9:18; 19:13, R.V., "lay" (A.V., "put"); 19:15; Mark 5:23; 6:5; 7:32; 8:23, R.V., "laid" (A.V., "put"); so in ver. 25; 16:18; Luke 4:40; 13:13; Acts 6:6; 8:17, 19; 9:12 and17, R.V., "laying" (A.V., "putting"); 13:3; 19:6; 28:8; in some mss. in Rev. 1:17, see No. 1, (*d*); of laying hands on a person by way of public recognition, 1 Tim. 5:22; of a shepherd's laying a sheep on his shoulders, Luke 15:5; of laying the Cross on Christ's shoulders, Luke 23:26; of laying on stripes, Acts 16:23; wood on a fire, 28:3; metaphorically, of laying burdens on men's shoulders, Matt. 23:4; similarly of giving injunctions, Acts 15:28 (cp. "put . . . upon" in ver. 10). See LADE, PUT, SET, SURNAME, WOUND.

NT: B.302d; CB.1246b; K.1176.
OT: nātan: S.5414; HR.535c.15a; H.1443; BD.678a.
sûm, sîm: S.7760; HR.535c.29; H.2243; BD.962c.
GEN. REF.: IS.3:94; NB.–; Z.–.

11. *anatithēmi* [ἀνατίθημι, 394], to put up or before (*ana*), is used in the Middle Voice of laying a case before an authority, Acts 25;14, R.V., "laid before," for A.V., "declared unto"; of setting forth a matter for consideration, Gal. 2:2, R.V., "laid before (them the gospel)," for A.V., "communicated unto." See COMMUNICATE, DECLARE. ¶

NT: B.62a; CB.–; K.57.
OT: ḥāram: S.2763; HR.83b.1; H.744; BD.355c.
GEN. REF.: –.

12. *prostithēmi* [προστίθημι, 4369], to put to, add, is used in the Passive Voice in Acts 13:36, "was laid" (unto his fathers), of the burial of David. See ADD, No. 2.

NT: B.718d; CB.1267b; K.1176.
OT: –.
GEN. REF.: –.

13. *ekteinō* [ἐκτείνω, 1614], to stretch out or forth, especially of the hand, is used of laying out anchors from a vessel, in Acts 27:30, R.V., "lay out" (A.V., "cast . . . out"). See CAST, *Notes*, STRETCH.

NT: B.245b; CB.1244a; K.219.
OT: nāṭāh: S.5186; HR.442a.7; H.1352; BD.639d.
shālaḥ: S.7971; HR.442a.16a; H.2394; BD.1018a.
GEN. REF.: –.

14. *keimai* [κεῖμαι, 2749], to be laid, to lie, is used as the Passive Voice of *tithēmi*, to put, and is translated by some part of the verb to be laid in Matt. 3:10 and Luke 3:9, of an axe; Luke 12:19, of goods; John 21:9, where the verb has been omitted from the translation, after the words "a fire of coals" (for *epikeimai*, of the fish, see No. 15); 1 Cor. 3:11, of Christ, as a foundation. See APPOINT, LIE, MADE (be), SET.

NT: B.426c; CB.1254c; K.425.
OT: sûm, sîm: S.7760; HR.758b.7; H.2243; BD.962c.
GEN. REF.: IS.3:94; NB.–; Z.–.

Notes: (1) In Luke 23:53, the R.V. has "had lain" (intransitive: see LIE), for A.V., "was laid."

(2) In Luke 24:12, some mss. have the verb, with reference to the linen cloths (the clause is absent in the best mss.); the translation should be "lying," not as A.V., "laid."

(3) In John 11:41, the verb is not found in the best mss.

15. *epikeimai* [ἐπίκειμαι, 1945], to be placed, to lie on (*epi*, upon, and No. 14), is translated by the verb to be laid upon, in John 21:9, of a fish; in 1 Cor. 9:16, of necessity. See IMPOSED, INSTANT, LIE, PRESS.

NT: B.294c; CB.–; K.425.
OT: nātan: S.5414; HR.523a.3; H.1443; BD.678a.
GEN. REF.: IS.3:94; NB.–; Z.–.

16. *apokeimai* [ἀπόκειμαι, 606], to be laid away, or up, is used of money in a napkin, Luke 19:20; metaphorically, of a hope, Col. 1:5; the crown of righteousness, 2 Tim. 4:8. In Heb. 9:27, said of physical death, it is translated "it is appointed" (R.V. marg., "laid up"). See APPOINT. ¶

NT: B.92d; CB.–; K.425.
OT: shîlōh: S.7886; HR.132c.2; H.2376; BD.1010a.
GEN. REF.: –.

17. *thēsaurizō* [θησαυρίζω, 2343], to lay up, store up (akin to *thēsauros*, a treasury, a storehouse, a treasure), is used of laying up treasures, on earth, Matt. 6:19; in Heaven, ver. 20; in the last days, Jas. 5:3, R.V., "ye have laid up your treasure" (A.V., "ye have heaped treasure together"); in Luke 12:21, "that layeth up treasure (for himself)"; in 1 Cor. 16:2, of money for needy ones (here the present participle is translated "in store," lit., 'treasuring,' or 'storing,' the 'laying by' translating the preceding verb *tithēmi*, see No. 1); in 2 Cor. 12:14, negatively, of children for parents; metaphorically, of laying up wrath, Rom. 2:5, "treasurest up." In 2 Pet. 3:7 the Passive Voice is used of the heavens and earth as "stored up" for fire, R.V. (marg., "stored" with fire), A.V., "kept in store." See STORE, TREASURE. ¶

NT: B.361b; CB.1272b; K.333.
OT: 'āṣar: S.686; HR.651b.1; H.154; BD.69d.
ṣābar: S.6651; HR.651b.2; H.840d; BD.840d.
GEN. REF.: –.

18. *trachēlizō* [τραχηλίζω, 5136], to seize and twist the neck (from *trachēlos*, the throat), was used of wrestlers, in the sense of taking by the throat. The word is found in Heb. 4:13, "laid open," R.V. (A.V., "opened"). The literal sense of the word seems to be 'with the head thrown back and the throat exposed.' Various suggestions have been made as to the precise significance of the word in this passage. Some have considered that the metaphor is from the manner of treating victims about to be sacrificed. Little help, however, can be derived from these considerations. The context serves to explain the meaning and the R.V. rendering is satisfactory. ¶

NT: B.824d; CB.–; K.–.
OT: –.
GEN. REF.: –.

Notes: (1) In Acts 25:7, A.V., *pherō*, to bear, bring, is rendered "laid . . . (complaints)," R.V., "bringing . . . (charges)."

(2) In Mark 7:8, A.V., *aphiēmi*, to leave, is translated "laying aside" (R.V., "ye leave").

(3) For *epilambanō*, to lay hold, see HOLD, No. 7.

For **LAY WAIT** see **LIE IN WAIT**

For **LAYING** (Acts 9:24) see **PLOT**

LAY WASTE

lumainomai [λυμαίνομαι, 3075], to maltreat. to outrage (from *lumē*, a brutal outrage), is translated "laid waste" (the church), in Acts 8:3, R.V. (A.V., "made havock of"). ¶

NT: B.481c; CB.–; K.540.
OT: shāḥat: S.7843; HR.889b.6; H.2370; BD.1007d.
GEN. REF.: –.

LAYING ON

epithesis [ἐπίθεσις, 1936], a laying on (*epi*, on, *tithēmi*, to put), is used in the N.T. (*a*) of the laying on of hands by the Apostles, accompanied by the impartation of the Holy Spirit in outward demonstration, in the cases of those in Samaria who had believed, Acts 8:18; such supernatural manifestations were signs especially intended to give witness to Jews as to the facts of Christ and the faith; they were thus temporary; there is no record of their continuance after the time and circumstances narrated in Acts 19 (in ver. 6 of which the corresponding verb *epitithēmi* is used; see below), nor was the gift delegated by the Apostles to others (see LAY, Nos. 1 and 10; (*b*) of the similar act by the elders of a church on occasions when a member of a church was set apart for a particular work, having given evidence of qualifications necessary for it, as in the case of Timothy, 1 Tim. 4:14; of the impartation of a spiritual gift through the laying on of the hands of the Apostle Paul, 2 Tim. 1:6, R.V., "laying" (A.V., "putting"); cp. the verb *epitithēmi* in Acts 6:6, on the appointment of the Seven, and in the case of Barnabas and Saul, 13:3; also in 19:6; (*c*) in Heb. 6:2, the doctrine of the laying on of hands refers to the act enjoined upon an Israelite in connection, e.g., with the peace offerings, Lev. 3:2, 8, 13; 4:29, 33; upon the priests in connection with the sin offering, 4:4; 16:21; upon the elders, 4:15; upon a ruler, 4:24. ¶

The principle underlying the act was that of identification on the part of him who did it with the animal or person upon whom the hands were laid. In the Sept., 2 Chron. 25:27; Ezek. 23:11. ¶

NT: B.293a; CB.1246b; K.1176.
OT: 'ᵃgābāh: S.5691; HR.520a.1; H.1559b; BD.721d.
GEN. REF.: IS.2:611; NB.–; Z.–.

Note: For the laying of Christ's hands on the sick, see LAY, No. 10.

LEAD, LED

1. *agō* [ἄγω, 71], to bear, bring, carry, lead, is translated by the verb to lead, e.g., in Mark

13:11; Luke 4:1; 4:9, R.V.; 4:29; 22:54; 23:1, A.V. only; 23:32; John 18:28 (present tense, R.V.); Acts 8:32; metaphorically in Rom. 2:4, of the goodness of God; 8:14 and Gal. 5:18, of the Spirit of God; 1 Cor. 12:2, of the powers of darkness instigating to idolatry; 2 Tim. 3:6, of divers lusts (in some mss., *aichmalōteuō*). In Luke 24:21 *agō* is used of the passing (or spending) of a day, and translated "it is (now the third day)"; here the verb is probably to be taken impersonally, according to idiomatic usage, in the sense 'there is passing the third day.' See BRING, No. 10, KEEP, *Note* (2).

NT: B.14b; CB.1233c; K.–.
OT: bô': S.935; HR.9a.1b; H.212; BD.97c.
hālak: S.1980; HR.9a.3a; H.498; BD.229d.
GEN. REF.: –.

2. *anagō* [ἀνάγω, 321], to lead up (*ana*, up), is used of Christ in being led up by the Spirit into the wilderness, Matt. 4:1; Luke 4:5 (A.V., "taking up"); by the elders of the people into their council, Luke 22:66, "led away." See BRING, No. 11.

NT: B.53a; CB.–; K.–.
OT: 'ālāh: S.5927; HR.75b.6b; H.1624; BD.748a.
GEN. REF.: –.

3. *apagō* [ἀπάγω, 520], to lead away (*apo*, away), is used of a way leading to destruction, Matt. 7:13; to life, ver. 14; of those who led Christ away from Gethsemane, Mark 14:44; in some mss., John 18:13, to Annas (the best mss. have No. 1 here); to Caiaphas, Matt. 26:57; Mark 14:53; to Pilate, Matt. 27:2; to the Praetorium, Mark 15:16; to crucifixion, Matt. 27:31; Luke 23:26; in some mss. John 19:16; of leading an animal away to watering, Luke 13:15; of being led away to idolatry, 1 Cor. 12:2, R.V., "led away" (A.V., "carried away"). Some mss. have it in Acts 24:7 (A.V., "took away"). It is translated "bring" in 23:17. In 12:19 it signifies to put to death. See BRING, No. 12, DEATH, C, No. 3. ¶

NT: B.79c; CB.–; K.–.
OT: hālak: S.1980; HR.115b.5; H.498; BD.229d.
nāhag: S.5090; HR.115b.8; H.1309,1310; BD.624a.
GEN. REF.: –.

4. *periagō* [περιάγω, 4013], used transitively, denotes to lead about, 1 Cor. 9:5. For the intransitive use, see GO, No. 9.

NT: B.645c; CB.–; K.–.
OT: sābab: S.5437; HR.1121b.2; H.1456; BD.685b.
'ābar: S.5674; HR.1121b.3; H.1556; BD.716d.
GEN. REF.: –.

5. *pherō* [φέρω, 5342], to bear, carry, is used metaphorically of a gate, as leading to a city, Acts 12:10. See BRING, No. 1.

NT: B.854d; CB.1264a; K.1252.
OT: –.
GEN. REF.: –.

6. *hodēgeō* [ὁδηγέω], to lead the way: see GUIDE, B, No. 1.

7. *eisagō* [εἰσάγω, 1521], to bring into, is translated "to be led into" in Acts 21:37, A.V. (R.V., "to be brought into"). See BRING, A, No. 13.

NT: B.232b; CB.–; K.–.
OT: bô': S.935; HR.407c.2b; H.212; BD.97c.
GEN. REF.: –.

8. *sunapagō* [συναπάγω, 4879], always in the Passive Voice, to be carried or led away with, is translated "being led away with" in 2 Pet. 3:17, A.V. (R.V., "being carried away with"). See CARRY.

NT: B.784d; CB.–; K.–.
OT: lāqaḥ: S.3947; HR.1312a.1; H.1124; BD.542c.
GEN. REF.: –.

9. *exagō* [ἐξάγω, 1806], to lead out, is rendered by the verb to lead, out or forth, in Mark 15:20 (in some mss. in 8:23, the best have *ekpherō*, to bring out); Luke 24:50; John 10:3; Acts 7:36, 40 (A.V. "brought"), and 13:17, R.V.; Acts 21:38; Heb. 8:9. See BRING, No. 14.

NT: B.271c; CB.–; K.–.
OT: yāṣā': S.3318; HR.483a.4b; H.893; BD.422b.
GEN. REF.: –.

10. *anapherō* [ἀναφέρω, 399], to carry or lead up, is translated "leadeth . . . up" in the A.V. of Mark 9:2 (R.V. "bringeth . . . up"). See BRING, No. 2.

NT: B.63a; CB.1235b; K.1252.
OT: 'ālāh: S.5927; HR.84c.10b; H.1624; BD.748a.
qāṭar: S.6999; HR.84c.12; H.2011; BD.882d.
GEN. REF.: –.

11. *eispherō* [εἰσφερω, 1533], to bring in, or into, is translated "lead (us not) into," in Matt. 6:13 and Luke 11:4 (R.V., "bring . . . into"), of temptation. See BRING, No. 4.

NT: B.233d; CB.1243b; K.1252.
OT: bô': S.935; HR.415a.2b; H.212; BD.97c.
GEN. REF.: –.

12. *planaō* [πλανάω, 4105], to lead astray (akin to *planē*, a wandering), is translated "lead . . . astray," metaphorically, in Matt. 24:4, 5, 11 and Mark 13:5, 6 (A.V., "deceive").

NT: B.665b; CB.1265a; K.857.
OT: tā'āh: S.8582; HR.1139b.16; H.2531; BD.1073b.
GEN. REF.: –.

13. *apoplanaō* [ἀποπλανάω, 635], to cause to go astray (*apo*, away from, and No. 12), is used metaphorically of leading into error, Mark 13:22, R.V., "lead astray" (A.V., "seduce"); Passive Voice in 1 Tim. 6:10 (A.V., "erred"). ¶

NT: B.97b; CB.1237a; K.857.
OT: nāṭāh: S.5186; HR.139c.2; H.1352; BD.639d.
nādaḥ: S.5080; HR.139c.1; H.1304; BD.623a.
GEN. REF.: –.

Notes: (1) In Rev. 13:10, some mss. have *sunagō*, to bring together, translated "leadeth (into captivity)," A.V. and R.V. marg. (R.V. text, "is for").

(2) For the verb *diagō*, to lead a life, 1 Tim. 2:2, see LIVE, No. 7.

(3) For *thriambeuō*, to "lead in triumph," 2 Cor. 2:14, R.V., see TRIUMPH.

(4) See also HAND (lead by the).

For **LEADERS** (Matt. 15:14) see **GUIDE**

LEAF

phullon [φύλλον, 5444], a leaf (originally *phulion*, Lat., *folium*; Eng., folio, foliaceous, foliage, foliate, folious, etc.), is found in Matt. 21:19; 24:32; Mark 11:13 (twice); 13:28; Rev. 22:2. ¶

NT: B.869a; CB.1264c; K.—.
OT: ʻāleh: S.5929; HR.1446a.1; H.1624a; BD.750a.
GEN. REF.: IS.3:96; NB.—; Z.—.

LEAN

1. *anakeimai* [ἀνάκειμαι, 345], to be laid up, to lie, is used of reclining at table, and translated "leaning (on Jesus' bosom)" in the A.V. of John 13:23, R.V., "reclining" (for ver. 25 see No. 2). In ver. 28, it is translated "at the table," lit., 'of (those) reclining.' See GUEST, RECLINE, SIT, TABLE (at the).

NT: B.55d; CB.1235a; K.425.
OT: —.
GEN. REF.: —.

2. *anapiptō* [ἀναπίπτω, 377], lit., to fall back (*ana*, back, *piptō*, to fall), is used of reclining at a repast and translated "leaning back, (as he was, on Jesus' breast)" in John 13:25, R.V. (the A.V. follows the mss. which have *epipiptō*, and renders it 'lying'); in 21:20, "leaned back," the Apostle's reminder of the same event in his experience. See SIT.

NT: B.59c; CB.1235b; K.—.
OT: kāraʻ: S.3766; HR.81b.1; H.1044; BD.502c.
GEN. REF.: —.

LEAP

1. *hallomai* [ἅλλομαι, 242], to leap (akin to *halma*, a leap), is used (*a*) metaphorically, of the springing up of water, John 4:14; (*b*) literally, of the leaping of healed cripples, Acts 3:8 (2nd part); 14:10. ¶

NT: B.39d; CB.1249a; K.—.
OT: dālag: S.1801; HR.55c.1; H.430; BD.194c.
GEN. REF.: —.

2. *skirtaō* [σκιρτάω, 4640], to leap, is found in Luke 1:41, 44, and 6:23, there translated "leap for joy"; in 1:44 the words "for joy" are expressed separately. ¶

NT: B.755d; CB.—; K.1046.
OT: pôsh: S.6335; HR.1274b.1; H.1751,1752; BD.807d.
rāqad: S.7540; HR.1274b.3; H.2214; BD.955a.
GEN. REF.: IS.1:856; NB.—; Z.—.

3. *exallomai* [ἐξάλλομαι, 1814], to leap up (lit., out, *ek*, and No. 1), is said in Acts 3:8 (1st part) of the cripple healed by Peter (cp. No. 1, above). ¶

NT: B.272c; CB.—; K.—.
OT: rāqad: S.7540; HR.487a.4; H.2214; BD.955a.
GEN. REF.: IS.1:856; NB.—; Z.—.

4. *ephallomai* [ἐφάλλομαι, 2177], to leap upon (*epi*, upon, and No. 1), is said of the demoniac in Acts 19:16. ¶

NT: B.330a; CB.—; K.—.
OT: ṣalēaḥ: S.6743; HR.585b.1; H.1916,1917; BD.852b.
GEN. REF.: —.

LEARN, LEARNED (be)

1. *manthanō* [μανθάνω, 3129], denotes (*a*) to learn (akin to *mathētēs*, a disciple), to increase one's knowledge, or be increased in knowledge, frequently to learn by enquiry, or observation, e.g., Matt. 9:13; 11:29; 24:32; Mark 13:28; John 7:15; Rom. 16:17; 1 Cor. 4:6; 14:35; Phil 4:9; 2 Tim. 3:14; Rev. 14:3; said of learning Christ, Eph. 4:20, not simply the doctrine of Christ, but Christ Himself, a process not merely of getting to know the Person but of so applying the knowledge as to walk differently from the rest of the Gentiles; (*b*) to ascertain, Acts 23:27, R.V., "learned" (A.V., "understood"); Gal. 3:2, "This only would I learn from you," perhaps with a tinge of irony in the enquiry, the answer to which would settle the question of the validity of the new Judaistic gospel they were receiving; (*c*) to learn by use and practice, to acquire the habit of, be accustomed to e.g., Phil. 4:11; 1 Tim. 5:4, 13; Tit. 3:14; Heb. 5:8. See UNDERSTAND.

NT: B.490b; CB.1257c; K.552.
OT: lāmad: S.3925; HR.895b.4a,b; H.1116; BD.540c.
GEN. REF.: —.

2. *ginōskō* [γινώσκω, 1097], to know by observation and experience, is translated to learn, in the R.V. of Mark 15:45; John 12:9. See ALLOW.

NT: B.160d; CB.1248b; K.119.
OT: yādaʻ: S.3045; HR.267a.4a; H.848; BD.393b.
GEN. REF.: —.

3. *akriboō* [ἀκριβόω, 198], to learn carefully, is so translated in Matt. 2:7, 16, R.V. (A.V., "diligently enquired"). ¶

NT: B.33b; CB.—; K.—.
OT: —.
GEN. REF.: —.

4. *mueō* [μυέω, 3453], to initiate into mysteries, is translated "I have learned the secret" (Passive Voice, perfect tense) in Phil. 4:12, R.V. (A.V., "I am instructed"). See INSTRUCT. ¶

NT: B.529a; CB.1259b; K.615.
OT: —.
GEN. REF.: —.

Note: Paideuō, to teach, instruct, train, is translated "instructed" in Acts 7:22, R.V. (A.V., "learned"); in 1 Tim. 1:20, "(that) they might be taught," A.V., "(that) they may learn."

LEARNING (Noun)

1. *gramma* [γράμμα, 1121], a letter, is used in the plural in Acts 26:24, with the meaning "learning," "(thy much) learning (doth turn thee to madness)," R.V., possibly an allusion to the Jewish Scriptures, to which the Apostle had been appealing; in John 7:15, "(How knoweth this Man) letters" (A.V. marg., "learning"), the succeeding phrase "not having learned" is illustrated in the papyri, where it indicates inability to write. See BILL.
NT: B.165d; CB.1248c; K.128.
OT: –.
GEN. REF.: –.

2. *didaskalia* [διδασκαλία, 1319], teaching, instruction (akin to *didaskō*, to teach), is translated "learning" in Rom. 15:4. See DOCTRINE.
NT: B.191c; CB.1241b; K.161.
OT: lāmad: S.3925; HR.316c.2; H.1116; BD.540c.
GEN. REF.: –.

LEAST

1. *elachistos* [ἐλάχιστος, 1646], least, is a superlative degree formed from the word *elachus*, little, the place of which was taken by *mikros* (the comparative degree being *elassōn*, less); it is used of (*a*) size, Jas. 3:4; (*b*) amount; of the management of affairs, Luke 16:10 (twice); 19:17, "very little"; (*c*) importance, 1 Cor. 6:2, "smallest (matters)"; (*d*) authority: of commandments, Matt. 5:19; (*e*) estimation, as to persons, Matt. 5:19 (2nd part); 25:40, 45; 1 Cor. 15:9; as to a town, Matt. 2:6; as to activities or operations, Luke 12:26; 1 Cor. 4:3, "a very small thing." ¶
NT: B.248d; CB.1244a; K.593.
OT: –.
GEN. REF.: IS.3:97; NB.–; Z.–.

2. *elachistoteros* [ἐλαχιστότερος, 1647], a comparative degree formed from No. 1, is used in Eph. 3:8, "less than the least." ¶
NT: B.248d; CB.1244a; K.–.
OT: –.
GEN. REF.: IS.3:97; NB.–; Z.–.

3. *mikros* [μικρός, 3398], small, little, is translated "the least" in Acts 8:10 and Heb. 8:11, with reference to rank or influence. See LITTLE, A, No. 1.
NT: B.521a; CB.1258c; K.593.
OT: mᵉʿaṭ: S.4592; HR.926c.3; H.1228a; BD.589d.
qāṭān: S.6996; HR.926c.5; H.2009a,b; BD.881d.
GEN. REF.: IS.3:97; NB.–; Z.–.

4. *mikroteros* [μικρότερος, 3398], the comparative of No. 3, is used of (*a*) size, Matt. 13:32, A.V., "the least," R.V., "less"; Mark 4:31 [cp. No. 1 (*a*)]; (*b*) estimation, Matt. 11:11 and Luke 7:28, A.V., "least," R.V., "but little," marg., "lesser" (in the Kingdom of Heaven), those in the Kingdom itself being less than John the Baptist [cp. No. 1 (*e*)]; Luke 9:48. See LESS. ¶
NT: B.521a; CB.1258c; K.–.
OT: –.
GEN. REF.: IS.3:97; NB.–; Z.–.

Notes: (1) In 1 Cor. 6:4, A.V., *exoutheneō*, in the Passive Voice, to be of no account, is translated "is least esteemed" (R.V., "are of no account"); see ACCOUNT.

(2) In Luke 19:42, the adverbial phrase *kai ge*, "at least," is found in some mss.; the R.V. follows those in which it is absent.

(3) In 1 Cor. 9:2, A.V., the phrase *alla ge* is rendered "doubtless"; R.V., "at least."

(4) In Acts 5:15, the phrase *k'an* (for *kai ean*, even if) denotes "at the least."

LEATHERN

dermatinos [δερμάτινος, 1193], denotes of skin, leathern (from *derma*, skin, hide of beasts, akin to *derō*, to flay; whence Eng., derm, dermal, dermatology); it is translated "leathern" in Matt. 3:4, of John the Baptist's girdle; in Mark 1:6, R.V. (A.V., "of a skin"). See SKIN. ¶
NT: B.175c; CB.–; K.–.
OT: ʿôr: S.5785; HR.291c.1; H.1589a; BD.736a.
GEN. REF.: IS.3:97; NB.92; Z.3:900.

LEAVE, LEFT

(*a*) *In the sense of leaving, abandoning, forsaking.*

1. *aphiēmi* [ἀφίημι, 863], *apo*, from, and *hiēmi*, to send, has three chief meanings, (*a*) to send forth, let go, forgive; (*b*) to let, suffer, permit; (*c*) to leave, leave alone, forsake, neglect. It is translated by the verb to leave (*c*), in Matt. 4:11; 4:20, 22, and parallel passages; 5:24; 8:15, and parallel passages; 8:22, R.V., "leave (the dead)," A.V., "let," and the parallel passage; 13:36, R.V., "left (the multitude)," A.V., "sent . . . away"; 18:12; 19:27, and parallel passages, R.V., "we have left" (A.V., "we have forsaken"); so ver. 29; 22:22, 25; 23:23, R.V., "have left undone" (A.V., "have omitted," in the 1st part, "leave undone" in the second); 23:38, and the parallel passage; 24:2, 40, 41, and parallel pasages; 26:56, R.V., "left"; Mark 1:18, "left"; 1:31; 7:8, R.V., "ye leave"; 8:13; 10:28, 29; 12:12, 19-22; 13:34; Luke 10:30; 11:42 (in some mss.); Luke 12:39, R.V. "have left," A.V. "have suffered" (No. 9 in Matt. 24:43); John 4:3, 28, 52; 8:29; 10:12; 14:18, 27; 16:28, 32; Rom. 1:27; 1 Cor. 7:11, R.V., "leave" (A.V., "put away"); 7:13 (A.V. and R.V.); Heb. 2:8; 6:1; Rev. 2:4. See FORGIVE.
NT: B.125c; CB.1236b; K.88.
OT: nûaḥ: S.5117; HR.183b.4; H.1323; BD.628a.
ʿāzab: S.5800; HR.183b.9; H.1594,1595; BD.736d.
GEN. REF.: –.

2. *aniēmi* [ἀνίημι, 447], *ana*, back and *hiēmi*, to send, denotes to let go, loosen, forbear; it is translated "I will (never) leave (thee)" in Heb. 13:5. See FORBEAR.

NT: B.69d; CB.—; K.60.
OT: rāphāh: S.7503; HR.102b.11c; H.2198; BD.951c.
nāśā': S.5375; HR.102b.8; H.1421; BD.669d.
GEN. REF.: —.

3. *kataleipō* [καταλείπω, 2641], to leave behind (*kata*, down, *leipō*, to leave), is everywhere rendered by the verb to leave except in the following: the A.V. of Rom. 11:4, "I have reserved" (R.V., "I have left"); Heb. 11:27, "he forsook"; 2 Pet. 2:15, A.V., "have forsaken," R.V., "forsaking." See FORSAKE, RESERVE.

NT: B.413c; CB.1254a; K.523.
OT: 'āzab: S.5800; HR.736a.11; H.1594,1595; BD.736d.
shā'ar: S.7604; HR.736a.17a,b; H.2307,2308; BD.983d.
GEN. REF.: —.

4. *apoleipō* [ἀπολείπω, 620], to leave behind (*apo*, from), is used (*a*) in the Active Voice, of leaving behind a cloak, 2 Tim. 4:13; a person, 2 Tim. 4:20; of abandoning a principality (by angels), Jude 6, R.V.; (*b*) in the Passive Voice, to be reserved, to remain, Heb. 4:6, 9; 10:26, See REMAIN, No. 3. ¶ In the papyri it is used as a technical term in wills (Moulton and Milligan, Vocab.).

NT: B.94d; CB.—; K.—.
OT: yātar: S.3498; HR.136b.3; H.836; BD.451a.
'āzab: S.5800; HR.136b.4; H.1594,1595; BD.736d.
GEN. REF.: —.

5. *enkataleipō* [ἐγκαταλείπω, 1459], lit., to leave behind in (*en*, in, and No. 3), signifies (*a*) to leave behind, Rom. 9:29, "a seed"; (*b*) to abandon, forsake, translated by the verb to leave in Acts 2:27, 31 (in some mss., No. 3) of the soul of Christ; in the following, by the verb to forsake, Matt. 27:46; Mark 15:34; 2 Cor. 4:9; 2 Tim. 4:10, 16; Heb. 10:25; 13:5 (see No. 2 in the same ver.). See FORSAKE. ¶

NT: B.215d; CB.—; K.—.
OT: 'āzab: S.5800; HR.365a.8a; H.1594,1595; BD.736d.
GEN. REF.: —.

6. *hupoleipō* [ὑπολείπω, 5275], to leave remaining, lit., to leave under (*hupo*), is used in the Passive Voice in Rom. 11:3, of a survivor. ¶

NT: B.845c; CB.1252b; K.—.
OT: yātar: S.3498; HR.1415a.4; H.836; BD.451a.
shā'ar: S.7604; HR.1415a.9; H.2307,2308; BD.983d.
GEN. REF.: —.

7. *perileipō* [περιλείπω, 4035], to leave over, is used in the Passive Voice in 1 Thess. 4:15, 17, R.V., "that are left" (A.V., "that remain"), lit., 'left over,' i.e., the living believers at the Lord's return. See REMAIN. ¶

NT: B.648c; CB.1263b; K.—.
OT: shā'ar: S.7604; HR.1124b.1; H.2307,2308; BD.983d.
GEN. REF.: —.

8. *pauō* [παύω, 3973], to make to cease, is used in the Middle Voice, signifying to cease, leave off, and is translated "had left" in Luke 5:4; "left" in Acts 21:32; elsewhere, to cease. See CEASE.

NT: B.638a; CB.—; K.—.
OT: kālāh: S.3615; HR.1112b.3; H.982-984; BD.477b.
shābat: S.7673; HR.1112b.13; H.2323; BD.991d.
GEN. REF.: —.

9. *eaō* [ἐάω, 1439], signifies (*a*) to let, permit, suffer, e.g., Matt. 24:43; (*b*) to leave, Acts 23:32, of leaving horsemen; 27:40, of leaving anchors in the sea, R.V. [A.V., "committed (themselves)"]. See COMMIT, SUFFER.

NT: B.212c; CB.—; K.—.
OT: sh^{e}baq (Aramaic): S.7662; HR.361a.8; H.3018; BD.1114c.
nûaḥ: S.5117; HR.361a.4; H.1323; BD.628a.
GEN. REF.: —.

10. *hupolimpanō* [ὑπολιμπάνω, 5277], *limpanō* being a late form for *leipō*, to leave, is used in 1 Pet. 2:21, "leaving (us an example)." ¶

NT: B.845d; CB.—; K.—.
OT: —.
GEN. REF.: —.

11. *perisseuō* [περισσεύω, 4052], to be over and above (the number), hence, to be or remain over, is translated "was left," in Matt. 15:37, A.V. (R.V., "remained over," as in 14:20; Luke 9:17; John 6:12 and ver. 13, where the A.V. adds "and above"), of the broken fragments after the feeding of the multitudes. See ABOUND.

NT: B.650c; CB.1263c; K.828.
OT: yātar: S.3498; HR.1126b.1a; H.836; BD.451a.
marbît: S.4768; HR.1126b.2; H.2103d; BD.916b.
GEN. REF.: —.

Note: The corresponding noun, *perisseuma*, that which is over and above, is used in the plural in Mark 8:8, R.V., "(of broken pieces) that remained over," A.V., "(of the broken meat) that was left," lit., 'of fragments of broken pieces.' See REMAIN.

12. *ekballō* [ἐκβάλλω, 1544], to cast out (*ek*, from, *ballō*, to cast), to drive out, is used in the sense of rejecting or leaving out, in Rev. 11:2, as to the measuring of the court of the Temple (marg., "cast without"). See CAST, No. 5.

NT: B.237b; CB.—; K.91.
OT: gārash: S.1644; HR.420c.3b; H.388; BD.176c.
shālak: S.7993; HR.420c.21; H.2398; BD.1020d.
GEN. REF.: —.

(*b*) *In the sense of giving leave.*

epitrepō [ἐπιτρέπω, 2010], lit. denotes to turn to (*epi*, upon, to, *trepō*, to turn), and so (*a*) to commit, entrust (not in N.T.); (*b*) to permit, give leave, send, of Christ's permission to the unclean spirits to enter the swine, Mark 5:13; in Luke 8:32, R.V., "give . . . leave," "gave . . . leave" (A.V., "suffer" and "suffered"); in John 19:38, of Pilate's permission to Joseph to take away the body of the Lord; in Acts 21:39, of Paul's request to the chief captain to permit him to address the people, R.V., "give . . . leave" (for A.V., "suffer"); in 21:40, "he had given him leave" (A.V., ". . . licence"). See LET, LIBERTY, LICENCE, PERMIT, SUFFER.

NT: B.303c; CB.–; K.–.
OT: –.
GEN. REF.: –.

(*c*) *In the sense of taking leave of, bidding farewell to.*

1. *apotassō* [ἀποτάσσω, 657], used in the Middle Voice in the N.T., lit. signifies to arrange oneself off (*apo*, from, *tassō*, to arrange); hence, to take leave of, Mark 6:46, R.V., "had taken leave of" (A.V., "had sent . . . away"); Acts 18:18; 18:21, R.V., "taking his leave of" (A.V., "bade . . . farewell"); 2 Cor. 2:13; in Luke 9:61, "to bid farewell"; in Luke 14:33 it has its other meaning "renouncing" (A.V., "forsaking"). See FAREWELL, FORSAKE, RENOUNCE. ¶

NT: B.100d; CB.–; K.1156.
OT: –.
GEN. REF.: –.

2. *apaspazomai* [ἀπασπάζομαι, —], to embrace, salute, take leave of (*apo*, from, *aspazomai*, to salute), is used in Acts 21:6, A.V., "when we had taken our leave" (R.V., "bade . . . farewell"). Some mss. have the simple verb *aspazomai*. ¶

NT: B.81d; CB.–; K.84.
OT: –.
GEN. REF.: –.

LEAVEN (Noun and Verb)

A. Noun.

zumē [ζύμη, 2219], leaven, sour dough, in a high state of fermentation, was used in general in making bread. It required time to fulfil the process. Hence, when food was required at short notice, unleavened cakes were used, e.g., Gen. 18:6; 19:3; Ex. 12:8. The Israelites were forbidden to use leaven for seven days at the time of Passover, that they might be reminded that the Lord brought them out of Egypt "in haste," Deut. 16:3, with Ex. 12:11; the unleavened bread, insipid in taste, reminding them, too, of their afflictions, and of the need of self-judgment, is called "the bread of affliction." Leaven was forbidden in all offerings to the Lord by fire, Lev. 2:11; 6:17. Being bred of corruption and spreading through the mass of that in which it is mixed, and therefore symbolizing the pervasive character of evil, leaven was utterly inconsistent in offerings which typified the propitiatory sacrifice of Christ.

In the O.T. leaven is not used in a metaphorical sense. In the N.T. it is used (*a*) metaphorically (1) of corrupt doctrine, Matt. 13:33 and Luke 13:21, of error as mixed with the truth (there is no valid reason for regarding the symbol here differently from its application elsewhere in the N.T.); Matt. 16:6, 11; Mark 8:15 (1st part); Luke 12:1; that the Kingdom of heaven is likened to leaven, does not mean that the Kingdom is leaven. The same statement, as made in other parables, shows that it is the whole parable which constitutes the similitude of the Kingdom; the history of Christendom confirms the fact that the pure meal of the doctrine of Christ has been adulterated with error; (2) of corrupt practices, Mark 8:15 (2nd part), the reference to the Herodians being especially applied to their irreligion; 1 Cor. 5:7, 8; (*b*) literally, in Matt. 16:12, and in the general statements in 1 Cor. 5:6 and Gal. 5:9, where the implied applications are to corrupt practice and corrupt doctrine respectively. ¶

NT: B.340a; CB.1273c; K.302.
OT: ḥāmēṣ: S.2557; HR.599b.1; H.679a; BD.329d.
sᵉʾôr: S.7603; HR.599b.2; H.2229; BD.959a.
GEN. REF.: IS.3:97; NB.725; Z.3:901.

B. Verb.

zumoō [ζυμόω, 2220], signifies to leaven, to act as leaven, Passive Voice in Matt. 13:33 and Luke 13:21; Active Voice in 1 Cor. 5:6 and Gal. 5:9. ¶

NT: B.340a; CB.1273c; K.302.
OT: ḥāmēṣ: S.2556; HR.599b.1a; H.679; BD.329d.
GEN. REF.: IS.3:97; NB.725; Z.3:901.

For **LED** see **LEAD**

LEE

Note: This forms part of the R.V. rendering of two verbs, (1) *hupopleō*, to sail under (i.e., under the lee of), from *hupo*, under, *pleō*, to sail, Acts 27:4, 7 (A.V., "sailed under"); ¶ (2) *hupotrechō*, to run in under (in navigation), to run under the lee of (*hupo*, and a form *hupodramōn*, used as an aorist participle of the verb), Acts 27:16, R.V., "running under the lee of" (A.V., "running under"). See RUN, SAIL. ¶

For **LEFT (Verb)** see **LEAVE**

LEFT (Adjective)

1. *aristeros* [ἀριστερός, 710], is used (*a*) of the left hand, in Matt. 6:3, the word "hand" being understood; in connection with the armour of righteousness, in 2 Cor. 6:7, "(on the right hand and) on the left," lit., '(of the weapons . . . the right and) the left'; (*b*) in the phrase "on the left," formed by *ex* (for *ek*), from, and the genitive plural of this adjective, Mark 10:37 (some mss. have No. 2 here); Luke 23:33. ¶

NT: B.106c; CB.1237c; K.–.
OT: sᵉmōʾl: S.8040; HR.157c.1a,b; H.2267a; BD.969d.
GEN. REF.: IS.3:100; NB.–; Z.–.

2. *euōnumos* [εὐώνυμος, 2176], lit., of good name, or omen (*eu*, well, *onoma*, a name), a word adopted to avoid the ill-omen attaching to the left (omens from the left being unlucky, but a good name being desired for them, cp, *aristeros*, lit., 'better of two,' euphemistic for the ill-omened *laios* and *skaios*; cp., too, the Eng., sinister, from the Latin word meaning 'left'), is used euphemistically for No. 1, either (*a*) simply as an adjective in Rev. 10:2, of the left foot; in Acts 21:3, "on the left" (lit., 'left'); or (*b*) with the preposition *ex* (for *ek*), signifying on the left hand, Matt. 20:21, 23; 25:33, 41; 27:38; Mark 10:40 (for ver. 37, in some mss., see No. 1); 15:27. ¶

NT: B.329d; CB.1247b; K.—.
OT: sᵉmō'l: S.8040; HR.585a.2a; H.2267a; BD.969d.
GEN. REF.: IS.3:100; NB.—; Z.—.

LEG

skelos [σκέλος, 4628], the leg from the hip downwards, is used only of the breaking of the legs of the crucified malefactors, to hasten their death, John 19:31-33 (a customary act, not carried out in the case of Christ, in fulfilment of Ex. 12:46; Numb. 9:12). The practice was known as *skelokopia* (from *koptō*, to strike), or, in Latin, *crurifragium* (from *crus*, a leg, and *frango*, to break). ¶

NT: B.753c; CB.—; K.—.
OT: regel: S.7272; HR.1268c.4a; H.2113a; BD.919c.
shôq: S.7785; HR.1268c.5a; H.2350a; BD.1003b.
GEN. REF.: IS.3:100; NB.728; Z.3:907.

LEGION

legiōn [λεγιών, 3003], otherwise spelt *legeōn*, a legion, occurs in Matt. 26:53, of angels; in Mark 5:9, 15, and Luke 8:30, of demons. Among the Romans a legion was primarily a chosen (*lego*, to choose) body of soldiers divided into ten cohorts, and numbering from 4,200 to 6,000 men (Gk. *speira*, see BAND). In the time of our Lord it formed a complete army of infantry and cavalry, of upwards of 5,000 men. The legions were not brought into Judaea till the outbreak of the Jewish war (A.D. 66), as they were previously employed in the frontier Provinces of the Empire. Accordingly in its N.T. use the word has its other and more general significance of a large number. ¶

NT: B.467d; CB.—; K.505.
OT: —.
GEN. REF.: IS.3:101; NB.728; Z.3:907.

LEISURE (to have)

eukaireō [εὐκαιρέω, 2119], to have leisure or opportunity (*eu*, well, *kairos*, a time or season), is translated "they had . . . leisure" in Mark 6:31; in Acts 17:21, "spent their time" (R.V., marg., "had leisure for"); in 1 Cor. 16:12, "he shall have opportunity," R.V. (A.V., ". . . convenient time"). See CONVENIENT, OPPORTUNITY, SPEND. ¶ This verb differs from *scholazō*, to have leisure; it stresses the opportunity of doing something, whereas *scholazō* stresses the leisure for engaging in it, e.g., 1 Cor. 7:5, "(that) ye may give yourselves to."

NT: B.321b; CB.1247b; K.—.
OT: —.
GEN. REF.: —.

LEND, LENDER

A. Verbs.

1. *daneizō* [δανείζω, —], is translated to lend in Luke 6:34, 35: see BORROW.

2. *kichrēmi* [κίχρημι, 5531], or *chraō* (χράω), to lend, is used in the aorist (or 'point') tense, Active Voice, in Luke 11:5, in the request, "lend me three loaves." The radical sense of the verb is to furnish what is needful (akin to *chreia*, which means both use and need, and to *chrē*, it is needful). Hence it is distinct from No. 1, the basic idea of which is to lend on security or return. ¶

NT: B.433a; CB.—; K.—.
OT: shā'al: S.7592; HR.765c.2; H.2303; BD.981b.
GEN. REF.: IS.3:102; NB.304; Z.2:79.

B. Noun.

danistēs or *daneistēs* [δανειστής, 1157], denotes a money-lender (akin to A, No. 1), translated "lender" in Luke 7:41, R.V. (A.V., "creditor"). ¶ In the Sept., 2 Kings 4:1; Ps. 109:11; Prov. 29:13. ¶

NT: B.170d; CB.1240b; K.—.
OT: nāshāh: S.5383; HR.285a.1; H.1427; BD.674b.
GEN. REF.: IS.3:102; NB.304; Z.2:79.

LENGTH

mēkos [μῆκος, 3372], length, from the same root as *makros*, long (see FAR, LONG), occurs in Eph. 3:18 and Rev. 21:16 (twice). ¶

NT: B.518c; CB.—; K.—.
OT: 'ōrek: S.753; HR.921b.1a; H.162a; BD.73d.
GEN. REF.: —.

LENGTH (at)

pote [ποτέ, 4218], is translated "at length" in Rom. 1:10, where the whole phrase "if by any means now at length" suggests not only ardent desire but the existence of difficulties for a considerable time. See AFORETIME.

NT: B.695a; CB.1266b; K.—.
OT: —.
GEN. REF.: —.

LEOPARD

pardalis [πάρδαλις, 3917], denotes a leopard or a panther, an animal characterized by swiftness of movement and sudden spring, in Dan. 7:6 symbolic of the activities of Alexander the Great, and the formation of the Grecian Kingdom, the third seen in the vision there recorded. In Rev. 13:2 the imperial power, described there also as a "beast," is seen to concentrate in himself the characteristics of those mentioned in Dan. 7. ¶

NT: B.623d; CB.1262b; K.—.
OT: nāmēr: S.5246; HR.1065c.1a; H.1372a; BD.649c.
GEN. REF.: IS.3:102; NB.729; Z.3:909.

LEPER

lepros [λεπρός, 3015], an adjective, primarily used of psoriasis, characterized by an eruption of rough, scaly patches; later, leprous, but chiefly used as a noun, a leper, Matt. 8:2; 10:8; 11:5; Mark 1:40; Luke 4:27; 7:22; 17:12; especially of Simon, mentioned in Matt. 26:6; Mark 14:3. ¶

NT: B.472a; CB.1256c; K.529.
OT: ṣāra': S.6879; HR.874a.1; H.1971; BD.863d.
GEN. REF.: IS.3:103; NB.314; Z.2:138.

LEPROSY

lepra [λέπρα, 3014], akin to *lepros* (above), is mentioned in Matt. 8:3; Mark 1:42; Luke 5:12, 13. ¶ In the removal of other maladies the verb to heal (*iaomai*) is used, but in the removal of leprosy, the verb to cleanse (*katharizō*, save in the statement concerning the Samaritan, Luke 17:15, "when he saw that he was healed." Matt. 10:8 and Luke 4:27 indicate that the disease was common in the nation. Only twelve cases are recorded in the N.T., but these are especially selected. For the Lord's commands to the leper mentioned in Matthew 8 and to the ten in Luke 17, see Lev. 14:2-32.

NT: B.472a; CB.1256c; K.529.
OT: ṣāra'at: S.6883; HR.873c.1a; H.1971a; BD.863d.
GEN. REF.: IS.3:103; NB.314; Z.2:138.

LESS

1. *elassōn* [ἐλάσσων, 1640], serves as a comparative degree of *mikros*, little (see LEAST), and denotes 'less' in (*a*) quality, as of wine, John 2:10, "worse"; (*b*) age, Rom. 9:12, "younger"; 1 Tim. 5:9, "under" neuter, adverbially); (*c*) rank, Heb. 7:7. See UNDER, WORSE, YOUNG. ¶

NT: B.248a; CB.1244a; K.—.
OT: —.
GEN. REF.: —.

2. *mikroteros* [μικρότερος, 3398], the comparative of *mikros*, is translated "less" in Matt. 13:32, R.V. (A.V., "least"), and Mark 4:31. See LEAST.

NT: B.521a; CB.—; K.—.
OT: —.
GEN. REF.: —.

3. *hēssōn* [ἥσσων, 2276], inferior, is used in the neuter adverbially in 2 Cor. 12:15, "the less." See WORSE.

NT: B.349a; CB.—; K.—.
OT: —.
GEN. REF.: —.

LEST

1. *mē* [μή, 3361], a negative particle, often used as a conjunction, is frequently translated "lest," e.g., Mark 13:36 (in ver. 5, R.V., "that no," for A.V., "let"); Acts 13:40; 23:10.

NT: B.515d; CB.1258a; K.—.
OT: —.
GEN. REF.: —.

2. *hina mē* [ἵνα μή, 2443 (*hina*)], in order that not, is rendered "lest," e.g., in Matt. 17:27; in some instances the R.V. renders the phrase "that . . . not," e.g., Luke 8:12, or "that . . . no," 1 Cor. 9:12 (A.V., "lest").

NT: B.378a; CB.1250c; K.366.
OT: —.
GEN. REF.: —.

3. *mēpote* or *mē pote* [μήποτε, 3379], denotes lest ever, lest perhaps, lest at any time, e.g., Matt. 4:6; "lest haply," Matt. 7:6, R.V. (A.V., "lest"), and in 13:15 (A.V., "lest at any time"); in 25:9, R.V., "peradventure" (A.V., "lest"). The R.V. does not translate this simply by "lest," as in the A.V.; see further, e.g., in Matt. 27:64; Mark 14:2; Luke 12:58; the addition of *pote* requires the fuller rendering.

NT: B.519b; CB.1258b; K.—.
OT: —.
GEN. REF.: —.

Note: In Luke 14:29, the conjunctive phrase *hina mēpote*, "lest haply," is used.

4. *mēpōs*, or *mē pōs* [μήπως, 3381], used as a conjunction, denotes lest somehow, lest haply, lest by any means, e.g., 2 Cor. 2:7, R.V., "lest by any means" (A.V., "lest perhaps"); so 12:20 (twice) and Gal. 4:11 (A.V., "lest"); in 1 Thess. 3:5 (A.V., "lest by some means").

NT: B.519c; CB.—; K.—.
OT: —.
GEN. REF.: —.

5. *mēpou*, or *mē pou* [μήπου, 3361, 4225], lest perhaps, is used in Acts 27:29, R.V., "lest haply" (A.V., "lest").

NT: B.519c; CB.—; K.—.
OT: —.
GEN. REF.: —.

Note: In 2 Cor. 4:4, A.V., the phrase *eis* (unto) *to* (the) *mē* (not), i.e., 'in order that . . . not,' is rendered "lest (the light) . . . should"; R.V., "that (the light) . . . should not."

LET (alone, go)

1. *aphiēmi* [ἀφίημι, 863], for the meanings of which see LEAVE, No. 1, frequently denotes to let, suffer, permit, e.g., Matt. 5:40 (translated "let . . . have"); 7:4; 13:30; 15:14; 27:49 and Mark 15:36, R.V., "let be;" probably short for 'let us see' (Moulton and Milligan, Vocab.); Mark 7:27; 11:6 ("let . . . go"); 14:6 ("let . . . alone"); so Luke 13:8; John 11:48; in Acts 5:38 (where some mss. have *eaō*, to permit, let, suffer); in John 11:44 and 18:8 ("let"); 1 Cor. 7:11, 12, R.V., "let . . . leave;" A.V., "let . . . put away"; 7:13 ("let . . . leave").

NT: B.125c; CB.1236b; K.88.
OT: ḥādal: S.2308; HR.183b.1; H.609; BD.292d.
nûaḥ: S.5117; HR.183b.4; H.1323; BD.628a.
GEN. REF.: –.

2. *epitrepō* [ἐπιτρέπω, 2010], for the meanings of which see LEAVE (*b*), is translated "let (me)" in Luke 9:61, A.V., R.V., "suffer (me)."

NT: B.303c; CB.–; K.–.
OT: –.
GEN. REF.: –.

3. *apoluō* [ἀπολύω, 630], signifies to set free, release, loose (*apo*, from, *luō*, to loose), e.g., Luke 13:12; John 19:10; forgive, Luke 6:37; to release, dismiss, send away, translated to let go, e.g., in Luke 14:4; in some mss. 22:68; in Luke 23:22, John 19:12 and Acts 3:13, A.V., "let . . . go" (R.V., "release"); in Acts 4:21, "they let . . . go"; in ver. 23 (Passive Voice), "being let go"; 5:40; in 15:33, A.V., "let go" (R.V., "dismissed"); 16:35, 36; 17:9; in 23:22, R.V., "let . . . go" (A.V., "let . . . depart"); in 28:18, A.V., "let . . . go" (R.V., "set . . . at liberty"). See DISMISS.

NT: B.96c; CB.1237a; K.–.
OT: gārash: S.1644; HR.138c.2; H.388; BD.176c.
GEN. REF.: –.

4. *eaō* [ἐάω, 1439], to let, occurs in Acts 27:32. See SUFFER.

NT: B.212c; CB.–; K.–.
OT: rāphāh: S.7503; HR.361a.7; H.2198; BD.951c.
shᵉbaq (Aramaic): S.7662; HR.361a.8b; H.3018; BD.1114c.
GEN. REF.: –.

Note: In Acts 2:29, the impersonal verb *exesti*, it is permitted, it is lawful, is rendered "let me," A.V. (R.V. and A.V., marg., "I may").

For **LET** (A.V. in Rom. 1:13 and 2 Thess. 2:7) see **HINDER** and **RESTRAIN**

LET DOWN

1. *kathiēmi* [καθίημι, 2524], to send, or let down (*kata*, down, *hiēmi*, to send), is translated to let down, with reference to (*a*) the paralytic in Luke 5:19; (*b*) Saul of Tarsus, Acts 9:25; (*c*) the great sheet in Peter's vision, 10:11 and 11:5. ¶

NT: B.390b; CB.–; K.–.
OT: –.
GEN. REF.: –.

2. *chalaō* [χαλάω, 5465], to slacken, loosen, let loose, denotes in the N.T., to let down, to lower; it is used with reference to (*a*) the paralytic, in Mark 2:4, cp. No. 1 (*a*); (*b*) Saul of Tarsus, Acts 9:25, "lowering" [see also No. 1 (*b*); 2 Cor. 11:33, "was I let down" (Passive Voice); (*c*) nets, LUke 5:4, 5 (in the latter, R.V., "nets"; A.V., "net"); (*d*) the gear of a ship, Acts 27:17, R.V., "they lowered (the gear)," A.V., "they strake (sail)"; (*e*) a ship's boat, ver. 30, R.V., "lowered" (A.V., "let down"). See LOWER, STRIKE. ¶

NT: B.874b; CB.–; K.–.
OT: –.
GEN. REF.: –.

LET OUT

ekdidōmi [ἐκδίδωμι, 1554], primarily, to give out, give up, surrender (*ek*, out, from, *didōmi*, to give), denotes to let out for hire; in the N.T. it is used, in the Middle Voice, with the meaning to let out to one's advantage, in the parable of the husbandman and his vineyard, Matt. 21:33, 41; Mark 12:1; Luke 20:9, A.V., "let . . . forth"; R.V., "let . . . out." ¶

NT: B.238c; CB.–; K.–.
OT: nātan: S.5414; HR.422a.4; H.1443; BD.678a.
GEN. REF.: –.

LETTER

1. *gramma* [γράμμα, 1121], primarily denotes that which is traced or drawn, a picture; then, that which is written, (*a*) a character, letter of the alphabet, 2 Cor. 3:7, "written," lit., '(in) letters'; Gal. 6:11; here the reference is not to the length of the Epistle (Paul never uses *gramma*, either in the singular or the plural, of his Epistles; of these he uses *epistolē*, No. 2), but to the size of the characters written by his own hand (probably from this verse to the end, as the use of the past tense, "I have written," is, according to Greek idiom, the equivalent of our 'Iam writing'). Moreover, the word for "letters" is here in the dative case, *grammasin*, 'with (how large) letters'; (*b*) a writing, a written document, a bond (A.V., "bill") Luke 16:6, 7; (*c*) a letter, by way of correspondence, Acts 28:21; (*d*) the Scriptures of the O.T., 2 Tim. 3:15; (*e*) learning, John 7:15, "letters"; Acts 26:24, "(much) learning" (lit., 'many letters'); in the papyri an illiterate person is often spoken of as one who does not know letters, "which never means anything else than inability to

write" (Moulton and Milligan); (*f*) "the letter," the written commandments of the Word of God, in contrast to the inward operation of the Holy Spirit under the New Covenant, Rom. 2:27, 29; 7:6; 2 Cor. 3:6; (*g*) the books of Moses, John 5:47. ¶

NT: B.165b; CB.1248c; K.128.
OT: miktāb: S.4385; HR.275a.2d; H.1053c; BD.508b.
sēpher: S.5612; HR.275a.3; H.1540a; BD.706d.
GEN. REF.: IS.3:106; NB.1341; Z.—.

2. *epistolē* [ἐπιστολή, —], see EPISTLE

For **LEVEL** see **PLACE**, *Note* (4)

For **LEWD** and **LEWDNESS** see **VILE** and **VILLANY**

LIAR

A. Nouns.

pseustēs [ψεύστης, 5583], a liar, occurs in John 8:44, 55; Rom. 3:4; 1 Tim. 1:10; Tit. 1:12; 1 John 1:10; 2:4, 22; 4:20; 5:10. ¶

NT: B.892c; CB.1267c; K.1339.
OT: kāzab: S.3576; HR.1485b.1a; H.970; BD.469b.
kāzāb: S.3577; HR.1485b.1b; H.970a; BD.469c.
GEN. REF.: IS.3:128; NB.734; Z.3:926.

B. Adjective.

pseudēs [ψευδής, 5571], lying, false (Eng., pseudo-), rendered "false" in Acts 6:13 and in the R.V. of Rev. 2:2 (A.V., "liars"), is used as a noun, "liars," in Rev. 21:8. See FALSE. ¶

NT: B.891c; CB.1267c; K.1339.
OT: kāzāb: S.3577; HR.1484b.1b; H.970a; BD.469c.
shāw': S.7723; HR.1484b.3; H.2338a; BD.996a.
sheqer: S.8267; HR.1484b.4; H.2461a; BD.1055b.
GEN. REF.: IS.3:128; NB.734; Z.3:926.

Note: Many compound nouns are formed by the prefix *pseudo-*: see, e.g., APOSTLES, BRETHREN, CHRISTS, PROPHETS, TEACHERS, WITNESS.

LIBERAL, LIBERALITY, LIBERALLY

A. Noun.

1. *haplotēs* [ἁπλοτής, 572], denotes (*a*) simplicity, sincerity, unaffectedness (from *haplous*, single, simple, in contrast to *diplous*, double), Rom. 12:8, "simplicity"; 2 Cor. 11:3 (in some mss. in 1:12); Eph. 6:5 and Col. 3:22, "singleness"; (*b*) simplicity as manifested in generous giving, "liberality," 2 Cor. 8:2; 9:11 (A.V., "bountifulness," R.V. marg., "singleness"); 9:13 (A.V., "liberal"). See BOUNTY, No. 2. ¶

NT: B.85d; CB.1249b; K.65.
OT: tōm: S.8537; HR.122c.2; H.2522a; BD.1070d.
GEN. REF.: IS.3:118; NB.—; Z.—.

2. *charis* [χάρις, —], is rendered "liberality" in 1 Cor. 16:3, A.V. See BOUNTY, No. 3.

B. Adverb.

haplōs [ἁπλῶς, 574], liberally, with singleness of heart, is used in Jas. 1:5 of God as the gracious and liberal Giver. The word may be taken either (*a*) in a logical sense, signifying unconditionally, simply, or (*b*) in a moral sense, generously; for the double meaning compare A, No. 1. ¶ On this passage Hort writes as follows: "Later writers comprehend under the one word the whole magnanimous and honourable type of character in which singleness of mind is the central feature."

NT: B.86b; CB.1249b; K.—.
OT: battōm: S.8537; HR.123a.1; H.2522a; BD.1070d.
GEN. REF.: IS.3:118; NB.—; Z.—.

LIBERTY

1. *anesis* [ἄνεσις, 425], a loosening, relaxation, is translated "liberty" in Acts 24:23, A.V. See INDULGENCE.

NT: B.65b; CB.—; K.60.
OT: —.
GEN. REF.: IS.3:118; NB.732; Z.—.

2. *aphesis* [ἄφεσις, 859], dismissal, release, forgiveness, is rendered "liberty" in the A.V. of Luke 4:18, R.V., "release." See FORGIVENESS.

NT: B.125a; CB.1236b; K.88.
OT: —.
GEN. REF.: IS.3:118; NB.732; Z.3:920.

4. *exousia* [ἐξουσία, 1849], authority, right, is rendered "liberty" in 1 Cor. 8:9 (marg., "power"), "this liberty of yours," or 'this right which you assert.' See AUTHORITY.

NT: B.277d; CB.1247c; K.238.
OT: —.
GEN. REF.: IS.3:118; NB.732; Z.—.

B. Adjective.

eleutheros [ἐλεύθερος, 1658], is rendered "at liberty" in 1 Cor. 7:39, A.V. (R.V. "free"). See FREE.

NT: B.250d; CB.1244b; K.224.
OT: ḥaphshî: S.2670; HR.452b.1; H.717c; BD.344d.
GEN. REF.: IS.3:118; NB.732; Z.3:920.

C. Verbs.

1. *apoluō* [ἀπολύω, 630], for the meanings of which see LET, No. 3, is translated "to set at liberty" in Acts 26:32 and Heb. 13:23. See DISMISS.

NT: B.96c; CB.1237a; K.—.
OT: —.
GEN. REF.: IS.3:118; NB.732; Z.3:920.

2. *apostellō* [ἀποστέλλω, 649], to send away, is translated "to set at liberty" in Luke 4:18. See SEND.

NT: B.98c; CB.1237a; K.67.
OT: —.
GEN. REF.: IS.3:118; NB.732; Z.—.

Note: In Acts 27:3, A.V., *epitrepō* is rendered "gave . . . liberty" (R.V. "gave . . . leave"). See LEAVE (*b*).

For **LICENCE** (in Acts 21:40 and 25:16, A.V.) see **LEAVE** (*b*) and **OPPORTUNITY**, A, No. 3

LICK

epileichō [ἐπιλείχω, —], to lick over (*epi*, over, *leichō*, to lick), is said of the dogs in Luke 16:21. Some mss. have *apoleichō*, to lick off. ¶

NT: B.295c; CB.—; K.—.
OT: —.
GEN. REF.: —.

LIE (falsehood: Noun and Verb)

A. Nouns.

1. *pseudos* [ψεῦδος, 5579], a falsehood, lie (see also under LIAR), is translated "lie" in John 8:44 (lit., 'the lie'); Rom. 1:25, where it stands by metonymy for an idol, as, e.g., in Isa. 44:20; Jer. 10:14; 13:25; Amos 2:4 (plural); 2 Thess. 2:11, with special reference to the lie of ver. 4, that man is God (cp. Gen. 3:5); 1 John 2:21, 27; Rev. 21:27; 22:15; in Eph. 4:25, A.V., "lying," R.V., "falsehood," the practice: in Rev. 14:5, R.V., "lie" (some mss. have *dolos*, "guile," A.V.); 2 Thess. 2:9, where "lying wonders" is, lit., 'wonders of falsehood,' i.e., wonders calculated to deceive (cp. Rev. 13:13-15), the purpose being to deceive people into the acknowledgement of the spurious claim to deity on the part of the Man of Sin. ¶

NT: B.892b; CB.1267c; K.1339.
OT: sheqer: S.8267; HR.1485a.4; H.2461a; BD.1055b.
kaḥash: S.3585; HR.1485a.2a; H.975a; BD.471c.
GEN. REF.: IS.3:128; NB.734; Z.3:926.

Note: In Rom. 1:25 the lie or idol is the outcome of pagan religion; in 1 John 2:21, 22 the lie is the denial that Jesus is the Christ; in 2 Thess. 2:11 the lie is the claim of the Man of Sin.

2. *pseusma* [ψεῦσμα, 5582], a falsehood, or an acted lie, Rom. 3:7, where "my lie" is not idolatry, but either the universal false attitude of man toward God or that with which his detractors charged the Apostle; the former seems to be the meaning. ¶

NT: B.892c; CB.—; K.1339.
OT: —.
GEN. REF.: IS.3:118; NB.734; Z.3:926.

B. Adjectives.

1. *pseudologos* [ψευδολόγος, 5573], denotes speaking falsely (*pseudēs*, false, *logos*, a word) in 1 Tim. 4:2, where the adjective is translated "that speak lies," R.V. (A.V., "speaking lies") and is applied to "demons," the actual utterances being by their human agents. ¶

NT: B.891c; CB.1267c; K.—.
OT: —.
GEN. REF.: IS.3:118; NB.734; Z.3:926.

2. *apseudēs* [ἀψευδής, 893], denotes free from falsehood (*a*, negative, *pseudēs*, false), truthful, Tit. 1:2, of God, "who cannot lie." ¶

NT: B.129c; CB.1237b; K.1339.
OT: —.
GEN. REF.: IS.3:118; NB.—; Z.—.

C. Verb.

pseudō [ψεύδω, 5574], to deceive by lies (always in the Middle Voice in the N.T.), is used (*a*) absolutely, in Matt 5:L11, falsely," lit., "lying (A.V., marg.); Rom. 9:1; 2 Cor. 11:31; Gal. 1:20; Col 3:9 (where the verb is followed by the preposition *eis*, to); 1 Tim. 2:7; Heb. 6:18; Jas. 3:14 (where it is followed by the preposition *kata*, against); 1 John 1:6; Rev. 3:9; (*b*) transitively, with a direct object (without a preposition following), Acts 5:3 (with the accusative case), "to lie to (the Holy Ghost)," R.V. marg., "deceive"; ver. 4 (with the dative case) "thou hast (not) lied (unto men, but unto God)."

NT: B.891d; CB.1267c; K.1339.
OT: kāḥash: S.3584; HR.1484b.4; H.975; BD.471a.
kāzab: S.3576; HR.1484b.2; H.970; BD.469b.
GEN. REF.: IS.3:118; NB.734; Z.3:926.

LIE (to lie down, on, upon)

1. *keimai* [κεῖμαι, 2749], to be laid, to lie, used as the Passive Voice of *tithēmi*, to lay (see LAY, No. 14), is said (*a*) of the Child Jesus, Luke 2:12, 16; (*b*) of the dead body of the Lord, Matt. 28:6; John 20:12; in Luke 23:53, "had . . . lain," R.V., A.V., "was laid" [see LAY, No. 14, *Note* (1)], in the tomb as hitherto empty; (*c*) of the linen cloths, John 20:5, 6, 7; (*d*) figuratively of a veil as lying upon the hearts of the Jews, 2 Cor. 3:15, R.V., "lieth" (A.V., "is"); (*e*) metaphorically, of the world as lying in the evil one, 1 John 5:19, R.V.; (*f*) of the Heavenly City, Rev. 21:16. For other instances in which the rendering is in the Passive Voice, see LAY, No. 14. See APPOINT.

NT: B.426c; CB.1254c; K.425.
OT: yā'ad: S.3259; HR.758b.3; H.878; BD.416d.
sîm, sûm: S.7760; HR.758b.7; H.2243; BD.962c.
GEN. REF.: —.

2. *katakeimai* [κατάκειμαι, 2621], to lie down (*kata*, down, and No. 1), is used of the sick, Mark 1:30; 2:4; Luke 5:25; John 5:3, 6; Acts 28:8; in Acts 9:33 it is rendered "had kept (his bed)," lit., 'lying (on a bed).' See SIT.

NT: B.411c; CB.—; K.425.
OT: shākab: S.7901; HR.733a.1; H.2381; BD.1011d.
GEN. REF.: IS.3:128; NB.—; Z.—.

3. *ballo* [βάλλω, 906], to throw, cast, is used in the Passive Voice, with reference to the sick, with the meaning to be laid, to lie, in Matt. 8:6, "(my servant) lieth (in the house)," lit., 'is laid';

8:14, "lying," R.V. (A.V., "laid"); 9:2, "lying (on a bed)," See CAST.
NT: B.130d; CB.1238b; K.91.
OT: —.
GEN. REF.: —.

4. *epikeimai* [ἐπίκειμαι, 1945], to lie upon, be laid upon, is translated with this meaning, intransitively in John 11:38 and Acts 27:20; transitively, in the Passive Voice, in John 21:9 and 1 Cor. 9:16. See IMPOSED.
NT: B.294c; CB.—; K.425.
OT: —.
GEN. REF.: —.

Notes: (1) In Mark 5:40, some mss. have the verb *anakeimai*, to be laid up, translated "was lying," A.V. In the most authentic the word is absent.

(2) In Acts 27:12, A.V., *blepō*, to look, is rendered "lieth," of the situation of the haven Phoenix (A.V., Phenice); R.V., "looketh."

(3) In John 11:17, A.V., the verb *echō*, to have, to hold, used with *en*, in, signifying to be in a certain condition, is translated "had *lain*" (R.V., "had been").

(4) In John 13:25, *anapiptō*, lit., to fall back (some mss. have *epipiptō*, lit., to fall upon, hence the A.V., "lying"), is used of John's position at the table, R.V., "leaning back (. . . on Jesus' breast)."

LIE IN WAIT

A. Verb.

enedreuō [ἐνεδρεύω, 1748], to lie in wait for, to lay wait for (from *en*, in, and *hedra*, a seat, cp. B), occurs in Luke 11:54, "laying wait for"; Acts 23:21, "there lie in wait for." ¶
NT: B.264c; CB.—; K.—.
OT: 'ārab: S.693; HR.472a.1a; H.156; BD.70b.
GEN. REF.: —.

Note: In Acts 23:30, the word *epiboulē*, a plot, necessitates the R.V. "(that there would be) a plot." For Eph. 4:14, A.V., see WILES.

B. Noun.

enedra or *enedron* [ἐνέδρα, 1747, 1749], akin to A, a lying in wait, an ambush, occurs in Acts 23:16 (where some mss. have the form *enedron*); 25:3, "laying wait," lit., 'making an ambush.' ¶ In the Sept., Josh. 8:7, 9; Ps. 10:8. ¶
NT: B.264c; CB.1245a; K.—.
OT: 'ārab: S.693; HR.472a.1a; H.156; BD.70b.
ma'ᵃrāb: S.3993; HR.472a.1b; H.156e; BD.70d.
GEN. REF.: —.

LIFE, LIVING, LIFETIME, LIFE-GIVING

A. Nouns.

1. *zōē* [ζωή, 2222], (Eng., zoo, zoology) is used in the N.T. "of life as a principle, life in the absolute sense, life as God has it, that which the Father has in Himself, and which He gave to the Incarnate Son to have in Himself, John 5:26, and which the Son manifested in the world, 1 John 1:2. From this life man has become alienated in consequence of the Fall, Eph. 4:18, and of this life men become partakers through faith in the Lord Jesus Christ, John 3:15, who becomes its Author to all such as trust in Him, Acts 3:15, and who is therefore said to be 'the life' of the believer, Col. 3:4, for the life that He gives He maintains, John 6:35, 63. Eternal life is the present actual possession of the believer because of his relationship with Christ, John 5:24; 1 John 3:14, and that it will one day extend its domain to the sphere of the body is assured by the Resurrection of Christ, 2 Cor. 5:4; 2 Tim. 1:10. This life is not merely a principle of power and mobility, however, for it has moral associations which are inseparable from it, as of holiness and righteousness. Death and sin, life and holiness, are frequently contrasted in the Scriptures.

"*Zōē* is also used of that which is the common possession of all animals and men by nature, Acts 17:25; 1 John 5:16, and of the present sojourn of man upon the earth with reference to its duration, Luke 16:25; 1 Cor. 15:19; 1 Tim. 4:8; 1 Pet. 3:10. 'This life' is a term equivalent to 'the gospel,' 'the faith,' 'Christianity,' Acts 5:20."*

Death came through sin, Rom. 5:12, which is rebellion against God. Sin thus involved the forfeiting of the life. "The life of the flesh is in the blood," Lev. 17:11. Therefore the impartation of life to the sinner must be by a death caused by the shedding of that element which is the life of the flesh. "It is the blood that maketh atonement by reason of the life" (*id.*, R.V.). The separation from God caused by the forfeiting of the life could be removed only by a sacrifice in which the victim and the offerer became identified. This which was appointed in the typical offerings in Israel received its full accomplishment in the voluntary sacrifice of Christ. The shedding of the blood in the language of Scripture involves the taking or the giving of the life. Since Christ had no sins of

*From Notes on Galatians by Hogg and Vine, pp. 324, 325.

his own to die for, His death was voluntary and vicarious, John 10:15 with Isa. 53:5, 10, 12; 2 Cor. 5:21. In His sacrifice He endured the Divine judgment due to man's sin. By this means the believer becomes identified with Him in His deathless life, through His resurrection, and enjoys conscious and eternal fellowship with God.

NT: B.340b; CB.1273c; K.290.
OT: ḥay: S.2416; HR.599c.4; H.644a; BD.311c.
ḥayyāh: S.2416; HR.599c.3b; H.644a; BD.312c.
GEN. REF.: IS.3:129; NB.735; Z.3:927.

2. *bios* [βίος, 979], (cp. Eng. words beginning with *bio-*), is used in three respects (*a*) of the period or duration of life, e.g., in the A.V. of 1 Pet. 4:3, "the time past of our life" (the R.V. follows the mss. which omit "of our life"); Luke 8:14; 2 Tim. 2:4; (*b*) of the manner of life, life in regard to its moral conduct, 1 Tim. 2:2; 1 John 2:16; (*c*) of the means of life, livelihood, maintenance, living, Mark 12:44; Luke 8:43; 15:12, 30; 21:4; 1 John 3:17, "goods," R.V. (A.V., "good"). See GOODS. ¶

NT: B.141d; CB.1239a; K.290.
OT: yôm: S.3117; HR.220b.3a; H.852; BD.398a.
GEN. REF.: IS.3:129; NB.735; Z.3:927.

Note: "While *zōē* is life intensive . . . *bios* is life extensive. . . . In *bios*, used as manner of life, there is an ethical sense often inhering which, in classical Greek at least, *zōē* does not possess." In Scripture *zōē* is "the nobler word, expressing as it continually does, all of highest and best which the saints possess in God" (Trench, Syn. §xxvii).

3. *psuchē* [ψυχή, 5590], besides its meanings, heart, mind, soul, denotes life in two chief respects, (*a*) breath of life, the natural life, e.g., Matt. 2:20; 6:25; Mark 10:45; Luke 12:22; Acts 20:10; Rev. 8:9; 12:11 (cp. Lev. 17:11; Esth. 8:11); (*b*) the seat of personality, e.g., Luke 9:24, explained in ver. 25 as "own self." See list under SOUL. See also HEART, MIND.

NT: B.893b; CB.1267c; K.1342.
OT: nephesh: S.5315; HR.1486a.4; H.1395a; BD.659b.
GEN. REF.: IS.3:129; NB.735; Z.3:927.

Notes: (1) "Speaking generally, *psuchē*, is the individual life, the living being, whereas *zōē*, is the life of that being, cp. Ps. 66:9, 'God . . . which holdeth our soul (*psuchē*) in life (*zōē*),' and John 10:10, 'I came that they may have life (*zōē*),' with ver. 11, 'The Good Shepherd layeth down His life (*psuchē*) for the sheep.' "*

(2) In Rev. 13:15, A.V., *pneuma*, breath, is translated "life" (R.V., "breath").

(3) In 2 Cor. 1:8, "we despaired even of life," the verb *zaō*, to live, is used in the Infinitive Mood, as a noun, and translated "life" (lit., 'living'). In Heb. 2:15 the Infinitive Mood of the same verb is translated "lifetime."

4. *biōsis* [βίωσις, 981], from *bioō*, to spend one's life, to live, denotes a manner of life, Acts 26:4. ¶

NT: B.142a; CB.–; K.–.
OT: –.
GEN. REF.: IS.3:129; NB.735; Z.3:927.

5. *agōgē* [ἀγωγή, 72], a manner of life, 2 Tim. 3:10; see CONDUCT.

NT: B.14d; CB.1233c; K.20.
OT: –.
GEN. REF.: IS.3:129; NB.735; Z.3:927.

6. *anastrophē* [ἀναστροφή, 391], behaviour, conduct, is translated "manner of life" (A.V., "conversation") in the R.V. of Gal. 1:13; 1 Tim. 4:12; 1 Pet. 1:18; 3:16; "living," in 1 Pet. 1:15. See BEHAVIOUR.

NT: B.61c; CB.1235b; K.1093.
OT: –.
GEN. REF.: IS.3:129; NB.735; Z.3:927.

B. Adjectives.

1. *biōtikos* [βιωτικός, 982], pertaining to life (*bios*), is translated "of this life," in Luke 21:34, with reference to cares; in 1 Cor. 6:3, "(things) that pertain to this life," and ver. 4, "(things) pertaining to this life," i.e., matters of this world, concerning which Christians at Corinth were engaged in public lawsuits one with another; such matters were to be regarded as relatively unimportant in view of the great tribunals to come under the jurisdiction of saints hereafter. Moulton and Milligan (Vocab.) illustrate the word from phrases in the papyri, e.g., "business (documents)"; "business concerning my livelihood"; "(stories) of ordinary life." ¶

NT: B.142a; CB.1239a; K.–.
OT: –.
GEN. REF.: IS.3:129; NB.735; Z.3:927.

2. *apsuchos* [ἄψυχος, 895], denotes lifeless, inanimate (*a*, negative, and *psuchē*, see A, No. 3), "without life," 1 Cor. 14:7. ¶

NT: B.129c; CB.–; K.–.
OT: –.
GEN. REF.: –.

C. Verb.

zōopoieō [ζωοποιέω, 2227], to make alive, cause to live, quicken (from *zōē*, life, and *poieō*, to make), is used as follows:

"(*a*) of God as the Bestower of every kind of life in the universe, 1 Tim. 6:13 (*zōogoneō*, to preserve alive, is the alternative reading adopted by most editors; see LIVE, No. 6), and, particularly, of resurrection life, John 5:21; Rom. 4:17; (*b*) of Christ, who also is the Bestower of resurrection life, John 5:21 (2nd part); 1 Cor. 15:45; cp. ver. 22; (*c*) of the

* From Notes on Thessalonians by Hogg and Vine, p. 325.

resurrection of Christ in "the body of His glory," 1 Pet. 3:18; (*d*) of the power of reproduction inherent in seed, which presents a certain analogy with resurrection, 1 Cor. 15:36; (*e*) of the 'changing,' or 'fashioning anew,' of the bodies of the living, which corresponds with, and takes place at the same time as, the resurrection of the dead in Christ, Rom. 8:11; (*f*) of the impartation of spiritual life, and the communication of spiritual sustenance generally, John 6:63; 2 Cor. 3:6; Gal. 3:21." ¶ * See QUICKEN, and cp. *sunzōopoieō*, to quicken together with, Eph. 2:5 and Col. 2:13. ¶

NT: B.341d; CB.1273c; K.290.
OT: ḥāyāh: S.2421; HR.601c.1; H.644; BD.310d.
GEN. REF.: IS.3:129; NB.735; Z.3:927.

Notes: (1) For the verb *diagō*, to lead a life, see LIVE, No. 7.

(2) For *politeuō*, in Phil. 1:27, R.V., "let your manner of life be," see LIVE, No. 8.

LIFT

1. *egeirō* [ἐγείρω, 1453], to awaken, raise up, is used in Matt. 12:11, of lifting a sheep out of a pit. In the following the R.V. has "raised" for A.V., "lifted"; Mark 1:31; 9:27; Acts 3:7. See ARISE, AWAKE, RAISE.

NT: B.214c; CB.1242c; K.195.
OT: qûm: S.6965; HR.364a; H.1999; BD.877c.
'ûr: S.5782; HR.364a.8d; H.1587; BD.734d.
GEN. REF.: IS.3:134; NB.–; Z.–.

2. *airō* [αἴρω, 142], signifies (*a*) to raise, take up, lift, draw up, (*b*) to bear, carry, (*c*) to take or carry away. It is used of lifting up the voice, Luke 17:13; Acts 4:24; eyes, John 11:41; hand, Rev. 10:5. See AWAY, BEAR, CARRY, DOUBT, A, No. 6, LOOSE, PUT, No. 17, REMOVE, TAKE.

NT: B.24b; CB.1234a; K.28.
OT: nāsā': S.5375; HR.34c.14a; H.1421; BD.669d.
GEN. REF.: IS.3:134; NB.–; Z.–.

3. *epairō* [ἐπαίρω, 1869], to lift up, raise (*epi*, upon, and No. 2), is used of lifting up the eyes, Matt. 17:8; Luke 6:20; 16:23; 18:13; John 4:35; 6:5; 17:1; the head, Luke 21:28; the hands, Luke 24:50; 1 Tim. 2:8; the voice, Luke 11:27; Acts 2:14; 14:11; 22:22; a foresail, Acts 27:40 ("hoisting," R.V.); metaphorically, of the heel, John 13:18, as of one lifting up the foot before kicking; the expression indicates contempt and violence; in the Passive Voice, Acts 1:9, of Christ's Ascension, "was taken up"; 2 Cor. 10:5, "is exalted" (with pride); 11:20, "exalteth himself." See EXALT, HOIST, TAKE. ¶

NT: B.281d; CB.–; K.28.
OT: nāsā': S.5375; HR.505a.14a-d; H.1421; BD.669d.
rûm: S.7311; HR.505a.20; H.2133; BD.926c.
GEN. REF.: IS.3:134; NB.–; Z.–.

4. *hupsoō* [ὑψόω, 5312], to lift or raise up (akin to *hupsos*, height), is rendered by the verb to lift up in John 3:14, of the brazen serpent; of Christ in crucifixion (*id.*), and 8:28; 12:32, 34; metaphorically, to exalt, lift up, e.g., Jas. 4:10, A.V., "shall lift . . . up," R.V., "shall exalt." See EXALT.

NT: B.850d; CB.1252b; K.1241.
OT: rûm: S.7311; HR.1422a.13a-d; H.2133; BD.926c.
gābah: S.1361; HR.1422a,3a,b; H.305; BD.146d.
GEN. REF.: IS.3:134; NB.–; Z.–.

5. *anistēmi* [ἀνίστημι, 450], to raise up (*ana*, up, *histēmi*, to cause to stand), is translated "lifted (her) up," in Acts 9:41, A.V.; R.V., "raised (her) up." See ARISE, RAISE.

NT: B.70a; CB.1235c; K.60.
OT: qûm: S.6965; HR.102c,8a,c; H.1999; BD.877c.
GEN. REF.: IS.3:134; NB.–; Z.–.

6. *anorthoō* [ἀνορθόω, 461], to set upright (*ana*, up, *orthos*, straight), is used of lifting up "hands that hang down," Heb. 12:12; of setting up a building, restoring ruins, Acts 15:16 (cp., e.g., 2 Sam. 7:13, 16; 1 Chron. 17:12; Jer. 10:12; often so used in the papyri); of the healing of the woman with a spirit of infirmity, Luke 13:13, "was made straight" (for ver. 11, see No. 7). See SET, STRAIGHT. ¶

NT: B.72c; CB.–; K.–.
OT: kûn: S.3559; HR.108b.2; H.964; BD.465c.
GEN. REF.: –.

7. *anakuptō* [ἀνακύπτω, 352], to lift oneself up, is used (*a*) of the body, Luke 13:11; John 8:7, 10; (*b*) metaphorically, of the mind, to look up, to be elated, Luke 21:28 (followed by No. 3, "lift up"); an instance is found in the papyri in which a person speaks of the impossibility of ever looking up again in a certain place, for very shame (Moulton and Milligan, Vocab.). ¶ In the Sept., Job 10:15. ¶

NT: B.56c; CB.–; K.–.
OT: nāsā': S.5375; HR.78c.1; H.1421; BD.670b.
GEN. REF.: IS.3:134; NB.–; Z.–.

LIGHT, Noun and Verb (bring to, give), LIGHTEN

A. Nouns.

1. *phōs* [φῶς, 5457], akin to *phaō*, to give light (from roots *pha*— and *phan*—, expressing light as seen by the eye, and, metaphorically, as reaching the mind, whence *phainō*, to make to appear, *phaneros*, evident, etc.); cp. Eng., phosphorus (lit., light-bearing). "Primarily light is a luminous emanation, probably of force, from certain bodies, which enables the eye to discern form and colour. Light requires an organ adapted for its reception (Matt. 6:22). Where the eye is absent, or where it has become impaired from any cause, light is useless. Man, naturally, is incapable of receiving spiritual light inasmuch as he lacks the capacity for

*From Notes on Galatians by Hogg and Vine, pp. 154, 155.

spiritual things, 1 Cor. 2:14. Hence believers are called 'sons of light,' Luke 16:8, not merely because they have received a revelation from God, but because in the New Birth they have received the spiritual capacity for it.

"Apart from natural phenomena, light is used in Scripture of (*a*) the glory of God's dwelling-place, 1 Tim. 6:16; (*b*) the nature of God, 1 John 1:5; (*c*) the impartiality of God, Jas. 1:17; (*d*) the favour of God, Ps. 4:6; of the King, Prov. 16:15; of an influential man, Job 29:24; (*e*) God, as the illuminator of His people, Isa. 60:19, 20; (*f*) the Lord Jesus as the illuminator of men, John 1:4, 5, 9; 3:19; 8:12; 9:5; 12:35, 36, 46; Acts 13:47; (*g*) the illuminating power of the Scriptures, Ps. 119:105; and of the judgments and commandments of God, Isa. 51:4; Prov. 6:23, cp. Ps. 43:3; (*h*) the guidance of God, Job 29:3; Ps. 112:4; Isa. 58:10; and, ironically, of the guidance of man, Rom. 2:19; (*i*) salvation, 1 Pet. 2:9; (*j*) righteousness, Rom. 13:12; 2 Cor. 11:14, 15; 1 John 2:9, 10; (*k*) witness for God, Matt. 5:14, 16; John 5:35; (*l*) prosperity and general well-being, Esth. 8:16; Job 18:18; Isa. 58:8-10."*

NT: B.871c; CB.1264b; K.1293.
OT: 'ôr: S.216; HR.1450b.1a; H.52a; BD.21c.
GEN. REF.: IS.3:134; NB.739; Z.3:932.

2. *phōstēr* [φωστήρ, 5458], denotes a luminary, light, or light-giver; it is used figuratively of believers, as shining in the spiritual darkness of the world, Phil. 2:15; in Rev. 21:11 it is used of Christ as the Light reflected in and shining through the Heavenly City (cp. ver. 23). ¶ In the Sept., Gen. 1:14, 16. ¶

NT: B.872c; CB.1264b; K.1293.
OT: zōhar: S.2096; HR.1451b.1; H.531a; BD.264a.
GEN. REF.: IS.3:134; NB.739; Z.3:932.

3. *phōtismos* [φωτισμός, 5436], an illumination, light, is used metaphorically in 2 Cor. 4:4, of the light of the Gospel, and in ver. 6, of the knowledge of the glory of God. ¶ In the Sept., Job 3:9; Psa. 27:1; 44:3; 78:14; 90:8; 139:11. ¶

NT: B.873c; CB.1264b; K.1293.
OT: 'ôr: S.216; HR.1451c.1a; H.52a; BD.21c.
GEN. REF.: IS.3:134; NB.739; Z.3:932.

4. *phengos* [φέγγος, 5338], brightness, lustre, is used of the light of the moon, Matt. 24:29; Mark 13:24; of a lamp, Luke 11:33 (some mss. have *phōs*, here). ¶

NT: B.854c; CB.1264a; K.—.
OT: nōgah: S.5051; HR.1426a.3; H.1290a; BD.618b.
GEN. REF.: IS.3:134; NB.739; Z.3:932.

5. *luchnos* [λύχνος, —], a hand-lamp: see LAMP.

6. *lampas* [λαμπάς, —], a torch: see LAMP.

B. Verbs.

1. *phōtizō* [φωτίζω, 5461], used (*a*) intransitively, signifies to shine, give light, Rev. 22:5; (*b*) transitively, (1) to illumine, to light, enlighten, to be lightened, Luke 11:36; Rev. 21:23; in the Passive Voice, Rev. 18:1; metaphorically, of spiritual enlightenment, John 1:9; Eph. 1:18; 3:9, "to make . . . see"; Heb. 6:4; 10:32, "ye were enlightened," R.V. (A.V., ". . . illuminated"); (2) to bring to light, 1 Cor. 4:5 (of God's act in the future); 2 Tim. 1:10 (of God's act in the past). See ENLIGHTEN, ILLUMINATE. ¶

NT: B.872d; CB.1264b; K.1293.
OT: 'ôr: S.215; HR.1451c.1a; H.52; BD.21a.
GEN. REF.: IS.3:134; NB.739; Z.3:932.

2. *epiphauskō* [ἐπιφαύσκω, 2017], or possibly *epiphauō*, to shine forth, is rendered "shall give . . . light," in Eph. 5:14, A.V. (R.V., "shall shine upon"), of the glory of Christ, illumining the believer who fulfils the conditions, so that being guided by His light he reflects His character. See SHINE. ¶ Cp. *epiphōskō*, to dawn (really a variant form of *epiphauskō*).

NT: B.304c; CB.—; K.1293.
OT: hālal: S.1984; HR.538a.2; H.499,500; BD.237c.
GEN. REF.: IS.3:134; NB.739; Z.3:932.

3. *lampō* [λάμπω, 2989], to give the light of a torch, is rendered "giveth light" in Matt. 5:15, A.V. (R.V., "shineth"). See SHINE.

NT: B.466a; CB.1256c; K.497.
OT: nāgah: S.5050; HR.853a.2a; H.1290; BD.618b.
nōgah: S.5051; HR.853a.2b; H.1290a; BD.618b.
GEN. REF.: IS.3:134; NB.739; Z.3:932.

4. *epiphainō* [ἐπιφαίνω, 2014], transitively, to show forth (*epi*, upon, *phainō*, to cause to shine), is used intransitively and metaphorically in Luke 1:79, and rendered "to give light," A.V. (R.V., "to shine upon"). See APPEAR, SHINE.

NT: B.304a; CB.1246a; K.1244.
OT: 'ôr: S.215; HR.537c.1; H.52; BD.21a.
GEN. REF.: IS.3:134; NB.739; Z.3:932.

5. *haptō* [ἅπτω, —], to kindle a fire and so give light: see KINDLE, No. 1, *Note*.

6. *kaiō* [καίω, —], to burn, is translated "do (men) light" in Matt. 5:15. See BURN.

7. *astraptō* [ἀστράπτω, 797], to flash forth, lighten as lightning (akin to *astrapē*, lightning), occurs in Luke 17:24; 24:4 (A.V. "shining"; R.V., "dazzling"). See DAZZLING.

NT: B.118b; CB.—; K.—.
OT: bāraq: S.1299; HR.173c.1; H.287; BD.140b.
GEN. REF.: IS.3:136; NB.739; Z.3:934.

Note: In Luke 2:32, A.V., the noun *apokalupsis*, an unveiling, revelation, preceded by *eis*, unto, with a view to, is rendered "to lighten" (R.V., "for revelation"; marg., "(the) unveiling"). See REVELATION.

* From Notes on Thessalonians by Hogg and Vine, pp. 159, 160.

C. Adjective.

phōteinos [φωτεινός, 5460], from *phōs* (A, No. 1), bright, is rendered "full of light" in Matt. 6:22; Luke 11:34, 36 (twice), figuratively, of the single-mindedness of the eye, which acts as the lamp of the body; in Matt. 17:5, "bright," of a cloud. See BRIGHT. ¶

NT: B.872d; CB.1264b; K.1293.
OT: —.
GEN. REF.: IS.3:134; NB.739; Z.3:932.

LIGHT (to light upon)

Notes: (1) In Matt. 3:16, A.V., *erchomai*, to come, is translated "lighting"; R.V., "coming."

(2) In Rev. 7:16, A.V., *piptō*, to fall, is translated "shall . . . light" (R.V., "shall . . . strike"). See STRIKE.

(3) For Acts 27:41, R.V., see FALL, B. No. 8.

LIGHT, LIGHTEN (as to weight)

A. Adjective.

elaphros [ἐλαφρός, 1645], light in weight, easy to bear, is used of the burden imparted by Christ, Matt. 11:30; of affliction, 2 Cor. 4:17. ¶

NT: B.248c; CB.—; K.—.
OT: qālal: S.7043; HR.449a.2b,c; H.2028; BD.886a.
qal: S.7031; HR.449a.2a; H.2028a; BD.886d.
GEN. REF.: —.

B. Verb.

kouphizō [κουφίζω, 2893], to make light, lighten (the adjective *kouphos*, not in N.T., denotes slight, light, empty), is used of lightening the ship, in Acts 27:38.

NT: B.447b; CB.—; K.—.
OT: qālal: S.7043; HR.781a.2; H.2028; BD.886a.
GEN. REF.: —.

Note: For the phrase in ver. 18, A.V., "they lightened the ship," see FREIGHT.

C. Noun.

elaphria [ἐλαφρία, —], lightness, 2 Cor. 1:17, A.V.: see FICKLENESS.

LIGHT OF (make), LIGHTLY

ameleō [ἀμελέω, 272], denotes (*a*) to be careless, not to care (*a*, negative, and *melei*, an impersonal verb, signifying it is a care: see CARE, Matt. 22:5, "they made light of (it)," lit., 'making light of (it),' aorist participle, indicating the definiteness of their decision. See NEGLECT, NEGLIGENT, REGARD.

NT: B.44d; CB.—; K.—.
OT: —.
GEN. REF.: —.

Note: In Mark 9:39, A.V., the adverb *tachu*, quickly, is translated "lightly" (R.V., "quickly"). See QUICKLY.

LIGHTNING

astrapē [ἀστραπή, 796], denotes (*a*) lightning (akin to LIGHT, B, No. 7), Matt. 24:27; 28:3; Luke 10:18; 17:24; in the plural, Rev. 4:5; 8:5; 11:19; 16:18; (*b*) "bright shining," or shining brightness, Luke 11:36. See SHINING. ¶

NT: B.118b; CB.1238a; K.86.
OT: bārāq: S.1300; HR.173c.1; H.287a; BD.140c.
GEN. REF.: IS.3:136; NB.739; Z.3:934.

LIKE, LIKE (as to, unto), (be) LIKE, (make) LIKE, LIKE (things), LIKEN

A. Adjectives.

1. *homoios* [ὅμοιος, 3664], like, resembling, such as, the same as, is used (*a*) of appearance or form, John 9:9; Rev. 1:13, 15; 2:18; 4:3 (twice), 6, 7; 9:7 (twice), 10, 19; 11:1; 13:2, 11; 14:14; (*b*) of ability, condition, nature, Matt. 22:39; Acts 17:29; Gal. 5:21, "such like," lit., 'and the (things) similar to these'; 1 John 3:2; Rev. 13:4; 18:18; 21:11, 18; (*c*) of comparison in parables, Matt. 13:31, 33, 44, 45, 47; 20:1; Luke 13:18, 19, 21; (*d*) of action, thought, etc., Matt. 11:16; 13:52; Luke 6:47, 48, 49; 7:31, 32; 12:36; John 8:55; Jude 7. ¶

NT: B.566c; CB.1251a; K.684.
OT: —.
GEN. REF.: —.

2. *isos* [ἴσος, 2470], equal (the same in size, quality, etc.), is translated "like," of the gift of the Spirit, Acts 11:17. See EQUAL, MUCH (AS).

NT: B.381a; CB.1253a; K.370.
OT: —.
GEN. REF.: —.

3. *paromoios* [παρόμοιος, 3946], much like (*para*, beside, and No. 1), is used in Mark 7:13, in the neuter plural, "(many such) like things." ¶

NT: B.629b; CB.1262c; K.—.
OT: —.
GEN. REF.: —.

B. Verbs.

1. *homoioō* [ὁμοιόω, 3666], to make like (akin to A, No. 1), is used (*a*) especially in the parables, with the significance of comparing, likening, or, in the Passive Voice, 'being likened,' Matt. 7:24, 26; 11:16; 13:24; 18:23; 22:2 (R.V., "likened"); 25:1; Mark 4:30; Luke 7:31; 13:18, R.V., "liken" (A.V., "resemble"); ver. 20; in several of these instances the point of resemblance is not a specific detail, but the whole circumstances of the parable; (*b*) of making like, or, in the Passive Voice, of being made or becoming like, Matt. 6:8; Acts 14:11, "in the likeness of (men)," lit., 'being made like' (aorist participle, Passive); Rom. 9:29; Heb. 2:17, of Christ in being "made like" unto His brethren,

i.e., in partaking of human nature, apart from sin (cp. ver. 14). ¶
NT: B.567b; CB.1251a; K.684.
OT: dāmāh: S.1819; HR.993a.2; H.437; BD.197d.
GEN. REF.: IS.3:137; NB.–; Z.–.

2. *eoika* [ἔοικα, 1503], a perfect tense with a present meaning (from an obsolete present, *eikō*), denotes to be like, to resemble, Jas. 1:6, 23. ¶ In the Sept., Job 6:3, 25. ¶
NT: B.280a; CB.1245b; K.–.
OT: –.
GEN. REF.: –.

3. *paromoiazō* [παρομοιάζω, 3945], to be like (from *para*, by, and a verbal form from *homoios*, A, No. 1), is used in Matt. 23:27 (perhaps with intensive force), in the Lord's comparison of the scribes and Pharisees to whitened sepulchres. ¶
NT: B.629b; CB.1262c; K.684.
OT: –.
GEN. REF.: –.

4. *aphomoioō* [ἀφομοιόω, 871], to make like (*apo*, from, and No. 1), is used in Heb. 7:3, of Melchizedek as "made like" the Son of God, i.e., in the facts related and withheld in the Genesis record. ¶
NT: B.127b; CB.1236c; K.684.
OT: –.
GEN. REF.: –.

Note: For the A.V. of Rom. 1:23, "made like," see LIKENESS, No. 1.

C. Adverbs.

1. *hōs* [ὡς, 5613], used as a relative adverb of manner, means as, like as, etc. and is translated "like," e.g., in Matt. 6:29; Mark 4:31; Luke 12:27; in Acts 3:22 and 7:37 (see R.V., marg.); in 8:32 (2nd part), R.V., "as" (A.V., "like"); Rev. 2:18, R.V. (the rendering should have been "as" here); 18:21, R.V., "as it were" (A.V., "like"); 21:11, 2nd part (ditto).
NT: B.897a; CB.1251b; K.–.
OT: –.
GEN. REF.: –.

2. *hōsper* [ὥσπερ, 5618], just as, is rendered "like as" in Rom. 6:4.
NT: B.899c; CB.1251b; K.–.
OT: –.
GEN. REF.: –.

Notes: (1) In Heb. 4:15, the phrase *kath' homoiotēta* (*kata*, according to, *homoiotēs*, a likeness, i.e., 'after the similitude'), is rendered "like as," in the statement that Christ has been tempted in all points "like as we are, yet without sin"; this may mean either 'according to the likeness of our temptations,' or 'in accordance with His likeness to us.'

(2) In the following the most authentic mss. have *hōs*, as, for *hōsei*, like, in the A.V.; Mark 1:10; Luke 3:22; John 1:32; Rev. 1:14.

(3) In John 7:46, A.V., the combination of the adverb *houtōs*, thus, with *hōs*, as, is translated "like," R.V. "(never man) so (spake)."

(4) For "in like manner" see MANNER.

(5) In 1 Thess. 2:14, A.V., *ta auta*, the same (things), is translated "like (things)," R.V., "the same (things)."

For (DID NOT) LIKE, Rom. 1:28, A.V., see REFUSE, No. 3

LIKEMINDED

1. *isopsuchos* [ἰσόψυχος, 2473], lit., of equal soul (*isos*, equal, *psuchē*, the soul), is rendered "like-minded" in Phil. 2:20. ¶ In the Sept., Psa. 55:13. ¶
NT: B.381b; CB.1253a; K.–.
OT: –.
GEN. REF.: –.

2. *homophrōn* [ὁμόφρων, 3675], (*homos*, the same, *phrēn*, the mind), occurs in 1 Pet. 3:8, R.V., "likeminded" (A.V., "of one mind").
NT: B.569c; CB.–; K.–.
OT: –.
GEN. REF.: –.

Note: In Rom. 15:5; Phil. 2:2, *phroneō to auto*, to think the same thing, is translated, A.V., "be likeminded" (R.V., "be of the same mind").

LIKENESS, LIKENESS OF (in the)

1. *homoiōma* [ὁμοίωμα, 3667], denotes that which is made like something, a resemblance, (*a*) in the concrete sense, Rev. 9:7, "shapes" (R.V., marg., "likenesses"); (*b*) in the abstract sense, Rom. 1:23, R.V., "(for) the likeness (of an image)"; the A.V. translates it as a verb, "(into an image) made like to"; the association here of the two words *homoiōma* and *eikōn* (see IMAGE) serves to enhance the contrast between the idol and "the glory of the incorruptible God," and is expressive of contempt; in 5:14, "(the) likeness of Adam's transgression" (A.V., "similitude"); in 6:5, "(the) likeness (of His death); in 8:3, "(the) likeness (of sinful flesh); in Phil. 2:7, "the likeness of men." "The expression 'likeness of men' does not of itself imply, still less does it exclude or diminish, the reality of the nature which Christ assumed. That . . . is declared in the words 'form of a servant.' 'Paul justly says *in the likeness of men*, because, in fact, Christ, although certainly perfect Man (Rom. 5:15; 1 Cor. 15:21; 1 Tim. 2:5), was, by reason of the Divine nature present in Him, not simply and merely man . . . but the Incarnate Son of God' " (Gifford, quoting Meyer). See SHAPE. ¶ Ch. LIKE, B, (*b*).
NT: B.567c; CB.1251a; K.684.
OT: dᵉmût: S.1823; HR.993a.1a; H.437a; BD.198b.
tabᵉnît: S.8403; HR.993a.6; H.255d; BD.125d.
tᵉmûnāh: S.8544; HR.993a.7; H.1191b; BD.568b.
GEN. REF.: IS.3:137; NB.–; Z.–.

2. *homoiōsis* [ὁμοίωσις, 3669], a making like, is translated "likeness" in Jas. 3:9, R.V. (A.V., "similitude"). ¶

NT: B.568a; CB.1251a; K.684.
OT: dᵉmût: S.1823; HR.993b.1a; H.437a; BD.198b.
GEN. REF.: IS.3:137; NB.—; Z.—.

3. *homoiotēs* [ὁμοιοτής, 3665], is translated "likeness" in Heb. 7:15, R.V. (A.V., "similitude").

NT: B.567a; CB.1251a; K.684.
OT: mîn: S.4327; HR.993a.1; H.1191a; BD.568b.
GEN. REF.: IS.3:137; NB.—; Z.—.

4. *antitupon* [ἀντίτυπον, 499], is rendered "after a true likeness," in 1 Pet. 3:21, R.V. (marg., "in the antitype"). See FIGURE, No. 2.

NT: B.76a; CB.1236a; K.1193.
OT: —.
GEN. REF.: IS.3:137; NB.—; Z.—.

LIKEWISE

1. *homoiōs* [ὁμοίως, 3668], in like manner (from the adjective *homoios*, see LIKE, A, No. 1), is rendered "likewise" in the A.V. of Matt. 22:26; 27:41, Luke 10:32; 16:25; John 5:19; Jas. 2:25; 1 Pet. 3:1, 7; Jude 8; Rev. 8:12 (in all these the R.V. has "in like manner"); in the following, A.V. and R.V. have "likewise"; Matt. 26:35; Luke 5:33; 6:31; 10:37; 17:28, 31; 22:36; John 6:11; 21:13; Rom. 1:27; 1 Pet. 5:5. ¶ See MANNER, SO.

NT: B.567d; CB.1251a; K.—.
OT: —.
GEN. REF.: —.

2. *hōsautōs* [ὡσαύτως, 5615], a strengthened form of *hōs*, as, denotes in like manner, just so, likewise; it is sometimes translated "likewise," e.g., Matt. 20:5; 21:30.

NT: B.899b; CB.—; K.—.
OT: —.
GEN. REF.: —.

3. *kai* [καί, 2532], and, even, is translated "likewise" in the A.V. and R.V. of Matt. 20:10 (last *kai* in the verse), more lit., 'even they'; elsewhere the R.V. has "also," for the A.V., "likewise," Matt. 18:35; 24:33; Luke 3:14; 17:10; 19:19; 21:31; Acts 3:24; 1 Cor. 14:9; Col. 4:16; 1 Pet. 4:1; in Matt. 21:24, the A.V. has "in like wise" (R.V., "likewise").

NT: B.391d; CB.1253a; K.—.
OT: —.
GEN. REF.: —.

4. *paraplēsiōs* [παραπλησίως, 3898], from *para*, beside, and the adjective *plēsios*, near (akin to the adverb *pelas*, near, hard by), is used in Heb. 2:14, A.V., "likewise" (R.V., "in like manner"), expressing the true humanity of Christ in partaking of flesh and blood. ¶

NT: B.621c; CB.—; K.—.
OT: —.
GEN. REF.: —.

Notes: (1) In Matt. 17:12 and Rom. 6:11, A.V., the adverb *houtōs*, thus, so, is translated "likewise" (R.V., "so"); in Luke 15:7 and 10, A.V., "likewise," R.V., "even so"; in Luke 14:33, A.V., followed by *oun*, therefore, it is rendered "so likewise" (R.V., "so therefore").

LILY

krinon [κρίνον, 2918], occurs in Matt. 6:28 and Luke 12:27; in the former the Lord speaks of "the lilies of the field"; the lily referred to was a flower of rich colour, probably including the Gladiolus and Iris species. The former "grow among the grain, often overtopping it and illuminating the broad fields with their various shades of pinkish purple to deep violet purple and blue. . . . Anyone who has stood among the wheat fields of Galilee . . . will see at once the appropriateness of our Saviour's allusion. They all have a reedy stem, which, when dry, would make such fuel as is used in the ovens. The beautiful Irises . . . have gorgeous flowers, and would suit our Saviour's comparison even better than the above. But they are plants of pasture grounds and swamps, and seldom found in grain fields. If, however, we understand by 'lilies of the field' simply wild lilies, these would also be included in the expression. Our Saviour's comparison would then be like a 'composite photograph,' a reference to all the splendid colours and beautiful shapes of the numerous wild plants comprehended under the name 'lily'" (G. E. Post, in Hastings' Bib. Dic.).

NT: B.451a; CB.—; K.—.
OT: shôshannāh: S.7799; HR.788c.3c; H.2356; BD.1004b.
peraḥ: S.6525; HR.788c.2; H.1813a; BD.827b.
GEN. REF.: IS.3:137; NB.1004; Z.3:935.

For **LIMIT**, in Heb. 4:7, A.V., see **DEFINE**

For **LINE** see **PROVINCE**, No. 2

For **LINEAGE** in Luke 2:4, A.V., see **FAMILY**

LINEN, LINEN CLOTH, FINE LINEN

1. *sindōn* [σινδών, 4616], was a fine linen cloth, an article of domestic manufacture (Prov. 31:24) used (*a*) as a garment or wrap, the "linen cloth" of Mark 14:51, 52; (*b*) as shrouds or winding sheets, Matt. 27:59; Mark 15:46, R.V., "linen cloth," for A.V., "linen"; Luke 23:53 (ditto). ¶ In the Sept., Judg. 14:12, "(thirty) sheets"; Prov. 31:24 (see above). ¶ The Mishna (the Great Collection of legal decisions by the

ancient Rabbis) records that the material was sometimes used for curtains.

NT: B.751c; CB.1269a; K.–.
OT: sādîn: S.5466; HR.1267a.1; H.1466; BD.690b.
GEN. REF.: IS.3:139; NB.740; Z.3:937.

2. *linon* [λίνον, 3043], denotes (*a*) flax, Matt. 12:20; (*b*) linen, in Rev. 15:6, A.V.; the best texts have *lithos*, "stone," R.V. See FLAX.

NT: B.475b; CB.–; K.–.
OT: pēshet: S.6593; HR.879b.2a; H.1849; BD.833d.
GEN. REF.: IS.3:139; NB.740; Z.3:937.

3. *othonion* [ὀθόνιον, 3608], a piece of fine linen, is used in the plural, of the strips of cloth with which the body of the Lord was bound, after being wrapped in the *sindōn*, Luke 24:12; John 19:40; 20:5, 6, 7. ¶ In the Sept., Judg. 14:13, "changes of raiment"; Hos. 2:5, 9. ¶ The word is a diminutive of *othonē*, a sheet (see SHEET).

NT: B.555c; CB.–; K.–.
OT: pēshet: S.6593; HR.967c.2; H.1849; BD.833d.
sādîn: S.5466; HR.967c.1; H.1466; BD.690b.
GEN. REF.: IS.3:139; NB.740; Z.3:937.

4. *bussos* [βύσσος, 1040], fine linen, made from a special species of flax, a word of Aramaean origin, used especially for the Syrian *byssus* (Arab. *bûs* is still used for native linen). Cp. Heb. *bûs*, in all O.T. passages quoted here, except Ezek. 27:7; Syriac *bûsâ* in Luke 16:19. It is the material mentioned in 1 Chron. 4:21, wrought by the house of Ashbea; 15:27, *bussinos*, No. 5 (David's robe); 2 Chron. 3:14, *bussos* (the veil of the Temple); 5:12, *bussinos* (the clothing of the Levite singers); Esth. 1:6 (the cords of the hangings in the king's garden); 8:15 (Mordecai's dress); Ezek. 27:7 (*bussos*, in Syrian trade with Tyre). In the N.T., Luke 16:19, the clothing of the "rich man." ¶

NT: B.148d; CB.–; K.–.
OT: shēsh: S.8336; HR.232b.4; H.2473,2379a; BD.1058c.
GEN. REF.: IS.3:139; NB.740; Z.3:937.

5. *bussinos* [βύσσινος, 1039], an adjective formed from No. 4, denoting made of fine linen. This is used of the clothing of the mystic Babylon, Rev. 18:12, 16, and of the suitable attire of the Lamb's wife, 19:8, 14, figuratively describing "the righteous acts of the saints." The presumption of Babylon is conspicuous in that she arrays herself in that which alone befits the Bride of Christ. ¶ For examples of the use in the Sept. see No. 4.

NT: B.148d; CB.–; K.–.
OT: shēsh: S.8336; HR.232b.4a; H.2473,2379a; BD.1058c.
bûṣ: S.948; HR.232b.2; H.219; BD.101b.
GEN. REF.: IS.3:139; NB.740; Z.3:937.

LINGER

argeō [ἀργέω, 691], to be idle, to linger (akin to *argos*, idle: see *katargeō*, under ABOLISH), is used negatively regarding the judgment of the persons mentioned in 2 Pet. 2:3. ¶ In the Sept., Ezra 4:24; Eccles. 12:3. ¶

NT: B.104c; CB.–; K.76.
OT: bᵉṭēl: S.989; HR.153a1.a; H.2625; BD.1084b.
bāṭal: S.988; HR.153a.1b; H.235; BD.105d.
GEN. REF.: –.

LION

leōn [λέων, 3023], occurs in 2 Tim. 4:17, probably figurative of the imminent peril of death, the figure being represented by the whole phrase, not by the word "lion" alone; some suppose the reference to be to the lions of the amphitheatre; the Greek commentators regarded the lion as Nero; others understand it to be Satan. The language not improbably recalls that of Psa. 22:21 and Dan. 6:20. The word is used metaphorically, too, in Rev. 5:5, where Christ is called "the Lion of the tribe of Judah." Elsewhere it has the literal meaning, Heb. 11:33; 1 Pet. 5:8; Rev. 4:7; 9:8, 17; 10:3; 13:2. ¶ Taking the O.T. and N.T. occurrences the allusions are to the three great features of the lion, (1) its majesty and strength, indicative of royalty, e.g., Prov. 30:30, (2) its courage, e.g., Prov. 28:1, (3) its cruelty, e.g., Psa. 22:13.

NT: B.472d; CB.1256c; K.531.
OT: ʾᵃrî: S.738; HR.874c.1a; H.158a; BD.71c.
ʾaryēh: S.738; HR.874c.1b; H.158a; BD.71d.
GEN. REF.: IS.3:141; NB.741; Z.3:939.

LIP

cheilos [χεῖλος, 5491], is used (*a*) of the organ of speech, Matt. 15:8 and Mark 7:6, where honouring with the lips, besides meaning empty words, may have reference to a Jewish custom of putting to the mouth the tassel of the tallith (the woollen scarf wound round the head and neck during prayer), as a sign of acceptance of the Law from the heart; Rom. 3:13; 1 Cor. 14:21 (from Isa. 28:11, 12, speaking of the Assyrian foe as God's message to disobedient Israel); Heb. 13:15; 1 Pet. 3:10; (*b*) metaphorically, of the brink or edge of things, as of the sea shore, Heb. 11:12, lit., 'the shore (of the sea).' ¶

NT: B.879c; CB.1239c; K.–.
OT: sāphāh: S.8193; HR.1456a.5; H.2278a; BD.973c.
GEN. REF.: IS.3:142; NB.742; Z.3:941.

LIST (Verb)

1. *thelō* [θέλω, 2309], to will, wish, is translated by the verb to list in Matt. 17:12; Mark 9:13; John 3:8. See DESIRE, B, No. 6.

NT: B.354d; CB.1271c; K.318.
OT: –.
GEN. REF.: IS.3:143; NB.–; Z.–.

2. *boulomai* [βούλομαι, 1014], to will, be minded, is translated "listeth" in Jas. 3:4 (R.V. "willeth"). See DESIRE, B, No. 7.
NT: B.146a; CB.1239b; K.108.
OT: —.
GEN. REF.: IS.3:143; NB.—; Z.—.

LITTLE

A. Adjectives.

1. *mikros* [μικρός, 3398], little, small (the opposite of *megas*, great), is used (*a*) of persons, with regard to (1) station, or age, in the singular, Mark 15:40, of James "the less" (R.V. marg., "little"), possibly referring to age; Luke 19:3; in the plural, little ones, Matt. 18:6, 10, 14; Mark 9:42; (2) rank or influence, e.g., Matt. 10:42 (see context); Acts 8:10; 26:22, "small," as in Rev. 11:18; 13:16; 19:5, 18; 20:12; (*b*) of things, with regard to (1) size, e.g., Jas. 3:5 (some mss. have No. 2 here); (2) quantity, Luke 12:32; 1 Cor. 5:6; Gal. 5:9; Rev. 3:8; (3) time, John 7:33; 12:35; Rev. 6:11; 20:3. See B, No. 1. See LEAST, SMALL.
NT: B.521a; CB.1258c; K.593.
OT: qāṭān: S.6996; HR.926c.5; H.2009a,b; BD.881d.
mᵉʻaṭ: S.4592; HR.926c.3; H.1228a; BD.589d.
GEN. REF.: —.

2. *oligos* [ὀλίγος, 3641], little, few (the opposite of *polus*, much), is translated "short" in Rev. 12:12; in the neut. sing., e.g., 2 Cor. 8:15. For Jas. 3:5, see No. 1. See FEW, SHORT, SMALL.
NT: B.563c; CB.1260c; K.682.
OT: mᵉʻaṭ: S.4592; HR.986b.4; H.1228a; BD.589d.
GEN. REF.: —.

3. *brachus* [βραχύς, 1024], short, is used to some extent adverbially of (*a*) time, with the preposition *meta*, after, Luke 22:58, "(after) a little while"; in Acts 5:34, without a preposition, R.V., "a little while" (A.V., "a little space"); in Heb. 2:7, 9, "a little" (A.V. marg. in ver. 7, and R.V. marg., in both, "a little while"), where the writer transfers to time what the Sept. in Psa. 8:5 says of rank; (*b*) of quantity, John 6:7; in Heb. 13:22, preceded by the preposition *dia*, by means of, and with *logōn*, words (genitive plural) understood, "(in) few words"; (*c*) of distance, Acts 27:28, R.V., "a little space" (A.V., "a little further"). See FEW, FURTHER, SPACE. ¶
NT: B.147b; CB.1239b; K.—.
OT: mᵉʻaṭ: S.4592; HR.230c.1; H.1228a; BD.589d.
GEN. REF.: —.

4. *elachistos* [ἐλάχιστος, 1646], which serves as the superlative of No. 1, is translated "a very little" in Luke 19:17. See LEAST.
NT: B.248d; CB.1244a; K.593.
OT: māʻaṭ: S.4591; HR.448b.2; H.1228; BD.589b.
GEN. REF.: —.

Note: For *mikroteros*, "but little," see LEAST, No. 4.

B. Adverbs.

1. *mikron* [μικρόν, 3397], the neuter of A, No. 1, is used adverbially (*a*) of distance, Matt. 26:39; Mark 14:35; (*b*) of quantity, 2 Cor. 11:1, 16; (*c*) of time, Matt. 26:73, "a while"; Mark 14:70; John 13:33, "a little while"; 14:19; 16:16-9; Heb. 10:37, with the repeated *hoson*, "how very," lit., 'a little while, how little, how little!' See WHILE. ¶
NT: B.521a; CB.1258c; K.593.
OT: mᵉʻaṭ: S.4592; HR.926c.3; H.1228a; BD.589d.
qāṭān: S.6996; HR.926c.5; H.2009a,b; BD.881d.
GEN. REF.: —.

2. *oligon* [ὀλίγον, 3641], the neuter of A, No. 2, is used adverbially of (*a*) time, Mark 6:31, "a while"; 1 Pet. 1:6, R.V., "a little while (A.V., "a season"); 5:10, R.V., "a little while" (A.V., "a while"); Rev. 17:10, R.V., "a little while" (A.V., "a short space"); (*b*) space, Mark 1:19; Luke 5:3; (*c*) extent, with the preposition *pros*, for, in 1 Tim. 4:8, R.V., "(for) a little" (A.V., and R.V. marg., "little"), where, while the phrase might refer to duration (as A.V. marg.), yet the antithesis "for all things" clearly indicates extent, i.e., 'physical training is profitable towards few objects in life.' See BRIEFLY, FEW, SEASON, C, *Note*.
NT: B.563c; CB.1260c; K.682.
OT: mᵉʻaṭ: S.4592; HR.986b.4; H.1228a; BD.589d.
GEN. REF.: —.

3. *metriōs* [μετρίως, 3357], moderately, occurs in Acts 20:12, "a little." ¶
NT: B.515a; CB.—; K.—.
OT: —.
GEN. REF.: —.

For (NO) **LITTLE** see **COMMON**, B, *Note* (3)

LIVE

1. *zaō* [ζάω, 2198], to live, be alive, is used in the N.T. of "(*a*) God, Matt. 16:16; John 6:57; Rom. 14:11; (*b*) the Son in Incarnation, John 6:57; (*c*) the Son in Resurrection, John 14:19; Acts 1:3; Rom. 6:10; 2 Cor. 13:4; Heb. 7:8; (*d*) spiritual life, John 6:57; Rom. 1:17; 8:13*b*; Gal. 2:19, 20; Heb. 12:9; (*e*) the present state of departed saints, Luke 20:38; 1 Pet. 4:6; (*f*) the hope of resurrection, 1 Pet. 1:3; (*g*) the resurrection of believers, 1 Thess. 5:10; John 5:25; Rev. 20:4, and of unbelievers, ver. 5, cp. ver. 13; (*h*) the way of access to God through the Lord Jesus Christ, Heb. 10:20; (*i*) the manifestation of Divine power in support of Divine authority, 2 Cor. 13:4*b*; cp. 12:10, and 1 Cor. 5:5; (*j*) bread, figurative of the Lord Jesus, John 6:51; (*k*) a stone, figurative of the Lord Jesus, 1 Pet. 2:4; (*l*) water, figurative of

the Holy Spirit, John 4:10; 7:38; (*m*) a sacrifice figurative of the believer, Rom. 12:1; (*n*) stones, figurative of the believer, 1 Pet. 2:5; (*o*) the oracles, *logion*, Acts 7:38, and word, *logos*, Heb. 4:12; 1 Pet. 1:23, of God; (*p*) the physical life of men, 1 Thess. 4:15; Matt. 27:63; Acts 25:24; Rom. 14:9; Phil. 1:21 (in the infinitive mood used as a noun, with the article, 'living'), 22; 1 Pet. 4:5; (*g*) the maintenance of physical life, Matt. 4:4; 1 Cor. 9:14; (*r*) the duration of physical life, Heb. 2:15; (*s*) the enjoyment of physical life, 1 Thess. 3:8; (*f*) the recovery of physical life from the power of disease, Mark 5:23; John 4:50; (*u*) the recovery of physical life from the power of death, Matt. 9:18; Acts 9:41; Rev. 20:5; (*v*) the course, conduct, and character of men, (1) good, Acts 26:5; 2 Tim. 3:12; Tit. 2:12; (2) evil, Luke 15:13; Rom. 6:2; 8:13*a*; 2 Cor. 5:15*b*; Col. 3:7; (3) undefined, Rom. 7:9; 14:7; Gal. 2:14; (*w*) restoration after alienation, Luke 15:32.

NT: B.336a; CB.1273b; K.290.
OT: ḥāyāh: S.2421; HR.594c.2; H.644; BD.310d.
ḥay: S.2416; HR.594c.3; H.644a; BD.311d.
GEN. REF.: IS.3:146; NB.—; Z.—.

Note: In 1 Thess. 5:10, to live means to experience that change, 1 Cor. 15:51, which is to be the portion of all in Christ who will be alive upon the earth at the Parousia of the Lord Jesus, cp. John 11:25, and which corresponds to the resurrection of those who had previously died in Christ, 1 Cor. 15:52-54.

"2. *sunzaō* [συνζάω, 4800], to live together with (*sun*, with, and *zaō*, to live), may be included with *zaō* in the above analysis as follows: (*g*) Rom. 6:8; 2 Tim. 2:11; (*s*), 2 Cor. 7:3. ¶

NT: B.775c; CB.—; K.1102.
OT: —.
GEN. REF.: —.

"3. *anazaō* [ἀναζάω, 326], *ana*, again, and *zaō*, denotes 'to live again,' 'to revive,' Luke 15:24; cp. (*w*) in list above, and Rom. 7:9, to manifest activity again." ¶ *

NT: B.53c; CB.1235b; K.290.
OT: —.
GEN. REF.: —.

Note: Zaō is translated "quick" (i.e., "living") in Acts 10:42; 2 Tim. 4:1; 1 Pet. 4:5; in Heb. 4:12, A.V. (R.V., "living").

4. *bioō* [βιόω, 980], to spend life, to pass one's life, is used in 1 Pet. 4:2. ¶

NT: B.142a; CB.1239a; K.290.
OT: ḥāyāh: S.2421; HR.220b.2; H.644; BD.310d.
GEN. REF.: IS.3:146; NB.—; Z.—.

5. *anastrephō* [ἀναστρέφω, 390], used metaphorically, in the Middle Voice, to conduct oneself, behave, live, is translated to live, in Heb. 13:18 ("honestly"); in 2 Pet. 2:18 ("in error"). See ABIDE, BEHAVE, etc.

NT: B.61b; CB.1235b; K.1093.
OT: shûb: S.7725; HR.82b.8a; H.2340; BD.996d.
GEN. REF.: —.

6. *zōogoneō* [ζωογονέω, 2225], denotes to preserve alive (from *zōos*, alive, and *ginomai*, to come to be, become, be made); in Luke 17:33, "shall preserve (it)," i.e., his life, R.V. marg., "save (it) alive"; cp. the parallels *sōzō*, to save, in Matt. 16:25, and *phulassō*, to keep, in John 12:25; in Acts 7:19, "live," negatively of the efforts of Pharaoh to destroy the babes in Israel; in 1 Tim. 6:13, according to the best mss. (some have *zōopoieō*, to cause to live), "quickeneth" (R.V., marg., "preserveth . . . alive," the preferable rendering). See PRESERVE, QUICKEN. ¶

NT: B.341c; CB.1273c; K.290.
OT: ḥāyāh: S.2421; HR.601b.1a,b; H.644; BD.310d.
GEN. REF.: —.

7. *diagō* [διάγω, 1236], is used of time in the sense of passing a life, 1 Tim. 2:2, "(that) we may lead (a tranquil and quiet, R.V.) life"; Tit. 3:3, "living (in malice and envy)." ¶

NT: B.182c; CB.—; K.—.
OT: 'ābar: S.5674; HR.299c.3; H.1556; BD.716d.
GEN. REF.: —.

8. *politeuō* [πολιτεύω, 4176], to be a citizen (*politēs*), to live as a citizen, is used metaphorically of conduct as in accordance with the characteristics of the heavenly community; in Acts 23:1, "I have lived"; in Phil. 1:27, "let your anner of life (A.V., conversation) be." See CITIZENSHIP, No. 4, *Note.* ¶

NT: B.686c; CB.1266a; K.906.
OT: —.
GEN. REF.: IS.3:146; NB.—; Z.—.

9. *huparchō* [ὑπάρχω, 5225], to be in existence, to be, is translated "live (delicately)" in Luke 7;25. See BEING.

NT: B.838a; CB.—; K.—.
OT: ḥāyāh: S.1961; HR.1406b.1; H.491; BD.224a.
GEN. REF.: IS.3:146; NB.—; Z.—.

Note: In 1 Cor. 9:13, A.V., *esthiō*, to eat, is translated "live of." In Tim. 5:6 the A.V. renders *spatalaō* "liveth in pleasure."

LIVE, LONG

makrochronios [μακροχρόνιος, 3118], an adjective denoting of long duration, long-lived (*makros*, long, *chronos*, time), is used in Eph. 6:3, "(that thou mayest) live long," lit., '(that thou mayest be) long-lived.' ¶ In the Sept., Ex. 20:12; Deut. 4:40; 5:16; 17:20. ¶

NT: B.488c; CB.—; K.—.
OT: 'ārak: S.748; HR.894a.1,2; H.162; BD.73c.
GEN. REF.: —.

* From Notes on Thessalonians by Hogg and Vine, pp. 173, 174.

LIVELY

Note: This is the A.V. translation of the present participle of the verb *zaō*, to live, in three passages, in each of which the R.V. has "living," Acts 7:38; 1 Pet. 1:3; 2:5.

For **LIVING** see **BEHAVIOUR**, B, No. 1, **LIFE**, No's 2, 6 and **LIVE**, No. 3, *Note*

For **LIVING CREATURES** see **BEAST**

LO!

1. *ide* [ἴδε, 2396], an aorist or point tense, marking a definite point of time, of the imperative mood of *eidon*, to see (taken as part of *horaō*, to see), is used as an interjection, addressed either to one or many persons, e.g., Matt. 25:20, 22, 25; John 1:29, 36, 47; Gal. 5:2, the only occurrence outside Matthew, Mark and John. See BEHOLD, SEE.

NT: B.369b; CB.1252c; K.—.
OT: rā'āh: S.7200; HR.669b.13a; H.2095; BD.906b.
GEN. REF.: —.

2. *idou* [ἰδού, 2400], a similar tense of No. 1, but in the Middle Voice, e.g., Matt. 1:20, 23; very frequent in the Synoptists and Acts and the Apocalypse.

NT: B.370d; CB.1252c; K.—.
OT: hinnēh: S.2009; HR.673c.7b; H.510a; BD.243d.
GEN. REF.: —.

For **LOAF** see **BREAD**

LOCUST

akris [ἀκρίς, 200], occurs in Matt. 3:4 and Mark 1:6, of the animals themselves, as forming part of the diet of John the Baptist; they are used as food; the Arabs stew them with butter, after removing the head, legs and wings. In Rev. 9:3, 7, they appear as monsters representing Satanic agencies, let loose by Divine judgments inflicted upon men for five months, the time of the natural life of the locust. For the character of the judgment see the whole passage. ¶

NT: B.33c; CB.1234b; K.—.
OT: 'arbeh: S.697; HR.50c.1; H.2103a; BD.916a.
GEN. REF.: IS.3:149; NB.743; Z.3:948.

LODGE, LODGING

A. Verbs.

1. *aulizomai* [αὐλίζομαι, 835], properly, to lodge in a courtyard (*aulē*, see COURT, No. 2), then, to lodge in the open, denotes, in the N.T., to pass the night, to lodge anywhere, Matt. 21:17; Luke 21:37, R.V., "lodged" (A.V., "abode") ¶ See the metaphorical use in the Sept. and the Heb. of Psa. 30:5, '(weeping) may come in to lodge (at even),' i.e., as a passing stranger. See ABIDE.

NT: B.121c; CB.—; K.—.
OT: lûn, lîn: S.3885; HR.178b.3; H.1096; BD.533c.
GEN. REF.: IS.2:826; NB.—; Z.3:951.

2. *kataskēnoō* [κατασκηνόω, 2681], to pitch one's tent (*kata*, down, *skēnē*, a tent), is rendered to lodge, of birds, in Matt. 13:32; Mark 4:32; Luke 13:19. In Acts 2:26, it is used of the body of the Lord in the tomb, as dwelling in hope, R.V., "shall dwell" (marg., "tabernacle"), A.V., "shall rest." See DWELL, REST. ¶ Cp. *kataskēnōsis*, a roosting place.

NT: B.418c; CB.1254b; K.1040.
OT: shākan: S.7931; HR.744b.5a,b; H.2387; BD.1014d.
GEN. REF.: —.

3. *kataluō* [καταλύω, 2647], in one of its meanings, signifies to unloose (*kata*, down, *luō*, to loose), unyoke, as of horses, etc., hence intransitively, to take up one's quarters, to lodge, Luke 9:12; 19:7, R.V., "to lodge" (A.V., "to be a guest"). See COME, Note (7) (come to nought), DESTROY, DISSOLVE, OVERTHROW, THROW. Cp. *kataluma*, a guest chamber, inn.

NT: B.414b; CB.1254a; K.543.
OT: lûn, lîn: S.3885; HR.738b.6a; H.1096; BD.533c.
shābat: S.7673; HR.738b.12; H.2323; BD.991d.
GEN. REF.: IS.2:826; NB.—; Z.3:951.

4. *xenizō* [ξενίζω, 3579], to receive as a guest (*xenos*, a guest, stranger), to entertain, lodge, is used in the Active Voice in Acts 10:23; 28:7, R.V., "entertained" (A.V., "lodged"); Heb. 13:2, "have entertained"; in the Passive Voice, Acts 10:6 (lit., 'he is entertained'), 18, 32; 21:16. Its other meaning, to think strange, is found in 1 Pet. 4:4, 12. See ENTERTAIN, STRANGE.

NT: B.547d; CB.1273b; K.661.
OT: —.
GEN. REF.: IS.2:826; NB.—; Z.—.

B. Noun.

xenia [ξενία, 3578], akin to A, No. 4, denotes (*a*) hospitality, entertainment, Philm. 22; (*b*) by metonymy, a place of entertainment, a lodging-place, Acts 28:23 (some put Philm. 22 under this section). ¶

NT: B.547b; CB.1273b; K.661.
OT: —.
GEN. REF.: IS.2:826.

For **LOFT**, Acts 20:9, see **STORY**

LOINS

osphus [ὀσφύς, 3751], is used (*a*) in the natural sense in Matt. 3:4; Mark 1:6; (*b*) as the seat of generative power, Heb. 7:5, 10; metaphorically in Acts 2:30; (*c*) metaphorically, (1) of girding the loins in readiness for active service for the Lord, Luke 12:35; (2) the same, with truth, Eph. 6:14, i.e., bracing up oneself so as to maintain perfect sincerity and reality as the counteractive in Christian character against hypocrisy and falsehood; (3) of girding the loins of the mind, 1 Pet. 1:13, R.V., "girding," suggestive of the alertness necessary for sobriety and for setting one's hope perfectly on "the grace to be brought . . . at the revelation of Jesus Christ" (the present participle, "girding," is introductory to the rest of the verse). ¶

NT: B.587d; CB.1261b; K.736.
OT: matᵉnayim: S.4975; HR.1023c.4; H.1267a; BD.608a.
GEN. REF.: IS.3:154; NB.–; Z.3:958.

LONG (Adjective and Adverb)

A. Adjectives.

1. *makros* [μακρός, 3117], is used of long prayers (Matt. 23:14, in some mss.), Mark 12:40; Luke 20:47. It denotes "far" in Luke 15:13; 19:12. See Far. ¶

NT: B.488c; CB.–; K.–.
OT: 'ārak: S.748; HR.893c.1c; H.162; BD.73c.
'ārōk: S.752, HR.893c.1a; H.162c; BD.74a.
'ārēk: S.750; HR.893c.1d; H.162b; BD.74a.
GEN. REF.: –.

2. *hikanos* [ἱκανός, 2425], sufficient, much, long, is used with *chronos*, time, in Luke 8:27; in 20:9 and 23:8 (A.V., "*season*") the plural is used, lit., 'long times'; Acts 8:11; 14:3. See Able (Ability), C, No. 2, Many, Much.

NT: B.374b; CB.1250c; K.361.
OT: –.
GEN. REF.: –.

3. *polus* [πολύς, 4183], much, is used with *chronos*, time, in Matt. 25:19; John 5:6; in Acts 27:21, with *asitia*, A.V., "long abstinence," R.V., "long without food." See Common, Note (1).

NT: B.687c; CB.1266a; K.–.
OT: rab: S.7227; HR.1181b.9a; H.2099a,b; BD.912d.
GEN. REF.: –.

4. *tosoutos* [τοσοῦτος, 5118], so long, is used with *chronos* in John 14:9 and Heb. 4:7.

NT: B.823b; CB.–; K.–.
OT: –.
GEN. REF.: –.

5. *posos* [πόσος, 4214], how much, is used with *chronos*, in Mark 9:21, "how long time," R.V. (A.V., "how long ago").

NT: B.694b; CB.–; K.–.
OT: –.
GEN. REF.: –.

6. *hosos* [ὅσος, 3745], how much, so much, is used after the preposition *epi* (*eph'*), and as an adjective qualifying *chronos*, signifying "for so long time," in Rom. 7:1; 1 Cor. 7:39; Gal. 4:1; see also B, No. 4.

NT: B.586b; CB.1251b; K.–.
OT: –.
GEN. REF.: –.

Notes: (1) In Acts 14:28, A.V., the adjective *oligos*, little, with the negative *ou*, not, and qualifying *chronos*, is rendered "long time"; R.V., "no little (time)."

(2) For the comparative adjective, *pleiōn*, see Longer, B.

B. Adverbs.

1. *polus* [πολύς, 4183], in one or other of its neuter forms, singular or plural, is used (*a*) of degree, greatly, much, many, e.g., Mark 1:45; (*b*) of time, e.g., Acts 27:14. Cp. A, No. 3. See Great, Much, Oft, Sore, Straitly, While.

NT: B.687c; CB.1266a; K.–.
OT: rab: S.7227; HR.1181b.9a; H.2099a,b; BD.912d.
GEN. REF.: –.

2. *eph' hikanon* [ἐφ' ἱκανόν, —], lit., 'unto much (time)', is rendered "a long while" in Acts 20:11. Cp. A, No. 2.

NT: B.374b; CB.–; K.–.
OT: –.
GEN. REF.: –.

3. *heōs pote* [ἕως, 4219 ποτε], lit., 'until when?' signifies "how long?" Matt. 17:17 (twice); Mark 9:19 (twice); Luke 9:41; John 10:24; Rev. 6:10.

NT: B.695a; CB.–; K.–.
OT: –.
GEN. REF.: –.

4. *eph' hoson* [ἐφ' ὅσον, 3745 ηοσοσ], signifies so long as, as long as (*epi*, upon, *hosos*, how much), Matt. 9:15; Mark 2:19; 2 Pet. 1:13. See Inasmuch, No. 2.

NT: B.586b; CB.–; K.–.
OT: –.
GEN. REF.: –.

Notes: (1) For the adverb Longer, see below.

(2) In 2 Pet. 2:3, A.V., the adverb *ekpalai*, "from of old," R.V. (*ek*, from, *palai*, of old, formerly), is translated "of a long time."

LONG (Verb), LONG (after, for), LONGING

A. Verb.

epipotheō [ἐπιποθέω, 1971], to long for greatly (a strengthened form of *potheō*, to long for, not found in the N.T.), is translated "I long," in Rom. 1:11; in 2 Cor. 5:2, R.V., "longing" (A.V., "earnestly desiring"); in 1 Thess. 3:6 and 2 Tim. 1:4, R.V., "longing" (A.V., "desiring greatly"); to long after, in 2 Cor. 9:14; Phil. 1:8; 2:26; to long for, in 1 Pet. 2:2, R.V. (A.V., "desire"); Jas. 4:5, R.V., "long." See Desire. ¶

NT: B.297d; CB.1246a; K.–.
OT: yā'ab: S.2968; HR.526c.4; H.828; BD.383b.
kāsaph: S.3700; HR.526c.5; H.1015; BD.493d.
'ārag: S.6165; HR.526c.6; H.1691; BD.788b.
GEN. REF.: –.

B. Adjective.

epipothētos [ἐπιπόθητος, 1973], akin to A, and an intensive form of *pothētos*, desired,

greatly desired, "longed for," is used in Phil. 4:1. ¶
NT: B.298a; CB.–; K.–.
OT: –.
GEN. REF.: –.

C. Nouns.

1. *epipothia* [ἐπιποθία, 1974], a longing (akin to A and B), is found in Rom. 15:23, R.V., "longing" (A.V., "great desire"). See DESIRE. ¶
NT: B.298a; CB.1246a; K.–.
OT: –.
GEN. REF.: –.

2. *epipothēsis* [ἐπιπόθησις, 1972], a longing (perhaps stressing the process more than No. 1), is found in 2 Cor. 7:7, R.V., "longing" (A.V., "earnest desire"); 7:11, R.V., "longing" (A.V., "vehement desire"). ¶
NT: B.298a; CB.1246a; K.–.
OT: –.
GEN. REF.: –.

LONGER

A. Adverbs.

1. *eti* [ἔτι, 2089], yet, as yet, still, is translated "longer" in Luke 16:2 (with separate negative); "any longer" in Rom. 6:2. See ALSO, EVEN, FURTHER, MORE, MOREOVER, STILL, THENCEFORTH, YET.
NT: B.315c; CB.1247a; K.–.
OT: 'ôd: S.5750; HR.561a.11; H.1576a; BD.728c.
GEN. REF.: –.

2. *ouketi* [οὐκέτι, 3765], no more, no longer (*ou*, not, *k*, euphonic, and No. 1), is rendered "no longer" in the R.V. of Mark 7:12 (A.V., "no more"); John 15:15, R.V. (A.V., "henceforth not"); Rom. 14:15, R.V. (A.V., "now . . . not"); Gal. 2:20, R.V. (A.V., "yet not"); Gal. 3:25; 4:7 (A.V., "no more"); Philm. 16 (A.V., "not now"). See HENCEFORTH, MORE, NOW, YET.
NT: B.592c; CB.–; K.–.
OT: 'ôd (w. neg.): S.5750; HR.1030a.6b; H.1576a; BD.728c.
GEN. REF.: –.

3. *mēketi* [μηκέτι, 3371], also means no more, no longer, but generally suggests what is a matter of thought or supposition, whereas No. 1 refers to what is a matter of fact. It is rendered "any longer" in Acts 25:24; "no longer," in Mark 2:2, R.V., "no longer (room)," A.V., "no (room)"; 2 Cor. 5:15, R.V. (A.V., "not henceforth"); Eph. 4:14, R.V. (A.V., "no more"); 4:17, R.V. (A.V., "henceforth . . . not"); 1 Thess. 3:1, 5; 1 Tim. 5:23; 1 Pet. 4:2. See (negatively) HENCEFORTH, HENCEFORWARD, HEREAFTER, NO MORE.
NT: B.518c; CB.–; K.–.
OT: –.
GEN. REF.: –.

4. *pleion* [πλεῖον, 4119], the neuter of *pleiōn*, more, the comparative degree of *polu*, much, is rendered "longer" in Acts 20:9, R.V. (A.V., "long").
NT: B.689a; CB.1265b; K.–.
OT: –.
GEN. REF.: –.

B. Adjective.

pleiōn [πλείων, 4119], more (cp. A, No. 4), is used with *chronos*, time, in Acts 18:20, "a longer time," R.V. (A.V., "longer").
NT: B.689a; CB.–; K.–.
OT: –.
GEN. REF.: –.

LONGSUFFERING (Noun and Verb)

A. Noun.

makrothumia [μακροθυμία, 3115], forbearance, patience, longsuffering (*makros*, long, *thumos*, temper), is usually rendered "longsuffering," Rom. 2:4; 9:22; 2 Cor. 6:6; Gal. 5:22; Eph. 4:2; Col. 1:11; 3:12; 1 Tim. 1:16; 2 Tim. 3:10; 4:2; 1 Pet. 3:20; 2 Pet. 3:15; "patience" in Heb. 6:12 and Jas. 5:10. See PATIENCE, and Note under FORBEAR. ¶
NT: B.488b; CB.1257c; K.550.
OT: 'ōrek: S.753; HR.893c.la; H.162a; BD.73d.
GEN. REF.: IS.–; NB.745; Z.3:958.

B. Verb.

makrothumeō [μακροθυμέω, 3114], akin to A, to be patient, longsuffering, to bear with, lit., to be long-tempered, is rendered by the verb to be longsuffering in Luke 18:7, R.V. (A.V., "bear long"); in 1 Thess. 5:14, R.V. (A.V., "be patient"); so in Jas. 5:7, 8; in 2 Pet. 3:9, A.V. and R.V., "is longsuffering." See BEAR, No. 14, ENDURE, PATIENT, SUFFER.
NT: B.488a; CB.1257c; K.550.
OT: 'ārak: S.748; HR.893c.la; H.162; BD.73c.
GEN. REF.: IS.–; NB.745; Z.3:958.

Note: "Longsuffering is that quality of self-restraint in the face of provocation which does not hastily retaliate or promptly punish; it is the opposite of anger, and is associated with mercy, and is used of God, Ex. 34:6 (Sept.); Rom. 2:4; 1 Pet. 3:20. Patience is the quality that does not surrender to circumstances or succumb under trial; it is the opposite of despondency and is associated with hope, 1 Thess. 1:3; it is not used of God."*

LOOK

A. Verbs.

1. *blepō* [βλέπω, 991], primarily, to have sight, to see, then, observe, discern, perceive, frequently implying special contemplation (cp.

* From Notes on Thessalonians by Hogg and Vine, pp. 183, 184.

No. 4), is rendered by the verb to look in Luke 9:62, "looking (back)"; John 13:22 "(the disciples) looked (one on another)"; Acts 1:9, R.V., "were looking" (A.V., "beheld"); 3:4, "look (on us)"; 27:12, R.V., "looking," A.V., "that lieth (towards)," of the haven Phenix; Eph. 5:15, R.V., "look (therefore carefully how ye walk)," A.V., "see (that ye walk circumspectly)"; Rev. 11:9 and 18:9, R.V., "look upon" (A.V., "shall see"). See BEHOLD.

NT: B.143b; CB.1239a; K.706.
OT: rā'āh: S.7200; HR.221a.10a; H.2095; BD.906b.
pānāh: S.6437; HR.221a.7a; H.1782; BD.815a.
GEN. REF.: IS.3:155; NB.–; Z.–.

2. *anablepō* [ἀναβλέπω, 308], denotes (*a*) to look up (*ana*, up, and No. 1), e.g., Matt. 14:19; Mark 8:24 (in some mss. ver. 25); (*b*) to recover sight, e.g., Matt. 11:5; 20:34, R.V., "received their sight"; John 9:11. See SIGHT. Cp. *anablepsis*, recovering of sight, Luke 4:18.

NT: B.50d; CB.1235a; K.–.
OT: nāsā': S.5375; HR.73b.3a; H.1421; BD.669d.
GEN. REF.: IS.3:156; NB.–; Z.–.

3. *periblepō* [περιβλέπω, 4017], to look about, or round about, on (*peri*, around, and No. 1), is used in the Middle Voice, Mark 3:5, 34; 5:32; 9:8; 10:23; 11:11; Luke 6:10. ¶

NT: B.646b; CB.–; K.–.
OT: pānāh: S.6437; HR.1122b.3; H.1782; BD.815a.
nābaṭ: S.5027; HR.1122b.1; H.1282; BD.613c.
GEN. REF.: IS.3:156; NB.–; Z.–.

4. *apoblepō* [ἀποβλέπω, 578], signifies to look away from (*apo*) all else at one object; hence, to look stedfastly, Heb. 11:26, R.V., "he looked" (A.V., "he had respect"). ¶ Cp. No. 8.

NT: B.89a; CB.1236c; K.–.
OT: pānāh: S.6437; HR.125c.2; H.1782; BD.815a.
rā'āh: S.7200; HR.125c.4; H.2095; BD.906b.
GEN. REF.: IS.3:156; NB.–; Z.–.

5. *emblepō* [ἐμβλέπω, 1689], to look at (*en*, in, and No. 1), is translated to look upon in Mark 10:27; 14:67; Luke 22:61; John 1:36. This verb implies a close, penetrating look, as distinguished from Nos. 6 and 9. See BEHOLD, No. 3, GAZE, SEE, No. 6.

NT: B.254c; CB.1244b; K.–.
OT: nābaṭ: S.5027; HR.455c.1; H.1282; BD.613c.
pānāh: S.6437; HR.455c.2; H.1782; BD.815a.
rā'āh: S.7200; HR.455c.3; H.2095; BD.906b.
GEN. REF.: IS.3:156; NB.–; Z.–.

6. *epiblepō* [ἐπιβλέπω, 1914], to look upon (*epi*, upon), is used in the N.T. of favourable regard, Luke 1:48, R.V., "he hath looked upon" (A.V., "hath regarded"), of the low estate of the Virgin Mary; in 9:38, in a request to the Lord to look upon an afflicted son; in Jas. 2:3, R.V., "ye have regard" (A.V., ". . . respect"), of having a partial regard for the well-to-do. See REGARD, RESPECT. ¶

NT: B.290b; CB.–; K.–.
OT: nābaṭ: S.5027; HR.516c.4; H.1282; BD.613c.
pānāh: S.6437; HR.516c.8; H.1782; BD.815a.
rā'āh: S.7200; HR.516c.11; H.2095; BD.906b.
GEN. REF.: IS.3:156; NB.–; Z.–.

7. *eidon* [εἶδον, 3708], used as the aorist tense of *horaō*, to see, in various senses, is translated to look, in the A.V. of John 7:52, R.V., "see"; Rev. 4:1 (R.V., "I saw"); so in 6:8; 14:1, 14 (as in A.V. of ver. 6), and 15:5. See BEHOLD, CONSIDER, HEED, No. 2, PERCEIVE, SEE, SHEW.

NT: B.220c; CB.1243a; K.706.
OT: rā'āh: S.7200; HR.1005a.8a,b; H.2095; BD.906b.
GEN. REF.: IS.3:156; NB.–; Z.–.

8. *aphoraō* [ἀφοράω, 872], to look away from one thing so as to see another (*apo*, from, and No. 7), to concentrate the gaze upon, occurs in Phil. 2:23, "I shall see"; Heb. 12:2, "looking." ¶

NT: B.127b; CB.–; K.–.
OT: –.
GEN. REF.: –.

9. *epeidon* [ἐπεῖδον, 1896], denotes to look upon (*epi*, upon), (*a*) favourably, Luke 1:25; (*b*) unfavourably, in Acts 4:29. ¶

NT: B.284b; CB.–; K.–.
OT: –.
GEN. REF.: IS.3:156; NB.–; Z.–.

10. *parakuptō* [παρακύπτω, 3879], lit. and primarily, to stoop sideways (*para*, aside, *kuptō*, to bend forward), denotes to stoop to look into, Luke 24:12, "stooping and looking in" (A.V., "stooping down"); John 20:5, 11; metaphorically in Jas. 1:25, of looking into the perfect law of liberty; in 1 Pet. 1:12 of things which the angels desire "to look" into. ¶

NT: B.619b; CB.–; K.784.
OT: shāqaph: S.8259; HR.1061b.2; H.2457; BD.1055a.
GEN. REF.: IS.3:156; NB.–; Z.–.

11. *anakuptō* [ἀνακύπτω, 352], to lift oneself up (*ana*, up), is translated "look up" in Luke 21:28, of being elated in joyous expectation (followed by *epairō*, to lift up). See LIFT.

NT: B.56d; CB.–; K.–.
OT: nāsā': S.5375; HR.78c.1; H.1421; BD.669d.
GEN. REF.: IS.3:156; NB.–; Z.–.

12. *skopeō* [σκοπέω, 4648], to look at, consider (Eng., scope), implying mental consideration, is rendered "while we look . . . at" in 2 Cor. 4:18; "looking to" (A.V., "on") in Phil. 2:4. See HEED, MARK.

NT: B.756d; CB.1269b; K.1047.
OT: –.
GEN. REF.: IS.3:156; NB.–; Z.–.

13. *episkopeō* [ἐπισκοπέω, 1983], lit., to look upon (*epi*, and No. 12), is rendered "looking carefully" in Heb. 12:15, R.V. (A.V., "looking diligently"), *epi* being probably intensive here; in 1 Pet. 5:2, to exercise the oversight, to visit, care for. See OVERSIGHT. ¶

NT: B.298d; CB.1246a; K.244.
OT: dārash: S.1875; HR.528c.1; H.455; BD.205a.
pāqad: S.6485; HR.528c.4; H.1802; BD.823a.
GEN. REF.: –.

14. *episkeptomai* [ἐπισκέπτομαι, 1980], a later form of No. 13, to visit, has the meaning of seeking out, and is rendered "look ye out" in Acts 6:3. See Visit.
NT: B.298c; CB.1246a; K.244.
OT: pāqad: S.6485; HR.527c.5a; H.1802; BD.823a.
GEN. REF.: –.

15. *atenizō* [ἀτενίζω, 816], to look fixedly, gaze, is translated "looking stedfastly" in Luke 22:56, R.V. (A.V., ". . . earnestly"); in Acts 1:10, "looking stedfastly"; in 3:12, A.V., "look . . . earnestly" (R.V., "fasten ye your eyes," as in 3:4 and 11:6); so in the R.V. of 6:15; 10:4; 13:9; 14:9; in 7:55, "looked up stedfastly"; in 23:1, "looking stedfastly on" (A.V., "earnestly beholding"); in 2 Cor. 3:7, R.V., "look stedfastly" (A.V., "stedfastly behold"); in 3:13, R.V., ditto (A.V., "stedfastly look"). In Luke 4:20, "were fastened" (*ophthalmoi*, eyes, being used separately). See Behold, No. 10. ¶
NT: B.119d; CB.1238a; K.–.
OT: –.
GEN. REF.: IS.3:156; NB.–; Z.–.

16. *theaomai* [θεάομαι, 2300], to behold (of careful contemplation), is translated "look" in John 4:35, of looking on the fields; in 1 John 1:1, A.V. (R.V., "we beheld"), of the Apostles' personal experiences of Christ in the days of His flesh, and the facts of His Godhood and Manhood. See Behold, No. 8.
NT: B.353a; CB.1271c; K.706.
OT: rā'āh: S.7200; HR.627c.1; H.2095; BD.906b.
GEN. REF.: IS.3:156; NB.–; Z.–.

17. *theōreō* [θεωρέω, 2334], to look at, gaze at, behold, is translated "looking on" in Mark 15:40, A.V. (R.V., "beholding"). See Behold, No. 6.
NT: B.368a; CB.1272a; K.706.
OT: rā'āh: S.7200; HR.649b.4; H.2095; BD.906b.
ḥ[a]zāh (Aramaic): S.2370; HR.649b.2c; H.–; BD.1092c.
GEN. REF.: IS.3:156; NB.–; Z.–.

B. Noun.

horasis [ὅρασις, 3706], akin to A, No. 7, denotes (*a*) a vision (so the associated noun *horama*, e.g., Acts 7:31; *horasis* signifies especially the act of seeing, *horama* that which is seen), Acts 2:17; Rev. 9:17; (*b*) an appearance, Rev. 4:3, translated "to look upon" (twice in the R.V.; in the second instance the A.V. has "in sight"). ¶
NT: B.577c; CB.1251a; K.706.
OT: mar'eh: S.4758; HR.1007b.4a,c,d; H.2095i; BD.909c.
ḥāzôn: S.2377; HR.1007b.2a; H.633a; BD.302d.
GEN. REF.: IS.3:156; NB.–; Z.–.

LOOK (for), LOOKING (after, for)

A. Verbs.

1. *prosdokaō* [προσδοκάω, 4328], to await, expect (*pros*, to or towards, *dokeō*, to think, be of opinion), is translated to look for, e.g., in Matt. 11:3; 2 Pet. 3:12, 13, 14; the R.V. renders it by the verb to expect, to be in expectation, in some instances, as does the A.V. in Luke 3:15; Acts 3:5. See Expect.
NT: B.712c; CB.1267a; K.943.
OT: sābar: S.7663; HR.1213b.2; H.2232; BD.960b.
GEN. REF.: IS.3:156; NB.–; Z.–.

2. *prosdechomai* [προσδέχομαι, 4327], to receive favourably, also means to expect, and is rendered to look for, e.g., in Luke 2:38; 23:51; Acts 24:15, R.V. (A.V., "allow"); Tit. 2:13; Jude 21. See Accept, A, No. 3, Allow, No. 4.
NT: B.712a; CB.1267a; K.146.
OT: rāṣah: S.7521; HR.1212c.8a; H.2207; BD.953a.
qābal: S.6901; HR.1212c.6; H.1980; BD.867a.
GEN. REF.: IS.3:156; NB.–; Z.–.

3. *ekdechomai* [ἐκδέχομαι, 1551], primarily to receive from another, hence, to expect, to await, is translated "he looked for" in Heb. 11:10; in 1 Cor. 16:11, A.V., "I look for" (R.V., "I expect"). See Expect, No. 1.
NT: B.238b; CB.1243c; K.146.
OT: –.
GEN. REF.: IS.3:156; NB.–; Z.–.

Notes: (1) In Phil. 3:20 and Heb. 9:28, A.V., *apekdechomai* (the verb in the preceding No. extended by *apo*, from), to await or expect eagerly, is translated "look for" (R.V., "wait for"; so A.V. everywhere else). See Wait.

(2) In Acts 28:6, A.V., *prosdokaō*, to expect, is translated "they looked" (R.V., "they expected"), and "they had looked" (R.V., "they were long in expectation").

B. Nouns.

1. *prosdokia* [προσδοκία, 4329], akin to A, No. 1, is translated "a looking after" in Luke 21:26, A.V. (R.V., "expectation," as in Acts 12:11, A.V. and R.V.). See Expectation. ¶
NT: B.712c; CB.–; K.943.
OT: sēber: S.7664; HR.1213a.2; H.2232a; BD.960b.
GEN. REF.: IS.3:156; NB.–; Z.–.

2. *ekdochē* [ἐκδοχή, 1561], akin to A, No. 3, is translated "looking for" in Heb. 10:27, A.V. See Expectation. ¶
NT: B.239c; CB.1243c; K.–.
OT: –.
GEN. REF.: IS.3:156; NB.–; Z.–.

LOOK (to)

1. *blepō* [βλέπω, 991], to look (see Look, No. 1), has the meaning of taking heed, looking to oneself, in 2 John 8. See Heed.
NT: B.143b; CB.1239a; K.706.
OT: rā'āh: S.7200; HR.221a.10a; H.2095; BD.906b.
pānāh: S.6437; HR.221a.7a; H.1782; BD.815a.
GEN. REF.: IS.3:156; NB.–; Z.–.

2. *horaō* [ὁράω, 3708], to see (see Look, No. 7), has the meaning of seeing to or caring for a thing in Matt. 27:4, "see (thou to it)"; in Acts 18:15, "look to it (yourselves)"; the future (sing. *opsei*, plural, *opsesthe*), is used for the tense

which is wanting in *horaō*, and stands for the imperative.

NT: B.577c; CB.1251a; K.706.
OT: rā'āh: S.7200; HR.1005a.8a,b; H.2095; BD.906b.
GEN. REF.: IS.3:156; NB.—; Z.—.

LOOSE

A. Verbs.

1. *luō* [λύω, 3089], denotes (*a*) to loose, unbind, release, (1) of things, e.g., in Acts 7:33, R.V., "loose (the shoes)," A.V., "put off"; Mark 1:7; (2) of animals, e.g., Matt. 21:2; (3) of persons, e.g., John 11:44; Acts 22:30; (4) of Satan, Rev. 20:3, 7, and angels, Rev. 9:14, 15; (5) metaphorically, of one diseased, Luke 13:16; of the marriage tie, 1 Cor. 7:27; of release from sins, Rev. 1:5 (in the most authentic mss.); (*b*) to loosen, break up, dismiss, dissolve, destroy; in this sense it is translated to loose in Acts 2:24, of the pains of death; in Rev. 5:2, of the seals of a roll. See BREAK, DESTROY, DISSOLVE, MELT, PUT (off), UNLOOSE.

NT: B.483c; CB.1257b; K.543.
OT: pātaḥ: S.6605; HR.889a.5; H.1854,1855; BD.834d.
nātar: S.5425; HR.889a.3; H.1448; BD.684a.
GEN. REF.: —.

2. *apoluō* [ἀπολύω, 630], *apo*, from, and No. 1, denotes (*a*) to set free, release, translated "loosed" in Luke 13:12, of deliverance from an infirmity; in Matt. 18:27, A.V., "loosed" (R.V., "released"), of a debtor; (*b*) to let go, dismiss, e.g., Matt. 14:15, 22. See DEPART, DISMISS, DIVORCE, FORGIVE, LET (go), LIBERTY, PUT (away), RELEASE, SEND (away).

NT: B.96c; CB.1237a; K.—.
OT: gārash: S.1644; HR.138c.2; H.388; BD.176c.
GEN. REF.: —.

3. *aniēmi* [ἀνίημι, 447], to send back (*ana*, back, *hiēmi*, to send), to leave, forbear, is translated to loose, in Acts 16:26, of the loosening of bonds; 27:40, rudder-bands. Elsewhere, Eph. 6:9; Heb. 13:5. See FORBEAR, LEAVE. ¶

NT: B.69d; CB.—; K.60.
OT: rāphāh: S.7503; HR.102b.11c; H.2198; BD.951d.
nāsā': S.5375; HR.102b.8; H.1421; BD.669d.
GHEN. REF.:—.

4. *anagō* [ἀνάγω, —]: see LAUNCH.

Notes: (1) In Acts 27:13, A.V., *airō*, to lift, is translated "loosing (thence)" (R.V., "they weighed anchor").

(2) For *katargeō*, translated "she is loosed" in Rom. 7:2, A.V. (R.V. "discharged"), see ABOLISH.

B. Noun.

lusis [λύσις, 3080], a loosening (akin to A, No. 1), 1 Cor. 7:27, of divorce, is translated "to be loosed," lit., 'loosing.' In the second part of the verse the verb *luō* is used. ¶ In the Sept., Eccles. 8:1, with the meaning "interpretation." ¶

NT: B.482b; CB.1257b; K.—.
OT: pēsher: S.6592; HR.890a.1; H.1847; BD.833d.
GEN. REF.: —.

LORD, LORDSHIP

A. Nouns.

1. *kurios* [κύριος, 2962], properly an adjective, signifying having power (*kuros*) or authority, is used as a noun, variously translated in the N.T., "'Lord,' 'master,' 'Master,' 'owner,' 'Sir,' a title of wide significance, occurring in each book of the N.T. save Tit. and the Epp. of John. It is used (*a*) of an owner, as in Luke 19:33, cp. Matt. 20:8; Acts 16:16; Gal. 4:1; or of one who has the disposal of anything, as the Sabbath, Matt. 12:8; (*b*) of a master, i.e., one to whom service is due on any ground, Matt. 6:24; 24:50; Eph. 6:5; (*c*) of an Emperor or King, Acts 25:26; Rev. 17:14; (*d*) of idols, ironically, 1 Cor. 8:5, cp. Isa. 26:13; (*e*) as a title of respect addressed to a father, Matt. 21:30, a husband, 1 Pet. 3:6, a master, Matt. 13:27; Luke 13:8, a ruler, Matt. 27:63, an angel, Acts 10:4; Rev. 7:14; (*f*) as a title of courtesy addressed to a stranger, John 12:21; 20:15; Acts 16:30; from the outset of His ministry this was a common form of address to the Lord Jesus, alike by the people, Matt. 8:2; John 4:11, and by His disciples, Matt. 8:25; Luke 5:8; John 6:68; (*g*) *kurios* is the Sept. and N.T. representative of Heb. Jehovah ('Lord' in Eng. versions), see Matt. 4:7; Jas. 5:11, e.g., of *adon*, Lord, Matt. 22:44, and of *Adonay*, Lord, 1:22; it also occurs for *Elohim*, God, 1 Pet. 1:25.

"Thus the usage of the word in the N.T. follows two main lines: One—*a-f*, customary and general, the other, *g*, peculiar to the Jews, and drawn from the Greek translation of the O.T.

"Christ Himself assumed the title, Matt. 7:21, 22; 9:38; 22:41-45; Mark 5:19 (cp. Ps. 66:16; the parallel passage, Luke 8:39, has 'God'); Luke 19:31; John 13:13, apparently intending it in the higher senses of its current use, and at the same time suggesting its O.T. associations.

"His purpose did not become clear to the disciples until after His resurrection, and the revelation of His Deity consequent thereon. Thomas, when he realised the significance of the presence of a mortal wound in the body of a living man, immediately joined with it the absolute title of Deity, saying, 'My Lord and my God,' John 20:28. Thereafter, except in Acts

10:4 and Rev. 7:14, there is no record that *kurios* was ever again used by believers in addressing any save God and the Lord Jesus; cp. Acts 2:47 with 4:29, 30.

"How soon and how completely the lower meaning had been superseded is seen in Peter's declaration in his first sermon after the resurrection, 'God hath made Him — Lord,' Acts 2:36, and that in the house of Cornelius, 'He is Lord of all,' 10:36; cp. Deut. 10:14; Matt. 11:25; Acts 17:24. In his writings the implications of his early teaching are confirmed and developed. Thus Ps. 34:8, 'O taste and see that Jehovah is good,' is applied to the Lord Jesus, 1 Pet. 2:3, and 'Jehovah of Hosts, Him shall ye sanctify,' Isa. 8:13, becomes 'sanctify in your hearts Christ as Lord,' 3:15.

"So also James who uses *kurios* alike of God, 1:7 (cp. v. 5); 3:9; 4:15; 5:4, 10, 11, and of the Lord Jesus, 1:1 (where the possibility that *kai* is intended epexegetically, i.e. = even, cp. 1 Thess. 3:11, should not be overlooked); 2:1 (lit., 'our Lord Jesus Christ of glory,' cp. Ps. 24:7; 29:3; Acts 7:2; 1 Cor. 2:8); 5:7, 8, while the language of 4:10; 5:15, is equally applicable to either.

"Jude, v. 4, speaks of 'our only — Lord, Jesus Christ,' and immediately, v. 5, uses 'Lord' of God (see the remarkable marg. here), as he does later, vv. 9, 14.

"Paul ordinarily uses *kurios* of the Lord Jesus, 1 Cor. 1:3, e.g., but also on occasion, of God, in quotations from the O.T., 1 Cor. 3:20, e.g., and in his own words, 1 Cor. 3:5, cp. v. 10. It is equally appropriate to either in 1 Cor. 7:25; 2 Cor. 3:16; 8:21; 1 Thess. 4:6, and if 1 Cor. 11:32 is to be interpreted by 10:21, 22, the Lord Jesus is intended, but if by Heb. 12:5-9, then *kurios* here also = God. 1 Tim. 6:15, 16 is probably to be understood of the Lord Jesus, cp. Rev. 17:14.

"Though John does not use 'Lord' in his Epp., and though, like the other Evangelists, he ordinarily uses the personal Name in his narrative, yet he occasionally speaks of Him as 'the Lord,' John 4:1; 6:23; 11:2; 20:20; 21:12.

"The full significance of this association of Jesus with God under the one appellation, 'Lord,' is seen when it is remembered that these men belonged to the only monotheistic race in the world. To associate with the Creator one known to be a creature, however exalted, though possible to Pagan philosophers, was quite impossible to a Jew.

"It is not recorded that in the days of His flesh any of His disciples either addressed the Lord, or spoke of Him, by His personal Name. Where Paul has occasion to refer to the facts of the gospel history he speaks of what the Lord Jesus said, Acts 20:35, and did, 1 Cor. 11:23, and suffered, 1 Thess. 2:15; 5:9, 10. It is our Lord Jesus who is coming, 1 Thess. 2:19, etc. In prayer also the title is given, 3:11; Eph. 1:3; the sinner is invited to believe on the Lord Jesus, Acts 16:31; 20:21, and the saint to look to the Lord Jesus for deliverance, Rom. 7:24, 25, and in the few exceptional cases in which the personal Name stands alone a reason is always discernible in the immediate context.

"The title 'Lord,' as given to the Saviour, in its full significance rests upon the resurrection, Acts 2:36; Rom. 10:9; 14:9, and is realised only in the Holy Spirit, 1 Cor. 12:3."*

NT: B.458d; CB.1256b; K.486.
OT: y^{e}hôwāh: S.3068; HR.800b.11a; H.484a; BD.217d.
’^{e}lōhîm: S.430; HR.800b.18b; H.93c; BD.43a.
’ēl: S.410; HR.800b.4a; H.93a; BD.42a,c.
GEN. REF.: IS.3:157; NB.477; Z.3:959.

2. *despotēs* [δεσπότης, 1203], a master, lord, one who possesses supreme authority, is used in personal address to God in Luke 2:29; Acts 4:24; Rev. 6:10; with reference to Christ, 2 Pet. 2:1; Jude 4; elsewhere it is translated "master," "masters," 1 Tim. 6:1, 2; 2 Tim. 2:21 (of Christ); Tit. 2:9; 1 Pet. 2:18. See MASTER. ¶

NT: B.176c; CB.1240c; K.145.
OT: ’ādôn: S.113; HR.292c; H.27b; BD.10d.
GEN. REF.: IS.3:157; NB.477; Z.3:959.

Note: For *rabboni*, rendered "Lord" in the A.V. of Mark 10:51, see RABBONI.

3. *megistan* [μεγιστάν, 3175], akin to *megistos*, greatest, the superlative degree of *megas*, great, denotes chief men, nobles; it is rendered "lords" in Mark 6:21, of nobles in Herod's entourage; "princes" in Rev. 6:15 and 18:23, R.V. (A.V., "great men"). ¶

NT: B.498c; CB.1258a; K.—.
OT: sar: S.8269; HR.907a.5; H.2295a; BD.978a.
rabr^{e}bān (Aramaic): S.7261; HR.907a.4; H.2984c; BD.1112b.
GEN. REF.: IS.3:157; NB.—; Z.—.

B. Verbs.

1. *kurieuō* [κυριεύω, 2961], denotes to be lord of, to exercise lordship over, Luke 22:25; Rom. 6:9, 14; 7:1; 14:9; 2 Cor. 1:24; 1 Tim. 6:15; see DOMINION, B, No. 1. ¶

NT: B.458c; CB.1256b; K.486.
OT: māshal: S.4910; HR.800a.4; H.1258,1259; BD.605c.
GEN. REF.: IS.3:157; NB.—; Z.—.

* From Notes on Thessalonians by Hogg and Vine, p. 25.

2. *katakurieuō* [κατακυριεύω, 2634], a strengthened form of No. 1, is rendered "lording it" in 1 Pet. 5:3, R.V.: see DOMINION, B, No. 2.

NT: B.412c; CB.1254a; K.486.
OT: kābash: S.3533; HR.735a.3; H.951; BD.461b.
māshal: S.4910; HR.735a.4; H.1258,1259; BD.605c.
GEN. REF.: –.

C. Adjective.

kuriakos [κυριακός, 2960], from *kurios* (A, No. 1), signifies pertaining to a lord or master; 'lordly' is not a legitimate rendering for its use in the N.T., where it is used only of Christ; in 1 Cor. 11:20, of the Lord's Supper, or the Supper of the Lord (see FEAST); in Rev. 1:10, of the Day of the Lord (see DAY, No. 1). ¶

NT: B.458c; CB.1256b; K.486.
OT: –.
GEN. REF.: –.

LOSE, (Suffer) LOSS, LOST

1. *apollumi* [ἀπόλλυμι, 622], signifies (I) In the Active Voice, (*a*) to destroy, destroy utterly, kill, e.g., Matt. 10:28; Mark 1:24; 9:22; (*b*) to lose utterly, e.g., Matt. 10:42, of losing a reward; Luke 15:4 (1st part), of losing a sheep; Luke 9:25, of losing oneself (of the loss of well-being hereafter); metaphorically, John 6:39, of failing to save; 18:9, of Christ's not losing His own; (II) in the Middle Voice, (*a*) to perish, of things, e.g., John 6:12 "(that nothing) be lost"; of persons, e.g., Matt. 8:25, "we perish"; of the loss of eternal life, usually (always in the R.V.) translated to perish, John 3:16; 17:12, A.V., "is lost," R.V., "perished"; 2 Cor. 4:3, "are perishing," A.V., "are lost" (see PERISH); (*b*) to be lost, e.g., Luke 15:4 (2nd part), "which is lost"; metaphorically, from the relation between shepherd and flock, of spiritual destitution and alienation from God, Matt. 10:6, "(the) lost (sheep)" of the house of Israel; Luke 19:10 (the perfect tense translated "lost" is here intransitive). See DESTROY.

NT: B.95a; CB.1237a; K.67.
OT: 'ābad: S.6; HR.136c.1; H.2; BD.1b.
shāḥat: S.7843; HR.136c.33; H.2370; BD.1007d.
kārat: S.3772; HR.136c.13; H.1048; BD.503c.
GEN. REF.: IS.3:170; NB.–; Z.–.

2. *zēmioō* [ζημιόω, 2210], to damage (akin to *zēmia*, damage, e.g., Acts 27:10, 21), is used in the N.T., in the Passive Voice, signifying to suffer loss, forfeit, lose, Matt. 16:26; Mark 8:36, of losing one's soul or life; Luke 9:25, R.V., "forfeit (his own self)," A.V., "be cast away" (for the preceding verb see No. 1); 1 Cor. 3:15, "he shall suffer loss," i.e., at the Judgment-Seat of Christ (see ver. 13 with 2 Cor. 5:10); 2 Cor. 7:9, "(that) ye might suffer loss," R.V. (A.V., "might receive damage"); though the Apostle did regret the necessity of making them sorry by his letter, he rejoiced that they were made sorry after a godly sort, and that they thus suffered no spiritual loss, which they would have done had their sorrow been otherwise than after a godly manner; in Phil. 3:8, "I suffered the loss (of all things)," R.V., i.e., of all things which he formerly counted gain (especially those in verses 5 and 6, to which the article before "all things" points). See CAST, FORFEIT. ¶

NT: B.338c; CB.1273c; K.299.
OT: 'ānash: S.6064; HR.594c.2; H.1659; BD.778d.
GEN. REF.: IS.3:170; NB.–; Z.–.

LOSS

1. *zēmia* [ζημία, 2209], akin to No. 2, above, is used in Acts 27:10, R.V., "loss" (A.V., "damage"); ver. 21, A.V. and R.V., "loss," of ship and cargo; in Phil. 3:7, 8 of the Apostle's estimate of the things which he formerly valued, and of all things on account of "the excellency of the knowledge of Christ Jesus." ¶

NT: B.338c; CB.1273c; K.299.
OT: 'ōnesh: S.6066; HR.594c.1; H.1659a; BD.778d.
GEN. REF.: IS.3:170; NB.–; Z.–.

2. *apobolē* [ἀποβολή, 580], lit., casting away (*apo*, away, *ballō*, to cast), is translated "loss" in Acts 27:22; in Rom. 11:15, "casting away," of the temporary exclusion of the nation of Israel from its position of Divine favour, involving the reconciling of the world (i.e., the provision made through the gospel, which brings the world within the scope of reconciliation). ¶

NT: B.89a; CB.–; K.–.
OT: –.
GEN. REF.: –.

3. *hēttēma* [ἥττημα, 2275], denotes a defect, loss, Rom. 11:12, R.V., "loss," A.V., "diminishing" (for the meaning of which in regard to Israel see No. 2); 1 Cor. 6:7, R.V., "defect" (A.V., "fault"). See DEFECT.

NT: B.349c; CB.1250b; K.–.
OT: –.
GEN. REF.: –.

Note: For "suffer loss" see LOSE, No. 2.

LOT, LOTS

A. Noun.

klēros [κλῆρος, 2819], denotes (*a*) an object used in casting or drawing lots, which consisted of bits, or small tablets, of wood or stone (the probable derivation is from *klaō*, to break); these were sometimes inscribed with the names of persons, and were put into a receptacle or a garment (a lap, Prov. 16:33), from which they were cast, after being shaken together; he whose lot first fell out was the one chosen. The method was employed in a variety of circumstances, e.g., of dividing or assigning property, Matt. 27:35; Mark 15:24; Luke 23:34; John 19:24 (cp., e.g., Numb. 26:55); of appointing to office, Acts 1:26 (cp., e.g., 1 Sam. 10:20); for other occurrences in the O.T., see, e.g., Josh. 7:14 (the earliest instance in Scripture); Lev. 16:7-10; Esth. 3:7; 9:24; (*b*) what is obtained by lot, an allotted portion, e.g., of the ministry allotted to the Apostles, Acts 1:17, R.V., "portion," marg., "lot" (A.V., "part"); in some mss. ver. 25, A.V., "part" (the R.V. follows those which have *topos*, "place"); Acts 8:21; it is also used like *klēronomia*, an inheritance, in Acts 26:18, of what God has in grace assigned to the sanctified; so Col. 1:12; in 1 Pet. 5:3 it is used of those the spiritual care of, and charge over, whom is assigned to elders, R.V., "the charge allotted to you" (plural, lit., 'the charges'), A.V., "(God's) heritage." From *klēros* the word "clergy" is derived (a transposition in the application of the term). See CHARGE, No. 4. ¶

NT: B.435b; CB.1255b; K.442.
OT: gôrāl: S.1486; HR.770a.1; H.381a; BD.174a.
naḥalāh: S.5159; HR.770a.6; H.1342a; BD.635a.
GEN. REF.: IS.3:172; NB.321; Z.3:988.

B. Verb.

lanchanō [λαγχάνω, 2975], denotes (*a*) to draw lots, John 19:24; (*b*) to obtain by lot, to obtain, Luke 1:9, "his lot was," lit., 'he received by lot,' i.e., by Divine appointment; Acts 1:17, of the portion allotted by the Lord to His Apostles in their ministry (cp. A, above); 2 Pet. 1:1, "that have obtained (a like precious faith)," i.e., by its being allotted to them, not by acquiring it for themselves, but by Divine grace (an act independent of human control, as in the casting of lots). See OBTAIN. ¶

NT: B.462a; CB.1256c; K.495.
OT: lākad: S.3920; HR.840b.1; H.1115; BD.539d.
GEN. REF.: –.

Note: For divide by lot see DIVIDE.

LOUD

megas [μέγας, 3173], great, is used, besides other meanings, of intensity, as, e.g., of the force of a voice, e.g., Matt. 27:46, 50; in the following the R.V. has "great" for the A.V., "loud," Rev. 5:2, 12; 6:10; 7:2, 10; 8:13; 10:3; 12:10; 14:7, 9, 15, 18. See GREAT.

NT: B.497c; CB.1258a; K.573.
OT: gādôl: S.1419; HR.902c.2a; H.315d; BD.152d.
GEN. REF.: –.

LOVE (Noun and Verb)

A. Verbs.

1. *agapaō* [ἀγαπάω, 25], and the corresponding noun *agapē* (B, No. 1 below) present "the characteristic word of Christianity, and since the Spirit of revelation has used it to express ideas previously unknown, enquiry into its use, whether in Greek literature or in the Septuagint, throws but little light upon its distinctive meaning in the N.T. Cp., however, Lev. 19:18; Deut. 6:5.

"*Agapē* and *agapaō* are used in the N.T. (*a*) to describe the attitude of God toward His Son, John 17:26; the human race, generally, John 3:16; Rom. 5:8 and to such as believe on the Lord Jesus Christ, particularly, John 14:21; (*b*) to convey His will to His children concerning their attitude one toward another, John 13:34, and toward all men, 1 Thess. 3:12; 1 Cor. 16:14; 2 Pet. 1:7; (*c*) to express the essential nature of God, 1 John 4:8.

"Love can be known only from the actions it prompts. God's love is seen in the gift of His Son, 1 John 4:9, 10. But obviously this is not the love of complacency, or affection, that is, it was not drawn out by any excellency in its objects, Rom. 5:8. It was an exercise of the Divine will in deliberate choice, made without assignable cause save that which lies in the nature of God Himself, cp. Deut. 7:7, 8.

"Love had its perfect expression among men in the Lord Jesus Christ, 2 Cor. 5:14; Eph. 2:4; 3:19; 5:2; Christian love is the fruit of His Spirit in the Christian, Gal. 5:22.

"Christian love has God for its primary object, and expresses itself first of all in implicit obedience to His commandments, John 14:15, 21, 23; 15:10;. 1 John 2:5; 5:3; 2 John 6. Self-will, that is, self-pleasing, is the negation of love to God.

"Christian love, whether exercised toward the brethren, or toward men generally, is not an impulse from the feelings, it does not always run with the natural inclinations, nor does it spend itself only upon those for whom some affinity is discovered. Love seeks the welfare of all, Rom. 15:2, and works no ill to any, 13:8-10; love seeks opportunity to do good to 'all men, and especially toward them that are of the household of the faith,' Gal. 6:10. See further 1 Cor. 13 and Col. 3:12-14."*

* From Notes on Thessalonians by Hogg and Vine, p. 105.

In respect of *agapaō* as used of God, it expresses the deep and constant love and interest of a perfect Being towards entirely unworthy objects, producing and fostering a reverential love in them towards the Giver, and a practical love towards those who are partakers of the same, and a desire to help others to seek the Giver. See BELOVED.

NT: B.46; CB.1233b; K.5.
OT: 'āhēb: S.157; HR.5b.la; H.29; BD.12c.
GEN. REF.: IS.3:173; NB.752; Z.3:989.

2. *phileō* [φιλέω, 5368], is to be distinguished from *agapaō* in this, that *phileō* more nearly represents tender affection. The two words are used for the love of the Father for the Son, John 3:35 (No. 1), and 5:20 (No. 2); for the believer, 14:21 (No. 1) and 16:27 (No. 2); both, of Christ's love for a certain disciple, 13:23 (No. 1), and 20:2 (No. 2). Yet the distinction between the two verbs remains, and they are never used indiscrimiantely in the same passage; if each is used with reference to the same objects, as just mentioned, each word retains its distinctive and essential character.

Phileō is never used in a command to men to love God; it is, however, used as a warning in 1 Cor. 16:22; *agapaō* is used instead, e.g., Matt. 22:37; Luke 10:27; Rom. 8:28; 1 Cor. 8:3; 1 Pet. 1:8; 1 John 4:21. The distinction between the two verbs finds a conspicuous instance in the narrative of John 21:15-17. The context itself indicates that *agapaō* in the first two questions suggests the love that values and esteems (cp. Rev. 12:11). It is an unselfish love, ready to serve. The use of *phileō* in Peter's answers and the Lord's third question, conveys the thought of cherishing the Object above all else, of manifesting an affection characterised by constancy, from the motive of the highest veneration. See also Trench, Syn., §xii.

Again, to love (*phileō*) life, from an undue desire to preserve it, forgetful of the real object of living, meets with the Lord's reproof, John 12:25. On the contrary, to love life (*agapaō*) as used in 1 Pet. 3:10, is to consult the true interests of living. Here the word *phileō* would be quite inappropriate.

NT: B.859b; CB.1264a; K.1262.
OT: 'āhēb: S.157; HR.1430b.1; H.29; BD.12c.
nāshaq: S.5401; HR.1430b.2; H.–; BD.676b.
GEN. REF.: IS.3:173; NB.752; Z.3:989.

Note: In Mark 12:38, A.V., *thelō*, to wish, is translated "love" (R.V., "desire").

B. Nouns.

1. *agapē* [ἀγάπη, 26], the significance of which has been pointed out in connection with A, No. 1, is always rendered "love" in the R.V. where the A.V. has "charity," a rendering nowhere used in the R.V.; in Rom. 14:15, where the A.V. has "charitably," the R.V., adhering to the translation of the noun, has "in love."

NT: B.5b; CB.1233b; K.5.
OT: 'ahᵃbāh: S.160; HR.6c.1; H.29c; BD.13b.
GEN. REF.: IS.3:173; NB.752; Z.3:989.

Note: In the two statements in 1 John 4:8 and 16, "God is love," both are used to enjoin the exercise of love on the part of believers. While the former introduces a declearation of the mode in which God's love has been manifested (vv. 9, 10), the second introduces a statement of the identification of believers with God in character, and the issue at the Judgment-Seat hereafter (ver. 17), an identification represented ideally in the sentence "as He is, so are we in this world."

2. *philanthrōpia* [φιλανθρωπία, 5363], denotes, lit., love for man (*phileō* and *anthrōpos*, man); hence, kindness, Acts 28:2; in Tit. 3:4, "(His) love toward man." ¶ Cp. the adverb *philanthrōpōs*, humanely, kindly, Acts 27:3. ¶ See KINDNESS.

NT: B.858d; CB.1264a; K.1261.
OT: –.
GEN. REF.: –.

Note: For *philarguria*, love of money, 1 Tim. 6:10, see MONEY (love of). For *philadelphia*, see BROTHER, Note (1).

LOVE-FEASTS

agapē [ἀγάπη, 26], is used in the plural in Jude 12, and in some mss. in 2 Pet. 2:13; R.V. marg., "many ancient authorities read 'deceivings,' " (*aputais*); so the A.V. These love-feasts arose from the common meals of the early churches (cp. 1 Cor. 11:21). They may have had this origin in the private meals of Jewish households, with the addition of the observance of the Lord's Supper. There were, however, similar common meals among the pagan religious brotherhoods. The evil dealt with at Corinth (l.c.) became enhanced by the presence of immoral persons, who degraded the feasts into wanton banquets, as mentioned in 2 Pet. and Jude. In later times the *agapē* became detached from the Lord's Supper.

NT: B.5b; CB.1233b; K.5.
OT: 'ahᵃbāh: S.160; HR.6c.1; H.29c; BD.13b.
GEN. REF.: IS.3:173; NB.754; Z.1:66.

LOVELY

prosphilēs [προσφιλής, 4375], pleasing, agreeable, lovely (*pros*, toward, *phileō*, to love),

occurs in Phil. 4:8. ¶ In the Sept., Esth. 5:1 (3rd sentence). ¶
NT: B.720b; CB.—; K.—.
OT: —.
GEN. REF.: IS.3:177; NB.—; Z.—.

LOVER

This is combined with other words, forming compound adjectives as follows:

1. *philotheos* [φιλόθεος, 5377], a lover of God, 2 Tim. 3:4. ¶
NT: B.860c; CB.1264b; K.—.
OT: —.
GEN. REF.: IS.3:177; NB.—; Z.—.

2. *philoxenos* [φιλόξενος, 5382], loving strangers (*xenia*, hospitality), translated "a lover of hospitality" in Tit. 1:8, A.V. (R.V., "given to h."); elsewhere, in 1 Tim. 3:2; 1 Pet. 4:9. See HOSPITALITY. ¶
NT: B.860d; CB.1264b; K.661.
OT: —.
GEN. REF.: IS.3:177; NB.—; Z.—.

3. *philagathos* [φιλάγαθος, 5358], loving that which is good (*agathos*), Tit. 1:8, "a lover of good," R.V. ¶
NT: B.858b; CB.1264a; K.3.
OT: —.
GEN. REF.: IS.3:177; NB.—; Z.—.

Note: The negative *aphilagathos* is found in 2 Tim. 3:3, "no lovers of good." ¶

4. *philarguros* [φιλάργυρος, 5366], loving money (*arguros*, silver), translated "lovers of money" in Luke 16:14; 2 Tim. 3:2, R.V. (A.V., "covetous"). See COVETOUS. ¶
NT: B.859a; CB.1264a; K.—.
OT: —.
GEN. REF.: IS.3:177; NB.—; Z.—.

5. *philautos* [φίλαυτος, 5367], loving oneself, 2 Tim. 3:2, R.V. ¶
NT: B.859a; CB.1264a; K.—.
OT: —.
GEN. REF.: IS.3:177; NB.—; Z.—.

6. *philēdonos* [φιλήδονος, 5369], loving pleasure (*hēdonē*, pleasure), 2 Tim. 3:4, "lovers of pleasure." ¶
NT: B.859c; CB.1264a; K.303.
OT: —.
GEN. REF.: IS.3:177; NB.—; Z.—.

Note: For loving warmly, Rom. 12:10, see AFFECTION, B, No. 2. ¶

For *aphilarguros*, no lover of money, 1 Tim. 3:3, R.V., and Heb. 13:5, R.V., see COVETOUS. ¶

LOW (to bring, to make), LOW (estate, degree)

A. Verb.

tapeinoō [ταπεινόω, 5013], to bring low, to humble, is translated "shall be brought low" in Luke 3:5. See HUMBLE.
NT: B.804c; CB.1271a; K.1152.
OT: kānaʻ: S.3665; HR.1334c.10; H.1001; BD.488b.
ʻānāh: S.6031; HR.1334c.14a-f; H.1651,1652; BD.776a.
shāphēl: S.8231; HR.1335a.20; H.2449; BD.1050a.
GEN. REF.: IS.3:177; NB.—; Z.—.

B. Adjective.

tapeinos [ταπεινός, 5011], denotes of low degree or estate, Rom. 12:16, "things that are lowly," R.V. (A.V., "men of low estate"). See BASE, DEGREE, ESTATE, HUMBLE, LOWLY.
NT: B.804a; CB.1271a; K.1152.
OT: shāphāl: S.8217; HR.1334b.11a; H.2445c; BD.1050c.
ʻānî: S.6041; HR.1334b.7a; H.1652d; BD.776d.
GEN. REF.: IS.3:177; NB.—; Z.—.

C. Noun.

tapeinōsis [ταπείνωσις, 5014], abasement, humiliation, low estate, is translated "low estate" in Luke 1:48; in Jas. 1:10, "that he is made low," lit., 'in his abasement.' See HUMILIATION.
NT: B.805a; CB.1271a; K.1152.
OT: ʻᵒnî: S.6040; HR.1335c.2a; H.1652e; BD.777a.
GEN. REF.: IS.3:177; NB.—; Z.—.

LOWER (Adjective, and Verb, to make), LOWEST

A. Adjectives.

1. *katōteros* [κατώτερος, 2737], the comparative degree of *katō*, beneath, is used in Eph. 4:9, of Christ's descent into "the lower parts of the earth"; two of the various interpretations of this phrase are (1) that the earth is in view in contrast to heaven, (2) that the region is that of Hades, the Sheol of the O.T. Inasmuch as the passage is describing the effects not merely of the Incarnation but of the Death and Resurrection of Christ, the second interpretation is to be accepted; cp., e.g., Ps. 16:10; 63:9; where the Sept. has the superlative; 139:15; Acts 2:31. Moreover, as Westcott says, it is most unlikely that the phrase would be used to describe the earth. The word *merē* (plural of *meros*), "parts," would have no force in such a meaning. ¶
NT: B.425a; CB.1254c; K.422.
OT: taḥtî: S.8482; HR.757a.1b; H.2504b; BD.1066b.
GEN. REF.: —.

2. *eschatos* [ἔσχατος, 2078], last, utmost, lowest, is rendered "lowest" in Luke 14:9, 10, of the lowest place at a meal. See LAST.
NT: B.313d; CB.1246c; K.264.
OT: 'aḥᵃrôn: S.314; HR.558a.1c; H.68e; BD.30d.
'aḥᵃrît: S.319; HR.558a.1d; H.68f; BD.31a.
GEN. REF.: —.

B. Verb.

elattoō [ἐλαττόω, 1642], denotes to make less (*elattōn*, less) and is used in the Active Voice in Heb. 2:7, "Thou madest (Him) . . . lower," and in the Passive in ver. 9, "was made . . . lower," and John 3:30, "(I must) decrease," (lit., 'be made less'). ¶
NT: B.248b; CB.—; K.—.
OT: ḥāsēr: S.2637; HR.448b.1a,b; H.705; BD.341a.
māʻaṭ: S.4591; HR.448b.2; H.1228; BD.589b.
GEN. REF.: —.

For **LOWER (Verb, to let down)** see **LET DOWN**, No. 2 (*d*)

LOWLINESS, LOWLY

A. Noun.

tapeinophrosunē [ταπεινοφροσύνη, 5012], lowliness of mind, humbleness, is translated "lowliness" or "lowliness of mind" in Acts 20:19, R.V.; Eph. 4:2; Phil. 2:3. See HUMBLENESS OF MIND.

NT: B.804c; CB.1271a; K.1152.
OT: –.
GEN. REF.: IS.3:177; NB.–; Z.–.

B. Adjective.

tapeinos [ταπεινός, —], low, lowly: see HUMBLE and LOW, B.

LOWRING (to be)

stugnazō [στυγνάζω, 4768], to have a gloomy, sombre appearance (akin to *stugnos*, sombre, gloomy, from a root *stug*—, to hate; cp. *stugētos*, hateful, Tit. 3:3), is said of the human countenance, Mark 10:22, R.V., "his countenance fell" (A.V., "he was sad"); of the sky, Matt. 16:3, "lowring." See COUNTENANCE, Note (3). ¶ In the Sept., Ezek. 27:35; 28:19; 32:10. ¶

NT: B.771d; CB.–; K.–.
OT: shāmēm: S.8074; HR.1297c.1; H.2409; BD.1030d.
GEN. REF.: –.

LUCRE (filthy)

A. Noun.

kerdos [κέρδος, 2771], gain (cp. *kerdainō*, to gain, get gain), is translated "gain" in Phil. 1:21 and 3:7; "lucre" in Tit. 1:11 (preceded by *aischros*, filthy). See GAIN. ¶

NT: B.429c; CB.1255a; K.428.
OT: –.
GEN. REF.: IS.3:178; NB.–; Z.3:998.

B. Adjective.

aischrokerdēs [αἰσχροκερδής, 146], denotes greedy of base gains (*aischros*, and A, as above), 1 Tim. 3:8, "greedy of filthy lucre"; so the R.V. in Tit. 1:7, A.V., "(given to) filthy lucre." In some mss. 1 Tim. 3:3. ¶

NT: B.25a; CB.1234a; K.–.
OT: –.
GEN. REF.: IS.3:178; NB.–; Z.–.

aischrokerdōs [αἰσχροκερδῶς, 147], denotes 'from eagerness for base gain,' 1 Pet. 5:2, "for filthy lucre." ¶

NT: B.25b; CB.–; K.–.
OT: –.
GEN. REF.: IS.3:178; NB.–; Z.–.

LUKEWARM

chliaros [χλιαρός, 5513], tepid, warm (akin to *chliō*, to become warm, not found in the N.T. or Sept.), is used metaphorically in Rev. 3:16, of the state of the Laodicean church, which afforded no refreshment to the Lord, such as is ministered naturally by either cold or hot water. ¶

NT: B.882c; CB.1239c; K.296.
OT: –.
GEN. REF.: –.

LUMP

phurama [φύραμα, 5445], denotes that which is mixed or kneaded (*phuraō*, to mix); hence, a lump, either of dough, Rom. 11:16 (cp. Numb. 15:21); 1 Cor. 5:6, 7; Gal. 5:9 (see under LEAVEN); of potter's clay, Rom. 9:21. ¶

NT: B.869a; CB.1264c; K.–.
OT: mish'eret: S.4863; HR.1446b.1; H.1252; BD.602b.
GEN. REF.: –.

For **LUNATIC** see **EPILEPTIC**

LUST (Noun and Verb)

A. Nouns.

1. *epithumia* [ἐπιθυμία, 1939) denotes strong desire of any kind, the various kinds being frequently specified by some adjective (see below). The word is used of a good desire in Luke 22:15; Phil. 1:23, and 1 Thess. 2:17 only. Everywhere else it has a bad sense. In Rom. 6:12 the injunction against letting sin reign in our mortal body to obey the lust thereof, refers to those evil desires which are ready to express themselves in bodily activity. They are equally the lusts of the flesh, Rom. 13:14; Gal. 5:16, 24; Eph. 2:3; 2 Pet. 2:18; 1 John 2:16, a phrase which describes the emotions of the soul, the natural tendency towards things evil. Such lusts are not necessarily base and immoral, they may be refined in character, but are evil if inconsistent with the will of God.

Other descriptions besides those already mentioned are:— "of the mind," Eph. 2:3; "evil (desire)," Col. 3:5; "the passion of," 1 Thess. 4:5, R.V.; "foolish and hurtful," 1 Tim. 6:9; "youthful," 2 Tim. 2:22; "divers," 2 Tim. 3:6 and Tit. 3:3; "their own," 2 Tim. 4:3; 2 Pet. 3:3; Jude 16; "worldly," Tit. 2:12; "his own," Jas. 1:14; "your former," 1 Pet. 1:14, R.V.; "fleshly," 2:11; "of men," 4:2; "of defilement," 2 Pet. 2:10; "of the eyes," 1 John 2:16; of the world ("thereof"), ver. 17; "their own ungodly," Jude 18. In Rev. 18:14 "(the fruits) which thy soul lusted after" is, lit., 'of thy soul's lust.' See DESIRE, A, No. 1 (where associated words are noted).

NT: B.293b; CB.1246b; K.339.
OT: ta'ᵃwāh: S.8378; HR.521a.1d; H.40d; BD.16c.
ḥᵃmûdāh: S.2530; HR.521a.3c; H.673; BD.326d.
GEN. REF.: IS.3:186; NB.759; Z.3:1008.

2. *orexis* [ὄρεξις, 3715], lit., a reaching or stretching after (akin to *oregomai*, to stretch oneself out, reach after), a general term for every kind of desire, is used in Rom. 1:27, "lust." ¶

NT: B.580a; CB.1261a; K.727.
OT: —.
GEN. REF.: IS.3:186; NB.759; Z.3:1008.

3. *hēdonē* [ἡδονή, 2237], pleasure, is translated "lusts," in the A.V. of Jas. 4:1, 3 (R.V., "pleasures"). See PLEASURE.

NT: B.344b; CB.1249c; K.303.
OT: —.
GEN. REF.: IS.3:186; NB.759; Z.3:1008.

Note: In 1 Thess. 4:5, A.V., *pathos*, passion (R.V., "passion"), is translated "lust," which is the better rendering of the next word *epithumia*, rendered "concupiscence." *Pathos* is described by Trench as "the diseased condition out of which *epithumia* springs." In 1 Cor. 12:6, *epithumētēs*, a luster after, is rendered to lust.

B. Verb.

epithumeō [ἐπιθυμέω, 1937], akin to A, No. 1, has the same twofold meaning as the noun, namely (*a*) to desire, used of the Holy Spirit against the flesh, Gal. 5:17 (see below); of the Lord Jesus, Luke 22:15, "I have desired"; of the holy angels, 1 Pet. 1:12; of good men, for good things, Matt. 13:17; 1 Tim. 3:1; Heb. 6:11; of men, for things without moral quality, Luke 15:16; 16:21; 17:22; Rev. 9:6; (*b*) of evil desires, in respect of which it is translated to lust in Matt. 5:28; 1 Cor. 10:6; Gal. 5:17 (1st part; see below); Jas. 4:2; to covet, Acts 20:23; Rom. 7:7; 13:9. See COVET, DESIRE, B, No. 2. ¶

NT: B.293a; CB.1246b; K.339.
OT: 'āwāh: S.183; HR.520b.1a,b; H.40; BD.16a.
ḥāmad: S.2530; HR.520b.4; H.673; BD.326b.
GEN. REF.: IS.3:186; NB.759; Z.3:1008.

Notes: (1) In Gal. 5:17, in the statement, "the flesh lusteth against the Spirit, and the Spirit against the flesh," the Holy Spirit is intended, as in the preceding verse. To walk by the Spirit involves the opposition here referred to. The verb "lusteth" is not repeated in the second part of the statement, but must in some way be supplied. Since in modern English the word "lust" is used exclusively in a bad sense, it is unsuitable as a translation of *epithumeō*, where the word is used in a good sense. As the rendering "desire" is used of the Lord Jesus (as mentioned above), it may be best so understood here in respect of the Holy Spirit.

(2) In James 4:5 the R.V. translates correctly in giving two questions, each of a rhetorical character, asked by way of remonstrance. The first draws attention to the fact that it is impossible for the Scripture to speak in vain; the second to the impossibility that the Holy Spirit, whom God has caused to dwell in the believer, should "long (unto envying)," *epipotheō* (A.V., "lust"). Here again, not the human spirit is in view, but the Spirit of God; cp. 1 Cor. 6:19. See LONG.

For **LYING** (falsehood) see **LIE**, and for **LYING** (in wait) see **LIE IN WAIT**

M

MAD, MADNESS

A. Verbs.

1. *mainomai* [μαίνομαι, 3105], to rage, be mad, is translated by the verb to be mad in John 10:20; Acts 12:15; 26:24, 25; 1 Cor. 14:23; see BESIDE ONESELF, No. 2.

NT: B.486b; CB.1257b; K.548.
OT: hālal: S.1984; HR.892a.1; H.499,500; BD.237d,239b.
shāga': S.7696; HR.892a.2; H.2328; BD.993c.
GEN. REF.: IS.3:211; NB.—; Z.—.

2. *emmainomai* [ἐμμαίνομαι, 1693], an intensive form of No. 1, prefixed by *en*, in, implying fierce rage, to be furious against; it is rendered "being exceedingly mad" in Acts 26:11 (cp. 9:1). ¶

NT: B.255a; CB.—; K.—.
OT: —.
GEN. REF.: —.

B. Nouns.

1. *mania* [μανία, 3130], akin to A, and transliterated into English, denotes frenzy, madness, Acts 26:24 "(thy much learning doth turn thee to) madness," R.V.; A.V., "(doth make thee) mad." ¶

NT: B.490d; CB.1257c; K.—.
OT: masṭēmāh: S.4895; HR.895c.1; H.2251a; BD.966b.
GEN. REF.: IS.3:211; NB.—; Z.4:29.

2. *anoia* [ἄνοια, 454], lit., without understanding (*a*, negative, *nous*, mind, understanding), denotes folly, 2 Tim. 3:9, and this finding its expression in violent rage, Luke 6:11. See FOLLY. ¶

NT: B.70d; CB.1235c; K.636.
OT: 'iwwelet: S.200; HR.105a.1; H.44c; BD.17c.
GEN. REF.: IS.3:211; NB.–; Z.–.

3. *paraphronia* [παραφρονία, 3913], madness (from *para*, contrary to, and *phrēn*, the mind), is used in 2 Pet. 2:16. ¶ Cp. *paraphroneō*, 2 Cor. 11:23, 'I speak like one distraught.' ¶

NT: B.623c; CB.–; K.–.
OT: –.
GEN. REF.: IS.3:211; NB.–; Z.–.

MADE (be)

A. Verbs.

1. *ginomai* [γίνομαι, 1096], to become, is sometimes translated by the Passive Voice of the verb to make, e.g., Matt. 9:16; John 1:3 (three times), 10; 8:33; Rom. 11:9; 1 Cor. 1:30; 3:13; 4:9, 13; Eph. 2:13; 3:7; Phil. 2:7 (but R.V. marg., "becoming"); Col. 1:23, 25; Heb. 5:5; 6:4; 7:12, 16, 21, 26; 11:3; Jas. 3:9; 1 Pet. 2:7. In many places the R.V. translates otherwise, and chiefly by the verb to become, e.g., Matt. 25:6, "there is"; 27:24, "was arising"; John 1:14, "became"; John 2:9, "become"; Rom. 1:3, "born"; 2:25, "is become"; 10:20, "became"; Gal. 3:13, "having become"; 4:4, "born" (twice); Heb. 3:14, "are become"; 7:22, "hath . . . become."

NT: B.158a; CB.1248b; K.117.
OT: hāyāh: S.1961; HR.256b.6d; H.491; BD.224a.
GEN. REF.: –.

2. *keimai* [κεῖμαι, 2749], to lie, is sometimes used as the Passive Voice of *tithēmi*, to put; it is translated "is (not) made" in 1 Tim. 1:9, of the Law, where a suitable rendering would be 'is (not) enacted.'

NT: B.426c; CB.1254c; K.425.
OT: –.
GEN. REF.: –.

Notes: (1) In 2 Pet. 2:12, A.V., the verb *gennaō*, to beget, in the Passive Voice, to be born, is translated "made" (R.V., "born").

(2) In Luke 3:5, A.V. (3rd statement), the future tense of *eimi*, to be, is translated "shall be made" (R.V., "shall become"); in the next sentence there is nothing in the original representing "*shall be* made."

(3) In Acts 16:13, A.V., the infinitive mood of *eimi*, to be, is translated "to be made" (of prayer), R.V., "there was (a place of prayer)."

(4) For the translation of words in which the Eng. "made" forms a part of another verb, see under those words, e.g., CONFESSION, KNOWN, LIKE, LOW, PAYMENT, RICH, SUBJECT.

B. Noun.

poiēma [ποίημα, 4161], whence Eng., poem, denotes that which is made (from *poieō*, to do, make), Rom. 1:20, "the things that are made"; Eph. 2:10, "(His) workmanship." ¶

NT: B.683b; CB.1265c; K.895.
OT: maʿaseh: S.4639; HR.1168b.1; H.1708a; BD.795c.
GEN. REF.: –.

MAGISTRATE

1. *stratēgos* [στρατηγός, 4755], besides its application to the captain of the Temple (see CAPTAIN), denotes a magistrate or governor, Acts 16:20, 22, 35, 36, 38. These were, in Latin terminology, the *duumviri* or *praetores*, so called in towns which were Roman colonies. They were attended by lictors or "serjeants," who executed their orders. In the circumstances of Acts 16 they exceeded their powers, in giving orders for Roman "citizens" to be scourged; hence they became suppliants. See CAPTAIN.

NT: B.770c; CB.1270a; K.1091.
OT: sāgān: S.5461; HR.1295b.3a; H.1461; BD.688c.
sar: S.8269; HR.1295b.5; H.2295a; BD.978a.
GEN. REF.: IS.3:219; NB.771; Z.4:38.

2. *archōn* [ἄρχων, 758], a ruler, denotes, in Luke 12:58, a local authority, a magistrate, acting in the capacity of one who received complaints, and possessing higher authority than the judge, to whom the magistrate remits the case. See CHIEF, PRINCE, RULER.

NT: B.113d; CB.1237b; K.81.
OT: nāśîʾ: S.5387; HR.166b.17; H.1421b,c; BD.672b.
rōʾsh: S.7218; HR.166b.26; H.2097; BD.910c.
sar: S.8269; HR.166b.30a; H.2295a; BD.978a.
GEN. REF.: IS.3:219; NB.771; Z.4:38.

Notes: (1) In Luke 12:11, A.V., *archē*, a beginning, rule, principality, is translated "magistrates"; the word, however, denotes rulers in general: hence the R.V., "rulers."

(2) For the A.V. of Tit. 3:1, "to obey magistrates," see OBEY, B, No. 3.

MAGNIFICENCE

megaleiotēs [μεγαλειότης, 3168], denotes splendour, magnificence (from *megaleios*, magnificent, "mighty," Acts 2:11, *megas*, great), translated "magnificence" in Acts 19:27, of the splendour of the goddess Diana. In Luke 9:43, R.V. (A.V., "mighty power"); in 2 Pet. 1:16, "majesty." In the papyri writings it is frequent as a ceremonial title. ¶

NT: B.496d; CB.1258a; K.573.
OT: tiph'eret: S.8597; HR.901b.2; H.1726b; BD.802c.
GEN. REF.: IS.3:221; NB.–; Z.–.

MAGNIFY

megalunō [μεγαλύνω, 3170], to make great (*megas*), is translated to magnify in Luke 1:46; in ver. 58, R.V., "had magnified (His mercy),"

A.V., "had shewed great (mercy)"; Acts 5:13; 10:46; 19:17; 2 Cor. 10:15, R.V. (A.V., "we shall be enlarged"), i.e., by their faith in its practical effect he will be so assisted to enlarge the scope of his Gospel ministry and carry its message to regions beyond them; in Phil. 1:20, of the magnifying of Christ by him in his body, i.e., in all his activities and ways. In Matt. 23:5, it signifies to enlarge. See ENLARGE. ¶

NT: B.497a; CB.1258a; K.573.
OT: gādal: S.1431; HR.902a.2a-f; H.315; BD.152a.
GEN. REF.: IS.3:221; NB.—; Z.—.

Note: In Rom. 11:13, A.V., the verb *doxazō*, to glorify, is translated "I magnify (my office);" R.V., "I glorify (my ministry)." See GLORIFY.

MAID, MAIDEN, MAIDSERVANT

1. *pais* [παῖς, 3816], a child, denotes a maid or maiden in Luke 8:51 and 54, R.V., "maiden" in both places. See CHILD, MANSERVANT, SERVANT, SON, YOUNG MAN.

NT: B.604c; CB.1261c; K.759.
OT: —.
GEN. REF.: IS.3:224; NB.—; Z.4:41.

2. *paidiskē* [παιδίσκη, 3814], a diminutive of No. 1, is translated "maid," "maids," in the A.V. and R.V. in Mark 14:66, 69; Luke 22:56; in the R.V. (A.V., "damsel"), in Matt. 26:69; John 18:17; Acts 12:13; 16:16; in Luke 12:45, "maidservants" (A.V. "maidens"); in Gal. 4:22, 23, 30, 31, R.V., "handmaid" (A.V., "bondmaid" or "bondwoman"). See BONDMAID, DAMSEL. ¶

NT: B.604b; CB.1261c; K.—.
OT: 'āmāh: S.519; HR.1048b.1; H.112; BD.51a.
shiphḥāh: S.8198; HR.1048b.4; H.2442a; BD.1046c.
GEN. REF.: IS.3:224; NB.—; Z.4:41.

3. *korasion* [κοράσιον, 2877], a colloquial, familiar term, is translated "maid" in Matt. 9:24, 25, A.V. (R.V., "damsel"). See DAMSEL, No. 1.

NT: B.444b; CB.1255c; K.—.
OT: na'arāh: S.5291; HR.779c.2a; H.1389c; BD.655a.
GEN. REF.: IS.3:224; NB.—; Z.4:41.

MAIMED

1. *anapēros*, or *anapeiros* [ἀνάπηρος, 376], crippled, maimed (from *ana*, up, and *pēros*, disabled in a limb), is found in Luke 14:13, 21. ¶

NT: B.59c; CB.—; K.—.
OT: —.
GEN. REF.: IS.3:225; NB.—; Z.—.

2. *kullos* [κυλλός, 2948], denotes crooked, crippled (akin to *kuliō*, to roll): in Matt. 15:30, 31, translated "maimed"; so in 18:8, A.V. (R.V., "halt") and Mark 9:43 (A.V. and R.V.). See HALT. ¶

NT: B.457b; CB.1256b; K.—.
OT: —.
GEN. REF.: IS.3:225; NB.—; Z.—.

For **MAINSAIL** see **FORESAIL**

MAINTAIN

proistēmi [προΐστημι, 4291], to preside, rule, also means to maintain, Tit. 3:8 and 14, "to maintain (good works);" R.V. marg., "profess honest occupations" (A.V., marg. . . "trades"). The usage of the phrase *kala erga* (good works) in the Pastoral Epistles is decisive for the rendering "good works," here. See OVER (to be), RULE.

NT: B.707a; CB.1266c; K.—.
OT: —.
GEN. REF.: —.

MAJESTY

1. *megaleiotēs* [μεγαλειότης, —]: See MAGNIFICENCE.

2. *megalōsunē* [μεγαλωσύνη, 3172], from *megas*, great, denotes greatness, majesty; it is used of God the Father, signifying His greatness and dignity, in Heb. 1:3, "the Majesty (on high);" and 8:1, "the Majesty (in the Heavens)"; and in an ascription of praise acknowledging the attributes of God in Jude 25. ¶

NT: B.497b; CB.1258a; K.573.
OT: gōdel: S.1433; HR.902c.3a; H.315b; BD.152d.
gᵉdûllāh: S.1420; HR.902c.3b; H.315e; BD.153c.
rᵉbû (Aramaic): S.7238; HR.902c.4; H.2985a; BD.1112c.
GEN. REF.: IS.3:225; NB.—; Z.—.

MAKE

1. *poieō* [ποιέω, 4160], to do, to make, is used in the latter sense (*a*) of constructing or producing anything, of the creative acts of God, e.g., Matt. 19:4 (2nd part); Acts 17:24; of the acts of human beings, e.g., Matt. 17:4; Acts 9:39; (*b*) with nouns denoting a state or condition, to be the author of, to cause, e.g., peace, Eph. 2:15; Jas. 3:18, stumblingblocks, Rom. 16:17; (*c*) with nouns involving the idea of action (or of something accomplished by action), so as to express the idea of the verb more forcibly (the Middle Voice is commonly used in this respect, suggesting the action as being of special interest to the doer); for the Active Voice see, e.g., Mark 2:23, of making one's way, where the idea is not that the disciples made a path through the standing corn, but simply that they went, the phrase being equivalent to going, "(they began) as they went (to pluck the ears)"; other instances of the Active are Rev. 13:13, 14; 16:14; 19:20; for the Middle Voice (the 'dynamic' or 'subjective' Middle), see, e.g., John 14:23, "will make Our abode"; in Acts 20:24, "none of these things move me," lit.,

'I make account of none of these things'; 25:17, "I made no delay," R.V.; Rom. 15:26; Eph. 4:16; Heb. 1:2; 2 Pet. 1:10; (*d*) to make ready or prepare, e.g., a dinner, Luke 14:12; a supper, John 12:2; (*e*) to acquire, provide a thing for oneself, Matt. 25:16; Luke 19:18; (*f*) to render or make one or oneself anything, or cause a person or thing to become something, e.g., Matt. 4:19; 12:16, "make (Him known)"; John 5:11, 15, to make whole; 16:2, lit., 'they shall make (you put out of the synagogue)'; Eph. 2:14; Heb. 1:7; to change one thing into another, Matt. 21:13; John 2:16; 4:46; 1 Cor. 6:15; (*g*) to constitute one anything, e.g., Acts 2:36; (*h*) to declare one or oneself anything, John 5:18, "making (Himself equal with God)"; 8:53; 10:33; 19:7, 12; 1 John 1:10; 5:10; (*i*) to make one do a thing, e.g., Luke 5:34; John 6:10; Rev. 3:9. See DO, No. 1, and other renderings there.

NT: B.680d; CB.1265c; K.895.
OT: ʿāsāh: S.6213; HR.1154a.33a; H.1708,1709; BD.793c.
GEN. REF.: IS.3:225; NB.–; Z.–.

2. *tithēmi* [τίθημι, 5087], to put, is used in the same way as No. 1 (*f*), Matt. 22:44; Mark 12:36; Luke 20:43; Acts 2:35; 1 Cor. 9:18 (of making the Gospel without charge); Heb. 1:13; 10:13; 2 Pet. 2:6; as No. 1 (*g*), Acts 20:28; Rom. 4:17. See APPOINT, No. 3.

NT: B.815d; CB.1272c; K.1176.
OT: nātan: S.5414; HR.1348c.16; H.1443; BD.678b.
sûm, sîm: S.7760; HR.1348c.25a; H.2243; BD.962c.
GEN. REF.: –.

3. *diatithēmi* [διατίθημι, 1303], to covenant, is rendered "I will make" (the noun *diathēkē*, a covenant, being expressed additionally), in the Middle Voice, in Acts 3:25; Heb. 8:10 and 10:16, lit., 'I will covenant' (see R.V., marg.). See APPOINT, No. 4.

NT: B.189d; CB.1241b; K.157.
OT: kārat: S.3772; HR.313b.1; H.1048; BD.503c.
GEN. REF.: –.

4. *kathistēmi* [καθίστημι, 2525], to set down, set in order, appoint, is used in the same way as No. 1 (*g*) in Acts 7:10, 27, 35; Heb. 7:28, A.V. (R.V., "appointeth"); as No. 1 (*f*) in Rom. 5:19 (twice). See APPOINT, No. 2.

NT: B.390b; CB.1254c; K.387.
OT: pāqad: S.6485; HR.702c.15a-d; H.1802; BD.823b.
sûm, sîm: S.7760; HR.703c.19; H.2243; BD.962c.
GEN. REF.: –.

5. *sunistēmi* [συνίστημι, 4921], to commend, prove, establish, is used in Gal. 2:18, much as in No. 1 (*g*), "I make myself (a transgressor)," i.e., 'I constitute (or prove) myself etc.' See APPROVE, No. 2.

NT: B.790c; CB.1270c; K.1120.
OT: –.
GEN. REF.: –.

6. *didōmi* [δίδωμι, 1325], to give, is used in 2 Thess. 3:9 in much the same sense as No. 1 (*g*), "to make (ourselves an ensample)"; in Rev. 3:9 (1st part), R.V., "I will give," the sense is virtually the same as *poieō* in the 2nd part of the verse, see No. 1 (*i*). See GIVE.

NT: B.192c; CB.1241c; K.166.
OT: nātan: S.5414; HR.317b.26a; H.1443; BD.678b.
GEN. REF.: –.

7. *epiteleō* [ἐπιτελέω, 2005], to complete, is translated "to make" in Heb. 8:5 (1st part), R.V. marg., "complete" [in the 2nd part No. 1 is used in sense (*a*)]. See ACCOMPLISH.

NT: B.302b; CB.–; K.–.
OT: kālāh: S.3615; HR.535a.4; H.982-984; BD.477b,478a.
ʿāsāh: S.6213; HR.535a.5; H.1708,1709; BD.793c.
GEN. REF.: IS.3:225; NB.–; Z.–.

8. *sunteleō* [συντελέω, 4931], to end, fulfil, is translated "I will make" in Heb. 8:8; said of the new covenant. See END.

NT: B.792a; CB.1271a; K.1161.
OT: kālāh: S.3615; HR.1319b.7b; H.982-984; BD.477b,478a.
tāmam: S.8552; HR.1319b.16a; H.2522; BD.1070b.
GEN. REF.: –.

9. *eimi* [εἰμί, 1510], to be, is translated "make" in Mark 12:42, lit., 'which is (a farthing).'

NT: B.222d; CB.1243a; K.206.
OT: –.
GEN. REF.: –.

10. *prospoieō* [προσποιέω, 4364], primarily, to claim, is used in the Middle Voice with the meaning to make as if, in Luke 24:28, of the Lord's action regarding the two on the way to Emmaus. ¶ In the Sept., 1 Sam. 21:13; Job 19:14. ¶

NT: B.718b; CB.–; K.–.
OT: –.
GEN. REF.: –.

11. *katechō* [κατέχω, 2722], to hold fast (*kata*, down, intensive, *echō*, to hold) is used of making for a place, in Acts 27:40, R.V., "they made for" (A.V., "they made toward"). See HOLD.

NT: B.422c; CB.1254b; K.286.
OT: –.
GEN. REF.: –.

12. *prokatartizō* [προκαταρτίζω, 4294], to render fit (fitted; *artos*, a joint) beforehand, is used in 2 Cor. 9:5, "to make up beforehand." ¶

NT: B.707c; CB.1266c; K.–.
OT: –.
GEN. REF.: –.

Notes: (1) In Heb. 9:2, A.V., *kataskeuazō*, to prepare, is translated "made" (R.V., "prepared").

(2) In Eph. 2:15, A.V., *ktizō*, to create, is translated "make" (R.V., "create").

(3) In Acts 26:16, A.V., *procheirizō*, to determine, choose, is translated "make" (R.V., "appoint").

(4) In Gal. 3:16, A.V., *erō*, to speak, is translated "were . . . made" (R.V. "were . . . spoken").

(5) In Luke 14:31, A.V., *sumballō*, to meet with, in hostile sense, is rendered in combination with the phrase *eis polemon*, in war, "to make war"; R.V., "to encounter (in war)."

(6) In Rom. 14:19 "the things which make for peace" is, lit., 'the things of peace.'

(7) In Acts 22:1 the verb "I make" represents no word in the original, lit., 'hear now my defence unto you.'

(8) The Eng. verb to make forms with many other verbs a rendering of single Greek verbs which are given under the respective headings.

(9) For "made," Luke 19:16, R.V., see GAIN, *Note* (1).

MAKER

dēmiourgos [δημιουργός, 1217], lit., one who works for the people (from *dēmos*, people, *ergon*, work; an ancient inscription speaks of the magistrates of Tarsus as *dēmiourgoi*: the word was formerly used thus regarding several towns in Greece; it is also found used of an artist), came to denote, in general usage, a builder or maker, and is used of God as the Maker of the Heavenly City, Heb. 11:10. In that passage the first word of the two, *technitēs*, denotes an architect, designer, the second, *dēmiourgos*, is the actual Framer; the city is the archetype of the earthly one which God chose for His earthly people. ¶ Cp. *Ktistēs*, creator.

NT: B.178d; CB.1240c; K.149.
OT: –.
GEN. REF.: –.

For **TENT-MAKER** see Vol. IV, p. 118

MALE

arsēn or *arrēn* [ἄρσην, 730], is translated "men" in Rom. 1:27 (three times); "man child" in Rev. 12:5 (ver. 13 in some mss.); "male" in Matt. 19:4; Mark 10:6; Luke 2:23; Gal. 3:28, "(there can be no) male (and female)," R.V., i.e., sex-distinction does not obtain in Christ; sex is no barrier either to salvation or the development of Christian graces. See MAN ¶.

NT: B.109d; CB.1237c; K.–.
OT: zākār: S.2145; HR.160c.4; H.551e; BD.271b.
GEN. REF.: IS.3:229; NB.–; Z.–.

MALEFACTOR

1. *kakourgos* [κακοῦργος, 2557], an adjective, lit., evil-working (*kakos*, evil, *ergon*, work), is used as a noun, translated "malefactor (-s)" in Luke 23:32, 33, 39, and in the R.V. in 2 Tim. 2:9 (A.V., "evil doer"). See EVIL, B, *Note* (1). In the Sept., Prov. 21:15. ¶

NT: B.398b; CB.1253b; K.391.
OT: (pō'ēl) 'āwen: S.205; HR.711c.1; H.48a; BD.20a.
GEN. REF.: IS.2:211; NB.–; Z.–.

2. *kakopoios* [κακοποιός, 2555], an adjective, lit., doing evil, is used in 1 Pet. 2:12, 14; 3:16 (in some mss.); 4:15. See EVIL, B, No. 5. ¶

NT: B.397c; CB.1253b; K.391.
OT: rā'a': S.7489; HR.709b.2; H.2191,2192; BD.949b.
GEN. REF.: IS.2:211; NB.–; Z.–.

MALICE, MALICIOUSNESS, MALICIOUS

kakia [κακία, 2549], badness in quality (the opposite of *aretē*, excellence), "the vicious character generally" (Lightfoot), is translated "malice" in 1 Cor. 5:8; 14:20; Eph. 4:31; Col. 3:8; Tit. 3:3; 1 Pet. 2:1, A.V. (R.V., "wickedness"; marg., "malice"); "maliciousness" in Rom. 1:29; in 1 Pet. 2:16, A.V. (R.V., "wickedness"; marg., "malice"). Elsewhere, Matt. 6:34; Acts 8:22; Jas. 1:21 (R.V. marg., "malice"). See EVIL, B, No. 1. ¶

NT: B.397a; CB.1253a; K.391.
OT: rā'āh: S.7451; HR.708a.11d; H.2191; BD.949a.
GEN. REF.: IS.3:230; NB.775; Z.–.

Note: In 2 John 10, A.V., *ponēros*, evil, wicked (see EVIL, A, No. 2), is translated "malicious" (R.V., "wicked").

MALIGNITY

kakoētheia [κακοήθεια, 2550], lit., bad manner or character (*kakos*, bad, *ēthos*, manner), hence, an evil disposition that tends to put the worst construction on everything, malice, malevolence, craftiness, occurs in Rom. 1:29, as the accompaniment of *dolos*, guile. ¶

NT: B.397b; CB.–; K.391.
OT: –.
GEN. REF.: IS.3:230; NB.–; Z.–.

MAMMON

mamōnas [μαμωνᾶς, 3126], a common Aramaic word for riches, akin to a Hebrew word signifying to be firm, stedfast (whence Amen), hence, that which is to be trusted; Gesenius regards it as derived from a Heb. word signifying "treasure" (Gen. 43:23); it is personified in Matt. 6:24; Luke 16:9, 11, 13. ¶

NT: B.490a; CB.1257c; K.552.
OT: –.
GEN. REF.: IS.3:232; NB.775; Z.4:47.

MAN (see also MEN)

1. *anthrōpos* [ἄνθρωπος, 444], is used:

(*a*) generally, of a human being, male or female, without reference to sex or nationality, e.g., Matt. 4:4; 12:35; John 2:25;

(*b*) in distinction from God, e.g., Matt. 19:6; John 10:33; Gal. 1:11; Col. 3:23;

(*c*) in distinction from animals etc., e.g., Luke 5:10;

(*d*) sometimes, in the plural, of men and women, people, e.g., Matt. 5:13, 16; in Mark 11:2 and 1 Tim. 6:16, lit., 'no one of men';

(*e*) in some instances with a suggestion of human frailty and imperfection, e.g., 1 Cor. 2:5; Acts 14:15 (2nd part);

(*f*) in the phrase translated "after man," "after the manner of men," "as a man" (A.V.), lit. 'according to (*kata*) man,' is used only by the Apostle Paul, of "(1) the practices of fallen humanity, 1 Cor. 3:3; (2) anything of human origin, Gal. 1:11; (3) the laws that govern the administration of justice among men, Rom. 3:5; (4) the standard generally accepted among men, Gal. 3:15; (5) an illustration not drawn from Scripture, 1 Cor. 9:8; (6) probably = 'to use a figurative expression' (see A.V., marg.), i.e., to speak evil of men with whom he had contended at Ephesus as 'beasts' (cp. 1 Cor. 4:6), 1 Cor. 15:32; Lightfoot prefers 'from worldly motives'; but the other interpretation, No. (4), seems to make better sense. See also Rom. 6:19, where, however, the Greek is slightly different, *anthrōpinos*, 'pertaining to mankind';" the meaning is as Nos. (5) and (6).*

(*g*) in the phrase "the inward man," the regenerate person's spiritual nature personified, the inner self of the believer, Rom. 7:22, as approving of the Law of God; in Eph. 3:16, as the sphere of the renewing power of the Holy Spirit; in 2 Cor. 4:16 (where *anthrōpos* is not repeated), in contrast to "the outward man," the physical frame, the man as cognizable by the senses; the "inward" man is identical with "the hidden man of the heart," 1 Pet. 3:4.

(*h*) in the expressions "the old man," "the new man," which are confined to Paul's Epistles, the former standing for the unregenerate nature personified as the former self of a believer, which, having been crucified with Christ, Rom. 6:6, is to be apprehended practically as such, and to be "put off," Eph. 4:22; Col. 3:9, being the source and seat of sin; the latter, "the new man," standing for the new nature personified as the believer's regenerate self, a nature "created in righteousness and holiness of truth," Eph. 4:24, and having been "put on" at regeneration, Col. 3:10, being "renewed after the image of Him that created him," it is to be "put on" in practical apprehension of these facts.

(*i*) often joined with another noun, e.g., Matt. 11:19, lit., 'a man, a glutton'; 13:52, lit., 'a man, a householder'; 18:23, "a certain king," lit., 'a man, a king.'

(*j*) as equivalent simply to 'a person,' or 'one,' whether man or woman, e.g., Acts 19:16; Rom. 3:28; Gal. 2:16; Jas. 1:19; 2:24; 3:8 (like the pronoun *tis*, someone; *tis* is rendered "man" in Matt. 8:28); or, again (as *tis* sometimes signifies), "a man," e.g., Matt. 17:14; Luke 13:19.

(*k*) definitely, with the article, of some particular person, Matt. 12:13; Mark 3:3, 5; or with the demonstrative pronoun and the article, e.g., Matt. 12:45; Luke 14:30. For the phrase "the Son of man" see SON OF MAN. For "the man of sin," 2 Thess. 2:3, see INIQUITY, No. 1.

(*l*) in the phrase "the man of God," 2 Tim. 3:17, not used as an official designation, nor denoting a special class of believers, it specifies what every believer should be, namely, a person whose life and conduct represent the mind of God and fulfil His will; so in 1 Tim. 6:11, "O man of God." Some regard this in the O.T. sense as of a prophet acting in a distinctive character, possessed of Divine authority; but the context is of such a general character as to confirm the more extended designation here.

NT: B.68a; CB.1236a; K.59.
OT: 'ādām: S.120; HR.96b.1; H.25a; BD.9a.
'îsh: S.376; HR.96b.2; H.83a; BD.35c.
GEN. REF.: IS.1:131; NB.776; Z.4:48.

Notes: (1) In Gal. 3:28, the R.V. adds the italicised word "man" ("ye all are one *man* in Christ Jesus"), in accordance with Eph. 2:15, which speaks of Jew and Gentile as becoming "one new man" in Christ. The figure is closely analogous to that of "the body." In these two passages "one" is masculine, i.e., 'one person'; in John 10:30; 11:52; 17:21, 22, 23, "one" is neuter, 'one thing,' as in 1 Cor. 3:8; 11:5. The first two, in Gal. 3 and Eph. 2, express vital union, present and eternal; in John 17 the union is moral, a process in course of accomplishment.

(2) For *philanthrōpia*, Tit. 3:4, "(His) love toward man," see KIND, C, No. 2.

(3) In Rev. 9:20, the R.V. translates the genitive plural of *anthrōpos* with the article, "mankind" (A.V., "the men"); it might have been rendered '(the rest) of men.'

2. *anēr* [ἀνήρ, 435], is never used of the female sex; it stands:

(*a*) in distinction from a woman, Acts 8:12; 1 Tim. 2:12; as a husband, Matt. 1:16; John 4:16; Rom. 7:2; Tit. 1:6;

* From Notes on Galatians by Hogg and Vine, p. 139.

(*b*) as distinct from a boy or infant, 1 Cor. 13:11; metaphorically in Eph. 4:13;

(*c*) in conjunction with an adjective or noun, e.g., Luke 5:8, lit., 'a man, a sinner'; 24:19, lit., 'a man, a prophet'; often in terms of address, e.g., Acts 1:16; 13:15, 26; 15:7, 13, lit., 'men, brethren'; with gentilic or local names (virtually a title of honour), e.g., Acts 2:14; 22:3, lit., 'Judaean men,' 'a Judaean man'; 3:12; 5:35, lit., 'Israelite men'; 17:22, 'Athenian men'; 19:35, lit., 'Ephesian men'; in Acts 14:15 it is used in addressing a company of men, without any descriptive term. In this verse, however, the distinction between *anēr* and *anthrōpos* (2nd part) is noticeable; the use of the latter comes under No. 1 (*e*);

(*d*) in general, a man, a male person (used like the pronoun *tis*, No. 3), "a man" (i.e., a certain man), e.g., Luke 8:41; in the plural, Acts 6:11.

NT: B.66c; CB.1235c; K.59.
OT: 'îsh: S.376; HR.88a.2; H.83a; BD.35c.
'enôsh: S.582; HR.88a.3a; H.136a; BD.60d.
GEN. REF.: IS.1:131; NB.776; Z.4:48.

3. *tis* [τις, 5100], some one, a certain one, is rendered "a man," a certain man, e.g., in Matt. 22:24; Mark 8:4, A.V. (R.V., "one"); 12:19; John 3:3, 5; 6:50; 14:23; 15:6, 13; Acts 13:41, A.V. (R.V., 'one'); 1 Cor. 4:2; 1 Tim. 1:8; 2 Tim. 2:5, 21; Jas. 2:14, 18; 1 Pet. 2:19; 1 John 4:20.

NT: B.819d; CB.1272c; K.—.
OT: 'îsh: S.376; HR.1354a.2; H.83a; BD.35c.
GEN. REF.: IS.1:131; NB.776; Z.4:48.

4. *arrēn* and *arsēn* [ἄρσην, —]: see MALE.

5. *teleios* [τέλειος, 5046], perfect, is translated "men" in 1 Cor. 14:20, R.V. marg., "of full age," A.V. marg., "perfect, or, of a ripe age." See PERFECT.

NT: B.809a; CB.1271b; K.1161.
OT: —.
GEN. REF.: —.

Note: In many cases the word "man" is combined with an adjective to translate one word in the original. These will be found under various other headings.

For MAN-CHILD see MALE

MAN'S, OF MAN, MANKIND (see also MEN)

anthrōpinos [ἀνθρώπινος, 442], human, belonging to man (from *anthrōpos*, see MAN, No. 1), is used:

(*a*) of man's wisdom, in 1 Cor. 2:13 (some mss. have it in ver. 4, where indeed it is implied; see, however, the R.V.);

(*b*) of "man's judgement," 1 Cor. 4:3 (marg., "day": see DAY);

(*c*) of "mankind," Jas. 3:7, lit., "the human nature," R.V. marg. (A.V. marg., "nature of man");

(*d*) of human ordinance, 1 Pet. 2:13; Moulton and Milligan show from the papyri how strongly antithetic to the Divine the use of the word is in this respect;

(*e*) of temptation, 1 Cor. 10:13, R.V., "such as man can bear" (A.V., "such as is common to man"), i.e., such as must and does come to men;

(*f*) of men's hands, Acts 17:25;

(*g*) in the phrase "after the manner of men," Rom. 6:19. ¶

NT: B.67d; CB.1236a; K.59.
OT: 'ādām: S.120; HR.96b.1; H.25a; BD.9a.
GEN. REF.: IS.1:131; NB.776; Z.4:48.

Notes: (1) In Luke 16:12, A.V., *allotrios*, belonging to another (*allos*, another), here used asd a pronoun, is translated "another man's" (R.V., "another's"); so, as an adjective, in Rom. 14:4; 15:20; 2 Cor. 10:15, 16 (in this last the R.V. omits "man").

(2) In Acts 27:22 there is no word representing "*man's*"; the R.V. has "of life."

(3) In Rom. 5:17, the R.V. rightly has "the trespass of the one," for A.V., "one man's offence."

MANGER

phatnē [φάτνη, 5336], a manger, Luke 2:7, 12, 16, also denotes a stall, 13:15. ¶ So in the Sept., the word denoted not only a manger but, by metonymy, the stall or "crib" (Prov. 14:4) containing the manger.

NT: B.854b; CB.—; K.1251.
OT: 'ēbûs: S.18; HR.1425b.1; H.10a; BD.7b.
GEN. REF.: IS.3:237; NB.779; Z.4:66.

MANIFEST (Adjective and Verb)

A. Adjectives.

1. *emphanēs* [ἐμφανής, 1717], manifest (akin to *emphainō*, to show in, to exhibit; *en*, in, *phainō*, to cause to shine), is used:

(*a*) literally in Acts 10:40, R.V. "(gave Him to be made) manifest";

(*b*) metaphorically in Rom. 10:20, "(I was made) manifest." See OPENLY. ¶ Cp. B, No. 2.

NT: B.257c; CB.1244b; K.—.
OT: dārash: S.1875; HR.460c.2; H.455; BD.205a.
yāda': S.3045; HR.460c.3; H.848; BD.393b.
GEN. REF.: IS.3:238; NB.—; Z.—.

2. *phaneros* [φανερός, 5318], open to sight, visible, manifest (the root *phan*—, signifying shining, exists also in No. 1), is translated "manifest" in Luke 8:17; Acts 4:16; 7:13, R.V. (A.V., "known"); Rom. 1:19; 1 Cor. 3:13; 11:19; 14:25; Gal. 5:19; Phil. 1:13; 1 Tim. 4:15 (A.V.,

"appear"); 1 John 3:10. See APPEAR, B, *Note* (2), KNOW, B, No. 2, OPENLY, OUTWARDLY.

NT: B.852b; CB.1263c; K.1244.
OT: yāda': S.3045; HR.1424a.3a; H.848; BD.393b.
GEN. REF.: IS.3:238; NB.–; Z.–.

3. *aphanēs* [ἀφανής, 852], denotes unseen, hidden, Heb. 4:13, "not manifest" (*a*, negative, and *phainō*). ¶ In the Sept., Neh. 4:8; Job 24:20. ¶

NT: B.124c; CB.–; K.–.
OT: –.
GEN. REF.: –.

Notes: (1) In 1 Cor. 15:27, A.V. *dēlos*, evident, is translated "manifest" (R.V., "evident").

(2) So with *ekdēlos*, 2 Tim. 3:9, an intensive form of *dēlos*, signifying quite evident. ¶

(3) In 1 Tim. 5:25, A.V., *prodēlos*, evident beforehand, clearly evident, is translated "manifest beforehand" (R.V., "evident"); see EVIDENT.

(4) For "manifest token," see TOKEN.

B. Verbs.

1. *phaneroō* [φανερόω, 5319], to make visible, clear, manifest, known (akin to A, No. 2), is used especially in the writings of the Apostles John and Paul), occurring 9 times in the Gospel, 9 times in 1 John, 2 in Rev.; in the Pauline Epistles (including Heb.) 24 times; in the other Gospels, only in Mark, 3 times; elsewhere in 1 Pet. 1:20; 5:4.

The true meaning is to uncover, lay bare, reveal. The following are variations in the rendering, which should be noted: Mark 16:12, 14 (R.V., "was manifested," A.V., "appeared"); John 21:1 (R.V., "manifested," A.V., "shewed"; cp. ver. 14); Rom. 1:19 (R.V., "manifested," A.V., "hath shewed"); 2 Cor. 3:3 (R.V., "being made manifest," A.V., "are manifestly declared"); 2 Cor. 5:10; 7:12 and Rev. 3:18 (R.V., "be made manifest," A.V., "appear"); 2 Cor. 11:6 (R.V., "we have made it manifest," A.V., "we have been throughly made manifest"); Col. 1:26 (R.V., "hath it been manifested," A.V., "is made manifest"); 3:4 (R.V., "be manifested," A.V., "appear"; so 1 Pet. 5:4); 1 Tim. 3:16 (R.V., "was manifested," A.V., "was manifest"); 2 Tim. 1:10 (R.V., "hath . . . been manifested," A.V., "is . . . made manifest"; cp. Rom. 16:26; 2 Cor. 4:10, 11; 1 Pet. 1:20); Heb. 9:26 (R.V., "hath He been manifested," A.V., "hath He appeared"); 1 John 2:28; 3:2 (R.V., "is . . . made manifest," A.V., "doth appear"). See APPEAR, A, No. 4.

NT: B.852d; CB.1263c; K.1244.
OT: gālāh: S.1540; HR.1424b.1; H.350; BD.162d.
GEN. REF.: IS.3:238; NB.–; Z.–.

2. *emphanizō* [ἐμφανίζω, 1718], akin to A, No. 1, is translated to manifest, make manifest, in John 14:21, 22; Heb. 11:14, R.V.; see APPEAR, A, No. 5.

NT: B.257c; CB.1244b; K.1244.
OT: yāda': S.3045; HR.460c.2; H.848; BD.393b.
rā'āh: S.7200; HR.460c.4; H.2095; BD.906b.
GEN. REF.: IS.3:238; NB.–; Z.–.

Note: For the adverb *phanerōs*, manifestly, see EVIDENTLY, OPENLY.

MANIFESTATION

phanerōsis [φανέρωσις, 5321], a manifestation (akin to *phaneros* and *phaneroō*; see MANIFEST), occurs in 1 Cor. 12:7 and 2 Cor. 4:2. ¶

NT: B.853b; CB.1263c; K.1244.
OT: –.
GEN. REF.: IS.3:238; NB.–; Z.–.

Note: In Rom. 8:19, A.V., *apokalupsis*, an uncovering, laying bare, revealing, revelation, is translated "manifestation" (R.V., "revealing"). See REVELATION.

MANIFOLD

1. *poikilos* [ποικίλος, 4164], varied, is translated "manifold" in 1 Pet. 1:6; 4:10 and in Jas. 1:2, R.V. (A.V., "divers"). See DIVERS, A, No. 2.

NT: B.683c; CB.–; K.901.
OT: –.
GEN. REF.: IS.3:238; NB.–; Z.–.

2. *polupoikilos* [πολυποίκιλος, 4182], much varied (*polus*, much, and No. 1), is said of the wisdom of God, in Eph. 3:10. ¶

NT: B.687b; CB.–; K.901.
OT: –.
GEN. REF.: IS.3:238; NB.–; Z.–.

3. *pollaplasiōn* [πολλαπλασίων, 4179], many times more (from *polus*, much), occurs in Luke 18:30, "manifold more," and in many ancient authorities in Matt. 19:29 (R.V., marg.; some editions in text); A.V. and R.V. text, "a hundredfold," translating *hekatontaplasiona*. ¶

NT: B.686d; CB.–; K.–.
OT: –.
GEN. REF.: IS.3:238; NB.–; Z.–.

For **MANKIND** see **MAN,** No. 1, *Note* (3), **MAN'S** (c), **ABUSERS**

MANNA

manna [μάννα, 3131], the supernaturally provided food for Israel during their wilderness journey (for details see Ex. 16 and Numb. 11). The Hebrew equivalent is given in Ex. 16:15, R.V. marg., "*man hu*." The translations are, R.V., "what is it?"; A.V. and R.V. marg., "it is manna." It is described in Ps. 78:24, 25 as "the corn of heaven" and "the bread of the mighty," R.V. text and A.V. marg. ("angels' food," A.V. text), and in 1 Cor. 10:3, as "spiritual meat."

The vessel appointed to contain it as a perpetual memorial, was of gold, Heb. 9:4, with Ex. 16:33. The Lord speaks of it as being typical of Himself, the true Bread from Heaven, imparting eternal life and sustenance to those who by faith partake spiritually of Him, John 6:31-35. The "hidden manna" is promised as one of the rewards of the overcomer, Rev. 2:17; it is thus suggestive of the moral excellence of Christ in His life on earth, hid from the eyes of men, by whom He was "despised and rejected"; the path of the overcomer is a reflex of His life.

None of the natural substances called manna is to be identified with that which God provided for Israel. ¶

NT: B.490d; CB.1257c; K.563.
OT: mān: S.4478; HR.895c.1; H.1208,1209; BD.577b.
GEN. REF.: IS.3:239; NB.–; Z.4:68.

MANNER

A. Nouns.

1. *ethos* [ἔθος, 1485], a habit, custom (akin to the verb *ethō*, to be accustomed), is always translated "custom" in the R.V. ("manner" in the A.V. of John 19:40; Acts 15:1; 25:16; Heb. 10:25). See CUSTOM, No. 1.

NT: B.218d; CB.1247a; K.202.
OT: –.
GEN. REF.: –.

2. *ēthos* [ἦθος, 2239], primarily a haunt, abode, then, a custom, manner, occurs in the plural in 1 Cor. 15:33, i.e., ethical conduct, morals. ¶

NT: B.344c; CB.1247a; K.–.
OT: –.
GEN. REF.: –.

3. *tropos* [τρόπος, 5158], a turning, fashion, manner, character, way of life, is translated "manner" in Acts 1:11, with reference to the Lord's Ascension and Return; in Jude 7, of the similarity of the evil of those mentioned in vv. 6 and 7. See CONVERSATION, MEANS, WAY.

NT: B.827b; CB.1273a; K.–.
OT: –.
GEN. REF.: –.

Note: In Acts 15:11, the phrase *kath' hon tropon*, 'according to what manner,' is translated "in like manner as," R.V. (A.V., "even as").

4. *tupos* [τύπος, 5179], a mark or impress, is translated "manner" in Acts 23:25. See FORM, No. 3.

NT: B.829d; CB.1273b; K.1193.
OT: –.
GEN. REF.: –.

5. *akribeia* [ἀκρίβεια, 195], exactness, precision (akin to *akribēs*, exact, careful; see *akriboō*, to enquire carefully, and *akribōs*, carefully), occurs in Acts 22:3, R.V., "strict manner" (A.V., "perfect manner"). ¶

NT: B.33a; CB.–; K.–.
OT: yaṣīb (Aramaic): S.3330; HR.50c.1; H.2773a; BD.1096a.
GEN. REF.: IS.3:240; NB.–; Z.–.

Notes: (1) The verb *ethō*, to be accustomed, has a perfect tense *eiōtha*, with a present meaning, the neuter of the participle of which, *eiōthos*, used with the article, signifies "custom," Luke 4:16. In Acts 17:2 the A.V. translates it "manner" (R.V., "custom"). See CUSTOM, WONT.

(2) For *agōgē*, in 2 Tim. 3:10, A.V., "manner of life" (R.V., "conduct"), see CONDUCT.

(3) For *anastrophē*, "manner of life," see LIFE, A, No. 6; cp. LIVE, No. 5. *Agōge* suggests conduct according to one's leading; *anastrophē*, conduct as one goes about and mingles with others.

B. Adjectives and Pronouns.

1. *potapos* [ποταπός, 4217], primarily, from what country, then, of what sort, is rendered "what manner of man," Matt. 8:27: so 2 Pet. 3:11; Mark 13:1 (twice); Luke 1:29; 7:39; 1 John 3:1. ¶

NT: B.694d; CB.–; K.–.
OT: –.
GEN. REF.: –.

2. *poios* [ποῖος, 4169], of what sort, is translated "by what manner of (death)" in John 21:19, R.V., (A.V., "by what"); in Acts 7:49, "what manner of (house)"; Rom. 3:27, "what manner of law"; 1 Cor. 15:35, "what manner of body."

NT: B.684c; CB.–; K.–.
OT: –.
GEN. REF.: –.

3. *hoios* [οἷος, 3634], a relative pronoun, signifying what sort of or manner of, is translated by the latter phrase in 1 Thess. 1:5; some mss. have it in Luke 9:55, as in A.V.; the R.V. follows those in which it is absent.

NT: B.562c; CB.1251a; K.–.
OT: –.
GEN. REF.: –.

4. *hopoios* [ὁποῖος, 3697], is rendered "what manner of" in 1 Thess. 1:9; Jas. 1:24. See SORT, A.

NT: B.575d; CB.–; K.–.
OT: –.
GEN. REF.: –.

C. Adverbs.

1. *polutropōs* [πολυτρόπως, 4187], lit., 'much turning' (*polus*, much, *tropos*, a turning), 'in many ways (or manners),' is rendered "in divers manners" in Heb. 1:1. ¶

NT: B.690c; CB.–; K.–.
OT: –.
GEN. REF.: –.

2. *houtōs* or *houtō* [οὕτως, 3779], thus, in this way, is rendered "after this manner" in Matt. 6:9; 1 Pet. 3:5; Rev. 11:5. See So, Thus.
NT: B.597c; CB.—; K.—.
OT: —.
GEN. REF.: —.

3. *hōsautōs* [ὡσαύτως, 5615], a strengthened form of *hōs*, thus, signifies just so, likewise, in like manner e.g., 1 Tim. 2:9; in the following the R.V. has "in like manner," for A.V., "likewise"; Mark 14:31; Luke 22:20; Rom. 8:26; 1 Tim. 3:8; 5:25; in Luke 20:31 the R.V. has "likewise," A.V., "in like manner." See Likewise.
NT: B.899b; CB.—; K.—.
OT: —.
GEN. REF.: —.

4. *homoiōs* [ὁμοίως, 3668], akin to the adjective *homoios*, like, signifies in like manner, equally; in the following the R.V. has "in like manner" for A.V., "likewise"; Matt. 27:41; Mark 4:16; 15:31; Luke 10:32; 13:3; 16:25; John 5:19; (Heb. 9:21;) Jas. 2:25; 1 Pet. 3:1, 7; Rev. 8:12; in Rev. 2:15 the A.V. "which thing I hate" translates a variant reading (*ho misō*). See Likewise, So.
NT: B.567d; CB.1251a; K.684.
OT: —.
GEN. REF.: IS.3:241; NB.—; Z.—.

5. *pōs* [πῶς, 4459], how, is translated "after what manner" in Acts 20:18. See Means.
NT: B.732a; CB.—; K.—.
OT: —.
GEN. REF.: —.

Note: For *paraplēsiōs*, Heb. 2:14, R.V., see Likewise, No. 4.

D. Preposition.

kata [κατά, 2596], according to, is translated "after the manner" in John 2:6, i.e., 'in accordance with'; in Rom. 3:5; 1 Cor. 3:3; 9:8, R.V., "after the manner of" (A.V., "as").
NT: B.405c; CB.1253c; K.—.
OT: —.
GEN. REF.: —.

E. Verb.

tropophoreō [τροποφορέω, 5159], to bear another's manners, is translated "suffered He (their) manners" in Acts 13:18. For this and the alternative reading see Bear, No. 8. ¶
NT: B.827c; CB.—; K.—.
OT: nāśā': S.5375; HR.1376b.1; H.1421; BD.669d.
GEN. REF.: —.

Notes: (1) In the following the phrase *kata tauta*, or *kata ta auta*, lit., 'according to the same things,' is translated "in (the) like (R.V., same) manner," Luke 6:23; ver. 26, R.V. (A.V., "so"); 17:30, R.V., "after the same manner" (A.V., "even thus").

(2) In Phil. 2:18 the phrase *to . . . auto*, lit., 'the same (thing),' used adverbially, is translated "in the same manner," R.V. (A.V., "for the same cause").

(3) In Mark 13:29, A.V., *kai*, also (so R.V.), is translated "in like manner."

(4) In Acts 15:23 some mss. have the demonstrative pronoun *tode* used adverbially and rendered "after this manner" (A.V.). The R.V., adhering to the mss. in which it is absent, inserts the word "*thus*" in italics.

(5) In Acts 25:20 a phrase lit. rendered '(as to) the enquiry concerning these things' (or according to some mss. 'this person,' whether "Jesus" or "Paul," ver. 19), is translated "of such manner of questions," A.V. (R.V., "how to inquire concerning these things").

(6) In Luke 1:66, A.V., *ara*, "then" (so R.V.), is rendered freely "(what) manner."

(7) In Luke 24:17, A.V., the pronoun *tis*, who, what, in the plural (R.V., "what" is translated what manner of"; similarly, in the singular in Mark 4:41; Luke 8:25 (R.V., "who"); John 7:36.

(8) In Gal. 2:14, A.V., the adverb *ethnikōs*, in Gentile fashion (*ethnos*, a nation: in the plural, Gentiles or nations), is translated "after the manner of Gentiles" (R.V., "as do . . ").

(9) In Matt. 12:31; Luke 11:42; Rev. 18:12, A.V., *pas*, "every" (so R.V.), is translated "all manner."

MANSERVANT

pais [παῖς, 3816], a child, boy, youth, also means a servant, attendant; in Luke 12:45 it is used in the plural "menservants," in contrast to *paidiskē*, a maidservant. See Child, No. 4.
NT: B.604c; CB.1261c; K.759.
OT: 'ebed: S.5650; HR.1049a.9a; H.1553; BD.713d.
GEN. REF.: IS.3:241; NB.—; Z.—.

MANSIONS

monē [μονή, 3438], primarily a staying, abiding (akin to *menō*, to abide), denotes an abode (Eng., manor, manse, etc.), translated "mansions" in John 14:2; "abode" in ver. 23. There is nothing in the word to indicate separate compartments in Heaven; neither does it suggest temporary resting-places on the road. ¶
NT: B.527a; CB.1259b; K.581.
OT: —.
GEN. REF.: IS.3:241; NB.780; Z.4:69.

MANSLAYERS

androphonos [ἀνδροφόνος, 409], from *anēr*, a man, and *phoneus*, a murderer, occurs in the plural in 1 Tim. 1:9. ¶
NT: B.64a; CB.—; K.—.
OT: —.
GEN. REF.: IS.3:241; NB.—; Z.—.

MANTLE

peribolaion [περιβόλαιον, 4018], lit., that which is thrown around, is translated "mantle" in Heb. 1:12, R.V. (A.V., "vesture.") See Covering, Veil

NT: B.646c; CB.1263b; K.–.
OT: k^esût: S.3682; HR.1122b.2a; H.1008b; BD.492b.
GEN. REF.: IS.3:242; NB.–; Z.–.

MANY

1. *polus* [πολύς, 4183], much, many, great, is used especially of number when its significance is "many," e.g., Matt. 8:30; 9:10; 13:17; so the R.V. of Matt. 12:15, where some mss. follow the word by *ochloi*, multitudes; 1 Cor. 12:12; Rev. 1:15; it is more frequently used as a noun, "many (persons)," e.g., Matt. 3:7; 7:22; 22:14; with the article, "the many," e.g., Matt. 24:12, R.V.; Mark 9:26, R.V., "the more part" (A.V. "many"); Rom. 5:15, 19 (twice), R.V.; 12:5; 1 Cor. 10:17; ver. 33, R.V.; so 2 Cor. 2:17; in 1 Cor. 11:30, R.V., "not a few." In Luke 12:47 it is translated "many stripes," the noun being understood. See Great, Much.

NT: B.687c; CB.1266a; K.–.
OT: rab: S.7227; HR.1181b.9a; H.2099a,b; BD.913c.
rôb: S.7230; HR.1181b.9b; H.2099c; BD.913d.
rābab: S.7231; HR.1181b.9c; H.2099; BD.912c.
GEN. REF.: –.

Notes: (1) In Luke 23:8 some mss. have *polla*, "many things," though it is absent from the most authentic; see the R.V.

(2) In Mark 6:20 the R.V., following the mss. which have *aporeō*, to be perplexed, translates *polla* by "much"; some mss. have *poieō*, to do; hence A.V., "did many things."

(3) In Gal. 4:27 the plural of *polus*, with *mallon*, more, is translated "more" in the R.V. (A.V., "many more"), lit., 'many are the children of the desolate more than of her that etc.,' the phrase implying that both should have many children, but the desolate more than the other.

(4) In John 7:40 there is no word in the original representing "*some*" or "many."

2. *pleiōn* [πλείων, 4119], more, greater, the comparative of No. 1, is translated "many" in Acts 2:40; 13:31; 21:10; 24:17; 25:14; 27:20; 28:23 (A.V.; R.V., " in great number"); with the article, "most," R.V. (or rather, 'the more part'), Acts 19:32; 1 Cor. 10:5, and Phil. 1:14 (for A.V., "many," an important change); in 2 Cor. 2:6, R.V., "the many" (marg., "the more"); so 4:15; in 9:2, "very many" (marg., "the more part"); in Heb. 7:23, R.V., "many in number" (A.V., "many"). See Greater, More.

NT: B.687c; CB.–; K.–.
OT: rab: S.7227; HR.1181b,9a; H.2099a,b; BD.913c.
rôb: S.7230; HR.1181b.9b; H.2099c; BD.913d.
rābab: S.7231; HR.1181b.9c; H.2099; BD.912c.
GEN. REF.: –.

3. *hikanos* [ἱκανός, 2425], sufficient, when used of number sometimes signifies many, suggesting a sufficient number, (*a*) with nouns, Luke 8:32; 23:9; Acts 9:23, 43; 20:8; 27:7; (*b*) absolutely, some noun being understood, e.g. Acts 12:12; 14:21; 19:19; 1 Cor. 11:30. See Able, C, No.2.

NT: B.374b; CB.1250c; K.361.
OT: day: S.1767; HR.683c.2; H.425; BD.191b.
shadday: S.7706; HR.683c.9; H.2333; BD.994d.
GEN. REF.: –.

4. *hosos* [ὅσος, 3745], how much, how many, how great, as much as, as many as, is translated "as many as," e.g., in Matt. 14:36; Mark 3:10; Luke 9:5, R.V. (A.V., "whosoever"); Acts 2:39; in 9:16, R.V., "how many things" (A.V., "how great things"); in Rom. 6:3, the R.V. renders it by "all we who" (A.V., "so many of us as"), a necessary alteration, not singling out some believers from others, as if some were not baptized, but implying what was recognized as true of all (see Acts 18:8); in 2 Cor. 1:20, R.V., "how many soever be" (A.V., "all"). See All, C.

NT: B.586b; CB.1251b; K.–.
OT: –.
GEN. REF.: –.

5. *posos* [πόσος, 4214], how much, how great, how many, has the last meaning in Matt. 15:34; 16:9, 10; 27:13 ("how many things"); Mark 6:38; 8:5, 19, 20; 15:4 ("how many things"); Luke 15:17; Acts 21:20. See Great.

NT: B.694b; CB.–; K.–.
OT: –.
GEN. REF.: –.

6. *tosoutos* [τοσοῦτος, 5118], so great, so much, so many, (*a*) qualifying a noun, is rendered "these many (years)" in Luke 15:29; "so many," John 12:37; 1 Cor. 14:10; (*b*) without a noun, John 6:9; 21:11; Gal. 3:4, "so many things." See Great.

NT: B.823b; CB.–; K.–.
OT: –.
GEN. REF.: –.

Note: In John 17:2, A.V., the neuter of *pas*, all followed by the neuter of the relative pronoun 'what,' and then by the plural of the personal pronoun, is translated "to as many as" (R.V., "whatsoever . . . to them").

MARAN-ATHA

maran-atha [μαρὰν ἀθά, 3134], an expression used in 1 Cor. 16:22, is the Greek spelling for two Aramaic words, formerly supposed by some to be an imprecatory utterance or "a curse reinforced by a prayer," an idea contrary to the intimations conveyed by its use in early Christian documents, e.g., "The Teaching of the Apostles," a document of the beginning of the 2nd cent., and in the "Apostolic Constitutions" (vii. 26), where it is used as follows: "Gather us all together into Thy Kingdom which Thou hast prepared. Maranatha, Hosanna to the Son of David; blessed is He that cometh etc."

The first part, ending in 'n,' signifies 'Lord'; as to the second part, the "Fathers" regarded it as a past tense, "has come." Modern expositors take it as equivalent to a present, "cometh," or future, "will come." Certain Aramaic scholars regard the last part as consisting of 'tha,' and regard the phrase as an ejaculation, 'Our Lord, come,' or 'O Lord, come.' The character of the context, however, indicates that the Apostle is making a statement rather than expressing a desire or uttering a prayer.

As to the reason why it was used, most probably it was a current ejaculation among early Christians, as embodying the consummation of their desires.

"At first the title *Marana* or *Maran*, used in speaking to and of Christ was no more than the respectful designation of the Teacher on the part of the disciples." After His resurrection they used the title of or to Him as applied to God, "but it must here be remembered that the Aramaic-speaking Jews did not, save exceptionally, designate God as 'Lord'; so that in the 'Hebraist' section of the Jewish Christians the expression 'our Lord' (*Marana*) was used in reference to Christ only" (Dalman, *The Words of Jesus*). ¶

NT: B.491b; CB.1257c; K.563.
OT: –.
GEN. REF.: IS.3:243; NB.781; Z.4:70.

MARBLE

marmaros [μάρμαρος, 3139], primarily denoted any glistering stone (from *marainō*, to glisten); hence, marble, Rev. 18:12. ¶

NT: B.492c; CB.–; K.–.
OT: –.
GEN. REF.: IS.3:243; NB.824; Z.4:71.

MARINERS

nautēs [ναύτης, 3492], a seaman, mariner, sailor (from *naus*, a ship, Eng., nautical), is translated "sailors" in Acts 27:27, 30, R.V. (A.V., "shipmen"); in Rev. 18:17, R.V., "mariners" (A.V., "sailors"). ¶

NT: B.534c; CB.–; K.–.
OT: –.
GEN. REF.: –.

MARK (Noun)

1. *charagma* [χάραγμα, 5480], denotes a stamp, impress, translated "mark" in Rev. 13:16, 17, etc. See GRAVEN.

NT: B.876a; CB.1239b; K.1308.
OT: –.
GEN. REF.: IS.3:248; NB.786; Z.4:90.

2. *stigma* [στίγμα, 4742], denotes a tattooed mark or a mark burnt in, a brand (akin to *stizō*, to prick), translated "marks" in Gal. 6:17. ¶ "It is probable that the Apostle refers to the physical sufferings he had endured since he began to proclaim Jesus as Messiah and Lord [e.g., at Lystra and Philippi]. It is probable, too, that this reference to his scars was intended to set off the insistence of the Judaizers upon a body-mark which cost them nothing. Over against the circumcision they demanded as a proof of obedience to the law he set the indelible tokens, sustained in his own body, of his loyalty to the Lord Jesus. As to the origin of the figure, it was indeed customary for a master to brand his slaves, but this language does not suggest that the Apostle had been branded by His Master. Soldiers and criminals also were branded on occasion; but to neither of these is the case of Paul as here described analogous. The religious devotee branded himself with the peculiar mark of the god whose cult he affected; so was Paul branded with the marks of his devotion to the Lord Jesus. It is true such markings were forbidden by the law, Lev. 19:28, but then Paul had not inflicted these on himself.

"The marks of Jesus cannot be taken to be the marks which the Lord bears in His body in consequence of the Crucifixion; they were different in character."*

NT: B.768c; CB.1270a; K.1086.
OT: nequdāh: S.5351; HR.1291a.1; H.1410c; BD.667a.
GEN. REF.: IS.3:248; NB.786; Z.4:90.

3. *skopos* [σκοπός, 4649], primarily a watcher, a watchman (as in the Sept., e.g., Ezek. 3:17), then, a mark on which to fix the eye (akin to *skopeō*, to look at), is used metaphorically in Phil. 3:14, of an aim or object, R.V., "goal." See GOAL. ¶

NT: B.756d; CB.1269b; K.1047.
OT: ṣāphāh: S.6822; HR.1275c.3; H.1950; BD.859b.
GEN. REF.: IS.3:248; NB.786; Z.4:90.

* From Notes on Galatians by Hogg and Vine, p. 344.

MARK (Verb)

1. *epechō* [ἐπέχω, 1907], to hold upon (*epi*, upon, *echō*, to hold), signifies (like *parechō*) to hold out, Phil. 2:16, of the word of life; then, to hold one's mind towards, to observe, translated "marked" in Luke 14:7, of the Lord's observance of those who chose the chief seats. See HEED, HOLD, STAY.

NT: B.285c; CB.–; K.–.
OT: –.
GEN. REF.: IS.3:248; NB.–; Z.–.

2. *skopeō* [σκοπέω, 4648], to look at, behold, watch, contemplate, (akin to *skopos*, a mark, see Noun above), is used metaphorically of looking to, and translated "mark" in Rom. 16:17, of a warning against those who cause divisions, and in Phil. 3:17, of observing those who walked after the example of the Apostle and his fellow-workers, so as to follow their ways. See HEED, *Note* (1), LOOK.

NT: B.756d; CB.1269b; K.1047.
OT: –.
GEN. REF.: IS.3:248; NB.–; Z.–.

MARKET, MARKET-PLACE

agora [ἀγορά, 58], primarily an assembly, or, in general, an open space in a town (akin to *ageirō*, to bring together), became applied, according to papyri evidences, to a variety of things, e.g., a judicial assembly, a market, or even supplies, provisions (Moulton and Milligan, Vocab.). In the N.T. it denotes a place of assembly, a public-place or forum, a market-place. A variety of circumstances, connected with it as a public gathering-place, is mentioned, e.g., business dealings such as the hiring of labourers, Matt. 20:3, the buying and selling of goods, Mark 7:4 (involving risk of pollution); the games of children, Matt. 11:16; Luke 7:32; exchange of greetings, Matt. 23:7; Mark 12:38; Luke 11:43; 20:46; the holding of trials, Acts 16:19; public discussions, Acts 17:17. Mark 6:56 records the bringing of the sick there. The word always carries with it the idea of publicity, in contrast to private circumstances.

The R.V. always translates it "market-place" or in the plural. The A.V. sometimes changes the rendering to "markets" and translates it "streets" in Mark 6:56. See STREET. ¶

NT: B.12c; CB.1233c; K.–.
OT: 'izzābôn: S.5801; HR.16b.1; H.1594b; BD.738a.
shûq: S.7784; HR.16b.2; H.2350b; BD.1003b.
GEN. REF.: IS.3:260; NB.786; Z.4:91.

MARRED

Note: In Mark 2:22, *apollumi*, to destroy, perish, is found in the most authentic mss. as applying both to the wine and the wine skins, R.V., "perisheth"; the A.V. follows the mss. which tell of the wine being "spilled" (*ekcheō*, to pour out), and the skins (A.V., "bottles") being "marred." See DESTROY, No. 1.

MARRIAGE (give in), MARRY

A. Noun.

gamos [γάμος, 1062], a marriage, wedding, or wedding feast, is used to denote (*a*) the ceremony and its proceedings, including the marriage feast, John 2:1, 2; of the marriage ceremony only, figuratively, Rev. 19:7, as distinct from the marriage feast (ver. 9); (*b*) the marriage feast, R.V. in Matt. 22:2, 3, 4, 9; in ver. 8, 10, "wedding"; in 25:10, R.V.,"marriage feast"; so Luke 12:36; 14:8; in Matt. 22:11, 12, the "wedding garment" is, lit., 'a garment of a wedding.' In Rev. 19, where, under the figure of a marriage, the union of Christ, as the Lamb of God, with His Heavenly Bride is so described, the marriage itself takes place in Heaven during the Parousia, ver. 7 (the aorist or point tense indicating an accomplished fact; the Bride is called "His wife"); the marriage feast or supper is to take place on earth, after the Second Advent, ver. 9. That Christ is spoken of as the Lamb points to His atoning sacrifice as the ground upon which the spiritual union takes place. The background of the phraseology lies in the O.T. description of the relation of God to Israel, e.g., Is. 54:4, ff.; Ezek. 16:7, ff.; Hos. 2:19; (*c*) marriage in general, including the married state, which is to be "had in honour," Heb. 13:4, R.V. ¶

NT: B.151b; CB.1248a; K.111.
OT: mishteh: S.4960; HR.234a.1; H.2477c; BD.1059c.
GEN. REF.: IS.3:261; NB.786; Z.4:92.

Note: Among the Jews the marriage-supper took place in the husband's house and was the great social event in the family life. Large hospitality, and resentment at the refusal of an invitation, are indicated in Matt. 22:1-14. The marriage in Cana exhibits the way in which a marriage feast was conducted in humbler homes. Special honour attached to the male friends of the bridegroom, "the sons of the bride-chamber," Matt. 9:15, R.V. (see BRIDE-CHAMBER). At the close the parents conducted the bride to the nuptial chamber (cp. Judg. 15:1).

B. Verbs.

1. *gameō* [γαμέω, 1060], to marry (akin to A), is used (*a*) of the man, Matt. 5:32; 19:9, 10; 22:25 (R.V.; A.V., "married a wife"); ver. 30; 24:38; Mark 6:17; 10:11; 12:25; Luke 14:20; 16:18; 17:27, R.V., "married" (A.V., "married wives"); 20:34, 35; 1 Cor. 7:28 (1st part); ver. 33; (*b*) of the woman, in the Active Voice, Mark 10;12; 1 Cor. 7:28 (last part); ver. 34; 1 Tim. 5:11, 14; in the Passive Voice, 1 Cor. 7:39; (*c*) of both sexes, 1 Cor. 7:9, 10, 36; 1 Tim. 4:3. ¶

NT: B.150d; CB.1248a; K.111.
OT: –.
GEN. REF.: IS.3:261; NB.786; Z.4:92.

2. *gamizō* [γαμίζω, —], to give in marriage, is used in the Passive Voice in Matt. 22:30 (2nd clause), some mss. have No. 5 here; Mark 12:25 (No. 3 in some mss.); Luke 17:27 (No. 5 in some mss.); 20:35 (last word), Passive (Nos. 3 and 4 in some mss.); in the Active Voice Matt. 24:38 (Nos. 3 and 5 in some mss.); further, of giving a daughter in marriage, 1 Cor. 7:38 (twice), R.V. (No. 5 in some mss.), which, on the whole, may be taken as the meaning. In this part of the Epistle, the Apostle was answering a number of questions on matters about which the church at Corinth had written to him, and in this particular matter the formal transition from marriage in general to the subject of giving a daughter in marriage, is simple. Eastern customs naturally would involve the inclusion of the latter in the enquiry and the reply. ¶

NT: B.151a; CB.1248a; K.–.
OT: –.
GEN. REF.: IS.3:261; NB.786; Z.4:92.

3. *gamiskō* [γαμίσκω, 1061], an alternative for No. 2, Luke 20:34 (some mss. have No. 4); in some mss. in Mark 12:25; Luke 20:35. ¶

NT: B.151b; CB.1248a; K.–.
OT: –.
GEN. REF.: IS.3:261; NB.786; Z.4:92.

4. *ekgamiskō* [ἐκγαμίσκω, 1548], to give out in marriage (*ek*, out, and No. 3): see Nos. 2 and 3.

NT: –.
OT: –.
GEN. REF.: –.

5. *ekgamizō* [ἐκγαμίζω, —], an alternative for No. 4: see Nos. 2 and 3. ¶

6. *epigambreuō* [ἐπιγαμβρεύω, 1918], to take to wife after (*epi*, upon, *gambros*, a connection by marriage), signifies to marry (of a deceased husband's next of kin, Matt. 22;24). ¶ Cp. Gen. 38:8.

NT: B.290c; CB.–; K.–.
OT: ḥātan: S.2859; HR.517c.1; H.781b; BD.368d.
GEN. REF.: IS.3:261; NB.786; Z.–.

Note: In Rom. 7:3 (twice) and ver. 4, A.V., *ginomai*, to become (here, to become another man's), is translated "be married" (R.V., "be joined).

MARROW

muelos [μυελός, 3452], marrow, occurs in Heb. 4:12, where, by a natural metaphor, the phraseology changes from the material to the spiritual. ¶

NT: B.528d; CB.–; K.–.
OT: ḥēleb: S.2459; HR.936b.1; H.651a; BD.316d.
GEN. REF.: IS.3:266; NB.–; Z.4:102.

For MARTYR see WITNESS

MARVEL (Noun and Verb), MARVELLOUS

A. Noun.

thauma [θαῦμα, 2295], a wonder (akin to *theaomai*, to gaze in wonder), is found in the most authentic mss. in 2 Cor. 11:14 (some mss. have the adjective *thaumastos*: see C, below), "(no) marvel"; in Rev. 17:6, R.V., "wonder" (A.V., "admiration"), said of John's astonishment at the vision of the woman described as Babylon the Great. ¶ In the Sept., Job 17:8; 18:20; in some mss., 20:8 and 21:5. ¶ Cp. *teras*, a wonder; *sēmeion*, a sign; *thambos*, wonder; *ekstasis*, amazement.

NT: B.352a; CB.1271c; K.31b.
OT: ḥizzayôn: S.2384; HR.626c.1; H.633e; BD.303b.
shāmēm: S.8074; HR.626c.3; H.2409; BD.1030d.
GEN. REF.: IS.3:267; NB.–; Z.4:103.

B. Verbs.

1. *thaumazō* [θαυμάζω, 2296], signifies to wonder at, marvel (akin to A); the following are R.V. differences from the A.V.: Luke 2:33, "were marvelling" for "marvelled"; Luke 8:25 and 11:14, "marvelled" for "wondered"; 9:43, "were marvelling" for "wondered"; 2 Thess. 1:10, "marvelled at" for "admired" (of the Person of Christ at the time of the shining forth of His Parousia, at the Second Advent). See WONDER.

NT: B.352b; CB.1271c; K.316.
OT: nāśā': S.5375; HR.626c.7a; H.1421; BD.669d.
shāmēm: S.8074; HR.626c.9; H.2409; BD.1030d.
GEN. REF.: IS.3:267; NB.–; Z.4:103.

Note: In Matt 9:8, A.V. translates this verb: R.V., *phobeō*, "were afraid;"

2. *ekthaumazō* [ἐκθαυμάζω, 1537, 2296], a strengthened form of No. 1 (*ek*, intensive), is found in the best mss. in mark 12:17, R.V., "wondered greatly" (some mss. have No. 1). ¶

NT: B.240b; CB.1244a; K.–.
OT: –.
GEN. REF.: –.

C. Adjective.

thaumastos [θαυμαστός, 2298], marvellous (akin to A and B), is said (*a*) of the Lord's doing in making the rejected Stone the Head of the corner, Matt. 21:42; Mark 12:11; (*b*) of the erstwhile blind man's astonishment that the

Pharisees knew not from whence Christ had come, and yet He had given him sight, John 9:30, R.V., "the marvel," A.V., "a marvellous thing"; (*c*) of the spiritual light into which believers are brought, 1 Pet. 2:9; (*d*) of the vision of the seven angels having the seven last plagues, Rev. 15:1; (*e*) of the works of God, 15:3. ¶

NT: B.352d; CB.1271c; K.316.
OT: yārē: S.3372; HR.627b.3; H.907, 908; BD.431a.
pālā': S.6381; HR.627b.6a; H.1768; BD.810c.
pele': S.6382; HR.627b.6c; H.1768a; BD.810b.
GEN. REF.: IS.3:267; NB.—; Z.4:103.

MASTER (Noun and Verb)

A. Nouns.

1. *didaskalos* [*διδάσκαλος*, 1320], a teacher (from *didaskō*, to teach), is frequently rendered "Master" in the four Gospels, as a title of address to Christ, e.g., Matt. 8:19; Mark 4:38 (there are more instances in Luke than in the other Gospels); John 1:38, where it interprets "Rabbi"; 20:16, where it interprets "Rabboni." It is used by Christ of Himself in Matt. 23:8 (see No. 6) and John 13:13, 14; by others concerning Him, Matt. 17:24; 26:18; Mark 5:35; 14:14; Luke 8:49; 22:11; John 11:28. In John 3:10, the Lord uses it in addressing Nicodemus, R.V., "the teacher" (A.V., "a master"), where the article does not specify a particular teacher, but designates the member of a class; for the class see Luke 2:46, "the doctors" (R.V., marg., "teachers"). It is used of the relation of a disciple to his master, in Matt. 10:24, 25; Luke 6:40. It is not translated "masters" in the rest of the N.T., save in the A.V. of Jas. 3:1 "(be not many) masters," where obviously the R.V. "teachers" is the meaning. See TEACHER.

NT: B.191c; CB.1241b; K.161.
OT: —.
GEN. REF.: IS.—; NB.794; Z.4:118.

2. *kurios* [*κύριος*, 2962], a lord, one who exercises power, is translated "masters" in Matt. 6:24; 15:27; Mark 13:35; Luke 16:13; Acts 16:16, 19; Rom. 14:4, A.V. (R.V., "lord"); Eph. 6:5, 9 (twice), the 2nd time of Christ; so in Col. 3:22; 4:1. See LORD.

NT: B.458d; CB.1256b; K.486.
OT: 'ēl: S.410; HR.800b.4a; H.93a; BD.42a,c.
y^{e}hôwāh: S.3068; HR.800b.11a; H.484c; BD.217d.
'^{e}lōhîm: S.430; HR.800b.18b; H.93c; BD.43a.
GEN. REF.: IS.3:278; NB.794; Z.4:119.

3. *despotēs* [*δεσπότης*, 1203], one who has "absolute ownership and uncontrolled power," is translated "masters" in 1 Tim. 6:1, 2; Tit. 2:9; 1 Pet. 2:18; of Christ, 2 Tim. 2:21; 2 Pet. 2:1, R.V. (for A.V., "Lord"); in Jude 4, R.V., it is applied to Christ" (our only) Master (and Lord, Jesus Christ)," A.V. "(the only) Lord (God)"; in Rev. 6:10, R.V., in an address to God, "O Master" (A.V., "O Lord"). It is rendered "Lord" in Luke 2:29 and Acts 4:24. See LORD. ¶

NT: B.176c; CB.1240c; K.145.
OT: 'ādôn: S.113; HR.292c.1a; H.27b; BD.10d.
'^{a}dōnay: S.113; HR.292c.1b; H.27b; BD.10d.
GEN. REF.: IS.3:278; NB.794; Z.4:118.

Note: For "master of the house," see GOODMAN.

4. *rabbei* [*ῥαββεί*, 4461], was an Aramaic word signifying "my master," a title of respectful address to Jewish teachers.

"The Aramaic word *rabbei*, transliterated into Greek, is explicitly recognized as the common form of address to Christ, Matt. 26:25 (cp., however, ver. 22, *kurios*); 26:49; Mark 9:5, but Matt. 17:4, *kurios*" (Dalman, *The Words of Jesus*).

In the following the R.V. has "Rabbi" for A.V. "Master"; Matt. 26:25, 49; Mark 9:5; 11:21; 14:45; John 4:31; 9:2; 11:8. In other passages the A.V. has "Rabbi," Matt. 23:7, 8; John 1:38, 49; 3:2, 26; 6:25. ¶

NT: B.733a; CB.1268a; K.982.
OT: rab (Aramaic): S.7229; HR.—; H.2984a; BD.1112b.
GEN. REF.: IS.3:278; NB.794; Z.4:119.

Note: The form *Rabbounei* (*Rabboni*), in Mark 10:51, is retained in the R.V. (for A.V., "Lord"); in John 20:16, in both A.V. and R.V. This title is said to be Galilean; hence it would be natural in the lips of a woman of Magdala. It does not differ materially from Rabbi. ¶

5. *epistatēs* [*ἐπιστάτης*, 1988], denotes a chief, a commander, overseer, master. It is used by the disciples in addressing the Lord, in recognition of His authority rather than His instruction (Nos. 1 and 6); it occurs only in Luke: 5:5; 8:24, 45; 9:33, 49; 17:13. ¶ In the Sept., 2 Kings 25:19; 2 Chron. 31:12; Jer. 36:26; 52:25. ¶

NT: B.300b; CB.1246a; K.248.
OT: pāqîd: S.6496; HR.529c.4; H.1802c; BD.824b.
nāgîd: S.5057; HR.529c.1; H.1289b; BD.617d.
sar: S.8269; HR.529c.6; H.2295a; BD.978a.
GEN. REF.: IS.3:278; NB.794; Z.4:119.

Note: "The form *epistata* . . . alongside of the commoner *didaskale* is . . . a Greek synonym for the latter, and both are to be traced back to the Aramaic *rabbei*." Christ forbade His disciples to allow themselves to be called *rabbi*, "on the ground that He alone was their Master, Matt. 23:8. In reference to Himself the designation was expressive of the real relation between them. The form of address 'Good Master' He, however, refused to allow, Mark 10:17, 18 . . . in the mouth of the speaker it was mere insolent flattery . . . the Lord was unwilling that anyone should thoughtlessly deal with such an epithet; and here, as always, the honour due to the Father was the first consideration with Him . . . The primitive community never ventured to call Jesus 'Our Teacher' after He had been exalted to the Throne of God. The title *rabbi*, expressing the relation of the disciple to the teacher, vanished from use; and there remained only the designation *maran*, the servant's appropriate acknowledgement of his Lord" (Dalman).

6. *kathēgētēs* [καθηγητής, 2519], properly a guide (akin to *kathēgeomai*, to go before, guide; *kata*, down, *hēgeomai*, to guide), denotes a master, a teacher, Matt. 23:10 (twice); some mss. have it in ver. 8, where the most authentic have No. 1. ¶

NT: B.388d; CB.—; K.—.
OT: —.
GEN. REF.: IS.3:278; NB.794; Z.—.

7. *kubernētēs* [κυβερνήτης, 2942], the pilot or steersman of a ship, or, metaphorically, a guide or governor (akin to *kubernaō*, to guide: Eng., govern is connected; cp. *kubernēsis*, a steering, pilotage, 1 Cor. 12:28, "governments"), is translated "master" in Acts 27:11; "shipmaster" in Rev. 18:17. ¶ In the Sept., Prov. 23:34; Ezek. 27:8, 27, 28. ¶

NT: B.456c; CB.1256b; K.—.
OT: ḥōbēl: S.2259; HR.796a.1; H.592c; BD.287a.
GEN. REF.: IS.—; NB.794; Z.—.

B. Verb.

katakurieuō [κατακυριεύω, 2634], to exercise lordship (*kata*, down upon, *kurios*, a lord), is translated "mastered" in Acts 19:16, R.V., of the action of the evil spirit on the sons of Sceva (A.V., "overcame"). In translating the word *amphoterōn* by its primary meaning, "both," the R.V. describes the incident as referring to two only. It has been shown, however, that in the period of the *Koinē* (see Foreword to Vol. I) *amphoteroi*, "both," was no longer restricted to two persons. Ramsay ascribes the abruptness of the word here to the vivid narrative of an eye witness. See DOMINION, LORD, LORDSHIP.

NT: B.412c; CB.1254a; K.486.
OT: kābash: S.3533; HR.735a.3; H.951; BD.461b.
rādāh: S.7287; HR.735a.6; H.2121, 2122; BD.921d.
māshal: S.4910; HR.735a.4; H.1258, 1259; BD.605c.
GEN. REF.: IS.3:278; NB.794; Z.—.

MASTERBUILDER

architektōn [ἀρχιτέκτων, 753], from *archē*, rule, beginning, and *tektōn*, an artificer (whence Eng., architect), a principal artificer, is used figuratively by the Apostle in 1 Cor. 3:10, of his work in laying the foundation of the local church in Corinth, inasmuch as the inception of the spiritual work there devolved upon him. The examples from the papyri and from inscriptions, as illustrated by Moulton and Milligan, show that the word had a wider application than our "architect," and confirm the rendering "masterbuilder" in this passage, which is of course borne out by the context. ¶

NT: B.113b; CB.1237b; K.—.
OT: ḥārāsh: S.2796; HR.1666.1; H.760a; BD.360d.
GEN. REF.: IS.3:278; NB.—; Z.—.

MATTER, MATTERS

1. *logos* [λόγος, 3056], a word, speech, discourse, account, hence also that which is spoken of, a matter, affair, thing, is translated "matter" in Mark 1:45; Acts 8:21; 15:6; 19:38; in the R.V. of Phil. 4:15, "in the matter of" (A.V., "concerning"). See ACCOUNT.

NT: B.477a; CB.1257a; K.505.
OT: dābār: S.1697; HR.881c.2a; H.399a; BD.182a.
GEN. REF.: —.

2. *pragma* [πρᾶγμα, 4229], akin to *prassō*, to do, denotes (*a*) that which has been done, a deed, translated "matters" in Luke 1:1, R.V. (A.V., "things"); "matter" in 2 Cor. 7:11; (*b*) that which is being done, an affair, translated "matter" in Rom. 16:2, R.V. (A.V., "business"); 1 Cor. 6:1, in a forensic sense, a law-suit (frequently found with this meaning in the papyri); 1 Thess. 4:6, "in the matter," i.e., the matter under consideration, which, as the preceding words show, is here the sin of adultery. See BUSINESS, B, *Note* (1), THING

NT: B.697a; CB.1266b; K.927.
OT: dābār: S.1697; HR.1199c.1; H.399a; BD.182a.
GEN. REF.: —.

3. *enklēma* [ἔγκλημα, 1462], an accusation, charge, Acts 25:16, R.V., "matter laid against him"; elsewhere, Acts 23:29, "charge"; see ACCUSATION, A, No. 3. ¶

NT: B.216b; CB.1245a; K.394.
OT: —.
GEN. REF.: —.

Notes: (1) In Gal. 2:6, the statement "it maketh no matter" translates the verb *diapherō*, to bear asunder, make a difference, with *ouden*, nothing, used adverbially, i.e., 'it makes no difference (to me)'; his commission from the Lord relieved him of responsibility to the authority of the Apostles.

(2) In 1 Cor. 9:11, R.V., the neuter of the adjective *megas*, great, is translated "a great matter" (A.V., "a great thing").

(3) In Jas. 3:5, A.V., *hulē*, a wood, forest, is translated "a matter" (R.V., and A.V. marg., "wood"). In older English the word "matter" actually meant "wood" (like its Latin original, *materia*).

(4) In Acts 17:32, the A.V. adds "*matter*" to the pronoun "this," R.V., "(concerning) this."

(5) In 2 Cor. 8:19, R.V., the phrase, lit., 'in this grace' is translated "in *the matter of* (A.V., with) this grace."

(6) In 2 Cor. 8:20, R.V., the phrase, lit., 'in this bounty' is translated "in *the matter of* this bounty" (A.V., "in this abundance").

(7) In 2 Cor. 9:5, the phrase, lit., 'as a bounty' is amplified to "as a matter of bounty."

(8) For 1 Pet. 4:15 see BUSYBODY. See also OTHER, THIS, THESE, WEIGHTIER, WRONG.

MAY, MAYEST, MIGHT

1. *dunamai* [δύναμαι, 1410], to be able, have power, whether by personal ability, permission, or opportunity, is sometimes rendered "may" or "might," e.g., Matt. 26:9; Mark 14:5; Acts 17:19; 1 Thess. 2:6. In the following the R.V. substitutes "can," "canst," "couldst," for the A.V., e.g., Matt. 26:42; Mark 4:32; 14:7; Luke 16:2; Acts 24:11; 25:11; 27:12; 1 Cor. 7:21; 14:31 (here the alteration is especially important, as not permission for all to prophesy, but ability to do so, is the meaning); Eph. 3:4. In the following the R.V. substitutes the verb to be able, Acts 19:40; 24:8; Rev. 13:17. See ABLE, B, No. 1.

NT: B.207a; CB.1242b; K.186.
OT: yākōl: S.3201; HR.353a.4a; H.866; BD.407b.
GEN. REF.: –.

2. *exesti* [ἔξεστι, 1832], it is permitted, lawful (*eimi*, to be, prefixed by *ek*, from), is rendered "(I) may" in Acts 2:29, R.V. [A.V., "let (me)"]; in Acts 21:37, "may (I)," lit., 'is it permitted (me to speak)?' Some mss. have it in 8:37, "thou mayest" (A.V.). See LAWFUL.

NT: B.275b; CB.1247c; K.–.
OT: –.
GEN. REF.: –.

3. *isōs* [ἴσως, 2481], equally (from the adjective *isos*, equal), is translated "it may be" in Luke 20:13 (i.e., 'perhaps'). ¶

NT: B.384a; CB.–; K.–.
OT: –.
GEN. REF.: –.

4. *tunchanō* [τυγχάνω, 5177], to meet with, reach, obtain, denotes, intransitively, to happen, chance, befall; used impersonally with the conjunction *ei*, if, it signifies 'it may be,' 'perhaps,' e.g., 1 Cor. 14:10; 15:37, "it may chance"; 16:6.

NT: B.829b; CB.–; K.1191.
OT: –.
GEN. REF.: –.

Notes: (1) In Matt. 8:28, A.V., *ischuō*, to have strength, be strong, be well able, is translated "might" (R.V., "could").

(2) "May," "might," sometimes translate the prepositional phrase *eis*, unto, with the definite article, followed by the infinitive mood of some verb, expressing purpose, e.g., Acts 3:19, "may be blotted out," it., 'unto the blotting out of'; Rom. 3:26, "that he might be," lit., 'unto his being'; so 8:29; 2 Cor. 1:4, "that we may be able," lit., 'unto our being able'; Eph. 1:18, "that ye may know," lit., 'unto your knowing'; Acts 7:19; Rom. 1:11; 4:16; 12:2; 15:13; Phil. 1:10; 1 Thess. 3:10, 13; 2 Thess. 1:5; 2:6, 10; Heb. 12:10. In Luke 20:20 the best mss have *hōste*, "so as to," R.V., as, e.g., in 1 Pet. 1:21. Sometimes the article with the infinitve mood without a preceding preposition, expresses result, e.g., Luke 21:22; Acts 26:18 (twice), "that they may turn," R.V.; cp. Rom. 6:6; 11:10; 1 Cor. 10:13; Phil. 3:10, "that I may know"; Jas. 5:17.

(3) The phrases "may be," "might be," are frequently the rendering of the verb to be, in the subjunctive or optative moods, preceded by a conjunction introducing a condition, or expressing a wish or purpose, e.g., Matt. 6:4; John 14:3; 17:11. Sometimes the phrase translates simply the infinitive mood of the verb *eimi*, to be, e.g., Luke 8:38, lit., 'to be (with Him)'; so the R.V. in 2 Cor. 5:9; in 2 Cor. 9:5, "that (the same) might be," lit., '(the same) to be.'

(4) In Heb. 7:9 the phrase *hōs* ('so') *epos* ('a word') *eipein* ('to say'), i.e., lit., 'so to say a word' is an idiom, translated in the R.V., "so to say" (A.V., "if I may so say"); the Eng. equivalent is 'one might almost say.'

ME

Notes: (1) The pronoun, whether alone or with some English preposition, e.g., of, to, for, in, translates one or other of the oblique cases of *ego*, 'I.'

(2) In Philm. 13 the reflexive pronoun *emauton*, myself, is translated "me," governed by the preposition *pros*, with, lit., 'with myself.'

(3) In Tit. 1:3, for the A.V., "is committed unto me," the R.V. has "I was intrusted."

(4) In Phil. 2:23, "how it will go with me," is, lit., 'the (things) concerning me.'

(5) The phrase *en emoi*, 'in me,' is used (*a*) instrumentally (*en*, instrumental, by or through), e.g., 2 Cor. 13:3; (*b*) subjectively, 'within me,' e.g., Gal. 2:20; (*c*) objectively, 'in my case,' e.g., 1 Cor. 9:15; 14:11; Gal. 1:16, 24; 1 Tim. 1:16.

(6) In Luke 22:19 the possessive pronoun *emos*, my, is rendered "of Me," lit., '(into) My (remembrance).'

MEAL

aleuron [ἄλευρον, 224], meal (akin to *aleuō*, to grind, and therefore, lit., 'what is ground'), occurs in Matt. 13:33; Luke 13:21. ¶

NT: B.35c; CB.–; K.–.
OT: qemah: S.7058; HR.52c.1; H.2033a; BD.887d.
GEN. REF.: IS.3:290; NB.798; Z.4:142.

MEAN (Adjective)

asēmos [ἄσημος, 767], lit., without mark (*a*, negative, *sēma*, a mark), i.e., undistinguished, obscure, was applied by the Apostle Paul negatively, to his native city, Tarsus, Acts 21:39. ¶ Moulton and Milligan (Vocab.) have a note as follows: "This word occurs perpetually in the papyri to denote a man who is 'not distinguished' from his neighbours by the convenient scars on eyebrow or arm or right shin, which identify so many individuals in formal documents." Deissmann suggests that the word may have been the technical term for "uncircumcised," among the Greek Egyptians. In another papyrus document a pair of silver bracelets are described as of "unstamped" (*asēmos*) silver.

NT: B.115a; CB.–; K.1015.
OT: –.
GEN. REF.: IS.3:292; NB.–; Z.–.

MEAN (Verb)

1. *eimi* [εἰμί, 1510], to be, in certain of its forms, has an explicative force, signifying to denote, to import, e.g., Matt. 9:13; 12:7, "(what this) meaneth," lit. '(what this) is'; Luke 18:36, "meant" (lit., 'might be'); Acts 10:17, "might mean," R.V. (lit., 'might be'); in Luke 15:26 the R.V. keeps to the verb to be, "(what these things) might be" (A.V., "meant"). In Acts 2:12 the verb to be is preceded by *thelō*, to will, and the phrase is translated "(what) meaneth (this)," lit., '(what) does (this) will to be?' in 17:20, lit., '(what do these things) will to be?'

NT: B.222d; CB.1243a; K.206.
OT: –.
GEN. REF.: –.

2. *legō* [λέγω, 3004], to say, sometimes has the significance of meaning something; so the R.V. in 1 Cor. 1:12; A.V., "(this) I say."

NT: B.468a; CB.1256c; K.505.
OT: 'āmar: S.559; HR.863c.1a; H.118; BD.55c.
GEN. REF.: IS.3:292; NB.–; Z.–.

Notes: (1) In Acts 27:2, A.V., *mellō*, to be about to, is translated "meaning" (R.V., "was about to"), with reference to the ship (according to the best mss.).

(2) In Acts 21:13, A.V., *poieō*, to do, is translated "(what) mean ye (to weep); "R.V., "(what) do ye, (weeping)."

(3) The abbreviated original in 2 Cor. 8:13 is rendered by the italicised additions, A.V., "*I mean* (not);" R.V., "*I say* (not) *this*." Cp. the R.V. italics in Mark 6:2.

MEANING

dunamis [δύναμις, 1411], power, force, is used of the significance or force of what is spoken, 1 Cor. 14:11. See MIGHT, POWER.

NT: B.207b; CB.1242b; K.186.
OT: ḥayil: S.2428; HR.350a.11; H.624a; BD.298c.
GEN. REF.: –.

MEANS (by all, by any, etc.)

1. *pantōs* [πάντως, 3843], an adverb from *pas*, all, denoting wholly, altogether, entirely, is used in 1 Cor. 9:22, "by all means." When the Apostle says, "I am become all things to all men, that I may by all means save some," he is simply speaking of his accommodating himself to various human conditions consistently with fidelity to the truth, with no unscriptural compliance with men, but in the exercise of self denial; "by all means" refers to the preceding context from ver. 18, and stresses his desire to be used in the salvation of some. It is found in Acts 21:22, R.V., "certainly." Some mss. have the word in this sense in Acts 18:21 (A.V.). See ALTOGETHER, B, No. 1.

NT: B.609b; CB.–; K.–.
OT: –.
GEN. REF.: –.

2. *pōs* [πως, 4458], at all, somehow, in any way, is used after the conjunction (*a*) *ei*, if, meaning 'if by any means,' e.g., Acts 27:12; Rom. 1:10; 11:14; Phil. 3:11; (*b*) *mē*, lest, 'lest by any means,' e.g., 1 Cor. 8:9; 9:27; 2 Cor. 2:7, R.V. (A.V., "perhaps"); 9:4, R.V. (A.V., "haply"); 11:3; 12:20, R.V.; Gal. 2:2; 4:11, R.V. (A.V., "lest"); 1 Thess. 3:5 (A.V., "lest by some means").

NT: B.732b; CB.–; K.–.
OT: –.
GEN. REF.: –.

3. *ek* [ἐκ, 1537], out of, from, by, suggesting the source from which something is done, is sometimes rendered "by means of," e.g., Luke 16:9, R.V., "by means of (the mammon of unrighteousness)"; A.V., "of"; 2 Cor. 1:11, "by (the) means of (many)."

NT: B.234a; CB.1243b; K.–.
OT: –.
GEN. REF.: –.

4. *dia* [διά, 1223], by, by means of, when followed by the genitive case, is instrumental, e.g., 2 Pet. 3:6, R.V., "by which means" (A.V., "whereby").

NT: B.179b; CB.1241a; K.149.
OT: –.
GEN. REF.: –.

5. *pōs* [πῶς, 4459], an interrogative adverb (different from No. 2), how, in what way, Luke 8:36, A.V., "by what means," R.V., "how"; so John 9:21; cp. *Note* (4) below.
NT: B.732b; CB.–; K.–.
OT: –.
GEN. REF.: –.

Notes: (1) In Luke 5:18 the A.V. adds the word "*means*" in italics.

(2) The word *tropos*, a manner, way, is sometimes used in a prepositional phrase, e.g., 2 Thess. 2:3, A.V., "by any means," R.V., "in any wise," lit., 'in any manner'; 3:16, A.V., "by all means," R.V. "in all ways," lit., 'in every manner.'

(3) The double negative *ou mē*, i.e., 'no not,' 'not at all,' is translated "by no means," Matt. 5:26; in Luke 10:19, "by any means," A.V. (R.V., "in any wise"); Luke 12:59, R.V., "by no means" (A.V., "not").

(4) In Acts 4:9, the phrase *en*, in or by, with *tini* (from *tis*, who), lit., "in whom" (R.V., marg.), is translated "by what means."

(5) In Heb. 9:15, R.V., the verb *ginomai*, to come to be, become, take place, used in its 2nd aorist participle, is rightly translated "(a death) having taken place"; A.V., "by means of (death)."

(6) In Rev. 13:14, R.V., *dia*, followed by the accusative case, is rightly translated "by reason of," i.e., 'on account of' (A.V., wrongly, "by *the means of*").

For **MEANWHILE** see **WHILE**

MEASURE (Noun and Verb)

A. Nouns.

1. *metron* [μέτρον, 3358], denotes (I) that which is used for measuring, a measure, (*a*) of a vessel, figuratively, Matt. 23:32; Luke 6:38 (twice); in John 3:34, with the preposition *ek*, "(He giveth not the Spirit) by measure," R.V. (which is a necessary correction; the italicized words "*unto him*," A.V. detract from the meaning). Not only had Christ the Holy Spirit without measure but God so gives the Spirit through Him to others. It is the Ascended Christ who gives the Spirit to those who receive His testimony and set their seal to this, that God is true. The Holy Spirit is imparted neither by degrees, nor in portions, as if He were merely an influence, He is bestowed Personally upon each believer, at the time of the new birth; (*b*) of a graduated rod or rule for measuring, figuratively, Matt. 7:2; Mark 4:24; literally, Rev. 21:15 (in the best mss.; see the R.V.); ver. 17; (II) that which is measured, a determined extent, a portion measured off, Rom. 12:3; 2 Cor. 10:13 (twice); Eph. 4:7, "(according to the) measure (of the gift of Christ)"; the gift of grace is measured and given according to the will of Christ; whatever the endowment, His is the bestowment and the adjustment; ver. 13, "the measure (of the stature of the fulness of Christ)," the standard of spiritual stature being the fulness which is essentially Christ's; ver. 16, "(according to the working in due) measure (of each several part)," i.e., according to the effectual working of the ministration rendered in due measure by every part. ¶
NT: B.515a; CB.1258c; K.590.
OT: middāh: S.4060; HR.918b.1; H.1146b; BD.551c.
'êphāh: S.374; HR.918b.5a; H.82; BD.35b.
GEN. REF.: IS.3:294; NB.1319; Z.5:916.

2. *meros* [μέρος, 3313], a part, portion, is used with the preposition *apo*, from, with the meaning "in some measure," Rom. 15:15, R.V. (A.V., ". . . sort") See COAST, PART.
NT: B.505b; CB.1258b; K.585.
OT: –.
GEN. REF.: IS.–; NB.1319; Z.–.

3. *saton* [σάτον, 4568], is a Hebrew dry measure (Heb., *seah*), about a peck and a half, Matt. 13:33; Luke 13:21; "three measures" would be the quantity for a baking (cp. Gen. 18:6; Judg. 6:19; 1 Sam. 1:24; the "ephah" of the last two passages was equal to three *sata*). ¶
NT: B.745b; CB.–; K.–.
OT: s^{e}'āh: S.5429; HR.–; H.1452; BD.684b.
GEN. REF.: IS.3:294; NB.1319; Z.5:916.

4. *koros* [κόρος, 2884], denotes a *cor*, the largest Hebrew dry measure (ten *ephahs*), containing about 11 bushels, Luke 16:7; the hundred measures amounted to a very considerable quantity. ¶
NT: B.444d; CB.–; K.–.
OT: kōr: S.3734; HR.–; H.1031; BD.499d.
GEN. REF.: IS.3:294; NB.1319; Z.5:916.

5. *batos* [βάτος, 943], denotes a *bath*, a Jewish liquid measure (the equivalent of an *ephah*), containing between 8 and 9 gallons, Luke 16:6. ¶
NT: B.137c; CB.–; K.–.
OT: bat: S.1324; HR.215a.1; H.298a; BD.144c.
GEN. REF.: IS.3:294; NB.1319; Z.5:916.

6. *choinix* [χοῖνιξ, 5518], a dry measure of rather less than a quart, about "as much as would support a person of moderate appetite for a day," occurs in Rev. 6:6 (twice). Usually eight *choenixes* could be bought for a *denarius* (about 9½d); this passage predicts circumstances in which the *denarius* is the price of one *choenix*. ¶ In the Sept., Ezek. 45:10, 11, where it represents the Heb. *ephah* and *bath*. ¶
NT: B.883b; CB.–; K.–.
OT: bat: S.1324; HR.1472a.1; H.298a; BD.144c.
GEN. REF.: IS.3:294; NB.1319; Z.5:916.

Notes: (1) In 2 Cor. 10:14, A.V., *huperekteinō*, to stretch out overmuch, is translated "we stretch (not ourselves) beyond measure," (R.V., ". . . overmuch)."

(2) In 2 Cor. 11:9, R.V., *prosanaplēroō*, to fill up by adding to, to supply fully, is translated "supplied the measure" (A.V., "supplied"). See SUPPLY.

(3) For the phrases in the A.V., "beyond measure," Gal. 1:13; "out of measure," 2 Cor. 1:8, see ABUNDANCE, A, No. 4, EXCEL, B.

(4) In Mark 6:51, some mss. have the phrase *ek perissou*, "beyond measure (A.V.).

(5) For the phrase "be exalted above measure," 2 Cor. 12:7, A.V., see EXALT, A, No. 4.

B. Adverbs.

1. *huperballontōs* [ὑπερβαλλόντως, 5234], beyond measure (*huper*, over, beyond, *ballō*, to throw; for the verb *huperballō*, see EXCEEDING), is rendered "above measure" in 2 Cor. 11:23. ¶

NT: B.840a; CB.–; K.1230.
OT: –.
GEN. REF.: –.

2. *perissōs* [περισσῶς, 280], Mark 10:26; see EXCEED, B, No.4.

3. *huperperissōs* [ὑπερπερισσῶς, —], Mark 7:37: see ABUNDANCE D, No. 3. ¶

C. Adjective.

ametros [ἄμετρος, 280], without measure (*a*, negative, and A, No. 1), is used in the neuter plural in an adverbial phrase in 2 Cor. 10:13, 15, *eis ta ametra*, lit., 'unto the (things) without measure,' R.V., "(we will not glory) beyond our measure"; A.V., "(we will not boast) of things without measure," referring to the sphere Divinely appointed for the Apostle as to his Gospel ministry; this had reached to Corinth, and by the increase of the faith of the church there, would extend to regions beyond. His opponents had no scruples about intruding into the spheres of other men's work. ¶

NT: B.45c; CB.1234c; K.590.
OT: –.
GEN. REF.: –.

D. Verbs.

1. *metreō* [μετρέω, 3354], to measure (akin to A, No. 1), is used (*a*) of space, number, value, etc., Rev. 11:1, 2; 21:15, 16, 17; metaphorically, 2 Cor. 10:12; (*b*) in the sense of measuring out, giving by measure, Matt. 7:2, "ye mete" (some mss. have No. 2); Mark 4:24; in some mss. in Luke 6:38 (see No. 2). ¶

NT: B.514c; CB.1258c; K.590.
OT: mādad: S.4058; HR.918a.1; H.1146; BD.551a.
GEN. REF.: IS.3:294; NB.1319; Z.–.

2. *antimetreō* [ἀντιμετρέω, 488], to measure in return (*anti*, back, in return and No. 1), is used in the Passive Voice, and found in some mss. in Matt. 7:2 (the most authentic have No. 1); in Luke 6:38 the most authentic have this verb. ¶ It is not found in the Sept.

NT: B.75b; CB.–; K.–.
OT: –.
GEN. REF.: –.

MEAT

1. *brōma* [βρῶμα, 1033], food (akin to *bibrōskō*, to eat, John 6:13 ¶), solid food in contrast to milk, is translated "food" in Matt. 14:15, R.V. (A.V., "victuals"); "meats," Mark 7:19; 1 Cor. 6:13 (twice); 1 Tim. 4:3; Heb. 9:10; 13:9; "meat," John 4:34; Rom. 14:15 (twice), 20; 1 Cor. 3:2; 8:8, 13; 10:3; "food," R.V., for A.V., "meat," Luke 3:11; 9:13. ¶

NT: B.148a; CB.1239b; K.111.
OT: 'ōkel: S.400; HR.231b.1a; H.85a; BD.38a.
ma'ᵃkāl: S.3978; HR.231b.1c; H.85d; BD.38b.
GEN. REF.: IS.–; NB.–; Z.2:581.

2. *brōsis* [βρῶσις, 1035], akin to No. 1, denotes (*a*) the act of eating, 1 Cor. 8:4 (see EAT); (*b*) food, translated "meat" in John 4:32 (for ver. 34, see No. 1); 6:27 (twice, the second time metaphorically, of spiritual food); 6:55, R.V., marg., "(true) meat"; Rom. 14:17, A.V., "meat," R.V., "eating"; Col. 2:16; in Heb. 12:16, R.V., "mess of meat," A.V., "morsel of meat"; in 2 Cor. 9:10, "food"; in Matt. 6:19, 20, "rust." See EAT, EATING, B. ¶

NT: B.148b; CB.1239b; K.111.
OT: 'ākal: S.398; HR.231c.1b; H.85; BD.37a.
ma'ᵃkāl: S.3978; HR.231c.1f; H.85d; BD.38b.
GEN. REF.: IS.–; NB.–; Z.2:581.

3. *brōsimos* [βρώσιμος, 1034], eatable, Luke 24:41, A.V., "any meat" (R.V., "anything to eat"). See EAT, C. ¶

NT: B.148b; CB.1239b; K.–.
OT: ma'ᵃkāl: S.3978; HR.231c.1; H.85d; BD.38b.
GEN. REF.: IS.–; NB.–; Z.2:581.

4. *trophē* [τροφή, 5160], nourishment, food, is translated "meat" in the A.V. (R.V. "food") except in two instances. See FOOD, No. 1.

NT: B.827d; CB.–; K.–.
OT: 'ōkel: S.400; HR.1376b.1; H.85a; BD.38a.
leḥem: S.3899; HR.1376b.4; H.1105a; BD.536d.
GEN. REF.: IS.–; NB.–; Z.2:581.

5. *phagō* [φάγω, 5315], to eat, is used as a noun, in the infinitive mood, and translated "meat" in Matt. 25:35, 42 (lit., 'to eat'); in Luke 8:55 the R.V. translates it literally, "to eat" (A.V., "meat"). See EAT, No. 2.

NT: B.312b; CB.–; K.–.
OT: 'ākal: S.398; HR.554a.1a; H.85; BD.37a.
GEN. REF.: IS.–; NB.–; Z.2:581.

6. *trapeza* [τράπεζα, 5132], a table (Eng., trapeze), is used, by metonymy, of the food on the table, in Acts 16:34 (R.V., marg., "a table"),

and translated "meat"; cp. "table" in Rom. 11:9; 1 Cor. 10:21. See TABLE.

NT: B.824b; CB.1273a; K.1187.
OT: shulḥān: S.7979; HR.1369b.4; H.2395a; BD.1020b.
GEN. REF.: —.

Notes: (1) For *prosphagion*, John 21:5, A.V., "any meat," see EAT, B, No. 2.

(2) In Luke 12:42, *sitometrion* denotes a measured portion of food (*sitos*, food, *metrios*, within measure).

(3) In Matt. 15:37 and Mark 8:8, the A.V. translates the plural of *klasma*, a broken piece (from *klaō*, to break), "broken meat" (R.V., "broken pieces").

(4) In John 12:2, R.V., *anakeimai*, to recline at table, is translated "sat at meat" (A.V., "sat at the table"); in Mark 6:26, R.V., according to the best mss., "sat at meat," some have *sunanakeimai* (A.V., "sat with him"); in Mark 6:22, R.V., *sunanakeimai*, to recline at table together, is translated "that sat at meat with him."

(5) In Acts 15:29, A.V., the neuter plural of *eidōlothutos*, sacrificed to idols, is translated "meats offered to idols" (R.V., "things . . ."; as elsewhere in the A.V.). See IDOLS (offered to.)

(6) For *kataklinō*, to sit down to (recline at) meat, see SIT, No. 7.

MEDIATOR

mesitēs [μεσίτης, 3316], lit., a go-between (from *mesos*, middle, and *eimi*, to go), is used in two ways in the N.T., (*a*) one who mediates between two parties with a view to producing peace, as in 1 Tim. 2:5, though more than mere mediatorship is in view, for the salvation of men necessitated that the Mediator should Himself possess the nature and attributes of Him towards whom He acts, and should likewise participate in the nature of those for whom He acts (sin apart); only by being possessed both of Deity and humanity could He comprehend the claims of the one and the needs of the other; further, the claims and the needs could be met only by One who, Himself being proved sinless, would offer Himself an expiatory sacrifice on behalf of men; (*b*) one who acts as a guarantee so as to secure something which otherwise would not be obtained. Thus in Heb. 8:6; 9:15; 12:24 Christ is the Surety of "the better covenant," "the new covenant," guaranteeing its terms for His people.

In Gal. 3:19 Moses is spoken of as a mediator, and the statement is made that "a mediator is not a mediator of one," ver. 20, that is, of one party. Here the contrast is between the promise given to Abraham and the giving of the Law. The Law was a covenant enacted between God and the Jewish people, requiring fulfilment by both parties. But with the promise to Abraham, all the obligations were assumed by God, which is implied in the statement, "but God is one." ¶ In the Sept., Job 9:33, "daysman." ¶

NT: B.506d; CB.1258b; K.585.
OT: bayin: S.996; HR.912c.1; H.239a; BD.107b.
GEN. REF.: IS.3:299; NB.802; Z.4:150.

MEDITATE

1. *meletaō* [μελετάω, 3191], primarily, to care for (akin to *meletē*, care; cp *melei*, it is a care), denotes (*a*) to attend to, practise, 1 Tim. 4:15, R.V., "be diligent in" (A.V., "meditate upon"); to practise is the prevalent sense of the word, and the context is not against this significance in the R.V. rendering; some mss. have it in Mark 13:11; (*b*) to ponder, imagine, Acts 4:25. See IMAGINE ¶

NT: B.500b; CB.—; K.—.
OT: hāgāh: S.1897; HR.908b.3a; H.467; BD.211c.
sîaḥ: S.7878; HR.908b.4; H.2255; BD.967a.
GEN. REF.: IS.3:305; NB.802; Z.4:163.

2. *promeletaō* [προμελετάω, 4304], to premeditate, is used in Luke 21:14. ¶

NT: B.708c; CB.—; K.—.
OT: —.
GEN. REF.: IS.3:305; NB.802; Z.4:163.

Note: In the corresponding passage in Mark 13:11, the most authentic mss. have the verb *promerimnaō*, to be anxious beforehand (R.V.); see No. 1.

For MEDDLER see BUSYBODY

MEEK, MEEKNESS

A. Adjective.

praüs or *praos* [πραΰς, 4239], denotes gentle, mild, meek; for its significance see the corresponding noun, below, B. Christ uses it of His own disposition, Matt. 11:29; He gives it in the third of His Beatitudes, 5:5; it is said of Him as the King Messiah, 21:5, from Zech. 9:9; it is an adornment of the Christian profession, 1 Pet. 3:4. ¶ Cp. *ēpios*, gentle, of a soothing disposition, 1 Thess. 2:7; 2 Tim. 2:24. ¶

NT: B.698d; CB.1266b; K.929.
OT: ʿānāw: S.6035; HR.1201a.1a; H.1652a; BD.776c.
ʿānî: S.6041; HR.1201a.1c; H.1652d; BD.776d.
GEN. REF.: IS.3:307; NB.804; Z.4:163.

B. Nouns.

1. *praütēs*, or *praotēs* [πραΰτης, 4240], an earlier form, denotes meekness. In its use in Scripture, in which it has a fuller, deeper significance than in non-scriptural Greek writings, it consists not in a person's "outward behaviour only; nor yet in his relations to his

fellow-men; as little in his mere natural disposition. Rather it is an inwrought grace of the soul; and the exercises of it are first and chiefly towards God. It is that temper of spirit in which we accept His dealings with us as good, and therefore without disputing or resisting; it is closely linked with the word *tapeinophrosunē* [humility], and follows directly upon it, Eph. 4:2; Col. 3:12; cp. the adjectives in the Sept. of Zeph. 3:12, "meek and lowly"; . . . it is only the humble heart which is also the meek, and which, as such, does not fight against God and more or less struggle and contend with Him. This meekness, however, being first of all a meekness before God, is also such in the face of men, even of evil men, out of a sense that these, with the insults and injuries which they may inflict, are permitted and employed by Him for the chastening and purifying of His elect" (Trench, Syn. § xlii). In Gal. 5:23 it is associated with *enkrateia*, self-control.

The meaning of *praütēs* "is not readily expressed in English, for the terms meekness, mildness, commonly used, suggest weakness and pusillanimity to a greater or less extent, whereas *praütēs* does nothing of the kind. Nevertheless, it is difficult to find a rendering less open to objection than 'meekness'; 'gentleness' has been suggested, but as *praütēs* describes a condition of mind and heart, and as 'gentleness' is appropriate rather to actions, this word is no better than that used in both English Versions. It must be clearly understood, therefore, that the meekness manifested by the Lord and commended to the believer is the fruit of power. The common assumption is that when a man is meek it is because he cannot help himself; but the Lord was 'meek' because he had the infinite resources of God at His command. Described negatively, meekness is the opposite to self-assertiveness and self-interest; it is equanimity of spirit that is neither elated nor cast down, simply because it is not occupied with self at all.

"In 2 Cor. 10:1 the Apostle appeals to the 'meekness . . . of Christ.' Christians are charged to show 'all meekness toward all men,' Tit. 3:2, for meekness becomes 'god's elect,' Col. 3:12. To this virtue the 'man of God' is urged; he is to 'follow after meekness' for his own sake, 1 Tim. 6:11 (the best texts have No. 2 here, however), and in his service, and more especially in his dealings with the 'ignorant and erring,' he is to exhibit 'a spirit of meekness,' 1 Cor. 4:21, and Gal. 6:1; even 'they that oppose themselves' are to be corrected in meekness, 2 Tim. 2:25. James exhorts his 'beloved brethren' to 'receive with meekness the implanted word,' 1:21. Peter enjoins 'meekness' in setting forth the grounds of the Christian hope, 3:15."* ¶

NT: B.699a; CB.1266b; K.929.
OT: 'anwāh: S.6038; HR.1201b.1a; H.1652b; BD.776c.
'ānāh: S.6031; HR.1201b.1b; H.1651,1652; BD.776b.
GEN. REF.: IS.3:307; NB.804; Z.4:163.

2. *praüpathia* [πραϋπαθία, —], a meek disposition, meekness (*praus*, meek, *paschō*, to suffer), is found in the best texts in 1 Tim. 6:11. ¶

NT: B.698d; CB.1266b; K.798.
OT: —.
GEN. REF.: —.

MEET (Adjective and Verb)

A. Adjectives.

1. *axios* [ἄξιος, 514], has the meaning of being of weight, value, worth; also befitting, becoming, right on the ground of fitness, e.g., Matt. 3:8, A.V., "meet" (R.V., "worthy"); so Acts 26:20; Luke 3:8 ("worthy"); 23:41 ("due reward"). See REWARD, WORTHY.

NT: B.78a; CB.1238b; K.63.
OT: shāwāh: S.7737; HR.113a.3; H.2342; BD.1000c.
GEN. REF.: —.

2. *hikanos* [ἱκανός, 2425], sufficient, competent, fit, is translated "meet" in 1 Cor. 15:9. See ENOUGH, SUFFICIENT.

NT: B.374b; CB.1250c; K.361.
OT: day: S.1767; HR.683c.2; H.425; BD.191b.
GEN. REF.: —.

3. *kalos* [καλός, 2570], good, is translated "meet" in Matt. 15:26 and Mark 7:27. See GOOD.

NT: B.400b; CB.1253b; K.402.
OT: ṭôb: S.2896; HR.715b.2a; H.793a; BD.373c.
GEN. REF.: —.

4. *euthetos* [εὔθετος, 2111], well-placed, is translated "meet" in Heb. 6:7: see FIT.

NT: B.320b; CB.—; K.—.
OT: —.
GEN. REF.: —.

Note: In Phil. 1:7 and 2 Pet. 1:13, A.V., *dikaios*, just, is translated "meet" (R.V., "right"). For "meet . . . for use," 2 Tim. 2:21, see USE, *Note*.

B. Verbs.

1. *dei* [δεῖ, 1163], an impersonal verb, it is necessary, one must, is translated "it was meet," in Luke 15:32; in Rom. 1:27, A.V., "was meet" (R.V., "was due"). See DUE, B, No. 2.

NT: B.172a; CB.1240b; K.140.
OT: —.
GEN. REF.: —.

2. *hikanoō* [ἱκανόω, 2427], to render fit, meet, to make sufficient, is translated "hath

* From Notes on Galatians by Hogg and Vine, pp. 294, 295.

made . . . meet" in Col. 1:12; in 2 Cor. 3:6, R.V., "made . . . sufficient" (A.V., "hath made . . . able"). See ABLE. ¶

NT: B.374d; CB.1250c; K.361.
OT: rab: S.7227; HR.684a.3; H.2099a,b; BD.912d,913b.
GEN. REF.: –.

MEET (Verb), MEET WITH, MET

A. Verbs.

1. *apantaō* [ἀπαντάω, 528], to go to meet, to meet (*apo*, from, *antaō*, to meet with, come face to face with), is used in Mark 14:13 and Luke 17:12. Some mss. have this verb for No. 3 in Matt. 28:9; Mark 5:2; Luke 14;31; John 4:51; Acts 16:16. ¶

NT: B.80c; CB.1236b; K.–.
OT: pāga': S.6293; HR.117a.1; H.1731; BD.803b.
GEN. REF.: IS.3:308; NB.–; Z.–.

2. *sunantaō* [συναντάω, 4876], to meet with, lit., to meet together with (*sun*, with and *antaō*, see No. 1), is used in Luke 9:37 (in ver. 18, in some mss.); 22:10; Acts 10:25; Heb. 7:1, 10; metaphorically in Acts 20:22 ("shall befall"). See BEFALL.

NT: B.784c; CB.1270c; K.–.
OT: pāga': S.6293; HR.1311a.6; H.1731; BD.803b.
qārā': S.7122; HR.1311a.10a; H.2064; BD.896d.
GEN. REF.: IS.3:308; NB.–; Z.–.

3. *hupantaō* [ὑπαντάω, —], to go to meet, to meet, has the same meaning as No. 1, and is used in Matt. 8:28; Luke 8:27; John 11:20, 30, and, in the most authentic mss., in Matt. 28:9; Mark 5:2; Luke 14:31 (of meeting in battle); John 4:51; 12:18 and Acts 16:16 (see No. 1). ¶

NT: –.
OT: –.
GEN. REF.: –.

4. *paratunchanō* [παρατυγχάνω, 3909], to happen to be near or present, to chance to be by (*para*, beside, near, *tunchanō*, to happen), occurs in Acts 17:17, "met with (him)." ¶

NT: B.623a; CB.–; K.–.
OT: –.
GEN. REF.: –.

5. *sumballō* [συμβάλλω, 4820], to confer, to fall in with, meet with, is translated "met" in Acts 20:14, R.V. (A.V., "met with"), of the Apostle Paul's meeting his companions at Assos. See CONFER, No. 3.

NT: B.777b; CB.–; K.–.
OT: –.
GEN. REF.: –.

B. Nouns.

1. *hupantēsis* [ὑπάντησις, 5222], a going to meet (akin to A, No. 3), preceded by the preposition *eis*, unto, lit., 'unto a meeting,' translated "to meet," is found in John 12:13, and in the most authentic mss. in Matt. 8:34 (see No. 3) and 25:1 (see No. 2). ¶

NT: B.837d; CB.1252a; K.419.
OT: qārā': S.7122; HR.1406b.2; H.2064; BD.896d.
pānîm: S.6440; HR.1406b.1; H.1782a; BD.815d.
GEN. REF.: IS.3:308; NB.–; Z.–.

2. *apantēsis* [ἀπάντησις, 529], a meeting (akin to A, No. 1), occurs in Matt. 25:6 (in some mss. in ver. 1, and in 27:32, in some mss.); Acts 28:15; 1 Thess. 4:17. It is used in the papyri of a newly arriving magistrate. "It seems that the special idea of the word was the official welcome of a newly arrived dignitary" (Moulton, Greek Test. Gram. Vol. I, p. 14.

NT: B.80c; CB.1236b; K.64.
OT: liqra't: S.7122; HR.117b.3; H.2064; BD.896d.
GEN. REF.: IS.3:308; NB.–; Z.–.

3. *sunantēsis* [συνάντησις, 4877], a coming to meet with (akin to A, No. 2), is found in some mss. in Matt. 8:34, of the coming out of all the people of a city to meet the Lord (see No. 1). ¶

NT: B.784c; CB.–; K.–.
OT: qārā': S.7122; HR.1311c.3; H.2064; BD.896d.
GEN. REF.: IS.3:308; NB.–; Z.–.

MELODY (Verb)

psallō [ψάλλω, 5567], primarily to twitch, twang, then, to play a stringed instrument with the fingers, and hence, in the Sept., to sing with a harp, sing psalms, denotes, in the N.T., to sing a hymn, sing praise; in Eph. 5:19, "making melody" (for the preceding word *adō*, see SING). Elsewhere it is rendered "sing," Rom. 15:9; 1 Cor. 14:15; in Jas. 5:13, R.V., "let him sing praise" (A.V., "let him sing psalms"). See SING. ¶

NT: B.891a; CB.1267b; K.1225.
OT: zāmar: S.2167; HR.1483a.1; H.558; BD.274a.
nāgan: S.5059; HR.1483a.2a; H.1291.1; BD.618d.
GEN. REF.: IS.3:313; NB.–; Z.–.

MELT

tēkō [τήκω, 5080], to melt, melt down, is used in the Passive Voice in 2 Pet. 3:12, "shall melt" (lit., 'shall be melted'), of the elements (Eng., 'thaw' is etymologically connected). ¶

NT: B.814b; CB.1271b; K.–.
OT: māsas: S.4549; HR.1348a.8a; H.1223; BD.587d.
S.4743; HR.1348a.9a; H.1237; BD.597d.
GEN. REF.: IS.3:314; NB.–; Z.–.

Note: In verse 10, the A.V. "shall melt" represents the verb *luō*, to loosen, dissolve (R.V., "shall be dissolved," Passive Voice); so in vv. 11, 12.

MEMBER

melos [μέλος, 3196], a limb of the body, is used (*a*) literally, Matt. 5:29, 30; Rom. 6:13 (twice), 19 (twice); 7:5, 23 (twice); 12:4 (twice); 1 Cor. 12:12 (twice), 14, 18-20, 22, 25, 26 (twice); Jas. 3:5, 6; 4:1; in Col. 3:5, "mortify therefore your members which are upon the earth"; since our bodies and their members belong to the earth, and are the instruments of sin, they are referred to as such (cp. Matt. 5:29, 30; Rom. 7:5, 23, mentioned above); the putting to death is not physical, but ethical; as the physical members have distinct individualities, so those evils, of which the physical members are agents, are by analogy regarded as examples of the way in which the members work if not put to death; this is not precisely the same as "the old man," ver. 9, i.e., the old nature, though there is a connection; (*b*) metaphorically, of believers as members of Christ, 1 Cor. 6:15 (1st part); of one another, Rom. 12:5 (as with the natural illustration, so with the spiritual analogy, there is not only vital unity, and harmony in operation, but diversity, all being essential to effectivity; the unity is not due to external organization but to common and vital union in Christ); there is stress in ver. 5 upon "many" and "in Christ" and "members"; 1 Cor. 12:27 (of the members of a local church as a body); Eph. 4:25 (of the members of the whole Church as the mystical body of Christ); in 1 Cor. 6:15 (2nd part), of one who practises fornication.

NT: B.501c; CB.1258b; K.577.
OT: nētaḥ: S.5409; HR.909b.2; H.1441a; BD.677c.
GEN. REF.: IS.3:314; NB.—; Z.4:178.

MEMORIAL

mnēmosunon [μνημόσυνον, 3422], denotes a memorial, that which keeps alive the memory of someone or something (from *mnēmōn*, mindful), Matt. 26:13; Mark 14:9; Acts 10:4 ¶

NT: B.525b; CB.1259a; K.—.
OT: zēker: S.2143; HR.931c.1a; H.551a; BD.271a.
zikkarôn: S.2146; HR.931c.1b; H.551b; BD.272a.
'azkārāh: S.234; HR.931c.1c; H.551d; BD.272b.
GEN. REF.: IS.3:315; NB.—; Z.4:179.

For **MEMORY (keep in)** see **KEEP**, *Note* (8)

MEN

Notes: (1) For this plural see the nouns under MAN.

(2) For *anthrōpinos*, e.g., Rom. 6:19, "after the manner of men," see MAN'S No. 1.

(3) For the phrase *kat' anthrōpen*, "after the manner of men," see MAN, No. 1 (*f*).

(4) The phrase "quit you like men," 1 Cor. 16:13, translates the verb *andrizō*, in the Middle Voice, to play the man (a verb illustrated in the papyri).

(5) See also ALL, GOOD, GREAT, LOW (estate), THESE, (*of*) WAR.

MEN-PLEASERS

anthrōpareskos [ἀνθρωπάρεσκος, 441], an adjective signifying studying to please men (*anthrōpos*, man, *areskō*, to please), designates, "not simply one who is pleasing to men . . ., but one who endeavours to please men and not God" (Cremer). It is used in Eph. 6:6 and Col. 3:22. ¶ In the Sept., Psa. 53:5. ¶

NT: B.67d; CB.1236a; K.77.
OT: —.
GEN. REF.: IS.3:319; NB.—; Z.—.

MENSERVANTS

pais [παῖς, —], for the meanings of which see CHILD, No. 4, is translated "menservants" in Luke 12:45.

NT: —.
OT: —.
GEN. REF.: —.

MEN-STEALERS

andrapodistēs [ἀνδραποδιστής, 405], a slave-dealer, kidnapper, from *andrapodon*, a slave captured in war, a word found in the plural in the papyri, e.g., in a catalogue of property and in combination with *tetrapoda*, four-footed things (*andrapodon*, *anēr*, a man, *pous*, a foot); *andrapodon* "was never an ordinary word for slave; it was too brutally obvious a reminder of the principle which made quadruped and human chattels differ only in the number of their legs" (Moulton and Milligan, Vocab.). The verb *andrapodizō* supplied the noun "with the like odious meaning,"which appears in 1 Tim. 1:10. ¶

NT: B.63d; CB.1235b; K.—.
OT: —.
GEN. REF.: —.

MEND

katartizō [καταρτίζω, 2675], from *kata*, down, intensive and *artios*, fit, has three meanings, (*a*) to mend, repair, Matt. 4:21; Mark 1:19, of nets; (*b*) to complete, furnish completely, equip, prepare, Luke 6:40; Rom. 9:22; Heb. 11:3 and in the Middle Voice, Matt. 21:16; Heb. 10:5; (*c*) ethically, to prepare, perfect, Gal. 6:1; 1 Thess. 3:10; 1 Pet. 5:10; Heb. 13:21; and in the Passive Voice, 1 Cor. 1:10; 2 Cor. 13:11. See FIT, FRAME, JOIN, PERFECT, PREPARE, RESTORE. ¶

NT: B.417d; CB.1254b; K.80.
OT: kûn: S.3559; HR.743b.3; H.964; BD.465c.
kᵉlal (Aramaic): S.3635; HR.743b.4; H.2788; BD.1097a.
GEN. REF.: —.

MENTION (Noun and Verb)

A. Noun.

mneia [μνεία, 3417], remembrance, mention (akin to *mimnēskō*, to remind, remember), is always used in connection with prayer, and translated "mention" in Rom. 1:9; Eph. 1:16;

1 Thess. 1:2; Philm. 4, in each of which it is preceded by the verb to make; "remembrance" in Phil. 1:3; 1 Thess. 3:6; 2 Tim. 1:3. Some mss. have it in Rom. 12:13, instead of *chreiais*, necessities. See REMEMBRANCE. ¶ Cp. *mnēmē*, memory, remembrance, 2 Pet. 1:15. ¶

NT: B.524b; CB.1259a; K.596.
OT: zākar: S.2142; HR.931a.1-4; H.551; BD.269c.
GEN. REF.: —.

B. Verb.

mnēmoneuō [μνημονεύω, 3421], which most usually means to call to mind, remember, signifies to make mention of, in Heb. 11:22. See REMEMBER.

NT: B.525a; CB.1259a; K.596.
OT: zākar: S.2142; HR.931c.1a; H.551; BD.269c.
GEN. REF.: —.

MERCHANDISE (Noun, and Verb, to make)

A. Nouns.

1. *emporia* [ἐμπορία, 1711], denotes commerce, business, trade [akin to No. 2, and to *emporos*, one on a journey (*en*, in, *poros*, a journey), a merchant], occurs in Matt. 22:5. ¶

NT: B.256d; CB.—; K.—.
OT: saḥar: S.5504; HR.459a.2a; H.1486a; BD.695c.
rᵉkullāh: S.7404; HR.459a.3c; H.2165a; BD.940b.
rākal: S.7402; HR.459a.3b; H.2165; BD.940b.
GEN. REF.: IS.3:321; NB.—; Z.4:187.

2. *emporion* [ἐμπόριον, 1712], denotes a trading-place, exchange (Eng., emporium), John 2:16, "(a house) of merchandise." ¶

NT: B.257a; CB.—; K.—.
OT: rākal: S.7402; HR.459a.1; H.2165; BD.940b.
zānāh: S.2181; HR.459a.3; H.563; BD.275c.
GEN. REF.: IS.3:321; NB.—; Z.4:187.

3. *gomos* [γόμος, 1117], is translated "merchandise" in Rev. 18:11, 12: see BURDEN, A, No. 3.

NT: B.164d; CB.—; K.—.
OT: massā': S.4853; HR.274b.1; H.1421e; BD.672c.
GEN. REF.: IS.—; NB.—; Z.4:187.

B. Verb.

emporeuomai [ἐμπορεύομαι, 1710], primarily signifies to travel, especially for business; then, to traffic, trade, Jas. 4:13; then, to make a gain of, make merchandise of, 2 Pet. 2:3. ¶

NT: B.256d; CB.1244b; K.—.
OT: sāḥar: S.5503; HR.459a.3a; H.1486; BD.695b.
rākal: S.7402; HR.459a.4; H.2165; BD.940b.
GEN. REF.: IS.3:321; NB.—; Z.4:187.

MERCHANT

emporos [ἔμπορος, 1713], denotes a person on a journey (*poros*, a journey), a passenger on shipboard; then, a merchant, Matt. 13:45; Rev. 18:3, 11, 15, 23. ¶

NT: B.257a; CB.—; K.—.
OT: sāḥar: S.5503; HR.459a.2a; H.1486; BD.695b.
rākal: S.7402; HR.459a.3; H.2165; BD.940b.
GEN. REF.: IS.3:321; NB.—; Z.4:187.

MERCIFUL (Adjective, and Verb, to be), MERCY (Noun, and Verb, to have, etc.)

A. Nouns.

1. *eleos* [ἔλεος, 1656], "is the outward manifestation of pity; it assumes need on the part of him who receives it, and resources adequate to meet the need on the part of him who shows it. It is used (*a*) of God, who is rich in mercy, Eph. 2:4, and who has provided salvation for all men, Tit. 3:5, for Jews, Luke 1:72, and Gentiles, Rom. 15:9. He is merciful to those who fear him, Luke 1:50, for they also are compassed with infirmity, and He alone can succour them. Hence they are to pray boldly for mercy, Heb. 4:16, and if for themselves, it is seemly that they should ask for mercy for one another, Gal. 6:16; 1 Tim. 1:2. When God brings His salvation to its issue at the Coming of Christ, His people will obtain His mercy, 2 Tim. 1:16; Jude 21; (*b*) of men; for since God is merciful to them, He would have them show mercy to one another, Matt. 9:13; 12:7; 23:23; Luke 10:37; Jas. 2:13.

"Wherever the words mercy and peace are found together they occur in that order, except in Gal. 6:16. Mercy is the act of God, peace is the resulting experience in the heart of man. Grace describes God's attitude toward the law-breaker and the rebel; mercy is His attitude toward those who are in distress."*

"In the order of the manifestation of God's purposes of salvation grace must go before mercy . . . only the forgiven may be blessed. . . . From this it follows that in each of the apostolic salutations where these words occur, grace precedes mercy, 1 Tim. 1:2; 2 Tim. 1:2; Tit. 1:4 (in some mss.); 2 John 3" (Trench, Syn. § xlvii).

NT: B.250a; CB.1244a; K.222.
OT: ḥesed: S.2617; HR.451a.2; H.686a,699a; BD.338c.
ḥēn: S.2580; HR.451a.1a; H.694a; BD.336b.
GEN. REF.: IS.3:322; NB.809; Z.4:188.

2. *oiktirmos* [οἰκτιρμός, 3628], pity, compassion for the ills of others, is used (*a*) of God, Who is "the Father of mercies," 2 Cor. 1:3; His mercies are the ground upon which believers are to present their bodies a living sacrifice, holy, acceptable to God, as their reasonable service, Rom. 12:1; under the Law he who set it at nought died without compassion, Heb. 10:28; (*b*) of men; believers are to feel and exhibit compassions one toward one toward

* From Notes on Galatians by Hogg and Vine, pp. 340, 341.

another, Phil. 2:1, R.V. "compassions," and Col. 3:12, R.V. "(a heart) of compassion"; in these two places the word is preceded by No. 3, rendered "tender mercies" in the former, and "a heart" in the latter, R.V. ¶

NT: B.561d; CB.1260c; K.680.
OT: raḥam (îm): S.7356; HR.983a.2a; H.2146a; BD.933b.
GEN. REF.: IS.3:322; NB.809; Z.4:188.

3. *splanchnon* [σπλάγχνον, 4698], affections, the heart, always in the plural in the N.T., has reference to feelings of kindness, goodwill, pity, Phil. 2:1, R.V., "tender mercies"; see AFFECTION, No. 2, and BOWELS.

NT: B.763a; CB.1269c; K.1067.
OT: beṭen: S.990; HR.1284c.1; H.236a; BD.105d.
raḥam (îm): S.7356; HR.1284c.2; H.2146a; BD.933b.
GEN. REF.: IS.3:322; NB.809; Z.4:188.

Note: In Acts 13:34 the phrase, lit., 'the holy things, the faithful things (of David)' is translated, "the holy and sure *blessings*," R.V.; the A.V., following the mss. in which the words "holy and" are absent, has "the sure mercies," but notices the full phrase in the margin.

B. Verbs.

1. *eleeō* [ἐλεέω, 1653], akin to A, No. 1, signifies, in general, to feel sympathy with the misery of another, and especially sympathy manifested in act, (*a*) in the Active Voice, to have pity or mercy on, to shew mercy to, e.g., Matt. 9:27; 15:22; 17:15; 18:33; 20:30, 31 (three times in Mark, four in Luke); Rom. 9:15, 16, 18; 11:32; 12:8; Phil. 2:27; Jude 22, 23; (*b*) in the Passive Voice, to have pity or mercy shown one, to obtain mercy, Matt. 5:7; Rom. 11:30, 31; 1 Cor. 7:25; 2 Cor. 4:1; 1 Tim. 1:13, 16; 1 Pet. 2:10.

NT: B.249c; CB.1244a; K.222.
OT: ḥānan: S.2603; HR.449c.6a; H.694,695; BD.335d.
rāḥam: S.7355; HR.449c.14; H.2146; BD.933c.
GEN. REF.: IS.3:322; NB.809; Z.4:188.

2. *oikteirō* [οἰκτείρω, 3627], akin to A, No. 2, to have pity on (from *oiktos*, pity: *oi*, an exclamation, = oh!), occurs in Rom. 9:15 (twice), where it follows No. 1 (twice); the point established there and in Ex. 33:19, from the Sept. of which it is quoted, is that the mercy and compassion shown by God are determined by nothing external to His attributes. Speaking generally *oikteirō* is a stronger term than *eleeō*. ¶

NT: B.561d; CB.1260c; K.680.
OT: ḥānan: S.2603; HR.982c.1; H.694,695; BD.335d.
rāḥam: S.7355; HR.982c.4; H.2146; BD.933c.
GEN. REF.: IS.3:322; NB.809; Z.4:188.

3. *hilaskomai* [ἱλάσκομαι, 2433], in profane Greek meant to conciliate, appease, propitiate, cause the gods to be reconciled; their goodwill was not regarded as their natural condition, but as something to be earned. The heathen believed their gods to be naturally alienated in feeling from man. In the N.T. the word never means to conciliate God; it signifies (*a*) to be propitious, merciful, Luke 18:13, in the prayer of the publican; (*b*) to expiate, make propitiation for, Heb. 2:17, "make propitiation."

That God is not of Himself already alienated from man, see John 3:16. His attitude toward the sinner does not need to be changed by his efforts. With regard to his sin, an expiation is necessary, consistently with God's holiness and for His righteousness' sake, and that expiation His grace and love have provided in the atoning Sacrifice of His Son; man, himself a sinner, justly exposed to God's wrath (John 3:36), could never find an expiation. As Lightfoot says, "when the N.T. writers speak at length on the subject of Divine wrath, the hostility is represented, not as on the part of God, but of men." Through that which God has accomplished in Christ, by His death, man, on becoming regenerate, escapes the merited wrath of God. The making of this expiation [(*b*) above], with its effect in the mercy of God (*a*) is what is expressed in *hilaskomai*. ¶ The Sept. uses the compound verb *exilaskomai*, e.g., Gen. 32:20; Ex. 30:10, 15, 16; 32:30, and frequently in Lev. and Numb. See PROPITIATION.

NT: B.375c; CB.1250c; K.362.
OT: kipper (from kāphar):
S.3722; HR.684b.1; H.1023-1026; BD.497b.
sālaḥ: S.5545; HR.684b.3; H.1505; BD.699b.
GEN. REF.: IS.3:322; NB.809; Z.4:188.

C. Adjectives.

1. *eleēmōn* [ἐλεήμων, 1655], merciful, akin to A, No. 1, not simply possessed of pity but actively compassionate, is used of Christ as a High Priest, Heb. 2:17, and of those who are like God, Matt. 5:7 (cp. Luke 6:35, 36, where the R.V., "sons" is to be read, as representing characteristics resembling those of their Father). ¶

NT: B.250a; CB.1244a; K.222.
OT: ḥannûn: S.2587; HR.450c.1; H.694d; BD.337a.
GEN. REF.: IS.3:322; NB.809; Z.4:188.

2. *oiktirmōn* [οἰκτίρμων, 3629], pitiful, compassionate for the ills of others, a stronger term than No. 1 (akin to A, No. 2), is used twice in Luke 6:36, "merciful" (of the character of God, to be expressed in His people); Jas. 5:11, R.V., "merciful," A.V., "of tender mercy." ¶

NT: B.561d; CB.1260c; K.680.
OT: raḥûm: S.7349; HR.983a.2a; H.2146c; BD.933d.
GEN. REF.: IS.3:322; NB.809; Z.4:188.

3. *hileōs* [ἵλεως, 2436], propitious, merciful (akin to B, No. 3), was used in profane Greek just as in the case of the verb (which see). There is nothing of this in the use of the word in Scripture. The quality expressed by it there essentially appertains to God, though man is undeserving of it. It is used only of God, Heb.

8:12; in Matt. 16:22, "Be it far from Thee" (Peter's word to Christ) may have the meaning given in the R.V. marg., "(God) have mercy on Thee," lit., 'propitious to Thee' (A.V. marg., "Pity Thyself") ¶ Cp. the Sept., 2 Sam. 20:20; 23:17.

NT: B.376a; CB.1250c; K.362.
OT: ḥālîl (āh): S.2486; HR.684c.1; H.661c; BD.321a.
sālaḥ: S.5545; HR.684c.8; H.1505; BD.699b.
GEN. REF.: IS.3:322; NB.809; Z.4:188.

4. *aneleos* or *anileōs* [ἀνέλεος or ἀνίλεως, 448], unmerciful, merciless (*a*, negative, *n*, euphonic, and A, No. 1, or C, No. 3), occurs in Jas. 2:13, said of judgment on him who shows no mercy. ¶

NT: B.64c; CB.1235c; K.222.
OT: –.
GEN. REF.: –.

MERCY-SEAT

hilastērion [ἱλαστήριον, 2435], the lid or cover of the ark of the Covenant, signifies the Propitiatory, so called on account of the expiation made once a year on the great day of atonement, Heb. 9:5. For the formation see Ex. 25:17-21. The Heb. word is *kapporeth*, the cover, a meaning connected with the covering or removal of sin (Psa. 32:1) by means of expiatory sacrifice. This mercy-seat, together with the ark, is spoken of as the footstool of God, 1 Chron. 28:2; cp. Ps. 99:5; 132:7. The Lord promised to be present upon it and to commune with Moses "from above the mercy-seat, from between the two cherubim," Ex. 25:22 (see CHERUBIM). In the Sept. the word *epithēma*, which itself means a cover, is added to *hilastērion*; *epithēma* was simply a translation of *kapporeth*; accordingly, *hilastērion*, not having this meaning, and being essentially connected with propitiation, was added. Eventually *hilastērion* stood for both. In 1 Chron. 28:11 the Holy of Holies is called "the House of the Kapporeth" (see R.V., marg.).

Through His voluntary expiatory sacrifice in the shedding of His blood, under Divine judgment upon sin, and through His Resurrection, Christ has become the Mercy-Seat for His people. See Rom. 3:25, and see PROPITIATION, B, No. 1. ¶

NT: B.375d; CB.1250c; K.362.
OT: kappōret: S.3727; HR.684c.1; H.1023c; BD.498c.
GEN. REF.: IS.3:323; NB.1232; Z.4:190.

MERRY (to be, to make)

1. *euphrainō* [εὐφραίνω, 2165], in the Active Voice, to cheer, make glad, 2 Cor. 2:2, is used everywhere else in the Passive Voice, signifying, to be happy, rejoice, make merry, and translated to be merry in Luke 12:19; 15:23, 24, 29, 32; in 16:19, "fared (sumptuously)"; in Rev. 11:10, "make merry." See FARE, GLAD, REJOICE.

NT: B.327c; CB.1247b; K.278.
OT: sāmēaḥ: S.8056; HR.581b.19a; H.2268a; BD.970c.
GEN. REF.: IS.3:327; NB.–; Z.–.

2. *euthumeō* [εὐθυμέω, 2114], from *eu*, well, and *thumos*, the soul, as the principle of feeling, especially strong feeling, signifies to make cheerful; it is used intransitively in the N.T., to be of good cheer, Acts 27:22, 25; in Jas. 5:13, R.V., "is (any) cheerful?" (A.V., ". . . merry?"). See CHEER. ¶

NT: B.320d; CB.–; K.–.
OT: –.
GEN. REF.: –.

MESS

brōsis [βρῶσις, 1035], eating, food, is translated "mess of meat" in Heb. 12:16, R.V. (A.V., "morsel of meat"). See FOOD, MEAT, No. 2.

NT: B.148b; CB.1239b; K.111.
OT: 'ākal: S.398; HR.231c.1b; H.85; BD.37a.
ma'ᵃkāl: S.3978; HR.231c.1f; H.85d; BD.38b.
GEN. REF.: –.

MESSAGE

1. *angelia* [ἀγγελία, 31], akin to *angellō*, to bring a message, proclaim, denotes a message, proclamation, news, 1 John 1:5 [some mss. have *epangelia*: see *Note* (1)]; 1 John 3:11, where the word is more precisely defined (by being followed by the conjunction "that," expressing the purpose that we should love one another) as being virtually equivalent to an order. ¶

NT: B.7a; CB.1235c; K.10.
OT: shᵉmû'āh: S.8052; HR.7b.3; H.2412d; BD.1035b.
GEN. REF.: –.

Notes: (1) *Epangelia* (*epi*, upon, and No. 1), a promise, is found in some mss. in 1 John 1:5, "message" (see No. 1). See PROMISE.

(2) In Luke 19:14, A.V., *presbeia*, is translated "a message"; R.V., "an ambassage," as in 14:32. See AMBASSAGE. ¶

2. *akoē* [ἀκοή, 189], hearing, also denotes the thing heard, a message; in 1 Thess. 2:13, it is associated with *logos*, a word, lit., 'the word of hearing' (R.V. marg.), R.V. "the word of the message," A.V., "the word . . . which ye heard"; so in Heb. 4:2, R.V., "the word of hearing" (A.V., "the word preached"). See HEARING.

NT: B.30d; CB.1234b; K.34.
OT: shāma': S.8085; HR.44b.1a; H.2412; BD.1033b.
shᵉmû'āh: S.8052; HR.44.1d; H.2412d; BD.1035b.
shēma': S.8088; HR.44.1f; H.2412b; BD.1034d.
GEN. REF.: –.

3. *kērugma* [κήρυγμα, 2782], that which is proclaimed by a herald, a proclamation, preaching, is translated "the message" in Tit. 1:3, R.V. (A.V., "preaching"). See PREACHING.

NT: B.430d; CB.1255a; K.430.
OT: qôl: S.6963; HR.763b.1; H.1998a,2028b; BD.876d.
qᵉrî'āh: S.7150; HR.763b; H.2063c; BD.896d.
GEN. REF.: —.

MESSENGER

1. *angelos* [ἄγγελος, 32], a messenger, an angel, one sent, is translated "messenger," of John the Baptist, Matt. 11:10; Mark 1:2; Luke 7:27; in the plural, of John's messengers, 7:24; of those whom Christ sent before Him when on His journey to Jerusalem, 9:52; of Paul's "thorn in the flesh," "a messenger of Satan," 2 Cor. 12:7; of the spies as received by Rahab, Jas. 2:25. See ANGEL.

NT: B.7a; CB.1235c; K.12.
OT: mal'āk: S.4397; HR.7b.7; H.1068a; BD.521c.
GEN. REF.: IS.3:329; NB.—; Z.4:196.

2. *apostolos* [ἀπόστολος, 652], an apostle, is translated "messengers" in 2 Cor. 8:23, regarding Titus and "the other brethren," whom Paul describes to the Church at Corinth as "messengers of the churches," in respect of offerings from those in Macedonia for the needy in Judaea; in Phil. 2:25, of Epaphroditus as the "messenger" of the church at Philippi to the Apostle in ministering to his need; R.V. marg. in each case, "apostle." See APOSTLE.

NT: B.99c; CB.1237a; K.67.
OT: shālaḥ: S.7971; HR.145b.1; H.2394; BD.1018a.
GEN. REF.: IS.3:329; NB.—; Z.4:196.

For METE see MEASURE

For MID see MIDST

MIDDAY

Note: In Acts 26:13, "at midday" translates the adjective *mesos*, middle, and the noun *hēmera*, a day, in a combined adverbial phrase. See MIDST.

For MIDDLE see WALL

MIDNIGHT

mesonuktion [μεσονύκτιον, 3317], an adjective denoting at, or of, midnight, is used as a noun in Mark 13:35; Luke 11:5; Acts 16:25; 20:7. ¶

NT: B.507a; CB.1258b; K.—.
OT: nesheph: S.5399; HR.912c.2; H.1434a; BD.676a.
GEN. REF.: IS.3:351; NB.—; Z.—.

Note: In Matt. 25:6 "at midnight" translates the adjective *mesos* and noun *nux*, night, in the combined adverbial phrase. In Acts 27:27 "about midnight" translates an adverbial phrase consisting of *kata*, towards, followed by *mesos*, middle and *nux*, night, with the article, lit., 'towards (the) middle of the night.' See MIDST.

MIDST

A. Adjective and Adverb.

mesos [μέσος, 3319], an adjective denoting middle, in the middle or midst, is used in the following, in which the English requires a phrase, and the adjectival rendering must be avoided; Luke 22:55, "Peter sat in the midst of them," lit., 'a middle one of (them)'; Luke 23:45, of the rending of the veil "in the midst"; here the adjective idiomatically belongs to the verb "was rent," and is not to be taken literally, as if it meant 'the middle veil'; John 1:26, "in the midst of you (standeth One)," R.V. (lit., 'a middle One'); Acts 1:18, where the necessity of avoiding the lit. rendering is obvious. Cp. the phrases "at midday," "at midnight" (see MIDDAY, MIDNIGHT, above).

NT: B.507b; CB.1258b; K.—.
OT: tāwek: S.8432; HR.913a.6a,b; H.2498; BD.1063c.
tîkōn: S.8484; HR.913a.6c; H.2498a; BD.1064a.
GEN. REF.: —.

Notes: (1) *Mesos* is used adverbially, in prepositional phrases, (*a*) *ana m.*, e.g., 1 Cor. 6:5, "between"; Matt. 13:25, "among"; Rev. 7:17, "in the midst"; (*b*) *dia m.*, e.g., Luke 4:30; 17:11, "through the midst"; (*c*) *en m.*, Luke 10:3, R.V., "in the midst," A.V., "among"; so 22:27; 1 Thess. 2:7; with the article after *en*, e.g., Matt. 14:6, R.V., "in the midst," A.V., "before"; (*d*) *eis m.*, Mark 14:60, "in the midst"; with the article, e.g., Mark 3:3, "forth" (lit., 'into the midst'); (*e*) *ek m.*, "out of the way," lit., 'out of the midst,' Col. 2:14; 2 Thess. 2:7, where, however, removal is not necessarily in view; there is no accompanying verb signifying removal, as in each of the other occurrences of the phrase; with the article, e.g., 1 Cor. 5:2; 2 Cor. 6:17; see WAY; (*f*) *kata m.*, Acts 27:27, "about mid(night)."

(2) The neuter, *meson*, is used adverbially in Matt. 14:24, in some mss., "in the midst (of the waves)"; in Phil. 2:15 in the best mss. (where some mss. have *en m.* . . .).

(3) For Rev. 8:13, see HEAVEN, A, No. 2.

B. Verb.

mesoō [μεσόω, 3322], to be in the middle, is used of time in John 7:14, translated "when it was . . . the midst (of the feast)," lit., '(the feast) being in the middle.' ¶

NT: B.508b; CB.—; K.—.
OT: ḥᵃṣî: S.2677; HR.913a.1a; H.719b; BD.345c.
maḥᵃṣît: S.4276; HR.913a.1b; H.719e; BD.345d.
tîkôn: S.8484; HR.913a.1c; H.2498a; BD.1064a.
GEN. REF.: —.

MIGHT (Noun), MIGHTY, MIGHTILY, MIGHTIER

A. Nouns.

1. *dunamis* [δύναμις, 1411], power, (*a*) used relatively, denotes inherent ability, capability, ability to perform anything, e.g., Matt. 25:15, "ability"; Acts 3:12, "power"; 2 Thess. 1:7, R.V., "(angels) of His power" (A.V., "mighty"); Heb. 11:11, R.V., "power" (A.V., "strength"); see ABILITY; (*b*) used absolutely, denotes (1) power to work, to carry something into effect, e.g., Luke 24:49; (2) power in action, e.g., Rom. 1:16; 1 Cor. 1:18; it is translated "might" in the A.V. of Eph. 1:21 (R.V., "power"); so 3:16; Col. 1:11 (1st clause); 2 Pet. 2:11; in Rom. 15:19, A.V., this noun is rendered "mighty"; R.V., "(in the) power of signs." The R.V. consistently avoids the rendering "might" for *dunamis*; the usual rendering is "power." Under this heading comes the rendering "mighty works," e.g., Matt. 7:22, R.V. (A.V., "wonderful works"); 11:20-23; singular number in Mark 6:5; in Matt. 14:2 and Mark 6:14 the R.V. has "powers"; in 2 Cor. 12:12, R.V., "mighty works" (A.V., "mighty deeds"). See MIRACLE, especially POWER.

NT: B.207b; CB.1242b; K.186.
OT: ḥayil: S.2428; HR.350a.11; H.624a; BD.298c.
ṣābā': S.6635; HR.350a.25; H.1865a,b; BD.838d.
GEN. REF.: IS.3:926; NB.–; Z.–.

Note: Dunamis, power, is to be distinguished from *exousia*, the right to exercise power. See DOMINION, *Note*.

2. *ischus* [ἰσχύς, 2479], denotes might, strength, power, (*a*) inherent and in action as used of God, Eph. 1:19, R.V., "(the strength, *kratos*, of His) might," A.V., "(His mighty) power," i.e., power (over external things) exercised by strength; Eph. 6:10, "of His might"; 2 Thess. 1:9, R.V., "(from the glory) of His might" (A.V. "power"); Rev. 5:12, R.V., "might" (A.V., "strength"); 7:12, "might"; (*b*) as an endowment, said (1) of angels, 2 Pet. 2:11; here the order is No. 2 and No. 1, R.V., "might and power," which better expresses the distinction than the A.V., "power and might"; in some mss. in Rev. 18:2 it is said of the voice of an angel [see E, (*c*)]; the most authentic mss. have the adjective *ischuros*, "mighty"; (2) of men, Mark 12:30, 33; Luke 10:27 (R.V. and A.V., "strength," in all three verses); 1 Pet. 4:11, R.V., "strength" (A.V., "ability": this belongs rather to No. 1). Either 'strength' or 'might' expresses the true significance of *ischus*. See ABILITY, POWER, STRENGTH. ¶

NT: B.383c; CB.1253a; K.378.
OT: kōaḥ: S.3581; HR.694b.16; H.971.1; BD.470c.
'az: S.5794; HR.694b.21a; H.1596a; BD.738c.
ḥayil: S.6635; HR.694b.13; H.624a; BD.298c.
GEN. REF.: IS.3:926; NB.–; Z.–.

Notes: (1) In Luke 9:43, A.V., *megaleiotēs*, greatness, majesty, is translated "mighty power" (R.V., "majesty").

(2) Cp. *kratos* (see POWER).

B. Adjectives.

1. *dunatos* [δυνατός, 1415], powerful, mighty (akin to A, No. 1), is used, with that significance, (1) of God, Luke 1:49, "mighty"; Rom. 9:22, "power" (here the neuter of the adjective is used with the article, as a noun, equivalent to *dunamis*); frequently with the meaning "able" (see ABLE, C, No. 1); (2) of Christ, regarded as a prophet, Luke 24:19 ("in deed and word"); (3) of men: Moses, Acts 7:22 ("in his words and works"); Apollos, 18:24, "in the Scriptures"; of those possessed of natural power, 1 Cor. 1:26; of those possessed of spiritual power, 2 Cor. 10:4. For the shades of meaning in the translation "strong," see Rom. 15:1; 2 Cor. 12:10; 13:9. For Rev. 6:15, see No. 2, below; see STRONG. See also POSSIBLE.

NT: B.208c; CB.1242b; K.186.
OT: gibbôr: S.1368; HR.355c.6c; H.310b; BD.150a.
ḥayil: S.6635; HR.355c.9a; H.624a; BD.298c.
GEN. REF.: IS.3:926; NB.–; Z.–.

2. *ischuros* [ἰσχυρός, 2478], strong, mighty (akin to A, No. 2, and with corresponding adjectival significance), is usually translated "strong"; "mighty" in Luke 15:14 (of a famine); Rev. 19:6 (of thunders); 19:18 (of men): in the following, where the A.V. has "mighty," the R.V. substitutes "strong," 1 Cor. 1:27; Rev. 6:15 (A.V., "mighty men"); 18:10, 21; Heb. 11:34, R.V., "(waxed) mighty" (A.V., "valiant"). See BOISTEROUS, POWERFUL, STRONG (where the word is analysed).

NT: B.383a; CB.1253a; K.378.
OT: gibbôr: S.1368; HR.693b.10a; H.310b; BD.150a.
ḥāzāq: S.2389; HR.693b.13a; H.636a; BD.305c.
'az: S.5794; HR.693b.17a; H.1596a; BD.738c.
GEN. REF.: IS.3:926; NB.–; Z.–.

3. *ischuroteros* [ἰσχυρότερος, 2478], stronger, mightier, the comparative degree of No. 2, is translated "mightier" in Matt. 3:11; Mark 1:7; Luke 3:16; "stronger" in Luke 11:22; 1 Cor. 1:25; 10:22. See STRONG. ¶

NT: B.383a; CB.1253a; K.–.
OT: –.
GEN. REF.: IS.3:926; NB.–; Z.–.

4. *biaios* [βίαιος, 972], violent (from *bia*, force, violence, strength, found in Acts 5:26;

21:35; 24:7; 27:41 ¶). Occurs in Acts 2:2, of wind. ¶

NT: B.141a; CB.1239a; K.—.
OT: 'az: S.5794; HR.218a.2; H.1596a; BD.738c.
GEN. REF.: IS.3:926; NB.—; Z.—.

5. *krataios* [κραταιός, 2900], strong, mighty (akin to *kratos*, strength, relative and manifested power: see MIGHTILY, below), is found in 1 Pet. 5:6, of the "mighty" hand of God. ¶

NT: B.448b; CB.1256a; K.466.
OT: ḥāzāq: S.2389; HR.782a.4b; H.636a; BD.305c.
'az: S.5794; HR.782a.7a; H.1596a; BD.738c.
'ōz: S.5797; HR.782a.7b; H.1596b; BD.738d.
GEN. REF.: IS.3:926; NB.—; Z.—.

6. *megaleios* [μεγαλεῖος, 3167], is rendered "mighty" in Acts 2:11, R.V. See WONDERFUL, *Note* (2).

NT: B.496d; CB.1258a; K.—.
OT: gādôl: S.1419; HR.901b.1b; H.315d; BD.152d.
gōdel: S.1433; HR.901b.1a; H.315b; BD.152d.
GEN. REF.: IS.3:926; NB.—; Z.—.

Notes: (1) In Luke 1:52, A.V., *dunastēs*, a potentate, prince, is translated "mighty" (R.V., "princes").

(2) In Rev. 6:13, A.V., *megas*, great, is translated "mighty" (R.V., "great"), of a wind.

(3) In Rev. 16:18, A.V., *tēlikoutos*, so great (when said of things), is translated "so mighty" (R.V., "so great"), of an earthquake.

C. Verb.

dunateō [δυνατέω, 1414], to be powerful (akin to A, No. 1 and B. No. 1), is found in the most authentic mss. in Rom. 14:4 (some have *dunatos*, B, No. 1), R.V. "(the Lord) hath power," A.V., "(God) is able"; similarly, as regard mss., in 2 Cor. 9:8, where the R.V. and A.V. have "(God) is able"; in 2 Cor. 13:3, A.V., "is mighty," R.V., "is powerful" (according to the general significance of *dunamis*). ¶

NT: B.208c; CB.1242b; K.186.
OT: —.
GEN. REF.: IS.3:926; NB.—; Z.—.

Note: In Gal. 2:8, A.V., *energeō*, to work, work in (*en*, in, *ergon*, work), is first translated "wrought effectually," then "was mighty in" (R.V., "wrought for," in both places; the probable meaning is 'in me'). See EFFECTUAL, WORK

D. Adverb.

eutonōs [εὐτόνως, 2159], vigorously, vehemently (*eu*, well, *teinō*, to stretch), is translated "mightily" in Acts 18:28, A.V., of the power of Apollos in 'confuting' the Jews (R.V., "powerfully"); in Luke 23:10 it is rendered "vehemently." See POWERFUL, VEHEMENTLY. ¶ In the Sept., Josh. 6:7, "(let them sound) loudly." ¶

NT: B.327b; CB.—; K.—.
OT: —.
GEN. REF.: —.

E. Phrases.

The following phrases signify "mightily":

(*a*) *en dunamei*, Col. 1:29, of the inward power of God's working, lit., "in power," as R.V. marg. (*en*, in, and A, No. 1);

(*b*) *kata kartos*, Acts 19:20, of the increase of the word of the Lord in a place, lit., 'according to might';

(*c*) in Rev. 18:2 some mss. have *en ischui*, lit., 'in strength' (*en*, in, and A, No. 2), of the voice of an angel.

MILE

milion [μίλιον, 3400], a Roman mile, a word of Latin origin (1680 yards), is used in Matt. 5:41. ¶

NT: B.521d; CB.—; K.—.
OT: —.
GEN. REF.: IS.3:354; NB.1319; Z.5:915.

MILK

gala [γάλα, 1051], is used (*a*) literally, 1 Cor. 9:7; (*b*) metaphorically, of rudimentary spiritual teaching, 1 Cor. 3:2; Heb. 5:12, 13; 1 Pet. 2:2; here the meaning largely depends upon the significance of the word *logikos*, which the A.V. renders "of the word," R.V. "spiritual." While *logos* denotes a word, the adjective *logikos* is never used with the meaning assigned to it in the A.V., nor does the context in 1:23 compel this meaning. While it is true that the Word of God, like milk, nourished the soul, and this is involved in the exhortation, the only other occurrence in the N.T. is Rom. 12:1, where it is translated "reasonable," i.e., rational, intelligent (service), in contrast to the offering of an irrational animal; so here the nourishment may be understood as of that spiritually rational nature which, acting through the regenerate mind, develops spiritual growth. God's Word is not given so that it is impossible to understand it, or that it requires a special class of men to interpret it; its character is such that the Holy Spirit who gave it can unfold its truths even to the young convert. Cp. 1 John 2:27. ¶

NT: B.149c; CB.1248a; K.111.
OT: ḥālāb: S.2461; HR.233b.1a; H.650a; BD.316b.
GEN. REF.: IS.3:355; NB.822; Z.—.

MILL

mulōn [μύλων, 3459], denotes a mill-house, where the millstone is, Matt. 24:41; some mss. have *mulos* (see next word). ¶ In the Sept., Jer. 52:11, "grinding house" (lit., 'house of a mill'). ¶

NT: B.529c; CB.—; K.—.
OT: —.
GEN. REF.: IS.3:355; NB.823; Z.4:227.

MILLSTONE

A. Noun.

mulos [μύλος, 3458], denotes a hand-mill, consisting of two circular stones, one above the other, the lower being fixed. From the centre of the lower a wooden pin passes through a hole in the upper, into which the grain is thrown, escaping as flour between the stones and falling on a prepared material below them. The handle is inserted into the upper stone near the circumference. Small stones could be turned by one woman (mill-grinding was a work deemed fit only for women and slaves; cp. Judg. 16:21); larger ones were turned by two (cp. Matt. 24:41, under MILL), or more.

Still larger ones were turned by an ass (*onikos*), Matt. 18:6, R.V., "a great millstone" (marg., "a millstone turned by an ass"), indicating the immediate and overhwleming drowning of one who causes one young believer to stumble; Mark 9:42 (where some mss. have *lithos mulikos*, a stone of a mill, as in Luke 17:2); Rev. 18:22 (some mss. have it in ver. 21, see below). ¶

NT: B.529b; CB.1259b; K.—.
OT: rēḥeh: S.7347; HR.936c.1; H.2144a; BD.932d.
GEN. REF.: IS.3:355; NB.823; Z.4:227.

B. Adjectives.

1. *mulikos* [μυλικός, 3457], 'of a mill,' occurs in Luke 17:2 (see above). ¶

NT: B.529b; CB.1259b; K.—.
OT: —.
GEN. REF.: IS.3:355; NB.823; Z.—.

2. *mulinos* [μύλινος, 3458], made of millstone, is used with *lithos*, a stone; and with the adjective *megas*, great, in the best mss. in Rev. 18:21 (some have the word *mulos*; see A). ¶

NT: B.529b; CB.1259b; K.—.
OT: —.
GEN. REF.: IS.3:355; NB.823; Z.—.

MIND (Noun and Verb)

A. Nouns.

1. *nous* [νοῦς, 3563], mind, denotes, speaking generally, the seat of reflective consciousness, comprising the faculties of perception and understanding, and those of feeling, judging and determining.

Its use in the N.T. may be analysed as follows: it denotes (*a*) the faculty of knowing, the seat of the understanding, Luke 24:45; Rom. 1:28; 14:5; 1 Cor. 14:15, 19; Eph. 4:17; Phil. 4:7; Col. 2:18; 1 Tim. 6:5; 2 Tim. 3:8; Tit. 1:15; Rev. 13:18; 17:9; (*b*) counsels, purpose, Rom. 11:34 (of the mind of God); 12:2; 1 Cor. 1:10; 2:16, twice (1) of the thoughts and counsels of God, (2) of Christ, a testimony to His Godhood; Eph. 4:23; (*c*) the new nature, which belongs to the believer by reason of the new birth, Rom. 7:23, 25, where it is contrasted with "the flesh," the principle of evil which dominates fallen man. Under (*b*) may come 2 Thess. 2:2, where it stands for the determination to be stedfast amidst afflictions, through the confident expectation of the day of rest and recompense mentioned in the first chapter. ¶

NT: B.544c; CB.1260a; K.636.
OT: lēbāb: S.3824; HR.950c.2; H.1071a; BD.523a.
GEN. REF.: IS.3:362; NB.—; Z.4:229.

2. *dianoia* [διάνοια, 1271], lit. a thinking through, or over, a meditation, reflecting, signifies (*a*) like No. 1, the faculty of knowing, understanding, or moral reflection, (1) with an evil significance, a consciousness characterized by a perverted moral impulse, Eph. 2:3 (plural); 4:18; (2) with a good significance, the faculty renewed by the Holy Spirit, Matt. 22:37; Mark 12:30; Luke 10:27; Heb. 8:10; 10:16; 1 Pet. 1:13; 1 John 5:20; (*b*) sentiment, disposition (not as a function but as a product); (1) in an evil sense, Luke 1:51, "imagination"; Col. 1:21; (2) in a good sense, 2 Pet. 3:1. ¶

NT: B.187a; CB.1241b; K.636.
OT: lēb: S.3820; HR.306c.3a; H.1071a; BD.524b.
lēbāb: S.3824; HR.306c.3b; H.1071a; BD.523a.
GEN. REF.: IS.3:362; NB.—; Z.4:229.

3. *ennoia* [ἔννοια, 1771], an idea, notion, intent, is rendered "mind" in 1 Pet. 4:1; see INTENT.

NT: B.267a; CB.1245b; K.636.
OT: bînāh: S.998; HR.475c.1a; H.239b; BD.108a.
m^{e}zimmāh: S.4209; HR.475c.4; H.556c; BD.273c.
GEN. REF.: IS.3:362; NB.—; Z.4:229.

4. *noēma* [νόημα, 3540], thought, design, is rendered "minds" in 2 Cor. 3:14; 4:4; 11:3; Phil. 4:7; se DEVICE, No. 2.

NT: B.540d; CB.1259c; K.636.
OT: —.
GEN. REF.: IS.3:362; NB.—; Z.4:229.

5. *gnomē* [γνώμη, 1106], a purpose, judgment, opinion, is translated "mind" in Philm. 14 and Rev. 17:13. See JUDGMENT, No. 4.

NT: B.163a; CB.1248b; K.119.
OT: ṭ^{e}'ēm (Aramaic): S.2942; HR.273a.2b; H.2757a; BD.1094c.
GEN. REF.: IS.—; NB.—; Z.4:229.

6. *phronēma* [φρόνημα, 5427], denotes what one has in the mind, the thought (the content of the process expressed in *phroneō*, to have in mind, to think); or an object of thought; in Rom. 8:6 (A.V., "to be carnally minded" and "to be spiritually minded"), the R.V., adhering to the use of the noun, renders by "the mind of the flesh," in vv. 6 and 7, and "the mind of the spirit," in ver. 6. In ver. 27 the word is used of the mind of the Holy Spirit. ¶

NT: B.866c; CB.1264c; K.1277.
OT: —.
GEN. REF.: IS.3:362; NB.—; Z.4:229.

Notes: (1) This word is to be distinguished from *phronēsis*, which denotes an understanding, leading to right action, prudence, Luke 1:17; Eph. 1:8. ¶

(2) In three places, Acts 14:2; Phil. 1:27; Heb. 12:3, the A.V. translates *psuchē*, the soul, by "mind" (R.V., "soul").

B. Verbs.

1. *phroneō* [φρονέω, 5426], signifies (*a*) to think, to be minded in a certain way; (*b*) to think of, be mindful of. It implies moral interest or reflection, not mere unreasoning opinion. Under (*a*) it is rendered by the verb to mind in the following: Rom. 8:5, "(they that are after the flesh) do mind (the things of the flesh)"; 12:16, "be of (the same) mind," lit., 'minding the same,' and "set (not) your mind on," R.V., A.V., "mind (not)"; 15:5, "to be of (the same) mind," R.V., (A.V., "to be likeminded"); so the R.V. in 2 Cor. 13:11, A.V., "be of (one) mind"; Gal. 5:10, "ye will be (none otherwise) minded"; Phil. 1:7, R.V., "to be (thus) minded," A.V., "to think (this)"; 2:2, R.V., "be of (the same) mind," A.V., " be likeminded," and "being . . . of (one) mind," lit., 'minding (the one thing)'; 2:5, R.V., "have (this) mind," A.V., "let (this) mind be," lit., 'mind this'; 3:15, "let us . . . be (thus) minded," and "(if) . . . ye are (otherwise) minded" (some mss. have the verb in ver. 16); 3:19, "(who) mind (earthly things)"; 4:2, "be of (the same) mind"; Col. 3:2, R.V. and A.V. marg., "set your mind," lit., 'mind (the things above),' A.V., "set your affection." See CAREFUL, B, No. 6, REGARD, SAVOUR, THINK, UNDERSTAND

NT: B.866a; CB.1264c; K.1277.
OT: bîn: S.995; HR.1439a.1; H.239; BD.106c.
ḥākam: S.2449; HR.1439a.2; H.647; BD.314b.
GEN. REF.: IS.3:362; NB.–; Z.4:229.

2. *anamimnēskō* [ἀναμιμνήσκω, 363], to remind, call to remembrance (*ana*, up, *mimnēskō*, to remind), is translated "called to mind," in Mark 14:72 (Passive Voice). See REMEMBRANCE.

NT: B.57d; CB.1235a; K.–.
OT: zākar: S.2142; HR.79c.1; H.551; BD.269c.
GEN. REF.: IS.3:362; NB.–; Z.4:229.

Note: The lengthened form *epanamimnēskō* is used in Rom. 15:15, A.V., "putting (you) in mind"; R.V., "putting (you) again (*epi*) in remembrance." ¶

3. *hupomimnēskō* [ὑπομιμνήσκω, 5279], to cause one to remember, put one in mind (*hupo*, under), is translated "put (them) in mind" in Tit. 3:1. See REMEMBER, REMEMBRANCE.

NT: B.846a; CB.1252b; K.–.
OT: zākar: S.2142; HR.1416a.1; H.551; BD.269c.
GEN. REF.: IS.3:362; NB.–; Z.4:229.

4. *hupotithēmi* [ὑποτίθημι, 5294], lit., to place under (*hupo*, under, *tithēmi*, to place), to lay down (of risking the life, Rom. 16:4), also denotes to suggest, put into one's mind, 1 Tim. 4:6, R.V., "put . . . in mind" (A.V., "put . . . in remembrance"). See LAY. ¶

NT: B.848b; CB.–; K.–.
OT: –.
GEN. REF.: –.

5. *sōphroneō* [σωφρονέω, 4993], signifies (*a*) to be of sound mind, or in one's right mind, sober-minded (*sōzō, to save, phrēn*, the mind), Mark 5:15 and Luke 8:35, "in his right mind"; 2 Cor. 5:13, R.V., "we are of sober mind" (A.V., "we be sober"); (*b*) to be temperate, self-controlled, Tit. 2:6, to be sober-minded"; 1 Pet. 4:7, R.V., "be ye . . . of sound mind" (A.V., "be ye sober"). See also Rom. 12:3. See SOBER. ¶

NT: B.802a; CB.1296b; K.1150.
OT: –.
GEN. REF.: IS.3:362; NB.–; Z.–.

Note: In Acts 20:13, A.V., *mellō*, to be about to, to intend, is translated "minding" (R.V., "intending"). See INTEND.

C. Adjective.

homophrōn [ὁμόφρων, 3675], agreeing, of one mind (*homos*, same, *phrēn*, the mind), is used in 1 Pet. 3:8. ¶

NT: B.569c; CB.–; K.–.
OT: –.
GEN. REF.: –.

Notes: (1) For the noun *sōphronismos*, in 2 Tim. 1:7, see DISCIPLINE. ¶

(2) In Rom. 15:6, A.V., the adverb *homothumadon*, of one accord, is translated "with one mind" (R.V., "of one accord"). See ACCORD.

(3) See also CAST, CHANGE, DOUBTFUL, FERVENT, FORWARDNESS, HUMBLENESS, HUMILITY, LOWLINESS, READINESS, READY, WILLING.

MINDED

1. *phroneō* [φρονέω, —]: see MIND, B, No. 1.

2. *boulomai* [βούλομαι, 1014], to wish, will, desire, purpose (akin to *boulē*, counsel, purpose), is translated "was minded" in Matt. 1:19; Acts 15:37, R.V. (A.V., "determined"); 18:27, R.V. (A.V., "was disposed"); 19:30, R.V. (A.V., "would have"); 5:33, R.V., "were minded" (A.V., "took counsel"); 18:15, R.V., "I am (not) minded (to be)," A.V., "I will (be no)"; Heb. 6:17, "being minded," R.V. (A.V., "willing"), said of God. see COUNSEL.

NT: B.146a; CB.1239b; K.108.
OT: ḥāphēṣ: S.2654; HR.226b.5a,b; H.712; BD.342c.
mā'ēn (with negative): S.3985; HR.226b.8; H.1138; BD.549b.
GEN. REF.: –.

2. *bouleuō* [βουλεύω, 1011], to take counsel, is translated to be minded in Acts 27:39; 2 Cor. 1:17, Middle Voice in each case. See COUNSEL, B, No. 1.

NT: B.145c; CB.1239b; K.—.
OT: yā'aṣ: S.3289; HR.227a.6; H.887; BD.419c.
GEN. REF.: —.

Note: For the noun *phronēma* in Rom. 8:6, see MIND, A, No. 6.

MINDFUL OF (to be)

1. *mimnēskō* [μιμνήσκω, 5403], the tenses of which are from the older verb *mnaomai*, signifies to remind; but in the Middle Voice, to remember, to be mindful of, in the sense of caring for, e.g., Heb. 2:6, "Thou art mindful"; in 13.3, "remember"; in 2 Tim. 1:4, R.V., "remembering" (A.V., "being mindful of"); so in 2 Pet. 3:2. See REMEMBER.

NT: B.522b; CB.1259a; K.596.
OT: zākar: S.2142; HR.927c.1; H.551; BD.269c.
GEN. REF.: IS.3:362; NB.—; Z.—.

2. *mnēmoneuō* [μνημονεύω, 3421], to call to mind, remember, is rendered "they had been mindful" in Heb. 11:15. See MENTION, B, REMEMBER.

NT: B.525a; CB.1259a; K.596.
OT: zākar: S.2142; HR.931c.1a; H.551; BD.269c.
GEN. REF.: IS.3:362; NB.—; Z.—.

For MINE, MINE OWN (self), see MY

MINGLE

1. *mignumi* [μίγνυμι, 3396], to mix, mingle (from a root *mik*; Eng., *mix* is akin), is always in the N.T. translated to mingle, Matt. 27:34; Luke 13:1; Rev. 8:7; 15:2. ¶

NT: B.499c; CB.—; K.—.
OT: 'ārab: S.6148; HR.926c.2; H.1686; BD.786c.
GEN. REF.: —.

2. *kerannumi* [κεράννυμι, 2767], to mix, to mingle, chiefly of the diluting of wine, implies "a mixing of two things, so that they are blended and form a compound, as in wine and water, whereas *mignumi* (No. 1) implies a mixing without such composition, as in two sorts of grain" (Liddell and Scott, Lex.). It is used in Rev. 18:6 (twice); in 14:10, R.V., "prepared" (marg., "mingled"; A.V., "poured out"), lit., 'mingled,' followed by *akratos*, unmixed, pure (*a*, negative, and *kratos*, an adjective, from this verb *kerannumi*), the two together forming an oxymoron, the combination in one phrase of two terms that are ordinarily contradictory. ¶

NT: B.429a; CB.1255a; K.—.
OT: māsak: S.4537; HR.759c.1; H.1220; BD.587c.
GEN. REF.: —.

Note: For the verb *smurnizō*, to mingle with myrrh, Mark 15:23, see MYRRH.

MINISTER (Noun and Verb)

A. Nouns.

1. *diakonos* [διάκονος, 1249], a servant, attendant, minister, deacon, is translated "minister" in Mark 10:43; Rom. 13:4 (twice); 15:8; 1 Cor. 3:5; 2 Cor. 3:6; 6:4; 11:15 (twice); Gal. 2:17; Eph. 6:21; Col. 1:7, 23, 25; 4:7; 1 Thess. 3:2; 1 Tim. 4:6. See DEACON.

NT: B.184c; CB.1241a; K.152.
OT: na'ar: S.5288; HR.303b.1; H.1389a; BD.654d.
shārat: S.8334; HR.303b.2; H.2472; BD.1058a.
GEN. REF.: IS.3:364; NB.825; Z.4:233.

2. *leitourgos* [λειτουργός, 3011], denoted among the Greeks, firstly, one who discharged a public office at his own expense, then, in general, a public servant, minister. In the N.T. it is used (*a*) of Christ, as a "Minister of the sanctuary" (in the Heavens), Heb. 8:2; (*b*) of angels, Heb. 1:7. (Psa. 104:4); (*c*) of the Apostle Paul, in his evangelical ministry, fulfilling it as a serving-priest, Rom. 15:16; that he used it figuratively and not in an ecclesiastical sense, is obvious from the context; (*d*) of Epaphroditus, as ministering to Paul's needs on behalf of the church at Philippi, Phil. 2:25; here, representative service is in view; (*e*) of earthly rulers, who though they do not all act consciously as servants of God, yet discharge functions which are the ordinance of God, Rom. 13:6. ¶

NT: B.471b; CB.1256c; K.526.
OT: shārat: S.8334; HR.873b.2; H.2472; BD.1058a.
GEN. REF.: IS.3:364; NB.825; Z.4:233.

3. *hupēretēs* [ὑπηρέτης, 5257], properly an under rower (*hupo*, under, *eretēs*, a rower), as distinguished from *nautēs*, a seaman (a meaning which lapsed from the word), hence came to denote any subordinate acting under another's direction; in Luke 4:20, R.V., "attendant," A.V., "minister," it signifies the attendant at the Synagogue service; in Acts 13:5, it is said of John Mark, R.V., "attendant," A.V., "minister"; in Acts 26:16, "a minister," it is said of Paul as a servant of Christ in the Gospel; so in 1 Cor. 4:1, where the Apostle associates others with himself, as Apollos and Cephas, as "ministers of Christ." See ATTEND, C, OFFICER.

NT: B.842c; CB.1252a; K.1231.
OT: 'ebed: S.5650; HR.1411c.2; H.1553a; BD.713d.
GEN. REF.: IS.3:364; NB.825; Z.4:233.

Note: Other synonymous nouns are *doulos*, a bondservant; *oiketēs*, a household servant; *misthios*, a hired servant; *misthōtos* (ditto); *pais*, a boy, a household servant. For all these see SERVANT. Speaking broadly, *diakonos* views a servant in relation to his work; *doulos*, in relation to his master; *hupēretēs*, in relation to his superior; *leitourgos*, in relation to public service.

B. Verbs.

1. *diakoneō* [διακονέω, 1247], akin to A, No. 1, signifies to be a servant, attendant, to serve, wait upon, minister. In the following it is translated to minister, except where to serve is mentioned: it is used (*a*) with a general significance, e.g., Matt. 4:11; 20:28; Mark 1:13; 10:45; John 12:26 ("serve," twice); Acts 19:22; Philm. 13; (*b*) of waiting at table, ministering to the guests, Matt. 8:15; Luke 4:39; 8:3; 12:37; 17:8, "serve"; 22:26, "serve," ver. 27, "serveth," twice; the 2nd instance, concerning the Lord, may come under (*a*); so of women preparing food, etc., Mark 1:31; Luke 10:40, "serve"; John 12:2, "served"; (*c*) of relieving one's necessities, supplying the necessaries of life, Matt. 25:44; 27:55; Mark 15:41; Acts 6:2, "serve"; Rom. 15:25; Heb. 6:10; more definitely in connection with such service in a local church, 1 Tim. 3:10, 13 [there is nothing in the original representing the word "office"; R.V., "let them serve as deacons," "they that have served (well) as deacons"]; (*d*) of attending, in a more general way, to anything that may serve another's interests, as of the work of an amanuensis, 2 Cor. 3:3 (metaphorical): of the conveyance of material gifts for assisting the needy, 2 Cor. 8:19, 20, R.V., "is ministered" (A.V., "is administered"); of a variety of forms of service, 2 Tim. 1:18; of the testimony of the O.T. prophets, 1 Pet. 1:12; of the ministry of believers one to another in various ways, 1 Pet. 4:10, 11 (not here of discharging ecclesiastical functions). ¶

NT: B.184a; CB.1241a; K.152.
OT: —.
GEN. REF.: IS.3:364; NB.825; Z.4:233.

Note: In Heb. 1:14, A.V. (2nd part), the phrase *eis diakonian* is translated "to minister," R.V., "to do service," lit., 'for service'; for the noun "ministering" in the 1st part, see MINISTERING, B.

2. *leitourgeō* [λειτουργέω, 3008], (akin to A, No. 2), in classical Greek, signified at Athens to supply public offices at one's own cost, to render public service to the State; hence, generally, to do service, said, e.g., of service to the gods. In the N.T. (see Note below) it is used (*a*) of the prophets and teachers in the church at Antioch, who "ministered to the Lord," Acts 13:2; (*b*) of the duty of churches of the Gentiles to minister in "carnal things" to the poor Jewish saints at Jerusalem, in view of the fact that the former had "been made partakers" of the "spiritual things" of the latter, Rom. 15:27; (*c*) of the official service of priests and Levites under the Law, Heb. 10:11 (in the Sept., e.g., Ex. 29:30; Numb. 16:9). ¶

NT: B.470c; CB.1256c; K.526.
OT: shārat: S.8334; HR.872c.4; H.2472; BD.1058a.
'ābad: S.5647; HR.872c.2a; H.1553; BD.712b.
GEN. REF.: IS.3:364; NB.825; Z.4:233.

Note: The synonymous verb *latreuō* (properly, to serve for hire), which is used in the Sept. of the service of both priests and people (e.g., Ex. 4:3; Deut. 10:12, and in the N.T., e.g., Heb. 8:5), and, in the N.T., of Christians in general, e.g., Rev. 22:3, is to be distinguished from *leitourgeō*, which has to do with the fulfilment of an office, the discharge of a function, something of a representative character (Eng., liturgy).

3. *hupēreteō* [ὑπηρετέω, 5256], to do the service of a *hupēretēs* (see A, No. 3), properly, to serve as a rower on a ship, is used (*a*) of David, as serving the counsel of God in his own generation, Acts 13:36, R.V., expressive of the lowly character of his service for God; (*b*) of Paul's toil in working with his hands, and his readiness to avoid any pose of ecclesiastical superiority, Acts 20:34; (*c*) of the service permitted to Paul's friends to render to him, 24:23. ¶

NT: B.842c; CB.1252a; K.1231.
OT: —.
GEN. REF.: IS.3:364; NB.825; Z.4:233.

4. *hierourgeō* [ἱερουργέω, 2418], to minister in priestly service (akin to *hierourgos*, a sacrificing priest, a word not found in the Sept. or N.T.; from *hieros*, sacred, and *ergon*, work), is used by Paul metaphorically of his ministry of the Gospel, Rom. 15:16; the offering connected with his priestly ministry is "the offering up of the Gentiles," i.e., the presentation by Gentile converts of themselves to God. ¶ The Apostle uses words proper to the priestly and Levitical ritual, to explain metaphorically his own priestly service. Cp. *prosphora*, "offering up," and *leitourgos* in the same verse.

NT: B.373c; CB.1250c; K.349.
OT: —.
GEN. REF.: IS.—; NB.825; Z.4:233.

5. *parechō* [παρέχω, 3930], to furnish, provide, supply, is translated "minister" in 1 Tim. 1:4, of the effect of 'fables and endless genealogies.' See BRING, A, No. 21.

NT: B.626b; CB.—; K.—.
OT: —.
GEN. REF.: —.

6. *ergazomai* [*ἐργάζομαι*, 2038], to work, work out, perform, is translated "minister" in 1 Cor. 9:13; the verb is frequently used of business, or employment, and here the phrase means 'those employed in sacred things' or 'those who are assiduous in priestly functions.' See COMMIT, A, No. 1.

NT: B.306d; CB.1246c; K.251.
OT: 'ābad: S.5647; HR.540c.8a; H.1553; BD.712b.
pā'al: S.6466; HR.590c.11a; H.1792; BD.821b.
GEN. REF.: IS.3:364,365; NB.—; Z.—.

Notes: (1) The verb *chorēgeō*, rendered "minister" in the A.V. of 2 Cor. 9:10, and the strengthened form *epichorēgeō*, rendered by the same verb in the A.V. of 2 Cor. 9:10; Gal. 3:5; Col. 2:19; 2 Pet. 1:11, in ver. 5, "add," are always translated to supply in the R.V. Both verbs suggest an abundant supply, and are used of material or of spiritual provision. See SUPPLY.

(2) In Eph. 4:29, A.V., *didōmi*, to give, is translated "minister" (R.V., "give").

MINISTERING, MINISTRATION MINISTRY

A. Nouns.

1. *diakonia* [*διακονία*, 1248], the office and work of a *idakonos* (see MINISTER, A, No. 1), service, ministry, is used (*a*) of domestic duties, Luke 10:40; (*b*) of religious and spiritual ministration, (1) of apostolic ministry, e.g., Acts 1:17, 25; 6:4; 12:25; 21:19; Rom. 11:13, R.V. (A.V., "office"); (2) of the service of believers, e.g., Acts 6:1; Rom. 12:7; 1 Cor. 12:5, R.V., "ministrations" (A.V., "administrations"); 1 Cor. 16:15; 2 Cor. 8:4; 9:1; 9:12, R.V., "ministration"; ver. 13; Eph. 4:12, R.V., "ministering" (A.V., "the ministry," not in the sense of an ecclesiastical function); 2 Tim. 4:11, R.V., "(for) ministering"; collectively of a local church, Acts 11:29, "relief" (R.V. marg., "for ministry"); Rev. 2:19, R.V., "ministry" (A.V., "service"); of Paul's service on behalf of poor saints, Rom. 15:31; (3) of the ministry of the Holy Spirit in the Gospel, 2 Cor. 3:8; (4) of the ministry of angels, Heb. 1:14, R.V., "to do service" (A.V., "to minister"); (5) of the work of the Gospel, in general, e.g., 2 Cor. 3:9, "of righteousness"; 5:18, "of reconciliation"; (6) of the general ministry of a servant of the Lord in preaching and teaching, Acts 20:24; 2 Cor. 4:1; 6:3; 11:8; 1 Tim. 1:12, R.V., "(to His) service"; 2 Tim. 4:5; undefined in Col. 4:17; (7) of the Law, as a ministration of death, 2 Cor. 3:7; of condemnation, 3:9. ¶

NT: B.184b; CB.1241a; K.152.
OT: na'ar: S.5288; HR.303b.1; H.1389a; BD.654d.
shārat: S.8334; HR.303b.2; H.2472; BD.1058a.
GEN. REF.: IS.3:364,365; NB.826; Z.4:233.

2. *leitourgia* [*λειτουργία*, 3009], akin to *leitourgos* (see MINISTER, A, No. 2), to which the meanings of *leitourgia* correspond, is used in the N.T. of sacred ministrations, (*a*) priestly, Luke 1:23; Heb. 8:6; 9:21; (*b*) figuratively, of the practical faith of the members of the church at Philippi regarded as priestly sacrifice, upon which the Apostle's life-blood might be poured out as a libation, Phil. 2:17; (*c*) of the ministration of believers one to another, regarded as priestly service, 2 Cor. 9:12; Phil. 2:30. See SERVICE. ¶

NT: B.471a; CB.1256c; K.526.
OT: '^{a}bōdāh: S.5656; HR.873b.2; H.1553c; BD.715a.
GEN. REF.: IS.3:364,365; NB.826; Z.4:233.

B. Adjective.

leitourgikos [*λειτουργικός*, 3010], of or pertaining to service, ministering, is used in Heb. 1:14, of angels as "ministering spirits" (for the word "do service" in the next clause, see A, No. 1). ¶ In the Sept., Ex. 31:10; 39:13; Numb. 4:12, 26; 7:5; 2 Chron. 24:14. ¶

NT: B.471b; CB.1256c; K.526.
OT: '^{a}bōdāh: S.5656; HR.873b.1; H.1553c; BD.715a.
shārēt: S.8335; HR.873b.2; H.2472a; BD.1058b.
GEN. REF.: IS.3:364,365; NB.826; Z.4:233.

MINSTREL

mousikos [*μουσικός*, 3451], is found in Rev. 18:22, R.V., "minstrels" (A.V., "musicians"); inasmuch as other instrumentalists are mentioned, some word like "minstrels" is necessary to make the distinction, hence the R.V.; Bengel and others translate it 'singers.' Primarily the word denoted 'devoted to the Muses' (the nine goddesses who presided over the principal departments of letters), and was used of anyone devoted to or skilled in arts and sciences, or 'learned.' ¶

NT: B.528d; CB.1259b; K.—.
OT: z^{e}mar (Aramaic): S.2164; HR.935c.1; H.557a; BD.1091c.
shîr: S.7891; HR.935c.2; H.2378; BD.1010c.
GEN. REF.: —.

MINT

hēduosmon [*ἡδύοσμον*, 2238], an adjective denoting sweet-smelling (*hēdus*, sweet, *osmē*, a smell), is used as a neuter noun signifying mint, Matt. 23:23; Luke 11:42. ¶

NT: B.344b; CB.1249c; K.—.
OT: —.
GEN. REF.: IS.3:371; NB.1006; Z.4:241.

MIRACLE

1. *dunamis* [*δύναμις*, 1411], power, inherent ability, is used of works of a supernatural origin and character, such as could not be produced by natural agents and means. It is translated "miracles" in the R.V. and A.V. in Acts 8:13

(where variant readings give the words in different order); 19:11; 1 Cor. 12:10, 28, 29; Gal. 3:5; A.V. only, in Acts 2:22 (R.V., "mighty works"); Heb. 2:4 (R.V., "powers"). In Gal. 3:5, the word may be taken in its widest sense, to include miracles both physical and moral. See MIGHT, A, No. 1, POWER, WORK.

NT: B.207b; CB.1242b; K.186.
OT: ḥayil: S.2428; HR.350a.11; H.624a; BD.298c.
ṣābā': S.6635; HR.350a.25; H.1865a,b; BD.838d.
GEN. REF.: IS.3:371; NB.828; Z.4:241.

2. *sēmeion* [σημεῖον, 4592], a sign, mark, token (akin to *sēmainō*, to give a sign; *sēma*, a sign), is used of miracles and wonders as signs of Divine authority; it is translated "miracles" in the R.V. and A.V. of Luke 23:8; Acts 4:16, 22; most usually it is given its more appropriate meaning "sign," "signs," e.g., Matt. 12:38, 39, and in every occurrence in the Synoptists, except Luke 23:8; in the following passages in John's Gospel the R.V. substitutes "sign" or "signs" for the A.V., "miracle" or "miracles"; 2:11, 23; 3:2; 4:54; 6:2, 14, 26; 7:31; 9:16; 10:41; 11:47; 12:18, 37; the A.V. also has "signs" elsewhere in this Gospel; in Acts, R.V., "signs," A.V., "miracles," in 6:8; 8:6; 15:12; elsewhere only in Rev. 13:14; 16:14; 19:20. See SIGN, TOKEN, WONDER.

NT: B.747d; CB.1268c; K.1015.
OT: 'ôt: S.226; HR.1263b.1a; H.41a; BD.16c.
nēs: S.5264; HR.1263b.5; H.1379; BD.651c.
GEN. REF.: IS.3:371; NB.828; Z.4:241.

MIRE

borboros [βόρβορος, 1004], mud, filth, occurs in 2 Pet. 2:22. ¶ In the Sept., Jer. 38:6 (twice), of the mire in the dungeon into which Jeremiah was cast. ¶

NT: B.145a; CB.1239b; K.–.
OT: ṭîṭ: S.2916; HR.224c.1; H.796a; BD.376c.
GEN. REF.: IS.3:381; NB.–; Z.–.

MIRROR

esoptron [ἔσοπτρον, 2072], rendered "glass" in the A.V., is used of any surface sufficiently smooth and regular to reflect rays of light uniformly, and thus produce images of objects which actually in front of it appear to the eye as if they were behind it. Mirrors in Biblical times were, it seems, metallic; hence the R.V. adopts the more general term "mirror"; in 1 Cor. 13:12, spiritual knowledge in this life is represented metaphorically as an image dimly perceived in a mirror; in Jas. 1:23, the "law of liberty" is figuratively compared to a mirror; the hearer who obeys not is like a person who, having looked into the mirror, forgets the reflected image after turning away; he who obeys is like one who gazes into the mirror and retains in his soul the image of what he should be. ¶

NT: B.313b; CB.1246c; K.27,264.
OT: –.
GEN. REF.: IS.3:382; NB.831; Z.4:251.

Note: For the verb *katoptrizō*, to reflect as a mirror (some regard it as meaning 'beholding in a mirror'), in 2 Cor. 3:18, see BEHOLD, No. 12.

For MISCHIEF, Acts 13:10, see VILLANY

MISERABLE, MISERABLY, MISERY

A. Adjectives.

1. *eleeinos* [ἐλεεινός, 1652], pitiable, miserable (from *eleos*, mercy, pity; see MERCY), is used in Rev. 3:17, in the Lord's description of the church at Laodicea; here the idea is probably that of a combination of misery and pitiableness. ¶

NT: B.249c; CB.1244a; K.–.
OT: –.
GEN. REF.: –.

Note: For the comparative degree *eleeinoteros*, rendered "most pitiable" in 1 Cor. 15:19, R.V. (A.V., "most miserable"), see PITIABLE.

2. *kakos* [κακός, 2556], bad, evil, is translated "miserable" in Matt. 21:41, R.V. (A.V., "wicked"). See BAD.

NT: B.397d; CB.1253b; K.391.
OT: ra': S.7451; HR.709b.13b; H.2191; BD.948c.
rā'āh: S.7451; HR.709b.13c; H.2191; BD.949a.
GEN. REF.: IS.2:206; NB.400; Z.2:420.

B. Adverb.

kakōs [κακῶς, 2560], badly, ill, is translated "miserably" in Matt. 21:41 (see A, No. 2). Adhering to the meaning 'evil,' and giving the designed stress, the sentence may be rendered, 'evil (as they are) he will evilly destroy them.'

NT: B.398c; CB.1253b; K.–.
OT: 'ārar: S.779; HR.712a.2a; H.168; BD.76c.
qālal: S.7043; HR.712a.2b; H.2028; BD.886b.
GEN. REF.: IS.–; NB.400; Z.2:420.

C. Noun.

talaipōria [ταλαιπωρία, 5004], hardship, suffering, distress (akin to *talaipōros*, wretched, Rom. 7:24; Rev. 3:17, ¶ and to *talaipōreō*, in the Middle Voice, to afflict oneself, in Jas. 4:9, "be afflicted" ¶), is used as an abstract noun, "misery," in Rom. 3:16; as a concrete noun, 'miseries,' in Jas. 5:1. ¶

NT: B.803b; CB.1271a; K.–.
OT: shōd: S.7701; HR.1333a.6a; H.2331a; BD.994c.
shādad: S.7703; HR.1333a.6b; H.2331; BD.994a.
GEN. REF.: –.

MIST

1. *achlus* [ἀχλύς, 887], a mist, especially a dimness of the eyes, is used in Acts 13:11. "In

the single place of its N.T. use it attests the accuracy in the selection of words, and not least of medical words, which 'the beloved physician' so often displays. For him it expresses the mist of darkness . . . which fell on the sorcerer Elymas, being the outward and visible sign of the inward spiritual darkness which would be his portion for a while in punishment for his resistance to the truth" (Trench, Syn., § c). ¶
NT: B.128b; CB.–; K.–.
OT: –.
GEN. REF.: IS.3:385; NB.–; Z.4:252.

2. *homichlē* [ὁμίχλη, —], a mist (not so thick as *nephos* and *nephelē*, a cloud), occurs in 2 Pet. 2:17 (1st part), R.V., "mists"; some mss. have *nephelai*, "clouds" (A.V.). ¶
NT: B.565d; CB.1251a; K.–.
OT: ḥōshek: S.2822; HR.991b.1; H.769a; BD.365a.
'êphāh: S.5890; HR.991b.3; H.1583d; BD.734a.
'ᵃrāphel: S.6205; HR.991b.4; H.1701b; BD.791d.
GEN. REF.: IS.3:385; NB.–; Z.4:252.

3. *zophos* [ζόφος, 2217], is rendered "mist" in the A.V. of 2 Pet. 2:17 (2nd part), R.V., "blackness"; 'murkiness' would be a suitable rendering. For this and other synonymous terms see BLACKNESS, DARKNESS.
NT: B.339d; CB.–; K.–.
OT: –.
GEN. REF.: –.

MITE

lepton [λεπτόν, 3016], the neuter of the adjective *leptos*, signifying, firstly, peeled, then, fine, thin, small, light, became used as a noun, denoting a small copper coin, often mentioned in the Mishna as proverbially the smallest Jewish coin. It was valued at ⅛th of the Roman *as*, and the 1/128th part of the *denarius*: its legal value was about one third of an English farthing; Mark 12:42 lit. reads 'two *lepta*, which make a *kodrantēs* (a *quadrans*)'; in Luke 12:59 'the last *lepton*' corresponds in effect to Matt. 5:26, 'the uttermost *kodrantēs*,' "farthing"; elsewhere Luke 21:2; see FARTHING. ¶
NT: B.472a; CB.1256c; K.–.
OT: –.
GEN. REF.: IS.3:386; NB.840; Z.–.

MIXED (with)

Note: In Heb. 4:2, A.V., *sunkerannumi*, lit., to mix with (*sun*, with, *kerannumi*, see MINGLE, No. 2), is so translated; R.V., "were (not) united (by faith) with" [A.V., "(not) being mixed . . . in], as said of persons; in 1 Cor. 12:24 "hath tempered." See TEMPER TOGETHER. ¶

MIXTURE

migma [μίγμα, 3395], a mixture (akin to *mignumi*, to mix, mingle: see MINGLE, No. 1), occurs in John 19:39 (some mss. have *heligma*, a roll). ¶
NT: B.521a; CB.–; K.–.
OT: –.
GEN. REF.: –.

Note: In Rev. 14:10, A.V., *akratos* (*a*, negative, and *kerannumi*, to mingle) is translated "without mixture" (R.V., "unmixed"). ¶ In the Sept., Psa. 75:8; Jer. 32:1. ¶

MOCK, MOCKER, MOCKING

A. Verbs.

1. *empaizō* [ἐμπαίζω, 1702], a compound of *paizō*, to play like a child (*pais*), to sport, jest, prefixed by *en*, in or at, is used only in the Synoptists, and, in every instance, of the mockery of Christ, except in Matt. 2:16 (there in the sense of deluding, or deceiving, of Herod by the wise men) and in Luke 14:29, of ridicule cast upon the one who after laying a foundation of a tower is unable to finish it. The word is used (*a*) prophetically by the Lord, of His impending sufferings, Matt. 20:19; Mark 10:34; Luke 18:32; (*b*) of the actual insults inflicted upon Him by the men who had taken Him from Gethsemane, Luke 22:63; by Herod and his soldiers, Luke 23:11; by the soldiers of the governor, Matt. 27:29, 31; Mark 15:20; Luke 23:36; by the chief priests, Matt. 27:41; Mark 15:31. ¶
NT: B.255d; CB.1244b; K.758.
OT: 'ālal: S.5953; HR.456b.3; H.1627,1628; BD.759d.
ṣāḥaq: S.6711; HR.456b.4; H.1905; BD.850b.
GEN. REF.: IS.3:398; NB.–; Z.4:268.

2. *muktērizō* [μυκτηρίζω, 3456], from *muktēr*, the nose, hence, to turn up the nose at, sneer at, treat with contempt, is used in the Passive Voice in Gal. 6:7, where the statement "God is not mocked" does not mean that men do not mock Him (see Prov. 1:30, where the Sept. has the same verb); the Apostle vividly contrasts the essential difference between God and man. It is impossible to impose upon Him who discerns the thoughts and intents of the heart. ¶
NT: B.529b; CB.1259b; K.614.
OT: lā'ag: S.3932; HR.936c.5; H.1118; BD.541b.
bûz: S.936; HR.936c.2a; H.213; BD.100b.
GEN. REF.: IS.3:398; NB.–; Z.4:268.

Note: Ekmuktērizō, a strengthened form of the above, to scoff at, is used in Luke 16:14 and 23:35 (R.V., "scoffed at"; A.V., "derided"). See DERIDE, SCOFF. ¶

3. *chleuazō* [χλευάζω, 5512], to jest, mock, jeer at (from *chleuē*, a jest), is said of the ridicule of some of the Athenian philosophers at the Apostle's testimony concerning the resurrection of the dead, Acts 17:32. ¶
NT: B.882c; CB.–; K.–.
OT: –.
GEN. REF.: IS.3:398; NB.–; Z.4:268.

4. *diachleuazō* [διαχλευάζω, —], an intensive form of No. 3, to scoff at, whether by gesture or word, is said of those who jeered at the testimony given on the day of Pentecost, Acts 2:13 (some mss. have No. 3.). ¶
NT: B.191a; CB.—; K.—.
OT: —.
GEN. REF.: IS.3:398; NB.—; Z.—.

B. Nouns.

1. *empaiktēs* [ἐμπαίκτης, 1703], a mocker (akin to A, No. 1), is used in 2 Pet. 3:3, R.V., "mockers" (A.V., "scoffers"); Jude 18, R.V. and A.V., "mockers." ¶ In the Sept., Is. 3:4. ¶
NT: B.255d; CB.—; K.758.
OT: taʿalûlîm: S.8586; HR.456c.1; H.1627; BD.760c.
GEN. REF.: IS.3:398; NB.—; Z.4:268.

2. *empaigmos* [ἐμπαιγμός, 1701], the act of the *empaiktēs*, a mocking, is used in Heb. 11:36, "mockings." ¶ In the Sept., Psa. 38:7; Ezek. 22:4. ¶
NT: B.255d; CB.—; K.758.
OT: qallāsāh: S.7048; HR.456b.2; H.2029b; BD.887b.
GEN. REF.: IS.3:398; NB.—; Z.4:268.

3. *empaigmonē* [ἐμπαιγμονή, —], an abstract noun, mockery, is used in 2 Pet. 3:3 (some mss. omit it, as in A.V.): (see also No. 1, above). ¶
NT: B.255d; CB.1244b; K.758.
OT: —.
GEN. REF.: IS.3:398; NB.—; Z.4:268.

For **MODERATION**, Phil. 4:5, A.V., see **FORBEARANCE**, C, No. 2

MODEST

kosmios [κόσμιος, 2887], orderly, well-arranged, decent, modest (akin to *kosmos*, in its primary sense as harmonious arrangement, adornment; cp. *kosmikos*, of the world, which is related to *kosmos* in its secondary sense as the world), is used in 1 Tim. 2:9 of the apparel with which Christian women are to adorn themselves; in 3:2 (R.V., "orderly"; A.V., "of good behaviour"), of one of the qualifications essential for a bishop or overseer. "The well-ordering is not of dress and demeanour only, but of the inner life, uttering indeed and expressing itself in the outward conversation" (Trench, Syn., § xcii). ¶ In the Sept., Eccl. 12:9. ¶
NT: B.445c; CB.1255c; K.459.
OT: —.
GEN. REF.: —.

MOISTURE

ikmas [ἰκμάς, 2429], moisture (probably from an Indo-European root *sik*— indicating wet), is used in Luke 8:6. ¶ In the Sept., Job 26:14; Jer. 17:8. ¶
NT: B.375a; CB.—; K.—.
OT: yûbal: S.3105; HR.684b.1; H.835b; BD.385b.
GEN. REF.: —.

MOMENT

A. Nouns.

1. *atomos* [ἄτομος, 823], lit. means indivisible (from *a*, negative, and *temnō*, to cut; Eng., atom); hence it denotes a moment, 1 Cor. 15:52. ¶
NT: B.120b; CB.1238b; K.—.
OT: —.
GEN. REF.: IS.3:402; NB.—; Z.—.

2. *stigmē* [στιγμή, 4743], a prick, a point (akin to *stizō*, to prick), is used metaphorically in Luke 4:5, of a moment, with *chronos*, "a moment (of time)." ¶
NT: B.768c; CB.—; K.—.
OT: petaʿ: S.6621; HR.1291b.1; H.1859; BD.837b.
GEN. REF.: IS.3:402; NB.—; Z.—.

Note: It is to be distinguished from *stigma*, a mark or brand, Gal. 6:17, which is however, also connected with *stizō*.

B. Adverb.

parautika [παραυτίκα, 3910], the equivalent of *parauta*, immediately (not in the N.T.), i.e., *para auta*, with *ta pragmata* understood, 'at the same circumstances,' is used adjectivally in 2 Cor. 4:17 and translated "which is but for a moment"; the meaning is not, however, simply that of brief duration, but that which is present with us now or immediate (*para*, beside, with), in contrast to the future glory; the clause is, lit., 'for the present lightness (i.e., light burden, the adjective *elaphron*, light, being used as a noun) of (our) affliction.' ¶ This meaning is confirmed by its use in the Sept. of Psa. 70:3, '(let them be turned back) immediately,' where the rendering could not be 'for a moment.' ¶
NT: B.623b; CB.—; K.—.
OT: —.
GEN. REF.: IS.3:402; NB.—; Z.—.

MONEY

1. *argurion* [ἀργύριον, 694], properly, a piece of silver, denotes (*a*) silver, e.g., Acts 3:6; (*b*) a silver coin, often in the plural, "pieces of silver," e.g., Matt. 26:15; so 28:12, where the meaning is 'many, (*hikanos*) pieces of silver'; (*c*) money; it has this meaning in Matt. 25:18, 27; 28:15; Mark 14:11; Luke 9:3; 19:15, 23; 22:5; Acts 8:20 (here the R.V. has "silver").
NT: B.104d; CB.1237c; K.—.
OT: keseph: S.3701; HR.153b.1a; H.1015a; BD.494a.
GEN. REF.: IS.3:402; NB.836; Z.—.

Note: In Acts 7:16, for the A.V., "(a sum of) money," the R.V. has "(a price in) silver." See SILVER.

2. *chrēma* [χρῆμα, 5536], lit., a thing that one uses (akin to *chraomai*, to use), hence, (*a*) wealth, riches, Mark 10:23, 24; Luke 18:24; (*b*) money, Acts 4:37, singular number, a sum of

money; plural in 8:18, 20; 24:26. ¶ See RICHES.

NT: B.885c; CB.1240a; K.1319.
OT: n^{e}kāsîm: S.5233; HR.1474b.4; H.1367; BD.647d.
keseph: S.3701; HR.1474b.2; H.1015a; BD.494a.
GEN. REF.: IS.3:402; NB.836; Z.–.

3. *chalkos* [χαλκός, 5475], copper, is used, by metonymy, of copper coin, translated "money," in Mark 6:8; 12:41. See BRASS.

NT: B.875a; CB.1239b; K.–.
OT: n^{e}ḥōshet: S.5178; HR.1453b.1b; H.1349a,1350a; BD.638d.
GEN. REF.: IS.3:402; NB.–; Z.–.

4. *kerma* [κέρμα, 2772], primarily a slice (akin to *keirō*, to cut short), hence, a small coin, change, is used in the plural in John 2:15, "the changers' money," proably considerable heaps of small coins. ¶

NT: B.429d; CB.–; K.–.
OT: –.
GEN. REF.: IS.–; NB.839; Z.–.

5. *nomisma* [νόμισμα, 3546], primarily that which is established by custom (*nomos*, a custom, law), hence, the current coin of a state, currency, is found in Matt. 22:19, "(tribute) money." ¶ In the Sept., Neh. 7:71. ¶

NT: B.541d; CB.–; K.–.
OT: dark^{e}môn: S.1871; HR.947a.1; H.453c; BD.204b.
GEN. REF.: IS.3:402; NB.839; Z.–.

Note: In Matt. 17:27, A.V., *statēr* (a coin, estimated at a little over three shillings, equivalent to four *drachmae*, the temple-tax for two persons), is translated "piece of money" (R.V., "shekel"). See SHEKEL. ¶

For **MONEY-CHANGER, CHANGER OF MONEY,** see **CHANGER**

MONEY (love of)

philarguria [φιλαργυρία, 5365], from *phileō*, to love, and *arguros*, silver, occurs in 1 Tim. 6:10 (cp. *philarguros*, covetous, avaricious). Trench contrasts this with *pleonexia*, covetousness. See under COVET, COVETOUSNESS. ¶

NT: B.859a; CB.1264a; K.–.
OT: –.
GEN. REF.: IS.3:410; NB.–; Z.–.

MONTH, MONTHS

1. *mēn* [μήν, 3376], connected with *mēnē*, the moon, akin to a Sanskrit root *mā*—, to measure (the Sanskrit *māsa* denotes both moon and month, cp., e.g., Lat. *mensis*, Eng., moon and month, the moon being in early times the measure of the month). The interval between the 17th day of the second month (Gen. 7:11) and the 17th day of the seventh month, is said to be 150 days (8:3, 4), i.e., five months of 30 days each; hence the year would be 360 days (cp. Dan. 7:25; 9:27; 12:7 with Rev. 11:2, 3; 12:6, 14; 13:5; whence we conclude that 3½ years or 42 months = 1260 days, i.e., one year = 360 days); this was the length of the old Egyptian year; later, five days were added to correspond to the solar year. The Hebrew year was as nearly solar as was compatible with its commencement, coinciding with the new moon, or first day of the month. This was a regular feast day, Numb. 10:10; 28:11-14; the Passover coincided with the full moon (the 14th of the month Abib: see PASSOVER).

Except in Gal. 4:10; Jas. 5:17; Rev. 9:5, 10, 15; 11:2; 13:5; 22:2, the word is found only in Luke's writings, Luke 1:24, 26, 36, 56; 4:25; Acts 7:20; 18:11; 19:8; 20:3; 28:11, examples of Luke's care as to accuracy of detail. ¶

NT: B.518d; CB.1258b; K.591.
OT: ḥōdesh: S.2320; HR.922a.1; H.613b; BD.294b.
GEN. REF.: IS.1:575; NB.178; Z.1:689.

2. *trimēnos* [τρίμηνος, 5150], an adjective, denoting of three months (*tri*, for *treis*, three, and No. 1), is used as a noun, a space of three months, in Heb. 11:23. ¶

NT: B.826b; CB.–; K.–.
OT: ḥōdesh (pl.): S.2320; HR.1373a.1; H.613b; BD.294b.
GEN. REF.: IS.1:575; NB.178; Z.1:689.

3. *tetramēnos* [τετράμηνος, 5072], an adjective, denoting of four months (*tetra*, for *tessares*, four, and No. 1), is used as a noun in John 4:35 (where *chronos*, time, may be understood). ¶

NT: B.813d; CB.–; K.–.
OT: ḥōdesh (pl.): S.2320; HR.1347b.1; H.613b; BD.294b.
GEN. REF.: IS.1:575; NB.178; Z.1:689.

MOON

1. *selēnē* [σελήνη, 4582], from *selas*, brightness (the Heb. words are *yarēach*, wandering, and *lebānāh*, white), occurs in Matt. 24:29; Mark 13:24; Luke 21:25; Acts 2:20; 1 Cor. 15:41; Rev. 6:12; 8:12; 12:1; 21:23. In Rev. 12:1, "the moon under her feet" is suggestive of derived authority, just as her being clothed with the sun is suggestive of supreme authority; everything in the symbolism of the passage centres in Israel. In 6:12 the similar symbolism of the sun and moon is suggestive of the supreme authority over the world, and of derived authority, at the time of the execution of Divine judgments upon nations at the close of the present age. ¶

NT: B.746d; CB.1268c; K.–.
OT: yārēaḥ: S.3394; HR.1262b.1; H.913a; BD.437a.
l^{e}bānāh: S.3842; HR.1262b.2; H.1074c; BD.526b.
GEN. REF.: IS.3:410; NB.841; Z.1:689;4:417.

2. *neomēnia* [νεομηνία, 3561], or *noumēnia*, denoting a new moon (*neos*, new, *mēn*, a month: see MONTH), is used in Col. 2:16, of a Jewish festival. ¶ Judaistic tradition added special features in the liturgy of the synagogue in

connection with the observance of the first day of the month, the new moon time.

In the O.T. the R.V. has "new moon" for A.V., "month" in Numb. 29:6; 1 Sam. 20:27; Hos. 5:7. For the connection with feast days see Lev. 23:24; Numb. 10:10; 29:1; Psa. 81:3.

NT: B.535d; CB.1259c; K.591.
OT: ḥōdesh: S.2320; HR.950b.1-4; H.613b; BD.294b.
GEN. REF.: IS.3:410; NB.841; Z.4:272,417.

For **MOOR** see **DRAW**, B, *Note* (1)

MORE

A. Adverbs.

1. *mallon* [μᾶλλον, 3123], the comparative degree of *mala*, very, very much, is used (*a*) of increase, "more," with qualifying words, with *pollǭ*, much, e.g., Mark 10:48, "the more (a great deal)"; Rom. 5:15, 17, "(much) more"; Phil. 2:12 (ditto); with *posǭ*, how much, e.g., Luke 12:24; Rom. 11:12; with *tosoutǭ*, by so much, Heb. 10:25; (*b*) without a qualifying word, by way of comparison, "the more," e.g., Luke 5:15, "so much the more"; John 5:18, "the more"; Acts 5:14 (ditto); Phil. 1:9; 1 Thess. 4:1, 10, "more and more"; 2 Pet. 1:10, R.V., "the more" (A.V., "the rather"); in Acts 20:35, by a periphrasis, it is translated "more (blessed)"; in Gal. 4:27, "more (than)," lit., 'rather (than)'; (*c*) with qualifying words, similarly to (*a*), e.g., Mark 7:36. See RATHER.

NT: B.489a; CB.1257c; K.—.
OT: —.
GEN. REF.: —.

2. *eti* [ἔτι, 2089], yet, as yet, still, used of degree is translated "more" in Matt. 18:16, "(one or two) more"; Heb. 8:12 and 10:17, "(will I remember no) more"; 10:2, "(no) more (conscience)"; 11:32, "(what shall I) more (say)?" Rev. 3:12, "(he shall go out thence no) more"; 7:16, "(no) more" and "any more"; 9:12, A.V., "more" (R.V., "hereafter"); 18:21-23, "(no) more," "any more" (5 times); 20:3, "(no) more"; 21:1, 4 (twice); 22:3. See ALSO, No. 2.

NT: B.315c; CB.1247a; K.—.
OT: —.
GEN. REF.: —.

3. *ouketi* [οὐκέτι, 3765], *ouk*, not, and No. 2, combined in one word, is translated "no more," e.g., in Matt. 19:6; Luke 15:19, 21; Acts 20:25, 38; Eph. 2:19. See HENCEFORTH, HEREAFTER, LONGER, NOW, *Note* (2).

NT: B.592c; CB.—; K.—.
OT: —.
GEN. REF.: —.

4. *perissoteron* [περισσότερον, 4054], the neuter of the comparative degree of *perissos*, more abundant, is used as an adverb, "more," e.g., Luke 12:4; 2 Cor. 10:8, A.V. (R.V., "abundantly"); Heb. 7:15, R.V., "more abundantly" (A.V., "far more"). See ABUNDANTLY, C, No. 2.

NT: B.651c; CB.1263c; K.828.
OT: —.
GEN. REF.: —.

Note: For the corresponding adverbs *perissōs* and *perissoterōs*, see ABUNDANTLY, EXCEEDINGLY.

5. *meizon* [μεῖζον, 3187], the neuter of *meizōn*, greater, the comparative degree of *megas*, great, is used as an adverb, and translated "the more" in Matt. 20:31. See GREATER.

NT: B.497c; CB.1258a; K.—.
OT: —.
GEN. REF.: —.

6. *huper* [ὑπέρ, 5228], a preposition, over, above, etc., is used as an adverb in 2 Cor. 11:23, "(I) more."

NT: B.838b; CB.1252a; K.1228.
OT: —.
GEN. REF.: —.

7. *hoson* [ὅσον, 3745], neuter of *hosos*, how much, is used adverbially in Mark 7:36 (1st part), "the more."

NT: B.586b; CB.1251b; K.—.
OT: —.
GEN. REF.: —.

B. Adjectives (*some with adverbial uses*).

1. *pleiōn* [πλείων, 4119], the comparative degree of *polus*, much, is used (*a*) as an adjective, e.g., John 15:2; Acts 24:11, R.V., "(not) more (than)" (A.V., "yet but"); Heb. 3:3; (*b*) as a noun, or with a noun understood, e.g., Matt. 20:10; Mark 12:43; Acts 19:32 and 27:12, "the more part"; 1 Cor. 9:19; (*c*) as an adverb, Matt. 5:20, "shall exceed," lit., '(shall abound) more (than)'; 26:53; Luke 9:13. See ABOVE, No. 3, *Note*, GREATER.

NT: B.687c; CB.1265b; K.—.
OT: rab: S.7227; HR.1181b.9a; H.2099a,b; BD.912d.
rōb: S.7230; HR.1181b.9b; H.2099c; BD.913d.
rābab: S.7231; HR.1181b.9c; H.2099; BD.912c.
GEN. REF.: —.

2. *perissos* [περισσός, 4053], more than sufficient, over and above, abundant (a popular substitute for No. 3), is translated "more," e.g., in Matt. 5:37, 47. In John 10:10 the neuter form is rendered "more abundantly," A.V., R.V., "abundantly" (marg., "abundance").

NT: B.651b; CB.1263c; K.828.
OT: yeter: S.3499; HR.1126c.1a; H.936a; BD.451d.
yôtēr: S.3148; HR.1126c.1c; H.936d; BD.452c.
yātar: S.3498; HR.1126.1d; H.936; BD.451a.
GEN. REF.: —.

3. *perissoteros* [περισσότερος, 4055], the comparative degree of No. 2, is translated "much more (than a prophet)" in Matt. 11:9, R.V. (A.V., "more"); in Luke 7:26 both R.V. and A.V. have "much more." See ABUNDANT, C.

NT: B.651c; CB.1263c; K.828.
OT: —.
GEN. REF.: —.

Notes: (1) In Matt. 25:20 (2nd part), A.V., *allos*, "other" (so the R.V.), is translated "more."

(2) In Jas. 4:6, A.V., the adjective *meizōn*, greater (see A, No. 5, above), is translated "more (grace)" (R.V. marg., "a greater grace"). See GRACE (at end).

(3) Various uses of the word "more" occur in connection with other words, especially in the comparative degree. The phrase "more than" translates certain prepositions and particles: in Rom. 1:25, A.V., *para*, beside, compared with, is translated "more than" (R.V., "rather than"); cp. Rom. 12:3; *huper*, over, above, "more than," in Matt. 10:37 (twice); in Philm. 21, A.V., "more than" (R.V., "beyond"). In Mark 14:5, A.V., *epanō*, above, is translated "more than" (R.V., "above"). In Luke 15:7 the particle *ē*, than, is necessarily rendered "more than"; cp. Luke 17:2 and 1 Cor. 14:19, "rather than." In Mark 8:14, the conjunction *ei*, if, with the negative *mē*, lit., 'if not,' signifying 'except,' is translated "more than (one loaf)."

MOREOVER

1. *eti* [ἔτι, 2089], yet, as yet, still, is translated "moreover" in Acts 2:26; in 21:28, R.V. (A.V., "further"); Heb. 11:36. See MORE, A, No. 2.

NT: B.315c; CB.1247a; K.–.
OT: –.
GEN. REF.: –.

2. *kai* [καί, 2532], and, is translated "moreover" in Acts 24:6; in the A.V., where the R.V. has "and," Acts 19:26.

NT: B.391d; CB.1253a; K.–.
OT: –.
GEN. REF.: –.

3. *de* [δέ, 1161], a particle signifying 'and' or 'but,' is translated "moreover" in Matt. 18:15, A.V. (R.V., "and"); Acts 11:12 (R.V., "and"); Rom. 5:20, A.V. (R.V., "but"); 8:30 ("and"); 1 Cor. 15:1 (R.V., "now"); 2 Cor. 1:23 (R.V., "but"); 2 Pet. 1:15 (R.V., "yea").

NT: B.171c; CB.–; K.–.
OT: –.
GEN. REF.: –.

4. *alla kai* [ἀλλὰ καί, 235 (alla)], but also, yea even, is translated "moreover" in Luke 24:22, R.V. (A.V., "yea, and"; in 16:21, A.V., "moreover" (R.V., "yea, even").

NT: B.38a; CB.–; K.–.
OT: –.
GEN. REF.: –.

5. *de kai* [δὲ καί, —], but also, is translated "moreover" in 1 Tim. 3:7.

NT: –.
OT: –.
GEN. REF.: –.

6. *kai . . . de* [καὶ . . . δέ, —], is translated "moreover" in Heb. 9.21.

NT: –.
OT: –.
GEN. REF.: –.

7. *loipon* [λοιπόν, 3063], the neuter of the adjective *loipos*, the rest, used adverbially, most usually rendered "finally," is translated "moreover" in 1 Cor. 4:2 (some mss. have *ho de loipon*, lit., 'but what is left,' A.V., "moreover," for *hōde loipon*, "here, moreover," as in the R.V.). See FINALLY.

NT: B.479d; CB.1257b; K.–.
OT: yeter: S.3499; HR.888a.1c; H.936a; BD.451d.
GEN. REF.: –.

Note: In 1 Cor. 10:1, A.V., *gar*, 'for,' is translated "moreover" (R.V., "for"); the R.V. is important here, as it introduces a reason for what has preceded in chap. 9, whereas "moreover" may indicate that a new subject is being introduced; this incorrect rendering tends somewhat to dissociate the two passages, whereas *gar* connects them intimately.

MORNING (in the, early in the)

A. Adjectives.

1. *prōïos* [πρώϊος, 4405], early, at early morn (from *pro*, before), is used as a noun in the feminine form *prōïa*, "morning" in Matt. 27:1 and John 21:4 (in some mss. in Matt. 21:18 and John 18:28, for B, No. 1, which see). Its adjectival force is retained by regarding it as qualifying the noun *hōra*, an hour, i.e., 'at an early hour.' ¶

NT: B.724d; CB.–; K.–.
OT: bōqer: S.1242; HR.1235b.1a; H.274c; BD.133c.
GEN. REF.: IS.3:413; NB.–; Z.–.

2. *prōïnos* [πρώϊνος, 4407], a later form of No. 1, qualifies *astēr*, star, in Rev. 2:28 and 22:16 (where some mss. have No. 3). That Christ will give to the overcomer "the morning star" indicates a special interest for such in Himself, as He thus describes Himself in the later passage. For Israel He will appear as "the sun of righteousness"; as the morning Star which precedes He will appear for the Rapture of the Church. ¶

NT: B.707a; CB.1266c; K.–.
OT: bōqer: S.1242; HR.1235a.1; H.274c; BD.133c.
GEN. REF.: IS.3:413; NB.–; Z.–.

3. *orthrinos* or *orthrios* [ὀρθρινός, 3720], pertaining to dawn or morning, in some mss. in Rev. 22:16 (see No. 2); see DAWN, B, *Note*.

NT: B.580c; CB.–; K.–.
OT: shākam: S.7925; HR.1011b.1; H.2386; BD.1014c.
GEN. REF.: IS.3:413; NB.–; Z.–.

B. Adverb.

prōï [πρωΐ, 4404], early, is translated "in the morning" in Matt. 16:3; 20:1 (with *hama*, "early"); 21:18; Mark 1:35; 11:20; 13:35; 15:1; "early" in Mark 16:2 (with *lian*, very; A.V., "early in the morning"); 16:9; Matt. 21:18 and

John 18:28 (in the best texts, for A, No. 1); 20:1; Acts 28:23 (with *apo*, from). ¶

NT: B.724d; CB.–; K.–.
OT: (ba) bōqer: S.1242; HR.1234b.1b; H.274c; BD.133c.
GEN. REF.: IS.3:413; NB.–; Z.–.

C. Noun.

orthros [ὄρθρος, 3722], denotes daybreak, dawn, Luke 24:1; John 8:2; Acts 5:21; see DAWN, B. ¶

NT: B.580c; CB.–; K.–.
OT: shaḥar: S.7837; HR.1011b.3; H.2369a; BD.1007b.
shākam: S.7925; HR.1011b.5e; H.2386; BD.1014c.
GEN. REF.: IS.3:413; NB.–; Z.–.

D. Verb.

orthrizō [ὀρθρίζω, 3719], to do anything early in the morning, is translated "came early in the morning," in Luke 21:38. ¶

NT: B.580c; CB.–; K.–.
OT: shākam: S.7925; HR.1011a.2; H.2386; BD.1014c.
shāḥar: S.7836; HR.1011a.1; H.2369; BD.1007c.
GEN. REF.: IS.3:413; NB.–; Z.–.

MORROW

1. *aurion* [αὔριον, 839], an adverb denoting to-morrow, is used (*a*) with this meaning in Matt. 6:30; Luke 12:28; 13:32, 33; Acts 23:15 (in some mss.), 20; 25:22; 1 Cor. 15:32; Jas. 4:13; (*b*) with the word *hēmera*, day, understood (occurring thus in the papyri), translated as a noun, "(the) morrow," Matt. 6:34 (twice); Luke 10:35; Acts 4:3 (A.V., "next day"); 4:5; Jas. 4:14. ¶

NT: B.122a; CB.–; K.–.
OT: māḥar: S.4279; HR.179a.1a; H.1185a; BD.563d.
GEN. REF.: IS.4:870; NB.–; Z.–.

2. *epaurion* [ἐπαύριον, 1887], *epi*, upon, and No. 1, is used as in (*b*) above; the R.V. always translates it "on (the) morrow"; in the following the A.V. has "(the) next day," Matt. 27:62; John 1:29, 35 ("the next day after"); 12:12; Acts 14:20; 21:8; 25:6; "(the) day following," John 1:43; 6:22; "the morrow after," Acts 10:24.

NT: B.283d; CB.–; K.–.
OT: māḥᵒrāt: S.4283; HR.508c.1b; H.1185b; BD.564a.
GEN. REF.: IS.4:870; NB.–; Z.–.

Note: In Acts 25:17, A.V., the adverb *hexēs*, next, successively, in order, is translated "on (the) morrow." See NEXT.

For **MORSEL** see **MEAT**, No. 2

MORTAL, MORTALITY

thnētos [θνητός, 2349], subject or liable to death, mortal (akin to *thnēskō*, to die), occurs in Rom. 6:12, of the body, where it is called "mortal," not simply because it is liable to death, but because it is the organ in and through which death carries on its death-producing activities; in 8:11, the stress is on the liability to death, and the quickening is not reinvigoration but the impartation of life at the time of the Rapture, as in 1 Cor. 15:53, 54 and 2 Cor. 5:4 (R.V., "what is mortal"; A.V., "mortality"); in 2 Cor. 4:11, it is applied to the flesh, which stands, not simply for the body, but the body as that which consists of the element of decay, and is thereby death-doomed. Christ's followers are in this life delivered unto death, that His life may be manifested in that which naturally is the seat of decay and death. That which is subject to suffering is that in which the power of Him who suffered here is most manifested. ¶

NT: B.362d; CB.1272b; K.312.
OT: 'ādām: S.120; HR.654a.1; H.25a; BD.9a.
ḥay: S.2416; HR.654a.2; H.644a; BD.311d.
mût: S.4191; HR.654a.3; H.1169; BD.559b.
GEN. REF.: IS.3:414; NB.–; Z.4:276.

MORTIFY

1. *thanatoō* [θανατόω, 2289], to put to death (from *thanatos*, death, akin to *thnētos*, mortal, see above), is translated "mortify" in Rom. 8:13 (Amer. R.V., "put to death"); in 7:4, "ye were made dead" (Passive Voice), betokens the act of God on the believer, through the Death of Christ; here in 8:13 it is the act of the believer himself, as being responsible to answer to God's act, and to put to death "the deeds of the body." See DEATH, C, No. 1.

NT: B.351c; CB.1271c; K.312.
OT: mût: S.4191; HR.625a.4c,d; H.1169; BD.559b.
hārag: S.2026; HR.625a.2; H.514; BD.246d.
GEN. REF.: IS.3:415; NB.–; Z.–.

2. *nekroō* [νεκρόω, 3499], to make dead (from *nekros*, see DEAD, A), is used figuratively in Col. 3:5 and translated "mortify" (Amer. R.V., "put to death"). See DEAD, B, No. 1.

NT: B.535c; CB.1259c; K.627.
OT: –.
GEN. REF.: IS.3:415; NB.–; Z.–.

MOST

1. *pleion* [πλεῖον, 4119], the neuter of *pleiōn*, more, is used adverbially and translated "most" (of degree) in Luke 7:42 (without the article); in ver. 43 (with the article, 'the most'); 1 Cor. 10:5, R.V., "most" (A.V., "many"); Phil. 1:14 (ditto). See MORE.

NT: B.687c; CB.1265b; K.–.
OT: rab: S.7227; HR.1181b.9a; H.2099a,b; BD.912d.
rôb: S.7230; HR.1181b.9b; H.2099c; BD.913d.
rābab: S.7231; HR.1181b.9c; H.2099; BD.912c.
GEN. REF.: –.

2. *pleistos* [πλεῖστος, 4118], the superlative degree of *polus*, is used (*a*) as an adjective in Matt. 11:20; 21:8, R.V., "(the) most part of" (A.V., "a very great"); (*b*) in the neuter, with the article, adverbially, "at the most," 1 Cor. 14:27; (*c*) as an elative (i.e., intensively) in Mark 4:1

(in the best mss.; some have *polus*), "a very great (multitude)."

NT: B.687c; CB.–; K.–.
OT: rab: S.7227; HR.1181b.9a; H.2099a,b; BD.912d.
rôb: S.7230; HR.1181b.9b; H.2099c; BD.913d.
rābab: S.7231; HR.1181b.9c; H.2099; BD.912c.
GEN. REF.: –.

3. *malista* [*μάλιστα*, 3122], an adverb, the superlative of *mala*, very, is translated "most of all" in Acts 20:38. See ESPECIALLY.

NT: B.488d; CB.–; K.–.
OT: –.
GEN. REF.: –.

Note: For combinations in the translation of other words, see BELIEVE, C *Note* (4), EXCELLENT, GLADLY, HIGH, STRAITEST.

MOTE

karphos [*κάρφος*, 2595], a small, dry stalk, a twig, a bit of dried stick (from *karphō*, to dry up), or a tiny straw or bit of wool, such as might fly into the eye, is used metaphorically of a minor fault, Matt. 7:3, 4, 5; Luke 6:41, 42 (twice), in contrast with *dokos*, a beam supporting the roof of a building (see BEAM). ¶ In the Sept., Gen. 8:11. ¶

NT: B.405c; CB.–; K.–.
OT: ṭārāph: S.2965; HR.725b.1; H.827a; BD.383a.
GEN. REF.: IS.4:594; NB.850; Z.4:296.

MOTH

sēs [*σής*, 4597], denotes a clothes moth, Matt. 6:19, 20; Luke 12:33. ¶ In Job 4:19 "crushed before the moth" alludes apparently to the fact that woollen materials, riddled by the larvae of moths, become so fragile that a touch demolishes them. In Job 27:18 "He buildeth his house as a moth" alludes to the frail covering which a larval moth constructs out of the material which it consumes. The rendering "spider" (marg.) seems an attempt to explain a difficulty.

NT: B.749b; CB.1269a; K.1025.
OT: ʿāsh: S.6211; HR.1265b.2; H.2931; BD.799c.
sās: S.5580; HR.1265b.1; H.1524; BD.703b.
GEN. REF.: IS.3:426; NB.850; Z.4:296.

MOTH-EATEN

sētobrōtos [*σητόβρωτος*, 4598], from *sēs*, a moth, and *bibrōskō*, to eat, is used in Jas. 5:2. ¶ In the Sept. Job 13:28. ¶

NT: B.749c; CB.–; K.1025.
OT: ʿāsh: S.6211; HR.1265b.1; H.2931; BD.799c.
GEN. REF.: IS.3:426; NB.–; Z.–.

MOTHER

1. *mētēr* [*μήτηρ*, 3384], is used (*a*) of the natural relationship, e.g., Matt. 1:18; 2 Tim. 1:5; (*b*) figuratively, (1) of one who takes the place of a mother, Matt. 12:49, 50; Mark 3:34, 35; John 19:27; Rom. 16:13; 1 Tim. 5:2; (2) of the Heavenly and spiritual Jerusalem, Gal. 4:26, which is "free" (not bound by law imposed externally, as under the Law of Moses), "which is our mother" (R.V.), i.e., of Christians, the metropolis, mother-city, used allegorically, just as the capital of a country is "the seat of its government, the centre of its activities, and the place where the national characteristics are most fully expressed"; (3) symbolically, of Babylon, Rev. 17:5, as the source from which has proceeded the religious harlotry of mingling pagan rites and doctrines with the Christian faith.

NT: B.520a; CB.1258c; K.592.
OT: ʾēm: S.517; HR.924a.1; H.115a; BD.51c.
GEN. REF.: IS.3:426; NB.415; Z.2:496.

Note: In Mark 16:1 the article, followed by the genitive case of the name "James," the word "mother" being omitted, is an idiomatic mode of expressing the phrase "the mother of James."

2. *mētrolōas*, or *mētralōas* [*μητραλῴας*, 3389], denotes a matricide (No. 1, and *aloiaō*, to smite); 1 Tim. 1:9, "murderers of mothers"; it probably has, however, the broader meaning of "smiters" (R.V., marg.), as in instances elsewhere than the N.T. ¶

NT: B.520c; CB.–; K.–.
OT: –.
GEN. REF.: –.

3. *amētōr* [*ἀμήτωρ*, 282], without a mother (*a*, negative, and No. 1), is used in Heb. 7:3, of the Genesis record of Melchizedek, certain details concerning him being purposely omitted, in order to conform the description to facts about Christ as the Son of God. The word has been found in this sense in the writings of Euripides the dramatist and Herodotus the historian. See also under FATHER. ¶

NT: B.46a; CB.1234c; K.–.
OT: –.
GEN. REF.: –.

MOTHER-IN-LAW

penthera [*πενθερά*, 3994], the feminine of *pentheros* (a father-in-law), occurs in Matt. 8:14; 10:35; Mark 1:30; Luke 4:38; 12:53 (twice). ¶

NT: B.642c; CB.–; K.–.
OT: ḥāmôt: S.2545; HR.1117c.1; H.674b; BD.327a.
ḥōtenet (from ḥōtēn): S.2859; HR.1117c.2; H.781b; BD.368c.
GEN. REF.: IS.4:77; NB.–; Z.–.

For **MOTION**, Rom. 7:5, A.V., see **PASSION**

MOUNT, MOUNTAIN

oros [*ὄρος*, 3735], is used (*a*) without specification, e.g., Luke 3:5 (distinct from *bounos*, a hill, see HILL, No. 3); John 4:20; (*b*) of the Mount of Transfiguration, Matt. 17:1, 9;

Mark 9:2, 9; Luke 9:28, 37 (A.V., "hill"); 2 Pet. 1:18; (*c*) of Zion, Heb. 12:22; Rev. 14:1; (*d*) of Sinai, Acts 7:30, 38; Gal. 4:24, 25; Heb. 8:5; 12:20; (*e*) of the Mount of Olives, Matt. 21:1; 24:3; Mark 11:1; 13:3; Luke 19:29, 37; 22:39; John 8:1; Acts 1:12; (*f*) of the hill districts as distinct from the lowlands, especially of the hills above the Sea of Galilee, e.g., Matt. 5:1; 8:1; 18:12; Mark 5:5; (*g*) of the mountains on the east of Jordan and those in the land of Ammon and the region of Petra, etc., Matt. 24:16; Mark 13:14; Luke 21:21; (*h*) proverbially, of overcoming difficulties, or accomplishing great things, 1 Cor. 13:2; cp. Matt. 17:20; 21:21; Mark 11:23; (*i*) symbolically, of a series of the imperial potentates of the Roman Dominion, past and future, Rev. 17:9. See HILL.

NT: B.582a; CB.1261b; K.732.
OT: har: S.2022; HR.1014b.2b; H.517a; BD.249a.
GEN. REF.: IS.2:714; NB.850; Z.—.

MOURN, MOURNING

A. Verbs.

1. *koptō* [κόπτω, 2875], to cut or beat, used in the Middle Voice of beating the breast or head in mourning (cp. Luke 23:27), is translated "shall mourn" in Matt. 24:30. See BEWAIL, No. 2, CUT, WAIL.

NT: B.444a; CB.1255c; K.453.
OT: sāphad: S.5594; HR.779a.10a; H.1530; BD.704c.
GEN. REF.: IS.3:64; NB.170; Z.4:302.

2. *pentheō* [πενθέω, 3996], to mourn for, lament, is used (*a*) of mourning in general, Matt. 5:4; 9:15; Luke 6:25; (*b*) of sorrow for the death of a loved one, Mark 16:10; (*c*) of mourning for the overthrow of Babylon and the Babylonish system, Rev. 18:11, 15, R.V., "mourning" (A.V., "wailing"); ver. 19 (ditto); (*c*) of sorrow for sin or for condoning it, Jas. 4:9; 1 Cor. 5:2; (*d*) of grief for those in a local church who show no repentance for evil committed, 2 Cor. 12:21, R.V., "mourn" (A.V., "bewail"). See BEWAIL, No. 3. ¶

NT: B.642c; CB.1263a; K.825.
OT: 'ābal: S.56; HR.1117b.1a,c; H.6; BD.5b.
GEN. REF.: IS.3:64; NB.170; Z.4:302.

3. *thrēneō* [θρηνέω, 2354], to lament, wail (akin to *thrēnos*, a lamentation, a dirge), is used (*a*) in a general sense, of the disciples during the absence of the Lord, John 16:20, "lament"; (*b*) of those who sorrowed for the sufferings and the impending crucifixion of the Lord, Luke 23:27, "lamented"; the preceding word is *koptō* (No. 1); (*c*) of mourning as for the dead, Matt. 11:17, R.V., "wailed" (A.V., "have mourned"); Luke 7:32 (ditto). See BEWAIL, *Note* (1). ¶

NT: B.363b; CB.1272b; K.335.
OT: yālal: S.3213; HR.654c.4a; H.868; BD.410a.
GEN. REF.: IS.3:64; NB.170; Z.4:302.

Notes: (1) Trench points out that *pentheō* is often joined with *klaiō*, to weep, 2 Sam. 19:1; Mark 16:10; Jas. 4:9; Rev. 18:15, indicating that *pentheō* is used especially of external manifestation of grief (as with *koptō* and *thrēneō*), in contrast to *lupeomai*, which may be used of inward grief (Syn. §xlv); though in Classical Greek *pentheō* was used of grief without violent manifestations (Grimm-Thayer).

(2) Among the well-to-do it was common to hire professional mourners (men and women), who accompanied the dead body to the grave with formal music and the singing of dirges. At the death of Jairus' daughter male flute-players were present, Matt. 9:23 (see, however, Jer. 9:17).

B. Nouns.

1. *odurmos* [ὀδυρμός, 3602], lamentation, mourning, is translated "mourning" in Matt. 2:18 and 2 Cor. 7:7: see BEWAIL, *Note* (2). ¶

NT: B.555b; CB.1260b; K.673.
OT: tamᵉrûr: S.8563; HR.967c.1; H.1248h; BD.601b.
GEN. REF.: —; NB.170; Z.4:302.

2. *penthos* [πένθος, 3997], akin to A, No. 2, mourning, is used in Jas. 4:9; Rev. 18:7 (twice), R.V., "mourning" (A.V., "sorrow"); ver. 8, "mourning"; 21:4, R.V., "mourning" (A.V., "sorrow"). See SORROW. ¶

NT: B.642d; CB.1263a; K.825.
OT: 'ēbel: S.60; HR.1118a.1a; H.6a; BD.5c.
GEN. REF.: IS.—; NB.170; Z.4:302.

MOUTH

A. Noun.

stoma [στόμα, 4750], akin to *stomachos* (which originally meant a throat, gullet), is used (*a*) of the mouth of man, e.g., Matt. 15:11; of animals, e.g., Matt. 17:27; 2 Tim. 4:17 (figurative); Heb. 11:33; Jas. 3:3; Rev. 13:2 (2nd occurrence); (*b*) figuratively, of inanimate things, of the "edge" of a sword, Luke 21:24; Heb. 11:34; of the earth, Rev. 12:16; (*c*) figuratively, of the mouth, as the organ of speech, (1) of Christ's words, e.g., Matt. 13:35; Luke 11:54; Acts 8:32; 22:14; 1 Pet. 2:22; (2) of human, e.g., Matt. 18:16; 21:16; Luke 1:64; Rev. 14:5; as emanating from the heart, Matt. 12:34; Rom. 10:8, 9; of prophetic ministry through the Holy Spirit, Luke 1:70; Acts 1:16; 3:18; 4:25; of the destructive policy of two world potentates at the end of this age, Rev. 13:2, 5, 6; 16:13 (twice); of shameful speaking, Eph. 4:29 and Col. 3:8; (3) of the Devil speaking as a dragon or serpent, Rev. 12:15, 16; 16:13; (*d*) figuratively, in the phrase "face to face" (lit., 'mouth to mouth'), 2 John 12; 3 John

14; (*e*) metaphorically, of the utterances of the Lord, in judgment, 2 Thess. 2:8; Rev. 1:16; 2:16; 19:15, 21; of His judgment upon a local church for its lukewarmness, Rev. 3:16; (*f*) by metonymy, for speech, Matt. 18:16; Luke 19:22; 21:15; 2 Cor. 13:1.

NT: B.69c; CB.1270a; K.1089.
OT: peh: S.6310; HR.1292b.1; H.1738; BD.804d.
GEN. REF.: IS.3:428; NB.851; Z.4:307.

Note: In Acts 15:27, *logos*, a word, is translated "word of mouth," R.V. (A.V., "mouth," marg., "word").

B. Verb.

epistomizō [ἐπιστομίζω, 1993], to bridle (*epi*, upon, and A), is used metaphorically of stopping the mouth, putting to silence, Tit. 1:11. ¶ Cp. *phrassō*, to stop, close, said of stopping the mouths of men, in Rom. 3:19. See STOP.

NT: B.301a; CB.—; K.—.
OT: —.
GEN. REF.: —.

MOVE, MOVED, MOVER, MOVING, UNMOVEABLE

A. Verbs.

1. *kineō* [κινέω, 2795], to set in motion, move (hence, e.g., Eng. kinematics, kinetics, cinema), is used (*a*) of wagging the head, Matt. 27:39; Mark 15:29; (*b*) of the general activity of the human being, Acts 17:28; (*c*) of the moving of mountains, Rev. 6:14, in the sense of removing, as in Rev. 2:5, of removing a lampstand (there figuratively of causing a local church to be discontinued); (*d*) figuratively, of exciting, stirring up feelings and passions, Acts 21:30 (Passive Voice); 24:5, "a mover"; (*e*) of moving burdens, Matt. 23:4. See REMOVE, WAG. ¶ Cp. *sunkineō*, to stir up, Acts 6:12. ¶

NT: B.432c; CB.—; K.435.
OT: nûa': S.5128; HR.765b.7; H.1328; BD.631a.
GEN. REF.: —.

2. *metakineō* [μετακινέω, 3334], in the Active Voice, to move something away (not in the N.T.; in the sept., e.g., Deut. 19:14; Is. 54:10); in the Middle Voice, to remove oneself, shift, translated in the Passive in Col. 1:23, "be . . . not moved away (from the hope of the gospel)." ¶

NT: B.511b; CB.—; K.435.
OT: mûṭ: S.4131; HR.916a.1; H.1158; BD.556c.
nûs: S.5127; HR.916a.3; H.1327; BD.630c.
nûa': S.5128; HR.916a.4; H.1328; BD.631a.
GEN. REF.: —.

3. *seiō* [σείω, 4579], to shake, move to and fro, usually of violent concussion (Eng., seismic, seismograph, seismology), is said (*a*) of the earth as destined to be shaken by God, Heb. 12:26; (*b*) of a local convulsion of the earth, at the Death of Christ, Matt. 27:51, "did quake"; (*c*) of a fig tree, Rev. 6:13; (*d*) metaphorically, to stir up with fear or some other emotion, Matt. 21:10, of the people of a city; 28:4, of the keepers or watchers, at the Lord's tomb, R.V., "did quake" (A.V., "did shake"). ¶

NT: B.746c; CB.1268c; K.1014.
OT: rā'ash: S.7493; HR.1261c.5; H.2195; BD.950a.
GEN. REF.: —.

4. *saleuō* [σαλεύω, 4531], to shake, properly of the action of a stormy wind, then, to render insecure, stir up, is rendered "I should (not) be moved" in Acts 2:25, in the sense of being cast down or shaken from a sense of security and happiness, said of Christ, in a quotation from Psa. 16:8. See SHAKE, STIR (up).

NT: B.740c; CB.1268b; K.996.
OT: mûṭ: S.4131; HR.1257c.9; H.1158; BD.556c.
nûa': S.5128; HR.1257c.14; H.1328; BD.631a.
GEN. REF.: —.

5. *sainō* [σαίνω, 4525], properly, of dogs, to wag the tail, fawn; hence, metaphorically of persons, to disturb, disquiet, 1 Thess. 3:3, Passive Voice, "(that no man) be moved (by these afflictions)." Some have suggested the primary meaning, to be wheedled, befooled, by pleasing utterances; but Greek interpreters regard it as synonymous with No. 3, or with *tarassō*, to disturb, and this is confirmed by the contrast with "establish" in ver. 2, and "stand fast" in ver. 8. A variant reading gives the verb *siainesthai*, to be disheartened, unnerved. ¶

NT: B.740a; CB.—; K.994.
OT: —.
GEN. REF.: —.

6. *pherō* [φέρω, 5342], to bear, carry, is rendered "being moved" in 2 Pet. 1:21, signifying that they were 'borne along,' or impelled, by the Holy Spirit's power, not acting according to their own wills, or simply expressing their own thoughts, but expressing the mind of God in words provided and ministered by Him.

NT: B.854d; CB.1264a; K.1252.
OT: bô': S.935; HR.1426c.3b; H.212; BD.97c.
nāśā': S.5375; HR.1426c.17; H.1421; BD.669d.
GEN. REF.: —.

Notes: (1) In Mark 15:11, A.V., *anaseiō*, to shake to and fro, stir up, is translated "moved" (R.V., "stirred up," as in Luke 23:5, A.V. and R.V.). ¶

(2) In Acts 20:24 some mss. have a phrase translated "none of these things move me." The text for which there is most support gives the rendering "but I hold not my life of any account, as dear unto myself." Field suggests a reading, the translation of which is, 'neither make I account of anything, nor think my life dear unto myself.'

(3) In 1 Cor. 15:34, for the more literal A.V., "I speak this to your shame," the R.V. has "I speak this to move you to shame."

(4) For "moved with godly fear" see FEAR, D, No. 2.

(5) See also COMPASSION, ENVY, FEAR, INDIGNATION.

B. Adjectives.

1. *asaleutos* [ἀσάλευτος, 761], unmoved, immoveable (from *a*, negative, and A, No. 4), is translated "unmoveable" in Acts 27:41; "which cannot be moved" in Heb. 12:28, A.V. (R.V., "that cannot be shaken"). ¶ In the Sept., Ex. 13:16; Deut. 6:8; 11:18. ¶

NT: B.114b; CB.1237c; K.—.
OT: ṭôṭāphôt: S.2903; HR.169c.1; H.804a; BD.377d.
GEN. REF.: —.

2. *ametakinētos* [ἀμετακίνητος, 277], firm, immoveable (*a*, negative, and A, No. 2), is used in 1 Cor. 15:58. ¶

NT: B.45c; CB.—; K.—.
OT: —.
GEN. REF.: —.

C. Noun.

kinēsis [κίνησις, 2796], a moving (akin to A, No. 1), is found in John 5:3 (in many ancient authorities, R.V., marg.), of the moving of the water at the pool of Bethesda. ¶

NT: B.432d; CB.—; K.—.
OT: —.
GEN. REF.: —.

MOW

amaō [ἀμάω, 270], to mow, is translated "mowed" in Jas. 5:4, R.V. (A.V., "have reaped down"). "The cognate words seem to shew that the sense of cutting or mowing was original, and that of gathering-in secondary" (Liddell and Scott, Lex.). ¶

NT: B.44c; CB.—; K.—.
OT: qāṣar: S.7114; HR.60c.1; H.2061,2062; BD.894b.
GEN. REF.: IS.3:429; NB.—; Z.—.

MUCH

1. *polus* [πολύς, 4183], is used (*a*) as an adjective of degree, e.g., Matt. 13:5, "much (earth)"; Acts 26:24, "much (learning)"; in ver. 29, in the answer to Agrippa's "with but little persuasion," some texts have *pollǭ* (some *megalǭ*, 'with great'), R.V., "(whether with little or) with much"; of number, e.g., Mark 5:24, R.V., "a great (multitude)," A.V., "much (people)"; so Luke 7:11; John 12:12; Rev. 19:1, etc.; (*b*) in the neuter singular form (*polu*), as a noun, e.g., Luke 16:10 (twice); in the plural (*polla*), e.g., Rom. 16:6, 12, "(laboured) much," lit., 'many things'; (*c*) adverbially, in the neuter singular, e.g., Acts 18:27; James 5:16; Matt. 26:9 (a genitive of price); in the plural, e.g., Mark 5:43, R.V., "much" (A.V., "straitly"); Mark 9:26, R.V., "much" (A.V., "sore"); John 14:30; and with the article, Acts 26:24; Rom. 15:22; 1 Cor. 16:19; Rev. 5:4. See GREAT.

NT: B.687c; CB.1266a; K.—.
OT: rab: S.7227; HR.1181b.9a; H.2099a,b; BD.912d.
rôb: S.7230; HR.1181b.9b; H.2099c; BD.913d.
rābab: S.7231; HR.1181b.9c; H.2099; BD.912c.
GEN. REF.: —.

2. *hikanos* [ἱκανός, 2425], enough, much, many, is translated "much," e.g., in Luke 7:12 (in some mss. Acts 5:37; see the R.V.); Acts 11:24, 26; 19:26; 27:9. See ABLE, ENOUGH, A, No. 2, GREAT, LARGE, MANY, MEET, SECURITY, SORE, SUFFICIENT, WORTHY.

NT: B.374b; CB.1250c; K.361.
OT: day: S.1767; HR.683c.2; H.425; BD.191b.
shadday: S.7706; HR.683c.9; H.2333; BD.994d.
GEN. REF.: —.

Notes: (1) For "much more," "so much the more," see MORE.

(2) In John 12:9, the R.V. has "the common people" for "much people."

(3) In Acts 27:16, A.V., *ischuō*, to be able, with *molis*, scarcely, is translated "had much work" (R.V., "were able, with difficulty").

(4) In Luke 19:15, A.V., the pronoun *ti*, "what" (R.V.), is translated "how much."

(5) The adjective *tosoutos*, so great, so much, is translated "so much (bread)," in Matt. 15:33, plural, R.V., "so many (loaves)"; in the genitive case, of price, in Acts 5:8, "for so much"; in the dative case, of degree, in Heb. 1:4, R.V., "by so much" (A.V., "so much"); so in Heb. 10:25; in Heb. 7:22 "by so much" translates the phrase *kata tosouto*; in Rev. 18:7, "so much."

(6) See DISPLEASED, EXHORTATION, PERPLEX, SPEAKING, WORK.

MUCH (AS)

Notes: (1) In Luke 6:34 the phrase *ta isa*, lit., 'the equivalent (things),' is translated "as much" (of lending, to receive back the equivalent).

(2) In Rom. 1:15, the phrase *to kat' eme*, lit., 'the (thing) according to me,' signifies "as much as in me is"; cp. the A.V. marg. in 1 Pet. 5:2 [lit., 'the (extent) in, or among, you'; the text takes the word 'flock' as understood, the marg. regards the phrase as adverbially idiomatic]; in Rom. 12:18 "as much as in you lieth" translates a similar phrase, lit., 'the (extent) out of you.'

(3) In Heb. 12:20, A.V., *kai ean* (contracted to *k'an*), "if even" (R.V.), is translated "and if so much as."

(4) The negatives *oude* and *mēde*, "not even" (R.V.) are translated "not so much as" in the A.V. in Mark 2:2; Luke 6:3 and 1 Cor. 5:1; in

the following the R.V. and A.V. translate them "not so much as;" Mark 3:20 (some mss. have *mēte*, with the same meaning); Acts 19:2; in Mark 6:31 "no (leisure) so much as."

(5) In Rom. 3:12, *heōs*, as far as, even unto, is translated "so much as" in the R.V.; the A.V. supplies nothing actually corresponding to it.

(6) In John 6:11 *hosos* denotes "as much as."

MULTIPLY

1. *plēthunō* [πληθύνω, 4129], used (*a*) transitively, denotes to cause to increase, to multiply, 2 Cor. 9:10; Heb. 6:14 (twice); in the Passive Voice, to be multiplied, Matt. 24:12, R.V., "(iniquity) shall be multiplied" (A.V., "shall abound"); Acts 6:7; 7:17; 9:31; 12:24; 1 Pet. 1:2; 2 Pet. 1:2; Jude 2; (*b*) intransitively it denotes to be multiplying, Acts 6:1, R.V., "was multiplying" (A.V., "was multiplied"). See ABUNDANCE, B, No. 5. ¶

NT: B.669a; CB.1265b; K.866.
OT: rābāh: S.7235; HR.1141b.10a-c; H.2103,2104; BD.915a.
GEN. REF.: –.

2. *pleonazō* [πλεονάζω, 4121], used intransitively, to abound, is translated "being multiplied" in the R.V. of 2 Cor. 4:15 (A.V., "abundant"); the Active Voice, aorist tense, here would be more accurately rendered 'having superabounded' or 'superabounding' or 'multiplying.' See ABUNDANCE, B, No. 3.

NT: B.667b; CB.1265b; K.864.
OT: 'ādaph: S.5736; HR.1141c.3; H.1568; BD.727a.
rābāh: S.7235; HR.1141c.4a,b; H.2103,2104; BD.915a.
GEN. REF.: –.

MULTITUDE

1. *ochlos* [ὄχλος, 3793], is used frequently in the four Gospels and the Acts; elsewhere only in Rev. 7:9; 17:15; 19:1, 6; it denotes (*a*) a crowd or multitude of persons, a throng, e.g., Matt. 14:14, 15; 15:33; often in the plural, e.g., Matt. 4:25; 5:1; with *polus*, much or great, it signifies "a great multitude," e.g., Matt. 20:29, or "the common people," Mark 12:37, perhaps preferably 'the mass of the people.' Field supports the meaning in the text, but either rendering is suitable. The mass of the people was attracted to Him (for the statement "heard Him gladly" cp. what is said in Mark 6:20 of Herod Antipas concerning John the Baptist); in John 12:9, "the common people," R.V., stands in contrast with their leaders (ver. 10); Acts 24:12, R.V., "crowd"; (*b*) the populace, an unorganised multitude, in contrast to *dēmos*, the people as a body politic, e.g., Matt. 14:5; 21:26; John 7:12 (2nd part); (*c*) in a more general sense, a multitude or company, e.g., Luke 6:17, R.V., "a (great) multitude (of His disciples)," A.V., "the company"; Acts 1:15, "a multitude (of persons)," R.V., A.V., "the number (of names)"; Acts 24:18, R.V., "crowd" (A.V., "multitude"). See COMPANY, No. 1, NUMBER.

NT: B.600c; CB.1260b; K.750.
OT: hāmôn: S.1995; HR.1043a.1; H.505a; BD.242b.
qāhāl: S.6951; HR.1043a.5; H.1991a; BD.874c.
GEN. REF.: IS.3:431; NB.–; Z.–.

2. *plēthos* [πλῆθος, 4128], lit., a fulness, hence, a large company, a multitude, is used (*a*) of things: of fish, Luke 5:6; John 21:6; of sticks ("bundle"), Acts 28:3; of stars and of sand, Heb. 11:12; of sins, Jas. 5:20; 1 Pet. 4:8; (*b*) of persons, (1) a multitude: of people, e.g., Mark 3:7, 8; Luke 6:17; John 5:3; Acts 14:1; of angels, Luke 2:13; (2) with the article, the whole number, the multitude, the populace, e.g., Luke 1:10; 8:37; Acts 5:16; 19:9; 23:7; a particular company, e.g., of disciples, Luke 19:37; Acts 4:32; 6:2, 5; 15:30; of elders, priests, and scribes, 23:7; of the Apostles and the elders of the church in Jerusalem, Acts 15:12. See ASSEMBLY, No. 3, BUNDLE, No. 2, COMPANY, No. 5.

NT: B.668b; CB.1265b; K.866.
OT: rôb: S.7230; HR.1142c.11a; H.2099c; BD.913d.
hāmôn: S.1995; HR.1142c.3; H.505a; BD.242b.
GEN. REF.: IS.3:431; NB.–; Z.–.

Note: In Luke 12:1, A.V., the phrase, lit., 'the myriads of the multitude' is translated "an innumerable multitude of people" (where "people" translates No. 1, above), R.V., "the many thousands of the multitude" (where "multitude" translates No. 1).

MURDER

phonos [φόνος, 5408], is used (*a*) of a special act, Mark 15:7; Luke 23:19, 25; (*b*) in the plural, of murders in general, Matt. 15:19; Mark 7:21 (Gal. 5:21, in some inferior mss.); Rev. 9:21; in the singular, Rom. 1:29; (*c*) in the sense of slaughter, Heb. 11:37, "they were slain with the sword," lit., '(they died by) slaughter (of the sword)'; in Acts 9:1, "slaughter." See SLAUGHTER. ¶

NT: B.864d; CB.1264b; K.–.
OT: dām: S.1818; HR.1437c.1; H.436; BD.196b.
ḥereb: S.2719; HR.1437c.2; H.732a; BD.352b.
peger: S.6297; HR.1437c.3; H.1732a; BD.803d.
GEN. REF.: IS.3:434; NB.275; Z.1:1032.

Note: In Matt. 19:18, A.V., *phoneuō*, to kill (akin to *phoneus*, see below), is translated "thou shalt do (no) murder" (R.V., "thou shalt (not) kill"). See K, ILL, SLAY.

MURDERER

1. *phoneus* [φονεύς, 5406], akin to *phoneuō* and *phonos* (see above), is used (*a*) in a general sense, in the singular, 1 Pet. 4:15; in the plural,

Rev. 21:8; 22:15; (*b*) of those guilty of particular acts, Matt. 22:7; Acts 3:14, lit. 'a man (*anēr*), a murderer'; 7:52; 28:4. ¶
NT: B.864c; CB.–; K.–.
OT: –.
GEN. REF.: IS.3:434; NB.275; Z.1:1032.

2. *anthropoktonos* [ἀνθρωποκτόνος, 443], an adjective, lit., 'manslaying,' used as a noun, a manslayer, murderer (*anthrōpos*, a man, *kteinō*, to slay), is used of Satan, John 8:44; of one who hates his brother, and who, being a murderer, has not eternal life, 1 John 3:15 (twice). ¶
NT: B.68a; CB.–; K.–.
OT: –.
GEN. REF.: IS.3:434; NB.275; Z.1:1032.

3. *patroloas* (or *patral—*) [πατρολῴας, 3964], a murderer of one's father, occurs in 1 Tim. 1:9. ¶
NT: B.637a; CB.–; K.–.
OT: –.
GEN. REF.: IS.3:434; NB.275; Z.–.

Note: For *sikarios*, in the plural, "murderers," in Acts 21:38, see ASSASSIN. ¶ See MOTHER, No. 2.

MURMUR, MURMURING

A. Verbs.

1. *gonguzō* [γογγύζω, 1111], to mutter, murmur, grumble, say anything in a low tone (Eng., gong), an onomatopoeic word, representing the significance by the sound of the word, as in the word "murmur" itself, is used of the labourers in the parable of the householder, Matt. 20:11; of the scribes and Pharisees, against Christ, Luke 5:30; of the Jews, John 6:41, 43; of the disciples, 6:61; of the people, 7:32 (of debating secretly); of the Israelites, 1 Cor. 10:10 (twice), where it is also used in a warning to believers. ¶ In the papyri it is used of the murmuring of a gang of workmen; also in a remark interposed, while the Emperor (late 2nd cent. A.D.) was interviewing a rebel, that the Romans were then murmuring (Moulton and Milligan, Vocab.).
NT: B.164b; CB.–; K.125.
OT: lûn: S.3885; HR.274a.3b,c; H.1096; BD.534a.
GEN. REF.: IS.3:435; NB.–; Z.–.

2. *diagonguzō* [διαγογγύζω, 1234], lit., to murmur through (*dia*, i.e., through a whole crowd, or among themselves), is always used of indignant complaining, Luke 15:2; 19:7. ¶
NT: B.182c; CB.–; K.125.
OT: lûn: S.3885; HR.299c.1; H.1096; BD.534a.
GEN. REF.: IS.3:435; NB.–; Z.–.

3. *embrimaomai* [ἐμβριμάομαι, 1690], is rendered "murmured against" in Mark 14:5; it expresses indignant displeasure: see CHARGE, C, No. 4.
NT: B.254d; CB.1244b; K.–.
OT: –.
GEN. REF.: –.

Note: For *stenazō*, Jas. 5:9, R.V., "murmur," see GRIEVE, No. 3.

B. Noun.

gongusmos [γογγυσμός, 1112], a murmuring, muttering (akin to A, No. 1), is used (*a*) in the sense of secret debate among people, John 7:12 (as with the verb in ver. 32); (*b*) of displeasure or complaining (more privately than in public), said of Grecian Jewish converts against Hebrews, Acts 6:1; in general admonitions, Phil. 2:14; 1 Pet. 4:9, R.V., "murmuring" (A.V., "grudging"). ¶
NT: B.164c; CB.–; K.125.
OT: t^{e}lunnāh: S.8519; HR.274b.2; H.1097a; BD.534b.
GEN. REF.: IS.3:435; NB.–; Z.–.

MURMURER

gongustēs [γογγυστής, 1113], a murmurer (akin to A, No. 1, and B, above), one who complains, is used in Jude 16, especially perhaps of utterances against God (see ver. 15). ¶
NT: B.164c; CB.–; K.125.
OT: –.
GEN. REF.: IS.3:435; NB.–; Z.–.

For MUSING (*dialogizomai*, in Luke 3:15, A.V.) see REASON (Verb)

MUSIC

sumphōnia [συμφωνία, 4858], lit., a sounding together (Eng., symphony), occurs in Luke 15:25. ¶ In the Sept., Dan. 3:5, 7, 10, 15, for Aramaic *sumpônyâ* (not in ver. 7), itself a loan word from the Greek; translated "dulcimer" (R.V., marg., "bagpipe") ¶
NT: B.781a; CB.1270b; K.1287.
OT: sûmpōnyāh (Aramaic): S.5481; HR.1306c.1a; H.2887; BD.1104a.
GEN. REF.: IS.3:436; NB.852; Z.4:311.

For MUSICIAN, Rev. 18:22, A.V., see MINSTREL

MUST

1. *dei* [δεῖ, 1163], an impersonal verb, signifying 'it is necessary' or 'one must,' 'one ought,' is found most frequently in the Gospels, Acts and the Apocalypse, and is used (*a*) of a necessity lying in the nature of the case, e.g., John 3:30; 2 Tim. 2:6; (*b*) of necessity brought about by circumstances, e.g., Matt. 26:35, R.V., "must," A.V., "should"; John 4:4; Acts 27:21; "should"; 2 Cor. 11:30; in the case of Christ, by reason of the Father's will, e.g., Luke 2:49; 19:5; (*c*) of necessity as to what is required that something may be brought about, e.g., Luke 12:12, "ought"; John 3:7; Acts 9:6; 1 Cor. 11:19;

Heb. 9:26; (*d*) of a necessity of law, duty, equity, e.g., Matt. 18:33, "shouldest"; 23:23, "ought"; Luke 15:32, "it was meet"; Acts 15:5, "it is needful" (R.V.); Rom. 1:27, R.V., "was due;" A.V., "was meet" (of a recompense due by the law of God); frequently requiring the rendering "ought;" e.g., Rom. 8:26; 12:3; 1 Cor. 8:2; (*e*) of necessity arising from the determinate will and counsel of God, e.g., Matt. 17:10; 24:6; 26:54; 1 Cor. 15:53, especially regarding the salvation of men through the Death, Resurrection and Ascension of Christ, e.g., John 3:14; Acts 3:21; 4:12. See BEHOVE, No. 2 (where see the differences in the meanings of synonymous words), MEET, NEED, NEEDFUL, OUGHT, SHOULD.

NT: B.172a; CB.1240b; K.140.
OT: –.
GEN. REF.: –.

2. *opheilō* [ὀφείλω, 3784], to owe, is rendered "must . . . needs" in 1 Cor. 5:10. See BEHOVE, No. 1.

NT: B.598d; CB.1261a; K.746.
OT: –.
GEN. REF.: –.

Notes: (1) In Mark 14:49, A.V., the conjunction *hina* with the subjunctive mood, in order that, is represented by "must" (R.V., "that . . . might").

(2) In Heb. 13:17, A.V., the future participle of *apodidōmi*, to give, is translated "they that must give" (R.V., "they that shall give").

(3) In 2 Pet. 1:14, A.V., the verb to be, with *apothesis*, a putting off, is translated "I must put off;" R.V., "(the) putting off . . . cometh;" lit., 'is (swift).'

(4) Sometimes the infinitive mood of a verb, with or without the article, is necessarily rendered by a phrase involving the word "must;" e.g., 1 Pet. 4:17, A.V., "must (begin)"; or "should;" Heb. 4:6, R.V., "should" (A.V. "must").

(5) Sometimes the subjunctive mood of a verb, used as a deliberative, is rendered "must;" etc., John 6:28, "(what) must (we do);" R.V. (A.V., "shall").

MUSTARD

sinapi [σίναπι, 4615], a word of Egyptian origin, is translated "mustard seed" in the N.T. "The conditions to be fulfilled by the mustard are that it should be a familiar plant, with a very small seed, Matt. 17:20; Luke 17:6, sown in the earth, growing larger than garden herbs, Matt. 13:31, having large branches, Mark 4:31, . . . attractive to birds, Luke 13:19 [R.V., '(became) a tree']. The cultivated mustard is *sinapis nigra*. The seed is well known for its minuteness. The mustards are annuals, reproduced with extraordinary rapidity . . . In fat soil they often attain a height of 10 or 12 feet, and have branches which attract passing birds" (A. E. Post, in Hastings' Bib. Dic.). ¶

The correct R.V. translation in Matt. 13:32, "greater than the herbs;" for the A.V., "greatest among herbs" (the mustard is not a herb), should be noted.

As the parable indicates, Christendom presents a sort of Christianity that has become conformed to the principles and ways of the world, and the world has favoured this debased Christianity. Contrast the testimony of the N.T., e.g., in John 17:14; Gal. 6:14; 1 Pet. 2:11; 1 John 3:1.

NT: B.751c; CB.1269a; K.1027.
OT: –.
GEN. REF.: IS.3:449; NB.1006; Z.4:324.

MUTUAL

Note: This is the A.V. rendering of the phrase *en allēlois* in Rom. 1:12, translated in the R.V., "each of us by the other's (faith)." See OTHER, No. 5.

MUZZLE

phimoō [φιμόω, 5392], to close the mouth with a muzzle (*phimos*), is used (*a*) of muzzling the ox when it treads out the corn, 1 Cor. 9:9, A.V., "muzzle the mouth of;" R.V., "muzzle;" and 1 Tim. 5:18, with the lesson that those upon whom spiritual labour is bestowed should not refrain from ministering to the material needs of those who labour on their behalf; (*b*) metaphorically, of putting to silence, or subduing to stillness, Matt. 22:12, 34; Mark 1:25; 4:39; Luke 4:35; 1 Pet. 2:15. See PEACE (hold), SILENCE. ¶

NT: B.861d; CB.–; K.–.
OT: ḥāsam: S.2629; HR.1432c.1; H.702; BD.340c.
GEN. REF.: IS.3:450; NB.–; Z.4:325.

MY (MINE)

emos [ἐμός, 1699], a possessive adjective of the first person, often used as a possessive pronoun with greater emphasis than the oblique forms of *egō* (see below), a measure of stress which should always be observed; it denotes (I) subjectively, (*a*) what I possess, e.g., John 4:34; 7:16 (1st part); 13:35; 1 Cor. 16:21; Gal. 6:11; Col. 4:18 (1st clause); as a pronoun, absolutely (i.e., not as an adjective), e.g., Matt. 20:15; 25:27; Luke 15:31, R.V., "(all that is) mine;" A.V., "(all that) I have"; John 16:14, 15;

17:10; (*b*) 'proceeding from me,' e.g., Mark 8:38; John 7:16 (2nd part); 8:37 (here the repetition of the article with the pronoun, after the article with the noun, lends special stress to the pronoun; more lit., 'the word, that which is mine'); so in John 15:12. Such instances are to be distinguished from the less emphatic order where the pronoun comes between the article and the noun, as in John 7:16, already mentioned; (*c*) in the phrase 'it is mine' (i.e., 'it rests with me'), e.g., Matt. 20:23; Mark 10:40; (II) objectively, pertaining or relating to me: (*a*) 'appointed for me,' e.g., John 7:6, "My time" (with the repeated article and special stress just referred to); (*b*) equivalent to an objective genitive ('of me') e.g., Luke 22:19, "(in remembrance) of Me" (lit., 'in My remembrance'); so 1 Cor. 11:24.

NT: B.255c; CB.1244b; K.—.
OT: —.
GEN. REF.: —.

Notes: (1) This pronoun frequently translates oblique forms of the first personal pronoun *egō*, I, e.g., of me, to me. These instances are usually unemphatic, always less so than those under *emos* (above).

(2) For "my affairs" and "my state" see AFFAIR, *Notes.*

(3) In Matt. 26:12, "for My burial" translates a phrase consisting of the preposition *pros* (towards) governing the article with the infinitive mood, aorist tense, of *entaphiazō*, to bury, followed by the personal pronoun "Me," as the object, where the infinitive is virtually a noun, lit., 'towards the burying (of) Me.'

(4) In 1 Tim. 1:11, "was committed to my trust" is, lit., '(with) which I was entrusted' (*pisteuō*, to entrust).

MYRRH

A. Noun.

smurna [σμύρνα, 4666], whence the name Smyrna, a word of Semitic origin, Heb., *mōr*, from a root meaning bitter, is a gum resin from a shrubby tree, which grows in Yemen and neighbouring regions of Africa; the fruit is smooth and somewhat larger than a pea. The colour of myrrh varies from pale reddish-yellow to reddish-brown or red. The taste is bitter, and the substance astringent, acting as an antiseptic and a stimulant. It was used as a perfume, Ps. 45:8, where the language is symbolic of the graces of the Messiah; Prov. 7:17; S. of Sol. 1:13; 5:5; it was one of the ingredients of the "holy anointing oil" for the priests, Ex. 30:23 (R.V., "flowing myrrh"); it was used also for the purification of women, Esth. 2:12; for embalming, John 19:39; as an anodyne (see B); it was one of the gifts of the Magi, Matt. 2:11. ¶

NT: B.758d; CB.1269b; K.1055.
OT: môr: S.4753; HR.1278b.1; H.1248b; BD.600d.
GEN. REF.: IS.3:450; NB.856; Z.4:326.

B. Verb.

smurnizō [σμυρνίζω, 4669], is used transitively in the N.T., with the meaning to mingle or drug with myrrh, Mark 15:23; the mixture was doubtless offered to deaden the pain (Matthew's word "gall" suggests that myrrh was not the only ingredient). Christ refused to partake of any such means of alleviation; He would retain all His mental power for the complete fulfilment of the Father's will. ¶

NT: B.759a; CB.1269b; K.1055.
OT: —.
GEN. REF.: IS.3:450; NB.856; Z.4:326.

MYSELF

1. *emautou* [ἐμαυτοῦ, 1683], a reflexive pronoun, of the first person, lit., of myself, is used (*a*) frequently after various prepositions, e.g., *hupo*, under, Matt. 8:9; Luke 7:8; R.V., "under myself"; *peri*, concerning, John 5:31; 8:14, 18; Acts 24:10; *apo*, from, John 5:30; 7:17, R.V., "from" (A.V., "of," which is ambiguous); so ver. 28; 8:28, 42; 10:18; 14:10 (R.V., "from"); *pros*, unto, John 12:32, R.V., "unto Myself"; 14:3; Philm. 13, "with me"; *eis*, to, 1 Cor. 4:6; *huper*, on behalf of, 2 Cor. 12:5; *ek* (*ex*), out of, or from, John 12:49, R.V., "from Myself"; (*b*) as the direct object of a verb, Luke 7:7; John 8:54; 14:21; 17:19; Acts 26:2; 1 Cor. 4:3; 9:19; 2 Cor. 11:7, 9; Gal. 2:18; Phil. 3:13; (*c*) in other oblique cases of the pronoun, without a preposition, e.g., Acts 20:24, "unto" (or to); 26:9, "with" (or 'to'); Rom. 11:4, R.V., "for" (A.V., "to"); 1 Cor. 4:4, R.V., "against myself" (A.V., inaccurately, "by"); in all these instances the pronoun is in the dative case; in 1 Cor. 10:33, "mine own" (the genitive case); in 1 Cor. 7:7, "I myself" (the accusative case). ¶

NT: B.253d; CB.—; K.—.
OT: —.
GEN. REF.: —.

2. *autos* [αὐτός, 846], self (*a*) with *egō*, I, "I myself," Luke 24:39; Acts 10:26; Rom. 7:25; 9:3; 2 Cor. 10:1; 12:13; (*b*) without the personal pronoun, Acts 24:16 (as the subject of a verb); in the nominative case, Acts 25:22; 1 Cor. 9:27; Phil. 2:24; in the genitive case, Rom. 16:2, R.V., "of mine own self."

NT: B.122c; CB.1238b; K.—.
OT: —.
GEN. REF.: —.

MYSTERY

mustērion [μυστήριον, 3466], primarily that which is known to the *mustēs*, the initiated (from *mueō*, to initiate into the mysteries; cp. Phil. 4:12, *mueomai*, "I have learned the secret," R.V.). In the N.T. it denotes, not the mysterious (as with the Eng. word), but that which, being outside the range of unassisted natural apprehension, can be made known only by Divine revelation, and is made known in a manner and at a time appointed by God, and to those only who are illumined by His Spirit. In the ordinary sense a mystery implies knowledge withheld; its Scriptural significance is truth revealed. Hence the terms especially associated with the subject are "made known," "manifested," "revealed," "preached," "understand," "dispensation." The definition given above may be best illustrated by the following passage: "the mystery which hath been hid from all ages and generations: but now hath it been manifested to His saints" (Col. 1:26, R.V.). It is used of:

"(*a*) spiritual truth generally, as revealed in the gospel, 1 Cor. 13:2; 14:2 [cp. 1 Tim. 3:9]. Among the ancient Greeks 'the mysteries' were religious rites and ceremonies practised by secret societies into which anyone who so desired might be received. Those who were initiated into these 'mysteries' became possessors of certain knowledge, which was not imparted to the uninitiated, and were called 'the perfected,' cp. 1 Cor. 2:6-16 where the Apostle has these 'mysteries' in mind and presents the gospel in contrast thereto; here 'the perfected' are, of course, the believers, who alone can perceive the things revealed;

(*b*) Christ, who is God Himself revealed under the conditions of human life, Col. 2:2; 4:3, and submitting even to death, 1 Cor. 2:1 [in some mss., for *marturion*, testimony], 7, but raised from among the dead, 1 Tim. 3:16, that the will of God to co-ordinate the universe in Him, and subject it to Him, might in due time be accomplished, Eph. 1:9 (cp. Rev. 10:7), as is declared in the gospel, Rom. 16:25; Eph. 6:19;

(*c*) the Church, which is Christ's Body, i.e., the union of redeemed men with God in Christ, Eph. 5:32 [cp. Col. 1:27];

(*d*) the rapture into the presence of Christ of those members of the Church which is His Body who shall be alive on the earth at His Parousia, 1 Cor. 15:51;

(*e*) the operation of those hidden forces that either retard or accelerate the Kingdom of Heaven (i.e., of God), Matt. 13:11; Mark 4:11;

(*f*) the cause of the present condition of Israel, Rom. 11:25;

(*g*) the spirit of disobedience to God, 2 Thess. 2:7; Rev. 17:5, 7; cp. Eph. 2:2."*

To these may be added (*h*) the seven local churches, and their angels, seen in symbolism, Rev. 1:20;

(*i*) the ways of God in grace, Eph. 3:9. The word is used in a comprehensive way in 1 Cor. 4:1.†

NT: B.530a; CB.1259b; K.615.
OT: rāz (Aramaic): S.7328; HR.937c.1; H.2993; BD.1112d.
GEN. REF.: IS.3:451; NB.856; Z.4:327.

* From Notes on Thessalonians by Hogg and Vine, pp. 256, 257.

† See The Twelve Mysteries of Scripture by Vine.

N

NAIL (Noun and Verb)

A. Noun.

hēlos [ἧλος, 2247], occurs in the remarks of Thomas regarding the print of the nails used in Christ's crucifixion, John 20:25. ¶

NT: B.345d; CB.—; K.—.
OT: masmēr: S.4548; HR.607b.2; H.1518b; BD.702c.
GEN. REF.: IS.3:479; NB.861; Z.4:358.

B. Verb.

prosēloō [προσηλόω, 4338], to nail to (*pros*, to, and a verbal form of A), is used in Col. 2:14, in which the figure of a bond (ordinances of the Law) is first described as cancelled, and then removed; the idea in the verb itself is not that of the cancellation, to which the taking out of the way was subsequent, but of nailing up the removed thing in triumph to the Cross. The Death of Christ not only rendered the Law useless as a means of salvation, but gave public demonstration that it was so. ¶

NT: B.714d; CB.—; K.—.
OT: —.
GEN. REF.: IS.3:479; NB.—; Z.—.

NAKED (Adjective and Verb), NAKEDNESS

A. Adjective.

gumnos [γυμνός, 1131], signifies (*a*) unclothed, Mark 14:52; in ver. 51 it is used as a noun ("*his*" and "*body*" being italicised); (*b*) scantily or poorly clad, Matt. 25:36, 38, 43, 44; Acts 19:16 (with torn garments); Jas. 2:15; (*c*) clad in the undergarment only (the outer being laid aside), John 21:7 (see CLOTHING); (*d*) metaphorically, (1) of a bare seed, 1 Cor. 15:37; (2) of the soul without the body, 2 Cor. 5:3; (3) of things exposed to the all-seeing eye of God, Heb. 4:13; (4) of the carnal condition of a local church, Rev. 3:17; (5) of the similar state of an individual, 16:15; (*e*) of the desolation of religious Babylon, 17:16. ¶

NT: B.167d; CB.1248c; K.133.
OT: ʿērōm: S.5903; HR.278a.4b; H.1588b; BD.735d.
ʿarōm: S.6174; HR.278a.4c; H.1698; BD.736a.
GEN. REF.: IS.3:480; NB.–; Z.4:360.

B. Verb.

gumniteuō [γυμνιτεύω, 1130], to be naked or scantily clad (akin to A), is used in 1 Cor. 4:11. In the *Koinē* writings (see Preface to Vol. 1) it is used of being light-armed. ¶

NT: B.167d; CB.–; K.–.
OT: –.
GEN. REF.: IS.3:480; NB.–; Z.4:360.

C. Noun.

gumnotēs [γυμνότης, 1132], nakedness (akin to A), is used (*a*) of want of sufficient clothing, Rom. 8:35; 2 Cor. 11:27; (*b*) metaphorically, of the nakedness of the body, said of the condition of a local church, Rev. 3:18. ¶

NT: B.168a; CB.1248c; K.133.
OT: ʿērōm: S.5903; HR.278b.1; H.1588b; BD.735d.
GEN. REF.: IS.3:480; NB.–; Z.4:360.

NAME

A. Noun.

onoma [ὄνομα, 3686], is used (I) in general of the name by which a person or thing is called, e.g., Mark 3:16, 17, "(He) surnamed," lit., '(He added) the name'; 14:32, lit., '(of which) the name (was); 'Luke 1:63; John 18:10; sometimes translated "named," e.g., Luke 1:5, "named (Zacharias)," lit., 'by name'; in the same verse, "named (Elizabeth)," lit., 'the name of her,' an elliptical phrase, with 'was' understood; Acts 8:9, R.V., "by name," 10:1; the name is put for the reality in Rev.3:1; in Phil. 2:9, the Name represents 'the title and dignity' of the Lord, as in Eph. 1:21 and Heb. 1:4;

(II) for all that a name implies, of authority, character, rank, majesty, power, excellence, etc., of everything that the name covers: (*a*) of the Name of God as expressing His attributes, etc., e.g., Matt. 6:9; Luke 1:49; John 12:28; 17:6, 26; Rom. 15:9; 1 Tim. 6:1; Heb. 13:15; Rev. 13:6; (*b*) of the Name of Christ, e.g., Matt. 10:22; 19:29; John 1:12; 2:23; 3:18; Acts 26:9; Rom. 1:5; Jas. 2:7; 1 John 3:23; 3 John 7; Rev. 2:13; 3:8; also the phrases rendered 'in the name'; these may be analysed as follows: (1) representing the authority of Christ, e.g., Matt. 18:5 (with *epi*, 'on the ground of My authority'); so Matt. 24:5 (falsely) and parallel passages; as substantiated by the Father, John 14:26; 16:23 (last clause), R.V.; (2) in the power of (with *en*, in), e.g., Mark 16:17; Luke 10:17; Acts 3:6; 4:10; 16:18; Jas. 5:14; (3) in acknowledgement or confession of, e.g., Acts 4:12; 8:16; 9:27, 28; (4) in recognition of the authority of (sometimes combined with the thought of relying or resting on), Matt. 18:20; cp. 28:19; Acts 8:16; 9:2 (*eis*, into); John 14:13; 15:16; Eph. 5:20; Col. 3:17; (5) owing to the fact that one is called by Christ's Name or is identified with Him, e.g. 1 Pet. 4:14 (with *en*, in); with *heneken*, for the sake of, e.g., Matt. 19:29; with *dia*, on account of, Matt. 10:22; 24:9; Mark 13:13; Luke 21:17; John 15:21; 1 John 2:12; Rev. 2:3 (for 1 Pet. 4:16, see *Note* below);

(III) as standing, by metonymy, for persons, Acts 1:15; Rev. 3:4; 11:13 (R.V., "persons").

NT: B.570d; CB.1260c; K.694.
OT: shēm: S.8034; HR.995b.3a; H.2405; BD.1027c.
GEN. REF.: IS.3:480; NB.861; Z.4:360.

Note: In Mark 9:41, the use of the phrase *en* with the dative case of *onoma* (as in the best mss.) suggests the idea of 'by reason of' or 'on the ground of' (i.e., 'because ye are My disciples'); 1 Pet. 4:16, R.V., "in this Name" (A.V., "on this behalf"), may be taken in the same way.

B. Verbs.

1. *onomazō* [ὀνομάζω, 3687], denotes (*a*) to name, mention, or address by name, Acts 19:13, R.V., "to name" (A.V., "to call"); in the Passive Voice, Rom. 15:20; Eph. 1:21; 5:3; to make mention of the Name of the Lord in praise and worship, 2 Tim. 2:19; (*b*) to name, call, give a name to, Luke 6:13, 14; Passive Voice, 1 Cor. 5:11, R.V., "is named" (A.V., "is called"); Eph. 3:15 (some mss. have the verb in this sense in Mark 3:14 and 1 Cor. 5:1). See CALL, Note (1). ¶

NT: B.573d; CB.1261a; K.694.
OT: zākar: S.2142; HR.999c.1; H.551; BD.269c.
qārāʾ: S.7121; HR.999c.3; H.2063; BD.894d.
GEN. REF.: IS.3:480; NB.861; Z.4:360.

2. *eponomazō* [ἐπονομάζω, 2028], to call by a name, surname (*epi*, on, and No. 1), is used in

Rom. 2:17, Passive Voice, R.V., "bearest the name of" (A.V., "art called"). See CALL, *Note* (1). ¶
NT: B.305c; CB.1246b; K.694.
OT: qārā': S.7121; HR.539a.3a; H.2063; BD.894d.
GEN. REF.: IS.3:480; NB.861; Z.4:360.

3. *prosagoreuō* [προσαγορεύω, 4316], primarily denotes to address, greet, salute; hence, to call by name, Heb. 5:10, R.V., "named (of God a High Priest)" (A.V., "called"), expressing the formal ascription of the title to Him whose it is; "called" does not adequately express the significance. Some suggest the meaning 'addressed,' but this is doubtful. The reference is to Ps. 110:4, a prophecy confirmed at the Ascension. ¶ In the Sept., Deut. 23:6. ¶
NT: B.711a; CB.—; K.—.
OT: —.
GEN. REF.: —.

4. *kaleō* [καλέω, 2564], to call, is translated "named" in Acts 7:58, R.V. (A.V., "whose name was"). See CALL, No. 1 (*b*).
NT: B.398d; CB.1253b; K.394.
OT: qārā': S.7121; HR.712c.9a; H.2063; BD.894d.
GEN. REF.: IS.3:480; NB.861; Z.4:360.

Notes: (1) In Luke 19:2, A.V., *kaleō*, to call (with the dative case of *onoma*, 'by name'), is translated "named" (R.V., "called by name"); in Luke 2:21, A.V., the verb alone is rendered "named" (R.V., "called").

(2) In Matt. 9:9 and Mark 15:7, A.V., the verb *legō*, to speak, to call by name, is rendered "named" (R.V., "called"). See CALL, No. 9.

NAMELY

Notes: (1) In Rom. 13:9, the preposition *en*, in, with the article, lit., 'in the,' is translated "namely."

(2) In 1 Cor. 7:26 the R.V., "*namely*," and A.V., "*I say*," do not translate anything in the original, but serve to reintroduce the phrase "that this is good."

NAPKIN

soudarion [σουδάριον, 4676], for which see HANDKERCHIEF, is translated "napkin" in Luke 19:20; John 11:44; 20:7. In Luke 19:20 the reference may be to a towel or any kind of linen cloth or even a sort of head-dress, any of which might be used for concealing money.
NT: B.759c; CB.—; K.—.
OT: —.
GEN. REF.: IS.3:490; NB.504; Z.4:372.

NARRATIVE

diēgēsis [διήγησις, 1335], translated "a declaration" in the A.V. of Luke 1:1, denotes a "narrative," R.V. (akin to *diēgeomai*, to set out in detail, recount, describe). See DECLARE, B, *Note* (1). ¶ In the Sept., Judg. 7:15; Hab. 2:6. ¶
NT: B.195a; CB.1241c; K.303.
OT: ḥîdāh: S.2420; HR.330a.1; H.616a; BD.295b.
mispār: S.4557; HR.330a.2; H.1540e; BD.708d.
GEN. REF.: —.

NARROW

A. Adjective.

stenos [στενός, 4728], from a root *sten-*, seen in *stenazō*, to groan, *stenagmos*, groaning (Eng., stenography, lit., narrow writing), is used figuratively in Matt. 7:13, 14, of the gate which provides the entrance to eternal life, narrow because it runs counter to natural inclinations, and "the way" is similarly characterized; so in Luke 13:24 (where the more intensive word *agōnizomai*, "strive," is used); R.V. "narrow" (A.V., "strait") in each place. Cp. *stenochōreō*, to be straitened, and *stenochōria*, narrowness, anguish, distress. ¶
NT: B.766b; CB.1270a; K.1077.
OT: ṣar: S.6862; HR.1288c.3; H.1973-1975; BD.865a.
m^{e}ṣād: S.4679; HR.1288c.2a; H.1885c; BD.844d.
GEN. REF.: —.

B. Verb.

thlibō [θλίβω, 2346], to press, is translated "narrow" in Matt. 7:14, A.V., lit., 'narrowed' (R.V., "straitened"; the verb is in the perfect participle, Passive Voice), i.e., hemmed in, like a mountain gorge; the way is 'rendered narrow' by the Divine conditions, which make it impossible for any to enter who think the entrance depends upon self-merit, or who still incline towards sin, or desire to continue in evil. See AFFLICT, No. 4.
NT: B.362a; CB.1272b; K.334.
OT: ṣar: S.6862; HR.652b.10c; H.1973-1975; BD.865a.
ṣārar: S.6887; HR.652b.10b; H.1973-1974; BD.864c.
GEN. REF.: —.

NATION

1. *ethnos* [ἔθνος, 1484], originally a multitude, denotes (*a*) a nation or people, e.g., Matt. 24:7; Acts 10:35; the Jewish people, e.g., Luke 7:5; 23:2; John 11:48, 50-52; Acts 10:22; 24:2, 10, 17; in Matt. 21:43, the reference is to Israel in its restored condition; (*b*) in the plural, the nations as distinct from Israel. See GENTILES.
NT: B.218b; CB.1246c; K.201.
OT: gôy: S.1471; HR.368b.4; H.326e; BD.156c.
'am: S.5971; HR.368b.13; H.1640a,e; BD.766b.
GEN. REF.: IS.3:492; NB.—; Z.4:375.

2. *genos* [γένος, —], a race: see KIND (Noun).

3. *allophulos* [ἀλλόφυλος, 246], foreign, of another race (*allos*, another, *phulon*, a tribe), is used in Acts 10:28, "one of another nation." ¶
NT: B.41a; CB.—; K.43.
OT: p^{e}leshet: S.6429,6430; HR.57c.3; H.—; BD.814b.
GEN. REF.: —.

Note: For Phil. 2:15, *genea* (A.V., "nation," R.V., "generation"), see AGE.

NATURAL, NATURALLY

A. Adjectives.

1. *phusikos* [φυσικός, 5446], originally signifying produced by nature, inborn, from *phusis*, nature (see below), cp. Eng., physical, physics, etc., dentoes (*a*) according to nature, Rom. 1:26, 27; (*b*) governed by mere natural instincts, 2 Pet. 2:12, R.V., "(born) mere animals," A.V. and R.V. marg., "natural (brute beasts)." ¶

NT: B.869a; CB.1264c; K.1283.
OT: –.
GEN. REF.: IS.3:496; NB.869; Z.4:386.

2. *psuchikos* [ψυχικός, 5591], belonging to the *psuchē*, soul (as the lower part of the immaterial in man), natural, physical, describes the man in Adam and what pertains to him (set in contrast to *pneumatikos*, spiritual), 1 Cor. 2:14; 15:44 (twice), 46 (in the latter used as a noun); Jas. 3:15, "sensual" (R.V. marg., "natural" or "animal"), here relating perhaps more especially to the mind, a wisdom in accordance with, or springing from, the corrupt desires and affections; so in Jude 19. ¶

NT: B.894b; CB.1267c; K.1342.
OT: –.
GEN. REF.: IS.3:496; NB.869; Z.4:386.

B. Noun.

genesis [γένεσις, 1078], birth, is used in Jas. 1:23, of the "natural face," lit., 'the face of his birth,' "what God made him to be" (Hort). See GENERATION, NATURE, No. 2.

NT: B.154c; CB.1248a; K.117.
OT: tôlēdōt: S.8435; HR.237a.3d; H.867g; BD.410a.
GEN. REF.: IS.3:496; NB.869; Z.4:386.

Note: In Rom. 11:21, 24 the preposition *kata*, according to, with the noun *phusis*, nature, is translated "natural," of branches, metaphorically describing members of the nation of Israel.

C. Adverb.

phusikōs [φυσικῶς, 5447], naturally, by nature (akin to A, No. 1), is used in Jude 10. ¶

NT: B.869b; CB.1264c; K.1283.
OT: –.
GEN. REF.: IS.3:496; NB.869; Z.4:386.

Note: In Phil. 2:20, A.V., *gnēsiōs*, sincerely, honourably, truly (from the adjective *gnēsios*, true, sincere, genuine; see, e.g., Phil. 4:3), is translated "naturally" (R.V., "truly"; marg., "genuinely"). ¶

NATURE

1. *phusis* [φύσις, 5449], from *phuō*, to bring forth, produce, signifies (*a*) the nature (i.e., the natural powers or constitution) of a person or thing, Eph. 2:3; Jas. 3:7 ("kind"); 2 Pet. 1:4; (*b*) origin, birth, Rom. 2:27, one who by birth is a Gentile, uncircumcised, in contrast to one who, though circumcised, has become spiritually uncircumcised by his iniquity; Gal. 2:15; (*c*) the regular law or order of nature, Rom. 1:26, against nature (*para*, against); 2:14, adverbially, "by nature" (for 11:21, 24, see NATURAL, *Note*); 1 Cor. 11:14; Gal. 4:8, "by nature (are no gods)," here "nature" is the emphatic word, and the phrase includes demons, men regarded as deified, and idols; these are gods only in name (the negative, *mē*, denies not simply that they were gods, but the possibility that they could be). ¶

NT: B.869b; CB.1264c; K.1280.
OT: –.
GEN. REF.: IS.3:496; NB.869; Z.4:386.

2. *genesis* [γένεσις, 1078], is used in the phrase in Jas. 3:6, "the wheel of nature," R.V. (marg., "birth"). Some regard this as the course of birth or of creation, or the course of man's nature according to its original Divine purpose; Mayor (on the Ep. of James) regards *trochos* here as a wheel, "which, catching fire from the glowing axle, is compared to the wide-spreading mischief done by the tongue," and shows that "the fully developed meaning" of *genesis* denotes "the incessant change of life . . . the sphere of this earthly life, meaning all that is contained in our life." The significance, then, would appear to be the whole round of human life and activity. Moulton and Milligan illustrate it in this sense from the papyri. See NATURAL, B.

NT: B.154c; CB.1248a; K.117.
OT: tôlēdôt: S.8435; HR.237a.3d; H.867g; BD.410a.
GEN. REF.: IS.3:496; NB.869; Z.4:386.

For **NAUGHTINESS,** Jas. 1:21, A.V., see **WICKEDNESS**

NAY

1. *ou* [οὐ, 3756], no, not, expressing a negation absolutely, is rendered "nay," e.g., in Matt. 5:37; 13:29; John 7:12, A.V. (R.V., "not so"); Acts 16:37; 2 Cor. 1:17, 18, 19; Jas. 5:12.

NT: B.590a; CB.–; K.–.
OT: –.
GEN. REF.: –.

2. *ouchi* [οὐχί, 3780], a strengthened form of No. 1, is used, e.g., in Luke 12:51; 13:3, 5; 16:30; Rom. 3:27.

NT: B.598b; CB.–; K.–.
OT: –.
GEN. REF.: –.

3. *alla* [ἀλλά, 235], but, to mark contrast or opposition, is rendered "nay" in Rom. 3:31,

R.V., "nay" (A.V., "yea"); in 7:7, R.V., "howbeit" (A.V., "nay"); 8:37; 1 Cor. 3:2, R.V.; 6:8; 12:22; in Heb. 3:16, R.V., "nay" (A.V., "howbeit").

NT: B.38a; CB.–; K.–.
OT: –.
GEN. REF.: –.

4. *menounge* [μενοῦνγε, 3304], (i.e., *men oun ge*), nay rather, is rendered "nay but" in Rom. 9:20 (in Rom. 10:18 and Phil. 3:8, "yea verily," A.V., "yea doubtless"). See YEA.

NT: B.503c; CB.–; K.–.
OT: –.
GEN. REF.: –.

NEAR (Adverb), NEAR (come, draw), NEARER

A. Adverbs.

1. *engus* [ἐγγύς, 1451], near, nigh, is used (*a*) of place, e.g., Luke 19:11, "nigh"; John 3:23; 11:54, "near"; 6:19, 23, "nigh"; metaphorically in Rom. 10:8; Eph. 2:13, 17, "nigh"; (*b*) of time, e.g., Matt. 24:32, 33, "nigh"; so Luke 21:30, 31; as a preposition, Heb. 6:8, "nigh unto (a curse)," and 8:13, "nigh unto (vanishing away)." See HAND (at), NIGH, READY.

NT: B.214a; CB.1245a; K.194.
OT: qārôb: S.7138; HR.363c.4; H.2065d; BD.898b.
GEN. REF.: IS.3:503; NB.–; Z.–.

2. *enguteron* [ἐγγύτερον, 1452], the comparative degree of No. 1, and the neuter of the adjective *enguteros*, used adverbially, occurs in Rom. 13:11. ¶

NT: B.214a; CB.–; K.–.
OT: –.
GEN. REF.: –.

3. *plēsion* [πλησίον, 4139], near, close by, neighbouring (the neuter of the adjective *plēsios*, used as an adverb), occurs in John 4:5. See NEIGHBOUR.

NT: B.672c; CB.1265b; K.872.
OT: rēaʿ: S.1453; HR.1148b.10a; H.2186; BD.945d.
GEN. REF.: –.

B. Adjective.

anankaios [ἀναγκαῖος, 316], necessary, is used, in a secondary sense, of persons connected by bonds of nature or friendship, with the meaning 'intimate,' in Acts 10:24, "(his) near (friends)"; it is found in this sense in the papyri. See NECESSARY, NEEDFUL.

NT: B.52b; CB.1235b; K.55.
OT: –.
GEN. REF.: –.

C. Verbs.

1. *engizō* [ἐγγίζω, 1448], transitively, to bring near (not in N.T.; in the Sept., e.g., Gen. 48:10; Is. 5:8); intransitively, to draw near, e.g., Matt. 21:34; Luke 18:40; 19:41, R.V., "draw nigh"; see APPROACH, A.

NT: B.213c; CB.1245a; K.194.
OT: nāgash: S.5066; HR.362b.11; H.1297; BD.620c.
qārab: S.7126; HR.362b.13a-c; H.2065; BD.897b.
qārôb: S.7138; HR.362b.13f; H.2065d; BD.898b.
GEN. REF.: IS.3:503; NB.–; Z.–.

2. *proserchomai* [προσέρχομαι, 4334], to come to, go to, is translated "drew near" in Acts 7:31 and Heb. 10:22. See COME, No. 10.

NT: B.713a; CB.1267a; K.257.
OT: nāgash: S.5066; HR.1213c.7a; H.1297; BD.620c.
qārab: S.7126; HR.1213c.10a; H.2065; BD.897b.
GEN. REF.: IS.3:503; NB.–; Z.–.

3. *prosagō* [προσάγω, 4317], is used (*a*) transitively, to bring, Acts 16:20; 1 Pet. 3:18; (*b*) intransitively, to draw near, in the latter sense in Acts 27:27. ¶

NT: B.711b; CB.–; K.20.
OT: nāgash: S.5066; HR.1211a.6; H.1297; BD.620c.
qārab: S.7126; HR.1211b.11; H.2065; BD.897b.
GEN. REF.: IS.3:503; NB.–; Z.–.

NECESSARY

1. *anankaios* [ἀναγκαῖος, 316], necessary (from *anankē*, necessity; see below), is so rendered in Acts 13:46; 1 Cor. 12:22; 2 Cor. 9:5; Phil. 2:25; Tit. 3:14; Heb. 8:3, R.V. (A.V., "of necessity"); for Acts 10:24, "near friends," see NEAR, B. ¶

NT: B.52a; CB.1235b; K.55.
OT: –.
GEN. REF.: –.

2. *anankē* [ἀνάγκη, 318], a necessity (see No. 1), is rendered "(it was) necessary" in Heb. 9:23, lit., 'it was a necessity.' See DISTRESS, A, No. 1

NT: B.52b; CB.1235b; K.55.
OT: mᵉṣûqāh: S.4691; HR.76a.6b; H.1895a; BD.848a.
ṣar: S.6862; HR.76a.7a; H.1973-1975; BD.865a.
ṣārāh: S.6869; HR.76a.7b; H.1973c,1974b; BD.865b.
GEN. REF.: –.

3. *epanankēs* [ἐπανάγκης, 1876], an adjective akin to the preceding, with *epi*, used intensively, found only in the neuter form, is used as an adverb signifying 'of necessity' and translated as an adjective in Acts 15:28, "necessary," lit., '(things) of necessity.' ¶

NT: B.282c; CB.–; K.–.
OT: –.
GEN. REF.: –.

Note: For the A.V. of Acts 28:10 see NEED, A, No.1.

NECESSITY (-TIES)

1. *anankē* [ἀνάγκη, 318], signifies (*a*) a necessity, what must needs be (see NEEDS), translated "necessity" (in some mss. in Luke 23:17) in 1 Cor. 7:37; 9:16; 2 Cor. 9:7 (with *ek*, out of); Philm. 14 (with *kata*, according to); Heb. 7:12; 9:16; (*b*) distress, pain, translated "necessities" in 2 Cor. 6:4; 12:10. See DISTRESS, No. 1, and the synonymous words there, and NEEDS, NEEDFUL (also CONSTRAIN, Note).

NT: B.52b; CB.1235b; K.55.
OT: mᵉṣûqāh: S.4691; HR.76a.6b; H.1895e; BD.848a.
ṣar: S.6862; HR.76a.7a; H.1973-1975; BD.865a.
sārāh: S.6869; HR.76a.7b; H.1973c,1974b; BD.865b.
GEN. REF.: –.

2. *chreia* [χρεία, 5532], a need, and almost always so translated, is used in the plural in Acts 20:34, "necessities"; Rom. 12:13, R.V. (A.V., "necessity"); in Phil. 4:16, A.V., "necessity," R.V., "need." See NEED, NEEDFUL.

NT: B.884d; CB.1240a; K.–.
OT: ḥ^ashaḥ (Aramaic): S.2818; HR.1474a.3; H.2746; BD.1093d.
hashhût (Aramaic): S.2819; HR.1474a.1; H.2746b; BD.1093d.
ṣōrek: S.6878; HR.1474a.2; H.1970b; BD.863d.
GEN. REF.: –.

NECK

trachēlos [τράχηλος, 5137], is used (*a*) literally, Matt. 18:6; Mark 9:42; Luke 17:2; of embracing, Luke 15:20; Acts 20:37; (*b*) metaphorically, in Acts 15:10, of putting a yoke upon; Rom. 16:4, singular in the original, '(laid down their) neck,' indicating the figurative use of the term rather than the literal. Prisca and Aquila in some way had risked their lives for the Apostle (the phrase is found with this significance in the papyri). ¶

NT: B.825a; CB.1273a; K.–.
OT: ṣawwā'r: S.6677; HR.1370b.4a; H.1897a; BD.848b.
GEN. REF.: IS.3:509; NB.874; Z.4:400.

NEED, NEEDS, NEEDFUL

A. Nouns.

1. *chreia* [χρεία, 5532], denotes a need, in such expressions as 'there is a need'; or 'to have need of' something, e.g., Matt. 3:14; 6:8; 9:12, R.V., "(have no) need," A.V., "need (not)," the R.V. adheres to the noun form; so in 14:16; Mark 14:63; Luke 5:31; 22:71; Eph. 4:28; 1 Thess. 4:9; in the following, however, both R.V. and A.V. use the verb form, to need (whereas the original has the verb *echō*, to have, with the noun *chreia* as the object, as in the instances just mentioned): Luke 15:7; John 2:25; 13:10; 16:30; 1 Thess. 1:8; 1 John 2:27; Rev. 22:5; in all these the verb to have could well have been expressed in the translation.

In Luke 10:42 it is translated "needful," where the "one thing" is surely not one dish, or one person, but is to be explained according to Matt. 6:33 and 16:26. In Eph. 4:29, for the A.V., "(to) the use (of edifying)," the R.V. more accurately has "(for edifying) as the need may be," marg., "the building up of the need," i.e., 'to supply that which needed in each case'; so Westcott, who adds "The need represents a gap in the life which the wise word 'builds up,' fills up solidly and surely." In Phil. 4:19 the R.V. has "every need of yours" (A.V., "all your need"); in 1 Thess. 4:12, R.V., "need" (A.V., "lack"); in Acts 28:10, R.V., "(such things) as we needed" (A.V., "as were necessary"), lit., 'the things for the needs (plural).' See BUSINESS, A, No. 1, LACK, NECESSITY, USE, WANT.

NT: B.884d; CB.1240a; K.–.
OT: ḥ^ashaḥ (Aramaic): S.2818; HR.1474a.3; H.2746; BD.1093d.
ḥashḥût (Aramaic): S.2819; HR.1474a.1; H.2746b; BD.1093d.
ṣōrek: S.6878; HR.1474a.2; H.1970b; BD.863d.
GEN. REF.: –.

2. *anankē* [ἀνάγκη, 318], a necessity, need, is translated "it must needs be" in Matt. 18:7, with the verb 'to be' understood (according to the best mss.); in Luke 14:18, "I must needs" translates the verb *echō*, to have, with this noun as the object, lit., 'I have need'; in Rom. 13:5 "(*ye*) must needs," lit., '(it is) necessary (to be subject).' See NECESSARY, No. 2, NECESSITY, No. 1. See also DISTRESS.

NT: B.52b; CB.1235b; K.55.
OT: m^eṣûqāh: S.4691; HR.76a,b; H.1895e; BD.848a.
ṣar: S.6862; HR.76a,7a; H.1973-1975; BD.865a.
ṣārāh: S.6869; HR.76a.7b; H.1973c,1974b; BD.865b.
GEN. REF.: –.

B. Verbs.

1. *chrēzō* [χρῄζω, 5535], to need, to have need of (akin to *chrē*, it is necessary, fitting), is used in Matt. 6:32; Luke 11:8; 12:30; Rom. 16:2, R.V., "may have need" (A.V., "hath need"); 2 Cor. 3:1. ¶

NT: B.885b; CB.1240a; K.–.
OT: –.
GEN. REF.: –.

2. *dei* [δεῖ, 1163], an impersonal verb, signifying 'it is necessary,' is rendered "must needs" in Mark 13:7; John 4:4; Acts 1:16, A.V. (R.V., "it was needful"); 17:3, A.V. (R.V., "it behoved"); (in some mss. in Acts 21:22); 2 Cor. 11:30; 12:1; in Acts 15:5, "it was needful."

NT: B.172a; CB.1240b; K.140.
OT: –.
GEN. REF.: –.

3. *deon* [δέον, 1163], the neuter of the present participle of No. 2, is used as a noun, signifying that which is needful, due, proper, in 1 Pet. 1:6, with the meaning 'need,' "(if) need (be)," with the verb to be understood. See OUGHT.

NT: B.172a; CB.1240c; K.140.
OT: –.
GEN. REF.: –.

4. *prosdeomai* [προσδέομαι, 4326], to want besides, to need in addition (*pros*, besides, *deomai*, to want), is used in Acts 17:25, "(as though) He needed (anything)"; the literal sense of *pros* is not to be stressed. ¶ In the Sept., Prov. 12:9, "lacking (bread)." ¶

NT: B.712a; CB.1267a; K.143.
OT: ḥāsēr: S.2637; HR.1212c.1; H.705; BD.341a.
GEN. REF.: –.

5. *opheilō* [ὀφείλω, 3784], to owe, be bound, obliged to do something, is translated "must ye needs," in 1 Cor. 5:10; in 7:36 it is used impersonally, signifying 'it is due,' and followed by the infinitive mood of *ginomai*, to become, to occur, come about, lit. 'it is due to become,'

translated "(if) need (so) require." See BEHOVE, BOUND, DEBT, DUE, DUTY, GUILTY, INDEBTED, MUST, OUGHT, OWE.

NT: B.598d; CB.1261a; K.746.
OT: ḥôb: S.2326; HR.1039a.2; H.614a; BD.295a.
nāshā': S.5378; HR.1039a.4a,b; H.1424; BD.673d.
GEN. REF.: –.

Note: In Phil. 4:12, A.V., *hustereō*, to come short, fail, to be in want, is translated "to suffer need" (R.V., "to be in want"). See BEHIND.

C. Adjectives.

1. *anankaioteros* [ἀναγκαιότερος, 316], the comparative degree of *anankaios*, necessary, is translated "more needful" in Phil. 1:24. See NECESSARY, No. 1.

NT: B.52a; CB.1235b; K.55.
OT: –.
GEN. REF.: –.

2. *epitēdeios* [ἐπιτήδειος, 2006], primarily, suitable, convenient, then, useful, necessary, is translated "needful" in Jas. 2:16, neuter plural, 'necessaries.' ¶ In the Sept., 1 Chron. 28:2, "suitable." ¶

NT: B.302d; CB.–; K.–.
OT: –.
GEN. REF.: –.

Note: In Heb. 4:16 *eukairos*, timely, seasonable, qualifying the noun *boētheia*, help, is translated "time of need," lit., 'for opportune help.' See CONVENIENT.

NEEDLE

1. *rhaphis* [ῥαφίς, 4476], from *rhaptō*, to sew, occurs in Matt. 19:24; Mark 10:25. ¶

NT: B.734c; CB.–; K.–.
OT: –.
GEN. REF.: IS.3:510; NB.–; Z.4:401.

2. *belonē* [βελόνη, —], akin to *belos*, a dart, denotes a sharp point, hence, a needle, Luke 18:25 (some mss. have No. 1). ¶

NT: B.139b; CB.–; K.–.
OT: –.
GEN. REF.: IS.3:510; NB.–; Z.4:401.

Note: The idea of applying 'the needle's eye' to small gates seems to be a modern one; there is no ancient trace of it. The Lord's object in the statement is to express human impossibility and there is no need to endeavour to soften the difficulty by taking the needle to mean anything more than the ordinary instrument. Mackie points out (Hastings' Bib. Dic.) that "an attempt is sometimes made to explain the words as a reference to the small door, a little over 2 feet square, in the large heavy gate of a walled city. This mars the figure without materially altering the meaning, and receives no justification from the language and traditions of Palestine."

NEGLECT, NEGLIGENT

1. *ameleō* [ἀμελέω, 272], denotes (*a*) to be careless, not to care (*a*, negative, *melei*, it is a care; from *melō*, to care, to be a care), Matt. 22:5, "made light of"; (*b*) to be careless of, neglect, 1 Tim. 4:14; Heb. 2:3; 8:9. "I regarded (them) not." See LIGHT OF (make), REGARD. ¶ (In the Sept., Jer. 4:17; 38:32. ¶)

NT: B.44d; CB.–; K.–.
OT: mārāh: S.4784; HR.65b.2; H.1242; BD.598a.
GEN. REF.: –.

2. *paratheōreō* [παραθεωρέω, 3865], primarily, to examine side by side, compare (*para*, beside, *theōreō*, to look at), hence, to overlook, to neglect, is used in Acts 6:1, of the neglect of widows in the daily ministration in Jerusalem. ¶

NT: B.616b; CB.–; K.–.
OT: –.
GEN. REF.: –.

Note: In 2 Pet. 1:12, some mss. have No. 1, hence the A.V., "I will not be negligent"; the R.V. follows those which have the future tense of *mellō*, to be ready. See READY. For "neglect to hear" see HEAR, No. 7.

For NEGLECTING (Col. 2:23) see SEVERITY

NEIGHBOUR

1. *geitōn* [γείτων, 1069], lit., one living in the same land, denotes a neighbour, always plural in the N.T., Luke 14:12; 15:6, 9; John 9:8. ¶

NT: B.153c; CB.–; K.–.
OT: shākēn: S.7934; HR.235b.2b; H.2387b; BD.1015c.
GEN. REF.: IS.3:517; NB.876; Z.4:408.

2. *perioikos* [περίοικος, 4040], an adjective, lit., dwelling around (*peri*, around, *oikos*, a dwelling), is used as a noun in Luke 1:58, "neighbours." ¶

NT: B.648d; CB.–; K.–.
OT: shākēn: S.7934; HR.1124c.4; H.2387b; BD.1015c.
sābîb: S.5439; HR.1124c.3; H.1456b; BD.686d.
GEN. REF.: IS.3:517; NB.876; Z.4:408.

3. *plēsion* [πλησίον, 4139], the neuter of the adjective *plēsios* (from *pelas*, near), is used as an adverb accompanied by the article, lit., 'the (one) near'; hence, one's neighbour; see refs. below.

This and Nos. 1 and 2 have a wider range of meaning than that of the Eng. word neighbour. There were no farmhouses scattered over the agricultural areas of Palestine; the populations, gathered in villages, went to and fro to their toil. Hence domestic life was touched at every point by a wide circle of neighbourhood. The terms for neighbour were therefore of a very comprehensive scope. This may be seen from the chief characteristics of the privileges and duties of neighbourhood as set forth in Scripture, (*a*) its helpfulness, e.g., Prov. 27:10; Luke 10:36; (*b*) its intimacy, e.g., Luke 15:6, 9 (see No. 1); Heb. 8:11; (*c*) its sincerity and sanctity, e.g., Ex. 22:7, 10; Prov. 3:29; 14:21; Rom. 13:10; 15:2; Eph. 4:25; Jas. 4:12. The N.T. quotes and expands the command in Lev. 19:18, to love one's neighbour as oneself; see, e.g., Matt. 5:43; 19:19; 22:39; Mark 12:31, 33; Luke 10:27; Gal. 5:14; Jas. 2:8. See also Acts 7:27.

NT: B.672c; CB.1265b; K.872.
OT: rēa': S.7453; HR.1148b.10a; H.2186a; BD.945a.
GEN. REF.: IS.3:517; NB.876; Z.4:408.

Note: In Rom. 13:8, for *heteron*, another, R.V. has "his neighbour."

NEIGHBOURHOOD

Note: This, in Acts 28:7, R.V., translates a phrase consisting of the dative plural of the article followed by *peri*, around, governed by the preposition *en*, in, "in the neighbourhood of (that place)," A.V., "in the (same quarters)," lit., 'in the (parts) around (that place).'

NEITHER See † p. 1

For NEITHER AT ANY TIME, Luke 15:29, see NEVER

For NEPHEWS see GRANDCHILDREN

NEST

kataskēnōsis [κατασκήνωσις, 2682], properly an encamping, taking up one's quarters, then, a lodging, abode (*kata*, down over, *skēnē*, a tent), is used of birds' nests in Matt. 8:20 and Luke 9:58. ¶ In the Sept., 1 Chron. 28:2, "the building"; Ezek. 37:27, "(My) tabernacle." ¶

The word *nossia*, signifying a brood, Luke 13:34, used in the Sept. to denote a nest, e.g., in Deut. 22:6; 32:11, signifies the actual receptacle built by birds in which to lay their eggs (having special reference to the prospective brood); but the word *kataskēnōsis*, used by the Lord, denotes a resting or roosting place. This lends force to His comparison. Not only was He without a home, He had not even a lodging-place (cp. *kataskēnoō*, to lodge, e.g., Matt. 13:32; Acts 2:26, R.V. marg., 'shall tabernacle'; see LODGE).

NT: B.418c; CB.1254b; K.—.
OT: bānāh S.1129; HR.744c.1; H.255; BD.124a.
mishkān: S.4908; HR.744c.2; H.2387c; BD.1015c.
GEN. REF.: IS.3:523; NB.978; Z.—.

NET

1. *amphiblēstron* [ἀμφίβληστρον, 293], lit., something thrown around (*amphi*, around, *ballō*, to throw), denotes a casting-net, a somewhat small net, cast over the shoulder, spreading out in a circle and made to sink by weights, Matt. 4:18 (in some mss. in Mark 1:16: the best have the verb *amphiballō* alone). ¶

NT: B.47b; CB.—; K.—.
OT: ḥērem: S.2764; HR.67c.1; H.744a; BD.357a.
makmōr: S.4364; HR.67c.2a; H.995b; BD.485c.
mikmeret: S.4365; HR.67c.2b; H.995c; BD.485c.
GEN. REF.: IS.3:524; NB.—; Z.4:412.

2. *diktuon* [δίκτυον, 1350], a general term for a net (from an old verb *dikō*, to cast: akin to *diskos*, a quoit), occurs in Matt. 4:20, 21; Mark 1:18, 19; Luke 5:2, 4-6; John 21:6, 8, 11 (twice). ¶ In the Sept. it was used for a net for catching birds, Prov. 1:17, in other ways, e.g., figuratively of a snare, Job. 18:8; Prov. 29:5.

NT: B.198c; CB.—; K.—.
OT: reshet: S.7568; HR.335c.2; H.920c; BD.440b.
sᵉbākāh: S.7639; HR.335c.3b; H.2230b; BD.959a.
GEN. REF.: IS.3:523; NB.879; Z.4:412.

3. *sagēnē* [σαγήνη, 4522], denotes a drag-net, a *seine*; two modes were employed with this, either by its being let down into the water and drawn together in a narrowing circle, and then into the boat, or as a semicircle drawn to the shore, Matt. 13:47, where Nos. 1 and 2 would not have suited so well. The Greek historian Herodotus uses the corresponding verb *sagēneuō* of a device by which the Persians are said to have cleared a conquered island of its inhabitants. ¶

NT: B.739c; CB.—; K.—
OT: ḥerem: S.2764; HR.1257a.1; H.744a; BD.357a.
mikmeret: S.4365; HR.1257a.2a; H.995c; BD.485c.
GEN. REF.: IS.3:523; NB.879; Z.4:412.

NEVER

1. *oudepote* [οὐδέποτε, 3763], from *oude*, not even, and *pote*, at any time, is used in definite negative statements, e.g., Matt. 7:23; 1 Cor. 13:8; Heb. 10:1, 11, or questions, e.g., Matt. 21:16, 42; in Luke 15:29 (1st part), R.V., "never" (A.V., "neither . . . at any time"); A.V. and R.V., "never" (2nd part).

NT: B.592b; CB.—; K.—.
OT: —.
GEN. REF.: —.

2. *mēdepote* [μηδέποτε, 3368], virtually the same as No. 1, the negative *mē*, however, conveying a less strong declarative negation, 2 Tim. 3:7. ¶

NT: B.518b; CB.—; K.—.
OT: —.
GEN. REF.: —.

3. *oudepō* [οὐδέπω, 3764], not yet, is translated "never (man) yet" in John 19:41 ("man" representing the idiomatically used negative

pronoun *oudeis*, 'no one'); some mss. have it in Luke 23:53, instead of *oupō*, not yet.
NT: B.592; CB.—; K.—.
OT: ṭerem: S.2962; HR.1029c.1; H.826; BD.382a.
GEN. REF.: —.

Notes: (1) In Mark 14:21, A.V., the negative particle *ouk*, not, is translated "never" (R.V., "not"); the negative particle *mē*, not (which suggests non-existence when the existence was after all possible, or even probable, in contrast to *ou*, which implies non-existence absolutely), is translated "never" in John 7:15, A.V. and R.V.

(2) The phrase *eis ton aiona*, for ever (not to be rendered literally, 'unto the age,' see ETERNAL), preceded by the double negative *ou mē*, denotes 'never,' John 4:14; 8:51, 52; 10:28; 11:26; 13:8; so, preceded by *ouk*, not, in Mark 3:29.

(3) In 2 Pet. 1:10, "never" is the translation of *ou mē pote*, i.e., 'by no means ever'; so with the double negative followed by the extended word *pōpote*, i.e., 'by no means not even at any time,' John 6:35 (2nd part).

(4) *Pōpote* follows *oudeis*, no one, in the dative case ('to no man') in John 8:33, R.V., "never yet" (A.V., "never"); so in Luke 19:30, where *oudeis* is in the nominative case, R.V., "no man ever yet" (A.V., "yet never man").

NEVERTHELESS: see † p. 1

NEW

1. *kainos* [καινός, 2537], denotes new, of that which is unaccustomed or unused, not new in time, recent, but new as to form or quality, of different nature from what is contrasted as old. " 'The new tongues,' *kainos*, of Mark 16:17 are the 'other tongues,' *heteros*, of Acts 2:4. These languages, however, were 'new' and 'different,' not in the sense that they had never been heard before, or that they were new to the hearers, for it is plain from v. 8 that this is not the case; they were new languages to the speakers, different from those in which they were accustomed to speak.

"The new things that the Gospel brings for present obedience and realization are: a new covenant, Matt. 26:28 in some texts; a new commandment, John 13:34; a new creative act, Gal. 6:15; a new creation, 2 Cor. 5:17; a new man, i.e., a new character of manhood, spiritual and moral, after the pattern of Christ, Eph. 4:24; a new man, i.e., 'the Church which is His (Christ's) body,' Eph. 2:15.

"The new things that are to be received and enjoyed hereafter are: a new name, the believer's, Rev. 2:17; a new name, the Lord's, Rev. 3:12; a new song, Rev. 5:9; a new Heaven and a new Earth, Rev. 21:1; the new Jerusalem, Rev. 3:12; 21:2; 'And He that sitteth on the Throne said, Behold, I make all things new,' Rev. 21:5."*

Kainos is translated "fresh" in the R.V. of Matt. 9:17; Mark 2:22 (in the best texts) and Luke 5:38, of wineskins. Cp. *kainotēs*, newness (below).
NT: B.394a; CB.1253a; K.388.
OT: hādāsh: S.2319; HR.705b.2; H.613a; BD.294a.
GEN. REF.: IS.3:526; NB.—; Z.4:415.

2. *neos* [νέος, 3501], signifies new in respect of time, that which is recent; it is used of the young, and so translated, especially the comparative degree "younger"; accordingly what is *neos* may be a reproduction of the old in quality or character. *Neos* and *kainos* are sometimes used of the same thing, but there is a difference, as already indicated. Thus the "new man" in Eph. 2:15 (*kainos*) is new in differing in character; so in 4:24 (see No. 1); but the "new man" in Col. 3:10 (*neos*) stresses the fact of the believer's new experience, recently begun, and still proceeding. "The old man in him . . . dates as far back as Adam; a new man has been born, who therefore is fitly so called" [i.e., *neos*], Trench, Syn. §lx. The new Covenant in Heb. 12:24 is new (*neos*) compared with the Mosaic, nearly fifteen hundred years before; it is new (*kainos*) compared with the Mosaic, which is old in character, ineffective, 8:8, 13; 9:15.

The new wine of Matt. 9:17; Mark 2:22; Luke 5:37-39; is *neos*, as being of recent production; the new wine of the Kingdom, Matt. 26:29; Mark 14:25; is *kainos*, since it will be of a different character from that of this world. The rendering "new" (*neos*) is elsewhere used metaphorically in 1 Cor. 5:7, "a new lump." See YOUNG, YOUNGER.
NT: B.535d; CB.1259c; K.628.
OT: ṣā'îr: S.6810; HR.942a.7c; H.1948a; BD.859a.
qāṭān: S.6996; HR.942a; H.2009a,b; BD.881d.
'ābîb: S.24; HR.942a.1; H.1b; BD.1a.
GEN. REF.: IS.3:526; NB.—; Z.4:415.

3. *prosphatos* [πρόσφατος, 4372], originally signifying freshly slain, acquired the general sense of new, as applied to flowers, oil, misfortune, etc. It is used in Heb. 10:20 of the "living way" which Christ "dedicated for us . . . through the veil . . . His flesh" (which stands for His expiatory death by the offering of His body, ver. 10). ¶ In the Sept., Numb.

* From Notes on Galatians by Hogg and Vine, pp. 337, 338.

6:3; Deut. 32:17; Psa. 81:9; Eccl. 1:9. ¶ Cp. the adverb *prosphatōs*, lately, recently, Acts 18:2. ¶
NT: B.719c; CB.1267b; K.950.
OT: zûr: S.2114; HR.1222c.1; H.541; BD.266b.
ḥādāsh: S.2319; HR.1222c.2; H.613a; BD.294a.
laḥ: S.3892; HR.1222c.3; H.1102a; BD.535a.
GEN. REF.: IS.3:526; NB.—; Z.4:415.

Note: In Matt. 9:16 and Mark 2:21, A.V., *agnaphos* is translated "new" (R.V., "undressed"). Moulton and Milligan give an instance in the papyri of its use in respect of a "new white shirt." See UNDRESSED. ¶

For NEWBORN, 1 Pet. 2:2, see BEGET, C. No. 2

NEWNESS

kainotēs [καινότης, 2538], akin to *kainos*, is used in the phrases (*a*) "newness of life," Rom. 6:4, i.e., life of a new quality (see NEW, No. 1); the believer, being a new creation (2 Cor. 5:17), is to behave himself consistently with this in contrast to his former manner of life; (*b*) newness of the spirit, R.V., Rom. 7:6, said of the believer's manner of serving the Lord. While the phrase stands for the new life of the quickened spirit of the believer, it is impossible to dissociate this (in an objective sense) from the operation of the Holy Spirit, by whose power the service is rendered. ¶
NT: B.394c; CB.1253a; K.388.
OT: —.
GEN. REF.: IS.3:526; NB.—; Z.4:415.

NEXT

1. *hexēs* [ἑξῆς, 1836], an adverb (akin to *echō*, to have) denoting 'in order,' successively, next, is used adjectivally, qualifying the noun "day" in Luke 9:37; Acts 21:1, R.V., "next" (A.V., "following"); 25:17, R.V., "next" (A.V., "on the morrow"); in 27:18, with *hēmera*, day, understood; in Luke 7:11, in the best mss., with the word *chronos*, time, understood, "soon afterwards" (marg., "on the next day," according to some ancient authorities). See AFTER, FOLLOW, *Note* (3), MORROW.
NT: B.276a; CB.—; K.—.
OT: —.
GEN. REF.: —.

2. *metaxu* [μεταξύ, 3342], signifies between, "next," in Acts 13:42. See BETWEEN, No. 2.
NT: B.512d; CB.—; K.—.
OT: —.
GEN. REF.: —.

3. *echō* [ἔχω, 2192], to have, in the Middle Voice, sometimes signifies to be next to, said of towns, in Mark 1:38; of a day, Acts 21:26; in 20:15 (2nd part), *hēmera*, day, is unexpressed. See HAVE.
NT: B.331d; CB.1242c; K.286.
OT: —.
GEN. REF.: —.

4. *erchomai* [ἔρχομαι, 2064], to come, is used in the present participle in Acts 13:44, "(the) next (sabbath)." See COME.
NT: B.310b; CB.1246b; K.257.
OT: bô': S.935; HR.548b.5a; H.212; BD.97c.
GEN. REF.: —.

Note: In Acts 7:26, A.V., *epeimi*, to come on or after, used with *hēmera*, day, is translated "next" (R.V., "following"); so with *hēmera*, understood, Acts 16:11; 20:15 (1st part); in 21:18, R.V. and A.V., "following."

NEXT DAY

Notes: (1) For *aurion*, to-morrow, translated "next day" in Acts 4:3, and *epaurion*, on the morrow, Matt. 27:62; John 1:29, 35; 12:12; Acts 14:20; 25:6, see MORROW.

(2) For *echō*, Acts 20:15, see NEXT, No. 3.

(3) For *epeimi*, without the noun *hēmera*, "day," see NEXT (end of Note).

(4) In Acts 20:15 (mid. of verse) *heteros*, other, signifies "next," with *hēmera*, understood.

(5) In Acts 28:13 (end of ver.) the adjective *deuteraios*, second, is used in the masculine plural adverbially, signifying "the second (day)," R.V., A.V., "the next (day)."

NIGH

A. Adverbs.

1. *engus* [ἐγγύς, 1451], nigh or near, is translated in both ways in Matt. 24:32, 33 and Mark 13:28, 29, A.V. (R.V., "nigh" in both); in Acts 1:12, with *echon*, present participle neuter of *echō*, to have, R.V., "nigh unto . . . off" (A.V., "from"). See NEAR, No. 1.
NT: B.214a; CB.1245a; K.194.
OT: qārôb: S.7138; HR.363c.4; H.2065d; BD.898b.
GEN. REF.: IS.3:503; NB.—; Z.—.

2. *paraplēsion* [παραπλήσιον, 3897], the neuter of the adjective *paraplēsios*, *para*, beside, *plēsios*, near, nearly resembling, is translated "nigh unto," with reference to death, in Phil. 2:27. ¶
NT: B.621c; CB.1262b; K.—.
OT: —.
GEN. REF.: —.

B. Verb.

engizō [ἐγγίζω, —]: see APPROACH.

C. Preposition.

para [παρά, 3844], beside, alongside of, is translated "nigh unto" in Matt. 15:29; in Mark 5:21, R.V., "by" (A.V., "nigh unto").
NT: B.609c; CB.1261c; K.771.
OT: —.
GEN. REF.: —.

Note: In Mark 5:11, A.V., *pros*, towards, on the side of, is translated "nigh unto (the mountain)," R.V., "on (the mountain) side"; the swine were not simply near the mountain.

NIGHT (by, in the)

nux [νύξ, 3571], is used (I) literally, (*a*) of the alternating natural period to that of the day, e.g., Matt. 4:2; 12:40; 2 Tim. 1:3; Rev. 4:8; (*b*) of the period of the absence of light, the time in which something takes place, e.g., Matt. 2:14 (27:64, in some mss.); Luke 2:8; John 3:2 (7:50, in some mss.); Acts 5:19; 9:25; (*c*) of point of time, e.g., Matt. 14:27 (in some mss.), 30; Luke 12:20; Acts 27:23; (*d*) of duration of time, e.g., Luke 2:37; 5:5; Acts 20:31; 26:7 (note the difference in the phrase in Mark 4:27); (II) metaphorically, (*a*) of the period of man's alienation from God, Rom. 13:12; 1 Thess. 5:5, lit., 'not of night,' where "of" means 'belonging to'; cp. "of the Way," Acts 9:2; "of shrinking back" and "of faith," Heb. 10:39, marg.; (*b*) of death, as the time when work ceases, John 9:4.

NT: B.546b; CB.1260b; K.661.
OT: layil: S.3915; HR.954c.1a; H.1111; BD.538c.
GEN. REF.: IS.3:535; NB.—; Z.4:436.

NIGHT AND A DAY (A)

nuchthēmeros [νυχθήμερος, 3574], an adjective denoting lasting a night and a day (from *nux*, night, and *hēmera*, a day), is used in 2 Cor. 11:25, in the neuter gender, as a noun, the object of the verb *poieō*, to do, lit., 'I have done a night-and-a-day.' ¶

NT: B.547a; CB.—; K.—.
OT: —.
GEN. REF.: IS.3:535; NB.—; Z.—.

NINE

ennea [ἐννέα, 1767], is found in Luke 17:17, and in connection with "ninety" (see below). ¶

NT: B.267a; CB.—; K.—.
OT: —.
GEN. REF.: —.

NINETY

enenēkonta, or *ennēn*— [ἐνενήκοντα, 1768], is found in Matt. 18:12, 13; Luke 15:4, 7. ¶

NT: B.265a; CB.—; K.—.
OT: —.
GEN. REF.: —.

NINTH

enatos, or *enn*— [ἔνατος, 1766], is found in reference (*a*) to the ninth hour (3 o'clock, p.m.) in Matt. 20:5; 27:45, 46; Mark 15:33, 34; Luke 23:44; Acts 3:1; 10:3, 30; (*b*) to the topaz as the ninth foundation of the city wall in the symbolic vision in Rev. 21 (ver. 20). ¶

NT: B.262a; CB.—; K.—.
OT: tēsha': S.8672; HR.469a.1a; H.2551; BD.1077c.
GEN. REF.: —.

NO: see † p. 1

NO LONGER, NO MORE

1. *ouketi* [οὐκέτι, 3765], a negative adverb of time, signifies no longer, no more (*ou*, not, *k*, euphonic, *eti* longer), denying absolutely and directly, e.g., Matt. 19:6; John 4:42, "now . . . not"; 6:66; Acts 20:25, 38; 2 Cor. 1:23, A.V., "not as yet"; Eph. 2:19; with another negative, to strengthen the negation, e.g., Matt. 22:46; Mark 14:25; 15:5, R.V., "no more (anything)," A.V., "yet . . . no (thing)"; Acts 8:39; Rev. 18:11, 14.

NT: B.592c; CB.—; K.—.
OT: 'ôd (w. neg.): S.5750; HR.1030a.6b; H.1576a; BD.728c.
GEN. REF.: —.

2. *mēketi* [μηκέτι, 3371], with the same meaning as No. 1, but generally expressing a prohibition, e.g., Matt. 21:19; John 5:14; Rom. 14:13; Eph. 4:28; 1 Tim. 5:23; 1 Pet. 4:2; indicating some condition expressed or implied, e.g., 1 Thess. 3:5; or non-existence, when the existence might have been possible under certain conditions, e.g., Mark 1:45; 2:2, R.V., "no longer" (A.V., "no"). See HENCEFORTH.

NT: B.518c; CB.—; K.—.
OT: —.
GEN. REF.: —.

Notes: (1) The double negative *ou mē*, by no means, in no wise, followed by *eti*, longer, still, yet, is rendered "no more" in Heb. 8:12; 10:17; Rev. 3:12.

(2) In John 15:4, A.V., *houtōs*, so, followed by *oude*, neither, is translated "no more" (R.V., "so neither").

NO MAN, NO ONE, NEITHER ANY MAN

Note: Oudeis and *mēdeis*, no one, no man, are related to one another in much the same way as indicated above under *ouketi* and *mēketi*. Instances of *oudeis* are Matt. 6:24; 9:16; 24:36 (R.V., "no one"); John 1:18; 3:2, 13, 32; 14:6 and 16:22 (R.V., "no one"); 2 Cor. 7:2 (thrice); Heb. 12:14; 1 John 4:12; Rev. 2:17, R.V., "no one"; so 5:3, 4; 19:12; in 3:7, 8 and 15:8 (R.V., "none"); in 7:9 and 14:3, "no man." In all these cases "man" stands for "person." The spelling *outheis* occurs occasionally in the mss.; Westcott and Hort adopt it in 2 Cor. 11:8, in the genitive case *outhenos*.

Instances of *mēdeis* are Matt. 8:4 (almost all those in the Synoptists are cases of prohibition or admonition); Acts 9:7; Rom. 12:17; 1 Cor. 3:18, 21; Gal. 6:17; Eph. 5:6; Col. 2:18; 1 Thess. 3:3; 1 Tim. 4:12; Rev. 3:11, R.V., "no one."

Notes: (1) In some mss. the negative *mē* and the indefinite pronoun *tis*, some one, anyone, appear as one word, *mētis* (always separated in the best mss.), e.g., Matt. 8:28, "no man"; so in 1 Cor. 16:11; 2 Cor. 11:16; 2 Thess. 2:3. The words are separated also in Matt. 24:4; 2 Cor. 8:20 (R.V., "any man," after "avoiding"); Rev. 13:17. These instances represent either impossibility or prohibition (see under No Longer, No. 2); contrast *ouch* (i.e., *ou*) . . . *tis* in Heb. 5:4, "no man (taketh)," where a direct negative statement is made.

(2) In 2 Cor. 11:10 the negative *ou*, "not," is translated "no man" (A.V. marg. "not"); in 1 Cor. 4:6, e.g., the negative *mē* is translated "no one"; in Rom. 14:13, the negative *mē*, used in an admonition, is translated "no man."

NO WISE (in), ANYWISE (in)

1. *ou mē* [οὐ μή, 3756 (*ou*)], a double negative, strongly expressing a negation, is translated "in no wise" in Matt. 5:18, 20, R.V. (A.V., "in no case"); 10:42; Luke 18:17; John 6:37; Acts 13:41; Rev. 21:27; in Matt. 13:14 (twice, R.V.; A.V., "not"); so in Mark 9:1; Luke 9:27; John 4:48; Acts 28:26 (twice); 1 Thess. 4:15; in Luke 10:19, R.V. "(nothing) . . . in any wise" (A.V., "by any means").

NT: B.517c; CB.–; K.–.
OT: –.
GEN. REF.: –.

Note: In 2 Thess. 2:3, R.V., "(no man) . . . in any wise" (A.V., "by any means"), the double negative is *mē* . . . *mēdena*.

2. *oudamōs* [οὐδαμῶς, 3760], akin to the adjective *oudamos*, not even one (not in the N.T.), denotes by no means, in no wise, Matt. 2:6. ¶

NT: B.591b; CB.–; K.–.
OT: –.
GEN. REF.: –.

3. *ou pantōs* [οὐ πάντως, 3843 (*pantōs*)], lit., 'not altogether,' i.e., 'wholly not' (from *pas*, all), is rendered "in no wise" in Rom. 3:9.

NT: B.609c; CB.–; K.–.
OT: –.
GEN. REF.: –.

Note: In Luke 13:11 the phrase *eis to panteles*, lit., unto the complete end (*pas*, all, *telos*, an end), i.e., completely, utterly, preceded by the negative *mē*, is translated "in no wise" ('who was utterly unable to lift herself up'). Cp. Heb. 7:25, where the same phrase is used without a negative, signifying "to the uttermost."

For **ON THIS WISE** see **THUS** (*b*)

NOBLE

1. *eugenēs* [εὐγενής, 2104], an adjective, lit., well born (*eu*, well, and *genos*, a family, race), (*a*) signifies noble, 1 Cor. 1:26; (*b*) is used with *anthrōpos*, a man, i.e., a nobleman, in Luke 19:12. ¶ In the Sept., Job 1:3. ¶

NT: B.319a; CB.1247b; K.–.
OT: gādôl: S.1419; HR.569a.1; H.315d; BD.152d.
GEN. REF.: IS.3:546; NB.–; Z.4:449.

2. *eugenesteros* [εὐγενέστερος, 2104], the comparative degree of No. 1, occurs in Acts 17:11, "more noble," i.e., more noble-minded. ¶

NT: B.319a; CB.–; K.–.
OT: –.
GEN. REF.: IS.3:546; NB.–; Z.4:449.

3. *kratistos* [κράτιστος, 2903], is translated "most noble" in the A.V. of Acts 24:3 and 26:25 (R.V., "most excellent"). See Excellent.

NT: B.449a; CB.1256a; K.–.
OT: ṭôb: S.2896; HR.785a.2a; H.793a; BD.373c.
GEN. REF.: IS.–; NB.–; Z.4:449.

NOBLEMAN

basilikos [βασιλικός, 937], an adjective, royal, belonging to a king (*basileus*), is used of the command, 'thou shalt love thy neighbour as thyself,' "the royal law," Jas. 2:8; this may mean a law which covers or governs other laws and therefore has a specially regal character (as Hort suggests), or because it is made by a King (a meaning which Deissmann assigns) with whom there is no respect of persons; it is used with the pronoun *tis*, a certain one, in John 4:46, 49, of a courtier, one in the service of a king, "a nobleman" (some mss. have the noun *basiliskos*, a petty king, in these two verses). It is used of a country in Acts 12:20, "the king's (country)," and of royal apparel in ver. 21. See King, Royal. ¶

NT: B.136d; CB.1238c; K.97.
OT: melek: S.4428; HR.214a.1a; H.1199a; BD.572d.
GEN. REF.: IS.–; NB.–; Z.4:449.

Note: For *eugenēs* in Luke 19:12, see Noble, No. 1.

NOISE

A. Adverb.

rhoizēdon [ῥοιζηδόν, 4500], from *rhoizos*, the whistling of an arrow, signifies 'with rushing sound,' as of roaring flames, and is used in 2 Pet. 3:10, of the future passing away of the heavens. ¶

NT: B.737a; CB.–; K.–.
OT: –.
GEN. REF.: IS.3:547; NB.–; Z.4:449.

B. Verbs.

1. *akouō* [ἀκούω, 191], to hear, is translated "it was noised" in Mark 2:1 (Passive Voice), of the rapid spread of the information that Christ was "in the house" in Capernaum. See Hear.

NT: B.31d; CB.1234b; K.34.
OT: shāmaʿ: S.8085; HR.45a.8a; H.2412; BD.1033b.
GEN. REF.: –.

2. *dialaleō* [διαλαλέω, 1255], lit., to speak through, is rendered "were noised abroad" in Luke 1:65. See COMMUNE.

NT: B.185c; CB.–; K.–.
OT: –.
GEN. REF.: –.

Notes: (1) In Rev. 6:1, A.V., *phōnē*, a voice or sound, is translated "noise" (R.V., "voice"); it is used with *ginomai* in Acts 2:6, A.V., "(this) was noised abroad," R.V., "(this) sound was heard."

(2) In Matt. 9:23, A.V., *thorubeō*, to make a tumult or uproar, in the Middle Voice, as in Mark 5:39 and Acts 20:10, is translated "making a noise" (R.V., "making a tumult"). See ADO, TROUBLE, TUMULT, UPROAR.

NOISOME

kakos [κακός, 2556], evil, is translated "noisome" in Rev. 16:2. See BAD.

NT: B.397d; CB.1253b; K.391.
OT: ra'a': S.7489; HR.709b.13a; H.2191,2192; BD.949b.
rā': S.7451; HR.709b.13b; H.2191; BD.948c.
rā'āh: S.7451; HR.709b.13c; H.2191; BD.949a.
GEN. REF.: IS.3:547; NB.–; Z.–.

For NONE see NO MAN

NOON

mesēmbria [μεσημβρία, 3314], lit., middle-day (*mesos*, middle, and *hēmera*, a day), signifies (*a*) noon, Acts 22:6; (*b*) the south, Acts 8:26. ¶

NT: B.506d; CB.–; K.–.
OT: ṣōhar: S.6672; HR.912c.3; H.1883a,b; BD.843d.
GEN. REF.: IS.3:550; NB.–; Z.4:451.

NOR: see † p. 1

NORTH

borras [βορρᾶς, 1005], primarily Boreas, the North Wind, came to denote the north (cp. Borealis), Luke 13:29; Rev. 21:13. ¶

NT: B.145b; CB.–; K.–.
OT: ṣāphôn: S.6828; HR.224c.1a; H.1953b; BD.860d.
GEN. REF.: IS.3:550; NB.–; Z.4:451.

NORTH EAST, NORTH WEST

chōros [χῶρος, 5566], Lat., *corus*, the Latin name for the north-west wind, hence, the north-west, occurs in Acts 27:12, A.V., R.V., "(north-east and) south-east," as the N.W. wind blows towards the S.E. ¶

NT: B.891c; CB.1240a; K.–.
OT: –.
GEN. REF.: IS.–; NB.–; Z.4:451.

Note: In the same ver., *lips*, the south-west (lit., Libyan) wind, hence, the south-west (so A.V.) is rendered "north-east" in R.V., as the S.W. wind blows towards the N.E. The difficulty is that Lutro (commonly identified with Phoenix) faces E., not W. But there is a harbour opposite Lutro which does look S.W. and N.W., bearing the name Phineka (R.V. marg. renders the whole phrase literally). This seems the best solution.

NOT: see † p. 1

NOTABLE, OF NOTE

1. *gnōstos* [γνωστός, 1110], an adjective, signifying 'known' (from *ginōskō*, to know), is used (*a*) as an adjective, most usually translated "known," whether of facts, e.g., Acts 1:19; 2:14; 4:10; or persons, John 18:15, 16; it denotes "notable" in Acts 4:16, of a miracle; (*b*) as a noun, "acquaintance," Luke 2:44 and 23:49. See ACQUAINTANCE, KNOWN.

NT: B.164b; CB.1248b; K.119.
OT: yāda': S.3045; HR.274a.1a,b; H.848; BD.393b.
GEN. REF.: IS.3:552; NB.–; Z.–.

2. *episēmos* [ἐπίσημος, 1978], primarily meant bearing a mark, e.g., of money, 'stamped,' 'coined,' (from *epi*, upon, and *sēma*, a mark, a sign; cp. *sēmainō*, to give a sign, signify, indicate, and *sēmeioō*, to note; see below); it is used in the N.T., metaphorically, (*a*) in a good sense, Rom. 16:7, "of note," illustrious, said of Andronicus and Junias (*b*) in a bad sense, Matt. 27:16, "notable," of the prisoner Barabbas. ¶ In the Sept., Gen. 30:42; Esth. 5:4; 8:13, toward the end of the verse, "a distinct (day)." ¶

NT: B.298b; CB.–; K.1015.
OT: qāshar: S.7194; HR.527b.1; H.2090; BD.905a.
GEN. REF.: IS.3:552; NB.–; Z.–.

3. *epiphanēs* [ἐπιφανής, 2016], illustrious, renowned, notable (akin to *epiphainō*, to show forth, appear; Eng., epiphany), is translated "notable" in Acts 2:20, of the great Day of the Lord. The appropriateness of this word (compared with Nos. 1 and 2) to that future occasion is obvious. ¶

NT: B.304b; CB.1246a; K.1244.
OT: yārē': S.3372; HR.538a.1; H.907,908; BD.431a.
GEN. REF.: IS.3:552; NB.–; Z.–.

NOTE (Verb)

sēmeioō [σημειόω, 4593], from *sēmeion*, a sign, token, signifies to mark, to note, in the Middle Voice, to note for oneself, and is so used in 2 Thess. 3:14, in an injunction to take cautionary note of one who refuses obedience to the Apostle's word by the Epistle. ¶ In the Sept. Ps. 5:6. ¶

NT: B.748d; CB.–; K.1015.
OT: nāsā': S.5375; HR.1264a.1; H.1421; BD.669d.
GEN. REF.: IS.3:552; NB.–; Z.–.

NOTHING

1. *ouden* [οὐδέν, 3762], the neuter of *oudeis*, no one, occurs, e.g., in Matt. 5:13; 10:26; 23:16; adverbially, e.g., in Matt. 27:24; 2 Cor. 12:11 (1st part), "in nothing"; 1 Tim. 4:4; in the dative case, after *en*, "in," Phil. 1:20. Westcott and Hort adopt the spelling *outhen* in Luke 22:35; 23:14; Acts 15:9; 19:27; 26:26; 1 Cor. 13:2.

NT: B.591d; CB.1261b; K.—.
OT: 'îsh (w. neg.): S.376; HR.1028b.3b; H.83a; BD.35c.
me'ûmāh (w. neg.): S.3972; HR.1028b.10; H.1136; BD.548d.
GEN. REF.: —.

2. *mēden* [μηδέν, 3367], the neuter of *mēdeis*, no one, is related to No. 1, in the same way as the masculine genders are; so with the negatives *ou* and *mē*, not, in all their usage and connections (see under NO MAN). Thus it is found, not in direct negative statements, as with No. 1, but in warnings, prohibitions, etc., e.g., Matt. 27:19; Acts 19:36; in expressions conveying certain impossibilities, e.g., Acts 4:21; comparisons, e.g., 2 Cor. 6:10; intimating a supposition to the contrary, 1 Tim. 6:4; adverbially, e.g., 2 Cor. 11:5, "not a whit." Westcott and Hort adopt the spelling *mēthen* in Acts 27:33.

NT: B.518a; CB.1258a; K.—.
OT: 'îsh (w. neg.): S.376; HR.920c.3; H.83a; BD.35c.
GEN. REF.: —.

3. *ou* [οὐ, 3756], not, is translated "nothing" in Luke 8:17; 11:6; 1 Cor. 9:16; 2 Cor. 8:15 (in each case, an absolute and direct negative).

NT: B.590a; CB.—; K.—.
OT: —.
GEN. REF.: —.

4. *mē* [μή, 3361], not, is translated "nothing" in John 6:39 in a clause expressing purpose; in the A.V. of Luke 7:42 (R.V., "not"), in a temporal clause.

NT: B.515d; CB.1258a; K.—.
OT: —.
GEN. REF.: —.

5. *ou . . . ti* [οὐ . . . τί, 5100 (*ti*)], followed by the subjunctive mood, "(have) nothing (to eat)," lit., '(they have) not what (they should eat),' in Matt. 15:32 (in some mss. in Mark 6:36); Mark 8:2; the phrase conveys more stress than the simple negative (No. 3).

NT: B.—; CB.—; K.—.
OT: —.
GEN. REF.: —.

6. *mē . . . ti* [μὴ . . . τί, —], followed by the subjunctive mood, "(they had) nothing (to eat)," R.V., "(having) nothing (to eat)," A.V., lit., 'not (having) what (they should eat),' in Mark 8:1; the negative is *mē* here because it is attached to a participle, 'having'; whereas in No. 5 the negative *ou* is attached to the indicative mood, 'they have.'

NT: —.
OT: —.
GEN. REF.: —.

7. *mē ti* [μή τι, —], lit., 'not anything,' not used in simple, direct negations (see under NO MAN), occurs in John 6:12 in a clause of purpose; in 1 Cor. 4:5, in a prohibition.

NT: —.
OT: —.
GEN. REF.: —.

8. *oude ti* [οὐδέ τι, 3761], not even anything, is found in 1 Tim. 6:7 (2nd part); it is a more forceful expression than the simple *ouden* in the 1st part of the verse, as if to say, 'it is a fact that we brought nothing into the world, and most certainly we can carry out not even the slightest thing, whatever we may have possessed.'

NT: —.
OT: —.
GEN. REF.: —.

Notes: (1) For "nothing" in Luke 1:37, A.V., see WORD, No. 2 (R.V.).

(2) In John 11:49 the double negative *ouk* (not) . . . *ouden* (nothing) is translated "nothing at all."

(3) In Acts 11:8 *pan*, everything, with *oudepote*, not even ever, is rendered "nothing . . . ever," R.V., A.V., "nothing . . . at any time."

(4) In 1 Cor. 1:19, A.V., *atheteō*, to set aside, make void, reject, is translated "I will bring to nothing" (R.V., "will I reject").

For **NOTICE BEFORE,** 2 Cor. 9:5, A.V., see **AFOREPROMISED**

NOTWITHSTANDING

Note: This is the A.V. rendering of (I) *alla*, but, in Rev. 2:20 (R.V., "but"); (2) *plēn*, howbeit, yet, except that, in Luke 10:11, 20, and Phil. 1:18 (R.V., "only that"); in 4:14, A.V., "notwithstanding" (R.V., "howbeit").

NOUGHT (for, bring to, come to, set at)

A. Pronoun.

ouden [οὐδέν, 3762], nothing (the neuter of *oudeis*, no one), is translated "nought" in Acts 5:36. See NOTHING.

NT: B.591d; CB.1261b; K.—.
OT: 'îsh (w. neg.): S.376; HR.1028b.3b; H.83a; BD.35c.
me'ûmāh (w. neg.): S.3972; HR.1028b.10; H.1136; BD.548d.
GEN. REF.: —.

B. Adverb.

dōrean [δωρεάν, 1432], freely, as a gift, is translated "for nought" in Gal. 2:21, R.V. (A.V., "in vain"); in 2 Thess. 3:8, in a denial by the Apostle that he lived on the hospitality of others at Thessalonica. See FREELY.

NT: B.210c; CB.1242a; K.166.
OT: ḥinnām: S.2600; HR.358c.1; H.694b; BD.336c.
GEN. REF.: —.

C. Verbs.

1. *katargeō* [καταργέω, 2673], is used in 1 Cor. 1:28, "(that) He might bring to nought"; 1 Cor. 2:6 (Passive Voice in the original); 1 Cor. 6:13, R.V., "will bring to nought" (A.V. "will destroy"); so 2 Thess. 2:8 and Heb. 2:14. See Abolish.

NT: B.417b; CB.1254b; K.76.
OT: b^{e}ṭēl (Aramaic): S.989; HR.743a.1; H.2625; BD.1084b.
GEN. REF.: —.

2. *exoutheneō* [ἐξουθενέω, 1848], to set at nought, treat with utter contempt, despise, is translated "set at nought" in Luke 18:9, R.V. (A.V., "despised"); in 23:11, "set (Him) at nought"; "was set at nought" in Acts 4:11; in Rom. 14:3, R.V., "set at nought" (A.V., "despise"); ver. 10, "set at nought." See Account, Despise.

NT: B.277c; CB.1247c; K.—.
OT: bāzāh: S.959; HR.500b.3; H.224; BD.102b.
mā'as: S.3988; HR.500b.6a; H.1139,1140; BD.549b.
GEN. REF.: —.

3. *exoudeneō* or *exoudenoō* [ἐξουδενέω, 1847], has the same meaning as No. 2, and is virtually the same word (*outhen* being another form of *ouden*, nothing), i.e., to treat as nothing (*ex*, intensive), and is translated "be set at nought" in Mark 9:12. ¶

NT: B.277c; CB.1247c; K.—.
OT: bāzāh: S.959; HR.500b.3; H.224; BD.102b.
mā'as: S.3988; HR.500b.6a; H.1139,1140; BD.549b.
GEN. REF.: —.

4. *ekpiptō* [ἐκπίπτω, 1601], to fall out, is used in Rom. 9:6 in the sense of falling from its place, failing, of the word of God, R.V., "hath come to nought" (A.V., "hath taken none effect"). See Fall.

NT: B.243d; CB.1243c; K.846.
OT: nābēl: S.5034; HR.439b.2; H.1286; BD.615b.
nāphal: S.5307; HR.439b.3a; H.1392; BD.656c.
GEN. REF.: —.

5. *atheteō* [ἀθετέω, 114], to set aside, reject, is translated "set at nought" in Heb. 10:28, R.V. (A.V., "despised"); so Jude 8. See Nothing, *Note* (4).

NT: B.21a; CB.1238a; K.1176.
OT: bāgad: S.898; HR.29b.1; H.198; BD.93c.
pāsha‘: S.6586; HR.29b.12; H.1846; BD.833b.
GEN. REF.: —.

Notes: (1) In Acts 5:38, A.V., *kataluō*, lit.; to loosen down, hence, to overthrow, is translated "it will come to nought" (R.V., "it will be overthrown"). See Destroy.

(2) In Rev. 18:17, A.V., *erēmoō*, to make desolate, is translated "is come to nought" (R.V., "is made desolate"). See Desolate.

(3) In Acts 19:27, A.V, the accusative case of *apelegmos*, confutation, disrepute, preceded by the verb *erhcomai*, to come, and *eis*, unto or into, is translated "be set at nought" (R.V., "come into disrepute"). See Disrepute. ¶

NOURISH, NOURISHMENT

1. *trephō* [τρέφω, 5142], to rear, feed, nourish, is translated by the verb to nourish in Jas. 5:5 (of luxurious living); Rev. 12:14 (of God's care for Israel against its enemies); so ver. 6, R.V. (A.V., "feed"); in Acts 12:20, R.V., "was fed" (A.V., "was nourished"). See Feed.

NT: B.825c; CB.—; K.—.
OT: ḥāyāh: S.2421; HR.1371b.5; H.644; BD.310d.
GEN. REF.: IS.3:553; NB.—; Z.—.

2. *anatrephō* [ἀνατρέφω, 397], to nurse, bring up (*ana*, up, and No. 1), is translated "nourished" in Acts 7:20 (A.V., "nourished up"); in 21, "nourished," A.V. and R.V. See Bring.

NT: B.62d; CB.—; K.—.
OT: —.
GEN. REF.: —.

3. *ektrephō* [ἐκτρέφω, 1625], *ek*, from, out of, and No. 1, primarily used of children, to nurture, rear, is translated "nurture" of the care of one's own flesh, Eph. 5:29, and in Eph. 6:4, R.V. (A.V., "bring . . . up"). See Bring. ¶

NT: B.246c; CB.1244a; K.—.
OT: qādal: S.1431; HR.443c.1; H.315; BD.152a.
GEN. REF.: IS.3:553; NB.—; Z.—.

4. *entrephō* [ἐντρέφω, 1789], to train up, nurture, is used metaphorically, in the Passive Voice, in 1 Tim. 4:6, of being nourished in the faith. ¶

NT: B.269d; CB.—; K.—.
OT: —.
GEN. REF.: IS.3:553; NB.—; Z.—.

For NOURISHMENT MINISTERED, Col. 2:19, see SUPPLY

NOVICE

neophutos [νεόφυτος, 3504], an adjective, lit., newly-planted (from *neos*, new, and *phuō*, to bring forth, produce), denotes a new convert, neophyte, novice, 1 Tim. 3:6, of one who by inexperience is unfitted to act as a bishop or overseer in a church. ¶ In the Sept., Job 14:9; Psa. 128:3; 144:12; Is. 5:7. ¶

NT: B.536c; CB.1259c; K.—.
OT: neṭa‘: S.5194; HR.943a.1a; H.1354a; BD.642c.
n^{e}ṭi‘îm: S.5195; HR.943a.1b; H.1354b; BD.642d.
GEN. REF.: IS.3:553; NB.—; Z.4:452.

NOW

A. Adverbs.

1. *nun* [νῦν, 3568], is used (*a*) of time, the immediate present, whether in contrast to the past, e.g., John 4:18; Acts 7:52, or to the future, e.g., John 12:27; Rom. 11:31; sometimes with the article, singular or plural, e.g., Acts 4:29; 5:38; (*b*) of logical sequence, often partaking also of the character of (*a*), now therefore, now

however, as it is, e.g., Luke 11:39; John 8:40; 9:41; 15:22, 24; 1 Cor. 5:11, R.V., marg., "as it is."

NT: B.545c; CB.1260a; K.658.
OT: 'attāh: S.6258; HR.951c.9a; H.1650c; BD.773d.
GEN. REF.: IS.3:553; NB.–; Z.–.

Note: Under (*a*) comes the phrase in 2 Cor. 8:14, with *kairos*, a time, all governed by *en*, in, or at, A.V., "now at this time" (R.V., "at this present time").

2. *nuni* [νυνί, 3570], a strengthened form of No. 1, is used (*a*) of time, e.g., Acts 22:1 (in the best mss.); 24:13; Rom. 6:22; 15:23, 25; (*b*) with logical import, e.g., Rom. 7:17; 1 Cor. 13:13, which some regard as temporal (*a*); but if this is the significance, "the clause means, 'but faith, hope, love, are our abiding possession now in this present life.' The objection to this rendering is that the whole course of thought has been to contrast the things which last only for the present time with the things which survive. And the main contrast so far has been between love and the special [then] present activity of prophecy, tongues, knowledge. There is something of disappointment, and even of bathos, in putting as a climax to these contrasts the statement that in this present state faith, hope, love abide; that is no more than can be said of [the then existing] prophecies, tongues and knowledge. If there is to be a true climax the 'abiding' must cover the future as well as the present state. And that involves as a consequence that *nuni* must be taken in its logical meaning, i.e., 'as things are,' 'taking all into account' . . . This logical sense of *nuni* . . . is enforced by the dominant note of the whole passage" (R. St. John Parry, in the Camb. Greek Test.).

It is certain that love will continue eternally; and hope will not cease at the Parousia of Christ, for hope will ever look forward to the accomplishment of God's eternal purposes, a hope characterised by absolute assurance; and where hope is in exercise faith is its concomitant. Faith will not be lost in sight.

NT: B.546b; CB.1260b; K.–.
OT: 'attāh: S.6258; HR.951c.9a; H.1650c; BD.773d.
GEN. REF.: IS.3:553; NB.–; Z.–.

3. *ēdē* [ἤδη, 2235], denotes already, now already, "the subjective present, with a suggested reference to some other time, or to some expectation" (Thayer), e.g., Matt. 3:10; 14:24; Luke 11:7; John 6:17; Rom. 1:10; 4:19; 13:11; Phil. 4:10.

NT: B.344a; CB.1242c; K.–.
OT: kebār: S.3528; HR.604b.2; H.947c; BD.460c.
'attāh: S.6258; HR.604b.3; H.1650c; BD.773d.
GEN. REF.: IS.3:553; NB.–; Z.–.

4. *arti* [ἄρτι, 737], expressing coincidence, and denoting strictly present time, signifies 'just now,' this moment, in contrast (*a*) to the past, e.g., Matt. 11:12; John 2:10; 9:19, 25; 13:33; Gal. 1:9, 10; (*b*) to the future, e.g., John 13:37; 16:12, 31; 1 Cor. 13:12 (cp. No. 2 in ver. 13); 2 Thess. 2:7; 1 Pet. 1:6, 8; (*c*) sometimes without necessary reference to either, e.g., Matt. 3:15; 9:18; 26:53; Gal. 4:20; Rev. 12:10.

NT: B.110b; CB.1237c; K.658.
OT: 'attāh: S.6258; HR.161a.1; H.1650c; BD.773d.
GEN. REF.: IS.3:553; NB.–; Z.–.

5. *aparti* [ἀπάρτι, 534], sometimes written separately, *ap'arti*, i.e., *apo*, from, and No. 4, denotes 'from now,' henceforth, John 13:19; 14:7; Rev. 14:13. See HENCEFORTH. ¶

NT: B.81a; CB.–; K.–.
OT: –.
GEN. REF.: –.

6. *loipon* [λοιπόν, 3063], the neuter of *loipos*, the rest, from now, is used adverbially with the article and translated "now" in Mark 14:41.

NT: B.479d; CB.1257b; K.–.
OT: yeter: S.3499; HR.888a.1c; H.936a; BD.451d.
GEN. REF.: –.

B. Conjunctions and Particles.

1. *oun* [οὖν, 3767], therefore, so then, is sometimes used in continuing a narrative, e.g., Acts 1:18; 1 Cor. 9:25; or resuming it after a digression, usually rendered "therefore," e.g., Acts 11:19; 25:1, R.V. (A.V., "now"). In the following it is absent from the best mss., Mark 12:20; Luke 10:36; John 16:19; 18:24; 19:29.

NT: B.592d; CB.–; K.–.
OT: –.
GEN. REF.: –.

Note: In 2 Cor. 5:20 *oun* is simply "therefore," as in R.V. (A.V., "now then").

2. *de* [δέ, 1161], but, and, now, often implying an antithesis, is rendered "now" in John 19:23; 1 Cor. 10:11; 15:50; Gal. 1:20; Eph. 4:9; in Acts 27:9 (1st part), R.V., "and" (A.V., "now"); in Gal. 4:1, R.V., "but" (A.V., "now").

NT: B.171c; CB.–; K.–.
OT: –.
GEN. REF.: –.

3. *dē* [δή, 1211], a consecutive particle, giving stress to the word or words to which it is attached, sometimes with hardly any exact Eng. equivalent, is translated "now" in Luke 2:15, in the words of the shepherds; in Acts 15:36, R.V. (A.V., "and"). Some mss. have it in 2 Cor. 12:1; see R.V. marg.

NT: B.178b; CB.–; K.–.
OT: –.
GEN. REF.: –.

Notes: (1) In 1 Cor. 4:7, A.V., B, No. 2, followed by *kai*, and, is translated "now" (R.V., "but").

(2) In Rom. 14:15 and Philm. 16, A.V., *ouketi*, no longer, is translated "now . . . not" and "not now" (R.V., "no longer"); cp. John 4:42 and 21:6, "now . . . not."

(3) The particle *ara*, then, expressing a more informal inference than *oun* (B, No. 1 above), is often in Paul's Epistles coupled with *oun*, the phrase meaning "so then," as A.V. and R.V. in Rom. 7:3, 25; 9:16; 14:12; in R.V. only (A.V., "therefore"), Rom. 5:18; 8:12; 9:18; 14:19; Gal. 6:10; 1 Thess. 5:6; 2 Thess. 2:15. In Eph. 2:19 the A.V. renders it "now therefore."

(4) In 1 Tim. 1:4, the R.V., "*so do I now*" (A.V., "*so do*") is added to complete the sentence.

(5) In Heb. 9:9, R.V., the perfect participle of *enistēmi*, to be present, is translated "(the time) *now* present" (A.V., "then present," which misses the meaning). See COME, (AT) HAND, PRESENT.

NUMBER

A. Nouns.

1. *arithmos* [ἀριθμός, 706], number, a number (Eng., arithmetic, etc.), occurs in Luke 22:3; John 6:10; Rom. 9:27; elsewhere five times in Acts, ten times in the Apocalypse.

NT: B.106b; CB.1237c; K.78.
OT: mispār: S.4557; HR.156c.7b; H.1540e; BD.708d.
GEN. REF.: IS.3:556; NB.–; Z.–.

2. *ochlos* [ὄχλος, 3793], a multitude, is translated "number" in Luke 6:17, R.V. (A.V., "multitude"); in Mark 10:46 and Acts 1:15 the renderings are reversed. See COMMON, COMPANY, CROWD, MULTITUDE, PEOPLE.

NT: B.600c; CB.1260b; K.750.
OT: hāmôn: S.1995; HR.1043a.1; H.505a; BD.242b.
qāhāl: S.6951; HR.1043a.5; H.1991a; BD.874c.
GEN. REF.: IS.3:556; NB.–; Z.–.

B. Verbs.

1. *arithmeō* [ἀριθμέω, 705], akin to A, is found in Matt. 10:30; Luke 12:7; Rev. 7:9. ¶

NT: B.106b; CB.1237c; K.78.
OT: sāphar: S.5608; HR.156b.4; H.1540; BD.707d.
GEN. REF.: IS.3:556; NB.–; Z.–.

2. *katarithmeō* [καταριθμέω, 2674], to number or count among (*kata*, and No. 1), is used in Acts 1:17. ¶

NT: B.417c; CB.–; K.–.
OT: mispār: S.4557; HR.743a.3; H.1540e; BD.708d.
GEN. REF.: IS.3:556; NB.–; Z.–.

3. *enkrinō* [ἐγκρίνω, 1469], to reckon among (*en*, in, *krinō*, to judge or reckon), is translated "to number . . . (ourselves) with" in 2 Cor. 10:12 (R.V. marg., "to judge ourselves among or . . . with"), of the Apostle's dissociation of himself and his fellow-missionaries from those who commended themselves. ¶

NT: B.216d; CB.–; K.469.
OT: –.
GEN. REF.: –.

4. *sunkatapsēphizō* [συγκαταψηφίζω, 4785], to vote or reckon (one) a place among (*sun*, with or among, *kata*, down, and *psēphizō*, to count or vote, originally with pebbles, *psēphos*, a pebble), is used of the numbering of Matthias with the eleven Apostles, Acts 1:26. ¶

NT: B.773c; CB.–; K.1341.
OT: –.
GEN. REF.: –.

Notes: (1) Some mss. have verse 28 in Mark 15 (A.V., where *logizomai*, to reckon, is translated "He was numbered."

(2) For *katalegō* 1 Tim. 5:9 (A.V., "let . . . be taken into the number"), see TAKE, *Note* (18).

(3) In Mark 5:13 see the italicised words in R.V.

(4) In Heb. 7:23, R.V., the adjective *pleiōn*, more, many, is translated "many in number" (A.V., "many"); in Acts 28:23, R.V., "a great number" (A.V., "many").

NURSE

trophos [τροφός, 5162], translated "nurse" in 1 Thess. 2:7, there denotes a nursing mother, as is clear from the statement "cherisheth her own children"; this is also confirmed by the word *ēpios*, gentle (in the same verse), which was commonly used of the kindness of parents towards children. Cp. *trephō*, to bring up (see NOURISH).

NT: B.827d; CB.1273a; K.–.
OT: yānaq: S.3243; HR.1376c.1; H.874; BD.413b.
GEN. REF.: IS.3:568; NB.–; Z.4:469.

For **NURTURE** (Eph. 6:4) see **CHASTENING**

O

OATH

1. *horkos* [ὅρκος, 3727], is primarily equivalent to *herkos*, a fence, an enclosure, that which restrains a person; hence, an oath. The Lord's command in Matt. 5:33 was a condemnation of the minute and arbitrary restrictions imposed by the scribes and Pharisees in the matter of adjurations, by which God's Name was profaned. The injunction is repeated in Jas. 5:12. The language of the Apostle Paul, e.g., in Gal. 1:20 and 1 Thess. 5:27 was not inconsistent with Christ's prohibition, read in the light of its context. Contrast the oaths mentioned in Matt. 14:7, 9; 26:72; Mark 6:26.

Heb. 6:16 refers to the confirmation of a compact among men, guaranteeing the discharge of liabilities; in their disputes "the oath is final for confirmation." This is referred to in order to illustrate the greater subject of God's oath to Abraham, confirming His promise; cp. Luke 1:73; Acts 2:30. ¶ Cp. the verbs *horkizō*, and *exorkizō*, under ADJURE.

NT: B.581c; CB.1251b; K.729.
OT: shᵉbû'āh: S.7621; HR.1013b.2b; H.2318a; BD.989d.
GEN. REF.: IS.3:572; NB.902; Z.4:476.

2. *horkōmosia* [ὁρκωμοσία, 3728], denotes an affirmation on oath (from No. 1 and *omnumi*, to swear). This is used in Heb. 7:20, 21 (twice), 28, of the establishment of the Priesthood of Christ, the Son of God, appointed a Priest after the order of Melchizedek, and "perfected for evermore." ¶ In the Sept., Ezek. 17:18, 19. ¶

NT: B.581c; CB.1251b; K.729.
OT: 'ālāh: S.423; HR.1013c.1; H.91a; BD.46d.
GEN. REF.: IS.3:572; NB.902; Z.4:476.

Note: For *anathematizō* in Acts 23:21, A.V., "have bound (themselves) with an oath," see CURSE.

OBEDIENCE, OBEDIENT, OBEY

A. Nouns.

1. *hupakoē* [ὑπακοή, 5218], obedience (*hupo*, under, *akouō*, to hear), is used (*a*) in general, Rom. 6:16 (1st part), R.V., "(unto) obedience," A.V., "(to) obey"; here obedience is not personified, as in the next part of the verse, "servants . . . of obedience" [see (*c*)], but is simply shown to be the effect of the presentation mentioned; (*b*) of the fulfilment of apostolic counsels, 2 Cor. 7:15; 10:6; Philm. 21; (*c*) of the fulfilment of God's claims or commands, Rom. 1:5 and 16:26, "obedience of faith," which grammatically might be objective, to the faith (marg.), or subjective, as in the text. Since faith is one of the main subjects of the Epistle, and is the initial act of obedience in the new life, as well as an essential characteristic thereof, the text rendering is to be preferred; Rom. 6:16 (2nd part); 15:18, R.V. "(for) the obedience," A.V., "(to make) obedient"; 16:19; 1 Pet. 1:2, 14, R.V., "(children of) obedience," i.e., characterized by obedience, A.V., "obedient (children)"; ver. 22, R.V., "obedience (to the truth)," A.V., "obeying (the truth)"; (*d*) of obedience to Christ (objective), 2 Cor. 10:5; (*e*) of Christ's obedience, Rom. 5:19 (referring to His death; cp. Phil. 2:8); Heb. 5:8, which refers to His delighted experience in constant obedience to the Father's will (not to be understood in the sense that he learned to obey). ¶

NT: B.837a; CB.1251c; K.34.
OT: 'ᵃnāwāh: S.6037; HR.1405c.1; H.1652b; BD.776c.
GEN. REF.: IS.2:649; NB.904; Z.4:482.

2. *hupotagē* [ὑποταγή, 5292], subjection (*hupo*, under, *tassō*, to order), is translated "obedience" in 2 Cor. 9:13, R.V. (A.V., "subjection"). See SUBJECTION.

NT: B.847d; CB.1252b; K.1156.
OT: –.
GEN. REF.: IS.2:649; NB.–; Z.–.

B. Verbs.

1. *hupakouō* [ὑπακούω, 5219], to listen, attend (as in Acts 12:13), and so, to submit, to obey, is used of obedience (*a*) to God, Heb. 5:9; 11:8; (*b*) to Christ, by natural elements, Matt. 8:27; Mark 1:27; 4:41; Luke 8:25; (*c*) to disciples of Christ, Luke 17:6; (*d*) to the faith, Acts 6:7; the Gospel, Rom. 10:16; 2 Thess. 1:8; Christian doctrine, Rom. 6:17 (as to a form or mould of teaching); (*e*) to apostolic injunctions, Phil. 2:12; 2 Thess. 3:14; (*f*) to Abraham by Sarah, 1 Peter. 3:6; (*g*) to parents by children, Eph. 6:1; Col. 3:20; (*h*) to masters by servants, Eph. 6:5; Col. 3:22; (*i*) to sin, Rom. 6:12; (*j*) in general, Rom. 6:16. ¶

NT: B.837b; CB.1251c; K.34.
OT: shāma': S.8085; HR.1405c.7a; H.2412; BD.1033b.
'ānāh: S.6031; HR.1405c.3a; H.1651,1652; BD.776a.
GEN. REF.: IS.2:649; NB.904; Z.4:482.

2. *peithō* [πείθω, 3982], to persuade, to win over, in the Passive and Middle Voices, to be persuaded, to listen to, to obey, is so used with this meaning, in the Middle Voice, e.g., in Acts 5:36, 37 (in ver. 40, Passive Voice, "they agreed"), Rom. 2:8; Gal. 5:7; Heb. 13:17; Jas. 3:3. The obedience suggested is not by sub-

mission to authority, but resulting from persuasion.

"*Peithō* and *pisteuō*, 'to trust,' are closely related etymologically; the difference in meaning is that the former implies the obedience that is produced by the latter, cp. Heb. 3:18, 19, where the disobedience of the Israelites is said to be the evidence of their unbelief. Faith is of the heart, invisible to men; obedience is of the conduct and may be observed. When a man obeys God he gives the only possible evidence that in his heart he believes God. Of course it is persuasion of the truth that results in faith (we believe because we are persuaded that the thing is true, a thing does not become true because it is believed), but *peithō*, in N.T. suggests an actual and outward result of the inward persuasion and consequent faith."* See ASSURANCE, B, No. 3.

NT: B.639a; CB.1263a; K.818.
OT: bāṭah: S.982; HR.1114b.2a; H.233; BD.105a.
GEN. REF.: IS.2:649; NB.904; Z.4:482.

3. *peitharcheō* [πειθαρχέω, 3980], to obey one in authority (No. 2, and *archē*, rule), is translated "obey" in Acts 5:29, 32; "to be obedient," Tit. 3:1, R.V. (A.V., "to obey magistrates"); in Acts 27:21, "hearkened." See HEARKEN. ¶

NT: B.638d; CB.1263a; K.818.
OT: shᵉmaʻ (Aramaic): S.8086; HR.1114b.1; H.3040; BD.1116b.
GEN. REF.: IS.2:649; NB.904; Z.4:482.

4. *apeitheō* [ἀπειθέω, 544], to disobey, be disobedient (*a*, negative, and No. 2), is translated "obey not" in Rom. 2:8; 1 Pet. 3:1; 4:17. See DISOBEDIENT.

NT: B.82c; CB.1236b; K.818.
OT: mārāh: S.4784; HR.119c.6; H.1242; BD.598a.
sārar: S.5639; HR.119c.9; H.–; BD.710d.
GEN. REF.: IS.2:649; NB.–; Z.–.

Note: In 1 Cor. 14:34, A.V., *hupotassō*, to be in subjection (R.V.), is translated "to be under obedience"; so Tit. 2:5, R.V. "being in subjection" (A.V., "obedient"); and ver. 9, R.V. (A.V., "to be obedient"). See SUBJECTION.

C. Adjective.

hupēkoos [ὑπήκοος, 5255], obedient (akin to A, No. 1), giving ear, subject, occurs in Acts 7:39, R.V., "(would not be) obedient," A.V., "(would not) obey"; 2 Cor. 2:9; Phil. 2:8, where the R.V. "*even*" is useful as making clear that the obedience was not to death but to the Father. ¶

NT: B.842b; CB.1252a; K.34.
OT: shāmaʻ: S.8085; HR.1411c.3; H.2412; BD.1033b.
GEN. REF.: IS.2:649; NB.904; Z.4:482.

For the verb **OBJECT,** Acts 24:19, see **ACCUSATION,** B, No. 4.

For **OBJECTS**, R.V., in Acts 17:23, see **WORSHIP**

OBSERVATION, OBSERVE

A. Noun.

paratērēsis [παρατήρησις, 3907], attentive watching (akin to *paratēreō*, to observe), is used in Luke 17:20, of the manner in which the Kingdom of God (i.e., the operation of the spiritual Kingdom in the hearts of men) does not come, "in such a manner that it can be watched with the eyes" (Grimm-Thayer), or, as A.V. marg., "with outward show." ¶

NT: B.622c; CB.1262b; K.1174.
OT: –.
GEN. REF.: IS.3:578; NB.–; Z.–.

B. Verbs.

1. *anatheōreō* [ἀναθεωρέω, 333], to observe carefully, consider well (*ana*, up, intensive, and *theōreō*, to behold), is used in Acts 17:23, R.V., "observed" (of Paul's notice of the objects of Athenian worship), and Heb. 13:7, "considering." See BEHOLD. ¶

NT: B.54c; CB.–; K.–.
OT: –.
GEN. REF.: IS.3:578; NB.–; Z.–.

2. *tēreō* [τηρέω, —]: see KEEP, No. 1.

3. *suntēreō* [συντηρέω, —]: see KEEP, No. 3.

4. *paratēreō* [παρατηρέω, 3906], to watch closely, observe narrowly (*para*, used intensively, and No. 2), is translated "ye observe" in Gal. 4:10, where the Middle Voice suggests that their religious observance of days etc. was not from disinterested motives, but with a view to their own advantage. See WATCH. Cp. *phroneō* (to think), "regardeth" in Rom. 14:6, where the subject is connected with the above, though the motive differs.

NT: B.622c; CB.1262b; K.1174.
OT: zāmam: S.2161; HR.1065a.1; H.556; BD.273a.
shāmar: S.8104; HR.1065a.2; H.2414; BD.1036b.
GEN. REF.: IS.3:578; NB.–; Z.–.

5. *phulassō* [φυλάσσω, —]: see KEEP, No. 4.

6. *poieō* [ποιέω, —], to do, is translated "to observe" in Acts 16:21. See DO.

OBTAIN, OBTAINING

A. Verbs.

1. *tunchanō* [τυγχάνω, 5177], to meet with, light upon, also signifies to obtain, attain to, reach, get (with regard to things), translated to obtain in Acts 26:22, of "the help that is from God"; 2 Tim. 2:10, of "the salvation which is in Christ Jesus with eternal glory"; Heb. 8:6,

* From Notes on Thessalonians by Hogg and Vine, pp. 254, 255.

of the ministry obtained by Christ; 11:35, of "a better resurrection." See CHANCE.
NT: B.829b; CB.–; K.1191.
OT: māṣā: S.4672; HR.1378a.1; H.2033; BD.592c.
GEN. REF.: –.

2. *epitunchanō* [ἐπιτυγχάνω, 2013], primarily, to light upon (*epi*, upon and No. 1), denotes to obtain, Rom. 11:7 (twice); Heb. 6:15; 11:33; Jas. 4:2. ¶
NT: B.303d; CB.–; K.–.
OT: –.
GEN. REF.: –.

3. *lanchanō* [λαγχάνω, 2975], to obtain by lot, is translated "that have obtained" in 2 Pet. 1:1; in Acts 1:17, A.V., "had obtained" (R.V., "received"), with *klēros*, a lot or portion. See LOTS.
NT: B.462a; CB.1256c; K.495.
OT: lākad: S.3920; HR.840b.1; H.1115; BD.539d.
GEN. REF.: –.

4. *ktaomai* [κτάομαι, 2932], to procure for oneself, get, gain, acquire, is translated "obtained" in Acts 1:18, R.V. (A.V., "purchased"); 8:20, R.V. (A.V., "may be purchased"); 22:28. See POSSESS, PROVIDE, PURCHASE.
NT: B.455a; CB.1256a; K.–.
OT: qānāh: S.7069; HR.793b.9a; H.2039; BD.888d.
GEN. REF.: –.

5. *krateō* [κρατέω, 2902], to be strong, also means to get possession of, obtain, e.g., in Acts 27:13, "they had obtained (their purpose)." See HOLD.
NT: B.448c; CB.1256a; K.466.
OT: ḥāzaq: S.2388; HR.783a,6a-c; H.636; BD.304a.
'āḥaz: S.270; HR.783a.2a; H.64; BD.28a.
GEN. REF.: –.

6. *lambanō* [λαμβάνω, 2983], to take, to receive, is translated by the verb to obtain in 1 Cor. 9:25; Phil. 3:12, R.V., "(not that) I have (already) obtained" (contrast *katantaō*, to attain, ver. 11); Moule translates it 'not that I have already received,' i.e., the prize; the verb does not signify to attain; Heb. 4:16, A.V., "obtain." See ACCEPT, No. 4.
NT: B.464a; CB.1256c; K.495.
OT: lāqaḥ: S.3947; HR.847a.11a; H.1124; BD.542c.
nāśā': S.5375; HR.847a.17a; H.1421; BD.669d.
GEN. REF.: –.

7. *heuriskō* [εὑρίσκω, 2147], denotes to find; in the Middle Voice, to find for oneself, to procure, get, obtain, with the suggestion of accomplishing the end which had been in view; so in Heb. 9:12, "having obtained (eternal redemption)."
NT: B.324d; CB.1250b; K.–.
OT: māṣā': S.4672; HR.576c.8a; H.2033; BD.592c.
GEN. REF.: –.

Notes: (1) In 1 Cor. 9:24, A.V., *katalambanō*, a strengthened form of No. 6 (*kata*, used intensively), is translated "obtain" (R.V., "attain").

(2) In Heb. 11:2, 4, 39, A.V., *martureō*, to bear witness, and in the Passive Voice, to have witness borne to one, is translated to obtain a good report, or to obtain witness (R.V., "had witness borne"). See WITNESS.

(3) For the A.V. of Heb. 1:4, "He hath by inheritance obtained" (R.V., "He hath inherited"), and of Eph. 1:11, see INHERIT.

(4) For the phrase to obtain mercy, the Passive Voice of *eleeō* in Matt. 5:7; Rom. 11:30, 31; 1 Cor. 7:25; 2 Cor. 4:1 (R.V.); 1 Tim. 1:13, 16; 1 Pet. 2:10 (twice), see MERCY.

B. Noun.

peripoiēsis [περιποίησις, 4047], lit., a making around (*peri*, around, *poieō*, to do or make), denotes (*a*) the act of obtaining anything, as of salvation in its completeness, 1 Thess. 5:9; 2 Thess. 2:14; (*b*) a thing acquired, an acquisition, possession, Eph. 1:14, R.V., "(*God's* own) possession" [some would put this under (*a*)]; so 1 Pet. 2:9, R.V., A.V., "a peculiar (people)"; cp. Is. 43:21; (*c*) preservation; this may be the meaning in Heb. 10:39, "saving" (R.V. marg., "gaining"); cp. the corresponding verb in Luke 17:33 (in the best texts), "preserve." ¶ In the Sept. the noun has the meaning (*b*) in Hag. 2:10 and Mal. 3:17, (*c*) in 2 Chron. 14:13. ¶
NT: B.650a; CB.1263b; K.–.
OT: miḥyāh: S.4241; HR.1125c.1; H.644b; BD.313c.
s[e]gullāh: S.5459; HR.1125c.2; H.1460a; BD.688c.
GEN. REF.: –.

OCCASION

aphormē [ἀφορμή, 874], properly a starting point, was used to denote a base of operations in war. In the N.T. it occurs as follows: "(*a*) the Law provided sin with a base of operations for its attack upon the soul, Rom. 7:8, 11; (*b*) the irreproachable conduct of the Apostle provided his friends with a base of operations against his detractors, 2 Cor. 5:12; (*c*) by refusing temporal support at Corinth he deprived these detractors of their base of operations against him, 2 Cor. 11:12; (*d*) Christian freedom is not to provide a base of operations for the flesh, Gal. 5:13; (*e*) unguarded behaviour on the part of young widows (and the same is true of all believers) would provide Satan with a base of operations against the faith, 1 Tim. 5:14."* ¶

The word is found frequently in the papyri with meanings which illustrate those in the N.T. In the Sept., Prov. 9:9; Ezek. 5:7. ¶
NT: B.127c; CB.1236c; K.730.
OT: –.
GEN. REF.: IS.3:578; NB.–; Z.–.

* From Notes on Galatians by Hogg and Vine, p. 269.

Notes: (1) For the R.V. renderings "occasion (or 'occasions') of stumbling," "occasion of falling," see FALLING, B, *Note* (3), OFFENCE.

(2) In 2 Cor. 8:8, A.V., the phrase "by occasion of" translates the preposition *dia*, through, by means of (R.V., "through").

For **OCCUPATION**, Acts 18:3, A.V., see **TRADE**

Notes: The phrase "of like occupation" in Acts 19:25 translates the phrase *peri* (about) *ta* (the) *toiauta* (such things), i.e., lit., '(occupied) about such things.'

OCCUPY

peripateō [περιπατέω, 4043], to walk, is sometimes used of the state in which one is living, or of that to which a person is given, e.g., Heb. 13:9, "(meats, wherein they that) occupied themselves," R.V. (marg., "walked"; A.V., "have been occupied"), i.e., exercising themselves about different kinds of food, regarding some as lawful, others as unlawful (referring especially to matters of the ceremonial details of the law).

NT: B.649a; CB.1263b; K.804.
OT: hālak: S.1980; HR.1125a.2a-c; H.—; BD.229d.
GEN. REF.: IS.3:579; NB.—; Z.—.

Notes: (1) For "occupy," in the A.V. of Luke 19:13, see TRADE

(2) For "occupieth," in the A.V. of 1 Cor. 14:16, see FILL, No. 2.

ODOUR

osmē [ὀσμή, 3744], a smell, an odour (akin to *ozō*, to smell), is translated "odour" in John 12:3; it is used metaphorically in Eph. 5:2, R.V., "an odour (of a sweet smell)," A.V., "(a sweet smelling) savour," of the effects Godward of the Sacrifice of Christ; in Phil. 4:18 of the effect of sacrifice, on the part of those in the church at Philippi, who sent material assistance to the Apostle in his imprisonment. The word is translated "savour" in 2 Cor. 2:14, 16 (twice). ¶

NT: B.586a; CB.1261b; K.735.
OT: rēaḥ: S.7381; HR.1018c.3; H.2131b; BD.926a.
GEN. REF.: IS.3:579; NB.—; Z.4:503.

Notes: For *thumiama*, incense, translated "odours" in the A.V. of Rev. 5:8 (R.V., "incense"), see INCENSE. For *Amōmon* (quoted in R.V. marg. in the latinized form *amomum*) in Rev. 18:13, see SPICE.

OF

Notes: (1) In addition to the rendering of a number of prepositions, "of" translates the genitive case of nouns, with various shades of meaning. Of these the subjective and objective are mentioned here, which need careful distinction. Thus the phrase "the love of God," e.g., in 1 John 2:5 and 3:16, is subjective, signifying "God's love"; in 1 John 5:3, it is objective, signifying our love to God. Again, "the witness of God," e.g., 1 John 5:9, is subjective, signifying the witness which God Himself has given; in Rev. 1:2, 9, and 19:10, e.g., "the testimony of Jesus" is objective, signifying the testimony borne to Him. In the A.V. "the faith of" is sometimes ambiguous; with reference to Christ it is objective, i.e., faith in Him, not His own faith, in the following passages in which the R.V., "in" gives the correct meaning; Rom. 3:22; Gal. 2:16 (twice), 20, R.V., "I live in faith, the faith which is in the Son of God"; 3:22; Eph. 3:12; Phil. 3:9 (cp. Col. 2:12, "faith in the working of God"). In Eph. 2:20, "the foundation of the apostles and prophets" is subjective, i.e., the foundation laid by the apostles and prophets ("other foundation can no man lay than . . . Jesus Christ," 1 Cor. 3:11).

(2) In the A.V. of John 16:13, "He shall not speak of Himself," the preposition is *apo*, "from," as in the R.V.; the Spirit of God often speaks of Himself in Scripture, the Lord's assurance was that the Holy Spirit would not be the Source of His utterances. So with regard to Christ's utterances, John 7:17, R.V., "I speak from (*apo*) Myself"; and 14:10.

(3) In John 6:46; 15:15; 17:7; Acts 17:9, the R.V., "from" is to be observed, as rightly translating *para* (A.V., "of").

(4) The following are instances in which "of" translates *ek*, or *ex*, out of, from, Matt. 21:25 (R.V., "from"); 1 Cor. 1:30; 15:6; 2 Cor. 5:1 (R.V., "from"); Jas. 4:1.

(5) In the following, *peri*, concerning, is so translated in the R.V. (for A.V., "of"), e.g., Acts 5:24; 1 Cor. 1:11; 1 John 1:1 (the R.V. is important); cp. John 16:8.

(6) *Epi*, over, is so translated in Matt. 18:13, R.V.; "concerning" in Acts 4:9.

(7) *Huper*, on behalf of, is so rendered in 2 Cor. 7:4, R.V. (A.V., "of").

(8) For *hupo*, by, see the R.V. of Matt. 1:22; 2:16; 11:27; Luke 9:7; Acts 15:4; 1 Cor. 14:24; 2 Cor. 8:19; Phil. 3:12.

(9) For other prepositions, etc., see † p. 1.

OFF: see † p. 1

OFFENCE

A. Nouns.

1. *skandalon* [σκάνδαλον, 4625], originally was "the name of the part of a trap to which the bait is attached, hence, the trap or snare itself, as in Rom. 11:9, R.V., 'stumblingblock,' quoted from Psa. 69:22, and in Rev. 2:14, for Balaam's device was rather a trap for Israel than a stumblingblock to them, and in Matt. 16:23, for in Peter's words the Lord perceived a snare laid for Him by Satan.

"In N.T. *skandalon* is always used metaphorically, and ordinarily of anything that arouses prejudice, or becomes a hindrance to others, or causes them to fall by the way. Sometimes the hindrance is in itself good, and those stumbled by it are the wicked."*

Thus it is used (*a*) of Christ in Rom. 9:33, "(a rock) of offence"; so 1 Pet. 2:8; 1 Cor. 1:23 (A.V. and R.V., "stumblingblock"), and of His Cross, Gal. 5:11 (R.V., ditto); of the "table" provided by God for Israel, Rom. 11:9 (see above); (*b*) of that which is evil, e.g., Matt. 13:41, R.V., "things that cause stumbling" (A.V., "things that offend"), lit., 'all stumblingblocks'; 18:7, R.V., "occasions of stumbling" and "occasion"; Luke 17:1 (ditto); Rom. 14:13, R.V., "an occasion of falling" (A.V., "an occasion to fall"), said of such a use of Christian liberty as proves a hindrance to another; 16:17, R.V., "occasions of stumbling," said of the teaching of things contrary to sound doctrine; 1 John 2:10, "occasion of stumbling," of the absence of this in the case of one who loves his brother and thereby abides in the light. Love, then, is the best safeguard against the woes pronounced by the Lord upon those who cause others to stumble. See FALL, B, *Note* (3). ¶ Cp. the Sept. in Hos. 4:17, "Ephraim partaking with idols hath laid stumblingblocks in his own path."

NT: B.753a; CB.1269a; K.1036.
OT: môqēsh: S.4170; HR.1268b.3; H.906c; BD.430c.
miksĥôl: S.4383; HR.1268b.4; H.1050c; BD.506a.
GEN. REF.: IS.3:580; NB.1220; Z.4:504.

2. *proskomma* [πρόσκομμα, 4348], an obstacle against which one may dash his foot (akin to *proskoptō*, to stumble or cause to stumble; *pros*, to or against, *koptō*, to strike), is translated "offence" in Rom. 14:20, in ver. 13, "a stumblingblock," of the spiritual hindrance to another by a selfish use of liberty (cp. No. 1 in the same verse); so in 1 Cor. 8:9. It is used of Christ, in Rom. 9:32, 33, R.V., "(a stone) of stumbling," and 1 Pet. 2:8, where the A.V. also has this rendering. ¶ Cp. the Sept. in Ex. 23:33, "these (the gods of the Canaanites) will be an offence (stumblingblock) unto thee."

NT: B.716b; CB.1267a; K.946.
OT: môqēsh: S.4170; HR.1217a.1; H.906c; BD.430c.
negeph: S.5063; HR.1217a.2; H.1294a; BD.620a.
GEN. REF.: IS.3:580; NB.1220; Z.4:504.

3. *proskopē* [προσκοπή, 4349], like No. 2, and formed from the same combination, occurs in 2 Cor. 6:3, R.V., "occasion of stumbling" (A.V., "offence"), something which leads others into error or sin. ¶ Cp. the Sept. in Prov. 16:18, "a haughty spirit (becomes) a stumblingblock" (i.e., to oneself).

NT: B.716b; CB.1267b; K.946.
OT: —.
GEN. REF.: IS.—; NB.—; Z.4:504.

Notes: (1) In the A.V. of Rom. 4:25; 5:15 (twice), 16, 17, 18, 20, *paraptōma*, a trespass, is translated "offence." See TRESPASS.

(2) In 2 Cor. 11:7, A.V., *hamartia*, a sin, is translated "an offence." See SIN.

B. Adjective.

aproskopos [ἀπρόσκοπος, 677], akin to A, No. 3, with *a*, negative, prefixed, is used (*a*) in the Active sense, not causing to stumble, in 1 Cor. 10:32, metaphorically of refraining from doing anything to lead astray either Jews or Greeks or the church of God (i.e., the local chuch), R.V., "no occasion of stumbling" (A.V., "none offence"); (*b*) in the Passive sense, blameless, without stumbling, Acts 24:16, "(a conscience) void of offence"; Phil. 1:10, "void of (A.V., without) offence." The adjective is found occasionally in the papyri writings. ¶

NT: B.102c; CB.1237b; K.946.
OT: —.
GEN. REF.: IS.3:580; NB.—; Z.—.

OFFEND

skandalizō [σκανδαλίζω, 4624], from *skandalon* (OFFENCE, No. 1), signifies to put a snare or stumblingblock in the way, always metaphorically in the N.T., in the same ways as the noun, which see. It is used 14 times in Matthew, 8 in Mark, twice in Luke, twice in John; elsewhere in 1 Cor. 8:13 (twice) and 2 Cor. 11:29. It is absent in the most authentic mss. in Rom. 14:21. The R.V. renders it by the verb to stumble, or cause to stumble, in every place save the following, where it uses the verb to offend, Matt. 13:57; 15:12; 26:31, 33; Mark 6:3; 14:27, 29.

NT: B.752d; CB.1269a; K.1036.
OT: kāshal: S.3782; HR.1268b.1; H.1050; BD.505b.
GEN. REF.: IS.3:580; NB.1220; Z.4:504.

Notes: (1) In Jas. 2:10; 3:2 (twice), A.V., *ptaiō*, to stumble, is translated "offend"; see FALL, STUMBLE.

* From Notes on Galatians by Hogg and Vine, p. 262.

(2) In Acts 25:8, A.V., *hamartanō*, to sin, is translated "have I offended"; see SIN.

OFFENDER

opheiletēs [ὀφειλέτης, 3781], a debtor, is translated "offenders" in Luke 13:4, R.V. (R.V. and A.V. marg., "debtors"; A.V., "sinners"). See DEBTOR.

NT: B.598b; CB.1261a; K.746.
OT: –.
GEN. REF.: IS.3:580; NB.–; Z.–.

Note: In Acts 25:11, A.V., *adikeō*, to do wrong, is translated "be an offender" (R.V., "am a wrong-doer").

OFFER, OFFERING

A. Verbs.

1. *prospherō* [προσφέρω, 4374], primarily, to bring to (*pros*, to, *pherō*, to bring), also denotes to offer, (*a*) of the sacrifice of Christ Himself, Heb. 8:3; of Christ in virtue of his High Priesthood (R.V., "This *high priest*"; A.V., "this man") 9:14, 25 (negative), 28; 10:12; (*b*) of offerings under, or according to, the Law, e.g., Matt. 8:4; Mark 1:44; Acts 7:42; 21:26; Heb. 5:1, 3; 8:3; 9:7, 9; 10:1, 2, 8, 11; (*c*) of offerings previous to the Law, Heb. 11:4, 17 (of Isaac by Abraham); (*d*) of gifts offered to Christ, Matt. 2:11, R.V., "offered" (A.V., "presented unto"); (*e*) of prayers offered by Christ, Heb. 5:7; (*f*) of the vinegar offered to Him in mockery by the soldiers at the Cross, Luke 23:36; (*g*) of the slaughter of disciples by persecutors, who think they are 'offering' service to God, John 16:2, R.V. (A.V., "doeth"); (*h*) of money offered by Simon the sorcerer, Acts 8:18. See BRING, A, No. 8, DEAL WITH, No. 2.

NT: B.719c; CB.1267a; K.1252.
OT: qārab: S.7126; HR.1222c.8a; H.2065; BD.897a.
bô': S.935; HR.1222c.1; H.212; BD.97c.
GEN. REF.: IS.4:260; NB.1113; Z.–.

2. *anapherō* [ἀναφέρω, 399], primarily, to lead or carry up (*ana*), also denotes to offer, (*a*) of Christ's sacrifice, Heb. 7:27; (*b*) of sacrifices under the Law, Heb. 7:27; (*c*) of such previous to the Law, Jas. 2:21 (of Isaac by Abraham); (*d*) of praise, Heb. 13:15; (*e*) of spiritual sacrifices in general, 1 Pet. 2:5. See BEAR, No. 3, BRING, A, No. 2.

NT: B.63a; CB.1235b; K.1252.
OT: 'ālāh: S.5927; HR.84c.10b; H.1624; BD.748a.
qāṭar: S.6999; HR.84c.12; H.2011; BD.882d.
GEN. REF.: IS.4:260; NB.1113; Z.–.

3. *didōmi* [δίδωμι, 1325], to give, is translated "to offer" in Luke 2:24; in Rev. 8:3, A.V., "offer" (R.V., "add"; marg., "give"). See GIVE.

NT: B.192c; CB.1241c; K.166.
OT: nātan: S.5414; HR.377b.26a; H.1443; BD.678a.
GEN. REF.: IS.4:260; NB.–; Z.–.

4. *parechō* [παρέχω, 3930], to furnish, offer, present, supply, is used in Luke 6:29, of offering the other cheek to be smitten after receiving a similar insult; for the A.V. marg., in Acts 17:31, see ASSURANCE, A, No. 1. See BRING, A, No. 21.

NT: B.626b; CB.–; K.–.
OT: 'ābar: S.5674; HR.1068c.11a; H.1556; BD.716d.
GEN. REF.: –.

5. *spendō* [σπένδω, 4689], to pour out as a drink offering, make a libation, is used figuratively in the Passive Voice in Phil. 2:17, "offered" (R.V. marg., "poured out as a drink offering"; A.V. marg., "poured forth"). In 2 Tim. 4:6, "I am already being offered," R.V. (marg., "poured out as a drink-offering"), the Apostle is referring to his approaching death, upon the sacrifice of his ministry. ¶ This use of the word is exemplified in the papyri writings.

NT: B.761c; CB.1269c; K.–.
OT: nāsak: S.5258; HR.1282b.1a-d; H.1375,1377; BD.650c.
GEN. REF.: –.

Notes: (1) In Luke 11:12, A.V., *epididōmi*, to give (*epi*, over, in the sense of instead of, and No. 3), is translated "will he offer" (R.V., and A.V. marg., "will he give").

(2) In Acts 7:41, A.V., *anagō*, to lead up or bring up, is rendered "offered" (R.V., "brought").

(3) In Acts 15:29; 21:25 and 1 Cor. 8:1, 4, 10; 10:19, A.V., *eidōlothutos*, sacrificed to idols, is translated "offered to idols" (*thuō* denotes to sacrifice). See SACRIFICE.

B. Nouns.

1. *prosphora* [προσφορά, 4376], lit., a bringing to (akin to A, No. 1), hence an offering, in the N.T. a sacrificial offering, (*a*) of Christ's sacrifice, Eph. 5:2; Heb. 10:10 (of His body); 10:14; negatively, of there being no repetition, 10:18; (*b*) of offerings under, or according to, the Law, Acts 21:26; Heb. 10:5, 8; (*c*) of gifts in kind conveyed to needy Jews, Acts 24:17; (*d*) of the presentation of believers themselves (saved from among the Gentiles) to God, Rom. 15:16. ¶

NT: B.720b; CB.1267b; K.1252.
OT: minḥāh: S.4503; HR.1223b.1; H.1214a; BD.585a.
pānîm: S.6440; HR.1223b.2; H.1782a; BD.815d.
GEN. REF.: IS.4:260; NB.1113; Z.5:194.

2. *holokautōma* [ὁλοκαύτωμα, —], a burnt offering: see BURNT.

3. *anathēma* [ἀνάθημα, 334], denotes a gift set up in a temple, a votive offering (*ana*, up, *tithēmi*, to place), Luke 21:5, R.V. "offerings" (A.V., "gifts"). ¶ Cp. *anathema* (see CURSE).

NT: B.54c; CB.1235b; K.57.
OT: ḥērem: S.2764; HR.77a,1a; H.744a; BD.356a.
GEN. REF.: –.

Notes: (1) In Luke 21:4, A.V., the plural of *dōron*, a gift, is translated "offerings" (R.V., "gifts").

(2) In Rom. 8:3 and Heb. 13:11, the R.V., "*as an offering*" is added to complete the sacrificial meaning of *peri*.

OFFICE

A. Nouns.

1. *praxis* [πρᾶξις, 4234], a doing, deed (akin to *prassō*, to do or practise), also denotes an acting or function, translated "office" in Rom. 12:4. See DEED.
NT: B.697d; CB.1266b; K.927.
OT: derek: S.1870; HR.1200c.1; H.453a; BD.202c.
pō'al: S.6467; HR.1200c.2; H.1792a; BD.821c.
GEN. REF.: –.

2. *hierateia* [ἱερατεία, 2405], or *hieratia*, denotes a priest's office, Luke 1:9; Heb. 7:5, R.V., "priest's office" (A.V., "office of the priesthood"). ¶
NT: B.371d; CB.1250b; K.349.
OT: k^{e}hunnāh: S.3550; HR.678c.2b; H.959b; BD.464d.
GEN. REF.: IS.3:581; NB.–; Z.–.

B. Verb.

hierateuō [ἱερατεύω, 2407], to officiate as a priest (akin to A, No. 2), is translated "he executed the priest's office" in Luke 1:8. The word is frequent in Inscriptions. ¶
NT: B.371d; CB.1250b; K.349.
OT: kāhan: S.3547; HR.679a.1b; H.959; BD.464c.
GEN. REF.: IS.3:581; NB.–; Z.–.

Notes: (1) In Rom. 11:13, A.V., *diakonia*, a ministry, is translated "office" (R.V., "ministry").

(2) In Acts 1:20, R.V., *episkopē*, an overseership, is translated "office" (marg., "overseership"; A.V., "bishoprick").

(3) In 1 Tim. 3:1, the word "office," in the phrase "the office of a bishop," has nothing to represent it in the original; the R.V. marg. gives "overseer" for "bishop," and the phrase lit., is 'overseership'; so in vv. 10, 13, where the A.V. has "use (and 'used') the office of a deacon," the R.V. rightly omits "office," and translates the verb *diakoneō*, to serve, "let them serve as deacons" and "(they that) have served (well) as deacons."

OFFICER

1. *hupēretēs* [ὑπηρέτης, 5257], for the original of which see MINISTER, A, No. 3, is translated "officer," with the following applications, (*a*) to a magistrate's attendant, Matt. 5:25; (*b*) to officers of the Synagogue, or officers or bailiffs of the Sanhedrin, Matt. 26:58; Mark 14:54, 65; John 7:32, 45, 46; 18:3, 12, 18, 22; 19:6; Acts 5:22, 26. See MINISTER, SERVANT.
NT: B.842c; CB.1252a; K.1231.
OT: 'ebed: S.5650; HR.1411c.2; H.1553a; BD.713d.
GEN. REF.: IS.3:582; NB.–; Z.4:504.

2. *praktōr* [πράκτωρ, 4233], lit., one who does, or accomplishes (akin to *prassō*, to do), was used in Athens of one who exacts payment, a collector (the word is frequently used in the papyri of a public accountant); hence, in general, a court officer, an attendant in a court of justice (so Deissmann); the word is used in Luke 12:58 (twice). ¶ In the Sept., Isa. 3:12. ¶
NT: B.697d; CB.1266b; K.927.
OT: nāgash: S.5066; HR.1200b.1; H.1297; BD.620c.
GEN. REF.: IS.3:582; NB.–; Z.4:504.

OFFSCOURING

peripsēma [περίψημα, 4067], that which is wiped off (akin to *peripsaō*, to wipe off all round; *peri*, around, *psaō*, to wipe), hence, offscouring, is used metaphorically in 1 Cor. 4:13. This and the synonymous word *perikatharma*, refuse, rubbish, "were used especially of condemned criminals of the lowest classes, who were sacrificed as expiatory offerings . . . because of their degraded life" (Lightfoot). ¶
NT: B.653c; CB.1263c; K.833.
OT: s^{e}ḥî: S.5501; HR.1128c; H.1483a,1484; BD.695a.
GEN. REF.: IS.3:584; NB.–; Z.4:512.

OFFSPRING

1. *gennēma* [γέννημα, 1081], akin to *gennaō*, to beget, denotes the offspring of men and animals, Matt. 3:7; 12:34; 23:33; Luke 3:7, R.V., "offspring" (A.V., "generation"). See FRUIT. ¶
NT: B.155d; CB.1248a; K.114.
OT: t^{e}bû'āh: S.8398; HR.238c.9; H.835h; BD.100a.
p^{e}rî: S.6529; HR.238c.8b; H.1809a; BD.826b.
GEN. REF.: IS.3:584; NB.–; Z.–.

2. *genos* [γένος, 1085], a race, family (akin to *ginomai*, to become), denotes an offspring, Acts 17:28, 29; Rev. 22:16. See GENERATION, KIND.
NT: B.156b; CB.1248b; K.117.
OT: mîn: S.4327; HR.239b.4; H.1191a; BD.568b.
'am: S.5971; HR.239b.6; H.1640a,e; BD.766b.
GEN. REF.: IS.3:584; NB.–; Z.–.

OFT, OFTEN, OFTENER, OFTENTIMES, OFT-TIMES

A. Adverbs.

1. *pollakis* [πολλάκις, 4178], akin to *polus*, much, many, is variously translated, e.g., "oft-times," Matt. 17:15 (A.V., "oft," 2nd part); "many times," 2 Cor. 8:22, R.V. (A.V., "oftentimes"); "oft," 2 Cor. 11:23; "often" (ver. 26).
NT: B.686d; CB.–; K.–.
OT: –.
GEN. REF.: IS.3:584; NB.–; Z.–.

2. *polla* [πολλά, 4183], the neuter plural of *polus*, is translated "oft" in Matt. 9:14; some ancient authorities omit it here (see R.V. marg.);

in Rom. 15:22, with the article, R.V., "these many times" (A.V., "much").

NT: B.687c; CB.–; K.–.
OT: –.
GEN. REF.: IS.3:584; NB.–; Z.–.

3. *posakis* [ποσάκις, 4212], an interrogative numeral adverb, how many times, how oft (or often)? occurs in Matt. 18:21; 23:37; Luke 13:34. ¶

NT: B.694b; CB.–; K.–.
OT: –.
GEN. REF.: IS.3:584; NB.–; Z.–.

4. *hosakis* [ὁσάκις, 3740], a relative adverb, as often (or oft) as, 1 Cor. 11:25, 26; Rev. 11:6. ¶

NT: B.585b; CB.1251b; K.–.
OT: –.
GEN. REF.: IS.3:584; NB.–; Z.–.

5. *pukna* [πυκνά, 4437], the neuter plural of *puknos* (see B), used adverbially, is translated "often" in Luke 5:33.

NT: B.729a; CB.–; K.–.
OT: –.
GEN. REF.: IS.3:584; NB.–; Z.–.

6. *puknoteron* [πυκνότερον, 4437], the neuter singular of the comparative degree of *puknos* (cp. No. 5, and see B), very often, or so much the oftener, Acts 24:26, "the oftener." ¶

NT: B.729a; CB.–; K.–.
OT: –.
GEN. REF.: IS.3:584; NB.–; Z.–.

Notes: (1) In Luke 8:29, the phrase *pollois chronois*, lit., 'many times,' is translated "oftentimes" (R.V. marg., "of a long time").

(2) For the rendering "oft" in Mark 7:3, see DILIGENTLY, D, No. 2.

B. Adjective.

puknos [πυκνός, 4437], primarily signifies close, compact, solid; hence, frequent, often, 1 Tim. 5:23. Cp. A, Nos. 5 and 6.

NT: B.729a; CB.–; K.–.
OT: –.
GEN. REF.: IS.3:584; NB.–; Z.–.

OIL

elaion [ἔλαιον, 1637], olive-oil, is mentioned over 200 times in the Bible. Different kinds were known in Palestine. The "pure," R.V. (A.V., "beaten"), mentioned in Ex. 27:20; 29:40; Lev. 24:2; Numb. 28:5 (now known as virgin oil) extracted by pressure, without heat, is called "golden" in Zech. 4:12. There were also inferior kinds. In the N.T. the uses mentioned were (*a*) for lamps, in which the oil is a symbol of the Holy Spirit, Matt. 25:3, 4, 8; (*b*) as a medicinal agent, for healing, Luke 10:34; (*c*) for anointing at feasts, Luke 7:46; (*d*) on festive occasions, Heb. 1:9, where the reference is probably to the consecration of kings; (*e*) as an accompaniment of miraculous power, Mark 6:13, or of the prayer of faith, Jas. 5:14. For its general use in commerce, see Luke 16:6; Rev. 6:6; 18:13. ¶

NT: B.247d; CB.1244a; K.221.
OT: shemen: S.8081; HR.447a.4; H.2410c; BD.1032a.
GEN. REF.: IS.3:585; NB.905; Z.4:513.

OINTMENT

muron [μύρον, 3464], a word derived by the ancients from *murō*, to flow, or from *murra*, myrrh-oil (it is probably of foreign origin; see MYRRH). The ointment is mentioned in the N.T. in connection with the anointing of the Lord on the occasions recorded in Matt. 26:7, 9, 12; Mark 14:3, 4; Luke 7:37, 38, 46; John 11:2; 12:3 (twice), 5. The alabaster cruse mentioned in the passages in Matthew, Mark and Luke was the best of its kind, and the spikenard was one of the costliest of perfumes. Ointments were used in preparing a body for burial, Luke 23:56 ("ointments"). Of the act of the woman mentioned in Matt. 26:6-13, the Lord said, "she did it to prepare Me for burial"; her devotion led her to antedate the customary ritual after death, by showing both her affection and her understanding of what was impending. For the use of the various kinds of ointments as articles of commerce, see Rev. 18:13. ¶

NT: B.529d; CB.1259b; K.615.
OT: shemen: S.8081; HR.937b.3a; H.2410c; BD.1032a.
mirqaḥat: S.4841; HR.937b.2b; H.2215g; BD.955c.
GEN. REF.: IS.3:586; NB.906; Z.4:516.

OLD

A. Adjectives.

1. *archaios* [ἀρχαῖος, 744], original, ancient (from *archē*, a beginning; Eng., archaic, archaeology, etc.), is used (*a*) of persons belonging to a former age, "(to) them of old time," Matt. 5:21, 33, R.V.; in some mss. ver. 27; the R.V. rendering is right; not ancient teachers are in view; what was said to them of old time was "to be both recognized in its significance and estimated in its temporary limitations, Christ intending His words to be regarded not as an abrogation, but a deepening and fulfilling" (Cremer); of prophets, Luke 9:8, 19; (*b*) of time long gone by, Acts 15:21; (*c*) of days gone by in a person's experience, Acts 15:7, "a good while ago," lit., 'from old (days),' i.e., from the first days onward in the sense of originality, not age; (*d*) of Mnason, "an early disciple," Acts 21:16, R.V., not referring to age, but to his being one of the first who had accepted the Gospel from the beginning of its proclamation; (*e*) of things which are old in relation to the new, earlier things in contrast to things present, 2 Cor. 5:17, i.e., of what

characterized and conditioned the time previous to conversion in a believer's experience, R.V., "they are become new," i.e., they have taken on a new complexion and are viewed in an entirely different way; (*f*) of the world (i.e., the inhabitants of the world) just previous to the Flood, 2 Pet. 2:5; (*g*) of the Devil, as "that old serpent," Rev. 12:9; 20:2, old, not in age, but as characterized for a long period by the evils indicated. ¶

NT: B.111b; CB.1237b; K.81.
OT: qedem: S.6924; HR.162c.4a; H.1988a; BD.869c.
qadmōnî: S.6930; HR.162c.4c; H.1988e; BD.870c.
GEN. REF.: –.

Note: For the difference between this and No. 2, see below.

2. *palaios* [παλαιός, 3820], akin to C, No. 1 (Eng., palaeology, etc.), of what is of long duration, old in years, etc., a garment, wine (in contrast to *neos*; see NEW), Matt. 9:16, 17; Mark 2:21, 22 (twice); Luke 5:36, 37, 39 (twice); of the treasures of Divine truth, Matt. 13:52 (compared with *kainos*: see NEW); of what belongs to the past, e.g., the believer's former self before his conversion, his "old man," old because it has been superseded by that which is new, Rom. 6:6; Eph. 4:22 (in contrast to *kainos*); Col. 3:9 (in contrast to *neos*); of the covenant in connection with the Law, 2 Cor. 3:14; of leaven, metaphorical of moral evil, 1 Cor. 5:7, 8 (in contrast to *neos*); of that which was given long ago and remains in force, an old commandment, 1 John 2:7 (twice), that which was familiar and well known in contrast to that which is fresh (*kainos*). ¶

NT: B.605d; CB.1261c; K.769.
OT: yāshān: S.3465; HR.1051b.3; H.928b; BD.445d.
'attîq: S.6267; HR.1051b.5; H.1721d; BD.801c.
GEN. REF.: –.

Note: Palaios denotes old, "without the reference to beginning and origin contained in *archaios*" (Abbott-Smith), a distinction observed in the papyri (Moulton and Milligan). While sometimes any difference seems almost indistinguishable, yet "it is evident that wherever an emphasis is desired to be laid on the reaching back to a beginning, whatever that beginning may be, *archaios* will be preferred (e.g., of Satan, Rev. 12:9; 20:2, see No. 1). That which . . . is old in the sense of more or less worn out . . . is always *palaios*" (Trench).

3. *presbuteros* [πρεσβύτερος, 4245], older, elder, is used in the plural, as a noun, in Acts 2:17, "old men." See ELDER.

NT: B.699c; CB.1266b; K.931.
OT: zāqēn: S.2205; HR.1201c.3; H.574b; BD.278c.
GEN. REF.: IS.3:587; NB.–; Z.–.

B. Nouns.

1. *gerōn* [γέρων, 1088], denotes an old man (from the same root comes Eng., grey), John 3:4. ¶

NT: B.157a; CB.1248b; K.–.
OT: zāqēn: S.2205; HR.240a.1; H.574b; BD.278c.
GEN. REF.: IS.3:587; NB.–; Z.–.

2. *presbutēs* [πρεσβύτης, 4246], "an old man," Luke 1:18, is translated "aged" in Tit. 2:2; Philm. 9 (for this, however, see the R.V. marg. See AGED.

NT: B.700d; CB.1266b; K.931.
OT: zāqēn: S.2205; HR.1202c.1; H.574b; BD.278c.
GEN. REF.: IS.3:587; NB.–; Z.–.

3. *gēras* [γῆρας, 1094], old age, occurs in Luke 1:36. ¶

NT: B.157d; CB.–; K.–.
OT: z^equnîm: S.2208; HR.255c.1c; H.574e; BD.279a.
ziqnāh: S.2209; HR.255c.1b; H.574d; BD.279a.
sêbāh: S.7872; HR.255c.3b; H.2253b; BD.966c.
GEN. REF.: IS.3:587; NB.–; Z.–.

Note: Augustine (quoted by Trench, §cvii, 2) speaks of the distinction observed among Greeks, that *presbutēs* conveys the suggestion of gravity.

C. Adverbs.

1. *palai* [πάλαι, 3819], denotes long ago, of old, Heb. 1:1, R.V., "of old time" (A.V., "in time past"); in Jude 4, "of old"; it is used as an adjective in 2 Pet. 1:9, "(his) old (sins)," lit., 'his sins of old.' See WHILE.

NT: B.605c; CB.1261c; K.769.
OT: rāḥôq: S.7350; HR.1051a.1; H.2151b; BD.935b.
GEN. REF.: –.

2. *ekpalai* [ἔκπαλαι, 1597], from of old, for a long time (*ek*, from, and No. 1), occurs in 2 Pet. 2:3, R.V., "from of old" (A.V., "of a long time"); 3:5. See LONG, B, *Note* (2).

NT: B.243c; CB.–; K.–.
OT: –.
GEN. REF.: –.

Note: In 1 Pet. 3:5, A.V., the particle *pote*, once, formerly, ever, sometime, is translated "in the old time" (R.V., "aforetime"); in 2 Pet. 1:21, "in old time" (R.V., "ever"), A.V. marg., "at any time."

D. Verbs.

1. *palaioō* [παλαιόω, 3822], akin to A, No. 2, denotes, in the Active Voice, to make or declare old, Heb. 8:13 (1st part); in the Passive Voice, to become old, of things worn out by time and use, Luke 12:33; Heb. 1:11, "shall wax old," lit., 'shall be made old,' i.e., worn out; in 8:13 (2nd part), R.V., "is becoming old" (A.V. "decayeth"); here and in the 1st part of the

verse, the verb may have the meaning to abrogate; for the next verb in the verse, see No. 2. ¶

NT: B.606a; CB.1261c; K.769.
OT: bālāh: S.1086; HR.1051b.1a,b; H.246; BD.115a.
'ātaq: S.6275; HR.1051b.4; H.1721; BD.801a.
GEN. REF.: —.

2. *gēraskō* [γηράσκω, 1095], from *gēras*, old age (akin to B, No. 1), to grow old, is translated "thou shalt be old," in John 21:18; "waxeth aged," Heb. 8:13, R.V. (A.V., "waxeth old"). ¶

NT: B.158a; CB.1248b; K.—.
OT: zāqēn: S.2205; HR.256a.1; H.574b; BD.278c.
GEN. REF.: IS.3:587; NB.—; Z.—.

Notes: (1) In John 8:57, *echō*, to have, is used with "fifty years" as the object, signifying, "Thou art (not yet fifty years) old," lit., 'Thou hast not yet fifty years.'

(2) In Mark 5:42, R.V., the verb *eimi*, to be, with the phrase 'of twelve years' is translated "was . . . old" (A.V., 'was *of the age* of').

OLDNESS

palaiotēs [παλαιότης, 3821], from *palaios* (see A, No. 2, above), occurs in Rom. 7:6, of "the letter," i.e., the law, with its rules of conduct, mere outward conformity to which has yielded place in the believer's service to a response to the inward operation of the Holy Spirit. The word is contrasted with *kainotēs*, newness. ¶

NT: B.606a; CB.1261c; K.769.
OT: —.
GEN. REF.: —.

OLD WIVES'

graōdēs [γραώδης, 1126], an adjective, signifying old-womanish (from *graus*, an old woman), is said of fables, in 1 Tim. 4:7. ¶

NT: B.167b; CB.—; K.—.
OT: —.
GEN. REF.: —.

OLIVES (OLIVE BERRIES), OLIVE TREE

1. *elaia* [ἐλαία, 1636], denotes (*a*) an olive tree, Rom. 17, 24; Rev. 11:4 (plural); the Mount of Olives was so called from the numerous olive-trees there, and indicates the importance attached to such; the Mount is mentioned in the N.T. in connection only with the Lord's life on earth, Matt. 21:1; 24:3; 26:30; Mark 11:1; 13:3; 14:26; Luke 19:37; 22:39; John 8:1; (*b*) an olive, Jas. 3:12, R.V. (A.V., "olive berries"). ¶

NT: B.247d; CB.1244a; K.221.
OT: zayit: S.2132; HR.446c.1; H.548; BD.268b.
GEN. REF.: IS.3:588; NB.907; Z.4:528.

2. *elaiōn* [ἐλαιών, 1638], an olive-grove or olive-garden, the ending —*on*, as in this class of noun, here indicates "a place set with trees of the kind designated by the primitive" (Thayer); hence it is applied to the Mount of Olives, Luke 19:29; 21:37; Acts 1:12 ("Olivet"); in the first two of these and in Mark 11:1, some mss. have the form of the noun as in No. 1. ¶

NT: B.248a; CB.1244a; K.—.
OT: zayit: S.2132; HR.447c.1; H.548; BD.268b.
GEN. REF.: IS.3:588; NB.907; Z.4:528.

3. *kallielaios* [καλλιέλαιος, 2565], the garden olive (from *kallos*, beauty, and No. 1), occurs in Rom. 11:24, "a good olive tree." ¶

NT: B.400a; CB.1253b; K.—.
OT: —.
GEN. REF.: IS.—; NB.907; Z.4:528.

4. *agrielaios* [ἀγριέλαιος, 65], an adjective (from *agrios*, growing in the fields, wild, and No. 1), denoting 'of the wild olive,' is used as a noun in Rom. 11:17, 24, "a wild olive tree" (R.V., in the latter verse). ¶

NT: B.13b; CB.1233c; K.—.
OT: —.
GEN. REF.: IS.3:589; NB.—; Z.4:528.

For OMITTED (Matt. 23:23, A.V.) see LEAVE (undone), No. 1

For OMNIPOTENT (Rev. 19:6) see ALMIGHTY

ON: see †, p. 1

ONCE (at; for all)

1. *hapax* [ἅπαξ, 530], denotes (*a*) once, one time, 2 Cor. 11:25; Heb. 9:7, 26, 27; 12:26, 27; in the phrase "once and again," lit., 'once and twice,' Phil. 4:16; 1 Thess. 2:18; (*b*) once for all, of what is of perpetual validity, not requiring repetition, Heb. 6:4; 9:28; 10:2; 1 Pet. 3:18; Jude 3, R.V., "once for all" (A.V., "once"); ver. 5 (ditto); in some mss. 1 Pet. 3:20 (so the A.V.). ¶

NT: B.80c; CB.1249b; K.64.
OT: 'eḥād: S.259; HR.118a.1; H.61; BD.25c.
pa'am: S.6471; HR.118a.2; H.1793a; BD.821d.
GEN. REF.: —.

2. *ephapax* [ἐφάπαξ, 2178], a strengthened form of No. 1 (*epi*, upon), signifies (*a*) once for all, Rom. 6:10; Heb. 7:27, R.V. (A.V., "once"); 9:12 (ditto); 10:10; (*b*) at once, 1 Cor. 15:6. ¶

NT: B.300a; CB.1245c; K.64.
OT: —.
GEN. REF.: —.

3. *pote* [ποτέ, 4218], denotes once upon a time, formerly, sometime, e.g., Rom. 7:9; Gal. 1:23, 1st part, R.V., "once" (A.V., "in times past"); 2nd part, A.V., and R.V., "once"; Gal. 2:6, R.V. marg., "what they once were" (to be preferred to the text, "whatsoever they were"), the reference probably being to the association of the twelve Apostles with the Lord during His ministry on earth; upon this their partisans

based their claim for the exclusive authority of these Apostles, which Paul vigorously repudiated; in Eph. 5:8, R.V., "once" (A.V., "sometimes"). See AFORETIME, LAST, LENGTH (at), TIME (past).

NT: B.695a; CB.1266b; K.–.
OT: –.
GEN. REF.: –.

Note: In Luke 23:18, A.V., *pamplēthei*, denoting with the whole multitude (*pas*, all, *plēthos*, a multitude), is rendered "all at once," R.V., "all together"). ¶

ONE

A. Numeral.

heis [εἷς, 1520], the first cardinal numeral, masculine (feminine and neuter nominative forms are *mia* and *hen*, respectively), is used to signify (1) (*a*) one in contrast to many, e.g., Matt. 25:15; Rom. 5:18, R.V., "(through) one (trespass)," i.e., Adam's transgression, in contrast to the "one act of righteousness," i.e., the Death of Christ (not as A.V., "the offence of one," and "the righteousness of one"); (*b*) metaphorically, union and concord, e.g., John 10:30; 11:52; 17:11, 21, 22; Rom. 12:4, 5; Phil. 1:27; (2) emphatically, (*a*) a single (one), to the exclusion of others, e.g., Matt. 21:24; Rom. 3:10; 1 Cor. 9:24; 1 Tim. 2:5 (twice); (*b*) one, alone, e.g., Mark 2:7, R.V. (A.V., "only"); 10:18; Luke 18:19; (*c*) one and the same, e.g., Rom. 3:30, R.V., "God is one," i.e., there is not one God for the Jew and one for the Gentile; cp. Gal. 3:20, which means that in a promise there is no other party; 1 Cor. 3:8; 11:5; 12:11; 1 John 5:8 (lit., 'and the three are into one,' i.e., united in one and the same witness); (3) a certain one, in the same sense as the indefinite pronoun *tis* (see B, No. 1), e.g., Matt. 8:19, R.V., "a (scribe)," marg., "one (scribe)," A.V., "a certain (scribe)"; 19:16, "one"; in Rev. 8:13, R.V. marg., "one (eagle)"; *heis tis* are used together in Luke 22:50; John 11:49; this occurs frequently in the papyri (Moulton, Prol., p. 96); (4) distributively, with *hekastos*, each, i.e., every one, e.g., Luke 4:40; Acts 2:6, "every man" (lit., 'every one'); in the sense of 'one . . . and one,' e.g., John 20:12; or one . . . followed by *allos* or *heteros*, the other, e.g., Matt. 6:24; or by a second *heis*, e.g., Matt. 24:40, R.V., "one"; John 20:12; in Rom. 12:5 *heis* is preceded by *kata* (*kath'*) in the sense of "severally (members) one (of another)," R.V. (A.V. "every one . . ."); cp. Mark 14:19; in 1 Thess. 5:11 the phrase in the 2nd part, "each other," R.V. (A.V., "one another"), is, lit., 'one the one'; (5) as an ordinal number, equivalent to *prōtos*, first, in the phrase "the first day of the week," lit. and idiomatically, 'one of sabbaths,' signifying 'the first day after the sabbath,' e.g., Matt. 28:1; Mark 16:2; Acts 20:7; 1 Cor. 16:2. Moulton remarks on the tendency for certain cardinal numerals to replace ordinals (Prol., p. 96).

NT: B.228a; CB.1249c; K.214.
OT: 'eḥād: S.259; HR.–; H.61; BD.25c.
GEN. REF.: IS.3:558; NB.–; Z.–.

B. Pronouns.

1. *tis* [τις, 5100], an indefinite pronoun signifying a certain one, some one, any one, one (the neuter form *ti* denotes a certain thing), is used (*a*) like a noun, e.g., Acts 5:25; 19:32; 21:34; 1 Cor. 3:4; or with the meaning 'someone,' e.g., Acts 8:31, R.V., "some one" (A.V., "some man"); Rom. 5:7; (*b*) as an adjective; see CERTAIN, *Note* (3), SOME.

NT: B.819d; CB.1272c; K.–.
OT: 'îsh: S.376; HR.1354a.2; H.83a; BD.35d.
GEN. REF.: –.

2. *hos* [ὅς, 3739], as a relative pronoun, signifies "who"; as a demonstrative pronoun, "this," or "the one" in contrast with "the other," or "another," e.g., Rom. 14:2, A.V. (R.V., "one man"); 1 Cor. 12:8.

NT: B.583b; CB.–; K.–.
OT: –.
GEN. REF.: –.

Notes: (1) The R.V. often substitutes "one" for "man," e.g., Matt. 17:8 (*oudeis*, no one); 1 Cor. 3:21 (i.e., 'no person'); 1 Cor. 15:35; 1 Thess. 5:15; 2 Tim. 4:16; 1 John 2:27; 3:3.

(2) The pronoun *houtos* is sometimes translated "this one," e.g., Luke 7:8.

(3) In 1 Pet. 3:8, A.V., *homophrōn*, "likeminded" (R.V.), is translated "of one mind" (lit., 'of the same mind').

(4) In Acts 7:26, "at one," is, lit., 'unto peace' (see PEACE).

(5) For "every one" in Acts 5:16 see EVERY, No. 2.

(6) In Mark 9:26 *nekros*, dead, is translated "one dead."

(7) In Acts 2:1 "in one place" translates *epi to auto*, lit., 'to the same,' which may mean 'for the same (purpose)'; in 1 Cor. 11:20 and 14:23, the R.V. translates it "together."

(8) In Mark 1:7, A.V., the article *ho*, the, is rendered "one" (R.V., "he that").

(9) In Mark 7:14, A.V., the plural of *pas*, "all" (so R.V.), is translated "every one"; in Matt. 5:28, A.V., *pas*, with the article, is translated "whosoever" (R.V. "every one who").

(10) In Acts 1:24, A.V., "whether" is, lit., and as the R.V., "the one whom."

(11) In 2 Thess. 2:7, the article is rendered "one that," R.V. (A.V., "he who").

See also ACCORD, CONSENT, B, No. 1, END, C *Note* (6), EYE (with one), GREAT, HOLY, LITTLE, MIND, NATION, WICKED.

ONE ANOTHER or ONE . . . ANOTHER, ONE . . . THE OTHER

Notes: (1) This translates a number of words and phrases, (*a*) *allēlōn*, a reciprocal pronoun in the genitive plural, signifying of, or from, one another (akin to *allos*, another), e.g., Matt. 25:32; John 13:22; Acts 15:39; 19:38; 1 Cor. 7:5; Gal. 5:17; the accusative *allēlous* denotes "one another," e.g., Acts 7:26, lit., 'why do ye wrong one another?'; 2 Thess. 1:3, R.V.; in Eph. 4:32 and Col. 3:13, e.g., R.V., "each other"; in 1 Thess. 5:15, "one (toward) another," R.V.; the dative *allēlois* denotes "one to another," e.g., Luke 7:32; (*b*) different forms of the plural of *heautou*, of himself, used as a reciprocal pronoun, e.g., Eph. 5:19, R.V., "one to another" (A.V., and R.V. marg., "to yourselves"); see also *Note* (5); (*c*) *allos pros allon*, "one to another," Acts 2:12; (*d*) *allos . . . heteros*, 1 Cor. 12:8 (for the difference between *allos* and *heteros*, see ANOTHER); (*e*) *hos men . . . hos de* (in various forms of the pronoun), lit., 'this indeed . . . but that,' e.g., Luke 23:33; Rom. 9:21; 14:5; 1 Cor. 11:21; 2 Cor. 2:16; Phil. 1:16, 17; (*f*) *heteros . . . heteros*, one . . . another, 1 Cor. 15:40.

(2) In Matt. 24:2; Mark 13:2; Luke 19:44, and 21:6, "one (stone upon) another" is, lit., 'stone upon stone.'

(3) In Heb. 10:25, "*one another*" is necessarily added in English to complete the sense of *parakaleō*, to exhort.

(4) In 1 Pet. 3:8, A.V., "one of another" represents nothing in the original (the R.V., "compassionate" sufficiently translates the adjective *sumpathēs*: see COMPASSION, C.).

(5) In Mark 9:10, A.V., *pros heautous*, "among yourselves" (R.V.), is translated "one with another."

(6) In 1 Tim. 5:21, A.V., the accusative case of *prosklisis*, partiality, preceded by *kata*, according to, is translated "preferring one before another" (R.V., "prejudice"; marg., "preference," lit., 'according to partiality').

ONLY

Adjectives.

1. *monos* [μόνος, 3441], alone, solitary, is translated "only," e.g., in Matt. 4:10; 12:4; 17:8; 1 Cor. 9:6; 14:36; Phil. 4:15; Col. 4:11; 2 John 1; it is used as an attribute of God in John 5:44; 17:3; Rom. 16:27; 1 Tim. 1:17; 1 Tim. 6:15, 16; Jude 4, 25; Rev. 15:4. See ALONE, A.

NT: B.527c; CB.1259b; K.–.
OT: l^ebad: S.905; HR.933b.3a; H.201a; BD.94c.
GEN. REF.: –.

2. *monogenēs* [μονογενής, 3439], only begotten (No. 1 and *genos*, offspring), has the meaning "only," of human offspring, in Luke 7:12; 8:42; 9:38; the term is one of endearment, as well as of singleness. For Heb. 11:17 see ONLY BEGOTTEN.

NT: B.527b; CB.1259b; K.606.
OT: yāḥîd: S.3173; HR.933a.1a; H.858a; BD.402d.
GEN. REF.: IS.–; NB.–; Z.4:538.

B. Adverbs.

1. *monon* [μόνον, 3441], the neuter of A, No. 1, only, exclusively, is translated "only," e.g., in Matt. 5:47; 8:8; John 5:18; 11:52; 12:9; 13:9; frequently in Acts, Romans and Galatians. See ALONE, B, No. 1.

NT: B.527c; CB.1259b; K.–.
OT: l^ebad: S.905; HR.933b.3a; H.201a; BD.94c.
GEN. REF.: –.

2. *plēn* [πλήν, 4133], howbeit, except that, is translated "only that" in the R.V. of Phil. 1:18 (A.V., "notwithstanding"); "only" in 3:16 (A.V., "nevertheless").

NT: B.669b; CB.1265b; K.–.
OT: 'ak: S.389; HR.1145c.3; H.84; BD.36c.
raq: S.7535; HR.1145c.19; H.2218a; BD.956b.
GEN. REF.: –.

Notes: (1) In Mark 2:7, A.V., *heis*, "one" (so R.V.), is translated "only"; in Jas. 4:12, R.V., "one only" (A.V., "one").

(2) For "only that" in Acts 21:25, A.V., see the R.V.

(3) The conjunction *ei*, if, with the negative *mē*, not, is translated "but only" in Luke 4:26, R.V. (A.V., "save"); 4:27 (A.V., "saving"); "only" in 1 Cor. 7:17 (A.V., "but"); in some mss. in Acts 21:25 (A.V. "save only").

ONLY BEGOTTEN

monogenēs [μονογενής, 3439], is used five times, all in the writings of the Apostle John, of Christ as the Son of God; it is translated "only begotten" in Heb. 11:17 of the relationship of Isaac to Abraham.

With reference to Christ, the phrase "the only begotten from the Father," John 1:14, R.V. (see also the marg.), indicates that as the Son of God He was the sole representative of the Being and character of the One who sent Him. In the original the definite article is omitted both before "only begotten" and before "Father," and its absence in each case serves to lay stress upon the characteristics referred to in the terms used. The Apostle's object is to demonstrate what sort of glory it was that he and his fellow-Apostles had seen. That he is not merely making a comparison with earthly relationships is indicated by *para*, "from." The glory was that of a unique relationship and the word "begotten" does not imply a beginning of His Sonship. It suggests relationship indeed, but must be distinguished from generation as applied to man.

We can only rightly understand the term "the only begotten" when used of the Son, in the sense of unoriginated relationship. "The begetting is not an event of time, however remote, but a fact irrespective of time. The Christ did not *become*, but necessarily and eternally *is* the Son. He, a Person, possesses every attribute of pure Godhood. This necessitates eternity, absolute being; in this respect He is not 'after' the Father" (Moule). The expression also suggests the thought of the deepest affection, as in the case of the O.T. word *yachid*, variously rendered, "only one," Gen. 22:2, 12; "only son," Jer. 6:26; Amos 8:10; Zech. 12:10; "only beloved," Prov. 4:3, and "darling," Psa. 22:20; 35:17.

In John 1:18 the clause "The Only Begotten Son, which is in the bosom of the Father," expresses both His eternal union with the Father in the Godhead and the ineffable intimacy and love between them, the Son sharing all the Father's counsels and enjoying all His affections. Another reading is *monogenēs Theos*, 'God only-begotten.' In John 3:16 the statement, "God so loved the world that he gave His Only Begotten Son," must not be taken to mean that Christ became the Only Begotten Son by Incarnation. The value and the greatness of the gift lay in the Sonship of Him who was given. His Sonship was not the effect of His being given. In John 3:18 the phrase "the Name of the Only Begotten Son of God" lays stress upon the full revelation of God's character and will, His love and grace, as conveyed in the Name of One who, being in a unique relationship to Him, was provided by Him as the Object of faith. In 1 John 4:9 the statement "God hath sent His Only Begotten Son into the world" does not mean that God sent out into the world one who at His birth in Bethlehem had become His Son. Cp. the parallel statement, "God sent forth the Spirit of His Son," Gal. 4:6, R.V., which could not mean that God sent forth One who became His Spirit when he sent Him. ¶

NT: B.527b; CB.1259b; K.606.
OT: yāḥîd: S.3173; HR.933a.1a; H.858a; BD.402d.
GEN. REF.: IS.3:606; NB.—; Z.4:538.

For **ONSET** Acts 14:5, R.V., see **ASSAULT** and **IMPULSE**

For **ONWARD**, 2 John 9, R.V., see **GO**, No. 10

OPEN, OPENING (For **OPENLY**, see below)

A. Verbs.

1. *anoigō* [ἀνοίγω, 455], is used (1) transitively, (*a*) literally, of a door or gate, e.g., Acts 5:19; graves, Matt. 27:52; a sepulchre, Rom. 3:13; a book, e.g., Luke 4:17 (some mss. have No. 4); Rev. 5:2-5; 10:8; the seals of a roll, e.g., Rev. 5:9; 6:1; the eyes, Acts 9:40; the mouth of a fish, Matt. 17:27; "the pit of the abyss," Rev. 9:2, R.V.; heaven and the heavens, Matt. 3:16; Luke 3:21; Acts 10:11 (for 7:56, see No. 2); Rev. 19:11; "the temple of the tabernacle of the testimony in heaven," Rev. 15:5; by metonymy, for that which contained treasures, Matt. 2:11; (*b*) metaphorically, e.g., Matt. 7:7, 8; 25:11; Rev. 3:7; Hebraistically, to open the mouth, of beginning to speak, e.g., Matt. 5:2; 13:35; Acts 8:32, 35; 10:34; 18:14; Rev. 13:6 (cp. e.g., Numb. 22:28; Job 3:1; Isa. 50:5); and of recovering speech, Luke 1:64; of the earth opening, Rev. 12:16; of the opening of the eyes, Acts 26:18; the ears, Mark 7:35 (in the best mss.; some have No. 2); (2) intransitively (perfect tense, active, in the Greek), (*a*) literally, of the heaven, John 1:51, R.V., "opened"; (*b*) metaphorically, of speaking freely, 2 Cor. 6:11.

NT: B.70d; CB.1235c; K.—.
OT: pātaḥ: S.6605; HR.105b.8a,b; H.1854,1855; BD.834d.
GEN. REF.: IS.3:607; NB.—; Z.—.

2. *dianoigō* [διανοίγω, 1272], to open up completely (*dia*, through, intensive, and No. 1), is used (*a*) literally, Luke 2:23; Acts 7:56, in the best mss.; (*b*) metaphorically, of the eyes, Mark 7:34; Luke 24:31; of the Scriptures, ver. 32 and Acts 17:3; of the mind, Luke 24:45, R.V. (A.V., "understanding"); of the heart, Acts 16:14. ¶

NT: B.187b; CB.1241b; K.—.
OT: peṭer: S.6363; HR.307b.3a; H.1764a,b; BD.809d.
pāqaḥ: S.6491; HR.307b.6; H.1803; BD.824c.
pātaḥ: S.6605; HR.307b.8; H.1854,1855; BD.834d.
GEN. REF.: IS.3:607; NB.—; Z.—.

3. *agō* [ἄγω, 71], to lead, or to keep or spend a day, is so used in Acts 19:38: see KEEP, *Note* (2).

NT: B.14b; CB.1233c; K.—.
OT: bô': S.935; HR.9a.1b; H.212; BD.97c.
hālak: S.1980; HR.9a.3b; H.498; BD.229d.
nāhag: S.5090; HR.9a.14; H.1309,1310; BD.624a.
GEN. REF.: —.

4. *anaptussō* [ἀναπτύσσω, 380], to unroll (*ana*, back, *ptussō*, to roll), is found in some mss.

in Luke 4:17 (of the roll of Isaiah), and translated "He had opened" (A.V.); see No. 1. ¶

NT: B.60a; CB.—; K.—.
OT: pāras: S.6566; HR.81c.3; H.1832; BD.831a.
kāsāh: S.3680; HR.81c.1; H.1008; BD.491b.
GEN. REF.: IS.3:607; NB.—; Z.—.

Notes: (1) For Heb. 4:13, "laid open," R.V. (A.V., "opened") see LAY, No. 18.

(2) In 2 Cor. 3:18, A.V., *anakaluptō*, to unveil, is translated "open" (R.V., "unveiled," which consistently continues the metaphor of the veil upon the heart of Israel).

(3) In Mark 1:10, A.V., *schizō*, to rend or split, is translated "opened," of the heavens, R.V., "rent asunder," A.V. marg., "cloven, or, rent."

(4) For *prodēlos*, in 1 Tim. 5:24, A.V., "open beforehand," see EVIDENT, A, No. 3.

(5) For "be opened" see EPHPHATHA.

(6) For "open (your hearts)," 2 Cor. 7:2, R.V., see RECEIVE, No. 18.

B. Nouns.

1. *anoixis* [ἄνοιξις, 457], an opening (akin to A, No. 1), is used in Eph. 6:19, metaphorically of the opening of the mouth as in A, No. 1 (2), (*b*). ¶

NT: B.71c; CB.1235c; K.—.
OT: —.
GEN. REF.: —.

2. *ope* [ὀπή, 3692], an opening, a hole, is used in Jas. 3:11, of the orifice of a fountain: see CAVE, HOLE, PLACE.

NT: B.574d; CB.—; K.—.
OT: ḥōr: S.2356; HR.1001b.3; H.758a; BD.359d.
GEN. REF.: —.

OPENLY

1. *parrhēsia* [παρρησία, 3954], freedom of speech, boldness, is used adverbially in the dative case and translated "openly" in Mark 8:32, of a saying of Christ; in John 7:13, of a public statement; in 11:54 of Christ's public appearance; in 7:26 and 18:20, of His public testimony; preceded by the preposition *en*, in, John 7:4, lit., 'in boldness' (cp. ver. 10, R.V., "publicly"). See BOLD, B.

NT: B.630c; CB.1262c; K.794.
OT: —.
GEN. REF.: IS.3:880; NB.—; Z.—.

2. *phanerōs* [φανερῶς, 5320], manifestly, openly: see EVIDENT, B.

NT: B.853a; CB.1263c; K.1244.
OT: —.
GEN. REF.: IS.3:880; NB.—; Z.—.

Notes: (1) In Gal. 3:1, "openly set forth" translates the verb *prographō*, lit., 'to write before,' as of the O.T., Rom. 15:4 (cp. Jude 4), and of a previous letter, Eph. 3:3. In Gal. 3:1, however, "it is probably used in another sense, unexampled in the Scriptures but not uncommon in the language of the day, = 'proclaimed,' 'placarded,' as a magistrate proclaimed the fact that an execution had been carried out, placarding his proclamation in a public place. The Apostle carries on his metaphor of the 'evil eye'; as a preventive of such mischief it was common to post up charms on the walls of houses, a glance at which was supposed to counteract any evil influence to which a person may have been subjected. 'Notwithstanding,' he says, in effect, 'that the fact that Christ had been crucified was placarded before your very eyes in our preaching, you have allowed yourselves to be . . . fascinated by the enemies of the Cross of Christ, when you had only to look at Him to escape their malignant influence'; cp. the interesting and instructive parallel in Num. 21:9."*

(2) In some mss. in Matt. 6:4, 6, 18, the phrase *en tǭ phanerǭ*, lit., 'in the manifest,' is found (A.V., "openly"); see the R.V.

(3) For *emphanēs*, rendered "openly" in Acts 10:40, A.V., see MANIFEST.

(4) In Acts 16:37, A.V., the dative case of the adjective *dēmosios*, belonging to the people (*dēmos*, a people), "public" (so R.V.), used adverbially, is translated "openly"; in 18:28 and 20:20, "publicly." For the adjective itself, "public," see Acts 5:18. See PUBLIC. ¶

For **OPERATION** see **WORKING**

OPPORTUNITY (lack)

A. Nouns.

1. *kairos* [καιρός, 2540], primarily, a due measure, is used of a fixed and definite period, a time, season, and is translated "opportunity" in Gal. 6:10 and Heb. 11:15. See SEASON, TIME, WHILE.

NT: B.394c; CB.1253a; K.389.
OT: 'ēt: S.6256; HR.706a.8; H.1650b; BD.773b.
mô'ēd: S.4150; HR.706a.4; H.878b; BD.417b.
pa'am: S.6471; HR.706a.9; H.1793a; BD.821d.
GEN. REF.: —.

2. *eukairia* [εὐκαιρία, 2120], a fitting time, opportunity (*eu*, well, and No. 1), occurs in Matt. 26:16 and Luke 22:6. ¶ Cp. *eukairos*, seasonable; see CONVENIENT.

NT: B.321b; CB.1247b; K.389.
OT: 'ēt: S.6256; HR.571c.1; H.1650b; BD.773b.
GEN. REF.: —.

3. *topos* [τόπος, 5117], a place, is translated "opportunity" in Acts 25:16, R.V. (A.V., "licence"). See PLACE, ROOM.

NT: B.822b; CB.1273a; K.1184.
OT: māqôm: S.4725; HR.1364b.8; H.1999b; BD.879d.
GEN. REF.: —.

* From Notes on Galatians by Hogg and Vine, pp. 106, 107.

B. Verbs.

1. *eukaireō* [*εὐκαιρέω*, 2119], to have time or leisure (akin to A, No. 2), is translated "he shall have opportunity" in 1 Cor. 16:12, R.V. (A.V., "convenient time"). See LEISURE.

NT: B.321b; CB.1247b; K.–.
OT: –.
GEN. REF.: –.

2. *akaireomai* [*ἀκαιρέομαι*, 170], to have no opportunity (*a*, negative, and *kairos*, season), occurs in Phil. 4:10. ¶

NT: B.29b; CB.1234a; K.–.
OT: –.
GEN. REF.: –.

OPPOSE

1. *antikeimai* [*ἀντίκειμαι*, —]: see ADVERSARY, B.

2. *antitassō* [*ἀντιτάσσω*, 498], is used in the Middle Voice in the sense of setting oneself against (*anti*, against, *tassō*, to order, set), opposing oneself to, Acts 18:6; elsewhere rendered by the verb to resist, Rom. 13:2; Jas. 4:6; 5:6; 1 Pet. 5:5. See RESIST. ¶

NT: B.76a; CB.–; K.–.
OT: nāsā': S.5375; HR.112a.2; H.1421; BD.669d.
shît: S.7896; HR.112a.4; H.2380; BD.1011a.
GEN. REF.: –.

3. *antidiatithēmi* [*ἀντιδιατίθημι*, 475], signifies to place oneself in opposition, oppose (*anti*, against, *dia*, through, intensive, *tithēmi*, to place), 2 Tim. 2:25. The A.V. and R.V. translate this as a Middle Voice, "them (A.V., those) that oppose themselves." Field (*Notes on the Trans. of the N.T.*) points out that in the only other known instance of the verb it is Passive. The sense is practically the same if it is rendered 'those who are opposed.' ¶

NT: B.74a; CB.–; K.–.
OT: –.
GEN. REF.: –.

OPPOSITIONS

antithesis [*ἀντίθεσις*, 477], a contrary position (*anti*, against, *tithēmi*, to place; Eng., antithesis), occurs in 1 Tim. 6:20. ¶

NT: B.74b; CB.–; K.–.
OT: –.
GEN. REF.: –.

OPPRESS

1. *katadunasteuō* [*καταδυναστεύω*, 2616], to exercise power over (*kata*, down, *dunastēs*, a potentate: *dunamai*, to have power), to oppress, is used, in the Passive Voice, in Acts 10:38; in the Active, in Jas. 2:6. ¶

NT: B.410c; CB.–; K.–.
OT: yānāh: S.3238; HR.731a.3; H.873; BD.413a.
'āshaq: S.6231; HR.731a.10; H.1713; BD.798d.
kābash: S.3533; HR.731a.4; H.951; BD.461b.
GEN. REF.: IS.3:609; NB.–; Z.–.

2. *kataponeō* [*καταπονέω*, —]: see DISTRESS, B, No. 4.

OR: see † p. 1

ORACLE

logion [*λόγιον*, 3051], a diminutive of *logos*, a word, narrative, statement, denotes a Divine response or utterance, an oracle; it is used of (*a*) the contents of the Mosaic Law, Acts 7:38; (*b*) all the written utterances of God through O.T. writers, Rom. 3:2; (*c*) the substance of Christian doctrine, Heb. 5:12; (*d*) the utterances of God through Christian teachers, 1 Pet. 4:11. ¶

NT: B.476c; CB.1257a; K.505.
OT: 'imrāh: S.565; HR.880c.1b; H.118b; BD.57a.
GEN. REF.: IS.3:999; NB.912; Z.–.

Note: Divine oracles were given by means of the breastplate of the High Priest, in connection with the service of the Tabernacle, and the Sept. uses the associated word *logeion* in Ex. 28:15, to describe the breastplate.

ORATION

dēmēgoreō [*δημηγορέω*, 1215], from *dēmos*, the people and *agoreuō*, to speak in the public assembly, to deliver an oration, occurs in Acts 12:21. ¶

NT: B.178d; CB.–; K.–.
OT: –.
GEN. REF.: IS.3:611; NB.–; Z.–.

ORATOR

rhētōr [*ῥήτωρ*, 4489], from an obsolete present tense, *rheō*, to say (cp. Eng., rhetoric), denotes a public speaker, an orator, Acts 24:1, of Tertullus. Such a person, distinct from the professional lawyer, was hired, as a professional speaker, to make a skilful presentation of a case in court. His training was not legal but rhetorical. ¶

NT: B.735d; CB.1268b; K.–.
OT: –.
GEN. REF.: IS.3:611; NB.912; Z.4:542.

ORDAIN

1. *tithēmi* [*τίθημι*, —], to put: see APPOINT, No. 3.

2. *kathistēmi* [*καθίστημι*, 2525], from *kata*, down, or over against, and *histēmi*, to cause to stand, to set, is translated to ordain in the A.V. of Tit. 1:5; Heb. 5:1; 8:3. See APPOINT, No. 2.

NT: B.390b; CB.1254c; K.387.
OT: nāṣab: S.5324; HR.702c.12; H.1398; BD.662a.
pāqad: S.6485; HR.702c.15a-d; H.1802; BD.823a.
sûm, sîm: S.7760; HR.703a.19; H.2243; BD.962c.
GEN. REF.: IS.3:612; NB.913; Z.4:542.

3. *tassō* [τάσσω, 5021], is translated to ordain, in Acts 13:48 and Rom. 13:1. See APPOINT, No. 5.
NT: B.805d; CB.1271a; K.1156.
OT: nātan: S.5414; HR.1337a.6; H.1443; BD.678a.
sûm, sîm: S.7760; HR.1337a.11; H.2243; BD.962c.
GEN. REF.: IS.3:612; NB.—; Z.4:542.

4. *diatassō* [διατάσσω, 1299], is translated to ordain in 1 Cor. 7:17; 9:14; Gal. 3:19, the last in the sense of 'administered.' Cp. *diatagē*, under DISPOSITION. See APPOINT, No. 6.
NT: B.189c; CB.1241b; K.1156.
OT: sîm: S.7760; HR.313a.7; H.2243; BD.962c.
ḥāqaq: S.2710; HR.313a.3; H.728; BD.349a.
GEN. REF.: IS.3:612; NB.—; Z.4:542.

5. *horizō* [ὁρίζω, 3724], is twice used of Christ as Divinely "ordained" to be the Judge of men, Acts 10:42; 17:31. See DETERMINE, No. 2.
NT: B.580d; CB.1251b; K.728.
OT: geᵉbûl: S.1366; HR.1011c.2a; H.307a; BD.147d.
GEN. REF.: IS.3:612; NB.—; Z.—.

6. *krinō* [κρίνω, 2919], to divide, separate, decide, judge, is translated "ordained" in Act 16:4, of the decrees by the Apostles and elders in Jerusalem. See JUDGE.
NT: B.451b; CB.1256a; K.469.
OT: shāphaṭ: S.8199; HR.787b.10a; H.2443; BD.1047a.
rîb: S.7378; HR.787b.8a; H.2159; BD.936b.
GEN. REF.: IS.—; NB.—; Z.4:542.

Notes: (1) In 1 Cor. 2:7, A.V., *proorizō*, to foreordain (see R.V.) is translated "ordained." See DETERMINE, No. 3.

(2) In Mark 3:14, A.V., *poieō*, to make, is translated "ordained" (R.V., "appointed").

(3) In Heb. 9:6, A.V., *kataskeuazō*, to prepare (so R.V.), is translated "were . . . ordained." See PREPARE.

(4) In Acts 14:23, A.V., *cheirotoneō*, to appoint (R.V.), is translated "they had ordained." See APPOINT, No. 11.

(5) In Eph. 2:10, A.V., *proetoimazō*, to prepare before, is translated "hath before ordained" (R.V., "afore prepared"); see PREPARE.

(6) In Jude 4, A.V., *prographō*, lit., to write before, is translated "were before . . . ordained" (R.V., "were . . . set forth"). See SET (forth).

(7) In Acts 1:22, A.V., *ginomai*, to become, is translated "be ordained" (R.V., "become").

(8) In Rom. 7:10, A.V., "*ordained*" represents no word in the original (see R.V.).

ORDER (Noun and Verb)

A. Nouns.

1. *taxis* [τάξις, 5010], an arranging, arrangement, order (akin to *tassō*, to arrange, draw up in order), is used in Luke 1:8 of the fixed succession of the course of the priests; of due order, in contrast to confusion, in the gatherings of a local church, 1 Cor. 14:40; of the general condition of such, Col. 2:5 (some give it a military significance here); of the Divinely appointed character or nature of a priesthood, of Melchizedek, as foreshadowing that of Christ, Heb. 5:6, 10; 6:20; 7:11 (where also the character of the Aaronic priesthood is set in contrast); 7:17 (in some mss., ver. 21). ¶
NT: B.803d; CB.1271a; K.—.
OT: maḥᵃneh: S.4264; HR.1334b.4; H.690e; BD.334a.
tôrāh: S.8451; HR.1334b.9; H.910d; BD.435d.
GEN. REF.: IS.3:613; NB.—; Z.—.

2. *tagma* [τάγμα, 5001], a more concrete form of No. 1, signifying that which has been arranged in order, was especially a military term, denoting a company; it is used metaphorically in 1 Cor. 15:23 of the various classes of those who have part in the first resurrection. ¶
NT: B.802d; CB.—; K.1156.
OT: degel: S.1714; HR.1333a.1; H.402a; BD.186b.
GEN. REF.: IS.3:613; NB.—; Z.—.

B. Verbs.

1. *anatassomai* [ἀνατάσσομαι, 392], to arrange in order (*ana*, up, and the Middle Voice of *tassō*, to arrange), is used in Luke 1:1, A.V., "to set forth in order" (R.V., "to draw up"); the probable meaning is to bring together and so arrange details in order. ¶
NT: B.61d; CB.1235b; K.—.
OT: —.
GEN. REF.: —.

2. *diatassō* [διατάσσω, 1299], to appoint, arrange, charge, give orders to, is used, in the Middle Voice, in Acts 24:23, "gave order" (R.V.); 1 Cor. 11:34, "will I set in order"; in the Active Voice, in 1 Cor. 16:1, "I gave order" (R.V.). See COMMAND, No. 1.
NT: B.189c; CB.1241b; K.1156.
OT: sîm: S.7760; HR.313a.7; H.2243; BD.962c.
ḥāqaq: S.2710; HR.313a.3; H.728; BD.349a.
GEN. REF.: IS.3:613; NB.—; Z.—.

3. *epidiorthoō* [ἐπιδιορθόω, 1930], to set in order (*epi*, upon, *dia*, through, intensive, and *orthos*, straight), is used in Tit. 1:5, in the sense of setting right again what was defective, a commission to Titus, not to add to what the Apostle himself had done, but to restore what had fallen into disorder since the Apostle had laboured in Crete; this is suggested by the *epi*. ¶
NT: B.292b; CB.—; K.—.
OT: —.
GEN. REF.: —.

C. Adverb.

kathexēs [καθεξῆς, 2517], is translated "in order" in Luke 1:3; Acts 11:4, R.V. (A.V., "by order"); Acts 18:23. See AFTERWARD, No. 3.
NT: B.388d; CB.—; K.—.
OT: —.
GEN. REF.: —.

Note: In 2 Cor. 11:32, R.V., the phrase "in order to" (as with the A.V., "desirous to") represents nothing in the original: the infinitive mood of the verb *piazō* expresses the purpose, viz., "to take."

ORDERLY

kosmios [κόσμιος, 2887], an adjective signifying decent, modest, orderly (akin to *kosmos*, order, adornment), is translated "modest" in 1 Tim. 2:9; "orderly" in 3:2, R.V. (A.V., "of good behaviour"). See MODEST.

NT: B.445c; CB.1255c; K.459.
OT: –.
GEN. REF.: –.

Note: For *stoicheō*, in Acts 21:24, "thou walkest orderly," see WALK.

ORDINANCE

A. Nouns.

1. *dikaiōma* [δικαίωμα, —]: see JUSTIFICATION, No. 2.

2. *diatagē* [διαταγή, 1296], is translated "ordinances," in Rom. 13:2. See DISPOSITION.

NT: B.189b; CB.–; K.1156.
OT: –.
GEN. REF.: –.

3. *dogma* [δόγμα, 1378], is translated "ordinances" in Eph. 2:15 and Col. 2:14. See DECREE.

NT: B.201c; CB.1242a; K.178.
OT: dāt: S.1881; HR.339b.2; H.458; BD.206c.
GEN. REF.: IS.3:614; NB.305; Z.4:543.

4. *ktisis* [κτίσις, 2937], a creation, creature, is translated "ordinance" in 1 Pet. 2:13. See CREATE, B, No. 1.

NT: B.455d; CB.1256a; K.481.
OT: –.
GEN. REF.: –.

Note: In 1 Cor. 11:2, A.V., *paradosis*, a tradition (marg., and R.V., "traditions"), is translated "ordinances." See TRADITION.

B. Verb.

dogmatizō [δογματίζω, 1379], akin to A, No. 3, to decree, signifies, in the Middle Voice, to subject oneself to an ordinance, Col. 2:20. ¶ In the Sept., Esth. 3:9; in some texts, Dan. 2:13, 15. ¶

NT: B.201d; CB.1242a; K.178.
OT: dāt: S.1881; HR.339b.1b; H.458; BD.206c.
kātab: S.3789; HR.339b.2; H.1053; BD.507a.
GEN. REF.: IS.–; NB.–; Z.4:543.

OTHER

1. *allos* [ἄλλος, 243], indicates numeral distinction of objects of similar character, and is used (*a*) absolutely, e.g., Matt. 20:3 (plural); (*b*) attached to a noun, e.g., Matt. 21:36; (*c*) with the article, e.g. Matt. 5:39; 1 Cor. 14:29 (plural, R.V.); in Matt. 13:5; Luke 9:19; John 9:9, e.g., R.V., "others" (A.V., "some"); in Matt. 25:20, R.V., "other" (A.V., "beside them . . . more"). See ANOTHER, MORE, B, *Note* (1), SOME.

NT: B.39d; CB.1234c; K.43.
OT: 'eḥād: S.259; HR.56b.1; H.61; BD.25c.
'aḥēr: S.312; HR.56b.2; H.68a; BD.29c.
GEN. REF.: –.

2. *heteros* [ἕτερος, 2087], indicates either numerical distinction, e.g., Luke 4:43; 5:7; or generic distinction, different in character, etc., e.g., Luke 9:29, "(the fashion of His countenance) was altered," lit., 'became other'; 23:32, "two others, (malefactors)," R.V., where the plural serves to make the necessary distinction between them and Christ; Acts 2:4; 19:39 ("other matters"); 1 Cor. 14:21, A.V., "other" (R.V., "strange"); 2 Cor. 11:4 (2nd and 3rd parts, R.V., "different"; in the 1st clause, *allos*, "another"). For the distinction between this and No. 1, see under ANOTHER.

NT: B.315a; CB.1250a; K.265.
OT: 'aḥēr: S.312; HR.560a.4a; H.68a; BD.29c.
GEN. REF.: –.

3. *loipos* [λοιπός, 3062], signifies remaining, the rest. It is translated "other," or "others," e.g., in Matt. 25:11; Mark 4:19; Luke 18:9; 24:10 (in ver. 9, "the rest"); but in Luke 8:10; Acts 28:9; Rom. 1:13; 1 Cor. 9:5; Eph. 2:3; 1 Thess. 4:13; 5:6; 1 Tim. 5:20, e.g., the R.V. renders this word "the rest" (A.V., "other" or "others"); in Eph. 4:17, some mss. have *loipa*, neuter plural, A.V., "other (Gentiles)"; see the R.V. See REMNANT, REST (the).

NT: B.479d; CB.1257b; K.–.
OT: yeter: S.3499; HR.888a.1c; H.936a; BD.451b.
GEN. REF.: –.

4. *allotrios* [ἀλλότριος, 245], belonging to another, not one's own, is translated "other men's" in 2 Cor. 10:15; 1 Tim. 5:22; in Heb. 9:25, R.V., "not his own" (A.V., "of others"). See ALIEN, MAN'S, *Note* (1), STRANGE, STRANGER.

NT: B.40c; CB.1234c; K.43.
OT: nēkār: S.5236; HR.57a.4a; H.1368b; BD.648c.
nākᵉrî: S.5237; HR.57a.4c; H.1368c; BD.648d.
GEN. REF.: –.

5. *allēlōn* [ἀλλήλων, 240], in Rom. 1:12, used in the dative case, is translated in the R.V. "(each of us by the) other's" (A.V., "mutual"); the accusative is translated "other" in Phil. 2:3. See MUTUAL and ONE ANOTHER.

NT: B.39c; CB.1234c; K.–.
OT: –.
GEN. REF.: –.

6. *heis* [εἷς, 1520], one, is sometimes translated "other" when expressing the second of a pair, e.g., Matt. 24:40, A.V. (R.V., "one"). See ONE, A (4).

NT: B.228a; CB.1249c; K.214.
OT: 'eḥād: S.259; HR.–; H.61; BD.25c.
GEN. REF.: –.

7. *ekeinos* [ἐκεῖνος, 1565], signifying that one, implying remoteness as compared with *houtos*, this, is translated "the other," e.g., in Matt. 23:23; Luke 11:42; 18:14.
NT: B.239b; CB.1243c; K.—.
OT: hû', hî': S.1931; HR.428a.6a-d; H.480; BD.214d.
GEN. REF.: —.

Notes: (1) In Acts 26:22, A.V., *ouden ektos*, lit., 'nothing besides' is translated "none other things" (R.V., "nothing but").

(2) The plural of the definite article is translated "others" in Acts 17:32; in Jude 23, A.V., "others" (R.V., "some").

(3) In Luke 24:1, the plural of *tis*, a certain one, is found in some mss., and translated "certain others" in the A.V.

For OTHER SIDE and OTHER WAY see SIDE and WAY

OTHERWISE

1. *allos* [ἄλλος, 243], is used, in its neuter form, *allo*, in Gal. 5:10, lit., 'another thing,' with the meaning "otherwise." See OTHER, No. 1.
NT: B.39d; CB.1234c; K.43.
OT: 'eḥād: S.259; HR.56b.1; H.61; BD.25c.
'aḥēr: S.312; HR.56b.2; H.68a; BD.29c.
GEN. REF.: —.

2. *allōs* [ἄλλως, 247], the adverb corresponding to No. 1, is translated "otherwise" in 1 Tim. 5:25; the contrast is not with works that are not good (No. 3 would signify that), but with good works which are not evident. ¶
NT: B.41a; CB.1234c; K.—.
OT: —.
GEN. REF.: —.

3. *heterōs* [ἑτέρως, 2088], is used in Phil. 3:15, "otherwise (minded)," i.e. differently minded. ¶ Contrast No. 2, and for the corresponding difference between the adjectives *allos* and *heteros*, see ANOTHER.
NT: B.315c; CB.1250a; K.—.
OT: —.
GEN. REF.: —.

4. *epei* [ἐπεί, 1893], when used of time, means since or when; used of cause, it means since, because; used elliptically it means otherwise or else; "otherwise" in Rom. 11:6 (the 2nd part of the ver. is absent from the most authentic mss.); ver. 22; in Heb. 9:17, A.V., "otherwise (it is of no strength at all)," R.V., "for (doth it ever avail?)." See ELSE.
NT: B.284a; CB.—; K.—.
OT: —.
GEN. REF.: —.

Note: The phrase *ei*, if, *de*, but, *mēge*, not indeed, i.e., 'but if not indeed,' is translated "otherwise" in the A.V. of Matt. 6:1; Luke 5:36 (R.V., "else," in each place); in 2 Cor. 11:16, A.V., "if otherwise" (R.V., "but if *ye do*"). See also TEACH.

For the pronoun OUGHT (A.V.) see AUGHT

OUGHT (Verb)

1. *dei* [δεῖ, 1163], denotes 'it is necessary,' one must; in Luke 24:26, A.V., "ought" (R.V., "behoved it"); the neuter of the present participle, used as a noun, is translated "things which they ought (not)" in 1 Tim. 5:13; in Acts 19:36, "ye ought" (see NEED). See MUST, No. 1.
NT: B.172a; CB.1240b; K.140.
OT: —.
GEN. REF.: —.

2. *opheilō* [ὀφείλω, 3784], to owe, is translated "ought," with various personal pronouns, in John 13:14; 19:7; Acts 17:29; Rom. 15:1; Heb. 5:3, A.V. (R.V., "he is bound"); 5:12; 1 John 3:16; 4:11; 3 John 8; with other subjects in 1 Cor. 11:7, 10; 2 Cor. 12:14; Eph. 5:28; 1 John 2:6. See BEHOVE, OWE, etc.
NT: B.598d; CB.1261a; K.746.
OT: ḥôb: S.2326; HR.1039a.2; H.614a; BD.295a.
nāshā': S.5378; HR.1039a.4a; H.1424; BD.673d.
GEN. REF.: —.

3. *chrē* [χρή, 5534], an impersonal verb (akin to *chraomai*, to use), occurs in Jas. 3:10, "(these things) ought (not so to be)," lit., 'it is not befitting, these things so to be.' ¶
NT: B.885b; CB.1240a; K.—.
OT: —.
GEN. REF.: —.

OUR, OURS

Notes: (1) This usually translates *hēmōn*, the genitive of *hēmeis*, "we," lit., 'of us,' e.g., Matt. 6:9, 11, 12. It is translated "ours," e.g., in Mark 12:7; Luke 20:14; 1 Cor. 1:2; 2 Cor. 1:14.

(2) In 1 John 4:17, the phrase *meta hēmōn*, rendered "our (love)" in the A.V., is accurately translated in the R.V. "(herein is love made perfect) with us," i.e., Divine love in Christ finds its expression in our manifestation of it to others.

(3) In Luke 17:5, "increase our faith" is, lit., 'add faith to us.'

(4) In Luke 24:22, "of our company" is, lit., 'from among us.'

(5) *Hēmeteros*, a possessive pronoun, more emphatic than *hēmeis*, is used in Luke 16:12, in the best mss. (some have *humeteros*, 'your own'); Acts 2:11; 24:6, in some mss.; 26:5; 2 Tim. 4:15; Tit. 3:14, "ours"; 1 John 1:3; 2:2, "ours."

(6) In Luke 23:41, "of our deeds," is, lit., 'of what things we practised.'

(7) In 1 Cor. 9:10, "for our sake," R.V. (twice), is, lit., 'on account of us.'

OUR OWN

1. *heautōn* [ἑαυτῶν, 1438], is sometimes used as a reflexive pronoun of the 1st person plural, signifying our own selves, translated "our own" in 1 Thess. 2:8, lit., '(the souls) of ourselves.'

NT: B.211d; CB.1249b; K.–.
OT: –.
GEN. REF.: –.

2. *idios* [ἴδιος, 2398], one's own, signifies "our own" in Acts 3:12; 1 Cor. 4:12; in Acts 2:8, with *hēmōn*, forming a strong possessive, lit., 'each in his own language of us.'

NT: B.369c; CB.1252c; K.–.
OT: –.
GEN. REF.: –.

OURSELVES

Notes: (1) This translates (*a*) *autoi*, the plural of *autos*, self, used emphatically either alone, e.g., John 4:42; Rom. 8:23 (1st part); 2 Cor. 1:4 (last part); 1:9, R.V., "we ourselves" (1st part); or joined with the plural pronouns, e.g., *hēmeis*, we, Rom. 8:23 (2nd part); (*b*) the plural *hemeis* alone, e.g., Tit. 3:3; in 2 Cor. 4:7, R.V., *ex hēmōn*, is translated "from ourselves" (A.V., "of us"); (*c*) *heautōn*, governed by the preposition *apo*, from, e.g., 2 Cor. 3:5 (1st part), lit., 'from ourselves' ("of ourselves," in the text); (*d*) *heautois*, the dative case of (*c*), e.g., Rom.15:1; governed by *en*, in, 2 Cor. 1:9 (1st part); by *epi*, on (2nd part); (*e*) *heautous*, the accusative case, e.g., Acts 23:14; 2 Cor. 3:1; 4:2, 5.

(2) In Acts 6:4, A.V., *proskartereō*, to continue stedfastly (R.V.), is translated "give ourselves continually."

(3) In 2 Cor. 10:12, A.V., *enkrinō*, to number (R.V.), is translated "to make ourselves of the number."

OUT, OUT OF

Notes: (1) The preposition *ek* (or *ex*), which frequently signifies "out of" or "from the midst of," has a variety of meanings, among which is "from," as virtually equivalent to *apo*, away from, e.g., 2 Cor. 1:10, "who delivered us out of so great a death, and will deliver"; since death was not actually experienced, but was impending, *ek* here does not signify "out of the midst of." In Acts 12:7 it is used in the statement "his chains fell off from his hands." In Matt. 17:9 it is used of descending from a mountain, not 'out of'; "we are not to suppose that they had been in a cave" (Dr. A. T. Robertson, *Gram. of the Greek N.T.*). In 1 Thess. 1:10, "even Jesus, which delivereth us from the wrath to come," R.V., the question whether *ek* here means 'out of the midst of' or 'away from,' is to be determined by some statement of Scripture where the subject is specifically mentioned; this is provided, e.g., in 5:9, the context of which makes clear that believers are to be delivered from (not 'out of') the Divine wrath to be executed on the nations at the end of the present age.

(2) For the phrase *ek mesou*, "out of the way," see MIDST, *Note* (1), (*e*).

(3) In Luke 8:4, A.V., the phrase *kata polin* is translated "out of every city" (R.V., "of every city," to be taken in connection with "they").

(4) *Ektos*, outside of, is translated "out of" in 2 Cor. 12:2; in 12:3 the best mss. have *chōris*, "apart from," R.V. (A.V., *ektos*, "out of").

(5) For other prepositions, and adverbs, see † p. 1.

OUTER

exōteros [ἐξώτερος, 1857], the comparative degree of *exō*, without, is used of the outer darkness, Matt. 8:12; 22:13; 25:30. ¶

NT: B.280a; CB.–; K.–.
OT: ḥûṣ: S.2351; HR.501c.2; H.627a; BD.299d.
GEN. REF.: –.

OUTGO

proerchomai [προέρχομαι, 4281], to go forward, go in advance, outgo, is used of time in Mark 6:33, "outwent," of the people who in their eagerness reached a spot earlier than Christ and His disciples. See GO, No. 17.

NT: B.705b; CB.1266c; K.–.
OT: 'ābar: S.5674; HR.1206a.1; H.1556; BD.716d.
GEN. REF.: –.

OUTRUN

protrechō [προτρέχω, 4390], primarily, to run forward (*pro*, forward or before, *trechō*, to run), is used with *tachion*, more quickly, in John 20:4, "outran," R.V. (A.V., "did outrun"), lit., 'ran forward more quickly'; in Luke 19:4, "he ran on before," R.V. (A.V., "ran before"). See RUN. ¶ In the Sept., 1 Sam. 8:11; in some texts, Job 41:13, "destruction runneth before him," in the Eng. Versions, ver. 22. ¶

NT: B.722b; CB.–; K.–.
OT: dûṣ: S.1750; HR.1231b.1; H.416; BD.189b.
rûṣ: S.7323; HR.1231b.2; H.2137; BD.930a.
GEN. REF.: –.

OUTSIDE

1. *exōthen* [ἔξωθεν, 1855], an adverb formed from *exō*, without, properly signifies 'from without,' Mark 7:18 (in ver. 15 it is used as a preposition); with the article it is equivalent to a noun, "the outside," Matt. 23:25 (for ver. 27,

see OUTWARD, No. 2); Luke 11:39; in ver. 40, R.V., "the outside" (A.V., "that which is without"). See OUTWARD, OUTWARDLY, WITHOUT.
NT: B.279d; CB.—; K.—.
OT: ḥûṣ: S.2351; HR.502b.2; H.627a; BD.299d.
GEN. REF.: IS.3:622; NB.—; Z.—.

2. *ektos* [ἐκτός, 1622], is once used with the article, "the outside," Matt. 23:26. See EXCEPT, No. 1.
NT: B.246a; CB.—; K.—.
OT: —.
GEN. REF.: —.

OUTWARD, OUTWARDLY

1. *exō* [ἔξω, 1854], without, is used metaphorically of the physical frame, "the outward man," 2 Cor. 4:16. See WITHOUT.
NT: B.279b; CB.1247c; K.240.
OT: ḥûṣ: S.2351; HR.501c.2; H.627a; BD.299d.
GEN. REF.: —.

2. *exōthen* [ἔξωθεν, 1855], is translated "outward" in Matt. 23:27 (R.V., "outwardly"); it is used with the article, adjectivally, in 1 Pet. 3:3, of outward adorning. See OUTSIDE, No. 1.
NT: B.279d; CB.—; K.—.
OT: ḥûṣ: S.2351; HR.502b.2; H.627a; BD.299d.
GEN. REF.: —.

Notes: (1) The phrase *en tō phanerō*, lit., 'in the open' (manifest), is rendered "outwardly" in Rom. 2:28.

(2) For "with outward shew," A.V., marg., Luke 17:20, see OBSERVATION.

(3) For the A.V., of 2 Cor. 10:7, "outward appearance," see FACE, No. 1.

OVEN

klibanos [κλίβανος, 2823], is mentioned in Matt. 6:30 and Luke 12:28. The form of oven commonly in use in the east indicates the kind in use as mentioned in Scripture. A hole is sunk in the ground about 3 feet deep and somewhat less in diameter. The walls are plastered with cement. A fire is kindled inside, the fuel being grass, or dry twigs, which heat the oven rapidly and blacken it with smoke and soot (see Lam. 5:10). When sufficiently heated the surface is wiped, and the dough is moulded into broad thin loaves, placed one at a time on the wall of the oven to fit its concave inner circle. The baking takes a few seconds. Such ovens are usually outside the house, and often the same oven serves for several families (Lev. 26:26). An oven of this sort is doubtless referred to in Ex. 8:3 (see Hastings, Bib. Dic.). ¶
NT: B.436b; CB.—; K.—.
OT: tannûr: S.8574; HR.771a.1; H.2526; BD.1072a.
GEN. REF.: IS.3:622; NB.—; Z.4:554.

OVER, OVER AGAINST:
see Note † p. 1

OVER (to be, to have)

1. *proistēmi* [προΐστημι, 4291], lit., 'to stand before,' hence to lead, to direct, attend to, is translated 'rule,' with reference to the family, in 1 Tim. 3:4, 5, 12; with reference to the church, in Rom. 12:8; 1 Thess. 5:12, "are over"; 1 Tim. 5:17. In Tit. 3:8, 14, it signifies to maintain. See MAINTAIN. ¶
NT: B.707a; CB.1266c; K.—.
OT: —.
GEN. REF.: —.

2. *pleonazō* [πλεονάζω, 4121], used intransitively, signifies to abound, to superabound; in 2 Cor. 8:15 it is used with the negative *ou*, "had nothing over," lit., 'had not more' (*pleon*, the comparative degree of *polus*, much).
NT: B.667b; CB.1265b; K.864.
OT: 'ādaph: S.5736; HR.1141c.3; H.1568; BD.727a.
rābāh: S.7235; HR.1141c.4; H.2103,2104; BD.915a.
GEN. REF.: —.

For OVERBOARD, Acts 27:18, R.V., see FREIGHT, and, in 27:43, R.V., see CAST, No. 11.

OVERCHARGE

1. *bareō* [βαρέω, 916], or *barunō*, is rendered "overcharged" in Luke 21:34. See BURDEN, B, No. 1.
NT: B.133c; CB.1238c; K.95.
OT: —.
GEN. REF.: —.

2. *epibareō* [ἐπιβαρέω, 1912], is rendered "overcharge" in 2 Cor. 2:5, A.V. See BURDEN, B, No. 2, and PRESS.
NT: B.290b; CB.1245c; K.—.
OT: —.
GEN. REF.: IS.3:622; NB.—; Z.—.

OVERCOME

1. *nikaō* [νικάω, 3528], is used (*a*) of God, Rom. 3:4 (a law term), R.V., "mightest prevail"; (*b*) of Christ, John 16:33; Rev. 3:21; 5:5; 17:14; (*c*) of His followers, Rom. 12:21 (2nd part); 1 John 2:13, 14; 4:4; 5:4, 5; Rev. 2:7, 11, 17, 26; 3:5, 12, 21; 12:11; 15:2; 21:7; (*d*) of faith, 1 John 5:4; (*e*) of evil (Passive Voice), Rom. 12:21; (*f*) of predicted human potentates, Rev. 6:2; 11:7; 13:7. ¶
NT: B.539a; CB.1259c; K.634.
OT: nāṣaḥ: S.5329; HR.945b.3; H.1402; BD.663d.
GEN. REF.: IS.3:622; NB.—; Z.—.

2. *hēttaomai* [ἡττάομαι, 2274], to be made inferior, be enslaved, is rendered "is (are) overcome," in 2 Pet. 2:19, 20. See INFERIOR.
NT: B.349c; CB.—; K.—.
OT: ḥātat: S.2865; HR.620b.3; H.784; BD.369a.
GEN. REF.: IS.3:622; NB.—; Z.—.

3. *katakurieuō* [κατακυριεύω, 2634], is translated "overcome" in Acts 19:16; see MASTER, B.

NT: B.412c; CB.1254a; K.486.
OT: kābash: S.3533; HR.735a.3; H.951; BD.461b.
māshal: S.4910; HR.735a.4; H.1258,1259; BD.605c.
rādāh: S.7287; HR.735a.6; H.2121,2122; BD.921d.
GEN. REF.: –.

OVERFLOW, OVERFLOWING

A. Verbs.

1. *huperperisseuō* [ὑπερπερισσεύω, 5248], to abound more exceedingly, Rom. 5:20, is used in the Middle Voice in 2 Cor. 7:4, R.V., "I overflow (with joy)," A.V., "I am exceeding (joyful)." See ABUNDANCE, B, No. 2.

NT: B.841d; CB.1252a; K.828.
OT: –.
GEN. REF.: –.

2. *katakluzō* [κατακλύζω, 2626], to inundate, deluge (*kata*, down, *kluzō*, to wash or dash over, said, e.g., of the sea), is used in the Passive Voice in 2 Pet. 3:6, of the Flood. ¶

NT: B.411d; CB.–; K.–.
OT: shāṭaph: S.7857; HR.734a.1; H.2373; BD.1009a.
GEN. REF.: –.

B. Noun.

perisseia [περισσεία, 4050], is translated "overflowing" in Jas. 1:21, R.V. See ABUNDANCE, A, No. 2.

NT: B.650c; CB.1263c; K.828.
OT: yitrôn: S.3504; HR.1126b.1a; H.936f; BD.452c.
GEN. REF.: –.

OVERLAY

perikaluptō [περικαλύπτω, 4028], denotes to cover around, cover up, or over; it is translated "overlaid" in Heb. 9:4. See BLINDFOLD, COVER.

NT: B.647d; CB.–; K.–.
OT: kāsāh: S.3680; HR.1124a.2; H.1008; BD.491b.
sākak: S.5526; HR.1124a.3; H.1475,1492,2259,2260; BD.696d.
GEN. REF.: –.

OVERLOOK

hupereidon [ὑπερεῖδον, 5237], to overlook (an aorist form), is used in Acts 17:30, R.V. (A.V., "winked at"), i.e., God bore with them without interposing by way of punishment, though the debasing tendencies of idolatry necessarily developed themselves. ¶

NT: B.841c; CB.–; K.–.
OT: –.
GEN. REF.: –.

OVERMUCH

perissoteros [περισσότερος, 4055], the comparative degree of *perissos*, abundant, is translated "overmuch" in 2 Cor. 2:7. See ABUNDANCE, C, No. 2.

NT: B.651c; CB.1263c; K.828.
OT: –.
GEN. REF.: –.

Notes: (1) In 2 Cor. 10:14, R.V., the verb *huperekteinō*, to stretch out over, is translated "we stretch (not ourselves) overmuch" (A.V., . . . beyond *our measure*"). See STRETCH. ¶

(2) In 2 Cor. 12:7 (twice), R.V., *huperairō*, in the Middle Voice, to uplift oneself, is translated "I should (not) be exalted overmuch," A.V., ". . . above measure." See EXALT.

OVER-RIPE

xērainō [ξηραίνω, 3583], denotes to dry up, wither, translated in Rev. 14:15, "over-ripe," R.V. (A.V., "ripe"), said figuratively of the harvest of the earth, symbolizing the condition of the world, political, especially connected with Israel (Joel 3:9, 14), and religious, comprehensive of the whole scene of Christendom (Matt. 13:38). Dee DRY.

NT: B.548c; CB.1273b; K.–.
OT: yābēsh: S.3001; HR.957a.2; H.837; BD.386b.
GEN. REF.: –.

For OVERSEER see BISHOP

OVERSHADOW

1. *episkiazō* [ἐπισκιάζω, 1982], to throw a shadow upon (*epi*, over, *skia*, a shadow), to overshadow, is used (*a*) of the bright cloud at the Transfiguration, Matt. 17:5; Mark 9:7; Luke 9:34; (*b*) metaphorically of the power of "the Most High" upon the Virgin Mary, Luke 1:35; (*c*) of the Apostle Peter's shadow upon the sick, Acts 5:15. ¶

NT: B.298d; CB.1246a; K.1044.
OT: sākak: S.5526; HR.528c.1; H.1475,1492,2259,2260; BD.696d.
shākan: S.7931; HR.528c.2; H.2387; BD.1014d.
GEN. REF.: –.

2. *kataskiazō* [κατασκιάζω, 2683], lit., to shadow down, is used of the "overshadowing" (R.V.) of the cherubim of glory above the mercy-seat, Heb. 9:5 (A.V., "shadowing"). ¶

NT: B.418d; CB.–; K.–.
OT: –.
GEN. REF.: –.

OVERSIGHT (exercise, take)

episkopeō [ἐπισκοπέω, 1983], lit., to look upon (*epi*, upon, *skopeō*, to look at, contemplate), is found in 1 Pet. 5:2 (some ancient authorities omit it), "exercising the oversight," R.V. (A.V., "taking . . ."); "exercising" is the right rendering; the word does not imply the entrance upon such responsibility, but the fulfilment of it. It is not a matter of assuming a position, but of the discharge of the duties.

The word is found elsewhere in Heb. 12:15, "looking carefully," R.V. See LOOK. ¶ Cp. *episkopē* in 1 Tim. 3:1 (see BISHOP, No. 2).

NT: B.298d; CB.1246a; K.244.
OT: pāqad: S.6485; HR.528c.4; H.1802; BD.823a.
dārash: S.1875; HR.528c.1; H.455; BD.205a.
GEN. REF.: IS.3:623; NB.—; Z.4:555.

OVERTAKE

1. *katalambanō* [καταλαμβάνω, 2638], to lay hold of, has the significance of overtaking, metaphorically, in John 12:35 (R.V., "overtake," A.V., "come upon") and 1 Thess. 5:4. See APPREHEND, No. 1.

NT: B.412d; CB.1254a; K.495.
OT: lākad: S.3920; HR.735a.6; H.1115; BD.539d.
nāsag: S.5381; HR.735a.11; H.1422; BD.673b.
GEN. REF.: —.

2. *prolambanō* [προλαμβάνω, 4301], to anticipate (*pro*, before, *lambanō*, to take), is used of the act of Mary, in Mark 14:8 [see COME, *Note* (2)]; of forestalling the less favoured at a social meal, 1 Cor. 11:21; of being overtaken in any trespass, Gal. 6:1, where the meaning is not that of detecting a person in the act, but of his being caught by the trespass, through his being off his guard (see 5:21 and contrast the premeditated practice of evil in 5:26). The modern Greek Version is 'even if a man, through lack of circumspection, should fall into any sin.' See TAKE. ¶

NT: B.708b; CB.1266c; K.495.
OT: —.
GEN. REF.: —.

OVERTHROW (Noun and Verb)

A. Noun.

katastrophē [καταστροφή, 2692], lit., a turning down (*kata*, down, *strophē*, a turning; Eng., catastrophe), is used (*a*) literally, 2 Pet. 2:6; (*b*) metaphorically, 2 Tim. 2:14, "subverting," i.e., the overthrowing of faith. ¶ Cp. *kathairesis*, a pulling down, 2 Cor. 10:4, 8; 13:10. ¶

NT: B.419b; CB.—; K.1093.
OT: 'êd: S.343; HR.746a.1; H.38c; BD.15c.
shādad: S.7703; HR.746a.5; H.2331; BD.994a.
sōph: S.5490; HR.746a.3; H.1478a; BD.693a.
GEN. REF.: —.

B. Verbs.

1. *katastrephō* [καταστρέφω, 2690], akin to A, lit. and primarily, to turn down or turn over, as, e.g., the soil, denotes to overturn, overthrow, Matt. 21:12; Mark 11:15; in Acts 15:16, Passive Voice, "ruins," lit., 'the overthrown (things) of it' (some mss. have *kataskaptō*, to dig down). See RUIN. ¶

NT: B.419a; CB.—; K.1093.
OT: hāphak: S.2015; HR.745c.1a; H.512; BD.245b.
GEN. REF.: —.

2. *anastrephō* [ἀναστρέφω, —], is found in some mss. in John 2:15 (see No. 3). See ABIDE, No. 8.

3. *anatrepō* [ἀνατρέπω, 396], lit., to turn up or over (*ana*, up, *trepō*, to turn), to upset, is used (*a*) literally, in the most authentic mss., in John 2:15 (see No. 2); (*b*) metaphorically, in 2 Tim. 2:18, "overthrow (the faith of some)"; in Tit. 1:11, R.V., "overthrow (whole houses)," A.V., "subvert . . . ;" i.e., households. Moulton and Milligan (Vocab.) give an apt illustration from a 2nd cent. papyrus, of the complete upsetting of a family by the riotous conduct of a member. ¶

NT: B.62c; CB.—; K.—.
OT: hādaph: S.1920; HR.84b.2; H.476; BD.213c.
dāḥāh: S.1760; HR.84b.1; H.420; BD.190d.
kāphāh: S.3711; HR.84b.3; H.1018; BD.495c.
GEN. REF.: —.

4. *kataluō* [καταλύω, 2647], lit., to loosen down, signifies to overthrow in Acts 5:38, R.V., "it will be overthrown" (A.V., "it will come to nought"); Rom. 14:20, R.V., "overthrow" (A.V., "destroy"). See DESTROY.

NT: B.414b; CB.1254a; K.543.
OT: —.
GEN. REF.: —.

5. *katastrōnnumi* [καταστρώννυμι, 2693], primarily, to strew or spread over (*kata*, down, *strōnnumi*, or *strōnnuō*, to spread), then, to overthrow, has this meaning in 1 Cor. 10:5, "they were overthrown." ¶ In the Sept., Numb. 14:16; Job 12:23. ¶

NT: B.419b; CB.—; K.—.
OT: shāḥaṭ: S.7819; HR.746a.1; H.—; BD.1006a.
shāṭaḥ: S.7849; HR.746a.2; H.—; BD.1008d.
GEN. REF.: —.

OWE

A. Verbs.

1. *opheilō* [ὀφείλω, 3784], to owe, to be a debtor (in the Passive Voice, to be owed, to be due), is translated by the verb to owe in Matt. 18:28 (twice); Luke 7:41; 16:5, 7; Rom. 13:8; in 15:27, R.V., "they (Gentile converts) owe it" (A.V., "it is their duty"); Philm. 18. See BEHOVE, DEBT, DUTY, GUILTY, INDEBTED, MUST, NEED, OUGHT.

NT: B.598d; CB.1261a; K.746.
OT: ḥôb: S.2326; HR.1039a.2; H.614a; BD.295a.
nāshā': S.5378; HR.1039a.4a; H.1424; BD.673d.
GEN. REF.: —.

2. *prosopheilō* [προσοφείλω, 4359], to owe besides (*pros*, in addition, and No. 1), is used in Philm. 19, "thou owest (to me even thine own self) besides," i.e., 'thou owest me already as much as Onesimus' debt, and in addition even thyself' (not 'thou owest me much more').

NT: B.717d; CB.—; K.—.
OT: —.
GEN. REF.: —.

B. Noun.

opheiletēs [ὀφειλέτης, 3781], a debtor (akin to A, No. 1), is translated "which owed" in Matt. 18:24, lit., 'a debtor (of ten thousand talents).' See DEBTOR.

NT: B.598b; CB.1261a; K.746.
OT: —.
GEN. REF.: —.

OWN (Adjective)

Notes: (1) *Gnēsios*, primarily, lawfully begotten, and hence 'true,' 'genuine,' is translated "own" in the A.V. of 1 Tim. 1:2 and Tit. 1:4 (R.V., "true"). See SINCERITY, TRUE.

(2) In Acts 5:4, "was it not thine own?" is, lit., 'did it not remain (*menō*) to thee?'

(3) In Jude 6 (1st part), A.V., *heautōn*, of themselves, "their own" (R.V.), is rendered "their"; in the 2nd part, R.V., *idios*, one's own, is translated "their proper" (A.V., "their own").

(4) In Gal. 1:14, R.V., *sunēlikiōtēs*, is rendered "of mine own age" (A.V., "my equals"; marg., "equals in years"). ¶

(5) For "its own" in 1 Tim. 2:6, R.V., see DUE, A.

(6) For association with other words see ACCORD, BUSINESS, COMPANY, CONCEITS, COUNTRY.

OWNER

1. *kurios* [κύριος, 2962], one having power (*kuros*) or authority, a lord, master, signifies an owner in Luke 19:33. See LORD, MASTER, SIR.

NT: B.458d; CB.1256b; K.486.
OT: 'ēl: S.410; HR.800b.4a; H.93a; BD.42a.
yᵉhôwāh: S.3068; HR.800b.11a; H.484a; BD.217d.
'ᵉlōhîm: S.430; HR.800b.18a; H.93c; BD.43b.
GEN. REF.: —.

2. *nauklēros* [ναύκληρος, 3490], a ship owner (*naus*, a ship, *klēros*, a lot), a shipmaster, occurs in Acts 27:11, "(the) owner of the ship." ¶

NT: B.534b; CB.—; K.—.
OT: —.
GEN. REF.: —.

OWNETH

Note: In Acts 21:11, "that owneth this girdle," is lit., 'whose is (*esti*) this girdle.'

OX

1. *bous* [βοῦς, 1016], denotes an ox or a cow, Luke 13:15; 14:5, 19; John 2:14, 15; 1 Cor. 9:9 (twice); 1 Tim. 5:18. ¶

NT: B.146c; CB.1239b; K.—.
OT: bāqār: S.1241; HR.229a.2; H.274a; BD.133a.
pārāh: S.6510; HR.229a.3b; H.1830b; BD.831a.
shôr: S.7794; HR.229a.5a; H.2355a; BD.1004a.
GEN. REF.: IS.3:624; NB.—; Z.1:764.

2. *tauros* [ταῦρος, 5022], Latin *taurus*, is translated "oxen" in Matt. 22:4 and Acts 14:13; "bulls" in Heb. 9:13 and 10:4. ¶

NT: B.806b; CB.1271a; K.—.
OT: shôr: S.7794; HR.1337c.5; H.2355a; BD.1004a.
par: S.6499; HR.1337c.4; H.1831a; BD.830d.
GEN. REF.: IS.3:624; NB.—; Z.1:764.

P

PAIN (Noun and Verb)

A. Nouns.

1. *ponos* [πόνος, 4192], is translated "pain" in Rev. 16:10; 21:4; "pains" in 16:11. See LABOUR.

NT: B.691c; CB.1266a; K.—.
OT: 'āwen: S.205; HR.1188b.1; H.48a; BD.19d.
'āmal: S.5999; HR.1188b.9; H.1639a; BD.765d.
GEN. REF.: IS.3:628; NB.—; Z.—.

2. *ōdin* [ὠδίν, 5604], a birth pang, travail-pain, is rendered "travail," metaphorically, in Matt. 24:8 and Mark 13:8, R.V. (A.V., "sorrows"); by way of comparison, in 1 Thess. 5:3; translated "pains (of death)," Acts 2:24 (R.V., "pangs"). See SORROW, TRAVAIL. ¶ Cp. *ōdinō*, to travail in birth.

NT: B.895c; CB.1260b; K.1353.
OT: ḥēbel: S.2256; HR.1492b.1; H.592b; BD.286d.
ḥîl: S.2427; HR.1492b.2a; H.623b; BD.297d.
hûl: S.2342; HR.1492b.2b; H.623; BD.296d.
GEN. REF.: IS.3:628; NB.—; Z.—.

B. Verb.

basanizō [βασανίζω, 928], primarily signifies to rub on the touchstone, to put to the test (from *basanos*, a touchstone, a dark stone used in testing metals); hence, to examine by torture, and, in general to distress; in Rev. 12:2, "in pain," R.V. (A.V., "pained"), in connection with parturition. See TORMENT. (In the Sept., 1 Sam. 5:3. ¶).

NT: B.134c; CB.1238c; K.96.
OT: —.
GEN. REF.: —.

Note: For Rom. 8:22, "travaileth in pain together," see TRAVAIL.

For **PAINFULNESS** (2 Cor. 11:27, A.V.) see **TRAVAIL**

PAIR

zeugos [ζεῦγος, 2201], a yoke (akin to *zeugnumi*, to yoke), is used (*a*) of beasts, Luke 14:19; (*b*) of a pair of anything; in Luke 2:24, of turtledoves. See YOKE. ¶
NT: B.337b; CB.1273c; K.–.
OT: ṣemed: S.6776; HR.594a.2; H.1927a; BD.855a.
GEN. REF.: –.

Note: In Rev. 6:5, A.V., *zugos*, a yoke (akin to *zeugos*), is translated "a pair of balances" (R.V., "a balance"). See BALANCE, YOKE.

PALACE

1. *aulē* [αὐλή, 833], a court, dwelling, palace: see COURT.
NT: B.121b; CB.1238b; K.–.
OT: ḥāṣēr: S.2691; HR.177b.2b; H.722a,723a; BD.347b.
GEN. REF.: IS.3:629; NB.917; Z.4:561.

2. *praitōrion* [πραιτώριον, 4232], signified originally a general's (praetor's) tent. Then it was applied to the council of army officers; then to the official residence of the Governor of a Province; finally, to the imperial bodyguard. In the A.V. the word appears only once, Mark 15:16, "the hall, called Praetorium" (R.V., "within the court which is the Praetorium," marg., "palace"); in the Greek of the N.T. it also occurs in Matt. 27:27, A.V., "the common hall," marg., "the governor's house"; R.V., "palace," see marg.; John 18:28 (twice), A.V., "the hall of judgment"; and "judgment hall," marg., "Pilate's house," R.V., "palace"; 18:33 and 19:9, A.V., "judgment hall," R.V., "palace," see marg.; so in Acts 23:35; in Phil. 1:13, A.V., "in all the palace," marg., "Caesar's court," R.V., "throughout the whole praetorian guard," marg., "in the whole Praetorium."

"In the Gospels the term denotes the official residence in Jerusalem of the Roman governor, and the various translations of it in our versions arose from a desire either to indicate the special purpose for which that residence was used on the occasion in question, or to explain what particular building was intended. But whatever building the governor occupied was the Praetorium. It is most probable that in Jerusalem he resided in the well-known palace of Herod. . . . Pilate's residence has been identified with the castle of Antonia, which was occupied by the regular garrison. The probability is that it was the same as Herod's palace. Herod's palace in Caesarea was used as the Praetorium there, and the expression in Acts 23:35, marg., 'Herod's praetorium,' is abbreviated from 'the praetorium of Herod's palace.' " (Hastings' Bib. Dic.).

In Phil. 1:13, marg., "the whole Praetorium" has been variously explained. It has been spoken of as 'the palace,' in connection with 4:22, where allusion is made to believers who belong to Caesar's household. Others have understood it of the barracks of the praetorian guard, but Lightfoot shows that this use of the word cannot be established, neither can it be regarded as referring to the barracks of the palace guard. The phrase 'and to all the rest' in 1:13 indicates that persons are meant. Mommsen, followed by Ramsay (*St. Paul the Traveller*, p. 357) regards it as improbable that the Apostle was committed to the praetorian guard and holds the view that Julius the centurion, who brought Paul to Rome, belonged to a corps drafted from legions in the provinces, whose duty it was to supervise the corn supply and perform police service, and that Julius probably delivered his prisoners to the Commander of his corps. Eventually Paul's case came before the praetorian council, which is the praetorium alluded to by the Apostle, and the phrase "to all the rest" refers to the audience of the trial. ¶
NT: B.697c; CB.–; K.–.
OT: –.
GEN. REF.: IS.–; NB.917; Z.4:561.

Note: Some scholars, believing that this Epistle was written during an Ephesian imprisonment, take the Praetorium here to be the residence in Ephesus of the Proconsul of the Province of Asia, and "Caesar's household" to be the local Imperial Civil Service (Deissmann etc.).

PALE

chlōros [χλωρός, 5515], pale green, is translated "pale" (of a horse) in Rev. 6:8, symbolizing death. See GREEN.
NT: B.882d; CB.1240a; K.–.
OT: yereq: S.3418; HR.1471c.2a; H.918a; BD.438d.
laḥ: S.3892; HR.1471c.4; H.1102a; BD.535a.
GEN. REF.: –.

PALM (of the hand)

Note: For *rhapizō*, to strike with a rod or with the palm of the hand, Matt. 26:67 (cp. 5:39), see SMITE. ¶ For *rhapisma*, a blow, with *didōmi*, to give, translated "did strike (and, struck) . . . with the palm of his hand" (A.V., in Mark 14:65; John 18:22), see BLOW.

PALM (palm tree)

phoinix [φοῖνιξ, 5404], denotes the date palm; it is used of palm trees in John 12:13, from which branches were taken; of the branches themselves in Rev. 7:9. ¶ The palm gave its name to Phoenicia and to Phoenix in Crete, Acts 27:12, R.V. Jericho was the city of palm trees, Deut. 34:3; Judg. 1:16; 3:13; 2 Chron. 28:15. They were plentiful there in the time of Christ.

NT: B.864b; CB.1264b; K.—.
OT: tāmār: S.8558; HR.1436c.1a; H.2523; BD.1071c.
timōrāh: S.8561; HR.1436c.1c; H.2523c; BD.1071c.
GEN. REF.: IS.3:649; NB.1294; Z.4:586.

PALSY (sick of)

A. Adjective.

paralutikos [παραλυτικός, 3885], paralytic, sick of the palsy, is found in Matt. 4:24 (R.V., "palsied"); 8:6; 9.2 (twice), 6; Mark 2:3, 4, 5, 9, 10; in some mss. Luke 5:24 (see B). ¶

NT: B.620b; CB.1262a; K.—.
OT: —.
GEN. REF.: IS.3:649; NB.—; Z.4:587.

B. Verb.

paraluō [παραλύω, 3886], lit., to loose from the side, hence, to set free, is used in the Passive Voice of being enfeebled by a paralytic stroke, palsied, Luke 5:18, R.V., "palsied" (A.V., "taken with a palsy"); 5:24 (ditto), in the best mss.; Acts 8:7 (ditto); 9:33, R.V., "he was palsied" (A.V., "was sick of the palsy"); Heb. 12:12, R.V., "palsied (knees)," A.V., "feeble." See FEEBLE. ¶

NT: B.620b; CB.1262a; K.—.
OT: rāphāh: S.7503; HR.1062a.13; H.2198; BD.951c.
kāshal: S.3782; HR.1062a.6; H.1050; BD.505b.
GEN. REF.: IS.3:649; NB.—; Z.4:587.

For **PANGS**, Acts 2:24, R.V., see **PAIN**

For **PAPS** see **BREAST**

PAPER

chartēs [χάρτης, 5489], a sheet of paper made of strips of papyrus (whence Eng., "paper"), Eng., chart, charter, etc.; the word is used in 2 John 12. ¶ The papyrus reed grew in ancient times in great profusion in the Nile and was used as a material for writing. From Egypt its use spread to other countries and it was the universal material for writing in general in Greece and Italy during the most flourishing periods of their literature.

The pith of the stem of the plant was cut into strips, placed side by side to form a sheath. Another layer was laid upon this at right angles to it. The two layers were united by moisture and pressure and frequently with the addition of glue. The sheets, after being dried and polished, were ready for use. Normally, the writing is on that side of the papyrus on which the fibres lie horizontally, parallel to the length of the roll, but where the material was scarce the writer used the other side also (cp. Rev. 5:1). Papyrus continued to be used until the seventh cent., A.D., when the conquest of Egypt by the Arabs led to the disuse of the material for literary purposes and the use of vellum till the 12th century.

NT: B.879b; CB.—; K.—.
OT: m^e^gillāh: S.4039; HR.1456a.1; H.353m; BD.166b.
GEN. REF.: IS.3:651; NB.1344; Z.—.

PARABLE

1. *parabolē* [παραβολή, 3850], lit. denotes a placing beside (akin to *paraballō*, to throw or lay beside, to compare). It signifies a placing of one thing beside another with a view to comparison (some consider that the thought of comparison is not necessarily contained in the word). In the N.T. it is found outside the Gospels, only in Heb. 9:9 and 11:19. It is generally used of a somewhat lengthy utterance or narrative drawn from nature or human circumstances, the object of which is to set forth a spiritual lesson, e.g., those in Matt. 13 and Synoptic parallels; sometimes it is used of a short saying or proverb, e.g., Matt. 15:15; Mark 3:23; 7:17; Luke 4:23; 5:36; 6:39. It is the lesson that is of value; the hearer must catch the analogy if he is to be instructed (this is true also of a proverb). Such a narrative or saying, dealing with earthly things with a spiritual meaning, is distinct from a fable, which attributes to things what does not belong to them in nature.

Christ's parables most frequently convey truths connected with the subject of the Kingdom of God. His withholding the meaning from His hearers as He did from the multitudes, Matt. 13:34, was a Divine judgment upon the unworthy.

Two dangers are to be avoided in seeking to interpret the parables in Scripture, that of ignoring the important features, and that of trying to make all the details mean something.

NT: B.612a; CB.1262a; K.773.
OT: māshāl: S.4912; HR.1056a.1a; H.1258a; BD.605a.
GEN. REF.: IS.3:655; NB.932; Z.4:590.

2. *paroimia* [παροιμία, 3942], denotes a wayside saying (from *paroimos*, by the way), a byword, maxim, or problem, 2 Pet. 2:22. The word is sometimes spoken of as a parable, John 10:6, i.e., a figurative discourse (R.V. marg.,

"proverb"); see also 16:25, 29, where the word is rendered "proverbs" (marg. "parables") and "proverb." ¶

NT: B.629b; CB.1262b; K.790.
OT: māshāl: S.4912; HR.1072a.1; H.1258a; BD.605a.
GEN. REF.: IS.3:655; NB.–; Z.4:590.

PARADISE

paradeisos [παράδεισος, 3857], is an Oriental word, first used by the historian Xenophon, denoting the parks of Persian kings and nobles. It is of Persian origin (Old Pers. *pairidoeza*, akin to Gk. *peri*, around, and *teichos*, a wall) whence it passed into Greek. See the Sept., e.g., in Neh. 2:8; Eccl. 2:5; S. of Sol. 4:13. The Sept. translators used it of the garden of Eden, Gen. 2:8, and in other respects, e.g., Numb. 24:6; Is. 1:30; Jer. 29:5; Ezek. 31:8, 9.

In Luke 23:43, the promise of the Lord to the repentant robber was fulfilled the same day; Christ, at His death, having committed His spirit to the Father, went in spirit immediately into Heaven itself, the dwelling place of God (the Lord's mention of the place as Paradise must have been a great comfort to the malefactor; to the oriental mind it expressed the sum total of blessedness). Thither the Apostle Paul was caught up, 2 Cor. 12:4, spoken of as "the third heaven" (ver. 3 does not introduce a different vision), beyond the heavens of the natural creation (see Heb. 4:14, R.V., with reference to the Ascension). The same region is mentioned in Rev. 2:7, where the "tree of life," the figurative antitype of that in Eden, held out to the overcomer, is spoken of as being in "the Paradise of God" (R.V.), marg., "garden," as in Gen. 2:8. ¶

NT: B.614a; CB.1262a; K.777.
OT: gan: S.1588; HR.1057c.1a; H.367a; BD.171a.
GEN. REF.: IS.3:660; NB.934; Z.4:598.

For **PARCEL** see **GROUND**, No. 4

PARCHMENT

membrana [μεμβράνα, 3200], is a Latin word, properly an adjective, from *membrum*, a limb, but denoting skin, parchment. The Eng. word 'parchment' is a form of *pergamena*, an adjective signifying 'of Pergamum,' the city in Asia Minor where parchment was either invented or brought into use. The word *membrana* is found in 2 Tim. 4:13, where Timothy is asked to bring to the Apostle "the books, especially the parchments." The writing material was prepared from the skin of the sheep or goat. The skins were first soaked in lime for the purpose of removing the hair, and then shaved, washed, dried, stretched and ground or smoothed with fine chalk or lime and pumice-stone. The finest kind is called vellum, and is made from the skins of calves or kids. ¶

NT: B.502a; CB.–; K.–.
OT: –.
GEN. REF.: IS.3:663; NB.1343; Z.–.

PARENTS

1. *goneus* [γονεύς, 1118], a begetter, a father (akin to *ginomai*, to come into being, become), is used in the plural in the N.T., Matt. 10:21; Mark 13:12; six times in Luke (in Luke 2:43, R.V., "His parents," A.V., "Joseph and His mother"); six in John; elsewhere, Rom. 1:30; 2 Cor. 12:14 (twice); Eph. 6:1; Col. 3:20; 2 Tim. 3:2. ¶

NT: B.165a; CB.–; K.–.
OT: –.
GEN. REF.: –.

2. *progonos* [πρόγονος, 4269], an adjective signifying born before (*pro*, before, and *ginomai*, see No. 1), is used as a noun, in the plural, (*a*) of ancestors, "forefathers," 2 Tim. 1:3; (*b*) of living parents, 1 Tim. 5:4. See FOREFATHER. ¶

NT: B.704a; CB.–; K.–.
OT: –.
GEN. REF.: –.

3. *patēr* [πατήρ, 3962], a father, is used in Heb. 11:23, in the plural, of both father and mother, the "parents" of Moses. See FATHER.

NT: B.635a; CB.1262c; K.805.
OT: 'āb: S.1; HR.1105a.1a; H.4a; BD.3a.
GEN. REF.: IS.2:285; NB.416; Z.2:504.

PART (Noun, a portion; Verb, to give or divide, partake)

A. Nouns.

1. *meros* [μέρος, 3313], denotes (*a*) a part, portion, of the whole, e.g., John 13:8; Rev. 20:6; 22:19; hence, a lot or destiny, e.g., Rev. 21:8; in Matt. 24:51 and Luke 12:46, "portion"; (*b*) a part as opposite to the whole, e.g., Luke 11:36; John 19:23; 21:6, "side"; Acts 5:2; 23:6; Eph. 4:16; Rev. 16:19; a party, Acts 23:9; the divisions of a province, e.g., Matt. 2:22; Acts 2:10; the regions belonging to a city, e.g., Matt. 15:21, R.V., "parts" (A.V., "coasts"); 16:13 (ditto); Mark 8:10, A.V. and R.V., "parts"; "the lower parts of the earth," Eph. 4:9; this phrase means the regions beneath the earth (see LOWER, A, No. 1); (*c*) a class, or category (with *en*, in, "in respect of"), Col. 2:16; "in this respect," 2 Cor. 3:10; 9:3, R.V. (A.V., "in this behalf"). See BEHALF, COAST, CRAFT, PIECE, PORTION, RESPECT.

NT: B.505d; CB.1258b; K.585.
OT: qāṣeh: S.7097; HR.911c.16a; H.2053a.c; BD.892a.
GEN. REF.: IS.3:670; NB.–; Z.–.

2. *meris* [*μερίς*, 3310], denotes (*a*) a part or portion, Luke 10:42; Acts 8:21; 2 Cor. 6:15 (R.V., "portion"); in Col. 1:12, "partakers," lit., 'unto the part of'; (*b*) a district or division, Acts 16:12, R.V., "district" (A.V., "part"). See DISTRICT, PARTAKER. ¶

NT: B.505a; CB.1258b; K.—.
OT: ḥēleq: S.2506; HR.911a.1a; H.669a; BD.324a.
ḥelqāh: S.2513; HR.911a.1b; H.670c; BD.324c.
mānāh: S.4490; HR.911a.2a; H.1213a; BD.584b.
GEN. REF.: IS.3:670; NB.—; Z.—.

3. *klima* [*κλίμα*, 2824], primarily an incline, slope (Eng., clime, climate), is used of a region, Rom. 15:23, A.V., "parts" (R.V., "regions"); 2 Cor. 11:10, A.V. and R.V., "regions"; Gal. 1:21 (ditto). See REGION. ¶

NT: B.436b; CB.—; K.—.
OT: pinnāh: S.6438; HR.771a.1; H.1783a; BD.819c.
GEN. REF.: —.

4. *eschatos* [*ἔσχατος*, 2078], an adjective signifying last, utmost, extreme, is often used as a noun; in Acts 13:47, R.V., "uttermost part" (A.V., "ends"). See END, LAST, LOWEST, UTTERMOST.

NT: B.313c; CB.1246c; K.—.
OT: 'aḥ^{a}rôn: S.314; HR.558a.1c; H.68e; BD.30d.
'aḥ^{a}rît: S.319; HR.558a.1d; H.68f; BD.31a.
GEN. REF.: —.

5. *topos* [*τόπος*, 5117], a place, is translated "parts" in Acts 16:3, R.V. (A.V., "quarters"). See PLACE, etc.

NT: B.822b; CB.1273a; K.1184.
OT: māqôm: S.4725; HR.1364b.8; H.1999b; BD.879d.
GEN. REF.: —.

6. The plural of the article, followed first by the particle *men*, indeed, and then by *de*, but, is translated "part . . . and part" in Acts 14:4.

7. *peras* [*πέρας*, 4009], an end, boundary, is translated, "utmost parts" in the A.V. of Matt. 12:42 and Luke 11:31. See END, A, No. 3.

NT: B.644a; CB.1263b; K.—.
OT: qēṣ: S.7093; HR.1120a.6a; H.2060a; BD.893d.
'ephem: S.657; HR.1120a.1; H.147a; BD.67a.
GEN. REF.: —.

Notes: (1) *Meros* is used with certain prepositions in adverbial phrases, (*a*) with *ana*, used distributively, 1 Cor. 14:27, "in turn," R.V., A.V., "by course"; (*b*) with *kata*, according to, Heb. 9:5, R.V., "severally" (A.V., "particularly"); (*c*) with *apo*, from, "in part," Rom. 11:25; 2 Cor. 1:14; 2:5 (see also MEASURE); (*d*) with *ek*, from, 1 Cor. 13:9, 10, 12; in 1 Cor. 12:27, R.V., "severally," marg., "each in his part" (A.V., "in particular").

(2) In Mark 4:38 and Acts 27:41, A.V., *prumna*, a stern, is translated "hinder part" (R.V., "stern").

(3) In Acts 1:17, A.V., *klēros*, a lot, is translated "part" (R.V., "portion"; marg., "lot"), of that portion allotted to Judas in the ministry of the Twelve. See INHERITANCE, LOT.

(4) In Acts 1:25, where the best mss. have *topos*, a place, R.V., "(to take) the place (in this ministry)," some texts have *klēros*, which the A.V. translates "part."

(5) In Mark 9:40, A.V., the preposition *huper*, on behalf of, is translated "on (our) part," R.V., "for (us)."

(6) In 1 Pet. 4:14, A.V., "on (their) part," "on (your) part," represents the preposition *kata*, according to, followed by the personal pronouns; the statements are not found in the most authentic mss.

(7) In Acts 9:32, A.V., the phrase *dia pantōn*, lit., 'through all,' is rendered "throughout all *quarters*" (R.V., "throughout all parts").

(8) In 1 Cor. 12:23, the R.V. has "*parts*" for "*members*"; A.V. and R.V. have "*parts*" in the end of the ver.; see also ver. 24.

(9) In 2 Cor. 10:16, the R.V. translates the neuter plural of the article "the parts" (A.V., "the *regions*").

(10) For "inward part" see INWARD.

B. Verbs.

1. *merizō* [*μερίζω*, 3307], to divide, to distribute (akin to A, No. 1), is translated "divided (A.V., gave) a . . . part" in Heb. 7:2, R.V. See DEAL.

NT: B.504c; CB.1258b; K.—.
OT: ḥālaq: S.2505; HR.910c.2a-c; H.669; BD.323c.
nāḥal: S.5157; HR.910c.5a,b; H.1342; BD.635c.
GEN. REF.: IS.3:671; NB.—; Z.—.

2. *metechō* [*μετέχω*, 3348], to partake of, share in, Heb. 2:14: see PARTAKE.

NT: B.514a; CB.1258c; K.286.
OT: —.
GEN. REF.: —.

3. *paraginomai* [*παραγίνομαι*, 3854], to be beside, support (*para*, beside, *ginomai*, to become), is rendered "took (my) part" in 2 Tim. 4:16 (A.V., "stood with"); some mss. have *sunparaginomai*. See COME, No. 13, GO, PRESENT (to be).

NT: B.613c; CB.—; K.—.
OT: bô': S.935; HR.1056c.1a; H.212; BD.97c.
GEN. REF.: —.

Notes: (1) In Rev. 6:8, *tetartos*, a fourth, is rendered "the fourth part."

(2) See GREATER, HINDER, INWARD, MORE, TENTH, THIRD, UTMOST, UTTERMOST.

PART (Verb, to separate)

1. *diamerizō* [*διαμερίζω*, 1266], to part among, to distribute, is translated by the verb to part (*a*) in the Middle Voice, with reference to the Lord's garments, Matt. 27:35, 1st part (in some mss., 2nd part); Mark 15:24; Luke 23:34; John 19:24; (*b*) in the Active Voice, of the proceeds of the sale of possessions and

goods, Acts 2:45; (*c*) in the Passive Voice in Acts 2:3, of the "parting asunder" (R.V.) of tongues like fire (A.V., "cloven"). See CLOVEN, DIVIDE, No. 7.

NT: B.186d; CB.–; K.–.
OT: ḥālaq: S.2505; HR.305c.1b; H.669; BD.323c.
GEN. REF.: IS.3:671; NB.–; Z.–.

2. *diistēmi* [διΐστημι, 1339], to set apart, separate (*dia*, apart, *histēmi*, to cause to stand), is used in the Active Voice in Luke 24:51, R.V., "He parted (from them)," A.V., "was parted." See GO, SPACE.

NT: B.195b; CB.–; K.–.
OT: ḥālaq: S.2505; HR.330b.2; H.669; BD.323c.
pārad: S.6504; HR.330b.4; H.1806; BD.825b.
GEN. REF.: IS.3:671; NB.–; Z.–.

3. *apospaō* [ἀποσπάω, 645], to draw off or tear away, is used in the Passive Voice in Luke 22:41, R.V., "He was parted" (A.V., "was withdrawn"), lit. 'He was torn away,' indicating the reluctance with which Christ parted from the loving sympathy of the disciples. Moulton and Milligan suggest that the ordinary use of the verb does not encourage this stronger meaning, but since the simpler meaning is not found in the N.T., except in Acts 21:1, and since the idea of withdrawal is expressed in Matt. by *anachōreō*, Luke may have used *apospaō* here in the stronger sense. See DRAW, A, No. 6.

NT: B.98a; CB.–; K.–.
OT: nātaq: S.5423; HR.141a.2; H.1447; BD.683c.
nātash: S.5428; HR.141a.3; H.1451; BD.684c.
GEN. REF.: IS.3:671; NB.–; Z.–.

4. *chōrizō* [χωρίζω, 5563], in Philm. 15, R.V., "parted": see DEPART, No. 13.

NT: B.890a; CB.1240a; K.–.
OT: bādal: S.914; HR.1482b.2; H.203; BD.95a.
pārad: S.6504; HR.1482b.4; H.1806; BD.825b.
GEN. REF.: IS.3:671; NB.–; Z.–.

5. *apochōrizō* [ἀποχωρίζω, 673], to part from, Acts 15:39, R.V.: see DEPART, No. 14.

NT: B.102b; CB.–; K.–.
OT: miphqād: S.4662; HR.150a.1; H.1802g; BD.824c.
GEN. REF.: –.

PARTAKE, PARTAKER

A. Nouns.

1. *koinōnos* [κοινωνός, 2844], an adjective, signifying having in common (*koinos*, common), is used as a noun, denoting a companion, partner, partaker, translated "partakers" in Matt. 23:30; 1 Cor. 10:18, A.V. (see COMMUNION, B); 2 Cor. 1:7; Heb. 10:33, R.V. (see COMPANION, No. 2); 2 Pet. 1:4; "partaker" in 1 Pet. 5:1. See PARTNER.

NT: B.439c; CB.1255b; K.447.
OT: ḥāber: S.2270; HR.775b.1a; H.598c; BD.288d.
ḥᵃberet: S.2278; HR.775b.1b; H.598d; BD.289a.
GEN. REF.: –.

2. *sunkoinōnos* [συγκοινωνός, 4791], denotes partaking jointly with (*sun*, and No. 1), Rom. 11:17, R.V. "(didst become) partaker with them" (A.V., "partakest"); 1 Cor. 9:23, R.V., "a joint partaker," i.e., with the Gospel, as co-operating in its activity; the A.V. misplaces the "with" by attaching it to the superfluous italicised pronoun "*you*"; Phil. 1:7, "partakers with (me of grace)," R.V., and A.V. marg.; not as A.V. text, "partakers (of my grace)"; Rev. 1:9, "partaker with (you in the tribulation, etc.)," A.V., "companion." See COMPANION. ¶

NT: B.774b; CB.1270c; K.447.
OT: –.
GEN. REF.: –.

3. *metochos* [μέτοχος, —]: see FELLOW, No. 3, PARTNER.

4. *summetochos* [συμμέτοχος, 4830], partaking together with (*sun*, with, and No. 3), is used as a noun, a joint-partaker, Eph. 3:6, R.V., "fellow-partakers" (A.V., "partakers"); in 5:7, R.V. and A.V., "partakers." ¶

NT: B.778c; CB.–; K.286.
OT: –.
GEN. REF.: –.

Notes: (1) For *antilambanō*, to partake of, rendered "partakers" in 1 Tim. 6:2, A.V., see B, No. 4.

(2) For the phrase "to be partakers," Col. 1:12, see PART, A, No. 2.

B. Verbs.

1. *koinōneō* [κοινωνέω, 2841], to have a share of, to share with, take part in (akin to A, No. 1), is translated to be partaker of in 1 Tim. 5:22; Heb. 2:14 (1st part), A.V., "are partakers of," R.V., "are sharers in" (for the 2nd part see No. 3); 1 Pet. 4:13; 2 John 11, R.V., "partaketh in" (A.V., "is partaker of"); in the Passive Voice in Rom. 15:27. See COMMUNICATE, DISTRIBUTE.

NT: B.438c; CB.1255b; K.447.
OT: ḥābar: S.2266; HR.775a.3a,b; H.598; BD.287d.
GEN. REF.: –.

2. *sunkoinōneō* [συγκοινωνέω, —]: see FELLOWSHIP, B, No. 2.

3. *metechō* [μετέχω, 3348], to partake of, share in (*meta*, with, *echō*, to have), akin to A, No. 3, is translated "of partaking" in 1 Cor. 9:10, R.V. (A.V., "be partaker of"); "partake of" in 9:12, R.V. (A.V., "be partakers of"); so in 10:17, 21; in ver. 30 "partake"; in Heb. 2:14, the A.V. "took part of" is awkward; Christ "partook of" flesh and blood, R.V.; cp. No. 1 in this verse; in Heb. 5:13, metaphorically, of receiving elementary spiritual teaching, R.V., "partaketh of (milk)," A.V., "useth"; in Heb. 7:13, it is said of Christ (the antitype of Melchizedek) as 'belonging to' (so R.V.) or 'partaking of' (R.V. marg.) another tribe than that of Levi (A.V., "pertaineth to"). See PERTAIN, USE. ¶ See PARTNER, *Note*.

NT: B.514a; CB.1258c; K.286.
OT: –.
GEN. REF.: –.

4. *antilambanō* [ἀντιλαμβάνω, 482], to take hold of, to lay hold of something before one, has the meaning to partake of in 1 Tim. 6:2, R.V., "partake of," marg., "lay hold of," A.V., "are . . . partakers of" (*anti*, in return for, *lambanō*, to take or receive); the benefit mentioned as partaken of by the masters would seem to be the improved quality of the service rendered; the benefit of redemption is not in view here. See HELP.

NT: B.74c; CB.—; K.—.
OT: ḥāzaq: S.2388; HR.110c.2b; H.636; BD.304a.
sā'ad: S.5582; HR.110c.8; H.1525; BD.703c.
GEN. REF.: —.

5. *metalambanō* [μεταλαμβάνω, 3335], to have, or get, a share of, is translated to be partaker (or partakers) of in 2 Tim. 2:6 and Heb. 12:10. See EAT, HAVE, RECEIVE, TAKE.

NT: B.511b; CB.1258b; K.495.
OT: —.
GEN. REF.: —.

6. *summerizō* [συμμερίζω, 4829], primarily, to distribute in shares (*sun*, with, *meros*, a part), in the Middle Voice, to have a share in, is used in 1 Cor. 9:13, A.V, "are partakers with (the altar)," R.V., "have their portion with," i.e., they feed with others on that which, having been sacrificed, has been placed upon an altar; so the believer feeds upon Christ (who is the altar in Heb. 13:10). ¶

NT: B.778c; CB.—; K.—.
OT: ḥālaq: S.2505; HR.1304b.1; H.669; BD.323c.
GEN. REF.: —.

PARTIAL, PARTIALITY

A. Verb.

diakrinō [διακρίνω, 1252], to separate, distinguish, discern, judge, decide (*dia*, asunder, *krinō*, to judge), also came to mean to be divided in one's mind, to hesitate, doubt, and had this significance in Hellenistic Greek (though not so found in the Sept.). For the A.V., "are ye (not) partial" in Jas. 2:4, see DIVIDE, No. 4. " 'This meaning seems to have had its beginning in near proximity to Christianity.' It arises very naturally out of the general sense of making distinctions." (Moulton and Milligan).

NT: B.185a; CB.1241a; K.469.
OT: shāphaṭ: S.8199; HR.304a.8a; H.2443; BD.1047a.
dîn: S.1777; HR.304a.4a; H.426; BD.192a.
GEN. REF.: —.

B. Noun.

prosklisis [πρόσκλισις, 4346], denotes inclination (*pros*, towards, *klinō*, to lean); it is used with *kata* in 1 Tim. 5:21, lit., 'according to partiality.' ¶

NT: B.716a; CB.—; K.—.
OT: —.
GEN. REF.: —.

C. Adjective.

adiakritos [ἀδιάκριτος, 87], primarily signifies not to be parted (*a*, negative, and an adjectival form akin to A), hence, without uncertainty, or indecision, Jas. 3:17, A.V., "without partiality" (marg. "wrangling"), R.V., "without variance" (marg., "Or, doubtfulness Or, partiality"). See VARIANCE. ¶ In the Sept., Prov. 25:1. ¶

NT: B.17a; CB.1233a; K.469.
OT: —.
GEN. REF.: —.

For **PARTICULAR** and **PARTICULARLY** see **EVERY**, No. 3, **SEVERALLY**

Note: In Acts 21:19, for the A.V. "particularly" the R.V. has "one by one," translating the phrase lit., 'according to each one.'

For **PARTING** see **HIGHWAY**

PARTITION

phragmos [φραγμός, 5418], primarily a fencing in (akin to *phrassō*, to fence in, stop, close), is used metaphorically in Eph. 2:14, of "the middle wall of partition"; "the partition" is epexegetic of "the middle wall," i.e., 'the middle wall, namely, the partition' between Jew and Gentile. J. A. Robinson suggests that Paul had in mind the barrier between the outer and inner courts of the Temple, notices fixed to which warned Gentiles not to proceed further on pain of death (see Josephus, *Antiq*. xv. 11. 5; *B. J.* v. 5. 2; vi. 2. 4; cp. Acts 21:29). See HEDGE.

NT: B.865c; CB.1264b; K.—.
OT: gādēr: S.1447; HR.1438b.1a; H.318a; BD.154d.
pereṣ: S.6556; HR.1438b.4; H.1826a; BD.829c.
GEN. REF.: IS.—; NB.—; Z.4:603.

PARTLY

Notes: (1) In the statement "I partly believe it," 1 Cor. 11:18, "partly" represents the phrase '*meros* (part) *ti* (some),' used adverbially, i.e., 'in some part,' 'in some measure.'

(2) In Heb. 10:33, "partly . . . partly" is a translation of the antithetic phrases '*touto men*, this indeed,' and '*touto de*, but this,' i.e., 'on the one hand . . . and on the other hand.'

PARTNER

1. *koinōnos* [κοινωνός, 2844], an adjective, signifying having in common (*koinos*), is used

as a noun, "partners" in Luke 5:10, "partner" in 2 Cor. 8:23; Philm. 17 (in spiritual life and business). See COMMUNION, B, COMPANION, No. 2, PARTAKER.

NT: B.439c; CB.1255b; K.447.
OT: ḥābēr: S.2270; HR.775a.1a; H.598c; BD.288d.
ḥᵃberet: S.2278; HR.775a.1b; H.598d; BD.289a.
GEN. REF.: –.

2. *metochos* [*μέτοχος*, 3353], an adjective, signifying having with, sharing, is used as a noun, "partners" in Luke 5:7. See FELLOW, PARTAKER.

NT: B.514c; CB.1258c; K.286.
OT: ḥābēr: S.2270; HR.918a.1a; H.598c; BD.288d.
ḥābār: S.2266; HR.918a.1b; H.598; BD.287d.
GEN. REF.: –.

Note: Koinōnos stresses the fact of having something in common, *metochos*, the fact of sharing; the latter is less thorough in effect than the former.

PASS, COME TO PASS (see *Notes* below)

1. *parerchomai* [*παρέρχομαι*, 3928], from *para*, by, *erchomai*, to come or go, denotes (I), literally, to pass, pass by, (*a*) of persons, Matt. 8:28; Mark 6:48; Luke 18:37; Acts 16:8; (*b*) of things, Matt. 26:39, 42; of time, Matt. 14:15; Mark 14:35; Acts 27:9, A.V., "past" (R.V., "gone by"); 1 Pet. 4:3; (II), metaphorically, (*a*) to pass away, to perish, Matt. 5:18; 24:34, 35; Mark 13:30, 31; Luke 16:17; 21:32, 33; 2 Cor. 5:17; Jas. 1:10; 2 Pet. 3:10; (*b*) to pass by, disregard, neglect, pass over, Luke 11:42; 15:29, "transgressed." For the meaning to come forth or come, see Luke 12:37; 17:7, R.V. (Acts 24:7 in some mss.). See COME, No. 9. ¶

NT: B.625d; CB.1262b; K.257.
OT: ʿābar: S.5674; HR.1068c.11a; H.1556; BD.716d.
GEN. REF.: IS.3:674; NB.–; Z.4:604.

2. *dierchomai* [*διέρχομαι*, 1330], denotes to pass through or over, (*a*) of persons, e.g., Matt. 12:43, R.V., "passeth (A.V., walketh) through"; Mark 4:35, A.V., "pass (R.V., go) over"; Luke 19:1, 4; Heb. 4:14, R.V., "passed through" (A.V. "into"); Christ passed through the created heavens to the Throne of God; (*b*) of things, e.g., Matt. 19:24, "to go through"; Luke 2:35, "shall pierce through" (metaphorically of a sword). See COME, No. 5.

NT: B.194c; CB.1241c; K.257.
OT: ʿābar: S.5674; HR.328c.10a; H.1556; BD.716d.
hālak: S.1980; HR.328c.4a,c; H.498; BD.229d.
GEN. REF.: IS.3:674; NB.–; Z.4:604.

3. *aperchomai* [*ἀπέρχομαι*, 565], to go away, is rendered to pass in Rev. 9:12; 11:14; "passed away" in Rev. 21:4. See DEPART, No. 4.

NT: B.84c; CB.1236b; K.257.
OT: hālak: S.1980; HR.121a.5a; H.498; BD.229d.
GEN. REF.: IS.3:674; NB.–; Z.–.

4. *proerchomai* [*προέρχομαι*, 4281], to go forward, is translated "passed on" in Acts 12:10. See GO.

NT: B.705b; CB.1266c; K.–.
OT: ʿābar: S.5674; HR.1206a.1; H.1556; BD.716d.
GEN. REF.: IS.3:674; NB.–; Z.4:604.

5. *antiparerchomai* [*ἀντιπαρέρχομαι*, 492], denotes to pass by opposite to (*anti*, over against, and No. 1), Luke 10:31, 32. ¶

NT: B.75c; CB.–; K.–.
OT: –.
GEN. REF.: IS.3:674; NB.–; Z.–.

6. *diabainō* [*διαβαίνω*, 1224], to step across, cross over, is translated "to pass" in Luke 16:26 (of passing across the fixed gulf: for the A.V. in the 2nd part of the ver., see No. 13); in Heb. 11:29, "passed through." See COME, No. 18.

NT: B.181c; CB.–; K.–.
OT: ʿābar: S.5674; HR.298a.5a; H.1556; BD.716d.
GEN. REF.: IS.3:674; NB.–; Z.4:604.

7. *metabainō* [*μεταβαίνω*, 3327], to pass over from one place to another (*meta*, implying change), is translated "we have passed out of" (A.V., "from") in 1 John 3:14, R.V., as to the change from death to life. See REMOVE, No. 1.

NT: B.510c; CB.1258b; K.90.
OT: –.
GEN. REF.: IS.3:674; NB.–; Z.–.

8. *anastrephō* [*ἀναστρέφω*, 390], lit., to turn back (*ana*, back, *strephō* to turn), in the Middle Voice, to conduct oneself, behave, live, is translated "pass (the time)" in 1 Pet. 1:17. See ABIDE, No. 8.

NT: B.61b; CB.1235b; K.1093.
OT: shûb: S.7725; HR.82b.8a; H.2340; BD.996d.
GEN. REF.: –.

9. *paragō* [*παράγω*, 3855], to pass by, pass away, in Matt. 9:9, R.V., "passed by" (A.V., "forth"), is used in the Middle Voice in 1 John 2:8, R.V., "is passing away" (A.V., "is past"), of the passing of spiritual darkness through the light of the Gospel, and in ver. 17 of the world. See DEPART, No. 2.

NT: B.613d; CB.–; K.20.
OT: ʿābar: S.5674; HR.1056b.2; H.1556; BD.716d.
GEN. REF.: IS.3:674; NB.–; Z.4:604.

10. *paraporeuomai* [*παραπορεύομαι*, 3899], primarily, to go beside, accompany (*para*, beside, *poreuomai*, to proceed), denotes to go past, pass by, Matt. 27:39; Mark 9:30, "passed through" (some mss. have *poreuomai*); 11:20; 15:29; in Mark 2:23, "going . . . through." See GO. ¶

NT: B.621c; CB.–; K.–.
OT: ʿābar: S.5674; HR.1063b.2; H.1556; BD.716d.
GEN. REF.: IS.3:674; NB.–; Z.4:604.

11. *diaporeuomai* [*διαπορεύομαι*, 1279], to pass across, journey through, is used in the Middle Voice, translated "pass by" in Luke 18:36, A.V., R.V., "going by." See GO.

NT: B.187d; CB.–; K.–.
OT: hālak: S.1980; HR.308b.4a-c; H.498; BD.229d.
ʿābar: S.5674; HR.308b.6; H.1556; BD.716d.
GEN. REF.: IS.3:674; NB.–; Z.4:604.

12. *huperballō* [ὑπερβάλλω, —], in Eph. 3:19, "passeth": see EXCEED, A, No. 1.

13. *huperechō* [ὑπερέχω, —], "passeth" in Phil. 4:7: see BETTER (be), No. 4.

14. *diaperaō* [διαπεράω, 1276], to pass over, cross over (used in Luke 16:26, 2nd part: see No. 6): see CROSS.

NT: B.187c; CB.—; K.—.
OT: ʿābar: S.5674; HR.307c.1; H.1556; BD.716d.
GEN. REF.: IS.3:674; NB.—; Z.4:604.

15. *diodeuō* [διοδεύω, 1353], to travel through, or along (*dia*, through, *hodos*, a way), is translated "they had passed through" in Acts 17:1, lit., 'having passed through'; in Luke 8:1, "He went about," R.V. (A.V., "throughout"). ¶

NT: B.198d; CB.—; K.—.
OT: ʿābar: S.5674; HR.336a.1; H.1556; BD.716d.
GEN. REF.: IS.3:674; NB.—; Z.4:604.

16. *chōreō* [χωρέω, 5562], used intransitively, signifies to make room, retire, pass; in Matt. 15:17, R.V., "passeth (into the belly)," A.V., "goeth." See COME, No. 24.

NT: B.889c; CB.1240a; K.—.
OT: —.
GEN. REF.: IS.3:674; NB.—; Z.—.

17. *katargeō* [καταργέω, 2673], is translated "was passing away" in 2 Cor. 3:7 (A.V., "was to be done away"); "passeth away" in 3:11, R.V. (A.V., "is done away"). See ABOLISH.

NT: B.417b; CB.1254b; K.76.
OT: beṭēl: S.989; HR.743a.1; H.2625; BD.1084b.
GEN. REF.: IS.3:674; NB.—; Z.—.

18. *paroichomai* [παροίχομαι, 3944], to have passed by, to be gone by, is used in Acts 14:16, of past generations, A.V., "(in times) past," R.V., "(in the generations) gone by." ¶

NT: B.629b; CB.—; K.—.
OT: —.
GEN. REF.: —.

Notes: (1) *Ginomai*, to become, take place, is often translated to come to pass; frequently in the Synoptic Gospels and Acts (note the R.V. of Luke 24:21); elsewhere in John 13:19; 14:22, R.V., "(what) is come to pass . . .?" A.V., "(how) is it . . .?"; 14:29 (twice); 1 Thess. 3:4; Rev. 1:1.

(2) In Acts 2:17, 21; 3:23 and Rom. 9:26, the A.V. translates the future of *eimi*, to be, "it shall come to pass" (R.V., "it shall be").

(3) In Acts 5:15, A.V., *erchomai*, to come, is translated "passing by" (R.V., "came by").

(4) For the A.V., "passing" in Acts 27:8, see COASTING, C.

(5) In Mark 6:35, A.V., "the time is far passed" (R.V., "the day is . . . far spent") is, lit., 'the hour is much (*polus*).'

(6) For *huperakmos* in 1 Cor. 7:36, R.V., "past the flower of her age," see FLOWER.

PASSING OVER

paresis [πάρεσις, 3929], primarily a letting go, dismissal (akin to *pariēmi*, to let alone, loosen), denotes a passing by or praetermission (of sin), a suspension of judgment, or withholding of punishment, Rom. 3:25, R.V., "passing over" (A.V., "remission"), with reference to sins committed previously to the propitiatory sacrifice of Christ, the passing by not being a matter of Divine disregard but of forbearance. ¶

NT: B.626b; CB.1262b; K.88.
OT: —.
GEN. REF.: —.

PASSION

A. Nouns.

1. *pathēma* [πάθημα, 3804], a suffering or a passive emotion, is translated "passions" in Rom. 7:5, R.V., "(sinful) passions," A.V., "motions," and Gal. 5:24, R.V.; see AFFECTION, A, No. 3, AFFLICT, B, No. 3.

NT: B.602b; CB.1262c; K.798.
OT: —.
GEN. REF.: IS.3:674; NB.936; Z.4:604.

2. *pathos* [πάθος, —]: see AFFECTION, A, No. 1.

B. Verb.

paschō [πάσχω, 3958], to suffer, is used as a noun, in the aorist infinitive with the article, and translated "passion" in Acts 1:3, of the suffering of Christ at Calvary. See SUPPER.

NT: B.633d; CB.1262c; K.798.
OT: ḥālāh: S.2470; HR.1103a.1; H.655; BD.317c.
GEN. REF.: IS.3:674; NB.—; Z.4:604.

C. Adjective.

homoiopathēs [ὁμοιοπαθής, 3663], of like feelings or affections (*homoios*, like, and A, No. 2; Eng., homoeopathy), is rendered "of like passions" in Acts 14:15 (R.V. marg., "nature"); in Jas. 5:17, R.V., ditto (A.V., "subject to like passions"). ¶

NT: B.566c; CB.1251a; K.798.
OT: —.
GEN. REF.: —.

PASSOVER

pascha [πάσχα, 3957], the Greek spelling of the Aramaic word for the Passover, from the Hebrew *pāsach*, to pass over, to spare, a feast instituted by God in commemoration of the deliverance of Israel from Egypt, and anticipatory of the expiatory sacrifice of Christ. The word signifies (I) the Passover Feast, e.g., Matt. 26:2; John 2:13, 23; 6:4; 11:55; 12:1; 13:1; 18:39; 19:14; Acts 12:4; Heb. 11:28; (II) by metonymy, (*a*) the Paschal Supper, Matt. 26:18, 19; Mark 14:16; Luke 22:8, 13; (*b*) the Paschal lamb, e.g.,

Mark 14:12 (cp. Ex. 12:21); Luke 22:7; (*c*) Christ Himself, 1 Cor. 5:7.
NT: B.633b; CB.1262c; K.797.
OT: pesaḥ: S.6453; HR.1103a.1; H.1786a; BD.820a.
GEN. REF.: IS.3:675; NB.936; Z.4:605.

PAST

A. Verbs.

1. *ginomai* [*γίνομαι*, 1096], to become, come to pass, is translated "was past" in Luke 9:36, A.V., and R.V. marg. (R.V., "came"), of the voice of God the Father at the Transfiguration; "is past," 2 Tim. 2:18.
NT: B.158a; CB.1248b; K.117.
OT: —.
GEN. REF.: —.

2. *diaginomai* [*διαγίνομαι*, 1230], *dia*, through, a stronger form than No. 1, used of time, denotes to intervene, elapse, pass, Mark 16:1, "was past"; Acts 5:13, R.V., "were passed"; 27:9, "was spent." ¶
NT: B.182b; CB.—; K.—.
OT: —.
GEN. REF.: —.

3. *proginomai* [*προγίνομαι*, 4266], to happen before (*pro*, before, and No. 1), is used in Rom. 3:25, A.V., "that are past" (R.V., "done aforetime"), of sins committed in times previous to the atoning sacrifice of Christ (see PASSING OVER). ¶
NT: B.703c; CB.1266c; K.—.
OT: —.
GEN. REF.: —.

Note: For the past tense of the verb to pass, see PASS, e.g., Nos. 1 and 17.

B. Particle.

pote [*ποτέ*, 4218], once, formerly, sometime, is translated "in time (or times) past," in Rom. 11:30; Gal. 1:13; ver. 23, A.V. (R.V., "once"); Eph. 2:2, 11 (R.V., "aforetime"); ver. 3 (R.V., "once"); Philm. 11 (R.V., "aforetime"); 1 Pet. 2:10.
NT: B.695a; CB.1266b; K.—.
OT: —.
GEN. REF.: —.

PASTOR

poimēn [*ποιμήν*, 4166], a shepherd, one who tends herds or flocks (not merely one who feeds them), is used metaphorically of Christian "pastors," Eph. 4:11. Pastors guide as well as feed the flock; cp. Acts 20:28, which, with ver. 17, indicates that this was the service committed to elders (overseers or bishops); so also in 1 Pet. 5:1, 2, "tend the flock . . . exercising the oversight," R.V.; this involves tender care and vigilant superintendence. See SHEPHERD.
NT: B.684a; CB.1265c; K.901.
OT: rā'āh: S.7462; HR.1169b.1; H.2185,2186; BD.944d.
GEN. REF.: IS.3:679; NB.—; Z.4:611.

PASTURE

nomē [*νομή*, 3542], denotes (*a*) pasture, pasturage, figuratively in John 10:9; (*b*) grazing, feeding, figuratively in 2 Tim. 2:17, of the doctrines of false teachers, lit., 'their word will have feeding as a gangrene.' See EAT. ¶
NT: B.541a; CB.1260a; K.—.
OT: mir'eh: S.4829; HR.946b.2a; H.2185b; BD.945c.
mar'ît: S.4830; HR.946b.2b; H.2185c; BD.945c.
nāweh: S.5116; HR.946b.3b; H.1322a-c; BD.627c.
GEN. REF.: IS.3:687; NB.—; Z.—.

PATH

1. *tribos* [*τρίβος*, 5147], a beaten track (akin to *tribō*, to rub, wear down), a path, is used in Matt. 3:3; Mark 1:3; Luke 3:4. ¶
NT: B.826b; CB.—; K.—.
OT: m^{e}sillāh: S.4546; HR.1372b.3; H.1506a; BD.700c.
'ōraḥ: S.734; HR.1372b.1; H.161a; BD.73a.
nātîb, n^{e}tîbāh: S.5410; HR.1372b.5; H.1440a,b; BD.677b.
GEN. REF.: IS.3:687; NB.—; Z.4:618.

2. *trochia* [*τροχία*, 5163], the track of a wheel (*trochos*, a wheel; *trechō*, to run), hence, a track, path, is used figuratively in Heb. 12:13. ¶ In the Sept., Prov. 2:15; 4:11, 26, 27; 5:6, 21; in some texts, Ezek. 27:19. ¶
NT: B.828a; CB.—; K.—.
OT: ma'gāl: S.4570; HR.1376c.1; H.1560f; BD.722d.
GEN. REF.: IS.3:687; NB.—; Z.—.

PATIENCE, PATIENT, PATIENTLY

A. Nouns.

1. *hupomonē* [*ὑπομονή*, 5281], lit., an abiding under (*hupo*, under, *menō*, to abide), is almost invariably rendered "patience." "Patience, which grows only in trial, Jas. 1:3, may be passive, i.e., = endurance, as, (*a*) in trials, generally, Luke 21:19 (which is to be understood by Matt. 24:13); cp. Rom. 12:12; Jas. 1:12; (*b*) in trials incident to service in the gospel, 2 Cor. 6:4; 12:12; 2 Tim. 3:10; (*c*) under chastisement, which is trial viewed as coming from the hand of God our Father, Heb. 12:7; (*d*) under undeserved affliction, 1 Pet. 2:20; or active, i.e. = persistence, perseverance, as (*e*) in well doing, Rom. 2:7 (A.V., 'patient continuance'); (*f*) in fruit bearing, Luke 8:15; (*g*) in running the appointed race, Heb. 12:1.

"Patience perfects Christian character, Jas. 1:4, and fellowship in the patience of Christ is therefore the condition upon which believers are to be admitted to reign with Him, 2 Tim. 2:12; Rev. 1:9. For this patience believers are 'strengthened with all power,' Col. 1:11, 'through His Spirit in the inward man,' Eph. 3:16.

"In 2 Thess. 3:5, the phrase 'the patience of Christ,' R.V., is possible of three interpretations, (*a*) the patient waiting for Christ, so A.V.

paraphrases the words, (*b*) that they might be patient in their sufferings as Christ was in His, see Heb. 12:2, (*c*) that since Christ is 'expecting till His enemies be made the footstool of His feet,' Heb. 10:13, so they might be patient also in their hopes of His triumph and their deliverance. While a too rigid exegesis is to be avoided, it may, perhaps, be permissible to paraphrase: 'the Lord teach and enable you to love as God loves, and to be patient as Christ is patient.' "*

In Rev. 3:10, "the word of My patience" is the word which tells of Christ's patience, and its effects in producing patience on the part of those who are His (see above on 2 Thess. 3:5).

NT: B.846b; CB.1252b; K.581.
OT: miqweh: S.4723; HR.1416b.1a; H.1994c; BD.876a.
tiqwāh: S.8615; HR.1416b.1b; H.1994d.e; BD.876b.
GEN. REF.: IS.3:689; NB.938; Z.4:619.

2. *makrothumia* [μακροθυμία, 3115], longsuffering (see B, No. 2), is rendered "patience" in Heb. 6:12; Jas. 5:10; see LONGSUFFERING.

NT: B.488b; CB.1257c; K.550.
OT: 'ōrek'appîm: S.753,639; HR.893c.1; H.162a,133a; BD.73d,60b.
GEN. REF.: IS.3:688; NB.938; Z.4:619.

B. Verbs.

1. *hupomenō* [ὑπομένω, 5278], akin to A, No. 1, (*a*) used intransitively, means to tarry behind, still abide, Luke 2:43; Acts 17:14; (*b*) transitively, to wait for, Rom. 8:24 (in some mss.), to bear patiently, endure, translated "patient" (present participle) in Rom. 12:12; "ye take it patiently," 1 Pet. 2:20 (twice). See also under A, No. 1.

NT: B.845d; CB.1252b; K.581.
OT: yāḥal: S.3176; HR.1415c.4; H.859; BD.403d.
qāwāh: S.6960; HR.1415c.8; H.1994,1995; BD.875c.
GEN. REF.: IS.3:689; NB.938; Z.4:619.

2. *makrothumeō* [μακροθυμέω, 3114], akin to A, No. 2, to be long-tempered, is translated to have patience, or to be patient, in Matt. 18:26, 29; 1 Thess. 5:14, A.V. (R.V., "be longsuffering"); Jas. 5:7 (1st part, "be patient"; 2nd part, R.V., "being patient," A.V., "hath long patience"); in Heb. 6:15, R.V., "having (A.V., after he had) patiently endured." See LONGSUFFERING.

NT: B.488a; CB.1257c; K.550.
OT: 'ārak: S.748; HR.893b.1a; H.162; BD.73c.
GEN. REF.: IS.3:689; NB.938; Z.4:619.

C. Adjectives.

Notes: (1) For *epieikēs*, translated "patient" in 1 Tim. 3:3, A.V., see GENTLE.

(2) For *anexikakos*, translated "patient" in 2 Tim. 2:24, A.V., see FORBEAR. ¶

D. Adverb.

makrothumōs [μακροθύμως, 3116], akin to A, No. 2, and B, No. 2, denotes "patiently," Acts 26:3. ¶

NT: B.488c; CB.1257c; K.550.
OT: –.
GEN. REF.: IS.3:689; NB.938; Z.4:619.

PATRIARCH

patriarchēs [πατριάρχης, 3966], from *patria*, a family, and *archō*, to rule, is found in Acts 2:29; 7:8, 9; Heb. 7:4. ¶ In the Sept., 1 Chron. 24:31; 27:22; 2 Chron. 19:8; 23:20; 26:12. ¶

NT: B.636d; CB.–; K.–.
OT: 'āb: S.1; HR.1111c.1,2; H.4a; BD.3a.
GEN. REF.: IS.3:690; NB.939; Z.4:620.

PATTERN

A. Nouns.

1. *tupos* [τύπος, 5179], is translated "pattern" in Tit. 2:7, A.V.; Heb. 8:5 (A.V. and R.V.). See ENSAMPLE.

NT: B.829d; CB.1273b; K.1193.
OT: ṣelem: S.6754; HR.1378b.1; H.1923a; BD.853d.
tabnît: S.8403; HR.1378b.2; H.255d; BD.125d.
GEN. REF.: IS.3:695; NB.–; Z.–.

2. *hupotupōsis* [ὑποτύπωσις, 5296], is translated "pattern" in 1 Tim. 1:16, A.V.; 2 Tim. 1:13, R.V. See ENSAMPLE, FORM. ¶

NT: B.848c; CB.1252b; K.1193.
OT: –.
GEN. REF.: IS.3:695; NB.–; Z.–.

3. *hupodeigma* [ὑπόδειγμα, 5262], is translated "patterns" in Heb. 9:23, A.V. See COPY.

NT: B.844a; CB.1252b; K.141.
OT: –.
GEN. REF.: IS.3:695; NB.–; Z.–.

B. Adjective.

antitupos [ἀντίτυπος, 499], is translated "like in pattern" in Heb. 9:24, R.V. See FIGURE, No. 2.

NT: B.76a; CB.1236a; K.1193.
OT: –.
GEN. REF.: –.

PAVEMENT

lithostrōtos [λιθόστρωτος, 3038], an adjective, denoting paved with stones (*lithos*, a stone, and *strōnnuō*, to spread), especially of tessellated work, is used as a noun in John 19:13, of a place near the Praetorium in Jerusalem, called Gabbatha, a Greek transliteration of an Aramaic word. ¶ In the Sept., 2 Chron. 7:3; Esth. 1:6; S. of Sol. 3:10. ¶

NT: B.454d; CB.–; K.–.
OT: riṣpāh: S.7531; HR.878b.1a; H.2210a,2211a; BD.954b.
rāṣaph: S.7528; HR.818b.1b; H.2210; BD.954b.
GEN. REF.: IS.3:730; NB.445; Z.4:665.

* From Notes on Thessalonians by Hogg and Vine, pp. 222, 285.

PAY (Verb), PAYMENT

1. *apodidōmi* [ἀποδίδωμι, 591], to give back, to render what is due, to pay, used of various obligations in this respect, is translated to pay, to make payment, in Matt. 5:26; 18:25 (twice), 26, 28, 29, 30, 34; 20:8, R.V. (A.V., "give"). See DELIVER.

NT: B.90b; CB.1236c; K.166.
OT: shûb: S.7725; HR.126b.8; H.2340; BD.996d.
mākar: S.4376; HR.126b.3; H.1194; BD.569a.
shālēm: S.7999; HR.126b.9; H.2401c; BD.1022b.
GEN. REF.: IS.3:730; NB.—; Z.—.

2. *teleō* [τελέω, 5055], to bring to an end, complete, fulfil, has the meaning to pay in Matt. 17:24 and Rom. 13:6. See ACCOMPLISH.

NT: B.810d; CB.1271b; K.1161.
OT: kālāh: S.3615; HR.1342c.3; H.982-984; BD.477b.
GEN. REF.: —.

Notes: (1) In Matt. 23:23, A.V., *apodekatoō*, to tithe, is translated "ye pay tithe" (R.V., "ye tithe").

(2) In Heb. 7:9, *dekatoō* (Passive Voice), to pay tithe, is translated "hath paid tithes," R.V. (perfect tense). See TITHE.

PEACE, PEACEABLE, PEACEABLY

A. Noun.

eirēnē [εἰρήνη, 1515], "occurs in each of the books of the N.T., save 1 John and save in Acts 7:26 ['(at) one again'] it is translated "peace" in the R.V. It describes (*a*) harmonious relationships between men, Matt. 10:34; Rom. 14:19; (*b*) between nations, Luke 14:32; Acts 12:20; Rev. 6:4; (*c*) friendliness, Acts 15:33; 1 Cor. 16:11; Heb. 11:31; (*d*) freedom from molestation, Luke 11:21; 19:42; Acts 9:31 (R.V., 'peace,' A.V., 'rest'); 16:36; (*e*) order, in the State, Acts 24:2 (R.V., 'peace,' A.V., 'quietness'); in the churches, 1 Cor. 14:33; (*f*) the harmonised relationships between God and man, accomplished through the gospel, Acts 10:36; Eph. 2:17; (*g*) the sense of rest and contentment consequent thereon, Matt. 10:13; Mark 5:34; Luke 1:79; 2:29; John 14:27; Rom. 1:7; 3:17; 8:6; in certain passages this idea is not distinguishable from the last, Rom. 5:1."*

"The God of peace" is a title used in Rom. 15:33; 16:20; Phil. 4:9; 1 Thess. 5:23; Heb. 13:20; cp. 1 Cor. 14:33; 2 Cor. 13:11. The corresponding Heb. word *shalom* primarily signifies wholeness; see its use in Josh. 8:31, "unhewn"; Ruth 2:12, "full"; Neh. 6:15, "finished"; Is. 42:19, marg., "made perfect." Hence there is a close connection between the title in 1 Thess. 5:23 and the word *holoklēros*, "entire," in that verse. In the Sept. *shalom* is often rendered by *sōtēria*, salvation, e.g., Gen. 26:31; 41:16; hence the "peace-offering" is called the "salvation offering." Cp. Luke 7:50; 8:48. In 2 Thess. 3:16, the title "the Lord of peace" is best understood as referring to the Lord Jesus. In Acts 7:26, "would have set them at one" is, lit., 'was reconciling them (conative imperfect tense, expressing an earnest effort) into peace.'

NT: B.227c; CB.1243a; K.207.
OT: shālôm: S.7965; HR.401b.6a; H.2401a; BD.1022d.
GEN. REF.: IS.3:731; NB.956; Z.4:666.

B. Verbs.

1. *eirēneuō* [εἰρηνεύω, 1514], primarily, to bring to peace, reconcile, denotes in the N.T., to keep peace or to be at peace: in Mark 9:50, R.V., the Lord bids the disciples "be at peace" with one another, gently rebuking their ambitious desires; in Rom. 12:18 (R.V., "be at peace," A.V., "live peaceably") the limitation "if it be possible, as much as in you lieth," seems due to the phrase "with all men," but is not intended to excuse any evasion of the obligation imposed by the command; in 2 Cor. 13:11 it is rendered "live in peace," a general exhortation to believers; in 1 Thess. 5:13, "be at peace (among yourselves)." ¶

NT: B.227a; CB.1243a; K.207.
OT: shālam: S.7999; HR.401b.3a,b; H.2401c; BD.1023d.
shālôm: S.7965; HR.401b.3c; H.2401a; BD.1022d.
shāqaṭ: S.8252; HR.401b.4; H.2453; BD.1052d.
GEN. REF.: IS.3:731; NB.956; Z.4:666.

2. *eirēnopoieō* [εἰρηνοποιέω, 1517], to make peace (*eirēnē*, and *poieō*, to make), is used in Col. 1:20. ¶ In the Sept., Prov. 10:10. ¶

NT: B.228a; CB.1243a; K.207.
OT: —.
GEN. REF.: IS.3:731; NB.956; Z.—.

C. Adjective.

eirēnikos [εἰρηνικός, 1516], akin to A, denotes peaceful. It is used (*a*) of the fruit of righteousness, Heb. 12:11, "peaceable" (or 'peaceful') because it is produced in communion with God the Father, through His chastening; (*b*) of "the wisdom that is from above," Jas. 3:17. ¶

NT: B.228a; CB.1243a; K.207.
OT: shelem: S.8002; HR.402c.2d; H.2401b; BD.1023b.
shālôm: S.7999; HR.402c.2b; H.2401c; BD.1023d.
GEN. REF.: IS.3:731; NB.956; Z.4:666.

Note: In 1 Tim. 2:2, A.V., *hēsuchios*, quiet, is translated "peacable" (R.V., "quiet").

PEACE (hold one's)

1. *sigaō* [σιγάω, 4601], signifies (*a*) used intransitively, to be silent (from *sigē*, silence),

* From Notes on Thessalonians by Hogg and Vine, p. 154.

translated to hold one's peace, in Luke 9:36; 18:39; 20:26; Acts 12:17; 15:13 (in ver. 12, "kept silence"; similarly rendered in 1 Cor. 14:28, 30, A.V., "hold his peace," 34); (*b*) used transitively, to keep secret; in the Passive Voice, to be kept secret, Rom. 16:25, R.V., "hath been kept in silence." See SECRET, SILENCE.

NT: B.749c; CB.—; K.—.
OT: ḥāshāh: S.2814; HR.1265c.4; H.768; BD.364c.
ḥārash: S.2790; HR.1265c.3; H.760; BD.361a.
GEN. REF.: IS.3:731; NB.—; Z.—.

2. *siōpaō* [σιωπάω, 4623], to be silent or still, to keep silence (from *siōpē*, silence), is translated to hold one's peace, in Matt. 20:31; 26:63; Mark 3:4; 9:34; 10:48; 14:61; Luke 19:40; Acts 18:9; in the Lord's command to the sea, in Mark 4:39, it is translated "peace" (for the next word "be still" see No. 4); in Luke 1:20, R.V., "thou shalt be silent" (A.V., "dumb"). See DUMB, B. ¶

NT: B.752c; CB.—; K.—.
OT: ḥārash: S.2790; HR.1267c.6; H.760; BD.361a.
ḥāshāh: S.2814; HR.1267c.7; H.768; BD.364c.
dāmam: S.1826; HR.1267c.3; H.439; BD.198d.
GEN. REF.: IS.3:731; NB.—; Z.—.

3. *hēsuchazō* [ἡσυχάζω, 2270], signifies to be still; it is used of holding one's peace, being silent, Luke 14:4; Acts 11:18; 21:14, "we ceased." See CEASE, A, No. 3, QUIET.

NT: B.349a; CB.1250; K.—.
OT: shāqaṭ: S.8252; HR.620a.11; H.2453; BD.1052d.
GEN. REF.: —.

4. *phimoō* [φιμόω, 5392], to muzzle, is used metaphorically in the Passive Voice, in Mark 1:25 and Luke 4:35, "hold thy peace"; in Mark 4:39, "be still." See MUZZLE.

NT: B.861d; CB.—; K.—.
OT: ḥāsam: S.2629; HR.1432c.1; H.702; BD.340c.
GEN. REF.: —.

PEACEMAKER

eirēnopoios [εἰρηνοποιός, 1518], an adjective signifying peace-making (*eirēnē*, and *poieō*, to make), is used in Matt. 5:9, "peacemakers." Cp. PEACE, B, No. 2. ¶

NT: B.228a; CB.1243a; K.207.
OT: —.
GEN. REF.: IS.3:733; NB.—; Z.4:668.

PEARL

margaritēs [μαργαρίτης, 3135], a pearl (Eng., Margaret), occurs in Matt. 7:6 (proverbially and figuratively); 13:45, 46; 1 Tim. 2:9; Rev. 17:4; 18:12, 16; 21:21 (twice). ¶

NT: B.491c; CB.1257c; K.564.
OT: —.
GEN. REF.: IS.3:734; NB.633; Z.4:668.

For **PECULIAR** see **POSSESSION**, B, No. 3, and C

PEN

kalamos [κάλαμος, 2563], a reed, reed-pipe, flute, staff, measuring rod, is used of a writing-reed or pen in 3 John 13. This was used on papyrus. Different instruments were used on different materials; the *kalamos* may have been used also on leather. "Metal pens in the form of a reed or quill have been found in the so-called Grave of Aristotle at Eretria." See REED.

NT: B.398d; CB.1253b; K.—.
OT: qāneh: S.7070; HR.712b.3; H.2040a; BD.889c.
GEN. REF.: IS.3:738; NB.1344; Z.—.

PENCE, PENNY, PENNYWORTH

dēnarion [δηνάριον, 1220], a Roman coin, a *denarius*, a little less than the value of the Greek *drachmē* (see PIECE), now estimated as amounting to about 9½d.* in the time of our Lord, occurs in the singular, e.g., Matt. 20:2; 22:19; Mark 12:15; Rev. 6:6; in the plural, e.g., Matt. 18:28; Mark 14:5; Luke 7:41; 10:35; John 12:5; "pennyworth" in Mark 6:37 and John 6:7, lit., '(loaves of two hundred) pence.'

NT: B.179b; CB.—; K.—.
OT: —.
GEN. REF.: IS.3:406; NB.838; Z.—.

PENTECOST

pentēkostos [πεντηκοστός, 4005], an adjective denoting fiftieth, is used as a noun, with "day" understood, i.e., the fiftieth day after the Passover, counting from the second day of the Feast, Acts 2:1; 20:16; 1 Cor. 16:8. ¶ For the Divine instructions to Israel see Ex. 23:16; 34:22; Lev. 23:15-21; Num. 28:26-31; Deut. 16:9-11.

NT: B.643a; CB.1263a; K.—.
OT: ḥ^{a}mishshîm: S.2572; HR.1119a.1; H.686c; BD.332b.
GEN. REF.: IS.3:757; NB.964; Z.4:692.

For **PENURY** (Luke 21:4, A.V., R.V., "want") see **LACK**

PEOPLE

1. *laos* [λαός, 2992], is used of (*a*) the people at large, especially of people assembled, e.g., Matt. 27:25; Luke 1:21; 3:15; Acts 4:27; (*b*) a people of the same race and language, e.g., Rev. 5:9; in the plural, e.g., Luke 2:31; Rom. 15:11; Rev. 7:9; 11:9; especially of Israel, e.g., Matt. 2:6; 4:23; John 11:50; Acts 4:8; Heb. 2:17; in distinction from their rulers and priests, e.g.,

* 1d. = 25 cents (approximately).

Matt. 26:5; Luke 20:19; Heb. 5:3; in distinction from Gentiles, e.g., Acts 26:17, 23; Rom. 15:10; (*c*) of Christians as the people of God, e.g., Acts 15:14; Tit. 2:14; Heb. 4:9; 1 Pet. 2:9.

NT: B.466c; CB.1256c; K.499.
OT: ʻam: S.5971; HR.853b.14; H.1640a,e; BD.766b.
GEN. REF.: IS.3:759; NB.965; Z.–.

2. *ochlos* [ὄχλος, 3793], a crowd, throng: see CROWD, MULTITUDE.

NT: B.600c; CB.1260b; K.750.
OT: hāmôn: S.1995; HR.1043a.1; H.505a; BD.242b.
qāhāl: S.6951; HR.1043a.5; H.1991a; BD.874c.
ʻam: S.5971; HR.1043a.4; H.1640a,e; BD.766b.
GEN. REF.: IS.3:759; NB.965; Z.–.

3. *dēmos* [δῆμος, 1218], the common people, the people generally (Eng., demagogue, democracy, etc.), especially the mass of the people assembled in a public place, Acts 12:22; 17:5; 19:30, 33. ¶

NT: B.179a; CB.1240c; K.149.
OT: mishpāḥāh: S.4940; HR.296a.1; H.2442b; BD.1046c.
GEN. REF.: IS.3:759; NB.–; Z.–.

4. *ethnos* [ἔθνος, 1484], denotes (*a*) a nation, e.g., Matt. 24:7; Acts 10:35; the Jewish people, e.g., Luke 7:5; Acts 10:22; 28:19; (*b*) in the plural, the rest of mankind in distinction from Israel or the Jews, e.g., Matt. 4:15; Acts 28:28; (*c*) the people of a city, Acts 8:9; (*d*) Gentile Christians, e.g., Rom. 10:19; 11:13; 15:27; Gal. 2:14. See GENTILES, NATION.

NT: B.218b; CB.1246c; K.201.
OT: ʻam: S.5971; HR.368b.13; H.1640a,e; BD.766b.
gôy: S.1471; HR.368b.4; H.326e; BD.156c.
GEN. REF.: IS.3:759; NB.965; Z.–.

5. *anthrōpos* [ἄνθρωπος, 444], man, without distinction of sex (cp. *anēr*, a male), is translated "people" in John 6:10, R.V. (A.V., "men").

NT: B.68a; CB.1236a; K.59.
OT: ʼādām: S.120; HR.96b.1; H.25a; BD.9a.
ʼîsh: S.376; HR.96b.2; H.83a; BD.35c.
GEN. REF.: IS.3:760; NB.–; Z.–.

PERADVENTURE

A. Adverb.

tacha [τάχα, 5029], primarily quickly (from *tachus*, quick), signifies "peradventure" in Rom. 5:7; in Philm. 15, "perhaps." See PERHAPS. ¶

NT: B.806c; CB.–; K.–.
OT: –.
GEN. REF.: –.

B. Conjunction.

mēpote [μήποτε, 3379], often written as two words, usually signifies lest ever, lest haply, haply; in indirect questions, 'if haply' or 'whether haply,' e.g., Luke 3:15, R.V.; in Matt. 25:9, R.V., "peradventure" (A.V., "lest"); "if peradventure," in 2 Tim. 2:25. See HAPLY.

NT: B.519b; CB.1258b; K.–.
OT: –.
GEN. REF.: –.

PERCEIVE

1. *ginōskō* [γινώσκω, 1097], to know by experience and observation, is translated to perceive in Matt. 12:15, R.V. (A.V., "knew"); 16:8; 21:45; 22:18; 26:10, R.V., (A.V., "understood"); Mark 8:17; 12:12 and 15:10, R.V. (A.V., "knew"); so Luke 9:11; 18:34; in Luke 7:39, R.V. (A.V., "known"); 20:19 (cp. No. 7 in ver. 23); John 6:15; 8:27, R.V. (A.V., "understood"); 16:19, R.V. (A.V., "knew"); Acts 23:6; Gal. 2:9; in 1 John 3:16, A.V., "perceive" (R.V., "know," perfect tense, lit., 'we have perceived,' and therefore know). See KNOW.

NT: B.160d; CB.1248b; K.119.
OT: yādaʻ: S.3045; HR.267a.4a; H.848; BD.393b.
GEN. REF.: –.

2. *epiginōskō* [ἐπιγινώσκω, 1921], a strengthened form of No. 1, to gain a full knowledge of, to become fully acquainted with, is translated to perceive in Mark 5:30, R.V. (A.V., "knowing"); Luke 1:22; 5:22; Acts 19:34, R.V. (A.V., "knew"). See ACKNOWLEDGE, KNOW.

NT: B.291a; CB.1245c; K.119.
OT: yādaʻ: S.3045; HR.517c.2a; H.848; BD.393b.
nākar: S.5234; HR.517c.3b; H.1368; BD.647d.
GEN. REF.: –.

3. *eidon* [εἶδον, 3708], (akin to *oida*, to know), an aorist form used to supply that tense of *horaō*, to see, is translated to perceive in Matt. 13:14; Mark 4:12; Acts 28:26; in Luke 9:47, A.V. (R.V., "saw"); in Acts 14:9, A.V., "perceiving" (RV., "seeing"). See BEHOLD, No. 1.

NT: B.220c; CB.1243a; K.706.
OT: –.
GEN. REF.: –.

4. *theōreō* [θεωρέω, 2334], to be a spectator of, look at, discern, is translated to perceive in John 4:19 (indicating the woman's earnest contemplation of the Lord); so Acts 17:22; in John 12:19, R.V., "behold" (A.V., "perceive ye"). See BEHOLD, No. 6.

NT: B.360a; CB.1272a; K.706.
OT: ḥᵃzāh (Aramaic): S.2370; HR.649b.2c; H.–; BD.1092c.
rāʼāh: S.7200; HR.649b.4; H.2095; BD.906b.
GEN. REF.: –.

5. *aisthanomai* [αἰσθάνομαι, 143], to perceive, to notice, understand, is used in Luke 9:45, R.V., "(that they should not) perceive," A.V., "(that) they perceived . . . (not)." ¶

NT: B.24d; CB.1234a; K.29.
OT: yādaʻ: S.3045; HR.36b.3; H.848; BD.393b.
bîn: S.995; HR.36b.1; H.239; BD.106c.
GEN. REF.: –.

6. *noeō* [νοέω, 3539], to perceive with the mind, to understand, is translated to perceive in Matt. 15:17, R.V. (A.V., "understand"); so 16:9, 11; John 12:40; Rom. 1:20; Eph. 3:4; in Mark 7:18 and 8:17, A.V. and R.V., "perceive." See CONSIDER, No. 4.

NT: B.540b; CB.1259c; K.636.
OT: bîn: S.995; HR.946a.1; H.239; BD.106c.
GEN. REF.: –.

7. *katanoeō* [κατανοέω, 2657], a strengthened form of No. 6, to take note of, consider carefully, is translated to perceive in Luke 6:41, A.V. (R.V., "considerest"); 20:23; Acts 27:39, R.V. (A.V., "discovered"). See BEHOLD, No. 11.
NT: B.415a; CB.1254a; K.636.
OT: nābaṭ: S.5027; HR.739c.3; H.1282; BD.613c.
rā'āh: S.7200; HR.739c.5; H.2095; BD.906b.
GEN. REF.: –.

8. *katalambanō* [καταλαμβάνω, 2638], to lay hold of, apprehend, comprehend, is translated to perceive in Acts 4:13; 10:34. See APPREHEND, No. 1.
NT: B.412d; CB.1254a; K.495.
OT: –.
GEN. REF.: –.

Notes: (1) In Mark 12:28 the best mss. have *oida*, to know (so R.V.), for *eidon*, to see, perceive (A.V.).

(2) In Acts 8:23, A.V., *horaō*, to see, is translated "I perceive" (R.V., "I see").

(3) In 2 Cor. 7:8, A.V., *blepō*, to look at, consider, see, is translated "I perceive" (R.V., "I see").

(4) In Acts 23:29, A.V., *heuriskō*, to find, is translated "perceived" (R.V., "found").

For **PERDITION** see **DESTRUCTION,** No. 1

PERFECT (Adjective and Verb), PERFECTLY

A. Adjectives.

1. *teleios* [τέλειος, 5046], signifies having reached its end (*telos*), finished, complete, perfect. It is used (I) of persons, (*a*) primarily of physical development, then, with ethical import, fully grown, mature, 1 Cor. 2:6; 14:20 ("men"; marg., "of full age"); Eph. 4:13; Phil. 3:15; Col. 1:28; 4:12; in Heb. 5:14, R.V., "full-grown" (marg., "perfect"), A.V., "of full age" (marg., "perfect"); (*b*) complete, conveying the idea of goodness without necessary reference to maturity of what is expressed under (*a*), Matt. 5:48; 19:21; Jas. 1:4 (2nd part); 3:2. It is used thus of God in Matt. 5:48; (II) of things, complete, perfect, Rom. 12:2; 1 Cor. 13:10 (referring to the complete revelation of God's will and ways, whether in the completed Scriptures or in the hereafter); Jas. 1:4 (of the work of patience); ver. 25; 1 John 4:18. ¶
NT: B.809a; CB.1271b; K.1161.
OT: shālēm: S.8003; HR.1342c.1b; H.2401; BD.1023d.
tāmîm: S.8549; HR.1342c.3a; H.2522d; BD.1071a.
tōm: S.8537; HR.1342c.3b; H.2522a; BD.1070d.
GEN. REF.: IS.3:764; NB.966; Z.4:697.

2. *teleioteros* [τελειότερος, 5047], the comparative degree of No. 1, is used in Heb. 9:11, of the very presence of God. ¶
NT: B.809a; CB.1271b; K.1161.
OT: –.
GEN. REF.: IS.3:764.

3. *artios* [ἄρτιος, 739], is translated "perfect" in 2 Tim. 3:17: see COMPLETE, B.
NT: B.110c; CB.1237c; K.80.
OT: –.
GEN. REF.: IS.3:764; NB.–; Z.4:697.

B. Verbs.

1. *teleioō* [τελειόω, 5048], to bring to an end by completing or perfecting, is used (I) of accomplishing (see FINISH, FULFIL); (II) of bringing to completeness, (*a*) of persons: of Christ's assured completion of His earthly course, in the accomplishment of the Father's will, the successive stages culminating in His Death, Luke 13:32; Heb. 2:10, to make Him perfect, legally and officially, for all that he would be to His people on the ground of His sacrifice; cp. 5:9; 7:28, R.V., "perfected" (A.V., "consecrated"); of His saints, John 17:23, R.V., "perfected" (A.V., "made perfect"); Phil. 3:12; Heb. 10:14; 11:40 (of resurrection glory); 12:23 (of the departed saints); 1 John 4:18; of former priests (negatively), Heb. 9:9; similarly of Israelites under the Aaronic priesthood, 10:1; (*b*) of things, Heb. 7:19 (of the ineffectiveness of the Law); Jas. 2:22 (of faith made perfect by works); 1 John 2:5, of the love of God operating through him who keeps His word; 4:12, of the love of God in the case of those who love one another; 4:17, of the love of God as "made perfect with" (R.V.) those who abide in God, giving them to be possessed of the very character of God, by reason of which 'as He is, even so are they in this world.'
NT: B.809d; CB.1271b; K.1161.
OT: mālē': S.4390; HR.1343a.3; H.1195; BD.569d.
tāmam: S.8552; HR.1343a.7; H.2522; BD.1070b.
GEN. REF.: IS.3:764; NB.966; Z.4:697.

2. *epiteleō* [ἐπιτελέω, 2005], to bring through to the end (*epi*, intensive, in the sense of 'fully,' and *teleō*, to complete), is used in the Middle Voice in Gal. 3:3, "are ye (now) perfected," continuous present tense, indicating a process, lit., 'are ye now perfecting yourselves'; in 2 Cor. 7:1, "perfecting (holiness)"; in Phil. 1:6, R.V., "will perfect (it)," A.V., "will perform." See ACCOMPLISH, No. 4.
NT: B.302b; CB.–; K.1161.
OT: kālāh: S.3615; HR.535a.4; H.982-984; BD.477b.
GEN. REF.: IS.3:764; NB.–; Z.4:697.

3. *katartizō* [καταρτιζω, 2675], to render fit, complete (*artios*), "is used of mending nets, Matt. 4:21; Mark 1:19, and is translated 'restore' in Gal. 6:1. It does not necessarily imply,

however, that that to which it is applied has been damaged, though it may do so, as in these passages; it signifies, rather, right ordering and arrangement, Heb. 11:3, 'framed'; it points out the path of progress, as in Matt. 21:16; Luke 6:40; cp. 2 Cor. 13:9; Eph. 4:12, where corresponding nouns occur. It indicates the close relationship between character and destiny, Rom. 9:22, 'fitted.' It expresses the pastor's desire for the flock, in prayer, Heb. 13:21, and in exhortation, 1 Cor. 1:10, R.V., 'perfected' (A.V., 'perfectly joined'); 2 Cor. 13:11, as well as his conviction of God's purpose for them, 1 Pet. 5:10. It is used of the Incarnation of the Word in Heb. 10:5, 'prepare,' quoted from Ps. 40:6 (Sept.), where it is apparently intended to describe the unique creative act involved in the Virgin Birth, Luke 1:35. In 1 Thess. 3:10 it means to supply what is necessary, as the succeeding words show."* See FIT, B, No. 3. ¶

NT: B.417d; CB.1254b; K.80.
OT: kᵉlal (Aramaic): S.3635; HR.743b.4; H.2788; BD.1097a.
kûn: S.3559; HR.743b.3; H.964; BD.465c.
GEN. REF.: IS.3:764; NB.—; Z.4:697.

Note: Cp. *exartizō*, rendered "furnished completely," in 2 Tim. 3:17, R.V.; see ACCOMPLISH, No. 1.

C. Adverbs.

1. *akribōs* [ἀκριβῶς, 199], accurately, is translated "perfectly" in 1 Thess. 5:2, where it suggests that Paul and his companions were careful ministers of the Word. See ACCURATELY, and see *Note* (2) below.

NT: B.33b; CB.—; K.—.
OT: yāṭab: S.3190; HR.50c.1; H.863; BD.405c.
GEN. REF.: —.

2. *akribesteron* [ἀκριβέστερον, 197], the comparative degree of No. 1, Acts 18:26; 23:15: see CAREFULLY, EXACTLY.

NT: B.33b; CB.—; K.—.
OT: —.
GEN. REF.: —.

3. *teleiōs* [τελείως, 5049], perfectly, is so translated in 1 Pet. 1:13, R.V. (A.V., "to the end"), of setting one's hope on coming grace. See END ¶

NT: B.810b; CB.1271b; K.—.
OT: —.
GEN. REF.: IS.3:764; NB.966; Z.4:697.

Notes: (1) In Rev. 3:2, A.V., *plēroō*, to fulfil, is translated "perfect" (R.V., "fulfilled").

(2) For the adverb *akribōs* in Luke 1:3, A.V., see ACCURATELY; in Acts 24:22, A.V., see EXACT.

(3) For the noun *akribeia* in Acts 22:3, see MANNER.

PERFECTION, PERFECTING (noun), PERFECTNESS

A. Nouns.

1. *katartisis* [κατάρτισις, 2676], a making fit, is used figuratively in an ethical sense in 2 Cor. 13:9, R.V., "perfecting" (A.V., "perfection"), implying a process leading to consummation (akin to *katartizō*, see PERFECT, B, No. 3). ¶

NT: B.418a; CB.1254b; K.80.
OT: —.
GEN. REF.: IS.3:764; NB.966; Z.4:697.

2. *katartismos* [καταρτισμός, 2677], denotes, in much the same way as No. 1, a fitting or preparing fully, Eph. 4:12. ¶

NT: B.418a; CB.1254b; K.80.
OT: —.
GEN. REF.: IS.3:764; NB.966; Z.4:697.

3. *teleiōsis* [τελείωσις, 5050], denotes a fulfilment, completion, perfection, an end accomplished as the effect of a process, Heb. 7:11; in Luke 1:45, R.V., "fulfilment" (A.V., "performance"). ¶

NT: B.810b; CB.1271b; K.1161.
OT: millu'îm: S.4394; HR.1343a.1; H.1195e; BD.571b.
GEN. REF.: IS.3:764; NB.966; Z.4:697.

4. *teleiotēs* [τελειότης, 5047], denotes much the same as No. 3, but stressing perhaps the actual accomplishment of the end in view, Col. 3:14, "perfectness"; Heb. 6:1, "perfection." ¶ In the Sept., Judg. 9:16, 19; Prov. 11:3; Jer. 2:2. ¶

NT: B.809c; CB.1271b; K.1161.
OT: tāmîm: S.8549; HR.1342c.1a; H.2522d; BD.1071a.
GEN. REF.: IS.3:764; NB.966; Z.4:697.

B. Verb.

telesphoreō [τελεσφορέω, 5052], to bring to a completion or an end in view (*telos*, an end, *pherō*, to bear), is said of plants, Luke 8:14. ¶

NT: B.810c; CB.—; K.—.
OT: —.
GEN. REF.: —.

PERFORM, PERFORMANCE

1. *teleō* [τελέω, 5055], to finish, is translated "performed" in Luke 2:39, A.V.: see ACCOMPLISH, No. 3.

NT: B.810d; CB.1271b; K.1161.
OT: kālāh: S.3615; HR.1342c.3; H.982-984; BD.477b.
GEN. REF.: IS.3:766; NB.—; Z.—.

2. *apoteleō* [ἀποτελέω, 658], to bring to an end, accomplish, is translated "I perform" in Luke 13:32, R.V. (A.V., "I do"); some mss. have No. 3; In Jas. 1:15, it is used of sin, "fullgrown" R.V. (A.V., "finished"). See FINISH, *Note* 2. ¶

NT: B.100d; CB.—; K.—.
OT: —.
GEN. REF.: IS.3:766; NB.—; Z.—.

* From Notes on Thessalonians by Hogg and Vine, p. 101.

3. *epiteleō* [ἐπιτελέω, 2005], Rom. 15:28, A.V., "performed" (R.V., "accomplished"); 2 Cor. 8:11, A.V., "perform" (R.V., "complete"); Phil. 1:6, A.V., "perform" (R.V., "perfect"): see ACCOMPLISH, No. 4.

NT: B.302b; CB.—; K.1161.
OT: kālāh: S.3615; HR.535a.4; H.982-984; BD.477b.
GEN. REF.: IS.3:766; NB.—; Z.—.

4. *poieō* [ποιέω, 4160], to do, is translated "to perform" in Rom. 4:21; in Luke 1:72, A.V. (R.V., "to shew"). See SHEW.

NT: B.680d; CB.1265c; K.895.
OT: 'āsāh: S.6213; HR.1154a.33a; H.1708,1709; BD.793c.
GEN. REF.: IS.3:766; NB.—; Z.—.

5. *apodidōmi* [ἀποδίδωμι, 591], to give back, or in full, is translated "thou . . . shalt perform" in Matt. 5:33. See DELIVER, No.3.

NT: B.90d; CB.1236c; K.166.
OT: shûb: S.7725; HR.126b.8b; H.2340; BD.996d.
GEN. REF.: IS.3:766; NB.—; Z.—.

Notes: (1) In Rom. 7:18, A.V., *katergazomai*, to work, is translated "to perform" (R.V., "to do"; marg., "work").

(2) In Luke 1:20, A.V., *ginomai*, to come to pass (R.V.) is translated "shall be performed."

(3) For "performance" in Luke 1:45, see FULFILMENT.

PERHAPS

1. *tacha* [τάχα, 5029], is translated "perhaps" in Philm. 15. See PERADVENTURE.

NT: B.806c; CB.—; K.—.
OT: —.
GEN. REF.: —.

2. *ara* [ἄρα, 686], a particle, 'then,' sometimes marking a result about which some uncertainty is felt, is translated "perhaps" in Acts 8:22.

NT: B.103d; CB.1237b; K.75.
OT: —.
GEN. REF.: —.

Note: In 2 Cor. 2:7, A.V., *pōs*, anyhow, "by any means" (R.V.), is translated "perhaps."

PERIL, see DANGER, Note: PERILOUS see GRIEVOUS

PERISH

1. *apollumi* [ἀπόλλυμι, 622], to destroy, signifies, in the Middle Voice, to perish, and is thus used (*a*) of things, e.g., Matt. 5:29, 30; Luke 5:37; Acts 27:34, R.V., "perish" (in some texts *piptō*, to fall, as A.V.); Heb. 1:11; 2 Pet. 3:6; Rev. 18:14 (2nd part), R.V., "perished" (in some texts *aperchomai*, to depart, as A.V.); (*b*) of persons, e.g., Matt. 8:25; John 3:(15), 16; 10:28; 17:12, R.V., "perished" (A.V., "is lost"); Rom. 2:12; 1 Cor. 1:18, lit., 'the perishing,' where the perfective force of the verb implies the completion of the process of destruction (Moulton, *Proleg.*, p. 114); 8:11; 15:18; 2 Pet. 3:9; Jude 11. For the meaning of the word see DESTROY, No. 1.

NT: B.95a; CB.1237a; K.67.
OT: 'ābad: S.6; HR.136c.1a-c; H.2; BD.1b.
kārat: S.3772; HR.136c.13; H.1048; BD.503c.
shāḥat: S.7843; HR.136c.33a,b; H.2370; BD.1007d.
GEN. REF.: IS.3:770; NB.—; Z.—.

2. *sunapollumi* [συναπόλλυμι, 4881], in the Middle Voice, denotes to perish together (*sun*, with, and No. 1), Heb. 11:31. ¶

NT: B.785a; CB.—; K.—.
OT: sāphāh: S.5595; HR.1312a.2; H.1531; BD.705a.
GEN. REF.: —.

3. *apothnēskō* [ἀποθνήσκω, 599], to die; in Matt. 8:32 "perished." See DIE, No. 2.

NT: B.91b; CB.1237b; K.312.
OT: mût: S.4191; HR.128a.4a; H.1169; BD.559b.
GEN. REF.: IS.3:770; NB.—; Z.—.

4. *aphanizō* [ἀφανίζω, 853], to make unseen (*a*, negative, *phainō*, to cause to appear), in the Passive Voice, is translated "perish" in Acts 13:41 (R.V., marg., "vanish away"). See DISFIGURE.

NT: B.124c; CB.1236b; K.—.
OT: shāmad: S.8045; HR.181b.20a,b; H.2406; BD.1029a.
shāmēm: S.8074; HR.181b.21a-c; H.2409; BD.1030d.
GEN. REF.: —.

5. *diaphtheirō* [διαφθείρω, 1311], to corrupt, is rendered "perish" in 2 Cor. 4:16, A.V. (R.V., "is decaying"). See CORRUPT, No. 3, DECAY.

NT: B.190c; CB.1241b; K.1259.
OT: shāḥat: S.7843; HR.314c.6b,c; H.2370; BD.1007d.
GEN. REF.: —.

Notes (1) In Acts 8:20, "(thy money) perish" is a translation of a phrase, lit, 'be unto destruction,' *apōleia*; see DESTRUCTION, B, (II), No. 1.

(2) In Col. 2:22, "to perish" is a translation of the phrase *eis pthoran*, lit., 'unto corruption'; see CORRUPT, B, No. 1.

(3) For "shall utterly perish," in 2 Pet. 2:12, A.V., see CORRUPT, B, No. 1 (*b*).

For PERJURED PERSON see FORSWEAR

PERMISSION

sungnōmē [συγγνώμη, 4774], lit., a joint opinion, mind or understanding (*sun*, with, *gnōmē*, an opinion), a fellow-feeling, hence, a concession, allowance, is translated "permission," in contrast to "commandment," in 1 Cor. 7:6. ¶

NT: B.773a; CB.—; K.119.
OT: —.
GEN. REF.: —.

PERMIT

epitrepō [ἐπιτρέπω, 2010], lit., to turn to (*epi*, to, *trepō*, to turn), to entrust, signifies to permit, Acts 26:1; 1 Cor. 14:34; 1 Cor. 16:7; 1 Tim.

2:12, R.V. "permit" (A.V., "suffer"); Heb. 6:3. See LEAVE.

NT: B.303c; CB.–; K.–.
OT: –.
GEN. REF.: –.

For PERNICIOUS, 2 Pet. 2:2, A.V., see LASCIVIOUS

PERPLEX, PERPLEXITY

A. Verbs.

1. *aporeō* [ἀπορέω, 639], is rendered "perplexed" in 2 Cor. 4:8, and in the most authentic mss. in Luke 24:4; see DOUBT, A, No. 1.

NT: B.97c; CB.–; K.–.
OT: sārar: S.6887; HR.140a.6; H.1973,1974; BD.865c.
pārar: S.6565; HR.140a.5; H.1803,1831; BD.830c.
mûk: S.4134; HR.140a.3; H.1159; BD.557b.
GEN. REF.: –.

2. *diaporeō* [διαπορέω, 1280], "was much perplexed" in Luke 9:7; see DOUBT, A, No. 2.

NT: B.187d; CB.–; K.–.
OT: –.
GEN. REF.: –.

B. Noun.

aporia [ἀπορία, 640], akin to A, No. 1, is translated "perplexity" in Luke 21:25 (lit., 'at a loss for a way,' *a*, negative, *poros*, a way, resource), of the distress of nations, finding no solution to their embarrassments; papyri illustrations are in the sense of being at one's wit's end, at a loss how to proceed, without resources. ¶

NT: B.97d; CB.–; K.–.
OT: behālāh: S.928; HR.140a.1; H.207a; BD.96d.
pārar: S.6565; HR.140a.4; H.1830,1831; BD.830c.
GEN. REF.: –.

PERSECUTE, PERSECUTION

A. Verbs.

1. *diōkō* [διώκω, 1377], has the meanings (*a*) to put to flight, drive away, (*b*) to pursue, whence the meaning to persecute, Matt. 5:10-12, 44; 10:23; 23:34; Luke 11:49 (No. 2 in some mss.); 21:12; John 5:16; 15:20 (twice); Acts 7:52; 9:4, 5, and similar passages; Rom. 12:14; 1 Cor. 4:12; 15:9; 2 Cor. 4:9, A.V. (R.V., "pursued"); Gal. 1:13, 23; 4:29; Gal. 5:11, R.V., "am . . . persecuted" (A.V., "suffer persecution"); so 6:12; Phil. 3:6; 2 Tim. 3:12, "shall suffer persecution"; Rev. 12:13. See FOLLOW, PURSUE.

NT: B.201b; CB.1242a; K.177.
OT: rādaph: S.7291; HR.338b.10a; H.2124; BD.922c.
GEN. REF.: IS.3:771; NB.968; Z.4:704.

2. *ekdiōkō* [ἐκδιώκω, 1559], *ek*, out, and No. 1, is used in 1 Thess. 2:15, A.V., "persecuted" (R.V., "drave out"). See also No. 1, See DRIVE, No. 2. ¶

NT: B.239a; CB.1243c; K.–.
OT: rādaph: S.7291; HR.423b.6; H.2124; BD.922c.
ṭrad: S.2957; HR.423b.3; H.2759; BD.1094c.
GEN. REF.: IS.3:771; NB.–; Z.4:704.

B. Noun.

diōgmos [διωγμός, 1375], akin to A, No. 1, occurs in Matt. 13:21; Mark 4:17; 10:30; Acts 8:1; 13:50; Rom. 8:35; 2 Cor. 12:10; 2 Thess. 1:4; 2 Tim. 3:11, twice (for ver. 12, see A, No. 1). ¶ In the Sept., Prov. 11:19; Lam. 3:19. ¶

NT: B.201a; CB.1242a; K.–.
OT: rādaph: S.7291; HR.338b.2; H.2124; BD.922c.
GEN. REF.: IS.3:771; NB.–; Z.4:704.

Note: In Acts 11:19, A.V., *thlipsis*, "tribulation" (R.V.), is translated "persecution."

PERSECUTOR

diōktēs [διώκτης, 1376], akin to *diōkō* (see above), occurs in 1 Tim. 1:13. ¶

NT: B.201b; CB.1242a; K.–.
OT: –.
GEN. REF.: IS.3:771; NB.–; Z.4:704.

PERSEVERANCE

proskarterēsis [προσκαρτέρησις, 4343], occurs in Eph. 6:18. Cp. the verb (and the formation) under ATTEND, No. 2. ¶

NT: B.715d; CB.1267a; K.417.
OT: –.
GEN. REF.: IS.3:776; NB.969; Z.4:709.

PERSON

1. *prosōpon* [πρόσωπον, 4383], for the meaning of which see APPEARANCE, No. 2, is translated "person" or "persons" in Matt. 22:16; Mark 12:14; Luke 20:21; 2 Cor. 1:11; 2 Cor. 2:10; Gal. 2:6; Jude 16, lit., '(admiring, or shewing respect of, R.V.) persons.'

NT: B.720d; CB.1267b; K.950.
OT: pānîm: S.6440; HR.1223c.6; H.1782a; BD.815d.
GEN. REF.: IS.3:780; NB.–; Z.–.

2. *anthrōpos* [ἄνθρωπος, 444], a generic name for man, is translated "persons" in Rev. 11:13, R.V. (A.V., "men").

NT: B.68a; CB.1236a; K.59.
OT: 'ādām: S.120; HR.96b.1; H.25a; BD.9a.
'îsh: S.376; HR.96b.2; H.83a; BD.35c.
GEN. REF.: IS.3:780; NB.–; Z.–.

Notes: (1) In Heb. 1:3, A.V., *hupostasis*, substance, is translated "person"; see SUBSTANCE.

(2) In Matt. 27:24, R.V., *toutou*, "of this . . . (man)," is translated "of this . . . person" (A.V.).

(3) In Philm. 12, the pronoun *autos*, he, placed in a position of strong emphasis, is translated "in his own person," R.V., stressing the fact that in spite of the Apostle's inclination to retain Onesimus, he has sent him, as being, so to speak, 'his very heart,' instead of adopting some other method.

(4) In 1 Cor. 5:13, A.V., the adjective *ponēros*, wicked, used as a noun, is translated "wicked person" (R.V., ". . . man").

(5) In 2 Pet. 2:5, A.V., *ogdoos*, "eighth," is translated "the (lit., an) eighth *person*" (R.V., " with seven others").

(6) Various adjectives are used with the word "persons," e.g., devout, perjured, profane.

PERSONS (respect of)

A. Nouns.

1. *prosōpolēmptēs* [προσωπολήμπτης, 4381], denotes a respecter of persons (*prosōpon*, a face or person, *lambanō*, to lay hold of), Acts 10:34. ¶

NT: B.720d; CB.1267b; K.950.
OT: –.
GEN. REF.: –.

2. *prosōpolēmpsia* (in inferior texts without the letter m) [προσωποληµψία, 4382], denotes respect of persons, partiality (akin to No. 1), the fault of one who, when responsible to give judgment, has respect to the position, rank, popularity, or circumstances of men, instead of their intrinsic conditions, preferring the rich and powerful to those who are not so, Rom. 2:11; Eph. 6:9; Col. 3:25; Jas. 2:1. ¶

NT: B.720d; CB.1267b; K.950.
OT: –.
GEN. REF.: –.

B. Verb.

prosōpolēmpteō [προσωποληµπτέω, 4380], to have respect of persons (see above), occurs in Jas. 2:9. ¶

NT: B.720c; CB.1267b; K.950.
OT: –.
GEN. REF.: –.

C. Adverb.

aprosōpolēmptōs [ἀπροσωπολήμπτως, 678], without respect of persons, impartially (*a*, negative), occurs in 1 Pet. 1:17. ¶

NT: B.102c; CB.1237b; K.950.
OT: –.
GEN. REF.: –.

PERSUADE

1. *peithō* [πείθω, 3982], in the Active Voice, signifies to apply persuasion, to prevail upon or win over, to persuade, bringing about a change of mind by the influence of reason or moral considerations, e.g., in Matt. 27:20; 28:14; Acts 13:43; 19:8; in the Passive Voice, to be persuaded, believe (see BELIEVE, No. 2, and OBEY), e.g., Luke 16:31; 20:6; Acts 17:4, R.V. (A.V., "believed"); 21:14; 26:26; Rom. 8:38; 14:14; 15:14; 2 Tim. 1:5, 12; Heb. 6:9; 11:13, in some mss.; 13:18, R.V. (A.V., "trust"). See ASSURANCE, B, No. 3.

NT: B.639a; CB.1263a; K.818.
OT: bāṭah: S.982; HR.1114b.2a; H.233; BD.105a.
GEN. REF.: IS.3:801; NB.–; Z.–.

Note: For Acts 26:28, A.V., "thou persuadest," see FAIN, *Note*.

2. *anapeithō* [ἀναπείθω, 374], to persuade, induce, in an evil sense (*ana*, back, and No. 1), is used in Acts 18:13. ¶ In the Sept., Jer. 29:8. ¶

NT: B.59b; CB.–; K.–.
OT: –.
GEN. REF.: IS.3:801; NB.–; Z.–.

Note: For *plērophoreō*, rendered "being fully persuaded," in Rom. 4:21 and 14:5, A.V., see ASSURANCE, B, No. 2.

PERSUASIVE, PERSUASIVENESS

A. Adjective.

peithos [πειθός, 3981], an adjective (akin to *peithō*), not found elsewhere, is translated "persuasive" in 1 Cor. 2:4, R.V. (A.V., "enticing"); see ENTICE, B. ¶

NT: B.639a; CB.1263a; K.818.
OT: –.
GEN. REF.: –.

B. Noun.

pithanologia [πιθανολογία, 4086], persuasiveness of speech, is used in Col. 2:4, R.V. See ENTICE, B, *Note*. ¶

NT: B.657b; CB.1265a; K.–.
OT: –.
GEN. REF.: –.

PERSUASION

peismonē [πεισμονή, 3988], akin to *peithō*, is used in Gal. 5:8, where the meaning is 'this influence that has won you over, or that seems likely to do so'; the use of *peithō*, in the sense of to obey, in ver. 7, suggests a play upon words here. ¶

NT: B.641b; CB.1263a; K.818.
OT: –.
GEN. REF.: IS.3:801; NB.–; Z.–.

PERTAIN TO

metechō [μετέχω, 3348], Heb. 7:13, A.V.; see BELONG, *Note* (*c*), PARTAKE, B, No. 3.

NT: B.514a; CB.1258c; K.286.
OT: –.
GEN. REF.: –.

Notes: (1) In Rom. 15:17, the phrase *ta pros*, lit., 'the (things) towards' is translated "things pertaining to," R.V. (A.V., "those things which pertain to"); in Heb. 2:17 and 5:1, R.V. and A.V., "things pertaining to."

(2) In Acts 1:3, A.V., the phrase *ta peri*, "the (things) concerning" (R.V.), is translated "the things pertaining to."

(3) In Rom. 9:4, the R.V. rightly translates the relative pronoun *hōn*, lit., 'of whom' (from *hos*, who), by "whose is" (A.V., "to whom *pertaineth*").

(4) In Rom. 4:1, A.V., *kata*, "according to" (R.V.), is translated "as pertaining to."

(5) For 1 Cor. 6:3, 4, see LIFE, B, No. 1.

PERVERSE, PERVERT

1. *apostrephō* [ἀποστρέφω, 654], to turn away (*apo*, from, *strephō*, to turn), is used metaphorically in the sense of perverting in Luke 23:14 (cp. No. 2 in ver. 2). See BRING, No. 22.

NT: B.100b; CB.1237a; K.1093.
OT: hāphak: S.2015; HR.916c.1; H.512; BD.245b.
GEN. REF.: IS.3:802; NB.—; Z.—.

2. *diastrephō* [διαστρέφω, 1294], to distort, twist (*dia*, through, and *strephō*), is translated to pervert in Luke 23:2 (cp. No. 1 in ver. 14); Acts 13:10 [in ver. 8, "to turn aside" (A.V., "away")]; in the perfect participle, Passive Voice, it is translated "perverse," lit., 'turned aside,' 'corrupted,' in Matt. 17:17; Luke 9:41; Acts 20:30; Phil. 2:15. ¶

NT: B.189a; CB.—; K.1093.
OT: tahpukāh: S.8419; HR.312a.1d; H.512f; BD.246c.
'āwat: S.5791; HR.312a.6; H.1591; BD.736c.
'āqash: S.6140; HR.312a.9a; H.1684; BD.786a.
GEN. REF.: IS.3:802; NB.—; Z.—.

3. *metastrephō* [μεταστρέφω, 3344], to transform into something of an opposite character (*meta*, signifying a change, and *strephō*,) as the Judaizers sought to "pervert the gospel of Christ," Gal. 1:7; cp. "the sun shall be turned into darkness," Acts 2:20; laughter into mourning and joy to heaviness, Jas. 4:9. See TURN. ¶

NT: B.513b; CB.—; K.1093.
OT: hāphak: S.2015; HR.916c.1; H.512; BD.245b.
GEN. REF.: IS.3:802; NB.—; Z.—.

4. *ekstrephō* [ἐκστρέφω, 1612], to turn inside out (*ek*, out), to change entirely, is used metaphorically in Tit. 3:11. R.V., "is perverted" (A.V., "is subverted"). See SUBVERT. ¶

NT: B.245b; CB.—; K.—.
OT: hāphak: S.2015; HR.441c.1a; H.512; BD.245b.
tahpukāh: S.8419; HR.441c.1b; H.512f; BD.246c.
hephek: S.2016; HR.441c.1c; H.512a; BD.246a.
GEN. REF.: IS.3:802; NB.—; Z.—.

Note: For "perverse disputings," 1 Tim. 6:5, A.V., see DISPUTE, A, No. 3.

PESTILENCE, PESTILENT FELLOW

loimos [λοιμός, 3061], a pestilence, any deadly infectious malady, is used in the plural in Luke 21:11 (in some mss., Matt.24:7); in Acts 24:5, metaphorically, "a pestilent fellow." See FELLOW. ¶

NT: B.479d; CB.—; K.—.
OT: beliyya'al: S.1100; HR.887c.1; H.246g; BD.116a.
lûṣ: S.3887; HR.887c.2a,b; H.1113; BD.539b.
GEN. REF.: IS.3:802; NB.1001; Z.4:720.

PETITION

aitēma [αἴτημα, 155], from *aiteō*, to ask, is rendered "petitions" in 1 John 5:15: see ASK, B, and cp. the distinction between A, Nos. 1 and 2. ¶ Cp. *deēsis* (see PRAYER).

NT: B.26b; CB.1234a; K.30.
OT: sheʼēlāh: S.7596; HR.38a.2a; H.2303a; BD.982c.
GEN. REF.: IS.3:819; NB.—; Z.—.

PHARISEES

pharisaios [φαρισαῖος, 5330], from an Aramaic word *peras* (found in Dan. 5:28), signifying to separate, owing to a different manner of life from that of the general public. The Pharisees and Sadducees appear as distinct parties in the latter half of the 2nd cent. B.C., though they represent tendencies traceable much earlier in Jewish history, tendencies which became pronounced after the return from Babylon (537 B.C.). The immediate progenitors of the two parties were, respectively, the Hasidaeans and the Hellenizers; the latter, the antedecents of the Sadducees, aimed at removing Judaism from its narrowness and sharing in the advantages of Greek life and culture. The Hasidaeans, a transcription of the Hebrew *chasidim*, i.e., pious ones, were a society of men zealous for religion, who acted under the guidance of the scribes, in opposition to the godless Hellenizing party; they scrupled to oppose the legitimate High Priest even when he was on the Greek side. Thus the Hellenizers were a political sect, while the Hasidaeans, whose fundamental principle was complete separation from non-Jewish elements, were the strictly legal party among the Jews, and were ultimately the more popular and influential party. In their zeal for the Law they almost deified it and their attitude became merely external, formal, and mechanical. They laid stress, not upon the righteousness of an action, but upon its formal correctness. Consequently their opposition to Christ was inevitable; His manner of life and teaching was essentially a condemnation of theirs; hence His denunciation of them, e.g., Matt. 6:2, 5, 16; 15:7 and chapter 23.

While the Jews continued to be divided into these two parties, the spread of the testimony of the Gospel must have produced what in the public eye seemed to be a new sect, and in the extensive development which took place at Antioch, Acts 11:19-26, the name "Christians" seems to have become a popular term applied to the disciples as a sect, the primary cause, however, being their witness to Christ (see CALL, A, No. 11). The opposition of both Pharisees and Sadducees (still mutually antagonistic, Acts 23:6-10) against the new

"sect" continued unabated during apostolic times.
NT: B.853c; CB.1263c; K.1246.
OT: —.
GEN. REF.: IS.3:822; NB.981; Z.4:745.

PHILOSOPHER

philosophos [φιλόσοφος, 5386], lit., loving wisdom (*philos*, loving, *sophia*, wisdom), occurs in Acts 17:18. ¶
NT: B.861b; CB.1264b; K.1269.
OT: 'ashshāph: S.825; HR.1432b.1; H.181; BD.80b.
GEN. REF.: IS.3:850; NB.—; Z.—.

PHILOSOPHY

philosophia [φιλοσοφία, 5385], denotes the love and pursuit of wisdom, hence, philosophy, the investigation of truth and nature; in Col. 2:8, the so-called philosophy of false teachers. "Though essentially Greek as a name and as an idea, it had found its way into Jewish circles . . . Josephus speaks of the three Jewish sects as three 'philosophies' . . . It is worth observing that this word, which to the Greeks denoted the highest effort of the intellect, occurs here alone in Paul's writings . . . the Gospel had deposed the term as inadequate to the higher standard whether of knowledge or of practice, which it had introduced" (Lightfoot). ¶
NT: B.861b; CB.1264a; K.1269.
OT: —.
GEN. REF.: IS.3:850; NB.—; Z.4:776.

PHYLACTERY

phulaktērion [φυλακτήριον, 5440], primarily an outpost, or fortification (*phulax*, a guard), then, any kind of safeguard, became used especially to denote an amulet. In the N.T. it denotes a prayer-fillet, a phylactery, a small strip of parchment, with portions of the Law written on it; it was fastened by a leathern strap either to the forehead or to the left arm over against the heart, to remind the wearer of the duty of keeping the commandments of God in the head and in the heart; cp. Ex. 13:16; Deut. 6:8; 11:18. It was supposed to have potency as a charm against evils and demons. The Pharisees broadened their phylacteries to render conspicuous their superior eagerness to be mindful of God's Law, Matt. 23:5. ¶
NT: B.868a; CB.1264c; K.—.
OT: —.
GEN. REF.: IS.3:864; NB.995; Z.4:786.

PHYSICIAN

iatros [ἰατρός, 2395], akin to *iaomai*, to heal, a physician, occurs in Matt. 9:12; Mark 2:17; 5:26; Luke 4:23; 5:31 (in some mss., 8:43); Col. 4:14. ¶
NT: B.368d; CB.1252c; K.344.
OT: rāphāh': S.7495; HR.669a.1b; H.2196; BD.950c.
marpē': S.4832; HR.669a.1a; H.2196c; BD.951b.
GEN. REF.: IS.3:865; NB.315; Z.4:788.

PIECE

1. *epiblēma* [ἐπίβλημα, 1915], primarily denotes that which is thrown over, a cover (*epi*, over, *ballō*, to throw); then, that which is put on, or sewed on, to cover a rent, a patch, Matt. 9:16; Mark 2:21; in the next sentence, R.V., "that which should fill" (A.V., "the new piece that filled"), there is no word representing "piece" (lit., 'the filling,' *plērōma*); see FILL, B; Luke 5:36. ¶
NT: B.290c; CB.—; K.—.
OT: —.
GEN. REF.: —.

2. *drachmē* [δραχμή, 1406], a *drachma*, firstly, an Attic weight, as much as one can hold in the hand (connected with *drassomai*, to grasp with the hand, lay hold of, 1 Cor. 3:19), then, a coin, nearly equal to the Roman *denarius* (see PENNY), is translated "pieces of silver" in Luke 15:8, 1st part; "piece," 2nd part and ver. 9. ¶
NT: B.206c; CB.—; K.—.
OT: darkᵉmôn: S.1871; HR.349a.1b; H.453c; BD.204a.
beqa': S.1235; HR.349a.2; H.271a; BD.132b.
sheqel: S.8255; HR.349a.3; H.2454a; BD.1053c.
GEN. REF.: —.

3. *meros* [μέρος, 3313], a part, is translated "a piece (of a broiled fish)" in Luke 24:42. See BEHALF, PART.
NT: B.505d; CB.1258b; K.585.
OT: —.
GEN. REF.: —.

4. *klasma* [κλάσμα, 2801], a broken piece (from *klaō*, to break), is used of the broken pieces from the feeding of the multitudes, R.V., "broken pieces," A.V., "fragments," Matt. 14:20; Mark 6:43; 8:19, 20; Luke 9:17; John 6:12, 13; in Matt. 15:37 and Mark 8:8, R.V., "broken pieces" (A.V., "broken meat"). ¶
NT: B.433b; CB.1255b; K.437.
OT: pēlaḥ: S.6400; HR.766c.1; H.1773a; BD.812a.
pat: S.6596; HR.766c.2a; H.1850; BD.837d.
GEN. REF.: IS.3:866; NB.—; Z.—.

5. *argurion* [ἀργύριον, 694], which frequently denotes "money," also represents a silver coin, of the value of a shekel or *tetradrachmon* (four times the *drachmē*, see No. 2); it is used in the plural in Matt. 26:15; 27:3-9. In Acts 19:19, "fifty thousand pieces of silver," is, lit., 'fifty thousand of silver' (probably drachmas). See MONEY, SILVER.
NT: B.104d; CB.1237c; K.—.
OT: keseph: S.3701; HR.153b.1a; H.1015a; BD.494a.
GEN. REF.: IS.3:402; NB.—; Z.—.

Notes: (1) In Acts 27:44, for A.V., "*broken pieces*," the R.V. translates *epi* (on) *tinōn* (certain things) *tōn* (the, i.e., those namely) by "on *other* things"; there is no word in the original representing "pieces."

(2) For the phrase to break to (in) pieces, Matt. 21:44, R.V., and Mark 5:4, see BREAK, A, Nos. 10 and 5 respectively.

(3) In Luke 14:18, A.V., *agros*, a field (R.V.), is translated "a piece of ground."

(4) In Matt. 17:27, A.V., *statēr*, a shekel (R.V.), a *tetradrachmon* (see No. 5, above), is translated "a piece of money."

PIERCE

1. *diikneomai* [διικνέομαι, 1338], to go through, penetrate (*dia*, through, *ikneomai*, to go), is used of the power of the Word of God, in Heb. 4:12, "piercing." ¶ In the Sept., Ex. 26:28. ¶

NT: B.195b; CB.—; K.—.
OT: bāraḥ: S.1272; HR.330b.1; H.284; BD.137d.
GEN. REF.: IS.3:866; NB.—; Z.—.

2. *dierchomai* [διέρχομαι, 1330], to go through, is translated "shall pierce through" in Luke 2:35. See COME, No. 5.

NT: B.194c; CB.1241c; K.257.
OT: 'ābar: S.5674; HR.328c.10a; H.1556; BD.716d.
GEN. REF.: IS.3:866; NB.—; Z.—.

3. *ekkenteō* [ἐκκεντέω, 1574], primarily, to prick out (*ek*, out, *kenteō*, to prick), signifies to pierce, John 19:37; Rev. 1:7. ¶

NT: B.240c; CB.—; K.216.
OT: dāqar: S.1856; HR.432c.1; H.449; BD.201a.
GEN. REF.: IS.3:866; NB.—; Z.—.

4. *nussō* [νύσσω, 3572], to pierce or pierce through, often of inflicting severe or deadly wounds, is used of the piercing of the side of Christ, John 19:34 (in some mss., Matt. 27:49). ¶

NT: B.547a; CB.—; K.—.
OT: —.
GEN. REF.: IS.3:866; NB.—; Z.—.

5. *peripeirō* [περιπείρω, 4044], to put on a spit, hence, to pierce, is used metaphorically in 1 Tim. 6:10, of torturing one's soul with many sorrows, "have pierced (themselves) through." ¶

NT: B.649d; CB.—; K.—.
OT: —.
GEN. REF.: IS.3:866.

PIETY (to shew)

eusebeō [εὐσεβέω, 2151], to reverence, to show piety towards any to whom dutiful regard is due (akin to *eusebēs*, pious, godly, devout), is used in 1 Tim. 5:4 of the obligation on the part of children and grandchildren (R.V.) to express in a practical way their dutifulness "towards their own family"; in Acts 17:23 of worshipping God. See WORSHIP. ¶

NT: B.326b; CB.1247b; K.1010.
OT: —.
GEN. REF.: IS.3:867; NB.995; Z.—.

For **PIGEON** see **DOVE**, No. 1

PILGRIM

parepidēmos [παρεπίδημος, 3927], an adjective signifying 'sojourning in a strange place, away from one's own people' (*para*, from, expressing a contrary condition, and *epidēmeō*, to sojourn; *dēmos*, a people), is used of O.T. saints, Heb. 11:13, "pilgrims" (coupled with *xenos*, a foreigner); of Christians, 1 Pet. 1:1, "sojourners (of the Dispersion)," R.V.; 2:11, "pilgrims" (coupled with *paroikos*, an alien, sojourner); the word is thus used metaphorically of those to whom Heaven is their own country, and who are sojourners on earth. ¶

NT: B.625d; CB.1262b; K.149.
OT: tôshāb: S.8453; HR.1068c.1; H.922d; BD.444c.
GEN. REF.: IS.—; NB.997; Z.4:793.

PILLAR

stulos [στύλος, 4769], a column supporting the weight of a building, is used (*a*) metaphorically, of those who bear responsibility in the churches as of the elders in the church at Jerusalem, Gal. 2:9; of a local church as to its responsibility, in a collective capacity, to maintain the doctrines of the faith by teaching and practice, 1 Tim. 3:15; some would attach this and the next words to the statement in ver. 16; the connection in the Eng. Versions seems preferable; (*b*) figuratively in Rev. 3:12, indicating a firm and permanent position in the spiritual, heavenly and eternal Temple of God; (*c*) illustratively, of the feet of the angel in the vision in Rev. 10:1, seen as flames rising like columns of fire indicative of holiness and consuming power, and thus reflecting the glory of Christ as depicted in 1:15; cp. Ezek. 1:7. ¶

NT: B.772a; CB.1270b; K.1096.
OT: 'ammûd: S.5982; HR.1297c.4b; H.1637c; BD.765a.
qeresh: S.7175; HR.1297c.5; H.2079a; BD.903c.
GEN. REF.: IS.3:869; NB.—; Z.4:793.

PILLOW

proskephalaion [προσκεφάλαιον, 4344], denotes a pillow, a cushion for the head (*pros*, to, *kephalē*, a head), Mark 4:38 (R.V., "cushion"). ¶ In the Sept., Ezek. 13:18. ¶

NT: B.715d; CB.—; K.—.
OT: keset: S.3704; HR.1217a.1; H.1009a; BD.492c.
GEN. REF.: IS.—; NB.999; Z.4:796.

PINE AWAY

xērainō [ξηραίνω, 3583], to dry up, wither, is rendered "pineth away" in Mark 9:18. See DRY.

NT: B.548c; CB.1273b; K.—.
OT: yābēsh: S.3001; HR.957a.2; H.837; BD.386b.
GEN. REF.: IS.3:872; NB.—; Z.—.

PINNACLE

pterugion [πτερύγιον, 4419], denotes (*a*) a little wing (diminutive of *pterux*, a wing); (*b*) anything like a wing, a turret, battlement, of the temple in Jerusalem, Matt. 4:5 and Luke 4:9 (of the *hieron*, the entire precincts, or parts of the main building, as distinct from the *naos*, the sanctuary). This "wing" has been regarded (1) as the apex of the sanctuary, (2) the top of Solomon's porch, (3) the top of the Royal Portico, which Josephus describes as of tremendous height (*Antiq*. xv. 11.5). ¶ It is used in the Sept. of the fins of fishes, e.g., Lev. 11:9-12; of the part of a dress, hanging down in the form of a wing, Ruth 3:9; 1 Sam. 24:5.

NT: B.727b; CB.1267c; K.—.
OT: kānāph: S.3671; HR.1238a.1; H.1003a; BD.489b.
sᵉnappîr: S.5579; HR.1238a.2; H.1523; BD.703b.
GEN. REF.: IS.3:872; NB.999; Z.4:799.

PIPE (Noun and Verb)

A. Noun.

aulos [αὐλός, 836], a wind instrument, e.g., a flute (connected with *aēmi*, to blow), occurs in 1 Cor. 14:7. ¶

NT: B.121c; CB.—; K.—.
OT: ḥālîl: S.2485; HR.178c.1; H.660d; BD.319d.
GEN. REF.: IS.—; NB.853; Z.4:320.

B. Verb.

auleō [αὐλέω, 836], to play on an *aulos*, is used in Matt. 11:17; Luke 7:32; 1 Cor. 14:7 (2nd part). ¶

NT: B.121b; CB.1238b; K.—.
OT: —.
GEN. REF.: IS.—; NB.853; Z.4:320.

For PIPERS, Rev. 18:22, A.V., see FLUTE-PLAYERS

PIT

1. *phrear* [φρέαρ, 5421], a well, dug for water (distinct from *pēgē*, a fountain), denotes a pit in Rev. 9:1, 2, R.V., "the pit (of the abyss)," "the pit," i.e., the shaft leading down to the abyss, A.V., "(bottomless) pit"; in Luke 14:5, R.V., "well" (A.V., "pit"); in John 4:11, 12, "well." See WELL. ¶

NT: B.865d; CB.1264c; K.—.
OT: bᵉ'ēr: S.875; HR.1438b.1; H.1949a; BD.91c.
GEN. REF.: IS.3:874; NB.1000; Z.4:802.

2. *bothunos* [βόθυνος, 999], is rendered "pit" in Matt. 12:11: see DITCH.

NT: B.144d; CB.—; K.—.
OT: paḥat: S.6354; HR.224b.3; H.1761a; BD.809b.
GEN. REF.: IS.3:874; NB.1000; Z.4:802.

3. *abussos* [ἄβυσσος, —]: see BOTTOMLESS, B.

4. *hupolēnion* [ὑπολήνιον, 5276], denotes a vessel or trough beneath a winepress, to receive the juice, Mark 12:1, R.V., "a pit for the winepress" (A.V., "*a place for* . . . the wine-fat"). ¶

NT: B.845c; CB.—; K.531.
OT: yeqeb: S.3342; HR.1415c.1; H.900a; BD.428c.
GEN. REF.: IS.3:874; NB.—; Z.—.

Note: For "pits," 2 Pet. 2:4, R.V., see CHAIN *Note* (1).

PITCH (Verb)

pēgnumi [πήγνυμι, 4078], to make fast, to fix (cp. *prospēgnumi*, Acts 2:23, of crucifixion), is used of pitching a tent; in Heb. 8:2, of the "true tabernacle," the Heavenly and spiritual, which "the Lord pitched." ¶

NT: B.656a; CB.1263a; K.—.
OT: nāṭāh: S.5186; HR.1130c.4; H.1352; BD.639d.
tāqa': S.8628; HR.1130c.10; H.2541; BD.1075b.
GEN. REF.: IS.—; NB.—; Z.4:803.

PITCHER

keramion [κεράμιον, 2765], an earthen vessel (*keramos*, potter's clay), a jar or jug, occurs in Mark 14:13; Luke 22:10. ¶

NT: B.428d; CB.1255a; K.—.
OT: gābîa': S.1375; HR.759c.2; H.309b; BD.149b.
bat: S.1324; HR.759c.1; H.298a; BD.144c.
GEN. REF.: IS.3:875; NB.—; Z.4:803.

PITIABLE (most)

eleeinoteros [ἐλεεινότερος, 1652], the comparative degree of *eleeinos*, miserable, pitiable (*eleos*, pity), is used in 1 Cor. 15:19, "most pitiable" (R.V.), 'more pitiable than all men.' See MISERABLE. ¶

NT: B.249c; CB.1244a; K.—.
OT: —.
GEN. REF.: IS.—.

PITIFUL, PITY

1. *polusplanchnos* [πολύσπλαγχνος, 4184], denotes very pitiful or full of pity (polus, much, *splanchnon*, the heart; in the plural, the affections), occurs in Jas. 5:11, R.V., "full of pity." ¶

NT: B.689d; CB.1266a; K.1067.
OT: —.
GEN. REF.: IS.3:876; NB.—; Z.—.

2. *eusplanchnos* [εὔσπλαγχνος, 2155], compassionate, tenderhearted, lit., 'of good heartedness' (*eu*, well, and *splanchnon*), is translated "pitiful" in 1 Pet. 3:8, A.V., R.V., "tenderhearted," as in Eph. 4:32. ¶

NT: B.326c; CB.1247b; K.1067.
OT: —.
GEN. REF.: IS.3:876; NB.—; Z.—.

PLACE (Noun, Verb, Adverb)

A. Nouns.

1. *topos* [τόπος, 5117], Eng., topic, topography etc., is used of a region or locality, frequently in the Gospels and Acts; in Luke 2:7

and 14:22, "room"; of a place which a person or thing occupies, a couch at table, e.g., Luke 14:9, 10, R.V., "place" (A.V., "room"); of the destiny of Judas Iscariot, Acts 1:25; of the condition of the "unlearned" or non-gifted in a church gathering, 1 Cor. 14:16, R.V., "place"; the sheath of a sword, Matt. 26:52; a place in a book, Luke 4:17; see also Rev. 2:5; 6:14; 12:8; metaphorically, of condition, occasion, opportunity Acts 25:16, R.V., "opportunity" (A.V., "licence"); Rom. 12:19; Eph. 4:27. See OPPORTUNITY, ROOM.

NT: B.822b; CB.1273a; K.1184.
OT: māqôm: S.4725; HR.1364b.8; H.1999b; BD.879d.
GEN. REF.: IS.3:877; NB.–; Z.–.

2. *chōrion* [χωρίον, 5564], a region (a diminutive of *chōra*, a land, country), is used of Gethsemane, Matt. 26:36; Mark 14:32. See FIELD.

NT: B.890b; CB.1240a; K.–.
OT: kerem: S.3754; HR.1482c.1; H.1040a; BD.501c.
GEN. REF.: –.

3. *huperochē* [ὑπεροχή, 5247], "high place," 1 Tim. 2:2: see AUTHORITY, No. 3.

NT: B.841d; CB.–; K.1230.
OT: qômāh: S.6967; HR.1411a.1; H.1999a; BD.879b.
GEN. REF.: –.

4. *periochē* [περιοχή, 4042], primarily a circumference, compass (*peri*, around, *echō*, to have), hence denotes a portion circumscribed, that which is contained, and in reference to a writing or book, a portion or passage of its contents, Acts 8:32, "(the) place." ¶

NT: B.648d; CB.–; K.–.
OT: m^eṣûdāh: S.4686; HR.1125a.2b; H.1885g,i; BD.845a.
māṣôr: S.4692; HR.1125a.3; H.1898a; BD.848d.
GEN. REF.: –.

5. *akroatērion* [ἀκροατήριον, 201], denotes a place of audience (*akroaomai*, to listen), Acts 25:23, "place of hearing." ¶

NT: B.33c; CB.–; K.–.
OT: –.
GEN. REF.: –.

6. *prōtoklisia* [πρωτοκλισία]: see CHIEF, B, No. 7.

Notes: (1) For *opē*, a hole, Jas. 3:11, A.V., "place," see OPENING: see also CAVE.

(2) For "place of toll," Matt. 9:9; Mark 2:14, see CUSTOM (TOLL), No. 2.

(3) In Heb. 4:5 "in this place" is, lit., 'in this,' i.e., 'in this (passage).'

(4) In Luke 6:17, R.V., *topos*, with *pedinos*, level, is translated "level place" (A.V., "plain").

(5) For *amphodon*, rendered "a place where two ways met," Mark 11:4 (R.V., "the open street"), see STREET. ¶

(6) For *erēmia*, a desert place, see DESERT, A.

(7) In 1 Cor. 11:20 and 14:23, A.V., the phrase *epi to auto*, lit., 'to the same,' is translated "into one place," R.V., "together"; perhaps = 'in assembly.'

(8) For "secret place," Luke 11:33, A.V., see CELLAR.

(9) For "place of prayer," Acts 16:13, R.V., see PRAYER.

(10) For Phil. 1:13 (A.V., "in all other places"), R.V., "to all the rest," see PALACE.

(11) For "rocky places," Mark 4:16, see ROCKY.

B. Verbs.

1. *anachōreō* [ἀναχωρέω, 402], to withdraw (*ana*, back, *chōreō*, to make room, retire), is translated "give place" in Matt. 9:24. See DEPART, No. 10.

NT: B.63c; CB.1235a; K.–.
OT: bāraḥ: S.1272; HR.85c.1; H.284; BD.137d.
nûs: S.5127; HR.85c.3; H.1327; BD.630c.
GEN. REF.: –.

2. *eikō* [εἴκω, 1502], to yield, give way, is rendered "gave place" in Gal. 2:5. ¶

NT: B.222a; CB.1243a; K.–.
OT: –.
GEN. REF.: –.

3. *ginomai* [γίνομαι, 1096], to become, take place, is translated "(a death) having taken place" in Heb. 9:15, R.V., A.V., "by means of (death)," referring, not to the circumstances of a testamentary disposition, but to the sacrifice of Christ as the basis of the new covenant.

NT: B.158a; CB.1248b; K.117.
OT: –.
GEN. REF.: –.

Note: For *chōreō* in John 8:37, A.V., "hath . . . place," see COURSE, B.

C. Adverbs, etc.

1. *hōde* [ὡδε, 5602], here, hither, is translated "to (unto, R.V.) this place" in Luke 23:5. See HERE.

NT: B.895a; CB.–; K.–.
OT: pōh: S.6311; HR.1491b.5; H.1739; BD.805d.
GEN. REF.: –.

2. *pantachou* [πανταχοῦ, 3837], everywhere, is translated "in all places" in Acts 24:3. See EVERYWHERE, No. 2.

NT: B.608b; CB.–; K.–.
OT: –.
GEN. REF.: –.

Notes: (1) For "in divers places," Matt. 24:7, etc., see DIVERS, B, *Note.*

(2) In the following the R.V. gives the correct meaning: in Mark 6:10, *ekeithen*, "thence" (A.V., "from that place"); in Heb. 2:6 and 4:4, *pou*, "somewhere" (A.V., "in a certain place"); in Matt. 12:6, *hōde*, "here" (A.V., "in this place"); in Mark 6:10, *hopou ean*, "wheresoever" (A.V., "in what place soever").

(3) The adjective *entopios*, "of that place," occurs in Acts 21:12. ¶

(4) In Jas. 2:3 *kalōs*, well (A.V., marg.), is rendered "in a good place." See DWELLING, HEAVENLY, HOLY, MARKET, SKULL, STEEP, YONDER.

PLAGUE

1. *mastix* [μάστιξ, 3148], a whip, scourge, Acts 22:24, "by scourging"; Heb. 11:36, "scourgings," is used metaphorically of disease or suffering, Mark 3:10; 5:29, 34; Luke 7:21. See SCOURGING. ¶

NT: B.495b; CB.1257c; K.571,655.
OT: shôt: S.7752; HR.898b.6; H.2344a; BD.1002a.
nega': S.5061; HR.898b.2; H.1293a; BD.619c.
GEN. REF.: IS.3:878; NB.1001; Z.4:804.

2. *plēgē* [πληγή, 4127], a stripe, wound (akin to *plēssō*, to smite), is used metaphorically of a calamity, a plague, Rev. 9:20; 11:6; 15:1, 6, 8; 16:9, 21 (twice); 18:4, 8; 21:9; 22:18. See STRIPE, WOUND.

NT: B.668a; CB.1265a; K.—.
OT: makkāh: S.4347; HR.1142b.3a; H.1364d; BD.646d.
m^{a}ggēphāh: S.4046; HR.1142b.5b; H.1294b; BD.620a.
GEN. REF.: IS.3:878; NB.1001; Z.4:804.

For PLAIN (Noun) see PLACE, A, *Note* (4)

PLAIN (Adverb), PLAINLY, PLAINNESS

1. *orthōs* [ὀρθῶς, 3723], rightly (from *orthos*, straight), is translated "plain," in Mark 7:35, of restored speech. See RIGHTLY.

NT: B.580d; CB.1261b; K.727.
OT: —.
GEN. REF.: IS.3:880; NB.—; Z.—.

2. *parrhēsia* [παρρησία, 3954], boldness, is used adverbially in its dative case and rendered "plainly" in John 10:24; 11:14; 16:25; 16:29 (with *en*, lit., 'in plainness'). See BOLD, B, where see also "plainness of speech," 2 Cor. 3:12, R.V.

NT: B.630c; CB.1262c; K.794.
OT: —.
GEN. REF.: IS.3:880; NB.—; Z.—.

PLAIT

plekō [πλέκω, 4120], to weave, twist, plait, is used of the crown of thorns inflicted on Christ, Matt. 27:29; Mark 15:17; John 19:2. ¶

NT: B.667b; CB.—; K.—.
OT: ^{c}ābōt: S.5688; HR.1141c.1; H.1558b; BD.721c.
GEN. REF.: IS.3:881; NB.—; Z.1:646.

For PLAITING (of the hair) see BRAIDED, *Note* (1)

For PLANK see BOARD

PLANT (Noun, Verb, Adjective)

A. Noun.

phuteia [φυτεία, 5451], firstly, a planting, then that which is planted, a plant (from *phuō*, to bring forth, spring up, grow, *phuton*, a plant), occurs in Matt. 15:13. ¶ In the Sept., 2 Kings 19:29; Ezek. 17:7; Mic. 1:6. ¶

NT: B.870a; CB.1264c; K.—.
OT: nāṭa': S.5193; HR.1446c.1a; H.1354; BD.642b.
mattā': S.4302; HR.1446c.1b; H.1354c; BD.642d.
GEN. REF.: IS.3:882; NB.—; Z.—.

B. Verb.

phuteuō [φυτεύω, 5452], to plant, is used (*a*) literally, Matt. 21:33; Mark 12:1; Luke 13:6; 17:6, 28; 20:9; 1 Cor. 9:7; (*b*) metaphorically, Matt. 15:13; 1 Cor. 3:6, 7, 8. ¶

NT: B.870a; CB.1264c; K.—.
OT: nāṭa': S.5193; HR.1446c.1a; H.1354; BD.642b.
GEN. REF.: IS.3:882; NB.—; Z.—.

C. Adjective.

sumphutos [σύμφυτος, 4854], firstly, congenital, innate (from *sumphuō*, to make to grow together), then, planted or grown along with, united with, Rom. 6:5, A.V., "planted together," R.V., "united with *Him*," indicating the union of the believer with Christ in experiencing spiritually "the likeness of His death." See UNITED. ¶ Cp. *emphutos*, Jas. 1:21, R.V., "implanted" (marg., "inborn"). See ENGRAFTED.

NT: B.780d; CB.1270b; K.1102.
OT: bāṣar: S.1219; HR.1306c.1a; H.270; BD.130d.
bāṣîr: S.1210; HR.1306c.1b; H.270f; BD.131b.
GEN. REF.: —.

PLATTER

1. *paropsis* [παροψίς, 3953], firstly, a side-dish of dainties (*para*, beside, *opson*, cooked); then, the dish itself, Matt. 23:25; ver. 26, in some mss. ¶

NT: B.630b; CB.—; K.—.
OT: —.
GEN. REF.: IS.—; NB.—; Z.4:810.

2. *pinax* [πίναξ, 4094], is translated platter in Luke 11:39; see CHARGER.

NT: B.658c; CB.—; K.—.
OT: —.
GEN. REF.: IS.3:884; NB.—; Z.4:810.

PLAY

paizō [παίζω, 3815], properly, to play as a child (*pais*), hence denotes to play as in dancing and making merry, 1 Cor. 10:7. ¶ Cp. *empaizō*, to mock.

NT: B.604c; CB.1261c; K.758.
OT: sāḥaq: S.7832; HR.1049a.3; H.1905c; BD.965d.
GEN. REF.: —.

PLEAD

entunchanō [ἐντυγχάνω, 1793], to make petition, is used of the pleading of Elijah against Israel, Rom. 11:2, R.V., "pleadeth with" (A.V., "maketh intercession to"). See DEAL WITH, INTERCESSIONS.

NT: B.270a; CB.1245b; K.1191.
OT: qᵉrēb (Aramaic): S.7127; HR.481b.1; H.2978; BD.1111c.
GEN. REF.: IS.3:884; NB.–; Z.–.

PLEASE, PLEASING (Noun), WELL-PLEASING, PLEASURE

A. Verbs.

1. *areskō* [ἀρέσκω, 700], signifies (*a*) to be pleasing to, be acceptable to, Matt. 14:6; Mark 6:22; Acts 6:5; Rom. 8:8; 15:2; 1 Cor. 7:32-34; Gal. 1:10; 1 Thess. 2:15; 4:1 (where the preceding *kai*, "and," is epexegetical, 'even,' explaining the 'walking,' i.e., Christian manner of life, as 'pleasing God'; in Gen. 5:22, where the Hebrew has "Enoch walked with God," the Sept. has "Enoch pleased God"; cp. Mic. 6:8; Heb. 11:5); 2 Tim. 2:4; (*b*) to endeavour to please, and so, to render service, doing so evilly in one's own interests, Rom. 15:1, which Christ did not, ver. 3; or unselfishly, 1 Cor. 10:33; 1 Thess. 2:4. This sense of the word is illustrated by Moulton and Milligan (Vocab.) from numerous Inscriptions, especially describing "those who have proved themselves of use to the commonwealth." ¶

NT: B.105c; CB.1237c; K.77.
OT: ṭôb: S.2895; HR.155c.2a,b; H.793; BD.373a.
yāṭab: S.3190; HR.155c.2c-e; H.863; BD.405c.
GEN. REF.: IS.3:885; NB.–; Z.–.

2. *euaresteō* [εὐαρεστέω, 2100], signifies to be well-pleasing (*eu*, well, and a form akin to No. 1); in the Active Voice, Heb. 11:5, R.V., "he had been well-pleasing (unto God)," A.V., "he pleased"; so ver. 6; in the Passive Voice, Heb. 13:16. ¶

NT: B.318c; CB.1247a; K.77.
OT: hālak: S.1980; HR.568c.1; H.498; BD.229d,235c.
GEN. REF.: IS.3:885; NB.–; Z.–.

3. *eudokeō* [εὐδοκέω, 2106], signifies (*a*) to be well pleased, to think it good [*eu*, well, and *dokeō*, see *Note* (1) below], not merely an understanding of what is right and good as in *dokeō*, but stressing the willingness and freedom of an intention or resolve regarding what is good, e.g., Luke 12:32, "it is (your Father's) good pleasure"; so Rom. 15:26, 27, R.V.; 1 Cor. 1:21; Gal. 1:15; Col. 1:19; 1 Thess. 2:8, R.V., "we were well pleased" (A.V., "we were willing"); this meaning is frequently found in the papyri in legal documents; (*b*) to be well pleased with, or take pleasure in, e.g., Matt. 3:17; 12:18; 17:5; 1 Cor. 10:5; 2 Cor. 12:10; 2 Thess. 2:12; Heb. 10:6, 8, 38; 2 Pet. 1:17.

NT: B.319b; CB.1247a; K.273.
OT: rāṣāh: S.7521; HR.569a.9a; H.2207; BD.953a.
GEN. REF.: IS.3:885; NB.–; Z.–.

4. *thelō* [θέλω, 2309], to will, wish, desire, is translated "it pleased (Him)" in 1 Cor. 12:18; 15:38, R.V. See DESIRE, B, No. 6.

NT: B.354d; CB.1271c; K.318.
OT: ḥāphēṣ: S.2654; HR.628b.8a,b; H.712; BD.342c.
rāṣāh: S.7521; HR.628b.12a; H.2207; BD.953a.
GEN. REF.: IS.3:885; NB.–; Z.–.

5. *spatalaō* [σπαταλάω, 4684], to live riotously, is translated "giveth herself to pleasure" in 1 Tim. 5:6, R.V. (A.V., "liveth in pleasure"); "taken your pleasure" in Jas. 5:5, A.V., "been wanton." ¶

NT: B.761a; CB.–; K.–.
OT: –.
GEN. REF.: IS.3:885; NB.–; Z.–.

Notes: (1) In Acts 15:22, A.V., *dokeō*, to seem good to (R.V.), is translated "it pleased" (in some mss., ver. 34); in Heb. 12:10, A.V., "(after their own) pleasure," R.V., "(as) seemed good (to them)."

(2) For *suneudokeō*, rendered "have pleasure in" in Rom. 1:32, A.V., see CONSENT, No. 6.

(3) For *truphaō*, rendered "lived in pleasure" in Jas. 5:5, A.V., see DELICATELY.

B. Adjectives.

1. *arestos* [ἀρεστός, 701], denotes pleasing, agreeable, John 8:29, R.V., "(the things that are) pleasing," A.V., "(those things that) please"; A.V. and R.V. in 1 John 3:22; in Acts 6:2, "fit" (R.V. marg., "pleasing"); 12:3, "it pleased," lit., 'it was pleasing.' See FIT. ¶

NT: B.105d; CB.1237c; K.77.
OT: yāshār: S.3477; HR.156a.3; H.930a; BD.449a.
ṭôb: S.2895; HR.156a.2; H.793; BD.373a.
GEN. REF.: IS.3:885; NB.–; Z.–.

2. *euarestos* [εὐάρεστος, 2101], *eu*, well, and No. 1, is translated "well-pleasing" in the R.V. except in Rom. 12:1, 2 (see marg., however). See ACCEPT, B, No. 4.

NT: B.318d; CB.1247a; K.77.
OT: –.
GEN. REF.: IS.3:885; NB.–; Z.–.

C. Noun.

areskeia (or *-ia*) [ἀρεσκεία, 699], a "pleasing," a giving pleasure, Col. 1:10, of the purpose Godward of a walk worthy of the Lord (cp. 1 Thess. 4:1). It was used frequently in a bad sense in classical writers. Moulton and Milligan illustrate from the papyri its use in a favourable sense, and Deissmann (*Bible Studies*) from an inscription. ¶ In the Sept., Prov. 31:30. ¶

NT: B.105c; CB.1237c; K.77.
OT: ḥēn: S.2580; HR.154b.1; H.694a; BD.336b.
GEN. REF.: IS.3:885; NB.–; Z.–.

PLEASURE

A. Nouns.

1. *hēdonē* [ἡδονή, 2237], pleasure, is used of the gratification of the natural desire or sinful desires (akin to *hēdomai*, to be glad, and *hēdeōs*, gladly), Luke 8:14; Tit. 3:3; Jas. 4:1, 3, R.V., "pleasures" (A.V., "lusts"); in the singular, 2 Pet. 2:13. See LUST. ¶

NT: B.344b; CB.1249c; K.303.
OT: ṭa'am: S.2940; HR.604b.1; H.815a; BD.381a.
GEN. REF.: IS.3:885; NB.–; Z.4:810.

2. *eudokia* [εὐδοκία, 2107], good pleasure (akin to *eudokeō*, PLEASE, No. 3), Eph. 1:5, 9; Phil. 2:13; 2 Thess. 1:11. See DESIRE, A, No. 2.

NT: B.319c; CB.1247a; K.273.
OT: rāṣôn: S.7522; HR.569b.1a; H.2207a; BD.953c.
GEN. REF.: IS.3:885; NB.–; Z.4:810.

3. *apolausis* [ἀπόλαυσις, 619], enjoyment, is used with *echō*, to have, and rendered "enjoy the pleasures" (lit., 'pleasure') in Heb. 11:25. See ENJOY.

NT: B.94d; CB.–; K.–.
OT: –.
GEN. REF.: IS.3:885; NB.–; Z.–.

Notes: (1) In Rev. 4:11, A.V., *thelēma*, a will, is translated "(for Thy) pleasure," R.V., "(because of Thy) will."

(2) For *charis*, translated "pleasure" in the A.V. of Acts 24:27 and 25:9, see FAVOUR, A.

B. Adjective.

philēdonos [φιλήδονος, 5369], loving pleasure (*philos*, loving, and A, No. 1), occurs in 2 Tim. 3:4, R.V., "lovers of pleasure" (A.V., ". . . pleasures"). See LOVER. ¶

NT: B.859c; CB.1264a; K.303.
OT: –.
GEN. REF.: IS.3:885; NB.–; Z.–.

Note: In 1 Tim. 5:6 the R.V. renders *spatalaō* "giveth herself to pleasure."

PLENTEOUS

polus [πολύς, 4183], much, is rendered "plenteous" in Matt. 9:37, of a harvest of souls, and Luke 10:2, R.V. (A.V., "great"). See GREAT.

NT: B.687c; CB.1266a; K.–.
OT: rab: S.7227; HR.1181b.9a; H.2099a,b; BD.912d.
rōb: S.7230; HR.1181b.9b; H.2099c; BD.913d.
rābab: S.7231; HR.1181b.9c; H.2099; BD.912c.
GEN. REF.: IS.3:887; NB.–; Z.–.

PLENTIFULLY

Note: This translates the prefix *eu* (well) of the verb *euphoreō*, to produce well, in Luke 12:16, "brought forth plentifully." ¶

PLOT

epiboulē [ἐπιβουλή, 1917], lit., a plan against (*epi*, against, *boulē*, a counsel, plan), is translated "plot" in the R.V. (A.V., "laying await" and "lying in wait") in Acts 9:24; 20:3, 19; 23:30. ¶

NT: B.290c; CB.1245c; K.–.
OT: –.
GEN. REF.: IS.3:889; NB.–; Z.–.

PLOUGH, PLOW

A. Noun.

arotron [ἄροτρον, 723], from *aroō*, to plough, occurs in Luke 9:62. ¶

NT: B.108b; CB.–; K.–.
OT: 'ēt: S.855; HR.159c.1; H.192a; BD.88a.
môrag: S.4173; HR.159c.2; H.1165; BD.558d.
GEN. REF.: IS.3:889-890; NB.19; Z.4:812.

B. Verb.

arotriaō [ἀροτριάω, 722], akin to A, a later form of *aroō*, to plough, occurs in Luke 17:7 and 1 Cor. 9:10. ¶

NT: B.108b; CB.–; K.–.
OT: ḥārash: S.2790; HR.159b.1; H.760; BD.360b.
GEN. REF.: IS.3:889-890; NB.–; Z.4:812.

PLUCK (out)

1. *tillō* [τίλλω, 5089], is used of plucking off ears of corn, Matt. 12:1; Mark 2:23; Luke 6:1. ¶ In the Sept., Isa. 18:7. ¶

NT: B.817a; CB.–; K.–.
OT: māraṭ: S.4803; HR.1352c.1a,b; H.1244; BD.598d.
GEN. REF.: –.

2. *harpazō* [ἁρπάζω, 726], to seize, snatch, is rendered "pluck" in John 10:28, 29, A.V., R.V., "snatch." For the meaning, see CATCH, No. 1.

NT: B.109a; CB.1249b; K.80.
OT: gāzal: S.1497; HR.160a.1; H.337; BD.159d.
ṭāraph: S.2963; HR.160a.3a; H.827; BD.382d.
GEN. REF.: –.

3. *exaireō* [ἐξαιρέω, 1807], to take out (*ex* for *ek*, out, *haireō*, to take), is translated "pluck out," of the eye as the occasion of sin, in Matt. 5:29; 18:9, indicating that, with determination and promptitude, we are to strike at the root of unholy inclinations, ridding ourselves of whatever would stimulate them. Cp. *Note* (2) below. See DELIVER, No. 8.

NT: B.272a; CB.–; K.–.
OT: nāṣal: S.5337; HR.484c.8a; H.1404; BD.664c.
GEN. REF.: –.

4. *exorussō* [ἐξορύσσω, 1846], to dig out or up, is rendered "ye would have plucked out (your eyes)" in Gal. 4:15, an indication of their feelings of gratitude to, and love for, the Apostle. The metaphor affords no real ground for the supposition of a reference to some weakness of his sight, and certainly not to the result of his temporary blindness at his conversion, the recovery from which must have been as complete as the infliction. There would be some reason for such an inference had the pronoun "ye" been stressed; but the stress is on the word "eyes"; their devotion prompted a readiness to

part with their most treasured possession on his behalf. For Mark 2:4 see BREAK, No. 14, DIG, No. 1, *Note* (2). ¶ In the Sept., 1 Sam. 11:2; Prov. 29:22. ¶

NT: B.277c; CB.—; K.—.
OT: nāqar: S.5365; HR.500a.1; H.1418; BD.669b.
GEN. REF.: —.

5. *ekrizoō* [ἐκριζόω, 1610], to pluck up by the roots (*ek*, out, *rhiza*, a root), is so translated in Jude 12 (figuratively), and in the A.V. in Luke 17:6, R.V., "rooted up"; "root up", Matt. 13:29; "shall be rooted up," 15:13. See ROOT. ¶

NT: B.244d; CB.1244a; K.985.
OT: ʻāqar: S.6131; HR.441a.3a; H.1681,1682; BD.785c.
nātash: S.5428; HR.441a.2; H.1451; BD.684c.
GEN. REF.: —.

Notes: (1) In Mark 5:4, A.V., *diaspaō*, to rend asunder (R.V.), is translated "plucked asunder," said of chains.

(2) In Mark 9:47, A.V., *ekballō*, to cast out (R.V.), is translated "pluck . . . out." Cp. No. 3, above.

POET

poiētēs [ποιητής, 4163], primarily a maker, later a doer (*poieō* to make, to do), was used, in classical Greek, of an author, especially a poet; so Acts 17:28. See DOER.

NT: B.683b; CB.1265c; K.895.
OT: —.
GEN. REF.: IS.3:891; NB.—; Z.4:813.

POINT, POINTS

A. Phrases.

Notes: (1) In Heb. 4:15, "in all points" represents the phrase *kata* with the neuter plural of *pas*, all, lit., 'according to all (things).'

(2) 'to be at the point of death' is a translation (*a*) of the verb *mellō*, to be about, with *teleutaō*, to end one's life, die, Luke 7:2; see DIE, No. 4; (*b*) of *mellō* with *apothnēskō*, to die, John 4:47; (*c*) of the phrase mentioned under DEATH, C, *Note*.

(3) In Jas. 2:10, *en heni* (the dative case of *heis*, one), lit., 'in one,' is rendered "in one *point*."

B. Noun.

kephalaion [κεφάλαιον, 2774], the neuter of the adjective *kephalaios*, of the head, is used as a noun, signifying (*a*) a sum, amount, of money, Acts 22:28; (*b*) a chief point, Heb. 8:1, not the summing up of the subject, as the A.V. suggests, for the subject was far from being finished in the Epistle; on the contrary, in all that was being set forth by the writer "the chief point" consisted in the fact that believers have "a High Priest" of the character already described. See SUM. ¶

NT: B.429d; CB.1255a; K.—.
OT: rō'sh: S.7218; HR.760c.1a; H.2097; BD.910c.
GEN. REF.: —.

C. Verb.

dēloō [δηλόω, 1213], to make plain (*dēlos*, evident), is translated "did point unto" in 1 Pet. 1:11, R.V. (A.V., "did signify"), of the operation of "the Spirit of Christ" in the prophets of the Old Testament in pointing on to the time and its characteristics, of the sufferings of Christ and subsequent glories. See SHEW, SIGNIFY.

NT: B.178c; CB.1240c; K.148.
OT: yādaʻ: S.3045; HR.295c.3; H.848; BD.393b.
ḥᵃwāh (Aramaic): S.2324; HR.295c.2b; H.2722; BD.1092b.
GEN. REF.: —.

POISON

ios [ἰός, 2447], denotes something active as (*a*) rust, as acting on metals, affecting their nature, Jas. 5:3; (*b*) poison, as of asps, acting destructively on living tissues, figuratively of the evil use of the lips as the organs of speech, Rom. 3:13; so of the tongue, Jas. 3:8. ¶

NT: B.378d; CB.1252c; K.368.
OT: ḥel'āh: S.2457; HR.687a.2; H.649a; BD.316a.
GEN. REF.: IS.3:899; NB.1009; Z.4:814.

For POLLUTE see DEFILE, A, No. 1

POLLUTION

alisgēma [ἀλίσγημα, 234], akin to a late verb *alisgeō*, to pollute, denotes a pollution, contamination, Acts 15:20, "pollutions of idols," i.e., all the contaminating associations connected with idolatry including meats from sacrifices offered to idols. ¶

NT: B.37d; CB.1234c; K.—.
OT: —.
GEN. REF.: IS.3:900; NB.—; Z.4:815.

Note: For *miasma*, A.V., "pollutions," in 2 Pet. 2:20, see DEFILEMENT, B, No. 1. ¶

POMP

phantasia [φαντασία, 5325], as a philosophic term, denoted an imagination; then, an appearance, like *phantasma*, an apparition; later, a show, display, pomp (Eng., phantasy), Acts 25:23. ¶ In the Sept., Hab. 2:18; 3:10; Zech. 10:1. ¶

NT: B.853b; CB.1263c; K.—.
OT: ḥāzîz: S.2385; HR.1424b.1; H.635a; BD.304a.
GEN. REF.: IS.3:902; NB.—; Z.—.

PONDER

sumballō [συμβάλλω, 4820], to throw together, confer, etc., has the meaning to ponder, i.e., to put one thing with another in considering circumstances, in Luke 2:19. See CONFER.

NT: B.777b; CB.—; K.—.
OT: —.
GEN. REF.: IS.3:902; NB.—; Z.—.

POOL

kolumbēthra [κολυμβήθρα, 2861], denotes a swimming pool (akin to *kolumbaō*, to swim, Acts 27:43), John 5:2 (ver. 4 in some mss.), 7; 9:7 (ver. 11 in some mss.). ¶

NT: B.442c; CB.—; K.—.
OT: bᵉrēkāh: S.1295; HR.777b.1; H.285c; BD.140a.
GEN. REF.: IS.3:904; NB.—; Z.4:819.

POOR

A. Adjectives.

1. *ptōchos* [πτωχός, 4434], for which see BEG, B, has the broad sense of "poor," (*a*) literally, e.g., Matt. 11:5; 26:9, 11; Luke 21:3 (with stress on the word, 'a conspicuously poor widow'); John 12:5, 6, 8; 13:29; Jas. 2:2, 3, 6; the poor are constantly the subjects of injunctions to assist them, Matt. 19:21; Mark 10:21; Luke 14:13, 21; 18:22; Rom. 15:26; Gal. 2:10; (*b*) metaphorically, Matt. 5:3; Luke 6:20; Rev. 3:17.

NT: B.728b; CB.1268a; K.969.
OT: dal: S.1800; HR.1239b.2a; H.433a; BD.195c.
'ānî: S.6041; HR.1239b.4a; H.1652d; BD.776d.
GEN. REF.: IS.3:905; NB.1016; Z.4:819.

2. *penichros* [πενιχρός, 3998], akin to B, needy, poor, is used of the widow in Luke 21:2 (cp. No. 1, of the same woman, in ver. 3); it is used frequently in the papyri. ¶ In the Sept., Ex. 22:25; Prov. 28:15; 29:7. ¶

NT: B.642d; CB.1263a; K.824.
OT: dal: S.1800; HR.1118b.1; H.433a; BD.195c.
'ānî: S.6041; HR.1118b.2; H.1652d; BD.776d.
GEN. REF.: IS.3:905; NB.1016; Z.4:819.

B. Noun.

penēs [πένης, 3993], a labourer (akin to *penomai*, to work for one's daily bread), is translated "poor" in 2 Cor. 9:9. ¶

NT: B.642c; CB.1263a; K.824.
OT: 'ebyôn: S.34; HR.1117a.1; H.3a; BD.2d.
'ānî: S.6041; HR.1117a.6b; H.1652d; BD.776d.
GEN. REF.: IS.3:905; NB.1016; Z.4:819.

C. Verb.

ptōcheuō [πτωχεύω, 4433], to be poor as a beggar (akin to A, No. 1), to be destitute, is said of Christ in 2 Cor. 8:9. ¶

NT: B.728a; CB.1268a; K.969.
OT: dālal: S.1809; HR.1239b.1; H.433; BD.195c.
yārash: S.3423; HR.1239b.2; H.920; BD.439a.
GEN. REF.: IS.3:905,906; NB.1016; Z.4:819.

PORCH

1. *stoa* [στοά, 4745], a portico, is used (*a*) of the porches at the pool of Bethesda, John 5:2; (*b*) of the covered colonnade in the Temple, called Solomon's porch, John 10:23; Acts 3:11; 5:12, a portico on the eastern side of the temple; this and the other porches existent in the time of Christ were almost certainly due to Herod's restoration. Cp. *Stoics* (Acts 17:18), 'philosophers of the porch.' ¶

NT: B.768d; CB.1270a; K.—.
OT: 'attîq: S.862; HR.1291c.1; H.191a; BD.87d.
riṣpāh: S.7531; HR.1291c.3; H.2210a,2211a; BD.954b.
GEN. REF.: IS.3:908; NB.1010; Z.4:821.

2. *pulōn* [πυλών, 4440], akin to *pulē*, a gate (Eng., pylon), is used of a doorway, porch or vestibule of a house or palace, Matt. 26:71. In the parallel passage Mark 14:68, No. 3 is used, and *pulōn* doubtless stands in Matt. 26 for *proaulion*. See GATE, No. 2.

NT: B.729c; CB.1268a; K.974.
OT: petaḥ: S.6607; HR.1242a.2; H.1854a; BD.835d.
sha'ar: S.8179; HR.1242a.3; H.2437a; BD.1044c.
GEN. REF.: IS.3:908; NB.1010; Z.4:821.

3. *proaulion* [προαύλιον, 4259], the exterior court or vestibule, between the door and the street, in the houses of well-to-do folk, Mark 14:68, "porch" (R.V. marg., "forecourt"). ¶

NT: B.702d; CB.—; K.—.
OT: —.
GEN. REF.: IS.3:908; NB.1010; Z.—.

PORTER

thurōros [θυρωρός, 2377], a door-keeper (*thura*, a door, *ouros*, a guardian), is translated "porter" in Mark 13:34; John 10:3; it is used of a female in John 18:16, 17, translated "(her) that kept the door." ¶ In the Sept., 2 Sam. 4:6; 2 Kings 7:11; Ezek. 44:11. ¶

NT: B.366a; CB.—; K.—.
OT: shō'ēr: S.7778; HR.664a.2; H.2437b; BD.1045b.
pᵉquddāh: S.6486; HR.664a.1; H.1802a; BD.824a.
GEN. REF.: IS.—; NB.—; Z.4:821.

PORTION

A. Nouns.

1. *meros* [μέρος, 3313], a part, is translated "portion" in Matt. 24:51; Luke 12:46; 15:12. See PART.

NT: B.505d; CB.—; K.585.
OT: —.
GEN. REF.: —.

2. *klēros* [κλῆρος, 2819], a lot, is translated "portion" in Acts 1:17, R.V. See CHARGE, INHERITANCE, LOT.

NT: B.435b; CB.1255b; K.442.
OT: gôrāl: S.1486; HR.770a.2; H.381a; BD.174a.
naḥᵃlāh: S.5159; HR.770a.6; H.1342a; BD.635a.
GEN. REF.: IS.3:909; NB.—; Z.—.

3. *meris* [μερίς, 3310], a part, is translated "portion" in 2 Cor. 6:15, R.V. See PART.

NT: B.505a; CB.1258b; K.—.
OT: ḥēleq: S.2506; HR.911a.1; H.669a; BD.324a.
mānāh: S.4490; HR.911a.2; H.1213a; BD.584b.
GEN. REF.: IS.3:909; NB.—; Z.—.

Note: For "portion of food," Luke 12:42, R.V., see FOOD, No. 4.

B. Verb.

summerizō [συμμερίζω, 4829], to have a part with (akin to A, No. 3), is translated "have their portion with" in 1 Cor. 9:13, R.V. See PARTAKER. ¶

NT: B.778c; CB.—; K.—.
OT: ḥālaq: S.2505; HR.1304b.1; H.669; BD.323c.
GEN. REF.: IS.3:909; NB.—; Z.—.

C. Adverb.

polumerōs [πολυμερῶς, 4181], signifies 'in many parts' or portions (*polus*, many, and A, No. 1), Heb. 1:1, R.V. (A.V., "at sundry times"). ¶

NT: B.687b; CB.—; K.—.
OT: —.
GEN. REF.: —.

POSSESS, POSSESSION

A. Verbs.

1. *katechō* [κατέχω, 2722], to hold fast, hold back, signifies to possess, in 1 Cor. 7:30 and 2 Cor. 6:10. See HOLD.

NT: B.422c; CB.1254b; K.286.
OT: 'āḥaz: S.270; HR.750c.1; H.64; BD.28a.
ḥāzaq: S.2388; HR.750c.5; H.636; BD.304a.
GEN. REF.: IS.3:910; NB.—; Z.—.

2. *ktaomai* [κτάομαι, 2932], to procure for oneself, acquire, obtain, hence, to possess (akin to B, No. 1), has this meaning in Luke 18:12 and 1 Thess. 4:4; in Luke 21:19, R.V., "ye shall win" (A.V., "possess ye"), where the probable meaning is 'ye shall gain the mastery over your souls,' i.e., instead of giving way to adverse circumstances. See OBTAIN.

NT: B.455a; CB.1256a; K.—.
OT: qānāh: S.7069; HR.793b.9a; H.2039; BD.888d.
GEN. REF.: IS.3:910; NB.—; Z.—.

3. *huparchō* [ὑπάρχω, 5225], to be in existence, and, in a secondary sense, to belong to, is used with this meaning in the neuter plural of the present participle with the article signifying one's possessions, "the things which he possesseth," Luke 12:15; Acts 4:32; in Heb. 10:34, R.V., "possessions" (A.V., "goods"); cp. B, No. 4. See GOODS.

NT: B.838a; CB.—; K.—.
OT: miqneh: S.4735; HR.1406b.4h; H.2039b; BD.889b.
r^{e}kûsh: S.7399; HR.1406b.4l; H.2167b; BD.940d.
GEN. REF.: —.

4. *daimonizomai* [δαιμονίζομαι, 1139], to be possessed of a demon or demons: see DEMON, B.

NT: B.169a; CB.1240b; K.137.
OT: —.
GEN. REF.: IS.—; NB.1010; Z.2:92.

Note: In Acts 8:7 and 16:16, A.V., *echō*, have, is translated to be possessed of, in the sense of No. 4, above, R.V., "had" and "having."

B. Nouns.

1. *ktēma* [κτῆμα, 2933], akin to A, No. 2, denotes a possession, property, Matt. 19:22; Mark 10:22; Acts 2:45; 5:1. ¶

NT: B.455b; CB.1256a; K.—.
OT: kerem: S.3754; HR.793c.2a; H.1040a; BD.501c.
naḥ^{a}lāh: S.5159; HR.793c.3; H.1342a; BD.635a.
GEN. REF.: IS.3:910; NB.—; Z.—.

2. *kataschesis* [κατάσχεσις, 2697], primarily a holding back (akin to A, No. 1), then, a holding fast, denotes a possession, Acts 7:5, or taking possession, ver. 45, with the article, lit., 'in the (i.e., their) taking possession.' ¶

NT: B.419c; CB.—; K.—.
OT: '^{a}huzzāh: S.272; HR.746b.1; H.64a; BD.28c.
GEN. REF.: IS.3:910; NB.—; Z.—.

3. *peripoiēsis* [περιποίησις, 4047], an obtaining, an acquisition, is translated (*God's* own) possession" in Eph. 1:14, R.V., which may mean 'acquisition,' A.V., "purchased possession"; 1 Pet. 2:9, R.V., "*God's* own possession," A.V., "a peculiar (people)." See OBTAIN.

NT: B.650a; CB.1263b; K.—.
OT: miḥyāh: S.4241; HR.1125c.1; H.644b; BD.313c.
s^{e}gullāh: S.5459; HR.1125c.2; H.1460a; BD.688c.
GEN. REF.: IS.3:910; NB.—; Z.—.

4. *huparxis* [ὕπαρξις, 5223], primarily subsistence (akin to A, No. 3), later denoted substance, property, "possession" in Heb. 10:34, R.V. (A.V., "substance"). See GOODS, SUBSTANCE.

NT: B.837d; CB.1252a; K.—.
OT: hôn: S.1952; HR.1406b.1; H.487a; BD.223c.
r^{e}kûsh: S.7399; HR.1406b.4; H.2167b; BD.940d.
GEN. REF.: IS.3:910; NB.—; Z.—.

Note: In Acts 28:7, A.V., *chōria*, lands (R.V.), is translated "possessions."

C. Adjective.

periousios [περιούσιος, 4041], of one's own possession, one's own, qualifies the noun *laos*, people, in Tit. 2:14, A.V., "peculiar," see R.V. ¶ In the Sept., Ex. 19:5; 23:22; Deut. 7:6; 14:2; 26:18. ¶

NT: B.648d; CB.—; K.828.
OT: s^{e}gullāh: S.5459; HR.1125a.1; H.1460a; BD.688c.
GEN. REF.: IS.3:910; NB.—; Z.—.

POSSESSOR

ktētōr [κτήτωρ, 2935], a possessor, an owner (akin to *ktaomai*, see POSSESS, No. 2), occurs in Acts 4:34. ¶

NT: B.455c; CB.—; K.—.
OT: —.
GEN. REF.: IS.3:910; NB.—; Z.—.

POSSIBLE

A. Adjective.

dunatos [δυνατός, 1415], strong, mighty, powerful, able (to do), in its neuter form signifies "possible," Matt. 19:26; 24:24; 26:39; Mark 9:23; 10:27; 13:22; 14:35, 36; Luke

18:27; Acts 2:24; 20:16 (27:39, in some mss.; *dunamai*, to be able, in the most authentic, R.V., "they could"); Rom. 12:18; Gal. 4:15. See ABLE.

NT: B.208c; CB.1242b; K.186.
OT: gibbôr: S.1368; HR.355c.6c; H.310b; BD.150a.
ḥayil: S.2428; HR.355c.9a; H.624a; BD.298c.
GEN. REF.: –.

B. Verb.

eimi [εἰμί, 1510], to be, is used in the third person singular, impersonally, with the meaning "it is possible," negatively in 1 Cor. 11:20, R.V. (A.V., "it is not"), and Heb. 9:5, "we cannot," lit., 'it is not possible.'

NT: B.222d; CB.1243a; K.206.
OT: –.
GEN. REF.: –.

Note: For Heb. 10:4, A.V., "it is not possible," see IMPOSSIBLE.

POT

1. *xestēs* [ξέστης, 3582], was a Sicilian corruption of the Latin liquid measure *sextaurius*, about a pint; in Mark 7:4 (ver. 8 also in some mss.) it denotes a pitcher, of wood or stone. ¶

NT: B.548b; CB.–; K.–.
OT: –.
GEN. REF.: IS.3:912; NB.–; Z.–.

2. *stamnos* [στάμνος, 4713], primarily an earthen jar for racking off wine, hence, any kind of jar, occurs in Heb. 9:4. ¶

NT: B.764b; CB.–; K.–.
OT: baqbuk: S.1228; HR.1286c.1; H.273a; BD.132d.
GEN. REF.: IS.–; NB.–; Z.4:829.

For **POTENTATE**, used of God, 1 Tim. 6:15, see **AUTHORITY**, No. 4

POTTER

A. Noun.

kerameus [κεραμεύς, 2763], a potter (from *kerannumi*, to mix, akin to *keramos*, potter's clay), is used (*a*) in connection with the "potter's field," Matt. 27:7, 10; (*b*) illustratively of the potter's right over the clay, Rom. 9:21, where the introductory "or" suggests the alternatives that either there must be a recognition of the absolute discretion and power of God, or a denial that the potter has power over the clay. There is no suggestion of the creation of sinful beings, or of the creation of any simply in order to punish them. What the passage sets forth is God's right to deal with sinful beings according to His own counsel. ¶

NT: B.428d; CB.1255a; K.–.
OT: yāṣar: S.3335; HR.759b.1; H.898; BD.427c.
GEN. REF.: IS.3:919; NB.–; Z.4:824.

B. Adjective.

keramikos [κεραμικός, 2764], denotes 'of (or made by) a potter' (Eng., ceramic), earthen, Rev. 2:27. ¶

NT: B.428d; CB.1255a; K.–.
OT: peḥār (Aramaic): S.6353; HR.759c.1; H.2937; BD.1108b.
GEN. REF.: IS.–; NB.–; Z.4:824.

POUND

1. *litra* [λίτρα, 3046] was a Sicilian coin, the equivalent of a Latin *libra* or *as* (whence the metric unit, litre); in the N.T. it is used as a measure of weight, a pound, John 12:3; 19:39. ¶

NT: B.475d; CB.–; K.–.
OT: –.
GEN. REF.: IS.4:1055; NB.–; Z.5:921.

2. *mina* [μνᾶ, 3414], a Semitic word, both a weight and a sum of money, 100 shekels (cp. 1 Kings 10:17, *maneh*; Dan. 5:25, 26, *mene*), in Attic Greek 100 *drachmai*, in weight about 15 oz., in value near about £4 1s. 3d. (see PIECE), occurs in Luke 19:13, 16 (twice), 18 (twice), 20, 24 (twice), 25. ¶

NT: B.524a; CB.–; K.–.
OT: māneh: S.4488; HR.931a.2; H.1213b; BD.584b.
GEN. REF.: IS.4:1052; NB.1320; Z.5:920.

POUR

1. *ballō* [βάλλω, 906], to throw, is used of pouring liquids, Matt. 26:12, R.V., marg., "cast" (of ointment); John 13:5 (of water). See CAST, No. 1.

NT: B.130d; CB.1238b; K.91.
OT: nāphal: S.5307; HR.189c.6b; H.1392; BD.656c.
GEN. REF.: –.

2. *katacheō* [καταχέω, 2708], to pour down upon (*kata*, down, *cheō*, to pour), is used in Matt. 26:7 (cp. No. 1 in ver. 12) and Mark 14:3, of ointment. ¶

NT: B.420c; CB.–; K.–.
OT: yāṣaq: S.3332; HR.748c.1; H.897; BD.427a.
nāṭāh: S.5186; HR.748c.2; H.1352; BD.639d.
GEN. REF.: –.

3. *ekcheō* [ἐκχέω, 1632], to pour out (*ek*, out), is used (*a*) of Christ's act as to the changers' money, John 2:15; (*b*) of the Holy Spirit, Acts 2:17, 18, 33, R.V., "He hath poured forth" (A.V., ". . . shed forth"); Tit. 3:6, R.V., "poured out" (A.V., "shed"); (*c*) of the emptying of the contents of the bowls (A.V., vials) of Divine wrath, Rev. 16:1-4, 8, 10, 12, 17; (*d*) of the shedding of the blood of saints by the foes of God, Rev. 16:6, R.V., "poured out" (A.V., "shed"); some mss. have it in Acts 22:20. See RUN, SHED, SPILL.

NT: B.247b; CB.1243b; K.220.
OT: shāphak: S.8210; HR.445c.12; H.2444; BD.1049b.
GEN. REF.: –.

4. *ekchunō* [ἐκχύνω, 1632], or *ekchunnō*, a Hellenistic form of No. 3, is used of the blood of Christ, Luke 22:20, R.V., "is poured out" (A.V., "is shed"); of the Holy Spirit, Acts 10:45. See GUSH OUT, RUN, SHED, SPILL.
NT: B.247c; CB.1243b; K.220.
OT: –.
GEN. REF.: –.

5. *epicheō* [ἐπιχέω, 2022], to pour upon (*epi*), is used in Luke 10:34, of the oil and wine used by the good Samaritan on the wounds of him who had fallen among robbers. ¶
NT: B.305a; CB.–; K.–.
OT: yāṣaq: S.3332; HR.538c.2; H.897; BD.427a.
GEN. REF.: –.

Note: For the A.V., "poured out" in Rev. 14:10 (R.V., "prepared"), see MINGLE, No. 2.

POVERTY

ptōcheia [πτωχεία, 4432], destitution (akin to *ptōcheuō*, see POOR, is used of the poverty which Christ voluntarily experienced on our behalf, 2 Cor. 8:9; of the destitute condition of saints in Judaea, ver. 2; of the condition of the church in Smyrna, Rev. 2:9, where the word is used in a general sense. Cp. synonymous words under POOR. ¶
NT: B.728a; CB.1268a; K.969.
OT: ʿᵒnî: S.6040; HR.1239b.2; H.1652e; BD.777a.
GEN. REF.: IS.3:921; NB.1016; Z.4:830.

For **POWDER** see **GRIND**

POWER (Noun, and Verb, to have, bring under)

A. Nouns.

1. *dunamis* [δύναμις, 1411], for the different meanings of which see ABILITY, MIGHT, is sometimes used, by metonymy, of persons and things, e.g., (*a*) of God, Matt. 26:64; Mark 14:62; (*b*) of angels, e.g., perhaps in Eph. 1:21, R.V., "power," A.V., "might" (cp. Rom. 8:38; 1 Pet. 3:22); (*c*) of that which manifests God's power: Christ, 1 Cor. 1:24; the Gospel, Rom. 1:16; (*d*) of mighty works (R.V., marg., "power" or "powers"), e.g., Mark 6:5, "mighty work"; so 9:39, R.V. (A.V., "miracle"); Acts 2:22 (ditto); 8:13, "miracles"; 2 Cor. 12:12, R.V., "mighty works" (A.V., "mighty deeds").
NT: B.207b; CB.1242b; K.186.
OT: ḥayil: S.2428; HR.350a.11; H.624a; BD.298c.
ṣābā': S.6635; HR.350a.25; H.1865a,b; BD.838d.
GEN. REF.: IS.3:926,927; NB.1017; Z.4:830.

Note: For different meanings of synonymous terms, see *Note* under DOMINION, A, No. 1.

2. *exousia* [ἐξουσία, 1849], denotes freedom of action, right to act; used of God, it is absolute, unrestricted, e.g., Luke 12:5 (R.V., marg., "authority"); in Acts 1:7 'right of disposal' is what is indicated; used of men, authority is delegated. Angelic beings are called "powers" in Eph. 3:10 (cp. 1:21); 6:12; Col. 1:16; 2:15 (cp. 2:10). See AUTHORITY, No. 1, see also PRINCIPALITY.
NT: B.277d; CB.1247c; K.238.
OT: memshālāh: S.4475; HR.500c.2; H.1259c; BD.606a.
shālṭān (Aramaic): S.7981; HR.500c.3b; H.3034; BD.1115d.
GEN. REF.: IS.3:926,927; NB.1017; Z.4:830.

3. *ischus* [ἰσχύς, 2479], ability, force, strength, is nowhere translated "power" in the R.V. (A.V. in 2 Thess. 1:9). See ABILITY, No. 2.
NT: B.383a; CB.1253a; K.378.
OT: kōaḥ: S.3581; HR.694b.16; H.971.1; BD.470d.
ḥayil: S.2428; HR.694b.13; H.624a; BD.298c.
GEN. REF.: IS.3:926,927; NB.1017; Z.4:830.

4. *kratos* [κράτος, 2904], is translated "power" in the R.V. and A.V. in 1 Tim. 6:16; Heb. 2:14; in Eph. 1:19 (last part); 6:10, A.V., "power" (R.V., "strength"): see DOMINION, A, No. 1, STRENGTH, A, No. 3.
NT: B.449a; CB.1256a; K.466.
OT: ʿōz: S.5797; HR.784a.6; H.1596b; BD.738d.
'ammiṣ: S.533; HR.784a.2; H.117d; BD.55c.
GEN. REF.: IS.3:926,927; NB.1017; Z.4:830.

5. *dunaton* [δυνατόν, 1415], the neuter of the adjective *dunatos*, powerful (akin to No. 1), is used as a noun with the article in Rom. 9:22, "(to make His) power (known)." See ABLE.
NT: B.208c; CB.1242b; K.186.
OT: gibbôr: S.1368; HR.355c.6c; H.310b; BD.150a.
ḥayil: S.2428; HR.355c.9a; H.624a; BD.298c.
GEN. REF.: IS.3:926,927; NB.1017; Z.4:830.

6. *archē* [ἀρχή, 746], a beginning, rule, is translated "power" in Luke 20:20, A.V. (R.V., "rule"). See BEGINNING, B.
NT: B.111d; CB.1237b; K.81.
OT: rō'sh: S.7218; HR.164a.20a; H.2097e; BD.910c.
rē'shît: S.7225; HR.164a.20c; H.2097e; BD.912a.
tᵉḥillāh: S.8462; HR.164a.23; H.661d; BD.321a.
GEN. REF.: –.

B. Verb.

exousiazō [ἐξουσιάζω, 1850], to exercise authority (akin to A, No. 2), is used (*a*) in the Active Voice, Luke 22:25, R.V., "have authority" (A.V., "exercise authority"), of the power of rulers; 1 Cor. 7:4 (twice), of marital relations and conditions; (*b*) in the Passive Voice, 1 Cor. 6:12, to be brought under the power of a thing; here, this verb and the preceding one connected with it, *exesti*, present a paranomasia, which Lightfoot brings out as follows: 'All are within my power; but I will not put myself under the power of any one of all things.' See AUTHORITY, B, No. 1. ¶
NT: B.279a; CB.1247c; K.238.
OT: shālaṭ: S.7980; HR.501b.2a,b; H.2396; BD.1020c.
shallîṭ: S.7989; HR.501b.2c; H.2396a; BD.1020c.
GEN. REF.: IS.3:926; NB.1017; Z.4:830.

Notes: (1) In Rev. 13:14, 15, A.V., *didōmi*, to give, is translated "(he) had power"; R.V., "it was given (him)" and "it was given *unto him*"; the A.V. misses the force of the permissive will of God in the actings of the Beast.

(2) In Rom. 16:25, A.V., *dunamai*, to be able, is translated "that is of power" (R.V., "that is able"). See ABLE.

(3) The subject of power in Scripture may be viewed under the following heads: (*a*) its original source, in the Persons in the Godhead; (*b*) its exercise by God in creation, its preservation and its government; (*c*) special manifestations of Divine power, past, present and future; (*d*) power existent in created beings, other than man, and in inanimate nature; (*e*) committed to man, and misused by him; (*f*) committed to those who, on becoming believers, were empowered by the Spirit of God, are indwelt by Him, and will exercise it hereafter for God's glory.

POWERFUL, POWERFULLY

A. Adjectives.

1. *energēs* [ἐνεργής, —]: see ACTIVE.

2. *ischuros* [ἰσχυρός, 2478], strong, mighty, akin to *ischus* (see POWER, A, No. 3), is translated "powerful" in 2 Cor. 10:10, A.V. (R.V., "strong"). See STRONG.

NT: B.383a; CB.1253a; K.378.
OT: gibbôr: S.1368; HR.693b.10a; H.310b; BD.150a.
'āṣûm: S.6099; HR.693b.19; H.1673d; BD.783a.
'ēl: S.410; HR.693b.5; H.93a; BD.42b.
GEN. REF.: IS.3:926; NB.1017; Z.4:830.

B. Adverb.

eutonōs [εὐτόνως, 2159], signifies vigorously, vehemently (*eu*, well, *teinō*, to stretch), Luke 23:10, "vehemently," of the accusation of the chief priests and scribes against Christ; Acts 18:28, R.V., "powerfully" (A.V., "mightily"), of Apollos in confuting Jews. ¶ In the Sept., Josh. 6:8. ¶

NT: B.327b; CB.—; K.—.
OT: (ba)shôphār(ôt): S.7782; HR.581a.1; H.2449c; BD.1051c.
GEN. REF.: —.

Note: For "is powerful," 2 Cor. 13:3, R.V., see MIGHTY, C.

For **PRACTICES** see **COVETOUS**, B, No. 3

PRACTISE

prassō [πράσσω, 4238], is translated by the verb to practise in the R.V. in the following passages (the A.V. nowhere renders the verb thus): John 3:20 (marg.); 5:29 (marg.); Acts 19:19; Rom. 1:32 (twice); 2:1, 2, 3; 7:15, 19; Gal. 5:21. See DO, No. 2.

NT: B.698b; CB.1266b; K.927.
OT: 'āsāh: S.6213; HR.1201a.3; H.1708,1709; BD.793c.
pā'al: S.6466; HR.1201a.4; H.1792; BD.821b.
GEN. REF.: —.

For **PRAETORIUM** and **PRAETORIAN GUARD** see **PALACE**

PRAISE

A. Nouns.

1. *ainos* [αἶνος, 136], primarily a tale, narration, came to denote praise; in the N.T. only of praise to God, Matt. 21:16; Luke 18:43. ¶

NT: B.23d; CB.1234a; K.27.
OT: hālal: S.1984; HR.34b.1; H.499,500; BD.237d.
GEN. REF.: IS.3:930; NB.1018; Z.4:834.

2. *epainos* [ἔπαινος, 1868], a strengthened form of No. 1 (*epi*, upon), denotes approbation, commendation, praise; it is used (*a*) of those on account of, and by reason of, whom as God's heritage, praise is to be ascribed to God, in respect of His glory (the exhibition of His character and operations), Eph. 1:12; in ver. 14, of the whole company, the Church, viewed as "*God's* own possession" (R.V.); in ver. 6, with particular reference to the glory of His grace towards them; in Phil. 1:11, as the result of "the fruits of righteousness" manifested in them through the power of Christ; (*b*) of praise bestowed by God, upon the Jew spiritually (Judah = praise), Rom. 2:29; bestowed upon believers hereafter at the Judgment-Seat of Christ, 1 Cor. 4:5 (where the definite article indicates that the praise will be exactly in accordance with each person's actions); as the issue of present trials, "at the revelation of Jesus Christ," 1 Pet. 1:7; (*c*) of whatsoever is praiseworthy, Phil. 4:8; (*d*) of the approbation by churches of those who labour faithfully in the ministry of the Gospel, 2 Cor. 8:18; (*e*) of the approbation of well-doers by human rulers, Rom. 13:3; 1 Pet. 2:14. ¶

NT: B.281c; CB.1245b; K.242.
OT: t^{e}hillāh: S.8416; HR.504c.3; H.500c; BD.239d.
ḥemdāh: S.2532; HR.504c.2; H.673b; BD.326c.
GEN. REF.: IS.3:930; NB.—; Z.4:834.

3. *ainesis* [αἴνεσις, 133], praise (akin to No. 1), is found in Heb. 13:15, where it is metaphorically represented as a sacrificial offering. ¶

NT: B.23c; CB.1234a; K.—.
OT: tôdāh: S.8426; HR.33c.1b; H.847b; BD.392d.
t^{e}hillāh: S.8416; HR.33c.2b; H.500c; BD.239d.
GEN. REF.: IS.3:930; NB.—; Z.4:834.

Notes: (1) In 1 Pet. 2:9, A.V., *aretē*, virtue, excellence, is translated "praises" (R.V., "excellencies").

(2) In the following the A.V. translates *doxa*, glory, by "praise" (R.V., "glory"); John 9:24, where "give glory to God" signifies 'confess thy sins' (cp. Josh. 7:19, indicating the genuine

confession of facts in one's life which gives glory to God); 12:43 (twice); 1 Pet. 4:11.

B. Verbs.

1. *aineō* [αἰνέω, 134], to speak in praise of, to praise (akin to A, No. 1), is always used of praise to God, (*a*) by angels, Luke 2:13; (*b*) by men, Luke 2:20; 19:37; 24:53; Acts 2:20, 47; 3:8, 9; Rom. 15:11 (No. 2 in some texts); Rev. 19:5. ¶

NT: B.23c; CB.1233a; K.27.
OT: hālal: S.1984; HR.33a.2a; H.499,500; BD.237d.
yādāh: S.3034; HR.33a.3; H.847; BD.392a.
GEN. REF.: IS.3:930; NB.1018; Z.4:834.

2. *epaineō* [ἐπαινέω, 1867], akin to A, No. 2, is rendered "praise," 1 Cor. 11:2, 17, 22: see COMMEND, No. 1.

NT: B.281c; CB.1245b; K.—.
OT: hālal: S.1984; HR.504c.1; H.499,500; BD.237d.
shābaḥ: S.7623; HR.504c.2; H.2312,2313; BD.986c.
GEN. REF.: IS.3:930; NB.1018; Z.4:834.

3. *humneō* [ὑμνέω, 5214], denotes (*a*) transitively, to sing, to laud, sing to the praise of (Eng., hymn), Acts 16:25, A.V., "sang praises" (R.V., "singing hymns"); Heb. 2:12, R.V., "will I sing (Thy) praise," A.V., "will I sing praise (unto Thee)," lit., 'I will hymn Thee'; (*b*) intransitively, to sing, Matt. 26:30; Mark 14:26, in both places of the singing of the paschal hymns (Psa. 113-118, and 136), called by Jews the Great Hallel. ¶

NT: B.836b; CB.1251b; K.1225.
OT: hālal: S.1984; HR.1405a.1; H.499,500; BD.237d.
shîr: S.7891; HR.1405a.6; H.2378; BD.1010c.
GEN. REF.: IS.3:930; NB.1018; Z.4:834.

4. *psallō* [ψάλλω, 5567], primarily, to twitch or twang (as a bowstring, etc.), then, to play (a stringed instrument with the fingers), in the Sept., to sing psalms, denotes, in the N.T., to sing a hymn, sing praise; in Jas. 5:13, R.V., "sing praise" (A.V., "sing psalms"). See MELODY, SING.

NT: B.891a; CB.1267b; K.1225.
OT: zāmar: S.2167; HR.1483a.1; H.558; BD.274a.
nāgan: S.5059; HR.1483a.2; H.1291.1; BD.618c.
GEN. REF.: IS.3:930; NB.1018; Z.4:834.

5. *exomologeō* [ἐξομολογέω, 1843], in Rom. 15:9, R.V., "will I give praise" (A.V., and R.V. marg., "I will confess"): see CONFESS, A, No. 2 (*c*).

NT: B.277a; CB.—; K.687.
OT: yādāh: S.3034; HR.499a.3b; H.847; BD.392a.
GEN. REF.: IS.3:930; NB.1018; Z.—.

Note: In Luke 1:64, A.V., *eulogeō*, to bless, is translated "praised" (R.V., "blessing").

PRATE

phluareō [φλυαρέω, 5396], signifies to talk nonsense (from *phluō*, to babble; cp. the adjective *phluaros*, babbling, garrulous, "tattlers," 1 Tim. 5:13), to raise false accusations, 3 John 10. ¶

NT: B.862b; CB.—; K.—.
OT: —.
GEN. REF.: —.

PRAY, PRAYER

A. Verbs.

1. *euchomai* [εὔχομαι, 2172], to pray (to God), is used with this meaning in 2 Cor. 13:7; ver. 9, R.V., "pray" (A.V., "wish"); Jas. 5:16; 3 John 2, R.V., "pray" (A.V., wish). Even when the R.V. and A.V. translate by "I would," Acts 26:29, or "wished for," Acts 27:29 (R.V., marg., "prayed"), or "could wish," Rom. 9:3 (R.V., marg., "could pray"), the indication is that prayer is involved. ¶

NT: B.329b; CB.1247a; K.279.
OT: nādar: S.5087; HR.583c.4a; H.1308; BD.623d.
'ātar: S.6279; HR.583c.7; H.1722; BD.801c.
GEN. REF.: IS.3:931; NB.1019; Z.4:835.

2. *proseuchomai* [προσεύχομαι, 4336], to pray, is always used of prayer to God, and is the most frequent word in this respect, especially in the Synoptists and Acts, once in Romans, 8:26; in Ephesians, 6:18; in Philippians, 1:9; in 1 Timothy, 2:8; in Hebrews, 13:18; in Jude, ver. 20. For the injunction in 1 Thess. 5:17, see CEASE, C.

NT: B.713b; CB.1267a; K.279.
OT: pālal: S.6419; HR.1214a.3b; H.1776; BD.813a.
GEN. REF.: IS.3:931; NB.1019; Z.4:835.

3. *erōtaō* [ἐρωτάω, 2065], to ask, is translated by the verb to pray in Luke 14:18, 19; 16:27; John 4:31; 14:16; 16:26; 17:9, 15, 20; in Acts 23:18, R.V., "asked" (A.V. "prayed"); in 1 John 5:16, R.V., "should make request" (A.V. "shall pray"). See ASK, A, No. 2.

NT: B.311d; CB.1246c; K.262.
OT: shā'al: S.7592; HR.553b.3; H.2303; BD.981b.
GEN. REF.: IS.3:931; NB.1019; Z.4:835.

4. *deomai* [δέομαι, 1189], to desire, in 2 Cor. 5:20; 8:4, R.V., "beseech" (A.V., "pray"): see BESEECH, No. 3.

NT: B.175a; CB.1240c; K.144.
OT: ḥānan: S.2603; HR.288a.8a-c; H.694,695; BD.335d.
GEN. REF.: IS.3:931; NB.1019; Z.4:835.

Notes: (1) *Parakaleō*, to call to one's aid, is rendered by the verb to pray in the A.V. in the following: Matt. 26:53 (R.V., "beseech"); so Mark 5:17, 18; Acts 16:9; in 24:4, R.V., "intreat"; in 27:34, R.V., "beseech." See BESEECH, No. 1.

(2) In 1 Thess. 5:23 and 2 Tim. 4:16, there is no word in the original for "I Pray," see the R.V.

B. Nouns.

1. *euchē* [εὐχή, 2171], akin to A, No. 1, denotes a prayer, Jas. 5:15; a vow, Acts 18:18 and 21:23. See VOW. ¶

NT: B.329b; CB.1247a; K.279.
OT: neder, nēder: S.5088; HR.584b.2b; H.1308a; BD.623d.
nēzer: S.5145; HR.584b.3b; H.1340a; BD.634b.
GEN. REF.: IS.3:931; NB.1019; Z.4:835.

2. *proseuchē* [προσευχή, 4335], akin to A, No. 2, denotes (*a*) prayer (to God), the most frequent term, e.g., Matt. 21:22; Luke 6:12, where the phrase is not to be taken literally as if it meant, 'the prayer of God' (subjective genitive), but objectively, "prayer to God." In Jas. 5:17, "He prayed fervently," R.V., is, lit., 'he prayed with prayer' (a Hebraistic form); in the following the word is used with No. 3: Eph. 6:18; Phil. 4:6; 1 Tim. 2:1; 5:5; (*b*) "a place of prayer," Acts 16:13, 16, a place outside the city wall, R.V.

NT: B.713b; CB.1267a; K.279.
OT: t^{e}phillāh: S.8605; HR.1214c.3; H.1776a; BD.813c.
GEN. REF.: IS.3:931; NB.1019; Z.4:835.

3. *deēsis* [δέησις, 1162], primarily a wanting, a need (akin to A, No. 4), then, an asking, entreaty, supplication, in the N.T. is always addressed to God and always rendered "supplication" or "supplications" in the R.V.; in the A.V. "prayer," or "prayers," in Luke 1:13; 2:37; 5:33; Rom. 10:1; 2 Cor. 1:11; 9:14; Phil. 1:4 (in the 2nd part, "request"); 1:19; 2 Tim. 1:3; Heb. 5:7; Jas. 5:16; 1 Pet. 3:12.

NT: B.171d; CB.1240b; K.143.
OT: t^{e}ḥinnāh: S.8467; HR.285c.8a; H.694f; BD.337c.
taḥ^{a}nûn: S.8469; HR.285c.8b; H.694g; BD.337c.
rinnāh: S.7440; HR.285c.5; H.2179c; BD.943c.
GEN. REF.: IS.3:931; NB.1019; Z.4:835.

4. *enteuxis* [ἔντευξις, 1783], is translated "prayer" in 1 Tim. 4:5; see INTERCESSION.

NT: B.268d; CB.1245b; K.1191.
OT: —.
GEN. REF.: IS.3:931; NB.1019; Z.—.

Notes: (1) *Proseuchē* is used of prayer in general; *deēsis* stresses the sense of need; it is used sometimes of request from man to man.

(2) In the papyri *enteuxis* is the regular word for a petition to a superior. For the synonymous word *aitēma* see PETITION; for *hiketēria*, Heb. 5:7, see SUPPLICATION.

(3) "Prayer is properly addressed to God the Father, Matt. 6:6; John 16:23; Eph. 1:17; 3:14, and the Son, Acts 7:59; 2 Cor. 12:8; but in no instance in the N.T. is prayer addressed to the Holy Spirit distinctively, for whereas the Father is in Heaven, Matt. 6:9, and the Son is at His right hand, Rom. 8:34, the Holy Spirit is in and with the believers, John 14:16, 17.

"Prayer is to be offered in the Name of the Lord Jesus, John 14:13, that is, the prayer must accord with His character, and must be presented in the same spirit of dependence and submission that marked Him, Matt. 11:26; Luke 22:42.

"The Holy Spirit, being the sole interpreter of the needs of the human heart, makes His intercession therein; and inasmuch as prayer is impossible to man apart from His help, Rom. 8:26, believers are exhorted to pray at all seasons in the Spirit, Eph. 6:18; cp. Jude 20, and Jas. 5:16, the last clause of which should probably be read 'the inwrought [i.e., by the Holy Spirit] supplication of a righteous man availeth much' (or 'greatly prevails,' *ischuō*, as in Acts 19:16, 20).

"None the less on this account is the understanding to be engaged in prayer, 1 Cor. 14:15, and the will, Col. 4:12; Acts 12:5 (where 'earnestly' is, lit., 'stretched out') and so in Luke 22:44.

"Faith is essential to prayer, Matt. 21:22; Mark 11:24; Jas. 1:5-8, for faith is the recognition of, and the committal of ourselves and our matters to, the faithfulness of God.

"Where the Jews were numerous, as at Thessalonica, they had usually a Synagogue, Acts 17:1; where they were few, as at Philippi, they had merely a *proseuchē*, or 'place of prayer,' of much smaller dimensions, and commonly built by a river for the sake of the water necessary to the preliminary ablutions prescribed by Rabbinic tradition, Acts 16:13, 16."*

PREACH, PREACHING

A. Verbs.

1. *euangelizō* [εὐαγγελίζω, 2097], is almost always used of the good news concerning the Son of God as proclaimed in the Gospel [exceptions are, e.g., Luke 1:19; 1 Thess. 3:6, in which the phrase "to bring (or shew) good (or glad) tidings" does not refer to the Gospel]; Gal. 1:8 (2nd part). With reference to the Gospel the phrase to bring, or declare, good, or glad, tidings is used in Acts 13:32; Rom. 10:15; Heb. 4:2.

In Luke 4:18 the R.V. "to preach good tidings" gives the correct quotation from Isaiah, rather than the A.V. "to preach the Gospel." In the Sept. the verb is used of any message intended to cheer the hearers, e.g., 1 Sam. 31:9; 2 Sam. 1:20. See GOSPEL, B, No. 1.

NT: B.317b; CB.1247a; K.—.
OT: bāsar: S.1319; HR.568b.1a; H.291; BD.142a.
GEN. REF.: IS.3:940; NB.1023; Z.4:844.

2. *kērussō* [κηρύσσω, 2784], signifies (*a*) to be a herald, or, in general, to proclaim, e.g., Matt. 3:1; Mark 1:45, "publish"; in Luke 4:18, R.V., "to proclaim," A.V., "to preach"; so verse 19; Luke 12:3; Acts 10:37; Rom. 2:21; Rev. 5:2. In 1 Pet. 3:19 the probable reference is, not to glad tidings (which there is no real evidence that Noah preached, nor is there evidence that the

* From Notes on Thessalonians by Hogg and Vine, pp. 189, 190.

spirits of antediluvian people are actually "in prison"), but to the act of Christ after His resurrection in proclaiming His victory to fallen angelic spirits; (*b*) to preach the Gospel as a herald, e.g., Matt. 24:14; Mark 13:10, R.V., "be preached" (A.V., "be published"); 14:9; 16:15, 20; Luke 8:1; 9:2; 24:47; Acts 8:5; 19:13; 28:31; Rom. 10:14, present participle, lit., '(one) preaching,' "a preacher"; 10:15 (1st part); 1 Cor. 1:23; 15:11 12; 2 Cor. 1:19; 4:5; 11:4; Gal. 2:2; Phil. 1:15; Col. 1:23; 1 Thess. 2:9; 1 Tim. 3:16; (*c*) to preach the word, 2 Tim. 4:2 (of the ministry of the Scriptures, with special reference to the Gospel). See PROCLAIM, PUBLISH.

NT: B.431b; CB.1255a; K.430.
OT: qārā': S.7121; HR.763c.5a; H.2063; BD.894d.
GEN. REF.: IS.3:940; NB.1023; Z.4:844.

3. *proeuangelizomai* [*προευαγγελίζομαι*, —]: see GOSPEL, B, No. 2.

4. *prokērussō* [*προκηρύσσω*, 4296], lit., to proclaim as a herald (*pro*, before, and No. 2), is used in Acts 13:24, "had first preached." Some mss. have the verb in Acts 3:20; for the best see APPOINT, No. 12. ¶

NT: B.707d; CB.—; K.430.
OT: —.
GEN. REF.: IS.3:940; NB.1023; Z.4:844.

5. *parrhēsiazomai* [*παρρησιάζομαι*, 3955], to be bold in speech, is translated to preach boldly in Acts 9:27 (2nd part); in ver. 29, R.V. (A.V., "he spake boldly"). See BOLD, A, No. 2.

NT: B.631a; CB.1262c; K.794.
OT: —.
GEN. REF.: IS.3:940; NB.1023; Z.—.

Notes: (1) For *diangellō*, translated "preach" in Luke 9:60, see DECLARE, A, No. 3.

(2) *Katangellō*, to proclaim, is always so translated in the R.V.; the A.V. renders it by to preach in Acts 4:2; 13:5, 38; 15:36; 17:3, 13; 1 Cor. 9:14; Col. 1:28.

(3) *Laleō*, to speak, is translated "preached," Mark 2:2, A.V., "preached" (R.V., "spake"); in Acts 8:25, 1st part, A.V. (R.V., "spoken"); so in 13:42 and 14:25; "preaching" in Acts 11:19, A.V., but what is indicated here is not a formal preaching by the believers scattered from Jerusalem, but a general testimony to all with whom they came into contact; in 16:6, R.V., "to speak" (A.V., "to preach").

(4) For *dialegomai*, in A.V. of Acts 20:7, 9, see DISCOURSE.

(5) For A.V., "preached" in Heb. 4:2 (2nd part), see HEARING.

(6) In Rom. 15:19 *plēroō*, to fulfil (R.V., marg.), is rendered 'I have fully preached.'

B. Nouns.

kērugma [*κήρυγμα*, 2782], a proclamation by a herald (akin to A, No. 2), denotes a message, a preaching (the substance of what is preached as distinct from the act of preaching), Matt. 12:41; Luke 11:32; Rom. 16:25; 1 Cor. 1:21; 2:4; 15:14; in 2 Tim. 4:17 and Tit. 1:3, R.V., "message," marg., "proclamation," A.V., "preaching." See MESSAGE. ¶ In the Sept., 2 Chron. 30:5; Prov. 9:3; Jonah 3:2. ¶

NT: B.430d; CB.1255a; K.430.
OT: qôl: S.6963; HR.763b.1; H.1998a,2028b; BD.876d.
q^{e}rî'āh: S.7150; HR.763b.2; H.2063c; BD.896c.
GEN. REF.: IS.3:940; NB.1023; Z.4:844.

Note: In 1 Cor. 1:18, A.V., *logos*, a word, is translated "preaching," R.V., "the word (of the Cross)," i.e., not the act of preaching, but the substance of the testimony, all that God has made known concerning the subject. For Heb. 4:2, A.V., see HEAR, B, No. 1.

PREACHER

kērux [*κῆρυξ*, 2783], a herald (akin to A, No. 2 and B, above), is used (*a*) of the preacher of the Gospel, 1 Tim. 2:7; 2 Tim. 1:11; (*b*) of Noah, as a preacher of righteousness, 2 Pet. 2:5. ¶

NT: B.431a; CB.1255a; K.430.
OT: kārôb (Aramaic): S.3744; HR.763c.1; H.2802; BD.1097d.
GEN. REF.: IS.3:942; NB.1023; Z.4:844.

Notes: (1) For "a preacher," in Rom. 10:14, where the verb *kērussō* is used, see PREACH, A, No. 2.

(2) *Kērux* indicates the preacher as giving a proclamation; *euangelistēs* points to his message as glad tidings; *apostolos* suggests his relationship to Him by whom he is sent.

PRECEDE

phthanō [*φθάνω*, 5348], to anticipate, to come sooner, is translated "shall (in no wise) precede" in 1 Thess. 4:15, R.V. (A.V., "prevent"), i.e., 'shall in no wise obtain any advantage over' (the verb does not convey the thought of a mere succession of one event after another); the Apostle, in reassuring the bereaved concerning their departed fellow-believers, declares that, as to any advantage, the dead in Christ will "rise first." See ATTAIN, No. 3, COME, No. 32.

NT: B.856d; CB.1264c; K.1258.
OT: nāga': S.5060; HR.1429b.5b; H.1293; BD.619a.
m^{e}ṭā': S.4291; HR.1429b.4; H.2825; BD.1100a.
GEN. REF.: —.

PRECEPT

1. *entolē* [ἐντολή, 1785], a commandment, is translated "precept" in Mark 10:5 (R.V., "commandment"); so Heb. 9:19. See COMMANDMENT No. 2.

NT: B.269a; CB.1245b; K.234.
OT: miṣwāh: S.4687; HR.479b.4; H.1887b; BD.846b.
GEN. REF.: IS.3:943; NB.–; Z.–.

2. *entalma* [ἔνταλμα, 1778], is always translated "precepts" in the R.V.; see COMMANDMENT, No. 3.

NT: B.268b; CB.–; K.–.
OT: miṣwāh: S.4687; HR.476c.2; H.1887b; BD.846b.
GEN. REF.: IS.3:943; NB.–; Z.–.

PRECIOUS, PRECIOUSNESS

1. *timios* [τίμιος, 5093], translated "precious," e.g., in Jas. 5:7; 1 Pet. 1:19; 2 Pet. 1:4; in 1 Cor. 3:12, A.V. (R.V., "costly"): see COSTLY, B, No. 1, DEAR, No. 1.

NT: B.818a; CB.1272c; K.–.
OT: yāqār: S.3368; HR.1353c.2a; H.905a; BD.429d.
GEN. REF.: IS.3:944; NB.–; Z.–.

2. *entimos* [ἔντιμος, 1784], "precious," 1 Pet. 2:4, 6: see DEAR, No. 2.

NT: B.268d; CB.1245b; K.–.
OT: ḥôr: S.2715; HR.479a.2; H.757a; BD.359d.
yāqar: S.3365; HR.479a.3a,b; H.905; BD.429c.
yāqār: S.3368; HR.479a.3c; H.905a; BD.429d.
GEN. REF.: IS.3:944; NB.–; Z.–.

3. *polutelēs* [πολυτελής, 4185], very expensive, translated "very precious" in Mark 14:3, A.V. (R.V., "very costly"): see COSTLY, B, No. 2.

NT: B.690a; CB.1266a; K.–.
OT: yāqār: S.–; HR.1185; H.–; BD.–.
GEN. REF.: IS.3:944; NB.–; Z.–.

4. *polutimos* [πολύτιμος, 4186], of great value; comparative degree in 1 Pet. 1:7; see COSTLY, B, No. 3, DEAR, No. 1 (for a less authentic reading).

NT: B.690a; CB.–; K.–.
OT: –.
GEN. REF.: IS.3:944; NB.–; Z.–.

5. *barutimos* [βαρύτιμος, 927], of great value, exceeding precious (*barus*, weighty, *timē*, value), is used in Matt. 26:7. ¶

NT: B.134b; CB.1238c; K.–.
OT: –.
GEN. REF.: –.

6. *isotimos* [ἰσότιμος, 2472], of equal value, held in equal honour (*isos*, equal, and *timē*), is used in 2 Pet. 1:1, "a like precious (faith)," R.V. (marg., "an equally precious"). ¶

NT: B.381b; CB.1253a; K.370.
OT: –.
GEN. REF.: –.

Note: In 1 Pet. 2:7, A.V., the noun *timē*, is translated "precious" (R.V., "preciousness"). See HONOUR, No. 1.

PREDESTINATE

proorizō [προορίζω, —]: see DETERMINE.

Note: This verb is to be distinguished from *proginōskō*, to foreknow; the latter has special reference to the persons foreknown by God; *proorizō* has special reference to that to which the subjects of His foreknowledge are predestinated. See FOREKNOW, A and B.

PRE-EMINENCE (to have the)

1. *prōteuō* [πρωτεύω, 4409], to be first (*prōtos*), to be pre-eminent, is used of Christ in relation to the Church, Col. 1:18. ¶

NT: B.725a; CB.1267b; K.965.
OT: gādal: S.1431; HR.1235b.1a; H.315; BD.152a.
nāsā': S.5375; HR.1235b.1b; H.1421; BD.669d.
GEN. REF.: IS.3:951; NB.–; Z.–.

2. *philoprōteuō* [φιλοπρωτεύω, 5383], lit., to love to be pre-eminent (*philos*, loving), to strive to be first, is said of Diotrephes, 3 John 9. ¶

NT: B.860d; CB.1264a; K.–.
OT: –.
GEN. REF.: IS.3:952; NB.–; Z.–.

PREFER, PREFERRING

proēgeomai [προηγέομαι, 4285], to go before and lead, is used in Rom. 12:10, in the sense of taking the lead in showing deference one to another, "(in honour) preferring one another." ¶

NT: B.706a; CB.–; K.303.
OT: liphnê (paneh): S.6440; HR.1206b.1; H.1782a; BD.816d,815d.
(bᵉ)rō'sh: S.7218; HR.1206b.2; H.2097; BD.910c.
GEN. REF.: –.

Notes: (1) In John 1:15, 30, A.V., *ginomai*, to become, is translated "is preferred" (R.V., "is become"); some mss. have it again in ver. 27.

(2) For *prokrima*, 1 Tim. 5:21 (A.V., "preferring one before another"), see PREJUDICE.

PREJUDICE

prokrima [πρόκριμα, 4299], denotes prejudging (akin to *prokrinō*, to judge beforehand), 1 Tim. 5:21, R.V., "prejudice" (marg., "preference"), preferring one person, another being put aside, by unfavourable judgment due to partiality. ¶

NT: B.708a; CB.1266c; K.469.
OT: –.
GEN. REF.: –.

PREMEDITATE

Note: This is the A.V. rendering of *meletaō*, to care for, which occurs in some mss. in Mark 13:11, "(neither) do ye premeditate." It is absent from the best mss. See IMAGINE.

PREPARATION, PREPARE, PREPARED

A. Nouns.

1. *hetoimasia* [ἑτοιμασία, 2091], denotes (*a*) readiness, (*b*) preparation; it is found in Eph. 6:15, of having the feet shod with the preparation of the Gospel of peace; it also has the meaning of firm footing (foundation), as in the Sept. of Ps. 89:14 (R.V., "foundation"); if that is the meaning in Eph. 6:15, the Gospel itself is to be the firm footing of the believer, his walk being worthy of it and therefore a testimony in regard to it. See READY. ¶

NT: B.316c; CB.1250b; K.266.
OT: kûn: S.3559; HR.564c.1a; H.964; BD.465c.
 mākôn: S.4349; HR.564c.1c; H.964c; BD.467c.
GEN. REF.: —.

2. *paraskeuē* [παρασκευή, 3904], denotes preparation, equipment. The day on which Christ died is called "the Preparation" in Mark 15:42 and John 19:31; in John 19:42 "the Jews' Preparation," R.V.; in 19:14 it is described as "the Preparation of the Passover"; in Luke 23:54, R.V., "the day of the Preparation (and the Sabbath drew on)." The same day is in view in Matt. 27:62, where the events recorded took place on "the day after the Preparation" (R.V.). The reference would be to the 6th day of the week. The title arose from the need of preparing food etc. for the Sabbath. Apparently it was first applied only to the afternoon of the 6th day; later, to the whole day. In regard to the phraseology in John 19:14, many hold this to indicate the preparation for the paschal feast. It probably means 'the Preparation day,' and thus falls in line with the Synoptic Gospels. In modern Greek and ecclesiastical Latin, *Parascevē* = Friday. ¶

NT: B.622b; CB.1262b; K.989.
OT: ʿ^{a}bōdāh: S.5656; HR.1064a.1; H.1553c; BD.715a.
GEN. REF.: IS.3:953; NB.1026; Z.4:848.

B. Verbs.

1. *hetoimazō* [ἑτοιμάζω, 2090], to prepare, make ready, is used (I) absolutely, e.g., Mark 14:15; Luke 9:52; (II) with an object, e.g., (*a*) of those things which are ordained (1) by God, such as future positions of authority, Matt. 20:23; the coming Kingdom, 25:34; salvation personified in Christ, Luke 2:31; future blessings, 1 Cor. 2:9; a city, Heb. 11:16; a place of refuge for the Jewish remnant, Rev. 12:6; Divine judgments on the world, Rev. 8:6; 9:7, 15; 16:12; eternal fire, for the Devil and his angels, Matt. 25:41; (2) by Christ: a place in Heaven for His followers, John 14:2, 3; (*b*) of human preparation for the Lord, e.g., Matt. 3:3; 26:17, 19; Luke 1:17 ("make ready"), 76; 3:4, A.V. (R.V., "make ye ready"); 9:52 ("to make ready"); 23:56; Rev. 19:7; 21:2; in 2 Tim. 2:21, of preparation of oneself for "every good work"; (c) of human preparations for human objects, e.g., Luke 12:20, R.V., "thou hast prepared" (A.V., "provided"); Acts 23:23; Philm. 22.

NT: B.316a; CB.1250b; K.266.
OT: kûn: S.3559; HR.563c.5; H.964; BD.465c.
GEN. REF.: —.

2. *katartizō* [καταρτίζω, 2675], to furnish completely, prepare, is translated "didst Thou prepare" in Heb. 10:5 (A.V., "hast thou prepared"), of the body of the Lord Jesus. See FIT, B, No. 3.

NT: B.417d; CB.1254b; K.80.
OT: k^{e}lal: S.3635; HR.743b.4; H.2788; BD.1097a.
 kûn: S.3559; HR.743b.3; H.964; BD.465c.
GEN. REF.: —.

3. *kataskeuazō* [κατασκευάζω, 2680], to prepare, make ready (*kata*, used intensively, *skeuē*, equipment), is so translated in Matt. 11:10; Mark 1:2; Luke 1:17; 7:27; Heb. 9:2, R.V. (A.V., "made"); 9:6, R.V. (A.V., "were . . . ordained"); 11:7; 1 Pet. 3:20. See BUILD, No. 5.

NT: B.418b; CB.1254b; K.—.
OT: bārā': S.1254; HR.744a.1; H.278; BD.135a.
 'āsāh: S.6213; HR.744a.5; H.1708,1709; BD.793c.
GEN. REF.: —.

4. *paraskeuazō* [παρασκευάζω, 3903], to prepare, make ready (*para*, beside), is used of making ready a meal, Acts 10:10; in the Middle Voice, of preparing oneself for war, 1 Cor. 14:8, R.V.; in the Passive Voice, of preparing an offering for the needy, 2 Cor. 9:2, "hath been prepared," R.V. (A.V., "was ready"); ver. 3, "ye may be prepared," R.V. (A.V., "ye may be ready"). See READY. ¶

NT: B.622a; CB.1262b; K.—.
OT: pālas: S.6424; HR.1064a.6; H.1777; BD.814a.
 qādash: S.6942; HR.1064a.7; H.1990; BD.872d.
GEN. REF.: IS.3:953; NB.1026; Z.4:848.

5. *proetoimazō* [προετοιμάζω, 4282], to prepare beforehand (*pro*, before, and No. 1), is used of good works which God "afore prepared," for fulfilment by believers, Eph. 2:10, R.V. (A.V., "hath before ordained," marg., "prepared"); of "vessels of mercy," as "afore prepared" by God "unto glory," Rom. 9:23. See ORDAIN. ¶

NT: B.705b; CB.1266c; K.266.
OT: —.
GEN. REF.: —.

Notes: (1) Etymologically, the difference between *hetoimazō* and *paraskeuazō*, is that the former is connected with what is real (*etumos*) or ready, the latter with *skeuos*, an article ready to hand, an implement, vessel.

(2) in Mark 14:15, A.V. *hetoimos*, ready, is translated "prepared" (R.V., "ready"). It is absent in some mss. See READY.

For **PRESBYTERY** see **ELDER**, A and B

PRESENCE

A. Nouns.

1. *prosōpon* [*πρόσωπον*, —]: see FACE, No. 1 (also APPEARANCE, No. 2).

2. *parousia* [*παρουσία*, —]: see COMING (Noun), No. 3.

B. Adverbs and Prepositions.

1. *emprosthen* [*ἔμπροσθεν*, —]; see BEFORE, A, No. 4.

2. *enōpion* [*ἐνώπιον*, 1799], is translated "in the presence of" in Luke 1:19; 13:26; 14:10; 15:10; John 20:30; Rev. 14:10 (twice); in 1 Cor. 1:29, A.V., "in His presence" (R.V., "before God"): see BEFORE, A, No. 9.

NT: B.270c; CB.1245b; K.—.
OT: —.
GEN. REF.: IS.3:955; NB.—; Z.—.

3. *katenōpion* [*κατενώπιον*, 2714], *kata*, down, and No. 2, in the very presence of, is translated "before the presence of" in Jude 24. See BEFORE, A, No. 10.

NT: B.421b; CB.1254b; K.—.
OT: —.
GEN. REF.: IS.3:955; NB.—; Z.—.

4. *apenanti* [*ἀπέναντι*, 561], over against, opposite to, is translated "in the presence of" in Acts 3:16. See BEFORE, A, No. 7.

NT: B.84a; CB.—; K.—.
OT: —.
GEN. REF.: IS.3:955; NB.—; Z.—.

PRESENT (to be)

A. Verbs.

1. *pareimi* [*πάρειμι*, 3918], signifies (*a*) to be by, at hand or present, of persons, e.g., Luke 13:1; Acts 10:33; 24:19; 1 Cor. 5:3; 2 Cor. 10:2, 11; Gal. 4:18, 20; of things, John 7:6, of a particular season in the Lord's life on earth, "is (not yet) come," or 'is not yet at hand'; Heb. 12:11, of chastening "(for the) present" (the neuter of the present participle, used as a noun); in 13:5 "such things as ye have" is, lit., 'the things that are present'; 2 Pet. 1:12, of the truth "(which) is with (you)" (not as A.V., "the present truth," as if of special doctrines applicable to a particular time); in ver. 9 "he that lacketh" is lit., 'to whom are not present'; (*b*) to have arrived or come, Matt. 26:50, "thou art come," R.V.; John 11:28; Acts 10:21; Col. 1:6.

NT: B.624a; CB.1262b; K.791.
OT: bô': S.935; HR.1065c.2; H.212; BD.97c.
GEN. REF.: IS.3:957; NB.—; Z.—.

2. *enistēmi* [*ἐνίστημι*, 1764], to set in, or, in the Middle Voice and perfect tense of the Active V., to stand in, be present, is used of the present in contrast with the past, Heb. 9:9, where the R.V. correctly has "(for the time) *now* present" (for the incorrect A.V., "then pr."); in contrast to the future, Rom. 8:38; 1 Cor. 3:22; Gal. 1:4, "present"; 1 Cor. 7:26, where "the present distress" is set in contrast to both the past and the future; 2 Thess. 2:2, where the R.V., "is *now* present" gives the correct meaning (A.V., incorrectly, "is at hand"); the saints at Thessalonica, owing to their heavy afflictions, were possessed of the idea that "the day of the Lord," R.V. (not as A.V., "the day of Christ"), had begun; this mistake the Apostle corrects; 2 Tim. 3:1, "shall come" See COME, No. 26. ¶

NT: B.266d; CB.—; K.234.
OT: 'āmad: S.5975; HR.475a.1; H.1637; BD.763c.
GEN. REF.: IS.3:957; NB.—; Z.—.

3. *ephistēmi* [*ἐφίστημι*, 2186], to set over, stand over, is translated "present" in Acts 28:2. See ASSAULT, A, COME, No. 27.

NT: B.330d; CB.—; K.—.
OT. nāṣab. S.5324, HR.585c.6; H.1398; BD.662a.
'āmad: S.5975; HR.585c.11; H.1637; BD.763c.
GEN. REF.: IS.3:957; NB.—; Z.—.

4. *paraginomai* [*παραγίνομαι*, 3854], to be beside (*para*, by, *ginomai*, to become), is translated "were present" in Acts 21:18. See COME, No. 13.

NT: B.613c; CB.—; K.—.
OT: bô': S.935; HR.1056c.1; H.212; BD.97c.
GEN. REF.: IS.3:957; NB.—; Z.—.

5. *parakeimai* [*παράκειμαι*, 3873], to lie beside (*para*, and *keimai*, to lie), to be near, is translated "is present" in Rom. 7:18, 21. ¶

NT: B.617d; CB.—; K.425.
OT: —.
GEN. REF.: —.

6. *sumpareimi* [*συμπάρειμι*, 4840], to be present with (*sun*, with, and No. 1), is used in Acts 25:24. ¶

NT: B.779a; CB.—; K.—.
OT: —.
GEN. REF.: —.

B. Adverbs.

1. *arti* [*ἄρτι*, 737], just, just now, this moment, is rendered "(this) present (hour)" in 1 Cor. 4:11; in 1 Cor. 15:6, R.V., "now" (A.V., "this present"). See NOW.

NT: B.110b; CB.1237c; K.658.
OT: 'attāh: S.6258; HR.161a.1; H.1650c; BD.773d.
GEN. REF.: —.

2. *nun* [*νῦν*, 3568], now, is translated "present," with reference to this age or period ("world"), in Rom. 8:18; 11:5; 2 Tim. 4:10; Tit. 2:12. See HENCEFORTH, NOW.

NT: B.545c; CB.1260a; K.658.
OT: 'attāh: S.6258; HR.951c.9a; H.1650c; BD.773d.
GEN. REF.: —.

Notes: (1) *Endēmeō*, to be at home, is so rendered in 2 Cor. 5:6 (A.V. and R.V.); in vv. 8, 9, R.V., "at home" (A.V., "present"). See HOME.

(2) In John 14:25, A.V., *menō*, to abide, is translated "being present" (R.V., "abiding").

(3) In Luke 5:17 the R.V. has "with Him," for A.V., italicised, "*present*."

PRESENT (Verb)

1. *paristēmi* [παρίστημι, 3936], denotes, when used transitively, to place beside (*para*, by, *histēmi*, to set), to present, e.g., Luke 2:22; Acts 1:3, "He shewed (Himself)"; 9:41; 23:33; Rom. 6:13 (2nd part), R.V., "present," A.V., "yield"; so 6:19 (twice); 12:1; 2 Cor. 4:14; 11:2; Eph. 5:27; Col. 1:22, 28; 2 Tim. 2:15, R.V. (A.V., "shew"). See Shew.

NT: B.627c; CB.1262b; K.788.
OT: 'āmad: S.5975; HR.1070c.6; H.1637; BD.763c.
nāṣab: S.5324; HR.1070c.5; H.1398; BD.662a.
GEN. REF.: IS.3:957; NB.–; Z.–.

2. *paristanō* [παριστάνω, 3936], a late present form of No. 1, is used in Rom. 6:13 (1st part) and ver. 16, R.V., "present" (A.V., "yield").

NT: B.627c; CB.1262b; K.788.
OT: –.
GEN. REF.: –.

Notes: (1) In Jude 24, A.V., *histēmi*, to cause to stand, to set, is translated "to present" (R.V., "to set").

(2) In Matt. 2:11, A.V., *prospherō*, to offer, is translated "presented" (R.V., "offered").

For **PRESENTLY** see **FORTHWITH**, No. 1, and **IMMEDIATELY**, No. 1

PRESERVE

1. *tēreō* [τηρέω, 5083], is translated to preserve in 1 Thess. 5:23, where the verb is in the singular number, as the threefold subject, "spirit and soul and body," is regarded as the unit, constituting the person. The aorist or 'point' tense regards the continuous preservation of the believer as a single, complete act, without reference to the time occupied in its accomplishment; in Jude 1, A.V. (R.V., "kept"). See Keep, No. 1.

NT: B.814d; CB.1271b; K.1174.
OT: shāmar: S.8104; HR.1348b.7; H.2414; BD.1036b.
nāṣar: S.5341; HR.1348b.2; H.1407; BD.665c.
GEN. REF.: –.

2. *suntēreō* [συντηρέω, —]: see Keep, No. 3.

3. *zōogoneō* [ζωογονέω, 2225], to preserve alive: see Live, No. 6.

NT: B.341c; CB.1273c; K.290.
OT: ḥāyāh: S.2421; HR.601b.1; H.644; BD.310d.
GEN. REF.: –.

4. *phulassō* [φυλάσσω, 5442], to guard, protect, preserve, is translated "preserved" in 2 Pet. 2:5, R.V. (A.V., "saved"). See Guard.

NT: B.868b; CB.1264c; K.1280.
OT: shāmar: S.8104; HR.1441c.11a; H.2414; BD.1036b.
GEN. REF.: –.

Note: In 2 Tim. 4:18, A.V., *sōzō*, to save, is translated "will preserve" (R.V., "will save").

For **PRESS (Noun)** see **CROWD**, A

PRESS (Verb)

A. Verbs.

1. *thlibō* [θλίβω, 2346], to press, distress, trouble, is translated "pressed" in 2 Cor. 4:8, R.V. (A.V., "troubled"). See Afflict, No. 4.

NT: B.362a; CB.1272b; K.334.
OT: ṣārar: S.6887; HR.652b.10a-c; H.1973,1974; BD.865c.
lāḥaṣ: S.3905; HR.652b.4; H.1106; BD.537d.
GEN. REF.: –.

2. *apothlibō* [ἀποθλίβω, 598], translated "press" in Luke 8:45 (end): see Crush.

NT: B.91b; CB.–; K.–.
OT: lāḥaṣ: S.3905; HR.128a.1; H.1106; BD.537d.
GEN. REF.: IS.3:958; NB.–; Z.–.

3. *biazo* [βιάζω, 971], in the Middle Voice, to press violently or force one's way into, is translated "presseth" in Luke 16:16, A.V., R.V., "entereth violently," a meaning confirmed by the papyri. Moulton and Milligan also quote a passage from D. S. Sharp's *Epictetus and the N.T.*, speaking of "those who (try to) force their way in"; the verb suggests forceful endeavour. See Enter, *Note* (3), Violence, B. No. 2.

NT: B.140c; CB.1239a; K.–.
OT: pāraṣ: S.6555; HR.218a.6; H.1826; BD.829b.
pāṣar: S.6484; HR.218a.5; H.1801; BD.823a.
GEN. REF.: IS.3:958; NB.–; Z.–.

4. *sunechō* [συνέχω, 4912]: for the significance of this in Acts 18:5, "was constrained by the word," R.V., i.e., Paul felt the urge of the word of his testimony to the Jews in Corinth, see Constrain, No. 3. It is used with No. 1. in Luke 8:45, R.V., "press" (A.V., "throng").

NT: B.789a; CB.1270c; K.1117.
OT: 'āṣar: S.6113; HR.1315b.12a,b; H.1675; BD.783c.
GEN. REF.: IS.3:958; NB.–; Z.–.

5. *enechō* [ἐνέχω, 1758], lit., to hold in, also signifies to set oneself against, be urgent against, as the scribes and Pharisees were regarding Christ, Luke 11:53, R.V., "to press upon," marg., "set themselves vehemently against" (A.V., "to urge"). See Entangle, No. 3.

NT: B.265d; CB.1245a; K.286.
OT: sāṭam: S.7852; HR.473a.1; H.2251; BD.966b.
GEN. REF.: IS.3:958; NB.–; Z.–.

6. *epikeimai* [ἐπίκειμαι, 1945], to lie upon, press upon, is rendered "pressed upon" in Luke 5:1. See Imposed.

NT: B.294c; CB.–; K.425.
OT: –.
GEN. REF.: –.

7. *epipiptō* [ἐπιπίπτω, 1968], to fall upon, is rendered "pressed upon" in Mark 3:10. See Fall, B, No. 5.

NT: B.297c; CB.–; K.–.
OT: nāphal: S.5307; HR.526b.4a; H.1392; BD.656c.
GEN. REF.: –.

8. *bareō* [βαρέω, 916], to weigh down, burden, is rendered "we were pressed" in 2 Cor. 1:8, A.V. (R.V., "we were weighed down"). See BURDEN, B, No. 1.
NT: B.133c; CB.1238c; K.95.
OT: kābēd: S.3513; HR.190c.1; H.943; BD.457a.
GEN. REF.: –.

9. *epibareō* [ἐπιβαρέω, 1912], 2 Cor. 2:5, R.V., "I press (not) too heavily" (A.V., "overcharge"). See BURDEN, B, No. 2, OVERCHARGE.
NT: B.290b; CB.1245c; K.–.
OT: –.
GEN. REF.: –.

10. *piezō* [πιέζω, 4085], to press down together, is used in Luke 6:38, "pressed down," of the character of the measure given in return for giving. ¶ In the Sept., Mic. 6:15. ¶
NT: B.657b; CB.–; K.–.
OT: dārak: S.1869; HR.1132c.2; H.453; BD.201d.
GEN. REF.: –.

11. *diōkō* [διώκω, 1377], to pursue, is used as a metaphor from the footrace, in Phil. 3:12, 14, of speeding on earnestly, R.V., "I press on." See FOLLOW, No. 7.
NT: B.201b; CB.1242a; K.177.
OT: rādaph: S.7291; HR.338b.10a; H.2124; BD.922c.
GEN. REF.: IS.3:958; NB.–; Z.–.

12. *pherō* [φέρω, 5342], to bear, carry, is used in the Passive Voice in Heb. 6:1, "let us . . . press on," R.V., lit., 'let us be borne on' (A.V., "go on"). See GO, *Note* (2), (*h*).
NT: B.854d; CB.1264a; K.1252.
OT: bô': S.935; HR.1426c.3b; H.212; BD.97c.
nāśā': S.5375; HR.1426c.17; H.1421; BD.669d.
GEN. REF.: –.

B. Noun.

epistasis [ἐπίστασις, —], primarily a stopping, halting (as of soldiers), then, an incursion, onset, rush, pressure (akin to *ephistēmi*, to set upon), is so used in 2 Cor. 11:28, "(that which) presseth upon (me)," A.V., "cometh upon," lit., '(the daily) pressure (upon me)'; some have taken the word in its other meaning 'attention,' which perhaps is accounted for by the variant reading of the pronoun (*mou*, 'my' instead of *moi*, 'to me,' 'upon me'), but that does not adequately describe the pressure or onset due to the constant call upon the Apostle for all kinds of help, advice, counsel, exhortation, decisions as to difficulties, disputes, etc. Cp. the other occurrence of the word in Acts 24:12, "stirring up," R.V. (A.V., "raising"), lit. 'making a stir' (in some mss., *episustasis*). See COME, *Notes* at end (9). ¶
NT: B.300b; CB.–; K.–.
OT: –.
GEN. REF.: –.

For **PRESUMPTUOUS** see **DARING**, B

PRETENCE

prophasis [πρόφασις, —]: see CLOKE (Pretence), No. 2

PREVAIL

1. *ischuō* [ἰσχύω, 2480], to be strong, powerful, is translated to prevail in Acts 19:16, 20; Rev. 12:8. See ABLE, B, No. 4.
NT: B.383d; CB.1253a; K.378.
OT: ḥāzaq: S.2388; HR.692c.6a-c; H.636; BD.304a.
GEN. REF.: –.

2. *katischuō* [κατισχύω, 2729], to be strong against (*kata*, against, and No. 1), is used in Matt. 16:18, negatively of the gates of Hades; in Luke 21:36 (in the most authentic mss.; some have *kataxioō*, to count worthy; see A.V.), of prevailing to escape judgments at the close of this age; in Luke 23:23, of the voices of the chief priests, rulers and people against Pilate regarding the crucifixion of Christ. ¶
NT: B.424a; CB.1254c; K.378.
OT: ḥāzaq: S.2388; HR.751b.7; H.636; BD.304a.
GEN. REF.: –.

3. *ōpheleō* [ὠφελέω, 5623], to benefit, do good, profit, is translated "prevailed" in Matt. 27:24, R.V. (A.V., "could prevail"), of the conclusion formed by Pilate concerning the determination of the chief priests, elders and people. The meaning of the verb with the negative is better expressed by the phrase 'he would do no good'; so in John 12:19, "ye prevail (nothing)," lit., 'ye are doing no good.' See ADVANTAGE, BETTERED, PROFIT.
NT: B.900c; CB.1261a; K.–.
OT: yā'al: S.3276; HR.1497b.1; H.882; BD.418c.
GEN. REF.: –.

4. *nikaō* [νικάω, 3528], to conquer, prevail, is used as a law term in Rom. 3:4, "(that) Thou . . . mightest prevail [A.V., 'overcome'] (when Thou comest into judgment)"; that the righteousness of the judge's verdict compels an acknowledgement on the part of the accused, is inevitable where God is the Judge. God's promises to Israel provided no guarantee that an unrepentant Jew would escape doom. In Rev. 5:5, A.V., "hath prevailed" (R.V., "hath overcome"). See CONQUER, No. 1.
NT: B.539a; CB.1259c; K.634.
OT: nāṣaḥ: S.5329; HR.945b.3; H.1402; BD.663d.
GEN. REF.: –.

For **PREVENT**, 1 Thess. 4:15, A.V., see **PRECEDE**: Matt. 17:25, A.V., see **SPEAK** No. 11

PRICE

A. Noun.

timē [τιμή, 5092], denotes a valuing, hence, objectively, (*a*) price paid or received, Matt. 27:6, 9; Acts 4:34 (plural); 5:2, 3; 7:16, R.V., "price (in silver)," A.V., "sum (of money)"; 19:19 (plural); 1 Cor. 6:20; 7:23; (*b*) value, honour, preciousness. See HONOUR, PRECIOUSNESS.

NT: B.817b; CB.1272c; K.1181.
OT: ʿērek: S.6187; HR.1353a.10; H.1694a; BD.789d.
y^{e}qār: S.3367; HR.1353a.4a; H.2775a; BD.1096a.
GEN. REF.: IS.3:959; NB.—; Z.—.

B. Verb.

timaō [τιμάω, 5091], to fix the value, to price, is translated "was priced" and "did price" in the R.V. of Matt. 27:9 (A.V., "was valued" and "did value"). See HONOUR.

NT: B.817a; CB.1272c; K.1181.
OT: kābēd: S.3513; HR.1353a.3a; H.943; BD.457a.
ʿārak: S.6186; HR.1353a.5a; H.1694; BD.789b.
GEN. REF.: IS.3:959; NB.—; Z.—.

C. Adjectives.

1. *polutelēs* [πολυτελής, 4185], "of great price," 1 Pet. 3:4: see COST, B, No. 2.

NT: B.690a; CB.1266c; K.—.
OT: yāqār: S.3368; HR.1185c.1; H.905a; BD.429d.
GEN. REF.: —.

2. *polutimos* [πολύτιμος, 4186], "of great price," Matt. 13:46: see COST, B, No. 3.

NT: B.690a; CB.—; K.—.
OT: —.
GEN. REF.: —.

For **PRICK** (Noun) see GOAD

PRICK (Verb)

katanussō [κατανύσσω, 2660], primarily, to strike or prick violently, to stun, is used of strong emotion, in Acts 2:37 (Passive Voice), "they were pricked (in their heart)." ¶ Cp. *katanuxis*, stupor; torpor of mind, Rom. 11:8. ¶

NT: B.415c; CB.—; K.419.
OT: dāmam: S.1826; HR.739c.2; H.439; BD.198d.
GEN. REF.: IS.3:960; NB.—; Z.—.

PRIDE

A. Nouns.

1. *alazonia* (or *—eia*) [ἀλαζονία, 212], is translated "pride" in 1 John 2:16, A.V. See BOAST, B, No. 2, VAINGLORY.

NT: B.34c; CB.1234b; K.36.
OT: —.
GEN. REF.: IS.3:960; NB.1027; Z.4:848.

2. *huperēphania* [ὑπερηφανία, 5243], pride, Mark 7:22: see HAUGHTY. ¶

NT: B.841a; CB.1252a; K.1231.
OT: ga'^{a}wāh: S.1346; HR.1409c.2a; H.299d; BD.144d.
gā'ôn: S.1347; HR.1409c.2b; H.299e; BD.144d.
GEN. REF.: IS.3:960; NB.1027; Z.4:848.

B. Verb.

tuphoō [τυφόω, 5187], "lifted up with pride," 1 Tim. 3:6, A.V. (R.V., "puffed up"). See HIGH-MINDED.

NT: B.831a; CB.—; K.—.
OT: —.
GEN. REF.: —.

PRIEST

1. *hiereus* [ἱερεύς, 2409], one who offers sacrifice and has the charge of things pertaining thereto, is used (*a*) of a priest of the pagan god Zeus, Acts 14:13; (*b*) of Jewish priests, e.g., Matt. 8:4; 12:4, 5; Luke 1:5, where allusion is made to the 24 courses of priests appointed for service in the Temple (cp. 1 Chron. 24:4ff.); John 1:19; Heb. 8:4; (*c*) of believers, Rev. 1:6; 5:10; 20:6. Israel was primarily designed as a nation to be a kingdom of priests, offering service to God, e.g., Ex. 19:6; the Israelites having renounced their obligations, Ex. 20:19, the Aaronic priesthood was selected for the purpose, till Christ came to fulfil His ministry in offering up Himself; since then the Jewish priesthood has been abrogated, to be resumed nationally, on behalf of Gentiles, in the Millennial Kingdom, Is. 61:6; 66:21. Meanwhile all believers, from Jews and Gentiles, are constituted "a kingdom of priests," Rev. 1:6 (see above), "a holy priesthood," 1 Pet. 2:5, and "royal," ver. 9. The N.T. knows nothing of a sacerdotal class in contrast to the laity; all believers are commanded to offer the sacrifices mentioned in Rom. 12:1; Phil. 2:17; 4:18; Heb. 13:15, 16; 1 Pet. 2:5; (*d*) of Christ, Heb. 5:6; 7:11, 15, 17, 21; 8:4 (negatively); (*e*) of Melchizedek, as the foreshadower of Christ, Heb. 7:1, 3.

NT: B.372a; CB.1250b; K.349.
OT: kōhēn: S.3548; HR.679a.1a; H.959a; BD.463a.
GEN. REF.: IS.3:965; NB.1028; Z.4:849.

2. *archiereus* [ἀρχιερεύς, 749], designates (*a*) the high priests of the Levitical order, frequently called "chief priests" in the N.T., and including ex-high priests and members of high priestly families, e.g., Matt. 2:4; 16:21; 20:18; 21:15; in the singular, a "high priest," e.g., Abiathar, Mark 2:26; Annas and Caiaphas, Luke 3:2, where the R.V. rightly has "in the high-priesthood of A. and C." (cp. Acts 4:6). As to the combination of the two in this respect, Annas was the high priest from A.D. 7-14, and, by the time referred to, had been deposed for some years; his son-in-law, Caiaphas, the fourth high priest since his deposition, was appointed about A.D. 24. That Annas was still called the high priest is explained by the facts (1) that by

the Mosaic law the high-priesthood was held for life, Numb. 35:25; his deposition was the capricious act of the Roman procurator, but he would still be regarded legally and religiously as high priest by the Jews; (2) that he probably still held the office of deputy-president of the Sanhedrin (cp. 2 Kings 25:18); (3) that he was a man whose age, wealth and family connections gave him a preponderant influence, by which he held the real sacerdotal power; indeed at this time the high-priesthood was in the hands of a clique of some half dozen families; the language of the writers of the Gospels is in accordance with this, in attributing the high-priesthood rather to a caste than a person; (4) the high priests were at that period mere puppets of Roman authorities who deposed them at will, with the result that the title was used more loosely than in former days.

The Divine institution of the priesthood culminated in the high priest, it being his duty to represent the whole people, e.g., Lev. 4:15, 16; ch. 16. The characteristics of the Aaronic high priests are enumerated in Heb. 5:1-4; 8:3; 9:7, 25; in some mss., 10:11 (R.V., marg.); 13:11.

(*b*) Christ is set forth in this respect in the Ep. to the Hebrews, where He is spoken of as "a high priest," 4:15; 5:5, 10; 6:20; 7:26; 8:1, 3 (R.V.); 9:11; "a great high priest," 4:14; "a great priest," 10:21; "a merciful and faithful high priest," 2:17; "the Apostle and high priest of our confession," 3:1, R.V.; "a high priest after the order of Melchizedek," 5:10. One of the great objects of this Epistle is to set forth the superiority of Christ's High Priesthood as being of an order different from and higher than the Aaronic, in that He is the Son of God (see especially 7:28), with a priesthood of the Melchizedek order. Seven outstanding features of His priesthood are stressed, (1) its character, 5:6, 10; (2) His commission, 5:4, 5; (3) His preparation, 2:17; 10:5; (4) His sacrifice, 8:3; 9:12, 14, 27, 28; 10:4-12; (5) His sanctuary, 4:14; 8:2; 9:11, 12, 24; 10:12, 19; (6) His ministry, 2:18; 4:15; 7:25; 8:6; 9:15, 24; (7) its effects, 2:15; 4:16; 6:19, 20; 7:16, 25; 9:14, 28; 10:14-17, 22, 39; 12:1; 13:13-17.

NT: B.112d; CB.1237b; K.349.
OT: kōhēn: S.3548; HR.165b.1; H.959a; BD.463a.
GEN. REF.: IS.3:965; NB.1028; Z.4:849.

Note: In Acts 4:6 the adjective *hieratikos*, high priestly, is translated "of the high priest."

PRIESTHOOD, PRIEST'S OFFICE

A. Nouns.

1. *hierateuma* [ἱεράτευμα, 2406], denotes a priesthood (akin to *hierateuō*, see below), a body of priests, consisting of all believers, the whole Church (not a special order from among them), called "a holy priesthood," 1 Pet. 2:5; "a royal priesthood," ver. 9; the former term is associated with offering spiritual sacrifices, the latter with the royal dignity of shewing forth the Lord's excellencies (R.V.). ¶ In the Sept., Ex. 19:6; 23:22. ¶

NT: B.371d; CB.1250b; K.349.
OT: kōhēn: S.3548; HR.679a.1; H.959a; BD.463a.
GEN. REF.: IS.3:965; NB.1028; Z.4:849.

2. *hierōsunē* [ἱερωσύνη, 2420], a priesthood, signifies the office, quality, rank and ministry of a priest, Heb. 7:11, 12, 24, where the contrasts between the Levitical priesthood and that of Christ are set forth. ¶ In the Sept., 1 Chron. 29:22. ¶

NT: B.373c; CB.1250c; K.349.
OT: kōhēn: S.3548; HR.683c.1; H.959a; BD.463a.
GEN. REF.: IS.3:965; NB.1028; Z.4:849.

3. *hierateia* [ἱερατεία, 2405], a priesthood, denotes the priest's office, Luke 1:9; Heb. 7:5, R.V., "priest's office." ¶

NT: B.371d; CB.1250b; K.349.
OT: kᵉhunnāh: S.3550; HR.678c.2b; H.959b; BD.464d.
GEN. REF.: IS.3:965; NB.1028; Z.4:849.

B. Verb.

hierateuō [ἱερατεύω, 2407], signifies to officiate as a priest, Luke 1:8, "he executed the priest's office." ¶

NT: B.371d; CB.1250b; K.349.
OT: kāhan: S.3547; HR.679a.1; H.959; BD.464e.
GEN. REF.: IS.3:965; NB.1028; Z.4:849.

PRINCE

1. *archēgos* [ἀρχηγός, 747] primarily an adjective signifying originating, beginning, is used as a noun, denoting a founder, author, prince or leader, Acts 3:15, "Prince" (marg., "Author"); 5:31; see AUTHOR, No. 2.

NT: B.112c; CB.1237b; K.81.
OT: rō'sh: S.7218; HR.165a.8a; H.2097; BD.910c.
GEN. REF.: IS.–; NB.1034; Z.4:867.

2. *archōn* [ἄρχων, 758], the present participle of the verb *archō*, to rule denotes a ruler, a prince. It is used as follows ("p" denoting "prince," or "princess"; "r," "ruler" or "rulers"): (*a*) of Christ, as "the Ruler (A.V.), Prince) of the kings of the earth," Rev. 1:5; (*b*) of rulers of nations, Matt. 20:25, R.V., "r," A.V., "p"; Acts 4:26, "r"; 7:27, "r"; 7:35, "r" (twice); (*c*) of judges and magistrates, Acts 16:19, "r"; Rom. 13:3; "r"; (*d*) of members of the Sanhedrin, Luke 14:1, R.V., "r" (A.V., "chief"); 23:13, 35, "r"; so 24:20; John 3:1; 7:26, 48; 12:42, R.V., "r" (A.V., "chief r."); "r" in Acts 3:17; 4:5, 8; 13:27; 14:5; (*e*) of rulers of synagogues, Matt. 9:18, 23, "r"; so Luke 8:41; 18:18; (*f*) of the Devil, as "prince" of this world, John 12:31; 14:30; 16:11; of the power of the air,

Eph. 2:2, "the air" being that sphere in which the inhabitants of the world live and which, through the rebellious and godless condition of humanity, constitutes the seat of his authority; (*g*) of Beelzebub, the prince of the demons, Matt. 9:24; 12:24; Mark 3:22; Luke 11:15. See CHIEF, B, No. 10. ¶

NT: B.113d; CB.1237b; K.81.
OT: nāśî': S.5387; HR.166b.17; H.1421b,c; BD.672b.
rō'sh: S.7218; HR.166b.26; H.2097; BD.910c.
sar: S.8269; HR.166b.30a; H.2295a; BD.978a.
GEN. REF.: IS.3:970; NB.1034; Z.4:867.

3. *hēgemōn* [ἡγεμών, 2232], a leader, ruler, is translated "princes" (i.e., leaders) in Matt. 2:6: see GOVERNOR, A, No. 1.

NT: B.343b; CB.1249c; K.—.
OT: 'allûph: S.441; HR.603c.2; H.109b; BD.49b.
sar: S.8269; HR.603c.5; H.2295a; BD.978a.
GEN. REF.: IS.3:970; NB.1034; Z.4:867.

Note: For *megistan*, Rev. 6:15; 18:23, R.V., "princes," see LORD, No. 3.

PRINCIPAL

prōtos [πρῶτος, 4413], first, is translated "principal men" in the R.V. of Luke 19:47 and Acts 25:2. See CHIEF, A.

NT: B.725b; CB.1267b; K.965.
OT: ri'shôn: S.7223; HR.1235c.3a; H.2097c; BD.911c.
GEN. REF.: IS.3:971; NB.—; Z.—.

Note: In Acts 25:23 the phrase *kat' exochēn*, lit., 'according to eminence,' is translated "principal (men)"; *exochē*, primarily a projection (akin to *exechō*, to stand out), is used here metaphorically of eminence. ¶ In the Sept., Job 39:28. ¶

PRINCIPALITY

archē [ἀρχή, 746], beginning, government, rule, is used of supramundane beings who exercise rule, called "principalities"; (*a*) of holy angels, Eph. 3:10, the Church in its formation being to them the great expression of "the manifold (or 'much-varied') wisdom of God"; Col. 1:16; (*b*) of evil angels, Rom. 8:38; Col. 2:15, some would put this under (*a*), but see SPOIL, B, No. 4; (*a*) and (*b*) are indicated in Col. 2:10. In Eph. 1:21, the R.V. renders it "rule" (A.V., "principality") and in Tit. 3:1, "rulers" (A.V., "principalities"). In Jude 6, R.V., it signifies, not the first estate of fallen angels (as A.V.), but their authoritative power, "their own" indicating that which had been assigned to them by God, which they left, aspiring to prohibited conditions. See BEGIN, B.

NT: B.111d; CB.1237b; K.81.
OT: rō'sh: S.7218; HR.164a.20a; H.2097; BD.910c.
rē'shît: S.7225; HR.164a.20c; H.2097e; BD.912a.
shālṭān: S.7985; HR.164a.22; H.3034a; BD.1115d.
GEN. REF.: IS.3:971; NB.—; Z.4:869.

PRINCIPLES

1. *archē* [ἀρχή, 746], beginning, is used in Heb. 6:1, in its relative significance, of the beginning of the thing spoken of; here "the first principles of Christ," lit., 'the account (or word) of the beginning of Christ,' denotes the teaching relating to the elementary facts concerning Christ. See BEGIN, B.

NT: B.111d; CB.1237b; K.81.
OT: rē'shît: S.7225; HR.164a.20c; H.2097e; BD.912a.
tᵉḥillāh: S.8462; HR.164a.23; H.661d; BD.321a.
GEN. REF.: IS.3:971; NB.—; Z.—.

2. *stoicheion* [στοιχεῖον, 4747], is translated "principles" in Heb. 5:12. See ELEMENTS.

NT: B.768d; CB.1270a; K.1087.
OT: —.
GEN. REF.: IS.3:973; NB.—; Z.—.

PRINT

tupos [τύπος, 5179], for which see ENSAMPLE, No. 1, is translated "print" in John 20:25 (twice), of the marks made by the nails in the hands of Christ.

NT: B.829d; CB.1273b; K.1193.
OT: tabnît: S.8403; HR.1378b.2; H.255d; BD.125d.
GEN. REF.: —.

PRISON, PRISON-HOUSE

1. *desmōtērion* [δεσμωτήριον, 1201], a place of bonds (from *desmos*, a bond, *deō*, to bind), a prison, occurs in Matt. 11:2; in Acts 5:21, 23 and 16:26, R.V., "prison-house" (A.V., "prison"). ¶

NT: B.176b; CB.1240c; K.—.
OT: sōhar: S.5470; HR.292b.2; H.1468b; BD.690c.
'āsîr: S.615; HR.292b.1a; H.141b; BD.64a.
GEN. REF.: IS.3:973; NB.1035; Z.4:869.

2. *phulakē* [φυλακή, 5438], for the various meanings of which see CAGE, denotes a prison, e.g., Matt. 14:10; Mark 6:17; Acts 5:19; 2 Cor. 11:23; in 2 Cor. 6:5 and Heb. 11:36 it stands for the condition of imprisonment; in Rev. 2:10; 18:2, "hold" (twice, R.V., marg., "prison"; in the 2nd case, A.V., "cage"); 20:7.

NT: B.867d; CB.1264c; K.1280.
OT: mishmār: S.4929; HR.1440c.2b; H.2414f; BD.1038b.
mishmeret: S.4931; HR.1440c.2c; H.2414g; BD.1038b.
GEN. REF.: IS.3:973; NB.1035; Z.4:869.

3. *tērēsis* [τήρησις, 5084], a watching, keeping, then, a place of keeping, is translated "prison" in Acts 5:18, A.V. (R.V., "ward"). See KEEPING, B.

NT: B.815c; CB.1271b; K.1174.
OT: —.
GEN. REF.: IS.3:973; NB.—; Z.4:869.

Notes: (1) For *oikēma* in Acts 12:7, A.V., "prison," see CELL.

(2) In Matt. 4:12, A.V., *paradidōmi*, to betray, deliver up, is translated "was cast into prison" (R.V., "was delivered up"); see BETRAY. In Mark 1:14, A.V., "was put in prison," R.V., as in Matt. 4:12; see PUT, No. 12.

For **PRISON-KEEPER** see **JAILOR**

PRISONER

1. *desmios* [δέσμιος, 1198], an adjective, primarily denotes binding, bound, then, as a noun, the person bound, a captive, prisoner (akin to *deō*, to bind), Matt. 27:15, 16; Mark 15:6; Acts 16:25, 27; 23:18; 25:14, R.V. (A.V., "in bonds"), 27; 28:16, 17; Eph. 3:1; 4:1; 2 Tim. 1:8; Philm. 1, 9; in Heb. 10:34 and 13:3, "in bonds." See BOND, No. 2. ¶

NT: B.176a; CB.1240c; K.145.
OT: 'āssîr: S.616; HR.292a.1b; H.141c; BD.64b.
GEN. REF.: IS.3:973; NB.1035; Z.4:869.

Note: The prison at Jerusalem (Acts 5) was controlled by the priests and probably attached to the high priest's palace, or the temple. Paul was imprisoned at Jerusalem in the fort Antonia, Acts 23:10; at Caesarea, in Herod's Praetorium, 23:35; probably his final imprisonment in Rome was in the Tullianum dungeon.

2. *desmōtēs* [δεσμώτης, —], akin to No. 1, occurs in Acts 27:1, 42. ¶

3. *sunaichmalōtos* [συναιχμάλωτος, 4869], a fellow-prisoner, primarily one of fellow-captives in war (from *aichmē*, a spear, and *haliskomai*, to be taken), is used by Paul of Andronicus and Junias, Rom. 16:7; of Epaphras, Philm. 23; of Aristarchus, Col. 4:10, on which Lightfoot remarks that probably his relations with the Apostle in Rome excited suspicion and led to a temporary confinement, or that he voluntarily shared his captivity by living with him. ¶

NT: B.783c; CB.1270b; K.31.
OT: —.
GEN. REF.: IS.3:973; NB.—; Z.4:869.

PRIVATE, PRIVATELY

A. Adjective.

idios [ἴδιος, 2398], one's own, is translated "private" in 2 Pet. 1:20 (see under INTERPRETATION). See BUSINESS, B.

NT: B.369c; CB.1252c; K.—.
OT: —.
GEN. REF.: —.

B. Adverbial Phrase.

kat' idian [κατ' ἰδίαν, —], is translated "privately" in Matt. 24:3; Mark 4:34, R.V. (A.V., "when they were alone"); 6:32 (A.V. only); 7:33, R.V.; 9:28; 13:3; Luke 10:23; Acts 23:19; Gal. 2:2. Contrast 2:14.

NT: B.370b; CB.—; K.—.
OT: —.
GEN. REF.: —.

PRIVILY

lathra [λάθρᾳ, 2977], secretly, covertly (from a root *lath—* indicating unnoticed, unknown, seen in *lanthanō*, to escape notice, *lēthē*, forgetfulness), is translated "privily" in Matt. 1:19; 2:7; Acts 16:37; "secretly" in John 11:28 (in some mss., Mark 5:33). See SECRETLY. ¶

NT: B.462c; CB.—; K.—.
OT: (ba)mistār: S.4565; HR.840c.2a; H.155ld; BD.712c.
(ba)sēter: S.5643; HR.840c.2b; H.155la; BD.712a.
GEN. REF.: —.

Note: In Gal. 2:4, *pareisaktos*, an adjective (akin to *pareisagō*, lit., to bring in beside, i.e., secretly, from *para*, by the side, *eis*, into, *agō*, to bring), is used, "privily brought in," R.V. (A.V., "unawares etc."), i.e., as spies or traitors. Strabo, a Greek historian contemporary with Paul, uses the word of enemies introduced secretly into a city by traitors within. ¶ In the same verse the verb *pareiserchomai* (see COME, No. 8) is translated "came in privily," of the same Judaizers, brought in by the circumcision party to fulfil the design of establishing the ceremonial law, and thus to accomplish the overthrow of the faith; cp. in Jude 4 the verb *pareisduō* (or *—dunō*), to slip in secretly, steal in, R.V., "crept in privily" (A.V., ". . . unawares"). See CREEP, No. 2.

PRIVY

sunoida [σύνοιδα, —]: see KNOW, No. 6

PRIZE

1. *brabeion* [βραβεῖον, 1017], a prize bestowed in connection with the games (akin to *brabeus*, an umpire, and *brabeuō*, to decide, arbitrate, "rule," Col. 3:15), 1 Cor. 9:24, is used metaphorically of the reward to be obtained hereafter by the faithful believer, Phil. 3:14; the preposition *eis*, "unto," indicates the position of the goal. The prize is not "the high calling," but will be bestowed in virtue of, and relation to, it, the heavenly calling, Heb. 3:1, which belongs to all believers and directs their minds and aspirations heavenward; for the prize see especially 2 Tim. 4:7, 8. ¶

NT: B.146d; CB.1239b; K.110.
OT: —.
GEN. REF.: IS.3:976; NB.—; Z.—.

2. *harpagmos* [ἁρπαγμός, 725], akin to *harpazō*, to seize, carry off by force, is found in Phil. 2:6, "(counted it not) a prize," R.V. (marg., "a thing to be grasped"), A.V., "(thought it not) robbery"; it may have two meanings, (*a*) in the Active sense, the act of seizing, robbery, a meaning in accordance with a rule connected with its formation; (*b*) in the Passive sense, a thing held as a prize. The subject is capably treated by Gifford in "*The Incarnation*," pp. 28, 36, from which the following is quoted:

"In order to express the meaning of the clause quite clearly, a slight alteration is required in the R.V., 'Counted it not a prize to be on an equality with God.' The form 'to be' is ambiguous and easily lends itself to the erroneous notion that to be on equality with God was something to be acquired in the future. The rendering 'counted it not a prize that He was on an equality with God,' is quite as accurate and more free from ambiguity. . . . Assuming, as we now may, that the equality was something which Christ possessed prior to His Incarnation, and then for a time resigned, we have . . . to choose between two meanings of the word *harpagmos:* (1) with the active sense 'robbery' or 'usurpation' we get the following meaning: 'Who *because* He was subsisting in the essential form of God, did not regard it as any usurpation that He was on an equality of glory and majesty with God, *but yet* emptied Himself of that co-equal glory. . . .' (2) The passive sense gives a different meaning to the passage: 'Who *though* He was subsisting in the essential form of God, *yet* did not regard His being on an equality of glory and majesty with God as a prize and a treasure to be held fast, *but* emptied himself thereof.'

After reviewing the arguments *pro* amd *con* Gifford takes the latter to be the right meaning, as conveying the purpose of the passage "to set forth Christ as the supreme example of humility and self-renunciation."

NT: B.108c; CB.1249b; K.80.
OT: –.
GEN. REF.: –.

Note: For *katabrabeuō* (*kata*, down, and *brabeuō*, see No. 1), translated "rob (you) of your prize," Col. 2:18, see BEGUILE, Note.

For **PROBATION**, R.V. in Rom. 5:4, see **EXPERIENCE**, No. 2

PROCEED

1. *ekporeuomai* [ἐκπορεύομαι, 1607], to go forth, is translated to proceed out of in Matt. 4:4; 15:11, R.V.; 15:18; Mark 7:15, R.V.; 7:20, R.V.; 7:21; 7:23, R.V.; Luke 4:22; John 15:26; Eph. 4:29; Rev. 1:16, R.V.; 4:5; 9:17, 18, R.V. (A.V., "issued"); 11:5; 19:15, R.V.; 19:21, A.V. (R.V., "came forth"); 22:1. See COME, No. 33, GO, *Note* (1).

NT: B.244b; CB.1244a; K.915.
OT: yāṣā': S.3318; HR.439c.5a; H.893; BD.422b.
GEN. REF.: –.

2. *exerchomai* [ἐξέρχομαι, 1831], is translated "proceed" in Matt. 15:19, A.V. (R.V., "come forth"); John 8:42, R.V., "came forth"; Jas. 3:10. The verb to proceed is not so suitable. See COME, No. 3.

NT: B.274b; CB.1247c; K.257.
OT: yāṣā': S.3318; HR.491c.5a; H.893; BD.422b.
GEN. REF.: –.

3. *prokoptō* [προκόπτω, 4298], lit., to cut forward (a way), is translated "will proceed" in 2 Tim. 2:16, R.V. (A.V., "will increase") and "shall proceed" (both Versions) in 3:9. See INCREASE.

NT: B.707d; CB.1266c; K.939.
OT: –.
GEN. REF.: –.

4. *prostithēmi* [προστίθημι, 4369], to put to, to add, is translated "proceeded" in Acts 12:3 (a Hebraism). See ADD, No. 2.

NT: B.718d; CB.1267b; K.1176.
OT: yāsaph: S.3254; HR.1221a.4a-c; H.876; BD.414d.
GEN. REF.: –.

PROCLAIM

1. *kērussō* [κηρύσσω, 2784], is translated to proclaim in the R.V., for A.V., to preach, in Matt. 10:27; Luke 4:19; Acts 8:5; 9:20. See PREACH, No. 2.

NT: B.431b; CB.1255a; K.430.
OT: qārā': S.7121; HR.763c.5a; H.2063; BD.894d.
GEN. REF.: IS.3:977; NB.–; Z.–.

2. *katangellō* [καταγγέλλω, 2605], to declare, proclaim, is translated to proclaim in the R.V., for A.V., to shew, in Acts 16:17; 26:23; 1 Cor. 11:26, where the verb makes clear that the partaking of the elements at the Lord's Supper is a proclamation (an evangel) of the Lord's Death; in Rom. 1:8, for A.V., "spoken of"; in 1 Cor. 2:1, for A.V., "declaring." See also PREACH, *Note* (2), and DECLARE, A, No. 4.

NT: B.409b; CB.1254a; K.10.
OT: –.
GEN. REF.: IS.3:977; NB.–; Z.–.

3. *plērophoreō* [πληροφορέω, 4135], to bring in full measure (*plērēs*, full, *pherō*, to bring), hence, to fulfil, accomplish, is translated "might be fully proclaimed," in 2 Tim. 4:17, R.V., with *kērugma*, marg., "proclamation" (A.V. ". . . known"). See ASSURE, B, No. 2, BELIEVE, C, *Note* (4), FULFIL, No. 6, KNOW, *Note* (2), PERSUADE, No. 2, *Note*, PROOF.

NT: B.670b; CB.1265b; K.867.
OT: mālē': S.4390; HR.1148b.1; H.1195; BD.569d.
GEN. REF.: IS.3:977; NB.–; Z.–.

PROCONSUL

anthupatos [ἀνθύπατος, 446], from *anti*, instead of, and *hupatos*, supreme, denotes a consul, one acting in place of a consul, a proconsul, the governor of a senatorial province (i.e., one which had no standing army). The proconsuls were of two classes, (*a*) ex-consuls, the rulers of the provinces of Asia and Africa, who were therefore proconsuls, (*b*) those who were ex-praetors or proconsuls of other senatorial provinces (a praetor being virtually the same as a consul). To the former belonged the proconsuls at Ephesus, Acts 19:38 (A.V., "deputies"); to the latter, Sergius Paulus in Cyprus, Acts 13:7, 8, 12, and Gallio at Corinth, 18:12. In the N.T. times Egypt was governed by a prefect. Provinces in which a standing army was kept were governed by an imperial legate (e.g., Quirinius in Syria, Luke 2:2): see GOVERNOR, A, No. 1. ¶

NT: B.69c; CB.1236a; K.–.
OT: –.
GEN. REF.: IS.3:978; NB.1036; Z.4:870.

Note: Anthupateō, to be proconsul, is in some texts in Acts 18:12.

PROFANE (Adjective and Verb)

A. Adjective.

bebēlos [βέβηλος, 952], primarily, permitted to be trodden, accessible (from *bainō*, to go, whence *bēlos*, a threshold), hence, unhallowed, profane (opposite to *hieros*, sacred), is used of (*a*) persons, 1 Tim. 1:9; Heb. 12:16; (*b*) things, 1 Tim. 4:7; 6:20; 2 Tim. 2:16. "The natural antagonism between the profane and the holy or divine grew into a moral antagonism. . . . Accordingly *bebēlos* is that which lacks all relationship or affinity to God" (Cremer, who compares *koinos*, common, in the sense of ritual uncleanness). ¶

NT: B.138d; CB.–; K.104.
OT: ḥōl: S.2455; HR.216b.1a; H.623a,661a; BD.320d.
ḥālal: S.2490; HR.216b.1b; H.660,661; BD.320a.
GEN. REF.: IS.3:979; NB.–; Z.4:872.

B. Verb.

bebēloō [βεβηλόω, 953], primarily, to cross the threshold (akin to A, which see), hence, to profane, pollute, occurs in Matt. 12:5 and Acts 24:6 (the latter as in 21:28, 29; cp. DEFILE, A, No. 1, PARTITION). ¶

NT: B.138d; CB.–; K.104.
OT: ḥālal: S.2490; HR.216b.1c; H.660,661; BD.320a.
GEN. REF.: IS.3:979; NB.–; Z.4:872.

PROFESS, PROFESSION

A. Verbs.

1. *epangellō* [ἐπαγγέλλω, 1861], to announce, proclaim, profess, is rendered to profess in 1 Tim. 2:10, of godliness, and 6:21, of "the knowledge . . . falsely so called." See PROMISE.

NT: B.280d; CB.1245b; K.240.
OT: 'āmar: S.559; HR.503c.1; H.118; BD.55c.
GEN. REF.: IS.3:980; NB.–; Z.–.

2. *homologeō* [ὁμολογέω, 3670], is translated to profess in Matt. 7:23 and Tit. 1:16; in 1 Tim. 6:12, A.V. (R.V., "confess"). See CONFESS.

NT: B.568a; CB.1251a; K.687.
OT: yādāh: S.3034; HR.993c.1; H.847; BD.392a.
GEN. REF.: IS.3:980; NB.–; Z.–.

3. *phaskō* [φάσκω, 5335], to affirm, assert: see AFFIRM, No. 3.

NT: B.854b; CB.–; K.–.
OT: –.
GEN. REF.: IS.3:980; NB.–; Z.–.

B. Noun.

homologia [ὁμολογία, 3671], akin to A, No. 2, confession, is translated "profession" and "professed" in the A.V. only. See CONFESS.

NT: B.568d; CB.1251a; K.687.
OT: –.
GEN. REF.: IS.3:980; NB.1036; Z.–.

PROFIT (Noun and Verb), PROFITABLE, PROFITING

A. Nouns.

1. *ōpheleia* [ὠφέλεια, 5622], primarily denotes assistance; then, advantage, benefit, "profit," Rom. 3:1. See ADVANTAGE, No. 3.

NT: B.900b; CB.1261a; K.–.
OT: beṣa': S.1215; HR.1497a.1; H.267a; BD.130c.
yā'al: S.3276; HR.1497a.2; H.882; BD.418c.
GEN. REF.: IS.3:980; NB.–; Z.–.

2. *ophelos* [ὄφελος, 3786], "profit" in Jas. 2:14, 16: see ADVANTAGE, No. 2.

NT: B.599b; CB.–; K.–.
OT: yā'al: S.3276; HR.1039b.1; H.882; BD.418c.
GEN. REF.: IS.3:980; NB.–; Z.–.

3. *sumpheron* [συμφέρον, —], the neuter form of the present participle of *sumpherō* (see B, No. 1), is used as a noun with the article in Heb. 12:10, "(for our) profit"; in some mss. in 1 Cor. 7:35 and 10:33 (see No. 4); in 1 Cor. 12:7, preceded by *pros*, with a view to, towards, translated "to profit withal," lit., 'towards the profiting.' ¶

NT: B.780b; CB.–; K.–.
OT: –.
GEN. REF.: –.

4. *sumphoros* [σύμφορος, —], akin to No. 3, an adjective, signifying profitable, useful, expedient, is used as a noun, and found in the best texts, with the article, in 1 Cor. 7:35 (see No. 3) and 10:33 (1st part), the word being understood in the 2nd part. ¶

NT: B.780b; CB.–; K.1252.
OT: –.
GEN. REF.: –.

5. *prokopē* [προκοπή, 4297], translated "profiting" in 1 Tim. 4:15, A.V. (R.V., "progress"); see FURTHERANCE.

NT: B.707d; CB.1266c; K.939.
OT: –.
GEN. REF.: –.

B. Verbs.

1. *sumpherō* [συμφέρω, 4851], to be "profitable," Matt. 5:29, 30; Acts 20:20: see EXPEDIENT.

NT: B.780b; CB.–; K.1252.
OT: –.
GEN. REF.: IS.3:980; NB.–; Z.–.

2. *ōpheleō* [ὠφελέω, 5623], akin to A, No. 1, is translated 'to profit' in Matt. 15:5; 16:26;

Mark 7:11; 8:36; Luke 9:25, R.V.; John 6:63; Rom. 2:25; 1 Cor. 13:3; 14:6; Gal. 5:2; Heb. 4:2; 13:9. See ADVANTAGE, BETTERED, PREVAIL.

NT: B.900c; CB.1261a; K.—.
OT: yā 'al: S.3276; HR.1497b.1; H.882; BD.418c.
GEN. REF.: IS.3:980; NB.—; Z.—.

3. *prokoptō* [προκόπτω, 4298], is translated "I profited" in Gal. 1:14, A.V. See ADVANCE.

NT: B.707d; CB.1266c; K.939.
OT: —.
GEN. REF.: —.

C. Adjectives.

1. *chrēsimos* [χρήσιμος, 5539], useful (akin to *chraomai*, to use), is translated as a noun in 2 Tim. 2:14, "to (no) profit," lit., 'to (nothing) profitable.' ¶

NT: B.885d; CB.—; K.—.
OT: beṣa': S.1215; HR.1474c.1; H.267a; BD.130c.
GEN. REF.: IS.3:980; NB.—; Z.—.

2. *euchrēstos* [εὔχρηστος, 2173], useful, serviceable (*eu*, well, *chrēstos*, serviceable, akin to *chraomai*, see No. 1), is used in Philm. 11, "profitable," in contrast to *achrēstos*, "unprofitable" (*a*, negative), with a delightful play upon the name "Onesimus," signifying "profitable" (from *onēsis*, profit), a common name among slaves. Perhaps the prefix *eu* should have been brought out by some rendering like 'very profitable,' 'very serviceable,' the suggestion being that whereas the runaway slave had done great disservice to Philemon, now after his conversion, in devotedly serving the Apostle in his confinement, he had thereby already become particularly serviceable to Philemon himself, considering that the latter would have most willingly rendered service to Paul, had it been possible. Onesimus, who had belied his name, was now true to it on behalf of his erstwhile master, who also owed his conversion to the Apostle.

It is translated "meet for (the master's) use" in 2 Tim. 2:21; "useful" in 4:11, R.V. (A.V., "profitable"). See USEFUL. ¶ In the Sept., Prov. 31:13. ¶

NT: B.329c; CB.—; K.—.
OT: ḥēpheṣ: S.2656; HR.584c.1; H.712b; BD.343a.
GEN. REF.: —.

3. *ōphelimos* [ὠφέλιμος, 5624], useful, profitable (akin to B, No. 2), is translated "profitable" in 1 Tim. 4:8, both times in the R.V. (A.V., "profiteth" in the 1st part), of physical exercise, and of godliness; in 2 Tim. 3:16 of the God-breathed Scriptures; in Tit. 3:8, of maintaining good works. ¶

NT: B.900d; CB.—; K.—.
OT: —.
GEN. REF.: IS.3:980; NB.—; Z.—.

PROGRESS

prokopē [προκοπή, 4297], is translated "progress" in Phil. 1:12, 25 and 1 Tim. 4:15: see FURTHERANCE. ¶

NT: B.707d; CB.1266c; K.939.
OT: —.
GEN. REF.: —.

PROLONG

parateinō [παρατείνω, 3905], to stretch out along (*para*, along, *teinō*, to stretch), is translated "prolonged" in Acts 20:7, R.V., of Paul's discourse: see CONTINUE, *Note* (1). ¶

NT: B.622c; CB.—; K.—.
OT: māshak: S.4900; HR.1065a.3; H.1257; BD.604a.
GEN. REF.: —.

PROMISE (Noun and Verb)

A. Nouns.

1. *epangelia* [ἐπαγγελία, 1860], primarily a law term, denoting a summons (*epi*, upon, *angellō*, to proclaim, announce), also meant an undertaking to do or give something, a promise. Except in Acts 23:21 it is used only of the promises of God. It frequently stands for the thing promised, and so signifies a gift graciously bestowed, not a pledge secured by negotiation; thus, in Gal. 3:14, "the promise of the Spirit" denotes 'the promised Spirit': cp. Luke 24:49; Acts 2:33 and Eph. 1:13; so in Heb. 9:15, "the promise of the eternal inheritance" is 'the promised eternal inheritance.' On the other hand, in Acts 1:4, "the promise of the Father," is the promise made by the Father.

In Gal. 3:16, the plural "promises" is used because the one promise to Abraham was variously repeated (Gen. 12:1-3; 13:14-17; 15:18; 17:1-14; 22:15-18), and because it contained the germ of all subsequent promises; cp. Rom. 9:4; Heb. 6:12; 7:6; 8:6; 11:17. Gal. 3 is occupied with showing that the promise was conditional upon faith and not upon the fulfilment of the Law. The Law was later than, and inferior to, the promise, and did not annul it, ver. 21; cp. 4:23, 28. Again, in Eph. 2:12, "the covenants of the promise" does not indicate different covenants, but a covenant often renewed, all centring in Christ as the promised Messiah-Redeemer, and comprising the blessings to be bestowed through Him.

In 2 Cor. 1:20 the plural is used of every promise made by God: cp. Heb. 11:33; in 7:6, of special promises mentioned. For other applications of the word, see, e.g., Eph. 6:2; 1 Tim. 4:8; 2 Tim. 1:1; Heb. 4:1; 2 Pet. 3:4, 9; in 1 John 1:5 some mss. have this word, instead of *angelia*, "message."

The occurrences of the word in relation to Christ and what centres in Him, may be arranged under the headings (1) the contents of the promise, e.g., Acts 26:6; Rom. 4:20; 1 John 2:25; (2) the heirs, e.g., Rom. 9:8; 15:8; Gal. 3:29; Heb. 11:9; (3) the conditions, e.g., Rom. 4:13, 14; Gal. 3:14-22; Heb. 10:36.

NT: B.280c; CB.1245b; K.240.
OT: –.
GEN. REF.: IS.3:981; NB.1036; Z.4:872.

2. *epangelma* [ἐπάγγελμα, 1862], denotes a promise made, 2 Pet. 1:4; 3:13. ¶

NT: B.281a; CB.1245b; K.240.
OT: –.
GEN. REF.: IS.3:981; NB.1036; Z.–.

B. Verbs.

1. *epangellō* [ἐπαγγέλλω, 1861], to announce, proclaim, has in the N.T. the two meanings to profess and to promise, each used in the Middle Voice; to promise (*a*) of promises of God, Acts 7:5; Rom. 4:21; in Gal. 3:19, Passive Voice; Tit. 1:2; Heb. 6:13; 10:23; 11:11; 12:26; Jas. 1:12; 2:5; 1 John 2:25; (*b*) made by men, Mark 14:11; 2 Pet. 2:19. See PROFESS.

NT: B.280d; CB.1245b; K.240.
OT: 'āmar: S.559; HR.503c.1; H.118; BD.55c.
GEN. REF.: IS.3:981; NB.1036; Z.4:870.

2. *proepangellō* [προεπαγγέλλω, 4279], in the Middle Voice, to promise before (*pro*, and No. 1), occurs in Rom. 1:2; 2 Cor. 9:5. See AFOREPROMISED. ¶

NT: B.705b; CB.1266c; K.240.
OT: –.
GEN. REF.: IS.3:981; NB.1036; Z.–.

3. *homologeō* [ὁμολογέω, 3670], to agree, confess, signifies to promise in Matt. 14:7. See CONFESS.

NT: B.568a; CB.1251a; K.687.
OT: nādar: S.5087; HR.993c.2; H.1308; BD.623d.
GEN. REF.: IS.3:981; NB.1036; Z.–.

Note For *exomologeō* in Luke 22:6, see CONSENT, No. 1.

PRONOUNCE

legō [λέγω, 3004], to say, declare, is rendered "pronounceth (blessing)" in Rom. 4:6, R.V., which necessarily repeats the verb in ver. 9 (it is absent from the original), for A.V., "*cometh*" (italicised). See ASK, A, No. 6, DESCRIBE, No. 2, SAY.

NT: B.468a; CB.1256c; K.505.
OT: 'āmar: S.559; HR.863c.1a; H.118; BD.55c.
GEN. REF.: –.

PROOF

1. *dokimē* [δοκιμή, —]: see EXPERIENCE, No. 2.

2. *dokimion* [δοκίμιον, 1383], a test, a proof, is rendered "proof" in Jas. 1:3, R.V. (A.V., "trying"); it is regarded by some as equivalent to *dokimeion*, a crucible, a test; it is the neuter form of the adjective *dokimios*, used as a noun, which has been taken to denote the means by which a man is tested and proved (Mayor), in the same sense as *dokimē* (No. 1) in 2 Cor. 8:2; the same phrase is used in 1 Pet. 1:7, R.V., "the proof (of your faith)," A.V., "the trial"; where the meaning probably is 'that which is approved [i.e., as genuine] in your faith'; this interpretation, which was suggested by Hort, and may hold good for Jas. 1:3, has been confirmed from the papyri by Deissmann (*Bible Studies*, p. 259, ff). Moulton and Milligan (Vocab.) give additional instances. ¶

NT: B.203a; CB.1242a; K.181.
OT: zāqaq: S.2212; HR.340a.1; H.576; BD.279b.
ʿalîl: S.5948; HR.340a.4; H.1628b; BD.760d.
GEN. REF.: –.

3. *endeixis* [ἔνδειξις, 1732]: see DECLARE, B. Cp. the synonymous word *endeigma*, a token, 2 Thess. 1:5, which refers rather to the thing proved, while *endeixis* points to the act of proving.

NT: B.262d; CB.1244c; K.–.
OT: –.
GEN. REF.: IS.3:983; NB.–; Z.–.

4. *tekmērion* [τεκμήριον, 5039], a sure sign, a positive proof (from *tekmar*, a mark, sign), occurs in Acts 1:3, R.V., "proofs" (A.V., "infallible proofs"; a proof does not require to be described as infallible, the adjective is superfluous). ¶

NT: B.808a; CB.1271b; K.–.
OT: –.
GEN. REF.: –.

Note: For the A.V. in 2 Tim. 4:5, "make full proof," R.V., "fulfil" (*plērophoreō*), see FULFIL.

PROPER

1. *asteios* [ἀστεῖος, 791], is translated "proper" in Heb. 11:23, R.V., "goodly": see BEAUTIFUL, No. 2.

NT: B.117c; CB.–; K.–.
OT: –.
GEN. REF.: –.

2. *idios* [ἴδιος, 2398], one's own, is found in some mss. in Acts 1:19, A.V., "proper"; in 1 Cor. 7:7, R.V., "own" (A.V., "proper"); in Jude 6, R.V., "their proper (habitation)," A.V. "their own."

NT: B.369c; CB.1252c; K.–.
OT: –.
GEN. REF.: IS.3:983; NB.–; Z.–.

PROPHECY, PROPHESY, PROPHESYING

A. Noun.

prophēteia [προφητεία, 4394], signifies the speaking forth of the mind and counsel of God (*pro*, forth, *phēmi*, to speak: see PROPHET); in the N.T. it is used (*a*) of the gift, e.g., Rom. 12:6;

1 Cor. 12:10; 13:2; (*b*) either of the exercise of the gift or of that which is prophesied, e.g., Matt. 13:14; 1 Cor. 13:8; 14:6, 22 and 1 Thess. 5:20, "prophesying (s)"; 1 Tim. 1:18; 4:14; 2 Pet. 1:20, 21; Rev. 1:3; 11:6; 19:10; 22:7, 10, 18, 19. ¶

"Though much of O.T. prophecy was purely predictive, see Micah 5:2, e.g., and cp. John 11:51, prophecy is not necessarily, nor even primarily, fore-telling. It is the declaration of that which cannot be known by natural means, Matt. 26:68, it is the forth-telling of the will of God, whether with reference to the past, the present, or the future, see Gen. 20:7; Deut. 18:18; Rev. 10:11; 11:3. . . .

"In such passages as 1 Cor. 12:28; Eph. 2:20, the 'prophets' are placed after the 'Apostles,' since not the prophets of Israel are intended, but the 'gifts' of the ascended Lord, Eph. 4:8, 11; cp. Acts 13:1; . . . .; the purpose of their ministry was to edify, to comfort, and to encourage the believers, 1 Cor. 14:3, while its effect upon unbelievers was to show that the secrets of a man's heart are known to God, to convict of sin, and to constrain to worship, vv. 24, 25.

"With the completion of the canon of Scripture prophecy apparently passed away, 1 Cor. 13:8, 9. In his measure the teacher has taken the place of the prophet, cp. the significant change in 2 Pet. 2:1. The difference is that, whereas the message of the prophet was a direct revelation of the mind of God for the occasion, the message of the teacher is gathered from the completed revelation contained in the Scriptures."*

NT: B.722d; CB.1267a; K.952.
OT: nᵉbû'āh: S.5016; HR.1231c.2; H.1277b; BD.612c.
ḥāzôn: S.2377; HR.1231c.1; H.633a; BD.302d.
GEN. REF.: IS.3:984; NB.1036; Z.4:875.

B. Adjective.

prophētikos [προφητικός, 4397], of or relating to prophecy, or proceeding from a prophet, prophetic, is used of the O.T. Scriptures, Rom. 16:26, "of the prophets," lit., '(by) prophetic (Scriptures)'; 2 Pet. 1:19, "the word of prophecy (*made* more sure)," i.e., confirmed by the Person and work of Christ (A.V., "a more sure etc."), lit., 'the prophetic word.' ¶

NT: B.724b; CB.1267a; K.952.
OT: –.
GEN. REF.: IS.3:984; NB.1036; Z.4:875.

C. Verb.

prophēteuō [προφητεύω, 4395], to be a prophet, to prophesy, is used (*a*) with the primary meaning of telling forth the Divine counsels, e.g., Matt. 7:22; 26:68; 1 Cor. 11:4, 5; 13:9; 14:1, 3-5, 24, 31, 39; Rev. 11:3; (*b*) of foretelling the future, e.g., Matt. 15:7; John 11:51; 1 Pet. 1:10; Jude 14.

NT: B.723a; CB.1267a; K.952.
OT: nābā': S.5012; HR.1231c.2a,b; H.1277; BD.612a.
GEN. REF.: IS.3:984; NB.1036; Z.4:875.

PROPHET

1. *prophētēs* [προφήτης, 4396], one who speaks forth or openly (see PROPHECY, A), a proclaimer of a divine message, denoted among the Greeks an interpreter of the oracles of the gods.

In the Sept. it is the translation of the word *rôeh*, a seer; 1 Sam. 9:9, indicating that the prophet was one who had immediate intercourse with God. It also translates the word *nābhî*, meaning either one in whom the message from God springs forth or one to whom anything is secretly communicated. Hence, in general, the prophet was one upon whom the Spirit of God rested, Numb. 11:17-29, one, to whom and through whom God speaks, Numb. 12:2; Amos 3:7, 8. In the case of the O.T. prophets their messages were very largely the proclamation of the Divine purposes of salvation and glory to be accomplished in the future; the prophesying of the N.T. prophets was both a preaching of the Divine counsels of grace already accomplished and the fore-telling of the purposes of God in the future.

In the N.T. the word is used (*a*) of the O.T. prophets, e.g., Matt. 5:12; Mark 6:15; Luke 4:27; John 8:52; Rom. 11:3; (*b*) of prophets in general, e.g., Matt. 10:41; 21:46; Mark 6:4; (*c*) of John the Baptist, Matt. 21:26; Luke 1:76; (*d*) of prophets in the churches, e.g., Acts 13:1; 15:32; 21:10; 1 Cor. 12:28, 29; 14:29, 32, 37; Eph. 2:20; 3:5; 4:11; (*e*) of Christ, as the afore-promised Prophet, e.g., John 1:21; 6:14; 7:40; Acts 3:22; 7:37, or, without the article, and, without reference to the Old Testament, Mark 6:15, Luke 7:16; in Luke 24:19 it is used with *anēr*, a man; John 4:19; 9:17; (*f*) of two witnesses yet to be raised up for special purposes, Rev. 11:10, 18; (*g*) of the Cretan poet Epimenides, Tit. 1:12; (*h*) by metonymy, of the writings of prophets, e.g., Luke 24:27; Acts 8:28.

NT: B.723b; CB.1267a; K.952.
OT: nābî': S.5030; HR.1232b.2a; H.1277a; BD.611c.
GEN. REF.: IS.3:984; NB.1036; Z.4:875.

2. *pseudoprophētēs* [ψευδοπροφήτης, 5578], a false prophet, is used of such (*a*) in O.T. times,

* From Notes on Thessalonians by Hogg and Vine, pp. 196, 197.

Luke 6:26; 2 Pet. 2:1; (*b*) in the present period since Pentecost, Matt. 7:15; 24:11, 24; Mark 13:22; Acts 13:6; 1 John 4:1; (*c*) with reference to a false prophet destined to arise as the supporter of the "beast" at the close of this age, Rev. 16:13; 19:20; 20:10 (himself described as "another beast," 13:11). ¶

NT: B.892a; CB.1267c; K.952.
OT: nābî': S.5030; HR.1485a.1; H.1277a; BD.611c.
GEN. REF.: IS.3:984; NB.1036; Z.4:875.

PROPHETESS

prophētis [προφῆτις, 4398], the feminine of *prophētēs* (see above), is used of Anna, Luke 2:36; of the self-assumed title of "the woman Jezebel" in Rev. 2:20. ¶

NT: B.724b; CB.1267a; K.952.
OT: n^{e}bî'āh: S.5031; HR.1233c.1; H.1277c; BD.612c.
GEN. REF.: IS.3:984; NB.1045; Z.4:874,877.

PROPITIATION

A. Verb.

hilaskomai [ἱλάσκομαι, 2433], was used amongst the Greeks with the significance to make the gods propitious, to appease, propitiate, inasmuch as their good will was not conceived as their natural attitude, but something to be earned first. This use of the word is foreign to the Greek Bible, with respect to God, whether in the Sept. or in the N.T. It is never used of any act whereby man brings God into a favourable attitude or gracious disposition. It is God who is propitiated by the vindication of His holy and righteous character, whereby, through the provision He has made in the vicarious and expiatory sacrifice of Christ, He has so dealt with sin that He can shew mercy to the believing sinner in the removal of his guilt and the remission of his sins.

Thus in Luke 18:13 it signifies to be propitious or merciful to (with the person as the object of the verb), and in Heb. 2:17 to expiate, to make propitiation for (the object of the verb being sins); here the R.V., "to make propitiation" is an important correction of the A.V., "to make reconciliation." Through the propitiatory sacrifice of Christ, he who believes upon Him is by God's own act delivered from justly deserved wrath, and comes under the covenant of grace. Never is God said to be reconciled, a fact itself indicative that the enmity exists on man's part alone, and that it is man who needs to be reconciled to God, and not God to man. God is always the same and, since He is Himself immutable, His relative attitude does change towards those who change. He can act differently towards those who come to Him by faith, and solely on the ground of the propitiatory sacrifice of Christ, not because He has changed, but because He ever acts according to His unchanging righteousness.

The expiatory work of the Cross is therefore the means whereby the barrier which sin interposes between God and man is broken down. By the giving up of His sinless life sacrificially, Christ annuls the power of sin to separate between God and the believer.

In the O.T. the Hebrew verb *kaphar* is connected with *kopher*, a covering (see MERCY-SEAT), and is used in connection with the burnt offering, e.g., Lev. 1:4; 14:20; 16:24, the guilt offering, e.g., Lev. 5:16, 18, the sin offering, e.g., Lev. 4:20, 26, 31, 35, the sin offering and burnt offering together, e.g., Lev. 5:10; 9:7, the meal offering and peace offering, e.g., Ezek. 45:15, 17, as well as in other respects. It is used of the ram offered at the consecration of the high priest, Ex. 29:33, and of the blood which God gave upon the altar to make propitiation for the souls of the people, and that because "the life of the flesh is in the blood," Lev. 17:11, and "it is the blood that maketh atonement by reason of the life" (R.V.). Man has forfeited his life on account of sin and God has provided the one and only way whereby eternal life could be bestowed, namely, by the voluntary laying down of His life by His Son, under Divine retribution. Of this the former sacrifices appointed by God were foreshadowings.

NT: B.375c; CB.1250c; K.362.
OT: kipper (kāphar): S.3722; HR.684b.1; H.1023-1026; BD.497b.
sālaḥ: S.5545; HR.684b.3; H.1505; BD.699b.
GEN. REF.: IS.3:1004; NB.1046; Z.4:903.

B. Nouns.

1. *hilastērion* [ἱλαστήριον, 2435], akin to A, is regarded as the neuter of an adjective signifying propitiatory. In the Sept. it is used adjectivally in connection with *epithēma*, a cover, in Ex. 25:17 and 37:6, of the lid of the ark (see MERCY-SEAT), but it is used as a noun (without *epithēma*), of locality, in Ex. 25:18, 19, 20, 21, 22; 31:7; 35:12; 37:7, 8, 9; Lev. 16:2, 13, 14, 15; Numb. 7:89, and this is its use in Heb. 9:5.

Elsewhere in the N.T. it occurs in Rom. 3:25, where it is used of Christ Himself; the R.V. text and punctuation in this verse are important: "whom God set forth *to be* a propitiation, through faith, by His blood." The phrase "by His blood" is to be taken in immediate connection with "propitiation." Christ, through His expiatory death, is the Personal means by whom God shows the mercy of His justifying grace to the sinner who believes. His "blood" stands for the voluntary giving up of His life, by the shedding of His blood in expiatory sacrifice, under Divine judgment righteously due to us as sinners, faith being the sole condition on man's part.

NT: B.375d; CB.1250c; K.362.
OT: kappōret: S.3727; HR.684c.1; H.1023c; BD.498c.
GEN. REF.: IS.3:1004; NB.1046; Z.4:903.

Note: "By metonymy, 'blood' is sometimes put for 'death,' inasmuch as, blood being essential to life, Lev. 17:11, when the blood is shed life is given up, that is, death takes place. The fundamental principle on which God deals with sinners is expressed in the words 'apart from shedding of blood,' i.e., unless a death takes place, 'there is no remission' of sins, Heb. 9:22.

"But whereas the essential of the type lay in the fact that blood was shed, the essential of the antitype lies in this, that the blood shed was that of Christ. Hence, in connection with Jewish sacrifices, 'the blood' is mentioned without reference to the victim from which it flowed, but in connection with the great antitypical sacrifice of the N.T. the words 'the blood' never stand alone; the One Who shed the blood is invariably specified, for it is the Person that gives value to the work; the saving efficacy of the Death depends entirely upon the fact that He Who died was the Son of God."*

2. *hilasmos* [ἱλασμός, 2434], akin to *hileōs* (merciful, propitious), signifies an expiation, a means whereby sin is covered and remitted. It is used in the N.T. of Christ Himself as "the propitiation," in 1 John 2:2 and 4:10, signifying that He Himself, through the expiatory sacrifice of His Death, is the Personal means by whom God shows mercy to the sinner who believes on Christ as the One thus provided. In the former passage He is described as "the propitiation for our sins; and not for ours only, but also for the whole world." The italicised addition in the A.V., "*the sins of*," gives a wrong interpretation. What is indicated is that provision is made for the whole world, so that no one is, by Divine pre-determination, excluded from the scope of God's mercy; the efficacy of the propitiation, however, is made actual for those who believe. In 4:10, the fact that God "sent His Son to be the propitiation for our sins," is shown to be the great expression of God's love toward man and the reason why Christians should love one another. ¶ In the Sept., Lev. 25:9; Numb. 5:8; 1 Chron. 28:20; Ps. 130:4; Ezek. 44:27; Amos 8:14. ¶

NT: B.375c; CB.1250c; K.362.
OT: kippurîm: S.3725; HR.684c.2; H.1023b; BD.498c.
sᵉlîḥāh: S.5547; HR.684c.4; H.1505b; BD.699c.
GEN. REF.: IS.3:1004; NB.1046; Z.4:903.

PROPORTION

analogia [ἀναλογία, 356], Eng., analogy, signified in classical Greek "the right relation, the coincidence or agreement existing or demanded according to the standard of the several relations, not agreement as equality" (Cremer). It is used in Rom. 12:6, where "let us prophesy according to the proportion of our faith," R.V., recalls v. 3. It is a warning against going beyond what God has given and faith receives. This meaning, rather than the other rendering, "according to the analogy of the faith," is in keeping with the context. The word *analogia* is not to be rendered literally. "Proportion" here represents its true meaning. The fact that there is a definite article before "faith" in the original does not necessarily afford an intimation that the faith, the body of Christian doctrine, is here in view. The presence of the definite article is due to the fact that faith is an abstract noun. The meaning "the faith" is not relevant to the context. ¶

NT: B.57b; CB.1235a; K.56.
OT: —.
GEN. REF.: IS.3:1005; NB.—; Z.—.

PROSELYTE

prosēlutos [προσήλυτος, 4339], akin to *proserchomai*, to come to, primarily signifies one who has arrived, a stranger; in the N.T. it is used of converts to Judaism, or foreign converts to the Jewish religion, Matt. 23:15; Acts 2:10; 6:5; 13:43. ¶ There seems to be no connexion necessarily with Palestine, for in Acts 2:10 and 13:43 it is used of those who lived abroad. Cp. the Sept., e.g., in Ex. 22:21; 23:9; Deut. 10:19, of the "stranger" living among the children of Israel.

NT: B.715a; CB.1267a; K.943.
OT: gēr: S.1616; HR.1216a.1; H.330a; BD.158a.
GEN. REF.: IS.3:1005; NB.1047; Z.4:905.

PROSPER

euodoō [εὐοδόω, 2137], to help on one's way (*eu*, well, *hodos*, a way or journey), is used in the Passive Voice signifying to have a prosperous journey, Rom. 1:10; metaphorically, to prosper, be prospered, 1 Cor. 16:2, R.V., "(as)

* From Notes on Thessalonians by Hogg and Vine, p. 168.

he may prosper," A.V., "(as God) hath prospered (him)," lit., 'in whatever he may be prospered,' i.e., in material things; the continuous tense suggests the successive circumstances of varying prosperity as week follows week; in 3 John 2, of the prosperity of physical and spiritual health. ¶

NT: B.323d; CB.—; K.666.
OT: ṣālēaḥ: S.6743; HR.575c.3b; H.1916,1917; BD.852b.
GEN. REF.: IS.3:1011; NB.—; Z.—.

PROTEST

Note: In 1 Cor. 15:31, "I protest by" is a rendering of *nē*, a particle of strong affirmation used in oaths. ¶ In the Sept., Gen. 42:15, 16. ¶

PROUD

huperēphanos [ὑπερήφανος, 5244], signifies showing oneself above others, pre-eminent (*huper*, above, *phainomai*, to appear, be manifest); it is always used in Scripture in the bad sense of arrogant, disdainful, proud, Luke 1:51; Rom. 1:30; 2 Tim. 3:2; Jas. 4:6; 1 Pet. 5:5. ¶

NT: B.841b; CB.1252a; K.1231.
OT: zēd: S.2086; HR.1410a.3; H.547a; BD.267d.
GEN. REF.: IS.3:960; NB.—; Z.—.

Note: For the A.V. renderings of the verb *tuphoō*, in 1 Tim. 3:6; 6:4; 2 Tim. 3:4, see HIGH-MINDED.

PROVE

A. Verbs.

1. *dokimazō* [δοκιμάζω, 1381], prove, with the expectation of approving, is translated to prove in Luke 14:19; Rom. 12:2; 1 Cor. 3:13, R.V. (A.V., "shall try"); 11:28, R.V. (A.V., "examine"); 2 Cor. 8:8, 22; 13:5; Gal. 6:4; Eph. 5:10; 1 Thess. 2:4 (2nd part), R.V. (A.V., "trieth"); 5:21; 1 Tim. 3:10; in some mss., Heb. 3:9 (the most authentic have the noun *dokimasia*, a proving ¶); 1 Pet. 1:7, R.V. (A.V., "tried"); 1 John 4:1, R.V. (A.V., "try"). See APPROVE.

NT: B.202c; CB.1242a; K.181.
OT: bāḥan: S.974; HR.339c.1; H.230; BD.103c.
GEN. REF.: IS.3:983; NB.—; Z.—.

2. *apodeiknumi* [ἀποδείκνυμι, 584], to show forth, signifies to prove in Acts 25:7. See APPROVE, No. 3.

NT: B.89c; CB.1236c; K.—.
OT: —.
GEN. REF.: IS.3:983; NB.—; Z.—.

3. *paristēmi* [παρίστημι, 3936], to present, signifies to prove in Acts 24:13. See COMMEND, No. 4.

NT: B.627c; CB.1262b; K.788.
OT: —.
GEN. REF.: IS.3:983; NB.—; Z.—.

4. *peirazō* [πειράζω, 3985], to try, either in the sense of attempting, e.g., Acts 16:7, or of testing, is rendered "to prove" in John 6:6. See EXAMINE, TEMPT.

NT: B.640b; CB.1263a; K.822.
OT: nāsāh: S.5254; HR.1115c.1; H.1373; BD.650a.
GEN. REF.: IS.3:983; NB.—; Z.—.

5. *sumbibazō* [συμβιβάζω, 4822], to join together, signifies to prove in Acts 9:22. See COMPACTED, No. 2.

NT: B.777d; CB.—; K.1101.
OT: yāda‘: S.3045; HR.1303b.2; H.848; BD.393b.
yārāh: S.3384; HR.1303b.3; H.910; BD.434d.
GEN. REF.: IS.3:983; NB.—; Z.—.

6. *sunistēmi* or *sunistanō* [συνίστημι, 4921], to commend, to prove, is translated "I prove (myself a transgressor)" in Gal. 2:18 (A.V., "I make"). See COMMEND.

NT: B.790c; CB.1270c; K.1120.
OT: —.
GEN. REF.: IS.3:983; NB.—; Z.—.

B. Noun.

peirasmos [πειρασμός, 3986], (*a*) a trying, testing, (*b*) a temptation, is used in sense (*a*) in 1 Pet. 4:12, with the preposition *pros*, towards or with a view to, R.V., "to prove" (A.V., "to try"), lit., 'for a testing.' See TEMPTATION.

NT: B.640d; CB.1263a; K.822.
OT: massāh: S.4531; HR.1116a.1; H.1223b; BD.650b.
GEN. REF.: IS.3:983; NB.—; Z.—.

Notes: (1) In Luke 10:36, R.V. *ginomai*, to become, come to be, is translated "proved (neighbour)," A.V., "was . . . ;" so in Heb. 2:2.

(2) In Rom. 3:9, A.V., *proaitiaomai*, to accuse beforehand, is translated "we have before proved" (marg., "charged"); for the R.V., see CHARGE, C, No. 9.

For **PROVERB** see **PARABLE**, No. 2

PROVIDE, PROVIDENCE, PROVISION

A. Verbs.

1. *hetoimazō* [ἑτοιμάζω, 2090], to prepare, is translated "hast provided" in Luke 12:20, A.V. see PREPARE.

NT: B.316a; CB.1250b; K.266.
OT: kûn: S.3559; HR.563c.5; H.964; BD.465c.
GEN. REF.: —.

2. *ktaomai* [κτάομαι, 2932], to get, to gain, is rendered "provide" in Matt. 10:9. See OBTAIN, POSSESS.

NT: B.455a; CB.1256a; K.—.
OT: qānāh: S.7069; HR.793b.9a; H.2039; BD.888d.
GEN. REF.: —.

3. *paristēmi* [παρίστημι, 3936], to present, signifies to provide in Acts 23:24. See COMMEND, PROVE, No. 3.

NT: B.627c; CB.1262b; K.788.
OT: —.
GEN. REF.: —.

4. *problepō* [προβλέπω, 4265], to foresee, is translated "having provided" in Heb. 11:40. See FORESEE. ¶

NT: B.703c; CB.—; K.—.
OT: rā'āh: S.7200; HR.1205c.1; H.2095; BD.906b.
GEN. REF.: —.

5. *pronoeō* [προνοέω, 4306], to take thought for, provide, is translated "provide . . . for" in 1 Tim. 5:8; in Rom. 12:17 and 2 Cor. 8:21, R.V., to take thought for (A.V., to provide). ¶

NT: B.708c; CB.1266c; K.636.
OT: bîn: S.995; HR.1207c.1; H.239; BD.106c.
GEN. REF.: —.

Note: In Luke 12:33, A.V., *poieō*, to make (R.V.), is translated "provide."

B. Noun.

pronoia [πρόνοια, 4307], forethought (*pro*, before, *noeō*, to think), is translated "providence" in Acts 24:2; "provision" in Rom. 13:14. ¶

NT: B.708d; CB.1266c; K.636.
OT: —.
GEN. REF.: —.

PROVINCE

1. *eparcheia* or *-ia* [ἐπαρχεία, 1885], was a technical term for the administrative divisions of the Roman Empire. The original meaning was the district within which a magistrate, whether consul or praetor, exercised supreme authority. The word *provincia* acquired its later meaning when Sardinia and Sicily were added to the Roman territories, 227 B.C. On the establishment of the Empire the proconsular power over all provinces was vested in the Emperor. Two provinces, Asia and Africa, were consular, i.e., held by ex-consuls; the rest were praetorian. Certain small provinces, e.g. Judaea and Cappadocia, were governed by procurators. They were usually districts recently added to the Empire and not thoroughly Romanized. Judaea was so governed in the intervals between the rule of native kings; ultimately it was incorporated in the province of Syria. The province mentioned in Acts 23:34 and 25:1 was assigned to the jurisdiction of an *eparchos*, a prefect or governor (cp. GOVERNOR, PROCONSUL). ¶ In the Sept., Esth. 4:11. ¶

NT: B.283c; CB.—; K.—.
OT: m^e^dînāh: S.4082; HR.508b.1; H.426d; BD.193d.
GEN. REF.: IS.3:1025; NB.1052; Z.4:923.

2. *kanōn* [κανών, 2583], originally denoted a straight rod, used as a ruler or measuring instrument, or, in rare instances, the beam of a balance, the secondary notion being either (*a*) of keeping anything straight, as of a rod used in weaving, or (*b*) of testing straightness, as a carpenter's rule; hence its metaphorical use to express what serves to measure or determine anything. By a common transition in the meaning of words, that which measures, was used for what was measured; thus a certain space at Olympia was called a *kanōn*. So in music, a canon is a composition in which a given melody is the model for the formation of all the parts. In general the word thus came to serve for anything regulating the actions of men, as a standard or principle. In Gal. 6:16, those who "walk by this rule (*kanōn*)" are those who make what is stated in vv. 14 and 15 their guiding line in the matter of salvation through faith in Christ alone, apart from works, whether following the principle themselves or teaching it to others. In 2 Cor. 10:13, 15, 16, it is translated "province," R.V. (A.V., "rule" and "line of things"; marg., "line"; R.V. marg., "limit" or "measuring rod." Here it signifies the limits of the responsibility in gospel service as measured and appointed by God. ¶

NT: B.403a; CB.1253b; K.414.
OT: —.
GEN. REF.: —.

For **PROVING** (*elenchos*) see **REPROOF**, A

PROVOCATION, PROVOKE

A. Nouns.

1. *parapikrasmos* [παραπικρασμός, 3894], from *para*, amiss or from, used intensively, and *pikrainō*, to make bitter (*pikros*, sharp, bitter), provocation, occurs in Heb. 3:8, 15. ¶ In the Sept., Psa. 95:8. ¶

NT: B.621b; CB.1262b; K.839.
OT: m^e^rîbāh: S.4808; HR.1063b.1; H.2159c; BD.937b.
GEN. REF.: IS.3:1028; NB.—; Z.4:924.

2. *paroxusmos* [παροξυσμός, 3948], denotes a stimulation (Eng., paroxysm), (cp. B, No. 2): in Heb. 10:24, "to provoke," lit., 'unto a stimulation (of love).' See CONTENTION, No. 2.

NT: B.629c; CB.1262c; K.791.
OT: qeṣeph: S.7110; HR.1072b.1; H.2058a; BD.893c.
GEN. REF.: IS.3:1028; NB.—; Z.—.

B. Verbs.

1. *parapikrainō* [παραπικραίνω, 3893], to embitter, provoke (akin to A, No. 1), occurs in Heb. 3:16. ¶

NT: B.621a; CB.1262b; K.839.
OT: mārāh: S.4784; HR.1063a.3a,b; H.1242; BD.598a.
kā'as: S.3707; HR.1063a.1; H.1016; BD.494d.
GEN. REF.: IS.3:1028; NB.—; Z.4:924.

2. *paroxunō* [παροξύνω, 3947], primarily, to sharpen (akin to A, No. 2), is used metaphorically, signifying to rouse to anger, to provoke, in the Passive Voice, in Acts 17:16, R.V., "was provoked" (A.V., "was stirred"); in 1 Cor. 13:5,

R.V., "is not provoked" (the word "easily" in A.V., represents no word in the original). See STIR. ¶

NT: B.629c; CB.1262c; K.791.
OT: qāṣaph: S.7107; HR.1072a.14; H.2058; BD.893b.
rāgaz: S.7264; HR.1072a.15; H.2112; BD.919a.
GEN. REF.: IS.3:1028; NB.–; Z.–.

3. *erethizō* [ἐρεθίζω, 2042], to excite, stir up, provoke, is used (*a*) in a good sense in 2 Cor. 9:2, A.V., "hath provoked;" R.V., "hath stirred up"; (*b*) in an evil sense in Col. 3:21, "provoke." See STIR. ¶

NT: B.308d; CB.–; K.–.
OT: gārāh: S.1624; HR.544b.1; H.378; BD.173a.
mārāh: S.4784; HR.544b.2; H.1242; BD.598a.
GEN. REF.: IS.3:1028; NB.–; Z.–.

4. *parorgizō* [παροργίζω, 3949], to provoke to wrath: see ANGER, B, No. 2.

NT: B.629c; CB.1262c; K.716.
OT: kā'am: S.3707; HR.1072b.2; H.1016; BD.494d.
GEN. REF.: IS.3:1028; NB.–; Z.–.

5. *parazēloō* [παραζηλόω, 3863], to provoke to jealousy: see JEALOUSY.

NT: B.616a; CB.–; K.297.
OT: qānā': S.7065; HR.1059c.2; H.2038; BD.888c.
ḥārāh: S.2734; HR.1059c.1; H.736; BD.354a.
GEN. REF.: IS.3:1028; NB.–; Z.4:924.

6. *apostomatizō* [ἀποστοματίζω, 653], in classical Greek meant to speak from memory, to dictate to a pupil (*apo*, from, *stoma*, a mouth); in later Greek, to catechize; in Luke 11:53, "to provoke (Him) to speak." ¶

NT: B.100b; CB.–; K.–.
OT: –.
GEN. REF.: IS.3:1028; NB.–; Z.–.

7. *prokaleō* [προκαλέω, 4292], to call forth, as to a contest, hence to stir up what is evil in another, occurs in the Middle Voice in Gal. 5:26. ¶

NT: B.707b; CB.–; K.394.
OT: –.
GEN. REF.: IS.3:1028; NB.–; Z.–.

PRUDENCE, PRUDENT

A. Nouns.

1. *phronēsis* [φρόνησις, 5428], akin to *phroneō*, to have understanding (*phrēn*, the mind), denotes practical wisdom, prudence in the management of affairs. It is translated "wisdom" in Luke 1:17; "prudence" in Eph. 1:8. See WISDOM. ¶

NT: B.866c; CB.1264c; K.1277.
OT: ḥokmāh: S.2451; HR.1439a.3; H.647a; BD.315b.
bînāh: S.998; HR.1439a.1a; H.239b; BD.108a.
tᵉbûnāh: S.8394; HR.1439a.1b; H.239c; BD.108a.
GEN. REF.: IS.3:1029; NB.–; Z.–.

2. *sunesis* [σύνεσις, 4907], understanding, is rendered "prudence" in 1 Cor. 1:19, R.V. (A.V., "understanding"); it suggests quickness of apprehension, the penetrating consideration which precedes action. Cp. B, in the same verse. See KNOWLEDGE, UNDERSTANDING.

NT: B.788c; CB.1270c; K.1119.
OT: bînāh: S.998; HR.1314a.1c; H.239b; BD.108a.
tᵉbûnāh: S.8394; HR.1314a.1d; H.239c; BD.108a.
sēkel, sekel: S.7922; HR.1314a.6b; H.2263a; BD.968c.
GEN. REF.: IS.3:1029; NB.–; Z.–.

B. Adjective.

sunetos [συνετός, 4908], signifies intelligent, sagacious, understanding (akin to *suniēmi*, to perceive), translated "prudent" in Matt. 11:25, A.V. (R.V., "understanding"); Luke 10:21 (ditto); Acts 13:7, R.V., "(a man) of understanding"; in 1 Cor. 1:19, "prudent," R.V. and A.V. ¶ Cp. *asunetos*, "without understanding."

NT: B.788d; CB.1270c; K.1119.
OT: bîn: S.995; HR.1315a.1; H.239; BD.106c.
ḥākām: S.2450; HR.1315a.2; H.647b; BD.314c.
sākal: S.7919; HR.1315a.7; H.2263,2264; BD.968a.
GEN. REF.: IS.3:1029; NB.–; Z.–.

PSALM

psalmos [ψαλμός, 5568], primarily denoted a striking or twitching with the fingers (on musical strings); then, a sacred song, sung to musical accompaniment, a psalm. It is used (*a*) of the O.T. book of Psalms, Luke 20:42; 24:44; Acts 1:20; (*b*) of a particular psalm, Acts 13:33 (cp. ver. 35); (*c*) of psalms in general, 1 Cor. 14:26; Eph. 5:19; Col. 3:16. ¶

NT: B.891b; CB.1267c; K.1225.
OT: mizmôr: S.4210; HR.1483b.1b; H.558c; BD.274c.
GEN. REF.: IS.3:1029; NB.1053; Z.4:924.

Note: For *psallō*, rendered "let him sing psalms" in Jas. 5:13, see MELODY, SING.

PUBLIC, PUBLICLY

A. Adjective.

dēmosios [δημόσιος, 1219], belonging to the people (*dēmos*, the people), is translated "public" in Acts 5:18, R.V., "public (ward)," A.V., "common (prison)."

NT: B.179a; CB.1240c; K.–.
OT: –.
GEN. REF.: –.

B. Adverbs.

phanerōs [φανερῶς, —]: see OPENLY, No. 2.

Note: For a form of *dēmosios* used as an adverb, "publicly," see OPENLY, *Note* (4).

PUBLICAN

telōnēs [τελώνης, 5057], primarily denoted a farmer of the tax (from *telos*, toll, custom, tax), then, as in the N.T., a subsequent subordinate of such, who collected taxes in some district, a tax-gatherer; such were naturally hated intensely by the people; they are classed with "sinners," Matt. 9:10, 11; 11:9; Mark 2:15, 16; Luke 5:30; 7:34; 15:1; with harlots Matt. 21:31, 32; with "the Gentile," Matt. 18:17; some mss have it in Matt. 5:47, the best have *ethnikoi*, "Gentiles." See also Matt. 5:46; 10:3; Luke 3:12; 5:27, 29; 7:29; 18:10, 11, 13. ¶

NT: B.812b; CB.1271b; K.1166.
OT: –.
GEN. REF.: IS.3:1050; NB.1064; Z.5:606.

Note: For *architelōnēs*, a chief publican, see CHIEF, B, No. 4.

PUBLISH

1. *kērussō* [κηρύσσω, 2784], to be a herald, to proclaim, preach, is translated to publish in Mark 1:45; 5:20; 7:36; 13:10, A.V. (R.V., "preached"); Luke 8:39. See PREACH, PROCLAIM.

NT: B.431b; CB.1255a; K.430.
OT: qārā': S.7121; HR.763c.5a; H.2063; BD.894d.
GEN. REF.: –.

2. *diapherō* [διαφέρω, 1308], to bear through, is translated "was published" in Acts 13:49, A.V. (R.V., "was spread abroad"). See BETTER (be), No. 1.

NT: B.190b; CB.–; K.1252.
OT: –.
GEN. REF.: –.

3. *ginomai* [γίνομαι, 1096], to become, come to be, is translated "was published" in Acts 10:37, lit., 'came to be.'

NT: B.158a; CB.1248b; K.117.
OT: –.
GEN. REF.: –.

4. *diangellō* [διαγγέλλω, 1229], to publish abroad, is so translated in Luke 9:60, R.V. (A.V., "preach"), and Rom. 9:17. See DECLARE, A, No. 3.

NT: B.182b; CB.1241b; K.10.
OT: sāphar: S.5608; HR.299b.2; H.1540; BD.707d.
GEN. REF.: –.

PUFF (up)

1. *phusioō* [φυσιόω, 5448], to puff up, blow up, inflate (from *phusa*, bellows), is used metaphorically in the N.T., in the sense of being puffed up with pride, 1 Cor. 4:6, 18, 19; 5:2; 8:1; 13:4; Col. 2:18. ¶

NT: B.869b; CB.1264c; K.–.
OT: –.
GEN. REF.: –.

2. *tuphoō* [τυφόω, 5187], is always rendered to puff up in the R.V. See HIGH-MINDED, PROUD.

NT: B.831a; CB.–; K.–.
OT: –.
GEN. REF.: –.

PULL (down)

kathaireō [καθαιρέω, 2507], to take down, is translated "I will pull down" in Luke 12:18. See DESTROY, No. 3.

NT: B.386c; CB.1254b; K.380.
OT: dûsh: S.1758; HR.697c.1; H.419; BD.190b.
GEN. REF.: –.

Notes: (1) In Jude 23, A.V., *harpazō*, to seize, snatch away, is rendered "pulling . . . out." See SNATCH.

(2) In Acts 23:10, A.V., *diaspaō*, to rend or tear asunder, is translated "should have been pulled in pieces" (R.V., "should be torn in pieces").

(3) *ekballō*, to cast out, is translated to pull out in Matt. 7:4 and Luke 6:42 (twice), A.V. (R.V., "cast out"). See CAST, No. 5.

(4) For *anaspaō*, rendered "pull out" in Luke 14:5, A.V., see DRAW, No. 5.

(5) For *kathairesis*, a casting down, 2 Cor. 10:4, see CAST, A, No. 14, *Note*.

PUNISH

1. *kolazō* [κολάζω, 2849], primarily denotes to curtail, prune, dock (from *kolos*, docked); then, to check, restrain, punish; it is used in the Middle Voice in Acts 4:21; Passive Voice in 2 Pet. 2:9, A.V., to be punished (R.V., "under punishment," lit., 'being punished'), a futurative present tense. ¶

NT: B.440c; CB.1255c; K.451.
OT: –.
GEN. REF.: IS.3:1051; NB.–; Z.4:954.

2. *timōreō* [τιμωρέω, 5097], primarily, to help, then, to avenge (from *timē*, value, honour, and *ouros*, a guardian), i.e., to help by redressing injuries, is used in the Active Voice in Acts 26:11, R.V., "punishing" (A.V., "I punished"); Passive V. in 22:5, lit., '(that) they may be punished.' Cp. No. 5, below. ¶

NT: B.818c; CB.–; K.–.
OT: shākal: S.7921; HR.1354a.1; H.2385; BD.1013b.
GEN. REF.: IS.3:1051; NB.–; Z.–.

Note: For 2 Thess. 1:9, "shall suffer punishment," R.V., see JUSTICE. See SUFFER, *Note* (10).

PUNISHMENT

1. *ekdikēsis* [ἐκδίκησις, —]: for 1 Pet. 2:14, A.V., "punishment" (R.V., "vengeance"), see AVENGE, B, No. 2.

2. *epitimia* [ἐπιτιμία, 2009], in the N.T. denotes penalty, punishment, 2 Cor. 2:6. ¶ Originally it signified the enjoyment of the rights and privileges of citizenship; then it became used of the estimate (*timē*) fixed by a judge on the infringement of such rights, and hence, in general, a penalty.

NT: B.303c; CB.1246b; K.249.
OT: –.
GEN. REF.: IS.3:1051; NB.–; Z.–.

3. *kolasis* [κόλασις, 2851], akin to *kolazō* (PUNISH, No. 1), punishment, is used in Matt. 25:46, "(eternal) punishment," and 1 John 4:18, "(fear hath) punishment," R.V. (A.V., "torment"), which there describes a process, not merely an effect; this kind of fear is expelled by perfect love; where God's love is being perfected in us, it gives no room for the fear of meeting with His reprobation; the punishment referred to is the immediate consequence of the

sense of sin, not a holy awe but a slavish fear, the negation of the enjoyment of love. ¶

NT: B.440d; CB.1255b; K.451.
OT: mikshôl: S.4383; HR.776b.1; H.1050c; BD.506a.
GEN. REF.: IS.3:1051; NB.—; Z.4:954.

4. *dikē* [δίκη, 1349], justice, or the execution of a sentence, is translated "punishment" in Jude 7, R.V. (A.V., "vengeance"). See JUSTICE.

NT: B.198c; CB.1242a; K.168.
OT: rîb: S.7378; HR.335b.6; H.2159; BD.936b.
nāqam: S.5358; HR.335b.5b; H.1413; BD.667d.
GEN. REF.: IS.3:1051; NB.—; Z.—.

5. *timōria* [τιμωρία, 5098], primarily help (see PUNISH, No. 2), denotes vengeance, punishment, Heb. 10:29. ¶

NT: B.818d; CB.—; K.—.
OT: mahᵃlumôt: S.4112; HR.1354a.1; H.502c; BD.240d.
GEN. REF.: IS.3:1051; NB.—; Z.—.

Note: The distinction, sometimes suggested, between No. 3 as being disciplinary, with special reference to the sufferer, and No. 5, as being penal, with reference to the satisfaction of him who inflicts it, cannot be maintained in the *koinē* Greek of N.T. times.

PURCHASE

1. *ktaomai* [κτάομαι, —]: see OBTAIN, A, No. 4.

2. *peripoieō* [περιποιέω, 4046], signifies to gain or get for oneself, purchase; Middle Voice in Acts 20:28 and 1 Tim. 3:13 (R.V., "gain"); see GAIN.

NT: B.650a; CB.1263b; K.—.
OT: rākash: S.7408; HR.1125c.7; H.2167; BD.940d.
GEN. REF.: IS.3:1054; NB.—; Z.—.

3. *agorazō* [ἀγοράζω, 59], is rendered to purchase in the R.V. of Rev. 5:9; 14:3, 4. See BUY, No. 1.

NT: B.12d; CB.1233c; K.19.
OT: shābar: S.7666; HR.16b.5; H.2322; BD.991c.
qānāh: S.7069; HR.16b.4; H.2039; BD.888d.
GEN. REF.: IS.3:1054; NB.—; Z.—.

Note: For *peripoiēsis*, "purchased possession," Eph. 1:14, see POSSESSION.

PURE, PURENESS, PURITY

A. Adjectives.

1. *hagnos* [ἁγνός, 53], pure from defilement, not contaminated (from the same root as *hagios*, holy), is rendered "pure" in Phil. 4:8; 1 Tim. 5:22; Jas. 3:17; 1 John 3:3; see CHASTE.

NT: B.11d; CB.1249a; K.19.
OT: ṭāhôr: S.2889; HR.16b.3; H.792d; BD.373a.
GEN. REF.: IS.3:1054; NB.—; Z.4:958.

2. *katharos* [καθαρός, 2513], pure, as being cleansed, e.g., Matt. 5:8; 1 Tim. 1:5; 3:9; 2 Tim. 1:3; 2:22; Tit. 1:15; Heb. 10:22; Jas. 1:27; 1 Pet. 1:22; Rev. 15:6; 21:18; 22:1 (in some mss.). See CHASTE, *Note*, CLEAN, A.

NT: B.388a; CB.1254b; K.381.
OT: ṭāhôr: S.2889; HR.698c.5; H.792d; BD.372a.
ṭāhēr: S.2891; HR.698c.15; H.792; BD.373a.
GEN. REF.: IS.3:1054; NB.—; Z.4:958.

Note: In 1 Pet. 1:22 the A.V., "with a pure heart," follows those mss. which have this adjective (R.V., "from the heart").

3. *eilikrinēs* [εἰλικρινής, 1506], signifies unalloyed, pure; (*a*) it was used of unmixed substances; (*b*) in the N.T. it is used of moral and ethical purity, Phil. 1:10, "sincere"; so the R.V. in 2 Pet. 3:1 (A.V., "pure"). Some regard the etymological meaning as 'tested by the sunlight' (Cremer). ¶ See CHASTE, *Note*, SINCERE.

NT: B.222d; CB.—; K.—.
OT: —.
GEN. REF.: IS.3:1055; NB.—; Z.—.

Note: Wine mixed with water may be *hagnos*, not being contaminated; it is not *katharos*, when there is the admixture of any element even though the latter is pure in itself.

B. Nouns.

1. *hagnotēs* [ἁγνότης, 54], the state of being *hagnos* (A, No. 1), occurs in 2 Cor. 6:6, "pureness"; 11:3, in the best mss., "(and the) purity," R.V. ¶

NT: B.12a; CB.1249a; K.19.
OT: —.
GEN. REF.: IS.3:1054; NB.—; Z.4:958.

2. *hagneia* [ἁγνεία, 47], synonymous with No. 1, "purity," occurs in 1 Tim. 4:12; 5:2, where it denotes the chastity which excludes all impurity of spirit, manner, or act. ¶

NT: B.10d; CB.1249a; K.18.
OT: ṭāhᵒrāh: S.2893; HR.15c.1; H.792c; BD.372d.
GEN. REF.: IS.3:1054; NB.—; Z.4:958.

PURGE

1. *kathairō* [καθαίρω, 2508], akin to *katharos* (see PURE, A, No. 2), to cleanse, is used of pruning, John 15:2, A.V., "purgeth" (R.V., "cleanseth"). ¶ In the Sept., 2 Sam. 4:6; Isa. 28:27; Jer. 38:28. ¶

NT: B.386d; CB.1254b; K.381.
OT: nātaṣ: S.5422; HR.697b.7; H.1446; BD.683b.
GEN. REF.: IS.3:1054; NB.—; Z.—.

2. *ekkathairō* [ἐκκαθαίρω, 1571], to cleanse out, cleanse thoroughly, is said of purging out leaven, 1 Cor. 5:7; in 2 Tim. 2:21, of purging oneself from those who utter "profane babblings," vv. 16-18. ¶

NT: B.240b; CB.1243c; K.381.
OT: bāʿar: S.1197; HR.432a.1; H.263; BD.128d.
ṣāraph: S.6884; HR.432a.3; H.1972; BD.864a.
GEN. REF.: IS.3:1056; NB.—; Z.—.

3. *diakathairō* [διακαθαίρω, 1223, 2508], to cleanse thoroughly, is translated "will throughly purge" in Luke 3:17, A.V. (R.V., "thoroughly to cleanse"; less authentic mss. have No. 5). ¶

NT: B.183d; CB.—; K.—.
OT: —.
GEN. REF.: IS.3:1054; NB.—; Z.—.

4. *katharizō* [καθαρίζω, 2511], to cleanse, make clean, is translated "purging (all meats),"

in Mark 7:19, A.V., R.V., "making (all meats) clean"; Heb. 9:14, A.V., "purge" (R.V., "cleanse"); so 9:22 (for ver. 23, see PURIFY) and 10:2. See CLEAN, B, No. 1.

NT: B.387b; CB.1254b; K.381.
OT: ṭāhēr: S.2891; HR.698a.5a-c; H.792; BD.373a.
GEN. REF.: IS.3:1056; NB.–; Z.4:958.

5. *diakatharizō* [διακαθαρίζω, 1245], to cleanse thoroughly, is translated "will throughly purge" in Matt. 3:12, A.V. See CLEAN, B, No. 2. Cp. the synonymous verb No. 3. ¶

NT: B.183d; CB.–; K.–.
OT: –.
GEN. REF.: –.

Notes: (1) For Heb. 1:3, A.V., "had purged," see PURIFICATION.

(2) For the A.V. rendering of the noun *katharismos*, cleansing, "that he was purged," see CLEAN, C, No. 1.

PURIFICATION, PURIFY, PURIFYING

A. Nouns.

1. *katharismos* [καθαρισμός, 2512], is rendered a cleansing (akin to No. 4, above), Mark 1:44; Luke 5:14; in Heb. 1:3, R.V., "purification."

NT: B.387d; CB.1254b; K.381.
OT: ṭāhᵒrāh: S.2893; HR.698c.2b; H.792c; BD.372d.
GEN. REF.: IS.3:1054; NB.–; Z.–.

2. *katharotēs* [καθαρότης, 2514], cleansing, Heb. 9:13. See CLEAN, C, No. 2. ¶

NT: B.388b; CB.1254b; K.381.
OT: ṭōhar: S.2892; HR.699c.1; H.792a; BD.372d.
GEN. REF.: IS.3:1054; NB.–; Z.4:958.

3. *hagnismos* [ἁγνισμός, 49], denotes a ceremonial purification, Acts 21:26, for the circumstances of which with reference to the vow of a Nazirite (R.V), see Numb. 6:9-13. ¶

NT: B.11a; CB.1249a; K.19.
OT: nēzer: S.5145; HR.16a.5; H.1340a; BD.634b.
ḥaṭṭā't: S.2403; HR.16a.1; H.638e; BD.308b.
ṭāhēr: S.2891; HR.16a.2; H.792; BD.373a.
GEN. REF.: IS.3:1054; NB.–; Z.4:958.

B. Verbs.

1. *hagnizō* [ἁγνίζω, 48], akin to *hagnos*, pure (see CHASTE), to purify, cleanse from defilement, is used of purifying (*a*) ceremonially, John 11:55; Acts 21:24, 26 (cp. No. 3 above); 24:18; (*b*) morally, the heart, Jas. 4:8; the soul, 1 Pet. 1:22; oneself, 1 John 3:3. ¶

NT: B.11a; CB.1249a; K.19.
OT: qādash: S.6942; HR.15c.4; H.1990; BD.872d.
ṭāhēr: S.2891; HR.15c.2; H.792; BD.373a.
GEN. REF.: IS.3:1054; NB.–; Z.4:958.

2. *katharizō* [καθαρίζω, 2511], to cleanse, make free from admixture, is translated to purify in Acts 15:9, A.V. (R.V., "cleansing"); Tit. 2:14; Heb. 9:23, A.V. (R.V., "cleansed"). See CLEAN, B, No. 1.

NT: B.387b; CB.1254b; K.381.
OT: ṭāhēr: S.2891; HR.698a.5a-c; H.792; BD.373a.
GEN. REF.: IS.3:1054; NB.–; Z.4:958.

PURLOIN

nosphizō [νοσφίζω, 3557], is translated "purloining" in Tit. 2:10. See KEEP, A, No. 10.

NT: B.543d; CB.–; K.–.
OT: –.
GEN. REF.: IS.3:1057; NB.–; Z.–.

PURPLE

A. Noun.

porphura [πορφύρα, 4209], originally denoted the purple-fish, then, purple dye (extracted from certain shell fish): hence, a purple garment, Mark 15:17, 20; Luke 16:19; Rev. 18:12. ¶

NT: B.694a; CB.1266a; K.–.
OT: 'argāmān: S.713; HR.1195b.1a; H.157b; BD.71a.
'argᵉwān: S.710; HR.1195b.1b; H.157b; BD.71a.
GEN. REF.: IS.3:1057; NB.–; Z.4:960.

B. Adjective.

porphureos [πορφύρεος, 4210], purple, a reddish purple, is used of the robe put in mockery on Christ, John 19:2, 5; in Rev. 17:4 (in the best texts; some have No. 1); 18:16, as a noun (with *himation*, a garment, understood). ¶

NT: B.694b; CB.–; K.–.
OT: 'argāmān: S.713; HR.1195b.1; H.157b; BD.71a.
GEN. REF.: IS.3:1057; NB.–; Z.4:960.

PURPLE (seller of)

porphuropōlis [πορφυρόπωλις, 4211], denotes a seller of purple fabrics (from *porphura*, and *pōleō*, to sell), Acts 16:14. ¶

NT: B.694a; CB.–; K.–.
OT: –.
GEN. REF.: IS.3:1057; NB.–; Z.4:960.

PURPOSE (Noun and Verb)

A. Nouns.

1. *boulēma* [βούλημα, 1013], a purpose or will (akin to *boulomai*, to will, wish, purpose), a deliberate intention, occurs in Acts 27:43, "purpose"; Rom. 9:19, "will"; 1 Pet. 4:3, in the best mss. (some have *thelēma*), A.V., "will," R.V., "desire." See WILL. ¶

NT: B.145d; CB.1239b; K.108.
OT: da'at: S.1847; HR.228b.1; H.848c; BD.395c.
GEN. REF.: IS.3:1058; NB.–; Z.–.

2. *prothesis* [πρόθεσις, 4286], a setting forth (used of the "shewbread"), a purpose (akin to B, No. 3), is used (*a*) of the purposes of God, Rom. 8:28; 9:11; Eph. 1:11; 3:11; 2 Tim. 1:9; (*b*) of human purposes, as to things material, Acts 27:13; spiritual, Acts 11:23; 2 Tim. 3:10. See SHEWBREAD.

NT: B.706a; CB.1267b; K.1176.
OT: 'ērek: S.6187; HR.1206b.1a; H.1694a; BD.789d.
maᵃreket: S.4635; HR.1206b.1b; H.1694e; BD.790b.
GEN. REF.: IS.3:1058; NB.–; Z.4:961.

3. *gnōmē* [γνώμη, 1106], an opinion, purpose, judgment, is used in the genitive case with *ginomai*, to come to be, in Acts 20:3, "he purposed," A.V. (R.V., "he determined"), lit., 'he came to be of purpose.'

NT: B.163a; CB.1248b; K.119.
OT: ṭᵉʿēm (Aramaic): S.2942; HR.273a.2b; H.2757a; BD.1094c.
GEN. REF.: IS.3:1058; NB.–; Z.–.

Notes: The following phrases are translated with the word "purpose": (*a*) *eis auto touto*, "for this same (or very) purpose," lit., 'unto this same (thing),' Rom. 9:17; Eph. 6:22; Col. 4:8; (*b*) *eis touto*, "for this purpose," Acts 26:16, A.V. (R.V., "to this end"), lit., 'unto this'; so 1 John 3:8; (*c*) *eis ti*, "to what purpose," Matt. 26:8, lit., 'unto what'; Mark 14:4, R.V., "to what purpose" (A.V., "why").

B. Verbs.

1. *bouleuō* [βουλεύω, 1011], to take counsel, resolve, always in the Middle Voice in the N.T., to take counsel with oneself, to determine with oneself, is translated "I purpose" in 2 Cor. 1:17 (twice). See COUNSEL, B, No. 1.

NT: B.145c; CB.1239b; K.–.
OT: yāʿaṣ: S.3289; HR.227a.6; H.887; BD.419c.
GEN. REF.: IS.3:1058; NB.–; Z.–.

2. *tithēmi* [τίθημι, 5087], to put, place, is used in the Middle Voice in Acts 19:21, "purposed," in the sense of resolving.

NT: B.815d; CB.1272c; K.1176.
OT: –.
GEN. REF.: IS.3:1058; NB.–; Z.–.

3. *protithēmi* [προτίθημι, 4388], to set before, set forth (*pro*, before, and No. 2, akin to A, No. 2), is used in Rom. 3:25, "set forth," R.V. marg., "purposed," A.V. marg., "foreordained," Middle Voice, which lays stress upon the Personal interest which God had in so doing; either meaning, to set forth or to purpose, would convey a Scriptural view, but the context bears out the former as being intended here; in Rom. 1:13, "I purposed"; Eph. 1:9, "He purposed (in Him)," R.V. See SET. ¶

NT: B.722b; CB.1267b; K.1176.
OT: ʿārak: S.6186; HR.1231a.4; H.1694; BD.789b.
shît: S.7896; HR.1231a.6; H.2380; BD.1011a.
GEN. REF.: IS.3:1058; NB.–; Z.–.

4. *poieō* [ποιέω, 4160], to make, is translated "He purposed" in Eph. 3:11 (for the noun *prothesis*, in the same verse, see A, No. 2). See DO, No. 1.

NT: B.680d; CB.1265c; K.895.
OT: –.
GEN. REF.: –.

5. *proaireō* [προαιρέω, 4255], to bring forth or forward, or, in the Middle Voice, to take by choice, prefer, purpose, is translated "He hath purposed" in 2 Cor. 9:7, R.V. (A.V., "he purposed"). ¶

NT: B.702d; CB.–; K.–.
OT: –.
GEN. REF.: –.

For **PURSE** see **BAG**, No. 2. and *Note*

PURSUE

diōkō [διώκω, 1377], to put to flight, pursue, persecute, is rendered to pursue in 2 Cor. 4:9, R.V. (A.V., "persecute"), and is used metaphorically of seeking eagerly after peace in 1 Pet. 3:11, R.V. (A.V., "ensue"). See FOLLOW.

NT: B.201b; CB.1242a; K.177.
OT: rādaph: S.7291; HR.338b.10a; H.2124; BD.922c.
GEN. REF.: –.

PUT

1. *tithēmi* [τίθημι, 5087], to place, lay, set, put, is translated to put in Matt. 5:15; 12:18; in Matt. 22:44, R.V., "put (underneath Thy feet)"; Mark 4:21 (1st part), in the 2nd part, R.V., "put" (in some texts, No. 4, A.V., "set"); 10:16, A.V. (R.V., "laying"); Luke 8:16 (1st part); 2nd part, R.V. (A.V., "setteth"); 11:33; John 19:19; Acts 1:7, A.V. (R.V., "set"); 4:3; 5:18, 25; 12:4; Rom. 14:13; 1 Cor. 15:25; 2 Cor. 3:13; 1 Tim. 1:12, A.V. (R.V., "appointing"); Rev. 11:9, A.V. (R.V., "laid"). See APPOINT, No. 3.

NT: B.815d; CB.1272c; K.1176.
OT: sûm, sîm: S.7760; HR.1348c.25a; H.2243; BD.962c.
GEN. REF.: –.

2. *peritithēmi* [περιτίθημι, 4060], to put around or on (*peri*, around, and No. 1), is so used in Matt. 27:28; Mark 15:17, R.V., "put on" (A.V., ". . . about"); 15:36; John 19:29. See BESTOW, No. 5.

NT: B.652c; CB.–; K.–.
OT: sûm, sîm: S.7760; HR.1127c.14; H.2243; BD.962c.
GEN. REF.: –.

3. *paratithēmi* [παρατίθημι, 3908], to set before (*para*, beside or before), is rendered to put forth (of a parable) in Matt. 13:24, 31, A.V. (R.V., "set before"). See SET.

NT: B.622d; CB.–; K.1176.
OT: sûm, sîm: S.7760; HR.1065a.7a; H.2243; BD.962c.
GEN. REF.: –.

4. *epitithēmi* [ἐπιτίθημι, 2007], to put on, upon, is so rendered in Matt. 19:13, A.V. (R.V., "lay"); so Mark 7:32; 8:25 (some mss. have No. 1, here); Matt. 21:7; 27:29; John 9:15; 19:2 (1st part); Acts 9:12 (R.V., "laying . . . on"); 15:10. See ADD, No. 1.

NT: B.302d; CB.1246b; K.1176.
OT: sûm, sîm: S.7760; HR.535c.29; H.2243; BD.962c.
sāmak: S.5564; HR.535c.17; H.1514; BD.701d.
GEN. REF.: –.

5. *apotithēmi* [ἀποτίθημι, 659], always in the Middle Voice in the N.T. to put off (*apo*) from oneself, is rendered "to put away" in the R.V. in the following: Eph. 4:22 (A.V., "put off"); Col. 3:8 (A.V., ditto); Eph. 4:25; Jas. 1:21 (A.V.,

"laying apart"); 1 Pet. 2:1 (A.V., "laying aside"). See CAST, No. 16.

NT: B.101a; CB.1237b; K.—.
OT: nûaḥ: S.5117; HR.148c.1; H.1323; BD.628a.
GEN. REF.: —.

6. *ballō* [*βάλλω*, 906], to throw, cast, put, is translated to put, in Matt. 9:17 (twice); 25:27; 27:6; Mark 2:22; 7:33; Luke 5:37; John 5:7; 12:6; 13:2 (of putting into the heart by the Devil); 18:11 (of putting up a sword); 20:25 (R.V. twice, A.V., "put" and "thrust"); ver. 27, R.V.; Jas. 3:3; Rev. 2:24 (R.V., "cast"). See CAST, No. 1.

NT: B.130d; CB.1238b; K.91.
OT: sûm, sîm: S.7760; HR.189c.14; H.2243; BD.962c.
shālak: S.7993; HR.189c.16; H.2398; BD.1020d.
nāphal: S.5307; HR.189c.6; H.1392; BD.656c.
GEN. REF.: —.

Note: blēteos (a gerundive form from *ballō*), meaning '(that which) one must put', is found in Luke 5:38, and, in some mss., Mark 2:22. ¶

7. *ekballō* [*ἐκβάλλω*, 1544], to cast out, is translated to put forth or out in Matt. 9:25; Mark 5:40 (Luke 8:54 in some mss.); John 10:4; Acts 9:40. See CAST, No. 5.

NT: B.237b; CB.1243b; K.91.
OT: gārash: S.1644; HR.420c.3; H.388; BD.176c.
yāṣā': S.3318; HR.420c.8; H.893; BD.422b.
GEN. REF.: —.

8. *epiballō* [*ἐπιβάλλω*, 1911], to put to or unto, is so translated in Matt. 9:16; Luke 5:36; 9:62; in Acts 12:1, R.V., "put forth (his hands)," A.V., "stretched forth." See CAST, No. 7.

NT: B.289d; CB.—; K.91.
OT: sûm, sîm: S.7760; HR.516a.15; H.2243; BD.962c.
shît: S.7896; HR.516a.17; H.2380; BD.1011a.
shālaḥ: S.7971; HR.516a.18a; H.2394; BD.1018a.
GEN. REF.: —.

9. *periballō* [*περιβάλλω*, 4016], to put or throw around, is translated "put on" in John 19:2, A.V. (R.V., "arrayed . . . in"). See CAST, No. 10, CLOTHE, No. 6.

NT: B.646a; CB.—; K.—.
OT: lābash: S.3847; HR.1121c.3; H.1075; BD.527d.
kāsāh: S.3680; HR.1121c.2; H.1008; BD.491b.
GEN. REF.: —.

10. *proballō* [*προβάλλω*, 4261], to put forward, is so used in Acts 19:33. See SHOOT FORTH.

NT: B.702d; CB.—; K.—.
OT: —.
GEN. REF.: —.

11. *didōmi* [*δίδωμι*, 1325], to give, is rendered to put in Luke 15:22, of the ring on the returned prodigal's finger; 2 Cor. 8:16 and Rev. 17:17, of putting into the heart by God; Heb. 8:10, of laws into the mind (A.V., marg., "give"); 10:16, of laws on (R.V.; A.V., "into") the heart. See GIVE.

NT: B.192c; CB.1241c; K.166.
OT: nātan: S.5414; HR.317b.26a; H.1443; BD.678a.
GEN. REF.: —.

12. *paradidōmi* [*παραδίδωμι*, 3860], to give or hand over, is rendered "put in prison" in Mark 1:14, A.V. (R.V., "delivered up"). See BETRAY.

NT: B.614b; CB.1262a; K.166.
OT: nātan: S.5414; HR.1058a.16; H.1443; BD.678a.
sāgar: S.5462; HR.1058a.17; H.1462; BD.688d.
GEN. REF.: —.

13. *poieō* [*ποιέω*, 4160], to do, make, is translated "to put" (with *exō* "forth") in Acts 5:34, lit., 'do (them) outside.'

NT: B.680d; CB.1265c; K.895.
OT: —.
GEN. REF.: —.

14. *chōrizō* [*χωρίζω*, 5563], to separate, divide (cp. *chōris*, apart, separate from), is translated to put asunder in Matt. 19:6; Mark 10:9, of putting away a wife.

NT: B.890a; CB.1240a; K.—.
OT: bādal: S.914; HR.1482b.2; H.203; BD.95a.
GEN. REF.: —.

15. *ekphuō* [*ἐκφύω*, 1631], to cause to grow out, put forth (*ek*, out, *phuō*, to bring forth, produce, beget), is used of the leaves of a tree, Matt. 24:32; Mark 13:28, "putteth forth." ¶

NT: B.247a; CB.—; K.—.
OT: —.
GEN. REF.: —.

16. *apoluō* [*ἀπολύω*, 630], to set free, let go, is rendered to put away in reference to one who is betrothed, Matt. 1:19; a wife, 5:31, 32 (twice; in 2nd part, R.V.; A.V., "is divorced"); 19:3, 7, 8, 9 (twice); Mark 10:2, 4, 11, 12; Luke 16:18 (twice). See DISMISS.

NT: B.96c; CB.1237a; K.—.
OT: gārash: S.1644; HR.138c.2; H.388; BD.176c.
hālak: S.1980; HR.138c.3; H.498; BD.229d.
GEN. REF.: —.

Note: In 1 Cor. 7:11, 12, A.V., *aphiēmi*, to send away, is translated to put away (R.V., "leave"), of the act of the husband toward the wife; in ver. 13, "leave," of the act of the wife toward the husband.

17. *airō* [*αἴρω*, 142], to take up, remove, is rendered "put away," of bitterness, wrath, anger, clamour, railing and malice, Eph. 4:31; in 1 Cor. 5:2 of the Divine effects of church discipline. See BEAR, No. 9.

NT: B.24b; CB.1234a; K.28.
OT: nāsā': S.5375; HR.34c.14a; H.1421; BD.669d.
GEN. REF.: —.

18. *exairō* [*ἐξαίρω*, 1808], to put away from the midst of (*ek*, from, and No. 17), is used of church discipline, 1 Cor. 5:13. ¶

NT: B.272a; CB.—; K.—.
OT: nāsa': S.5265; HR.485a.22; H.1380; BD.652a.
sûr: S.5493; HR.485a.27; H.1480; BD.693b.
kārat: S.3772; HR.485a.15; H.1048; BD.503c.
GEN. REF.: —.

19. *katargeō* [*καταργέω*, 2673], is rendered "I put away" in 1 Cor. 13:11; in 15:24, A.V., "shall have put down" (R.V., "abolished"). See ABOLISH.

NT: B.417b; CB.1254b; K.76.
OT: bᵉṭēl: S.989; HR.743a.1; H.2625; BD.1084b.
GEN. REF.: —.

20. *kathaireō* [καθαιρέω, 2507], to take down, put down, is rendered "He hath put down" in Luke 1:52. See CAST, A, No. 14.
NT: B.386c; CB.1254b; K.381.
OT: –.
GEN. REF.: –.

21. *apostellō* [ἀποστέλλω, 649], to send forth (*apo*, from or forth, *stellō*, to send), is said of using the sickle, Mark 4:29, R.V., "he putteth forth," marg., "sendeth forth" (A.V., "putteth in". (See SEND, SET.)
NT: B.98c; CB.1237a; K.67.
OT: shālaḥ: S.7971; HR.141b.13a-c; H.2394; BD.1018a.
GEN. REF.: –.

22. *apekduō* [ἀπεκδύω, 554], to strip off clothes or arms, is used in the Middle Voice in the N.T., Col. 2:15, R.V., "having put off from Himself," (A.V., "having spoiled"): in 3:9, "ye have put off," of "the old man" (see MAN). See SPOIL. ¶
NT: B.83c; CB.1236b; K.192.
OT: –.
GEN. REF.: –.

23. *methistēmi* or *methistanō* [μεθίστημι, 3179], to change, remove (*meta*, implying change, *histēmi*, to cause to stand), is used of putting a man out of his stewardship, Luke 16:4 (Passive Voice). See REMOVE, TRANSLATE, TURN (away).
NT: B.498d; CB.–; K.–.
OT: sûr: S.5493; HR.907b.4; H.1480; BD.693b.
ᵃdāh: S.5709; HR.907b.5; H.2898; BD.1105b.
GEN. REF.: –.

24. *anagō* [ἀνάγω, 321], to lead or bring up, is used nautically of 'putting out to sea,' Acts 27:2, 4, R.V. See LAUNCH.
NT: B.53a; CB.–; K.–.
OT: 'ālāh: S.5927; HR.75b.6b; H.1624; BD.748a.
GEN. REF.: –.

25. *epanagō* [ἐπανάγω, 1877], to bring up or back, is used in the same sense as No. 24, in Luke 5:3, 4. See LAUNCH.
NT: B.282d; CB.–; K.–.
OT: –.
GEN. REF.: –.

26. *enduō* [ἐνδύω, 1746], used in the Middle Voice, of putting on oneself, or on another, is translated to put on (*a*) literally, Matt. 6:25; 27:31; Mark 6:9; 15:20; Luke 12:22; 15:22; (*b*) metaphorically, of putting on the armour of light, Rom. 13:12; the Lord Jesus Christ, 13:14; Christ, Gal. 3:27; incorruption and immortality (said of the body of the believer), 1 Cor. 15:53, 54; the new man, Eph. 4:24; Col. 3:10; the whole armour of God, Eph. 6:11; the breastplate of righteousness, 6:14, R.V.; the breastplate of faith and love, 1 Thess. 5:8; various Christian qualities, Col. 3:12. See CLOTHE, No. 2.
NT: B.264a; CB.1245a; K.192.
OT: lābash: S.3847; HR.471a.2; H.1075; BD.527d.
GEN. REF.: –.

27. *embibazō* [ἐμβιβάζω, 1688], to put in (*en* in, *bibazō*, not found in the N.T.), is used of putting persons on board ship, Acts 27:6. ¶ In the Sept., 2 Kings 9:28; Prov. 4:11. ¶
NT: B.254c; CB.–; K.–.
OT: dārak: S.1869; HR.455c.1; H.453; BD.201d.
rākab: S.7392; HR.455c.2; H.2163; BD.938d.
GEN. REF.: –.

28. *probibazō* [προβιβάζω, 4264], to put forward, hence, to induce, incite, is rendered "being put forward" in Matt. 14:8, R.V. (A.V., "being before instructed"). ¶ In the Sept., Ex. 35:34; Deut. 6:7. ¶
NT: B.703c; CB.–; K.–.
OT: yārāh: S.3384; HR.1205c.1; H.910; BD.434d.
GEN. REF.: –.

29. *apostrephō* [ἀποστρέφω, 654], to turn away, remove, return, is used of 'putting up again' a sword into its sheath, Matt. 26:52. See BRING, A, No. 22.
NT: B.100b; CB.1237a; K.1093.
OT: shûb: S.7725; HR.145b.24a,d; H.2340; BD.996d.
GEN. REF.: –.

Notes: (1) *Ekteinō*, to stretch forth (always so translated in the R.V., save in Acts 27:30, "lay out," of anchors), is rendered to put forth in the A.V. of Matt. 8:3; Mark 1:41; Luke 5:13.

(2) In Luke 14:7, A.V., *legō*, to speak (see R.V.), is translated "He put forth."

(3) In Acts 13:46, A.V., *apōtheō*, to thrust away (R.V.), is rendered "put . . . from"; in 1 Tim. 1:19, A.V., "having put away" (R.V., "having thrust from"), Middle Voice in each; so in Acts 7:27, A.V. and R.V., "thrust away." See CAST, No. 13, THRUST.

(4) For "to put away" in Heb. 9:26, see PUTTING, *Note* (below).

(5) In Acts 7:33, A.V., *luō*, to loose (R.V.), is translated "put off." See LOOSE.

(6) For the A.V. of *hupotassō*, "put under" in 1 Cor. 15:27, 28; Eph. 1:22; Heb. 2:8, see SUBJECT, and for the connected negative adjective *anupotaktos*, rendered "not put under" in Heb. 2:8, A.V., see DISOBEDIENT, B, (*Note*).

(7) In John 19:29, A.V., *prospherō*, to bring to, is translated "they put it to (His mouth)," R.V., "they brought it . . ."

(8) For *anamimnēskō*, to put in remembrance, 1 Cor. 4:17, R.V., see REMEMBRANCE.

(9) For *apokteinō*, to kill, rendered "put to death" in Mark 14:1, etc., see DEATH, C, No. 4.

(10) For 1 Thess. 2:4, A.V., "to be put in trust," see INTRUST.

(11) For the phrase "put . . . to . . . account" in Philm. 18, see ACCOUNT, A, No. 2.

(12) In Acts 15:9, A.V., *diakrinō*, to make a distinction (R.V.), is translated "put (no) difference."

(13) In Matt. 9:16, A.V., *plērōma*, the fulness or filling, is rendered "(that) which is put in to fill it up," R.V., "(that) which should fill it up." See FILL.

(14) For *paradeigmatizō*, to put to an open shame, Heb. 6:6, see SHAME.

(15) For *phimoō*, to put to silence, see SILENCE.

(16) For "I will put My trust," Heb. 2:13, see TRUST.

PUTTING

1. *endusis* [ἔνδυσις, 1745], a putting on (akin to *enduō*, PUT, No. 26), is used of apparel, 1 Pet. 3:3. ¶ In the Sept., Esth. 5:1; Job 41:4. ¶

NT: B.263d; CB.—; K.—.
OT: lᵉbûsh: S.3830; HR.472a.1; H.1075a; BD.528c.
GEN. REF.: —.

2. *epithesis* [ἐπίθεσις, 1936], a putting on (akin to *epitithēmi*, PUT, No. 4), is used of the putting or laying on of hands; in 2 Tim. 1:6, R.V., "laying" (A.V., "putting"). See LAYING ON.

NT: B.293a; CB.1246b; K.1176.
OT: —.
GEN. REF.: —.

3. *apothesis* [ἀπόθεσις, 595], a putting off or away (akin to *apotithēmi*, PUT, No. 5), is used metaphorically in 1 Pet. 3:21, of the "putting away" of the filth of the flesh; in 2 Pet. 1:14, R.V., of "the putting off" of the body (as a tabernacle) at death (A.V., "I must put off"). ¶

NT: B.91a; CB.1237b; K.—.
OT: —.
GEN. REF.: —.

4. *apekdusis* [ἀπέκδυσις, 555], a putting off, stripping off (akin to *apekduō*, PUT, No. 22), is used in Col. 2:11, of "the body of the flesh" (R.V., an important rendering). ¶

NT: B.83c; CB.1236b; K.192.
OT: —.
GEN. REF.: —.

Note: For *athetēsis*, a putting away, translated "to put away" in Heb. 9:26, lit., '(unto) a setting aside,' see DISANNUL, B. ¶

Q

QUAKE

1. *entromos* [ἔντρομος, 1790], an adjective signifying trembling with fear (*en*, in, *tremō*, to tremble), is used with *eimi*, to be, in Heb. 12:21 (some mss. have *ektromos*, with the same meaning), "I quake," lit., 'I am trembling.' It is used with *ginomai*, to become, in Acts 7:32, "trembled," lit., 'became trembling,' and 16:29, R.V., "trembling for fear" (A.V., "came trembling"). See TREMBLE. ¶

NT: B.269d; CB.—; K.—.
OT: rā'ad: S.7460; HR.481a.1; H.2184; BD.944c.
rā'ash: S.7493; HR.481a.2; H.2195; BD.950a.
GEN. REF.: IS.4:5; NB.—; Z.—.

2. *seiō* [σείω, 4579], "did quake," Matt. 27:51, and 28:4, R.V. (A.V., "did shake"). See MOVE, No. 3, SHAKE, TREMBLE.

NT: B.746c; CB.1268c; K.1014.
OT: rā'ash: S.7493; HR.1261c.5; H.2195; BD.950a.
GEN. REF.: IS.4:5; NB.—; Z.—.

For **QUARREL** see **COMPLAINT**, No. 2, and **SET**, No. 15, Mark 6:19, R.V.

QUARTER

pantothen [πάντοθεν, 3840], from all sides, is translated "from every quarter" in Mark 1:45. See EVERY SIDE, ROUND ABOUT.

NT: B.608d; CB.—; K.—.
OT: —.
GEN. REF.: —.

Notes: (1) In Rev. 20:8, A.V., *gōnia*, an angle, corner, is rendered "quarter" (R.V., "corner").

(2) In Acts 16:3, A.V., *topois*, "parts" (R.V.) is translated "quarters."

(3) In Acts 9:32 the phrase *dia pantōn*, lit., 'throughout all,' is rendered "throughout all parts," R.V. (*meros*, a part, being understood), A.V., "throughout all *quarters*."

(4) for "quarters" in Acts 28:7, A.V., see NEIGHBOURHOOD.

QUATERNION

tetradion [τετράδιον, 5069], a group of four (*tetra*—, four), occurs in Acts 12:4. A quaternion was a set of four men occupied in the work of a guard, two soldiers being chained to the prisoner and two keeping watch; alternatively one of the four watched while the other three slept. The night was divided into four watches of three hours each; there would be one quaternion for each watch by day and by night. ¶ Cp. the "guard" in Matt. 27:65 and 28:11.

NT: B.813c; CB.1271c; K.—.
OT: —.
GEN. REF.: IS.4:608; NB.—; Z.—.

QUEEN

basilissa [βασίλισσα, 938], the feminine of *basileus*, a king, is used (*a*) of the Queen of Sheba, Matt. 12:42; Luke 11:31; of Candace, Acts 8:27; (*b*) metaphorically, of Babylon, Rev. 18:7. ¶

NT: B.137a; CB.1238c; K.97.
OT: malkāh: S.4436; HR.214a.2a; H.1199b; BD.573c.
GEN. REF.: IS.4:7; NB.1068; Z.5:3.

QUENCH, UNQUENCHABLE

A. Verb.

sbennumi [σβέννυμι, 4570], is used (*a*) of quenching fire or things on fire, Matt. 12:20, quoted from Is. 42:3, figurative of the condition of the feebie; Heb. 11:34; in the Passive Voice, Matt. 25:8, of torches (see LAMP), R.V., "are going out," lit., 'are being quenched'; of the retributive doom hereafter of sin unrepented of and unremitted in this life, Mark 9:48 (in some mss. in vv. 44, 46); (*b*) metaphorically, of quenching the fire-tipped darts of the evil one, Eph. 6:16; of quenching the Spirit, by hindering His operations in oral testimony in the church gatherings of believers, 1 Thess. 5:19. "The peace, order, and edification of the saints were evidence of the ministry of the Spirit among them, 1 Cor. 14:26, 32, 33, 40, but if, through ignorance of His ways, or through failure to recognise, or refusal to submit to, them, or through impatience with the ignorance or self-will of others, the Spirit were quenched, these happy results would be absent. For there was always the danger that the impulses of the flesh might usurp the place of the energy of the Spirit in the assembly, and the endeavour to restrain this evil by natural means would have the effect of hindering His ministry also. Apparently then, this injunction was intended to warn believers against the substitution of a mechanical order for the restraints of the Spirit."* ¶ Cp. S. of Sol. 8:7.

NT: B.745b; CB.1268c; K.1009.
OT: kābāh: S.3518; HR.1261a.2; H.944; BD.459c.
dā'ak: S.1846; HR.1261a.1; H.445; BD.200a.
GEN. REF.: IS.4:11; NB.—; Z.—.

B. Adjective.

asbestos [ἄσβεστος, 762], not quenched (*a*, negative, and A), is used of the doom of persons described figuratively as "chaff," Matt. 3:12 and Luke 3:17, "unquenchable"; of the fire of Gehenna (see HELL), Mark 9:43, R.V, "unquenchable fire" (in some mss. ver. 45). ¶ In the Sept., Job 20:26. ¶

NT: B.114b; CB.1237c; K.—.
OT: nāphaḥ (with negative): S.5301; HR.169c.1; H.1390; BD.655d.
GEN. REF.: —.

QUESTION (Noun and Verb), QUESTIONING

A. Nouns.

1. *zētēsis* [ζήτησις, 2214], primarily a seeking, search (*zēteō*, to seek), for which see DISPUTATION, is used in John 3:25; Acts 25:20, R.V., "(being perplexed) how to inquire (concerning these things)," A.V. "(because I doubted of such manner) of questions," lit., 'being perplexed as to the enquiry (or discussion) concerning these things'; in 1 Tim. 1:4 (in some mss.); 6:4; 2 Tim. 2:23; Tit. 3:9. See INQUIRY.

NT: B.339b; CB.1273c; K.300.
OT: —.
GEN. REF.: IS.4:11; NB.—; Z.—.

2. *zētēma* [ζήτημα, —], synonymous with No. 1, but, generally speaking, suggesting in a more concrete form the subject of an enquiry, occurs in Acts 15:2; 18:15; 23:29; 25:19; 26:3. ¶

3. *logos* [λόγος, 3056], a word, is translated "question" in Matt. 21:24 (A.V., "thing"); in Mark 11:29 (R.V., marg., "word") and Luke 20:3, A.V., "one thing"; there is no word in the original for "one," hence the R.V., "a question."

NT: B.477a; CB.1257a; K.505.
OT: dābār: S.1697; HR.881c.2a; H.399a; BD.182a.
GEN. REF.: IS.4:11; NB.—; Z.—.

4. *ekzētēsis* [ἐκζήτησις, 1537, 2214], a questioning, is found in the best texts in 1 Tim. 1:4 (see R.V.); cp. No. 1. ¶

NT: B.240b; CB.1244a; K.—.
OT: —.
GEN. REF.: —.

Notes: (1) In Matt. 22:41, there is no word in the original for "question."

(2) For *suzētēsis* or *sunzētēsis*, a questioning together (*sun*, with), see DISPUTATION.

(3) In Acts 19:40, A.V., *enkaleō*, to bring a charge against, is translated "to be called in question" (R.V., "to be accused").

B. Verbs.

1. *suzēteō* [συζητέω, 4802] or *sunzēteō*, to search together (cp. *Note*, above), to discuss, dispute, is translated to question (or q. with or together) in Mark 1:27; 8:11; 9:10, 14, 16; 12:28, R.V. (A.V., "reasoning together"); Luke 22:23, R.V. (A.V., "enquire"); 24:15, R.V. (A.V., "reasoned"). See DISPUTE, B, No. 3, INQUIRE, REASON.

NT: B.775d; CB.—; K.1099.
OT: bāqash: S.1245; HR.1301a.1; H.276; BD.134c.
GEN. REF.: IS.4:11; NB.—; Z.—.

2. *eperōtaō* [ἐπερωτάω, 1905], to ask, is translated "asked . . . a question," in Matt.

*From Notes on Thessalonians, by Hogg and Vine, p. 196.

22:35, 41; in Luke 2:46, "asking . . . questions"; "questioned" in Luke 23:9. See ASK, A, No. 3.
NT: B.285b; CB.1245c; K.262.
OT: shā'al: S.7592; HR.510b.4; H.2303; BD.981b.
GEN. REF.: IS.4:11; NB.–; Z.–.

For **QUICK**, see **DISCERN**, C, **LIVE** No. 3, *Note*

QUICKEN

1. *zōopoieō* [ζωοποιέω, 2227], to make alive: see LIFE, C.
NT: B.341d; CB.1273c; K.290.
OT: ḥāyāh: S.2421; HR.601c.1; H.644; BD.310d.
GEN. REF.: IS.4:11; NB.–; Z.5:5.

2. *zōogoneō* [ζωογονέω, 2225], to endue with life, produce alive, preserve alive: see LIVE, No. 6.
NT: B.341c; CB.1273c; K.290.
OT: ḥāyāh: S.2421; HR.601c.1; H.644; BD.310d.
GEN. REF.: IS.4:11; NB.–; Z.5:5.

3. *suzōopoieō* [συζωοποιέω, 4806] or *sunzōopoieō*, to quicken together with, make alive with (*sun*, with and No. 1), is used in Eph. 2:5; Col. 2:13, of the spiritual life with Christ, imparted to believers at their conversion. ¶
NT: B.776a; CB.1271a; K.1102.
OT: –.
GEN. REF.: IS.4:11; NB.–; Z.–.

QUICKLY

1. *tachu* [ταχύ, 5035], the neuter of *tachus*, swift, quick, signifies quickly, Matt. 5:25; 28:7, 8; Mark 9:39, R.V. (A.V., "lightly"); Luke 15:22; John 11:29; Rev. 2:16 (ver. 5 in some mss.); 3:11; 11:14; 22:7, 12, 20. See LIGHTLY. ¶
NT: B.807b; CB.1271a; K.–.
OT: māhar: S.4116; HR.1339a.2a; H.1152; BD.554c.
mᵉhērāh: S.4120; HR.1339a.2b; H.1152d; BD.555b.
GEN. REF.: –.

2. *tacheion* [τάχειον, 5032], the comparative degree of No. 1, is translated "quickly" in John 13:27; "out(ran)" in 20:4, R.V., lit., '(ran before) more quickly (than Peter)'; "shortly" in 1 Tim. 3:14 and Heb. 13:23; in 13:19, "(the) sooner." See SHORTLY. ¶
NT: B.806d; CB.–; K.–.
OT: –.
GEN. REF.: –.

3. *tacheōs* [ταχέως, 5030], akin to No. 1, is translated "quickly" in Luke 14:21; 16:6; John 11:31, R.V.; "shortly" in 1 Cor. 4:19; Phil. 2:19, 24; 2 Tim. 4:9; with a suggestion of rashness in the following, Gal. 1:6, R.V., "quickly" (A.V., "soon"); 2 Thess. 2:2; and 1 Tim. 5:22, "hastily," (A.V., "suddenly"). See HASTILY, C. ¶
NT: B.806d; CB.–; K.–.
OT: māhar: S.4116; HR.1338a.1a; H.1152; BD.554c.
mᵉhērāh: S.4120; HR.1338a.1b; H.1152d; BD.555d.
GEN. REF.: –.

4. *en tachei* [ἐν τάχει, 5034], lit., in, or with, swiftness, with speed (*en*, in, and the dative case of *tachos*, speed), is translated "quickly" in Acts 12:7; 22:18; "speedily" in Luke 18:8; "shortly" in Acts 25:4; Rom. 16:20; 1 Tim. 3:14 in some texts; Rev. 1:1; 22:6. In the last two places, "with speed" is probably the meaning. See SHORTLY, SPEEDILY. ¶
NT: B.807a; CB.–; K.–.
OT: –.
GEN. REF.: –.

QUICKSANDS

Note: This is the A.V. rendering in Acts 27:17 of *Surtis*, "Syrtis" (R.V.). The Syrtes, Major and Minor, lie on the North coast of Africa, between the headlands of Tunis and Barca. They have been regarded as dangerous to mariners from very early times, both from the character of the sands and from the cross currents of the adjoining waters. In the voyage described in this chapter the vessel had left the shelter of the island of Cauda and was drifting before the N.E. wind Euraquilo. The mariners might well fear that they would be driven on the Syrtes on the leeward of their course. The changing character of the tempest, however, drove them into the sea of Adria. ¶

QUIET, QUIETNESS

A. Adjectives.

1. *ēremos* [ἤρεμος, 2263], quiet, tranquil, occurs in 1 Tim. 2:2, R.V., "tranquil" (A.V., "quiet"); it indicates tranquillity arising from without. ¶
NT: B.348b; CB.–; K.–.
OT: midbār: S.4057; HR.545a.5; H.399k,l; BD.184c.
GEN. REF.: IS.4:11; NB.–; Z.–.

2. *hēsuchios* [ἡσύχιος, 2272], has much the same meaning as No. 1, but indicates tranquillity arising from within, causing no disturbance to others. It is translated "quiet" in 1 Tim. 2:2, R.V. (A.V., "peaceable"); "quiet" in 1 Pet. 3:4, where it is associated with "meek," and is to characterize the spirit or disposition. See PEACEABLE. ¶
NT: B.349c; CB.1250a; K.–.
OT: –.
GEN. REF.: IS.4:11; NB.–; Z.–.

B. Verbs.

1. *hēsuchazō* [ἡσυχάζω, 2270], akin to A, No. 2, to be still, to live quietly: see CEASE, A, No. 3. ¶
NT: B.349a; CB.1250a; K.–.
OT: shāqaṭ: S.8252; HR.620a.11; H.2453; BD.1052d.
GEN. REF.: IS.4:11; NB.–; Z.–.

2. *katastellō* [καταστέλλω, 2687], denotes to quiet: see APPEASE.
NT: B.419a; CB.–; K.1074.
OT: –.
GEN. REF.: IS.4:11; NB.–; Z.–.

C. Nouns.

1. *eirēnē* [εἰρήνη, 1515], peace, is translated "quietness" in Acts 24:2, A.V. (R.V., "peace"). See PEACE (*e*).

NT: B.227a; CB.1243a; K.207.
OT: shālôm: S.7965; HR.401b.6a; H.2401a; BD.1022d.
GEN. REF.: —.

2. *hēsuchia* [ἡσυχία, 2271], akin to A, No. 2, and B, No. 1, denotes quietness, 2 Thess. 3:12; it is so translated in the R.V. of 1 Tim. 2:11, 12 (A.V., "silence"); in Acts 22:2, R.V., "(they were the more) quiet," A.V., "(they kept the more) silence," lit., 'they kept quietness the more.' ¶

NT: B.349b; CB.1250a; K.—.
OT: shāqaṭ: S.8252; HR.620b.4a; H.2453; BD.1052d
sheqeṭ: S.8253; HR.620b.4b; H.2453a; BD.1053b.
GEN. REF.: IS.4:11; NB.—; Z.—.

QUIT

1. *apallassō* [ἀπαλλάσσω, 525], to free from, is used in the Passive Voice in Luke 12:58, R.V., "to be quit" (A.V., "to be delivered"). See DELIVER, A, No. 6.

NT: B.80a; CB.1236b; K.40.
OT: sûr: S.5493; HR.116b.3; H.1480; BD.693b.
GEN. REF.: —.

2. *andrizō* [ἀνδρίζω, 407], signifies to make a man of (*anēr*, a man); in the Middle Voice, in 1 Cor. 16:13, to play the man, "quit you like men." ¶

NT: B.64a; CB.1235b; K.59.
OT: ḥāzaq: S.2388; HR.86b.2; H.636; BD.304a.
GEN. REF.: IS.4:13; NB.—; Z.—.

R

RABBI

rabbei or *rabbi* [ῥαββεί, 4461], from a word *rab*, primarily denoting "master" in contrast to a slave; this with the added pronominal suffix signified "my master" and was a title of respect by which teachers were addressed. The suffix soon lost its specific force, and in the N.T. the word is used as courteous title of address. It is applied to Christ in Matt. 26:25, 49; Mark 9:5; 11:21; 14:45; John 1:38 (where it is interpreted as *didaskalos*, "master," marg., "teacher" (see also "Rabboni" in John 20:16); ver. 49; 3:2; 4:31; 6:25; 9:2; 11:8; to John the Baptist in John 3:26. In Matt. 23:7, 8 Christ forbids his disciples to covet or use it. In the latter verse it is again explained as *didaskalos*, "master" (some mss. have *kathēgētēs*, a guide). ¶

NT: B.733a; CB.1268a; K.982.
OT: rab: S.7227; HR.—; H.2099a,b; BD.913c.
GEN. REF.: IS.4:30; NB.1072; Z.5:16.

RABBONI

rabbounei or *rabbōni* [ῥαββουνεί, 4462], formed in a similar way to the above, was an Aramaic form of a title almost entirely applied to the president of the Sanhedrin, if such was a descendant of Hillel. It was even more respectful than Rabbi, and signified 'My great master'; in its use in the N.T. the pronominal force of the suffix is apparently retained (contrast Rabbi above); it is found in Mark 10:51 in the best texts, R.V., "Rabboni" (A.V., "Lord"), addressed to Christ by blind Bartimaeus, and in John 20:16 by Mary Magdalene, where it is interpreted by *didaskalos*, "Master" (marg., "Teacher"). ¶

NT: B.733a; CB.1268a; K.982.
OT: rab: S.7227; HR.—; H.2099a,b; BD.913c.
GEN. REF.: IS.4:30; NB.1072; Z.5:16.

For **RABBLE** see **COURT**, No. 1

RACA

raka [ῥακά, 4469], is an Aramaic word akin to the Heb. *rêq*, empty, the first *a* being due to a Galilaean change. In the A.V. of 1611 it was spelt *racha*; in the edition of 1638, *raca*. It was a word of utter contempt, signifying empty, intellectually rather than morally, empty-headed, like Abimelech's hirelings, Judg. 9:4, and the "vain" man of Jas. 2:20. As condemned by Christ, Matt. 5:22, it was worse than being angry, inasmuch as an outrageous utterance is worse then a feeling unexpressed or somewhat controlled in expression; it does not indicate such a loss of self-control as the word rendered "fool," a godless, moral reprobate. ¶

NT: B.733d; CB.1268a; K.983.
OT: rēq: S.7386; HR.—; H.2161a; BD.938a.
GEN. REF.: IS.2:856; NB.1073; Z.5:17.

For **RACE (kindred)** see **KIND**

RACE (contest)

1. *agōn* [ἀγών, 73], is translated "race" in Heb. 12:1, one of the modes of athletic contest, this being the secondary meaning of the word. See CONFLICT.

NT: B.15a; CB.1233c; K.20.
OT: lā'āh: S.3811; HR.18c.1; H.1066; BD.521a.
GEN. REF.: IS.4:31; NB.—; Z.2:397.

2. *stadion* [στάδιον, 4712], a stadium, denotes a racecourse, 1 Cor. 9:24. The stadium (about 600 Greek feet or ⅛ of a Roman mile) was the length of the Olympic course. See FURLONG.

NT: B.764a; CB.—; K.—.
OT: —.
GEN. REF.: IS.4:31; NB.—; Z.—.

Note: No. 1 signifies the race itself; No. 2 the course.

RAGE, RAGING

A. Verb.

phruassō [φρυάσσω, 5433], was primarily used of the snorting, neighing and prancing of horses; hence, metaphorically, of the haughtiness and insolence of men, Acts 4:25. ¶ In the Sept., Psa. 2:1. ¶

NT: B.867b; CB.—; K.—.
OT: —.
GEN. REF.: —.

B. Noun.

kludōn [κλύδων, 2830], a billow, surge (akin to *kluzō*, "to wash over," said of the sea; cp. *kludōnizomai*, to be tossed by the waves, Eph. 4:14), is translated "raging" in Luke 8:24; in Jas. 1:6, R.V., "surge" (A.V., "wave"). ¶

NT: B.436d; CB.—; K.—.
OT: sā'ar: S.5590; HR.772b.1a; H.1528b; BD.704a.
sa'ar: S.5591; HR.772b.1b; H.1528; BD.704b.
GEN. REF.: —.

Note: In Jude 13, A.V., the adjective *agrios*, wild, is translated "raging" (R.V., "wild"). See WILD.

RAIL, RAILER, RAILING

A. Verb.

blasphēmeō [βλασφημέω, 987], to blaspheme, rail, revile (for the meanings of which see BLASPHEME), is translated to rail at, or on, in Matt. 27:39, R.V. (A.V., "reviled"); Mark 15:29; Luke 23:39; 2 Pet. 2:10, R.V. (A.V., "to speak evil of"); 2:12, R.V. (A.V., "speak evil of"). Cp. *loidoreō*, to revile (see REVILE), and B, No. 2 and C, No. 2.

NT: B.142c; CB.1239a; K.107.
OT: nādaph: S.5086; HR.221a.1; H.1307; BD.623c.
nā'aṣ: S.5006; HR.221a.3; H.1274; BD.610d.
GEN. REF.: IS.4:35; NB.—; Z.—.

B. Nouns.

1. *blasphēmia* [βλασφημία, 988], is translated "railings" in Matt. 15:19, R.V.; 1 Tim. 6:4, A.V. and R.V.; "railing" in Mark 7:22, R.V.; Col. 3:8, R.V.; Jude 9, A.V. and R.V., lit., 'judgment of railing'; in Eph. 4:31, R.V. (A.V., "evil speaking"). See BLASPHEMY.

NT: B.143a; CB.1239a; K.107.
OT: ne'āṣāh: S.5007; HR.221a.1; H.1274a,b; BD.611a.
GEN. REF.: IS.4:35; NB.—; Z.—.

2. *loidoria* [λοιδορία, 3059], abuse, railing, reviling, is rendered "reviling" in the R.V., 1 Pet. 3:9 (twice); in 1 Tim. 5:14, A.V. marg., "for their reviling." See REVILE, C. ¶

NT: B.479c; CB.1257a; K.538.
OT: rîb: S.7378; HR.887c.2a; H.2159; BD.936b.
m^erîbāh: S.4808; HR.887c.2b; H.2159c; BD.937b.
GEN. REF.: IS.4:35; NB.—; Z.—.

C. Adjectives.

1. *blasphēmos* [βλάσφημος, —], akin to A, and B, No. 1; see BLASPHEME, C.

2. *loidoros* [λοίδορος, 3060], an adjective denoting reviling, railing (akin to B, No. 2), is used as a noun, "a railer," 1 Cor. 5:11. See REVILE.

NT: B.479c; CB.1257b; K.538.
OT: mādôn: S.4066; HR.887c.1; H.426c; BD.193b.
GEN. REF.: IS.4:35; NB.—; Z.—.

RAIMENT

Notes: (1) For *himation*, rendered "raiment" in Matt. 17:2, A.V. (R.V., "garments"), so Matt. 27:31; Mark 9:3; Luke 23:34; John 19:24; Acts 22:20; Rev. 3:5, 18; 4:4; A.V. and R.V., Acts 18:6, see CLOTHING, No. 2 and ROBE. *Himatismos* is rendered "raiment" in Luke 9:29; *enduma* in Matt. 3:4; 6:25, 28; 28:3 and Luke 12:23. For *esthēs*, translated "raiment" in Jas. 2:2 (2nd part), A.V., see APPAREL.

(2) For *skepasma*, a covering, rendered "raiment" in 1 Tim. 6:8, A.V., see COVER, B, No. 2.

RAIN (Noun and Verb)

A. Nouns.

1. *huetos* [ὑετός, 5205], from *huō*, to rain, is used especially, but not entirely, of showers, and is found in Acts 14:17; 28:2; Heb. 6:7; Jas. 5:7 (see EARLY AND LATTER); 5:18; Rev. 11:6 (see B). ¶

NT: B.833b; CB.1251c; K.—.
OT: māṭār: S.4306; HR.1384a.2; H.1187a; BD.564b.
geshem: S.1653; HR.1384a.1; H.389a; BD.177c.
GEN. REF.: IS.4:35; NB.1074; Z.5:27.

2. *brochē* [βροχή, 1028], akin to B, below, lit., a wetting, hence, rain, is used in Matt. 7:25, 27. ¶ In the Sept., Ps. 68:9; 105:32. ¶ It is found in the papyri in connection with irrigation in Egypt (Deissmann, *Light from the Ancient East*).

NT: B.147d; CB.1239b; K.—.
OT: geshem: S.1653; HR.231b.1; H.389a; BD.177c.
GEN. REF.: IS.4:35; NB.1074; Z.5:27.

B. Verb.

brechō [βρέχω, 1026], akin to A, No. 2, signifies (*a*) to wet, Luke 7:38, 44, R.V. (A.V., to wash); (*b*) to send rain, Matt. 5:45; to rain, Luke 17:29 (of fire and brimstone); Jas. 5:17, used impersonally (twice); Rev. 11:6, where *huetos* (A, No. 1) is used as the subject, lit., '(that) rain rain (not)'. ¶

NT: B.147c; CB.1239b; K.–.
OT: māṭar: S.4305; HR.230c.3b; H.1187; BD.565a.
GEN. REF.: IS.4:35; NB.1074; Z.–.

RAINBOW

iris [ἶρις, 2463], whence Eng., iris, the flower, describes the rainbow seen in the heavenly vision, "round about the throne, like an emerald to look upon," Rev. 4:3, emblematic of the fact that, in the exercise of God's absolute sovereignty and perfect counsels, He will remember His covenant concerning the earth (Gen. 9:9-17); in Rev. 10:1, "the rainbow," R.V., the definite article suggests a connection with the scene in 4:3; here it rests upon the head of an angel who declares that "there shall be delay no longer" (ver. 6, R.V. marg., the actual meaning); the mercy to be shown to the earth must be preceded by the execution of Divine judgments upon the nations who defy God and His Christ. Cp. Ezek. 1:28. ¶

NT: B.380c; CB.1253a; K.369.
OT: qeshet: S.7198; HR.1363c.3; H.2093; BD.905d.
GEN. REF.: IS.4:36; NB.1075; Z.5:28.

RAISE (up)

1. *egeirō* [ἐγείρω, 1453], for the various meanings of which see ARISE, No. 3, is used (*a*) of raising the dead, Active and Passive Voices, e.g., of the resurrection of Christ, Matt. 16:21; 17:23; 20:19, R.V.; 26:32, R.V., "(after) I am raised up" (A.V., ". . . risen again"); Luke 9:22; 20:37; John 2:19; Acts 3:15; 4:10 [not 5:30, see (*c*) below]; 10:40 [not 13:23 in the best texts, see (*c*) below]; 13:30, 37; Rom. 4:24, 25; 6:4, 9; 7:4; 8:11 (twice); 8:34, R.V.; 10:9; 1 Cor. 6:14, (1st part); 15:13, 14, R.V.; 15:15 (twice), 16, 17; 15:20, R.V.; 2 Cor. 4:14; Gal. 1:1; Eph. 1:20; Col. 2:12; 1 Thess. 1:10; 1 Pet. 1:21; in 2 Tim. 2:8, R.V., "risen"; (*b*) of the resurrection of human beings, Matt. 10:8; 11:5; Matt. 27:52, R.V. (A.V., "arose"); Mark 12:26, R.V.; Luke 7:22; John 5:21; 12:1, 9, 17; Acts 26:8; 1 Cor. 15:29 and 32, R.V.; 15:35, 42, 43 (twice), 44, 52; 2 Cor. 1:9; 4:14; Heb. 11:19; (*c*) of raising up a person to occupy a place in the midst of a people, said of Christ, Acts 5:30; in 13:23, A.V. only (the best texts have *agō*, to bring, R.V., "hath . . . brought"); of David, Acts 13:22 (for ver. 33 see No. 2); (*d*) metaphorically, of a horn of salvation, Luke 1:69; (*e*) of children, from stones, by creative power, Luke 3:8; (*f*) of the Temple, as the Jews thought, John 2:20, R.V., "wilt Thou raise (it) up" (A.V., "rear"); (*g*) of lifting up a person, from physical infirmity, Mark 1:31, R.V., "raised . . . up" (A.V., "lifted"); so 9:27; Acts 3:7; 10:26, R.V. (A.V., "took"); Jas. 5:15, "shall raise . . . up"; (*h*) metaphorically, of raising up affliction, Phil. 1:17, R.V. (in the best texts; the A.V., ver. 16, following those which have *epipherō*, has "to add"). See AWAKE, No. 1.

NT: B.214c; CB.1242c; K.195.
OT: qûm: S.6965; HR.364a.12; H.1999; BD.877c.
'ûr: S.5782; HR.364a.8; H.1587; BD.734d.
GEN. REF.: IS.4:36; NB.–; Z.–.

2. *anistēmi* [ἀνίστημι, 450], for the various applications of which see ARISE, No. 1, is translated to raise or raise up, (*a*) of the resurrection of the dead by Christ, John 6:39, 40, 44, 54; (*b*) of the resurrection of Christ from the dead, Acts 2:24 (for ver. 30 see R.V., *kathizō*, to set, as in the best texts); 2:32; 13:34, see (*c*) below; Acts 17:31; (*c*) of raising up a person to occupy a place in the midst of a nation, said of Christ, Acts 3:26; 7:37; 13:33, R.V., "raised up Jesus," not here by resurrection from the dead, as the superfluous "again" of the A.V. would suggest; this is confirmed by the latter part of the verse, which explains the raising up as being by way of His Incarnation, and by the contrast in ver. 34, where stress is laid upon His being raised "from the dead," the same verb being used; (*d*) of raising up seed, Matt. 22:24; (*e*) of being raised from natural sleep, Matt. 1:24, A.V., "being raised" (R.V., "arose"); here some mss. have *diegeirō*, to arouse completely; see ARISE, No. 4.

NT: B.70a; CB.–; K.60.
OT: qûm: S.6965; HR.102c.8a-c; H.1999; BD.877c.
GEN. REF.: IS.4:36; NB.–; Z.–.

Note: For the contrast between No. 1 and No. 2 see ARISE, No. 3 (parag. 2).

3. *exegeirō* [ἐξεγείρω, 1825], *ek*, out of, and No. 1, is used (*a*) of the resurrection of believers, 1 Cor. 6:14 [2nd part; see No. 1 (*a*) for the 1st part]; (*b*) of raising a person to public position, Rom. 9:17, "did I raise thee up," R.V., said of Pharaoh. ¶

NT: B.273d; CB.–; K.195.
OT: 'ûr: S.5782; HR.490b.11a-d; H.1587; BD.734d.
qûm: S.6965; HR.490b.12; H.1999; BD.877c.
yāqaṣ: S.3364; HR.490b.6; H.904; BD.429c.
GEN. REF.: IS.4:36; NB.–; Z.–.

4. *exanistēmi* [ἐξανίστημι, 1817], *ek*, out of, and No. 2, is used of raising up seed, Mark 12:19; Luke 20:28; elsewhere, Acts 15:5, to rise up. See RISE. ¶

NT: B.272d; CB.1247c; K.60.
OT: qûm: S.6965; HR.487c.6; H.1999; BD.877c.
GEN. REF.: IS.4:36; NB.–; Z.–.

5. *sunegeirō* [συνεγείρω, 4891], to raise together (*sun*, with, and No. 1), is used of the believer's spiritual resurrection with Christ, Eph. 2:6; Passive Voice in Col. 2:12, R.V., "ye were . . . raised (with Him)," A.V., "ye are risen"; so 3:1. See RISE.

NT: B.785d; CB.1270c; K.1102.
OT: 'ûr: S.5782; HR.1313a.1; H.1587; BD.734d.
'āzab: S.5800; HR.1313a.2; H.1594,1595; BD.736d.
GEN. REF.: IS.4:36; NB.–; Z.–.

Notes: (1) In Acts 13:50, A.V., *epegeirō*, to rouse up, excite, is translated "raised" (R.V., "stirred up," as in A.V. and R.V. in 14:2).

(2) In Acts 24:12, *poieō*, to make, is used with *epistasis*, a collection of people, and translated "stirring up (a crowd)," R.V., lit., 'making a collection (of a crowd)'; some mss. have *episustasis*, a riotous throng, A.V., "raising up (the people)."

(3) In Heb. 11:35, A.V., the noun *anastasis*, a resurrection, preceded by *ex* (i.e., *ek*), out of, or by, instrumental, is translated "raised to life again" (a paraphrase), R.V., "by a resurrection."

For **RAN** see **RUN**

RANKS

prasia [πρασιά, 4237], a garden-bed or plot (probably from *prason*, a leek), is used metaphorically in Mark 6:40 of ranks of persons arranged in orderly groups. ¶

NT: B.698b; CB.–; K.–.
OT: –.
GEN. REF.: –.

RANSOM

1. *lutron* [λύτρον, 3083], lit., a means of loosing (from *luō*, to loose), occurs frequently in the Sept., where it is always used to signify equivalence. Thus it is used of the ransom for a life, e.g., Ex. 21:30, of the redemption price of a slave, e.g., Lev. 19:20, of land, 25:24, of the price of a captive, Isa. 45:13. In the N.T. it occurs in Matt. 20:28 and Mark 10:45; where it is used of Christ's gift of Himself as "a ransom for many." Some interpreters have regarded the ransom price as being paid to Satan; others, to an impersonal power such as death, or evil, or "that ultimate necessity which has made the whole course of things what it has been." Such ideas are largely conjectural, the result of an attempt to press the details of certain Old Testament illustrations beyond the actual statements of new Testament doctrines.

That Christ gave up His life in expiatory sacrifice under God's judgment upon sin and thus provided a ransom whereby those who receive Him on this ground obtain deliverance from the penalty due to sin, is what Scripture teaches. What the Lord states in the two passages mentioned involves this essential character of His death. In these passages the preposition is *anti*, which has a vicarious significance, indicating that the ransom holds good for those who, accepting it as such, no longer remain in death since Christ suffered death in their stead. The change of preposition in 1 Tim. 2:6, where the word *antilutron*, a substitutionary ransom, is used, is significant. There the preposition is *huper*, on behalf of, and the statement is made that He "gave Himself a ransom for all," indicating that the ransom was provisionally universal, while being of a vicarious character. Thus the three passages consistently show that while the provision was universal, for Christ died for all men, yet it is actual for those only who accept God's conditions, and who are described in the Gospel statements as "the many." The giving of His life was the giving of His entire Person, and while His death under Divine judgment was alone expiatory, it cannot be dissociated from the character of His life which, being sinless, gave virtue to His death and was a testimony to the fact that His death must be of a vicarious nature. ¶

NT: B.482c; CB.1257b; K.543.
OT: g^{e}'ullāh: S.1353; HR.890a.1a; H.300b; BD.145b.
kōpher: S.3724; HR.890a.2; H.1025b; BD.497a.
p^{e}dûyim: S.6302; HR.890a.4d; H.1734a; BD.804b.
GEN. REF.: IS.4:44; NB.1078; Z.5:38.

2. *antilutron* [ἀντίλυτρον, —], 1 Tim. 2:6. See under No. 1. ¶

For **RASH, RASHLY** see **HEADSTRONG**

RATHER

A. Adverb.

mallon [μᾶλλον, 3123], the comparative degree of *mala*, very, very much, is frequently translated "rather," e.g., Matt. 10:6, 28; 1 Cor. 14:1, 5; sometimes followed by "than," with a connecting particle, e.g., Matt. 18:13 ("more than"); or without, e.g., John 3:19; Acts 4:19, R.V. (A.V., "more"); in 1 Cor. 9:12, A.V., "rather" (R.V., "yet more"); 12:22, R.V., "rather" (A.V., "more"); 2 Cor. 3:9 (ditto);

Philm. 16 (ditto); in 2 Pet. 1:10, A.V., "the rather" (R.V., "the more"). See MORE.
NT: B.489a; CB.1257c; K.–.
OT: –.
GEN. REF.: –.

B. Verb.

thelō [θέλω, 2309], to will, wish, is translated "I had rather" in 1 Cor. 14:19. See DESIRE, B, No. 6.
NT: B.354d; CB.1271c; K.318.
OT: 'ābāh: S.14; HR.628a.1; H.3; BD.2c.
ḥāphēṣ: S.2654; HR.628a.8; H.712; BD.342c.
rāṣôn: S.7522; HR.628a.12b; H.2207a; BD.953c.
GEN. REF.: –.

C. Preposition.

para [παρά, 3844], beyond, in comparison with, is translated "rather than" in Rom. 1:25, R.V. (A.V., "more than"; marg., "rather").
NT: B.609c; CB.1261c; K.771.
OT: –.
GEN. REF.: –.

D. Conjunction.

alla [ἀλλά, 235], but, on the contrary, is translated "and rather" in Luke 17:8. ¶
NT: B.38a; CB.–; K.–.
OT: –.
GEN. REF.: –.

Notes: (1) In Heb. 13:19, A.V., *perissoterōs*, "the more exceedingly" (R.V.), is translated "the rather."

(2) In Luke 11:41 and 12:31, A.V., *plēn*, an adverb signifying yet, howbeit, is translated "rather" (R.V., "howbeit").

(3) In Rom. 3:8, A.V., the negative particle *mē*, "not," is translated with "*rather*" in italics (R.V., "why not").

(4) In Luke 10:20, A.V., "rather rejoice," there is no word in the original for "rather" (see the R.V.).

RAVEN

korax [κόραξ, 2876], a raven (perhaps onomatopoeic, representing the sound), occurs in the plural in Luke 12:24. The Heb. *oreb* and the Arabic *ghurab* are from roots meaning 'to be black'; the Arabic root also has the idea of leaving home. Hence the evil omen attached to the bird. It is the first bird mentioned in the Bible, Gen. 8:7. Christ used the ravens to illustrate and enforce the lesson of God's provision and care. ¶
NT: B.444b; CB.–; K.–.
OT: 'ōrēb: S.6158; HR.779c.1; H.1690a; BD.788b.
GEN. REF.: IS.4:48; NB.156; Z.5:40.

RAVENING

A. Adjective.

harpax [ἅρπαξ, 727], an adjective signifying rapacious, is translated "ravening" (of wolves) in Matt. 7:15: see EXTORT, C.
NT: B.109b; CB.1249b; K.–.
OT: ṭāraph: S.2963; HR.160a.1; H.827; BD.382d.
GEN. REF.: IS.4:49; NB.–; Z.–.

B. Noun.

harpagē [ἁρπαγή, 724], is translated "ravening" in Luke 11:39, A.V.: see EXTORT, B, No. 1.
NT: B.109b; CB.1249b; K.–.
OT: gāzēl: S.1498; HR.159a.1a; H.337a; BD.160a.
g^ezēlāh: S.1500; HR.159a.1b; H.337b; BD.160a.
shālal: S.7997; HR.159a.3; H.2399,2400; BD.1021d.
GEN. REF.: IS.4:49; NB.–; Z.–.

REACH

1. *akoloutheō* [ἀκολουθέω, 190], to follow, is translated "have reached," in Rev. 18:5, of the sins of Babylon. Some mss. have the verb *kollaomai*, to cleave together, R.V., marg.; see FOLLOW. ¶
NT: B.31a; CB.1234b; K.33.
OT: hālak: S.1980; HR.443.b; H.498; BD.229d.
GEN. REF.: –.

2. *oregō* [ὀρέγω, 3713], to reach or stretch out, is rendered "reached after" in 1 Tim. 6:10, R.V.; see DESIRE, B, No. 5.
NT: B.579d; CB.1261a; K.727.
OT: –.
GEN. REF.: –.

3. *pherō* [φέρω, 5342], to bear, carry, is used of reaching forth the hand in John 20:27 (twice). See BEAR, No. 2.
NT: B.854d; CB.1264a; K.1252.
OT: bō': S.935; HR.1426c.3b; H.212; BD.97c.
GEN. REF.: –.

4. *ephikneomai* [ἐφικνέομαι, 2185], to come to, reach, is used in 2 Cor. 10:13, 14. ¶
NT: B.330c; CB.–; K.–.
OT: –.
GEN. REF.: –.

5. *katantaō* [καταντάω, 2658], to come to a place, is translated "reach" in Acts 27:12, R.V. (A.V., "attain to"). See COME, No. 28.
NT: B.415b; CB.1254a; K.419.
OT: –.
GEN. REF.: –.

Note: In Phil. 3:13, A.V., *epekteinō*, in the Middle Voice, to stretch forward, is translated "reaching forth" (R.V., "stretching forward").

READ, READING

A. Verb.

anaginōskō [ἀναγινώσκω, 314], primarily, to know certainly, to know again, recognize (*ana*, again, *ginōskō*, to know), is used of reading written characters, e.g., Matt. 12:3, 5; 21:16; 24:15; of the private reading of Scripture, Acts 8:28, 30, 32; of the public reading of Scripture, Luke 4:16; Acts 13:27; 15:21; 2 Cor. 3:15; Col. 4:16 (thrice); 1 Thess. 5:27; Rev. 1:3. In 2 Cor. 1:13 there is a purposive play upon words; firstly, "we write none other things unto you, than what ye read (*anaginōskō*) "signifies that there is no hidden or mysterious meaning in his Epistles; whatever doubts may have arisen and been expressed in this respect, he means what he says; then follows the similar verb *epiginōskō*, to acknowledge, "or even acknowledge, and I hope ye will acknowledge unto the end." The *paronomasia* can hardly be reproduced in English. Similarly, in 3:2 the verb *ginōskō*, to know, and *anaginōskō*, to read, are put in that order, and metaphorically applied to the church at Corinth as being an epistle, a message to the world, written by the Apostle and his fellow-missionaries, through their ministry of the gospel and the consequent change in the lives of the converts, an epistle "known and read of all men." For other instances of *paronomasia* see, e.g., Rom. 12:3, *phroneō, huperphroneō, sōphroneō*; 1 Cor. 2:13, 14, *sunkrinō, anakrinō*; 2 Thess. 3:11, *ergazomai*, and *periergazomai*; 1 Cor. 7:31, *chraomai* and *katachraomai*; 11:31, *diakrinō* and *krinō*; 12:2, *agō* and *apagō*; Phil. 3:2, 3, *katatomē* and *peritomē*.

NT: B.51c; CB.1235a; K.55.
OT: qārā': S.7121; HR.75e.2a,b; H.2063; BD.894d.
GEN. REF.: IS.4:49; NB.—; Z.—.

B. Noun.

anagnōsis [ἀνάγνωσις, 320], in non-Biblical Greek denoted recognition or a survey (the latter foud in the papyri); then, reading; in the N.T. the public reading of Scripture, Acts 13:15; 2 Cor. 3:14; 1 Tim. 4:13, where the context makes clear that the reference is to the care required in reading the Scriptures to a company, a duty ever requiring the exhortation "take heed." Later, readers in churches were called *anagnōstai*. ¶ In the Sept., Neh. 8:8. ¶

NT: B.52d; CB.1235a; K.55.
OT: miqrā': S.4744; HR.76b.1; H.2063d; BD.896d.
GEN. REF.: IS.4:49; NB.—; Z.—.

READINESS

1. *prothumia* [προθυμία, 4288], eagerness, willingness, readiness (*pro*, forward, *thumos*, mind, disposition, akin to *prothumos*, READY, A, No. 2), is translated "readiness of mind" in Acts 17:11, "readiness" in 2 Cor. 8:11; in ver. 12, R.V. (A.V., "a willing mind"); in ver. 19, R.V. "(our) readiness," A.V., "(your) ready mind"; in 9:2, R.V., "readiness" (A.V., "forwardness of . . . mind"; see FORWARDNESS, *Note* (4). ¶

NT: B.706c; CB.1267b; K.937.
OT: —.
GEN. REF.: —.

2. *hetoimos* [ἕτοιμος, 2092], an adjective (see READY, A, No. 1), is used with *echō*, to have, and *en*, in, idiomatically, as a noun, in 2 Cor. 10:6, R.V., "being in readiness" (A.V., "having in readiness"), of the Apostle's aim for the church to be obedient to Christ. Cp. READY, C.

NT: B.316c; CB.1250b; K.266.
OT: kûn: S.3559; HR.564c.la; H.964; BD.465c.
mākôn: S.4349; HR.564c.lc; H.964c; BD.467c.
GEN. REF.: —.

READY

A. Adjectives.

1. *hetoimos* [ἕτοιμος, 2092], prepared, ready (akin to *hetoimasia*, preparation), is used (*a*) of persons, Matt. 24:44; 25:10; Luke 12:40; 22:33; Acts 23:15, 21 (for 2 Cor. 10:6, see above); Tit. 3:1; 1 Pet. 3:15; (*b*) of things, Matt. 22:4 (2nd part), 8; Mark 14:15, R.V., "ready" (A.V., "prepared"); Luke 14:17; John 7:6; 2 Cor. 9:5; 10:16, R.V., "things ready" (A.V., "things made ready"); 1 Pet. 1:5. See PREPARE, No. 5, *Note* (2). ¶

NT: B.316c; CB.1250b; K.266.
OT: kûn: S.3559; HR.564c.la; H.964; BD.465c.
mākôn: S.4349; HR.564c.lc; H.964c; BD.467c.
GEN. REF.: —.

2. *prothumos* [πρόθυμος, 4289], predisposed, willing (akin to *prothumia*, see READINESS), is translated "ready" in Rom. 1:15, expressive of willingness, eagerness: in Mark 14:38, R.V., "willing" (A.V., "ready"); in Matt. 26:41, "willing." See WILLING. ¶

NT: B.706c; CB.—; K.937.
OT: nādîb: S.5081; HR.1206c.2; H.1299b; BD.622a.
GEN. REF.: —.

B. Verbs.

1. *mellō* [μέλλω, 3195], to be about to, is translated to be ready in 2 Pet. 1:12, R.V., where the future indicates that the Apostle will be prepared, as in the past and the present, to remind his readers of the truths they know (some mss. have *ouk amelēsō*, "I will not be negligent," A.V.; cp., however, ver. 15. Field, in *Notes on the Translation of the N.T.,* suggests that the true reading is *melēsō*, the future of *melō*, to be a care, or an object of care); in Rev. 3:2, R.V., "were ready" (some texts have the present tense, as in the A.V.). Elsewhere, where the A.V. has the rendering to be ready, the R.V. gives renderings in accordance with the usual significance as follows: Luke 7:2, "was . . . at the point of"; Acts 20:7, "intending"; Rev. 12:4, "about (to)."

NT: B.500d; CB.1258a; K.—.
OT: —.
GEN. REF.: —.

2. *hetoimazō* [ἑτοιμάζω, 2090], make ready: see PREPARE, B, No. 1.

NT: B.316a; CB.1250b; K.266.
OT: kûn: S.3559; HR.563c.5; H.964; BD.465c.
GEN. REF.: —.

3. *paraskeuazō* [παρασκευάζω, 3903], to prepare, make ready: see PREPARE, B, No. 4.
NT: B.622a; CB.1262b; K.—.
OT: qādash: S.6942; HR.1064a.7; H.1990; BD.872d.
GEN. REF.: —.

Note: On the difference between No. 2 and No. 3, see PREPARE, *Note* (1) under No. 5.

C. Adverb.

hetoimōs [ἑτοίμως, 2093], readily (akin to A, No. 1), is used with *echō*, to have, lit., 'to have readily,' i.e., to be in readiness, to be ready, Acts 21:13; 2 Cor. 12:14; 1 Pet. 4:5. ¶
NT: B.316d; CB.—; K.—.
OT: 'āsparnā' (Aramaic): S.629; HR.565a.1; H.2594; BD.1082a.
GEN. REF.: —.

Notes: (1) In Heb. 8:13, A.V. *engus*, near, is translated "ready" (R.V., "nigh"). See NIGH.

(2) For "ready to distribute," 1 Tim. 6:18, see DISTRIBUTE, B.

(3) In 2 Tim. 4:6, A.V., *spendomai*, "I am being offered," R.V., with *ēdē*, "already," is translated "I am now ready to be offered." See OFFER.

(4) In 1 Pet. 5:2 *prothumōs*, willingly, with alacrity, is rendered "of a ready mind." ¶

REAP

therizō [θερίζω, 2325], to reap (akin to *theros*, summer, harvest), is used (*a*) literally, Matt. 6:26; 25:24, 26; Luke 12:24; 19:21, 22; Jas.5:4 (2nd part), A.V., "have reaped"; (*b*) figuratively or in proverbial expressions, John 4:36 (twice), 37, 38, with immediate reference to bringing Samaritans into the Kingdom of God, in regard to which the disciples would enjoy the fruits of what Christ Himself had been doing in Samaria; the Lord's words are, however, of a general application in respect of such service; in 1 Cor. 9:11, with reference to the right of the Apostle and his fellow-missionaries to receive material assistance from the church, a right which he forbore to exercise; in 2 Cor. 9:6 (twice), with reference to rendering material help to the needy, either "sparingly" or "bountifully," the reaping being proportionate to the sowing; in Gal. 6:7, 8 (twice), of reaping "corruption," with special reference, according to the context, to that which is naturally shortlived transient (though the statement applies to every form of sowing to the flesh), and of reaping eternal life (characteristics and moral qualities being in view), as a result of sowing "to the Spirit," the reference probably being to the new nature of the believer, which is, however, under the controlling power of the Holy Spirit, ver. 9, the reaping (the effect of well doing) being accomplished, to a limited extent, in this life, but in complete fulfilment at and beyond the Judgment-Seat of Christ; diligence or laxity here will then produce proportionate results; in Rev. 14:15 (twice), 16, figurative of the discriminating judgment Divinely to be fulfilled at the close of this age, when the wheat will be separated from the tares (see Matt. 13:30). ¶
NT: B.359b; CB.1272b; K.332.
OT: qāṣar: S.7114; HR.648c.4a; H.2061,2062; BD.894b.
GEN. REF.: IS.4:50; NB.—; Z.5:41.

For **REAP DOWN**, Jas. 5:4, see **MOW**

REAPER

theristēs [θεριστής, 2327], a reaper (akin to *therizō*, see above), is used of angels in Matt. 13:30, 39. ¶
NT: B.359c; CB.1272b; K.—.
OT: —.
GEN. REF.: IS.4:50; NB.—; Z.5:41.

For **REAR UP**, John 2:20, see **RAISE**, No. 1. (*f*)

REASON (Noun)

logos [λόγος, 3056], a word, etc., has also the significance of the inward thought itself, a reckoning, a regard, a reason, translated "reason" in Acts 18:14, in the phrase "reason would," *kata logon*, lit., 'according to reason (I would bear with you)'; in 1 Pet. 3:15, "a reason (concerning the hope that is in you)." See WORD.
NT: B.477a; CB.1257; K.505.
OT: dābār: S.1697; HR.881c.2a; H.399a; BD.182a.
GEN. REF.: IS.4:51; NB.—; Z.—.

Note: In Acts 6:2, A.V., the adjective *arestos*, pleasing, agreeable, is translated "reason" (R.V., "fit," marg., "pleasing"). See FIT, No. 2.

For the prepositions rendered **BY REASON OF** see † p. 1

REASON (Verb)

1. *dialogizomai* [διαλογίζομαι, 1260], to bring together different reasons and reckon them up, to reason, is used in the N.T. (*a*) chiefly of thoughts and considerations which are more or less objectionable, e.g., of the disciples who reasoned together, through a mistaken view of Christ's teaching regarding leaven, Matt. 16:7, 8 and Mark 8:16, 17; of their reasoning as to who was the greatest among them, Mark 9:33, R.V., "were ye reasoning," A.V., "ye disputed" (for ver. 34, see DISPUTE); of the Scribes and Pharisees in criticising Christ's claim to forgive sins, Mark 2:6,

8 (twice) and Luke 5:21, 22; of the chief priests and elders in considering how to answer Christ's question regarding John's baptism, Matt. 21:25; Mark 11:31 (some mss. have *logizomai*, here, which is nowhere else rendered "to reason"); of the wicked husbandmen, and their purpose to murder the heir and seize his inheritance, Luke 20:14; of the rich man who "reasoned" within himself, R.V. (A.V., "thought"), as to where to bestow his fruits, Luke 12:17 (some mss. have it in John 11:50, the best have *logizomai*; see ACCOUNT, No. 4); (*b*) of considerations not objectionable, Luke 1:29, "cast in (her) mind"; 3:15, R.V., and A.V., marg., "reasoned" (A.V., "mused"). See CAST, No. 15, DISPUTE, B, No. 2. ¶

NT: B.186a; CB.1241b; K.155.
OT: ḥāshab: S.2803; HR.304c.2; H.767; BD.362d.
GEN. REF.: IS.4:51; NB.—; Z.—.

2. *dialegomai* [*διαλέγομαι*, 1256], to think different things with oneself, to ponder, then, to dispute with others, is translated to reason in Acts 17:2, A.V. and R.V.; 17:17, R.V.; 18:4, 19, A.V. and R.V.; 19:8, 9, R.V.; 24:25, A.V. and R.V.; Heb. 12:5, R.V., "reasoneth (with you)," A.V., "speaketh (unto you)." See DISPUTE, B, No. 1.

NT: B.185c; CB.1241a; K.155.
OT: dābar: S.1696; HR.304b.1; H.399; BD.180b.
rîb: S.7378; HR.304b.2; H.2159; BD.936b.
GEN. REF.: IS.4:51; NB.—; Z.—.

3. *sullogizomai* [*συλλογίζομαι*, 4817], to compute (*sun*, with, and *logizomai*; cp. Eng., syllogism), also denotes to reason, and is so rendered in Luke 20:5. ¶

NT: B.777a; CB.—; K.—.
OT: ḥāshab: S.2803; HR.1302c.2; H.767; BD.362d.
bîn: S.995; HR.1302c.1; H.239; BD.106c.
GEN. REF.: IS.4:51; NB.—; Z.—.

4. *suzēteō* [*συζητέω*, 4802], to seek or examine together (*sun*, with, *zēteō*, to seek), to discuss, is translated "reasoning" in Mark 12:28, A.V. (R.V., "questioning"); similarly in Luke 24:15. See DISPUTE, B, No. 3.

NT: B.775d; CB.—; K.1099.
OT: bāqash: S.1245; HR.1301b.1; H.276; BD.134c.
GEN. REF.: —.

REASONABLE

logikos [*λογικός*, 3050], pertaining to the reasoning faculty, reasonable, rational, is used in Rom. 12:1, of the service (*latreia*) to be rendered by believers in presenting their bodies "a living sacrifice, holy, acceptable to God." The sacrifice is to be intelligent, in contrast to those offered by ritual and compulsion; the presentation is to be in accordance with the spiritual intelligence of those who are new creatures in Christ and are mindful of "the mercies of God." For the significance of the word in 1 Pet. 2:2, see under MILK. ¶

NT: B.476c; CB.1257a; K.505.
OT: —.
GEN. REF.: IS.4:51; NB.—; Z.—.

REASONING

dialogismos [*διαλογισμός*, 1261], a thought, reasoning, inward questioning [akin to *dialogizomai*, see REASON (Verb), No. 1], is translated "reasoning" or "reasonings" in Luke 5:22, R.V. (A.V., "thoughts"); 9:46; ver. 47, R.V. (A.V., "thoughts"); 24:38 (A.V., "thoughts"); Rom. 1:21 (A.V., "imaginations"); 1 Cor. 3:20 (A.V., "thoughts"). See DISPUTE, A, No. 1.

NT: B.186a; CB.1241b; K.155.
OT: maḥªshābāh: S.4284; HR.305a.2; H.767d; BD.364b.
ra'yôn: S.7476; HR.305a.4b; H.2998b; BD.1113b.
GEN. REF.: IS.4:51; NB.—; Z.—.

Note: In those mss. which contain Acts 28:29, occurs *suzētēsis*, a disputation, which is translated "reasoning" (A.V.). ¶

REBUKE (Verb and Noun)

A. Verbs.

1. *epitimaō* [*ἐπιτιμάω*, 2008], primarily, to put honour upon, then, to adjudge, hence signifies to rebuke. Except for 2 Tim. 4:2 and Jude 9, it is confined in the N.T. to the Synoptic Gospels, where it is frequently used of the Lord's rebukes to (*a*) evil spirits, e.g., Matt. 17:18; Mark 1:25; 9:25; Luke 4:35, 41; 9:42; (*b*) winds, Matt. 8:26; Mark 4:39; Luke 8:24; (*c*) fever, Luke 4:39; (*d*) disciples, Mark 8:33; Luke 9:55; contrast Luke 19:39. For rebukes by others see Matt. 16:22; 19:13; 20:31; Mark 8:32; 10:13; 10:48, R.V., "rebuked" (A.V., "charged"); Luke 17:3; 18:15, 39; 23:40. See CHARGE, C, No. 7.

NT: B.303b; CB.1246b; K.249.
OT: gā'ar: S.1605; HR.537a.1; H.370; BD.172a.
GEN. REF.: IS.4:52; NB.—; Z.—.

2. *elenchō* [*ἐλέγχω*, 1651], to convict, refute, reprove, is translated to rebuke in the A.V. of the following (the R.V. always has the verb to reprove): 1 Tim. 5:20; Tit. 1:13; 2:15; Heb. 12:5; Rev. 3:19. See CONVICT, No. 1.

NT: B.249b; CB.1244a; K.221.
OT: yākaḥ: S.3198; HR.449b.3a; H.865; BD.406d.
GEN. REF.: IS.4:52; NB.—; Z.—.

Note: While *epitimaō* signifies simply a rebuke which may be either undeserved, Matt. 16:22, or ineffectual, Luke 23:40, *elenchō* implies a rebuke which carries conviction.

3. *epiplēssō* [*ἐπιπλήσσω*, 1969], to strike at (*epi*, upon or at, *plēssō*, to strike, smite), hence, to rebuke, is used in the injunction against rebuking an elder, 1 Tim. 5:1. ¶

NT: B.297d; CB.—; K.—.
OT: —.
GEN. REF.: IS.4:52; NB.—; Z.—.

Note: In Phil. 2:15, the best texts have *amōmos*, without blemish (*a*, negative, *mōmos*, a blemish, a moral disgrace), R.V., "without blemish"; some mss. have *amōmētos* (*a*, negative, and *mōmaomai*, to blame), A.V., "without rebuke." Contrast *amemptos* in the same verse, blameless on account of absence of inconsistency or ground of reproof, whereas *amōmos* indicates absence of stain or blemish. We may have blemish, with freedom from blame.

B. Noun.

elenxis [ἔλεγξις, 1649], akin to A, No. 2, denotes rebuke; in 2 Pet. 2:16, it is used with *echō*, to have, and translated "he was rebuked," lit., 'he had rebuke.' ¶ In the Sept., Job 21:4, "reproof"; 23:2, "pleading." ¶

NT: B.249a; CB.1244a; K.221.
OT: sîaḥ: S.7879; HR.449a.1; H.2255a; BD.967a.
GEN. REF.: IS.4:52; NB.—; Z.—.

For **RECEIPT** see **CUSTOM (Toll)**, No. 2

RECEIVE, RECEIVING

A. Verbs.

1. *lambanō* [λαμβάνω, 2983], denotes either to take, or to receive, (I) literally, (*a*) without an object, in contrast to asking, e.g., Matt. 7:8; Mark 11:24, R.V., "have received" (the original has no object); (*b*) in contrast to giving, e.g., Matt. 10:8; Acts 20:35; (*c*) with objects, whether things, e.g., Mark 10:30; Luke 18:30, in the best mss. (some have No. 4); John 13:30; Acts 9:19, R.V., "took" (A.V., "received"); 1 Cor. 9:25, R.V., "receive" (A.V., "obtain"); or persons, e.g., John 6:21; 13:20; 16:14, R.V., "take"; 2 John 10; in Mark 14:65, R.V., "received (Him with blows of their hands)"; this has been styled a vulgarism; (II) metaphorically, of the word of God, Matt. 13:20; Mark 4:16; the sayings of Christ, John 12:48; the witness of Christ, John 3:11; a hundredfold in this life, and eternal life in the world to come, Mark 10:30; mercy, Heb. 4:16, R.V., "may receive" (A.V., "may obtain"); a person (*prosōpon*, see FACE), Luke 20:21, "acceptest," and Gal. 2:6, "accepteth," an expression used in the O.T. either in the sense of being gracious or kind to a person, e.g., Gen. 19:21; 32:20, or (negatively) in the sense of being impartial, e.g., Lev. 19:15; Deut. 10:17; this latter is the meaning in the two N.T. passages just mentioned. See ACCEPT, A, No. 4, TAKE, etc.

Lambanō and *prosōpon* are combined in the nouns *prosōpolēmpsia*, respect of persons, and *prosōpolēmptēs*, respecter of persons, and in the verb *prosōpolēmptō*, to have respect of persons: see PERSON.

NT: B.464a; CB.1256c; K.495.
OT: lāqaḥ: S.3947; HR.847a.11a; H.1124; BD.542c.
nāśā': S.5375; HR.847a.17a; H.1421; BD.669d.
GEN. REF.: —.

2. *paralambanō* [παραλαμβάνω, 3880], to receive from another (*para*, from beside), or to take, signifies to receive, e.g., in Mark 7:4; John 1:11; 14:3; 1 Cor. 11:23; 15:1, 3; Gal. 1:9, 12; Phil. 4:9; Col. 2:6; 4:17; 1 Thess. 2:13 (1st part); 4:1; 2 Thess. 3:6; Heb. 12:28. See TAKE.

NT: B.619b; CB.1262a; K.495.
OT: lāqaḥ: S.3947; HR.1061b.2; H.1124; BD.542c.
yārash: S.3423; HR.1061b.1a; H.2633; BD.439a.
GEN. REF.: —.

3. *analambanō* [ἀναλαμβάνω, 353], to take up (*ana*), to take to oneself, receive, is rendered to receive in Mark 16:19; Acts 1:2, 11, 22, R.V., "He was received up" (A.V., "taken"); 10:16; 1 Tim. 3:16. See TAKE.

NT: B.56d; CB.1235a; K.495.
OT: nāśā': S.5375; HR.78c.5; H.1421; BD.669d.
lāqaḥ: S.3947; HR.78c.3a; H.1124; BD.542c.
GEN. REF.: —.

4. *apolambanō* [ἀπολαμβάνω, 618], signifies to receive from another, (*a*) to receive as one's due (for Luke 18:30, see No. 1); Luke 23:41; Rom. 1:27; Col. 3:24; 2 John 8; (*b*) without the indication of what is due, Luke 16:25; Gal. 4:5 (in some mss. 3 John 8, for No. 7); (*c*) to receive back, Luke 6:34 (twice); 15:27. For its other meaning, to take apart, Mark 7:33, see TAKE. ¶

NT: B.94b; CB.1237a; K.—.
OT: lāqaḥ: S.3947; HR.136a.1; H.1124; BD.542c.
GEN. REF.: —.

5. *proslambanō* [προσλαμβάνω, 4355], denotes to take to oneself (*pros*, to) or to receive, always in the Middle Voice, signifying a special interest on the part of the receiver, suggesting a welcome, Acts 28:2; Rom. 14:1, 3; 15:7; Philm. 12 (in some mss.; the best omit it); ver. 17. See TAKE.

NT: B.717b; CB.1267b; K.495.
OT: lāqaḥ: S.3947; HR.1218b.2; H.1124; BD.542c.
GEN. REF.: —.

6. *metalambanō* [μεταλαμβάνω, 3335], to have or get a share of, partake of (*meta*, with), is rendered "receiveth" in Heb. 6:7. See EAT, HAVE, PARTAKE, TAKE. In the Sept., Esth. 5:1. ¶

NT: B.511b; CB.1258b; K.495.
OT: —.
GEN. REF.: —.

7. *hupolambanō* [ὑπολαμβάνω, 5274], to take or bear up (*hupo*, under), to receive, is rendered "received" in Acts 1:9, of the cloud

at the Ascension; in 3 John 8, R.V., "welcome" (A.V., "receive"). See ANSWER, B, No. 3, SUPPOSE, WELCOME.

NT: B.845b; CB.1252b; K.495.
OT: –.
GEN. REF.: –.

8. *dechomai* [δέχομαι, 1209], to receive by deliberate and ready reception of what is offered, is used of (*a*) taking with the hand, taking hold, taking hold of or up, e.g., Luke 2:28, R.V., "he received (Him)," A.V., "took he (Him) up"; 16:6, 7; 22:17; Eph. 6:17; (*b*) receiving, said of a place receiving a person, of Christ into the Heavens, Acts 3:21; or of persons in giving access to someone as a visitor, e.g., John 4:45; 2 Cor. 7:15; Gal. 4:14; Col. 4:10; by way of giving hospitality, etc., e.g., Matt. 10:14, 40 (four times), 41 (twice); 18:5; Mark 6:11; 9:37; Luke 9:5, 48, 53; 10:8, 10; 16:4; ver. 9, of reception, "into the eternal tabernacles," said of followers of Christ who have used "the mammon of unrighteousness" to render assistance to ("make . . . friends of") others; of Rahab's reception of the spies, Heb. 11:31; of the reception, by the Lord, of the spirit of a departing believer, Acts 7:59; of receiving a gift, 2 Cor. 8:4 (in some mss.; R.V. follows those which omit it); of the favourable reception of testimony and teaching, etc., Luke 8:13; Acts 8:14; 11:1; 17:11; 1 Cor. 2:14; 2 Cor. 8:17; 1 Thess. 1:6; 2:13, where *paralambanō* (No. 2) is used in the 1st part, "ye received," *dechomai* in the 2nd part, "ye accepted," R.V. (A.V., "received"), the former refers to the ear, the latter, adding the idea of appropriation, to the heart; Jas. 1:21; in 2 Thess. 2:10, "the love of the truth," i.e., love for the truth; cp. Matt. 11:14, "if ye are willing to receive it," an elliptical construction frequent in Greek writings; of receiving, by way of bearing with, enduring, 2 Cor. 11:16; of receiving by way of getting, Acts 22:5; 28:21; of becoming partaker of benefits, Mark 10:15; Luke 18:17; Acts 7:38; 2 Cor. 6:1; 11:4 (last clause "did accept": cp. *lambanō* in previous clauses); Phil. 4:18. ¶

NT: B.177b; CB.1240b; K.146.
OT: lāqaḥ: S.3947; HR.294c.4; H.1124; BD.542c.
rāṣāh: S.7521; HR.294c.7; H.2207; BD.953a.
GEN. REF.: –.

Note: There is a certain distinction between *lambanō* and *dechomai* (more pronounced in the earlier, classical use), in that in many instances *lambanō* suggests a self-prompted taking, whereas *dechomai* more frequently indicates "a welcoming or an appropriating reception" (Grimm-Thayer).

9. *anadechomai* [ἀναδέχομαι, 324], to receive gladly, is used in Acts 28:7, of the reception by Publius of the shipwrecked company in Melita; in Heb. 11:17, of Abraham's reception of God's promises, R.V., "gladly (*ana*, up, regarded as intensive) received." Moulton and Milligan point out the frequency of this verb in the papyri in the legal sense of taking the responsibility of something, becoming security for, undertaking, and say "The predominance of this meaning suggests its application in Heb. 11:17. The statement that Abraham had 'undertaken,' 'assumed the responsibility of,' the promises, would not perhaps be alien to the thought." The responsibility would surely be that of his faith in receiving the promises. In Classical Greek it had the meaning of receiving, and it is a little difficult to attach any other sense to the circumstances, save perhaps that Abraham's faith undertook to exercise the assurance of the fulfilment of the promises. ¶

NT: B.53c; CB.–; K.–.
OT: –.
GEN. REF.: –.

10. *apodechomai* [ἀποδέχομαι, 588], to welcome, to accept gladly (*apo*, from), to receive without reserve, is used (*a*) literally, Luke 8:40, R.V., "welcomed"; 9:11 (in the best texts, some have No. 8); Acts 18:27; 21:17; 28:30; (*b*) metaphorically, Acts 2:41; 24:3, "we accept," in the sense of acknowledging, the term being used in a tone of respect. See ACCEPT, A No. 2. ¶

NT: B.90a; CB.1236c; K.146.
OT: –.
GEN. REF.: –.

11. *eisdechomai* [εἰσδέχομαι, 1523], to receive into (*eis*), is used only in 2 Cor. 6:17, where the verb does not signify to accept, but to admit (as antithetic to "come ye out," and combining Isa. 52:11 with Zeph. 3:20). ¶

NT: B.232c; CB.1243b; K.146.
OT: qābaṣ: S.6908; HR.410a.1a,b; H.1983; BD.867c.
GEN. REF.: –.

12. *epidechomai* [ἐπιδέχομαι, 1926], lit., to accept besides (*epi*, upon), to accept (found in the papyri, of accepting the terms of a lease), is used in the sense of accepting in 3 John 9; in ver. 10, in the sense of receiving with hospitality, in each verse said negatively concerning Diotrephes. ¶

NT: B.292a; CB.–; K.–.
OT: –.
GEN. REF.: –.

13. *paradechomai* [παραδέχομαι, 3858], to receive or admit with approval (*para*, beside), is used (*a*) of persons, Acts 15:4 (in some texts, No. 10); Heb. 12:6; (*b*) of things, Mark 4:20, A.V., "receive" (R.V., "accept"); Acts 16:21;

22:18; 1 Tim. 5:9. ¶ In the Sept., Ex. 23:1; Prov. 3:12. ¶

NT: B.614b; CB.–; K.–.
OT: nāsā': S.5375; HR.1058a.1; H.1421; BD.669d.
rāṣāh: S.7521; HR.1058a.2; H.2207; BD.953a.
GEN. REF.: –.

14. *prosdechomai* [προσδέχομαι, 4327], to receive to oneself, to receive favourably, also to look for, wait for, is used of receiving in Luke 15:2; Rom. 16:2; Phil. 2:29. See ACCEPT, A, No. 3, ALLOW, LOOK (for), TAKE, WAIT.

NT: B.712a; CB.1267a; K.146.
OT: rāṣāh: S.7521; HR.1212c.8; H.2207; BD.953a.
GEN. REF.: –.

15. *hupodechomai* [ὑποδέχομαι, 5264], denotes to receive under one's roof (*hupo*, under), receive as a guest, entertain hospitably, Luke 10:38; 19:6; Acts 17:7; Jas. 2:25. ¶

NT: B.844b; CB.–; K.–.
OT: –.
GEN. REF.: –.

16. *komizō* [κομίζω, 2865], denotes to bear, carry, e.g., Luke 7:37; in the Middle Voice, to bear for oneself, hence (*a*) to receive, Heb. 10:36; 11:13 (in the best texts; some have *lambanō*, No. 1), 39; 1 Pet. 1:9; 5:4; in some texts in 2 Pet. 2:13 (in the best mss. *adikeomai*, "suffering wrong," R.V.); (*b*) to receive back, recover, Matt. 25:27; Heb. 11:19; metaphorically, of requital, 2 Cor. 5:10; Col. 3:25, of 'receiving back again' by the believer at the Judgment-Seat of Christ hereafter, for wrong done in this life; Eph. 6:8, of receiving, on the same occasion, "whatsoever good thing each one doeth," R.V.; see BRING, No. 20. ¶

NT: B.442d; CB.1255c; K.–.
OT: nāsā': S.5375; HR.777b.3; H.1421; BD.669d.
GEN. REF.: –.

17. *apechō* [ἀπέχω, 568], denotes (*a*) transitively, to have in full, to have received; so the R.V. in Matt. 6:2, 5, 16 (for A.V., "they have"); Luke 6:24, A.V., and R.V.; in all these instances the present tense (to which the A.V. incorrectly adheres in the Matt. 6 verses) has a perfective force, consequent upon the combination with the prefix *apo* (from), not that it stands for the perfect tense, but that it views the action in its accomplished result; so in Phil. 4:18, where the A.V. and R.V. translate it "I have"; in Philm. 15, "(that) thou shouldest have (him for ever)," A.V., "shouldest receive"; see HAVE, No. 2, and the reference to illustrations from the papyri of the use of the Verb in receipts; (*b*) intransitively, to be away, distant, used with *porrō*, far, Matt. 15:8; Mark 7:6; with *makran*, far off, afar, Luke 7:6; 15:20; without an accompanying adverb, Luke 24:13, "which was from." See ABSTAIN, ENOUGH, HAVE.

NT: B.84d; CB.1236b; K.286.
OT: rāḥaq: S.7368; HR.122a.9,10b; H.2151; BD.934d.
rāḥôq: S.7350; HR.122a.10a; H.2151b; BD.935b.
GEN. REF.: –.

18. *chōreō* [χωρέω, 5562], to give space, make room for (*chōra*, a place), is used metaphorically, of receiving with the mind, Matt. 19:11, 12; into the heart, 2 Cor. 7:2, R.V., "open your hearts," marg., "make room" (A.V., "receive"). See COME, No. 24, CONTAIN, No. 1, COURSE, B.

NT: B.889c; CB.1240a; K.–.
OT: kûl: S.3557; HR.1482; H.962; BD.465a.
GEN. REF.: –.

19. *lanchanō* [λαγχάνω, 2975], to obtain by lot, is translated "received" in Acts 1:17; R.V. (A.V., "had obtained"). See LOT.

NT: B.462a; CB.1256c; K.495.
OT: lākad: S.3920; HR.840b.1; H.1115; BD.539d.
GEN. REF.: –.

Notes: (1) In Mark 2:2, A.V., *chōreō* is translated "there was (no) room to receive" [R.V., "there was (no longer) room (for)."

(2) In Rev. 13:16, A.V., *didōmi* is translated "to receive" (marg., "to give them"), R.V., "(that) there be given (them)."

(3) In 2 Cor. 7:9, A.V., *zēmioō*, to suffer loss (R.V.), is translated "ye might receive damage."

(4) In Luke 7:22, R.V., *anablepō*, to recover sight, is translated "receive their sight" (A.V., "see").

(5) For "received (R.V., hath taken) tithes," Heb. 7:6, see TITHE.

(6) For *eleeō*, in the Passive Voice, 2 Cor. 4:1, A.V., "having received mercy" (R.V., "obtained"), see MERCY.

(7) For *patroparadotos*, in 1 Pet. 1:18, A.V., "*received* by tradition from your fathers," see HANDED DOWN.

(8) In the A.V. of Matt. 13:19, 20, 22, 23, *speirō*, to sow seed, is translated "received seed"; see SOW.

B. Nouns.

1. *lēpsis* or *lēmpsis* [λῆμψις, 3028], a receiving (akin to *lambanō*, A, No. 1), is used in Phil. 4:15. ¶ In the Sept., Prov. 15:27, 29. ¶

NT: B.473a; CB.–; K.–.
OT: mattānāh: S.4979; HR.876a.1; H.1443c; BD.682b.
GEN. REF.: –.

2. *analē(m)psis* [ἀνάλημψις, 354], a taking up (*ana*, up, and No. 1), is used in Luke 9:51 with reference to Christ's Ascension; "that He should be received up" is, lit., 'of the receiving up (of Him).' ¶

NT: B.57a; CB.1235a; K.495.
OT: –.
GEN. REF.: –.

3. *metalē(m)psis* [μετάλημψις, 3336], a participation, taking, receiving, is used in 1 Tim. 4:3, in connection with food, "to be received," lit., 'with a view to (*eis*) reception.' ¶

NT: B.511c; CB.1258b; K.495.
OT: –.
GEN. REF.: –.

4. *proslē(m)psis* [πρόσλημψις, 4356], *pros,* to, and No. 1, is used in Rom. 11:15, of the restoration of Israel. ¶
NT: B.717c; CB.1267b; K.495.
OT: –.
GEN. REF.: –.

RECKON, RECKONING

1. *logizomai* [λογίζομαι, 3049], is properly used (*a*) of numerical calculation, e.g., Luke 22:37; (*b*) metaphorically, by a reckoning of characteristics or reasons, to take into account, Rom. 2:26, "shall . . . be reckoned," R.V. (A.V., "counted"), of reckoning uncircumcision for circumcision by God's estimate in contrast to that of the Jew regarding his own condition (ver. 3); in 4:3, 5, 6, 9, 11, 22, 23, 24, of reckoning faith for righteousness, or reckoning righteousness to persons, in all of which the R.V. uses the verb to reckon instead of the A.V. to count or to impute; in ver. 4 the subject is treated by way of contrast between grace and debt, which latter involves the reckoning of a reward for works; what is owed as a debt cannot be reckoned as a favour, but the faith of Abraham and his spiritual children sets them outside the category of those who seek to be justified by self-effort, and, *vice versa,* the latter are excluded from the grace of righteousness bestowed on the sole condition of faith; so in Gal. 3:6 (R.V., "was reckoned," A.V., "was accounted"); since Abraham, like all the natural descendants of Adam, was a sinner, he was destitute of righteousness in the sight of God; if, then, his relationship with God was to be rectified (i.e., if he was to be justified before God), the rectification could not be brought about by works of merit on his part; in Jas. 2:23, R.V., "reckoned," the subject is viewed from a different standpoint (see under JUSTIFICATION, B, last four paragraphs); for other instances of reckoning in this respect see Rom. 9:8, R.V., "are reckoned" (A.V., "are counted"); 2 Cor. 5:19, R.V., "(not) reckoning (trespasses)," A.V., "imputing"; (*c*) to consider, calculate, translated to reckon in Rom. 6:11; 8:36; 2 Cor. 10:11, R.V., "let (such a one) reckon (this)"; (*d*) to suppose, judge, deem, translated to reckon in Rom. 2:3, "reckonest thou (this)," R.V. (A.V., "thinkest"); 3:28 (A.V., "we conclude"); 8:18; 2 Cor. 11:5 (A.V., "I suppose"); see ACCOUNT, A, No. 4, CONSIDER, No. 6, COUNT, No. 3, SUPPOSE; (*e*) to purpose, decide, 2 Cor. 10:2, R.V., "count" (A.V., "think"); see COUNT, No. 3.
NT: B.475d; CB.1257a; K.536.
OT: ḥāshab: S.2803; HR.880a.2a-c; H.767; BD.362d.
GEN. REF.: IS.4:54; NB.–; Z.–.

2. *legō* [λέγω, 3004], to say, speak, also has the meaning to gather, reckon, account, used in this sense in Heb. 7:11, R.V., "be reckoned" (A.V., "be called"). See ASK, A, No. 6.
NT: B.468a; CB.1256c; K.505.
OT: 'āmar: S.559; HR.863c.1a; H.118; BD.55c.
GEN. REF.: IS.4:54; NB.–; Z.–.

3. *sunairō* [συναιρω, 4868], to take up together (*sun,* with, *airō,* to take), is used with the noun *logos,* an account, signifying to settle accounts, Matt. 18:23, R.V., "make a reckoning" (A.V., "take account"); ver. 24, A.V. and R.V., "to reckon" (*logos* being understood); 25:19, R.V., "maketh a reckoning" (A.V., "reckoneth"). This phrase occurs not infrequently in the papyri in the sense of settling accounts (see DEISSMANN, *Light from the Ancient East,* 118). ¶ In the Sept., the verb occurs in its literal sense in Ex. 23:5, "thou shalt help to raise" (lit., 'raise with'). ¶
NT: B.783c; CB.–; K.–.
OT: –.
GEN. REF.: –.

RECLINE

anakeimai [ἀνάκειμαι, 345], lit., and in classical usage, to be laid up, laid, denotes, in the N.T., to recline at table; it is translated "reclining" in John 13:23, R.V. (A.V., "leaning"); cp. *anapiptō* in ver. 25, R.V., "leaning back." See also ver. 12, marg. See LEAN, SIT, TABLE (at the).
NT: B.55d; CB.1235a; K.425.
OT: –.
GEN. REF.: IS.4:54; NB.–; Z.–.

For **RECOMMEND**, Acts 14:26; 15:40, A.V., see **COMMEND**, No. 2

RECOMPENCE, RECOMPENSE

A. Nouns.

1. *antapodoma* [ἀνταπόδομα, 468], akin to *antapodidōmi,* to recompense (see below), lit., a giving back in return (*anti,* in return, *apo,* back, *didōmi,* to give), a requital, recompence, is used (*a*) in a favourable sense, Luke 14:12; (*b*) in an unfavourable sense, Rom. 11:9, indicating that the present condition of the Jewish nation is the retributive effect of their transgressions, on account of which that which was designed as a blessing ("their table") has become a means of judgment. ¶
NT: B.73a; CB.1236a; K.166.
OT: gᵉmûl: S.1576; HR.109b.1; H.360a; BD.168b.
GEN. REF.: IS.4:54; NB.–; Z.–.

2. *antapodosis* [ἀνταπόδοσις, 469], derived, like No. 1, from *antapodidōmi,* is rendered "recompense" in Col. 3:24, R.V. (A.V., "reward"). ¶
NT: B.73a; CB.1236a; K.166.
OT: gᵉmûl: S.1576; HR.109b.1a; H.360a; BD.168b.
shillûm: S.7966; HR.109b.4a; H.2401h; BD.1024b.
GEN. REF.: IS.4:54; NB.–; Z.–.

3. *antimisthia* [ἀντιμισθία, 489], a reward, requital (*anti*, in return, *misthos*, wages, hire), is used (*a*) in a good sense, 2 Cor. 6:13; (*b*) in a bad sense, Rom. 1:27. ¶

NT: B.75b; CB.1236a; K.599.
OT: –.
GEN. REF.: –.

4. *misthapodosia* [μισθαποδοσία, 3405], a payment of wages (from *misthos*, see No. 3, and *apodidōmi*, B, No. 2), a recompence, is used (*a*) of reward, Heb. 10:35; 11:26; (*b*) of punishment, Heb. 2:2. ¶ Cp. *misthapodotēs*, a rewarder, Heb. 11:6. ¶

NT: B.523a; CB.1259a; K.599.
OT: –.
GEN. REF.: –.

B. Verbs.

1. *antapodidōmi* [ἀνταποδίδωμι, 467], akin to A, No. 1 and No. 2, to give back as an equivalent, to requite, recompense (the *anti* expressing the idea of a complete return), is translated "render" in 1 Thess. 3:9, here only in the N.T. of thanksgiving to God (cp. the Sept. of Ps. 116:12); elsewhere it is used of recompense, "whether between men (but in that case only of good, not of evil, see No. 2 in 1 Thess. 5:15), Luke 14:14 *a*, cp. the corresponding noun in v. 12; or between God and evil-doers, Rom. 12:19, R.V. (A.V., "repay"); Heb. 10:30, cp. the noun in Rom. 11:9; or between God and those who do well, Luke 14:14 *b*; Rom. 11:35, cp. the noun in Col. 3:24; in 2 Thess. 1:6 both reward and retribution are in view."* ¶

NT: B.73a; CB.1236a; K.166.
OT: shālam: S.7999; HR.108c.5a-c; H.2401c; BD.1023d.
gāmal: S.1580; HR.108c.2a; H.360; BD.168a.
shûb: S.7725; HR.108c.4; H.2340; BD.996d.
GEN. REF.: IS.4:54; NB.–; Z.–.

2. *apodidōmi* [ἀποδίδωμι, 591], to give up or back, restore, return, is translated "shall recompense" in the R.V. of Matt. 6:4, 6, 18 (A.V., "shall reward"); in Rom. 12:17, A.V., "recompense" (R.V., "render"); in 1 Thess. 5:15, "render." See DELIVER, GIVE, PAY, PERFORM, RENDER, REPAY, REQUITE, RESTORE, REWARD, SELL, YIELD.

NT: B.90b; CB.1236c; K.166.
OT: mākar: S.4376; HR.126b.3; H.1194; BD.569a.
shûb: S.7725; HR.126b.8; H.360; BD.168a.
shālēm: S.7999; HR.126b.9; H.2401c; BD.1023d.
GEN. REF.: IS.4:54; NB.–; Z.–.

RECONCILE, RECONCILIATION

A. Verbs.

1. *katallassō* [καταλλάσσω, 2644], properly denotes to change, exchange (especially of money); hence, of persons, to change from enmity to friendship, to reconcile. With regard to the relationship between God and man, the use of this and connected words shows that primarily reconciliation is what God accomplishes, exercising His grace towards sinful man on the ground of the death of Christ in propitiatory sacrifice under the judgment due to sin, 2 Cor. 5:19, where both the verb and the noun are used (cp. No. 2, in Col. 1:21). By reason of this men in their sinful condition and alienation from God are invited to be reconciled to Him; that is to say, to change their attitude, and accept the provision God has made, whereby their sins can be remitted and they themselves be justified in His sight in Christ.

Rom. 5:10 expresses this in another way: "For if, while we were enemies, we were reconciled to God through the death of His Son . . ."; that we were "enemies" not only expresses man's hostile attitude to God but signifies that until this change of attitude takes place men are under condemnation, exposed to God's wrath. The death of His Son is the means of the removal of this, and thus we "receive the reconciliation," ver. 11, R.V. This stresses the attitude of God's favour toward us. The A.V. rendering "atonement" is incorrect. Atonement is the offering itself of Christ under Divine judgment upon sin. We do not receive atonement. What we do receive is the result, namely, "reconciliation."

The removal of God's wrath does not contravene His immutability. He always acts according to His unchanging righteousness and loving-kindness, and it is because He changes not that His relative attitude does change towards those who change. All His acts show that He is Light and Love. Anger, where there is no personal element, is a sign of moral health if, and if only, it is accompanied by grief. There can be truest love along with righteous indignation, Mark 3:5, but love and enmity cannot exist together. It is important to distinguish "wrath" and "hostility." The change in God's relative attitude toward those who receive the reconciliation only proves His real unchangeableness. Not once is God said to be reconciled. The enmity is alone on our part. It was we who needed to be reconciled to God, not God to us, and it is propitiation, which His righteousness and mercy have provided, that makes the reconciliation possible to those who receive it.

When the writers of the N.T. speak upon the subject of the wrath of God, "the hostility is represented not as on the part of God, but of man. And this is the reason why the Apostle

* From Notes on Thessalonians by Hogg and Vine, p. 226.

never uses *diallassō* [a word used only in Matt. 5:24, in the N.T.] in this connection, but always *katallassō*, because the former word denotes mutual concession after mutual hostility [frequently exemplified in the Sept.], an idea absent from *katallassō*" (Lightfoot, *Notes on the Epistles of Paul*, p. 288).

The subject finds its great unfolding in 2 Cor. 5:18-20, which states that God "reconciled us (believers) to Himself through Christ," and that "the ministry of reconciliation" consists in this, "that God was in Christ reconciling the world unto Himself." The insertion of a comma in the A.V. after the word "Christ" is misleading; the doctrine stated here is not that God was in Christ (the unity of the Godhead is not here in view), but that what God has done in the matter of reconciliation He has done in Christ, and this is based upon the fact that "Him who knew no sin He made to be sin on our behalf; that we might become the righteousness of God in Him." On this ground the command to men is "be ye reconciled to God."

The verb is used elsewhere in 1 Cor. 7:11, of a woman returning to her husband. ¶

NT: B.414a; CB.1254a; K.40.
OT: —.
GEN. REF.: IS.4:55; NB.1077; Z.5:44.

2. *apokatallassō* [ἀποκαταλλάσσω, 604], to reconcile completely (*apo*, from, and No. 1), a stronger form of No. 1, to change from one condition to another, so as to remove all enmity and leave no impediment to unity and peace, is used in Eph. 2:16, of the reconciliation of believing Jew and Gentile "in one body unto God through the Cross"; in Col. 1:21 not the union of Jew and Gentile is in view, but the change wrought in the individual believer from alienation and enmity, on account of evil works, to reconciliation with God; in ver. 20 the word is used of the Divine purpose to reconcile through Christ "all things unto Himself . . . whether things upon the earth, or things in the heavens," the basis of the change being the peace effected "through the blood of His Cross." It is the Divine purpose, on the ground of the work of Christ accomplished on the Cross, to bring the whole universe, except rebellious angels and unbelieving man, into full accord with the mind of God, Eph. 1:10. Things "under the earth," Phil. 2:10, are subdued, not reconciled. ¶

NT: B.92c; CB.1237a; K.40.
OT: —.
GEN. REF.: IS.4:55; NB.1077; Z.5:44.

3. *diallassō* [διαλλάσσω, 1259], to effect an alteration, to exchange, and hence, to reconcile, in cases of mutual hostility yielding to mutual concession, and thus differing from No. 1 (under which see Lightfoot's remarks), is used in the Passive Voice in Matt. 5:24, which illustrates the point. There is no such idea as "making it up" where God and man are concerned. ¶

NT: B.186a; CB.1241a; K.40.
OT: sûr: S.5493; HR.304c.1; H.1480; BD.693b.
rāṣāh: S.7521; HR.304c.3; H.2207; BD.953a.
GEN. REF.: IS.4:55; NB.1077; Z.5:44.

B. Noun.

katallagē [καταλλαγή, 2643], akin to A, No. 1, primarily an exchange, denotes reconciliation, a change on the part of one party, induced by an action on the part of another; in the N.T., the reconciliation of men to God by His grace and love in Christ. The word is used in Rom. 5:11 and 11:15. The occasioning cause of the world-wide proclamation of reconciliation through the Gospel, was the casting away (partially and temporarily) of Israel. A new relationship Godward is offered to the Gentiles in the Gospel. The word also occurs in 2 Cor. 5:18, 19, where "the ministry of reconciliation" and "the word of reconciliation" are not the ministry of teaching the doctrine of expiation, but that of beseeching men to be reconciled to God on the ground of what God has wrought in Christ. See No. 1, above. ¶

NT: B.414a; CB.1254a; K.40.
OT: —.
GEN. REF.: IS.4:55; NB.1077; Z.5:44.

Note: In the O.T. in some passages the A.V. incorrectly has "reconciliation," the R.V. rightly changes the translation to "atonement," e.g., Lev. 8:15; Ezek. 45:20, R.V., "make atonement for" (A.V., "reconcile").

For **RECONCILIATION (MAKE)**, Heb. 2:17, A.V., see **PROPITIATION**

For **RECORD** (A.V.) see **TESTIFY**, No. 3, **TESTIMONY**, No. 2

RECOVER

1. *sōzō* [σώζω, 4982], to save, is sometimes used of healing or restoration to health, the latter in John 11:12, R.V., "he will recover," marg., "be saved" (A.V., "he shall do well"). See HEAL, PRESERVE, SAVE, WHOLE.

NT: B.798a; CB.1269c; K.1132.
OT: yāsha': S.3467; HR.1328b.5b; H.929; BD.446b.
mālaṭ: S.4422; HR.1328b.6b; H.1198; BD.572b.
nāṣal: S.5337; HR.1328b.7; H.1404; BD.664c.
GEN. REF.: —.

2. *ananēphō* [ἀνανήφω, 366], to return to soberness, as from a state of delirium or drunkenness (*ana*, back, or again, *nēphō*, to be

sober, to be wary), is used in 2 Tim. 2:26, "may recover themselves" (R.V. marg., "return to soberness," A.V. marg., "awake"), said of those who, opposing the truth through accepting perversions of it, fall into the snare of the Devil, becoming intoxicated with error; for these recovery is possible only by "repentance unto the knowledge of the truth." For a translation of the verse see CAPTIVE, B, No. 3. ¶

NT: B.58b; CB.1235b; K.–.
OT: –.
GEN. REF.: –.

Notes: (1) For "recovering of sight," Luke 4:18, see SIGHT.

(2) In Mark 16:18, the phrase *echō kalōs*, lit., 'to have well,' i.e., "to be well," is rendered "they shall recover."

RED

A. Adjectives.

1. *purrhos* [πυρρός, 4450], denotes fire-coloured (*pur*, fire), hence, fiery red, Rev. 6:4; 12:3, in the latter passage said of the Dragon, indicative of the cruelty of the Devil. ¶

NT: B.731c; CB.1268a; K.975.
OT: 'ādōm: S.122; HR.1246a.1; H.26b; BD.10b.
GEN. REF.: IS.1:732; NB.–; Z.5:46.

2. *eruthros* [ἐρυθρός, 2063], denotes red (the ordinary colour); the root *rudh—* is seen, e.g., in the Latin *rufus*, Eng., ruby, ruddy, rust, etc. It is applied to the Red Sea, Acts 7:36; Heb. 11:29. ¶ The origin of the name is uncertain; it has been regarded as due, e.g., to the colour of the corals which cover the Red Sea bed or line its shores, or to the tinge of the mountains which border it, or to the light of the sky upon its waters.

NT: B.310b; CB.–; K.–.
OT: sûph: S.5488; HR.548b.2; H.1479; BD.693a.
GEN. REF.: IS.4:58; NB.1077; Z.5:46.

B. Verb.

purrhazō [πυρράζω, 4449], to be fiery red (akin to A, No. 1), is used of the sky, Matt. 16:2, 3. ¶ In the Sept., *purrhizō*, Lev. 13:19, 42, 43, 49; 14:37. ¶

NT: B.731b; CB.1268a; K.–.
OT: '^{a}damdām: S.125; HR.1246a.1; H.26g; BD.10c.
GEN. REF.: IS.–; NB.–; Z.5:46.

REDEEM, REDEMPTION

A. Verbs.

1. *exagorazō* [ἐξαγοράζω, 1805], a strengthened form of *agorazō*, to buy (see BUY, No. 1), denotes to buy out (*ex* for *ek*), especially of purchasing a slave with a view to his freedom. It is used metaphorically (*a*) in Gal. 3:13 and 4:5, of the deliverance by Christ of Christian Jews from the Law and its curse; what is said of *lutron* (RANSOM, No. 1) is true of this verb and of *agorazō*, as to the Death of Christ, that Scripture does not say to whom the price was paid; the various suggestions made are purely speculative; (*b*) in the Middle Voice, to buy up for oneself, Eph. 5:16 and Col. 4:5, of "buying up the opportunity" (R.V. marg.; text, "redeeming the time," where "time" is *kairos*, a season, a time in which something is seasonable), i.e., making the most of every opportunity, turning each to the best advantage since none can be recalled if missed. ¶

NT: B.271b; CB.1247b; K.19.
OT: z^{e}ban (Aramaic): S.2084; HR.484a.1; H.2702; BD.1091a.
GEN. REF.: IS.4:62; NB.–; Z.5:49.

Note: In Rev. 5:9; 14:3, 4, A.V., *agorazō*, to purchase (R.V.) is translated "redeemed." See PURCHASE.

2. *lutroō* [λυτρόω, 3084], to release on receipt of ransom (akin to *lutron*, a ransom), is used in the Middle Voice, signifying to release by paying a ransom price, to redeem (*a*) in the natural sense of delivering, Luke 24:21, of setting Israel free from the Roman yoke; (*b*) in a spiritual sense, Tit. 2:14, of the work of Christ in redeeming men "from all iniquity" (*anomia*, lawlessness, the bondage of self-will which rejects the will of God); 1 Pet. 1:18 (Passive Voice), "ye were redeemed," from a vain manner of life, i.e., from bondage to tradition. In both instances the Death of Christ is stated as the means of redemption. ¶

NT: B.482d; CB.1257b; K.543.
OT: gā'al: S.1350; HR.890a.1a; H.300; BD.145b.
pādāh: S.6299; HR.890a.3a; H.1734; BD.804a.
GEN. REF.: IS.4:62; NB.1078; Z.5:49.

Note: While both No. 1 and No. 2 are translated to redeem, *exagorazō* does not signify the actual redemption, but the price paid with a view to it, *lutroō* signifies the actual deliverance, the setting at liberty.

B. Nouns.

1. *lutrōsis* [λύτρωσις, 3085], a redemption (akin to A, No. 2), is used (*a*) in the general sense of deliverance, of the nation of Israel, Luke 1:68, R.V., "wrought redemption"; 2:38; (*b*) of the redemptive work of Christ, Heb. 9:12, bringing deliverance through His death, from the guilt and and power of sin. ¶ In the Sept., Lev. 25:29, 48; Numb. 18:16; Judg. 1:15; Ps. 49:8; 111:9; 130:7; Isa. 63:4. ¶

NT: B.483a; CB.1257b; K.543.
OT: g^{e}'ullāh: S.1353; HR.890c.1a; H.300b; BD.145d.
p^{e}dût: S.6304; HR.890c.2c; H.1734b; BD.804b.
pidyôn: S.6306; HR.890c.2b; H.1734c; BD.804b.
GEN. REF.: IS.4:62; NB.1078; Z.5:49.

2. *apolutrōsis* [ἀπολύτρωσις, 629], a strengthened form of No. 1, lit., a releasing, for (i.e., on payment of) a ransom. It is used of (*a*) "deliverance" from physical torture, Heb.

11:35, see DELIVER, B, No. 1; (*b*) the deliverance of the people of God at the Coming of Christ with His glorified saints, "in a cloud with power and great glory," Luke 21:28, a redemption to be accomplished at the 'outshining of His Parousia,' 2 Thess. 2:8, i.e., at His Second Advent; (*c*) forgiveness and justification, redemption as the result of expiation, deliverance from the guilt of sins, Rom. 3:24, "through the redemption that is in Christ Jesus"; Eph. 1:7, defined as "the forgiveness of our trespasses," R.V.; so Col. 1:14, "the forgiveness of our sins," indicating both the liberation from the guilt and doom of sin and the introduction into a life of liberty, "newness of life" (Rom. 6:4); Heb. 9:15, "for the redemption of the transgressions that were under the first covenant," R.V., here "redemption of" is equivalent to 'redemption from,' the genitive case being used of the object from which the redemption, is effected, not from the consequence of the transgressions, but from the transgressions themselves; (*d*) the deliverance of the believer from the presence and power of sin, and of his body from bondage to corruption, at the Coming (the Parousia in its inception) of the Lord Jesus, Rom. 8:23; 1 Cor. 1:30; Eph. 1:14; 4.30. ¶ See also PROPITIATION.

NT: B.96a; CB.1237a; K.543.
OT: —.
GEN. REF.: IS.4:62; NB.1079; Z.5:49.

For **REBOUND**, 2 Cor. 4:15 (R.V., "abound"), see **ABUNDANCE**, B, No. 1 (*c*)

REED

kalamos [κάλαμος, 2563], denotes (*a*) the reed mentioned in Matt. 11:7; 12:20; Luke 7:24, the same as the Heb., *qāneh* (among the various reeds in the O.T.), e.g., Isa. 42:3, from which Matt. 12:20 is quoted (cp. Job 40:21; Ezek. 29:6, a reed with jointed, hollow stalk); (*b*) a reed-staff, staff, Matt. 27:29, 30, 48; Mark 15:19, 36 (cp. *rhabdos*, a rod; in 2 Kings 18:21, *rhabdos kalaminē*); (*c*) a measuring reed or rod, Rev. 11:1; 21:15, 16; (*d*) a writing reed, a pen, 3 John 13; see PEN. ¶

NT: B.398d; CB.1253b; K.—.
OT: qāneh: S.7070; HR.712b.3; H.2040a; BD.889c.
GEN. REF.: IS.4:63; NB.1079; Z.5:51.

REFINED

puroomai [πυρόομαι, 4448], to burn, is translated "refined," as of metals, in Rev. 1:15 and 3:18, R.V. (A.V., "burned," and "tried"). See BURN, No. 4.

NT: B.731b; CB.1268a; K.—.
OT: sāraph: S.6884; HR.1245c.3; H.1972; BD.864a.
GEN. REF.: IS.4:64; NB.1080; Z.5:52.

For **REFLECTING**, 2 Cor. 3:18, R.V., see **BEHOLD**, No. 12

REFORMATION

diorthōsis [διόρθωσις, 1357], properly, a making straight (*dia*, through, *orthos*, straight; cp. *diorthōma* in Acts 24:2; see CORRECTION, No. 1), denotes a "reformation" or reforming, Heb. 9:10; the word has the meaning either (*a*) of a right arrangement, right ordering, or, more usually, (*b*) of restoration, amendment, bringing right again; what is here indicated is a time when the imperfect, the inadequate, would be superseded by a better order of things, and hence the meaning (*a*) seems to be the right one; it is thus to be distinguished from that of Acts 24:2, mentioned above. ¶ The word is used in the papyri in the other sense of the rectification of things, whether by payments or manner of life.

NT: B.199a; CB.1242a; K.727.
OT: —.
GEN. REF.: IS.4:65; NB.—; Z.—.

REFRAIN

1. *pauō* [παύω, 3973], to stop, is used in the Active Voice, in the sense of making to cease, restraining in 1 Pet. 3:10, of causing the tongue to refrain from evil; elsewhere in the Middle Voice, see CEASE, No. 1.

NT: B.638a; CB.—; K.—.
OT: kālāh: S.3615; HR.1112b.3b; H.982-984; BD.477b.
shābat: S.7673; HR.1112b.13b; H.2323; BD.991d.
GEN. REF.: —.

2. *aphistēmi* [ἀφίστημι, 868], to cause to depart, is used intransitively, in the sense of departing from, refraining from, Acts 5:38. See DEPART, No. 20.

NT: B.126d; CB.1236b; K.88.
OT: sûr: S.5493; HR.184b.27b; H.1480; BD.693b.
GEN. REF.: —.

REFRESH, REFRESHING

A. Verbs.

1. *anapauō* [ἀναπαύω, 373], to give intermission from labour, to give rest, refresh (*ana*, back, *pauō*, to cause to cease), is translated to refresh in 1 Cor. 16:18; 2 Cor. 7:13; Philm. 7, 20. See REST.

NT: B.58d; CB.1235b; K.56.
OT: nûaḥ: S.5117; HR.80b.3a-c; H.1323; BD.628a.
rābaṣ: S.7257; HR.80b.6; H.2109; BD.918b.
shākan, shākēn: S.7931; HR.80b.12; H.2387; BD.1014d.
GEN. REF.: IS.4:65; NB.—; Z.—.

2. *sunanapauomai* [συναναπαύομαι, 4875], to lie down, to rest with (*sun*, with, and No. 1 in the Middle Voice), is used metaphorically of being refreshed in spirit with others, in Rom. 15:32, A.V., "may with (you) be refreshed" (R.V., ". . . find rest"). ¶ In the Sept., Isa. 11:6. ¶

NT: B.784b; CB.–; K.–.
OT: rābaṣ: S.7257; HR.1311a.1; H.2109; BD.918b.
GEN. REF.: IS.4:65; NB.–; Z.–.

3. *anapsuchō* [ἀναψύχω, 404], to make cool, refresh (*ana*, back, *psuchō*, to cool), is used in 2 Tim. 1:16 (cp. B). ¶ In the papyri it is used of taking relaxation.

NT: B.63d; CB.1235b; K.1342.
OT: nāphash: S.5314; HR.86a.3; H.1395; BD.661c.
rāwaḥ: S.7304; HR.86a.4; H.2132; BD.926b.
GEN. REF.: IS.4:65; NB.–; Z.–.

Note: In Acts 27:3, the verb *tunchanō*, to obtain or receive, with the object *epimeleia*, care, is translated "to refresh himself" (R.V., marg., "to receive attention," i.e., to enjoy the kind attention of his friends).

B. Noun.

anapsuxis [ἀνάψυξις, 403], a refreshing (akin to A, No. 3), occurs in Acts 3:19. ¶ In the Sept., Ex. 8:15. ¶ In the papyri it is used of obtaining relief.

NT: B.63c; CB.1235b; K.1342.
OT: rᵉwāḥāh: S.7309; HR.86a.1; H.2132b; BD.926c.
GEN. REF.: IS.4:65; NB.–; Z.–.

For **REFUGE** see **FLEE**, No. 3

REFUSE (Verb)

1. *arneomai* [ἀρνέομαι, 720], to deny, renounce, reject, in late Greek came to signify to refuse to acknowledge, to disown, and is translated to refuse in Acts 7:35; Heb. 11:24. See DENY, No. 1.

NT: B.107d; CB.1237c; K.79.
OT: kāḥash: S.3584; HR.159b.1; H.975; BD.471a.
GEN. REF.: IS.4:67; NB.–; Z.–.

2. *paraiteomai* [παραιτέομαι, 3868], for the various meanings of which see AVOID, No. 3, denotes to refuse in Acts 25:11; 1 Tim. 4:7; 5:11; 2 Tim. 2:23, R.V. (A.V., "avoid"); Tit. 3:10, R.V. (marg., "avoid"; A.V., "reject"); Heb. 12:25 (twice), perhaps in the sense of begging off. See EXCUSE, INTREAT, REJECT.

NT: B.616c; CB.1262a; K.30.
OT: –.
GEN. REF.: IS.4:67; NB.–; Z.–.

3. *dokimazō* [δοκιμάζω, 1381), to prove, to approve, used with a negative in Rom. 1:28, is translated "they refused," R.V. (A.V., "they did not like"); R.V. marg., "did not approve." See APPROVE, No. 1.

NT: B.202c; CB.1242a; K.181.
OT: –.
GEN. REF.: –.

Notes: (1) For *parakouō*, to refuse to hear, R.V. in Matt. 18:17 (twice), see HEAR, A, No. 7.

(2) In 1 Tim. 4:4, A.V., *apoblētos*, "rejected" (R.V.), is translated "refused." See REJECT.

REGARD

1. *blepō* [βλέπω, 991], to behold, look, perceive, see, has the sense of regarding by way of partiality, in Matt. 22:16 and Mark 12:14. See BEHOLD, No. 2.

NT: B.143b; CB.1239a; K.706.
OT: rā'āh: S.7200; HR.221a.10a; H.2095; BD.906b.
pānāh: S.6437; HR.221a.7a; H.1782; BD.815a.
pāneh: S.6440; HR.221a.8; H.1782a; BD.815d.
GEN. REF.: –.

2. *entrepō* [ἐντρέπω, 1788], to turn about (*en*, in, *trepō*, to turn), is metaphorically used of putting to shame, e.g., 1 Cor. 4:14; in the Middle Voice, to reverence, regard, translated "regard" in Luke 18:2, 4. See ASHAMED, REVERENCE, SHAME.

NT: B.269c; CB.–; K.–.
OT: kālam: S.3637; HR.480c.2; H.987; BD.483c.
kāna': S.3665; HR.480c.4; H.1001; BD.488b.
GEN. REF.: –.

3. *phroneō* [φρονέω, 5426], to think, set the mind on, implying moral interest and reflection, is translated to regard in Rom. 14:6 (twice); the second part in the A.V. represents an interpolation and is not part of the original. The Scripture does not speak of not regarding a day. See CARE, B, No. 6, MIND, SAVOUR, THINK, UNDERSTAND.

NT: B.866a; CB.1264c; K.1277.
OT: ḥākam: S.2449; HR.1439a.2; H.647; BD.314b.
bîn: S.995; HR.1439a.2; H.239; BD.106b.
GEN. REF.: –.

4. *epiblepō* [ἐπιβλέπω, 1914], to look upon (*epi*, upon, and No. 1), in the N.T. to look on with favour, is used in Luke 1:48, A.V., "hath regarded" (R.V., "hath looked upon"); in Jas. 2:3, R.V., "ye have regard to" (A.V., "ye have respect to"). See LOOK, No. 6, RESPECT.

NT: B.290b; CB.–; K.–.
OT: pānāh: S.6437; HR.516c.8a; H.1782; BD.815a.
nābaṭ: S.5027; HR.516c.4; H.1282; BD.613c.
rā'āh: S.7200; HR.516c.11; H.2095; BD.906b.
GEN. REF.: –.

5. *oligōreō* [ὀλιγωρέω, 3643], denotes to think little of (*oligos*, little, *ōra*, care), to regard lightly, Heb. 12:5, R.V. (A.V., "despise"). See DESPISE, *Note* (3). ¶ In the Sept., Prov. 3:11. ¶

NT: B.564a; CB.1260c; K.–.
OT: mā'as: S.3988; HR.987a.1; H.1139,1140; BD.549b.
GEN. REF.: –.

6. *prosechō* [προσέχω, 4337], to take or give heed, is translated "they had regard" in Acts 8:11, A.V. (R.V., "they gave heed"). See ATTEND, No. 1.

NT: B.714b; CB.1267a; K.–.
OT: qāshab: S.7181; HR.1215a.16a; H.2084; BD.904a.
shāmar: S.8104; HR.1215a.19; H.2414; BD.1036b.
GEN. REF.: –.

7. *ameleō* [ἀμελέω, 272], not to care, is translated "I regarded . . . not" in Heb. 8:9. See NEGLECT.

NT: B.44d; CB.—; K.—.
OT: mārāh: S.4784; HR.65b.2; H.1242; BD.598a.
GEN. REF.: —.

Notes: (1) In Gal. 6:4, R.V., *eis*, into, is translated "in regard of (himself)," A.V., "in"; so in 2 Cor. 10:16; Eph. 5:32.

(2) In Rom. 6:20, the dative case of *dikaiosunē*, righteousness, signifies, not "from righteousness," A.V., but "in regard of righteousness," R.V., lit., 'free to righteousness'; i.e., righteousness laid no sort of bond upon them, they had no relation to it in any way.

(3) In 2 Cor. 8:4 the accusative case of *charis* and *koinōnia* is, in the best texts, used absolutely, i.e., not as the objects of an expressed verb; hence the R.V., "in regard to" (A.V., "that we would receive," where the verb is the result of a supplementary gloss).

(4) For "not regarding" in Phil. 2:30, A.V. (R.V., "hazarding"), see HAZARD, No. 2.

REGENERATION

1. *palingenesia* [παλιγγενεσία, 3824], new birth (*palin*, again, *genesis*, birth), is used of spiritual regeneration, Tit. 3:5, involving the communication of a new life, the two operating powers to produce which are "the word of truth," Jas. 1:18; 1 Pet. 1:23, and the Holy Spirit, John 3:5,6; the *loutron*, the laver, the washing, is explained in Eph. 5:26, "having cleansed it by the washing (*loutron*) of water with the word."

The new birth and regeneration do not represent successive stages in spiritual experience, they refer to the same event but view it in different aspects. The new birth stresses the communication of spiritual life in contrast to antecedent spiritual death; regeneration stresses the inception of a new state of things in contrast with the old; hence the connection of the use of the word with its application to Israel, in Matt. 19:28. Some regard the *kai* in Tit. 3:5 as epexegetic, 'even'; but, as Scripture marks two distinct yet associated operating powers, there is not sufficient ground for this interpretation. See under EVEN.

In Matt. 19:28 the word is used, in the Lord's discourse, in the wider sense, of the "restoration of all things" (Acts 3:21, R.V.), when, as a result of the Second Advent of Christ, Jehovah 'sets His King upon His holy hill of Zion' (Ps. 2:6), and Israel, now in apostasy, is restored to its destined status, in the recognition and under the benign sovereignty of its Messiah. Thereby will be accomplished the deliverance of the world from the power and deception of Satan and from the despotic and antichristian rulers of the nations. This restitution will not in the coming Millennial age be universally a return to the pristine condition of Edenic innocence previous to the Fall, but it will fulfil the establishment of God's Covenant with Abraham concerning his descendants, a veritable re-birth of the nation, involving the peace and prosperity of the Gentiles. That the worldwide subjection to the authority of Christ will not mean the entire banishment of evil, is clear from Rev. 20:7, 8. Only in the new heavens and earth, "wherein dwelleth righteousness," will sin and evil be entirely absent. ¶

NT: B.606a; CB.1261c; K.117.
OT: —.
GEN. REF.: IS.4:67; NB.1080; Z.5:52.

REGION

1. *chōra* [χώρα, 5561], a space lying between two limits, a country, land, is translated "region" in Matt. 4:16; Luke 3:1; Acts 8:1; 13:49; 16:6; 18:23, R.V. In the last three passages it has the technical sense of a subdivision of a Roman Province, Lat. *regio*; as also No. 2 in Acts 14:6. See COUNTRY, No. 3.

NT: B.889b; CB.1240a; K.—.
OT: 'ereṣ: S.776; HR.1481a.4; H.167; BD.75d.
m^edînāh: S.4082; HR.1481a.5; H.426d; BD.193d.
GEN. REF.: IS.4:71; NB.—; Z.—.

2. *perichōros* [περίχωρος, 4066], a country or region round about (*peri*), is translated "region round about" in Matt. 3:5; 14:35, R.V.; Mark 1:28 (in some mss. Mark 6:55); Luke 3:3, R.V.; 4:14; 4:37, R.V.; 7:17; Acts 14:6 (see No. 1). See COUNTRY, No. 4.

NT: B.653c; CB.—; K.—.
OT: kikkār: S.3603; HR.1128b.2a; H.—; BD.503a.
ḥebel: S.2256; HR.1128b.1; H.592b; BD.286c.
pelek: S.6418; HR.1128b.5; H.1775a; BD.813a.
GEN. REF.: IS.4:71; NB.—; Z.—.

3. *klima* [κλίμα, 2824], an inclination, slope, is translated "regions" in Rom. 15:23, R.V.; 2 Cor. 11:10; Gal. 1:21. See PART, A, No. 3. ¶

NT: B.436b; CB.—; K.—.
OT: —.
GEN. REF.: IS.4:71; NB.—; Z.—.

Note: For "*regions* beyond," 2 Cor. 10:16, A.V., see PART, A, *Note* (9).

REGRET

A. Verb.

metamelomai [μεταμέλομαι, 3338], to regret, to repent one, is translated to regret in 2 Cor. 7:8, R.V. (twice), A.V., "repent." See REPENT.

NT: B.511c; CB.1258c; K.589.
OT: nāḥam: S.5162; HR.916b.3; H.1344; BD.636d.
GEN. REF.: —.

B. Adjective.

ametamelētos [ἀμεταμέλητος, 278], not repented of (*a*, negative, and A), is translated "which bringeth no regret" in 2 Cor. 7:10, R.V., said of repentance (A.V., "not to be repented of"); elsewhere, in Rom. 11:29. See REPENT. ¶

NT: B.45c; CB.1234c; K.589.
OT: –.
GEN. REF.: –.

For **REGULAR**, Acts 19:39, R.V., see **LAW**, C, No. 2

REHEARSE

1. *anangellō* [ἀναγγέλλω, 312], to bring back word (*ana*, back, *angellō*, to announce), is translated to rehearse in Acts 14:27; 15:4, R.V. See ANNOUNCE.

NT: B.51b; CB.1235b; K.10.
OT: nāgad: S.5046; HR.74a.10; H.1289; BD.616c.
GEN. REF.: –.

2. *exēgeomai* [ἐξηγέομαι, 1834], primarily, to lead, show the way, is used metaphorically with the meaning to unfold, declare, narrate, and is translated to rehearse in the R.V. of Luke 24:35; Acts 10:8; 15:12, and 14, R.V. See DECLARE, No. 8.

NT: B.275d; CB.1247c; K.303.
OT: sāphar: S.5608; HR.495b.3; H.1540; BD.707d.
GEN. REF.: –.

Note: In Acts 11:4, the A.V. translates the Middle Voice of *archō*, to begin, "rehearsed . . . from the beginning," R.V., "began, (and)."

REIGN (Verb and Noun)

1. *basileuō* [βασιλεύω, 936], to reign, is used (I) literally, (*a*) of God, Rev. 11:17; 19:6, in each of which the aorist tense (in the latter, translated "reigneth") is "ingressive," stressing the point of entrance; (*b*) of Christ, Luke 1:33; 1 Cor. 15:25; Rev. 11:15; as rejected by the Jews, Luke 19:14, 27; (*c*) of the saints, hereafter, 1 Cor. 4:8 (2nd part), where the Apostle, casting a reflection upon the untimely exercise of authority on the part of the church at Corinth, anticipates the due time for it in the future (see No. 2); Rev. 5:10; 20:4, where the aorist tense is not simply of a "point" character, but "constative," that is, regarding a whole action as having occurred, without distinguishing any steps in its progress (in this instance the aspect is future); ver. 6; 22:5; (*d*) of earthly potentates, Matt. 2:22; 1 Tim. 6:15, where "kings" is, lit., 'them that reign'; (II) metaphorically, (*a*) of believers, Rom. 5:17, where "shall reign in life" indicates the activity of life in fellowship with Christ in His sovereign power, reaching its fulness hereafter; 1 Cor. 4:8 (1st part), of the carnal pride that laid claim to a power not to be exercised until hereafter; (*b*) of Divine grace, Rom. 5:21; (*c*) of sin, Rom. 5:21; 6:12; (*d*) of death, Rom. 5:14, 17. ¶

NT: B.136c; CB.1238c; K.97.
OT: mālak: S.4427; HR.194c.3; H.1199,1200; BD.573d.
GEN. REF.: IS.4:74; NB.–; Z.–.

2. *sumbasileuō* [συμβασιλεύω, 4821], to reign together with (*sun*, with, and No. 1), is used of the future reign of believers together and with Christ in the Kingdom of God in manifestation, 1 Cor. 4:8 (3rd part); of those who endure 2 Tim. 2:12, cp. Rev. 20:6. ¶

NT: B.777c; CB.1270b; K.97,1102.
OT: –.
GEN. REF.: IS.4:74; NB.–; Z.–.

Notes: (1) In Rom. 15:12, A.V., *archō*, to rule (R.V.), is translated "to reign."

(2) In Rev. 17:18, *echō*, to have, with *basileia*, a kingdom, is translated "reigneth," lit., 'hath a kingdom,' suggestive of a distinction between the sovereignty of mystic Babylon and that of ordinary sovereigns.

(3) In Luke 3:1, *hēgemonia*, rule, is rendered "reign." ¶

REINS

nephros [νεφρός, 3510], a kidney (Eng., nephritis, etc.), usually in the plural, is used metaphorically of the will and the affections, Rev. 2:23, "reins" (cp. Ps. 7:9; Jer. 11:20; 17:10; 20:12). The feelings and emotions were regarded as having their seat in the kidneys. ¶

NT: B.537a; CB.1259c; K.630.
OT: kilyāh: S.3629; HR.944a.1; H.983a; BD.480b.
GEN. REF.: IS.3:13; NB.690; Z.3:790.

REJECT

A. Verbs.

1. *apodokimazō* [ἀποδοκιμάζω, 593], to reject as the result of examination and disapproval (*apo*, away from, *dokimazō*, to approve), is used (*a*) of the rejection of Christ by the elders and chief priests of the Jews, Matt. 21:42; Mark 8:31; 12:10; Luke 9:22; 20:17; 1 Pet. 2:4, 7 (A.V., "disallowed"); by the Jewish people, Luke 17:25; (*b*) of the rejection of Esau from inheriting "the blessing," Heb. 12:17. See DISALLOW. Cp. and contrast *exoutheneō*, Acts 4:11. See DESPISE.

NT: B.90d; CB.1236c; K.181.
OT: mā'as: S.3988; HR.127c.1; H.1139,1140; BD.549b.
GEN. REF.: IS.4:74; NB.–; Z.–.

2. *atheteō* [ἀθετέω, 114], properly, to do away with what has been laid down, to make *atheton* (i.e., without place, *a*, negative, *tithēmi*, to place), hence, besides its meanings to set aside, make void, nullify, disannul, signifies to reject; in Mark 6:26, regarding Herod's pledge to

Salome, it almost certainly has the meaning 'to break faith with' (cp. the Sept. of Jer. 12:6, and Lam. 1:2, "dealt treacherously"). Moulton and Milligan illustrate this meaning from the papyri. Field suggests 'disappoint.' In Mark 7:9 "ye reject (the commandment)" means 'ye set aside'; in Luke 7:30, "ye reject" may have the meaning of nullifying or making void the counsel of God; in Luke 10:16 (four times), "rejecteth," R.V. (A.V., "despiseth"); "rejecteth" in John 12:48; "reject" in 1 Cor. 1:19 (A.V., "bring to nothing"); 1 Thess. 4:8, to despise, where the reference is to the charges in ver. 2; in 1 Tim. 5:12, R.V., "have rejected" (A.V., "have cast off"). See DESPISE, *Notes* (1), DISANNUL, No. 1.

NT: B.21a; CB.1238a; K.1176.
OT: bāgad: S.898; HR.29b.1; H.198; BD.93c.
pāsha': S.6586; HR.29b.12; H.1846; BD.833b.
mārad: S.4775; HR.29b.7; H.1240; BD.597c.
GEN. REF.: IS.4:74; NB.—; Z.—.

3. *ekptuō* [ἐκπτύω, 1609], to spit out (*ek*, out, and *ptuō*, to spit), i.e., to abominate, loathe, is used in Gal. 4:14, "rejected" (marg., "spat out"), where the sentence is elliptical: 'although my disease repelled you, you did not refuse to hear my message.' ¶

NT: B.244d; CB.1244a; K.216.
OT: —.
GEN. REF.: —.

4. *paraiteomai* [παραιτέομαι, 3868], besides the meanings to beg from another, Mark 15:6 (in the best texts); to entreat that . . . not, Heb. 12:19; to beg off, ask to be excused, Luke 14:18, 19; 12:25 (see REFUSE, No. 2), is translated to reject in Tit. 3:10, A.V. See EXCUSE, INTREAT, REFUSE.

NT: B.616c; CB.1262a; K.30.
OT: —.
GEN. REF.: —.

B. Adjectives.

1. *adokimos* [ἀδόκιμος, 96], not standing the test (see CAST, C), is translated "rejected" in 1 Cor. 9:27, R.V.; Heb. 6:8, A.V. and R.V. See REPROBATE.

NT: B.18c; CB.1233a; K.181.
OT: sîg: S.5509; HR.27b.1; H.1469a; BD.691a.
GEN. REF.: —.

2. *apoblētos* [ἀπόβλητος, 579], lit., cast away (*apo*, from, *ballō*, to throw), occurs in 1 Tim. 4:4, R.V., "rejected" (A.V., "refused"). See REFUSE. ¶

NT: B.89a; CB.—; K.—.
OT: —.
GEN. REF.: —.

REJOICE

1. *chairō* [χαίρω, 5463], to rejoice, is most frequently so translated. As to this verb, the following are grounds and occasions for rejoicing, on the part of believers: in the Lord, Phil. 3:1; 4:4; His Incarnation, Luke 1:14; His power, Luke 13:17; His presence with the Father, John 14:28; His presence with them, John 16:22; 20:20; His ultimate triumph, 8:56; hearing the gospel, Acts 13:48; their salvation, Acts 8:39; receiving the Lord, Luke 19:6; their enrolment in Heaven, Luke 10:20; their liberty in Christ, Acts 15:31; their hope, Rom. 12:12 (cp. Rom. 5:2; Rev. 19:7); their prospect of reward, Matt. 5:12; the obedience and godly conduct of fellow-believers, Rom. 16:19, R.V., "I rejoice" (A.V., "I am glad"); 2 Cor. 7:7, 9; 13:9; Col. 2:5; 1 Thess. 3:9; 2 John 4; 3 John 3; the proclamation of Christ, Phil. 1:18; the gospel harvest, John 4:36; suffering with Christ, Acts 5:41; 1 Pet. 4:13; suffering in the cause of the gospel, 2 Cor. 13:9 (1st part); Phil. 2:17 (1st part); Col. 1:24; in persecutions, trials and afflictions, Matt. 5:12; Luke 6:23; 2 Cor. 6:10; the manifestation of grace, Acts 11:23; meeting with fellow-believers, 1 Cor. 16:17, R.V., "I rejoice"; Phil. 2:28; receiving tokens of love and fellowship, Phil. 4:10; the rejoicing of others, Rom. 12:15; 2 Cor. 7:13; learning of the well-being of others, 2 Cor. 7:16. See FAREWELL, GLAD, GREETING, etc.

NT: B.873b; CB.1239b; K.1298.
OT: sāmaḥ: S.8055; HR.1452a.7a; H.2268; BD.970a.
gîl: S.1523; HR.1452a.2; H.346; BD.162a.
GEN. REF.: —.

2. *sunchairō* [συγχαίρω, 4796], to rejoice with (*sun*, and No. 1), is used of rejoicing together in the recovery of what was lost, Luke 15:6, 9; in suffering in the cause of the gospel, Phil. 2:17 (2nd part), 18; in the joy of another, Luke 1:58, in the honour of fellow-believers, 1 Cor. 12:26; in the triumph of the truth, 1 Cor. 13:6, R.V., "rejoiceth with." ¶

NT: B.775a; CB.1270c; K.1298.
OT: ṣāḥaq: S.6711; HR.1301a.1; H.1905; BD.850b.
GEN. REF.: —.

3. *agalliaō* [ἀγαλλιάω, 21], to rejoice greatly, to exult, is used, (I) in the Active Voice, of rejoicing in God, Luke 1:47; in faith in Christ, 1 Pet. 1:8, R.V. (Middle V. in some mss.), "ye rejoice greatly"; in the event of the marriage of the Lamb, Rev. 19:7, "be exceeding glad," R.V.; (II) in the Middle Voice, (*a*) of rejoicing in persecutions, Matt. 5:12 (2nd part); in the light of testimony for God, John 5:35; in salvation received through the gospel, Acts 16:34, "he rejoiced greatly," R.V.; in salvation ready to be revealed, 1 Pet. 1:6; at the revelation of His glory, 1 Pet. 4:13, "with exceeding joy," lit., 'ye may rejoice (see No. 1) exulting'; (*b*) of Christ's rejoicing (greatly) "in the Holy Spirit," Luke 10:21, R.V.; said of His praise, as foretold in Ps. 16:9, quoted in Acts 2:26 (which follows

the Sept., "My tongue"); (*c*) of Abraham's rejoicing, by faith, to see Christ's day, John 8:56. ¶

NT: B.3d; CB.1233b; K.—.
OT: gîl: S.1523; HR.4c.1; H.346; BD.162a.
rānan: S.7442; HR.4c.6b; H.2134,2179; BD.943a.
'ālaz: S.5937; HR.4c.4a; H.1625; BD.759c.
GEN. REF.: —.

4. *euphrainō* [εὐφραίνω, 2165], in the Active Voice, to cheer, gladden (*eu*, well, *phrēn*, the mind), signifies in the Passive Voice to rejoice, make merry; it is translated to rejoice in Acts 2:26, R.V., "was glad," A.V., "did . . . rejoice," of the heart of Christ as foretold in Ps. 16:9 [cp. No. 3, II (*b*)]; in Acts 7:41, of Israel's idolatry; in Rom. 15:10 (quoted from the Sept. of Deut. 32:43, where it is a command to the Gentiles to rejoice with the Jews in their future deliverance by Christ from all their foes, at the establishment of the Messianic Kingdom) the Apostle applies it to the effects of the gospel; in Gal. 4:27 (touching the barrenness of Sarah as referred to in Is. 54:1, and there pointing to the ultimate restoration of Israel to God's favour, cp. 51:2), the word is applied to the effects of the gospel, in that the progeny of grace would greatly exceed the number of those who had acknowledged allegiance to the Law; grace and faith are fruitful, law and works are barren as a means of salvation; in Rev. 12:12, it is used in a call to the heavens to rejoice at the casting out of Satan and the inauguration of the Kingdom of God in manifestation and the authority of His Christ; in 18:20, of a call to heaven, saints, apostles, prophets, to rejoice in the destruction of Babylon. See GLAD, No. 3, MERRY, No. 1.

NT: B.327c; CB.1247b; K.278.
OT: sāmēaḥ, sāmaḥ: S.8055; HR.581b.19a-c; H.2268; BD.970a.
GEN. REF.: —.

5. *kauchaomai* [καυχάομαι, 2744], to boast, to glory, is rendered to rejoice, (*a*) Rom. 5:2, in hope of the glory of God; (*b*) 5:3, R.V. (A.V. "glory"), in tribulation; (*c*) 5:11, R.V. (A.V., "we joy"), in God; (*d*) Phil. 3:3, R.V., "glory" (A.V., "rejoice") in Christ Jesus; (*e*) Jas. 1:9 (R.V., "glory," A.V., "rejoice"), the brother of low degree in his high estate; the rich brother in being made low; (*f*) Jas. 4:16, of evil glorying. See GLORY (to boast).

NT: B.425c; CB.1254c; K.423.
OT: hālal: S.1984; HR.757b.2; H.499,500; BD.237d.
'ālaz: S.5937; HR.757b.3; H.1625; BD.759c.
GEN. REF.: —.

Notes: (1) In Jas. 2:13, A.V., *katakauchaomai*, to glory, boast against, is translated "rejoiceth against" (R.V., "glorieth against"). See GLORY (to boast), A, No. 2.

(2) The nouns *kauchēma, kauchēsis*, signifying glorying, boasting, are always so rendered in the R.V., where the A.V. has "rejoicing," the former in 2 Cor. 1:14; Gal. 6:4; Phil. 1:26; 2:16; Heb. 3:6; the latter in 1 Cor. 15:31; 2 Cor. 1:12; 1 Thess. 2:19; Jas. 4:16. See GLORY, B, Nos. 1 and 2.

RELEASE

apoluō [ἀπολύω, 630], to loose from, is translated to release in Matt. 18:27, R.V. (A.V., "loosed"); 27:15, 17, 21, 26; Mark 15:6, 9, 11, 15; Luke 6:37 (twice), R.V. (A.V., "forgive" and "ye shall be forgiven"); 23:16 (ver. 17, in some mss.), 18, 20, 25; 23:22, R.V. (A.V., "let . . . go"); John 18:39 (twice); 19:10; in 19:12, in the 1st part, A.V. and R.V.; in the 2nd part, R.V., "release" (A.V., "let . . . go"); so in Acts 3:13. See DEPART, DISMISS.

NT: B.96c; CB.1237a; K.—.
OT: gārash: S.1644; HR.138c.2; H.388; BD.176c.
GEN. REF.: IS.4:78; NB.—; Z.—.

Note: For *aphesis*, "release," Luke 4:18, R.V., see DELIVERANCE.

RELIEF

1. *diakonia* [διακονία, 1248], ministry, is translated "relief" in Acts 11:29 [R.V., marg., "for (*eis*) ministry"].

NT: B.184b; CB.1241a; K.152.
OT: na'ar: S.5288; HR.303b.1; H.1389a; BD.654d.
shārat: S.8334; HR.303b.2; H.2472; BD.1058a.
GEN. REF.: —.

2. *anesis* [ἄνεσις, 425], a loosening, relaxation (akin to *aniēmi*, to send away, let go, loosen), is translated "relief" in 2 Cor. 2:13 and 7:5 (A.V., "rest"). See REST.

NT: B.65b; CB.—; K.60.
OT: —.
GEN. REF.: —.

RELIEVE

eparkeō [ἐπαρκέω, 1884], signifies to be strong enough for, and so either to ward off, or to aid, to relieve (a strengthened form of *arkeō*, which has the same three meanings, *epi* being intensive); it is used in 1 Tim. 5:10, 16 (twice). ¶

NT: B.283c; CB.—; K.—.
OT: —.
GEN. REF.: —.

RELIGION

1. *thrēskeia* [θρησκεία, 2356], signifies religion in its external aspect (akin to *thrēskos*, see below), religious worship, especially the ceremonial service of religion; it is used of the religion of the Jews, Acts 26:5; of the "worshipping" of angels, Col. 2:18, which they themselves repudiate (Rev. 22:8, 9); "there was an officious parade of humility in selecting these

lower beings as intercessors rather than appealing directly to the Throne of Grace" (Lightfoot); in Jas. 1:26, 27 the writer purposely uses the word to set in contrast that which is unreal and deceptive, and the "pure religion" which consists in visiting "the fatherless and widows in their affliction," and in keeping oneself "unspotted from the world." He is "not herein affirming . . . these offices to be the sum total, nor yet the great essentials, of true religion, but declares them to be the body, the *thrēskeia*, of which godliness, or the love of God, is the informing soul" (Trench). ¶

NT: B.363b; CB.1272b; K.337.
OT: –.
GEN. REF.: IS.4:78; NB.1083; Z.–.

2. *deisidaimonia* [δεισιδαιμονία, 1175], primarily denotes fear of the gods (from *deidō*, to fear, *daimōn*, a pagan deity, Eng., demon), regarded whether as a religious attitude, or, in its usual meaning, with a condemnatory or contemptuous significance, superstition. That is how Festus regarded the Jews' religion, Acts 25:19, A.V. and R.V. marg., "superstition" (R.V., "religion"). See RELIGIOUS, *Note* (1), and under SUPERSTITIOUS. ¶

NT: B.173c; CB.–; K.137.
OT: –.
GEN. REF.: IS.4:78; NB.–; Z.–.

Notes: (1) *Thrēskeia* is external, *theosebeia* is the reverential worship of God (see GODLINESS), *eusebeia* is piety (see GODLINESS), *eulabeia* the devotedness arising from godly fear (see FEAR).

(2) For "the Jews' religion," Gal. 1:13, 14, see JEWS, B.

RELIGIOUS

thrēskos [θρῆσκος, 2357], religious, careful of the externals of divine service, akin to *thrēskeia* (see above), is used in Jas. 1:26. ¶

NT: B.363c; CB.1272b; K.337.
OT: –.
GEN. REF.: IS.4:78; NB.1083; Z.–.

Notes: (1) For *deisidaimōn*, Acts 17:22, R.V., marg., "religious," see SUPERSTITIOUS.

(2) For "religious (proselytes)," A.V. in Acts 13:43, see DEVOUT, No. 3.

REMAIN

1. *menō* [μένω, 3306], to stay, abide, is frequently rendered to remain, e.g., Matt. 11:23; Luke 10:7; John 1:33, A.V. (R.V., "abiding"); 9:41 (in 15:11, the best texts have the verb to be, see R.V.); 15:16, A.V. (R.V., "abide"); 19:31; Acts 5:4 (twice), R.V., "whiles it remained, did it (not) remain (thine own)?"; 27:41; 1 Cor. 7:11; 15:6; 2 Cor. 3:11, 14; 9:9, A.V. (R.V., "abideth"); Heb. 12:27; 1 John 3:9. See ABIDE.

NT: B.503c; CB.1258b; K.581.
OT: yāshab: S.3427; HR.910a.7; H.922; BD.442a.
'āmad: S.5975; HR.910a.12; H.1637; BD.763c.
qûm: S.6965; HR.910a.15a; H.1999; BD.877c.
GEN. REF.: –.

2. *diamenō* [διαμένω, 1265], to remain throughout (*dia*, through, and No. 1), is translated to remain in Luke 1:22; Heb. 1:11, A.V. (R.V., "Thou continuest"). See CONTINUE, No. 4.

NT: B.186c; CB.–; K.–.
OT: 'āmad: S.5975; HR.305c.6; H.1637; BD.763c.
GEN. REF.: –.

3. *apoleipō* [ἀπολείπω, 620], in the Passive Voice, to be reserved, to remain, is translated "remaineth" in Heb. 4:6, 9; 10:26. See LEAVE, No. 4.

NT: B.94d; CB.–; K.–.
OT: yātar: S.3498; HR.136b.3; H.836; BD.451a.
GEN. REF.: IS.4:130,131; NB.–; Z.–.

4. *perileipō* [περιλείπω, 4035], to leave over, used in the Middle Voice, is translated "remain" in 1 Thess. 4:15, 17, A.V. (R.V., "are left"), where it stands for the living believers at the coming (the beginning of the Parousia) of Christ. ¶

NT: B.648c; CB.1263b; K.–.
OT: shā'ar: S.7604; HR.1124b.1; H.2307,2308; BD.983d.
GEN. REF.: IS.4:130,131; NB.–; Z.–.

5. *perisseuō* [περισσεύω, 4052], to abound, to be over and above, to remain over, is rendered "(that which) remained over" in Matt. 14:20, R.V.; and Luke 9:17, R.V. (A.V., "remained"); John 6:12, 13 (A.V., ". . . over and above"). See ABUNDANCE, B, No. 1.

NT: B.650c; CB.1263c; K.828.
OT: yātar: S.3498; HR.1126b.1a; H.836; BD.451a.
GEN. REF.: IS.4:130,131; NB.–; Z.–.

Notes: (1) In Mark 8:8, *perisseuma*, an abundance, is used in the plural, R.V., "(of broken pieces) that remained over" (A.V., "that was left").

(2) In 1 Cor. 7:29, A.V., *to loipon*, lit., '(as to) what is left,' '(as for) the rest,' is translated "it remaineth" (R.V., "henceforth"); in Rev. 3:2, *ta loipa*, the plural, "the things that remain."

REMEMBER, REMEMBRANCE, REMINDED

A. Verbs.

1. *mimnēskō* [μιμνήσκω, 3403], from the older form *mnaomai*, in the Active Voice signifies to remind; in the Middle Voice, to remind oneself of, hence, to remember, to be mindful of; the later form is found only in the present tense, in Heb. 2:6, "are mindful of," and 13:3, "remember"; the perfect tense in 1 Cor. 11:2 and in 2 Tim. 1:4 (R.V., "remembering," A.V., "being mindful of"), is used with a

present meaning. R.V. variations from the A.V. are, in Luke 1:54, R.V., "that He might remember" (A.V., "in remembrance of"); 2 Pet. 3:2, "remember" (A.V., "be mindful of"); Rev. 16:19 (Passive Voice), "was remembered" (A.V., "came in remembrance"). The Passive Voice is used also in Acts 10:31, A.V. and R.V., "are had in remembrance." See MINDFUL OF (to be).

NT: B.522b; CB.1259a; K.–.
OT: zākar: S.2142; HR.927c.1; H.551; BD.269c.
GEN. REF.: IS.4:129; NB.–; Z.–.

2. *mnēmoneuō* [μνημονεύω, 3421], signifies to call to mind, remember; it is used absolutely in Mark 8:18; everywhere else it has an object, (*a*) persons, Luke 17:32; Gal. 2:10; 2 Tim. 2:8, where the R.V. rightly has "remember Jesus Christ, risen from the dead"; Paul was not reminding Timothy (nor did he need to) that Christ was raised from the dead (A.V.), what was needful for him was to remember (to keep in mind) the One who rose, the Source and Supplier of all his requirements; (*b*) things, e.g., Matt. 16:9; John 15:20; 16:21; Acts 20:35; Col. 4:18; 1 Thess. 1:3; 2:9; Heb. 11:15, "had been mindful of"; 13:7; Rev. 18:5; (*c*) a clause, representing a circumstance etc., John 16:4; Acts 20:31; Eph. 2:11; 2 Thess. 2:5; Rev. 2:5; 3:3; in Heb. 11:22 it signifies to make mention of. See MENTION. ¶

NT: B.525a; CB.1259a; K.596.
OT: zākar: S.2142; HR.931c.1a; H.551; BD.269c.
GEN. REF.: IS.4:129; NB.–; Z.–.

3. *anamimnēskō* [ἀναμιμνῄσκω, 363], *ana*, back, and No. 1, signifies in the Active Voice to remind, call to one's mind, 1 Cor. 4:17, "put (A.V., bring) . . . into remembrance"; so 2 Tim. 1:6; in the Passive Voice, to remember, call to (one's own) mind, Mark 11:21, "calling to remembrance"; 14:72, "called to mind"; 2 Cor. 7:15, "remembereth"; Heb. 10:32, "call to remembrance." ¶

NT: B.57d; CB.1235a; K.–.
OT: zākar: S.2142; HR.79c.1; H.551; BD.269c.
GEN. REF.: IS.4:129; NB.–; Z.–.

4. *hupomimnēskō* [ὑπομιμνῄσκω, 5279], signifies to cause one to remember, put one in mind of (*hupo*, under, often implying suggestion, and No. 1), John 14:26, "shall . . . bring . . . to (your) remembrance"; 2 Tim. 2:14, "put . . . in remembrance"; Tit. 3:1, "put . . . in mind"; 3 John 10, R.V., "I will bring to remembrance" (A.V., "I will remember"); Jude 5, "to put . . . in remembrance." In Luke 22:61 it is used in the Passive Voice, "(Peter) remembered," lit., 'it was put in mind.' ¶

NT: B.846a; CB.1252b; K.–.
OT: zākar: S.2142; HR.1416a.1; H.551; BD.269c.
GEN. REF.: IS.4:129; NB.–; Z.–.

5. *epanamimnēskō* [ἐπαναμιμνῄσκω, 1878], to remind again (*epi*, upon, and No. 3), is used in Rom. 15:15, R.V., "putting (you) again in remembrance," A.V., "putting (you) in mind." See MIND. ¶

NT: B.282d; CB.–; K.–.
OT: –.
GEN. REF.: –.

Note: In 1 Tim. 4:6, A.V., *hupotithēmi*, to lay under, to suggest, is translated "put . . . in remembrance" (R.V., "put . . . in mind"). See MIND.

B. Nouns.

1. *anamnēsis* [ἀνάμνησις, 364], a remembrance (*ana*, up, or again, and A, No. 1), is used (*a*) in Christ's command in the institution of the Lord's Supper, Luke 22:19; 1 Cor. 11:24, 25, not 'in memory of' but in an affectionate calling of the Person Himself to mind; (*b*) of the remembrance of sins, Heb. 10:3, R.V., "a remembrance" (A.V., "a remembrance again"; but the prefix *ana* does not here signify again); what is indicated, in regard to the sacrifices under the law, is not simply an external bringing to remembrance, but an awakening of mind. ¶ In the Sept., Lev. 24:7; Numb. 10:10; Pss. 38 and 70, Titles. ¶

NT: B.58a; CB.1235a; K.56.
OT: zākar: S.2142; HR.80a.1a; H.551; BD.269c.
zikkārôn: S.2146; HR.80a.1c; H.551b; BD.272a.
GEN. REF.: IS.4:129; NB.–; Z.–.

2. *hupomnēsis* [ὑπόμνησις, 5280], denotes a reminding, a reminder; in 2 Tim. 1:5 it is used with *lambanō*, to receive, lit., 'having received a reminder,' R.V., "having been reminded" (A.V., "when I call to remembrance"); in 2 Pet. 1:13 and 3:1, "remembrance." ¶

NT: B.846b; CB.1252b; K.56.
OT: t^{e}hillāh: S.8416; HR.1416b.1; H.500c; BD.239d.
GEN. REF.: IS.4:129; NB.–; Z.–.

Note: A distinction has been drawn between Nos. 1 and 2, in that *anamnēsis* indicates an unassisted recalling, *hupomnēsis*, a remembrance prompted by another.

3. *mneia* [μνεία, 3417], denotes a remembrance, or a mention. See MENTION.

NT: B.524b; CB.1259a; K.596.
OT: zākar: S.2142; HR.931a.1-4; H.551; BD.269c.
GEN. REF.: IS.4:129; NB.–; Z.–.

4. *mnēmē* [μνήμη, 3420], denotes a memory (akin to *mnaomai*, A, No. 1), remembrance, mention, 2 Pet. 1:15, "remembrance"; here, however, it is used with *poieō*, to make (Middle Voice), and some suggest that the meaning is 'to make mention.' ¶

NT: B.524d; CB.1259a; K.596.
OT: zēker: S.2143; HR.931b.1a; H.551a; BD.271a.
GEN. REF.: IS.4:129; NB.–; Z.–.

REMISSION, REMIT

A. Nouns.

1. *aphesis* [ἄφεσις, 859], a dismissal, release (from *aphiēmi*, B), is used of the forgiveness of sins and translated "remission" in Matt. 26:28; Mark 1:4; Luke 1:77; 3:3; 24:47; Acts 2:38; 5:31 (A.V., "forgiveness"); 10:43; 13:38, R.V. (A.V., "forgiveness"); 26:18 (ditto); Heb. 9:22; 10:18. See FORGIVE, B, and A, No. 1.

NT: B.125a; CB.1236b; K.88.
OT: d^{e}rôr: S.1865; HR.182b.3; H.454b; BD.204d.
GEN. REF.: IS.2:340; NB.–; Z.2:596.

2. *paresis* [πάρεσις, 3929], a passing by of debt or sin, Rom. 3:25, A.V., "remission" (R.V. and A.V. marg., "passing over"). See PASSING OVER ¶

NT: B.626b; CB.1262b; K.88.
OT: –.
GEN. REF.: IS.2:340; NB.–; Z.–.

Note: No. 2 is a matter of forbearance, No. 1 a matter of grace.

B. Verb.

aphiēmi [ἀφίημι, 863], to send away (akin to A, No. 1), is translated to remit in John 20:23 (twice), A.V. (R.V., to forgive). Scripture makes clear that the Lord's words could not have been intended to bestow the exercise of absolution, which Scripture declares is the prerogative of God alone. There is no instance in the N.T. of this act on the part of the Apostles. The words are to be understood in a "declarative" sense; the statement has regard to the effects of their ministry of the gospel, with its twofold effects of remission or retention. They could not, nor could anyone subsequently, forgive sins, any more than that Joseph actually restored the butler to his office and hanged the baker (Gen. 41:13), or any more than that the prophets actually accomplished things when they declared that they were about to be done (Jer. 1:10; Ezek. 43:3). See FORGIVE, No. 1.

NT: B.125c; CB.1236b; K.88.
OT: nāsā': S.5375; HR.183b.6; H.1421; BD.669d.
sālaḥ: S.5545; HR.183b.8a,b; H.1505; BD.699b.
GEN. REF.: IS.2:340; NB.–; Z.2:596.

REMNANT

1. *loipos* [λοιπός, 3062], an adjective (akin to *leipō*, to leave) signifying remaining, is used as a noun and translated "the rest" in the R.V., where the A.V. has "the remnant," Matt. 22:6; Rev. 11:13; 12:17; 19:21. See OTHER, RESIDUE, REST (the).

NT: B.479d; CB.1257b; K.–.
OT: yeter: S.3499; HR.888a.1c; H.936a; BD.451d.
sh^{e}'ār: S.7605; HR.888a.4a; H.2307a; BD.984b.
sh^{e}'ērît: S.7611; HR.888a.4c; H.2307b; BD.984c.
GEN. REF.: IS.4:130,131; NB.588; Z.5:61.

2. *leimma* [λεῖμμα, 3005], that which is left (akin to *leipō*, to leave), a remnant, is used in Rom. 11:5, "there is a remnant," more lit., 'there has come to be a remnant,' i.e., there is a spiritual remnant saved by the gospel from the midst of apostate Israel. While in one sense there has been and is a considerable number, yet, compared with the whole nation, past and present, the remnant is small, and as such is an evidence of God's electing grace (see ver. 4). ¶ In the Sept., 2 Kings 19:4. ¶

NT: B.470b; CB.1256c; K.523.
OT: sh^{e}'ērît: S.7611; HR.872b.1; H.2307b; BD.984c.
GEN. REF.: IS.4:130,131; NB.574ff; Z.5:61.

3. *hupoleimma* [ὑπόλειμμα, 5259, 3005], *hupo*, under, signifying diminution, and No. 2, is used in Rom. 9:27: some mss. have *kataleimma*, which has virtually the same meaning (*kata*, down, behind), a remnant, where the contrast is drawn between the number of Israel as a whole, and the small number in it of those who are saved through the Gospel. The quotation is chiefly from the Sept. of Isa. 10:22, 23, with a modification recalling Hosea 1:10, especially with regard to the word "number." The return of the remnant is indicated in the name "Shear-Jashub," see Isa. 7:3, marg. The primary reference was to the return of a remnant from captivity to their own land and to God Himself; here the application is to the effects of the gospel. There is stress on the word "remnant." ¶

NT: B.845c; CB.1252b; K.523.
OT: sh^{e}'ērît: S.7611; HR.1415a.2c; H.2307b; BD.984c.
sh^{e}'ār: S.7605; HR.1415a.2b; H.2307a; BD.984b.
shā'ar: S.7604; HR.1415a.2a; H.2307,2308; BD.983d.
GEN. REF.: IS.4:130,131; NB.574ff; Z.5:61.

REMOVE, REMOVING

A. Verbs.

1. *metabainō* [μεταβαίνω, 3327], to pass over from one place to another (*meta*, implying change, and *bainō*, to go), is translated to remove in Matt. 17:20 (twice). See PASS, No. 7.

NT: B.510c; CB.1258b; K.90.
OT: –.
GEN. REF.: –.

2. *methistēmi* [μεθίστημι, 3179], is used transitively in the sense of causing to remove, in Acts 13:22, of the removing of King Saul, by bringing about his death; in 1 Cor. 13:2, of removing mountains. See PUT, No. 23, TRANSLATE, TURN.

NT: B.498d; CB.–; K.–.
OT: sûr: S.5493; HR.907b.4; H.1480; BD.693b.
'^{a}dāh: S.5709; HR.907b.5; H.2898; BD.1105b.
GEN. REF.: –.

3. *metatithēmi* [μετατίθημι, 3346], to remove a person or thing from one place to another (*meta*, implying change, *tithēmi*, to put), e.g.,

Acts 7:16, "were carried over," signifies, in the Middle Voice, to change oneself, and is so used in Gal. 1:6 "(I marvel that) ye are . . . removing," R.V. (not as A.V., "removed"); the present tense suggests that the defection of the Galatians from the truth was not yet complete and would continue unless they changed their views. The Middle Voice indicates that they were themselves responsible for their declension, rather than the Judaizers who had influenced them. See CARRY, No. 5.

NT: B.513c; CB.1258c; K.1176.
OT: sûg: S.5472; HR.917a.3; H.1469; BD.690d
sût: S.5496; HR.917a.4; H.1481; BD.694d.
GEN. REF.: –.

4. *parapherō* [παραφέρω, 3911], lit., to bring to or before (*para*, beside, *pherō*, to carry), to take or carry away, is translated "remove" in the Lord's prayer in Gethsemane, Mark 14:36, R.V. (A.V., "take away"); Luke 22:42. See TAKE. In the Sept., 1 Sam. 21:13. ¶

NT: B.623b; CB.–; K.–.
OT: hālal: S.1984; HR.1065b.1; H.499,500; BD.237d,239b.
ʿābar: S.5674; HR.1065b.2; H.1556; BD.716d.
GEN. REF.: –.

5. *metoikizō* [μετοικίζω, 3351], to remove to a new abode, cause to migrate (*meta*, implying change, *oikos*, a dwelling place), is translated "removed" in Acts 7:4; "I will carry . . . away" (ver. 43). See CARRYING AWAY, B.

NT: B.514b; CB.–; K.–.
OT: gālāh: S.1540; HR.918a.1; H.350; BD.162d.
GEN. REF.: –.

6. *apochōrizō* [ἀποχωρίζω, 673], to separate, part asunder, is used in the Passive Voice in Rev. 6:14, "(the heaven) was removed," R.V. (A.V., "departed"). See DEPART, No. 14.

NT: B.102b; CB.–; K.–.
OT: –.
GEN. REF.: –.

Notes: (1) In Matt. 21:21 and Mark 11:23, *airō*, to lift, take up, is translated "be thou removed" (R.V., "be thou taken up").

(2) In Rev. 2:5, A.V., *kineō*, to move (R.V.), is translated "will remove." See MOVE.

B. Noun.

metathesis [μετάθεσις, 3331], change of position (transliterated in Eng., metathesis, a transposition of the letter of a word), from *meta*, implying change, and *tithēmi*, to place, is used only in Hebrews and translated "removing" in 12:27; "translation" in 11:5; "change" in 7:12. See CHANGE, A. ¶

NT: B.511a; CB.1258c; K.1176.
OT: –.
GEN. REF.: –.

REND, RENT (Verb and Noun)

A. Verbs.

1. *rhēgnumi* [ῥήγνυμι, 4486], to tear, rend, is translated to rend in Matt. 7:6, of swine. See BREAK, A, No. 6.

NT: B.735a; CB.–; K.–.
OT: bāqaʿ: S.1234; HR.1248c.1a-c; H.271; BD.131d.
qāraʿ: S.7167; HR.1248c.5; H.2074; BD.902b.
GEN. REF.: –.

2. *diarrhēssō*, or *diarēssō* [διαρήσσω, 1284], a late form of *diarrhēgnumi*, to break asunder, rend (*dia*, through, and No. 1), is used of rending one's garments, Matt. 26:65; Mark 14:63; Acts 14:14. See BREAK, A, No. 7.

NT: B.188a; CB.–; K.–.
OT: bāqaʿ: S.1234; HR.309a.2; H.271; BD.131d.
qāraʿ: S.7167; HR.309a.7a,b; H.2074; BD.902b.
GEN. REF.: –.

3. *perirrhēgnumi*, or *perirēgnumi* [περιρήγνυμι, 4048], to tear off all round (*peri*, around), is said of garments in Acts 16:22. ¶

NT: B.650b; CB.–; K.–.
OT: –.
GEN. REF.: –.

4. *schizō* [σχίζω, 4977], to split, rend open, translated to rend in Matt. 27:51 (twice); Mark 1:10, R.V., "rent asunder" (A.V., "open"); 15:38; Luke 5:36, R.V., "rendeth (from)"; the A.V. follows the mss. which omit it in the 1st part of this verse; 23:45; John 19:24; 21:11, R.V., "rent" (A.V., "broken"), of a net. See BREAK, A, No. 12.

NT: B.797b; CB.1268c; K.1130.
OT: bāqaʿ: S.1234; HR.1327c.1; H.271; BD.131d.
qāraʿ: S.7167; HR.1327c.2; H.2074; BD.902b.
GEN. REF.: –.

5. *diaspaō* [διασπάω, 1288], to tear asunder, is translated "rent asunder" in Mark 5:4, R.V. (A.V., "plucked asunder"); for Acts 23:10, see TEAR. ¶

NT: B.188c; CB.–; K.–.
OT: nātaq: S.5423; HR.310c.3; H.1447; BD.683c.
GEN. REF.: –.

Note: In Mark 9:26, A.V., *sparassō*, to tear (R.V.), is rendered "rent." See TEAR.

B. Noun.

schisma [σχίσμα, 4978], a rent, division (akin to A, No. 4), signifies a rent in wineskins in Matt. 9:16; Mark 2:21. See DIVISION, No. 3.

NT: B.797c; CB.1268c; K.1130.
OT: –.
GEN. REF.: –.

RENDER

1. *apodidōmi* [ἀποδίδωμι, 591], to give up or back, is translated to render, (*a*) of righteous acts, (1) human, Matt. 21:41; 22:21; Mark 12:17; Luke 16:2, R.V. (A.V., "give"); Luke 20:25; Rom. 13:7; 1 Cor. 7:3; (2) Divine, Matt. 16:27, R.V., "shall render" (A.V., "shall reward"), an important R.V. change; Rom. 2:6; 2 Tim. 4:14, R.V. (A.V., "reward"); Rev. 18:6 (ditto); 22:12,

R.V. (A.V., "give"); (*b*) of unrighteous acts, Rom. 12:17, R.V. (A.V., "recompense"); 1 Thess. 5:15; 1 Pet. 3:9. See DELIVER, A, No. 3, RECOMPENSE, B, No. 2.
NT: B.90b; CB.1236c; K.166.
OT: shûb: S.7725; HR.126b.8; H.2340; BD.996d.
shālēm: S.7999; HR.126b.9; H.2401c; BD.1022b.
GEN. REF.: –.

2. *antapodidōmi* [ἀνταποδίδωμι, 467], to give in return for, is translated "render" in 1 Thess. 3:9. See RECOMPENSE, REPAY.
NT: B.73a; CB.1236a; K.166.
OT: shûb: S.7725; HR.108c.4; H.2340; BD.996d.
shālam: S.7999; HR.108c.5a,b; H.2401c; BD.1022b.
gāmal: S.1580; HR.108c.2a; H.360; BD.168a.
GEN. REF.: –.

3. *parechō* [παρέχω, 3930], to furnish, provide, supply, is translated "render" in Col. 4:1, R.V. (A.V., "give"), of what is due from masters to servants. See GIVE, No. 8.
NT: B.626b; CB.–; K.–.
OT: –.
GEN. REF.: –.

4. *didōmi* [δίδωμι, 1325], to give, is translated "rendering" in 2 Thess. 1:8, R.V. (A.V., "taking"), of the Divine execution of vengeance at the revelation of Christ from heaven hereafter. See GIVE, No. 1.
NT: B.192c; CB.1241c; K.166.
OT: nātan: S.5414; HR.317b.26; H.1443; BD.678a.
GEN. REF.: –.

RENEW, RENEWING (Verb and Noun)

A. Verbs.

1. *anakainoō* [ἀνακαινόω, 341], to make new (*ana*, back or again, *kainos*, new, not recent but different), to renew, is used in the Passive Voice in 2 Cor. 4:16, of the daily renewal of "the inward man" (in contrast to the physical frame), i.e., of the renewal of spiritual power; in Col. 3:10, of "the new man" (in contrast to the old unregenerate nature), which "is being renewed unto knowledge," R.V. (cp. No. 3 in Eph. 4:23), i.e., the true knowledge in Christ, as opposed to heretical teachings. ¶
NT: B.55c; CB.1235a; K.388.
OT: –.
GEN. REF.: IS.4:135; NB.–; Z.–.

Note: This word has not been found elsewhere in Greek writings as yet, though No. 2 is, which would prevent the supposition that the Apostle coined a new word.

2. *anakainizō* [ἀνακαινίζω, 340], is a variant form of No. 1, used in Heb. 6:6, of the impossibility of renewing to repentance those Jews who professedly adhered to the Christian faith, if, after their experiences of it (not actual possession of its regenerating effects), they apostatized into their former Judaism. ¶ In the Sept., 2 Chron. 15:8; Ps. 39:2; 103:5; 104:30; Lam. 5:21. ¶
NT: B.55b; CB.1235a; K.388.
OT: ḥādash: S.2318; HR.78a.1; H.613; BD.293d.
GEN. REF.: IS.4:135; NB.–; Z.–.

3. *ananeoō* [ἀνανεόω, 365], to renew, make young (*ana*, as in No. 1, and *neos*, recent, not different), is used in Eph. 4:23, "be renewed (in the spirit of your mind)." The renewal here mentioned is not that of the mind itself in its natural powers of memory, judgment and perception, but 'the spirit of the mind,' which, under the controlling power of the indwelling Holy Spirit, directs its bent and energies Godward in the enjoyment of "fellowship with the Father and with His Son, Jesus Christ," and of the fulfilment of the will of God. ¶ The word is frequent in inscriptions and in the papryi.
NT: B.58a; CB.1235b; K.628.
OT: –.
GEN. REF.: IS.4:135; NB.–; Z.–.

B. Noun.

anakainōsis [ἀνακαίνωσις, 342], akin to A, No. 1, a renewal, is used in Rom. 12:2, "the renewing (of your mind)," i.e., the adjustment of the moral and spiritual vision and thinking to the mind of God, which is designed to have a transforming effect upon the life; in Tit. 3:5, where "the renewing of the Holy Spirit" is not a fresh bestowment of the Spirit, but a revival of His power, developing the Christian life; this passage stresses the continual operation of the indwelling Spirit of God; the Romans passage stresses the willing response on the part of the believer. ¶
NT: B.55c; CB.1235a; K.388.
OT: –.
GEN. REF.: IS.4:135; NB.–; Z.–.

RENOUNCE

1. *apeipon* [ἀπεῖπον, 550], lit., to tell from (*apo*, from, *eipon*, an aorist form used to supply parts of *legō*, to say), signifies to renounce, 2 Cor. 4:2 (Middle Voice), of disowning "the hidden things of shame." ¶ In the Sept. of 1 Kings 11:2 it signifies to forbid, a meaning found in the papyri. The meaning to renounce may therefore carry with it the thought of forbidding the approach of the things disowned.
NT: B.83b; CB.–; K.–.
OT: 'āmar: S.559; HR.120a.1; H.118; BD.55c.
mā'as: S.3988; HR.120a.3; H.1139,1140; BD.549b.
GEN. REF.: –.

2. *apotassō* [ἀποτάσσω, 657], to set apart, to appoint, a meaning found in the papyri (*apo*, from, *tassō*, to arrange), is used in the Middle Voice in the sense either of taking leave of, e.g.,

Acts 18:18, or forsaking, Luke 14:33, R.V., "renounceth" (A.V., "forsaketh"). See FORSAKE, LEAVE.
NT: B.100d; CB.–; K.1156.
OT: yā'ash: S.2976; HR.148c.1; H.833; BD.384c.
GEN. REF.: –.

REPAY

1. *apodidōmi* [ἀποδίδωμι, 591], to give back, is translated "I will repay" in Luke 10:35. See DELIVER, A, No. 3, RECOMPENSE, B, No. 2, RENDER, No. 1.
NT: B.90b; CB.1236c; K.166.
OT: shûb: S.7725; HR.126b.8b; H.2340; BD.996d.
mākar: S.4376; HR.126b.3a; H.1194; BD.569a.
shālēm: S.7999; HR.126b.9; H.2401c; BD.1022a.
GEN. REF.: –.

2. *antapodidōmi* [ἀνταποδίδωμι, 467], to give in return for, is translated "I will repay" in Rom. 12:19, A.V. (R.V., "I will recompense"). See RECOMPENSE, B, No. 1, RENDER, No. 2.
NT: B.73a; CB.1236a; K.166.
OT: gāmal: S.1580; HR.108c.2a; H.360; BD.168a.
shûb: S.7725; HR.108c.4; H.2340; BD.996d.
shālēm: S.7999; HR.108c.5a,b; H.2401c; BD.1022a.
GEN. REF.: –.

3. *apotinō* or *apotiō* [ἀποτίνω, 661], signifying to pay off (*apo*, off, *tinō*, to pay a fine), is used in Philm. 19, of Paul's promise to repay whatever Onesimus owed Philemon, or to whatever extent the runaway slave had wronged his master. ¶ The verb is very common in the papyri, e.g., in a contract of apprenticeship the father has to pay a forfeit for each day of the son's absence from work. Moulton and Milligan, who draw this and other illustrations in the way of repayment, point out that "this verb is stronger than *apodidōmi* (No. 1), and carries with it the idea of repayment by way of a fine or punishment, a fact which lends emphasis to its use in Philm. 19."
NT: B.101b; CB.–; K.–.
OT: shālēm: S.7999; HR.149a.3; H.2401c; BD.1022a.
GEN. REF.: –.

REPENT, REPENTANCE

A. Verbs.

1. *metanoeō* [μετανοέω, 3340], lit., to perceive afterwards (*meta*, after, implying change, *noeō*, to perceive; *nous*, the mind, the seat of moral reflection), in contrast to *pronoeō*, to perceive beforehand, hence signifies to change one's mind or purpose, always, in the N.T., involving a change for the better, an amendment, and always, except in Luke 17:3, 4, of repentance from sin. The word is found in the Synoptic Gospels (in Luke, nine times), in Acts five times, in the Apocalypse twelve times, eight in the messages to the churches, 2:5 (twice), 16, 21 (twice), R.V., "she willeth not to repent" (2nd part); 3:3, 19 (the only churches in those chapters which contain no exhortation in this respect are those at Smyrna and Philadelphia); elsewhere only in 2 Cor. 12:21. See also the general *Note* below.
NT: B.511d; CB.1258c; K.636.
OT: shûb: S.7725; HR.916b.2; H.2340; BD.996d.
GEN. REF.: IS.4:135; NB.1083; Z.5:62.

2. *metamelomai* [μεταμέλομαι, 3338], *meta*, as in No. 1, and *melō*, to care for, is used in the Passive Voice with Middle Voice sense, signifying to regret, to repent oneself, Matt. 21:29, R.V., "repented himself"; ver. 32, R.V., "ye did (not) repent yourselves" (A.V., "ye repented not"); 27:3, "repented himself"; 2 Cor. 7:8 (twice), R.V., "regret" in each case; Heb. 7:21, where alone in the N.T. it is said (negatively) of God. ¶
NT: B.511c; CB.1258c; K.589.
OT: nāḥam: S.5162; HR.916b.3; H.1344; BD.636d.
GEN. REF.: IS.4:135; NB.1083; Z.–.

B. Adjective.

ametamelētos [ἀμεταμέλητος, 278], not repented of, unregretted (*a*, negative, and a verbal adjective of A, No. 2), signifies 'without change of purpose'; it is said (*a*) of God in regard to his "gifts and calling," Rom. 11:29; (*b*) of man, 2 Cor. 7:10, R.V., "[repentance (*metanoia*, see C)] . . . which bringeth no regret" (A.V., "not to be repented of"); the difference between *metanoia* and *metamelomai*, illustrated here, is briefly expressed in the contrast between repentance and regret. ¶
NT: B.45c; CB.1234c; K.636.
OT: –.
GEN. REF.: –.

C. Noun.

metanoia [μετάνοια, 3341], after-thought, change of mind, repentance, corresponds in meaning to A, No. 1, and is used of repentance from sin or evil, except in Heb. 12:17, where the word "repentance" seems to mean, not simply a change of Isaac's mind, but such a change as would reverse the effects of his own previous state of mind. Esau's birthright-bargain could not be recalled, it involved an irretrievable loss.

As regards repentance from sin, (*a*) the requirement by God on man's part is set forth, e.g., in Matt. 3:8; Luke 3:8; Acts 20:21; 26:20; (*b*) the mercy of God in giving repentance or leading men to it is set forth, e.g., in Acts 5:31; 11:18; Rom. 2:4; 2 Tim. 2:25. The most authentic mss. omit the word in Matt. 9:13 and Mark 2:17, as in the R.V.
NT: B.512c; CB.1258c; K.636.
OT: –.
GEN. REF.: IS.4:135; NB.1083; Z.5:62.

Note: In the O.T., repentance with reference to sin is not so prominent as that change of mind or purpose, out of pity for those who have been affected by one's action, or in whom the results of the action have not fulfilled expectations, a repentance attributed both to God and to man, e.g., Gen. 6:6; Ex. 32:14 (that this does not imply anything contrary to God's immutability, but that the aspect of His mind is changed toward an object that has itself changed, see under RECONCILE).

In the N.T. the subject chiefly has reference to repentance from sin, and this change of mind involves both a turning from sin and a turning to God. The parable of the prodigal son is an outstanding illustration of this. Christ began His ministry with a call to repentance, Matt. 4:17, but the call is addressed, not as in the O.T. to the nation, but to the individual. In the Gospel of John, as distinct from the Synoptic Gospels, referred to above, repentance is not mentioned, even in connection with John the Baptist's preaching; in John's Gospel and 1st Epistle the effects are stressed, e.g., in the new birth, and, generally, in the active turning from sin to God by the exercise of faith (John 3:3; 9:38; 1 John 1:9) as in general.

REPETITIONS (use vain)

battalogeō or *battologeō* [βατταλογέω, 945], to repeat idly, is used in Matt. 6:7, "use (not) vain repetitions"; the meaning to stammer is scarcely to be associated with this word. The word is probably from an Aramaic phrase and onomatopoeic in character. The rendering of the Sinaitic Syriac is "Do not be saying *battalatha*, idle things," i.e., meaningless and mechanically repeated phrases, the reference being to pagan (not Jewish) modes of prayer. *Battalos*, "the Gabbler," was a nickname for Demosthenes, the great orator, assigned to him by his rivals. ¶

NT: B.137d; CB.1239a; K.103.
OT: –.
GEN. REF.: –.

REPLY

antapokrinomai [ἀνταποκρίνομαι, 470], is translated "repliest against" in Rom. 9:20 (*anti*, against, *apokrinomai*, to answer); in Luke 14:6, "answer again." See ANSWER, B, No. 2. ¶

NT: B.73b; CB.–; K.469.
OT: ʻānāh: S.6030; HR.109b.1; H.1650,1653; BD.772c.
GEN. REF.: –.

REPORT (Noun and Verb)

A. Nouns.

1. *akoē* [ἀκοή, 189], a hearing, is translated "report" in John 12:38 and Rom. 10:16, and in the R.V. of Matt. 4:24; 14:1; Mark 1:28. See HEARING, B, No. 1.

NT: B.30d; CB.1234b; K.34.
OT: shāmaʻ: S.8085; HR.44b.1a; H.2412; BD.1033b.
shᵉmûʻāh: S.8052; HR.44b.1d; H.2412d; BD.1035b.
shēmaʻ: S.8088; HR.44b.1f; H.2412b; BD.1034b.
GEN. REF.: –.

2. *euphēmia* [εὐφημία, 2162], a good report, good reputation (*eu*, well, *phēmē*, a saying or report), is used in 2 Cor. 6:8. Contrast No. 3. ¶

NT: B.327c; CB.–; K.–.
OT: –.
GEN. REF.: –.

3. *dusphēmia* [δυσφημία, 1426], evil-speaking, defamation (*dus-*, an inseparable prefix, the opposite to *eu*, well, see No. 2), is used in 2 Cor. 6:8. ¶

NT: B.209d; CB.–; K.–.
OT: –.
GEN. REF.: –.

4. *logos* [λόγος, 3056], a word, is translated "report," i.e., a story, narrative; in Luke 5:15 (A.V., "fame"); 7:17 (A.V., "rumour"); Acts 11:22 (A.V., "things"). See WORD.

NT: B.477a; CB.1257a; K.505.
OT: dābār: S.1697; HR.881c.2a; H.399a; BD.182a.
GEN. REF.: –.

Note: For *marturia*, rendered "report" in 1 Tim. 3:7, A.V., see TESTIMONY, WITNESS.

B. Adjective.

euphēmos [εὔφημος, 2163], akin to A, No. 2, primarily, uttering words or sounds of good omen, then, avoiding ill-omened words, and hence fair-sounding, "of good report," is so rendered in Phil. 4:8. ¶

NT: B.327c; CB.–; K.–.
OT: –.
GEN. REF.: –.

C. Verbs.

1. *martureō* [μαρτυρέω, 3140], to be a witness, bear witness, testify, signifies, in the Passive Voice, to be well testified of, to have a good report, Acts 6:3, "of good (A.V., honest) report," lit., 'being well testified of'; 10:22; 16:2; 22:12; 1 Tim. 5:10; in Heb. 11:2, 39, A.V., "obtained a good report" (R.V., "had witness borne to them"); in 3 John 12, A.V., "hath good report" (R.V., "hath the witness"), lit., 'witness hath been borne.' See TESTIFY, WITNESS.

NT: B.492c; CB.1257c; K.564.
OT: ʻēd: S.5707; HR.896b.1c; H.1576b; BD.729c.
GEN. REF.: –.

2. *apangellō* [ἀπαγγέλλω, 518], to report (*apo*, from, *angellō*, to give a message), announce, declare (by a messenger, speaker, or writer), is translated "reported" in Acts 4:23; 16:36, R.V. (A.V., "told"); ver. 38 (some mss. have No. 3; A.V., "told"); "report" in 1 Cor. 14:25, A.V. (R.V., "declaring"); 1 Thess. 1:9, R.V., "report" (A.V., "shew"); so Acts 28:21. See DECLARE, No. 2.

NT: B.79b; CB.1236b; K.10.
OT: nāgad: S.5046; HR.113c.2; H.1289; BD.616c.
GEN. REF.: –.

3. *anangellō* [ἀναγγέλλω, 312], to bring back word, in later Greek came to have the same meaning as No. 2, to announce, declare; it is translated "are reported" in 1 Pet. 1:12, A.V. (R.V., "have been announced"). See DECLARE, No. 1.
NT: B.51b; CB.1235b; K.10.
OT: nāgad: S.5046; HR.74a.10a; H.1289; BD.616c.
GEN. REF.: –.

4. *akouō* [ἀκούω, 191], to hear, is used in the Passive Voice, impersonally, in 1 Cor. 5:1, lit., 'it is heard' or 'there is heard,' translated "it is reported." See HEAR.
NT: B.31d; CB.1234b; K.34.
OT: shāma': S.8085; HR.45a.8a; H.2412; BD.1033b.
GEN. REF.: –.

5. *blasphēmeō* [βλασφημέω, 987], to speak slanderously, impiously, profanely (*blaptō*, to injure, and *phēmē*, a saying), is translated "we be slanderously reported" in Rom. 3:8 (Passive Voice). See BLASPHEME, B.
NT: B.142c; CB.1239a; K.107.
OT: gādaph: S.1442; HR.221a.1; H.317; BD.154c.
na'aṣ: S.5006; HR.221a.3; H.1274; BD.610d
GEN. REF.: –.

Note: In Matt. 28:15, A.V., *diaphēmizō*, to spread abroad (*dia*, throughout, *phēmē*, a saying, report), is translated "is commonly reported" (R.V., "was spread abroad"). See BLAZE ABROAD.

REPROACH (Noun and Verb), REPROACHFULLY

A. Nouns.

1. *oneidismos* [ὀνειδισμός, 3680], a reproach, defamation, is used in Rom. 15:3; 1 Tim. 3:7; Heb. 10:33; 11:26; 13:13. ¶
NT: B.570b; CB.1260c; K.693.
OT: ḥerpāh: S.2781; HR.994c.3; H.749a; BD.357d.
GEN. REF.: –.

2. *oneidos* [ὄνειδος, 3681], akin to No. 1, is used in Luke 1:25 in the concrete sense of a matter of reproach, a disgrace. ¶ To have no children was, in the Jewish mind, more than a misfortune, it might carry the implication that this was a Divine punishment for some secret sin. Cp. Gen. 30:1; 1 Sam. 1:6-10.
NT: B.570b; CB.1260c; K.693.
OT: ḥerpāh: S.2781; HR.995a.2; H.749a; BD.357d.
GEN. REF.: –.

3. *atimia* [ἀτιμία, 819], dishonour, is translated "reproach" in 2 Cor. 11:21, A.V. (R.V., "disparagement"). See DISHONOUR, SHAME, VILE.
NT: B.120a; CB.1238b; K.–.
OT: k^elimmāh: S.3639; HR.175c.3b; H.987a; BD.484a.
qālôn: S.7036; HR.175c.5c; H.2024a; BD.885d.
GEN. REF.: –.

Note: In 2 Cor. 12:10, A.V., *hubris*, insolence, injury, is translated "reproaches" (R.V., "injuries"). See HARM.

B. Verbs.

1. *oneidizō* [ὀνειδίζω, 3679], akin to A, Nos. 1 and 2, signifies (*a*), in the Active Voice, to reproach, upbraid, Matt. 5:11, R.V., "shall reproach" (A.V., "shall revile"); 11:20, "to upbraid"; 27:44, R.V., "cast . . . reproach" [A.V., "cast . . . in (His) teeth"]; Mark 15:32, R.V., "reproached" (A.V., "reviled"); 16:14, "upbraided"; Luke 6:22, "shall reproach"; Rom. 15:3; Jas. 1:5, "upbraideth"; (*b*) in the Passive Voice, to suffer reproach, be reproached, 1 Tim. 4:10 (in some mss. in the 2nd part); 1 Pet. 4:14. ¶
NT: B.570a; CB.1260c; K.693.
OT: ḥāraph: S.2778; HR.994b.2; H.749-751; BD.357c.
GEN. REF.: IS.4:139; NB.–; Z.–.

2. *hubrizō* [ὑβρίζω, 5195], akin to *hubris* (see A, *Note*), used transitively, denotes to outrage, insult, treat insolently; it is translated "Thou reproachest" in Luke 11:45. The word is much stronger than to reproach; the significance is 'Thou insultest (even us),' i.e., who are superior to ordinary Pharisees. The lawyer's imputation was unjust; Christ's rebuke was not *hubris*, insult. What He actually said was by way of reproach (*oneidizō*). See DESPITEFULLY.
NT: B.831d; CB.1251c; K.1200.
OT: qālal: S.7043; HR.1379c.3; H.2028; BD.886b.
GEN. REF.: IS.4:139; NB.–; Z.–.

Notes: (1) For *anepilēptos*, "without reproach," R.V., in 1 Tim. 3:2; 5:7; 6:14, see BLAMELESS, B, No. 5.

(2) In 1 Tim. 5:14, A.V., *loidoria*, reviling (R.V.), used in the genitive case with *charin*, in respect of, "for," is translated "reproachfully" (R.V., "for reviling"). Cp. *loidoreō*, to revile. See RAILING.

REPROBATE

adokimos [ἀδόκιμος, 96], signifying 'not standing the test,' rejected (*a*, negative, *dokimos*, approved), was primarily applied to metals (cp. Is. 1:22); it is used always in the N.T. in a Passive sense, (*a*) of things, Heb. 6:8, "rejected," of land that bears thorns and thistles; (*b*) of persons, Rom. 1:28, of a "reprobate mind," a mind of which God cannot approve, and which must be rejected by Him, the effect of refusing "to have God in *their* knowledge"; in 1 Cor. 9:27 (for which see CAST, REJECTED); 2 Cor. 13:5, 6, 7, where the R.V. rightly translates the adjective "reprobate" (A.V., "reprobates"), here the reference is to the great test as to whether Christ is in a person; in 2 Tim. 3:8 of those "reprobate concerning the faith," i.e., men whose moral sense is perverted and whose minds are beclouded with their own specula-

tions; in Tit. 1:16, of the defiled, who are "unto every good work reprobate," i.e., if they are put to the test in regard to any good work (in contrast to their profession), they can only be rejected. ¶ In the Sept., Prov. 25:4; Isa. 1:22. ¶
NT: B.18c; CB.1233a; K.181.
OT: sîg: S.5509; HR.27b.1; H.1469a; BD.691a.
GEN. REF.: IS.4:139; NB.1085; Z.5:66.

REPROOF, REPROVE

A. Noun.

elegmos [ἐλεγμός, --], a reproof (akin to B), is found in the best texts in 2 Tim. 3:16 (some mss. have *elenchos*, which denotes a proof, proving, test, as in Heb. 11:1, "proving," R.V. marg., "test"). ¶ Cp. *elenxis*, rebuke, 2 Pet. 2:16 (lit., 'had rebuke'). ¶
NT: B.249a; CB.1244a; K.221.
OT: mar: S.4751; HR.449a.3; H.1248a.c; BD.600c.
tôkēḥāh: S.8433; HR.449a.2b; H.865a,b; BD.407b.
tôkaḥat: S.8433; HR.449a.2c; H.865a,b; BD.407b.
GEN. REF.: IS.4:139; NB.–; Z.–.

B. Verb.

elenchō [ἐλέγχω, 1651], to convict, rebuke, reprove, is translated to reprove in Luke 3:19; John 3:20, R.V. marg., "convicted"; the real meaning here is "exposed" (A.V., marg., "discovered"); Eph. 5:11, 13, where to expose is again the significance; in John 16:8, A.V., "will reprove" (R.V., "will convict"); in 1 Cor. 14:24, R.V., "reproved" (A.V., "convinced"); in the following the R.V. has 'to reprove,' for A.V., 'to rebuke,' 1 Tim. 5:20; Tit. 2:15; Heb. 12:5; Rev. 3:19; for synonymous words see CONVICT and REBUKE.
NT: B.249b; CB.1244a; K.221.
OT: yākaḥ: S.3198; HR.449b.3a; H.865; BD.406d.
GEN. REF.: IS.4:139; NB.–; Z.–.

REPUTATION, REPUTE

dokeō [δοκέω, 1380], signifies (*a*) to be of opinion (akin to *doxa*, an opinion), to suppose, e.g., Luke 12:51; 13:2 (see SUPPOSE); (*b*) to seem, to be reputed; in Gal. 2:2, R.V., "who were of repute" (A.V., "which were of reputation"); in 2:6 (twice), and 9, R.V., "were reputed" and "were of repute" (A.V., "seemed"); in each case the present participle of the verb with the article is used, lit., '(well) thought of' by them, persons held in consideration; in ver. 6, R.V., "(those) who were reputed to be somewhat" (A.V., "who seemed to be somewhat"); so ver. 9, where there is no irony [cp. the rendering "are accounted" in Mark 10:42 (i.e., not rulers nominally)], Paul recognized that James, Cephas, and John were, as they were reputed by the church at Jerusalem, its responsible guides; (*c*) impersonally, to think, to seem good. See SEEM and THINK.

The first meaning, to suppose, implies a subjective opinion based on thought; the second meaning, exemplified in the Galatians passages, expresses, from the standpoint of the observer, his own judgment about a matter (Trench, Syn., § lxxx).
NT: B.201d; CB.1242a; K.178.
OT: ṭôb: S.2895; HR.339b.3a; H.793; BD.373a.
GEN. REF.: IS.4:140; NB.–; Z.–.

Notes: (1) In Acts 5:34, A.V., *timios*, honoured, had in honour (R.V.), is translated "had in reputation."

(2) In Phil. 2:29, A.V., *entimos*, honourable, with *echō*, to have, i.e., to hold in honour, is translated "hold . . . in reputation" (R.V., "hold . . . in honour").

(3) For *kenoō*, in Phil. 2:7, A.V., "made (Himself) of no reputation," see EMPTY.

REQUEST (Noun and Verb)

A. Nouns.

1. *aitēma* [αἴτημα, 155], denotes that which has been asked for (akin to *aiteō*, to ask); in Luke 23:24, R.V., "what they asked for" (A.V., "as they required"), lit., 'their request (should be done, *ginomai*)'; in Phil. 4:6, "requests"; in 1 John 5:15 "petitions." See PETITION, REQUIRE. ¶
NT: B.26b; CB.1234a; K.30.
OT: sh^{e}'ēlāh: S.7596; HR.38a.2; H.2303a; BD.982c.
GEN. REF.: –.

2. *deēsis* [δέησις, 1162], an asking, entreaty, supplication, is translated "request" in Phil. 1:4, A.V. (R.V., "supplication"). See PRAYER, SUPPLICATION.
NT: B.171d; CB.1240b; K.143.
OT: t^{e}ḥinnāh: S.8467; HR.285c.8a; H.694f; BD.337c.
taḥ^{a}nûn: S.8469; HR.285c.8b; H.694g; BD.337c.
GEN. REF.: –.

B. Verbs.

1. *deomai* [δέομαι, 1189], akin to A, No. 2, to beseech, pray, request, is translated to make request in Rom. 1:10. See BESEECH, No. 3.
NT: B.175a; CB.1240c; K.144.
OT: ḥānan: S.2603; HR.288a.8c; H.694,695; BD.335d.
GEN. REF.: –.

2. *aiteō* [αἰτέω, 154], to ask, is translated to make request in Col. 1:9, R.V. (A.V., "to desire"). See ASK, No. 1.
NT: B.25d; CB.1234a; K.30.
OT: shā'al: S.7592; HR.37c.3; H.2303; BD.981b.
GEN. REF.: –.

3. *erōtaō* [ἐρωτάω, 2065], to ask, is translated to make request in 1 John 5:16. See ASK, No. 2 and remarks on the difference between Nos. 1 and 2.
NT: B.311d; CB.1246c; K.262.
OT: sha'al: S.7592; HR.553b.3a; H.2303; BD.981b.
GEN. REF.: –.

REQUIRE

1. *zēteō* [ζητέω, 2212], to seek, seek after, also signifies to require, demand, "shall be required," Luke 12:48; in 1 Cor. 4:2, "it is required (in stewards)." See DESIRE, *Note* (2), ENDEAVOUR, GO, *Note* (2) (*a*), SEEK.

NT: B.338d; CB.1273c; K.300.
OT: bāqash: S.1245; HR.597a.6a; H.276; BD.134c.
dārash: S.1875; HR.597a.8a; H.455; BD.205a.
GEN. REF.: IS.4:140; NB.—; Z.—.

2. *ekzēteō* [ἐκζητέω, 1567], to seek out (*ek*, out, and No. 1), also denotes to demand, require, Luke 11:50, 51, of executing vengeance for the slaughter of the prophets (cp. 2 Sam. 4:11; Ezek. 3:18). See SEEK.

NT: B.240a; CB.1244a; K.300.
OT: dārash: S.1875; HR.430c.3a; H.455; BD.205a.
bāqash: S.1245; HR.430c.2; H.276; BD.134c.
GEN. REF.: IS.4:140; NB.—; Z.—.

3. *apaiteō* [ἀπαιτέω, 523], to ask back, demand back (*apo*, from, or back, *aiteō*, to ask), is translated "shall be required" in Luke 12:20, lit., 'do they require,' in the impersonal sense; elsewhere, Luke 6:30, to ask again. ¶ It is used in the papyri frequently in the sense of demanding, making demands.

NT: B.80a; CB.1236b; K.30.
OT: nāgas: S.5065; HR.116b.1; H.1296; BD.620b.
GEN. REF.: IS.4:140; NB.—; Z.—.

4. *prassō* [πράσσω, 4238], to do, practise, perform, is used financially in the sense of exacting payment, in Luke 19:23. See EXTORT, A.

NT: B.698b; CB.1266b; K.927.
OT: nāgas: S.5065; HR.1201a.2; H.1296; BD.620b.
GEN. REF.: —.

Notes: (1) In Luke 23:23, A.V., *aiteō*, to ask (Middle Voice) is translated "requiring" (R.V., "asking"); so in 1 Cor. 1:22 (Active Voice), A.V., "require" (R.V., "ask").

(2) In Luke 23:24, A.V., the noun *aitēma* (see REQUEST), that which is asked for, is translated "as they required" (R.V., "what they asked for").

(3) In 1 Cor. 7:36 the rendering "need so requireth" (R.V.) represents the phrase *houtōs* (thus) *opheilei* (it ought) *genesthai* (to become, i.e., to be done).

REQUITE

amoibē [ἀμοιβή, 287], a requital, recompence (akin to *ameibomai*, to repay, not found in the N.T.), is used with the verb *apodidōmi*, to render, in 1 Tim. 5:4, and translated "to requite." ¶ This use is illustrated in the papyri by way of making a return, conferring a benefaction in return for something (Moulton and Milligan).

NT: B.46c; CB.—; K.—.
OT: —.
GEN. REF.: —.

RESCUE

exaireō [ἐξαιρέω, 1807], to take out (*ek*, from, *haireō*, to take), is used of delivering from persons and circumstances, and translated "rescued" in Acts 23:27. See DELIVER, No. 8, PLUCK.

NT: B.271d; CB.—; K.—.
OT: nāsa': S.5265; HR.485a.22a; H.1380; BD.652a.
sûr: S.5493; HR.485a.27; H.1480; BD.693b.
GEN. REF.: IS.4:141; NB.—; Z.—.

For **RESEMBLE**, Luke 13:18, A.V., see **LIKEN**, B, No. 1

RESERVE

tēreō [τηρέω, 5087], to guard, keep, preserve, give heed to, is translated to reserve, (*a*) with a happy issue, 1 Pet. 1:4; (*b*) with a retributive issue, 2 Pet. 2:4; ver. 9, A.V. (R.V., "keep"); 2:17; 3:7; Jude 6, A.V. (R.V., "hath kept"); ver. 13; (*c*) with the possibility either of deliverance or execution, Acts 25:21, A.V. (R.V., "kept"). See KEEP.

NT: B.814d; CB.1271b; K.1174.
OT: shāmar: S.8104; HR.1348b.7; H.2414; BD.1036b.
nāṣar: S.5341; HR.1348b.2; H.1407; BD.665c.
GEN. REF.: —.

Note: In Rom. 11:4, A.V., *kataleipō*, to leave behind, leave remaining, is translated "I have reserved" (R.V., "I have left"). See LEAVE.

RESIDUE

kataloipos [κατάλοιπος, 2645], an adjective denoting 'left remaining' (*kata*, after, behind, *leipō*, to leave), akin to the verb in the *Note* above, is translated "residue" in Acts 15:17, from the Sept. of Amos 9:12. ¶

NT: B.414b; CB.1254a; K.—.
OT: yeter: S.3499; HR.738a.3a; H.936a; BD.451d.
sh^e'ērît: S.7611; HR.738a.5c; H.2307b; BD.984c.
GEN. REF.: IS.4:142; NB.—; Z.—.

Note: In Mark 16:13, A.V., the plural of *loipos*, left, is translated "residue" (R.V., "rest").

RESIST

1. *anthistēmi* [ἀνθίστημι, 436], to set against (*anti*, against, *histēmi*, to cause to stand), used in the Middle (or Passive) Voice and in the intransitive 2nd aorist and perfect Active, signifying to withstand, oppose, resist, is translated to resist in Matt. 5:39; Acts 6:10, A.V. (R.V., "withstand"); Rom. 9:19, A.V. (R.V., "withstandeth"); 13:2 (2nd and 3rd parts; for 1st part, see No. 3), A.V. (R.V., "withstandeth" and "withstand"); Gal. 2:11, R.V. (A.V., "withstood"); 2 Tim. 3:8 (2nd part), A.V. (R.V., "withstand"); Jas. 4:7; 1 Pet. 5:9, A.V. (R.V.,

"withstand"); to withstand in Acts 13:8; Eph. 6:13; 2 Tim. 3:8 (1st part); 4:15. ¶
NT: B.67b; CB.—; K.—.
OT: yaṣab: S.3320; HR.95c.7a; H.894; BD.426a.
nāṣab: S.5324; HR.95c.7b; H.1398; BD.662a.
'āmad: S.5975; HR.95c.9; H.1637; BD.763c.
GEN. REF.: —.

2. *antikathisetēmi* [ἀντικαθίστημι, 478], to stand firm against (*anti*, against, *kathistēmi*, to set down, *kata*), is translated "ye have (not) resisted" in Heb. 12:4. ¶ In the Sept., Deut. 31:21; Josh. 5:7; Mic. 2:8. ¶
NT: B.74b; CB.—; K.—.
OT: qûm: S.6965; HR.110c.2; H.1999; BD.877c.
GEN. REF.: —.

3. *antitassō* [ἀντιτάσσω, 498], *anti*, against, *tassō*, to arrange, originally a military term, to range in battle against, and frequently so found in the papyri, is used in the Middle Voice signifying to set oneself against, resist, (*a*) of men, Acts 18:6, "opposed themselves"; elsewhere to resist, of resisting human potentates, Rom. 13:2; (*b*) of God, Jas. 4:6; 5:6, negatively, of leaving persistent evildoers to pursue their self-determined course, with eventual retribution; 1 Pet. 5:5. See OPPOSE. ¶
NT: B.76a; CB.—; K.—.
OT: nāśā': S.5375; HR.112a.2; H.1421; BD.669d.
shît: S.7896; HR.112a.4; H.2380; BD.1011a.
GEN. REF.: —.

4. *antipiptō* [ἀντιπίπτω, 496], lit., and primarily, to fall against or upon (*anti*, against, *piptō*, to fall), then, to strive against, resist, is used in Acts 7:51; of resisting the Holy Spirit. ¶
NT: B.75d; CB.—; K.—.
OT: shûb: S.7725; HR.111c.3; H.2340; BD.996d.
GEN. REF.: —.

RESOLVE

ginōskō [γινώσκω, 1097], to come to know, perceive, realize, is used in the 2nd aorist tense in Luke 16:4. "I am resolved," expressing the definiteness of the steward's realization, and his consequent determination of his course of action. See KNOW.
NT: B.160d; CB.1248b; K.119.
OT: yāda': S.3045; HR.267a.4a; H.848; BD.393b.
GEN. REF.: —.

RESORT

1. *erchomai* [ἔρχομαι, 2064], to come, is translated "resorted" in Mark 2:13; in John 10:41 (R.V., "came"). See COME, No. 1.
NT: B.310b; CB.1246b; K.257.
OT: bô': S.935; HR.548b.5a; H.212; BD.97c.
GEN. REF.: —.

2. *epiporeuomai* [ἐπιπορεύομαι, 1975], to travel or journey to a place (*epi*, to, *poreuomai*, to go), is translated "resorted" in Luke 8:4, R.V. (A.V., "were come"). ¶
NT: B.298a; CB.—; K.—.
OT: 'ābar: S.5674; HR.527a.2; H.1556; BD.716d.
GEN. REF.: —.

3. *sunagō* [συνάγω, 4863], to gather or bring together (*sun*, with, *agō*, to bring), in the Passive Voice, to be gathered or come together, is translated "resorted" in John 18:2 (the aorist tense expressing repeated action viewed cumulatively). See ASSEMBLE, GATHER, LEAD, *Note* (1).
NT: B.782a; CB.1270b; K.—.
OT: qābaṣ: S.6908; HR.1307b.34; H.1983; BD.867c.
GEN. REF.: —.

Notes: (1) In the A.V. of John 18:20 and Acts 16:13, *sunerchomai*, to come together (R.V.), is translated to resort.

(2) In Mark 10:1, A.V., *sumporeuomai*, to come together (R.V.), is translated "resort."

RESPECT (Noun and Verb)

A. Noun.

meros [μέρος, 3313], a part, has occasionally the meaning of a class or category, and, used in the dative case with *en*, in, signifies 'in respect of,' 2 Cor. 3:10, "in (this) respect"; 9:3, R.V., A.V., "in (this) behalf"; Col. 2:16, "in respect of (a feast day)."
NT: B.505d; CB.1258b; K.585.
OT: —.
GEN. REF.: —.

B. Verbs.

1. *apoblepō* [ἀποβλέπω, 578], to look away from all else at one object (*apo*, from), hence, to look stedfastly, is translated "he had respect" in Heb. 11:26, A.V. (R.V., "looked"). See LOOK.
NT: B.89a; CB.1236c; K.—.
OT: pānāh: S.6437; HR.125c.2; H.1782; BD.815a.
rā'āh: S.7200; HR.125c.4; H.2095; BD.906b.
GEN. REF.: IS.4:142; NB.—; Z.—.

2. *epiblepō* [ἐπιβλέπω, 1914], to look upon (*epi*), is translated "have respect" in Jas. 2:3 (R.V. "regard"); see LOOK, No. 6.
NT: B.290b; CB.—; K.—.
OT: pānāh: S.6437; HR.516c.8a; H.1782; BD.815a.
rā'āh: S.7200; HR.516c.11; H.2095; BD.906b.
nābat: S.5027; HR.516c.4; H.1282; BD.613c.
GEN. REF.: IS.4:142; NB.—; Z.—.

Notes: (1) The following prepositions are translated "in respect of: "*peri*, concerning, in John 16:8, R.V.; *epi*, upon, over, in Heb. 11:4, R.V.; marg., 'over (his gifts)'; *kata*, in regard to, in Phil. 4:11.

(2) For "respect of persons" and "respecter of persons" see PERSON.

REST (Noun and Verb)

A. Nouns.

1. *anapausis* [ἀνάπαυσις, 372], cessation, refreshment, rest (*ana*, up, *pauō*, to make to cease), the constant word in the Sept. for the Sabbath rest, is used in Matt. 11:29; here the contrast seems to be to the burdens imposed by

the Pharisees. Christ's rest is not a rest from work, but in work, "not the rest of inactivity but of the harmonious working of all the faculties and affections — of will, heart, imagination, conscience — because each has found in God the ideal sphere for its satisfaction and development" (J. Patrick, in Hastings' Bib. Dic.); it occurs also in Matt. 12:43; Luke 11:24; Rev. 4:8, R.V., "(they have no) rest" [A.V., "(they) rest (not)"], where the noun is the object of the verb *echō*, to have; so in 14:11. ¶

NT: B.58d; CB.1235b; K.56.
OT: shabbātôn: S.7677; HR.80c.4c; H.2323d; BD.992d.
mānôaḥ: S.4494; HR.80c.1b; H.1323e; BD.629d.
mᵉnûḥāh: S.4496; HR.80c.1c; H.1323f; BD.629d.
GEN. REF.: IS.4:142; NB.1085; Z.5:68.

2. *katapausis* [κατάπαυσις, 2663], in classical Greek, denotes a causing to cease or putting to rest; in the N.T., rest, repose; it is used (*a*) of God's rest, Acts 7:49; Heb. 3:11, 18; 4:1, 3 (twice), R.V. (1st part), "that rest" (the A.V., "rest," is ambiguous), 5, 11; (*b*) in a general statement, applicable to God and man, 4:10. ¶

NT: B.415d; CB.1254a; K.419.
OT: shābat: S.7676; HR.741a.3; H.2323b; BD.992a.
mānôaḥ: S.4494; HR.741a.2c; H.1323e; BD.629d.
mᵉnûḥāh: S.4496; HR.741a.2d; H.1323f; BD.629d.
GEN. REF.: IS.4:142; NB.1085; Z.5:68.

3. *anesis* [ἄνεσις, 425], for the significance of which see EASE, b, is translated "rest" in 2 Cor. 2:13, A.V. (R.V., "relief"); 7:5 (ditto); in 2 Thess. 1:7, the subject is not the rest to be granted to the saints, but the Divine retribution on their persecutors; hence the phrase "and to you that are afflicted rest with us," is an incidental extension of the idea of recompense, and to be read parenthetically. The time is not that at which the saints will be relieved of persecution, as in 1 Thess. 4:15-17, when the Parousia of Christ begins, but that at which the persecutors will be punished, namely, at the epiphany (or out-shining) of His Parousia (2 Thess. 2:8). For similar parentheses characteristic of epistolary writings see ver. 10; 1 Thess. 1:6; 2:15, 16.

NT: B.65b; CB.—; K.60.
OT: —.
GEN. REF.: IS.4:142; NB.—; Z.—.

4. *sabbatismos* [σαββατισμός, 4520], a Sabbath-keeping, is used in Heb. 4:9, R.V., "a sabbath rest," A.V. marg., "a keeping, of a sabbath" (akin to *sabbatizō*, to keep the sabbath, used, e.g., in Ex. 16:30, not in the N.T.); here the sabbath-keeping is the perpetual sabbath rest to be enjoyed uninterruptedly by believers in their fellowship with the Father and the Son, in contrast to the weekly Sabbath under the Law. Because this sabbath rest is the rest of God Himself, 4:10, its full fruition is yet future, though believers now enter into it. In whatever way they enter into Divine rest, that which they enjoy is involved in an indissoluble relation with God. ¶

NT: B.739a; CB.1268b; K.989.
OT: —.
GEN. REF.: IS.4:142; NB.—; Z.—.

5. *koimēsis* [κοίμησις, 2838], a resting, reclining (akin to *keimai*, to lie), is used in John 11:13, of natural sleep, translated "taking rest," R.V. ¶

NT: B.437d; CB.—; K.—.
OT: —.
GEN. REF.: IS.4:142; NB.—; Z.—.

Note: In Acts 9:31, A.V., *eirēnē*, peace (R.V.), is translated "rest."

B. Verbs.

1. *anapauō* [ἀναπαύω, 373], akin to A, No. 1, in the Active Voice, signifies to give intermission from labour, to give rest, to refresh, Matt. 11:28; 1 Cor. 16:18, "have refreshed"; Philm. 20, "refresh"; Passive Voice, to be rested, refreshed, 2 Cor. 7:13, "was refreshed"; Philm. 7, "are refreshed"; in the Middle Voice, to take or enjoy rest, Matt. 26:45; Mark 6:31; 14:41; Luke 12:19, "take thine ease"; 1 Pet. 4:14; Rev. 6:11; 14:13. See REFRESH. ¶ In the papyri it is found as an agricultural term, e.g., of giving land rest by sowing light crops upon it. In inscriptions it is found on gravestones of Christians, followed by the date of death (Moulton and Milligan).

NT: B.58d; CB.1235b; K.56.
OT: nûaḥ: S.5117; HR.80b.3a; H.1323; BD.628a.
rābaṣ: S.7257; HR.80b.6; H.2109; BD.918b.
shākan: S.7931; HR.80b.12a; H.2387; BD.1014d.
GEN. REF.: IS.4:142; NB.1085; Z.5:68.

2. *katapauō* [καταπαύω, 2664], akin to A, No. 2, used transitively, signifies to cause to cease, restrain, Acts 14:18; to cause to rest, Heb. 4:8; intransitively, to rest, Heb. 4:4, 10. See CEASE, A, No. 6, RESTRAIN. ¶

NT: B.416a; CB.1254a; K.419.
OT: shābat: S.7673; HR.740c.11; H.2323; BD.991d.
nûah: S.5117; HR.740c.7; H.1323; BD.628a.
GEN. REF.: IS.4:142; NB.1085; Z.5:68.

3. *episkēnoō* [ἐπισκηνόω, 1981) to spread a tabernacle over (*epi*, upon, *skēnē*, a tent), is used metaphorically in 2 Cor. 12:9, "may rest upon (me)," R.V., marg., "cover," "spread a tabernacle over." ¶

NT: B.298d; CB.1246a; K.1040.
OT: —.
GEN. REF.: IS.4:142; NB.1085; Z.—.

4. *kataskēnoō* [κατασκηνόω, 2681], to pitch one's tent, lodge, is translated "shall rest," in Acts 2:26, A.V. (R.V., "shall dwell"). See LODGE.

NT: B.418c; CB.1254b; K.1040.
OT: shākan: S.7931; HR.744c.5a; H.2387; BD.1014d.
GEN. REF.: IS.4:142; NB.1085; Z.—.

5. *hēsuchazō* [ἡσυχάζω, 2270], to be still, to rest from labour, is translated "they rested" in Luke 23:56. See PEACE (hold one's), No. 3.

NT: B.349a; CB.1250a; K.–.
OT: shāqaṭ: S.8252; HR.620a.11; H.2453; BD.1052d.
GEN. REF.: IS.4:142; NB.1085; Z.–.

6. *epanapauō* [ἐπαναπαύω, 1879], to cause to rest, is used in the Middle Voice, metaphorically, signifying to rest upon (*epi*, upon, and No. 1), in Luke 10:6 and Rom. 2:17. ¶

NT: B.–; CB.1245b; K.56.
OT: nûah: S.5117; HR.506b.1; H.1323; BD.628a.
sha'an: S.8172; HR.506b.2; H.2434; BD.1043d.
GEN. REF.: IS.4:142; NB.1085; Z.5:68.

Note: For "find rest," Rom. 15:32, R.V., see REFRESH, No. 2.

REST (the)

1. *loipos* [λοιπός, 3062], remaining (for which see REMNANT), is frequently used to mean "the rest," and is generally so translated in the R.V. (A.V., "others" in Luke 8:10; Acts 28:9; Eph. 2:3; 1 Thess. 4:13; 5:6; 1 Tim. 5:20; A.V., "other" in Luke 18:11; Acts 17:9; Rom. 1:13; 2 Cor. 12:13; 13:2; Gal. 2:13; Phil. 1:13; 4:3); the neut. plur., lit., 'remaining things,' is used in Luke 12:26; 1 Cor. 11:34.

NT: B.479d; CB.1257b; K.–.
OT: yeter: S.3499; HR.888a.1c; H.936a; BD.451d.
sh^{e}'ār: S.7605; HR.888a.4a; H.2307a; BD.984b.
sh^{e}'ērît: S.7611; HR.888a.4c; H.2307b; BD.984c.
GEN. REF.: IS.4:142; NB.–; Z.–.

2. *epiloipos* [ἐπίλοιπος, 1954], signifying still left, left over (*epi*, over, and No. 1), is used in the neuter with the article in 1 Pet. 4:2, "the rest (of your time)." ¶

NT: B.295d; CB.–; K.–.
OT: yeter: S.3499; HR.525a.1b; H.936a; BD.451d.
sh^{e}'ār: S.7605; HR.525a.2b; H.2307a; BD.984b.
sh^{e}'ērît: S.7611; HR.525a.2c; H.2307b; BD.984c.
GEN. REF.: IS.4:142; NB.–; Z.–.

For **RESTITUTION** see **RESTORATION**

RESTLESS

akatastatos [ἀκατάστατος, 182], unsettled, unstable, disorderly (*a*, negative, *kathistēmi*, to set in order), is translated "unstable" in Jas. 1:8; "restless" in 3:8, R.V. [in the latter, the A.V. "unruly" represents the word *akataschetos*, signifying 'that cannot be restrained' (*a*, negative, *katechō*, to hold down, restrain). In the Sept., Job 31:11 ¶]. See UNRULY, UNSTABLE. ¶ In the Sept., Isa. 54:11. ¶

NT: B.30b; CB.–; K.387.
OT: sā'ar: S.5590; HR.44a.1; H.1528b; BD.704a.
GEN. REF.: –.

RESTORATION

apokatastasis [ἀποκατάστασις, 605], from *apo*, back, again, *kathistēmi*, to set in order, is used in Acts 3:21, R.V., "restoration" (A.V., "restitution"). See under REGENERATION, concerning Israel in its regenerated state hereafter. In the papyri it is used of a temple cell of a goddess, a repair of a public way, the restoration of estates to rightful owners, a balancing of accounts. Apart from papyri illustrations the word is found in an Egyptian reference to a consummating agreement of the world's cyclical periods, an idea somewhat similar to that in the Acts passage (Moulton and Milligan). ¶

NT: B.30a; CB.–; K.–.
OT: –.
GEN. REF.: IS.4:144; NB.1085; Z.–.

RESTORE

1. *apodidōmi* [ἀποδίδωμι, 591], to give back, is translated "I restore" in Luke 19:8. See DELIVER, A, No. 3.

NT: B.90b; CB.1236c; K.166.
OT: shûb: S.7725; HR.126b.8b; H.2340; BD.996d.
shālēm: S.7999; HR.126b.9; H.2401c; BD.1022a.
mākar: S.4376; HR.126b.3a; H.1194; BD.569a.
GEN. REF.: IS.4:144; NB.–; Z.–.

2. *apokathistēmi* or the alternative form *apokathistanō* [ἀποκαθίστημι, 600], is used (*a*) of restoration to a former condition of health, Matt. 12:13; Mark 3:5; 8:25; Luke 6:10; (*b*) of the Divine restoration of Israel and conditions affected by it, including the renewal of the Covenant broken by them, Matt. 17:11; Mark 9:12; Acts 1:6; (*c*) of giving or bringing a person back, Heb. 13:19. ¶ In the papyri it is used of financial restitution, of making good the breaking of a stone by a workman by his substituting another, of the reclamation of land, etc. (Moulton and Milligan).

NT: B.91d; CB.1237a; K.65.
OT: shûb: S.7725; HR.131b.5a-c; H.2340; BD.996d.
GEN. REF.: IS.4:144; NB.–; Z.–.

3. *katartizō* [καταρτίζω, 2675], to mend, to furnish completely, is translated "restore" in Gal. 6:1, metaphorically, of the restoration, by those who are spiritual, of one overtaken in a trespass, such a one being as a dislocated member of the spiritual body. The tense is the continuous present, suggesting the necessity for patience and perseverance in the process. See FIT, MEND, PERFECT.

NT: B.417d; CB.1254b; K.80.
OT: kûn: S.3559; HR.743b.3; H.964; BD.465c.
k^{e}lal (Aramaic): S.3635; HR.743b.4; H.2788; BD.1097a.
GEN. REF.: IS.4:144; NB.–; Z.–.

RESTRAIN

1. *katapauō* [καταπαύω, —]; see REST, B, No. 2.

2. *katechō* [κατέχω, 2722], to hold fast or down, is translated "restraineth" in 2 Thess. 2:6 and 7. In ver. 6 lawlessness is spoken of as being restrained in its development: in ver. 7 "one that restraineth" is, lit., 'the restrainer' (the article with the present participle, 'the restraining one'); this may refer to an individual, as in the similar construction in 1 Thess. 3:5, "the tempter" (cp. 1:10, lit., 'the Deliverer'); or to a number of persons presenting the same characteristics, just as 'the believer' stands for all believers, e.g., Rom. 9:33; 1 John 5:10. Ver. 6 speaks of a principle, ver. 7 of the principle as embodied in a person or series of persons; cp. what is said of "the power" in Rom. 13:3, 4, a phrase representing all such rulers. Probably such powers, i.e, 'constituted governments,' are the restraining influence here intimated (specifications being designedly withheld). For an extended exposition see Notes on Thessalonians, by Hogg and Vine, pp. 254-261.

NT: B.422c; CB.1254b; K.286.
OT: 'āḥaz: S.270; HR.750c.1; H.64; BD.28a.
ḥāzaq: S.2388; HR.750c.5; H.636; BD.304a.
GEN. REF.: IS.4:144; NB.—; Z.—.

RESURRECTION

1. *anastasis* [ἀνάστασις, 386], denotes (I) a raising up, or rising (*ana*, up, and *histēmi*, to cause to stand), Luke 2:34, "the rising up"; the A.V. "again" obscures the meaning; the Child would be like a stone against which many in Israel would stumble while many others would find in its strength and firmness a means of their salvation and spiritual life; (II) of resurrection from the dead, (*a*) of Christ, Acts 1:22; 2:31; 4:33; Rom. 1:4; 6:5; Phil. 3:10; 1 Pet. 1:3; 3:21; by metonymy, of Christ as the Author of resurrection, John 11:25; (*b*) of those who are Christ's at His Parousia (see COMING), Luke 14:14, "the resurrection of the just"; Luke 20:33, 35, 36; John 5:29 (1st part), "the resurrection of life"; 11:24; Acts 23:6; 24:15 (1st part); 1 Cor. 15:21, 42; 2 Tim. 2:18; Heb. 11:35 (2nd part), see RAISE, *Note* (3); Rev. 20:5, "the first resurrection"; hence the insertion of "is" stands for the completion of this resurrection, of which Christ was "the firstfruits"; 20:6; (*c*) of "the rest of the dead," after the Millennium (cp. Rev. 20:5); John 5:29 (2nd part), "the resurrection of judgment"; Acts 24:15 (2nd part), "of the unjust"; (*d*) of those who were raised in more immediate connection with Christ's resurrection, and thus had part already in the first resurrection, Acts 26:23, and Rom. 1:4 (in each of which "dead" is plural; see Matt. 27:52); (*e*) of the resurrection spoken of in general terms, Matt. 22:23; Mark 12:18; Luke 20:27; Acts 4:2; 17:18; 23:8; 24:21; 1 Cor. 15:12, 13; Heb. 6:2; (*f*) of those who were raised in O.T. times, to die again, Heb. 11:35 (1st part), lit., 'out of resurrection.' ¶

NT: B.60b; CB.1235b; K.60.
OT: qûm: S.6965; HR.82a.1a; H.1999; BD.877c.
qîmāh: S.7012; HR.82a.1b; H.1999d; BD.879c.
GEN. REF.: IS.4:145; NB.1086; Z.5:70.

2. *exanastasis* [ἐξανάστασις, 1815], *ek*, from or out of, and No. 1, Phil. 3:11, followed by *ek*, lit., 'the out-of-resurrection from among the dead.' For the significance of this see ATTAIN, No. 1. ¶

NT: B.272d; CB.1247c; K.60.
OT: —.
GEN. REF.: IS.4:145; NB.1086; Z.—.

3. *egersis* [ἔγερσις, 1454], a rousing (akin to *egeirō*, to arouse, to raise), is used of the resurrection of Christ, in Matt. 27:53. ¶

NT: B.215b; CB.1242c; K.195.
OT: qûm: S.6965; HR.361b.1; H.1999; BD.877c.
GEN. REF.: IS.4:145; NB.1086; Z.5:70.

RETAIN

krateō [κρατέω, 2902], to be strong, obtain, hold, hold fast, is translated to retain, of sins, John 20:23 (twice); see on REMIT. See HOLD, KEEP, OBTAIN, TAKE.

NT: B.448c; CB.1256a; K.466.
OT: 'āḥaz: S.270; HR.783a.2a; H.64; BD.28a.
ḥāzaq: S.2388; HR.783a.6a-c; H.636; BD.304a.
GEN. REF.: IS.4:154; NB.—; Z.—.

Notes: (1) In Philm. 13, A.V., *katechō*, to hold fast, hold back, detain, is translated to retain (R.V., to keep).

(2) In Rom. 1:28, A.V., *echō*, "to have" (R.V.), is translated "to retain."

RETURN

1. *analuō* [ἀναλύω, 360], to depart in Phil. 1:23, signifies to return in Luke 12:36, used in a simile of the return of a lord for his servants after a marriage feast (R.V.). See DEPART, No. 16. ¶

NT: B.57c; CB.1235a; K.543.
OT: —.
GEN. REF.: IS.4:159; NB.—; Z.—.

2. *anastrephō* [ἀναστρέφω, 390], to turn back, is translated to return in Acts 5:22 and 15:16. See ABIDE, BEHAVE.

NT: B.61b; CB.1235b; K.1093.
OT: shûb: S.7725; HR.82b.8a; H.2340; BD.996d.
GEN. REF.: IS.4:159; NB.—; Z.—.

3. *epistrephō* [ἐπιστρέφω, 1994], to turn about, or towards, is translated to return in Matt. 12:44; 24:18; Mark 13:16, R.V. (A.V., "turn back again"); Luke 2:39; 8:55, R.V. (A.V.,

"came again"); 17:31; Acts 15:36, R.V. (A.V., "go again"). See CONVERT, A, No. 2, TURN.

NT: B.301a; CB.1246a; K.1093.
OT: shûb: S.7725; HR.531a.18a-c; H.2340; BD.996d.
pānāh: S.6437; HR.531a.16; H.1782; BD.815a.
GEN. REF.: IS.4:159; NB.–; Z.–.

4. *hupostrephō* [ὑποστρέφω, 5290], to turn behind, or back (*hupo*, under), is translated to return (in some texts in Mark 14:40) in Luke 1:56; 2:20, 43; ver. 45, R.V. (A.V., "turned back again"); 4:1, 14; 7:10, 8:37; 10:17; 11:24, A.V. (R.V., "I will turn back"); 17:18; 19:12; 23:48, 56; Acts 1:12; 12:25; 13:13; 13:34; 20:3; 21:6; 22:17, R.V. (A.V., "was come again"); 23:32; Gal. 1:17; Heb. 7:1. See TURN (back).

NT: B.847c; CB.–; K.–.
OT: shûb: S.7725; HR.1417b.4a; H.2340; BD.996d.
GEN. REF.: IS.4:159; NB.–; Z.–.

5. *anakamptō* [ἀνακάμπτω, 344], to turn or bend back, occurs in Matt. 2:12; Luke 10:6 (i.e., as if it was unsaid); Acts 18:21; Heb. 11:15. ¶

NT: B.55c; CB.–; K.–.
OT: shûb: S.7725; HR.78b.2; H.2340; BD.996d.
GEN. REF.: IS.4:159; NB.–; Z.–.

5. *epanagō* [ἐπανάγω, 1877], to bring up or back (primarily a nautical term for putting to sea; see LAUNCH, PUT), is used intransitively, in Matt. 21:18, "He returned."

NT: B.282d; CB.–; K.–.
OT: –.
GEN. REF.: IS.4:159; NB.–; Z.–.

Note: In Luke 19:15, A.V., *epanerchomai*, to come back again (R.V.) is translated "returned." See COME, No. 4.

REVEAL

1. *apokaluptō* [ἀποκαλύπτω, 601], signifies to uncover, unveil (*apo*, from, *kaluptō*, to cover); both verbs are used in Matt. 10:26; in Luke 12:2, *apokaluptō* is set in contrast to *sunkaluptō*, to cover up, cover completely. "The N.T. occurrences of this word fall under two heads, subjective and objective. The subjective use is that in which something is presented to the mind directly, as, (*a*) the meaning of the acts of God, Matt. 11:25; Luke 10:21; (*b*) the secret of the Person of the Lord Jesus, Matt. 16:17; John 12:38; (*c*) the character of God as Father, Matt. 11:27; Luke 10:22; (*d*) the will of God for the conduct of His children, Phil. 3:15; (*e*) the mind of God to the prophets of Israel, 1 Pet. 1:12, and of the Church, 1 Cor. 14:30; Eph. 3:5.

"The objective use is that in which something is presented to the senses, sight or hearing, as, referring to the past, (*f*) the truth declared to men in the gospel, Rom. 1:17; 1 Cor. 2:10; Gal. 3:23; (*g*) the Person of Christ to Paul on the way to Damascus, Gal. 1:16; (*h*) thoughts before hidden in the heart, Luke 2:35; referring to the future, (*i*) the coming in glory of the Lord Jesus, Luke 17:30; (*j*) the salvation and glory that await the believer, Rom. 8:18; 1 Pet. 1:5; 5:1; (*k*) the true value of service, 1 Cor. 3:13; (*l*) the wrath of God (at the Cross, against sin, and, at the revelation of the Lord Jesus, against the sinner), Rom. 1:18; (*m*) the Lawless One, 2 Thess. 2:3, 6, 8."* ¶

NT: B.92a; CB.1236c; K.405.
OT: gālāh: S.1540; HR.131c.1a-d; H.350; BD.162d.
GEN. REF.: IS.4:161; NB.1090; Z.5:86.

2. *chrēmatizō* [χρηματίζω, 5537], to give Divine admonition, instruction, revelation, is translated "it had been revealed," in Luke 2:26. See ADMONITION, B, No. 3. CALL.

NT: B.885c; CB.1240a; K.1319.
OT: dābar: S.1696; HR.1474c.1; H.399; BD.180b.
GEN. REF.: IS.4:161; NB.–; Z.–.

REVELATION

apokalupsis [ἀποκάλυψις, 602], an uncovering (akin to *apokaluptō*; see above), "is used in the N.T. of (*a*) the drawing away by Christ of the veil of darkness covering the Gentiles, Luke 2:32; cp. Isa. 25:7; (*b*) 'the mystery,' the purpose of God in this age, Rom. 16:25; Eph. 3:3; (*c*) the communication of the knowledge of God to the soul, Eph. 1:17; (*d*) an expression of the mind of God for the instruction of the church, 1 Cor. 14:6, 26, for the instruction of the Apostle Paul, 2 Cor. 12:1, 7; Gal. 1:12, and for his guidance, Gal. 2:2; (*e*) the Lord Jesus Christ, to the saints at His Parousia, 1 Cor. 1:7, R.V. (A.V., 'coming'); 1 Pet. 1:7, R.V. (A.V., 'appearing'), 13; 4:13; (*f*) the Lord Jesus Christ when He comes to dispense the judgments of God, 2 Thess. 1:7; cp. Rom. 2:5; (*g*) the saints, to the creation, in association with Christ in His glorious reign, Rom. 8:19, R.V., 'revealing' (A.V., 'manifestation'); (*h*) the symbolic forecast of the final judgments of God, Rev. 1:1 (hence the Greek title of the book, transliterated 'Apocalypse' and translated 'Revelation')."† See APPEARING, COMING, LIGHTEN, B, *Note*, MANIFESTATION. ¶

NT: B.92b; CB.1236c; K.405.
OT: –.
GEN. REF.: IS.4:161; NB.1090; Z.5:86.

REVEL, REVELLING

1. *truphē* [τρυφή, 5172], luxuriousness, daintiness, revelling, is translated freely by the verb "to revel" in 2 Pet. 2:13, R.V. (A.V., "to riot"), lit., 'counting revelling in the daytime a pleasure.' In Luke 7:25 it is used with *en*, in,

* From Notes on Galatians by Hogg and Vine, pp. 41, 42.

† From Notes on Thessalonians by Hogg and Vine, pp. 228, 229.

and translated "delicately." See DELICATELY, RIOT. ¶

NT: B.828d; CB.—; K.—.
OT: 'ēden: S.5730; HR.1377c.1a; H.1568a; BD.726c.
ma'adannîm: S.4574; HR.1377c.1b; H.1568d; BD.726d.
GEN. REF.: IS.4:171; NB.—; Z.—.

2. *kōmos* [κῶμος, 2970], a revel, carousal, the concomitant and consequence of drunkenness, is used in the plural, Rom. 13:13, translated by the singular, R.V., "revelling" (A.V., "rioting"); Gal. 5:21 and 1 Pet. 4:3, "revellings." See RIOT.

NT: B.461d; CB.1255c; K.—.
OT: —.
GEN. REF.: IS.4:171; NB.—; Z.—.

Note: For *entruphaō*, 2 Pet. 2:13, R.V., "to revel," see SPORTING.

For REVENGE and REVENGER see AVENGE and AVENGER

REVERENCE (Noun and Verb)

A. Verbs.

1. *entrepō* [ἐντρέπω, 1788], lit., to turn in (i.e., upon oneself), to put to shame, denotes, when used in the Passive Voice to feel respect for, to show deference to, to reverence, Matt. 21:37; Mark 12:6; Luke 20:13; Heb. 12:9. See ASHAMED, A, No. 4, REGARD.

NT: B.269c; CB.—; K.—.
OT: kālam: S.3637; HR.480c.2; H.987; BD.483c.
kāna': S.3665; HR.480c.4; H.1001; BD.488b.
GEN. REF.: —.

2. *phobeō* [φοβέω, 5399], to fear, is used in the Passive Voice in the N.T.; in Eph. 5:33 of reverential fear on the part of a wife for a husband, A.V., "reverence" (R.V., "fear"). See FEAR, D, No. 1.

NT: B.862b; CB.1264b; K.1272.
OT: yārē': S.3372; HR.1433b.9; H.907,908; BD.431a.
GEN. REF.: IS.4:177; NB.—; Z.5:99.

B. Noun.

eulabeia [εὐλάβεια, 2124], caution, reverence, is translated "reverence" in Heb. 12:28 (1st part in the best mss; some have *aidōs*). See FEAR.

NT: B.321d; CB.1247b; K.275.
OT: d^e'āgāh: S.1674; HR.572a.1; H.393a; BD.178c.
GEN. REF.: IS.4:177; NB.—; Z.5:99.

REVERENT

hieroprepēs [ἱεροπρεπής, 2412], suited to a sacred character, reverend (*hieros*, sacred, *prepō*, to be fitting), is translated "reverent" in Tit. 2:3, R.V. (A.V., "as becometh holiness"). See BECOME, B. ¶

NT: B.372d; CB.1250b; K.—.
OT: —.
GEN. REF.: IS.4:177; NB.—; Z.—.

REVILE, REVILING, REVILER

A. Verbs.

1. *loidoreō* [λοιδορέω, 3058], denotes to abuse, revile, John 9:28; Acts 23:4; 1 Cor. 4:12; 1 Pet. 2:23 (1st clause). ¶

NT: B.479c; CB.1257a; K.538.
OT: rîb: S.7378; HR.887b.2; H.2159; BD.936b.
GEN. REF.: IS.4:177; NB.—; Z.—.

2. *oneidizō* [ὀνειδίζω, 3679], to reproach, upbraid, is translated to revile in Matt. 5:11, A.V., and Mark 15:32 (R.V., "reproach"). See REPROACH.

NT: B.570a; CB.1260c; K.693.
OT: ḥāraph: S.2778; HR.994b.2; H.749-751; BD.357c.
GEN. REF.: IS.4:177; NB.—; Z.—.

3. *blasphēmeō* [βλασφημέω, 987], to speak profanely, rail at, is translated "reviled" in Matt. 27:39, A.V., (R.V., "railed on"); Luke 22:65, R.V., "reviling" (A.V., "blasphemously").

NT: B.142c; CB.1239a; K.107.
OT: gādaph: S.1442; HR.221a.1; H.317; BD.154c.
GEN. REF.: IS.4:177; NB.—; Z.—.

4. *antiloidoreō* [ἀντιλοιδορέω, 486], to revile back or again (*anti*, and No. 1), is found in 1 Pet. 2:23 (2nd clause). ¶

NT: B.75a; CB.1236a; K.538.
OT: —.
GEN. REF.: IS.4:177; NB.—; Z.—.

Note: For *epēreazō*, 1 Pet. 3:16, R.V., "revile," see ACCUSE, B, No. 3.

B. Adjective.

loidoros [λοίδορος, 3060], akin to A, No. 1, abusive, railing, reviling, is used as a noun, 1 Cor. 5:11, R.V., "a reviler" (A.V., "a railer"); 6:10, "revilers." ¶ In the Sept., Prov. 25:24; 26:21; 27:15. ¶

NT: B.479c; CB.1257b; K.538.
OT: midyān: S.4079; HR.887c.1; H.426c; BD.193b.
GEN. REF.: IS.4:177; NB.—; Z.—.

C. Noun.

loidoria [λοιδορία, 3059], akin to A, No. 1, and B, abuse, railing, is used in 1 Tim. 5:14, R.V., "for (*charin*, for the sake of) reviling" (A.V., "to speak reproachfully" — a paraphrase); 1 Pet. 3:9 (twice), R.V., "reviling" (A.V., "railing"). See RAIL, B. ¶

NT: B.479c; CB.1257a; K.538.
OT: rîb: S.7379; HR.887c.2a; H.2159a; BD.936d.
GEN. REF.: IS.4:177; NB.—; Z.—.

REVIVE

1. *anathallō* [ἀναθάλλω, 330], to flourish anew (*ana*, again, anew, *thallō*, to flourish or blossom), hence, to revive, is used metaphorically in Phil. 4:10, R.V., "ye have revived (your thought for me)," A.V., "(your care of me) hath flourished again." ¶ In the Sept., Psa. 28:7; Ezek. 17:24; Hos. 8:9. ¶

NT: B.54a; CB.—; K.—.
OT: pāraḥ: S.6524; HR.77a.2; H.1813-1815; BD.827a.
'ālaz: S.5937; HR.77a.1; H.1625; BD.759c.
GEN. REF.: IS.4:178; NB.—; Z.—.

2. *anazaō* [ἀναζάω, 326], to live again (*ana*, and *zaō*, to live), to regain life, is used of moral revival, Luke 15:24, "is alive again"; (*b*) of sin, Rom. 7:9, "revived," lit., 'lived again' i.e., it sprang into activity, manifesting the evil inherent in it; here sin is personified, by way of contrast to the man himself. Some mss. have it in Rom. 14:9, for *zaō*, as in the R.V., which italicises "*again*." ¶

NT: B.53d; CB.1235b; K.290.
OT: pāraḥ: S.6524; HR.76c.1; H.1813-1815; BD.827a.
GEN. REF.: IS.4:178; NB.–; Z.–.

REWARD (Noun and Verb)

A. Noun.

misthos [μισθός, 3408], primarily wages, hire, and then, generally, reward, (*a*) received in this life, Matt. 5:46; 6:2, 5, 16; Rom. 4:4; 1 Cor. 9:17, 18; of evil rewards, Acts 1:18; see also HIRE; (*b*) to be received hereafter, Matt. 5:12; 10:41 (twice), 42; Mark 9:41; Luke 6:23, 35; 1 Cor. 3:8, 14; 2 John 8; Rev. 11:18; 22:12. See WAGES.

NT: B.523b; CB.1259a; K.599.
OT: sākar: S.7939; HR.930a.6a; H.2264.1b; BD.969a.
maskōret: S.4909; HR.930a.6b; H.2264.1d; BD.969b.
GEN. REF.: IS.4:179; NB.1095; Z.5:99.

Notes: (1) In Luke 23:41, *axios*, worthy, befitting, used in the plur., is rendered "the due reward," lit., 'things worthy.'

(2) For *antapodosis*, rendered "reward" in Col. 3:24, A.V., see RECOMPENSE.

(3) For *katabrabeuō*, to rob of a reward, Col. 2:18, see BEGUILE, *Note*, and ROB.

B. Verb.

apodidōmi [ἀποδίδωμι, 591], to give back, is nowhere translated to reward in the R.V.; A.V., Matt. 6:4, 6, 18 (see RECOMPENSE, B. No. 2); Matt. 16:27; 2 Tim. 4:14; Rev. 18:6 (see RENDER).

NT: B.90b; CB.1236c; K.166.
OT: shûb: S.7725; HR.126b.8b; H.2340; BD.996d.
shālēm: S.7999; HR.126b.9; H.2401c; BD.1022a.
mākar: S.4376; HR.126b.3a; H.1194; BD.569a.
GEN. REF.: IS.4:179; NB.1095; Z.–.

REWARDER

misthapodotēs [μισθαποδότης, 3406], one who pays wages (*misthos*, wages, *apo*, back, *didōmi*, to give), is used by metonymy in Heb. 11:6, of God, as the "Rewarder" of those who "seek after Him" (R.V.). ¶ Cp. *misthapodosia*, recompence.

NT: B.523a; CB.1259a; K.599.
OT: –.
GEN. REF.: IS.4:179; NB.–; Z.–.

RICH, RICHES, RICHLY, RICH MAN

A. Adjective.

plousios [πλούσιος, 4145], akin to B, C, No. 1, rich, wealthy, is used (I) literally, (*a*) adjectivally (with a noun expressed separately) in Matt. 27:57; Luke 12:16; 14:12; 16:1, 19; (without a noun), 18:23; 19:2; (*b*) as a noun, singular, a rich man (the noun not being expressed), Matt. 19:23, 24; Mark 10:25; 12:41; Luke 16:21, 22; 18:25; Jas. 1:10, 11, "the rich," "the rich (man)"; plural, Mark 12:41, lit., 'rich (ones)'; Luke 6:24 (ditto); 21:1; 1 Tim. 6:17, "(them that are) rich," lit., '(the) rich'; Jas. 2:6, R.V., "the rich"; 5:1, R.V., "ye rich"; Rev. 6:15 and 13:16, R.V., "the rich"; (II) metaphorically, of God, Eph. 2:4 ("in mercy"); of Christ, 2 Cor. 8:9; of believers, Jas. 2:5, R.V., "(*to be*) rich (in faith)"; Rev. 2:9, of spiritual enrichment generally; 3:17, of a false sense of enrichment. ¶

NT: B.673c; CB.1265b; K.873.
OT: 'āshîr: S.6223; HR.1150b.3a; H.1714b; BD.799b.
GEN. REF.: IS.4:185; NB.–; Z.5:909.

B. Verbs.

1. *plouteō* [πλουτέω, 4147], to be rich, in the aorist or point tense, to become rich, is used (*a*) literally, Luke 1:53, "the rich," present participle, lit., '(ones or those) being rich'; 1 Tim. 6:9, 18; Rev. 18:3, 15, 19 (all three in the aorist tense); (*b*) metaphorically, of Christ, Rom. 10:12 (the passage stresses the fact that Christ is Lord; see ver. 9, and the R.V.); of the enrichment of believers through His poverty, 2 Cor. 8:9 (the aorist tense expressing completeness, with permanent results); so in Rev. 3:18, where the spiritual enrichment is conditional upon righteousness of life and conduct (see GOLD, No. 2); of a false sense of enrichment, 1 Cor. 4:8 (aorist), R.V., "ye are become rich" (A.V., "ye are rich"); Rev. 3:17 (perfect tense, R.V., "I . . . have gotten riches," A.V., "I am . . . increased with goods"), see GOODS, *Note* (3); of not being rich toward God, Luke 12:21. ¶

NT: B.673d; CB.1265b; K.873.
OT: 'āshar: S.6238; HR.1150c.2a; H.1714; BD.799a.
'āshîr: S.6223; HR.1150c.2c; H.1714b; BD.799b.
GEN. REF.: IS.4:185; NB.–; Z.5:909.

2. *ploutizō* [πλουτίζω, 4148], to make rich, enrich, is rendered "making (many) rich" in 2 Cor. 6:10 (metaphorical of enriching spiritually). See ENRICH.

NT: B.674a; CB.1265b; K.873.
OT: 'āshar: S.6238; HR.1150c.1; H.1714; BD.799a.
GEN. REF.: IS.4:185; NB.–; Z.5:909.

C. Nouns.

1. *ploutos* [πλοῦτος, 4149], is used in the singular (I) of material riches, used evilly, Matt. 13:22; Mark 4:19; Luke 8:14; 1 Tim. 6:17; Jas. 5:2; Rev. 18:17; (II) of spiritual and moral riches, (*a*) possessed by God and exercised towards men, Rom. 2:4, "of His goodness and forbearance and longsuffering"; 9:23 and Eph. 3:16, "of His glory" (i.e., of its manifestation in grace towards believers); Rom. 11:33, of His wisdom and knowledge; Eph. 1:7 and 2:7, "of His grace"; 1:18, "of the glory of His inheritance in the saints"; 3:8, "of Christ"; Phil. 4:19, "in glory in Christ Jesus," R.V.; Col. 1:27, "of the glory of this mystery . . . Christ in you, the hope of glory"; (*b*) to be ascribed to Christ, Rev. 5:12; (*c*) of the effects of the gospel upon the Gentiles, Rom. 11:12 (twice); (*d*) of the full assurance of understanding in regard to the mystery of God, even Christ, Col. 2:2, R.V.; (*e*) of the liberality of the churches of Macedonia, 2 Cor. 8:2 (where "the riches" stands for the spiritual and moral value of their liberality); (*f*) of "the reproach of Christ" in contrast to this world's treasures, Heb. 11:26. ¶

NT: B.674b; CB.1265b; K.873.
OT: ‘ōsher: S.6239; HR.1150c.7a; H.1714a; BD.799b.
GEN. REF.: IS.4:185; NB.—; Z.5:909.

2. *chrēma* [χρῆμα, 5536], what one uses or needs (*chraomai*, to use), a matter, business, hence denotes riches, Mark 10:23, 24; Luke 18:24; see MONEY, No. 2.

NT: B.885c; CB.1240a; K.1319.
OT: n^{e}kāsîm: S.5233; HR.1474b.4; H.1367; BD.647d.
GEN. REF.: IS.4:185; NB.—; Z.—.

D. Adverb.

plousiōs [πλουσίως, 4146], richly, abundantly, akin to A, is used in Col. 3:16; 1 Tim. 6:17; Tit. 3:6, R.V., "richly" (A.V., "abundantly"); 2 Pet. 1:11 (ditto). ¶

NT: B.673d; CB.1265b; K.—.
OT: —.
GEN. REF.: IS.4:185; NB.—; Z.5:909.

For **RID** see **CARE**, A, No. 1, *Note*

RIDE

epibainō [ἐπιβαίνω, 1910], to go upon (*epi*, upon, *bainō*, to go), is used of Christ's riding into Jerusalem, Matt. 21:5, R.V., "riding" (A.V., "sitting"). See COME, No. 16.

NT: B.289d; CB.—; K.—.
OT: rākab: S.7392; HR.515c.10; H.2163; BD.938c.
GEN. REF.: —.

RIGHT (opp. to left), RIGHT HAND, RIGHT SIDE

dexios [δεξιός, 1188], an adjective, used (*a*) of the right as opposite to the left, e.g., Matt. 5:29, 30; Rev. 10:5, R.V., "right hand"; in connection with armour (figuratively), 2 Cor. 6:7; with *en*, followed by the dative plural, Mark 16:5; with *ek*, and the genitive plural, e.g., Matt. 25:33, 34; Luke 1:11; (*b*) of giving the right hand of fellowship, Gal. 2:9, betokening the public expression of approval by leaders at Jerusalem of the course pursued by Paul and Barnabas among the Gentiles; the act was often the sign of a pledge, e.g., 2 Kings 10:15; 1 Chron. 29:24, marg.; Ezra 10:19; Ezek. 17:18; figuratively Lam. 5:6; it is often so used in the papyri; (*c*) metaphorically of power or authority, Acts 2:33 with *ek*, signifying "on," followed by the genitive plural, Matt. 26:64; Mark 14:62; Heb. 1:13; (*d*) similarly of a place of honour in the Messianic Kingdom, Matt. 20:21; Mark 10:37.

NT: B.174c; CB.1241a; K.143.
OT: yāmîm: S.3225; HR.290a.2a; H.872a; BD.411c.
y^{e}mānî: S.3233; HR.290a.2c; H.872d; BD.412b.
GEN. REF.: IS.4:191; NB.—; Z.—.

RIGHT (not wrong — Noun and Adjective), RIGHTLY

A. Noun.

exousia [ἐξουσία, 1849], authority, power, is translated "right" in the R.V., for A.V. "power," in John 1:12; Rom. 9:21; 1 Cor. 9:4, 5, 6, 12 (twice), 18; 2 Thess. 3:9, where the right is that of being maintained by those among whom the ministers of the gospel had laboured, a right possessed in virtue of the 'authority' given them by Christ, Heb. 13:10; Rev. 22:14.

Exousia first denotes freedom to act and then authority for the action. This is first true of God, Acts 1:7. It was exercised by the Son of God, as from, and in conjunction with, the Father when the Lord was upon earth, in the days of His flesh, Matt. 9:6; John 10:18, as well as in resurrection, Matt. 28:18; John 17:2. All others hold their freedom to act from God (though some of them have abused it), whether angels, Eph. 1:21, or human potentates, Rom. 13:1. Satan offered to delegate his authority over earthly kingdoms to Christ, Luke 4:6, who, though conscious of His right to it, refused, awaiting the Divinely appointed time. See AUTHORITY, No. 1, and for various synonyms see DOMINION, No. 1, *Note*.

NT: B.277d; CB.1247c; K.238.
OT: memshālāh: S.4475; HR.500c.2; H.1259c; BD.606a.
shālṭān (Aramaic): S.7985; HR.500c.3b; H.3034a; BD.1115d.
GEN. REF.: IS.4:191; NB.—; Z.—.

B. Adjectives.

1. *dikaios* [δίκαιος, 1342], just, righteous, that which is in accordance with *dikē*, rule,

right, justice, is translated "right" in Matt. 20:4; ver. 7, A.V. only (R.V. omits, according to the most authentic mss., the clause having been inserted from ver. 4, to the detriment of the narrative); Luke 12:57; Acts 4:19; Eph. 6:1; Phil. 1:7, R.V. (A.V., "meet"); 2 Pet. 1:13 (A.V., "meet"). See JUST, RIGHTEOUS.

NT: B.195c; CB.1241c; K.168.
OT: ṣādîq: S.6662; HR.330c.10b; H.1879c; BD.843a.
GEN. REF.: IS.4:191; NB.–; Z.5:104.

2. *euthus* [εὐθύς, 2117], straight, hence, metaphorically, right, is so rendered in Acts 8:21, of the heart; 13:10, of the ways of the Lord; 2 Pet. 2:15. See STRAIGHT.

NT: B.321a; CB.1247b; K.–.
OT: yāshar: S.3474; HR.571a.2a,b; H.930; BD.448c.
yāshār: S.3477; HR.571a.2c; H.930a; BD.449a.
GEN. REF.: IS.4:191; NB.–; Z.5:104.

C. Adverb.

orthōs [ὀρθῶς, 3723], rightly (akin to *orthos*, straight, direct), is translated "plain" in Mark 7:35; in Luke 7:43 and 20:21, "rightly"; in Luke 10:28, "right." ¶

NT: B.580d; CB.1261b; K.–.
OT: yāṭab: S.3190; HR.1011c.1a; H.863; BD.405c.
tôb: S.2896; HR.1011c.1b; H.793a; BD.373c.
GEN. REF.: IS.4:191; NB.–; Z.–.

Notes: (1) For "right mind" see MIND, B, No. 5.

(2) For the A.V., "rightly" in 2 Tim. 2:15, see DIVIDE, A, No. 8.

RIGHTEOUS, RIGHTEOUSLY

A. Adjective.

dikaios [δίκαιος, 1342], signifies 'just,' without prejudice or partiality, e.g., of the judgment of God, 2 Thess. 1:5, 6; of His judgments. Rev. 16:7; 19:2; of His character as Judge, 2 Tim. 4:8; Rev. 16:5; of His ways and doings, Rev. 15:3. See further under JUST, A, No. 1, RIGHT, B, No. 1.

In the following the R.V. substitutes "righteous" for the A.V. "just"; Matt. 1:19; 13:49; 27:19, 24; Mark 6:20; Luke 2:25; 15:7; 20:20; 23:50; John 5:30; Acts 3:14; 7:52; 10:22; 22:14; Rom. 1:17; 7:12; Gal. 3:11; Heb. 10:38; Jas. 5:6; 1 Pet. 3:18; 2 Pet. 2:7; 1 John 1:9; Rev. 15:3.

NT: B.195c; CB.1241c; K.168.
OT: ṣadîq: S.6662; HR.330c.10b; H.1879c; BD.843a.
GEN. REF.: IS.4:192; NB.–; Z.5:104.

B. Adverb.

dikaiōs [δικαίως, 1346], is translated "righteously" in 1 Cor. 15:34, R.V., "(awake up) righteously," A.V., "(awake to) righteousness"; 1 Thess. 2:10, R.V. (A.V., "justly") Tit. 2:12; 1 Pet. 2:23. See JUSTLY

NT: B.198b; CB.1241c; K.–.
OT: ṣedeq: S.6664; HR.335a.2; H.1879a; BD.841c.
GEN. REF.: IS.4:192; NB.–; Z.5:104.

Notes: (1) In Rev. 22:11 the best texts have *dikaiosunē*, righteousness, with *poieō*, to do, R.V., "let him do righteousness"; the A.V. follows those which have the Passive Voice of *dikaioō* and renders it "let him be righteous," lit., 'let him be made righteous.'

(2) *Dikaiokrisia*, "righteous judgment" (*dikaios*, and *krisis*), occurs in Rom. 2:5. ¶

RIGHTEOUSNESS

1. *dikaiosunē* [δικαιοσύνη, 1343], is the character or quality of being right or just; it was formerly spelled 'rightwiseness,' which clearly expresses the meaning. It is used to denote an attribute of God, e.g., Rom. 3:5, the context of which shews that "the righteousness of God" means essentially the same as His faithfulness, or truthfulness, that which is consistent with His own nature and promises; Rom. 3:25, 26 speaks of His righteousness as exhibited in the Death of Christ, which is sufficient to shew men that God is neither indifferent to sin nor regards it lightly. On the contrary, it demonstrates that quality of holiness in Him which must find expression in His condemnation of sin.

"*Dikaiosunē* is found in the sayings of the Lord Jesus, (*a*) of whatever is right or just in itself, whatever conforms to the revealed will of God, Matt. 5:6, 10, 20; John 16:8, 10; (*b*) whatever has been appointed by God to be acknowledged and obeyed by man, Matt. 3:15; 21:32; (*c*) the sum total of the requirements of God, Matt. 6:33; (*d*) religious duties, Matt. 6:1 (distinguished as almsgiving, man's duty to his neighbour, vv. 2-4, prayer, his duty to God, vv. 5-15, fasting, the duty of self-control, vv. 16-18.

"In the preaching of the Apostles recorded in Acts the word has the same general meaning. So also in Jas. 1:20; 3:18, in both Epp. of Peter, 1st John and the Revelation. In 2 Pet. 1:1, 'the righteousness of our God and Saviour Jesus Christ,' is the righteous dealing of God with sin and with sinners on the ground of the Death of Christ. 'Word of righteousness,' Heb. 5:13, is probably the gospel, and the Scriptures as containing the gospel, wherein is declared the righteousness of God in all its aspects.

"This meaning of *dikaiosunē*, right action, is frequent also in Paul's writings, as in all five of its occurrences in Rom. 6; Eph. 6:14, etc. But for the most part he uses it of that gracious gift of God to men whereby all who believe on the Lord Jesus Christ are brought into right relationship with God. This righteousness is unattainable by obedience to any law, or by any merit of man's own, or any other condition than that of faith in Christ.... The man who trusts in Christ becomes 'the righteousness of God in Him,' 2 Cor. 5:21, i.e., becomes in Christ all that God requires a man to be, all that he could never be in himself. Because Abraham accepted the Word of God, making it his own by that act of the mind and spirit which is called faith, and, as the sequel showed, submitting himself to its control, therefore God accepted him as one who fulfilled the whole of His requirements, Rom. 4:3....

"Righteousness is not said to be imputed to the believer save in the sense that faith is imputed ('reckoned' is the better word) for righteousness. It is clear that in Rom. 4:6, 11, 'righteousness reckoned' must be understood in the light of the context, 'faith reckoned for righteousness,' vv. 3, 5, 9, 22. 'For' in these places is *eis*, which does not mean 'instead of,' but 'with a view to.' The faith thus exercised brings the soul into vital union with God in Christ, and inevitably produces righteousness of life, that is, conformity to the will of God."*

NT: B.196b; CB.1241c; K.168.
OT: ṣᵉdāqāh: S.6666; HR.332c.10c; H.1879b; BD.842a.
ṣedeq: S.6664; HR.332c.10b; H.1879a; BD.841c.
GEN. REF.: IS.4:192; NB.1097; Z.5:104.

2. *dikaiōma* [δικαίωμα, 1345], is the concrete expression of righteousness: see JUSTIFICATION, A, No. 2.

NT: B.198a; CB.1241c; K.168.
OT: ḥōq: S.2706; HR.334b.2a; H.728a; BD.349b.
ḥuqqāh: S.2708; HR.334b.2b; H.728b; BD.349d.
mishpāt: S.4941; HR.334b.4; H.2443c; BD.1048b.
GEN. REF.: IS.4:192; NB.1097; Z.5:104.

Note: In Heb. 1:8, A.V., *euthutēs*, straightness, uprightness (akin to *euthus*, straight, right), is translated "righteousness" (R.V., "uprightness"; A.V., marg., "rightness, or straightness").

RING

daktulios [δακτύλιος, 1146], a finger-ring, occurs in Luke 15:22. ¶

NT: B.170a; CB.1240b; K.140.
OT: ṭabba'at: S.2885; HR.284b.2; H.789a; BD.371c.
GEN. REF.: IS.4:196; NB.—; Z.5:119.

Note: Chrusodaktulios, an adjective signifying "with a gold ring," a gold-ringed (person), from *chrusos*, gold, and *daktulos*, a finger, occurs in Jas. 2:2. ¶

RINGLEADER

prōtostatēs [πρωτοστάτης, 4414], one who stands first (*prōtos*, first, *histēmi*, to cause to stand), was used of soldiers, one who stands in the front rank; hence, metaphorically, a leader, Acts 24:5. ¶

NT: B.726c; CB.1267b; K.—.
OT: —.
GEN. REF.: IS.4:197; NB.—; Z.—.

RIOT, RIOTING, RIOTOUS, RIOTOUSLY

A. Nouns.

1. *asōtia* [ἀσωτία, 810], prodigality, a wastefulness, profligacy (*a*, negative, *sōzō*, to save), is rendered "riot" in Eph. 5:18, R.V. (A.V., "excess"); Tit. 1:6 and 1 Pet. 4:4 (A.V. and R.V., "riot"). The corresponding verb is found in a papyrus writing, telling of 'riotous living' (like the adverb *asōtōs*, see B). ¶ In the Sept., Prov. 28:7. ¶ Cp. the synonymous word *aselgeia* (under LASCIVIOUSNESS).

NT: B.119c; CB.—; K.87.
OT: zālal: S.2151; HR.175a.1; H.553; BD.272d.
GEN. REF.: IS.4:197; NB.—; Z.—.

2. *kōmos* [κῶμος, 2970], a revel, is rendered "rioting" in Rom. 13:13, A.V.; see REVEL.

NT: B.461a; CB.1255c; K.—.
OT: —.
GEN. REF.: IS.4:197; NB.—; Z.—.

3. *truphē* [τρυφή, 5172], luxuriousness, is rendered "riot" in 2 Pet. 2:13, A.V.; see DELICATELY, REVEL.

NT: B.828d; CB.—; K.—.
OT: 'ēden: S.5730; HR.1377c.1a; H.1568a; BD.726c.
ma'ᵃdannîm: S.4574; HR.1377c.1b; H.1568d; BD.726d.
GEN. REF.: IS.4:197; NB.—; Z.—.

4. *stasis* [στάσις, 4714], primarily a standing (akin to *histēmi*, to cause to stand), then an insurrection, is translated "riot" in Acts 19:40, R.V. (A.V., "uproar"). See DISSENSION, INSURRECTION, SEDITION, UPROAR.

NT: B.764c; CB.1270a; K.1070.
OT: —.
GEN. REF.: IS.4:197; NB.—; Z.—.

B. Adverb.

asōtōs [ἀσώτως, 811], wastefully (akin to A, No. 1), is translated "with riotous living" in Luke 15:13; though the word does not necessarily signify 'dissolutely,' the parable narrative makes clear that this is the meaning here. ¶ In the Sept., Prov. 7:11. ¶

NT: B.119c; CB.1238a; K.—.
OT: —.
GEN. REF.: —.

Note: The verb *ekchunō*, a Hellenistic form of *ekcheō* (though the form actually used is the regular classical aorist passive of *ekcheō*), to pour out, shed, is translated "ran riotously" in Jude 11, R.V. (A.V., "ran greedily"); see POUR, SHED.

* From Notes on Galatians by Hogg and Vine, pp. 246, 247.

RIPE (to be fully)

1. *akmazō* [ἀκμάζω, 187], to be at the prime (akin to *akmē*, a point), to be ripe, is translated "are fully ripe" in Rev. 14:18. ¶

NT: B.30d; CB.1234b; K.—.
OT: —.
GEN. REF.: —.

2. *xērainō* [ξηραίνω, 3583], to dry up, wither, is used of ripened crops in Rev. 14:15, R.V., "over-ripe," A.V., "ripe" (marg., "dried"). See DRY, B, OVER-RIPE, WITHER.

NT: B.548c; CB.1273b; K.—.
OT: yābēsh: S.3001; HR.957a.2; H.837; BD.386b.
GEN. REF.: —.

3. *paradidōmi* [παραδίδωμι, 3860], to give over, commit, deliver, etc., also signifies to permit; in Mark 4:29, of the ripe condition of corn, R.V., and A.V. marg., "is ripe"; R.V. marg., "alloweth" (the nearest rendering); A.V., "is brought forth."

NT: B.614b; CB.1262a; K.166.
OT: nātan: S.5414; HR.1058a.16a; H.1443; BD.678a.
GEN. REF.: —.

RISE, RISING

Notes: (1) For the various verbs *anistēmi, exanistēmi, egeirō, anabainō, anatellō, sunephistēmi*, see under ARISE.

(2) For the A.V., "should rise" in Acts 26:23, see RESURRECTION.

(3) *Exanistēmi*, transitively, to raise up (*ek*, out, from, out of), is used intransitively in Acts 15:5, "there rose up," i.e., from the midst of a gathered company. See RAISE.

(4) For the A.V. and R.V. of *sunegeirō*, to raise together with, and in the Passive Voice in Col. 2:12; 3:1, see RAISE.

(5) For the word "rising," which is used to translate the verbs *anatellō* in mark 16:2, and *anistēmi*, in Mark 9:10, see under ARISE, Nos. 9 and 1 respectively.

(6) For *katephistēmi*, Acts 18:12, R.V., see INSURRECTION, B.

(7) *Epanistamai*, to rise up against, occurs in Matt. 10:21; Mark 13:12. ¶

(8) *Anastasis*, is rendered "rising up" in Luke 2:34, R.V.

RIVER

potamos [ποταμός, 4215], denotes (*a*) a stream, Luke 6:48, 49; (*b*) a flood or floods, Matt. 7:25, 27; (*c*) a river, natural, Matt. 3:6, R.V.; Mark 1:5; Acts 16:13; 2 Cor. 11:26, R.V. (A.V., "waters"); Rev. 8:10; 9:14; 16:4, 12; symbolical, Rev. 12:15 (1st part), R.V., "river" (A.V., "flood"); so ver. 16; 22:1, 2 (cp. Gen. 2:10; Ezek. 47); figuratively, John 7:38, the effects of the operation of the Holy Spirit in and through the believer. See FLOOD, WATER. ¶

NT: B.694c; CB.1266b; K.921.
OT: yᵉʾōr: S.2975; HR.1196a.1; H.832; BD.384b.
nāhār: S.5104; HR.1196a.2a; H.1315a; BD.625c.
GEN. REF.: IS.4:197; NB.1098; Z.4:120.

Note: For *potamophorētos* in Rev. 12:15, see FLOOD, B.

ROAR, ROARING

A. Verbs.

1. *mukaomai* [μυκάομαι, 3455], properly of oxen, an onomatopoeic word, to low, bellow, is used of a lion, Rev. 10:3. ¶

NT: B.529b; CB.—; K.—.
OT: —.
GEN. REF.: —.

2. *ōruomai* [ὠρύομαι, 5612], to howl or roar, onomatopoeic, of animals or men, is used of a lion, 1 Pet. 5:8, as a simile of Satan. ¶

NT: B.897a; CB.—; K.—.
OT: shā'ag: S.7580; HR.1494a.1a; H.2300; BD.980c.
GEN. REF.: —.

B. Noun.

ēchos [ἦχος, 2279], a noise or sound (Eng., echo), is used of the roaring of the sea in Luke 21:25, in the best mss., "for the roaring (of the sea and the billows)," R.V.; some mss. have the present participle of *ēcheō*, to sound, A.V., "(the sea and the waves) roaring." See RUMOUR, SOUND.

NT: B.349d; CB.1242c; K.—.
OT: hāmôn: S.1995; HR.620c.2; H.505a; BD.242b.
GEN. REF.: —.

ROB

1. *sulaō* [συλάω, 4813], to plunder, spoil, is translated "I robbed" in 2 Cor. 11:8. ¶ Cp *sulagōgeō*, to make spoil of, Col. 2:8. ¶

NT: B.776c; CB.1270b; K.—.
OT: —.
GEN. REF.: —.

2. *katabrabeuō* [καταβραβεύω, 2603], to give judgment against, to condemn (*kata*, against, and *brabeus*, an umpire; cp. *brabeion*, a prize in the games, 1 Cor. 9:24; Phil. 3:14, and *brabeuō*, to act as an umpire, arbitrate, Col. 3:15), occurs in Col. 2:18, R.V., "let (no man) rob (you) of your prize" (A.V., ". . . beguile . . . of your reward"), said of false teachers who would frustrate the faithful adherence of the believers to the truth, causing them to lose their reward. Another rendering closer to the proper meaning of the word, as given above, is 'let no man decide for or against you; (i.e., without any notion of a prize); this suitably follows the word "judge" in ver. 16, i.e., 'do not give yourselves up to the judgment and decision of any man' (A.V., marg., "judge against"). ¶

NT: B.409b; CB.1254a; K.—.
OT: —.
GEN. REF.: —.

ROBBER

1. *lēstēs* [ληστής, 3027], a robber, brigand (akin to *leia*, booty), one who plunders openly and by violence (in contrast to *kleptēs*, a thief, see below), is always translated "robber" or "robbers" in the R.V., as the A.V. in John 10:1, 8; 18:40; 2 Cor. 11:26; the A.V. has "thief" or "thieves" in Matt. 21:13, and parallel passages; 26:55, and parallel passages; 27:38, 44 and Mark 15:27; Luke 10:30, 36; but "thief" is the meaning of *kleptēs*. See THIEF.

NT: B.473a; CB.1256c; K.532.
OT: gᵉdûd: S.1416; HR.876a.1; H.313a; BD.151a.
pārîs: S.6530; HR.876a.2; H.1826b; BD.829d.
GEN. REF.: IS.4:203; NB.–; Z.–.

2. *hierosulos* [ἱερόσυλος, 2417], an adjective signifying robbing temples (*hieron*, a temple, and *sulaō*, to rob), is found in Acts 19:37. ¶ Cp. *hierosuleō*, to rob a temple, Rom. 2:22, A.V., "commit sacrilege." ¶

NT: B.373c; CB.1250c; K.–.
OT: –.
GEN. REF.: IS.4:132; NB.–; Z.–.

For ROBBERY see PRIZE

ROBE

1. *stolē* [στολή, 4749], for which see CLOTHING, No. 8, is translated "robe" in Mark 16:5, R.V. (A.V., "garment"); "long robes" in Luke 20:46.

NT: B.769c; CB.1270a; K.1088.
OT: beged: S.899; HR.1291c.3; H.198a; BD.93d.
lᵉbûsh: S.3830; HR.1291c.7; H.1075a; BD.528c.
GEN. REF.: IS.4:204; NB.–; Z.5:130.

2. *chlamus* [χλαμύς, 5511], a cloak, is translated "robe" in Matt. 27:28, 31. See CLOTHING, *Note* (4). ¶

NT: B.882b; CB.–; K.–.
OT: –
GEN. REF.: IS.4:204; NB.–; Z.5:130.

3. *himation* [ἱμάτιον, 2440], is translated "robe" in the A.V. of John 19:2, 5 (R.V., "garment"). See APPAREL, No. 2, CLOTHING, No. 2, GARMENT.

NT: B.376b; CB.1250c; K.–.
OT: beged: S.899; HR.685a.1; H.198a; BD.93d.
simlāh: S.8071; HR.685a.11; H.2270a; BD.971a.
GEN. REF.: IS.4:204; NB.–; Z.5:130.

4. *esthēs* [ἐσθής, 2066], apparel, is translated "robe" in Luke 23:11 (R.V., "apparel"). See APPAREL, No. 1.

NT: B.312b; CB.1246c; K.–.
OT: –.
GEN. REF.: IS.4:204; NB.–; Z.–.

ROCK

1. *petra* [πέτρα, 4073], denotes a mask of rock, as distinct from *petros*, a detached stone or boulder, or a stone that might be thrown or easily moved. For the nature of *petra*, see Matt. 7:24, 25; 27:51, 60; Mark 15:46; Luke 6:48 (twice), a type of a sure foundation (here the true reading is as in the R.V., "because it had been well builded"); Rev. 6:15, 16 (cp. Is. 2:19, ff.; Hos. 10:8); Luke 8:6, 13, used illustratively; 1 Cor. 10:4 (twice), figuratively, of Christ; in Rom. 9:33 and 1 Pet. 2:8, metaphorically, of Christ; in Matt. 16:18, metaphorically, of Christ and the testimony concerning Him; here the distinction between *petra*, concerning the Lord Himself, and *petros*, the Apostle, is clear (see above). ¶

NT: B.654a; CB.1263c; K.834.
OT: sûr: S.6697; HR.1129c.3a; H.1901a; BD.849c.
selaʿ: S.5553; HR.1129c.2; H.1508a; BD.700d.
GEN. REF.: IS.4:205; NB.1098; Z.5:132.

2. *spilas* [σπιλάς, 4694], a rock or reef, over which the sea dashes, is used in Jude 12, "hidden rocks," R.V., metaphorical of men whose conduct is a danger to others. ¶ A late meaning ascribed to it is that of "spots," (A.V.), but that rendering seems to have been influenced by the parallel passage in 2 Pet. 2:13, where *spiloi*, "spots," occurs.

NT: B.762c; CB.–; K.–.
OT: –.
GEN. REF.: –; NB.–; Z.5:132.

ROCKY

petrōdēs [πετρώδης, 4075], rock-like (*petra*, a rock, *eidos*, a form, appearance), is used of rock underlying shallow soil, Matt. 13:5, 20, R.V., "the rocky places" (A.V., "stony places"); Mark 4:5, R.V., "the rocky ground" (A.V., "stony ground"); ver. 16, R.V., "rocky places" (A.V., "stony ground"). ¶

NT: B.655c; CB.1263c; K.–.
OT: –.
GEN. REF.: IS.4:205; NB.–; Z.–.

Note: In Acts 27:29, A.V., the phrase *tracheis topoi*, lit., 'rough places,' is translated "rocks" (R.V., "rocky ground").

ROD

A. Noun.

rhabdos [ῥάβδος, 4464], a staff, rod, sceptre, is used (*a*) of Aaron's rod, Heb. 9:4; (*b*) a staff used on a journey, Matt. 10:10, R.V., "staff" (A.V., "staves"); so Luke 9:3; Mark 6:8, "staff"; Heb. 11:21, "staff"; (*c*) a ruler's staff, a "sceptre," Heb. 1:8 (twice); elsewhere a rod, Rev. 2:27; 12:5; 19:15; (*d*) a rod for chastisement (figuratively), 1 Cor. 4:21; (*e*) a measuring rod, Rev. 11:1. See STAFF. ¶

NT: B.733b; CB.1268a; K.982.
OT: maṭṭeh: S.4294; HR.1247a.2; H.1352b; BD.641c.
maqqēl: S.4731; HR.1247a.3; H.1236; BD.596b.
shēbeṭ: S.7626; HR.1247a.6; H.2314a; BD.986d.
GEN. REF.: IS.4:206; NB.1098; Z.5:132.

B. Verb.

rhabdizō [ῥαβδίζω, 4463], to beat with a rod, is used in Acts 16:22, R.V., "to beat . . . with rods"; 2 Cor. 11:25. The rods were those of the Roman lictors or "serjeants" (*rhabdouchos*, lit., rod-bearers); the Roman beating with rods is distinct from the Jewish infliction of stripes. ¶ In the Sept., Judg. 6:11; Ruth 2:17. ¶ Cp. Matt. 26:67, R.V. marg.; John 18:22 (A.V. marg., and R.V. marg.); 19:3, R.V. marg.; see SMITE.

NT: B.733b; CB.1268a; K.982.
OT: ḥābaṭ: S.2251; HR.1247a.1; H.591; BD.286a.
GEN. REF.: IS.4:206; NB.1098; Z.5:132.

ROLL (Noun and Verb)

A. Verbs.

1. *apokuliō* or *apokulizō* [ἀποκυλίω, 617], to roll away (*apo*, from, *kuliō*, to roll; cp. Eng., cylinder, etc.), is used of the sepulchre-stone, Matt. 28:2; Mark 16:3 (ver. 4 in some mss.; see No. 2); Luke 24:2. ¶ In the Sept., Gen. 29:3, 8, 10. ¶

NT: B.94b; CB.—; K.—.
OT: gālal: S.1556; HR.136a.1; H.353; BD.164b.
GEN. REF.: —.

2. *anakuliō* [ἀνακυλίω, 303; 2947], to roll up or back (*ana*), is found in the best texts, in Mark 16:4 (see No. 1). ¶

NT: B.56c; CB.—; K.—.
OT: —.
GEN. REF.: —.

3. *proskuliō* [προσκυλίω, 4351], to roll up or to (*pros*), is used in Matt. 27:60; Mark 15:46, of the sepulchre-stone. ¶

NT: B.716c; CB.—; K.—.
OT: —.
GEN. REF.: —.

4. *heilissō* or *helissō* [ἑλίσσω, 1507], to roll, or roll up, is used (*a*) of the rolling up of a mantle, illustratively of the heavens, Heb. 1:12, R.V.; (*b*) of the rolling up of a scroll, Rev. 6:14, illustratively of the removing of the heaven. ¶

NT: B.251b; CB.—; K.—.
OT: gālal: S.1556; HR.453a.1; H.353; BD.164b.
ḥālaph: S.2498; HR.453a.3; H.666; BD.322a.
GEN. REF.: —.

5. *entulissō* [ἐντυλίσσω, 1794], to wrap up, roll round or about, is translated "rolled up" in John 20:7, R.V., of the cloth or "napkin" that had been wrapped around the head of the Lord before burial. Both the R.V. and the A.V., "wrapped together," might suggest that this cloth had been rolled or wrapped up and put in a certain part of the tomb at the Lord's resurrection, whereas, as with the body wrappings, the head cloth was lying as it had been rolled round His head, an evidence, to those who looked into the tomb, of the fact of His resurrection without any disturbance of the wrappings either by friend or foe or when the change took place. It is followed by *en*, in, and translated "wrapped" in Matt. 27:59, a meaning and construction which Moulton and Milligan illustrate from the papyri; in Luke 23:53 it is followed by the dative of the noun *sindōn*, linen cloth, used instrumentally. See WRAP. ¶

NT: B.270b; CB.—; K.—.
OT: —.
GEN. REF.: —.

B. Noun.

kephalis [κεφαλίς, 2777], lit., a little head (a diminutive of *kephalē*, a head; Lat., *capitulum*, a diminutive of *caput*), hence, a capital of a column, then, a roll (of a book), occurs in Heb. 10:7, R.V., "in the roll" (A.V., "in the volume"), lit., 'in the heading of the scroll' (from Ps. 40:7). ¶

NT: B.430c; CB.1255a; K.—.
OT: m^e^gillāh: S.4039; HR.763a.4; H.353m; BD.166b.
GEN. REF.: IS.4:363; NB.1344; Z.5:313.

ROMAN

rhōmaios [Ῥωμαῖος, 4514], occurs in John 11:48; Acts 2:10, R.V., "from Rome" (A.V., "of Rome"); 16:21, 37, 38; 22:25, 26, 27, 29; 23:27; 25:16; 28:17. ¶ For a note on Roman citizenship see CITIZEN, No. 3.

NT: B.738c; CB.—; K.—.
OT: —.
GEN. REF.: —.

ROOF

stegē [στέγη, 4721], a covering (*stegō*, to cover), denotes, a roof, Mark 2:4; said of entering a house, Matt. 8:8; Luke 7:6. ¶

NT: B.765d; CB.—; K.1073.
OT: mikseh: S.4372; HR.1288a.1; H.1008c; BD.492c.
GEN. REF.: IS.2:771; NB.—; Z.5:171.

ROOM

A. Nouns.

1. *topos* [τόπος, 5117], a place, is translated "room" in Luke 2:7 and 14:22, i.e., place; in the A.V. in Luke 14:9, 10, R.V., "place" (of a couch at a feast); of a position or condition which a person occupies, 1 Cor. 14:16 (R.V., "place"). See OPPORTUNITY, PLACE.

NT: B.822b; CB.1273a; K.1184.
OT: māqôm: S.4725; HR.1364b.8; H.1999b; BD.879d.
GEN. REF.: IS.4:236; NB.—; Z.—.

2. *prōtoklisia* [πρωτοκλισία, 4411], the chief reclining place at table, is rendered "uppermost rooms," in Matt. 23:6, A.V. (R.V., "chief place"); in Mark 12:39, "uppermost rooms," A.V. (R.V., "chief places"); in Luke 14:7, "chief rooms," A.V. (R.V., "chief seats"); in ver. 8, A.V., "highest room" (R.V., "chief seat"); in 20:46, A.V., "highest seats" (R.V., "chief seats"). See CHIEF, B, No. 7, PLACE, No. 5. ¶

NT: B.725b; CB.1267b; K.965.
OT: —.
GEN. REF.: —.

3. *anagaion* or *anōgeon* [ἀνάγαιον, 508], an upper room (*ana*, above, *gē*, ground), occurs in Mark 14:15; Luke 22:12, a chamber, often over a porch, or connected with the roof, where meals were taken and privacy obtained. ¶
NT: B.51a; CB.—; K.—.
OT: —.
GEN. REF.: —.

4. *huperōon* [ὑπερῷον, 5253], the neuter of the adjective *huperoos*, upper (from *huper*, above), used as a noun, denoted in classical Greek an upper storey or room where the women resided; in the Sept. and the N.T., an upper chamber, a roof-chamber, built on the flat roof of the house, Acts 1:13, R.V., "upper chamber" (A.V., "upper room"); see CHAMBER, No. 2.
NT: B.842b; CB.—; K.—.
OT: ᵃliyyāh S.5944; HR.1411b.1a; H.1624f; BD.751a.
GEN. REF.: —.

B. Verb.

chōreō [χωρέω, 5562], to make room, is translated "there was . . . room" in Mark 2:2. See CONTAIN, No. 1.
NT: B.889c; CB.1240a; K.—.
OT: —.
GEN. REF.: —.

C. Preposition.

anti [ἀντί, 473], in place of, instead of, is translated "in the room of" in Matt. 2:22.
NT: B.73c; CB.1236a; K.61.
OT: —.
GEN. REF.: —.

Notes: (1) In Luke 12:17, A.V., *pou*, anywhere or where, with a negative, is translated "no room" (R.V., " not where").

(2) In Acts 24:27, A.V., *diadochos*, a successor, with *lambanō*, to receive, is translated "came into (Felix') room," R.V., "(Felix) was succeeded by." *Diadochos* often meant a deputy, a temporary successor. ¶

ROOT

A. Noun.

rhiza [ῥίζα, 4491], is used (*a*) in the natural sense, Matt. 3:10; 13:6, 21; Mark 4:6, 17; 11:20; Luke 3:9; 8:13; (*b*) metaphorically (1) of cause, origin, source, said of persons, ancestors, Rom. 11:16, 17, 18 (twice); of things, evils, 1 Tim. 6:10, R.V., of the love of money as a root of all "kinds of evil" (marg., "evils"; A.V., "evil"); bitterness, Heb. 12:15; (2) of that which springs from a root, a shoot, said of offspring, Rom. 15:12; Rev. 5:5; 22:16. ¶
NT: B.736a; CB.1268b; K.985.
OT: shōresh: S.8328; HR.1251c.5; H.2471a; BD.1057c.
GEN. REF.: IS.4:236; NB.—; Z.5:171.

B. Verbs.

1. *rhizoō* [ῥιζόω, 4492], to cause to take root, is used metaphorically in the Passive Voice in Eph. 3:17, of being rooted in love; Col. 2:7, in Christ, i.e., in the sense of being firmly planted, or established. ¶ In the Sept., Is. 40:24; Jer. 12:2. ¶
NT: B.736b; CB.1268b; K.985.
OT: shārash: S.8327; HR.1252a.1; H.2471; BD.1057d.
GEN. REF.: IS.4:236; NB.—; Z.—.

2. *ekrizoō* [ἐκριζόω, 1610], to root out or up (*ek*, out, and No. 1), is rendered to root up in Matt. 13:29; 15:13; see PLUCK.
NT: B.244d; CB.1244a; K.985.
OT: nātash: S.5428; HR.441a.2; H.1451; BD.684c.
'āqar: S.6131; HR.441a.3a; H.1681, 1682; BD.785c.
shōresh: S.8328; HR.441a.4; H.2471a; BD.1057c.
GEN. REF.: IS.4:236; NB.—; Z.—.

ROPE

schoinion [σχοινίον, 4979], a diminutive of *schoinos*, a rush, is used of the small cords of which Christ made a scourge, John 2:15; of the ropes of a boat, Acts 27;32. See CORD. ¶
NT: B.797d; CB.—; K.—.
OT: ḥebel: S.2256; HR.1328a.1; H.592b; BD.286c.
GEN. REF.: IS.4:237; NB.252; Z.5:172.

For **ROSE** see **RISE**

ROUGH

1. *sklēros* [σκληρός, 4642], hard, is translated "rough" in Jas. 3:4, R.V., of winds (A.V., "fierce"). See AUSTERE, FIERCE, *Note* (1).
NT: B.756a; CB.1269a; K.816.
OT: qāsheh: S.7186; HR.1274b.4a; H.2085a; BD.904c.
GEN. REF.: —.

2. *trachus* [τραχύς, 5138], rough, uneven, is used of paths, Luke 3:5; of rocky places, Acts 27:29. See ROCKY. ¶
NT: B.825c; CB.1273a; K.—.
OT: rekes: S.7406; HR.1371a.2; H.2166a; BD.940c.
GEN. REF.: —.

ROUND, ROUND ABOUT

1. *kuklothen* [κυκλόθεν, 2943], from *kuklos*, a circle, ring (Eng., cycle, etc.), occurs in Rev. 4:3, 4; in ver. 8, R.V., "round about," with reference to the eyes. ¶
NT: B.456d; CB.—; K.—.
OT: sābîb: S.5439; HR.796b.2a,b,d; H.1456b; BD.686d.
GEN. REF.: —.

2. *pantothen* [πάντοθεν, 3840) on all sides (from *pas*, all), is translated "round about" in Heb. 9:4. See EVERYWHERE, No. 3.
NT: B.608d; CB.—; K.—.
OT: —.
GEN. REF.: —.

3. *perix* [πέριξ, 4038], from the preposition *peri*, around, occurs in Acts 5:16, "round about" (of cities). ¶
NT: B.648d; CB.—; K.—.
OT: —.
GEN. REF.: —.

4. *kuklō* [κύκλῳς, 2945], the dative case of the noun *kuklos*, a ring, is used as an adverb, and translated "round about" in Mark 3:34, A.V. (R.V., "round"); 6:6, 36; Luke 9:12; Rom. 15:19; Rev. 4:6; 7:11. ¶
NT: B.456d; CB.—; K.—.
OT: —.
GEN. REF.: —.

Note: For combinations with other words see, e.g., COME, No. 38, COUNTRY, A, No. 6, A, No. 4, DWELL, No. 5, GO, No. 9, HEDGE, LOOK, A, No. 3, REGION, SHINE, STAND, B, No. 5.

ROUSE

exupnos [ἔξυπνος, 1853], roused out of sleep (*ek*, out of, *hupnos*, sleep), occurs in Acts 16:27. ¶ Cp. *exupnizō*, AWAKE, No. 4.
NT: B.279b; CB.—; K.1233.
OT: —.
GEN. REF.: —.

ROW (Verb)

elaunō [ἐλαύνω, 1643], to drive, is used of rowing or sailing a boat, Mark 6:48; John 6:19. See DRIVE.
NT: B.248c; CB.—; K.—.
OT: shayiṭ: S.7885; HR.448c.4; H.2344c; BD.1002b.
GEN. REF.: —.

ROYAL

1. *basileios* [βασίλειος, 934], from *basileus*, a king, is used in 1 Pet. 2:9 of the priesthood consisting of all believers. ¶ Cp. Luke 7:25, for which see COURT, No. 3. In the Sept., Ex. 19:6; 23:22; Deut. 3:10 ¶.
NT: B.136a; CB.1238c; K.97.
OT: mamlākāh: S.4467; HR.194c.1; H.1199f; BD.575a.
GEN. REF.: IS.4:238; NB.—; Z.—.

2. *basilikos* [βασιλικός, 937], belonging to a king, is translated "royal" in Acts 12:21; Jas. 2:8. See KING B, No. 2, NOBLEMAN.
NT: B.136d; CB.1238c; K.97.
OT: melek: S.4428; HR.214a.1a-c; H.1199a; BD.572d.
GEN. REF.: IS.4:238; NB.—; Z.—.

RUB

psōchō [ψώχω, 5597], to rub, to rub to pieces, is used in Luke 6:1. ¶
NT: B.894d; CB.—; K.—.
OT: —.
GEN. REF.: —.

RUDDER

pēdalion [πηδάλιον, 4079], a rudder (akin to *pēdos*, the blade of an oar), occurs in Jas. 3:4, R.V., "rudder" (A.V., "helm"), and Acts 27:40, plural, R.V., "(the bands of) the rudders," A.V., "the rudder (bands)." ¶

The *pēdalia* were actually steering paddles, two of which were used as rudders in ancient ships.
NT: B.656a; CB.—; K.—.
OT: —.
GEN. REF.: IS.4:238; NB.—; Z.—.

RUDE

idiōtēs [ἰδιώτης, 2399], for which see IGNORANT, No. 4, is translated "rude" in 2 Cor. 11:6.
NT: B.370c; CB.1252c; K.348.
OT: —.
GEN. REF.: —.

RUDIMENTS

stoicheion [στοιχεῖον, 4747], one of a row or series, is translated "rudiments" in the R.V. of Gal. 4:3, 9; Heb. 5:12, and the A.V. and R.V. of Col. 2:8, 20. See ELEMENTS.
NT: B.768d; CB.1270a; K.1087.
OT: —.
GEN. REF.: IS.1:57; NB.—; Z.—.

RUE

pēganon [πήγανον, 4076], a shrubby plant with yellow flowers and a heavy smell, cultivated for medicinal purposes, is mentioned in Luke 11:42. ¶
NT: B.655d; CB.1263a; K.—.
OT: —.
GEN. REF.: IS.4:239; NB.1006; Z.5:174.

RUIN

1. *rhēgma* [ῥῆγμα, 4485], akin to *rhēgnumi*, to break, denotes a cleavage, fracture (so in the Sept., e.g., 1 Kings 11:30, 31); by metonymy, that which is broken, a ruin, Luke 6:49. ¶
NT: B.735a; CB.—; K.—.
OT: qᵉra'îm: S.7168; HR.1248c.2; H.2074a; BD.902d.
GEN. REF.: IS.4:239; NB.—; Z.—.

2. *katestrammena* [κατεστραμμένα, 2690], the neuter plural, perfect participle, Passive, of *katastrephō*, to overturn, is translated "ruins" in Acts 15:16; cp. DIG, No. 3. See OVERTHROW.
NT: B.419b; CB.—; K.1093.
OT: —.
GEN. REF.: IS.4:239; NB.—; Z.—.

RULE (Noun and Verb)

A. Nouns.

1. *archē* [ἀρχή, 746], a beginning etc., denotes rule, Luke 20:20, R.V., "rule" (A.V., "power"); 1 Cor. 15:24; Eph. 1:21, R.V., "rule" (A.V., "principality"). See BEGINNING, B.
NT: B.111d; CB.1237b; K.81.
OT: mamlākāh: S.4467; HR.163c.10; H.1199f; BD.575a.
rō'sh: S.7218; HR.164a.20a; H.2097; BD.910c.
GEN. REF.: IS.4:240; NB.—; Z.—.

2. *kanōn* [κανών, 2583], is translated "rule" in the A.V. of 2 Cor. 10:13, 15; in Gal. 6:16, A.V.

and R.V.; in Phil. 3:16, A.V. (R.V., in italics): see PROVINCE, No. 2.
NT: B.403a; CB.1253b; K.414.
OT: –.
GEN. REF.: IS.4:240; NB.–; Z.–.

B. Verbs.

1. *archō* [ἄρχω, 757], (akin to A, No. 1), in the Active Voice denotes to rule, Mark 10:42 and Rom. 15:12, R.V., "to rule" (A.V., "to reign"). See BEGIN, A, No. 1.
NT: B.113c; CB.1237b; K.81.
OT: māshal: S.4910; HR.163a.6; H.1258,1259; BD.605c.
GEN. REF.: IS.4:240; NB.–; Z.5:175.

2. *oikodespoteō* [οἰκοδεσποτέω, 3616], from *oikos*, a house, and *despotēs*, a master, signifies to rule the household; so the R.V. in 1 Tim. 5:14 (A.V., "guide the house"). See GUIDE, B, *Note* (1). ¶ Cp. *oikodespotēs*, a householder.
NT: B.558a; CB.1260b; K.145.
OT: –.
GEN. REF.: IS.4:240; NB.–; Z.–.

3. *proistēmi* [προΐστημι, 4291], lit., 'to stand before,' hence, to lead, attend to (indicating care and diligence), is translated to rule (Middle Voice), with reference to a local church, in Rom. 12:8; perfect Active in 1 Tim. 5:17; with reference to a family, 1 Tim. 3:4 and 12 (Middle Voice); ver. 5 (2nd aorist, Active). See MAINTAIN.
NT: B.707a; CB.1266c; K.–.
OT: –.
GEN. REF.: IS.4:240; NB.–; Z.–.

4. *hēgeomai* [ἡγέομαι, 2233], to lead, is translated to rule in Heb. 13:7, 17, 24 (A.V. marg., in the first two, "are the guides" and "guide,"
NT: B.343c; CB.1249c; K.303.
OT: nāgîd: S.5057; HR.602c.21; H.1289b; BD.617d.
rō'sh: S.7218; HR.602c.31; H.2097; BD.910c.
GEN. REF.: IS.4:240; NB.490; Z.5:175.

5. *poimaino* [ποιμαίνω, 4165], to act as a shepherd, tend flocks, is translated to rule in Rev. 2:27; 12:5; 19:15, all indicating that the governing power exercised by the Shepherd is to be of a firm character; in Matt. 2:6, A.V., "shall rule" (R.V., "shall be shepherd of"). See FEED.
NT: B.683d; CB.1265c; K.901.
OT: rā'āh: S.7462; HR.1169a.2a; H.2185,2186; BD.944d.
GEN. REF.: IS.4:241; NB.–; Z.–.

6. *brabeuō* [βραβεύω, 1018], properly, to act as an umpire (*brabeus*), hence, generally, to arbitrate, decide, Col. 3:15, "rule" (R.V., marg., "arbitrate"), representing "the peace of Christ" (R.V.) as deciding all matters in the hearts of believers; some regard the meaning as that of simply directing, controlling, ruling. ¶ Cp. *katabrabeuō*l see ROB.
NT: B.146c; CB.1239b; K.110.
OT: –.
GEN. REF.: IS.4:240; NB.–; Z.–.

RULER

1. *archōn* [ἄρχων, 758], a ruler, chief, prince, is translated "rulers," e.g., in 1 Cor. 2:6, 8, R.V. (A.V., "princes"); "ruler," Rev. 1:5 (A.V., "prince"). See MAGISTRATE, PRINCE, No. 2.
NT: B.113d; CB.1237b; K.81.
OT: nāsî': S.5387; HR.166b.17; H.1421b,c; BD.672b.
rō'sh: S.7218; HR.166b.26; H.2097; BD.910c.
sar: S.8269; HR.166b.30a; H.2295a; BD.978a.
GEN. REF.: IS.4:241; NB.490; Z.5:175.

2. *archē* [ἀρχή, 746], a rule, sovereignty, is rendered "rulers" in Luke 12:11, R.V. (A.V., "magistrates"). See BEGINNING.
NT: B.111d; CB.1237b; K.81.
OT: mamlākāh: S.4467; HR.163c.10; H.1199f; BD.575a.
rō'sh: S.7218; HR.163c.20a; H.2097; BD.910c.
GEN. REF.: IS.4:241; NB.490; Z.–.

3. *kosmokratōr* [κοσμοκράτωρ, 2888], denotes a ruler of this world (contrast *pantokratōr*, almighty). In Greek literature, in Orphic hymns, etc., and in Rabbinic writings, it signifies a ruler of the whole world, a world-lord. In the N.T. it is used in Eph. 6:12, "the world-rulers (of this darkness)," R.V., A.V., "the rulers (of the darkness) of this world." The context ("not against flesh and blood") shows that not earthly potentates are indicated, but spirit powers, who, under the permissive will of God, and in consequence of human sin, exercise Satanic and therefore antagonistic authority over the world in its present condition of spiritual darkness and alienation from God. The suggested rendering 'the rulers of this dark world' is ambiguous and not phraseologically requisite. Cp. John 12:31; 14:30; 16:11; 2 Cor. 4:4. ¶
NT: B.445c; CB.1255c; K.466.
OT: –.
GEN. REF.: IS.4:241; NB.–; Z.5:175.

4. *politarchēs* [πολιτάρχης, 4173], a ruler of a city (*polis*, a city, *archō*, to rule), a politarch, is used in Acts 17:6, 8, of the magistrates in Thessalonica, before whom the Jews, with a mob of market idlers, dragged Jason and other converts, under the charge of showing hospitality to Paul and Silas, and of treasonable designs against the Emperor. Thessalonica was a "free" city and the citizens could choose their own politarchs. The accuracy of Luke has been vindicated by the use of the term, for while classical authors use the terms *poliarchos* and *politarchos* of similar rulers, the form used by Luke is supported by inscriptions discovered at Thessalonica, one of which mentions Sosipater, Secundus, and Gaius among the politarchs, names occurring as those of Paul's companions. Prof. Burton of Chicago, in a paper on "The Politarchs," has recorded 17 inscriptions which attest their existence,

thirteen of which belong to Macedonia and five presumably to Thessalonica itself, illustrating the influence of Rome in the municipal organization of the place. ¶

NT: B.686a; CB.1265c; K.–.
OT: –.
GEN. REF.: –.

5. *architriklinos* [ἀρχιτρίκλινος, 755], denotes the superintendent of a banquet, whose duty lay in arranging the tables and food (*archē*, ruler, *triklinos*, lit., a room with three couches), John 2:8, 9. ¶

NT: B.113b; CB.–; K.–.
OT: –.
GEN. REF.: IS.–; NB.491; Z.–.

Notes: (1) In Mark 13:9 and Luke 21:12, A.V., *hēgemōn*, a leader, a governor of a Province, is translated "ruler" (R.V., "governor"). See GOVERNOR, PRINCE, No. 3.

(2) For ruler of the synagogue, see SYNAGOGUE.

(3) In Matt. 24:45, A.V., *kathistēmi*, to appoint, is translated "hath made ruler" (R.V., "hath set"); so in ver. 47; 25:21, 23; Luke 12:42, 44.

RUMOUR

1. *akoē* [ἀκοή, 189], a hearing, is translated "rumour" in Matt. 24:6; Mark 13:7. See HEARING, B, No. 1.

NT: B.30d; CB.1234b; K.34.
OT: shāma': S.8085; HR.44a.1a; H.2412; BD.1033b.
shemû'āh: S.8052; HR.44a.1d; H.2412d; BD.1035b.
shēma': S.8088; HR.44a.1f; H.2412b; BD.1034d.
GEN. REF.: –.

2. *ēchos* [ἦχος, 2279], a noise, sound, is translated "rumour" in Luke 4:37, R.V. (A.V., "fame"). See ROAR, SOUND.

NT: B.349d; CB.1242c; K.–.
OT: hāmôn: S.1995; HR.620c.2; H.505a; BD.242b.
GEN. REF.: –.

Note: In Luke 7:17, A.V., *logos*, a word, is translated "rumour" (R.V., "report").

RUN, RAN

1. *trechō* [τρέχω, 5143], to run, is used (*a*) literally, e.g., Matt. 27:48 (*dramōn*, an aorist participle, from an obsolete verb *dramō*, but supplying certain forms absent from *trechō*, lit., 'having run,' 'running,' expressive of the decisiveness of the act); the same form in the indicative mood is used, e.g., in Matt. 28:8; in the Gospels the literal meaning alone is used; elsewhere in 1 Cor. 9:24 (twice in 1st part); Rev. 9:9. A.V., "running" (R.V., "rushing"); (*b*) metaphorically, from the illustration of runners in a race, of either swiftness or effort to attain an end, Rom. 9:16, indicating that salvation is not due to human effort, but to God's sovereign right to exercise mercy; 1 Cor. 9:24 (2nd part), and ver. 26, of persevering activity in the Christian course with a view to obtaining the reward; so Heb. 12:1; in Gal. 2:2 (1st part), R.V., "(lest) I should be running," continuous present tense, referring to the activity of the special service of his mission to Jerusalem; (2nd part), "had run," aorist tense, expressive of the continuous past, referring to the activity of his antagonism to the Judaizing teachers at Antioch, and his consent to submit the case to the judgment of the church in Jerusalem; in 5:7 of the erstwhile faithful course doctrinally of the Galatian believers; in Phil. 2:16, of the Apostle's manner of life among the Philippian believers; in 2 Thess. 3:1, of the free and rapid progress of "the word of the Lord."

NT: B.825d; CB.1273a; K.1189.
OT: rûṣ: S.7323; HR.1371c.2a; H.2137; BD.930a.
GEN. REF.: IS.4:242; NB.–; Z.–.

2. *prostrechō* [προστρέχω, 4370], to run to (*pros*, to, and No. 1), as used in Mark 9:15; 10:17; Acts 8:30. ¶

NT: B.719b; CB.–; K.–.
OT: rûṣ: S.7323; HR.1222b.1; H.2137; BD.930a.
GEN. REF.: IS.4:242; NB.–; Z.–.

3. *peritrechō* [περιτρέχω, 4063], to run about (*peri*, around, and No. 1), is used in Mark 6:55, R.V., "ran round about" (A.V., "ran through"). ¶

NT: B.653a; CB.–; K.–.
OT: shûṭ: S.7751; HR.1128a.1; H.2344; BD.1001d.
GEN. REF.: IS.4:242; NB.–; Z.–.

4. *suntrechō* [συντρέχω, 4936], to run together with (*sun*, with), is used (*a*) literally, Mark 6:33; Acts 3:11; (*b*) metaphorically, 1 Pet. 4:4, of running a course of evil with others. ¶ In the Sept., Psa. 50:18. ¶

NT: B.793a; CB.1271a; K.–.
OT: rāṣāh: S.7521; HR.1321a.1; H.2207; BD.953a.
GEN. REF.: IS.4:242; NB.–; Z.–.

5. *protrechō* [προτρέχω, 4390], to run before, Luke 19:4: see OUTRUN.

NT: B.722b; CB.–; K.–.
OT: rûṣ: S.7323; HR.1231b.1,2; H.2137; BD.930a.
GEN. REF.: IS.4:242; NB.–; Z.–.

6. *eistrechō* [εἰστρέχω, 1532], to run in (*eis*, in) occurs in Acts 12:14. ¶

NT: B.233d; CB.–; K.–.
OT: –.
GEN. REF.: –.

7. *hupotrechō* [ὑποτρέχω, 5295], to run under (*hupo*, under), is used nautically in Acts 27:16. ¶

NT: B.848b; CB.–; K.–.
OT: –.
GEN. REF.: –.

8. *episuntrechō* [ἐπισυντρέχω, 1998], to run together again (*epi*, upon, or again, and No. 4), occurs in Mark 9:25. ¶

NT: B.301d; CB.–; K.–.
OT: –.
GEN. REF.: –.

9. *ekchunnō* or *ekchunō* [ἐκχύννω, 1632], to shed, is translated "ran riotously" in Jude 11, R.V. (A.V., "ran greedily"). See RIOTOUSLY, *Note*. See SHED, SPILL.
NT: B.247b; CB.1243b; K.220.
OT: –.
GEN. REF.: –.

10. *huperekchunnō* [ὑπερεκχύννω, 5240], a late form of *huperekcheō*, to overflow, is rendered "running over" in Luke 6:38. ¶
NT: B.840d; CB.–; K.–.
OT: –.
GEN. REF.: –.

11. *epikellō* or *epokellō* [ἐπικέλλω, 2027], to drive upon, is used in Acts 27:41 of running a ship ashore. ¶
NT: B.294d; CB.–; K.–.
OT: –.
GEN. REF.: –.

Notes: (1) *Hormaō*, to set in motion, urge on, but intransitively, to hasten on, rush, is always translated to rush in the R.V.; A.V., "ran violently," Matt. 8:32; Mark 5:13; Luke 8:33; "ran," Acts 7:57; "rushed," 19:29. See RUSH. ¶

(2) In Acts 21:30, *sundromē*, a running together, with *ginomai*, to become, take place, is translated "ran together," lit., 'a running together took place.'

(3) In Matt. 9:17, A.V., *ekcheō*, to pour out, used in the Passive Voice (R.V., "is spilled"), is translated "runneth out."

(4) In Acts 14:14, R.V., *ekpēdaō*, to spring forth, is translated "sprang forth" (this verb is found in the papyri); the A.V., "ran in" translates the mss. which have *eispēdaō*, to spring in.

(5) *Katatrechō*, to run down, occurs in Acts 21:32. ¶

RUSH, RUSHING

1. *hormaō* [ὁρμάω, –], for which see RUN, *Note* (1), with refs., is akin to *hormē* (see ASSAULT) and *hormēma*, a rushing (see VIOLENCE).

2. *pherō* [φέρω, 5342], to bear, is used in the present participle, Passive Voice, in Acts 2:2, and translated "rushing," R.V., "the rushing (of a mighty wind)," A.V., "a rushing (mighty wind)," lit., 'a violent wind borne (along).'
NT: B.854d; CB.1264a; K.1252.
OT: nāsā': S.5375; HR.1426c.17; H.1421; BD.669d.
GEN. REF.: –.

3. *trechō* [τρέχω, 5143], to run, is translated "rushing (to war)" in Rev. 9:9, R.V., A.V., "running (to battle)."
NT: B.825d; CB.1273a; K.1189.
OT: rûṣ: S.7323; HR.1371c.2a; H.2137; BD.930a.
GEN. REF.: IS.4:242; NB.–; Z.–.

RUST (Noun and Verb)

A. Nouns.

1. *brōsis* [βρῶσις, 1035], an eating (akin to *bibrōskō*, to eat), is used metaphorically to denote "rust" in Matt. 6:19, 20. See EAT, B. No. 1, FOOD, MEAT, MORSEL.
NT: B.148b; CB.1239b; K.111.
OT: 'akal: S.398; HR.231c.1b; H.85; BD.37a.
ma'ᵃkal: S.3978; HR.231c.1f; H.85d; BD.38b.
GEN. REF.: IS.4:243; NB.–; Z.–.

2. *ios* [ἰός, 2447], poison, denotes rust in Jas. 5:3. See POISON.
NT: B.378d; CB.1252c; K.368.
OT: ḥel'āh: S.2457; HR.687a.2; H.649a; BD.316a.
GEN. REF.: IS.4:243; NB.–; Z.5:175.

B. Verb.

katioō [κατιόω, 2728], an intensive form of *ioō*, to poison (akin to A, No. 2), strengthened by *kata*, down, to rust over, and in the Passive Voice, to become rusted over, occurs in Jas. 5:3, R.V., "are rusted" (A.V., "are cankered"). ¶ Cp. *gangraina*, a gangrene, 2 Tim. 2:17, R.V. ¶
NT: B.424a; CB.–; K.–.
OT: –.
GEN. REF.: IS.4:243; NB.–; Z.–.

S

SABACHTHANI

sabachthanei [σαβαχθανεί, 4518], an Aramaic word signifying 'Thou hast forsaken Me,' is recorded as part of the utterance of Christ on the Cross, Matt. 27:46; Mark 15:34, a quotation from Ps. 22:1. Recently proposed renderings which differ from those of the A.V. and R.V. have not been sufficiently established to require acceptance.
NT: B.738b; CB.–; K.–.
OT: shᵉbaq (Aramaic): S.7662; HR.–; H.3018; BD.1114c.
GEN. REF.: IS.1:61; NB.–; Z.2:280.

SABAOTH

sabaōth [σαβαώθ, 4519], is the transliteration of a Hebrew word which denotes hosts or armies, Rom. 9:29; Jas. 5:4. ¶ While the word "hosts" probably had special reference to angels, the title "the LORD of hosts" became used to designate Him as the One who is supreme over all the innumerable hosts of spiritual agencies, or of what are described as "the armies of heaven." Eventually it was used as equivalent to 'the LORD all-sovereign.' In the prophetical books of the O.T. the Sept. sometimes has *Kurios Sabaōth* as the equivalent of "the LORD of hosts," sometimes *Kurios Pantokratōr*; in Job, it uses *Pantokratōr* to render the Hebrew Divine title *Shadday* (see ALMIGHTY).

NT: B.738b; CB.1268b; K.–.
OT: ṣᵉbā'ôt: S.6635; HR.1256a.1; H.1865a,b; BD.838c,839b.
GEN. REF.: IS.2:507; NB.480; Z.2:763.

SABBATH

1. *sabbaton* [σάββατον, 4521], or *sabbata*: the latter, the plural form, was transliterated from the Aramaic word, which was mistaken for a plural; hence the singular, *sabbaton*, was formed from it. The root means to cease, desist (Heb., *shābath*; cp. Arab., *sabata*, to intercept, interrupt); the doubled *b* has an intensive force, implying a complete cessation or a making to cease, probably the former. The idea is not that of relaxation or refreshment, but cessation from activity.

The observation of the seventh day of the week, enjoined upon Israel, was 'a sign' between God and His earthly people, based upon the fact that after the six days of creative operations He rested, Ex. 31:16, 17, with 20:8-11. The O.T. regulations were developed and systematized to such an extent that they became a burden upon the people (who otherwise rejoiced in the rest provided) and a byword for absurd extravagance. Two treatises of the Mishna (the *shabbāth* and *'Ērūbin*) are entirely occupied with regulations for the observance; so with the discussions in the Gemara, on Rabbinical opinions. The effect upon current opinion explains the antagonism roused by the Lord's cures wrought on the Sabbath, e.g., Matt. 12:9-13; John 5:5-16, and explains the fact that on a Sabbath the sick were brought to be healed after sunset, e.g., Mark 1:32. According to Rabbinical ideas, the disciples, by plucking ears of corn (Matt. 12:1; Mark 2:23), and rubbing them (Luke 6:1), broke the sabbath in two respects; for to pluck was to reap, and to rub was to thresh. The Lord's attitude towards the sabbath was by way of freeing it from these vexatious traditional accretions by which it was made an end in itself, instead of a means to an end (Mark 2:27).

In the Epistles the only direct mentions are in Col. 2:16, "a sabbath day," R.V. (which rightly has the singular, see 1st parag., above), where it is listed among things that were "a shadow of the things to come" (i.e., of the age introduced at Pentecost), and in Heb. 4:4-11, where the perpetual *sabbatismos* is appointed for believers (see REST); inferential references are in Rom. 14:5 and Gal. 4:9-11. For the first three centuries of the Christian era the first day of the week was never confounded with the sabbath; the confusion of the Jewish and Christian institutions was due to declension from apostolic teaching.

NT: B.739a; CB.1268b; K.989.
OT: shabbāt: S.7676; HR.1256b.1a; H.2323b; BD.992a.
GEN. REF.: IS.4:247; NB.1110; Z.5:181.

Notes: (1) In Matt 12:1 and 11, where the plural is used, the A.V. (as the R.V.) rightly has the singular, "the sabbath day"; in ver. 5 the A.V. has the plural (see above). Where the singular is used the R.V. omits the word "day," ver. 2; 24:20; Mark 6:2; Luke 6:1 ("on a sabbath"); 14:3; John 9:14 ("it was the sabbath on the day when . . ."). As to the use or omission of the article the omission does not always require the rendering 'a sabbath'; it is absent, e.g., in Matt. 12:2.

(2) In Acts 16:13, "on the sabbath day," is, lit., 'on the day of the sabbath' (plural).

(3) For Matt. 28:1, see LATE.

(4) For "the first day of the week" see ONE, A, (5).

2. *prosabbaton* [προσάββατον, 4315], signifies "the day before the sabbath" (*pro*, before, and No. 1), Mark 15:42; some mss. have *prin*, before, with *sabbaton* separately). ¶

NT: B.711a; CB.–; K.–.
OT: shabbāt: S.7676; HR.1211a.1; H.2323b; BD.992a.
GEN. REF.: IS.4:247; NB.1110; Z.5:181.

SACKCLOTH

sakkos [σάκκος, 4526], a warm material woven from goat's or camel's hair, and hence of a dark colour, Rev. 6:12; Jerome renders it *saccus cilicinus* (being made from the hair of the black goat of Cilicia, the Romans called it *cilicium*); cp. Isa. 50:3; it was also used for saddle-cloths, Jos. 9:4; also for making sacks, e.g., Gen. 42:25, and for garments worn as expressing mourning or penitence, Matt. 11:21;

Luke 10:13, or for purposes of prophetic testimony, Rev. 11:3. ¶

NT: B.740a; CB.—; K.995.
OT: saq: S.8242; HR.1257b.1; H.2282a; BD.974b.
GEN. REF.: IS.4:256; NB.1112; Z.5:192.

SACRED

hieros [ἱερός, 2413], denotes consecrated to God, e.g., the Scriptures, 2 Tim. 3:15, R.V., "sacred" (A.V. "holy"); it is used as a noun in the neuter plural in 1 Cor. 9:13, R.V., "sacred things" (A.V., "holy things"). ¶ The neuter singular, *hieron*, denotes a temple. See TEMPLE. For a comparison of this and synonymous terms see HOLY, B, No. 1 (*b*) and *Note* (2).

NT: B.372d; CB.1250b; K.349.
OT: miqdāsh: S.4720; HR.683a.4; H.1990f; BD.874a.
GEN. REF.: IS.4:258; NB.—; Z.—.

SACRIFICE (Noun and Verb)

A. Noun.

thusia [θυσία, 2378], primarily denotes the act of offering; then, objectively, that which is offered (*a*) of idolatrous sacrifice, Acts 7:41; (*b*) of animal or other sacrifices, as offered under the Law, Matt. 9:13; 12:7; Mark 9:49; 12:33; Luke 2:24; 13:1; Acts 7:42; 1 Cor. 10:18; Heb. 5:1; 7:27 (R.V., plural); 8:3; 9:9; 10:1, 5, 8 (R.V., plural), 11; 11:4; (*c*) of Christ; in His sacrifice on the Cross, Eph. 5:2; Heb. 9:23, where the plural antitypically comprehends the various forms of Levitical sacrifices in their typical character; 9:26; 10:12, 26; (*d*) metaphorically, (1) of the body of the believer, presented to God as a living sacrifice, Rom. 12:1; (2) of faith, Phil. 2:17; (3) of material assistance rendered to servants of God, Phil. 4:18; (4) of praise, Heb. 13:15; (5) of doing good to others and communicating with their needs, Heb. 13:16; (6) of spiritual sacrifices in general, offered by believers as a holy priesthood, 1 Pet. 2:5. ¶

NT: B.366b; CB.1272c; K.342.
OT: zebaḥ: S.2077; HR.664a.2b; H.525a; BD.257b.
mimḥāh: S.4503; HR.664a.4; H.1214a; BD.585a.
GEN. REF.: IS.4:261; NB.1113; Z.5:199.

B. Verb.

thuō [θύω, 2380], is used of sacrificing by slaying a victim, (*a*) of the sacrifice of Christ, 1 Cor. 5:7, R.V., "hath been sacrificed" (A.V., "is sacrificed"); (*b*) of the Passover sacrifice, Mark 14:12, R.V., "they sacrificed" (A.V., "they killed"); Luke 22:7, R.V., "(must) be sacrificed;" A.V., "(must) be killed"; (*c*) of idolatrous sacrifices, Acts 14:13, 18; 1 Cor. 10:20 (twice). See KILL, No. 3.

NT: B.367a; CB.1272c; K.342.
OT: zābaḥ: S.2076; HR.659a.1; H.525; BD.256d.
shāḥaṭ: S.7819; HR.659a.4a; H.2362; BD.1006a.
GEN. REF.: IS.4:261; NB.1113; Z.5:199.

Note: For *eidōlothutos*, sacrificed to idols, see IDOLS (offered to), No. 1.

For SACRILEGE see ROBBER, No. 2, Rom. 2:22

For SAD see COUNTENANCE

For SADDUCEES see under PHARISEES

SAFE, SAFELY, SAFETY

A. Adjective.

asphalēs [ἀσφαλής, 804], certain, secure, safe (from *a*, negative, and *sphallō*, to trip up), is translated "safe" in Phil. 3:1. See CERTAIN, B.

NT: B.119a; CB.1238a; K.87.
OT: —.
GEN. REF.: IS.4:281; NB.—; Z.—.

B. Nouns.

1. *asphaleia* [ἀσφάλεια, 803], certainty, safety (akin to A), is translated "safety" in Acts 5:23; 1 Thess. 5:3. See CERTAIN, A.

NT: B.118d; CB.1238a; K.87.
OT: bāṭaḥ: S.982; HR.174b.1a; H.233; BD.105a.
beṭaḥ: S.983; HR.174b.1b; H.233a; BD.105b.
GEN. REF.: IS.4:281; NB.—; Z.—.

2. *sōtēria* [σωτηρία, 4991], salvation, is translated "safety" in Acts 27:34, R.V. (A.V., "health"). See HEALTH, *Note*.

NT: B.801b; CB.1269c; K.1132.
OT: yēsha‘: S.3468; HR.1331b.1a; H.929a; BD.447a.
y^{e}shû‘āh: S.3444; HR.1331b.1b; H.929b; BD.447b.
t^{e}shû‘āh: S.8668; HR.1331b.5; H.929e; BD.448b.
GEN. REF.: IS.4:281,291; NB.—; Z.—.

C. Adverb.

asphalōs [ἀσφαλῶς, 806], safely (akin to A, and B, No. 1), is so rendered in Mark 14:44 and Acts 16:23. See ASSURANCE, C. In the Sept., Gen. 34:25. ¶

NT: B.119b; CB.1238a; K.87.
OT: beṭaḥ: S.983; HR.174c.1; H.233a; BD.105b.
GEN. REF.: IS.4:281; NB.—; Z.—.

D. Verbs.

1. *diasōzō* [διασώζω, 1295], to bring safely through danger, and, in the Passive Voice, to come safe through (*dia*, through, *sōzō*, to save), is translated "bring safe" in Acts 23:24; "escaped safe" in 27:44. See ESCAPE, HEAL, SAVE, WHOLE.

NT: B.189a; CB.1241b; K.—.
OT: mālaṭ: S.4422; HR.312b.3; H.1198; BD.572b.
sārîd: S.8300; HR.312b.6b; H.2285a; BD.975a.
GEN. REF.: IS.4:281; NB.—; Z.—.

2. *hugiainō* [ὑγιαίνω, 5198], to be sound, healthy (Eng., hygiene, etc.), is translated "safe and sound" in Luke 15:27, lit., 'being healthy.' See HEALTH, SOUND, WHOLE.

NT: B.832b; CB.1251c; K.1202.
OT: shālôm: S.7965; HR.1380b.1b; H.2401a; BD.1022d.
GEN. REF.: IS.4:281; NB.—; Z.—.

For **SAIL** (Noun, Acts 27:17, A.V.) see **GEAR**

SAIL (Verb)

1. *pleō* [πλέω, 4126], to sail, occurs in Luke 8:23; Acts 21:3; 27:2, 6, 24; Rev. 18:17, R.V., "saileth" (for the A.V. see COMPANY, A, No. 7). ¶

NT: B.668a; CB.—; K.—.
OT: bô': S.935; HR.1141c.1; H.212; BD.97c.
GEN. REF.: IS.4:282; NB.—; Z.—.

2. *apopleō* [ἀποπλέω, 636], to sail away (*apo*, from, and No. 1), occurs in Acts 13:4; 14:26; 20:15; 27:1. ¶

NT: B.97c; CB.—; K.—.
OT: —.
GEN. REF.: IS.4:282; NB.—; Z.—.

3. *ekpleō* [ἐκπλέω, 1602], to sail from, or thence (*ek*, from), occurs in Acts 15:39; 18:18; 20:6. ¶

NT: B.244a; CB.—; K.—.
OT: —.
GEN. REF.: IS.4:282; NB.—; Z.—.

4. *parapleō* [παραπλέω, 3896], to sail by (*para*), occurs in Acts 20:16. ¶

NT: B.621b; CB.—; K.—.
OT: —.
GEN. REF.: IS.4:282; NB.—; Z.—.

5. *diapleō* [διαπλέω, 1277], to sail across (*dia*, through), occurs in Acts 27:5. ¶

NT: B.187c; CB.—; K.—.
OT: —.
GEN. REF.: IS.4:282; NB.—; Z.—.

6. *hupopleō* [ὑποπλέω, 5284], to sail under (*hupo*), i.e., under the lee of, occurs in Acts 27:4, 7. ¶

NT: B.846d; CB.—; K.—.
OT: —.
GEN. REF.: IS.4:282; NB.—; Z.—.

7. *anagō* [ἀνάγω, 321], to lead up, is used of putting to sea, Acts 13:13; 16:11; 18:21; 20:3, 13; 21:1; 27:21; 28:10, 11; see LAUNCH.

NT: B.53a; CB.—; K.—.
OT: 'ālāh: S.5927; HR.75b.6b; H.1624; BD.748a.
GEN. REF.: IS.4:282; NB.—; Z.—.

8. *paralegō* [παραλέγω, 3881], to lay beside (*para*), is used in the Middle Voice, of sailing past in Acts 27:8, R.V., "coasting along" (A.V., "passing"); ver. 13, R.V., "sailed along" (A.V., "sailed"). ¶

NT: B.619d; CB.—; K.—.
OT: —.
GEN. REF.: IS.4:282; NB.—; Z.—.

9. *diaperaō* [διαπεράω, 1276], to cross over, is translated "sailing over" in Acts 21:2, A.V. (R.V., "crossing over"). See PASS.

NT: B.187c; CB.—; K.—.
OT: 'ābar: S.5674; HR.307c.1; H.1556; BD.716d.
GEN. REF.: —.

10. *braduploeō* [βραδυπλοέω, 1020], to sail slowly (*bradus*, slow, *plous*, a voyage), occurs in Acts 27:7. ¶

NT: B.147a; CB.—; K.—.
OT: —.
GEN. REF.: IS.4:282; NB.—; Z.—.

For **SAILING** see **VOYAGE**

For **SAILORS** see **MARINERS**

SAINT(S)

hagios [ἅγιος, 40], for the meaning and use of which see HOLY, B, No. 1, is used as a noun in the singular in Phil. 4:21, where *pas*, "every," is used with it. In the plural, as used of believers, it designates all such and is not applied merely to persons of exceptional holiness, or to those who, having died, were characterized by exceptional acts of saintliness. See especially 2 Thess. 1:10, where "His saints" are also described as "them that believed," i.e., the whole number of the redeemed. They are called "holy ones" in Jude 14, R.V. For the term as applied to the Holy Spirit see HOLY SPIRIT. See also SANCTIFY.

NT: B.9b; CB.1249a; K.14.
OT: qōdesh: S.6944; HR.12a.15; H.1990a; BD.871c.
qādôsh: S.6918; HR.12a.12; H.1990b; BD.872c.
miqdāsh: S.4720; HR.12a.6; H.1990f; BD.874a.
GEN. REF.: IS.4:282; NB.530; Z.5:216.

Notes: (1) In Rev. 15:3 the R.V. follows those texts which have *aiōnōn*, "ages," and assigns the reading *ethnōn*, "nations," to the margin; the A.V. translates those which have the inferior reading *hagiōn*, "saints," and puts "nations" and "ages" in the margin.

(2) In Rev. 18:20, the best texts have *hagioi* and *apostoloi*, each with the article, each being preceeded by *kai*, "and," R.V., "and ye saints, and ye apostles"; the A.V., "and ye holy apostles" follows those mss. from which the 2nd *kai* and the article are absent.

(3) In Rev. 22:21, the R.V. follows those mss. which have *hagiōn*, with the article, "(with) the saints"; the A.V. those which simply have *pantōn*, all, but adds "you" (R.V., marg., "with all").

SAKE (for the): see † p. 1

SALT (Noun, Adjective and Verb), SALTNESS

A. Noun.

halas [ἅλας, 217], a late form of *hals* (found in some mss. in Mark 9:49), is used (*a*) literally in Matt. 5:13 (2nd part); Mark 9:50 (1st part, twice); Luke 14:34 (twice); (*b*) metaphorically, of believers, Matt. 5:13 (1st part); of their character and condition, Mark 9:50 (2nd part); of wisdom exhibited in their speech, Col. 4:6. ¶

Being possessed of purifying, perpetuating and antiseptic qualities, salt became emblematic of fidelity and friendship among eastern nations. To eat of a person's salt and so to share his hospitality is still regarded thus among the Arabs. So in Scripture, it is an emblem of the covenant between God and His people, Num. 18:19; 2 Chron. 13:5; so again when the Lord says "Have salt in yourselves, and be at peace one with another" (Mark 9:50). In the Lord's teaching it is also symbolic of that spiritual health and vigour essential to Christian virtue and counteractive of the corruption that is in the world, e.g., Matt. 5:13, see (*b*) above. Food is seasoned with salt (see B); every meal offering was to contain it, and it was to be offered with all offerings presented by Israelites, as emblematic of the holiness of Christ, and as betokening the reconciliation provided for man by God on the ground of the Death of Christ, Lev. 2:13. To refuse God's provision in Christ and the efficacy of His expiatory sacrifice is to expose oneself to the doom of being "salted with fire," Mark 9:49.

While salt is used to fertilize soil, excess of it on the ground produces sterility (e.g., Deut. 29:23; Judg. 9:45; Jer. 17:6; Zeph. 2:9).

NT: B.35a; CB.1249a; K.36.
OT: melaḥ: S.4417; HR.59b.1b; H.1197a; BD.571d.
GEN. REF.: IS.4:286; NB.1125; Z.5:220.

B. Verb.

halizō [ἁλίζω, 233], akin to A, signifies to sprinkle or to season with salt, Matt. 5:13; Mark 9:49 (see under A), ¶ Cp. SAVOUR, B.

NT: B.37d; CB.1249a; K.–.
OT: mālaḥ: S.4414; HR.54b.1; H.1196,1197; BD.572a.
GEN. REF.: IS.4:286; NB.–; Z.–.

C. Adjectives.

1. *halukos* [ἁλυκός, 252], occurs in Jas. 3:12, "salt (water)." ¶

NT: B.41b; CB.1249a; K.–.
OT: melaḥ: S.4417; HR.60a.1; H.1197a; BD.571d.
GEN. REF.: IS.4:286; NB.–; Z.5:220.

2. *analos* [ἄναλος, 358], denotes saltless (*a*, negative, *n*, euphonic, and A), insipid, Mark 9:50, "have lost its saltness," lit., "have become (*ginomai*) saltless (*analos*)"; cp. *mōrainō* in Luke 14:34 (see SAVOUR, B).

NT: B.57b; CB.1235a; K.–.
OT: –.
GEN. REF.: IS.4:286; NB.–; Z.–.

For **SALUTATION** and **SALUTE** see **GREET**

SALVATION

A. Nouns.

1. *sōtēria* [σωτηρία, 4991], denotes deliverance, preservation, salvation. Salvation is used in the N.T. (*a*) of material and temporal deliverance from danger and apprehension, (1) national, Luke 1:69, 71; Acts 7:25, R.V. marg., "salvation" (text, "deliverance"); (2) personal, as from the sea, Acts 27:34; R.V., "safety" (A.V., "health"); prison, Phil. 1:19; the flood, Heb. 11:7; (*b*) of the spiritual and eternal deliverance granted immediately by God to those who accept His conditions of repentance and faith in the Lord Jesus, in whom alone it is to be obtained, Acts 4:12, and upon confession of Him as Lord, Rom. 10:10; for this purpose the gospel is the saving instrument, Rom. 1:16; Eph. 1:13 (see further under SAVE); (*c*) of the present experience of God's power to deliver from the bondage of sin, e.g., Phil. 2:12, where the special, though not the entire, reference is to the maintenance of peace and harmony; 1 Pet. 1:9; this present experience on the part of believers is virtually equivalent to sanctification; for this purpose, God is able to make them wise, 2 Tim. 3:15; they are not to neglect it, Heb. 2:3; (*d*) of the future deliverance of believers at the Parousia of Christ for His saints, a salvation which is the object of their confident hope, e.g., Rom. 13:11; 1 Thess. 5:8, and ver. 9, where salvation is assured to them, as being deliverance from the wrath of God destined to be executed upon the ungodly at the end of this age (see 1 Thess. 1:10); 2 Thess. 2:13; Heb. 1:14; 9:28; 1 Pet. 1:5; 2 Pet. 3:15; (*e*) of the deliverance of the nation of Israel at the Second Advent of Christ at the time of 'the epiphany (or shining forth) of His Parousia' (2 Thess. 2:8); Luke 1:71; Rev. 12:10; (*f*) inclusively, to sum up all the blessings bestowed by God on men in Christ through the Holy Spirit, e.g., 2 Cor. 6:2; Heb. 5:9; 1 Pet. 1:9, 10; Jude 3; (*g*) occasionally, as standing virtually for the Saviour, e.g., Luke 19:9; cp. John 4:22 (see SAVIOUR); (*h*) in ascriptions of praise to God, Rev. 7:10, and as that which it is His prerogative to bestow, 19:1 (R.V.).

NT: B.801b; CB.1269c; K.1132.
OT: yēsha': S.3468; HR.1331b.1a; H.929a; BD.447a.
yᵉshû'āh: S.3444; HR.1331b.1b; H.929b; BD.447b.
tᵉshû'āh: S.8668; HR.1331b.5; H.929e; BD.448b.
GEN. REF.: IS.4:287; NB.1126; Z.5:221.

2. *sōtērion* [σωτήριον, 4992], the neuter of the adjective (see B), is used as a noun in Luke 2:30; 3:6, in each of which it virtually stands for the Saviour, as in No. 1 (*g*); in Acts 28:28, as in No. 1 (*b*); in Eph. 6:17, where the hope of salvation [see No. 1 (*d*)] is metaphorically described as a helmet. ¶

NT: B.801d; CB.1269c; K.1132.
OT: yᵉshû'āh: S.3444; HR.1332a.1b; H.929b; BD.447b.
shelem: S.8002; HR.1332a.2b; H.2401b; BD.1023b.
GEN. REF.: IS.4:287; NB.1126; Z.5:221.

B. Adjective.

sōtērios [σωτήριος, 4992], saving, bringing salvation, describes the grace of God, in Tit. 2:11. ¶

NT: B.801d; CB.1269c; K.1132.
OT: shelem: S.8002; HR.1332c.1; H.2401b; BD.1023b.
GEN. REF.: IS.4:287; NB.1126; Z.5:221.

SAME

1. *autos* [αὐτός, 846], denotes 'the same' when preceded by the article, and either with a noun following, e.g., Mark 14:39; Phil. 1:30; 1 Cor. 12:4, or without, e.g., Matt. 5:46, 47; Rom. 2:1; Phil. 2:2; 3:1; Heb. 1:12; 13:8. It is thus to be distinguished from uses as a personal and a reflexive pronoun.

NT: B.122d; CB.1238b; K.–.
OT: –.
GEN. REF.: –.

2. *houtos* [οὗτος, 3778], this (person or thing), or he (and the feminine and neuter forms), is sometimes translated "the same," e.g., John 3:2, 26; 7:18; Jas. 3:2; sometimes the R.V. translates it by "this" or "these," e.g., John 12:21, "these" (A.V., "the same"); 2 Cor. 8:6, "this" (A.V., "the same").

NT: B.596b; CB.1251b; K.–.
OT: –.
GEN. REF.: –.

SANCTIFICATION, SANCTIFY

A. Noun.

hagiasmos [ἁγιασμός, 38], sanctification, is used of (*a*) separation to God, 1 Cor. 1:30; 2 Thess. 2:13; 1 Pet. 1:2; (*b*) the course of life befitting those so separated, 1 Thess. 4:3, 4, 7; Rom. 6:19, 22; 1 Tim. 2:15; Heb. 12:14. ¶ "Sanctification is that relationship with God into which men enter by faith in Christ, Acts 26:18; 1 Cor. 6:11, and to which their sole title is the death of Christ, Eph. 5:25, 26; Col. 1:22; Heb. 10:10, 29; 13:12.

"Sanctification is also used in N.T. of the separation of the believer from evil things and ways. This sanctification is God's will for the believer, 1 Thess. 4:3, and His purpose in calling him by the gospel, ver. 7; it must be learned from God, ver. 4, as He teaches it by His Word, John 17:17, 19; cp. Ps. 17:4; 119:9, and it must be pursued by the believer, earnestly and undeviatingly, 1 Tim. 2:15; Heb. 12:14. For the holy character, *hagiōsunē*, 1 Thess. 3:13, is not vicarious, i.e., it cannot be transferred or imputed, it is an individual possession, built up, little by little, as the result of obedience to the Word of God, and of following the example of Christ, Matt. 11:29; John 13:15; Eph. 4:20; Phil. 2:5, in the power of the Holy Spirit, Rom. 8:13; Eph. 3:16.

"The Holy Spirit is the Agent in sanctification, Rom. 15:16; 2 Thess. 2:13; 1 Pet. 1:2; cp. 1 Cor. 6:11. . . . The sanctification of the Spirit is associated with the choice, or election, of God; it is a Divine act preceding the acceptance of the Gospel by the individual."*

For synonymous words see HOLINESS.

NT: B.9a; CB.1249a; K.14.
OT: miqdāsh: S.4720; HR.11c.1; H.1990f; BD.874a.
qādash: S.6942; HR.11c.4; H.1990; BD.872d.
qōdesh: S.6944; HR.11c.5; H.1990a; BD.871c.
GEN. REF.: IS.4:321; NB.1139; Z.5:264.

B. Verb.

hagiazō [ἁγιάζω, 37], to sanctify, "is used of (*a*) the gold adorning the Temple and of the gift laid on the altar, Matt. 23:17, 19; (*b*) food, 1 Tim. 4:5; (*c*) the unbelieving spouse of a believer, 1 Cor. 7:14; (*d*) the ceremonial cleansing of the Israelites, Heb. 9:13; (*e*) the Father's Name, Luke 11:2; (*f*) the consecration of the Son by the Father, John 10:36; (*g*) the Lord Jesus devoting Himself to the redemption of His people, John 17:19; (*h*) the setting apart of the believer for God, Acts 20:32; cp. Rom. 15:16; (*i*) the effect on the believer of the Death of Christ, Heb. 10:10, said of God, and 2:11; 13:12, said of the Lord Jesus; (*j*) the separation of the believer from the world in his behaviour — by the Father through the Word, John 17:17, 19; (*k*) the believer who turns away from such things as dishonour God and His gospel, 2 Tim. 2:21; (*l*) the acknowledgment of the Lordship of Christ, 1 Pet. 3:15.

"Since every believer is sanctified in Christ Jesus, 1 Cor. 1:2, cp. Heb. 10:10, a common N.T. designation of all believer is 'saints,' *hagioi*, i.e., 'sanctified' or 'holy ones.' Thus sainthood, or sanctification is not an attainment, it is the state into which God, in grace, calls sinful men, and in which they begin their course as Christians, Col. 3:12; Heb. 3:1."†

NT: B.8c; CB.1249a; K.14.
OT: qādash: S.6942; HR.10c.7; H.1990; BD.872d.
GEN. REF.: IS.4:321; NB.1139; Z.5:264.

SANCTUARY

1. *hagion* [ἅγιον, 39], the neuter of the adjective *hagios*, holy, is used of those structures which are set apart to God, (*a*) of the Tabernacle in the wilderness, Heb. 9:1, R.V., "its sanctuary, *a sanctuary* of this world" (A.V., "a worldly

* From Notes on Thessalonians by Hogg and Vine, pp. 115, 271.

† From Notes on Thessalonians by Hogg and Vine, pp. 113, 114.

sanctuary"); in ver. 2 the outer part is called "the Holy place," R.V. (A.V., "the sanctuary"); here the neuter plural *hagia* is used, as in verse 3.

Speaking of the absence of the article, Westcott says "The anarthrous form Ἅγια (literally *Holies*) in this sense appears to be unique, as also ἅγια ἁγίων below, if indeed the reading is correct. Perhaps it is chosen to fix attention on the character of the sanctuary as in other cases. The plural suggests the idea of the sanctuary with all its parts: cp. Moulton-Winer, p. 220." In their margin, Westcott and Hort prefix the article *ta* to *hagia* in vv. 2 and 3. In ver. 3 the inner part is called "the Holy of Holies," R.V. (A.V., "the holiest of all"); in ver. 8, "the holy place" (A.V., "the holiest of all"), lit., '(the way) of the holiest'; in ver. 24 "a holy place," R.V. (A.V., "the holy places"), neuter plural; so in ver. 25, "the holy place" (A.V. and R.V.), and in 13:11, R.V., "the holy place" (A.V., "the sanctuary"); in all these there is no separate word *topos*, place, as of the Temple in Matt. 24:15; (*b*) of "Heaven itself," i.e., the immediate presence of God and His Throne, Heb. 8:2, "the sanctuary" (R.V., marg., "holy things"); the neut. plur. with the article points to the text as being right, in view of 9:24, 25 and 13:11 (see above), exegetically designated "the true tabernacle"; neut. plur. in 9:12, "the holy place"; so 10:19, R.V. (A.V., "the holiest"; there are no separate compartments in the antitypical and Heavenly sanctuary), into which believers have "boldness to enter" by faith. ¶

NT: B.9b; CB.1249a; K.14.
OT: qōdesh: S.6944; HR.12a.15; H.1990a; BD.871c.
qādôsh: S.6918; HR.12a.12; H.1990b; BD.872c.
miqdāsh: S.4720; HR.12a.6; H.1990f; BD.874a.
GEN. REF.: IS.4:321; NB.1141; Z.5:264.

2. *naos* [ναός, 3485], is used of the inner part of the Temple in Jerusalem, in Matt. 23:35, R.V., "sanctuary." See TEMPLE.

NT: B.533b; CB.1259b; K.625.
OT: hêkāl: S.1964; HR.939a.4a; H.493; BD.228a.
GEN. REF.: –.

SAND

ammos [ἄμμος, 285], sand or sandy ground, describes (*a*) an insecure foundation, Matt. 7:26; (*b*) numberlessness, vastness, Rom. 9:27; Heb. 11:12; Rev. 20:8; (*c*) symbolically in Rev. 13:1, R.V., the position taken up by the Dragon (not, as in the A.V., by John), in view of the rising of the Beast out of the sea (emblematic of the restless condition of nations; see SEA). ¶

NT: B.46b; CB.–; K.–.
OT: ḥôl: S.2344; HR.66a.1; H.623a; BD.297c.
'āphār: S.6083; HR.66a.2; H.1664a; BD.779c.
GEN. REF.: IS.4:331; NB.1142; Z.5:267.

SANDAL

sandalion [σανδάλιον, 4547], a diminutive of *sandalon*, probably a Persian word, Mark 6:9; Acts 12:8. The sandal usually had a wooden sole bound on by straps round the instep and ankle. ¶

NT: B.742a; CB.–; K.702.
OT: na'al: S.5275; HR.1259a.1; H.1383a; BD.653a.
GEN. REF.: IS.4:491; NB.–; Z.5:268.

SAPPHIRE

sappheiros [σάπφειρος, 4552], is mentioned in Rev. 21:19 (R.V., marg., "*lapis lazuli*") as the second of the foundations of the wall of the heavenly Jerusalem (cp. Is. 54:11). ¶ It was one of the stones in the high priest's breastplate, Ex. 28:18; 39:11; as an intimation of its value see Job 28:16; Ezek. 28:13. See also Ex. 24:10; Ezek. 1:26; 10:1. The sapphire has various shades of blue, and ranks next in hardness to the diamond.

NT: B.742c; CB.1268b; K.–.
OT: sappîr: S.5601; HR.1259b.1; H.1535; BD.705d.
GEN. REF.: IS.4:629; NB.633; Z.–.

SARDIUS, SARDINE (A.V.)

sardion or *sardinos* [σάρδιον, 4555], denotes the sardian stone. *Sardius* is the word in the best texts in Rev. 4:3 (R.V., "a sardius"), where it formed part of the symbolic appearance of the Lord on His Throne, setting forth His glory and majesty in view of the judgment to follow. There are two special varieties, one a yellowish brown, the other a transparent red (like a cornelian). The beauty of the stone, its transparent brilliance, the high polish of which it is susceptible, made it a favourite among the ancients. It forms the sixth foundation of the wall of the heavenly Jerusalem, Rev. 21:20. ¶

NT: B.742d; CB.1268b; K.–.
OT: shōham: S.7718; HR.1259b.2; H.2337; BD.995d.
'ōdem: S.124; HR.1259b.1; H.26c; BD.10b.
GEN. REF.: IS.4:626,629; NB.633; Z.5:274.

SARDONYX

sardonux [σαρδόνυξ, 4557], a name which indicates the formation of the gem, a layer of sard, and a layer of onyx, marked by the red of the sard and the white of the onyx. It was used among the Romans both for cameos and for signets. It forms the fifth foundation of the wall of the heavenly Jerusalem, Rev. 21:20. ¶

NT: B.742d; CB.1268b; K.–.
OT: –.
GEN. REF.: IS.–; NB.633; Z.5:278.

SATAN

satanas [Σατανᾶς, 4567], a Greek form derived from the Aramaic (Heb., *Sātān*), an adversary, is used (*a*) of an angel of Jehovah in Num. 22:22 (the first occurrence of the word in the O.T.); (*b*) of men, e.g., 1 Sam. 29:4; Psa. 38:20; 71:13; four in Ps. 109; (*c*) of Satan, the Devil, some seventeen or eighteen times in the O.T.; in Zech. 3:1, where the name receives its interpretation, "to be (his) adversary," R.V. (see marg.; A.V., "to resist him").

In the N.T. the word is always used of Satan, the adversary (*a*) of God and Christ, e.g., Matt. 4:10; 12:26; Mark 1:13; 3:23, 26; 4:15; Luke 4:8 (in some mss.); 11:18; 22:3; John 13:27; (*b*) of His people, e.g., Luke 22:31; Acts 5:3; Rom. 16:20; 1 Cor. 5:5; 7:5; 2 Cor. 2:11; 11:14; 12:7; 1 Thess. 2:18; 1 Tim. 1:20; 5:15; Rev. 2:9, 13 (twice), 24; 3:9; (*c*) of mankind, Luke 13:16; Acts 26:18; 2 Thess. 2:9; Rev. 12:9; 20:7.

His doom, sealed at the Cross, is foretold in its stages in Luke 10:18; Rev. 20:2, 10. Believers are assured of victory over him, Rom. 16:20.

The appellation was given by the Lord to Peter, as a Satan-like man, on the occasion when he endeavoured to dissuade Him from death, Matt. 16:23; Mark 8:33. ¶

Satan is not simply the personification of evil influences in the heart, for he tempted Christ, in whose heart no evil thought could ever have arisen (John 14:30; 2 Cor. 5:21; Heb. 4:15); moreover his personality is asserted in both the O.T. and the N.T., and especially in the latter, whereas if the O.T. language was intended to be figurative, the N.T. would have made this evident. See DEVIL.

NT: B.744d; CB.1268c; K.1007.
OT: sāṭān: S.7854; HR.—; H.2252a; BD.966b.
GEN. REF.: IS.4:340; NB.1145; Z.5:282.

SATISFY

1. *chortazō* [χορτάζω, 5526], to fill or satisfy with food, is translated "satisfy" in Mark 8:4, A.V. (R.V., "to fill"). See FILL, No. 8.

NT: B.883d; CB.1240a; K.—.
OT: sāba': S.7646; HR.1472c.1; H.2231; BD.959b.
GEN. REF.: IS.4:344; NB.—; Z.—.

2. *empiplēmi* or *emplēthō* [ἐμπίπλημι, 1705], to fill up, fill full, satisfy (*en*, in, *pimplēmi* or *plēthō*, to fill), is used metaphorically in Rom. 15:24, of taking one's fill of the company of others, R.V., "I shall have been satisfied" (A.V., "I be . . . filled"). See FILL, No. 6.

NT: B.256a; CB.1244b; K.840.
OT: mālē': S.4390; HR.457a.3a-c; H.1195; BD.569d.
sāba': S.7646; HR.457a.6a-c; H.2231; BD.959b.
GEN. REF.: IS.4:344; NB.—; Z.—.

For **SATISFYING**, Col. 2:23, A.V., see **INDULGENCE**

For **SAVE** (Preposition) see † p. 1

SAVE, SAVING

A. Verbs.

1. *sōzō* [σώζω, 4982], to save, is used (as with the noun *sōtēria*, salvation) (*a*) of material and temporal deliverance from danger, suffering, etc., e.g., Matt. 8:25; Mark 13:20; Luke 23:35; John 12:27; 1 Tim. 2:15; 2 Tim. 4:18 (A.V., "preserve"); Jude 5; from sickness, Matt. 9:22, "made . . . whole" (R.V., marg., "saved"); so Mark 5:34; Luke 8:48; Jas. 5:15; (*b*) of the spiritual and eternal salvation granted immediately by God to those who believe on the Lord Jesus Christ, e.g., Acts 2:47, R.V. "(those that) were being saved"; 16:31; Rom. 8:24, R.V., "were we saved"; Eph. 2:5, 8; 1 Tim. 2:4; 2 Tim. 1:9; Tit. 3:5; of human agency in this, Rom. 11:14; 1 Cor. 7:16; 9:22; (*c*) of the present experiences of God's power to deliver from the bondage of sin, e.g., Matt. 1:21; Rom. 5:10; 1 Cor. 15:2; Heb. 7:25; Jas. 1:21; 1 Pet. 3:21; of human agency in this, 1 Tim. 4:16; (*d*) of the future deliverance of believers at the Second Coming of Christ for His saints, being deliverance from the wrath of God to be executed upon the ungodly at the close of this age and from eternal doom, e.g., Rom 5:9; (*e*) of the deliverance of the nation of Israel at the Second Advent of Christ, e.g., Rom. 11:26; (*f*) inclusively for all the blessings bestowed by God on men in Christ, e.g., Luke 19:10; John 10:9; 1 Cor. 10:33; 1 Tim. 1:15; (*g*) of those who endure to the end of the time of the great tribulation, Matt. 10:22; Mark 13:13; (*h*) of the individual believer, who, though losing his reward at the Judgment-Seat of Christ hereafter, will not lose his salvation, 1 Cor. 3:15; 5:5; (*i*) of the deliverance of the nations at the Millennium, Rev. 21:24 (in some mss.). See SALVATION.

NT: B.798a; CB.1269c; K.1132.
OT: yāsha': S.3467; HR.1328b.5b; H.929; BD.446b.
mālaṭ: S.4422; HR.1328b.6b; H.1198; BD.572b.
nāṣal: S.5337; HR.1328b.7; H.1404; BD.664c.
GEN. REF.: IS.4:287; NB.—; Z.5:221.

2. *diasōzō* [διασώζω, 1295], to bring safely through (*dia*, through, and No. 1), is used (*a*) of the healing of the sick by the Lord, Matt. 14:36, R.V., "were made whole" (A.V. adds "perfectly"); Luke 7:3; (*b*) of bringing safe to a destination, Acts 23:24; (*c*) of keeping a person safe, 27:43; (*d*) of escaping through the perils of shipwreck, 27:44; 28:1, 4, Passive Voice; (*e*) through the Flood, 1 Pet. 3:20. See ESCAPE, WHOLE. ¶

NT: B.189a; CB.1241b; K.—.
OT: mālaṭ: S.4422; HR.312b.3; H.1198; BD.572b.
sārîd: S.8300; HR.312b.6b; H.2285a; BD.975a.
GEN. REF.: IS.4:287; NB.—; Z.5:221.

Note: In 2 Pet. 2:5, A.V., *phulassō*, to guard, keep, preserve, is translated "saved" (R.V., "preserved"). In Luke 17:33 some mss. have *sōzō* (A.V., "save"), for the R.V.: see GAIN, B, No. 3. For "save alive," Luke 17:33, R.V., see LIVE, No. 6.

B. Noun.

peripoiēsis [περιποίησις, 4047], (*a*) preservation, (*b*) acquiring or gaining something, is used in this latter sense in Heb. 10:39, translated "saving" (R.V. marg., "gaining"); the reference here is to salvation in its completeness. See OBTAIN, POSSESSION.

NT: B.650a; CB.1263b; K.—.
OT: miḥyāh: S.4241; HR.1125c.1; H.644b; BD.313c.
s^{e}gullāh: S.5459; HR.1125c.2; H.1460a; BD.688c.
GEN. REF.: —.

Note: In Heb. 11:7 *sōtēria* is rendered "saving." See SALVATION.

SAVING (Preposition)

parektos [παρεκτός, 3924], used as a preposition, denotes "saving," Matt. 5:32 (in some mss., 19:9). See EXCEPT. ¶

NT: B.625a; CB.1262b; K.—.
OT: —.
GEN. REF.: —.

Note: In Luke 4:27 and Rev. 2:17, A.V., *ei mē* (lit., 'if not'), is translated "saving" (R.V., "but only" and "but").

SAVIOUR

sōtēr [σωτήρ, 4990], a saviour, deliverer, preserver, is used (*a*) of God, Luke 1:47; 1 Tim. 1:1; 2:3; 4:10 (in the sense of Preserver, since He gives "to all life and breath and all things"); Tit. 1:3; 2:10; 3:4; Jude 25; (*b*) of Christ, Luke 2:11; John 4:42; Acts 5:31; 13:23 (of Israel); Eph. 5:23 (the Sustainer and Preserver of the Church, His "body"); Phil. 3:20 (at His return to receive the Church to Himself); 2 Tim. 1:10 (with reference to His Incarnation, "the days of His flesh"); Tit. 1:4 (a title shared, in the context, with God the Father); 2:13, R.V., "our great God and Saviour Jesus Christ," the pronoun "our," at the beginning of the whole clause, includes all the titles; Tit. 3:6; 2 Pet. 1:1, "our God and Saviour Jesus Christ," R.V., where the pronoun "our," coming immediately in connection with "God," involves the inclusion of both titles as referring to Christ, just as in the parallel in ver. 11, "our Lord and Saviour Jesus Christ" (A.V. and R.V.); these passages are therefore a testimony to His Deity; 2 Pet. 2:20; 3:2, 18; 1 John 4:14. ¶

NT: B.800c; CB.1269c; K.1132.
OT: yāsha': S.3467; HR.1331a.1a; H.929; BD.446b.
y^{e}shû'āh: S.3444; HR.1331a.1b; H.929b; BD.447b.
yēsha': S.3468; HR.1331a.1c; H.929a; BD.447a.
GEN. REF.: IS.4:291ff; NB.—; Z.5:291.

SAVOUR (Noun and Verb)

A. Nouns.

1. *euōdia* [εὐωδία, 2175], fragrance (*eu*, well, *ozō*, to smell), is used metaphorically (*a*) of those who in the testimony of the gospel are to God "a sweet savour of Christ," 2 Cor. 2:15; (*b*) of the giving up of His life by Christ for us, an offering and a sacrifice to God for an odour (*osmē*, see No. 2) of "a sweet smell," Eph. 5:2, R.V. [A.V., "a sweet smelling (savour)"]; (*c*) of material assistance sent to Paul from the church at Philippi "(an odour) of a sweet smell," Phil. 4:18. In all three instances the fragrance is that which ascends to God through the Person, and as a result of the Sacrifice, of Christ. ¶

NT: B.329d; CB.1247b; K.285.
OT: nîḥōaḥ: S.5207; HR.584c.1; H.1323c; BD.629b.
GEN. REF.: IS.3:579; NB.1148; Z.4:503.

2. *osmē* [ὀσμή, 3744], a smell, odour (from *ozō*, to smell; Eng., ozone), is translated "odour" in John 12:3; it is used elsewhere in connection with No. 1, in the three passages mentioned, as of an odour accompanying an acceptable sacrifice; in 2 Cor. 2:14, 16 (twice), of the "savour" of the knowledge of Christ through Gospel testimony, in the case of the perishing "a savour from death unto death," as of that which arises from what is dead (the spiritual condition of the unregenerate); in the case of the saved "a savour from life unto life," as from that which arises from what is instinct with life (the spiritual condition of the regenerate); in Eph. 5:2, "a (sweetsmelling) savour"; in Phil. 4:18, "an odour (of a sweet smell)"; cp. No. 1. See ODOUR. ¶

NT: B.586a; CB.1261b; K.735.
OT: rêaḥ: S.7381; HR.1018c.3; H.2131b; BD.926b.
GEN. REF.: IS.3:579; NB.1148; Z.4:503.

B. Verb.

mōrainō [μωραίνω, 3471], primarily, to be foolish, is used of salt that has lost its savour, Matt. 5:13; Luke 14:34. See FOOLISH, B, No. 1.

NT: B.531b; CB.1259b; K.620.
OT: bā'ar: S.1197; HR.938b.1; H.263; BD.129c.
sākal: S.5528; HR.938b.2; H.1493; BD.698a.
GEN. REF.: —.

Note: In the A.V. of Matt. 16:23 and Mark 8:33, *phroneō*, to think, to mind, is translated "thou savourest" (R.V., "thou mindest").

SAW ASUNDER

prizō or *priō* [πρίζω, 4249], to saw asunder, occurs in Heb. 11:37. Some have seen here a reference to the tradition of Isaiah's martyrdom under Manasseh. ¶ In the Sept., Amos 1:3. ¶ Cp. *diapriō*, to cut to the heart, Acts 5:33; 7:54. ¶

NT: B.701a; CB.—; K.—.
OT: —.
GEN. REF.: IS.4:347; NB.—; Z.—.

SAY

1. *legō* [λέγω, 3004], primarily, to pick out, gather, chiefly denotes to say, speak, affirm, whether of actual speech, e.g., Matt. 11:17, or of unspoken thought, e.g., Matt. 3:9, or of a message in writing, e.g., 2 Cor. 8:8. The 2nd aorist form *eipon* is used to supply that tense, which is lacking in *legō*.

Concerning the phrase "he answered and said," it is a well known peculiarity of Hebrew narrative style that a speech is introduced, not simply by 'and he said,' but by prefixing "and he answered" (*apokrinomai*, with *eipon*). In Matt. 14:27, "saying," and Mark 6:50, "and saith," emphasis is perhaps laid on the fact that the Lord, hitherto silent as He moved over the lake, then addressed His disciples. That the phrase sometimes occurs where no explicit question has preceded (e.g., Matt. 11:25; 17:4; 28:5; Mark 11:14; 12:35; Luke 13:15; 14:3; John 5:17, 19), illustrates the use of the Hebrew idiom.

NT: B.468a; CB.1256c; K.505.
OT: 'āmar: S.559; HR.863c.1a; H.118; BD.55c.
GEN. REF.: —.

Note: A characteristic of *legō* is that it refers to the purport or sentiment of what is said as well as the connection of the words; this is illustrated in Heb. 8:1, R.V., "(in the things which) we are saying," A.V., "(which) we have spoken." In comparison with *laleō* (No. 2), *legō* refers especially to the substance of what is said, *laleō*, to the words conveying the utterance; see, e.g., John 12:49, "what I should say (*legō*, in the 2nd aorist subjunctive form *eipō*), and what I should speak (*laleō*)"; ver. 50, "even as the Father hath said (*legō*, in the perfect form *eirēke*) unto Me, so I speak" (*laleō*); cp. 1 Cor. 14:34, "saith (*legō*) the law"; ver. 35, "to speak" (*laleō*). Sometimes *laleō* signifies the utterance, as opposed to silence, *legō* declares what is said; e.g., Rom. 3:19, "what things soever the law saith (*legō*), it speaketh (*laleō*) to them that are under the law"; see also Mark 6:50; Luke 24:6. In the N.T. *laleō* never has the meaning to chatter.

2. *laleō* [λαλέω, 2980], to speak, is sometimes translated to say; in the following where the A.V. renders it thus, the R.V. alters it to the verb to speak, e.g., John 8:25 (3rd part), 26; 16:6; 18:20 (2nd part), 21 (1st part); Acts 3:22 (2nd part); 1 Cor. 9:8 (1st part); Heb. 5:5; in the following the R.V. uses the verb to say, John 16:18; Acts 23:18 (2nd part); 26:22 (2nd part); Heb. 11:18. See *Note* above, and SPEAK, TALK, TELL, UTTER.

NT: B.463a; CB.1256b; K.505.
OT: dābar: S.1696; HR.841c.2c; H.399; BD.180b.
GEN. REF.: —.

3. *phēmi* [φημί, 5346], to declare, say, (*a*) is frequently used in quoting the words of another, e.g., Matt. 13:29; 26:61; (*b*) is interjected into the recorded words, e.g., Acts 23:35; (*c*) is used impersonally, 2 Cor. 10:10.

NT: B.856b; CB.1264a; K.—.
OT: —.
GEN. REF.: —.

4. *eirō* [εἴρω, after 1518], an obsolete verb, has the future tense *ereō*, used, e.g., in Matt. 7:4; Luke 4:23 (2nd part); 13:25 (last part); Rom. 3:5; 4:1; 6:1; 7:7 (1st part); 8:31; 9:14, 19, 20, 30; 11:19; 1 Cor. 15:35; 2 Cor. 12:6; Jas. 2:18. The perfect is used, e.g., in John 12:50; see No. 1, *Note*. The 1st aorist passive, "it was said," is used in Rom. 9:12, 26; Rev. 6:11. See SPEAK, No. 13.

NT: —.
OT: —.
GEN. REF.: —.

5. *proeipon* [προεῖπον, 4302] and *proereō*, to say before, used as aorist and future respectively of *prolegō* (*pro*, before, and No. 1), is used (*a*) of prophecy, e.g., Rom. 9:29; 'to tell before,' Matt. 24:25; Mark 13:23; "were spoken before," 2 Pet. 3:2; Jude 17; (*b*) of saying before, 2 Cor. 7:3; 13:2, R.V. (A.V., to tell before and foretell); Gal. 1:9; 5:21; in 1 Thess. 4:6, "we forewarned," R.V. See FORETELL, FOREWARN, TELL.

NT: B.704d; CB.—; K.—.
OT: —.
GEN. REF.: —.

6. *anteipon* [ἀντεῖπον, —], to say against (*anti*, against, and No. 1), is so rendered in Acts 4:14. See GAINSAY.

NT: B.73b; CB.—; K.—.
OT: —.
GEN. REF.: —.

Notes: (1) *Phaskō*, to affirm, assert, is translated "saying" in Acts 24:9, A.V. (R.V., "affirming"), and Rev. 2:2 in some mss. (A.V.). See AFFIRM, No. 3.

(2) In Acts 2:14, A.V., *apophthengomai*, to speak forth (R.V.), is rendered "said."

(3) The phrase *tout 'esti* (i.e., *touto esti*), "that is," is so translated in Matt. 27:46, R.V. (A.V., "that is to say"); so Acts 1:19; in Heb. 9:11 and

10:20, A.V. and R.V., "that is to say"; in Mark 7:11 the phrase is *ho esti*, lit., 'which is'; the phrase *ho legetai*, lit., 'which is said,' John 1:38 and 20:16, is rendered "which is to say."

(4) In Luke 7:40 and Acts 13:15, the imperative mood of *eipon* and *legō*, respectively, is rendered "say on."

(5) In Mark 6:22, A.V., *autēs*, "herself," R.V., is rendered "the said."

(6) In Heb. 5:11, "we have many things to say" is, lit., 'much (*polus*) is the word (or discourse, *logos*) for us.'

SAYING

1. *logos* [λόγος, 3056], a word, as embodying a conception or idea, denotes among its various meanings, a saying, statement or declaration, uttered (*a*) by God; R.V., "word" or "words" (A.V., "saying"), e.g., in John 8:55; Rom. 3:4; Rev. 19:9; 22:6, 7, 9, 10; (*b*) by Christ, e.g., Mark 8:32; 9:10; 10:22; Luke 9:28; John 6:60; 21:23; the R.V. appropriately substitutes "word" or "words" for A.V., "saying" or "sayings," especially in John's Gospel, e.g., 7:36, 40; 8:51, 52; 10:19; 14:24; 15:20; 18:9, 32; 19:13; (*c*) by an angel, Luke 1:29; (*d*) by O.T. prophets, John 12:38 (R.V., "word"); Rom. 13:9 (ditto); 1 Cor. 15:54; (*e*) by the Apostle Paul in the Pastoral Epp., 1 Tim. 1:15; 3:1; 4:9; 2 Tim. 2:11; Tit. 3:8; (*f*) by other men, Mark 7:29; Acts 7:29; John 4:37 (in general). See ACCOUNT, and especially WORD.

NT: B.477a; CB.1257a; K.505.
OT: dābār: S.1697; HR.881c.2a; H.399a; BD.182a.
GEN. REF.: –.

2. *rhēma* [ῥῆμα, 4487], that which is said, a word, is rendered "saying" or "sayings" in Mark 9:32; Luke 1:65; 2:17, 50, 51; 7:1; 9:45 (twice); 18:34. See WORD.

NT: B.735b; CB.1268a; K.505.
OT: dābār: S.1697; HR.1249a.2a; H.399a; BD.182a.
GEN. REF.: –.

Note: In Acts 14:18, "with these sayings" is, lit., 'saying (*legō*) these things.' For *lalia*, "saying," John 4:42. A.V., see SPEECH, No. 2.

SCALE

lepis [λεπίς, —], from *lepō*, to peel, occurs in Acts 9:18. ¶

For **SCARCE, SCARCELY** see **DIFFICULTY**

SCARLET

kokkinos [κόκκινος, 2847], is derived from *kokkos*, used of the 'berries' (clusters of the eggs of an insect) collected from the *ilex coccifera*; the colour, however, is obtained from the cochineal insect, which attaches itself to the leaves and twigs of the coccifera oak; another species is raised on the leaves of the *cactus ficus*. The Arabic name for this insect is *qirmiz*, whence the word crimson. It is used (*a*) of scarlet wool, Heb. 9:19; cp., in connection with the cleansing of a leper, Lev. 14:4, 6, "scarlet"; with the offering of the red heifer, Numb. 19:6; (*b*) of the robe put on Christ by the soldiers, Matt. 27:28; (*c*) of the "beast" seen in symbolic vision in Rev. 17:3, "scarlet-coloured"; (*d*) of the clothing of the "woman" as seen sitting on the "beast," 17:4; (*e*) of part of the merchandise of Babylon, 18:12; (*f*) figuratively, of the glory of the city itself, 18:16; the neuter is used in the last three instances. ¶

NT: B.440b; CB.1255b; K.450.
OT: tôlēʻāh: S.8438; HR.775c.3b; H.2516b; BD.1069a.
shānî: S.8144; HR.775c.2; H.2420a; BD.1040c.
GEN. REF.: IS.1:732; NB.–; Z.5:292.

SCATTER

A. Verbs.

1. *skorpizō* [σκορπίζω, 4650], is used in Matt. 12:30; Luke 11:23; John 10:12; 16:32; 2 Cor. 9:9, R.V. See DISPERSE, No. 2. ¶

NT: B.757a; CB.1269b; K.1048.
OT: zārāh: S.2219; HR.1275c.2; H.579; BD.279d.
pûṣ: S.6327; HR.1275c.4; H.1745-6,1800; BD.806d.
GEN. REF.: –.

2. *diaskorpizō* [διασκορπίζω, 1287], to scatter abroad, is rendered to scatter in Matt. 25:24, 26, R.V. (A.V., "strawed"); 26:31; Mark 14:27; Luke 1:51; John 11:52; Acts 5:37, R.V. See DISPERSE, No. 3.

NT: B.188b; CB.1241b; K.1048.
OT: zārāh: S.2219; HR.310b.4; H.579; BD.279d.
pûṣ: S.6327; HR.310b.10; H.1745-6,1800; BD.806d.
GEN. REF.: –.

3. *diaspeirō* [διασπείρω, 1289], to scatter abroad (*dia*, throughout, *speirō*, to sow seed), is used in Acts 8:1, 4; 11:19, all of the church in Jerusalem scattered through persecution; the word in general is suggestive of the effects of the scattering in the sowing of the spiritual seed of the Word of life. See DISPERSE, No. 4. ¶

NT: B.188c; CB.1241b; K.–.
OT: zārāh: S.2219; HR.310c.1; H.579; BD.279d.
pûṣ: S.6327; HR.310c.6; H.1475-6,1800; BD.806d.
GEN. REF.: –.

4. *rhiptō* [ῥίπτω, 4496], to throw, cast, hurl, to be cast down, prostrate, is used in Matt. 9:36 of people who were scattered as sheep without a shepherd. See CAST, No. 2, THROW.

NT: B.736c; CB.–; K.987.
OT: shālak: S.7993; HR.1252b.10a; H.2398; BD.1020d.
GEN. REF.: –.

5. *likmaō* [λικμάω, 3039], to winnow (*likmow*, a winnowing-fan), is rendered "will scatter . . . as dust" in Matt. 21:44 and Luke 20:18, R.V. (A.V., "will grind . . . to powder"). See GRIND, *Note*. ¶

NT: B.474d; CB.–; K.535.
OT: zārāh: S.2219; HR.878b.1a-c; H.579; BD.279d.
GEN. REF.: –.

6. *dialuō* [διαλύω, 1262], to dissolve, is translated "scattered" in Acts 5:36, A.V.; see DISPERSE, No. 1. ¶
NT: B.186b; CB.1241b; K.–.
OT: –.
GEN. REF.: –.

B. Noun.

diaspora [διασπορά, 1290], a dispersion, is rendered "scattered abroad" in Jas. 1:1, A.V.; "scattered" in 1 Pet. 1:1, A.V.; see DISPERSION, B.
NT: B.188c; CB.1241b; K.156.
OT: nādaḥ: S.5080; HR.311a.5; H.1304; BD.623a.
GEN. REF.: IS.1:962; NB.–; Z.2:119.

For **SCEPTRE** see **ROD**

SCHISM

schisma [σχίσμα, 4978], a rent, division, is translated "schism" in 1 Cor. 12:25, metaphorically of the contrary condition to that which God has designed for a local church in 'tempering the body together' (ver. 24), the members having "the same care one for another" ("the same" being emphatic). See DIVISION, No. 3, RENT.
NT: B.797c; CB.1268c; K.1130.
OT: –.
GEN. REF.: IS.4:351; NB.–; Z.5:293.

SCHOOL

scholē [σχολή, 4981], (whence Eng., school) primarily denotes leisure, then, that for which leisure was employed, a disputation, lecture; hence, by metonymy, the place where lectures are delivered, a school, Acts 19:9. ¶
NT: B.798a; CB.–; K.–.
OT: –.
GEN. REF.: –.

For **SCHOOLMASTER**, Gal. 3:24, 25, see **INSTRUCTOR**, B. No. 1

SCIENCE

gnōsis [γνῶσις, 1108], is translated "science" in the A.V. of 1 Tim. 6:20; the word simply means "knowledge" (R.V.), where the reference is to the teaching of the Gnostics (lit., the knowers) 'falsely called knowledge'. Science in the modern sense of the word, viz., the investigation, discovery and classification of secondary laws, is unknown in Scripture. See KNOW, C, No. 1.
NT: B.163d; CB.1248b; K.119.
OT: da'at: S.1847; HR.273c.1b; H.848c; BD.359c.
GEN. REF.: IS.3:48; NB.–; Z.–.

SCOFF

ekmuktērizō [ἐκμυκτηρίζω, 1592], to hold up the nose in derision at (*ek*, from, used intensively, *muktērizō*, to mock; from *muktēr*, the nose), is translated "scoffed at" in Luke 16:14, R.V. (A.V., "derided"), of the Pharisees in their derision of Christ on account of His teaching; in 23:35 (ditto), of the mockery of Christ on the Cross by the rulers of the people. ¶ In the Sept., Ps. 2:4; 22:7; 35:16. ¶
NT: B.243b; CB.1243c; K.614.
OT: lā'ag: S.3932; HR.438b.1a,b; H.1118; BD.541b.
GEN. REF.: IS.4:356; NB.–; Z.5:296.

For **SCOFFERS**, 2 Pet. 3:3, A.V., see **MOCKERS**

SCORCH, SCORCHING

A. Verb.

kaumatizō [καυματίζω, 2739], to scorch (from *kauma*, heat), is used (*a*) of seed that had not much earth, Matt. 13:6; Mark 4:6; (*b*) of men, stricken retributively by the sun's heat, Rev. 16:8, 9. ¶
NT: B.425b; CB.1254c; K.423.
OT: –.
GEN. REF.: IS.4:357; NB.–; Z.–.

B. Noun.

kausōn [καύσων, 2742], burning heat (akin to *kaiō*, to burn), is translated "scorching heat" in Matt. 20:12 (A.V., "heat"); Luke 12:55 (ditto); in Jas. 1:11, R.V., "scorching wind" (A.V., "burning heat"), here the reference is to a hot wind from the east (cp. Job 1:19). See HEAT. ¶ In the Sept., Job 27:21; Jer. 18:17; 51:1; Ezek. 17:10; 19:12; Hos. 12:1; 13:15; Jonah 4:8. ¶
NT: B.425c; CB.–; K.423.
OT: qādîm: S.6921; HR.757b.1; H.1988d; BD.870b.
GEN. REF.: IS.4:357; NB.–; Z.–.

For **SCORN** see **LAUGH**

SCORPION

skorpios [σκορπίος, 4651], akin to *skorpizō*, to scatter (which see), is a small animal (the largest of the several species is 6 in. long) like a lobster, but with a long tail, at the end of which is its venomous sting; the pain, the position of the sting and the effect are mentioned in Rev. 9:3, 5, 10. The Lord's rhetorical question as to the provision of a scorpion instead of an egg, Luke 11:12, is, firstly, an allusion to the egg-like shape of the creature when at rest; secondly, an indication of the abhorrence with which it is regarded. In Luke 10:19, the Lord's assurance to the disciples of the authority given them by Him to tread upon serpents and scorpions conveys the thought of victory over spiritually antagonistic forces, the powers of darkness, as is shown by His reference to the "power of the enemy" and by the context in vv. 17, 20. ¶

NT: B.757a; CB.1269b; K.—.
OT: ʿaqrāb: S.6137; HR.1276a.1; H.1683; BD.785d.
GEN. REF.: IS.4:357; NB.1149; Z.5:297.

SCOURGE (Noun and Verb)

A. Noun.

phragellion [φραγέλλιον, 5416], a whip (from Latin, *flagellum*), is used of the scourge of small cords which the Lord made and employed before cleansing the Temple, John 2:15. However He actually used it, the whip was in itself a sign of authority and judgment. ¶

NT: B.865b; CB.1264b; K.—.
OT: —.
GEN. REF.: IS.4:358; NB.1150; Z.5:297.

B. Verbs.

1. *phragelloō* [φραγελλόω, 5417], (akin to A: Latin, *flagello*; Eng., flagellate), is the word used in Matt. 27:26, and Mark 15:15, of the scourging endured by Christ and administered by the order of Pilate. Under the Roman method of scourging, the person was stripped and tied in a bending posture to a pillar, or stretched on a frame. The scourge was made of leathern thongs, weighted with sharp pieces of bone or lead, which tore the flesh of both the back and the breast (cp. Psa. 22:17). Eusebius (*Chron.*) records his having witnessed the suffering of martyrs who died under this treatment. ¶

NT: B.865b; CB.1264b; K.—.
OT: —.
GEN. REF.: IS.4:358; NB.1150; Z.5:297.

Note: In John 19:1 the scourging of Christ is described by Verb No. 2, as also in His prophecy of His sufferings, Matt. 20:19; Mark 10:34; Luke 18:33. In Acts 22:25 the similar punishment about to be administered to Paul is described by Verb No. 3 (the scourging of Roman citizens was prohibited by the Porcian law of 197, B.C.).

2. *mastigoō* [μαστιγόω, 3146], akin to *mastix* (see below), is used (*a*) as mentioned under No. 1; (*b*) of Jewish scourgings, Matt. 10:17 and 23:34; (*c*) metaphorically, in Heb. 12:6, of the chastening by the Lord administered in love to His spiritual sons. ¶

NT: B.495a; CB.1257c; K.571.
OT: nākāh: S.5221; HR.898a.3; H.1364; BD.645a.
nāgaʿ: S.5060; HR.898a.2; H.1293; BD.619a.
GEN. REF.: IS.4:358; NB.1150; Z.5:297.

Note: The Jewish method of scourging, as described in the Mishna, was by the use of three thongs of leather, the offender receiving thirteen stripes on the bare breast and thirteen on each shoulder, the "forty stripes save one," as administered to Paul five times (2 Cor. 11:24). See also SCOURGINGS (below).

3. *mastizō* [μαστίζω, 3147], akin to No. 2, occurs in Acts 22:25 (see No. 1, above). ¶ In the Sept., Numb. 22:25. ¶

NT: B.495a; CB.1257c; K.571.
OT: nākāh: S.5221; HR.898b.1; H.1364; BD.645a.
GEN. REF.: IS.4:358; NB.1150; Z.5:297.

SCOURGING (-S)

mastix [μάστιξ, 3148], a whip, scourge, is used (*a*) with the meaning scourging, in Acts 22:24, of the Roman method (see above, B, No. 1, *Note*); (*b*) in Heb. 11:36, of the sufferings of saints in the O.T. times. Among the Hebrews the usual mode, legal and domestic, was that of beating with a rod (see 2 Cor. 11:25); (*c*) metaphorically, of disease or suffering: see PLAGUE, No. 1.

NT: B.495b; CB.1257c; K.571,655.
OT: shôṭ: S.7752; HR.898b.6; H.2344a; BD.1002a.
negaʿ: S.5061; HR.898b.2; H.1293a; BD.619c.
GEN. REF.: IS.4:358; NB.1150; Z.5:297.

SCRIBE (-S)

grammateus [γραμματεύς, 1122], from *gramma*, a writing, denotes a scribe, a man of letters, a teacher of the law; the scribes are mentioned frequently in the Synoptists, especially in connection with the Pharisees, with whom they virtually formed one party (see Luke 5:21), sometimes with the chief priests, e.g., Matt. 2:4; Mark 8:31; 10:33; 11:18, 27; Luke 9:22. They are mentioned only once in John's Gospel, 8:3, three times in the Acts, 4:5; 6:12; 23:9; elsewhere only in 1 Cor. 1:20, in the singular. They were considered naturally qualified to teach in the Synagogues, Mark 1:22. They were ambitious of honour, e.g., Matt. 23:5-11, which they demanded especially from their pupils, and which was readily granted them, as well as by the people generally. Like Ezra (Ezra 7:12), the scribes were found originally among the priests and Levites. The priests being the official interpreters of the Law, the scribes ere long became an independent company; though they never held political power, they became leaders of the people.

Their functions regarding the Law were to teach it, develop it, and use it in connection with the Sanhedrin and various local courts. They also occupied themselves with the sacred writings both historical and didactic. They attached the utmost importance to ascetic elements, by which the nation was especially separated from the Gentiles. In their régime piety was reduced to external formalism. Only that was of value which was governed by external precept. Life under them became a burden; they themselves sought to evade certain of their own precepts, Matt. 23:16, ff.; Luke 11:46; by their traditions the Law, instead of being a help in moral and spiritual life, became an instrument for preventing true access to God, Luke 11:52. Hence the Lord's stern denunciations of them and the Pharisees (see PHARISEES).

NT: B.165d; CB.1248c; K.127.
OT: shōṭēr: S.7860; HR.275b.5; H.2374a; BD.1009c.
sōphēr: S.5608; HR.275b.2a; H.1540; BD.708b.
GEN. REF.: IS.4:359; NB.1151; Z.5:298.

Note: The word *grammateus* is used of the town clerk in Ephesus, Acts 19:35.

For **SCRIP** see **WALLET**

SCRIPTURE

1. *graphē* [γραφή, 1124], akin to *graphō*, to write (Eng., graph, graphic, etc.), primarily denotes a drawing, painting; then a writing (*a*) of the O.T. Scriptures, (1) in the plural, the whole, e.g., Matt. 21:42; 22:29; John 5:39; Acts 17:11; 18:24; Rom. 1:2, where "the prophets" comprises the O.T. writers in general; 15:4; 16:26, lit., 'prophetic writings,' expressing the character of all the Scriptures; (2) in the singular in reference to a particular passage, e.g., Mark 12:10; Luke 4:21; John 2:22; 10:35 (though applicable to all); 19:24, 28, 36, 37; 20:9; Acts 1:16; 8:32, 35; Rom. 4:3; 9:17; 10:11; 11:2; Gal. 3:8, 22; 4:30; 1 Tim. 5:18, where the 2nd quotation is from Luke 10:7, from which it may be inferred that the Apostle included Luke's Gospel as "Scripture" alike with Deuteronomy, from which the first quotation is taken; in reference to the whole, e.g. Jas. 4:5 (see R.V., a separate rhetorical question from the one which follows); in 2 Pet. 1:20, "no prophecy of Scripture," a description of all, with special application to the O.T. in the next verse; (*b*) of the O.T. Scriptures (those accepted by the Jews as canonical) and all those of the N.T. which were to be accepted by Christians as authoritative, 2 Tim. 3:16; these latter were to be discriminated from the many forged epistles and other religious writings already produced and circulated in Timothy's time. Such discrimination would be directed by the fact that "every Scripture," characterized by inspiration of God, would be profitable for the purposes mentioned; so the R.V. The A.V. states truth concerning the completed Canon of Scripture, but that was not complete when the Apostle wrote to Timothy.

The Scriptures are frequently personified by the N.T. writers (as by the Jews, John 7:42), (*a*) as speaking with Divine authority, e.g., John 19:37; Rom. 4:3; 9:17, where the Scripture is said to speak to Pharaoh, giving the message actually sent previously by God to him through Moses; Jas. 4:5 (see above); (*b*) as possessed of the sentient quality of foresight, and the active power of preaching, Gal. 3:8, where the Scripture mentioned was written more than four centuries after the words were spoken. The Scripture, in such a case, stands for its Divine Author with an intimation that it remains perpetually characterized as the living voice of God. This Divine agency is again illustrated in Gal. 3:22 (cp. ver. 10 and Matt 11:13).

NT: B.166a; CB.1248c; K.128.
OT: k[e]tāb: S.3791; HR.277c.1b; H.1053a; BD.508b.
GEN. REF.: IS.4:361; NB.1151; Z.5:302.

2. *gramma* [γράμμα, 1121], a letter of the alphabet, etc. is used of the Holy Scriptures in 2 Tim. 3:15. For the various uses of this word see LETTER.

NT: B.165b; CB.1248c; K.128.
OT: sēpher: S.5612; HR.275a.3; H.1540a; BD.706d.
GEN. REF.: IS.4:361; NB.1151; Z.5:302.

SCROLL

biblion [βιβλίον, 975], the diminutive of *biblos*, a book, is used in Rev. 6:14, of a scroll, the rolling up of which illustrates the removal of the heaven. See BOOK, No. 2.

NT: B.141b; CB.1239a; K.106.
OT: sēpher: S.5612; HR.218b.4c; H.1540a; BD.706d.
GEN. REF.: IS.4:363; NB.1344; Z.5:313.

SEA

1. *thalassa* [θάλασσα, 2281], is used (*a*) chiefly literally, e.g., the Red Sea, Acts 7:36; 1 Cor. 10:1; Heb. 11:29; the sea of Galilee or Tiberias, Matt. 4:18; 15:29; Mark 6:48, 49, where the acts of Christ testified to His Deity; John 6:1; 21:1; in general, e.g., Luke 17:2; Acts 4:24; Rom. 9:27; Rev. 16:3; 18:17; 20:8, 13; 21:1; in combination with No. 2, Matt. 18:6; (*b*) metaphorically, of the ungodly men described in Jude 13 (cp. Is. 57:20); (*c*) symbolically, in the apocalyptic vision of "a glassy sea like unto crystal," Rev. 4:6, emblematic of the fixed purity and holiness of all that appertains to the authority and judicial dealings of God; in 15:2, the same, "mingled with fire," and, standing by it (R.V.) or on it (A.V. and R.V. marg.), those who had "come vic-

torious from the beast" (chapt. 13); of the wild and restless condition of nations, Rev. 13:1 (see 17:1, 15), where "he stood" (R.V.) refers to the dragon, not John (A.V.); from the midst of this state arises the beast, symbolic of the final Gentile power dominating the federated nations of the Roman world (see Dan., chapts. 2, 7, etc.).

NT: B.350a; CB.1271c; K.—.
OT: yām: S.3220; HR.621a.2; H.871a; BD.410d.
GEN. REF.: IS.4:366; NB.1153; Z.5:316.

Note: For the change from "the sea" in Deut. 30:13, to "the abyss" in Rom. 10:7, see BOTTOM, B.

2. *pelagos* [πέλαγος, 3989], the deep sea, the deep, is translated "the depth" in Matt. 18:6, and is used of the Sea of Cilicia in Acts 27:5. See DEPTH, No. 2. ¶ *Pelagos* signifies "the vast expanse of open water," *thalassa*, "the sea as contrasted with the land" (Trench, Syn., § xiii).

NT: B.641b; CB.—; K.—.
OT: —.
GEN. REF.: IS.4:366; NB.1153; Z.5:316.

B. Adjectives.

1. *enalios* [ἐνάλιος, 1724], "in the sea," lit., of, or belonging to, the salt water (from *hals*, salt), occurs in Jas. 3:7. ¶

NT: B.261d; CB.—; K.—.
OT: —.
GEN. REF.: —.

2. *paralios* [παράλιος, 3882], by the sea, Luke 67:17: see COAST. ¶

NT: B.620a; CB.—; K.—.
OT: yām: S.3220; HR.1061c.3,4; H.871a; BD.410d.
GEN. REF.: IS.4:366; NB.1153; Z.5:316.

3. *parathalassios* [παραθαλάσσιος, 3864], by the sea, Matt. 4:13, see COAST, *Note* 2. ¶

NT: B.616a; CB.—; K.—.
OT: yām: S.3220; HR.1059c.1,2; H.871a; BD.410d.
GEN. REF.: IS.4:366; NB.1153; Z.5:316.

4. *dithalassos* [διθάλασσος, 1337], primarily signifies divided into two seas (*dis*, twice, and *thalassa*); then, dividing the sea, as of a reef or rocky projection running out into the sea, Acts 27:41.

NT: B.195a; CB.—; K.—.
OT: —.
GEN. REF.: —.

SEAL (Noun and Verb)

A. Noun.

sphragis [σφραγίς, 4973], denotes (*a*) a seal or signet, Rev. 7:2, "the seal of the living God," an emblem of ownership and security, here combined with that of destination (as in Ezek. 9:4), the persons to be sealed being secured from destruction and marked for reward; (*b*) the impression of a seal or signed, (1) literal, a seal on a book or roll, combining with the ideas of security and destination those of secrecy and postponement of disclosures, Rev. 5:1, 2, 5, 9; 6:1, 3, 5, 7, 9, 12; 8:1; (2) metaphorical, Rom. 4:11, said of circumcision, as an authentication of the righteousness of Abraham's faith, and an external attestation of the covenant made with him by God; the Rabbis called circumcision "the seal of Abraham"; in 1 Cor. 9:2, of converts as a seal or authentication of Paul's apostleship; in 2 Tim. 2:19, "the firm foundation of God standeth, having this seal, The Lord knoweth them that are His," R.V., indicating ownership, authentication, security and destination, "and, Let every one that nameth the Name of the Lord depart from unrighteousness," indicating a ratification on the part of the believer of the determining counsel of God concerning him; Rev. 9:4 distinguishes those who will be found without the seal of God on their foreheads [see (*a*) above and B, No. 1]. ¶

NT: B.796c; CB.1269c; K.1127.
OT: ḥōtām: S.2368; HR.1327b.1; H.780a; BD.368a.
GEN. REF.: IS.4:369; NB.1153; Z.5:319.

B. Verbs.

1. *sphragizō* [σφραγίζω, 4972], to seal (akin to A), is used to indicate (*a*) security and permanency (attempted but impossible), Matt. 27:66; on the contrary, of the doom of Satan, fixed and certain, Rev. 20:3, R.V., "sealed it over"; (*b*) in Rom. 15:28, "when . . . I have . . . sealed to them this fruit," the formal ratification of the ministry of the churches of the Gentiles in Greece and Galatia to needy saints in Judaea, by Paul's faithful delivery of the gifts to them; this material help was the fruit of his spiritual ministry to the Gentiles, who on their part were bringing forth the fruit of their having shared with them in spiritual things; the metaphor stresses the sacred formalities of the transaction (Deissmann illustrates this from the papyri of Fayyum, in which the sealing of sacks guarantees the full complement of the contents); (*c*) secrecy and security and the postponement of disclosure, Rev. 10:4; in a negative command, 22:10; (*d*) ownership and security, together with destination, Rev. 7:3, 4, 5 (as with the noun in ver. 2; see A); the same three indications are conveyed in Eph. 1:13, in the metaphor of the sealing of believers by the gift of the Holy Spirit, upon believing (i.e., at the time of their regeneration, not after a lapse of time in their spiritual life, "having also believed" — not as A.V., "after that ye believed" —; the aorist-participle marks the definiteness and completeness of the act of faith); the idea of destination is stressed by the phrase "the Holy Spirit of promise" (see also ver. 14); so 4:30, "ye were

sealed unto the day of redemption"; so in 2 Cor. 1:22, where the Middle Voice intimates the special interest of the Sealer in His act; (*e*) authentication by the believer, (by receiving the witness of the Son) of the fact that "God is true," John 3:33; authentication by God in sealing the Son as the Giver of eternal life (with perhaps a figurative allusion to the impress of a mark upon loaves), 6:27. ¶

NT: B.796b; CB.1269c; K.1127.
OT: ḥātam: S.2856; HR.1327a.1a; H.780; BD.367c.
GEN. REF.: IS.4:369; NB.1153; Z.5:319.

Note: In Rev. 7, after the 5th verse (first part) the original does not repeat the mention of the sealing except in ver. 8 (last part) (hence the omission in the R.V.).

2. *katasphragizō* [κατασφραγίζω, 2696], No. 1, strengthened by *kata*, intensive, is used of the book seen in the vision in Rev. 5:1, R.V., "close sealed (with seven seals)," the successive opening of which discloses the events destined to take place throughout the period covered by chapters 6 to 19. ¶ In the Sept., Job 9:7; 37:7. ¶

NT: B.419c; CB.1254b; K.1127.
OT: ḥātam: S.2856; HR.746b.1; H.780; BD.367c.
GEN. REF.: IS.4:369; NB.1153; Z.5:319.

SEAM (without)

araphos or *arrhaphos* [ἄραφος, 729], denotes "without seam" (*a*, negative, and *rhaptō*, to sew), John 19:23. ¶

NT: B.104b; CB.—; K.—.
OT: —.
GEN. REF.: IS.4:375; NB.—; Z.—.

SEARCH

1. *eraunaō* or *ereunaō*, an earlier form, [ἐραυνάω, 2045], to search, examine, is used (*a*) of God, as searching the heart, Rom. 8:27; (*b*) of Christ, similarly, Rev. 2:23; (*c*) of the Holy Spirit, as searching all things, 1 Cor. 2:10, acting in the spirit of the believer; (*d*) of the O.T. prophets, as searching their own writings concerning matters foretold of Christ, testified by the Spirit of Christ in them, 1 Pet. 1:11 (cp. No. 2); (*e*) of the Jews, as commanded by the Lord to search the Scriptures, John 5:39, A.V., and R.V. marg., "search," R.V. text, "ye search," either is possible grammatically; (*f*) of Nicodemus as commanded similarly by the chief priests and Pharisees, John 7:52. ¶

NT: B.306c; CB.1246b; K.255.
OT: ḥāphas: S.2664; HR.544c.2; H.716; BD.344b.
ḥāqar: S.2713; HR.544c.3; H.729; BD.350c.
GEN. REF.: IS.4:381; NB.—; Z.—.

2. *exeraunaō* [ἐξεραυνάω, 1830], a strengthened form of No. 1 (*ek*, or *ex*, out), to search out, is used in 1 Pet. 1:10, "searched diligently"; cp. No. 1 (*d*). ¶

NT: B.274b; CB.—; K.255.
OT: ḥāphas: S.2664; HR.491b.1; H.716; BD.344b.
ḥāqar: S.2713; HR.491b.3; H.729; BD.350c.
nāṣar: S.5341; HR.491b.5; H.1407; BD.665c.
GEN. REF.: IS.4:381; NB.—; Z.—.

3. *exetazō* [ἐξετάζω, 1833], to examine closely, inquire carefully (from *etazō*, to examine), occurs in Matt. 2:8, R.V., "search out"; so Matt. 10:11, R.V.: see INQUIRE, No. 4.

NT: B.275c; CB.—; K.—.
OT: dārash: S.1875; HR.495a.2; H.455; BD.205a.
bāḥan: S.974; HR.495a.1; H.230; BD.103c.
GEN. REF.: IS.4:381; NB.—; Z.—.

Note: For *anakrinō*, rendered "searched" in Acts 17:11, A.V., see EXAMINE.

For SEARED see BRANDED

SEASON (Noun)

A. Nouns.

1. *kairos* [καιρς, 2540], primarily, due measure, fitness, proportion, is used in the N.T. to signify a season, a time, a period possessed of certain characteristics, frequently rendered "time" or "times"; in the following the R.V. substitutes "season" for the A.V. "time," thus distinguishing the meaning from *chronos* (see No. 2): Matt. 11:25; 12:1; 14:1; 21:34; Mark 11:13; Acts 3:19; 7:20; 17:26; Rom. 3:26; 5:6; 9:9 13:11; 1 Cor. 7:5; Gal. 4:10; 1 Thess. 2:17, lit., 'for a season (of an hour)'; 2 Thess. 2:6; in Eph. 6:18, "at all seasons" (A.V., "always"); in Tit. 1:3, "His own seasons" (marg., "its"; A.V., "in due times"); in the preceding clause *chronos* is used.

The characteristics of a period are exemplified in the use of the term with regard, e.g., to harvest, Matt. 13:30; reaping, Gal. 6:9; punishment, Matt. 8:29; discharging duties, Luke 12:42; opportunity for doing anything, whether good, e.g., Matt. 26:18; Gal. 6:10 ("opportunity"); Eph. 5:16; or evil, e.g., Rev. 12:12; the fulfilment of prophecy, Luke 1:20; Acts 3:19; 1 Pet. 1:11; a time suitable for a purpose, Luke 4:13, lit., 'until a season'; 2 Cor. 6:2; see further under No. 2. See ALWAYS, *Note*, OPPORTUNITY, TIME, WHILE.

NT: B.394c; CB.1253a; K.389.
OT: ‘ēt: S.6256; HR.706a.8; H.1650b; BD.773b.
pa‘am: S.6471; HR.706a.9; H.1793a; BD.821d.
mô‘ēd: S.4150; HR.706a.4; H.878b; BD.417b.
GEN. REF.: IS.4:375; NB.—; Z.—.

2. *chronos* [χρόνος, 5550], whence Eng. words beginning with chron—, denotes a space of time, whether long or short; (*a*) it implies duration, whether longer, e.g., Acts 1:21, "(all the) time"; Acts 13:18; 20:18, R.V., "(all the) time" (A.V., "at all seasons"); or shorter, e.g.,

Luke 4:5; (*b*) it sometimes refers to the date of an occurrence, whether past, e.g., Matt. 2:7, or future, e.g., Acts 3:21; 7:17.

Broadly speaking, *chronos* expresses the duration of a period, *kairos* stresses it as marked by certain features; thus in Acts 1:7, "the Father has set within His own authority" both the times (*chronos*), the lengths of the periods, and the season (*kairos*), epochs characterized by certain events; in 1 Thess. 5:1, "times" refers to the length of the interval before the Parousia takes place (the presence of Christ with the saints when he comes to receive them to Himself at the Rapture), and to the length of time the Parousia will occupy; "seasons" refers to the special features of the period before, during, and after the Parousia.

Chronos marks quantity, *kairos*, quality. Sometimes the distinction between the two words is not sharply defined as, e.g., in 2 Tim. 4:6, though even here the Apostle's "departure" signalizes the time (*kairos*). The words occur together in the Sept. only in Dan. 2:21 and Eccl. 3:1. *Chronos* is rendered "season" in Acts 19:22, A.V. (R.V., "a while"); 20:18 (R.V., "all the time," see above); Rev. 6:11. A.V. (R.V., "time"); so 20:3. In Luke 23:8 it is used with *hikanos* in the plural, R.V., "(of a long) time," more lit., '(for a sufficient number) of times.'

In Rev. 10:6 *chronos* has the meaning "delay" (R.V., marg.), an important rendering for the understanding of the passage (the word being akin to *chronizō*, to take time, to linger, delay, Matt. 24:48; Luke 12:45). See DELAY, B, *Note*, SPACE, TIME, WHILE.

NT: B.887d; CB.1240b; K.1337.
OT: yôm: S.3117; HR.1476b.2; H.852; BD.398a.
'ēt: S.6256; HR.1476b.3; H.1650b; BD.773b.
'ôlām: S.5769; HR.1476b.8; H.1631a; BD.761d.
GEN. REF.: IS.4:375; NB.—; Z.—.

3. *hōra* [ὥρα, 5610], an hour, is translated "season" in John 5:35; 2 Cor. 7:8; Philm. 15: see HOUR.

NT: B.896a; CB.1251a; K.1355.
OT: 'ēt: S.6256; HR.1493b.5; H.1650b; BD.773b.
GEN. REF.: IS.4:375; NB.—; Z.—.

B. Adjective.

proskairos [πρόσκαιρος, 4340], temporary, transient, is rendered "for a season" in Heb. 11:25. See TEMPORAL, TIME, WHILE.

NT: B.715b; CB.1267a; K.389.
OT: —.
GEN. REF.: IS.4:375; NB.—; Z.—.

C. Adverbs.

1. *akairōs* [ἀκαίρως, 171], denotes "out of season," unseasonably (akin to *akairos*, unseasonable, *a*, negative, and A, No. 1), 2 Tim. 4:2. ¶

NT: B.29b; CB.1234a; K.—.
OT: —.
GEN. REF.: —.

2. *eukairōs* [εὐκαίρως, 2122], "in season" (*eu*, well), 2 Tim. 4:2; it occurs also in Mark 14:11, "conveniently." ¶

NT: B.321c; CB.1247b; K.389.
OT: —.
GEN. REF.: —.

Note: For *oligon*, 1 Pet. 1:6, A.V., "for a season," see WHILE.

SEASON (Verb)

artuō [ἀρτύω, 741], to arrange, make ready (cp. *artios*, fitted), is used of seasoning, Mark 9:50; Luke 14:34; Col. 4:6. ¶

NT: B.111a; CB.1237c; K.—.
OT: —.
GEN. REF.: IS.4:376; NB.—; Z.—.

SEAT (Noun and Verb)

A. Nouns.

1. *kathedra* [καθέδρα, 2515], from *kata*, down, and *hedra*, a seat, denotes a seat (Eng., cathedral), a chair; Matt. 21:12; Mark 11:15; of teachers, Matt. 23:2. ¶

NT: B.388b; CB.1254c; K.—.
OT: môshāb: S.4186; HR.699c.1a; H.922c; BD.444a.
yāshab: S.3427; HR.699c.1b; H.922; BD.442a.
shebet: S.7675; HR.699c.1c; H.922a; BD.443d.
GEN. REF.: IS.4:376; NB.—; Z.5:324.

2. *prōtokathedria* [πρωτοκαθεδρία, 4410], the first seat, Matt. 23:6; Mark 12:39; Luke 11:43; 20:46; see CHIEF, No. 6. Cp. ROOM. ¶

NT: B.725b; CB.1267b; K.—.
OT: —.
GEN. REF.: —.

Note: For *thronos*, sometimes translated "seat" in the A.V., see THRONE.

B. Verb.

kathēmai [κάθημαι, 2521], to sit, be seated, is translated "shall . . . be seated" in Luke 22:69, R.V.; "is seated," Col. 3:1, R.V. (A.V., "shall . . . sit" and "sitteth"). See SIT.

NT: B.389b; CB.1254c; K.386.
OT: yāshab: S.3427; HR.700b.3a; H.922; BD.442a.
GEN. REF.: IS.4:376; NB.—; Z.—.

SECOND, SECONDARILY, SECONDLY

1. *deuteros* [δεύτερος, 1208], denotes second in order with or without the idea of time, e.g., Matt. 22:26, 39; 2 Cor. 1:15; Rev. 2:11; in Rev. 14:8, R.V. only ("a second angel"); it is used in the neuter, *deuteron*, adverbially, signifying a second time, e.g., John 3:4; 21:16; Acts 7:13; Rev. 19:3, R.V. (A.V., "again"); Jude 5, "afterward" (R.V., marg., "the second time"); used with *ek* (of) idiomatically, the preposition

signifying "for (the second time)," Mark 14:72; John 9:24 and Acts 11:9, R.V. (A.V., "again"); Heb. 9:28; in 1 Cor. 12:28, A.V., "secondarily," R.V., "secondly."

NT: B.177a; CB.1241a; K.–.
OT: shēnî: S.8145; HR.293b.9a; H.2421b; BD.1041b.
GEN. REF.: –.

Note: In Acts 13:33 some mss. have *prōtos*, "(in the) first (psalm)"; the 1st and 2nd Psalms were originally one, forming a prologue to the whole book; hence the numbering in the Sept.

2. *deuteraios* [δευτεραῖος, 1206], an adjective with an adverbial sense (from No. 1), is used in Acts 28:13, R.V., "on the second day" (A.V., "the next day"), lit., 'second day (persons we came).' ¶

NT: B.177a; CB.–; K.–.
OT: –.
GEN. REF.: –.

Note: In Luke 6:1, the A.V. translates those mss. which have *deuteroprōtos*, lit., 'second-first,' said of a sabbath (see R.V. marg.). ¶

SECRET, SECRETLY

A. Adjectives.

1. *kruptos* [κρυπτός, 2927], secret, hidden (akin to *kruptō*, to hide), Eng., crypt, cryptic etc., is used as an adjective and rendered "secret" in Luke 8:17, A.V. (R.V., "hid"); in the neuter, with *en*, in, as an adverbial phrase, "in secret," with the article, Matt. 6:4, 6 (twice in each ver.); without the article, John 7:4, 10; 18:20; in the neuter plural, with the article, "the secrets (of men)," Rom. 2:16; of the heart, 1 Cor. 14:25; in Luke 11:33, A.V., "a secret place" (R.V., "cellar"). See CELLAR, HIDDEN, INWARDLY.

NT: B.454a; CB.1256a; K.476.
OT: 'āṭam: S.331; HR.792c.1; H.73; BD.31d.
sātar: S.5641; HR.792c.5a; H.1551; BD.711b.
kāsāh: S.3680; HR.792c.3; H.1008; BD.491b.
GEN. REF.: IS.4:377; NB.–; Z.–.

2. *apokruphos* [ἀπόκρυφος, 614], (whence Apocrypha), hidden, is translated "kept secret" in Mark 4:22, A.V. (R.V., "made secret"); "secret" in Luke 8:17, R.V. (A.V., "hid"). See HIDE, B, No. 2.

NT: B.93d; CB.1237a; K.476.
OT: sēter: S.5643; HR.134c.3a; H.1551a; BD.712a.
mistār: S.4565; HR.134c.3c; H.1551d; BD.712c.
GEN. REF.: IS.4:377; NB.–; Z.–.

3. *kruphaios* [κρυφαῖος, —], occurs in the best mss. in Matt. 6:18 (twice; some have No. 1). ¶

NT: B.454d; CB.1256a; K.476.
OT: mistār: S.4565; HR.793a.1; H.1551d; BD.712c.
GEN. REF.: IS.4:377; NB.–; Z.–.

B. Adverbs.

1. *kruphē* [κρυφῃ, 2931], akin to A, No. 1, secretly, in secret, is used in Eph. 5:12. ¶

NT: B.454d; CB.1256a; K.476.
OT: sātar: S.5641; HR.793a.3a; H.1551; BD.711b.
(ba) sēter: S.5643; HR.793a.3b,c; H.1551a; BD.712a.
GEN. REF.: –.

2. *lathra* [λάθρᾳ, 2977], akin to *lanthanō*, to escape notice, be hidden, is translated "secretly" in John 11:28. See PRIVILY.

NT: B.462c; CB.–; K.–.
OT: (ba) sēter: S.5643; HR.840c.2b; H.1551a; BD.712a.
(ba) mistār: S.4565; HR.840c.2a; H.1551d; BD.712c.
GEN. REF.: IS.4:377; NB.–; Z.–.

C. Verb.

kruptō [κρύπτω, 2928], to hide, is translated "secretly" in John 19:38 [perfect participle, Passive Voice, lit., '(but) having been hidden'], referring to Nicodemus as having been a secret disciple of Christ; in Matt. 13:35, A.V., it is translated "kept secret" (R.V., "hidden").

NT: B.454b; CB.1256a; K.476.
OT: ḥābā': S.2244; HR.791c.1a-e; H.588a; BD.285a.
sātar: S.5641; HR.791c.9a-d; H.1551; BD.711b.
GEN. REF.: IS.4:377; NB.–; Z.–.

Notes: (1) For *tameion*, translated "secret chambers" in Matt. 24:26, see CHAMBER, No. 1.

(2) For the A.V. rendering of *sigaō*, in Rom. 16:25, "kept secret," see PEACE (hold one's), No. 2, and SILENCE.

(3) For "I have learned the secret," see LEARN, No. 4.

SECT

hairesis [αἵρεσις, 139], a choosing, is translated "sect"; throughout the Acts, except in 24:14, A.V., "heresy" (R.V., "sect"); it properly denotes a predilection either for a particular truth, or for a perversion of one, generally with the expectation of personal advantage; hence, a division and the formation of a party or sect in contrast to the uniting power of "the truth," held *in toto*; a sect is a division developed and brought to an issue; the order "divisions, heresies" (marg. "parties") in "the works of the flesh" in Gal. 5:19-21 is suggestive of this. See HERESY.

NT: B.23d; CB.1249a; K.27.
OT: nᵉdābāh: S.5071; HR.36a.1; H.1299a; BD.621d.
GEN. REF.: IS.4:378; NB.519; Z.5:328.

SECURE (Verb)

perikratēs [περικρατής, 4031], an adjective, signifies 'having full command of' (*peri*, around, about, *krateō*, to be strong, to rule); it is used with *ginomai*, to become, in Acts 27:16, R.V., "to secure (the boat)," A.V., "to come by." ¶

NT: B.648b; CB.–; K.–.
OT: –.
GEN. REF.: –.

Note: In Matt. 28:14, A.V., *amerimnos*, without anxiety, with *poieō*, to make, is translated "we will . . . secure (you)," R.V., "we will . . . rid (you) of care." The Eng. "secure" is derived from the Latin *se*, free from, and *cura*, care. See CARE.

SECURITY

hikanos [ἱκανός, 2425], sufficient, is used in its neuter form with the article, as a noun, in Acts 17:9, "(when they had taken) security," i.e., satisfaction, lit., 'the sufficient.' The use of *hikanos* in this construction is a Latinism in Greek. See Moulton, Proleg., p. 20. Probably the bond given to the authorities by Jason and his friends included an undertaking that Paul would not return to Thessalonica. Any efforts to have the bond cancelled were unsuccessful; hence the reference to the hindrance by Satan (1 Thess. 2:18). See ABLE, C, No. 2.

NT: B.374b; CB.1250c; K.361.
OT: day: S.1767; HR.683c.2; H.425; BD.191b.
shadday: S.7706; HR.683c.9; H.2333; BD.994d.
GEN. REF.: –.

SEDITION

A. Nouns.

1. *stasis* [στάσις, 4714], a dissension, an insurrection, is translated "sedition" in Acts 24:5, A.V. (R.V., "insurrections"). See DISSENSION, INSURRECTION.

NT: B.764c; CB.1270a; K.1070.
OT: –.
GEN. REF.: –.

2. *dichostasia* [διχοστασία, 1370], lit., a standing apart (*dicha*, asunder, apart, *stasis*, a standing), hence a dissension, division, is translated "seditions" in Gal. 5:20, A.V. See DIVISION, No. 2.

NT: B.200b; CB.1241b; K.88.
OT: –.
GEN. REF.: IS.4:379; NB.–; Z.–.

B. Verb.

anastatoō [ἀναστατόω, 387], to excite, unsettle, 'to stir up to sedition,' is so translated in Acts 21:38, R.V. (A.V., "madest an uproar"); in 17:6, "have turned (the world) upside down," i.e., causing tumults; in Gal. 5:12, R.V., "unsettle" (A.V., "trouble"), i.e., by false teaching (here in the continuous present tense, lit., 'those who are unsettling you'). The word was supposed not to have been used in profane authors. It has been found, however, in several of the papyri writings. See TURN, UNSETTLE. ¶

NT: B.61a; CB.–; K.–.
OT: dûsh (Aramaic): S.1759; HR.82a.1; H.2670; BD.1087c.
GEN. REF.: –.

SEDUCE, SEDUCING

A. Verbs.

1. *planaō* [πλανάω, 4105], to cause to wander, lead astray, is translated to seduce in 1 John 2:26, A.V. (R.V., "lead . . . astray"); in Rev. 2:20, to seduce. See DECEIT, C, No. 6.

NT: B.665b; CB.1265a; K.857.
OT: tā'āh: S.8582; HR.1139b.16; H.2531; BD.1073b.
GEN. REF.: IS.4:379; NB.–; Z.–.

2. *apoplanaō* [ἀποπλανάω, 635], is translated "seduce" in Mark 13:22 (R.V., "lead astray"); see LEAD, No. 13.

NT: B.97b; CB.1237a; K.857.
OT: nāṭāh: S.5186; HR.139c.2; H.1352; BD.639d.
nādaḥ: S.5080; HR.139c.1; H.1304; BD.623a.
GEN. REF.: IS.4:379; NB.–; Z.–.

B. Adjective.

planos [πλάνος, 4105], akin to A, lit., wandering, then, deceiving, is translated "seducing" in 1 Tim. 4:1. See DECEIVER, No. 1.

NT: B.666a; CB.1265a; K.857.
OT: mᵉshûgāh: S.4879; HR.1140b.1; H.2341a; BD.1000c.
GEN. REF.: –.

For SEDUCERS see IMPOSTORS

SEE, SEEING

A. Verbs.

1. *blepō* [βλέπω, 991], to have sight, is used of bodily vision, e.g., Matt. 11:4; and mental, e.g., Matt. 13:13, 14; it is said of God the Father in Matt. 6:4, 6, 18; of Christ as seeing what the Father doeth, John 5:19. It especially stresses the thought of the person who sees. For the various uses see BEHOLD, No. 2; see *Note* below.

NT: B.143b; CB.1239a; K.706.
OT: rā'āh: S.7200; HR.221a.10a; H.2095; BD.906b.
pānāh: S.6437; HR.221a.7a; H.1782; BD.815a.
pāneh: S.6440; HR.221a.8; H.1782a; BD.815d.
GEN. REF.: IS.4:379; NB.–; Z.–.

2. *horaō* [ὁράω, 3708], with the form *eidon*, serving for its aorist tense, and *opsomai*, for its future tense (Middle Voice), denotes to see, of bodily vision, e.g., John 6:36; and mental, e.g., Matt. 8:4; it is said of Christ as seeing the Father, John 6:46, and of what He had seen with the Father, 8:38. It especially indicates the direction of the thought to the object seen. See BEHOLD, No. 1.

NT: B.577c; CB.1251a; K.706.
OT: rā'āh: S.7200; HR.1005a.8a,b; H.2095; BD.906b.
GEN. REF.: IS.4:379; NB.–; Z.–.

Note: "*Horaō* and *blepō* both denote the physical act: *horaō*, in general, *blepō*, the single look; *horaō* gives prominence to the discerning mind, *blepō* to the particular mood or point. When the physical side recedes, *horaō* denotes perception in general (as resulting principally from vision) . . . *Blepō*, on the other hand, when its physical side recedes, gets a purely outward sense, look (open, incline) towards [as of a situation]" (Schmidt, Grimm-Thayer).

3. *aphoraō* [ἀφοράω, 872], with *apeidon* serving as the aorist tense, to look away from one thing so as to see another (*apo*, from, and No. 2), as in Heb. 12:2, simply means to see in Phil. 2:23. ¶

NT: B.127b; CB.–; K.–.
OT: rā'āh: S.7200; HR.122b.1; H.2095; BD.906b.
GEN. REF.: IS.4:379; NB.–; Z.–.

4. *kathoraō* [καθοράω, 2529], lit., to look down (*kata*, and No. 2), denotes to discern clearly, Rom. 1:20, "are clearly seen." ¶ In the Sept., Numb. 24:2; Job 10:4; 39:26. ¶
NT: B.391a; CB.1254c; K.—.
OT: rā'āh: S.7200; HR.704b.1; H.2095; BD.906b.
GEN. REF.: IS.4:379; NB.—; Z.—.

5. *diablepō* [διαβλέπω, 1227], to see clearly (*dia*, through, and No. 1), is used in Matt. 7:5; Luke 6:42; in Mark 8:25, R.V., "he looked stedfastly" (No. 6 is used in the next clause; No. 1 in ver. 24, and No. 2 in the last part). ¶
NT: B.181d; CB.—; K.—.
OT: —.
GEN. REF.: —.

6. *emblepō* [ἐμβλέπω, 1689], to look at (*en*, in, and No. 1), used of earnestly looking, is translated "saw" in Mark 8:25 (last part); "could (not) see" in Acts 22:11. See BEHOLD, No. 3.
NT: B.254c; CB.1244b; K.—.
OT: nābaṭ: S.5027; HR.455c.1b; H.1282; BD.613c.
pānāh: S.6437; HR.455c.2; H.1782; BD.815a.
rā'āh: S.7200; HR.455c.3; H.2095; BD.906b.
GEN. REF.: IS.4:379; NB.—; Z.—.

7. *anablepō* [ἀναβλέπω, 308], to look up, is translated "see," of the blind, in Luke 7:22, A.V. (R.V., "receive their sight"). See SIGHT.
NT: B.50d; CB.1235a; K.—.
OT: nāsā': S.5375; HR.73b.3a; H.1421; BD.669d,670c.
GEN. REF.: IS.4:379; NB.—; Z.—.

8. *theaomai* [θεάομαι, 2300], to view attentively, to see with admiration, desire, or regard, stresses more especially the action of the person beholding, as with No. 1, in contrast to No. 2; it is used in Matt. 11:7 (R.V., "to behold"), while *idein*, the infinitive of *eidon* (see under No. 2), is used in the questions in the next two verses; in verse 7 the interest in the onlooker is stressed, in vv. 8, 9, the attention is especially directed to the object seen. The verb is translated to see in the A.V. and R.V. of Matt. 6:1; Mark 16:11, 14; John 6:5; Acts 8:18 (in some mss.); 21:27; Rom. 15:24; elsewhere, for the A.V., to see, the R.V. uses the verb to behold, bringing out its force more suitably. See BEHOLD, No. 8.
NT: B.353a; CB.1271c; K.706.
OT: rā'āh: S.7200; HR.627c.1; H.2095; BD.906b.
GEN. REF.: IS.4:379; NB.—; Z.—.

9. *theōreō* [θεωρέω, 2334], denotes to be a spectator of, indicating the careful perusal of details in the object; it points especially, as in No. 1, to the action of the person beholding, e.g., Matt. 28:1; the R.V. frequently renders it by to behold, for the A.V., to see, e.g., John 14:17, 19; 16:10, 16, 17, 19. The difference between this verb and Nos. 1 and 2 is brought out in John 20:5, 6, 8; in ver. 5 *blepō* is used of John's sight of the linen cloths in the tomb, without his entering in; he saw at a glance the Lord was not there; in ver. 6 the closer contemplation by Peter is expressed in the verb *theōreō*. But in ver. 8 the grasping by John of the significance of the undisturbed cloths is denoted by *eidon* (see No. 2, and see WRAP).
NT: B.360a; CB.1272a; K.706.
OT: rā'āh: S.7200; HR.649b.4; H.2095; BD.906b.
ḥāzāh: S.2372; HR.649b.2; H.633; BD.302b.
GEN. REF.: IS.4:379; NB.—; Z.—.

10. *muōpazō* [μυωπάζω, 3467], to be short-sighted (*muō*, to shut, *ōps*, the eye; cp. Eng., myopy, myopic: the root *mu* signifies a sound made with closed lips, e.g., in the words mutter, mute), occurs in 2 Pet. 1:9, R.V. "seeing only what is near" (A.V., "and cannot see afar off"); this does not contradict the preceding word "blind," it qualifies it; he of whom it is true is blind in that he cannot discern spiritual things, he is near-sighted in that he is occupied in regarding wordly affairs. ¶
NT: B.531a; CB.—; K.—.
OT: —.
GEN. REF.: IS.4:379; NB.—; Z.—.

11. *phainō* [φαίνω, 5316], to cause to appear, and in the Passive Voice, to appear, be manifest, is rendered "(that) they may be seen" in Matt. 6:5; "it was (never so) seen," 9:33. See APPEAR.
NT: B.851b; CB.1263c; K.1244.
OT: 'ôr: S.215; HR.1423a.1a; H.52; BD.21a.
rā'āh: S.7200; HR.1423a.10; H.2095; BD.906b.
GEN. REF.: IS.4:379; NB.—; Z.—.

Notes: (1) For *ide* and *idou*, regularly rendered "behold" in the R.V., see BEHOLD, No. 4.

(2) For *optanō*, in Acts 1:3, A.V., "being seen," see APPEAR, A, No. 7.

(3) For *historeō*, in Gal. 1:18, A.V., to see, see VISIT.

(4) For *prooraō*, and *proeidon*, to see before, see FORESEE.

(5) For "make . . . see" see ENLIGHTEN.

B. Noun.

blemma [βλέμμα, 990], primarily, a look, a glance (akin to A, No. 1), denotes sight, 2 Pet. 2:8, rendered "seeing"; some interpret it as meaning "look"; Moulton and Milligan illustrate it thus from the papyri; it seems difficult, however to take the next word "hearing" (in the similar construction) in this way. ¶
NT: B.143b; CB.—; K.—.
OT: —.
GEN. REF.: —.

SEED

1. *sperma* [σπέρμα, 4690], akin to *speirō*, to sow (Eng., sperm, spermatic etc.), has the following usages, (*a*) agricultural and botanical, e.g., Matt. 13:24, 27, 32 (for the A.V. of vv. 19, 20, 22, 23, see SOW, as in the R.V.); 1 Cor.

15:38; 2 Cor. 9:10; (*b*) physiological, Heb. 11:11; (*c*) metaphorical and by metonymy for offspring, posterity, (1) of natural offspring, e.g., Matt. 22:24, 25, R.V., "seed" (A.V., "issue"); John 7:42; 8:33, 37; Acts 3:25; Rom. 1:3; 4:13, 16, 18; 9:7 (twice), 8, 29; 11:1; 2 Cor. 11:22; Heb. 2:16; 11:18; Rev. 12:17; Gal. 3:16, 19, 29; in the 16th ver., "He saith not, And to seeds, as of many; but as of one, And to thy seed, which is Christ," quoted from the Sept. of Gen. 13:15 and 17:7, 8, there is especial stress on the word "seed," as referring to an individual (here, Christ) in fulfilment of the promises to Abraham — a unique use of the singular. While the plural form "seeds," neither in Hebrew nor in Greek, would have been natural any more than in English (it is not so used in Scripture of human offspring; its plural occurrence is in 1 Sam. 8:15, of crops), yet if the Divine intention had been to refer to Abraham's natural descendants, another word could have been chosen in the plural, such as 'children'; all such words were, however, set aside, 'seed' being selected as one that could be used in the singular, with the purpose of showing that the "seed" was Messiah. Some of the Rabbis had even regarded "seed," e.g., in Gen. 4:25 and Is. 53:10, as referring to the Coming One. Descendants were given to Abraham by other than natural means, so that through him Messiah might come, and the point of the Apostle's argument is that since the fulfilment of the promises of God is secured alone by Christ, they only who are "in Christ" can receive them; (2) of spiritual offspring, Rom. 4:16, 18; 9:8; here "the children of the promise are reckoned for a seed" points, firstly, to Isaac's birth as being not according to the ordinary course of nature but by Divine promise, and, secondly, by analogy, to the fact that all believers are children of God by spiritual birth; Gal. 3:29.

As to 1 John 3:9, "his seed abideth in him," it is possible to understand this as meaning that children of God (His seed) abide in Him, and do not go on doing (practising) sin (the verb to commit does not represent the original in this passage). Alternatively, the seed signifies the principle of spiritual life as imparted to the believer, which abides in him without possibility of removal or extinction; the child of God remains eternally related to Christ, he who lives in sin has never become so related, he has not the principle of life in him. This meaning suits the context and the general tenor of the Epistle.

NT: B.761d; CB.1269c; K.1065.
OT: zera': S.2233; HR.1282b.1a; H.582a; BD.282a.
GEN. REF.: IS.4:380; NB.1157; Z.5:328.

2. *sporos* [σπόρος, 4703], akin to No. 1, properly, a sowing, denotes seed sown, (*a*) natural, Mark 4:26, 27; Luke 8:5, 11 (the natural being figuratively applied to the Word of God); 2 Cor. 9:10 (1st part); (*b*) metaphorically of material help to the needy, 2 Cor. 9:10 (2nd part), R.V., "(your) seed for sowing" (A.V., "seed sown"). ¶

NT: B.763b; CB.1269c; K.1065.
OT: zera': S.2233; HR.1285b.1a; H.582a; BD.282a.
GEN. REF.: IS.4:380; NB.1157; Z.5:328.

3. *spora* [σπορά, 4701], akin to No. 1, and like No. 2, a sowing, seedtime, denotes seed sown, 1 Pet. 1:23, of human offspring. ¶ In the Sept., 2 Kings 19:29. ¶

NT: B.763b; CB.1269c; K.1065.
OT: zāra': S.2232; HR.1285b.1; H.582; BD.281b.
GEN. REF.: IS.4:380; NB.1157; Z.5:328.

SEEING, SEEING THAT (conjunction), see † p. 1

SEEK

1. *zēteō* [ζητέω, 2212], signifies (*a*) to seek for, e.g., Matt. 7:7, 8; 13:45; Luke 24:5; John 6:24; of plotting against a person's life, Matt. 2:20; Acts 21:31; Rom. 11:3; metaphorically, to seek by thinking, to seek how to do something, or what to obtain, e.g., Mark 11:18; Luke 12:29; to seek to ascertain a meaning, John 16:19, "do ye inquire"; to seek God, Acts 17:27, R.V.; Rom. 10:20; (*b*) to seek or strive after, endeavour, to desire, e.g., Matt. 12:46, 47, R.V., "seeking" (A.V., "desiring"); Luke 9:9, R.V., "sought" (A.V., "desired"); John 7:19, R.V., "seek ye" (A.V., "go ye about"); so ver. 20; Rom. 10:3, R.V., "seeking" (A.V., "going about"); of seeking the kingdom of God and His righteousness, in the sense of coveting earnestly, striving after, Matt. 6:33; "the things that are above," Col. 3:1; peace, 1 Pet. 3:11; (*c*) to require or demand, e.g., Mark 8:12; Luke 11:29 (some mss. have No. 4); 1 Cor. 4:2, "it is required"; 2 Cor. 13:3, "ye seek." See ABOUT, B, *Note*, DESIRE, B, *Note* (2), ENDEAVOUR, GO, *Note* (2) (*a*), INQUIRE, REQUIRE.

NT: B.338d; CB.1273c; K.300.
OT: bāqash: S.1245; HR.597a.6a; H.276; BD.134c.
dārash: S.1875; HR.597a.8; H.455; BD.205a.
GEN. REF.: IS.4:381; NB.—; Z.—.

2. *anazēteō* [ἀναζητέω, 327], to seek carefully (*ana*, up, used intensively, and No. 1), is used of searching for human beings, difficulty in the effort being implied, Luke 2:44, 45 (some mss. have No. 1 in the latter ver.); Acts 11:25; numerous illustrations of this particular

meaning in the papyri are given by Moulton and Milligan. ¶ In the Sept., Job 3:4; 10:6. ¶
NT: B.53d; CB.–; K.–.
OT: bāqash: S.1245; HR.77a.1; H.276; BD.134c.
dārash: S.1875; HR.77a.2; H.455; BD.205a.
GEN. REF.: IS.4:381; NB.–; Z.–.

3. *ekzēteō* [ἐκζητέω, 1567], signifies (*a*) to seek out (*ek*) or after, to search for; e.g., God, Rom. 3:11; the Lord, Acts 15:17; in Heb. 11:6, R.V., "seek after" (A.V., "diligently seek"); 12:17, R.V., "sought diligently" (A.V., "sought carefully"); 1 Pet. 1:10, R.V., "sought" (A.V., "have inquired"), followed by *exeraunaō*, to search diligently; (*b*) to require or demand, Luke 11:50, 51. See INQUIRE, *Note* (3), REQUIRE. ¶
NT: B.240a; CB.1244a; K.300.
OT: bāqash: S.1245; HR.430c.2; H.276; BD.134c.
dārash: S.1875; HR.430c.3a; H.455; BD.205a.
GEN. REF.: IS.4:381; NB.–; Z.–.

4. *epizēteō* [ἐπιζητέω, 1934], to seek after (directive, *epi*, towards), is always rendered in the R.V., by some form of the verb to seek, Acts 13:7, "sought" (A.V., "desired"); 19:39, "seek" (A.V., "inquire"); Phil. 4:17, "seek for" (A.V., "desire"), twice; elsewhere, Matt. 6:32; 12:39; 16:4; Mark 8:12 (in some texts); Luke 12:30; Acts 12:19; Rom. 11:7; Heb. 11:14; 13:14. See DESIRE, INQUIRE. ¶
NT: B.292d; CB.1246b; K.300.
OT: dārash: S.1875; HR.520a.2; H.455; BD.205a.
bāqash: S.1245; HR.520a.1; H.276; BD.134c.
GEN. REF.: IS.4:381; NB.–; Z.–.

5. *oregō* [ὀρέγω, 3713], to reach out, or after, used in the Middle Voice is translated "seeketh" in 1 Tim. 3:1, R.V., of 'seeking overseership' (A.V., "desireth"). See DESIRE, No. 5.
NT: B.579d; CB.1261a; K.–.
OT: –.
GEN. REF.: –.

Note: For the R.V. renderings of *zēloō*, in Gal. 4:17, 18, "they zealously seek," "ye may seek," "to be zealously sought," see AFFECT, *Note*, and ZEALOUS.

SEEM

dokeō [δοκέω, 1380], denotes (*a*) to be of opinion (akin to *doxa*, opinion), e.g., Luke 8:18, R.V., "thinketh" (A.V., "seemeth"); so 1 Cor. 3:18; to think, suppose, Jas. 1:26, R.V., "thinketh himself" (A.V., "seem"); see SUPPOSE, THINK; (*b*) to seem, to be reputed, e.g., Acts 17:18; 1 Cor. 11:16; 12:22; 2 Cor. 10:9; Heb. 4:1; 12:11; for Gal. 2:2, 6, 9, see REFUTE; (*c*) impersonally (1) to think (see THINK, (2) to seem good, Luke 1:3; Acts 15:22, R.V., "it seemed good" (A.V., "it pleased"); 15:25, 28 (ver. 34 in some mss.); in Heb. 12:10, the neuter of the present participle is used with the article, lit., 'the (thing) seeming good,' R.V., "(as) seemed good," A.V., "after (their own) pleasure." See ACCOUNT, No. 1.
NT: B.201d; CB.1242a; K.178.
OT: ḥāshab: S.2803; HR.339b.3; H.767; BD.362d.
GEN. REF.: –.

Notes: In Matt. 11:26 and Luke 10:21, *eudokia*, good pleasure, satisfaction (*eu*, well, and *dokeō*), is used with *ginomai*, to become, and translated "it seemed good," A.V. (R.V., "it was well-pleasing").

(2) In Luke 24:11, A.V., *phainō*, to appear (Passive Voice), is translated "seemed" (R.V., "appeared").

For **SEEMLY**, R.V., see **COMELY**, B, and *Note* (2)

Note: In 1 Pet. 2:12, R.V., *kalos*, good, fair, is rendered "seemly."

SEIZE

1. *sullambanō* [συλλαμβάνω, 4815], lit., to take together (*sun*, with, *lambanō*, to take or lay hold of), chiefly signifies to seize as a prisoner; in the following the R.V. substitutes the more suitable and forceful verb, to seize, for A.V., to take: Matt. 26:55; Mark 14:48; Luke 22:54; John 18:12; Acts 12:3; 23:27; 26:21; in Acts 1:16, R.V. and A.V., "took." See CATCH, No. 8, CONCEIVE, HELP.
NT: B.776d; CB.1270b; K.1101.
OT: tāphas: S.8610; HR.1301c.7; H.2538; BD.1074c.
lākad: S.3920; HR.1301c.3; H.1115; BD.539d.
GEN. REF.: –.

2. *sunarpazō* [συναρπάζω, 4884], is translated "seized" in the R.V. of Luke 8:29; Acts 6:12; 19:29; see CATCH, No. 7.
NT: B.785b; CB.–; K.–.
OT: lāqaḥ: S.3947; HR.1312c.1; H.1124; BD.542c.
GEN. REF.: –.

Note: In Matt. 21:38, the best texts have *echō*, to have (to take, R.V.); some have *katechō*, to lay hold of (A.V.; "seize on").

SELF, SELVES

1. *automatos* [αὐτόματος, 844], of oneself (Eng., automatic, automaton, etc.), is used in Mark 4:28; Acts 12:10. See ACCORD, B, No. 2. ¶
NT: B.122c; CB.1238b; K.–.
OT: –.
GEN. REF.: –.

2. *autos* [αὐτός, 846], he, also means self, in the reflexive pronouns myself, thyself, himself, etc. (see, e.g., HE), expressing distinction, exclusion, etc.; it is usually emphatic in the nominative case, e.g., Luke 6:42; 11:4; John 18:28; Rom. 8:16, R.V., "Himself."
NT: B.122c; CB.1238b; K.–.
OT: –.
GEN. REF.: –.

Note: In John 16:27, "the Father Himself (*autos*)," Field (*Notes on the Translation of the N.T.*) remarks that *autos* stands for *automatos*.

For **SELF-CONDEMNED** see **CONDEMN**, C, No. 1

SELF-CONTROL (without)

akratēs [ἀκρατής, 193], powerless (*a*, negative, *kratos*, strength), is rendered "without self-control," in 2 Tim. 3:3, R.V.; see INCONTINENT. ¶

NT: B.33a; CB.1234b; K.196.
OT: —.
GEN. REF.: IS.4:386; NB.—; Z.—.

SELFSAME

Notes: (1) In 2 Cor. 5:5, A.V., *auto touto*, this thing itself, "this very thing," R.V., is rendered "the selfsame"; in 2 Cor. 7:11, R.V. and A.V., "this selfsame thing."

(2) In Matt. 8:13, A.V., *ekeinos*, with the article, "that," R.V., is rendered "that selfsame."

(3) In 1 Cor. 12:11, A.V., the article with *autos*, "the same," R.V., is rendered "the selfsame."

SELF-WILLED

authadēs [αὐθάδης, 829], self-pleasing (*autos*, self, *hēdomai*, to please), denotes one who, dominated by self-interest, and inconsiderate of others, arrogantly asserts his own will, "self-willed," Tit. 1:7; 2 Pet. 2:10 (the opposite of *epieikēs*, gentle, e.g., 1 Tim. 3:3), "one so far overvaluing any determination at which he has himself once arrived that he will not be removed from it" (Trench, who compares and contrasts *philautos*, loving self, selfish; Syn. § xciii). ¶ In the Sept., Gen. 49:3, 7; Prov. 21:24. ¶

NT: B.120d; CB.—; K.87.
OT: yāhîr: S.3093; HR.176c.1; H.851a; BD.397d.
GEN. REF.: IS.4:1064; NB.—; Z.—.

SELL

1. *pōleō* [πωλέω, 4453], to exchange or barter, to sell, is used in the latter sense in the N.T., six times in Matthew, three in Mark, six in Luke; in John only in connection with the cleansing of the Temple by the Lord, 2:14, 16; in Acts only in connection with the disposing of property for distribution among the community of believers, 4:34, 37; 5:1; elsewhere, 1 Cor. 10:25; Rev. 13:17.

NT: B.731c; CB.1265c; K.—.
OT: mākar: S.4376; HR.1246b.1; H.1194; BD.569a.
GEN. REF.: IS.1:562,565; NB.—; Z.—.

2. *pipraskō* [πιπράσκω, 4097], from an earlier form, *peraō*, to carry across the sea for the purpose of selling or to export, is used (*a*) literally, Matt. 13:46; 18:25; 26:9; Mark 14:5; John 12:5; Acts 2:45; 4:34; 5:4; (*b*) metaphorically, Rom. 7:14, "sold under sin," i.e., as fully under the domination of sin as a slave is under his master; the statement evinces an utter dissatisfaction with such a condition; it expresses, not the condemnation of the unregenerate state, but the evil of bondage to a corrupt nature, involving the futility of making use of the Law as a means of deliverance. ¶

NT: B.659a; CB.1265a; K.846.
OT: mākar: S.4376; HR.1135c.1; H.1194; BD.569a.
GEN. REF.: IS.1:562; NB.—; Z.—.

3. *apodidōmi* [ἀποδίδωμι, 591], to give up or back, also means, in the Middle Voice, to give up of one's own will; hence, to sell; it is so used in Peter's question to Sapphira as to selling the land, Acts 5:8; of the act of Joseph's brothers, 7:9; of Esau's act in selling his birthright, Heb. 12:16.

NT: B.90b; CB.1236c; K.166.
OT: mākar: S.4376; HR.126b.3; H.1194; BD.569a.
GEN. REF.: IS.1:562; NB.—; Z.—.

Note: In Jas. 4:13, A.V., *emporeuomai*, to trade (R.V.), is rendered "buy and sell."

For **SELLER** see **PURPLE**

SENATE

gerousia [γερουσία, 1087], a council of elders (from *gerōn*, an old man, a term which early assumed a political sense among the Greeks, the notion of age being merged in that of dignity), is used in Acts 5:21, apparently epexegetically of the preceding word *sunedrion*, "council," the Sanhedrin. ¶

NT: B.156d; CB.1248b; K.—.
OT: zāqēn: S.2205; HR.240a.1; H.574b; BD.278c.
GEN. REF.: IS.4:392; NB.1159; Z.5:338.

SEND

1. *apostellō* [ἀποστέλλω, 649], lit., to send forth (*apo*, from), akin to *apostolos*, an apostle, denotes (*a*) to send on service, or with a commission, (1) of persons; Christ, sent by the Father, Matt. 10:40; 15:24; 21:37; Mark 9:37; 12:6; Luke 4:18, 43; 9:48; 10:16; John 3:17; 5:36, 38; 6:29, 57; 7:29; 8:42; 10:36; 11:42; 17:3, 8, 18 (1st part), 21, 23, 25; 20:21; Acts 3:20 (future); 3:26; 1 John 4:9, 10, 14; the Holy Spirit, Luke 24:49 (in some texts; see No. 3); 1 Pet. 1:12; Rev. 5:6; Moses, Acts 7:35; John the Baptist, John 1:6; 3:28; disciples and apostles, e.g., Matt. 10:16; Mark 11:1; Luke 22:8; John 4:38; 17:18 (2nd part); Acts 26:17;

servants, e.g., Matt. 21:34; Luke 20:10; officers and officials, Mark 6:27; John 7:32; Acts 16:35; messengers, e.g., Acts 10:8, 17, 20; 15:27; evangelists, Rom. 10:15; angels, e.g., Matt. 24:31; Mark 13:27; Luke 1:19, 26; Heb. 1:14; Rev. 1:1; 22:6; demons, Mark 5:10; (2) of things, e.g., Matt. 21:3; Mark 4:29, R.V., marg., "sendeth forth," text, "putteth forth" (A.V., ". . . in"); Acts 10:36; 11:30; 28:28; (*b*) to send away, dismiss, e.g., Mark 8:26; 12:3; Luke 4:18, "to set (at liberty)." See *Note* below, No. 2.

NT: B.98c; CB.1237a; K.67.
OT: shālaḥ: S.7971; HR.140b.13a-c; H.2394; BD.1018a.
GEN. REF.: IS.4:393; NB.–; Z.–.

2. *pempō* [πέμπω, 3992], to send, is used (*a*) of persons: Christ, by the Father, Luke 20:13; John 4:34; 5:23, 24, 30, 37; 6:38, 39, (40), 44; 7:16, 18, 28, 33; 8:16, 18, 26, 29; 9:4; 12:44, 45, 49; 13:20 (2nd part); 14:24; 15:21; 16:5; Rom. 8:3; the Holy Spirit, John 14:26; 15:26; 16:7; Elijah, Luke 4:26; John the Baptist, John 1:33; disciples and apostles, e.g., Matt. 11:2; John 20:21; servants, e.g., Luke 20:11, 12; officials, Matt. 14:10; messengers, e.g., Acts 10:5, 32, 33; 15:22, 25; 2 Cor. 9:3; Eph. 6:22; Phil. 2:19, 23, 25; 1 Thess. 3:2, 5; Tit. 3:12; a prisoner, Acts 25:25, 27; potentates, by God, 1 Pet. 2:14; an angel, Rev. 22:16; demons, Mark 5:12; (*b*) of things, Acts 11:29; Phil. 4:16; 2 Thess. 2:11; Rev. 1:11; 11:10; 14:15, 18, R.V., "send forth" (A.V., "thrust in").

NT: B.641d; CB.1263a; K.67.
OT: shālaḥ: S.7971; HR.1116b.2; H.2394; BD.1018a.
GEN. REF.: IS.4:393; NB.–; Z.–.

Notes: (1) *Pempō* is a more general term than *apostellō*; *apostellō* usually "suggests official or authoritative sending" (Thayer). A comparison of the usages mentioned above shows how nearly (in some cases practically quite) interchangeably they are used and yet on close consideration the distinction just mentioned is discernible; in the Gospel of John, cp. *pempō* in 5:23, 24, 30, 37, *apostellō* in 5:33, 36, 38; *pempō* in 6:38, 39, 44, *apostellō* in 6:29, 57; the two are not used simply for the sake of variety of expression. *Pempō* is not used in the Lord's prayer in chapt. 17, whereas *apostellō* is used six times.

(2) The sending of the Son by the Father was from the glory which He had with the Father into the world, by way of the Incarnation, not a sending out into the world after His birth, as if denoting His mission among and His manifestation to the people. "Hofmann, in support of his view that Jesus is called the Son of God only in virtue of His being born of man, vainly urges that the simple accusative after *apostellō* also denotes what the Person is or becomes by being sent. What he states is true but only when the name of the object spoken of is chosen to correspond with the purposed mission, as e.g., in Mark 1:2; Luke 14:32; 19:14. We can no more say, 'God sent Jesus that He should be His Son' than we can render 'he sent his servants,' Matt. 21:34, in this manner. That the Sonship of Christ is anterior to His mission to the world . . . is clear from John 16:28; cp. especially also the double accusative in 1 John 4:14, 'the Father sent the Son the Saviour of the world.' The expression that Jesus is sent by God denotes the mission which He has to fulfil and the authority which backs Him" (Cremer, *Lexicon of N.T. Greek*).

3. *exapostellō* [ἐξαποστέλλω, 1821], denotes (*a*) to send forth: of the Son by God the Father, Gal. 4:4; of the Holy Spirit, 4:6; Luke 24:49 in the best texts (some have No. 1); an angel, Acts 12:11; the ancestors of Israel, Acts 7:12; Paul to the Gentiles, 22:21; of the word of salvation, 13:26 (some mss. have No. 1); (*b*) to send away, Luke 1:53; 20:10, 11; Acts 9:30; 11:22; 17:14. ¶

NT: B.273a; CB.1247c; K.67.
OT: shālaḥ: S.7971; HR.488a.8a-c; H.2394; BD.1018a.
GEN. REF.: IS.4:393; NB.–; Z.–.

4. *anapempō* [ἀναπέμπω, 375], denotes (*a*) to send up (*ana*, up, and No. 2), to a higher authority, Luke 23:7, 15; Acts 25:21 (in the best texts; some have No. 2); this meaning is confirmed by examples from the papyri (Moulton and Milligan), by Diessmann (*Bible Studies*, p. 229); see also Field, *Notes on the Trans. of the N.T.*; (*b*) to send back, Luke 23:11; Philm. 12. ¶

NT: B.59b; CB.–; K.–.
OT: –.
GEN. REF.: IS.4:393; NB.–; Z.–.

5. *ekpempō* [ἐκπέμπω, 1599], denotes to send forth (*ek*, out of), Acts 13:4, "being sent forth"; 17:10, "sent away." ¶

NT: B.243c; CB.–; K.–.
OT: shālaḥ: S.7971; HR.439a.1; H.2394; BD.1018a.
GEN. REF.: IS.4:393; NB.–; Z.–.

6. *ballō* [βάλλω, 906], to cast, throw, is translated "to send (peace)" in Matt. 10:34 (twice), (R.V., marg., "cast"). See CAST.

NT: B.130d; CB.1238b; K.91.
OT: nāphal: S.5307; HR.189c.6b; H.1392; BD.656c,658a.
shālaḥ: S.7971; HR.189c.16; H.2394; BD.1018a.
GEN. REF.: IS.4:393; NB.–; Z.–.

7. *ekballō* [ἐκβάλλω, 1544], to cast out, or send out, is translated "sent out" in Mark 1:43, R.V. (A.V., "sent away"), and in A.V. and R.V. in Jas. 2:25. See CAST, No. 5.

NT: B.237b; CB.1243b; K.91.
OT: gārash: S.1644; HR.420c.3b; H.388; BD.176c.
shālaḥ: S.7971; HR.420c.21; H.2394; BD.1018a.
GEN. REF.: IS.4:393; NB.–; Z.–.

8. *apoluō* [ἀπολύω, 630], to set free, to let go, is translated to send away in Matt. 14:15, 22, 23; Mark 6:36, 45; 8:3, 9; Luke 8:38; Acts 13:3, where the sending is not that of commissioning, but of letting go, intimating that they would gladly have retained them (contrast *ekpempō*, the act of commissioning by the Holy Spirit in ver. 4).

NT: B.96c; CB.1237a; K.—.
OT: gārash: S.1644; HR.138c.2; H.388; BD.176c.
GEN. REF.: —.

9. *metapempō* [μεταπέμπω, 3343], to send after or for, fetch (*meta*, after), is used only in the Acts; in the Middle Voice, translated to send for in 10:22, 29 (2nd part: Passive Voice in the 1st part); 20:1, R.V. only (some texts have *proskaleō*); 24:24, 26; 25:3; in 10:5 and 11:13, R.V., "fetch." See FETCH. ¶

NT: B.513b; CB.—; K.—.
OT: lāqaḥ: S.3947; HR.916c.1; H.1124; BD.542c.
GEN. REF.: —.

10. *bruō* [βρύω, 1032], to be full to bursting, was used of the earth in producing vegetation, of plants in putting forth buds; in Jas. 3:11 it is said of springs gushing with water, "(doth the fountain) send forth . . .?" ¶

NT: B.148a; CB.—; K.—.
OT: —.
GEN. REF.: —.

11. *sunapostellō* [συναποστέλλω, 4882], to send along with, is used in 2 Cor. 12:18. ¶ In the Sept., Ex. 33:2, 12. ¶

NT: B.785a; CB.—; K.—.
OT: shālaḥ: S.7971; HR.1312b.1; H.2394; BD.1018a.
GEN. REF.: —.

12. *sunpempō* [συνπέμπω, 4842], to send along with, is used in 2 Cor. 8:18, 22. ¶

NT: B.779b; CB.—; K.—.
OT: —.
GEN. REF.: —.

Notes: (1) In Matt. 13:36, A.V., *aphiēmi*, to leave, is translated "he sent . . . away" (R.V., "he left"); so in Mark 4:36, A.V., "they had sent away," R.V., "leaving."

(2) In Mark 6:46, *apotassomai*, to take leave of (R.V.) is translated "He had sent . . . away."

(3) In John 13:16 *apostolos* is rendered "one (A.V., he) that is sent," R.V. marg., "an apostle."

(4) *Paristēmi* is rendered "send" in Matt. 26:53, R.V.

For **SENSELESS** see **FOOLISH**, No. 4

SENSES

aisthētērion [αἰσθητήριον, 145], sense, the faculty of perception, the organ of sense (akin to *aisthanomai*, to perceive), is used in Heb. 5:14, "senses," the capacities for spiritual apprehension. ¶ In the Sept., Jer. 4:19. '(I am pained . . . in the) sensitive powers (of my heart).' ¶

NT: B.25a; CB.1234a; K.29.
OT: qîr: S.7023; HR.36c.1; H.2022; BD.885a.
GEN. REF.: —.

For **SENSUAL** see **NATURAL**, A, No. 2

SENTENCE

A. Nouns.

1. *krima* [κρίμα, 2917], a judgment, a decision passed on the faults of others, is used especially of God's judgment upon men, and translated "sentence" in 2 Pet. 2:3, R.V. (A.V., "judgment"). See JUDGMENT, No. 2.

NT: B.450c; CB.1256a; K.469.
OT: mishpāṭ: S.4941; HR.786b.7b; H.2443c; BD.1048b.
GEN. REF.: IS.4:397; NB.—; Z.—.

2. *katadikē* [καταδίκη, —], a judicial sentence, condemnation, is translated "sentence" in Acts 25:15, R.V. (A.V., "judgment"); some mss. have *dikē*. ¶

NT: B.410b; CB.1254a; K.418.
OT: —.
GEN. REF.: IS.4:397; NB.—; Z.—.

3. *apokrima* [ἀπόκριμα, 610], is translated "sentence" in 2 Cor. 1:9, A.V. (R.V., "answer"). See ANSWER, No. 2. ¶

NT: B.93b; CB.—; K.469.
OT: —.
GEN. REF.: IS.4:397; NB.—; Z.—.

B. Verbs.

1. *krinō* [κρίνω, 2919], to judge, to adjudge, is translated "(my) sentence is" in Acts 15:19, A.V., R.V., "(my) judgment is," lit., 'I (*egō*, emphatic) judge,' introducing the substance or draft of a resolution. See JUDGE, B, No. 1.

NT: B.451b; CB.1256a; K.469.
OT: shāphaṭ: S.8199; HR.787b.10a; H.2443; BD.1047a.
dîn: S.1777; HR.787b.3a; H.426; BD.192a.
GEN. REF.: IS.4:397; NB.—; Z.—.

2. *epikrinō* [ἐπικρινω, 1948], to give sentence, is used in Luke 23:24. ¶

NT: B.295a; CB.—; K.—.
OT: —.
GEN. REF.: —.

SEPARATE

A. Verbs.

1. *aphorizō* [ἀφορίζω, 873], to mark off by bounds (*apo*, from, *horizō*, to determine; *horos*, a limit), to separate, is used of "(*a*) the Divine action in setting men apart for the work of the gospel, Rom. 1:1; Gal. 1:15; (*b*) the Divine judgment upon men, Matt. 13:49; 25:32; (*c*) the separation of Christians from unbelievers, Acts 19:9; 2 Cor. 6:17; (*d*) the separation of believers by unbelievers, Luke 6:22; (*e*) the withdrawal of Christians from their brethren, Gal. 2:12. In

(*c*) is described what the Christian must do, in (*d*) what he must be prepared to suffer, and in (*e*) what he must avoid." ¶ *

NT: B.127b; CB.1236c; K.728.
OT: gābal: S.1379; HR.185c.3; H.307; BD.148b.
bādal: S.914; HR.185c.1a; H.203; BD.95a.
GEN. REF.: IS.4:398; NB.–; Z.–.

2. *chōrizō* [χωρίζω, 5563], to put asunder, separate, is translated to separate in Rom. 8:35, 39; in the Middle Voice, to separate oneself, depart (see DEPART); in the Passive Voice in Heb. 7:26, R.V., "separated" (A.V., "separate"), the verb here relates to the resurrection of Christ, not, as A.V. indicates, to the fact of His holiness in the days of His flesh; the list is progressive in this respect that the first three qualities apply to His sinlessness, the next to His Resurrection, the last to His Ascension. See PUT, No. 14.

NT: B.890a; CB.1240a; K.–.
OT: bādal: S.914; HR.1482b.2; H.203; BD.95a.
GEN. REF.: IS.4:398; NB.–; Z.–.

3. *apodiorizō* [ἀποδιορίζω, 592], to mark off (*apo*, from, *dia*, asunder, *horizō*, to limit), hence denotes metaphorically to make separations, Jude 19, R.V. (A.V., "separate themselves"), of persons who make divisions (in contrast with ver. 20); there is no pronoun in the original representing "themselves." ¶

NT: B.90d; CB.–; K.728.
OT: –.
GEN. REF.: –.

B. Preposition.

chōris [χωρίς, 5565], apart from, without (cp. *aneu*, without, a rarer word than this), is translated "separate from" in Eph. 2:12 (A.V., "without"). See APART, BESIDE, WITHOUT.

NT: B.890c; CB.1240a; K.–
OT: –.
GEN. REF.: –.

For **SEPARATIONS** see No. 3, above

SEPULCHRE

1. *taphos* [τάφος, 5028], akin to *thaptō*, to bury, originally a burial, then, a place for burial, a tomb, occurs in Matt. 23:27; ver. 29, R.V. (A.V., "tombs"); 27:61, 64, 66; 28:1; metaphorically, Rom 3:13 ¶

NT: B.806b; CB.1271a; K.–.
OT: qeber: S.6913; HR.1338a.1a; H.1984a; BD.868b.
GEN. REF.: IS.4:870; NB.–; Z.5:347,767.

2 and 3. *mnēma* [μνῆμα, —] and *mnēmeion* [μνημεῖον, —): see GRAVE.

SERGEANT (-S)

rhabdouchos [ῥαβδοῦχος, 4465], a rod-bearer (*rhabdos*, a rod, *echō*, to hold), one who carries a staff of office, was, firstly, an umpire or judge, later, a Roman lictor, Acts 16:35, 38. The duty of these officials was to attend Roman magistrates to execute their orders, especially administering punishment by scourging or beheading; they carried as their sign of office the fasces (whence "Fascist"), a bundle of rods with an axe inserted. At Philippi they acted under the *stratēgoi* or *praetors* (see MAGISTRATE, No. 1). ¶

NT: B.733c; CB.1268a; K.982.
OT: –.
GEN. REF.: IS.3:900; NB.1161; Z.5:349.

SERPENT

1. *ophis* [ὄφις, 3789]: the characteristics of the serpent as alluded to in scripture are mostly evil (though Matt. 10:16 refers to its caution in avoiding danger); its treachery, Gen. 49:17; 2 Cor. 11:3; its venom, Psa. 58:4; 1 Cor. 10:9; Rev. 9:19; its skulking, Job 26:13; its murderous proclivities, e.g., Psa. 58:4; Prov. 23:32; Eccl. 10:8, 11; Amos 5:19; Mark 16:18; Luke 10:19; the Lord used the word metaphorically of the Scribes and Pharisees, Matt. 23:33 (cp. *echidna*, viper, in Matt. 3:7; 12:34). The general aspects of its evil character are intimated in the Lord's rhetorical question in Matt. 7:10 and Luke 11:11. Its characteristics are concentrated in the arch-adversary of God and man, the Devil, metaphorically described as the serpent, 2 Cor. 11:3; Rev. 12:9, 14, 15; 20:2. The brazen serpent lifted up by Moses was symbolical of the means of salvation provided by God, in Christ and His vicarious death under the Divine judgment upon sin, John 3:14. While the living serpent symbolizes sin in its origin, hatefulness and deadly effect, the brazen serpent symbolized the bearing away of the curse and the judgment of sin; the metal was itself figurative of the righteousness of God's judgment. ¶

NT: B.600a; CB.1261a; K.748.
OT: nāḥāsh: S.5175; HR.1042b.2; H.1347a; BD.638a.
GEN. REF.: IS.4:417; NB.1164; Z.5:356.

2. *herpeton* [ἑρπετόν, 2062], a creeping thing (from *herpō*, to creep), a reptile, is rendered "serpents" in Jas. 3:7, A.V. (R.V., "creeping things," as elsewhere). See CREEP, B.

NT: B.310b; CB.–; K.–.
OT: remes: S.7431; HR.548a.3a; H.2177a; BD.943a.
chereṣ: S.8318; HR.548a.4; H.2467a; BD.1056d.
GEN. REF.: IS.4:417; NB.1164; Z.5:356.

SERVANT

A. Nouns.

1. *doulos* [δοῦλος, 1401], an adjective, signifying 'in bondage,' Rom. 6:19 (neuter plural, agreeing with *melē*, members), is used as a noun, and as the most common and general

* From Notes on Galatians by Hogg and Vine, p. 83.

word for "servant," frequently indicating subjection without the idea of bondage; it is used (*a*) of natural conditions, e.g., Matt. 8:9; 1 Cor. 7:21, 22 (1st part); Eph. 6:5; Col. 4:1; 1 Tim. 6:1; frequently in the four Gospels; (*b*) metaphorically of spiritual, moral and ethical conditions: servants (1) of God, e.g., Acts 16:17; Tit. 1:1; 1 Pet. 2:16; Rev. 7:3; 15:3; the perfect example being Christ Himself, Phil. 2:7; (2) of Christ, e.g., Rom. 1:1; 1 Cor. 7:22 (2nd part); Gal. 1:10; Eph. 6:6; Phil. 1:1; Col. 4:12; Jas. 1:1; 2 Pet. 1:1; Jude 1; (3) of sin, John 8:34 (R.V., "bondservants"); Rom. 6:17, 20; (4) of corruption, 2 Pet. 2:19 (R.V., "bondservants"); cp. the verb *douloō* (see B). See BONDMAN.

NT: B.205c; CB.1242b; K.182.
OT: 'ebed: 5650; HR.346b.2b; H.1553a; BD.713d.
GEN. REF.: IS.4:419; NB.1166; Z.5:358.

2. *diakonos* [διάκονος, 1249], for which see DEACON and *Note* there on synonymous words, is translated "servant" or "servants" in Matt. 22:13 (R.V. marg., "ministers"); 23:11 (R.V. marg., ditto); Mark 9:35, A.V. (R.V., "minister"); John 2:5, 9; 12:26; Rom. 16:1.

NT: B.184c; CB.1241a; K.152.
OT: na'ar: S.5288; HR.303b.1; H.1389a; BD.654d.
shārat: S.8334; HR.303b.2; H.2472; BD.1058a.
GEN. REF.: IS.4:419; NB.1166; Z.5:358.

3. *pais* [παῖς, 3816], for which see CHILD, No. 4, also denotes an attendant; it is translated "servant" (*a*) of natural conditions, in Matt. 8:6, 8, 13; 14:2; Luke 7:7 ("menservants" in 12:45); 15:26; (*b*) of spiritual relation to God, (1) of Israel, Luke 1:54; (2) of David, Luke 1:69; Acts 4:25; (3) of Christ, so declared by God the Father, Matt. 12:18; spoken of in prayer, Acts 4:27, 30, R.V. (A.V., "child"); the argument advanced by Dalman for the rendering "Child" in these passages, is not sufficiently valid as against the R.V., "Servant" in Acts 4, and the A.V. and R.V. in Matt. 12 (cp., e.g., the use of *pais* in the Sept. of Gen. 41:38; Jer. 36:24). The Matt. 12 passage by direct quotation, and the Acts 4 passages by implication, refer to the ideal "Servant of Jehovah" (Sept., *pais Kuriou*), of Is. 42:1 and following passages, thus identifying the Servant with the Lord Jesus; for the same identification, cp. Acts 8:35.

NT: B.604c; CB.1261c; K.759.
OT: na'ar: S.5288; HR.1049a.8a; H.1389a; BD.654d.
'ebed: S.5650; HR.1049a.9a; H.1553a; BD.713d.
GEN. REF.: IS.4:419; NB.1166; Z.5:358.

4. *oiketēs* [οἰκέτης, 3610], a house-servant (*oikeō*, to dwell, *oikos*, a house), is translated "servant" in Luke 16:13 (R.V. marg., "household-servant"); so Rom. 14:4 and 1 Pet. 2:18; in Acts 10:7, A.V. and R.V., "household-servants." ¶

NT: B.557a; CB.1260b; K.—.
OT: 'ebed: S.5650; HR.969a.1; H.1553a; BD.713d.
GEN. REF.: IS.4:419; NB.1166; Z.5:358.

5. *hupēretēs* [ὑπηρέτης, 5257], for which see MINISTER, No. 3, and OFFICER, is translated "servants" in the A.V. of Matt. 26:58; Mark 14:65 (R.V., "officers"); in John 18:36, A.V. and R.V. (R.V., marg., "officers").

NT: B.842c; CB.1252a; K.1231.
OT: 'ebed: S.5650; HR.1411c.2; H.1553a; BD.713d.
GEN. REF.: IS.4:419; NB.1166; Z.5:358.

6. *therapōn* [θεράπον, 2324], akin to *therapeuō*, to serve, to heal, an attendant, servant, is a term of dignity and freedom, used of Christ in Heb. 3:5. ¶

NT: B.359b; CB.1272b; K.331.
OT: 'ebed: S.5650; HR.648b.3; H.1553a; BD.713d.
GEN. REF.: IS.4:419; NB.1166; Z.5:358.

7. *sundoulos* [σύνδουλος, 4889], a fellow-servant, is used (*a*) of natural conditions, Matt. 18:28, 29, 31, 33; 24:49; (*b*) of servants of the same Divine Lord, Col. 1:7; 4:7; Rev. 6:11; of angels, Rev. 19:10; 22:9. ¶

NT: B.785d; CB.1270c; K.182.
OT: kᵉnāt (Aramaic): S.3675; HR.1313a.1; H.2793; BD.1097c.
GEN. REF.: IS.—; NB.—; Z.5:358.

Note: For *misthios* and *misthōtos*, see HIRED SERVANT.

B. Verb.

douloō [δουλόω, 1402], to enslave, to bring into bondage (akin to A, No. 1), e.g., 1 Cor. 9:19, R.V., "I brought (myself) under bondage (to all)," A.V., "I made myself servant," denotes in the Passive Voice, to be brought into bondage, to become a slave or servant, rendered "ye became servants (of righteousness)" in Rom. 6:18; "being . . . become servants (to God)," ver. 22. See BONDAGE, B, No. 2.

NT: B.206b; CB.—; K.182.
OT: 'ābad: S.5647; HR.348b.1; H.1553; BD.712b.
GEN. REF.: IS.4:419; NB.1166; Z.5:358.

SERVE

1. *diakoneō* [διακονέω, 1247], to minister (akin to *diakonos*, No. 2, above), to render any kind of service, is translated to serve, e.g., in Luke 10:40; 12:37; 17:8; 22:26, 27 (twice); see MINISTER, B, No. 1.

NT: B.184a; CB.1241a; K.152.
OT: —.
GEN. REF.: IS.4:419; NB.1166; Z.5:358.

2. *douleuō* [δουλεύω, 1398], to serve as a *doulos* (No. 1, above), is used (*a*) of serving God (and the impossibility of serving mammon also), Matt. 6:24 and Luke 16:13; Rom. 7:6; in the gospel, Phil. 2:22; (*b*) Christ, Acts 20:19; Rom. 12:11; 14:18; 16:18; Eph. 6:7; Col. 3:24; (*c*) the Law of God, Rom. 7:25; (*d*) one another, Gal. 5:13, R.V., "be servants to" (A.V., "serve"); (*e*) a father, Luke 15:29 (with a suggestion of acting as a slave); (*f*) earthly masters, Matt. 6:24; Luke 16:13; 1 Tim. 6:2, R.V., "serve"; (*g*) the younger by the elder, Rom. 9:12; (*h*) of being

in bondage to a nation, Acts 7:7; Gal. 4:25, to the Romans, actually, though also spiritually to Judaizers; (*i*) to idols, Gal. 4:8, R.V., "were in bondage" (A.V., "did service"); (*j*) to "the weak and beggarly rudiments," ver. 9 (R.V.), "to be in bondage" (aorist tense in the best texts, suggesting 'to enter into bondage'), i.e., to the religion of the Gentiles ("rudiments" being used in ver. 3 of the religion of the Jews); (*k*) sin, Rom. 6:6, R.V., "be in bondage" (A.V., "serve"); (*l*) "divers lusts and pleasures," Tit. 3:3; (*m*) negatively, to any man — a proud and thoughtless denial by the Jews, John 8:33. ¶

NT: B.205a; CB.1242b; K.182.
OT: 'ābad: S.5647; HR.345a.1a; H.1553; BD.712b.
GEN. REF.: IS.4:419; NB.1166; Z.5:358.

3. *latreuō* [λατρεύω, 3000], primarily to work for hire (akin to *latris*, a hired servant), signifies (1) to worship, (2) to serve; in the latter sense it is used of service (*a*) to God, Matt. 4:10; Luke 1:74 ("without fear"); 4:8; Acts 7:7; 24:14, R.V., "serve" (A.V., "worship"); 26:7; 27:23; Rom. 1:9 ("with my spirit"); 2 Tim. 1:3; Heb. 9:14; 12:28, A.V., "we may serve," R.V., "we may offer service"; Rev. 7:15, (*b*) to God and Christ ("the Lamb"), Rev. 22:3; (*c*) in the tabernacle, Heb. 8:5, R.V.; 13:10; (*d*) to "the host of heaven," Acts 7:42, R.V., "to serve" (A.V., "to worship"); (*e*) to "the creature," instead of the Creator, Rom. 1:25, of idolatry: see WORSHIP.

NT: B.467c; CB.1256c; K.503.
OT: 'ābad: S.5647; HR.863a.2a; H.1553; BD.712b.
pᵉlaḥ: S.6399; HR.863a.3a; H.2940; BD.1108c.
GEN. REF.: IS.4:419; NB.1166; Z.5:358.

Note: In Luke 2:37 the R.V. has "worshipping," for A.V., "served"; in Heb. 9:9, "the worshipper," for A.V., "that did the service."

4. *hupēreteō* [ὑπηρετέω, 5256], for which see MINISTER, B, No. 3, is translated to serve in Acts 13:36; there is a contrast intimated between the service of David, lasting for only a generation, and the eternal character of Christ's ministry as the One who not having seen corruption was raised from the dead.

NT: B.842c; CB.1252a; K.1231.
OT: –.
GEN. REF.: –.

SERVICE, SERVING

1. *diakonia* [διακονία, 1248], is rendered "service" in Rom. 15:31, A.V.; "serving" in Luke 10:40. See MINISTRY, A, No. 1.

NT: B.184b; CB.1241a; K.152.
OT: na'ar: S.5288; HR.303b.1; H.1389a; BD.654d.
shārat: S.8334; HR.303b.2; H.2472; BD.1058a.
GEN. REF.: IS.4:419; NB.–; Z.5:362.

2. *leitourgia* [λειτουργία, 3009], is rendered "service" in 2 Cor. 9:12; Phil. 2:17, 30. See MINISTRY, A, No. 2.

NT: B.471a; CB.1256c; K.526.
OT: ᵃbōdāh: S.5656; HR.873b.2; H.1553c; BD.715a.
GEN. REF.: IS.4:419; NB.–; Z.5:362.

3. *latreia* [λατρεία, 2999], akin to *latreuō* (see No. 3, above), primarily hired service, is used (*a*) of the service of God in connection with the Tabernacle, Rom. 9:4; Heb. 9:1, "Divine service"; ver. 6, plural, R.V., "services" (A.V., "service," and, in italics, "*of God*"); (*b*) of the intelligent service of believers in presenting their bodies to God, a living sacrifice, Rom. 12:1, R.V. marg., "worship"; (*c*) of imagined service to God by persecutors of Christ's followers, John 16:2. ¶

NT: B.467b; CB.1256c; K.503.
OT: ᵃbōdāh: S.5656; HR.863a.1; H.1553c; BD.715a.
GEN. REF.: IS.4:419; NB.–; Z.5:362.

Note: For "soldier on service," 2 Tim. 2:3, R.V., see SOLDIER, B.

SET

A. Verbs.

1. *histēmi* [ἵστημι, 2476], to cause to stand, is translated to set in Matt. 4:5 (aorist tense in the best texts; some have the present, as in A.V.); 18:2; 25:33; Mark 9:36; Luke 4:9; 9:47; John 8:3; Acts 4:7; 5:27; 6:6; ver. 13, "set up"; 22:30; in Jude 24, R.V., "to set" (A.V., "to present"). See ABIDE, No. 10.

NT: B.381d; CB.1250c; K.1082.
OT: 'āmad: S.5975; HR.689a.26a-c; H.1637; BD.763c.
qûm: S.6965; HR.689a.28a-c; H.1999; BD.877c.
GEN. REF.: –.

2. *kathistēmi* [καθίστημι, 2525], lit., to set down (*kata*, down, and No. 1), to appoint, constitute, is translated to set in Matt. 24:45, 47; 25:21, 23, R.V. (A.V., "made"); so Luke 12:42, 44; it is found in some mss. in Heb. 2:7, and translated "set over" (A.V.). See APPOINT, No. 2.

NT: B.390b; CB.1254c; K.387.
OT: sûm, sîm: S.7760; HR.703a.19; H.2243; BD.962c.
GEN. REF.: –.

3. *tithēmi* [τίθημι, 5087], to put, to place, is translated to set in Acts 1:7, of times and seasons (A.V., "put"); Acts 13:47; Rev. 10:2; "setteth on" (of wine) in John 2:10, R.V. (A.V., "doth set forth"); in the A.V. of Mark 4:21 (2nd part) and in Luke 8:16 it is rendered "set" (R.V., "put"), of a lamp (some texts have No. 6 in both). In Mark 4:30 it is used of setting forth by parable the teaching concerning the Kingdom of God, R.V., "shall we set (it) forth" (A.V., "compare"). See APPOINT, No. 3.

NT: B.815d; CB.1272c; K.1176.
OT: sûm, sîm: S.7760; HR.1348c.25; H.2243; BD.962c.
nātan: S.5414; HR.1348c.16; H.1443; BD.678a.
GEN. REF.: –.

4. *paratithēmi* [παρατίθημι, 3908], to place beside (*para*, beside, and No. 3), to set forth, of a parable, Matt. 13:24, R.V. (A.V., "put forth"); to set before, of food, Mark 6:41; 8:6 (twice), 7; Luke 9:16; 10:8; 11:6; Acts 16:34; 1 Cor. 10:27. See ALLEGE, No. 1, PUT, No. 3.
NT: B.622d; CB.–; K.1176.
OT: sûm, sîm: S.7760; HR.1065a.7a; H.2243; BD.962c.
GEN. REF.: –.

5. *perititēmi* [περιτίθημι, 4060], to place or put around (*peri*, around, and No. 3), is translated to set about (of a hedge) in Mark 12:1. See BESTOW, No. 5, PUT.
NT: B.652c; CB.–; K.–.
OT: sûm, sîm: S.7760; HR.1127; H.2243; BD.962c.
nātan: S.5414; HR.1127; H.1443; BD.678a.
GEN. REF.: –.

6. *epitithēmi* [ἐπιτίθημι, 2007], to put, set or lay upon, is used of the placing over the head of Christ on the Cross "His accusation," Matt. 27:37, "set up"; of attacking a person, Acts 18:10, "shall set on." See ADD, No. 1.
NT: B.302d; CB.1246b; K.1176.
OT: nātan: S.5414; HR.535c.15a; H.1443; BD.678a.
sûm, sîm: S.7760; HR.535c.29; H.2243; BD.962c.
GEN. REF.: –.

7. *protithēmi* [προτίθημι, 4388], to set before (*pro*, before, and No. 3), is used in the Middle Voice, translated "set forth," of Christ, in Rom. 3:25 (R.V. marg., "purposed"). See PURPOSE, B, No. 3.
NT: B.722b; CB.1267b; K.1176.
OT: 'ārak: S.6186; HR.1231a.4; H.1694; BD.789b.
sûm: S.7760; HR.1231a.5; H.2243; BD.962c.
shît: S.7896; HR.1231a.6; H.2380; BD.1011a.
GEN. REF.: –.

8. *didōmi* [δίδωμι, 1325], to give, is translated "I have set before" in Rev. 3:8 (R.V. marg., "given"). See GIVE.
NT: B.192c; CB.1241c; K.166.
OT: nātan: S.5414; HR.317b.26; H.1443; BD.678a.
GEN. REF.: –.

9. *kathizō* [καθίζω, 2523], used transitively, signifies to cause to sit down, set, appoint, translated to set in Acts 2:30, R.V. (A.V., incorrectly, "to sit"); in 1 Cor. 6:4, of appointing, i.e., obtaining the services of, judges in lawcourts; in Eph. 1:20, R.V., "made (Him) to sit" (A.V., "set").
NT: B.389d; CB.1254c; K.386.
OT: yāshab: S.3427; HR.701c.4a; H.922; BD.442a.
GEN. REF.: –.

Note: In Heb. 8:1, *kathizō* is used intransitively, R.V., "sat down" (A.V., "is set"); so in 12:2, R.V., "hath sat down" (A.V., "is set down"); Rev. 3:21, R.V., "I . . . sat down" (A.V., "am set down"). So *epikathizō* in Matt. 21:7 (last part), R.V., "He sat" [some mss. have the plural in a transitive sense, A.V., "they set (Him)]." See SIT, No. 8.

10. *tassō* [τάσσω, 5021], to arrange, assign, order, is translated "set (under authority)" in Luke 7:8. In 1 Cor. 16:15, R.V., "have set (themselves)," A.V., "addicted." See APPOINT, No. 5.
NT: B.805d; CB.1271a; K.1156.
OT: sûm, sîm: S.7760; HR.1337a.11; H.2243; BD.962c.
GEN. REF.: –.

11. *anatassomai* [ἀνατάσσομαι, 392], to arrange in order, draw up in order (*ana*, up, and the Middle Voice of No. 10), occurs in Luke 1:1, A.V., "to set forth in order," R.V., "to draw up." See DRAW, No. 9. ¶
NT: B.61d; CB.1235b; K.–.
OT: –.
GEN. REF.: –.

12. *dunō* [δύνω, 1416], to sink into, is used of the setting of the sun, Mark 1:32, "did set"; Luke 4:40, "was setting." The sun, moon and stars were conceived of as sinking into the sea when they set. ¶
NT: B.209a; CB.1242b; K.–.
OT: –.
GEN. REF.: –.

13. *sunallassō* [συναλλάσσω, —], to reconcile (*sun*, together, *allassō*, to change or exchange), is translated "he . . . would have set (them at one, lit., 'into peace') again" in Acts 7:26 (the imperfect tense being conative, expressing an attempt); some mss. have *sunelaunō*, to drive together, force together.¶
NT: B.784d; CB.–; K.–.
OT: –.
GEN. REF.: –.

14. *katangellō* [καταγγέλλω, 2605], to declare, proclaim, is translated "set forth" in Acts 16:21, R.V. (A.V., "teach"); "set I forth" in Acts 17:23, R.V. (A.V., "declare I"). See DECLARE, No. 4. ¶
NT: B.409b; CB.1254a; K.10.
OT: –.
GEN. REF.: –.

15. *enechō* [ἐνέχω, 1758], to hold in, has a secondary significance of setting oneself against a person, being urgent against, Mark 6:19; Luke 11:53 (R.V., marg.). See ENTANGLE, No. 3, QUARREL, URGE.
NT: B.265d; CB.1245a; K.286.
OT: sāṭam: S.7852; HR.473a.1; H.2251; BD.966b.
GEN. REF.: –.

16. *propempō* [προπέμπω, 4311], lit. to send forward (*pro*, forward, *pempō*, to send), is translated "set forward" in Tit. 3:13, R.V. (A.V., "bring") and in 3 John 6, R.V. (.A.V., "bring forward"), of practical assistance to servants of God in their journeys. See ACCOMPANY, No. 4.
NT: B.709b; CB.–; K.–.
OT: –.
GEN. REF.: –.

17. *apodeiknumi* [ἀποδείκνυμι, 584], to show forth, declare, is translated "set forth" in 1 Cor. 4:9, here, a technical term, used for exhibiting gladiators in an arena, "last of all" referring to the grand finale, to make the most thrilling sport for the spectators (cp. 15:32); prophets and others had preceded the apostles in the spec-

tacle; in 2 Thess. 2:4 it is used of the man of sin, who will "set (himself) forth (as God)," A.V., "shewing." Elsewhere Acts 2:22; 25:7. See APPROVE, PROVE. ¶ The word is frequently used in the papyri of the proclamation of the accession of a king or the appointment of an official. Cp. *apodeixis*, "demonstration," 1 Cor. 2:4. ¶

NT: B.89c; CB.1236c; K.—.
OT: rā'āh: S.7200; HR.126a.1; H.2095; BD.906b.
shᵉlēṭ: S.7981; HR.126a.2; H.3034; BD.1115c.
GEN. REF.: —.

18. *epibibazō* [ἐπιβιβάζω, 1913], to place upon, is used of causing persons to mount animals for riding, Luke 10:34; 19:35; Acts 23:24. ¶

NT: B.290b; CB.—; K.—.
OT: rākab: S.7392; HR.516c.3; H.2163; BD.938c.
GEN. REF.: —.

19. *stērizō* [στηρίζω, 4741], to fix, establish, is rendered "He stedfastly set (His face)" in Luke 9:51. See ESTABLISH, No. 1.

NT: B.768a; CB.1270a; K.1085.
OT: sāmak: S.5564; HR.1290c.6a; H.1514; BD.701d.
sûm, sîm: S.7760; HR.1290c.9; H.2243; BD.962c.
GEN. REF.: —.

20. *anorthoō* [ἀνορθόω, 461], to set straight, set up (*ana*, up, *orthos*, straight), is used in Acts 15:16 in God's promise to set up the fallen tabernacle (*skēnē*, tent) of David. The word is used in the papyri of rearing buildings again. See LIFT, No. 6, STRAIGHT.

NT: B.72c; CB.—; K.—.
OT: kûn: S.3559; HR.108b.2; H.964; BD.465c.
GEN. REF.: —.

21. *keimai* [κεῖμαι, 2749], to lie, to be laid (used as the Passive Voice of *tithēmi*, No. 3), is translated to be set, e.g., in Matt. 5:14 (of a city); Luke 2:34 (of Christ); John 2:6 (of waterpots); 19:29 (of a vessel of vinegar); Phil. 1:16, R.V. (ver. 17, A.V.) (of the Apostle Paul); Rev. 4:2 (of the Throne in Heaven). See APPOINT, LAY, LIE.

NT: B.426c; CB.1254c; K.425.
OT: sûm, sîm: S.7760; HR.758b.7; H.2243; BD.962c.
yā'ad: S.3259; HR.758b.3; H.878; BD.416d.
GEN. REF.: —.

22. *anakeimai* [ἀνάκειμαι, 345], to be laid up (*ana*, up), to recline at a meal, is so used in John 6:11, "(to them) that were set down." See LEAN, LIE, *Note* (1), SIT, No. 3.

NT: B.55d; CB.1235a; K.425.
OT: —.
GEN. REF.: —.

23. *prokeimai* [πρόκειμαι, 4295], signifies (*a*) to be set before (*pro*, before, and No. 21), and is so rendered in Heb. 6:18 of the hope of the believer; 12:1, of the Christian race; ver. 2, of the joy set before Christ in the days of His flesh and at His death; (*b*) to be set forth, said of Sodom and Gomorrah, in Jude 7. It is used elsewhere in 2 Cor. 8:12, for which see FIRST, D, *Note* (2). ¶

NT: B.707c; CB.1266c; K.425.
OT: pānîm: S.6440; HR.1207b.1; H.1782a; BD.815d.
GEN. REF.: —.

24. *prographō* [προγράφω, 4270], to write before, is translated "were set forth (unto this condemnation)" in Jude 4, R.V. (A.V., "ordained"); the evil teachers were 'designated of old for this judgment' (cp. 2 Pet. 2:3). For the meaning of this verb in Gal. 3:1, R.V., "openly set forth," see OPENLY, No. 2, *Note*. See WRITE.

NT: B.704a; CB.1266c; K.128.
OT: —.
GEN. REF.: —.

Adjective.

taktos [τακτός, 5002], an adjective (from *tassō*, A, No. 10), ordered, fixed, "set," is said of an appointed day, in Acts 12:21. ¶ In the Sept., Job 12:5. ¶

NT: B.803a; CB.—; K.—.
OT: —.
GEN. REF.: —.

Notes: (1) For "to set at liberty" (*apoluō* and *apostellō*), see LIBERTY.

(2) In Acts 21:2, A.V., *anagō*, to set sail (R.V.), is translated "set forth"; see LAUNCH.

(3) In Luke 22:55, A.V., *sunkathizō*, to sit down together (R.V.), is translated "were set down together." See SIT, No. 10.

(4) For Acts 7:5, "to set his foot on," see FOOT, A, No. 1, *Note*.

(5) In Acts 13:9, A.V., *atenizō*, to look fixedly, gaze, is rendered "set his eyes on" (R.V., "fastened his eyes on"). See FASTEN, No. 1.

(6) In Matt. 27:19, A.V., *kathēmai*, to sit, is rendered "he was set down" (R.V., "he was sitting"). See SIT, No. 1.

(7) In John 13:12, A.V., *anapiptō*, to recline at table, is translated "was set down" (R.V., "sat down"; marg., "reclined"). See RECLINE.

(8) In Matt. 27:66 there is no word in the Greek representing the A.V. "setting"; the R.V. has "the guard being with them," lit., 'with (*meta*) the guard.'

(9) The verb is combined with other words, e.g., AFFECTION, FIRE, MIND, NOUGHT, ORDER, SEAL, UPROAR, VARIANCE.

SETTER FORTH

katangeleus [καταγγελεύς, 2604], a proclaimer, herald (akin to *katangellō*, to proclaim), is used in Acts 17:18, "a setter forth (of strange gods)." It is found in Inscriptions in connection with proclamations made in public places. ¶

NT: B.409b; CB.1254a; K.10.
OT: —.
GEN. REF.: —.

SETTLE

tithēmi [τίθημι, 5087], to put, place, is translated "settle (it therefore in your hearts)" in Luke 21:14, Active Voice in the best texts (some have the Middle), the aorist tense signifying complete decision, i.e., 'resolve' (not 'consider'); cp. Acts 5:4, to conceive in the heart, and contrast Luke 1:66, 'to lay up' (both have aorist tense, Middle Voice). See APPOINT, No. 3.

NT: B.815d; CB.1272c; K.1176.
OT: sûm, sîm: S.7760; HR.1348c.25; H.2243; BD.962c.
nātan: S.5414; HR.1348c.16; H.1443; BD.678a.
GEN. REF.: IS.4:424; NB.—; Z.—.

Notes: (1) In 1 Pet. 5:10, some texts have *themelioō*, to lay a foundation, used metaphorically, and translated "settle," A.V.

(2) In Col. 1:23, A.V., *hedraios*, lit., seated (*hedra*, a seat), is translated "settled" (R.V., "stedfast").

(3) For *epiluō* see DETERMINE, No. 4.

SEVEN

hepta [ἑπτά, 2033], whence Eng. words beginning with hept—, corresponds to the Heb. *sheba'* (which is akin to *sāba'*, signifying to be full, abundant), sometimes used as an expression of fulness, e.g., Ruth 4:15: it generally expresses completeness, and is used most frequently in the Apocalypse; it is not found in the Gospel of John, nor between the Acts and the Apocalypse, except in Heb. 11:30 (in Rom. 11:4 the numeral is *heptakischilioi*, seven thousand); in Matt. 22:26 it is translated "seventh" (marg., "seven").

NT: B.306b; CB.1250a; K.249.
OT: sheba': S.7651; HR.—; H.2319; BD.987d.
GEN. REF.: IS.3:559; NB.898; Z.—.

Note: In 2 Pet. 2:5, R.V., "Noah with seven others" is a translation into idiomatic English of the Greek idiom "Noah the eighth *person*" (so A.V., translating literally). See EIGHTH.

SEVENTH

hebdomos [ἕβδομος, 1442], occurs in John 4:52; Heb. 4:4 (twice); Jude 14; Rev. 8:1; 10:7; 11:15; 16:17; 21:20. ¶

NT: B.213a; CB.—; K.249.
OT: shᵉbî'î: S.7637; HR.361c.1a; H.2319a; BD.988c.
GEN. REF.: —.

SEVEN TIMES

heptakis [ἑπτάκις, 2034], occurs in Matt. 18:21, 22; Luke 17:4 (twice). ¶

NT: B.306b; CB.1250a; K.249.
OT: sheba': S.7651; HR.539c.1a,c; H.2319; BD.988c.
GEN. REF.: IS.3:559; NB.898; Z.—.

SEVENTY

hebdomēkonta [ἑβδομήκοντα, 1440], occurs in Luke 10:1, 17; in Acts 7:14 it precedes *pente*, five, lit., 'seventy-five,' rendered "threescore and fifteen"; for the details see FIFTEEN, *Note* (1); in 23:23 it is translated "threescore and ten"; in 27:37 it precedes *hex*, six, lit., 'seventy-six,' rendered "threescore and sixteen." ¶

NT: B.212d; CB.1249b; K.249.
OT: shib'îm: S.7657; HR.—; H.2319b; BD.988c.
GEN. REF.: IS.—; NB.898; Z.—.

SEVENTY TIMES

hebdomēkontakis [ἑβδομηκοντάκις, 1441], occurs in Matt. 18:22, where it is followed by *hepta*, seven, "seventy times seven"; R.V. marg. has "seventy times and seven," which many have regarded as the meaning; cp. Gen. 4:24 (Winer, in Winer-Moulton, Gram., p. 314, remarks that while this would be the strict meaning, it "would not suit the passage"; his translator, W. F. Moulton, in a footnote, expresses the opinion that it would. So also J. H. Moulton, Prol., p. 98, says: "A definite *allusion* to the Genesis story is highly probable: Jesus pointedly sets against the natural man's craving for seventy-sevenfold revenge the spiritual man's ambition to exercise the privilege of seventy-sevenfold forgiveness").

The Lord's reply "until seventy times seven" was indicative of completeness, the absence of any limit, and was designed to turn away Peter's mind from a merely numerical standard. God's forgiveness is limitless; so should man's be. ¶

NT: B.213a; CB.—; K.249.
OT: shib'îm: S.7657; HR.361c.1; H.2319b; BD.988c.
GEN. REF.: —.

SEVER

1. *katargeō* [καταργέω, 2673], lit., to reduce to inactivity (see ABOLISH, where all the occurrences are given), is rendered "ye are severed (from Christ)" in Gal. 5:4, R.V.; the aorist tense indicates that point of time at which there was an acceptance of the Judaistic doctrines; to those who accepted these Christ would be of no profit, they were as branches severed from the tree.

NT: B.417b; CB.1254b; K.76.
OT: bᵉṭēl (Aramaic): S.989; HR.743a.1; H.2625; BD.1084b.
GEN. REF.: IS.4:428; NB.—; Z.—.

2. *aphorizō* [ἀφορίζω, 873], to separate from, is used of the work of the angels at the end of this age, in severing the wicked from among the righteous, Matt. 13:49, a pre-millennial act

quite distinct from the Rapture of the Church as set forth in 1 Thess. 4. See DIVIDE, No. 1.
NT: B.127b; CB.1236c; K.728.
OT: bādal: S.914; HR.185c.1a; H.203; BD.95a.
pārad: S.6504; HR.185c.14; H.1806; BD.825b.
GEN. REF.: IS.4:428; NB.–; Z.–.

SEVERAL

idios [ἴδιος, 2398], one's own, is translated "several (ability)," in Matt. 25:15.
NT: B.369c; CB.1252c; K.–.
OT: –.
GEN. REF.: IS.4:428; NB.–; Z.–.

Note: For Rev. 21:21, "the several gates," R.V., see EVERY, No. 3.

SEVERALLY

idiᾳ [ἰδίᾳ, 2398], the dative case, feminine, of *idios* (see above), is used adverbially, signifying "severally," in 1 Cor. 12:11.
NT: B.369c; CB.1252c; K.–.
OT: –.
GEN. REF.: –.

Notes: (1) In Rom. 12:5, *kata* (*kath'*) followed by the numeral *heis*, one, and preceded by the article, signifies "severally," R.V. (A.V., "every one"). Cp. EVERY, *Note* (1).

(2) In 1 Cor. 12:27, R.V., the phrase *ek merous*, lit., out of a part (*meros*), is rendered "severally" (A.V., "in particular").

(3) In Heb. 9:5, R.V., the phrase *kata meros*, lit., according to a part, is rendered "severally."

(4) For Eph. 5:33, R.V., "severally," see EVERY, No. 3.

SEVERITY

1. *apotomia* [ἀποτομία, 663], steepness, sharpness (*apo*, off, *temnō*, to cut; *tomē*, a cutting), is used metaphorically in Rom. 11:22 (twice) of "the severity of God," which lies in His temporary retributive dealings with Israel. ¶ In the papyri it is used of exacting to the full the provisions of a statute. Cp. the adverb *apotomōs*, sharply (which see).
NT: B.101c; CB.–; K.1169.
OT: –.
GEN. REF.: –.

2. *apheidia* [ἀφειδία, 857], primarily extravagance (*a*, negative, *pheidomai*, to spare), hence, unsparing treatment, severity, is used in Col. 2:23, R.V., "severity (to the body)," A.V., "neglecting of" (marg., "punishing, not sparing"); here it refers to ascetic discipline; it was often used among the Greeks of courageous exposure to hardship and danger. ¶
NT: B.124d; CB.–; K.–.
OT: –.
GEN. REF.: –.

SEW

epiraptō or *epirrhaptō* [ἐπιράπτω, 1976], (*epi*, upon, *rhaptō*, to sew or stitch), is used in Mark 2:21. ¶
NT: B.298a; CB.–; K.987.
OT: –.
GEN. REF.: IS.4:428; NB.–; Z.–.

SHADOW (Noun)

1. *skia* [σκιά, 4639], is used (*a*) of a shadow, caused by the interception of light, Mark 4:32, Acts 5:15; metaphorically of the darkness and spiritual death of ignorance, Matt. 4:16; Luke 1:79; (*b*) of the image or outline cast by an object, Col. 2:17, of ceremonies under the Law; of the Tabernacle and its appurtenances and offerings, Heb. 8:5; of these as appointed under the Law, Heb. 10:1. ¶
NT: B.755d; CB.1269a; K.1044.
OT: ṣēl: S.6738; HR.1274a.1; H.1921a; BD.853b.
GEN. REF.: IS.4:439; NB.1168; Z.5:368.

2. *aposkiasma* [ἀποσκίασμα, 644], a shadow, is rendered "shadow that is cast" in Jas. 1:17, R.V.; the A.V. makes no distinction between this and No. 1. The probable significance of this word is overshadowing or shadowing-over (which *apo* may indicate), and this with the genitive case of *tropē*, "turning," yields the meaning 'shadowing-over of mutability' implying an alternation of shadow and light; of this there are two alternative explanations, namely, overshadowing (1) not caused by mutability in God, or (2) caused by change in others, i.e., "no changes in this lower world can cast a shadow on the unchanging Fount of light" [Mayor, who further remarks, "The meaning of the passage will then be, 'God is alike incapable of change (*parallagē*) and incapable of being changed by the action of others' "].
NT: B.98a; CB.–; K.1044.
OT: –.
GEN. REF.: IS.4:439; NB.–; Z.–.

For **SHADOWING**, Heb. 9:5, A.V., see **OVERSHADOW**

SHAKE

1. *saleuō* [σαλεύω, 4531], to agitate, shake, primarily of the action of stormy winds, waves, etc., is used (*a*) literally, of a reed, Matt. 11:7; Luke 7:24; a vessel, shaken in filling, Luke 6:38; a building, Luke 6:48; Acts 4:31; 16:26; the natural forces of the heavens and heavenly bodies, Matt. 24:29; Mark 13:25; Luke 21:26; the earth, Heb. 12:26, "shook"; (*b*) metaphorically, (1) of shaking so as to make insecure,

Heb. 12:27 (twice); (2) of casting down from a sense of security, Acts 2:25, "I should (not) be moved"; (3) to stir up (a crowd), Acts 17:13; (4) to unsettle, 2 Thess. 2:2, "(to the end that) ye be not (quickly) shaken (from your mind)," i.e., from their settled conviction and the purpose of heart begotten by it, as to the return of Christ before the Day of the Lord begins; the metaphor may be taken from the loosening of a ship from its moorings by a storm. See MOVE, STIR. ¶

NT: B.740c; CB.1268b; K.996.
OT: mûṭ, môṭ: S.4131; HR.1257c.9; H.1158; BD.556d.
nûa': S.5128; HR.1257c.14; H.1328; BD.631a.
GEN. REF.: IS.4:441; NB.–; Z.–.

2. *seiō* [σείω, 4579], to shake to and fro, is rendered to shake in Matt. 28:4, A.V.; Heb. 12:26, A.V.; Rev. 6:13, A.V. and R.V.; see MOVE, No. 3.

NT: B.746c; CB.1268c; K.1014.
OT: rā'ash: S.7493; HR.1261c.5; H.2195; BD.950a.
GEN. REF.: IS.4:441; NB.–; Z.–.

3. *apotinassō* [ἀποτινάσσω, 660], to shake off (*apo*, from, *tinassō*, to shake), is used in Luke 9:5, of dust from the feet; Acts 28:5, of a viper from the hand. ¶ In the Sept., Judg. 16:20; 1 Sam. 10:2; Lam. 2:7. ¶

NT: B.101b; CB.1237b; K.–.
OT: nāṭash: S.5203; HR.149a.1; H.1357; BD.643c.
nā'ar: S.5287; HR.149a.3; H.1388; BD.654c.
GEN. REF.: IS.4:441; NB.–; Z.–.

4. *ektinassō* [ἐκτινάσσω, 1621], to shake out, is used of shaking off the dust from the feet, Matt. 10:14; Mark 6:11; Acts 13:51; of shaking out one's raiment, Acts 18:6. ¶

NT: B.245d; CB.1244a; K.–.
OT: nā'ar: S.5287; HR.443b.3; H.1388; BD.654c.
GEN. REF.: IS.4:441; NB.–; Z.–.

SHALL

mellō [μέλλω, 3195], to be about (to be or do), is used of purpose, certainty, compulsion or necessity. It is rendered simply by "shall" or "should" (which frequently represent elsewhere part of the future tense of the verb) in the following (the R.V. sometimes translates differently, as noted): Matt. 16:27 (1st part), lit., 'is about to come'; 17:12, 22; 20:22; R.V., "am about"; 24:6; Mark 13:4 (2nd part), R.V., "are about"; Luke 9:44; 21:7 (2nd part), R.V., "are about"; ver. 36; Acts 23:3; 24:15; 26:2, R.V., "I am (to)"; Rom. 4:24; 8:13 (1st part), R.V., "must"; ver. 18; 2 Tim. 4:1; Heb. 1:14; 10:27; Jas. 2:12, R.V., "are to"; 1 Pet. 5:1; Rev. 1:19; 2:10 (1st and 2nd parts), R.V., "art about," "is about"; 3:10, R.V., "is (to)"; 17:8 (1st part), R.V., "is about." See ABOUT, B.

NT: B.500d; CB.1258a; K.–.
OT: –.
GEN. REF.: –.

Notes: (1) The use of shall, shalt, is frequently part of the rendering of a future tense of a verb.

(2) The phrase "it shall come to pass" is the rendering of the future tense of *eimi*, to be, in Acts 2:17, 21; 3:23; Rom. 9:26.

SHAMBLES

makellon [μάκελλον, 3111], a term of late Greek borrowed from the Latin *macellum*, denotes a meat-market, translated "shambles" in 1 Cor. 10:25. The word is found in the *koinē*, or vernacular Greek covering the time of the N.T., illustrating this passage (see Deissmann, *Light from the Ancient East*, 274). A plan, drawn by Lietzmann, of a forum in Pompeii, shows both the slaughter-house and the meat-shop next to the chapel of Caesar. Some of the meat which had been used for sacrificial purposes was afterwards sold in the markets. The Apostle enjoins upon the believer to enter into no enquiry, so as to avoid the troubling of conscience (contrast ver. 28). ¶

NT: B.487b; CB.–; K.549.
OT: –.
GEN. REF.: IS.3:260; NB.1169; Z.5:372.

SHAME (Noun, and Verb)

A. Nouns.

1. *atimia* [ἀτιμία, 819], signifies (*a*) shame, disgrace, Rom. 1:26, "vile (passions)," R.V., lit., '(passions) of shame'; 1 Cor. 11:14 (*b*) dishonour, e.g., 2 Tim. 2:20, where the idea of disgrace or shame does not attach to the use of the word; the meaning is that while in a great house some vessels are designed for purposes of honour, others have no particular honour (*timē*) attached to their use (the prefix *a* simply negatives the idea of honour). See DISHONOUR.

NT: B.120a; CB.1238b; K.–.
OT: qālôn: S.7036; HR.175c.5c; H.2024a; BD.885d.
k^elimmāh: S.3639; HR.175c.3b; H.987a; BD.484a.
GEN. REF.: IS.4:447; NB.1169; Z.–.

2. *aischunē* [αἰσχύνη, —]: see ASHAMED, B, No. 1.

3. *entropē* [ἐντροπή, —], 1 Cor. 6:5 and 15:34. See ASHAMED, B, No. 2. ¶

4. *aschēmosunē* [ἀσχημοσύνη, 808], denotes (*a*) "unseemliness," Rom. 1:27, R.V. (A.V., "that which is unseemly"); (*b*) shame, nakedness, Rev. 16:15, a euphemism for No. 2. ¶

NT: B.119b; CB.–; K.–.
OT: 'er^ewāh: S.6172; HR.174c.2a; H.1692b; BD.788d.
GEN. REF.: IS.–; NB.1169; Z.–.

B. Adjective.

aischros [αἰσχρός, 150], base, shameful (akin to *aischos*, shame), of that which is opposed to modesty or purity, is translated as a noun in

1 Cor. 11:6; 14:35, A.V. (R.V., "shameful"); Eph. 5:12; in Tit. 1:11, "filthy (lucre)," lit., 'shameful (gain).' See FILTHY. ¶

NT: B.25b; CB.1234a; K.29.
OT: ra': S.7451; HR.36c.1a; H.2191; BD.948a.
GEN. REF.: IS.4:447; NB.1169; Z.—.

C. Verbs.

1. *atimazō* [ἀτιμάζω, 818], to dishonour, put to shame (akin to A, No. 1): see DISHONOUR, C, No. 1.

NT: B.120a; CB.1238b; K.—.
OT: bāzāh: S.959; HR.175c.1b; H.224; BD.102b.
qālāh: S.7034; HR.175c.6a; H.2024; BD.885c.
qālal: S.7043; HR.175c.6c; H.2028; BD.886b.
GEN. REF.: IS.4:447; NB.1169; Z.—.

2. *entrepō* [ἐντρέπω, 1788], lit., to turn in upon, to put to shame (akin to A, No. 3), is translated "to shame (you)" in 1 Cor. 4:14. See ASHAMED, A, No. 4.

NT: B.269c; CB.—; K.—.
OT: kālam: S.3637; HR.480c.2; H.987; BD.483c.
kāna': S.3665; HR.480c.4; H.1001; BD.488b.
GEN. REF.: IS.4:447; NB.1169; Z.—.

3. *kataischunō* [καταισχύνω, 2617], to put to shame (*kata*, perhaps signifying utterly), is translated "ye . . . shame (them)" in 1 Cor. 11:22, A.V., R.V., "ye . . . put (them) to shame." (See ASHAMED, A, No. 3.

NT: B.410d; CB.1254a; K.29.
OT: bôsh: S.954; HR.731c.1a,b; H.222; BD.101c.
kālam: S.3665; HR.731c.4; H.1001; BD.488b.
GEN. REF.: IS.4:447; NB.1169; Z.5:372.

4. *paradeigmatizō* [παραδειγματίζω, 3856], signifies to set forth as an example (*para*, beside, *deiknumi*, to show), and is used in Heb. 6:6 of those Jews, who, though attracted to, and closely associated with, the Christian faith, without having experienced more than a tasting of the heavenly gift and partaking of the Holy Ghost (not actually receiving Him), were tempted to apostatize to Judaism, and, thereby crucifying the Son of God a second time, would "put Him to an open shame." So were criminals exposed. ¶ In the Sept., Numb. 25:4; Jer. 13:22; Ezek. 28:17. ¶

NT: B.614a; CB.1262a; K.141.
OT: ḥāmas: S.2554; HR.1057c.1; H.678; BD.329b.
yāqa': S.3363; HR.1057c.2; H.903; BD.429b.
GEN. REF.: —.

SHAMEFASTNESS (A.V., SHAMEFACEDNESS)

aidōs [αἰδώς, 127], a sense of shame, modesty, is used regarding the demeanour of women in the church, 1 Tim. 2:9 (some mss. have it in Heb. 12:28 for *deos*, "awe": here only in N.T.). "Shamefastness is that modesty which is 'fast' or rooted in the character . . . The change to 'shamefacedness' is the more to be regretted because shamefacedness . . . has come rather to describe an awkward diffidence, such as we sometimes call sheepishness" (Davies; *Bible English*, p. 12).

As to *aidōs* and *aischunē* (see ASHAMED, B, No. 1), *aidōs* is more objective, having regard to others; it is the stronger word. "*Aidōs* would always restrain a good man from an unworthy act, *aischunē* would sometimes restrain a bad one" (Trench, Syn. §§ xix, xx).

NT: B.22b; CB.1233c; K.26.
OT: —.
GEN. REF.: IS.—; NB.1169; Z.—.

SHAMEFULLY (ENTREAT)

Note: This forms part of the rendering of (*a*) *atimazō*, Mark 12:4, Luke 20:11, see DISHONOUR, C, No. 1, ENTREAT, *Note*, HANDLE, No. 4; (*b*) *hudrizō*, to insult, Acts 14:5, R.V.; 1 Thess. 2:2, "were (R.V., having been) shamefully entreated." See SPITEFULLY.

SHAPE

1. *eidos* [εἶδος, 1491], rendered "shape" in the A.V. of Luke 3:22 and John 5:37: see FORM, No. 4.

NT: B.221b; CB.1243a; K.202.
OT: mar'āh: S.4759; HR.375c.1; H.2095g,h; BD.909b.
tō'ar: S.8389; HR.375c.8; H.2491a; BD.1061b.
GEN. REF.: —.

2. *homoiōma* [ὁμοίωμα, 3667], rendered "shapes" in Rev. 9:7: see LIKENESS, No. 1.

NT: B.567c; CB.1251a; K.684.
OT: d^emût: S.1823; HR.993a.1a; H.437a; BD.198b.
tabnît: S.8403; HR.993a.6; H.255d; BD.125d.
t^emûnāh: S.8544; HR.999a.7; H.1191b; BD.568b.
GEN. REF.: —.

For **SHARERS** (Heb. 2:14) see **PARTAKE**, B, No. 1.

SHARP, SHARPER, SHARPLY, SHARPNESS

A. Adjectives.

1. *oxus* [ὀξύς, 3691], denotes (*a*) sharp (Eng., *oxy*—), said of a sword, Rev. 1:16; 2:12; 19:15; of a sickle, 14:14, 17, 18 (twice); (*b*) of motion, swift, Rom. 3:15. See SWIFT. ¶

NT: B.574c; CB.—; K.701.
OT: ḥad: S.2299; HR.1001a.1a; H.605a; BD.292b.
GEN. REF.: —.

2. *tomos* [τομός, 5114], akin to *temnō*, to cut [Eng., (ana)tomy, etc.], is used metaphorically in the comparative degree, *tomōteros*, in Heb. 4:12, of the Word of God. ¶

NT: B.822a; CB.—; K.—.
OT: —.
GEN. REF.: —.

B. Adverb.

apotomōs [ἀποτόμως, 664], signifies abruptly, curtly, lit., in a manner that cuts (*apo*, from *temnō*, to cut), hence sharply, severely, 2 Cor. 13:10, R.V., "(that I may not . . . deal)

sharply," A.V., "(use) sharpness"; the pronoun "you" is to be understood, i.e., 'that I may not use (or deal with) . . . sharply'; Tit. 1:13, of rebuking. ¶ Cp. *apotomia*, severity.
NT: B.101c; CB.–; K.–.
OT: –.
GEN. REF.: –.

SHAVE

xuraō [ξυράω, 3587], a late form of *xureō*, from *xuron*, a razor, occurs in Acts 21:24 (Middle Voice), in connection with a vow (Numb. 6: 2-18; cp. Acts 18:18: see SHEAR); 1 Cor. 11:5, 6 (2nd part in each).
NT: B.549c; CB.–; K.–.
OT: gālaḥ: S.1548; HR.959c.1a; H.351; BD.164a.
GEN. REF.: IS.4:454; NB.–; Z.5:378.

SHE

Note: The words under HE in their feminine forms are used for this pronoun.

SHEAR, SHEARER, SHORN

keirō [κείρω, 2751], is used (*a*) of shearing sheep, Acts 8:32, "shearer," lit., 'the (one) shearing'; (*b*) in the Middle Voice, to have one's hair cut off, be shorn, Acts 18:18; 1 Cor. 11:6 (twice; cp. *xuraō*, to shave; see above). ¶
NT: B.427a; CB.–; K.–.
OT: gāzaz: S.1494; HR.758b.1; H.336; BD.159c.
GEN. REF.: IS.4:455; NB.–; Z.–.

SHEATH

thēkē [θήκη, 2336], a place to put something in (akin to *tithēmi*, to put), a receptacle, chest, case, is used of the sheath of a sword, John 18:11. ¶
NT: B.360b; CB.1271c; K.–.
OT: bayit: S.1004; HR.649c.1; H.241; BD.108c,109c.
GEN. REF.: IS.4:456; NB.–; Z.–.

SHED

1. *ekcheō* [ἐκχέω, 1632], to pour out, is translated to shed or to shed forth in Acts 2:33; Tit. 3:6, A.V.; of shedding blood in murder, Rom. 3:15. See POUR, No. 3.
NT: B.247b; CB.1243b; K.220.
OT: shāphak: S.8210; HR.445c.12a; H.2444; BD.1049b.
GEN. REF.: IS.4:462; NB.–; Z.–.

2. *ekchunō*, or *ekchunnō* [ἐκχύνω, 1632], a later form of No. 1, is used of the voluntary giving up of His life by Christ through the shedding of His blood in crucifixion as an atoning sacrifice, Matt. 26:28; Mark 14:24; Luke 22:30, A.V., "is shed," R.V., "is poured out"; these passages do not refer to the effect of the piercing of His side (which took place after His Death); of the murder of servants of God, Matt. 23:35; Luke 11:50; Acts 22:20 (in the best texts; others have No. 1); of the love of God in the hearts of believers through the Holy Spirit, Rom. 5:5. For the 'pouring out' of the Holy Spirit, Acts 10:45, see POUR, No. 4. (The form in the last two passages might equally well come from No. 1, above.) See GUSH OUT, RUN, SPILL.
NT: B.247b; CB.1243b; K.220.
OT: –.
GEN. REF.: IS.4:462; NB.–; Z.–.

SHEEP

1. *probaton* [πρόβατον, 4263], from *probainō*, to go forward, i.e., of the movement of quadrupeds, was used among the Greeks of small cattle, sheep and goats; in the N.T., of sheep only (*a*) naturally, e.g., Matt. 12:11, 12; (*b*) metaphorically, of those who belong to the Lord, the lost ones of the house of Israel, Matt. 10:6; of those who are under the care of the Good Shepherd, e.g., Matt. 26:31; John 10:1, lit., 'the fold of the sheep,' and vv. 2-27; 21:16, 17 in some texts; Heb. 13:20; of those who in a future day, at the introduction of the Millennial Kingdom, have shewn kindness to His persecuted earthly people in their great tribulation, Matt. 25:33; of the clothing of false shepherds, Matt. 7:15; (*c*) figuratively, by way of simile, of Christ, Acts 8:32; of the disciples, e.g., Matt. 10:16; of true followers of Christ in general, Rom. 8:36; of the former wayward condition of those who had come under His Shepherd care, 1 Pet. 2:25; of the multitudes who sought the help of Christ in the days of His flesh, Matt. 9:36; Mark 6:34.
NT: B.703a; CB.1266c; K.936.
OT: ṣō'n: S.6629; HR.1240b.2a; H.1864a; BD.838a.
GEN. REF.: IS.4:463; NB.1174; Z.5:385.

2. *probation* [προβάτιον, —], a diminutive of No. 1, a little sheep, is found in the best texts in John 21:16, 17 (some have No. 1); distinct from *arnia*, lambs (ver. 15), but used as a term of endearment. ¶
NT: B.703a; CB.–; K.936.
OT: –.
GEN. REF.: IS.4:463; NB.–; Z.–.

Note: For "keeping sheep," Luke 17:7, R.V., see CATTLE.

For SHEEPFOLD see FOLD

SHEEP GATE, SHEEP MARKET

probatikos [προβατικός, 4262], an adjective, used in the grammatically feminine form, in John 5:2, to agree with *pulē*, a gate, understood, R.V., "sheep *gate*" (not with *agora*, a market, A.V., "sheep *market*"). ¶ In the Sept., Neh. 3:1, 32; 12:39. ¶ This sheep gate was near the

Temple; the sacrifices for the Temple probably entered by it.
NT: B.703a; CB.–; K.–.
OT: sō'n: S.6629; HR.1204b.1; H.1864a; BD.838a.
GEN. REF.: IS.4:465; NB.–; Z.5:388.

SHEEPSKIN

mēlōtē [μηλωτή, 3374], from *mēlon*, a sheep or goat, occurs in Heb. 11:37. ¶ In the Sept., 1 Kings 19:13, 19; 2 Kings 2:8, 13, 14. ¶
NT: B.518d; CB.–; K.591.
OT: 'aderet: S.155; HR.922a.1; H.28c; BD.12b.
GEN. REF.: IS.4:466; NB.–; Z.5:388.

SHEET

othonē [ὀθόνη, 3607], primarily denoted fine linen, later, a sheet, Acts 10:11; 11:5. ¶ Cp. *tohonion*, linen.
NT: B.555c; CB.–; K.–.
OT: –.
GEN. REF.: IS.4:466; NB.–; Z.–.

SHEKEL, HALF SHEKEL

1. *statēr* [στατήρ, 4715], a *tetradachmon* or four *drachmae*, originally 224 grains, in Tyrian currency, but reduced in weight somewhat by the time recorded in Matt. 17:24; the value was about three shillings, and would pay the Temple tax for two persons, Matt. 17:27, R.V., "shekel" (A.V., "a piece of money"); in some mss., 26:16; see MONEY, *Note*. ¶
NT: B.764c; CB.1270a; K.–.
OT: –.
GEN. REF.: IS.–; NB.840; Z.–.

2. *didrachmon* [δίδραχμον, 1323], a half-shekel (i.e., *dis*, twice, *drachmē*, a drachma, the coin mentioned in Luke 15:8, 9), was the amount of the tribute in the 1st cent., A.D., due from every adult Jew for the maintenance of the Temple services, Matt. 17:24 (twice). ¶ This was based on Ex. 30:13, 24 (see also 38: 24-26; Lev. 5:15; 27:3, 25; Numb. 3:47; 50; 7:13 ff.; 18:16).
NT: B.192c; CB.1241c; K.–.
OT: sheqel: S.8255; HR.328a.2; H.2454a; BD.1053c.
GEN. REF.: IS.4:1053; NB.840; Z.–.

SHEPHERD

poimēn [ποιμήν, 4166], is used (*a*) in its natural significance, Matt. 9:36; 25:32; Mark 6:34; Luke 2:8, 15, 18, 20; John 10:2, 12; (*b*) metaphorically of Christ, Matt. 26:31; Mark 14:27; John 10:11, 14, 16; Heb. 13:20; 1 Pet. 2:25; (*c*) metaphorically of those who act as pastors in the churches, Eph. 4:14. ¶ See PASTOR.
NT: B.684c; CB.1265c; K.901.
OT: rā'āh: S.7462; HR.1169b.1; H.2185,2186; BD.944d.
GEN. REF.: IS.4:463; NB.1175; Z.5:397.

For **CHIEF SHEPHERD** see **CHIEF**, B, No. 3.

SHEW (SHOW)

1. *deiknumi*, or *deiknuō* [δείκνυμι, 1166], denotes (*a*) to shew, exhibit, e.g., Matt. 4:8; 8:4; John 5:20; 20:20; 1 Tim. 6:15; (*b*) to shew by making known, Matt. 16:21; Luke 24:40; John 14:8, 9; Acts 10:28; 1 Cor. 12:31; Rev. 1:1; 4:1; 22:6; (*c*) to shew by way of proving, Jas. 2:18; 3:13.
NT: B.172c; CB.1240c; K.141.
OT: rā'āh: S.7200; HR.286a.12b; H.2095; BD.906b.
GEN. REF.: –.

2. *anadeiknumi* [ἀναδείκνυμι, 322], signifies (*a*) to lift up and shew, shew forth, declare (*ana*, up, and No. 1), Acts 1:24; (*b*) to appoint, Luke 10:1. See APPOINT, No. 14. ¶
NT: B.53b; CB.1235c; K.141.
OT: mānāh: S.4487; HR.76c.2; H.1213; BD.584a.
GEN. REF.: –.

3. *endeiknumi* [ἐνδείκνυμι, 1731], signifies (1) to shew forth, prove (Middle Voice), said (*a*) of God as to His power, Rom, 9:17; His wrath, 9:22; the exceeding riches of His grace, Eph. 2:7; (*b*) of Christ, as to His longsuffering, 1 Tim. 1:16; (*c*) of Gentiles, as to "the work of the Law written in their hearts," Rom. 2:15; (*d*) of believers, as to the proof of their love, 2 Cor. 8:24; all good fidelity, Tit. 2:10; meekness, 3:2; love toward God's Name, Heb. 6:10; diligence in ministering to the saints, ver. 11; (2) to manifest by evil acts, 2 Tim. 4:14, "did (me much evil)," marg., "shewed." ¶
NT: B.262c; CB.–; K.–.
OT: –.
GEN. REF.: –.

4. *epideiknumi* [ἐπιδείκνυμι, 1925], *epi*, upon, intensive, and No. 1, signifies (*a*) to exhibit, display, Matt. 16:1; 22:19; 24:1; Luke 17:14 (in some mss. 24:40; No. 1 in the best texts); in the Middle Voice, to display, with a special interest in one's own action, Acts 9:39; (*b*) to point out, prove, demonstrate, Acts 18:28; Heb. 6:17. ¶
NT: B.291d; CB.–; K.–.
OT: bō': S.935; HR.518c.1; H.212; BD.97c,98d.
GEN. REF.: –.

5. *hupodeiknumi* [ὑποδείκνυμι, 5263], primarily, to shew secretly (*hupo*, under), or by tracing out, hence, to make known, warn, is translated to shew in Luke 6:47; Acts 9:16; in 20:35, A.V. (R.V., "I gave . . . an example"). See EXAMPLE, WARN.
NT: B.844b; CB.–; K.–.
OT: nāgad: S.5046; HR.1413a.5; H.1289; BD.616c.
GEN. REF.: –.

6. *poieō* [ποιέω, 4160], to make, to do, is translated "He hath shewed" in Luke 1:51; "to shew (mercy)," ver. 72, R.V. (A.V., "perform"); "shewed (mercy)," 10:37; John 6:30, A.V., "shewest Thou," R.V., "doest Thou (for a sign)"; Acts 7:36, A.V., "shewed," R.V.,

"wrought"; Jas. 2:13, "shewed (no mercy)"; in Mark 13:22 in the best texts (some have *didōmi*), "shall shew (signs)." See Do, No. 1.
NT: B.680d; CB.1265c; K.895.
OT: 'āsāh: S.6213; HR.1154a.33a; H.1708,1709; BD.793c.
GEN. REF.: –.

7. *mēnuō* [μηνύω, 3377], to disclose, make known (what was secret), is rendered to shew in Luke 20:37; 1 Cor. 10:28; in a forensic sense, John 11:57; Act 23:30, R.V. (A.V., "it was told"). See TELL. ¶
NT: B.519a; CB.–; K.–.
OT: –.
GEN. REF.: –.

8. *paristēmi* [παρίστημι, 3936], to shew, in Acts 1:3; 2 Tim. 2:15; (A.V.: see PRESENT, No. 1.
NT: B.627c; CB.1262b; K.788.
OT: 'āmad: S.5975; HR.1070c.6a,b; H.1637; BD.763c.
yāṣab: S.3320; HR.1070c.3; H.894; BD.426a.
nāṣab: S.5324; HR.1070c.5; H.1398; BD.662a.
GEN. REF.: –.

9. *parechō* [παρέχω, 3930], to afford, give, shew, etc., in the Active Voice, is translated "shewed" in Acts 28:2; in the Middle Voice, "shewing" in Tit. 2:7 (1st part). See BRING, No. 21.
NT: B.626b; CB.–; K.–.
OT: –.
GEN. REF.: –.

10. *exangellō* [ἐξαγγέλλω, 1804], to tell out, proclaim abroad, to publish completely (*ek*, or *ex*, out, *angellō*, to proclaim), is rendered "shew forth" in 1 Pet. 2:9; it indicates a complete proclamation (verbs compounded with *ek* often suggest what is to be done fully). ¶
NT: B.271b; CB.1247c; K.10.
OT: sāphar: S.5608; HR.483a.2b; H.1540; BD.707d.
GEN. REF.: –.

11. *didōmi* [δίδωμι, 1325], to give, is rendered to shew in Matt. 24:24. See also No. 6.
NT: B.192c; CB.1241c; K.166.
OT: –.
GEN. REF.: –.

Notes: The A.V. translates the following words by the verb to shew in the passages indicated. The R.V. gives the better renderings:

(1) *apodeiknumi* (to demonstrate), 2 Thess. 2:4, "setting (himself) forth," see SET, No. 17;

(2) *anangellō* (to declare), Matt. 11:4, "tell"; John 16: 13-15, "declare"; 16:25, "shall tell"; Acts 19:18 and 20:20, "declaring";

(3) *katangellō*, Acts 16:17; 26:23; 1 Cor. 11:26, "proclaim"; in the last passage the partaking of the elements at the Lord's Supper is not a showing forth of His death, but a proclamation of it;

(4) *phaneroō*, John 7:4; 21:1 (twice), 14; Rom. 1:19, to manifest;

(5) *dēloō*, (to make plain), 2 Pet. 1:14, "signify";

(6) *diēgeomai* (to recount), Luke 8:39, "declare";

(7) *emphanizō* (to manifest), Acts 23:22, "hast signified";

(8) *euangelizō*, Luke 1:19, "to bring glad tidings";

(9) *katatithēmi* (to lay up), Acts 24:27, "to gain";

(10) *legō* (to tell), 1 Cor. 15:51, "I tell";

(11) *energeō*, Matt. 14:2 and Mark 6:14, "work";

(12) *ōphthē* (lit., 'was seen'), Acts 7:26, "He appeared";

(13) *ginomai* (to become), Acts 4:22, "was wrought";

(14) in Acts 10:40, *emphanēs*, manifest, with *didōmi* to give, and *ginomai*, to become, "gave . . . to be made manifest" (A.V. "shewed . . . openly");

(15) *apangellō* (to announce), Matt. 11:4, "tell"; 12:18, "declare"; 28:11, "told"; Luke 14:21, "told"; Acts 26:20, "declared"; 28:21, "report" 1 Thess. 1:9, "report"; 1 John 1:2, "declare";

(16) In Luke 1:58, A.V., *megalunō*, to magnify (R.V.), is rendered "shewed great."

(17) See also SHEWING.

For **SHEW BEFORE** see **FORESHEW**

SHEWBREAD

Note: The phrase rendered "the shewbread" is formed by the combination of the nouns *prothesis*, a setting forth (*pro*, before, *tithēmi*, to place) and *artos*, a loaf (in the plural), each with the article, Matt. 12:4; Mark 2:26 and Luke 6:4, lit., 'the loaves of the setting forth'; in Heb. 9:2, lit., 'the setting forth of the loaves.' ¶ The corresponding O.T. phrases are lit., 'bread of the face,' Ex. 25:30, i.e., the presence, referring to the Presence of God (cp. Isa. 63:9 with Ex. 33:14, 15); 'the bread of ordering,' 1 Chron. 9:32, marg. In Numb. 4:7 it is called "the continual bread"; in 1 Sam. 21:4, 6, "holy bread" (A.V., "hallowed"). In the Sept. of 1 Kings 7:48, it is called "the bread of the offering" (*prosphora*, a bearing towards). The twelve loaves, representing the tribes of Israel, were set in order every Sabbath day before the Lord, "on the behalf of the children," Lev. 24:8, R.V. (marg., and A.V., "from"), "an everlasting covenant." The loaves symbolized the fact that on the basis of the sacrificial atonement of the Cross, believers are accepted before God, and nourished by Him in the Person of Christ. The shewbread was partaken of by the priests, as representatives of the nation. Priesthood now being co-extensive with all who belong to Christ, 1 Pet. 2:5, 9, He, the Living Bread, is the nourishment of all, and where He is, there, representatively, they are.

SHEWING

anadeixis [ἀνάδειξις, 323], a shewing forth (*ana*, up or forth, and *deiknumi*, to show), is translated "shewing" in Luke 1:80. ¶

NT: B.53c; CB.1235a; K.141.
OT: –.
GEN. REF.: –.

Note: For "shewing," Rom. 3:25, 26, R.V., see DECLARE, B.

SHIELD

thureos [θυρεός, 2375], formerly meant a stone for closing the entrance of a cave; then, a shield, large and oblong, protecting every part of the soldier; the word is used metaphorically of faith, Eph. 6:16, which the believer is to take up 'in (*en* in the original) all' (all that has just been mentioned), i.e., as affecting the whole of his activities. ¶

NT: B.366a; CB.1272c; K.702.
OT: māgēn: S.4043; HR.663c.1; H.367c; BD.171b.
GEN. REF.: IS.4:1040; NB.82; Z.1:318.

SHINE, SHINING

A. Verbs.

1. *phainō* [φαίνω, 5316], to cause to appear, denotes, in the Active Voice, to give light, shine, John 1:5; 5:35; in Matt. 24:27, Passive Voice; so Phil. 2:15, R.V., "ye are seen" (for A.V., "ye shine"); 2 Pet. 1:19 (Active); so 1 John 2:8; Rev. 1:16; in 8:12 and 18:23 (Passive); 21:23 (Active). See APPEAR.

NT: B.851b; CB.1263c; K.1244.
OT: rā'āh: S.7200; HR.1423a.10; H.2095; BD.906b.
'ôr: S.215; HR.1423a.1a; H.52; BD.21a.
GEN. REF.: IS.4:481; NB.–; Z.–.

2. *epiphainō* [ἐπιφαίνω, 2014], to shine upon (*epi*, upon, and No. 1), is so translated in Luke 1:79, R.V. (A.V., "to give light"). See APPEAR, No. 2.

NT: B.304a; CB.1246a; K.1244.
OT: 'ûr, 'ôr: S.215; HR.537c.1; H.52; BD.21a.
GEN. REF.: –.

3. *lampō* [λάμπω, 2989], to shine as a torch, occurs in Matt. 5:15, 16; 17:2; Luke 17:24; Acts 12:7; 2 Cor. 4:6 (twice). ¶ : see LIGHT, B, No. 3.

NT: B.466a; CB.1256c; K.497.
OT: nāgah: S.5050; HR.853a.2a; H.1290; BD.618b.
GEN. REF.: IS.4:481; NB.–; Z.–.

4. *stilbō* [στίλβω, 4744], to shine, glisten, is used in Mark 9:3 of the garments of Christ at His Transfiguration, R.V., "glistering," A.V., "shining." ¶ Cp. *exastraptō*, "dazzling," in Luke 9:29, R.V.

NT: B.768d; CB.–; K.1087.
OT: lahab: S.3851; HR.1291b.1; H.1077, 1077a; BD.529a.
ṣāhēb: S.6668; HR.1291b.2; H.1880; BD.843c.
GEN. REF.: –.

5. *eklampō* [ἐκλάμπω, 1584], to shine forth (*ek*, out, and No. 3), is used in Matt. 13:43, of the future shining forth of the righteous "in the Kingdom of their Father." ¶

NT: B.242a; CB.1243c; K.497.
OT: 'ûr, 'ôr: S.215; HR.435a.1; H.52; BD.21a.
zāhar: S.2094; HR.435a.2; H.531,532; BD.263d.
nāgah: S.5050; HR.435a.3; H.1290; BD.618b.
GEN. REF.: IS.4:481; NB.–; Z.–.

6. *perilampō* [περιλάμπω, 4034], to shine around (*peri*, around, and No. 3), is used in Luke 2:9, "shone round about," of the glory of the Lord; so in Acts 26:13, of the light from Heaven upon Saul of Tarsus. ¶

NT: B.648c; CB.1263b; K.497.
OT: –.
GEN. REF.: IS.4:481; NB.–; Z.–.

7. *periastraptō* [περιαστράπτω, 4015], to flash around, shine round about (*peri*, and *astrapē*, shining brightness), is used in Acts 9:3 and 22:6 of the same circumstance as in 26:13 (No. 6). ¶

NT: B.645d; CB.–; K.–.
OT: –.
GEN. REF.: IS.4:481; NB.–; Z.–.

8. *epiphauskō* or *epiphauō* [ἐπιφαύσκω, 2017], to shine forth, is used figuratively of Christ upon the slumbering believer who awakes and arises from among the dead, Eph. 5:14, R.V., "shall shine upon thee" (A.V., "shall give thee light"). ¶

NT: B.304c; CB.–; K.1293.
OT: hālal: S.1984; HR.538a.2; H.499,500; BD.237d.
GEN. REF.: IS.4:481; NB.–; Z.–.

B. Noun.

astrapē [ἀστραπή, 796], denotes (*a*) lightning, (*b*) bright shining, of a lamp, Luke 11:36. See LIGHTNING. Cp. No. 7, above, and *Note* (1) below.

NT: B.118a; CB.1238a; K.86.
OT: bārāq: S.1300; HR.173c.1; H.287a; BD.140c.
GEN. REF.: –.

Notes: (1) In Luke 24:4, A.V., *astraptō*, to lighten, is translated "shining" (R.V., "dazzling").

(2) In 2 Cor. 4:4, A.V., *augazō*, to shine forth, is translated "shine" (R.V., "dawn"). ¶

SHIP, SHIPPING

1. *ploion* [πλοῖον, 4143], akin to *pleō*, to sail, a boat or a ship, always rendered appropriately "boat" in the R.V. in the Gospels; "ship" in the Acts; elsewhere, Jas. 3:4; Rev. 8:9; 18:17 (in some mss.), 19. See BOAT, No. 2.

NT: B.673b; CB.–; K.–.
OT: 'oniyyāh: S.591; HR.1150a.1a; H.125b; BD.58b.
GEN. REF.: IS.4:482; NB.1178; Z.5:410.

2. *ploiarion* [πλοιάριον, 4142], a diminutive form of No. 1, is translated "ship" in the A.V. of Mark 3:9; 4:36 and John 21:8; "(took) shipping" in John 6:24, A.V., R.V. "(got into the) boats." See BOAT, No. 1.
NT: B.673b; CB.—; K.—.
OT: —.
GEN. REF.: IS.4:482; NB.—; Z.5:410.

3. *naus* [ναῦς, 3491], denotes a ship (Lat. *navis*, Eng. nautical, naval, etc.), Acts 27:41. ¶ *Naus*, in classical Greek the ordinary word for a ship, survived in Hellenistic Greek only as a literary word, but disappeared from popular speech (Moulton, Proleg., p. 25). Blass (*Philology of the Gospels*, p. 186) thinks the solitary Lucan use of *naus* was due to a reminiscence of the Homeric phrase for beaching a ship.
NT: B.534c; CB.—; K.—.
OT: ʾᵒniyyāh: S.591; HR.940a.1b; H.125b; BD.58b.
GEN. REF.: IS.4:482; NB.1169; Z.5:410.

Note: For *epibainō*, Acts 21:6, "we took ship," see TAKE, *Note* (16).

For **OWNER OF THE SHIP** see **OWNER**, No. 2

For **SHIPMEN** see **MARINERS**

For **SHIPMASTER** see **MASTER**, A, No. 7

SHIPWRECK

nauageō [ναυαγέω, 3489], signifies (*a*) literally, to suffer shipwreck (*naus*, a ship, *agnumi*, to break), 2 Cor. 11:25; (*b*) metaphorically, to make shipwreck, 1 Tim. 1:19, "concerning the faith," as the result of thrusting away a good conscience (both verbs in this ver. are in the aorist tense, signifying the definiteness of the acts). ¶
NT: B.534b; CB.1259b; K.627.
OT: —.
GEN. REF.: —.

For **SHIVERS** (Rev. 2:27) see **BREAK**, A, No. 5

For **SHOD** see **BIND**, No. 3

SHOE

hupodēma [ὑπόδημα, 5266], denotes a sole bound under the foot (*hupo*, under, *deō*, to bind; cp. *hupodeō*, to bind under), a sandal, always translated "shoes," e.g., Matt. 3:11; 10:10; Mark 1:7.
NT: B.844c; CB.—; K.702.
OT: naʿal: S.5275; HR.1413b.1b; H.1383a; BD.653a.
GEN. REF.: IS.4:491; NB.—; Z.5:419.

SHOOT FORTH

proballō [προβάλλω, 4261], lit., to throw before, is used of the putting forth of leaves, blossom, fruit, said of trees in general, Luke 21:30, "shoot forth." See PUT (forward), Acts 19:33. ¶
NT: B.702d; CB.—; K.—.
OT: yārāh: S.3384; HR.1204a.2; H.910; BD.434d.
shālaḥ: S.7971; HR.1204a.4; H.2394; BD.1018a.
GEN. REF.: —.

Note: In Mark 4:32, A.V., *poieō*, to do, make, is rendered "shooteth out," R.V., "putteth out."

For **SHORE** see **BEACH** and **LIP**

For **SHORT** (Adjective and Adverb) see **LITTLE**, A, No. 2 and B, No. 2

Note: In 1 Thess. 2:17, "a short season," is lit., 'a season of an hour' (*hōra*; see HOUR, SEASON, No. 1.

SHORT (come, cut), SHORTEN

1. *koloboō* [κολοβόω, 2856], denotes to cut off, amputate (*kolobos*, docked); hence, to curtail, shorten, said of the shortening by God of the time of the great tribulation, Matt. 24:22 (twice); Mark 13:20 (twice). ¶ In the Sept., 2 Sam. 4:12. ¶
NT: B.442a; CB.1255c; K.452.
OT: qāṣaṣ: S.7112; HR.777a.1; H.2060; BD.893c.
GEN. REF.: IS.4:493; NB.—; Z.—.

2. *sustellō* [συστέλλω, 4958], denotes (*a*) to draw together (*sun*, together, *stellō*, to bring, gather), to contract, shorten, 1 Cor. 7:29, R.V., "(the time) is shortened" (A.V., ". . . is short"); the coming of the Lord is always to be regarded as nigh for the believer, who is to be in constant expectation of His return, and thus is to keep himself from being the slave of earthly conditions and life's relationships; (*b*) to wrap up, of enshrouding a body for burial, Acts 5:6, R.V., "they wrapped (A.V., wound) . . . up." ¶
NT: B.795a; CB.—; K.1074.
OT: —.
GEN. REF.: —.

3. *suntemnō* [συντέμνω, 4932], primarily, to cut in pieces (*sun*, together, *temnō*, to cut), then, to cut down, cut short, is used metaphorically in Rom. 9:28 (twice in some texts), "the Lord will execute His word (*logos*, not work, as A.V.) upon the earth, finishing it and cutting it short," i.e., in the fulfilment of His judgments pronounced upon Israel, a remnant only being saved; the cutting short of His word is suggestive of the summary and decisive character of the Divine act. ¶
NT: B.792b; CB.—; K.—.
OT: hāraṣ: S.2782; HR.1320b.1; H.752; BD.358c.
GEN. REF.: —.

Note: For *hustereō*, to come short, fall short, see FALL, No. 10.

SHORTLY

1. *eutheōs* [εὐθέως, 2112], straightway, directly, is translated "shortly" in 3 John 14. The general use of the word suggests something sooner than "shortly." See FORTHWITH, STRAIGHTWAY.

NT: B.320b; CB.1247b; K.—.
OT: pit'ōm: S.6597; HR.570b.1; H.1859a; BD.837b.
GEN. REF.: —.

2. *tacheōs* [ταχέως, —]: see QUICKLY, No. 3.

3. *tacheion* [τάχειον, —]: see QUICKLY, No. 2.

4. *en tachei* [ἐν τάχει, —]: see QUICKLY, No. 4.

Note: In 2 Pet. 1:14, A.V., *tachinos*, an adjective denoting swift (akin to the above), is translated "shortly" (R.V., "swiftly"), lit., 'the putting off of my tabernacle is swift' (i.e., in its approach). Cp. 2:1.

SHOULD

Note: This is frequently part of the translation of the tense of a verb. Otherwise it translates the following:

1. *mellō* [μέλλω, 3195], to be about to (for the significance of which see SHALL), e.g., Mark 10:32, R.V., "were to"; Luke 19:11, R.V., "was to"; "should" in 22:23; 24:21; John 6:71; 7:39, R.V., "were to"; 11:51; 12:4, 33; 18:32; Acts 11:28; 23:27, R.V., "was about (to be slain)"; 1 Thess. 3:4, R.V., "are to"; Rev. 6:11. See ABOUT, B.

NT: B.500d; CB.1258a; K.—.
OT: —.
GEN. REF.: —.

2. *dei* [δεῖ, 1163], it needs, it should, e.g., Matt. 18:33; Acts 27:21. See MUST.

NT: B.177c; CB.1240b; K.148.
OT: —.
GEN. REF.: —.

Note: In 1 Cor. 9:10, A.V., *opheilō*, to owe, is rendered "should" (R.V., "ought to").

SHOULDER

ōmos [ὦμος, 5606], occurs in Matt. 23:4 and Luke 15:5, and is suggestive (as in the latter passage) of strength and safety. ¶

NT: B.895d; CB.—; K.—.
OT: kātēph: S.3802; HR.1493a.1; H.1059; BD.509b.
shᵉkem: S.7926; HR.1493a.3; H.2386a; BD.1014a.
GEN. REF.: IS.4:493; NB.—; Z.5:420.

SHOUT (Noun and Verb)

A. Noun.

keleusma [κέλευσμα, 2752], a call, summons, shout of command (akin to *keleuō*, to command), is used in 1 Thess. 4:16 of the shout with which (*en*, in, denoting the attendant circumstances) the Lord will descend from heaven at the time of the Rapture of the saints (those who have fallen asleep, and the living) to meet Him in the air. The shout is not here said to be His actual voice, though this indeed will be so (John 5:28). ¶ In the Sept., Prov. 30:27, "(the locusts . . . at the) word of command (march in rank)." ¶

NT: B.427b; CB.1254c; K.426.
OT: —.
GEN. REF.: —.

B. Verb.

epiphōneō [ἐπιφωνέω, 2019], to call out (*epi*, upon, *phōneō*, to utter a sound), is translated "shouted" in Acts 12:22, R.V. (A.V., "gave a shout"). See CRY, B, No. 8.

NT: B.304d; CB.1246a; K.—.
OT: —.
GEN. REF.: IS.4:493; NB.—; Z.—.

SHOW (Noun)

logos [λόγος, 3056], a word, is sometimes used of mere talk, the talk which one occasions; hence, repute, reputation; this seems to be the meaning in Col. 2:23, translated "a show (A.V. 'shew') of wisdom," i.e., 'a reputation for wisdom,' rather than 'appearance,' 'reason' etc. See WORD.

NT: B.477a; CB.1257a; K.505.
OT: —.
GEN. REF.: —.

Note: In Luke 20:47, A.V., *prophasis*, a pretence (R.V.), is translated "shew." See CLOKE (Pretence), No. 2.

SHOW (make a)

1. *deigmatizō* [δειγματίζω, 1165], to make a show of, expose, is used in Col. 2:15 of Christ's act regarding the principalities and powers, displaying them "as a victor displays his captives or trophies in a triumphal procession" (Lightfoot). Some regard the meaning as being that He showed the angelic beings in their true inferiority (see under TRIUMPH). For its other occurrence, Matt. 1:19, see EXAMPLE, B, No. 1.

NT: B.172c; CB.1240c; K.141.
OT: —.
GEN. REF.: —.

2. *euprosōpeō* [εὐπροσωπέω, 2146], denotes to look well, make a fair show (*eu*, well, *prosōpon*, a face), and is used in Gal. 6:12, "to make a fair show (in the flesh)," i.e., to make a display of religious zeal. Deissmann illustrates

the metaphorical use of this word from the papyri in *Light from the Ancient East*, p. 96. ¶
NT: B.324c; CB.–; K.950.
OT: –.
GEN. REF.: –.

Note: For *paratērēsis*, A.V. marg. in Luke 17:20, "outward shew," see OBSERVATION. ¶

SHOWER

ombros [ὄμβρος, 3655], denotes a heavy shower, a storm of rain, Luke 12:54. ¶
NT: B.565b; CB.1260c; K.–.
OT: –.
GEN. REF.: IS.4:494; NB.–; Z.–.

For SHRANK and SHRINK see DRAW (*B*), No. 4

SHRINE

naos [ναός, 3485], the inmost part of a temple, a shrine, is used in the plural in Acts 19:24, of the silver models of the pagan shrine in which the image of Diana (Greek Artemis) was preserved. The models were large or small, and were signs of wealth and devotion on the part of purchasers. The variety of forms connected with the embellishment of the image provided "no little business" for the silversmiths. See TEMPLE.
NT: B.533b; CB.1259b; K.625.
OT: hêkāl: S.1964; HR.939a.4a; H.493; BD.228a.
GEN. REF.: IS.4:494; NB.–; Z.5:421.

SHUDDER

phrissō [φρίσσω, 5425], primarily, to be rough, to bristle, then, to shiver, shudder, tremble, is said of demons, Jas. 2:19, R.V., "shudder" (A.V., "tremble"). ¶ Cp. Matt. 8:29, indicating a cognizance of their appointed doom.
NT: B.866a; CB.–; K.–.
OT: –.
GEN. REF.: –.

For SHUN see AVOID, No. 4 and DRAW, (*B*), No. 4

SHUT, SHUT UP

1. *kleiō* [κλείω, 2808], is used (*a*) of things material, Matt. 6:6; 25:10; Luke 11:7; John 20:19, 26; Acts 5:23; 21:30; Rev. 20:3; figuratively, 21:25; (*b*) metaphorically, of the Kingdom of Heaven, Matt. 23:13; of heaven, with consequences of famine, Luke 4:25; Rev. 11:6; of compassion, 1 John 3:17, R.V. (A.V., "bowels *of compassion*"); of the blessings accruing from the promises of God regarding David, Rev. 3:7; of a door for testimony, 3:8. ¶
NT: B.434a; CB.1255b; K.–.
OT: sāgar: S.5462; HR.767a.3; H.1462; BD.688d.
GEN. REF.: –.

2. *apokleiō* [ἀποκλείω, 608], to shut fast (*apo*, away from, and No. 1), is used in Luke 13:25, expressing the impossibility of entrance after the closing. ¶
NT: B.93a; CB.–; K.–.
OT: sāgar: S.5462; HR.132b.2; H.1462; BD.688d.
GEN. REF.: –.

3. *katakleiō* [κατακλείω, 2623], lit., to shut down (the *kata* has, however, an intensive use), signifies to shut up in confinement, Luke 3:20; Acts 26:10. ¶ In the Sept., Jer. 32:3. ¶
NT: B.411c; CB.–; K.–.
OT: kālā': S.3607; HR.733b.1; H.980; BD.476b.
GEN. REF.: –.

4. *sunkleiō* [συγκλείω, –]: see INCLOSE

SICK, SICKLY, SICKNESS

A. Verbs.

1. *astheneō* [ἀσθενέω, 770], lit., to be weak, feeble (*a*, negative, *sthenos*, strength), is translated to be sick, e.g., in Matt. 10:8, "(the) sick"; 25:36; ver. 39 in the best texts (some have B, No. 1); Mark 6:56; Luke 4:40; 7:10 (R.V. omits the word); 9:2; John 4:46; 5:3, R.V. (A.V., "impotent folk"); ver. 7; 6:2, R.V. (A.V., "were diseased"); 11:1-3, 6; Acts 9:37; 19:12; Phil. 2:26, 27; 2 Tim. 4:20; Jas. 5:14. See DISEASED, B, No. 1, IMPOTENT, and, especially, WEAK.
NT: B.115b; CB.1238a; K.83.
OT: kāshal: S.3782; HR.172a.7a,b; H.1050; BD.505b.
GEN. REF.: IS.4:498; NB.–; Z.–.

2. *kamnō* [κάμνω, 2577], primarily, to work, hence, from the effect of constant work, to be weary, Heb. 12:3, is rendered "(him) that is sick," in Jas. 5:15, R.V., A.V. "(the) sick." The choice of this verb instead of the repetition of No. 1 (ver. 14, see above), is suggestive of the common accompaniment of sickness, weariness of mind (which is the meaning of this verb), which not infrequently hinders physical recovery; hence this special cause is here intimated in the general idea of sickness. In some mss. it occurs in Rev. 2:3. ¶ In the Sept., Job 10:1; 17:2. ¶
NT: B.402a; CB.–; K.–.
OT: –.
GEN. REF.: IS.4:498; NB.–; Z.–.

3. *sunechō* [συνέχω, 4912], to hold in, hold fast, is used, in the Passive Voice, of being seized or afflicted by ills, Acts 28:8, "sick" (of the father of Publius, cp. Matt. 4:24; Luke 4:38, "taken with"). See CONSTRAIN, No. 3.
NT: B.789a; CB.1270c; K.1117.
OT: –.
GEN. REF.: –.

Notes: (1) *Noseō*, to be sick, is used metaphorically of mental ailment, in 1 Tim. 6:4, "doting" (marg., "sick").

(2) The adverb *kakōs*, evilly, ill, with *echō*, to hold, to have, is rendered to be sick, in Matt. 4:24, R.V., "that were sick"; 8:16; 9:12; 14:35 and Mark 1:32, R.V. (A.V., "diseased"); 1:34; 2:17; 6:55; Luke 5:31; 7:2.

(3) For "sick of the palsy," Luke 5:24; Acts 9:33, see PALSY (sick of).

B. Adjectives.

1. *asthenēs* [ἀσθενής, 772], lit., without strength, hence, feeble, weak, is used of bodily debility, Matt. 25:43 (for ver. 39, see A, No. 1), 44; some texts have it in Luke 9:2 (the best omit it, the meaning being to heal in general); 10:9; Acts 5:15, 16; in 4:9 it is rendered "impotent." See FEEBLE, IMPOTENT, WEAK.

NT: B.115c; CB.1238a; K.83.
OT: dal: S.1800; HR.172b.3; H.433a; BD.195c.
'ānî: S.6041; HR.172b.7a; H.1652d; BD.776d.
rāpeh: S.7504; HR.172b.10; H.2198a; BD.952a.
GEN. REF.: IS.4:499; NB.—; Z.—.

2. *arrhōstos* [ἄρρωστος, 732], feeble, sickly (*a*, negative, *rhōnnumi*, to be strong), is translated "sick" in Matt. 14:14; Mark 16:18; "sick folk" in Mark 6:5; "that were sick" in 6:13; "sickly" in 1 Cor. 11:30, here also of the physical state. ¶ In the Sept., 1 Kings 14:5; Mal. 1:8. ¶

NT: B.109d; CB.—; K.—.
OT: ḥālāh: S.2470; HR.160b.1; H.655; BD.317c.
GEN. REF.: IS.4:499; NB.—; Z.—.

C. Nouns.

1. *astheneia* [ἀσθένεια, 769], weakness, sickness (akin to A, No. 1 and B, No. 1), is translated "sickness" in John 11:4. See DISEASE, No. 1, INFIRMITY, WEAKNESS.

NT: B.115a; CB.1238a; K.83.
OT: kāshal: S.3782; HR.172a.1a; H.1050; BD.505b.
'aṣṣebet: S.6094; HR.172a.2; H.1666d; BD.781a.
GEN. REF.: IS.4:499; NB.—; Z.—.

2. *nosos* [νόσος, —]: see DISEASE, No. 3.

SICKLE

drepanon [δρέπανον, 1407], a pruning-hook, a sickle (akin to *drepō*, to pluck), occurs in Mark 4:29; Rev. 14:14, 15, 16, 17, 18 (twice), 19. ¶

NT: B.206d; CB.1242b; K.—.
OT: mazmērāh: S.4211; HR.349a.4; H.559c; BD.275a.
maggāl: S.4038; HR.349a.3; H.1292a; BD.618c.
GEN. REF.: IS.4:499; NB.—; Z.5:426.

SIDE

A. Noun.

pleura [πλευρά, 4125], a side (cp. Eng., pleurisy), is used of the side of Christ, into which the spear was thrust, John 19:34; 20:20, 25, 27 (some mss. have it in Matt. 27:49; see R.V. marg.); elsewhere, in Acts 12:7. ¶

NT: B.668a; CB.—; K.—.
OT: ṣēla': S.6763; HR.1142a.8; H.1924a; BD.854b.
ṣad: S.6654; HR.1142a.7; H.1876a; BD.841a.
GEN. REF.: —.

B. Adverb.

peran [πέραν, 4008], an adverb, signifying beyond, on the other side, is used (*a*) as a preposition and translated "on the other side of," e.g., in Mark 5:1; Luke 8:22; John 6:1, R.V.; 6:22, 25; (*b*) as a noun with the article, e.g., Matt. 8:18, 28; 14:22; 16:5. See BEYOND, No. 2.

NT: B.643d; CB.—; K.—.
OT: 'ēber: S.5676; HR.1119b.2a; H.1556a; BD.719b.
GEN. REF.: —.

Notes: (1) In Luke 9:47, the preposition *para*, by the side of, with the dative case of the pronoun *heautou*, is rendered "by His side," R.V. (A.V., "by Him").

(2) See also EITHER, EVERYWHERE, No. 3, HIGHWAY, RIGHT.

SIFT

siniazō [σινιάζω, 4617], to winnow, sift (*sinion*, a sieve), is used figuratively in Luke 22:31. ¶

NT: B.751d; CB.1269a; K.1028.
OT: —.
GEN. REF.: IS.4:505; NB.—; Z.—.

SIGH

1. *stenazō* [στενάζω, 4727], to groan, is translated "He sighed" in Mark 7:34. See GRIEF, GROAN.

NT: B.766b; CB.1270a; K.1076.
OT: 'ānaḥ: S.584; HR.1288b.3; H.127; BD.58d.
'ānaq: S.602; HR.1288b.4; H.134; BD.60b.
GEN. REF.: —.

2. *anastenazō* [ἀναστενάζω, 389], to sigh deeply (*ana*, up, suggesting 'deep drawn,' and No. 1), occurs in Mark 8:12. ¶ In the Sept., Lam. 1:4. ¶

NT: B.61b; CB.—; K.—.
OT: 'ānaḥ: S.584; HR.82a.1; H.127; BD.58d.
GEN. REF.: —.

SIGHT

A. Nouns.

1. *eidos* [εἶδος, 1491], is translated "sight" in 2 Cor. 5:7; see APPEARANCE, No. 1.

NT: B.221a; CB.1243a; K.202.
OT: mar'eh: S.4758; HR.375c.1; H.2095i; BD.909c.
tō'ar: S.8389; HR.375c.8; H.2491a; BD.1061b.
GEN. REF.: —.

2. *theōria* [θεωρία, 2335], denotes a spectacle, a sight (akin to *theōreō*, to gaze, behold; see BEHOLD), in Luke 23:48. ¶

NT: B.360b; CB.1272a; K.—.
OT: —.
GEN. REF.: —.

3. *horama* [ὅραμα, 3705], that which is seen (akin to *horaō*, to see), besides its meaning, a vision, appearance, denotes a sight, in Acts 7:31. See VISION.

NT: B.577b; CB.1251a; K.706.
OT: ḥāzôn: S.2377; HR.1004c.1a; H.633a; BD.302d.
mar'eh: S.4758; HR.1004c.4b; H.2095i; BD.909c.
GEN. REF.: –.

4. *ophthalmos* [ὀφθαλμός, 3788], an eye (Eng., ophthalmic, etc.), in Acts 1:9 is translated "sight" (plur., lit., 'eyes'). See EYE.

NT: B.599b; CB.1261a; K.706.
OT: 'ayin: S.5869; HR.1039b.2; H.1612a,1613; BD.744a.
GEN. REF.: –.

5. *anablepsis* [ἀνάβλεψις, 309], denotes "recovering of sight" (*ana*, again, *blepō*, to see), Luke 4:18. ¶ In the Sept., Isa. 61:1. ¶

NT: B.51a; CB.–; K.–.
OT: pᵉqaḥ-qôaḥ: S.6495; HR.73b.1; H.1803b; BD.824d.
GEN. REF.: –.

Notes: (1) For *horasis* (akin to No. 3), translated "in sight" in Rev. 4:3, A.V. (R.V., "to look upon"), see LOOK, B.

(2) In Luke 7:21, the infinitive mood of *blepō*, to see, is used as a noun, "(He bestowed, A.V., 'gave') sight." In Acts 9:9 it is used in the present participle with *mē*, not, "without sight" (lit., 'not seeing').

(3) In Heb. 12:21 *phantazomai*, to make visible, is used in the present participle as a noun, with the article, "(the) sight." ¶

(4) In Luke 21:11, A.V., *phobētron* (or *phobēthron*), plur., is translated "fearful sights" (R.V., "terrors"). ¶

B. Verb.

anablepō [ἀναβλέπω, 308], to look up, also denotes to receive or recover sight (akin to A, No. 5), e.g., Matt. 11:5; 20:34; Mark 10:51, 52; Luke 18:41-43; John 9:11, 15, 18 (twice); Acts 9:12, 17, 18; 22:13.

NT: B.50d; CB.1235a; K.–.
OT: nāśā': S.5375; HR.73b.3; H.1421; BD.669d.
GEN. REF.: –.

SIGHT OF (in the)

1. *enōpion* [ἐνώπιον, 1799], for which see BEFORE, No. 9, is translated 'in the sight of' in the R.V. (for A.V., "before") in Luke 12:6; 15:18; 16:15; Acts 7:46; 10:33; 19:19; 1 Tim. 5:4, 21; 2 Tim. 2:14; 4:1; Rev. 13:12. The R.V. is more appropriate in most passages, as giving the real significance of the word.

NT: B.270c; CB.1245b; K.–.
OT: –.
GEN. REF.: –.

2. *katenōpion* [κατενώπιον, 2714], see BEFORE, No. 10, is translated "in the sight of" in 2 Cor. 2:17 (in some texts); Col. 1:22, A.V.

NT: B.421b; CB.1254b; K.–.
OT: –.
GEN. REF.: –.

3. *emprosthen* [ἔμπροσθεν, 1715], see BEFORE, No. 4, is translated "in the sight of" in Matt. 11:26; Luke 10:21; 1 Thess. 1:3, A.V.

NT: B.257a; CB.1244b; K.–.
OT: liphnê (pāneh): S.6440; HR.459b.3c; H.1782a; BD.815d,816d.
GEN. REF.: –.

4. *enantion* [ἐναντίον, 1726], see BEFORE, No. 5, is translated "in the sight of" in Acts 7:10.

NT: B.261d; CB.1244c; K.–.
OT: –.
GEN. REF.: –.

5. *enanti* [ἔναντι, 1725], see BEFORE, No. 6, is translated "in the sight of" in Acts 8:21, A.V.

NT: B.261d; CB.1244c; K.–.
OT: –.
GEN. REF.: –.

6. *katenanti* [κατέναντι, 2713], see BEFORE, No. 8, is found in the best texts in 2 Cor. 12:19, "in the sight of," R.V., and in 2:17.

NT: B.421b; CB.–; K.–.
OT: –.
GEN. REF.: –.

SIGN

1. *sēmeion* [σημεῖον, 4592], a sign, mark, indication, token, is used (*a*) of that which distinguished a person or thing from others, e.g., Matt. 26:48; Luke 2:12; Rom. 4:11; 2 Cor. 12:12 (1st part); 2 Thess. 3:17, "token," i.e., his autograph attesting the authenticity of his letters; (*b*) of a sign as a warning or admonition, e.g., Matt. 12:39, "the sign of (i.e., consisting of) the prophet Jonas"; 16:4; Luke 2:34; 11:29, 30; (*c*) of miraculous acts (1) as tokens of Divine authority and power, e.g., Matt. 12:38, 39 (1st part); John 2:11, R.V., "signs"; 3:2 (ditto); 4:54, "(the second) sign," R.V.; 10:41 (ditto); 20:30; in 1 Cor. 1:22, "the Jews ask for signs," R.V., indicates that the Apostles were met with the same demand from Jews as Christ had been: "signs were vouchsafed in plenty, signs of God's power and love, but these were not the signs which they sought. . . . They wanted signs of an outward Messianic Kingdom, of temporal triumph, of matrial greatness for the chosen people. . . . with such cravings the Gospel of a 'crucified Messiah' was to them a stumblingblock indeed" (Lightfoot); 1 Cor. 14:22; (2) by demons, Rev. 16:14; (3) by false teachers or prophets, indications of assumed authority, e.g., Matt. 24:24; Mark 13:22; (4) by Satan through his special agents, 2 Thess. 2:9; Rev. 13:13, 14; 19:20; (*d*) of tokens portending future events, e.g., Matt. 24:3, where "the sign of the Son of Man" signifies, subjectively, that the Son of Man is Himself the sign of what He is about to do; Mark 13:4; Luke 21:7, 11, 25; Acts 2:19; Rev. 12:1, R.V.; 12:3, R.V.; 15:1.

Signs confirmatory of what God had accomplished in the atoning sacrifice of Christ, His resurrection and ascension, and of the sending of the Holy Spirit, were given to the Jews for their recognition, as at Pentecost, and supernatural acts by apostolic ministry, as well as by the supernatural operations in the churches, such as the gift of tongues and prophesyings; there is no record of the continuance of these latter after the circumstances recorded in Acts 19:1-20.

NT: B.747d; CB.1268c; K.1015.
OT: 'ôt: S.226; HR.1263b.1a; H.41a; BD.16c.
GEN. REF.: IS.4:505; NB.1185; Z.5:429.

2. *parasēmos* [παράσημος, 3902], an adjective meaning 'marked at the side' (*para*, beside, *sēma*, a mark), is used in Acts 28:11 as a noun denoting the figure-head of a vessel. ¶

NT: B.622a; CB.—; K.—.
OT: —.
GEN. REF.: —.

SIGNS (to make)

enneuō [ἐννεύω, 1770], to nod to (*en*, in, *neuō*, to nod), denotes to make a sign to in Luke 1:62. ¶ In the Sept., Prov. 6:13; 10:10. ¶

NT: B.267a; CB.—; K.—.
OT: qāraṣ: S.7169; HR.475c.1; H.2075; BD.902d.
GEN. REF.: IS.4:505; NB.—; Z.—.

Note: For *dianeuō*, Luke 1:22, R.V., see BECKON, No. 2.

For **SIGNIFICATION**, 1 Cor. 14:10, see **DUMB**, No. 2

SIGNIFY

1. *sēmainō* [σημαίνω, 4591], to give a sign, indicate (*sēma*, a sign: cp. SIGN, No. 1), to signify, is so translated in John 12:33; 18:32; 21:19; Acts 11:28; 25:27; Rev. 1:1, where perhaps the suggestion is that of expressing by signs. ¶

NT: B.747c; CB.1268c; K.1015.
OT: yāda': S.3045; HR.1263a.2a; H.848; BD.393b,394d.
yᵉda' (Aramaic): S.3046; HR.1263a.2b; H.2765; BD.1095a.
GEN. REF.: IS.—; NB.—; Z.5:429.

2. *dēloō* [δηλόω, 1213], to make plain (*dēlos*, evident), is translated to signify in 1 Cor. 1:11, R.V., "it hath been signified" (A.V., "declared"); Heb. 9:8; 12:27; 1 Pet. 1:11, A.V. (R.V., "point unto"); 2 Pet. 1:14, R.V., "signified" (A.V., "hath shewed"). See POINT (unto).

NT: B.178c; CB.1240c; K.148.
OT: yāda': S.3045; HR.295c.3c; H.848; BD.393b,394d.
yᵉda' (Aramaic): S.3046; HR.295c.3d; H.2765; BD.1095a.
ḥᵃwāh: S.2324; HR.295c.2; H.2722; BD.1092b.
GEN. REF.: —.

3. *emphanizō* [ἐμφανίζω, 1718], to manifest, make known, is translated "signify" in Acts 23:15; ver. 22, R.V. (A.V., "hath shewed"). See APPEAR, No. 5.

NT: B.257c; CB.1244b; K.1244.
OT: yāda': S.3045; HR.460c.2; H.848; BD.393b,394d.
rā'āh: S.7200; HR.460c.4; H.2095; BD.906b.
GEN. REF.: —.

Note: In Acts 21:26, A.V., *diangellō*, to announce, is rendered "to signify" (R.V., "declaring").

SILENCE

A. Noun.

sigē [σιγή, 4602], occurs in Acts 21:40; Rev. 8:1, where the silence is introductory to the judgments following the opening of the seventh seal. ¶

NT: B.749d; CB.—; K.—.
OT: —.
GEN. REF.: IS.4:509; NB.—; Z.—.

Note: For *hēsuchia*, A.V., "silence," in Acts 22:2 and 1 Tim. 2:11, 12, see QUIETNESS.

B. Verbs.

1. *phimoō* [φιμόω, 5392], to muzzle, is rendered "to put to silence" in Matt. 22:34; 1 Pet. 2:15. See MUZZLE, PEACE (hold), SPEECHLESS, STILL.

NT: B.861d; CB.—; K.—.
OT: ḥāsam: S.2629; HR.1432b.1; H.702; BD.340c.
GEN. REF.: IS.4:509; NB.—; Z.—.

2. *sigaō* [σιγάω, 4601], to be silent: see PEACE (hold), No. 1.

NT: B.749c; CB.—; K.—.
OT: ḥārash: S.2790; HR.1265c.3; H.760; BD.361a.
ḥāshāh: S.2814; HR.1265c.4; H.768; BD.364c.
GEN. REF.: IS.4:509; NB.—; Z.—.

For **SILENT**, Luke 1:20, R.V., see **DUMB**, B

SILK

sērikos or *sirikos* [σιρικός, 4596], silken, an adjective derived from the *Sēres*, a people of India, who seem to have produced silk originally as a marketable commodity, is used as a noun with the article, denoting silken fabric, Rev. 18:12. ¶

NT: B.751d; CB.—; K.—.
OT: —.
GEN. REF.: IS.4:510; NB.1186; Z.5:434.

For **SILLY**, 2 Tim. 3:6, see **WOMAN**, No. 2

SILVER

A. Nouns.

1. *argurion* [ἀργύριον, 694], is rendered "silver" in Acts 3:6; 8:20, R.V. (A.V., "money"); 20:33; 1 Cor. 3:12 (metaphorical); 1 Pet. 1:18. See MONEY, PIECE.

NT: B.104d; CB.1237c; K.—.
OT: keseph: S.3701; HR.153b.1a; H.1015a; BD.494a.
GEN. REF.: IS.4:512; NB.825; Z.5:437.

2. *arguros* [ἄργυρος, 696], akin to *argos*, shining, denotes silver. In each occurrence in the N.T. it follows the mention of gold, Matt. 10:9; Acts 17:29; Jas. 5:3; Rev. 18:12. ¶

NT: B.105a; CB.1237c; K.–.
OT: keseph: S.3701; HR.155b.1a; H.1015a; BD.494a.
kᵉsaph: S.3702; HR.155b.1b; H.2794; BD.1097c.
GEN. REF.: IS.4:512; NB.825; Z.5:437.

Note: For *drachmē*, Luke 15:8, see PIECE.

B. Adjective.

argureos [ἀργύρεος, 693], signifies made of silver, Acts 19:24; 2 Tim. 2:20; Rev. 9:20. ¶

NT: B.105a; CB.–; K.–.
OT: keseph: S.3701; HR.153a.1a; H.1015a; BD.494a.
GEN. REF.: IS.4:512; NB.825; Z.5:437.

SILVERSMITH

argurokopos [ἀργυροκόπος, 695], from *arguros* (see above) and *koptō*, to beat, occurs in Acts 19:24. ¶ In the Sept., Judg. 17:4; Jer. 6:29. ¶

NT: B.105a; CB.–; K.–.
OT: ṣāraph: S.6884; HR.155b.1; H.1972; BD.864a.
GEN. REF.: IS.4:513; NB.–; Z.5:438.

SIMILITUDE

Note: For *homoiōma*, rendered "similitude" in Rom. 5:14, A.V., see LIKENESS, No. 1. For *homoiotēs*, "similitude" in Heb. 7:15, A.V., see LIKE, C, *Note* (1), and LIKENESS, No. 3. For *homoiōsis*, "similitude" in Jas. 3:9, A.V., see LIKENESS, No. 2.

For **SIMPLE** see **GUILELESS**, No. 2, and **HARMLESS**

For **SIMPLICITY** see **LIBERALITY**

SIN (Noun and Verb)

A. Nouns.

1. *hamartia* [ἁμαρτία, 266], is, lit., a missing of the mark, but this etymological meaning is largely lost sight of in the N.T. It is the most comprehensive term for moral obliquity. It is used of sin as (*a*) a principle or source of action, or an inward element producing acts, e.g., Rom. 3:9; 5:12, 13, 20; 6:1, 2; 7:7 (abstract for concrete); 7:8 (twice), 9, 11, 13, "sin, that it might be shewn to be sin," i.e., 'sin became death to me, that it might be exposed in its heinous character': in the last clause, "sin might become exceeding sinful," i.e., through the holiness of the Law, the true nature of sin was designed to be manifested to the conscience;

(*b*) a governing principle or power, e.g., Rom. 6:6, "(the body) of sin," here sin is spoken of as an organized power, acting through the members of the body, though the seat of sin is in the will (the body is the organic instrument); in the next clause, and in other passages, as follows, this governing principle is personified, e.g., Rom. 5:21; 6:12, 14, 17; 7:11, 14, 17, 20, 23, 25; 8:2; 1 Cor. 15:56; Heb. 3:13; 11:25; 12:4; Jas. 1:15 (2nd part);

(*c*) a generic term (distinct from specific terms such as No. 2, yet sometimes inclusive of concrete wrong doing, e.g., John 8:21, 34, 46; 9:41; 15:22, 24; 19:11); in Rom. 8:3, "God, sending His own Son in the likeness of sinful flesh," lit., 'flesh of sin,' the flesh stands for the body, the instrument of indwelling sin [Christ, pre-existently the Son of God, assumed human flesh, "of the substance of the Virgin Mary"; the reality of incarnation was His, without taint of sin (for *homoiōma*, likeness, see LIKENESS)], "and *as an offering* for sin," i.e., 'a sin-offering' (so the Sept., e.g., in Lev. 4:32; 5:6, 7, 8, 9), "condemned sin in the flesh," i.e., Christ, having taken human nature, sin apart (Heb. 4:15), and having lived a sinless life, died under the condemnation and judgment due to our sin; for the generic sense see further, e.g., Heb. 9:26; 10:6, 8, 18; 13:11; 1 John 1:7, 8; 3:4 (1st part; in the 2nd part, sin is defined as "lawlessness," R.V.), 8, 9; in these verses the A.V. use of the verb to commit is misleading; not the committal of an act is in view, but a continuous course of sin, as indicated by the R.V., "doeth." The Apostle's use of the present tense of *poieō*, to do, virtually expresses the meaning of *prassō*, to practise, which John does not use (it is not infrequent in this sense in Paul's Epp., e.g., Rom. 1:32, R.V.; 2:1; Gal. 5:21; Phil. 4:9); 1 Pet. 4:1 (singular in the best texts), lit., 'has been made to cease from sin,' i.e., as a result of suffering in the flesh, the mortifying of our members, and of obedience to a Saviour who suffered in flesh. Such no longer lives in the flesh, "to the lusts of men, but to the will of God"; sometimes the word is used as virtually equivalent to a condition of sin, e.g., John 1:29, "the sin (not sins) of the world"; 1 Cor. 15:17; or a course of sin, characterized by continuous acts, e.g., 1 Thess. 2:16; in 1 John 5:16 (2nd part) the R.V. marg., is probably to be preferred, "there is sin unto death," not a special act of sin, but the state or condition producing acts; in ver. 17, "all unrighteousness is sin" is not a definition of sin (as in 3:4), it gives a specification of the term in its generic sense;

(*d*) a sinful deed, an act of sin, e.g., Matt. 12:31; Acts 7:60; Jas. 1:15 (1st part); 2:9; 4:17; 5:15, 20; 1 John 5:16 (1st part).

NT: B.43a; CB.1249b; K.44.
OT: ḥaṭṭa't: S.2403; HR.62a.2e; H.638e; BD.308b.
'āwōn: S.5771; HR.62a.6; H.1577a; BD.730d.
pesha': S.6588; HR.62a.8b; H.1846a; BD.833b.
GEN. REF.: IS.4:518; NB.1189; Z.5:444.

Notes: (1) Christ is predicated as having been without sin in every respect, e.g., (*a*), (*b*), (*c*) above, 2 Cor. 5:21 (1st part); 1 John 3:5; John 14:30; (*d*) John 8:46; Heb. 4:15; 1 Pet. 2:22.

(2) In Heb. 9:28 (2nd part) the reference is to a sin offering.

(3) In 2 Cor. 5:21, "Him . . . He made to be sin" indicates that God dealt with Him as He must deal with sin, and that Christ fulfilled what was typified in the guilt offering.

(4) For the phrase "man of sin" in 2 Thess. 2:3, see INIQUITY, No. 1.

2. *hamartēma* [ἁμάρτημα, 265], akin to No. 1, denotes an act of disobedience to Divine law [as distinct from No. 1 (*a*), (*b*), (*c*)]; plural in Mark 3:28; Rom. 3:25; 2 Pet. 1:9, in some texts; sing. in Mark 3:29 (some mss. have *krisis*, A.V., "damnation"); 1 Cor. 6:18. ¶

NT: B.42d; CB.1249b; K.44.
OT: ḥaṭṭā't: S.2403; HR.62a.1b; H.638e; BD.308b.
'āwōn: S.5771; HR.62a.2; H.1577a; BD.730d.
pesha': S.6588; HR.62a.3; H.1846a; BD.833b.
GEN. REF.: IS.4:518; NB.1189; Z.5:444.

Notes: (1) For *paraptōma*, rendered "sins" in the A.V. in Eph. 1:7; 2:5; Col. 2:13 (R.V., "trespass"), see TRESPASS. In Jas. 5:16, the best texts have No. 1 (R.V., "sins").

(2) For synonymous terms see DISOBEDIENCE, ERROR, FAULT, INIQUITY, TRANSGRESSION, UNGODLINESS.

B. Adjective.

anamartētos [ἀναμάρτητος, 361], without sin (*a*, negative, *n*, euphonic, and C, No. 1), is found in John 8:7. ¶ In the Sept., Deut. 29:19. ¶

NT: B.42d; CB.—; K.51.
OT: —.
GEN. REF.: —.

C. Verbs.

1. *hamartanō* [ἁμαρτάνω, 264], lit., to miss the mark, is used in the N.T. (*a*) of sinning against God, (1) by angels, 2 Pet. 2:4; (2) by man, Matt. 27:4; Luke 15:18, 21 (Heaven standing, by metonymy, for God); John 5:14; 8:11; 9:2, 3; Rom. 2:12 (twice); 3:23; 5:12, 14, 16; 6:15; 1 Cor. 7:28 (twice), 36; 15:34; Eph. 4:26; 1 Tim. 5:20; Tit. 3:11; Heb. 3:17; 10:26; 1 John 1:10; in 2:1 (twice), the aorist tense in each place, referring to an act of sin; on the contrary, in 3:6 (twice), 8, 9, the present tense indicates, not the committal of an act, but the continuous practice of sin [see on A, No. 1 (*c*)]; in 5:16 (twice) the present tense indicates the condition resulting from an act, "unto death" signifying 'tending towards death'; (*b*) against Christ, 1 Cor. 8:12; (*c*) against man, (1) a brother, Matt. 18:15, R.V., "sin" (A.V., "trespass"); ver. 21; Luke 17:3, 4, R.V., "sin" (A.V., "trespass"); 1 Cor. 8:12; (2) in Luke 15:18, 21, against the father by the prodigal son, "in thy sight" being suggestive of befitting reverence; (*d*) against Jewish law, the Temple and Caesar, Acts 25:8, R.V., "sinned" (A.V., "offended"); (*e*) against one's own body, by fornication, 1 Cor. 6:18; 1 Cor. 6:18; (*f*) against earthly masters by servants, 1 Pet. 2:20, R.V., "(when) ye sin (and are buffeted for it)," A.V., "(when ye be buffeted) for your faults," lit., 'having sinned.' ¶

NT: B.42b; CB.1249a; K.44.
OT: ḥāṭā': S.2398; HR.60c.2a; H.638; BD.306c.
GEN. REF.: IS.4:518; NB.1189; Z.5:444.

2. *proamartanō* [προαμαρτάνω, 4258], to sin previously (*pro*, before, and No. 1), occurs in 2 Cor. 12:21; 13:2, R.V. in each place, "have sinned heretofore" (so A.V. in the 2nd; in the 1st, "have sinned already"). ¶

NT: B.702c; CB.—; K.—.
OT: —.
GEN. REF.: —.

SINCE: see † p. 1

SINCERE, SINCERELY, SINCERITY

A. Adjectives.

1. *adolos* [ἄδολος, 97], guileless, pure, is translated "sincere" in 1 Pet. 2:2, A.V., "without guile," R.V. See GUILELESS, No. 1.

NT: B.18c; CB.1233a; K.—.
OT: —.
GEN. REF.: —.

2. *gnēsios* [γνήσιος, 1103], true, genuine, sincere, is used in the neuter, as a noun, with the article, signifying "sincerity," 2 Cor. 8:8 (of love). See OWN, TRUE.

NT: B.162d; CB.1248b; K.125.
OT: —.
GEN. REF.: IS.4:528; NB.—; Z.—.

3. *eilikrinēs* [εἰλικρινής, —]: see PURE, A, No. 3.

B. Adverb.

hagnōs [ἁγνῶς, 55], denotes with pure motives, akin to words under PURE, A, No. 1, and B, Nos. 1 and 2, and is rendered "sincerely" in Phil. 1:17, R.V. (ver. 16, A.V.). ¶

NT: B.12a; CB.1249a; K.19.
OT: —.
GEN. REF.: IS.4:528; NB.—; Z.—.

C. Noun.

eilikrinia (or —*eia*) [εἰλικρινία, 1505], akin to A, No. 3, denotes sincerity, purity; it is described metaphorically in 1 Cor. 5:8 as "unleavened (bread)"; in 2 Cor. 1:12, "sincerity (of God)," R.V., A.V., "(godly) sincerity," it describes a quality possessed by God, as that which is to characterize the conduct of believers; in

2 Cor. 2:17 it is used of the rightful ministry of the Scriptures. ¶
NT: B.222d; CB.–; K.–.
OT: –.
GEN. REF.: IS.4:528; NB.–; Z.5:450.

Notes: (1) For 2 Cor. 8:8, see A, No. 2.

(2) In Eph. 6:24, A.V., *aphtharsia*, incorruption, is translated "sincerity" (R.V., "uncorruptness," A.V. marg., "incorruption"); some inferior mss. have it in Tit. 2:7, A.V.; the R.V. follows those in which it is absent.

SINFUL

hamartōlos [ἁμαρτωλός, 268], an adjective, akin to *hamartanō*, to sin, is used as an adjective, "sinful" in Mark 8:38; Luke 5:8; 19:7 (lit., 'a sinful man'); 24:7; John 9:16, and 24 (lit., 'a man sinful'); Rom. 7:13, for which see SIN, A, No. 1 (*a*). Elsewhere it is used as a noun: see SINNER. The noun is frequently found in a common phrase in sepulchral epitaphs in the S.W. of Asia Minor, with the threat against any desecrator of the tomb, 'let him be as a sinner before the subterranean gods' (Moulton and Milligan).
NT: B.44a; CB.1249b; K.51.
OT: rāshā': S.7563; HR.64b.5a; H.2222b; BD.957b.
ḥaṭṭā': S.2400; HR.64b.1b; H.638b; BD.308b.
GEN. REF.: IS.–; NB.–; Z.5:444.

Notes: (1) In Rom. 8:3, "sinful flesh" is, lit., 'flesh of sin' (R.V. marg.): see SIN, No. 1 (*c*).

(2) For the R.V. of Rom. 7:5, "sinful passions," see PASSION, No. 1.

SING, SINGING

1. *ą̄dō* [ᾄδω, 103], is used always of praise to God, (*a*) intransitively, Eph. 5:19; Col. 3:16; (*b*) transitively, Rev. 5:9; 14:3; 15:3. ¶
NT: B.19b; CB.1233a; K.24.
OT: shîr: S.7891; HR.19a.3a,b; H.2378; BD.1010c.
GEN. REF.: –.

2. *psallō* [ψάλλω, –]: see MELODY.

3. *humneō* [ὑμνέω, –]: see HYMN, B.

SINGLE

haplous [ἁπλοῦς, 573], simple, single, is used in a moral sense in Matt. 6:22 and Luke 11:34, said of the eye; singleness of purpose keeps us from the snare of having a double treasure and consequently a divided heart. ¶ The papyri provide instances of its use in other than the moral sense, e.g., of a marriage dowry, to be repaid pure and simple by a husband (Moulton and Milligan). In the Sept., Prov. 11:25. ¶
NT: B.86a; CB.1249b; K.65.
OT: –.
GEN. REF.: –.

SINGLENESS

1. *aphelotēs* [ἀφελότης, 858], denotes simplicity, Acts 2:46, "singleness," for which Moulton and Milligan, from papyri examples, suggest "unworldly simplicity"; the idea here is that of an unalloyed benevolence expressed in act. ¶
NT: B.124d; CB.–; K.–.
OT: –.
GEN. REF.: –.

2. *haplotēs* [ἁπλότης, –]: see BOUNTY, No. 2.

SINK

1. *buthizō* [βυθίζω, 1036], is used literally in Luke 5:7. See DROWN, No. 1.
NT: B.148c; CB.–; K.–.
OT: –.
GEN. REF.: –.

2. *katapontizō* [καταποντίζω, 2670], is translated to sink in Matt. 14:30 (Passive Voice). See DROWN, No. 3.
NT: B.417a; CB.–; K.–.
OT: bāla': S.1104; HR.742a.1; H.251; BD.118a.
shāṭaph: S.7857; HR.742a.3; H.2373; BD.1009a.
GEN. REF.: –.

3. *tithēmi* [τίθημι, 5087], to put, is rendered "let . . . sink" in Luke 9:44, R.V. ("let . . . sink down," A.V.). See APPOINT, LAY.
NT: B.815d; CB.1272c; K.1176.
OT: –.
GEN. REF.: –.

Note: In Acts 20:9 (2nd part), A.V., *katapherō*, to bear down, is translated "he sunk down" (R.V., "being borne down"); in the 1st part it is rendered "being fallen," A.V., "borne down," R.V.

SINNER

hamartōlos [ἁμαρτωλός, 268], lit., one who misses the mark (a meaning not to be pressed), is an adjective, most frequently used as a noun (see SINFUL); it is the most usual term to describe the fallen condition of men; it is applicable to all men, Rom. 5:8, 19. In the Synoptic Gospels the word is used not infrequently, by the Pharisees, of publicans (tax-collectors) and women of ill repute, e.g., "a woman which was in the city, a sinner," Luke 7:37; "a man that is a sinner," 19:7. In Gal. 2:15, in the clause "not sinners of the Gentiles," the Apostle is taking the Judaizers on their own ground, ironically reminding them of their claim to moral superiority over Gentiles; he proceeds to show that the Jews are equally sinners with Gentiles.
NT: B.44a; CB.1249b; K.51.
OT: rāshā': S.7563; HR.64b.5a; H.2222b; BD.957b.
ḥaṭṭā': S.2400; HR.64b.1b; H.638b; BD.308b.
GEN. REF.: IS.4:529; NB.–; Z.5:444.

Note: In Luke 13:4, A.V., *opheiletēs*, a debtor, is translated "sinners" (R.V., "offenders"; R.V. and A.V. marg., "debtors").

SIR(-S)

1. *kurios* [κύριος, —]: see LORD.

2. *anēr* [ἀνήρ, 435], a man, is translated "sirs" in Acts 7:26; 14:15; 19:25; 27:10, 21, 25. See MAN.

NT: B.66c; CB.1235c; K.59.
OT: 'îsh: S.376; HR.88a.2; H.83a; BD.35c.
'enôsh: S.582; HR.88a.3a; H.136a; BD.60d.
GEN. REF.: IS.4:529; NB.—; Z.—.

Note: In John 21:5 the A.V. marg. has "sirs" for *paidia*, "children."

SISTER

adelphē [ἀδελφή, 79], is used (*a*) of natural relationship, e.g., Matt. 19:29; of the sisters of Christ, the children of Joseph and Mary after the Virgin Birth of Christ, e.g., Matt. 13:56; (*b*) of spiritual kinship with Christ, an affinity marked by the fulfilment of the will of the Father, Matt. 12:50; Mark 3:35; of spiritual relationship based upon faith in Christ, Rom. 16:1; 1 Cor. 7:15; 9:5, A.V. and R.V. marg.; Jas. 2:15; Philm. 2, R.V.

NT: B.15d; CB.1233a; K.22.
OT: 'āḥot: S.269; HR.19b.1; H.62c; BD.27d.
GEN. REF.: IS.4:534; NB.—; Z.—.

Note: In Col. 4:10, A.V., *anepsios* (cp. Lat., *nepos*, whence Eng., nephew), a cousin (so, R.V.), is translated "sister's son." See COUSIN. ¶

SIT

1. *kathēmai* [κάθημαι, 2521], is used (*a*) of the natural posture, e.g., Matt. 9:9, most frequently in the Apocalypse, some 32 times; frequently in the Gospels and Acts; elsewhere only in 1 Cor. 14:30; Jas. 2:3 (twice); and of Christ's position of authority on the throne of God, Col. 3:1, A.V., "sitteth" (R.V., "is, seated"); Heb. 1:13 (cp. Matt. 22:44; 26:64 and parallel passages in Mark and Luke, and Acts 2:34); often as antecedent or successive to, or accompanying, another act (in no case a superfluous expression), e.g., Matt. 15:29; 27:36; Mark 2:14; 4:1; (*b*) metaphorically in Matt. 4:16 (twice); Luke 1:79; of inhabiting a place (translated "dwell"), Luke 21:35; Rev. 14:6, R.V. marg., "sit" (in the best texts: some have *katoikeō*, to dwell). See DWELL.

NT: B.389b; CB.1254c; K.386.
OT: yāshab: S.3427; HR.700b.3a; H.922; BD.442a.
GEN. REF.: IS.4:736; NB.—; Z.—.

2. *sunkathēmai* [συγκάθημαι, 4775], to sit with (*sun*, with, and No. 1), occurs in Mark 14:54; Acts 26:30. ¶ In the Sept., Ps. 101:6, "dwell." ¶

NT: B.773a; CB.—; K.—.
OT: yāshab: S.3427; HR.1299a.1; H.922; BD.442a.
GEN. REF.: IS.4:376; NB.—; Z.—.

3. *anakeimai* [ἀνάκειμαι, 345], to recline at table (*ana*, up, *keimai*, to lie), is rendered to sit at meat in Matt. 9:10 (R.V., marg., "reclined"); 26:7; 26:20, R.V., "He was sitting at meat" (A.V., "He sat down"); Mark 16:14; in some mss. Luke 7:37 (see No. 5); 22:27 (twice); in Mark 14:18, "sat"; in John 6:11, "were set down"; John 12:2 in the best texts (see No. 4). See GUEST, LEAN, LIE, *Note* (1), SET, No. 22, TABLE at the).

NT: B.55d; CB.1235a; K.425.
OT: —.
GEN. REF.: IS.4:376; NB.—; Z.—.

4. *sunanakeimai* [συνανάκειμαι, 4873], to recline at table with or together (*sun* and No. 3), to sit at meat or at table with, occurs in Matt. 9:10, "sat down"; 14:9; Mark 2:15, R.V., "sat down with" (A.V., "sat . . . together with"); 6:22; Luke 7:49; 14:10, 15; John 12:2 (in some texts). ¶

NT: B.784b; CB.—; K.425.
OT: —.
GEN. REF.: IS.4:376; NB.—; Z.—.

5. *katakeimai* [κατάκειμαι, 2621], to lie down (*kata*, down, and *keimai*, cp. No. 3), is used of reclining at a meal, Mark 2:15; 14:3; Luke 5:29, R.V., "were sitting at meat" (A.V., "sat down"); 7:37 (in the best texts); 1 Cor. 8:10. See KEEP, LIE.

NT: B.411c; CB.—; K.425.
OT: shākab: S.7901; HR.733a.1; H.2381; BD.1011d.
GEN. REF.: IS.4:376; NB.—; Z.—.

6. *anaklinō* [ἀνακλίνω, 347], to cause to recline, make to sit down, is used in the Active Voice, in Luke 12:37 (also in 2:7, of 'laying' the infant Christ in the manger); in the Passive, Matt. 8:11; 14:19; Mark 6:39 (in the best texts); in some texts, Luke 7:36 and 9:15 (see No. 7); 13:29. See LAY.

NT: B.56a; CB.—; K.—.
OT: —.
GEN. REF.: —.

7. *kataklinō* [κατακλίνω, 2625], is used only in connection with meals, (*a*) in the Active Voice, to make recline, Luke 9:14, 15 (in the best texts); in the Passive Voice, to recline, Luke 7:36 (in the best texts), "sat down to meat"; 14:8; 24:30 (R.V., "had sat down . . . to meat"). ¶

NT: B.411d; CB.—; K.—.
OT: kāra': S.3766; HR.733c.1; H.1044; BD.502c.
GEN. REF.: —.

8. *kathizō* [καθίζω, 2523], is used (*a*) transitively, to make sit down, Acts 2:30 (see also SET, No. 9); (*b*) intransitively, to sit down, e.g., Matt. 5:1, R.V., "when (He) had sat down" (A.V., "was set"); 19:28; 20:21, 23; 23:2; 25:31;

26:36; Mark 11:2, 7; 12:41; Luke 14:28, 31; 16:6; John 19:13; Acts 2:3 (of the tongues of fire); 8:31; 1 Cor. 10:7; 2 Thess. 2:4, "he sitteth," aorist tense, i.e., 'he takes his seat' (as, e.g., in Mark 16:19); Rev. 3:21 (twice), R.V., "to sit down" and "sat down"; 20:4.

NT: B.389d; CB.1254c; K.386.
OT: yāshab: S.3427; HR.701c.4a; H.922; BD.442a.
GEN. REF.: IS.4:376; NB.–; Z.–.

9. *parakathezomai* [παρακαθέζομαι, 3869], to sit down beside (*para*), in a Passive Voice form, occurs in the best mss. in Luke 10:39. ¶ Some texts have the verb *parakathizō*, to set beside, Active form in Middle sense.

NT: B.616d; CB.–; K.–.
OT: –.
GEN. REF.: –.

10. *sunkathizō* [συγκαθίζω, 4776], denotes (*a*) transitively, to make to sit together, Eph. 2:6; (*b*) intransitively, Luke 22:55, R.V., "had sat down together" (A.V., "were set down"). ¶

NT: B.773b; CB.–; K.1102.
OT: yāshab: S.3427; HR.1299a.1; H.922; BD.442a.
rābaṣ: S.7257; HR.1299a.2; H.2109; BD.918b.
GEN. REF.: IS.4:376; NB.–; Z.–.

11. *anakathizō* [ἀνακαθίζω, 339], to set up, is used intransitively, to sit up, of two who were raised from the dead, Luke 7:15; Acts 9:40. ¶

NT: B.55b; CB.–; K.–.
OT: –.
GEN. REF.: –.

12. *anapiptō* [ἀναπίπτω, 377], to fall back (*ana*, back, *piptō*, to fall), denotes, in the N.T., to recline for a repast, Matt. 15:35; Mark 6:40; 8:6; Luke 11:37; 14:10; 17:7; 22:14; John 6:10 (twice); 13:12; in John 13:25 and 21:20 it is used of leaning on the bosom of Christ. See LEAN. ¶ In the Sept., Gen. 49:9. ¶

NT: B.59c; CB.1235b; K.–.
OT: kāra': S.3766; HR.81b.1; H.1044; BD.502c.
GEN. REF.: –.

13. *kathezomai* [καθέζομαι, 2516], to sit (down), is used in Matt. 26:55; Luke 2:46; John 4:6; 11:20; 20:12; Acts 6:15. ¶

NT: B.388c; CB.1254c; K.386.
OT: yāshab: S.3427; HR.699c.1; H.922; BD.442a.
GEN. REF.: IS.4:376; NB.–; Z.–.

Note: For *epibainō*, "sitting upon," Matt. 21:5, A.V., see RIDE.

SIX

hex [ἕξ, 1803], whence Eng. prefix, *hex-*, is used separately from other numerals in Matt. 17:1; Mark 9:2; Luke 4:25; 13:14; John 2:6; 12:1, Acts 11:12; 18:11; Jas. 5:17; Rev. 4:8. It sometimes suggests incompleteness, in comparison with the perfect number seven.

NT: B.271b; CB.1250b; K.–.
OT: shēsh: S.8337; HR.–; H.2336a; BD.995c.
GEN. REF.: IS.3:559; NB.–; Z.–.

Notes: (1) In combination with *tessarakonta*, forty, it occurs in John 2:20; with *hebdomēkonta*, seventy, Acts 27:37, "(two hundred) three-score and sixteen."

(2) It forms the first syllable of *hexēkonta*, sixty (see below), and *hexakosioi*, six hundred, Rev. 13:18 (see SIXTY, *Note*); 14:20.

SIXTH

hektos [ἕκτος, 1623], is used (*a*) of a month, Luke 1:26, 36; (*b*) an hour, Matt. 20:5; 27:45 and parallel passages; John 4:6; (*c*) an angel, Rev. 9:13, 14; 16:12; (*d*) a seal of a roll, in vision, Rev. 6:12; (*e*) of the sixth precious stone, the sardius, in the foundations of the wall of the heavenly Jerusalem, Rev. 21:20.

NT: B.246a; CB.–; K.–.
OT: shishshî: S.8345; HR.443b.1c; H.2336b; BD.995d.
GEN. REF.: –.

SIXTY, SIXTYFOLD

hexēkonta [ἑξήκοντα, 1835], occurs in Matt. 13:8, R.V. (A.V., "sixtyfold"); 13:23; Mark 4:8, where the R.V. and A.V. reverse the translation, as in Matt. 13:8, while in Mark 4:20 the R.V. has "sixtyfold," A.V., "sixty"; in Rev. 13:18, R.V., "sixty" (A.V., "threescore"). It is rendered "threescore" in Luke 24:13; 1 Tim. 5:9; Rev. 11:3; 12:6. ¶

NT: B.276a; CB.–; K.–.
OT: shishshîm: S.8346; HR.–; H.2336c; BD.995d.
GEN. REF.: –.

Note: In Rev. 13:18, the number of the "Beast," the human potentate destined to rule with Satanic power the ten-kingdom league at the end of this age, is given as "six hundred and sixty and six" (R.V.), and described as "the number of (a) man." The number is suggestive of the acme of the pride of fallen man, the fullest development of man under direct Satanic control, and standing in contrast to seven as the number of completeness and perfection.

SKIN

askos [ἀσκός, 779], a leather bottle, wineskin, occurs in Matt. 9:17 (four times); Mark 2:22 (four times); Luke 5:37 (three times), 38; in each place, R.V., "wineskins" or "skins," for A.V., "bottles." A whole goatskin, for example, would be used with the apertures bound up, and when filled, tied at the neck. They were tanned with acacia bark and left hairy on the outside. New wines, by fermenting, would rend old skins (cp. Josh. 9:13; Job 32:19). Hung in the smoke to dry, the skin-bottles become shrivelled (see Ps. 119:83). ¶

NT: B.116c; CB.–; K.–.
OT: ḥēmet: S.2573; HR.172c.1; H.689a; BD.332d.
nō'd: S.4997; HR.172c.2a; H.1270; BD.609d.
GEN. REF.: IS.4:535; NB.–; Z.–.

Note: For "(a girdle) of a skin," Mark 1:6, see Leathern.

SKULL

kranion [κρανίον, 2898], Lat., *cranium* (akin to *kara*, the head), is used of the scene of the Crucifixion, Matt. 27:33; Mark 15:22; John 19:17; in Luke 23:33, R.V., "(the place which is called) The skull," A.V., "Calvary" (from Latin *calvaria*, a skull: marg., "the place of a skull"). The locality has been identified by the traces of the resemblance of the hill to a skull. ¶ In the Sept., Jud. 9:53; 2 Kings 9:35. ¶

NT: B.448a; CB.—; K.—.
OT: gulgōlet: S.1538; HR.782a.1; H.3531; BD.166b.
GEN. REF.: IS.4:536; NB.—; Z.—.

For **SKY** see **HEAVEN**

SLACK (Verb), SLACKNESS

A. Verb.

bradunō [βραδύνω, 1019], used intransitively signifies to be slow, to tarry (*bradus*, slow), said negatively of God, 2 Pet. 3:9, "is (not) slack"; in 1 Tim. 3:15, translated "(if) I tarry." See Tarry. ¶ In the Sept., Gen. 43:10; Deut. 7:10; Isa. 46:13. ¶

NT: B.147a; CB.—; K.—.
OT: 'āḥar: S.309; HR.229c.1; H.68; BD.29b.
māhah: S.4102; HR.229c.2; H.1150; BD.554c.
GEN. REF.: —.

B. Noun.

bradutēs [βραδυτής, 1022], slowness (akin to A), is rendered "slackness" in 2 Pet. 3:9. ¶

NT: B.147a; CB.—; K.—.
OT: —.
GEN. REF.: —.

SLANDERER

diabolos [διάβολος, 1228], an adjective, slanderous, accusing falsely, is used as a noun, translated "slanderers" in 1 Tim. 3:11, where the reference is to those who are given to finding fault with the demeanour and conduct of others, and spreading their innuendos and criticisms in the church; in 2 Tim. 3:3, R.V. (A.V., "false accusers"); Tit. 2:3 (ditto); see Accuser, Devil.

NT: B.182a; CB.1241a; K.150.
OT: sāṭān: S.7854; HR.299b.2; H.2252a; BD.966b.
GEN. REF.: IS.4:537; NB.1236; Z.—.

For **SLANDEROUSLY** see **REPORT**, C, No. 5

SLAUGHTER

1. *sphagē* [σφαγή, 4967], is used in two quotations from the Sept., Acts 8:32 from Isa. 53:7, and Rom. 8:36 from Psa. 44:22; in the latter the quotation is set in a strain of triumph, the passage quoted being an utterance of sorrow. In Jas. 5:5 there is an allusion to Jer. 12:3, the luxurious rich, getting wealth by injustice, spending it on their pleasures, are "fattening themselves like sheep unconscious of their doom." ¶

NT: B.795d; CB.—; K.1125.
OT: h^{a}rēgāh: S.2028; HR.1324a.1b; H.514b; BD.247c.
ṭebaḥ: S.2874; HR.1324a.3b; H.786a; BD.370d.
GEN. REF.: IS.4:537; NB.—; Z.—.

2. *kopē* [κοπή, 2871], a stroke (akin to *koptō*, to strike, to cut), signifies a smiting in battle, in Heb. 7:1. ¶ In the Sept., Gen. 14:17; Deut. 28:25; Josh. 10:20. ¶

NT: B.443c; CB.—; K.—.
OT: nākāh: S.5221; HR.778b.2a; H.1364; BD.645a.
makkāh: S.4347; HR.778b.2b; H.1364d; BD.646d.
nāgaph: S.5062; HR.778b.1; H.1294; BD.619d.
GEN. REF.: IS.4:537; NB.—; Z.—.

3. *phonos* [φόνος, 5408], a killing, murder, is rendered "slaughter" in Acts 9:1; see Murder.

NT: B.864d; CB.1264b; K.—.
OT: ḥereb: S.2719; HR.1437c.2; H.732a; BD.352b.
peh: S.6310; HR.1437c.4; H.1738; BD.804d.
GEN. REF.: IS.4:539; NB.—; Z.—.

SLAVE

sōma [σῶμα, 4983], a body, is translated "slaves" in Rev. 18:13 (R.V. and A.V. marg., "bodies"), an intimation of the unrighteous control over the bodily activities of slaves; the next word "souls" stands for the whole being. See Body.

NT: B.799a; CB.1269b; K.1140.
OT: —.
GEN. REF.: —.

SLAY, SLAIN, SLEW

1. *apokteinō* [ἀποκτείνω, 615], the usual word for to kill, is so translated in the R.V. wherever possible (e.g., for A.V., to slay, in Luke 11:49; Acts 7:52; Rev. 2:13; 9:15; 11:13; 19:21); in the following the verb to kill would not be appropriate, Rom. 7:11, "slew," metaphorically of sin, as using the commandment; Eph. 2:16, "having slain," said metaphorically of the enmity between Jew and Gentile. See Kill, No. 1.

NT: B.93d; CB.1237a; K.—.
OT: hārag: S.2026; HR.135a.2a; H.514; BD.246d.
mût: S.4191; HR.135a.4c; H.1169; BD.559b.
GEN. REF.: IS.4:546; NB.—; Z.—.

Note: Some mss. have it in John 5:16 (A.V., "to slay").

2. *anaireō* [ἀναιρέω, 337], to take away, destroy, kill, is rendered to slay in Matt. 2:16; Acts 2:23; 5:33, 36; 9:29, A.V. (R.V., to kill); 10:39; 13:28; 22:20; 23:15, R.V.; in 2 Thess. 2:8 the best texts have this verb (for *analiskō*, to consume, A.V. and R.V. marg.); hence the R.V.,

"shall slay," of the destruction of the man of sin. See KILL, No. 2.
NT: B.54d; CB.—; K.—.
OT: hārag: S.2026; HR.77b.2a; H.514; BD.246d.
mût: S.4191; HR.77b.4b; H.1169; BD.559b.
nākāh: S.5221; HR.77b.6; H.1364; BD.645a.
GEN. REF.: IS.4:546; NB.—; Z.—.

3. *sphazō* or *sphattō* [σφάττω, 4969], to slay, especially of victims for sacrifice (akin to *sphagē*: see SLAUGHTER), is used (*a*) of taking human life, 1 John 3:12 (twice); Rev. 6:4, R.V., "slay" (A.V., "kill"); in 13:3, probably of assassination, R.V., "smitten (unto death)," A.V., "wounded (to death)," R.V. marg., "slain"; 18:24; (*b*) of Christ, as the Lamb of sacrifice, Rev. 5:6, 9, 12; 6:9; 13:8. See KILL, No. 7. ¶
NT: B.796a; CB.1269c; K.1125.
OT: shāḥaṭ: S.7819; HR.1324b.4a; H.2362; BD.1006a.
ṭābaḥ: S.2873; HR.1324b.3a; H.786; BD.370b.
GEN. REF.: IS.4:546; NB.—; Z.—.

4. *katasphazō* [κατασφάζω, 2695], to kill off (*kata*, used intensively, and No. 3), is used in Luke 19:27. ¶ In the Sept., Ezek. 16:40; Zech. 11:5. ¶
NT: B.419c; CB.—; K.—.
OT: hārag: S.2026; HR.746b.2; H.514; BD.246d.
bātaq: S.1333; HR.746b.1; H.296; BD.144a.
GEN. REF.: IS.4:546; NB.—; Z.—.

5. *diacheirizō* [διαχειρίζω, 1315], to lay hands on, kill, is translated "slew" in Acts 5:30. See KILL, No. 6.
NT: B.191a; CB.—; K.—.
OT: —.
GEN. REF.: —.

6. *phoneuō* [φονεύω, 5407], to kill, to murder, is rendered "ye slew" in Matt. 23:35. See KILL, No. 4.
NT: B.864c; CB.—; K.—.
OT: rāṣah: S.7523; HR.1437a.4; H.2208; BD.953d.
hārag: S.2026; HR.1437a.1a; H.514; BD.246d.
hākāh: S.5221; HR.1437a.3; H.1364; BD.645a.
GEN. REF.: IS.4:546; NB.—; Z.—.

Note: For *thuō*, Acts 11:7, A.V., "slay" (R.V., "kill"), see KILL, No. 3.

For **SLAIN BEASTS** see **BEAST**, No. 5

For **SLEEP** see **ASLEEP**

SLEIGHT

kubia (or *-eia*) [κυβία, 2940], denotes dice-playing (from *kubos*, a cube, a die as used in gaming); hence, metaphorically, trickery, sleight, Eph. 4:14. The Eng. word is connected with 'sly' (not with slight). ¶
NT: B.456c; CB.—; K.—.
OT: —.
GEN. REF.: IS.1:836; NB.1199; Z.—.

For **SLIP** see **DRIFT**

SLOTHFUL

1. *nōthros* [νωθρός, 3576], indolent, sluggish, is rendered "slothful" in Heb. 6:12, A.V. See DULL, and synonymous words there, and SLUGGISH.
NT: B.547c; CB.—; K.661.
OT: ḥāshōk: S.2823; HR.956b.1; H.769b; BD.365b.
GEN. REF.: IS.4:550; NB.—; Z.—.

2. *oknēros* [ὀκνηρός, 3636], shrinking, irksome, is translated "slothful" in Matt. 25:26, and Rom. 12:11, where "in diligence not slothful," R.V., might be rendered 'not flagging in zeal.' See GRIEVOUS, *Note* (2).
NT: B.563a; CB.—; K.681.
OT: 'āṣēl: S.6102; HR.985b.1a; H.1672a; BD.782b.
GEN. REF.: IS.4:550; NB.—; Z.—.

SLOW

bradus [βραδύς, 1021], is used twice in Jas. 1:19, in an exhortation to be slow to speak and slow to wrath; in Luke 24:25, metaphorically of the understanding. ¶
NT: B.147a; CB.—; K.—.
OT: —.
GEN. REF.: IS.—; NB.—; Z.5:461.

Note: For "slow" (*argos*) in Tit. 1:12, see IDLE.

For **SLOWLY** (sailed) see **SAIL**, No. 10

SLUGGISH

nōthros [νωθρός, 3576], for which see SLOTHFUL, is translated "sluggish" in Heb. 6:12, R.V.; here it is set in contrast to confident and constant hope; in 5:11 ("dull") to vigorous growth in knowledge. See DULL. ¶
NT: B.547c; CB.—; K.661.
OT: ḥāshōk: S.2823; HR.956b.1; H.769b; BD.365b.
GEN. REF.: IS.4:550; NB.—; Z.5:461.

For **SLUMBER (Noun)** see **STUPOR**

SLUMBER (Verb)

nustazō [νυστάζω, 3573], denotes to nod to sleep (akin to *neuō*, to nod), fall asleep, and is used (*a*) of natural slumber, Matt. 25:5; (*b*) metaphorically in 2 Pet. 2:3, negatively, of the destruction awaiting false teachers. ¶
NT: B.547a; CB.—; K.—.
OT: nûm: S.5123; HR.956a.2; H.1325; BD.630b.
GEN. REF.: —.

SMALL

1. *mikros* [μικρός, 3398], little, small (of age, quantity, size, space), is translated "small" in Acts 26:22; Rev. 11:18; 13:16; 19:5, 18; 20:12. See LITTLE.
NT: B.521a; CB.1258c; K.593.
OT: me'aṭ: S.4592; HR.926c.3; H.1228a; BD.589d.
qāṭān: S.6996; HR.926c.5; H.2009a,b; BD.881d.
GEN. REF.: —.

2. *oligos* [ὀλίγος, 3641], little, small (of amount, number, time), is translated "small" in Acts 12:18; 15:2; 19:23; ver. 24, A.V. (R.V., "little"); 27:20.
NT: B.563c; CB.1260c; K.682.
OT: m^e^'aṭ: S.4592; HR.986b.4; H.1228a; BD.589d.
GEN. REF.: –.

Notes: (1) For "very small" and "smallest" see LEAST.

(2) For combinations with other words, see CORD, FISH, ISLAND.

For SMELL see SAVOUR

SMELLING

osphrēsis [ὄσφρησις, 3750], denotes the sense of smell, 1 Cor. 12:17, "smelling." ¶
NT: B.587c; CB.–; K.–.
OT: –.
GEN. REF.: IS.4:551; NB.–; Z.–.

SMITE

1. *patassō* [πατάσσω, 3960], to strike, smite, is used (I) literally, of giving a blow with the hand, or fist or a weapon, Matt. 26:51, R.V., "smote" (A.V., "struck"); Luke 22:49, 50; Acts 7:24; 12:7; (II) metaphorically, (*a*) of judgment meted out to Christ, Matt. 26:31; Mark 14:27; (*b*) of the infliction of disease, by an angel, Acts 12:23; of plagues to be inflicted upon men by two Divinely appointed witnesses, Rev. 11:6; (*c*) of judgment to be executed by Christ upon the nations, Rev. 19:15, the instrument being His Word, described as a sword, ¶
NT: B.634d; CB.1262c; K.804.
OT: nākāh: S.5221; HR.1103b.9a; H.1364; BD.645a.
GEN. REF.: IS.4:551; NB.–; Z.–.

2. *tuptō* [τύπτω, 5180], to strike, smite, beat, is rendered to smite in Matt. 24:49, A.V. (R.V., "beat"); 27:30; Mark 15:19; Luke 6:29; 18:13; in some texts in 22:64 (1st part: R.V. omits; for the 2nd part see No. 3); 23:48; Acts 23:2, 3 (twice). See BEAT, No. 2.
NT: B.830b; CB.1273b; K.1195.
OT: nākāh: S.5221; HR.1378b.4; H.1364; BD.645a.
GEN. REF.: IS.4:551; NB.–; Z.–.

3. *paiō* [παίω, 3817], signifies to strike or smite (*a*) with the hand or fist, Matt. 26:68; Luke 22:64 (see No. 2); (*b*) with a sword, Mark 14:47; John 18:10, A.V. (R.V., "struck"); (*c*) with a sting, Rev. 9:5, "striketh." ¶
NT: B.605b; CB.–; K.–.
OT: nākāh: S.5221; HR.1048c.5; H.1364; BD.645a.
GEN. REF.: IS.4:551; NB.–; Z.–.

4. *derō* [δέρω, 1194], to flay, to beat, akin to *derma*, skin, is translated to smite in Luke 22:63, A.V. (R.V., "beat"); John 18:23; 2 Cor. 11:20. See BEAT, No. 1.
NT: B.175d; CB.1240c; K.–.
OT: pāshaṭ: S.6584; HR.291b.1; H.1845; BD.832d.
GEN. REF.: –.

5. *plēssō* [πλήσσω, 4141], akin to *plēgē*, a plague, stripe, wound, is used figuratively of the effect upon sun, moon and stars, after the sounding of the trumpet by the fourth angel, in the series of Divine judgments upon the world hereafter, Rev. 8:12. ¶
NT: B.673a; CB.–; K.–.
OT: nākāh: S.5221; HR.1149c.3b-d; H.1364; BD.645a.
GEN. REF.: IS.4:551; NB.–; Z.–.

6. *rhapizō* [ῥαπίζω, 4474], primarily to strike with a rod (*rhapis*, a rod), then, to strike the face with the palm of the hand or the clenched fist, is used in Matt. 5:39; 26:67, where the marg. of A.V. and R.V. has "with rods." Cp. *rhapisma*, *Note* (2), below. ¶
NT: B.734b; CB.1268a; K.–.
OT: –.
GEN. REF.: –.

7. *kataballō* [καταβάλλω, 2598], to cast down, is translated "smitten down" in 2 Cor. 4:9, R.V. See CAST, No. 8.
NT: B.408d; CB.1253c; K.–.
OT: nāphal: S.5307; HR.728c.4b; H.1392; BD.656c.
GEN. REF.: –.

8. *proskoptō* [προσκόπτω, 4350], to beat upon, is translated "smote upon" in Matt. 7:27. See BEAT, No. 6.
NT: B.716b; CB.1267b; K.946.
OT: nāgaph: S.5062; HR.1217b.2; H.1294; BD.619d.
GEN. REF.: IS.4:551; NB.–; Z.–.

9. *sphazō* [σφάζω, 4969], to slay, is translated "smitten unto death" in Rev. 13:3; see KILL, SLAY.
NT: B.796a; CB.1269c; K.1125.
OT: shāḥaṭ: S.7819; HR.1324b.4a; H.2362; BD.1006a.
ṭābaḥ: S.2873; HR.1324b.3a; H.786; BD.370b.
GEN. REF.: –.

Notes: (1) In Matt. 26:51, A.V., *aphaireō*, to take away, take off, is translated "smote off" (R.V., "struck off").

(2) The noun *rhapisma*, a blow, in the plural, as the object of *didōmi*, to give, in John 19:3 is translated "smote (Him) with their hands" (R.V., "struck etc."), lit., 'gave . . . blows' (R.V. marg., "with rods"); in 18:22 (where the phrase is used with the singular of the noun) the R.V. renders it "struck . . . with his hand" (A.V., "struck . . . with the palm of his hand"), marg. of both, "with a rod."

The same word is used in Mark 14:65, "(received Him) with blows (of their hands)," R.V. [A.V., "did strike Him with the palms (of their hands)," R.V. margin, "strokes of rods"]. See BLOW (Noun). ¶ Cp. No. 6, above, re Matt. 26:67.

SMOKE (Noun and Verb)

A. Noun.

kapnos [καπνός, 4586], smoke, occurs in Acts 2:19 and 12 times in the Apocalypse. ¶

NT: B.403b; CB.—; K.—.
OT: ʻāshān: S.6227; HR.718c.1; H.1712a; BD.798c.
GEN. REF.: IS.4:554; NB.—; Z.5:462.

B. Verb.

tuphō [τύφω, 5188], to raise a smoke [akin to *tuphos*, smoke (not in the N.T.), and *tuphoō*, to puff up with pride, see HIGH-MINDED], is used in the Passive Voice in Matt. 12:20, "smoking (flax)," lit., 'caused to smoke,' of the wick of a lamp which has ceased to burn clearly, figurative of mere nominal religiousness without the Spirit's power. ¶ The Sept. uses the verb *kapnizō* (akin to A).

NT: B.831c; CB.—; K.—.
OT: —.
GEN. REF.: —.

SMOOTH

leios [λεῖος, 3006], smooth, occurs in Luke 3:5, figurative of the change in Israel from self-righteousness, pride and other forms of evil, to repentance, humility and submission. ¶ In the Sept., Gen. 27:11; 1 Sam. 17:40; Prov. 2:20; 12:13; 26:23; Isa. 40:4. ¶

NT: B.470b; CB.—; K.523.
OT: ḥālāq: S.2509; HR.872b.1a; H.670; BD.325b.
ḥalluq: S.2512; HR.872b.1b; H.670d; BD.325c.
GEN. REF.: —.

Note: Chrēstologia (*chrēstos*, good, *legō*, to speak) is rendered "smooth . . . (speech)," in Rom. 16:18, R.V. (A.V., "good words"). ¶

SNARE

1. *pagis* [παγίς, 3803], a trap, a snare (akin to *pēgnumi*, to fix, and *pagideuō*, to ensnare, which see), is used metaphorically of (*a*) the allurements to evil by which the Devil ensnares one, 1 Tim. 3:7; 2 Tim. 2:26; (*b*) seductions to evil, which ensnare those who "desire to be rich," 1 Tim. 6:9; (*c*) the evil brought by Israel upon themselves by which the special privileges Divinely granted them and centring in Christ, became a snare to them, their rejection of Christ and the Gospel being the retributive effect of their apostasy, Rom. 11:9; (*d*) of the sudden judgments of God to come upon those whose hearts are "overcharged with surfeiting, and drunkenness, and cares of this life," Luke 21:34 (ver. 35 in A.V.). ¶

NT: B.602a; CB.1261b; K.752.
OT: paḥ: S.6341; HR.1044b.5a; H.1759a,b; BD.809a.
môqēsh: S.4170; HR.1044b.2b; H.906c; BD.430c.
reshet: S.7568; HR.1044b.6; H.920c; BD.440b.
GEN. REF.: IS.4:556; NB.1200; Z.5:464.

2. *brochos* [βρόχος, 1029], a noose, slip-knot, halter, is used metaphorically in 1 Cor. 7:35, "a snare" (R.V., marg., "constraint," "noose"). ¶ In the Sept., Prov. 6:5; 7:21; 22:25. ¶

NT: B.147d; CB.—; K.—.
OT: môqēsh: S.4170; HR.231b.3; H.906c; BD.430c.
GEN. REF.: IS.4:556; NB.1200; Z.5:464.

SNATCH

harpazō [ἁρπάζω, 726], to snatch, is translated to snatch in the R.V. only, in Matt. 13:19, A.V., "catcheth away"; John 10:12, A.V., "catcheth"; 10:28, 29, A.V., "pluck"; Jude 23, A.V., "pulling." See CATCH, No. 1.

NT: B.109a; CB.1249b; K.80.
OT: gāzal: S.1497; HR.160a.1; H.337; BD.159d.
ṭāraph: S.2963; HR.160a.3a; H.827; BD.382d.
GEN. REF.: —.

SNOW

chiōn [χιών, 5510], occurs in Matt. 28:3; Rev. 1:14. Some mss. have it in Mark 9:3 (A.V.). ¶

NT: B.882b; CB.1239c; K.—.
OT: sheleg: S.7950; HR.1471b.1a; H.2391a; BD.1017a.
GEN. REF.: IS.4:557; NB.1200; Z.5:464.

SO

Notes: (1) *Houtōs* or *houtō*, thus, is the usual word (see THUS).

(2) Some form of *houtos*, this, is sometimes rendered "so," e.g., Acts 23:7; Rom. 12:20.

(3) It translates *homoiōs*, likewise, e.g., in Luke 5:10; *oun*; therefore, e.g., John 4:40, 53.

(4) For "so many as," see MANY; for "so much as," see MUCH.

(5) *Sumbainō*, when used of events, signifies to come to pass, happen; in Acts 21:35 it is rendered "so it was." See BEFALL, HAPPEN.

(6) In 1 Pet. 3:17, *thelō*, to will, is translated "should so will," lit., 'willeth.'

(7) In 2 Cor. 12:16, the imperative mood, 3rd person singular, of *eimi*, to be, is used impersonally, and signifies "be it so."

(8) In Heb. 7:9 *epos*, a word, is used in a phrase rendered "so to say"; see WORD, *Note* (1).

(9) In 1 Tim. 3:11, *hōsautōs*, likewise, is translated "even so."

(1) *Hōs*, as, is rendered "so" in Heb. 3:11 (R.V., "as"). For association with other words see † p. 1.

SOBER, SOBERLY, SOBERMINDED

A. Adjective.

sōphrōn [σώφρων, 4998], denotes of sound mind (*sōzō*, to save, *phrēn*, the mind); hence,

self-controlled, soberminded, always rendered "soberminded" in the R.V.; in 1 Tim. 3:2 and Tit. 1:8, A.V., "sober"; in Tit. 2:2, A.V., "temperate"; in 2:5, A.V., "discreet." ¶
NT: B.802c; CB.1269b; K.1150.
OT: –.
GEN. REF.: IS.4:558; NB.–; Z.–.

Note: For *nēphalios* (akin to B, No. 1), translated "sober" in 1 Tim. 3:11; Tit. 2:2, see TEMPERATE.

B. Verbs.

1. *nēphō* [νήφω, 3525], signifies to be free from the influence of intoxicants; in the N.T., metaphorically, it does not in itself imply watchfulness, but is used in association with it, 1 Thess. 5:6, 8; 2 Tim. 4:5; 1 Pet. 1:13; 4:7, R.V. (A.V., "watch"); 5:8. ¶ Cp. *eknēphō* and *ananēphō*, under AWAKE, No. 3 and *Note.*
NT: B.538d; CB.1259c; K.633.
OT: –.
GEN. REF.: IS.4:558; NB.–; Z.–.

2. *sōphroneō* [σωφρονέω, 4993], akin to A, is rendered to think soberly, Rom. 12:3; to be sober, 2 Cor. 5:13; to be soberminded, Tit. 2:6; in 1 Pet. 4:7, A.V. "be ye sober" (R.V., "of sound mind"); see MIND, B, No. 5.
NT: B.802a; CB.1269b; K.1150.
OT: –.
GEN. REF.: IS.4:558; NB.–; Z.–.

3. *sōphronizō* [σωφρονίζω, 4994], denotes to cause to be of sound mind, to recall to one's senses; in Tit. 2:4, R.V., it is rendered "they may train" (A.V., "they may teach . . . to be sober," marg., "wise"); "train" expresses the meaning more adequately; the training would involve the cultivation of sound judgment and prudence. ¶
NT: B.802b; CB.–; K.1150.
OT: –.
GEN. REF.: IS.4:558; NB.–; Z.–.

C. Adverb.

sōphronōs [σωφρόνως, 4996], akin to A and B, Nos. 2 and 3, soberly, occurs in Tit. 2:12; it suggests the exercise of that self-restraint that governs all passions and desires, enabling the believer to be conformed to the mind of Christ. ¶
NT: B.802c; CB.1269b; K.–.
OT: –.
GEN. REF.: IS.4:558; NB.–; Z.–.

Note: For the phrase to think soberly, see B, No. 2.

SOBERNESS, SOBRIETY

sōphrosunē [σωφροσύνη, 4997], denotes soundness of mind (see SOBER, A), Acts 26:25, "soberness"; 1 Tim. 2:9, 15, "sobriety"; 'sound judgment' practically expresses the meaning; "it is that habitual inner self-government, with its constant rein on all the passions and desires, which would hinder the temptation to these from arising, or at all events from arising in such strength as would overbear the checks and barriers which *aidōs* (shamefastness) opposed to it" (Trench Syn. § xx, end). ¶
NT: B.802c; CB.1269b; K.1150.
OT: –.
GEN. REF.: IS.4:558; NB.–; Z.–.

For SOFT see EFFEMINATE

For SOFTLY see BLOW (Verb), No. 2

SOJOURN, SOJOURNER, SOJOURNING

A. Verbs.

1. *paroikeō* [παροικέω, 3939], denotes to dwell beside, among or by (*para*, beside, *oikeō*, to dwell); then, to dwell in a place as a *paroikos*, a stranger (see below), Luke 24:18, R.V., "Dost thou (alone) sojourn . . .?" [marg., "Dost thou sojourn (alone)" is preferable], A.V., "art thou (only) a stranger?" (*monos*, alone, is an adjective, not an adverb); in Heb. 11:9, R.V., "he became a sojourner" (A.V., "he sojourned"), the R.V. gives the force of the aorist tense. ¶
NT: B.628d; CB.1262b; K.788.
OT: gûr: S.1481; HR.1071a.1a; H.330,332; BD.157c.
GEN. REF.: IS.4:561; NB.1219; Z.–.

2. *epidēmeō* [ἐπιδημέω, 1927], is rendered to sojourn in Acts 17:21, R.V.,
NT: B.292a; CB.–; K.–.
OT: –.
GEN. REF.: –.

B. Adjectives.

1. *paroikos* [πάροικος, 3941], an adjective, akin to A, No.1, lit., dwelling near (see above), then, foreign, alien (found with this meaning in Inscriptions), hence, as a noun, a sojourner, is used with *eimi*, to be, in Acts 7:6, "should sojourn," lit., 'should be a sojourner'; in 7:29, R.V., "sojourner" (A.V., "stranger"); in Eph. 2:19, R.V., "sojourners" (A.V., "foreigners"), the preceding word rendered "strangers" is *xenos*; in 1 Pet. 2:11, R.V., ditto (A.V., "strangers"). ¶
NT: B.629a; CB.1262b; K.788.
OT: gēr: S.1616; HR.1071c.2a; H.330a; BD.158a.
tôshāb: S.8453; HR.1071c.4; H.922d; BD.444c.
GEN. REF.: IS.4:561; NB.1219; Z.5:468.

2. *apodēmos* [ἀπόδημος, 590], gone abroad (*apo*, from, *dēmos*, people), signifies "sojourning in another country," Mark 13:34, R.V. (A.V., "taking a far journey"). ¶
NT: B.90b; CB.–; K.–.
OT: –.
GEN. REF.: –.

3. *parepidēmos* [παρεπίδημος, 3927], sojourning in a strange place, is used as a noun,

denoting a sojourner, an exile, 1 Pet. 1:1, R.V., "sojourners" (A.V., "strangers"). See PILGRIM. ¶
NT: B.625d; CB.1262b; K.149.
OT: tôshāb: S.8453; HR.1068c.1; H.922d; BD.444c.
GEN. REF.: IS.4:561; NB.1219; Z.5:468.

C. Noun.

paroikia [παροικία, 3940], a sojourning (akin to A and B, Nos. 1, occurs in Acts 13:17, rendered "they sojourned," R.V., A.V., "dwelt as strangers," lit., 'in the sojourning'; in 1 Pet. 1:17, "sojourning." ¶
NT: B.629a; CB.1262b; K.788.
OT: māgôr: S.4033; HR.1071c.2a; H.330c; BD.158c.
mᵉgûrāh: S.4035; HR.1071c.2b; H.330d; BD.158c.
gûr: S.1481; HR.1071c.2c; H.330,332; BD.157c.
GEN. REF.: IS.4:561; NB.–; Z.–.

SOLDIER

A. Nouns.

1. *stratiōtēs* [στρατιώτης, 4757], a soldier, is used (*a*) in the natural sense, e.g., Matt. 8:9; 27:27; 28:12; Mark 15:16; Luke 7:8; 23:36; six times in John; thirteen times in Acts; not again in the N.T.; (*b*) metaphorically of one who endures hardship in the cause of Christ, 2 Tim. 2:3.
NT: B.770d; CB.1270a; K.1091.
OT: –.
GEN. REF.: IS.4:565; NB.–; Z.–.

2. *strateuma* [στράτευμα, 4753], an army, is used to denote a company of soldiers in Acts 23:10; in ver. 27, R.V., "the soldiers," A.V., "an army"; in Luke 23:11 (plural), R.V., "soldiers," A.V., "men of war." See ARMY.
NT: B.770b; CB.1270a; K.1091.
OT: –.
GEN. REF.: IS.4:565; NB.–; Z.–.

3. *sustratiōtēs* [συστρατιώτης, 4961], a fellow-soldier (*sun*, with, and No. 1), is used metaphorically in Phil. 2:25 and Philm. 2, of fellowship in Christian service. ¶
NT: B.795b; CB.–; K.1091.
OT: –.
GEN. REF.: IS.4:565; NB.–; Z.–.

B. Verb.

strateuō [στρατεύω, 4754], always in the Middle Voice in the N.T., is used (*a*) literally of serving as a soldier, Luke 3:14, "soldiers" (R.V., marg., "soldiers on service," present participle); 1 Cor. 9:7, R.V., "(what) soldier . . . serveth," A.V., "(who) goeth a warfare"; 2 Tim. 2:4, R.V., "soldier on service," A.V., "man that warreth," lit., 'serving as a soldier'; (*b*) metaphorically, of spiritual conflict: see WAR.
NT: B.770b; CB.1270a; K.–.
OT: yāṣā': S.3318; HR.1295a.1; H.893; BD.422b,424a.
ṣābā': S.6633; HR.1295a.3; H.1865; BD.838c.
GEN. REF.: IS.4:565; NB.84; Z.–.

Notes: (1) For *spekoulatōr*, Mark 6:27, R.V., "soldier of his guard," see GUARD. ¶

(2) In 2 Tim. 2:4 *stratologeō* is rendered "hath chosen (him) to be a soldier," A.V. (R.V., "enrolled (him) as a soldier"). ¶

SOLID

stereos [στερεός, 4731], for which see FIRM, No. 2, has the meaning "solid" in Heb. 5:12, 14, of food (A.V., "strong"). As solid food requires more powerful digestive organs than are possessed by a babe, so a fuller knowledge of Christ (especially here with reference to His Melchizedek priesthood) required that exercise of spiritual intelligence which is derived from the practical appropriation of what had already been received.
NT: B.766d; CB.1270a; K.1077.
OT: –.
GEN. REF.: –.

For **SOLITARY**, Mark 1:35, A.V., see **DESERT**, B

SOME, SOMEONE, SOMETHING, SOMEWHAT

Notes: (1) Various forms of the article and certain pronouns, followed by the particles *men* and *de* denote "some." These are not enumerated here.

(2) The indefinite pronoun *tis* in its singular or plural forms, frequently means "some," "some one" (translated "some man," in the A.V., e.g., of Acts 8:31; 1 Cor. 15:35), or "somebody," Luke 8:46; the neuter plural denotes "some things" in 2 Pet. 3:16; the singular denotes "something," e.g., Luke 11:54; John 13:29 (2nd part); Acts 3:5; 23:18; Gal. 6:3, where the meaning is 'anything,' as in 2:6, "somewhat." It is translated "somewhat," in the more indefinite sense, in Luke 7:40; Acts 23:20; 25:26; 2 Cor. 10:8; Heb. 8:3. See also ONE, B, No. 1.

(3) *Meros*, a part, a measure, preceded by the preposition *apo*, from, is translated "in some measure" in Rom. 15:15, R.V. (A.V., "in some sort"), and ver. 24 (A.V., "somewhat").

(4) In the following *alloi*, others ("some" in the A.V.), is translated "others" in the R.V., Matt. 13:5, 7; Mark 4:7 ("other"); 8:28; Luke 9:19; John 9:9. Followed by a correlative expression it denotes "some," e.g., Acts 19:32; 21:34; see OTHER, No. 1.

For **SOMETIMES** see **TIME**

SOMEWHERE

pou [πού, 4225], a particle, signifies "somewhere" in Heb. 2:6 and 4:4, R.V. (A.V., "in a certain place"); the writer avoids mentioning the place to add stress to his testimony. See HAPLY, No. 5, VERILY.

NT: B.696a; CB.1266b; K.—.
OT: —.
GEN. REF.: —.

SON

huios [υἱός, 5207], primarily signifies the relation of offspring to parent (see John 9:18-20; Gal. 4:30). It is often used metaphorically of prominent moral characteristics (see below). "it is used in the N.T. of (*a*) male offspring, Gal. 4:30; (*b*) legitimate, as opposed to illegitimate, offspring, Heb. 12:8; (*c*) descendants, without reference to sex, Rom. 9:27; (*d*) friends attending a wedding, Matt. 9:15; (*e*) those who enjoy certain privileges, Acts 3:25; (*f*) those who act in a certain way, whether evil, Matt. 23:31, or good, Gal. 3:7; (*g*) those who manifest a certain character, whether evil, Acts 13:10; Eph. 2:2, or good, Luke 6:35; Acts 4:36; Rom. 8:14; (*h*) the destiny that corresponds with the character, whether evil, Matt. 23:15; John 17:12; 2 Thess. 2:3, or good, Luke 20:36; (*i*) the dignity of the relationship with God whereinto men are brought by the Holy Spirit when they believe on the Lord Jesus Christ, Rom. 8:19; Gal. 3:26. . . .

"The Apostle John does not use *huios*, 'son,' of the believer, he reserves that title for the Lord; but he does use *teknon*, 'child,' as in his Gospel, 1:12; 1 John 3:1, 2: Rev. 21:7 (*huios*) is a quotation from 2 Sam. 7:14.

"The Lord Jesus used *huios* in a very significant way, as in Matt. 5:9, 'Blessed are the peacemakers, for they shall be called the sons of God,' and vv. 44, 45, 'Love your enemies, and pray for them that persecute you; that ye may be (become) sons of your Father which is in heaven.' The disciples were to do these things, not in order that they might become children of God, but that, being children (note 'your Father' throughout), they might make the fact manifest in their character, might 'become sons.' See also 2 Cor. 6:17, 18.

"As to moral characteristics, the following phrases are used: (*a*) sons of God, Matt. 5:9, 45; Luke 6:35; (*b*) sons of the light, Luke 16:8; John 12:36; (*c*) sons of the day, 1 Thess. 5:5; (*d*) sons of peace, Luke 10:6; (*e*) sons of this world, Luke 16:8; (*f*) sons of disobedience, Eph. 2:2; (*g*) sons of the evil one, Matt. 13:38, cp. 'of the Devil,' Acts 13:10; (*h*) son of perdition, John 17:12; 2 Thess. 2:3. It is also used to describe characteristics other than moral, as: (*i*) sons of the resurrection, Luke 20:36; (*j*) sons of the Kingdom, Matt. 8:12; 13:38; (*k*) sons of the bridechamber, Mark 2:19; (*l*) sons of exhortation, Acts 4:36; (*m*) sons of thunder, Boanerges, Mark 3:17."*

NT: B.833c; CB.1251c; K.—.
OT: bēn: S.1121; HR.1384c.3; H.254; BD.119d.
GEN. REF.: IS.4:570; NB.416; Z.—.

Notes: (1) For the synonyms *teknon* and *teknion* see under CHILD. The difference between believers as 'children of God' and as 'sons of God' is brought out in Rom. 8:14-21. The Spirit bears witness with their spirit that they are "children of God," and, as such, they are His heirs and joint-heirs with Christ. This stresses the fact of their spiritual birth (vv. 16, 17). On the other hand, "as many as are led by the Spirit of God, these are sons of God," i.e., 'these and no other.' Their conduct gives evidence of the dignity of their relationship and their likeness to His character.

(2) *Pais* is rendered "son" in John 4:51. For Acts 13:13, 26 see below.

The Son of God

In this title the word Son is used sometimes (*a*) of relationship, sometimes (*b*) of the expression of character. "Thus, e.g., when the disciples so addressed Him, Matt. 14:33; 16:16; John 1:49, when the centurion so spoke of Him, Matt. 27:54, they probably meant that (*b*) He was a manifestation of God in human form. But in such passages as Luke 1:32, 35; Acts 13:33, which refer to the humanity of the Lord Jesus, . . . the word is used in sense (*a*).

"The Lord Jesus Himself used the full title on occasion, John 5:25; 9:35 [some mss. have 'the Son of man'; see R.V. marg.]; 11:4, and on the more frequent occasions on which He spoke of Himself as 'the Son,' the words are to be understood as an abbreviation of 'the Son of God,' not of 'the Son of Man'; this latter he always expressed in full; see Luke 10:22; John 5:19, etc.

"John uses both the longer and shorter forms of the title in his Gospel, see 3:16-18; 20:31, e.g., and in his Epistles; cp. Rev. 2:18. So does the writer of Hebrews, 1:2; 4:14; 6:6, etc. An eternal relation subsisting between the Son and the Father in the Godhead is to be understood.

* From Notes on Galatians by Hogg and Vine, pp. 167-169, and on Thessalonians, pp. 158, 159.

because He at any time began to derive His being from the Father (in which case He could not be co-eternal with the Father), but because He is and ever has been the expression of what the Father is; cp. John 14:9, 'he that hath seen Me hath seen the Father.' The words of Heb. 1:3, 'Who being the effulgence of His (God's) glory, and the very image of His (God's) substance' are a definition of what is meant by 'Son of God.' Thus absolute Godhead, not Godhead in a secondary or derived sense, is intended in the title."*

Other titles of Christ as the Son of God are: "His Son," 1 Thess. 1:10 (in Acts 13:13, 26, R.V., *pais* is rendered "servant"); "His own Son," Rom. 8:32; "My beloved Son," Matt. 3:17; "His Only Begotten Son," John 3:16; "the Son of His love," Col. 1:13.

"The Son is the eternal object of the Father's love, John 17:24, and the sole Revealer of the Father's character, John 1:14; Heb. 1:3. The words, 'Father' and 'Son,' are never in the N.T. so used as to suggest that the Father existed before the Son; the Prologue to the Gospel according to John distinctly asserts that the Word existed 'in the beginning,' and that this Word is the Son, Who 'became flesh and dwelt among us.' "†

In addressing the Father in His prayer in John 17 He says, "Thou lovedst Me before the foundation of the world." Accordingly in the timeless past the Father and the Son existed in that relationship, a relationship of love, as well as of absolute Deity. In this passage the Son gives evidence that there was no more powerful plea in the Father's estimation than that co-eternal love existing between the Father and Himself.

The declaration "Thou art My Son, this day have I begotten Thee," Psa. 2:7, quoted in Acts 13:33; Heb. 1:5; 5:5, refers to the birth of Christ, not to His resurrection. In Acts 13:33 the verb "raise up" is used of the raising up of a person to occupy a special position in the nation, as of David in verse 22 (so of Christ as a Prophet in 3:22 and 7:37). The word "again" in the A.V. in ver. 33 represents nothing in the original. The R.V. rightly omits it. In ver. 34 the statement as to the resurrection of Christ receives the greater stress in this respect through the emphatic contrast to that in ver. 33 as to His being raised up in the nation, a stress imparted by the added words "from the dead." Accordingly ver. 33 speaks of His Incarnation, ver. 34 of His resurrection.

In Heb. 1:5, that the declaration refers to the Birth is confirmed by the contrast in verse 6. Here the word "again" is rightly placed in the R.V., "when He again bringeth in the Firstborn into the world." This points on to His Second Advent, which is set in contrast to His first Advent, when God brought His Firstborn into the world the first time (see FIRSTBORN).‡

So again in Heb. 5:5, where the High Priesthood of Christ is shown to fulfil all that was foreshadowed in the Levitical priesthood, the passage stresses the facts of His humanity, the days of His flesh, His perfect obedience and His sufferings.

Son of Man

In the N.T. this is a designation of Christ, almost entirely confined to the Gospels. Elsewhere it is found in Acts 7:56, the only occasion where a disciple applied it to the Lord and in Rev. 1:13; 14:14 (see below).

"Son of Man" is the title Christ used of Himself; John 12:34 is not an exception, for the quotation by the multitude was from His own statement. The title is found especially in the Synoptic Gospels. The occurrences in John's Gospel, 1:51; 3:13, 14; 5:27; 6:27, 53, 62; 8:28 (9:35 in some texts); 12:23, 34 (twice); 13:31, are not parallel to those in the Synoptic Gospels. In the latter the use of the title falls into two groups, (*a*) those in which it refers to Christ's humanity, His earthly work, sufferings and death, e.g., Matt. 8:20; 11:19; 12:40; 26:2, 24; (*b*) those which refer to His glory in resurrection and to that of His future Advent, e.g., Matt. 10:23; 13:41; 16:27, 28; 17:9; 24:27, 30 (twice), 37, 39, 44.

While it is a Messianic title it is evident that the Lord applied it to Himself in a distinctive way, for it indicates more than Messiahship, even universal headship on the part of One who is Man. It therefore stresses His manhood, manhood of a unique order in comparison with all other men, for He is declared to be of heaven,

* From Notes on Galatians by Hogg and Vine, pp. 99, 100.

† From Notes on Thessalonians by Hogg and Vine, pp. 46, 47.

‡ The Western text of Luke 3:22 reads "Thou art My Son, this day have I begotten Thee," instead of "Thou art My beloved son, in Thee I am well pleased." There is probably some connection between this and those early heresies which taught that our Lord's Deity began at His Baptism.

1 Cor. 15:47, and even while here below; was "the Son of Man, which is in Heaven," John 3:13. As the Son of Man He must be appropriated spiritually as a condition of possessing eternal life, John 6:53. In His death, as in His life, the glory of His Manhood was displayed in the absolute obedience and submission to the will of the Father (12:23, 13:31), and, in view of this, all judgment has been committed to Him, who will judge in full understanding experimentally of human conditions, sin apart, and will exercise the judgment as sharing the nature of those judged, John 5:22, 27. Not only is He man, but He is "Son of man," not by human generation but, according to the Semitic usage of the expression, partaking of the characteristics (sin apart) of manhood belonging to the category of mankind. Twice in the Apocalypse, 1:13 and 14:14, He is described as "One like unto a Son of man," R.V. (A.V., ". . . the Son of Man"), cp. Dan. 7:13. He who was thus seen was indeed the Son of Man, but the absence of the article in the original serves to stress what morally characterizes Him as such. Accordingly in these passages He is revealed, not as the Person known by the title, but as the One who is qualified to act as the Judge of all men. He is the same Person as in the days of His flesh, still continuing His humanity with His Deity. The phrase "like unto" serves to distinguish Him as there seen in His glory and majesty in contrast to the days of His humiliation.

SONG

ōdē [ᾠδή, 5603], an ode, song, is always used in the N.T. (as in the Sept.), in praise of God or Christ; in Eph. 5:19 and Col. 3:16 the adjective "spiritual" is added, because the word in itself is generic and might be used of songs anything but spiritual; in Rev. 5:9 and 14:3 (1st part) the descriptive word is "new" (*kainos*, new in reference to character and form: see NEW), a song, the significance of which was confined to those mentioned (ver. 3, and 2nd part); in 15:3 (twice), "the song of Moses . . . and the song of the Lamb," the former as celebrating the deliverance of God's people by His power, the latter as celebrating redemption by atoning sacrifice. ¶

NT: B.895a; CB.1260b; K.24.
OT: shîr: S.7892; HR.1492a.6a; H.2378a,b; BD.1010b.
shîrāh: S.7892; HR.1492a.6b; H.2378a,b; BD.1010c.
GEN. REF.: IS.4:581; NB.–; Z.–.

For **SOON** see **IMMEDIATELY**, No. 1 and **QUICKLY**, No. 3.

AS SOON AS: see † p. 1

For **SOONER** see **QUICKLY**, No. 2

SOOTHSAYING

manteuomai [μαντεύομαι, 3132], to divine, practise divination (from *mantis*, a seer, diviner), occurs in Acts 16:16. ¶ The word is allied to *mainomai*, to rave, and *mania*, fury displayed by those who were possessed by the evil spirit (represented by the pagan god or goddess) while delivering their oracular messages. Trench (Syn. § vi) draws a distinction between this verb and *prophēteuō*, not only as to their meanings, but as to the fact of the single occurrence of *manteuomai* in the N.T., contrasted with the frequency of *prophēteuō*, exemplifying the avoidance by N.T. writers of words the employment of which "would tend to break down the distinction between heathenism and revealed religion."

NT: B.491a; CB.1257c; K.–.
OT: qāsam: S.7080; HR.896a.1a; H.2044; BD.890c.
GEN. REF.: IS.–; NB.320; Z.–.

SOP

psōmion [ψωμίον, 5596], a diminutive of *psōmos*, a morsel, denotes a fragment, a sop (akin to *psōmizō*; see FEED), John 13:26 (twice), 27, 30. It had no connection with the modern meaning of sop, something given to pacify (as in the classical expression 'a sop to Cerberus'). ¶

NT: B.894d; CB.–; K.–.
OT: –.
GEN. REF.: IS.–; NB.–; Z.5:494.

SORCERER

1. *magos* [μάγος, 3097], (*a*) one of a Median caste, a magician: see WISE; (*b*) a wizard, sorcerer, a pretender to magic powers, a professor of the arts of witchcraft, Acts 13:6, 8 where Bar-Jesus was the Jewish name, Elymas, an Arabic word meaning "wise." Hence the name Magus, "the magician," originally applied to Persian priests. In the Sept., only in Dan. 2:2, 10, of the "enchanters," R.V. (A.V., "astrologers"), of Babylon. The superior Greek version of Daniel by Theodotion has it also at 1:20; 2:27; 4:7; 5:7, 11, 15. ¶

NT: B.484d; CB.1257b; K.547.
OT: 'ashshāq: S.825; HR.891b.1; H.181; BD.80b.
GEN. REF.: IS.3:213; NB.766; Z.2:148.

2. *pharmakos* [φαρμακός, 5333], an adjective signifying 'devoted to magical arts,' is used as a noun, a sorcerer, especially one who uses drugs, potions, spells, enchantments, Rev. 21:8,

in the best texts (some have *pharmakeus*), and 22:15. ¶
NT: B.854b; CB.1264a; K.–.
OT: ḥartummîm: S.2748; HR.1425a.2a; H.738b; BD.355a.
kāshaph: S.3784; HR.1425a.3a; H.1051; BD.506c.
GEN. REF.: IS.3:213; NB.766; Z.2:146.

SORCERY

A. Nouns.

1. *pharmakia* (or *-eia*) [φαρμακία, 5331], (Eng., pharmacy etc.) primarily signified the use of medicine, drugs, spells; then, poisoning; then, sorcery, Gal. 5:20, R.V., "sorcery" (A.V., "witchcraft"), mentioned as one of "the works of the flesh." See also Rev. 9:21; 18:23. ¶ In the Sept., Ex. 7:11, 22; 8:7, 18; Isa. 47:9, 12. ¶ In sorcery, the use of drugs, whether simple or potent, was generally accompanied by incantations and appeals to occult powers, with the provision of various charms, amulets, etc., professedly designed to keep the applicant or patient from the attention and power of demons, but actually to impress the applicant with the mysterious resources and powers of the sorcerer.
NT: B.854a; CB.1263c; K.–.
OT: kesheph: S.3785; HR.1425a.1; H.1051a; BD.506c.
lāṭ: S.3909; HR.1425a.2b; H.1092a; BD.532a.
GEN. REF.: IS.3:213; NB.766; Z.2:146.

2. *magia* (or *-eia*) [μαγία, 3095], the magic art, is used in the plural in Acts 8:11, "sorceries" (see SORCERER, No. 1). ¶
NT: B.484b; CB.1257b; K.547.
OT: –.
GEN. REF.: IS.3:213; NB.766; Z.–.

B. Verb.

mageuō [μαγεύω, 3096], akin to A, No. 2, to practise magic, Acts 8:9, "used sorcery," is used as in A, No. 2, of Simon Magnus. ¶
NT: B.484c; CB.1257b; K.547.
OT: –.
GEN. REF.: IS.3:213; NB.766; Z.–.

SORE (Noun, Adjective, Adverb), SORER

A. Noun.

helkos [ἕλκος, 1668], a sore or ulcer (primarily a wound), occurs in Luke 16:21; Rev. 16:2, 11. ¶
NT: B.251c; CB.–; K.–.
OT: sheḥîn: S.7822; HR.453b.1; H.2364a; BD.1006c.
GEN. REF.: IS.4:585; NB.–; Z.5:495.

B. Verb.

helkoō [ἑλκόω, 1669], to wound, to ulcerate, is used in the Passive Voice, signifying to suffer from sores, to be "full of sores," Luke 16:20 (perfect participle). ¶
NT: B.251c; CB.–; K.–.
OT: –.
GEN. REF.: –.

C. Adjectives.

1. *hikanos* [ἱκανός, 2425], used of things, occasionally denotes "much," translated "sore" in Acts 20:37, lit., 'there was much weeping of all.' See ABLE, C, No. 2.
NT: B.374b; CB.1250c; K.361.
OT: –.
GEN. REF.: –.

2. *cheirōn* [χείρων, 5501], worse (used as a comparative degree of *kakos*, evil), occurs in Heb. 10:29, "sorer." See WORSE.
NT: B.881b; CB.–; K.–.
OT: –.
GEN. REF.: –.

D. Adverbs.

1. *lian* [λίαν, 3029], very, exceedingly, is translated "sore" in Mark 6:51 (of amazement). See EXCEED, B, No. 1.
NT: B.473b; CB.1257a; K.–.
OT: m^{e}'ōd: S.3966; HR.876a.1; H.1134; BD.547a.
GEN. REF.: –.

2. *sphodra* [σφόδρα, 4970], very, very much, is translated "sore" in Matt. 17:6 (of fear). See GREATLY, *Note* (1).
NT: B.796a; CB.1269c; K.–.
OT: m^{e}'ōd: S.3966; HR.1325a.2a; H.1134; BD.547a.
GEN. REF.: –.

Notes: (1) For the A.V., "sore vexed" in Matt. 17:15, see GRIEVOUSLY, B, No. 2, *Note* (2).

(2) In Luke 2:9 *megas*, great, is used with *phobos*, fear, as the object of the verb to fear, "(they were) sore (afraid)," lit., '(they feared) a great (fear).'

(3) In Mark 9:26, A.V., *polla*, much (R.V.), the neuter plur. of *polus*, used as an adverb, is translated "sore."

(4) In Matt. 21:15, *aganakteō*, to be moved with indignation (R.V.), is translated "they were sore displeased."

(5) For the R.V., "sore troubled," Matt. 26:37 and Mark 14:33 (A.V., "very heavy"), see TROUBLE, B, No. 12.

(6) For A.V., "were sore amazed" in Mark 14:33, see AMAZE, B, No. 4.

(7) In Luke 9:39, R.V., *suntribō*, to break, bruise, is rendered "bruiseth sorely." See BREAK, A, No. 5.

(8) In Mark 9:6, *ekphobos* is rendered "sore afraid."

SORROW (Noun and Verb), SORROWFUL

A. Nouns.

1. *lupē* [λύπη, 3077], grief, sorrow, is translated "sorrow" in Luke 22:45; John 16:6, 20-22; Rom. 9:2, R.V. (A.V., "heaviness");

2 Cor. 2:1, R.V.; 2:3, 7; 7:10 (twice); Phil. 2:27 (twice). See GRIEF.

NT: B.482a; CB.1257b; K.540.
OT: 'eṣeb: S.6089; HR.889c.3a; H.1666a,1667a; BD.780c.
'iṣṣābôn: S.6093; HR.889c.3b; H.1666e; BD.781a.
yāgôn: S.3015; HR.889c.2; H.839a; BD.387b.
GEN. REF.: IS.4:585; NB.–; Z.5:495.

2. *odunē* [ὀδύνη, 3601], pain, consuming grief, distress, whether of body or mind, is used of the latter, Rom. 9:2, R.V., "pain"; 1 Tim. 6:10. ¶

NT: B.555b; CB.1260b; K.673.
OT: yāgôn: S.3015; HR.967a.8; H.839a; BD.387b.
'āwen: S.205; HR.967a.2; H.48a; BD.19d.
ballāhāh: S.1091; HR.967a.3; H.247a; BD.117a.
GEN. REF.: IS.4:585; NB.–; Z.–.

2. *ōdin* [ὠδίν, 5604], a birth-pang, travail, pain, "sorrows," Matt. 24:8; Mark 13:8; see PAIN, A, No. 2.

NT: B.895c; CB.1260b; K.1353.
OT: ḥîl: S.2427; HR.1492b.2a; H.623b; BD.297d.
ḥēbel: S.2256; HR.1492b.1; H.592b; BD.286d.
GEN. REF.: IS.4:585; NB.–; Z.–.

4. *penthos* [πένθος, 3997], mourning, "sorrow," Rev. 18:7 (twice); 21:4: see MOURN.

NT: B.642d; CB.1263a; K.825.
OT: 'ēbel: S.60; HR.1118a.1a; H.6a; BD.5c.
GEN. REF.: –.

B. Verbs.

1. *lupeō* [λυπέω, 3076], akin to A, No. 1: see GRIEF, B, No. 1, SORRY, A (below).

NT: B.481c; CB.1257b; K.540.
OT: rāgaz: S.7264; HR.889b.10; H.2112; BD.919a.
'āṣab: S.6087; HR.889b.8; H.1666,1667; BD.780c.
GEN. REF.: IS.4:585; NB.–; Z.5:495.

2. *odunaō* [ὀδυνάω, 3600], to cause pain (akin to A, No. 2), is used in the Middle Voice in Luke 2:48; Acts 20:38: see ANGUISH, B, No. 3.

NT: B.555a; CB.–; K.–.
OT: ḥîl: S.2427; HR.967a.2; H.623b; BD.297d.
dāweh: S.1739; HR.967; H.411b; BD.188c.
GEN. REF.: IS.4:585; NB.–; Z.–.

C. Adjectives.

1. *perilupos* [περίλυπος, 4036], very sad, deeply grieved (*peri*, intensive), is used in Matt. 26:38 and Mark 14:34, "exceeding sorrowful"; Mark 6:26; Luke 18:23 (ver. 24 in some mss.). ¶

NT: B.648c; CB.–; K.540.
OT: ḥārāh: S.2734; HR.1124c.1; H.736; BD.354a.
shāḥaḥ: S.7817; HR.1124c.2; H.2361; BD.1005d.
GEN. REF.: IS.4:585; NB.–; Z.–.

2. *alupos* [ἄλυπος, 253], denotes free from grief (*a*, negative, *lupē*, grief), comparative degree in Phil. 2:28, "less sorrowful," their joy would mean the removal of a burden from his heart. ¶

NT: B.41a; CB.–; K.540.
OT: –.
GEN. REF.: –.

SORRY

A. Verb.

lupeō [λυπέω, 3076], is rendered to be sorry (Passive Voice) in Matt. 14:9, A.V. (R.V., "grieved"); 17:23; 18:31; 2 Cor. 2:2 [1st part, Active V., "make sorry" (as in 7:8, twice); 2nd part, Passive]; 2:4, R.V., "made sorry"; 9:9 and 11, R.V., "ye were made sorry." See GRIEVE, B, No. 1.

NT: B.481c; CB.1257b; K.540.
OT: rāgaz: S.7264; HR.889b.10; H.2112; BD.919a.
'āṣab: S.6087; HR.889b.8; H.1666,1667; BD.780c.
GEN. REF.: IS.4:585; NB.–; Z.5:495.

B. Adjective.

perilupos [περίλυπος, 4036], is translated "exceeding sorry" in Mark 6:26: see SORROWFUL, C, No. 1.

NT: B.648c; CB.–; K.540.
OT: ḥārāh: S.2734; HR.1124c.1; H.736; BD.354a.
shāḥaḥ: S.7817; HR.1124c.2; H.2361; BD.1005d.
GEN. REF.: IS.4:585; NB.–; Z.–.

SORT

A. Adjective.

hopoios [ὁποῖος, 3697], of what sort, is so rendered in 1 Cor. 3:13. See MANNER, SUCH AS, WHAT.

NT: B.575d; CB.–; K.–.
OT: –.
GEN. REF.: –.

B. Noun.

meros [μέρος, 3313], a part, is used with *apo*, from, in Rom. 15:15 and rendered "(in some) sort," A.V. (R.V., ". . . measure"). See BEHALF.

NT: B.505d; CB.1258b; K.585.
OT: –.
GEN. REF.: –.

Note: See BASE, No. 3, GODLY, C, *Notes* (2) and (3).

For **SOUGHT** see **SEEK**

SOUL

psuchē [ψυχή, 5590], denotes the breath, the breath of life, then the soul, in its various meanings. The N.T. uses "may be analysed approximately as follows:

(*a*) The natural life of the body, Matt. 2:20; Luke 12:22; Acts 20:10; Rev. 8:9; 12:11; cp. Lev. 17:11; 2 Sam. 14:7; Esth. 8:11; (*b*) the immaterial, invisible part of man, Matt. 10:28; Acts 2:27; cp. 1 Kings 17:21; (*c*) the disembodied (or 'unclothed' or 'naked,' 2 Cor. 5:3, 4) man, Rev. 6:L9; (*d*) the seat of personality, Luke 9:24, explained as = 'own self,' ver. 25; Heb. 6:19; 10:39; cp. Isa. 53:10 with 1 Tim. 2:6; (*e*) the seat of the sentient element in man, that by which he perceives, reflects, feels, desires, Matt. 11:29; Luke 1:46; 2:35; Acts 14:2, 22; cp. Ps. 84:2; 139:14; Isa. 26:9; (*f*) the seat of will and purpose, Matt. 22:37; Acts 4:32; Eph. 6:6; Phil. 1:27; Heb. 12:3; cp. Num. 21:4; Deut. 11:13; (*g*) the seat of appetite, Rev. 18:14; cp.

Ps. 107:9; Prov. 6:30; Isa. 5:14 ('desire'); 29:8; (*h*) persons, individuals, Acts 2:41, 43; Rom. 2:9; Jas. 5:20; 1 Pet. 3:20; 2 Pet. 2:14; cp. Gen. 12:5; 14:21 ('persons'); Lev. 4:2 ('any one'); Ezek. 27:13; of dead bodies, Num. 6:6, lit., 'dead soul'; and of animals, Lev. 24:18, lit., 'soul for soul'; (*i*) the equivalent of the personal pronoun, used for emphasis and effect:— 1st person, John 10:24 ('us'); Heb. 10:38; cp. Gen 12:13; Num. 23:10; Jud. 16:30; Ps. 120:2 ('me'); 2nd person, 2 Cor. 12:15; Heb. 13:17; Jas. 1:21; 1 Pet. 1:9; 2:25; cp. Lev. 17:11; 26:15; 1 Sam. 1:26; 3rd person, 1 Pet. 4:19; 2 Pet. 2:8; cp. Ex. 30:12; Job 32:2, Heb. 'soul,' Sept. 'self'; (*j*) an animate creature, human or other, 1 Cor. 15:45; Rev. 16:3; cp. Gen. 1:24; 2:7, 19; (*k*) 'the inward man,' the seat of the new life, Luke 21:19 (cp. Matt. 10:39); 1 Pet. 2:11; 3 John 2.

"With (*j*) compare *a-psuchos*, soulless, inanimate, 1 Cor. 14:7. ¶

"With (*f*) compare *di-psuchos*, two-souled, Jas. 1:8; 4:8; ¶ *oligo-psuchos*, feeble-souled, 1 Thess. 5:14; ¶ *iso-psuchos*, like-souled, Phil. 2:20; ¶ *sum-psuchos*, joint-souled ('with one accord'), Phil. 2:2. ¶

"The language of Heb. 4:12 suggests the extreme difficulty of distinguishing between the soul and the spirit, alike in their nature and in their activities. Generally speaking the spirit is the higher, the soul the lower element. The spirit may be recognised as the life principle bestowed on man by God, the soul as the resulting life constituted in the individual, the body being the material organism animated by soul and spirit. . . .

"Body and soul are the constituents of the man according to Matt. 6:25; 10:28; Luke 12:20; Acts 20:10; body and spirit according to Luke 8:55; 1 Cor. 5:3; 7:34; Jas. 2:26. In Matt. 26:38 the emotions are associated with the soul, in John 13:21 with the spirit; cp. also Ps. 42:11 with 1 Kings 21:5. In Ps. 35:9 the soul rejoices in God, in Luke 1:47 the spirit.

"Apparently, then, the relationships may be thus summed up, '*Sōma*, body, and *pneuma*, spirit, may be separated, *pneuma* and *psuchē*, soul, can only be distinguished' (Cremer)."*

NT: B.893b; CB.1267c; K.1342.
OT: nephesh: S.5315; HR.1486a.4; H.1395a; BD.659b.
GEN. REF.: IS.4:587; NB.1208; Z.5:496.

SOUND (Noun and Verb)

A. Nouns.

1. *phōnē* [φωνή, 5456], most frequently "a voice," is translated "sound" in Matt. 24:31 (A.V. marg., "voice"); John 3:8, A.V. (R.V., "voice"); so 1 Cor. 14:7 (1st part), 8; Rev. 1:15; 18:22 (2nd part, R.V., "voice"); A.V. and R.V., in 9:9 (twice); in Acts 2:6, R.V., "(this) sound (was heard)," A.V., "(this) was noised abroad."

NT: B.870c; CB.1264b; K.1287.
OT: qôl: S.6963; HR.1447b.10a; H.1998a,2028b; BD.876d.
GEN. REF.: IS.4:589; NB.–; Z.–.

2. *ēchos* [ἦχος, 2279], a noise, a sound of any sort (Eng., echo), is translated "sound" in Acts 2:2; Heb. 12:19. See ROARING, B, RUMOUR.

NT: B.349d; CB.1242c; K.–.
OT: tāqaʿ: S.8628; HR.620c.4a; H.2541; BD.1075b.
tēqaʿ: S.8629; HR.620c.4b; H.2541a; BD.1075d.
hāmôn: S.1995; HR.620c.2; H.505a; BD.242b.
GEN. REF.: –.

3. *phthongos* [φθόγγος, 5353], akin to *phthengomai*, to utter a voice, occurs in Rom. 10:18; 1 Cor. 14:7. ¶ In the Sept., Psa. 19:4. ¶

NT: B.857c; CB.–; K.–.
OT: –.
GEN. REF.: –.

B. Verbs.

1. *ēcheō* [ἠχέω, 2278], akin to A, No. 2, occurs in 1 Cor. 13:1, "sounding (brass)"; in some mss.; Luke 21:25. See ROARING. ¶

NT: B.349c; CB.1242c; K.311.
OT: hāmāh: S.1993; HR.620c.2; H.505; BD.242a.
GEN. REF.: –.

2. *exēcheō* [ἐξηχέω, 1837], to sound forth as a trumpet or thunder (*ex*, out, and No. 1), is used in 1 Thess. 1:8, "sounded forth," Passive Voice, lit., 'has been sounded out.' ¶ In the Sept., Joel 3:14. ¶

NT: B.276a; CB.–; K.–.
OT: hāmôn: S.1995; HR.495c.1; H.505a; BD.242b.
GEN. REF.: –.

3. *salpizō* [σαλπίζω, 4537], to sound a trumpet (*salpinx*), occurs in Matt. 6:2; 1 Cor. 15:52, "the trumpet shall sound"; Rev. 8:6-8, 10, 12, 13; 9:1, 13; 10:7; 11:15. ¶

NT: B.741a; CB.1268b; K.997.
OT: tāqaʿ: S.8628; HR.1258c.3; H.2541; BD.1075b.
GEN. REF.: –.

4. *bolizō* [βολίζω, 1001], to heave the lead (*bolis*, that which is thrown or hurled, akin to *ballō*, to throw; sounding-lead), to take soundings, occurs in Acts 27:28 (twice). ¶

NT: B.144d; CB.–; K.–.
OT: –.
GEN. REF.: –.

Note: In Luke 1:44, A.V., *ginomai*, to become, is rendered "sounded" (R.V., "came").

SOUND (Adjective), BE SOUND

A. Adjective.

hugiēs [ὑγιής, 5199], whole, healthy, is used metaphorically of "sound speech," Tit. 2:8. See WHOLE.

NT: B.832c; CB.1251c; K.1202.
OT: ḥay: S.2416; HR.1380c.1; H.644a; BD.311d.
(bᵉ) shālôm: S.7965; HR.1380c.2; H.2401a; BD.1022d.
GEN. REF.: –.

* From Notes on Thessalonians by Hogg and Vine, pp. 205-207.

B. Verb.

hugiainō [ὑγιαίνω, 5198], to be healthy, sound in health (Eng., hygiene etc.), translated "safe and sound" in Luke 15:27, is used metaphorically of doctrine, 1 Tim. 1:10; 2 Tim. 4:3; Tit. 1:9; 2:1; of words, 1 Tim. 6:3, R.V. (A.V., "wholesome," R.V. marg., "healthful"); 2 Tim. 1:13; "in the faith," Tit. 1:13 (R.V. marg., "healthy"); "in faith," Tit. 2:2 (R.V. marg., ditto).

NT: B.832b; CB.1251c; K.1202.
OT: shālôm: S.7965; HR.1380b.1b; H.2401a; BD.1022d.
GEN. REF.: IS.4:589; NB.—; Z.—.

Note: For "sound mind" in 2 Tim. 1:7, A.V., see DISCIPLINE; in 1 Pet. 4:7 (A.V., "sober"), see MIND, B, No. 5.

SOUNDNESS

holoklēria [ὁλοκυηρία, 3647], completeness, soundness (akin to *holoklēros*, see ENTIRE), occurs in Acts 3:16. ¶ In the Sept., Isa. 1:6. ¶

NT: B.564c; CB.—; K.442.
OT: mᵉtôm: S.4974; HR.989a.1; H.2522e; BD.1071b.
GEN. REF.: —.

SOUTH, SOUTH WIND

notos [νότος, 3558], denotes (*a*) the south wind, Luke 12:55; Acts 27:13; 28:13; (*b*) south, as a direction, Luke 13:29; Rev. 21:13; (*c*) the South, as a region, Matt. 12:42; Luke 11:31. ¶

NT: B.544a; CB.1260a; K.—.
OT: negeb: S.5045; HR.949c.3; H.1288a; BD.616a.
têmān: S.8486; HR.949c.5; H.872e; BD.412c.
GEN. REF.: IS.4.590; NB.—; Z.5:498.

Note: For *mesēmbria*, Acts 8:26, see NOON.

SOUTH WEST

lips [λίψ, 3047], lit., Libyan, denotes the S.W. wind, Acts 27:12, "(looking) north-east (and south-east)," R.V., lit., '(looking down) the south-west wind (and down the north-west wind)'; to look down a wind was to look in the direction in which it blows. A S.W. wind blows towards the N.E.; the aspect of the haven answers to this. See also under NORTH EAST, NORTH WEST. ¶

NT: B.475d; CB.—; K.—.
OT: negeb: S.5045; HR.879c.3; H.1288a; BD.616a.
têmān: S.8486; HR.879c.4; H.872e; BD.412c.
GEN. REF.: —.

SOW (Noun)

hus [ὑς, 5300], swine (masc. or fem.), is used in the fem. in 2 Pet. 2:22. ¶

NT: B.848d; CB.1252b; K.—.
OT: ḥᵃzîr: S.2386; HR.1418b.1; H.637a; BD.306b.
GEN. REF.: IS.4:673; NB.—; Z.—.

SOW (Verb), SOWER

speirō [σπείρω, 4687], to sow seed, is used (1) literally, especially in the Synoptic Gospels; elsewhere, 1 Cor. 15:36, 37; 2 Cor. 9:10, "the sower"; (2) metaphorically, (*a*) in proverbial sayings, e.g., Matt. 13:3, 4; Luke 19:21, 22; John 4:37; 2 Cor. 9:6; (*b*) in the interpretation of parables, e.g., Matt. 13:19-23 (in these vv., R.V., "was sown," for A.V., "received seed"); (*c*) otherwise as follows: of sowing "spiritual things" in preaching and teaching, 1 Cor. 9:11; of the interment of the bodies of deceased believers, 1 Cor. 15:42-44; of ministering to the necessities of others in things temporal (the harvest being proportionate to the sowing), 2 Cor. 9:6, 10 (see above); of sowing to the flesh, Gal. 6:7, 8 ("that" in ver. 7 is emphatic, 'that and that only,' what was actually sown); in ver. 8, *eis*, "unto," signifies 'in the interests of'; of the "fruit of righteousness" by peacemakers, Jas. 3:18.

NT: B.761b; CB.1269c; K.1065.
OT: zāraʿ: S.2232; HR.1282a.2a,b; H.582; BD.281b.
GEN. REF.: IS.4:590; NB.—; Z.—.

SPACE

A. Noun.

diastēma [διάστημα, 1292], an interval, space (akin to B), is used of time in Acts 5:7. ¶

NT: B.188d; CB.—; K.—.
OT: migrāsh: S.4054; HR.311c.7; H.388c; BD.177b.
gizrāh: S.1508; HR.311c.5; H.340c; BD.160d.
rewaḥ: S.7305; HR.311c.10; H.2132a; BD.926c.
GEN. REF.: —.

B. Verb.

diistēmi [διίστημι, 1339], to set apart, separate (*dia*, apart, *histēmi*, to cause to stand), see A, is rendered "after the space of" in Luke 22:59; in Acts 27:28, with *brachu*, a little, R.V., "after a little space" (A.V., "when they had gone a little further"). See PART.

NT: B.195b; CB.—; K.—.
OT: ḥālaq: S.2505; HR.330b.2; H.669; BD.323c.
pārad: S.6504; HR.330b.4; H.1806; BD.825b.
GEN. REF.: —.

Notes: (1) In Acts 15:33 and Rev. 2:21, A.V., *chronos*, time (R.V.), is translated "space."

(2) In Acts 19:8 and 10, *epi*, for or during (of time), is translated "for the space of"; in 19:34, "about the space of."

(3) In Acts 5:34, A.V., *brachu* (the neuter of *brachus*, short), used adverbially, is translated "a little space" (R.V. ". . . while").

(4) In Gal. 2:1, *dia*, through, is rendered "after the space of," R.V., stressing the length of the period mentioned (a.v., "after," which would represent the preposition *meta*).

(5) In Jas. 5:17 there is no word in the original representing the phrase "by the space of," A.V. (R.V., "for").

(6) In Rev. 14:20, A.V., *apo*, away from, is translated "by the space of" (R.V., "as far as").

(7) In Rev. 17:10, A.V., *oligon*, "a little while" (R.V.), is rendered "a short space."

SPARE, SPARINGLY

A. Verbs.

pheidomai [φείδομαι, 5339], to spare, i.e., to forego the infliction of that evil or retribution which was designed, is used with a negative in Acts 20:29; Rom. 8:32; 11:21 (twice); 2 Cor. 13:2; 2 Pet. 2:4, 5; positively, in 1 Cor. 7:28; 2 Cor. 1:3; rendered "forbear" in 2 Cor. 12:6. See FORBEAR. ¶

NT: B.854d; CB.–; K.–.
OT: ḥûs: S.2347; HR.1426a.1a; H.626; BD.299b.
ḥāmal: S.2550; HR.1426a.2a; H.676; BD.328a.
GEN. REF.: IS.4:592; NB.–; Z.–.

Note: In Luke 15:17, *perisseuō*, to abound, have abundance, is translated "have enough and to spare."

B. Adverb.

pheidomenōs [φειδομένως, 5340], akin to A, "sparingly," occurs in 2 Cor. 9:6 (twice), of sowing and reaping. ¶

NT: B.854d; CB.1264a; K.–.
OT: –.
GEN. REF.: IS.4:592; NB.–; Z.–.

SPARROW

strouthion [στρουθίον, 4765], a diminutive of *strouthos*, a sparrow, occurs in Matt. 10:29, 31; Luke 12:6, 7. ¶

NT: B.771c; CB.1270b; K.1096.
OT: ṣippôr: S.6833; HR.1297a.3; H.1959a; BD.861d.
GEN. REF.: IS.4:593; NB.154; Z.5:500.

SPEAK

1. *legō* [λέγω, —], to say, speak: see SAY, No. 1.

2. *laleō* [λαλέω, 2980], for which say SAY, No. 2, is used several times in 1 Cor. 14; the command prohibiting women from speaking in a church gathering vv. 34, 35, is regarded by some as an injunction against chattering, a meaning which is absent from the use of the verb everywhere else in the N.T.; it is to be understood in the same sense as in vv. 2, 3-6, 9, 11, 13, 18, 19, 21, 23, 27-29, 39.

NT: B.463a; CB.1256b; K.505.
OT: dābar: S.1696; HR.841c.2c; H.399; BD.180b.
GEN. REF.: –.

3. *proslaleō* [προσλαλέω, 4354], to speak to or with (*pros*, to, and No. 2), is used in Acts 13:43 and 28:20. ¶

NT: B.717b; CB.–; K.–.
OT: dābar: S.1696; HR.1218b.1; H.399; BD.180b.
GEN. REF.: –.

4. *phthengomai* [φθέγγομαι, 5350], to utter a sound or voice, is translated to speak in Acts 4:18; 2 Pet. 2:16; in 2:18, A.V., "speak" (R.V., "utter").

NT: B.857a; CB.–; K.–.
OT: nābaʻ: S.5042; HR.1429c.2; H.1287; BD.615d.
ʻānāh: S.6030; HR.1429c.3; H.1650,1653; BD.772c.
sîaḥ: S.7878; HR.1429c.4; H.2255; BD.967a.
GEN. REF.: –.

5. *apophthengomai* [ἀποφθέγγομαι, 669], to speak forth (*apo*, forth, and No. 4), is so rendered in Acts 2:14, R.V. (A.V., "said"), and 26:25; in 2:2 it denotes to give utterance. ¶

NT: B.102a; CB.1237a; K.75.
OT: nābāʼ: S.5012; HR.150a.2a; H.1277; BD.612a.
nābaʻ: S.5042; HR.150a.3; H.1287; BD.615d.
ʻānan: S.6049; HR.150a.4; H.1655,1656; BD.778a.
GEN. REF.: –.

6. *antilegō* [ἀντιλέγω, 483], to speak against, is so rendered in Luke 2:34; John 19:12; Acts 13:45, A.V. (R.V., "contradicted"); 28:19, 22. See CONTRADICT, GAINSAY.

NT: B.74d; CB.–; K.–.
OT: rîb: S.7378; HR.111a.2; H.2159; BD.936b.
GEN. REF.: –.

7. *katalaleō* [καταλαλέω, 2635], synonymous with No. 6 (*kata*, against, and No. 2), is always translated to speak against in the R.V. See BACKBITER, *Note*.

NT: B.413b; CB.1254a; K.495.
OT: dābar: S.1696; HR.735a.2; H.399; BD.180b.
GEN. REF.: –.

8. *kakologeō* [κακολογέω, 2551], to speak evil: see CURSE, B, No. 4.

NT: B.397b; CB.1253b; K.391.
OT: –.
GEN. REF.: –

9. *sullaleō* [συλλαλέω, 4814], to speak together (*sun*, with, and No. 2), is rendered "spake together" in Luke 4:36, R.V. See COMMUNE, No. 3, CONFER, No. 2, TALK.

NT: B.776d; CB.–; K.–.
OT: dābar: S.1696; HR.1301c.1; H.399; BD.180b.
sîaḥ: S.7878; HR.1301c.2; H.2255; BD.967a.
GEN. REF.: –.

10. *proeipon* [προεῖπον, 4302], to speak or say before (a 2nd aorist tense from an obsolete present), is rendered to speak before in Acts 1:16; 2 Pet. 3:2; Jude 17. See FORETELL.

NT: B.704d; CB.–; K.–.
OT: –.
GEN. REF.: –.

11. *prophthanō* [προφθάνω, 4399], to anticipate (an extension, by *pro*, before, of *phthanō*, which has the same meaning), is rendered "spake first" in Matt. 17:25, R.V. (A.V., "prevented"). ¶

NT: B.724b; CB.–; K.1258.
OT: qādam: S.6923; HR.1233c.1; H.1988; BD.869d.
GEN. REF.: –.

12. *prosphōneō* [προσφωνέω, 4377], to address, call to, is rendered "spake unto" (or "to") in Luke 23:20; Acts 21:40; 22:2; "to call

unto" (or "to") in Matt. 11.16; Luke 6:13; 7:32, 13:12. ¶
NT: B.720c; CB.–; K.–.
OT: –.
GEN. REF.: –.

13. *eirō* [εἴρω, 3004], for which see SAY, No. 4, has a 1st aorist, passive participle *rhēthen*, "spoken" or "spoken of," used in Matt. 1:22; 2:15, 17, 23; 3:3; 4:14; 8:17; 12:17; 13:35; 21:4; 22:31; 24:15; 27:9 (in some texts in 27:35 and Mark 13:14).

Notes: (1) In Heb. 12:5, A.V., *dialegomai*, to discuss, to reason, is translated "speaketh" (R.V., "reasoneth").

(2) In Heb. 12:25, A.V. *chrēmatizō*, to warn, instruct, is translated "spake" (R.V., "warned"): see ADMONISH.

(3) In Eph. 4:31, A.V., *blasphēmia* is translated "evil speaking": see RAILING

(4) In Heb. 12:19, *prostithēmi*, to put to, add, used with *logos*, a word, is rendered "(that no word) more should be spoken," R.V. [A.V., "(that) the word should (not) be spoken (to them) any more"].

(5) In Acts 26:24, A.V., *apologeomai*, to make a defence (R.V.), is rendered "spake for himself." See ANSWER, B. No. 4.

(6) In Rom. 15:21. A.V., *anangellō*, to bring back word (R.V., "tidings . . . came"), is translated "he was . . . spoken of."

(7) For "is spoken of" in Rom. 1:8, A.V., see PROCLAIM, No. 2.

(8) For "spake out" in Luke 1:42, A.V., see VOICE, *Note*.

(9) In Gal. 4:15, there is no verb in the original for the A.V., "ye spake of" (see R.V.).

(10) For "spoken against" in Acts 19:36 see GAINSAY, C.

(11) For "speak reproachfully," 1 Tim. 5:14, see REVILE, C.

(12) In Acts 21:3, A.V., *ginōskō* is translated "speak," R.V., "know."

SPEAKER (chief)

Note: In Acts 14:12 the verb *hēgeomai*, to lead the way, be the chief, is used in the present participle with the article (together equivalent to a noun), followed by the genitive case of *logos*, speech, with the article, the phrase being rendered "the chief speaker," lit., 'the leader of the discourse.' See CHIEF, C.

SPEAKING (evil, much)

polulogia [πολυλογία, 4180], loquacity, "much speaking" (*polus*, much, *logos*, speech), is used in Matt. 6:7. ¶ In the Sept., Prov. 10:19. ¶
NT: B.687b; CB.–; K.911.
OT: (rōb) d^ebārîm: S.1697; HR.1181a.1; H.399a; BD.182a,183b.
GEN. REF.: –.

Note: For "evil speaking(s)," in Eph. 4:31, see RAILING; in 1 Pet. 2:1, see BACKBITING. For "shameful speaking" see COMMUNICATION, B, *Note*.

SPEAR

lonchē [λόγχη, 3057], primarily a spear-head, then, a lance or spear, occurs in John 19:34; some texts have it in Matt. 27:49. ¶ As to John 19:29, there is an old conjecture, mentioned by Field (*Notes on the Trans. of the N.T.*), to the effect that the sponge was put on a spear (*hussos*, a javelin, the Roman *pilum*, instead of *hussōpos*, hyssop).
NT: B.479b; CB.–; K.–.
OT: rōmaḥ: S.7420; HR.887b.5; H.2172; BD.942b.
GEN. REF.: IS.4:1036; NB.84; Z.1:318.

SPEARMAN

dexiolabos [δεξιολάβος, 1187], from *dexios*, the right (hand), and *lambanō*, to lay hold of, is used in the plural in Acts 23:23, "spearmen." Some texts have *dexiobolos*, one who throws with his right hand (*ballō*, to throw), 'right-handed slingers.' ¶
NT: B.174c; CB.–; K.–.
OT: –.
GEN. REF.: –.

SPECIAL

Note: Tuchōn, the 2nd aorist participle of *tunchanō*, to happen, meet with, chance, is used with a negative signifying 'not common or ordinary,' special, Acts 19:11; so in 28:2. See COMMON, B, *Note* (3).

For **SPECIALLY** see **ESPECIALLY**

SPECTACLE

theatron [θέατρον, 2302], akin to *theaomai*, to behold, denotes (*a*) a theatre (used also as a place of assembly), Acts 19:29, 31; (*b*) a spectacle, a show, metaphorically in 1 Cor. 4:9. See THEATRE. ¶
NT: B.353c; CB.1271c; K.318.
OT: –.
GEN. REF.: IS.4:824; NB.–; Z.–.

SPEECH

1. *logos* [λόγος, 3056], akin to *legō* (SPEAK, No. 1.), most frequently rendered 'word' (for an analysis see WORD), signifies speech, as follows: (*a*) discourse, e.g., Luke 20:20, R.V., "speech" (A.V., "words"); Acts 14:12 (see SPEAKER); 20:7; 1 Cor. 2:1, 4; 4:19, A.V. (R.V., "word"); 2 Cor. 10:10; (*b*) the faculty of speech, e.g., 2 Cor. 11:6; (*c*) the manner of speech, e.g., Matt. 5:37, R.V., "speech" (A.V., "communication"); Col. 4:6; (*d*) manner of instruction, Tit. 2:8; 1 Cor. 14:9, R.V. (A.V., "words"); Eph. 4:29, R.V. (A.V., "communication"). See SAYING.

NT: B.477a; CB.1257a; K.505.
OT: dābār: S.1697; HR.881c.2a; H.399a; BD.182a.
GEN. REF.: IS.4:594; NB.—; Z.—.

2. *lalia* [λαλιά, 2981], akin to *laleō* (SPEAK, No. 2), denotes talk, speech, (*a*) of a dialect, Matt. 26:73; Mark 14:70; (*b*) utterances, John 4:42, R.V., "speaking" (A.V., "saying"); 8:43. ¶

NT: B.464a; CB.1256c; K.—.
OT: dābār: S.1697; HR.846c.2a; H.399a; BD.182a.
GEN. REF.: IS.4:594; NB.—; Z.—.

3. *eulogia* [εὐλογία, 2129], has the meaning fair speaking, flattering speech in Rom. 16:18, R.V., "fair speech" (A.V., "fair speeches"). See BLESSING, C, No. 1.

NT: B.322d; CB.1247b; K.—.
OT: b^e^rākāh: S.1293; HR.574b.2d; H.285b; BD.139c.
GEN. REF.: —.

4. *chrēstologia* [χρηστολογία, 5542], which has a similar meaning to No. 3 occurs with it in Rom. 16:18 [R.V., "smooth . . . (speech)"]. See SMOOTH, *Note*. ¶

NT: B.886a; CB.1240a; K.1320.
OT: —.
GEN. REF.: —.

Notes: (1) For "persuasiveness of speech," Col. 2:4, R.V., see PERSUASIVE, B.

(2) In Acts 14:11 "the speech of Lycaonia" translates the adverb *Lukaonisti*. Lycaonia was a large country in the centre and south of the plateau of Asia Minor; the villages retained the native language, but cities like Lystra probably had a Seleucid tone in their laws and customs (Ramsay on Galatians).

SPEECHLESS

1. *eneos* (or *enneos*) [ἐνεός, 1769], dumb, speechless, occurs in Acts 9:7. ¶ In the Sept., Prov. 17:28; Isa. 56:10. ¶

NT: B.265a; CB.—; K.—.
OT: 'illēm: S.483; HR.472c.1; H.102c; BD.48a.
GEN. REF.: IS.4:594; NB.—; Z.—.

2. *kōphos* [κωφός, 2974], which means either deaf or dumb (see DEAF), is translated "speechless" in Luke 1:22.

NT: B.462a; CB.1255c; K.—.
OT: ḥērēsh: S.2795; HR.840c.2; H.761a; BD.361b.
GEN. REF.: —.

Note: For *phimoō*, translated "he was speechless" in Matt. 22:12, see MUZZLE, SILENCE.

SPEED, SPEEDILY

Notes: (1) In Acts 17:15 "with all speed" is the rendering of the phrase *hōs*, as, *tachista*, most speedily (the superlative of *tachu*, speedily), i.e., as speedily as possible.

(2) For "speedily," *en tachei*, in Luke 18:8, see QUICKLY, No. 4.

(3) For "God speed" see GREETING, A, No. 2.

SPEND, SPENT

1. *dapanaō* [δαπανάω, 1159], denotes (*a*) to expend, spend, Mark 5:26 [for Acts 21:24 see CHARGE, Note (5)]: 2 Cor. 12:15 (1st part: for "be spent," see No. 2); (*b*) to consume, squander, Luke 15:14; Jas. 4:3. See CONSUME, *Note*. ¶

NT: B.171a; CB.—; K.—.
OT: —.
GEN. REF.: —.

2. *ekdapanaō* [ἐκδαπανάω, 1550], lit., to spend out (*ek*), an intensive form of No. 1, to spend entirely, is used in 2 Cor. 12:15, in the Passive Voice, with reflexive significance, to spend oneself out (for others), "will . . . be spent," R.V. marg., "spent out" (see No. 1). ¶

NT: B.238b; CB.—; K.—.
OT: —.
GEN. REF.: —.

3. *prosdapanaō* [προσδαπανάω, 4325], to spend besides (*pros*, and No. 1), is used in Luke 10:35, "thou spendest more." ¶

NT: B.712a; CB.—; K.—.
OT: —.
GEN. REF.: —.

4. *prosanaliskō* [προσαναλίσκω, 4321], to spend besides, a strengthened form of *analiskō*, to expend, consume (see CONSUME, No. 1), occurs in most texts in Luke 8:43. ¶

NT: B.711c; CB.—; K.—.
OT: —.
GEN. REF.: —.

5. *diaginomai* [διαγίνομαι, 1230], used of time, to intervene, elapse, is rendered "was spent" in Acts 27:9. See PAST.

NT: B.182b; CB.—; K.—.
OT: —.
GEN. REF.: —.

6. *prokoptō* [προκόπτω, 4298], to cut forward a way, advance, is translated "is far spent," in Rom. 13:12, said metaphorically of "the night," the whole period of man's alienation from God. Though the tense is the aorist, it must not be rendered 'was far spent,' as if it referred, e.g., to Christ's first Advent. The aorist is here perfective. See ADVANCE.

NT: B.707d; CB.1266c; K.939.
OT: —.
GEN. REF.: —.

7. *klinō* [κλίνω, 2827], to lean, decline, is said of the decline of day in Luke 24:29, "is (now) far spent," lit., 'has declined.' See Bow (Verb).
NT: B.436c; CB.–; K.–.
OT: nāṭāh: S.5186; HR.771a.7; H.1352; BD.639d.
GEN. REF.: –.

8. *ginomai* [γίνομαι, 1096], to become, occur, is rendered "was far spent" in Mark 6:35, lit., 'much hour (i.e., many an hour) having taken place.'
NT: B.158a; CB.1248b; K.117.
OT: –.
GEN. REF.: –.

9. *poieō* [ποιέω, 4160], to do, is translated "have spent (*but* one hour)," in Matt. 20:12, R.V. (A.V., "have wrought") lit., as in the Eng., idiom, 'have done one hour'; so in Acts 20:3, R.V., "when he had spent (lit., 'had done') three months" (A.V., "abode").
NT: B.680d; CB.1265c; K.895.
OT: –.
GEN. REF.: –.

10. *eukaireō* [εὐκαιρέω, 2119], to have leisure or devote one's leisure to, is translated "spent their time," in Acts 17:21. See Leisure.
NT: B.321b; CB.1247b; K.–.
OT: –.
GEN. REF.: –.

11. *chronotribeō* [χρονοτριβέω, 5551], to spend time (*chronos*, time, *tribō*, to rub, to wear out), occurs in Acts 20:16. ¶
NT: B.888c; CB.1240b; K.–.
OT: –.
GEN. REF.: –.

Note: Polus, much, is rendered "far spent" (twice in Mark 6:35, R.V.

SPEW (A.V., SPUE)

emeō [ἐμέω, 1692], to vomit (cp. Eng., emetic), is used in Rev. 3:16, figuratively of the Lord's utter abhorrence of the condition of the church at Laodicea. ¶ In the Sept., Isa. 19:14. ¶
NT: B.254d; CB.1244b; K.–.
OT: qî': S.6958; HR.456a.1; H.2014; BD.883c.
GEN. REF.: –.

SPICE(S)

1. *arōma* [ἄρωμα, 759], spice, occurs in Mark 16:1, R.V., "spices" (A.V., "sweet sp."); Luke 23:56; 24:1; John 19:40. ¶ A papyrus document has it in a list of articles for a sacrifice.
NT: B.114a; CB.1237c; K.–.
OT: bōshem: S.1314; HR.169b.1; H.290a; BD.141d.
GEN. REF.: IS.4:596; NB.1209; Z.5:501.

2. *amōmon* [ἄμωμον, —], *amomum*, probably a word of Semitic origin, a fragrant plant of India, is translated "spice" in Rev. 18:13, R.V. (A.V., "odours"). ¶
NT: B.47d; CB.1234c; K.619.
OT: –.
GEN. REF.: IS.4:596; NB.–; Z.–.

SPIKENARD

nardos [νάρδος, 3487], is derived, through the Semitic languages (Heb. *nērd*, Syriac *nardin*), from the Sanskrit *nalada*, a fragrant oil, procured from the stem of an Indian plant. The Arabs call it the Indian spike. The adjective *pistikos* is attached to it in the N.T., Mark 14:3; John 12:3; *pistikos*, if taken as an ordinary Greek word, would signify 'genuine.' There is evidence, however, that it was regarded as a technical term. It has been suggested that the original reading was *pistakēs*, i.e., the *Pistacia Terebinthus*, which grows in Cyprus, Syria, Palestine, etc., and yields a resin of very fragrant odour, and in such inconsiderable quantities as to be very costly. "Nard was frequently mixed with aromatic ingredients . . . so when scented with the fragrant resin of the *pistakē* it would quite well be called *nardos pistakēs*" (E. N. Bennett, in the *Classical Review* for 1890, Vol. iv, p. 319. The oil used for the anointing of the Lord's head was worth about £12, and must have been of the most valuable kind. ¶ In the Sept., S. of Sol. 1:12; 4:13, 14. ¶
NT: B.534a; CB.–; K.–.
OT: nēred: S.5373; HR.939c.1; H.1420; BD.669d.
GEN. REF.: IS.3:490; NB.1210; Z.5:502.

SPILL

ekchunnō (or *ekchunō* [ἐκχύννω, 1632], to pour out, shed, is rendered "be spilled" in Luke 5:37. See Pour, Shed.
NT: B.247b; CB.1243b; K.220.
OT: –.
GEN. REF.: –.

Note: Some texts have *ekcheō* in Mark 2:22 (so A.V.). The form in Luke 5:37 might also come from *ekcheō*.

SPIN

nēthō [νήθω, 3514], to spin, is found in Matt. 6:28 and Luke 12:27, of the lilies of the field (see Lily. ¶
NT: B.537c; CB.–; K.–.
OT: ṭāwāh: S.2901; HR.944b.1a; H.794; BD.376a.
maṭweh: S.4299; HR.944b.1b; H.794a; BD.376a.
GEN. REF.: IS.4:597; NB.1210; Z.5:502.

SPIRIT

pneuma [πνεῦμα, 4151], primarily denotes the wind (akin to *pneō*, to breathe, blow); also breath; then, especially the spirit, which, like the wind, is invisible, immaterial and powerful. The N.T. uses of the word may be analysed approximately as follows:

"(*a*) the wind, John 3:8 (where marg. is, perhaps, to be preferred); Heb. 1:7; cp. Amos

4:13, Sept.; (*b*) the breath, 2 Thess. 2:8; Rev. 11:11; 13:15; cp. Job 12:10, Sept.; (*c*) the immaterial, invisible part of man, Luke 8:55; Acts 7:59; 1 Cor. 5:5; Jas. 2:26; cp. Ecc. 12:7, Sept.; (*d*) the disembodied (or 'unclothed,' or 'naked,' 2 Cor. 5:3, 4) man, Luke 24:37, 39; Heb. 12:23; 1 Pet. 4:6; (*e*) the resurrection body, 1 Cor. 15:45; 1 Tim. 3:16; 1 Pet. 3:18; (*f*) the sentient element in man, that by which he perceives, reflects, feels, desires, Matt. 5:3; 26:41; Mark 2:8; Luke 1:47, 80; Acts 17:16; 20:22; 1 Cor. 2:11; 5:3, 4; 14:4, 15; 2 Cor. 7:1; cp. Gen. 26:35; Isa. 26:9; Ezek. 13:3; Dan. 7:15; (*g*) purpose, aim, 2 Cor. 12:18; Phil. 1:27; Eph. 4:23; Rev. 19:10; cp. Ezra 1:5; Ps. 78:8; Dan. 5:12; (*h*) the equivalent of the personal pronoun, used for emphasis and effect: 1st person, 1 Cor. 16:18; cp. Gen 6:3; 2nd person, 2 Tim. 4:22; Philm. 25; cp. Ps. 139:7; 3rd person, 2 Cor. 7:13; cp. Isa. 40:13; (*i*) character, Luke 1:17; Rom. 1:4; cp. Num. 14:24; (*j*) moral qualities and activities: bad, as of bondage, as of a slave, Rom. 8:15; cp. Isa. 61:3; stupor, Rom. 11:8; cp. Isa. 29:10; timidity, 2 Tim. 1:7; cp. Josh. 5:1; good, as of adoption, i.e., liberty as of a son, Rom. 8:15; cp. Ps. 51:12; meekness, 1 Cor. 4:21; cp. Prov. 16:19; faith, 2 Cor. 4:13; quietness, 1 Pet. 3:4; cp. Prov. 14:29; (*k*) the Holy Spirit, e.g., Matt. 4:1 (see below); Luke 4:18; (*l*) 'the inward man' (an expression used only of the believer, Rom. 7:22; 2 Cor. 4:16; Eph. 3:16); the new life, Rom. 8:4-6, 10, 16; Heb. 12:9; cp. Psa. 51.10; (*m*) unclean spirits, demons, Matt. 8:16; Luke 4:33; 1 Pet. 3:19; cp. 1 Sam. 18:10; (*n*) angels, Heb. 1:14; cp. Acts 12:15; (*o*) divine gift for service, 1 Cor. 14:12, 32; (*p*) by metonymy, those who claim to be depositories of these gifts, 2 Thess. 2:2; 1 John 4:1-3; (*q*) the significance, as contrasted with the form, of words, or of a rite, John 6:63; Rom. 2:29; 7:6; 2 Cor. 3:6; (*r*) a vision, Rev. 1:10; 4:2; 17:3; 21:10."*

NT: B.674c; CB.1265b; K.876.
OT: rûaḥ: S.7307; HR.1151c.3; H.2131a; BD.924c.
GEN. REF.: IS.4:599; NB.1211; Z.5:503.

Notes: (1) For *phantasma*, rendered "spirit," Matt. 14:26; Mark 6:49, A.V., see APPARITION.

(2) For the distinction between spirit and soul, see under SOUL, last three paragraphs.

The Holy Spirit

The Holy Spirit is spoken of under various titles in the N.T. ('Spirit' and 'Ghost' are renderings of the same word *pneuma*; the advantage of the rendering 'Spirit' is that it can always be used, whereas 'Ghost' always requires the word 'Holy' prefixed.) In the following list the omission of the definite article marks its omission in the original (concerning this see below): "Spirit, Matt. 22:43; Eternal Spirit, Heb. 9:14; the Spirit, Matt. 4:1; Holy Spirit, Matt. 1:18; the Holy Spirit, Matt. 28:19; the Spirit, the Holy, Matt. 12:32; the Spirit of promise, the Holy, Eph. 1:13; Spirit of God, Rom. 8:9; Spirit of (the) living God, 2 Cor. 3:3; the Spirit of God, 1 Cor. 2:11; the Spirit of our God, 1 Cor. 6:11; the Spirit of God, the Holy, Eph. 4:30; the Spirit of glory and of God, 1 Pet. 4:14; the Spirit of Him that raised up Jesus from the dead (i.e., God), Rom. 8:11; the Spirit of your Father, Matt. 10:20; the Spirit of His Son, Gal. 4:6; Spirit of (the) Lord, Acts 8:39; the Spirit of (the) Lord, Acts 5:9; (the) Lord, (the) Spirit, 2 Cor. 3:18; the Spirit of Jesus, Acts 16:7; Spirit of Christ, Rom. 8:9; the Spirit of Jesus Christ, Phil. 1:19; Spirit of adoption, Rom. 8:15; the Spirit of truth, John 14:17; the Spirit of life, Rom. 8:2; the Spirit of grace, Heb. 10:29."†

The use or absence of the article in the original where the Holy Spirit is spoken of, cannot always be decided by grammatical rules, nor can the presence or absence of the article alone determine whether the reference is to the Holy Spirit. Examples where the Person is meant when the article is absent are Matt. 22:43 (the article is used in Mark 12:36); Acts 4:25, R.V. (absent in some texts); 19:2, 6; Rom. 14:17; 1 Cor. 2:4; Gal. 5:25 (twice); 1 Pet. 1:2. Sometimes the absence is to be accounted for by the fact that *Pneuma* (like *Theos*) is substantially a proper name, e.g., in John 7:39. As a general rule the article is present where the subject of the teaching is the Personality of the Holy Spirit, e.g., John 14:26, where He is spoken of in distinction from the Father and the Son. See also 15:26 and cp. Luke 3:22.

In Gal. 3:3, in the phrase "having begun in the Spirit," it is difficult to say whether the reference is to the Holy Spirit or to the quickened spirit of the believer; that it possibly refers to the latter is not to be determined by the absence of the article, but by the contrast with "the flesh"; on the other hand, the contrast may be between the Holy Spirit who in the believer sets His seal on the perfect work of Christ, and the flesh which seeks to better

* From Notes on Thessalonians by Hogg and Vine, pp. 204, 205.

† From Notes on Galatians by Hogg and Vine, p. 193.

itself by works of its own. There is no preposition before either noun, and if the reference is to the quickened spirit it cannot be dissociated from the operation of the Holy Spirit. In Gal. 4:29 the phrase "after the Spirit" signifies 'by supernatural power,' in contrast to "after the flesh," i.e., 'by natural power,' and the reference must be to the Holy Spirit; so in 5:17.

The full title with the article before both *pneuma* and *hagios* (the "resumptive" use of the article), lit., 'the Spirit the Holy,' stresses the character of the Person, e.g., Matt. 12:32; Mark 3:29; 12:36; 13:11; Luke 2:26, 10:21 (R.V.); John 14:26; Acts 1:16; 5:3; 7:51; 10:44, 47; 13:2; 15:28; 19:6; 20:23, 28; 21:11; 28:25; Eph. 4:30; Heb. 3:7; 9:8; 10:15.

The Personality of the Spirit is emphasized at the expense of strict grammatical procedure in John 14:26; 15:26; 16:8, 13, 14, where the emphatic pronoun *ekeinos*, "He," is used of Him in the masculine, whereas the noun *pneuma* is neuter in Greek, while the corresponding word in Aramaic, the language in which our Lord probably spoke, is feminine (*rûchâ*, cf. Heb. *rûach*). The rendering "itself" in Rom. 8:16, 26, due to the Greek gender, is corrected to "Himself" in the R.V.

The subject of the Holy Spirit in the N.T. may be considered as to His Divine attributes; His distinct Personality in the Godhead; His operation in connection with the Lord Jesus in His Birth, His life, His baptism, His Death; His operations in the world; in the Church; His having been sent at Pentecost by the Father and by Christ; His operations in the individual believer; in local churches; His operations in the production of Holy Scripture; His work in the world, etc.

SPIRITUAL

A. Adjective.

pneumatikos [πνευματικός, 4152], "always connotes the ideas of invisibility and of power. It does not occur in the Sept. nor in the Gospels; it is in fact an after-Pentecost word. In the N.T. it is used as follows: (*a*) the angelic hosts, lower than God but higher in the scale of being than man in his natural state, are 'spiritual hosts,' Eph. 6:12; (*b*) things that have their origin with God, and which, therefore, are in harmony with His character, as His law is, are 'spiritual,' Rom. 7:14; (*c*) 'spiritual' is prefixed to the material type in order to indicate that what the type sets forth, not the type itself, is intended, 1 Cor. 10:3, 4; (*d*) the purposes of God revealed in the gospel by the Holy Spirit, 1 Cor. 2:13a, and the words in which that revelation is expressed, are 'spiritual,' 13b, matching, or combining, spiritual things with spiritual words [or, alternatively, 'interpreting spiritual things to spiritual men,' see (*e*) below]; 'spiritual songs' are songs of which the burden is the things revealed by the Spirit, Eph. 5:19; Col. 3:16; 'spiritual wisdom and understanding' is wisdom in, and understanding of, those things, Col. 1:9; (*e*) men in Christ who walk so as to please God are 'spiritual,' Gal. 6:1; 1 Cor. 2:13b [but see (*d*) above], 15; 3:1; 14:37; (*f*) the whole company of those who believe in Christ is a 'spiritual house,' 1 Pet. 2:5a; (*g*) the blessings that accrue to regenerate men at this present time are called 'spiritualities,' Rom. 15:27; 1 Cor. 9:11; 'spiritual blessings,' Eph. 1:3; 'spiritual gifts,' Rom. 1:11; (*h*) the activities Godward of regenerate men are 'spiritual sacrifices,' 1 Pet. 2:5b; their appointed activities in the churches are also called 'spiritual gifts,' lit., 'spiritualities,' 1 Cor. 12:1; 14:1; (*i*) the resurrection body of the dead in Christ is 'spiritual,' i.e., such as is suited to the heavenly environment, 1 Cor. 15:44; (*j*) all that is produced and maintained among men by the operations of the Spirit of God is 'spiritual,' 1 Cor. 15:46. . . .

"The spiritual man is one who walks by the Spirit both in the sense of Gal. 5:16 and in that of 5:25, and who himself manifests the fruit of the Spirit in his own ways. . . .

"According to the Scriptures, the 'spiritual' state of soul is normal for the believer, but to this state all believers do not attain, nor when it is attained is it always maintained. Thus the Apostle, in 1 Cor. 3:1-3, suggests a contrast between this spiritual state and that of the babe in Christ, i.e., of the man who because of immaturity and inexperience has not yet reached spirituality, and that of the man who by permitting jealousy, and the strife to which jealousy always leads, has lost it. The spiritual state is reached by diligence in the Word of God and in prayer; it is maintained by obedience and self-judgment. Such as are led by the Spirit are spiritual, but, of course, spirituality is not a fixed or absolute condition, it admits of growth; indeed growth in 'the grace and knowledge of our Lord and Saviour Jesus Christ,' 2 Pet. 3:18, is evidence of true spirituality."*

NT: B.678d; CB.1265c; K.876.
OT: —.
GEN. REF.: IS.4:599; NB.1211; Z.5:503.

* From Notes on Galatians by Hogg and Vine, pp. 308-310.

B. Adverb.

pneumatikōs [πνευματικῶς, 4153], spiritually, occurs in 1 Cor. 2:14, with the meaning as (*j*) above, and Rev. 11:8, with the meaning as in (*c*). Some mss. have it in 1 Cor. 2:13. ¶

NT: B.679b; CB.1265c; K.–.
OT: –.
GEN. REF.: IS.4:599; NB.1211; Z.5:503.

Notes: (1) In Rom. 8:6, the R.V. rightly renders the noun *pneuma* "(the mind) of the spirit," A.V., "spiritual (mind)."

(2) In 1 Cor. 14:12 the plural of *pneuma*, "spirits," R.V., marg., stands for "spiritual *gifts*" (text).

(3) In 1 Pet. 2:2, the R.V. renders *iogikos* "spiritual."

SPIT

1. *ptuō* [πτύω, 4429], to spit, occurs in Mark 7:33; 8:23; John 9:6. ¶ In the Sept., Numb. 12:14. ¶

NT: B.727d; CB.–; K.–.
OT: yāraq: S.3417; HR.1238c.1; H.918,919; BD.439a.
GEN. REF.: IS.4:604; NB.1214; Z.5:509.

2. *emptuō* [ἐμπτύω, 1716], to spit upon (*en*, in, and No. 1), occurs in Matt. 26:67; 27:30; Mark 10:34; 14:65; 15:19; Luke 18:32. ¶ In the Sept., Numb. 12:14, in some texts; Deut. 25:9. ¶

NT: B.257c; CB.–; K.–.
OT: yāraq: S.3417; HR.1238c.1; H.918,919; BD.439a.
GEN. REF.: IS.4:604; NB.1214; Z.5:509.

SPITEFULLY (ENTREAT)

hubrizō [ὑβρίζω, 5195], used transitively, denotes to outrage, treat insolently; to entreat shamefully in Matt. 22:6, R.V. (A.V., "spitefully"); so in Luke 18:32, R.V.; in Acts 14:5 (A.V., "use despitefully"); in 1 Thess. 2:2, A.V. and R.V.; in Luke 11:45, "reproachest." See DESPITEFULLY, ENTREAT, REPROACH, SHAMEFULLY. ¶

NT: B.831d; CB.1251c; K.1200.
OT: qālal: S.7043; HR.1379c.3; H.2028; BD.886b.
GEN. REF.: –.

SPITTLE

ptusma [πτύσμα, 4427], akin to *ptuō*, to spit, occurs in John 9:6. ¶

NT: B.727d; CB.–; K.–.
OT: –.
GEN. REF.: IS.4:604; NB.1214; Z.–.

SPOIL (Noun and Verb), SPOILING

A. Nouns.

1. *skulon* [σκῦλον, 4661], used in the plural, denotes arms stripped from a foe; "spoils" in Luke 11:22. ¶

NT: B.758b; CB.–; K.–.
OT: shālāl: S.7998; HR.1227b.3; H.2400a; BD.1021d.
GEN. REF.: IS.4:604; NB.–; Z.5:509.

2. *akrothinion* [ἀκροθίνιον, 205], primarily the top of a heap (*akros*, highest, top, and *this*, a heap), hence firstfruit offerings, and in war the choicest spoils, Heb. 7:4. ¶

NT: B.33d; CB.–; K.–.
OT: –.
GEN. REF.: IS.4:604; NB.–; Z.–.

3. *harpagē* [ἁρπαγή, 724], pillage, is rendered "spoiling" in Heb. 10:34. See EXTORT, B, No. 1.

NT: B.108b; CB.1249b; K.–.
OT: gāzēl: S.1498; HR.159c.1a; H.337a; BD.160a.
g^{e}zēlāh: S.1500; HR.159c.1b; H.337b; BD.160a.
shalal: S.7998; HR.159c.3; H.2400a; BD.1021d.
GEN. REF.: IS.4:604; NB.–; Z.5:509.

B. Verbs.

1. *diarpazō* [διαρπάζω, 1283], to plunder, is found in Matt. 12:29, 2nd part (the 1st has *harpazō*, in the best texts), lit., '(then) he will completely (*dia*, intensive) spoil (his house)'; Mark 3:27 (twice). ¶

NT: B.188b; CB.–; K.–.
OT: gāzal: S.1497; HR.308c.2; H.337; BD.159d.
bāzaz: S.962; HR.308c.1b; H.225; BD.102d.
GEN. REF.: IS.4:604; NB.–; Z.5:509.

2. *harpazō* [ἁρπάζω, 726], to seize, snatch away, is rendered "spoil" in Matt. 12:29a (see No. 1). See CATCH, No. 1.

NT: B.109a; CB.1249b; K.80.
OT: gāzal: S.1497; HR.160a.1; H.337; BD.159d.
ṭāraph: S.2963; HR.160a.3a; H.827; BD.382d.
GEN. REF.: IS.4:604; NB.–; Z.–.

3. *sulagōgeō* [συλαγωγέω, 4812], to carry off as spoil, lead captive (*sulē*, spoil, *ago*, to lead), is rendered "maketh spoil of" in Col. 2:8, R.V. (A.V., "spoil"), rather 'carry you off as spoil.' The false teacher, through his "philosophy and vain deceit," would carry them off as so much booty. ¶

NT: B.776c; CB.1270b; K.–.
OT: –.
GEN. REF.: –.

4. *apekduō* [ἀπεκδύω, 554], in the Middle Voice is translated "having spoiled" in Col. 2:15, A.V., R.V., "having put off from Himself (the principalities and the powers)." These are regarded by some as the unsinning angels, because they are mentioned twice before in the Epistle (1:16; 2:10). It is also argued that the verb *apekduō*, rendered "having put off from Himself," in 2:15, is used in a somewhat different sense in 3:9. Such representations do not form a sufficiently cogent reason for regarding the principalities and the powers here mentioned as those of light, rather than those of darkness.

Others think that the reference is to the holy angels, which were in attendance at the giving of the Law (Acts 7:53; Gal. 3:19), and that Christ wrought His work on the Cross, without any such attendance, or, again, that, even apart from the Law and its circumstances, the Lord stripped Himself of those who usually ministered to Him, as, e.g., in the wilderness and in the Garden of Gethsemane.

The exposition given by Lightfoot and others seems to be the right one. There is no doubt that Satan and his hosts gathered together to attack the soul of Christ, while He was enduring, in propitiatory sacrifice, the judgment due to our sins, and fulfilling the great work of redemption. There is an intimation of this in Psa. 22:21, "Save Me from the lion's mouth; yea, from the horns of the wild-oxen" (cp. vv. 12, 13). Doubtless the powers of darkness gathered against the Lord at that time, fiercely assaulting Him to the utmost of their power. He Himself had said, "This is your hour, and the power of darkness" (Luke 22:53). The metaphor of putting off from Himself these powers need not be pressed to the extent of regarding them as a garment clinging about Him. It seems to stand simply as a vivid description of His repulsion of their attack and of the power by which He completely overthrew them.

NT: B.83c; CB.1236b; K.192.
OT: –.
GEN. REF.: –.

SPONGE

spongos [σπόγγος, 4699], was the medium by which vinegar was carried to the mouth of Christ on the Cross, Matt. 27:48; Mark 15:36; John 19:29. ¶

NT: B.763b; CB.–; K.–.
OT: –.
GEN. REF.: IS.4:605; NB.–; Z.5.510.

SPORTING

entruphaō [ἐντρυφάω, 1792], occurs in 2 Pet. 2:13 (R.V., "revel").

NT: B.270a; CB.–; K.–.
OT: ʿādan: S.5727; HR.481a.1; H.1568; BD.726c.
ʿānāg: S.6026; HR.481a.2; H.1648; BD.772b.
GEN. REF.: IS.4:605; NB.–; Z.–.

SPOT (Noun and Verb)

1. *spilos* [σπῖλος, 4696], a spot or stain, is used metaphorically (*a*) of moral blemish, Eph. 5:27; (*b*) of lascivious and riotous persons, 2 Pet. 2:13. ¶

NT: B.762d; CB.–; K.–.
OT: –.
GEN. REF.: IS.4:606; NB.–; Z.–.

2. *spilas* [σπιλάς, 4694], is rendered "spots" in Jude 12, A.V.: see ROCK, No. 2.

NT: B.762c; CB.–; K.–.
OT: –.
GEN. REF.: IS.4:606; NB.–; Z.–.

B. Verb.

spiloō [σπιλόω, 4695], akin to A, No. 1, is used in Jude 23, in the clause "hating even the garment spotted by the flesh," the garment representing that which, being brought into contact with the polluting element of the flesh, becomes defiled: see CLOTHING, No. 3 (last par.). See DEFILE, No. 4.

NT: B.762d; CB.–; K.–.
OT: –.
GEN. REF.: IS.4:606; NB.–; Z.–.

C. Adjective.

aspilos [ἄσπιλος, 784], unspotted, unstained (*a*, negative, and A), is used of a lamb, 1 Pet. 1:19; metaphorically, of keeping a commandment without alteration and in the fulfilment of it, 1 Tim. 6:14; of the believer in regard to the world, Jas. 1:27, and free from all defilement in the sight of God, 2 Pet. 3:14. ¶

NT: B.117a; CB.1238a; K.85.
OT: –.
GEN. REF.: IS.4:606; NB.–; Z.–.

Note: For *amōmos*, in Heb. 9:14, A.V., see BLEMISH, B.

SPREAD

1. *strōnnuō* or *strōnnumi* [στρωννύω, 4766], to spread, is so rendered in Matt. 21:8, R.V., twice; Mark 11:8, R.V., once. See FURNISH.

NT: B.771c; CB.–; K.–.
OT: yāṣaʿ: S.3331; HR.1297b.2; H.896; BD.426d.
rāphad: S.7502; HR.1297b.7; H.2197; BD.951c.
GEN. REF.: IS.4:606; NB.–; Z.–.

2. *hupostrōnnuō* [ὑποστρωννύω, 5291], to spread under (*hupo*), of clothes, is used in Luke 19:36. ¶

NT: B.847c; CB.–; K.–.
OT: yāṣaʿ: S.3331; HR.1417b.1; H.896; BD.426d.
GEN. REF.: IS.4:606; NB.–; Z.–.

3. *dianemō* [διανέμω, 1268], to distribute, is used in the Passive Voice in Acts 4:17, "spread," lit., 'be spread about' (*dia*). ¶ In the Sept., Deut. 29:26, to assign or divide (concerning the worship of other gods). ¶

NT: B.186d; CB.–; K.–.
OT: ḥālaq: S.2505; HR.306b.1; H.669; BD.323c.
GEN. REF.: IS.4:606; NB.–; Z.–.

4. *diapherō* [διαφέρω, 1308], to carry about, spread abroad: see PUBLISH, No. 2; for other meanings of the word see BETTER (be), No. 1.

NT: B.190b; CB.–; K.1252.
OT: –.
GEN. REF.: IS.4:606; NB.–; Z.–.

5. *ekpetannumi* [ἐκπετάννυμι, 1600], to spread out (as a sail), is rendered "did I spread

out" in Rom. 10:21, R.V. (A.V., "I have stretched forth"). ¶
NT: B.243d; CB.–; K.–.
OT: –.
GEN. REF.: –.

Notes: (1) In Mark 1:28 and 1 Thess. 1:8, A.V., *exerchomai,* to go out or forth (R.V.), is rendered to spread abroad.

(2) In Mark 6:14, A.V., *ginomai,* to become, with *phaneros,* manifest, is translated "had spread abroad" (R.V., "had become known").

(3) In 2 Cor. 8:18, the R.V. "*is spread*" (A.V., "*is*") represents nothing in the original.

(4) For R.V., "spread His tabernacle over," Rev. 7:15, see DWELL, No. 9.

(5) For Mark 1:45, see BLAZE ABROAD.

SPRING (Noun and Verb)

A. Verbs.

1. *ginomai* [γίνοαι, 1096], to become, is used in the best texts in Heb. 11:12, "sprang" (some have *gennaō,* in the Passive Voice, rendered in the same way.)
NT: B.158a; CB.1248b; K.117.
OT: –.
GEN. REF.: –.

2. *anatellō* [ἀνατέλλω, 393], to arise, is rendered by the verb to spring, or spring up, in Matt. 4:16 and Heb. 7:14. See ARISE, No. 9.
NT: B.62a; CB.1235b; K.57.
OT: sāmaḥ: S.6779; HR.83a.10a-c; H.1928; BD.855b.
zāraḥ: S.2224; HR.83a.2; H.580; BD.280b.
pāraḥ: S.6524; HR.83a.8; H.1813-1815; BD.827a.
GEN. REF.: –.

3. *exanatellō* [ἐξανατέλλω, 1816], *ek* or *ex,* out, and No. 2, is used of the springing up of seeds, Matt. 13:5; Mark 4:5 (No. 7 in ver. 8). ¶
NT: B.272d; CB.–; K.–.
OT: ṣāmaḥ: S.6779; HR.487c.2; H.1928; BD.855b.
zāraḥ: S.2224; HR.487c.1; H.580; BD.280b.
GEN. REF.: –.

4. *phuō* [φύω, 5453], used transitively, to bring forth, produce, denotes, in the Passive Voice, to spring up, grow, of seed, Luke 8:6, 8, A.V., "was sprung up" and "sprang up" (R.V., "grew"); in the Active Voice, intransitively, in Heb. 12:15, of a root of bitterness. See GROW. ¶
NT: B.870b; CB.1264c; K.–.
OT: nāṭa': S.5193; HR.1440c.1; H.1354; BD.642b.
pārāh: S.6509; HR.1440c.3; H.1809; BD.826a.
ṣāmaḥ: S.6779; HR.1440c.4; H.1928; BD.855b.
GEN. REF.: –.

5. *sumphuō* [συμφύω, 4855], to cause to grow together (*sun,* with, and No. 4), occurs in Luke 8:7, R.V., "grew with," A.V., "sprang up with." ¶
NT: B.780d; CB.–; K.–.
OT: –.
GEN. REF.: –.

6. *blastanō* [βλαστάνω, 985], to sprout, is rendered to spring up in Matt. 13:26, of tare-blades, and Mark 4:27, of seed. See BRING, A, No. 26, BUD.
NT: B.142b; CB.1239a; K.–.
OT: sāmaḥ: S.6779; HR.220c.6; H.1928; BD.855b.
dāshā': S.1876; HR.220c.2; H.456; BD.205d.
GEN. REF.: –.

7. *anabainō* [ἀναβαίνω, 305], to go up, is rendered "sprang up" in Matt. 13:7, A.V., of thorns, and Mark 4:8, of seed (R.V., "grew up"). See GROW, No. 4.
NT: B.50a; CB.1235a; K.90.
OT: pārāh: S.6509; HR.70a.13; H.1809; BD.826a.
'ālāh: S.5927; HR.70a.11a; H.1624; BD.748a.
GEN. REF.: –.

8. *hallomai* [ἅλλομαι, 242], to leap, spring, is rendered "springing up," of well water, in John 4:14, figurative of the Holy Spirit in the believer. See LEAP.
NT: B.39d; CB.–; K.–.
OT: dālag: S.1801; HR.55c.1; H.430; BD.194c.
sālad: S.5539; HR.55c.2; H.1501; BD.698d.
ṣālēaḥ: S.6743; HR.55c.3; H.1916,1917; BD.852b.
GEN. REF.: –.

9. *eispēdaō* [εἰσπηδάω, 1530], to spring or leap in, occurs in Acts 16:29, "sprang in." ¶ In the Sept., Amos 5:19. ¶
NT: B.233c; CB.–; K.–.
OT: bō': S.935; HR.414a.1; H.212; BD.97c.
GEN. REF.: –.

10. *ekpēdaō* [ἐκπηδάω, —], to spring forth, occurs in Acts 14:14, in the best texts. See RUN, *Note* (4).
NT: B.243d; CB.–; K.–.
OT: zānaq: S.2187; HR.439a.1; H.566; BD.276c.
GEN. REF.: –.

B. Noun.

pēgē [πηγή, 4077], is rendered "springs" in 2 Pet. 2:17, R.V.: see FOUNTAIN.
NT: B.655d; CB.1263a; K.837.
OT: 'ayin: S.5869; HR.1130b.5a; H.1612a,1613; BD.745a.
GEN. REF.: –.

Note: For *epiginomai,* Acts 28:13, see BLOW (verb).

SPRINKLE, SPRINKLING

A. Verb.

rhantizō [ῥαντίζω, 4472], to sprinkle (a later form of *rhainō*), is used in the Active Voice in Heb. 9:13, of sprinkling with blood the unclean, a token of the efficacy of the expiatory sacrifice of Christ, His blood signifying the giving up of His life in the shedding of His blood (cp. 9:22) under Divine judgment upon sin (the voluntary act to be distinguished from that which took place after His death in the piercing of His side); so again in vv. 19, 21 (see B); in Heb. 10:22, Passive Voice, of the purging (on the ground of the same efficacy) of the hearts of believers from an evil conscience. This application of the blood of Christ is necessary for believers, in respect of their committal of sins, which on that ground receive forgiveness, 1 John 1:9. In Mark 7:4, the verb is found in the Middle Voice "in some ancient authorities" (R.V. marg.) instead of *baptizō*. In Rev. 19:13, the R.V., "sprinkled" follows those texts which have *rhantizō* (marg., "some anc. auth. read 'dipped in.' " *baptō*; so Nestle's text). ¶ This requires mention as a variant text in Rev. 19:13 under DIP.

NT: B.734a; CB.1268a; K.984.
OT: nāzāh: S.5137; HR.12248a.2; H.1335,1336; BD.633b.
ḥāṭā': S.2398; HR.1248a.1; H.638; BD.306c.
GEN. REF.: IS.4:606; NB.—; Z.—.

B. Nouns.

1. *rhantismos* [ῥαντισμός, 4473], sprinkling, akin to A, is used of the sprinkling of the blood of Christ, in Heb. 12:24 and 1 Pet. 1:2, an allusion to the use of the blood of sacrifices, appointed for Israel, typical of the sacrifice of Christ (see under A). ¶

NT: B.734b; CB.1268a; K.984.
OT: niddāh: S.5079; HR.1248a.1; H.1302a; BD.622c.
GEN. REF.: IS.4:606; NB.—; Z.—.

2. *proschusis* [πρόσχυσις, 4378], a pouring or sprinkling upon, occurs in Heb. 11:28, of the sprinkling of the blood of the Passover lamb. ¶

NT: B.720c; CB.1267a; K.—.
OT: —.
GEN. REF.: IS.4:606; NB.—; Z.—.

For SPUE see SPEW

SPY (Noun and Verb)

A. Nouns.

1. *enkathetos* [ἐγκάθετος, 1455], an adjective denoting suborned to lie in wait (*en*, in, *kathiēmi*, to send down), is used as a noun in Luke 20:20, "spies." ¶ In the Sept., Job. 19:12; 31:9. ¶

NT: B.215b; CB.—; K.—.
OT: 'ārab: S.693; HR.364b.1; H.156; BD.70b.
GEN. REF.: IS.4:607; NB.—; Z.—.

2. *kataskopos* [κατάσκοπος, 2685], denotes a spy (*kata*, down, signifying closely, and *skopeō*, to view), Heb. 11:31. ¶

NT: B.418d; CB.1254b; K.1047.
OT: rāgal: S.7270; HR.745a.1; H.2113; BD.920a.
GEN. REF.: IS.4:607; NB.—; Z.—.

kataskopeō [κατασκοπέω, 2684], to view closely (akin to A, No. 2), spy out, search out with a view to overthrowing, is used in Gal. 2:4. ¶ In the Sept., 2 Sam. 10:3; 1 Chron. 19:3. ¶

NT: B.418d; CB.—; K.1047.
OT: rāgal: S.7270; HR.745a.2; H.2113; BD.920a.
rā'āh: S.7200; HR.745a.1; H.2095; BD.906b.
GEN. REF.: IS.4:607; NB.—; Z.—.

For STABLISH see ESTABLISH

STAFF, STAVES

1. *rhabdos* [ῥάβδος, 4464], rendered "staff" or "staves" in Matt. 10:10, parallel passages, and Heb. 11:21: see ROD

NT: B.733b; CB.1268a; K.982.
OT: maqqēl: S.4731; HR.1247a.3; H.1236; BD.596b.
maṭṭeh: S.4294; HR.1247a.2; H.1352b; BD.641c.
shēbeṭ: S.7626; HR.1247a.6; H.2314a; BD.986d.
GEN. REF.: IS.4:608; NB.1098; Z.5:510.

2. *xulon* [ξύλον, 3586], wood, then, anything made of wood, e.g., a cudgel or staff, is rendered "staves" in Matt. 26:47, 55 and parallel passages. See STOCKS, TREE, WOOD.

NT: B.549a; CB.1273b; K.665.
OT: 'ēṣ: S.6086; HR.958a.3a; H.1670a; BD.781c.
GEN. REF.: IS.—; NB.—; Z.5:510.

For STAGGER see WAVER

STAIR

anabathmos [ἀναβαθμός, 304], an ascent (akin to *anabainō*, to go up), denotes a flight of stairs, Acts 21:35, 40. These were probably the steps leading down from the castle of Antonia to the Temple. (See Josephus, *B.J.*, v., 5, 8.) ¶ In the Sept., it is used, e.g., in the titles of the Songs of Ascents, Psa. 120-134.

NT: B.50a; CB.—; K.—.
OT: ma'alāh: S.4609; HR.70a.1; H.1624l,m; BD.752a.
GEN. REF.: IS.4:609; NB.—; Z.5:511.

For STALL see MANGER

STANCH

histēmi [ἵστημι, 2476], transitively, to cause to stand, is used intransitively (to stand still) in Luke 8:44, translated "stanched." See STAND.

NT: B.381d; CB.1250c; K.1082.
OT: —.
GEN. REF.: —.

STAND (Noun and Verb), STANDING, STOOD

A. Noun.

luchnia [λυχνία, 3087], a lampstand, is translated "stand" in Matt. 5:15 and parallel passages (A.V., "candlestick"). See LAMP-STAND.

NT: B.483a; CB.1257b; K.542.
OT: mᵉnôrāh: S.4501; HR.891a.1; H.1333c; BD.633a.
GEN. REF.: —.

B. Verbs.

1. *histēmi* [ἵστημι, 2476], (*a*) transitively, denotes to cause to stand, to set; in the Passive Voice, to be made to stand, e.g., Matt. 2:9, lit., 'was made to stand'; so Luke 11:18; 19:8 (Col. 4:12 in some mss.); in Rev. 13:1 the R.V. follows the best texts, "he stood" (not as A.V., "I stood"); the reference is to the Dragon. In the Middle Voice, to take one's stand, place oneself,

e.g., Rev. 18:15; (*b*) intransitively, in the 2nd aorist and perfect Active, to stand, stand by, stand still, e.g., Matt. 6:5; 20:32, "stood still"; in Luke 6:8, "stand forth" and "stood forth"; metaphorically, to stand firm, John 8:44 (negatively), in the truth (see No. 7); Rom. 5:2, in grace; 1 Cor. 15:1, in the gospel; Rom. 11:20, "by thy faith," R.V.; 2 Cor. 1:24, "by faith" (marg., "by your faith"); of stedfastness, 1 Cor. 7:37; Eph. 6:11, 13, 14; Col. 4:12 [some mss. have the Passive, see (*a*)]. See APPOINT, ESTABLISH, SET.

NT: B.381d; CB.1250c; K.1082.
OT: ʻāmad: S.5975; HR.689a.26a-c; H.1637; BD.763c.
qûm: S.6965; HR.689a.28a-d; H.1999; BD.877c.
GEN. REF.: –.

2. *anistēmi* [ἀνίστημι, 450], to raise, intransitively, to rise, is translated to stand up in Matt. 12:41, R.V.; Mark 14:60; Luke 4:16; 10:25; Acts 1:15; 5:34; 10:26; 11:28; 13:16; in 14:10; "stand upright." See ARISE, No. 1.

NT: B.70a; CB.1235c; K.60.
OT: qûm: S.6965; HR.102c.8a; H.1999; BD.877c.
GEN. REF.: –.

3. *ephistēmi* [ἐφίστημι, 2186], (*epi*, upon, and No. 1), used intransitively, denotes to stand upon or by, be present, Luke 2:9 and Acts 12:7, "stood by," R.V. (A.V., "came upon"); Luke 4:39, "stood over"; 24:4 and Acts 23:11, "stood by"; Acts 10:17, "stood"; 22:13, "standing by (me)," R.V.; so ver. 20, A.V. and R.V. See ASSAULT, COME, No. 27, HAND (AT), B, *Note* (2), INSTANT, PRESENT.

NT: B.330c; CB.–; K.–.
OT: qûm: S.6965; HR.585c.13; H.1999; BD.877c.
ʻāmad: S.5975; HR.585c.11a; H.1637; BD.763c.
nāṣab: S.5324; HR.585c.6; H.1398; BD.662a.
GEN. REF.: –.

4. *paristēmi* [παρίστημι, 3936], intransitively, denotes to stand by or beside (*para*, by, and No. 1), Mark 14:47, 69, 70; 15:35, 39 (R.V., "stood by"); Luke 19:24; John 18:22; 19:26; Acts 1:10; 9:39; 23:2, 4; 27:23; in 27:24, "stand before"; in 4:10, "doth . . . stand here"; in Luke 1:19, "stand"; Rom. 14:10, "we shall . . . stand before" (Middle Voice); 2 Tim. 4:17, R.V., "stood by" (A.V., ". . . with"). See COMMEND, No. 4.

NT: B.627c; CB.1262b; K.788.
OT: ʻāmad: S.5975; HR.1070c.6; H.1637; BD.763c.
nāṣab: S.5324; HR.1070c.5; H.1398; BD.662a.
GEN. REF.: –.

5. *periistēmi* [περιίστημι, 4026], intransitively, to stand around (*peri*, is so used in John 11:42; Acts 25:7. See Acts 25:7. See AVOID, No. 4.

NT: B.647c; CB.–; K.–.
OT: nāṣab: S.5324; HR.1123c.1; H.1398; BD.662a.
sābab: S.5437; HR.1123c.2; H.1456; BD.685b.
GEN. REF.: –.

6. *sunistēmi* [συνίστημι, 4921], intransitively, denotes to stand with (*sun*), Luke 9:32; for 2 Pet. 3:5, A.V., "standing," see COMPACTED, No. 1: for other meanings see APPROVE, A, No. 2.

NT: B.790c; CB.1270c; K.1120.
OT: qāhal: S.6950; HR.1317a.10; H.1991; BD.874d.
GEN. REF.: –.

7. *stēkō* [στήκω, 4739], a late present tense from *hestēka*, the perfect of *histēmi*, is used (*a*) literally, Mark 3:31; 11:25; John 1:26, in the best texts (in some texts Rev. 12:4); (*b*) figuratively, Rom. 14:4, where the context indicates the meaning 'standeth upright' rather than that of acquittal; of standing fast, 1 Cor. 16:13, "in the faith," i.e., by adherence to it; Gal. 5:1, in freedom from legal bondage; Phil. 1:27, "in one spirit"; Phil. 4:1 and 1 Thess. 3:8, "in the Lord," i.e, in the willing subjection to His authority; 2 Thess. 2:15, in the Apostle's teaching; some mss. have it in John 8:44, the most authentic have *histēmi*, R.V., "stood" (A.V., "abode"). ¶

NT: B.767d; CB.–; K.1082.
OT: ʻāmad: S.5975; HR.1290b.3; H.1637; BD.763c.
kûn: S.3559; HR.1290b.2; H.964; BD.465c.
GEN. REF.: –.

8. *menō* [μένω, 3306], to abide, remain, is rendered "might stand," in Rom. 9:11, of the purpose of God, i.e., might abide for the permanent recognition of its true character. See ABIDE, No. 1.

NT: B.503c; CB.1258b; K.581.
OT: ʻāmad: S.5975; HR.910a.12; H.1637; BD.763c.
qûm: S.3559; HR.910a.15a; H.964; BD.465c.
GEN. REF.: –.

9. *kukloō* [κυκλόω, 2944], "stood round about," Acts 14:20: see COMPASS, No. 2.

NT: B.456d; CB.–; K.–.
OT: sābab: S.5437; HR.798b.3a; H.1456; BD.685b.
GEN. REF.: –.

Notes: (1) In Mark 3:3, *egeirō*, to raise, followed by the phrase *eis to meson*, 'into the midst,' is translated "stand forth."

(2) In 2 Tim. 4:16, A.V., *paraginomai* (in some texts, *sumparaginomai*), to come up to assist, is rendered "stood with (me)," R.V., "took (my) part."

(3) In Heb. 9:8, R.V., "is . . . standing" (A.V., "was . . . standing") represents the phrase *echō*, to have, *stasis*, a standing, lit., 'has a standing.'

(4) For "stand . . . in jeopardy" see DANGER.

STAR

1. *astēr* [ἀστήρ, 792], a star, Matt. 2:2-10; 24:29; Mk. 13:25; 1 Cor. 15:41; Rev. 6:13; 8:10-12; 9:1; 12:1, 4, is used metaphorically, (*a*) of Christ, as "the morning star," figurative of the approach of the day when He will appear as the "sun of righteousness," to govern the earth in peace, an event to be preceded by the Rapture of the Church, Rev. 2:28; 22:16, the

promise of the former to the overcomer being suggestive of some special personal interest in Himself and His authority; (*b*) of the angels of the seven churches, Rev. 1:16, 20; 2:1; 3:1; (*c*) of certain false teachers, described as "wandering stars," Jude 13, as if the stars, intended for light and guidance, became the means of deceit by irregular movements. ¶

NT: B.117c; CB.1238a; K.86.
OT: kôkāb: S.3556; HR.173b.1; H.942a; BD.456c.
GEN. REF.: IS.4:611; NB.1214; Z.–.

2. *astron* [ἄστρον, 798], practically the same as No. 1, is used (*a*) in the sing. in Acts 7:43, "the star of the god Rephan," R.V., the symbol or "figure," probably of Saturn, worshipped as a god, apparently the same as Chiun in Amos 5:26 (Rephan being the Egyptian deity corresponding to Saturn, Chiun the Assyrian); (*b*) in the plur., Luke 21:25; Acts 27:20; Heb. 11:12. ¶

NT: B.118b; CB.1238a; K.86.
OT: kôkāb: S.3556; HR.173c.2a; H.942a; BD.456c.
GEN. REF.: IS.4:611; NB.1214; Z.–.

For **STATE** see **ESTATE**, Notes

For **STATURE** see **AGE**, A, No. 3

For **STAVES** see **STAFF**

STAY

1. *katechō* [κατέχω, 2722], to hold fast, hold back, is used in the sense of detaining in Luke 4:42, "would have stayed (Him)," R.V. See HOLD.

NT: B.422c; CB.1254b; K.286.
OT: 'āhaz: S.270; HR.750c.1; H.64; BD.28a.
ḥāzaq: S.2388; HR.750c.5; H.636; BD.304a.
GEN. REF.: –.

2. *epechō* [ἐπέχω, 1907], has the meaning to wait in a place, to stay, in Acts 19:22. See HEED, HOLD, MARK.

NT: B.285c; CB.–; K.–.
OT: yāḥal: S.3176; HR.511a.5; H.859; BD.403d.
GEN. REF.: –.

3. *kōluō* [κωλύω, 2967], to hinder, is rendered "stayed" in Act 27:43, R.V. (A.V., "kept"); so in 2 Pet. 2:16, R.V. (A.V., "forbad"). See HINDER ¶

NT: B.461b; CB.1255c; K.–.
OT: kālā': S.3607; HR.839b.1; H.980; BD.476b.
māna': S.4513; HR.839b.3; H.1216; BD.586a.
GEN. REF.: –.

For **STEADFAST** see **STEDFAST**

STEAL

kleptō [κλέπτω, 2813], to steal, akin to *kleptēs*, a thief (cp. Eng., kleptomania), occurs in Matt. 6:19, 20; 19:18; 27:64; 28:13; Mark 10:19; Luke 18:20; John 10:10; Rom. 2:21 (twice); 13:9; Eph. 4:28 (twice). ¶

NT: B.434c; CB.1255b; K.441.
OT: gānab: S.1589; HR.767b.1a; H.364; BD.170b.
GEN. REF.: IS.4:614; NB.–; Z.–.

STEDFAST, STEDFASTLY, STEDFASTNESS

A. Adjectives.

1. *bebaios* [βέβαιος, 949], firm, secure (akin to *bainō*, to go), is translated "stedfast" in 2 Cor. 1:7; Heb. 2:2; 3:14, A.V. (R.V., "firm"); 6:19. See FIRM, FORCE, SURE.

NT: B.138b; CB.1239a; K.103.
OT: –.
GEN. REF.: IS.4:613; NB.–; Z.–.

2. *hedraios* [ἑδραῖος, 1476], primarily denotes seated (*hedra*, a seat); hence, stedfast, metaphorical of moral fixity, 1 Cor. 7:37; 15:58; Col. 1:23, R.V. (A.V., "settled"). ¶

NT: B.217d; CB.1249c; K.200.
OT: –.
GEN. REF.: IS.4:613; NB.–; Z.–.

3. *stereos* [στερεός, 4731], firm, is rendered "stedfast" in 1 Pet. 5:9. See FIRM, No. 2.

NT: B.766d; CB.1270a; K.1077.
OT: ṣûr: S.6697; HR.1289a.7a; H.1901a; BD.849c.
ṣar: S.6862; HR.1289a.7b; H.1973-1975; BD.866a.
ḥāzāq: S.2389; HR.1289a.4; H.636a; BD.305c.
GEN. REF.: –.

B. Nouns.

1. *stereōma* [στερέωμα, 4733], primarily a support, foundation, denotes strength, stedfastness, Col. 2:5. ¶ In the Sept., in Gen. 1:6, and Ezek. 1:22, it is used of the firmament, which was believed to be a solid canopy. The corresponding Heb. word *rāqîa'* means 'expanse,' from *rāqa',* to spread out.

NT: B.766d; CB.–; K.1077.
OT: rāqîa': S.7549; HR.1289b.2; H.2217a; BD.956a.
GEN. REF.: IS.–; NB.–; Z.5:514.

2. *stērigmos* [στηριγμός, 4740], a setting firmly, supporting, then fixedness, stedfastness (akin to *stērizō*, to establish), is used in 2 Pet. 3:17. ¶

NT: B.768a; CB.–; K.1085.
OT: –.
GEN. REF.: IS.–; NB.–; Z.5:514.

Note: For STEDFASTLY see BEHOLD, No. 10, CONTINUE, No. 9, FASTEN, No. 1, LOOK, No. 15, SET, No. 19.

STEEP

krēmnos [κρημνός, 2911], a steep bank (akin to *kremannumi*, to hang), occurs in Matt. 8:32; Mark 5:13; Luke 8:33, R.V., "the steep" (A.V., "a steep place"). ¶ In the Sept., 2 Chron. 25:12. ¶

NT: B.450b; CB.–; K.–.
OT: sela': S.5553; HR.785c.1; H.1508a; BD.700d.
GEN. REF.: –.

For **STEERSMAN** see **GOVERNOR**, B, *Note*

STEP (Noun and Verb)

A. Noun.

ichnos [ἴχνος, 2487], a footstep, a track, is used metaphorically of the steps (*a*) of Christ's conduct, 1 Pet. 2:21; (*b*) of Abraham's faith, Rom. 4:12; (*c*) of identical conduct in carrying on the work of the Gospel, 2 Cor. 12:18. ¶

NT: B.384b; CB.—; K.379.
OT: kaph: S.3709; HR.696b.3; H.1022a; BD.496a.
GEN. REF.: —.

B. Verb.

katabainō [καταβαίνω, 2597], to go, or come, down, is translated "steppeth down" in John 5:7. See COME, No. 19.

NT: B.408b; CB.1253c; K.90.
OT: yārad: S.3381; HR.727a.8a; H.909; BD.432c.
GEN. REF.: —.

Note: Many ancient authorities have the passage in the A.V. in John 5:4, which contains *embainō*, rendered "stepped in." See COME, No. 21.

STERN

prumna [πρύμνα, 4403], the feminine form of the adjective *prumnos*, hindmost, is rendered "stern" in Acts 27:29; and in the R.V. in ver. 41 and Mark 4:38. See PART, A, *Note* (2). ¶

NT: B.724d; CB.—; K.—.
OT: —.
GEN. REF.: —.

STEWARD, STEWARDSHIP

A. Nouns.

1. *oikonomos* [οἰκονόμος, 3623], primarily denoted the manager of a household or estate (*oikos*, a house, *nemō*, to arrange), a steward (such were usually slaves or freedmen), Luke 12:42; 16:1, 3, 8; 1 Cor. 4:2; Gal. 4:2, R.V. (A.V., "governors"); in Rom. 16:23, the "treasurer" (R.V.) of a city (see CHAMBERLAIN, *Note*); it is used metaphorically, in the wider sense, of a steward in general, (*a*) of preachers of the Gospel and teachers of the Word of God, 1 Cor. 4:1; (*b*) of elders or bishops in churches, Tit. 1:7; (*c*) of believers generally, 1 Pet. 4:10. ¶

NT: B.560a; CB.1260b; K.674.
OT: ('al-) habbayit: S.1004; HR.973a.1; H.241; BD.108c,110b.
GEN. REF.: IS.4:617; NB.1216; Z.5:516.

2. *epitropos* [ἐπίτροπος, 2012], is rendered "steward" in Matt. 20:8; Luke 8:3: see GUARDIAN.

NT: B.303d; CB.1246b; K.—.
OT: —.
GEN. REF.: IS.4:617; NB.1216; Z.5:516.

3. *oikonomia* [οἰκονομία, 3622], is rendered "stewardship" in Luke 16:2, 3, 4, and in the R.V. in 1 Cor. 9:17; see DISPENSATION

NT: B.559c; CB.1260b; K.674.
OT: memshālāh: S.4475; HR.973a.1; H.1259c; BD.606c.
GEN. REF.: IS.4:617; NB.1216; Z.—.

B. Verb.

oikonomeō [οἰκονομέω, 3621], akin to A, Nos. 1 and 3, signifies to be a house steward, Luke 16:2. ¶ In the Sept., Psa. 112:5. ¶

NT: B.559c; CB.1260b; K.674.
OT: kûl: S.3557; HR.973a.1; H.962; BD.465a.
GEN. REF.: IS.4:617; NB.1216; Z.5:516.

STICK

phruganon [φρύγανον, 5434], denotes a dry stick (from *phrugō*, to parch); in the plural, brushwood, Acts 28:3. ¶

NT: B.867b; CB.—; K.—.
OT: qash: S.7179; HR.1440a.3; H.2091a; BD.905d.
GEN. REF.: —.

STICK FAST

ereidō [ἐρείδω, 2043], primarily to prop, fix firmly, is used intransitively in Acts 27:41 of a ship driving ashore, R.V., "struck." ¶

NT: B.308d; CB.—; K.—.
OT: tāmak: S.8551; HR.544c.4; H.2520; BD.1069c.
GEN. REF.: —.

STIFFNECKED

sklērotrachēlos [σκληροτράχηλος, 4644], from *sklēros*, harsh, hard, *trachēlos*, a neck, is used metaphorically in Acts 7:51. ¶

NT: B.756b; CB.1269a; K.816.
OT: (qᵉsheh-) 'ōreph: S.6203; HR.1274c.1a; H.1700a; BD.791b.
GEN. REF.: IS.4:619; NB.—; Z.5:516.

STILL (Verb)

phimoō [φιμόω, 5392], in the Passive Voice is rendered "be still" in Mark 4:39: see MUZZLE.

NT: B.861d; CB.—; K.—.
OT: ḥāsam: S.2629; HR.1432c.1; H.702; BD.340c.
GEN. REF.: IS.4:619; NB.—; Z.—.

STILL (Adverb)

eti [ἔτι, 2089], yet, as yet, still, is translated "still" in the R.V. in 1 Cor. 12:31; 2 Cor. 1:10; Gal 1:10 and 5:11; A.V. and R.V. in Rev. 22:11 (four times), where the word indicates the permanent character, condition and destiny of the unrighteous and the filthy, the righteous and the holy (for the verbs see the R.V.); in John 11:30, the best mss. have the word; so R.V. (A.V. omits).

NT: B.315c; CB.1247a; K.—.
OT: 'ôd: S.5750; HR.561a.11; H.1576a; BD.728c.
GEN. REF.: —.

Note: For combinations see ABIDE, IGNORANCE, B, No. 1, STAND.

For STING see GOAD

STINK

ozō [ὄζω, 3605], to emit a smell (cp. Eng., ozone), occurs in John 11:39. ¶ In the Sept., Ex. 8:14. ¶

NT: B.555c; CB.–; K.–.
OT: bā'ash: S.887; HR.967c.1; H.195; BD.92d.
GEN. REF.: –.

STIR, STIR UP (Noun and Verb)

A. Noun.

tarachos [τάραχος, 5017], akin to *tarachē*, trouble, and *tarassō*, to trouble, is rendered "stir" in Acts 12:18; 19:23. ¶

NT: B.805c; CB.1271a; K.–.
OT: mᵉhûmāh: S.4103; HR.1337a.2; H.486a; BD.223b.
ballāhāh: S.1091; HR.1337a.1; H.247a; BD.117a.
'ākar: S.5916; HR.1337a.3; H.1621; BD.747c.
GEN. REF.: –.

B. Verbs.

1. *anazōpureō* [ἀναζωπυρέω, 329], denotes to kindle afresh, or keep in full flame (*ana*, up, or again, *zōos*, alive, *pur*, fire), and is used metaphorically in 2 Tim. 1:6, where "the gift of God" is regarded as a fire capable of dying out through neglect. ¶ The verb was in common use in the vernacular of the time.

NT: B.54a; CB.–; K.–.
OT: ḥāyāh: S.2421; HR.77a.1; H.644; BD.310d.
GEN. REF.: –.

2. *epegeirō* [ἐπεγείρω, 1892], "stirred up" in Acts 14:2. See RAISE.

NT: B.284a; CB.–; K.–.
OT: qûm: S.6965; HR.509a.4; H.1999; BD.877c.
'ûr: S.5782; HR.509a.3; H.1587; BD.734d.
GEN. REF.: –.

3. *diegeirō* [διεγείρω, 1326], "stir up" in 2 Pet. 1:13; 3:1; see ARISE, No. 4.

NT: B.193d; CB.–; K.–.
OT: –.
GEN. REF.: –.

4. *seiō* [σείω, 4579], to move to and fro, is rendered "was stirred" in Matt. 21:10, R.V. (A.V., "was moved"). See MOVE, QUAKE, SHAKE.

NT: B.746c; CB.1268c; K.1014.
OT: rā'ash: S.7493; HR.1261c.5; H.2195; BD.950a.
GEN. REF.: –.

5. *anaseiō* [ἀνασείω, 383], primarily denotes to shake back or out, move to and fro; then, to stir up, used metaphorically in Mark 15:11, R.V., "stirred . . . up" (A.V., "moved"), and Luke 3:14; 23:5. ¶

NT: B.60a; CB.1235b; K.–.
OT: –.
GEN. REF.: –.

6. *saleuō* [σαλεύω, 4531], "stirred up" in Acts 17:13: see SHAKE.

NT: B.740c; CB.1268b; K.996.
OT: môṭ: S.4131; HR.1257c.9; H.1158; BD.556d.
nû'a: S.5128; HR.1257c.14; H.1328; BD.631a.
GEN. REF.: –.

7. *parotrunō* [παροτρύνω, 3951], from *para*, used intensively, beyond measure, and *otrunō*, to urge on, rouse, occurs in Acts 13:50, "stirred up." ¶

NT: B.629d; CB.–; K.–.
OT: –.
GEN. REF.: –.

8. *sunkineō* [συγκινέω, 4787], to move together (*sun*, together, *kineō*, to move), to stir up, excite, is used metaphorically in Acts 6:12. ¶

NT: B.773d; CB.–; K.–.
OT: –.
GEN. REF.: –.

9. *suncheō* [συγχέω, 4797], to pour together, is used metaphorically in Acts 21:27, "stirred up." See CONFOUND, B, No. 1.

NT: B.775a; CB.–; K.–.
OT: rāgaz: S.7264; HR.1301a.9; H.2112; BD.919a.
bālal: S.1101; HR.1301a.1; H.248; BD.117b.
GEN. REF.: –.

10. *paroxunō* [παροξύνω, 3947], "stirred" in Acts 17:16: see PROVOKE, No. 2.

NT: B.629c; CB.1262c; K.791.
OT: qāṣaph: S.7107; HR.1072a.14; H.2058; BD.893b.
rāgaz: S.7264; HR.1072a.15; H.2112; BD.919a.
GEN. REF.: –.

11. *erethizō* [ἐρεθίζω, 2042], "hath stirred" in 2 Cor. 9:2, R.V. See PROVOKE, No. 3.

NT: B.308d; CB.–; K.–.
OT: gārāh: S.1624; HR.544b.1; H.378; BD.173b.
mārāh: S.4784; HR.544b.2; H.1242; BD.598a.
GEN. REF.: –.

12. *anastatoō* [ἀναστατόω, 387], to excite, unsettle (akin to *anistēmi*, to raise up, and *anastasis*, a raising), is used (*a*) of stirring up to sedition, and tumult, Acts 17:6, "turned . . . upside down"; 21:38, R.V., "stirred up to sedition," A.V., "madest an uproar"; (*b*) to upset by false teaching, Gal. 5:12, R.V., "unsettle" (A.V., "trouble"). ¶

NT: B.61a; CB.–; K.–.
OT: dûsh (Aramaic): S.1759; HR.82a.1; H.2670; BD.1087c.
GEN. REF.: –.

Note: In Acts 24:12, *poieō*, to make, with *epistasis*, a stopping (in some texts *episustasis*, signifies to collect (a crowd), A.V., "raising up (the people)," R.V., "stirring up (a crowd)." See COME, *Note* (9).

For STOCK see KIND

STOCKS

xulon [ξύλον, 3586], wood, is used of stocks in Acts 16:24. See STAFF, TREE, WOOD

NT: B.549a; CB.1273b; K.665.
OT: 'ēṣ: S.6086; HR.958a.3a; H.1670a; BD.781c.
GEN. REF.: IS.4:620; NB.1216; Z.5:518.

STOMACH

stomachos [στόμαχος, 4751], properly a mouth, an opening, akin to *stoma*, a mouth, denotes the stomach in 1 Tim. 5:23. ¶

NT: B.770a; CB.–; K.–.
OT: –.
GEN. REF.: IS.4:622; NB.1217; Z.5:520.

STONE (Noun, Verb, and Adjective)

A. Nouns.

1. *lithos* [λίθος, 3037], is used (I) literally, of (*a*) the stones of the ground, e.g., Matt. 4:3, 6; 7:9; (*b*) tombstones, e.g., Matt. 27:60, 66; (*c*) building stones, e.g., Matt. 21:42; (*d*) a millstone, Luke 17:2; cp. Rev. 18:21 (see MILLSTONE); (*e*) the tables (or tablets) of the Law, 2 Cor. 3:7; (*f*) idol images, Acts 17:29; (*g*) the treasures of commercial Babylon, Rev. 18:12, 16; (II) metaphorically, of (*a*) Christ, Rom. 9:33; 1 Pet. 2:4, 6, 8; (*b*) believers, 1 Pet. 2:5; (*c*) spiritual edification by Scriptural teaching, 1 Cor. 3:12; (*d*) the adornment of the foundations of the wall of the spiritual and heavenly Jerusalem, Rev. 21:19; (*e*) the adornment of the seven angels in Rev. 15:6, R.V. (so the best texts; some have *linon*, linen, A.V.); (*f*) the adornment of religious Babylon, Rev. 17:4; (III) figuratively, of Christ Rev. 4:3; 21:11, where "light" stands for 'Light-giver' (*phōstēr*).

NT: B.474b; CB.1257a; K.534.
OT: 'eben: S.68; HR.876c.1a; H.9; BD.6b.
GEN. REF.: IS.4:622; NB.1217; Z.–.

2. *psēphos* [ψῆφος, 5586], a smooth stone, a pebble, worn smooth as by water, or polished (akin to *psaō*, to rub), denotes (*a*) by metonymy, a vote (from the use of pebbles for this purpose; cp. *psēphizō*, to count), Acts 26:10, R.V. (A.V., "voice"); (*b*) a (white) stone to be given to the overcomer in the church at Pergamum, Rev. 2:17 (twice); a white stone was often used in the social life and judicial customs of the ancients; festal days were noted by a white stone, days of calamity by a black; in the courts a white stone indicated acquittal, a black condemnation. A host's appreciation of a special guest was indicated by a white stone with the name or a message written on it; this is probably the allusion here. ¶

NT: B.892c; CB.–; K.–.
OT: ḥāṣāṣ: S.2687; HR.1485c.1; H.721a; BD.346b.
ṣōr: S.6864; HR.1485c.3; H.1975b; BD.866a.
GEN. REF.: –.

Note: In John 1:42 *petros* stands for the proper name, Peter, as the R.V. (A.V., "a stone"; marg., "Peter"); *petros* denotes a piece of a rock, a detached stone or boulder, in contrast to *petra*, a mass of rock. See ROCK

B. Verbs.

1. *lithoboleō* [λιθοβολέω, 3036], to pelt with stones (A, No. 1, and *ballō*, to throw), to stone to death, occurs in Matt. 21:35; 23:37; Luke 13:34 (John 8:5 in some mss.: see No. 2); Acts 7:58, 59; 14:5; Heb. 12:20. ¶

NT: B.474a; CB.–; K.533.
OT: sāqal: S.5619; HR.876c.1; H.1541; BD.709c.
GEN. REF.: IS.4:630; NB.1218; Z.5:524.

2. *lithazō* [λιθάζω, 3034], to stone, virtually equivalent to No. 1, but not stressing the casting, occurs in John 8:5 (in the most authentic mss.); 10:31-33; 11:8; Acts 5:26; 14:19; 2 Cor. 11:25; Heb. 11:37. ¶

NT: B.473d; CB.–; K.533.
OT: sāqal: S.5619; HR.876b.1; H.1541; BD.709c.
GEN. REF.: IS.4:630; NB.1218; Z.5:524.

3. *katalithazō* [καταλιθάζω, 2642], an intensive form of No. 2, to cast stones at, occurs in Luke 20:6. ¶

NT: B.413d; CB.–; K.533.
OT: –.
GEN. REF.: IS.4:630; NB.1218; Z.5:524.

C. Adjective.

lithinos [λίθινος, 3035], of stone (akin to A, No. 1), occurs in John 2:6; 2 Cor. 3:3; Rev. 9:20. ¶

NT: B.474a; CB.1257a; K.534.
OT: 'eben: S.68; HR.876b.1; H.9; BD.6b.
GEN. REF.: IS.4:622; NB.1217; Z.–.

For STONY see ROCKY

STOOP

1. *kuptō* [κύπτω, 2955], to bow the head, stoop down, occurs in Mark 1:7; John 8:6, 8. ¶

NT: B.458a; CB.–; K.–.
OT: qādad: S.6915; HR.799c.3; H.1985; BD.869a.
GEN. REF.: –.

2. *parakuptō* [παρακύπτω, 3879], is rendered to stoop down in Luke 24:12; John 20:5, 11, R.V., "stooping and looking in": see LOOK, No. 10.

NT: B.619b; CB.–; K.784.
OT: shāqaph: S.8259; HR.1061b.2; H.2457; BD.1054c.
GEN. REF.: –.

STOP

1. *phrassō* [φράσσω, 5420], to fence in (akin to *phragmos*, a fence), close, stop, is used (*a*) metaphorically, in Rom. 3:19, of preventing all excuse from Jew and Gentile, as sinners; in 2 Cor. 11:10, lit., 'this boasting shall not be stopped to me'; Passive Voice in both; (*b*) physically, of the mouths of lions, Heb. 11:33 (Active Voice). ¶

NT: B.865c; CB.1264b; K.–.
OT: 'āṭam: S.331; HR.1438b.1; H.73; BD.31d.
sāṭam: S.5640; HR.1438b.4; H.1550; BD.711a.
GEN. REF.: –.

2. *sunechō* [συνέχω, 4912], to hold together, is rendered "stopped (their ears)" in Acts 7:57. See HOLD.

NT: B.789a; CB.1270c; K.1117.
OT: 'āṣar: S.6113; HR.1315b.12a,b; H.1675; BD.783c.
GEN. REF.: –.

3. *epistomizō* [ἐπιστομίζω, 1993], to stop the mouth, Tit. 1:11: see MOUTH, B. ¶

NT: B.301a; CB.–; K.–.
OT: –.
GEN. REF.: –.

STORE (Verb)

1. *thēsaurizō* [θησαυρίζω, 2343], to lay up, store up, is rendered "in store" (lit., 'storing'), with a view to help a special case of need, 1 Cor. 16:2; said of the heavens and earth in 2 Pet. 3:7, R.V., "have been stored up (for fire)," marg., "stored (with fire)," A.V., "kept in store (reserved unto fire)." See LAY, No. 17, TREASURE.

NT: B.361b; CB.1272b; K.333.
OT: 'āṣar: S.686; HR.651b.1; H.154; BD.69d.
ṣābar: S.6651; HR.651b.2; H.1874; BD.840d.
GEN. REF.: –.

2. *apothēsaurizō* [ἀποθησαυρίζω, 597], to treasure up, store away (*apo*, is used in 1 Tim. 6:19, of "laying up in store" a good foundation for the hereafter by being rich in good works. ¶

NT: B.91b; CB.–; K.–.
OT: –.
GEN. REF.: –.

For STORE-HOUSE, STORE-CHAMBER, see CHAMBER

STORM

lailaps [λαῖλαψ, 2978], a hurricane, whirlwind, is rendered "storm" in Mark 4:37; Luke 8:23; 2 Pet. 2:17, R.V. (A.V., "tempest"). See TEMPEST. ¶

NT: B.462d; CB.1256b; K.–.
OT: sûphāh: S.5492; HR.841a.1; H.1478b; BD.693a.
sa'ar: S.5591; HR.841a.2a; H.1528b; BD.704b.
s^e'ārāh: S.5591; HR.841a.2b; H.1528; BD.704b.
GEN. REF.: IS.4:631; NB.–; Z.–.

STORY

tristegos [τρίστεγος, 5152], an adjective denoting of three stories (*treis*, three, *stegē*, a roof), occurs in Acts 20:9 (with *oikēma*, a dwelling, understood), R.V. "the third story" (A.V., "the third loft"). ¶

NT: B.826c; CB.–; K.–.
OT: –.
GEN. REF.: IS.4:632; NB.–; Z.–.

STRAIGHT

A. Adjectives.

1. *euthus* [εὐθύς, 2117], direct, straight, right, is translated "straight," figuratively, of the paths of the Lord, Matt. 3:3; Mark 1:3; Luke 3:4; in ver. 5 of the rectification of the crooked, with reference to moral transformation; in Acts 9:11, the name of a street in Damascus, still one of the principal thoroughfares. See RIGHT.

NT: B.321a; CB.1247b; K.–.
OT: yāshar: S.3474; HR.571a.2a; H.930; BD.448c.
yāshār: S.3477; HR.571a.2c; H.930a; BD.449a.
GEN. REF.: IS.4:633; NB.–; Z.5:526.

2. *orthos* [ὀρθός, 3717], used of height, denotes "upright," Acts 14:10; of line of direction, figuratively, said of paths of righteousness, Heb. 12:13. ¶

NT: B.580b; CB.1261b; K.727.
OT: yāshār: S.3477; HR.1010c.2c; H.930a; BD.449a.
GEN. REF.: IS.4:633; NB.–; Z.–.

B. Verbs.

1. *euthunō* [εὐθύνω, 2116], akin to A, No. 1, is used of the directing of a ship by the steersman, Jas. 3:4 (see GOVERNOR, B, *Note*); metaphorically, of making straight the way of the Lord, John 1:23. ¶

NT: B.320d; CB.–; K.–.
OT: yāshar: S.3474; HR.570c.1; H.930; BD.448c.
nāṭāh: S.5186; HR.570c.2; H.1352; BD.639d.
GEN. REF.: IS.4:633; NB.–; Z.–.

2. *anorthoō* [ἀνορθόω, 461], to set up, make straight: see LIFT, No. 6.

NT: B.72c; CB.–; K.–.
OT: kûn: S.3559; HR.108b.2; H.964; BD.465c.
GEN. REF.: –.

For STRAIGHT COURSE, see COURSE, B, *Note* (1)

For STRAIGHTWAY see FORTHWITH, Nos. 1, 2, 3, and IMMEDIATELY, No. 1

STRAIN OUT

diülizō [διϋλίζω, 1368], primarily denotes to strain thoroughly (*dia*, through, intensive, *hulizō*, to strain), then, to strain out, as through a sieve or strainer, as in the case of wine, so as to remove the unclean midge, Matt. 23:24, R.V. (A.V., "strain at"). ¶ In the Sept., Amos 6:6. ¶

NT: B.200b; CB.–; K.–.
OT: –.
GEN. REF.: IS.4:634; NB.–; Z.–.

For the Adjective STRAIT see NARROW

STRAIT (be in a), STRAITENED

1. *sunechō* [συνέχω, 4912], to hold together, constrain, is translated "I am in a strait" in Phil. 1:23 (Passive Voice), i.e., being restricted on both sides, under a pressure which prevents a definite choice; so in Luke 12:50, "(how) am I straitened," i.e., pressed in. See CONSTRAIN, A, No. 3.

NT: B.789a; CB.1270c; K.1117.
OT: 'āṣar: S.6113; HR.1315b.12a,b; H.1675; BD.783c.
GEN. REF.: IS.4:634; NB.–; Z.–.

2. *stenochōreō* [στενοχωρέω, 4729], to be pressed for room (*stenos*, narrow, *chōros*, a space) is rendered to be straitened in 2 Cor. 4:8, R.V. (A.V., "distressed"); 6:12 (twice). See ANGUISH, B, No. 1. ¶

NT: B.766c; CB.1270a; K.1077.
OT: ṣārar: S.6887; HR.1288c.3; H.1973,1974; BD.864c.
'ûṣ: S.213; HR.1288c.1; H.51; BD.21a.
GEN. REF.: IS.4:634; NB.–; Z.–.

3. *thlibō* [θλίβω, 2346], for which see AFFLICT, No. 4, is used in the perfect participle Passive of a narrowed way, in Matt. 7:14, R.V., "straitened," A.V., "narrow," of the way "that leadeth unto life," i.e., hemmed in like a narrow gorge between rocks.

NT: B.362a; CB.1272b; K.334.
OT: lāḥaṣ: S.3906; HR.652b.4; H.1106a; BD.537d.
ṣārar: S.6887; HR.652b.10b; H.1973,1974; BD.864c.
ṣar: S.6862; HR.652b.10c; H.1973-1975; BD.865a.
GEN. REF.: IS.4:634; NB.–; Z.–.

STRAITEST

akribestatos [ἀκριβέστατος, 196], the superlative degree of *akribēs*, accurate, exact (cp. *akribōs*, see ACCURATELY and associated words there), occurs in Acts 26:5, "the straitest (sect)," R.V. (A.V., "most straitest"). ¶

NT: B.–; CB.–; K.–.
OT: –.
GEN. REF.: –.

STRAITLY

Notes: (1) For *polla*, A.V., "straitly" in Mark 3:12; 5:43, see MUCH (R.V.).

(2) In Acts 4:17 some mss. have *apeilē*, a threat, with *apeileō* (Middle Voice), lit., 'let us threaten them with a threat,' A.V., "let us straitly threaten"; the best texts omit the noun (so R.V.). Moulton and Milligan (Vocab.), arguing for the presence of the noun, consider that it "clearly reflects the literal rendering of a Semitic original reported to Luke from an eye-witness — was it Paul?"

(3) A similar construction, *parangellō* with the noun *parangelia*, occurs in Acts 5:28, "we straitly charged you," lit., 'we charged you with a charge.' See CHARGE, A, No. 6.

(4) For *embrimaomai*, A.V., "charge straitly" (R.V., "strictly") in Matt. 9:30; Mark 1:43, see CHARGE, C, No. 4.

For **STRAKE**, Acts 27:17, A.V. (R.V., "lowered"), see **LET DOWN**, No. 2.

STRANGE

A. Adjectives.

1. *xenos* [ξένος, 3581], denotes (*a*) foreign, alien, Acts 17:18, of gods; Heb. 13:9, of doctrines; (*b*) unusual, 1 Pet. 4:12, 2nd part, of the fiery trial of persecution (for 1st part, see B). See STRANGER.

NT: B.548a; CB.1273b; K.661.
OT: nākrî: S.5237; HR.957a.3; H.1368c; BD.648d.
gēr: S.1616; HR.957a.2; H.330a; BD.158a.
GEN. REF.: IS.4:635; NB.–; Z.5:526.

2. *allotrios* [ἀλλότριος, 245], denotes (*a*) belonging to another (*allos*), see MAN'S, *Note* (1); (*b*) alien, foreign, strange, Acts 7:6; Heb. 11:9, A.V., R.V., "(a *land*) not his own." See ALIEN, STRANGER.

NT: B.40c; CB.1234c; K.43.
OT: nēkār: S.5236; HR.57a.4a; H.1368b; BD.648c.
nākrî: S.5237; HR.57a.4c; H.1368c; BD.648d.
GEN. REF.: IS.4:635; NB.–; Z.5:526.

3. *paradoxos* [παράδοξος, 3861], contrary to received opinion (*para*, beside, *doxa*, opinion; Eng. paradox, — ical), is rendered "strange things" in Luke 5:26. ¶

NT: B.615d; CB.–; K.178.
OT: –.
GEN. REF.: IS.4:635; NB.–; Z.–.

4. *exō* [ἔξω, 1854], outside, is rendered "strange" in Acts 26:11, A.V.: see FOREIGN.

NT: B.279b; CB.1247c; K.240.
OT: ḥûṣ: S.2351; HR.501c.2; H.627a; BD.299c.
GEN. REF.: –.

Note: In 1 Cor. 14:21 (1st part), R.V., *heteroglōssos*, signifying of a different tongue (*heteros*, another, *glōssa*, a tongue) is translated "of strange (A.V., other) tongues." ¶

B. Verb.

xenizō [ξενίζω, 3579], denotes to think something strange, 1 Pet. 4:4, 12, Passive Voice, i.e., 'they are surprised,' and 'be (not) surprised'; in Acts 17:20, the present participle, Active, is rendered "strange," i.e., 'surprising.' See ENTERTAIN, LODGE.

NT: B.547d; CB.1273b; K.661.
OT: –.
GEN. REF.: IS.4:635; NB.–; Z.5:526.

STRANGER

A. Adjectives (used as nouns).

1. *xenos* [ξένος, 3581], strange (see No. 1 above), denotes a stranger, foreigner, Matt. 25:35, 38, 43, 44; 27:7; Acts 17:21; Eph. 2:12, 19; Heb. 11:13; 3 John 5.

NT: B.548a; CB.1273b; K.661.
OT: nākrî: S.5237; HR.957a.3; H.1368c; BD.648d.
gēr: S.1616; HR.957a.2; H.330a; BD.158a.
GEN. REF.: IS.4:635; NB.–; Z.5:526.

2. *allotrios* [ἀλλότριος, 245], "strangers," Matt. 17:25, 26; John 10:5 (twice): see No. 2, above.

NT: B.40c; CB.1234c; K.43.
OT: nēkār: S.5236; HR.57a.4a; H.1368b; BD.648c.
nākrî: S.5237; HR.57a.4c; H.1368c; BD.648d.
GEN. REF.: IS.4:635; NB.–; Z.5:526.

3. *allogenēs* [ἀλλογενής, 241], (*allos*, another, *genos*, a race) occurs in Luke 17:18, of a Samaritan. Moulton and Milligan illustrate the use of the word by the inscription on the Temple barrier, "let no foreigner enter within the screen and enclosure surrounding the sanctuary"; according to Mommsen this inscription was cut by the Romans: cp. PARTITION. ¶

NT: B.39c; CB.1234c; K.43.
OT: nēkār: S.5236; HR.55c.3a; H.1368b; BD.648c.
zûr: S.2114; HR.55c.1; H.541; BD.266b.
GEN. REF.: IS.–; NB.–; Z.5:526.

Notes: (1) For *paroikos*, in A.V., see SOJOURN, B, No. 1. For *parepidēmos*, in A.V., see PILGRIM.

(2) The pronoun *heteros*, other, is translated "strangers" in 1 Cor. 14:21 (2nd part), R.V. (A.V., "other"); cp. STRANGE, A, *Note*.

B. Verb.

xenodocheō [ξενοδοχέω, 3580], to receive strangers (*xenos*, No. 1, above, and *dechomai*, to receive), occurs in 1 Tim. 5:10, R.V., "(if) she hath used hospitality to strangers," A.V., "(if) she have lodged strangers." ¶

NT: B.548a; CB.1273b; K.661.
OT: –.
GEN. REF.: –.

Note: For *epidēmeō*, in A.V., see SOJOURNER, A, No. 2. For *paroikeō*, in A.V., see SOJOURN, A, No. 1.

C. Noun.

philoxenia [φιλοξενία, 5381], love of strangers, occurs in Rom. 12:13, "hospitality," and Heb. 13:2, R.V., "to shew love unto strangers," A.V., "to entertain strangers." See ENTERTAIN, *Note*. ¶

NT: B.860d; CB.1264b; K.661.
OT: –.
GEN. REF.: IS.4:635; NB.–; Z.–.

Note: For *paroikia* in Acts 13:17, see SOJOURN, C.

STRANGLED

pniktos [πνικτός, 4156], from *pnigo*, to choke, occurs in Acts 15:20, 29; 21:25, of the flesh of animals killed by strangling, without shedding their blood (see, e.g., Lev. 17:13, 14). ¶

NT: B.679d; CB.1265c; K.895.
OT: –.
GEN. REF.: IS.4:636; NB.–; Z.–.

For **STRAWED** see **FURNISH** and **SCATTER**, No. 2

For **STREAM** see **RIVER**

STREET

1. *plateia* [πλατεῖα, 4113], grammatically the feminine of *platus*, broad, is used as a noun (*hodos*, a way, being understood, i.e., a broad way), a street, Matt. 6:5; 12:19 (in some texts, Mark 6:56); Luke 10:10; 13:26; 14:21; Acts 5:15; Rev. 11:8; 21:21; 22:2. ¶

NT: B.666d; CB.1265a; K.–.
OT: r^{e}ḥôb: S.7339; HR.1140c.2; H.2143d; BD.932a.
GEN. REF.: IS.4:636; NB.–; Z.–.

2. *amphodon* [ἄμφοδον, 296], properly a way around (*amphi*, around, *hodos*, a way), occurs in Mark 11:4, R.V., "the open street" (A.V., "where two ways met"). ¶

NT: B.47c; CB.–; K.–.
OT: –.
GEN. REF.: IS.4:636; NB.–; Z.–.

Note: For *rhumē*, see LANE. For *agora*, see MARKET.

STRENGTH, STRENGTHEN

A. Nouns.

1. *dunamis* [δύναμις, 1411], is rendered "strength" in the R.V. and A.V. of Rev. 1:16; elsewhere the R.V. gives the word its more appropriate meaning "power," for A.V., "strength," 1 Cor. 15:56; 2 Cor. 1:8; 12:9; Heb. 11:11; Rev. 3:8; 12:10. See ABILITY, No. 1, POWER, No. 1.

NT: B.207b; CB.1242b; K.186.
OT: ḥayil: S.2428; HR.350a.11; H.624a; BD.298c.
ṣābā': S.6635; HR.350a.25; H.1865a,b; BD.838d.
GEN. REF.: IS.4:637; NB.–; Z.–.

2. *ischus* [ἰσχύς, 2479], ability, strength, is rendered "strength" in Mark 12:30, 33; Luke 10:27; in Rev. 5:12, A.V. (R.V., "might"). See ABILITY, No. 2, MIGHT.

NT: B.383c; CB.1253a; K.378.
OT: kōaḥ: S.3581; HR.694b.16; H.971.1; BD.470c.
hayil: S.2428; HR.694b.13; H.624a; BD.298c.
GEN. REF.: IS.4:637; NB.–; Z.–.

3. *kratos* [κράτος, 2904], force, might, is rendered "strength" in Luke 1:51, R.V. and A.V.; R.V., "strength" (A.V., "power") in Eph. 1:19 and 6:10. See DOMINION, No. 1, POWER, No. 4.

NT: B.449a; CB.1256a; K.466.
OT: ḥāzaq: S.2388; HR.784a.4; H.636; BD.304a.
'ōz: S.5797; HR.784a.6; H.1596b; BD.738d.
'ammîṣ: S.533; HR.784a.2; H.117d; BD.55c.
GEN. REF.: IS.4:637; NB.–; Z.–.

Note: In Rev. 17:13, A.V., *exousia*, freedom of action, is rendered "strength" (R.V., "authority").

B. Verbs.

1. *dunamoō* [δυναμόω, 1412], to strengthen, occurs in Col. 1:11, and in the best texts in Heb. 11:34, "were made strong" (some have No. 2); some have it in Eph. 6:10 (the best have No. 2). ¶ In the Sept., Psa. 52:7; 68:28; Eccl. 10:10; Dan. 9:27. ¶

NT: B.208c; CB.1242b; K.186.
OT: gābar: S.1396; HR.353a.1; H.310; BD.149c.
'āzaz: S.5810; HR.353a.2; H.1596; BD.738b.
GEN. REF.: IS.4:637; NB.–; Z.–.

2. *endunamoō* [ἐνδυναμόω, 1743], to make strong, is rendered "increased . . . in strength" in Acts 9:22; to strengthen in Phil. 4:13; 2 Tim. 2:1, R.V., "be strengthened"; 4:17. See ENABLE, STRONG, B.

NT: B.263d; CB.1245a; K.186.
OT: lābash: S.3847; HR.472a.1; H.1075; BD.527d.
'āzaz: S.5810; HR.472a.2; H.1596; BD.738b.
GEN. REF.: –.

3. *ischuō* [ἰσχύω, 2480], akin to A, No. 2, to have strength, is so rendered in Mark 5:4, R.V. (A.V., "could"); in Luke 16:3, R.V., "I have not strength to" (A.V., "I cannot"). See AVAIL.

NT: B.383d; CB.1253a; K.378.
OT: ḥāzaq: S.2388; HR.692c.6a-c; H.636; BD.304a.
gābar: S.1396; HR.692c.5a; H.310; BD.149c.
gibbôr: S.1368; HR.692c.5b; H.310b; BD.150a.
GEN. REF.: –.

4. *enischuō* [ἐνισχύω, 1765], akin to A, No. 2, a strengthened form of No. 3, is used in Luke 22:43 and Acts 9:19. ¶

NT: B.266d; CB.1245a; K.—.
OT: ḥāzaq: S.2388; HR.475a.4a-c; H.636; BD.304a.
GEN. REF.: —.

5. *krataioō* [κραταιόω, 2901], to strengthen, is rendered "to be strengthened" in Eph. 3:16. See STRONG, B.

NT: B.448b; CB.1256a; K.466.
OT: ḥāzaq: S.2388; HR.782b.3; H.636; BD.304a.
'āzaz: S.5810; HR.782c.7a-c; H.1596; BD.738b.
GEN. REF.: —.

6. *sthenoō* [σθενόω, 4599], from *sthenōs*, strength, occurs in 1 Pet. 5:10, in a series of future tenses, according to the best texts, thus constituting Divine promises. ¶

NT: B.749c; CB.—; K.—.
OT: —.
GEN. REF.: —.

Note: (1) For *ischuō*, Heb. 9:17, see AVAIL.

(2) For *stērizō*, Luke 22:32, see ESTABLISH, No. 1.

(3) For *stereoō*, Acts 3:7, see ESTABLISH, No. 2.

(4) *Epistērizō* is found in some texts in Acts 18:23, A.V., "strengthening." See CONFIRM, A, No. 2, ESTABLISH, No. 1.

(5) For "without strength," Rom. 5:6, A.V., see WEAK.

STRETCH

1. *ekteinō* [ἐκτείνω, 1614], to stretch out or forth, is so rendered in Matt. 12:13 (twice), 49; 14:31; 26:51; Mark 3:5 (twice); Luke 6:10; in Matt. 8:3; Mark 1:41 and Luke 5:13, R.V. (A.V., "put forth"); Luke 22:53; John 21:18; Acts 4:30; 26:1. For Acts 27:30 see LAY, No. 13. ¶

NT: B.245b; CB.1244a; K.219.
OT: shālaḥ: S.7971; HR.442a.16a; H.2394; BD.1018a.
nāṭāh: S.5186; HR.442a.7a; H.1352; BD.639d.
GEN. REF.: —.

2. *epekteinō* [ἐπεκτείνω, 1901], an intensive form of No. 1 (*epi*, forth), is used in Phil. 3:13, R.V., "stretching forward" (A.V., "reaching forth"), a metaphor probably from the foot race (rather than the chariot race), so Lightfoot, who quotes Bengel's paraphrase, 'the eye goes before and draws on the hand, the hand goes before and draws on the foot.' ¶

NT: B.284d; CB.—; K.—.
OT: —.
GEN. REF.: —.

3. *huperekteinō* [ὑπερεκτείνω, 5239], to stretch out beyond (*huper*, over, and No. 1), occurs in 2 Cor. 10:14, R.V., "we stretch (not) . . . overmuch" (A.V., ". . . beyond *our measure*"). ¶

NT: B.840d; CB.—; K.219.
OT: —.
GEN. REF.: —.

Note: For *ekpetannumi*, Rom. 10:21, see SPREAD, No. 5. For *epiballō*, Acts 12:1, see PUT, No. 8.

STRICKEN (in years)

probainō [προβαίνω, 4260], to go forward, is used metaphorically of age, in Luke 1:7, 18, with the phrases "in their (her) days," translated "well stricken in years" (see marg.); in 2:36, "of a great age" (marg., "advanced in many days"). See GO, No. 20.

NT: B.702d; CB.1266c; K.—.
OT: bō': S.935; HR.1204a.1; H.212; BD.97c.
GEN. REF.: —.

For **STRICT**, R.V., see **MANNER**, A, No. 5. For **STRICTLY**, R.V., see **STRAITLY**

STRIFE

1. *eris* [ἔρις, 2054], strife, contention, is the expression of enmity, Rom. 1:29, R.V., "strife" (A.V., "debate"); 13:13; 1 Cor. 1:11, "contentions" (R.V. and A.V.); 3:3; 2 Cor. 12:20, R.V., "strife" (A.V., "debates"); Gal. 5:20, R.V., "strife" (A.V., "variance"); Phil. 1:15; 1 Tim. 6:4; Tit. 3:9, R.V., "strifes" (A.V., "contentions"). See CONTENTION, A, No. 1. ¶

NT: B.309c; CB.1246c; K.—.
OT: —.
GEN. REF.: —.

2. *erithia* (or *-eia*) [ἐριθία, —]: see FACTION.

3. *antilogia* [ἀντιλογία, —], "strife," Heb. 6:16, A.V.: see DISPUTE, A, No. 4.

4. *machē* [μάχη, —], "strifes," 2 Tim. 2:23: see FIGHTING, A.

5. *philoneikia* [φιλονεικία, —], "strife," Luke 22:24, A.V.: see CONTENTION, A, No. 3. ¶

6. *logomachia* [λογομαχία, —], "strife of words," 1 Tim. 6:4: see DISPUTE, A, No. 2. ¶

STRIKE

Note: (1) In Rev. 7:16, *piptō*, to fall, is rendered "strike" in the R.V., A.V., "light (on)."

(2) In Acts 27:41, *ereidō*, to fix firmly, is used of a ship driving ashore, R.V., "struck" (A.V., "stuck fast"). ¶

(3) For *paiō*, to smite, Rev. 9:5, A.V., "striketh," see SMITE, No. 3.

(4) For *patassō*, to smite, Matt. 26:51, A.V., "struck," see SMITE, No. 1.

(5) For *chalaō*, to let go, Acts 27:17, A.V., "strake," see LET DOWN, No. 2.

(6) In Luke 22:64 some mss. have *tuptō*, to beat, imperfect tense, 'they were beating.'

(7) For *rhapizō*, Matt. 26:67, and *rhapisma*, Mark 14:65, see BLOW, SMITE, No. 6 and *Note* (2). Some mss. have *ballō*, "struck."

STRIKER

plēktēs [πλήκτης, 4131], a striker, a brawler (akin to *plēssō*, to strike, smite), occurs in 1 Tim. 3:3; Tit. 1:7. ¶

NT: B.669b; CB.–; K.–.
OT: –.
GEN. REF.: –.

For STRING see BOND, No. 1

STRIP

ekduō [ἐκδύω, 1562], to take off, strip off, is used especially of clothes, and rendered to strip in Matt. 27:28 (some mss. have *enduō*, to clothe), and Luke 10:30; to take off, Matt. 27:31; Mark 15:20; figuratively, 2 Cor. 5:4, "unclothed" (Middle Voice), of putting off the body at death (the believer's state of being unclothed does not refer to the body in the grave but to the spirit, which awaits the "body of glory" at the resurrection). ¶

NT: B.239b; CB.1243c; K.192.
OT: pāshaṭ: S.6584; HR.423c.2; H.1845; BD.832d.
GEN. REF.: –.

STRIPE

1. *mōlōps* [μώλωψ, 3468], a bruise, a wound from a stripe, is used in 1 Pet. 2:24 (from the Sept. of Is. 53:5), lit., in the original, 'by whose bruise,' not referring to Christ's scourging, but figurative of the stroke of Divine judgment administered vicariously to Him on the Cross (a comforting reminder to these Christian servants, who were not infrequently buffeted, ver. 20, by their masters). ¶

NT: B.531a; CB.1259a; K.619.
OT: ḥabbûrāh: S.2250; HR.938a.1; H.598g; BD.289a.
GEN. REF.: –.

2. *plēgē* [πληγή, 4127], a blow, stripe, wound (akin to *plēssō*, to strike, and *plēktēs*, a striker), is rendered "stripes" in Luke 12:48 (the noun is omitted in the original in ver. 47 and the 2nd part of ver. 48); Acts 16:23, 33; 2 Cor. 6:5; 11:23. See PLAGUE, WOUND.

NT: B.668a; CB.1265a; K.–.
OT: makkāh: S.4347; HR.1142b.3a; H.1364d; BD.646d.
maggēphāh: S.4046; HR.1142b.5b; H.1294b; BD.620a.
GEN. REF.: –.

STRIVE

1. *agōnizomai* [ἀγωνίζομαι, 75], to contend (Eng., agonize), is rendered to strive in Luke 13:24; 1 Cor. 9:25; Col. 1:29; 4:12, R.V. (A.V., "labouring fervently"). In 1 Tim. 4:10, the best texts have this verb (R.V., "strive") for *oneidizomai*, to suffer reproach, A.V.; see FIGHT, B, No. 1.

NT: B.15b; CB.1233c; K.20.
OT: shᵉdar (Aramaic): S.7712; HR.18c.2; H.3021; BD.1114c.
GEN. REF.: IS.4:637; NB.–; Z.–.

2. *machomai* [μάχομαι, 3164], to fight, to quarrel, dispute, is rendered to strive in John 6:52; Acts 7:26; 2 Tim. 2:24. See FIGHT, B, No. 3.

NT: B.496c; CB.1257b; K.573.
OT: rîb: S.7378; HR.900c.6; H.2159; BD.936d.
nāṣāh: S.5327; HR.900c.5; H.1399-1401; BD.663c.
GEN. REF.: IS.4:637; NB.–; Z.–.

3. *diamachomai* [διαμάχομαι, 1264], to struggle against (*dia*, intensive, and No. 2), is used of contending in an argument, Acts 23:9, "strove." ¶

NT: B.186c; CB.–; K.–.
OT: lāḥam: S.3898; HR.305c.1; H.1104; BD.535b.
GEN. REF.: –.

4. *erizō* [ἐρίζω, —], to wrangle, strive (*eris*, strife), is used in Matt. 12:19. ¶

NT: –
OT: –.
GEN. REF.: –.

5. *logomacheō* [λογομαχέω, —], to strive about words (*logos*, a word, and No. 2), is used in 2 Tim. 2:14. ¶

NT: –.
OT: –.
GEN. REF.: –.

6. *antagōnizomai* [ἀνταγωνίζομαι, 464], to struggle against (*anti*), is used in Heb. 12:4, "striving against." ¶

NT: B.72d; CB.1236a; K.20.
OT: –.
GEN. REF.: –.

7. *sunagōnizomai* [συναγωνίζομαι, 4865], to strive together with (*sun*), is used in Rom. 15:30. ¶

NT: B.783b; CB.1270b; K.–.
OT: –.
GEN. REF.: IS.4:637; NB.–; Z.–.

8. *sunathleō* [συναθλέω, 4866], to strive together, Phil. 1:27: see LABOUR, B, No. 3.

NT: B.783b; CB.1270c; K.25.
OT: –.
GEN. REF.: IS.4:637; NB.–; Z.–.

Notes: (1) In 2 Tim. 2:5, A.V., *athleō*, to contend in games, wrestle (*athlos*, a contest), is rendered "strive." See CONTEND.

(2) For *philotimeomai*, Rom. 15:20, see AIM.

For STRIVINGS, Tit. 3:9, A.V., see FIGHTING

STROLLING

perierchomai [περιέρχομαι, 4022], to go about, as an itinerant (*peri*, around, *erchomai*, to go), is used of certain Jews in Acts 19:13, R.V., "strolling" (A.V., "vagabond"). See COMPASS, No. 6, WANDER.

NT: B.646d; CB.1263b; K.257.
OT: sābab: S.5437; HR.1123a.1; H.1456; BD.685b.
GEN. REF.: –.

STRONG, STRONGER

A. Adjectives.

1. *dunatos* [δυνατός, 1415], powerful, mighty, is translated "strong," in Rom. 15:1, where the "strong" are those referred to in ch. 14, in contrast to "the weak in faith," those who have scruples in regard to eating meat and the observance of days; 2 Cor. 12:10, where the strength lies in bearing sufferings in the realization that the endurance is for Christ's sake; 2 Cor. 13:9, where "ye are strong" implies the good spiritual condition which the Apostle desires for the church at Corinth in having nothing requiring his exercise of discipline (contrast No. 2 in 1 Cor. 4:10). See ABLE, C, No. 1, MIGHTY, POSSIBLE, POWER.

NT: B.208c; CB.1242b; K.186.
OT: gibbôr: S.1368; HR.355c.6a; H.310b; BD.150a.
ḥayil: S.2428; HR.355c.9a; H.624a; BD.298c.
GEN. REF.: IS.3:926; NB.—; Z.—.

2. *ischuros* [ἰσχυρός, 2478], strong, mighty, is used of (*a*) persons: (1) God, Rev. 18:8; (2) angels, Rev. 5:2; 10:1; 18:21; (3) men, Matt. 12:29 (twice) and parallel passages; Heb. 11:34, A.V., "valiant" (R.V., "mighty"); Rev. 6:15 (in the best texts; some have No. 1); 19:18, "mighty"; metaphorically, (4) the church at Corinth, 1 Cor. 4:10, where the Apostle reproaches them ironically with their unspiritual and self-complacent condition; (5) of young men in Christ spiritually strong, through the Word of God, to overcome the evil one, 1 John 2:14; of (*b*) things: (1) wind, Matt. 14:30 (in some mss.), "boisterous"; (2) famine, Luke 15:14; (3) things in the mere human estimate, 1 Cor. 1:27; (4) Paul's letters, 2 Cor. 10:10; (5) the Lord's crying and tears, Heb. 5:7; (6) consolation, 6:18; (7) the voice of an angel, Rev. 18:2 (in the best texts; some have *megas*, "great"); (8) Babylon, Rev. 18:10; (9) thunderings, Rev. 19:6. See BOISTEROUS, MIGHTY.

NT: B.383a; CB.1253a; K.378.
OT: gibbôr: S.1368; HR.693b.10a; H.310b; BD.150a.
ḥāzāq: S.2389; HR.693b.13a; H.636a; BD.305c.
'az: S.5794; HR.693b.17a; H.1596a; BD.738c.
GEN. REF.: IS.3:926; NB.—; Z.—.

3. *ischuroteros* [ἰσχυρότερος, 2478], the comparative degree of No. 2, is used (*a*) of Christ, Matt. 3:11; Mark 1:7; Luke 3:16; (*b*) of "the weakness of God," as men without understanding regard it, 1 Cor. 1:25; (*c*) of a man of superior physical strength, Luke 11:22; (*d*) in 1 Cor. 10:22, in a rhetorical question, implying the impossibility of escaping the jealousy of God when it is kindled. ¶

NT: B.383a; CB.1253a; K.—.
OT: gibbôr: S.1368; HR.693b.10a; H.310b; BD.150a.
ḥāzāq: S.2389; HR.693b.13a; H.636a; BD.305c.
'az: S.5794; HR.693b.17a; H.1596a; BD.738c.
GEN. REF.: IS.3:926; NB.—; Z.—.

Notes: (1) For "strong delusion," 2 Thess. 2:11, A.V., see ERROR, No. 1.

(2) For "strong (meat)," Heb. 5:12, 14, A.V., see SOLID.

B. Verbs.

1. *endunamoō* [ἐνδυναμόω, 1743], to make strong (*en*, in, *dunamis*, power), to strengthen, is rendered "waxed strong" in Rom. 4:20, R.V. (A.V., "was strong"); "be strong," Eph. 6:10; "were made strong," Heb. 11:34. See ENABLE, STRENGTH, B, No. 2.

NT: B.263c; CB.1245a; K.186.
OT: lābash: S.3847; HR.472a.1; H.1075; BD.527d.
'āzaz: S.5810; HR.472a.2; H.1596; BD.738b.
GEN. REF.: —.

2. *krataioō* [κραταιόω, 2901], to strengthen (akin to *kratos*, strength), is rendered (a) to wax strong, Luke 1:80; 2:40; "be strong," 1 Cor. 16:13, lit., 'be strengthened'; "to be strengthened," Eph. 3:16 (Passive Voice in each place). See STRENGTHEN. ¶

NT: B.448b; CB.1256a; K.466.
OT: hāzaq: S.2388; HR.782b.3a-d; H.636; BD.304a.
'āzaz: S.5810; HR.782c.7a; H.1596; BD.738b.
GEN. REF.: IS.3:926; NB.—; Z.—.

3. *stereoō* [στερεόω, —]: see ESTABLISH, No. 2.

STRONGHOLDS

ochurōma [ὀχύρωμα, 3794], a stronghold, fortress (akin to *ochuroō*, to make firm), is used metaphorically in 2 Cor. 10:4, of those things in which mere human confidence is imposed. ¶

NT: B.601b; CB.1260b; K.752.
OT: mibṣār: S.4013; HR.1043c.3c; H.270g; BD.131b.
GEN. REF.: IS.4:640; NB.—; Z.—.

STUBBLE

kalamē [καλάμη, 2562], a stalk of corn, denotes straw or stubble; in 1 Cor. 3:12, metaphorically of the effect of the most worthless form of unprofitable doctrine, in the lives and conduct of those in a church who are the subjects of such teaching; the teachings received and the persons who receive them are associated; the latter are "the doctrine exhibited in concrete form" (Lightfoot). ¶

NT: B.398c; CB.—; K.—.
OT: qash: S.7179; HR.712b.3; H.2091a; BD.905d.
GEN. REF.: IS.4:640; NB.1220; Z.5:527.

For **STUCK** see **STICK**

STUDY

Notes: For *philotimeomai*, "study," 1 Thess. 4:11, see AIM. For *spoudazō*, 2 Tim. 2:15, A.V., see DILIGENCE, B, No. 1.

For **STUFF**, Luke 17:31, A.V., see **GOODS**, No. 4.

STUMBLE

1. *proskoptō* [προσκόπτω, 4350], to strike against, is used of stumbling, (*a*) physically, John 11:9, 10; (*b*) metaphorically, (1) of Israel in regard to Christ, whose Person, teaching, and atoning Death, and the Gospel relating thereto, were contrary to all their ideas as to the means of righteousness before God, Rom. 9:32; 1 Pet. 2:8; (2) of a brother in the Lord in acting against the dictates of his conscience, Rom. 14:21. See BEAT, No. 6.

NT: B.716b; CB.1267b; K.946.
OT: kāshal: S.3782; HR.1217b.1; H.1050; BD.505b.
nāgaph: S.5062; HR.1217b.2; H.1294; BD.619d.
GEN. REF.: IS.—; NB.1220; Z.—.

2. *ptaiō* [πταίω, 4417], to cause to stumble, signifies, intransitively, to stumble, used metaphorically in Rom. 11:11, in the sense (*b*) (1) in No. 1; with moral significance in Jas. 2:10 and 3:2 (twice), R.V., "stumble" (A.V., "offend"); in 2 Pet. 1:10, R.V., "stumble" (A.V., "fall"). ¶

NT: B.727a; CB.1267c; K.968.
OT: nāgaph: S.5062; HR.1237c.2; H.1294; BD.619d.
GEN. REF.: —.

Note: For *aptaistos*, "from stumbling," Jude 24, R.V., see FALL, B, *Note* (6).

For **STUMBLING, STUMBLING BLOCK, STUMBLING-STONE**, see **OFFENCE**, A, Nos. 1, 2, 3 and B

STUPOR

katanuxis [κατάνυξις, 2659], a pricking (akin to *katanussō*, to strike or prick violently, Acts 2:37), is used in Rom. 11:8, R.V., "stupor" (A.V., "slumber"). It is suggested that this meaning arose from the influence of the verb *katanustazō*, to nod or fall asleep (Field, *Notes on the Translation of the N.T.*). Evidently what is signified is the dulling of the spiritual sense. ¶ In the Sept., Psa. 60:3; Isa. 29:10. ¶

NT: B.415c; CB.—; K.419.
OT: tardēmāh: S.8639; HR.739c.1; H.2123a; BD.922b.
tar'ēlāh: S.8653; HR.739c.2; H.2188c; BD.947a.
GEN. REF.: —.

SUBDUE

katagōnizomai [καταγωνίζομαι, 2610], primarily, to struggle against (*kata*, against, *agōn*, a contest), came to signify to conquer, Heb. 11:33, "subdued." ¶

NT: B.410a; CB.1254a; K.20.
OT: —.
GEN. REF.: —.

Note: For *hupotassō*, A.V., to subdue, in 1 Cor. 15:28 and Phil. 3:21, see SUBJECT.

SUBJECT, SUBJECTION (Verb, Adjective, Noun)

A. Verb.

hupotassō [ὑποτάσσω, 5293], primarily a military term, to rank under (*hupo*, under, *tassō*, to arrange), denotes (*a*) to put in subjection, to subject, Rom. 8:20 (twice); in the following, the R.V., has to subject for A.V., to put under, 1 Cor. 15:27 (thrice), 28 (3rd clause); Eph. 1:22; Heb. 2:8 (4th clause); in 1 Cor. 15:28 (1st clause), for A.V. "be subdued"; in Phil. 3:21, for A.V., "subdue"; in Heb. 2:5, A.V., "hath . . . put in subjection"; (*b*) in the Middle or Passive Voice, to subject oneself, to obey, be subject to, Luke 2:51; 10:17, 20; Rom. 8:7; 10:3, R.V., "did (not) subject themselves" [A.V., "have (not) submitted themselves"]; 13:1, 5; 1 Cor. 14:34, R.V., "be in subjection" (A.V., "be under obedience"); 15:28 (2nd clause); 16:16, R.V., "be in subjection" (A.V., "submit, etc."); so Col. 3:18; Eph. 5:21, R.V., "subjecting yourselves" (A.V., "submitting, etc."); ver. 22, R.V. in italics, according to the best texts; ver. 24, "is subject"; Tit. 2:5, 9, R.V., "be in subjection" (A.V., "be obedient"); 3:1, R.V., "to be in subjection" (A.V., "to be subject"); Heb. 12:9, "be in subjection"; Jas. 4:7, R.V., "be subject" (A.V., "submit yourselves"); so 1 Pet. 2:13; ver. 18, R.V., "be in subjection"; so 3:1, A.V. and R.V.; ver. 5, similarly; 3:22, "being made subject"; 5:5, R.V., "be subject" (A.V., "submit yourselves"); in some texts in the 2nd part, as A.V. See OBEDIENT, SUBMIT.

NT: B.847d; CB.—; K.1156.
OT: dāmam: S.1826; HR.1417b.3; H.439; BD.198d.
kābash: S.3533; HR.1417b.4; H.951; BD.461b.
māshal: S.4910; HR.1417b.5; H.1258,1259; BD.605c.
GEN. REF.: IS.4:643; NB.—; Z.—.

Note: For *doulagōgeō*, 1 Cor. 9:27, A.V., "bring into subjection," see BONDAGE, B, No. 3. For *anupotaktos*, "not subject," Heb. 2:8, see DISOBEDIENT, B, *Note*.

B. Adjective.

enochos [ἔνοχος, 1777], held in, bound by, in Heb. 2:15, "subject to": see DANGER, B, No. 1.

NT: B.267d; CB.1245b; K.286.
OT: dām: S.1818; HR.476c.2a; H.436; BD.196b.
GEN. REF.: IS.4:643; NB.—; Z.—.

Note: For "subject to like passions," Jas. 5:17, A.V., see PASSION.

C. Noun.

hupotagē [ὑποταγή, 5292], subjection, occurs in 2 Cor. 9:13; Gal. 2:5; 1 Tim. 2:11; 3:4. ¶

NT: B.847d; CB.1252b; K.1156.
OT: —.
GEN. REF.: IS.4:643; NB.—; Z.—.

SUBMIT

hupeikō [ὑπείκω, 5226], to retire, withdraw (*hupo*, under, *eikō*, to yield), hence, to yield, submit, is used metaphorically in Heb. 13:17, of submitting to spiritual guides in the churches. ¶

NT: B.838b; CB.—; K.—.
OT: —.
GEN. REF.: —.

Note: For *hupotassō*, see SUBJECT, A.

SUBORN

hupoballō [ὑποβάλλω, 5260], to throw or put under, to subject, denoted to suggest; whisper, prompt; hence, to instigate, translated "suborned" in Acts 6:11. To suborn in the legal sense is to procure a person who will take a false oath. The idea of making suggestions is probably present in this use of the word. ¶

NT: B.843d; CB.—; K.—.
OT: —.
GEN. REF.: IS.4:377; NB.—; Z.—.

SUBSTANCE

1. *ousia* [οὐσία, 3776], derived from a present participial form of *eimi*, to be, denotes substance, property, Luke 15:12, 13, R.V., "substance," A.V., "goods" and "substance." ¶

NT: B.596a; CB.1261b; K.—.
OT: —.
GEN. REF.: —.

2. *huparchonta* [ὑπάρχοντα, 5224], the neuter plural of the present participle of *huparchō*, to be in existence, is used as a noun with the article, signifying one's goods, and translated "substance" in Luke 8:3. See GOODS, POSSESS, A, No. 3.

NT: B.838a; CB.1252a; K.—.
OT: miqneh: S.4735; HR.1406b.4h; H.2039b; BD.889b.
rᵉkûsh: S.7399; HR.1406b.4l; H.2167b; BD.940d.
GEN. REF.: IS.4:644; NB.—; Z.—.

3. *huparxis* [ὕπαρξις, 5223], existence (akin to No. 2), possession: see POSSESS, B, No. 4.

NT: B.837d; CB.1252a; K.—.
OT: hôn: S.1952; HR.1406b.1; H.487a; BD.223c.
rᵉkûsh: S.7399; HR.1406b.4; H.2167b; BD.940d.
GEN. REF.: IS.4:644; NB.—; Z.—.

4. *hupostasis* [ὑπόστασις, 5287], for which see CONFIDENCE, A, No. 2, is translated "substance" (*a*) in Heb. 1:3, of Christ as "the very image" of God's "substance"; here the word has the meaning of the real nature of that to which reference is made in contrast to the outward manifestation (see the preceding clause); it speaks of the Divine essence of God existent and expressed in the revelation of His Son. The A.V., "person" is an anachronism; the word was not so rendered till the 4th cent. Most of the earlier Eng. versions have "substance"; (*b*) in Heb. 11:1 it has the meaning of confidence, "assurance" (R.V.), marg., "the giving substance to," A.V., "substance," something that could not equally be expressed by *elpis*, hope.

NT: B.847b; CB.1252b; K.1237.
OT: yᵉqûm: S.3351; HR.1417a.2; H.1999f; BD.879c.
sôd: S.5475; HR.1417a.7; H.1471a; BD.691c.
rāqam: S.7551; HR.1417a.8; H.2216; BD.955c.
GEN. REF.: —.

SUBTILLY

katasophizomai [κατασοφίζομαι, 2686], to deal subtilly (from *kata*, against, under, *sophos*, wise, subtle, used in the Sept. in 2 Sam. 13:3, of Jonadab), occurs in Acts 7:19. ¶ In the Sept., Ex. 1:10. ¶

NT: B.418c; CB.—; K.—.
OT: ḥākam: S.2449; HR.745a.1; H.647; BD.314b.
GEN. REF.: —.

SUBTILTY

Note: For *dolos*, Matt. 26:4; Acts 13:10, see GUILE. For *panourgia*, 2 Cor. 11:3, see CRAFTINESS

SUBVERT, SUBVERTING

A. Verb.

anaskeuazō [ἀνασκευάζω, 384], primarily, to pack up baggage (*ana*, up *skeuos*, a vessel), hence, from a military point of view, to dismantle a town, to plunder, is used metaphorically in Acts 15:24, of unsettling or subverting the souls of believers. In the papyri it is used of going bankrupt. ¶

NT: B.60b; CB.—; K.—.
OT: —.
GEN. REF.: IS.4:647; NB.—; Z.—.

Note: For *anatrepō*, Tit. 1:11, see OVERTHROW, B, No. 3. For *ekstrephō*, Tit. 3:11, see PERVERT, No. 4.

B. Noun.

katastrophē [καταστροφή, 2692], an overthrow, 2 Pet. 2:6 (Eng., catastrophe), is rendered "subverting" in 2 Tim. 2:14. See OVERTHROW. ¶

NT: B.419b; CB.—; K.1093.
OT: 'ēd: S.343; HR.746a.1; H.38c; BD.15c.
shādad: S.7703; HR.746a.5; H.2331; BD.994a.
GEN. REF.: IS.4:647; NB.—; Z.—.

For **SUCCEED**, Acts 24:27, R.V., see **ROOM**, *Note* (2)

For **SUCCOUR** see **HELP**, B, No. 4

SUCCOURER

prostatis [προστάτις, 4368], a feminine form of *prostatēs*, denotes a protectress, patroness; it is used metaphorically of Phoebe in Rom. 16:2. It is a word of dignity, evidently chosen instead of others which might have been used (see, e.g., under HELPER), and indicates the high esteem with which she was regarded, as one who had been a protectress of many.

Prostatēs was the title of a citizen in Athens, who had the responsibility of seeing to the welfare of resident aliens who were without civic rights. Among the Jews it signified a wealthy patron of the community. ¶

NT: B.718d; CB.—; K.—.
OT: —.
GEN. REF.: —.

For **SUCH** see † p. 1

SUCH AS

Notes: (1) In Acts 2:47, A.V., the article with the present participle, Passive, of *sōzō*, to save, lit., the (ones), i.e., those, being saved, is translated "such as (should be saved)"; the R.V., "those that (were being saved)," gives the correct meaning, marking the kind of persons who were added to the company;

(2) "such as" is a rendering of certain relative pronouns: *hoios*, what sort of, e.g., Matt. 24:21; 2 Cor. 12:20 (twice); Rev. 16:18; *hostis*, whoever, e.g., Mark 4:20; *hopoios*, of what sort, preceded by *toioutos*, of such a sort, Acts 26:29;

(3) *deina*, Matt. 26:18, denotes such a one (whom one cannot, or will not, name). ¶

(4) In Heb. 13:5, "such things as ye have" represents the phrase *ta paronta*,' the (things) present' (present participle of *pareimi*);

(5) in Luke 11:41, *ta enōnta*, A.V., "such things as ye have," lit., 'the (things) within' (*eneimi*, to be in), R.V., "those things which are within" (A.V. marg., "as you are able," R.V., marg., "ye can"), perhaps signifying not outward things such as lustrations, but 'what things ye have within your cups and platters,' i.e., your possessions.

SUCK (GIVE SUCK), SUCKLING

thēlazō [θηλάζω, 2337], from *thēlē*, a breast, is used (*a*) of the mother, to suckle, Matt. 24:19; Mark 13:17; Luke 21:23; in some texts in 23:29 (the best have *trephō*); (*b*) of the young, to suck, Matt. 21:16, "sucklings"; Luke 11:27. ¶

NT: B.360c; CB.—; K.—.
OT: yānaq: S.3243; HR.650a.1; H.874; BD.413b.
GEN. REF.: —.

SUDDEN, SUDDENLY

A. Adjective.

aiphnidios [αἰφνίδιος, 160], sudden, occurs in 1 Thess. 5:3, where it has the place of emphasis at the beginning of the sentence, as *olethros*, destruction, which the adjective qualifies, has at the end; in Luke 21:34, it is used adverbially, R.V., "suddenly" (A.V., "unawares"). See UNAWARES. ¶

NT: B.26d; CB.—; K.—.
OT: —.
GEN. REF.: —.

B. Adverbs.

1. *aphnō* [ἄφνω, 869], suddenly, occurs in Acts 2:2; 16:26; 28:6. ¶

NT: B.127a; CB.—; K.—.
OT: pit'ōm: S.6597; HR.185b.1; H.1859a; BD.837b.
GEN. REF.: —.

2. *exaiphnēs* [ἐξαίφνης, 1810], a strengthened form, akin to No. 1, occurs in Mark 13:36; Luke 2:13; 9:39; Acts 9:3; 22:6. ¶

NT: B.272b; CB.—; K.—.
OT: pit'ōm: S.6597; HR.486b.2; H.1859a; BD.837b.
GEN. REF.: —.

3. *exapina* [ἐξάπινα, 1819], a later form of No. 2, occurs in Mark 9:8. ¶

NT: B.273a; CB.—; K.—.
OT: pit'ōm: S.6597; HR.488a.2; H.1859a; BD.837b.
GEN. REF.: —.

Note: For *tacheōs* in 1 Tim. 5:22, A.V., "suddenly," R.V., "hastily," see QUICKLY, No. 3.

For **SUE** see **LAW**, B, No. 2

SUFFER

A. Verbs.

(*a*) *to permit*

1. *eaō* [ἐάω, 1439], to let, permit, is translated to suffer in Matt. 24:43; Luke 4:41; 22:51; Acts 14:16; 16:7; 19:30; 28:4; 1 Cor. 10:13. See LEAVE (*a*) No. 9, LET, No. 4.

NT: B.212c; CB.—; K.—.
OT: —.
GEN. REF.: —.

2. *proseaō* [προσεάω, 4330], to permit further (*pros*, and No. 1), occurs in Acts 27:7. ¶

NT: B.712d; CB.—; K.—.
OT: —.
GEN. REF.: —.

3. *epitrepō* [ἐπιτρέπω, 2010], for which see LEAVE, (*b*), is rendered to suffer in A.V. and R.V. in Matt. 8:21; Mark 10:4; Luke 9:59; Acts 28:16; R.V. only, Luke 9:61 (A.V., "let"); A.V. only, Acts 21:39; in some texts, Matt. 8:31, A.V. only. See LIBERTY, C, *Note*, PERMIT.

NT: B.303c; CB.—; K.—.
OT: 'āzab: S.5800; HR.537b.2; H.1594,1595; BD.736d.
GEN. REF.: IS.4:649; NB.—; Z.—.

4. *aphiēmi* [ἀφίημι, 863], to send away, signifies to permit, suffer, in Matt. 3:15 (twice); Matt. 19:14; 23:13; Mark 1:34; 5:19, 37; 10:14; 11:16; Luke 8:51; 12:39, A.V. (R.V., "left"); 18:16; John 12:7, R.V., A.V. and R.V. marg., "let (her) alone"; Rev. 11:9. See FORGIVE.

NT: B.125c; CB.1236b; K.88.
OT: sālaḥ: S.5545; HR.183b.8; H.1505; BD.699b.
nûaḥ: S.5117; HR.183b.4; H.1323; BD.628a.
GEN. REF.: IS.4:649; NB.—; Z.—.

Notes: (1) In Acts 2:27 and 13:35, A.V., *didōmi*, to give (R.V.), is rendered to suffer.

(2) In 1 Cor. 6:7, A.V., *apostereō*, in the Passive Voice, is rendered "*suffer yourselves to* be defrauded" (R.V., "be defrauded").

(3) For *kōluō* in Heb. 7:23, A.V., "were not suffered," see HINDER.

(*b*) *to endure suffering*

1. *anechō* [ἀνέχω, 430], in the Middle Voice, to bear with, is rendered to suffer in Matt. 17:17 and parallel passages; A.V. only, 1 Cor. 4:12 (R.V., "endure"); 2 Cor. 11:19, 20 and Heb. 13:22 (R.V., "bear with"). See BEAR, ENDURE.

NT: B.65d; CB.1235b; K.58.
OT: 'āphaq: S.662; HR.87c.1; H.149; BD.67c.
GEN. REF.: –.

2. *paschō* [πάσχω, 3958], to suffer, is used (I) of the sufferings of Christ (*a*) at the hands of men, e.g., Matt. 16:21; 17:12; 1 Pet. 2:23; (*b*) in His expiatory and vicarious sacrifice for sin, Heb. 9:26; 13:12; 1 Pet. 2:21; 3:18; 4:1; (*c*) including both (*a*) and (*b*), Luke 22:15; 24:26, 46; Acts 1:3, "passion"; 3:18; 17:3; Heb. 5:8; (*d*) by the antagonism of the evil one, Heb. 2:18; (II) of human suffering, (*a*) of followers of Christ, Acts 9:16; 2 Cor. 1:6; Gal. 3:4; Phil. 1:29; 1 Thess. 2:14; 2 Thess. 1:5; 2 Tim. 1:12; 1 Pet. 3:14, 17; 5:10; Rev. 2:10; in identification with Christ in His crucifixion, as the spiritual ideal to be realized, 1 Pet. 4:1; in a wrong way, 4:15; (*b*) of others, physically, as the result of demoniacal power, Matt. 17:15, R.V., "suffereth (grievously)," A.V., "is (sore) vexed"; cp. Mark 5:26; in a dream, Matt. 27:19; through maltreatment, Luke 13:2; 1 Pet. 2:19, 20; by a serpent (negatively), Acts 28:5, R.V., "took" (A.V., "felt": see FEEL, *Note*); (*c*) of the effect upon the whole body through the suffering of one member, 1 Cor. 12:26, with application to a church.

NT: B.633d; CB.1262c; K.798.
OT: ḥālāh: S.2470; HR.1103a.1; H.655; BD.317c.
GEN. REF.: IS.4:649; NB.–; Z.–.

3. *propaschō* [προπάσχω, 4310], to suffer before (*pro*, and No. 2), occurs in 1 Thess. 2:2. ¶

NT: B.709b; CB.–; K.798.
OT: –.
GEN. REF.: IS.4:649; NB.–; Z.–.

4. *sumpaschō* [συμπάσχω, 4841], to suffer with (*sun*, and No. 2), is used in Rom. 8:17 of suffering with Christ; in 1 Cor. 12:26 of joint suffering in the members of the body. ¶

NT: B.779b; CB.1270b; K.798,1102.
OT: –.
GEN. REF.: IS.4:649; NB.–; Z.–.

5. *hupechō* [ὑπέχω, 5254], to hold under (*hupo*, under, *echō*, to have or hold), is used metaphorically in Jude 7 of suffering punishment. ¶ In the Sept., Ps. 89:50; Lam. 5:7. ¶

NT: B.842b; CB.–; K.–.
OT: sābal: S.5445; HR.1411c.2; H.1458; BD.687d.
GEN. REF.: –.

6. *kakoucheō* [κακουχέω, 2558], to ill-treat (*kakos*, evil, and *echō*, to have), is used in the Passive Voice in Heb. 11:37, R.V., "evil entreated" (A.V., "tormented"); in 13:3, R.V., "are evil entreated" (A.V., "suffer adversity"). ¶

NT: B.398b; CB.–; K.–.
OT: 'ānāh: S.6031; HR.711c.1; H.1651,1652; BD.776a.
GEN. REF.: –.

7. *sunkakoucheomai* [συγκακουχέομαι, 4778], to endure adversity with, is used in Heb. 11:25 (*sun*, with, and No. 6), R.V., "to be evil entreated with," A.V., "to suffer affliction with." ¶

NT: B.773b; CB.–; K.–.
OT: –.
GEN. REF.: –.

8. *makrothumeō* [μακροθυμέω, 3114], is rendered "suffereth long" in 1 Cor. 13:4. See PATIENCE.

NT: B.488a; CB.1257c; K.550.
OT: 'ārak: S.748; HR.893b.1a; H.162; BD.73c.
GEN. REF.: –.

9 *adikeō* [ἀδικέω, 91], to do wrong, injustice (*a*, negative, *dikē*, right), is used in the Passive Voice in 2 Pet. 2:13, R.V., "suffering wrong" (some texts have *komizō*, to receive, A.V.); there as a play upon words here which may be brought out thus, 'being defrauded (of the wages of fraud),' a use of the verb illustrated in the papyri. See HURT.

NT: B.17c; CB.1233a; K.22.
OT: 'āwāh: S.5753; HR.24c.11c; H.1577; BD.730c.
'āshaq: S.6231; HR.24c.15; H.1713; BD.798c.
GEN. REF.: –.

Notes: (1) In 1 Cor. 9:12, A.V., *stegō*, to bear up under, is translated "suffer" (R.V., "bear"); see BEAR, No. 11.

(2) For *hupomenō*, rendered to suffer in 2 Tim. 2:12, see ENDURE, No. 2.

(3) For suffer hardship, suffer trouble, see HARDSHIP, Nos. 1 and 2.

(4) For suffer need, Phil. 4:12, see WANT.

(5) For suffer loss, 2 Cor. 7:9, R.V., see LOSE, No. 2.

(6) For suffer persecution, see PERSECUTION.

(7) For suffer shipwreck, see SHIPWRECK.

(8) For *tropophoreō* in Acts 13:18 "suffered . . . manners," see MANNER, E.

(9) For "suffereth violence," *biazō*, see FORCE, B, No. 1, VIOLENCE, B, No. 2.

(10) In 2 Thess. 1:9, R.V., *tinō*, to pay a penalty, is rendered "shall suffer (punishment)." ¶

B. Adjective.

pathētos [παθητός, 3805], akin to *paschō*, denotes one who has suffered, or subject to suffering, or destined to suffer; it is used in the last sense of the suffering of Christ, Acts 26:23. ¶

NT: B.602d; CB.1262c; K.798.
OT: –.
GEN. REF.: –.

SUFFERING

pathēma [πάθημα, 3804], is rendered "sufferings" in the R.V. (A.V., "afflictions") in 2 Tim. 3:11; Heb. 10:32; 1 Pet. 5:9; in Gal. 5:24, "passions" (A.V., "affections"). See AFFLICTION, B, No. 3.

NT: B.602b; CB.1262c; K.798.
OT: –.
GEN. REF.: IS.4:649; NB.–; Z.–.

Note: For *kakopatheia*, Jas. 5:10, R.V., "suffering," see AFFLICTION, B, No. 1.

SUFFICE, SUFFICIENT

A. Verbs.

1. *arkeō* [ἀρκέω, 714], to suffice, is rendered "is sufficient" in John 6:7; 2 Cor. 12:9; "it sufficeth" in John 14:8. See CONTENT, ENOUGH.

NT: B.107a; CB.1237c; K.78.
OT: hôn: S.1952; HR.158a.2; H.487a; BD.223c.
GEN. REF.: –.

Note: For 1 Pet. 4:3, see B, No. 2.

2. *hikanoō* [ἱκανόω, 2427], to make sufficient, render fit, is translated "made (us) sufficient" in 2 Cor. 3:6, R.V. (A.V., "hath made . . . able"). See ABLE, B, No. 6, *Note*.

NT: B.374d; CB.1250c; K.361.
OT: rab: S.7227; HR.684a.3; H.2099a,b; BD.912d.
GEN. REF.: –.

B. Adjectives.

1. *hikanos* [ἱκανός, 2425], akin to A, No. 2, enough, sufficient, fit, etc. is translated "sufficient" in 2 Cor. 2:6, 16; 3:5. See ABLE, C, No. 2.

NT: B.374b; CB.1250c; K.361.
OT: hôn: S.1952; HR.683c.3; H.487a; BD.223c.
GEN. REF.: –.

2. *arketos* [ἀρκετός, 713], akin to A, No. 1, used with *eimi*, to be, is translated "may suffice" in 1 Pet. 4:3. See ENOUGH, A, No. 1.

NT: B.107a; CB.1237c; K.78.
OT: –.
GEN. REF.: –.

SUFFICIENCY

1. *autarkeia* [αὐτάρκεια, 841], (*autos*, self, *arkeō*, see A, above; Eng., autarchy), "contentment," 1 Tim. 6:6, is rendered "sufficiency" in 2 Cor. 9:8. ¶

NT: B.122b; CB.1238b; K.78.
OT: –.
GEN. REF.: –.

2. *hikanotēs* [ἱκανότης, 2426], is rendered "sufficiency" in 2 Cor. 3:5. ¶

NT: B.374d; CB.1250c; K.361.
OT: –.
GEN. REF.: –.

For SUIT (make), Acts 25:24, R.V., see DEAL WITH, *Note* (1)

SUM (Noun), SUM UP

A. Noun.

Note: For *kephalaion*, Acts 22:28; Heb. 8:1, see POINT, B. ¶ For *timē*, Acts 7:16, see PRICE, A.

B. Verb.

anakephalaioō [ἀνακεφαλαιόω, 346], to sum up, gather up (*ana*, up, *kephalē*, a head), to present as a whole, is used in the Passive Voice in Rom. 13:9, R.V., "summed up" (A.V., "briefly comprehended"), i.e., the one commandment expresses all that the Law enjoins, and to obey this one is to fulfil the Law (cp. Gal. 5:14); Middle Voice in Eph. 1:10, R.V., "sum up" (A.V., "gather together"), of God's purpose to sum up all things in the heavens and on the earth in Christ, a consummation extending beyond the limits of the Church, though the latter is to be a factor in its realization. ¶

NT: B.55d; CB.–; K.–.
OT: –.
GEN. REF.: –.

SUMMER

theros [θέρος, 2330], akin to *therō*, to heat, occurs in Matt. 24:32; Mark 13:28; Luke 21:30. ¶

NT: B.359d; CB.1272b; K.–.
OT: qayiṣ: S.7019; HR.649b.1; H.2020a; BD.884d.
GEN. REF.: IS.4:375; NB.–; Z.5:540.

SUMPTUOUS, SUMPTUOUSLY

A. Adjective.

lampros [λαμπρός, 2986], bright, is rendered "sumptuous" in Rev. 18:14, R.V. See BRIGHT, GOODLY, *Note*.

NT: B.465d; CB.1256c; K.497.
OT: –.
GEN. REF.: –.

B. Adverb.

lamprōs [λαμπρῶς, 2988], the corresponding adverb, is used in Luke 16:19, "sumptuously." ¶

NT: B.466a; CB.1256c; K.–.
OT: –.
GEN. REF.: –.

SUN

hēlios [ἥλιος, 2246], whence Eng. prefix helio–, is used (*a*) as a means of the natural benefits of light and heat, e.g., Matt. 5:45, and power, Rev. 1:16; (*b*) of its qualities of brightness and glory, e.g., Matt. 13:43; 17:2; Acts 26:13; 1 Cor. 15:41; Rev. 10:1; 12:1; (*c*) as a means of destruction, e.g., Matt. 13:6; Jas. 1:11; of physical misery, Rev. 7:16; (*d*) as a means of judgment, e.g., Matt. 24:29; Mark 13:24; Luke 21:25; 23:45; Acts 2:20; Rev. 6:12; 8:12; 9:2; 16:8.

NT: B.345c; CB.1249c; K.–.
OT: shemesh: S.8121; HR.606b.9; H.2417a; BD.1039a.
GEN. REF.: IS.4:662; NB.1223; Z.5:540.

Note: In Rev. 7:2 and 16:12, *anatolē*, rising, used with *hēlios*, is translated "sunrising," R.V. (A.V., "east").

For **SUNDER (Asunder)** see **CUT**, No. 6

For **SUNDRY** see **PORTION**, C

SUP

deipneō [δειπνέω, 1172], to sup (said of taking the chief meal of the day), occurs in Luke 17:8; 22:20 (in the best texts), lit., '(the) supping'; so 1 Cor. 11:25; metaphorically in Rev. 3:20, of spiritual communion between Christ and the faithful believer. ¶

NT: B.173b; CB.1240c; K.143.
OT: lāḥam: S.3898; HR.288a.1; H.1104; BD.536d.
GEN. REF.: –.

For **SUPERFLUITY** see **ABUNDANCE**, A, No. 2, B, No. 1

SUPERFLUOUS

perissos [περισσός, 4053], abundant, more than sufficient, is translated "superfluous" in 2 Cor. 9:1. See ABUNDANT, C, No. 1, ADVANTAGE, MORE, B, No. 2.

NT: B.651b; CB.1263c; K.828.
OT: yeter: S.3499; HR.1126c.1a; H.936a; BD.451d.
yātar: S.3498; HR.1126c.1d; H.936; BD.451a.
yôtēr: S.3148; HR.1126c.1c; H.936d; BD.452c.
GEN. REF.: –.

SUPERSCRIPTION

epigraphē [ἐπιγραφή, 1923], lit., an over-writing (*epi*, over, *graphō*, to write) (the meaning of the anglicized Latin word "superscription"), denotes an inscription, a title. On Roman coins the Emperor's name was inscribed, Matt. 22:20; Mark 12:16; Luke 20:24. In the Roman Empire, in the case of a criminal on his way to execution, a board on which was inscribed the cause of his condemnation, was carried before him or hung round his neck; the inscription was termed a title (*titlos*). The four Evangelists state that at the crucifixion of Christ the title was affixed to the cross, Mark (15:26) and Luke (23:38) call it a "superscription"; Mark says it was "written over" (*epigraphō*, the corresponding verb). Matthew calls it "His accusation"; John calls it "a title" (a technical term). The wording varies: the essential words are the same, and the variation serves to authenticate the narratives, shewing that there was no consultation leading to an agreement as to the details. See further under TITLE. ¶

NT: B.291c; CB.1245c; K.–.
OT: –.
GEN. REF.: IS.4:864; NB.1224; Z.–.

For **SUPERSTITION** see **RELIGION**

SUPERSTITIOUS

deisidaimōn [δεισιδαίμων, 1174], reverent to the deity (*deidō*, to fear; *daimōn*, a demon, or pagan god), occurs in Acts 17:22 in the comparative degree, rendered "somewhat superstitious," R.V. (A.V., "too s."), a meaning which the word sometimes has; others, according to its comparative form, advocate the meaning 'more religious (than others),' 'quite religious' (cp. the noun in 25:19). This is supported by Ramsay, who renders it 'more than others respectful of what is divine'; so Deissmann in *Light from the Ancient East*, and others. It also agrees with the meaning found in Greek writers; the context too suggests that the adjective is used in a good sense; perhaps, after all, with kindly ambiguity (Grimm-Thayer). An ancient epitaph has it in the sense of 'reverent' (Moulton and Milligan). ¶

NT: B.173d; CB.1240c; K.137.
OT: –.
GEN. REF.: IS.4:665; NB.–; Z.5:543.

SUPPER

deipnon [δεῖπνον, 1173], denotes a supper or feast (for an analysis of the uses see FEAST, No. 2). In John 13:2 the R.V., following certain texts, has "during supper" (A.V., "supper being ended").

NT: B.173b; CB.1240c; K.143.
OT: patbāg: S.6598; HR.288a.2; H.1851; BD.834a.
GEN. REF.: IS.3:291; NB.–; Z.–.

Note: For "supper" in Luke 22:20 see SUP.

SUPPLICATION

1. *deēsis* [δέησις, 1162], is always translated "supplication," or the plural, in the R.V. See PRAYER, B, No. 3.

NT: B.171d; CB.1240b; K.143.
OT: t^eḥinnāh: S.8467; HR.285c.8a; H.694f; BD.337c.
taḥ^anûn: S.8469; HR.285c.8b; H.694g; BD.337c.
GEN. REF.: –.

2. *hiketēria* [ἱκετηρία, 2428], is the feminine form of the adjective *hiketērios*, denoting 'of a suppliant,' and used as a noun, formerly an

olive-branch carried by a suppliant (*hiketēs*), then later, a supplication, used with No. 1 in Heb. 5:7. ¶ In the Sept., Job 40:22 (Eng. Vers. 41:3). ¶

NT: B.375a; CB.1250c; K.362.
OT: —.
GEN. REF.: —.

SUPPLY (Noun and Verb)

A. Verbs.

1. *chorēgeō* [χορηγέω, 5524], primarily, among the Greeks, signified to lead a stage chorus or dance (*choros*, and *hēgeomai*, to lead), then, to defray the expenses of a chorus; hence, later, metaphorically, to supply, 2 Cor. 9:10 (2nd part; see also No. 2), R.V., "supply" (A.V. "minister"); 1 Pet. 4:11, R.V., "supplieth" (A.V., "giveth"). See GIVE, *Note* (4), MINISTER, B, *Note* (1). ¶

NT: B.883d; CB.—; K.—.
OT: kûl: S.3557; HR.1472b.2; H.962; BD.465a.
GEN. REF.: IS.4:666; NB.—; Z.—.

2. *epichorēgeō* [ἐπιχορηγέω, 2023], to supply fully, abundantly (a strengthened form of No. 1), is rendered to supply in the R.V. of 2 Cor. 9:10 (1st part) and Gal. 3:5 (for A.V., to minister), where the present continuous tense speaks of the work of the Holy Spirit in all His ministrations to believers individually and collectively; in Col. 2:19, R.V., "being supplied" (A.V., "having nourishment ministered"), of the work of Christ as the Head of the Church His body; in 2 Pet. 1:5, "supply" (A.V., "add"); in ver. 11, "shall be . . . supplied" (A.V., "shall be ministered"), of the reward hereafter which those are to receive, in regard to positions in the Kingdom of God, for their fulfilment here of the conditions mentioned. ¶

NT: B.305a; CB.—; K.—.
OT: —.
GEN. REF.: IS.4:666; NB.—; Z.—.

Note: In 2 Cor. 9:10 (see Nos. 1 and 2 above) the stronger verb No. 2 is used where the will and capacity to receive are in view.

3. *anaplēroō* [ἀναπληρόω, 378], to fill up, fulfil, is rendered to supply in 1 Cor. 16:17 and Phil. 2:30. See FILL, FULFIL, OCCUPY.

NT: B.59c; CB.1235b; K.867.
OT: mālē': S.4390; HR.81b.1; H.1195; BD.569d.
GEN. REF.: —.

4. *prosanaplēroō* [προσαναπληρόω, 4322], to fill up by adding to, to supply fully (*pros*, to, and No. 3), is translated "supplieth" in 2 Cor. 9:12, A.V. (R.V., "filleth up the measure of"); in 11:9, R.V. and A.V., "supplied." ¶

NT: B.711d; CB.1267a; K.—.
OT: —.
GEN. REF.: IS.4:666; NB.—; Z.—.

Note: In Phil. 4:19, A.V., *plēroō*, to fulfil (R.V.), is rendered "shall supply."

B. Noun.

epichorēgia [ἐπιχορηγία, 2024], a full supply, occurs in Eph. 4:16, "supplieth," lit., 'by the supply of every joint,' metaphorically of the members of the Church, the Body of which Christ is the Head, and Phil. 1:19, "the supply (of the Spirit of Jesus Christ)," i.e., 'the bountiful supply'; here "of the Spirit" may be taken either in the subjective sense, the Giver, or the objective, the Gift. ¶

NT: B.305b; CB.—; K.—.
OT: —.
GEN. REF.: IS.4:666; NB.—; Z.—.

SUPPORT

Notes: (1) In Acts 20:35, A.V., *antilambanomai*, to help (R.V.), is translated "support." See HELP, B, No. 1.

(2) In 1 Thess. 5:14, *antechomai* signifies to support: see HOLD, No. 3.

SUPPOSE

1. *nomizō* [νομίζω, 3543], to consider, suppose, think, is rendered to suppose in Matt. 20:10; Luke 2:34; 3:23; Acts 7;25; 14:19; 16:27; 21:29; 1 Tim. 6:5; in 1 Cor. 7:26, A.V. (R.V., "I think"); in Acts 16:13, the R.V. adheres to the meaning "to suppose," "(where) we supposed (there was a place of prayer)"; this word also signifies 'to practise a custom' (*nomos*) and is commonly so used by Greek writers. Hence the A.V., "was wont (to be made)"; it is rendered to think in Matt. 5:17; 10:34; Acts 8:20; 17:29; 1 Cor. 7:36. See THINK. ¶

NT: B.541a; CB.1260a; K.—.
OT: —.
GEN. REF.: —.

2. *dokeō* [δοκέω, 1380], to be of opinion, is translated to suppose in Mark 6:49; Luke 24:37; John 20:15; Acts 27:13; in the following, A.V. "suppose," R.V., "think," Luke 12:51; 13:2; Heb. 10:29. It is most frequently rendered to think, always in Matthew; always in John, except 11:31, "supposing," R.V. [where the best texts have this verb (for *legō*, A.V., "saying")], and 20:15 (see above).

NT: B.201d; CB.1242a; K.178.
OT: —.
GEN. REF.: —.

3. *hupolambanō* [ὑπολαμβάνω, 5274], when used of mental action, signifies to suppose, Luke 7:43, and Acts 2:15. See ANSWER, RECEIVE.

NT: B.845b; CB.1252b; K.495.
OT: —.
GEN. REF.: —.

4. *huponoeō* [ὑπονοέω, 5282], to suspect, to conjecture, is translated "suppose ye" in Acts

13:25, R.V. (A.V., "think ye"); "I supposed" in 25:18. See DEEM.

NT: B.846d; CB.—; K.636.
OT: s^ebar (Aramaic): S.5452; HR.1416b.1; H.2883; BD.1104a.
GEN. REF.: —.

5. *oiomai* or *oimai* [οἴομαι, 3633], signifies to expect, imagine, suppose; it is rendered to suppose in John 21:25; Phil. 1:17, R.V. (A.V., ver. 16, "thinking"); "think" in Jas. 1:7. See THINK. ¶

NT: B.562c; CB.—; K.—.
OT: —.
GEN. REF.: —.

Notes: (1) In 2 Cor. 11:5, A.V., *logizomai*, to reckon (R.V.), is rendered "I suppose"; so in 1 Pet. 5:12, A.V., R.V., "(as) I account (him)"; Silvanus was not supposed by Peter to be faithful, he was reckoned or regarded so.

(2) In Phil. 2:25, A.V., *hēgeomai*, to reckon, deem, is rendered "I supposed" (R.V., "I counted").

SUPREME

huperechō [ὑπερέχω, 5242], to be superior, to excel, is translated "supreme" in 1 Pet. 2:13: see EXCEL, No. 3.

NT: B.840d; CB.1252a; K.1230.
OT: 'ādaph: S.5736; HR.1409b.5; H.1568; BD.727a.
'āmēṣ: S.553; HR.1409b.2; H.117; BD.54d.
GEN. REF.: —.

SURE

A. Adjective.

1. *asphalēs* [ἀσφαλής, 804], safe, is translated "sure" in Heb. 6:19. See CERTAIN, B.

NT: B.119a; CB.1238a; K.87.
OT: —.
GEN. REF.: IS.4:666; NB.—; Z.—.

2. *bebaios* [βέβαιος, 949], firm, stedfast, is used of (*a*) God's promise to Abraham, Rom. 4:16; (*b*) the believer's hope, Heb. 6:19, "stedfast"; (*c*) the hope of spiritual leaders regarding the welfare of converts, 2 Cor. 1:7, "stedfast"; (*d*) the glorying of the hope, Heb. 3:6, "firm"; (*e*) the beginning of our confidence, 3:14, R.V., "firm" (A.V., "stedfast"); (*f*) the Law given at Sinai, Heb. 2:2, "stedfast"; (*g*) the testament (or covenant) fulfilled after a death, 9:17, "of force"; (*h*) the calling and election of believers, 2 Pet. 1:10, to be made "sure" by the fulfilment of the injunctions in vv. 5-7; (*i*) the word of prophecy, "*made* more sure," 2 Pet. 1:19, R.V., A.V., "a more sure (word of prophecy)"; what is meant is not a comparison between the prophecies of the O.T. and N.T., but that the former have been confirmed in the Person of Christ (vv. 16-18). See FIRM. ¶

NT: B.138a; CB.1239a; K.103.
OT: —.
GEN. REF.: IS.4:666; NB.—; Z.—.

3. *pistos* [πιστός, 4103], faithful, is translated "sure" in Acts 13:34. See FAITHFUL.

NT: B.664c; CB.1265a; K.849.
OT: 'āman: S.539; HR.1138c.1a; H.116; BD.52d.
GEN. REF.: IS.4:666; NB.—; Z.—.

Note: In 2 Tim. 2:19, A.V., *stereos*, firm, is translated "sure," and connected with "standeth," R.V., "the firm (foundation of God standeth)," i.e., 'however much the faith may be misrepresented or denied, the firm foundation of God's knowledge and truth, with its separating power, remains.'

B. Verb.

asphalizō [ἀσφαλίζω, 805], to make safe or sure (akin to A, No. 1), is rendered to make sure in Matt. 27:64, 65, 66, of the sepulchre of Christ; elsewhere, Acts 16:24, of making feet fast in the stocks. See FAST. ¶

NT: B.119a; CB.1238a; K.87.
OT: ḥāzaq: S.2388; HR.174b.1; H.636; BD.304a.
GEN. REF.: IS.4:666; NB.—; Z.—.

Note: In the A.V. of John 16:30; Rom. 2:2 and 15:29, the verb *oida*, to know, is translated to be sure (R.V., in each place, to know). So with *ginōskō*, to know, in John 6:69. For the difference between the verbs see KNOW.

SURELY

Notes: (1) In the A.V. of Matt. 26:73; Mark 14:70; John 17:8, *alēthōs*, truly, is rendered "surely" (R.V., "of a truth"); so *pantōs*, at all events, altogether, in Luke 4:23 (R.V., "doubtless"), and *nai*, yea, in Rev. 22:20 (R.V., "yea").

(2) In Heb. 6:14, "surely" represents the phrase *ei mēn* (so the best texts; some have *ē mēn*).

(3) For Luke 1:1, A.V., see BELIEVE, C, *Note* (4).

(4) For "surely" in 2 Pet. 2:12, R.V., see CORRUPT, A, No. 2 (*b*).

SURETY (Noun)

enguos [ἔγγυος, 1450], primarily signifies bail, the bail who personally answers for anyone, whether with his life or his property (to be distinguished from *mesitēs*, a mediator); it is used in Heb. 7:22, "(by so much also hath Jesus become) the Surety (of a better covenant)," referring to the abiding and unchanging character of His Melchizedek priesthood, by reason of which His suretyship is established by God's oath (vv. 20, 21). As the Surety, He is the Personal guarantee of the terms of the new and better covenant, secured on the ground of His perfect sacrifice (ver. 27). ¶

NT: B.214a; CB.1245a; K.194.
OT: —.
GEN. REF.: IS.—; NB.—; Z.5:543.

For **SURETY (of a)**, Acts 12:11, A.V., see **TRUE**, D, No. 1

SURFEITING

kraipalē [κραιπάλη, 2897], signifies the giddiness and headache resulting from excessive wine-bibbing, a drunken nausea, "surfeiting," Luke 21:34. ¶ Trench (Syn. § lxi) distinguishes this and the synonymous words, *methē*, drunkenness, *oinophlugia*, wine-bibbing (A.V., "excess of wine," 1 Pet. 4:3), *kōmos*, revelling.

NT: B.448a; CB.1255c; K.—.
OT: —.
GEN. REF.: IS.—; NB.—; Z.5:543.

For **SURGE**, Jas. 1:6, R.V., see **RAGE** and **WAVE**

For **SURMISE, SURMISINGS**, see **DEEM**

SURNAME

epikaleō [ἐπικαλέω, 1941], to put a name upon (*epi*, upon, *kaleō*, to call), to surname, is used in this sense in the Passive Voice, in some texts in Matt. 10:3 (it is absent in the best); in Luke 22:3, in some texts (the best have *kaleō*, to call); Acts 1:23; 4:36; 10:5, 18, 32; 11:13; 12:12, 25; in some texts, 15:22 (the best have *kaleō*).

NT: B.294a; CB.1245c; K.394.
OT: qārā': S.7121; HR.521b.5a; H.2063; BD.894d.
GEN. REF.: IS.4:667; NB.—; Z.5:543.

Notes: (1) In Mark 3:16, 17, "He surnamed" is a translation of *epitithēmi*, to put upon, to add to, with *onoma*, a name, as the object.

(2) In Acts 15:37, A.V., *kaleō*, to call (R.V., "called"), is rendered "whose surname was."

(3) The verb *eponomazō*, translated "bearest the name" in Rom. 2:17, R.V., finds a literal correspondence in the word 'surname' (*epi*, upon, = *sur*), and had this significance in Classical Greek. ¶

For **SURPASS**, 2 Cor. 3:10, see **EXCEED**, A, No. 1

For **SUSPENSE (hold in)** see **DOUBT**, No. 6

SUSTENANCE

chortasma [χόρτασμα, 5527], fodder (akin to *chortazō*, to feed, fill, see FEED, No. 4), is used in the plural in Acts 7:11, "sustenance." ¶ In the Sept., Gen. 24:25, 32; 42:27; 43:24; Deut. 11:15; Judg. 19:19. ¶

NT: B.884a; CB.1240a; K.—.
OT: mispô': S.4554; HR.1473a.1; H.1529a; BD.704c.
GEN. REF.: —.

SWADDLING-CLOTHES

sparganoō [σπαργανόω, 4683], to swathe (from *sparganon*, a swathing-band), signifies to wrap in swaddling-clothes in Luke 2:7, 12. The idea that the word means 'rags' is without foundation. ¶ In the Sept., Job 38:9; Ezek. 16:4. ¶

NT: B.760d; CB.—; K.—.
OT: ḥātal: S.2853; HR.1281c.1a; H.779; BD.367c.
ḥ^{a}tullāh: S.2854; HR.1281c.1b; H.779a; BD.367c.
GEN. REF.: IS.4:670; NB.—; Z.5:547.

SWALLOW (Verb)

katapinō [καταπίνω, 2666], to drink down (*kata* and *pinō*, to drink), to swallow, is used with this meaning (*a*) physically, but figuratively, Matt. 23:24; Rev. 12:16; (*b*) metaphorically, in the Passive Voice, of death (by victory), 1 Cor. 15:54; of being overwhelmed by sorrow, 2 Cor. 2:7; of the mortal body (by life), 5:4. See DEVOUR, No. 3, DROWN, No. 2.

NT: B.416b; CB.1254b; K.841.
OT: bāla': S.1104; HR.741c.1a-c; H.251; BD.118a.
GEN. REF.: —.

SWEAR, SWORN

omnumi [ὄμνυμι, 3660], or *omnuō* [ὀμνύω], is used of affirming or denying by an oath, e.g., Matt. 26:74; Mark 6:23; Luke 1:73; Heb. 3:11 18; 4:3; 7:21; accompanied by that by which one swears, e.g., Matt. 5:34, 36; 23:16; Heb. 6:13, 16; Jas. 5:12; Rev. 10:6. Cp. ADJURE.

NT: B.565d; CB.1260c; K.—.
OT: shāba': S.7650; HR.991b.2a; H.2318; BD.989a.
GEN. REF.: IS.4:670; NB.902; Z.4:476.

Note: For "false swearers," 1 Tim. 1:10, see FORSWEAR.

SWEAT

hidrōs [ἱδρώς, 2402], is used in Luke 22:44. ¶ In the Sept., Gen. 3:19. ¶

NT: B.371c; CB.—; K.—.
OT: zē'āh: S.2188; HR.678c.1; H.857b; BD.402c.
GEN. REF.: IS.4:671; NB.—; Z.5:547.

SWEEP

saroō [σαρόω, 4563], occurs in Matt. 12:44; Luke 11:25; 15:8. ¶

NT: B.744c; CB.—; K.—.
OT: —.
GEN. REF.: —.

SWEET

glukus [γλυκύς, 1099], (cp. Eng., glycerine, glucose), occurs in Jas. 3:11, 12 (A.V., "fresh" in this verse); Rev. 10:9, 10. ¶

NT: B.162a; CB.1248b; K.–.
OT: mātôq: S.4966; HR.271a.2a; H.1268c; BD.608d.
meteq: S.4986; HR.271a.2b; H.1268a; BD.608d.
GEN. REF.: IS.4:671; NB.–; Z.–.

For SWEET SMELLING see SAVOUR, No. 1

SWELL, SWOLLEN

pimprēmi [πίμπρημι, 4092], primarily, to blow, to burn, later came to denote to cause to swell, and, in the Middle Voice, to become swollen, Acts 28:6. ¶ In the Sept., Numb. 5:21, 22, 27. ¶

NT: B.658b; CB.–; K.–.
OT: –.
GEN. REF.: IS.4:672; NB.–; Z.–.

Note: Some, connecting the word *prēnēs* in Acts 1:18 with *pimprēmi*, give it the meaning 'swelling up': see HEADLONG.

SWELLING

1. *phusiōsis* [φυσίωσις, 5450], denotes a puffing up, swelling with pride (akin to *phusioō*, to puff up), 2 Cor. 12:20, "swellings." ¶

NT: B.870a; CB.–; K.–.
OT: –.
GEN. REF.: –.

2. *huperonkos* [ὑπέρογκος, 5246], an adjective denoting of excessive weight or size, is used metaphorically in the sense of immoderate, especially of arrogant speech, in the neuter plural, virtually as a noun, 2 Pet. 2:18; Jude 16, "great swelling words," doubtless with reference to Gnostic phraseology. ¶

NT: B.841c; CB.–; K.–.
OT: pele': S.6382; HR.1410c.2a; H.1768a; BD.810b.
pālā': S.6381; HR.1410c.2b; H.1768; BD.810c.
GEN. REF.: –.

SWERVE

astocheō [ἀστοχέω, 795], to miss the mark, is translated "having swerved" in 1 Tim. 1:6. See ERR, No. 3. Moulton and Milligan illustrate the use of the verb from the papyri, e.g., of a man in extravagant terms bewailing the loss of a pet fighting-cock, "(I am distraught, for my cock) has failed (me)."

NT: B.118a; CB.1238a; K.–.
OT: –.
GEN. REF.: –.

SWIFT, SWIFTLY

1. *oxus* [ὀξύς, 3691], denotes "swift" in Rom. 3:15. See SHARP.

NT: B.574c; CB.–; K.–.
OT: ḥad: S.2299; HR.1001a.1a; H.605a; BD.292c.
hādad: S.2300; HR.1001a.1b; H.605; BD.292c.
GEN. REF.: –.

2. *tachus* [ταχύς, 5036], swift, speedy, is used in Jas. 1:19. ¶ Cp. *tacheōs*, *tachu* and *tacheion*, quickly, *tachos*, quickness, speed.

NT: B.807b; CB.1271a; K.–.
OT: māhar: S.4116; HR.1339a.2a; H.1152; BD.554d.
GEN. REF.: –.

3. *tachinos* [ταχινός, 5031], a poetical and late form of No. 2, of swift approach, is used in 2 Pet. 1:14, R.V., "swiftly" (A.V., "shortly"), lit., '(the putting off of my tabernacle is) swift,' i.e., imminent; in 2:1, "swift (destruction)." ¶ In the Sept.; Prov. 1:16; Is. 59:7; Hab. 1:6. ¶

NT: B.807a; CB.1271a; K.–.
OT: māhar: S.4116; HR.1338b.1; H.1152; BD.554d.
GEN. REF.: –.

SWIM

1. *kolumbaō* [κολυμβάω, 2860], to dive, plunge, into the sea, hence, to swim, occurs in Acts 27:43. ¶ Cp. *kolumbēthra*, a pool.

NT: B.442c; CB.–; K.–.
OT: –.
GEN. REF.: IS.4:672; NB.–; Z.–.

2. *ekkolumbaō* [ἐκκολυμβάω, 1579], to swim out of (*ek*), occurs in Acts 27:42. ¶

NT: B.241d; CB.–; K.–.
OT: –.
GEN. REF.: IS.4:672; NB.–; Z.–.

SWINE

choiros [χοῖρος, 5519], a swine, is used in the plural, in the Synoptic Gospels only, Matt. 7:6; 8:30, 31, 32; Mark 5:11-13, 16; Luke 8:32, 33; Luke 15:15, 16. It does not occur in the O.T. ¶

NT: B.883b; CB.1240a; K.–.
OT: –.
GEN. REF.: IS.4:673; NB.1224; Z.5:548.

SWORD

1. *machaira* [μάχαιρα, 3162], a short sword or dagger (distinct from No. 2), e.g., Matt. 26:47, 51, 52 and parallel passages; Luke 21:24; 22:38, possibly a knife (Field, *Notes on the Translation of the N.T.*); Heb. 4:12 (see TWO-EDGED); metaphorically and by metonymy, (*a*) for ordinary violence, or dissensions, that destroy peace, Matt. 10:34; (*b*) as the instrument of a magistrate or judge, e.g., Rom. 13:4; (*c*) of the Word of God, "the sword of the Spirit," probing the conscience, subduing the impulses to sin, Eph. 6:17.

NT: B.496b; CB.1257b; K.572.
OT: ḥereb: S.2719; HR.899c.3; H.732a; BD.352b.
GEN. REF.: IS.4:1037; NB.83; Z.1:316.

2. *rhomphaia* [ῥομφαία, 4501], a word of somewhat doubtful origin, denoted a Thracian weapon of large size, whether a sword or spear is not certain, but usually longer than No. 1; it occurs (*a*) literally in Rev. 6:8; (*b*) metaphorically, as the instrument of anguish, Luke 2:35; of judgment, Rev. 1:16; 2:12, 16; 19:15, 21,

probably figurative of the Lord's judicial utterances. ¶
NT: B.737a; CB.1268b; K.987.
OT: ḥereb: S.2719; HR.1253a.2; H.732a; BD.352b.
GEN. REF.: IS.4:1037; NB.83; Z.1:316.

SYCAMINE

sukaminos [συκάμινος, 4807], occurs in Luke 17:6. ¶ It is generally recognized as the Black Mulberry, with fruit like blackberries. The leaves are too tough for silkworms and thus are unlike the White Mulberry. Neither kind is the same as the Mulberry of 2 Sam. 5:23, 24, etc. The town Haifa was called Sycaminopolis, from the name of the tree.
NT: B.776a; CB.–; K.1100.
OT: shiqmāh: S.8256; HR.1301b.1; H.2455; BD.1054a.
GEN. REF.: IS.4:674; NB.1294; Z.5:548.

SYCAMORE

sukomorea [συκομορέα, 4809], occurs in Luke 19:4. ¶ This tree is of the fig species, with leaves like the mulberry and fruit like the fig. It is somewhat less in height than the sycamine and spreads to cover an area from 60 to 80 feet in diameter. It is often planted by the roadside, and was suitable for the purpose of Zacchaeus. Seated on the lowest branch he was easily within speaking distance of Christ.
NT: B.776b; CB.–; K.1100.
OT: –.
GEN. REF.: IS.4:674; NB.1294; Z.5:548.

SYNAGOGUE

sunagōgē [συναγωγή, 4864], properly a bringing together (*sun*, together, *agō*, to bring), denoted (*a*) a gathering of things, a collection, then, of persons, an assembling, of Jewish religious gatherings, e.g., Acts 9:2; an assembly of Christian Jews, Jas. 2:2, R.V., "synagogue" (A.V., marg.; text, "assembly"); a company dominated by the power and activity of Satan, Rev. 2:9; 3:9 (*b*) by metonymy, the building in which the gathering is held, e.g. Matt. 6:2; Mark 1:21. The origin of the Jewish synagogue is probably to be assigned to the time of the Babylonish exile. Having no Temple, the Jews assembled on the sabbath to hear the Law read, and the practice continued in various buildings after the return. Cp. Ps. 74:8.
NT: B.782d; CB.1270b; K.1108.
OT: ʿēdāh: S.5712; HR.1309b.13; H.812a; BD.417a.
qāhāl: S.6951; HR.1309b.17a; H.1991a; BD.874c.
GEN. REF.: IS.4:676; NB.1227; Z.5:555.

SYNAGOGUE (put out of the)

aposunagōgos [ἀποσυνάγωγος, 656], an adjective denoting 'expelled from the congregation', excommunicated, is used (*a*) with *ginomai*, to become, be made, John 9:22; 12:42; (*b*) with *poieō*, to make, John 16:2. This excommunication involved prohibition not only from attendance at the synagogue, but from all fellowship with Israelites. ¶
NT: B.100d; CB.1237b; K.1108.
OT: –.
GEN. REF.: –.

SYNAGOGUE (ruler of the)

archisunagōgos [ἀρχισυνάγωγος, 752], denotes the administrative official, with the duty of preserving order and inviting persons to read or speak in the assembly, Mark 5:22, 35, 36, 38; Luke 8:49; 13:14; Acts 13:15; "chief ruler" (A.V.) in Acts 18:8, 17. ¶
NT: B.113b; CB.–; K.1108.
OT: –.
GEN. REF.: IS.4:681; NB.1228; Z.5:563.

Note: In Luke 8:41, "ruler of the synagogue" represents *archōn*, ruler, followed by the genitive case of the article and *sunagōgē*.

SYROPHOENICIAN

surophoinikissa or *surophunissa* [Συροφοινίκισσα, 4949], occurs in Mark 7:26 as the national name of a woman called "a Canaanitish woman" in Matt. 15:22, i.e., not a Jewess but a descendant of the early inhabitants of the coast-land of Phoenicia. The word probably denoted a Syrian residing in Phoenicia proper. ¶ There is a tradition that the woman's name was Justa and her daughter Bernice (*Clementine Homilies*, ii:19; iii:73). In Acts 21:2, 3, the two parts of the term are used interchangeably.
NT: B.794b; CB.–; K.–.
OT: –.
GEN. REF.: IS.4:694; NB.1230; Z.5:569.

T

TABERNACLE

1. *skēnē* [σκηνή, 4633], a tent, booth, tabernacle, is used of (*a*) tents as dwellings, Matt. 17:4; Mark 9:5; Luke 9:33; Heb. 11:9, A.V., "tabernacles" (R.V., "tents"); (*b*) the Mosaic Tabernacle, Acts 7:44; Heb. 8:5; 9:1 (in some mss.); 9:8, 21 termed "the tent of meeting," R.V. (i.e., where the people were called to meet God), a preferable description to "the tabernacle of the congregation," as in the A.V. in the O.T.; the outer part, 9:2, 6; the inner sanctuary, 9:3; (*c*) the Heavenly prototype, Heb. 8:2; 9:11; Rev. 13:6; 15:5; 21:3 (of its future descent); (*d*) the eternal abodes of the saints, Luke 16:9, R.V., "tabernacles" (A.V., "habitations"); (*e*) the temple in Jerusalem, as continuing the service of the tabernacle, Heb. 13:10; (*f*) the house of David, i.e., metaphorically of his people, Acts 15:16; (*g*) the portable shrine of the god Moloch, Acts 7:43. ¶

NT: B.754c; CB.1269a; K.1040.
OT: 'ōhel: S.168; HR.1271a.1; H.32a; BD.13d.
mishkān: S.4908; HR.1271a.3; H.2387c; BD.1015c.
GEN. REF.: IS.4:698; NB.1231; Z.5:572.

2. *skēnos* [σκῆνος, 4636], the equivalent of No. 1, is used metaphorically of the body as the tabernacle of the soul, 2 Cor. 5:1, 4. ¶

NT: B.755b; CB.1269a; K.1040.
OT: –.
GEN. REF.: IS.4:698; NB.1231; Z.5:572.

3. *skēnōma* [σκήνωμα, 4638], occurs in Acts 7:46; 2 Pet. 1:13, 14; see HABITATION, No. 6. ¶

NT: B.755c; CB.1269a; K.1040.
OT: 'ōhel: S.168; HR.1273b.1; H.32a; BD.13d.
mishkān: S.4908; HR.1273b.3; H.2387a; BD.1015c.
GEN. REF.: IS.4:698; NB.1231; Z.5:572.

4. *skēnopēgia* [σκηνοπηγία, 4634], properly the setting up of tents or dwellings (No. 1, and *pēgnumi*, to fix), represents the word "tabernacles" in "the feast of tabernacles," John 7:2. ¶ This feast, one of the three Pilgrimage Feasts in Israel, is called "the feast of ingathering" in Ex. 23:16; 34:22; it took place at the end of the year, and all males were to attend at the tabernacle with their offerings. In Lev. 23:34; Deut. 16:13, 16; 31:10; 2 Chron. 8:13; Ezra 3:4 (cp. Neh. 8:14-18), it is called "the feast of tabernacles" (or booths, *sukkôth*), and was appointed for seven days at Jerusalem from the 15th to the 22nd Tishri (approximately October), to remind the people that their fathers dwelt in these in the wilderness journeys. Cp. Numb. 29:15-38, especially vers. 35-38, for the regulations of the eighth or "last day, the great day of the feast" (John 7:37).

NT: B.754d; CB.1269a; K.1040.
OT: sukkāh: S.5521; HR.1273a.1; H.1492d; BD.697c.
GEN. REF.: –.

Note: For *skēnoō*, to spread a tabernacle over, Rev. 7:15, R.V., see DWELL, No. 9.

TABLE

1. *trapeza* [τράπεζα, 5132], is used of (*a*) a dining-table, Matt. 15:27; Mark 7:28; Luke 16:21; 22:21, 30; (*b*) the table of shewbread, Heb. 9:2; (*c*) by metonymy, of what is provided on the table (the word being used of that with which it is associated), Acts 16:34; Rom. 11:9 (figurative of the special privileges granted to Israel and centring in Christ); 1 Cor. 10:21 (twice), "the Lord's table," denoting all that is provided for believers in Christ on the ground of His Death (and thus expressing something more comprehensive than the Lord's Supper); "the table of demons," denoting all that is partaken of by idolaters as the result of the influence of demons in connection with their sacrifices; (*d*) a money-changer's table, Matt. 21:12; Mark 11:15; John 2:15; (*e*) a bank, Luke 19:23 (cp. *trapezitēs*: see BANKERS); (*f*) by metonymy for the distribution of money, Acts 6:2. See BANK. ¶

NT: B.824b; CB.1273a; K.1187.
OT: shulḥān: S.7979; HR.1369b.4; H.2395a; BD.1020b.
GEN. REF.: IS.4:706; NB.1235; Z.5:583.

2. *plax* [πλάξ, 4109], primarily denotes anything flat and broad, hence, a flat stone, a tablet, 2 Cor. 3:3 (twice); Heb. 9:4. ¶

NT: B.666a; CB.–; K.–.
OT: lûaḥ: S.3871; HR.1140b.1; H.1091a; BD.531c.
GEN. REF.: IS.4:706; NB.1235; Z.5:583.

Note: Some texts have the word *klinē*, a couch, in Mark 7:4 (A.V., "tables").

TABLE (at the)

anakeimai [ἀνάκειμαι, 345], to recline at a meal table, is rendered "sat at the table" in John 12:2, A.V., R.V., "sat at meat" (some texts have *sunanakeimai*); "sat," of course does not express the actual attitude; in John 13:23, R.V., "at the table reclining"; A.V., "leaning"; in 13:28, "at the table" (A.V. and R.V.), lit., 'of (those) reclining.'

NT: B.55d; CB.1235a; K.425.
OT: –.
GEN. REF.: –.

For **TABLET** see **WRITING TABLET**

TACKLING

skeuē [σκευή, 4631], denotes gear, equipment, tackling (of a ship), Acts 27:19. ¶

NT: B.754a; CB.–; K.–.
OT: –.
GEN. REF.: –.

TAIL

oura [οὐρά, 3769], the tail of an animal, occurs in Rev. 9:10 (twice), 19; 12:4. ¶

NT: B.593c; CB.–; K.–.
OT: zānab: S.2180; HR.1031a.1; H.562a; BD.275b.
GEN. REF.: IS.4:716; NB.–; Z.–.

TAKE

1. *lambanō* [λαμβάνω, 2983], to take, lay hold of, besides its literal sense, e.g., Matt. 5:40; 26:26, 27, is used metaphorically, of fear, in taking hold of people, Luke 7:16, R.V. (A.V., "came . . . on"); of sin in "finding (occasion)," R.V. (A.V., "taking"), Rom. 7:8, 11, where sin is viewed as the corrupt source of action, an inward element using the commandment to produce evil effects; of the power of temptation, 1 Cor. 10:13; of taking an example, Jas. 5:10; of taking peace from the earth, Rev. 6:4; of Christ in taking the form of a servant, Phil. 2:7; of taking rightful power (by the Lord, hereafter), Rev. 11:17. See ACCEPT, No. 4.

NT: B.464a; CB.1256c; K.495.
OT: lāqaḥ: S.3947; HR.847a.11a; H.1124; BD.542c.
nāśā': S.5375; HR.847a.17a; H.1421; BD.669d.
GEN. REF.: –.

2. *analambanō* [ἀναλαμβάνω, 353], signifies (*a*) to take up (*ana*), e.g., Acts 1:2, 11, 22 (R.V., "received"); (*b*) to take to oneself, Acts 7:43; or to one's company, 20:13, 14; 23:31; 2 Tim. 4:11; of taking up spiritual armour, Eph. 6:13, 16. See RECEIVE.

NT: B.56d; CB.1235a; K.495.
OT: lāqaḥ: S.3947; HR.78c.3a; H.1124; BD.542c.
nāśā': S.5375; HR.78c.5; H.1421; BD.669d.
GEN. REF.: –.

3. *apolambanō* [ἀπολαμβάνω, 618], besides its common meaning, to receive, denotes to take apart or aside, Mark 7:33, Middle Voice. It is frequent in the papyri, and, in the sense of separation or drawing aside, is illustrated in a message of sorrow, concerning the non-arrival of one who with others had been 'shut up' as recluses in a temple (Moulton and Milligan, Vocab.). See RECEIVE.

NT: B.94b; CB.1237a; K.–.
OT: lāqaḥ: S.3947; HR.136a.1; H.1124; BD.542c.
GEN. REF.: –.

4. *epilambanō* [ἐπιλαμβάνω, 1949], in the Middle Voice, to lay hold of, take hold of, is used literally, e.g., Mark 8:23; Luke 9:47; 14:4; metaphorically, e.g., Heb. 8:9, "(I) took them (by the hand)": for other instances in each respect see HOLD, No. 7.

NT: B.295a; CB.1246a; K.495.
OT: 'āḥaz: S.270; HR.523c.1; H.64; BD.28a.
ḥāzaq: S.2388; HR.523c.2; H.636; BD.304a.
GEN. REF.: –.

5. *katalambanō* [καταλαμβάνω, 2638], to lay hold of, is rendered to take, in Mark 9:18; John 8:3, 4. See APPREHEND.

NT: B.412d; CB.1254a; K.495.
OT: lākad: S.3920; HR.735a.6; H.1115; BD.539d.
nāsag: S.5381; HR.735a.11; H.1422; BD.673b.
GEN. REF.: –.

6. *metalambanō* [μεταλαμβάνω, 3335], to get, or have, a share of, is rendered "to take (food)" in Acts 2:46, R.V. (A.V., "did eat;" see EAT, *Note*); 27:33, i.e., to share it together. See HAVE, PARTAKE, RECEIVE).

NT: B.511d; CB.1258b; K.495.
OT: –.
GEN. REF.: –.

7. *paralambanō* [παραλαμβάνω, 3880], besides its meaning to receive, denotes to take to (or with) oneself, of taking a wife, e.g., Matt. 1:20, 24; of taking a person or persons with one, e.g., Matt. 2:13, 14, 20, 21; 4:5, 8; of demons, 12:45; of Christ and His disciples, 17:1; 20:17; Mark 9:2; 10:32; 14:33; of witnesses, Matt. 18:16; of the removal of persons from the earth in judgment, when "the Son of Man is revealed," Matt. 24:40, 41; Luke 17:34, 35 (cp. the means of the removal of corruption, in ver. 37); of the taking of Christ by the soldiers for scourging, Matt. 27:27, R.V., and to crucifixion, John 19:16; see also Acts 15:39; 16:33; 21:24, 26, 32; 23:18. See RECEIVE.

NT: B.619b; CB.1262a; K.495.
OT: lāqaḥ: S.3947; HR.1061b.2; H.1124; BD.542c.
yārash: S.3423; HR.1061b.1a; H.920; BD.439a.
GEN. REF.: –.

8. *sumparalambanō* [συμπαραλαμβάνω, 4838], *sun*, with, and No. 7, denotes to take along with oneself, as a companion, Acts 12:25; 15:37, 38; Gal. 2:1. ¶

NT: B.779a; CB.–; K.–.
OT: sāphāh: S.5595; HR.1304c.1; H.1531; BD.705a.
GEN. REF.: –.

9. *proslambanō* [προσλαμβάνω, 4355], to take to oneself (*pros*), is used of food, Acts 27:33-36; of persons, of Peter's act toward Christ, Matt. 16:22; Mark 8:32; for evil purposes, Acts 17:5; for good purposes, 18:26. See RECEIVE.

NT: B.717b; CB.1267b; K.495.
OT: lāqaḥ: S.3947; HR.1218b.2; H.1124; BD.542c.
GEN. REF.: –.

10. *prolambanō* [προλαμβάνω, 4301], is rendered to take before in 1 Cor. 11:21. See COME, *Note* (2) at end, OVERTAKE.

NT: B.708b; CB.1266c; K.495.
OT: –.
GEN. REF.: –.

11. *sullambanō* [συλλαμβάνω, 4815], to seize, take, is rendered to take in Matt. 26:55 and Mark 14:48, A.V. (R.V., "seize"); Luke 5:9; Acts 1:16; in 12:3 and 23:27, A.V. (R.V., "seize"). See CATCH, CONCEIVE, HELP.
NT: B.776d; CB.1270b; K.1101.
OT: lākad: S.3920; HR.1301c.3a; H.1115; BD.539d.
tāphas: S.8610; HR.1301c.7a; H.2538; BD.1074c.
GEN. REF.: –.

12. *airō* [αἴρω, 142], to lift, carry, take up or away, occurs very frequently with its literal meanings. In John 1:29 it is used of Christ as "the Lamb of God, which taketh away the sin of the world," not the sins, but sin, that which has existed from the time of the Fall, and in regard to which God has had judicial dealings with the world; through the expiatory sacrifice of Christ the sin of the world will be replaced by everlasting righteousness; cp. the plural, "sins," in 1 John 3:5. Righteous judgment was "taken away" from Christ at human tribunals, and His life, while voluntarily given by Himself (John 10:17, 18), was "taken (from the earth)," Acts 8:33 (quoted from the Sept. of Isa. 53:8). In John 15:2 it is used in the Lord's statement "Every branch in Me that beareth not fruit, He taketh it away." This does not contemplate members of the "body" of Christ, but those who (just as a graft which being inserted, does not "abide" or "strike") are merely professed followers, giving only the appearance of being joined to the parent stem.

The Law described in Col. 2:14 as "the bond written in ordinances that was against us," Christ "took" out of the way at His Cross. In 1 Cor. 5:2, *airō* is used in the best texts (some have No. 14), of the Divine judgment which would have been exercised in 'taking away' from the church the incestuous delinquent, had they mourned before God. See AWAY, BEAR, No. 9, etc.
NT: B.24b; CB.1234a; K.28.
OT: nāsā': S.5375; HR.34c.14a; H.1421; BD.669d.
GEN. REF.: –.

13. *apairō* [ἀπαίρω, 522], to lift off (*apo*, from, and No. 12), is used, in the Passive Voice, of Christ, metaphorically as the Bridegroom of His followers, Matt. 9:15; Mark 2.20; Luke 5:35. ¶
NT: B.79d; CB.–; K.–.
OT: nāsa': S.5265; HR.115c.2a; H.1380; BD.652a.
GEN. REF.: –.

14. *exairō* [ἐξαίρω, 1808], to take away, is used of putting away a person in church discipline, 1 Cor. 5:13; for this verb as a variant reading in ver. 2, see No. 12. ¶
NT: B.272a; CB.–; K.–.
OT: nāsa': S.5265; HR.485a.22a; H.1380; BD.652a.
kārat: S.3772; HR.485a.15a-c; H.1048; BD.503c.
sûr: S.5493; HR.485a.27; H.1480; BD.693b.
GEN. REF.: –.

15. *epairō* [ἐπαίρω, 1869], to lift, raise, is used in the Passive Voice and rendered "He was taken up" in Acts 1:9. See EXALT, HOIST, LIFT.
NT: B.281d; CB.–; K.28.
OT: nāsā': S.5375; HR.505a; H.1421; BD.669d.
GEN. REF.: –.

16. *anaireō* [ἀναιρέω, 337], to take up (*ana*, up, and *haireō*, to take), is used of Pharaoh's daughter in taking up the infant Moses, Acts 7:21; of God's act in taking away the typical animal sacrifices under the Law, Heb. 10:9. See DEATH, C, No. 2, KILL, SLAY.
NT: B.54d; CB.–; K.–.
OT: hārag: S.2026; HR.77b.2a; H.514; BD.246d.
mût: S.4191; HR.77b.4b; H.1169; BD.559b.
GEN. REF.: –.

17. *aphaireō* [ἀφαιρέω, 851], to take away (*apo*), is used with this meaning in Luke 1:25; 10:42; 16:3; Rom. 11:27, of the removal of the sins of Israel; Heb. 10:4, of the impossibility of the removal of sins by offerings under the Law; in Rev. 22:19 (twice). See CUT, No. 8.
NT: B.124b; CB.1236b; K.–.
OT: sûr: S.5493; HR.180a.23b; H.1480; BD.693b.
rûm: S.7311; HR.180a.32; H.2133; BD.926c.
GEN. REF.: –.

18. *kathaireō* [καθαιρέω, 2507], to take down (*kata*), besides its meaning of putting down by force, was the technical term for the removal of the body after crucifixion, Mark 15:36, 46; Luke 23:53; Acts 13:29. See CAST, No. 14.
NT: B.386c; CB.–; K.–.
OT: –.
GEN. REF.: –.

19. *periaireō* [περιαιρέω, 4014], to take away that which surrounds (*peri*, around), is used (*a*) literally, of casting off anchors, Acts 27:40, R.V. (A.V., "having taken up"); 28:13 in some texts, for *perierchomai*, to make a circuit; (*b*) metaphorically, of taking away the veil off the hearts of Israel, 2 Cor. 3:16; of hope of rescue, Acts 27:20; of sins (negatively), Heb. 10:11. ¶
NT: B.645d; CB.–; K.–.
OT: sûr: S.5493; HR.1121b.4a,b; H.1480; BD.693b.
GEN. REF.: –.

20. *dechomai* [δέχομαι, 1209], to receive, is rendered "take (thy bond, R.V., A.V., bill)" in Luke 16:6, 7; "take (the helmet of salvation)," Eph. 6:17, suggesting a heartiness in the taking. See ACCEPT, No. 1, RECEIVE.
NT: B.177b; CB.1240b; K.146.
OT: lāqaḥ: S.3947; HR.294c.4; H.1124; BD.542c.
rāṣāh: S.7521; HR.294c.7; H.2207; BD.953a.
GEN. REF.: –.

21. *prosdechomai* [προσδέχομαι, 4327], to receive favourably, is rendered "took" in Heb. 10:34. See ACCEPT, No. 3.
NT: B.712a; CB.1267a; K.146.
OT: rāṣāh: S.7521; HR.1212c.8; H.2207; BD.953a.
GEN. REF.: –.

22. *krateō* [κρατέω, 2902], to take hold of, get possession of, is translated to take in Matt.

9:25; 22:6; 26:4; Mark 1:31; 5:41; 9:27; 14:1, 44, 46, 49; Luke 8:54; Act 24:6. See HOLD, No. 6.

NT: B.448c; CB.1256a; K.466.
OT: ḥāzaq: S.2388; HR.783a.6c; H.636; BD.304a.
'āḥaz: S.270; HR.783a.2a; H.64; BD.28a.
GEN. REF.: —.

23. *drassomai* [δράσσομαι, 1405], to grasp with the hand, take hold of, is used metaphorically in 1 Cor. 3:19, "taketh (the wise in their craftiness)." ¶

NT: B.206c; CB.—; K.—.
OT: qāmaṣ: S.7061; HR.348c.2; H.2036; BD.888a.
GEN. REF.: —.

24. *didōmi* [δίδωμι, 1325], to give, found in the best texts in Mark 3:6, is rendered "took (counsel)"; some have *poieō*, to make.

NT: B.192c; CB.1241c; K.166.
OT: —.
GEN. REF.: —.

25. *katechō* [κατέχω, 2722], to hold, is rendered "to take (the lowest place)" in Luke 14:9. See HOLD.

NT: B.422c; CB.1254b; K.286.
OT: 'āḥaz: S.270; HR.750c.1; H.64; BD.28a.
ḥāzaq: S.2388; HR.750c.5; H.636; BD.304a.
GEN. REF.: —.

26. *piazō* [πιάζω, 4084], to lay or take hold of forcefully, is always rendered to take in the R.V. See APPREHEND, No. 2.

NT: B.657a; CB.—; K.—.
OT: 'āḥaz: S.270; HR.1132c.1; H.64; BD.28a.
GEN. REF.: —.

27. *parapherō* [παραφέρω, 3911], to bear away (*para*, aside, *pherō*, to bear), remove, is rendered "take away" in Mark 14:36, A.V., R.V., "remove," as in Luke 22:42. See REMOVE. ¶

NT: B.623b; CB.—; K.—.
OT: 'ābar: S.5674; HR.1065b.2; H.1556; BD.716d,718a.
GEN. REF.: —.

28. *echō* [ἔχω, 2192], to have, to hold, is used in Matt. 21:46 in the sense of regarding a person as something, "they took (Him) for (a prophet)." See HAVE. ¶

NT: B.331d; CB.1242c; K.286.
OT: —.
GEN. REF.: —.

29. *sunagō* [συνάγω, 4863], to bring together, is used of taking a person into one's house receiving hospitality, "took . . . in," Matt. 25:35, 38, 43; so in Acts 11:26, R.V., "were gathered together," A.V., "assembled"; perhaps the meaning is 'they were entertained.' See ASSEMBLE, BESTOW, GATHER.

NT: B.782a; CB.1270b; K.—.
OT: 'āsaph: S.622; HR.1307b.1a,b; H.140; BD.62a.
qābaṣ: S.6908; HR.1307b.34; H.1983; BD.867c.
GEN. REF.: —.

30. *ekduō* [ἐκδύω, 1562], to take off a garment from a person, is so rendered with reference to the soldiers' treatment of Christ, Matt. 27:31; Mark 15:20. See STRIP.

NT: B.239a; CB.1243c; K.192.
OT: pāshaṭ: S.6584; HR.423c.2; H.1845; BD.832d.
GEN. REF.: —.

31. *ekballō* [ἐκβάλλω, 1544], has the meaning to bring or take out in Luke 10:35, "took out (two pence)," a word perhaps chosen to express the wholeheartedness of the act (lit., to throw out). See CAST, No. 5.

NT: B.237a; CB.1243b; K.91.
OT: gārash: S.1644; HR.420c.3a,b; H.388; BD.176c.
GEN. REF.: —.

32. *bastazō* [βαστάζω, 941], to bear, lift, is used of taking up stones, John 10:31. As to Matt. 3:11, Moulton and Milligan supply evidences from the vernacular that the word signified to take off (the sandals), which confirms Mark's word *luō*, to unloose (1:7). See BEAR, No. 1.

NT: B.137b; CB.1238c; K.102.
OT: nāsā': S.5375; HR.215a.2; H.1421; BD.669d.
GEN. REF.: —.

33. *epicheireō* [ἐπιχειρέω, 2021], to take in hand (*epi*, upon, *cheir*, the hand), to attempt, take upon oneself, is rendered "have taken in hand," Luke 1:1; "took upon (them)," Acts 19:13. See GO, No. 30.

NT: B.304d; CB.—; K.—.
OT: —.
GEN. REF.: —.

34. *ginomai* [γίνομαι, 1096], to become, to come to be, is rendered "he be taken" in 2 Thess. 2:7, lit., '(until) he, or it, become' (for a treatment of the whole passage see Notes on Thess. by Hogg and Vine).

NT: B.158a; CB.1248b; K.117.
OT: —.
GEN. REF.: —.

Notes: (1) For *sunairō* in Matt. 18:23, see RECKON.

(2) Some texts have *apagō*, to take away, in Acts 24:7.

(3) In John 6:24, A.V., *embainō*, to enter, is rendered "took (shipping)," R.V., "got into (the boats)."

(4) In 2 Thess. 1:8, A.V., *didōmi*, to give (R.V., "rendering"), is translated "taking."

(5) In Rom. 3:5, A.V., *epipherō*, to bring against, is rendered "taketh (vengeance)," R.V., "visiteth (with wrath)."

(6) In Luke 4:5, *anagō*, to lead up (R.V., "led"), is rendered "took up."

(7) In Acts 10:26, A.V., *egeirō*, to raise (R.V.), is rendered "took . . . up."

(8) For taking up baggage, Acts 21:15, see BAGGAGE.

(9) For "taken from" in 1 Thess. 2:17, A.V., see BEREAVED, No. 1.

(10) *Sunechō* is translated "taken with" in Matt. 4:24; Luke 4:38; 8:37. See HOLDEN.

(11) In 2 Pet. 2:12 "to be taken" translates the phrase *eis halōsin*, lit., 'for capture' (*halōsis*, a taking).

(12) In 1 Pet. 2:20, *hupomenō*, to endure, is rendered "ye take . . . patiently."

(13) In Matt. 11:12; John 6:15; Acts 23:10 *harpazō* (see CATCH) is rendered "take . . . by force."

(14) For *apotassomai*, to take leave of, see LEAVE, (*c*) No. 1.

(15) For *apaspazomai*, rendered to take leave of in Acts 21:6, A.V., See LEAVE, (*c*) No. 2.

(16) In Acts 21:6 some mss. have *epibainō*, A.V., "we took ship" (R.V., *embainō*, "we went on board"): cp. *Note* (3), above.

(17) For "untaken" in 2 Cor. 3:14 see UNLIFTED.

(18) In 1 Tim. 5:9, A.V., *katalegō* is rendered to take into the number (R.V., "be enrolled"). ¶

(19) For "take . . . to record" see TESTIFY. See also CARE, HEED, JOURNEY, THOUGHT (to take).

TALENT

A. Noun.

talanton [*τάλαντον*, 5007], originally a balance, then, a talent in weight, was hence a sum of money in gold or silver equivalent to a talent. The Jewish talent contained 3,000 shekels of the sanctuary, e.g., Ex. 30:13 (about 114 lbs.). In N.T. times the talent was not a weight of silver, but the Roman-Attic talent, comprising 6,000 denarii or drachms, and equal to about £240. It is mentioned in Matthew only, 18:24; 25:15, 16, 20 (twice in the best texts), 22 (thrice), 24, 25, 28 (twice). In 18:24 the vastness of the sum, 10,000 talents (£2,400,000), indicates the impossibility of man's clearing himself, by his own efforts, of the guilt which lies upon him before God. ¶

NT: B.803c; CB.–; K.–.
OT: kikkār: S.3603; HR.1333c.2a; H.–; BD.503a.
GEN. REF.: –.

Note: That the talent denoted something weighed has provided the meaning of the Eng. word as a gift or ability, especially under the influence of the Parable of the Talents (Matt. 25:14-30).

B. Adjective.

talantiaios [*ταλαντιαῖος*, 5006], denotes 'of a talent's weight,' Rev. 16:21. ¶

NT: B.803b; CB.–; K.–.
OT: –.
GEN. REF.: –.

For TALES see TALK

TALITHA

taleitha or *talitha* [*ταλειθά*, 5008], an Aramaic feminine meaning 'maiden,' Mark 5:41, has been variously transliterated in the N.T. Greek mss. *Koumi* or *Koum* (Heb. and Aram., *qûm*, arise), which follows, is interpreted by "I say unto thee, arise." *Koum* is the better attested word; so in the Talmud, where this imperative occurs "seven times in one page" (Edersheim, *Life and Times of Jesus*, i, p. 631). ¶

NT: B.803c; CB.1271a; K.–.
OT: –.
GEN. REF.: IS.4:716; NB.1236; Z.5:589.

TALK (Noun and Verb)

A. Nouns.

1. *logos* [*λόγος*, 3056], a word, is translated "talk" in Matt. 22:15; Mark 12:13. See ACCOUNT, B.

NT: B.477a; CB.1257a; K.505.
OT: dābār: S.1697; HR.881c.2a; H.399a; BD.182a.
GEN. REF.: –.

2. *lēros* [*λῆρος*, 3026], denotes foolish talk, nonsense, Luke 24:11, R.V., "idle talk" (A.V., "idle tales"). ¶

NT: B.473a; CB.–; K.–.
OT: –.
GEN. REF.: –.

B. Verbs.

1. *laleō* [*λαλέω*, 2980], to speak, say, is always translated to speak in the R.V., where the A.V. renders it by to talk, Matt. 12:46; Mark 6:50; Luke 24:32; John 4:27 (twice); 9:37; 14:30; Acts 26:31; Rev. 4:1; 17:1; 21:9, 15. The R.V. rendering is preferable; the idea of chat or chatter is entirely foreign to the N.T., and should never be regarded as the meaning in 1 Cor. 14:34, 35. See COMMUNE, *Note*, SAY, No. 1, *Note*, and No. 2, SPEAK.

NT: B.463a; CB.1256b; K.505.
OT: dābar: S.1696; HR.841c.2c; H.399; BD.180b.
GEN. REF.: –.

2. *sullaleō* [*συλλαλέω*, 4814], to speak with (*sun*), is translated to talk with, Matt. 17:3; Mark 9:4; Luke 9:30. See CONFER, No. 2.

NT: B.776c; CB.–; K.–.
OT: dābar: S.1696; HR.1301c.1; H.399; BD.180b.
GEN. REF.: –.

3. *homileō* [*ὁμιλέω*, 3656], to be in company with, consort with (*homilos*, a throng; *homilia*, company), hence, to converse with, is rendered to talk with, Acts 20:11. See COMMUNE, No. 2.

NT: B.565c; CB.–; K.–.
OT: dābar: S.1696; HR.991a.1; H.399; BD.180b.
hālak: S.1980; HR.991a.2; H.498; BD.229d.
GEN. REF.: –.

4. *sunomileō* [*συνομιλέω*, 4926], to converse, talk with, occurs in Acts 10:27. ¶

NT: B.791c; CB.–; K.–.
OT: –.
GEN. REF.: –.

TALKERS (vain)

mataiologos [*ματαιολόγος*, 3151], an adjective denoting talking idly (*mataios*, vain,

idle, *legō*, to speak), is used as a noun (plural) in Tit. 1:10. ¶
NT: B.495c; CB.1258a; K.571.
OT: –.
GEN. REF.: –.

TALKING (vain, foolish)

1. *mataiologia* [ματαιολογία, 3150], a noun corresponding to the above, is used in 1 Tim. 1:6, R.V., "vain talking" ("vain jangling"). ¶
NT: B.495c; CB.1258a; K.571.
OT: –.
GEN. REF.: –.

2. *mōrologia* [μωρολογία, 3473], from *mōros*, foolish, dull, stupid, and *legō*, is used in Eph. 5:4; it denotes more than mere idle talk. Trench describes it as "that 'talk of fools' which is foolishness and sin together" (Syn. § xxxiv). ¶
NT: B.531b; CB.1259b; K.620.
OT: –.
GEN. REF.: –.

TAME

damazō [δαμάζω, 1150], to subdue, tame, is used (*a*) naturally in Mark 5:4 and Jas. 3:7 (twice); (*b*) metaphorically, of the tongue, in Jas. 3:8. ¶ In the Sept., Dan. 2:40. ¶
NT: B.170b; CB.–; K.–.
OT: ḥᵃshal (Aramaic): S.2827; HR.284c.1; H.2748; BD.1094a.
GEN. REF.: –.

TANNER

burseus [βυρσεύς, 1038], a tanner (from *bursa*, a hide), occurs in Acts 9:43; 10:6, 32. ¶
NT: B.148d; CB.–; K.–.
OT: –.
GEN. REF.: IS.–; NB.92; Z.5:595.

For **TARE (Verb)** see **TEAR**

TARES

zizanion [ζιζάνιον, 2215], is a kind of darnel, the commonest of the four species, being the bearded, growing in the grain fields, as tall as wheat and barley, and resembling wheat in appearance. It was credited among the Jews with being degenerate wheat. The Rabbis called it "bastard." The seeds are poisonous to man and herbivorous animals, producing sleepiness, nausea, convulsions and even death (they are harmless to poultry). The plants can be separated out, but the custom, as in the parable, is to leave the cleaning out till near the time of harvest, Matt. 13:25-27, 29, 30, 36, 38, 40. ¶ The Lord describes the tares as "the sons of the evil *one*"; false teachings are indissociable from their propagandists. For the Lord's reference to the Kingdom see KINGDOM.
NT: B.339c; CB.1273c; K.–.
OT: –.
GEN. REF.: IS.4:1045; NB.1238; Z.5:596.

TARRY

1. *menō* [μένω, 3306], to abide, is translated by the verb to abide, in the R.V., for A.V., to tarry, in Matt. 26:38; Mark 14:34; Luke 24:29; John 4:40; Acts 9:43; 18:20; the R.V. retains the verb to tarry in John 21:22, 23; in Acts 20:5, A.V., "tarried" (R.V., "were waiting"). Some mss. have it in Acts 20:15 (A.V., "tarried"). See ABIDE.
NT: B.503c; CB.1258b; K.581.
OT: 'āmad: S.5975; HR.910a.14; H.1637; BD.763c.
qûm: S.6965; HR.910a.15a; H.1999; BD.877c.
qāwāh: S.6960; HR.910a.14; H.1994; BD.875c.
GEN. REF.: –.

2. *epimenō* [ἐπιμένω, 1961], to abide, continue, a strengthened form of No. 1, is translated to tarry in Acts 10:48; 21:4, 10; 28:12, 14; 1 Cor. 16:7, 8; Gal. 1:18, R.V. (A.V., "abode"). See ABIDE, No. 2.
NT: B.296b; CB.1246a; K.–.
OT: māhah: S.4102; HR.525c.1; H.1150; BD.554c.
GEN. REF.: –.

3. *hupomenō* [ὑπομένω, 5278], to endure, is rendered "tarried behind" in Luke 2:43. See ENDURE, No. 2.
NT: B.845d; CB.1252b; K.581.
OT: qāwāh: S.6960; HR.1415c.8; H.1994,1995; BD.875c.
GEN. REF.: –.

4. *prosmenō* [προσμένω, 4357], to abide still, continue, is translated "tarried" in Acts 18:18, suggesting patience and stedfastness in remaining after the circumstances which preceded; in 1 Tim. 1:3, R.V., "to tarry" (A.V., "to abide still"). See ABIDE, No. 6.
NT: B.717c; CB.1267b; K.581.
OT: ḥûl: S.2342; HR.1218c.1; H.623; BD.298c.
GEN. REF.: –.

5. *diatribō* [διατρίβω, 1304], for which see ABIDE, No. 7, is invariably rendered to tarry, in the R.V.; A.V., twice, John 3:22; Acts 25:6; "continued" in John 11:54; Acts 15:35; "abode," Acts 12:19; 14:3, 28; 20:6; "abiding," 16:12; "had been," 25:14. ¶
NT: B.190a; CB.–; K.–.
OT: gûr: S.1481; HR.314a.1; H.330,332; BD.157c.
yāshab: S.3427; HR.314a.2; H.922; BD.442a.
GEN. REF.: –.

6. *chronizō* [χρονίζω, 5549], to spend or while away time; to tarry, Matt. 25:5; Luke 1:21; Heb. 10:37. See DELAY, No. 2.
NT: B.887d; CB.1240b; K.–.
OT: 'āḥar: S.309; HR.1476a.1b; H.68; BD.29b.
GEN. REF.: –.

7. *bradunō* [βραδύνω, 1019], to be slow (*bradus*, slow), is rendered "I tarry long," 1 Tim. 3:15; "is . . . slack," 2 Pet. 3:9. ¶
NT: B.147a; CB.–; K.–.
OT: 'āḥar: S.309; HR.229c.1; H.68; BD.29b.
māhah: S.4102; HR.229c.2; H.1150; BD.554c.
GEN. REF.: –.

8. *kathizō* [καθίζω, 2523], to make to sit down, or, intransitively, to sit down, is translated "tarry ye" in Luke 24:49. See SIT.
NT: B.389d; CB.1254c; K.386.
OT: yāshab: S.3427; HR.701c.4a; H.922; BD.442a.
GEN. REF.: –.

9. *mellō* [μέλλω, 3195], to be about to, is rendered "(why) tarriest thou?" in Acts 22:16. See ABOUT, B.
NT: B.500d; CB.1258a; K.–.
OT: –.
GEN. REF.: –.

10. *ekdechomai* [ἐκδέχομαι, 1551], to expect, await (*ek*, from, *dechomai*, to receive), is translated "tarry" in 1 Cor. 11:33, A.V. (R.V., "wait"). See EXPECT, LOOK, WAIT.
NT: B.238b; CB.1243c; K.146.
OT: –.
GEN. REF.: –.

Notes: (1) In Acts 27:33, A.V., *prosdokaō*, to wait, look for, is translated "have tarried" (R.V., "wait").

(2) In Acts 15:33, *poieō*, to make or do, is used with *chronos*, time, A.V., "they had tarried a space," R.V., "they had spent some time."

TASTE

geuō [γεύω, 1089], to make to taste, is used in the Middle Voice, signifying to taste (*a*) naturally, Matt. 27:34; Luke 14:24; John 2:9; Col. 2:21; (*b*) metaphorically, of Christ's tasting death, implying His Personal experience in voluntarily undergoing death, Heb. 2:9; of believers (negatively) as to tasting of death, Matt. 16:28; Mark 9:1; Luke 9:27; John 8:52; of tasting the heavenly gift (different from receiving it), Heb. 6:4; "the good word of God, and the powers of the age to come," 6:5; "that the Lord is gracious," 1 Pet. 2:3. See EAT.
NT: B.157a; CB.–; K.–.
OT: tā'am: S.2938; HR.240a.2; H.815; BD.380d.
GEN. REF.: IS.4:738; NB.–; Z.–.

TATTLER

phluaros [φλύαρος, 5397], babbling, garrulous (from *phluō*, to babble: cp. *phluareō*, to prate against), is translated "tattlers" in 1 Tim. 5:13. ¶
NT: B.862b; CB.–; K.–.
OT: –.
GEN. REF.: IS.2:536; NB.–; Z.–.

TAUGHT (Adjective)

1. *didaktos* [διδακτός, 1318], primarily what can be taught, then, taught, is used (*a*) of persons, John 6:45; (*b*) of things, 1 Cor. 2:13 (twice), "(not in words which man's wisdom) teacheth, (but which the Spirit) teacheth," lit., '(not in words) taught (of man's wisdom, but) taught (of the Spirit).' ¶
NT: B.191b; CB.1241b; K.161.
OT: limmud: S.3928; HR.316c.1; H.1116a; BD.541a.
GEN. REF.: IS.4:743; NB.–; Z.–.

2. *theodidaktos* [θεοδίδακτος, 2312], God-taught (*Theos*, God, and No. 1), occurs in 1 Thess. 4:9, lit., 'God-taught (persons)'; while the missionaries had taught the converts to love one another, God had Himself been their Teacher. Cp. John 6:45 (see No. 1). ¶
NT: B.356b; CB.–; K.322.
OT: –.
GEN. REF.: –.

For TAXED, TAXING see ENROL, ENROLMENT

TEACH

A. Verbs.

1. *didaskō* [διδάσκω, 1321], is used (*a*) absolutely, to give instruction, e.g., Matt. 4:23; 9:35; Rom. 12:7; 1 Cor. 4:17; 1 Tim. 2:12; 4:11; (*b*) transitively, with an object, whether persons, e.g., Matt. 5:2; 7:29, and frequently in the Gospels and Acts, or things taught, e.g., Matt. 15:9; 22:16; Acts 15:35; 18:11; both persons and things, e.g., John 14:26; Rev. 2:14, 20.
NT: B.192a; CB.1241c; K.161.
OT: lāmad: S.3925; HR.316c.8b; H.1116; BD.540c.
GEN. REF.: IS.4:743; NB.–; Z.–.

2. *paideuō* [παιδεύω, 3811], to instruct and train: see INSTRUCT, No. 2.
NT: B.603d; CB.1261c; K.753.
OT: yāsar: S.3256; HR.1047a.4b-d; H.877; BD.415d.
GEN. REF.: –.

3. *katēcheō* [κατηχέω, 2727], for which see INFORM, No. 2, INSTRUCT, No. 1, is rendered to teach in 1 Cor. 14:19, A.V. (R.V., "instruct"); Gal. 6:6 (twice).
NT: B.423d; CB.1254b; K.422.
OT: –.
GEN. REF.: IS.4:743.

4. *heterodidaskaleō* [ἑτεροδιδασκαλέω, 2085], to teach a different doctrine (*heteros*, "different," to be distinguished from *allos*, another of the same kind: see ANOTHER), is used in 1 Tim. 1:3; 6:3, R.V., A.V., "teach (no) other d." and "teach otherwise," of what is contrary to the faith. ¶
NT: B.314d; CB.1250a; K.161.
OT: –.
GEN. REF.: IS.4:743; NB.–; Z.–.

Notes: (1) For *mathēteuō*, to teach, in the A.V. of Matt. 28:19; Acts 14:21, see DISCIPLE, B.

(2) In Acts 16:21, A.V., *katangellō*, to declare, preach, is rendered "teach" (R.V., "set forth").

(3) For "teacheth" in 1 Cor. 2:13, see TAUGHT, No. 1 (*b*).

B. Adjective.

didaktikos [διδακτικός, 1317], skilled in teaching (akin to No. 1 above: Eng., didactic), is translated "apt to teach" in 1 Tim. 3:2; 2 Tim. 2:24. ¶

NT: B.191b; CB.1241b; K.161.
OT: –.
GEN. REF.: IS.4:743; NB.–; Z.–.

TEACHER, FALSE TEACHERS

1. *didaskalos* [διδάσκαλος, 1320], is rendered "teacher" or "teachers" in Matt. 23:8, by Christ, of Himself; in John 3:2 of Christ; of Nicodemus in Israel, 3:10, R.V.; of teachers of the truth in the churches, Acts 13:1; 1 Cor. 12:28, 29; Eph. 4:11; Heb. 5:12; Jas. 3:1, R.V.; by Paul of his work among the churches, 1 Tim. 2:7; 2 Tim. 1:11; of teachers, wrongfully chosen by those who have "itching ears," 2 Tim. 4:3. See MASTER, RABBI.

NT: B.191c; CB.1241b; K.161.
OT: –.
GEN. REF.: IS.4:743; NB.–; Z.5:607.

2. *kalodidaskalos* [καλοδιδάσκαλος, 2567], denotes a teacher of what is good (*kalos*), Tit. 2:3. ¶

NT: B.400a; CB.1253b; K.161.
OT: –.
GEN. REF.: IS.4:743; NB.–; Z.–.

3. *pseudodidaskalos* [ψευδοδιδάσκαλος, 5572], a false teacher, occurs in the plural in 2 Pet. 2:1. ¶

NT: B.891c; CB.1267c; K.161.
OT: –.
GEN. REF.: IS.4:743; NB.–; Z.–.

For TEACHING (Noun) see DOCTRINE, Nos. 1 and 2

TEARS

dakruon or *dakru* [δάκρυον, 1144], akin to *dakruō*, to weep, is used in the plural, Mark 9:24; Luke 7:38, 44 (with the sense of washing therewith the Lord's feet); Acts 20:19, 31; 2 Cor. 2:4; 2 Tim. 1:4; Heb. 5:7; 12:17; Rev. 7:17; 21:4. ¶

NT: B.170a; CB.–; K.–.
OT: dim'āh: S.1832; HR.284a.1; H.442b; BD.199c.
GEN. REF.: IS.4:745; NB.–; Z.5:611.

TEAR, TORN

1. *sparassō* [σπαράσσω, 4682], denotes to tear, rend, convulse, Mark 1:26; 9:20 (in some mss.), 26, R.V., "having . . . torn" (A.V., "rent"); Luke 9:39. ¶ In the Sept., 2 Sam. 22:8, of the foundations of heaven; Jer. 4:18, of the heart. ¶

NT: B.760d; CB.–; K.–.
OT: gā'ash: S.1607; HR.1281c.1; H.371; BD.172b.
hāmāh: S.1993; HR.1281c.2; H.505; BD.242a.
GEN. REF.: –.

2. *susparassō* [συσπαράσσω, 4952], to tear violently (*sun*, with, intensive), convulse completely, a strengthened form of No. 1, is used in Mark 9:20, in the best texts (some have No. 1); Luke 9:42. ¶

NT: B.794c; CB.–; K.–.
OT: –.
GEN. REF.: –.

3. *diaspaō* [διασπάω, 1288], to break or tear asunder, is translated "should be torn in pieces" in Acts 23:10, R.V. (A.V., ". . . pulled . . ."). See REND, No. 5.

NT: B.188c; CB.–; K.–.
OT: nātaq: S.5423; HR.310c.3; H.1447; BD.683c.
GEN. REF.: –.

4. *rhēgnumi* [ῥήγνυμι, 4486], to break, is rendered "teareth" in Mark 9:18, A.V. (R.V., "dasheth . . . down"). See HINDER, No. 1.

NT: B.735a; CB.–; K.–.
OT: qāra': S.7167; HR.1248c.5; H.2074; BD.902b.
GEN. REF.: –.

TEDIOUS (to be)

enkoptō [ἐνκόπτω, 1465], to hinder, is rendered to be tedious in Acts 24:4, of detaining a person unnecessarily. See HINDER, No. 1.

NT: B.216c; CB.1245a; K.453.
OT: –.
GEN. REF.: –.

For TEETH see TOOTH

TELL

1. *legō* [λέγω, 3004], and the 2nd aorist form *eipon*, used to supply this tense in *legō*, are frequently translated to tell, e.g., Matt. 2:13, R.V., "I tell," A.V., "I bring (thee) word"; 10:27. See SAY, No. 1.

NT: B.468a; CB.1256c; K.505.
OT: 'āmar: S.559; HR.863c.1a; H.118; BD.55c.
GEN. REF.: –.

2. *laleō* [λαλέω, 2980], for which see SAY, No. 2, is usually rendered to speak, in the R.V. (for A.V., to tell), e.g., Matt. 26:13; Luke 1:45; 2:17, 18, 20; Acts 11:14; 27:25; but R.V. and A.V., to tell in John 8:40; Acts 9:6; 22:10.

NT: B.463a; CB.1256b; K.505.
OT: dābar: S.1696; HR.841c.2c; H.399; BD.180b.
GEN. REF.: –.

3. *eklaleō* [ἐκλαλέω, 1583], to speak out (*ek*), is translated "tell" in Acts 23:22. ¶

NT: B.242a; CB.–; K.–.
OT: –.
GEN. REF.: –.

4. *eirō* [εἴρω, fut. of 3004], for which see SAY, No. 4, is rendered to tell in Matt. 21:24; Mark 11:29; John 14:29; Rev. 17:7.

NT: B.468a; CB.–; K.–.
OT: –.
GEN. REF.: –.

5. *apangellō* [ἀπαγγέλλω, 518], to announce, declare, report (usually as a messenger), is

frequently rendered to tell, e.g., Matt. 8:33; 14:12. See BRING, No. 36.
NT: B.79b; CB.1236b; K.10.
OT: nāgad: S.5046; HR.113c.2; H.1289; BD.616c.
GEN. REF.: –.

6. *anangellō* [ἀναγγέλλω, 312], to bring back word, announce, is sometimes rendered to tell, e.g., John 5:15; 2 Cor. 7:7. See DECLARE, No. 1.
NT: B.51b; CB.1235b; K.10.
OT: nāgad: S.5046; HR.74a.10; H.1289; BD.616c.
GEN. REF.: –.

7. *diēgeomai* [διηγέομαι, 1334], for which see DECLARE, No. 6, is rendered to tell, in the A.V. and R.V., in Mark 9:9; Heb. 11:32.
NT: B.195a; CB.1241c; K.–.
OT: sāphar: S.5608; HR.329c.5b; H.1540; BD.707d.
GEN. REF.: –.

8. *exēgeomai* [ἐξηγέομαι, 1834], for which see DECLARE, No. 8, is translated "told" in Luke 24:35, A.V. (R.V., "rehearsed").
NT: B.275d; CB.1247c; K.303.
OT: sāphar: S.5608; HR.495b.3; H.1540; BD.707d.
GEN. REF.: –.

9. *diasapheō* [διασαφέω, 1285], to make clear (*dia*, throughout, *saphēs*, clear), explain fully, is translated "told" in Matt. 18:31. See EXPLAIN.
NT: B.188a; CB.–; K.–.
OT: bēʾēr: S.874; HR.309c.1; H.194; BD.91b.
GEN. REF.: –.

10. *mēnuō* [μηνύω, 3377], is rendered "told" in Acts 23:30, A.V.: see SHEW, No. 7.
NT: B.519a; CB.–; K.–.
OT: –.
GEN. REF.: –.

11. *proeirō* (*prolegō*) [προείρω, 4280], to tell before, is so rendered in Matt. 24:25: see FORETELL, FOREWARN.
NT: B.708b; CB.–; K.–.
OT: –.
GEN. REF.: –.

Note: In the following, *oida*, to know, is translated "tell" in the A.V. (R.V., "know"), Matt. 21:27; Mark 11:33; Luke 20:7; John 3:8; 8:14; 16:18; 2 Cor. 12:2.

TEMPER TOGETHER

sunkerannumi [συγκεράννυμι, 4786], to mix or blend together, is used in 1 Cor. 12:24, of the combining of the members of the human body into an organic structure, as illustrative of the members of a local church (see ver. 27, where there is no definite article in the original). See MIXED (with).
NT: B.773d; CB.1270c; K.–.
OT: ʿārab: S.6151; HR.1299b.1; H.2927; BD.1107d.
GEN. REF.: –.

TEMPERANCE, TEMPERATE

A. Noun.

enkrateia [ἐγκράτεια, 1466], from *kratos*, strength, occurs in Acts 24:25; Gal. 5:23; 2 Pet. 1:6 (twice), in all of which it is rendered "temperance"; the R.V. marg., "self-control" is the preferable rendering, as temperance is now limited to one form of self-control; the various powers bestowed by God upon man are capable of abuse; the right use demands the controlling power of the will under the operation of the Spirit of God; in Acts 24:25 the word follows "righteousness," which represents God's claims, self-control being man's response thereto; in 2 Pet. 1:6, it follows "knowledge," suggesting that what is learnt requires to be put into practice. ¶
NT: B.216c; CB.1245a; K.196.
OT: –.
GEN. REF.: IS.–; NB.1241; Z.5:336.

B. Adjectives.

1. *enkratēs* [ἐγκρατής, 1468], akin to A, denotes exercising self-control, rendered "temperate" in Tit. 1:8. ¶
NT: B.216d; CB.1245a; K.196.
OT: –.
GEN. REF.: IS.–; NB.1241; Z.–.

2. *nēphalios* [νηφάλιος, 3524], for which see SOBER, is translated "temperate" in 1 Tim. 3:2, R.V. (A.V., "vigilant"); in 3:11 and Tit. 2:2, R.V. (A.V., "sober"). ¶
NT: B.538d; CB.1259c; K.633.
OT: –.
GEN. REF.: IS.4:558; NB.1242; Z.–.

Note: In Tit. 2:2, A.V., *sōphrōn*, sober, is rendered "temperate" (R.V., "soberminded").

C. Verb.

enkrateuomai [ἐγκρατεύομαι, 1467], akin to A and B, No. 1, rendered "is temperate" in 1 Cor. 9:25, is used figuratively of the rigid self-control practised by athletes with a view to gaining the prize. See CONTINENCY.
NT: B.216c; CB.1245a; K.196.
OT: ʾāphaq: S.662; HR.366c.1; H.149; BD.67c.
GEN. REF.: –; NB.1241; Z.–.

TEMPEST

1. *thuella* [θύελλα, 2366], a hurricane, cyclone, whirlwind (akin to *thuō*, to slay, and *thumos*, wrath), is used in Heb. 12:18. ¶ In the Sept., Ex. 10:22; Deut. 4:11; 5:22. ¶
NT: B.365a; CB.–; K.–.
OT: ʿărāphel: S.6205; HR.659c.1; H.1701b; BD.791d.
GEN. REF.: IS.4:631; NB.–; Z.–.

2. *seismos* [σεισμός, 4578], a shaking (Eng., seismic, etc.), is used of a tempest in Matt. 8:24. See EARTHQUAKE.
NT: B.746b; CB.1268c; K.1014.
OT: raʿash: S.7494; HR.1262b.2; H.2195a; BD.950b.
GEN. REF.: IS.4:631; NB.–; Z.–.

3. *cheimōn* [χειμών, 5494], winter, a winter storm, hence, in general, a tempest, is so rendered in Acts 27:20. See WEATHER, WINTER.
NT: B.879d; CB.–; K.–.
OT: geshem: S.1653; HR.1457c.1; H.389a; BD.177c.
GEN. REF.: IS.4:631; NB.–; Z.–.

4. *lailaps* [λαῖλαψ, 2978], "a tempest," 2 Pet. 2:17, A.V.: see STORM.

NT: B.462d; CB.1256b; K.—.
OT: sûphāh: S.5492; HR.841a.1; H.1478b; BD.693a.
sa'ar: S.5591; HR.841a.2; H.1528; BD.704b.
s[e]'ārāh: S.5591; HR.841a.3; H.1528; BD.704b.
GEN. REF.: IS.4:631; NB.—; Z.—.

Note: For "tossed with a tempest," Acts 27:18, A.V., see LABOUR, B, No. 2.

TEMPESTUOUS

tuphōnikos [τυφωνικός, 5189], from *tuphōn*, a hurricane, typhoon, is translated "tempestuous" in Acts 27:14. ¶

NT: B.831c; CB.—; K.—.
OT: —.
GEN. REF.: —.

TEMPLE

1. *hieron* [ἱερόν, 2411], the neuter of the adjective *hieros*, sacred, is used as a noun denoting a sacred place, a temple, that of Artemis (Diana), Acts 19:27; that in Jerusalem, Mark 11:11, signifying the entire building with its precincts, or some part thereof, as distinct from the *naos*, the inner sanctuary (see No. 2); apart from the Gospels and Acts, it is mentioned only in 1 Cor. 9:13. Christ taught in one of the courts, to which all the people had access. *Hieron* is never used figuratively. The Temple mentioned in the Gospels and Acts was begun by Herod in B.C. 20, and destroyed by the Romans in A.D. 70.

NT: B.372b; CB.1250b; K.349.
OT: miqdāsh: S.4720; HR.683a.4; H.1990f; BD.874a.
GEN. REF.: IS.4:759; NB.1242; Z.5:622.

2. *naos* [ναός, 3485], a shrine or sanctuary, was used (*a*) among the heathen, to denote the shrine containing the idol, Acts 17:24; 19:24 (in the latter, miniatures); (*b*) among the Jews, the sanctuary in the Temple, into which only the priests could lawfully enter, e.g., Luke 1:9, 21, 22; Christ, as being of the tribe of Judah, and thus not being a priest while upon the earth (Heb. 7:13, 14; 8:4), did not enter the *naos*; for 2 Thess. 2:4 see *Note* (below); (*c*) by Christ metaphorically, of His own physical body, John 2:19, 21; (*d*) in apostolic teaching, metaphorically, (1) of the Church, the mystical Body of Christ, Eph. 2:21; (2) of a local church, 1 Cor. 3:16, 17; 2 Cor. 6:16; (3) of the present body of the individual believer, 1 Cor. 6:19; (4) of the Temple seen in visions in the Apocalypse, 3:12; 7:15; 11:19; 14:15, 17; 15:5, 6, 8; 16:1, 17; (5) of the Lord God Almighty and the Lamb, as the Temple of the new and Heavenly Jerusalem, Rev. 21:22. See SANCTUARY and HOLY, B (*b*), par. 4.

NT: B.533b; CB.1259b; K.625.
OT: hêkāl: S.1964; HR.939a.4a; H.493; BD.228a.
GEN. REF.: IS.4:759; NB.1242; Z.5:622.

Notes: (1) The temple mentioned in 2 Thess. 2:4 (*naos*), as the seat of the Man of Sin, has been regarded in different ways. The weight of Scripture evidence is in favour of the view that it refers to a literal temple in Jerusalem, to be reconstructed in the future (cp. Dan. 11:31 and 12:11, with Matt. 24:15). For a fuller examination of the passage, see Notes on Thessalonians by Hogg and Vine, pp. 250-252.

(2) For *oikos*, rendered "temple," Luke 11:51, A.V., see HOUSE, No. 1.

TEMPLE-KEEPER

neōkoros [νεωκόρος, 3511], Acts 19:35, R.V., and A.V. marg., "temple-keeper" (A.V., "worshipper"), is used in profane Greek of one who has charge of a temple. Coin inscriptions show that it was an honorary title given to certain cities, especially in Asia Minor, where the cult of some god or of a deified human potentate had been established, here to Ephesus in respect of the goddess Artemis. Apparently the Imperial cult also existed at Ephesus. Josephus applies the word to Jews as worshippers, but this is not the meaning in Acts 19. ¶

NT: B.537b; CB.1259c; K.—.
OT: —.
GEN. REF.: —.

TEMPORAL

proskairos [πρόσκαιρος, 4340], for a season (*pros*, for, *kairos*, a season), is rendered "temporal" in 2 Cor. 4:18. See SEASON, WHILE.

NT: B.715b; CB.1267a; K.389.
OT: —.
GEN. REF.: —.

TEMPT

A. Verbs.

1. *peirazō* [πειράζω, 3985], signifies (1) to try, attempt, assay (see TRY); (2) to test, try, prove, in a good sense, said of Christ and of believers, Heb. 2:18, where the context shows that the temptation was the cause of suffering to Him, and only suffering, not a drawing away to sin, so that believers have the sympathy of Christ as their High Priest in the suffering which sin occasions to those who are in the enjoyment of communion with God; so in the similar passage in 4:15; in all the temptations which Christ endured, there was nothing within Him that answered to sin. There was no sinful infirmity in Him. While He was truly man, and His Divine nature was not in any way inconsistent with His Manhood, there was nothing in Him such as is produced in us by the sinful nature

which belongs to us; in Heb. 11:37, of the testing of O.T. saints; in 1 Cor. 10:13, where the meaning has a wide scope, the verb is used of testing as permitted by God, and of the believer as one who should be in the realization of his own helplessness and his dependence upon God (see PROVE, TRY); in a bad sense, to tempt (*a*) of attempts to ensnare Christ in His speech, e.g., Matt. 16:1; 19:3; 22:18, 35, and parallel passages; John 8:6; (*b*) of temptations to sin, e.g., Gal. 6:1, where one who would restore an erring brother is not to act as his judge, but as being one with him in liability to sin, with the possibility of finding himself in similar circumstances, Jas. 1:13, 14 (see note below); of temptations mentioned as coming from the Devil, Matt. 4:1, and parallel passages; 1 Cor. 7:5; 1 Thess. 3:5 (see TEMPTER; (*c*) of trying or challenging God, Acts 15:10; 1 Cor. 10:9 (2nd part); Heb. 3:9; the Holy Spirit, Acts 5:9: cp. No. 2.

NT: B.640b; CB.1263a; K.822.
OT: nāsāh: S.5254; HR.1115c.1; H.1373; BD.650a.
GEN. REF.: IS.4:784; NB.1250; Z.5:669.

Note: *"James 1:13-15 seems to contradict other statements of Scripture in two respects, saying (*a*) that 'God cannot be tempted with evil,' and (*b*) that 'He Himself tempteth no man.' But God tempted, or tried, Abraham, Heb. 11:17, and the Israelites tempted, or tried, God, 1 Cor. 10:9. Ver. 14, however, makes it plain that, whereas in these cases the temptation or trial, came from without, James refers to temptation, or trial, arising within, from uncontrolled appetites and from evil passions, cp Mark 7:20-23. But though such temptation does not proceed from God, yet does God regard His people while they endure it, and by it tests and approves them."

2. *ekpeirazō* [ἐκπειράζω, 1598], an intensive form of the foregoing, is used in much the same way as No. 1 (2) (*c*), in Christ's quotation from Deut. 6:16, in reply to the Devil, Matt. 4:7; Luke 4:12; so in 1 Cor. 10:9, R.V., "the Lord" (A.V., "Christ"); of the lawyer who tempted Christ, Luke 10:25. ¶ In the Sept., Deut. 6:16; 8:2, 16; Ps. 78:18. ¶ Cp. *dokimazō* (see PROVE).

NT: B.243c; CB.1243c; K.822.
OT: nāsāh: S.5254; HR.438c.1; H.1373; BD.650a.
GEN. REF.: IS.4:784; NB.1250; Z.5:669.

B. Adjective.

apeirastos [ἀπείραστος, 551], untempted, untried (*a*, negative, and A, No. 1), occurs in Jas. 1:13, with *eimi*, to be, "cannot be tempted," 'untemptable' (Mayor). ¶

NT: B.83b; CB.–; K.822.
OT: –.
GEN. REF.: IS.4:784; NB.–; Z.–.

TEMPTATION

peirasmos [πειρασμός, 3986], akin to A, above, is used of (1) trials with a beneficial purpose and effect, (*a*) of trials or temptations, Divinely permitted or sent, Luke 22:28; Acts 20:19; Jas. 1:2; 1 Pet. 1:6; 4:12, R.V., "to prove," A.V., "to try"; 2 Pet. 2:9 (singular); Rev. 3:10, R.V., "trial" (A.V., "temptation"); in Jas. 1:12, "temptation" apparently has meanings (1) and (2) combined (see below), and is used in the widest sense; (*b*) with a good or neutral significance, Gal. 4:14, of Paul's physical infirmity, "a temptation" to the Galatian converts, of such a kind as to arouse feelings of natural repugnance; (*c*) of trials of a varied character, Matt. 6:13 and Luke 11:4, where believers are commanded to pray not to be led into such by forces beyond their own control; Matt. 26:41; Mark 14:38; Luke 22:40, 46, where they are commanded to watch and pray against entering into temptations by their own carelessness or disobedience; in all such cases God provides "the way of escape," 1 Cor. 10:13 (where *peirasmos* occurs twice). (2) of trial definitely designed to lead to wrong doing, temptation, Luke 4:13; 8:13; 1 Tim. 6:9; (3) of trying or challenging God, by men, Heb. 3:8. ¶

NT: B.640d; CB.1263a; K.822.
OT: massāh: S.4531; HR.1116a.1; H.1223b; BD.650b.
GEN. REF.: IS.4:784; NB.1250; Z.5:669.

TEMPTER

Note: The present participle of *peirazō*, to tempt, preceded by the article, lit., 'the (one) tempting,' is used as a noun, describing the Devil in this character, Matt. 4:3; 1 Thess. 3:5. ¶

TEN

deka [δέκα, 1176], whence the Eng. prefix *deca-*, is regarded by some as the measure of human responsibility, e.g., Luke 19:13, 17; Rev. 2:10; it is used in a figurative setting in Rev. 12:3; 13:1; 17:3, 7, 12, 16.

NT: B.173d; CB.1240c; K.143.
OT: –.
GEN. REF.: IS.3:560; NB.–; Z.–.

Notes: (1) In Acts 23:23, *hebdomēkonta*, seventy, is translated "threescore and ten."

*From Notes on Thessalonians by Hogg and Vine, p. 97.

(2) For "ten thousand" see THOUSAND.

For TEND, John 21:16; 1 Pet. 5:2, R.V., see FEED, No. 2

TENDER

hapalos [ἁπαλός, 527], soft, tender, is used of the branch of a tree, Matt. 24:32; Mark 13:28. ¶

NT: B.80b; CB.–; K.–.
OT: –.
GEN. REF.: IS.4:790; NB.–; Z.–.

Note: For Luke 1:78, "tender mercy"; Phil. 1:8; 2:1, "tender mercies," see BOWELS.

For TENDER-HEARTED see PITIFUL, No. 2

TENTH

1. *dekatos* [δέκατος, 1182], an adjective from *deka*, ten, occurs in John 1:39; Rev. 11:13; 21:20. ¶

NT: B.174a; CB.1240c; K.–.
OT: 'ᵃsîrî: S.6224; HR.289a.1b; H.1711f; BD.798a.
ma'ᵃśēr: S.4643; HR.289a.1c; H.1711i; BD.798b.
'issārôn: S.6241; HR.289a.1f; H.1711h; BD.798a.
GEN. REF.: IS.5:861; NB.–; Z.–.

2. *dekatē* [δεκάτη, 1181], grammatically the feminine form of No. 1, with *meris*, a part, understood, is used as a noun, translated "a tenth part" in Heb. 7:2, "a tenth," ver. 4; "tithes" in vv. 8, 9. ¶

NT: B.174a; CB.1240c; K.–.
OT: 'ᵃsîrî: S.6224; HR.289a.1b; H.1711f; BD.798a.
ma'ᵃśēr: S.4643; HR.289a.1c; H.1711i; BD.798d.
'issārôn: S.6241; HR.289a.1f; H.1711h; BD.798a.
GEN. REF.: IS.5:861; NB.–; Z.–.

For TENTS see TABERNACLE, No. 1.

TENT-MAKERS

skēnopoios [σκηνοποιός, 4635], an adjective, 'tent-making' (*skēnē*, a tent, *poieō*, to make), is used as a noun in Acts 18:3. ¶

NT: B.755a; CB.1269a; K.1040.
OT: –.
GEN. REF.: IS.4:792; NB.–; Z.5:677.

TERM

prothesmios [προθέσμιος, 4287], an adjective denoting appointed beforehand (*pro*, before, *tithēmi*, to put, appoint: see APPOINT, No. 3, *Note*), is used as a noun, *prothesmia* (grammatically feminine, with *hēmera*, a day, understood), as in Greek law, a day appointed before, Gal. 4:2, R.V., "the term appointed," i.e., 'a stipulated date' (A.V., "the time appointed"). ¶

NT: B.706b; CB.–; K.–.
OT: –.
GEN. REF.: –.

TERRESTRIAL

epigeios [ἐπίγειος, 1919], on earth, earthly (*epi*, on, *gē*, the earth), is rendered "terrestrial" in 1 Cor. 15:40 (twice), in contrast to *epouranios*, heavenly. See EARTHLY, No. 2.

NT: B.290c; CB.1245c; K.116.
OT: –.
GEN. REF.: –.

For TERRIBLE, Heb. 12:21, see FEARFUL, B, No. 1

TERRIFY

A. Verbs.

1. *ptoeō* [πτοέω, 4422], to terrify, is used in the Passive Voice, Luke 21:9; 24:37. ¶

NT: B.727c; CB.–; K.–.
OT: ḥātat: S.2865; HR.1238c.2a,b; H.784; BD.369a.
GEN. REF.: IS.4:793; NB.–; Z.–.

2. *ekphobeō* [ἐκφοβέω, 1629], to frighten away (*ek*, out, *phobos*, fear), occurs in 2 Cor. 10:9. ¶

NT: B.247a; CB.–; K.–.
OT: ḥārad: S.2729; HR.445b.1; H.735; BD.353b.
GEN. REF.: IS.4:793; NB.–; Z.–.

3. *pturō* [πτύρω, 4426], to scare, Phil. 1:28: see AFFRIGHTED, B, No. 1. ¶

NT: B.727d; CB.–; K.–.
OT: –.
GEN. REF.: –.

B. Adjective.

emphobos [ἔμφοβος, 1719], terrified, is so rendered in the R.V. of Acts 24:25. See TREMBLE.

NT: B.257d; CB.–; K.–.
OT: –.
GEN. REF.: IS.4:793; NB.–; Z.–.

TERROR

1. *phobos* [φόβος, 5401], fear, is rendered "terror" in Rom. 13:3; in 2 Cor. 5:11 and 1 Pet. 3:14, A.V. (R.V., "fear"). See FEAR, No. 1.

NT: B.863c; CB.1264b; K.1272.
OT: 'êmāh: S.367; HR.1435c.1a; H.80b; BD.33d.
yir'āh: S.3374; HR.1435c.4a; H.907b; BD.432a.
pāḥad: S.6343; HR.1435c.6; H.1756a; BD.808b.
GEN. REF.: IS.4:793; NB.–; Z.–.

2. *phobētron* [φόβητρον, 5400], that which causes fright, a terror, is translated "terrors" in Luke 21:11, R.V. (A.V., "fearful sights"). ¶ See FEAR, A, *Note*. For *ptoēsis*, see AMAZEMENT.

NT: B.863c; CB.1264b; K.–.
OT: ḥāgā': S.2283; HR.1435c.1; H.602b; BD.291b.
GEN. REF.: IS.4:793; NB.–; Z.–.

For TESTAMENT see COVENANT

TESTATOR

diatithēmi [διατίθημι, 1303], to arrange, dispose, is used only in the Middle Voice in the N.T.; in Heb. 9:16, 17, the present participle with the article, lit., 'the (one) making a testament (or covenant),' virtually a noun, "the testator" (the covenanting one); it is used of making a covenant in 8:10 and 10:16 and Acts 3:25. In covenant-making, the sacrifice of a victim was customary (Gen. 15:10; Jer. 34:18, 19). He who made a covenant did so at the cost of a life. While the terminology in Heb. 9:16, 17 has the appearance of being appropriate to the circumstances of making a will, there is excellent reason for adhering to the meaning 'covenant-making.' The rendering "the death of the testator" would make Christ a Testator, which He was not. He did not die simply that the terms of a testamentary disposition might be fulfilled for the heirs. Here He who is "the Mediator of a new covenant" (ver. 15) is Himself the Victim whose death was necessary. The idea of making a will destroys the argument of ver. 18. In spite of various advocacies of the idea of a will, the weight of evidence is confirmatory of what Hatch, in *Essays in Biblical Greek*, p. 48, says: "There can be little doubt that the word (*diathēkē*) must be invariably taken in this sense of 'covenant' in the N.T., and especially in a book . . . so impregnated with the language of the Sept. as the Epistle to the Hebrews" (see also Westcott, and W. F. Moulton). We may render somewhat literally thus: 'For where a covenant (is), a death (is) necessary to be brought in of the one covenanting; for a covenant over dead ones (victims) is sure, since never has it force when the one covenanting lives' [Christ being especially in view]. The writer is speaking from a Jewish point of view, not from that of the Greeks. "To adduce the fact that in the case of wills the death of the testator is the condition of validity, is, of course, no proof at all that a death is necessary to make a covenant valid. . . . To support his argument, proving the necessity of Christ's death, the writer adduces the general law that he who makes a covenant does so at the expense of life" (Marcus Dods). See APPOINT, MAKE.

NT: B.189d; CB.1241b; K.157.
OT: kārat: S.3772; HR.313b.1; H.1048; BD.503c.
GEN. REF.: IS.–; NB.264,267; Z.–.

TESTIFY

1. *martureō* [μαρτυρέω, 3140], for which see WITNESS, is frequently rendered to bear witness, to witness, in the R.V., where A.V. renders it to testify, John 2:25; 3:11, 32; 5:39; 15:26; 21:24; 1 Cor. 15:15; Heb. 7:17; 11:4; 1 John 4:14; 5:9; 3 John 3. In the following, however, the R.V., like the A.V., has the rendering to testify, John 4:39, 44; 7:7; 13:21; Acts 26:5; Rev. 22:16, 18, 20.

NT: B.492c; CB.1257c; K.564.
OT: 'ûd: S.5749; HR.896b.1b; H.1576; BD.729d.
'ēd: S.5707; HR.896b.1c; H.1576b; BD.729c.
GEN. REF.: IS.4:797; NB.–; Z.–.

2. *epimartureō* [ἐπιμαρτυρέω, 1957], to bear witness to (a strengthened form of No. 1), is rendered "testifying" in 1 Pet. 5:12. ¶

NT: B.296a; CB.1246a; K.564.
OT: 'ûd: S.5749; HR.525b.1; H.1576; BD.729d.
GEN. REF.: IS.4:797; NB.–; Z.–.

3. *marturomai* [μαρτύρομαι, 3143], primarily, to summon as witness, then, to bear witness (sometimes with the suggestion of solemn protestation), is rendered to testify in Acts 20:26, R.V. (A.V., "I take . . . to record"); 26:22, in the best texts (some have No. 1), R.V.; Gal. 5:3; Eph. 4:17; 1 Thess. 2:11, in the best texts (some have No. 1), R.V., "testifying" (A.V., "charged"). ¶

NT: B.494a; CB.1257c; K.564.
OT: –.
GEN. REF.: IS.4:797; NB.–; Z.–.

4. *diamarturomai* [διαμαρτύρομαι, 1263], to testify or protest solemnly, an intensive form of No. 3, is translated to testify in Luke 16:28; Acts 2:40; 8:25; 10:42; 18:5; 20:21, 23, 24; 23:11; 28:23; 1 Thess 4:6; Heb. 2:6; to charge in 1 Tim. 5:21; 2 Tim. 2:14; 4:1. ¶

NT: B.186c; CB.1241b; K.564.
OT: 'ûd: S.5749; HR.305b.3; H.1576; BD.729d.
GEN. REF.: IS.4:797; NB.–; Z.–.

5. *promarturomai* [προμαρτύρομαι, 4303], to testify beforehand, occurs in 1 Pet. 1:11, where the pronoun "it" should be "He" (the "it" being due to the grammatically neuter form of *pneuma*; the Personality of the Holy Spirit requires the masculine pronoun). ¶

NT: B.708c; CB.–; K.564.
OT: –.
GEN. REF.: IS.4:797; NB.–; Z.–.

Note: In Rev. 22:18 some texts have *summartureō*, to bear witness with. See WITNESS.

TESTIMONY

1. *marturion* [μαρτύριον, 3142], a testimony, witness, is almost entirely translated "testimony" in both A.V. and R.V. The only place where both have "witness" is Acts 4:33. In Acts 7:44 and Jas. 5:3, the R.V. has "testimony" (A.V., "witness").

In 2 Thess. 1:10, "our testimony unto you," R.V., refers to the fact that the missionaries, besides proclaiming the truths of the gospel, had borne witness to the power of these truths. *Kērugma*, the thing preached, the message, is objective, having especially to do with the effect on the hearers; *marturion* is mainly subjective, having to do especially with the preacher's personal experience. In 1 Tim. 2:6 the R.V. is important, "the testimony (i.e., of the gospel) *to be borne* in its own times," i.e., in the times

Divinely appointed for it, namely, the present age, from Pentecost till the Church is complete. In Rev. 15:5, in the phrase, "the temple of the tabernacle of the testimony in Heaven," the testimony is the witness to the rights of God, denied and refused on earth, but about to be vindicated by the exercise of the judgments under the pouring forth of the seven bowls or vials of Divine retribution. See WITNESS.

NT: B.493d; CB.1257c; K.564.
OT: mô'ēd: S.4150; HR.896c.1; H.878b; BD.417b.
'ēdāh: S.5713; HR.896c.2b; H.1576c,e; BD.729d,730a.
'ēdût: S.5715; HR.896c.2c; H.1576f; BD.730b.
GEN. REF.: IS.4:797; NB.—; Z.5:682.

2. *marturia* [μαρτυρία, 3141], witness, evidence, testimony, is almost always rendered "witness" in the R.V. (for A.V., "testimony" in John 3:32, 33; 5:34; 8:17; 21:24, and always for A.V., "record," e.g., 1 John 5:10, 11), except in Acts 22:18 and in the Apocalypse, where both, with one exception, have "testimony," 1:2, 9; 6:9; 11:7; 12:11, 17; 19:10 (twice); 20:4 (A.V., "witness"). In 19:10, "the testimony of Jesus" is objective, the testimony or witness given to Him (cp. 1:2, 9; as to those who will bear it, see Rev. 12:17, R.V.). The statement "the testimony of Jesus is the spirit of prophecy," is to be understood in the light, e.g., of the testimony concerning Christ and Israel in the Psalms, which will be used by the godly Jewish remnant in the coming time of "Jacob's Trouble." All such testimony centres in and points to Christ. See WITNESS.

NT: B.493c; CB.1257c; K.564.
OT: 'ēd: S.5707; HR.896b.2a; H.1576b; BD.729c.
'ēdût: S.5715; HR.896b.2b; H.1576f; BD.730b.
mô'ēd: S.4150; HR.896b.1; H.878b; BD.417b.
GEN. REF.: IS.4:797; NB.—; Z.5:682.

TETRARCH

A. Noun.

tetraarchēs or *tetrarchēs* [τετραάρχης, 5076], denotes one of four rulers (*tetra*, four, *archē*, rule), properly, the governor of the fourth part of a region; hence, a dependent princeling, or any petty ruler subordinate to kings or ethnarchs; in the N.T., Herod Antipas, Matt. 14:1; Luke 3:19; 9:7; Acts 13:1. ¶

NT: B.814a; CB.—; K.—.
OT: —.
GEN. REF.: IS.4:798; NB.1253; Z.5:683.

B. Verb.

tetraarcheō or *tetrarcheō* [τετρααρχέω, 5075], to be a tetrarch, occurs in Luke 3:1 (thrice), of Herod Antipas, his brother Philip and Lysanias. Antipas and Philip each inherited a fourth part of his father's dominions. Inscriptions bear witness to the accuracy of Luke's details. ¶

NT: B.814a; CB.—; K.—.
OT: —.
GEN. REF.: IS.4:798; NB.—; Z.5:683.

THAN: see † p. 1

THANK, THANKS (Noun and Verb), THANKFUL, THANKFULNESS, THANKSGIVING, THANKWORTHY

A. Nouns.

1. *charis* [χάρις, 5485], for the meanings of which see GRACE, No. 1, is rendered "thank" in Luke 6:32, 33, 34; in 17:9, "doth he thank" is lit., 'hath he thanks to'; it is rendered "thanks (be to God)" in Rom. 6:17, R.V. (A.V., "God be thanked"); "thanks" in 1 Cor. 15:57; in 1 Tim. 1:12 and 2 Tim. 1:3, "I thank" is, lit., 'I have thanks'; "thankworthy," 1 Pet. 2:19, A.V. (R.V., "acceptable"). See ACCEPT, D, No. 2.

NT: B.877b; CB.1239c; K.1298.
OT: ḥēn: S.2580; HR.1455a.2; H.694a; BD.336b.
GEN. REF.: IS.4:822; NB.—; Z.—.

2. *eucharistia* [εὐχαριστία, 2169], *eu*, well, *charizomai*, to give freely (Eng., eucharist), denotes (*a*) gratitude, "thankfulness," Acts 24:3; (*b*) giving of thanks, thanksgiving, 1 Cor. 14:16; 2 Cor. 4:15; 9:11, 12 (plur.); Eph. 5:4; Phil. 4:6; Col. 2:7; 4:2; 1 Thess. 3:9 ("thanks"); 1 Tim. 2:1 (plur.); 4:3, 4; Rev. 4:9, "thanks"; 7:12. ¶

NT: B.328c; CB.1247a; K.1298.
OT: —.
GEN. REF.: IS.4:822; NB.—; Z.—.

B. Verbs.

1. *eucharisteō* [εὐχαριστέω, 2168], akin to A, No. 2, to give thanks, (*a*) is said of Christ, Matt. 15:36; 26:27; Mark 8:6; 14:23; Luke 22:17, 19; John 6:11, 23; 11:41; 1 Cor. 11:24; (*b*) of the Pharisee in Luke 18:11 in his self-complacent prayer; (*c*) is used by Paul at the beginning of all his Epistles, except 2 Cor. (see, however, *eulogētos* in 1:3), Gal., 1 Tim., 2 Tim. (see, however, *charin echō*, 1:3), and Tit., (1) for his readers, Rom. 1:8; Eph. 1:16; Col. 1:3; 1 Thess. 1:2; 2 Thess. 1:3 (cp. 2:13); virtually so in Philm. 4; (2) for fellowship shown, Phil. 1:3; (3) for God's gifts to them, 1 Cor. 1:4; (*d*) is recorded (1) of Paul elsewhere, Acts 27:35; 28:15; Rom. 7:25; 1 Cor. 1:14; 14:18; (2) of Paul and others, Rom. 16:4; 1 Thess. 2:13; of himself, representatively, as a practice, 1 Cor. 10:30; (3) of others, Luke 17:16; Rom. 14:6 (twice); 1 Cor. 14:17; Rev. 11:17; (*e*) is used in admonitions to the saints, the Name of the Lord Jesus suggesting His character and example, Eph. 5:20; Col. 1:12; 3:17; 1 Thess. 5:18; (*f*) as the expression of a purpose, 2 Cor. 1:11, R.V.; (*g*) negatively of the ungodly, Rom. 1:21. ¶ Thanksgiving is the expression of joy Godward,

and is therefore the fruit of the Spirit (Gal. 5:22); believers are encouraged to abound in it (e.g., Col. 2:7, and see C. below).

NT: B.328a; CB.1247a; K.1298.
OT: –.
GEN. REF.: IS.4:822; NB.–; Z.–.

2. *exomologeō* [ἐξομολογέω, 1843], in the Middle Voice, signifies to make acknowledgment, whether of sins (to confess), or in the honour of a person, as in Rom. 14:11; 15:9 (in some mss. in Rev. 3:5); this is the significance in the Lord's address to the Father, "I thank (Thee)," in Matt. 11:25 and Luke 10:21, the meaning being 'I make thankful confession' or 'I make acknowledgment with praise.' See CONFESS, No. 2, CONSENT, PROMISE.

NT: B.277a; CB.–; K.687.
OT: yādāh: S.3034; HR.499a.3b; H.847; BD.392a.
GEN. REF.: IS.4:822; NB.–; Z.–.

3. *anthomologeomai* [ἀνθομολογέομαι, 437], to acknowledge fully, to celebrate fully (*anti*) in praise with thanksgiving, is used of Anna in Luke 2:38. ¶

NT: B.67b; CB.–; K.687.
OT: yādāh: S.3034; HR.96a.1; H.847; BD.392a.
shᵉbaḥ (Aramaic): S.7624; HR.96a.2; H.3014; BD.1114b.
GEN. REF.: IS.4:822; NB.–; Z.–.

Note: For *homologeō*, rendered "giving thanks" in Heb. 13:15 (R.V., "make confession"), see CONFESS, A, No. 1 (*d*).

C. Adjective.

eucharistos [εὐχάριστος, 2170], primarily, gracious, agreeable (as in the Sept., Prov. 11:16, of a wife, who brings glory to her husband ¶), then grateful, thankful, is so used in Col. 3:15. ¶

NT: B.329a; CB.1247a; K.1298.
OT: ḥēn: S.2580; HR.583c.1; H.694a; BD.336b.
GEN. REF.: IS.4:822; NB.–; Z.–.

THAT (Conjunction, etc.): see † p. 1

For THAT (Demonstrative Pronoun), see THIS

THEATRE

theatron [θέατρον, 2302], a theatre, was used also as a place of assembly, Acts 19:29, 31; in 1 Cor. 4:9 it is used of a show or spectacle. See SPECTACLE. ¶

NT: B.353c; CB.1271c; K.318.
OT: –.
GEN. REF.: IS.4:824; NB.1270; Z.5:714.

THEE

Note: This translates the oblique forms of the pronoun *su*, thou. In 2 Tim. 4:11, it translates the reflexive pronoun *seautou*, thyself.

THEFT

1. *klopē* [κλοπή, 2829], akin to *kleptō*, to steal, is used in the plural in Matt. 15:19; Mark 7:22. ¶

NT: B.436d; CB.–; K.–.
OT: gānab: S.1589; HR.772b.1a,b; H.364; BD.170b.
gannāb: S.1590; HR.772b.1c; H.364b; BD.170c.
GEN. REF.: IS.4:614; NB.–; Z.–.

2. *klemma* [κλέμμα, 2809], a thing stolen, and so, a theft, is used in the plural in Rev. 9:21. ¶ In the Sept., Gen. 31:39; Ex. 22:3, 4. ¶

NT: B.434b; CB.–; K.–.
OT: gānab: S.1589; HR.767b.1a; H.364; BD.170b.
gᵉnēbāh: S.1591; HR.767b.1b; H.364a; BD.170c.
GEN. REF.: IS.4:614; NB.–; Z.–.

THEIR, THEIRS

Note: These pronouns are the rendering of (1) *autōn*, the genitive plur. of *autos*, he, e.g., Matt. 2:12; (2) *heautōn*, of themselves, the genitive plur. of *heautou*, of himself, e.g., Matt. 8:22; Rom. 16:4, 18, "their own"; or the accusative plur. *heautous*, e.g., 2 Cor. 8:5, "their own selves"(for John 20:10, see HOME, A, No. 3); (3) *idious*, the accusative plur. of *idios*, one's own, e.g., 1 Cor. 14:35, "their own"; (4) *toutōn*, lit., 'of these,' the gen. plur. of *houtos*, this, Rom. 11:30, "their (disobedience)"; (5) *ekeinōn*, the gen. plur. of *ekeinos*, that one (emphatic), e.g., 2 Cor. 8:14 (twice), "their," lit., 'of those'; 2 Tim. 3:9, "theirs."

THEM, THEMSELVES

Note: These translate the plural, in various forms, of (1) *autos* [see (1) above], e.g., Matt. 3:7; (2) *heatou* [see (2) above], e.g., Matt 15:30; (3) *houtos* (*toutous*) [see (4) above], e.g., Acts 21:24; (4) *eikeinos* [see (5) above], e.g., Matt. 13:11. Regarding *allēlōn*, of one another, and its other forms, the R.V. substitutes "one another" for the A.V. "themselves" in Mark 8:16; 9:34; Luke 4:36; John 6:52; 11:56; 16:17; 19:24; Acts 26:31; 28:4; Rom. 2:15, but adheres to the rendering "themselves" in Mark 15:31; Acts 4:15; 28:25.

THEN

1. *tote* [τότε, 5119], a demonstrative adverb of time, denoting at that time, is used (*a*) of concurrent events, e.g., Matt. 2:17; Gal. 4:8, "at that time"; ver. 29, "then"; 2 Pet. 3:6, "(the world) that then was," lit., '(the) then (world)'; (*b*) of consequent events, then, thereupon, e.g., Matt. 2:7; Luke 11:26; 16:16; "[from (A.V., since)] that time"; John 11:14; Acts 17:14; (*c*) of things future, e.g., Matt. 7:23; 24:30 (twice), 40; eight times in ch. 25; 1 Cor. 4:5; Gal. 6:4; 1 Thess. 5:3; 2 Thess. 2:8. It occurs 90 times in Matthew, more than in all the rest of the N.T. together.

NT: B.823d; CB.1273a; K.–.
OT: 'āz: S.227; HR.1367c.2a; H.54; BD.23a.
GEN. REF.: –.

2. *eita* [εἶτα, 1534], denotes sequence (*a*) of time, then, next, Mark 4:17, R.V., "then"; 4:28,

in some texts; 8:25, R.V., "then" (A.V., "after that"); Luke 8:12; John 13:5; 19:27; 20:27; in some texts in 1 Cor. 12:28; 1 Cor. 15:5, 7, 24; 1 Tim 2:13; 3:10; Jas. 1:15; (*b*) in argument, Heb. 12:9, "furthermore." ¶

NT: B.233d; CB.1243b; K.–.
OT: –.
GEN. REF.: –.

3. *epeita* [ἔπειτα, 1899], is used only of sequence, thereupon, thereafter, then (in some texts, Mark 7:5; *kai*, "and," in the best); Luke 16:7; John 11:7; 1 Cor. 12:28, R.V., "then" (A.V., "after that"); 15:6 and 7 (ditto); ver. 23, R.V., A.V., "afterward" (No. 2 in ver. 24); ver. 46 (ditto); Gal. 1:18; ver. 21, R.V. (A.V., "afterwards"); 2:1; 1 Thess. 4:17; Heb. 7:2, R.V. (A.V., "after that"); ver. 27, Jas. 3:17; 4:14. See AFTER. ¶

NT: B.284c; CB.–; K.–.
OT: –.
GEN. REF.: –.

4. *loipon* [λοιπόν, 3063], finally, for the rest, the neuter of *loipos*, (the) rest, used adverbially, is rendered "then" in Acts 27:20, A.V. (R.V., "now.").

NT: B.479d; CB.1257b; K.–.
OT: –.
GEN. REF.: –.

5. *oun* [οὖν, 3767], a particle expressing sequence or consequence, is rendered "then," e.g., Matt. 22:43; 27:22; Luke 11:13.

NT: B.592d; CB.–; K.–.
OT: –.
GEN. REF.: –.

6. *oukoun* [οὐκοῦν, 3766], an adverb formed from *ouk*, not, *oun*, therefore, with the negative element dropped, meaning 'so then,' is used in John 18:37. ¶

NT: B.592d; CB.–; K.–.
OT: –.
GEN. REF.: –.

Notes: (1) In James 2:24, where in some texts the inferential particle *toinun*, therefore, occurs, the A.V. renders it by "then" (R.V. follows the superior mss. which omit it).

(2) For conjunctions (*ara*, so; *de*, but; *gar*, for; *kai*, and; *te*, and), sometimes translated "then," see † p. 1.

THENCE (from)

ekeithen [ἐκεῖθεν, 1564], is used (*a*) of place, e.g., Matt. 4:21, "from thence"; 5:26; in Acts 20:13, "there"; often preceded by *kai*, written *kàkeithen*, e.g., Mark 9:30 and Luke 11:53 (in the best texts); Acts 7:4; 14:26; (*b*) of time, Acts 13:21, "and afterward." See AFTER.

NT: B.239b; CB.–; K.–.
OT: mishshām: S.8033; HR.427b.2a; H.2404; BD.1027c.
GEN. REF.: –.

Note: In Acts 28:13, *hothen*, from whence, is translated "from thence."

THENCEFORTH

eti [ἔτι, 2089], yet, still, further, is rendered "thenceforth" in Matt. 5:13.

NT: B.315c; CB.1247a; K.–.
OT: –.
GEN. REF.: –.

Notes: (1) In Luke 13:9, R.V., the phrase *eis to mellon*, lit., 'unto the about to be' (*mellō*, to be about to), is translated "thenceforth" (A.V., "after that").

(2) In John 19:12, A.V., *ek toutou*, from this, is translated "from thenceforth" (R.V., "upon this").

THERE, THITHER

1. *ekei* [ἐκεῖ, 1563], signifies (*a*) there, e.g., Matt. 2:13, frequently in the Gospels; (*b*) thither, e.g., Luke 17:37; in Rom. 15:24, "thitherward."

NT: B.239a; CB.1243c; K.–.
OT: shām: S.8033; HR.423c.8a; H.2404; BD.1027a.
GEN. REF.: –.

2. *ekeise* [ἐκεῖσε, 1566], properly, 'thither,' signifies "there" in Acts 21:3; 22:5. ¶ In the Sept., Job 39:29. ¶

NT: B.240a; CB.–; K.–.
OT: mishshām: S.8033; HR.430c.1; H.2404; BD.1027a.
GEN. REF.: –.

3. *ekeithen* [ἐκεῖθεν, 1564], thence, is rendered "there" in Acts 20:13. See THENCE.

NT: B.239b; CB.–; K.–.
OT: mishshām: S.8033; HR.427b.2a; H.2404; BD.1027c.
GEN. REF.: –.

4. *enthade* [ἐνθάδε, 1759], here, hither, is rendered "there" in Acts 10:18. See HERE, HITHER.

NT: B.266a; CB.–; K.–.
OT: –.
GEN. REF.: –.

5. *autou* [αὐτοῦ, 847], the genitive case, neuter, of *autos*, he, lit., 'of it,' is used as an adverb, "there," in Acts 18:19; 21:4 (in some texts in 15:34). See HERE.

NT: B.124a; CB.–; K.–.
OT: –.
GEN. REF.: –.

Notes: (1) In Luke 24:18 and Acts 9:38, "there" translates the phrase *en autę̄*, 'in it.'

(2) In John 21:9, "there" is used to translate the verb *keimai*.

(3) In Matt. 24:23 (2nd part), A.V., *hōde*, "here" (R.V.), is translated "there."

(4) In Acts 17:21, "there" forms part of the translation of *epidēmeō*, to sojourn, "sojourning there," R.V. ("which were there," A.V.).

THEREABOUT

Note: The phrase *peri toutou*, 'concerning this,' is rendered "thereabout" in Luke 24:4.

THEREAT

Note: The phrase *di' autēs*, lit., 'by (*dia*) it,' is rendered "thereat" in Matt. 7:13, A.V. (R.V., "thereby").

THEREBY

Notes: (1) *Di' autēs* (see above) occurs in Matt. 7:13; John 11:4; Heb. 12:11.

(2) *Dia tautēs*, by means of this, "thereby," occurs in Heb. 12:15; 13:2.

(3) *En autę̄*, in, or by, it, is rendered "thereby" in Rom. 10:5; *en autǭ* in Eph. 2:16 (some texts have *en heautǭ*, 'in Himself'); 1 Pet. 2:2.

THEREFORE, † p. 1

THEREIN, THEREINTO, THEREOF, THEREON, THEREOUT, THERETO, THEREUNTO, THEREUPON, THEREWITH

Note: These translate various phrases consisting of a preposition with forms of either the personal pronoun *autos*, he, or the demonstrative *houtos*, this.

For THESE see THIS

THEY, THEY THEMSELVES

Note: When not forming part of the translation of the 3rd pers., plur. of a verb, (1) these translate the plural of the pronouns under HE, in their various forms, *autos, houtos, ekeinos, heautou*.

(2) In Acts 5:16, *hoitines*, the plural of *hostis*, anyone who, is translated "they"; so in 23:14, translated "and they"; in 17:11, "in that they" (some texts have it in Matt. 25:3).

(3) Sometimes the plural of the article is rendered "they," e.g., Phil. 4:22; Heb. 13:24; in 1 Cor. 11:19, "they which are (approved)" is, lit., 'the approved'; in Gal. 2:6, "they . . . (who were of repute)," R.V.

For THICK see GATHER, A, No. 8

THIEF, THIEVES

1. *kleptēs* [κλέπτης, 2812], is used (*a*) literally, Matt. 6:19, 20; 24:43; Luke 12:33, 39; John 10:1, 10; 12:6; 1 Cor. 6:10; 1 Pet. 4:15; (*b*) metaphorically of false teachers, John 10:8; (*c*) figuratively, (1) of the Personal coming of Christ, in a warning to a local church, with most of its members possessed of mere outward profession and defiled by the world, Rev. 3:3; in retributive intervention to overthrow the foes of God, 16:15; (2) of the Day of the Lord, in Divine judgment upon the world, 2 Pet. 3:10 and 1 Thess. 5:2, 4; in ver. 2, according to the order in the original "the word 'night' is not to be read with 'the day of the Lord,' but with 'thief,' i.e., there is no reference to the time of the coming, only to the manner of it. To avoid ambiguity the phrase may be paraphrased, 'so comes as a thief in the night comes.' The use of the present tense instead of the future emphasises the certainty of the coming. . . . The unexpectedness of the coming of the thief, and the unpreparedness of those to whom he comes, are the essential elements in the figure; cp. the entirely different figure used in Matt. 25:1-13." ¶ *

NT: B.434b; CB.1255b; K.441.
OT: gannāb: S.1590; HR.767c.1b; H.364b; BD.170c.
GEN. REF.: IS.4:614; NB.–; Z.–.

2. *lēstēs* [λῃστής, 3027], is frequently rendered "thieves" in the A.V., e.g., Matt. 21:13. See ROBBER.

NT: B.473a; CB.1256c; K.532.
OT: gᵉdûd: S.1416; HR.876a.1; H.313a; BD.151a.
GEN. REF.: IS.4:614; NB.–; Z.–.

THIGH

mēros [μηρός, 3382], occurs in Rev. 19:16; Christ appears there in the manifestation of His judicial capacity and action hereafter as the Executor of Divine vengeance upon the foes of God; His Name is spoken of figuratively as being upon His thigh (where the sword would be worn; cp. Ps. 45:3), emblematic of His strength to tread down His foes, His action being the exhibition of His Divine attributes of righteousness and power. ¶

NT: B.519d; CB.1258b; K.585.
OT: yārēk: S.3409; HR.923c.2a; H.916a; BD.437d.
GEN. REF.: IS.4:838; NB.–; Z.5:729.

For THINE see THY

THING(S)

1. *logos* [λόγος, 3056], a word, an account, etc., is translated "thing" in Matt. 21:24, A.V. (1st part), and Luke 20:3, A.V., R.V., "question", (in Matt. 21:24, 2nd part, "these things" translates *tauta*, the neut. plur. of *houtos*, this); Luke 1:4; Acts 5:24, A.V. (R.V., "words") See ACCOUNT.

NT: B.477a; CB.1257a; K.505.
OT: dābār: S.1697; HR.881c.2a; H.399a; BD.182a.
GEN. REF.: –.

* From Notes on Thessalonians by Hogg and Vine, pp. 153, 154.

2. *pragma* [πρᾶγμα, 4229], for which see MATTER, No. 2, is translated "thing" in Matt. 18:19, as part of the word "anything," lit., 'every thing'; Luke 1:1, A.V. only; Acts 5:4; in Heb. 6:18; 10:1, and 11:1, "things." See BUSINESS, MATTER, WORK

NT: B.697a; CB.1266b; K.927.
OT: dābār: S.1697; HR.1199c.1; H.399a; BD.182a.
GEN. REF.: —.

3. *rhēma* [ῥῆμα, 4487], a saying, word, is translated "thing" in Luke 2:15; ver. 19, A.V. (R.V., "saying"); in Acts 5:32, "things." See SAYING.

NT: B.735b; CB.1268a; K.505.
OT: dābār: S.1697; HR.1249a.2a; H.399a; BD.182a.
GEN. REF.: —.

Notes: (1) The neuter sing. and plur. of the article are frequently rendered "the thing" and "the things"; so with *tauta*, "these things," the neut. plur. of *houtos*, this.

(2) So in the case of the neut. plur. of certain pronouns and adjectives without nouns, e.g., all, base, heavenly, which.

(3) When "thing" represents a separate word in the original, it is a translation of one or other of Nos. 1, 2, 3, above.

(4) In Phil. 2:10, "*things*" is added in italics to express the meaning of the three adjectives.

THINK

1. *dokeō* [δοκέω, 1380], to suppose, to think, to form an opinion, which may be either right or wrong, is sometimes rendered to think, e.g., Matt. 3:9; 6:7; see ACCOUNT, No. 1, SUPPOSE, No. 2.

NT: B.201d; CB.1242a; K.178.
OT: —.
GEN. REF.: IS.4:839; NB.—; Z.—.

2. *hēgeomai* [ἡγέομαι, 2233], for which see ACCOUNT, No. 3, is rendered to think in Acts 26:2; 2 Cor. 9:5, "I thought"; Phil. 2:6, A.V. (R.V., "counted"); 2 Pet. 1:13.

NT: B.343c; CB.—; K.303.
OT: —.
GEN. REF.: IS.4:839; NB.—; Z.—.

3. *noeō* [νοέω, 3539], to perceive, understand, apprehend, is rendered "think" in Eph. 3:20. See PERCEIVE, UNDERSTAND.

NT: B.540b; CB.1259c; K.636.
OT: bîn: S.995; HR.946a.1; H.239; BD.106c.
GEN. REF.: IS.4:839; NB.—; Z.—.

4. *huponoeō* [ὑπονοέω, 5289], to suppose, surmise (*hupo*, under, and No. 3), is rendered to think in Acts 13:25, A.V. (R.V., "suppose"). See DEEM.

NT: B.846d; CB.—; K.636.
OT: sᵉbar (Aramaic): S.5452; HR.1416b.1; H.2883; BD.1104a.
GEN. REF.: IS.4:839; NB.—; Z.—.

5. *logizomai* [λογίζομαι, 3049], to reckon, is rendered to think, in Rom. 2:3, A.V. (R.V., "reckonest"); 1 Cor. 13:5, A.V., R.V., "taketh (not) account of);" i.e., love does not reckon up or calculatingly consider the evil done to it (something more than refraining from imputing motives); 13:11, "I thought"; in the following, for the A.V., to think, in 2 Cor. 3:5, R.V., "to account"; 10:2 (twice), "count"; 10:7, "consider"; 10:11, "reckon"; 12:6, "account." In Phil. 4:8, "think on (these things)," it signifies 'make those things the subjects of your thoughtful consideration,' or 'carefully reflect on them' (R.V. marg., "take account of"). See ACCOUNT, A, No. 4.

NT: B.475d; CB.1257a; K.536.
OT: ḥāshab: S.2803; HR.880a.2; H.767; BD.362a.
GEN. REF.: IS.4:839; NB.—; Z.—.

6. *nomizō* [νομίζω, 3543], to suppose, is sometimes rendered to think, e.g., Matt. 5:17. See SUPPOSE, No. 1.

NT: B.541a; CB.1260a; K.—.
OT: —.
GEN. REF.: IS.4:839; NB.—; Z.—.

7. *phroneō* [φρονέω, 5426], to be minded in a certain way (*phrēn*, the mind), is rendered to think, in Rom. 12:3 (2nd and 3rd occurrences), R.V., "not to think of himself more highly (*huperphroneō*, see No. 13) than he ought to think (*phroneō*); but so to think (*phroneō*) as to think soberly [*sōphroneō*, see *Note* (3)]"; the play on words may be expressed by a literal rendering somewhat as follows: 'not to over-think beyond what it behoves him to think, but to think unto sober-thinking'; in 1 Cor. 4:6, some inferior texts have this verb, hence the A.V. "to think"; in the best texts, it is absent, hence the R.V., puts "*go*" in italics; lit., the sentence is 'that ye might learn the (i.e., the rule) not beyond what things have been written.' The saying appears to be proverbial, perhaps a Rabbinical adage. Since, however, *graphō*, to write, was a current term for framing a law or an agreement (so Diessman, *Bible Studies*, and Moulton and Milligan, *Vocab.*), it is quite possible that the Apostle's meaning is 'not to go beyond the terms of a teacher's commission, thinking more of himself than the character of his commission allows'; this accords with the context and the whole passage, 3:1-4:5. In Phil. 1:7, A.V., "to think" (R.V., "to be . . . minded"). See AFFECTION, B, *Note* (1) and list there.

NT: B.866a; CB.1264c; K.1277.
OT: bîn: S.995; HR.1439a.1; H.239; BD.106c.
ḥākam: S.2449; HR.1439a.2; H.647; BD.314b.
GEN. REF.: IS.4:839; NB.—; Z.—.

8. *oiomai* or *oimai* [οἴομαι, 3633], to imagine, is rendered "I suppose" in John 21:25; "thinking" in Phil. 1:17, R.V. (ver. 16, A.V., "supposing"); "let (not that man) think," Jas. 1:7. See SUPPOSE ¶

NT: B.562c; CB.—; K.—.
OT: —.
GEN. REF.: IS.4:839; NB.—; Z.—.

9. *phainō* [φαίνω, 5316], in the Passive Voice, to appear, is rendered "(what) think (ye)" in Mark 14:64, lit., 'what does it appear to you?' See APPEAR, No. 1.
NT: B.851b; CB.1263c; K.1244.
OT: 'ôr: S.215; HR.1423a.1a; H.52; BD.21a.
rā'āh: S.7200; HR.1423a.10; H.2095; BD.906b,908a.
GEN. REF.: IS.4:839; NB.–; Z.–.

10. *eudokeō* [εὐδοκέω, 2106], to be well-pleasing, is rendered "we thought it good" in 1 Thess. 3:1. See PLEASE.
NT: B.319b; CB.1247a; K.273.
OT: rāṣāh: S.7521; HR.569a.9; H.2207; BD.953a.
GEN. REF.: –.

11. *axioō* [ἀξιόω, 515], to regard as worthy (*axios*), to deem it suitable, is rendered "thought (not) good" in Acts 15:38. See WORTHY, B.
NT: B.78c; CB.1238b; K.63.
OT: –.
GEN. REF.: IS.4:839; NB.–; Z.–.

12. *enthumeomai* [ἐνθυμέομαι, 1760], to reflect on, ponder, is used in Matt. 1:20; 9:4: see No. 14. Cp. *enthumēsis*, consideration (see THOUGHT). ¶
NT: B.266a; CB.1245b; K.–.
OT: dāmāh: S.1819; HR.473c.1; H.437; BD.197d.
zāmam: S.2161; HR.473c.2; H.556; BD.273a.
GEN. REF.: IS.4:839; NB.–; Z.–.

13. *huperphroneō* [ὑπερφρονέω, 5252], to be overproud, high-minded, occurs in Rom. 12:3, rendered "to think of himself more highly." See No. 7. ¶
NT: B.842a; CB.1252a; K.–.
OT: –.
GEN. REF.: IS.4:839; NB.–; Z.–.

14. *dienthumeomai* [διενθυμέομαι, —], to consider deeply (*dia*, through, and No. 12), is used of Peter in Acts 10:19, in the bext texts (some have No. 12). ¶
NT: B.194a; CB.–; K.–.
OT: –.
GEN. REF.: –.

15. *epiballō* [ἐπιβάλλω, 1911], to throw oneself upon, is used metaphorically in Mark 14:72, "when he thought thereon (he wept)," lit., 'thinking thereon,' but to think is an exceptional sense of the word (see BEAT, CAST, LAY, PUT); hence various suggestions have been made. Field, following others, adopts the meaning 'putting (his garment) over (his head),' as an expression of grief. Others regard it as having here the same meaning as *archomai*, to begin (at an early period, indeed, *archomai* was substituted in the text for the authentic *epiballō*); Moulton confirms this from a papyrus writing. Another suggestion is to understand it as with *dianoian*, mind, i.e., 'casting his mind thereon.'
NT: B.289d; CB.–; K.91.
OT: –.
GEN. REF.: –.

Notes: (1) In Acts 26:8, A.V., *krinō*, to judge, reckon, is translated "should it be thought" (R.V., "is it judged").

(2) In Luke 12:17, A.V., *dialogizomai*, to reason (R.V., "reasoned"), is translated "thought."

(3) In Rom. 12:3, *sōphroneō*, "to think soberly," R.V., is, lit., 'unto sober-thinking,' the infinitive mood of the verb being used as a noun (A.V. marg., "to sobriety"): cp. No. 7. See SOBER, B, No. 2.

THIRD, THIRDLY

tritos [τρίτος, 5154], is used (*a*) as a noun, e.g., Luke 20:12, 31; in Rev. 8:7-12 and 9:15, 18, "the third part," lit., 'the third'; (*b*) as an adverb, with the article, "the third time," e.g., Mark 14:41; John 21:17 (twice); without the article, lit., 'a third time,' e.g., John 21:14; 2 Cor. 12:14; 13:1; in enumerations, in Matt. 26:44, with *ek*, from, lit., 'from the third time' (the *ek* indicates the point of departure, especially in a succession of events, cp. John 9:24; 2 Pet. 2:8); absolutely, in the accusative neuter, in 1 Cor. 12:28, "thirdly"; (*c*) as an adjective (its primary use), e.g., in the phrase "the third heaven," 2 Cor. 12:2 [cp. HEAVEN, A, No. 1 (*c*) PARADISE]; in the phrase "the third hour," Matt. 20:3; Mark 15:25; Acts 2:15 (". . . of the day"); 23:23 (". . . of the night"); in a phrase with *hēmera*, a day, "on the third day" (i.e., 'the next day but one'), e.g., Matt. 16:21; Luke 24:46; Acts 10:40; in this connection the idiom "three days and three nights," Matt. 12:40, is explained by ref. to 1 Sam. 30:12, 13, and Esth. 4:16 with 5:1; in Mark 9:31 and 10:34, the R.V., "after three days," follows the texts which have this phrase, the A.V., "the third day," those which have the same phrase as in Matt. 16:2, etc.
NT: B.826c; CB.1273a; K.1188.
OT: shᵉlīshî: S.7992; HR.1373c.1a; H.2403b; BD.1026a.
shilshôm: S.8032; HR.1373c.2; H.2403c; BD.1026b.
GEN. REF.: IS.4:840; NB.–; Z.–.

Note: For "third story," Acts 20:9, R.V., see STORY.

THIRST (Noun and Verb), THIRSTY (to be), ATHIRST

A. Noun.

dipsos [δίψος, 1373], thirst (cp. Eng., dipsomania), occurs in 2 Cor. 11:27. ¶
NT: B.200d; CB.1242a; K.177.
OT: ṣāmā': S.6772; HR.338b.1a; H.1926a; BD.854d.
GEN. REF.: IS.4:840; NB.–; Z.–.

B. Verb.

dipsaō [διψάω, 1372], is used (*a*) in the natural sense, e.g., Matt. 25:25, 37, 42; in ver. 44, "athirst" (lit., 'thirsting'); John 4:13, 15; 19:28; Rom. 12:20; 1 Cor. 4:11; Rev. 7:16; (*b*) figuratively, of spiritual thirst, Matt. 5:6; John

4:14; 6:35; 7:37; in Rev. 21:6 and 22:17, "that is athirst."

NT: B.200c; CB.1242a; K.177.
OT: sāmē': S.6770; HR.338a.4a,b; H.1926; BD.854c.
GEN. REF.: IS.4:840; NB.—; Z.—.

THIRTY, THIRTYFOLD

triakonta [τριάκοντα, 5144], is usually rendered "thirty," e.g., Matt. 13:23; "thirtyfold," in Matt. 13:8, A.V. only; in Mark 4:8, R.V. only; in Mark 4:20, A.V. and R.V.

NT: B.826a; CB.—; K.—.
OT: —.
GEN. REF.: —.

THIS, THESE

Note: The singular and plural translate various forms of the following: (1) *houtos*, which is used (*a*) as a noun, this one, followed by no noun, e.g., Matt. 3:17; translated in Luke 2:34, "this *child*"; in 1 Cor. 5:3, R.V., "this thing" (A.V., "this deed"); for "this fellow" see FELLOW, *Note* (3); in Acts 17:32 the R.V. rightly omits "*matter*"; in Heb. 4:5 "*place*" is italicized; it is frequently rendered "this man," e.g., Matt. 9:3; John 6:52; "of this sort," 2 Tim. 3:6, A.V. (R.V., "of these"); (*b*) as an adjective with a noun, either with the article and before it, e.g., Matt. 12:32, or after the noun (which is preceded by the article), e.g., Matt. 3:9 and 4:3, "these stones"; or without the article often forming a predicate, e.g., John 2:11; 2 Cor. 13:1; (2) *ekeinos*, that one, rendered "this" in Matt. 24:43; (3) *autos*, he, rendered "this" in Matt. 11:14, lit., 'he'; in John 12:7, A.V. (R.V., "it"); in the feminine, Luke 13:16; (4) the article *ho*, Matt. 21:21 (*to*, the neuter), A.V. (R.V., "what"); in Rom. 13:9 (1st part); Gal. 5:14; Heb. 12:27, the article *to* is virtually equivalent to 'the following.'

The demonstrative pronouns THAT and the plural THOSE translate the same pronouns (1), (2), (3) mentioned above. In Heb. 7:21, A.V., "those" translates the article, which requires the R.V., "they."

THISTLE

tribolos [τρίβολος, 5146], occurs in Matt. 7:16 and Heb. 6:8 (A.V., "briers"). ¶ In the Sept., Gen. 3:18; 2 Sam. 12:31; Prov. 22:5; Hos. 10:8. ¶ Cp. THORNS.

NT: B.826a; CB.1273a; K.—.
OT: dardar: S.1863; HR.1372b.1; H.454e; BD.205a.
GEN. REF.: IS.4:842; NB.—; Z.5:731.

For THITHER, THITHERWARD see THERE

Note: In John 7:34, 36, A.V., *hopou*, "where" (R.V.), is amplified by the italicized word "*thither*."

For THONG see LATCHET

THORN, THORNS (of)

A. Nouns.

1. *akantha* [ἄκανθα, 173], a brier, a thorn (from *akē*, a point), is always used in the plural in the N.T., Matt. 7:16 and parallel passage in Luke 6:44; Matt. 13:7 (twice), 22 and parallels in Mark and Luke; in Matt. 27:29 and John 19:2, of the crown of thorns placed on Christ's head (see also B) in mock imitation of the garlands worn by emperors. They were the effects of the Divine curse on the ground (Gen. 3:18; contrast Is. 55:13). The thorns of the crown plaited by the soldiers, are usually identified with those of the *Zizyphus spina Christi*, some 20 feet high or more, fringing the Jordan and abundant in Palestine; its twigs are flexible. Another species, however, the Arabian *qundaul*, crowns of which are plaited and sold in Jerusalem as representatives of Christ's crown, seems likely to be the one referred to. The branches are easily woven and adapted to the torture intended. The word *akantha* occurs also in Heb. 6:8. ¶

NT: B.29c; CB.1234a; K.—.
OT: qôs: S.6975; HR.43c.5; H.2003a; BD.881a.
shayit: S.7898; HR.43c.6; H.2380c; BD.1011d.
GEN. REF.: IS.4:842; NB.—; Z.5:736.

2. *skolops* [σκόλοψ, 4647], originally denoted anything pointed, e.g., a stake; in Hellenistic vernacular, a thorn (so the Sept., in Numb. 33:55; Ezek. 28:24; Hos. 2:6 ¶), 2 Cor. 12:7, of the Apostle's "thorn in the flesh"; his language indicates that it was physical, painful, humiliating; it was also the effect of Divinely permitted Satanic antagonism; the verbs rendered "that I should (not) be exalted overmuch" (R.V.) and "to buffet" are in the present tense, signifying recurrent action, indicating a constantly repeated attack. Lightfoot interprets it as "a stake driven through the flesh," and Ramsay agrees with this. Most commentators adhere to the rendering "thorn." Field says "there is no doubt that the Alexandrine use of *skolops* for thorn is here intended, and that the ordinary meaning of 'stake' must be rejected." What is stressed is not the metaphorical size, but the acuteness of the suffering and its effects. Attempts to connect this with the circumstances of Acts 14:19 and Gal. 4:13 are speculative. ¶

NT: B.756c; CB.1269a; K.1047.
OT: sûr: S.5518; HR.1275b.1; H.1489,1490; BD.696c.
sillôn S.5544; HR.1275b.2; H.1504; BD.699b.
sēk: S.7899; HR.1275b.3; H.2262a; BD.968a.
GEN. REF.: IS.4:842; NB.—; Z.—.

B. Adjective.

akanthinos [ἀκάνθινος, 174], of thorns (from A, No. 1), is used in Mark 15:17 and John 19:5. ¶ In the Sept., Isa. 34:13. ¶

NT: B.29c; CB.1234a; K.—.
OT: sîr: S.5518; HR.43c.1; H.1489,1490; BD.696c.
GEN. REF.: IS.4:842; NB.—; Z.5:736.

THOROUGHLY (THROUGHLY)

Note: This is usually part of the translation of a verb, e.g., CLEANSE, FURNISH, PURGE. In 2 Cor. 11:6, the phrase *en panti*, "in everything," R.V., is translated "throughly" in the A.V.

For THOSE see THIS (last part of *Note*)

THOU

Note: Frequently this forms part of the translation of a verb in the 2nd person, singular. Otherwise it translates (*a*) the pronoun *su*, used for emphasis or contrast, e.g., John 1:19, 21 (twice), 25, 42 (twice); 8:5, 13, 25, 33, 48, 52, 53; Acts 9:5; in addressing a person or place, e.g., Matt. 2:6; Luke 1:76; John 17:5; perhaps also in the phrase *su eipas*, "thou hast said," e.g., Matt. 26:64 (sometimes without emphasis, e.g., Acts 13:33); (*b*) in the oblique cases, e.g., the dative *soi*, lit., to thee, e.g., Matt. 17:25, "what thinkest thou?" (lit., 'what does it seem to thee?'); (*c*) *autos*, self, e.g., Luke 6:42; Acts 21:24, "thou thyself"; (*d*) the reflexive pronoun, *seauton*, Rom. 2:19, "thou thyself."

THOUGH: see † p. 1

For THOUGHT (Verb) see THINK

THOUGHT (Noun)

1. *epinoia* [ἐπίνοια, 1963], a thought by way of a design (akin to *epinoeō*, to contrive, *epi*, intensive, *noeō*, to consider), is used in Acts 8:22. ¶ In the Sept., Jer. 20:10. ¶

NT: B.296c; CB.1246a; K.—.
OT: —.
GEN. REF.: —.

2. *noēma* [νόημα, 3540], a purpose, device of the mind (akin to *noeō*, see No. 1), is rendered "thought" in 2 Cor. 10:5, "thoughts" in Phil. 4:7, R.V.: see DEVICE, No. 2.

NT: B.540d; CB.1259c; K.636.
OT: —.
GEN. REF.: IS.4:839; NB.—; Z.—.

3. *dianoēma* [διανόημα, 1270], a thought, occurs in Luke 11:17, where the sense is that of machinations. ¶

NT: B.187a; CB.1241b; K.636.
OT: mahᵃshābāh: S.4284; HR.306c.2; H.767d; BD.364b.
GEN. REF.: IS.4:839; NB.—; Z.—.

4. *enthumēsis* [ἐνθύμησις, 1761], is translated "thoughts" in Matt. 9:4; 12:25; Heb. 4:12: see DEVICE, No. 1.

NT: B.266a; CB.1245b; K.339.
OT: —.
GEN. REF.: IS.4:839; NB.—; Z.—.

5. *logismos* [λογισμός, 3053], is translated "thoughts" in Rom. 2:15: see IMAGINATION, No. 1.

NT: B.476d; CB.1257a; K.536.
OT: mahᵃshābāh: S.4284; HR.881a.1a; H.767d; BD.364b.
GEN. REF.: IS.4:839; NB.—; Z.—.

6. *dialogismos* [διαλογισμός, 1261], reasoning, is translated "thoughts" in Matt. 15:19; Mark 7:21; Luke 2:35; 6:8; in 5:22, A.V., R.V., "reasonings"; in 9:47, A.V., R.V., "reasoning," and 24:38, A.V., R.V., "reasonings"; so 1 Cor. 3:20; in Luke 9:46, A.V. and R.V., "reasoning"; "thoughts" in Jas. 2:4, A.V. and R.V. See DISPUTE, IMAGINATION, REASONING.

NT: B.186a; CB.1241a; K.155.
OT: mahᵃshābāh: S.4284; HR.305a.2; H.767d; BD.364b.
GEN. REF.: IS.4:839; NB.—; Z.—.

THOUGHT (to take)

1. *merimnaō* [μεριμνάω, 3309], denotes to be anxious, careful. For the A.V., to take thought, the R.V. substitutes to be anxious in Matt. 6:25, 27, 28, 31, 34; 10:19; Luke 12:11, 22, 25, 26. See CARE, B, No. 1.

NT: B.505a; CB.1258b; K.584.
OT: dā'ag: S.1672; HR.911a.1; H.393; BD.178b.
rāgaz: S.7264; HR.911a.5; H.2112; BD.919a.
GEN. REF.: —.

2. *promerimnaō* [προμεριμνάω, 4305], to be anxious beforehand, occurs in Mark 13:11. ¶

NT: B.708c; CB.1266c; K.584.
OT: —.
GEN. REF.: —.

3. *phroneō* [φρονέω, 5426]: for Phil. 4:10, R.V., "ye did take thought," see CARE, B, No. 6.

NT: B.866a; CB.1264c; K.1277.
OT: sākal: S.7919; HR.1439a.3; H.2263,2264; BD.968a.
bîn: S.995; HR.1439a.1; H.239; BD.106c.
GEN. REF.: IS.4:839; NB.—; Z.—.

4. *pronoeō* [προνοέω, 4306], to provide, is rendered to take thought in Rom. 12:17 and 2 Cor. 8:21. See PROVIDE.

NT: B.708c; CB.—; K.636.
OT: bîn: S.995; HR.1207c.1; H.239; BD.106c.
GEN. REF.: IS.4:839; NB.—; Z.—.

THOUSAND (-S)

1. *chilioi* [χίλιοι, 5507], a thousand, occurs in 2 Pet. 3:8; Rev. 11:3; 12:6; 14:20; 20:2-7. ¶

NT: B.882a; CB.1239c; K.1316.
OT: 'eleph: S.505; HR.1469a.1; H.109a; BD.48d.
GEN. REF.: IS.3:557; NB.890; Z.3:560.

2. *chilias* [χιλιάς, 5505], one thousand, is always used in the plural, *chiliades*, but translated in the sing. everywhere, except in the phrase "thousands of thousands," Rev. 5:11.

NT: B.882a; CB.1239c; K.1316.
OT: 'eleph: S.505; HR.1469a.1; H.109a; BD.48d.
GEN. REF.: IS.3:557; NB.890; Z.3:560.

Notes: (1) The following compounds of No. 1 represent different multiples of a thousand: *dischilioi*, 2,000, Mark 5:13; ¶ *trischilioi*, 3,000, Acts 2:41; ¶ *tetrakischilioi*, 4,000, Matt. 15:38; 16:10; Mark 8:9, 20; Acts 21:38; ¶ *pentakischilioi*, 5,000, Matt. 14:21; 16:9; Mark 6:44; 8:19; Luke 9:14; John 6:10; ¶ *heptakischilioi*, 7,000, Rom. 11:4. ¶

(2) *Murias*, a myriad, a vast number, "many thousands," Luke 12:1, R.V.; Acts 21:20; it also denotes 10,000, Acts 19:19, lit., 'five ten-thousands'; Jude 14, "ten thousands"; in Rev. 5:11 "ten thousand times ten thousand" is, lit., 'myriads of myriads'; in Rev. 9:16 in the best texts, *dismuriades muriadōn*, "twice ten thousand times ten thousand" R.V. (A.V., "two hundred thousand thousand"): see INNUMERABLE.

(3) *murioi* (the plur. of *murios*), an adjective signifying numberless, is used in this indefinite sense in 1 Cor. 4:15 and 14:19; it also denotes the definite number "ten thousand," Matt. 18:24. ¶

THREATEN

1. *apeileō* [ἀπειλέω, 546], is used of Christ, negatively, in 1 Pet. 2:23; in the Middle Voice, Acts 4:17, where some texts have the noun *apeilō* in addition, hence the A.V., "let us straitly threaten," lit., 'let us threaten . . . with threatening' (see THREATENING). ¶ (See also STRAITLY.)

NT: B.82d; CB.—; K.—.
OT: gā'ar: S.1605; HR.120a.1; H.370; BD.172a.
zā'am: S.2194; HR.120a.2; H.568; BD.276d.
GEN. REF.: —.

2. *prosapeileō* [προσαπειλέω, 4324], to threaten further (*pros*, and No. 1) occurs in the Middle Voice in Acts 4:21. ¶

NT: B.711d; CB.—; K.—.
OT: —.
GEN. REF.: —.

THREATENING

apeilē [ἀπειλή, 547], akin to *apeileō* (see above), occurs in Acts 4:29 (in some mss. ver. 17); 9:1; Eph. 6:9. ¶

NT: B.83a; CB.—; K.—.
OT: g^{e}'ārāh: S.1606; HR.120a.2b; H.370a; BD.172a.
GEN. REF.: —.

THREE

treis [τρεῖς, 5140], is regarded by many as a number sometimes symbolically indicating fulness of testimony or manifestation, as in the Three Persons in the Godhead, cp. 1 Tim. 5:19; Heb. 10:28; the mention in 1 John 5:7 is in a verse which forms no part of the original; no Greek ms. earlier than the 14th century contained it; no version earlier than the 5th cent. in any other language contains it, nor is it quoted by any of the Greek or Latin "Fathers" in their writings on the Trinity. That there are those who bear witness in Heaven is not borne out by any other Scripture. It must be regarded as the interpolation of a copyist.

In Mark 9:31 and 10:34 the best texts have *meta treis hemeras*, "after three days," which idiomatically expresses the same thing as *tę̄ tritę̄ hēmerą*, "on the third day," which some texts have here, as, e.g., the phrase "the third day" in Matt. 17:23; 20:19; Luke 9:22; 18:33, where the repetition of the article lends stress to the number, lit., 'the day the third'; 24:7, 46; Acts 10:40. For THREE TIMES see THRICE.

NT: B.825b; CB.1273a; K.1188.
OT: shālōsh: S.7969; HR.1371a; H.2403a; BD.1025c.
GEN. REF.: IS.3:558; NB.896; Z.3:558.

THREE HUNDRED

triakosioi [τριακόσιοι, —], occurs in Mark 14:5 and John 12:5. ¶

For THREESCORE see SIXTY and SEVENTY

For THREE THOUSAND see THOUSAND

THRESH

aloaō [ἀλοάω, 248], to thresh, is so rendered in 1 Cor. 9:10; in ver. 9 and 1 Tim. 5:18, "that treadeth out the corn." ¶

NT: B.41a; CB.—; K.—.
OT: dûsh: S.1758; HR.59a.1; H.419; BD.190b.
GEN. REF.: IS.4:844; NB.—; Z.3:738.

THRESHING-FLOOR

halōn [ἅλων, 257], a threshing-floor, is so translated in Matt. 3:12, and Luke 3:17, R.V. (A.V., "floor"), perhaps by metonymy for the grain. ¶

NT: B.41d; CB.1249a; K.—.
OT: gōren: S.1637; HR.60a.3; H.383a; BD.175b.
GEN. REF.: IS.4:844; NB.—; Z.5:738.

For THREW see THROW

THRICE

tris [τρίς, 5151], occurs in Matt. 26:34, 75 and parallel passages; in Acts 10:16 and 11:10, preceded by *epi*, up to; 2 Cor. 11:25 (twice); 12:8.

NT: B.826b; CB.1273a; K.1188.
OT: (shālōsh) p^{e}'āmîm: S.6470; HR.1373; H.1793; BD.821d,822a.
GEN. REF.: —.

THROAT (Noun) to take by the (Verb)

A. Noun.

larunx [λάρυγξ, 2995], a throat (Eng., larynx), is used metaphorically of speech in Rom. 3:13. ¶

NT: B.467b; CB.–; K.503.
OT: gārôn: S.1627; HR.862c.1; H.378a; BD.173c.
ḥēk: S.2441; HR.862c.2; H.692a; BD.335a.
GEN. REF.: –.

B. Verb.

pnigō [πνίγω, 4155], to choke, is rendered "took . . . by the throat" in Matt. 18:28. See CHOKE, No. 1.

NT: B.679d; CB.1265c; K.895.
OT: bā'at: S.1204; HR.1153b.1; H.265; BD.129d.
GEN. REF.: –.

THRONE

1. *thronos* [θρόνος, 2362], a throne, a seat of authority, is used of the throne (*a*) of God, e.g., Heb. 4:16, "the throne of grace," i.e., from which grace proceeds; 8:1; 12:2; Rev. 1:4; 3:21 (2nd part); 4:2 (twice); 5:1; frequently in Rev.; in 20:12, in the best texts, "the throne" (some have *Theos*, "God," A.V.); cp. 21:3; Matt. 5:34; 23:22; Acts 7:49; (*b*) of Christ, e.g., Heb. 1:8; Rev. 3:21 (1st part); 22:3; His seat of authority in the Millennium, Matt. 19:28 (1st part); (*c*) by metonymy for angelic powers, Col. 1:16; (*d*) of the Apostles in Millennial authority, Matt. 19:28 (2nd part); Luke 22:30; (*e*) of the elders in the Heavenly vision, Rev. 4:4 (2nd and 3rd parts), R.V., "thrones" (A.V., "seats"); so 11:16; (*f*) of David, Luke 1:32; Acts 2:30; (*g*) of Satan, Rev. 2:13, R.V., "throne" (A.V., "seat"); (*h*) of "the beast," the final and federal head of the revived Roman Empire, Rev. 13:2; 16:10.

NT: B.364b; CB.1272b; K.338.
OT: kissē': S.3678; HR.655b.3a; H.1007; BD.490c.
GEN. REF.: IS.4:844; NB.1274; Z.5:740.

2. *bēma* [βῆμα, 968], for which see JUDGMENT-SEAT, is used of the throne or tribunal of Herod, Acts 12:21.

NT: B.140b; CB.1239a; K.–.
OT: migdāl: S.4026; HR.217c.1; H.351f,g; BD.153d.
midrāk: S.4096; HR.217c.2; H.453b; BD.204a.
GEN. REF.: IS.4:844; NB.–; Z.5:740.

THRONG (Verb)

1. *thlibō* [θλίβω, 2346], to press, is rendered "throng," Mark 3:9. See AFFLICT, No. 4.

NT: B.362a; CB.1272b; K.334.
OT: lāḥaṣ: S.3905; HR.652b.4; H.1106; BD.537c.
GEN. REF.: –.

2. *sunthlibō* [συνθλίβω, 4918], to press together, on all sides (*sun*, together, and No. 1), a strengthened form, is used in Mark 5:24, 31. ¶

NT: B.790a; CB.–; K.–.
OT: rāṣaṣ: S.7533; HR.1316b.1; H.2212; BD.954c.
GEN. REF.: –.

3. *sumpnigō* [συμπνίγω, 4846], to choke, is used of thronging by a crowd, Luke 8:42. See CHOKE, No. 3.

NT: B.779d; CB.1270b; K.895.
OT: –.
GEN. REF.: –.

Note: For *sunechō*, to hold together, press together, Luke 8:45 (A.V., "throng"), see PRESS.

THROUGH and THROUGHOUT

see † p. 1

For THROUGHLY see THOROUGHLY

THROW

1. *ballō* [βάλλω, 906], to cast, to throw, is rendered to throw in Mark 12:42, A.V. (R.V., "cast"); so Acts 22:23 (2nd part); to throw down, Rev. 18:21 (2nd part), A.V. (R.V., "cast down"). See CAST, No. 1.

NT: B.130d; CB.1238b; K.91.
OT: nāphal: S.5307; HR.189c.6b; H.1392; BD.656c,658a.
shālak: S.7993; HR.189c.16; H.2398; BD.1020d.
GEN. REF.: –.

2. *rhiptō* [ῥίπτω, 4496], to hurl, throw, throw off, is rendered "had thrown . . . down" in Luke 4:35, R.V. (A.V., "had thrown"). See CAST, No. 2.

NT: B.736c; CB.–; K.987.
OT: shālak: S.7993; HR.1252b.10; H.2398; BD.1020d.
GEN. REF.: –.

2. *katakrēmnizō* [κατακρημνίζω, 2630], to throw over a precipice (*krēmnos*), cast down headlong, is rendered "throw . . . down" in Luke 4:29 (A.V., "cast . . . down headlong"). ¶

NT: B.412a; CB.–; K.–.
OT: shālak: S.7993; HR.734c.1; H.2398; BD.1020d.
GEN. REF.: –.

4. *kataluō* [καταλύω, 2647], lit., to loosen down, is rendered to throw down (of the stones of the Temple) in Matt. 24:2 and parallel passages. See DESTROY, No. 5.

NT: B.414b; CB.1254a; K.543.
OT: –.
GEN. REF.: –.

THRUST

1. *ballō* [βάλλω, 906], for which cp. THROW, No. 1, is rendered to thrust in John 20:25, 27, A.V. (R.V., "put"); Acts 16:24, A.V. (R.V., "cast"); so Rev. 14:16, 19. See CAST, No. 1.

NT: B.130d; CB.1238b; K.91.
OT: nāphal: S.5307; HR.189c.6b; H.1392; BD.656c,658a.
shālak: S.7993; HR.189c.16; H.2398; BD.1020d.
GEN. REF.: –.

2. *ekballō* [ἐκβάλλω, 1544], to cast out, is rendered "thrust . . . out" in Luke 4:29, A.V. (R.V., "cast . . . forth"); so 13:28 and Acts 16:37. See CAST, No. 5.

NT: B.237b; CB.1243b; K.91.
OT: gārash: S.1644; HR.420c.3b; H.388; BD.176c.
yāṣā': S.3318; HR.420c.8; H.893; BD.422b.
GEN. REF.: –.

3. *apōtheō* [ἀπωθέω, 683], to thrust away, is used in the Middle Voice, to thrust away from oneself, and translated "thrust away" in Acts 7:27, 39; "thrust . . . from," 13:46, R.V. (A.V., "put . . . from"); "having thrust from them," 1 Tim. 1:19, R.V. (A.V., "having put away"). See CAST, No. 13.

NT: B.103b CB.—; K.75.
OT: zānaḥ: S.2186; HR.151a.10; H.564; BD.276b.
mā'as: S.3988; HR.151a.11; H.1139,1140; BD.549b.
GEN. REF.: —.

4. *katatoxeuō* [κατατοξεύω, 2700], to strike down with an arrow, shoot dead, occurs in Heb. 12:20 in some mss. (in a quotation from Ex. 19:13, Sept.). ¶

NT: B.419d; CB.—; K.—.
OT: yārāh: S.3384; HR.747a.1; H.910; BD.434c.
GEN. REF.: —.

Notes: (1) In Matt. 11:23 and Luke 10:15 the best texts have *katabainō*, to go down (R.V.), instead of *katabibazō*, in the Passive Voice, to be thrust down or brought down (A.V.).

(2) In Acts 27:39, A.V., *exōtheō*, to drive out, is rendered "to thrust in," R.V., "drive (the ship) upon (it [i.e., the beach])."

(3) In Rev. 14:15, 18, A.V., *pempō*, to send (R.V., "send forth"), is translated "thrust in."

(4) For Luke 5:3, A.V., see LAUNCH, No. 2.

THUNDER, THUNDERING

brontē [βροντή, 1027]: in Mark 3:17 "sons of thunder" is the interpretation of Boanērges, the name applied by the Lord to James and John; their fiery disposition is seen in 9:38 and Luke 9:54; perhaps in the case of James it led to his execution. The name and its interpretation have caused much difficulty; some suggest the meaning 'the twins.' It is however most probably the equivalent of the Aramaic *benê regesh*, 'sons of tumult'; the latter of the two words was no doubt used of thunder in Palestinian Aramaic; hence the meaning "the sons of thunder"; the cognate Hebrew word *ragash*, to rage, is used in Ps. 2:1 and there only. In John 12:29 *brontē* is used with *ginomai*, to take place, and rendered "it had thundered"; lit., 'there was thunder'; elsewhere, Rev. 4:5; 6:1; 8:5; 10:3, 4; 11:19; 14:2; 16:18; 19:6. ¶

NT: B.147c; CB.1239b; K.110.
OT: ra'am: S.7482; HR.231a.1; H.2189a; BD.947b.
GEN. REF.: IS.4:845; NB.—; Z.5:741.

THUS

houtōs or *houtō* [οὕτως, 3779], in this way, so, thus, is used (*a*) with reference to what precedes, e.g., Luke 1:25; 2:48; (*b*) with reference to what follows, e.g., Luke 19:31, rendered "on this wise," in Matt. 1:18; John 21:1, and before quotations, Acts 7:6; 13:34; Rom. 10:6, A.V. (R.V., "thus"); Heb. 4:4; (*c*) marking intensity, rendered "so," e.g., Gal. 1:6; Heb. 12:21; Rev. 16:18; (*d*) in comparisons, rendered "so," e.g., Luke 11:30; Rom. 5:15. See FASHION, B, LIKEWISE, *Note* (1), MANNER, C, No. 2, SO, *Note* (1).

NT: B.597c; CB.—; K.—.
OT: kēn: S.3651; HR.1035c.13a; H.964a,b; BD.485d.
GEN. REF.: —.

Notes: (1) *Touto*, the neuter of *houtos*, this, is translated "thus" in 2 Cor. 1:17; 5:14; Phil. 3:15; the neuter plural, *tauta*, these things, e.g., in Luke 18:11; 19:28; John 9:6; 11:43; 13:21; 20:14; Acts 19:41.

(2) *Tade*, these things (the neuter plural of *hode*, this), is translated "thus" in Acts 21:11.

(3) In Luke 17:30, A.V., *kata tauta*, lit., 'according to these things,' is rendered "thus" (R.V., "after the same manner," follows the reading *kata ta auta*, lit., 'according to the same things').

THY, THINE, THINE OWN, THYSELF

Note: These are translations of (1) the possessive pronoun *sos*, and its inflections, e.g., Matt. 7:3 (1st part); it is used as a noun with the article, in the phrases *to son*, "that which is thine," Matt. 20:14; 25:25, "thine own"; *hoi soi*, "thy friends," Mark 5:19; *ta sa*, "thy goods," Luke 6:30, lit., 'the thine'; (2) one of the oblique cases of *su*, thou; *sou*, of thee, e.g., Matt. 1:20; 7:3 (2nd part), "thine own"; *soi*, to thee, e.g., Mark 5:9; with *menō*, to remain, Acts 5:4 (1st part), "thine own," lit., 'remain to thee'; in Matt. 26:18, *pros se*, "at thy house," lit., 'with thee'; (3) *seauton*, "(as) thyself," Rom. 13:9; *seautou*, of thyself, e.g., Matt. 4:6; *seautǭ*, to thyself, Acts 16:28; (4) *heautou* (with *apo*, from), John 18:34; "of thyself," lit., 'from thyself'; (5) *autos*, self, is sometimes used for "thyself," e.g., Luke 6:42.

THYINE (WOOD)

thuīnos [θύϊνος, 2367], is akin to *thuia*, or *thua*, an African aromatic and coniferous tree; in Rev. 18:12 it describes a wood which formed part of the merchandise of Babylon; it was valued by Greeks and Romans for tables, being hard, durable and fragrant (A.V. marg., "sweet"). ¶

NT: B.365a; CB.—; K.—.
OT: —.
GEN. REF.: IS.4:349; NB.1294; Z.5:744.

TIDINGS

A. Noun.

phasis [φάσις, 5334], akin to *phēmi*, to speak, denotes information, especially against fraud or other delinquency, and is rendered "tidings" in Acts 21:31. ¶
NT: B.854b; CB.–; K.–.
OT: –.
GEN. REF.: –.

Note: In Acts 11:22, A.V., *logos*, a word, a "report" (R.V.), is rendered "tidings."

B. Verbs.

1. *euangelizō* [εὐαγγελίζω, 2097], is used of any message designed to cheer those who receive it; it is rendered to bring, declare, preach, or show good or glad tidings, e.g., Luke 1:19; 2:10; 3:18, R.V.; 4:43, R.V.; 7:22, R.V.; 8:1; Acts 8:12 and 10:36, R.V.; 14:15, R.V.; in 1 Thess. 3:6, "brought us glad (A.V., good) tidings"; in Heb. 4:2, R.V., "we have had good tidings preached"; similarly, 4:6; in 1 Pet. 1:25 *rhēma*, a word, is coupled with this verb, "the word of good tidings which was preached," R.V. (A.V., "the word which by the gospel is preached"). See PREACH, A, No. 1.
NT: B.317b; CB.1247a; K.267.
OT: bāsar: S.1319; HR.568b.1a; H.291; BD.142a.
GEN. REF.: IS.2:475; NB.–; Z.–.

2. *anangellō* [ἀναγγέλλω, 312], to announce, declare, is rendered "(no) tidings . . . came," in Rom. 15:21, R.V., A.V., "was (not) spoken of." See TELL.
NT: B.51b; CB.1235b; K.10.
OT: nāgad: S.5046; HR.74a.10; H.1289; BD.616c.
GEN. REF.: –.

TIE

1. *deō* [δέω, 1210], to bind, is rendered to tie in Matt. 21:2; Mark 11:2, 4; Luke 19:30. See BIND
NT: B.177c; CB.1240c; K.148.
OT: ʾāsar: S.631; HR.287b.1a; H.141; BD.63c.
GEN. REF.: –.

2. *proteinō* [προτείνω, 4385], to stretch out or forth, is used of preparations for scourging, Acts 22:25, R.V., "had tied (him) up" (A.V., "bound"). ¶
NT: B.721d; CB.–; K.–.
OT: –.
GEN. REF.: –.

TILES, TILING

keramos [κέραμος, 2766], potter's clay, or an earthen vessel, denotes in the plural "tiles" in Luke 5:19, R.V., A.V., "tiling." ¶ In the Sept., 2 Sam. 17:28. ¶
NT: B.429a; CB.1255a; K.–.
OT: yāṣar: S.3335; HR.759c.1; H.898; BD.427c.
GEN. REF.: IS.4:851; NB.1277; Z.–.

For **TILL** (Conjunction) see † p.1

TILL

geōrgeō [γεωργέω, 1090], to till the ground, is used in the Passive Voice in Heb. 6:7, R.V., "it is tilled" (A.V., ". . .dressed"). ¶ Moulton and Milligan point out that, agriculture being the principal industry in Egypt, this word and its cognates (*geōrgion*, see HUSBANDRY, and *geōrgos*, see HUSBANDMAN) are very common in the papyri with reference to the cultivation of private allotments and the crown lands.
NT: B.157b; CB.–; K.–.
OT: –.
GEN. REF.: –.

TIME

A. Nouns.

1. *chronos* [χρόνος, 5550], denotes a space of time, whether short, e.g., Matt. 2:7; Luke 4:5, or long, e.g., Luke 8:27; 20:9; or a succession of times, shorter, e.g., Acts 20:18, or longer, e.g., Rom. 16:25, R.V., "times eternal"; or duration of time, e.g., Mark 2:19, 2nd part, R.V., "while" (A.V., "as long as"), lit., 'for whatever time.' For a fuller treatment see SEASON, A, No. 2.
NT: B.887d; CB.1240b; K.1337.
OT: yôm: S.3117; HR.1476b.2; H.852; BD.398a.
ʿôlām: S.5769; HR.1476b.8; H.1631a; BD.761d.
ʿēt: S.6256; HR.1476b.3; H.1650b; BD.773b.
GEN. REF.: IS.4:852; NB.1277; Z.–.

2. *kairos* [καιρός, 2540], primarily due measure, due proportion, when used of time, signified a fixed or definite period, a season, sometimes an opportune or seasonable time, e.g., Rom. 5:6, R.V., "season"; Gal. 6:10, "opportunity," In Mark 10:30 and Luke 18:30, "this time" (*kairos*), i.e., in this lifetime, is contrasted with 'the coming age.' In 1 Thess. 5:1, "the times and the seasons," "times" (*chronos*) refers to the duration of the interval previous to the Parousia of Christ and the length of time it will occupy (see COMING, No. 3, Vol. 1, top of p. 209), as well as other periods; "seasons" refers to the characteristics of these periods. See SEASON, A, No. 1, and the contrasts between *chronos* and *kairos* under SEASON, A, No. 2.
NT: B.394c; CB.1253a; K.389.
OT: ʿēt: S.6256; HR.706a.8; H.1650b; BD.773b.
môʿēd: S.4150; HR.706a.4; H.878b; BD.417b.
GEN. REF.: IS.4:852; NB.1277; Z.–.

3. *hōra* [ὥρα, 5610], primarily, any time or period fixed by nature, is translated "time" in Matt. 14:15; Luke 14:17; Rom. 13:11, "high time"; in the following the R.V. renders it "hour," for A.V., "time," Matt. 18:1; Luke 1:10; John 16:2, 4, 25; 1 John 2:18 (twice); Rev. 14:15; in Mark 6:35, R.V., "day"; in 1 Thess. 2:17,

R.V., "a short (season)," lit., '(the season, A.V., time) of an hour.' See HOUR.

NT: B.896a; CB.1251a; K.1355.
OT: 'ēt: S.6256; HR.1493b.5; H.1650b; BD.773b.
GEN. REF.: IS.—; NB.1277; Z.—.

B. Adverbs.

1. *pōpote* [πώποτε, 4455], ever yet, is rendered "at any time" in John 1:18; 5:37; 1 John 4:12. For Luke 15:29 see *Note* (14) below. See NEVER.

NT: B.732a; CB.1266a; K.—.
OT: —.
GEN. REF.: —.

2. *ēdē* [ἤδη, 2235], already, now, is translated "by this time" in John 11:39. See ALREADY

NT: B.344a; CB.1242c; K.—.
OT: k[e]bār: S.3528; HR.604b.2; H.947c; BD.460c.
'attāh: S.6258; HR.604b.3; H.1650c; BD.773d.
GEN. REF.: —.

3. *palai* [πάλαι, 3819], long ago, of old, is rendered "of old time" in Heb. 1:1 (A.V., "in time past"). See OLD.

NT: B.605c; CB.1261c; K.769.
OT: (l[e]mē) rāḥôq: S.7350; HR.1051a.1; H.2151b; BD.935b.
mē'āz: S.227; HR.1051a.2; H.54; BD.23b.
GEN. REF.: —.

Notes: (1) In Luke 9:51 and Acts 8:1, A.V., *hēmera*, a day, is translated "time," in the former, plural, R.V., "the days"; in Luke 23:7 (plural), R.V. "(in these) days," A.V., "(at that) time."

(2) In 1 Tim. 6:19 the phrase *eis to mellon*, lit., 'unto the about-to-be,' i.e., 'for the impending (time),' is rendered "against the time to come."

(3) In 1 Cor. 16:12, A.V., *nun*, "now" (R.V.), is rendered "at this time"; in Acts 24:25, the phrase *to nun echon*, lit., 'the now having,' is rendered "at this time" (the verb is adjectival); the phrase is more expressive than the simple "now." Cp. *heōs tou nun*, "until now," Matt. 24:21 and Mark 13:19, R.V., A.V., "unto (this time)."

(4) For *polumerōs*, strangely rendered "at sundry times," in Heb. 1:1, A.V., see PORTION, C.

(5) For "long time," see LONG.

(6) For "nothing . . . at any time," see NOTHING, *Note* (3).

(7) For *proskairos*, rendered "for a time" in Mark 4:17, A.V., see SEASON, WHILE.

(8) In Matt., *apo tote*, "from that time," lit., 'from then,' occurs thrice, 4:17; 16:21; 26:16; in Luke 16:16, R.V. (A.V., "since that time"); in John 6:66, A.V., "from that time" translates *ek toutou*, lit., 'from, or out of, this,' R.V., "upon this."

(9) In Luke 4:27, the preposition *epi* signifies "in the time of."

(10) For *genea*, rendered "times" in Acts 14:16, "time" in 15:21, see AGE, No. 2 (R.V., "generations").

(11) For "at every time," 2 Pet. 1:15, R.V., see ALWAYS, No. 2.

(12) For "in time of need," Heb. 4:16, see CONVENIENT, and NEED, C, *Note*.

(13) In Heb. 2:1, *pote* signifies "at any time"; in 1 Pet. 3:5, "in the old time"; in 2 Pet. 1:21, "in old time." See PAST. In the following where the A.V. has "sometimes" the R.V. has "once" in Eph. 2:13 and 5:8; "aforetime" in Tit. 3:3.

(14) In Luke 15:29, A.V., "*oudepote*," never, is rendered "neither . . . at any time" (R.V., "never").

(15) For *eukaireō*, to spend time, Acts 17:21, see SPEND, No. 10.

(16) For *chronotribeō*, to spend time, see SPEND, No. 11.

(17) For *prolegō*, rendered "told . . . in time past," in Gal. 5:21, A.V., see FOREWARN.

(18) In Luke 12:1, "in the mean time" is a rendering of the phrase *en hois*, lit., 'in which (things or circumstances).'

(19) In Rev. 5:11 there is no word representing "times": see THOUSAND, *Note* (2).

(20) In Gal. 4:2 *prothesmios* (in its feminine form, with *hēmera*, day, understood) is rendered "time appointed." (see APPOINT, No. 3 and *Note*, TERM).

For **TINKLING** see **CLANGING**

TIP

akron [ἄκρον, 206], the top, an extremity, is translated "tip" in Luke 16:24. See END, C, *Note* (6), TOP.

NT: B.34a; CB.—; K.—.
OT: qāṣeh: S.7097; HR.51b.6a; H.2053a,c; BD.892a.
GEN. REF.: —.

For **TITHES** (Noun) see **TENTH**

TITHE (Verb)

1. *dekatoō* [δεκατόω, 1183], from *dekatos*, tenth, in the Active Voice denotes to take tithes of, Heb. 7:6, R.V., "hath taken (A.V., received) tithes"; in the Passive, to pay tithes, 7:9, R.V., "hath paid (A.V., payed) tithes." ¶ In the Sept., Neh. 10:37. ¶

NT: B.174b; CB.1240c; K.—.
OT: 'āsar: S.6237; HR.289c.1; H.1711c; BD.797c.
GEN. REF.: IS.4:861; NB.—; Z.—.

2. *apodekatoō* [ἀποδεκατόω, 586], denotes (*a*) to tithe (*apo*, from, *dekatos*, tenth), Matt. 23:23 (A.V., "pay tithe of"); Luke 11:42; in

Luke 18:12 (where the best texts have the alternative form *apodekateuō*), "I give tithes"; (*b*) to exact tithes from, Heb. 7:5. ¶
NT: B.89d; CB.1236c; K.–.
OT: 'āsar: S.6237; HR.126b.1; H.1711c; BD.797c.
GEN. REF.: IS.4:861; NB.–; Z.–.

3. *apodekateuō* [ἀποδεκατεύω, —], to give tithes, in Luke 18:12 (some texts have No. 2). ¶
NT: B.89d; CB.1236c; K.–.
OT: –.
GEN. REF.: IS.4:861; NB.–; Z.–.

Note: Heb. 7:4-9 shows the superiority of the Melchizedek priesthood to the Levitical, in that (1) Abraham, the ancestor of the Levites, paid tithes, to Melchizedek (Gen. 14:20); (2) Melchizedek, whose genealogy is outside that of the Levites, took tithes of Abraham, the recipient himself of the Divine promises; (3) whereas death is the natural lot of those who receive tithes, the death of Melchizedek is not recorded; (4) the Levites who receive tithes virtually paid them through Abraham to Melchizedek.

TITLE

titlos [τίτλος, 5102], from Latin *titulus*, is used of the inscription above the Cross of Christ, John 19:19, 20. See SUPERSCRIPTION. ¶
NT: B.820d; CB.1272c; K.–.
OT: –.
GEN. REF.: IS.4:864; NB.1224; Z.–.

TITTLE

keraia or *kerea* [κεραία, 2762], a little horn (*keras*, a horn), was used to denote the small stroke distinguishing one Hebrew letter from another. The Rabbis attached great importance to these; hence the significance of the Lord's statements in Matt. 5:18 and Luke 16:17, charging the Pharisees with hypocrisy, because, while professing the most scrupulous reverence to the Law, they violated its spirit.

Grammarians used the word to denote the accents in Greek words. ¶
NT: B.428d; CB.1255a; K.–.
OT: –.
GEN. REF.: IS.1:985; NB.665; Z.1:985.

For **TO** see † p. 1

TO-DAY, THIS DAY

sēmeron [σήμερον, 4594], an adverb (the Attic form is *tēmeron*), akin to *hēmera*, a day, with the prefix *t* originally representing a pronoun. It is used frequently in Matthew, Luke and Acts; in the last it is always rendered "this day"; also in Heb. 1:5, and the R.V. of 5:5 (A.V., "to day") in the same quotation; "to-day" in 3:7, 13, 15; 4:7 (twice); 13:8; also Jas. 4:13.

The clause containing *sēmeron* is sometimes introduced by the conjunction *hoti*, 'that,' e.g., Mark 14:30; Luke 4:21; 19:9; sometimes without the conjunction, e.g., Luke 22:34; 23:43, where "to-day" is to be attached to the next statement, "shalt thou be with Me"; there are no grammatical reasons for the insistence that the connection must be with the statement "Verily I say unto thee," nor is such an idea necessitated by examples from either the Sept. or the N.T.; the connection given in the A.V. and R.V. is right.

In Rom. 11:8 and 2 Cor. 3:14, 15, the lit. rendering is 'unto the to-day day,' the emphasis being brought out by the R.V., "unto (until) this very day."

In Heb. 4:7, the "to-day" of Ps. 95:7 is evidently designed to extend to the present period of the Christian faith.
NT: B.749a; CB.1269a; K.1024.
OT: yôm: S.3117; HR.1264a.1-11; H.852; BD.398a.
GEN. REF.: –.

TOGETHER

1. *homou* [ὁμοῦ, 3674], used in connection with place, in John 21:2; Acts 2:1 (in the best texts), R.V., "together" (A.V., "with one accord," translating the inferior reading *homothumadon*: see ACCORD, A), is used without the idea of place in John 4:36; 20:4. ¶
NT: B.569b; CB.–; K.–.
OT: yaḥad: S.3162; HR.994a.1; H.858b; BD.403a.
'eḥād: S.259; HR.994a.2; H.61; BD.25c.
GEN. REF.: –.

2. *hama* [ἅμα, 260], at once, is translated "together" in Rom. 3:12; 1 Thess. 4:17; 5:10. See EARLY, *Note*, WITHAL.
NT: B.42a; CB.1249a; K.–.
OT: –.
GEN. REF.: –.

Notes: (1) For *pamplēthei*, Luke 23:18, R.V., see ONCE, *Note*.

(2) In 1 Thess. 5:11, A.V., *allēlous*, "one another" (R.V.), is rendered "yourselves together"; in Luke 23:12, A.V., *meta allēlōn*, lit., with one another, is rendered "together" (R.V., "with each other"); so in Luke 24:14, A.V., *pros allēlous*, R.V., "with each other."

(3) In the following, "together" translates the phrase *epi to auto*, lit., 'to (upon, or for) the same,' Matt. 22:34; Luke 17:35; Acts 1:15; 2:44 (3:1, in some texts); 4:26; 1 Cor. 7:5; 14:23, R.V.: see PLACE, A, *Note* (7).

(4) In Acts 14:1, it translates *kata to auto*, 'at the same'; it may mean 'in the same way' (i.e., as they had entered the synagogue at Pisidian Antioch).

(5) In many cases "together" forms part of another word.

TOIL (Verb and Noun)

A. Verbs.

1. *kopiaō* [κοπιάω, 2872], to be weary, to labour, is rendered to toil in Matt. 6:28; Luke 5:5 (12:27, in some mss.); in 1 Cor. 4:12, R.V. (A.V., "we labour"). See LABOUR.

NT: B.443c; CB.1255c; K.453.
OT: yāga': S.3021; HR.778b.6a; H.842; BD.388a.
GEN. REF.: IS.4:868; NB.–; Z.–.

2. *basanizō* [βασανίζω, 928], primarily, to rub on the touchstone, to put to the test, then, to examine by torture (*basanos*, touchstone, torment), hence denotes to torture, torment, distress; in the Passive Voice it is rendered "toiling" in Mark 6:48, A.V. (R.V., "distressed"). See PAIN, TORMENT, VEX.

NT: B.134c; CB.1238c; K.96.
OT: –.
GEN. REF.: –.

B. Noun.

kopos [κόπος, 2873], labour, trouble, is rendered "toil" in Rev. 2:2, R.V. (A.V., "labour"). See LABOUR.

NT: B.443c; CB.1255c; K.453.
OT: 'āmal: S.5998; HR.778c.7; H.1639; BD.765c.
'āwen: S.205; HR.778c.1; H.48a; BD.19d.
GEN. REF.: IS.4:868; NB.–; Z.–.

TOKEN

1. *sēmeion* [σημεῖον, 4592], a sign, token or indication, is translated "token" in 2 Thess. 3:17, of writing of the closing salutations, the Apostle using the pen himself instead of his amanuensis, his autograph attesting the authenticity of his Epistles. See MIRACLE, SIGN.

NT: B.747d; CB.1268c; K.1015.
OT: 'ôt: S.226; HR.1263b.1a; H.41a; BD.16c.
nēs: S.5251; HR.1263b.5; H.1379a; BD.651d.
GEN. REF.: –.

2. *sussēmon* [σύσσημον, 4953], a fixed sign or signal, agreed upon with others (*sun*, with), is used in Mark 14:44, "a token." ¶ In the Sept., Judg. 20:38, 40; Is. 5:26; 49:22; 62:10. ¶

NT: B.794d; CB.–; K.1015.
OT: nēs: S.5251; HR.1323b.2; H.1379a; BD.651d.
mas'ēt: S.4864; HR.1323b.1; H.1421h; BD.673a.
GEN. REF.: –.

3. *endeigma* [ἔνδειγμα, 1730], a plain token, a proof (akin to *endeiknumi*, to point out, prove), is used in 2 Thess. 1:5, "a manifest token," said of the patient endurance and faith of the persecuted saints at Thessalonica, affording proof to themselves of their new life, and a guarantee of the vindication by God of both Himself and them (see No. 4, *Note*). ¶

NT: B.262c; CB.–; K.–.
OT: –.
GEN. REF.: –.

4. *endeixis* [ἔνδειξις, 1732], a pointing out, showing forth, is rendered "evident token" in Phil. 1:28. See DECLARE, B, PROOF. Cp. *apodeixis*, 1 Cor. 2:4.

NT: B.262d; CB.1244c; K.–.
OT: –.
GEN. REF.: –.

Note: No. 4 refers to the act or process of proving, No. 3 to the thing proved. While the two passages, Phil. 1:28 and 2 Thess. 1:5, contain similar ideas, *endeigma* indicates the token as acknowledged by those referred to; *endeixis* points more especially to the inherent veracity of the token.

TOLERABLE

anektos [ἀνεκτός, 414], (akin to *anechō*, in the Middle Voice, to endure, see ENDURE, No. 5) is used in its comparative form, *anektoteros*, in Matt. 10:15; 11:22, 24; Luke 10:12, 14; some texts have it in Mark 6:11. ¶

NT: B.64c; CB.1235c; K.58.
OT: –.
GEN. REF.: –.

For **TOLL** see **CUSTOM (Toll)**

TOMB

1. *mnēmeion* [μνημεῖον, 3419], is almost invariably rendered "tomb" or "tombs" in the R.V., never "grave," sometimes "sepulchre"; in the A.V., "tomb" in Matt. 8:28; 27:60; Mark 5:2; 6:29. See GRAVE, No. 1, SEPULCHRE.

NT: B.524c; CB.1259a; K.596.
OT: qeber: S.6913; HR.931b.1a; H.1984a; BD.868d.
GEN. REF.: IS.4:870; NB.–; Z.5:767.

2. *mnēma* [μνῆμα, 3418], rendered "tombs" in Mark 5:3, 5; Luke 8:27: see GRAVE, No. 2, SEPULCHRE.

NT: B.524c; CB.1259a; K.596.
OT: qeber: S.6913; HR.931b.1a; H.1984a; BD.868d.
GEN. REF.: IS.4:870; NB.–; Z.5:767.

3. *taphos* [τάφος, 5028], akin to *thaptō*, to bury, is translated "tombs" in Matt. 23:29; elsewhere "sepulchre." See SEPULCHRE.

NT: B.806b; CB.1271a; K.–.
OT: qeber: S.6913; HR.1338a.1a; H.1984a; BD.868d.
GEN. REF.: IS.4:870; NB.–; Z.5:767.

TO-MORROW

aurion [αὔριον, 839], is used either without the article, e.g., Matt. 6:30; 1 Cor. 15:32; Jas. 4:13; or with the article in the feminine form, to agree with *hēmera*, day, e.g., Matt. 6:34; Acts 4:3, R.V., "the morrow" (A.V., "next day"); Jas. 4:14; preceded by *epi*, on, e.g., Luke 10:35; Acts 4:5.

NT: B.122a; CB.–; K.–.
OT: māhār: S.4279; HR.179a.1a; H.1185a; BD.563d.
GEN. REF.: IS.4:870; NB.–; Z.–.

TONGUE (-S)

A. Nouns.

1. *glōssa* [γλῶσσα, 1100], is used of (1) the "tongues . . . like as of fire" which appeared at Pentecost; (2) the tongue, as an organ of speech, e.g., Mark 7:33; Rom. 3:13; 14:11; 1 Cor. 14:9; Phil. 2:11; Jas. 1:26; 3:5, 6, 8; 1 Pet. 3:10; 1 John 3:18; Rev. 16:10; (3) (*a*) a language, coupled with *phulē*, a tribe, *laos*, a people, *ethnos*, a nation, seven times in the Apocalypse, 5:9; 7:9; 10:11; 11:9; 13:7; 14:6; 17:15; (*b*) the supernatural gift of speaking in another language without its having been learnt; in Acts 2:4-13 the circumstances are recorded from the view-point of the hearers; to those in whose language the utterances were made it appeared as a supernatural phenomenon; to others, the stammering of drunkards; what was uttered was not addressed primarily to the audience but consisted in recounting "the mighty works of God"; cp. 2:46; in 1 Cor., chapters 12 and 14, the use of the gift of tongues is mentioned as exercised in the gatherings of local churches; 12:10 speaks of the gift in general terms, and couples with it that of "the interpretation of tongues"; chapt. 14 gives instruction concerning the use of the gift, the paramount object being the edification of the church; unless the tongue was interpreted the speaker would speak "not unto men, but unto God," ver. 2; he would edify himself alone, ver. 4, unless he interpreted, ver. 5, in which case his interpretation would be of the same value as the superior gift of prophesying, as he would edify the church, vv. 4-6; he must pray that he may interpret, ver. 13; if there were no interpreter, he must keep silence, ver. 28, for all things were to be done "unto edifying," ver. 26. "If I come . . . speaking with tongues, what shall I profit you," says the Apostle (expressing the great object in all oral ministry), "unless I speak to you either by way of revelation, or of knowledge, or of prophesying, or of teaching?" (ver. 6). Tongues were for a sign, not to believers, but to unbelievers, ver. 22, and especially to unbelieving Jews (see ver. 21): cp. the passages in the Acts.

There is no evidence of the continuance of this gift after Apostolic times nor indeed in the later times of the Apostles themselves; this provides confirmation of the fulfilment in this way of 1 Cor. 13:8, that this gift would cease in the churches, just as would "prophecies" and "knowledge" in the sense of knowledge received by immediate supernatural power (cp. 14:6). The completion of the Holy Scriptures has provided the churches with all that is necessary for individual and collective guidance, instruction, and edification.

NT: B.162b; CB.1248b; K.123.
OT: lāshôn: S.3956; HR.271b.2a; H.1131a; BD.546a.
GEN. REF.: IS.4:870; NB.1285; Z.5:775.

2. *dialektos* [διάλεκτος, 1258], language (Eng., dialect), is rendered "tongue" in the A.V. of Acts 1:19; 2:6, 8; 21:40; 22:2; 26:14. See LANGUAGE. ¶

NT: B.185d; CB.1241a; K.—.
OT: lāshôn: S.3956; HR.304c.1; H.1131a; BD.546a.
GEN. REF.: IS.4:870; NB.1285; Z.5:775.

B. Adjective.

heteroglōssos [ἑτερόγλωσσος, 2084], is rendered "strange tongues" in 1 Cor. 14:21, R.V. (*heteros*, another of a different sort — see ANOTHER — and A, No. 1), A.V., "other tongues." ¶

NT: B.314d; CB.1250a; K.123.
OT: —.
GEN. REF.: IS.4:870; NB.—; Z.5:775.

C. Adverb.

hebraisti (or *ebraisti*, Westcott and Hort), [Ἑβραϊστί, 1447], denotes (*a*) "in Hebrew," Rev. 9:11, R.V. (A.V., "in the Hebrew tongue"); so 16:16; (*b*) in the Aramaic vernacular of Palestine, John 5:2, A.V., "in the Hebrew tongue" (R.V., "in Hebrew"); in 19:13, 17, A.V., "in the Hebrew" (R.V., "in Hebrew") in ver. 20, A.V. and R.V., "in Hebrew"; in 20:16, R.V. only, "in Hebrew (Rabboni)." ¶

NT: B.213c; CB.1249a; K.372.
OT: —.
GEN. REF.: —.

Note: Cp. *Hellēnisti*, "in Greek," John 19:20, R.V.; Acts 21:37, "Greek." ¶ See also *Rhōmaisti*, under LATIN.

TOOTH, TEETH

odous [ὀδούς, 3599], is used in the sing. in Matt. 5:38 (twice); elsewhere in the plural, of the gnashing of teeth, the gnashing being expressive of anguish and indignation, Matt. 8:12; 13:42, 50; 22:13; 24:51; 25:30; Mark 9:18; Luke 13:28; Acts 7:54; in Rev. 9:8, of the beings seen in a vision and described as locusts. ¶

NT: B.555a; CB.1260b; K.—.
OT: shēn: S.8127; HR.966c.1; H.2422a; BD.1042a.
GEN. REF.: IS.4:876; NB.—; Z.5:778.

TOP

A. Noun.

akron [ἄκρον, 206], for which see TIP, is used of Jacob's staff, Heb. 11:21.

NT: B.34a; CB.—; K.—.
OT: —.
GEN. REF.: —.

B. Phrases.

Note: In Matt. 27:51 and Mark 15:38, *apo anōthen*, "from the top" (lit., 'from above'), is used of the upper part of the Temple veil. In John 19:23, the different phrase *ek tōn anōthen* is used of the weaving of the Lord's garment (the *chitōn*: see CLOTHING), lit., 'from the parts above.'

TOPAZ

topazion [τοπάζιον, 5116], is mentioned in Rev. 21:20, as the ninth of the foundation stones of the wall of the Heavenly Jerusalem; the stone is of a yellow colour (though there are topazes of other colours) and is almost as hard as the diamond. It has the power of double refraction, and when heated or rubbed becomes electric. ¶ In the Sept., Ex. 28:17; 39:10; Job 28:19; Ps. 119:127, "(gold and) topaz"; Ezek. 28:13. ¶

NT: B.822b; CB.1273a; K.–.
OT: piṭdām: S.6357; HR.1364b.2; H.1762; BD.809b.
GEN. REF.: IS.4:629; NB.633; Z.5:779.

TORCH

lampas [λαμπάς, 2985], a torch, is used in the plur. and translated "torches" in John 18:3; in Rev. 8:10, R.V., "torch" (A.V., "lamp"). See LAMP.

NT: B.465c; CB.1256c; K.497.
OT: lappîd: S.3940; HR.852c.1; H.1122a; BD.542a.
GEN. REF.: IS.4:879; NB.1287; Z.5:780.

TORMENT (Noun and Verb)

A. Nouns.

1. *basanismos* [βασανισμός, 929], akin to *basanizō* (see TOIL, No. 2), is used of Divine judgments in Rev. 9:5; 14:11; 18:7, 10, 15. ¶

NT: B.134c; CB.1238c; K.96.
OT: –.
GEN. REF.: IS.4:880; NB.–; Z.–.

2. *basanos* [βάσανος, 931], primarily a touchstone, employed in testing metals, hence, torment, is used (*a*) of physical diseases, Matt. 4:24: (*b*) of a condition of retribution in Hades, Luke 16:23, 28.

NT: B.134d; CB.1238c; K.96.
OT: k^e^limmāh: S.3639; HR.191c.2; H.987a; BD.484a.
GEN. REF.: IS.4:880; NB.–; Z.–.

Note: In 1 John 4:18, A.V., *kolasis*, "punishment" (R.V.), is rendered "torment." See PUNISHMENT, No. 3.

B. Verbs.

1. *basanizō* [βασανίζω, 928], for which see TOIL, No. 2, is translated to torment, (*a*) of sickness, Matt. 8:6; (*b*) of the doom of evil spirits, Mark 5:7; Luke 8:28; (*c*) of retributive judgments upon impenitent mankind at the close of this age, Rev. 9:5; 11:10; (*d*) upon those who worship the Beast and his image and receive the mark of his name, 14:10; (*e*) of the doom of Satan and his agents, 20:10.

NT: B.134c; CB.1238c; K.96.
OT: –.
GEN. REF.: IS.4:880; NB.–; Z.–.

2. *kakoucheō* [κακουχέω, 2558], to treat evilly, in the Passive Voice is translated "tormented" in Heb. 11:37, A.V. (R.V., "evil entreated"). See SUFFER, No. 6.

NT: B.398b; CB.–; K.–.
OT: –.
GEN. REF.: –.

3. *odunaō* [ὀδυνάω, 3600], for which see ANGUISH, B, No. 3. in the Passive Voice is rendered "I am (thou art) tormented" in Luke 16:24, 25, A.V.

NT: B.555a; CB.–; K.–.
OT: ḥîl: S.2427; HR.967a.2; H.623b; BD.297d.
GEN. REF.: –.

TORMENTOR

basanistēs [βασανιστής, 930], properly, a torturer (akin to *basanizō*, see TORMENT, B), one who elicits information by torture, is used of jailors, Matt. 18:34. ¶

NT: B.134d; CB.1238c; K.96.
OT: –.
GEN. REF.: IS.4:880; NB.–; Z.5:780.

TORTURE (Verb)

tumpanizō [τυμπανίζω, 5178], primarily denotes to beat a drum (*tumpanon*, a kettledrum, Eng., tympanal, tympanitis, tympanum), hence, to torture by beating, to beat to death, Heb. 11:35. ¶ In the Sept., 1 Sam. 21:13. "(David) drummed (upon the doors of the city)." ¶ The tympanum as an instrument of torture seems to have been a wheelshaped frame upon which criminals were stretched and beaten with clubs or thongs.

NT: B.829d; CB.–; K.–.
OT: –.
GEN. REF.: IS.4:880; NB.–; Z.–.

TOSS

1. *rhipizō* [ῥιπίζω, 4494], primarily to fan a fire (*rhipis*, a fan, cp, *rhipē*, twinkling), then, to make a breeze, is used in the Passive Voice in Jas. 1:6, "tossed," of the raising of waves by the wind. ¶

NT: B.736b; CB.1268b; K.–.
OT: –.
GEN. REF.: –.

2. *kludōnizomai* [κλυδωνίζομαι, 2831], signifies to be tossed by billows (*kludōn*, a billow); metaphorically, in Eph. 4:14, of an unsettled condition of mind influenced and agitated by one false teaching and another, and characterized by that immaturity which lacks the firm conviction begotten by the truth. ¶ In the Sept., Isa. 57:20. ¶

NT: B.436d; CB.–; K.–.
OT: gārash: S.1644; HR.772b.1; H.388; BD.176c.
GEN. REF.: –.

Note: For "being . . . tossed," Acts 27:18, see LABOUR, B, No. 2.

TOUCH (Verb)

1. *haptō* [ἅπτω, 681], primarily, to fasten to, hence, of fire, to kindle, denotes, in the Middle Voice (*a*) to touch, e.g., Matt. 8:3, 15; 9:20, 21, 29; (*b*) to cling to, lay hold of, John 20:17; here the Lord's prohibition as to clinging to Him was indicative of the fact that communion with Him would, after His ascension, be by faith, through the Spirit; (*c*) to have carnal intercourse with a woman, 1 Cor. 7:1; (*d*) to have fellowship and association with unbelievers, 2 Cor. 6:17; (*e*) (negatively) to adhere to certain Levitical and ceremonial ordinances, in order to avoid contracting external defilement, or to practise rigorous asceticism, all such abstentions being of "no value against the indulgence of the flesh," Col. 2:21, A.V. (R.V., "handle"); (*f*) to assault, in order to sever the vital union between Christ and the believer, said of the attack of the Evil One, 1 John 5:18. See HANDLE, No. 2, KINDLE, LIGHT.

NT: B.102d; CB.1249b; K.–.
OT: –.
GEN. REF.: –.

2. *thinganō* [θιγγάνω, 2345], to touch, a lighter term than No. 1, though Heb. 11:28 approximates to it, in expressing the action of the Destroyer of the Egyptian firstborn; in Heb. 12:20 it signifies to touch, and is not to be interpreted by Ps. 104:32, "He toucheth (No. 1 in the Sept.) the hills and they smoke"; in Col. 2:21, R.V. (A.V., "handle"). See HANDLE, No. 2. ¶

NT: B.361d; CB.–; K.–.
OT: nāga': S.5060; HR.652a; H.1293; BD.619a.
GEN. REF.: –.

3. *prospsauō* [προσψαύω, 4379], to touch upon, to touch slightly, occurs in Luke 11:46. ¶

NT: B.720c; CB.–; K.–.
OT: –.
GEN. REF.: –.

4. *psēlaphaō* [ψηλαφάω, 5584], to feel, to handle, is rendered "that might be touched" in Heb. 12:18. See FEEL, No. 3, HANDLE, No. 1.

NT: B.892c; CB.–; K.–.
OT: mûsh: S.4184; HR.1485b.3; H.1168; BD.559b.
mâshash: S.4959; HR.1485b.4; H.1262; BD.606d.
GEN. REF.: –.

5. *katagō* [κατάγω, 2609], to bring down, is used of bringing a ship to land in Acts 27:3. See BRING, No. 16.

NT: B.410a; CB.–; K.–.
OT: –.
GEN. REF.: –.

6. *sumpatheō* [συμπαθέω, 4834], for which see COMPASSION, A, No. 3, is rendered "be touched with" in Heb. 4:15.

NT: B.778d; CB.1270b; K.798.
OT: –.
GEN. REF.: –.

7. *paraballō* [παραβάλλω, 3846], for which see ARRIVE, No. 4, COMPARE, No. 2, is rendered "touched at" in Acts 20:15, R.V.

NT: B.611d; CB.1262a; K.–.
OT: –.
GEN. REF.: –.

For **TOUCHING** (Preposition) see †, p. 1

For **TOWARD** (Preposition), see †, p. 1

TOWEL

lention [λέντιον, 3012], denotes "a linen cloth or towel" (Lat., *as used by the Lord, John 13:4, 5; it was commonly used by servants in a household.* ¶

NT: B.471c; CB.–; K.–.
OT: –.
GEN. REF.: IS.–; NB.–; Z.5:782.

TOWER

purgos [πύργος, 4444], is used of a watch-tower in a vineyard, Matt. 21:33; Mark 12:1; probably, too, in Luke 14:28 (cp. Is. 5:2); in Luke 13:4, of the tower in Siloam, the modern Silwan, which is built on a steep escarpment of rock. ¶

NT: B.730d; CB.–; K.980.
OT: migdāl: S.4026; HR.1244c.1; H.315f,g; BD.153d.
GEN. REF.: IS.4:881; NB.–; Z.5:782.

TOWN

1. *kōmopolis* [κωμόπολις, 2969], denotes a country town, Mark 1:38, a large village usually without walls. ¶

NT: B.461d; CB.–; K.–.
OT: –.
GEN. REF.: IS.4:882; NB.–; Z.5:782.

2. *kōmē* [κώμη, 2968], a village, or country town without walls. The R.V. always renders this "village" or "villages," A.V., "town" or "towns," Matt. 10:11; Mark 8:23, 26 (twice), 27; Luke 5:17; 9:6, 12; John 7:42; 11:1, 30. See VILLAGE.

NT: B.461d; CB.1255c; K.–.
OT: ḥāṣēr: S.2691; HR.839c.3; H.722a,723a; BD.347b.
GEN. REF.: IS.4:882; NB.236; Z.5:782.

TOWNCLERK

grammateus [γραμματεύς, 1122], a writer, scribe, is used in Acts 19:35 of a state clerk, an important official, variously designated, according to inscriptions found in Graeco-

Asiatic cities. He was responsible for the form of decrees first approved by the Senate, then sent for approval in the popular assembly, in which he often presided. The decrees having been passed, he sealed them with the public seal in the presence of witnesses. Such an assembly frequently met in the theatre. The Roman administration viewed any irregular or unruly assembly as a grave and even capital offence, as tending to strengthen among the people the consciousness of their power and the desire to exercise it. In the circumstances at Ephesus the townclerk feared that he might himself be held responsible for the irregular gathering. See SCRIBE.

NT: B.165d; CB.1248c; K.127.
OT: sāphar: S.5608; HR.275b.2a; H.1540; BD.707d.
shōṭēr: S.7860; HR.275b.5; H.2374a; BD.1009c.
GEN. REF.: IS.–; NB.1287; Z.5:783.

TRACE

A. Verb.

parakoloutheō [*παρακολουθέω*, 3877], to follow up, is used of investigating or tracing a course of events, Luke 1:3, where the writer, humbly differentiating himself from those who possessed an essential apostolic qualification, declares that he "traced the course of all things" (R.V.) about which he was writing (A.V., "having had . . . understanding, etc."). See FOLLOW, No. 5.

NT: B.618d; CB.1262a; K.33.
OT: –.
GEN. REF.: –.

B. Adjective.

anexichniastos [*ἀνεξιχνίαστος*, 421], signifies 'that cannot be traced out' (*a*, negative, *ex*, for *ek*, out, *ichnos*, a track), is rendered "past tracing out" in Rom. 11:33, R.V. (A.V., "past finding out"); in Eph. 3:8, "unsearchable." See FIND, *Note* (3), UNSEARCHABLE. ¶ In the Sept., Job 5:9; 9:10; 34:24. ¶

NT: B.65a; CB.–; K.58.
OT: ḥēqer: S.2714; HR.87b.1; H.729a; BD.350c.
GEN. REF.: –.

TRADE (Noun and Verb)

A. Verbs.

1. *ergazomai* [*ἐργάζομαι*, 2038], to work, is rendered "traded" in Matt. 25:16; in Rev. 18:17, A.V., "trade," R.V., "gain their living." See COMMIT, DO, LABOUR, B, *Note* (1), MINISTER, WORK.

NT: B.306d; CB.1246c; K.251.
OT: 'ābad: S.5647; HR.540c.8a; H.1553; BD.712b.
GEN. REF.: IS.4:883; NB.–; Z.–.

2. *pragmateuomai* [*πραγματεύομαι*, 4231], is rendered "trade ye" in Luke 19:13, R.V., which adds "*herewith*": see OCCUPY. ¶

NT: B.697b; CB.1266b; K.927.
OT: –.
GEN. REF.: IS.4:883; NB.–; Z.–.

3. *diapragmateuomai* [*διαπραγματεύομαι*, 1281], to accomplish by traffic, to gain by trading, occurs in Luke 19:15. ¶

NT: B.187d; CB.1241b; K.927.
OT: –.
GEN. REF.: IS.4:883; NB.–; Z.–.

4. *emporeuomai* [*ἐμπορεύομαι*, 1710], is rendered "trade" in Jas. 4:13, R.V.: see BUY, *Note*, MERCHANDISE, B.

NT: B.256d; CB.1244b; K.–.
OT: sāḥar: S.5503; HR.459a.3a; H.1486; BD.695b.
GEN. REF.: IS.4:883; NB.–; Z.–.

B. Nouns.

1. *technē* [*τέχνη*, 5078], an art (Eng., technique, technical), is used in Acts 18:3 (2nd part) of a "trade," R.V. (A.V., "occupation"). For the 1st part see *Note* below. See ART.

NT: B.814b; CB.1271a; K.–.
OT: ḥokmāh: S.2451; HR.1347c.1; H.647a; BD.315b.
ma'aseh: S.4639; HR.1347c.2; H.1708a; BD.795c.
GEN. REF.: –.

2. *meros* [*μέρος*, 3313], a portion, is used of a trade in Acts 19:27. See CRAFT, No. 5.

NT: B.505d; CB.1258b; K.585.
OT: –.
GEN. REF.: IS.4:883; NB.–; Z.–.

Note: For the adjective *homotechnos*, "of the same trade," Acts 18:3, 1st part, R.V., see CRAFT, No. 4. ¶

TRADITION

paradosis [*παράδοσις*, 3862], a handing down or on (akin to *paradidōmi*, to hand over, deliver), denotes a tradition, and hence, by metonymy, (*a*) the teachings of the Rabbis, interpretations of the law, which was thereby made void in practice, Matt. 15:2, 3, 6; Mark 7:3, 5, 8, 9, 13; Gal. 1:14; Col. 2:8; (*b*) of apostolic teaching, 1 Cor. 11:2, R.V., "traditions" (A.V., "ordinances"), of instructions concerning the gatherings of believers (instructions of wider scope than ordinances in the limited sense); in 2 Thess. 2:15, of Christian doctrine in general, where the Apostle's use of the word constitutes a denial that what he preached originated with himself, and a claim for its Divine authority (cp. *paralambanō*, to receive, 1 Cor. 11:23; 15:3); in 2 Thess. 3:6, it is used of instructions concerning everyday conduct. ¶

NT: B.615d; CB.1262a; K.166.
OT: –.
GEN. REF.: IS.4:883; NB.1290; Z.5:793.

For **TRAIN**, Tit. 2:4, R.V., see **SOBER**, B, No. 2

TRAITOR

prodotēs [*προδότης*, 4273], denotes a betrayer, traitor; the latter term is assigned to

Judas, virtually as a title, in Luke 6:16; in 2 Tim. 3:4 it occurs in a list of evil characters, foretold as abounding in the last days. See BETRAY, B.

NT: B.704c; CB.–; K.–.
OT: –.
GEN. REF.: –.

TRAMPLE

katapateō [καταπατέω, 2662], to tread down, trample under foot, is rendered "trample" in Matt. 7:6. See TREAD, No. 2.

NT: B.415d; CB.1254a; K.804.
OT: dārak: S.1869; HR.740b.5; H.453; BD.201d.
rāmam: S.7429; HR.740b.10a; H.2176; BD.942c.
rāphas: S.7511; HR.740b.11a; H.2199; BD.952c.
GEN. REF.: –.

TRANCE

ekstasis [ἔκστασις, 1611], for which see AMAZE, A, No. 1, denotes a trance in Acts 10:10; 11:5; 22:17, a condition in which ordinary consciousness and the perception of natural circumstances were withheld, and the soul was susceptible only to the vision imparted by God.

NT: B.245a; CB.1244a; K.217.
OT: –.
GEN. REF.: IS.4:886; NB.1291; Z.5:795.

For **TRANQUIL**, 1 Tim. 2:2, R.V., see **QUIET**, No. 1.

For **TRANSFER** (in a figure) see **FASHION**, C, No. 1, and **FIGURE**, *Note* (2).

TRANSFIGURE

metamorphoō [μεταμορφόω, 3339], to change into another form (*meta*, implying change, and *morphē*, form: see FORM, No. 1), is used in the Passive Voice (*a*) of Christ's transfiguration, Matt. 17:2; Mark 9:2; Luke (in 9:29) avoids this term, which might have suggested to Gentile readers the metamorphoses of heathen gods, and uses the phrase *egeneto heteron*, "was altered," lit., 'became (*ginomai*) different (*heteros*)'; (*b*) of believers, Rom. 12:2, "be ye transformed," the obligation being to undergo a complete change which, under the power of God, will find expression in character and conduct; *morphē* lays stress on the inward change, *schēma* (see the preceding verb in that verse, *suschēmatizō*) lays stress on the outward (see FASHION, No. 3, FORM, No. 2); the present continuous tenses indicate a process; 2 Cor. 3:18 describes believers as being "transformed (R.V.) into the same image" (i.e., of Christ in all His moral excellencies), the change being effected by the Holy Spirit. ¶

NT: B.511c; CB.1258c; K.607.
OT: –.
GEN. REF.: IS.4:886; NB.–; Z.5:796.

TRANSFORM

1. *metamorphoō* [μεταμορφόω, 3339], is rendered "transformed" in Rom. 12:2: see TRANSFIGURE.

NT: B.511c; CB.1258c; K.607.
OT: –.
GEN. REF.: IS.4:886; NB.–; Z.5:796.

2. *metaschēmatizō* [μετασχηματίζω, 3345], in the Passive Voice is rendered to be transformed in the A.V. of 2 Cor. 11:13, 14, 15: see FASHION, C, No. 1.

NT: B.513b; CB.1258c; K.1129.
OT: –.
GEN. REF.: –.

TRANSGRESS, TRANSGRESSION

A. Verbs.

1. *parabainō* [παραβαίνω, 3845], lit., to go aside (*para*), hence to go beyond, is chiefly used metaphorically of transgressing the tradition of the elders, Matt. 15:2; the commandment of God, 15:3; in Acts 1:25, of Judas, A.V., "by transgression fell" (R.V., "fell away"); in 2 John 9 some texts have this verb (A.V., "transgresseth"), the best have *proagō* (see GO, No. 10). ¶

NT: B.611c; CB.1262a; K.772.
OT: sûr: S.5493; HR.1055b.3; H.1480; BD.693b.
'ābar: S.5674; HR.1055b.4; H.1556; BD.716d.
sāṭāh: S.7847; HR.1055b.7; H.2250; BD.966b.
GEN. REF.: IS.4:889; NB.–; Z.–.

2. *huperbainō* [ὑπερβαίνω, 5233], lit., to go over (*huper*), used metaphorically and rendered "transgress" in 1 Thess. 4:6 (A.V., "go beyond"), i.e., of overstepping the limits separating chastity from licentiousness, sanctification from sin. ¶

NT: B.840a; CB.1252a; K.772.
OT: 'ābar: S.5674; HR.1409a.4; H.1556; BD.716d.
GEN. REF.: IS.4:889; NB.–; Z.–.

3. *parerchomai* [παρέρχομαι, 3928], to come by (*para*, by, *erchomai*, to come), pass over, and hence, metaphorically, to transgress, is so used in Luke 15:29. See COME, No. 9, PASS.

NT: B.625d; CB.1262b; K.257.
OT: 'ābar: S.5674; HR.1068c.11; H.1556; BD.716d.
GEN. REF.: IS.4:889; NB.–; Z.–.

B. Nouns.

1. *parabasis* [παράβασις, 3847], akin to A, No. 1, primarily a going aside, then, an overstepping, is used metaphorically to denote transgression (always of a breach of law); (*a*) of Adam, Rom. 5:14; (*b*) of Eve, 1 Tim. 2:14;

(*c*) negatively, where there is no law, since transgression implies the violation of law, none having been enacted between Adam's transgression and those under the Law, Rom. 4:15; (*d*) of transgressions of the Law, Gal. 3:19, where the statement "it was added because of transgressions" is best understood according to Rom. 4:15; 5:13 and 5:20; the Law does not make men sinners, but makes them transgressors; hence sin becomes "exceeding sinful," Rom. 7:7, 13. Conscience thus had a standard external to itself; by the Law men are taught their inability to yield complete obedience to God, that thereby they may become convinced of their need of a Saviour; in Rom. 2:23, R.V., "transgression (of the Law)," A.V., "breaking (the Law)"; Heb. 2:2, 9:15. ¶

NT: B.611d; CB.1262a; K.772.
OT: sēṭîm: S.7846; HR.1056a.1; H.2240a; BD.962b.
GEN. REF.: IS.4:889; NB.–; Z.5:797.

2. *paranomia* [παρανομία, 3892], law-breaking (*para*, contrary to, *nomos*, law), is rendered "transgression" in 2 Pet. 2:16, R.V. (A.V., "iniquity"). ¶

NT: B.621a; CB.–; K.646.
OT: mizmāh: S.4209; HR.1062b.1; H.556c; BD.273c.
ʿāwôn: S.5771; HR.1062b.2; H.1577a; BD.730d.
GEN. REF.: IS.4:889; NB.–; Z.–.

Note: In 1 John 3:4 (1st part), A.V., *poieō*, to do, with *anomia*, lawlessness, is rendered "transgresseth . . . the law" (R.V., "doeth . . . lawlessness"); in the 2nd part *anomia* alone is rendered "transgression of the law," A.V. (R.V., "lawlessness").

TRANSGRESSOR

1. *parabatēs* [παραβάτης, 3848], lit. and primarily, one who stands beside, then, one who oversteps the prescribed limit, a transgressor (akin to *parabainō*, to transgress, see above); so Rom. 2:25, R.V. (A.V., "a breaker"); ver. 27, R.V., "a transgressor" (A.V., "dost transgress"); Gal. 2:18; Jas. 2:9, 11. ¶

NT: B.612a; CB.1262a; K.772.
OT: –.
GEN. REF.: –.

Note: Hamartōlos, a sinner, one who misses the mark, is applicable to all men without distinction; *parabatēs* stresses the positive side of sin, and is applicable to those who received the Law.

2. *anomos* [ἄνομος, 459], without law (*a* —, negative), is translated "transgressors" in Luke 22:37 (in some texts, Mark 15:28), in a quotation from Isa. 53:12. See LAW, C, No. 3, LAWLESS, A.

NT: B.72a; CB.1235c; K.646.
OT: rāshāʿ: S.7563; HR.107c.16a; H.2222b; BD.957b.
reshaʿ: S.7562; HR.107c.16b; H.2222a; BD.957c.
GEN. REF.: –.

TRANSLATE, TRANSLATION

A. Verbs.

1. *methistēmi* or *methistanō* [μεθίστημι, 3179], to change, remove (*meta*, implying change, *histēmi*, to cause to stand), is rendered "hath translated" in Col. 1:13. See PUT, REMOVE, TURN (away).

NT: B.498d; CB.–; K.–.
OT: sûr: S.5493; HR.907b.4; H.1480; BD.693b.
ʿădāh (Aramaic): S.5709; HR.907b.5; H.2898; BD.1105b.
GEN. REF.: –.

2. *metatithēmi* [μετατίθημι, 3346], to transfer to another place (*meta*, see above, *tithēmi*, to put), is rendered to translate in Heb. 11:5 (twice). See CARRY, CHANGE, REMOVE, TURN.

NT: B.513c; CB.1258c; K.1176.
OT: sûg: S.5472; HR.917a.3; H.1469; BD.690d.
GEN. REF.: –.

B. Noun.

metathesis [μετάθεσις, 3331], a change of position (akin to A, No. 2), is rendered "translation" in Heb. 11:5. See CHANGE, REMOVING.

NT: B.511a; CB.1258c; K.1176.
OT: –.
GEN. REF.: IS.4:890; NB.–; Z.–.

For **TRANSPARENT,** Rev. 21:21, see **DAWN,** A, No. 2, *Note*

TRAP

thēra [θήρα, 2339], denotes a hunting, chase, then, a prey; hence, figuratively, of preparing destruction by a net or "trap," Rom. 11:9. ¶

NT: B.360a; CB.–; K.–.
OT: ṣayid: S.6718; HR.650b.2a; H.1885a,1886a; BD.844d.
GEN. REF.: IS.4:556; NB.–; Z.–.

TRAVAIL (Noun and Verb)

A. Nouns.

1. *mochthos* [μόχθος, 3449], labour, involving painful effort, is rendered "travail" in 2 Cor. 11:27, R.V. (A.V., "painfulness"); in 1 Thess. 2:9 and 2 Thess. 3:8 it stresses the toil involved in the work. ¶

NT: B.528d; CB.1259a; K.–.
OT: ʿāmāl: S.5999; HR.935c.4; H.1639a; BD.765d.
GEN. REF.: IS.4:890; NB.–; Z.–.

2. *ōdin* [ὠδίν, 5604], a birth pang, travail pain, is used illustratively in 1 Thess. 5:3 of the calamities which are to come upon men at the beginning of the Day of the Lord; the figure used suggests the inevitableness of the catastrophe. See PAIN, No. 2, SORROW.

NT: B.895c; CB.1260b; K.1353.
OT: ḥēbel: S.2256; HR.1492b.1; H.592b; BD.286d.
ḥîl: S.2427; HR.1492b.2a; H.623b; BD.297d.
GEN. REF.: IS.4:896; NB.–; Z.–.

B. Verbs.

1. *ōdinō* [ὠδίνω, 5605], akin to A, No. 2, is used negatively in Gal. 4:27, "(thou) that travailest (not);" quoted from Isa. 54:1; the Apostle applies the circumstances of Sarah and Hagar (which doubtless Isaiah was recalling) to show that, whereas the promise by grace had temporarily been replaced by the works of the Law (see Gal. 3:17), this was now reversed, and, in the fulfilment of the promise to Abraham, the number of those saved by the Gospel would far exceed those who owned allegiance to the Law. Isa. 54 has primary reference to the future prosperity of Israel restored to God's favour, but frequently the principles underlying events recorded in the O.T. extend beyond their immediate application.

In 4:19 the Apostle uses it metaphorically of a second travailing on his part regarding the churches of Galatia; his first was for their deliverance from idolatry (ver. 8), now it was for their deliverance from bondage to Judaism. There is no suggestion here of a second regeneration necessitated by defection. There is a hint of reproach, as if he was enquiring whether they had ever heard of a mother experiencing second birthpangs for her children.

In Rev. 12:2 the woman is figurative of Israel; the circumstances of her birth-pangs are mentioned in Isa. 66:7 (see also Micah 5:2, 3). Historically the natural order is reversed. The Man-child, Christ, was brought forth at His first Advent; the travail is destined to take place in "the time of Jacob's trouble," the "great tribulation," Matt. 24:21; Rev. 7:14. The object in 12:2 in referring to the Birth of Christ is to connect Him with His earthly people Israel in their future time of trouble, from which the godly remnant, the nucleus of the restored nation, is to be delivered (Jer. 30:7). ¶

NT: B.895d; CB.1260b; K.1353.
OT: ḥûl: S.2342; HR.1492c.3a; H.623; BD.296b.
ḥābal: S.2254; HR.1492c.2; H.592; BD.286b.
GEN. REF.: IS.4:896; NB.–; Z.–.

2. *sunōdinō* [συνωδίνω, 4944], to be in travail together, is used metaphorically in Rom. 8:22, of the whole creation. ¶

NT: B.793d; CB.–; K.–.
OT: –.
GEN. REF.: IS.4:896; NB.–; Z.–.

3. *tikto* [τίκτω, 5088], to beget, is rendered "travail" in John 16:21.

NT: B.816d; CB.1272c; K.–.
OT: –.
GEN. REF.: IS.4:890.

For **TRAVEL** (companions in), Acts 19:29, and **TRAVEL WITH,** 2 Cor. 8:19, see **COMPANION,** No. 1.

TRAVEL

dierchomai [διέρχομαι, 1330], to go or pass through, is translated "travelled" in Acts 11:19. See Come, No. 5.

NT: B.194c; CB.1241c; K.257.
OT: hālak: S.1980; HR.328c.4a-c; H.498; BD.229d.
GEN. REF.: –.

Note: For *apodēmeō*, rendered "travelling" in Matt. 25:14, A.V., see Go, No. 27.

TREAD, TRODE, TRODDEN

1. *pateō* [πατέω, 3961], is used (*a*) intransitively and figuratively, of treading upon serpents, Luke 10:19; (*b*) transitively, of treading on, down or under, of the desecration of Jerusalem by its foes, Luke 21:24; Rev. 11:2; of the avenging, by the Lord in Person hereafter, of this desecration and of the persecution of the Jews, in Divine retribution, metaphorically spoken of as the treading of the winepress of God's wrath, Rev. 14:20; 19:15 (cp. Isa. 63:2, 3). ¶

NT: B.634d; CB.1262c; K.804.
OT: dārak: S.1869; HR.1105a.3; H.453; BD.201d.
GEN. REF.: –.

2. *katapateō* [καταπατέω, 2662], to tread down, trample under foot, is used (*a*) literally, Matt. 5:13; 7:6; Luke 8:5; 12:1; (*b*) metaphorically, of 'treading under foot' the Son of God, Heb. 10:29, i.e., turning away from Him, to indulge in wilful sin. ¶

NT: B.415d; CB.1254a; K.804.
OT: rāmas: S.7429; HR.740b.10a; H.2176; BD.942c.
rāphas: S.7511; HR.740b.11a; H.2199; BD.952c.
dārak: S.1869; HR.740b.5; H.453; BD.201d.
GEN. REF.:–.

For TREADING out the corn, see **THRESH**

TREASURE (Noun and Verb)

A. Nouns.

1. *thēsauros* [θησαυρός, 2344], denotes (1) a place of safe keeping (possibly akin to *tithēmi*, to put), (*a*) a casket, Matt. 2:11; (*b*) a storehouse, Matt. 13:52; used metaphorically of the heart, Matt. 12:35, twice (R.V., "out of his treasure"); Luke 6:45; (2) a treasure, Matt. 6:19, 20, 21; 13:44; Luke 12:33, 34; Heb. 11:26; treasure (in heaven or the heavens), Matt. 19:21; Mark 10:21; Luke 18:22; in these expressions (which are virtually equivalent to that in Matt. 6:1, "with your Father which is in Heaven") the promise does not simply refer to the present life, but looks likewise to the hereafter; in 2 Cor. 4:7

it is used of "the light of the knowledge of the glory of God in the face of Jesus Christ," descriptive of the Gospel, as deposited in the earthen vessels of the persons who proclaim it (cp. ver. 4); in Col. 2:3, of the wisdom and knowledge hidden in Christ. ¶

NT: B.361c; CB.1272b; K.333.
OT: 'ôṣār: S.214; HR.651c.1a; H.154a; BD.69d.
GEN. REF.: IS.4:898,899; NB.–; Z.5:807.

2. *gaza* [γάζα, 1047], a Persian word, signifying royal treasure, occurs in Acts 8:27. ¶

NT: B.149b; CB.–; K.–.
OT: ginzîn: S.1595; HR.233a.2; H.365a; BD.170d.
GEN. REF.: IS.4:898,899; NB.–; Z.–.

B. Verb.

thēsaurizō [θησαυρίζω, 2343], akin to A, No. 1, is used metaphorically in Rom. 2:5 of treasuring up wrath. See LAY, No. 17.

NT: B.361b; CB.1272b; K.333.
OT: 'āṣar: S.686; HR.651b.1; H.154; BD.69d.
ṣābar: S.6651; HR.651b.2; H.1874; BD.840d.
ṣāphan: S.6845; HR.651b.3; H.1953; BD.860c.
GEN. REF.: IS.4:898,899; NB.–; Z.5:807.

For **TREASURER** see **CHAMBERLAIN**, *Note*

TREASURY

1. *gazophulakion* [γαζοφυλάκιον, 1049], from *gaza*, a treasure, *phulakē*, a guard, is used by Josephus for a special room in the women's court in the Temple in which gold and silver bullion was kept. This seems to be referred to in John 8:20; in Mark 12:41 (twice), 43 and Luke 21:1 it is used of the trumpet-shaped or ram's horn-shaped chests, into which the temple-offerings of the people were cast. There were 13 chests, six for such gifts in general, seven for distinct purposes. ¶

NT: B.149b; CB.1248a; K.–.
OT: lishkāh: S.3957; HR.233a.2a; H.1129a; BD.545c.
nishkāh: S.5393; HR.233a.2b.; H.1431; BD.675b.
GEN. REF.: IS.4:899; NB.–; Z.5:807,809.

2. *korbanas* [κορβανâw, 2878], signifying the place of gifts, denoted the Temple treasury, Matt. 27:6. See CORBAN. ¶

NT: B.444c; CB.1255c; K.459.
OT: –.
GEN. REF.: IS.4:899; NB.–; Z.–.

For **TREATED,** Acts 27:3, R.V., see **ENTREAT** (to deal with)

TREATISE

logos [λόγος, 3056], a word, denotes a treatise or written narrative in Acts 1:1. See WORD.

NT: B.477a; CB.1257a; K.505.
OT: dābār: S.1697; HR.881c.2a; H.399a; BD.182a.
GEN. REF.: –.

TREE

1. *dendron* [δένδρον, 1186], a living, growing tree (cp. Eng., rhododendron, lit., rose-tree), known by the fruit it produces, Matt. 12:33; Luke 6:44; certain qualities are mentioned in the N.T.; "a good tree," Matt. 7:17, 18; 12:33; Luke 6:43; "a corrupt tree" (ditto); in Jude 12, metaphorically, of evil teachers, "autumn trees (A.V., trees whose fruit withereth) without fruit, twice dead, plucked up by the roots," R.V.; in Luke 13:19, in some texts, "a great tree," A.V. (R.V., "a tree"); for this and Matt. 13:32 see MUSTARD; in Luke 21:29 the fig tree is illustrative of Israel, "all the trees" indicating Gentile nations.

NT: B.174c; CB.1240c; K.–.
OT: 'ēṣ: S.6086; HR.289c.3; H.1670a; BD.781c.
'îlān: S.363; HR.289c.1; H.2570; BD.1079a.
GEN. REF.: –.

2. *xulon* [ξύλον, 3586], wood, a piece of wood, anything made of wood (see STAFF, STOCKS), is used, with the rendering "tree," (*a*) in Luke 23:31, where "the green tree" refers either to Christ, figuratively of all His living power and excellencies, or to the life of the Jewish people while still inhabiting their land, in contrast to "the dry," a figure fulfilled in the horrors of the Roman massacre and devastation in A.D. 70 (cp. the Lord's parable in Luke 13:6-9; see Ezek. 20:47, and cp. 21:3); (*b*) of the Cross, the tree being the *stauros*, the upright pale or stake to which Romans nailed those who were thus to be executed, Acts 5:30; 10:39; 13:29; Gal. 3:13; 1 Pet. 2:24; (*c*) of the tree of life, Rev. 2:7; 22:2 (twice), 14, 19, R.V., A.V., "book." See WOOD.

NT: B.549a; CB.1273b; K.665.
OT: 'ēṣ: S.6086; HR.958a.3a; H.1670a; BD.781c.
GEN. REF.: IS.–; NB.–; Z.5:810.

TREMBLE, TREMBLING

A. Verbs.

1. *tremō* [τρέμω, 5141], to tremble, especially with fear, is used in Mark 5:33; Luke 8:47 (Acts 9:6, in some mss.); 2 Pet. 2:10, R.V., "they tremble (not)," A.V., "they are (not) afraid." ¶

NT: B.825b; CB.–; K.–.
OT: ḥārēd: S.2730; HR.1371b.2; H.735a; BD.353c.
GEN. REF.: IS.4:903; NB.–; Z.–.

2. *seiō* [σείω, 4579], to move to and fro, shake, is rendered "will I make to tremble" in Heb. 12:26, R.V. (A.V., "I shake"). See QUAKE, SHAKE.

NT: B.746c; CB.1268c; K.1014.
OT: rā'ash: S.7493; HR.1261c.5; H.2195; BD.950a.
GEN. REF.: IS.4:903; NB.–; Z.–.

Notes: (1) For *phrissō* in Jas. 2:19, A.V., "tremble," see SHUDDER.

(2) For the adjective *entromos*, trembling, Acts 7:32; 16:29, R.V., "trembling for fear," see QUAKE, No. 1.

(3) The adjective *emphobos*, used with *ginomai*, to become, is rendered "trembled" in Acts 24:25 (R.V., "was terrified"); in Luke 24:5, R.V., "they were affrighted," A.V., "they were afraid." See AFFRIGHTED, A.

B. Noun.

tromos [τρόμος, 5156], a trembling (akin to A, No. 1), occurs in Mark 16:8, R.V., "trembling (. . . had come upon them)"; 1 Cor. 2:3; 2 Cor. 7:15; Eph. 6:5; Phil. 2:12. ¶

NT: B.827a; CB.1273a; K.–.
OT: ra'ad: S.7461; HR.1374c.7; H.2184a; BD.944c.
paḥad: S.6343; HR.1374.c.5; H.1756a; BD.808b.
reṭeṭ: S.7374; HR.1374c.6; H.2156a; BD.936a.
GEN. REF.: IS.4:903; NB.–; Z.–.

TRENCH

charax [χάραξ, 5482], primarily a pointed stake, hence, a palisade or rampart, is rendered "trench" in Luke 19:43, A.V. (R.V., "bank;" marg., "palisade"). In A.D. 70, Titus, the Roman general, surrounded Jerusalem with a palisaded mound (Tyndale, *l.c.*, renders it "mound"). The Jews in one of their sorties destroyed this *charax*, after which Titus surrounded the city with a wall of masonry. ¶

NT: B.876b; CB.1239c; K.–.
OT: sōlᵉlāh: S.5550; HR.1454c.5; H.1506b; BD.700c.
muṣṣāb: S.4674; HR.1454c.2; H.1398d; BD.663a.
GEN. REF.: –.

TRESPASS (Noun and Verb)

A. Noun.

paraptōma [παράπτωμα, 3900], primarily a false step, a blunder (akin to *parapiptō*, to fall away, Heb. 6:6), lit., 'a fall beside,' used ethically, denotes a trespass, a deviation, from uprightness and truth, Matt. 6:14, 15 (twice); 18:35, in some mss.; Mark 11:25, 26; in Romans the R.V. substitutes "trespass" and "trespasses" for A.V., "offence" and "offences," 4:25, "for (i.e., because of) our trespasses"; 5:15 (twice), where the trespass is that of Adam (in contrast to the free gift of righteousness, ver. 17, a contrast in the nature and the effects); 5:16, where "of many trespasses" expresses a contrast of quantity; the condemnation resulted from one trespass, the free gift is "of (*ek*, expressing the origin, and throwing stress upon God's justifying grace in Christ) many trespasses"; ver. 17, introducing a contrast between legal effects and those of Divine grace; ver. 18, where the R.V., "through one trespass," is contrasted with "one act of righteousness"; this is important, the difference is not between one man's trespass and Christ's righteousness (as A.V.), but between two acts, that of Adam's trespass and the vicarious Death of Christ; ver. 20 [cp. TRANSGRESSION, B, No. 1 (*d*)]; in 2 Cor. 5:19, A.V. and R.V., "trespasses"; in Eph. 1:7, R.V., "trespasses" (A.V., "sins"); in 2:1, R.V., ("dead through your) trespasses," A.V., "(dead in) trespasses"; 2:5, R.V., "(dead through our) trespasses," A.V., "(dead in) sins"; so Col. 2:13 (1st part); in the 2nd part, A.V. and R.V., "trespasses."

In Gal. 6:1, R.V., "(in any) trespass" (A.V., "fault"), the reference is to "the works of the flesh" (5:19), and the thought is that of the believer's being found off his guard, the trespass taking advantage of him; in Jas. 5:16, A.V., "faults" (R.V., "sins" translates the word *hamartias*, which is found in the best texts), auricular confession to a priest is not in view here or anywhere else in Scripture; the command is comprehensive, and speaks either of the acknowledgment of sin where one has wronged another, or of the unburdening of a troubled conscience to a godly brother whose prayers will be efficacious, or of open confession before the church.

In Rom. 11:11, 12, the word is used of Israel's "fall," i.e., their deviation from obedience to God and from the fulfilment of His will (to be distinguished from the verb *ptaiō*, "fall," in the 1st part of ver. 11, which indicates the impossibility of recovery). See FALL, A, No. 2. ¶

NT: B.621c; CB.1262b; K.846.
OT: ma'al: S.4604; HR.1063c.2; H.1230a; BD.591b.
'āwel: S.5766; HR.1063c.3; H.1580a,b; BD.732b.
pesha': S.6588; HR.1063c.4; H.1846a; BD.833b.
GEN. REF.: IS.4:903; NB.1189; Z.5:444,811.

B. Verb.

hamartanō [ἁμαρτάνω, 264], to sin, is translated to trespass, in the A.V. of Matt. 18:15, and Luke 17:3, 4 (R.V., to sin).

NT: B.42b; CB.1249a; K.44.
OT: ḥāṭa': S.2398; HR.60c.2a; H.638; BD.306c.
GEN. REF.: IS.4:518; NB.1189; Z.5:444,811.

Note: For the different meanings of words describing sin, see SIN. *Paraptōma*, and *hamartēma* (a sinful deed) are closely associated, with regard to their primary meanings: *parabasis* seems to be a stronger term, as the breach of a known law (see TRANSGRESSION).

TRIAL

1. *dokimē* [δοκιμή, 1382], for which see EXPERIENCE, No. 2, is rendered "trial" in 2 Cor. 8:2, A.V. (R.V., "proof").

NT: B.202d; CB.1242a; K.181.
OT: –.
GEN. REF.: –.

2. *peira* [πεῖρα, 3984], a making trial, an experiment, is used with *lambanō*, to receive or take, in Heb. 11:29, rendered "assaying," and ver. 36, in the sense of 'having experience of' (akin to *peiraō*, to assay, to try), "had trial." In the Sept., Deut. 28:56. ¶

NT: B.640a; CB.1263a; K.822.
OT: nāsāh: S.5254; HR.1115c.2; H.1373; BD.650a.
massāh: S.4531; HR.1115c.1; H.1223b; BD.650b.
GEN. REF.: IS.4:904; NB.–; Z.–.

3. *peirasmos* [πειρασμός, 3986], akin to No. 2, is rendered "trials" in Acts 20:19, R.V. See TEMPTATION.

NT: B.640d; CB.1263a; K.822.
OT: massāh: S.4531; HR.1116a.1; H.1223b; BD.650b.
GEN. REF.: IS.4:904; NB.–; Z.5:669.

4. *purōsis* [πύρωσις, 4451], akin to *puroō*, to set on fire, signifies (*a*) a burning; (*b*) a refining, metaphorically in 1 Pet. 4:12, "fiery trial," or rather 'trial by fire,' referring to the refining of gold (1:7). See BURNING

NT: B.731c; CB.1268a; K.975.
OT: kûr: S.3564; HR.1246a.1; H.967b; BD.468b.
GEN. REF.: –.

Note: For *dokimion*, rendered "trial" in 1 Pet. 1:7, A.V., see PROOF, No. 2.

TRIBE (-S)

1. *phulē* [φυλή, 5443], a company of people united by kinship or habitation, a clan, tribe, is used (*a*) of the peoples of the earth, Matt. 24:30; in the following the R.V. has "tribe(-s)" for A.V., "kindred(-s)," Rev. 1:7; 5:9; 7:9; 11:9; 13:7; 14:6; (*b*) of the tribes of Israel, Matt. 19:28; Luke 2:36; 22:30; Acts 13:21; Rom. 11:1; Phil. 3:5; Heb. 7:13, 14; Jas. 1:1; Rev. 5:5; 7:4-8; 21:12. ¶

NT: B.868d; CB.1264c; K.1280.
OT: maṭṭeh: S.4294; HR.1444b.6; H.1352b; BD.641c.
mishpāḥāh: S.4940; HR.1444b.7; H.2442b; BD.1046c.
shebeṭ: S.7626; HR.1444b.8a; H.2314a; BD.986d.
GEN. REF.: IS.4:904; NB.–; Z.5:813.

2. *dōdekaphulos* [δωδεκάφυλος, 1429], an adjective signifying 'of twelve tribes' (*dōdeka*, twelve, and No. 1), used as a noun in the neuter, occurs in Acts 26:7. ¶

NT: B.210b; CB.–; K.192.
OT: –.
GEN. REF.: IS.4:904; NB.–; Z.–.

TRIBULATION

thlipsis [θλῖψις, 2347], for which see AFFLICTION, B, No. 4, is translated "tribulation" in the R.V. (for A.V., "affliction") in Mark 4:17; 13:19; plural in 2 Thess. 1:4, A.V., "tribulations," R.V., "afflictions"; in Acts 14:22 "many tribulations" (A.V., "much tribulation"); in Matt. 24:9, "unto tribulation" (A.V., "to be afflicted"); in 2 Cor. 1:4; 7:4; 2 Thess. 1:6, A.V., "tribulation" for R.V., "affliction"; R.V. and A.V., "tribulation(-s)," e.g., in Rom. 2:9; 5:3 (twice); 8:35; 12:12; Eph. 3:13; Rev. 1:9; 2:9, 10, 22.

In Rev. 7:14, "the great tribulation," R.V., lit., 'the tribulation, the great one' (not as A.V., without the article), is not that in which all saints share; it indicates a definite period spoken of by the Lord in Matt. 24:21, 29; Mark 13:19, 24, where the time is mentioned as preceding His Second Advent, and as a period in which the Jewish nation, restored to Palestine in unbelief by Gentile instrumentality, will suffer an unprecedented outburst of fury on the part of the antichristian powers confederate under the Man of Sin (2 Thess. 2:10-12; cp. Rev. 12:13-17); in this tribulation Gentile witnesses for God will share (Rev. 7:9), but it will be distinctly "the time of Jacob's trouble" (Jer. 30:7); its beginning is signalized by the setting up of the "abomination of desolation" (Matt. 24:15; Mark 13:14, with Dan. 11:31; 12:11).

NT: B.362b; CB.1272b; K.334.
OT: ṣārāh: S.6869; HR.652c.11a; H.1973c,1974d; BD.865b.
GEN. REF.: IS.4:913; NB.1296; Z.5:820.

Note: For the verb *thlibō*, in the Passive Voice rendered "suffer tribulation" in 1 Thess. 3:4, A.V. (R.V., "suffer affliction"), see AFFLICT, No. 4.

TRIBUTE

1. *phoros* [φόρος, 5411], akin to *pherō*, to bring, denotes tribute paid by a subjugated nation, Luke 20:22; 23:2; Rom. 13:6, 7. ¶

NT: B.865a; CB.1264b; K.1252.
OT: mas: S.4522; HR.1438a.4; H.1218; BD.586d.
GEN. REF.: IS.4:739; NB.1297,1298; Z.5:821.

2. *kēnsos* [κῆνσος, 2778], Lat. and Eng., census, denotes a poll tax, Matt. 17:25; 22:17, 19; Mark. 12:14. ¶

NT: B.430d; CB.1255a; K.–.
OT: –.
GEN. REF.: IS.–; NB.–; Z.5:821.

3. *didrachmon* [δίδραχμον, 1323], the half-shekel, is rendered "tribute" in Matt. 17:24 (twice): see SHEKEL, No. 2. ¶

NT: B.192c; CB.1241c; K.–.
OT: sheqel: S.8255; HR.328a.2; H.2454a; BD.1053c.
GEN. REF.: IS.–; NB.–; Z.5:821.

TRIM

kosmeō [κοσμέω, 2885], to arrange, adorn, is used of trimming lamps, Matt. 25:7. See ADORN, GARNISH.

NT: B.445a; CB.1255c; K.459.
OT: –.
GEN. REF.: –.

TRIUMPH

thriambeuō [θριαμβεύω, 2358], denotes (*a*) to lead in triumph, used of a conqueror with reference to the vanquished, 2 Cor. 2:14. Theodoret paraphrases it 'He leads us about here and there and displays us to all the world.' This is in agreement with evidences from various sources. Those who are led are not captives exposed to humiliation, but are displayed as the glory and devoted subjects of Him who leads (see the context). This is so even if there is a reference to a Roman "triumph." On such occasions the general's sons, with various officers, rode behind his chariot (Livy, xlv. 40). But there is no necessary reference here to a Roman "triumph" (Field, in *Notes on the Trans. of the N.T.*). The main thought is that of the display, "in Christ" being the sphere; its evidences are the effects of gospel testimony.

In Col. 2:15 the circumstances and subjects are quite different, and relate to Christ's victory over spiritual foes at the time of His Death; accordingly the reference may be to the triumphant display of the defeated. ¶

NT: B.363d; CB.1272b; K.337.
OT: —.
GEN. REF.: IS.4:922; NB.—; Z.—.

For **TRODE** see **TREAD**

TROUBLE (Noun and Verb)

A. Noun.

thlipsis [θλῖψις, 2347], for which see AFFLICTION, No. 4, and TRIBULATION, is rendered "trouble" in the A.V. of 1 Cor. 7:28 (R.V., "tribulation"); 2 Cor. 1:4 (2nd clause), 8 (R.V., "affliction").

NT: B.362b; CB.1272b; K.334.
OT: ṣārāh: S.6869; HR.652c.11a; H.1973c,1974d; BD.865b.
GEN. REF.: —.

Note: In some mss. *tarachē*, an agitation, disturbance, trouble, is found in Mark 13:8 (plur.) and John 5:4 (R.V. omits). ¶

B. Verbs.

1. *tarassō* [ταράσσω, 5015], akin to *tarachē* (A, *Note*), is used (1) in a physical sense, John 5:7 (in some mss. ver. 4), (2) metaphorically, (*a*) of the soul and spirit of the Lord, John 11:33, where the true rendering is 'He troubled Himself'; (*b*) of the hearts of disciples, 14:1, 27; (*c*) of the minds of those in fear or perplexity, Matt. 2:3; 14:26; Mark 6:50; Luke 1:12; 24:38; 1 Pet. 3:14; (*d*) of subverting the souls of believers, by evil doctrine, Acts 15:24; Gal. 1:7; 5:10; (*e*) of stirring up a crowd, Acts 17:8; ver. 13 in the best texts, "troubling (the multitudes)," R.V. ¶

NT: B.805b; CB.1271a; K.—.
OT: rāgaz: S.7264; HR.1336; H.2112; BD.919a.
bāhal: S.926; HR.1336a.1a; H.207; BD.96b.
GEN. REF.: —.

2. *diatarassō* [διαταράσσω, 1298], to agitate greatly (*dia*, throughout, and No. 1), is used of the Virgin Mary, Luke 1:29. ¶

NT: B.189b; CB.—; K.—.
OT: —.
GEN. REF.: —.

3. *ektarassō* [ἐκταράσσω, 1613], to throw into great trouble, agitate, is used in Acts 16:20, "do exceedingly trouble (our city)." ¶ In the Sept., Psa. 18:4; 88:16. ¶

NT: B.245b; CB.—; K.—.
OT: bā'at: S.1204; HR.442a.1; H.265; BD.129d.
GEN. REF.: —.

4. *thlibō* [θλίβω, 2346], to afflict, is rendered to trouble in the A.V., e.g., 2 Cor. 4:8 (R.V., "pressed"); 7:5, but never in the R.V.: see AFFLICT, No. 4, PRESS, STRAITENED, TRIBULATION.

NT: B.362a; CB.1272b; K.334.
OT: ṣārar: S.6887; HR.652b.10a-c; H.1973,1974; BD.865c.
lāḥaṣ: S.3905; HR.652b.4; H.1106; BD.537d.
GEN. REF.: —.

5. *enochleō* [ἐνοχλέω, 1776], from *en*, in, *ochlos*, a throng, crowd, is used in Heb. 12:15 of a root of bitterness; in Luke 6:18 (in the best texts; some have *ochleō*), R.V., "were troubled" (A.V., "were vexed"). ¶

NT: B.267b; CB.1245b; K.—.
OT: ḥālāh: S.2470; HR.476b.2; H.655; BD.317c.
GEN. REF.: —.

6. *parenochleō* [παρενοχλέω, 3926], to annoy concerning anything (*para*, and No. 5), occurs in Acts 15:19, "we trouble (not them)." ¶

NT: B.625c; CB.—; K.—.
OT: rāgaz: S.7264; HR.1068c.6; H.2112; BD.919a.
ḥārēd: S.2730; HR.1068c.2; H.735a; BD.353c.
lā'āh: S.3811; HR.1068c.3; H.1066; BD.521a.
GEN. REF.: —.

7. *skullō* [σκύλλω, 4660], primarily to flay, hence, to vex, annoy ("there was a time when the Greek, in thus speaking, compared his trouble to the pains of flaying alive," Moulton, *Proleg*, p. 89), is used in the Active Voice in Mark 5:35; Luke 8:49; in the Passive Voice, Matt. 9:36, in the best texts, R.V., "they were distressed" (some have *ekluō*, A.V., "they fainted"); in the Middle Voice, Luke 7:6, "trouble (not thyself)." ¶ The word is frequent in the papyri.

NT: B.758b; CB.—; K.—.
OT: —.
GEN. REF.: —.

8. *anastatoō* [ἀναστατόω, 387], is rendered "trouble" in Gal. 5:12, A.V.: see STIR, No. 12, TURN, No. 15, UPROAR.

NT: B.61a; CB.—; K.—.
OT: —.
GEN. REF.: —.

9. *thorubeō* [θορυβέω, 2350], akin to *thorubos*, a tumult, in the Middle Voice, to make

an uproar, is rendered "trouble not yourselves" in Acts 20:10, A.V. See ADO, TUMULT.

NT: B.362d; CB.1272b; K.–.
OT: bā'at: S.1204; HR.654a.1; H.265; BD.129d.
rā'al: S.7477; HR.654a.3; H.2188; BD.947a.
GEN. REF.: –.

10. *throeō* [θροέω, 2360], to make an outcry (*throos*, a tumult), is used in the Passive Voice, Matt. 24:6; Mark 13:7; Luke 24:37; 2 Thess. 2:2. ¶ In the Sept., S. of Sol. 5:4. ¶

NT: B.364a; CB.–; K.–.
OT: hāmāh: S.1993; HR.655b.1; H.505; BD.242a.
GEN. REF.: –.

11. *thorubazō* [θορυβάζω, —], to disturb, to trouble (akin to No. 9), is used in Luke 10:41, in the best texts (in some, *turbazō*, with the same meaning). ¶

NT: B.362d; CB.1272b; K.–.
OT: –.
GEN. REF.: –.

12. *adēmoneō* [ἀδημονέω, 85], to be much troubled, distressed (perhaps from *a*, negative, and *dēmōn*, knowing, the compound therefore originally suggesting bewilderment), is translated "sore troubled" in Matt. 26:37 and Mark 14:33, R.V. (A.V., "very heavy"); so the R.V. in Phil. 2:26 (A.V., "full of heaviness"); Lightfoot renders it "distressed," a meaning borne out in the papyri. See HEAVY. ¶

NT: B.16d; CB.–; K.–.
OT: –.
GEN. REF.: –.

13. *diaponeō* [διαπονέω, 1278], denotes to work out with toil, hence, to be "sore troubled"; so the R.V. in Acts 4:2 and 16:18 (A.V., "grieved") Mark 14:4 in some texts. ¶

NT: B.187c; CB.–; K.–.
OT: 'āṣab: S.6087; HR.308a.1; H.1666,1667; BD.780c.
GEN. REF.: –.

Notes: (1) The noun *kopos*, a striking, beating, then, laborious toil, trouble, used with *parechō*, to furnish, to supply, is rendered to trouble (lit., to give trouble to), in Matt. 26:10; Mark 14:6; Luke 11:7; 18:5; Gal. 6:17; the meaning is to embarrass a person by distracting his attention, or to give occasion for anxiety. In the last passage the Apostle expresses his determination not to allow the Judaizing teachers to distract him any further. See LABOUR, A, No. 1.

(2) For "suffer trouble" in 2 Tim. 2:9, see HARDSHIP.

TROW

Note: Some mss. have *dokeō*, to think, in Luke 17:9, A.V., "I trow (not)."

For **TRUCE-BREAKERS** see **IMPLACABLE**

TRUE, TRULY, TRUTH

A. Adjectives.

1. *alēthēs* [ἀληθής, 227], primarily, unconcealed, manifest (*a*, negative, *lēthō*, to forget, = *lanthanō*, to escape notice), hence, actual, true to fact, is used (*a*) of persons, truthful, Matt. 22:16; Mark 12:14; John 3:33; 7:18; 8:26; Rom. 3:4; 2 Cor. 6:8; (*b*) of things, true, conforming to reality, John 4:18, "truly," lit., 'true'; 5:31, 32; in the best texts, 6:55 (twice), "indeed"; 8:13, 14 (ver. 16 in some texts: see No. 2), 17; 10:41; 19:35; 21:24; Acts 12:9; Phil. 4:8; Tit. 1:13; 1 Pet. 5:12; 2 Pet. 2:22; 1 John 2:8, 27; 3 John 12. ¶

NT: B.36c; CB.1234b; K.37.
OT: 'emet: S.571; HR.53c.1; H.116k; BD.54a.
kûn: S.3559; HR.53c.3; H.964; BD.465c.
GEN. REF.: IS.4:926; NB.1301; Z.5:827.

2. *alēthinos* [ἀληθινός, 228], akin to No. 1, denotes true in the sense of real, ideal, genuine; it is used (*a*) of God, John 7:28 (cp. No. 1 in 7:18, above); 17:3; 1 Thess. 1:9; Rev. 6:10; these declare that God fulfils the meaning of His Name, He is "very God," in distinction from all other gods, false gods (*alēthēs*, see John 3:33 in No. 1, signifies that He is veracious, true to His utterances, He cannot lie); (*b*) of Christ, John 1:9; 6:32; 15:1; 1 John 2:8; 5:20 (thrice); Rev. 3:7, 14; 19:11; His judgment, John 8:16 (in the best texts, instead of No. 1); (*c*) God's words, John 4:37; Rev. 19:9; 21:5; 22:6; the last three are equivalent to No. 1; (*d*) His ways, Rev. 15:3; (*e*) His judgments, Rev. 16:7; 19:2; (*f*) His riches, Luke 16:11; (*g*) His worshippers, John 4:23; (*h*) their hearts, Heb. 10:22; (*i*) the witness of the Apostle John, John 19:35; (*j*) the spiritual, antitypical Tabernacle, Heb. 8:2; 9:24, not that the wilderness Tabernacle was false, but that it was a weak and earthly copy of the Heavenly. ¶

NT: B.37a; CB.1234b; K.37.
OT: 'emet: S.571; HR.54a.1c; H.116k; BD.54a.
yāshār: S.3474; HR.54a.2a; H.930; BD.448c.
shālēm: S.8003; HR.54a.4; H.2401; BD.1023d.
GEN. REF.: IS.4:926; NB.1301; Z.5:827.

Note: "*Alēthinos* is related to *alēthēs* as form to contents or substances; *alēthēs* denotes the reality of the thing, *alēthinos* defines the relation of the conception to the thing to which it corresponds = genuine" (Cremer).

3. *gnēsios* [γνήσιος, 1103], primarily lawfully begotten (akin to *ginomai*, to become), hence, true, genuine, sincere, is used in the Apostle's exhortation to his "true yoke-fellow" in Phil. 4:3. See OWN, SINCERITY.

NT: B.162d; CB.1248b; K.125.
OT: –.
GEN. REF.: –.

Note: In the A.V. of 2 Cor. 1:18 and 1 Tim. 3:1, *pistos*, "faithful" (R.V.), is translated "true."

B. Verb.

alētheuō [ἀληθεύω, 226], signifies to deal faithfully or truly with anyone (cp. Gen. 42:16, Sept., "whether ye deal truly or no"), Eph. 4:15, "speaking the truth"; Gal. 3:16, "I tell (you) the truth," where probably the Apostle is referring to the contents of his Epistle. ¶

NT: B.36c; CB.1234b; K.37.
OT: 'emet: S.571; HR.53c.1; H.116k; BD.54a.
shālam: S.7999; HR.53c.4; H.2401c; BD.1023d.
GEN. REF.: IS.4:926; NB.1301; Z.5:827.

C. Noun.

alētheia [ἀλήθεια, 225], truth, is used (*a*) objectively, signifying "the reality lying at the basis of an appearance; the manifested, veritable essence of a matter" (Cremer), e.g., Rom. 9:1; 2 Cor. 11:10; especially of Christian doctrine, e.g., Gal. 2:5, where "the truth of the Gospel" denotes the true teaching of the Gospel, in contrast to perversions of it; Rom. 1:25, where "the truth of God" may be 'the truth concerning God' or 'God whose existence is a verity'; but in Rom. 15:8 "the truth of God" is indicative of His faithfulness in the fulfilment of His promises as exhibited in Christ; the word has an absolute force in John 14:6; 17:17; 18:37, 38; in Eph. 4:21, where the R.V., "even as truth is in Jesus," gives the correct rendering, the meaning is not merely ethical truth, but truth in all its fulness and scope, as embodied in Him; He was the perfect expression of the truth; this is virtually equivalent to His statement in John 14:6; (*b*) subjectively, truthfulness, truth, not merely verbal, but sincerity and integrity of character, John 8:44; 3 John 3, R.V.; (*c*) in phrases, e.g., "in truth" (*epi*, on the basis of), Mark 12:14; Luke 20:21; with *en*, in, 2 Cor. 6:7; Col. 1:6; 1 Tim. 2:7, R.V. (A.V., "in . . . verity"); 1 John 3:18; 2 John 1, 3, 4.

NT: B.35d; CB.1234b; K.37.
OT: 'emet: S.571; HR.53a.2d; H.116k; BD.54a.
GEN. REF.: IS.4:926; NB.1301; Z.5:827.

Note: In Matt. 15:27, A.V., *nai*, "yea" (R.V.), is translated "truth."

D. Adverbs.

1. *alēthōs* [ἀληθῶς, 230], truly, surely, is rendered "of a truth" in Matt. 14:33; 26:73 and Mark 14:70, R.V. (A.V., "surely"); Luke 9:27; 12:44; 21:3; John 6:14; 7:40; 17:8, R.V., "of a truth" (A.V., "surely"); Acts 12:11, R.V. (A.V., "of a surety"); "in truth," 1 Thess. 2:13; "truly," Matt. 27:54; Mark 15:39. See INDEED, No. 3.

NT: B.37b; CB.1234b; K.—.
OT: 'emet: S.571; HR.54b.1e; H.116k; BD.54a.
'āmēn: S.543; HR.54b.1a; H.116b; BD.53b.
'umᵉnāh: S.552; HR.54b.1d; H.116i; BD.53d.
GEN. REF.: IS.4:926; NB.1301; Z.5:827.

2. *gnēsiōs* [γνησίως, 1104], sincerely, honourably (akin to A, No. 3), is rendered "truly" (marg., "genuinely") in Phil. 2:20 (A.V., "naturally"). ¶

NT: B.163a; CB.1248b; K.—.
OT: —.
GEN. REF.: —.

Notes: (1) The particles *ara*, *men*, and *de* are sometimes rendered "truly" in the A.V., but are differently rendered in the R.V.

(2) In 1 Cor. 14:25, A.V., *ontōs* (R.V., "indeed") is rendered "of a truth." See CERTAIN, C, No. 1, INDEED, No. 4.

(3) In John 20:30, A.V., the particle *oun*, therefore (R.V.), is rendered "truly."

TRUMP, TRUMPET

A. Noun.

salpinx [σάλπιγξ, 4536], is used (1) of the natural instrument, 1 Cor. 14:8; (2) of the supernatural accompaniment of Divine interpositions, (*a*) at Sinai, Heb. 12:19; (*b*) of the acts of angels at the Second Advent of Christ, Matt. 24:31; (*c*) of their acts in the period of Divine judgments preceding this, Rev. 8:2, 6, 13; 9:14; (*d*) of a summons to John to the presence of God, Rev. 1:10; 4:1; (*e*) of the act of the Lord in raising from the dead the saints who have fallen asleep and changing the bodies of those who are living, at the Rapture of all to meet Him in the air, 1 Cor. 15:52, where "the last trump" is a military allusion, familiar to Greek readers, and has no connection with the series in Rev. 8:6 to 11:15; there is a possible allusion to Num. 10:2-6, with reference to the same event, 1 Thess. 4:16, "the (lit., a) trump of God" (the absence of the article suggests the meaning 'a trumpet such as is used in God's service'). ¶

NT: B.741a; CB.1268b; K.997.
OT: hᵃṣōṣᵉrāh: S.2689; HR.1258b.1; H.726a; BD.348c.
shôphār: S.7782; HR.1258b.4; H.2449c; BD.1051c.
GEN. REF.: IS.4:439; NB.—; Z.4:320.

B. Verb.

salpizō [σαλπίζω, 4537], to sound a trumpet, Matt. 6:2; as in (2) (*c*) above, Rev. 8:6, 7, 8, 10, 12, 13; 9:1, 13; 10:7; 11:15; as in (2) (*e*), 1 Cor. 15:52. ¶

NT: B.741a; CB.1268b; K.997.
OT: tāqa': S.8628; HR.1258c.3; H.2541; BD.1075b.
GEN. REF.: IS.4:439; NB.—; Z.—.

TRUMPETER

salpistēs [σαλπιστής, 4538], occurs in Rev. 18:22. ¶

NT: B.741b; CB.1268b; K.997.
OT: –.
GEN. REF.: –.

TRUST (Noun and Verb)

A. Noun.

pepoithēsis [πεποίθμσις, 4006], is rendered "trust" in 2 Cor. 3:4, A.V.; see CONFIDENCE, No. 1.

NT: B.643b; CB.1263b; K.818.
OT: biṭṭāḥôn: S.986; HR.1119b.1; H.233c; BD.105c.
GEN. REF.: –.

B. Verbs.

1. *peithō* [πείθω, 3982], intransitively, in the perfect and pluperfect Active, to have confidence, trust, is rendered to trust in Matt. 27:43; Mark 10:24; Luke 11:22; 18:9; 2 Cor. 1:9; 10:7; Phil. 2:24; 3:4, A.V. (R.V., "to have confidence"); Heb. 2:13; in the present middle, Heb. 13:18, A.V. (R.V., "are persuaded"). See AGREE, No. 5, PERSUADE.

NT: B.639a; CB.1263a; K.818.
OT: bāṭaḥ: S.982; HR.1114b.2a; H.233; BD.105a.
beṭaḥ: S.983; HR.1114b.11b; H.233a; BD.105b.
GEN. REF.: IS.4:925; NB.–; Z.–.

2. *pisteuō* [πιστεύω, 4100], to entrust, or, in the Passive Voice, to be entrusted with, is rendered to commit to one's trust, in Luke 16:11; 1 Tim. 1:11; to be put in trust with, 1 Thess. 2:4, A.V. (R.V., "to be intrusted").

NT: B.660b; CB.1265a; K.849.
OT: 'āman: S.539; HR.1137c.1b; H.116; BD.52d.
GEN. REF.: IS.4:925; NB.–; Z.–.

Note: Wherever *elpizō*, to hope, is translated to trust in the A.V., the R.V. substitutes to hope. So *proelpizō*, to hope before. See HOPE.

For TRUTH see TRUE

TRY, TRIED

1. *dokimazō* [δοκιμάζω, 1381], is rendered to try in the A.V. in 1 Cor. 3:13; 1 Thess. 2:4; 1 Pet. 1:7; 1 John 4:1: see PROVE, No. 1.

NT: B.202c; CB.1242a; K.181.
OT: bāḥan: S.974; HR.339c.1; H.230; BD.103c.
GEN. REF.: –.

2. *peirazō* [πειράζω, 3985], is rendered to try in Heb. 11:17; Rev. 2:2, 10; 3:10. In Acts 16:7 it is rendered "assayed"; in 24:6, R.V., "assayed" (A.V., "hath gone about"): see GO, *Note* (2) (*b*). See EXAMINE, PROVE, TEMPT. Cp. *peiraō* in Acts 26:21, R.V., "assayed" (A.V., "went about"); see GO, *Note* (2) (*c*).

NT: B.640b; CB.1263a; K.822.
OT: nāsāh: S.5254; HR.1115c.1; H.1373; BD.650a.
GEN. REF.: –.

Notes: (1) In Rev. 3:18, A.V., *puroō*, in the Passive Voice, to be purified by fire (R.V., "refined"), is rendered "tried."

(2) For *dokimion*, Jas. 1:3, A.V., "trying," see PROOF.

(3) For *dokimos*, Jas. 1:12, A.V., "tried," see APPROVED.

(4) In 1 Pet. 4:12, A.V., the phrase *pros peirasmon*, lit., 'for trial,' i.e., for testing, is rendered "to try (you)," R.V., "to prove (you)."

TUMULT

1. *akatastasia* [ἀκαταστασία, 181], is rendered "tumults" in Luke 21:9, R.V.; 2 Cor. 6:5; 12:20. See CONFOUND, A, No. 1.

NT: B.30a; CB.1234b; K.387.
OT: midḥeh: S.4072; HR.44a.1; H.420b; BD.191c.
GEN. REF.: –.

2. *thorubos* [θόρυβος, 2351], a noise, uproar, tumult, is rendered "tumult" in Matt. 27:24 and Mark 5:38; in Matt. 26:5, R.V. (A.V., "uproar"), so in Mark 14:2; in Acts 20:1, "uproar," A.V. and R.V.; in 24:18, "tumult"; in 21:34, A.V., "tumult" (R.V., "uproar"). ¶

NT: B.363a; CB.1272b; K.–.
OT: hāmôn: S.1995; HR.654a.2; H.505a; BD.242b.
tᵉrû'āh: S.8643; HR.654a.6; H.2135b; BD.929d.
GEN. REF.: –.

Note: For *thorubeō*, R.V., to make a tumult, see NOISE, *Note* (2).

TURN

1. *strephō* [στρέφω, 4762], denotes (1) in the Active Voice, (*a*) to turn (something), Matt. 5:39; (*b*) to bring back, Matt. 27:3 (in the best texts; some have No. 2); (*c*) reflexively, to turn oneself, to turn the back to people, said of God, Acts 7:42; (*d*) to turn one thing into another, Rev. 11:6 (the only place where this word occurs after the Acts); (2) in the Passive Voice, (*a*) used reflexively, to turn oneself, e.g., Matt. 7:6; John 20:14, 16; (*b*) metaphorically, Matt. 18:3, R.V., "(except) ye turn" (A.V., ". . . be converted"); John 12:40 (in the best texts; some have No. 4). See CONVERT, A, No. 1.

NT: B.771a; CB.1270b; K.1093.
OT: hāphak: S.2015; HR.1296c.3; H.512; BD.245b.
sābab: S.5437; HR.1296c.4; H.1456; BD.685b.
shûb: S.7725; HR.1296c.7; H.2340; BD.996d.
GEN. REF.: –.

2. *apostrephō* [ἀποστρέφω, 654], denotes (*a*) to cause to turn away (*apo*), to remove, Rom. 11:26; 2 Tim 4:4 (1st clause); metaphorically, to turn away from allegiance, pervert, Luke 23:14; (*b*) to make to return, put back, Matt. 26:52; (*c*) in the Passive Voice, used reflexively, to turn oneself away from, Matt. 5:42; 2 Tim. 1:15; Tit. 1:14; Heb. 12:25; in the Active Voice, Acts 3:26. See PERVERT, PUT. ¶

NT: B.100b; CB.1237a; K.1093.
OT: shûb: S.7725; HR.145b.24a,b; H.2340; BD.996d.
sātar: S.5641; HR.145b.16b; H.1551; BD.711b.
GEN. REF.: –.

3. *diastrephō* [διαστρέφω, 1294], to distort (*dia*, asunder), is rendered "to turn aside," R.V. (A.V., ". . . away"), in Acts 13:8. See PERVERT, No. 2.

NT: B.189a; CB.—; K.1093.
OT: ʿāwat: S.5791; HR.312a.6; H.1591; BD.736c.
ʿāqash: S.6140; HR.312a.9a; H.1684; BD.786a.
tahpukāh: S.8419; HR.312a.1d; H.512f; BD.246c.
GEN. REF.: —.

4. *epistrephō* [ἐπιστρέφω, 1994], is used (*a*) transitively, to make to turn towards (*epi*), Luke 1:16, 17; Jas. 5:19, 20 (to convert); (*b*) intransitively, to turn oneself round, e.g., in the Passive Voice, Mark 5:30 (see RETURN); in the Active Voice, Matt. 13:15, R.V., "turn again" (A.V., "be converted"); Acts 11:21; 14:15; 15:19; 1 Thess. 1:9, "ye turned," the aorist tense indicating an immediate and decisive change, consequent upon a deliberate choice; conversion is a voluntary act in response to the presentation of truth. See CONVERT.

NT: B.301a; CB.1246a; K.1093.
OT: sābab: S.5437; HR.531a.12a-c; H.1456; BD.685b.
pānāh: S.6437; HR.531a.16a; H.1782; BD.815a.
shûb: S.7725; HR.531a.18a-c; H.2340; BD.996d.
GEN. REF.: —.

5. *metastrephō* [μεταστρέφω, 3344], signifies, in the Passive Voice, to be turned (of a change into something different, *meta*), in Acts 2:20 and Jas. 4:9: see PERVERT, No. 3.

NT: B.513b; CB.—; K.1093.
OT: hāphak: S.2015; HR.916c.1; H.512; BD.245b.
GEN. REF.: —.

6. *hupostrephō* [ὑποστρέφω, 5290], is used intransitively of turning back, behind (*hupo*), e.g., Luke 17:15, "turned back"; in 2:45, R.V., "returned": see RETURN.

NT: B.847a; CB.—; K.—.
OT: shûb: S.7725; HR.1417b.4; H.2340; BD.996d.
GEN. REF.: —.

7. *apobainō* [ἀποβαίνω, 576], to go from, is used metaphorically of events, to issue, turn out, Luke 21:13; Phil. 1:19. See GO, No. 21.

NT: B.88c; CB.—; K.—.
OT: —.
GEN. REF.: —.

8. *metagō* [μετάγω, 3329], to move from one side to another, is rendered to turn about in Jas. 3:3, 4. ¶

NT: B.510d; CB.—; K.—.
OT: —.
GEN. REF.: —.

9. *metatithēmi* [μετατίθημι, 3346], to change, is translated "turning (the grace of God)" in Jude 4. See CARRY, CHANGE, REMOVE, TRANSLATE.

NT: B.513c; CB.1258c; K.1176.
OT: sûg: S.5472; HR.917a.3; H.1469; BD.690d.
sût: S.5496; HR.917a.4; H.1481; BD.694c.
GEN. REF.: —.

10. *anakamptō* [ἀνακάμπτω, 344], *ana*, back, *kamptō*, to bend, is rendered "shall turn . . . again," in Luke 10:6. See RETURN.

NT: B.55c; CB.—; K.—.
OT: shûb: S.7725; HR.78b.2; H.2340; BD.996d.
GEN. REF.: —.

11. *ektrepō* [ἐκτρέπω, 1624], to cause to turn aside (*ek*, from, *trepō*, to turn), is used in the Passive Voice, with Middle sense, in 1 Tim. 1:6; 5:15; 6:20, R.V., "turning away" (A.V., "avoiding"); 2 Tim. 4:4 (2nd clause); Heb. 12:13, "be (not) turned out of the way" (R.V., marg., "put out of joint"); some adhere to the meaning to turn aside, go astray; the interpretation depends on the antithesis which follows, "but rather be healed" (R.V.), which is not the antithesis to turning aside or being turned out of the way; accordingly the marg. is to be preferred (the verb is often used medically). ¶ In the Sept., Amos 5:8. ¶

NT: B.246b; CB.1244a; K.—.
OT: hāphak: S.2015; HR.443c.1; H.512; BD.245b.
GEN. REF.: —.

12. *apotrepō* [ἀποτρέπω, 665], to cause to turn away (*apo*), is used in the Middle Voice in 2 Tim. 3:5. ¶

NT: B.101c; CB.1237b; K.—.
OT: —.
GEN. REF.: —.

13. *peritrepō* [περιτρέπω, 4062], to turn about (*peri*), is rendered "doth turn (thee to madness)" in Acts 26:24, R.V., A.V., "doth make (thee mad)." ¶

NT: B.653a; CB.—; K.—.
OT: —.
GEN. REF.: —.

14. *methistēmi* [μεθίστημι, 3179], is used metaphorically in Acts 19:26, "turned away (much people)." See PUT, REMOVE, TRANSLATE.

NT: B.498d; CB.—; K.—.
OT: sûr: S.5493; HR.907b.4; H.1480; BD.693b.
ʿadāh (Aramaic): S.5709; HR.907b.5; H.2898; BD.1105b.
GEN. REF.: —.

15. *anastatoō* [ἀναστατόω, 387], to stir up, excite, unsettle (*ana*, up, *histēmi*, to cause to stand), is rendered "have turned (the world) upside down" in Acts 17:6. See TROUBLE, UPROAR.

NT: B.61a; CB.—; K.—.
OT: —.
GEN. REF.: —.

16. *ginomai* [γίνομαι, 1096], to become, is rendered "shall be turned" in John 16:20 (of sorrow into joy).

NT: B.158a; CB.1248b; K.117.
OT: —.
GEN. REF.: —.

17. *ekklinō* [ἐκκλίνω, 1578], to turn aside (*ek*, from, *klinō*, to lean), is rendered "have . . . turned aside" in Rom. 3:12 (A.V., "are . . . gone out of the way"); 16:17, R.V., "turn away" (A.V., "avoid"); 1 Pet. 3:11, R.V., ditto (A.V., "eschew"). ¶

NT: B.241c; CB.—; K.—.
OT: nāṭāh: S.5186; HR.433c.11a,b; H.1352; BD.639d.
sûr: S.5493; HR.433c.15; H.1480; BD.693b.
GEN. REF.: —.

16. *diadechomai* [διαδέχομαι, 1237], to receive through another, to receive in turn (*dia*,

through, *dechomai*, to receive), occurs in Acts 7:45, R.V., "in their turn . . . when they entered" (A.V., "that came after"); the meaning here is 'having received (it) after,' i.e., as from Moses under Joshua's leadership. In the papyri the word is used similarly of visiting as deputy (see also Field, *Notes on the Trans. of the N.T.*, 116). ¶

NT: B.182c; CB.–; K.–.
OT: mishneh: S.4932; HR.300a.1; H.2421c; BD.1041c.
GEN. REF.: –.

Notes: (1) In Matt. 2:22, A.V., *anachōreō*, to retire, withdraw, is rendered "turned aside" (R.V., "withdrew").

(2) For "turned to flight," *klinō*, Heb. 11:34, see FLIGHT, B.

(3) For the phrase "by turn" in 1 Cor. 14:27 see COURSE, B, *Note* (3).

TURNING

tropē [τροπή, 5157], used especially of the revolution of the heavenly orbs (akin to *trepō*, to turn), occurs in Jas. 1:17, "(neither shadow) that is cast by turning," R.V. (A.V., "of turning"). For a more detailed treatment of the passage, see SHADOW, No. 2. ¶

NT: B.827a; CB.–; K.–.
OT: –.
GEN. REF.: –.

For **TURTLE-DOVE** see **DOVE**

For **TUTOR** see **GUARDIAN** and **INSTRUCTOR**, No. 1.

TWAIN, TWO

duo [δύο, 1417], is rendered "twain" in Matt. 5:41; 19:5, 6; 21:31; 27:21, 51; Mark 10:8 (twice); 15:38; in 1 Cor. 6:16 and Eph. 5:31, R.V. (A.V., "two"); Eph. 2:15; in Rev. 19:20, R.V. (A.V., "both").

NT: B.209c; CB.1242b; K.148,192.
OT: shᵉnayim: S.8147; HR.–; H.2421a; BD.1040d.
GEN. REF.: IS.3:558; NB.–; Z.–.

Notes: (1) In the following phrases the numeral is used distributively: (*a*) *ana duo*, "two apiece," John 2:6 (in some mss., Luke 9:3); in Luke 10:1, "two and two" ('by twos'); (*b*) *kata duo*, "by two," 1 Cor. 14:27; (*c*) *duo duo*, "by two and two," lit., 'two (and) two,' Mark 6:7 (not a Hebraism; the form of expression is used in the papyri); (*d*) *eis duo*, 'into two,' "in twain," Matt. 27:51 and Mark 15:38 (see above).

(2) In Luke 17:34 *duo* stands for "two men"; in ver. 35 for "two women."

TWELFTH

dōdekatos [δωδέκατος, 1428], occurs in Rev. 21:20. ¶

NT: B.210b; CB.–; K.192.
OT: shᵉnêm, 'āsar: S.8147; HR.358b.1; H.2421a; BD.1040d, 1041b.
GEN. REF.: IS.3:560; NB.–; Z.–.

TWELVE

dōdeka [δώδεκα, 1427], is used frequently in the Gospels for the twelve Apostles, and in Acts 6:2; 1 Cor. 15:5; Rev. 21:14b; of the tribes of Israel, Matt. 19:28; Luke 22:30; Jas. 1:1; Rev. 21:12c (cp. 7:5-8; 12:1); in various details relating to the Heavenly Jerusalem, Rev. 21:12-21; 22:2. The number in general is regarded as suggestive of Divine administration.

NT: B.210a; CB.1242a; K.192.
OT: shᵉnêm, 'āsar: S.8147; HR.–; H.2421a; BD.1040d, 1041b.
GEN. REF.: IS.3:560; NB.–; Z.–.

TWENTY

eikosi [εἴκοσι, 1501], occurs in Luke 14:31; John 6:19; Acts 1:15; 27:28; 1 Cor. 10:8; of the four and twenty elders, in Rev. 4:4 (twice), 10; 5:8; 11:16; 19:4 (combined in one numeral with *tessares*, four, in some mss.). ¶

NT: B.222a; CB.1243a; K.–.
OT: 'esrîm: S.6242; HR.–; H.1711e; BD.797d.
GEN. REF.: –.

TWICE

dis [δίσ, 1364], occurs in Mark 14:30, 72; Luke 18:12; Jude 12; combined with *muriades*, ten thousand, in Rev. 9:16; rendered "again" in Phil. 4:16 and 1 Thess. 2:18. See AGAIN. ¶

NT: B.199d; CB.–; K.–.
OT: paᶜᵃmayim: S.6471; HR.337b.1a; H.1793a; BD.821d, 822a.
GEN. REF.: –.

TWINKLING

rhipē [ῥιπή, 4493], akin to *rhiptō*, to hurl, was used of any rapid movement, e.g., the throw of a javelin, the rush of wind or flame; in 1 Cor. 15:52 of the twinkling of an eye. ¶

NT: B.736b; CB.1268b; K.–.
OT: –.
GEN. REF.: –.

For **TWO** see **TWAIN**

TWO-EDGED

distomos [δίστομος, 1366], lit., 'two-mouthed' (*dis*, and *stoma*, a mouth), was used of rivers and branching roads; in the N.T. of swords, Heb. 4:12; Rev. 1:16; 2:12, R.V., "two-edged" (A.V., "with two edges"). ¶ In the Sept., Judg. 3:16; Psa. 149:6; Prov. 5:4. ¶

NT: B.200a; CB.1242a; K.–.
OT: piyyôt: S.6310; HR.337b.2; H.1738; BD.804d, 805b.
GEN. REF.: –.

For TWOFOLD MORE see DOUBLE

TWO HUNDRED

diakosioi [διακόσιοι, 1250], occurs in Mark 6:37; John 6:7; 21:8; Acts 23:23 (twice); 27:37, "two hundred (threescore and sixteen)"; Rev. 11:3, "(a thousand) two hundred (and threescore)"; so 12:6. ¶

NT: B.185a; CB.–; K.–.
OT: –.
GEN. REF.: –.

Note: In Acts 27:37, some ancient authorities read "about three-score and sixteen souls" (R.V., margin). The confusion was quite natural when the word *diakosioi* was not written in full but represented by one Greek letter. The larger number is by no means improbable: Josephus sailed for Rome in A.D. 63 in a ship which had 600 on board (*Life*, ch. 3).

For TWO THOUSAND see THOUSAND, *Note* (1)

U

For UNAPPROACHABLE, 1 Tim. 6:16, R.V., see APPROACH, B

UNAWARES

Notes: (1) In Heb. 13:2, *lanthanō*, to escape notice, is used with the aorist participle of *xenizō*, to entertain, signifying "entertained . . . unawares" (an idiomatic usage common in classical Greek).

(2) For *aiphnidios*, "unawares," in Luke 21:34, A.V., see SUDDENLY.

(3) In Gal. 2:4, A.V., *pareisaktos*, brought in secretly, is rendered "unawares brought in." See PRIVILY, *Note*: cp. BRING, No. 17. ¶

(4) In Jude 4, A.V., *pareisdunō*, to slip in secretly, is rendered "crept in unawares." See CREEP, A, No. 2. ¶

UNBELIEF

1. *apistia* [ἀπιστία, 570], "unbelief" 12 times, but see BELIEF, C, *Note* (2) for references.

NT: B.85c; CB.1236c; K.849.
OT: –.
GEN. REF.: IS.4:942; NB.1304; Z.–.

2. *apeitheia* [ἀπείθεια, 543], is always rendered "disobedience" in the R.V.; in Rom. 11:30, 32 and Heb. 4:6, 11, A.V., "unbelief." See DISOBEDIENCE, A, No. 1.

NT: B.82c; CB.1236b; K.818.
OT: –.
GEN. REF.: IS.4:942; NB.1304; Z.–.

UNBELIEVER

apistos [ἄπιστος, 571], an adjective, is used as a noun, rendered "unbeliever" in 2 Cor. 6:15 and 1 Tim. 5:8, R.V.; plural in 1 Cor. 6:6 and 2 Cor. 6:14; A.V. only, Luke 12:46 (R.V., "unfaithful"). See BELIEF, C, *Note* (3), FAITHLESS, INCREDIBLE.

NT: B.85d; CB.1236c; K.849.
OT: –.
GEN. REF.: IS.4:942; NB.–; Z.–.

UNBELIEVING

A. Adjective.

apistos [ἄπιστος, —]: see BELIEF, C, *Note* (3).

B. Verb.

apeitheō [ἀπειθέω, —]: see DISBELIEVE, DISOBEDIENT, C.

UNBLAMEABLE, UNBLAMEABLY

A. Adjectives.

1. *amemptos* [ἄμεμπτος, 273], "unblameable" (from *a*, negative, and *memphomai*, to find fault), is so rendered in 1 Thess. 3:13, i.e., free from all valid charge. See BLAME, B, No. 3.

NT: B.45a; CB.1234c; K.–.
OT: tām: S.8535; HR.65b.6,7; H.2522c; BD.1070d.
GEN. REF.: –.

2. *amōmos* [ἄμωμος, —]: see BLEMISH, B.

B. Adverb.

amemptōs [ἀμέμπτως, 274], is used in 1 Thess. 2:10, "unblameably," signifying that no charge could be maintained, whatever charges might be made. See BLAME, C.

NT: B.45a; CB.1234c; K.–.
OT: –.
GEN. REF.: –.

For UNCEASING see CEASE, B. For UNCEASINGLY, R.V., in Rom. 1:9, see CEASE, C

UNCERTAIN, UNCERTAINLY, UNCERTAINTY

A. Adjective.

adēlos [ἄδηλος, 82], denotes (*a*) unseen; with the article, translated "which appear not" (*a*, negative, *dēlos*, evident), Luke 11:44; (*b*) "uncertain," indistinct, 1 Cor. 14:8. ¶ In the Sept., Ps. 51:6. ¶

NT: B.16c; CB.—; K.—.
OT: —.
GEN. REF.: IS.4:942; NB.—; Z.—.

B. Adverb.

adēlōs [ἀδήλως, 84], uncertainly (akin to A), occurs in 1 Cor. 9:26. ¶

NT: B.16d; CB.1233a; K.—.
OT: —.
GEN. REF.: IS.4:942; NB.—; Z.—.

C. Noun.

adēlotēs [ἀδηλότης, 83], uncertainty (akin to A and B), occurs in 1 Tim. 6:17, "(the) uncertainty (of riches)," R.V. (the A.V. translates it as an adjective, "uncertain"), i.e., riches the special character of which is their uncertainty; the Greek phrase is a rhetorical way of stressing the noun "riches"; when a genitive (here "of riches") precedes the governing noun (here "uncertainty") the genitive receives emphasis. ¶

NT: B.16d; CB.—; K.—.
OT: —.
GEN. REF.: IS.4:942; NB.—; Z.—.

UNCHANGEABLE

aparabatos [ἀπαράβατος, 531], is used of the priesthood of Christ, in Heb. 7:24, "unchangeable," unalterable, inviolable, R.V., marg. (a meaning found in the papyri); the more literal meaning in A.V. and R.V. margins, "that doth not pass from one to another," is not to be preferred. This active meaning is not only untenable, and contrary to the constant usage of the word, but does not adequately fit with either the preceding or the succeeding context. ¶

NT: B.80d; CB.1236b; K.772.
OT: —.
GEN. REF.: —.

For UNCIRCUMCISED and UNCIRCUMCISION see CIRCUMCISION

UNCLEAN

A. Adjectives.

1. *akathartos* [ἀκάθαρτος, 169], unclean, impure (*a*, negative, *kathairō*, to purify), is used (*a*) of unclean spirits, frequently in the Synoptists, not in John's Gospel; in Acts 5:16; 8:7; Rev. 16:13; 18:2a (in the 2nd clause the birds are apparently figurative of destructive Satanic agencies); (*b*) ceremonially, Acts 10:14, 28; 11:8; 1 Cor. 7:14; (*c*) morally, 2 Cor. 6:17, including (*b*), R.V.; "no unclean thing"; Eph. 5:5; Rev. 17:4, R.V., "the unclean things" (A.V. follows the texts which have the noun *akathartēs*, "the filthiness").

NT: B.29a; CB.1234b; K.381.
OT: ṭāmēʼ: S.2931; HR.42c.3a-c; H.809a; BD.379d.
GEN. REF.: IS.1:718; NB.238; Z.5:842.

2. *koinos* [κοινός, 2839], common, is translated "unclean" in Rom. 14:14 (thrice); in Rev. 21:27, R.V. (A.V., "that defileth," follows the inferior texts which have the verb *koinoō:* see B). See COMMON, DEFILE, C, UNHOLY, No. 2.

NT: B.438a; CB.1255b; K.447.
OT: ḥeber: S.2267; HR.775a.2; H.598a; BD.288c.
GEN. REF.: IS.1:718; NB.—; Z.5:842.

B. Verb.

koinoō [κοινόω, 2840], to make *koinos*, to defile, is translated "unclean" in Heb. 9:13, A.V., where the perfect participle, Passive, is used with the article, hence the R.V., "them that have been defiled." See DEFILE, A, No. 1.

NT: B.438b; CB.1255b; K.447.
OT: —.
GEN. REF.: IS.1:718; NB.—; Z.5:842.

C. Noun.

akatharsia [ἀκαθαρσία, 167], akin to A, No. 1, denotes uncleanness, (*a*) physical, Matt. 23:27 (instances in the papyri speak of tenants keeping houses in good condition); (*b*) moral, Rom. 1:24; 6:19; 2 Cor. 12:21; Gal. 5:19; Eph. 4:19; 5:3; Col. 3:5; 1 Thess. 2:3 (suggestive of the fact that sensuality and evil doctrine are frequently associated); 4:7. ¶

NT: B.28d; CB.1234b; K.381.
OT: ṭumʼāh: S.2932; HR.42b.1d; H.809b; BD.380a.
GEN. REF.: IS.1:718; NB.238; Z.5:842.

Note: In 2 Pet. 2:10, A.V., *miasmos*, a defilement, is rendered "uncleanness"; see DEFILEMENT, B, No. 2. ¶

For UNCLOTHED see STRIP

UNCOMELY

aschēmōn [ἀσχήμων, 809], shapeless (*a*, negative, *schēma*, a form), the opposite of *euschēmōn*, comely, is used in 1 Cor. 12:23. ¶ In the Sept., Gen. 34:7; Deut. 24:3. ¶

NT: B.119b; CB.1238a; K.—.
OT: nᵉbālāh: S.5039; HR.175a.1; H.1285b; BD.615a.
ʻerᵉwāh: S.6172; HR.175a.2; H.1692b; BD.788d.
GEN. REF.: —.

Note: For the verb *aschēmoneō*, rendered to behave oneself uncomely in 1 Cor. 7:36, A.V., see BEHAVE, No. 4.

UNCONDEMNED

akatakritos [ἀκατάκριτος, 178], rendered "uncondemned" in Acts 16:37; 22:25 (*a*, negative, *katakrinō*, to condemn), properly means 'without trial,' not yet tried. Sir W. M. Ramsay points out that the Apostle, in claiming his rights, would probably use the Roman phrase *re incognita*, i.e., 'without investigating our case' (*The Cities of St. Paul*, p. 225). ¶

NT: B.29d; CB.–; K.–.
OT: –.
GEN. REF.: –.

For **UNCORRUPTIBLE** see **CORRUPT**, C, No. 2. For **UNCORRUPTNESS**, see **CORRUPT**, B, No. 4

UNCOVER

apostegazō [ἀποστεγάζω, 648], signifies to unroof (*apo*, from, *stegē*, a roof), Mark 2:4. ¶

NT: B.98c; CB.–; K.–.
OT: –.
GEN. REF.: –.

For **UNCOVERED,** 1 Cor. 11:5, 13, see **UNVEILED**

For **UNCTION** see **ANOINT**, B

UNDEFILED

amiantos [ἀμίαντος, 283], undefiled, free from contamination (*a*, negative, *miainō*, to defile), is used (*a*) of Christ, Heb. 7:26; (*b*) of pure religion, Jas. 1:27; (*c*) of the eternal inheritance of believers, 1 Pet. 1:4; (*d*) of the marriage bed as requiring to be free from unlawful sexual intercourse, Heb. 13:4. ¶

NT: B.46b; CB.1234c; K.593.
OT: –.
GEN. REF.: IS.4:945; NB.–; Z.–.

UNDER, UNDERNEATH

1. *hupokatō* [ὑποκάτω, 5270], an adverb signifying under, is used as a preposition and rendered "under" in Mark 6:11; 7:28; Luke 8:16; Heb. 2:8; Rev. 5:3, 13; 6:9; 12:1; "underneath" in Matt. 22:44, R.V. (Mark 12:36 in some mss.); John 1:50, R.V., (A.V., "under"). ¶

NT: B.844d; CB.–; K.–.
OT: taḥat: S.8478; HR.1413c.2a; H.2504; BD.1065a.
GEN. REF.: –.

2. *katōterō* [κατωτέρω, 2736], the comparative degree of *katō*, below, beneath, occurs in Matt. 2:16, "under."

NT: B.425b; CB.1254c; K.–.
OT: taḥat: S.8478; HR.756c.2; H.2504; BD.1065a.
maṭṭāh: S.4295; HR.756c.1a; H.1352a; BD.641b.
GEN. REF.: –.

3. *elasson* [ἔλασσον, 1640], the neuter of the adjective *elassōn*, less, is used adverbially in 1 Tim. 5:9, "under" (or 'less than'). See LESS.

NT: B.248a; CB.–; K.–.
OT: –.
GEN. REF.: –.

Notes: (1) The preposition *epi*, upon, is rendered "under" in Heb. 7:11; 9:15; 10:28, A.V. (R.V., "on *the word of*").

(2) The preposition *en*, in, is rendered "under" in Matt. 7:6; Rom. 3:19 (1st part).

(3) The usual preposition is *hupo*.

UNDERGIRD

hupozōnnumi [ὑποζώννυμι, 5269], *hupo*, under, *zōnnumi*, to gird, is used of frapping a ship, Acts 27:17, bracing the timbers of a vessel by means of strong ropes. ¶

NT: B.844d; CB.–; K.–.
OT: –.
GEN. REF.: IS.4:945; NB.–; Z.–.

UNDERSTAND, UNDERSTOOD

A. Verbs.

1. *suniēmi* [συνίημι, 4920], primarily, to bring or set together, is used metaphorically of perceiving, understanding, uniting (*sun*), so to speak, the perception with what is perceived, e.g., Matt. 13:13-15, 19, 23, 51; 15:10; 16:12; 17:13, and similar passages in Mark and Luke; Acts 7:25 (twice); 28:26, 27; in Rom. 3:11, the present participle, with the article, is used as a noun, lit., 'there is not the understanding (one),' in a moral and spiritual sense; Rom. 15:21; 2 Cor. 10:12, R.V., "are (without) understanding," A.V., "are (not) wise"; Eph. 5:17, R.V., "understand." See CONSIDER, *Note* (2).

NT: B.790a; CB.1270c; K.1119.
OT: sākal: S.7919; HR.1316b.6b; H.2263,2264; BD.968a.
bîn: S.995; HR.1316b.1; H.239; BD.106c.
GEN. REF.: IS.4:945; NB.–; Z.–.

2. *noeō* [νοέω, 3539], to perceive, with the mind, as distinct from perception by feeling, is so used in Matt. 15:17, A.V., "understand," R.V., "perceive"; 16:9, 11; 24:15 (here rather perhaps in the sense of considering) and parallels in Mark (not in Luke); John 12:40; Rom. 1:20; 1 Tim. 1:7; Heb. 11:3; in Eph. 3:4, A.V., "may understand" (R.V., "can perceive"); 3:20, "think"; 2 Tim. 2:7, "consider." See CONSIDER, No. 4. ¶

NT: B.540b; CB.1259c; K.636.
OT: bîn: S.995; HR.946a.1; H.239; BD.106c.
sākal: S.7919; HR.946a.4; H.2263,2264; BD.968a.
GEN. REF.: IS.4:945; NB.–; Z.–.

3. *ginōskō* [γινώσκω, 1097], to know, to come to know, is translated to understand in the A.V. in Matt. 26:10 and John 8:27 (R.V., to perceive); A.V. and R.V. in John 8:43; 10:6; in 10:38, R.V. (in some texts *pisteuō*, A.V.,

"believe"); A.V. and R.V. in 12:16; 13:7, R.V., A.V., "know" (see *Note* under KNOW, No. 2); Acts 8:30; in Phil. 1:12, A.V., R.V., "know" (in some texts, Acts 24:11, A.V.). See KNOW, No. 1.

NT: B.160c; CB.1248b; K.119.
OT: yāda': S.3045; HR.267a.4; H.848; BD.393b.
GEN. REF.: IS.4:945; NB.—; Z.—.

4. *epistamai* [ἐπίσταμαι, 1987], to know well, is rendered to understand in Mark 14:68; Jude 10, R.V., and clause (A.V., "know"). See KNOW, No. 5.

NT: B.300a; CB.1246a; K.—.
OT: yāda': S.3045; HR.529b.2a; H.848; BD.393b.
GEN. REF.: IS.4:945; NB.—; Z.—.

5. *punthanomai* [πυνθάνομαι, 4441], to inquire, is rendered to understand in Acts 23:34. See INQUIRE.

NT: B.729c; CB.—; K.—.
OT: dārash: S.1875; HR.1242b.1; H.455; BD.205a.
GEN. REF.: —.

6. *gnōrizō* [γνωρίζω, 1107], to make known, is rendered "I give . . . to understand" in 1 Cor. 12:3. See KNOW, No. 8.

NT: B.163b; CB.1248b; K.119.
OT: yāda': S.3045; HR.273a.2; H.848; BD.393b.
GEN. REF.: IS.4:945; NB.—; Z.—.

7. *agnoeō* [ἀγνοέω, 50], to be ignorant, is rendered "they understood not" in Mark 9:32; Luke 9:45; in 2 Pet. 2:12, A.V., R.V., "they are ignorant of." See IGNORANT, B, No. 1.

NT: B.11a; CB.—; K.18.
OT: shāgāh: S.7686; HR.16a.6; H.2325; BD.993a.
shāgag: S.7683; HR.16a.5; H.2324; BD.992d.
GEN. REF.: —.

Notes: (1) In 1 Cor. 13:2, A.V., *oida*, to know, to perceive, is rendered "understand" (R.V., "know"); so in 14:16.

(2) For *manthanō*, rendered "understand" in Acts 23:27, A.V., see LEARN, No. 1.

(3) In 1 Cor. 13:11, A.V., *phroneō*, to be minded, is rendered "I understood" (R.V., "I felt").

(4) For *parakoloutheō*, Luke 1:3, A.V., "have perfect understanding of," see TRACE.

B. Adjectives.

1. *eusēmos* [εὔσημος, 2154], primarily denotes conspicuous or glorious (as in Ps. 81:3, Sept.; E.V., "solemn" ¶), then, distinct, clear to understanding, 1 Cor. 14:9, "easy to be understood" (A.V., marg., "significant"). ¶

NT: B.326c; CB.—; K.278.
OT: —.
GEN. REF.: —.

2. *dusnoētos* [δυσνόητος, 1425], hard to be understood (*dus*, a prefix like Eng., *mis-* or *un-*, and A, No. 2), occurs in 2 Pet. 3:16. ¶

NT: B.209d; CB.1242c; K.636.
OT: —.
GEN. REF.: —.

UNDERSTANDING

A. Nouns.

1. *nous* [νοῦς, 3563], for which see MIND, No. 1, is translated "understanding" in Luke 24:45, A.V. (R.V., "mind"); 1 Cor. 14:14, 15 (twice), 19; Phil. 4:7; Rev. 13:18.

NT: B.544c; CB.1260a; K.636.
OT: lēbāb: S.3824; HR.950c.2; H.1071a; BD.523a.
'ōzen: S.241; HR.950c.1; H.57a; BD.23d.
GEN. REF.: IS.4:945; NB.—; Z.—.

2. *sunesis* [σύνεσις, 4907], akin to *suniēmi*, to set together, to understand, denotes (*a*) the understanding, the mind or intelligence, Mark 12:33; (*b*) understanding, reflective thought, Luke 2:47; 1 Cor. 1:19, R.V., "prudence"; Eph. 3:4, R.V. (A.V., "knowledge"); Col. 1:9; 2:2; 2 Tim. 2:7 ¶ See PRUDENCE, No. 2.

NT: B.788c; CB.1270c; K.1119.
OT: bînāh: S.998; HR.1314a.1c; H.239b; BD.108a.
tᵉbûnāh: S.8394; HR.1314a.1d; H.239c; BD.108a.
GEN. REF.: IS.4:945; NB.—; Z.—.

3. *dianoia* [διάνοια, 1271], for which see MIND, No. 2, is rendered "understanding" in Eph. 4:18; 1 John 5:20 (in some texts, Eph. 1:18, A.V., for *kardia*, "heart," R.V.).

NT: B.187a; CB.1241b; K.636.
OT: lēbāb: S.3824; HR.306c.3b; H.1071a; BD.523a.
lēb: S.3820; HR.306c.3a; H.1071a; BD.524b.
GEN. REF.: IS.4:945; NB.—; Z.—.

B. Adjective.

asunetos [ἀσύνετος, 801], without understanding or discernment (*a*, negative, *sunetos*, intelligent, understanding), is translated "without understanding" in Matt. 15:16; Mark 7:18; Rom. 1:31; 10:19, R.V., "void of understanding" (A.V., "foolish"); in Rom. 1:21, R.V., "senseless" (A.V., "foolish"). ¶

NT: B.118c; CB.1238a; K.1119.
OT: nābāl: S.5036; HR.174a.2; H.1285a; BD.614d.
kᵉsîl: S.3684; HR.174a.1; H.1011c,e; BD.493a.
GEN. REF.: IS.4:945; NB.—; Z.—.

Note: In 1 Cor. 14:20, A.V., *phrēn*, the mind, is translated "understanding" (twice), R.V., "mind."

For **UNDONE (leave)** see **LEAVE**, No. 1

UNDRESSED

agnaphos [ἄγναφος, 46], uncarded (*a*, negative, *knaptō*, to card wool), is rendered "undressed," of cloth, in Matt. 9:16 and Mark 2:21, R.V. (A.V., "new"). ¶

NT: B.10d; CB.—; K.—.
OT: —.
GEN. REF.: —.

For **UNEQUALLY** see **YOKED**

UNFAITHFUL

apistos [ἄπιστος, 571], unbelieving, faithless, is translated "unfaithful" in Luke 12:46, R.V. (A.V., "unbelievers"). See BELIEF, C, *Note* (3), FAITHLESS, INCREDIBLE.

NT: B.85d; CB.1236c; K.849.
OT: –.
GEN. REF.: IS.2:276; NB.–; Z.–.

For **UNFEIGNED** see **DISSIMULATION**, C

For **UNFRUITFUL** see **FRUIT**, B, No. 2

UNGODLINESS, UNGODLY

A. Noun.

asebeia [ἀσέβεια, 763], impiety, ungodliness, is used of (*a*) general impiety, Rom. 1:18; 11:26; 2 Tim. 2:16; Tit. 2:12; (*b*) ungodly deeds, Jude 15, R.V., "works of ungodliness"; (*c*) of lusts or desires after evil things, Jude 18. It is the opposite of *eusebeia*, godliness. ¶

NT: B.114c; CB.1238a; K.1010.
OT: pesha': S.6588; HR.169c.11; H.1846a; BD.833b.
resha': S.7562; HR.169c.13a; H.2222a; BD.957c.
GEN. REF.: IS.4:946; NB.–; Z.–.

Note: Anomia is disregard for, or defiance of, God's laws; *asebeia* is the same attitude towards God's Person.

B. Adjective.

asebēs [ἀσεβής, 765], impious, ungodly (akin to A), without reverence for God, not merely irreligious, but acting in contravention of God's demands, Rom. 4:5; 5:6; 1 Tim. 1:9; 1 Pet. 4:18; 2 Pet. 2:5 (v. 6 in some mss.); 3:7; Jude 4, 15 (twice). ¶

NT: B.114c; CB.1238a; K.1010.
OT: rāshā': S.7563; HR.170b.14c; H.2222b; BD.957b.
GEN. REF.: IS.4:946; NB.–; Z.–.

C. Verb.

asebeō [ἀσεβέω, 764], akin to A and B, signifies (*a*) to be or live ungodly, 2 Pet. 2:6; (*b*) to commit ungodly deeds, Jude 15. ¶

NT: B.114c; CB.1238a; K.1010.
OT: rāsha': S.7561; HR.170a.8a,b; H.2222; BD.957d.
pāsha': S.6586; HR.170a.7; H.1846; BD.833b.
GEN. REF.: IS.4:946; NB.–; Z.–.

UNHOLY

1. *anosios* [ἀνόσιος, 462], (*a*, negative, *n*, euphonic, *hosios*, holy), unholy, profane, occurs in 1 Tim. 1:9; 2 Tim. 3:2. ¶ Cp. HOLY. In the Sept., Ezek. 22:9. ¶

NT: B.72c; CB.1235c; K.734.
OT: zimmāh: S.2154; HR.108b.1; H.556b; BD.273b.
GEN. REF.: –.

2. *koinon* [κοινόν, 2839], the neut of *koinos*, common, is translated "an unholy thing" in Heb. 10:29. See COMMON, DEFILE, C, UNCLEAN, A, No. 2.

NT: B.438a; CB.1255b; K.–.
OT: ḥeber: S.2267; HR.775a.2; H.598a; BD.288a.
GEN. REF.: –.

For **UNITED**, Rom. 6:5, R.V., see **PLANT**, C; in Heb. 4:2, see **MIXED (with)**, *Note*

UNITY

henotēs [ἑνότης, 1775], from *hen*, the neuter of *heis*, one, is used in Eph. 4:3, 13. ¶

NT: B.267c; CB.1250a; K.–.
OT: –.
GEN. REF.: IS.4:947; NB.–; Z.–.

UNJUST

adikos [ἄδικος, 94], not in conformity with *dikē*, right, is rendered "unjust" in the A.V. and R.V. in Matt. 5:45; Luke 18:11; Acts 24:15; elsewhere for the A.V. "unjust" the R.V. has "unrighteous." See UNRIGHTEOUS.

NT: B.18b; CB.1233a; K.22.
OT: sheqer: S.8267; HR.26c.18; H.2461a; BD.1055b.
ḥāmās: S.2555; HR.26c.3; H.678a; BD.329c.
GEN. REF.: –.

Note: For *adikeō*, to be unrighteous, or do unrighteousness, Rev. 22:11, R.V., and *adikia*, "unrighteous," Luke 16:8 and 18:6, R.V., see UNRIGHTEOUSNESS.

For **UNKNOWN** see **IGNORANCE**, B, No. 1, and **KNOW**, B, No. 4

UNLADE

apophortizō [ἀποφορτίζω, 670], to discharge a cargo (*apo*, from, *phortizō*, to load), is used in Acts 21:3. ¶

NT: B.102a; CB.–; K.–.
OT: –.
GEN. REF.: –.

UNLAWFUL

athemitos [ἀθέμιτος, 111], a late form for *athemistos* (*themis*, custom, right; in classical Greek, divine law), contrary to what is right, is rendered "an unlawful thing" (neuter) in Acts 10:28; in 1 Pet. 4:3, "abominable." ¶

NT: B.20d; CB.–; K.25.
OT: –.
GEN. REF.: –.

Note: For 2 Pet. 2:8, A.V., see LAWLESS.

UNLEARNED

1. *agrammatos* [ἀγράμματος, 62], lit., unlettered (*grammata*, letters: *graphō*, to write), Acts 4:13, is explained by Grimm-Thayer as meaning "unversed in the learning of the

Jewish schools"; in the papyri, however, it occurs very frequently in a formula used by one who signs for another who cannot write, which suggests that the rulers, elders and scribes regarded the Apostles as "unlettered" (Moulton and Milligan). ¶
NT: B.13b; CB.1233c; K.—.
OT: —.
GEN. REF.: IS.1:21; NB.—; Z.—.

2. *amathēs* [ἀμαθής, 261], unlearned (*manthanō*, to learn), is translated "unlearned" in 2 Pet. 3:16, A.V. (R.V., "ignorant"). ¶
NT: B.42b; CB.—; K.—.
OT: —.
GEN. REF.: IS.1:21; NB.—; Z.—.

3. *apaideutos* [ἀπαίδευτος, 521], uninstructed (*paideuō*, to train, teach), is translated "unlearned" in 2 Tim. 2:23, A.V. (R.V., "ignorant"). ¶
NT: B.79d; CB.1236a; K.753.
OT: kᵉsîl: S.5036; HR.115c.3; H.1285a; BD.614d.
nābāl: S.3684; HR.115c.5; H.1011c,e; BD.493a.
GEN. REF.: IS.1:21; NB.—; Z.—.

Note: For *idiōtēs*, rendered "unlearned" in 1 Cor. 14:16, 23, 24, see IGNORANT, No. 4.

For **UNLEAVENED** see **BREAD**, No. 2

For **UNLESS** see **EXCEPT**

UNLIFTED

anakaluptō [ἀνακαλύπτω, 343], to uncover, unveil, used in 2 Cor. 3:14 with the negative *mē*, not, is rendered "unlifted," R.V., A.V., "untaken away" (a paraphrase rather than translation); the R.V. marg., "remaineth, it not being revealed that it is done away," is not to be preferred. The best rendering seems to be, 'the veil remains unlifted (for it is in Christ that it is done away).' Judaism does not recognise the vanishing of the glory of the Law as a means of life, under God's grace in Christ. In 3:18 the R.V., "unveiled (face)" (A.V., "open"), continues the metaphor of the veil (vv. 13-17), referring to hindrances to the perception of spiritual realities, hindrances removed in the unveiling. ¶
NT: B.55c; CB.1235a; K.405.
OT: gālāh: S.1540; HR.78a.1a-c; H.350; BD.162d.
GEN. REF.: —.

UNLOOSE

luō [λύω, 3089], to loose, is rendered to unloose in Mark 1:7; Luke 3:16; John 1:27; in Acts 13:25, R.V.: see LOOSE.
NT: B.483c; CB.1257b; K.543.
OT: pātaḥ: S.6605; HR.889a.5; H.1854,1855; BD.834b.
nātar: S.5425; HR.889a.3; H.1448; BD.684a.
shᵉrā' (Aramaic): S.8271; HR.889a.7; H.3048; BD.1117b.
GEN. REF.: —.

UNMARRIED

agamos [ἄγαμος, 22], *a*, negative, *gameō*, to marry, occurs in 1 Cor. 7:8, 11, 32, 34. ¶
NT: B.4b; CB.1233b; K.—.
OT: —.
GEN. REF.: —.

UNMERCIFUL

aneleēmōn [ἀνελεήμων, 415], without mercy (*a*, negative, *n*, euphonic, *eleēmōn*, merciful), occurs in Rom. 1:21. ¶
NT: B.64c; CB.1235c; K.222.
OT: 'akzār: S.393; HR.86c.1a; H.971a; BD.470a.
'akzārî: S.394; HR.86c.1b; H.971b; BD.470a.
GEN. REF.: —.

For **UNMIXED**, Rev. 14:10, R.V., see **MIXTURE**, *Note*

For **UNMOVEABLE**, Acts 27:41, see **MOVE**, B, No. 1; in 1 Cor. 15:58, **MOVE**, B, No. 2

UNPREPARED

aparaskeuastos [ἀπαρασκεύαστος, 532], from *a*, negative, and *paraskeuazō* (see PREPARE, B, No. 4), occurs in 2 Cor. 9:4. ¶
NT: B.80d; CB.1236b; K.—.
OT: —.
GEN. REF.: —.

UNPROFITABLE, UNPROFITABLENESS

A. Adjectives.

1. *achreios* [ἀχρεῖος, 888], useless (*chreia*, use), unprofitable, occurs in Matt. 25:30 and Luke 17:10. ¶ In the Sept., 2 Sam. 6:22. ¶
NT: B.128c; CB.—; K.—.
OT: shāphāl: S.8217; HR.187c.1; H.2445c; BD.1050c.
GEN. REF.: —.

2. *achrēstos* [ἄχρηστος, 890], unprofitable, unserviceable (*chrēstos*, serviceable), is said of Onesimus, Philm. 11, antithetically to *euchrēstos*, profitable, with a play on the name of the converted slave (from *onēsis*, profit). ¶
NT: B.128c; CB.1233a; K.—.
OT: —.
GEN. REF.: —.

Note: Achreios is more distinctly negative than *achrēstos*, which suggests positively hurtful.

3. *alusitelēs* [ἀλυσιτελής, 255], not advantageous, not making good the expense involved (*lusitelēs*, useful), occurs in Heb. 13:17. ¶
NT: B.41c; CB.—; K.—.
OT: —.
GEN. REF.: —.

4. *anōphelēs* [ἀνωφελής, 512], not beneficial or serviceable (*a*, negative, *n*, euphonic, *ōpheleō*, to do good, to benefit), is rendered "unprofitable" in Tit. 3:9; in the neuter, used as a noun, "unprofitableness," Heb. 7:18, said of the Law

as not accomplishing that which the "better hope" could alone bring. ¶ In the Sept., Prov. 28:3; Isa. 44:10; Jer. 2:8. ¶

NT: B.77c; CB.–; K.–.
OT: yā'al (with neg.): S.3276; HR.113a.1; H.882; BD.418c.
GEN. REF.: –.

B. Verb.

achreoō, or *achreioō* [ἀχρεόω, 889], akin to A, No. 1, to make useless, occurs in Rom. 3:12, in the Passive Voice, rendered "they have . . . become unprofitable." ¶

NT: B.128c; CB.–; K.–.
OT: 'ālaḥ: S.444; HR.187c.1; H.98; BD.47a.
GEN. REF.: –.

FOR **UNQUENCHABLE** see **QUENCH**

UNREASONABLE

1. *alogos* [ἄλογος, 249], without reason, irrational, is rendered "unreasonable" in Acts 25:27. See BRUTE.

NT: B.41a; CB.1234c; K.505.
OT: ('ᵃral) sᵉphātayim: S.8193; HR.59b.2; H.2278a; BD.973c.
GEN. REF.: –.

2. *atopos* [ἄτοπος, 824], lit., 'out of place' (*topos*, a place), is translated "unreasonable" in 2 Thess. 3:2, where the meaning intended seems to be 'perverse,' 'truculent.' See AMISS.

NT: B.120c; CB.–; K.–.
OT: 'āwen: S.205; HR.176b.1; H.48a; BD.19d.
GEN. REF.: –.

For **UNREBUKEABLE** see **BLAME**, B, No. 5

UNRIGHTEOUS

adikos [ἄδικος, 94], not conforming to *dikē*, right, is translated "unrighteous" in Luke 16:10 (twice), R.V., 11; Rom. 3:5; 1 Cor. 6:1, R.V.; 6:9; Heb. 6:10; 1 Pet. 3:18, R.V.; 2 Pet. 2:9, R.V.: see UNJUST.

NT: B.18b; CB.1233a; K.22.
OT: sheqer: S.8267; HR.26c.18; H.2461a; BD.1055b.
ḥāmās: S.2555; HR.26c.3; H.678a; BD.329c.
GEN. REF.: –.

UNRIGHTEOUSNESS

A. Noun.

adikia [ἀδικία, 93], denotes (*a*) injustice, Luke 18:6, lit., 'the judge of injustice'; Rom. 9:14; (*b*) unrighteousness, iniquity, e.g., Luke 16:8, lit., "the steward of unrighteousness," R.V. marg., i.e., characterized by unrighteousness; Rom. 1:18, 29; 2:8; 3:5; 6:13; 1 Cor. 13:6, R.V., "unrighteousness"; 2 Thess. 2:10, "[with all (lit., in every) deceit] of unrighteousness," i.e., deceit such as unrighteousness uses, and that in every variety; Antichrist and his ministers will not be restrained by any scruple from words or deeds calculated to deceive; 2 Thess. 2:12, of those who have pleasure in it, not an intellectual but a moral evil; distaste for truth is the precursor of the rejection of it; 2 Tim. 2:19, R.V.; 1 John 1:9, which includes (*c*); (*c*) a deed or deeds violating law and justice (virtually the same as *adikēma*, an unrighteous act), e.g., Luke 13:27, "iniquity"; 2 Cor. 12:13, "wrong," the wrong of depriving another of what is his own, here ironically of a favour; Heb. 8:12, 1st clause, "iniquities," lit., 'unrighteousnesses' (plural, not as A.V.); 2 Pet. 2:13, 15, R.V., "wrong doing," A.V., "unrighteousness"; 1 John 5:17. See INIQUITY.

NT: B.17d; CB.1233a; K.22.
OT: 'āwōn: S.5771; HR.25b.21; H.1577a; BD.730d.
sheqer: S.8267; HR.25b.34; H.2461a; BD.1055b.
'awᵉlāh: S.5766; HR.25b.19; H.1580a,b; BD.732c.
GEN. REF.: –.

Notes: (1) In 2 Cor. 6:14, A.V., *anomia*, lawlessness, is translated "unrighteousness" (R.V., "iniquity").

(2) *Adikia* is the comprehensive term for wrong, or wrong-doing, as between persons; *anomia*, lawlessness, is the rejection of Divine law, or wrong committed against it.

B. Verb.

adikeō [ἀδικέω, 91], to do wrong, is rendered in Rev. 22:11, R.V., firstly, "he that is unrighteous," lit., 'the doer of unrighteousness' (present participle of the verb, with the article), secondly, "let him do unrighteousness (still)," the retributive and permanent effect of a persistent course of unrighteous-doing (A.V., "he that is unjust, let him be unjust"). See HURT, OFFENDER, *Note*, WRONG.

NT: B.17c; CB.1233a; K.22.
OT: 'āwāh: S.5753; HR.24c.11c; H.1577; BD.730c.
'āshaq: S.6231; HR.24c.15a,b; H.1713; BD.798d.
GEN. REF.: –.

For **UNRIPE, UNTIMELY,** see **FIG**, No. 2

UNRULY

1. *anupotaktos* [ἀνυπότακτος, 506], not subject to rule (*a*, negative, *n*, euphonic, *hupotassō*, to put in subjection), is used (*a*) of things, Heb. 2:8, R.V., "not subject" (A.V., "not put under"); (*b*) of persons, "unruly," 1 Tim. 1:9, R.V. (A.V., "disobedient"); Tit. 1:6, 10. See DISOBEDIENT, B, *Note*. ¶

NT: B.76d; CB.–; K.1156.
OT: –.
GEN. REF.: –.

2. *ataktos* [ἄτακτος, 813], is rendered "unruly" in 1 Thess. 5:14, A.V. (marg. and R.V., "disorderly"). See DISORDERLY, A. ¶
NT: B.119c; CB.–; K.1156.
OT: –.
GEN. REF.: –.

Note: In Jas. 3:8, some texts have *akataschetos*, 'that cannot be restrained,' A.V., "unruly": see RESTLESS. ¶

UNSEARCHABLE

1. *anexeraunētos*, or *anexereunētos* [ἀνεξεραύνητος, 419], *a*, negative, *n*, euphonic, *ex* (*ek*), out, *eraunaō*, to search, examine, is used in Rom. 11:33, of the judgments of God. ¶
NT: B.65a; CB.1235c; K.58.
OT: –.
GEN. REF.: –.

2. *anexichniastos* [ἀνεξιχνίαστος, 421], with the same prefixes as in No. 1, and an adjectival form akin to *ichneuō*, to trace out (*ichnos*, a footprint, a track), is translated "unsearchable" in Eph. 3:8, of the riches of Christ; in Rom. 11:33, "past tracing out," of the ways of the Lord (cp. No. 1, in the same verse). The ways of God are the outworkings of His judgment. Of the two questions in ver. 34, the first seems to have reference to No. 1, the second to No. 2. See FIND, *Note* (3), TRACE. ¶
NT: B.65a; CB.–; K.58.
OT: ḥēqer (with neg.): S.2714; HR.87b.1; H.729a; BD.350d.
GEN. REF.: –.

UNSEEMLINESS, UNSEEMLY

aschēmosunē [ἀσχημοσύνη, 808], from *aschēmōn*, unseemly, is rendered "unseemliness" in Rom. 1:27, R.V.: see SHAME, No. 4.
NT: B.119b; CB.–; K.–.
OT: 'erᵉwāh: S.6172; HR.174c.2a; H.1692b; BD.788d.
GEN. REF.: –.

Note: For "behave . . . unseemly" see BEHAVE, No. 4.

For **UNSETTLE**, Gal. 5:12, R.V., see **STIR**, No. 12

For **UNSKILFUL,** Heb. 5:13, see **EXPERIENCE**, No. 1

UNSPEAKABLE

1. *anekdiēgētos* [ἀνεκδιήγητος, 411], denotes inexpressible (*a*, negative, *n*, euphonic *ekdiēgeomai*, to declare, relate), 2 Cor. 9:15, "unspeakable" (of the gift of God); regarding the various explanations of the gift, it seems most suitable to view it as the gift of His Son. ¶
NT: B.64b; CB.–; K.–.
OT: –.
GEN. REF.: –.

2. *aneklalētos* [ἀνεκλάλητος, 412], denotes unable to be told out (*eklaleō*, to speak out), 1 Pet. 1:8, of the believer's joy. ¶
NT: B.64b; CB.–; K.–.
OT: –.
GEN. REF.: –.

3. *arrhētos* [ἄρρητος, 731], primarily, unspoken (*a*, negative, *rhētos*, spoken), denotes unspeakable, 2 Cor. 12:4, of the words heard by Paul when caught up into Paradise. ¶ The word is common in sacred inscriptions especially in connection with the Greek Mysteries; hence Moulton and Milligan suggest the meaning 'words too sacred to be uttered.'
NT: B.109c; CB.1237c; K.–.
OT: –.
GEN. REF.: –.

For **UNSPOTTED** see **SPOT**, C

UNSTABLE, UNSTEDFAST

1. *astēriktos* [ἀστήρικτος, 793], *a*, negative, *stērizō*, to fix, is used in 2 Pet. 2:14; 3:16, A.V., "unstable," R.V., "unstedfast." ¶
NT: B.118a; CB.–; K.1085.
OT: –.
GEN. REF.: –.

2. *akatastatos* [ἀκατάστατος, 182], from *kathistēmi*, to set in order, is rendered "unstable" in Jas. 1:8: see RESTLESS.
NT: B.30b; CB.–; K.387.
OT: sā'ar: S.5590; HR.44a.1; H.1528b; BD.704a.
GEN. REF.: –.

For **UNTAKEN AWAY**, 2 Cor. 3:14, A.V., see **UNLIFTED**

UNTHANKFUL

acharistos [ἀχάριστος, 884], denotes ungrateful, thankless (*charis*, thanks), Luke 6:35; 2 Tim. 3:2. ¶
NT: B.128b; CB.–; K.1298.
OT: –.
GEN. REF.: –.

UNTIL and **UNTO**: see † p. 1

For **UNTIMELY** see **FIG**, No. 2

For **UNTOWARD** see **CROOKED**

UNVEILED

akatakaluptos [ἀκατακάλυπτος, 177], uncovered (*a*, negative, *katakaluptō*, to cover), is used in 1 Cor. 11:5, 13, R.V., "unveiled," with reference to the injunction forbidding women to be unveiled in a church gathering. ¶ Whatever the character of the covering, it is to be on her head as "a sign of authority" (ver. 10), R.V., the meaning of which is indicated in ver. 3 in the matter of headships, and the reasons for which are given in vv. 7-9, and in the phrase "because of the angels," intimating their witness of, and interest in, that which betokens the headship of Christ. The injunctions were neither Jewish, which required men to be veiled in prayer, nor Greek, by which men and women were alike unveiled. The Apostle's instructions were "the commandment of the Lord" (14:37) and were for all the churches (vv. 33, 34).

NT: B.29d; CB.1234a; K.—.
OT: pāra‘: S.6544; HR.43c.1; H.1822-1824; BD.828d.
GEN. REF.: —.

Note: For the verb *anakaluptō*, rendered "unveiled" in 2 Cor. 3:18, R.V., see UNLIFTED (2nd ref.).

UNWASHEN

aniptos [ἄνιπτος, 449], unwashed (*a*, negative, *niptō*, to wash), occurs in Matt. 15:20; Mark 7:2 (ver. 5 in some mss.). ¶

NT: B.69d; CB.1235c; K.635.
OT: —.
GEN. REF.: IS.4:1022; NB.—; Z.—.

UNWILLING

Note: "I am unwilling" is the R.V. rendering of *thelō*, to will, with the negative *ou*, in 3 John 13 (A.V., "I will not").

UNWISE

1. *anoētos* [ἀνόητος, 453], is translated "unwise" in Rom. 1:14, A.V.; see FOOLISH, No. 2.

NT: B.70d; CB.1235c; K.636.
OT: ’^{e}wîl: S.191; HR.105a.1a; H.44a; BD.17b.
’iwwelet: S.200; HR.105a.1b; H.44c; BD.17c.
GEN. REF.: —.

2. *aphrōn* [ἄφρων, 878], is translated "unwise" in Eph. 5:17, A.V.; see FOOLISH, No. 1.

NT: B.127d; CB.1236c; K.1277.
OT: k^{e}sîl: S.3684; HR.186c.8a; H.1011c,e; BD.493a.
’^{e}wîl: S.191; HR.186c.1a; H.44a; BD.17b.
nābāl: S.5036; HR.186c.10; H.1285a; BD.614d.
GEN. REF.: —.

3. *asophos* [ἄσοφος, 781], *a*, negative, is rendered "unwise" in Eph. 5:15, R.V. (A.V., "fools"). ¶

NT: B.116c; CB.1238a; K.—.
OT: —.
GEN. REF.: —.

UNWORTHILY, UNWORTHY

A. Adverb.

anaxiōs [ἀναξίως, 371], is used in 1 Cor. 11:27, of partaking of the Lord's Supper unworthily, i.e., treating it as a common meal, the bread and cup as common things, not apprehending their solemn symbolic import. In the best texts the word is not found in ver. 29 (see R.V.). ¶

NT: B.58d; CB.1235b; K.—.
OT: —.
GEN. REF.: IS.4:1134; NB.—; Z.—.

B. Adjective.

anaxios [ἀνάξιος, 370], *a*, negative, *n*, euphonic, *axios*, worthy, is used in 1 Cor. 6:2. In modern Greek it signifies "incapable." ¶

NT: B.58c; CB.1235b; K.63.
OT: zālal: S.2151; HR.80b.1; H.553; BD.272d.
GEN. REF.: IS.4:1134; NB.—; Z.—.

Note: In Acts 13:46, "unworthy" represents the adjective *axios*, preceded by the negative *ouk*.

UP

Notes: (1) In Matt. 13:6 and Mark 4:6, A.V., *anatellō*, to rise (of the sun), is rendered "was up." See RISE.

(2) The adverb is used with numerous Eng. verbs to translate single Greek verbs. In John 11:41 and Heb. 12:15, however, the adverb *anō*, up, is used separately: see ABOVE, BRIM, HIGH.

For **UPBRAID** see **REPROACH**, B. No. 1

UPHOLD

pherō [φέρω, 5342], to bear, carry, uphold, is rendered "upholding" in Heb. 1:3. See BEAR.

NT: B.854d; CB.1264a; K.1252.
OT: nāśā’: S.5375; HR.1426c.17; H.1421; BD.669d,671a.
GEN. REF.: —.

UPON: see † p. 1

For **UPPER** see **CHAMBER**, **COUNTRY**, B, No. 1, **ROOM**

UPPERMOST

Note: In Luke 11:43 *prōtokathedria*, a chief seat, is translated "uppermost seats," A.V. (R.V., "chief seats"). In Matt. 23:6 and Mark 12:39, A.V., *prōtoklisia*, a chief place, is translated "uppermost rooms" (R.V., "chief place" and "chief places"). See CHIEF, B, Nos. 6 and 7.

UPRIGHT: see **STRAIGHT**, No. 2; UPRIGHTLY: see **WALK**, No. 6

UPRIGHTNESS

euthutēs [εὐθύτης, 2118], from *euthus*, straight, is rendered "uprightness" in Heb. 1:8, R.V., A.V., "righteousness," marg., "rightness," or, "straightness." ¶

NT: B.321b; CB.—; K.—.
OT: yōsher: S.3476; HR.571b.1b; H.930b; BD.449c.
mîshôr: S.4334; HR.571b.1d; H.930f; BD.449d.
mêshār (îm): S.4339; HR.571b.1e; H.930e; BD.449c.
GEN. REF.: IS.4:948; NB.—; Z.—.

For **UPROAR (Noun)**, *thorubos*, see **TUMULT**, and for *stasis* see **RIOT**

UPROAR (Verbs)

thorubeō [θορυβέω, 2350], used in the Middle Voice, denotes to make a noise or uproar, or, transitively, in the Active Voice, to trouble, throw into confusion, Acts 17:5. See ADO, NOISE, TROUBLE.

NT: B.362d; CB.1272b; K.–.
OT: rāʻal: S.7477; HR.654a.3; H.2188; BD.947a.
bāʻat: S.1204; HR.654a.1; H.265; BD.129d.
GEN. REF.: –.

Note: For *suncheō*, to confuse, Acts 21:31 (A.V., "was in an uproar"), see CONFUSION; for *anastatoō*, Acts 21:38 (A.V., "madest an uproar"), see STIR UP.

For **UPSIDE DOWN** see **TURN**, No. 15

URGE

Notes: (1) In Acts 13:50, A.V., *parotrunō*, to urge on (R.V.), is rendered "stirred up." ¶

(2) In Acts 13:43, *peithō*, to persuade, is rendered "urged," R.V. (A.V., "persuaded").

(3) For *enechō*, rendered "to urge" in Luke 11:53, A.V., see ENTANGLE, No. 3.

US

The oblique cases of *hēmeis*, we, are the genitive *hēmōn*, of us, the dative *hēmin*, to us, the accusative *hēmas*, us. When the nominative *hēmeis* is used, it is always emphatic, e.g., John 11:16, "(let) us (go)", lit., 'we, let us go'; 1 Thess. 5:8, "let us . . . be sober," lit., 'we . . . let us be sober.' Sometimes the oblique cases are governed by prepositions.

USE (Noun), USEFUL

1. *hexis* [ἕξις, 1838], akin to *echō*, to have, denotes habit, experience, "use," Heb. 5:14. ¶

NT: B.276b; CB.1250b; K.–.
OT: –.
GEN. REF.: –.

2. *chreia* [χρεία, 5532], need, is translated "uses" in Tit. 3:14; in Eph. 4:29, A.V., "(for the) use (of edifying)," R.V., "(as the) need (may be)." See NECESSITY, NEED.

NT: B.884d; CB.1240a; K.–.
OT: ḥªshḥû(t) (Aramaic): S.2819; HR.1474a.1; H.2746b; BD.1093d.
ḥªshaḥ: S.2818; HR.1474a.3; H.2746; BD.1093d.
GEN. REF.: –.

3. *chrēsis* [χρῆσις, 5540], use (akin to *chraomai*, to use), occurs in Rom. 1:26, 27. ¶

NT: B.885d; CB.–; K.–.
OT: –.
GEN. REF.: –.

Notes: (1) In 2 Tim. 2:21, the adjective *euchrēstos*, useful, serviceable (*eu*, well, *chraomai*, to use), is translated "meet for . . . use"; in 4:11, "useful," R.V. (A.V., "profitable"); in Philm. 11, "profitable." See PROFITABLE, B, No. 2. ¶

(2) In 1 Cor. 8:7 the best texts have the noun *sunētheia*, R.V., "being used," lit., 'by the custom (of the idol),' i.e., by being associated. See CUSTOM. In the Sept., Prov. 31:13. ¶ Contrast *achrēstos*, unprofitable, Philm. 11. ¶

USE (Verb)

1. *chraomai* [χράομαι, 5530], from *chrē*, it is necessary, denotes (*a*) to use, Acts 27:17; 1 Cor. 7:21, where "use it rather" means 'use your bondservice rather'; 7:31, where "they that use (this world)" is followed by the strengthened form *katachraomai*, rendered "abusing," or "using to the full" (R.V., marg.); 9:12, 15; 2 Cor. 1:17; 3:12; 13:10; 1 Tim. 1:8, of using the Law lawfully, i.e., agreeably to its designs; 1 Tim. 5:23; (*b*) deal with, Acts 27:3. See ENTREAT (to treat). Cp. the Active *chraō* (or *kichrēmi*), to lend, Luke 11:5. See LEND. ¶

NT: B.884b; CB.1240a; K.–.
OT: –.
GEN. REF.: –.

2. *echō* [ἔχω, 2192], to have, is rendered "using" in 1 Pet. 2:16 (marg., "having"); see HAVE.

NT: B.331d; CB.1242c; K.286.
OT: –.
GEN. REF.: –.

3. *anastrephō* [ἀναστρέφω, 390], chiefly denotes to behave, to live in a certain manner, rendered "(were so) used" in Heb. 10:33 (Passive Voice); the verb, however, does not mean to treat or use; here it has the significance of living amidst sufferings, reproaches etc. See ABIDE, BEHAVE, LIVE, OVERTHROW, PASS, RETURN.

NT: B.61b; CB.1235b; K.1093.
OT: –.
GEN. REF.: –.

Notes: (1) In Acts 19:19, A.V., *prassō*, to practise (R.V.), is rendered "used."

(2) For Heb. 5:13, A.V., "useth (milk)," see PARTAKE, B, No. 3.

(3) In 1 Thess. 2:5, "were we found using" is the rendering of the verb *ginomai*, to become, with the preposition *en*, in, governing the noun, "words (or speech) [of flattery]"; this idiomatic phrase signifies to be engaged in, to resort to. A rendering close to the meaning of the Greek is 'for neither at any time did we fall into the use of flattering speech'; cp. 1 Tim. 2:14, "fallen into transgression."

(4) To use is combined in Eng. with other words, e.g., DECEIT, DESPITEFULLY, HOSPITALITY, REPETITIONS.

USING

apochrēsis [ἀπόχρησις, 671], a strengthened form of *chrēsis*, a using, and signifying a misuse (akin to *apochraomai*, to use to the full, abuse), is translated "using" in Col. 2:22; the clause may be rendered 'by their using up.' "The unusual word was chosen for its expressiveness; the *chrēsis* here was an *apochrēsis*; the things could not be used without rendering them unfit for further use" (Lightfoot). ¶

NT: B.102a; CB.—; K.—.
OT: —.
GEN. REF.: —.

For **USURP** see **AUTHORITY**, B, No. 3

USURY

Note: The R.V., "interest," Matt. 25:27; Luke 19:23, is the preferable rendering of *tokos* here. See INTEREST. ¶

For **UTMOST PART** see **END**, A, No. 3

UTTER

1. *laleō* [λαλέω, 2980], to speak, is rendered to utter in 2 Cor. 12:4 and Rev. 10:3, 4 (twice). See PREACH, SAY, SPEAK, TALK, TELL.

NT: B.463a; CB.1256b; K.505.
OT: dābar: S.1696; HR.841a.2c; H.399; BD.180b.
GEN. REF.: —.

2. *ereugomai* [ἐρεύγομαι, 2044], primarily, to spit or spue out, or, of oxen, to bellow, roar, hence, to speak aloud, utter, occurs in Matt. 13:35. ¶ This affords an example of the tendency for certain words to become softened in force in late Greek.

NT: B.308d; CB.—; K.—.
OT: shā'ag: S.7580; HR.544c.2; H.2300; BD.980c.
GEN. REF.: —.

3. *aphiēmi* [ἀφίημι, 863], to send forth, is used of uttering a cry, Mark 15:37, of Christ's final utterance on the Cross, R.V., "uttered" (A.V., "cried"). See FORGIVE, LAY, *Note* (2), LEAVE, LET, OMITTED, PUT, REMIT, SUFFER, YIELD.

NT: B.125c; CB.1236b; K.88.
OT: —.
GEN. REF.: —.

4. *didōmi* [δίδωμι, 1325], to give, is translated "utter" in 1 Cor. 14:9. See GIVE.

NT: B.192c; CB.1241c; K.166.
OT: —.
GEN. REF.: —.

5. *phthengomai* [φθέγγομαι, 5350], to utter a sound or voice, is translated "uttering" in 2 Pet. 2:18, R.V.: see SPEAK, No. 4.

NT: B.857a; CB.—; K.—.
OT: 'ānāh: S.6030; HR.1429c.3; H.1650,1653; BD.772c.
GEN. REF.: —.

Notes: (1) In Rom. 8:26, *alalētos*, inexpressible (*a*, negative, *laleō*, to speak), is rendered "which cannot be uttered." ¶

(2) In Heb. 5:11, A.V., *dusermēneutos*, followed by *legō*, to speak, [translated "hard of interpretation" (R.V.), *dus* (whence *dys-* in Eng., dyspeptic, etc.), a prefix like Eng., un-, or mis-, and *hermēneuō*, to interpret], is rendered "hard to be uttered." ¶

UTTERANCE

logos [λόγος, 3056], a word, is translated "utterance" in 1 Cor. 1:5; 2 Cor. 8:7; Eph. 6:19. See WORD.

NT: B.477a; CB.1257a; K.505.
OT: dābār: S.1697; HR.881c.2a; H.399a; BD.182a.
GEN. REF.: —.

Notes: (1) In Col. 4:3, A.V., *logos* is rendered "(a door) of utterance."

(2) For *apophthengomai*, rendered "utterance" in Acts 2:4, see SPEAK, No. 5.

For **UTTERLY**, 1 Cor. 6:7, see **ACTUALLY**; 2 Pet. 2:12, see **CORRUPT**, A, No. 2 (*b*)

UTTERMOST

1. *panteles* [παντελές, 3838], the neuter of the adjective *pantelēs*, complete, perfect, used with *eis to* ('unto the'), is translated "to the uttermost" in Heb. 7:25, where the meaning may be 'finally'; in Luke 13:11 (negatively), "in no wise." ¶

NT: B.608c; CB.1261c; K.1161.
OT: —.
GEN. REF.: —.

2. *telos* [τέλος, 5056], an end, is rendered "the uttermost" in 1 Thess. 2:16, said of Divine wrath upon the Jews, referring to the prophecy of Deut. 28:15-68; the nation as such, will yet, however, be delivered (Rom. 11:26; cp. Jer. 30:4-11). The full phrase is *eis telos*, to the uttermost, which is probably the meaning in John 13:1, "to the end."

NT: B.811b; CB.1271b; K.1161.
OT: qēṣ: S.7093; HR.1344a.4a; H.2060a; BD.893d.
laneṣaḥ: S.5331; HR.1344a.6f; H.1402a; BD.664b.
GEN. REF.: —.

Notes: (1) For "uttermost (farthing)," Matt. 5:26, A.V., see LAST. For "uttermost" in Acts 24:22, see DETERMINE, No. 5.

(2) For "uttermost part (-s)," see END, A, No. 3 (*a*) and C (*b*).

V

For **VAGABOND** see **STROLLING**

For **VAIL** see **VEIL**

VAIN, IN VAIN, VAINLY

A. Adjectives.

1. *kenos* [κενός, 2756], empty, with special reference to quality, is translated "vain" (as an adjective) in Acts 4:25; 1 Cor. 15:10, 14 (twice); Eph. 5:6; Col. 2:8; Jas. 2:20; in the following the neuter, *kenon*, follows the preposition *eis*, in, and denotes "in vain," 2 Cor. 6:1; Gal. 2:2; Phil. 2:16 (twice); 1 Thess. 3:5. See EMPTY, B, where the applications are enumerated.

NT: B.427d; CB.1255a; K.426.
OT: rîq: S.7324; HR.759a.9a; H.2161; BD.937d.
rêqāh: S.7387; HR.759a.9c; H.2161c; BD.938b.
shāw': S.7723; HR.759a.10; H.2338a; BD.996a.
GEN. REF.: IS.4:963; NB.1308; Z.5:859.

2. *mataios* [μάταιος, 3152], void of result, is used of (*a*) idolatrous practices, Acts 14:15, R.V., "vain things" (A.V., "vanities"); (*b*) the thoughts of the wise, 1 Cor. 3:20; (*c*) faith, if Christ is not risen, 1 Cor. 15:17; (*d*) questionings, strifes, etc., Tit. 3:9; (*e*) religion, with an unbridled tongue, Jas. 1:26; (*f*) manner of life, 1 Pet. 1:18. ¶ For the contrast between No. 1 and No. 2 see EMPTY.

NT: B.495c; CB.1258a; K.571.
OT: shāw': S.7723; HR.898c.10; H.2338a; BD.996a.
hebel: S.1892; HR.898c.4; H.463a; BD.210c.
kāzāb: S.3577; HR.898c.7; H.970a; BD.469c.
GEN. REF.: IS.4:963; NB.1308; Z.5:859.

Note: For *mataiologoi*, Tit. 1:10, see TALKERS (vain). ¶

B. Verbs.

1. *mataioō* [ματαιόω, 3154], to make vain, or foolish, corresponding in meaning to A, No. 2, occurs in Rom. 1:21, "became vain." ¶

NT: B.495d; CB.1258a; K.571.
OT: hābal: S.1891; HR.899b.2; H.463; BD.211a.
sākal: S.5528; HR.899b.3; H.1493; BD.698a.
GEN. REF.: IS.4:963; NB.1308; Z.5:859.

2. *kenoō* [κενόω, 2758], to empty, corresponding to A, No. 1, is translated "should be in vain" in 2 Cor. 9:3, A.V. See EFFECT, EMPTY, VOID.

NT: B.428a; CB.1255a; K.426.
OT: 'āmal: S.535; HR.759b.1; H.114; BD.51b.
GEN. REF.: IS.4:963; NB.–; Z.–.

C. Adverbs.

1. *matēn* [μάτην, 3155], properly the accusative case of *matē*, a fault, a folly, signifies in vain, to no purpose, Matt. 15:9; Mark 7:7. ¶

NT: B.495d; CB.1258a; K.571.
OT: shāw': S.7723; HR.899c.4,6; H.2338a; BD.996a.
hebel: S.1892; HR.899c.2; H.463a; BD.210c.
GEN. REF.: IS.4:963; NB.1308; Z.5:859.

2. *dōrean* [δωρεάν, 1432], the accusative of *dōrea*, a gift, is used adverbially, denoting (*a*) freely (see FREE, D); (*b*) uselessly, "in vain," Gal. 2:21, A.V. (R.V., "for nought"). See CAUSE, A, under "*without a cause*."

NT: B.210c; CB.1242a; K.166.
OT: ḥinnām: S.2600; HR.358c.1; H.694b; BD.336c.
GEN. REF.: IS.4:963; NB.–; Z.5:859.

3. *eikē* [εἰκῇ, 1500], denotes (*a*) without cause, "vainly," Col. 2:18; (*b*) to no purpose, "in vain," Rom. 13:4; Gal. 3:4 (twice); 4:11. See CAUSE, A, *Note* (1), under "*without a cause*."

NT: B.221d; CB.1243a; K.203.
OT: –.
GEN. REF.: IS.4:963; NB.–; Z.5:859.

VAINGLORY, VAINGLORIOUS

A. Nouns.

1. *kenodoxia* [κενοδοξία, 2754], from *kenos*, vain, empty, *doxa*, glory, is used in Phil. 2:3. ¶

NT: B.427c; CB.1255a; K.426.
OT: –.
GEN. REF.: IS.4:963; NB.–; Z.–.

2. *alazoneia*, or *-ia* [ἀλαζονεία, 212], denotes boastfulness, vaunting, translated "vainglory" in 1 John 2:16, R.V. (A.V., "pride"); in Jas. 4:16, R.V., "vauntings" (A.V., "boastings"). Cp. *alazōn*, a boaster. ¶

NT: B.34c; CB.1234b; K.36.
OT: –.
GEN. REF.: –.

B. Adjective.

kenodoxos [κενόδοξος, 2755], akin to A, No. 1, is rendered "vainglorious" in Gal. 5:26, R.V. (A.V., "desirous of vain glory"). ¶

NT: B.427c; CB.1255a; K.426.
OT: –.
GEN. REF.: IS.4:963; NB.–; Z.–.

For **VALIANT** see **MIGHTY**, B, No. 2, **STRONG**, No. 2 (*a*) (3)

VALLEY

pharanx [φάραγξ, 5327], denotes a ravine or valley, sometimes figurative of a condition of loneliness and danger (cp. Psa. 23:4); the word occurs in Luke 3:5 (from the Sept. of Isa. 40:4). ¶

NT: B.853c; CB.–; K.–.
OT: naḥal: S.5158; HR.1424b.4; H.1343a,b; BD.636a.
gay': S.1516; HR.1424b.2; H.343; BD.161a.
GEN. REF.: IS.4:964; NB.1308; Z.5:860.

VALUE

A. Verb.

diapherō [διαφέρω, 1308], used intransitively, means to differ, to excel, hence to be

of more value, Matt. 6:26, R.V., "are (not) ye of (much) more value" (A.V., "better"); 12:12 and Luke 12:24, ditto; Matt. 10:31; Luke 12:7. See BETTER (be), CARRY, No. 4, DIFFER, DRIVE, No. 7, EXCELLENT, MATTER, *Note* (1), PUBLISH, No. 2.
NT: B.190b; CB.–; K.1252.
OT: –.
GEN. REF.: IS.4:965; NB.–; Z.–.

Note: For *timaō*, rendered to value in Matt. 27:9 (twice), A.V., see PRICE.

B. Noun.

timē [τιμή, 5092], denotes a valuing, a price, honour; in Col. 2:23, R.V., "(not of any) value (against the indulgence of the flesh)" [A.V., "(not in any) honour . . ."], i.e., the ordinances enjoined by human tradition are not of any value to prevent (*pros*, against; cp. Acts 26:14) indulgence of the flesh. See HONOUR, PRECIOUS, PRICE, SUM.
NT: B.817b; CB.1272c; K.1181.
OT: ʿērek: S.6187; HR.1353a.10; H.1694a; BD.789d.
yᵉqār: S.3366; HR.1353a.4a; H.905b; BD.430b.
GEN. REF.: IS.4:965; NB.–; Z.2:750.

VANISH, VANISHING

A. Verb.

aphanizō [ἀφανίζω, 853], to render unseen, is translated "vanisheth away" in Jas. 4:14 (Passive Voice, lit., 'is made to disappear'). See CONSUME, DISFIGURE, PERISH.
NT: B.124c; CB.1236b; K.–.
OT: shāmēm: S.8074; HR.181b.21a-c; H.2409; BD.1030d.
shāmad: S.8045; HR.181b.20a,b; H.2406; BD.1029a.
GEN. REF.: –.

Note: In 1 Cor. 13:8, A.V., *katargeō*, to abolish, is rendered "it shall vanish away" (R.V., ". . . be done away"). See ABOLISH.

B. Noun.

aphanismos [ἀφανισμός, 854], *a*, negative, *phainō*, to cause to appear (akin to A), occurs in Heb. 8:13, R.V., "(nigh unto) vanishing away"; the word is suggestive of abolition. ¶
NT: B.124d; CB.–; K.–.
OT: shammāh: S.8047; HR.182a.7a; H.2409d; BD.1031c.
shᵉmāmāh: S.8077; HR.182a.7b; H.2409b,c; BD.1031b.
GEN. REF.: –.

Note: In Luke 24:31, the adjective *aphantos* (akin to A and B), invisible, used with *ginomai*, to become, and followed by *apo*, from, with the plural personal pronoun, is rendered "He vanished out of their sight" (A.V., marg., "He ceased to be seen of them"), lit., 'He became invisible from them.' ¶

VANITY

mataiotēs [ματαιότης, 3153], emptiness as to results, akin to *mataios* (see EMPTY, VAIN), is used (*a*) of the creation, Rom. 8:20, as failing of the results designed, owing to sin; (*b*) of the mind which governs the manner of life of the Gentiles, Eph. 4:17; (*c*) of the "great swelling *words*" of false teachers, 2 Pet. 2:18. ¶
NT: B.495d; CB.1258a; K.571.
OT: hebel: S.1892; HR.899a.1a; H.463a; BD.210c.
shāwʾ: S.7723; HR.899a.4; H.2338a; BD.996a.
GEN. REF.: IS.4:965; NB.1308; Z.5:861.

Note: For *mataios*, in the neut. plur. in Acts 14:15, "vanities," see VAIN, A, No. 2 (*a*).

VAPOUR

atmis [ἀτμίς, 822], is used of smoke, Acts 2:19; figuratively of human life, Jas. 4:14. ¶
NT: B.120b; CB.–; K.–.
OT: ʿānān: S.6051; HR.176b.1; H.1655a; BD.777d.
ʿāshān: S.6227; HR.176b.2; H.1712a; BD.798c.
qîṭôr: S.7008; HR.176b.3; H.2011b; BD.882c.
GEN. REF.: IS.4:966; NB.–; Z.–.

VARIABLENESS, VARIATION

parallagē [παραλλαγή, 3883], denotes, in general, a change (Eng., *parallax*, the difference between the directions of a body as seen from two different points), a transmission from one condition to another; it occurs in Jas. 1:17, R.V., "variation" (A.V., "variableness"); the reference may be to the sun, which varies its position in the sky. ¶ In the Sept., 2 Kings 9:20. ¶
NT: B.620a; CB.–; K.–.
OT: shiggāʿwôn: S.7697; HR.1061c.1; H.2328a; BD.993d.
GEN. REF.: –.

VARIANCE

dichazō [διχάζω, 1369], to cut apart, divide in two, is used metaphorically in Matt. 10:35, "to set at variance." ¶
NT: B.200b; CB.–; K.–.
OT: –.
GEN. REF.: –.

Notes: (1) In Gal. 5:20, A.V., *eris*, strife (R.V.), is rendered "variance."

(2) For *adiakritos*, Jas. 3:17, R.V., "without variance" (marg., "doubtfulness, or partiality"), A.V., "without partiality" (marg., "without wrangling"), see PARTIAL. ¶

VAUNT (ONESELF)

perpereuomai [περπερεύομαι, 4068], to boast or vaunt oneself (from *perperos*, vainglorious, braggart, not in the N.T.), is used in 1 Cor. 13:4, negatively of love. ¶
NT: B.653d; CB.–; K.833.
OT: –.
GEN. REF.: –.

For VAUNTINGS see VAINGLORY

For VEHEMENT see DESIRE, A, No. 3

VEHEMENTLY

1. *deinōs* [δεινῶς, 1171], for which see GRIEVOUS, B, No. 1, is rendered "vehemently" in Luke 11:53.
NT: B.173b; CB.1240c; K.—.
OT: pālā': S.6381; HR.288a.1; H.1768; BD.810c.
ḥārāh: S.2734; HR.288a.2; H.736; BD.354a.
GEN. REF.: —.

2. *eutonōs* [εὐτόνως, 2159], vigorously, is translated "vehemently" in Luke 23:10, of accusations against Christ. See MIGHTY, D.
NT: B.327b; CB.—; K.—.
OT: —.
GEN. REF.: IS.4:967; NB.—; Z.—.

3. *ekperissōs* [ἐκπερισσῶς, 1537, 4053], formed from *ek*, out of, and the adverb *perissōs*, exceedingly, the more, is found in Mark 14:31, in the best texts (some have *ek perissou*, the genitive case of the adjective *perissos*, more), R.V., "exceeding vehemently" (A.V., "the more vehemently"), of Peter's protestation of loyalty; the R.V. gives the better rendering. ¶
NT: B.243c; CB.—; K.—.
OT: —.
GEN. REF.: IS.4:967; NB.—; Z.—.

Note: For "brake (A.V., beat) vehemently," Luke 6:48, 49, see BEAT, No. 8.

VEIL

1. *katapetasma* [καταπέτασμα, 2665], lit., that which is spread out (*petannumi*) before (*kata*), hence, a veil, is used (*a*) of the inner veil of the Tabernacle, Heb. 6:19; 9:3; (*b*) of the corresponding veil in the Temple, Matt. 27:51; Mark 15:38; Luke 23:45; (*c*) metaphorically of the "flesh" of Christ, Heb. 10:20, i.e., His body which He gave up to be crucified, thus by His expiatory Death providing means of the spiritual access of believers, the "new and living way," into the presence of God. ¶
NT: B.416a; CB.1254a; K.420.
OT: tārōket: S.6532; HR.741b.2; H.1818a; BD.827d.
māsāk: S.4539; HR.741b.1; H.1482a; BD.697a.
GEN. REF.: IS.—; NB.1232; Z.5:862.

2. *kalumma* [κάλυμμα, 2571], a covering, is used (*a*) of the veil which Moses put over his face when descending Mount Sinai, thus preventing Israel from beholding the glory, 2 Cor. 3:13; (*b*) metaphorically of the spiritually darkened vision suffered retributively by Israel, until the conversion of the nation to their Messiah takes place, vv. 14, 15, 16. See under UNLIFTED. ¶
NT: B.400d; CB.1253b; K.405.
OT: mikseh: S.4372; HR.716c.1b; H.1008c; BD.492c.
masweh: S.4533; HR.716c.2; H.1472b; BD.691d.
māsāk: S.4539; HR.716c.3; H.1482a; BD.697a.
GEN. REF.: IS.4:967; NB.—; Z.—.

3. *peribolaion* [περιβόλαιον, 4018], rendered "a veil" in the A.V. marg. of 1 Cor. 11:15: see COVER, B, No. 1, VESTURE. ¶
NT: B.646c; CB.1263b; K.—.
OT: k^{e}sût: S.3682; HR.1122b.2a; H.1008b; BD.492b.
l^{e}bûsh: S.3830; HR.1122b.3a; H.1075a; BD.528c.
malbûsh: S.4403; HR.1122b.3b; H.1075b; BD.528d.
GEN. REF.: —.

VENGEANCE

ekdikēsis [ἐκδίκησις, 1557], lit., '(that which proceeds) out of justice,' not, as often with human vengeance, out of a sense of injury or merely out of a feeling of indignation. The word is most frequently used of Divine vengeance, e.g., Rom. 12:19; Heb. 10:30. For a complete list see AVENGE, B, No. 2. The judgments of God are holy and right (Rev. 16:7), and free from any element of self-gratification or vindictiveness.
NT: B.238d; CB.1243c; K.215.
OT: n^{e}qāmāh: S.5360; HR.423a.2c; H.1413b; BD.668c.
nāqām: S.5359; HR.423a.2b; H.1413a; BD.668b.
shepheṭ: S.8201; HR.423a.4b; H.2443a; BD.1048a.
GEN. REF.: IS.4:968; NB.—; Z.5:863.

Notes: (1) *Dikē*, justice, is translated "vengeance" in the A.V. of Acts 28:4 and Jude 7: see JUSTICE.

(2) In Rom. 3:5, A.V., *orgē*, wrath (R.V.), is rendered "vengeance": see ANGER, WRATH.

For **VENOMOUS** see **BEAST**, No. 2

VERILY

1. *alēthōs* [ἀληθῶς, 230], truly (akin to *alētheia*, truth), is translated "verily" in 1 John 2:5. See INDEED, No. 3, SURELY, TRULY.
NT: B.37b; CB.1234b; K.—.
OT: 'um^{e}nāh: S.552; HR.54b.1d; H.116i; BD.53d.
'emet: S.571; HR.54b.1e; H.116k; BD.54a.
GEN. REF.: IS.4:923; NB.1301; Z.5:827.

2. *amēn* [ἀμήν, 281], the transliteration of a Heb. word = 'truth,' is usually translated "verily" in the four Gospels; in John's Gospel the Lord introduces a solemn pronouncement by the repeated word "verily, verily" twenty-five times. See AMEN.
NT: B.45c; CB.1234c; K.53.
OT: 'āmēn: S.543; HR.65c.1; H.116b; BD.53b.
GEN. REF.: IS.4:923; NB.—; Z.—.

3. *ontōs* [ὄντως, 3689], really (connected with *eimi*, to be), is rendered "verily" in Mark 11:32, R.V., and Gal. 3:21. See INDEED, No. 4.
NT: B.574a; CB.—; K.—.
OT: 'um^{e}nāh: S.552; HR.1000c.3; H.116i; BD.53d.
'ak: S.389; HR.1000c.1; H.84; BD.36c.
'ākēn: S.403; HR.1000c.2; H.86; BD.38c.
GEN. REF.: IS.4:923; NB.1301; Z.—.

Notes: (1) In Acts 16:37, *gar*, for, is translated "verily."

(2) In Heb. 2:16, *dēpou* (in some texts *dē pou*), a particle meaning of course, we know, is rendered "verily." ¶

(3) In Luke 11:51, A.V., *nai*, yea (R.V.), is translated "verily."

(4) The particle *men* (see INDEED, No. 1) is rendered "verily," e.g., in 1 Cor. 5:3; 14:17; Heb. 12:10; in the A.V., Heb. 3:5; 7:5, 18; 1 Pet. 1:20; in Acts 26:9 it is combined with *oun* (therefore): see YEA, No. 4.

For **VERITY**, 1 Tim. 2:7, A.V., see **TRUTH**

VERY

Notes: (1) When "very" forms part of the translation of numerous other words (e.g., act, bold, many, precious, sorrowful, well), there is no separate word in the original.

(2) For *sphodra*, exceedingly, sometimes rendered "very" in the A.V., see EXCEEDING, B, No. 2.

(3) Occasionally one of the forms of the pronoun *autos*, self, same, is translated "very"; the R.V. rendering is sometimes "himself" etc., e.g., 1 Thess. 5:23, "(The God of peace) Himself"; see, however, John 14:11, "(the) very (works)"; Rom. 13:6 and Phil. 1:6, "(this) very (thing)"; Heb. 10:1, "(the) very (image)"; and the R.V., "very" (A.V., "same") in Luke 12:12; 20:19; 24:13, 33; Acts 16:18; Rom. 9:17; Eph. 6:22.

(4) Sometimes it translates the conjunction *kai*, in the sense of "even," e.g., Matt. 10:30; in 24:24, A.V., "very" (R.V., "even"); Luke 12:59.

(5) In Philm. 12, R.V., "my very" translates the possessive pronoun *emos* (in the neuter plural, *ema*) used with emphasis.

(6) In Mark 8:1 some texts have *pampollou*, "very great," A.V. (from *pas*, all, *polus*, much), R.V., "a great *(pollou) multitude*" (after *palin*, again).

(7) For "very great" in Matt. 21:8 see GREAT, *Note* (6).

(8) The adverb *lian* is translated "very" in Mark 16:2; 2 Cor. 11:5; 12:11. See EXCEEDING, B, No. 1.

VESSEL

1. *skeuos* [σκεῦος, 4632], is used (*a*) of a vessel or implement of various kinds, Mark 11:16; Luke 8:16; John 19:29; Acts 10:11, 16; 11:5; 27:17 (a sail); Rom. 9:21; 2 Tim. 2:20; Heb. 9:21; Rev. 2:27; 18:12; (*b*) of goods or household stuff, Matt. 12:29 and Mark 3:27, "goods"; Luke 17:31, R.V., "goods" (A.V., "stuff"); (*c*) of persons, (1) for the service of God, Acts 9:15, "a (chosen) vessel"; 2 Tim. 2:21, "a vessel (unto honour)"; (2) the subjects of Divine wrath, Rom. 9:22; (3) the subjects of Divine mercy, Rom. 9:23; (4) the human frame, 2 Cor. 4:7; perhaps 1 Thess. 4:4; (5) a husband and wife, 1 Pet. 3:7; of the wife, probably, 1 Thess. 4:4; while the exhortation to each one "to possess himself of his own vessel in sanctification and honour" is regarded by some as referring to the believer's body [cp. Rom. 6:13; 1 Cor.9:27; see No. (4)], the view that the "vessel" signifies the wife, and that the reference is to the sanctified maintenance of the married state, is supported by the facts that in 1 Pet. 3:7 the same word *timē*, honour, is used with regard to the wife; again in Heb. 13:4, *timios*, honourable (R.V., "in honour") is used in regard to marriage; further, the preceding command in 1 Thess. 4 is against fornication, and the succeeding one (ver. 6) is against adultery. ¶ In Ruth 4:10, Sept., *ktaomai*, to possess, is used of a wife.

NT: B.754a; CB.1269a; K.1038.
OT: k^{e}lî: S.3627; HR.1269b.1; H.982g; BD.479b.
GEN. REF.: IS.3:919; NB.1310; Z.5:878.

2. *angos* [ἄγγος, —], denotes a jar or pail, Matt. 13:48, in the best texts (some have No. 3). It is used, in an inscription, of a cinerary urn. ¶

NT: B.8b; CB.—; K.—.
OT: k^{e}lî: S.3627; HR.9a.2; H.982g; BD.479b.
k^{e}lûb: S.3619; HR.9a.1; H.981b; BD.477b.
GEN. REF.: IS.3:919; NB.1310; Z.5:878.

3. *angeion* [ἀγγεῖον, 30], denotes a small vessel (a diminutive of No. 2), e.g., for carrying oil, Matt. 25:4. ¶

NT: B.6d; CB.—; K.—.
OT: —.
GEN. REF.: —.

Note: For *phaulos*, Jas. 3:16, R.V., see EVIL, A, No. 3.

VESTURE

1. *himation* [ἱμάτιον, 2440], an outer garment, is rendered "vesture" in Rev. 19:13, 16, A.V. (R.V., "garment"). See APPAREL, No. 2.

NT: B.376b; CB.1250c; K.—.
OT: beged: S.899; HR.685a.1; H.198a; BD.93d.
sîmlāh: S.8071; HR.685a.11; H.2270a; BD.971a.
GEN. REF.: IS.4:983; NB.1310; Z.5:880.

2. *himatismos* [ἱματισμός, 2441], used of clothing in general, is translated "vesture" in Matt. 27:35, A.V., in a quotation from Ps. 22:18 (R.V., following the better texts, omits the quotation); in John 19:24, A.V. and R.V.; see CLOTHING, No. 4.

NT: B.376d; CB.—; K.—.
OT: beged: S.899; HR.686a.1; H.198a; BD.93d.
l^{e}bûsh: S.3830; HR.686a.4a; H.1075a; BD.528c.
sîmlāh: S.8071; HR.686a.7; H.2270a; BD.971a.
GEN. REF.: IS.4:983; NB.1310; Z.5:880.

3. *peribolaion* [περιβόλαιον, 4018], is translated "vesture" in Heb. 1:12, A.V. (R.V., "mantle"). See COVER, B, No. 1.
NT: B.646c; CB.1263b; K.—.
OT: k^e^sût: S.3682; HR.1122b.2a; H.1008b; BD.492b.
l^e^bûsh: S.3830; HR.1122b.3a; H.1075a; BD.528c.
malbûsh: S.4403; HR.1122b.3b; H.1075b; BD.528d.
GEN. REF.: IS.4:983; NB.1310; Z.5:880.

VEX

1. *ochleō* [ὀχλέω, 3791], to disturb, trouble, is used in the Passive Voice, of being troubled by evil spirits, Acts 5:16. ¶
NT: B.600c; CB.—; K.—.
OT: —.
GEN. REF.: —.

2. *basanizō* [βασανίζω, 928], to torment, is translated "vexed" in 2 Pet. 2:8. See TORMENT.
NT: B.134c; CB.1238c; K.96.
OT: —.
GEN. REF.: IS.4:983; NB.—; Z.—.

Notes: (1) In Luke 6:18, the best texts have *enochleō*, R.V., "troubled." See TROUBLE, B, No. 5.

(2) In 2 Pet. 2:7, A.V., *kataponeō*, to wear down with toil, is translated "vexed." See DISTRESS, B, No. 4.

(3) In Acts 12:1, A.V., *kakoō*, to afflict (R.V.), is translated "to vex." See AFFLICT, No. 1.

(4) For Matt. 17:15, A.V., "vexed," see GRIEVOUSLY, B, *Note* (2).

For VIAL see BOWL

VICTORY, VICTORIOUS

A. Nouns.

1. *nikē* [νίκη, 3529], victory, is used in 1 John 5:4. ¶
NT: B.539c; CB.1259c; K.634.
OT: nēṣaḥ: S.5331; HR.945b.1; H.1402a; BD.664b.
GEN. REF.: —.

2. *nikos* [νῖκος, 3534], a later form of No. 1, is used in Matt. 12:20; 1 Cor. 15:54, 55, 57. ¶
NT: B.539d; CB.1259c; K.634.
OT: nēṣaḥ: S.5331; HR.945c.1; H.1402a; BD.664b.
GEN. REF.: —.

B. Verb.

nikaō [νικάω, 3528], to conquer, overcome, is translated "(them) that come victorious from" in Rev. 15:2, R.V. (A.V., "that had gotten the victory"). See CONQUER, OVERCOME, PREVAIL.
NT: B.539a; CB.1259c; K.634.
OT: nāṣaḥ: S.5329; HR.945b.3; H.—; BD.—.
GEN. REF.: IS.—; NB.—; Z.1:761.

VICTUALS

episitismos [ἐπισιτισμός, 1979], provisions, food (*epi*, upon, *sitizō*, to feed, nourish; *sitos*, food), is translated "victuals" in Luke 9:12. ¶
NT: B.298c; CB.—; K.—.
OT: ṣêdāh: S.6720; HR.527b.1; H.1886b; BD.845b.
GEN. REF.: —.

Note: In Matt. 14:15, A.V., *brōma*, food, meat, is translated "victuals" (R.V., "food"). See MEAT.

For VIGILANT, 1 Tim. 3:2, see TEMPERATE; 1 Pet. 5:8, see WATCHFUL

VILE

A. Noun.

atimia [ἀτιμία, 819], dishonour, is translated "vile" in Rom. 1:26, R.V., marg., "(passions) of dishonour." see DISHONOUR.
NT: B.120a; CB.1238b; K.—.
OT: k^e^limmāh: S.3639; HR.175c.3b; H.987a; BD.484a.
qālôn: S.7036; HR.175c.5c; H.2024a; BD.885d.
GEN. REF.: —.

B. Adjectives.

1. *rhuparos* [ῥυπαρός, 4508], filthy, dirty, is used (*a*) literally, of old shabby clothing, Jas. 2:2, "vile"; (*b*) metaphorically, of moral defilement, Rev. 22:11 (in the best texts). ¶ In the Sept., Zech. 3:3, 4. ¶
NT: B.738a; CB.1268b; K.—.
OT: ṣō': S.6674; HR.1255b.1; H.1883d; BD.844b.
GEN. REF.: —.

2. *ponēros* [πονηρός, 4190], evil, is translated "vile" in Acts 17:5, R.V. (A.V., "lewd"). See BAD, EVIL.
NT: B.690d; CB.1266a; K.912.
OT: ra': S.7451; HR.1186c.4a; H.2191; BD.948a.
GEN. REF.: IS.4:984; NB.—; Z.—.

Note: For "vile" in the A.V. of Phil. 3:21, see HUMILIATION.

VILLAGE

kōmē [κώμη, 2968], a village, or country town, primarily as distinct from a walled town, occurs in the Gospels; elsewhere only in Acts 8:25. The difference between *polis*, a city, and *kōmē*, is maintained in the N.T., as in Josephus. Among the Greeks the point of the distinction was not that of size or fortification, but of constitution and land. In the O.T. the city and the village are regularly distinguished. The Mishna makes the three distinctions, a large city, a city and a village.

The R.V. always substitutes "village(-s)" for A.V., "town(-s)," Matt. 10:11; Mark 8:23, 26, 27; Luke 5:17; 9:6, 12; John 7:42; 11:1, 30. See TOWN.
NT: B.461d; CB.1255c; K.—.
OT: ḥāṣēr: S.2691; HR.839c.3; H.722a,723a; BD.347b.
bat: S.1323; HR.839c.1; H.254b; BD.123a.
GEN. REF.: IS.4:984; NB.1310; Z.5:880.

VILLANY

1. *rhạdiourgia* [ῥᾳδιουργία, 4468], lit. and primarily denotes ease in working (*rhạdios*,

easy, *ergon*, work), easiness, laziness; hence recklessness, wickedness, Acts 13:10, R.V., "villany," A.V., "mischief." ¶ In the papyri it is used of theft.
NT: B.733c; CB.–; K.983.
OT: –.
GEN. REF.: IS.4:985; NB.–; Z.–.

2. *rhąadiourgēma* [ῥᾳδιούργημα, 4467], a reckless act (akin to No. 1), occurs in Acts 18:14, R.V., "villany" (A.V., "lewdness"). ¶
NT: B.733c; CB.–; K.983.
OT: –.
GEN. REF.: –.

VINE, VINTAGE

ampelos [ἄμπελος, 288], is used (*a*) lit., e.g., Matt. 26:29 and parallel passages; Jas. 3:12; (*b*) figuratively, (1) of Christ, John 15:1, 4, 5; (2) of His enemies, Rev. 14:18, 19, "the vine of the earth" (R.V., "vintage" in v. 19), probably figurative of the remaining mass of apostate Christendom. ¶
NT: B.46c; CB.1234c; K.54.
OT: gephen: S.1612; HR.66c.2; H.372a; BD.172a.
GEN. REF.: IS.4:986; NB.–; Z.5:882.

VINEDRESSER

ampelourgos [ἀμπελουργός, 289], a worker in a vineyard (from *ampelos*, a vine, and *ergon*), is rendered "vine-dresser" in Luke 13:7, R.V. (A.V., "dresser of the vineyard"). ¶
NT: B.47a; CB.1234c; K.–.
OT: kōrēm: S.3755; HR.67a.1; H.1040; BD.501d.
GEN. REF.: IS.4:986; NB.–; Z.–.

VINEGAR

oxos [ὄξος, 3690], akin to *oxus*, sharp, denotes sour wine, the ordinary drink of labourers and common soldiers; it is used in the four Gospels of the vinegar offered to the Lord at His crucifixion. In Matt. 27:34 the best texts have *oinos*, "wine" (R.V.). Some have *oxos* (A.V., vinegar), but Mark 15:23 (A.V. and R.V.) confirms the R.V. in the passage in Matthew. This, which the soldiers offered before crucifying, was refused by Him, as it was designed to alleviate His sufferings; the vinegar is mentioned in Mark 15:36; so Luke 23:36, and John 19:29, 30. ¶ In the Sept., Numb. 6:3; Ruth 2:14; Ps. 69:21; Prov. 25:20. ¶
NT: B.574b; CB.1261b; K.701.
OT: ḥōmeṣ: S.2558; HR.1001a.1; H.679b; BD.330a.
GEN. REF.: IS.4:987; NB.1312; Z.5:884.

VINEYARD

ampelōn [ἀμπελών, 290], is used 22 times in the Synoptic Gospels; elsewhere in 1 Cor. 9:7.
NT: B.47a; CB.1234c; K.–.
OT: kerem: S.3754; HR.67a.2; H.1040a; BD.501c.
GEN. REF.: IS.4:986; NB.1312; Z.5:882.

VIOLENCE, VIOLENT, VIOLENTLY

A. Nouns.

1. *bia* [βία, 970], denotes force, violence, said of men, Acts 5:26; 21:35; 24:7; of waves, 27:41. ¶
NT: B.140c; CB.1239a; K.–.
OT: kᵉbēdut: S.3517; HR.218a.3; H.943g; BD.459c.
perek: S.6531; HR.218a.4; H.1817a; BD.827d.
tōqeph: S.8633; HR.218a.6; H.2542a; BD.1076a.
GEN. REF.: IS.4:987; NB.–; Z.–.

2. *hormēma* [ὅρμημα, 3731], a rush (akin to *hormaō*, to urge on, to rush), is used of the fall of Babylon, Rev. 18:21, A.V., "violence," R.V., "mighty fall." ¶
NT: B.581d; CB.–; K.730.
OT: ʿebrāh: S.5678; HR.1014a.2; H.1556d; BD.720c.
GEN. REF.: IS.4:987; NB.–; Z.–.

3. *biastēs* [βιαστής, 973], a forceful or violent man, is used in Matt. 11:12. See FORCE, B, No. 1, *Note*. ¶
NT: B.141a; CB.1239a; K.105.
OT: –.
GEN. REF.: IS.4:988; NB.–; Z.–.

Note: In Heb. 11:34, A.V., *dunamis*, power (R.V.), is rendered "violence."

B. Verbs.

1. *diaseiō* [διασείω, 1286], to shake violently, is used in Luke 3:14, "do violence," including intimidation. ¶ In the Sept., Job 4:14. ¶
NT: B.188b; CB.1241b; K.–.
OT: pāḥad: S.6342; HR.309c.1; H.1756; BD.808b.
GEN. REF.: IS.4:987; NB.–; Z.–.

2. *biazō* [βιάζω, 971], in the Passive Voice, is rendered "suffereth violence" in Matt. 11:12; see FORCE, B, Nos. 1 and 2. Some, e.g., Cremer (Lexicon) and Dalman (*Words of Jesus*, pp. 139, ff.), hold that the reference is to the antagonism of the enemies of the Kingdom, but Luke 16:16 (Middle Voice: R.V., "entereth violently") indicates the meaning as referring to those who make an effort to enter the Kingdom in spite of violent opposition: see PRESS, A, No. 3. ¶
NT: B.140c; CB.1239a; K.–.
OT: pāraṣ: S.6555; HR.218a.6; H.1826; BD.829b.
pāṣar: S.6484; HR.218a.5; H.1801; BD.823a.
GEN. REF.: IS.4:987; NB.–; Z.–.

Note: For *hormaō*, rendered "ran violently," in Matt. 8:32 and parallels, see RUN, RUSH.

VIPER

echidna [ἔχιδνα, 2191], is probably a generic term for poisonous snakes. It is rendered "viper" in the N.T., (*a*) of the actual creature, Acts 28:3; (*b*) metaphorically in Matt. 3:7; 12:34; 23:33; Luke 3:7. ¶
NT: B.331d; CB.–; K.286.
OT: –.
GEN. REF.: IS.4:988; NB.–; Z.5:885.

VIRGIN

parthenos [παρθένος, 3933], is used (*a*) of the Virgin Mary, Matt. 1:23; Luke 1:27; (*b*) of the ten virgins in the parable, Matt. 25:1, 7, 11; (*c*) of the daughters of Philip the evangelist, Acts 21:9; (*d*) those concerning whom the Apostle Paul gives instructions regarding marriage, 1 Cor. 7:25, 28, 34; in vv. 36, 37, 38, the subject passes to that of 'virgin *daughters*' (R.V.), which almost certainly formed one of the subjects upon which the church at Corinth sent for instructions from the Apostle; one difficulty was relative to the discredit which might be brought upon a father (or guardian), if he allowed his daughter or ward to grow old unmarried. The interpretation that this passage refers to a man and woman already in some kind of relation by way of a spiritual marriage and living together in a vow of virginity and celibacy, is untenable if only in view of the phraseology of the passage; (*e*) figuratively, of a local church in its relation to Christ, 2 Cor. 11:2; (*f*) metaphorically, of chaste persons, Rev. 14:4. ¶

NT: B.627a; CB.1262c; K.786.
OT: b^{e}tûlāh: S.1330; HR.1070a.1a; H.295a; BD.143d.
'almāh: S.5959; HR.1070a.3; H.1627d; BD.761c.
GEN. REF.: IS.4:989; NB.1312; Z.5:885.

VIRGINITY

parthenia [παρθενία, 3932], akin to the above, occurs in Luke 2:36. ¶ In the Sept., Jer. 3:4. ¶

NT: B.626d; CB.1262c; K.–.
OT: h^{e}'ûrûm: S.5271; HR.1069c.1; H.1389d,e; BD.655b.
GEN. REF.: IS.4:989; NB.1312; Z.5:885.

VIRTUE

aretē [ἀρετή, 703], properly denotes whatever procures pre-eminent estimation for a person or thing; hence, intrinsic eminence, moral goodness, virtue, (*a*) of God, 1 Pet. 2:9, "excellencies" (A.V., "praises"); here the original and general sense seems to be blended with the impression made on others, i.e., renown, excellence or praise (Hort); in 2 Pet. 1:3, "(by His own glory and) virtue," R.V. (instrumental dative), i.e., the manifestation of His divine power; this significance is frequently illustrated in the papyri and was evidently common in current Greek speech; (*b*) of any particular moral excellence, Phil. 4:8; 2 Pet. 1:5 (twice), where virtue is enjoined as an essential quality in the exercise of faith, R.V., "(in your faith supply) virtue." ¶

NT: B.105d; CB.1237c; K.77.
OT: t^{e}hillāh: S.8416; HR.156a.2; H.500c; BD.239d.
hôd: S.1935; HR.156a.1; H.482a; BD.217a.
GEN. REF.: IS.4:993; NB.1312; Z.5:889.

Note: In the A.V. of Mark 5:30; Luke 6:19; 8:46, *dunamis*, "power" (R.V.), is rendered "virtue."

VISIBLE

horatos [ὁρατός, 3707], from *horaō*, to see, occurs in Col. 1:16. ¶

NT: B.577c; CB.1251a; K.706.
OT: mar'eh: S.4758; HR.1008b.1a; H.2095i; BD.909c.
rā'āh: S.7200; HR.1008b.1b; H.2095; BD.906b.
GEN. REF.: IS.4:993; NB.1312; Z.5:889.

VISION

1. *horama* [ὅραμα, 3705], that which is seen (*horaō*), denotes (*a*) a spectacle, sight, Matt. 17:9; Acts 7:31 ("sight"); (*b*) an appearance, vision, Acts 9:10 (ver. 12 in some mss.); 10:3, 17, 19; 11:5; 12:9; 16:9, 10; 18:9. ¶

NT: B.577b; CB.1251a; K.706.
OT: ḥāzôn: S.2377; HR.1004c.1a; H.633a; BD.303b.
mar'eh: S.4758; HR.1004c.4a; H.2095i; BD.909c.
massā': S.4853; HR.1004c.5; H.1421e; BD.672d.
GEN. REF.: IS.4:993; NB.1312; Z.5:889.

2. *horasis* [ὅρασις, 3706], sense of sight, is rendered "visions" in Acts 2:17; Rev. 9:17. See LOOK, B.

NT: B.577c; CB.1251a; K.706.
OT: ḥāzôn: S.2377; HR.1007b.2a; H.633a; BD.303b.
mar'eh: S.4758; HR.1007b.4a; H.2095i; BD.909c.
GEN. REF.: IS.4:993; NB.1312; Z.5:889.

3. *optasia* [ὀπτασία, 3701], (a late form of *opsis*, the act of seeing), from *optanō*, to see, a coming into view, denotes a vision in Luke 1:22; 24:23; Acts 26:19; 2 Cor. 12:1. ¶

NT: B.576c; CB.1261a; K.706.
OT: mar'āh: S.4759; HR.1004b.1c; H.2095a,h; BD.909b.
mar'eh: S.4758; HR.1004b.1b; H.2095i; BD.909c.
GEN. REF.: IS.4:993; NB.1312; Z.5:889.

VISIT

1. *episkeptomai* [ἐπισκέπτομαι, 1980], primarily, to inspect (a late form of *episkopeō*, to look upon, care for, exercise oversight), signifies (*a*) to visit with help, of the act of God, Luke 1:68, 78; 7:16; Acts 15:14; Heb. 2:6; (*b*) to visit the sick and afflicted, Matt. 25:36, 43; Jas. 1:27; (*c*) to go and see, pay a visit to, Acts 7:23; 15:36; (*d*) to look out certain men for a purpose, Acts 6:3. See LOOK. ¶

NT: B.298c; CB.1246a; K.244.
OT: pāqad: S.6485; HR.527c.5; H.1802; BD.823a.
GEN. REF.: IS.4:994; NB.–; Z.–.

Note: In the Sept., to visit with punishment, e.g., Psa. 89:32; Jer. 9:25.

2. *historeō* [ἱστορέω, 2477], from *histōr*, one learned in anything, denotes to visit in order to become acquainted with, Gal. 1:18, R.V., "visit" (A.V., "see"), R.V. marg., "become acquainted with." ¶

NT: B.383a; CB.1251a; K.377.
OT: –.
GEN. REF.: IS.4:994; NB.–; Z.–.

3. *epipherō* [ἐπιφέρω, 2018], for which see BRING, No. 6, is rendered "visiteth (with wrath)" in Rom. 3:5, R.V., A.V., "taketh (vengeance)."

NT: B.304c; CB.1246a; K.–.
OT: shālaḥ: S.7971; HR.538a.6; H.2394; BD.1018a.
GEN. REF.: –.

VISITATION

episkopē [ἐπισκοπή, 1984], for which see BISHOP, No. 2, denotes a visitation, whether in mercy, Luke 19:44, or in judgment, 1 Pet. 2:12.

NT: B.299a; CB.1246a; K.244.
OT: pāqad: S.6485; HR.528c.5a; H.1802; BD.823a.
pᵉquddāh: S.6486; HR.528c.5d; H.1802a; BD.824a.
GEN. REF.: IS.4:994; NB.–; Z.5:890.

For **VOCATION**, Eph. 4:1, see **CALL**, B

VOICE

phōnē [φωνή, 5456], a sound, is used of the voice (*a*) of God, Matt. 3:17; John 5:37; 12:28, 30; Acts 7:31; 10:13, 15; 11:7, 9; Heb. 3:7, 15; 4:7; 12:19, 26; 2 Pet. 1:17, 18; Rev. 18:4; 21:3; (*b*) of Christ, (1) in the days of His flesh, Matt. 12:19 (negatively); John 3:29; 5:25; 10:3, 4, 16, 27; 11:43; 18:37; (2) on the Cross, Matt. 27:46, and parallel passages; (3) from heaven, Acts 9:4, 7; 22:7, 9, 14; 26:14; Rev. 1:10, 12 (here, by metonymy, of the speaker), 15; 3:20; (4) at the resurrection "to life," John 5:28; 1 Thess. 4:16, where "the voice of the archangel" is, lit., 'a voice of an archangel,' and probably refers to the Lord's voice as being of an archangelic character; (5) at the resurrection to judgment, John 5:28 [not the same event as (4)]; (*c*) of human beings on earth, e.g., Matt. 2:18; 3:3; Luke 1:42, in some texts, A.V., "voice," and frequently in the Synoptists; (*d*) of angels, Rev. 5:11, and frequently in the Apocalypse; (*e*) of the redeemed in heaven, e.g., Rev. 6:10; 18:22; 19:1, 5; (*f*) of a pagan god, Acts 12:22; (*g*) of things, e.g., wind, John 3:8, R.V., "voice" (A.V., "sound"). See SOUND.

NT: B.870c; CB.1264a; K.1287.
OT: qôl: S.6963; HR.1447b.10a; H.1998a,2028b; BD.876d.
GEN. REF.: IS.4:997; NB.–; Z.–.

Notes: (1) In Luke 1:42 (1st part), A.V., *anaphōneō*, to lift up one's voice, is rendered "spake out," R.V., "lifted up (her) voice."

(2) In Acts 26:10, A.V., "I gave my voice" (R.V., ". . . vote"): see STONE, No. 2.

VOID

1. *kenoō* [κενόω, 2758], to empty, make of no effect, is rendered to make void, in Rom. 4:14; 1 Cor. 1:17, R.V.; 9:15; 2 Cor. 9:3, R.V. See EFFECT (of none), No. 3, EMPTY, VAIN, B, No. 2.

NT: B.428a; CB.1255a; K.426.
OT: 'āmal: S.535; HR.759b.1; H.114; BD.51b.
GEN. REF.: –.

2. *atheteō* [ἀθετέω, 114], for which see DISANNUL, No. 1, is rendered to make void in Gal. 2:21, R.V. (A.V., "frustrate"); 3:15, R.V.

NT: B.21a; CB.1238a; K.1176.
OT: bāgad: S.898; HR.29b.1; H.198; BD.93c.
mārad: S.4775; HR.29b.7; H.1240; BD.597c.
pāsha': S.6586; HR.29b.12; H.1846; BD.833b.
GEN. REF.: –.

3. *akuroō* [ἀκυρόω, 208], for which see DISANNUL, No. 2, is rendered to make void in Matt. 15:6; Mark 7:13, R.V.

NT: B.34b; CB.–; K.494.
OT: –.
GEN. REF.: IS.4:997; NB.–; Z.–.

Notes: (1) In Rom. 3:31, A.V., *katargeō* is translated to make void. See ABOLISH, EFFECT (of none), No. 2.

(2) See also IMPOSSIBLE, B, OFFENCE, UNDERSTANDING.

For **VOLUME** see **ROLL**, B

VOLUNTARY

Note: In Col. 2:18, *thelō* (for which see DESIRE, B, No. 6) is rendered "(in a) voluntary (humility)," present participle, i.e., "being a voluntary (in humility)," A.V. marg., R.V. marg., "of his own mere will (by humility)," *en*, in, being rendered as instrumental; what was of one's own mere will, with the speciousness of humility, would mean his being robbed of his prize.

VOMIT

exerama [ἐξέραμα, 1829], a vomit (from *exeraō*, to disgorge), occurs in 2 Pet. 2:22. ¶

NT: B.274b; CB.–; K.–.
OT: –.
GEN. REF.: –.

For **VOTE**, Acts 26:10, R.V., see **STONE**, No. 2

VOUCHSAFE

homologeō [ὁμολογέω, 3670], to agree, is found in the best texts in Acts 7:17, and rendered "vouchsafed," R.V., with reference to God's promise to Abraham; some mss. have *ōmosen*, "swore" (*omnumi*, to swear), as in A.V. See CONFESS, PROFESS, PROMISE, THANKS, B, *Note*.

NT: B.568a; CB.1251a; K.687.
OT: nādar: S.5087; HR.993c.2; H.1308; BD.623d.
shāba': S.7650; HR.993c.3; H.2318; BD.989a.
GEN. REF.: –.

VOW

euchē [εὐχή, 2171], denotes also a vow, Acts 18:18; 21:23, with reference to the vow of the Nazirite (wrongly spelt Nazarite), see Numb. 6, R.V.; in Jas. 5:15, "prayer." See PRAYER. ¶

NT: B.329b; CB.1247a; K.279.
OT: nēder: S.5088; HR.584b.2b; H.1308a; BD.623d.
nēzer: S.5145; HR.584b.3b; H.1340a; BD.634b.
GEN. REF.: IS.4:998; NB.1313; Z.5:890.

VOYAGE

ploos or *plous* [πλόος, 4144], is rendered a voyage (*pleō*, to sail) in Acts 27:10 (A.V. and R.V.); in 21:7, R.V. (A.V., "course"); in 27:9, R.V. (A.V., "sailing"). See COURSE, B, *Note* (4). ¶

NT: B.673c; CB.—; K.—.
OT: —.
GEN. REF.: —.

W

WAG

kineō [κινέω, 2795], to move, is used of those who mocked the Lord at His crucifixion, nodding their heads in the direction of the Cross as if sneering at this supposed ending of His career, Matt. 27:39; Mark 15:29. Cp. 2 Kings 19:21; Job 16:4; Psa. 22:7; 109:25; Is. 37:22. See MOVE, No. 1.

NT: B.432c; CB.—; K.435.
OT: nûaʿ: S.5128; HR.765b.7; H.1328; BD.631a.
GEN. REF.: —.

WAGES

1. *opsōnion* [ὀψώνιον, 3800], for which see CHARGE, A, No. 5, denotes (*a*) soldiers' pay, Luke 3:14; 1 Cor. 9:7 ("charges"); (*b*) in general, hire, wages of any sort, used metaphorically, Rom. 6:23, of sin; 2 Cor. 11:8, of material support which Paul received from some of the churches which he had established and to which he ministered in spiritual things; their support partly maintained him at Corinth, where he forebore to receive such assistance (vv. 9, 10). ¶

NT: B.602a; CB.1261a; K.752.
OT: —.
GEN. REF.: IS.4:1001; NB.—; Z.5:893.

2. *misthos* [μισθός, 3408], hire, is rendered "wages" in John 4:36; in 2 Pet. 2:15, A.V. (R.V., "hire"). See HIRE, A.

NT: B.523b; CB.1259a; K.599.
OT: sakar: S.7936; HR.930a.6a; H.2264.1; BD.968d.
maskōret: S.4909; HR.930a.6b; H.2264.1d; BD.969b.
GEN. REF.: IS.4:1001; NB.1314; Z.5:893.

WAIL, WAILING

Notes: (1) For *alalazō*, rendered to wail in Mark 5:38, see CLANGING.

(2) For *koptō*, rendered to wail in Rev. 1:7, A.V. (R.V., "shall mourn") and 18:9, R.V., "wail" (A.V., "lament"), see BEWAIL.

(3) For *pentheō*, rendered to wail in Rev. 18:15, 19, A.V., see MOURN.

(4) For *klauthmos*, rendered "wailing" in Matt. 13:42, 50, A.V., see WEEP.

(5) In Matt. 11:17 and Luke 7:32, A.V., *thrēneō*, to wail (R.V.), is rendered to mourn. See BEWAIL, *Note* (1), MOURN.

WAIT

1. *ekdechomai* [ἐκδέχομαι, 1551], for which see EXPECT, No. 1, is rendered to wait in John 5:3, A.V.; Acts 17:16; 1 Cor. 11:33, R.V.

NT: B.238b; CB.1243c; K.146.
OT: —.
GEN. REF.: IS.4:1003; NB.—; Z.—.

2. *apekdechomai* [ἀπεκδέχομαι, 553], to await or expect eagerly, is rendered to wait for in Rom. 8:19, 23, 25; 1 Cor. 1:7; Gal. 5:5; Phil. 3:20, R.V. (A.V., "look for"); Heb. 9:28, R.V. (A.V., "look for"), here "them that wait" represents believers in general, not a section of them; 1 Pet. 3:20 (in the best texts; some have No. 1). See LOOK (for), *Note* (1). ¶

NT: B.83c; CB.1236b; K.146.
OT: —.
GEN. REF.: IS.4:1003; NB.—; Z.—.

3. *prosdechomai* [προσδέχομαι, 4327], to look for with a view to favourable reception, is rendered to wait for in Mark 15:43; Luke 2:25; 12:36; 23:51. See LOOK (for), No. 2.

NT: B.712a; CB.1267a; K.146.
OT: rāṣāh: S.7521; HR.1212c.8; H.2207; BD.953a.
sābar: S.7663; HR.1212c.9; H.2232; BD.960b.
GEN. REF.: IS.4:1003; NB.—; Z.—.

4. *prosdokaō* [προσδοκάω, 4328], to await, is rendered to wait for in Luke 1:21; 8:40; Acts 10:24; in 27:33, R.V., "ye wait" (A.V., "have tarried"). See LOOK (for), No. 1.

NT: B.712c; CB.1267a; K.943.
OT: qāwāh: S.6960; HR.1213a.1; H.1994,1995; BD.875c.
sābar: S.7663; HR.1213a.2; H.2232; BD.960b.
GEN. REF.: IS.4:1003; NB.—; Z.—.

5. *anamenō* [ἀναμένω, 362], to wait for (*ana*, up, used intensively, and *menō*, to abide), is used in 1 Thess. 1:10, of waiting for the Son of God from heaven; the word carries with it

the suggestion of waiting with patience and confident expectancy. ¶

NT: B.57d; CB.1235a; K.—.
OT: qāwāh: S.6960; HR.79c.1; H.1994,1995; BD.875c.
GEN. REF.: IS.4:1003; NB.—; Z.—.

6. *perimenō* [περιμένω, 4037], to await an event, is used in Acts 1:4, of waiting for the Holy Spirit, "the promise of the Father." ¶ In the Sept., Gen. 49:18. ¶

NT: B.648c; CB.1263b; K.581.
OT: qāwāh: S.6960; HR.1124c.1; H.1994,1995; BD.875c.
GEN. REF.: IS.4:1002; NB.—; Z.—.

7. *proskartereō* [προσκαρτερέω, 4342], to continue stedfastly, is rendered to wait on, in Mark 3:9 and Acts 10:7. See CONTINUE, No. 9 (in the Sept., Numb. 13:21 ¶).

NT: B.715c; CB.1267a; K.417.
OT: ḥāzaq: S.2388; HR.1216c.1; H.636; BD.304a.
GEN. REF.: IS.4:1003; NB.—; Z.—.

8. *paredreuō* [παρεδρεύω, —], to sit constantly beside (*para*, beside, *hedra*, a seat), is used in the best texts in 1 Cor. 9:13, R.V., "wait upon (A.V., at) (the altar)." ¶ In the Sept., Prov. 1:21; 8:3. ¶

NT: B.624a; CB.—; K.—.
OT: —.
GEN. REF.: —.

Notes: (1) In 2 Thess. 3:5, A.V., *hupomonē*, patience (so R.V.), is rendered "patient waiting" (marg., "patience"). See PATIENCE.

(2) For "lie in wait" in Eph. 4:14, A.V., see WILES.

(3) For "lying in wait," Acts 20:19, A.V., and "laid wait," 20:3; 23:30, see PLOT.

WAKE

grēgoreō [γρηγορέω, 1127], translated "wake" in 1 Thess. 5:10, is rendered "watch" in the R.V. marg., as in the text in ver. 6, and the R.V. in the twenty-one other places in which it occurs in the N.T. (save 1 Pet. 5:8, "be watchful"). It is not used in the metaphorical sense of 'to be alive'; here it is set in contrast with *katheudō*, 'to sleep,' which is never used by the Apostle with the meaning 'to be dead' (it has this meaning only in the case of Jairus' daughter). Accordingly the meaning here is that of vigilance and expectancy as contrasted with laxity and indifference. All believers will live together with Christ from the time of the Rapture described in chap. 4; for all have spiritual life now, though their spiritual condition and attainment vary considerably. Those who are lax and fail to be watchful will suffer loss (1 Cor. 3:15; 9:27; 2 Cor. 5:10, e.g.), but the Apostle is not here dealing with that aspect of the subject. What he does make clear is that the Rapture of believers at the Second Coming of Christ will depend solely on the Death of Christ for them, and not upon their spiritual condition. The Rapture is not a matter of reward, but of salvation. See WATCH.

NT: B.167b; CB.1248c; K.195.
OT: shāqad: S.8245; HR.278a.2; H.2451; BD.1052a.
GEN. REF.: —.

WALK

1. *peripateō* [περιπατέω, 4043], is used (*a*) physically, in the Synoptic Gospels (except Mark 7:5); always in the Acts except in 21:21; never in the Pauline Epistles, nor in those of John; (*b*) figuratively, "signifying the whole round of the activities of the individual life, whether of the unregenerate, Eph. 4:17, or of the believer, 1 Cor. 7:17; Col. 2:6. It is applied to the observance of religious ordinances, Acts 21:21; Heb. 13:9, marg., as well as to moral conduct. The Christian is to walk in newness of life, Rom. 6:4, after the spirit, 8:4, in honesty, 13:13, by faith, 2 Cor. 5:7, in good works, Eph. 2:10, in love, 5:2, in wisdom, Col. 4:5, in truth, 2 John 4, after the commandments of the Lord, v. 6. And, negatively, not after the flesh, Rom. 8:4; not after the manner of men, 1 Cor. 3:3; not in craftiness, 2 Cor. 4:2; not by sight, 5:7; not in the vanity of the mind, Eph. 4:17; not disorderly, 2 Thess. 3:6."* See GO, *Note* (2) (*r*).

NT: B.649a; CB.1263b; K.804.
OT: hālak: S.1980; HR.1125a.2a-c; H.498; BD.229d.
GEN. REF.: IS.4:1003; NB.—; Z.5:894.

2. *poreuō* [πορεύω, 4198], for which see DEPART, No. 8, and GO, No. 1, is used in the Middle Voice and rendered to walk in Luke 1:6, of the general activities of life; so in Luke 13:33, A.V., "walk" (R.V., "go on My way"); Acts 9:31; 14:16; 1 Pet. 4:3; 2 Pet. 2:10; Jude 16, 18.

NT: B.692b; CB.1266a; K.—.
OT: hālak: S.1980; HR.1189a.3a; H.498; BD.229d.
GEN. REF.: IS.4:1003; NB.—; Z.5:894.

3. *emperipateō* [ἐμπεριπατέω, 1704], to walk about in, or among (*en*, in, and No. 1), is used in 2 Cor. 6:16, of the activities of God in the lives of believers. ¶

NT: B.256a; CB.1244b; K.804.
OT: hālak: S.1980; HR.456c.1; H.498; BD.229d.
GEN. REF.: IS.4:1003; NB.—; Z.5:894.

4. *stoicheō* [στοιχέω, 4748], from *stoichos*, a row, signifies to walk in line, and is used metaphorically of walking in relation to others (No. 1 is used more especially of the individual walk); in Acts 21:24, it is translated "walkest orderly"; in Rom. 4:12, "walk (in . . . steps)"; in Gal. 5:25 it is used of walking "by the Spirit," R.V., in an exhortation to keep step with one

* From Notes on Thessalonians by Hogg and Vine, p. 67.

another in submission of heart to the Holy Spirit, and therefore of keeping step with Christ, the great means of unity and harmony in a church (contrast No. 1 in ver. 16; ver. 25 begins a new section which extends to 6:10); in 6:16 it is used of walking by the rule expressed in vv. 14, 15; in Phil. 3:16 the reference is to the course pursued by the believer who makes "the prize of the high calling" the object of his ambition. ¶ In the Sept., Eccl. 11:6. ¶

NT: B.769c; CB.1270a; K.1087.
OT: kāshēr: S.3787; HR.1291c.1; H.1052; BD.506d.
GEN. REF.: IS.4:1003; NB.–; Z.–.

5. *dierchomai* [διέρχομαι, 1330], to go through (*dia*), is rendered to walk through in the A.V. of Matt. 12:43 and Luke 11:24 (R.V., "passeth through"). See COME, No. 5, PASS, No. 2.

NT: B.194c; CB.1241c; K.257.
OT: hālak: S.1980; HR.328c.4a-c; H.498; BD.229d.
yāṣā': S.3318; HR.328c.6; H.893; BD.422b.
'ābar: S.5674; HR.328c.10; H.1556; BD.716d.
GEN. REF.: IS.4:1003; NB.–; Z.5:894.

6. *orthopodeō* [ὀρθοποδέω, 3716], to walk in a straight path (*orthos*, straight, *pous*, a foot), is used metaphorically in Gal. 2:14, signifying a course of conduct by which one leaves a straight track for others to follow ("walked . . . uprightly"). ¶

NT: B.580a; CB.1261b; K.727.
OT: –.
GEN. REF.: –.

Note: In Mark 1:16, A.V., *paragō*, to pass along (R.V., "passing along"), is translated "walked."

WALL

1. *teichos* [τεῖχος, 5038], a wall, especially one around a town, is used (*a*) literally, Acts 9:25; 2 Cor. 11:33; Heb. 11:30; (*b*) figuratively, of the wall of the heavenly city, Rev. 21:12, 14, 15, 17, 18, 19. ¶

NT: B.808a; CB.1271b; K.–.
OT: ḥômāh: S.2346; HR.1339c.1; H.674e; BD.327b.
GEN. REF.: IS.–; NB.–; Z.5:894.

2. *toichos* [τοῖχος, 5109], a wall, especially of a house, is used figuratively in Acts 23:3, "(thou whited) wall." ¶

NT: B.821c; CB.1272c; K.–.
OT: qîr: S.7023; HR.1362c.5; H.2022; BD.885a.
GEN. REF.: –.

3. *mesotoichon* [μεσότοιχον, 3320], a partition wall (*mesos*, middle, and No. 2), occurs in Eph. 2:14, figuratively of the separation of Gentile from Jew in their unregenerate state, a partition demolished by the Cross for both on acceptance of the Gospel. Cp. PARTITION. ¶

NT: B.508a; CB.1258b; K.589.
OT: –.
GEN. REF.: –.

WALLET

pēra [πήρα, 4082], a traveller's leathern bag or pouch for holding provisions, is translated "wallet" in the R.V. (A.V., "scrip"), Matt. 10:10; Mark 6:8; Luke 9:3; 10:4; 22:35, 36. ¶ Deissmann (*Light from the Ancient East*) regards it as an alms-bag.

NT: B.656c; CB.1263b; K.–.
OT: –.
GEN. REF.: IS.1:403; NB.–; Z.5:894.

WALLOW (Verb and Noun)

A. Verb.

kuliō [κυλίω, 2947], in the Active Voice denotes to roll, roll along; in the Middle Voice in Mark 9:20, rendered "wallowed." ¶

NT: B.457b; CB.–; K.–.
OT: gālal: S.1556; HR.798c.1; H.353; BD.164b.
GEN. REF.: –.

B. Noun.

kulismos [κυλισμός, 2946], a rolling, wallowing, akin to A (some texts have *kulisma*), is used in 2 Pet. 2:22, of the proverbial sow that had been washed. ¶

NT: B.457b; CB.–; K.–.
OT: –.
GEN. REF.: –.

WANDER

A. Verb.

planaō [πλανάω, 4105], for which see DECEIT, C, No. 6, is translated to wander in Heb. 11:38, Passive Voice, lit., 'were made to wander.'

NT: B.666a; CB.1265a; K.857.
OT: tā'āh: S.8582; HR.1139b.16; H.2531; BD.1073b.
GEN. REF.: IS.4:1005; NB.–; Z.–.

Note: In the A.V. of 1 Tim. 5:13 and Heb. 11:37, *perierchomai*, to go about or around, is translated to wander about. See GO, No. 29.

B. Noun.

planētēs [πλανήτης, 4107], a wanderer (Eng., planet), is used metaphorically in Jude 13, of the evil teachers there mentioned as "wandering (stars)." ¶ In the Sept., Hos. 9:17. ¶

NT: B.666a; CB.1265a; K.857.
OT: nādad: S.5074; HR.1140a.1; H.1300; BD.622b.
GEN. REF.: IS.4:1005; NB.–; Z.–.

WANT (Noun and Verb)

A. Nouns.

1. *husterēsis* [ὑστέρησις, 5304], akin to B, No. 1 (below), occurs in Mark 12:14 and Phil. 4:11. ¶

NT: B.849c; CB.1252b; K.1240.
OT: –.
GEN. REF.: –.

2. *husterēma* [ὑστέρημα, 5305], denotes (more concretely than No. 1) (*a*) that which is lacking (see LACK); (*b*) need, poverty, want, rendered "want" in Luke 21:4 (A.V., "penury"); 2 Cor. 8:14 (twice); 9:12; 11:9 (2nd occurrence), R.V., "want" (A.V., "that which was lacking").
NT: B.849b; CB.1252b; K.1240.
OT: ḥesrôn: S.2642; HR.1418c.1a; H.705d; BD.341c.
GEN. REF.: –.

3. *chreia* [χρεία, 5532], is rendered "want" in Phil. 2:25, A.V. (R.V., "need"). See BUSINESS.
NT: B.884d; CB.1240a; K.–.
OT: ṣōrek: S.6878; HR.1474a.2; H.1970b; BD.863d.
GEN. REF.: –.

B. Verbs.

1. *hustereō* [ὑστερέω, 5302], signifies to be in want, Luke 15:14; 2 Cor. 11:9 (1st occurrence); Phil. 4:12, R.V. (A.V. "to suffer need"); in John 2:3, A.V., "wanted" (R.V., "failed"). See BEHIND, B, No. 1.
NT: B.849a; CB.1252b; K.1240.
OT: ḥāsēr: S.2637; HR.1418b.3a,b; H.705; BD.341a.
GEN. REF.: –.

2. *leipō* [λείπω, 3007], to leave, is rendered 'to be wanting' in Tit. 1:5 and 3:13, and in the A.V. in Jas. 1:4. See LACK, C, No. 3.
NT: B.470b; CB.1256c; K.–.
OT: –.
GEN. REF.: –.

WANTONNESS, WANTON, WANTONLY

A. Nouns.

1. *aselgeia* [ἀσέλγεια, 766], lasciviousness, licentiousness, is rendered "wantonness" in 2 Pet. 2:18, A.V.; see LASCIVIOUSNESS.
NT: B.114d; CB.1238a; K.83.
OT: –.
GEN. REF.: –.

2. *strēnos* [στρῆνος, 4764], insolent luxury, is rendered "wantonness" in Rev. 18:3, R.V. (marg., "luxury"; A.V., "delicacies," not a sufficiently strong rendering). ¶
NT: B.771c; CB.–; K.–.
OT: sha'ᵃnān: S.7600; HR.1297a.1; H.2304a; BD.983b.
GEN. REF.: IS.4:1013; NB.–; Z.–.

B. Verbs.

1. *strēniaō* [στρηνιάω, 4763], akin to A, No. 2, to run riot, is rendered "waxed wanton" in Rev. 18:7, R.V., and "lived wantonly" in ver. 8. See DELICATELY, *Note* (1). The root of the verb is seen in the Latin *strenuus*. ¶
NT: B.771c; CB.–; K.–.
OT: –.
GEN. REF.: IS.4:1013; NB.–; Z.–.

2. *katastrēniaō* [καταστρηνιάω, 2691], an intensive form of No. 1, to wax wanton against, occurs in 1 Tim. 5:11. ¶
NT: B.419b; CB.–; K.420.
OT: –.
GEN. REF.: IS.4:1013; NB.–; Z.–.

WAR (Verb and Noun)

A. Verbs.

1. *polemeō* [πολεμέω, 4170], (Eng., polemics), to fight, to make war, is used (*a*) literally, Rev. 12:7 (twice), R.V.; 13:4; 17:14; 19:11; (*b*) metaphorically, Rev. 2:16, R.V.; (*c*) hyperbolically, Jas. 4:2. See FIGHT, B, *Note* (1). ¶
NT: B.685a; CB.1265c; K.904.
OT: lāḥam: S.3898; HR.1170b.1b; H.1104; BD.535b.
GEN. REF.: IS.4:1013; NB.1315; Z.–.

2. *strateuō* [στρατεύω, 4754], used in the Middle Voice, to make war (from *stratos*, an encamped army), is translated to war in 2 Cor. 10:3; metaphorically, of spiritual conflict, 1 Tim. 1:18; 2 Tim. 2:3, A.V.; Jas. 4:1; 1 Pet. 2:11. See SOLDIER, B.
NT: B.770b; CB.1270a; K.1091.
OT: ṣābā': S.6633; HR.1295a.3; H.1865; BD.838c.
GEN. REF.: IS.4:1013; NB.–; Z.–.

3. *antistrateuomai* [ἀντιστρατεύομαι, 497], not found in the Active Voice *antistrateuō*, to make war against (*anti*), occurs in Rom. 7:23. ¶
NT: B.75d; CB.–; K.–.
OT: –.
GEN. REF.: IS.4:1013; NB.–; Z.–.

Note: For "men of war," Luke 23:11, A.V., see SOLDIER, No. 2.

B. Noun.

polemos [πόλεμος, 4171], war (akin to A, No. 1), is so translated in the R.V., for A.V., "battle," 1 Cor. 14:8; Rev. 9:7, 9; 16:14; 20:8; for A.V., "fight," Heb. 11:34; A.V. and R.V. in Jas. 4:1, hyperbolically of private quarrels; elsewhere, literally, e.g., Matt. 24:6; Rev. 11:7. See BATTLE.
NT: B.685a; CB.1265c; K.904.
OT: milḥāmāh: S.4421; HR.1172a.4a; H.1104c; BD.536a.
GEN. REF.: IS.4:1013; NB.1315; Z.–.

WARD

1. *phulakē* [φυλακή, 5438], a guard, is used of the place where persons are kept under guard (akin to *phulax*, a keeper), and translated "ward" in Acts 12:10. See CAGE, HOLD (Noun), IMPRISONMENT, PRISON, WATCH.
NT: B.867d; CB.1264c; K.1280.
OT: mishmār: S.4929; HR.1440c.2b; H.2414g; BD.1038b.
mishmeret: S.4931; HR.1440c.2c; H.2414g; BD.1038b.
maṭṭārāh: S.4307; HR.1440c.5; H.1356a; BD.643c.
GEN. REF.: IS.3:973; NB.1035; Z.4:869.

2. *tērēsis* [τήρησις, 5084], primarily denotes a watching (*tēreō*, to watch); hence imprisonment, ward, Acts 4:3 (A.V., "hold"); 5:18, R.V., "(public) ward" [A.V., "(common) prison"]. See HOLD (Noun), KEEPING, B, PRISON.
NT: B.815c; CB.1271b; K.1174.
OT: –.
GEN. REF.: IS.3:973; NB.1035; Z.4:869.

Note: For "were kept in ward," Gal. 3:23, see GUARD, B, No. 3, KEEP, No. 6.

WARE OF

phulassō [φυλάσσω, 5442], denotes to guard, watch; in 2 Tim. 4:15, "of (whom) be thou ware" (Middle Voice): see BEWARE, No. 3.
NT: B.868b; CB.1264c; K.1280.
OT: shāmar: S.8104; HR.1441a.11a,b; H.2414; BD.1036b.
GEN. REF.: –.

Note: For *sunoida*, translated "were ware" in Acts 14:6, A.V. (R.V., "became aware of it"), see KNOW, A, No. 6.

WARFARE

strateia, or *-tia* [στρατεία, 4756], primarily a host or army, came to denote a warfare, and is used of spiritual conflict in 2 Cor. 10:4; 1 Tim. 1:18. ¶
NT: B.770b; CB.1270a; K.1091.
OT: ṣābā': S.6633; HR.1295c.4; H.1865; BD.838c.
ḥayil: S.2428; HR.1295c.1; H.624a; BD.298c.
GEN. REF.: IS.4:1013; NB.–; Z.–.

Note: For the verb to go a warfare, 1 Cor. 9:7, A.V., see SOLDIER, B, No. 1.

WARM (Verb)

thermainō [θερμαίνω, 2328], to warm, heat (Eng. thermal etc.), when used in the Middle Voice, signifies to warm oneself, Mark 14:54, 67; John 18:18 (twice), 25; Jas. 2:16. ¶
NT: B.359c; CB.1272b; K.–.
OT: ḥāmam: S.2552; HR.649a.1a,b; H.677; BD.328c.
GEN. REF.: –.

WARN

1. *noutheteō* [νουθετέω, 3560], to put in mind, warn, is translated to warn in the A.V., in the passages mentioned under ADMONISH, B, No. 1 (which see); the R.V. always translates this word by the verb to admonish.
NT: B.544b; CB.1260a; K.636.
OT: yāsar: S.3256; HR.950b.2; H.877; BD.415d.
kāhāh: S.3543; HR.950b.3; H.957; BD.462d.
GEN. REF.: –.

2. *hupodeiknumi* [ὑποδείκνυμι, 5263], primarily, to show secretly (*hupo*, under, *deiknumi*, to show), hence, generally, to teach, make known, is translated to warn in Matt. 3:7; Luke 3:7; 12:5, R.V. (A.V., "forewarn"). See FOREWARN, *Note*, SHEW.
NT: B.844b; CB.–; K.–.
OT: nāgad: S.5046; HR.1413a.5; H.1289; BD.616c.
GEN. REF.: –.

3. *chrēmatizō* [χρηματίζω, 5537], for which see ADMONISH, B, No. 3, is translated to warn in Matt. 2:12, 22; Acts 10:22; Heb. 8:5, R.V. (A.V., "admonished"); 11:7; 12:25, R.V. (A.V., "spake").
NT: B.885c; CB.1240a; K.1319.
OT: –.
GEN. REF.: –.

WAS, WAST, WERE, WERT

Note: When not part of another verb, or phrase, these translate *eimi*, to be, e.g., Matt. 1:18, or the following: (*a*) *ginomai*, to become, e.g., Matt. 8:26; (*b*) *huparchō*, to exist, especially when referring to an already existing condition, e.g., Luke 8:41; Acts 5:4 (2nd part); 16:3; 27:12; Rom. 4:19, A.V., "when he was" (R.V., "he being"); (*c*) *echō*, to have, e.g., Acts 12:15; (*d*) *apechō*, to be away, to be distant, e.g., Luke 7:6; 24:13; (*e*) *mellō*, to be about to, e.g., Luke 19:4; Acts 21:27, 37, A.V. (R.V., "was about to"); (*f*) *sumbainō*, to come to pass, happen, e.g., Acts 21:35; (*g*) in Gal. 4:28, the preposition *kata*, according to, is rendered "was," in the phrase "as Isaac was," lit., 'like Isaac'; as Isaac's birth came by Divine interposition, so does the spiritual birth of every believer.

WASH

1. *niptō* [νίπτω, 3538], is chiefly used of washing part of the body, John 13:5, 6, 8 (twice, figuratively in 2nd clause), 12, 14 (twice); in 1 Tim. 5:10, including the figurative sense; in the Middle Voice, to wash oneself, Matt. 6:17; 15:2; Mark 7:3; John 9:7, 11, 15; 13:10. ¶ For the corresponding noun see BASON.
NT: B.540b; CB.1259c; K.635.
OT: rāḥaṣ: S.7364; HR.945c.2; H.2150; BD.934b.
GEN. REF.: IS.4:1022; NB.–; Z.–.

2. *aponiptō* [ἀπονίπτω, 633], to wash off, is used in the Middle Voice, in Matt. 27:24. ¶
NT: B.97a; CB.–; K.–.
OT: rāḥaṣ: S.7364; HR.139a.2; H.2150; BD.934b.
māḥāh: S.4229; HR.139a.1; H.1178,1179; BD.562a.
shāṭaph: S.7857; HR.139a.3; H.2373; BD.1009a.
GEN. REF.: IS.4:1022; NB.–; Z.–.

3. *louō* [λούω, 3068], signifies to bathe, to wash the body, (*a*) Active Voice, Acts 9:37; 16:33; (*b*) Passive Voice, John 13:10, R.V., "bathed" (A.V., "washed"); Heb. 10:22, lit., 'having been washed as to the body,' metaphorical of the effect of the Word of God upon the activities of the believer; (*c*) Middle Voice, 2 Pet. 2:22. Some inferior mss. have it instead of *luō*, to loose, in Rev. 1:5 (see R.V.). ¶
NT: B.480d; CB.1257b; K.538.
OT: rāḥaṣ: S.7364; HR.888b.1; H.2150; BD.934b.
GEN. REF.: IS.4:1022; NB.–; Z.–.

4. *apolouō* [ἀπολούω, 628], to wash off or away, is used in the Middle Voice, metaphorically, to wash oneself, in Acts 22:16, where the command to Saul of Tarsus to wash away his sins indicates that by his public confession, he would testify to the removal of his sins, and to the complete change from his past life; this 'washing away' was not in itself the actual remission of his sins, which had taken place at

his conversion; the Middle Voice implies his own particular interest in the act (as with the preceding verb. "baptize," lit., 'baptize thyself,' i.e., 'get thyself baptized'); the aorist tenses mark the decisiveness of the acts; in 1 Cor. 6:11, lit., 'ye washed yourselves clean'; here the Middle Voice (rendered in the Passive in A.V. and R.V., which do not distinguish between this and the next two Passives; see R.V. marg.) again indicates that the converts at Corinth, by their obedience to the faith, voluntarily gave testimony to the complete spiritual change Divinely wrought in them. ¶ In the Sept., Job 9:30. ¶

NT: B.96a; CB.1237a; K.–.
OT: rāḥaṣ: S.7364; HR.138c.1; H.2150; BD.934b.
GEN. REF.: IS.4:1022; NB.–; Z.–.

5. *plunō* [πλύνω, 4150], is used of washing inanimate objects, e.g., nets, Luke 5:2 (some texts have *apoplunō*); of garments, figuratively, Rev. 7:14; 22:14 (in the best texts; the A.V. translates those which have the verb *poieō*, to do, followed by *tas entolas autou*, "His commandments"). ¶

NT: B.674c; CB.1265b; K.–.
OT: kābas: S.3526; HR.1151b.2; H.946; BD.460a.
GEN. REF.: IS.4:1022; NB.–; Z.–.

6. *rhantizō* [ῥαντίζω, 4472], to sprinkle, is used in the Middle Voice in Mark 7:4, in some ancient texts, of the acts of the Pharisees in their assiduous attention to the cleansing of themselves after coming from the market place (some texts have *baptizō* here). See SPRINKLE.

NT: B.734a; CB.1268a; K.984.
OT: nāzāh: S.5137; HR.1248a.2; H.1335,1336; BD.633b.
GEN. REF.: –.

7. *brechō* [βρέχω, 1026], to wet, is translated to wash in Luke 7:38, 44, A.V.; the R.V., "to wet" and "hath wetted," gives the correct rendering. See RAIN, B.

NT: B.147c; CB.1239b; K.–.
OT: māṭar: S.4305; HR.230c.3; H.1187; BD.565a.
GEN. REF.: –.

8. *baptizō* [βαπτίζω, 907], is rendered "washed" in Luke 11:38. See BAPTIZE.

NT: B.131c; CB.1238c; K.92.
OT: ṭābal: S.2881; HR.190b.1; H.787,788; BD.371b.
GEN. REF.: IS.4:1022; NB.–; Z.–.

Note: With regard to Nos. 1, 3, 5, the Sept. of Lev. 15:11 contains all three with their distinguishing characteristics, No. 1 being used of the hands, No. 3 of the whole body, No. 5 of the garments.

WASHING

1. *baptismos* [βαπτισμός, 909], denotes the act of washing, ablution, with special reference to purification, Mark 7:4 (in some texts, ver. 8); Heb. 6:2, "baptisms"; 9:10, "washings." See BAPTISM. ¶

NT: B.132d; CB.1238c; K.92.
OT: –.
GEN. REF.: IS.1:11; NB.–; Z.–.

2. *loutron* [λουτρόν, 3067], a bath, a laver (akin to *louō*, see above), is used metaphorically of the Word of God, as the instrument of spiritual cleansing, Eph. 5:26; in Tit. 3:5, of "the washing of regeneration" (see REGENERATION). ¶ In the Sept., S. of Sol. 4:2; 6:6. ¶

NT: B.480c; CB.1257b; K.538.
OT: raḥṣāh: S.7367; HR.888c.1; H.2150b; BD.934d.
GEN. REF.: IS.4:1022; NB.–; Z.–.

WASTE (Noun and Verb)

A. Noun.

apōleia [ἀπώλεια, 684], destruction, is translated "waste" in Matt. 26:8; Mark 14:4. See DESTRUCTION, B, II, No. 1.

NT: B.103b; CB.1237a; K.67.
OT: 'ᵃbaddôn: S.11; HR.151c.1d; H.2d; BD.2b.
'ᵃbēdāh: S.9; HR.151c.1c; H.2b; BD.2b.
'êd: S.343; HR.151c.2; H.38c; BD.15c.
GEN. REF.: –.

B. Verbs.

1. *diaskorpizō* [διασκορπίζω, 1287], to scatter abroad, is used metaphorically of squandering property, Luke 15:13; 16:1. See DISPERSE, SCATTER.

NT: B.188b; CB.1241b; K.1048.
OT: pûṣ: S.6327; HR.310b.10; H.1745; BD.806d.
zārāh: S.2219; HR.310b.4; H.579; BD.279d.
GEN. REF.: –.

2. *portheō* [πορθέω, 4199], to ravage, is rendered "wasted" in Gal. 1:13, A.V.; see DESTROY, *Note*, HAVOCK.

NT: B.693a; CB.–; K.–.
OT: –.
GEN. REF.: –.

3. *lumainō* [λυμαίνω, 3075], to outrage, maltreat, is used in the Middle Voice in Acts 8:3, of Saul's treatment of the church, R.V., "laid waste" (A.V., "made havock of"). ¶

NT: B.481c; CB.–; K.–.
OT: –.
GEN. REF.: –.

WATCH (Noun and Verb), WATCHERS, WATCHFUL, WATCHINGS

A. Nouns.

1. *phulakē* [φυλακή, 5438], is used (*a*) with the meaning 'a watch,' actively, a guarding, Luke 2:8, lit., '(keeping, *phulassō*) watches'; (*b*) of the time during which guard was kept by night, a watch of the night, Matt. 14:25; 24:43; Mark 6:48; Luke 12:38. See CAGE, HOLD, IMPRISONMENT, PRISON.

NT: B.867d; CB.1264c; K.1280.
OT: mishmār: S.4929; HR.1440c.2b; H.2414f; BD.1038b.
mishmeret: S.4931; HR.1440c.2c; H.2414g; BD.1038b.
GEN. REF.: IS.4:1022; NB.1035; Z.4:869.

Note: Among the Jews the night was divided into three watches (see, e.g., Ex. 14:24; Judg. 7:19), and this continued on through Roman times. The Romans divided the night into four watches; this was recognized among the Jews (see Mark 13:35).

2. *koustōdia* [κουστωδία, 2892], from Lat., *custodia* (cp. Eng., custody), is rendered, "watch" in Matt. 27:65, 66 and 28:11, A.V.: see GUARD. ¶
NT: B.447b; CB.—; K.—.
OT: —.
GEN. REF.: IS.—; NB.1317; Z.—.

5. *agrupnia* [ἀγρυπνία, 70], sleeplessness (akin to B, No. 4), is rendered "watchings" in 2 Cor. 6:5; 11:27. ¶
NT: B.14a; CB.1233c; K.—.
OT: —.
GEN. REF.: IS.4:1022; NB.—; Z.—.

B. Verbs.

1. *grēgoreō* [γρηγορέω, 1127], to watch, is used (*a*) of keeping awake, e.g., Matt. 24:43; 26:38, 40, 41; (*b*) of spiritual alertness, e.g., Acts 20:31; 1 Cor. 16:13; Col. 4:2; 1 Thess. 5:6, 10 (for which see WAKE); 1 Pet. 5:8, R.V., "be watchful" (A.V., "be vigilant"); Rev. 3:2, 3; 16:15.
NT: B.167b; CB.1248c; K.195.
OT: shāqad: S.8245; HR.278a.2; H.2451; BD.1052a.
GEN. REF.: IS.4:1023; NB.—; Z.5:901.

2. *tēreō* [τηρέω, 5083], to keep, is rendered to watch, of those who kept guard at the Cross, Matt. 27:36, 54; 28:4, R.V., "watchers" (A.V., "keepers"), lit., 'the watching ones.' See HOLD, No. 8, KEEP, OBSERVE, PRESERVE, RESERVE.
NT: B.814d; CB.1271b; K.1174.
OT: shāmar: S.8104; HR.1348b.7; H.2414; BD.1036b.
nāṣar: S.5341; HR.1348b.2; H.1407; BD.665c.
GEN. REF.: IS.4:1023; NB.—; Z.4:869.

3. *paratēreō* [παρατηρέω, 3906], to observe, especially with sinister intent (*para*, near, and No. 2), is rendered to watch in Mark 3:2; Luke 6:7; 14:1; 20:20; Acts 9:24. See OBSERVE.
NT: B.622c; CB.1262b; K.1174.
OT: shāmar: S.8104; HR.1065a.2; H.2414; BD.1036b.
zāmam: S.2161; HR.1065a.1; H.556; BD.273a.
GEN. REF.: IS.4:1023; NB.—; Z.5:901.

4. *agrupneō* [ἀγρυπνέω, 69], to be sleepless (from *agreuō*, to chase, and *hupnos*, sleep), is used metaphorically, to be watchful, in Mark 13:33; Luke 21:36; Eph. 6:18; Heb. 13:17. The word expresses not mere wakefulness, but the watchfulness of those who are intent upon a thing. ¶
NT: B.14a; CB.1233c; K.195.
OT: shāqad: S.8245; HR.18a.2; H.2451; BD.1052a.
GEN. REF.: IS.4:1023; NB.—; Z.5:901.

5. *nēphō* [νήφω, 3525], to abstain from wine, is used metaphorically of moral alertness, and translated to watch, in the A.V. of 2 Tim. 4:5. See SOBER.
NT: B.538d; CB.1250b; K.633.
OT: —.
GEN. REF.: IS.—; NB.—; Z.5:901.

WATER (Noun and Verb), WATERING, WATERLESS

A. Noun.

hudōr [ὕδωρ, 5204], whence Eng. prefix, *hydro-*, is used (*a*) of the natural element, frequently in the Gospels; in the plural especially in the Apocalypse; elsewhere, e.g., Heb. 9:19; Jas. 3:12; in 1 John 5:6, that Christ "came by water and blood," may refer either (1) to the elements that flowed from His side on the Cross after His Death, or, in view of the order of the words and the prepositions here used, (2) to His baptism in Jordan and His Death on the Cross. As to (1), the water would symbolize the moral and practical cleansing effected by the removal of defilement by our taking heed to the Word of God in heart, life and habit; cp. Lev. 14, as to the cleansing of the leper. As to (2), Jesus the Son of God came on His mission by, or through, water and blood, namely, at His baptism, when He publicly entered upon His mission and was declared to be the Son of God by the witness of the Father, and at the Cross, when he publicly closed His witness; the Apostle's statement thus counteracts the doctrine of the Gnostics that the Divine *Logos* united Himself with the Man Jesus at His baptism, and left him at Gethsemane. On the contrary, He who was baptized and He who was crucified was the Son of God throughout in His combined Deity and humanity.

The word water is used symbolically in John 3:5, either (1) of the Word of God, as in 1 Pet. 1:23 (cp. the symbolic use in Eph. 5:26), or, in view of the preposition, *ek*, out of, (2) of the truth conveyed by baptism, this being the expression, not the medium, the symbol, not the cause, of the believer's identification with Christ in His Death, Burial and Resurrection. So the new birth is, in one sense, the setting aside of all that the believer was according to the flesh, for it is evident that there must be an entirely new beginning. Some regard the *kai*, "and," in John 3:5, as epexegetic, = 'even,' in which case the water would be emblematic of the Spirit, as in John 7:38 (cp. 4:10, 14), but not in 1 John 5:8, where the Spirit and the water are distinguished. "The water of life," Rev. 21:6 and 22:1, 17, is emblematic of the maintenance of spiritual life in perpetuity. In Rev. 17:1 the waters are symbolic of nations, peoples, etc.

NT: B.832d; CB.1251c; K.1203.
OT: mayim: S.4325; HR.1381a.1; H.1188; BD.565a.
GEN. REF.: IS.4:1024; NB.1317; Z.5:902.

Note: For *potamos*, rendered "waters" in 2 Cor. 11:26, see RIVER.

B. Verb.

potizō [ποτίζω, 4222], to give to drink, is used (*a*) naturally in Luke 13:15, "watering," with reference to animals; (*b*) figuratively, with reference to spiritual ministry to converts, 1 Cor. 3:6-8. See DRINK, B, No. 3.

NT: B.695d; CB.1266b; K.841.
OT: shāqāh: S.8248; HR.1197c.3; H.2452; BD.1052b.
GEN. REF.: –.

Notes: (1) For *hudropoteō*, to drink water, 1 Tim. 5:23, see DRINK, B, No. 5.

(2) For the adjective *anudros*, waterless (R.V.), without water, see DRY, No. 2.

WATERPOT

hudria [ὑδρία, —], occurs in John 2:6, 7; 4:28. ¶

NT: –.
OT: –.
GEN. REF.: –.

WAVE

1. *kuma* [κῦμα, 2949], from *kuō*, to be pregnant, to swell, is used (*a*) literally in the plural, Matt. 8:24; 14:24; Mark 4:37 (Acts 27:41, in some mss.); (*b*) figuratively, Jude 13. ¶

NT: B.457c; CB.–; K.–.
OT: gal: S.1530; HR.799a.2; H.353a; BD.164c.
GEN. REF.: –.

2. *salos* [σάλος, 4535], denotes a tossing, especially the rolling swell of the sea, Luke 21:25, A.V., "waves" (R.V., "billows"). ¶

NT: B.741a; CB.1268b; K.996.
OT: môṭ: S.4131; HR.1258a.2; H.1158; BD.556d.
sᵉʿārāh: S.5591; HR.1258a.5; H.1528; BD.704b.
GEN. REF.: –.

3. *kludōn* [κλύδων, 2830], a billow, is translated "wave" in Jas. 1:6, A.V. (R.V., "surge"); in Luke 8:24 it is translated "raging (of the water)." See RAGE, B. ¶

NT: B.436d; CB.–; K.–.
OT: sāʿar: S.5590; HR.772b.1a; H.1528b; BD.704a.
saʿar: S.5591; HR.772b.1b; H.1528; BD.704b.
GEN. REF.: –.

WAVER, WAVERING

A. Adjective.

aklinēs [ἀκλινής, 186], without bending (*a*, negative, *klinō*, to bend), occurs in Heb. 10:23, A.V., "without wavering," R.V., "that it waver not." ¶

NT: B.30c; CB.–; K.–.
OT: –.
GEN. REF.: –.

B. Verb.

diakrinō [διακρίνω, 1252], is rendered to waver in Rom. 4:20, R.V. (A.V., "staggered"); in Jas. 1:6 (twice). See DOUBT, No. 3.

NT: B.185a; CB.1241a; K.469.
OT: –.
GEN. REF.: –.

WAX

1. *prokoptō* [προκόπτω, 4298], for which see ADVANCE, is rendered to wax in 2 Tim. 3:13.

NT: B.707d; CB.1266c; K.939.
OT: –.
GEN. REF.: –.

2. *ginomai* [γίνομαι, 1096], to become, is translated "waxed" in Luke 13:19, A.V. (R.V., "became"); in Heb. 11:34, A.V. and R.V., "waxed": see COME, No. 12, etc.

NT: B.158a; CB.1248b; K.117.
OT: –.
GEN. REF.: –.

Note: This verb forms part of the translation of certain tenses of other verbs; see, e.g., BOLD, A, No. 2, COLD, C, CONFIDENT, B, No. 1, CORRUPT, A, No. 2, GROSS, OLD, D, No. 2, STRONG, B, No. 2, WANTON, B, Nos. 1 and 2, WEARY, No. 2, WROTH, No. 1.

WAY

1. *hodos* [ὁδός, 3598], denotes (*a*) a natural path, road, way, frequent in the Synoptic Gospels; elsewhere, e.g., Acts 8:26; 1 Thess. 3:11; Jas. 2:25; Rev. 16:12; (*b*) a traveller's way (see JOURNEY); (*c*) metaphorically, of a course of conduct, or way of thinking, e.g., of righteousness, Matt. 21:32; 2 Pet. 2:21; of God, Matt. 22:16, and parallels, i.e., the way instructed and approved by God; so Acts 18:26 and Heb. 3:10, "My ways" (cp. Rev. 15:3); of the Lord, Acts 18:25; "that leadeth to destruction," Matt. 7:13; ". . . unto life," 7:14; of peace, Luke 1:79; Rom. 3:17; of Paul's ways in Christ, 1 Cor. 4:17 (plural); "more excellent" (of love), 1 Cor. 12:31; of truth, 2 Pet. 2:2; of the right way, 2:15; of Balaam (*id*); of Cain, Jude 11; of a way consisting in what is from God, e.g., of life, Acts 2:28 (plural); of salvation, Acts 16:17; personified, of Christ as the means of access to the Father, John 14:6; of the course followed and characterized by the followers of Christ, Acts 9:2; 19:9, 23; 24:22. See HIGHWAY.

NT: B.553d; CB.1251a; K.666.
OT: derek: S.1870; HR.962b.3a; H.453a; BD.202c.
GEN. REF.: IS.4:1032; NB.–; Z.5:909.

Note: In Luke 5:19 and 19:4 the noun is not expressed in the original, but is understood.

2. *parodos* [πάροδος, 3938], a passing or passage, is used with *en*, in, 1 Cor. 16:7, "by the way" (lit., 'in passing'). ¶

NT: B.628d; CB.–; K.–.
OT: derek: S.1870; HR.1071a.1; H.453a; BD.202c.
hēlek: S.1982; HR.1071a.2; H.498a; BD.237a.
'ābar: S.5674; HR.1071a.3; H.1556; BD.716d.
GEN. REF.: IS.4:1032; NB.–; Z.5:909.

3. *tropos* [τρόπος, 5158], a turning, a manner, is translated "way" in Rom. 3:2, "(every) way"; Phil. 1:18, "(in every) way." See CONVERSATION, MANNER, MEANS.

NT: B.827b; CB.1273a; K.–.
OT: –.
GEN. REF.: IS.4:1032; NB.–; Z.–.

Notes: (1) In Jas. 1:11, A.V., *poreia*, a journey, a going, is rendered "ways" (R.V., "goings").

(2) In Heb. 12:17, *topos*, a place, is rendered in A.V. marg., "way (to change his mind)."

(3) For the A.V. rendering of *makran*, a good (or great) way off, Matt. 8:30; Luke 15:20, see FAR, B, No. 1.

(4) In Luke 14:32, *porrō* is rendered "a great way off."

(5) In Heb. 5:2, A.V., *planaō*, Middle Voice, to wander, is rendered "(them) that are out of the way," R.V., "(the) erring."

(6) In Col. 2:14 and 2 Thess. 2:7, *ek mesou*, is translated "out of the way"; see MIDST, *Note* (1) (*e*).

(7) For "two ways" in Mark 11:4, A.V., see STREET.

(8) In John 10:1, the adverb *allachothen*, from some other place (from *allos*, another), is translated "some other way."

(9) In 2 Pet. 3:1, the A.V. translates *en* "by way of" ("by," R.V.).

(10) In Gal. 2:5, the renderings "by," A.V., "in the way of," R.V., serve to express the dative case of *hupotagē*, subjection.

(11) For *propempō*, to bring on one's way, Acts 15:3; 21:5, and the A.V. of 2 Cor. 1:16 (R.V., "to be set forward on my journey"), see BRING, No. 25.

(12) *Aperchomai*, to go away, is rendered to go one's way, e.g., Matt. 13:25; 20:4; Mark 11:4; 12:12; Luke 19:32; John 11:46; Acts 9:17; Jas. 1:24: see GO, No. 14.

(13) In Luke 8:14, A.V., *poreuomai*, to go on one's way (R.V.), is rendered "go forth"; in 13:33, A.V., "walk" (R.V., "go on my way"); in Matt. 24:1, A.V., it is rendered "departed" (R.V., "was going on his way"): see DEPART, No. 8.

(14) In Acts 24:3, *pantę̄* is rendered "in all ways" (A.V., "always"). ¶

(15) In Rom. 3:12, A.V., *ekklinō*, to turn aside (R.V.), is rendered "are gone out of the way."

(16) See also ESCAPE, B, LASCIVIOUS.

WE

Note: When this is not part of the translation of a verb or phrase, it stands for some case of *hēmeis*, the plural of *egō*, I; this separate use of the pronoun is always emphatic. For "we ourselves," we OURSELVES.

WEAK, WEAKENED, WEAKER, WEAKNESS

A. Adjectives.

1. *asthenēs* [ἀσθενής, 772], lit., strengthless (see IMPOTENT), is translated "weak," (*a*) of physical weakness, Matt. 26:41; Mark 14:38; 1 Cor. 1:27; 4:10; 11:30 (a judgment upon spiritual laxity in a church); 2 Cor. 10:10; 1 Pet. 3:7 (comparative degree); (*b*) in the spiritual sense, said of the rudiments of Jewish religion, in their inability to justify anyone, Gal. 4:9; of the Law, Heb. 7:18; in Rom. 5:6, R.V., "weak" (A.V., "without strength"), of the inability of man to accomplish his salvation; (*c*) morally or ethically, 1 Cor. 8:7, 10; 9:22; (*d*) rhetorically, of God's actions according to the human estimate, 1 Cor. 1:25, "weakness," lit., 'the weak things of God.' See FEEBLE, SICK.

NT: B.115c; CB.1238a; K.83.
OT: dal: S.1800; HR.172b.3; H.433a; BD.195c.
'ānî: S.6041; HR.172b.7a; H.1652d; BD.776d.
rāpheh: S.7504; HR.172b.10; H.2198a; BD.952a.
GEN. REF.: –.

2. *adunatos* [ἀδύνατος, 102], lit., not powerful, is translated "weak" in Rom. 15:1, of the infirmities of those whose scruples arise through lack of faith (see 14:22, 23), in the same sense as No. 1 (*c*); the change in the adjective (cp. 14:1) is due to the contrast with *dunatoi*, the "strong," who have not been specifically mentioned as such in chap. 14. See IMPOSSIBLE

NT: B.19a; CB.1233a; K.186.
OT: dal: S.1800; HR.28a.3; H.433a; BD.195c.
'ebyôn: S.34; HR.28a.1; H.3a; BD.2d.
GEN. REF.: –.

B. Verb.

astheneō [ἀσθενέω, 770], to lack strength, is used in much the same way as A, No. 1, and translated "being . . . weak" in Rom. 4:19, A.V. (R.V., "being weakened"); 8:3; 14:1, 2 (in some texts, 1 Cor. 8:9); 2 Cor. 11:21, 29 (twice); 12:10; 13:3, 4, 9. See DISEASED, IMPOTENT, SICK.

NT: B.115b; CB.1238a; K.83.
OT: kāshal: S.3782; HR.172a.7a,b; H.1050; BD.505b.
dal: S.1800; HR.172a.4b; H.433a; BD.195c.
GEN. REF.: –.

C. Noun.

astheneia [ἀσθένεια, 769], for which see INFIRMITY, is rendered "weakness," of the body, 1 Cor. 2:3; 15:43; 2 Cor. 11:30, R.V.; 12:5 (plural, R.V.), 9, 10, R.V.; Heb. 11:34; in 2 Cor. 13:4, "He was crucified through weakness" is said in respect of the physical sufferings to which Christ voluntarily submitted in giving Himself up to the death of the Cross.

NT: B.115a; CB.1238a; K.83.
OT: kāshal: S.3782; HR.172a.1a; H.1050; BD.505b.
'aṣebet: S.6094; HR.172a.2; H.1666d; BD.781a.
GEN. REF.: –.

WEALTH

euporia [εὐπορία, 2142], primarily facility (*eu*, well, *poros*, a passage), hence plenty, wealth, occurs in Acts 19:25. ¶ Cp. *euporeō*, to be well provided for, to prosper, Acts 11:29. ¶

NT: B.324b; CB.–; K.–.
OT: ḥayil: S.2428; HR.576a.1; H.624a; BD.298c.
GEN. REF.: IS.4:186; NB.–; Z.–.

Note: In 1 Cor. 10:24, the A.V., "*wealth*," R.V., "*good*," is, lit., 'the (thing) of the other.'

WEAPONS

hoplon [ὅπλον, 3696], always in the plur., is translated "weapons" in John 18:3 and 2 Cor. 10:4, the latter metaphorically of those used in spiritual warfare. See ARMOUR, INSTRUMENTS.

NT: B.575c; CB.1251a; K.702.
OT: māgēn: S.4043; HR.1003c.3; H.367c; BD.171b.
nesheq: S.5402; HR.1003c.4; H.1436a; BD.676d.
GEN. REF.: –.

WEAR, WEARING

A. Verbs.

1. *phoreō* [φορέω, 5409], a frequentative form of *pherō*, to bear, and denoting repeated or habitual action, is chiefly used of clothing, weapons, etc., of soft raiment, Matt. 11:8; fine clothing, Jas. 2:3; the crown of thorns, John 19:5. See BEAR, No. 7.

NT: B.864d; CB.–; K.1252.
OT: –.
GEN. REF.: –.

2. *endiduskō* [ἐνδιδύσκω, 1737], to put on, is used in the Active Voice in Mark 15:17 (in good mss.; some have No. 3); in Luke 8:27 (Middle Voice), in some texts; the best have No. 3. For Luke 16:19, see CLOTHE, No. 3. ¶

NT: B.263a; CB.–; K.–.
OT: lābash: S.3847; HR.470b.1; H.1075; BD.527d.
GEN. REF.: –.

3. *enduō* [ἐνδύω, 1746], is rendered to wear in Luke 8:27 (Middle Voice; see No. 2). See CLOTHE, No. 2, PUT, No. 26.

NT: B.264a; CB.1245a; K.192.
OT: lābash: S.3847; HR.471a-2a,b; H.1075; BD.527d.
GEN. REF.: –.

4. *klinō* [κλίνω, 2827], to bend, decline, is used of a day, wearing away, Luke 9:12 (in 24:29, "is far spent"). See BOW, No. 4, FLIGHT, B, LAY, No. 6, SPEND.

NT: B.436c; CB.–; K.–.
OT: –.
GEN. REF.: –.

5. *hupōpiazō* [ὑπωπιάζω, 5299], is translated "wear (me) out" in Luke 18:5, R.V. (A.V., "weary"). For this and the somewhat different application in 1 Cor. 9:27, see BUFFET, No. 2. ¶

NT: B.848d; CB.1252b; K.1239.
OT: –.
GEN. REF.: –.

B. Noun.

perithesis [περίθεσις, 4025], a putting around or on (*peri*, around, *tithēmi*, to put), is used in 1 Pet. 3:3 of wearing jewels of gold (R.V.). ¶

NT: B.647c; CB.–; K.–.
OT: –.
GEN. REF.: –.

For **WEARINESS**, 2 Cor. 11:27, R.V., see **LABOUR**, No. 1

WEARY

1. *kopiaō* [κοπιάω, 2872], to grow weary, be beaten out (*kopos*, a beating, toil), is used of the Lord in John 4:6 (used in His own word "labour" in Matt. 11:28), in Rev. 2:3, R.V. See, LABOUR, TOIL.

NT: B.443c; CB.1255c; K.453.
OT: yāga': S.3021; HR.778b.6a; H.842; BD.388a.
'āmal: S.5998; HR.778b.11a; H.1639; BD.765c.
GEN. REF.: –.

2. *kamnō* [κάμνω, 2577], to be weary, is rendered to wax weary in Heb. 12:3, R.V. See FAINT, No. 3, SICK.

NT: B.402a; CB.–; K.–.
OT: –.
GEN. REF.: –.

3. *ekkakeō* or *enkakeō* [ἐκκακέω, 1573], for which see FAINT, No. 2, is rendered to be weary in Gal. 6:9; 2 Thess. 3:13.

NT: B.240c; CB.–; K.–.
OT: –.
GEN. REF.: –.

Note: For *hupōpiazō*, rendered to weary in Luke 18:5, A.V., see WEAR, A, No. 5.

WEATHER

1. *eudia* [εὐδία, 2105], akin to *eudios*, calm, denotes "fair weather," Matt. 16:2. ¶

NT: B.319a; CB.1247a; K.–.
OT: –.
GEN. REF.: IS.4:1043; NB.–; Z.–.

2. *cheimōn* [χειμών, 5494], winter, also a winter storm, is translated "foul weather" in Matt. 16:3. See TEMPEST, WINTER.

NT: B.879d; CB.–; K.–.
OT: geshem: S.1653; HR.1457c.1; H.389a; BD.177c.
GEN. REF.: IS.4:1043; NB.–; Z.–.

For **WEDDING** see **MARRIAGE**

WEEK

sabbaton [σάββατον, 4521], is used (*a*) in the plural in the phrase "the first day of the week," Matt. 28:1; Mark 16:2, 9; Luke 24:1; John 20:1, 19; Acts 20:7; 1 Cor. 16:2. For this idiomatic use of the word see ONE, A, (5); (*b*) in the singular, Luke 18:12, "twice in the week," lit., 'twice of the sabbath,' i.e., twice in the days after the sabbath. See SABBATH.

NT: B.739a; CB.1268b; K.989.
OT: shabbāt: S.7676; HR.1256b.1a; H.2323b; BD.992a.
GEN. REF.: IS.4:1045; NB.–; Z.1:689,692.

WEEP, WEEPING

A. Verbs.

1. *klaiō* [κλαίω, 2799], is used of any loud expression of grief, especially in mourning for the dead, Matt. 2:18; Mark 5:38, 39; 16:10; Luke 7:13; 8:52 (twice); John 11:31, 33 (twice); 20:11 (twice), 13, 15; Acts 9:39; otherwise, e.g., in exhortations, Luke 23:28; Rom. 12:15; Jas. 4:9; 5:1; negatively, "weep not," Luke 7:13; 8:52; 23:28; Rev. 5:5 (cp. Acts 21:13); in 18:9, R.V., "shall weep" (A.V., "bewail"). See BEWAIL.

NT: B.433a; CB.1255a; K.436.
OT: bākāh: S.1058; HR.766a.1a; H.243; BD.113b.
GEN. REF.: IS.4:1046; NB.–; Z.–.

2. *dakruō* [δακρύω, 1145], to shed tears (*dakruon*, a tear), is used only of the Lord Jesus, John 11:35. ¶

NT: B.170a; CB.–; K.–.
OT: bākāh: S.1058; HR.284a.1; H.243; BD.113b.
GEN. REF.: IS.4:1046; NB.–; Z.–.

Note: Other synonymous verbs are *thrēneō*, to mourn, of formal lamentation: see BEWAIL, *Note* (1); *alalazō*, to wail; *stenazō*, to groan (*oduromai*, to lament audibly, is not used in N.T.; see the noun *odurmos*, mourning).

B. Noun.

klauthmos [κλαυθμός, 2805], akin to A, No. 1, denotes weeping, crying, Matt. 2:18; 8:12; 13:42, 50, R.V. (A.V., "wailing"); 22:13; 24:51; 25:30; Luke 13:28; Acts 20:37. ¶

NT: B.433c; CB.1255b; K.436.
OT: b^ekî: S.1065; HR.767a.2b; H.243b; BD.113d.
GEN. REF.: IS.4:1046; NB.–; Z.–.

WEIGH, WEIGHT, WEIGHTY, WEIGHTIER

A. Verbs.

1. *bareō* [βαρέω, 916], to weigh down, is so rendered in 2 Cor. 1:8, R.V.; see BURDEN, B, No. 1.

NT: B.133c; CB.1238c; K.95.
OT: kābēd: S.3513; HR.190c.1; H.943; BD.457a.
GEN. REF.: –.

2. *histēmi* [ἵστημι, 2476], to cause to stand, is used in Matt. 26:15, R.V., "they weighed (unto)" (of pieces of silver), A.V., metaphorically, "covenanted (with)."

NT: B.381d; CB.1250c; K.1082.
OT: –.
GEN. REF.: –.

B. Nouns.

1. *baros* [βάρος, 922], akin to A, is rendered "weight" in 2 Cor. 4:17. See BURDEN, A, No. 1.

NT: B.133d; CB.1238c; K.95.
OT: kābōd: S.3520; HR.190c.1; H.943f; BD.459c.
GEN. REF.: IS.4:1046; NB.–; Z.–.

2. *onkos* [ὄγκος, 3591], denotes a bulk or mass; hence, metaphorically, an encumbrance, weight, Heb. 12:1. ¶

NT: B.553a; CB.1260c; K.666.
OT: –.
GEN. REF.: IS.4:1046; NB.–; Z.–.

C. Adjective.

barus [βαρύς, 926], heavy (akin to A and B, No. 1), is rendered "weighty" in 2 Cor. 10:10, of Paul's letters. The comparative degree is used in the neuter plural in Matt. 23:23, "(the) weightier matters (of the Law)." See GRIEVOUS, HEAVY.

NT: B.134b; CB.1238c; K.95.
OT: kābēd (Adjective): S.3515; HR.191b.2a; H.943a; BD.458a.
kābēd (Verb): S.3513; HR.191b.3; H.943; BD.457a.
GEN. REF.: IS.4:1046; NB.–; Z.–.

WELCOME

1. *apodechomai* [ἀποδέχομαι, 588], to receive gladly, is rendered to welcome in the R.V. of Luke 8:40; 9:11. See RECEIVE.

NT: B.90a; CB.1236c; K.146.
OT: –.
GEN. REF.: –.

2. *hupolambanō* [ὑπολαμβάνω, 5274], to take up, to entertain, is rendered "to welcome" in 3 John 8, R.V., of a hearty welcome to servants of God. See RECEIVE.

NT: B.845b; CB.1252b; K.495.
OT: 'ānāh: S.6030; HR.1414c.7a; H.1650,1653; BD.772c.
GEN. REF.: –.

WELL (Noun)

phrear [φρέαρ, 5421], a pit, is translated a "well" in John 4:11, 12. See PIT.

NT: B.865d; CB.1264c; K.–.
OT: b^e'ēr: S.875; HR.1438b.1; H.194a; BD.91c.
GEN. REF.: IS.4:1055; NB.1325; Z.5:925.

Note: For *pēgē*, translated "well" in John 4:6 (twice), 14; 2 Pet. 2:17, see FOUNTAIN.

WELL (Adverb)

1. *kalōs* [καλῶς, 2573], finely (akin to *kalos*, good, fair), is usually translated "well," indicating what is done rightly; in the Epistles it is most frequent in 1 Tim. (3:4, 12, 13; 5:17);

twice it is used as an exclamation of approval, Mark 12:32; Rom. 11:20; the comparative degree *kallion*, "very well;" occurs in Acts 25:10. See GOOD, C, No. 1.

NT: B.401b; CB.1253b; K.–.
OT: yāṭab: S.3190; HR.717b.1a,2b,3a; H.863; BD.405c.
ṭôb: S.2896; HR.717b.1b,3b; H.793a; BD.375a.
GEN. REF.: –.

Note: The neuter form of the adjective *kalos*, with the article and the present participle of *poieō*, to do, is translated "well-doing" in Gal. 6:9.

2. *eu* [εὐ, 2095], primarily the neuter of an old word, *eus*, noble, good, is used (*a*) with verbs, e.g., Mark 14:7, "do (*poieō*) . . . good"; Acts 15:29 (*prassō*); Eph. 6:3 (*ginomai*, to be); (*b*) in replies, good, "well done;" Matt. 25:21, 23; in Luke 19:17, *eu ge* (in the best texts). The word is the opposite of *kakōs*, evilly. See GOOD, C, No. 2. ¶

NT: B.317a; CB.1247c; K.–.
OT: yāṭab: S.3190; HR.568a.1a,2a,3a; H.863; BD.405c.
ṭôb: S.2896; HR.568a.2b; H.793a; BD.375a.
GEN. REF.: –.

Notes: (1) In 2 Tim. 1:18, *beltion*, the neuter form of what is used as the comparative degree of *agathos*, good, is used adverbially and translated "very well." ¶

(2) For John 2:10, "have well drunk" (R.V., "freely"), see DRINK, B, No. 2.

(3) *Hōs*, as, with *kai*, also (and), is rendered "as well as" in Acts 10:47 (*kathōs* in some mss.) and 1 Cor. 9:5.

(4) In Heb. 4:2 *kathaper*, even as, with *kai*, is translated "as well as": see EVEN, No. 8.

WELL (do), WELL-DOING

A. Verbs.

1. *agathopoieō* [ἀγαθοποιέω, 15], to do good (*agathos*, good, *poieō*, to do), is used (*a*) of such activity in general, 1 Pet. 2:15, "well-doing"; ver. 20, "do well"; 3:6, 17; 3 John 11, "doeth good"; (*b*) of acting for another's benefit, Mark 3:4; Luke 6:9, 33, 35. ¶

NT: B.2c; CB.1233b; K.–.
OT: yāṭab: S.3190; HR.1c.1; H.863; BD.405c.
GEN. REF.: –.

2. *kalopoieō* [καλοποιέω, 2569], to do well, excellently, act honourably (*kalos*, good, *poieō*, to do), occurs in 2 Thess. 3:13. ¶ The two parts of the word occur separately in Rom. 7:21; 2 Cor. 13:7; Gal. 6:9; Jas. 4:17.

NT: B.400b; CB.1253b; K.–.
OT: –.
GEN. REF.: –.

Notes: (1) The distinction between Nos. 1 and 2 follows that between *agathos* and *kalos* (see GOOD).

(2) In John 11:12, A.V., *sōzō* (Passive Voice, to be saved), is rendered "he shall do well" (R.V., "he will recover").

B. Noun.

agathopoiia [ἀγαθοποιΐα, 16], well-doing (akin to A, No. 1), occurs in 1 Pet. 4:19. ¶

NT: B.2c; CB.1233b; K.3.
OT: –.
GEN. REF.: –.

C. Adjective.

agathopoios [ἀγαθοποιός, 17], doing good, beneficent, is translated "them that do well" in 1 Pet. 2:14, lit., 'well-doing (ones).' ¶

NT: B.2c; CB.1233b; K.3.
OT: –.
GEN. REF.: –.

For **WELL-BELOVED** see **BELOVED**

WELL-NIGH

Note: This forms part of the translation of *sumplēroō*, to fulfil, in Luke 9:51, "were well-nigh" come (see COME, No. 36), and *plēroō*, to fulfil, in Acts 7:23, "was well-nigh . . .," lit., 'a time (of forty years) was fulfilled (to him)' (see FULFIL, A, No. 1).

WELL PLEASED

A. Noun.

eudokia [εὐδοκία, 2107], good pleasure, occurs in the genitive case in Luke 2:14, lit., "(men) of good pleasure" (so R.V. marg.), R.V., "(men) in whom He is well pleased" (the genitive is objective); the A.V., "good will (toward men)," follows the inferior texts which have the nominative. See DESIRE, PLEASURE, SEEM, WELL-PLEASING, WILL.

NT: B.319c; CB.1247a; K.273.
OT: rāṣôn: S.7522; HR.569b.1a; H.2207a; BD.953c.
GEN. REF.: –.

B. Verb.

eudokeō [εὐδοκέω, 2106], to be well pleased: see PLEASE, A, No. 3, WILLING, B, No. 3.

NT: B.319b; CB.1247a; K.273.
OT: rāṣāh: S.7521; HR.569a.9; H.2207; BD.953a.
GEN. REF.: –.

WELL-PLEASING

A. Adjective.

euarestos [εὐάρεστος, 2101], is used in Rom. 12:1, 2, translated "acceptable" (R.V. marg., "well-pleasing"); in the following the R.V. has "well-pleasing," Rom. 14:18; 2 Cor. 5:9; Eph. 5:10; in Phil. 4:18 and Col. 3:20 (R.V. and A.V.); in Tit. 2:9, R.V., "well-pleasing" (A.V., "please . . . well"); in Heb. 13:21, R.V. and A.V. See ACCEPTABLE. ¶

NT: B.318d; CB.1247a; K.77.
OT: –.
GEN. REF.: –.

B. Verb.

euaresteō [εὐαρεστέω, 2100], akin to A, is rendered to be well-pleasing in Heb. 11:5, 6, R.V. (A.V., "please"); in Heb. 13:16, "is well pleased." ¶

NT: B.318c; CB.1247a; K.77.
OT: hālak: S.1980; HR.568c.1; H.498; BD.229d,236a.
GEN. REF.: –.

C. Noun.

eudokia [εὐδοκία, 2107], lit., 'good pleasure,' is rendered "well-pleasing" in Matt. 11:26 and Luke 10:21. See DESIRE, PLEASURE, SEEM, WELL PLEASED, WILL.

NT: B.319c; CB.1247a; K.273.
OT: rāṣôn: S.7522; HR.569b.1a; H.2207a; BD.953c.
GEN. REF.: –.

For **WENT** see **GO**

WEST

dusmē [δυσμή, 1424], the quarter of the sun-setting (*dusis*, a sinking, setting; *dunō*, to sink), hence, the west, occurs in Matt. 8:11; 24:27; Luke 12:54 (some regard this as the sunset); 13:29; Rev. 21:13. ¶

NT: B.209d; CB.–; K.–.
OT: mābô': S.877; HR.357b.2b; H.194d; BD.99d.
ma'ᵃrāb: S.4628; HR.357b.5a; H.1689b; BD.788a.
'ᵃrābāh: S.6160; HR.357b.5d; H.1688d; BD.787b.
GEN. REF.: IS.1056; NB.–; Z.5:925.

For **WET**, Luke 7:38, 44, R.V., see **WASH**, No. 7

WHALE

kētos [κῆτος, 2785], denotes a huge fish, a sea-monster, Matt. 12:40. ¶ In the Sept., Gen. 1:21; Job 3:8; 9:13; 26:12; Jonah 1:17 (twice); 2:1, 10. ¶

NT: B.431d; CB.1255a; K.–.
OT: dāg: S.1709; HR.763c.1a; H.401a; BD.185c.
tannîn: S.8577; HR.763c.4; H.2528b; BD.1072c.
GEN. REF.: IS.–; NB.1325; Z.5:925.

WHAT

Notes: (1) Most frequently this is a translation of some form of the relative pronoun *hos* or the interrogative *tis*.

(2) Other words are (*a*) *hoios*, of what kind, e.g., 2 Cor. 10:11, R.V. (A.V., "such as"); 1 Thess. 1:5, "what manner of men"; 2 Tim. 3:11 (twice), lit., 'what sorts of things,' 'what sorts of persecutions'; (*b*) *poios*, what sort of, e.g., Matt. 21:23, 24, 27; 24:42, 43; Luke 5:19; 6:32-34; 20:2, 8; 24:19; John 12:33, "what manner of"; so in 18:32; 21:19; Rom. 3:27; 1 Cor. 15:35; in Jas. 4:14, "what"; 1 Pet. 2:20 and Rev. 3:3 (ditto); 1 Pet. 1:11, "what manner of"; (*c*) *hopoios*, "what sort of," 1 Cor. 3:13; "what manner of," 1 Thess. 1:9; (*d*) *hosos*, how great, Mark 6:30 (twice), R.V., "whatsoever"; Acts 15:12; Rom. 3:19, "what things soever"; Jude 10 (1st part), "what soever things," R.V.; (2nd part) "what"; (*e*) *posos*, how great, how much, 2 Cor. 7:11, "what (earnest care)," R.V. (*posos* here stands for the repeated words in the Eng. Versions, the adjective not being repeated in the original); (*f*) *hostis*, "what (things)," Phil. 3:7; (*g*) in Matt. 26:40, *houtōs*, thus, so, is used as an exclamatory expression, translated "What" (in a word immediately addressed by the Lord to Peter), lit., 'So'; (*h*) for *potapos*, rendered "what" in Mark 13:1 (2nd part), A.V., see MANNER; (*i*) in 1 Cor. 6:16, 19, A.V., the particle *ē*, "or" (R.V.), is rendered "What?"; in 1 Cor. 14:36, A.V. and R.V., "what?" (*j*) in 1 Cor. 11:22, *gar*, in truth, indeed, has its exclamatory use "What?"

(3) In John 5:19 "but what" translates a phrase, lit., 'if not anything.'

(4) In Matt. 8:33 "what" is, lit., 'the things' (neuter plural of the article).

WHATSOEVER

Note: For this see *Notes* on words under WHAT. Frequently by the addition of the particle *an*, or the conjunction *ean*, if, the phrase has the more general idea of "whatsoever," e.g., with *hos*, Matt. 10:11; with *hosos*, Matt. 17:12; with *hostis*, neuter form, Luke 10:35.

For **WHEAT** see **CORN**

For **WHEEL**, Jas. 3:6, R.V., see **COURSE**, A, No. 4.

For **WHEN, WHENCE, WHENSOEVER, WHERE,** etc., see † p. 1

WHEREFORE

Note: This represents (1) some phrases introduced by the preposition *dia*, on account of, *dia touto*, an account of this, e.g., Matt. 12:31; Rom. 5:12; Eph. 1:15; 3 John 10; *dia hēn* (the accusative feminine of *hos*, who), on account of which (*aitia*, a cause, being understood), e.g., Acts 10:21 (with *aitia*, expressed, Tit. 1:13; Heb. 2:11); *dia ti* on account of what? (sometimes as one word, *diati*), e.g., Luke 19:23; Rom. 9:32; 2 Cor. 11:11; Rev. 17:7; (2) *dio* = *dia ho* (the neuter of the relative pronoun *hos*), on account of which (thing), e.g., Matt. 27:8; Acts 15:19; 20:31; 24:26; 25:26; 27:25, 34; Rom. 1:24; 15:7; 1 Cor. 12:3; 2 Cor. 2:8; 5:9; 6:17; Eph. 2:11; 3:13; 4:8, 25; 5:14; Phil. 2:9; 1 Thess. 5:11; Philm. 8; Heb. 3:7, 10; 10:5; 11:16; 12:12, 28; 13:12; Jas. 1:21; 4:6; 1 Pet. 1:13; 2 Pet. 1:10, 12; 3:14; (3) *dioper*, for which very reason (a strengthened form of the preceding), 1 Cor. 8:13; 10:14 (14:13 in some mss.); ¶ (4) *hothen* (which denotes 'whence,' when used of direction or source, e.g., Matt. 12:44), used of cause and denoting 'wherefore' in Heb. 2:17; 3:1; 7:25; 8:3; (5) *ti*, what, why, John 9:27; Acts 22:30; Gal. 3:19, A.V. (R.V., "what"); (6) *heneka* with *tinos* (the genitive case of *ti*), because of what, Acts 19:32; (7) *charin* with *hou*, the genitive case, neuter of *hos*, for the sake of what, Luke 7:47; (8) *eis*, unto, with *ti*, what, Matt. 14:31; with *ho*, which (the accusative neuter of *hos*), 2 Thess. 1:11, A.V. (R.V., "to which end"); (9) *ara*, so, 2 Cor. 7:12, A.V. (R.V., "so"); with *ge*, at least, Matt. 7:20, A.V. (R.V., "therefore"); (10) *hina*, in order that, with *ti*, what, Matt. 9:4; (11) *toigaroun*, therefore, rendered "wherefore" in Heb. 12:1, A.V.; (12) in Matt. 26:50, *epi*, unto, with *ho*, as in No. (8) above, A.V., "wherefore (art thou come)?" R.V., "(*do* that) for which (thou art come)"; (13) *oun*, a particle expressing sequence or consequence, e.g., Matt. 24:26; Acts 6:3; (14) *hōste*, so that, "wherefore," e.g., Rom. 7:12, 13; 1 Cor. 10:12; 11:27, 33; 14:22, 39; 2 Cor. 5:16; Gal. 3:24; 4:7; Phil. 4:1; 1 Thess. 4:18; 1 Pet. 4:19.

WHETHER: see † p. 1

WHICH

Notes: (1) This is the translation of (*a*) the article with nouns, adjectives, numerals, participles, etc., e.g., "that which" etc.; (*b*) the relative pronoun *hos*, "who," in one of its forms (a frequent use); (*c*) *hostis*, whoever, differing from *hos* by referring to a subject in general, as one of a class, e.g., Rom. 2:15; Gal. 4:24 (twice); 5:19; Rev. 2:24; 20:4; (*d*) the interrogative pronoun *tis*, who? which?, e.g., Matt. 6:27; John 8:46; (*e*) *hoios*, of what kind, e.g., Phil. 1:30; (*f*) *poios*, the interrogative of (*e*), e.g., John 10:32; (*g*) *hosos*, whatsoever, etc.; plural, how many, translated "which" in Acts 9:39.

(2) In Acts 8:26, A.V., *hautē* (the feminine of *houtos*, this), "the same" (R.V.), is translated "which."

(3) In the triple title of God in Rev. 1:4, 8; 4:8, "which" is the translation, firstly, of the article with the present participle of *eimi*, to be, lit., 'the (One) being,' secondly, of the article with the imperfect tense of *eimi* (impossible of lit. translation, the title not being subject to grammatical change), thirdly, of the article with the present participle of *erchomai*, to come, lit., 'the coming (One)'; in 11:17 and 16:5 the wording of the A.V. and R.V. differs; in 11:17 the A.V. follows the inferior mss. by adding "and art to come" (R.V. omits); in 16:5, the A.V., "and shalt be," represents *kai* (and) followed by the article and the future participle of *eimi*, to be, lit., 'and the (One) about to be'; the R.V. substitutes the superior reading "Thou Holy One," lit., 'the holy (One)': see HOLY, B, No. 2.

(4) In Phil. 2:21, A.V., "the things of Jesus Christ" (R.V.), is rendered "the things which are Jesus Christ's."

WHILE, WHILES, WHILST

Notes: (1) See LITTLE, B, No. 1.

(2) In Matt. 13:21, *proskairos estin*, lit., 'is for a season,' is rendered "dureth (R.V., endureth) for a while."

(3) *Chronos*, time, is rendered "while" in Luke 18:4; John 7:33; 12:35 (1st part); 1 Cor. 16:7; *kairos*, a season, "a while," Luke 8:13; in Acts 19:22, R.V., "while" (A.V., "season"); for the different meanings of these words see SEASON.

(4) In Acts 18:18, A.V., "a good while," is, lit., 'sufficient days,' R.V., "many days."

(5) In Acts 28:6, A.V., *epi polu*, lit., 'upon much,' is rendered "a great while" (R.V., "long").

(6) For Mark 1:35 see DAY, B.

(7) In Mark 15:44 *palai*, long ago, is rendered "any while."

(8) In Acts 27:33 and Heb. 3:13 *achri* (or *achris*) followed by *hou*, the genitive case of the relative pronoun *hos*, lit., 'until which,' is rendered "while"; cp. *en hǭ*, in Mark 2:19; Luke 5:34; John 5:7; *en tǭ*, in Luke 1:21, R.V., "while"; in Heb. 3:15, "while it is said," is, lit., 'in the being said' (*en*, with the article and the pres. infin., Passive of *legō*); so, e.g., in Matt. 13:25.

(9) In Heb. 10:33, A.V., "whilst ye were made;" partly translating the present participle of *theatrizomai*, to become a gazing-stock, R.V., "being made"; in the 2nd part, *ginomai*, to become, is translated "whilst ye became;" A.V. (R.V., "becoming"). ¶

(10) The conjunction *heōs*, until, etc., has the meaning "while" in Matt. 14:22; Mark 6:45; 14:32; in some texts, John 9:4; 12:35, 36; with *hotou*, whatever (an oblique case, neuter, of *hostis*, whoever) "whiles;" Matt. 5:25.

(11) In Acts 20:11 *hikanos*, sufficient, is rendered "a long while."

(12) *Hōs*, as, "while" in Luke 24:32 (twice); John 12:35, 36; Acts 1:10; 10:17.

(13) *Hotan*, when, is rendered "while" in 1 Cor. 3:4, A.V. (R.V., "when").

(14) *Hote*, when, is rendered "while" in John 17:12; Heb. 9:17.

(15) In John 4:31 *metaxu*, between, used with *en tǭ*, 'in the,' is rendered "meanwhile"; in Rom. 2:15 *metaxu* is itself rendered "the mean while" (R.V., "between").

(16) In Acts 18:18, R.V., *hikanos* is rendered "many" (A.V., "good").

(17) In 1 Pet. 1:6, R.V., *oligon*, a little, is rendered "for a little while" (A.V., "for a season").

WHISPERER, WHISPERING

1. *psithuristēs* [ψιθυριστής, 5588], a whisperer, occurs in an evil sense in Rom. 1:29. ¶
NT: B.893a; CB.1267c K.—.
OT: —.
GEN. REF.: —.

2. *psithurismos* [ψιθυρισμός, 5587], a whispering, is used of secret slander in 2 Cor. 12:20. ¶ In the Sept., Eccl. 10:11, of a murmured enchantment. ¶
NT: B.892d; CB.1267c; K.—.
OT: lāḥash: S.3907; HR.1485c.1; H.1107; BD.538a.
GEN. REF.: IS.4:1058; NB.—; Z.—.

Note: Synonymous with No. 1 is *katalalos*, a backbiter (Rom. 1:30 ¶), the distinction being that this denotes one guilty of open calumny, *psithuristēs*, one who does it clandestinely.

For **WHIT** see **EVERY WHIT** and **NOTHING**, No. 2

WHITE (Adjective and Verb)

A. Adjective.

leukos [λευκός, 3022], is used of (*a*) clothing (sometimes in the sense of bright), Matt. 17:2; 28:3; Mark 9:3; 16:5; Luke 9:29; John 20:12; Acts 1:10; symbolically, Rev. 3:4, 5, 18; 4:4; 6:11; 7:9, 13; 19:14 (2nd part); (*b*) hair, Matt. 5:36; Christ's head and hair (in a vision; cp. Dan. 7:9), Rev. 1:14 (twice); ripened grain, John 4:35; a stone, Rev. 2:17, an expression of the Lord's special delight in the overcomer, the new name on it being indicative of a secret communication of love and joy; a horse (in a vision), 6:2; 19:11, 14 (1st part); a cloud, 14:14; the throne of God, 20:11. ¶
NT: B.472b; CB.1257a; K.530.
OT: lābān: S.3836; HR.874c.3; H.1074a,b; BD.526b.
GEN. REF.: IS.1:732; NB.—; Z.5:928.

Note: Lampros, bright, clear, is rendered "white" in Rev. 15:6, A.V., of "white (linen)" (R.V., "bright;" following those mss. which have *lithon*, stone); in 19:8 (R.V., "bright"). See BRIGHT, CLEAR, GOODLY, *Note*, GORGEOUS.

B. Verbs.

1. *leukainō* [λευκαίνω, 3021], to whiten, make white (akin to A), is used in Mark 9:3; figuratively in Rev. 7:14. ¶
NT: B.472b; CB.—; K.530.
OT: lābān: S.3835; HR.874b.1a; H.1074h; BD.526a.
lābān: S.3836; HR.874b.1b; H.1074a,b; BD.526b.
GEN. REF.: IS.1:732; NB.—; Z.5:928.

2. *koniaō* [κονιάω, 2867], from *konia*, dust, lime, denotes to whiten, whitewash, of tombs, Matt. 23:27; figuratively of a hypocrite, Acts 23:3. ¶ In the Sept., Deut. 27:2, 4; Prov. 21:9. ¶
NT: B.443a; CB.1255c; K.453.
OT: sîd: S.7875; HR.777c.1; H.2254a; BD.966d.
GEN. REF.: —.

WHITHER, WHITHERSOEVER, see † p. 1

WHO, WHOM, WHOSE

Notes: These are usually the translations of forms of the relative pronoun *hos*, or of the interrogative pronoun *tis*; otherwise of *hostis*, whoever, usually of a more general subject than *hos*, e.g., Mark 15:7; Luke 23:19; Gal. 2:4; *hosos*, as many as, Heb. 2:15; in Acts 13:7, A.V., *houtos*, this (man), is translated "who;" R.V., "the same."

WHOLE (made), WHOLLY, WHOLESOME

A. Adjectives.

1. *holos* [ὅλος, 3650], for which see ALL, A, No. 3, and ALTOGETHER, signifies "whole;" (*a*) with a noun, e.g., Matt. 5:29, 30; Mark 8:36; 15:1, 16, 33; Luke 11:36 (1st part), though *holon* may here be used adverbially with *phōteinon*, 'wholly light' [as in the 2nd part, R.V., "wholly (full of light)"]; John 11:50; 1 Cor. 12:17 (1st

part); 1 John 2:2; 5:19; (*b*) absolutely, as a noun, e.g., Matt. 13:33; 1 Cor., 12:17 (2nd part).
NT: B.564c; CB.1251a; K.682.
OT: kōl: S.3605; HR.989b.1a; H.985a; BD.481a.
GEN. REF.: –.

2. *pas* [πᾶς, 3956], for which see ALL, A, No. 1, is sometimes translated "the whole" when used with the article, e.g., Matt. 8:32, 34; Rom. 8:22.
NT: B.631a; CB.1262c; K.795.
OT: kōl: S.3605; HR.1073a.1; H.985a; BD.481a.
GEN. REF.: –.

3. *hapas* [ἅπας, 537], for which see ALL, A, No. 2, is rendered "the whole," e.g., in Luke 19:37; 23:1.
NT: B.81d; CB.1249b; K.795.
OT: kōl: S.3605; HR.118c.1a; H.985a; BD.481a.
GEN. REF.: –.

4. *holoklēros* [ὁλόκληρος, 3648], from No. 1 and *klēros*, a lot, is rendered "whole" in 1 Thess. 5:23: see ENTIRE.
NT: B.564c; CB.–; K.442.
OT: shālēm: S.8003; HR.989a.2; H.2401; BD.1023d.
tāmîm: S.8549; HR.989a.3; H.2512a; BD.1071a.
GEN. REF.: –.

5. *hugiēs* [ὑγιής, 5199], (cp. Eng., hygiene) is used especially in the Gospels of making sick folk "whole," Matt. 12:13; 15:31; Mark 3:5; 5:34; Luke 6:10; John 5:4, 6, 9, 11, 14, 15; 7:23; also Acts 4:10; of "sound (speech)," Tit. 2:8. See SOUND. ¶
NT: B.832a; CB.1251c; K.1202.
OT: ḥay: S.2416; HR.1380c.1; H.644a; BD.311d.
GEN. REF.: –.

6. *holotelēs* [ὁλοτελής, 3651], "wholly," 1 Thess. 5:23, is lit., 'whole-complete' (A, No. 1, and *telos*, an end), i.e., 'through and through'; the Apostle's desire is that the sanctification of the believer may extend to every part of his being. The word is similar in meaning to No. 4; *holoklēros* draws attention to the person as a whole, *holotelēs* to the several parts which constitute him. ¶
NT: B.565a; CB.–; K.682.
OT: –.
GEN. REF.: –.

Note: In 1 Tim. 4:15, the sentence freely rendered "give thyself wholly to them" is, lit., 'be in these (things).'

B. Verbs.

1. *hugiainō* [ὑγιαίνω, 5198], to be in good health, akin to A, No. 5, is rendered "they that are whole" in Luke 5:31; "whole" in 7:10 (present participle); "wholesome" in 1 Tim. 6:3, A.V. (R.V., "sound"; marg., "healthful"). See HEALTH, SOUND.
NT: B.832b; CB.1251c; K.1202.
OT: shālôm: S.7965; HR.1380b.1b; H.2401a; BD.1022d.
GEN. REF.: –.

2. *sōzō* [σώζω, 4982], to save, is sometimes rendered to make whole, and, in the Passive Voice, to be made whole, or to be whole, e.g., Matt. 9:21, 22 (twice), and parallel passages; Acts 4:9. See HEAL, SAVE.
NT: B.798a; CB.1269c; K.1132.
OT: shālēm: S.7999; HR.1328b.16; H.2401c; BD.1022a.
GEN. REF.: –.

3. *iaomai* [ἰάομαι, 2390], to heal, is rendered to make whole, Matt. 15:28; Acts 9:34, A.V. (R.V., "healeth"). See HEAL.
NT: B.368b; CB.1252c; K.344.
OT: rāphā': S.7495; HR.668a.3; H.2196; BD.950c.
GEN. REF.: IS.4:1059; NB.–; Z.–.

4. *ischuō* [ἰσχύω, 2480], to be strong, is rendered "they that are whole" in Matt. 9:12 and Mark 2:17. See ABLE, B, No. 4.
NT: B.383d; CB.1253a; K.378.
OT: –.
GEN. REF.: –.

5. *diasōzō* [διασώζω, 1295], to save thoroughly (*dia*), is used in the Passive Voice and rendered "were made whole" in Matt. 14:36, R.V. (A.V., "were made perfectly whole"). See ESCAPE, HEAL, SAVE.
NT: B.189a; CB.1241b; K.–.
OT: –.
GEN. REF.: –.

For **WHORE, WHOREMONGER** see **FORNICATION, HARLOT**

WHOSO, WHOSOEVER

Note: The same pronouns as those under WHO are used for the above, often with the addition of the particle *an* and a change of construction when a generalisation is expressed. Some texts in Mark 15:6 have *hosper*, a strengthened form of *hos*, A.V., "whomsoever." For sentences introduced by the conjunction *ei* or *ean*, if, see † p. 1.

WHY: see † p. 1

WICKED

1. *ponēros* [πονηρός, 4190], for which see BAD, No. 2, EVIL, A and B, No. 2, is translated "wicked" in the A.V. and R.V. in Matt. 13:49; 18:32; 25:26; Luke 19:22; Acts 18:14; 1 Cor. 5:13; in the following the R.V. substitutes "evil" for A.V., "wicked": Matt. 12:45 (twice); 13:19; 16:4; Luke 11:26; Col. 1:21; 2 Thess. 3:2; and in the following, where Satan is mentioned as "the (or that) evil one": Matt. 13:38; Eph. 6:16; 1 John 2:13, 14; 3:12 (1st part); 5:18; in ver. 19 for A.V., "wickedness"; he is so called also in A.V. and R.V. in John 17:15; 2 Thess. 3:3; A.V. only in Luke 11:4; in 3 John 10, A.V., the word is translated "malicious," R.V., "wicked."
NT: B.690d; CB.1266a; K.912.
OT: ra': S.7451; HR.1186c.4a; H.2191; BD.948a.
GEN. REF.: IS.4:1059; NB.1326; Z.–.

2. *athesmos* [ἄθεσμος, 113], lawless (*a*, negative, *thesmos*, law, custom), "wicked," occurs in 2 Pet. 2:7; 3:17. ¶ An instance of the use of the word is found in the papyri, where a father breaks off his daughter's engagement because he learnt that her fiancé was giving himself over to lawless deeds (Moulton and Milligan, Vocab.).

NT: B.21a; CB.—; K.25.
OT: —.
GEN. REF.: IS.4:1059; NB.1326; Z.—.

Notes: (1) In Matt. 21:41, A.V., *kakos* (for which see BAD, No. 1, EVIL, A, No. 1), is translated "wicked" (R.V., "miserable").

(2) In Acts 2:23 and 2 Thess. 2:8, A.V., *anomos*, "lawless" (R.V.), is translated "wicked."

WICKEDNESS

1. *ponēria* [πονηρία, 4189], akin to *ponēros* (see above, No. 1), is always rendered "wickedness" save in Acts 3:26: see INIQUITY, No. 4.

NT: B.690c; CB.1266a; K.912.
OT: rā'āh: S.7451; HR.1186b.4c; H.2191; BD.949a.
GEN. REF.: IS.4:1059; NB.1326; Z.—.

2. *kakia* [κακία, 2549], evil, is rendered "wickedness" in Acts 8:22; R.V. in Jas. 1:21, A.V., "naughtiness." See EVIL, B, No. 1, MALICE.

NT: B.397a; CB.1253a; K.391.
OT: rā'āh: S.7451; HR.708a.11d; H.2191; BD.949a.
GEN. REF.: IS.4:1059; NB.—; Z.—.

Notes: (1) For the A.V. of 1 John 5:19 see WICKED, No. 1.

(2) In Acts 25:5, A.V, the word *atopos* (R.V., "amiss") is incorrectly rendered "wickedness."

For WIDE see BROAD

WIDOW

chēra [χήρα, 5503], Matt. 28:13 (in some texts); Mark 12:40, 42, 43; Luke 2:37; 4:25, 26, lit., 'a woman a widow'; 7:12; 18:3, 5; 20:47; 21:2, 3; Acts 6:1; 9:39, 41; 1 Tim. 5:3 (twice), 4, 5, 11, 16 (twice); Jas. 1:27; 1 Tim. 5:9 refers to elderly widows (not an ecclesiastical "order"), recognized, for relief or maintenance by the church (cp. vv. 3, 16), as those who had fulfilled the conditions mentioned; where relief could be ministered by those who had relatives that were widows (a likely circumstance in large families), the church was not to be responsible; there is an intimation of the tendency to shelve individual responsibility at the expense of church funds. In Rev. 18:7, it is used figuratively of a city forsaken. ¶

NT: B.881c; CB.1239c; K.1313.
OT: 'almānāh: S.490; HR.1468a.1a; H.105; BD.48a.
GEN. REF.: IS.4:1060; NB.1326; Z.5:928.

WIFE, WIVES

1. *gunē* [γυνή, 1135], denotes (1) a woman, married or unmarried (see WOMAN); (2) a wife, e.g., Matt. 1:20; 1 Cor. 7:3, 4; in 1 Tim. 3:11, R.V., "women," the reference may be to the wives of deacons, as the A.V. takes it.

NT: B.168b; CB.1248c; K.134.
OT: 'ishshāh: S.802; HR.278b.1; H.137a; BD.61a.
GEN. REF.: IS.4:1089; NB.—; Z.—.

2. *gunaikeios* [γυναικεῖος, 1134], an adjective denoting womanly, female, is used as a noun in 1 Pet. 3:7, A.V., "wife," R.V., "woman." ¶

NT: B.168b; CB.1248c; K.—.
OT: 'ishshāh: S.802; HR.278b.1; H.137a; BD.61a.
GEN. REF.: IS.4:1089; NB.—; Z.—.

Note: In John 19:25 the article stands idiomatically for "the *wife* (of)"; in Matt. 1:6, the article is rendered "her *that had been the wife* (of)."

WIFE'S MOTHER

penthera [πενθερά, 3994], denotes a mother-in-law, Matt. 8:14; 10:35; Mark 1:30; Luke 4:38; 12:53 (twice). ¶

NT: B.642c; CB.—; K.—.
OT: ḥāmôt: S.2545; HR.1117c.1; H.674b; BD.327b.
GEN. REF.: —.

WILD

agrios [ἄγριος, 66], denotes (*a*) of or in fields (*agros*, hence, not domestic, said of honey, Matt. 3:4; Mark 1:6; (*b*) savage, fierce, Jude 13, R.V., metaphorically, "wild (waves)," A.V., "raging." ¶ It is used in the papyri of a malignant wound.

NT: B.13c; CB.1233c; K.—.
OT: sādeh: S.7704; HR.16c.6; H.2234a,b; BD.961b.
pere': S.6501; HR.16c.5; H.1805a; BD.825b.
GEN. REF.: —.

Note: In Rev. 6:8 the R.V. renders *thērion* (plural) "wild beasts" (A.V., "beasts").

WILDERNESS

1. *erēmia* [ἐρημία, 2047], an uninhabited place, is translated "wilderness" in the A.V. of Matt. 15:33 and Mark 8:4 (R.V., "a desert place"); R.V. and A.V., "wilderness" in 2 Cor. 11:26. See DESERT, A. (In the Sept., Is. 60:20; Ezek. 35:4, 9. ¶

NT: B.308d; CB.1246b; K.255.
OT: ḥārēb: S.2720; HR.545a.1a; H.731a; BD.351d.
ḥārbāh: S.2723; HR.545a.1b; H.731d; BD.352a.
shemāmāh: S.8077; HR.545a.2; H.2409b,c; BD.1031b.
GEN. REF.: IS.4:1062; NB.—; Z.—.

2. *erēmos* [ἔρημος, 2048], an adjective signifying desolate, deserted, lonely, is used as a noun, and rendered "wilderness" 32 times in the A.V.; in Matt. 24:26 and John 6:31, R.V.,

"wilderness" (A.V., "desert"). For the R.V., "deserts" in Luke 5:16 and 8:29 see DESERT, B.

NT: B.309a; CB.1246b; K.255.
OT: midbār: S.4057; HR.545a.5; H.399k,l; BD.184c.
negeb: S.5045; HR.545a.8; H.1288a; BD.616a.
shᵉmāmāh: S.8077; HR.545a.11d; H.2409b,c; BD.1031b.
GEN. REF.: IS.4:1062; NB.–; Z.5:931.

WILES

methodia or *-eia* [*μεθοδία*, 3180], denotes craft, deceit (*meta*, after, *hodos*, a way), a cunning device, a wile, and is translated "wiles (of error)" in Eph. 4:14, R.V. [A.V. paraphrases it, "they lie in wait (to deceive)"], lit., '(with a view to) the craft (singular) of deceit'; in 6:11, "the wiles (plural) (of the Devil.)" ¶

NT: B.499a; CB.1258c; K.666.
OT: –.
GEN. REF.: –.

WILFULLY

A. Adverb.

hekousiōs [*ἑκουσίως*, 1596], denotes voluntarily, willingly, Heb. 10:26, (of sinning) "wilfully"; in 1 Pet. 5:2, "willingly" (of exercising oversight over the flock of God). ¶

NT: B.243c; CB.–; K.221.
OT: (bi) nᵉdābāh: S.5071; HR.438c.1; H.1299a; BD.621d.
GEN. REF.: –.

B. Verb.

thelō [*θέλω*, 2309], to will, used in the present participle in 2 Pet. 3:5, is rendered "wilfully (forget)" in the R.V., A.V., "willingly (are ignorant of)," lit., 'this escapes them (i.e., their notice) willing (i.e. of their own will).' See WILL, C, No. 1, WILLING, B, No. 1.

NT: B.354d; CB.1271c; K.318.
OT: 'ābāh: S.14; HR.628b.1; H.3; BD.2c.
ḥāphēṣ: S.2654; HR.628b.8a; H.712; BD.342c.
mā'ēn (with neg.): S.3985; HR.628b.13b; H.1138; BD.549a.
GEN. REF.: –.

WILL, WOULD

A. Nouns.

1. *thelēma* [*θέλημα*, 2307], signifies (*a*) objectively, that which is willed, of the will of God, e.g., Matt. 18:14; Mark 3:35, the fulfilling being a sign of spiritual relationship to the Lord; John 4:34; 5:30; 6:39, 40; Acts 13:22, plural, 'my desires'; Rom. 2:18; 12:2, lit., 'the will of God, the good and perfect and acceptable'; here the repeated article is probably resumptive, the adjectives describing the will, as in the Eng. Versions; Gal. 1:4; Eph. 1:9; 5:17, "of the Lord"; Col. 1:9; 4:12; 1 Thess. 4:3; 5:18, where it means 'the gracious design,' rather than 'the determined resolve'; 2 Tim. 2:26; which should read 'which have been taken captive by him [(*autou*), i.e., by the Devil; the R.V., "by the Lord's servant" is an interpretation, it does not correspond to the Greek] unto His (*ekeinou*) will' (i.e., God's will; the different pronoun refers back to the subject of the sentence, viz., God); Heb. 10:10; Rev. 4:11, R.V., "because of Thy will"; of human will, e.g., 1 Cor. 7:37; (*b*) subjectively, the will being spoken of as the emotion of being desirous, rather than as the thing willed; of the will of God, e.g., Rom. 1:10; 1 Cor. 1:1; 2 Cor. 1:1; 8:5; Eph. 1:1, 5, 11; Col. 1:1; 2 Tim. 1:1; Heb. 10:7, 9, 36; 1 John 2:17; 5:14; of human will, e.g., John 1:13; Eph. 2:3, "the desires of the flesh"; 1 Pet. 4:3 (in some texts); 2 Pet. 1:21. See DESIRE, A, No. 5, PLEASURE, *Note* (1).

NT: B.354b; CB.1271c; K.318.
OT: ḥēpheṣ: S.2656; HR.629a.1c; H.712b; BD.343a.
rāṣôn: S.7522; HR.629a.4; H.2207a; BD.953c.
GEN. REF.: IS.4:1064; NB.–; Z.5:931.

2. *thelēsis* [*θέλησις*, 2308], denotes a willing, a wishing [similar to No. 1 (*b*)], Heb. 2:4. ¶

NT: B.354c; CB.1271c; K.318.
OT: ḥāphēṣ: S.2654; HR.629b.2; H.712; BD.342c.
rāṣôn: S.7522; HR.629b.4; H.2207a; BD.953c.
GEN. REF.: IS.4:1064; NB.–; Z.–.

3. *boulēma* [*βούλημα*, 1013], a deliberate design, that which is purposed, Rom. 9:19; 1 Pet. 4:3 (in the best texts). See PURPOSE, A, No. 1.

NT: B.145d; CB.1239b; K.108.
OT: dā'at: S.1847; HR.228b.1; H.848c; BD.395c.
GEN. REF.: IS.4:1064; NB.–; Z.5:931.

4. *eudokia* [*εὐδοκία*, 2107], (*eu*, well, *dokēo*), to think) is rendered "good will" in Luke 2:14, A.V. (see WELL PLEASED); Phil. 1:15: see DESIRE, PLEASURE, SEEM, WELL-PLEASING.

NT: B.319c; CB.1247a; K.273.
OT: rāṣôn: S.7522; HR.569b.1a; H.2207a; BD.953c.
GEN. REF.: IS.4:1064; NB.–; Z.–.

5. *eunoia* [*εὔνοια*, 2133], good will (*eu*, well, *nous*, the mind), occurs in Eph. 6:7 (in some texts, 1 Cor. 7:3). ¶

NT: B.323b; CB.–; K.636.
OT: –.
GEN. REF.: –.

Notes: (1) In Acts 13:36, A.V., *boulē*, "counsel" (R.V.), is translated "will."

(2) In Rev. 17:17, A.V., *gnōmē*, an opinion, R.V., "mind," is translated "will."

(3) For "will-worship," Col. 2:23, see WORSHIP, B, No. 2.

B. Adjectives.

1. *hekōn* [*ἑκών*, 1635], of free will, willingly, occurs in Rom. 8:20, R.V., "of its own will" (A.V., "willingly"); 1 Cor. 9:17, R.V., "of my own will" (A.V., "willingly"). ¶ In the Sept., Ex. 21:13; Job 36:19. ¶

NT: B.247d; CB.–; K.221.
OT: –.
GEN. REF.: –.

2. *akōn* [*ἄκων*, 210], *a*, negative, and No. 1, unwillingly, occurs in 1 Cor. 9:17, R.V., "not

of mine own will" (A.V., "against my will"). ¶ In the Sept., Job 14:17. ¶

NT: B.34b; CB.–; K.221.
OT: –.
GEN. REF.: –.

C. Verbs.

When "will" is not part of the translation of the future tense of verbs, it represents one of the following:

1. *thelō* [θέλω, 2309], for the force of which see Desire, B, No. 6, usually expresses desire or design; it is most frequently translated by "will" or "would"; see especially Rom. 7:15, 16, 18-21. In 1 Tim. 2:4, R.V., "willeth" signifies the gracious desire of God for all men to be saved; not all are willing to accept His condition, depriving themselves either by the self-established criterion of their perverted reason, or because of their self-indulgent preference for sin. In John 6:21, the A.V. renders the verb "willingly" (R.V., "they were willing"); in 2 Pet. 3:5, A.V., the present participle is translated "willingly" (R.V., "wilfully").

The following are R.V. renderings for the A.V., 'will': Matt. 16:24, 25, "would"; "wouldest," 19:21 and 20:21; "would," 20:26, 27; Mark 8:34, 35; 10:43, 44; "would fain," Luke 13:31; "would," John 6:67; "willeth," 7:17; in 8:44, "it is your will (to do)"; "wouldest," Rom. 13:3; "would," 1 Cor. 14:35 and 1 Pet. 3:10.

NT: B.354d; CB.1271c; K.318.
OT: 'ābāh: S.14; HR.628b.1; H.3; BD.2c.
ḥāphēṣ: S.2654; HR.628b.8a; H.712; BD.342c.
mā'ēn (with neg.): S.3985; HR.628b.13b; H.1138; BD.549a.
GEN. REF.: IS.4:1064; NB.–; Z.5:931.

2. *boulomai* [βούλομαι, 1014], for the force of which see Desire, B, No. 7, usually expresses the deliberate exercise of volition more strongly than No. 1, and is rendered as follows in the R.V., where the A.V. has "will": Matt. 11:27 and Luke 10:22, "willeth"; Jas. 4:4, "would"; in Jas. 3:4, R.V., "willeth" (A.V., "listeth"). In Jas. 1:18 the perfect participle is translated "of His own will," lit. "having willed."

NT: B.146a; CB.1239b; K.108.
OT: 'ābāh: S.14; HR.226b.1; H.3; BD.2c.
ḥāphēṣ: S.2654; HR.226b.5a; H.712; BD.342c.
mā'ēn (with neg.): S.3985; HR.226b.8a; H.1138; BD.549a.
GEN. REF.: IS.4:1064; NB.–; Z.5:931.

3. *mellō* [μέλλω, 3195], to be about to, is translated "will" in Matt. 2:13 and John 7:35 (twice); "wilt," John 14:22; "will," Acts 17:31; "wouldest," 23:20; "will," 27:10 and Rev. 3:16. See About, B.

NT: B.500d; CB.1258a; K.–.
OT: –.
GEN. REF.: –.

WILLING (Adjective and Verb)

A. Adjectives.

1. *prothumos* [πρόθυμος, 4289], is rendered "willing" in Matt. 26:41; Mark 14:38, R.V. See Ready, No. 2.

NT: B.706c; CB.–; K.937.
OT: nādîb: S.5081; HR.1206c.2; H.1299b; BD.622a.
GEN. REF.: –.

2. *hekousios* [ἑκούσιος, 1595], willing, is used with *kata* in Philm. 14, lit., 'according to willing,' R.V., "of free will" (A.V., "willingly"). ¶

NT: B.243b; CB.–; K.221.
OT: n^{e}dābāh: S.5071; HR.438c.2b; H.1299a; BD.621d.
GEN. REF.: –.

B. Verbs.

1. *thelō* [θέλω, 2309], is rendered "ye were willing" in John 5:35. See Will, C, No. 1.

NT: B.354d; CB.1271c; K.318.
OT: 'ābāh: S.14; HR.628b.1; H.3; BD.2c.
ḥāphēṣ: S.2654; HR.628b.8a; H.712; BD.342c.
mā'ēn (with neg.): S.3985; HR.628b.13b; H.1138; BD.549a.
GEN. REF.: IS.4:1064; NB.–; Z.5:931.

2. *boulomai* [βούλομαι, 1014], is rendered "(if) Thou be willing" in Luke 22:42; in 2 Pet. 3:9, A.V. (R.V., "wishing"). See Will, C, No. 2.

NT: B.146a; CB.1239b; K.108.
OT: 'ābāh: S.14; HR.226b.1; H.3; BD.2c.
ḥāphēṣ: S.2654; HR.226b.5a; H.712; BD.342c.
mā'ēn (with neg.): S.3985; HR.226b.8a; H.1138; BD.549a.
GEN. REF.: IS.4:1064; NB.–; Z.5:931.

3. *eudokeō* [εὐδοκέω, 2106], to be well pleased, to think it good, is rendered "we are willing" in 2 Cor. 5:8; in 1 Thess. 2:8, A.V., "we were willing" (R.V., "we were well pleased"). See Please, Pleasure.

NT: B.319b; CB.1247a; K.273.
OT: rāṣāh: S.7521; HR.569a.9; H.2207; BD.953a.
GEN. REF.: IS.4:1064; NB.–; Z.5:931.

Notes: (1) In 2 Cor. 8:3, A.V., *authairetos*, of one's own accord (R.V.), is rendered "willing of themselves"; in ver. 17, "of his own accord." See Accord. ¶

(2) For "willing to communicate," 1 Tim. 6:18, see Communicate, C.

For **WILLING MIND** see **READINESS**

WILLINGLY

Notes: (1) For *hekōn* see Will, B, No. 1.

(2) For *hekousiōs*, see Wilfully.

(3) For Philm. 14 see Willing, A, No. 2.

(4) For 2 Pet. 3:5 see Will, C, No. 1.

For **WIN** see **POSSESS**, A, No. 2.

WIND (Noun)

1. *anemos* [ἄνεμος, 417], besides its literal meaning, is used metaphorically in Eph. 4:14, of variable teaching. In Matt. 24:31 and Mark

13:27 the four winds stand for the four cardinal points of the compass; so in Rev. 7:1, "the four winds of the earth" (cp. Jer. 49:36; Dan. 7:2); the contexts indicate that these are connected with the execution of Divine judgments. Deissmann (*Bible Studies*) and Moulton and Milligan (Vocab.) illustrate the phrase from the papyri.

NT: B.64c; CB.1235c; K.—.
OT: rûaḥ: S.7307; HR.86c.1; H.2131a; BD.924c.
GEN. REF.: IS.4:1067; NB.1331; Z.5:934.

2. *pnoē* [πνοή, 4157], a blowing, blast (akin to *pneō*, to blow), is used of the rushing wind at Pentecost, Acts 2:2. See BREATH.

NT: B.680b; CB.1265c; K.876.
OT: nᵉshāmāh: S.5397; HR.1153b.2a; H.1433a; BD.675c.
GEN. REF.: IS.4:1067; NB.—; Z.5:934.

3. *pneuma* [πνεῦμα, 4151], is translated "wind" in John 3:8 (R.V., marg., "the Spirit breatheth," the probably meaning); in Heb. 1:7 the R.V. has "winds" for A.V., "spirits." See SPIRIT.

NT: B.674c; CB.1265b; K.876.
OT: rûaḥ: S.7307; HR.1151c.3; H.2131a; BD.924c.
GEN. REF.: IS.4:1067; NB.1331; Z.5:934.

Notes: (1) For *pneō*, to blow ("wind" in Acts 27:40), see BLOW, No. 1.

(2) For *anemizō*, Jas. 1:6, "driven by the wind," see DRIVE, No. 8. ¶

WIND (Verb)

1. *deō* [δέω, 1210], to bind, is translated "wound (it in linen clothes)," John 19:40, A.V., of the body of Christ (R.V., "bound"). See BIND, No. 1, TIE.

NT: B.177d; CB.1240c; K.148.
OT: 'āsar: S.631; HR.287b.1a; H.141; BD.63c.
GEN. REF.: —.

2. *sustellō* [συστέλλω, 4958], is translated "wound . . . up" in Acts 5:6 (R.V., "wrapped . . . round"). See SHORTEN, No. 2, WRAP.

NT: B.795a; CB.—; K.1074.
OT: —.
GEN. REF.: —.

3. *eneileō* [ἐνειλέω, 1750], to roll in, wind in, is used in Mark 15:46, of winding the cloth around the Lord's body, R.V., "wound" (A.V., "wrapped"). ¶

NT: B.264c; CB.—; K.—.
OT: lûṭ: S.3874; HR.472b.1; H.1092; BD.532c.
GEN. REF.: —.

WINDOW

thuris [θυρίς, 2376], a diminutive of *thura*, a door, occurs in Acts 20:9; 2 Cor. 11:33. ¶

NT: B.366a; CB.—; K.—.
OT: hallôn: S.2474; HR.663c.2; H.660c; BD.319d.
GEN. REF.: IS.4:1068; NB.—; Z.5:934.

WINE

1. *oinos* [οἶνος, 3631], is the general word for wine. The mention of the bursting of the wineskins, Matt. 9:17; Mark 2:22; Luke 5:37, implies fermentation. See also Eph. 5:18 (cp. John 2:10; 1 Tim. 3:8; Tit. 2:3). In Matt. 27:34, the R.V. has "wine" (A.V., "vinegar," translating the inferior reading *oxos*).

The drinking of wine could be a stumbling-block and the Apostle enjoins abstinence in this respect, as in others, so as to avoid giving an occasion of stumbling to a brother, Rom. 14:21. Contrast 1 Tim. 5:23, which has an entirely different connection. The word is used metaphorically (*a*) of the evils ministered to the nations by religious Babylon, 14:8; 17:2; 18:3; (*b*) of the contents of the cup of Divine wrath upon the nations and Babylon, Rev. 14:10; 16:19; 19:15.

NT: B.562a; CB.1260c; K.680.
OT: yayin: S.3196; HR.983c.2; H.864; BD.406b.
tîrōsh: S.8492; HR.983c.7; H.2505; BD.440d.
GEN. REF.: IS.4:1068; NB.1331; Z.5:935.

2. *gleukos* [γλεῦκος, 1098], denotes sweet "new wine," or must, Acts 2:13, where the accusation shows that it was intoxicant and must have been undergoing fermentation some time. ¶ In the Sept., Job 32:19. ¶

NT: B.162a; CB.1248b; K.—.
OT: yayin: S.3196; HR.270c.1; H.864; BD.406b.
GEN. REF.: IS.4:1069; NB.1332; Z.5:935.

Note: In instituting the Lord's Supper He speaks of the contents of the cup as the "fruit of the vine." So Mark 14:25.

For GIVEN TO WINE see BRAWLER, No. 1

WINE-BIBBER

oinopotēs [οἰνοπότης, 3630], a wine-drinker (*oinos*, and *potēs*, a drinker), is used in Matt. 11:19; Luke 7:34. ¶ In the Sept., Prov. 23:20. ¶

NT: B.562a; CB.1260c; K.—.
OT: sābā': S.5433; HR.983c.1; H.1455; BD.684d.
GEN. REF.: IS.4:1072; NB.—; Z.—.

For WINEBIBBINGS see EXCESS, *Note* (2)

WINEPRESS, WINE-FAT

1. *lēnos* [ληνός, 3025], denotes a trough or vat, used especially for the treading of grapes, Matt. 21:33. Not infrequently they were dug out in the soil or excavated in a rock, as in the rock-vats in Palestine to-day. In Rev. 14:19, 20 (twice) and 19:15 (where *oinos* is added, lit., 'the winepress of the wine') the word is used metaphorically with reference to the execution of Divine judgment upon the gathered foes of the Jews at the close of this age preliminary to the establishment of the Millennial kingdom. ¶

NT: B.473a; CB.—; K.531.
OT: yeqeb: S.3342; HR.875c.3; H.900a; BD.428c.
gat: S.1660; HR.875c.1a; H.841a; BD.387c.
GEN. REF.: IS.4:1072; NB.—; Z.—.

2. *hupolēnion* [ὑπολήνιον, 5276], was a vessel or trough beneath the press itself (*hupo*, beneath, and No. 1), for receiving the juice, Mark 12:1, R.V., "a pit for the winepress." ¶ In the Sept., Isa. 16:10; Joel 3:13; Hag. 2:16; Zech. 14:10. ¶

NT: B.845c; CB.—; K.531.
OT: yeqeb: S.3342; HR.1415c.1; H.900a; BD.428c.
GEN. REF.: IS.4:1072; NB.—; Z.—.

For **WINE-SKINS** see **SKIN**

WING

pterux [πτέρυξ, 4420], is used of birds, Matt. 23:37; Luke 13:34; symbolically in Rev. 12:14, R.V., "the two wings of the great eagle" (A.V., "two wings of a great eagle"), suggesting the definiteness of the action, the wings indicating rapidity and protection, an allusion, perhaps, to Ex. 19:4 and Deut. 32:11, 12; of the "living creatures" in a vision, Rev. 4:8; 9:9. ¶ Cp. *pterugion*, a pinnacle.

NT: B.727b; CB.1267c; K.—.
OT: kānāph: S.3671; HR.1238a.2; H.1003a; BD.489b.
GEN. REF.: IS.4:1072; NB.—; Z.5:938.

For **WINK AT** see **OVERLOOK**

WINTER (Noun and Verb)

A. Noun.

cheimōn [χειμών, 5494], denotes winter, in Matt. 24:20; Mark 13:18; John 10:22; 2 Tim. 4:21. See TEMPEST.

NT: B.879d; CB.—; K.—.
OT: geshem: S.1653; HR.1457c.1; H.389a; BD.177c.
GEN. REF.: IS.4:375; NB.—; Z.—.

B. Verb.

paracheimazō [παραχειμάζω, 3914], denotes to winter at a place (*para*, at, and A), Acts 27:12 (2nd part); 28:11; 1 Cor. 16:6; Tit. 3:12. ¶

NT: B.623c; CB.—; K.—.
OT: —.
GEN. REF.: IS.4:375; NB.—; Z.—.

Note: In Acts 27:12 (1st part) *paracheimasia*, a wintering, is rendered "(to) winter in." ¶

WIPE

1. *apomassō* [ἀπομάσσω, 631], to wipe off, wipe clean (*apo*, from, *massō*, to touch, handle), is used in the Middle Voice, of wiping dust from the feet, Luke 10:11. ¶

NT: B.96d; CB.—; K.—.
OT: —.
GEN. REF.: —.

2. *ekmassō* [ἐκμάσσω, 1591], to wipe out (*ek*), wipe dry, is used of wiping tears from Christ's feet, Luke 7:38, 44; John 11:2; 12:3; of Christ's wiping the disciples' feet, John 13:5. ¶

NT: B.243b; CB.—; K.—.
OT: —.
GEN. REF.: —.

3. *exaleiphō* [ἐξαλείφω, 1813], to wipe out or away (*ek*, or *ex*, out, *aleiphō*, to anoint), is used metaphorically of wiping away tears from the eyes, Rev. 7:17; 21:4. See BLOT OUT.

NT: B.272c; CB.1247b; K.—.
OT: māḥāh: S.4229; HR.486c.4; H.1178,1179; BD.562a.
GEN. REF.: —.

WISDOM

1. *sophia* [σοφία, 4678], is used with reference to (*a*) God, Rom. 11:33; 1 Cor. 1:21, 24; 2:7; Eph. 3:10; Rev. 7:12; (*b*) Christ, Matt. 13:54; Mark 6:2; Luke 2:40, 52; 1 Cor. 1:30; Col. 2:3; Rev. 5:12; (*c*) wisdom personified, Matt. 11:19; Luke 7:35; 11:49; (*d*) human wisdom (1) in spiritual things, Luke 21:15; Acts 6:3, 10; 7:10; 1 Cor. 2:6 (1st part); 12:8; Eph. 1:8, 17; Col. 1:9, R.V., "(spiritual) wisdom," 28; 3:16; 4:5; Jas. 1:5; 3:13, 17; 2 Pet. 3:15; Rev. 13:18; 17:9; (2) in the natural sphere, Matt. 12:42; Luke 11:31; Acts 7:22; 1 Cor. 1:17, 19, 20, 21 (twice), 22; 2:1, 4, 5, 6 (2nd part), 13; 3:19; 2 Cor. 1:12; Col. 2:23; (3) in its most debased form, Jas. 3:15, "earthly, sensual, devilish" (marg., "demoniacal"). ¶

NT: B.759c; CB.1269b; K.1056.
OT: ḥokmāh: S.2451; HR.1278c.3; H.647a; BD.315b.
GEN. REF.: IS.4:1074; NB.1333; Z.5:939.

2. *phronēsis* [φρόνησις, 5428], understanding, prudence, i.e., a right use of *phrēn*, the mind, is translated "wisdom" in Luke 1:17. See PRUDENCE.

NT: B.866c; CB.1264c; K.1277.
OT: ḥokmāh: S.2451; HR.1439a.3; H.647a; BD.315b.
tᵉbûnāh: S.8394; HR.1439a.1b; H.239c; BD.108a.
bînāh: S.998; HR.1439a.1a; H.239b; BD.108a.
GEN. REF.: IS.4:1074; NB.1333; Z.5:939.

Note: "While *sophia* is the insight into the true nature of things, *phronēsis* is the ability to discern modes of action with a view to their results; while *sophia* is theoretical, *phronēsis* is practical" (Lightfoot). *Sunesis*, understanding, intelligence, is the critical faculty; this and *phronēsis* are particular applications of *sophia*.

WISE, WISER, WISELY

A. Adjectives.

1. *sophos* [σοφός, 4680], is used of (*a*) God, Rom. 16:27; in 1 Tim. 1:17 and Jude 25 *sophos* is absent, in the best mss. (see the R.V.), the comparative degree, *sophōteros*, occurs in 1 Cor. 1:25, where "foolishness" is simply in the human estimate; (*b*) spiritual teachers in Israel, Matt. 23:34; (*c*) believers endowed with spiritual and practical wisdom, Rom. 16:19; 1 Cor. 3:10; 6:5; Eph. 5:15; Jas. 3:13; (*d*) Jewish teachers in the time of Christ, Matt. 11:25;

Luke 10:21; (*e*) the naturally learned, Rom. 1:14, 22; 1 Cor. 1:19, 20, 26, 27; 3:18-20. ¶

NT: B.760b; CB.1269b; K.1056.
OT: ḥākām: S.2450; HR.1280b.2a; H.647b; BD.314c.
ḥakkîm (Aramaic): S.2445; HR.1280b.2b; H.2729a; BD.1093a.
GEN. REF.: IS.4:1074; NB.1333; Z.—.

2. *phronimos* [φρόνιμος, 5429], prudent, sensible, practically wise, Matt. 7:24; 10:16; 24:45; 25:2, 4, 8, 9; Luke 12:42; 16:8 (comparative degree, *phronimōteros*); 1 Cor. 10:15; in an evil sense, "wise (in your own conceits)," lit., 'wise (in yourselves),' i.e., 'judged by the standard of your self-complacency,' Rom. 11:25; 12:16; ironically, 1 Cor. 4:10; 2 Cor. 11:19. ¶

NT: B.866d; CB.1264c; K.1277.
OT: tᵉbûnāh: S.8394; HR.1439b.1c; H.239c; BD.108a.
bîn: S.995; HR.1439b.1a; H.239; BD.106c.
ḥokmāh: S.2451; HR.1439b.2a; H.647a; BD.315b.
GEN. REF.: IS.4:1074; NB.1333; Z.5:939.

B. Noun.

magos [μάγος, 3097], denotes a Magian, one of a sacred caste, originally Median, who apparently conformed to the Persian religion while retaining their old beliefs; it is used in the plural, Matt. 2:1, 7, 16 (twice), "wise men." See also SORCERER.

NT: B.484d; CB.1257b; K.547.
OT: 'ashshaph: S.825; HR.891b.1; H.181; BD.80b.
GEN. REF.: —.

C. Verbs.

1. *sophizō* [σοφίζω, 4679], is rendered to make wise in 2 Tim. 3:15; see DEVISED.

NT: B.760b; CB.1269b; K.1056.
OT: ḥākam: S.2449; HR.1280a.2; H.647; BD.314b.
GEN. REF.: IS.4:1074; NB.1333; Z.5:939.

2. *suniēmi* or *suniō* [συνίημι, 4920], to perceive, understand, is used negatively in 2 Cor. 10:12, A.V., "are not wise" (R.V., "are without understanding"). See UNDERSTAND.

NT: B.790a; CB.1270c; K.1119.
OT: bîn: S.995; HR.1316b.1; H.239; BD.106c.
sākal: S.7919; HR.1316b.6; H.2263,2264; BD.968a.
GEN. REF.: IS.—; NB.—; Z.5:939.

D. Adverbs.

phronimōs [φρονίμως, 5430], wisely (akin to A, No. 2), occurs in Luke 16:8. ¶

NT: B.866d; CB.1264c; K.—.
OT: —.
GEN. REF.: —.

WISE (IN NO)

1. *ou mē* [οὐ μή, —], a double negative, expressing an emphatic negation, 'by no means,' is rendered "in no wise" in Matt. 10:42; Luke 18:17; John 6:37; Acts 13:41; Rev. 21:27.

NT: B.590a; CB.—; K.—.
OT: —.
GEN. REF.: —.

2. *pantōs* [πάντως, 3843], altogether, by all means, is used with the negative *ou* (not) in Rom. 3:9, stating a complete denial, rendered "No, in no wise." See ALL, B, 3, ALTOGETHER, B, 1.

NT: B.609b; CB.—; K.—.
OT: —.
GEN. REF.: —.

3. *panteles* [παντελές, 3838], the neuter of *pantelēs*, is used with the negative *mē*, and with *eis to*, 'unto the,' in Luke 13:11, and translated "in no wise," lit., 'not to the uttermost': see UTTERMOST, No. 1.

NT: B.608c; CB.1261c; K.1161.
OT: —.
GEN. REF.: —.

For WISE (ON THIS) see THUS

WISH

1. *euchomai* [εὔχομαι, 2172], is rendered to wish in Acts 27:29 (R.V. marg., "prayed"); so Rom. 9:3; in 2 Cor. 13:9 and 3 John 2, R.V., "pray"; see PRAY.

NT: B.329b; CB.1247a; K.—.
OT: nādar: S.5087; HR.583c.4a; H.1308; BD.623d.
'ātar: S.6279; HR.583c.7; H.1722; BD.801c.
GEN. REF.: IS.4:1085; NB.—; Z.—.

2. *boulomai* [βούλομαι, 1014], in Mark 15:15, R.V., is translated "wishing" (A.V., "willing"); so 2 Pet. 3:9; in Acts 25:22, R.V., "could wish" (A.V., "would"). See WILL, C, No. 2.

NT: B.146a; CB.1239b; K.108.
OT: 'ābāh: S.14; HR.226b.1; H.3; BD.2c.
ḥāphēṣ: S.2654; HR.226b.5a; H.712; BD.342c.
mā'ēn (with neg.): S.3985; HR.226b.8a; H.1138; BD.549a.
GEN. REF.: IS.4:1085; NB.—; Z.—.

3. *thelō* [θέλω, 2309], in 1 Cor. 16:7, R.V., is translated "wish" (A.V., "will"); Gal. 4:20, "I could wish" (A.V. "I desire"). See WILL, C, No. 1.

NT: B.354d; CB.1271c; K.318.
OT: 'ābāh: S.14; HR.628b.1; H.3; BD.2c.
ḥāphēṣ: S.2654; HR.628b.8a; H.712; BD.342c.
mā'ēn (with neg.): S.3985; HR.628b.13b; H.1138; BD.549a.
GEN. REF.: IS.4:1085; NB.—; Z.—.

WIST

oida (from *eidō*) [οἶδα, 1492], to know, in the pluperfect tense (with imperfect meaning) is rendered "wist" (the past tense of the verb to wit: cp. WOT) in Mark 9:6; 14:40; Luke 2:49; John 5:13; Acts 12:9; 23:5. See KNOW, No. 2.

NT: B.555d; CB.1260b; K.673.
OT: yāda': S.3045; HR.374b.1; H.848; BD.393b.
GEN. REF.: IS.4:1085; NB.—; Z.—.

WIT (TO)

A. Adverb.

hōs [ὡς, 5613], a relative adverb signifying 'as,' or 'how,' is used in 2 Cor. 5:19 to introduce the statement "that God was . . ." and rendered "to wit," lit., 'how.'

NT: B.897a; CB.1251b; K.—.
OT: —.
GEN. REF.: —.

B. Verb.

gnōrizō [γνωρίζω, 1107], to know, to make known, is rendered "we do (you) to wit" in 2 Cor. 8:1, A.V., R.V., "we make known (to you)." See KNOW, No. 8.

NT: B.163b; CB.1248b; K.119.
OT: yādaʻ: S.3045; HR.273a.2a-c; H.848; BD.393b.
yᵉdaʻ (Aramaic): S.3046; HR.273a.2d; H.2765; BD.1095a.
GEN. REF.: –.

Note: In Rom. 8:23 the italicized words "*to wit*" are added to specify the particular meaning of "adoption" there mentioned.

For WITCHCRAFT see SORCERY

WITH: see † p. 1

WITHAL

hama [ἅμα, 260], at the same time, is rendered "withal" in Acts 24:26, R.V. (A.V., "also"); 1 Tim. 5:13 (with *kai*, 'also'); Philm. 22.

NT: B.42a; CB.1249a; K.–.
OT: –.
GEN. REF.: –.

Notes: (1) In Eph. 6:16, R.V., the phrase *en pasin* (*en*, in, and the dative plural of *pas*, all) is rightly rendered "withal" (A.V., "above all"); the shield of faith is to accompany the use of all the other parts of the spiritual equipment.

(2) in 1 Cor. 12:7 *sumpherō* is rendered "profit withal." See EXPEDIENT, PROFIT, B, No. 1.

(3) In Acts 25:27, *kai*, also, is rendered "withal."

WITHDRAW

1. *hupostellō* [ὑποστέλλω, 5288], is translated "withdraw" in Gal. 2:12: see DRAW (*B*), No. 4.

NT: B.847b; CB.–; K.1074.
OT: kālāʼ: S.3607; HR.1417a.2; H.313a,b; BD.476b.
GEN. REF.: –.

2. *apospaō* [ἀποσπάω, 645], in the Passive Voice, is translated "was withdrawn" in Luke 22:41, A.V.: see PART (Verb), No. 3.

NT: B.98a; CB.–; K.–.
OT: nātaq: S.5423; HR.141a.2; H.1447; BD.683c.
nātash: S.5428; HR.141a.3; H.1451; BD.684c.
pārad: S.6504; HR.141a.5; H.1806; BD.825b.
GEN. REF.: –.

3. *anachōreō* [ἀναχωρέω, 402], is translated to withdraw in the R.V. of Matt. 2:22 and John 6:15; R.V. and A.V. in Matt. 12:15 and Mark 3:7. See DEPART, No. 10.

NT: B.63c; CB.1235a; K.–.
OT: bāraḥ: S.1272; HR.85c.1; H.284; BD.137d.
nûs: S.5127; HR.85c.3; H.1327; BD.630c.
GEN. REF.: –.

4. *hupochōreō* [ὑποχωρέω, 5298], to retire, is translated "withdrew Himself" in Luke 5:16; elsewhere in 9:10, R.V., "withdrew apart" (A.V., "went aside"). See GO, No. 16. ¶

NT: B.848c; CB.–; K.–.
OT: –.
GEN. REF.: –.

5. *stellō* [στέλλω, 4724], to bring together, gather up (used of furling sails), hence, in the Middle Voice, signifies to shrink from a person or thing, 2 Thess. 3:6, "withdraw"; elsewhere, 2 Cor. 8:20, "avoiding." See AVOID. ¶ Cp. No. 1.

NT: B.766a; CB.1270a; K.1074.
OT: –.
GEN. REF.: –.

Note: In 1 Tim. 6:5, some texts have *aphistēmi*, rendered "withdraw thyself," A.V.

WITHER (away)

xērainō [ξηραίνω, 3583], to dry up, parch, wither, is translated to wither, (*a*) of plants, Matt. 13:6; 21:19, 20; Mark 4:6; 11:20, R.V. (A.V., "dried up"), 21; Luke 8:6; John 15:6; Jas. 1:11; 1 Pet. 1:24; (*b*) of members of the body, Mark 3:1, and, in some texts, 3. See DRY, B, OVER-RIPE, PINE AWAY, RIPE.

NT: B.548c; CB.1273b; K.–.
OT: yābēsh: S.3001; HR.957a.2; H.837; BD.386b.
GEN. REF.: IS.4:1086; NB.–; Z.–.

Notes: (1) For the adjective *xēros*, dry, withered, see DRY, A, No. 1.

(2) For "whose fruit withereth," Jude 12, A.V., see AUTUMN.

WITHHOLD

kōluō [κωλύω, 2967], to hinder, restrain, is translated "withhold (not)" in Luke 6:29, R.V., A.V., "forbid (not) to take." See FORBID, HINDER, KEEP, *Note* (7), SUFFER, WITHSTAND.

NT: B.461b; CB.1255b; K.–.
OT: kālāʼ: S.3607; HR.839a.1; H.313a,b; BD.476b.
GEN. REF.: –.

Note: For "withholdeth" in 2 Thess. 2:6 see RESTRAIN.

WITHIN

Note: This is a translation of (*a*) *entos*: see INSIDE, No. 1; in Luke 17:21 the R.V. marg., "in the midst of," is to be preferred; the Kingdom of God was not in the hearts of the Pharisees; (*b*) *en*, of thinking or saying within oneself, e.g., Luke 7:39, 49 (marg., "among"); locally, e.g., Luke 19:44; (*c*) *esōthen*, 2 Cor. 7:5; Rev. 4:8; 5:1; "from within," Mark 7:21, 23; Luke 11:7; "within," Matt. 23:25; Luke 11:40, R.V. "inside"; in Matt. 23:27, 28, R.V., "inwardly"; (*d*) *esō*, John 20:26; Acts 5:23; 1 Cor. 5:12 (i.e., within the church); (*e*) *pros*, to, or with, in Mark 14:4, A.V., "within" (R.V., "among"); (*f*) dia, through, rendered "within (three days)" in Mark 14:58, A.V. (R.V., "in," looking through the time to the event, and in keeping with the metaphor of building); (*g*) *esōteros*, Heb. 6:19, the comparative degree of *esō*, used with the article translated "that within," lit., 'the inner (part of the veil),' i.e., inside: see INNER, No. 2; (*h*) in Luke 11:41, R.V., *eneimi*, to be in, is rendered "are within" (A.V., "ye have").

WITHOUT

Notes: (1) This is a translation of (*a*) *exō*, outside, e.g., Matt. 12:46, 47; "(them that are) without," 1 Cor. 5:12, 13; Col. 4:5; 1 Thess. 4:12 (the unregenerate); Heb. 13:11-13; (*b*) *exōthen*, from without, or without, e.g., Mark 7:15, 18; Luke 11:40; 2 Cor. 7:5; 1 Tim. 3:7; as a preposition, Rev. 11:2; (*c*) *chōris*, apart from, frequently used as a preposition, especially in Hebrews [4:15; 7:7, 20, 21; 9:7, 18, 22, 28; 11:6; in 11:40, R.V., "apart from" (A.V., "without"); 12:8, 14]; (*d*) *aneu* like *chōris*, but rarer, Matt. 10:29; Mark 13:2; 1 Pet. 3:1; 4:9; ¶ (*e*) *ater*, Luke 22:6, marg., "without (tumult)"; ver. 35; ¶ (*f*) *ektos*, out of, outside, 1 Cor. 6:18: see OTHER, OUT, OUTSIDE; (*g*) *parektos*, besides, in addition, 2 Cor. 11:28, "(those things that are) without," R.V., marg., "(the things which) I omit," or "(the things that come) out of course."

(2) In Acts 5:26, *ou*, not, *meta*, with, is rendered "without (violence)."

(3) In Acts 25:17, A.V., "without (any delay)" represents *poieō*, to make, and *mēdemian*, no, R.V., "I made no (delay)."

(4) For "without ceasing," Acts 12:5, A.V., see EARNESTLY, C, No. 1.

(5) In many nouns the negative prefix *a* forms part of the word and is translated "without."

WITHSTAND

1. *kōluō* [κωλύω, 2967], to hinder, is rendered "withstand" in Acts 11:17. See FORBID, HINDER.

NT: B.461b; CB.1255b; K.—.
OT: kālā': S.3607; HR.839a.1; H.313a,b; BD.476b.
GEN. REF.: —.

2. *anthistēmi* [ἀνθίστημι, 436], to set against, is translated to withstand in Acts 13:8 (Middle Voice); in the intransitive 2nd aorist, Active Voice, Eph. 6:13; 2 Tim. 3:8 (1st part; Middle Voice in 2nd part); 4:15. See RESIST.

NT: B.67b; CB.—; K.—.
OT: 'āmad: S.5975; HR.95c.9; H.1637; BD.763c.
yāṣab: S.3320; HR.95c.7a; H.894; BD.426a.
nāṣab: S.5324; HR.95c.7b; H.1398; BD.662a.
GEN. REF.: —.

WITNESS (Noun and Verb)

A. Nouns.

1. *martus* or *martur* [μάρτυς, 3144], (whence Eng., martyr, one who bears witness by his death) denotes one who can or does aver what he has seen or heard or knows; it is used (*a*) of God, Rom. 1:9; 2 Cor. 1:23; Phil. 1:8; 1 Thess. 2:5, 10 (2nd part); (*b*) of Christ, Rev. 1:5; 3:14; (*c*) of those who witness for Christ by their death, Acts 22:20; Rev. 2:13; Rev. 17:6; (*d*) of the interpreters of God's counsels, yet to witness in Jerusalem in the times of the Antichrist, Rev. 11:3; (*e*) in a forensic sense, Matt. 18:16; 26:65; Mark 14:63; Acts 6:13; 7:58; 2 Cor. 13:1; 1 Tim. 5:19; Heb. 10:28; (*f*) in a historical sense, Luke 11:48; 24:48; Acts 1:8, 22; 2:32; 3:15; 5:32; 10:39, 41; 13:31; 22:15; 26:16; 1 Thess. 2:10 (1st part); 1 Tim. 6:12; 2 Tim. 2:2; Heb. 12:1, "(a cloud) of witnesses," here of those mentioned in chapt. 11, those whose lives and actions testified to the worth and effect of faith, and whose faith received witness in Scripture; 1 Pet. 5:1. ¶

NT: B.494b; CB.1257c; K.564.
OT: 'ēd: S.5707; HR.897c.1; H.1576b; BD.729c.
GEN. REF.: IS.4:1086; NB.1335; Z.5:949.

2. *marturia* [μαρτυρία, 3141], testimony, a bearing witness, is translated "witness" in Mark 14:55, 56, 59; Luke 22:71; John 1:7, 19 (R.V.); 3:11, 32 and 33 (R.V.); 5:31, 32, 34 (R.V.), 36; R.V. in 8:13, 14, 17; 19:35; 21:24; A.V. in Tit. 1:13; A.V. and R.V. in 1 John 5:9 (thrice), 10a; R.V. in 10b, 11; 3 John 12: see TESTIMONY, No. 2.

NT: B.493c; CB.1257c; K.564.
OT: 'ēd: S.5707; HR.896b.2a; H.1576b; BD.729c.
mô'ēd: S.4150; HR.896b.1; H.878b; BD.417b.
GEN. REF.: IS.4:1086; NB.1335; Z.—.

3. *marturion* [μαρτύριον, 3142], testimony or witness as borne, a declaration of facts, is translated "witness" in Matt. 24:14, A.V.; Acts 4:33; 7:44 (A.V.); Jas. 5:3 (A.V.): see TESTIMONY, No. 1.

NT: B.493d; CB.1257c; K.564.
OT: mô'ēd: S.4150; HR.896c.1; H.878b; BD.417b.
'ēdāh: S.5713; HR.896c.2b; H.1576c,e; BD.730a.
'ēdût: S.5715; HR.896c.2c; H.1576f; BD.730b.
GEN. REF.: IS.4:1086; NB.1335; Z.—.

4. *pseudomartus* or *-tur* [ψευδομάρτυς, 5575], denotes a false witness, Matt. 26:60; 1 Cor. 15:15. ¶

NT: B.892a; CB.1267c; K.564.
OT: —.
GEN. REF.: —.

5. *pseudomarturia* [ψευδομαρτυρία, 5577], false witness, occurs in Matt. 15:19; 26:59. ¶

NT: B.892a; CB.1267c; K.564.
OT: —.
GEN. REF.: —.

B. Verbs.

1. *martureō* [μαρτυρέω, 3140], denotes (I) to be a *martus* (see A, No. 1), or to bear witness to, sometimes rendered to testify (see TESTIFY, No. 1); it is used of the witness (*a*) of God the Father to Christ, John 5:32, 37; 8:18 (2nd part); 1 John 5:9, 10; to others, Acts 13:22; 15:8; Heb. 11:2, 4 (twice), 5:39; (*b*) of Christ, John 3:11, 32; 4:44; 5:31; 7:7; 8:13, 14, 18 (1st part); 13:21; 18:37; Acts 14:3; 1 Tim. 6:13; Rev. 22:18, 20; of the Holy Spirit, to Christ, John 15:26; Heb. 10:15; 1 John 5:7, 8, R.V., which rightly omits the latter part of ver. 7 (it was a marginal gloss which crept into the original text: see THREE); it finds no support in Scripture; (*c*) of the Scriptures, to Christ, John 5:39; Heb. 7:8, 17; (*d*) of the works of Christ, to Himself, and of the circumstances connected with His Death, John 5:36; 10:25; 1 John 5:8; (*e*) of prophets and apostles, to the righteousness of God, Rom. 3:21; to Christ, John 1:7, 8, 15, 32, 34; 3:26; 5:33, R.V.; 15:27; 19:35; 21:24; Acts 10:43; 23:11; 1 Cor. 15:15; 1 John 1:2; 4:14; Rev. 1:2; to doctrine, Acts 26:22 (in some texts, so A.V.; see No. 2); to the Word of God, Rev. 1:2; (*f*) of others, concerning Christ, Luke 4:22; John 4:39; 12:17; (*g*) of believers to one another, John 3:28; 2 Cor. 8:3; Gal. 4:15; Col. 4:13; 1 Thess. 2:11 (in some texts: see No. 2); 3 John 3, 6, 12 (2nd part); (*h*) of the Apostle Paul concerning Israel, Rom. 10:2; (*i*) of an angel, to the churches, Rev. 22:16; (*j*) of unbelievers, concerning themselves, Matt. 23:31; concerning Christ, John 18:23; concerning others, John 2:25; Acts 22:5; 26:5; (II) to give a good report, to approve of, Acts 6:3; 10:22; 16:2; 22:12; 1 Tim. 5:10; 3 John 12 (1st part); some would put Luke 4:22 here. ¶

NT: B.492c; CB.1257c; K.564.
OT: 'ûd: S.5749; HR.896b.1b; H.1576; BD.728c.
'ēd: S.5707; HR.896b.1c; H.1576b; BD.729c.
GEN. REF.: IS.4:1086; NB.1335; Z.—.

2. *marturomai* [μαρτύρομαι, 3143], strictly meaning to summon as a witness, signifies to affirm solemnly, adjure, and is used in the Middle Voice only, rendered to testify in Acts 20:26, R.V. (A.V., "I take . . . to record"); 26:22, R.V., in the best texts [see No. 1 (*e*)]; Gal. 5:3; Eph. 4:17; 1 Thess. 2:11, in the best texts [see No. 1 (*g*)]. ¶

NT: B.494a; CB.1257c; K.564.
OT: —.
GEN. REF.: IS.4:1086; NB.1335; Z.—.

3. *summartureō* [συμμαρτυρέω, 4828], denotes to bear witness with (*sun*), Rom. 2:15, 8:16; 9:1. ¶

NT: B.778b; CB.1270b; K.564.
OT: —.
GEN. REF.: —.

4. *sunepimartureo* [συνεπιμαρτυρέω, 4901], denotes to join in bearing witness with others, Heb. 2:4. ¶

NT: B.787c; CB.—; K.564.
OT: —.
GEN. REF.: —.

5. *katamartureō* [καταμαρτυρέω, 2649], denotes to witness against (*kata*), Matt. 26:62; 27:13; Mark 14:60 (in some mss., 15:4, for *katēgoreō*, to accuse, R.V.). ¶

NT: B.414d; CB.1254a; K.564.
OT: 'ûd: S.5749; HR.739a.2; H.1576; BD.728c.
'ānāh: S.6030; HR.739a.3; H.1650,1653; BD.772c.
GEN. REF.: IS.—; NB.1335; Z.—.

6. *pseudomartureō* [ψευδομαρτυρέω, 5576], to bear false witness (*pseudēs*, false), occurs in Matt. 19:18; Mark 10:19; 14:56, 57; Luke 18:20; in some texts, Rom. 13:9. ¶

NT: B.891d; CB.1267c; K.564.
OT: 'ānāh: S.6030; HR.1485a.1; H.1650,1653; BD.772c.
GEN. REF.: —.

C. Adjectives.

amarturos [ἀμάρτυρος, 267], denotes without witness (*a*, negative, and *martus*), Acts 14:17. ¶

NT: B.44a; CB.—; K.—.
OT: —.
GEN. REF.: —.

WOE

ouai [οὐαί, 3759], an interjection, is used (*a*) in denunciation, Matt. 11:21; 18:7 (twice); eight times in ch. 23; 24:19; 26:24; Mark 13:17; 14:21; Luke 6:24, 25 (twice), 26; 10:13; six times in ch. 11; 17:1; 21:23; 22:22; 1 Cor. 9:16; Jude 11; Rev. 8:13 (thrice); 12:12; as a noun, Rev. 9:12 (twice); 11:14 (twice); (*b*) in grief, "alas;" Rev. 18:10, 16, 19 (twice in each). ¶

NT: B.591a; CB.1261b; K.—.
OT: —.
GEN. REF.: IS.4:1088; NB.1335; Z.—.

WOLF

lukos [λύκος, 3074], occurs in Matt. 10:16; Luke 10:3; John 10:12 (twice); metaphorically, Matt. 7:15; Acts 20:29. ¶

NT: B.481b; CB.1257b; K.540.
OT: zᵉ'ēb: S.2061; HR.889a.2; H.522; BD.255b.
GEN. REF.: IS.4:1088; NB.1336; Z.5:950.

WOMAN

1. *gunē* [γυνή, 1135], for which see also WIFE, is used of a woman unmarried or married, e.g., Matt. 11:11; 14:21; Luke 4:26, of a widow; Rom. 7:2; in the vocative case, used in addressing a woman, it is a term not of reproof or severity, but of endearment or respect, Matt. 15:28; John 2:4, where the Lord's words to His mother at the wedding in Cana, are neither rebuff nor rebuke. The

question is, lit., 'what to Me and to thee?' and the word "woman," the term of endearment, follows this. The meaning is 'There is no obligation on Me or you, but love will supply the need.' She confides in Him, He responds to her faith. There was lovingkindness in both hearts. His next words about 'His hour' suit this; they were not unfamiliar to her. Cana is in the path to Calvary; Calvary was not yet, but it made the beginning of signs possible. See also 4:21; 19:26.

In Gal. 4:4 the phrase "born of a woman" is in accordance with the subject there, viz., the real humanity of the Lord Jesus; this the words attest. They declare the method of His Incarnation and "suggest the means whereby that humanity was made free from the taint of sin consequent upon the Fall, viz., that He was not born through the natural process of ordinary generation, but was conceived by the power of the Holy Spirit . . . To have written 'born of a virgin' would have carried the argument in a wrong direction . . . Since that man is born of woman is a universal fact, the statement would be superfluous if the Lord Jesus were no more than man" (Notes on Galatians, by Hogg and Vine, pp. 184 f.).

NT: B.168b; CB.1248c; K.134.
OT: 'ishshāh: S.802; HR.278b.1; H.137a; BD.61a.
GEN. REF.: IS.4:1089; NB.1336; Z.5:950.

2. *gunaikarion* [γυναικάριον, 1133], a diminutive of No. 1, a little woman, is used contemptuously in 2 Tim. 3:6, a silly woman. ¶

NT: B.168b; CB.1248c; K.—.
OT: —.
GEN. REF.: IS.4:1089; NB.1336; Z.—.

3. *presbuteros* [πρεσβύτερος, 4245], elder, older, in the feminine plural, denotes "elder women" in 1 Tim. 5:2. See ELDER, A, No. 1.

NT: B.699d; CB.1266b; K.931.
OT: zāqēn: S.2205; HR.1201c.3; H.574b; BD.278c.
GEN. REF.: —.

4. *presbutis* [πρεσβῦτις, 4247], the feminine of *presbutēs*, aged, is used in the plural and translated "aged women" in Tit. 2:3. ¶

NT: B.700d; CB.1266b; K.—.
OT: —.
GEN. REF.: —.

5. *thēleia* [θήλεια, 2338], the feminine of the adjective *thēlus*, denotes female, and is used as a noun, Rom. 1:26, 27. See FEMALE.

NT: B.360c; CB.—; K.—.
OT: —.
GEN. REF.: —.

WOMB

1. *koilia* [κοιλία, 2836], denotes the womb, Matt. 19:12; Luke 1:15, 41, 42, 44; 2:21; 11:27; 23:29; John 3:4; Acts 3:2; 14:8; Gal. 1:15. See BELLY, No. 1.

NT: B.437b; CB.1255b; K.446.
OT: beṭen: S.990; HR.773a.1; H.236a; BD.105d.
mē'îm: S.4578; HR.773a.5a; H.1227a; BD.588d.
qereb: S.7130; HR.773a.6; H.2066a; BD.899a.
GEN. REF.: IS.4:1097; NB.1336; Z.—.

2. *gastēr* [γαστήρ, 1064], is rendered "womb" in Luke 1:31. See BELLY, No. 2.

NT: B.152c; CB.—; K.—.
OT: beṭen: S.990; HR.234b.1; H.236a; BD.105d.
hārāh (Verb): S.2029; HR.234b.2a; H.515; BD.247c.
hārāh (Adjective): S.2030; HR.234b.2b; H.515a; BD.248a.
GEN. REF.: IS.4:1097; NB.1336; Z.—.

3. *mētra* [μήτρα, 3388], the matrix (akin to *mētēr*, a mother), occurs in Luke 2:23; Rom. 4:19. ¶

NT: B.520b; CB.1258c; K.—.
OT: reḥem, raḥam: S.7358; HR.925b.2; H.2146a; BD.933a.
GEN. REF.: IS.4:1097; NB.1336; Z.—.

WONDER (Noun and Verb)

A. Nouns.

1. *teras* [τέρας, 5059], something strange, causing the beholder to marvel, is always used in the plural, always rendered "wonders," and generally follows *sēmeia*, "signs"; the opposite order occurs in Acts 2:22, 43; 6:8, R.V.; 7:36; in Acts 2:19 "wonders" occurs alone. A sign is intended to appeal to the understanding, a wonder appeals to the imagination, a power (*dunamis*) indicates its source as supernatural. "Wonders" are manifested as Divine operations in thirteen occurrences (9 times in Acts); three times they are ascribed to the work of Satan through human agents, Matt. 24:24; Mark 13:22 and 2 Thess. 2:9.

NT: B.812c; CB.1271b; K.1170.
OT: môphēt: S.4159; HR.1345a.1; H.152a; BD.68d.
GEN. REF.: IS.4:1100; NB.828; Z.—.

2. *thambos* [θάμβος, 2285], amazement, is rendered "wonder" in Acts 3:10. See AMAZE, A, No. 2.

NT: B.350c; CB.1271c; K.312.
OT: 'āyōm: S.366; HR.623b.1; H.80a; BD.33d.
ḥatḥat: S.2849; HR.623b.2; H.784e; BD.369d.
GEN. REF.: IS.4:1100; NB.—; Z.—.

Notes: (1) For *thauma*, a wonder (rendered "admiration" in Rev. 17:6, A.V.), see MARVEL.

(2) In Rev. 12:1, 3 and 13:13 *sēmeion*, a sign, is translated in the A.V., "wonder(s)," R.V., "sign(s)."

(3) In Acts 3:11 *ekthambos* (*ek*, intensive, and No. 2) is translated "greatly wondering." ¶

(4) For *pseudos*, 2 Thess. 2:9, "lying wonders," see FALSE, B. Cp. AMAZE, B, Nos. 3 and 4.

B. Verbs.

Note: For *thaumazō*, see MARVEL; for *existēmi*, Acts 8:13, A.V., see AMAZE, B, No. 1.

WONDERFUL (THING, WORK)

Notes: (1) In Matt. 7:22, A.V., *dunamis* (in the plural) is rendered "wonderful works" (R.V., "mighty works," marg., "powers"). See POWER.

(2) In Acts 2:11, A.V., the adjective *megaleios*, magnificent, in the neuter plural with the article, is rendered "the wonderful works" (R.V., "the mighty works"). ¶

(3) In Matt. 21:15, the neuter plural of the adjective *thaumasios*, wonderful, is used as a noun, "wonderful things," lit., 'wonders.'

WONT

ethō [ἔθω, 1486], to be accustomed, is used in the pluperfect tense (with imperfect meaning), *eiōtha*, rendered "was wont" in Matt. 27:15; Mark 10:1. See CUSTOM, B, No. 2, MANNER, A, *Note* (1).

NT: B.234a; CB.–; K.–.
OT: –.
GEN. REF.: –.

Notes: (1) In Mark 15:8, "he was wont to do," R.V., represents the imperfect tense of *poieō*, to do (A.V., "he had ever done").

(2) In Luke 22:39, A.V., *ethos*, a custom, preceded by *kata* and the article, lit., 'according to the (i.e., His) custom,' is translated "as He was wont" (R.V., "as His custom was"): see CUSTOM, A, No. 1.

(3) In Acts 16:13 the A.V., "was wont," translates the texts which have the Passive Voice of *nomizō* with its meaning to hold by custom; the R.V., "we supposed," translates the texts which have the imperfect tense, Active, with the meaning to consider, suppose.

WOOD

1. *xulon* [ξύλον, 3586], denotes timber, wood for any use, 1 Cor. 3:12; Rev. 18:12 (twice). See STAFF, STOCKS, TREE.

NT: B.549a; CB.1273b; K.665.
OT: 'ēṣ: S.6086; HR.958a.3a; H.1670a; BD.781c.
GEN. REF.: IS.–; NB.–; Z.5:955.

2. *hulē* [ὕλη, 5208], denotes a wood, a forest, Jas. 3:5 (A.V., "matter," marg., "wood"). ¶ See MATTER, *Note* (3).

NT: B.836a; CB.1251c; K.–.
OT: sukkāh: S.5521; HR.1405a.2; H.1492d; BD.697c.
GEN. REF.: –.

WOOL

erion [ἔριον, 2053], occurs in Heb. 9:19; Rev. 1:14. ¶

NT: B.309c; CB.–; K.–.
OT: ṣemer: S.6785; HR.547b.2; H.1931a; BD.856a.
GEN. REF.: IS.4:1101; NB.–; Z.5:955.

WORD

1. *logos* [λόγος, 3056], denotes (I) the expression of thought — not the mere name of an object — (*a*) as embodying a conception or idea, e.g., Luke 7:7; 1 Cor. 14:9, 19; (*b*) a saying or statement, (1) by God, e.g., John 15:25; Rom. 9:9; 9:28, R.V., "word" (A.V., "work"); Gal. 5:14; Heb. 4:12; (2) by Christ, e.g., Matt. 24:35 (plur.); John 2:22; 4:41; 14:23 (plur.); 15:20. In connection with (1) and (2) the phrase "the word of the Lord," i.e., the revealed will of God (very frequent in the O.T.), is used of a direct revelation given by Christ, 1 Thess. 4:15; of the gospel, Acts 8:25; 13:49; 15:35, 36; 16:32; 19:10; 1 Thess. 1:8; 2 Thess. 3:1; in this respect it is the message from the Lord, delivered with His authority and made effective by His power (cp. Acts 10:36); for other instances relating to the gospel see Acts 13:26; 14:3; 15:7; 1 Cor. 1:18, R.V.; 2 Cor. 2:17; 4:2; 5:19; 6:7; Gal. 6:6; Eph. 1:13; Phil. 2:16; Col. 1:5; Heb. 5:13; sometimes it is used as the sum of God's utterances, e.g., Mark 7:13; John 10:35; Rev. 1:2, 9; (*c*) discourse, speech, of instruction etc., e.g., Acts 2:40; 1 Cor. 2:13; 12:8; 2 Cor. 1:18; 1 Thess. 1:5; 2 Thess. 2:15; Heb. 6:1, R.V., marg.; doctrine, e.g., Matt. 13:20; Col. 3:16; 1 Tim. 4:6; 2 Tim. 1:13; Tit. 1:9; 1 John 2:7;

(II) The Personal Word, a title of the Son of God; this identification is substantiated by the statements of doctrine in John 1:1-18, declaring in verses 1 and 2 (1) His distinct and superfinite Personality, (2) His relation in the Godhead (*pros*, with, not mere company, but the most intimate communion), (3) His Deity; in ver. 3 His creative power; in ver. 14 His Incarnation ("became flesh," expressing His voluntary act; not as A.V., "was made"), the reality and totality of His human nature, and His glory "as of the only begotten from the Father," R.V. (marg., "an only begotten from a father"), the absence of the article in each place lending stress to the nature and character of the relationship; His was the Shekinah glory in open manifestation; ver. 18 consummates the identification: "the only-begotten Son (R.V. marg., many ancient authorities read 'God only begotten,'), which is in the bosom of the Father, He hath declared Him," thus fulfilling the significance of the title "*Logos*," the Word, the personal manifestation, not of a part of the Divine nature, but of the whole Deity (see IMAGE).

The title is used also in 1 John 1, "the Word of life" combining the two declarations in John

1:1 and 4 and Rev. 19:13 (for 1 John 5:7 see THREE).

NT: B.477a; CB.1257a; K.505.
OT: dābār: S.1697; HR.881c.2a; H.399a; BD.182a.
GEN. REF.: IS.4:1101; NB.1337; Z.5:956.

2. *rhēma* [ῥῆμα, 4487], denotes that which is spoken, what is uttered in speech or writing; in the singular, a word, e.g., Matt. 12:36; 27:14; 2 Cor. 12:4; 13:1; Heb. 12:19; in the plural, speech, discourse, e.g., John 3:34; 8:20; Acts 2:14; 6:11, 13; 11:14; 13:42; 26:25; Rom. 10:18; 2 Pet. 3:2; Jude 17; it is used of the gospel in Rom. 10:8 (twice), 17, R.V., "the word of Christ" (i.e., the word which preaches Christ); 10:18; 1 Pet. 1:25 (twice); of a statement, command, instruction, e.g., Matt. 26:75; Luke 1:37, R.V., "(no) word (from God shall be void of power)"; ver. 38; Acts 11:16; Heb. 11:3.

The significance of *rhēma* (as distinct from *logos*) is exemplified in the injunction to take "the sword of the Spirit, which is the word of God," Eph. 6:17; here the reference is not to the whole Bible as such, but to the individual scripture which the Spirit brings to our remembrance for use in time of need, a prerequisite being the regular storing of the mind with Scripture.

NT: B.735b; CB.1268a; K.505.
OT: dābār: S.1697; HR.1249a; H.399a; BD.182a.
GEN. REF.: IS.4:1101; NB.1337; Z.5:956.

Notes: (1) *Epos*, a word, is used in a phrase in Heb. 7:9, lit., '(as to say) a word,' R.V., "(so to) say," A.V., "(as I may so) say"; *logos* is reasoned speech, *rhēma*, an utterance, *epos*, "the articulated expression of a thought" (Abbott-Smith).

(2) In Rom. 16:18, A.V., *chrēstologia*, useful discourse (*chrēstos*, beneficial), is rendered "good words" [R.V., "smooth . . . (speech)"]. ¶

(3) For *logikos*, 1 Pet. 2:2 (R.V., "spiritual"), rendered "of the word," A.V., see MILK.

(4) For the verb *apangellō*, rendered to bring word, see BRING, No. 36.

(5) In Matt. 2:13, A.V., *eipon*, to tell (R.V.), is rendered "bring . . . word."

(6) For "enticing words," Col. 2:4, see ENTICE and PERSUASIVENESS.

(7) For "strifes of words," 1 Tim. 6:4, A.V., and "strive . . . about words," 2 Tim. 2:14, see STRIFE, STRIVE.

(8) For *suntomōs*, Acts 24:4, "A few words," see FEW, B. ¶ For the same phrase see FEW, A, Nos. 1 and 2.

WORK (Noun and Verb), WROUGHT

A. Nouns.

1. *ergon* [ἔργον, 2041], denotes (I) work, employment, task, e.g., Mark 13:34; John 4:34; 17:4; Acts 13:2; Phil. 2:30; 1 Thess. 5:13; in Acts 5:38 with the idea of enterprise; (II) a deed, act, (*a*) of God, e.g., John 6:28, 29; 9:3; 10:37; 14:10; Acts 13:41; Rom. 14:20; Heb. 1:10; 2:7; 3:9; 4:3, 4, 10; Rev. 15:3; (*b*) of Christ, e.g., Matt. 11:2, especially in John, 5:36; 7:3, 21; 10:25, 32, 33, 38; 14:11, 12; 15:24; Rev. 2:26; (*c*) of believers, e.g., Matt. 5:16; Mark 14:6; Acts 9:36; Rom. 13:3; Col. 1:10; 1 Thess. 1:3, "work of faith," here the initial act of faith at conversion (turning to God, ver. 9); in 2 Thess. 1:11, "*every* work of faith," R.V., denotes every activity undertaken for Christ's sake; 2:17; 1 Tim. 2:10; 5:10; 6:18; 2 Tim. 2:21; 3:17; Tit. 2:7, 14; 3:1, 8, 14; Heb. 10:24; 13:21; frequent in James, as the effect of faith [in 1:25, A.V., "(a doer) of the work," R.V., "(a doer) that worketh"]; 1 Pet. 2:12; Rev. 2:2 and in several other places in chapts. 2 and 3; 14:13; (*d*) of unbelievers, e.g., Matt. 23:3, 5; John 7:7; Acts 7:41 (for idols); Rom. 13:12; Eph. 5:11; Col. 1:21; Tit. 1:16 (1st part); 1 John 3:12; Jude 15, R.V.; Rev. 2:6, R.V.; of those who seek justification by works, e.g., Rom. 9:32; Gal. 3:10; Eph. 2:9; described as the works of the law, e.g., Gal. 2:16; 3:2, 5; dead works, Heb. 6:1; 9:14; (*e*) of Babylon, Rev. 18:6; (*f*) of the Devil, John 8:41; 1 John 3:8. See DEED.

NT: B.307d; CB.1246c; K.251.
OT: m^elā'kāh: S.4399; HR.541c.10; H.1068b; BD.521d.
^ca^bōdāh: S.5656; HR.541c.16b; H.1553c; BD.715a.
ma^{ca}seh: S.4639; HR.541c.19b; H.1708a; BD.795c.
GEN. REF.: IS.4:1107; NB.1337; Z.—.

2. *ergasia* [ἐργασία, 2039], denotes a work or business, also a working, performance, Eph. 4:19, where preceded by *eis*, to, it is rendered "to work" (marg., "to make a trade of"). See DILIGENCE, GAIN.

NT: B.307c; CB.1246b; K.251.
OT: m^elā'kāh: S.4399; HR.541b.1; H.1068b; BD.521d.
^ca^bōdāh: S.5656; HR.541b.3b; H.1553c; BD.715a.
GEN. REF.: IS.4:1107; NB.1337; Z.—.

Notes: (1) In Rom. 9:28, A.V., *logos*, a word (R.V.), is rendered "work."

(2) For *pragma*, Jas. 3:16, rendered "work" in the A.V., the R.V. has "deed."

(3) For *praxis*, a doing, Matt. 16:27, R.V. marg., A.V., "works," see DEED.

(4) For the A.V., "much work," Acts 27:16, see DIFFICULTY.

(5) For "workfellow," Rom. 16:21, A.V., see WORKER, No. 2.

(6) In Matt. 14:2 and Mark 6:14, A.V., *dunameis*, "powers," R.V., is translated "mighty works"; in Acts 2:22, R.V., "mighty works," A.V., "miracles."

(7) For "wonderful works" see WONDERFUL, *Note* (2).

B. Verbs.

1. *ergazomai* [ἐργάζομαι, 2038], is used (I) intransitively, e.g., Matt. 21:28; John 5:17; 9:4 (2nd part); Rom. 4:4, 5; 1 Cor. 4:12; 9:6; 1 Thess. 2:9; 4:11; 2 Thess. 3:8, 10-12 (for the play upon words in ver. 11 see BUSYBODY, A); (II) transitively, (*a*) to work something, produce, perform, e.g., Matt. 26:10, "she hath wrought"; John 6:28, 30; 9:4 (1st part); Acts 10:35; 13:41; Rom. 2:10; 13:10; 1 Cor. 16:10; 2 Cor. 7:10a, in the best texts, some have No. 2; Gal. 6:10, R.V., "let us work"; Eph. 4:28; Heb. 11:33; 2 John 8; (*b*) to earn by working, work for, John 6:27, R.V., "work" (A.V., "labour"). See COMMIT, DO, LABOUR, MINISTER, TRADE.

NT: B.306d; CB.1246c; K.251.
OT: ʿābad: S.5647; HR.540c.8a; H.1553; BD.712b.
pāʿal: S.6466; HR.540c.11a; H.1792; BD.821b.
GEN. REF.: IS.4:1107; NB.1337; Z.–.

2. *katergazomai* [κατεργάζομαι, 2716], an emphatic form of No. 1, signifies to work out, achieve, effect by toil, rendered to work (past tense, wrought) in Rom. 1:27; 2:9, R.V.; 4:15 (the Law brings men under condemnation and so renders them subject to Divine wrath); 5:3; 7:8, 13; 15:18; 2 Cor. 4:17; 5:5; 7:10 (see No. 1), 11; 12:12; Phil. 2:12, where "your own salvation" refers especially to freedom from strife and vainglory; Jas. 1:3, 20; 1 Pet. 4:3. See DO, No. 5.

NT: B.421c; CB.–; K.421.
OT: ʿābad: S.5647; HR.749b.4; H.1553; BD.712b.
ʿāsāh: S.6213; HR.749b.5; H.1708,1709; BD.793c.
pāʿal: S.6466; HR.749b.6; H.1792; BD.821b.
GEN. REF.: IS.4:1107; NB.1337; Z.–.

3. *energeō* [ἐνεργέω, 1754], lit., to work in (*en*, and A, No. 1), to be active, operative, is used of "(*a*) God, 1 Cor. 12:6; Gal. 2:8; 3:5; Eph. 1:11, 20; 3:20; Phil. 2:13a; Col. 1:29; (*b*) the Holy Spirit, 1 Cor. 12:11; (*c*) the Word of God, 1 Thess. 2:13 (Middle Voice; A.V., 'effectually worketh'); (*d*) supernatural power, undefined, Matt. 14:2; Mark 6:14; (*e*) faith, as the energizer of love, Gal. 5:6; (*f*) the example of patience in suffering, 2 Cor. 1:6; (*g*) death (physical) and life (spiritual), 2 Cor. 4:12; (*h*) sinful passions, Rom. 7:5; (*i*) the spirit of the Evil One, Eph. 2:2; (*j*) the mystery of iniquity, 2 Thess. 2:7."*

To these may be added (*k*) the active response of believers to the inworking of God, Phil. 2:13b, R.V., "to work (for)," A.V., "to do (of)"; (*l*) the supplication of the righteous, Jas. 5:16, R.V., "in its working" (A.V., "effectual fervent").

NT: B.265b; CB.1245a; K.251.
OT: pāʿal: S.6466; HR.473a.2a; H.1792; BD.821b.
GEN. REF.: IS.4:1107; NB.1337; Z.–.

4. *poieō* [ποιέω, 4160], to do, is rendered to work in Matt. 20:12, A.V. (R.V., "spent"); Acts 15:12, "had wrought"; 19:11; 21:19; Heb. 13:21; Rev. 16:14; 19:20; 21:27, A.V. (R.V., "maketh"; marg. "doeth"). See DO.

NT: B.680d; CB.1265c; K.895.
OT: ʿāsāh: S.6213; HR.1154a.33a; H.1708,1709; BD.793c.
GEN. REF.: IS.4:1107; NB.–; Z.–.

5. *sunergeō* [συνεργέω, 4903], to work with or together (*sun*), occurs in Mark 16:20; Rom. 8:28, "work together"; 1 Cor. 16:16, "helpeth with"; 2 Cor. 6:1, "workers together," present participle, 'working together'; the "*with Him*" represents nothing in the Greek; Jas. 2:22, "wrought with." See HELP. ¶

NT: B.787c; CB.1270c; K.1116.
OT: –.
GEN. REF.: –.

6. *ginomai* [γίνομαι, 1096], to become, take place, is rendered "wrought" in Mark 6:2; Acts 5:12, "were . . . wrought."

NT: B.158a; CB.1248b; K.117.
OT: –.
GEN. REF.: –.

WORKER, WORKFELLOW, FELLOW-WORKERS, WORKMAN

1. *ergatēs* [ἐργάτης, 2040], is translated "workers" in Luke 13:27 ("of iniquity"); 2 Cor. 11:13 ("deceitful"); Phil. 3:2 ("evil"); "workman," Matt. 10:10, A.V. (R.V., "labourer"); "workman," 2 Tim. 2:15; "workmen," Acts 19:25. See LABOURER.

NT: B.307c; CB.1246c; K.251.
OT: –.
GEN. REF.: IS.4:1111; NB.–; Z.–.

2. *sunergos* [συνεργός, 4904], denotes a worker with, and is rendered "workfellow" in Rom. 16:21, A.V., R.V., "fellow-worker"; in Col. 4:11, "fellow-workers" (see R.V.). See the R.V., "God's fellow-workers," in 1 Cor. 3:9. See COMPANION, HELPER, LABOURER, *Note*.

NT: B.787d; CB.1270c; K.1116.
OT: –.
GEN. REF.: IS.4:1111; NB.–; Z.–.

Note: For "workers at home," Tit. 2:5, see HOME, B.

WORKING

1. *energeia* [ἐνέργεια, 1753], (Eng., energy) is used (1) of the power of God, (*a*) in the resurrection of Christ, Eph. 1:19; Col. 2:12, R.V., "working" (A.V., "operation"); (*b*) in the

* From Notes on Galatians by Hogg and Vine, pp. 114, 115.

call and enduement of Paul, Eph. 3:7; Col. 1:29; (*c*) in His retributive dealings in sending "a working of error" (A.V., "strong delusion") upon those under the rule of the Man of Sin who receive not the love of the truth, but have pleasure in unrighteousness, 2 Thess. 2:11; (2) of the power of Christ (*a*) generally, Phil. 3:21; (*b*) in the Church, individually, Eph. 4:16; (3) of the power of Satan in energising the Man of Sin in his 'parousia,' 2 Thess. 2:9, "coming." ¶

NT: B.265a; CB.1245a; K.251.
OT: –.
GEN. REF.: –.

2. *energēma* [ἐνέργημα, 1755], what is wrought, the effect produced by No. 1, occurs in 1 Cor. 12:6, R.V., "workings" (A.V., "operations"); ver. 10. ¶

NT: B.265c; CB.1245a; K.251.
OT: –.
GEN. REF.: –.

For **WORKMANSHIP** see **MADE**, B

WORLD

1. *kosmos* [κόσμος, 2889], primarily order, arrangement, ornament, adornment (1 Pet. 3:3, see ADORN, B), is used to denote (*a*) the earth, e.g., Matt. 13:35; John 21:25; Acts 17:24; Rom. 1:20 (probably here the universe: it had this meaning among the Greeks, owing to the order observable in it); 1 Tim. 6:7; Heb. 4:3; 9:26; (*b*) the earth in contrast with Heaven, 1 John 3:17 (perhaps also Rom. 4:13); (*c*) by metonymy, the human race, mankind, e.g., Matt. 5:14; John 1:9 [here "that cometh (R.V., coming) into the world" is said of Christ, not of "every man"; by His coming into the world He was the light for all men]; ver. 10; 3:16, 17 (thrice), 19; 4:42, and frequently in Rom., 1 Cor. and 1 John; (*d*) Gentiles as distinguished from Jews, e.g., Rom. 11:12, 15, where the meaning is that all who will may be reconciled (cp. 2 Cor. 5:19); (*e*) the present condition of human affairs, in alienation from and opposition to God, e.g., John 7:7; 8:23; 14:30; 1 Cor. 2:12; Gal. 4:3; 6:14; Col. 2:8; Jas. 1:27; 1 John 4:5 (thrice); 5:19; (*f*) the sum of temporal possessions, Matt. 16:26; 1 Cor. 7:31 (1st part); (*g*) metaphorically, of the tongue as "a world (of iniquity)," Jas. 3:6, expressive of magnitude and variety.

NT: B.445d; CB.1255c; K.459.
OT: ʿᵃdî: S.5716; HR.780c.4; H.1566a; BD.725d.
ṣābāʾ: S.6633; HR.780c.6; H.1865; BD.838c.
GEN. REF.: IS.4:1112; NB.1338; Z.5:963.

2. *aiōn* [αἰών, 165], an age, a period of time, marked in the N.T. usage by spiritual or moral characteristics, is sometimes translated "world"; the R.V. marg. always has "age." The following are details concerning the world in this respect; its cares, Matt. 13:22; its sons, Luke 16:8; 20:34; its rulers, 1 Cor. 2:6, 8; its wisdom, 1 Cor. 1:20; 2:6; 3:18; its fashion, Rom. 12:2; its character, Gal. 1:4; its god, 2 Cor. 4:4. The phrase "the end of the world" should be rendered "the end of the age," in most places (see END, A, No. 2); in 1 Cor. 10:11, A.V., "the ends (*telē*) of the world," R.V., "the ends of the ages," probably signifies the fulfilment of the Divine purposes concerning the ages, in regard to the Church [this would come under END, A, No. 1, (*c*)]. In Heb. 11:3 [lit., 'the ages (have been prepared)'] the word indicates all that the successive periods contain; cp. 1:2.

Aiōn is always to be distinguished from *kosmos*, even where the two seem to express the same idea, e.g., 1 Cor. 3:18, *aiōn*, ver. 19, *kosmos*; the two are used together in Eph 2:2, lit., 'the age of this world.' For a list of phrases containing *aiōn*, with their respective meanings, see EVER, B.

NT: B.27b; CB.1234a; K.–.
OT: ʿôlām: S.5769; HR.39b.5a; H.1631a; BD.761d.
GEN. REF.: IS.4:1113; NB.–; Z.5:963.

3. *oikoumenē* [οἰκουμένη, 3625], the inhabited earth (see EARTH, No. 2), is used (*a*) of the whole inhabited world, Matt. 24:14; Luke 4:5; 21:26; Rom. 10:18; Heb. 1:6; Rev. 3:10; 16:14; by metonymy, of its inhabitants, Acts 17:31; Rev. 12:9; (*b*) of the Roman Empire, the world as viewed by the writer or speaker, Luke 2:1; Acts 11:28; 24:5; by metonymy, of its inhabitants, Acts 17:6; 19:27; (*c*) the inhabited world in a coming age, Heb. 2:5. ¶

NT: B.561b; CB.1260c; K.674.
OT: –.
GEN. REF.: IS.–; NB.–; Z.5:963.

Notes: (1) In Rev. 13:3, A.V., *gē*, the earth (R.V.), is translated "world."

(2) For phrases containing *aiōnios*, e.g., Rom. 16:25; 2 Tim. 1:9; Tit. 1:2, see ETERNAL, No. 2.

WORLDLY

kosmikos [κοσμικός, 2886], pertaining to this world, is used (*a*) in Heb. 9:1, of the tabernacle, A.V., "worldly," R.V., "of this world" (i.e., made of mundane materials, adapted to this visible world, local and transitory); (*b*) in Tit. 2:12, ethically, of "worldly lusts," or desires. ¶

NT: B.445b; CB.1255c; K.459.
OT: –.
GEN. REF.: –.

For **WORLD-RULERS**, Eph. 6:12, R.V., see **RULER**, No. 3

WORM

1. *skōlēx* [σκώληξ, 4663], a worm which preys upon dead bodies, is used metaphorically by the Lord in Mark 9:48; in some mss. vv. 44, 46, cp. Is. 66:24. The statement signifies the exclusion of the hope of restoration, the punishment being eternal. ¶

NT: B.758c; CB.–; K.1054.
OT: tôla': S.8438; HR.1278a.2a; H.2516b; BD.1068d.
tôlē'āh: S.8438; HR.1278a.2b; H.2516b; BD.1069a.
tôla'at: S.8438; HR.1278a.2c; H.2516b; BD.1069a.
GEN. REF.: IS.4:1116; NB.–; Z.5:968.

2. *skōlēkobrōtos* [σκωληκόβρωτος, 4662], denotes devoured by worms (*skōlēx*, and *bibrōskō*, to eat), Acts 12:23. ¶

NT: B.758c; CB.–; K.1054.
OT: –.
GEN. REF.: IS.4:1116; NB.–; Z.–.

WORMWOOD

apsinthos [ἄψινθος, 894], (Eng., absinth), a plant both bitter and deleterious, and growing in desolate places, figuratively suggestive of calamity (Lam. 3:15) and injustice (Amos 5:7), is used in Rev. 8:11 (twice; in the 1st part as a proper name). ¶

NT: B.129c; CB.1237b; K.–.
OT: –.
GEN. REF.: IS.4:1117; NB.1340; Z.5:969.

WORSE

A. Adjectives.

1. *cheirōn* [χείρων, 5501], used as the comparative degree of *kakos*, evil, describes (*a*) the condition of certain men, Matt. 12:45; Luke 11:26; 2 Pet. 2:20; (*b*) evil men themselves and seducers, 2 Tim. 3:13; (*c*) indolent men who refuse to provide for their own households, and are worse than unbelievers, 1 Tim. 5:8, R.V.; (*d*) a rent in a garment, Matt. 9:16; Mark 2:21; (*e*) an error, Matt. 27:64; (*f*) a person suffering from a malady, Mark 5:26; (*g*) a possible physical affliction, John 5:14; (*h*) a punishment, Heb. 10:29, "sorer." See SORE. ¶

NT: B.881b; CB.–; K.–.
OT: –.
GEN. REF.: –.

2. *elassōn* or *elattōn* [ἐλάσσων, 1640], is said of wine in John 2:10. See LESS.

NT: B.248a; CB.1244a; K.–.
OT: mā'aṭ: S.4591; HR.448b.3a,b; H.1228; BD.589b.
m^e'aṭ: S.4592; HR.448b.3c; H.1228a; BD.589d.
qāṭôn: S.6996; HR.448b.5; H.2009a,b; BD.882a.
GEN. REF.: –.

3. *hēssōn* or *hēttōn* [ἥσσων, 2276], less, inferior, used in the neuter, after *epi*, for, is translated "worse" in 1 Cor. 11:17; in 2 Cor. 12:15 the neuter, used adverbially, is translated "the less." ¶

NT: B.349a; CB.–; K.–.
OT: –.
GEN. REF.: –.

B. Verbs.

1. *hustereō* [ὑστερέω, 5302], is rendered "are we the worse" in 1 Cor. 8:8. See BEHIND, B, No. 1, COME, No. 39, DESTITUTE, FAIL, *Note* (2), LACK, WANT.

NT: B.849a; CB.1252b; K.1240.
OT: ḥāsēr: S.2637; HR.1418b.3a; H.705; BD.341c.
GEN. REF.: –.

2. *proechō* [προέχω, 2276], to hold before, promote, is rendered "are we better" in Rom. 3:9, A.V. (Passive Voice); R.V., "are we in worse case." See BETTER (be), *Note* (1). ¶

NT: B.705d; CB.–; K.–.
OT: –.
GEN. REF.: –.

WORSHIP (Verb and Noun), WORSHIPPING

A. Verbs.

1. *proskuneō* [προσκυνέω, 4352], to make obeisance, do reverence to (from *pros*, towards, and *kuneō*, to kiss), is the most frequent word rendered to worship. It is used of an act of homage or reverence (*a*) to God, e.g., Matt. 4:10; John 4:21-24; 1 Cor. 14:25; Rev. 4:10; 5:14; 7:11; 11:16; 19:10 (2nd part) and 22:9; (*b*) to Christ, e.g., Matt. 2:2, 8, 11; 8:2; 9:18; 14:33; 15:25; 20:20; 28:9, 17; John 9:38; Heb. 1:6, in a quotation from the Sept. of Deut. 32:43, referring to Christ's Second Advent; (*c*) to a man, Matt. 18:26; (*d*) to the Dragon, by men, Rev. 13:4; (*e*) to the Beast, his human instrument, Rev. 13:4, 8, 12; 14:9, 11; (*f*) the image of the Beast, 13:15; 14:11; 16:2; (*g*) to demons, Rev. 9:20; (*h*) to idols, Acts 7:43.

NT: B.716c; CB.1267b; K.948.
OT: shāḥāh: S.7812; HR.1217b.6; H.2360; BD.1005b.
s^egid (Aramaic): S.5457; HR.1217b.4b; H.2884; BD.1104a.
GEN. REF.: IS.4:1118; NB.1340; Z.5:969.

Note: As to Matt. 18:26, this is mentioned as follows, in the "List of readings and renderings preferred by the American Committee" (see R.V. *Classes of Passages*, IV): "At the word 'worship' in Matt. 2:2, etc., add the marginal note 'The Greek word denotes an act of reverence, whether paid to man (see chap. 18:26) or to God (see chap. 4:10).'" The Note to John 9:38 in the American Standard Version in this connection is most unsound; it implies that Christ was a creature. J. N. Darby renders the verb 'do homage' [see the Revised Preface to the Second Edition (1871) of his *New Translation*].

2. *sebomai* [σέβομαι, 4576], to revere, stressing the feeling of awe or devotion, is used of worship (*a*) to God, Matt. 15:9; Mark 7:7; Acts

16:14; 18:7, 13; (*b*) to a goddess, Acts 19:27. See DEVOUT, No. 3.
NT: B.746a; CB.1268c; K.1010.
OT: –.
GEN. REF.: –.

3. *sebazomai* [σεβάζομαι, 4573], akin to No. 2, to honour religiously, is used in Rom. 1:25. ¶
NT: B.745c; CB.1268c; K.1010.
OT: –.
GEN. REF.: –.

4. *latreuō* [λατρεύω, 3000], to serve, to render religious service or homage, is translated to worship in Phil. 3:3, "(who) worship (by the Spirit of God)," R.V., A.V., "(which) worship (God in the spirit)"; the R.V. renders it to serve (for A.V., to worship) in Acts 7:42; 24:14; A.V. and R.V., "(the) worshippers" in Heb. 10:2, present participle, lit., '(the ones) worshipping.' See SERVE.
NT: B.467c; CB.1256c; K.503.
OT: ʿābad: S.5647; HR.863a.2a; H.1553; BD.712b.
pᵉlaḥ (Aramaic): S.6399; HR.863a.3a; H.2940; BD.1108c.
GEN. REF.: IS.4:1118; NB.1340; Z.–.

5. *eusebeō* [εὐσεβέω, 2151], to act piously towards, is translated "ye worship" in Acts 17:23. See PIETY (to shew).
NT: B.326b; CB.1247b; K.1010.
OT: –.
GEN. REF.: –.

Notes: (1) The worship of God is nowhere defined in Scripture. A consideration of the above verbs shows that it is not confined to praise; broadly it may be regarded as the direct acknowledgement to God, of His nature, attributes, ways and claims, whether by the outgoing of the heart in praise and thanksgiving or by deed done in such acknowledgement.

(2) In Acts 17:25 *therapeuō,* to serve, do service to (so R.V.), is rendered "is worshipped." See CURE, HEAL.

B. Nouns.

1. *sebasma* [σέβασμα, 4574], denotes an object of worship (akin to A, No. 3); Acts 17:23 (see DEVOTION: in 2 Thess. 2:4, "that is worshipped"; every object of worship, whether the true God or pagan idols, will come under the ban of the Man of Sin. ¶
NT: B.745d; CB.1268c; K.1010.
OT: –.
GEN. REF.: –.

2. *ethelothrēskeia* (or *-ia*) [ἐθελοθρησκεία, 1479], will-worship (*ethelō,* to will, *thrēskeia,* worship), occurs in Col. 2:23, voluntarily adopted worship, whether unbidden or forbidden, not that which is imposed by others, but which one affects. ¶
NT: B.218a; CB.–; K.337.
OT: –.
GEN. REF.: –.

3. *thrēskeia* [θρησκεία, 2356], for which see RELIGION, is translated "worshipping" in Col. 2:18.
NT: B.363b; CB.1272b; K.337.
OT: –.
GEN. REF.: –.

Note: In Luke 14:10, A.V., *doxa,* "glory" (R.V.), is translated "worship."

WORSHIPPER

1. *proskunētēs* [προσκυνητής, 4353], akin to *proskuneō* (see WORSHIP, A, No. 1), occurs in John 4:23. ¶
NT: B.717b; CB.1267b; K.948.
OT: –.
GEN. REF.: IS.–; NB.1340; Z.–.

2. *neōkoros* [νεωκόρος, 3511], is translated "worshipper" in Acts 19:35, A.V.: see TEMPLE-KEEPER. ¶
NT: B.537b; CB.1259c; K.–.
OT: –.
GEN. REF.: –.

3. *theosebēs* [θεοσεβής, 2318], denotes 'reverencing God' (*theos,* God, *sebomai,* see WORSHIP, A, No. 2), and is rendered "a worshipper of God" in John 9:31. ¶ Cp. *theosebeia,* godliness, 1 Tim. 2:10. ¶
NT: B.358b; CB.1272b; K.331.
OT: yārēʾ: S.3372; HR.648a.1; H.907,908; BD.431a.
GEN. REF.: –.

Note: For Heb. 10:2, see WORSHIP, A, No. 4.

WORTHY, WORTHILY

A. Adjectives.

1. *axios* [ἄξιος, 514], of weight, worth, worthy, is said of persons and their deeds: (*a*) in a good sense, e.g., Matt. 10:10, 11, 13 (twice), 37 (twice), 38; 22:8; Luke 7:4; 10:7; 15:19, 21; John 1:27; Acts 13:25; 1 Tim. 5:18; 6:1; Heb. 11:38; Rev. 3:4; 4:11; 5:2, 4, 9, 12; (*b*) in a bad sense, Luke 12:48; 23:15; Acts 23:29; 25:11, 25; 26:31; Rom. 1:32; Rev. 16:6. See MEET, REWARD.
NT: B.78a; CB.1238b; K.63.
OT: shāwāh: S.7737; HR.113a.3; H.2342; BD.1000d.
mālēʾ: S.4390; HR.113a.2; H.1195; BD.569d.
GEN. REF.: IS.4:1133; NB.–; Z.–.

2. *hikanos* [ἱκανός, 2425], sufficient, is translated "worthy" in this sense in Matt. 3:11 (marg., "sufficient"); so 8:8; Mark 1:7; Luke 3:16; 7:6. See ABILITY, C, No. 2, etc.
NT: B.374b; CB.1250c; K.361.
OT: day: S.1767; HR.683c.2; H.425; BD.191b.
shadday: S.7706; HR.683c.9; H.2333; BD.994d.
GEN. REF.: IS.4:1133; NB.–; Z.–.

3. *enochos* [ἔνοχος, 1777], held in, bound by, is translated "worthy (of death)" in Matt. 26:66 and Mark 14:64, R.V. (marg., "liable to"; A.V., "guilty"). See DANGER.
NT: B.267b; CB.1245b; K.286.
OT: dām: S.1818; HR.476c.2; H.436; BD.196b.
GEN. REF.: IS.4:1133; NB.–; Z.–.

Notes: (1) In Jas. 2:7, A.V., *kalos*, good, fair, is translated "worthy" (R.V., "honourable").

(2) For the A.V. of Eph. 4:1; Col. 1:10; 1 Thess. 2:12, see C, below.

B. Verbs.

1. *axioō* [ἀξιόω, 515], to think or count worthy, is used (1) of the estimation formed by God (*a*) favourably, 2 Thess. 1:11, "may count (you) worthy (of your calling)," suggestive of grace (it does not say 'may make you worthy'); Heb. 3:3, "of more glory," of Christ in comparison with Moses; (*b*) unfavourably, 10:29, "of how much sorer punishment"; (2) by a centurion (negatively) concerning himself, Luke 7:7; (3) by a church, regarding its elders, 1 Tim. 5:17, where "honour" stands probably for 'honorarium,' i.e., material support. See also DESIRE, B, No. 1 (Acts 28:22), THINK (Acts 15:38). ¶

NT: B.78c; CB.1238b; K.63.
OT: b^{e}'ā' (Aramaic): S.1156; HR.113a.1a; H.2635; BD.1085a.
bāqash: S.1245; HR.113a.2a; H.276; BD.134c.
GEN. REF.: IS.4:1133; NB.—; Z.—.

2. *kataxioō* [καταξιόω, 2661], a strengthened form of No. 1, occurs in Luke 20:35; 21:36, in some texts; Acts 5:41; 2 Thess. 1:5. ¶ See ACCOUNT, A, No. 5.

NT: B.415c; CB.1254b; K.63.
OT: —.
GEN. REF.: IS.4:1133; NB.—; Z.—.

C. Adverb.

axiōs [ἀξίως, 516], worthily, so translated in the R.V. [with one exception, see (c)], for A.V., "worthy" and other renderings, (*a*) "worthily of God," 1 Thess. 2:12, of the Christian walk as it should be; 3 John 6, R.V., of assisting servants of God in a way which reflects God's character and thoughts; (*b*) "worthily of the Lord," Col. 1:10; of the calling of believers, Eph. 4:1, in regard to their "walk" or manner of life; (*c*) "worthy of the gospel of Christ," Phil. 1:27, of a manner of life in accordance with what the gospel declares; (*d*) "worthily of the saints," R.V., of receiving a fellow-believer, Rom. 16:2, in such a manner as befits those who bear the name of "saints." ¶ Deissmann (*Bible Studies*, pp. 248 ff.) shows from various inscriptions that the phrase "worthily of the god" was very popular at Pergamum.

NT: B.78d; CB.1238b; K.—.
OT: —.
GEN. REF.: IS.4:1133; NB.—; Z.—.

For **WORTHY DEEDS**, Acts 24:2, A.V., see **CORRECTION**

WOT

Note: This form, the 1st person singular and the plural of the present tense of an Anglo-Saxon verb *witan*, to see or to know (for the past tense cp. WIST), is a rendering of (1) *oida*, to know, in Acts 3:17; 7:40; Rom 11:2 (see KNOW, No. 2); (2) *gnōrizō*, to come to know, in Phil. 1:22 (see KNOW, No. 8).

WOULD

Notes: (1) This is often a translation of various inflections of a Greek verb. When it represents a separate word, it is always emphatic, and is a translation of one or other of the verbs mentioned under WILL.

(2) *Ophelon* (the 2nd aorist tense of *opheilō*, to owe) expresses a wish, "I would that," either impracticable, 1 Cor. 4:8, R.V. (A.V., "would to God"); or possible, 2 Cor. 11:1; Gal. 5:12; Rev. 3:15.

(3) *Euchomai*, to pray, with the particle *an*, expressing a strong desire with a remote possibility of fulfilment, is used in Acts 26:29, "I would (to God, that)."

WOUND (Noun and Verb)

A. Nouns.

trauma [τραῦμα, 5134], a wound, occurs in Luke 10:34. ¶

NT: B.824d; CB.—; K.—.
OT: peṣa': S.6482; HR.1369c.4; H.1799a; BD.822d.
ḥālāl: S.2491; HR.1369c.2; H.660a; BD.319c.
GEN. REF.: —.

Note: *Plēgē*, a blow, a stroke, is used in Luke 10:30 with *epitithēmi*, to lay on, lit., 'laid on blows,' R.V., "beat" (A.V., "wounded"). In Rev. 13:3, 12, *plēgē* is used with the genitive case of *thanatos*, death, lit., 'stroke of death,' R.V., "death-stroke" (A.V., "deadly wound"); the rendering "wound" does not accurately give the meaning; in ver. 14, with the genitive of *machaira*, a sword, A.V., "wound" (R.V., "stroke").

B. Verbs.

traumatizō [τραυματίζω, 5135], to wound (from A), occurs in Luke 20:12 and Acts 19:16. ¶

NT: B.824d; CB.—; K.—.
OT: ḥālal: S.2490; HR.1370b,2a,b; H.660,661; BD.319b.
ḥālāl: S.2491; HR.1370b.2c; H.660a; BD.319c.
pāṣa': S.6481; HR.1370b.3; H.1799; BD.822d.
GEN. REF.: —.

Note: In Rev. 13:3, A.V., *sphazō*, to slay, is translated "wounded," R.V., "smitten" (A.V. and R.V. marg., "slain").

For **WOUND** (wrapped) see **WIND** (Verb)

WOVEN

huphantos [ὑφαντός, 5307], from *huphainō*, to weave (found in good mss. in Luke 12:27), is used of Christ's garment, John 19:23. ¶

NT: B.849d; CB.—; K.—.
OT: ḥāshab: S.2803; HR.1419a.2; H.767; BD.362d.
'ārag: S.707; HR.1419a.1; H.157; BD.70d.
GEN. REF.: —.

WRANGLINGS

diaparatribē [διαπαρατριβή, —], found in 1 Tim. 6:5, denotes constant strife, 'obstinate contests' (Ellicott), 'mutual irritations' (Field), A.V., "perverse disputings" (marg., "gallings one of another"), R.V. "wranglings." Some texts have *paradiatribē*. The preposition *dia-* is used intensively indicating thoroughness, completeness. ¶ The simple word *paratribē* (not found in the N.T.), denotes hostility, enmity. See DISPUTE, No. 3.

NT: B.187c; CB.—; K.—.
OT: —.
GEN. REF.: —.

WRAP

1. *eneileō* [ἐνειλέω, 1750], to roll in, wind in, occurs in Mark 15:46; see WIND (Verb), No. 3. ¶

NT: B.264c; CB.—; K.—.
OT: lûṭ: S.3874; HR.472b.1; H.1092; BD.532a.
GEN. REF.: —.

2. *entulissō* [ἐντυλίσσο, 1794], to roll in, occurs in Matt. 27:59; Luke 23:53; John 20:7: see ROLL, No. 5. ¶

NT: B.270b; CB.—; K.—.
OT: —.
GEN. REF.: —.

3. *sustellō* [συστέλλω, 4958], to wrap or wind up, Acts 5:6; see WIND, No. 2; 1 Cor. 7:29, see SHORTEN, No. 2. ¶

NT: B.795a; CB.—; K.1074.
OT: —.
GEN. REF.: —.

WRATH

1. *orgē* [ὀργή, —]: see ANGER and *Notes* (1) and (2).

2. *thumos* [θυμός, 2372], hot anger, passion, for which see ANGER, *Notes* (1) and (2), is translated "wrath" in Luke 4:28; Acts 19:28; Rom. 2:8, R.V.; Gal. 5:20; Eph. 4:31; Col. 3:8; Heb. 11:27; Rev. 12:12; 14:8, 10, 19; 15:1, 7; 16:1; 18:3; "wraths" in 2 Cor. 12:20; "fierceness" in Rev. 16:19; 19:15 (followed by No. 1). ¶

NT: B.365b; CB.1272c; K.339.
OT: 'aph: S.639; HR.660c.1; H.133a; BD.60a.
ḥēmāh: S.2534; HR.660c.5c; H.860a; BD.404b.
GEN. REF.: IS.4:1134; NB.—; Z.5:990.

3. *parorgismos* [παροργισμός, 3950], occurs in Eph. 4:26: see ANGER, A, *Note* (2). ¶

NT: B.629d; CB.1262c; K.716.
OT: ka'as: S.3708; HR.1072c.1; H.1016a; BD.495b.
ne'āṣāh: S.5007; HR.1072c.2; H.1274a,b; BD.611a.
qeṣeph: S.7110; HR.1072c.3; H.2058a; BD.893c.
GEN. REF.: IS.4:1134; NB.—; Z.5:990.

Note: For the verb *parorgizō*, to provoke to wrath, Eph. 6:4, A.V., see ANGER, B, No. 2.

WREST

strebloō [στρεβλόω, 4761], to twist, to torture (from *streblē*, a winch or instrument of torture, and akin to *strephō*, to turn), is used metaphorically in 2 Pet. 3:16, of wresting the Scriptures on the part of the ignorant and unstedfast. ¶ In the Sept., 2 Sam. 22:27. ¶

NT: B.771a; CB.—; K.—.
OT: pātal: S.6617; HR.1296b.1; H.1857; BD.836c.
GEN. REF.: IS.4:1135; NB.—; Z.—.

WRESTLE, WRESTLING

palē [πάλη, 3823], a wrestling (akin to *pallō*, to sway, vibrate), is used figuratively in Eph. 6:12, of the spiritual conflict engaged in by believers, R.V., "(our) wrestling," A.V., "(we) wrestle." ¶

NT: B.606a; CB.—; K.770.
OT: —.
GEN. REF.: IS.—; NB.—; Z.5:995.

WRETCHED

talaipōros [ταλαίπωρος, 5005], distressed, miserable, wretched, is used in Rom. 7:24 and Rev. 3:17. ¶ Cp. *talaipōria*, misery, and *talaipōreō* (see AFFLICT).

NT: B.803b; CB.1271a; K.—.
OT: shādad: S.7703; HR.1333b.1,2 H.2331; BD.994a.
GEN. REF.: —.

WRINKLE

rhutis [ῥυτίς, 4512], from an obsolete verb *rhuō*, signifying to draw together, occurs in Eph. 5:27, describing the flawlessness of the complete Church, as the result of the love of Christ in giving Himself up for it, with the purpose of presenting it to Himself hereafter. ¶

NT: B.738b; CB.—; K.—.
OT: —.
GEN. REF.: IS.4:1133; NB.—; Z.—.

WRITE, WROTE, WRITTEN

A. Verbs.

1. *graphō* [γράφω, 1125], is used (*a*) of forming letters on a surface or writing material, John 8:6; Gal. 6:11, where the Apostle speaks of his having written with large letters in his own hand, which not improbably means that at this point he took the pen from his amanuensis and finished the Epistle himself; this is not negatived by the fact that the verb is in the

aorist or past definite tense, lit., 'I wrote,' for in Greek idiom the writer of a letter put himself beside the reader and spoke of it as having been written in the past; in Eng. we should say 'I am writing,' taking our point of view from the time at which we are doing it; cp. Philm. 19 (this Ep. is undoubtedly a holograph), where again the equivalent English translation is in the present tense (see also Acts 15:23; Rom. 15:15); possibly the Apostle, in Galatians, was referring to his having written the body of the Epistle but the former alternative seems the more likely; in 2 Thess. 3:17 he says that the closing salutation is written by his own hand and speaks of it as "the token in every Epistle" which some understand as a purpose for the future rather than a custom; see, however, 1 Cor. 16:21 and Col. 4:18. The absence of the token from the other Epistles of Paul can be explained differently, their authenticity not being dependent upon this; (*b*) to commit to writing, to record, e.g., Luke 1:63; John 19:21, 22; it is used of Scripture as a standing authority, "it is written," e.g., Mark 1:2; Rom. 1:17 (cp. 2 Cor. 4:13); (*c*) of writing directions or giving information, e.g., Rom. 10:5, "(Moses) writeth," R.V. (A.V., "describeth"); 15:15; 2 Cor. 7:12; (*d*) of that which contained a record or message, e.g., Mark 10:4, 5; John 19:19; 21:25; Acts 23:25.

NT: B.166c; CB.1248c; K.128.
OT: kātab: S.3789; HR.276a.3a; H.1053; BD.507a.
GEN. REF.: IS.4:1136; NB.1341; Z.—.

2. *epistellō* [ἐπιστέλλω, 1989], denotes to send a message by letter, to write word (*stellō*, to send; Eng., epistle), Acts 15:20; 21:25 (some mss. have *apostellō*, to send); Heb. 13:22. ¶

NT: B.300c; CB.1246a; K.1074.
OT: shālaḥ: S.7971; HR.529c.1; H.2394; BD.1018a.
GEN. REF.: —.

3. *prographō* [προγράφω, 4270], denotes to write before, Rom. 15:4 (in the best texts; some have *graphō*); Eph. 3:3. See SET (forth).

NT: B.704a; CB.1266c; K.128.
OT: —.
GEN. REF.: —.

4. *engraphō* [ἐγγράφω, 1449], denotes to write in, Luke 10:20; 2 Cor. 3:2, 3. ¶

NT: B.213d; CB.1245a; K.128.
OT: kātab: S.3789; HR.363b.1; H.1053; BD.507a.
GEN. REF.: IS.4:1136; NB.1342; Z.—.

5. *epigraphō* [ἐπιγράφω, 1924], is rendered to write over or upon (*epi*) in Mark 15:26; figuratively, on the heart, Heb. 8:10; 10:16; on the gates of the Heavenly Jerusalem, Rev. 21:12. See INSCRIPTION.

NT: B.291c; CB.1245c; K.—.
OT: kātab: S.3789; HR.518c.1; H.1053; BD.507a.
GEN. REF.: IS.4:1136; NB.1342; Z.—.

Notes: (1) For *apographō*, Heb. 12:23, A.V., "written," see ENROL.

(2) In 2 Cor. 3:7 "written" is a translation of *en*, in, with the dative plural of *gramma*, a letter, lit., 'in letters.'

B. Adjective.

graptos [γραπτός, 1123], from A, No. 1, written, occurs in Rom. 2:15. ¶

NT: —.
OT: —.
GEN. REF.: —.

WRITING

gramma [γράμμα, 1121], from *graphō*, to write, is rendered "writings" in John 5:47. See LETTER, No. 1.

NT: B.165b; CB.1248c; K.128.
OT: sēpher: S.5612; HR.275a.3; H.1540a; BD.706d.
kᵉtāb: S.3791; HR.275a.2b; H.1053a; BD.508b.
GEN. REF.: IS.4:1136; NB.—; Z.—.

Notes: (1) For *biblion*, "writing," A.V. in Matt. 19:7, see BILL, No. 1.

(2) In John 19:19, A.V., "the writing (was)" is a translation of the perfect participle, Passive Voice, of *graphō*, R.V., "(there was) written."

WRITING TABLET (A.V., WRITING TABLE)

pinakidion [πινακίδιον, 4093], occurs in Luke 1:63, a diminutive of *pinakis*, a tablet, which is a variant reading here. ¶

NT: B.658b; CB.—; K.—.
OT: —.
GEN. REF.: IS.4:1136; NB.—; Z.—.

WRONG (Noun and Verb), WRONG-DOER, WRONG-DOING

A. Nouns.

1. *adikia* [ἀδικία, 93], *a*, negative, *dikē*, right, is translated "wrong" in 2 Pet. 2:13 (2nd part), 15, R.V., "wrong-doing" (A.V., unrighteousness); in 2 Cor. 12:13, it is used ironically. See INIQUITY, UNJUST, UNRIGHTEOUSNESS.

NT: B.17d; CB.1233a; K.22.
OT: 'awᵉlāh: S.5766; HR.25b.19; H.1580a,b; BD.732c.
'āwōn: S.5771; HR.25b.21; H.1577a; BD.730d.
sheqer: S.8267; HR.25b.34; H.2461a; BD.1055b.
GEN. REF.: —.

2. *adikēma* [ἀδίκημα, 92], denotes a misdeed, injury, in the concrete sense (in contrast to No. 1), Acts 18:14, "a matter of wrong"; 24:20, R.V., "wrong-doing" (A.V., "evil doing"). See INIQUITY.

NT: B.17d; CB.1233a; K.22.
OT: 'āwōn: S.5771; HR.25a.4; H.1577a; BD.730d.
pesha': S.6588; HR.25a.6; H.1846a; BD.833b.
GEN. REF.: —.

B. Verb.

adikeō [ἀδικέω, 91], to do wrong, is used (*a*) intransitively, to act unrighteously, Acts 25:11,

R.V., "I am a wrong-doer" (A.V., ". . . an offender"); 1 Cor. 6:8; 2 Cor. 7:12 (1st part); Col. 3:25 (1st part); cp. Rev. 22:11 (see UNRIGHTEOUSNESS, B); (*b*) transitively, to wrong, Matt. 20:13; Acts 7:24 (Passive Voice), 26, 27, 25:10; 2 Cor. 7:2, ver. 12 (2nd part; Passive Voice); Gal. 4:12, "ye did (me no) wrong," anticipating a possible suggestion that his vigorous language was due to some personal grievance; the occasion referred to me that of His first visit; Col: 3:25 (2nd part), lit., 'what he did wrong', which brings consequences both in this life and at the Judgment-seat of Christ; Philm. 18; 2 Pet. 2:13 (1st part); in the Middle or Passive Voice, to take or suffer wrong, to suffer (oneself) to be wronged, 1 Cor. 6:7. See HURT, OFFENDER, UNJUST.

NT: B.17c; CB.1233a; K.22.
OT: 'āwāh: S.5753; HR.24c.11c; H.1577; BD.731c.
'āshaq: S.6231; HR.24c.15a; H.1713; BD.798d.
GEN. REF.: –.

WRONGFULLY

adikōs [ἀδίκως, 95], akin to the above, occurs in 1 Pet. 2:19. ¶

NT: B.18b; CB.1233a; K.–.
OT: sheqer: S.8267; HR.27b.7; H.2461a; BD.1055b.
GEN. REF.: –.

Note: For "exact wrongfully," Luke 3:14, R.V., see ACCUSE, B, No. 5.

WROTH (be)

1. *orgizō* [ὀργίζω, 3710], always in the Middle or Passive Voice in the N.T., is rendered "was (were) wroth" in Matt. 18:34; 22:7; Rev. 11:18, R.V., (A.V., "were angry"); 12:17, R.V., "waxed wroth." See ANGER, B, No. 1.

NT: B.579c; CB.1261a; K.–.
OT: ḥārāh: S.2734; HR.1010a.5a; H.736; BD.354a.
qāsaph: S.7107; HR.1010a.9; H.2058; BD.893b.
rāgaz: S.7264; HR.1010a.10; H.2112; BD.919a.
GEN. REF.: –.

2. *thumoō* [θυμόω, 2373], signifies to be very angry (from *thumos*, wrath, hot anger), to be stirred into passion, Matt. 2:16, of Herod (Passive Voice). ¶

NT: B.365c; CB.1272c; K.–.
OT: ḥārāh: S.2734; HR.662b.6,7; H.736; BD.354a.
qāsaph: S.7107; HR.662b.12; H.2058; BD.893b.
rāgaz: S.7264; HR.662b.14; H.2112; BD.919a.
GEN. REF.: –.

3. *cholaō* [χολάω, 5520], primarily, to be melancholy (*cholē*, gall), signifies to be angry, John 7:23, R.V., "are ye wroth" (A.V., ". . . angry"). ¶

NT: B.883b; CB.–; K.–.
OT: –.
GEN. REF.: –.

For **WROUGHT** see **WORK**

Y

YE, YOU, YOURSELVES, YOUR OWN SELVES

Notes: (1) These are most frequently the translations of various inflections of a verb; sometimes of the article before a nominative used as a vocative, e.g., Rev. 18:20, "ye saints, and ye apostles, and ye prophets" (lit., 'the saints, etc.'). When the 2nd person plural pronouns are used separately from a verb, they are usually one or other of the forms of *humeis*, the plural of *su*, "thou," and are frequently emphatic, especially when they are subjects of the verb, an emphasis always to be noticed, e.g., Matt. 5:13, 14, 48; 6:9, 19, 20; Mark 6:31, 37; John 15:27a; Rom. 1:6; 1 Cor. 3:17, 23; Gal. 3:28, 29a; Eph. 1:13a; 2:8; 2:11, 13; Phil. 2:18; Col. 3:4, 7a; 4:1; 1 Thess. 1:6; 2:10, 19, 20; 3:8; 2 Thess. 3:13; Jas. 5:8; 1 Pet. 2:9a; 1 John 2:20, 24 (1st and 3rd occurrences), 27a; 4:4; Jude 17, 20.

(2) The addition of *autoi*, yourselves, to the pronoun marks especial emphasis, e.g., Mark 6:31; John 3:28; 1 Cor. 11:13; 1 Thess. 4:9. Sometimes *autoi* is used without the pronoun, e.g., Luke 11:46, 52; Acts 2:22; 20:34; 1 Thess. 2:1; 3:3; 5:2; 2 Thess. 3:7; Heb. 13:3.

(3) The reflexive pronoun "yourselves" represents the various plural forms of the reflexive pronoun *heautou* (frequently governed by some preposition), e.g., Matt. 3:9; 16:8; 23:31; 25:9; Mark 9:50; Luke 3:8; 12:33, 57; 16:9; 21:30, "of your own selves"; 21:34; Acts 5:35; in Rom. 11:25, "in your own (conceits)," lit., 'in (*en*; some texts have *para*, among) yourselves'; so 12:16 (with *para*); 1 Pet. 4:8; Jude 20, 21; in Eph. 5:19, R.V., "one to another" (A.V., and R.V. marg., "to yourselves").

Note: In 1 Thess. 5:11, A.V., *allēlous*, "one another" (R.V.), is rendered "yourselves together."

YEA, YES

1. *nai* [ναί, 3483], a particle of affirmation, is used (*a*) in answer to a question, Matt. 9:28; 11:9; 13:51; 17:25; 21:16; Luke 7:26; John 11:27; 21:15, 16; Acts 5:8; 22:27; Rom. 3:29; (*b*) in assent to an assertion, Matt. 15:27, R.V. (A.V., "truth"); Mark 7:28; Rev. 14:13; 16:7, R.V. (A.V., "even so"); (*c*) in confirmation of an assertion, Matt. 11:26 and Luke 10:21, R.V. (A.V., "even so"); Luke 11:51, R.V. (A.V., "verily"); 12:5; Phil. 4:3 (in the best texts); Philm. 20; (*d*) in solemn asseveration, Rev. 1:7 (A.V. and R.V., "even so"); 22:20, R.V. (A.V., "surely"); (*e*) in repetition for emphasis, Matt. 5:37; 2 Cor. 1:17; Jas. 5:12; (*f*) singly in contrast to *ou*, "nay," 2 Cor. 1:18, 19 (twice), 20, "(the) yea," R.V. ¶

NT: B.532d; CB.—; K.—.
OT: —.
GEN. REF.: —.

2. *alla* [ἀλλά, 235], but, is translated "yea" in John 16:2; Rom. 3:31, A.V. (R.V., "nay"); 1 Cor. 4:3; 2 Cor. 7:11 (six times); Gal. 4:17, A.V. (R.V., "nay"); Phil. 1:18; 2:17; 3:8; Jas. 2:18.

NT: B.38a; CB.—; K.—.
OT: —.
GEN. REF.: —.

3. *kai* [καί, 2532], and, even, is rendered "yea," e.g., Luke 2:35; John 16:32; 1 Cor. 2:10; 2 Cor. 8:3; in Acts 7:43, A.V. (R.V., "and").

NT: B.391c; CB.1253a; K.—.
OT: —.
GEN. REF.: —.

4. *men oun* [μὲν οὖν, 3304], in some texts *menounge*, i.e., *men-oun-ge*, "yea rather," occurs, e.g., in Luke 11:28; in Rom. 10:18, "yea (A.V., yes) verily"; in Phil. 3:8, R.V., "yea verily" (A.V., "yea doubtless").

NT: B.503b; CB.—; K.—.
OT: —.
GEN. REF.: —.

Notes: (1) In 1 Cor. 15:15 the R.V. translates *kai* by "and" (A.V., "yea").

(2) In Luke 24:22 the R.V. translates *alla kai* "moreover" (A.V., "yea . . . and").

(3) In 1 Cor. 16:6, A.V., *ē kai*, "or even" (R.V.), is translated "yea, and."

(4) In 2 Cor. 5:16, A.V., the phrase *ei kai* (some texts have *ei de kai*) is translated "yea, though" (R.V., "even though").

(5) In Phil. 2:8, R.V., the particle *de*, but, is translated "yea" (A.V., "even").

YEAR

A. Nouns.

1. *etos* [ἔτος, 2094], is used (*a*) to mark a point of time at or from which events take place, e.g., Luke 3:1 (dates were frequently reckoned from the time when a monarch began to reign); in Gal. 3:17 the time of the giving of the Law is stated as 430 years after the covenant of promise given to Abraham; there is no real discrepancy between this and Ex. 12:40; the Apostle is not concerned with the exact duration of the interval; it certainly was not less than 430 years; the point of the argument is that the period was very considerable; Gal. 1:18 and 2:1 mark events in Paul's life; as to the former the point is that three years elapsed before he saw any of the Apostles; in 2:1 the 14 years may date either from his conversion or from his visit to Peter mentioned in 1:18; the latter seems the more natural (for a full discussion of the subject see Notes on Galatians by Hogg and Vine, pp. 55 ff.); (*b*) to mark a space of time, e.g., Matt. 9:20; Luke 12:19; 13:11; John 2:20; Acts 7:6, where the 400 years mark not merely the time that Israel was in bondage in Egypt, but the time that they sojourned or were strangers there (the R.V. puts a comma after the word "evil"); the Genevan Version renders Gen. 15:13 "thy posterity shall inhabit a strange land for 400 years"; Heb. 3:17; Rev. 20:2-7; (*c*) to date an event from one's birth, e.g., Mark 5:42; Luke 2:42; 3:23; John 8:57; Acts 4:22; 1 Tim. 5:9; (*d*) to mark recurring events, Luke 2:41 (with *kata*, used distributively); 13:7; (*e*) of an unlimited number, Heb. 1:12.

NT: B.316d; CB.—; K.—.
OT: shānāh: S.8141; HR.565a.3a; H.2419a; BD.1040a.
GEN. REF.: IS.1:575; NB.178; Z.1:689.

2. *eniautos* [ἐνιαυτός, 1763], originally a cycle of time, is used (*a*) of a particular time marked by an event, e.g., Luke 4:19; John 11:49, 51; 18:13; Gal. 4:10; Rev. 9:15; (*b*) to mark a space of time, Acts 11:26; 18:11; Jas. 4:13; 5:17; (*c*) of that which takes place every year, Heb. 9:7; with *kata* [cp. (*d*) above], Heb. 9:25; 10:1; 3. ¶

NT: B.266b; CB.1245a; K.—.
OT: shānāh: S.8141; HR.474a.1; H.2419a; BD.1040a.
GEN. REF.: IS.1:575; NB.178; Z.1:689.

3. *dietia* [διετία, 1333], denotes a space of two years (*dis*, twice, and No. 1), Acts 24:27; 28:30. ¶

NT: B.194d; CB.—; K.—.
OT: —.
GEN. REF.: —.

4. *trietia* [τριετία, 5148], denotes a space of three years (*treis*, three, and No. 1), Acts 20:31. ¶

NT: B.826b; CB.—; K.—.
OT: —.
GEN. REF.: —.

Note: In Luke 1:7, 18, *hēmera*, a day, is rendered "years."

B. Adjectives.

1. *dietēs* [διετής, 1332], akin to A, No. 3, denotes lasting two years, two years old, Matt. 2:16. ¶

NT: B.194d; CB.—; K.—.
OT: —.
GEN. REF.: —.

2. *hekatontaetēs* [ἑκατονταετής, 1541], denotes a hundred years old, Rom. 4:19. ¶

NT: B.236d; CB.—; K.—.
OT: shānāh: S.8141; HR.420b.1; H.2419a; BD.1040a.
GEN. REF.: IS.1:575; NB.178; Z.1:689.

C. Adverb.

perusi [πέρυσι, 4070], last year, a year ago (from *pera*, beyond), is used with *apo*, from 2 Cor. 8:10; 9:2. ¶

NT: B.653d; CB.1263c; K.—.
OT: —.
GEN. REF.: —.

Note: In Heb. 11:24, A.V., *ginomai*, to become, with *megas*, great, is rendered "when he was come to years" (R.V., "when he was grown up").

For YES, see YEA

YESTERDAY

echthes or *chthes* [ἐχθές, 5504], occurs in John 4:52; Acts 7:28; Heb. 13:8. ¶

NT: B.331b; CB.—; K.—.
OT: t^emôl: S.8543; HR.1468c.3a; H.2521; BD.1069d.
GEN. REF.: —.

YET

Notes: This represents (1) the adverb *eti*, implying addition or duration, e.g., Matt. 12:40; Rom. 3:7; 5:6, 8; 9:19; in Heb. 12:26, 27, "yet . . . more"; (2) *alla*, but, marking antithesis or transition, e.g., Mark 14:29; 1 Cor. 4:4, 15; 9:2; (3) *mentoi*, nevertheless, John 4:27; 20:5; (4) *akmēn*, even to this point of time (the accusative case of *akmē*, a point), Matt. 15:16; ¶ (5) *ouketi*, no longer, Mark 15:5, A.V., "yet . . . nothing" (R.V., "no more . . . anything"); 2 Cor. 1:23, A.V., "not as yet"; "yet not," e.g. Gal. 2:20, A.V.; (6) *oupō*, "not yet," John 7:39 and 1 Cor. 8:2 (*oudepō*, in some mss., A.V., "nothing yet"); *oudepō*, John 19:41, "never yet"; 20:9, "as yet . . . not"; (7) *mēpō*, not yet, Rom. 9:11; Heb. 9:8; ¶ (8) *kai*, and, even, also, "yet" in Luke 3:20; in Gal. 3:4, *ei ge kai*, A.V., "if . . . yet" (R.V., "if . . . indeed"); (9) *ge*, a particle meaning 'indeed,' "yet," Luke 11:8; (10) *oudeis pōpote*, 19:30, R.V., "no man ever yet," A.V., "yet never man," lit., 'no one at any time (yet)'; (11) the following, in which the R.V. gives the correct meaning for the A.V., "yet": *ēdē*, "now," Mark 13:28; *pote*, "ever," Eph. 5:29 (A.V., "ever yet"); *kai . . . de*, John 8:16, "yea and" (A.V., "and yet"); *ou pleious*, Acts 24:11, "not more"; (12) *mellō*, to be about to, "are yet," Rev. 8:13; (13) other combinations with AND, AS, NOR, NOT.

YIELD

1. *didōmi* [δίδωμι, 1325], to give, is translated to yield, i.e., to produce, in Matt. 13:8, R.V. (A.V., "brought forth"); Mark 4:7, 8. See GIVE.

NT: B.192c; CB.1241c; K.166.
OT: nātan: S.5414; HR.317b.26a; H.1443; BD.678a.
GEN. REF.: —.

2. *apodidōmi* [ἀποδίδωμι, 591], to give up or back, is translated to yield in Heb. 12:11; Rev. 22:2 (in each case, of bearing fruit). See DELIVER, A, No. 3, etc.

NT: B.90b; CB.1236c; K.166.
OT: mākar: S.4376; HR.126b.3a; H.1194; BD.569a.
shûb: S.7725; HR.126b.8b; H.2340; BD.996d.
shālēm: S.7999; HR.126b.9; H.2401c; BD.1022b.
GEN. REF.: —.

3. *paristēmi* or *paristanō* [παρίστημι, 3936], to present, is translated to yield in Rom. 6:13 (twice), 16, 19 (twice), R.V., to present, in each place. See COMMEND, etc.

NT: B.627c; CB.1262b; K.788.
OT: —.
GEN. REF.: —.

4. *poieō* [ποιέω, 4160], to make, to do, is translated "yield" in Jas. 3:12. See DO.

NT: B.680d; CB.1265c; K.895.
OT: —.
GEN. REF.: —.

5. *aphiēmi* [ἀφίημι, 863], to send away, is translated "yielded up (His spirit)" in Matt. 27:50 (cp. *paratithēmi*, "I commend," Luke 23:46, and *paradidōmi*, "He gave up," John 19:30). See FORGIVE, etc.

NT: B.125c; CB.1236b; K.88.
OT: nāsā': S.5375; HR.183b.6; H.1421; BD.669d.
'āzab: S.5800; HR.183b.9; H.1594,1595; BD.736d.
GEN. REF.: —.

6. *peithō* [πείθω, 3982], to persuade, in the Passive Voice, to be persuaded, is translated "do (not) thou yield," Acts 23:21. See PERSUADE.

NT: B.639a; CB.1263a; K.818.
OT: bāṭaḥ: S.982; HR.1114b.2a,14a; H.233; BD.105a.
beṭaḥ: S.983; HR.1114b.11a; H.233a; BD.105b.
GEN. REF.: —.

Note: In Acts 5:10, A.V., *ekpsuchō*, to breathe one's last, expire (*ek*, out, *psuchē*, the life), is translated "yielded up (R.V., gave up) the ghost." See GHOST (give up the), No. 2.

YOKE, YOKED

A. Noun.

1. *zugos* [ζυγός, 2218], a yoke, serving to couple two things together, is used (1) metaphorically, (*a*) of submission to authority, Matt. 11:29, 30, of Christ's yoke, not simply imparted by Him but shared with Him; (*b*) of bondage, Acts 15:10 and Gal. 5:1, of bondage to the Law as a supposed means of salvation;

(*c*) of bondservice to masters, 1 Tim. 6:1; (2) to denote a balance, Rev. 6:5. See BALANCE. ¶
NT: B.339d; CB.1273c; K.301.
OT: mō'zᵉnayim: S.2976; HR.599a.1a; H.833; BD.24d.
'ōl: S.5923; HR.599a.7; H.1628a; BD.760d.
GEN. REF.: IS.4:1164; NB.1352; Z.5:1022.

2. *zeugos* [ζεῦγος, 2201], a pair of animals, Luke 14:19. See PAIR.
NT: B.337b; CB.1273c; K.—.
OT: ṣemed: S.6776; HR.594a.2; H.1927a; BD.855a.
GEN. REF.: IS.4:1164; NB.1352; Z.5:1022.

B. Verb.

heterozugeō [ἑτεροζυγέω, 2086], to be unequally yoked (*heteros*, another of a different sort, and A, No. 1), is used metaphorically in 2 Cor. 6:14. ¶
NT: B.314d; CB.1250a; K.301.
OT: —.
GEN. REF.: IS.4:1165; NB.1352; Z.5:1022.

YOKE-FELLOW

sunzugos or *suzugos* [σύνζυγος, 4805], an adjective denoting yoked together, is used as a noun in Phil. 4:3, a yoke-fellow, fellow-labourer; probably here it is a proper name, Synzygus, addressed as "true," or genuine (*gnēsios*), i.e., properly so-called. ¶
NT: B.775d; CB.—; K.1099.
OT: —.
GEN. REF.: IS.4:1165; NB.—; Z.5:1023.

YONDER

ekei [ἐκεῖ, 1563], there, is rendered "yonder" in Matt. 26:36; "to yonder place," 17:20. See THERE, THITHER.
NT: B.239a; CB.1243c; K.—.
OT: shām: S.8033; HR.423c.8a; H.2404; BD.1027a.
GEN. REF.: —.

For YOU see YE

YOUNG, YOUNG (children, daughter, man, men, woman, women)

1. *neōteros* [νεώτερος, 3501], the comparative degree of *neos*, new, youthful, is translated "young" in John 21:18; in the plural, Acts 5:6, "young men" (marg., "younger"); Tit. 2:6, A.V., R.V., "younger men." See YOUNGER.
NT: B.535d; CB.1259c; K.—.
OT: —.
GEN. REF.: IS.4:1165; NB.—; Z.5:1023.

2. *neos* [νέος, 3501], in the feminine plural, denotes "young women," Tit. 2:4. See NEW, No. 2.
NT: B.535d; CB.1259c; K.628.
OT: qāṭān, qāṭōn: S.6996; HR.942a.7d; H.2009a,b; BD.881d,882b.
ṣā'îr: S.6810; HR.942a.7c; H.1948a; BD.859a.
na'ar: S.5288; HR.942a.7b; H.1389a; BD.654d.
GEN. REF.: IS.4:1165; NB.—; Z.—.

3. *neanias* [νεανίας, 3494], a young man, occurs in Acts 7:58; 20:9; 23:17, 18 (in some texts). ¶
NT: B.534c; CB.—; K.—.
OT: na'ar: S.5288; HR.940a.3a; H.1389a; BD.654d.
bāḥûr: S.970; HR.940a.1a; H.231a; BD.104c.
GEN. REF.: IS.4:1165; NB.—; Z.5:1023.

4. *neaniskos* [νεανίσκος, 3495], a diminutive of No. 3, a youth, a young man, occurs in Matt. 19:20, 22; Mark 14:51 (1st part; R.V. omits in 2nd part); 16:5; Luke 7:14; Acts 2:17; 5:10 (i.e., attendants); 23:18 (in the best texts), 22; 1 John 2:13, 14, of the second branch of the spiritual family. ¶
NT: B.534c; CB.1259c; K.—.
OT: na'ar: S.5288; HR.940b.4; H.1389a; BD.654d.
bāḥûr: S.970; HR.940b.2a; H.231a; BD.104c.
GEN. REF.: IS.4:1165; NB.—; Z.5:1023.

5. *nossos* or *neossos* [νοσσός, 3502], a young bird (akin to No. 2), is translated "young" in Luke 2:24. ¶ Cp. *nossia*, a brood, Luke 13:34, and the noun *nossion*, used in the neuter plural, *nossia*, in Matt. 23:37, "chickens"; *nossion* is the diminutive of *nossos*. ¶
NT: B.543d; CB.—; K.—.
OT: bēn: S.1121; HR.949c.2; H.254; BD.119d.
'ephrōaḥ: S.667; HR.949c.1; H.1813c; BD.827b.
GEN. REF.: —.

Notes: (1) In Acts 20:12, A.V., *pais*, a "lad" (R.V.), is translated "young man."

(2) In Mark 7:25, A.V., *thugatrion*, a diminutive of *thugatēr*, a daughter, is rendered "young (R.V., little) daughter."

(3) In Mark 10:13, A.V., *paidion*, in the neuter plural, is rendered "young (R.V., little) children."

(4) In Acts 7:19, A.V., *brephos*, in the neuter plural, is rendered "young children," R.V., "babes." See BABE, No. 1.

YOUNGER

1. *neōteros* [νεώτερος, 3501], for which see No. 1, above, occurs in Luke 15:12, 13; 22:26; 1 Tim. 5:1 ("younger men"); 5:2, feminine; ver. 11, "younger (widows)"; ver. 14, "younger (*widows*)," R.V., marg. and A.V., "younger (women)" (see WIDOW); 1 Pet. 5:5. For Tit. 2:6 see YOUNG, No. 1. ¶
NT: B.535d; CB.1259c; K.—.
OT: —.
GEN. REF.: IS.4:1165; NB.—; Z.—.

2. *elassōn* [ἐλάσσων, 1640], is rendered "younger" in Rom. 9:12: see LESS.
NT: B.248a; CB.1244a; K.—.
OT: mā'aṭ: S.4591; HR.448b.3a,b; H.1228; BD.589b.
mᵉ'aṭ: S.4592; HR.448b.3c; H.1228a; BD.589d.
qāṭōn: S.6996; HR.448b.5; H.2009a,b; BD.882a.
GEN. REF.: —.

YOUR, YOURS

Notes: (1) "Your" is most frequently the translation of *humōn*, lit., of you, the genitive plural of *su*, thou, you; it is translated "yours" in 1 Cor. 3:21, 22; in 8:9, "of yours"; 16:18; 2 Cor. 12:14. In the following the dative plural, *humin*, lit., 'to you,' is translated "your"; Luke 16:11, lit., '(who will entrust) to you'; in 21:15 "your adversaries" is, lit., '(those opposed) to you'; in 1 Cor. 6:5 and 15:34, A.V., "(I speak to) your (shame)," R.V., "(I say *this* to move) you (to shame)," is, lit., '(I speak unto a shame) to you.' The accusative plural, *humas*, preceded by *kata*, according to, is rendered in Acts 18:15 "your own (law)," R.V., A.V., "your (law)," lit., '(of the law) according to you,' with emphasis and scorn; in Eph. 1:15 the same construction is used of faith, but *kata* here means "among," as in the R.V., "(the faith . . . which is) among you," A.V., "your (faith)"; in John 14:26 "He shall . . . bring to your remembrance" is lit., 'He shall . . . put you in mind of.'

(2) The possessive pronoun, *humeteros*, your, is used in Luke 6:20; John 7:6; 8:17; 15:20; Acts 27:34; Rom. 11:31; 1 Cor. 15:31; 16:17; 2 Cor. 8:8; Gal. 6:13; in Luke 16:12, "your own." ¶

(3) In Rom. 16:19, A.V., the phrase *to epi humin*, lit., 'the (matter) over you,' is rendered "on your behalf" (R.V., "over you," following the mss. which omit the neuter article *to*).

YOUTH

neotēs [νεότης, 3503], from *neos*, new, occurs in Mark 10:20; Luke 18:21; Acts 26:4; 1 Tim. 4:12 (in some mss., Matt. 19:20). ¶

NT: B.536c; CB.1259c; K.–.
OT: –.
GEN. REF.: IS.4:1165; NB.–; Z.5:1023.

YOUTHFUL

neōterikos [νεωτερικός, 3512], from *neōteros*, the comparative degree of *neos*, new, is used especially of qualities, of lusts, 2 Tim. 2:22. ¶

NT: B.537b; CB.–; K.–.
OT: –.
GEN. REF.: IS.4:1165; NB.–; Z.–.

Z

ZEAL

zēlos [ζῆλος, 2205], denotes zeal in the following passages; John 2:17, with objective genitive, i.e., 'zeal for Thine house'; so in Rom. 10:2, "a zeal for God"; in 2 Cor. 7:7, R.V., "(your) zeal (for me)," A.V., "(your) fervent mind (toward me)"; used absolutely in 7:11; 9:2; Phil. 3:6 (in Col. 4:13 in some texts; the best have *ponos*, "labour," R.V.). See ENVY, *Note*, FERVENT, C, *Note* (2), INDIGNATION, A, *Note* (3), JEALOUSY.

NT: B.337c; CB.1273b; K.297.
OT: qin'āh: S.7068; HR.594a.1; H.2038a; BD.888b.
GEN. REF.: IS.4:1175; NB.–; Z.5:1036.

ZEALOUS

A. Noun.

zēlōtēs [ζηλωτής, 2207], is used adjectivally, of being zealous (*a*) "of the Law," Acts 21:20; (*b*) "towards God," lit., 'of God,' 22:3, R.V., "for God"; (*c*) "of spiritual gifts," 1 Cor. 14:12, i.e., for exercise of spiritual gifts (lit., 'of spirits,' but not to be interpreted literally); (*d*) "for (A.V., of) the traditions of my fathers," Gal. 1:14, of Paul's loyalty to Judaism before his conversion; (*e*) of good works," Tit. 2:14.

The word is, lit., 'a zealot,' i.e., an uncompromising partisan. The "Zealots" was a name applied to an extreme section of the Pharisees, bitterly antagonistic to the Romans. Josephus (*Antiq*. xviii. 1. 1, 6; *B.J*. ii. 8.1) refers to them as the "fourth sect of Jewish philosophy" (i.e., in addition to the Pharisees, Sadducees, and Essenes), founded by Judas of Galilee (cp. Acts 5:37). After his rebellion in A.D. 6, the Zealots nursed the fires of revolt, which, bursting out afresh in A.D. 66, led to the destruction of Jerusalem in 70. To this sect, Simon, one of the Apostles, had belonged, Luke 6:15; Acts 1:13. The equivalent Hebrew and Aramaic term was "Cananaean" (Matt. 10:4); this is not connected with Canaan, as the A.V. "Canaanite" would suggest, but is derived from Heb. *qannâ*, jealous. ¶

NT: B.338a; CB.1273b; K.297.
OT: qannā': S.7067; HR.594b.1a; H.2038b; BD.888d.
GEN. REF.: IS.4:1175; NB.1354; Z.5:1036.

B. Verbs.

1. *zēloō* [ζηλόω, 2206], to be jealous, also signifies to seek or desire eagerly; in Gal. 4:17, R.V., "they zealously seek (you)," in the sense of taking a very warm interest in; so in ver. 18,

Passive Voice, "to be zealously sought" (A.V., "to be zealously affected"), i.e., to be the object of warm interest on the part of others; some texts have this verb in Rev. 3:19 (see No. 2). See AFFECT, *Note,* COVET, DESIRE, ENVY, JEALOUS.

NT: B.338a; CB.1273b; K.297.
OT: qānā': S.7065; HR.594b.4a; H.2038; BD.888c.
GEN. REF.: IS.4:1175; NB.–; Z.5:1036.

2. *zēleuō* [ζηλεύω, --], a late and rare form of No. 1, is found in the best texts in Rev. 3:19, "be zealous." ¶

NT: B.337a; CB.1273b; K.–.
OT: –.
GEN. REF.: IS.4:1175; NB.–; Z.–.

Note: For *spoudazō*, Gal. 2:10, R.V., see DILIGENT, B, No. 1.

ADDITIONAL NOTES

ON THE PARTICLE **KAI** [*καί*]

(*a*) The particle *kai*, "and," chiefly used for connecting words, clauses and sentences (the copulative or connective use), not infrequently signifies "also." This is the *adjunctive*, or *amplificatory*, use, and it is to be distinguished from the purely copulative significance "and." A good illustration is provided in Matt. 8:9, in the words of the centurion, "I also am a man under authority." Other instances are Matt. 5:39, 40; 8:9; 10:18; 18:33; 20:4; Luke 11:49; 12:41, 54, 57; 20:3; John 5:26, "the Son also," R.V.; 7:3; 12:10; 14:1, 3, 7, 19; 15:9, 27; 17:24; Acts 11:17; Rom. 1:13; 6:11; 1 Cor. 7:3; 11:25; 15:30; Gal. 6:1; Phil. 4:12, "I know also," R.V.; 1 Thess. 3:12. In 1 Cor. 2:13 the *kai* phrase signifies 'which are the very things we speak, with the like power of the Holy Spirit.'

This use includes the meanings "so," or "just so," by way of comparison, as in Matt. 6:10, and "so also," e.g., John 13:33; cp. Rom. 11:16. In Heb. 7:26 the most authentic mss. have *kai* in the first sentence, which may be rendered 'for such a High Priest also became us.' Here it virtually has the meaning "precisely."

(*b*) Occasionally *kai* tends towards an *adversative* meaning, expressing a contrast, "yet," almost the equivalent of *alla*, "but"; see, e.g., Mark 12:12, 'yet they feared'; Luke 20:19; John 18:28, 'yet they themselves entered not.' Some take it in this sense in Rom. 1:13, where, however, it may be simply parenthetic. Sometimes in the English Versions the "yet" has been added in italics, as in 2 Cor. 6:8, 9, 10.

(*c*) In some passages *kai* has the meaning "and yet," e.g., Matt. 3:14, 'and yet comest Thou to me?'; 6:26, 'and yet (R.V. "and," A.V., "yet") your Heavenly Father feedeth them'; Luke 18:7, 'and yet He is longsuffering'; John 3:19, 'and yet men loved the darkness'; 4:20, 'and yet we say'; 6:49, 'and yet they died'; 1 Cor. 5:2, 'and yet ye are puffed up'; 1 John 2:9, 'and yet hateth his brother.' The same is probably the case in John 7:30, 'and yet no man laid hands on Him'; some rule this and similar cases out because of the negative in the sentence following the *kai*, but that seems hardly tenable.

(*d*) In some passages it has a *temporal* significance, "then." In Luke 7:12 the *kai*, which is untranslated in the English Versions, provides the meaning 'then, behold, there was carried out'; so Acts 1:10, 'then, behold, two men stood.' This use is perhaps due to the influence of the Septuagint, reflecting the Hebrew idiom, especially when *idou*, "behold" follows the *kai*.

(*e*) There is also the *inferential* use before a question, e.g., Mark 10:26, "then who can be saved?" R.V. This is commonly expressed by the English "and," as in Luke 10:29; John 9:36.

(*f*) Occasionally it has almost the sense of *hoti*, "that," e.g., Matt. 26:15 (first part); Mark 14:40 (last part); Luke 5:12, 17, where, if the *kai* had been translated, the clause might be rendered 'that, behold, a man . . . ,' lit., 'and behold . . . '; so ver. 17; see also 9:51, where *kai*, 'that,' comes before "He stedfastly set"; in 12:15, 'take heed that ye keep.' What is said under (*d*), regarding the influence of the Septuagint, is applicable also to this significance.

(*g*) Sometimes it has the consecutive meaning of "and so": e.g., Matt. 5:15, 'and so it shineth'; Phil. 4:7, 'and so the peace . . . '; Heb. 3:19, 'and so we see.'

(*h*) The *epexegetic* or *explanatory* use. This may be represented by the expressions 'namely,' 'again,' 'and indeed,' 'that is to say'; it is usually translated by 'and.' In such cases not merely an addition is in view. In Matt. 21:5, 'and upon a colt' means 'that is to say, upon a colt.' In John 1:16 the clause "and grace for grace" is explanatory of the "fulness." In John 12:48, "and receiveth not My sayings," is not simply an addition to "that rejecteth Me," it explains what the rejection involves, as the preceding verse shows. In Mark 14:1, "and the unleavened bread" is perhaps an instance, since the Passover feast is so defined in Luke 22:1. In Acts 23:6 the meaning is 'the hope, namely, the resurrection of the dead.' In Rom. 1:5 "grace and apostleship" may signify 'grace expressed in apostleship.' In Eph. 1:1 "and the faithful" does not mark a distinct class of believers, it defines "the saints"; but in this case it goes a little further than what is merely epexegetical, it adds a more distinctive epithet than the preceding and may be taken as meaning 'yes indeed.'

For the suggestion as to the epexegetic use of *kai* in John 3:5, 'water, even the Spirit,' see Vol. IV, p. 202, 11. 6-9.

In regard to Titus 3:5, "the renewing of the Holy Ghost" is co-ordinate with "the washing of regeneration," and some would regard it as precisely explanatory of that phrase, taking the *kai* as signifying 'namely.' Certainly the "renewing" is not an additional and separate impartation of the Holy Spirit; but the scope of the renewal is surely not limited to regeneration; the second clause goes further than what is merely epexegetic of the first. Just so in Rom. 12:2, "the renewing of your mind" is not a single act, accomplished once and for all, as in regeneration. See under RENEW, B. The Holy Ghost, as having been 'shed on us,' continues to act in renewing us, in order to maintain by His power the enjoyment of the relationship into which He has brought us. "The man is cleansed in connection with the new order of things; but the Holy Ghost is a source of an entirely new life, entirely new thoughts; not only of a new moral being, but of the communication of all that in which this new being develops itself . . . He ever communicates more and more of the things of this new world into which He has brought us . . . 'the renewing of the Holy Ghost' embraces all this . . . so that it is not only that we are born of Him, but that he works in us, communicating to us all that is ours in Christ" (J. N. Darby). Both the washing and the renewing are His work.

(*i*) The *ascensive* use. This is somewhat similar to the epexegetic significance. It represents, however, an advance in thought upon what precedes and has the meaning "even." The context alone can determine the occurrences of this use. The following are some instances. In Matt. 5:46, 47, the phrases "even the publicans" and "even the Gentiles" represent an extension of thought in regard to the manner of reciprocity exhibited by those referred to, in comparison with those who, like the Pharisees, were considered superior to them. In Mark 1:27, "even the unclean spirits" represents an advance in the minds of the people concerning Christ's miraculous power, in comparison with the authority exercised by the Lord in less remarkable ways. So in Luke 10:17. In Acts 10:45, the *kai*, rendered "also," in the phrase "on the Gentiles also," seems necessary to be regarded in the same way, in view of the amazement manifested by those of the circumcision, and thus the rendering will be 'even on the Gentiles was poured out the gift'; cp. 11:1.

In Rom. 13:5, the clause "but also for conscience sake" should probably be taken in this sense. In Gal. 2:13, the phrase "even Barnabas" represents an advance of thought in comparison with the waywardness of others; as much as to say, 'the Apostle's closest associate, from whom something different might be expected, was surprisingly carried away.' In Phil. 4:16 there are three occurrences of *kai*, the first ascensive, "even"; the second (untranslated) meaning "both," before the word "once"; the third meaning "and." In 1 Thess. 1:5, in the cause "and in the Holy Ghost," the *kai* rendered "and," is ascensive, conveying an extension of thought beyond "power"; that is to say, 'power indeed, but the power of the Holy Spirit.' In 1 Pet. 4:14 "the Spirit of God" is "the Spirit of glory." Here there is an advance in idea from the abstract to the Personal. The phrase "the Spirit of God" does more than define "the Spirit of glory"; it is explanatory but ascensive also.

When preceded or followed by the conjunction *ei*, "if," the phrase signifies "even if," or "if even," e.g., Mark 14:29; Phil. 2:17; 1 Pet. 3:1.

ON THE PARTICLE **DE** [$\delta\varepsilon$]

The particle *de* has two chief uses, (*a*) *continuative* or *copulative*, signifying 'and,' or 'in the next place,' (*b*) *adversative*, signifying 'but,' or 'on the other hand.' The first of these, (*a*), is well illustrated in the genealogy in Matt. 1:2-16, the line being simply reckoned from Abraham to Christ. So in 2 Cor. 6:15, 16, where the *de* anticipates a negative more precisely than would be the case if *kai* had been used. In 1 Cor. 15:35; Heb. 12:6, e.g., the *de* "and (scourgeth)" is purely copulative.

(*b*) The adversative use distinguishes a word or clause from that which precedes. This is exemplified, for instance, in Matt. 5:22, 28, 32; 34, 39, 44, in each of which the *egō*, "I," stands out with pronounced stress by way of contrast. This use is very common. In Matt. 23:4 the first *de* is copulative, "Yea, they bind heavy burdens" (R.V.), the second is adversative, "but they themselves will not . . ."

In John 3:1, R.V., it may not at first sight seem clear whether the *de*, "Now," is copulative, introducing an illustration of Christ's absolute knowledge, or adversative, signifying 'But.' In the former case the significance would be that, however fair the exterior might be, as exemplified in Nicodemus, he needs to be born again. In the latter case it introduces a contrast, in regard to Nicodemus, to what has just been stated, that "Jesus did not trust Himself" (2:24) to those mentioned in v. 23. And, inasmuch as He certainly did afford to Nicodemus the opportunity of learning the truths of the new birth and the Kingdom of God, as a result of which he became a disciple ("secret" though he was), he may be introduced in the Apostle's narrative as an exception to those who believed simply through seeing the signs accomplished by the Lord (2:23).

In Rom. 3:22, in the clause "even the righteousness," the *de* serves to annexe not only an explanation, defining "a righteousness of God" (v. 21, R.V.), but an extension of the thought; so in 9:30, "even the righteousness which is of faith."

In 1 Cor. 2:6, in the clause "yet a wisdom," an exception (not an addition) is made to what precedes; some would regard this as belonging to (*a*); it seems, however, clearly adversative. In 4:7 the first *de* is copulative, "and what has thou . . .?"; the second is adversative, "but if thou didst receive . . ."

In 1 Thess. 5:21 "many ancient authorities insert 'but' " (see R.V. marg.), so translating *de*, between the two injunctions "despise not prophesyings" and "prove all things," and this is almost certainly the correct reading. In any case the injunctions are probably thus contrastingly to be connected.

In 2 Pet. 1:5-7, after the first *de*, which has the meaning "yea," the six which follow, in the phrases giving virtues to be supplied, suggest the thought 'but there is something further to be done.' These are not merely connective, as expressed by the English "and," but adversative, as indicating a contrast to the possible idea that to add virtue to our faith is sufficient for the moral purpose in view.

De, in combination with the negatives *ou* and *mē* (*oude* and *mēde*, usually "but not," "and not," "neither," "nor,"), sometimes has the force of "even," e.g., *oude* in Matt. 6:29, "even Solomon . . . was not arrayed . . ."; Mark 6:31, lit., '(they had) not even leisure to eat'; Luke 7:9, lit., 'not even in Israel have I found such faith'; John 7:5, "For even His brethren did not believe on Him"; Acts 4:32, lit., 'not even one of them'; 1 Cor. 5:1, "not even among the Gentiles"; *mēde*, in Mark 2:2, "not even about the door"; 1 Cor. 5:11, lit., "with such a one not even to eat."

ON THE PREPOSITIONS **ANTI** [ἀντί] AND **HUPER** [ὑπέρ]

The basic idea of *anti* is "facing." This may be a matter of opposition, unfriendliness or antagonism, or of agreement. These meanings are exemplified in compounds of the preposition with verbs, and in nouns. The following are instances: *antiparerchomai* in Luke 10:31, 32, where the verb is rendered "passed by on the other side," i.e., of the road, but facing the wounded man; *antiballō* in Luke 24:17, where the *anti* suggests that the two disciples, in exchanging words (see R.V. marg.), turned to face one another, indicating the earnest nature of their conversation. The idea of antagonism is seen in *antidikos*, an adversary, Matt. 5:25, *antichristos*, antichrist, 1 John 4:3, etc.

There is no instance of the uncompounded preposition signifying "against." Arising from the basic significance, however, there are several other meanings attaching to the separate use of the preposition. In the majority of the occurrences in the N.T., the idea is that of "in the place of," "instead of," or of exchange; e.g., Matt. 5:38, "an eye for (*anti*) an eye"; Rom. 12:17, "evil for evil"; so 1 Thess. 5:15; 1 Pet. 3:9, and, in the same verse, "reviling for reviling." The ideas of substitution and exchange are combined, e.g., in Luke 11:11, "for a fish . . . a serpent"; Heb. 12:16, "for one mess of meat . . . his own birthright." So in Matt. 17:27, "a shekel (*statēr*) . . . for thee and Me;" where the phrase is condensed; that is to say, the exchange is that of the coin for the tax demanded from Christ and Peter, rather than for the persons themselves. So in 1 Cor. 11:15, where the hair is a substitute for the covering.

Of special doctrinal importance are Matt. 20:28; Mark 10:45, "to give His life a ransom (*lutron*) for (*anti*) many." Here the substitutionary significance, "instead of," is clear, as also with the compound *antilutron* in 1 Tim. 2:6, "who gave Himself a ransom (*antilutron*) for (*huper*) all"; here the use of *huper*, "on behalf of," is noticeable. Christ gave Himself as a ransom (of a substitutionary character), not instead of all men, but on behalf of *all*. The actual substitution, as in the passages in Matthew and Mark, is expressed by the *anti*, instead of, "*many*." The unrepentant man should not be told that Christ was his substitute, for in that case the exchange would hold good for him and though unregenerate he would not be in the place of death, a condition in which, however, he exists while unconverted. Accordingly the "many" are those who, through faith, are delivered from that condition. The substitutionary meaning is exemplified in Jas. 4:15, where the A.V. and R.V. render the *anti* "for that" (R.V., marg., "instead of").

In Heb. 12:2, "for (*anti*) the joy that was set before Him endured the cross," neither the thought of exchange nor that of substitution is conveyed; here the basic idea of facing is present. The cross and the joy faced each other in the mind of Christ and He chose the one with the other in view.

In John 1:16 the phrase "grace for grace" is used. The idea of 'following upon' has been suggested, as wave follows wave. Is not the meaning that the grace we receive corresponds to the grace inherent in Christ, out of whose fulness we receive it?

The primary meaning of *huper* is "over," "above." Hence, metaphorically, with the accusative case, it is used of superiority, e.g., Matt. 10:24, "above his master" (or teacher); or of measure in excess, in the sense of beyond, e.g., 1 Cor. 4:6, "beyond the things that are written"; or "than," after a comparative, e.g., Luke 16:8; Heb. 4:12; or "more than," after a verb, e.g., Matt. 10:37. With the genitive it means (1) on behalf of, in the interests of, e.g., of prayer, Matt. 5:44; of giving up one's life, and especially of Christ's so doing for man's redemption, e.g., John 10:15; 1 Tim. 2:6, 'on behalf of all' (see under *Anti*); 2 Thess. 2:1, 'in the interest of (i.e., 'with a view to correcting your thoughts about') the Coming.' The difficult passage, 1 Cor. 15:29, possibly comes here. With an alteration of the punctuation (feasible from the ms. point of view), the reference may be to baptism as taught elsewhere in the N.T., and the verse may read thus: 'Else what shall they do which are being baptized? (i.e., what purpose can they serve?); (it is) in the interest of the dead, if the dead are not raised at all. Why then are they baptized in the interest of them?' That is to say, they fulfil the ordinance in the interest of a Christ who is dead and in joint witness with (and therefore, in the interest of) believers who never will be raised, whereas an essential element in baptism is its testimony to the resurrection of Christ and of the believer.

In some passages *huper* may be used in the substitutionary sense, e.g., John 10:11, 15; Rom. 8:32; but it cannot be so taken in the majority of instances. Cp. 2 Cor. 5:15, in regard to which, while it might be said that Christ died in place of us, it cannot be said that Christ rose again in the place of us.

ON THE PREPOSITIONS **APO** [ἀπό] AND **EK** [ἐκ]

The primary meaning of *apo* is "off"; this is illustrated in such compounds as *apokaluptō*, to take the veil off, to reveal; *apokoptō*, to cut off; hence there are different shades of meaning, the chief of which is "from" or "away from," e.g., Matt. 5:29, 30; 9:22; Luke 24:31, lit., 'He became invisible from them'; Rom. 9:3.

The primary meaning of *ek* is "out of," e.g., Matt. 3:17, "a voice out of the heavens" (R.V.); 2 Cor. 9:7, lit., 'out of necessity.' Omitting such significances of *ek* as origin, source, cause, occasion, etc., our consideration will here be confined to a certain similarity between *apo* and *ek*. Since *apo* and *ek* are both frequently to be translated by "from" they often approximate closely in meaning. The distinction is largely seen in this, that *apo* suggests a starting point from without, *ek* from within; this meaning is often involved in *apo*, but *apo* does not give prominence to the "within-ness," as *ek* usually does. For instance, *apo* is used in Matt. 3:16, where the R.V. rightly reads "Jesus . . . went up straightway from the water"; in Mark 1:10 *ek* is used, "coming up out of the water"; *ek* (which stands in contrast to *eis* in v. 9) stresses more emphatically than *apo* the fact of His having been baptized in the water. In all instances where these prepositions appear to be used alternately this distinction is to be observed.

The literal meaning "out of" cannot be attached to *ek* in a considerable number of passages. In several instances *ek* obviously has the significance of 'away from'; and where either meaning seems possible, the context, or some other passage, affords guidance. The following are examples in which *ek* does not mean 'out of the midst of' or 'out from within,' but has much the same significance as *apo*: John 17:15, "that Thou shouldest keep them from the evil one"; 1 Cor. 9:19, "though I was free from all men"; 2 Cor. 1:10, "who delivered us from so great a death" (A.V.); 2 Pet. 2:21, "to turn back from the holy commandment"; Rev. 15:2, "them that had come victorious from the beast, and from his image, and from the number of his name" (*ek* in each case).

Concerning the use of *ek*, in 1 Thess. 1:10, "Jesus, which delivereth (the present tense, as in the R.V., is important) us from the wrath to come" [or, more closely to the original, 'our Deliverer (cp. the same phrase in Rom. 11:26) from the coming wrath'], the passage makes clear that the wrath signifies the calamities to be visited by God upon men when the present period of grace is closed. As to whether the *ek* here denotes 'out of the midst of' or 'preservation from,' this is determined by the statement in 5:9, that "God appointed us not unto wrath, but unto the obtaining of salvation"; the context there shows that the salvation is from the wrath just referred to. Accordingly the *ek* signifies 'preservation from' in the same sense as *apo*, and not 'out from the midst of.'

ON THE PREPOSITION **EN** [ἐν]

En, "in," is the most common preposition. It has several meanings, e.g., of place (e.g., Heb. 1:3, lit., 'on the right hand,' i.e., in that position), and time, e.g., in 1 Thess. 2:19; 3:13; 1 John 2:28, in each of which the phrase "at His coming" (inadequately so rendered, and lit., 'in His Parousia') combines place and time; the noun, while denoting a period, also signifies a presence involving accompanying circumstances, e.g., 1 Thess. 4:15.

Further consideration must here be confined to the instrumental use, often rendered "with" (though *en* in itself does not mean "with"), e.g., Matt. 5:13, "wherewith (lit., 'in what,' i.e., by what means) shall it be salted"; 7:2, "with what measure ye mete." Sometimes the instrumental is associated with the locative significance (which indeed attaches to most of its uses), e.g., Luke 22:49, "shall we smite with the sword?" the smiting being viewed as located in the sword; so in Matt. 26:52, "shall perish with the sword"; cp. Rev. 2:16; 6:8; 13:10. In Matt. 12:24, "by (marg., 'in') Beelzebub," indicates that the casting out is located in Beelzebub. Cp. Luke 1:51, "with His arm." In Heb. 11:37, the statement "they were slain with the sword" is, lit., 'they died by (*en*) slaughter of the sword.' There is a noticeable change in Rom. 12:21, from *hupo*, by, to *en*, with, in this instrumental and locative sense; the lit. rendering is 'be not overcome by (*hupo*) evil, but overcome evil with (*en*) good,' *en* expressing both means and circumstances. A very important instance of the instrumental *en* is in Rom. 3:25, where the R.V., "faith, by His blood," corrects the A.V., "faith in His blood," and the commas which the R.V. inserts are necessary. Thus the statement reads "whom God set forth to be a propitiation, through faith, by His blood." Christ is a propitiation, by means of His blood, i.e., His expiatory death. Faith is exercised in the living God, not in the blood, which provides the basis of faith.